The New Palgrave

A Dictionary of Economics

THE NEW PALGRAVE
A DICTIONARY OF ECONOMICS

EDITED BY

JOHN EATWELL

MURRAY MILGATE

PETER NEWMAN

Volume 4

Q to Z

M

THE MACMILLAN PRESS LIMITED, LONDON
THE STOCKTON PRESS, NEW YORK
MARUZEN COMPANY LIMITED, TOKYO

The New Palgrave: A Dictionary of Economics
Edited by John Eatwell, Murray Milgate and Peter Newman
in four volumes, 1987

Published in the United Kingdom by
THE MACMILLAN PRESS LIMITED, 1987
London and Basingstoke
Associated companies in Auckland, Delhi, Dublin, Gaborone, Hamburg, Harare, Hong Kong, Johannesburg, Kuala Lumpur, Lagos, Manzini, Melbourne, Mexico City, Nairobi, New York, Singapore, Tokyo.

Published in the United States of America and Canada by
THE STOCKTON PRESS, 1987
15 East 26th Street, New York, NY10010, USA

Published in Japan by
MARUZEN COMPANY LIMITED, 1987
3–10, Nihonbashi 2-Chome, Chuo-Ku, Tokyo 103, Japan

Reprinted 1988 (twice)

Library of Congress Cataloging-in-Publication Data
The New Palgrave: a dictionary of economics
Sequel to: Dictionary of political economy/Robert Harry Inglis Palgrave. 1910.
Bibliography: p.
Includes index.
1. Economics—Dictionaries. I. Eatwell, John.
II. Milgate, Murray. III. Newman, Peter K. 1928–.
IV. Palgrave, Robert Harry Inglis, Sir, 1827–1919.
Dictionary of political economy.
HB61.N49 330′.03′21 87–1946
ISBN 0-935859-10-1 (set)

British Library Cataloguing in Publication Data
The New Palgrave: a dictionary of economics
1. Economics—Dictionaries
I. Eatwell, John. II. Milgate, Murray
III. Newman, Peter.
330.03′21 HB61
ISBN 0-333-37235-2

Text keyboarded by Morton Word Processing Ltd, Scarborough, North Yorkshire.
Database management and text composition by Pergamon Orbit InfoLine Ltd, London.
Typeset by A. Wheaton & Co. Ltd, Exeter, Devon.
Printed and bound in Hong Kong.

Contents

LIST OF ENTRIES A – Z

One-line cross-references are shown in *italics*.

Q

qualitative economics. Qualitative economics comprises the analysis of economic systems for which qualitative information is available, that is, information about the direction of change (+, −, 0) of the values of the functional relations defining the system with respect to changes in the values of its variables. A distinction can be drawn between *purely* qualitative systems, namely, systems in which the only information available is such sign information, and mixed quantitative–qualitative systems which have quantitative information available as well.

Two classes of economic models have been the subject for most of the work done in qualitative economics: comparative statics models of the form $Ax=b$, and linear dynamic models of the form $\dot{x}=Ax$, where A is an $n \times n$ matrix, and x and b are $n \times 1$ vectors. In the comparative statics models, the problem is to sign (+, −, 0) the elements of the vector x, given information about the sign pattern of the matrix A and of the vector b. In the dynamic models, the problem is that of determining when there is asymptotic stability

$$\left(\lim_{t\to\infty} x(t) = 0\right),$$

given information about the sign pattern of the matrix A.

Rather complete results are known in the case of purely qualitative systems, while there are a number of special results for mixed systems. Literature surveys covering the former appear in Maybee and Quirk (1969), Allingham and Morishima (1973), and Maybee (1981), while Quirk (1981) presents a summary of stability results for both pure and mixed systems.

Qualitative hypotheses have been a part of economics from the earliest days of formal economic analysis, but it was only in the late 1930s that the first attempts were made to formalize the analysis of qualitative information in economic models, beginning with Hicks's (1939) model of general equilibrium of a competitive economy. In *Foundations of Economic Analysis*, Samuelson (1947) identified qualitative information, the maximization hypothesis, and the hypothesis of stability of equilibrium as the three fundamental sources of comparative statics theorems in neoclassical economics. Metzler (1945), Mosak (1944), and Morishima (1952) made basic contributions to the analysis of the comparative statics properties of the Hicksian model, and Arrow, Block and Hurwicz (1958, 1959) and McKenzie (1960) provided proofs of stability of the Hicksian model under the gross substitute case, a mixed quantitative–qualitative system.

In the *Foundations*, Samuelson suggested an elimination approach to analysing qualitative solvability, but the first formal work on the comparative statics properties of purely qualitative systems was due to Lancaster (1962, 1964, 1965), whose approach was generalized by Gorman (1964). The Gorman approach to the qualitative solvability problem is an iterative one, involving a nesting procedure whereby at any stage in the analysis the set of variables is partitioned into two disjoint non-empty sets. For the functional relation associated with that stage, the direction of change of its value with respect to the variables is weakly the same for all variables in a given set, and opposite to that for the variables in the other set. There is qualitative solvability if and only if this nested partitioning can be continued, exhausting all functional relations, until one element sets are reached.

Taking a different approach, Bassett, Maybee and Quirk (BMQ) (1968) provided the first proof of necessary and sufficient conditions for qualitative solvability of the comparative statics system $Ax=b$. The BMQ conditions use the notions of cycles and chains in matrices. A chain of length m from i to j $(i \neq j)$ in an $n \times n$ matrix A is a product of m elements of A, with the first term in the chain having a row index i and the last term a column index j, with the row index of any term in the product the same as the column index in the preceding term in the product, and with all row indices differing from one another. A cycle (of length $m+1$) is obtained by multiplying such a chain by the element a_{ji}.

The system $Ax=b$ is said to be qualitatively solvable if, given information as to the signs (+, −, 0) of the elements of A and b, one can solve for a unique sign pattern for the vector x. In analysing such a system, admissible qualitative operations are restricted to renumbering individual equations and/or variables, and multiplying individual equations and/or variables by −1. The BMQ conditions state that $Ax=b$ is qualitatively solvable if and only if by admissible qualitative operations the system can be put into the form $Cy=d$, where all diagonal elements in C are negative and all cycles in C are non-positive, while all the elements in d are non-negative. If the jth element in d is strictly positive, then all chains in C terminating in j must be non-negative. The solution vector y then has all elements non-positive.

Work on qualitative solvability in more recent years has been concerned primarily with the construction of efficient algorithms for testing for qualitative solvability (see Greenberg and Maybee, 1981; Lady, 1983; Ritschard, 1983), much of this utilizing the tools of graph theory. In addition some work has been done on the problem of partial qualitative solvability, that is, solving for the signs of one or more components of the vector x given sign information as to A and b. The problem of partial qualitative solvability has been resolved for the case where A is qualitatively non-singular but the problem has not been solved in general (see Quirk, 1972; Maybee, 1981; Lady, 1983).

In the purely qualitative case, analysis of the stability properties of the system $\dot{x}=Ax$ has been concerned with the derivation of conditions such that the matrix A can be judged a stable matrix (i.e. the real parts of its characteristic roots are all negative), simply from information as to the sign pattern of A. When every matrix with the same sign pattern as A is a stable matrix, then A is said to be a sign stable matrix, and the dynamic system $\dot{x}=Bx$ is asymptotically stable for any matrix B with the same sign pattern as A. In Quirk and Ruppert (QR) (1965), necessary and sufficient conditions for A to be a sign stable matrix were derived for the case where all the diagonal elements of A are negative. In this case, sign stability occurs if and only if (1) all cycles of length two in A are non-positive; and (2) all cycles of length greater than two in A are zero. The attempt by QR to extend this result to the case where zeros appear on the diagonal in A was shown to be incorrect by Jeffries, Klee and Van Den Driessche (1977), who proved the following general sign stability theorem:

> An $n \times n$ matrix A is sign stable if and only if the following conditions are satisfied: (1) all diagonal elements in A are non-positive; (2) all cycles in A of length two are non-positive; (3) all cycles in A of length greater than two are zero; (4) there exists a non-zero term in the expansion of the determinant of A; (5) in every R_A colouring of the undirected graph G_A all vertices are black.

Turning to mixed quantitative–qualitative models, most of the literature is concerned with the analysis of comparative statics or dynamic models of general equilibrium of a competitive economy. In the general equilibrium case, the functional relations describing the model are the excess demand functions of the economy, with the variables being the prices of the goods traded in the economy. As Sonnenschein (1973) has shown, the neoclassical maximization and convexity assumptions underlying the competitive model imply only three restrictions on the excess demand functions: homogeneity of degree zero in prices, Walras's Law, and continuity. The mixed quantitative–qualitative problems associated with general equilibrium models thus become the comparative statics and stability problems associated with models in which the signs, $(+, -, 0)$ of the partial derivatives of excess demands with respect to prices are known, while, in addition, the excess demand functions satisfy homogeneity and Walras's Law.

In *Value and Capital*, Hicks studied the comparative statics properties of his general equilibrium model for two qualitative cases, namely the case in which all goods are gross substitutes for one another, and the case where all goods obey the rule that substitutes of substitutes and complements of complements are substitutes, but substitutes of complements and complements of substitutes are complements. The first case is known as the gross substitute case, and the second as the Morishima case. In his work on comparative statics, Hicks introduced the special assumption that the matrix A of partial derivatives of excess demands with respect to prices (for non-numeraire goods) was characterized by 'perfect stability', which is equivalent to a situation in which all principal minors of the matrix A of odd order are negative and all principal minors of even order are positive. The term 'Hicksian stability' is generally used to refer to Hicks's notion of perfect stability.

In the case of an economy with three goods, Hicks developed his Three Laws of Comparative Statics for the gross substitute case, under the assumption that Hicksian stability is present: a shift in demand from numeraire to some other commodity, say commodity i, (1) increases the equilibrium price of good i; (2) increases the equlibrium prices of all other non-numeraire goods; (3) increases the equilibrium price of i proportionately more than any other equilibrium price. In the Morishima case, under Hicksian stability, a shift in demand from *numéraire* to commodity i increases the equilibrium price of good i, increases the equilibrium prices of substitutes for i, and decreases the equilibrium prices of complements for i.

Mosak (1944) showed that Hicks's Three Laws of Comparative Statics hold for an economy with n goods, given gross substitutability and Hicksian stability. Metzler (1945) showed that in the gross substitute case, Hicksian stability of the $n \times n$ matrix A of partial derivatives of non-numeraire excess demands with respect to prices is equivalent to the condition that the matrix A be a stable matrix, that is, the real parts of the characteristic roots of A are negative. Morishima (1952) showed that Hicksian stability of the $n \times n$ matrix A is equivalent to the condition that A is a stable matrix, given the Morishima sign pattern conditions, and that Hicks's comparative statics results for the Morishima case extended to the case of n goods. Debreu and Herstein (1953) pointed out that the Mosak–Metzler–Morishima results all could be derived from the Perron–Frobenius theorem (as can the Hawkins–Simon conditions for viability of an input–output matrix), noting that a Morishima matrix is similar to a gross substitute matrix. (The term 'Metzler matrix' is also often used to refer to a gross substitute matrix.)

If the excess demand functions for a competitive economy satisfy Walras's Law and/or homogeneity, then there is asymptotic stability of the dynamic system $\dot{x} = Ax$, representing the linearized version of the tâtonnement adjustment equations for non-numeraire prices in a competitive economy. Arrow, Block and Hurwicz (1958, 1959), in their classic treatment of stability of the competitive equilibrium, showed that there is global stability in the gross substitute case, that the competitive equilibrium is not stable when all goods are gross complements, and in addition showed that the competitive equilibrium is not stable when all commodities (including numeraire) obey the Morishima sign conditions. McKenzie (1960) used the theory of dominant diagonal matrices to develop a simple proof of global stability of the competitive equilibrium in the gross substitute case. Bassett, Habibagahi and Quirk (1968) showed that the only class of qualitatively specified matrices for which stability implies the dominant diagonal property is the class of Metzler and Morishima matrices.

It is not known at present what the complete class of qualitatively specified cases is such that under Walras's Law and homogeneity either qualitative solvability or dynamic stability can be proved. Quirk (1970) has shown that in the case of sign symmetry for all goods, including numeraire, it is only in the gross substitute case that stability can be proved simply from qualitative information coupled with Walras's Law and homogeneity. Solvability of the qualitative comparative statics model associated with the competitive equilibrium occurs under a wider range of cases, some of which are identified in Quirk (1969).

JAMES QUIRK

See also ADJUSTMENT PROCESSES AND STABILITY; COMPARATIVE STATICS; STABILITY.

BIBLIOGRAPHY

Allingham, M. and Morishima, M. 1973. Qualitative economics and comparative statics. In *Theory of Demand – Real and Monetary*, ed. M. Morishima et al., Oxford: Clarendon Press.

Arrow, K., Block, H. and Hurwicz, L. 1959. On the stability of the competitive equilibrium II. *Econometrica* 27, 82–109.

Arrow, K. and Hurwicz, L. 1958. On the stability of the competitive equilibrium I. *Econometrica* 26, 522–52.

Bassett, L., Habibagahi, H. and Quirk, J. 1967. Qualitative economics and Morishima matrices. *Econometrica* 35, 221–33.

Bassett, L., Maybee, J. and Quirk, J. 1968. Qualitative economics and the scope of the correspondence principle. *Econometrica* 36, 544–63.

Debreu, G. and Herstein, I. 1953. Non-negative square matrices. *Econometrica* 21, 597–607.

Gorman, W. 1964. More scope for qualitative economics. *Review of Economic Studies* 31, 65–8.

Greenberg, H. and Maybee, J. 1981. *Computer Assisted Analysis and Model Simplifications*. New York: Academic Press.

Hicks, J. 1939. *Value and Capital.* Oxford: Oxford University Press.
Jeffries, C., Klee, V. and Van Den Driessche, P. 1977. When is a matrix sign stable? *Canadian Journal of Mathematics* 29, 315–26.
Lady, G. 1983. The structure of qualitatively determinate relationships. *Econometrica* 51, 197–218.
Lancaster, K. 1962. The scope of qualitative economics. *Review of Economic Studies* 29, 99–123.
Lancaster, K. 1964. Partitionable systems and qualitative economics. *Review of Economic Studies* 31, 69–72.
Lancaster, K. 1965. The theory of qualitative economic systems. *Econometrica* 33, 395–408.
McKenzie, L. 1960. Matrices with dominant diagonals and economic theory. In *Mathematical Methods in the Social Sciences 1959*, ed. K. Arrow, S. Karlin and P. Suppes, Stanford: Stanford University Press.
Maybee, J. 1981. Sign solvability. In Greenberg and Maybee (1981), 201–57.
Maybee, J. and Quirk, J. 1969. Qualitative problems in matrix theory. *SIAM Review* 11, 30–51.
Metzler, L. 1945. Stability of multiple markets: the Hicks conditions. *Econometrica* 13, 277–92.
Morishima, M. 1952. On the laws of change of the price system in an economy which contains complementary commodities. *Osaka Economic Papers* 1, 101–13.
Mosak, J. 1944. *General Equilibrium Theory in International Trade.* Cowles Foundation Monograph No. 7, Bloomington: Principia.
Quirk, J. 1969. The competitive equilibrium: a qualitative analysis. In *Economic Models, Estimation and Risk Programming*, ed. K. Fox et al., Berlin: Springer-Verlag.
Quirk, J. 1970. Complementarity and stability of the competitive equilibrium. *American Economic Review* 60, 358–63.
Quirk, J. 1972. Qualitative economics. Mimeographed, Caltech.
Quirk, J. 1981. Qualitative stability of matrices and economic theory. In Greenberg and Maybee (1981), 113–64.
Quirk, J. and Ruppert, R. 1965. Qualitative economics and the stability of equilibrium. *Review of Economic Studies* 32, 311–26.
Ritschard, G. 1983. Computable qualitative comparative statics techniques. *Econometrica* 51, 1145–68.
Samuelson, P. 1947. *Foundations of Economic Analysis.* Cambridge, Mass.: Harvard University Press.
Sonnenschein, H. 1973. Do Walras's identity and continuity characterize the class of community excess demand functions? *Journal of Economic Theory* 6, 345–54.

quantity equations: early history. The idea that there exists a relationship between the available quantity of money and the general level of prices was translated into mathematical form in the 17th century by John Briscoe in his *Discourse on the Late Funds*... of 1694 where it was expressed as a relation between the stock of precious metals and the value of commodities exchanged. There was, however, no recognition of the role of the velocity of circulation in Briscoe's equation. There followed an equation by Henry Lloyd in 1771 in his *Essay on the Theory of Money* which similarly failed to incorporate any velocity term; perhaps betraying the mercantilist element in their thought. The inclusion of the latter had to await the work of early 19th-century writers, and came with the appearance of Klaus Kröncke's *Das Steuerwesen nach seiner Natur und seinen Wirtkungen untersucht* (1804), Joseph Lang's *Grundlinien der politischen Arithmetik* (1811), Luca Samuele Cagnazzi's *Elementi di Economia Politica* (1813), and Samuel Turner's *Letter Addressed to the Right Hon. Robert Peel* (1819). In 1840 the probabilist John Lubbock produced what is almost certainly the most sophisticated early version of the quantity equation in his anonymous *On Currency* where the possibility of differences in the velocity of circulation of different components of the available quantity of money is admitted. This, of course, is the same as recognising a problem as to the definition of the M in modern versions of the equation; something neglected in earlier versions. One might notice the comparatively unsophisticated uses to which these equations were put by their architects, the more so given the sophisticated understanding of monetary theory that existed at the time and which gained expression in the Bullionist controversy and the Banking school–Currency school debates. In this instance, the laws of algebra and those of economics still, it would seem, remained far apart.

Somewhat similar remarks might be made of other mid-19th-century versions; those of Levasseur, Bowen, Roscher, and Rau come to mind (though the last does have the distinction of writing a version of the equation with the now familiar symbols $MV = PQ$). It is rather with Walras and Simon Newcomb that the algebra began to catch up with the theory, and with Fisher and Pigou (early in this century) the two strands finally came together. Subsequent to this period, it is virtually impossible to separate developments in the quantity theory of money itself from developments in the mathematical formulations it is given. The same is not true of the early history of the quantity equation.

MURRAY MILGATE

BIBLIOGRAPHY

Humphrey, T.M. 1984. Algebraic quantity equations before Fisher and Pigou. Federal Reserve Bank of Richmond *Economic Review* 70(5), 13–22.

quantity of capital. *See* CAPITAL AS A FACTOR OF PRODUCTION.

quantity theory of money.

> Lowness of interest is generally ascribed to plenty of money. But... augmentation [in the quantity of money] has no other effect than to heighten the price of labour and commodities... In the progress toward these changes, the augmentation may have some influence, by exciting industry, but after the prices are settled... it has no manner of influence.
>
> [T]hough the high price of commodities be a necessary consequence of the increase of gold and silver, yet it follows not immediately upon that increase; but some time is required before the money circulates through the whole state.... In my opinion, it is only in this interval of intermediate situation, between the acquisition of money and rise of prices, that the increasing quantity of gold and silver is favourable to industry.... [W]e may conclude that it is of no manner of consequence, with regard to the domestic happiness of a state, whether money be in greater or less quantity. The good policy of the magistrate consists only in keeping it, if possible, still increasing...
>
> (David Hume, 1752).

In this survey, we shall first present a formal statement of the quantity theory, then consider the Keynesian challenge to the quantity theory, recent developments, and some empirical evidence. We shall conclude with a discussion of policy implications, giving special attention to the likely implications of the worldwide fiat money standard that has prevailed since 1971.

1. THE FORMAL THEORY

(a) NOMINAL VERSUS REAL QUANTITY OF MONEY. Implicit in the quotation from Hume, and central to all later versions of the quantity theory, is a distinction between the *nominal* quantity of money and the *real* quantity of money. The nominal quantity of money is the quantity expressed in whatever units are used to designate money – talents, shekels, pounds, francs, lira, drachmas, dollars, and so on. The real quantity of money is the quantity expressed in terms of the volume of goods and services the money will purchase.

There is no unique way to express either the nominal or the real quantity of money. With respect to the nominal quantity of money, the issue is what assets to include – whether only currency and coins, or also claims on financial institutions; and, if such claims are included, which ones should be, only deposits transferable by cheque, or also other categories of claims which in practice are close substitutes for deposits transferable by cheque. More recently, economists have been experimenting with the theoretically attractive idea of defining money not as the simple sum of various categories of claims but as a weighted aggregate of such claims, the weights being determined by one or another concept of the 'moneyness' of the various claims.

Despite continual controversy over the definition of 'money', and the lack of unanimity about relevant theoretical criteria, in practice, monetary economists have generally displayed wide agreement about the most useful counterpart, or set of counterparts, to the concept of 'money' at particular times and places (Friedman and Schwartz, 1970, pp. 89–197; Barnett, Offenbacher and Spindt, 1984; Spindt, 1985).

The real quantity of money obviously depends on the particular definition chosen for the nominal quantity. In addition, for each such definition, it can vary according to the set of goods and services in terms of which it is expressed. One way to calculate the real quantity of money is by dividing the nominal quantity of money by a price index. The real quantity is then expressed in terms of the standard basket whose components are used as weights in computing the price index – generally, the basket purchased by some representative group in a base year.

A different way to express the real quantity of money is in terms of the time duration of the flow of goods and services the money could purchase. For a household, for example, the real quantity of money can be expressed in terms of the number of weeks of the household's average level of consumption its money balances could finance or, alternatively, in terms of the number of weeks of its average income to which its money balances are equal. For a business enterprise, the real quantity of money it holds can be expressed in terms of the number of weeks of its average purchases, or of its average sales, or of its average expenditures on final productive services (net value added) to which its money balances are equal. For the community as a whole, the real quantity of money can be expressed in terms of the number of weeks of aggregate transactions of the community, or aggregate net output of the community, to which its money balances are equal.

The reciprocal of any of this latter class of measures of the real quantity of money is a velocity of circulation for the corresponding unit or group of units. For example, the ratio of the annual transactions of the community to its stock of money is the 'transactions velocity of circulation of money', since it gives the number of times the stock of money would have to 'turn over' in a year to accomplish all transactions. Similarly, the ratio of annual income to the stock of money is termed 'income velocity'. In every case, the real quantity of money is calculated at the set of prices prevailing at the date to which the calculation refers. These prices are the bridge between the nominal and the real quantity of money.

The quantity theory of money takes for granted, first, that the real quantity rather than the nominal quantity of money is what ultimately matters to holders of money and, second, that in any given circumstances people wish to hold a fairly definite real quantity of money. Starting from a situation in which the nominal quantity that people hold at a particular moment of time happens to correspond at current prices to the real quantity that they wish to hold, suppose that the quantity of money unexpectedly increases so that individuals have larger cash balances than they wish to hold. They will then seek to dispose of what they regard as their excess money balances by paying out a larger sum for the purchase of securities, goods, and services, for the repayment of debts, and as gifts, than they are receiving from the corresponding sources. However, they cannot as a group succeed. One man's spending is another man's receipts. One man can reduce his nominal money balances only by persuading someone else to increase his. The community as a whole cannot in general spend more than it receives; it is playing a game of musical chairs.

The attempt to dispose of excess balances will nonetheless have important effects. If prices and incomes are free to change, the attempt to spend more will raise total spending and receipts, expressed in nominal units, which will lead to a bidding up of prices and perhaps also to an increase in output. If prices are fixed by custom or by government edict, the attempt to spend more will either be matched by an increase in goods and services or produce 'shortages' and 'queues'. These in turn will raise the effective price and are likely sooner or later to force changes in customary or official prices.

The initial excess of nominal balances will therefore tend to be eliminated, even though there is no change in the nominal quantity of money, by either a reduction in the real quantity available to hold through price rises or an increase in the real quantity desired through output increases. And conversely for an initial deficiency of nominal balances.

Changes in prices and nominal income can be produced either by changes in the real balances that people wish to hold or by changes in the nominal balances available for them to hold. Indeed, it is a tautology, summarized in the famous quantity equations, that all changes in nominal income can be attributed to one or the other – just as a change in the price of any good can always be attributed to a change in either demand or supply. The quantity theory is not, however, this tautology. On an analytical level, it has long been an analysis of the factors determining the quantity of money that the community wishes to hold; on an empirical level, it has increasingly become the generalization that changes in desired real balances (in the demand for money) tend to proceed slowly and gradually or to be the result of events set in train by prior changes in supply, whereas, in contrast, substantial changes in the supply of nominal balances can and frequently do occur independently of any changes in demand. The conclusion is that substantial changes in prices or nominal income are almost always the result of changes in the nominal supply of money.

(b) QUANTITY EQUATIONS. Attempts to formulate mathematically the relations just presented verbally date back several centuries (Humphrey, 1984). They consist of creating identities equating a flow of money payments to a flow of exchanges of goods or services. The resulting quantity equations have proved a useful analytical device and have taken different forms as quantity theorists have stressed different variables.

The transactions form of the quantity equation. The most famous version of the quantity equation is doubtless the transactions version formulated by Simon Newcomb (1885) and popularized by Irving Fisher (1911):

$$MV = PT, \qquad (1)$$

or

$$MV + M'V' = PT. \qquad (2)$$

In this version the elementary event is a transaction – an exchange in which one economic actor transfers goods or services or securities to another actor and receives a transfer of money in return. The right-hand side of the equations corresponds to the transfer of goods, services, or securities; the left-hand side, to the matching transfer of money.

Each transfer of goods, services or securities is regarded as the product of a price and quantity; wage per week times number of weeks, price of a good times number of units of the good, dividend per share times number of shares, price per share times number of shares, and so on. The right-hand side of equations (1) and (2) is the aggregate of such payments during some interval, with P a suitably chosen *average* of the prices and T a suitably chosen *aggregate* of the quantities during that interval, so that PT is the total nominal value of the payments during the interval in question. The units of P are dollars (or other monetary unit) per unit of quantity; the units of T are number of unit quantities per period of time. We can convert the equation from an expression applying to an *interval* of time to one applying to a *point* in time by the usual limiting process of letting the interval for which we aggregate payments approach zero, and expressing T not as an aggregate but as a rate of flow. The magnitude T then has the dimension of quantity per unit time; the product of P and T, of dollars (or other monetary unit) per unit time.

T is clearly a rather special index of quantities: it includes service flows (man-hours, dwelling-years, kilowatt-hours) and also physical capital items yielding such flows (houses, electric-generating plants) and securities representing both physical capital items and such intangible capital items as 'goodwill'. Since each capital item or security is treated as if it disappeared from economic circulation once it is transferred, any such item that is transferred more than once in the period in question is implicitly weighted by the number of times it enters into transactions (its 'velocity of circulation', in strict analogy with the 'velocity of circulation' of money). Similarly, P is a rather special price index.

The monetary transfer analysed on the left-hand side of equations (1) and (2) is treated very differently. The money that changes hands is treated as retaining its identity, and all money, whether used in transactions during the time interval in question or not, is explicitly accounted for. Money is treated as a stock, not as a flow or a mixture of a flow and a stock. For a single transaction, the breakdown into M and V is trivial: the cash that is transferred is turned over once, or $V=1$. For all transactions during an interval of time, we can, in principle, classify the existing stock of monetary units according as each monetary unit entered into 0, 1, 2,... transactions – that is, according as the monetary unit 'turned over' 0, 1, 2,... times. The weighted average of these numbers of turnover, weighted by the number of dollars that turned over that number of times, is the conceptual equivalent of V. The dimensions of M are dollars (or other monetary unit); of V, number of turnovers per unit time; so, of the product, dollars per unit time.

Equation (2) differs from equation (1) by dividing payments into two categories: those effected by the transfer of hand-to-hand currency (including coin) and those effected by the transfer of deposits. In equation (2) M stands for the volume of currency and V for the velocity of currency, M' for the volume of deposits, and V' for the velocity of deposits.

One reason for the emphasis on this particular division was the persistent dispute about whether the term *money* should include only currency or deposits as well. Another reason was the direct availability of data on $M'V'$ from bank records of clearings or of debits to deposit accounts. These data make it possible to calculate V' in a way that is not possible for V.

Equations (1) and (2), like the other quantity equations we shall discuss, are intended to be identities – a special application of double-entry bookkeeping, with each transaction simultaneously recorded on both sides of the equation. However, as with the national income identities with which we are all familiar, when the two sides, or the separate elements on the two sides, are estimated from independent sources of data, many differences between them emerge. This statistical defect has been less obvious for the quantity equations than for the national income identities – with their standard entry 'statistical discrepancy' – because of the difficulty of calculating V directly. As a result, V in equation (1) and V and V' in equation (2) have generally been calculated as the numbers having the property that they render the equations correct. These calculated numbers therefore embody the whole of the counterpart to the 'statistical discrepancy'.

Just as the left-hand side of equation (1) can be divided into several components, as in equation (2), so also can the right-hand side. The emphasis on transactions reflected in this version of the quantity equation suggests dividing total transactions into categories of payments for which payment periods or practices differ: for example, into capital transactions, purchases of final goods and services, purchases of intermediate goods, and payments for the use of resources, perhaps separated into wage and salary payments and other payments. The observed value of V might well depend on the distribution of total payments among categories. Alternatively, if the quantity equation is interpreted not as an identity but as a functional relation expressing desired velocity as a function of other variables, the distribution of payments may well be an important set of variables.

The income form of the quantity equation. Despite the large amount of empirical work done on the transactions equations, notably by Irving Fisher (1911, pp. 280–318; 1919, pp. 407–9) and Carl Snyder (1934, pp. 278–91), the ambiguities of the concepts of 'transactions' and the 'general price level' – particularly those arising from the mixture of current and capital transactions – have never been satisfactorily resolved. More recently, national or social accounting has stressed income transactions rather than gross transactions and has explicitly if not wholly satisfactorily dealt with the conceptual and statistical problems involved in distinguishing between changes in prices and changes in quantities. As a result, since at least the work of James Angell (1936), monetary economists have tended to express the quantity equation in terms of income transactions rather than gross transactions. Let Y = nominal income, P = the price index implicit in estimating national income at constant prices, N = the number of persons in the population, y = per capita national income in constant prices, and $y' = Ny$ = national income at constant prices, so that

$$Y = PNy = Py'. \quad (3)$$

Let M represent, as before, the stock of money; but define V as the average number of times per unit time that the money stock is used in making *income* transactions (that is, payment for final productive services or, alternatively, for final goods and services) rather than all transactions. We can then write the quantity equation in income form as

$$MV = PNy = Py'. \quad (4)$$

or, if we desire to distinguish currency from deposit transactions, as

$$MV + M'V' = PNy. \quad (5)$$

Although the symbols P, V, and V' are used both in equations (4) and (5) and in equations (1) and (2), they stand for different concepts in each pair of equations. (In practice, gross national product often replaces national income in calculating velocity even though the logic underlying the equation calls for national income. The reason is the widespread belief that estimates of GNP are subject to less statistical error than estimates of national income.)

In the transactions version of the quantity equation, each intermediate transaction – that is, purchase by one enterprise from another – is included at the total value of the transaction, so that the value of wheat, for example, is included once when it is sold by the farmer to the mill, a second time when the mill sells flour to the baker, a third time when the baker sells bread to the grocer, a fourth time when the grocer sells bread to the consumer. In the income version, only the net value added by each of these transactions is included. To put it differently, in the transactions version, the elementary event is an isolated exchange of a physical item for money – an actual, clearly observable event. In the income version, the elementary event is a hypothetical event that can be inferred but is not directly observable. It is a complete series of transactions involving the exchange of productive services for final goods, via a sequence of money payments, with all the intermediate transactions in this income circuit netted out. The total value of all transactions is therefore a multiple of the value of income transactions only.

For a given flow of productive services or, alternatively, of final products (two of the multiple faces of income), the volume of transactions will be affected by vertical integration or disintegration of enterprises, which reduces or increases the number of transactions involved in a single income circuit, and by technological changes that lengthen or shorten the process of transforming productive services into final products. The volume of income will not be thus affected.

Similarly, the transactions version includes the purchase of an existing asset – a house or a piece of land or a share of equity stock – precisely on a par with an intermediate or final transaction. The income version excludes such transactions completely.

Are these differences an advantage or disadvantage of the income version? That clearly depends on what it is that determines the amount of money people want to hold. Do changes of the kind considered in the preceding paragraphs, changes that alter the ratio of intermediate and capital transactions to income, also alter in the same direction and by the same proportion the amount of money people want to hold? Or do they tend to leave this amount unaltered? Or do they have a more complex effect?

The transactions and income versions of the quantity theory involve very different conceptions of the role of money. For the transactions version, the most important thing about money is that it is transferred. For the income version, the most important thing is that it is held. This difference is even more obvious from the Cambridge cash-balance version of the quantity equation (Pigou, 1917). Indeed, the income version can perhaps best be regarded as a way station between the Fisher and the Cambridge version.

Cambridge cash-balance approach. The essential feature of a money economy is that an individual who has something to exchange need not seek out the double coincidence – someone who both wants what he has and offers in exchange what he wants. He need only find someone who wants what he has, sell it to him for general purchasing power, and then find someone who has what he wants and buy it with general purchasing power.

For the act of purchase to be separated from the act of sale, there must be something that everybody will accept in exchange as 'general purchasing power' – this aspect of money is emphasized in the transactions approach. But also there must be something that can serve as a temporary abode of purchasing power in the interim between sale and purchase. This aspect of money is emphasized in the cash-balance approach.

How much money will people or enterprises want to hold on the average as a temporary abode of purchasing power? As a first approximation, it has generally been supposed that the amount bears some relation to income, on the assumption that income affects the volume of potential purchases for which the individual or enterprise wishes to hold cash balances. We can therefore write

$$M = kPNy = kPy', \tag{6}$$

where M, N, P, y, and y' are defined as in equation (4) and k is the ratio of money stock to income – either the observed ratio so calculated as to make equation (6) an identity or the 'desired' ratio so that M is the 'desired' amount of money, which need not be equal to the actual amount. In either case, k is numerically equal to the reciprocal of the V in equation (4), the V being interpreted in one case as measured velocity and in the other as desired velocity.

Although equation (6) is simply a mathematical transformation of equation (4), it brings out sharply the difference between the aspect of money stressed by the transactions approach and that stressed by the cash-balance approach. This difference makes different definitions of money seem natural and leads to placing emphasis on different variables and analytical techniques.

The transactions approach makes it natural to define money in terms of whatever serves as the medium of exchange in discharging obligations. The cash-balance approach makes it seem entirely appropriate to include in addition such temporary abodes of purchasing power as demand and time deposits not transferable by check, although it clearly does not require their inclusion (Friedman and Schwartz, 1970, ch. 3).

Similarly, the transactions approach leads to emphasis on the mechanical aspect of the payments process: payments practices, financial and economic arrangements for effecting transactions, the speed of communication and transportation, and so on (Baumol, 1952; Tobin, 1956; Miller and Orr, 1966, 1968). The cash-balance approach, on the other hand, leads to emphasis on variables affecting the usefulness of money as an asset: the costs and returns from holding money instead of other assets, the uncertainty of the future, and so on (Friedman, 1956; Tobin, 1958).

Of course, neither approach enforces the exclusion of the variables stressed by the other. Portfolio considerations enter into the costs of effecting transactions and hence affect the most efficient payment arrangements; mechanical considerations enter into the returns from holding cash and hence affect the usefulness of cash in a portfolio.

Finally, with regard to analytical techniques, the cash-balance approach fits in much more readily with the general Marshallian demand-supply apparatus than does the transactions approach. Equation (6) can be regarded as a demand function for money, with P, N, and y on the right-hand side being three of the variables on which the quantity of money demanded depends and k symbolizing all the other variables, so that k is to be regarded not as a numerical constant but as itself a function of still other variables. For completion, the analysis requires another equation showing the supply of money as a function of these and other variables. The price level or the level of nominal income is then the resultant of the interaction of the demand and supply functions.

Levels versus rates of change. The several versions of the quantity equations have all been stated in terms of the levels of the variables involved. For the analysis of monetary change it is often more useful to express them in terms of rates of change. For example, take the logarithm of both sides of equation (4) and differentiate with respect to time. The result is

$$\frac{1}{M}\frac{dM}{dt}+\frac{1}{V}\frac{dV}{dt}=\frac{1}{P}\frac{dP}{dt}+\frac{1}{y'}\frac{dy'}{dt} \tag{7}$$

or, in simpler notation,

$$g_M+g_V=g_p+g_{y'}=g_{Y'}, \tag{8}$$

where g stands for the percentage rate of change (continuously compounded) of the variable denoted by its subscript. The same equation is implied by equation (6), with g_V replaced by $-g_k$.

The rate of change equations serve two very different purposes. First, they make explicit an important difference between a once-for-all change in the level of the quantity of money and a change in the rate of change of the quantity of money. The former is equivalent simply to a change of units – to substituting cents for dollars or pence for pounds – and hence, as is implicit in equations (4) and (6), would not be presumed to have any effect on real quantities, on neither V (nor k) nor y', but simply an offsetting effect on the price level, P. A change in the rate of change of money is a very different thing. It will tend, according to equations (7) and (8), to be accompanied by a change in the rate of inflation (g_P) which, as pointed out in section *d* below, affects the cost of holding money, and hence the desired real quantity of money. Such a change will therefore affect real quantities, V and g_V, y' and $g_{y'}$, as well as nominal and real interest rates.

The second purpose served by the rate of change equations is to make explicit the role of time, and thereby to facilitate the study of the effect of monetary change on the temporal pattern of response of the several variables involved. In recent decades, economists have devoted increasing attention to the short-term pattern of economic change, which has enhanced the importance of the rate of change versions of the quantity equations.

(c) THE SUPPLY OF MONEY. The quantity theory in its cash-balance version suggests organizing an analysis of monetary phenomena in terms of (1) the conditions determining supply (this section); (2) the conditions determining demand (section d below); and (3) the reconciliation of demand with supply (section e below).

The factors determining the nominal supply of money available to be held depend critically on the monetary system. For systems like those that have prevailed in most major countries during the past two centuries, they can usefully be analysed under three main headings termed the proximate determinants of the quantity of money: (1) the amount of high-powered money – specie plus notes or deposit liabilities issued by the monetary authorities and used either as currency or as reserves by banks; (2) the ratio of bank deposits to bank holdings of high-powered money; and (3) the ratio of the public's deposits to its currency holdings (Friedman and Schwartz, 1963b, pp. 776–98; Cagan, 1965; Burger, 1971; Black, 1975).

It is an identity that

$$M=H\cdot\frac{\frac{D}{R}\left(1+\frac{D}{C}\right)}{\frac{D}{R}+\frac{D}{C}}, \tag{9}$$

where H = high-powered money; D = deposits; R = bank reserves; C = currency in the hands of the public so that (D/R) is the deposit–reserve ratio; and (D/C) is the deposit–currency ratio. The fraction on the right-hand side of (9), i.e., the ratio of M to H, is termed the money multiplier, often a convenient summary of the effect of the two deposit ratios. The determinants are called proximate because their values are in turn determined by much more basic variables. Moreover, the same labels can refer to very different contents.

High-powered money is the clearest example. Until some time in the 18th or 19th century, the exact date varying from country to country, it consisted only of specie or its equivalent: gold, or silver, or cowrie shells, or any of a wide variety of commodities. Thereafter, until 1971, with some significant if temporary exceptions, it consisted of a mixture of specie and of government notes or deposit liabilities. The government notes and liabilities generally were themselves promises to pay specified amounts of specie on demand, though this promise weakened after World War I, when many countries promised to pay either specie or foreign currency. During the Bretton Woods periods after World War II, only the USA was obligated to pay gold, and only to foreign monetary agencies, not to individuals or other non-governmental entities; other countries obligated themselves to pay dollars.

Since 1971, the situation has been radically different. In every major country, high-powered money consists solely of fiat money – pieces of paper issued by the government and inscribed with the legend 'one dollar' or 'one pound' and the message 'legal tender for all debts public and private'; or book entries, labelled deposits, consisting of promises to pay such pieces of paper. Such a worldwide fiat (or irredeemable paper) standard has no precedent in history. The 'gold' that central banks still record as an asset on their books is simply the grin of a Cheshire cat that has disappeared.

Under an international commodity standard, the total quantity of high-powered money in any one country – so long as it remains on the standard – is determined by the balance of payments. The division of high-powered money between physical specie and the fiduciary component of government-issued promises to pay is determined by the policies of the monetary authorities. For the world as a whole, the total quantity of high-powered money is determined both by the policies of the various monetary authorities and the physical conditions of supply of specie. The latter provide a physical anchor for the quantity of money and hence ultimately for the price level.

Under the current international fiat standard, the quantity of high-powered money is determined solely by the monetary authorities, consisting in most countries of a central bank plus the fiscal authorities. What happens to the quantity of high-powered money depends on their objectives, on the institutional and political arrangements under which they operate, and the operating procedures they adopt. These are likely to vary considerably from country to country. Some countries (e.g., Hong Kong, Panama) have chosen to link their currencies rigidly to some other currency by pegging the exchange rate. For them, the amount of high-powered money is determined in the same way as under an international commodity standard – by the balance of payments.

The current system is so new that it must be regarded as in a state of transition. Some substitute is almost sure to emerge to replace the supply of specie as a long-term anchor for the price level, but it is not yet clear what that substitute will be (see section 5 below).

The deposit–reserve ratio is determined by the banking system subject to any requirements that are imposed by law or the monetary authorities. In addition to any such requirements, it depends on such factors as the risk of calls for conversion of bank deposits to high-powered money; the cost of acquiring additional high-powered money in case of need; and the returns from loans and investments, that is, the structure of interest rates.

The deposit–currency ratio is determined by the public. It depends on the relative usefulness to holders of money of deposits and currency and the relative cost of holding the one or the other. The relative cost in turn depends on the rates of interest received on deposits, which may be subject to controls imposed by law or the monetary authorities.

These factors determine the *nominal*, but not the *real*, quantity of money. The real quantity of money is determined by the interaction between the *nominal* quantity supplied and the *real* quantity demanded. In the process, changes in demand for real balances have feedback effects on the variables determining the nominal quantity supplied, and changes in nominal supply have feedback effects on the variables determining the real quantity demanded. Quantity theorists have generally concluded that these feedback effects are relatively minor, so that the *nominal* supply can generally be regarded as determined by a set of variables distinct from those that affect the *real* quantity demanded. In this sense, the nominal quantity can be regarded as determined primarily by supply, the real quantity, primarily by demand.

Instead of expressing the nominal supply in terms of the identity (9), it can also be expressed as a function of the variables that are regarded as affecting H, D/R, and D/C, such as the rate of inflation, interest rates, nominal income, the extent of uncertainty, perhaps also the variables that are regarded as determining the decisions of the monetary authorities. Such a supply function is frequently written as

$$M^S = h(R, Y, \ldots), \tag{10}$$

where R is an interest rate or set of interest rates, Y is nominal income, and the dots stand for other variables that are regarded as relevant.

(d) THE DEMAND FOR MONEY. The cash-balance version of the quantity theory, by stressing the role of money as an asset, suggests treating the demand for money as part of capital or wealth theory, concerned with the composition of the balance sheet or portfolio of assets.

From this point of view, it is important to distinguish between ultimate wealth holders, to whom money is one form in which they choose to hold their wealth, and enterprises, to whom money is a producer's good like machinery or inventories (Friedman, 1956; Laidler, 1985; Friedman and Schwartz, 1982).

Demand by ultimate wealth holders. For ultimate wealth holders the demand for money, in real terms, may be expected to be a function primarily of the following variables:

1. *Total wealth.* This is the analogue of the budget constraint in the usual theory of consumer choice. It is the total that must be divided among various forms of assets. In practice, estimates of total wealth are seldom available. Instead, income may serve as an index of wealth. However, it should be recognized that income as measured by statisticians may be a defective index of wealth because it is subject to erratic year-to-year fluctuations, and a longer-term concept, like the concept of permanent income developed in connection with the theory of consumption, may be more useful (Friedman, 1957, 1959).

The emphasis on income as a surrogate for wealth, rather than as a measure of the 'work' to be done by money, is perhaps the basic conceptual difference between the more recent analyses of the demand for money and the earlier versions of the quantity theory.

2. *The division of wealth between human and non-human forms.* The major asset of most wealth holders is personal earning capacity. However, the conversion of human into non-human wealth or the reverse is subject to narrow limits because of institutional constraints. It can be done by using current earnings to purchase non-human wealth or by using non-human wealth to finance the acquisition of skills, but not by purchase or sale of human wealth and to only a limited extent by borrowing on the collateral of earning power. Hence, the fraction of total wealth that is in the form of non-human wealth may be an additional important variable.

3. *The expected rates of return on money and other assets.* These rates of return are the counterparts to the prices of a commodity and its substitutes and complements in the usual theory of consumer demand. The nominal rate of return on money may be zero, as it generally is on currency, or negative, as it sometimes is on demand deposits subject to net service charges, or positive, as it sometimes is on demand deposits on which interest is paid and generally is on time deposits. The nominal rate of return on other assets consists of two parts: first, any currently paid yield, such as interest on bonds, dividends on equities, or cost, such as storage costs on physical assets, and, second, a change in the nominal price of the asset. The second part is especially important under conditions of inflation or deflation.

4. *Other variables determining the utility attached to the services rendered by money relative to those rendered by other assets – in Keynesian terminology, determining the value attached to liquidity proper.* One such variable may be one already considered – namely, real wealth or income, since the services rendered by money may, in principle, be regarded by wealth holders as a 'necessity', like bread, the consumption of which increases less than in proportion to any increase in income, or as a 'luxury', like recreation, the consumption of which increases more than in proportion.

Another variable that is important empirically is the degree of economic stability expected to prevail, since instability enhances the value wealth-holders attach to liquidity. This variable has proved difficult to express quantitatively although qualitative information often indicates the direction of change. For example, the outbreak of war clearly produces expectations of greater instability. That is one reason why a notable increase in real balances – that is, a notable decline in velocity – often accompanies the outbreak of war. Such a decline in velocity produced an initial *decline* in sensitive prices at the outset of both World War I and World War II – not the rise that later inflation would have justified.

The rate of inflation enters under item 3 as a factor affecting the cost of holding various assets, particularly currency. The variability of inflation enters here, as a major factor affecting the usefulness of money balances. Empirically, variability of inflation tends to increase with the level of inflation, reinforcing the negative effect of higher inflation on the quantity of money demanded.

Still another relevant variable may be the volume of trading in existing capital goods by ultimate wealth holders. The higher the turnover of capital assets, the larger the fraction of total assets people may find it useful to hold as cash. This variable corresponds to the class of transactions omitted in going from the transactions version of the quantity equation to the income version.

We can express this analysis in terms of the following

demand function for money for an individual wealth holder:

$$M^D = P \cdot f(y, w; R_M^*, R_B^*, R_E^*; u), \qquad (11)$$

where M, P, and y have the same meaning as in equation (6) except that they relate to a single wealth-holder (for whom $y = y'$); w is the fraction of wealth in non-human form (or, alternatively, the fraction of income derived from property); an asterisk denotes an expected value, so R_M^* is the expected nominal rate of return on money; R_B^* is the expected nominal rate of return on fixed-value securities, including expected changes in their prices; R_E^* is the expected nominal rate of return on physical assets, including expected changes in their prices; and u is a portmanteau symbol standing for other variables affecting the utility attached to the services of money. Though the expected rate of inflation is not explicit in equation (11), it is implicit because it affects the expected nominal returns on the various classes of assets, and is sometimes used as a proxy for R_E^*. For some purposes it may be important to classify assets still more finely – for example, to distinguish currency from deposits, long-term from short-term fixed-value securities, risky from relatively safe equities, and one kind of physical assets from another.

Furthermore, the several rates of return are not independent. Arbitrage tends to eliminate differences among them that do not correspond to differences in perceived risk or other nonpecuniary characteristics of the assets, such as liquidity. In particular, as Irving Fisher pointed out in 1896, arbitrage between real and nominal assets introduces an allowance for anticipated inflation into the nominal interest rate (Fisher, 1896; Friedman, 1956).

The usual problems of aggregation arise in passing from equation (11) to a corresponding equation for the economy as a whole – in particular, from the possibility that the amount of money demanded may depend on the distribution among individuals of such variables as y and w and not merely on their aggregate or average value. If we neglect these distributional effects, equation (11) can be regarded as applying to the community as a whole, with M and y referring to per capita money holdings and per capita real income, respectively, and w to the fraction of aggregate wealth in non-human form.

Although the mathematical equation may be the same, its significance is very different for the individual wealth-holder and the community as a whole. For the individual, all the variables in the equation other than his own income and the disposition of his portfolio are outside his control. He takes them, as well as the structure of monetary institutions, as given, and adjusts his nominal balances accordingly. For the community as a whole, the situation is very different. In general, the nominal quantity of money available to be held is fixed and what adjusts are the variables on the right-hand side of the equation, including an implicit underlying variable, the structure of monetary institutions, which, in the longer run, at least, adjusts itself to the tastes and preferences of the holders of money. A dramatic example is provided by the restructuring of the financial system in the US in the 1970s and 1980s.

In practice, the major problems that arise in applying equation (11) are the precise definitions of y and w, the estimation of *expected* rates of return as contrasted with actual rates of return, and the quantitative specification of the variables designated by u.

Demand for business enterprises. Business enterprises are not subject to a constraint comparable to that imposed by the total wealth of the ultimate wealth-holder. They can determine the total amount of capital embodied in productive assets, including money, to maximize returns, since they can acquire additional capital through the capital market.

A similar variable defining the 'scale' of the enterprise may, however, be relevant as an index of the productive value of different quantities of money to the enterprise. Lack of data has meant that much less empirical work has been done on the business demand for money than on an aggregate demand curve encompassing both ultimate wealth-holders and business enterprises. As a result, there are as yet only faint indications about the best variable to use: whether total transactions, net value added, net income, total capital in nonmoney form, or net worth.

The division of wealth between human and non-human form has no special relevance to business enterprises, since they are likely to buy the services of both forms on the market.

Rates of return on money and on alternative assets are, of course, highly relevant to business enterprises. These rates determine the net cost of holding money balances. However, the particular rates that are relevant may differ from those that are relevant for ultimate wealth-holders. For example, the rates banks charge on loans are of minor importance for wealth-holders yet may be extremely important for businesses, since bank loans may be a way in which they can acquire the capital embodied in money balances.

The counterpart for business enterprises of the variable u in equation (11) is the set of variables other than scale affecting the productivity of money balances. At least one subset of such variables – namely, expectations about economic stability and the variability of inflation – is likely to be common to business enterprises and ultimate wealth-holders.

With these interpretations of the variables, equation (11), with w excluded, can be regarded as symbolizing the business demand for money and, as it stands, symbolizing aggregate demand for money, although with even more serious qualifications about the ambiguities introduced by aggregation.

Buffer stock effects. In serving its basic function as a temporary abode of purchasing power, cash balances necessarily fluctuate, absorbing temporary discrepancies between the purchases and sales they mediate.

Though always recognized, this 'buffer stock' role of money has seldom been explicitly modelled. Recently, more explicit attention has been paid to the buffer stock notion in an attempt to explain anomalies that have arisen in econometric estimates of the short-run demand for money (Judd and Scadding, 1982; Laidler, 1984; Knoester, 1984).

(e) THE RECONCILIATION OF DEMAND WITH SUPPLY. Multiply equation (11) by N to convert it from a per capita to an aggregate demand function, and equate it to equation (10), omitting for simplicity the asterisks designating expected values, and letting R stand for a vector of interest rates:

$$M^S = h(R, Y, \ldots) = P \cdot N \cdot f(y, w, R, g_P, u). \qquad (12)$$

The result is quantity equation (6) in an expanded form. In principle, a change in any of the underlying variables that produces a change in M^S and disturbs a pre-existing equilibrium can produce offsetting changes in any of the other variables. In practice, as already noted earlier, the initial impact is likely to be on y and R, the ultimate impact predominantly on P.

A frequent criticism of the quantity theory is that its proponents do not specify the transmission mechanism between a change in M^S and the offsetting changes in other variables, that they rely on a black box connecting the input –

the nominal quantity of money – and the output – effects on prices and quantities.

This criticism is not justified insofar as it implies that the transmission mechanism for the quantity equation is fundamentally different from that for a demand–supply analysis of a particular product – shoes, or copper, or haircuts. In both cases the demand function for the community as a whole is the sum of demand functions for individual consumer or producer units, and the separate demand functions are determined by the tastes and opportunities of the units. In both cases, the supply function depends on production possibilities, institutional arrangements for organizing production, and the conditions of supply of resources. In both cases a shift in supply or in demand introduces a discrepancy between the amounts demanded and supplied *at the pre-existing price*. In both cases any discrepancy can be eliminated only by either a price change or some alternative rationing mechanism, explicit or implicit.

Two features of the demand–supply adjustment for money have concealed this parallelism. One is that demand–supply analysis for particular products typically deals with flows – number of pairs of shoes or number of haircuts per year – whereas the quantity equations deal with the stock of money at a point in time. In this respect the correct analogy is with the demand for, say, land, which, like money, derives its value from the flow of services it renders but has a purchase price and not merely a rental value. The second is the widespread tendency to confuse 'money' and 'credit', which has produced misunderstanding about the relevant price variable. The 'price' of money is the quantity of goods and services that must be given up to acquire a unit of money – the inverse of the price level. This is the price that is analogous to the price of land or of copper or of haircuts. The 'price' of money is not the interest rate, which is the 'price' of credit. The interest rate connects stocks with flows – the rental value of land with the price of land, the value of the service flow from a unit of money with the price of money. Of course, the interest rate may affect the quantity of money demanded – just as it may affect the quantity of land demanded – but so may a host of other variables.

The interest rate has received special attention in monetary analysis because, without quite realizing it, fractional reserve banks have created part of the stock of money in the course of serving as an intermediary between borrowers and lenders. Hence changes in the quantity of money have frequently occurred through the credit markets, in the process producing important transitory effects on interest rates.

On a more sophisticated level, the criticism about the transmission mechanism applies equally to money and to other goods and services. In all cases it is desirable to go beyond equality of demand and supply as defining a stationary equilibrium position and examine the variables that affect the quantities demanded and supplied and the dynamic temporal process whereby actual or potential discrepancies are eliminated. Examination of the variables affecting demand and supply has been carried farther for money than for most other goods or services. But for both, there is as yet no satisfactory and widely accepted description, in precise quantifiable terms, of the dynamic temporal process of adjustment. Much research has been devoted to this question in recent decades; yet it remains a challenging subject for research. (For surveys of some of the literature, see Laidler, 1985; Judd and Scadding, 1982.)

(f) FIRST-ROUND EFFECTS. Another frequent criticism of the quantity equations is that they neglect any effect on the outcome of the source of change in the quantity of money. In Tobin's words, the question is whether 'the genesis of new money makes a difference', in particular, whether 'an increase in the quantity of money has the same effect whether it is issued to purchase goods or to purchase bonds' (1974, p. 87).

Or, as John Stuart Mill put a very similar view in 1844, 'The issues of a *Government* paper, even when not permanent, will raise prices; because Governments usually issue their paper in purchases for consumption. If issued to pay off a portion of the national debt, we believe they would have no effect' (1844, p. 589).

Tobin and Mill are right that the way the quantity of money is increased affects the outcome in some measure or other. If one group of individuals receives the money on the first round, they will likely use it for different purposes than another group of individuals. If the newly printed money is spent on the first round for goods and services, it adds directly at that point to the demand for such goods and services, whereas if it is spent on purchasing debt, or simply held temporarily as a buffer stock, it has no immediate effect on the demand for goods and services. Such effects come later as the initial recipients of the 'new' money dispose of it. However, as the 'new' money spreads through the economy, any first-round effects tend to be dissipated. The 'new' money is merged with the old and is distributed in much the same way.

One way to characterize the Keynesian approach (see below) is that it gives almost exclusive importance to the first-round effect by putting primary emphasis on flows of spending rather than on stocks of assets. Similarly, one way to characterize the quantity-theory approach is to say that it gives almost no importance to first-round effects.

The empirical question is how important the first-round effects are compared with the ultimate effects. Theory cannot answer that question. The answer depends on how different are the reactions of the recipients of cash via alternative routes, on how rapidly a larger money stock is distributed through the economy, on how long it stays at each point in the economy, on how much the demand for money depends on the structure of government liabilities, and so on. Casual empiricism yields no decisive answer. Maybe the first-round effect is so strong that it dominates later effects; maybe it is highly transitory.

Despite repeated assertions by various authors that the first-round effect is significant, none, so far as I know, has presented any systematic empirical evidence to support that assertion. The apparently similar response of spending to changes in the quantity of money at widely separated dates in different countries and under diverse monetary systems establishes something of a presumption that the first-round effect is not highly significant. This presumption is also supported by several empirical studies designed to test the importance of the first-round effect (Cagan, 1972).

(g) THE INTERNATIONAL TRANSMISSION MECHANISM. From its very earliest days, the quantity theory was intimately connected with the analysis of the adjustment mechanism in international trade. A commodity standard, in which money is specie or its equivalent, was taken as the norm. Under such a standard, the supply of money in any one country is determined by the links between that country and other countries that use the same commodity as money. Under such a standard, the same theory explains links among money, prices, and nominal income in various parts of a single country – money, prices, and nominal income in Illinois and money, prices, and nominal income in the rest of the United States –

and the corresponding links among various countries. The differences between interregional adjustment and international adjustment are empirical: greater mobility of people, goods, and capital among regions than among countries, and hence more rapid adjustment.

According to the specie-flow mechanism developed by Hume and elaborated by Henry Thornton, David Ricardo and their successors, 'too' high a money stock in country A tends to make prices in A high relative to prices in the rest of the world, encouraging imports and discouraging exports. The resulting deficit in the balance of trade is financed by shipment of specie, which reduces the quantity of money in country A and increases it in the rest of the world. These changes in the quantity of money tend to lower prices in country A and raise them in the rest of the world, correcting the original disequilibrium. The process continues until price levels in all countries are at a level at which balances of payments are in equilibrium (which may be consistent with a continuing movement of specie, for example, from gold- or silver-producing countries to non-gold- or silver-producing countries, or between countries growing at different secular rates).

Another strand of the classical analysis has recently been revived under the title 'the monetary theory of the balance of payments'. The specie-flow mechanism implicitly assumes that prices adjust only in response to changes in the quantity of money produced by specie flows. However, if markets are efficient and transportation costs are neglected, there can be only a single price expressed in a common currency for goods traded internationally. Speculation tends to assure this result. Internally, competition between traded and nontraded goods tends to keep their relative price in line with relative costs. If these adjustments are rapid, 'the law of one price' holds among countries. If the money stock is not distributed among countries in such a way as to be consistent with the equilibrium prices, excess demands and supplies of money will lead to specie flows. Domestic nominal demand in a country with 'too' high a quantity of money will exceed the value of domestic output and the excess will be met by imports, producing a balance of payments deficit financed by the export of specie; and conversely in a country with too 'low' a quantity of money. Specie flows are still the adjusting mechanism, but they are produced by differences between demand for output in nominal terms and the supply of output at world prices rather than by discrepancies in prices. Putative rather than actual price differences are the spur to adjustment. This description is highly oversimplified, primarily because it omits the important role assigned to short- and long-term capital flows by all theorists – those who stress the specie-flow mechanism and even more those who stress the single-price mechanism (Frenkel, 1976; Frenkel and Johnson, 1976).

In practice, few countries have had pure commodity standards. Most have had a mixture of commodity and fiduciary standards. Changes in the fiduciary component of the stock of money can replace specie flows as a means of adjusting the quantity of money.

The situation is still different for countries that do not share a unified currency, that is, a currency in which only the name assigned to a unit of currency differs among countries. Changes in the rates of exchange between national currencies then serve to keep prices in various countries in the appropriate relation when expressed in a common currency. Exchange rate adjustments replace specie flows or changes in the quantity of domestically created money. And exchange rate changes too may be produced by actual or putative price differences or by short- or long-term capital flows. Moreover, especially during the Bretton Woods period (1945–71), but more recently as well, governments have often tried to avoid changes in exchange rates by seeking adjustment through subsidies to exports, obstacles to imports, and direct controls over foreign exchange transactions. These measures involved either implicit or explicit multiple rate systems and were accompanied by government borrowing to finance balance-of-payments deficits, or governmental lending to offset surpluses. They sometimes led to severe financial crises and major exchange rate adjustments – one reason the Bretton Woods system finally broke down in 1971. Since then, exchange rates have supposedly been free to float and to be determined in private markets. In practice, however, governments still intervene in an attempt to affect the exchange rates of their currencies, either directly by buying or selling their currency on the market, or indirectly, by adopting monetary or fiscal or trade policies designed to alter the market exchange rate. However, most governments no longer announce fixed parities for their currencies.

2 KEYNESIAN CHALLENGE TO THE QUANTITY THEORY

The depression of the 1930s produced a wave of scepticism about the relevance and validity of the quantity theory of money. The central banks of the world – the Federal Reserve in the forefront – proclaimed that, despite the teachings of the quantity theory, 'easy money' was proving to be ineffective in stemming the depression. They pointed to the low level of short-term interest rates as evidence of how 'easy' monetary policy was. Their claims seemed credible not only because of the confusion between 'lowness of interest' and 'plenty of money' pointed out by Hume but also because of the absence of readily available evidence on what was happening to the quantity of money. Most observers at the time did not know, as we do now, that the Federal Reserve permitted the quantity of money in the United States to decline by one-third between 1929 and 1933, and hence that the accompanying contraction in economic activity and deflation of prices was entirely consistent with the quantity theory. Monetary policy was incredibly 'tight' not 'easy'.

The scepticism about the quantity theory was further heightened by the publication of John Maynard Keynes's *The General Theory of Employment, Interest and Money* (Keynes, 1936) which offered an alternative interpretation of economic fluctuations in general and the depression in particular. Keynes emphasized spending on investment and the stability of the consumption function rather than the stock of money and the stability of the demand function for money. He relegated the forces embodied in the quantity theory to a minor role, and treated fiscal rather than monetary policy as the chief instrument for influencing the course of events. Received wisdom both inside and outside the economics profession became 'money does not matter'.

Keynes did not deny the validity of the quantity equation, in any of its forms – after all, he had been a major contributor to the quantity theory (Keynes, 1923). What he did was something very different. He argued that the demand for money, which he termed the liquidity-preference function, had a special form such that *under conditions of underemployment* the V in equation (4) and the k in equation (6) would be highly unstable and would passively adapt to whatever changes independently occurred in money income or the stock of money. Under such conditions, these equations, though entirely valid, were largely useless for policy or prediction. Moreover, he regarded such conditions as prevailing much, if not most of the time.

That possibility rested on two other key propositions. First, that, contrary to the teachings of classical and neoclassical economists, the *long-run equilibrium* position of an economy need not be characterized by 'full employment' of resources even if all prices are flexible. In his view, unemployment could be a deep-seated characteristic of an economy rather than simply a reflection of price and wage rigidity or transitory disturbances. This proposition has played an important role in promoting the acceptance of Keynesianism, especially by non-economists, even though, by now, it is widely accepted that, as a *theoretical* matter, the proposition is false. Keynes's error consisted in neglecting the role of wealth in the consumption function. There is no fundamental 'flaw in the price system' that makes persistent structural unemployment a possible or probable natural outcome of a fully operative market system (Haberler, 1941, pp. 242, 389, 403, 491–503; Pigou, 1947; Tobin, 1947; Patinkin, 1948; Johnson, 1961). The concept of 'underemployment equilibrium' has been replaced by the concept of a 'natural rate of unemployment' (see section 3 below).

Keynes's final key proposition was that, as an *empirical* matter, prices, especially wages, can be regarded as rigid – an institutional datum – for *short-run economic fluctuations*; in which case, the distinction between real and nominal magnitudes that is at the heart of the quantity theory is irrelevant for such fluctuations. This proposition, unlike the other two, did not conflict with the teachings of the quantity theory. Classical and neoclassical economists had long recognized that price and wage rigidity existed and contributed to unemployment during cyclical contractions, and to labour scarcity during cyclical booms. But to them, wage rigidity was a defect of the market; to Keynes, it was a rational response to the possibility of underemployment equilibrium (Keynes, 1936, pp. 269–71).

In his analysis of the demand for money (i.e., the form of equation (6) or (11)), Keynes treated the stock of money as if it were divided into two parts, one part, M_1, 'held to satisfy the transactions- and precautionary-motives', the other, M_2, 'held to satisfy the speculative-motive' (Keynes, 1936, p. 199). He regarded M_1 as a roughly constant fraction of income. He regarded the demand for M_2 as arising from '*uncertainty* as to the future course of the rate of interest' (Keynes, 1936, p. 168) and the amount demanded as depending on the relation between current rates of interest and the rates of interest expected to prevail in the future. Keynes, of course, recognized the existence of a whole complex of interest rates. However, for simplicity, he spoke in terms of 'the rate of interest', usually meaning by that the rate on long-term securities that were fixed in nominal value and that involved minimal risks of default – for example, government bonds. In a 'given state of expectations', the higher the current rate of interest, the lower would be the (real) amount of money that people would want to hold for speculative motives for two reasons: first, the greater would be the cost in terms of current earnings sacrificed by holding money instead of securities, and, second, the more likely it would be that interest rates would fall, and hence bond prices rise, and so the greater would be the cost in terms of capital gains sacrificed by holding money instead of securities.

To formalize Keynes's analysis in terms of the symbols we have used so far, we can write his demand (liquidity-preference) function as

$$M/P = M_1/P + M_2/P = k_1 y' + f(R - R^*, R^*) \quad (13)$$

where R is the current rate of interest, R^* is the rate of interest expected to prevail, and k_1, the analogue to the inverse of the income velocity of circulation of money, is treated as determined by payment practices and hence as a constant at least in the short run. Later writers in this tradition have argued that k_1 too should be regarded as a function of interest rates (Baumol, 1952; Tobin, 1956).

Although expectations are given great prominence in developing the liquidity function expressing the demand for M_2, Keynes and his followers generally did not explicitly introduce an expected interest rate into that function as is done in equation (13). For the most part, in practice, they treated the amount of M_2 demanded as a function simply of the current interest rate, the emphasis on expectations serving only as a reason for attributing instability to the liquidity function. Moreover, for the most part, they omitted P (and replaced y' by Y) because of their assumption that prices were rigid.

Except for somewhat different language, the analysis up to this point differs from that of earlier quantity theorists, such as Fisher, only by its subtle analysis of the role of expectations about future interest rates, its greater emphasis on current interest rates, and its narrower restriction of the variables explicitly considered as affecting the amount of money demanded.

Keynes's special twist concerned the empirical form of the liquidity-preference function at the low interest rates that he believed would prevail under conditions of underemployment equilibrium. Let the interest rate fall sufficiently low, he argued, and money and bonds would become perfect substitutes for one another; liquidity preference, as he put it, would become absolute. The liquidity-preference function, expressing the quantity of M_2 demanded as a function of the rate of interest, would become horizontal at some low but finite rate of interest. Under such circumstances, an increase in the quantity of money by whatever means would lead holders of money to seek to convert their additional cash balances into bonds, which would tend to lower the rate of interest on bonds. Even the slightest lowering would lead speculators with firm expectations to absorb the additional money balances by selling any bonds demanded by the initial holders of the additional money. The result would simply be that the community as a whole would hold the increased quantity of money without any change in the interest rate; k would be higher and V lower. Conversely, a decrease in the quantity of money would lead holders of bonds to seek to restore their money balances by selling bonds, but this would tend to raise the rate of interest, and even the slightest rise would induce the speculators to absorb the bonds offered.

Or, again, suppose nominal income increases or decreases for whatever reason. That will require an increase or decrease in M_1, which can come out of or be transferred to M_2 without any further effects. The conclusion is that, *under circumstances of absolute liquidity preference*, income can change without a change in M and M can change without a change in income. The holders of money are in metastable equilibrium, like a tumbler on its side on a flat surface; they will be satisfied with whatever the quantity of money happens to be.

Keynes regarded absolute liquidity preference as a strictly 'limiting case' of which, though it 'might become practically important in future', he knew 'of no example ... hitherto' (1936, p. 207). However, he treated velocity as if in practice its behaviour frequently approximated that which would prevail in this limiting case.

Keynes's disciples went much farther than Keynes himself. They were readier than he was to accept absolute liquidity preference as the actual state of affairs. More important, many argued that when liquidity preference was not absolute, changes in the quantity of money would affect only the interest rate on bonds and that changes in this interest rate in turn would have little further effect. They argued that both consumption expenditures and investment expenditures were nearly completely insensitive to changes in interest rates, so that a change in M would merely be offset by an opposite and compensatory change in V (or a change in the same direction in k), leaving P and y almost completely unaffected. In essence their argument consists in asserting that only paper securities are substitutes for money balances – that real assets never are (see Hansen, 1957, p. 50; Tobin, 1961).

The apparent success during the 1950s and 1960s of governments committed to a Keynesian full-employment policy in achieving rapid economic growth, a high degree of economic stability, and relatively stable prices and interest rates, for a time strongly reinforced belief in the initial Keynesian views about the unimportance of variations in the nominal quantity of money.

The 1970s administered a decisive blow to these views and fostered a revival of belief in the quantity theory. Rapid monetary growth was accompanied not only by accelerated inflation but also by rising, not falling, average levels of unemployment (Friedman, 1977), and by rising, not declining, interest rates. As Robert Lucas put it in 1981,

> Keynesian orthodoxy ... appears to be giving seriously wrong answers to the most basic questions of macroeconomic policy. Proponents of a class of models which promised $3\frac{1}{2}$ to $4\frac{1}{2}$ percent unemployment to a society willing to tolerate annual inflation rates of 4 to 5 percent have some explaining to do after a decade [i.e., the 1970s] such as we have just come through. A forecast error of this magnitude and central importance to policy has consequences (pp. 559–60).

This experience undermined the belief that the price level could be regarded as rigid – or at any rate as determined by forces unrelated to the quantity of money; that the nominal quantity of money demanded could be regarded as a function primarily of the nominal interest rate, and that absolute liquidity preference was the normal state of affairs. No teacher of elementary economics since the late 1970s can, as so many did in the 1940s, 1950s, and 1960s, draw on the blackboard a downward sloping liquidity-preference diagram with the nominal quantity of money on the horizontal axis and a nominal interest rate on the vertical axis and confidently proclaim that the only important effect of an increase in the nominal quantity of money would be to lower the rate of interest. The distinction between the nominal interest rate and the real interest rate introduced by Irving Fisher in 1896 has entered – or re-entered – received wisdom (Fisher, 1896).

Despite its subsidence, the Keynesian attack on the quantity theory has left its mark. It has reinforced the tendency, already present in the Cambridge approach, to stress the role of money as an asset and hence to regard the analysis of the demand for money as part of capital or wealth theory, concerned with the composition of the balance sheet or portfolio of assets. The Keynesian stress on autonomous spending and hence on fiscal policy remains important in its own right but also has led to greater emphasis on the effect of government fiscal policies on the demand for money. Keynes's stress on expectations has contributed to the rapid growth in the analysis of the role and formation of expectations in a variety of economic contexts. Conversely, the revival of the quantity theory has led Keynesian economists to treat changes in the quantity of money as an essential element in the analysis of short-term change.

Finally, the controversy between Keynesians and quantity theorists has led both groups to distinguish more sharply between long-run and short-run effects of monetary changes; between 'static' or 'long-run equilibrium' theory and the dynamics of economic change.

As Franco Modigliani put it in his 1976 presidential address to the American Economic Association, there are currently 'no serious analytical disagreements between leading monetarists [i.e., quantity theorists] and leading nonmonetarists [i.e., Keynesians]' (1977, p. 1).

However, there still remain important differences on an empirical level. These all centre on the dynamics of short-run change – the process whereby a change in the quantity of money affects aggregate spending and the role of fiscal variables in the process.

The Keynesians regard a change in the quantity of money as affecting in the first instance 'the' interest rate, interpreted as a market rate on a fairly narrow class of financial liabilities. They regard spending as affected only 'indirectly' as the changed interest rate alters the profitability and amount of investment spending, again interpreted fairly narrowly, and as investment spending, through the multiplier, affects total spending. Hence the emphasis they give in their analysis to the interest elasticities of the demand for money and of investment spending.

The quantity theorists, on the other hand, stress a much broader and more 'direct' impact of spending, saying, as in section 1a above, that individuals will seek 'to dispose of what they regard as their excess money balances by paying out a larger sum for the purchase of securities, goods, and services, for the repayment of debts, and as gifts than they are receiving from the corresponding sources'.

The two approaches can be readily reconciled on a formal level. Quantity theorists can describe the transmission mechanism as operating 'through' the balance sheet and 'through' changes in interest rates. The attempt by holders of money to restore or attain a desired balance sheet after an unexpected increase in the quantity of money tends initially to raise the prices of assets and reduce interest rates, which encourages spending to produce new assets and also spending on current services rather than on purchasing existing assets. This is how an initial effect on balance sheets gets translated into an effect on income and spending. The resulting increase in spending tends to raise prices of goods and services which, in turn, by lowering the real value of the quantity of money and of nominal assets, tends to eliminate the initial decline in interest rates, even overshooting in the process.

The difference between the quantity theorists and the Keynesians is less in the nature of the process than in the range of assets considered. The Keynesians tend to concentrate on a narrow range of marketable assets and recorded interest rates. The quantity theorists insist that a far wider range of assets and interest rates must be taken into account – such assets as durable and semi-durable consumer goods, structures, and other real property. As a result, the quantity theorists regard the market rates stressed by the Keynesians as only a small part of the total spectrum of rates that are relevant.

This difference in the assumed transmission mechanism is largely a by-product of the different assumptions about price. The rejection of absolute liquidity preference forced Keynes's followers to let the interest rate be flexible. This chink in the key assumption that prices are an institutional datum was minimized by interpreting the 'interest rate' narrowly, and market institutions made it easy to do so. After all, it is most unusual to quote the 'interest rate' implicit in the sales and rental prices of houses and automobiles, let alone furniture, household appliances, clothes, and so on. Hence the prices of these items continued to be regarded as an institutional datum, which forced the transmission process to go through an extremely narrow channel. On the side of the quantity theorists there was no such inhibition. Since they regard prices as flexible, though not 'perfectly' flexible, it was natural for them to interpret the transmission mechanism in terms of relative price adjustments over a broad area rather than in terms of narrowly defined interest rates.

Less important differences are the tendency for Keynesians to stress the short-run as opposed to the long-run impact of changes to a far greater extent than the quantity theorists; and, a related difference, to give greater scope to the first-round effect of changes in the quantity of money.

3 THE PHILLIPS CURVE AND THE NATURAL RATE HYPOTHESIS

A major postwar development that contributed greatly to the revival of the quantity theory grew out of criticism by quantity theorists of the 'Phillips curve' – an allegedly stable inverse relation between unemployment and the rate of change of nominal wages such that a high level of unemployment was accompanied by declining wages, a low level by rising wages. Though not formally linked to the Keynesian theoretical system, the Phillips curve was widely welcomed by Keynesians as helping to fill a gap in the system created by the assumption of rigid wages. In addition, it appeared to offer an attractive trade-off possibility for economic policy: a permanent reduction in the level of unemployment at the cost of a moderate sustained increase in the rate of inflation. The Keynesian assumption that prices and wages could be regarded as institutionally determined made it easy for them to accept a relation between a nominal magnitude (the rate of change of wages) and a real magnitude (unemployment).

By contrast, the quantity theory distinction between real and nominal magnitudes implies that the Phillips curve is theoretically flawed. The quantity of labour demanded is a function of real not nominal wages; and so is the quantity supplied. Under any given set of circumstances, there is an equilibrium level of unemployment corresponding to an equilibrium structure of *real* wage rates. A higher level of unemployment will put downward pressure on real wage rates; a lower level will put upward pressure on real wage rates. The level of unemployment consistent with the equilibrium structure of real wage rates has been termed the 'natural rate of unemployment' and defined as

> the level that would be ground out by the Walrasian system of general equilibrium equations, provided there is imbedded in them the actual structural characteristics of the labour and commodity markets, including market imperfections, stochastic variability in demands and supplies, the cost of gathering information about job vacancies and labour availabilities, the costs of mobility, and so on (Friedman, 1968, p. 8).

The nominal wage rate that corresponds to any given real wage rate depends on the level of prices. Whether that nominal wage rate is rising or falling depends on whether prices are rising or falling. If wages and prices change at the same rate, the real wage rate remains the same. Hence, in the long run, there need be no relation between the rate of change of *nominal* wages and the rate of change of *real* wages, and hence between the rate of change of nominal wages and the level of unemployment. In the long run, therefore, the Phillips curve will tend to be vertical at the natural rate of unemployment – a proposition that came to be termed the Natural Rate Hypothesis.

Over short periods, an *unanticipated* increase in inflation reduces real wages as viewed by employers, inducing them to offer higher nominal wages, which workers erroneously view as higher real wages. This discrepancy simultaneously encourages employers to offer more employment and workers to accept more employment, thereby reducing unemployment, which produces the inverse relation encapsulated in the Phillips curve. However, if the higher rate of inflation continues, the anticipations of workers and employers will converge and the decline in unemployment will be reversed. A negatively sloping Phillips curve is therefore a short-run phenomenon. Moreover, it will not be stable over time, since what matters is not the nominal rates of change of wages and prices but the difference between the actual and the *anticipated* rates of change. The emergence of stagflation in the 1970s quickly confirmed this analysis, leading to the widespread replacement of the original Phillips curve by an expectations-adjusted Phillips curve (Friedman, 1977).

Acceptance of the natural rate hypothesis has had far-reaching effects not only on received wisdom among economists but also on economic policy. It became widely recognized that expansionary monetary and fiscal policies at best gave only a temporary stimulus to output and employment and if long continued would be reflected primarily in inflation.

4 THE THEORY OF RATIONAL EXPECTATIONS

A subsequent theoretical development was the belated flowering of a seed planted in 1961 by John F. Muth, in a long-neglected article on 'Rational expectations and the theory of price movements' (Muth, 1961). The theory of rational expectations offers no special insight into stationary-state or long-run equilibrium analysis. Its contribution is to dynamics – short-run change, and hence potentially to stabilization policy.

It has long been recognized by writers of all persuasions that, as Abraham Lincoln put it over a century ago, 'you can't fool all of the people all of the time.' The tendency for the public to learn from experience and to adjust to it underlies David Hume's view that monetary expansion 'is favourable to industry' only in its initial stages, but that if it continues, it will come to be anticipated and will affect prices and nominal interest rates but not real magnitudes. It also underlies the companion view associated with the natural rate hypothesis that a 'full employment' policy in which monetary, or for that matter fiscal, measures are used to counteract any increase in unemployment will almost inevitably lead not simply to uneven inflation but to uneven inflation around a rising trend – a conclusion often illustrated by analogizing inflation to a drug of which the addict must take larger and larger doses to get the same kick.

Nonetheless, the importance of anticipations and how they are formed in determining the dynamic response to changes in money and other magnitudes remained largely implicit until Lucas and Sargent applied the Muth rational expectations idea explicitly to the reliability of econometric models of the economy and to stabilization policies (Fischer, 1980; Lucas, 1976; Lucas and Sargent, 1981).

The theory of rational expectations asserts that economic agents should be treated as if their anticipations fully incorporate both currently available information about the state of the world and a correct theory of the interrelationships among the variables. Anticipations formed in this way will on the average tend to be correct (a statement whose simplicity conceals fundamental problems of interpretation, Friedman and Schwartz, 1982, pp. 556–7).

The rational expectations hypothesis has far-reaching implications for the validity of econometric models. Suppose a statistician were able to construct a model that predicted highly accurately for a past period all relevant variables; also, that a monetary rule could be devised that if used during the past period with that model could have achieved a particular objective – say keeping unemployment between 4 and 5 per cent. Suppose now that that policy rule were adopted for the future. It would be nearly certain that the model for which the rule was developed would no longer work. The economic equivalent of the Heisenberg indeterminacy principle would take over. The model was for an economy without that monetary rule. Put the rule into effect and it will alter rational expectations and hence behaviour. Even without putting the rule into effect, the model would very likely continue to work only so long as its existence could be kept secret because if market participants learned about it they would use it in forming their rational expectations and thereby falsify it to a greater or lesser extent. Little wonder that every major econometric model is always being sent back to the drawing board as experience confounds it, or that their producers have reacted so strongly to the theory of rational expectations.

The implication of one variant of the theory that has received the most attention and generated the most controversy is the so-called neutrality hypothesis about stabilization policy – in particular, about discretionary monetary policy directed at promoting economic stability. Correct rational expectations of economic agents will include correct anticipation of any systematic monetary policy; hence such policy will be allowed for by economic agents in determining their behaviour. Given further the natural rate hypothesis, it follows that any systematic monetary policy will affect the behaviour only of nominal magnitudes and not of such real magnitudes as output and employment. The authorities can affect the course of events only by 'fooling' the participants, that is, by acting in an unpredictable, ad hoc way. But, in general, such strictly ad hoc intervention will destabilize the economy, not stabilize it, serving simply to introduce another series of random shocks into the economy to which participants must adapt and which reduce their ability to form precise and accurate expectations.

This is a highly oversimplified account of the rational expectations hypothesis and its implications. All otherwise valid models of the economy will not be falsified by being known. All real effects of systematic and announced governmental policies will not be rendered nugatory. Serious problems have arisen in formulating the hypothesis in a logically satisfactory way, and in giving it empirical content, especially in incorporating multi-valued rather than single-valued expectations and allowing for non-independence of events over time. Research in this area is exploding; rapid progress and many changes in received opinion can confidently be anticipated before the rational expectations revolution is fully domesticated.

5 EMPIRICAL EVIDENCE

There is perhaps no empirical regularity among economic phenomena that is based on so much evidence for so wide a range of circumstances as the connection between substantial changes in the quantity of money and in the level of prices. There are few if any instances in which a substantial change in the quantity of money per unit of output has occurred without a substantial change in the level of prices in the same direction. Conversely, there are few if any instances in which a substantial change in the level of prices has occurred without a substantial change in the quantity of money per unit of output in the same direction. And instances in which prices and the quantity of money have moved together are recorded for many centuries of history, for countries in every part of the globe, and for a wide diversity of monetary arrangements.

The statistical connection itself, however, tells nothing about direction of influence, and this is the question about which there has been the most controversy. A rise or fall in prices, occurring for whatever reason, could produce a corresponding rise or fall in the quantity of money, so that the monetary changes are a passive consequence. Alternatively, changes in the quantity of money could produce changes in prices in the same direction, so that control of the quantity of money implies control of prices. The second interpretation – that substantial changes in the quantity of money are both a necessary and a sufficient condition for substantial changes in the general level of prices – is strongly supported by the variety of monetary arrangements for which a connection between monetary and price movements has been observed. But of course this interpretation does not exclude a reflex influence of changes in prices on the quantity of money. The reflex influence is often important, almost always complex, and, depending on the monetary arrangements, may be in either direction.

Evidence from specie standards. Until modern times, money was mostly metallic – copper, brass, silver, gold. The most notable changes in its nominal quantity were produced by sweating and clipping, by governmental edicts changing the nominal values attached to specified physical quantities of the metal, or by discoveries of new sources of specie. Economic history is replete with examples of the first two and their coincidence with corresponding changes in nominal prices (Cipolla, 1956; Feavearyear, 1931). The specie discoveries in the New World in the 16th century are the most important example of the third. The association between the resulting increase in the quantity of money and the price revolution of the 16th and 17th centuries has been well documented (Hamilton, 1934).

Despite the much greater development of deposit money and paper money, the gold discoveries in Australia and the United States in the 1840s were followed by substantial price rises in the 1850s (Cairnes, 1873; Jevons, 1863). When growth of the gold stock slowed, and especially when country after country shifted from silver to gold (Germany in 1871–3, the Latin Monetary Union in 1873, the Netherlands in 1875–6) or returned to gold (the United States in 1879), world prices in terms of gold fell slowly but fairly steadily for about three decades. New gold discoveries in the 1880s and 1890s, powerfully reinforced by improved methods of mining and refining, particularly commercially feasible methods of using the cyanide process to extract gold from low-grade ore, led to much more rapid growth of the world gold stock. Further, no additional important countries shifted to gold. As a result, world prices in terms of gold rose by 25 to 50 per cent from the mid-1890s to 1914 (Bordo and Schwartz, 1984).

Evidence from great inflations. Periods of great monetary disturbances provide the most dramatic evidence on the role of the quantity of money. The most striking such periods are the hyperinflations after World War I in Germany, Austria, and Russia, and after World War II in Hungary and Greece, and the rapid price rises, if not hyperinflations, in many South

American and some other countries both before and after World War II. These 20th-century episodes have been studied more systematically than earlier ones. The studies demonstrate almost conclusively the critical role of changes in the quantity of money (Cagan, 1965; Meiselman, 1970; Sargent, 1982).

Substantial inflations following a period of relatively stable prices have often had their start in wartime, though recently they have become common under other circumstances. What is important is that something, generally the financing of extraordinary governmental expenditures, produces a more rapid growth of the quantity of money. Prices start to rise, but at a slower pace than the quantity of money, so that for a time the real quantity of money increases. The reason is twofold: first, it takes time for people to readjust their money balances; second, initially there is a general expectation that the rise in prices is temporary and will be followed by a decline. Such expectations make money a desirable form in which to hold assets, and therefore lead to an increase in desired money balances in real terms.

As prices continue to rise, expectations are revised. Holders of money come to expect prices to continue to rise, and reduce desired balances. They also take more active measures to eliminate the discrepancy between actual and desired balances. The result is that prices start to rise faster than the stock of money, and real balances start to decline (that is, velocity starts to rise). How far this process continues depends on the rate of rise in the quantity of money. If it remains fairly stable, real balances settle down at a level that is lower than the initial level but roughly constant – a constant expected rate of inflation implies a roughly constant level of desired real balances; in this case, prices ultimately rise at the same rate as the quantity of money. If the rate of money growth declines, inflation will follow suit, which will in turn lead to an increase in actual and desired real balances as people readjust their expectations; and conversely. Once the process is in full swing, changes in real balances follow with a lag changes in the rate of change of the stock of money. The lag reflects the fact that people apparently base their expectations of future rates of price change partly on an average of experience over the preceding several years, the period of averaging being shorter the more rapid the inflation.

In the extreme cases, those that have degenerated into hyperinflation and a complete breakdown of the medium of exchange, rates of price change have been so high and real balances have been driven down so low as to lead to the widespread introduction of substitute moneys, usually foreign currencies. At that point completely new monetary systems have had to be introduced.

A similar phenomenon has occurred when inflation has been effectively suppressed by price controls, so that there is a substantial gap between the prices that would prevail in the absence of controls and the legally permitted prices. This gap prevents money from functioning as an effective medium of exchange and also leads to the introduction of substitute moneys, sometimes rather bizarre ones like the cigarettes and cognac used in post-World War II Germany.

Other evidence. The past two decades have witnessed a literal flood of literature dealing with monetary phenomena. Expressed in broad terms, the literature has been of two overlapping types – qualitative and econometric – and has dealt with two overlapping sets of issues – static or long-term effects of monetary change and dynamic or cyclical effects.

Some broad findings are:

(1). For both long and short periods there is a consistent though not precise relation between the rate of growth of the quantity of money and the rate of growth of nominal income. If the quantity of money grows rapidly, so will nominal income, and conversely. This relation is much closer for long than for short periods.

Two recent econometric studies have tested the long-run effects using comparisons among countries for the post-World War II period. Lothian concludes his study for 20 countries for the period 1956–80:

> In this paper I have examined three sets of hypotheses associated with the quantity theory of money: the classical neutrality proposition [i.e., changes in the nominal quantity of money do not affect real magnitudes in the long run], the monetary approach to exchange rates [i.e., changes in exchange rates between countries reflect primarily changes in money per unit of output in the several countries], and the Fisher equation [i.e., differences in sustained rates of inflation produce corresponding differences in nominal interest rates]. The data are completely consistent with the first two and moderately supportive of the last (1985, p. 835).

Duck concludes his study for 33 countries and the period 1962 to 1982 – which uses overlapping data but substantially different methods:

> Its [the study's] findings suggest that (i) the real demand for money is reasonably well explained by a small number of variables, principally real income and interest rates; (ii) nominal income is closely related to the quantity of money, but is also related to the behaviour of other variables, principally interest rates; (iii) most changes in nominal income or its determinants are absorbed by price increases; (iv) even over a 20-year period some nominal income growth is to a significant degree absorbed by real output growth; (v) the evidence that expectations are rational is weak (1985, p. 33).

(2). These findings for the long run reflect a long-run real demand function for money involving, as Duck notes, a small number of variables, that is highly stable and very similar for different countries. The elasticity of this function with respect to real income is close to unity, occasionally lower, generally higher, especially for countries that are growing rapidly and in which the scope of the money economy is expanding. The elasticity with respect to interest rates is, as expected, negative but relatively low in absolute value. The real quantity demanded is not affected by the price level (i.e., there is no 'monetary illusion') (Friedman and Schwartz, 1982; Laidler, 1985).

(3). Over short periods, the relation between growth in money and in nominal income is often concealed from the naked eye partly because the relation is less close for short than long periods but mostly because it takes time for changes in monetary growth to affect income, and how long it takes is itself variable. Today's income growth is not closely related to today's monetary growth; it depends on what has been happening to money in the past. What happens to money today affects what is going to happen to income in the future.

(4). For most major Western countries, a change in the rate of monetary growth produces a change in the rate of growth of nominal income about six to nine months later. This is an average that does not hold in every individual case. Sometimes the delay is longer, sometimes shorter. In particular, it tends to be shorter under conditions of high and highly variable rates of monetary growth and of inflation.

(5). In cyclical episodes the response of nominal income, allowing for the time delay, is greater in amplitude than the change in monetary growth, so that velocity tends to rise during the expansion phase of a business cycle and to fall during the contraction phase. This reaction appears to be partly a response to the pro-cyclical pattern of interest rates; partly to the linkage of desired cash balances to permanent rather than measured income.

(6). The changed rate of growth of nominal income typically shows up first in output and hardly at all in prices. If the rate of monetary growth increases or decreases, the rate of growth of nominal income and also of physical output tends to increase or decrease about six to nine months later, but the rate of price rise is affected very little.

(7). The effect on prices, like that on income and output, is distributed over time, but comes some 12 to 18 months later, so that the total delay between a change in monetary growth and a change in the rate of inflation averages something like two years. That is why it is a long row to hoe to stop an inflation that has been allowed to start. It cannot be stopped overnight.

(8). Even after allowance for the delayed effect of monetary growth, the relation is far from perfect. There's many a slip over short periods 'twixt the monetary change and the income change.

(9). In the short run, which may be as long as three to ten years, monetary changes affect primarily output. Over decades, on the other hand, as already noted, the rate of monetary growth affects primarily prices. What happens to output depends on real factors: the enterprise, ingenuity and industry of the people; the extent of thrift; the structure of industry and government; the relations among nations, and so on. (In re points 3 to 9, Friedman and Schwartz, 1963a, 1963b; Friedman, 1961, 1977, 1984; Judd and Scadding, 1982.)

(10). One major finding has to do with severe depressions. There is strong evidence that a monetary crisis, involving a substantial decline in the quantity of money, is a necessary and sufficient condition for a major depression. Fluctuations in monetary growth are also systematically related to minor ups and downs in the economy, but do not play as dominant a role compared to other forces. As Friedman and Schwartz put it,

> Changes in the money stock are ... a consequence as well as an independent source of change in money income and prices, though, once they occur, they produce in their turn still further effects on income and prices. Mutual interaction, but with money rather clearly the senior partner in longer-run movements and in major cyclical movements, and more nearly an equal partner with money income and prices in shorter-run and milder movements – this is the generalization suggested by our evidence (1963b, p. 695; Friedman and Schwartz, 1963a; Cagan, 1965, pp. 296–8).

(11). A major unsettled issue is the short-run division of a change in nominal income between output and price. The division has varied widely over space and time and there exists no satisfactory theory that isolates the factors responsible for the variability (Gordon, 1980, 1981, 1982; Friedman and Schwartz, 1982, pp. 59–62).

(12). It follows from these propositions that *inflation is always and everywhere a monetary phenomenon* in the sense that it is and can be produced only by a more rapid increase in the quantity of money than in output. Many phenomena can produce temporary fluctuations in the rate of inflation, but they can have lasting effects only insofar as they affect the rate of monetary growth. However, there are many different possible reasons for monetary growth, including gold discoveries, financing of government spending, and financing of private spending. Hence, these propositions are only the beginning of an answer to the causes and cures for inflation. The deeper question is why excessive monetary growth occurs.

(13). Government spending may or may not be inflationary. It clearly will be inflationary if it is financed by creating money, that is, by printing currency or creating bank deposits. If it is financed by taxes or by borrowing from the public, the main effect is that the government spends the funds instead of the taxpayer or instead of the lender or instead of the person who would otherwise have borrowed the funds. Fiscal policy is extremely important in determining what fraction of total national income is spent by government and who bears the burden of that expenditure. It is also extremely important in determining monetary policy and, via that route, inflation. Essentially all major inflations, especially hyperinflations, have resulted from resort by governments to the printing press to finance their expenditures under conditions of great stress such as defeat in war or internal revolution, circumstances that have limited the ability of governments to acquire resources through explicit taxation.

(14). A change in monetary growth affects interest rates in one direction at first but in the opposite direction later on. More rapid monetary growth at first tends to lower interest rates. But later on, the resulting acceleration in spending and still later in inflation produces a rise in the demand for loans which tends to raise interest rates. In addition, higher inflation widens the difference between real and nominal interest rates. As both lenders and borrowers come to anticipate inflation, lenders demand, and borrowers are willing to offer, higher nominal rates to offset the anticipated inflation. That is why interest rates are highest in countries that have had the most rapid growth in the quantity of money and also in prices – countries like Brazil, Chile, Israel, South Korea. In the opposite direction, a slower rate of monetary growth at first raises interest rates but later on, as it decelerates spending and inflation, lowers interest rates. That is why interest rates are lowest in countries that *have had* the slowest rate of growth in the quantity of money – countries like Switzerland, Germany, and Japan.

(15). In the major Western countries, the link to gold and the resultant long-term predictability of the price level meant that until some time after World War II, interest rates behaved as if prices were expected to be stable and both inflation and deflation were unanticipated; the so-called Fisher effect was almost completely absent. Nominal returns on nominal assets were relatively stable; real returns unstable, absorbing almost fully inflation and deflation.

(16). Beginning in the 1960s, and especially after the end of Bretton Woods in 1971, interest rates started to parallel rates of inflation. Nominal returns on nominal assets became more variable; real returns on nominal assets, less variable (Friedman and Schwartz, 1982, pp. 10–11).

6. POLICY IMPLICATIONS

On a very general level the implications of the quantity theory for economic policy are straightforward and clear. On a more precise and detailed level they are not.

Acceptance of the quantity theory means that the quantity of money is a key variable in policies directed at controlling the level of prices or of nominal income. Inflation can be prevented if and only if the quantity of money per unit of output can be kept from increasing appreciably. Deflation can be prevented if and only if the quantity of money per unit of output can be kept from decreasing appreciably. This implication is by no means trivial. Monetary authorities have more frequently than not taken conditions in the credit market – rates of interest, availability of loans, and so on – as criteria of policy and have paid little or no attention to the quantity of money per se. The emphasis on credit as opposed to the quantity of money accounts both for the great contraction in the United States from 1929 to 1933, when the Federal Reserve System allowed the stock of money to decline by one-third, and for many of the post-World War II inflations.

The quantity theory has no such clear implication, even on this general level, about policies concerned with the growth of real income. Both inflation and deflation have proved consistent with growth, stagnation, or decline.

Passing from these general and vague statements to specific prescriptions for policy is difficult. It is tempting to conclude from the close average relation between changes in the quantity of money and changes in money income that control over the quantity of money can be used as a precision instrument for offsetting other forces making for instability in money income. Unfortunately the loose relation between money and income over short periods, the long and variable lag between changes in the quantity of money and other variables, and the often conflicting objectives of policy-makers precludes precise offsetting control.

An international specie standard leaves only limited scope for an independent monetary policy. Over any substantial period, the quantity of money is determined by the balance of payments. Capital movements plus time delays in the transmission of monetary and other impulses leave some leeway, which may be more or less extensive, depending on the importance of foreign transactions for a country and the sluggishness of response. As a result, monetary policy under an effective international specie standard has consisted primarily of banking policy, directed towards avoiding or relieving banking and liquidity crises (Bagehot, 1873).

Until 1971, departures from an international specie standard, at least by major countries, took place infrequently and only at times of crisis. Surveying such episodes, Fisher concluded in 1911 that 'irredeemable paper money has almost invariably proved a curse to the country employing it' (1911, p. 131), a generalization that has applied equally to most of the period since, certainly up to 1971, and that explains why such episodes were generally transitory.

The declining importance of the international specie standard and its final termination in 1971 have changed the situation drastically. 'Irredeemable paper money' is no longer an expedient grasped at in times of crisis; it is the normal state of affairs in countries at peace, facing no domestic crises, political or economic, and with governments fully capable of obtaining massive resources through explicit taxes. This is an unprecedented situation. We are in unexplored terrain.

As Keynes pointed out in 1923, monetary authorities cannot serve two masters: as he put it, 'we cannot keep *both* our own price level *and* our exchanges stable. And we are compelled to choose' (p. 126). Experience since has converted his dilemma into a trilemma. In principle, monetary authorities can achieve any two of the following three objectives: control of exchange rates, control of the price level, freedom from exchange controls. In practice, it has in fact proved impossible to achieve the first two by accepting exchange controls. Such controls have proved extremely costly and ultimately ineffective. The Bretton Woods system was ultimately wrecked on this trilemma. The attempts by many countries to pursue an independent monetary policy came into conflict with the attempt to maintain pegged exchange rates, leading to the imposition of exchange controls, repeated monetary crises, accompanied by large, discontinuous changes in exchange rates, and ultimately to the abandonment of the system in 1971.

Since then, most countries have had no formal commitment about exchange rates, which have been free to fluctuate and have fluctuated widely. Nonetheless, Keynes's dilemma is still alive and well. Monetary authorities have tried to influence the exchange rates of their currency and, at the same time, achieve internal objectives. The result has been what has been described as a system of managed floating.

One recent strand of policy discussions has consisted of attempts to devise a substitute for the Bretton Woods arrangements that would somehow combine the virtues of exchange rate stability with internal monetary stability. For example, one proposal, by McKinnon (1984), is for the USA, Germany, and Japan to fix exchange rates among their currencies and set a joint target for the rate of increase of the total quantity of money (or high-powered money) issued by the three countries together. So far, no such proposal has gained wide support among either economists or a wider public.

A different strand of policy discussions has been concerned with the instruments, targets, and objectives of monetary authorities. One element of the quantity theory approach that has had considerable influence is emphasis on the quantity of money as the appropriate intermediate target for monetary policy. Most major countries now (1985) follow the practice of announcing in advance their targets for monetary growth. That is so for the USA, Great Britain, Germany, Japan, Switzerland, and many others. The record of achievement of the announced targets varies greatly – from excellent to terrible. Recently, a considerable number of economists have favoured the use of nominal income (usually nominal gross national product) as the intermediate target. The common feature is the quantity theory emphasis on nominal magnitudes.

A more abstract strand of policy discussions has been concerned with the optimum quantity of money: what rate or pattern of monetary growth would in principle promote most effectively the long-run efficiency of the economic system – meaning by that a Pareto welfare optimum. This issue turns out to be closely related to a number of others, in particular the optimum behaviour of the price level; the optimum rate of interest; the optimum stock of capital, and the optimum structure of capital (Friedman, 1969, pp. 1–50).

One widely accepted answer is based on the observation that no real resource cost need be incurred in increasing the real quantity of money since that can be done by reducing the price level. The implication is that the optimum quantity of money is that at which the marginal benefit from increasing the real quantity is also zero. Various arrangements are possible that will achieve such an objective, of which perhaps the simplest, if money pays no interest, is a pattern of monetary growth involving a decline in the price level at a rate equal to the real interest rate (Mussa, 1977; Ihori, 1985).

This answer, despite its great theoretical interest, has had little practical consequence. Short-run considerations have understandably been given precedence to such a highly abstract long-run proposition.

Finally, there has been a literal explosion of discussion of the basic structure of the monetary system. One component derives from the belief that Fisher's generalization about irredeemable paper money will continue to hold for the present world fiat money system and that we are headed for a world monetary collapse ending in hyperinflation unless a specie (gold) standard is promptly restored. In the United States, this monetary belief was powerful enough to lead

Congress to establish a Commission on the Role of Gold. In its final report, 'the Commission concludes that, under present circumstances, restoring a gold standard does not appear to be a fruitful method for dealing with the continuing problem of inflation. ... We favour no change in the flexible exchange rate system' (Commission, 1982, vol. 1, pp. 17, 20). The testimony before the Commission revealed that agreement on a 'gold standard' concealed wide differences in the precise meaning of the phrase, varying from a system in which money consisted of full-bodied gold or warehouse receipts for gold to one in which the monetary authorities were instructed to regard the price of gold as one factor affecting their policy.

A very different component of the discussion has to do with possible alternatives to gold as a long-term anchor to the price level. This includes proposals for subjecting monetary authorities to more specific legislative or constitutional guidelines, varying from guidelines dealing with their objectives (price stability, rate of growth of nominal income, real interest rate, etc.) to guidelines specifying a specific rate of growth in money or high-powered money. Perhaps the most widely discussed proposal along this line is the proposal for imposing on the authorities the obligation to achieve a constant rate of growth in a specified monetary aggregate (Friedman, 1960, pp. 92–5; Commission, 1982, vol. 1, p. 17). Other proposals include freezing the stock of base money and eliminating discretionary monetary policy, and denationalizing money entirely, leaving it to the private market and a free banking system (Friedman, 1984; Friedman and Schwartz, 1986; Hayek, 1976; White, 1984a).

Finally, a still more radical series of proposals is that the unit of account be separated from the medium of exchange function, in the belief that financial innovation will establish an efficient payment system dispensing entirely with the use of cash. The specific proposals are highly sophisticated and complex, and have been sharply criticized. So far, their value has been primarily as a stimulus to a deeper analysis of the meaning and role of money. (For the proposals, see Black, 1970; Fama, 1980; Hall, 1982a, 1982b; Greenfield and Yeager, 1983; for the criticisms, see White, 1984b; McCallum, 1985).

One thing is certain: the quantity theory of money will continue to generate agreement, controversy, repudiation, and scientific analysis, and will continue to play a role in government policy during the next century as it has for the past three.

MILTON FRIEDMAN

BIBLIOGRAPHY

Angell, J.W. 1936. *The Behavior of Money*. New York: McGraw-Hill.

Bagehot, W. 1873. *Lombard Street*. London: Henry S. King.

Barnett, W.A., Offenbacher, E.K. and Spindt, P.A. 1984. The new Divisia monetary aggregates. *Journal of Political Economy* 92(6), December, 1049–85.

Baumol, W.J. 1952. The transactions demand for cash: an inventory theoretic approach. *Quarterly Journal of Economics* 66, November, 545–56.

Black, F. 1970. Banking and interest rates in a world without money: the effects of uncontrolled banking, *Journal of Bank Research* 1(3), Autumn, 2–20.

Black, H. 1975. The relative importance of determinants of the money supply: the British case. *Journal of Monetary Economics* 1(2), April, 25–64.

Bordo, M.D. and Schwartz, A.J. (eds) 1984. *A Retrospective on the Classical Gold Standard, 1821–1931*. Chicago: University of Chicago Press for the National Bureau of Economic Research.

Burger, A.E. 1971. *The Money Supply Process*. Belmont: Wadsworth.

Cagan, P. 1965. *Determinants and Effects of Changes in the Stock of Money, 1875–1960*. New York: Columbia University Press for the National Bureau of Economic Research.

Cagan, P. 1972. *The Channels of Monetary Effects on Interest Rates*. New York: National Bureau of Economic Research.

Cairnes, J.E. 1873. Essays on the gold question. In J.E. Cairnes, *Essays in Political Economy*, London: Macmillan.

Cipolla, C.M. 1956. *Money, Prices, and Civilization in the Mediterranean World, Fifth to Seventeenth Century*. Princeton: Princeton University Press.

Commission on the Role of Gold in the Domestic and International Monetary Systems. 1982. *Report to the Congress*, March. Washington, D.C.: The Commission.

Duck, N.W. 1985. Money, output and prices: an empirical study using long-term cross country data. Working Paper, University of Bristol, September.

Fama, E.F. 1980. Banking in the theory of finance. *Journal of Monetary Economics* 6(1), January, 39–57.

Feavearyear, A.E. 1931. *The Pound Sterling: a History of English Money*. 2nd edn, Oxford: Clarendon Press, 1963.

Fischer, S. (ed.) 1980. *Rational Expectations and Economic Policy*. Chicago: University of Chicago Press for the National Bureau of Economic Research.

Fisher, I. 1896. *Appreciation and Interest*. Ner York: American Economic Association.

Fisher, I. 1911. *The Purchasing Power of Money*. 2nd revised edn, 1926; reprinted New York: Kelley, 1963.

Fisher, I. 1919. Money, prices, credit and banking. *American Economic Review* 9, June, 407–9.

Frenkel, J.A. 1976. Adjustment mechanisms and the monetary approach to the balance of payments. In *Recent Issues in International Monetary Economics*, ed. E. Claassen and P. Salin, Amsterdam: North-Holland.

Frenkel, J.A. and Johnson, H.G. 1976. The monetary approach to the balance of payments: essential concepts and historical origins. In *The Monetary Approach to the Balance of Payments*, ed. J.A. Frenkel and H.G. Johnson, Toronto: University of Toronto Press.

Friedman, M. 1956. The quantity theory of money – a restatement. In *Studies in the Quantity Theory of Money*, ed. M. Friedman, Chicago: University of Chicago Press.

Friedman, M. 1957. *A Theory of the Consumption Function*. Princeton: Princeton University Press for the National Bureau of Economic Research.

Friedman, M. 1959. The demand for money: some theoretical and empirical results. *Journal of Political Economy* 67, August, 327–51. Reprinted as Occasional Paper No. 68, New York: National Bureau of Economic Research, and in Friedman (1969).

Friedman, M. 1960. *A Program for Monetary Stability*. New York: Fordham University Press.

Friedman, M. 1961. The lag in effect of monetary policy. *Journal of Political Economy* 69, October, 447–66. Reprinted in Friedman (1969).

Friedman, M. 1968. The role of monetary policy. *American Economic Review* 58(1), March, 1–17. Reprinted in Friedman (1969).

Friedman, M. 1969. *The Optimum Quantity of Money and Other Essays*. Chicago: Aldine.

Friedman, M. 1977. Inflation and unemployment (Nobel lecture). *Journal of Political Economy* 85(3), June, 451–72.

Friedman, M. 1984. Monetary policy for the 1980s. In *To Promote Prosperity: U.S. domestic policy in the mid-1980s*, ed. J.H. Moore, Stanford: Hoover Institution Press.

Friedman, M. and Schwartz, A.J. 1963a. Money and business cycles. *Review of Economics and Statistics* 45(1), Supplement, February, 32–64. Reprinted in Friedman (1969).

Friedman, M. and Schwartz, A.J. 1963b. *A Monetary History of the United States, 1867–1960*. Princeton: Princeton University Press for the National Bureau of Economic Research.

Friedman, M. and Schwartz, A.J. 1970. *Monetary Statistics of the United States*. New York: Columbia University Press for the National Bureau of Economic Research.

Friedman, M. and Schwartz, A.J. 1982. *Monetary Trends in the United States and the United Kingdom: Their Relation to Income, Prices, and Interest Rates, 1867–1975*. Chicago: University of Chicago Press for the National Bureau of Economic Research.

Friedman, M. and Schwartz, A.J. 1986. Has government any role in money? *Journal of Monetary Economics* 17(1), January, 37–62.

Gordon, R.J. 1980. A consistent characterization of a near-century of price behavior. *American Economic Review* 70(2), May, 243–49.
Gordon, R.J. 1981. Output fluctuations and gradual price adjustment. *Journal of Economic Literature* 19(2), June, 493–530.
Gordon, R.J. 1982. Price inertia and policy ineffectiveness in the United States, 1890–1980. *Journal of Political Economy* 90(6), December, 1087–117.
Greenfield, R.L. and Yeager, L.B. 1983. A laissez-faire approach to monetary stability. *Journal of Money, Credit, and Banking* 15(3), August, 302–15.
Haberler, G. 1941. *Prosperity and Depression*. 3rd edn, Geneva: League of Nations.
Hall, R.E. 1982a. Explorations in the gold standard and related policies for stabilizing the dollar. In *Inflation: Causes and Effects*, ed. R.E. Hall, Chicago: University of Chicago Press.
Hall, R.E. 1982b. 'Monetary trends in the United States and the United Kingdom': a review from the perspective of new developments in monetary economics. *Journal of Economic Literature* 20(4), December, 1552–6.
Hamilton, E.J. 1934. *American Treasure and the Price Revolution in Spain, 1501–1650*. Harvard Economic Studies, Vol. 43, New York: Octagon, 1965.
Hansen, A. 1957. *The American Economy*. New York: McGraw-Hill.
Hayek, F.A. 1976. *Denationalization of Money*. 2nd extended edn, London: Institute of Economic Affairs, 1978.
Hume, D. 1752. Of interest; of money. In *Essays, Moral, Political and Literary*, Vol. 1 of *Essays and Treatises*, a new edn, Edinburgh: Bell and Bradfute, Cadell and Davies, 1804.
Humphrey, T.M. 1984. Algebraic quantity equations before Fisher and Pigou. *Economic Review*, Federal Reserve Bank of Richmond 70(5), September–October, 13–22.
Ihori, T. 1985. On the welfare cost of permanent inflation. *Journal of Money, Credit, and Banking* 17(2), May, 220–31.
Jevons, W.S. 1863. A serious fall in the value of gold. In *Investigations in Currency and Finance*, 2nd edn, London: Macmillan, 1909.
Johnson, H.G. 1961. *The General Theory* after twenty-five years. *American Economic Association, Papers and Proceedings* 51, May, 1–17.
Judd, J.P. and Scadding, J.L. 1982. The search for a stable money demand function. *Journal of Economic Literature* 20(3), September, 993–1023.
Keynes, J.M. 1923. *A Tract on Monetary Reform*. Reprinted London: Macmillan for the Royal Economic Society, 1971.
Keynes, J.M. 1936. *The General Theory of Employment, Interest, and Money*. Reprinted London: Macmillan for the Royal Economic Society, 1973.
Knoester, A. 1984. Pigou and buffer effects in monetary economics. Discussion Paper 8406 G/M, Institute for Economic Research, Erasmus University, Rotterdam.
Laidler, D. 1984. The 'buffer stock' notion in monetary economics. *Economic Journal* 94, Supplement, 17–34.
Laidler, D. 1985. *The Demand for Money: theories, evidence, and problems*. 3rd edn, New York: Harper & Row.
Lothian, J.R. 1985. Equilibrium relationships between money and other economic variables. *American Economic Review* 75(4), September, 828–35.
Lucas, R.E., Jr. 1976. Econometric policy evaluation: a critique. *Journal of Monetary Economics* supplementary series 1, 19–46.
Lucas, R.E., Jr. 1981. Tobin and monetarism: a review article. *Journal of Economic Literature* 19(2), June, 558–67.
Lucas, R.E., Jr. and Sargent, T.J. (eds.) 1981. *Rational Expectations and Economic Practice*. 2 vols, Minneapolis: University of Minnesota Press.
McCallum, B. 1985. Bank deregulation, accounting systems of exchange and the unit of account: a critical review. *Carnegie-Rochester Conference Series on Public Policy* 23, Autumn.
McKinnon, R. 1984. *An International Standard for Monetary Stabilization*. Cambridge, Mass: MIT Press.
Meiselman, D. (ed.) 1970. *Varieties of Monetary Experience*. Chicago: University of Chicago Press.
Mill, J.S. 1844. Review of books by Thomas Tooke and R. Torrens. *Westminster Review*, June.
Miller, M.H. and Orr, D. 1966. A model of the demand for money by firms. *Quarterly Journal of Economics* 80(3), August, 413–35.
Miller, M.H. and Orr, D. 1968. The demand for money by firms: extensions of analytical results. *Journal of Finance* 23(5), December, 735–59.
Modigliani, F. 1977. The monetarist controversy, or should we forsake stabilization policies? *American Economic Review* 67(2), March, 1–19.
Mussa, M. 1977. The welfare cost of inflation and the role of money as a unit of account. *Journal of Money, Credit, and Banking* 9(2), May, 276–86.
Muth, J.F. 1961. Rational expectations and the theory of price movements. *Econometrica* 29, July, 315–35. Reprinted in Lucas and Sargent (1981).
Newcomb, S. 1885. *Principles of Political Economy*. New York: Harper & Brothers.
Patinkin, D. 1948. Price flexibility and full employment. *American Economic Review* 38, September, 543–64. Revised and reprinted in F.A. Lutz and L.W. Mints (American Economic Association), *Readings in Monetary Theory*, Homewood, Ill.: Irwin, 1951.
Phelps, E.S. 1967. Phillips curves, expectations of inflation, and optimal unemployment over time. *Economica* 34(135), August, 254–81.
Pigou, A.C. 1917. The value of money. *Quarterly Journal of Economics* 32, November, 38–65. Reprinted in F.A. Lutz and L.W. Mints (American Economic Association), *Readings in Monetary Theory*, Homewood, Ill.: Irwin, 1951.
Pigou, A.C. 1947. Economic progress in a stable environment. *Economica* 14(55), August, 180–88.
Sargent, T.J. 1982. The ends of four big inflations. In *Inflation: Causes and Effects*, ed. R.E. Hall, Chicago: University of Chicago Press.
Snyder, C. 1934. On the statistical relation of trade, credit, and prices. *Revue de l'Institut International de Statistique* 2, October, 278–91.
Spindt, P.A. 1985. Money is what money does: monetary aggregation and the equation of exchange. *Journal of Political Economy* 93(1), February, 1975–2204.
Tobin, J. 1947. Money wage rates and employment. In *The New Economics*, ed. S. Harris, New York: Knopf.
Tobin, J. 1956. The interest-elasticity of transactions demand for cash. *Review of Economics and Statistics* 38, August, 241–47.
Tobin, J. 1958. Liquidity preference as behavior toward risk. *Review of Economic Studies* 25, February, 65–86.
Tobin, J. 1961. Money, capital and other stores of value. *American Economic Review, Papers and Proceedings* 51, May, 26–37.
Tobin, J. 1974. Friedman's theoretical framework. In *Milton Friedman's Monetary Framework: a Debate with His Critics*, ed. R.J. Gordon, Chicago: University of Chicago Press.
White, L.H. 1984a. *Free Banking in Britain: Theory, Experience and Debate, 1800–1845*. New York: Cambridge University Press.
White, L.H. 1984b. Competitive payments systems and the unit of account. *American Economic Review* 74(4), September, 699–712.

quasi-concavity.

DEFINITION. A real function f defined on a convex subset C of a linear space E is said to be quasi-concave if

$$x, y \in C, \quad t \in [0,1] \Rightarrow f(tx + (1-t)y) \geqslant \mathrm{Min}[f(x), f(y)]. \quad (1)$$

A function g is said to be quasi-convex if $-g$ is quasi-concave. Concave functions are quasi-concave, convex functions are quasi-convex.

For all $\lambda \in R$, let $S(\lambda) = \{x : x \in C, f(x) \geqslant \lambda\}$. These sets are termed as the upper level sets of f. Upper level sets play an essential role in quasi-concavity. In particular, an alternative and useful way of characterizing quasi-concavity is to say that a function f is quasi-concave if all its upper level sets are convex.

Like concave functions, quasi-concave functions enjoy nice properties: the set of maximizing points is convex, the infimum of a family of quasi-concave functions is quasi-concave, if f is quasi-concave and k is a real non-decreasing function on R then $k \bigcirc f$ is quasi-concave. But, in contrast, a quasi-concave function is not necessarily continuous on the interior of its domain and the sum of quasi-concave functions is not quasi-concave in general.

Quasi-concavity was pioneered by De Finetti (1949), Fenchel (1953), Arrow and Enthoven (1961), Mangasarian (1965). It occurs in consumer theory where, under reasonable assumptions, a consumer's preferences can be represented by a quasi-concave utility function. In producer theory, production functions can also be reasonably assumed to be quasi-concave.

CHARACTERIZATIONS OF QUASI-CONCAVE DIFFERENTIABLE FUNCTIONS. For the sake of simplicity, we assume hereafter that E is the n-dimensional space R^n and C is an open convex set of R^n. Assume that f is differentiable on C, then f is quasi-concave on C iff

$$x, y \in C, \quad f(x) \leqslant f(y) \Rightarrow (y - x)\nabla f(x) \geqslant 0. \qquad (2)$$

Because quasi-concavity is often concerned with maximization problems, it would be suitable for f to achieve its maximum at each x so that $\nabla f(x) = 0$, but this is not so. A slight change of (2) leads to the following definition: a differentiable function f defined on the open convex set C is said to be pseudoconcave if

$$x, y \in C, \quad f(x) < f(y) \Rightarrow (y - x)\nabla f(x) > 0. \qquad (3)$$

Pseudoconcave functions are quasi-concave and concave functions are psuedoconcave. Actually, pseudoconcave functions are those quasi-concave functions which achieve their maximum at each point so that $\nabla f(x) = 0$.

Now, assume that f is twice differentiable on C. Then f is pseudoconcave iff

(a) $\quad x \in C, \quad v\nabla f(x) = 0 \Rightarrow v\nabla^2 f(x)v \leqslant 0,$

and

(b) $\quad$ if $\; x \in C, \quad \nabla f(x) = 0.$

then f achieves its maximum at x. Similarly, f is quasi-concave iff (a) holds and

(b′) if $\nabla f(x) = 0$, then for all $h \in R^n$ the function $t \rightarrow f(x + th)$ is quasi-concave.

Condition (a) can be formulated alternatively in terms of the bordered hessian of the function.

DUALITY. Assume that f is continuous and quasi-concave on the closed convex subset C of R^n, define

$$F(p, \lambda) = \mathrm{Inf}[px : x \in C, f(x) \geqslant \lambda],$$

and

$$G(p, r) = \mathrm{Sup}[f(x) : x \in C, px \leqslant r].$$

Then

$$f(x) = \mathrm{Inf}_{p}\,[G(p, px)]$$

$$= \mathrm{Inf}_{p}\,\mathrm{Sup}_{\lambda}\,[\lambda : F(p, \lambda) \leqslant px].$$

Thus, f can be generated from either F or G. The functions F and G each have a useful economic interpretation. Assume that C is the set of available commodities, p is the vector of commodity prices and the consumer's preferences are given by the utility function f. Then $F(p, \lambda)$ is the minimal cost to be paid by the consumer to get a value of utility greater than or equal to λ and $G(p, r)$ is the maximal value of utility that he can get for expenditure r. The function $p \rightarrow G(p, 1)$ is sometimes called the indirect utility function (Diewert, 1981, Crouzeix, 1983).

CONCAVIFIABILITY. If a consumer's preferences are represented by a continuous utility function u, then $f = k \bigcirc u$ when k is a real continuous increasing function on R is also a continuous utility function that represents these preferences; and all utility functions are of this kind. In many economic problems, it is extremely useful to know if there exists a concave utility function, but this is not true in general. The problem was initiated by De Finetti (1949) and Fenchel (1953), a recent reference is Kannai (1981). Dual functions are extremely useful here, thanks to the following characterization to concave functions: a continuous quasi-concave function f is concave iff for all p the function $\lambda \rightarrow F(p, \lambda)$ is convex or alternatively iff for all p the function $r \rightarrow G(p, r)$ is concave.

If preferences can be represented by a concave utility function, then they admit a concave utility function u such that for any other concave utility function v there exists a real increasing concave function k such that $v = k \bigcirc u$. This function is called (Debreu, 1976) a least concave utility. Least concave utility functions are useful in the context of decision making under uncertainty.

ADDITIVITY. The sum of quasi-concave functions is not quasi-concave, even when each are separable. Assume that the set C of commodities and a consumer's utility function have the following form

$$C = C_1 \times C_2 \times \cdots \times C_p,$$

$$u(x_1, x_2, \ldots, x_p) = u_1(x_1) + u_2(x_2) + \cdots + u_p(x_p) \qquad x_i C_i.$$

Assume that u is quasi-concave on C and that the functions u_i are not constant. Then all functions u_i are concave except perhaps one which is concavifiable (Debreu and Koopmans, 1982; Crouzeix and Lindberg, 1986). Quasi-concavity and additivity cannot be brought together without problems.

J.-P. CROUZEIX

BIBLIOGRAPHY

An important and up to date discussion of quasiconcavity and related topics with their applications for economics as well as for mathematical programming can be found in *Generalized Concavity in Optimization and Economics*, a collection of papers by several authors edited by S. Schaible and W.T. Ziemba (New York: Academic Press, 1981).

Arrow, K.J. and Enthoven, A.C. 1961. Quasi-concave programming. *Econometrica* 29(4), October, 779–800.

Crouzeix, J.P. 1983. Duality between direct and indirect utility functions. *Journal of Mathematical Economics* 12(2), 149–65.

Crouzeix, J.P. and Lindberg, P.O. 1986. Additively decomposed quasi-convex functions. *Mathematical Programming* 35(1), 42–57.

Debreu, G. 1976. Least concave utility functions. *Journal of Mathematical Economics* 3(2), 121–29.

Debreu, G. and Koopmans, T.C. 1982. Additively decomposed quasi-convex functions. *Mathematical Programming* 24(1), 1–38.

De Finetti, B. 1949. Sulle stratificazioni convesse. *Annali di matematica pura ed applicata*, Series IV, 30, 173–83.

Diewert, W.E. 1981. Generalized concavity in economics. In *Generalized Concavity in Optimization and Economics*, ed. S. Schaible and W.T. Ziemba, New York: Academic Press.

Fenchel, W. 1953. Convex cones, sets and functions. Mimeo, Princeton University.

Kannai, Y. 1981. Concave utility functions. In *Generalized Concavity in Optimization and Economics*, ed. S. Schaible and W.T. Ziemba, New York: Academic Press.

Mangasarian, O.L. 1965. Pseudo-convex functions. *SIAM Journal on Control* 3(2), 281–90.

quasi-contract. A quasi-contract may be defined as a transaction or state of facts to which the law, independently of the volition of the parties, annexes an obligation similar to that which would arise from a contract. The term, though a familiar one in Roman law, has only been recently adopted into English law. Yet a quasi-contract is clearly distinct from an implied contract, the term which was formerly used to cover both classes of obligations. When a man goes into a shop and orders goods, and nothing is said about the price, there is an implied contract to pay for them, for this is the intention of the parties. But the obligation of a principal in the absence of any agreement to indemnify his agent for anything done pursuant to his authority, is an instance of quasi-contract. The law annexes the obligation to the relationship between the parties.

[M.D. CHALMERS]

Reprinted from *Palgrave's Dictionary of Political Economy.*

BIBLIOGRAPHY

Anson, W.R. 1879. *On Contracts.* Book 6, Oxford: Oxford University Press.

quasi-rent. *See* MARSHALL, ALFRED.

Quesnay, François (1694–1774). Quesnay was born at Mère, Seine-et-Oise. He came from a family of humble origin, the eighth of thirteen children. His father Nicholas was a small merchant, and the family also had a piece of land; thanks to these two activities they were comfortably off. François Quesnay had no systematic education; at ten he could not even read, but early on he developed an interest in medicine. In 1711 he went to Paris for formal training in medicine and surgery. There he read Descartes and Malebranche, and the latter's *Recherche de la verité* had a profound impact on the young Quesnay. In 1717 he married Jeanne-Cathérine Dauphin who gave him four children, two of whom survived. He began his career at Mantes, a small town not far from Paris, and in the 1720s and 1730s he made his reputation as a surgeon, particularly with respect to bleeding techniques. In 1736 he published *l'Essai physique sur l'oeconomie animale*, his first major work. Quesnay was deeply involved in the polemic between surgeons and physicians which took place in the 1740s. At that time he was also physician to the Duke of Villeroy and through him and the Comtesse d'Estrades he met Madame de Pompadour, Louis XV's favourite. Quesnay became her private physician and established himself at Versailles. In 1752 he saved the Dauphin from smallpox, and in gratitude the King granted Quesnay a noble title and a sum of money which he used to buy an estate at Beauvoir in the Minervois for his son Blaise-Guillaume. In 1750 and 1751 Quesnay published the last of his medical works and became a member of the French Académie des Sciences and of the Royal Society in London.

In the early 1750s Quesnay became interested in economics and in particular, in agricultural matters. He was in contact with many important thinkers including D'Alembert and Diderot, Buffon, Helvetius and Condillac. He was induced to contribute to the *Encyclopédie*, for which he wrote two articles: *Evidence*, which appeared in Volume VI in January 1756, and *Fonction de l'âme* which was never published there since the *Encyclopédie* had been condemned by the government. Quesnay preferred to publish his articles anonymously. In 1756 he also published his article *Fermiers*, while in 1757 he wrote *Grains* for the seventh volume of the *Encyclopédie*. These two articles are Quesnay's first economic writings. He wrote three more pieces for the *Encyclopédie*: *Hommes*, *Impôts* and *Intérêt de l'argent*. But after the attack on the King's life at Damiens, the enemies of the *encyclopédistes* managed to obtain the repeal of its royal privilege and Quesnay, like Turgot, withdrew his three articles from publication. The third appeared 1766 in the *Journal de l'agriculture*; *Hommes* was published in 1908 by Etienne Bauer and *Impôts* appeared in 1902 thanks to Gustave Schelle.

In 1757 Quesnay met Victor Riquetti, Marquis de Mirabeau (see Hecht, 1958, p. 256). Mirabeau came from an old noble family and supported the view that the main cause of national wealth was the number of people. Quesnay convinced him that agriculture was much more important than population, because it produced the commodities which were necessary for men's subsistence, Mirabeau became the most faithful propagator of Quesnay's ideas, and this episode marks the beginning of the Physiocratic school.

In 1758 Quesnay published the *Questions intéressantes sur la population, l'agriculture et le commerce* and at the end of the same year he wrote the first edition of the *Tableau économique*. In the first half of 1759 this was followed by two other editions. The *Tableau*, printed in a limited edition at Versailles, was presented to Louis XV, who was apparently greatly impressed by Quesnay's strange schemes. Quesnay was also engaged in supervising Mirabeau's writings, which were designed to illustrate the rather obscure *Tableau*, and, more generally, to spread Physiocratic doctrine. Mirabeau's *Theorie de l'impôt*, the result of this close collaboration, appeared at the end of 1760. The reactions to this work and Mirabeau's consequent imprisonment convinced the two that it was better to work silently. Almost three years elapsed before Mirabeau published the *Philosophie rurale* in three volumes, in November 1763. There can be no doubt that Quesnay revised the entire work and wrote some chapters (Meek, 1962, p. 38).

The year 1763 marked the beginning of a period of active intervention by the Physiocrats in economic debates. Quesnay found new followers: Du Pont de Nemours, Mercier de La Rivière, Baudeau and Turgot, a good friend of the Physiocrats. Quesnay contributed to the development of physiocratic ideas with articles which appeared in the *Journal de l'agriculture* and after 1767 in the *Ephémérides du citoyen*. Among other works Quesnay wrote *Le droit naturel*, the *Mémoires sur les avantages de l'industrie et du commerce* and the *Dialogue sur les travaux des artisans*. In these latter works he discusses the sterility of industry and trade and the productivity of agriculture. The most famous of Quesnay's articles appeared in the *Journal de l'agriculture* of 1766 with the title *Analyse de la formule arithmétique du Tableau économique*, in which he presented a simplified version of the *Tableau*. This new *Tableau* was also used by Quesnay in the *Premier problème économique*, which appeared in the same periodical. Between 1767 and 1768 Quesnay published several articles in the *Ephémérides: Despotisme de la Chine*, *Analyse du gouvernment des Incas du Pérou*. In 1767 he also wrote the *Second problème économique* for the *Physiocratie*, a collection of his main writings prepared by Du Pont de Nemours. Between 1764 and 1767 Quesnay was the true master of the Physiocrats; new disciples joined the group and his ideas found some application in French economic policy. By 1768 the cultural and political impact of Physiocracy began to decline and Quesnay's theory was bitterly criticized. He spent his last years studying geometry, notwithstanding the advice of his friends and the fact that he was ridiculed by some of his enemies (Hecht, 1958, pp. 278–9). Quesnay died in December

1774 at Grand-Commun, a place not far away from Versailles, a few months after the death of Louis XV.

Quesnay was directly responsible for all the main aspects of Physiocratic thought and, in particular, for its economic analysis. Some Physiocrats contributed to the development and the explanation of particular aspects of the doctrine, but Quesnay was the one who put forward the most innovative concepts and the general framework in which they were inserted. The analysis of Quesnay's economic writings presents a peculiar problem; he did not write a single major text as a summary of his entire thought, but instead wrote small pieces, articles for the *Encyclopédie* and for the periodicals which were controlled by the Physiocrats (Vaggi, 1987, ch. 2, part 2). Thus usually he discussed only one economic issue at the time. This methodology is quite clear in his first works, where he presents the major features of Physiocratic economics, such as the role of farmers and capital in agriculture; the importance of commercial policies and free trade, the question of the fiscal system. But the same method of analysis characterizes the writings of the period 1766–8, where Quesnay had to defend his theory from the criticisms of many important thinkers of the time.

Correct interpretation of Quesnay's economics must take all his writings into account and cannot be limited to the analysis of the most famous. There are clear logical links between Quesnay's different works. On several occasions he himself indicates where these connections are to be found. Indeed, despite his method of writing on one specific issue at a time, the analytical structure of Quesnay's economics is clearly characterized by systematic cause-and-effect relationships. It is an important feature of Quesnay's thought that he explained economic facts and individual actions on the basis of a view of society as a general interrelated system. Therefore, he believed that all aspects of social life were linked together and that it was possible to find the underlying causal relationships, which were nothing else than the outcome of natural laws.

The role and significance of the *Tableau économique* within Quesnay's economics needs further clarification since this is the most important and famous work of Physiocracy and has often been regarded as a summary of the entire corpus of Physiocratic economics (Herlitz, 1961, p. 134; Fox-Genovese, 1976, p. 258). The *Tableau* has also been regarded as the analytical synthesis of the logical structure of Quesnay's economics, or at least as its most relevant aspect. In any case, all too often knowledge of Physiocracy is limited to the *Tableau économique*. However, the various types of *Tableau* elaborated by Quesnay between 1758 and 1766 cannot be analysed in isolation; by themselves they do not provide an exhaustive presentation of Physiocratic economics. An accurate understanding of Quesnay's theory and of the *Tableau* itself requires the study of his other writings. Some of these are particularly significant because they supplement the *Tableau*. For instance, Quesnay's first economic articles, *Hommes, Fermiers* and *Grains*, were written just before the *Tableau* and can be regarded as the basis on which the analysis of the *Tableau* is carried out. Quesnay's economics must be regarded as a mosaic, where all the inlays are necessary, though the *Tableau* is the central part of the picture.

The *Tableau économique* is one of those works in the history of economics which have often been regarded as an anticipation of modern theories. The *Tableau* has been considered a first rough presentation of Keynes's multiplier and as a sort of general equilibrium system of a Walrasian type (Schumpeter, 1954, p. 242). For others, the *Tableau* is an input–output table (Phillips, 1955, pp. 137–8). Because of the *Tableau*, Quesnay has been regarded as an early econometrician. The *Tableau* has also been interpreted as the first classical system of price determination, thus anticipating Marx's reproduction schemes and Sraffa's price system (Cartelier, 1976, p. 57).

There are two main reasons why the *Tableau* impressed Quesnay's contemporaries and later interpreters so much. The first is the 'obscurity' of the schemes, the second is the fact that there is not just one *Tableau* but many. The history of the *Tableau économique* begins at the end of 1758 with the first manuscript edition of the work, which included a table and a few pages of comments entitled *Remarques sur les variations de la distribution des revenus annuels d'une nation* comprising 22 remarks. The second edition, the first to be printed, followed a few months later (Kuczynski and Meek, 1972, pp. xvi-xviii). This *Tableau* is similar to the earlier one, but is now followed by 23 remarks which are very similar to the *Maximes générales* at the end of the 1757 article *Grains* and are entitled *Extrait des oeconomies royales de M. de Sully*. The third edition

TABLEAU ECONOMIQUE

Objects to be considered: (1) three kinds of expenditure; (2) their source; (3) their advances; (4) their distribution; (5) their effects; (6) their reproduction; (7) their relations with one another; (8) their relations with the population; (9) with agriculture; (10) with industry; (11) with trade; (12) with the total wealth of a nation.

PRODUCTIVE EXPENDITURE relative to agriculture, etc.	EXPENDITURE OF THE REVENUE after deduction of taxes, is divided between productive expenditure and sterile expenditure	*STERILE EXPENDITURE* relative to industry, etc.
Annual advances required to produce a revenue of 600^l are 600^l	**Annual** revenue	**Annual advances** for the works of sterile expenditure are

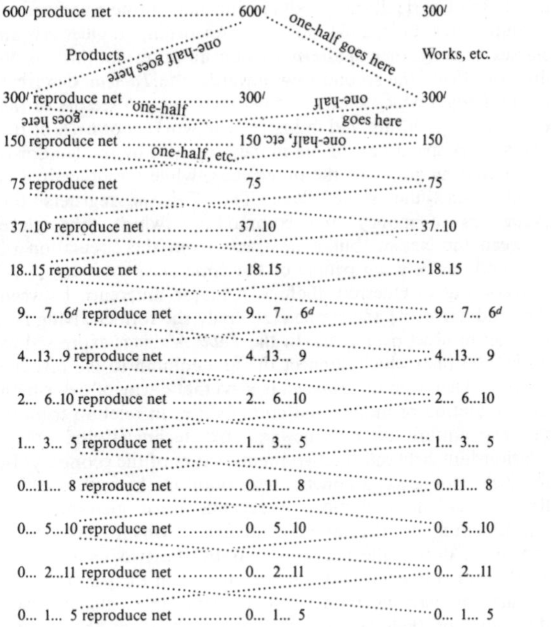
600^l produce net .... 600^l .... 300^l
one-half goes here
Products
one-half goes here
Works, etc.
300^l reproduce net .... 300^l .... 300^l
one-half
goes here
one-half
goes here
150 reproduce net .... 150 one-half, etc. 150
one-half, etc.
75 reproduce net 75 75
37..10^s reproduce net .... 37..10 .... 37..10
18..15 reproduce net .... 18..15 .... 18..15
9... 7...6^d reproduce net .... 9... 7... 6^d .... 9... 7... 6^d
4...13...9 reproduce net .... 4...13... 9 .... 4...13... 9
2... 6..10 reproduce net .... 2... 6...10 .... 2... 6...10
1... 3... 5 reproduce net .... 1... 3... 5 .... 1... 3... 5
0...11... 8 reproduce net .... 0...11... 8 .... 0...11... 8
0... 5...10 reproduce net .... 0... 5...10 .... 0... 5...10
0... 2...11 reproduce net .... 0... 2...11 .... 0... 2...11
0... 1... 5 reproduce net .... 0... 1... 5 .... 0... 1... 5

etc.

TOTAL REPRODUCED......600^l of revenue; in addition, the annual costs of 600^l and the interest on the original advances of the husbandman amounting to 300^l, which the land restores. Thus the reproduction is 1500^l, including the revenue of 600^l which forms the base of the calculation, abstraction being made of the taxes deducted and of the advances which their annual reproduction entails, etc. See the Explanation on the following page.

appeared in 1759, but then it disappeared for more than two centuries. It was rediscovered and published in 1965 by Marguerite Kuczynski (Kuczynski and Meek, 1972, pp. xxvff). The third edition of the *Tableau* is made up of the table itself plus an enlarged version of the *Extrait* with 24 remarks and long footnotes and a new text called *Explications du Tableau économique*. Clearly, Quesnay must have felt that more explanations of the scheme were required. All three editions present the original type of *Tableau*, which is characterized by three columns whose figures are related to each other by means of descending lines crossing the table. This is the so called zig-zag version of the *Tableau*.

A similar *Tableau* can also be found in the sixth part of Mirabeau's *L'ami des hommes*, published in 1760 (Mirabeau, 1758–60, vol. 2, pp. 118ff). The two side-columns give the annual advances of the productive sector – agriculture – and of the sterile sector – industry. The central column presents the revenue of the landlords and the way in which it is spent. In the first row of each column Quesnay writes the value of each of the three magnitudes at the beginning of the process of circulation of commodities and revenue. These figures are characterized by some peculiar ratios; the revenue and the annual advances of the productive class have the same value; these annual advances are twice as large as those of the sterile class. All the zig-zag *Tableaux* and most of the following ones have these ratios. Among the figures in the first row, particularly important is the value assumed by revenue, which is usually called the 'basis' of the *Tableau* because it determines all the other figures. The first zig-zag started with a revenue of 400 *livres*, while the next two editions had a revenue of 600 *livres*. The *Tableau* shows the effects of the expenditure of revenue on the other two classes. Quesnay generally assumes that landlords spend half of their revenue in the purchase of agricultural products and half in the purchase of manufactures (Eltis, 1984, pp. 20ff). According to Quesnay, all classes comply their pattern of consumption to this 50–50 division. From the second row onwards, the *Tableau* describes the exchanges which take place between the two sectors of the economy, agriculture and industry. The workers of each of the two sectors spend half of the money received by the landlords in purchasing goods of the other class, while the other half is spent inside the same class. The *Tableau* registers the exchanges of money and commodities which take place between the classes, but it abstracts from the circulation of commodities between people of the same class.

According to Quesnay there is a major difference between the productive and the sterile class, only the former giving rise to a net product over costs. In the *Tableau* this is expressed as horizontal lines which connect the first column to the revenue column. Therefore the *Tableau* is a synthetic way of describing the circulation of money and commodities in relation to both the expenditure of revenue and the technical and social relationships between the two main sectors of the economy. In the *Tableau* there is a concise description of the way in which the process of circulation of revenue must guarantee the reproduction of the annual advances which have been consumed during the previous year by the two sectors. The *Tableau's* iterative process is completed when the peasants and the artisans have no money left to spend, in particular when the value of their receipts is equal to that of the annual advances which have been used up. In fact, as a result of the sequence of exchanges, all three classes receive 600 *livres*, which is the sum of the figures from the second row to the bottom of each column. The productive and sterile class have recovered their annual advances, and the landlords have got back their revenue. Hence the process of circulation of commodities depends upon the technical requirements of production, which are described by the reconstruction of the means of production in each sector, and by a particular rule in the distribution of income, which states that the revenue accrues entirely to the owners of land. At the end of the process of circulation there are all the conditions needed to start a new productive cycle.

The *Tableau* also serves as a representation, and perhaps to Quesnay's mind also as a proof, that a surplus exists only in agriculture. The first two columns from the right show that agriculture reproduces its means of production plus a revenue for the landlords, and, for this reason, is regarded as a productive sector. Some problems arise with respect to the third column. The overall production of the sterile class is 600 *livres* and its annual advances are only 300 *livres*. However, Quesnay says that industrial activities are unproductive because they do not contribute to the landlords' revenue. But it is clear from the figures of the Tableau that at the end of the process of circulation the sterile class has 300 *livres* in excess of its advances. This derives from the assumption that each class spend half of its revenue in the purchase of the products of the other sector. In order to reconcile this result with the opinion that only agriculture yields a surplus, it is necessary to resort to some further considerations. Some commentators have pointed out that the *Tableau* does not include one particular act of exchange: the purchase by the sterile class of an amount of agricultural products whose value is 300 *livres* (Meek, 1962, pp. 275–7).

If this act of exchange is included in the picture the sterile class has no surplus left. Alternatively it has been said that in the *Tableau* the sterile class sells part of its output abroad in exchange for agricultural goods (Meek, 1962, p. 283; Gilibert, 1977, pp. 42–5). In any case industry does not seem to be as sterile as the Physiocrats maintain.

A few years after the first version, Quesnay slightly modified the *Tableau économique*. In the 1764 *Philosophie rurale* there are several *tableaux*, some of them are still of the zig-zag type but others have evolved into a new scheme which is called *Précis des résultats de la distribution representée dans le Tableau*, that is to say a summary of the *Tableau* itself (Mirabeau, 1764, vol. 1, p. 327). In the *Précis* Quesnay changed the 'basis' of the *Tableau*: the revenue and the annual advances of the productive class are now 2000 *livres*, the advances of the sterile class are still half this value. Above all there is no iterative process with the descending lines. Instead, Quesnay gives the final results of the circulation of commodities and of revenue. Only a few exchanges are indicated in the scheme and the first and last row are almost exactly alike; they show that the process of reproduction of revenue and both sectors' advances has been completed. The only difference between the first and last row is the annual output of industry, 2000 *livres*, and its annual advances, 1000 *livres*. Thus at first sight it would seem that the value of industrial output still exceeds that of its inputs. But there is an important difference between the zig-zag and the *Précis*; in this latter type of Tableau the advances of industry are entirely made up of agricultural commodities and do not include manufactures. Moreover, even though this does not appear in the diagram Quesnay now quite clearly states in the accompanying text that the artisans purchase 1000 *livres* of raw materials to transform them into manufactured goods. Therefore industry now uses 2000 *livres* of primary products to produce an output of equal value. There is no net product left.

Because of this new act of exchange between industry and agriculture, the output of the primary sector must rise in order to account for these 1000 *livres* of raw materials which go to industry. At the same time, farmers must buy 1000 *livres* of manufactured goods as a repayment for the raw materials which they sell to the artisans. In the *Précis* the farmers receive this 1000 *livres* of industrial products as 'interests' on their original advances (Meek, 1962, pp. 278–9). The third edition of the zig-zag already included these interests, but it was not at all clear whether these products came from industry, or, more probably from agriculture itself (Eltis, 1984, p. 26). The existence of these 1000 *livres* of industrial products which are purchased by the farmers is another reason why the *Tableau économique* cannot be regarded as a proof of the sterility of industry. The cultivation of land requires industrial goods, and this prevents agriculture from being considered as a self-sufficient sector. Industry produces part of the means of production of the primary sector, and therefore contributes, albeit indirectly, to the production of the net product.

The *Précis* is an intermediate step in the evolution of the *Tableau économique*, whose final version is the so called *Analyse de la formule arithmétique du Tableau économique* of 1766. This is also the most well-known version of the *Tableau* and it has been often confused with the original 1758 zig-zag. There are many similarities between the *Précis* and the *Analyse*. Both schemes give a concise representation of all transactions; and the advances of the sterile class are entirely made up of agricultural goods. But in the *Analyse* Quesnay explicitly includes the purchase of manufactured goods by farmers, as their 'interests'. Moreover, the *Analyse* is a very well-written article, which condenses both the scheme and the texts needed to explain it in a few pages, while in the *Philosophie rurale*, the *Précis* and its explanations run into many pages. In the *Analyse*, Quesnay gives the final explanation of the technicalities of the *Tableau*. The formula has become the true *Tableau économique*; this is the version which has been converted into an input–output table (Phillips, 1955), and which has been extensively analysed by modern economists (Tsuru, 1942).

The *Tableau* of the formula type works in the following way. Landlords receive two 'milliards' of *livres* from the farmers as their annual rent and spend this revenue half in the purchase of foodstuffs and half in that of manufactured goods. Artisans buy raw materials and necessaries of life from agriculture.

FORMULE DU TABLEAU ECONOMIQUE

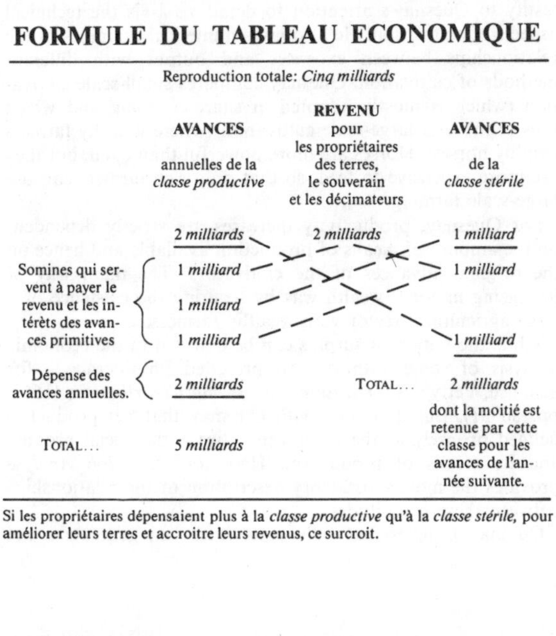

Si les propriétaires dépensaient plus à la *classe productive* qu'à la *classe stérile*, pour améliorer leurs terres et accroitre leurs revenus, ce surcroit.

Now the cultivators have the two milliards, one of which is used to buy the manufactured products which are necessary to maintain the initial value of the fixed capital of cultivation. The artisans need the necessities of life and one milliard goes back to the productive class. In the end one sees that industry has produced two milliards of products using two milliards of primary commodities as input. The total reproduction of agriculture is five milliards because the cultivators sell three milliards, one to the landlords and two to the artisans, but they also keep two milliards of output for themselves, to be used as raw materials and necessaries for future production. For Quesnay five 'milliards' is also the level of output in the whole economy, because the two milliards of manufactured goods are nothing more than reshaping of the same primary commodities which have been used as inputs. Of course this is a flaw in Quesnay's analysis; following his criterion, agricultural output should only be two milliards, because the overall means of production employed in agriculture amount to three milliards. Alternatively, the gross national product should include industrial output too, and its value would be seven milliards. This inconsistency in Quesnay's economics derives from his belief that industry cannot produce a surplus, a view by no means backed up by the figures of the formula-type *Tableau*, where it is quite clear that industrial products are used as inputs in agriculture (Meek, 1962, p. 154).

The *Analyse* has one further merit; from the very beginning Quesnay explicitly states all the hypotheses which characterize the economic system depicted in the *Tableau* (Meek, 1962, p. 298). The same assumptions can be found in Quesnay's comments and explanations in the other *Tableaux*, but in the *Analyse* they are grouped together in a few pages (Meek, 1962, pp. 151–3).

The main features of the economy described in the *Tableau* are as follows. First, in agriculture there are the best methods of cultivation, with large capital stock and high productivity, so that the annual advances can produce a surplus of the same size. A second assumption relates to the fiscal system; all duties and excises which exist in France ought to be substituted by a single tax on agricultural surplus. Third, free competition rules both in domestic and foreign trade in agricultural products, thus there is a *bon prix* for primary commodities and cultivation is a profitable activity. A fourth hypothesis relates to the landlords, who have made all the necessary ground advances, such as drainage, transport facilities etc. We could, of course, add other assumptions which clearly appear in the articles which precede the 1758 zig-zag. The State guarantees the ownership rights for all citizens and not only for landlords. In particular, the State protects the capital invested by cultivators as original advances (Kuczynski and Meek, 1972, pp. 7–8). Another assumption states that the landlords spend their revenue half in the purchase of foodstuffs and half in manufactures (ibid., p. 12). This hypothesis implies that in the *Tableau* the revenue is entirely consumed and is neither hoarded nor used to make financial investments, which are considered a sterile form of activity (ibid., pp. 4, 13).

It goes without saying that the society examined in the *Tableau* has little in common with the France of Louis XV. It is an ideal country where all reforms and economic measures advocated by the Physiocrats have already been implemented. This economic system is quite similar to the natural order of society. According to Quesnay, England is the country which most resembles this ideal society, and this explains why England is so prosperous and wealthy (see INED, 1958, vol. 2, pp. 474, 533). The *Tableau* is a normative benchmark for the government; it describes the circulation and distribution of the social product and surplus, and it shows the final effects of these exchanges on future production. The first zig-zag version of the *Tableau* (Table 1 above) and the *Analyse* are the most coherent descriptions of this ideal situation. In these works Quesnay highlights the normal and regular working conditions of an economic system which is a mirror of the natural order of society. From this point of view one could describe these *Tableaux* as types of equilibrium conditions, but no further similarity can be found with general equilibrium analysis (Meek, 1962, p. 292). But Quesnay is not interested in the conditions of logical consistency between *all* economic variables. He pinpoints *some specific* causal relationships which are regarded as particularly important for the development of the economy. Thus, even though the *Tableau* presents the mutual relationships between several aspects of the economy, Quesnay stresses the relationships of cause-and-effect affecting the increase in national wealth.

In several of his writings Quesnay uses the *Tableau* to study what happens when government regulations or the behaviour of landlords does not conform to this natural order. For instance, in the 1767 article *Second problème économique* he analyses the consequences of several forms of indirect taxation, and shows that these taxes are ultimately damaging (Meek, 1962, pp. 186ff). In an earlier article, a formula *Tableau* had been used to illustrate the beneficial effects of an increase in the prices of agricultural products (ibid., p. 168). The *Tableau* is also used to examine what happens when the landlords modify their pattern of consumption. The proprietors can modify the level of surplus through their decisions to spend more or less revenue on the purchase of agricultural products (Mirabeau, 1764, vol. 3, pp. 33–53). Quesnay uses the zig-zag version and the *Précis* to show that the higher the proportion of revenue which is spent in the consumption of primary goods the higher will be the surplus. From these articles, it emerges that Quesnay was always primarily concerned with the effects of different economic measures on gross and net output. Far from regarding the *Tableau* as a static scheme, Quesnay uses it to show the government ways of speeding up economic growth.

The *Tableau économique* is the most original aspect of Quesnay's economics, but it does not exhaust his economic theory. On the contrary, the assumptions on which the *Tableau* is built and, in general, the comments which supplement it show that the ideas of the Physiocrats are also to be found outside the *Tableau*. Many aspects of Quesnay's economics which are complementary to the *Tableau* are discussed in other writings. A peculiarity of the *Tableau* is the fact that it immediately conveys the view of the economy as a single system which must reproduce itself. The analysis of the conditions which have to be satisfied to guarantee this reproducibility is the main object of economic science. This analysis indicates the factors which lead to an increase of national wealth. The *Tableau* provides a schematic description of reproduction, which is based on the distinction between economic activities in a few major sectors. Moreover, social classes are distinguished according to their role in the process of production and expenditure of output and revenue. Thus there are two major sectors, agriculture and industry, and three main classes of people; two of them are identified with the above sector while the third is characterized by its ownership of the soil. In the *Tableau* Quesnay does not spend much time analysing another important social group, merchants, but this is due to the fact that in the *Tableau* natural order is assumed to rule. Professional traders should disappear in the ideal society where free competition rules in all markets. (INED, 1958, vol. 2, pp. 941–2; Spengler, 1958, p. 62).

The power of professional traders is one of the issues which is not discussed in the *Tableau*, but is investigated in other writings. In the *Tableau* merchants are hidden inside the sterile class. Another limitation is that in the *Tableau* Quesnay does not separate salaried workers from master entrepreneurs. This problem is discussed in other works, in particular in his article *Fermiers*, where the cultivators are clearly described as capitalist entrepreneurs (INED, 1958, vol. 2, pp. 427, 483). But in Quesnay's economics there is no complete analysis of the capitalistist relationship of production.

It must be noticed that the *Tableau*, and the entire economic theory of François Quesnay, is based on two main concepts, capital and net product. Quesnay uses the term *avances* to indicate all the commodities which exist at the beginning of the productive process and are the necessary inputs for production. These commodities are 'advanced' with respect to the output, but are part of the social product of the previous year. In order to satisfy the conditions of self-reproduction, the same commodities that are used up in production must also appear in the social product; otherwise production might come to a stop, or at the very least the level of activity would lower.

Given his belief that only the primary sector yields a net product, Quesnay concentrates his analysis on the advances of agriculture. In the *Analyse* Quesnay says that the advances of cultivation are made up of two milliards of annual advances and ten milliards of original advances. The former are entirely consumed during each productive process, and are a sort of circulating capital. Original advances last for more than one productive period and are subject to wear and tear, which is assumed to be worth one tenth of the initial stock. Therefore in the *Analyse* the value of the part of the social product needed to replace the capital goods which have worn out in production is equal to three milliards of livres. Quesnay calls this sum the annual returns, or *réprises*. Although the *Tableau* gives a concise and accurate description of all the types of advances, this issue is much more thoroughly dealt with in the articles written for the *Encyclopédie* just before the *Tableau*. In the article *Fermiers*, Quesnay examines all the different types of commodities that are required as inputs in the production of several primary commodities. These long lists of goods testify to Quesnay's attention to detail vis-à-vis the technical aspects of cultivation. He also gives numerical examples of the relationships between expenses and output with different methods of cultivation. Quesnay compares small-scale cultivation (which is mostly adopted in share-cropping and which uses oxen) with large-scale cultivation (where wealthy farmers employ horses). Horses are more powerful than oxen, but they are more expensive to feed, so that only rich farmers can use large-scale farming.

For Quesnay, productivity increases are strictly dependent on the amount of means of production available and hence on the original advances of the cultivators. The main way of increasing national wealth was by securing the existence of a large agricultural sector with wealthy farmers.

While the notion of surplus can be detected in the economic analysis of some authors who preceded Physiocracy – for instance, Petty's *A Treatise of Taxes and Contributions* (1662, pp. 30–31). But it is only with Quesnay that net product is defined precisely as the difference between the social product and its means of production. Here too the 1766 *Analyse* provides the most satisfactory description of the relationships between these magnitudes.

Quesnay believes that only agriculture can generate a net

product; this view is taken for granted in the various *Tableaux* but is widely discussed in the *Dialogue sur les travaux des artisans*. This is highly significant; it testifies that Quesnay was not satisfied simply with the accounting definition of surplus, but also attempted to explain its origin and then the factors which might led to its increase. The net product is the new wealth produced in each productive cycle. The main problem in Quesnay's analysis is of the nature of wealth and the ways in which it can be created. From this point of view Quesnay clearly set out the main economic issues which were subsequently examined by Adam Smith in the *Wealth of Nations*.

The concept of net product characterizes Quesnay's entire economic analysis and not just the *Tableau*. For instance in the 1757 article *Grains* he analyses the distribution of surplus between social classes; the Physiocratic theory of taxation is also built on the distinction between surplus and means of production. The notion of net product was the main analytical tool used by Quesnay to examine all the other important economic features in society. The idea of a single tax on rent is closely related to the determination of surplus. Rent is landlords' revenue, the landlords receiving the highest share of the net product of cultivation.

Agriculture is the only productive sector, and taxation of surplus is the only way of avoiding damage to future production. The stock of productive capital must not be reduced by taxes, otherwise it would be impossible to maintain the same level of activity as the previous year. Hence rent is the only taxable magnitude.

Quesnay's theory of circulation and distribution of income is also founded on the distinction between gross and net product. Part of the social product must circulate in such a way to replenish the means of production which have been consumed. As the *Tableau* clearly states the three milliards of returns to the cultivators depend on the methods of production. Hence the destination of output depends on the technical conditions which must be fulfilled to guarantee the self-sustaining character of the economic system. The other share of the social product is surplus; its distribution is not linked to technological factors, but customs and laws ascribe it to the landowners, including the Sovereign and the Church. This appropriation of the net product is a social rule which is part of the reproduction of the social and economic system of the *ancien régime*. Therefore the Physiocratic theory of the distribution of income is based on technical and social conditions.

The identification of agricultural surplus with rent is a simplification of Quesnay's theory of income distribution, which has led many interpreters of Physiocracy to deny any relevant role to the concept of profits (see Meek, 1962, pp. 279–80, 384). In *Grains* Quesnay describes the way in which the net product is distributed; the highest share accrues to the landlords and to the King, but part of the surplus also goes to the farmers (INED, 1958, vol. 2, p. 475). Profits are regarded as a share of the net product also in other writings (ibid., pp. 601, 566). Quesnay puts less emphasis on farmers' profits in his later works, but the main problem arises because in the different types of *Tableau* there is no clear mention of their existence.

This awkward aspect of Physiocratic theory has been interpreted in the following way. Land leases between landlords and farmers are renewed every nine years (Weulersse, 1910, vol. 1, p. 405). Before this renewal the cultivators keep the surplus of cultivation; therefore they receive the entire benefits due either to technical progress (which diminishes production costs) or to an increase in the price of primary goods. But when lease contracts come up for renewal the farmers compete with each other for the right to cultivate the soil, thus rents rise and eventually absorb the whole net product. Farmers' profits are only a temporary share of surplus, and they finally 'crystallize out' into rent (Meek, 1962, pp. 279–80). The *Tableau* describes the final situation, thus profits are not included in it because they are not a regular part of the net product. The farmers' gains are sometimes regarded as salaries of superintendence to remunerate their work as entrepreneurs. According to Meek, this solution has the advantage of being consistent with Quesnay's fiscal theory. Farmers must be exempted from taxation because their incomes are not part of the surplus, and are not fully disposable; only rent has this requisite. Other authors consider profits as part of the net product, which is then made up of two parts, profits and rent, but only the latter is disposable for taxation because profits must be reinvested in production (Woog, 1950, pp. 21–2).

Whatever interpretation one decides to accept it must be recognized that Quesnay was very ambiguous about farmers' profits. The fact that he played down their importance in his later writings is not necessarily due to the need for logical coherence, but can also be explained by his need to convince the nobles that cultivators would not become too rich and powerful (Vaggi, 1987, ch. 5, part 2). In any case it would be wrong to accuse Quesnay of failing to deal with profits. The true limitations of his analysis is the particular concept of profit he uses, namely 'profit upon alienation', a sort of windfall gain which exists simply because the cultivators are able to sell their products at a price higher than the cost of production. This notion can be traced back to mercantilist literature but was to be overturned by Turgot and Smith, who regarded profit as a rate on the capital invested (Groenewegen, 1971, pp. 333–4). In Quesnay's economics, profits have a precise economic role as the source of capital accumulation, because only the farmers can handle the increase in the original advances of cultivation. By means of a sustained process of investment in agriculture, cultivators transform part of the surplus of one productive cycle into the means of production of the next one. Even if farmers' profits were only a temporary share of net product, Quesnay's concept of profit is the notion which relates the three concepts of surplus, investments and capital accumulation. Moreover, Quesnay considers profits as the necessary stimulus to induce the cultivators to increase their advances; they act in consideration of profitability (INED, 1958, vol. 2, p. 807).

Another aspect of Quesnay's economics that is almost entirely ignored is his analysis of price determination. This interpretation too seems to derive from the fact that in the *Tableau économique* Quesnay does not openly discuss the question of value in exchange. The figures in the *Tableau* are in monetary terms, but they are currently interpreted as a proxy for physical magnitudes.

Many commentators have interpreted Quesnay's economics as a purely physical model: in agriculture the same goods are both the inputs and the outputs of the same process of production and the surplus can be measured simply as the difference between two physical quantities of agricultural product. The entire economic system can be described as a 'corn model' where the product and its means of production are homogeneous commodities; thus there is no need for a price theory. The manufactured products used in agriculture can simply be regarded as primary commodities which have changed shape thanks to the work of artisans (INED, 1958, vol. 2, p. 865).

Other authors maintain that prices exist in Physiocratic

economics and that the agricultural output and its means of production are heterogeneous goods. However, they believe that Quesnay took the exchange ratios between the products of industry and those of agriculture as given, and fixed.

A careful reading of Quesnay's writings show that he was very concerned about prices and changes in prices. This problem is not dealt with in the *Tableau*, but price theory is a necessary element in Quesnay's theory of the growth of national wealth. *Grains* and *Hommes* are the articles where Quesnay gave the clearest exposition of his price theory. Like many other economists before him, Quesnay separates the use value of commodities from their exchange value. In *Grains* he refers to a precise physical characteristic of a good which makes it suitable for the satisfaction of specific needs and desires. This is a sort of prerequisite which a good must have in order to be exchanged; there must be somebody willing to buy it. But the price of a commodity is independent of the utility derived from its consumption; use and exchange values are regulated by different laws (INED, 1958, vol. 2, p. 526). Quesnay singles out many concepts of price, which he uses to analyse the characteristics of the domestic and foreign trade of agricultural products. There is the *prix du vendeur*, which is the price paid by the merchant to the farmer. Besides this wholesale price, there is also the *prix de l'acheteur*, which governs the exchange between the merchant and the consumer. The retail price is always higher than the *prix du vendeur* which can also be called the 'current price' (ibid., p. 752). The difference between the two prices is the merchant's gain, whose activity damages both the consumers and the producers, because it depresses the 'current price' and raises the retail one (ibid., p. 947). National wealth must be measured by current prices, when a product leaves the first producer there is no further increase in wealth, hence the merchants' gains are a burden for the whole economy.

The merchants dominate the process of circulation of commodities because they are wealthy enough to stock the products of agriculture and wait for the best moments for their purchases and their sales. On the contrary the farmers must always sell the entire output, because they are too poor to wait (ibid., p. 985). Moreover, merchants usually enjoy exclusive rights, granted by the government, which give them a monopolistic position on certain markets. Free competition in domestic and foreign trade reduces merchants' profits and the difference between the retail and current price greatly diminishes; as was happening in England, where *laissez-faire* had already been implemented. The main purpose of free trade is that of raising the profitability of cultivation, without damaging the standard of living of consumers. This can be achieved thanks to the squeeze on merchants' profits. The merchants do not appear in the *Tableau*, even though they are mentioned in the accompanying texts. But here too one must remember that the *Tableau* describes an economy working according to natural laws, and free competition is one of the main features of natural order.

Quesnay was particularly interested in securing the free exportation of French corn. He believed that one of the main reasons for the backwardness of agriculture was the low level of the prices of its products. This fact made cultivation unprofitable, but domestic demand was not sufficient to raise these prices, because, on the whole, French consumers were too poor. In France there was lack of effective consumption (ibid., p. 824), and Quesnay clearly separates the concept of effective demand, which is the demand of those who actually pay for a product, from the generic desire to consume more. A similar distinction was later to be found in Adam Smith's economics. Because of the lack of purchasing power at home it is necessary to allow the exportation of corn, so that the 'current price' can rise. Quesnay's arguments in favour of free trade are that it will strictly sustain the effective demand and the price of primary commodities, in order to achieve a higher profitability for cultivation. The 'current price' of corn was a *bon prix* in England, where the farmers were stimulated to reinvest their profits. It is the existence of a *bon prix* which guarantees profits to farmers and new investments in agriculture. Therefore the main aim of commercial policy is to restrict the gains made by merchants and increase the profits made by farmers. Landlords will also benefit from these measures, because they will receive higher rents when their leases are renewed and, above all, rent will rise because capital accumulation increases the productivity of agriculture and its surplus (Mirabeau, 1764, vol. 2, pp. 366ff).

Another important concept of price in Physiocratic economics is that of *prix fondamental*. This price is the sum of the overall expenses incurred by the farmer in the production of one unit of corn, it includes wages, raw materials and the repayment of wear and tear on fixed capital. These three items make up the technical cost of cultivation but they do not exhaust the expenses of production. To go on farming, the farmer must also fulfill his obligations towards the landlords by paying them the rent. This payment was a necessary social condition of production in 18th-century France, and was the way in which the king and the aristocracy received part of the fruits of their land.

The fundamental price is the price level below which the farmer makes a loss and stops farming the soil (INED, 1958, vol. 2, p. 529; Du Pont, 1764, p. 18). This notion defines the lower limit of the current price, whose variations must be above the unit cost of production. If free competition rules in the process of circulation of commodities there is a positive difference between the current price and the fundamental one, which is the profit of the cultivator. In Quesnay's economics, theories of distribution and of value are closely related. Profits depend upon the technical conditions of cultivation, which influence the fundamental price, but are also affected by changes in the current price, which depend upon the state of the market for agricultural products and, in particular, on their effective demand.

Price theory is the final piece required to complete the picture of Quesnay's economic analysis of the ways of achieving growth and development. There are several steps to reach the well-ordered economy described in the *Tableau*. The implementation of free trade stimulates the effective demand for primary commodities and raises their current prices. This leads to higher profits for the farmers. If the fiscal system is based on the single tax on rent profits can be entirely reinvested in agriculture, thus raising the advances of cultivation. Capital accumulation in the productive sector of the economy leads to productivity increases. The surplus rises both in absolute terms as a share of the social product; more and more resources can be reinvested in production, and national wealth grows. Quesnay develops a theory of growth which is based on the notion of surplus, but he used other concepts to complete it. In this mosaic the *Tableau* was also designed to single out the ultimate effects of this process of growth, to show the nobles that they would receive the benefits of Physiocratic economic policy.

Quesnay's main contributions to economic science are certainly the concept of surplus and the *Tableau économique*. But one must also stress that for the first time there is a complete and relatively coherent theory designed to answer the most important problems of economic systems on the basis of a general analysis of all their main features. All economic issues are examined with the help of precise concepts and on the basis of a theoretical approach. Economic policy proposals derive from theoretical speculation, and are part of a single general model of the growth of national wealth. Finally all the aspects of Quesnay's economics are linked, in one way or the other, to his notion of surplus, which provides a sort of unifying thread to his thought. Quesnay can quite appropriately be regarded as the founder of that approach to the analysis of economic events which is called theory of surplus.

G. VAGGI

See also PHYSIOCRATS.

SELECTED WORKS

1756. Evidence. Fermiers. Grains. In *Encyclopédie, ou Dictionaire raisonné des sciences, des arts et des métiers*, Paris: Briasson, Vols 6 and 7. *Fermiers* trans. in Groenewegen (1983).

1759. *Tableau économique*. 3rd edn, Paris. Ed. M. Kuczynski and R. Meek, London: Macmillan, 1972.

1765. Hommes. Impôts. In *Encyclopédie*, Vol. 8. Reprinted. in INED (1958).

BIBLIOGRAPHY

Cartelier, J. 1976. *Surproduit et reproduction – la formation de l'économie politique classique*. Paris: Maspero.

Daire, E. 1846. *Physiocrates*. Paris: Librairie de Guillaumin.

Du Pont de Nemours, P.S. 1764. *De l'importation et de l'exportation des grains*. In *Collection des économistes et des réformateurs sociaux de la France*, Paris: Librairie Paul Geuthner, 1911.

Eltis, W.A. 1975. François Quesnay: a reinterpretation. 2. The theory of economic growth. *Oxford Economic Papers* 27(3), November, 327–51.

Eltis, W.A. 1984. *The Classical Theory of Economic Growth*. London: Macmillan.

Fox-Genovese, E. 1976. *The Origins of Physiocracy. Economic Revolution and Social Order in Eighteenth Century France*. Ithaca and London: Cornell University Press.

Gilibert, G. 1977. *Quesnay, la costruzione della macchina della prosperità*. Milan: Etas Libri.

Groenewegen, P.D. 1971. A re-interpretation of Turgot's theory of capital and interest. *Economic Journal* 83(2), June, 327–40.

Groenewegen, P.D. (ed.) 1983. *Quesnay. Farmers (1756)* and *Turgot. Sur la grande et la petite culture (1766)*. Reprints of Economic Classics, Series 2, No. 2, Sydney: University of Sydney.

Hecht, J. 1958. La vie de François Quesnay. INED, Vol. 1, Paris: Institut National d'Etudes Démographiques.

Herlitz, L. 1961. The *Tableau économique* and the doctrine of sterility. *Scandinavian Economic History Review* 1.

INED: 1958. *François Quesnay et la Physiocratie*. Ed. L. Salleron, Paris: Institut Nationale d'Etudes Démographiques, 2 vols.

Kuczynski, M. and Meek, R.L. 1972. *Quesnay's Tableau Economique*. London: Macmillan.

Marx, K. 1963. *Theories of Surplus Value*. London: Lawrence & Wishart.

Mirabeau, V.R. 1758–60. *L'ami des hommes ou traité de la population*. Reprinted, Aalen: Scientia Verlag, 1970.

Mirabeau, V.R. 1764. *Philosophie rurale, ou économie générale et politique de l'agriculture*. Amsterdam, chez les Libraires Associés. Reprinted, Aalen: Scientia Verlag, 1972.

Oncken, A. (ed.). 1888. *Oeuvres économiques et philosophiques de François Quesnay*. Paris: Jules Peelman.

Petty, W. 1662. *A Treatise of Taxes and Contributions*. In *The Economic Writings of Sir William Petty*, Vol. 1, ed. C.H. Hull. Cambridge: Cambridge University Press, 1899.

Phillips, A. 1955. The Tableau Economique as a simple Leontief model. *Quarterly Journal of Economics* 69, February, 137–44.

Schumpeter, J.A. 1954. *History of Economic Analysis*. London: Allen & Unwin.

Spengler, J.J. 1958. Quesnay philosophe, empiriste, économiste. In INED (1958), Vol. 1.

Tsuru, S. 1942. On reproduction schemes. In *The Theory of Capitalist Development*, ed. P. Sweezy, New York: Monthly Review Press.

Vaggi, G. 1987. *The Economics of François Quesnay*. London: Macmillan.

Weulersse, G. 1910. *Le mouvement physiocratique en France (de 1756 à 1770)*. Paris: Felix Alcan.

Woog, H. 1950. *The Tableau Economique of François Quesnay*. Berne: Franckle Verlag.

queueing theory. Queueing theory is about mathematical models of congestion and delay phenomena. Most of the models are stochastic and, until the 1970s, they described physical rather than economic characteristics. For example, there is more theory from which one could deduce the (probability) distribution of the number of items stored in an inventory system than there is to specify a pattern of tolls which is appropriate for a municipal road traffic network. Similarly, the theory for models of a single service facility, such as a post office, is more highly developed than the theory for networks of service facilities, such as a multi-access computer network. Recent and current research, often motivated by emerging technology in manufacturing and computer-based communication systems, is redressing the imbalances.

The prehistory of queueing theory is the history of probability theory through the first quarter of this century. The Poisson process, which emerged from modelling 19th-century deaths in the Prussian army due to mule kicks, is particularly important in queueing theory. The growth of telephone systems this century precipitated the birth and nurtured the childhood of the theory. In particular, C. Palm and A.K. Erlang in Denmark, F. Pollaczek in France and various researchers at Bell Telephone Laboratories in the US made seminal contributions. So the standard elements of queueing models are an abstraction of a telephone switchboard with human telephone operators. Syski (1960) is a somewhat outdated exposition of queueing theory from the point of view of telephony.

A 'single service facility' is the class of queueing models which correspond to a telephone switchboard. The jargon of telephony will be used here to describe these models. The canonical form of a queueing model of a single service facility has the following elements. The *arrival process* is the stochastic process of arriving calls for service. The *service regime* specifies the (probability) distribution of *service times* (durations of telephone calls), the matching of callers with servers, the priority rules (who is served next if there are more subscribers attempting to place calls than there are available operators) and the number of *servers* (number of operators). In a *loss system*, a caller receives a 'system busy signal' if all servers are busy; the caller is then *blocked* from entering the queueing system. In a *delay system*, a limited number of callers can wait until a server becomes free to process them.

The most common model analysed is a delay system with a Poisson arrival process, service times which are independent and identically distributed exponential random variables (which are independent too of the arrival process), calls are served on a first come, first served priority basis, and there is room for infinitely many callers to wait, if necessary. The *Kendall notation* (after D.G. Kendall) for this model is $M/M/c$ or $M/M/c/\infty$. In this notation, say $X/Y/c/n$, X refers to the arrival process, Y refers to the distribution of service times, c is the number of servers, and n is the number of calls which the system can contain. If $n = c$, the model is a loss system; if $n > c$, there is waiting room for $n - c$ callers (in addition to at most c callers being served). If $c = 1$, it is a *single-server* model; otherwise, it is a *multi-server* model. If X is written as GI, the arrival process is a renewal process (independent, identically distributed, non-negative interarrival times); a Poisson process is a renewal process, so GI includes M. If Y is written as G, no particular service-time distribution is assumed. If Y is written as M, the service-time distribution is exponential. If $n = \infty$, then n is often deleted in the notation.

The $GI/G/1$ model is mathematically challenging but it is thoroughly understood (see Cohen, 1969). Very little is known about the $GI/G/c/n$ model with $c > 1$. Current research utilizes martingale methods in the spirit of D.V. Lindley's random-walk analysis of $GI/G/1$. More generally, current research on descriptive queueing theory is more closely tied to underlying basic stochastic processes, such as renewal or stationary point processes, than was true in earlier years.

DESCRIPTIVE QUEUEING THEORY. The theory developed prior to the 1970s, concentrates on single-facility rather than network models, exact analytical solutions rather than approximate computational methods, and descriptive rather than normative theory. The principal induced random variables studied are the number of calls in the queueing system as a whole, the number of calls in queue waiting to be served, the lengths of time calls are held in the queue and in the system, the number of servers who are busy processing calls, and the cumulative fraction of arriving calls which are blocked from entering the system because it is full. These random variables are indexed by time or caller. *Transient analysis* concerns the moments of these random variable when the indices are finite. *Long-run, equilibrium*, and *stationary* analysis concerns the moments if the indices tend to infinity. Many applications utilize computer-based simulations to estimate the moments. Nevertheless, simulation and queueing theory are regarded as separate topics, and the former subject will not be discussed in this essay.

The usual goal is to provide a formula which specifies a moment. If necessary, Laplace transforms are sought as a surrogate for the following reason. Let X be a non-negative random variable with distribution function $F(\cdot)$ and kth moment and Laplace transform

$$E(X^k) = \int_0^\infty x^k \, \mathrm{d}F(x) \quad \text{and} \quad f(\theta) = \int_0^\infty \mathrm{e}^{-\theta x} \, \mathrm{d}F(x) = E(\mathrm{e}^{-\theta x})$$

where $E(\cdot)$ denotes expected value and θ is a complex number. Under rather general conditions, $E(X^k) = (-1)^k f^{(k)}(0)$ where $f^{(k)}(\theta)$ denotes the kth derivative. The essentially one-to-one correspondence between distribution functions and transforms is another reason to derive a transform. However, the numerical or analytical inversion of a transform or the differentiation above can be extremely formidable tasks; sometimes, a transform merely corresponds to an existence theorem concerning moments.

Many properties of $GI/G/c/n$ models have been derived by making specific assumptions about the distributions of interarrival times and service times and then analysing the detailed distributional properties of the induced stochastic processes. However, a few powerful results have been obtained by analysing the sample paths (or trajectories) of these stochastic processes; distributional assumptions can occasionally be avoided. The most important example of such a non-parametric result is the equation $L = \lambda W$ and its generalizations first proved by J.D.C. Little. In this equation, L, W, and λ are the respective long-run averages of the number of calls in the system, the amount of time which calls spend in the system and the rate per unit time at which calls arrive. This equation is valid for essentially all reasonably stable queueing-like models in which the three elements in the equation are well defined. In the particular case of $GI/G/c/n$, no particular assumptions are necessary concerning interarrival-time or service-time distributions. For example, the formula is valid for models with heterogeneous servers, multiple classes of arriving calls (some of which might arrive in groups), and interdependent service and arrival processes.

The Poisson process arises naturally in many applications because, as A.Y. Khintchine first proved, it is the limit process when a large number of independent point processes are combined. The arrival processes in many applications are aggregates of many independent inputs. The Poisson process is particularly useful because the 'memoryless' property of exponential random variables induces Markov processes. This property leads to some results which are valid for models regardless of the service time distribution. The best-known example is the *Pollaczek–Khintchine formula* for the $M/G/1$ model

$$L = \rho + [\rho^2(\sigma^2\mu^2 + 1)]/[2(1 - \rho)] \tag{1}$$

where μ^{-1} and σ^2 are the respective mean and variance of the service-time distribution and $\rho = \lambda/\mu$. A corresponding result is obtained for W by exploiting $L = \lambda W$. Formula (1) and other properties of $M/G/1$ are obtained by analysing the *embedded Markov chain* of the number of calls in the system at instants of time when calls are terminated and leave the system.

It is *not* generally true that the stationary distribution of a discrete-time process embedded in a continuous-time process yields the long-run time-average probabilities for the latter. However, Strauch's PASTA result (cf. Wolff, 1982) is that 'Poisson arrivals "see" time averages.' That is, the long-run distribution of the number of calls in a queueing model, as seen by the calls at their moments of arrival, is the same as the long-run continuous-time average probabilities if the arrival process is Poisson.

Queueing models with Poisson arrival processes and exponential service times, $M/M/c/n$ for example, are appealing because the number of calls in the system is a continuous-time Markov chain, which is also a birth–death process. Therefore, many operating characteristics of these models can be computed explicitly. It is tempting to use the computed quantities as 'guestimates' of the same operating characteristics in models which are *not* $M/M/c/n$ (and whose operating characteristics are too difficult to compute). Although such approximations can be poor, occasionally they are perfect! Recent and current research, under the label *insensitivity*, utilizes generalized semi-Markov processes to establish sufficient conditions for $M/M/c/n$ properties to be valid more generally (cf. Schassberger, 1978).

Calls in a network of queues may be serviced at a sequence of service centres. The diverse applications of such models include manufacturing, computer operating systems, communications networks, vehicular traffic and patients in hospitals. A typical patient's sequence of services might be admission, X-ray, surgery, recovery room, physical therapy, etc. The stochastic processes associated with networks of queues can be extremely complicated; so Markov process assumptions are usually made. The specific assumptions are that the interarrival times of exogenous arrivals and the internal service times are exponentially distributed, calls move between nodes according to a Markov chain, and each node can hold as many calls as necessary. This model is called a *Jackson network* after R.R.P. Jackson and J.R. Jackson.

J.R. Jackson obtained the surprising result that the steady-state distribution of the number of calls at each node in a Jackson network can be computed as if the nodes were independent $M/M/c$ queueing models. However, P.J. Burke confirmed the complexity of network models by showing that the flows between nodes in a Jackson network are *not* generally Poisson processes. See Disney and Konig (1985) for a survey of flows in queueing networks and Kelley (1979) for a somewhat dated treatise on the rapidly developing area of queueing networks.

The application of Jackson's result requires the computation of a normalizing constant; this task is burdensome and pressures modellers to build network models with relatively few nodes and calls. The first wave of widespread applications, during the 1970s, was directed at computer system performance evaluation. Extremely small and simplistic models were surprisingly effective in describing some features of these systems. This success spawned sub-disciplines in computer science and attracted the attention of analysts of 'flexible manufacturing systems', labelled FMS. Many papers continue to be written on the application of queueing network models to FMS, but their scientific basis has not yet been confirmed. Relatively few FMS have thus far been built and installed (prices of tens of millions US dollars are typical in 1986) and most of these are not yet heavily utilized. Data do not yet exist to confirm the existence of major stochastic elements in machine processing times or part interarrival times. It may turn out that the dominant issues to which modelling effort should be devoted are machine breakdowns (server reliability) and schedules of the input stream of work to be performed.

Explicit solutions of queueing models are often unavailable and, if obtainable, ill-suited to numerical calculation. Beginning with results by J.F.C. Kingman, numerous bounds on operating characteristics have been derived, and the approximate solution of queueing models is an active research area. The bounds initially obtained were valid for all distributions of service times and interarrival times and utilized only their means and variances. Since the actual values of operating characteristics usually depend on more than the first two moments of underlying distributions, it is unreasonable to expect the bounds to be close to actual values in all instances. So one direction of improvement of the bounds is to restrict the classes of underlying distribution; for example, to assume that the service-time distribution has a monotone hazard rate. This effort corresponds to research on the classical moment problem of Chebyshev and Markov (see Godwin, 1964), but linkages between the two literatures have only begun to be constructed.

Approximate solutions of queueing models have been sought in several ways. One class of approximations consists of an exact solution to an approximate model; these *system approximations* are obtained in an ad hoc manner, but their quality can be excellent (see earlier remarks on insensitivity; see also Stoyan, 1977, for a survey). Another class of approximations, initiated by D.L. Iglehart, approximates a queueing process with a diffusion process. Diffusion approximations can be particularly effective in studying queues in 'heavy traffic', i.e. $\rho = \lambda/(c\mu) \geqslant 1$ in $GI/G/c$ (see Whitt, 1974, for a survey). Diffusion approximations of queueing networks is an important but incompletely understood topic (see Harrison, 1985).

NORMATIVE QUEUEING THEORY. Few normative results in queueing theory existed prior to the 1970s. If a normative consideration arose in an application before then, it would typically be resolved superficially by appending a cost function to an expected-value formula such as (1) above. For example, the issue might have been posed as the selection of the service rate, μ, in an $M/G/1$ model. Suppose that $c(\mu)$ is the cost per unit time of the service process if the rate is μ, and h is the cost per unit time per customer in the system. Then the goal might have been to minimize the total average cost per unit time, namely $hL(\mu)+c(\mu)$, where the notation $L(\mu)$ for the left side of (1) makes the dependence on μ explicit. The numerical or analytical solution of such optimization problems yields little qualitative insight.

Less is known about the optimization of the design of queueing systems than about their optimal operation. Among the few unambiguous results is the (intuitive) superiority of a $GI/G/c$ system compared to c separate $GI/G/1$ facilities (μ being the same for all servers in both cases) unless there are pronounced diseconomies of scale. A more delicate issue is the trade-off between the service rate, μ, and the number of servers, c. Under what conditions are a few fast servers superior to many slow servers? S. Stidham Jr (1970) has established sufficient conditions for the optimality of a fast single server.

The order in which calls are serviced, namely the priority rule employed, is an important operational policy in many applications. First, Little's equation, $L = \lambda W$, implies that queue disciplines that do not affect L will leave the asymptotic mean waiting time unchanged. Examples of such disciplines are FIFO (first in, first out), LIFO (last in, first out) and random order of service. However, there are notable second moment effects. Among those disciplines which leave L, hence W, unchanged, the smallest (largest) variance of the asymptotic delay is achieved by FIFO (LIFO).

In some applications (manufacturing and main-frame computers, for example), it is feasible to interrupt a call's service and resume it later without losing the benefit of the service time already expended on the call; this is a *pre-empt resume* service regime. The SRPT (shortest remaining processing-time discipline) places into service at time t whichever call present at t has the smallest remaining service time. This presumes that the service times of calls are known on arrival, residual service times are known until service is completed, and a pre-empt resume regime exists. Let $X(t, \omega)$ be the number of calls in the system at time t if ω denotes the realization of arrival and service times. Then SRPT minimizes $X(t, \omega)$ for every t and ω if (a) the model does not admit disciplines which permit servers to remain idle while a call is in the system and not being served, and (b) the discipline employed will not affect arrival times or aggregate service times.

Until recently, it has been surprisingly difficult to characterize optimal policies for the number of servers which should be active in multi-server queueing models with costs of change. Consider a model with a Poisson arrival process, exponential service times, constant cost per unit time per call in the system, constant cost per unit time per busy server, and positive costs of activating a dormant server or deactivating an active server. By analogy with inventory theory, a policy which minimizes the average cost per unit time or the expected present value of the cost over an infinite horizon should have the following form. If C is the maximum number of servers who can be active, there are numbers $a_0 \leqslant a_1 \leqslant \cdots \leqslant a_C$ and $b_0 \leqslant \cdots \leqslant b_C$ with $a_c \leqslant b_c$ for all c, such that if c servers are active at time t and $X(t)$ calls are in the system, then no change should occur if $a_c \leqslant X(t) \leqslant b_c$; replace c with $c+1$ if $X(t) > b_c$; replace c with $c-1$ if $X(t) < a_c$. This problem is completely solved for $C = 1$ but has failed to yield to numerous investigations of $C > 1$. Lu and Serfozo (1983) have obtained the only continuous-time results which warrant optimism that the conjectured form of the solution is valid for $C \geqslant 1$.

Several writers have studied the regulation of queue size via prices. In one class of models initiated by P. Naor and developed by U. Yechiali and others, an exogenous arrival process generates callers who may choose to *balk* (i.e. refuse to enter the service facility) when they arrive and learn the price for entry then in effect. Each arriving call is assumed to employ a balking rule which is individually optimal. The price-maker's problem is to devise an optimal pricing policy. In this setting, a price policy may fluctuate with the number of calls in the system and, perhaps, other summaries of the past history of the process. The typical analysis contrasts the pricing policies which are socially and entrepreneurially optimal. Mendelson (1985) applies this body of results to the problem of pricing computer services. His and others' work demonstrates that new theory will emerge from studies of structured classes of pricing applications. In view of the general importance of the subject of pricing and congestion, the dearth of pricing results is striking.

The problem of routing calls in queueing networks is closely related to the issue of priority assignment. The former optimization problem arises in numerous applications, but it appears to be forbiddingly difficult. Little is known except for networks with two nodes and unidirectional flow; the subject of *stochastic scheduling* is closely related to this problem (see Pinedo and Schrage, 1982; Weiss, 1982). Crabill, Gross, and Magazine (1977) is a somewhat dated survey of normative queueing theory.

RESEARCH DIRECTIONS. Current research is often influenced by the explosive growth in computer usage. Many studies are directed at algorithms rather than analytical representations of transforms (Neuts, 1981). One finds stochastic models which have been devised with a view towards their non-parametric flexibility and their solution with computationally stable algorithms, and software which facilitates applications by encouraging the user to perform sensitivity analyses by varying the model structure as well as model parameters (see Ramakrishnan and Mitra (1982) and Whitt (1983). These directions are likely to be followed in the future in combination with the development of approximate methods which are computationally feasible for modelling much larger networks than are presently practical.

Tailoring theory to large classes of structured applications, such as communications, manufacturing and mainframe computer systems occurs increasingly often. This increased attention to special structure induced by an application encourages greater attention to modelling human behaviour in some important applications. An obvious and important by-product will be a more extensive and sophisticated theory of pricing and congestion. In particular, results may emerge in which, unlike present theory, arrival processes are influenced by callers' previous waiting-time experiences.

MATTHEW J. SOBEL

See also CONGESTION; OPERATIONS RESEARCH.

BIBLIOGRAPHY

Cohen, J.W. 1969. *The Single Server Queue.* New York: Wiley.

Cooper, R.B. 1981. *Introduction to Queueing Theory.* 2nd edn, New York: North-Holland.

Crabill, T.B., Gross, D. and Magazine, M.J. 1977. A classified bibliography of research on optimal design and control of queues. *Operations Research* 15, 304–18.

Disney, R.L. and Konig, D. 1985. Queueing networks – a survey of their random processes. *SIAM Review* 27(3), 335–403.

Godwin, H.J. 1964. *Inequalities on Distribution Functions.* London: Griffin.

Gross, D. and Harris, C.M. 1985. *Fundamentals of Queueing Theory.* 2nd edn, New York: Wiley.

Harrison, J.M. 1985. *Brownian Motion and Stochastic Flow Systems.* New York: Wiley.

Heyman, D.P. and Sobel, M.J. 1982. *Stochastic Models in Operations Research*, Vol. I: *Stochastic Processes and Operating Characteristics.* New York: McGraw-Hill.

Kelley, F.P. 1979. *Reversibility and Stochastic Networks.* New York: Wiley.

Lu, F.V. and Serfozo, R. 1983. M/M/1 queueing decision processes with monotone hysteretic optimal policies. *Operations Research* 32(5), 1116–32.

Mendelson, H. 1985. Pricing computer services: queueing effects. *Communications ACM* 28(3), March, 312–21.

Neuts, M.F. 1981. *Matrix-Geometric Solutions in Stochastic Models.* Baltimore: Johns Hopkins University Press.

Pinedo, M. and Schrage, L. 1982. Stochastic shop scheduling – a survey. In *Deterministic and Stochastic Scheduling*, ed. M.A.H. Dempster et al., Dordrecht: Reidel.

Ramakrishnan, K.G. and Mitra, D. 1982. An overview of PANACEA, a software package for analyzing Markovian queuing networks. *Bell Systems Technology Journal* 61(10), 2849–72.

Schassberger, R. 1978. Insensitivity of stationary probabilities in networks of queues. *Advances in Applied Probability* 10(4), 906–12.

Stidham, S., Jr. 1970. On the optimality of single-server queueing systems. *Operations Research* 18, 708–32.

Stoyan, D. 1977. Bounds and approximations in queueing through monotonicity and continuity. *Operations Research* 25, 851–63.

Syski, R. 1960. *Introduction to Congestion Theory in Telephone Systems.* Edinburgh and London: Oliver & Boyd.

Weiss, G. 1982. Multiserver stochastic scheduling. In *Deterministic and Stochastic Scheduling*, ed. M.A.H. Dempster et al., Dordrecht: Reidel.

Whitt, W. 1983. The queuing network analyzer. *Bell Systems Technology Journal* 62(9), 2779–816.

Whitt, W. 1974. Heavy traffic limit theorems for queues: a survey. In *Mathematical Methods in Queueing Theory*, ed. A.B. Clarke, New York: Springer-Verlag.

quotas and tariffs. Until the mid-1960s, it was commonly argued that quotas and tariffs were equivalent protective devices in terms of their effects on the volume of imports, domestic price, domestic output, and domestic consumption. Yet, at times they have been viewed as non-equivalent, as for instance revealed by the relative lenience of GATT rules toward tariffs vis-à-vis quotas.

Bhagwati (1965) initiated the discussion on the comparative properties of tariffs and quotas and showed that the equivalence result is restricted to cases that are characterized by competitive market structures. In the context of a partial equilibrium model, he demonstrated that the presence of monopoly power in production and/or in quota holdings would lead to a breakdown of the equivalence proposition. Since then, the relationship between quotas and tariffs has been examined within the general equilibrium framework and the non-equivalence result has been demonstrated under a variety of conditions, such as uncertainty and retaliation.

When the equivalence result holds in terms of the real equilibrium conditions, then the welfare implications of the two protective devices are also identical. However, when there is non-equivalence, it is important to know which policy instrument is preferable in achieving certain objectives such as keeping the level of imports at a certain level, revenue collection by the government or protecting a particular domestic industry. Thus, an extension of the literature has further investigated the welfare implications of employing quotas vs. tariffs as policy instruments when equivalence does not hold.

The classical equivalence argument can be demonstrated

with the use of the Marshallian diagram below where *DD* and *SS* are domestic demand and supply schedules for the importable good. Assuming that the importing country is small, the foreign supply curve S^w can be drawn horizontally at the C.I.F. landed price for imports, P^w. A tariff rate t^w will shift the S^w schedule to S^t. In the pre-tariff situation, *OA* and *AD* represent the quantity of domestic supply and the level of imports respectively. After the imposition of the tariff, the domestic supply will increase to *OB*, while the level of imports will be reduced to *BC*. Now, the prevailing domestic price P^d is equal to $P^w\ (1+t^w)$ with *OC* representing the level of domestic consumption.

Equivalence means that there is a quota-equivalent of the tariff rate t^w, so that the levels of domestic output, imports, domestic consumption and domestic price resulting from the imposition of the tariff rate t^w can alternatively be produced by the use of an import-quota restriction. If the tariff is replaced by a quota that corresponds to the level of imports associated with t^w, that is *BC*, the prevailing domestic price will be P^d, while P^w is the C.I.F. price of imports. In this case, P^dP^w/OP^w will represent an *implicit* tariff, which is equal to the *explicit* tariff rate t^w, while *OB* and *BC* correspond to the level of domestic supply and imports respectively. Thus, the quota restriction is an equivalent alternative to the tariff in terms of obtaining a given level of imports, domestic production, domestic price and consumption. Furthermore, the welfare effects of quotas and tariffs would be identical if the tariff revenue, equal to the shaded area, is spent in the same way as the rents received by the import licensees, also equal to the shaded area.

Bhagwati (1965) challenged the equivalence proposition by introducing imperfect market conditions into the analysis. He showed that for equivalence to hold in terms of the real variable and welfare effects, there must be perfect competition in the domestic and international markets. Furthermore, quota holdings must be allocated to quota holders under competitive conditions. If, for instance, the domestic supplier is a monopolist, for the same level of imports, output will be higher and domestic price lower with a tariff, than with a

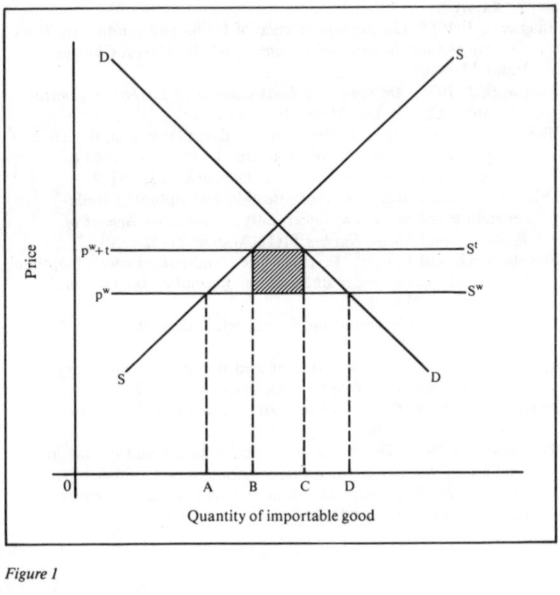

Figure 1

quota. The basic underlying reason for the non-equivalence in the presence of monopoly is the differential supply and demand shifts induced by the two alternative policies.

As Bhagwati (1978) later noted, the crucial assumption of the classical equivalence argument is that the supply and demand schedules are given. It is the violation of this implicit assumption that is common to the non-equivalence results under a variety of conditions, the presence of monopoly being only one of them.

In the general equilibrium context, Rodriguez (1974) and Tower (1975) took up the question of retaliation and showed that the two policy instruments will give rise to different dynamic processes. Earlier, Johnson (1953) had considered retaliation with optimum tariffs in a Cournot model, where each country sets its tariff optimally, taking the other country's tariff as given. He had showed that the retaliation process may lead to tariff cycles and to welfare improvement vis-à-vis free trade for a country exercising its monopoly power. In contrast, using an approach similar to Johnson's, Rodriguez (1974) and Tower (1975) demonstrated that optimum quota retaliation will lead asymptotically to the elimination of trade. The reason for this outcome is the fact that countries generate different offer curves when they retaliate, depending on whether they use tariffs or quotas as the retaliatory instrument. Given the neoclassical postulate that 'some trade is better than no trade', the analyses of Tower and Rodriguez also lead to the policy prescription that tariffs are preferable to quotas.

Both the Bhagwati demonstration and the Rodriguez–Tower analyses of non-equivalence are examples of shifts in demand and supply schedules *endogeneous* to the use of the trade policy instrument. There is yet another type of non-equivalence resulting from the exogeneous shifts in demand and supply schedules under conditions of uncertainty. This question was taken up Fishelson and Flatters (1975) and Pelcovitz (1976) within the partial equilibrium framework.

Fishelson and Flatters compare tariffs and quotas in the classical optimum tariff case, in which a large country facing a less than perfectly elastic foreign supply curve for its imports seeks to improve the terms of trade by restricting imports. They assume that in the absence of uncertainty, tariffs and quotas are exactly equivalent. They introduce uncertainty as stochastic behaviour attached independently to the domestic and foreign demand and supply functions for imports. The stochastic behaviour may result from random disturbances underlying the conditions of foreign and domestic supply and demand, or from random measurement error in determining the tariff and quota levels, or from rigidities in the legislative process. The analysis of Fishelson and Flatters reveals that when uncertainty is introduced, the two instruments are not generally equivalent in their welfare effects. Furthermore, they show that there is no basis for favouring one instrument over the other. The superiority of one instrument over the other depends on the precise source of the uncertainty and the properties of the relevant demand and supply functions. They conclude that tariffs are always preferable to quotas whenever the supply of imports is elastic, whereas quotas are more likely to be superior when the dominant source of uncertainty is due to foreign supply conditions and when the supply of imports is inelastic.

The Fishelson–Flatters analysis was significant not only in terms of introducing uncertainty as a stochastic process, but also because of the challenge it posed to the generally held presumption that tariffs are preferable to quotas under uncertainty since tariffs allow for more flexibility. It has been argued that when circumstances change so as to require a higher level of desired imports, if the initial level of desired imports had been achieved through a tariff, imports would be able to respond to the new conditions by increasing. This would not be possible under a quota system. In this context tariffs were presumed to be more desirable than quotas. Fishelson and Flatters pointed out that this reasoning ignores

> the possibility that under a given tariff structure the responsiveness of imports to a change in demand or supply may be such that the new level of imports overshoots the new optimal level by an amount greater than the amount by which the new optimum exceeds the old (quota) level of imports (Fishelson and Flatters 1975, p. 387).

Hence, depending on the conditions of uncertainty and supply and demand, it is possible that quotas are preferable to tariffs.

The ranking of optimal policies under conditions of uncertainty was further investigated by Pelcovitz (1976) in the case of a small country. While the Fishelson–Flatters analysis extended the discussion of non-equivalence of tariffs and quotas as welfare-maximizing policy instruments, using the classical optimum tariff problem, Pelcovitz compared quotas and tariffs as instruments for achieving a 'non-economic' objective, i.e. the constraining of expected imports to a prescribed level by a small country. The Pelcovitz analysis, thus, developed the (non)-equivalence literature in the direction of welfare ranking of tariffs and quotas in the presence of non-economic objectives, which are non-economic only in the sense that they refer to additional arguments in a social utility function other than the conventional ones of final consumption of goods and services. An alternative way of formulating such a problem is to treat these objectives as constraints in the social welfare maximization analysis. Examples of such objectives/constraints are achieving economic self-sufficiency, revenue raising on the part of the government, or achieving a certain level of production, consumption, export or import of a good, or achieving a certain level of employment in a particular industry. (As can be seen from these examples, the distinction between economic and non-economic objectives is an artificial one.)

Pelcovitz used a partial equilibrium model and showed that the tariff is not always preferable to a quota when the foreign demand curve is stochastic but the import demand curve is certain, while in the case of a stochastic import demand curve and a certain supply curve the tariff always dominates the quota. That is, given uncertainty, a tariff or quota that yields the same expected level of imports produces different social utility levels.

Indeed, the general result in the literature on quotas versus tariffs under uncertainty is that one policy will be the dominant one and most investigations then take as their point of departure the exact determination of the dominating policy under different circumstances. As pointed out above, the classical equivalence result applies in the case of a competitive market under certainty. However, Driscoll and Ford (1983) demonstrated that in the context of uncertainty it is also possible for quotas and tariffs to be equivalent if there is a feasibility of having quotas and tariffs *which are themselves state-contingent*.

Driscoll and Ford examined the case when the objective of policy is to maximize the net domestic consumers' surplus, with the constraint of achieving a certain expected level of output in the importables industry. This case is particularly relevant since very often the object of trade restriction is the protection of domestic industry.

Driscoll and Ford analysed trade restriction by the use of quotas and tariffs (the *ad valorem* and the specific tariff) not only when they are fixed policy instruments but also when they are state-contingent. The pre-existing literature had concentrated on fixed trade-restricting policies where the objective is to maximize the value of net domestic consumers' surplus subject to a constraint on the expected level of imports, the expected value of foreign exchange expenditure or the level of revenue raised by trade restriction, since it is not possible to have state-contingent policies under such constraints. In the case studied by Driscoll and Ford, such a policy is possible since the expected constraint does not directly contain the trade restricting instruments. Their analysis reveals that in the case of a fixed trade-restricting policy, a *specific* tariff is the optimal policy while the second best strategy would be the adoption of a quota rather than an *ad valorem* tariff, once more questioning the validity of the view that a tariff is superior to a quota due to the former's greater flexibility. Furthermore, any fixed trade-restricting policy can be dominated by its state-contingent counterpart and when state-contingent tariffs and quotas are feasible, *they can be equivalent*.

The analysis of quotas and tariffs has been recently extended in another direction to compare the monetary consequences of tariffs and quotas. The literature discussed so far gives no explicit consideration to money in the domestic economy. Blejer and Hillman (1982) and Kimbrough (1985) are examples of comparisons of tariffs and quotas in a monetary economy which point in the direction of non-equivalence results. This is another area which has yet to be further explored.

While orthodox economic theory has generally advocated free trade, quotas and tariffs have been extensively used particularly during periods of worldwide economic crisis. Their theoretical equivalence is now the exception rather than the rule and it is more important than ever to fully understand the differential impact of quotas and tariffs as policy instruments.

NILÜFER ÇAĞATAY

See also DEVALUATION; INTERNATIONAL TRADE; PROTECTION.

BIBLIOGRAPHY

Bhagwati, J. 1965. On the equivalence of tariffs and quotas. In *Trade, Growth and the Balance of Payments*, ed. R. Caves, Chicago: Rand McNally.

Bhagwati, J. 1978. *Anatomy and Consequences of Exchange Control Measures*. Cambridge, Mass.: Ballinger.

Blejer, M. and Hillman, A. 1982. On the dynamic non-equivalence of tariffs and quotas in the monetary model of the balance of payments. *Journal of International Economics* 13, 163–9.

Driscoll, N. and Ford, J. 1983. Protection and optimum trade-restricting policies under uncertainty. *Manchester School of Economic and Social Studies* 51(1), March, 21–32.

Fishelson, G. and Flatters, F. 1975. The (non)-equivalence of optimal tariffs and quotas under uncertainty. *Journal of International Economics* 5, 385–93.

Johnson, H. 1954. Optimum tariffs and retaliation. *Review of Economic Studies* 21, 142–53.

Kimbrough, K. 1985. Tariffs, quotas and welfare in a monetary economy. *Journal of International Economics* 19, 257–77.

Pelcovitz, M. 1976. Quotas versus tariffs. *Journal of International Economics* 6, 363–70.

Rodriguez, C. 1974. The non-equivalence of tariffs and quotas under retaliation. *Journal of International Economics* 4, 295–8.

Tower, A. 1975. The optimum quota and retaliation. *Review of Economic Studies* 42, 623–30.

R

race and economics. The concept of race enters formal economic theory through a range of areas primarily within labour economics. These include discrimination, inequality, human capital, labour market competition and segmentation, and class relations. The first substantive attention by neoclassical theory to the economic problems posed by race began with the work of Gary Becker in 1957 which approaches the subject from the standpoint of discrimination. (Race is addressed from a structural standpoint by Marx in *Capital*, Volume I, through his analysis of the impact of slavery and the slave trade on the working class of the United States.)

Subsequent to Becker there have been numerous theoretical advances and approaches towards an understanding of the role of race in the economy. There are three alternative formulations of the problem: (1) employer or employee discrimination; (2) labour supply; (3) competition between capitals and between capital and labour.

EMPLOYER/EMPLOYEE DISCRIMINATION. I. Becker presents race as a problem of 'taste' for discrimination or a 'distaste' for physical association with a particular race (his formulation would be equally applicable to any standard physical attribute such as sex). The taste for discrimination can come from the employer or employee. Becker's employer distaste model assumes two societies; B, which is relatively labour-abundant, and W, which is relatively capital-abundant. These two societies engage in voluntary trade with each other but with the capital of W having a distaste for working in physical proximity to B labour. Given the assumptions of a pure theory of international trade and without such distaste, B and W exchange their respective relatively abundant quantities until the marginal product of each factor is equal in both societies. However, because of the distaste or subjective preference of W employers, their utility function must be augmented to include the number of B workers and $dU_W < dL_B < 0$. The capital exported by W must receive a money return greater than the return on capital domestically employed. The differences between the return on domestic vs. exported capital is the return or compensation W employers feel they must have for being physically close to B labour. Since such compensation must be positive, discrimination reduces the quantity of W capital exported and the quantity of B labour exported.

Becker's model concludes that as a result of discrimination, W labour's money income increases and W capital's net income falls because with the reduction in W capitals exported and B labour imported, W labour works with more capital and W capital works with less labour.

> Since $f_{LL} < 0$ and $f_{KL} < 0$, the f_L, the wage of labor, rises under the described conditions. Since $f_{KL} < 0$, the f_{KW}, the money return to domestic capital, falls as more capital is employed (Becker, 1957).

In the absence of monopoly, discrimination would end if one employer did not have or did not exercise his distaste. This employer would reap abnormal profits thus forcing other competitors to follow, assuming the drive for profits is stronger than racial distaste.

II. A more advanced version of the employer discrimination model are 'statistical discrimination models' (Reich, 1981). Such models make discrimination by employers more 'rational' in their employee hirings than Becker's subjective preference criteria. Racial discrimination results from problems associated with the personnel costs of hiring, training and identifying productivity. Such costs give rise to discrimination in the normal pursuit of profits; consequently, discrimination persists.

Personnel costs affect racial employment in the following way. A Race A employer with few or no workers of Race B may want to employ some. However, the costs of hiring and training new workers would not be offset by Race B's lower wages. The costs are profit maximization considerations, therefore, racial inequality persists as an integral part of competition. Although marginal changes arc made, the tendency is for no major overhaul in the racial composition of any employer's work force.

Prejudiced perceptions of Race B workers' productivity influence Race A employer's queueing or prioritizing workers for employment. Since it is costly to determine productivity prior to employment, employers of Race A presume that all workers of race B are less productive than Race A workers. This presumably protects the employer because it is much more costly to hire an inefficient worker than to pass over a productive one. As a result, Race B workers are not hired or hired at a lower wage rate. Prejudiced perceptions may emerge from a variety of sources. Regardless, in this model, they provide a low cost screen in the employee search process.

III. Employee discrimination models are based on perceived and competing economic and racial interests. Such models require the ability of workers of Race A to obtain cooperation from employers and other actors in Race A to form a 'cartel' to discriminate against workers of Race B. The following characteristics describe this cartel arrangement (see Krueger, 1963; Bergmann, 1971):

1. Race A capital and labour combine to discriminate against Race B's labour even though Race A labour gains while Race A capital loses (as per Becker).
2. Racial income differences can be accounted for through Race A's political control which limits inputs into Race B's schooling and, thus, skills.
3. Further discrimination against Race B takes place through the cartel arrangement by restricting hiring, occupational mobility, wage payments, access to capital markets, and through price discrimination.
4. Race B's labour is 'crowded' into certain lower paying occupations through racial discrimination. This results in a depressed marginal product because excess labour is employed and, hence, wage rates are depressed.

The results reflected in the combination/cartel arrangements require critical institutional mechanisms to assure enforcement of the 'rules' of the cartel.

LABOUR SUPPLY. Race is a component of labour supply analysis primarily in relationship to human capital theory. Differences in the quantity/quality of human capital explains racial income differences. While the subjective demand for human capital by Race B may be the same as Race A's subjective demand for human capital, the objective capacity to invest is less due to lower initial endowments which may result from discrimination. Additionally the supply of human capital, e.g., education and health care, is likely to be less (Sowell, 1975).

Labour supply analyses of racial inequality tend to locate the discrimination problem outside of the economic area, generally focusing on education as the critical form of human capital. Contemporary analyses of racial inequality have raised the question of the inequality of demand for human capital in the form of education (Sowell, 1975). Accordingly, an emerging 'underclass', disproportionately of a particular race, has a low demand for education as a result of cultural variables which reject work at the prevailing wage rate. The important cultural variables can emerge from geographic dislocation such as migration from a rural to an urban setting, or from previous experience in the labour market.

COMPETITION. All of the previously discussed approaches to race involve competition theories. Marxian economists have also approached race from the standpoint of either structural conflict between capital and labour, or between capitalists, or both. The Marxian concepts of accumulation and class struggle provide the foundation of this approach to an analysis of race. Race is examined not only to understand racial inequality as in previously discussed formulations, but also to understand competition between firms and capital labour conflict (Baron, 1975; Harris, 1972; Reich, 1981; Sysmanski, 1975).

Racial inequality, in this framework, is the product of the pursuit of profits. Particularly, the pursuit of cheap resource markets gives economic rationality to the use of race as a means of cheapening the cost of Race B's labour. Institutional arrangements as suggested in the 'cartel' approach, and/or direct discrimination as suggested in the employer discrimination approach, may be the explicit manifestation of the pursuit of profits.

Racial inequality may also be a product of capital–labour conflict due to deliberate manipulation of Race B's access to employment by either capital or labour from Race A. In such instances, race is utilized to strengthen or weaken a particular side of the conflict. Capital may utilize cheaper labour from Race B to reduce labour's bargaining strength. Race A labour may join with Race B labour to prevent such tactics and, thereby, strengthen Race A labour's posture.

Race, in this framework, both influences and is influenced by economic processes. Often in this framework, racial inequality and the manipulation of race in competition/conflict is considered endemic to the competitive profit pursuit.

In the past 30 years there has been a dramatic increase in the attention of economic theory to race and race related issues. As indicated above, these approaches either focus on market imperfections or on the structural character of capitalism as explanations of racial discrimination and/or inequality. Most structuralist analyses also utilize race as a means of explaining the dynamics of economic processes.

H. STANBACK

BIBLIOGRAPHY

Baron, H. 1975. *The Demand for Black Labor*. Boston: New England.

Becker, G.S. 1957. *The Economics of Discrimination*. 2nd edn, Chicago: University of Chicago Press, 1971.

Bergmann, B. 1971. The effect on white incomes of discrimination in employment. *Journal of Political Economy* 71(2), March–April, 294–31.

Harris, D.J. 1972. The black ghetto as colony: a theoretical critique and alternative formulation. *Review of Black Political Economy* 2(4), Summer.

Krueger, A. 1963. The economics of discrimination. *Journal of Political Economy* 71, October, 481–6.

Reich, M. 1981. *Racial Inequality: A Political Economic Analysis*. Princeton: Princeton University Press.

Sowell, T. 1975. *Race and Economics*. New York: David McKay.

Sysmanski, A. 1975. Trends in economic discrimination against blacks in the U.S. working class. *Review of Radical Political Economics* 7(3), Fall, 1–21.

radical political economy. There is no simple generalization that can characterize the diverse and at times inconsistent principles and theories that comprise radical economics. As Martin Bronfenbrenner found in his 1970 review article, 'Radical economics in America' (Bronfenbrenner, 1970), it is much easier to establish what radical economists *do* than what radical economics *is*. This essay explores what radical economists do by examining both the common concerns that unite them and the theoretical disputes that divide them.

The basic common concerns, which were indeed the impetus for a revival of radical thought in the 1960s, are inequality and imperialism. Finding neoclassical theory either vacuous or apologetic in explaining the persistence of these phenomena, younger economists began to turn to the works of Marxian and other non-orthodox economists for insight and analysis. Among the many contemporary sources widely used as references, two of the most influential on imperialism were André Gunder Frank's *Capitalism and Underdevelopment in Latin America* (1967) and Harry Magdoff's *Age of Imperialism* (1969). Broader systemic analyses of the failures of capitalism that were extensively read and cited at the time include Baran and Sweezy's *Monopoly Capitalism* (1966) and Ernest Mandel's *Marxist Economic Theory* (1969).

As a direct result of the growing interest in non-neoclassical theory, the long-established journal *Monthly Review* was discovered by a new generation of sympathetic economists and a series of new journals appeared, including *The Review of Radical Political Economy*, *Socialist Review*, *New Left Review*, *Capital and Class* and *Politics and Society*. At the same time, prominent economists were working on and publishing in Marxian economic theory. In 1968, publication of a collection of works by economists such as Josef Steindl, Maurice Dobb and Wassily Leontief (Horowitz, 1968) reflected a new respectability of Marxian economic theory.

In the early years of the radical revival, the common concerns, coupled with a theoretical innocence and eclecticism, made for strange bedfellows. In the Union for Radical Political Economics (URPE), for example, Marxist and libertarian ideas were represented. But as theoretical sophistication grew, the differences between radicals, rather than their alliance in opposition to capitalism, came to the fore. What remains as the core of radical economics is the maintenance of class concerns while reformulating classical Marxian analysis. These reworkings of orthodox Marxian theory range from modest clarifications to models from which certain fundamental Marxian categories are conspicuously absent.

Beyond this most basic unity, radicals are divided on many theoretical and empirical issues. This account of radical political economy considers three related areas of radical thought in which reformulation and disagreement are most active: the connection between values and prices, the causes of economic crisis and the appropriateness to radical economics of the methodology of Keynes or Sraffa.

1. PRICE OR VALUE? The debate over the labour theory of value is analytically the primary debate in radical political economy. From positions in this debate follow positions on crisis theory and on the possibility of synthesis between class-based models and those of Sraffa, Keynes or neoclassical general equilibrium.

Briefly, the issue raised by reconsiderations of Marxian theory of value and surplus value is the relevance of labour-denominated values for explaining the rate of profit and prices. Defence of the labour theory of value is grounded in the nature of labour in a capitalist economy. Labour is a commodity like no other because it alone can be exploited. Only labour input can, even in the absence of market imperfections, be forced by social conditions to work longer than is necessary to reproduce its own value. The gap between the value produced by workers and the value received in wages is then surplus value, the absolute measure of exploitation. Surplus value thus carries with it an entire set of social relations between classes, and value theory highlights what is historically specific to the capitalist economy. From this perspective, only a value analysis, which expresses the inequality of classes in their access to means of production, can correctly analyse capitalism.

Surplus value is the technical centrepiece of this interpretation of Marxian economics, acting as a centre of gravity determining in the limit relative prices and the rate of profit. Value and surplus value therefore are seen to be necessary for both a theory of price and a theory of profit. What is still at issue within this approach, however, is the precise sense in which value does determine prices. With varying capital/labour ratios among sectors, with different turnover times for capital, with heterogeneous labour and with joint production, any simple correspondence between value and price disappears. More complicated correspondences have been developed, in particular iterative methods which transform values into prices in the case of differing capital/labour ratios (Shaikh, 1977), and joint production problems have been addressed (Morishima, 1973), but there are no universally accepted solutions to the problem of determining prices through values. One criticism of defences of the labour theory of value based on solutions to the transformation problem argues that Marx never intended to establish a simple transformation relation between value and prices. Rather, values and prices should be seen as an expression of the inherently contradictory realities of production and circulation (Mohun and Himmelweit, 1981). Value holds sway in production, while prices reign in circulation, and the two spheres are subject to different laws by virtue of their different forms. The use-value of the commodity labour-power is the key to understanding production and exploitation, but it is exchange value which determines prices. Equating value and price destroys Marx's complex distinction between use-value and exchange-value and so obscures the process of exploitation.

A related criticism is made of solutions to the problem of joint production, a case in which values of produced commodities may be negative. These solutions are based on the notion that labour embodied can be defined as a technical coefficient of production. But value, orthodox critics argue, is more than a purely physical relationship between inputs and outputs, so the joint production problem can be 'solved' only at the cost of giving up on the historically-specific concept of value as an expression of relations of production under *capitalism*. Value, then, is not a quantitative concept alone; it is also qualitative, representing the social realities of class inequality and conflict (Sweezy, 1981).

Those who would jettison the labour theory of value altogether while maintaining a class analysis argue on two grounds: the labour theory of value is inconsistent and it is redundant (Steedman, 1977). Inconsistency arguments expand on the difficulties of maintaining a labour theory of price with fixed capital and joint production. Redundancy arguments focus rather on the sufficiency of data on the real wage and the coefficients of the prevailing technique for determining prices and the rate of profit. Indeed, labour values are calculated from precisely these same data, so that labour values at best coexist with prices and the rate of profit, but in no way determine them. Hence, values are redundant to a surplus approach to explaining profit and prices. Moreover, these heterodox critics argue that *exploitation* does *not* depend upon a labour theory of value. One model of exploitation and class, developed by John Roemer (1982), finds that a general class-based theory of exploitation requires a new definition of labour values, a definition in which labour values are dependent upon exchange values, that is, upon prices. Turning the direction of determination around, Roemer concludes that the only way in which exploitation has any class content is when prices determine values. In addition, Roemer argues that any meaningful definition of exploitation must consider alternative possibilities open to workers. Under these conditions, if workers employed by capitalists cannot do better on their own (as is likely to be the case under increasing returns to scale), then workers are not exploited. These results are criticized on the grounds that Roemer's model, designed to compare exploitation across socio-economic systems (for example, capitalism and socialism), is not constructed around the *differentiae specificae* of capitalism. As a general theory of economic systems, it does not need a distinction between values and prices, which is necessary only to capture the essential contradiction of *capitalism*. Thus, by giving up on values, Roemer is only following the logic of an a-historical theory of exploitation. Adherents to the classical labour theory of value do not believe that his model invalidates the labour theory for analysing a *capitalist* economy.

2. CRISIS THEORY. To a large extent, positions on crisis theory follow from positions on the nature and role of the labour theory of value. The most orthodox, or 'fundamentalist' position is that the primary source of instability in capitalism is the tendency of the capital/labour ratio (measured in value terms and otherwise known as the organic composition of capital) to rise over time as capitalists substitute capital for labour. (For a compendium of radical crisis theory, see Union for Radical Political Economics, 1978.) The cost to capitalists of this substitution is that the base from which surplus value is extracted shrinks as machines replace exploitable workers. Thus the maximum profit (surplus) which capitalists can earn declines over time. This is clearly a long-run theory of crisis, since it is only the potential maximum profit which is affected, and also at any given time, other problems in the economy can affect profits. But in this view a falling rate of profit due to a rising organic composition of capital will always be the dominant constraint under which capitalists operate and the constraint will bind ever more tightly as capitalism develops. A critique of this position argues that capitalists will never *choose* a technique which reduces the rate of profit, whatever a labour theory of value argues about the ceiling on potential profits (Okishio, 1961). Other critics argue against any *a priori* tendency in one direction or another, but identify specific

structural changes in inter-industry relations which could lower the average profit rate (Rowthorn and Harris, 1985).

Radical views of crisis which are less closely tied to a labour theory of value still emphasize class conflict as the ultimate cause of crisis. The most prominent of this type of crisis theory is a social structure of accumulation approach, which views the periodic deep crises of capitalism as the result of accumulating rigidities in institutions which once resolved or at least mediated class tensions (Gordon, 1980; Mandel, 1980). At the centre of this story is the debilitating effect of class conflict on all capitalist institutions. Exacerbating the tendency to breakdown is the increasing interdependence of institutions in advanced capitalism: one weak link, like US international competitiveness, can undermine several other critical institutions. Although social structure theories of crisis tell a story of macroeconomic imbalance, theoretically a distinction between labour and labour-power is the crucial concept. Ultimately, capitalism cannot maintain stable institutions, particularly labour peace, because it cannot deliver the goods; it cannot grow smoothly. What retards growth is inefficiency, and the capitalist firm is inherently inefficient because it minimizes the cost of labour, not the use of labour power. In other words, when the capitalist firm maximizes profit it does *not* minimize the physical use of resources and hence is inefficient. Waste is thus argued to be an integral feature of capitalism (Bowles, Gordon and Weisskopf, 1983). Associated with this position is a large literature on the labour process in capitalism, which analyses the behaviour of the capitalist firm both historically and theoretically as a continuing search for a reconciliation of efficiency and profitability (Braverman, 1974; Edwards, 1979; Bluestone and Harrison, 1982).

Another institutional approach to explaining crisis highlights financial institutions. Here, money and credit arrangements are seen to be the most vulnerable institutions of advanced capitalism. The basic argument is that competition and the unplanned nature of capitalist production generate escalating demand for ever-growing credit emissions, which eventually cannot sustain their value in terms of the growth of real productive assets in the economy. This perspective rejects a one-sided emphasis on the labour process, or the point of production, as the source of crisis tendencies. It argues instead that production and circulation are mutually dependent, and that the role of credit is at least as important a determinant of growth in advanced capitalism as the ability of capitalists to wrest a surplus from their workers. Much of this work expands on Marx's theory of money by extending value analysis to non-produced commodities (de Brunhoff, 1976; Foley, 1982; Lipietz, 1982). Another branch remains agnostic on the relation between value and money, but argues that an important source of money emissions is the mediation of class conflict through inflation. Thus, periods of heightened class conflict are likely to be times of monetary instability (Rowthorn, 1977).

3. MARX, SRAFFA AND KEYNES. From the voluminous literature on this topic, only a brief taste of the most controversial issues can be offered here. The basic disagreement about reformulations of Marx is over what constitutes the irreducible core of Marxian analysis. In general, those who argue for synthesis between Marx and Sraffa or Keynes believe that the analytical core of Marxian theory is class exploitation and the historical materialist methodology, which defines historical epochs by relations between those who produce and those who appropriate surplus. But this methodology itself is not seen to imply surplus *value*. Surplus, minus the labour theory of value and surplus value, is then argued to be entirely consistent with the Sraffian model. Indeed, Steedman (1977) contends that because of its inconsistencies the labour theory of value is the major *impediment* to a materialist analysis of capitalism. Defenders argue, as noted above, that only a labour theory of value provides a meaningful concept of exploitation because of the special theoretical status it accords labour. Leaving surplus value out of a surplus theory leads to what these critics of a Sraffian synthesis call the characteristic neo-Ricardian emphasis on distribution rather than production to explain exploitation.

Models of capitalism which forge a Marx–Keynes synthesis find a theory of effective demand lacking in Marx. Without a theory of demand, a class analysis of crisis, for example, lacks coherence (Harris, 1978). In order for the reproduction of capitalism to proceed smoothly, not only must a surplus be generated in production, but a savings/investment balance must be achieved. A major effort at synthesis is presented in Marglin (1984), in which Keynesian principles of aggregate demand are reformulated and incorporated into a Marxian model to explain the relative shares going to capitalists and workers.

This account of radical political economics shows how wide and varied a field it is. There is currently no cohesive theoretical framework within which radicals work, nor is there agreement about what a legitimate framework might be. Nonetheless, radical economics has thrown up a distinctive research agenda revolving around class issues. Economics from history to general equilibrium theory has been rebuilt from the perspective of relations between labour and capital in a way that accepts Marxism as a starting point while at the same time reformulating classical Marxism into a modern radical world view.

DIANE FLAHERTY

BIBLIOGRAPHY

Baran, P.A. and Sweezy, P.M. 1966. *Monopoly Capital: An Essay on the American Economic and Social Order*. New York: Monthly Review Press.

Braverman, H. 1974. *Labor and Monopoly Capital*. New York: Monthly Review Press.

Bluestone, B. and Harrison, B. 1982. *The Deindustrialization of America*. New York: Basic Books.

Bowles, S. Gordon, D.M. and Weisskopf, T.E. 1983. *Beyond The Wasteland*. New York: Anchor Press/Doubleday.

Bronfenbrenner, M. 1970. Radical economics in America. *Journal of Economic Literature* 8(3), September, 747–66.

de Brunhoff, S. 1976. *Marx on Money*. New York: Urizen.

Edwards, R. 1979. *Contested Terrain*. New York: Basic Books.

Foley, D. 1982. The value of money, the value of labor power and the Marxian transformation problem. *Review of Radical Political Economy* 14(2), Summer, 37–47.

Frank, A.G. 1967. *Capitalism and Underdevelopment in Latin America; Historical Studies of Chile and Brazil*. New York: Monthly Review Press.

Gordon, D.M. 1980. Stages of accumulation and long economic cycles. In *Processes in the World System*, ed. T. Hopkins and I. Wallerstein, Beverly Hills: Sage.

Harris, D.J. 1978. *Capital Accumulation and Income Distribution*. Stanford: Stanford University Press.

Himmelweit, S. and Mohun, S. 1981. Real abstractions and anomalous assumptions. In I. Steedman et. al., *The Value Controversy*, London: Verso.

Horowitz, D. (ed.) 1968. *Marx and Modern Economics*. New York: Monthly Review Press.

Lipietz, A. 1982. Credit money: a condition permitting inflationary crisis. *Review of Radical Political Economy* 14(2), Summer, 49–57.

Magdoff, H. 1969. *The Age of Imperialism: The Economics of U.S. Foreign Policy*. New York: Monthly Review Press.

Mandel, E. 1969. *Marxist Economic Theory*. 2 vols, New York: Monthly Review Press.

Mandel, E. 1980. *Long Waves of Capitalist Development*. New York: Cambridge University Press.
Marglin, S.A. 1984. Growth, distribution and inflation: a centennial synthesis. *Cambridge Journal of Economics* 8(2), June, 115–44.
Morishima, M. 1973. *Marx's Economics*. Cambridge: Cambridge University Press.
Okishio, N. 1961. Technical changes and the rate of profit. *Kobe University Economic Review* 7, 85–99.
Roemer, J. 1982. *A General Theory of Exploitation and Class*. Cambridge, Mass.: Harvard University Press.
Rowthorn, R.E. 1977. Conflict, inflation and money. *Cambridge Journal of Economics* 1(3), September, 215–39.
Rowthorn, B. and Harris, D.J. 1985. The organic composition of capital and capitalist development. In *Rethinking Marxism: Essays for Harry Magdoff and Paul Sweezy*, ed. S. Resnick and R. Wolff, New York: Automedia.
Shaikh, A. 1977. Marx's theory of value and the 'transformation problem'. In *The Subtle Anatomy of Capitalism*, ed. J. Schwartz, Santa Monica: Goodyear.
Steedman, I. 1977. *Marx after Sraffa*. London: New Left Books.
Sweezy, P.M. 1981. Marxian value theory and crises. In I. Steedman et. al., *The Value Controversy*, London: Verso.
Union for Radical Political Economics, Economics Education Project. 1978. *U.S. Capitalism in Crisis*. New York: Union for Radical Political Economics.

Rae, John (1796–1872). John Rae was born in Aberdeen on 1 June 1796 into a merchant and shipping family. He graduated from the University of Aberdeen in 1815 and read medicine in the University of Edinburgh, but had to abandon his studies when his father's business failed in 1817. He emigrated to Canada in 1822 and turned to medical practice (whence 'Dr' Rae) and schoolteaching. He also participated in public affairs, but his career was shattered in 1848 when he was dismissed on spurious grounds after becoming embroiled in controversies about church control of education. Rae set out to start a new life first in California, and then the Hawaiian island of Maui. After another twenty years of farming, teaching, providing medical services to the natives, and serving as district judge and notary public, Rae went to live with a former pupil in New York, where he died on 12 July 1872.

None of Rae's many misfortunes and distractions could quell his scientific curiosity. He reported scientific experiments and inventions, lectured on scientific subjects, and wrote on public affairs, geology, and Polynesian language and customs (James, 1965). The only book he ever managed to get published, his *Statement of Some New Principles on the Subject of Political Economy* (1834), originally intended as an appendix to a larger work on the Natural History and Statistics of Canada, is one of the highlights of classical economic theory.

Rae's economics is rooted in a Natural History of Man which he had conceived in the tradition of Montesquieu, Turgot and the Scottish Enlightenment, but never came to execute. Political power and economic progress are seen to result not from the pursuit of self-interest, but to require 'social instincts' which create 'an intelligent and moral community' that furthers both the 'effective desire of accumulation' and the 'rational spirit of invention'. Charging Adam Smith with building his system exclusively on the pursuit of self-interest, and neglecting the role of inventions, Rae contended that economic activity is based primarily on an unselfish regard for the future. In consequence Rae emphasized the temporal aspect of economic activity, and developed a theory of capital accumulation and technical progress which goes far beyond what can be found in Adam Smith or other classical writers.

In language which Fisher was to take up, Rae argued that 'provident forethought' leads man to create 'instruments', that is, capital goods, in order to change the course of events. The sum total of such instruments constitutes the wealth of a society. All instruments are formed, directly or indirectly, by labour; all have the capacity to provide, directly or indirectly, for future wants; and they need time before they are finally exhausted (land being a special case). Rae assumes that the cost of production, and capacity, of any instrument can be measured, in a given society, in exogenously given wage units. All instruments whose capacity exceeds their cost of production can 'be arranged in ... a series, of which the orders are determined, by the proportions existing between the labour expended in the formation of instruments, the capacity given to them, and the time elapsing from the period of formation to that of exhaustion' (1834, p. 100). Rae expresses this 'order' by the time which elapses before the instrument has yielded twice its cost of production, i.e. by n in the expression $(1+r)^n=2$ where r is the internal rate of return of the quasi-rents associated with the instrument. Rae rejected working with the latter because it leads, in his view, to the assumption that the stock of all instruments is 'an homogeneous quantity' which he 'found to be the foundation of much of the contradictions, in which the reasonings on these subjects are involved' (1834, p. 197). His calculation rests on the assumption that every instrument can be associated with a unique rate of return. This need not be the case, but the possible multiplicity of internal rates of return does not affect his argument.

Rae argued that with knowledge stationary, both capital widening and capital deepening (i.e. increasing the durability of instruments) necessarily lower the internal rate of return. Nevertheless, capital goods will be created as long as their internal rate of return is higher than the 'effective desire of accumulation', or rate of time preference, which Rae also expresses in time periods, i.e. by m in the expression $(1+s)^m=2$ where s is the rate of time preference. Such time preference exists because life is finite and its end uncertain; and because 'passion' is often stronger than 'reason'. But it is counteracted by the concern for future generations, or what Rae called 'social and benevolent affections' (1834, p. 122), which depend on a healthy climate that increases life expectancy, or on social circumstances such as internal and external security, good government, etc. Hence the strength of the 'effective desire of accumulation', which Rae considers as much a social habit as an individual inclination, varies from one society to another. Variations from one person to another, Rae shows in an almost neoclassical manner, will be equalized by the exchange of instruments among them, so that a social rate of time preference can be juxtaposed to an internal rate of return which is equalized across different 'employments' by profit-seeking 'merchants'.

Rae defines the equality of the social rate of return with the social rate of time preference as a stationary state in which accumulation ceases. 'Gravitation' towards it is slow. In a comparative static analysis Rae shows that the division of labour – which he views as a consequence of the accumulation of capital rather than its cause, as Adam Smith did – reduces the time for which instruments lie idle, and consequently increases their quasi-rents; hence more instruments can be created before the stationary state is reached, and wealth is increased. Similarly, foreign trade is said to increase the productivity of instruments, while conspicuous consumption (his term) will lower the effective desire of accumulation. Rae also argues that as accumulation proceeds, more and more wealth will be tied up in instruments of increasing durability; hence the value of cash balances, and thus liquidity preference, will increase. But far and away the most important factor making for changes in the progress of accumulation was in Rae's view the progress of inventions. Apart from raising quasi-rents, and hence the internal rate of return, and thus providing scope for more accumulation, inventions also raise the value of existing capital goods. Obviously assuming that these Wicksell effects were positive, Rae placed such capital 'augmentation' alongside capital accumulation as a factor in creating wealth. Indeed, Rae ascribes to inventions a more important role for economic progress (and thus the creation of political power) than capital accumulation, and criticizes Adam Smith for emphasizing savings too much, and neglecting technical progress.

The policy conclusions Rae draws from his analysis are also used to controvert Adam Smith. Instead of pursuing a policy of non-intervention, the 'legislator' should stimulate foreign trade and technical progress, encourage the transfer of knowledge, tax luxuries, and use tariffs to protect infant industries.

It was in this sense that Rae tried to expose 'the fallacies of the system of free trade, and of some other doctrines maintained in the *Wealth of Nations*', as he announced on his title page. But, issued in the midst of a protectionist campaign, Rae's book was mistaken as a heavy-going anti-free-trade tract, and ignored. It did find a champion in Nassau Senior (Bowley, 1937, ch. 4) and through him in J.S. Mill, who quoted from it copiously in his *Principles* (1848), comparing Rae on accumulation to Malthus on population. But there the matter rested, except that it seems to have had a strong influence on Hearn's *Plutology* (1863). Rae was re-discovered by Mixter (1897) as a forerunner of Böhm-Bawerk, who acknowledged him as such (1900, ch. XI) despite some criticism. Together with a (botched, because re-arranged) reprint of Rae's book by Mixter (Rae, 1905), this brought Rae's work to the attention of capital theorists such as Irving Fisher (1907, 1930) who dedicated one of his main works to Rae, as well as Wicksell and Åkerman. It also influenced Schumpeter's (1911) concept of economic development, and Veblen's (1899) notion of conspicuous consumption.

In his criticism of Adam Smith, Rae did not go beyond Bentham (1787) and Lauderdale (1804). But he added poignancy because he derived it from a theory of economic development which was altogether novel. Based on a materialist conception of capital and a vintage-type approach complete with the distinction between capital goods and their value, Rae clearly separated the supply of from the demand for capital goods, and investigated their determinants. He saw but dimly the equality between discounted marginal returns and marginal costs, but he was clear about the equality of opportunities to invest to the 'inclination ... to yield up a present good'. He was quite clear, too, about the equality between the rate of return on capital and on money, and about what brought about such equalities: and also about the effects technical progress and the growth of knowledge have upon both demand and supply of capital. All this adds up to a remarkably original and creative performance which was, like that of Gossen, Cournot or Thünen, ahead of its time.

K.H. Hennings

SELECTED WORKS

1834. *Statement of Some New Principles on the Subject of Political Economy, Exposing the Fallacies of the System of Free Trade, and of some Other Doctrines Maintained in the 'Wealth of Nations'.* Boston: Hilliard Gray & Co.

1905. *The Sociological Theory of Capital, being a Complete Reprint of the New Principles of Political Economy 1834.* Ed. C.W. Mixter, New York: Macmillan.

BIBLIOGRAPHY

Åkerman, G. 1923–4. *Realkapital und Kapitalzins.* Stockholm: Centraltryckeriet.

Bentham, J. 1787. *Defence of Usury.* In *Jeremy Bentham's Economic Writings*, ed. W. Stark, London: George Allen and Unwin, 1952, Vol. I.

Birchler, U.W. 1980. *John Rae (1796–1872). Seine Theorie der wirtschaftlichen Entwicklung.* Bern: Lang.

Böhm-Bawerk, E.von. 1900. *Kapital und Kapitalzins*, Vol. I, *Geschichte und Kritik der Kapitalzines-Theorien.* 2nd edn, Innsbruck: Wagner. Trans. as: *Capital and Interest*, Vol. I, *History and Critique of Interest Theories*, South Holland, Ill.: Libertarian Press, 1959.

Bowley, M. 1937. *Nassau Senior and Classical Economics.* London: George Allen & Unwin.

Edmonson, N. 1970. John Rae and liquidity preference. *History of Political Economy* 2, 432–40.

Fisher, I. 1907. *The Rate of Interest.* New York: Macmillan.

Fisher, I. 1930. *The Theory of Interest.* New York: Macmillan.

Hearn, W.E. 1863. *Plutology, or the Theory of the Efforts to Satisfy Human Wants.* Melbourne: Robertson.

James, R.W. 1965. *John Rae, Political Economist. An Account of his Life and a Compilation of his Main Writings.* 2 vols, Toronto: University of Toronto Press.

Lauderdale, [J. Maitland] Earl of. 1804. *An Inquiry Into the Nature and Origin of Public Wealth.* Edinburgh: Constable.

Lehmann, H. 1937. *John Raes Werk, seine philosophischen und methodologischen Grundlagen.* Dresden: Dittert.

Mill, J.S. 1848. *Principles of Political Economy.* Ed. W.J. Ashley, London: Longmans, 1909.

Mixter, C.W. 1897. A forerunner of Böhm-Bawerk. *Quarterly Journal of Economics* 11, 161–90.

Mixter, C.W. 1902. Böhm-Bawerk on Rae. *Quarterly Journal of Economics* 16, 385–412.

Robbins, L. 1968. *The Theory of Economic Development in the History of Economic Thought.* London: Macmillan.

Schumpeter, J.A. 1911. *Theorie der wirtschaftlichen Entwicklung.* Leipzig: Duncker & Humblot. Trans. as *The Theory of Economic Development*, Cambridge, Mass.: Harvard University Press, 1934.

Spengler, J.J. 1959. John Rae on economic development: a note. *Quarterly Journal of Economics* 73, August, 393–406.

Veblen, T.B. 1899. *The Theory of the Leisure Class.* New York: Macmillan.

Rae, John (1845–1915). John Rae was born in Wick, Caithness, Scotland on 26 May 1845, the eldest son of William Rae who was for some years Provost of the town. Rae received his early education at Edinburgh Academy, before proceeding to university in the city. He graduated in 1866 with first class honours in philosophy. Rae was awarded an honorary doctorate in 1897 by his alma mater. He died on 19 April 1915, having spent the last fifteen years of his life in London, and was buried in Wick.

John Rae has been variously described as 'author and journalist' (1953, i. 582) and as 'economist, writer on socialism' (1966, i. p. 1057). He was certainly all of these, publishing numerous articles, notably in the *Fortnightly Review* (1885), the *Temple Bar* (1882, 1883, 1897), *MacMillan's Magazine* (1893) and the *National Review* (1889). The great bulk of his considerable output is to be found in the *Contemporary Review* (from 1880) of which he was assistant editor.

Rae's contributions to the *Contemporary Review* disclose an interest in at least five major areas. These include a review of contemporary literature on social philosophy (in seven parts), and a number of articles on the Socialism of Karl Marx and the Hegelians, Christian Socialism in Germany, and State Socialism and Social Reform. Rae also contributed articles on the crofting problem in the Highlands, supplementing these with pieces on the Highland Shealing (*Temple Bar*, 1883) and on the Scotch Village Community (*Fortnightly Review*, 1885). Rae wrote a number of articles on taxation and a review of recent economic literature. Finally, he addressed questions of industrial relations, in considering the implications of the eight-hour day in the context of unemployment and of foreign competition.

Rae's journalistic interests resulted in three major books. The first of these was entitled *Contemporary Socialism* (1884). This was followed by *Eight Hours for Work* (1894); a book which consisted largely of his articles on labour questions, supplemented by chapters on the connection between hours and wages, the eight-hour movement of 1833, and current legislative proposals.

John Rae is now best known for his admirable *Life of Adam Smith* (1895) which was favourably reviewed in *The Times* for 8 March 1895 as presenting a 'vivid picture' of his subject. The review also drew attention to the point that the book's real merit lay 'not in the originality of the matter, but in the patient industry, with which Mr Rae has collected his materials, old and new, and in the skill and judgement with which he has presented them to the reader'.

While more critical of Rae's scholarship (1965, p. 12), Jacob Viner has noted that Rae was a trained writer who made his *Life* 'an interesting and highly readable book' (p. 13). Viner also drew attention to the remarkable fact that 'As a comprehensive biography, it had no substantial predecessor. Seventy years after its publication, it still has no substantial successor' (1965, p. 5). These judgements are still valid.

ANDREW SKINNER

See also SMITH, ADAM.

SELECTED WORKS

1884. *Contemporary Socialism*. London and Wick: W. Isbister, 2nd edn, enlarged, London: Sonnenschein, 1891; 3rd edn (with additional chapter), London: Swan Sonnenschein, 1901; 4th edn, London: Swan Sonnenschein, 1908.

1894. *Eight Hours for Work*. London: Macmillan.

1895. *Life of Adam Smith*. London: Macmillan.

BIBLIOGRAPHY

Viner, J. 1965. Guide to John Rae's *Life of Adam Smith*. In Rae's *Life of Adam Smith*. New York: Kelley.

The Wellesley Index to Victorian Periodicals, 1824–1900. Vol. I, ed. W.E. Houghton, Toronto: Toronto University Press, 1966.

Who was Who 1897–1915, Vol. I. 4th edn, London: Adam & Charles Black, 1953.

Ramsey, Frank Plumpton (1903–1930). There are interesting parallels in the careers of Frank Ramsey and John von Neumann. Each was born in 1903, one the product of the 'High Intelligentsia of England' (Keynes, 1933, p. vii) and the other the son of a wealthy banker in Budapest (Ulam, 1976, p. 79). Each was a creative mathematician of high order but each also made major contributions to at least two other disciplines. Each wrote just three papers in economic theory, all six of which were of fundamental importance. Moreover, with one exception every one of these seminal papers had to wait many years for its proper recognition; even the exception – the utility theory set out in the Appendix to von Neumann and Morgenstern (1947) – at first encountered serious misunderstanding within the profession. Indeed, considering them purely as economists, one wonders how these two geniuses would fare today, when promotion and tenure so often depend on a good immediate showing in citation indexes and the like.

The three papers of Ramsey are in subjective probability and utility (1926), optimal taxation (1927), and optimal one-sector growth (1928), while those of von Neumann are in game theory (1928, 1944), optimal multi-sector growth (1937, 1945–6), and objective probability and utility (1947). It is quite striking that their work both on growth theory and on choice under uncertainty should be so complementary, especially since there is no evidence that von Neumann knew of Ramsey's work in either field.

Another and grievous similarity was that both men died early, Ramsey on 19 January 1930 of complications associated with jaundice, and von Neumann (twice Ramsey's age) on 8 February 1957 of cancer. Both losses were tragic, especially that of the 26-year-old Frank Ramsey, whose 'death at the height of his powers deprives Cambridge of one of its intellectual glories and contemporary philosophy of one of its profoundest thinkers' (Braithwaite's Introduction to Ramsey, 1931, p. ix).

I. LIFE

Frank Plumpton Ramsey was born in Cambridge on 22 February 1903. His father was a mathematician, Fellow and later President of Magdalene College (Harrod, 1951, pp. 141, 320), and his brother Michael became Archbishop of Canterbury. He was educated at Winchester and at Trinity College Cambridge, and was a Scholar of both those ancient foundations. In the autumn of 1924 he became Fellow of King's College and University Lecturer in Mathematics and soon afterwards married Lettice Baker, who had been a student in the Moral Sciences Tripos. After his death she became a founder of Ramsey and Muspratt, a firm of portrait photographers that has long been an Oxbridge institution. She survived into the 1980s, in vigorous old age.

In physical appearance Ramsey was tall and portly, the latter a feature he shared with von Neumann; 'I take no credit for weighing nearly 17 stone [238 pounds]' (1931, p. 291). All accounts agree as to his simplicity and modesty, qualities which are happily reflected in his engaging literary style. 'Ramsey reminds one of Hume more than of anyone else, particularly in his common sense and a sort of hard-headed practicality towards the whole business' (Keynes, 1933, p. 301). But his unfailing cheerfulness did not disguise 'the amazing, easy efficiency of the intellectual machine which ground away behind his wide temples and broad, smiling face' (ibid., p. 296). 'He comes down to earth, however, with a satisfying bump, and earth is certainly the natural element of my old friend Lettice,' (Partridge, 1981, p. 129).

RAMSEY AND WITTGENSTEIN. For many years it was thought that while still an undergraduate Ramsey assisted in the translation of the German text of Wittgenstein's *Tractatus Logico-Philosophicus* (1922). It now appears that 'the first draft of the translation was produced by F.P. Ramsey alone' (von Wright, 1982, p. 102). Just 19, he dictated it directly to a stenographer in the University Typing Office in Cambridge in the winter of 1921–2 (reminiscent, on a smaller scale, of the 19-year-old 'John S. Mill' beginning in 1825 to edit Bentham's massive *Rationale of Judicial Evidence*). Wittgenstein seems to have been pleased with Ramsey's translation (1973, p. 77), and a fast friendship was thereby established between the two philosophers that lasted for the rest of Ramsey's short life.

In September 1923 the *Tractatus* had been published for almost a year. Not only had Ramsey been its main translator but he had also written a long and penetrating review of it for *Mind* (reprinted in 1931, pp. 270-86). But still there were many passages which remained unclear to him. To remedy this he made a special journey to Austria, where Wittgenstein was teaching in the local school of a small village and living in spartan conditions. The eccentric philosopher and the brilliant undergraduate hit it off immediately. Ramsey stayed two weeks, spending every afternoon from 2 to 7 elucidating the great man's work: 'we get on about a page an hour' (ibid., p. 79).

In the several letters that Ramsey afterwards wrote to Wittgenstein we can glimpse what Keynes meant in referring to 'the simplicity of his feelings and reactions, half-alarming sometimes and occasionally almost cruel in their directness and literalness' (Keynes, 1933, p. 296). Consider for example these passages from his letters of 12 November and 20 December 1923 (Wittgenstein, 1973, pp. 81–3):

> I have not been doing much towards reconstructing mathematics; partly because I have been reading miscellaneous things, a little Relativity and a little Kant, and Frege ... But I am awfully idle; and most of my energy has been absorbed since January by an unhappy passion for a married woman, which produced such psychological disorder, that I nearly resorted to psychoanalysis, and should probably have gone at Christmas to live in Vienna for nine months and be analysed, had not I suddenly got better a fortnight ago, since when I have been happy and done a fair amount of work.
>
> I think I have solved all problems about finite integers, except such as are connected with the axiom of infinity, but I may well be wrong.
>
> [December 20th] I was silly to think I had solved those problems. I'm always doing that and finding it a mare's nest... *I have been trying to prove a proposition in the Mengenlehre* either $2^{\aleph_0} = \aleph_1$, or $2^{\aleph_0} \neq \aleph_1$, which it is no one knows but I have had no success (his italics).

In 1924 Ramsey actually did spend six months in Vienna in psychoanalysis (rarer then than now), after which 'I feel that people know far less about themselves than they imagine, and am not nearly so anxious to talk about myself as I used to be, having had enough of it to get bored,' (1931, p. 290). The mathematical problem referred to in his second letter was of course the famous Continuum Hypothesis. His lack of success in this is scarcely surprising, since in the 1960s Paul Cohen showed the Hypothesis to be an undecidable proposition within Zermelo–Fraenkel set theory (see e.g. Cohen, 1966). It was, incidentally, a continual disappointment to von Neumann that it was not him but his hero Kurt Gödel who made the startling discovery, in 1930–31, of the necessary existence of such undecidable propositions (Ulam, 1976, pp. 76, 80).

Wittgenstein returned to Cambridge early in 1929 and began those 'innumerable conversations' with Ramsey that are acknowledged in the Preface/Foreword (dated January 1945) to his *Philosophical Investigations* (1953, p. x). Unfortunately, these were cut short by Ramsey's tragic death, a moving account of which may be found in Frances Partridge's *Memories* (1981, 169–82); the grieving Wittgenstein was at Ramsey's bedside in the hospital until a few hours before he died.

The only other person acknowledged by name in the Preface to the *Investigations*, and for even greater help than Ramsey gave, was Piero Sraffa. The trio of Ramsey, Sraffa and Wittgenstein must have been a formidable discussion group indeed; a treasured piece of Cambridge folklore is a lunch at which the three of them discussed Keynes's theory of probability with its author. The odd pattern of belated recognition of intellectual indebtedness was continued in Sraffa's acknowledgement (1960, pp. vi-vii) of Ramsey's help, a mere thirty years after the fact.

II. WORKS

Ramsey's early work in philosophy was a continuation of the methods of Russell and Whitehead's *Principia*, but it is clear that the influence of Wittgenstein and the evolution of his own thinking were moving him towards the end of his life in a quite different, more pragmatic direction. These later contributions were left fragmentary and incomplete at his death, but a very brief account of them and their relations to modern philosophy may be gleaned from the first two Introductions to the revised edition (1978) of (1931).

In mathematics proper, as distinct from the foundations of mathematics, his main contribution is a fundamental theorem which appeared actually as a byproduct of a paper of 1928 on formal logic (reprinted in 1931, pp. 82–111). It reads (1931, p. 82):

> *Theorem* A. Let Γ be an infinite class, and u and r positive integers; and let all those sub-classes of Γ which have exactly r members, or, as we may say, let all r-combinations of the members of Γ be divided into μ mutually exclusive classes $C_i (i = 1, 2, \ldots, \mu)$, so that every r-combination is a member of one and only one C_i; then, assuming the Axiom of Selections [i.e. the Axiom of Choice], Γ must contain an infinite sub-class Δ such that all the r-combinations of the members of Δ belong to the same C_i.

This beautiful result was ignored until 1935, when it was essentially rediscovered by Paul Erdös and Esther Szekeres. Gradually, it led to the formation of a subdiscipline of Combinatorial Analysis known as *Ramsey Theory*, which already contains many hundreds of papers and is growing at a remarkable rate (see the survey by Graham, Rothschild and Spencer, 1980).

Ramsey's pioneering paper on optimal taxation seems to have been written in response to a request by Pigou to look into the problem (see Pigou, 1928, pp. 126–8) but his work on the theory of growth was apparently his alone, although greatly admired by and discussed with Keynes. These two sterling contributions are the subject of separate entries elsewhere in this Dictionary.

Mathematical expectation, probability and utility. The present discussion of Ramsey's great Chapter VII (1931, pp. 156–98) will consider it quite narrowly, as a contribution only to the theory of choice under uncertainty, and thus neglect the important question of its relation to traditional theories of probability. Ramsey himself adopted throughout a modest and peaceable tone towards probability theory, stressing that 'the meaning of probability in logic' may be quite different from 'its meaning in physics' (p. 157).

The chapter is entitled 'Truth and Probability' and dated 1926; presumably most of it was written then, in spite of a reference which bears the date 1927. It contains almost all of what he has to say on the subject, although further on in Chapter VIII and pages 256-7 there are a few unsystematic comments and glosses on the earlier work. The first ten pages form a critique of Keynes's theory of probability (1921), which may well have stimulated his own interest in the whole subject, so it is not until Section 3 that Ramsey begins his 'inquiry ... [into] ... the logic of partial belief'.

Ignoring here all his careful qualifications, the theory outlined in that Section begins as follows (pp. 172–4):

> The old-established way of measuring a person's belief is to propose a bet, and see what are the lowest odds which he will accept. This method I regard as fundamentally sound; ... I propose to take as a basis a general psychological theory ... that we act in the way we think most likely to realize the objects of our desires ... The question then arises how ... to take account of varying degrees of certainty in his beliefs. I suggest that we introduce as a law of psychology that his behaviour is governed by what is called the mathematical expectation; ... We thus define degree of belief in a way which *presupposes* the use of the mathematical expectation (my italics).

Ramsey was fully aware of the crucial dependence of his approach on mathematical expectation. Later in the *Foundations* he asks: 'The question ... why just this law of mathematical expectation. The answer to this is that if we use probability to measure utility, as explained in my paper, then consistency [for which see below] requires just this law' (p. 251).

Putting the matter in its crudest (and so necessarily inaccurate) form, mathematical expectation as a principle of choice involves the use for any risky line of action α of a 'probability' π_i and a 'valuation' v_i attached to each of the possible outcomes α_i that constitute α, in such a way that: (i) the expected valuation $E(\alpha)$ of α is $\Sigma\pi_i v_i$ (or an appropriate integral if α has infinitely many members, an alternative which Ramsey expressly rejects: pp. 183–4); and (ii) α is chosen rather than another risky line of action β if and only if $E(\alpha) > E(\beta)$.

Implicit in this crude form is a conflation between events and outcomes. Outcomes depend upon decisions and events, and it is in events and not outcomes that the randomness present is usually held to reside, so that given the occurrence of an event the relevant outcome on which it depends follows deterministically. Nevertheless, the randomness that inheres in the events may be transferred to the outcomes that are conditional upon those events. In the words of Arrow (1951; 1971, p. 26): 'no matter how complicated the structure of a game of chance is, we can always describe it by a single probability distribution of the final outcomes.'

Notice that because mathematical expectation depends linearly both on the probabilities and on the valuations, choice that follows this principle is made according to a *bilinear* form; there is however no necessity for the valuations of the possible outcome themselves to depend linearly upon those outcomes.

Essentially, given any two of the three concepts: mathematical expectation, probabilities and valuations, the remaining one follows more or less naturally. For example, in Daniel Bernoulli's account of the theory of risk (1738, 1954), the π_i are apparently given 'objectively', for example by the tosses of a coin. Wishing to preserve the principle of mathematical expectation, and citing the St Petersburg Paradox as evidence for the inappropriateness of using money itself as valuation, Bernoulli was thus led to a specific *utility function* to compute the correct valuations, this being a nonlinear (actually, concave) function of wealth. This did not in fact resolve the basic difficulty of the Paradox (which resides in unboundedness of the mathematical expectation) but it was a novel and important idea that was very influential.

A quite different approach was used by Bayes (1763, 1958), who actually *defined* probability in terms of mathematical expectation: 'The *probability of any event* is the ratio between the value at which an expectation depending on the happening of the event ought to be computed, and the value of the thing expected upon it's happening' (1958, p. 298; Jeffreys (1961, pp. 30–34) stresses the similarity here between Bayes and Ramsey). Possibly in ignorance of the earlier contribution, Bayes retained monetary valuations rather than replace them by Bernoullian utilities.

Both authors regarded the maximization of the mathematical expectation of gain as the appropriate principle of choice in an uncertain situation. But whereas Bernoulli accepted probabilities from the outside and altered the meaning of valuations so as to achieve consonance between the maximization of mathematical expectation and rational choice, Bayes started with the outside monetary valuations and thence determined probabilities so as to square rational choice with mathematical expectation.

Ramsey was more subtle. He effectively 'bootstrapped' both the valuations *and* the probabilities from mathematical expectation, at the small cost of: (a) a very general assumption about preferences; (b) an assumed existence of a certain kind of event; and (c) a further principle, original with him, that no agent's subjective probabilities should be *inconsistent*. To be inconsistent means that 'He could have a book made against him by a cunning better and would then stand to lose in any event' (1931; p. 182); this no-win situation is now usually called a *Dutch book*.

Sketch of a proof. Ramsey provided sufficient detail for a formal proof of the existence of valuations and probabilities to be constructed from his system of axioms, but he did not construct one himself. Such proofs, for varying circumstances, have been given by Davidson and Suppes (1956) and Vickers (1962), while more informal discussions may be found in Jeffrey (1965, 1983, ch. 3) and Luce and Suppes (1965, pp. 291–4). Only the merest sketch is attempted here, and its mild technical detail follows Davidson and Suppes (1956) rather than Ramsey's original treatment, which was couched mainly in the concepts of Wittgenstein's *Tractatus* and the language of Russell and Whitehead's *Principia*, both long since unfamiliar.

Ramsey begins by considering the case where the agent has 'certain [i.e. sure] beliefs about everything'. He then adopts assumption (a) above, which expressed in modern language says that the agent has a complete preference preordering over 'all possible courses of the world ... [though] ... we ... have no definite way of representing them by numbers' (1931, p. 176). Vickers points out that if different preferences can themselves be parts of different 'courses of the world' then the argument is ambiguous, and if not then the question is begged (1962, pp. 6-11); however, he shows how to resolve these problems by suitable amendment of Ramsey's definitions.

When 'the subject is capable of doubt' (p. 177), the theory proceeds by offering options. Suppose that the agent has two options: the first is α, in which he receives x if an event e occurs and a preferentially different outcome y if it does not; and the other is β, in which he receives r if e occurs and another outcome s if it does not. Assuming that probabilities $\pi(e)$ and $\pi(e')$ can be attached to the events e and to e' (the complement of e), respectively, and that valuations $v(x)$, $v(y)$, etc. can be placed on the outcomes x, y, r and s, then the principle of mathematical expectation says that α is better than, indifferent to, or worse than β, according as

$$\pi(e)v(x)+\pi(e')v(y) > ; = ; < \pi(e)v(r)+\pi(e')v(s) \qquad (1)$$

Ramsey's next assumption is (b) above, to the effect that there exists some event, say e^*, such that for *every* pair (m, n) of preferentially distinct outcomes the subject is indifferent between the option γ consisting of m if e^* and n if not e^*, and another option δ consisting of n if e^* and m if not e^*. According to the principle of mathematical expectation, this implies

$$\pi(e^*)v(m)+\pi(e^{*\prime})v(n)=\pi(e^*)v(n)+\pi(e^{*\prime})v(m) \quad (2)$$

Since m and n are preferentially distinct, their valuations must be such that $v(m)\neq v(n)$. Then from this and (2) it follows that necessarily

$$\pi(e^*)=\pi(e^{*\prime}) \quad (3)$$

Although quantitative probabilities have not yet been defined, (3) shows that there is a clear qualitative sense in which event e^* has a (subjective) probability of 1/2, *provided* that the subjective probabilities of an event and its complement sum to unity. Ramsey terms *ethically neutral* any event (in his language, proposition) that has the properties of e^*; the force of the word 'ethically' is not explained (p. 177). The assumption that such events (propositions) exist is perhaps the weakest part of his theory of choice under uncertainty, although before it is rejected out of hand the careful philosophical discussion of it by Vickers (1962) and the equally careful empirical applications of it discussed by Davidson and Suppes (1956) should be consulted.

Now take the case of (1) where e is an ethically neutral event e^*, and the option α is indifferent to the option β. Then from (1) and (3),

$$v(x)-v(r)=v(s)-v(y) \quad (4)$$

This says that differences in valuations can be equated, so that the latter are measurable by an *interval scale*; or what comes to the same thing, that they are measurable up to choice of unit and origin, so that for any other such scale μ, $\mu(\cdot)=\alpha+bv(\cdot)$, where $b>0$.

A valuation having been obtained in this fashion for each outcome, and assuming again that for any event e, $\pi(e)+\pi(e')=1$, it follows from the case of equality in (1) that

$$[\pi(e)]^{-1}=1+[v(x)-v(r)]/[v(s)-v(y)] \quad (5)$$

This gives a way of calculating the subjective probability $\pi(e)$ of any event, ethically neutral or not, in a way compatible simultaneously with the principle of mathematical expectation and with the valuations $v(\cdot)$ of the possible outcomes. Thus both valuations ('utilities') and subjective probabilities have been bootstrapped, in that order, from the simple assumptions (a) and (b), plus the assumption that any event and its negation have subjective probabilities that add up to one. Ramsey dispenses with this last, auxiliary assumption by means of his principle (c) of consistency, which in effect insists upon the impossibility of Dutch books.

Dutch books. Although his paper is crystal clear that consistency means that the subjective probabilities of any set of disjoint and exhaustive events must sum to one, and it is twice stated explicitly (pp. 182–3) that anyone who is not consistent in this sense can have a Dutch book made against him, Ramsey provided no formal proof of equivalence between these two ideas. Hence this result is usually attributed to de Finetti (1937), who gave a very neat proof. Not having read Ramsey's paper, de Finetti like Bayes worked with monetary valuations in his account of personal probability, though he admitted later (1964, p. 102 fn(a)) that 'Such a formulation could better, like Ramsey's, deal with expected *utilities*; I did not know of Ramsey's work before 1937, but I was aware of the difficulty of money bets.' What follows is a free adaptation of de Finetti's proof to Ramsey's problem.

Let there be n mutually incompatible and together exhaustive events e_i, e.g. the faces of a die. Suppose then that I, knowing your subjective probabilities π_i, offer you the following wager: If e_i occurs I pay you σ_i. In return, you pay me an initial stake of $\Sigma\pi_i\sigma_i$ valuation units, where the sum is taken over the n events. If you behave according to Ramsey's theory of choice under uncertainty, then you should be on the margin of accepting this wager, since for you to attach probability π_i to e_i is to say that you would be indifferent between the following offers: receive σ_i valuation units contingent on the occurrence of e_i, and the amount $\pi_i\sigma_i$ for sure. Since by hypothesis the e_i are exclusive events, the separate amounts $\pi_i\sigma_i$ may be added together.

If event e_h occurs, your gain is

$$\gamma_h=\sigma_h-\Sigma\pi_i\sigma_i \qquad h=1,2,\ldots,n \quad (6)$$

These are n linear equations, which can be put into matrix–vector notation. Writing g and s for the vectors of the γ_i and σ_i, respectively, I for the $n\times n$ identity matrix, and P for the matrix whose (i, j)th element is π_j, the equations (6) become

$$g=(I-P)s \quad (7)$$

Computation shows that $\det(I-P)=1-\Sigma\pi_i$. So if $\Sigma\pi_i\neq 1$, then for any desired vector of gains g stakes $s=(I-P)^{-1}g$ can be computed that will guarantee me the vector $-g$. In particular, I can specify g to be strictly negative, thus ensuring that you will lose whatever event occurs.

Conversely, suppose that your subjective probabilities are what de Finetti called coherent (and Ramsey, consistent), so that by definition $\Sigma\pi_i=1$. Then, multiplying each equation in (6) by π_h and adding over all events,

$$\Sigma\pi_h\gamma_h=\Sigma\pi_h\sigma_h-\Sigma\pi_h\Sigma\pi_i\sigma_i=0 \quad (8)$$

Since each $\pi_h\geqslant 0$ and their sum is non-zero, it follows from (8) that not all the γ_h can be negative. Hence the condition that your subjective probabilities π_i sum to one for all complete sets of incompatible events e_i, i.e. that you obey the rules of probability calculus, is necessary and sufficient in order that no Dutch book can be made against you.

The reception of 'Truth and Probability'. Ramsey's theory of choice under uncertainty was deeply original. Emile Borel, in his review (1924) of Keynes's theory of probability, had earlier sketched an interesting theory of subjective probability in terms of bets (note in particular his remark that 'the method of betting permits us in the majority of cases a numerical evaluation of probabilities that has exactly the same characteristics as the evaluation of prices by the methods of exchange' (1964, p. 57)), but nobody had come close to the depth and comprehensiveness of Ramsey's theory. He was characteristically modest about its range of application: 'I only claim for what follows approximate truth ... like Newtonian mechanics ... [it] can, I think, still be profitably used even though it is known to be false' (p. 173).

Perhaps because the theory was too original, such modesty did not help its author, any more than his high reputation as a philosopher. I can find no evidence that anyone, let alone any economist, took any serious notice of Ramsey's work until after von Neumann and Morgenstern's quite separate utility theory had appeared in 1947. The latter theory was very much in the Bernoullian tradition, in which the probabilities are given from outside, 'objectively'. Coupling these with a complete preference preordering for such alternatives, suitable continuity, and the principle of mathematical expectation in the form of the Independence Axiom, the authors were able to deduce the existence of a utility function, unique up to positive affine transformations, which gave valuations compatible both with the outside probabilities and that principle.

The first published reference to Ramsey's theory known to me appears in Little (1950, p. 29, fn1), who considered it 'essentially the same' as that of von Neumann and Morgenstern. Little's reference was soon followed by one in Arrow (1951), who acknowledged that Ramsey was brought to his attention by Norman Dalkey. Though complaining that 'Ramsey's work was none too clear' (1971, p. 26), Arrow did see that it originated 'a new stage' in decision theory, 'in which a priori probabilities are derived from behavior postulates' (1971, p. 22). Thereafter there was a gradual increase in the appreciation of Ramsey's contribution, although even as late as 1954 an excellent collection of papers on decision theory (Thrall, Coombs and Davis, 1954) contained not one reference to his work.

It is a common mistake to suppose that the line of descent in the theory of personal probability is direct from Ramsey to de Finetti (1937) to Savage (1954). We have seen that de Finetti did not know of Ramsey's work, his own remarkable contribution being very much in the Bayesian tradition which takes the valuations from outside and thence derives the probabilities. Moreover, a careful reading of Savage's fine book shows that Ramsey's influence was at best peripheral, the axiomatization of probabilities and valuations proceeding far more along the lines developed by de Finetti.

There have in fact been relatively few explicit exponents of Ramsey's approach. The most notable are probably Davidson and Suppes (e.g. 1956) and Anscombe and Aumann (1963), who used an interesting bootstrapping argument to go from assumed probabilities for what they called 'roulette' lotteries to valuations, and thence to subjective probabilities for the much wider class of 'horse' lotteries, all very much in the Ramsey manner.

The direct heirs to Ramsey's work have been few but there is no doubt that its influence has been pervasive, to such extent that chairs in decision theory at US business schools have been named after him (though with what warrant is hard to say). Arrow (1965, p. 57) claimed that all arguments involving the expected-utility hypothesis 'are only variations of Ramsey's', while Savage (1962, p. 10) wrote that the 'more thoroughgoing ... formulation of Ramsey (1931) ... is in no way obsolete'. Even now, not to experience that 'clear purity of illumination with which the writer's mind is felt by the reader to play about its subject' (Keynes on Ramsey, 1928) is a sad loss for the modern student.

PETER NEWMAN

See also EXPECTED UTILITY HYPOTHESIS; SUBJECTIVE PROBABILITY; VON NEUMANN, JOHN.

SELECTED WORKS

1926. Truth and probability. Chapter VII, pages 156–98 in (1931). Reprinted in (1978) and in Kyburg and Smokler (1964), 61–92.
1927. A contribution to the theory of taxation. *Economic Journal* 37, 47–61. Reprinted in (1978).
1928. A mathematical theory of saving. *Economic Journal* 38, 543–9. Reprinted in (1978).
1931. *The Foundations of Mathematics*. Edited by R.B. Braithwaite, with a Preface by G.E. Moore, London: Routledge & Kegan Paul.
1978. *Foundations*. Edited by D.H. Mellor, with Introductions by the editor, L. Mirsky, T.J. Smiley and J.R.N. Stone, London: Routledge & Kegan Paul.

BIBLIOGRAPHY

Anscombe, F.J. and Aumann, R.J. 1963. A definition of subjective probability. *Annals of Mathematical Statistics* 34, 199–205.
Arrow, K.J. 1951. Alternative approaches to the theory of choice in risk-taking situations. *Econometrica* 19, 404–37.
Arrow, K.J. 1965. *Aspects of the Theory of Risk-Bearing*. Helsinki: Yrjö Jahnsson Foundation.
Arrow, K.J. 1971. *Essays in the Theory of Risk-Bearing*. Chicago: Markham.
Bayes, T. 1763. An essay towards solving a problem in the doctrine of chances. *Philosophical Transactions of the Royal Society* 53, 370–418. Reprinted in *Biometrika* 45, (1958), 293–315.
Bernoulli, D. 1738. Specimen theoriae novae de mensura sortis. *Commentarii Academiae Scientiarum Imperialis Petropolitanae*, Vol. V, 175–92. Translated as 'Exposition of a new theory on the measurement of risk', *Econometrica* 22, 1954, 23–36.
Borel, E. 1924. A propos d'un traité de probabilité. *Revue Philosophique* 98, 321–36. Translated in Kyburg and Smokler (1964), 45–60.
Cohen, P.J. 1966. *Set Theory and the Continuum Hypothesis*. New York: W.A. Benjamin.
Davidson, D. and Suppes, P. 1956. A finitistic axiomatization of subjective probability and utility. *Econometrica* 24, 264–75.
de Finetti, B. 1937. La prévision, ses lois logiques, ses sources subjectives. *Annales de l'Institut Henri Poincaré* 7, 1–68. Translated in Kyburg and Smokler (1964), 93–158.
Graham, R.L., Rothschild, B.L. and Spencer, J.H. 1980. *Ramsey Theory*. New York: John Wiley & Sons.
Harrod, R.F. 1951. *The Life of John Maynard Keynes*. London: Macmillan.
Jeffrey, R.L. 1965. *The Logic of Decision*. New York: McGraw-Hill. 2nd edn, Chicago: University of Chicago Press, 1983.
Jeffreys, H. 1961. *Theory of Probability*. 3rd edn, Oxford: Clarendon Press.
Keynes, J.M. 1921. *A Treatise on Probability*. London: Macmillan.
Keynes, J.M. 1933. *Essays in Biography*. London: Macmillan.
Kyburg, H.E. and Smokler, H.E. (eds) 1964. *Studies in Subjective Probability*. New York: John Wiley & Sons.
Little, I.M.D. 1950. *A Critique of Welfare Economics*. Oxford: Clarendon Press.
Luce, R.D. and Suppes, P. 1965. Preference, utility, and subjective probability. In *Handbook of Mathematical Psychology*, Vol. III, ed. R.D. Luce, R.R. Bush and E. Galanter, New York: John Wiley & Sons, 249–410.
Neumann, J. von. 1928. Zur Theorie der Gesellschaftspiele. *Mathematische Annalen* 100, 295–320.
Neumann, J. von. 1937. Über ein ökonomisches Gleichungssystem und eine Verallgemeinerung des Brouwerschen Fixpunksatzes. *Ergebnisse eines mathematischen Kolloquiums* 8, 78–83. Translated as 'A model of general economic equilibrium', *Review of Economic Studies* 13, 1945–6, 1–9.
Neumann, J. von. and Morgenstern, O. 1944. *Theory of Games and Economic Behavior*. Princeton: Princeton University Press.
Neumann, J. von. and Morgenstern, O. 1947. 2nd edn of (1944).
Partridge, F. 1981. *Memories*. London: Victor Gollancz.
Pigou, A.C. 1928. *A Study in Public Finance*. London: Macmillan.
Savage, L.J. 1954. *The Foundations of Statistics*. New York: John Wiley & Sons.
Savage, L.J. et al. 1962. *The Foundations of Statistical Inference: A discussion*. London: Methuen.
Sraffa, P. 1960. *Production of Commodities by Means of Commodities*. Cambridge: Cambridge University Press.
Thrall, R.M., Coombs, C.H. and Davis, R.L. (eds) 1954. *Decision Processes*. New York: John Wiley & Sons.
Ulam, S.M. 1976. *Adventures of a Mathematician*. New York: Charles Scribner's Sons.
Vickers, J.M. 1962. A critical investigation of Frank Ramsey's Theory of Value and Belief. PhD dissertation in the Department of Philosophy, Stanford University.
Wittgenstein, L. 1922. *Tractatus Logico-Philosophicus*, with an Introduction by Bertrand Russell. London: Kegan Paul, Trench, Trubner & Co.
Wittgenstein, L. 1953. *Philosophical Investigations*. Translated by G.E. Anscombe, Oxford: Basil Blackwell.

Wittgenstein, L. 1973. *Letters to C.K. Ogden*. Edited by G.H. von Wright, Oxford: Basil Blackwell.
Wright, G.H. von. 1982. *Wittgenstein*. Minneapolis: University of Minnesota Press.

Ramsey model. Frank Plumpton Ramsey died at the age of 26 after making brilliant contributions to philosophy mathematical logic, and, of course, economics. His two contributions to economics both appeared in the *Economic Journal*, then edited by J.M. Keynes. The first, 'A Contribution to the Theory of Taxation', published in March, 1927, laid the foundation for the modern theory of commodity taxation. The second, the subject of this entry, was 'A Mathematical Theory of Saving', published in December, 1928. Keynes, in his obituary notice published two months after Ramsey's death, in the *Economic Journal* of March, 1930, described the latter as 'one of the most remarkable contributions to mathematical economics ever made, both in respect of the intrinsic importance and difficulty of its subject, the power and elegance of the technical methods employed, and the clear purity of illumination with which the writer's mind is felt by the reader to play about its subject'.

Ramsey asked how much of its income should a nation save and derived a remarkably simple rule, usually known as the Keynes–Ramsey Rule, as Keynes provided a non-technical argument for the result. The rule states that the rate of saving, multiplied by the marginal utility of consumption, should always be equal to the amount by which the total net rate of enjoyment of utility falls short of the maximum possible rate.

Ramsey's formulation of the problem served as a model for almost all subsequent studies of optimal economic growth, and, with the critical addition of a growing population, might have created neoclassical growth theory about thirty years before Solow's (1956) contribution. He assumed a one-good world, in which labour with a stock of capital would produce a flow of output, part of which was consumed, and the balance was saved and thereby added to the stock of capital. The objective, or criterion, was to achieve the maximum level of enjoyment, summing over all time, where enjoyment was the utility of consumption, $U(C)$, less the disutility of working, $V(L)$. Ramsey made three crucial assumptions which together allowed him to solve explicitly an otherwise intractable problem. He assumed that there was no population growth, no technical progress, and no discounting of utility, 'a practice which is ethically indefensible and arises merely from the weakness of the imagination' (Ramsey, 1928, p. 543). He further supposed that there was a 'maximum *obtainable* rate of enjoyment' called *Bliss*, B, either because of capital or consumption saturation. As neither population grows nor future utilities are discounted, Ramsey then argues, rather informally, that it must be desirable to save enough to eventually reach bliss, or approximate to it indefinitely. To stop short means foregoing a finite amount of utility, which, summed over an infinite time horizon, is infinitely costly. Formally, Ramsey deals with this problem of a potentially unbounded integral of utility (summed without discounting over infinite time) by *minimizing* the amount by which enjoyment falls short of bliss integrated throughout time:

$$\min \int_0^\infty [B - U(C) + V(L)]\,\mathrm{d}t \tag{1}$$

subject to

$$\frac{\mathrm{d}K}{\mathrm{d}t} + C = F(K, L). \tag{2}$$

Ramsey attacks the problem from two directions: economic and mathematical. His economic argument first solves for the relationship between consumption and the effort by equating the marginal disutility of labour to the product of the marginal product of labour and the marginal disutility of consumption. He then solves the basic arbitrage relationship equating the marginal utility of consuming a unit now with the marginal utility of consuming the product of investing the unit until the next instant of time. This key relationship implies that the marginal utility of consumption, $U'(C)$, must fall at the rate of interest, equal to the marginal product of capital, $\partial F/\partial K$. These two conditions, together with (2), the initial stock of capital, and a terminal condition as $t \rightarrow \infty$, produce a differential equation which can be integrated to give the result.

The mathematical approach observes that the calculus of variations gives the first two conditions directly, but also observes that the variable of integration in (1) can be changed from t to K by using (2) to give

$$\min \int_{K_0}^\infty \frac{B - U(C) + V(L)}{F(K, L) - C}\,\mathrm{d}K \tag{3}$$

and since C and L are arbitrary functions of K all that is needed to minimize the integrand is to set its partial derivations to zero. Differentiating with respect to C gives

$$F(K, L) - C = \frac{B - [U(C) - V(L)]}{U'(C)}. \tag{4}$$

The left-hand side of (4) is the rate of investment or saving, whilst the right-hand side is equal to bliss minus the additional rate of enjoyment, divided by the marginal utility of consumption, and the whole is the Keynes–Ramsey rule.

Ramsey concluded from this rule that the optimal rate of saving should be 'greatly in excess of that which anyone would normally suggest' and gave an illustration in which the savings rate should be 60 per cent of income. One of the main themes explored by later writers was whether this was a robust conclusion, or whether the optimal rate of saving was very sensitive to the simplifying assumptions – a theme which is discussed below. Ramsey recognized that discounting utility would destroy the simple reasoning which led to (4), and was thus anxious to have an ethical reason for rejecting it. He believed that population growth would argue for higher rates of saving whilst technical progress would have ambiguous effects – as proved to be the case in later formal models.

Ramsey drew attention to two remarkable features of the rule. The first is that the level of saving does not depend on the production function. The second is that it does not depend on the rate of interest, unless this is actually zero. In fact, the first feature is only apparently the case, for in (4), C will depend on the level of output, F, and since savings, given by the right-hand side, also depends on C, it will depend on F. In his section III, Ramsey clearly pointed out that the level of saving was motivated by the demand for future consumption, whilst the rate of interest was determined by the current stock of capital (in this one-sector model). In a concluding remark to this section he notes that 'in the accounting of a Socialist State the function of the rate of interest would be to ensure the wisest use of existing capital, not to serve in any direct way as a guide to the proportion of income which should be saved'. The second result does not survive in more general models which allow for utility discounting. Nevertheless, the arbitrage relationship does suggest a way in which the rate of interest can guide the rate of saving. If the rate of decline of the marginal utility of consumption is less than the rate of interest, taken to be the rate of return on investment, then the rate of saving is too low, and vice versa.

The main contribution of the paper was to pose a fruitful question – what should the rate of savings be – and propose a method of analysis – that of intertemporal welfare maximization using the techniques of dynamic optimization, in this case the calculus of variations. The main result was striking – the rate of saving should apparently be rather high. In addition to this contribution, the paper also contained various remarkable extensions. It considers the choice of savings rate for an individual facing constant factor prices, who wishes to optimize his lifetime consumption pattern, and as such provides a positive theory of life-cycle savings. It shows that if utility is to be discounted, then it must be discounted at a constant rate if one is to escape the contradiction 'that successive generations are motivated by the same system of preferences'. Later, Strotz (1956) would return to this issue and the related problem of dynamic consistency. Finally, Ramsey shows that if a society consists of individuals who differ in their rate of discount, and if it is in steady state, then the equilibrium would be attained by a division of society into two classes, the thrifty enjoying bliss and the improvident at the subsistence level. In short, he characterizes the long-run general equilibrium of a society of heterogeneous individuals.

Ramsey thus laid the foundations for the study of optimal accumulation and optimal growth, as well as the positive theory of savings and the rate of interest. Space precludes a full assessment of the subsequent work his paper stimulated, though Burmeister and Dobell's (1970) textbook lists 107 references in their chapter on optimal economic growth, and much has happened since that date. Instead we shall briefly mention some of the themes of this subsequent work.

Ramsey's model represented a significant advance on the classical analysis of stationary states, since it made possible the analysis of non-stationary time paths of capital accumulation, but ultimately his model would tend towards a stationary state. With the development of growth theory the profession acquired a more appealing concept of long-run equilibrium – that of steady growth. In due course this suggested the obvious extension to Ramsey's model of incorporating these dynamic features – population growth at the steady rate n and Harrod-neutral technical progress at a steady rate g. The instantaneous level of national welfare was variously taken as $U(C_t)$, $U(C_t/L_t)$, or, most satisfactorily, $L_t u(C_t/L_t)$, where L_t was the total population or workforce, and C_t was total consumption. Since welfare now depended on time, it made no drastic difference to include a utility discount rate, δ, and to propose a more general objective such as

$$W = \int_0^\infty U(C_t, t)\,\mathrm{d}t = \int_0^\infty L_t u(C_t/L_t)\,\mathrm{e}^{-\delta t}\,\mathrm{d}t. \qquad (5)$$

Steady growth now raised the question of the *existence* of an optimal savings policy in an acute form, for the integral in (5) might diverge unless δ was sufficiently large. Ramsey had faced a similar problem and avoided it by minimizing the shortfall from a reference path (or bliss). Similar devices were invoked to deal with divergent integrals, and much effort was expended on devising criteria of optimality and categorizing conditions under which an optimal savings plan existed, though many apparently reasonable problems nevertheless failed to possess an optimal savings plan, as Hammond and Mirrlees (1973) demonstrated. (They also give references to earlier discussions of the problem of non-existence.) They observe that no restrictions on the class of utility function will ensure existence, nor will any realistic restrictions on the production assumptions by themselves be enough to avoid the problem. They then argue that if we could specify a date after which events are of no significance, then the problem reduces to a finite horizon model, for which the utility integral would converge. Different people might disagree on the horizon date, but if the initial T_0 years of the plan were relatively insensitive to any horizon date later than some date T_1, then everyone would agree with the T year plan, and, in their language, the plan would be *agreeable*. Hammond and Mirrlees show that in the one good model with a general instantaneous utility function $U(C_t, t)$ the agreeable path is unique and locally optimal, and that if an optimal path exists it is agreeable. Establishing the existence of agreeable paths is, however, considerably easier than establishing the existence of optimal paths.

Whilst existence problems are important and raise intriguing philosophical problems (what if optimal growth paths do not exist?), they are not central to the economics of the problem. One of the key issues that has engaged the attention of subsequent researchers is whether the optimal savings rate is indeed as high as Ramsey argued (though, as Samuelson (1969) pointed out, Ramsey's conclusion depended on a particular choice of utility function). Certainly, Tinbergen (1956) was inclined to agree, but Mirrlees (1967) argued that Ramsey's model was seriously misleading, and that once population growth, technical progress and utility discounting were admitted, the initial value of the optimal rate of saving was typically very different from that implied by the Keynes–Ramsey rule. Once time enters the production function, it is no longer possible to obtain explicit solutions and an alternative solution strategy is required. Mirrlees argued that it was preferable to find the asymptotic form of the optimally developing economy in which output, consumption and consumption per head all grow at steady rates along a 'modified Golden Rule', and in which the savings rate is constant. The initial value of the savings rate could then be estimated by expanding around this asymptotic solution.

Mirrlees, in common with a large number of other optimal growth theorists, used a particular utility function – the iso-elastic form

$$\begin{aligned} u(c) &= -c^{1-v}, \qquad v > 1, \\ &= \log c, \qquad v = 1, \end{aligned} \qquad (6)$$

for which Ramsey's rule gives a savings rate of $1/v$ (providing an optimum exists). Mirrlees was impressed that for plausible values of the parameters of his model, the optimum savings rate was very different from the Ramsey value, and might be quite low. He also pointed out that the asymptotic solution, or the 'modified Golden Rule', would differ from the Golden Rule (according to which the rate of savings should equal the share of profit), if utilities were discounted – for the obvious reason that one would expect optimum policies to reflect the values regarding the distribution between generations.

Ramsey's model made skilful use of the classical calculus of variations, and in that vein Samuelson and Solow (1956) extended the model to deal with heterogeneous capital goods. In so doing they made possible two notable contributions to capital theory. The first was to argue that on the optimum path it was not too misleading to think in terms of an abstract quantity of capital – heterogeneity did not significantly alter the Ramsey theory. Second, the Hahn–Samuelson problem of the indeterminacy of equilibrium with capital heterogeneity disappeared on the optimal path, though the significance of this did not emerge until the paper by Hahn (1966).

As Samuelson and Solow pointed out, the classical calculus

of variations could be replaced by Hamiltonian methods which would be able to deal with inequality constraints. The powerful techniques of the Pontryagin Maximum Principle and Bellman's Dynamic Programming were in due course applied to various extensions of the Ramsey problem to good effect, and their advantages and interrelationships are well discussed in the textbook of Intriligator (1971). In both approaches shadow prices or co-state variables play an important role both in characterizing the solution and demonstrating the relationships between optimality, intertemporal efficiency, and a set of intertemporal (shadow) prices (prices on futures markets) which might be used to decentralize the optimum. These shadow prices have a natural interpretation, for they value the capital stock in terms of the objective function, that is social welfare or the utility of consumption. The price guides the instantaneous allocation of output between consumption and investment, for consumption should be increased, if possible, until its value (the marginal utility of consumption) falls to the value of investment, that is of the capital stock. The evolution of the price over time then satisfies the fundamental arbitrage relationship, so that asset holders obtain a return (including capital gains) on the asset equal to the return on other assets and to the return from delaying consumption.

The strengths of these alternative approaches are best appreciated in multisector models when there are constraints on reallocating resources. If investment goods are physically different from consumption goods, and capital is immobile between sectors then savings will be constrained by the feasible output of the investment goods sector, and the planners' problem is primarily one of choosing the allocation of investment between the two sectors. In such a model the rate of return on capital will depend on the level of investment, and Ramsey's observation that in his model the two are independent is shown to be a feature of the one-good assumption. With two sectors corner solutions are quite likely (in the early stages) and the inequality constraints require the extra power of the new approaches.

The shadow prices are arguably most useful for cost–benefit analysis, rather than the more ambitious planning problems which so engaged the attentions of optimal growth theorists in the 1960s. Little and Mirrlees (1969, 1974) and Newbery (1972) and Stern (1972) were concerned to develop methods for calculating shadow or accounting prices in dual economy models of developing countries in which the level of aggregate savings was constrained. The two key accounting prices on which optimal growth models can shed light are the wage rate and the rate of discount to use in investment projects. The former emerges from the constraints on the allocation of labour and on the level of wages which must be paid, whilst the latter is again given by an arbitrage relation, or the rate of change of the shadow price of capital itself. The arbitrage equation gives a differential equation for the shadow price which, together with the equation for saving and the accumulation of capital, can be numerically integrated backwards from the asymptotic solution. Modern computers allow this to be done quickly, as illustrated in Newbery (1972).

The arbitrage equation comes into its own in exhaustible resource models where the return to the exhaustible resource must, whilst it remains in the ground, take the form of a capital gain equal to the return on other assets. This rule, due originally to Hotelling (1931), and nicely exposited by Solow (1974), has achieved prominence since the dramatic rise in the oil price of 1973–4.

Although the revival of interest in the Ramsey model in the 1960s was initially motivated by the postwar popularity of national economic planning, a popularity which waned rapidly in the 1970s, the model and its successors remain useful for the more modest aims of characterizing intertemporal competitive equilibrium in asset markets, especially for exhaustible resources like oil and gas, and for providing a more satisfactory neoclassical theory of equilibrium growth with individually rational savers. The common feature of Ramsey's two contributions to economics was that they were normative, and postulated an additive (utilitarian) social welfare function as the objective to be maximized. Several writers have taken the natural step of combining both of Ramsey's two interests and enquiring what optimal tax (and monetary) policy should be in an intertemporal model in which savings and investment are affected by these policies. Arrow and Kurz (1969) were the first to explore these issues and the closely related issues of the problem of public investment criteria systematically in a growth model in which full optimality is not achieved.

Diamond (1973) extended their work to a model with many goods, and demonstrated the desirability (under constant returns) of equal efficiency, on average, between public and private production, even though aggregate efficiency was not desired. In particular the public and private sectors should use the same discount rates. Later work (surveyed, for example, by Kotlikoff, 1984) has explored the efficiency losses involved in an economy of intertemporal optimizing individuals in the presence of distortionary taxes on capital, and have used these estimates to rank alternative capital tax reform programmes – a compromise between the optimal tax approach of Diamond, and the need to incorporate more of the complex features of particular economies.

In short, if the central question which Ramsey addressed of the right level of saving and investment has fallen from favour recently, nevertheless the spirit of the Ramsey model with its emphasis on intertemporal optimization lives on strongly, whether it be in the study of the oil market, the derivation of public investment rules, or the reform of the corporate tax system.

DAVID M. NEWBERY

See also CALCULUS OF VARIATIONS; NEOCLASSICAL GROWTH THEORY; OPTIMAL SAVINGS.

BIBLIOGRAPHY

Arrow, K. and Kurz, M. 1969. Optimal public investment policy and controllability with fixed private savings ratio. *Journal of Economic Theory* 1(1), 141–77.

Burmeister, E. and Dobell, A.R. 1970. *Mathematical Theories of Economic Growth*. New York: Macmillan.

Chakravarty, S. 1969. *Capital and Development Planning*. Cambridge, Mass.: MIT Press.

Diamond, P.A. 1973. Taxation and public production in a growth setting. Ch. 10 in Mirrlees and Stern (1973).

Hahn, F.H. 1966. Equilibrium dynamics with heterogeneous capital goods. *Quarterly Journal of Economics* 80(4), November, 633–46.

Hammond, P.J. and Mirrlees, J.A. 1973. Agreeable plans. Ch. 13 in Mirrlees and Stern (1973).

Hotelling, H. 1931. The economics of exhaustible resources. *Journal of Political Economy* 39, 137–75.

Intriligator, M.D. 1971. *Mathematical Optimization and Economic Theory*. Englewood Cliffs, NJ: Prentice-Hall.

Kotlikoff, L.J. 1984. Taxation and savings: a neoclassical perspective. *Journal of Economic Literature* 22(4), 1576–629.

Little, I.M.D. and Mirrlees, J.A. 1969. *Manual of Industrial Project Analysis for Developing Countries*. Vol. II: *Social Cost Benefit Analysis*. Paris: OECD Development Centre.

Little, I.M.D. and Mirrlees, J.A. 1974. *Project Appraisal and Planning for Developing Countries*. London: Heinemann.

Mirrlees, J.A. 1967. Optimum growth when technology is changing. *Review of Economic Studies* 34(1), 95–124.
Mirrlees, J.A. and Stern, N.H. (eds) 1973. *Models of Economic Growth*. London: Macmillan.
Newbery, D.M.G. 1972. Public policy in the dual economy. *Economic Journal* 82, June, 567–90.
Ramsey, F.P. 1927. A contribution to the theory of taxation. *Economic Journal* 37, March, 47–61.
Ramsey, F.P. 1928. A mathematical theory of saving. *Economic Journal* 38, December, 543–59.
Samuelson, P.A. 1969. Foreword to Chakravarty (1969).
Samuelson, P.A. and Solow, R. 1956. A complete capital model involving heterogeneous capital goods. *Quarterly Journal of Economics* 70(4), November, 537–62.
Solow, R.M. 1956. A contribution to the theory of economic growth. *Quarterly Journal of Economics* 70(1), February, 65–94.
Solow, R.M. 1974. The economics of resources or the resources of economics. *American Economic Review Papers and Proceedings* 64(2), May, 1–14.
Stern, N.H. 1972. Optimum development in a dual economy. *Review of Economic Studies* 39(2), April, 171–84.
Strotz, R.H. 1956. Myopia and inconsistency in dynamic utility maximization. *Review of Economic Studies* 23(3), 165–80.
Tinbergen, J. 1956. The optimal rate of savings. *Economic Journal* 66, December, 603–9.

Ramsey pricing. Ramsey prices are prices that are Pareto optimal subject to a constraint on the total profits of a single supplier or group of suppliers. In particular, because a firm whose activities are characterized by scale economies will lose money if it sets the prices of its products equal to their marginal costs, Ramsey prices become for that firm the prices that are optimal (economically efficient) given the financial feasibility requirement that the firm's profits be non-negative. The same Ramsey prices can also be shown to be those necessary for maximization of the sum of consumers' and producers' surpluses.

The concept is named after Frank Ramsey, its discoverer, whose 1927 paper on the subject was one of several revolutionary contributions to economics, mathematics and philosophy this extraordinary man made before he died at the age of 26. Since then and until the 1970s, the principle was largely forgotten even though it was rediscovered and expanded upon by Pigou, Boiteux and Samuelson. In 1970 it was publicized and its history explored in an article by Baumol and Bradford, and the principle has since been widely recognized and accepted by economists and practitioners. As an illustration, in 1983 the Interstate Commerce Commission adopted Ramsey pricing as the underlying principle it would follow in the regulation of railroad rates.

Ramsey prices are an outstanding example of the use of pure economic theory to derive an operational solution to a difficult set of practical problems. It may also be as definitive as any available second-best theorem. The extraordinary achievement of the theorem lies in the very explicit formulae it is able to derive from so weak a premise – the Pareto optimality requirement that the prices be those which elicit such a set of outputs and purchase quantities that it is impossible to increase the welfare of any one individual without harming anyone else. Aside from the apparent weakness of this assumption, the definitive character of the Ramsey theorem is surprising in light of the conclusion suggested by much of the second-best literature, that where additional constraints are superimposed on the usual requirements of optimality, one can expect no simple and straightforward results to emerge.

THE RAMSEY THEOREM AND ITS INTERPRETATION. The Ramsey theorem is expressed in a variety of formulae all of which are essentially equivalent. Perhaps its simplest form asserts that when a producer supplies n commodities then Pareto optimality subject to a profit constraint requires the prices, p_j of these goods to satisfy

$$\frac{p_j - mc_j}{p_n - mc_n} = \frac{mr_j - mc_j}{mr_n - mc_n}, \qquad (j = 1, \ldots, n-1),$$

$$\sum_{j=1}^{n} p_j y_j = c(y_1, \ldots, y_n) + k \tag{1}$$

where mc_j and mr_j are, respectively, the marginal cost and marginal revenue of output j, $c(\cdot)$ is the supplier's total cost function and k is any constant.

In the special case in which none of the seller's goods is either a complement or a substitute in demand, the preceding relationship is easily shown to take the special form which is widely known as 'the inverse elasticity formula':

$$\frac{(p_j - mc_j)/p_j}{(p_n - mc_n)/p_n} = \frac{E_n}{E_j}, \qquad (j = 1, \ldots, n-1)$$

$$\sum p_i y_i = c(\cdot) + k, \tag{2}$$

where E_j is the price elasticity of demand for product j.

In the particular case where an optimum satisfies locally the requirements of constant returns to scale, so that marginal cost pricing yields zero economic profits exactly, then (for $k = 0$) conditions (1) and (2) are automatically transformed into the marginal cost pricing conditions

$$p_j = mc_j, \qquad (j = 1, \ldots, n). \tag{3}$$

It is easy to show that no prices can be Pareto optimal subject to the profit constraint indicated unless they satisfy (1). Moreover, as long as the proper concavity–convexity conditions hold, any prices which satisfy (1) will be consistent with Pareto optimality so constrained.

One can suggest in rough intuitive terms why constrained Pareto optimality requires prices which satisfy (1), or (2) – in the case of demand independence. The latter is perhaps the most illuminating case, and so it is useful to summarize the argument briefly.

As a starting point, one should recall that the reason marginal cost pricing is necessary for a 'first best' (unconstrained) optimum is that such prices equate the pecuniary cost to the consumer of purchasing an additional unit of the item and the economic cost of producing it, i.e. its marginal cost . Thus, when the consumer selects his purchases so as to maximize the utility he derives from a given outlay of money, he thereby automatically maximizes the utility derivable from a bundle of economic resources.

However, where returns to scale are not constant at the vector of purchases elicited by the prices $p_i = mc_i$ then the requirement $\Sigma p_i y_i = c(\cdot)$ will be violated by those marginal cost prices. Consequently, prices will have to deviate from marginal costs in some pattern that satisfies the profit constraint. Of course, every such deviation will affect consumer purchases, and so the quantities produced, making them depart in different degrees from the optimal quantities that would have been selected under marginal cost pricing. The objective is to cause the p_i to deviate from the mc_i in a manner that satisfies the profit constraint and yet distorts consumer purchases from their optimal levels as little as possible.

For this purpose, consider two of the pertinent commodities, i and j, with i's demand highly elastic and j's very inelastic. Start with $p_i = mc_i$ and $p_j = mc_j$ and assume that at those prices profits are negative. Because of the high demand elasticity of i

a small rise in p_i above mc_i will cause a relatively large 'distortion' in consumer demand from its Pareto optimal quantity. Moreover, also because of the high elasticity, the rise in p_i will yield a relatively small increase in revenue to help eliminate losses. In contrast, a similar percentage increase in p_j will cause a smaller percentage change in quantity of j demanded and a larger gain in revenue. Clearly less damage will be done to welfare if a larger share of the task of meeting the shortfall of total revenue relative to total cost is carried out via a rise in p_j, the price of the commodity with the more inelastic demand. This is, in essence, the logic of the inverse elasticity formula.

INFORMAL DERIVATION OF THE THEOREM. A simplified and rather informal derivation of the formulae is straightforward. For brevity only a single consumer and a single input, labour, is used in the following, but the proofs in the k consumer – m input cases are virtually identical. Let

y_i = the supplier's output of i $(i = 1, \ldots, n)$
x = the vector of outputs of all other goods
R = the available quantity of resource
r = unused resource (leisure)
p_i = the price of i
w = wage (price of leisure)
$U(y_1, \ldots, y_n, x, r)$ = the consumer's utility function
$C(y_1, \ldots, y_n)$ = the firm's input requirement function
$K(x)$ = the input requirement for production of x. Then, optimality requires maximization of

$$U(y_1, \ldots, y_n, x, r)$$

subject to the resource constraint

$$C(y_1, \ldots, y_n) + K(x) + r = R$$

and the budget constraint

$$\Sigma p_i y_i = wC(y_1, \ldots, y_n).$$

This yields the Lagrangian

$$L = U(\cdot) + \alpha[R - C(\cdot) - K(\cdot) - r] + \beta[\Sigma p_i y_i - wC(\cdot)]$$

Using the notation U_i for $\partial U/\partial y_i$, $U_r = \partial U/\partial r$, etc., we have the first order conditions

$$U_i - \alpha C_i + \beta(mr_i - wC_i) = 0, \tag{4}$$

where $mr_i = \partial \Sigma p_i y_i / \partial y_i$ is the marginal revenue of i, and

$$U_r - \alpha = 0. \tag{5}$$

Since consumer equilibrium requires equality between price ratios and marginal rates of substitution (the ratios of marginal utilities) we have

$$\frac{U_i}{p_i} = \frac{U_r}{w} = k, \qquad (i = 1, \ldots, n)$$

so that (5) yields $U_i = kw = \alpha$, and therefore (4) becomes

$$p_i - wC_i + (\beta/k)(mr_i - wC_i) = 0, \tag{6}$$

which, writing $mc_i = wC_i$, yields the general Ramsey formula (1). To obtain the inverse elasticity formula (2) we simply use a standard relationship for the case of independent demands,

$$mr_i = p_i(1 - 1/E_i),$$

substituting this into (6) we have

$$p_i - mc_i = (\beta/k)(p_i - mc_i - p_i/E_i),$$

or

$$(1 - \beta/k)(p_i - mc_i) = -(\beta/k)p_i/E_i$$

which immediately yields (2).

APPLICATIONS. Aside from its obvious connection with pricing by the firm, the theorem also has applications to the principles of taxation and to the general equilibrium analysis of the economy. Indeed, Frank Ramsey presented his result as a theorem on taxation rather than pricing. The point is that the theoretical concept of lump-sum taxes aside, any tax must be a levy on some sort of economic activity. Even if the price of that activity's product is equal to its marginal cost, the tax will in general drive a wedge between the two, particularly if the total tax revenue is required to meet some particular target. Thus the problem of determining the vector of tax rates on the economy's activities that will meet the overall revenue target with minimum social welfare loss is equivalent to determining the optimal vector of deviations between prices and marginal costs that will satisfy that revenue (budget) constraint. In sum, the search for the optimal (budget constrained) prices and the optimal (revenue constrained) tax rates are formally equivalent.

The analysis also has direct implications for general equilibrium theory, for it tells us that if lump-sum taxes are impossible, then a vector of (first best) marginal cost prices may also be ruled out for the economy as a whole. Indeed, such a first-best parametric price solution is possible only if, at the corresponding vector of activity levels (outputs), the production frontier happens to be locally linear and homogeneous (meaning, in the differentiable case, that it must be tangent to a hyperplane through the origin in input–output space).

For suppose this is not so – say, that there are increasing returns to scale at any such point. Then marginal cost pricing will yield negative profits for the economy, and suppliers as a class will be able to survive financially with such prices only if they receive subsidies. But subsidies must be paid for by taxes, and any such taxes on activities whose pretax prices equal their marginal costs must yield after tax prices which do not. In sum, one cannot escape the problem of finding the deviations of prices from their 'first best' magnitudes which meet the budget requirement that every subsidy must be covered by tax revenues. This, then, is the inescapable Ramsey problem for the entire economy if prices are parametric and no optimal output vector is a point of (at least local) linear homogeneity.

The case of diminishing returns poses corresponding problems, even though it is often thought to be compatible with competitive equilibrium and marginal cost pricing. As long as input quantities (including the input of entrepreneurship) can be expanded, marginal cost pricing will be incompatible with equilibrium at an optimal point because marginal cost pricing will then yield positive economic profits and the number of firms will therefore increase. There can be *no* finite number of firms at which this manifestation of disequilibrium ceases unless marginal cost pricing is abandoned. But then the best equilibrium prices in terms of Pareto optimality must again be the Ramsey prices.

In sum, Ramsey pricing is no mere artifact of regulation of industry or tax policy. It is deeply embedded in the logic of the general equilibrium mechanism.

HISTORY OF RAMSEY ANALYSIS. The basic theorem apparently first appeared in Frank Ramsey's classic article (1927). While the article has sometimes attracted the attention it deserved, it did not effectively convey to the profession the wider implications of its second-best pricing analysis. In 1928 A.C. Pigou, who had apparently posed the original issue to Ramsey, published a restatement of the theorem. Here, too, it was presented as a result on the principles of taxation and not related to pricing. Ursula Hicks (1947) independently provided a similar discussion.

Perhaps the first work on Ramsey theory that was expressed in terms of pricing issues occurred in the aftermath of Hotelling's (1938) classic paper on marginal cost pricing. There the author had advocated a system of subsidies to firms subject to scale economies, but he himself came to recognize the tax implications and the consequences for the overall optimality of the solution. He and J.R. Hicks discussed the problem, and Hicks emerged with an independently discovered Ramsey theorem, which was never published.

Early after World War II, two major contributions were made to the literature. Paul Samuelson (1951) prepared a memorandum for the US Treasury pointing out the logic of the Ramsey approach to taxation. As is to be expected, Samuelson's contribution was highly sophisticated and offered substantial original insights, but although widely circulated in public finance circles, it was never published. After having published a less sophisticated version of the theorem in 1951, Marcel Boiteux, now Directeur-Générale of Électricité de France, published a major article on the subject in 1956. It explicitly dealt with the topic as an issue in pricing policy for nationalized or regulated firms and derived its results directly from a Pareto optimality model. Moreover, it provided a result more general than the inverse elasticity form of the theorem on which Ramsey and Pigou had focused.

An even deeper exploration of the subject was provided by Diamond and Mirrlees (1971) as part of their continuing work on the theory of optimal taxation. Their papers are important not only because of their careful analysis but also because they played a major role in bringing the subject to the profession's attention. Within a year or two of the appearance of their articles and that of Baumol and Bradford (1970), 'everyone' in the profession was fully aware of the notion of Ramsey pricing and its logic. Since then there has been an explosion of writings on the subject and it occurs centrally or peripherally in a wide variety of fields.

An illustrative and perhaps surprising application which suggests the unexpected places in which the construct can turn up, is the 'weak invisible hand theorem', that occurs in the contestable markets literature (see Baumol, Bailey and Willig, 1977). That theorem states that if a monopolist who is constrained by a regulatory (or other) profit ceiling chooses to adopt the Ramsey price vector rather than some other set of prices that enable him to earn his allowed return, then under a fairly attractive set of assumptions the monopolist will be rewarded for his virtuous decision by being protected from entry by those prices. In other words, self-interest may impel a monopolist to adopt Ramsey prices because those prices are *sustainable* against entry, meaning that at those prices the monopolist will earn the profits that the constraint allows to him, but any rival firm that undertakes to enter the field will be predestined to lose money even if the incumbent undertakes no strategic (retaliatory) response.

Today Ramsey pricing is accepted as a basic proposition of microanalysis and appears with great frequency in new writings on the theory of the firm, industrial organization and public finance; it recurs regularly in the pricing discussions of American regulatory agencies.

WILLIAM J. BAUMOL

See also OPTIMAL TAXATION.

BIBLIOGRAPHY

Baumol, W.J. and Bradford, D.F. 1970. Optimal departures from marginal cost pricing. *American Economic Review* 60, June, 265–83.

Baumol, W.J., Bailey, E.E. and Willig, R.D. 1977. Weak invisible hand theorems on the sustainability of prices in a multiproduct monopoly. *American Economic Review* 67, June, 350–65.

Boiteux, M. 1956. Sur la géstion des monopoles publics astreints à l'équilibre budgétaire. *Econometrica* 24, January, 22–40.

Diamond, P.A. and Mirrlees, J.A. 1971. Optimal taxation and public production: II. *American Economic Review* 61, June, 261–78.

Hicks, U. 1947. *Public Finance*. London: Nisbet.

Hotelling, H. 1938. The general welfare in relation to problems of taxation and of railway and utility rates. *Econometrica* 6, July, 242–69.

Pigou, A.C. 1928. *A Study in Public Finance*. London: Macmillan.

Ramsey, F. 1927. A contribution to the theory of taxation. *Economic Journal* 37, March, 47–61.

Samuelson, P.A. 1951. Theory of optimal taxation. Unpublished memorandum for the US Treasury.

random coefficients. Random coefficients models generalize conventional fixed coefficients models to avoid inconsistent and inaccurate assessments of relationships among variables.

FIXED COEFFICIENTS MODELS. As Goldberger (1964, pp. 380–88) indicates, there are three alternative ways to formulate fixed coefficients models: (1) structural-form, (2) reduced-form, and (3) recursive-form. The view of the economic mechanism underlying these formulations is that there is a joint probability distribution of the current endogenous (random) variables $y_t^* = (y_{1t}^*, \ldots, y_{Lt}^*)'$ conditional on the values of the predetermined variables $x_t = (x_{1t}, \ldots, x_{Kt})'$. This conditional distribution may be written as

$$p(y_t | x_t, \boldsymbol{\theta}), \tag{1}$$

where $\boldsymbol{\theta}$ is a fixed parameter vector taking values in a parameter space Ω and Y is a sample space in which y_t takes on its values.

One way to specify this distribution is to postulate a reduced-form model. The vector $\boldsymbol{\theta}$ then includes the fixed coefficients as well as the disturbance variances and covariances of the reduced-form. Alternatively, one could postulate a structural-form model and then deduce the conditional distribution by transforming the structural-form into the reduced-form. Finally, one could postulate a model in recursive-form, thereby imposing upon the structural-form the triangularity restriction on the coefficients matrix of the endogenous variables and the diagonality restriction of the covariance matrix of the disturbances.

INACCURACIES AND INCONSISTENCIES. Regardless of the formulation postulated, the usefulness of fixed coefficients models is limited because of inherent inconsistencies and inaccuracies. For example, even when the fixed coefficients model is formulated in structural-form, the equations frequently are subjected to episodic breakdowns that are usually handled by judgemental 'add factors' and dummy variables. Even in those situations when microeconomic relationships remain invariant under changed circumstances, the corresponding macroeconomic relationships obtained by aggregating across individual units may not remain invariant, as shown by Swamy et al. (1982).

Besides these inaccuracies, the reduced-form is invariant under nonsingular transformations of the structural-form, see Goldberger (1964, p. 312). Different values of the structural parameters therefore imply the same conditional distribution so that the structural equations may not be identified. Yet, identification is a necessary condition for statistical consistency, see Gabrielsen (1978). Of course, one can achieve identification by imposing restrictions on the parameters of structural equations. But if these restrictions are over-identifying, they can be inconsistent, as shown by Conway et al. (1984, p. 7). Furthermore, there are cases in which the reduced-form parameters are also not identified without appropriate restrictions. Imposing identifying restrictions on the reduced-form parameters, however, may contradict the structural identifying restrictions, see Swamy (1980) and Swamy and Mehta (1983), leading to a logically inconsistent model. Surely no one would wish to construct this type of model, since as Boland convincingly argues, even if one cannot prove a model is true, to be true it must be at least logically consistent, see Swamy et al. (1985). Furthermore, if a model is logically inconsistent, the notion of the true value of a parameter and the related concept of statistical consistency do not apply.

Finally, according to Lane (1984), there are three possible interpretations of the elements of Ω:

(a) θ is compatible with the conditional distribution;
(b) Ω is an abstract set and θ merely indexes the conditional distribution;
(c) θ is a possible value for some 'real' physical parameter and function (1) is to be regarded as the distribution of the random quantity y^* (conditional on x) should θ be the true value of that parameter.

Interpretation (c) raises the difficult philosophical question: When and in what sense do 'real' physical parameters exist? Furthermore, must one believe that each structural parameter has a propensity to take a single value? It is difficult to believe that there are model-free physical quantities underlying each model parameter, without guidance as to what constitutes reality and how reality is linked to the mathematics embodied in specific models. Such guidance is impossible, however, because the truth status of a logically consistent model cannot be established, see Swamy et al. (1985). Thus, one never knows when interpretation (c) is appropriate. An appeal to statistical consistency based on the notion of the true values of parameters therefore cannot be made with any conviction.

Since interpretations (a) and (b) are defined solely in terms of the assumed (mathematical) model and do not necessarily refer to the physical reality that model is intended to represent, they are mathematically precise. However, interpretation (a) provides no scope for the mixture principle (that is, permitting an assumed underlying distribution for the parameters to affect the ultimate values of the endogenous variables), since only models whose sampling distributions are identical share 'the same Ω'. Fixed coefficients models thus apply only to situations when the model structure can be represented solely in terms of probability distributions on the sample space indexed by the fixed and unknown θ.

Interpretation (b), on the other hand, does provide wide scope for mixing. Indeed, any two fixed coefficients models with the same index set can be mixed. Consequently, if there exists a pair of observations, one from each model, yielding the same likelihood function on the index set Ω, the likelihood principle holds that the 'evidence' or 'inference' derived from the two models with these two observations must be identical. Yet, this conclusion may not only be incorrect, but is inconsistent with the Bayesian approach, as Lane (1984) points out.

In sum, the foundational status of a fixed coefficients model cannot be determined until Ω is interpreted. Depending upon whether one adopts interpretation (a), (b), or (c), fixed coefficients models are either devoid of interesting consequences (since θ is fixed and unknown), wrong (since inferences may be incorrect and unacceptable to Bayesians), or severely and ambiguously restricted in its domain of applicability (since the truth status of models cannot be known).

RANDOM COEFFICIENTS MODELS. A way to avoid the difficulties mentioned in the preceding section is to use the following random coefficients model (for earlier models, see Swamy (1971) and the references therein) developed by Swamy and Tinsley (1980):

$$\begin{aligned} &\text{(i)}\quad y_t^* = x_t'\beta_t^*;\\ &\text{(ii)}\quad \beta_t^* = Bz_t + J\xi_t^*;\\ &\text{(iii)}\quad \xi_t^* = \Phi\xi_{t-1}^* + v_t^*; \end{aligned} \tag{2}$$

with $E(v_t^*|z_t, x_t, \xi_{t-1}) = E(v_t^*) = 0$ for all z_t, x_t, and ξ_{t-1}, $E(v_t^* v_s^{*\prime}|z_t, x_t, \xi_{t-1}) = \Delta_v$ if $t = s$ and 0 if $t \neq s$. One element of each of x_t and z_t may be identically equal to 1 for all t, with the coefficients corresponding to these unit elements representing a random intercept and a constant vector, respectively. Although Swamy and Tinsley set $J = [I, 0, \ldots, 0]$, alternative choices for J are possible.

Since the disturbance term is indistinguishable from a time-dependent random element of β_t^* corresponsing to the unit element of x_t, both specifications are combined into a single element of β_t^*. When an equation is part of a larger model, regressors may be jointly determined with the regressand and hence correlated with the contemporaneous disturbance term, see Goldberger (1964, p. 292). If so, elements of x_t in equation (2) (i) are correlated with β_t^*, which means they also appear in z_t. Equation (2) (ii) admits such correlations. The term $J\xi_t^*$ is that part of β_t^* that is mean-independent of x_t and z_t.

Clearly, fixed coefficients models are special cases of random coefficients models. This is the case, for instance, when all the elements of β_t^* corresponding to the non-constant elements of x_t have zero variances and when the columns of B corresponding to the non-constant elements of z_t are null. Thus, in fixed coefficients models, the intercept but not the slopes may be interpreted as random, see Swamy (1970; 1971, p. 8).

When time series of cross-sections data are available, equation (2) has been generalized by Swamy and Mehta (1975) to

$$\begin{aligned} &\text{(i)}\quad y_{it}^* = x_{it}'\beta_{it}^* = \sum_{j=1}^{K} x_{jit}\beta_{jit}^*\\ &\text{(ii)}\quad \beta_{it}^* = \beta + \alpha_i^* + \xi_{it}^*, \end{aligned} \tag{3}$$

where i indexes cross-section observations, t indexes time series observations, the α_i^* are independently distributed with mean vector zero and constant covariance matrix Δ_α, the ξ_{it}^* are distributed with mean vector zero and a general covariance matrix Δ, the α_i^* are independent of the ξ_{it}^* and the β_{it}^* are mean-independent of the x_{it}.

Since these random coefficients models are designed to provide only a convenient approach to modelling relationships, they do not carry a metaphysical burden of 'reality' for the parameters they contain. Furthermore, equations (2) (ii) and (3) (ii) provide rich classes of coherent mixing functions. Swamy and Mehta (1975) and Swamy and Tinsley (1980) use data based methods to select the mixing functions, though purely subjective beliefs can form the basis for these functions. Based on these observations, the correct interpretation for the coefficients β_t^* and β_{it}^* is Lane's interpretation (b). Unlike fixed coefficients, random coefficients are not subject to inconsistent restrictions. Since the ultimate aim of inference is typically to generate an accurate prediction about the value of some future observables, Swamy and Lad (1985) employed a random coefficients model to generate predictions about the future values of stock prices based upon the current and past values of dividends. The resulting forcasts are substantially better than those obtained from the corresponding fixed coefficients model, demonstrating the potential gain in accuracy provided by this consistent approach to modelling relationships among variables.

In conclusion, rather than indicting fixed coefficients models, the comments presented here emphasize the shortcomings of that approach as compared with random coefficients models, thereby providing the researcher with more complete information when deciding upon an empirical model.

P.A.V.B. SWAMY AND J.R. BARTH

See also ESTIMATION.

BIBLIOGRAPHY

Conway, R.K., Swamy, P.A.V.B., Yanagida, J.F. and von zur Muehlen, P. 1984. The impossibility of causality testing. *Agricultural Economic Research* 36(3), Summer, 1–19.

Gabrielsen, A. 1978. Consistency and identifiability. *Journal of Econometrics* 8(2), October, 261–63.

Goldberger, A.S. 1964. *Econometric Theory*. New York: Wiley.

Lane, D.A. 1984. Discussion of the likelihood principle by J.O. Berger and R.L. Wolpert. Lecture Notes – Monograph Series, Vol. 6, Hayward, California, Institute of Mathematical Statistics.

Swamy, P.A.V.B. 1970. Efficient inference in a random coefficient regression model. *Econometrica* 38(2), March, 311–23.

Swamy, P.A.V.B. 1971. *Statistical Inference in Random Coefficient Regression Models*. New York: Springer-Verlag.

Swamy, P.A.V.B. 1980. A comparison of estimators for undersized samples. *Journal of Econometrics* 14(2), October, 161–81.

Swamy, P.A.V.B. and Lad, F. 1985. Forecasting stock prices with the stochastic coefficients models. Special Studies, Federal Reserve Board, Washington, DC.

Swamy, P.A.V.B. and Mehta, J.S. 1975. Baysian and non-Bayesian analysis of switching regressions and of random coefficient regression models. *Journal of the American Statistical Association* 70, Pt I, September, 593–602.

Swamy, P.A.V.B. and Mehta, J.S. 1983. Further results on Zellner's minimum expected loss and full information maximum likelihood estimators for undersized samples. *Journal of Business and Economic Statistics* 1(2), April, 154–62.

Swamy, P.A.V.B. and Tinsley, P.A. 1980. Linear prediction and estimation methods for regression models with stationary stochastic coefficients. *Journal of Econometrics* 12(2), February, 103–42.

Swamy, P.A.V.B., Barth, J.R. and Tinsley, P.A. 1982. The rational expectations approach to economic modelling. *Journal of Economic Dynamics and Control* 4(2), May, 125–47.

Swamy, P.A.V.B., Conway, R.K. and von zur Muehlen, P. 1985. The foundations of econometrics – are there any? (With discussion.) *Econometric Reviews* 4(1), November, 1–61.

randomization. Randomization refers to the selection of an element *a*, from a set *A*, according to some probability distribution P on *A*.

EXAMPLE 1. In the 1970 United States draft lottery it was necessary to order eligible males randomly for possible later induction into the armed services. In an attempt to do this fairly, capsules representing each day of the year were mixed in a large drum and selected by drawing. Those individuals with birthdays on the day corresponding to the first capsule drawn would be drafted first; those with birthdays corresponding to the second capsule drawn would be drafted second, and so on. The set *A* was thus the set of all sequences of capsules corresponding to days 1 through 366 of the year (1970 was a leap year). The sequence of capsules that was actually drawn began $a = (258, 115, 365, 45, 292, 250, \ldots)$.

The goal of the randomization was to be 'fair', so that any such sequence had the same chance of occurring. Choosing *a* according to the uniform probability distribution on *A* would have achieved this fairness, the uniform distribution being that which assigns equal probability to each *a* in *A*. Interestingly, the mixing process used with the capsules was not very good, and the capsules with large numbers ended up being drawn sooner than capsules with small numbers (on the average). Thus the actual randomization used was not the uniform distribution, and resulted in bias against individuals with late birthdays (see Rosenblatt and Filliben, 1971).

Randomization is very commonly used to select winners (or losers) as in example 1. Lotteries are the most common examples. There are also technical roles for randomization in such fields as statistics and game theory, and it is to these roles we now turn.

The use of randomization in statistics is very widespread, particularly in experimental design.

EXAMPLE 2. Two medical treatments A and B are to be tested, and 20 patients are available for the experiment. From the 20 patients, 10 are randomly selected using *simple random sampling* (i.e., the selection is done in such a way that any 10 people would have the same chance of being chosen). These 10 are given treatment A, with the remaining 10 being given treatment B.

The major reason for use of randomization in example 2 is to help prevent possible (unintentional) experimental bias. For instance, the doctors administering the treatments might well have feelings as to which treatment is better for a patient with given characteristics, and could (perhaps subconsciously) allow these feelings to affect the assignment of patients to treatment, if given that responsibility. Historical examples of (unintentional) experimenter-induced bias abound, to the extent that randomization of treatment assignment is now standard practice in most statistical experimentation. The statistician most responsible for the widespread adoption of randomization was R.A. Fisher (see Fisher, 1966).

Modes of randomization, considerably more complicated than that in example 2, are used in sophisticated experimental designs. The major reason for such sophistication is that, while random assignment of treatments can help prevent experimenter-induced bias, it can result in 'unlucky bias'. In example 2, for instance, the sickest people could (by bad luck) all end up in the group chosen to receive treatment A. To help prevent such an eventuality, and to reduce variance, randomization is often combined with use of *control* in experimental design. (See Cox, 1958; Fisher, 1966; and Anderson and McLean, 1974, for general discussions. Moore, 1979, gives an excellent nontechnical introduction to the subject.)

Another use of randomization in statistics, and also in game theory, is to choose an action or statistical answer randomly. The motivation in game theory is easiest to perceive.

EXAMPLE 3. Each of two players in a game is to choose 'odd' or 'even'. If their choices match, player I wins; otherwise player II wins. This game is to be played repeatedly.

It is clear that if either player falls into a recognizable pattern of choosing 'odd' or 'even', the other player can adapt his strategy to this pattern and win repeatedly. Thus it might be wise for the players to adopt *random* strategies, whereby their choice of 'odd' or 'even' is determined by a chance mechanism. For instance, a simple random strategy is to flip a fair coin, choosing 'odd' if a head occurs and 'even' if a tail occurs (and, of course, keeping the coin flip secret). This would correspond to choosing 'odd' and 'even' with probability 0.5 each.

In a general game having a set A of available strategies, a *randomized strategy* is simply a choice from A according to a probability distribution, P, on A. Each P corresponds to a different randomized strategy. (Some of these strategies can, of course, be quite bad.) Randomized strategies play a crucial role in game theory (cf. Thomas, 1984; and Berger, 1985).

Some proponents of the frequentist approach to statistics advocate use of randomized statistical strategies. The reason is that one could be in a situation where it is impossible, say, to find a statistical test having type I error probability of 0.05, unless one is willing, for certain data, to allow the possibility of deciding at random whether to accept or reject the hypothesis. This can put the statistician in the rather untenable position of having to flip a coin at the end of the analysis, with heads leading to 'rejection at the 0.05 level' and tails leading to acceptance. The careful experimenter, seeing the statistician draw conclusions from his data in this fashion, will not be thrilled. Use of randomized statistical strategies has thus never been very widespread.

Implementing a desired randomization is not as easy as one might expect; witness the fiasco described in example 1. The most common method used today is based on random number tables or random number generators in computers.

EXAMPLE 1 (CONT.). The most direct method of generating a uniform random sequence would be to label the days as 001, 002, 003,... , 366, and use a random number table or generator to obtain a sequence of three-digit random numbers. Simply list the three-digit random numbers in the order they occur (ignoring any three-digit numbers, other than those above, which happen to be generated). Note that it is necessary to label day 1 as 001, day 15 as 015, and so on; if the labels of the days were allowed to have different numbers of digits, they would have different probabilities of being generated. (Any one-digit number has three times the chance of being generated, by a uniform random number generator, as does a three-digit number.) See Moore (1979) for further discussion at an introductory level. Note that computers also have available software for generating probability randomizations other than the uniform.

JAMES O. BERGER

See also LIKELIHOOD; PROBABILITY.

BIBLIOGRAPHY

Anderson, V.L. and McLean, R.A. 1974. *Design of Experiments*. New York: Marcel Dekker.

Berger, J. 1985. *Statistical Decision Theory and Bayesian Analysis*. New York: Springer-Verlag.

Cox, D.R. 1958. *Planning of Experiments*. New York: Wiley.

Fisher, R.A. 1966. *The Design of Experiments*. 8th edn, New York: Hafner.

Moore, D.S. 1979. *Statistics, Concepts and Controversies*. San Francisco: Freeman.

Rosenblatt, J.R. and Filliben, J.J. 1971. Randomization and the draft lottery. *Science* 171, 306–8.

Thomas, L.C. 1984. *Games, Theory and Applications*. New York: Wiley.

random variables. Scientific statements often have a probabilistic element, for example, 'In population Ω the distribution of individual income, I, can be approximated by a log-normal distribution'. The formal interpretation of this statement requires a moderate amount of structure, such as,

The population Ω has n members, $\omega_1, \ldots, \omega_n$. Associated with each ω is an income, $I(\omega)$. Each ω has the same probability $P(\omega_i)$ of being observed so that $P(\omega_i) = 1/n$ for $i = 1, \ldots, n$. Finally, $P(I \leqslant t) \doteq F(t, \alpha, \beta, \gamma)$ for $-\infty < t < \infty$ where F is the 3-parameter log-normal distribution function.

For this formal description, the following terms are often used. The set of all *elementary events*, ω, that is Ω, is the *sample space*. A function, such as $I(\omega)$ defined on Ω, is called a *random variable*. The *distribution function* of $I(\omega)$ is given by the probabilities of the events that if ω_i is selected, then $I(\omega_i) \leqslant t$ as a function of t. In this example, $F(t, \alpha, \beta, \gamma)$ is a *model* for the distribution of I. The model contains unspecified *parameters*, α, β, γ, which could depend on units of measurement, the population, time, etc. The sign $\doteq$ indicates the approximation.

BASIC PROPERTIES OF RANDOM VARIABLES

In studying a random variable, $X(\omega)$, attention is focused on finding probabilities of events described in terms of $X(\omega)$, such as, $a \leqslant X(\omega) \leqslant b$, or in terms of concepts derived from those probabilities, such as, the average or *expected value* of $X(\omega)$, see (16). Other approaches could have been taken: the development could use expected value instead of probability as the basic concept, or the sample space concept could be omitted, proceeding directly to distribution functions. The approach taken here is in the mainstream. The theory requires a σ-field of sets, $\mathscr{F}$, whose members are subsets of Ω; that is, if $A \in \mathscr{F}$ then the complement of A is in $\mathscr{F}$, $\Omega \in \mathscr{F}$, and if $A_i \in \mathscr{F}$ for $i = 1, 2, \ldots$, then $\cup A_i \in \mathscr{F}$. The basic theory permits us to compute probabilities of events, B, only when $B \in \mathscr{F}$; these sets are called *measurable*. For the real line we select the smallest σ-field which includes all intervals of the form $(-\infty, t]$. Random variables must be *measurable*; that is, events defined in terms of a random variable must belong to $\mathscr{F}$. Thus, if X is a random variable, then for each t it is required that $\{\omega\colon X(\omega) \leqslant t\} \in \mathscr{F}$.

All probabilities of events determined in terms of $X(\omega)$ can be obtained from the *distribution function* of X, denoted by $F(t)$, where $F(t) = P(X \leqslant t)$ for $-\infty < t < \infty$.

The necessary and sufficient conditions for $F(t)$ to be a distribution function are:

(a) $F(s) \leqslant F(t)$ for $-\infty < s < t < \infty$.

(b) $\lim_{t \to -\infty} F(t) = 0$.

(c) $\lim_{t \to \infty} F(t) = 1$.

(d) $\lim_{x \to t^+} F(x) = F(t)$. (1)

Notice, F can be used to compute probabilities for events not of the form $X \leqslant t$, for examples,

$$P(X = t) = F(t) - \lim_{x \to t^-} F(x),$$

and

$$P(a \leqslant X \leqslant b) = F(b) - \lim_{x \to a^-} F(x).$$

Every distribution function has a unique decomposition of the form,

$$F = w_{\text{ac}} F_{\text{ac}} + w_{\text{s}} F_{\text{s}} + w_{\text{d}} F_{\text{d}}, \tag{2}$$

where $w_{\text{ac}} + w_{\text{s}} + w_{\text{d}} = 1$, $0 \leqslant w_{\text{ac}}$, w_{s}, w_{d}. Here F_{ac} is an *absolutely continuous* distribution function, that is, there exists a function f_{ac} such that

$$F_{\text{ac}}(t) = \int_{-\infty}^{t} f_{\text{ac}}(x)\,\mathrm{d}x \qquad -\infty < t < \infty. \tag{3}$$

Table 1. Discrete distributions

Name	Probability function	Support	Characteristic function	Mean	Variance
(1) Degenerate (x_0)	1	$x \in \{x_0\}$	e^{itx_0}	x_0	0
(2) Bernoulli (p) $B(p)$	$f(0) = 1-p$ $f(1) = p$	$x \in \{0, 1\}$ $0 \leqslant p \leqslant 1$	$1 - p + p\,e^{it}$	p	$p(1-p)$
(3) Binomial (n, p) $B(n, p)$	$\binom{n}{x} p^x (1-p)^{n-x}$	$x \in \{0, 1, \ldots, n\}$ n is a positive integer $0 \leqslant p \leqslant 1$	$(1 - p + p\,e^{it})^n$	np	$np(1-p)$
(4) Poisson (λ) $P(\lambda)$	$e^{-\lambda}\lambda^x/x!$	$x \in \{0, 1, \ldots\}$ $0 \leqslant \lambda$	$e^{-\lambda(1-e^{it})}$	λ	λ
(5) Geometric (p)	$(1-p)^{x-1}p$	$x \in \{1, 2, \ldots\}$ $0 < p \leqslant 1$	$\dfrac{p\,e^{it}}{1-(1-p)\,e^{it}}$	$\dfrac{1}{p}$	$\dfrac{1-p}{p^2}$
(6) Uniform (a) $U(a)$	$1/a$	$x \in \{1, 2, \ldots, n\}$ a is a positive integer	$\dfrac{e^{it}(1-e^{ita})}{a(1-e^{it})}$	$\dfrac{1+a}{2}$	$\dfrac{a^2-1}{12}$
(7) Hypergeometric	$\dfrac{\binom{n}{x}\binom{m}{r-x}}{\binom{m+n}{r}}$	$x \in \{0, 1, \ldots, \min(m, n)\}$ n, m, r non-negative integers with $r \leqslant m+n$		$\dfrac{rn}{m+n}$	$\left(\dfrac{m+n-r}{m+n-1}\right) r \dfrac{mn}{(m+n)^2}$
(8) Multinomial	$n! \prod_{j=1}^{J} (p_j^{x_j}/x_j!)$	$x_j = 0, 1, \ldots$ $\sum x_j = n$ $p_j \geqslant 0,\ j = 1, \ldots, J$ $\sum p_j = 1$	$\left(\sum p_j e^{it_j}\right)^n$	$EX_j = np_j$, $j = 1, \ldots, J$	$\sigma_j^2 = np_j(1-p_j)$ $\sigma_{jk} = -np_jp_k$ $j \neq k$

Table 2. Continuous distributions

Name	Density	Support	Characteristic function	Mean	Variance
(1) Exponential	e^{-x}	$x \in (0, \infty)$	$1/(1-it)$	1	1
(2) Logistic	$\dfrac{e^{-x}}{(1+e^{-x})^2}$	$x \in (-\infty, \infty)$	πt cosech πt	0	$\pi^2/3$
(3) Normal (0, 1) $N(0, 1)$	$\dfrac{1}{(2\pi)^{1/2}} e^{-x^2/2}$	$-\infty < x < \infty$	$e^{-t^2/2}$	0	1
(4) Uniform (0, 1) $U(0, 1)$	1	$x \in (0, 1)$	$(e^{it}-1)/it$	1/2	1/12
(5) Chi-Square (n) $\chi^2\,(n)$	$\dfrac{1}{2^{n/2}\Gamma(n/2)} e^{-x/2} x^{(n/2)-1}$	$x \in (0, \infty)$ $n \in (0, \infty)$	$(1-2it)^{-n/2}$	n	$2n$
(6) Cauchy	$[\pi(1+x^2)]^{-1}$	$x \in (-\infty, \infty)$	$e^{-\lvert t\rvert}$	See (16)	See (16)
(7) Student's $t(n)$ $t(n)$	$\dfrac{1}{n^{1/2}\mathscr{B}\left(\frac{1}{2}, \frac{n}{2}\right)} \left(1+\dfrac{x^2}{n}\right)^{-[(n+1)/2]}$	$x \in (-\infty, \infty)$ $n \in (0, \infty)$		0 if $n > 1$	$n/(n-2)$ if $n > 2$
(8) Fisher's $F(m, n)$ $F(m, n)$	$C \dfrac{x^{(m-2)/2}}{(n+mx)^{(n+m)/2}}$ with $C = \dfrac{m^{m/2}n^{n/2}}{\mathscr{B}(m/2, n/2)}$	$x \in (0, \infty)$ $m \in (0, \infty)$ $n \in (0, \infty)$		$\dfrac{n}{n-2}$ if $n > 2$	$\dfrac{2n^2(n+m-2)}{m(n-2)^2(n-4)}$ if $n > 4$
(9) Beta (a, b) $\beta(a, b)$	$\dfrac{x^{a-1}(1-x)^{b-1}}{\mathscr{B}(a, b)}$	$x \in (0, 1)$ $a, b \in (0, \infty)$		$\dfrac{a}{a+b}$	$\dfrac{ab}{(a+b)^2(a+b+1)}$
(10) Lognormal	$(2\pi x^2)^{-1/2} \exp[-(\ln x)^2/2]$	$x \in (0, \infty)$		$e^{1/2}$	$e^2 - e$
(11) Extreme value	$e^{-x-e^{-x}}$	$x \in (-\infty, \infty)$	$\Gamma(1-it)$	0.577	$\pi^2/6$
(12) Weibull	$cx^{c-1}e^{-x^c}$	$x \in (0, \infty)$ $c \in (0, \infty)$		$\Gamma(c^{-1}+1)$	$\Gamma(2c^{-1}+1) - [\Gamma(c^{-1}+1)]^2$
(13) Bivariate normal	See (61)				

The function f_{ac} is a *density*. Notice

$$f_{ac} \geqslant 0 \quad \text{and} \quad \int f_{ac} = 1.$$

The distribution function F_s is *singular* in that although it is not identically zero, its derivative exists and is zero almost everywhere. The distribution function F_d is *discrete*, that is, it is a right continuous step function with at most countably many jumps at $\{t_i\}$. The *probability function* f_d for F_d is zero everywhere except on $\{t_i\}$ where

$$f(t_i) = F(t_i) - \operatorname*{limit}_{x \to t_i^-} F(x).$$

The most common situations are the *discrete distributions* ($w_d = 1$) and the *(absolutely) continuous distributions* ($w_{ac} = 1$). In the discrete case the most common situation is the non-negative integer lattice, that is $\{t_i\} = \{i\}$ where the range of i is a set of non-negative integers, see Table 1.

In Table 1, x is used to designate a value of the random variable. All values that have a positive probability of occurrence are called the *support*. Also found in the 'support' column are specific restrictions on the constants or parameters of the probability function. In Table 1

$$A! = \Gamma(A+1) = \int_0^\infty x^A e^{-x}\,dx, \qquad A \geqslant -1, \tag{4}$$

and when A is a non-negative integer,

$$\binom{B}{A} = \frac{B(B-1)\cdots(B-A+1)}{A!}. \tag{5}$$

The name of a random variable or of a distribution, for example $B(p)$, is used also to represent the random variable. The symbol $\sim$ between two random variables means that they have the same distribution function, and in the case of discrete random variables, that they have the same probability function. Notice

$$B(1) \sim U(1) \sim \text{Degenerate}(1) \sim \text{Geometric}(1),$$

$$B(p) \sim B(1, p),$$

$$B(n, 0) \sim P(0) \sim \text{Degenerate}(0),$$

$$B(n, p) \sim n - B(n, 1-p).$$

In Table 2

$$\mathscr{B}(a, b) = \frac{\Gamma(a)\Gamma(b)}{\Gamma(a+b)}. \tag{6}$$

For the continuous distributions (Table 2), there are many interesting variations which arise from transformations (12). For example, $\sigma N(0, 1) + \mu$ with $\sigma \geqslant 0$ defines a normal random variable with expectation μ and variance σ^2, that is, $N(\mu, \sigma^2) \sim \sigma N(0, 1) + \mu$. The 3-parameter log-normal is obtained from Table 2(10) with the transformation $x = [(y - \alpha)/\beta]^\gamma$, $y > \alpha$, $\beta > 0$, $\gamma > 0$ and the real root is used. Two useful connections between discrete and continuous random variables are

$$P[B(n, p) \geqslant k] = P[\beta(k, n-k+1) \leqslant p] \quad \text{for } k = 0, \ldots, n, \quad 0 \leqslant p \leqslant 1, \tag{7}$$

and

$$P[P(\lambda) < a] = P[\chi^2(2a) \geqslant 2\lambda] \quad \text{for } a = 1, 2, \ldots \text{ and } \lambda > 0. \tag{8}$$

ELEMENTARY MANIPULATIONS OF RANDOM VARIABLES

An absolutely continuous distribution does not have a unique density; the value of an integral is not changed if the integrand is changed on a countable number of points or a set of Lebesgue measure 0.

For $0 < \alpha < 1$, the *α-percentile* of a random variable X, denoted by x_α, is defined by

$$x_\alpha = \inf\{x : F(x) \geqslant \alpha\}. \tag{9}$$

Deciles, quartiles and medians (50-percentiles) are special cases.

If $X = X(\omega)$ is a random variable, then for any (measurable) function $g(\cdot)$ one obtains the random variable

$$Y = Y(\omega) = g[X(\omega)] = g(X)$$

with

$$F_Y(y) = P(Y \leqslant y) = P[g(X) \leqslant y] = \int_{\{x:\, g(x) \leqslant y\}} dF_X(x). \tag{10}$$

where F_X is the distribution function of X. In the discrete case, the $\int$ is a summation and $dF(x)$ is the probability function. In the absolutely continuous case, $dF(x)$ becomes $f(x)\,dx$ where f is a density function.

If $g(\cdot)$ is a strictly increasing function,

$$F_Y(y) = F_X[g^{-1}(y)], \tag{11}$$

and further, in the absolutely continuous case when g', the derivative of g, is assumed to exist, then

$$f_Y(y) = f_X[g^{-1}(y)][dg^{-1}(y)/dy]. \tag{12}$$

If $g(x) = \mu + \sigma x$, and $\sigma > 0$, then

$$f_Y(y) = \sigma^{-1} f_X[(y - \mu)/\sigma]. \tag{13}$$

In this monotone increasing case

$$y_\alpha = g^{-1}(x_\alpha). \tag{14}$$

Notice, if g is strictly decreasing, then in (12) replace $(g^{-1})'$ by $|(g^{-1})'|$ and (14) becomes

$$y_\alpha = g^{-1}(x_{1-\alpha}). \tag{15}$$

The *expected value* of X, denoted by EX, is defined by

$$EX = \int_{-\infty}^{\infty} x\,dF(x) \quad \text{provided} \quad \int_{-\infty}^{\infty} |x|\,dF(x) < \infty; \tag{16}$$

this last condition is sometimes relaxed to either

$$-\int_{-\infty}^{0} x\,dF(x) < \infty \quad \text{or} \quad \int_0^\infty x\,dF(x) < \infty.$$

In the discrete case,

$$EX = \sum x f(x), \tag{17}$$

and in the absolutely continuous case,

$$EX = \int_{-\infty}^{\infty} x f(x)\,dx. \tag{18}$$

If $Y = g(X)$, then

$$EY = \int_{-\infty}^{\infty} g(x)\,dF_X(x). \tag{19}$$

So we write $Eg(X)$ and it is not necessary to compute $F_Y(y)$.

Assume $g(x)$ is *convex* on an interval I which includes the support of X; that is, for x_1 and $x_2 \in I$ and $\alpha \in [0, 1]$,

$$g[\alpha x_1 + (1-\alpha)x_2] \leqslant \alpha g(x_1) + (1-\alpha) g(x_2). \tag{20}$$

(If $g''(x) \geqslant 0$ for $x \in I$, then g is convex.) Then *Jensen's inequality* is:

$$Eg(X) \geqslant g(EX), \tag{21}$$

provided both expected values exist. In particular,

$$EX^2 \geqslant (EX)^2, \tag{22}$$

so the *variance*, denoted by σ^2 and defined by

$$\sigma^2 = EX^2 - (EX)^2, \tag{23}$$

satisfies $\sigma^2 \geqslant 0$. An equivalent definition is

$$\sigma^2 = E(X - EX)^2. \tag{24}$$

A continuous distribution is *unimodal* with mode x_0 if $F(x)$ is convex for $x \in (-\infty, x_0)$, and $1 - F(x)$ is convex for $x_0 \in (x, \infty)$. The discrete X is *unimodal* if there is a unique x which maximizes its probability function. The discrete examples (except for the uniform), for most choices of the parameters are unimodal, and when the probability function has several maximizing values, they are contiguous.

Following are results and definitions for often-used expectations, if they exist (16):

$$\textit{Mean of } X = \mu = EX. \tag{25}$$

$$k\textit{th moment of } X = \alpha_k = EX^k, \quad \text{so } \mu = \alpha_1. \tag{26}$$

$$k\textit{th absolute moment of } X = E|X|^k. \tag{27}$$

$$k\textit{th central moment of } X = \mu_k = E(X - \mu)^k,$$

$$\text{so that } \sigma^2 = \mu_2, \text{ see (24)}. \tag{28}$$

$$E\{N(0,1)\}^{2k+1} = 0,$$

and

$$E\{N(0,1)\}^{2k} = (2k)!/k!2^k \text{ for } k,$$

$$\text{a non-negative integer.} \tag{29}$$

Characteristic function of X, $\phi_X(t)$ or $\phi(t)$ is defined by

$$\phi(t) = E\,\mathrm{e}^{itX}. \tag{30}$$

Always $\phi(0) = 1$, $|\phi(t)| \leqslant 1$, ϕ is uniformly continuous in t, and there is a one-to-one correspondence between distribution functions and characteristic functions. This correspondence is made explicit by

The *inversion formula:* If ϕ is the characteristic function of X, then

$$F(x + \Delta) - F(x - \Delta) = \lim_{T \to \infty} \int_{-T}^{T} \frac{1}{\pi} \frac{\sin t\Delta}{t} \mathrm{e}^{-itx} \phi(t)\, \mathrm{d}t \tag{31}$$

provided $x - \Delta$ and $x + \Delta$ are continuity points of F.

$\phi(t)$ is a characteristic function if and only if ϕ is continuous, $\phi(0) = 1$ and ϕ is non-negative definite; that is, for all $n\,(\geqslant 1)$, $t_1, \ldots, t_n$, and $h_1, \ldots, h_n$

$$\sum_{j=1}^{n} \sum_{k=1}^{n} h_j \phi(t_j - t_k) \bar{h}_k \geqslant 0, \tag{32}$$

where $\bar{h}$ is the complex conjugate of h.

The characteristic function of X is real if and only if

$$X \sim -X; \tag{33}$$

that is, X has a symmetric (about 0) distribution.

If $Y = aX + b$, then

$$\phi_Y(t) = \mathrm{e}^{ibt} \phi_X(at). \tag{34}$$

If X and Y are independent (50), then

$$\phi_{X+Y}(t) = \phi_X(t)\phi_Y(t). \tag{35}$$

The *moment generating function of X* is $m(t) = E\mathrm{e}^{tX}$ and

$$\ln m(t) \text{ is the } \textit{cumulant generating function.} \tag{36}$$

If X has support on the non-negative integers, then the *probability generating function of X* is

$$\theta(t) = Et^X, \qquad \text{for } 0 \leqslant t \leqslant 1,$$

and

$$P(X = k) = \frac{1}{k!} \frac{\mathrm{d}^k \theta(t)}{\mathrm{d}t^k}\bigg|_{t=0}, \quad \text{for } k = 1, 2, \ldots. \tag{37}$$

If the kth moment of X exists, then

$$EX^k = \mathrm{d}^k m(t)/\mathrm{d}t^k|_{t=0} = i^{-k} \mathrm{d}^k \phi(t)/\mathrm{d}t^k|_{t=0},$$

$$\text{for } k = 1, 2, \ldots. \tag{38}$$

The *kth cumulant* is the kth derivative of the cumulant generating function evaluated at 0. For $P(\lambda)$ the cumulant generating function is $\lambda(\mathrm{e}^t - 1)$ so all the $P(\lambda)$ cumulants are λ. In general, the cumulants can be expressed in terms of the central moments and vice versa.

Many inequalities can be obtained from the *Markov inequality:*

If $P[g(X) \geqslant 0] = 1$ and $A > 0$,

$$\text{then } P[g(X) \geqslant A] \leqslant Eg(X)/A. \tag{39}$$

The *Chebychev inequality* is one consequence of

$$P(|X - \mu| \geqslant \lambda) \leqslant \frac{E|X - \mu|^p}{\lambda^p}, \quad \lambda > 0 \text{ and } p > 0, \tag{40}$$

and another is the *Bernstein inequality:* If $x \geqslant 0$, then

$$P(X \geqslant x) \leqslant \inf_{t \geqslant 0} [\mathrm{e}^{-xt} m(t)]. \tag{41}$$

SEVERAL RANDOM VARIABLES

To this point we have mentioned the possibility of several random variables being defined on the same Ω. Now the discussion will focus on two random variables, say $X_1 = X_1(\omega)$ and $X_2 = X_2(\omega)$, for example, X_1 could be Income and X_2 could be Savings. So if ω_0 is an individual, then $[X_1(\omega_0), X_2(\omega_0)]$ is the income and savings of ω_0.

The *distribution function* is defined by

$$F(x_1, x_2) = F_{X_1, X_2}(x_1, x_2) = P(X_1 \leqslant x_1 \text{ and } X_2 \leqslant x_2). \tag{42}$$

Notice,

$$\operatorname*{limit}_{x_1 \to -\infty} F(x_1, x_2) = \operatorname*{limit}_{x_2 \to -\infty} F(x_1, x_2) = 0, \tag{43}$$

$$F_{X_1}(x_1) = \operatorname*{limit}_{x_2 \to \infty} F(x_1, x_2),$$

$$F_{X_2}(x_2) = \operatorname*{limit}_{x_1 \to \infty} F(x_1, x_2), \tag{44}$$

$$F(x_1+\Delta, x_2+\epsilon)-F(x_1, x_2+\epsilon)-F(x_1+\Delta, x_2)+F(x_1, x_2)$$
$$= P(x_1 < X_1 \leqslant x_1+\Delta \text{ and } x_2 < X_2 \leqslant x_2+\epsilon) \geqslant 0, \quad (45)$$

when $\Delta \geqslant 0$ and $\epsilon \geqslant 0$, and

$$F \text{ is right continuous in each of its arguments.} \quad (46)$$

Conditions (43)–(46) are necessary and sufficient for F to be a distribution function; (45) is the analogue of $F(x)$ being an increasing function in the univariate case (1). The discrete bivariate distributions offer no surprises when compared to the univariate case, but there are many special cases of mixed continuous and discrete situations. And there are simple continuous examples where nothing like a density could exist, such as

$$F(x, y) = \begin{cases} 0, & \text{for } x+y \leqslant 1 \\ \min(x, 1)+\min(y, 1)-1, & \text{for } x+y \geqslant 1 \end{cases}. \quad (47)$$

The random variables X and Y, are said to have the *joint density*, $f(x, y)$, provided

$$F(x, y) = P(X \leqslant x, Y \leqslant y) = \int_{-\infty}^{x}\int_{-\infty}^{y} f(s, t)\, \mathrm{d}s\, \mathrm{d}t,$$
$$\text{for } -\infty < x < \infty \quad \text{and} \quad -\infty < y < \infty. \quad (48)$$

When continuous random variables are discussed, the usual meaning will be this absolutely continuous situation with a (joint) density.

The random variables X and Y are *independent* if and only if

$$P(X \in A, Y \in B) = P(X \in A)P(Y \in B), \quad (49)$$

for all measurable sets A and B. A necessary and sufficient condition for the independence of X and Y, is

$$F(x, y) = F_X(x)F_Y(y)$$
$$\text{for } -\infty < x < \infty \quad \text{and} \quad -\infty < y < \infty; \quad (50)$$

when there is a density or probability function, (50) is equivalent to

$$f(x, y) = f_X(x)f_Y(y)$$
$$\text{for } -\infty < x < \infty \quad \text{and} \quad -\infty < y < \infty. \quad (51)$$

The expected value of a function of several random variables, say $Z = g(X, Y)$, can be found from

$$EZ = Eg(X, Y) = \iint g(x, y)\, \mathrm{d}F(x, y). \quad (52)$$

Always,

$$E(aX+bY) = aEX + bEY, \quad (53)$$

and if X and Y are independent,

$$EXY = (EX)(EY), \quad (54)$$

provided both EX and EY exist. In these formulas one can replace X by $r(X)$ and Y by $s(Y)$ to obtain results, such as, (35) and (24). The *covariance* is defined by

$$\sigma_{X,Y} = E(X-\mu_X)(Y-\mu_Y) = EXY - \mu_X\mu_Y, \quad (55)$$

and the Pearson product moment *correlation* is defined by,

$$\rho_{X,Y} = \sigma_{X,Y}/\sigma_X\sigma_Y. \quad (56)$$

The Cauchy–Schwarz inequality is equivalent to $-1 \leqslant \rho \leqslant 1$. If X and Y are independent, then $\rho = 0$, but not conversely.

Assume the equations

$$u = u(x, y) \quad \text{and} \quad v = v(x, y) \quad (57)$$

have a unique inverse; that is,

$$x = x(u, v) \quad \text{and} \quad y = y(u, v) \quad (58)$$

and the *Jacobian* determinant,

$$J(x, y; u, v) = \det \begin{bmatrix} \dfrac{\partial x}{\partial u} & \dfrac{\partial y}{\partial u} \\ \dfrac{\partial x}{\partial v} & \dfrac{\partial y}{\partial v} \end{bmatrix}, \quad (59)$$

exists, is continuous and is never equal to 0. Then

$$f_{U,V}(u, v) = |J(x, y; u, v)| f_{X,Y}[x(u, v), y(u, v)]. \quad (60)$$

The above conditions are sufficient and in applications, even if they fail, a little analysis might show that (60) still holds. The linear transformation

$$Y_1 = \mu_1 + \sigma_1 X_1 \quad \text{and} \quad Y_2 = \mu_2 + \sigma_2[\rho X_1 + (1-\rho^2)^{1/2} X_2]$$

of X_1 and X_2, two independent $N(0, 1)$ variables, yields

$$f_{Y_1,Y_2}(y_1, y_2) = \frac{1}{2\pi}\frac{1}{\sigma_1\sigma_2(1-\rho^2)^{1/2}} \exp\left\{\frac{-1}{2(1-\rho^2)\sigma_1^2\sigma_2^2} \times [\sigma_2^2(y_1-\mu_1)^2 - 2\rho\sigma_1\sigma_2(y_1-\mu_1)(y_2-\mu_2) + \sigma_1^2(y_2-\mu_2)^2]\right\}, \quad (61)$$

or

$$(Y_1, Y_2) \sim N(\mu, \Sigma). \quad (62)$$

In (62) $N(\mu, \Sigma)$ is a *bivariate normal* random variable with mean vector μ and variance–covariance matrix Σ where

$$\mu = \begin{pmatrix} \mu_1 \\ \mu_2 \end{pmatrix} \quad \text{and} \quad \Sigma = \begin{pmatrix} \sigma_1^2 & \rho\sigma_1\sigma_2 \\ \rho\sigma_1\sigma_2 & \sigma_2^2 \end{pmatrix}.$$

From the general bivariate normal density (61), one can show $Y_1 \sim N(\mu_1, \sigma_1^2)$ and $Y_2 \sim N(\mu_2, \sigma_2^2)$. The random variables Y_1 and Y_2 are independent if and only if $\rho = 0$.

To finish this introduction to bivariate distributions, we introduce the conditional probability of A given B,

$$P(A \mid B) = \frac{P(A \text{ and } B)}{P(B)}, \quad (63)$$

provided $P(B) > 0$. When X and Y are discrete random variables (defined on the same sample space), the conditional probability function of X given Y, is defined accordingly

$$f_{X|Y}(x \mid y) = \frac{f_{X,Y}(x, y)}{f_Y(y)}, \quad (64)$$

provided $f_Y(y) > 0$. For each y-value, $f_{X|Y}$ will be a probability function, and conditional expectations are defined by

$$E(X \mid Y = y) = \sum x f_{X|Y}(x, y). \quad (65)$$

The function in (65) has y as its argument. If $y = Y(\omega)$, then the conditional expectation becomes a random variable denoted by $EX \mid Y$. The conditional density may be defined as in (64) for the continuous case as well. For the bivariate normal (61), the conditional distribution of Y_1 given $Y_2 = y_2$ is

$$N\left[\mu_1 + \rho\frac{\sigma_1}{\sigma_2}(y_2 - \mu_2), (1-\rho^2)\sigma_1^2\right]. \quad (66)$$

Conditioning on Y_2 reduces the variance of Y_1 and makes the expected value of Y_1 depend linearly on the specified value of Y_2 when $\rho \neq 0$.

ASYMPTOTIC THEOREMS FOR SUMS OF INDEPENDENT RANDOM VARIABLES

A random variable X with expectation μ is often observed near μ. And if there are several random variables, $X_1, \ldots, X_n$ each with expectation μ, then their average, $\bar{X}_n = \Sigma X_i/n$, should even be closer to μ. Now consider a sequence of random variables $X_1, \ldots, X_n, \ldots$, which are independent each with the same distribution and $EX_i = \mu$.

Weak Law of Large Numbers:

$$\lim_{n\to\infty} P(|\bar{X}_n - \mu| < \epsilon) = 1, \quad \text{for every } \epsilon > 0. \quad (67)$$

Strong Law of Large Numbers:

$$P\left(\lim_{n\to\infty} \bar{X}_n = \mu\right) = 1. \quad (68)$$

The mode of convergence in (67) is *in probability* or *weak*, and the mode of convergence in (68) is *with probability one* or *strong*. The difference between weak and strong statements is shown in the following example, $\bar{A}$ is the complement of A, and $\text{mod}_1\, a = r$ where $a = a' + r$ with a' an integer and $0 \leqslant r < 1$. Let:

$$Z_n(\omega) = \begin{cases} 0, & \text{if } \omega \in \bar{A}_n \\ 1, & \text{if } \omega \in A_n \end{cases}, \quad (69)$$

where $\Omega = (0, 1)$, $A_n = (\text{mod}_1\, \Sigma_1^n 1/i, \text{mod}_1\, \Sigma_1^{n+1} 1/i)$ and the probability of a set in Ω is the length of the set. Then $P(A_n) \to 0$ so that Z_n converges in probability to 0. Also, every ω is in an infinite number of A_n so that Z_n does *not* converge with probability one.

Strong convergence implies weak convergence; when the Strong Law of Large Numbers applies, so will the Weak Law of Large Numbers. A sequence of random variables Z_n is said to converge in *mean square* to μ if and only if

$$E(Z_n - \mu)^2 \to 0. \quad (70)$$

Mean square convergence implies weak convergence. A consequence of the Chebychev inequality is:

Assume for each i and j that $EX_i = \mu$, $\sigma_{X_i, X_j} = \sigma_{ij}$

and $\sum_{i=1}^{n}\sum_{j=1}^{n} \sigma_{ij}/n^2 \to 0$; then $\bar{X}_n \to \mu$ in probability. (71)

Another type of convergence is *in distribution*. The sequence of random variables $X_1, X_2, \ldots, X_n, \ldots$ converge in distribution to X if and only if

$$F_X(x) = \lim_{n\to\infty} F_{X_n}(x)$$

at all continuity points of F_X. It is expressed as $X_n \rightsquigarrow X$. Note X and X_n can be defined on different sample spaces Ω and Ω_n so $P(X \in A, X_n \in B)$ would not be defined. The symbol $X - X_n$ requires X and X_n to be defined on the same space. Thus the conclusion of (67) is $\bar{X}_n \rightsquigarrow$ degenerate (μ). Note $B(n, \lambda/n) \rightsquigarrow P(\lambda)$ for fixed λ.

Also, $X_n a \rightsquigarrow Y$ means there are sequences $\{a_n\}$ and $\{b_n\}$ such that $a_n X_n + b_n \rightsquigarrow Y$. The assumptions of (72) imply $\bar{X}_n a \rightsquigarrow N(0, 1)$, $\bar{X}_n a \rightsquigarrow \mu$, $\bar{X}_n a \rightsquigarrow 0$. Read $X_n \rightsquigarrow Y$ as 'the limiting distribution of $\{X_n\}$ is the distribution of Y' or 'X_n converges to Y in distribution'. And read $X_n a \rightsquigarrow Y$ as 'the *asymptotic* distribution of $\{X_n\}$ is the distribution of Y'.

Central Limit Theorem. If each X_i is independent and has the same distribution with finite mean μ and finite variance σ^2, then

$$n^{1/2}(\bar{X}_n - \mu)/\sigma \rightsquigarrow N(0, 1). \quad (72)$$

The Weak Law of Large Numbers probabilistically says that $(\bar{X}_n - \mu)$ is small, but the Central Limit Theorem gives a much stronger statement since it implies that $n^{1/2}(X_n - \mu)$ is not large in a probabilistic sense.

Berry–Essen Theorem. Assume and define:

(a) $X_1, \ldots, X_n$ are independent, and $EX_i = 0$.

(b) For each i write $\sigma_{X_i}^2 = \sigma_i^2$.

(c) $s_n^2 = \sum_{i=1}^{n} \sigma_i^2 > 0$.

(d) For each i, $\gamma_i = E|X_i|^\Delta < \infty$, for some $2 < \Delta \leqslant 3$.

(e) $\Gamma_n^\Delta = \sum_{i=1}^{n} \gamma_i$. (73)

Then there exists constants $C_\Delta (C_3 \leqslant 7.5)$ such that

$$\max_{-\infty<x<\infty} \left| P[n\bar{X}_n/s_n < x] - \int_{-\infty}^{x} \frac{1}{(2\pi)^{1/2}} e^{-t^2/2}\, dt \right| \leqslant C_\Delta(\Gamma_n/s_n)^\Delta.$$

When the random variables are identically distributed, $C_\Delta(\Gamma_n/s_n)^\Delta$ is proportional to $n^{[(2-\Delta)/2]}$ which might be small enough to give useful bounds.

Some tools useful in proving limit theorems are: (31) and (35).

Consider a sequence of distribution functions $\{F_i\}$ and the corresponding sequence of characteristic functions $\{\phi_i\}$. Assume there exists a function $\phi(t)$ which is continuous at 0 and

$$\phi(t) = \lim_{i\to\infty} \phi_i(t) \text{ for every } t.$$

Then,

(a) $\phi(t)$ is a characteristic function, and if $F(x)$ is the associated distribution function,

(b) $F(x) = \lim_{i\to\infty} F_i(x)$ at every x which is a continuity point of F. (74)

$(X_{n1}, X_{n2}) \rightsquigarrow (Y_1, Y_2)$ if and only if

$$t_1 X_{n1} + t_2 X_{n2} \rightsquigarrow t_1 Y_1 + t_2 Y_2 \quad (75)$$

for each pair of real numbers (t_1, t_2).

Slutsky's Theorem. If for each n, the random variables X_n, Y_n, Z_n are defined on the same sample space, and

(a) $X_n \rightsquigarrow X$,

(b) $Y_n \rightsquigarrow a$,

(c) $Z_n \rightsquigarrow b$; then $X_n Y_n + Z_n \rightsquigarrow aX + b$. (76)

Propagation of Error. Assume $[n^{1/2}(X_n-\mu_x), n^{1/2}(Y_n-\mu_y)]$ has a bivariate normal limiting distribution with mean vector (0, 0) and variance–covariance matrix

$$\begin{pmatrix}\sigma_{XX} & \sigma_{XY}\\ \sigma_{XY} & \sigma_{YY}\end{pmatrix},$$

and $H(x, y)$ has continuous first derivatives,

$$\left[H_x(x,y)=\frac{\partial H(x,y)}{\partial x},\ H_y(x,y)=\frac{\partial H(x,y)}{\partial y}\right]$$

in the neighbourhood of (μ_X, μ_Y); then

$$n^{1/2}[H(X_n, Y_n)-H(\mu_X,\mu_Y)] \rightsquigarrow N[0, H_x^2(\mu_X,\mu_Y)\sigma_X^2 + 2H_x(\mu_X,\mu_Y)H_y(\mu_X,\mu_Y)\sigma_{XY}+H_y^2(\mu_X,\mu_Y)\sigma_Y^2], \quad (77)$$

provided this variance is >0.

Although the limiting distribution of $n^{1/2}[H(X_n, Y_n)-H(\mu_X,\mu_Y)]$ exists and has finite moments, the moments of $H(X_n, Y_n)$ may not exist; for example, let $H(x)=1/x$ and X_n be the average of n independent $P(\lambda)$ variables. Then $H(EX_n)=1/\lambda$, and $EH(X_n)=\infty$ for every n.

Example: if

$$X_n \sim B(n,p) \quad \text{then} \quad n^{1/2}(X_n/n-p) \rightsquigarrow N[0, p(1-p)];$$

from (72) where $X_n=\Sigma_{i=1}^n Y_i$, with the Y_i independent Bernoulli (p) random variables. Now consider $H(x)=\arcsin(x)^{1/2}$ so that $H_x(x)=1/\{2[x(1-x)]^{1/2}\}$, and thus,

$$n^{1/2}[\arcsin(X_n/n)^{1/2}-\arcsin(p)] \rightsquigarrow N(0, 1/4). \quad (78)$$

The transformation is *variance stabilizing*.

There are many other classes of limit theorems, such as,

Law of the Iterated Logarithm: Assume

(a) $X_1, \ldots, X_n, \ldots$ are mutually independent with the same distribution.

(b) $EX_1=0$.

(c) $EX_1^2=1$. (79)

Then

$$P\left\{\overline{\lim_{n\to\infty}} \frac{\sum_{i=1}^n X_i}{[n\ln(\ln n)]^{1/2}}=(2)^{1/2}\right\}=1.$$

DISTRIBUTIONS RELATED TO THE NORMAL

Assume $X, X_1, X_2, \ldots, X_i, \ldots$ are independent $N(0, 1)$; then the following definitions, examples and theorems apply:

$$\bar{X}_n=\sum_1^n X_i/n \quad \text{and} \quad S_n^2=\sum_1^n (X_i-\bar{X}_n)^2/(n-1)$$

are independent, and

$$\bar{X}_n \sim N(0, 1/n), \quad S_n^2 \sim (n-1)^{-1}\chi^2(n-1). \quad (80)$$

A more general result is: $\bar{X}_n$ and $D_n(X_1, \ldots, X_n)$ are independent provided D_n is translation invariant; that is, $D_n(X_1, \ldots, X_n)=D_n(X_1+a, \ldots, X_n+a)$ for every a.

$$\sum_{i=1}^r X_i^2 \sim \chi^2(r) \text{ with } r \text{ a positive integer.} \quad (81)$$

If $\chi^2(r)$ and $\chi(s)^2$ are independent, then

$$\chi^2(r)+\chi^2(s) \sim \chi^2(r+s). \quad (82)$$

If X and $\chi^2(r)$ are independent, then

$$t=X/[\chi^2(r)/r]^{1/2} \quad (83)$$

has a t-distribution with r degrees of freedom, $t(r)$.

Student's Theorem: If $Y_1, \ldots, Y_n$ are independent $N(\mu, \sigma^2)$, then

$$\frac{n^{1/2}(\bar{Y}_n-\mu)^{1/2}}{\left[\frac{\sum(Y_i-\bar{Y}_n)^2}{n-1}\right]} \sim t(n-1). \quad (84)$$

$$\frac{\chi^2(n)-n}{(2n)^{1/2}} \rightsquigarrow N(0, 1). \quad (85)$$

$$t(n) \rightsquigarrow N(0, 1). \quad (86)$$

If $\chi^2(r)$ and $\chi^2(s)$ are independent, then

(a) $\beta=\dfrac{\chi^2(r)}{\chi^2(r)+\chi^2(s)}$ has a $\beta(r, s)$ distribution, and

(b) $F=\dfrac{[\chi^2(r)/r]}{[\chi^2(s)/s]}$ has an F-distribution with r and s degrees of freedom, $F(r, s)$. (87)

$$t^2(n) \sim F(1, n). \quad (88)$$

$$[F(r,s)]^{-1} \sim F(s, r). \quad (89)$$

$$rF(r,s) \underset{s\to\infty}{\rightsquigarrow} \chi^2(r). \quad (90)$$

Under the conditions of (84), if $n=n_1+n_2$, then

$$S_1^2/S_2^2 \sim F(n_1-1, n_2-1),$$

where

$$S_1^2=\sum_1^{n_1}\left[Y_i-\left(\sum_1^{n_1} Y_i/n_1\right)\right]^2\Big/(n_1-1),$$

and

$$S_2^2=\sum_{n_1+1}^{n}\left[Y_i-\left(\sum_{n_1+1}^{n} Y_i/n_2\right)\right]^2\Big/(n_2-1). \quad (91)$$

ORDER STATISTICS

In this section assume $X, X_1, \ldots, X_n$ are independent real-valued random variables; each X has density f and distribution function F. Further, let $\{X_i\}$, when arranged in order from smallest to largest, be denoted by $X_{(1)}, \ldots, X_{(n)}$.

For $1 \leqslant r \leqslant n$, the density of $X(r)$ is

$$f_{X_{(r)}}(x)=\frac{n!}{(r-1)!(n-r)!}F^{r-1}(x) \times [1-F(x)]^{n-r}f(x). \quad (92)$$

$$F_{X_{(n)}}(x)=F^n(x). \quad (93)$$

$$F_{X_{(1)}}(x)=1-[1-F(x)]^n. \quad (94)$$

If $1 \leqslant r < s \leqslant n$, then

$$f_{X_{(r)},X_{(s)}}(x,y)=\frac{n!}{(r-1)!(r-s-1)!(n-s)!}F^{r-1}(x) \times [F(y)-F(x)]^{s-r-1}[1-F(y)]^{n-s}f(x)f(y),$$

$$-\infty < x < y < \infty. \quad (95)$$

$$f_{X_{(1)}, X_{(2)}, \ldots, X_{(n)}}(y_1, y_2, \ldots, y_n) = n! \prod_1^n f(y_i),$$

$$-\infty < y_1 < y_2 \cdots < y_n < \infty. \quad (96)$$

Theorem: If

(a) f is continuous where $f = F'$.

(b) For specified α and β satisfying $0 < \alpha < \beta < 1$, define x_α and x_β as the unique solutions of $F(x) = \alpha$ and $F(x) = \beta$, respectively.

(c) $0 < f(x_\alpha) < \infty$ and $0 < f(x_\beta) < \infty$.

(d) $[m]$ is the largest integer not exceeding m.

Then,

$$n^{1/2}(X_{[\alpha n]} - x_\alpha, X_{[\beta n]} - x_\beta)$$

$$\rightsquigarrow N\left\{\begin{pmatrix}0\\0\end{pmatrix}, \begin{bmatrix} \dfrac{\alpha(1-\alpha)}{f^2(x_\alpha)} & \dfrac{\alpha(1-\beta)}{f(x_\alpha)f(x_\beta)} \\ \dfrac{\alpha(1-\beta)}{f(x_\alpha)f(x_\beta)} & \dfrac{\beta(1-\beta)}{f^2(x_\beta)} \end{bmatrix}\right\}. \quad (97)$$

Not all limit theorems involve sums of random variables (100). Theorem (97) appears to be an example, but consider the following:

$$P[X_{(k)} < x] = P\left\{\sum_1^n B_i[F(x)] \geqslant k\right\}, \quad (98)$$

where $B_1, \ldots, B_n$ are independent, Bernoulli $[F(x)]$ and $k = 1, 2, \ldots, n$.

Renyi Representation. If f is exponential [Table 2(1)], then

$$X_{(i)} = \sum_{j=1}^{i} Y_j/(n - j + 1), \quad (99)$$

where the $\{Y_j\}$ satisfy the same conditions as the $\{X_i\}$.

Extreme Value Theorem. If $a_n X_{(n)} + b_n a \rightsquigarrow Z$, then Z is one of three types, the principal ones being the Extreme Value [Table 2(11)] and Weibull [Table 2(12)]. In particular, if F is normal, then there exist sequences of constants $\{A_n\}$ and $\{B_n\}$ such that

$$A_n X_{(n)} + B_{(n)} \rightsquigarrow \text{extreme value [Table 2(11)]}. \quad (100)$$

FAILURE RATE (HAZARD RATE, FORCE OF MORTALITY, INTENSITY RATE)

Starting with Karl Pearson, families of distributions have been introduced to unify theory or applications. The exponential family (107) plays a central role in theoretical statistics, and the characterization of failure rates is central to the description of lifetimes of organizations, animals, equipment, etc.

Assume F satisfies:

(a) $F(0) = 0$; (b) $f(x) = F'(x)$ exists for all $x \geqslant 0$.

Then define the *failure rate*, $r(t)$, by

$$r(t) = \frac{f(t)}{1 - F(t)} \text{ for all } t \text{ such that } 1 - F(t) > 0. \quad (101)$$

The following classes of distributions are non-empty since the exponential [Table 2(1)] belongs to each of them. The names of the classes are suggestive of their applied interest.

IFR (DFR) – Increasing (Decreasing) Failure Rate:

$r(t)$ increases (decreases) for $t \geqslant 0$. (102)

IFRA(DFRA) – Increasing(Decreasing)FailureRateAverage:

$$\frac{1}{t}\int_0^t r(u)\,du \text{ increases (decreases) for all } t > 0. \quad (103)$$

NBU (NWU) – New Better (Worse) than Used:

$$[1 - F(x + y)] \leqslant (\geqslant) [1 - F(x)][1 - F(y)]$$

for all $x \geqslant 0$, $y \geqslant 0$. (104)

NBUE(NWUE) – New Better(Worse) than Used Expectation:

(a) $\mu = \int_0^\infty x f(x)\,dx = \int_0^\infty [1 - F(x)]\,dx < \infty\ (\leqslant \infty)$,

(b) $\int_t^\infty [1 - F(x)]\,dx \leqslant (\geqslant) \mu[1 - F(t)]$ for $t \geqslant 0$. (105)

The classes obey the following inclusion relations:

$$\text{IFR} \subset \text{IFRA} \subset \text{NBU} \subset \text{NBUE},$$

and

$$\text{DFR} \subset \text{DFRA} \subset \text{NWUC} \subset \text{NWUE}. \quad (106)$$

A Weibull random variable [Table 2(12)] is IFR if $c \geqslant 1$, and is DFR if $c \leqslant 1$. There are many analytic results associated with these classes, for example, if X and Y are independent and NBUE, then $Z \sim X + Y$ is NBUE; however, the analogous implication fails for NWU.

Exponential Family. (107)

Many of the examples of densities (or probability functions) are of the form:

$$\exp[a(x)b(\theta) + c(x) + d(\theta)], \quad (108)$$

where x is a possible value of the random variable, and θ is a parameter.

Statistical Sufficiency. If $X_1, \ldots, X_n$ are independent each with the same density of form (108), and $T = \Sigma\, a(X_i)$, then

$$f_{X_1, \ldots, X_n | T}(x_1, \ldots, x_n | T, \theta) \quad (109)$$

does not depend on θ; that is, for purposes of making inferences about θ, all of the information in the sample, $\{X_i\}$, is in the sufficient statistic, $\Sigma\, a(X_i)$.

Theorem: If X has density (108), $b(\cdot)$ is one to one, $b(\theta)$ is an interior point of $\{b(\theta) : d(\theta) \text{ is finite}\}$ and the derivatives denoted by ′ and ″ below exist. Then

(a) $Ea(X) = -d'(\theta)/b'(\theta)$.

(b) The Fisher information, I_θ, for a family of densities, $f(\cdot, \theta)$, is defined by

$$I_\theta = E\left[\frac{\partial \ln f(X_1, \theta)}{\partial \theta}\right]^2.$$

When X has a density in the form of (108),

$$I_\theta = -d''(\theta) + d'(\theta)[b''(\theta)/b'(\theta)].$$

When, as often happens, $b(\theta) = \theta$, the result becomes

$$I_\theta = -d''(\theta) = V[a(X)]. \quad (110)$$

Infinitely Divisible and Stable Random Variables. (111)

A random variable, X, is *infinitely divisible* if and only if for every positive integer, n, there exists independent and identically distributed random variables, $\{X_{ni}\}$, such that $X \sim X_{n1} + X_{n2} + \cdots + X_{nn}$. Normal, Poisson, Cauchy and exponential random variables are infinitely divisible. A random variable, X, is *stable* if and only if for each choice of $a_1 \geqslant 0$ and $a_2 \geqslant 0$, there exists $a > 0$ and b such that $aX + b \sim a_1 X_1 + a_2 X_2$, where X_1 and X_2 are independent and $X \sim X_1 \sim X_2$. Stable random variables are unimodal, absolutely continuous and infinitely divisible. Normal random variables are the only stable random variables with finite variance; Cauchy random variables are stable.

The function, $\phi(t)$, is the characteristic function of an infinitely divisible random variable if and only if it has the form

$$\log\phi(t) = itA - \frac{\sigma^2}{2}t^2 + \int_{-\infty}^{0-}\left(e^{itu} - 1 - \frac{itu}{1+u^2}\right)dM(u)$$

$$+ \int_{0+}^{\infty}\left(e^{itu} - 1 - \frac{itu}{1+u^2}\right)dN(u), \qquad (112)$$

where $M(u)$, $N(u)$ and σ^2 satisfy:

(a) $M(u)$ and $N(u)$ are non-decreasing on $(-\infty, 0)$ and $(0, \infty)$.

(b) $M(-\infty) = N(\infty) = 0$.

(c) $\int_{-\epsilon}^{0} u^2\,dM(u)$ and $\int_{0}^{\epsilon} u^2\,dN(u)$ are finite for every $\epsilon > 0$.

(d) $\sigma^2 \geqslant 0$.

The representation is unique. [Define $\log\phi(t)$ so that $\log\phi(0) = 0$.]

For stable random variables (112) must have either

(a) $\sigma^2 > 0$, $M(u) \equiv 0$, and $N(u) \equiv 0$, or

(b) $\sigma^2 = 0$, $M(u) = C_1|u|^{-\alpha}$ for $u < 0$,

$N(u) = -C_2 u^{-\alpha}$ for $u > 0$ where $0 < \alpha < 2$, $C_1 \geqslant 0$,

$C_2 \geqslant 0$ and $C_1 + C_2 > 0$. (113)

Conversely, functions satisfying these conditions are characteristic functions of stable random variables.

MIXTURES AND EXCHANGEABILITY

Assume the distribution of X depends on the random parameter θ. When $\theta = \theta_0$, let the conditional density of X be $f(x\,|\,\theta_0)$. Now assume θ is a random variable with density $f(\theta)$, and the marginal density of X is

$$f_X(x) = \int f(x\,|\,\theta)\,dF(\theta). \qquad (114)$$

Since $f_X(x)$ is a weighted combination of the conditional densities of X, it is called a *mixture*.

Example: Assume X is Poisson (λ) and $\lambda \sim$ exponential, then

$$f_X(x) = \int_0^{\infty} \frac{e^{-\lambda}\lambda^x}{x!} e^{-\lambda} = 2^{-x}, \quad x = 0, 1, \ldots. \qquad (115)$$

An interpretation of this example is that the λ associated with an individual reflects his accident-proneness, while X is the number of accidents.

Example: Let I be income and θ be sex. Then it is plausible that I given θ has a log-normal distribution with parameters dependent on θ. The marginal distribution of income would be of interest. The $P(\theta = \text{female})$ would have a simple sampling interpretation. The components of these examples appear in Bayesian models. (116)

A condition, not as restrictive as independence and identical distribution of random variables, is

$$f_{X_1,\ldots,X_n}(x_1, \ldots, x_n) \equiv f_{X_1,\ldots,X_n}[x_{\pi(1)}, \ldots, x_{\pi(n)}], \qquad (117)$$

where the identity holds for all $n \geqslant 1$ and all $n!$ permutations $[\pi(1), \ldots, \pi(n)]$ of $(1, \ldots, n)$. Random variables for which condition (117) holds are called *exchangeable random variables*. Note (117) is equivalent to the following generalization of (114):

$$f_{X_1,\ldots,X_n}(x_1, \ldots, x_n) = \int \prod_{i=1}^{n} f(x_i|\theta)\,dF(\theta). \qquad (118)$$

Now consider sequences of random variables, $\{X_i\}$, where in contrast to exchangeability the labels on the random variables, $\{i\}$, are important. Much of applied statistics is concerned with

$$X_a \sim \sum_{m=1}^{M} t_{am}\beta_m + \epsilon_a, \quad a = 1, \ldots, N, \qquad (119)$$

where the $\{\epsilon_a\}$ are independent and identically distributed. This is the regression model with M independent variables, $\{t_{am}\}$, and parameters $\{\beta_m\}$. Further complications involve structure on the errors.

(Strictly) Stationary: For every choice of k distinct integers $\{a_i\}$ and every integer t: (120)

$$(X_{a_1}, X_{a_2}, \ldots, X_{a_k}) \sim (X_{a_1+t}, X_{a_2+t}, \ldots, X_{a_k+t}) \qquad (121)$$

This implies, for every a, $X_a \sim X_0$, so the random variables are identically distributed but not necessarily independent.

Weakly Stationary:

(a) $EX_a = \mu$, and

(b) EX_a^2 is finite

(c) $\sigma_{a,b} = C(|a - b|)$. (122)

where, specifically, the function C will be of the form

$$C(k) = \sigma^2 \int_{-\pi}^{\pi} \cos k\omega\,dG(\omega), \quad k = 1, 2, \ldots. \qquad (123)$$

In (123) G is a distribution function with support in $(-\pi, \pi)$, and $G(\omega) + G(-\omega) = 1$ at continuity points of G. If a sequence is weakly stationary, then there is a random variable X such that

$$\lim_{n\to\infty} P(|\bar{X}_n - X| > \epsilon) = 0,$$

where $\epsilon > 0$ and $\bar{X}_n = (X_1 + \cdots + X_n)/n$.

BROWNIAN MOTION OR WIENER PROCESSES

Now consider a random variable for each $t \in [0, \infty)$, that is, an uncountably infinite number of random variables. The notation will be $X(t, \omega)$ or $X(t)$. In the above discussion of n random variables, each ω gives an n-dimensional vector $[X_1(\omega), \ldots, X_n(\omega)]$. In the current situation, each ω gives a curve $X(t, \omega)$, $0 \leqslant t$.

We will not consider continuous time stochastic processes, $X(t)$ for $0 \leqslant t$, in general, but we will report results for *Brownian motion* or *Wiener processes*.

Definition of (standard) Brownian motion:

(a) $X(0)=0$.

(b) The sample paths, $X(s, \omega)$ for $s \in [0, \infty)$, are continuous except for a set $A \in \Omega$ with $P(A)=0$.

(c) If $0 \leqslant t_1 < t_2 < \cdots < t_k$, then the random variables $X(t_i)-X(t_{i-1})$ are independent, and $X(t_i)-X(t_{i-1}) \sim N(0, t_i - t_{i-1})$ for $i=2,\ldots,k$. (124)

Some properties of Brownian motion are:

$$\text{If } 0 \leqslant s < t, \text{ then } [X(s), X(t)] \sim N\left[\begin{pmatrix}0\\0\end{pmatrix}, \begin{pmatrix}s & s\\ s & t\end{pmatrix}\right]. \quad (125)$$

The sample paths are differentiable on a set of Lebesgue measure 0 with probability one. (126)

If T replaces n and

$$X(T) \text{ replaces } \sum_{i=1}^{n} X_i, \text{ then (79) holds.} \quad (127)$$

For $a>0$ define T_a as the least t with $X(t) \geqslant a$. Then

$$P(T_a \leqslant t) = 2P[X(t) \geqslant a] = P[t^{1/2}|N(0,1)| \geqslant a]. \quad (128)$$

Assume $\mu < 0$ and define $W = \max_{0 \leqslant t}[X(t)+\mu t]$. Then,

$$P(W \geqslant w) = e^{2\mu w}, \quad w \geqslant 0. \quad (129)$$

Let T^* be the largest s such that $X(s)=0$ for $0 \leqslant s \leqslant t^*$. Then,

$$P(T^* \leqslant t_0) = (2/\pi)\arcsin(t_0/t^*)^{1/2} \text{ for } 0 \leqslant t_0 \leqslant t^*. \quad (130)$$

Assume $X_1, \ldots, X_n$ are independent, and each X_i has the same distribution, F. Define the empirical distribution, F_n, by

$$F_n(x) = (\text{number of } X_i \leqslant x)/n \text{ for } -\infty < x < \infty. \quad (131)$$

The Glivenko–Cantelli Lemma asserts that

$$P\left[\lim_{n\to\infty} \max_{-\infty<x<\infty} |F_n(x)-F(x)| = 0\right] = 1. \quad (132)$$

Further, if F is continuous, then for large values of n,

$$B_n(t) = n^{1/2}\{F_n[F^{-1}(t)] - t\} \text{ for } 0 \leqslant t \leqslant 1 \quad (133)$$

behaves asymptotically like a *Brownian bridge*,

$$B(t) = X(t) - tX(1), \quad 0 \leqslant t \leqslant 1, \quad (134)$$

where X is Brownian motion.

A consequence is

$$\lim_{n\to\infty} P\left[\max_{-\infty<x<\infty} (n)^{1/2}|F_n(x)-F(x)| \geqslant t\right] = 2\sum_{m=1}^{\infty}(-1)^{m+1}\exp[-2m^2t^2]. \quad (135)$$

The Glivenko–Cantelli Lemma (132) is a generalization of the strong law (68), and (133, 134) is a generalization of the central limit theorem (72).

Brownian motion also provides limit theorems for *random walks*. Let $X_1, \ldots, X_n, \ldots$ be independently and identically distributed random variables with mean μ and variance σ^2. Then

$$S_{tn} = \sum_{i=1}^{[tn]} X_i + (nt - [nt])X_{[nt]+1}, \quad n \geqslant 1, \quad 0 < t,$$

particularly when X is a lattice random variable, is called a *random walk*. Its large sample properties, n large, can be found by treating

$$\frac{S_{tn} - \mu tn}{(n\sigma^2)^{1/2}} \quad (136)$$

as a sequence of stochastic processes that behaves asymptotically as a Brownian motion, $X(t)$. Some properties of $X(t)$ that are of interest in this regard are:

$$\text{With probability 1, } X(t)=0 \text{ infinitely often.} \quad (137)$$

Assume T is a *stopping time*; that is, the event $T \leqslant t$ depends on the values of $X(s)$ only for $s \leqslant t$, and assume $ET < \infty$. Then

$$EX(T) = 0. \quad (138)$$

Notice this implies the stopping time in (128) does not have finite expectation.

The nonlimiting case yields Wald's equation,

$$ES_N = \mu EN, \quad (139)$$

where $\{N \leqslant n\}$ depends on $\{X_i\}$ for $i=1,\ldots,n$.

Assume $a<0<b$ and T is the least t such that $X(T) \leqslant a$ or $X(T) \geqslant b$. Then

$$P[X(T)=b] = \frac{|a|}{|a|+b} \quad \text{and} \quad ET = |a|b. \quad (140)$$

I. RICHARD SAVAGE

BIBLIOGRAPHY

Note. Some of the criteria used in selecting the references were clarity, availability and completeness. The Johnson and Kotz volumes are a storehouse of information about specific random variables, and Greenwood and Hartley gives extensive detail on available printed tables. The best entry to the current literature on random variables or other statistical-probabilistic topics is the *Current Index to Statistics* (published by the American Statistical Association and the Institute of Mathematical Statistics, 1984, volume 10, also available electronically as *MathScience* produced by the American Mathematics Society) which is a key-word, permuted-title index. Barlow and Proschan, David, Lukacs and Pollard are monographs on specialized topics. Comprehensive views of broad areas are given by Anderson, Chow and Teicher, Rao and Serfling. Ash gives a detailed mathematical setting for probability theory, and Lamperti quickly shows the power of the theory.

Anderson, T.W. 1984. *An Introduction to Multivariate Statistical Analysis*. 2nd edn, John Wiley, 1972.

Ash, R.B. 1972. *Real Analysis and Probability*. New York: Academic Press.

Barlow, R.E. and Proschan, F. 1975. *Statistical Theory of Reliability and Life Testing Probability Models*. New York: Holt, Rinehart and Winston.

Chow, Y.S. and Teicher, H. 1978. *Probability Theory: Independence Interchangeability, Martingales*. New York: Springer-Verlag.

David, H.A. 1981. *Order Statistics*. 2nd edn. New York: John Wiley.

Greenwood, J.A. and Hartley, H.O. 1962. *Guide to Tables in Mathematical Statistics*. Princeton: Princeton University Press.

Johnson, N.L. 1969. *Distributions in Statistics: Discrete Distributions*. Boston: Houghton Miffiin, chs 1–11.

Johnson, N.L. 1970a. *Continuous Distributions*, Vol.1. Boston: Houghton Mifflin, chs 12–24.

Johnson, N.L. 1970b. *Continuous Distributions*, Vol.2. Boston: Houghton Mifflin, chs 22–33.

Johnson, N.L. 1972. *Continuous Multivariate Distributions*. New York: John Wiley, chs 34–42.

Karlin, S. and Taylor, H.M. 1975. *A First Course in Stochastic Processes*. 2nd edn, New York: Academic Press.
Lamperti. J. 1966. *Probability; A Survey of Mathematical Theory*. New York: W.A. Benjamin.
Lukacs, E. 1970. *Characteristic Functions*. 2nd edn. New York: Hafner Publishing.
Pollard, D. 1984. *Convergence of Stochastic Processes*. New York: Springer-Verlag.
Rao, C. 1973. *Linear Statistical Inference and Its Applications*. 2nd edn, New York: John Wiley.
Serfling, R.J. 1980. *Approximation Theorems of Mathematical Statistics*. New York: John Wiley.

rank. All men are equal, but members of an organization are not. Organizations are associations of persons for the achievement of tasks that exceed the capacity of an individual. These tasks must, therefore, be subdivided and the subtasks assigned to certain individual organization members, the operatives.

SUPERVISION. Coordination of subtasks in an organization is (normally) not done through markets but is made a subtask in itself. A simple organization has but one coordinator, the boss, who supervises all operatives directly. Large organizations become possible if *supervision*, too, can be subdivided, supervised and coordinated. This cascading of supervision can, in principle, be carried to any length and no technical limits exist to the size of organizations. (Whether their effectiveness declines with size is another question, see below).

In small organizations the necessary subdivision and coordination can, in principle, be achieved also through mutual consultation and voluntary cooperation: partnerships and communes. Alternatively supervision may be rotated in order to restore equality, but at the expense of stripping the supervision of much of his/her power (as the example of Deans in European universities shows).

Organizations that rely on professional supervisors, or 'managers' for the discharging of the coordinator's job, are called *hierarchical* organizations. In their purest form, they are composed of operatives who do not supervise and supervisors who do no operative work. A ranking system is the outward manifestation of the supervisory structure that is the essential feature of hierarchical organizations, as will be shown now. The coordination of subtasks or of the division of labour in organizations thus relies on supervision as its key element: organizations coordinate through supervision. In practice, supervision can mean many things such as selection, induction, training, setting goals, assisting, monitoring, checking, correcting, evaluating, rewarding and firing.

The remarkable similarities between organizations in the face of the great differences in their tasks results, however, from the fact that formally and structurally supervision has the same properties in all hierarchical organizations.

Formally, supervision is a binary relationship which is acyclic. (This rules out 'mutual supervision' or any closed chain of supervision.) A single individual, the president, is distinguished by having no supervisor. All others report to one and only one organization member, their assigned supervisor. This principle of 'unity of command' is occasionally replaced by multiple supervision in the form of a functional division of supervision (as between administrative and research director) or of temporary assignment to task forces with special supervisors as in 'matrix management'.

The supervisory relationships may be pieced together in a 'directed graph' known as an *organizational chart*. On this chart every organization member is connected to the president through a unique *line of command*, and to every other organization member by official channels of communication coming together in some manager who directly or indirectly supervises both.

The organizational chart shows that there are at least three types of positions in any complex (i.e. not simple) organization: president (no supervisor), operatives (no subordinates) and intermediate supervisors. Further classifications may exist according to such functions as support and advisory (staff), but these, too, must be fitted into the supervisory structure that holds the organization together.

CONTROL. An organization member j is said to be *controlled* by another organization member i if i supervises j directly or indirectly through a chain of intermediate supervisors. Every supervisor controls a subset of the organization, a department, division, etc.

The president, in control of the entire organization, is usually made responsible for achieving the organization's task to an outside board of trustees, although he/she is exempt from day-to-day supervision.

The relationship $\rightarrow$, control, is by construction *transitive* (if supervisory chains exist from i to j and from j to k then this defines a supervisory chain from i to k). Control is *irreflexive*: not $i \rightarrow i$ because the relationship of supervision is irreflexive. Control is also *asymmetric*: if $i \rightarrow j$ then not $j \rightarrow i$, because the relationship of supervision is acyclic.

Any relationship with these properties defines a *strict partial ordering* in the set of organization members, the organization. It is partial because in any complex organization there exist two members such that neither controls the other. For purposes of supervision alone, and also for setting salary schedules that do not conflict with supervision and control relationships, this partial ordering would suffice. But interpersonal relationships in large organizations become more transparent when this partial ordering is extended to a complete ordering. In a complete ordering the following is true for any two organization members, i, j: i precedes j, j precedes i, or i and j are equivalent.

RANK. A complete ordering is another word for ranking. Such a ranking is *ordinal* and makes no statement about the 'degree' to which i precedes j.

If the complete ordering is to be made the basis of the salary or compensations structure, then the ranking system must be converted to a *cardinal* one. This is usually achieved by mapping the equivalence classes under the ordinal ranking onto the positive integers. (Example: executive ranks I–V, and GS ranks 1–18 in the Federal government.)

Even when ranks are not labelled numerically, but as titles arranged in well-defined sequences (secretary, under secretary, deputy under secretary, assistant secretary, deputy assistant secretary ...) this is equivalent to a numerical rank system.

ASSIGNMENT OF RANK. A number system $1, \ldots, r, \ldots, R$ generates unique ranks for all positions on the longest line of command (supervisory chain from the president to operatives). If all lines are equally long, the organization is 'balanced'. In nonbalanced organizations there is some choice in assigning ranks. The choice is constrained by the following *assignment principle*: a supervisor must have a strictly greater rank than any subordinate. Rank jumps may occur. Two simple methods of rank assignment are the following: in *counting up* all operatives are assigned rank 1 and each supervisor ranks one above the highest rank of any subordinate. Rank is then measured by the distance from the president. In *counting down*, each person is assigned a rank just one below his/her supervisor, possibly resulting in a rank for operatives above one. Counting up may be shown to result in the highest and counting down in the lowest ranks consistent with the assignment principle. While organization members may pressure for counting down, organizational efficiency – achieving a given task at minimum cost – is best served by counting up.

In some organizations a person's *permanent rank* ('rank in the job') assigned to the position on the organizational chart, is distinguished from his/her *temporary rank* ('rank in the man') which reflects a person's station in a career (see below) although ideally and normally the two ranks coincide.

Although a rank system is ultimately founded on supervision, ranks above the minimum may be assigned also to operatives (or staff or support persons) even in a system of counting up, to fit them into the salary structure.

ATTRIBUTES OF RANK. The main attributes of rank are: *power*, *prestige*, and *money income*.

Power is directly exercised over the organization members in the control set of the rank holder, the set of persons reached through a chain of supervision or command. Supervisory power in a hierarchical organization is, however, restricted by the formalities first spelled out by Max Weber in his definition and analysis of bureaucracy (1925).

For rank to be economically meaningful, compensation must increase with rank including: salary, bonus, stock options and the tax-exempt income generated by expense accounts, insurance, use of cars, paid leisure and recreation and other perquisites of rank. Utility is often a linear function of rank. Diminishing marginal utility and the progressive income tax imply that income should then be a convex function of rank. The simplest scheme is one where income grows at a constant rate with rank. In practice, salary schedules tend to combine an exponential with a linear function of rank. The growth factor differs widely between organizations and countries: from 5 per cent in the Chinese civil service to approximately 50 per cent in some American corporations. (Presidential compensation of $2 million compared to an operative's salary of $20,000 in the presence of twelve intervening ranks implies an average salary growth rate of 47 per cent.)

The question of the economic determinants of salary schemes is answered differently in the case of organizations that have no interaction with labour markets except at the entry level of rank one (church, military) and those that operate in competitive labour markets by hiring and firing personnel at all levels (see below).

Prestige, not properly an economic variable, is a residual category that reflects all attributes of rank other than power and money income. The prestige aspect may be expressed by such marks of rank as titles and the trappings of the office (size, location, furnishings, and number of windows).

SPAN OF CONTROL. The workload of a supervisor is best described by the number of subordinates under his/her immediate supervision: the *span of control*. This span may vary between departments and ranks. It is larger in supervising operatives than in supervising other managers. The literature on business organization recommends a lighter span for the president. The smaller the span, the more effective is supervision, *ceteris paribus*. The longer the chains of command, the less effective is top managements' control over operatives. But organizations with a given task size and given labour force (number of operatives) face a tradeoff between average span of control and number of ranks (Simon, 1948). The optimal span of control and hence the optimal number of ranks is thus the result of an economic choice rather than of purely technical considerations (such as complexity of the job), and depends also on relative wages. Given the span of control s and the number Q of operatives required to handle the organization's task, the number of managers M to perform the required supervision (including that of their own) is determined as $M=Q-1/S-1$. Efficient organizational design can then aim at keeping the ranks of management as low as possible. This may be constrained by the presence of rigid departmental boundaries which cannot be crossed by supervisory relationships.

Efficient organizational design is further complicated by the fact that ranks express not only a supervisory structure but also serve as an instrument of motivation when rank is considered a stage in a member's career. An analysis of optimal organizational structures, taking account of both the structural and the motivational side of ranks is part of ongoing research.

CAREERS. Ranks in an organization are not assigned once and for all. Beginners start in rank one and attain higher ranks in this or other organizations only through a process of screening, training, rotation, monitoring, and selection, designed to protect the organization from gross mismanagement and to discover the persons most productive in the higher ranks. Only when no significant differences of qualification persist after initial selection can promotions be reduced to a matter of seniority, which has been called the only truly objective method for advancement (Chapman, 1970).

Normal career expectations exist in many organizations. This means that promotion to the top rank in a given rank class is practically a matter of certainty, although the timing is not. Transition from one class to the next (lower to middle management, middle management to top management), is, however, rare and based on rigorous selection.

EXPECTED UTILITY OF A CAREER. Attainment of high rank is thus always beset by uncertainties, but probabilities of reaching the various levels may be calculated, given the number of ranking positions and the timing of promotions on the average, or conditional on the present age distribution of incumbents. A career is then a lottery in which the end positions may be considered the prizes. The economic value of a prospective career in an organization is then the expected utility of this lottery. Competition for personnel at the entry point to organizations must then equalize the expected utility of careers for qualified personnel in all organizations. This is confirmed by the fact that the calculated utility of careers in various federal agencies, the military, and universities in the USA all lie close together, and apart from the expected utility of government careers for candidates without college degrees (Beckmann, 1978, p. 109).

The economic value of a rank, that is, of a continuing career when a certain rank has been reached is then the expected utility of attaining various end positions conditional on the present rank. The incentive of a promotion depends both on the utility difference between the ranks and the probability of this promotion. This incentive is maximal for an intermediate value of the promotion probability.

When ranks are standardized between comparable organizations, for example, universities in the same prestige class, then the expected utility must be equal among organizations at all rank levels for which mobility exists. In the absence of prestige differences salary becomes a proxy variable or sufficient statistic for equivalent rank and this comparability carries over to markets for managers moving between organizations with different rank structures. Prestige differences between organizations imply now that the equivalent rank carries a lower salary in a more prestigious organization (as exemplified by the Ivy League universities).

Salary levels are determined by supply and demand at all levels. But in the long run both are dependent on the frequency distribution of ability. The unravelling of this complicated relationship constitutes another problem area of current research.

ALTERNATIVES TO HIERARCHY. Are there alternatives to hierarchical organization? Some organizations perform tasks that in principle could also be carried out by individuals on their own (artists, artisans, teachers, lawyers, scholars, inventors), but in fact organizations compete with individuals in almost every field or have even replaced them completely. Why and when are organizations superior to individual effort? Clearly when there are *increasing returns* to scale which can be reaped by organizations but not as well by individuals even with access to specialized capital goods through a rental market. Organizations are the best-known method of capturing returns to scale.

A more subtle and difficult question is whether and when subordination can be avoided by sharing the monitoring and coordinating work among the organizations members in a more equitable way. Partnerships exist and communes exemplify alternatives, but only to simple organizations. Their main attractions are freedom from bosses, and a more even distribution of rewards. But mutual supervision and the expected conformity to a high code of ethics may turn out to be even more oppressive. According to Samuel Johnson

> Subordination tends greatly to the happiness of men.... Were we all upon an equality, none of us would be happy, any more than single animals who enjoyed mere animal pleasure (Boswell, *London Journal*, 20 July 1763).

Modern democratic society, professing the principle of equality, considers rank to be a necessary evil, a means without substitute for running the complex organizations that play such an important part in modern life.

M.J. BECKMANN

See also HIERARCHY.

BIBLIOGRAPHY

Alchian, A.A. and Demsetz, H. 1972. Production, information costs, and economic organization. *American Economic Review* 62, 777–95.

Beckmann, M.J. 1978. Rank in organizations. In *Lecture Notes in Economics and Mathematical Systems* No. 161, Berlin and New York: Springer-Verlag.

Beckmann, M.J. 1983. *Tinbergen Lectures on Organization Theory.* Berlin and New York: Springer-Verlag.

Calvo, G. and Wellisz, S. 1978. Supervision, loss of control and the optimum size of the firm. *Journal of Political Economy* 86(5), 943–52.

Chapman, B. 1970. *The Profession of Government*. 4th edn, London: Unwin University Books.

Crémer, J. 1980. A partial theory of the optimal organization of bureaucracy. *Bell Journal of Economics* 11(2), 683–93.

Hess, J.D. 1983. *The Economics of Organization*. Amsterdam: North-Holland.

March, J. and Simon, H.A. 1958. *Organizations*. New York: Wiley.

Marschak, J. 1975. Economics of organizational systems. In *Man and Computer*, ed. T. Marvis, Amsterdam: North-Holland.

Mirrlees, J. 1976. The optimal structure of incentives and authority within an organization. *Bell Journal of Economics* 7, 105–31.

Radner, R. 1986. Decentralization and incentives. In *Information, Incentives, and Economic Mechanisms: Essays in Honor of Leonid Hurwicz*, ed. T. Groves, R. Radner, and S. Reiter, Minneapolis: University of Minnesota Press.

Rosen, S. 1982. Authority, control and the distribution of earnings. *Bell Journal of Economics* 13(2), 311–23.

Simon, H. 1948. *Administrative Behavior*. New York: Macmillan.

Simon, H. 1951. A formal theory of the employment relationship. *Econometrica* 19, 293–305.

Spence, A.M. 1975. Incentives, risk, and information: notes towards a theory of hierarchy. *Bell Journal of Economics* 6(2), Autumn, 552–79.

Tuck, R.H. 1954. *An Essay on the Economic Theory of Rank*. Oxford: Basil Blackwell.

Weber, M. 1925. *The Theory of Social and Economic Organization.* Trans. A.M. Henderson and T. Parsons, ed. T. Parsons, New York: Oxford University Press, 1947.

Williamson, O.E. 1975. *Markets and Hierarchies: Analysis and Antitrust Implications*. New York: Free Press.

Williamson, O.E. 1985. *The Economic Institutions of Capitalism*. New York: Free Press.

rankings. *See* ORDERINGS.

rank-order methods. *See* NON-PARAMETRIC METHODS.

rate of exploitation. According to Karl Marx, the proletariat, i.e. wage labourers, is exploited by the capitalists: behind the apparent freedom and equality of the partners in the wage contract, Marx sees a power inequality which results in the workers being exploited by the capitalists in the same sense in which the serfs were exploited by their feudal landlords, or slaves by their masters. The capitalists are able to compel the workers to produce a surplus product, which they appropriate as profits, not by virtue of any productive contribution of theirs, but simply owing to their superior bargaining position vis-à-vis the workers, deriving from their collective monopoly of the means of production. Much the same (although without using the term 'exploitation') had already been said by Adam Smith, who also anticipated Marx on the importance of the repressive state apparatus's support for the institution of private property.

This general perspective explains Marx's occasional use of the term 'rate of exploitation' as synonymous with 'rate of surplus value', the latter being the more frequently used term, whose meaning will now be clarified. The labour value of, or labour embodied in, a commodity is defined by Marx as the sum of the direct and indirect labour necessary to its production, i.e. of the live labour expended in its direct process of production plus the labour embodied in the means of production used up (according to the socially necessary conditions of production) in that same process. If the socially necessary live labour performed in the whole economy is L, and the labour embodied in the means of production used up to produce the total social product is C, then the labour value of the total social product is $L+C$, and of the net social product is again L (because the net social product is defined as the total social product minus that part of it which replaces the means of production used up, a part whose labour value is clearly C). If now V is the labour embodied in the part of the net social product going to the workers, then $S \equiv L-V$, the surplus labour, or surplus value, is the labour embodied in the surplus product. Under constant returns to scale, only V, instead of L, would be necessary to produce a net product equal to the workers' share only; hence Marx calls V the 'necessary' or 'paid' labour, and S the surplus or 'unpaid' labour, and divides in the same proportions the average working day in a 'paid' and an 'unpaid' part. The ratio S/V is what he calls 'rate of surplus value' or 'rate of exploitation'.

Given the techniques in use, S/V depends on the average wage basket, and its changes reflect changes in the balance of power between classes. Its importance for Marx lies in its being one of the two proximate determinants of the rate of profits, the other one being the average 'organic composition of capital', i.e. the ratio of what Marx called 'constant capital' (the labour value of the capital goods employed in the production process) to what Marx called 'variable capital' (the labour value of the wage goods, which for Marx are part of capital because he considered wages to be advanced, rather than paid at the end of the production period as is usually assumed nowadays), in other words the ratio (assuming for simplicity that all the capital goods utilized in the economy are circulating capital) C/V. The rate of exploitation and the organic composition of capital can also be defined for each industry: then $s+v$ is the live labour performed in that industry; s/v, the rate of exploitation, is the ratio of the surplus or 'unpaid' labour to the labour value of the real wages obtained by the workers in that industry, c the value of the capital goods employed; c/v the organic composition of capital; and the rate of profits is given by $r=s/(c+v)$ which can also be re-written as $r=(s/v)/[(c/v)+1]$. If – as Marx assumes in Volume I of *Capital* – commodities exchanged at prices proportional to labour values, then the rate of profits (assuming prices proportional to labour values) could be uniform across the different industries only if – what observation shows not to be true – c/v were uniform (s/v is, on the other hand, uniform if the hourly wage is uniform or, as Marx assumes, heterogeneous or differently paid labour is reduced to homogeneity on the basis of relative wages). Marx was thus able to understand, more clearly than anyone before him, why the tendency of profit rates towards uniformity will cause relative prices to deviate from relative labour values. He nonetheless thought that in the economy as a whole the deviations cancel out, and that the uniform rate of profits is therefore the same as the average rate of profits which would obtain if commodities did exchange at labour values, i.e. $r=S/(C+V)$, or $r=(S/V)/[(C/V)+1]$.

Thus, he thought, the influences on the rate of profits can be better understood by studying the way they affect the two ratios S/V and C/V. This he thought to be a useful distinction because it allowed one better to separate the effects on the rate of profits of various types of technological change (effects which could be seen to be important in so far as they affected C/V or – e.g. speedups – S/V) from the effects of the workers' struggles over the wage level or, given the *daily* wage, over the length of the working day (affecting S/V).

This role of the rate of exploitation as defined by Marx has been undermined by the subsequent analytical advances in the theory of prices of production, associated with the names of Dmitriev, Bortkiewicz, Sraffa and now many others. It has been seen that Marx's basic insight was correct in that the *data* (the technological conditions, i.e. the matrix of physical and labour inputs, and the average wage basket), from which individual labour values and the aggregate magnitudes S, V, C are derived, do suffice to determine the rate of profits and relative prices; but it has also been seen that Marx's formula $r=S/(C+V)$ is incorrect except in very special cases, and that, although it would be possible to find algorithms to determine the correct rate of profits and prices from individual labour values, the calculation of labour values is anyway superfluous, a direct determination of the rate of profits and prices from those data being possible and easier. New analytical instruments, e.g. the wage-profit frontier, allow a more rigorous study of the effects of changes in technology or in the real wage on the rate of profits than S/V and C/V (e.g. it has been seen that technical change may in some cases cause r to move in a direction opposite to what Marx's formula would lead one to expect), relegating – for the study of these problems – labour value magnitudes to historical importance only, in that they allowed Marx to determine prices and the rate of profits, and the effects of the main forces acting on them, in the only (imperfect) way concretely possible at the time (Garegnani, 1984).

Many marxists (e.g. Sweezy, Hunt, Nuti) defend the importance of labour values by arguing that these allow one to show that workers are exploited. It is often claimed, in this connection, that central to Marx's analysis was the so-called Fundamental Marxian Theorem, stating that the rate of profits is positive if and only if the rate of exploitation is positive (Morishima, 1974). This is a doubtful claim, since the theorem re-states, in terms of labour embodied, the obvious fact – accepted by all critics of Marx as well – that profits can only be positive if wages do not absorb the entire net product. To call the S/V ratio 'rate of exploitation' is not a *demonstration* that workers are exploited: e.g. the marginalist, or neoclassical, approach would have no quarrel with the Fundamental Marxian Theorem and yet would argue that workers are not exploited, because they receive their marginal products, i.e. as much as each of them is contributing to production, and in the same way a positive rate of profits does not emerge from domination but rather corresponds to the marginal product of capital, and is therefore a just reward to the sacrifice of postponed consumption which, through savings, creates the capital: the marginalist explanation of distribution thus implies that capitalists (i.e., in the marginalist approach, savers) do contribute to production. The required demonstration of the existence of exploitation appears rather to lie in the validity of Marx's different explanation of why the surplus product does not go to the workers, referred to above, now supported by the criticisms directed at the marginalist theory of distribution (Eatwell and Milgate, 1983).

The existence of exploitation is therefore not endangered by the demonstration, due to Steedman (1975), that the Fundamental Marxian Theorem cannot be generalized to the case of joint production, so long at least as labour values are defined as usual, i.e. as the prices (in terms of the wage) at a zero rate of profits (if A and B are the square matrices of input and output coefficients respectively, and l the labour input vector, then the vector of labour values k is determined by $kA+l=kB$; this expression is what the price equations $(pA+wl)(1+r)=pB$ collapse to if $r=0$ and $w=1$; without joint production one has $B=I$, the identity matrix, and hence $kA+l=k$). With joint production, some labour values may be negative, and the surplus product may then have a negative labour value, implying a negative rate of exploitation. An intuitive explanation is as follows. The labour value of a commodity is an employment multiplier, indicating by what amount total employment would change if (with constant returns) the net product of that commodity increased by 1 unit, the other net products remaining constant. If several commodities are jointly produced by several processes, an increase in the net product of only one commodity may require expanding some processes but contracting some others (no contraction could be necessary in the absence of joint products): the resulting total variation in employment need not be positive. If the rate of exploitation is negative, total employment would have to increase in order not to produce at all the surplus product. But, it would seem, there still is exploitation, because the surplus product is not going to the workers, while it would if the capitalists' domination were not preventing the wage from rising.

Morishima and others have counter-argued that the idea of a negative labour embodied in a (single or composite) commodity makes no sense, and have proposed to re-define (via linear programming) the labour embodied in a commodity as the minimum labour time necessary, with the known techniques, to produce a net product containing at least that commodity (but possibly other commodities as well; individual labour values are then no longer additive, the labour value of a bundle of wool and mutton is no longer the sum of the labour values of the wool and of the mutton). The surplus labour S^* is then the difference between L and the minimum labour V^* necessary to produce, with the available technical knowledge, a net product containing at least the total wage basket. The rate of exploitation is then re-defined as S^*/V^*: a notion, it would seem, only interesting for purposes of comparison of reality with possible utopias ('how much less workers could afford to work if the social goal were the minimization of their working time, given their consumption'). It is not impossible, anyway, that in extreme cases S^*/V^* be zero in spite of a positive surplus product, as shown by the following example: the economy produces only, and jointly, wool and mutton from sheep, the surplus product consists of all the wool and the real wages of all the mutton; the rate of profits might be positive too (Petri, 1980).

This and other recent attempts at re-defining labour values and the rate of exploitation cannot, it would seem, find support in Marx, where the role of labour values appears to have been only the determination of prices and of the rate of profits, as shown for example by the way labour values are determined: Marx, like Ricardo, determines labour values on the no-rent land, and reduces heterogeneous labour to homogeneity on the basis of relative wages (implying a rate of exploitation uniform by assumption for all kinds of labour; see Steedman, 1985): which is what he must do in order to argue that prices would be proportional to labour values were it not for the non-uniformity of the organic composition of capital. Nowadays, ethical aims, for example some measurement of the degree of suffering imposed upon workers by capitalism, are often implicit in the search for re-definitions of the rate of exploitation. This is not necessarily illegitimate, but should be clearly stated and distinguished from Marx's own project.

FABIO PETRI

See also SURPLUS VALUE.

BIBLIOGRAPHY

Bortkiewicz, L. von. 1907. Value and price in the Marxian system. Trans. in *International Economic Papers* No. 2, 5–60, 1952.

Dmitriev, V.K. 1974. *Economic Essays on Value, Competition and Utility*. Ed. D.M. Nuti, Cambridge: Cambridge University Press.

Eatwell, J. and Milgate, M. (eds) 1983. *Keynes's Economics and the Theory of Value and Distribution*. London: Duckworth.

Garegnani, P. 1984. Value and distribution in the classical economists and Marx. *Oxford Economic Papers* 36(2), June, 291–325.

Hunt, E.K. and Schwartz, J.G. (eds) 1972. *A Critique of Economic Theory*. Harmondsworth: Penguin.

Marx, K. 1867–94. *Capital*, Vols. I–III. Moscow: Progress Publishers, 1965–6.

Mainwaring, L. 1984. *Value and Distribution in Capitalist Economies. An Introduction to Sraffian Economics*. Cambridge: Cambridge University Press.

Morishima, M. 1974. Marx in the light of modern economic theory. *Econometrica* 42(4), July, 611–32.

Morishima, M. and Catephores, G. 1978. *Value, Exploitation and Growth*. London: McGraw-Hill.

Petri, F. 1980. Positive profits without exploitation: a note on the generalized fundamental marxian theorem. *Econometrica* 48(2), March, 531–3.

Sraffa, P. 1960. *Production of Commodities by Means of Commodities*. Cambridge: Cambridge University Press.

Steedman, I. 1975. Positive profits with negative surplus value. *Economic Journal* 85, March, 114–23.

Steedman, I. 1985. Heterogeneous labour, money wages, and Marx's theory. *History of Political Economy* 17(4), 551–74.

Steedman, I., Sweezy, P. et al. 1981. *The Value Controversy*. London: New Left Books.

rational behaviour. The concept of rational behaviour is frequently used in economic theory. The interest in this concept springs from two quite distinct motivations. First, insofar as economic exercises often take a prescriptive form, it is interesting to know how one could behave rationally in a given situation. This may be called the 'prescriptive motivation'. It should be warned that the prescription need not be necessarily of an ethical kind. Indeed, the prescriptive motivation is sometimes described in clearly non-ethical terms, involving the pursuit of self-interest only. In a classic presentation of this position, Harsanyi (1977) describes 'perfectly rational behaviour' in the context of game theory in the following terms:

> ... our theory is a *normative* (prescriptive) theory rather than a *positive* (descriptive) theory. At least formally and explicitly it deals with the question of how each player *should* act in order to promote his own interests most effectively in the game and not with the question of how he (or persons like him) *will* actually act in a game of this particular type (Harsanyi, 1977, p. 16).

The second motivation concerns the possible use of models of rational behaviour in explaining and predicting *actual* behaviour. This exercise is done, as it were, in two steps. The first step consists in characterizing rational behaviour and the second, following that, bases actual behaviour on rational behaviour. In this way the characterization of rational behaviour may end up specifying the predicted actual behaviour as well. This motivation underlies much of the theory of general equilibrium (see, for example, Edgeworth, 1881; Arrow, 1951; Debreu, 1959; Arrow and Hahn, 1971). The argument is that while actual behaviour can, in principle, take any form, it is reasonable to assume that much of the time it will, in fact, be of the kind that can be described as 'rational'.

In reviewing the theory of rational behaviour, this duality of motivations has to be borne in mind. Even though the primary concern of this essay is with the way rational behaviour has been characterized, the nature of the second motivation makes it imperative that the possible use of rational behaviour models for explaining and predicting actual behaviour must not be overlooked.

RATIONALIZABILITY, BINARINESS AND SELF-INTEREST. In the presence of uncertainty, rational behaviour requires an appreciation of possible variations in the outcome of any chosen action, and such behaviour must, therefore, be based on systematic reading of uncertainties regarding the outcome and ways of dealing with them. Rational behaviour under uncertainty will be presently taken up, but before that the more elementary case when there is no uncertainty has to be dealt with. In fact, behaviour under certainty can be formally seen as an extreme case of behaviour under uncertainty when the uncertainty in question is not only small but simply absent. In this sense, rational behaviour under certainty must be subsumed by any theory that deals with rational behaviour in the presence of uncertainty.

Although there are many different approaches to rational behaviour under certainty, it is fair to say that there are two *main* approaches to this question. The first emphasizes *internal consistency*: rationality of behaviour is identified with a requirement that choices from different subsets should correspond to each other in a cogent and systematic way. Various conditions of internal consistency have been proposed in the literature, but the one which seems to command most attention in formal economic theory is *binariness* which requires that the choices from different subsets can be seen as maximizing solutions from the respective subsets according to some binary relation R (often interpreted as 'preference', e.g. xRy standing for 'x being preferred or indifferent to y'). Or, to put it another way, rational behaviour, in this interpretation, amounts to our ability to find a binary relation R over the universal set of alternatives such that the choice from any particular subset of that universal set consists of exactly the R-maximal elements of that subset. Richter (1971) calls this 'rationalizability'.

In other formulations – still within the general approach of internal consistency – the condition of rationalizability has been relaxed, demanding only a part of the kind of consistency that binary maximization must entail. On the other hand, in some other formulations, the demands have been made stronger than that of maximization according to a binary relation by requiring further that the binary relation in question be an ordering, satisfying both completeness and transitivity.

An enormous variety of conditions of internal consistency have been proposed in the literature, but it can be shown that many of them are equivalent to each other, and indeed altogether they fall into a number of classes, with each class containing different, but essentially equivalent, demands. Such reductionist analyses can be found, for example, in Houthakker (1956), Uzawa (1956), Arrow (1959), Richter (1971), Sen (1971), Herzberger (1973), Suzumura (1983). For critiques (and arguments for the rejection of) the binary approach to rationality, see Kanger (1976), Gauthier (1985), Sen (1985a, 1986b) and Sugden (1985).

The second common approach to rational behaviour under certainty sees it in terms of reasoned pursuit of self-interest. The origins of this approach are often traced to Adam Smith, and it is frequently asserted that the father of modern economics saw human beings as tirelessly fostering their respective self-interests. As a piece of history of economic thought, this is, to say the least, dubious, since Adam Smith's (1776, 1790) belief in the hold of self-interest in some spheres of activity (e.g., exchange) was qualified by his conviction that many other motivations are important in human behaviour in general (on this see Winch, 1978; Brennan and Lomasky, 1985; and Sen, 1987). But it is certainly true that the assumption of the 'economic man' relentlessly pursuing self-interest in a fairly narrowly defined form has played a major part in the characterization of individual behaviour in economics for a very long time.

SELF-INTEREST AND CONSISTENCY. Rational behaviour in the form of maximization in pursuit of self-interest makes the analysis of individual behaviour a good deal more tractable than a less structured assumption would permit. This is certainly one of its appeals. In addition this behavioural assumption is also quite crucial for the derivation of certain central results in traditional and modern economic theory, for example, Pareto optimality of competitive equilibria and *vice versa* (Arrow, 1951; Debreu, 1959; Arrow and Hahn, 1971). This is sometimes called the 'Fundamental Theorem of Welfare Economics'. Roughly stated, it claims, first, that every perfectly competitive equilibrium (with each person maximizing utility, given the prices) under certain assumptions (such as no externalities) achieves Pareto optimality, and second, under a slightly different set of assumptions (including the requirement of no externalities, but also some additional requirements, e.g., the absence of increasing returns to scale), every Pareto optimal state is a perfectly competitive equilibrium with respect to some set of prices and some initial distribution of resources. This correspondence between Pareto optimality and competitive equilibria works neatly given individual self-interested behaviour precisely because Pareto optimality is one characteristic of self-interest maximization of a group, in the sense that in such a situation no one's self-interest can be further enhanced without hurting the self-interest of somebody else. It is the assumption of rational behaviour in the form of the pursuit of self-interest that established the close relationship between competitive equilibria and Pareto optimality (with price-taking behaviour and absence of externalities preventing people from getting in each other's way in their respective pursuit of self-interest). In this result and in many other similar ones, the particular characterization of rational behaviour chosen plays a strategically crucial role.

It can be argued that rational behaviour under the self-interest approach is a special case of that under the consistency approach. If a person does pursue self-interest, it may follow that his or her behaviour will have the consistency needed for maximization of a cogent function. On the other hand, a person can be consistent without necessarily maximizing self-interest, since the maximizing function may have a different interpretation altogether (e.g., the pursuit of some moral values or political goals). Thus internal consistency of choice may be taken to be necessary but not sufficient for self-interested behaviour. There is undoubtedly something in this way of seeing the correspondence between the two common approaches to rational behaviour.

However, that alleged correspondence is also somewhat misleading, since the nature of self-interest need not necessarily take the uncomplicated form of being binary in character. Strictly speaking, neither does the self-interest thesis entail the consistency thesis, nor of course the other way round. While this must, in general, be correct, nevertheless the way self-interest has been actually viewed in standard economic theory has made it clearly binary and more typically an ordering (and often seen as being numerically representable). If self-interest must take this form, then it would indeed be the case that the self-interest approach is just a special case of the consistency approach.

In some treatises on rational behaviour, the distance between the self-interest approach and the consistency approach is bridged by some careful definitions. For example, in the 'revealed preference theory', pioneered by Samuelson (1938), consistency is demanded in the form of the 'Weak Axiom of Revealed Preference', to wit: if x is chosen from a set containing y, then y will not be chosen from any set containing x. This type of consistency is, on its own, without a particular substantive interpretation, except that it corresponds generally to some kind of maximization. However, the term 'revealed preference' might indicate that the chosen alternative is always also the preferred one. Insofar as preference reflects self-interest (as is typically assumed to be the case), this established, through the terminology of 'revealed preference', what looks like a congruence of choice and self-interest.

The consistency entailed by the Weak Axiom of Revealed Preference does not, in general, entail transitivity, which is a property that might be thought to be a natural one to impose on the relation of self-interest. But that hole can be plugged by *either* demanding stronger conditions (such as Houthakker's, 1950, 'Strong Axiom of Revealed Preference'), *or* by demanding that the consistency of the Weak Axiom be satisfied over all finite subsets, which makes the strong axiom equivalent to the weak (on this see Arrow, 1959; Sen, 1971). One way or another, the consistency imposed by revealed preference axioms can lead to a 'preference' relation that has the regularity properties normally associated with the concept of self-interest, and then the gap between the two could be seen as fully bridged.

However, that entire bridging exercise is based on *defining* the relation of choice as a relation of 'preference' which happens to be 'revealed' by the act of choice. But that terminology is arbitrarily imposed, and it is possible that the binary relation of choice, even when fully transitive and complete, may in fact reflect neither the person's preference, nor his or her self-interest. There is, obviously, scope for methodological arguments on this point, and these issues have often been joined.

In the philosophical literature, it is common to distinguish between 'instrumental rationality' and 'substantive rationality' (see Latsis, 1976). It is clear that the self-interest view of rational behaviour is one of substantive rationality requiring that rational behaviour must take the form of pursuing some independently defined self-interest. Obviously, this characteristic of substantiveness is not satisfied by the theory of revealed preference, since there the identification of choice with preference or self-interest takes the form of *defining* the relation of choice as a relation of preference, which is not an independent way of characterizing preference or self-interest. But in other theories, the substantive exercise is carefully done, for example, in the typical general equilibrium theory (see Arrow, 1951; Debreu, 1959; Arrow and Hahn, 1971). The starting point of individual behaviour is, then, not a choice function but a utility function, representing the self-interest of the person in question. Choices follow from constrained maximization of that utility function. In this form, the substantive nature of the characterized rationality is strongly asserted, in the shape of pursuit of self-interest.

A number of criticisms have been recently made about the special nature of the assumption of self-interest maximization. Human beings may well have other motivations, and self-interest is just one of various things that a person might wish to pursue. Different types of criticisms of this substantive assumption have been made by such authors as Nagel (1970), Kornai (1971), Sen (1973, 1977, 1987), Scitovsky (1976), Leibenstein (1976), Schelling (1978), Wong (1978), Elster (1979, 1983), Hirschman (1982, 1983), McPherson (1982), Margolis (1982), Akerlof (1984), Schick (1984) and others.

If the assumption of self-interest maximization is seen as too narrow, it can be argued that merely requiring internal consistency is much too permissive. Indeed, it is tempting to think of the consistency approach as belonging to the 'instrumental' view of rationality. But this is not quite so, since the instrumental view requires that the person pursues some independently defined objective (even though the objective need not be based on self-interest only). In the consistency view there is no such independently defined function at all, and the binary relation that is precipitated by the choice function is a *reflection* of choice rather than a *determinant* of it. It is rather that the consistency approach opens the way to some instrumental view of rationality, involving the maximization of some objective function. Indeed, in this sense, the consistency approach can be seen as permissively admitting the approach of instrumental rationality implicit in the self-interest approach, where the objective function maximized happens to be the self-interest of the person in question.

The consistency approach can be criticized on grounds of inadequacy in characterizing rationality of behaviour. A person's choice function may be internally consistent in the sense that the different things chosen from different subsets correspond to each other in an apparently cogent and coherent way, but this does not in itself indicate that the person's behaviour is consistent with his or her aims or objectives. Indeed, a person who systematically does exactly the *opposite* of what has to be done for the pursuit of his or her objective function may end up producing a consistent choice behaviour, but the binary relation that will be revealed by the choices – the 'opposite' of the person's objective function – will be, clearly, at war with the goals and aims of that person. To describe such a person as behaving rationally would, obviously, lead to some interesting methodological difficulties.

MAXIMIZING, SATISFICING AND BOUNDED RATIONALITY. These problems with the standard views of rationality tend to undermine the very foundations of these approaches. Some other approaches have involved more qualified use of the standard presumptions. For example, Herbert Simon (1957, 1979) has argued powerfully that individuals may not actually *maximize* any function at all, and their behaviour may take the form of what has been called 'satisficing'. There are various ways of characterizing satisficing, but it can be thought of in terms of a person having a certain target level of achievement, which he or she will try to reach, but beyond which he or she may not try to improve the achievement any further.

There is a genuine problem of interpretation involved in analysing satisficing, and it can be argued that satisficing behaviour really is maximization according to an effectively incomplete relation, such that the states satisfying the target level of achievement are all put in a non-comparable class as far as choice behaviour is concerned. Maximization can indeed be defined in terms of such incomplete relations (see, for example, Debreu's 1959 analysis of 'maximal' sets based on 'pre-orderings'), and if it is seen in these terms, the gap between satisficing and maximizing may be, at least formally, reduced. However, the content of the claim of satisficing is that the person in question *can* tell between the different levels of achievement which are all beyond the target level required, and despite this discernibility, choice behaviour departs from relentless maximization of the level of achievement. In this version of the story, a substantial difference is indeed made by the notion of satisficing, and the implications of satisficing behaviour may, in this interpretation, be quite different from those of maximization.

Variations of the maximization assumption and the related consistency conditions can be justified by seeing the use of reason in human affairs in terms of what has been called 'bounded rationality'. In this structure human choice is seen not in terms of grand maximizing behaviour, but as a series of particular decisions, not fully integrated with each other, taken in situations of partial information and based on limited reflection. This approach has been developed by Herbert Simon (1957, 1979, 1983) both at a theoretical level and in the context of specific empirical applications. The results differ quite substantially from that of rational behaviour seen in terms of consistency, or in terms of optimization according to self-interest. As Simon (1983) puts it:

> Rationality of the sort described by the behavioural model [of bounded rationality] doesn't optimize, of course. Nor does it even guarantee that our decisions will be consistent. As a matter of fact, it is very easy to show that choices made by an organism having these characteristics will often depend on the order in which alternatives are presented (Simon, 1983, p. 23).

NATURAL SELECTION AND MOTIVES. Supporters of optimizing models have typically used two different types of arguments to defend the practice, against models of the kind characterized by 'bounded rationality' and other behavioural departures. One argument takes the direct form of arguing that human beings do optimize and take care to do so. The second argument suggests that natural selection will lead to this result: those who optimize do better, and those who do not, get eliminated by natural selection. For example, non-profit-maximizing firms may go to the wall, so that only the profit-maximizing ones may survive (see Friedman, 1953). This type of indirect justification of what has been called 'enforced maximization' has many pitfalls, since the analogy with natural selection in biology is at best tenuous (see Helm, 1984; Matthews, 1984), and the biological story itself is far from straightforward (Dawkins, 1982; Maynard Smith, 1982).

It is by no means clear that individual self-interest-maximizers will typically do relatively better in a group of people with diverse motivations. More importantly, when it comes to comparisons of survival of different *groups*, it can easily be the case that groups that emphasize values other than pure self-interest maximization might actually do better (see Sen, 1973, 1974, 1985b; Akerlof, 1984). It has been argued that economic success has often come more plentifully in cultures that emphasize norms of conduct quite different from that of persistent maximization of individual self-interest, focusing on other values (e.g., what Morishima, 1982, calls 'the Japanese ethos'; see also Dore, 1983). The relation between social norms and individual conduct is an enormously complex field, and the simple assumptions of self-interest maximization, or straightforward models of apparent 'consistency', may overlook important aspects of the individual-society relationships (see, for example, Hirschman, 1970, 1982). This is not to argue that 'natural selection' arguments are worthless in economics – they may be far from that – but the results of the selection may lack the simplicity demanded by supporters of simple optimization and may take a more complex form (see Hirshleifer, 1977; Helm, 1984; Matthews, 1984).

In assessing the overall value of standard models of rational behaviour, it is important to pay attention to the distinction made earlier between the value of these structures as representations of *rationality* and their usefulness in terms of predicting *actual* behaviour. Some of the deficiencies of the optimizing structure apply specifically to the latter. For example, models of 'bounded rationality' are often defended by claims of greater plausibility in explaining actual human conduct.

In fact, the entire enterprise of getting to actual behaviour via models of rationality may itself be seen as methodologically quite dubious. There is scope for argument here on both sides, since the unrealism of rational behaviour may be large, but the unrealism of any *specific kind* of 'irrational' behaviour could be larger still. Whether 'bounded rationality' is the right kind of compromise in getting a grip on actuality via limited use of rationality remains an interesting question.

REASON AND RATIONALITY. As far as the other objective of rational behaviour models is concerned, i.e., the ability of these models to capture the essence of rationality (no matter how people do actually behave), there are a number of complex philosophical issues underlying the question. It is easy enough to argue that mere internal consistency of choice cannot be adequate for rationality, nor can self-interest maximization be seen as uniquely rational in a way that pursuing other kinds of objectives (such as altruism, public spirit, class consciousness, group solidarity) must fail to be. What is much harder to do is to develop an alternative structure for rationality that would be regarded as satisfactory for the purpose of capturing what can be demanded of reason in human choice (whether or not it also serves the second purpose of giving us a good guess regarding actual behaviour). This question remains, to a great extent, an open one, which has been as yet rather inadequately explored.

Two difficulties, in particular, may be worth mentioning in this context. First, while 'instrumental rationality' must have some place in economics, and the role of reasoned choice of means for serving *given* ends cannot be dismissed, it is hard to believe that any kind of objectives – no matter how bizarre – must be seen as okay, i.e., not compromising the rationality of the person pursuing it. The need for rational assessment of objectives and preferences have been analysed by John Broome (1978), Derek Parfit (1984) and others, and both the procedural and substantive features of this type of assessment do deserve serious attention.

Second, even when goals are clearly given, the translation of these into actions depends on the pattern of social interdependence assumed in group behaviour, with members having partly divergent goals. As the discussions on the so-called 'Newcomb's problem' and other complex cases have brought out, the correct individual decision may not be entirely unproblematic even when there appears to exist a strictly dominant strategy (see Nozick, 1969; Brams, 1975; Levi, 1975; Gibbard and Harper, 1978; Jeffrey, 1983, among others). The nature of beliefs permits alternative interpretations of the nature of the decision problem, and this philosophical question is of relevance to decision problems in economics as much as it is in other fields of human choice.

The Prisoner's Dilemma has been frequently used in economic arguments to illustrate the nature of inefficiencies of atomistic non-cooperative behaviour when the interdependence incorporates both congruence and conflict of interests in such a way that the combination of each person's dominant strategies produces an outcome that is inferior in terms of the goals of everyone in the group (see Luce and Raiffa, 1957). Attempts to resolve the problem by assuming temporal repetition of the game have not been easy, since it can be demonstrated that with complete knowledge and standard optimizing behaviour, a finitely repeated Prisoner's Dilemma will continue to produce the inferior outcome throughout (Luce and Raiffa, 1957, pp. 97-101).

Such non-cooperative behaviour is, however, violated in many experimental games as well as in the usual readings of many real-life situations. The apparent dissonace between received theory and observed behaviour has been explained in a variety of ways in the large literature that has developed on the Prisoner's Dilemma. The 'ways out' have included relaxing the assumption of mutual knowledge, for example, introducing uncertainty about the number of times for which the game will be played, admitting ignorance of the players about other people's knowledge and motivation, limiting the range of alternative strategies that can be considered, and other relaxations (see Howard, 1971; Basu, 1977; Davis, 1977;

Radner, 1980; Smale, 1980; Kreps, Milgrom, Roberts and Wilson, 1982; Axelrod, 1984). Other analyses have emphasized more complex features of 'practical reasoning' involving various types of action ethics, sensitive beliefs, behavioural commitments, and instrumental use of reciprocity; see Sen (1974, 1985b), Watkins (1974, 1985), Levi (1975, 1986), Gauthier (1985), McClennen (1985). If it has done nothing else, the literature has at least brought out sharply the complexity of the nature of rationality in situations of interdependence as well as various conceptual and logistic difficulties in using models of rationality to understand the nature of actual behaviour.

It seems easy to accept that rationality involves many features that cannot be summarized in terms of some straightforward formula, such as binary consistency. But this recognition does not immediately lead to alternative characterizations that might be regarded as satisfactory, even though the inadequacies of the traditional assumptions of rational behaviour standardly used in economic theory have become hard to deny. It will not be an easy task to find replacements for the standard assumptions of rational behaviour – and related to it of actual behaviour – that can be found in the traditional economic literature, both because the identified deficiencies have been seen as calling for rather divergent remedies, and also because there is little hope of finding an alternative assumption structure that will be as simple and usable as the traditional assumptions of self-interest maximization, or of consistency of choice.

UNCERTAINTY AND EXPECTED UTILITY. The extension of the modelling of rational behaviour from certainty to uncertainty involves both (1) the characterization of uncertainty, and (2) taking note of uncertainty thus characterized in making actual decisions over alternative courses of actions. The model that has been most extensively used in this context is that of 'expected utility'. This takes the form of weighing the value of each of the outcomes by the respective probabilities of the different outcomes. The probability-weighted overall 'expected value', thus derived, is then maximized in this approach to rational choice under uncertainty.

The use of probability calculus involves interpretational problems as to what the probabilities stand for. While the view of probability as a measure of relative frequency is a natural one to consider, there is clearly much cogency in interpreting probability as a measure of the degree of belief (as argued by Fisher, 1921, and Keynes, 1921).

Actual decision-taking operations involve a reading of the likelihood of different outcomes and an assessment of the different outcomes in the light of the respective likelihoods. In a pioneering contribution in axiomatizing conjointly characterized probabilities and utilities, Frank Ramsey (1931) provided the structure (and a possible derivation) of the expected utility calculus. Another major contribution in this area came from Von Neumann and Morgenstern (1947). Given the probabilities of different outcomes, consistent and complete rankings of the possible lotteries over the outcomes (including lotteries of lotteries and so forth) permit the construction of cardinal utility functions for the respective rankings associated with the outcomes, provided the rankings in question satisfy certain regularity properties which were specified by Von Neumann and Morgenstern (see also Marschak, 1946). The assigned cardinal utility numbers of the respective outcomes, weighted by the respective probabilities, when summed together, yield the expected values of the lotteries, and provide numerical representations of the overall goodness of the respective lotteries. Rational behaviour under expected utility maximization takes the form of choosing that lottery which has the highest overall value, thus calculated. The expected utility approach can be and has been used extensively both in economic theory and in applied economics (see, for example, Friedman and Savage, 1948; Arrow, 1971).

INDEPENDENCE AND CONSISTENCY. The axioms underlying the derivation of expected utility maximization have been subjected to a good deal of examination and scrutiny. There is scope for disputation both about the exact content and the plausibility of the expected utility axioms (for a very helpful introduction see Luce and Raiffa, 1957; see also Fishburn, 1970, 1981).

The axiom that has perhaps attracted the most criticism is the so-called 'strong independence'. This independence condition can be stated in several different ways, but a rather immediate one is the following. If in a combined lottery over, say, lotteries L^1 and L^2, the latter L^2 is replaced by another lottery L^3 which is preferred to L^2 (leaving the probabilities and L^1 unchanged), then the modified combined lottery (over L^1 and L^3) would be preferred to the original one (over L^1 and L^2). And *vice versa*.

Another axiom, related to this one, is sometimes called 'the sure thing principle', which, in one version, requires that anything that raises the probability of the preferred component in a two-alternative lottery would improve the lottery. These axioms are implicit in expected utility maximization, even though the 'independence' condition can be dispensed with in a more limited ('locally' valid) version of expected utility behaviour (as has been shown by Mark Machina, 1982).

Various 'counter-examples' to expected utility maximization have been proposed in the literature, often on the basis of considering interesting 'hypothetical' cases, but sometimes on the basis of experimental observations as well. In assessing these objections, we must distinguish, once again, between the claims *to* rationality of this model, and the claims of the model to explain actual behaviour *via* rationality.

It is certainly clear that very often people do act in a way that cannot be made consistent with expected utility maximization. (An early critique, with an alternative framework for choice behaviour, came from Shackle, 1938, 1952.) Observations of behaviour and articulated judgements under uncertainty have indicated different types of violations of expected utility behaviour (see, for example, Kahneman, Slovik and Tversky, 1982). There seem to be problems both in risk perception as well as in the utilization of probability information in making actual decisions. These departures from rational behaviour in the form of expected utility maximization have considerable implications on the way economic models may have to be constructed involving uncertainty (on this see Arrow, 1982, 1983). As a framework for understanding actual behaviour, the merits and demerits of the expected utility model are certainly becoming clearer on the basis of recent work. But the 'bottom line' of overall judgement continues to vary. While some have been extremely sceptical, others (such as Harsanyi, 1977) continue to emphasize, with some justice, the usefulness of this model in 'explaining or predicting real-life human behaviour' (p. 16).

The need for departures – small or great – from the expected utility model in explaining *actual* behaviour does not, of course, settle the question of the rationality or irrationality of maximization of expected utility. However, a number of telling and powerful arguments have also been presented in the literature giving reasons for departing from 'consistency' of the kind demanded by the expected utility model (for arguments on both sides, see the collection of papers in Daboni, Montesano and Lines, 1986). Allais (1953) has followed up his empirical critique of expected utility model as representation of actual behaviour by arguments in favour of the reasonableness of the departures, and more arguments on this have been outlined in recent years (see Allais and Hagen, 1979; Stigum and Wenstop, 1983; and Daboni, Montesano and Lines, 1986). Also, the possibility of 'state-dependent utilities' has raised questions of a different sort, requiring reformulation of the original model (see Drèze, 1974).

One of the important considerations that the expected utility model may leave out consists of 'counterfactual' information. One's 'disappointment', 'regret', etc., may well depend on what one anticipated and what did not occur. Earlier discussions of such criteria as 'minimax regret' (see Savage, 1954) have been followed in recent years by various models of disappointment and regret (see, for example, Bell, 1982; Loomes and Sugden, 1982).

It is arguable that something which has not happened, but could have, should not really affect one's decision, and in particular, it is irrational to regret and sigh about what could have happened. But while it is indeed possible to argue that it is irrational to regret a past decision on the ground of what could have happened in the light of later information, nevertheless *if* it is the case that one would willy-nilly regret the past decision if it turns out to be unfortunate, then it is *not* in any sense obviously irrational to *recognize* that fact and take that inescapable feeling into account. Clarity of analysis requires that we distinguish between (1) the rationality of what psychology we ought to have, and (2) the rationality of decisions, taking note of what psychology we might not be able to escape. Many counter-examples to expected utility behaviour presented in the literature relate – directly or indirectly – to mental-state considerations, for example, Allais (1953), MacCrimmon (1968), Bernard (1974), Drèze (1974), Tversky (1975), Machina (1981), McClennen (1983) and others.

One reason why the inclusion of mental states among the influences on choice is resisted is the idea that mental state is a particular interpretation of *utility* of which another – alternative – interpretation is given by the numerical representation of choice, with which the expected utility model is concerned. In the context of utilitarianism, the mental-state utility and the numerical representation of choice can indeed be seen as *alternatives*, as they have been viewed in the ethical literature. However, in terms of the description of the world, both mental states and choices are distinct parts of the reality, and the acknowledgement of the existence of one does not deny the existence of the other. Indeed, it is not unreasonable to ask how each might relate to the other. The states of affairs over which choices may be considered (including choices over lotteries of those states) may, quite importantly, include the mental states of the parties involved.

On the other hand, including such mental states in the description of states of affairs makes the scope of such conditions as 'strong independence' rather limited. Varying an *alternative* lottery (e.g., L^3 vis-à-vis L^2) might affect the description of the 'prize' of a given lottery (L^1) through variations of mental states (now included in the outcome of L^1) related to considering and reflecting on the nature of the alternative (L^3 vis-à-vis L^2) and the corresponding disappointment, regret, etc. If L^1 is no longer 'the same' in the two cases, then 'strong independence' would make no demand. Thus 'strong independence' may be saved only at the cost of making it often trivially fulfilled (see Sen, 1985a). The same difficulty applies if strong independence is 'rescued' by including counterfactual information in describing states of affairs.

The basis of rationality implicit in expected utility calculation does, however, require descriptions of states of affairs in sufficient detail such that choices can be made taking all the relevant considerations into account. It can be argued, as indeed Peter Hammond (1986) has, that 'consequential' reasoning taking into account all the relevant considerations, will push us in the direction of expected utility maximization. The important question is whether the relevant considerations would include either counterfactuals or mental states, and if they do so, whether enough scope for the use of such conditions as 'strong independence' can be found to build up utility numbering in a way that would make the expected utility model work in practice. This is not a matter, obviously, of pure theory only, and much depends on the nature of people's psychology and what considerations might be regarded as rational, in taking note of the complexities of our psychology.

CONCLUDING REMARKS. Attempts at constructing models of rational behaviour have certainly played a creative part in reducing the untractability of unstructured assessment of (1) the demands of rationality, and (2) facts of actual behaviour. On the other hand, models of rational behaviour actually presented have tended to ignore some of the complexities that have to be faced. This problem arises even when no uncertainty is introduced into the picture.

Neither of the two standard views of rational behaviour – as 'consistent choice' or as 'self-interest maximization' – has emerged as being really adequate as representations of rationality or of actuality. Various suggestions as to the directions in which we might go were reviewed earlier. Although none of the suggestions are unproblematic, many fruitful avenues of investigation have certainly been identified in the critical literature.

These difficulties carry over to rational behaviour models accommodating uncertainty. The limitations of characterizing rational behaviour in terms of just internal consistency, as discussed in the context of choice under certainty, obviously would apply to the modelling of choice under uncertainty as well. Similarly, pursuit of self-interest cannot be seen as being *uniquely* rational in models of uncertainty, any more than they can be so seen when everything is certain. However, it is not really necessary that expected utility models be seen in terms of self-interest maximization, and indeed some writers, for example, Ramsey (1931), have explicitly repudiated that interpretation. In fact, what the expected utility models do concentrate on is 'consistency' in a very demanding sense, and in this context objections similar to the ones raised in models of choice *without* uncertainty can be raised *a fortiori* with uncertainty.

Rationality may be seen as demanding something other than just consistency of choices from different subsets. It must, at least, demand cogent relations between aims and objectives actually entertained by the person and the choices that the person makes. This problem is not eliminated by the terminological procedure of describing the cardinal representation of choices as the 'utility' of the person, since this does not give any independent evidence on what the person is aiming to do or trying to achieve.

A more difficult issue, as discussed in the context of certainty, concerns the *assessment* of aims and objectives pursued by a person, even if they are fully reflected in the choices actually made. As Patrick Suppes (1984) has put it, the standard normative model of expected utility 'can be satisfied by cognitive and moral idiots'. 'Put another way, the consistency of computations required by the expected-utility model does not guarantee the exercise of judgement and wisdom in the traditional sense' (pp. 207–8). Suppes argues in favour of moving to the Aristotelian view that the rational person acts 'in accordance with good reasons', and is not embarrassed by the fact that this leaves a certain amount of 'pluralism' in the possible approach to rationality.

In addition to those problems of rationality that are shared by models of certainty as well as uncertainty, there are some special problems that apply particularly to considerations of uncertain outcomes. The status of counterfactuals, and their influences on mental states, raise interesting and important questions as to what may or may not be relevant to take into account in rationally assessing alternative courses of action.

While these problems were addressed earlier on in this paper, one issue that has not yet received much attention here concerns the nature of uncertainty itself. Reference was made earlier to the distinction between interpreting probabilities as degrees of belief, and interpreting them as frequencies. There are also other issues (see, for example, Levi, 1982, 1987). Even the very idea of having beliefs about possible outcomes in the form of probabilities in a situation of partial ignorance raises some interesting philosophical questions. At the very least, it is possible to make a distinction that was made by Frank Knight (1921) between 'risk' and 'uncertainty', with probability distributions being specified in the case of the former but not in the latter case. Whether arguments such as 'insufficient reason' can permit one to *construct* probability distributions even when we do not start with them remains a hard question to settle.

The area of expectation formation is also one in which the demands of rationality are not easy to specify. In some models of rational behaviour, no requirements of rationality are imposed on expectations at all, and the problem of rationality arises only in taking note of the actual expectations in arriving at decisions regarding action. In models of 'adaptive expectations' a step is taken in the direction of making expectations responsive – in an intelligent way – on experience. What goes very much further than this is the assumption of 'rational expectation' by which each person anticipates what can, in some sense, be described as objective probabilities; see Muth (1961), Lucas and Sargent (1982).

This approach not only raises the question as to what the philosophical status of objective probabilities might be, but also whether it is really a matter of *rationality* as such whether one is successful in guessing what the objective probabilities are. It is fair to say that the assessment of models of 'rational expectation' cannot be based on the idea of rationality alone, since the demands of such a theory go well beyond the requirements of the use of reason, especially in a situation of ignorance. It is sensible enough to think that there are problems in models of behaviour in which such that people's expectations are systematically wrong, but to try to move from that recognition to one in which everyone manages to take note of objective probabilities fully is quite a dramatic step. Whether that step is worth taking in predicting actual behaviour might well be discussed and assessed in the light of the ability of such a theory to explain actual behaviour, but that, as we have already discussed, is a rather different problem from assessing the *rationality* as such of that behaviour.

In addition to the issue of the role of rationality involved in 'rational expectation' models, even the basic rational behaviour models (without such expectational assumptions), widely used in economics, raises, as we have seen, difficult – sometimes perplexing – questions. It is not hard to see the merit of trying to reduce a complex reality by characterizing rationality in rather narrow terms, but nor is it hard to fathom that such a narrowing might do grave injustice to the notion of rationality, which is, after all, one of the central concerns of human life.

We have to make a clear distinction between (1) what type of behaviour might be described as *rational*, and (2) what rational behaviour models might be useful in making predictions about *actual* behaviour. These different questions are not, of course, independent of each other. But the first step in pursuing their interrelations is to recognize the distinction between the two questions. What issues respectively arise in facing these distinct questions, and how they might possibly be related, were discussed earlier on in this paper in the light of the existing literature. There was, however, no escape from noting the fact that the existing literature is indeed deeply incomplete in that real difficulties have been identified without providing an adequate structure for solutions. The need to go beyond the existing literature is apparent enough, but where to go is less clear.

AMARTYA SEN

See also AXIOMATIC METHODS; ECONOMIC THEORY AND THE HYPOTHESIS OF RATIONALITY; PHILOSOPHY AND ECONOMICS; SOCIAL CHOICE; WELFARE ECONOMICS.

BIBLIOGRAPHY

Akerlof, G.A. 1984. *An Economic Theorist's Book of Tales.* Cambridge: Cambridge University Press.

Allais, M. 1953. Le comportement de l'homme rationnel devant le risque: critique de postulates et axiomes de l'école Américaine. *Econometrica* 21, October, 503–46.

Allais, M. and Hagen, O. (eds) 1979. *Expected Utility Hypotheses and the Allais Paradox: Contemporary Discussions of Decisions under Uncertainty with Allais' Rejoinder*. Dordrecht: Reidel.

Arrow, K.J. 1951. An extension of the basic theorems of classical welfare economics. In *Proceedings of the Second Berkeley Symposium of Mathematical Statistics*, ed. J. Neyman, Berkeley: University of California Press.

Arrow, K.J. 1959. Rational choice functions and orderings. *Economica* 26, May, 121–7.

Arrow, K.J. 1971. *Essays in the Theory of Risk-Bearing*. Amsterdam: North-Holland.

Arrow, K.J. 1982. Risk perception in psychology and economics. *Economic Inquiry* 20(1), 1–9.

Arrow, K.J. 1983. Behaviour under uncertainty and its implications for policy. In Stigum and Wenstop (1983).

Arrow, K.J. and Hahn, F.H. 1971. *General Competitive Analysis*. San Francisco: Holden-Day. Republished, Amsterdam: North-Holland, 1979.

Axelrod, R. 1984. *The Evolution of Cooperation*. New York: Academic Press.

Basu, K. 1977. Information and strategy in iterated Prisoners' Dilemma. *Theory and Decision* 8(3), 293–8.

Bell, D.E. 1982. Regret in decision making under uncertainty. *Operations Research* 30(5), 961–81.

Bernard, G. 1974. On utility functions. *Theory and Decision* 5(2), 205–42.

Brams, S.J. 1975. *Game Theory and Politics*. New York: Free Press.

Brennan, G, and Lomasky, L. 1985. The impartial spectator goes to Washington: toward a Smithian theory of economic behavior. *Economics and Philosophy* 1(2), October, 189–211.

Broome, J. 1978. Choice and value in economics. *Oxford Economic Papers* 30(3), November, 313–33.

Broome, J. 1984. Uncertainty and fairness. *Economic Journal* 94, 624–32.

Campbell, R. and Sowden, L. (eds) 1985. *Paradoxes of Rationality and Cooperation.* Vancouver: University of British Columbia Press.

Chipman, J.S., Hurwicz, L., Richter, M.K. and Sonnenschein, H.F. 1971. *Preferences, Utility, and Demand.* New York: Harcourt, Brace.
Daboni, L., Montesano, A. and Lines, M. (eds) 1986. *Recent Developments in the Foundations of Utility Theory and Risk.* Dordrecht: Reidel.
Davis, L.M. 1977. Prisoners, paradox and rationality. *American Philosophical Quarterly* 14. Also in Campbell and Sowden (1985).
Dawkins, R. 1982. *The Extended Phenotype.* Oxford: Clarendon Press.
Davidson, D., Suppes, P. and Siegel, S. 1957. *Decision Making: An Experimental Approach.* Stanford: Stanford University Press.
Debreu, G. 1959. *A Theory of Value.* New York: Wiley.
Dore, R. 1983. Goodwill and the spirit of market capitalism. *British Journal of Sociology* 34, December, 459–82.
Drèze, J.H. 1974. Axiomatic theories of choice, cardinal utility and subjective probability: a review. In *Allocation under Uncertainty: Equilibrium and Optimality*, ed. J.H. Drèze, London: Macmillan.
Edgeworth, F. 1881. *Mathematical Psychics.* London: Kegan Paul.
Elster, J. 1979. *Ulysses and the Sirens.* Cambridge: Cambridge University Press.
Elster, J. 1983. *Sour Grapes.* Cambridge: Cambridge University Press.
Fishburn, P.C. 1970. *Utility Theory and Decision Making.* New York: Wiley.
Fishburn, P.C. 1981. Subjective expected utility: a review of normative theories. *Theory and Decision* 31(2), 139–99.
Fisher, R.A. 1921. On the mathematical foundations of theoretical statistics. *Philosophical Transactions of the Royal Society of London*, Series A 222, April, 309–68.
Friedman, M. 1953. *Essays in Positive Economics.* Chicago: Chicago University Press.
Friedman, M. and Savage, L.J. 1948. The utility analysis of choices involving risk. *Journal of Political Economy* 56, August, 279–304.
Gauthier, D. 1985. Maximization constrained: the rationality of cooperation. In Campbell and Sowden (1985).
Gibbard, A. and Harper, W.L. 1978. Counterfactual and two kinds of expected utility. In Hooker, Leach and McClennen (1978).
Hammond, P.J. 1976. Changing tastes and coherent dynamic choice. *Review of Economic Studies* 43(1), February, 159–73.
Hammond, P.J. 1986. Consequentialism and rationality in dynamic choice under uncertainty. In *Social Choice and Public Decision Making: Essays in Honor of K.J. Arrow*, ed. W. Heller, D. Starrett and R. Starr, Vol. I, Cambridge: Cambridge University Press.
Harsanyi, J.C. 1977. *Rational Behaviour and Bargaining Equilibrium in Games and Social Situations.* Cambridge: Cambridge University Press.
Helm, D. 1984. Predictions and causes: a comparison of Friedman and Hicks on method. *Oxford Economic Papers* 36, Supplement, November, 118–34.
Herzberger, H. 1973. Ordinal preference and rational choice. *Econometrica* 41(2), March, 187–237.
Hirschman, A.O. 1970. *Exit, Voice, and Loyalty.* Cambridge, Mass.: Harvard University Press.
Hirschman, A.O. 1982. *Shifting Involvements.* Princeton: Princeton University Press.
Hirschman, A.O. 1983. Against parsimony: three easy ways of complicating some categories of economic discourse. *American Economic Review, Papers and Proceedings* 74(2), May, 89–96.
Hirshleifer, J. 1977. Economics from a biological viewpoint. *Journal of Law and Economics* 20(1), April, 1–52.
Hooker, C.A., Leach, J.J. and McClennen, E.F. (eds) 1978. *Foundations and Applications of Decision Theory.* Dordrecht: Reidel.
Houthakker, H.S. 1950. Revealed preference and the utility function. *Economica* 15, May, 159–74.
Houthakker, H.S. 1956. On the logic of preference and choice. In *Contributions to Logic and Methodology in Honor of J.J. Bochenski*, ed. A. Tymieniecka, Amsterdam: North-Holland.
Howard, N. 1971. *Paradoxes of Rationality.* Cambridge, Mass.: MIT Press.
Jeffrey, R.C. 1965. *The Logic of Decision.* New York: McGraw-Hill.
Jeffrey, R.C. 1983. *The Logic of Decision.* 2nd edn, Chicago: University of Chicago Press.
Kahneman, D. and Tversky, A. 1979. Prospect theory: an analysis of decisions under risk. *Econometrica* 47(2), March, 263–91.
Kahneman, D., Slovik, P. and Tversky, A. 1982. *Judgement under Uncertainty: Heuristics and Biases.* Cambridge: Cambridge University Press.
Kanger, S. 1976. Preference based on choice. Mimeographed, Uppsala University.
Keynes, J.M. 1921. *A Treatise on Probability.* London: Macmillan.
Knight, F. 1921. *Risk, Uncertainty and Profit.* New York: Houghton Mifflin.
Kornai, J. 1971. *Anti-Equilibrium.* Amsterdam: North-Holland.
Kreps, D.M., Milgrom, P., Roberts, J. and Wilson, R. 1982. Rational cooperation in the finitely repeated Prisoner's Dilemma. *Journal of Economic Theory* 27(2), August, 245–52.
Latsis, S.J. (ed.) 1976. *Method and Appraisal in Economics.* Cambridge: Cambridge University Press.
Leibenstein, H. 1976. *Beyond Economic Man: A New Foundation for Microeconomics.* Cambridge, Mass.: Harvard University Press.
Levi, I. 1975. Newcomb's many problems. *Theory and Decision* 6(2), 161–75.
Levi, I. 1982. Ignorance, probability and rational choice. *Synthése* 53(2), December, 287–417.
Levi, I. 1987. *Hard Choices.* Cambridge: Cambridge University Press.
Loomes, G. and Sugden, R. 1982. Regret theory: an alternative theory of rational choice. *Economic Journal* 92(368), December, 805–24.
Lucas, R.E. and Sargent, T.J. 1982. *Rational Expectation and Econometric Practice.* London: Allen & Unwin.
Luce, R.D. and Raiffa, H. 1957. *Games and Decisions.* New York: Wiley.
MacCrimmon, K.R. 1968. Descriptive and normative implications of decision theory postulates. In *Risk and Uncertainty*, ed. K. Borch and J. Mossin, London: Macmillan.
Machina, M. 1981. 'Rational' decision making vs. 'rational' decision modelling? *Journal of Mathematical Psychology* 24.
Machina, M. 1982. 'Expected utility' analysis without the independence axiom. *Econometrica* 50(2), March, 277–323.
McClennen, E.F. 1983. Sure-thing doubts. In Stigum and Wenstop (1983).
McClennen, E.F. 1985. Prisoner's dilemma and resolute choice. In Campbell and Sowden (1985).
McPherson, M.S. 1982. Mill's moral theory and the problem of preference change. *Ethics* 92(2), 252–73.
Margolis, H. 1982. *Selfishness, Altruism and Rationality.* Cambridge: Cambridge University Press.
Marschak, J. 1946. Von Neumann's and Morgenstern's new approach to static economics. *Journal of Political Economy* 54, April, 91–115.
Matthews, R.C.O. 1984. Darwinism and economic change. *Oxford Economic Papers* 36, Supplement, November, 91–117.
Maynard Smith, J. 1982. *Evolution and the Theory of Games.* Cambridge: Cambridge University Press.
Morishima, M. 1982. *Why Has Japan 'Succeeded'? Western Technology and Japanese Ethos.* Cambridge: Cambridge University Press.
Muth, J.F. 1961. Rational expectations and the theory of price movements. *Econometrica* 29, July, 315–35.
Nagel, T. 1970. *The Possibility of Altruism.* Oxford: Clarendon Press.
Nozick, R. 1969. Newcomb's problem and two principles of choice. In *Essays in Honor of Carl G. Hempel*, ed. N. Rescher, Dordrecht: Reidel.
Parfit, D. 1984. *Reasons and Persons.* Oxford: Clarendon Press.
Radner, R. 1980. Collusive behaviour in non-cooperative epsilon-equilibria of oligopolies with long but finite lives. *Journal of Economic Theory* 22(2), April, 136–54.
Ramsey, F.P. 1931. Truth and probability. In F.P. Ramsey, *The Foundations of Mathematics and other Logical Essays*, London: Kegan Paul.
Richter, M.K. 1971. Rational choice. In Chipman, Hurwicz, Richter and Sonnenschein (1971).
Samuelson, P.A. 1938. A note on the pure theory of consumers' behaviour. *Economica* 5, February, 61–71.
Savage, L.J. 1954. *The Foundations of Statistics.* New York: Wiley.
Schelling, T.C. 1978. *Micromotives and Macrobehavior.* New York: Norton.

Schelling, T.C. 1984. Self-command in practice, in policy, and in a theory of rational choice. *American Economic Review, Papers and Proceedings* 74(2), May, 1–11.
Schick, F. 1984. *Having Reasons: An Essay on Rationality and Sociality*. Princeton: Princeton University Press.
Scitovsky, T. 1976. *The Joyless Economy*. London: Oxford University Press.
Sen, A.K. 1971. Choice functions and revealed preference. *Review of Economic Studies* 38, July, 307–17.
Sen, A.K. 1973. Behaviour and the concept of preference. *Economica* 40, August, 241–59. Reprinted in Sen (1982).
Sen, A.K. 1974. Choice, orderings and morality. In *Practical Reason*, ed. S. Körner, Oxford: Blackwell. Reprinted in Sen (1982).
Sen, A.K. 1977. Rational fools: a critique of the behavioural foundations of economic theory. *Philosophy and Public Affairs* 6, Summer, 317–44. Reprinted in Sen (1982).
Sen, A.K. 1982. *Choice, Welfare and Measurement*. Oxford: Blackwell; Cambridge, Mass.: MIT Press.
Sen, A.K. 1985a. Rationality and uncertainty. *Theory and Decision* 18. Also in Daboni, Montesano and Lines (1985).
Sen, A.K. 1985b. Goals, commitment and identity. *Journal of Law, Economics and Organization* 1.
Sen, A.K. 1987. *On Ethics and Economics*. Oxford: Blackwell.
Shackle, G.L.S. 1938. *Expectations, Investment and Income*. Cambridge: Cambridge University Press.
Shackle, G.L.S. 1952. *Expectations in Economics*. 2nd edn, Cambridge: Cambridge University Press.
Simon, H.A. 1957. *Models of Man*. New York: Wiley.
Simon, H.A. 1979. *Models of Thought*. New Haven: Yale University Press.
Simon, H.A. 1983. *Reason in Human Affairs*. Oxford: Blackwell.
Smale, S. 1980. The Prisoner's Dilemma and dynamic systems associated to non-cooperative games. *Econometrica* 48(7), November, 1617–34.
Smith, A. 1776. *An Inquiry into the Nature and Causes of the Wealth of Nations*. Ed. by R.H. Campbell and A.S. Skinner, Oxford: Clarendon Press, 1976.
Smith, A. 1790. *The Theory of Moral Sentiments*. Ed. by D.D. Raphael and A.L. Macfie, Oxford: Clarendon Press, 1974.
Stigum, B.P. and Wenstop, F. (eds) *Foundations of Utility and Risk Theory with Applications*. Dordrecht: Reidel.
Sugden, R. 1985. Why be consistent? A critical analysis of consistency requirements in choice theory. *Economica* 52, May, 167–83.
Suppes, P. 1984. *Probabilistic Metaphysics*. Oxford: Blackwell.
Suzumura, K. 1983. *Rational Choice, Collective Decisions and Social Welfare*. Cambridge: Cambridge University Press.
Tversky, A. 1975. A critique of expected utility theory: descriptive and normative considerations. *Erkenntnis* 9, 163–73.
Uzawa, H. 1956. A note on preference and axioms of choice. *Annals of the Institute of Statistical Mathematics* 8(1), 35–40.
Von Neumann, J. and Morgenstern, O. 1947. *Theory of Games and Economic Behavior*. Princeton: Princeton University Press.
Watkins, J. 1974. Comment: self-interest and morality. In *Practical Reason*, ed. S. Körner, Oxford: Blackwell.
Watkins, J. 1985. Second thoughts on self-interest and mortality. In Campbell and Sowden (1985).
Winch, D. 1978. *Adam Smith's Politics*. Cambridge: Cambridge University Press.
Wong, S. 1978. *Foundations of Paul Samuelson's Revealed Preference Theory*. London: Routledge.

rational expectations. 'Rational Expectations' is an equilibrium concept that can be applied to dynamic economic models that have elements of 'self reference', that is, models in which the endogenous variables are influenced by the expectations about future values of those variables held by the agents in the model. The concept was introduced and applied by John F. Muth (1960, 1961) in two articles that interpreted some econometric distributed lag models. Muth used explicitly stochastic dynamic models, and brought to bear an extensive knowledge of classical linear prediction theory to interpret distributed lags in terms of economic parameters. For Muth, an econometric model with rational expectations possesses the defining property that the forecasts made by agents within the model are no worse than the forecasts that can be made by the economist who has the model. Muth's first concrete application of rational expectations was to find restrictions on a stochastic process for income that would render Milton Friedman's (1957) geometric distributed lag formula for permanent income an optimal predictor for income. Muth showed that if the first difference of income is a first order moving average process, then Friedman's formula is optimal for forecasting income over *any* horizon. The independence of this formula from the horizon makes precise the sense in which Friedman's formula extracts from past income an estimator of 'permanent' income. In working backwards from Friedman's formula to a process for income in this way, Muth touched Lucas's Critique (1976). Given *any* distributed lag for forecasting income, one can work backwards as Muth did and discover a stochastic process for income that makes that distributed lag an optimal predictor for income over some horizon. Solving a few such problems in the fashion of Muth quickly reveals the dependence of a distributed lag associated with forecasting the future on the form of the stochastic process that is being forecast. In 1963 Peter Whittle published a book that conveniently summarized and made more accessible to economists the classical linear prediction theory that Muth had used. That book reports and repeatedly applies the Wiener–Kolmogorov formula for the optimal j-step ahead predictor of a covariance stationary stochastic process x_t with moving average representation $x_t = c(L)\ \epsilon_t$. The Wiener–Kolmogorov formula displays the dependence of the optimal distributed lag for predicting future x on the form of $c(L)$. That dependence underlies Lucas's critique of econometric policy evaluation procedures that were common when Lucas composed his critique in 1973. Those procedures had assumed that distributed lags in behavioural relations would remain invariant with respect to alterations in government policy rules, alterations which took the form of changes in $c(L)$ for government policy instruments. Although the formulas in Whittle's book were used extensively by Nerlove (1967) to work out additional examples along the lines of Muth's, it was not until the writing of Lucas's Critique in 1973 and its publication in 1976 that the implications for econometric practice of Muth's ideas and the prediction formulas in Whittle began to be widely appreciated.

Lucas and Prescott (1971) did much to clarify the nature of rational expectations as an equilibrium concept, and also pointed the way to connecting the theory with observations. Lucas and Prescott described the partial equilibrium of an industry in which there exists a fixed number of identical firms, each subject to costs of adjustment for a single factor of production, capital. The industry faces a downward sloping demand curve for its output, which moves about randomly due to a demand shock that follows a Markov process. The representative firm maximizes the expected present value of its profits by choosing a contingency plan or strategy for its investment. In order that the firm's optimum problem be completely stated, it is necessary to describe what the firm believes about the laws of motion of variables that influence the firm's future returns even though they are beyond the firm's control. The price of output is such an uncontrollable variable, but the demand curve for output and the hypothesis of market clearing make price a function of the capital stock in the industry as a whole. To state the firm's decision problem requires, by way of completely describing the 'constraints' subject to which maximization occurs, that the firm's view about the law of motion of the aggregate capital stock be stated. The representative firm's optimum problem can then be solved, yielding a law of motion for the capital stock of the representative firm. Multiplying this law of motion by the number of firms then gives the actual law of motion for capital in the industry. In this way, the firm's optimization problem and the hypothesis of market clearing induce a mapping from a perceived law of motion to the actual law of motion for the industry's capital stock. A rational expectations equilibrium is a perceived law of motion that equals the actual law of motion for capital. That is, a rational expectations equilibrium is a fixed point of the mapping from a perceived law of motion to an actual law of motion for capital. Lucas and Prescott described conditions under which a unique fixed point exists. The equilibrium law of motion for capital induces a stochastic process for capital that assumes the form of a Markov process. Lucas and Prescott showed that this Markov process has the property that for any initial capital stock, capital converges in distribution to a unique invariant distribution. This assures satisfaction of some conditions that justify the asymptotic distribution theory underlying time series econometrics, in particular, the availability of some mean ergodic theorems that guarantee that sample moments converge to the corresponding population moments. Lucas and Prescott's model took a big step toward integrating theory and econometrics by generating an explicit mapping from *economic* parameters describing preferences, technology, and exogenous shocks to the population moments of observable sequences of economic time series. Roughly speaking, the task of econometrics under rational expectations is to 'invert' this mapping in order to make inferences about economic parameters on the basis of time series data.

Hansen and Sargent (1980) used linear versions of Lucas–Prescott models as a vehicle for working out econometric techniques for estimating rational expectations models. They describe how the statistical properties (e.g. consistency and asymptotic efficiency) desired for estimators of the model's economic parameters, parameters describing preferences, technology and shock processes, induce a metric for measuring distance between the sample moments from the time series data at hand and the population moments implied by the equilibrium of the model at given parameter values. Typical metrics are ones associated with the generalized method of moments and one associated with the normal likelihood function. Parameter estimates are obtained by minimizing the metric with respect to the parameter values, a nonlinear minimization problem. Econometric identification of parameters means uniqueness of the minimizer of distance between the theory and the observations. Identification is partially achieved by the rich set of cross-equation restrictions that the hypothesis of rational expectations imposes (the *same* parameters appear in many equations, in highly nonlinear ways). These cross-equation restrictions achieve identification differently than did the Cowles Commission's 'rank and order' conditions, which explicitly excluded cross-equation restrictions. There is a pervasive subversion of 'exclusion restrictions' in rational expectations models, and thus a breakdown of the neat division between 'supply' and 'demand' curves which underlay the 'exclusion' approach to identification.

Minimum distance estimation requires recomputing the equilibrium for each set of parameter values used during the descent along the metric. Except for linear models, Bellman's 'curse of dimensionality' makes it difficult to compute an equilibrium, so development of improved computational methods is currently an important research area. Sims (1985) and Novales (1984) suggested a promising method for solving rational expectations 'backwards'. Methods for computing equilibria are required not only for parameter estimation, but also for quantitatively evaluating the effects of proposed interventions, e.g., new policies for setting government instruments. A new government policy implies, via the cross-equation restrictions, new laws of motion for all of the endogenous variables in the models. It is no coincidence that full information estimation methods require calculations that are closely connected with those needed to evaluate policy. Hansen and Singleton (1982) suggested a short cut method capable of estimating the parameters of one preference or technology function by itself, without computing a full equilibrium. They pointed out that their method requires special restrictions on the stochastic process of disturbances to the function being estimated, and that their method does not estimate enough parameters to permit evaluating many kinds of interventions.

Lucas and Prescott's model can be used to study aspects of the theory of policy. Their model generates a stochastic process for output, price, and industry capital that exhibits recurrent but aperiodic 'cycles', as realizations of stochastic difference equations do. Thus Lucas and Prescott's model is an alternative to the 'cobweb' mechanism for generating fluctuations in commodity markets. Two-industry versions of the model can readily be constructed to model 'corn-hog' cycles. Models along the lines of Lucas and Prescott's reveal a different perspective on these cycles than do cobweb models. Lucas and Prescott show that, despite cyclical fluctuations, the equilibrium of their model is optimal in the sense that it maximizes the expected present value of consumer surplus net of producer surplus. Therefore, unlike cobweb models, in which cycles partly reflect erroneous and readily improved upon perceptions of private agents, matters cannot be improved by government interventions designed to smooth out the cycles. Government interventions, say in the form of taxes or subsidies, *matter* in the Lucas–Prescott model, but to evaluate their effects requires recomputing the equilibrium under alternative government policies. In order to rationalize a government intervention, Lucas and Prescott's model could be modified in either of two ways. One way would be to alter the specification of technology by adding a dynamic externality of the kind studied in a related context by Paul Romer (1983). Under such a specification, although the competitive rational expectations equilibrium without taxes is not optimal, there exists a strategy for administering distorting taxes that produces an optimal equilibrium. To compute the optimal government strategy requires knowledge of the parameters of technology and preferences that can be estimated via rational expectations econometrics. Another way to provide a role for the government would be simply to assume that as part of a plan for financing a stream of government expenditures the industry is assigned a particular present value of taxes that must be raised from it via distorting taxes.

For purposes of studying a variety of macroeconomic questions, researchers have used what can be interpreted as a version of Lucas and Prescott's model, suitably modified and reinterpreted to apply to an aggregative economy. Brock and Mirman (1972) analysed a centralized version of such an economy, which took the form of a stochastic version of a one-sector optimal growth model. The planner in their model seeks to maximize the expected discounted value of utility of consumption subject to a technology for transforming consumption over time via investment in physical capital. Brock and Mirman gave conditions under which the optimal plan for capital and consumption induces a stochastic process that converges in distribution, so that like Lucas and Prescott's model, theirs is prepared for rigorous treatment econometrically. It is possible to decentralize Brock and Mirman's model into an equivalent economy consisting of competitive firms and households who interact in markets for labour and capital and who have rational expectations about the evolution of the wages and interest rates that they face. Decentralized versions of Brock–Mirman models have been used to construct equilibrium theories of stock prices and interest rates, typically by computing particular shadow prices associated with the planning problem (Lucas, 1978; Brock, 1982). Decentralized versions of Brock and Mirman's model form the backbone of the modern version of 'real business cycle theory', which was initiated by Kydland and Prescott (1982). Since the stochastic optimal growth model has a stochastic difference equation for capital as its equilibrium, it shares with Lucas and Prescott's model the property that it readily generates realizations for capital, output and consumption that display recurrent but aperiodic fluctuations of the kind observed in aggregate time series data. Kydland and Prescott embarked on the task of taking seriously the possibility that the preferences and technology of a small stochastic optimal growth model could be specified so that it would approximate closely the moments of a list of important aggregate economic time series for the US, Kydland and Prescott have constructed several such models, each driven by a single unobserved shock, which they interpret as a disturbance to technology. This research strategy is charged with meaning, since it undertakes to explain aggregate time series data with a model whose equilibrium is optimal, and in which there is no government. The government is neither a contributing source to economic fluctuations nor a potential modifier of those fluctuations. Real business cycle models of this kind are capable of determining a long list of real variables, while remaining silent about all nominal variables.

A nontrivial role for government can be injected into such models by resorting either to a dynamic externality in the fashion of Romer (1983), or adding a public good or stream of government expenditures that must be financed via a tax that is distorting. A dynamic optimal taxation problem is typically posed by having the government behave as a dominant player in a dynamic game with a private sector that behaves competitively. In selecting an optimal tax strategy, the government takes into account the way in which private agents' decisions at time t depend on the government's strategy for setting taxes for all periods $s \geqslant t$. The government is supposed to maximize the expected discounted utility of a representative agent, taking as a constraint the mapping from the stochastic processes for tax rates to the equilibrium stochastic process for the economy. In some simple models in which there is no physical or human capital, Barro (1979) and Lucas and Stokey (1983) found that the solution of an optimal taxation problem had the characteristic of 'tax-smoothing', it being optimal to make taxes nearly a martingale even in the face of a highly unsmooth (erratic or cyclical) path for government purchases. In models with private capital, tax smoothing does not characterize the optimal solution. Instead, the optimal tax plan typically involves high taxes on existing capital, together with lower tax rates in the future. In models with physical capital, the government's optimal tax plan is time inconsistent. The source of the time inconsistency is that in future periods the government seems free to ignore, and is tempted to ignore, those constraints on the original problem that represented the effects of then future tax rates on initial rates of private investment. There are open problems on how to compute the solutions of dominant player games. There also remains disagreement about what to make of the time inconsistency of the solution of dominant player dynamic games. One line is to search for an alternative decentralization scheme that makes the time inconsistent solution 'self-enforcing'. Another line is to interpret time inconsistency of a solution as an indication that the wrong 'game' or mechanism is being used for analysing the environment under study.

Some version of a dominant player game with the government as dominant player frequently motivates building a rational expectations model. Models have been used for two strikingly different purposes. One is as a vehicle for giving the government advice for improving its strategy relative to the one used historically. Here the idea is that a new and different game from the one that has been played is to be recommended for the future, namely, the solution of the dominant player game under study. Another use is as positive models of historical government behaviour. Thus, Barro used his tax smoothing model as a device for understanding historical movements in taxes and government deficits, not as a source of recommendations for new policies. There is a logical difficulty in using a rational expectations model to give advice, stemming from the self-referential aspect of the model that threatens to absorb the economic advisor into the model. For suppose that the economist's advice is persuasive in the sense that it alters the probabilities attached to future government actions. Then the economist was not really using a rational expectations equilibrium to interpret the historical observations, having attributed to agents expectations about government policy that did not properly take into account his advice. This conundrum was discussed by Sargent and Wallace (1976) and Sargent (1984), and forms the basis for Sims's (1982) challenge to rational expectations econometrics. In dynamic rational expectations models, there are important ways in which the future influences the present, with an equilibrium simultaneously determining current outcomes and probability distributions of future events. That simultaneity is the source of the logical difficulties in using rational expectations models to give advice about government policy. To give advice in the form of an altered law of motion for government policy variables for an economy operating in real time seems to require some backing off from a full rational expectations equilibrium, usually in the subtle form of interpreting the historical data by assuming a (suboptimal) law of motion for government policy instruments which the economist will recommend be changed on the basis of his analysis.

The logical difficulty with using rational expectations models to give advice is of little practical concern in the context of a model whose equilibrium without government action is optimal, for example, the Kydland–Prescott model. But much work in rational expectations macroeconomics is directed at understanding situations in which government interventions have a role in altering or improving equilibrium outcomes. Especially in monetary economics, economies have been studied in which the grounds for government intervention go beyond those of public goods and distorting taxes discussed above. There is a large body of work constructing rational expectations models of economies with valued fiat currency. In their specification of technologies and preferences, these models all deviate in important ways from models in the style of Brock and Mirman. To model fiat currency requires leaving the Brock–Mirman model, which has no room for valued fiat currency because the economy functions well enough without it. A variety of models have been constructed which use spatial and/or temporal separation and heterogeneity of agents in order to create economic environments in which fiat currency is valued because it facilitates exchanges that cannot occur in its absence. Leading examples are the overlapping generations model of Samuelson (1958) and the 'turnpike' model of Townsend (1980). These economies typically have equilibria both with and without valued fiat currency, equilibria associated with different consumption allocations. Wallace (1981a, 1983) has used the overlapping generations model for analyzing a variety of legal regulations on financial intermediation, and for exploring equivalence classes of government policies that preserve allocations. That work attributes much importance to financial regulations in affecting allocations, and emphasizes the 'fiscal' and redistributional components to policies that have often been characterized as purely 'monetary'.

There often occur multiple equilibria in models with valued fiat currency. Wallace (1981b) has described a very weak fiscal intervention that eliminates suboptimal equilibria in an overlapping generations model. Wallace's scheme still permits there to exist multiple 'high interest rate' equilibria, all of which are optimal. Grandmont has studied models in which there is a very large number of such high interest rate equilibria, with different allocations, all of them optimal, having quite distinct distributions of wealth and welfare across and within generations. Grandmont (1985) has constructed deterministic versions of overlapping generations models that have multiple equilibria, many of them 'chaotic'. The private agents in the equilibria described by Grandmont have 'perfect foresight', experiencing no uncertainty about future price levels over any horizon. However, an econometrician who lacks exact prior information on the structure of the economy, and who observes a realization of a time series for the price level, plausibly concludes that the price level is a random process. The private agents in this model typically forecast far better than can the economist studying them. This situation reverses the asymmetry in forecasting abilities of the economist and the private agents which Muth challenged in the beginning.

THOMAS J. SARGENT

See also BUSINESS CYCLES; INFLATIONARY EXPECTATIONS; NEW 'CLASSICAL' MACROECONOMICS.

BIBLIOGRAPHY

Barro, R.J. 1979. On the determination of the public debt. *Journal of Political Economy* 87(5), October, 940–71.

Brock, W.A. 1982. Asset prices in a production economy. In *Economics of Information and Uncertainty*, ed. J.J. McCall, Chicago: University of Chicago Press, 1–43.

Brock, W.A. and Mirman, L. 1972. Optimal economic growth under uncertainty: the discounted case. *Journal of Economic Theory* 4(3), June, 479–513.

Friedman, M. 1957. *A Theory of the Consumption Function.* Princeton: Princeton University Press.

Grandmont, J.M. 1985. On endogenous competitive business cycles. *Econometrica* 53(5), 995–1045.

Hansen, L.P. and Sargent, T.J. 1980. Formulating and estimating dynamic linear rational expectations models. *Journal of Economic Dynamics and Control* 2(1), 7–46.

Hansen, L.P. and Singleton, K.J. 1982. Generalized instrumental variables estimation of nonlinear rational expectations models. *Econometrica* 50(5), September, 1269–86.

Kydland, F.E. and Prescott, E.C. 1982. Time to build and aggregate fluctuations. *Econometrica* 50(6), 1345–70.

Lucas, R.E., Jr. 1976. Econometric policy evaluation: a critique. In *The Phillips Curve and the Labor Market*, ed. K. Brunner and A. Meltzer, Vol. 1 of Carnegie-Rochester Conference on Public Policy, a supplementary series to the *Journal of Monetary Economics*, Amsterdam: North-Holland.

Lucas, R.E., Jr. 1978. Asset prices in an exchange economy. *Econometrica* 46(6), 1429–45.

Lucas, R.E., Jr. and Prescott, E.C. 1971. Investment under uncertainty. *Econometrica* 39(5), 659–81.

Lucas, R.E., Jr. and Stokey, N. 1983. Optimal fiscal and monetary policy in an economy without capital. *Journal of Monetary Economics* 12(1), July, 55–93.

Muth, J.F. 1960. Optimal properties of exponentially weighted forecasts. *Journal of The American Statistical Association* 55(290), 299–306.

Muth, J.F. 1961. Rational expectations and the theory of price movements. *Econometrica* 29(3), 315–35.

Nerlove, M. 1967. Distributed lags and unobserved components in economic time series. In W. Fellner et. al., *Ten Economic Studies in the Tradition of Irving Fisher*, New York: Wiley.

Novales, A. 1984. A stochastic monetary equilibrium model of the interest rate. Discussion paper, State University of New York at Stony Brook.

Romer, P.M. 1983. Externalities and increasing returns in dynamic competitive analysis. Working paper No. 8319, Department of Economics, University of Rochester.

Samuelson, P.A. 1958. An exact consumption-loan model of interest with or without the social contrivance of money. *Journal of Political Economy* 66(6), 467–82.

Sargent, T.J. 1984. Autoregressions, expectations, and advice. *American Economic Review* 74(2), May, 408–15.

Sargent, T.J. and Wallace, N. 1976. Rational expectations and the theory of economic policy. *Journal of Monetary Economics* 2(2), 169–83.

Sims, C.A. 1972. Money, income, and causality. *The American Economic Review* 62(4), 5–4052.

Sims, C.A. 1982. Policy analysis with econometric models. *Brookings Papers on Economic Activity* No. 1, 107–52.

Sims, C.A. 1985. Solving nonlinear stochastic equilibrium models backwards. Manuscript, University of Minnesota, Economic Research Center.

Townsend, R.M. 1980. Models of money with spatially separated agents. In *Models of Monetary Economics*, ed. J.H. Kareken and N. Wallace, Minneapolis: Federal Reserve Bank of Minneapolis, 265–305.

Wallace, N. 1981a. A Modigliani–Miller theorem for open market operations. *American Economic Review* 71(3), 267–74.

Wallace, N. 1981b. A hybrid fiat-commodity monetary system. *Journal of Economic Theory* 25(3), 421–30.

Wallace, N. 1983. A legal restrictions theory of the demand for 'money' and the role of monetary policy. *Federal Reserve Bank of Minneapolis Quarterly Review* 7(1), 1–7.

Whittle, P. 1983. *Prediction and Regulation by Linear Least-Square Methods*. 2nd edn revised, Minneapolis: University of Minnesota Press.

rational expectations: econometric implications. It has long been recognized that forecasts affect outcomes. Similarly, outcomes affect expectations. Thus, there is a mapping from expectations to outcomes and back to expectations and so from expectations to expectations. A rational expectations equilibrium is a fixed point of this mapping in which expectations generate outcomes which confirm the original expectations. A rational expectations equilibrium is a natural solution concept in a model with expectations. The heuristic reasoning is that outside rational expectations equilibria agents make systematic mistakes; expectations are not confirmed by outcomes in that the expectations are not correct on the average. Consequently, it is very plausible that outside rational expectations equilibria agents will eventually notice that they are making systematic mistakes and attempt to revise the way they forecast in order to eliminate the sources of the systematic errors. This suggests that agents are not in equilibrium until they have learned to form rational expectations.

Econometric analysis typically assumes that the econometrician is an outside observer: nothing which the econometrician does affects the data generation process. In particular, it is assumed that the forecasts based on the econometrician's estimated model do not influence the forecasts of the agents in the economy. By contrast, the agents in the economy are inside econometricians. If the agents' forecasts are derived from an estimated econometric model, then the data generation process changes when the agents update the parameter estimates or change the model specification. A single atomistic agent can act like the outside econometrician, but this is not so for agents as a whole. The collective impact of the forecasting activity of the agents is to change the data generation process; this is the essence of forecast feedback.

This entry concentrates on three topics which involve the econometric implications of rational expectations: solutions, estimation and learning. The issues surrounding the solutions are discussed in section 1 in the context of a second order linear expectational difference equation. Section 2 considers maximum likelihood and general method of moment estimators which can be used by an outside econometrician to estimate the parameters of a rational expectations model. The question of whether agents – inside econometricians – can learn to form rational expectations is addressed in section 3. The concluding comments are in section 4.

1. SOLUTIONS

A prototype for many rational expectations models is the second order expectational difference equation

$$E_t y_{t+1} - (\rho_1 + \rho_2) y_t + \rho_1 \rho_2 y_{t-1} = x_t \tag{1}$$

where t indexes the integers, $\{x_t\}$ and $\{y_t\}$ are scalar stochastic processes and where for expositional purposes ρ_1 and ρ_2 are assumed to be real numbers. The variable x is called the 'driving process' and '$E_t y_{t+1}$' is the forecast of y based on the information available at time t. The reduced form of the model is the solution of the equation which expresses y as a function of current and past values of x_t, which is the information available at time t. Second order expectational difference equations arise as necessary conditions for optima in linear-quadratic versions of costly adjustment models and in this context are called Euler equations. Examples can be found in Kennan (1979), Sargent (1979), Hansen and Sargent (1980), Eichenbaum (1983) and Hansen and Singleton (1982).

There is a long list of methods for finding solutions to linear expectational difference equations. These include 'state-space' techniques in Lucas (1972), 'methods of undetermined coefficients' in Muth (1961) and Aoki and Canzoneri (1979), 'forward and backward' solutions in Blanchard (1979) and Blanchard and Kahn (1980) and a 'method of undetermined coefficients in the frequency domain' in Saracoglu and Sargent (1978), Futia (1981) and Whiteman (1983).

The solutions presented below are those obtained by the approach of Whiteman (1983). This method is analytically straightforward and has the virtue that it finds all the solutions within a certain set. Whiteman assumes that the driving process is covariance stationary and looks for solutions with the same general structure as the driving process, that is, for solutions in the same 'space' as the driving process. The motivation for this approach is twofold. The first is that without any restrictions on the $\{x_t\}$ and without any side conditions there is a plethora of solutions. The second is that stationarity is assumed in the estimation theory for expectational difference equations.

The Whiteman solution technique employs four assumptions. First, x_t has a known Wold decomposition

$$x_t = \sum_{j=0}^{\infty} A_j \epsilon_{t-j} \tag{2}$$

with $\epsilon_t = x_t - E(x_t | x_{t-1}, x_{t-2}, \ldots)$, $\Sigma_{j=0}^{\infty} A_j^2 < \infty$ and the function $A(z) = \Sigma_{j=0}^{\infty} A_j z^j$ must be analytic on the open unit disk. Thus (2) can be written as

$$x_t = \sum_{j=0}^{\infty} A_j L^j \epsilon_t = A(L)\epsilon_t \tag{2'}$$

where L is the lag operator: $L^n = x_{t-n}$. Second, the solutions are in the space of the driving process (2) and are of the form

$$y_t = \sum_{j=0}^{\infty} C_j \epsilon_{t-j} = C(L)\epsilon_t. \tag{3}$$

Third, the forecasting procedure is rational and the forecasts are computed using the Wiener–Kolmogorov formula

$$\begin{aligned} E_t y_{t+1} &= E_t[C_0\epsilon_{t+1} + C_1\epsilon_t + C_2\epsilon_{t-1} + \cdots] \\ &= C_1\epsilon_t + C_2\epsilon_{t-1} + \cdots \\ &= [C(L) - C_0]L^{-1}\epsilon_t \end{aligned} \tag{4}$$

since $E_t\epsilon_{t+1} = 0$. Note that the forecast is computed using a solution to the model and hence is model consistent. Fourth, the rational expectations restrictions hold for all realizations of the driving process. Using (2), (3) and (4) equation (1) can be written as

$$[C(L) - C_0]L^{-1}\epsilon_t - (\rho_1 + \rho_2)C(L)\epsilon_t + \rho_1\rho_2 C(L)L\epsilon_t = A(L)\epsilon_t \tag{5}$$

where it is assumed that (5) holds for all realizations of $\{\epsilon_t\}$. The solutions are obtained by exploiting the property that the z transforms of the sequences represented in (5) must be identical as analytic functions on the open unit disk.

The solutions are now presented for the three cases corresponding to three different sets of values for the parameters ρ_1 and ρ_2. First suppose $|\rho_1| < 1, |\rho_2| < 1$. The Wold representation for the solutions $\{y_t\}$ is

$$y_t = \{(1 - \rho_1 L)(1 - \rho_2 L\}^{-1}\{A(L)L + C_0\}\epsilon_t \tag{6}$$

which can be written as

$$y_t = \{(1 - \rho_1 L)(1 - \rho_2 L)\}^{-1}\{L - C_0 A(L)^{-1}\}x_t \tag{6'}$$

provided that $\{x_t\}$ has an autoregressive representation. In this case the expectational difference equation (1) does not uniquely determine the solution $\{y_t\}$. For any finite value of C_0 (6) gives a process lying in the space of the driving process which satisfies equation (1). Since C_0 is a parameter in the forecasting formula the model does not completely determine the forecasting procedure of the agents.

The second case is $|\rho_1| < 1 < |\rho_2|$. In this case (1) and (2) determine a unique solution for y_t:

$$y_t = \{(1 - \rho_1 L)(1 - \rho_2 L)\}^{-1}\{(L - \rho_2^{-1}A(\rho_2^{-1})A(L)^{-1}\}x_t. \tag{7}$$

This case applies when (1) is interpreted as the Euler equation in a linear-quadratic costly adjustment model; see Kennan (1979).

The third case is where $1 < |\rho_1|, 1 < |\rho_2|$. In this case there is no solution lying in the space of the driving process.

There are several econometric implications of the solutions. First, the parameters of (6) and (7) depend on the parameters of both the driving process and the expectational difference equation. Thus, there are cross-equation restrictions between the parameters of the reduced form and the driving process.

Sargent (1981) has called the cross-equation restrictions the 'hallmark of rational expectations'. If x is a policy variable and if a change in policy is described by a change in the parameters of the x process, then a policy change induces a change in the values of the reduced form parameters. The consequence is that if the reduced form parameters are estimated from data generated by the existing policy regime, the resulting estimates may produce a misleading forecast of what will happen under a different policy regime. This point is spelled out in Lucas's (1976) critique of econometric policy evaluation. The connection between the notion of exogeneity and the Lucas critique is discussed by Engle, Hendry and Richard (1983). See also Sims (1982).

The second point is that when $|\rho_1| < 1$ and $|\rho_2| < 1$ there may be many stationary solutions in the space of the driving process. The nature and implication of the multiple solutions has been discussed by Gourieroux, Laffont and Monfort (1982), Broze, Gourieroux and Szafarz (1985) and Evans and Honkapohja (1986). A number of criteria have been proposed for eliminating some of the solutions. Examples include Taylor's (1977) 'minimum variance' criterion, which chooses the solution with the smallest variance, McCallum's (1983) 'minimum state variable' criterion, which chooses the solution which depends on the fewest other variables and Evans's (1985) 'expectational stability' criterion, which chooses solutions that are stable given a small deviation of the expectations functions from rational expectations equilibrium.

The search for selection criteria in linear rational expectations models has a resemblance to a parallel activity in game theory. Games of complete as well as incomplete information can have multiple equilibria. Several selection criteria – 'refinements' to the concept of Nash equilibrium – have been developed for the purpose of eliminating some of these equilibria. These criteria, or refinements, include Selten's (1965) 'subgame perfection', Selten's (1975) 'trembling hand perfection' and the Kohlberg and Mertens (1986) 'stability' criterion. It is difficult to find appealing arguments for eliminating solutions for linear rational expectations models when the expectational difference equation is not the first order condition to a well posed optimization problem.

Third, in the case of the unique solution (7) it is the relation between the C_j's and not the absolute size of these coefficients that is determined. This can be seen from the renormalization $C^* = C_0^{-1}C_j$ and $v_t^* = C_0^{-1}\epsilon_t$. The same rescaling procedure can be applied to the representation for x_t.

Fourth, the second order case is the simplest case where all three possibilities exist: many, one and no solutions in the space of a stationary driving process. The case of no solutions is of special interest since in empirical studies the estimation procedures assume that a stationary solution exists.

Fifth, there are solutions lying outside the space of the driving process, some of which are nonstationary. Nonstationary solutions exist whether or not the driving process is stationary.

2. ESTIMATION

The problem considered here is the estimation of a rational expectations model by an outside econometrician. Hansen (1982) has shown that under certain assumptions there are strongly consistent estimators for the parameters of linear and nonlinear rational expectations models. A key assumption is that the driving process and the solution are stationary and ergodic. This assumption again highlights the importance of the driving process.

A stationary and ergodic driving process $\{x_t\}$ is illustrated by the first order autoregressive process:

$$x_t = ax_{t-1} + \epsilon_t, \qquad |a| < 1, \tag{8}$$

where $\{\epsilon_t\}$ is independently identically normally distributed. The moving average representation of the $\{x_t\}$ process (8) is

$$x_t = (1 - aL)^{-1}\epsilon_t = A(L)\epsilon_t. \tag{8'}$$

If $\{y_t\}$ is in the space of the driving process, then it is also stationary and ergodic.

For empirical work the assumption of stationarity and ergodicity is a demanding one, especially for times series as opposed to cross-sectional series. Nelson and Plosser (1982) have provided evidence that a number of macroeconomic variables such as GNP and the money supply behave very similar to random walks or integrated processes rather than stationary processes about a trend. In practice the driving variables are often detrended. The detrending of a random walk produces a number of spurious effects. For example, Nelson and Kang (1981, 1983) have shown that regressing a trend-free random walk against a time trend will result in the misleading inference that the trend is significant and that the detrended series is serially correlated. Some examples of the empirical implications of trends versus random walks for rational expectations models are discussed in Deaton (1986). The general asymptotic theory for testing the random walk versus the time trend model has been recently developed by Durlauf and Phillips (1986). They examine analytically the effects of spuriously detrending random walks.

The fact that the driving process is stationary does not imply that the solution is stationary since the solution may not be in the space of the driving process. Hence there is the additional problem of testing whether the solution is stationary.

Turning to estimation, the objective is to estimate the parameters of the structural equation rather than the parameters of the driving process. The parameters of the expectational difference equation (1) are often interpreted as the coefficients of the utility function or production function of a representative agent or firm and hence it is these parameters which are of economic interest.

There are two approaches to the estimation of the structural parameters. One is to estimate the structural parameters via the reduced form. The estimates produced by the reduced form approach depend on the specification of the driving process and on which solution is selected. Suppose the driving process is the first order autoregression (8) and the parameters of equation (1) are estimated from the non-unique solution (6). Substituting $(1 - aL)^{-1}$ for $A(L)$ in (6) gives

$$y_t = \{(1 - \rho_1 L)(1 - \rho_2 L)\}^{-1}\{L + C_0(1 - aL)\}x_t, \tag{9}$$

which can be rearranged as

$$y_t = (\rho_1 + \rho_2)y_{t-1} - \rho_1\rho_2 y_{t-2} + C_0 x_t + (1 - C_0 a)x_{t-1}. \tag{9'}$$

Since (9′) is an exact relation the coefficients of (9′) can be calculated exactly from four sample points of the form $(y_{t'}, y_{t'-1}, y_{t'-2}, x_{t'}, x_{t'-1})$. Given the prior information $|\rho_1| < 1$ and $|\rho_2| < 1$ only the sum and the product of ρ_1 and ρ_2 can be identified from the data.

Assume next that $|\rho_1| < 1 < |\rho_2|$. Then substituting $(1 - aL)^{-1}$ for $A(L)$ in the unique solution (7) yields

$$y_t - \{(a - \rho_2)(1 - \rho_1 L)\}^{-1}x_t, \tag{10}$$

which can be rewritten as

$$y_t - \rho_1 y_{t-1} = (a - \rho_2)^{-1}x_t. \tag{10'}$$

The parameter a can be consistently estimated by applying least squares to (8). In this case (10) and (10′) are also exact relations so that the coefficients of y_{t-1} and x_t can be determined exactly from the two sample points (y_t, y_{t-1}, x_t) and (y_{t+1}, y_t, x_{t+1}). Given an estimate of a an estimate of ρ_2 is obtained from the coefficient of x_t in (10′) and the ρ_1 is determined exactly since it is the coefficient of y_{t-1} in (10′). In this case the prior information $|\rho_1| < 1 < |\rho_2|$ allows the parameters ρ_1 and ρ_2 to be identified.

In empirical studies the sample data does not satisfy exact relations such as (9′) and (10′). This has led to the construction of models based on stories where the agents have more information than the outside econometrician. For example, in a model in which agents face several driving variables, the econometrician may have observations on only some of the driving variables. This is illustrated by

$$E_t y_{t+1} - (\rho_1 + \rho_2) y_t + \rho_1 \rho_2 y_{t-1} = x_t = x'_t + \eta_t. \quad (11)$$

where the outside econometrician observes only x'_t. Whiteman calls (11) a 'perturbed equation'.

Observe that in the perturbed version of (9′) the parameters C_0 and a are over-identified since given an estimate of a from the driving process two estimates of C_0 can be calculated from the perturbed version of (9′) and also two estimates of a; one obtained from the driving process and one from (9′).

The coefficients of the perturbed equation (11) can be consistently estimated from the reduced form provided certain conditions are satisfied. As an illustration suppose the autoregression (8) is the driving process where the ϵ_t's and n_t's are serially and mutually independent. Applying least squares to the driving process and to the perturbed version of (10′) produces consistent estimates of the coefficients in these equations. A consistent estimate of the structural parameter ρ_2 is derived from the coefficient of x_t in the perturbed version of (10′) using the least squares estimate of the parameter a in the autoregression (8).

Asymptotically efficient estimators of the parameters of the driving process and the structure can be obtained by using the method of maximum likelihood. Hansen and Sargent (1980) show that the maximum likelihood estimator is asymptotically efficient only if it maximizes the joint likelihood function of the driving process and the reduced form.

Two problems are encountered using maximum likelihood. First, it is difficult to solve explicitly for the reduced form if structural equation is nonlinear and the driving process is complicated. For the case of nonlinear expectational difference equations Fair and Taylor (1983) have proposed an approximate maximum likelihood procedure which circumvents some of the computational difficulties of obtaining a complete characterization of the reduced form. In particular, they develop a method for solving numerically for the reduced form. The second is that the maximum likelihood estimator may not be consistent, or, if consistent, not efficient, when the model is misspecified. Hansen and Singleton (1982) present an example in which the maximum likelihood estimator fails to be consistent due to a misspecification of the stochastic properties of the driving process.

The other approach is to estimate the structural parameters directly. This approach applied to equation (1) can be motivated as follows. The difference between y_{t+1} and the conditional expectation $E_t y_{t+1}$ is

$$u_{t+1} = y_{t+1} - E_t y_{t+1} = [C(L) - (C(L) - C_0)]L^{-1}\epsilon_t$$
$$= C_0 \epsilon_{t+1}, \quad (12)$$

which implies that

$$E_t u_{t+1} = 0 \quad (12')$$

and hence that y_{t+1} is a conditionally unbiased estimate of the conditional expectation. This condition can be interpreted as the first order condition to a linear-quadratic optimization problem. By assumption the forecast error is orthogonal to the observed forecast and to any other variables in the information set of agents when the forecast is made. Substituting y_{t+1} for $E_t y_{t+1}$ in (1) and rearranging gives

$$y_{t+1} = (\rho_1 + \rho_2) y_t - \rho_1 \rho_2 y_{t-1} + x_t + u_{t+1}. \quad (13)$$

From (13) it is seen that the 'error' (12) introduced by the substitution is contemporaneously uncorrelated with the 'regressors' y_t, y_{t-1} and x_t provided that the ϵ_t's are serially uncorrelated. Thus, consistent estimates of the parameters ρ_1 and ρ_2 can be obtained by applying least squares to (13). If instead of (1) the starting point is the perturbed equation (11), least squares is consistent if the error η_t in (11) is independent of the error u_{t+1}. The direct structural approach was used by Kennan (1979) to estimate a perturbed version of an Euler equation.

Note that the value of C_0 and the variance of ϵ_{t+1} combine to determine the variance of the error (12) and that the direct structural approach gives a consistent estimate of the error variance. As a consequence, the value of C_0 in the multiple solutions case (6) is (implicitly) consistently estimated.

An alternative motivation for the direct structural approach exploits certain orthogonality conditions. Define

$$h(z_{t+1}, b_0) = y_{t+1} - (\rho_1 + \rho_2) y_t + \rho_1 \rho_2 y_{t-1} - x_t = 0 \quad (14)$$

where $z_{t+1} = (y_{t+1}, y_t, y_{t-1}, x_t)$ is the vector of variables and $b_0 = [(\rho_1 + \rho_2), (\rho_1 \rho_2)]$ is the vector of parameters in (1). Using these definitions (1) can be written as

$$E_t h(z_{t+1}, b_0) = 0 \quad (14')$$

so that given a set of variables $\{w_q\}$ in the agents' information set which are observed by the econometrician

$$E_t[h(z_{t+1}, b_0) w_{q,t}] = 0 \quad (15)$$

where the variables w_q can be thought of as instrumental variables. Taking the expectation of (15) over the variables in information set gives the unconditional expectation

$$EE_t[h(z_{t+1}, b_0) w_{q,t}] = E[h(z_{t+1}, b_0) w_{q,t}] = 0. \quad (15')$$

Hansen (1982) defines the general method of moments estimator of the true parameter b_0 as the estimator which makes the sample versions of the population orthogonality conditions (15′) as close to zero as possible according to some measure of distance. Examples of this method include the least squares procedure of Kennan (1979) and a variety of instrumental variable techniques. For identification there must be at least as many orthogonality conditions as parameters to be estimated.

The general method of moments estimators are in general less asymptotically efficient than maximum likelihood if the model is correctly specified. Heuristically, this is because the method of moments does not use all the stochastic properties of the driving process and all the orthogonality conditions. The chief advantages of the method of moments estimators are robustness to misspecification and computational convenience. The method is robust in the sense that the model does not have to be completely specified; in particular, it is not necessary to make precise assumptions about the stochastic properties of the driving process. The computational advantage is that least squares type procedures can be used and that the model does not have to be solved for the reduced form. Hence, the method is especially suited to the estimation of nonlinear rational expectations models. In many applications of interest the u_{t+1}'s are serially correlated and conditionally heteroskedastic. Hansen (1982) has also stated conditions under which the method is consistent in the presence of serial correlation and conditional heteroskedasticity.

3. LEARNING

One possible and appealing justification for the use of rational expectations is that agents learn to form rational expectations. There is a large literature on learning to form rational expectations, much of which is surveyed in Blume, Bray and Easley (1982). The literature falls into two parts: one is concerned with 'rational learning' in which the model is correctly specified and agents form rational expectations given knowledge of the model and estimates of its parameters. Examples include Townsend (1978, 1983), Brandenburger (1984) and Bray and Kreps (1986). Rational learning is the natural extension of the standard methodology, based on optimization, to learning. Bray and Kreps (1986) show that it also guarantees convergence to rational expectations equilibrium under quite mild assumptions. The case which have been studied suppose a substantial degree of insight and prior knowledge of the part of agents.

The other part of this literature assumes some degree of bounded rationality. Examples of this type include Bray (1982, 1983), Radner (1982) Frydman (1982), Bray and Savin (1986) Fourgeaud, Gourieroux and Pradel (1986) and Marcet and Sargent (1986). In the bounded rationality framework agents are assumed to learn using reasonable model specifications which are often correct in rational expectations equilibrium, but misspecified when there is learning.

Following the classic paper by Muth (1961), the cobweb model has been used in the discussion of expectations formation of Townsend (1978), Brandenburger (1984), Frydman (1982), Bray and Savin (1986), Fourgeaud, Gourieroux and Pradel (1986) and others. Townsend (1978) and Bray and Savin (1986) consider a continuum of firms producing a homogeneous good where the set of firms is the unit interval [0,1] indexed by i. The firms make their production decisions at each date t before the realization of an exogenous stochastic demand which depends linearly on p_t, the market clearing price of the good, and on an unobserved exogenous demand shock. Each firm has a quadratic cost function so that the optimal output of firm i at date t is proportional to p^e_{it}, the mean of firm i's prior on p_t at date t. Setting the average supply to the market equal to the demand gives

$$p_t = x_t'm + a\bar{p}^e_t + u_t \tag{16}$$

where x_t is a vector of exogenous supply shocks observable by firms when the production decision is made, u_t is the difference between the unobservable exogenous shocks in the demand and supply equations and

$$\bar{p}^e_t = \int_0^1 p^e_{it}\,di \tag{17}$$

is the average of the price expectations (prior means) of the firms. In Bray and Savin (1986) the description of the model is completed by assuming that the stochastic processes x_t and u_t are independently identically distributed random variables with bounded forth moments. The equation (16) is a special type of expectational difference equation called a 'withholding equation'. The simplest example of such an equation is

$$E_{t-1}y_t - \rho y_t = x_t. \tag{18}$$

The equation (16) is a perturbed version of (18) due to the addition of the error u_t. Withholding equations are very prevalent in the rational expectations literature. One reason is that a class of models stemming from the absolute versus relative-price confusion paradigm of Lucas (1972, 1975) employs (18). Another reason is that Muth's (1961) cobweb model produces such an equation. The unique solution y_t to (18) lying in the space of a driving process when the ϵ_t's are independently identically distributed is

$$y_t = (1-\rho)^{-1}x_t \tag{19}$$

provided ρ is not equal to unity. It is important to note that this unique solution exists regardless of the value of ρ. For further details see Whiteman (1983).

From (16) the rational expectations equilibrium price forecast is

$$p^e_{it} = x_t'm(1-a)^{-1} \tag{20}$$

for all i, provided a is not equal to unity. This solution is essentially the same as (19). Substituting this forecast in (16) the price in rational expectations equilibrium is the random variable

$$p_t = x_t'm(1-a)^{-1} + u_t. \tag{21}$$

Hence if agents know the numerical value of $m(1-a)^{-1}$ they can form rational expectations.

The learning procedure followed by agents should depend on how much they know about the model and the way other agents learn. Suppose all agents know the numerical value of a and can observe or infer $\bar{p}^e_t$. Then (16) can be written as $y_t = x_t'm + u_t$ where $y_t = p_t - a\bar{p}^e_t$ is an observable variable. This equation satisfies the assumptions of the standard linear model so that m can be consistently estimated using classical or Bayesian methods.

Townsend (1978) assumes that the agents are Bayesians who know a and have enough common knowledge to infer $\bar{p}^e_t$ and hence can use Bayesian methods to infer m. A similar result under weaker common knowledge assumption has been obtained by Brandenburger (1984). In Townsend and Brandenburger the agents know that they are in a market game where the actual price depends on the collective output decisions of all the firms. Each agent calculates the Bayesian Nash equilibrium price of the game at each date and uses this as the price forecast. These examples assume Bayesian learning based on correctly specified likelihood functions, that is, likelihood functions which take into account the forecast feedback.

By contrast, in Bray and Savin (1986) and Fourgeaud, Gourieroux and Pradel (1986) the agents do not know the value of a and use a misspecified model for forecasting price. The agents assume that

$$p_t = x_t b + u_t \tag{22}$$

and that (22) satisfies the assumptions of the standard linear model and estimate b using classical or Bayesian techniques. For simplicity, suppose that the agents are classical statisticians and that b is estimated after observing $(x_1, p_1), \ldots, (x_{t-1}, p_{t-1})$ by

$$b_{t-1} = \left[\sum_{j=1}^{t-1} x_j x_j'\right]^{-1}\left[\sum_{j=1}^{t-1} x_j p_j\right]. \tag{22}$$

The agent's forecast of p_t is $x_t' b_{t-1}$. Substituting this forecast into (16) gives

$$p_t = x_t'(m + ab_{t-1}) + u_t. \tag{23}$$

Equations (22) and (23) describe the true data generation process. Comparing (23) with (21) it is clear that agents are using a misspecified model since they are assuming that b in (21) is a constant when in fact the learning process induces a time-varying parameter $m + ab_{t-1}$. The specification (21) is not arbitrary since it would be correct in rational expectations equilibrium, that is, if the value $m(1-a)^{-1}$ were known and used in forecasting. On the other hand, the agents are not fully rational because they fail to employ the relevant model to deduce (16) and hence to deduce that the forecasting procedure based on (21) implies the time-varying parameter model (23), which in turn implies that the forecasting procedure based on (21) is inconsistent with the model.

It can be shown that b_t cannot converge to any other value than the rational expectations equilibrium value $m(1-a)^{-1}$ and that if $a < 1$, b_t strongly converges to $m(1-a)^{-1}$. In this case agents eventually learn how to form rational expectations. When $a < 1$ the demand curve crosses the supply curve from above, which is the standard economically plausible case. Fourgeaud, Gourieroux and Pradel (1986) and Marcet and Sargent (1986) present proofs for the case where b is estimated by least squares and Bray and Savin (1986) for the case where agents are Bayesian statisticians.

When $a > 1$ it appears that b_t does not converge. In this case b_t follows one of a variety of divergent processes including a random walk. The nonconvergence is due to the unstable cobweb since the driving process is stable.

The question of the rate of convergence of b_t to the rational expectations equilibrium value is of considerable interest and has been investigated by Bray and Savin (1986). If the rate of convergence is fast, then the learning procedure works in the sense of generating expectations which are very nearly rational in a short time. Rapid convergence justifies the use of the rational expectations equilibrium as a good asymptotic approximation to a learning process and encourages the application of rational expectations models to actual data.

If convergence is slow or does not appear to occur, then the agents will eventually detect that the model (21) is misspecified. As a consequence, the specification of the model may be revised. Whether the sequence of model revisions adopted by agents will eventually lead to rational expectations equilibrium is an open question.

Time-varying models are widely used in empirical studies. Since learning processes can generate data which closely mimics that generated by standard time-varying parameter models, learning is a potentially attractive explanation for the observed phenomenon of time-varying coefficients.

4. CONCLUDING COMMENTS

The implicit assumption made in the case of an outside econometrician estimating a rational expectations model is that the actions of the outside econometrician do not influence the agents in the economy. This is true if the model estimated by the econometrician is ignored by the agents. If the empirical work of the outside econometrician is in fact ignored, then this raises the question of the motivation for such work. On the other hand, if the outside econometrician's model specification and estimates do have influence, then it is no longer true that the outside econometrician is indeed outside the economy. In this situation the econometrician's model may be misspecified due to forecast feedback.

The stationarity of the driving process and the solution plays an important role in the analysis of the solutions and in the theory of estimation. Nonstationarity appears to be a characteristic of many macroeconomic time series. It is this which accounts for the popularity of time-varying parameter methods in econometrics. This nonstationarity may be in part a product of agents learning how to form rational expectations. Even if agents are fully rational in the sense that they can calculate the Bayesian Nash equilibrium, this does not rule out nonstationarity. The assumption of stationarity may not be consistent with the notion of agents learning to form rational expectations.

In the typical rational expectations model forecasting is assumed to be a costless activity. In practice forecasting is costly, if for no other reason, because it is a time consuming activity; agents may be playing many market games simultaneously or agents may be playing one game which involves substantial amounts of data collection and processing. This suggests that the choice of a forecasting procedure is the outcome of a constrained optimization problem. Thus the assumption of bounded rationality is not necessary to explain why agents do not forecast with all available information. Alternatively, bounded rationality can be interpreted as the result of a budget constraint. Rule of thumb forecasting procedures may closely approximate the procedures selected by constrained optimization. The time constraint also naturally suggests why there is a market for forecasting services. Given the opportunity cost of time it may be optimal for agents to buy forecasts rather than make their own. The econometricians who supply these forecasts are inside the economy which means that econometric modelling is complicated by the presence of forecast feedback. This in turn may explain why econometric models require frequent revision.

N.E. SAVIN

See also ECONOMETRICS; MACROECONOMETRIC MODELS.

BIBLIOGRAPHY

Aoki, A. and Canzoneri, M. 1979. Reduced forms of rational expectations models. *Quarterly Journal of Economics* 93, 59–71.

Blanchard, O.J. 1979. Backward and forward solutions for economies with rational expectations. *American Economic Review* 69, 114–18.

Blanchard, O.J. and Kahn, C.M. 1980. The solution of linear difference models under rational expectations. *Econometrica* 48, 1305–11.

Blume, L., Bray, M.M. and Easley, D. 1982. Introduction to the stability of rational expectations equilibrium. *Journal of Economic Theory* 26, 313–17.

Brandenburger, A. 1984. Information and learning in market games. Churchill College, Cambridge Mimeo, August 1984.

Bray, M.M. 1982. Learning estimation, and the stability of rational expectations. *Journal of Economic Theory* 26, 318–39.

Bray, M.M. 1983. Convergence to rational expectations equilibrium. In *Individual Forecasting and Aggregate Outcomes*, ed. R. Frydman and E.S. Phelps, Cambridge: Cambridge University Press.

Bray, M.M. and Kreps, D. 1986. Rational learning and rational expectations. In *Essays in Honour of K.J. Arrow*, ed, W. Heller, R. Starr and D. Starrett, Cambridge: Cambridge University Press.

Bray, M.M. and Savin, N.E. 1986. Rational expectations equilibria, learning and model specification. *Econometrica* 57, 1129–60.

Broze, L., Gourieroux, C. and Szafarz, A. 1985. Solutions of linear rational expectations models. *Econometric Theory* 1, 341–68.

Deaton, A. 1986. Life-cycle models of consumption: is the evidence consistent with the theory? Woodrow Wilson School, Princeton University, Mimeo.

Durlauf, S.N. and Phillips, P.C.B. 1986. Trends versus random walks in time series analysis. Cowles Foundation Discussion Paper No. 788.
Eichenbaum, M.S. 1983. A rational expectations equilibrium model of finished goods and employment. *Journal of Monetary Economics* 12, 259–77.
Engle, R.F., Hendry, D.F. and Richard, J.-F. 1983. Exogeneity. *Econometrica* 50, 227–304.
Evans, G. 1985. Expectational stability and multiple solutions in linear rational expectations models. *Quarterly Journal of Economics* 99, 1217–33.
Evans, G. and Honkapohja, S. 1986. A complete characterization of ARMA solutions to linear rational expectations models. *Review of Economic Studies* 53, 227–39.
Fair, R.C. and Taylor, J.B. 1983. Solution and maximum likelihood estimation of dynamic nonlinear rational expectations models. *Econometrica* 51, July, 1169–85.
Fourgeaud, C., Gourieroux, C. and Pradel, J. 1986. Learning procedure and convergence to rationality. *Econometrica*, 54, 845–68.
Frydman, R. 1982. Towards an understanding of market processes: individual expectations, learning and convergence to rational expectations equilibrium. *American Economic Review* 72, 652–68.
Futia, C.A. 1981. Rational expectations in stationary linear models. *Econometrica* 49, 171–92.
Gourieroux, C., Laffont, J.J. and Monfort, A. 1982. Rational expectations in linear models: analysis of solutions. *Econometrica* 50, 409–25.
Hansen, L.P. 1982. Large sample properties of generalized method of moments estimators. *Econometrica* 50, 1029–54.
Hansen, L.P. and Sargent, T.J. 1980. Formulating and estimating dynamic linear rational expectations. *Journal of Economic Dynamics and Control* 2, 7–46.
Hansen, L.P. and Singleton, K.J. 1982. Generalized instrumental variable estimation of nonlinear rational expectations models. *Econometrica* 50, 1269–86.
Kennan, J. 1979. The estimation of partial adjustment models with rational expectations. *Econometrica* 47, 1441–6.
Kohlberg, E. and Mertens, J.-F. 1986. On the strategic stability of equilibria. *Econometrica*, 57, 1003–38.
Lucas, R.E. Jr. 1972. Econometric testing of the natural rate hypothesis. In *Econometrics of Price Determination Conference*, ed. O. Eckstein, Washington, DC: Board of Governors of the Federal Reserve System.
Lucas, R.E. Jr. 1975. An equilibrium model of the business cycle. *Journal of Political Economy* 83, 1113–144.
Lucas, R.E. Jr. 1976. Econometric policy evaluation: a critique. In *The Phillips Curve and Labor Markets*, Carnegie-Rochester Conference on Public Policy, Vol. 1, ed. K. Brunner and A.H. Meltzer, Amsterdam: North-Holland.
Marcet, A. and Sargent, T.J. 1986. Convergence of least squares learning mechanisms in self referential linear stochastic models. University of Minnesota, Mimeo.
McCallum, B.T. 1983. On non-uniqueness in rational expectations models: an attempt at perspective. *Journal of Monetary Economics* 11, 139–68.
Muth, J.F. 1961. Rational expectations and the theory of price movements. *Econometrica* 29, 315–35.
Nelson, C.R. and Plosser, C. 1982. Trends and random walk in macroeconomic time series: some evidence and implications. *Journal of Monetary Economics* 10, 139–62.
Nelson, C.R. and Kang, H. 1981. Spurious periodicity in inappropriately detrended time series. *Econometrica* 49, 741–51.
Nelson, C.R. and Kang, H. 1983. Pitfalls in the use of time as an explanatory variable in regression. NBER Technical Working Paper No. 30.
Radner, R. 1982. Equilibrium under uncertainty. In *Handbook of Mathematical Economics*, Vol. II, ed. K.J. Arrow and M.D. Intriligator, Amsterdam: North-Holland.
Saracoglu, R. and Sargent, T.J. 1978. Seasonality and portfolio balance under rational expectations. *Journal of Monetary Economics* 4, 511–21.
Sargent, T.J. 1979. *Macroeconomic Theory*. New York: Academic Press.
Sargent, T.J. 1981. Interpreting economic time series. *Journal of Political Economy* 89, 403–10.
Selten, R. 1965. Spieltheoretische Behandlung eines Oligopomodells mit Nachfragetragheit. *Zeitschrift fur die Gesamte Staatswissenschaft* 122, 301–24.
Selten, R. 1975. A re-examination of the perfectness concept for equilibrium points in extensive games. *International Journal of Game Theory* 4, 25–55.
Sims, C.A. 1982. Policy analysis with econometric models. *Brookings Papers on Economic Activity* No. 1, 107–52.
Taylor, J.B. 1977. Conditions for unique solutions in stochastic macroeconomic models with rational expectations. *Econometrica* 45, 1337–85.
Townsend, R.M. 1978. Market anticipations, rational expectations and Bayesian analysis. *International Economic Review* 19, 481–94.
Townsend, R.M. 1983. Forecasting the forecasts of others. *Journal of Political Economy* 91, 545–88.
Whiteman, C.H. 1983. *Linear Rational Expectations Models*. Minneapolis: University of Minnesota Press.

rationalization of industry. Rationalization of industry is a term used to describe the changes, usually quite drastic, that are needed to correct a position of fundamental disequilibrium in an industry. The case most commonly associated with the problem is that of adjustments needed to correct overcapacity, but also involved are adjustments to correct substantial cost differences between firms arising from differences in technology or from variations in the efficiency with which a given technology is used.

We start with the case of overcapacity and ask why this state of affairs arose in the first place. There are several possible reasons which will be dealt with briefly because the main concern of this essay is with corrective mechanisms. First, overcapacity may have resulted from a fall in domestic demand brought about by a fall in world demand, or by a fall in the price of imports, or by a switch in demand to a close substitute. Second, it may be due to government policies aimed at stimulating production. Third, it may have arisen because the competitive process resulted in an overexpansion of capacity during a period of increasing demand. There is no convincing theoretical or empirical evidence to suggest that this is more likely to result in one type of industry structure than another. In perfectly competitive markets the problem hinges around the fact that, following an increase in demand, each firm bases its expansion plans on current market prices which are assumed to stay constant. In relation to long-run equilibrium these prices are too high in the case of output and too low in respect of inputs. If all firms are equally assiduous in spotting profitable expansion opportunities the result will be an overexpansion of capacity. This result may be avoided or at least ameliorated if there are speculators who have more accurate information than producers about the course of future prices so that speculative selling of the product reduces the extent of short-run price increases. The same result may obtain if producers hold large stocks which can be used to meet part of the increased demand. More important however is the likelihood that firms' capacity extensions will be staggered so that some bring additional output on to the market, thus depressing the price, before others have put their investment plans into effect. In oligopolistic industries a key factor is the importance that firms attach to customer goodwill and in particular the ability to meet orders promptly. As a result an important aspect of oligopolistic competition during an upswing is competition in capacity extensions. This tendency may be accentuated if capacity extensions are also used as a barrier to entry.

Whatever the reasons for the emergence of over-capacity can it not be left to market forces to correct the imbalance? Market forces will indeed tend to act as a corrective mechanism but intervention may yield a better outcome. This is because of two interrelated factors: the speed with which market forces work, and divergences between private and social costs and benefits.

From the point of view of maximizing the level of output in the economy market forces may, depending on circumstances, operate either too slowly or too quickly – too slowly, because in some industries the long run may be considerably longer for downward adjustments to the capital stock than for additions to it. In industries with high fixed costs prices may have to fall to a very low level before they fail to cover the operating costs of even the most inefficient firm. Typically such aggressive price competition will not occur in oligopolistic industries except perhaps in a severe and prolonged recession. The effectiveness of price competition in eliminating inefficient firms is further reduced if each firm has built up its own clientele. A fall in demand is therefore likely to affect all firms in an industry rather than be concentrated on the most inefficient. Even if aggressive price cutting does occur this does not necessarily mean the elimination of the tail of inefficient firms only; the outcome will also be affected by such factors as the financial resources that each firm has when the slump in demand occurs, and their degree of vertical integration and diversification. Finally, even if price competition does succeed in eliminating inefficient firms this does not necessarily mean any reduction in productive capacity since the plant of a firm that leaves an industry may be acquired by one of the survivors. If for these and other reasons it is indeed the case that resources are released very slowly from declining industries, and if these resources could be more profitably used elsewhere, there is a strong case for a planned rationalization scheme possibly backed by government financial inducements to speed up the process of adjustment.

In other circumstances, however, the optimum policy will be to slow down the process of adjustment. The arguments for contracting an industry are based on existing and expected profitability. Profit is the difference between the value of output produced and the cost of inputs used in production. Its use as an indicator of efficiency is valid if the price of a commodity reflects society's valuation of it (relative to other commodities) and if the cost of inputs reflects the social value of those inputs. When these conditions hold an enterprise making a profit is creating goods whose value is greater than the social value of the inputs used. If, therefore, the government intervenes to support an unprofitable industry it is destroying social value because the labour that is being kept in that industry could be more efficiently used elsewhere in the economy. The argument can be extended to cover competing imports. At an equilibrium exchange rate the price of imports is the value of domestically produced goods that have to be exported to pay for these imports. If the cost of an imported good is less than that of the domestically produced equivalent then the most efficient way of obtaining that good is to import it in exchange for other domestically produced goods.

The above analysis is wholly dependent on the assumptions made. If, for instance, wage rates are rigid in the industry requiring rationalization, contraction of the industry will result in unemployment. The labour market mechanism by which workers, especially those with specific skills, are re-employed elsewhere may work very slowly. There is thus a trade-off between the immediate loss of output resulting from the unemployment and the longer run benefits of transferring workers to more profitable activities. The optimal solution will involve some form of intervention that slows down the rate of decline. More generally, when rationalization leads to unemployment wages are no longer an accurate measure of the social value of labour; i.e the opportunity cost of labour, or the 'shadow wage', is below the market wage.

The case for slowing down the process of contraction is even stronger where the redundancies resulting from a rationalization programme are added to an already high level of unemployment. In these conditions the opportunity cost of certain types of labour may be zero, i.e. the employment of this labour is not preventing more efficient production taking place elsewhere in the economy. Furthermore, additional redundancies have a multiplier effect arising partly from the disruption of backward and forward linkages and partly from the reduced purchasing power available to the newly redundant.

Failure to appreciate the relevance of these considerations is all too common. For instance, in spite of a high level of unemployment and the low shadow wage of coal miners, a substantial programme of rationalization involving the closure of high cost pits was pursued in Britain in 1985 and 1986 on the basis of accounting rates of return. This was said to be necessary to adjust the industry to a lower level of demand for domestically produced coal and to make way for new investment. In the circumstances of this particular case, however, there are strong arguments which suggest that government intervention would have been economically justified to slow down the rate of contraction.

A theoretical issue of general importance in the economics of the rationalization of industry is the legitimacy of using a shadow wage in decisions relating to one particular industry. The use of a shadow wage has been challenged on a number of counts: (i) the shadow wage argument can only be applied to a handful of special cases, otherwise nobody would be paying taxes for common services from which they derive benefit; (ii) if the shadow wage argument were generalized the effect would be to slow down the rate of structural change; (iii) why should any one industry be singled out for special treatment?

Objections (i) and (ii) are based on a misunderstanding of the rationale of shadow pricing. The purpose of using a shadow wage in policy decisions is to correct for the existence of unemployment and to minimize the loss of output associated with it. Where there is large-scale unemployment there is no reason whatever why the shadow wage argument should not be applied across the board. In practical terms this would involve the use of a general labour subsidy the level of which would fall as the level of unemployment came down. The suggestion that structural change is impeded by shortage of labour at a time of high unemployment is implausible. Objection (iii) is a legitimate query, and indeed on grounds of efficiency a general labour subsidy is preferable to subsidizing high-cost units in a particular industry. However, in the absence of effective macroeconomic policies to bring down the level of unemployment recourse to shadow wages in closure decisions in a particular industry is justifiable on second-best grounds, particularly where that industry is concentrated geographically.

Government intervention in the rationalization of industry can thus be justified either to speed up the process or to slow it down. But the form of intervention is also important, a point that is well illustrated by reference to European attempts to rationalize agriculture and steel.

In agriculture, massive overproduction of products such as milk and cereals has been due to high price guarantees combined with technological advances. After half-hearted attempts to stem the flow of milk the European Commission in

1983 spelt out the options for a serious attack on the problem: either a price reduction or production quotas with a levy on excess production. In the event and largely for political reasons, quotas were introduced. The preference for quotas over price reductions has been justified on grounds of fairness: whereas price reductions would affect all producers a levy on excess production would affect only those producing the excess and in proportion to their contribution to overproduction. The most likely reason for choosing quotas however was that farmers, who traditionally dislike price cuts, may not readily have appreciated that quotas imply a hidden price reduction; the prices being a weighted average of the guaranteed price on the quota and the disposal price on excess deliveries.

Quotas, however, are an inefficient way of reducing overcapacity. The uneven treatment of producers is actually perverse, preventing efficient farms from expanding while encouraging inefficient farms to maintain production. A straightforward price cut on the other hand would be more easily absorbed by efficient farmers and more discouraging to the inefficient. The anomaly would also be avoided of farmers who had invested heavily in modern dairying facilities not having a quota because they were not in production on day one of the new regime. In addition quotas are administratively cumbersome as compared to a straightforward price reduction and they operate solely on the supply side of the market whereas a price cut would also stimulate demand.

Some of the drawbacks of quotas would be overcome if they were freely marketable, but there would still be a problem of equity. Those who are awarded a large quota are in effect given a valuable capital asset so that the system implies an arbitrary redistribution of wealth within the farm sector. The situation is most unfair on the tenant farmer who once he ceases milk production has no right over the quota, the entire capital being vested in the landowner.

The problems of overproduction in European agriculture would be more efficiently tackled by a gradual relaxation of price controls, with the farm sector supported by means of production subsidies financed out of taxation.

This example of the attempt to rationalize milk production in the European Economic Community draws attention to a general problem in rationalization schemes; that of allocating output between firms with different cost functions. Standard economic theory shows that where there are cost differences it is generally possible for a rationalization cartel to reallocate output so as to increase total industry profits. In the diagram, (Figure 1) D is the industry demand curve and MR industry marginal revenue. There are two firms, A and B, each with demand curve d and marginal revenue curve mr. The profit maximizing price for firm A is P_A and for B, P_B with outputs of A and B respectively. Industry profits are maximized where $\sigma MC = MR$, with market shares of A^* and B^* which equalizes the marginal costs of the two firms. This however requires that A, the high cost firm, accepts a big reduction in market share and in the profits on its own sales. There is clearly no incentive for A to go along with the rationalization scheme unless there is a profit-pooling arrangement and side payments which make it better off than it was before the rationalization scheme was introduced.

However even if a rationalization cartel can increase total industry profits and side payments are feasible it is by no means certain that high-cost firms will participate voluntarily. These firms will fear that by agreeing to a smaller market share they will suffer a loss of bargaining power and perhaps be even worse off than they would have been without cartelization. And once quotas have been agreed it can prove extraordinarily difficult for a firm to improve its market share

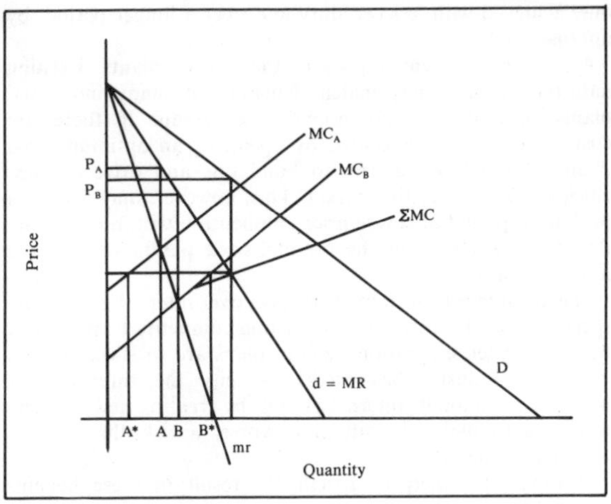

Figure 1

through the more efficient use of existing assets or through modernization of plant and equipment. Indeed one of the problems often encountered by cartels is that of matching overall capacity to demand without at the same time unduly inhibiting cost-reducing investments.

These problems have been encountered for instance within the European Coal and Steel Corporation (ECSC). An ECSC Plan to establish a voluntary European cartel in 1977 broke down in a price war. To restore order in the market the ECSC declared a 'manifest crisis', using its powers to compel adherence to quotas, and setting minimum prices for a range of steel products. This was very similar to the method of intervention in agriculture and is subject to the same criticism: firms which have made efforts to improve efficiency are penalized if they are unable to translate this into a larger market share. In its 1984/85 Annual Report the British Steel Corporation complained that, 'with demand for strip mill products markedly higher in the UK than elsewhere in the EEC, it was difficult to secure adequate quota to meet normal UK market share without incurring unacceptably high fines ... the quota position remains very unsatisfactory'.

Whatever the theoretical possibilities the general experience with cartels is that they tend to cement existing industry structure rather than help in achieving efficiency-enhancing structural changes.

Where cartelization is not feasible the obvious alternative route to greater industry discipline and the benefits of rationalization is through merger. Mergers may lead to benefits of increased specialization within plants and also to larger plants with associated economies of size. In this case, as with cartels, it has to be asked why, if substantial benefits exist, are they not realized through the mechanism of competition between rival producers. if efficiency can be increased by greater specialization within plants it should pay a firm to build up sales of a smaller range of products by offering lower prices on selected brands. However, if there is a great deal of overlap in the product-range of firms this may lead to competitive price-cutting across the board leaving all firms in the end with the same product-range but with lower prices and profits. By concentrating plants into a smaller number of firms mergers may result in economies of rationalization that could not be achieved, or at least could only achieved with less certainty and over a longer period, by internal growth.

A similar argument applies to the size of plants. Existing industry capacity may match demand but many individual plants may be of sub-optimal size. Again if there are cost-reductions to be secured by operating an optimum-sized plant it should pay a firm to build one and drive the less efficient units out of the market. This, however, may lead to a prolonged period of severe price competition with no certainty that the investment in the optimal-sized plants will yield a normal return.

The advantages which mergers have over internal growth are speed and safety. In the face of strong competition speed may be of the essence if rationalization plans are to succeed. And where an industry has excess capacity the safety factor becomes paramount. Internal growth by creating new capacity threatens to make the situation worse, a risk that can be avoided by merger.

However, for mergers actually to result in these benefits rationalization plans have to be implemented. Increased product specialization within plants and the replacement of sub-optimal plants by optimal sized ones are not brought about without conscious management decisions. Although the opportunity for executing rationalization plans may be enhanced by mergers empirical evidence suggests that the end result is often disappointing.

The rationalization of industry has always been a factor associated with structural change and shifting comparative advange. However the scale of the problem has tended to increase with the increasing importance of international competition. In an oligopolistic grouping consisting entirely of domestic firms a degree of cohesiveness can be expected which is unlikely to be matched in a group that transcends national boundaries. If this is so the pressures to adjust will be greater. Furthermore the problem may be accentuated by direct or indirect state aid to industry. Given the existence of state aid in one country others may feel forced to follow suit, or alternatively to impose some form of control on imports. Rationalization schemes may then turn out to be a cloak for 'beggar-my-neighbour' policies with one country endeavouring to throw a larger share of the burden of adjustment on to another.

This brings us back to the interrelationship between rationalization schemes and other policies – in particular macroeconomic policies and policies such as re-training schemes aimed at increasing the mobility of labour. Government intervention to slow down the rate of contraction of a declining industry is justified if it results in a higher overall level of output. The case for such intervention is strongest when alternative employment opportunities are few, i.e. at times of recession, and when labour is immobile because of specific skills and poor retraining facilities. However, actual experience of schemes, including government-supported rationalization cartels, designed to soften the effect of market forces suggests that they often result in serious allocative inefficiency. On the other hand, the more successful government policy is in maintaining a high level of employment and an adaptable labour force the weaker is the case for policies that slow down the structural change that is the outcome of market forces, and the greater the scope for government intervention that works with market forces rather than against them.

K.D. George

See also CARTELS; MANUFACTURING AND DE-INDUSTRIALIZATION.

BIBLIOGRAPHY

Allen, G.C. 1981. *The Japanese Economy*. London: Weidenfeld & Nicolson.

Caves, R.E. and Uekusa, M. 1976. *Industrial Organization in Japan*. Washington, DC: Brookings Institution.

Cowling, K. et. al. 1980. *Mergers and Economic Performance*. Cambridge: Cambridge University Press.

Dixit, A.K. 1980. The role of investment in entry-deterrence. *Economic Journal* 90, March, 75–106.

Duesenberry, J.S. 1958. *Business Cycles and Economic Growth*. New York: McGraw-Hill.

Foster, B.A. and Rees, R. 1983. The optimal rate of decline of an inefficient industry. *Journal of Public Economics* 22(2), November, 227–42.

George, K.D. and Mainwaring, L. (eds) 1988. *The Welsh Economy*. Cardiff: University of Wales Press.

George, K.D. and Joll, C. 1981. *Industrial Organisation; Competition Growth and Structural Change*. 3rd edn, London: George Allen & Unwin.

Jacquemin, A. (ed.) 1984. *European Industry: Public Policy and Corporate Strategy*. Oxford: Clarendon Press.

Osborne, D.K. 1976. Cartel problems. *American Economic Review* 66(5), December, 835–44.

Pinder, J. (ed.) 1982. *National Industrial Strategies and the World Economy*. Beckenham: Croom Helm.

Richardson, G.B. 1960. *Information and Investment*. Oxford: Oxford University Press.

Scherer, F.M. 1980. *Industrial Market Structure and Economic Performance*. 2nd edn, Boston: Houghton Mifflin.

Shaw, R.W. and Shaw, S.A. 1983. Excess capacity and rationalization in the West European synthetic fibers industry. *Journal of Industrial Economics* 32(2), December, 149–66.

rationed equilibria.

DEFINITION AND SCOPE. Equilibria with rationing, also called non-Walrasian equilibria, are a wide class of equilibrium concepts which generalize the traditional notion of Walrasian equilibrium by allowing markets not to clear (in the traditional sense) and therefore quantity rationing to be experienced. Their scope is best described by examining first Walrasian equilibrium as a reference.

In a Walrasian equilibrium by definition all markets clear, that is, demand equals supply for each good. This consistency of the actions of all agents is achieved by price movements solely. No rationing is experienced as each agent is able to exchange as much as he wants at the Walrasian equilibrium price system. As noted by Arrow (1959), there is a 'missing element' in the concept, in that, whereas quantity actions by the agents result from rational behaviour, market clearing is assumed axiomatically. Non-Walrasian theory thus simply abandons this last assumption, allowing prices to be determined by other mechanisms than market clearing. An almost immediate corollary is that in order to obtain equilibrium concepts, quantity signals and quantity adjustments will have to be introduced together with price adjustments. To summarize briefly, the Walrasian equilibrium concept is generalized in the following directions:

(1) More general price mechanisms are considered, ranging from full rigidity to full flexibility, with intermediate forms of imperfect competition. Moreover each market may have its own price determination scheme.

(2) Quantity signals are introduced in addition to price signals. They intervene in both demand-supply and price making behaviour.

(3) Equilibrium in the short run is achieved by quantity adjustments as well as by price adjustments.

(4) Expectations about the future concern not only price signals, but quantity signals as well.

HISTORY. Equilibria with rationing have a double ancestry: Keynes (1936) because he developed (at the macroeconomic level) a concept of equilibrium where adjustment was made by quantities (the level of income) as well as by prices, and Walras (1874) because he developed a model of general equilibrium with interdependent markets. The Walrasian model has been beautifully developed into a highly elaborate and rigorous concept, notably in Hicks (1939), Arrow and Debreu (1954), Debreu (1959), Arrow and Hahn (1971).

The gap between these two lines of thought was unfortunately total until the stimulating contributions of Clower (1965) and Leijonhufvud (1968), who reinterpreted Keynesian analysis in terms of labour market rationing and quantity adjustments. These insights were included in the first fixprice macroeconomic model by Barro and Grossman (1971) (1976).

Rigorous microeconomic concepts of equilibrium with quantity rationing were then developed: Drèze (1975) built an equilibrium concept with prices variable between preset limits; Benassy (1975a, 1977b, 1982) constructed an alternative concept of fixprice equilibrium, and introduced expectations into that framework. A third concept of fixprice equilibrium was built by Younès (1975). Benassy (1976, 1977a, 1982) also developed a non-Walrasian equilibrium concept with price makers which bridged the gap with another important line of work, that dealing with general equilibrium under imperfect competition, notably associated with the name of Negishi (1961).

Still other concepts of equilibria with rationing were proposed by Glustoff (1968), Hahn (1978), Böhm and Levine (1979), Heller and Starr (1979).

We shall now describe the main concepts of the theory. In order to set the stage and introduce notation, let us first describe the economy considered and the corresponding Walrasian equilibrium concept.

THE ECONOMY AND WALRASIAN EQUILIBRIUM. We shall describe the various concepts in the framework of an exchange economy. One good, which we shall call money, serves as numeraire, medium of exchange and reserve of value (non-monetary exchange has been considered in Benassy, 1975b). There are l markets where nonmonetary goods, indexed by $h = 1, \ldots, l$, are exchanged against money at the price p_h. Call p the l-dimensional vector of these prices. Agents are indexed by $i = 1, \ldots, n$. Agent i has an initial endowment of good h ω_{ih}, and of money $\bar{m}_i$. Call d_{ih} his purchase of good h, s_{ih} his sale of good h. Define $z_{ih} = d_{ih} - s_{ih}$ his net purchase of good h and z_i the vector of these net purchases. His final holdings of non-monetary goods and money are respectively

$$x_i = \omega_i + z_i \qquad m_i = \bar{m}_i - pz_i$$

and we shall assume that the agent has a utility function $U_i(x_i, m_i) = U_i(\omega_i + z_i, m_i)$ which we shall assume throughout strictly quasi-concave in its arguments.

Having described the economy, let us now turn to the notion of Walrasian equilibrium. As indicated above, each agent is assumed to be able to exchange as much as he wants on each market. He thus transmits demands and supplies which maximize his utility subject to the budget constraint, i.e. the Walrasian net demand function is the solution in z_i of the following programme:

$$\text{Maximize } U_i(\omega_i + z_i, m_i) \quad \text{s.t.}$$
$$pz_i + m_i = \bar{m}_i$$

This yields a vector of Walrasian net demands $z_i(p)$. A Walrasian equilibrium price vector p^* is defined by the condition that all markets clear, i.e.:

$$\sum_{i=1}^{n} z_i(p^*) = 0.$$

Transactions realized by agent i are simply equal to $z_i(p^*)$.

EQUILIBRIUM WITH BOUNDED PRICES. This concept, due to Drèze (1975), develops a notion of equilibrium valid when prices are subject to inequality constraints. We shall describe here, for simplicity of exposition, the case where absolute prices are subject to limits of the form:

$$\underline{p}_h \leqslant p_h \leqslant \bar{p}_h$$

Price limits linked to a price index were considered as well in Drèze (1975) (see also Van der Laan, 1980; Dehez and Drèze, 1984).

The basic idea behind this concept of equilibrium is that rationing becomes operative when prices hit one of the limits. The rationing considered will take the form of an upper bound on trades. (We shall see in the next section a possible justification for this type of rationing.) More specifically, as in Drèze (1975), consider a uniform rationing on each market, and call $\bar{d}_h$ the upper bound on purchases on market h, $\bar{s}_h$ the upper bound on sales. Net purchases of agent i on market h, z_{ih}, are thus limited to the interval:

$$-\bar{s}_h \leqslant z_{ih} \leqslant \bar{d}_h.$$

An equilibrium with price rigidities 'à la Drèze' can be now defined as a set of prices p_h^*, transactions z_{ih}^* and quantity constraints $\bar{d}_h$ and $\bar{s}_h$ such that:

(i) $\underline{p}_h \leqslant p_h^* \leqslant \bar{p}_h \quad \forall h$

(ii) $\sum_{i=1}^{n} z_{ih}^* = 0 \qquad \forall h$

(iii) The vector z_i^* is solution in z_i of

Maximize $U_i(\omega_i + z_i, m_i)$, s.t.

$$\begin{cases} pz_i + m_i = \bar{m}_i \\ -\bar{s}_{ih} \leqslant z_{ih} \leqslant \bar{d}_{ih} \quad \forall h \end{cases}$$

(iv) $\forall h \quad z_{ih}^* = \bar{d}_h$ for some i implies $z_{jh}^* > -\bar{s}_h \quad \forall j$

$z_{ih}^* = -\bar{s}_h$ for some i implies $z_{jh}^* < \bar{d}_h \quad \forall j$

(v) $\forall h \quad p_h < \bar{p}_h$ implies $z_{ih}^* < \bar{d}_h \qquad \forall i$

$p_h > \underline{p}_h$ implies $z_{ih}^* > -\bar{s}_h \quad \forall i$

Condition (i) simply reminds us that prices are bounded upward and downward. Condition (ii) says that transactions should be consistent on every market. Condition (iii) says that transactions must be individually rational, i.e. they must maximize utility subject to the budget constraint and quantity constraints on all markets. Condition (iv) says that rationing may affect either supply or demand, but not both simultaneously. This condition is usually presented as a condition of market by market efficiency. Note also that money is never rationed. This condition is aimed at suppressing trivial equilibria where all agents would be constrained to trade nothing. Condition (v) says that upward (downward) price rigidity must be binding if there is quantity rationing of demand (supply). It thus expresses in an intuitive way that quantity rationing is a substitute for price variations.

We should note at this stage that this concept contains as particular cases both a fixprice equilibrium concept (when both price limits are equal) and Walrasian equilibrium (when the lower bound is zero and the upper bound infinite).

Existence of such an equilibrium with uniform bounds on net trades was proved in Drèze (1975). The concept is easily extended to some non-uniform bounds (Grandmont and Laroque, 1976, Greenberg and Müller, 1979), but in this last case it is not specified in the concept how shortages are allocated among rationed demanders or rationed suppliers. We shall now study alternative concepts based on different premises which, in particular, make this more explicit. We shall now therefore study in more detail how transactions and quantity signals may be formed in a nonclearing market.

THE FUNCTIONING OF A NONCLEARING MARKET. In this and the two subsequent sections we shall study other non-Walrasian concepts due to Benassy (1975a, 1976, 1977b, 1982). A basic characteristic of these models is that a clear-cut difference is made between demands and supplies on the one hand, and the resulting transactions on the other. Agents express effective demands $\tilde{d}_{ih}$ or supplies $\tilde{s}_{ih}$ which are somehow signals to the market and the other agents, and which do not necessarily match on a specific market. However, the trading process will generate transactions, i.e. purchases d^*_{ih} and sales s^*_{ih} which identically balance on each market:

$$\sum_{i=1}^{n} d^*_{ih} = \sum_{i=1}^{n} s^*_{ih} \quad \forall h.$$

A rationing process is thus necessary, which may take various forms, such as uniform rationing, queueing, priority systems, proportional rationing, etc. . . . To be more explicit, define:

$$\tilde{z}_{ih} = \tilde{d}_{ih} - \tilde{s}_{ih}, \quad z^*_{ih} = d^*_{ih} - s^*_{ih}.$$

A rationing scheme on a market h is described by a set of n functions:

$$z^*_{ih} = F_{ih}(\tilde{z}_{1h}, \ldots, \tilde{z}_{nh}), \quad i = 1, \ldots, n \tag{1}$$

such that:

$$\sum_{i=1}^{n} F_{ih}(\tilde{z}_{1h}, \ldots, \tilde{z}_{nh}) \equiv 0.$$

We shall generally assume that F_{ih} is continuous, non-decreasing in $\tilde{z}_{ih}$ and non-increasing in the other arguments. Let us now examine a few possible properties. The first one is that of voluntary exchange, according to which no one can be forced to trade more than he wants, which is expressed by:

$$d^*_{ih} \leqslant \tilde{d}_{ih} \qquad s^*_{ih} \leqslant \tilde{s}_{ih}$$

or

$$z^*_{ih} \cdot \tilde{z}_{ih} \geqslant 0 \quad \text{and} \quad |z^*_{ih}| \leqslant |\tilde{z}_{ih}|$$

We shall now assume this property throughout. It allows to classify the agents in two categories: unrationed agents for which $z^*_{ih} = \tilde{z}_{ih}$, and rationed ones who trade less than they wanted. A second property we want to discuss is that of manipulability. A scheme is non-manipulable if an agent, when rationed, cannot increase the level of his transaction by increasing his demand or supply. Priority or uniform rationing schemes are non-manipulable, a proportional rationing scheme is manipulable. Rationing schemes which satisfy both voluntary exchange and non-manipulability can be expressed under the form:

$$d^*_{ih} = \min(\tilde{d}_{ih}, \bar{d}_{ih})$$
$$s^*_{ih} = \min(\tilde{s}_{ih}, \bar{s}_{ih}) \tag{2}$$

with:

$$\bar{d}_{ih} = G^d_{ih}(\tilde{z}_{1h}, \ldots, \tilde{z}_{nh})$$
$$\bar{s}_{ih} = G^s_{ih}(\tilde{z}_{1h}, \ldots, \tilde{z}_{nh}) \tag{3}$$

where $\bar{d}_{ih}$ and $\bar{s}_{ih}$, the quantity constraints faced by agent i, are actually functions only of demands other than $\tilde{z}_{ih}$ (hence the property of non-manipulability). We thus see that a rationing which takes the form of upper bounds on net trades results from both properties of voluntary exchange and non-manipulability, and we shall assume these in what follows (a more general theory covering other cases has been developed in Benassy, 1977b, 1982).

A third property which is often used, though it is not necessary for what follows, is that of market efficiency, according to which one should not find rationed demanders and rationed suppliers at the same time on a market. The intuitive idea behind it is that in an efficiently organized market a rationed buyer and a rationed seller should be able to meet, and would exchange until one of the two is not rationed. Of course this condition will be more often met in a small micro-market than on a large aggregated macro-market. Together with voluntary exchange it implies the 'short-side' rule according to which agents on the short side of the market may realize their desired transactions:

$$\tilde{z}_{ih}\left(\sum_j \tilde{z}_{jh}\right) \leqslant 0 \Rightarrow z^*_{ih} = \tilde{z}_{ih}.$$

FIXPRICE EQUILIBRIUM. The concept we shall describe here was developed in Benassy (1975a, 1977b, 1982). We have already seen in the previous section how transactions and quantity signals are formed in a market where effective demands and supplies have been expressed (equations (1) and (3)). All we need, in order, to obtain a fixprice equilibrium concept, is to show how optimal effective demands are expressed as a function of price and quantity signals.

For that each agent maximizes the utility of his transactions $U_i(\omega_i + z_i, m_i)$, knowing that the transactions he will obtain are related to his demands and supplies by formulas (2). A convenient solution (Benassy, 1977b, 1982) is to take the effective demand $\tilde{z}_{ih}$ as the solution (unique because of strict quasi-concavity) of the following programme:

Maximize $U_i(\omega_i + z_i, m_i)$ s.t.

$$\begin{cases} pz_i + m_i = \bar{m}_i \\ -\bar{s}_{ik} \leqslant z_{ik} \leqslant \bar{d}_{ik} \quad k \neq h \end{cases}$$

which yields an effective demand function denoted as $\zeta_{ih}(p, \bar{d}_i, \bar{s}_i)$, where $\bar{d}_i$ and $\bar{s}_i$ are the vectors of quantity constraints.

A fixprice equilibrium is now naturally defined as a set of effective demands, transactions and quantity constraints such that:

(a) $\quad \tilde{z}_{ih} = \zeta_{ih}(p, \bar{d}_i, \bar{s}_i) \quad \forall i, \forall h$

(b) $\quad z^*_{ih} = F_{ih}(\tilde{z}_{1h}, \ldots, \tilde{z}_{nh}) \quad \forall i, \forall h$

(c) $\quad \bar{d}_{ih} = G^d_{ih}(\tilde{z}_{1h}, \ldots, \tilde{z}_{nh}) \quad \forall i, \forall h$

$\quad \bar{s}_{ih} = G^s_{ih}(\tilde{z}_{1h}, \ldots, \tilde{z}_{nh}) \quad \forall i, \forall h$

Equilibria defined by these equations exist for all positive prices and rationing schemes satisfying voluntary exchange and non-manipulability (Benassy, 1975a, 1982). Because the concept includes an explicit description of the rationing procedure, the equilibrium is unique for a given price system and rationing scheme under fairly natural assumptions (Schulz, 1983).

Equilibria as defined above also possess the optimality properties one would naturally expect: they are consistent at the market level because of (b), and individually rational since effective demands have been constructed to yield optimal transactions, given price and quantity constraints. If moreover the rationing scheme on a market h is efficient, then no demanders and suppliers are rationed at the same time on that market. This last remark suggests that, even though their respective logics of construction are quite different, under the added assumption of market efficiency the Benassy and Drèze concepts should yield similar allocations at given prices. This was shown indeed by Silvestre (1982, 1983) for both exchange and productive economies. Some efficiency (and inefficiency) properties of the corresponding allocations are studied in the entry FIXPRICE MODELS.

NON-WALRASIAN EQUILIBRIA WITH PRICE MAKERS. At this stage, the theory is still in need of a description of price making by agents internal to the system. We shall now describe a concept dealing with that problem (Benassy, 1976, 1977a, 1982), which synthesizes the previous developments and the theory of general equilibrium with monopolistic competition, as developed notably by Negishi (1961, 1972).

As indicated in the entry DISEQUILIBRIUM ANALYSIS, the idea behind the modelling of price making in such models is that each price maker uses the prices he controls to 'manipulate' the quantity constraints he faces. To make things more precise, assume that agent i controls the price of a subset H_i of the goods, with H_i and H_j disjoint so that the price of each good is determined by one agent at most. Agent i thus sets a vector of prices p_i,

$$p_i = \{p_h | h \in H_i\}$$

He perceives that his sales constraint in a market h he controls, $\bar{s}_{ih}$ (this constraint is actually equal to the total demand of the other agents, since he is the only seller on that market) depends on the vector p_i through a function, the perceived demand curve, denoted as

$$\bar{S}_{ih}(p_i, \theta_i)$$

where θ_i is a vector of parameters. Symmetrically a demander who sets a price p_h has a perceived supply curve

$$\bar{D}_{ih}(p_i, \theta_i)$$

We assume that the parameters θ_i are estimated as a function of current signals p, $\bar{d}_i$, $\bar{s}_i$ (and of course any other signal available, including data of past periods. This formulation thus allows some learning about the demand curve). Because we are dealing with a general equilibrium concept, at equilibrium the perceived demand or supply curve must go through the observed point (Bushaw and Clower, 1957), i.e.

$$\bar{D}_{ih}(p_i, \theta_i) = \bar{d}_{ih}$$
$$\bar{S}_{ih}(p_i, \theta_i) = \bar{s}_{ih} \qquad (4)$$

We can now make explicit the procedure of price formation. Agent i, facing a price p_h and constraints $\bar{d}_{ih}$ and $\bar{s}_{ih}$ on markets $h \notin H_i$ will choose his price so as to maximize his utility, i.e. the solution in p_i to the programme

Maximize $U_i(\omega_i + z_i, m_i)$ s.t.

$$\begin{cases} pz_i + m_i = \bar{m}_i \\ -\bar{s}_{ih} \leqslant z_{ih} \leqslant \bar{d}_{ih}, \quad h \notin H_i \\ -\bar{S}_{ih}(p_i, \theta_i) \leqslant z_{ih} \leqslant \bar{D}_{ih}(p_i, \theta_i) \quad h \in H_i \end{cases}$$

which yields a function $\mathscr{P}_i^*(p, \bar{d}_i, \bar{s}_i)$ since the parameters θ_i are function of p, $\bar{d}_i$, $\bar{s}_i$. A non-Walrasian equilibrium with price makers is then simply defined as an equilibrium where quantities are optimal given prices and no price maker has interest in changing his price i.e.:

(a) The quantities $\tilde{z}_{ih}$, z_{ih}^*, $\bar{d}_{ih}$, $\bar{s}_{ih}$ form a fixprice equilibrium for p^*

(b) $p_i^* = \mathscr{P}_i^*(p^*, \bar{d}_i, \bar{s}_i) \qquad \forall i.$

We may note that under reasonable assumptions (though not necessarily always) a price maker will satisfy the demand addressed to him. Sufficient conditions are found in Benassy (1982).

We may note as a final remark that the consistency conditions (4) imposed on the parameters of the perceived demand and supply curves are minimal ones, which thus allows to cover a maximum number of cases, depending on the structure of information available to price makers. More demanding consistency conditions have been searched for (see notably the ideas of an objective demand curve in Nikaido (1975) or of rational conjectures in Hahn, 1978) but the problem has not yet received a general satisfactory solution, for lack of a well defined concept of a 'true' demand curve in a general equilibrium situation with price makers.

EXPECTATIONS AND NON-WALRASIAN EQUILIBRIA. Up to now we have dealt with an equilibrium structure in the period considered, implicitly a short-run one, but of course the economy extends further in the future, as we are reminded at least by the presence of money as a store of value. More generally the presence of stocks (inventories, capital goods, financial assets) makes it necessary to form expectations, and these will influence current equilibrium. How this occurs has been studied in Benassy (1975a, 1982), and we shall only briefly outline the method for dealing with that problem.

Each agent actually plans for the current and future periods. Expectations for future periods take the form of prices and quantity constraints (for price takers) or expected demand curves (for price makers). These may be deterministic or stochastic. These expectations are formed via expectations schemes, which link future price quantity expectations to all price quantity signals received in past and current periods. This formulation is thus quite general and covers any expectations scheme, 'rational' or not, based on actually available information.

By a standard dynamic programming technique, one can reduce the multi-period problem to a single period one, where the valuation of all stocks (and notably money) depends upon future expectations, and thus, via the expectations schemes, upon the current and past price-quantity signals, We are thus back to the one period formulation used in the previous section, with the only difference that current and past quantity signals must be added in the valuation functions. We should note that the inclusion of these expectations does not create any problem for the existence of an equilibrium when the prices are fully rigid, but may jeopardize existence when endogenous price setting is considered (see Benassy, 1982). We should also note that rational expectations are fully consistent with this type of model, as was pointed out in Neary and Stiglitz (1983).

The most important feature of the introduction of expectations in such models is that, whereas traditional market clearing models deal with price expectations only, these models deal with a richer menu of price and quantity expectations.

CONCLUDING REMARKS. The concepts of equilibria with rationing, or non-Walrasian equilibria, described in this entry represent a useful generalization of the traditional Walrasian equilibrium concept in several directions: whereas the Walrasian model covers by definition only the case where all markets clear, these concepts consider more general price mechanisms including full or partial price rigidities or imperfect competition. They introduce quantity signals in addition to price signals in demand-supply theory and mixed price-quantity adjustments in the short run. They integrate quantity expectations as well as price expectations. All this is done with the same rigorous methods which have proved successful in Walrasian theory. Besides their evident microeconomic interest, non-Walrasian equilibria have been widely used in macroeconomics (see, for example, Benassy, 1986), where they allow, for example, to study more rigorously states of the economy with involuntary unemployment.

A great strength of the theory is that it gives a rigorous framework within which one can predict which allocations will occur when prices are not the Walrasian ones. It also provides the first steps of a theory of endogenous price making, in line with the traditional theories of imperfect competition in general equilibrium. This theory is certainly called for new interesting developments and applications as new modes of price making without an auctioneer will be integrated within that framework.

JEAN-PASCAL BENASSY

See also DISEQUILIBRIUM ANALYSIS; FIXPRICE MODELS; GENERAL EQUILIBRIUM.

BIBLIOGRAPHY

Arrow, K.J. 1959. Towards a theory of price adjustment. In *The Allocation of Economic Resources*, ed. M. Abramowitz, Stanford: Stanford University Press.

Arrow, K.J. and Debreu, G. 1954. Existence of an equilibrium for a competitive economy. *Econometrica* 22, 265–90.

Arrow, K.J. and Hahn, F. 1971. *General Competitive Analysis*. San Francisco: Holden-Day.

Barro, R.J. and Grossman, H.I. 1971. A general disequilibrium model of income and employment. *American Economic Review* 61, 82–93.

Barro, R.J. and Grossman, H.I. 1976. *Money, Employment and Inflation*. Cambridge: Cambridge University Press.

Bellman, R. 1957. *Dynamic Programming*. Princeton: Princeton University Press.

Benassy, J.P. 1975a. Neo-Keynesian disequilibrium theory in a monetary economy. *Review of Economic Studies* 42, 502–23.

Benassy, J.P. 1975b. Disequilibrium exchange in barter and monetary economies. *Economic Inquiry* 13, 131–56.

Benassy, J.P. 1976. The disequilibrium approach to monopolistic price setting and general monopolistic equilibrium. *Review of Economic Studies* 43, 69–81.

Benassy, J.P. 1977a. A neokeynesian model of price and quantity determination in disequilibrium. In *Equilibrium and Disequilibrium in Economic Theory*, ed. G. Schwödiauer, Boston: D. Reidel.

Benassy, J.P. 1977b. On quantity signals and the foundations of effective demand theory. *Scandinavian Journal of Economics* 79, 147–68.

Benassy, J.P. 1982. *The Economics of Market Disequilibrium*. New York: Academic Press.

Benassy, J.P. 1986. *Macroeconomics: An Introduction to the Non-Walrasian Approach*. New York: Academic Press.

Böhm, V. and Levine, P. 1979. Temporary equilibria with quantity rationing. *Review of Economic Studies* 46, 361–77.

Bushaw, D.W. and Clower, R. 1957. *Introduction to Mathematical Economics*. Homewood, Ill.: Richard D. Irwin.

Clower, R.W. 1965. The Keynesian counterrevolution: a theoretical appraisal. In *The Theory of Interest Rates*, ed. F.H. Hahn and F.P.R. Brechling, London: Macmillan.

Debreu, G. 1959. *Theory of Value*. New York: Wiley.

Dehez, P. and Drèze, J.H. 1984. On supply constrained equilibria. *Journal of Economic Theory* 33, 172–82.

Drèze, J.H. 1975. Existence of an exchange equilibrium under price rigidities. *International Economic Review* 16, 301–20.

Glustoff, E. 1968. On the existence of a Keynesian equilibrium. *Review of Economic Studies* 35, 327–34.

Grandmont, J.M. and Laroque, G. 1976. On Keynesian temporary equilibria. *Review of Economic Studies* 43, 53–67.

Greenberg, J. and Müller, H. 1979. Equilibria under price rigidities and externalities. In *Game Theory and Related Topics*, ed. O. Moeschlin and D. Pallaschke, Amsterdam: North-Holland.

Hahn, F.H. 1978. On non-Walrasian equilibria. *Review of Economic Studies* 45, 1–17.

Heller, W.P. and Starr, R.M. 1979. Unemployment equilibrium with myopic complete information. *Review of Economic Studies* 46, 339–59.

Hicks, J.R. 1939. *Value and Capital*. Oxford: Clarendon Press. 2nd edn, 1946.

Keynes, J.M. 1936. *The General Theory of Money, Interest and Employment*. New York: Harcourt, Brace.

Leijonhufvud, A. 1968. *On Keynesian Economics and the Economics of Keynes*. Oxford: Oxford University Press.

Neary, J.P. and Stiglitz, J.E. 1983. Toward a reconstruction of Keynesian economics: expectations and constrained equilibria. *Quarterly Journal of Economics* 98, Supplement, 199–228.

Negishi, T. 1961. Monopolistic competition and general equilibrium. *Review of Economic Studies* 28, 196–201.

Negishi, T. 1972. *General Equilibrium Theory and International Trade*. Amsterdam: North-Holland.

Nikaido, H. 1975. *Monopolistic Competition and Effective Demand*. Princeton: Princeton University Press.

Schulz, N. 1983. On the global uniqueness of fixprice equilibria. *Econometrica* 51, 47–68.

Silvestre, J. 1982. Fixprice analysis of exchange economies. *Journal of Economic Theory* 26, 28–58.

Silvestre, J. 1983. Fixprice analysis in productive economies. *Journal of Economic Theory* 30, 401–9.

Triffin, R. 1940. *Monopolistic Competition and General Equilibrium Theory*. Cambridge, Mass.: Harvard University Press.

Van Der Laan G. 1980. Equilibrium under rigid prices with compensation for the consumers. *International Economic Review* 21, 63–74.

Walras, L. 1874. *Eléments d'économie politique pure*. Lausanne: Corbaz. Definitive edition translated by W. Jaffé: *Elements of Pure Economics*, London: Allen & Unwin, 1954.

Younès, Y. 1975. On the role of money in the process of exchange and the existence of a non-Walrasian equilibrium. *Review of Economic Studies* 42, 489–501.

rationing. The standard theory of consumer behaviour assumes that the consumer is free to purchase unlimited quantities of commodities at fixed prices, subject only to a linear budget constraint which derives from his given income or expenditure. By contrast, in many situations, consumers are constrained in the levels of particular commodities which they may consume. Such quantity constraints may impose consumption levels either below or above those levels that would be freely chosen: goods rationing in wartime illustrates the former, while examples of the latter include precommitted expenditures and unemployment (which may be viewed as 'forced consumption' of leisure). From an analytic point of view, the two cases are identical and may be described by the general term 'rationing'. Following a brief introduction, this article outlines the principal results of the microeconomic theory of rationing and then notes some of its recent applications. We concentrate throughout on 'simple' rationing (i.e., exogenous restrictions on the consumption of particular commodities); some work has also been done on 'points' rationing (where the consumer has a number of ration 'points' or 'coupons' to be allocated between a group of commodities) and there is an extensive literature on the general case of non-linear budget constraints, from both theoretical and empirical perspectives (see Hausman, 1985).

The prevalence of rationing in World War II Britain led to a great deal of work on its theoretical and empirical implications. (See the survey by Tobin, 1952.) A subsequent lapse of interest was followed by a revival in the 1970s, as the importance of quantity constraints began to be recognized in a number of areas. These included: empirical demand analysis, where the increased use of complete systems of demand equations drew attention to applications (such as consumer durables, labour supply, etc.) where the assumption of unconstrained choice is implausible, at least in the short run; public economics, where the increasingly sophisticated study of optimal public policy was extended to public goods (the consumption of which is predetermined from an individual consumer's point of view) and non-linear commodity taxation (of which government-imposed consumption quotas are a special but empirically important case); and macroeconomics, where the work of Clower (1965) and Barro and Grossman (1971) led to a reinterpretation of Keynes's contribution as the economics of 'general disequilibrium', in which the failure of prices to adjust faces agents with quantity constraints which 'spill over' to influence their behaviour in other markets. These areas remain the principal fields in which rationing theory has been applied.

The case where only two commodities are consumed misses many important aspects of rationing. Nevertheless, it serves to introduce most of the basic ideas. In Figure 1, the unconstrained optimal consumption bundle (x_0, y_0) is represented by point *A*, the point of tangency between the budget constraint *BC* and the highest attainable indifference curve, II. Suppose now that the consumer is faced with an additional constraint which stipulates that consumption of commodity y cannot exceed the level $\bar{y}$. The consumer is therefore forced to adjust consumption to the point *D*. Here, the budget constraint

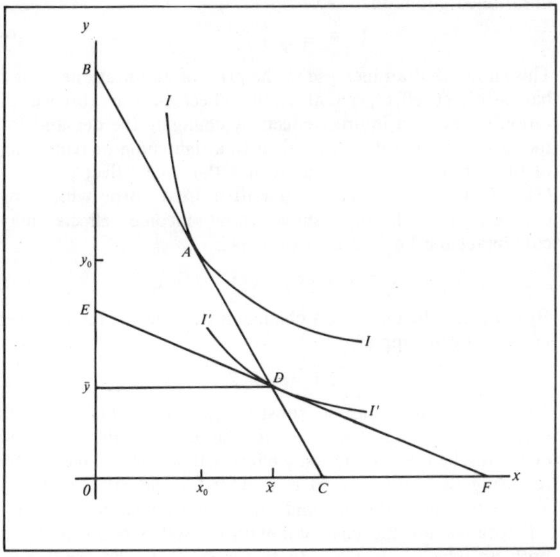

Figure 1

is still satisfied, consumption of y is constrained to equal $\bar{y}$, and expenditure has spilled over onto the unrationed commodity x, leading to a new higher consumption level $\tilde{x}$.

The rationed optimum at point *D* is of course extremely special because the number of commodities is the same as the number of independent binding constraints, so that the optimal consumption bundle is uniquely determined. In the more usual case, where there are fewer constraints than commodities, the consumer is free to allocate his uncommitted expenditure between a number of unrationed commodities, and a major focus of rationing theory has been on the manner in which this allocation, and its responsiveness to changes in exogenous variables, is affected by the presence of rationing. As the problem is usually formulated, this amounts to asking how the behaviour of a rationed consumer may be related to that of an unrationed one. One approach to answering this is to note that an unrationed consumer might *choose* to consume at point *D* under certain circumstances. Specifically, this would occur if the consumer were faced with a relative price ratio equal to the tangent to the indifference curve *I'I'* at *D*, and were given an adjusted level of income such that that point represented the unconstrained utility-maximizing consumption bundle. The hypothetical relative price ratio required is given by the slope of the line *EF*. Following Rothbarth (1941) and Neary and Roberts (1980), the difference between this and the actual price ratio is that the actual price of the rationed commodity must be replaced by its *virtual* price: that is, that price which would induce the consumer to purchase the ration level voluntarily. The advantage of this approach is that the effect of any exogenous shock on a rationed consumer may be decomposed into the sum of two effects on an orthodox unrationed consumer: the direct effect of the shock itself and the indirect effect arising from the induced change in the virtual price of the rationed good. (Note in passing that the terms 'virtual price' or 'demand price' are preferable to 'shadow price', since the latter risks confusion with the shadow price of the ration constraint which emerges from the consumer's maximization problem.)

It is clear that for non-zero virtual prices to be unique and well defined, it is necessary that the indifference curve at *D* be convex and differentiable. (Further technical details may be found in Neary and Roberts, 1980.) Provided assumptions on preferences sufficient to guarantee this are made, this approach may be extended to the general case where unrationed commodities are represented by a vector x and their prices by a vector p; while the commodity subject to a binding ration constraint is represented by a scalar y and its market price by q. (The analysis can easily be generalized to allow for more than one rationed commodity.) It is then straightforward to relate the Hicksian or compensated demand schedules for x in the presence of rationing to the corresponding unrationed schedules, since both are evaluated at the same utility level, that corresponding to the indifference curve *I'I'*:

$$\tilde{x}^c(p, \bar{y}, u) = x^c(p, \bar{q}, u). \qquad (1)$$

Here, x^c denotes compensated demands, and a tilde ($\sim$) denotes a demand schedule for unrationed commodities in the presence of the ration constraint $\bar{y}$. Of course, the virtual price $\bar{q}$ is not a parameter but is defined implicitly by the condition that it equate the unconstrained demand for y to the ration level $\bar{y}$:

$$\bar{y} = y^c(p, \bar{q}, u). \qquad (2)$$

Differentiating (1) and (2) now yields two important comparative statics results. Consider first the effect of a change in the ration level $\bar{y}$ on the demand for unrationed commodities x:

$$\tilde{x}_y^c = x_q^c (y_q^c)^{-1}, \tag{3}$$

where subscripts indicate partial derivatives (e.g., $\tilde{x}_y^c$ is the vector whose ith element gives the partial derivative of the rationed compensated demand function for x_i with respect to the level of the ration constraint). Since the compensated own-price derivative y_q^c is negative, the sign of (3) depends on the sign of x_q^c. Thus, a tightening of the ration constraint (a reduction in $\bar{y}$) raises the compensated demand for unrationed commodities which are net substitutes for y and reduces it for commodities which are net complements for y.

Next, consider the effects on the demand for x of changes in their own prices. Differentiating (1) and (2) and rearranging yields:

$$\tilde{x}_p^c - x_p^c = -x_q^c (y_q^c)^{-1} x_q^c. \tag{4}$$

This shows that the *difference* between the matrices of own-price responses of the unrationed commodities with and without rationing is a positive definite matrix. For any particular unrationed commodity, this implies that rationing *reduces* its responsiveness to its own price. This result is often referred to as the *Le Chatelier principle*, and was first introduced into economics by Samuelson (1947, pp. 36–9). Its limitations should be carefully noted: it relates only to a comparison of *compensated* demands (compare (10) below); and it requires that the derivatives of both rationed and unrationed demand schedules be evaluated at the same consumption bundle. (For example, in Figure 1, both demand schedules are evaluated at the consumption bundle given by point D, whereas the properties of the unrationed demand schedule at that point may differ considerably from its properties at the unconstrained consumption bundle *A*.) Despite these qualifications, the principle is often interpreted as implying in a general sense that the imposition of restrictions on some aspects of behaviour makes individuals less responsive to exogenous changes in their environment.

Equations (3) and (4) are two of the most important results in rationing theory. However, their simplicity depends crucially on the fact that they refer to the properties of compensated demand schedules. There is one special case where equation (3) holds exactly for uncompensated (Marshallian) as well as compensated (Hicksian) demands, namely where the ration 'just' binds, in the sense that the ration constraint $\bar{y}$ coincides exactly with the amount of y that would be demanded by an unrationed consumer (so that points *A* and *D* in Figure 1 coincide). This was the case for which Tobin and Houthakker (1950–1) derived their results in a classic paper. For strictly binding ration constraints, any exogenous change has additional income effects, and their implications were derived independently by Deaton (1981), Neary and Roberts (1980) and others.

To illustrate the additional income effects which strictly binding ration constraints introduce, refer again to Figure 1. The distance *OC* measures the consumer's actual income in terms of x, I/p or $\tilde{x} + (q/p)\bar{y}$. However, this income would not be sufficient to induce an unrationed consumer faced with prices p and $\tilde{q}$ to consume voluntarily at *D*; to do this they would need an income equal (in terms of good x) to the distance *OF*. Simple geometry shows that this distance equals $\tilde{x} + (\tilde{q}/p)\bar{y}$, or $[I + (\tilde{q} - q)\bar{y}]/p$. Hence, the uncompensated demands of the rationed consumer may be equated to the uncompensated demands of an unrationed consumer, provided the latter are evaluated at the virtual price $\tilde{q}$ and at a 'virtual income' $I + (\tilde{q} - q)\bar{y}$:

$$\tilde{x}(\bar{y}, p, q, I) = x[p, \tilde{q}, I + (\tilde{q} - q)\bar{y}]. \tag{5}$$

In addition, the virtual price and income must be such that they induce an uncompensated demand for the rationed good equal to the ration constraint, so that (2) must be replaced by:

$$\bar{y} = y[p, \tilde{q}, I + (\tilde{q} - q)\bar{y}]. \tag{6}$$

Differentiating (5) and (6) now yields the full effects of exogenous changes on the demand for unrationed commodities. Consider first the effect of a change in income:

$$\tilde{x}_I = x_I - \tilde{x}_y^c y_I. \tag{7}$$

Thus, an increase in income affects demands for unrationed goods in two ways: first, it has a direct effect identical to the effect of an income increase in the absence of rationing (though evaluated at the virtual prices and income of course); and secondly, by raising demand for the rationed good (assuming that y is normal so that y_I is positive), it is equivalent to a tightening of the ration constraint, and so has an indirect effect given by equation (3).

Consider next the effect of a change in the ration constraint. Differentiating (5) and (6) yields after some manipulation:

$$\tilde{x}_y = \tilde{x}_y^c + \tilde{x}_I(\tilde{q} - q). \tag{8}$$

This shows that a tightening of the ration constraint has a compensated or substitution effect given by (3) and an additional income effect, given by the last term in (8). This term vanishes if the virtual and actual price of the rationed good coincide, which corresponds to the case where the ration constraint 'just' binds. In the case illustrated in Figure 1, where the consumer would like to consume more of the rationed good, $\tilde{q}$ exceeds q, and so a tightening of the ration constraint, by lowering real income, tends to reduce the demand for all normal unrationed goods. (Of course, as already noted in discussing the diagram, the total effect must be an increase in spending on the unrationed goods as a group.)

Finally, the effect of changes in prices may be obtained in a similar manner. Firstly, for an increase in the prices of the unrationed goods themselves:

$$\tilde{x}_p = x_p - \tilde{x}_y^c y_p. \tag{9}$$

This shows that an increase in the price of an unrationed good has a direct effect, equal to its effect in the absence of rationing, and an indirect effect: by changing the demand for the rationed good it is equivalent to a tightening or relaxation of the ration constraint and so has the usual effect given by (3). Equation (9) may be rewritten in a form which, by comparison with (4), shows how income effects may counteract the Le Chatelier principle:

$$\tilde{x}_p - x_p = (\tilde{x}_p^c - x_p^c) + \tilde{x}_y^c y_I x. \tag{10}$$

By contrast, the effect of a change in the price of the rationed good is much simpler:

$$\tilde{x}_q = -\tilde{x}_I \bar{y}. \tag{11}$$

This price change has no substitution effect, which explains why q is not an argument in the compensated rationed demand schedules (1). Its only effect is to lower real income by requiring the consumer to pay more for the rationed good, and so it reduces the demand for normal unrationed goods.

Before leaving the basic comparative statics of rationing, a problem which is peculiar to this area should be mentioned. All the results which have been derived assume that the values of the exogenous variables are such that the ration constraint is a binding one. However, it is quite possible for a finite change in an exogenous variable to render the constraint non-binding. For example, in Figure 1, this would occur if the ration constraint $\bar{y}$ rose above the unconstrained demand $y(p, q, I)$. If this happens, the ration constraint ceases to be binding and the ordinary unconstrained demand functions become applicable. Shifts of 'regime' such as this dictate great care in applying rationing theory in cases where large finite changes in exogenous variables occur; and in applications where interest focuses on the interaction between constraints which impinge on different agents (such as fix-price macroeconomics).

Turning to applications of the theory, it is often desirable to impose further restrictions on the structure of preferences in order to derive stronger properties of the rationed demand functions. One such restriction with attractive implications is the assumption of *weak separability* between the rationed and unrationed commodities. This implies that the direct utility function $v(x, y)$ can be written in the form $U[f(x), y]$ where f is a scalar sub-utility function. In this case, it is unnecessary to work with virtual prices at all, since the constrained demand functions for the unrationed goods, $\tilde{x}(\bar{y}, p, q, I)$, take the special form $\tilde{X}(p, I - q\bar{y})$. This has the very strong implication that the level of the ration constraint has an income effect only, so that (8) simplifies to:

$$\tilde{x}_y = -\tilde{x}_I q. \qquad (8')$$

This specification is plausible in the case of some public goods (e.g., increased spending on national defence is unlikely to affect the pattern of demand for private goods). Unfortunately, in other applications, it has highly implausible implications. For example, if leisure is the rationed commodity, weak separability implies that all other goods must be substitutes for it, irrespective of the extent of unemployment. Nevertheless, some interesting work has been carried out using weakly separable specifications. For example, Ashenfelter (1977) estimated a complete system of demand equations for unemployed and employed households, whose preferences were characterized by a Stone-Geary utility function (which is additively, and therefore *a fortiori* weakly, separable).

More recently, attention has focused on deriving explicit forms for rationed demand functions which are tractable but not as restrictive as those implied by weak separability. As in the case of consumer theory in the absence of rationing, progress in this direction seems most likely not by specifying functional forms for the direct utility function but by adopting a dual approach, which takes the expenditure function as its starting point. In the presence of rationing the constrained expenditure function gives the minimum cost of attaining a given utility level:

$$\tilde{E}(\bar{y}, p, q, u) = \min_x [p'x + q\bar{y}: v(x, y) \geq u]. \qquad (12)$$

$$= p'\tilde{x}^c(\bar{y}, p, u) + q\bar{y}. \qquad (12')$$

Substituting from (1) and (2) yields, after some manipulation, the fundamental relationship between constrained and unconstrained expenditure functions:

$$\tilde{E}(\bar{y}, p, q, u) = E(p, \bar{q}, u) + (\bar{q} - q)\bar{y}. \qquad (13)$$

In principle, this identity permits the derivation of a matched pair of rationed and unrationed demand functions, characterizing the behaviour of the same consumer in both environments. Two interesting specifications of the expenditure function which permit this are investigated in the labour supply context by Deaton and Muellbauer (1981). Unfortunately, the derivation of such matched pairs of demand functions is not possible in general. An alternative approach is to specify a general functional form for the rationed expenditure function which imposes fewer restrictions on demand responses though at the cost of an inability to write the unrationed demand functions in closed form. This approach has been pursued by Deaton (1981), who derives a system of rationed demand functions which express budget shares as a linear function of the ration level and the logarithms of prices and real expenditure on unrationed goods. He shows that treating expenditure on housing as predetermined in this framework leads to more plausible results than when it is assumed to be unconstrained. (Specifically, the rationed system goes much of the way towards avoiding the implausible rejection of homogeneity in nominal variables, which has been found in many empirical studies of demand.)

A different type of application of rationing theory is to the calculation of the welfare costs associated with it. Attempts to do this in wartime Britain included Rothbarth (1940–1) and Nicholson (1942–3), who estimated the correction to the official price index required as a result of commodity rationing. Analytically, it is easily seen from (13) that a money measure of the additional cost of attaining a given utility level as a result of a small tightening of the ration level is given by the difference between the virtual and the market prices of the rationed good:

$$-\tilde{E}_y = \bar{q} - q. \qquad (14)$$

For finite changes in the degree of rationing it is possible to integrate over (14). Thus the calculation of consumer-surplus-type measures of changes in the cost of living as a result of changes in prices or ration levels need not pose any greater conceptual or empirical difficulties than they do in the absence of rationing.

Finally, within a utility-maximizing framework, it may be noted that rationing necessarily imposes a welfare loss. This consideration underlies the instinctive preference by most economists for the use of the price system as an allocation mechanism rather than direct controls, a preference which is supported by the two fundamental theorems of welfare economics. Nevertheless, in situations where the conditions for these theorems do not obtain, it may be possible to give a second-best justification for rationing. While work along these lines pertains more to public economics than to rationing theory per se, mention may be made of two especially interesting contributions. One is a paper by Weitzman (1977), who develops a model where the just distribution of a particular commodity on the basis of need alone is considered a socially desirable end in itself. He shows that rationing the commodity is preferable to allocating it via the price system if tastes are homogeneous but income is unevenly distributed. The other is a paper by Guesnerie and Roberts (1984), who show that, in a second-best world with given commodity taxes (so that consumer prices diverge from marginal social valuations), rationing is likely to be welfare improving.

J.P. Neary

See also DEMAND THEORY; LABOUR SUPPLY; LE CHATELIER PRINCIPLE.

BIBLIOGRAPHY

Ashenfelter, O. 1980. Unemployment as disequilibrium in a model of aggregate labour supply. *Econometrica* 48, 547–64.

Barro, R.J. and Grossman, H.I. 1971. A general disequilibrium model of income and employment. *American Economic Review* 61, 82–93.

Clower, R.W. 1965. The Keynesian counter-revolution: a theoretical appraisal. In *The Theory of Interest Rates*, ed. F.H. Hahn and F.P.R. Brechling, London: Macmillan.
Deaton, A.S. 1981. Theoretical and empirical approaches to consumer demand under rationing. In *Essays in the Theory and Measurement of Consumer Behaviour in Honour of Sir Richard Stone*, ed. A.S. Deaton, Cambridge: Cambridge University Press, 55–72.
Deaton, A. and Muellbauer, J. 1981. Functional forms for labour supply and commodity demands with and without quantity constraints. *Econometrica* 49, 1521–32.
Guesnerie, R. and Roberts, K.W.S. 1984. Effective policy tools and quantity controls. *Econometrica* 52, 59–86.
Hausman, J.A. 1985. The econometrics of nonlinear budget sets. *Econometrica* 53, 1255–82.
Neary, J.P. and Roberts, K.W.S. 1980. The theory of household behaviour under rationing. *European Economic Review* 13, 25–42.
Nicholson, J.L. 1942–3. Rationing and index numbers. *Review of Economic Studies* 10, 68–72.
Rothbarth, E. 1941. The measurement of changes in real income under conditions of rationing. *Review of Economic Studies* 8, 100–107.
Samuelson, P.A. 1947. *Foundations of Economic Analysis*. Cambridge, Mass.: Harvard University Press.
Tobin, J. 1952. A survey of the theory of rationing. *Econometrica* 20, 512–53.
Tobin, J. and Houthakker, H.S. 1950–51. The effects of rationing on demand elasticities. *Review of Economic Studies* 18, 140–53.
Weitzman, M. 1977. Is the price system or rationing more effective in getting a commodity to those who need it most? *Bell Journal of Economics* 8, 517–24.

Rau, Karl Heinrich (1792–1870). Rau was born in Erlangen and was a Lecturer (*Privatdozent*) and Professor (1816). In 1822 Rau was appointed to a chair of economics at the University of Freiburg. Involved in political affairs, as were many German professors in the 19th century, he was appointed a member of the upper Chamber of Baden and in 1848 was elected to the Frankfurt Assembly.

At first influenced by Cameralist ideas, Rau was one of the main mediators and defenders of Smith's 'system of natural liberty', whose central principles, abstractly exposed, he embodied in a rich supply of illustrative facts in his famous *Lehrbuch* (1826–37) yet without attempting to test his hypotheses empirically, i.e. to use factual materials as confirmation instead of pure description. To that extent he was not an original thinker. Yet he was a great teacher. Similar to Samuelson's *Economics* in our time, his bestselling textbook, published in eight editions (1862–9) was an authoritative work for the majority of economists teaching at German universities for several generations. Based on classical ideas, it thus shaped the economic and political *Weltbild* of future civil servants and lawyers.

Rau's tripartite division of economics, which was obviously influenced by Smith, was divided into three volumes, theory (economic laws), policy (*Polizeiwissenschaft*) and public finance; this division became the established tradition in the teaching of political economy at German universities and is divisive up to the present day. With the rise and the establishment of the German Historical School its stress on both the ethical aspect of economic issues, that is of the distribution of income and property, and on the historical character of economic principles, Rau's star faded although his work on public finance became the foundations of Wagner's famous treatise.

Viewed in a historical continuum, the Freiburg School (Eucken, Röpke, von Hayek), Erhard's liberal economic policy and, more recently, a group of German economists who are attempting to revive Smith's tripartite theory of order (ethics, economics and politics as an entity) all indirectly resume that thread of Rau's concept, although on a different analytical level (Recktenwald, 1985). In the light of a worldwide Smith renaissance in our epoch, Rau's editing function seems to merit secular attention.

H.C. Recktenwald

SELECTED WORKS

For a complete list, see C. Meitzel, *Handwörterbuch der Staatswissenschaft*, 4th edn, Vol. 6, Jena: G. Fischer, 1925.

1825. *Über die Kameralwissenschaft*. Heidelberg: Groos.
1826–37. *Lehrbuch der politischen Ökonomie*. 3 vols. 8th edn, Heidelberg: C.F. Winter.

BIBLIOGRAPHY

Recktenwald, H.C. (ed.) 1973. *Political Economy: A Historical Perspective*. London: Collier-Macmillan, particularly the introduction.
Recktenwald, H.C. (ed.) 1985. *Ethik, Wirtschaft und Staat: Adam Smiths politische Ökonomie heute*. Darmstadt: Wissenschaftliche Buchgesellschaft, particularly 110–20 and 345–90 and G.J. Stigler's and P.A. Samuelson's contributions.

Ravenstone, Piercy. Attention was drawn to a book bearing this author's name because it is mentioned in the Ricardo–Malthus–Mill correspondence. The true identity of the author is not known for certain, although Sraffa (1973), on the basis of two separate identifications in libraries, suggests it was Richard Puller (*fl.* 1789–1831); on the basis of internal evidence, Dorfman (1966) had previously suggested that the author was an Anglican clergyman, Edward Edwards.

The author has been classified (by Seligman and by Halévy) as a Socialist; as a Tory Democrat (by Beer); and as an Institutionalist (by W.C. Mitchell). The content of the work discussed by Ricardo is, however, essentially Physiocratic; there is no understanding of division of labour, productivity, or exchange; tradesmen add no value but simply pass wealth through their hands; and a large sterile class enjoys revenue generated by a productive class employed in agriculture. Property is perfectly justifiable where it originates in labour, but it has developed into an institution enabling the sterile class to live on the productivity of the productive class. This abstraction takes place through both rent and profits – capital is an imaginary concept designed to justify the revenue enjoyed as profit. Poverty is not caused by Malthusian population pressures – with remarkable self-confidence in the employment of arithmetical ratios, the author satisfied himself that the rate of population increase was everywhere constant – but to the abstraction of revenue for the sterile classes. Since debt service taxes were also used to this end, public debt was undesirable.

D.P. O'Brien

SELECTED WORKS

1821. *A Few Doubts as to the correctness of some opinions generally entertained on the subjects of Population and Political Economy*. London: J. Andrews. Reprinted with an introduction by J. Dorfman, New York: A.M. Kelley, 1966.
1824. *Thoughts on the Funding System and its Effects*. London: J. Andrews.

BIBLIOGRAPHY

Sraffa, P. (ed.) 1952, 1973. *The Works and Correspondence of David Ricardo*, Vols IX, XI. Cambridge: Cambridge University Press for the Royal Economic Society.

Raymond, Daniel. (1786–1849). The first American to publish a treatise on economic topics, Raymond was born in Connecticut but made his home in Baltimore, where he practised law. *Thoughts on Political Economy* (1820) was written to while away the time as the young attorney waited for clients. The book constituted a challenge to classical orthodoxy and as such was warmly received by the protectionists. To make his voice more resounding they tried (without success) to secure Raymond a professorship at the University of Maryland that they were willing to underwrite. Raymond was an original thinker, whose ideas reverberated in the later writings of Frederick List, the historical economists and the 20th-century literature on economic development.

Raymond's principal concern was national economic development and, unlike the classics, he placed the nation rather than the individual in the centre of his analysis. Following Lauderdale, he distinguished between national and individual wealth, but unlike Lauderdale, to whom usefulness was the characteristic feature of public wealth and scarcity that of private wealth, Raymond interpreted national wealth in terms of its 'capacity' to produce goods. This view opens up to government a central position in promoting economic development by means of tariff protection. Raymond also underlines the conflicts of interest among different groups in the economy and again calls on government for their resolution.

While Raymond's basic ideas reflect the influence of Alexander Hamilton, his distrust of paper money and bank credit echoes the related views of Jefferson. Raymond also was highly critical of corporations. These incongruities were bound to affect the impact of his work.

HENRY W. SPIEGEL

See also NATIONAL SYSTEM.

SELECTED WORKS

1819. *The Missouri Question.* Baltimore: Schaeffer & Maund.
1820. *Thoughts on Political Economy.* Baltimore: F. Lucas, Jr.
1828. *The American System.* Baltimore: Lucas & Deaver.
n.d. *The Elements of Constitutional Law.* 2nd edn, Baltimore: F. Lucas, Jr. and E.J. Cooder, 1832.

BIBLIOGRAPHY

Conkin, P.K. 1980. *Prophets of Prosperity: America's First Political Economists.* Bloomington: Indiana University Press.
Dorfman, J. 1946. *The Economic Mind in American Civilization 1606–1865.* New York: Viking.

Read, Samuel (*fl.* 1816–29). There is no biography of Samuel Read. Nothing is known of his life apart from his writings, which were all published between 1816 and 1829 in Edinburgh. The Preface of his principal work was annotated from Roslin, which is about eight miles south of Edinburgh.

Read's earlier tracts were on currency and government debt, plus a small pamphlet opposing Malthus on population. His major work was *An Inquiry into the Natural Grounds of Right to Vendible Property or Wealth*, published in 1829, in which he tried to put certain moral laws against the importance that economists attributed to material wealth. He used the utilitarian calculus as the basis for human action and the determination of economic justice, which included the natural right of the poor to public support. Labour he deemed the foundation and only certain measure of value. But wealth was more than just the product of labour, since accumulated capital and land also contributed to its production.

Read admitted Samuel Bailey's (1825) influence, but this extended only to showing the absurdity of reducing capital and the time needed for its production into mere labour expended; he did not follow Bailey on the relativity of value. With Bailey and some other Ricardian critics, Read objected to the theory that wages and profits varied inversely and he hinted at an abstinence factor in the supply of capital, thus predating Nassau Senior (1836).

Read was also somewhat ahead of the economists of his time in urging nationalization of local poor rates (i.e. the taxes necessary to support the unemployed, indigent, and other needy), but Samuel Whitbread had already proposed regularization of the poor relief rates in 1807.

R.M. RAUNER

SELECTED WORKS

1816. *On Money and the Bank Restriction Laws.* Edinburgh.
1818. *The Problem Solved; an explication of a plan of a safe, steady, and secure government paper currency, and legal tender.* Edinburgh.
1819. *Exposure of Certain Plagiarisms of J.R. McCulloch Esq., author of two essays on reduction of the interest of the National Debt, committed in the last published of those essays, the Scotsman Newspaper and the Edinburgh Review.* Edinburgh.
1821. *General Statement of an Argument on the Subject of Population in Answer to Mr. Malthus's Theory.* Edinburgh.
1829. *An Inquiry into the Natural Grounds of Right to Vendible Property or Wealth.* Edinburgh.

BIBLIOGRAPHY

Bailey, S. 1825. *A Critical Dissertation on the Nature, Measures, and Causes of Value; chiefly in reference to the writings of Mr. Ricardo and his followers.* London.
Senior, N. 1836. *An Outline of the Science of Political Economy.* London: Allen & Unwin.

real and nominal quantities. Adam Smith, in his *Inquiry into the Nature and Causes of the Wealth of Nations* of 1776, distinguished between the *nominal* price and the *real* price of commodities. He defined the nominal price of a commodity as its price in silver or gold and the real price as the quantity of labour which it can purchase or 'command'. In other words, he adopted the money wage of ordinary labour as his standard of value. Ever since the critical commentaries of Ricardo and Marx this choice of standard has been seen by many as evidence that Smith's measure and theory of value were confused or inconsistent (see Ricardo, *Works* I, pp. 14–15; Marx, 1861–63, I, pp. 69–77; II, pp. 200, 369; and Douglas, 1928). More recently there has been a rejection of the view that Smith confused labour embodied and labour commanded and, as Hollander says, 'the issue at hand, it is now generally recognized, corresponds to the modern "index number" problem of estimating changes in "real income" over space and time' (Hollander, 1973, p. 127; see also Schumpeter, 1954, p. 127 and Blaug, 1978, pp. 51–3).

Undoubtedly some of this criticism and disagreement arose because of the obscurity of Smith's account – his chapter 'On the real and nominal Price of Commodities or of their Price in Labour, and their Price in Money' has recently been described as 'arguably ... the most convoluted chapter ever to emerge from the pen of a great economist' (O'Brien, 1975, p. 82). However, if the *purpose* for which Smith wanted this measure of value, and the *assumptions* upon which he based it, are clearly identified then no serious confusions or inconsistencies are found, and the now widely accepted view that he adopted labour command as an index of general purchasing power can be dismissed.

SMITH'S LABOUR COMMAND MEASURE. In his treatment of value Smith focused on *changes* in relative price brought about in the process of technical change (see Bladen, 1975). Consequently he was concerned to find a 'standard by which we can compare the values of different commodities at all times and at all places' (Smith, 1776, I, v.17). He rejected gold and silver because their values vary due to changes in their method of production, and 'a commodity which is itself continually varying in its own value, can never be an accurate measure of the value of other commodities' (1776, I, v.7). It has seldom been noted that in choosing to measure the change in the value of a commodity by the change in the quantity of labour it can command Smith made a number of assumptions which served to lend a rational foundation to that choice: he adopted a set of assumptions which rendered changes in the labour *commanded* by a commodity roughly proportional to changes in the labour *embodied* in it.

First, Smith assumed that 'equal quantities of labour, at all times and places, may be said to be equal value to the labourer' (1776, I, v.7) – thus labour *time* is a good measure of ultimate dearness or difficulty of production. This assumption has indeed been noted by many commentators. Second, Smith assumed that the corn wage was constant over long periods (1776, I, v.15). Third, and most significant, was Smith's assumption that corn was produced at constant cost. He made only an oblique reference to this in chapter v of Book I (see 1776, I, v.16) but that scarcely excuses this crucial assumption being ignored in most commentaries (see, e.g. Bowley, 1973, p. 116) and openly denied in others (see Hollander, 1973, p. 130n). For, when he came to *use* his labour command or corn measure Smith made this assumption quite explicit –

> In every different stage of improvement, besides, the raising of equal quantities of corn in the same soil and climate, will, at an average, require nearly equal quantities of labour; or what comes to the same thing, the price of nearly equal quantities (1776, I, xi.e.28).

Furthermore, he stated clearly that this constant cost was the *basis* upon which his use of the labour or corn measure of value was founded (1776, I, xi.e.28).

THE OPERATION OF SMITH'S MEASURE. The assumptions outlined above lent a degree of logical validity to labour command or corn as a measure of *changes* in value. As Sylos-Labini points out, it is known 'that the variations of this standard correspond to those expressed by labour embodied if the distributive shares are constant' (Sylos-Labini, 1976, p. 206). It should be clear that the use by Smith of a labour commanded or corn measure to examine changes in value due to changes in methods of production depended not only on a constant corn wage but also on the constant production cost of corn. For without this is a change in the *real price* (labour command) of any given commodity could indicate not only a change in *its* value but also a change in the value of *corn*.

A numerical example can be constructed which illustrates the primary use of the labour command measure of value in the *Wealth of Nations*. Consider a *manufactured commodity* in the production of which improved techniques have reduced the amount of labour required (H) from 2 to 1.

	H	W	$H.W$	a	$P=(WH/a)$	P/W
time 1:	2	10	20	0.5	40	4
time 2:	1	10	10	0.5	20	2

A constant corn wage requires a constant money wage (W) of 10, given the unchanged production conditions of corn and an unchanged value of money. If the share of wages in the value of output (denoted a) is constant then the change (fall) in the value (of the manufacturer commodity) measured in labour commanded (P/W) will be proportional to its change measured in labour embodied (H). Both labour embodied and labour commanded will have been halved. Smith's major use of his measure of value in this fashion was in his long 'Digression concerning the variations in the value of silver' in chapter xi of Book I. There he challenged the conventional view that a high or low *money* price of goods in general – that is, a high or low value of silver – was an indicator of the level of economic development of a country (1776, I, xi. n. 2). Against this he argued that it was only from the high or low price of certain goods 'in proportion to that *of corn*' (i.e. their high or low *real price*) that 'we can infer, with a degree of probability that approaches almost to certainty, that it was rich or poor, that the greater part of its lands were improved or unimproved, and that it was either in a more or less barbarous state, or in a more or less civilized one' (1776, I, xi. n. 3).

In view of this demonstration that Smith's measure of value was designed precisely to deal with *changing* relative prices it is clear that the now widely accepted view that he saw the labour command value or real price of a given commodity or aggregate of commodities as an index of its *general purchasing power* must be dismissed. Indeed, it is a wonder that the spread of this interpretation was not long ago halted by Smith's own explicit statement that differential rates of productivity growth will sever any connection between changes in the value of an individual commodity as measured by labour commanded (or labour embodied) and changes in its purchasing power over other commodities in general (see Smith, 1776, I, viii. 4).

R. O'DONNELL

See also INDEX NUMBERS; REAL INCOME.

BIBLIOGRAPHY

Bladen, V.W. 1975. Command over labour: a study in misinterpretation. *Canadian Journal of Economics* 8(4), November, 504–19.

Blaug, M. 1978. *Economic Theory in Retrospect*. 3rd edn, Cambridge: Cambridge University Press.

Bowley, M. 1973. *Studies in the History of Economic Theory before 1870*. London: Macmillan.

Douglas, P. 1928. Adam Smith's theory of value and distribution. In J.M. Clark et al., *Adam Smith 1776–1926*, Chicago: University of Chicago Press.

Hollander, S. 1973. *The Economics of Adam Smith*. London: Heinemann.

Marx, K. 1861–63. *Theories of Surplus Value*. In 3 parts, London: Lawrence & Wishart, 1969–72.

O'Brien, D.P. 1975. *The Classical Economists*. Oxford: Clarendon Press.

Ricardo, D. 1821. *Principles of Political Economy*. In *Works and Correspondence of David Ricardo*, Vol. I, ed. P. Sraffa with the collaboration of M.H. Dobb, Cambridge: Cambridge University Press, 1951.

Schumpeter, J. 1954. *History of Economic Analysis*. London: George Allen & Unwin.

Smith, A. 1776. *An Inquiry into the Nature and Causes of the Wealth of Nations*. 2 vols, ed. R.H. Campbell and A.S. Skinner, Oxford: Clarendon Press, 1976.

Sylos-Labini, P. 1976. Competition: the product market. In *The Market and the State: Essays in Honour of Adam Smith*, ed. T. Wilson and A.S. Skinner, Oxford: Clarendon Press.

real balances. By the term 'real balances' is meant the real value of the money balances held by an individual or by the economy as a whole, as the case may be. The emphasis on real, as distinct from nominal, reflects the basic assumption that individuals are free of 'money illusion'. It is a corresponding property of any well-specified demand function for money that its dependent variable is real balances. Indeed, Keynes in his *Treatise on Money* (1930, vol. 1, p. 222) designated the variation on the Cambridge equation that he had presented in his *A Tract on Monetary Reform* (1923, ch. 3: 1) as 'The "Real-Balances" Quantity Equation'.

Implicit – and sometimes explicit – in the quantity-theory analysis of the effect of (say) an increase in the quantity of money is the assumption that the mechanism by which such an increase ultimately causes a proportionate increase in prices is through its initial effect in increasing the real value of money balances held by individuals and consequently increasing their respective demands for goods: that is, through what is now known as the 'real-balance effect'. This effect, however, was not assigned a role in the general-equilibrium system of equations with which writers of the interwar period attempted to describe the workings of a money economy. In particular, these writers mistakenly assumed that in order for their commodity demand functions to be free of money illusion, they had to fulfil the so-called 'homogeneity postulate', which stated that these functions depended only on relative prices, and so were not affected by a change in the absolute price level generated by an equi-proportionate change in all money prices (Leontief, 1936, p. 192). Thus they failed to take account of the effect of such a change on the real value of money balances and hence on commodity demands. This in turn led them to contend that there existed a dichotomy of the pricing process, with equilibrium relative prices being determined in the 'real sector' of the economy (as represented by the excess-demand equations for commodities), while the equilibrium absolute price level was determined in the 'monetary sector' (as represented by the excess-demand equation for money): (Modigliani, 1944, sec. 13). This, however, is an invalid dichotomy, for it leads to contradictory implications about the determinacy or, alternatively, stability of the absolute price level (Patinkin, 1965, ch. 8).

Nor was the real-balance effect taken account of in Keynes's *General Theory* and in the subsequent Hicks (1937)–Modigliani (1944) IS–LM exposition of this theory, which rapidly became the standard one of macroeconomic textbooks. According to this exposition, the only way in which a decline in wages and prices can increase employment is by its effect in increasing the real value of money balances, hence reducing the rate of interest, and hence (through its stimulating effect on investment) increasing the aggregate demand for goods and hence employment. A further and basic tenet of this exposition was that there was a minimum below which the rate of interest could not fall. So if the wage decline were to bring about a lowering of the rate of interest to this minimum before full-employment were reached, any further decline in the wage rate would be to no avail. In brief, the economy would then be caught in the 'liquidity trap'. And even though Keynes had stated in the *General Theory*, 'whilst this limiting case might become practically important in the future, I know of no example of it hitherto' (p. 207), the Keynesian theory of employment was for many years interpreted in terms of this 'trap'.

It was against this background that Pigou (1943, 1947) pointed out that the increase in the real value of money holdings generated by the wage and price decline increased the aggregate demand for goods directly, and not only indirectly through its downward effect on the rate of interest. Pigou's rationale was that individuals saved in order to accumulate a certain amount of wealth relative to their income, and that indeed the savings function depended inversely on the ratio of wealth to income. Correspondingly, as wages and prices declined, the real value of the monetary component of wealth increased and with it the ratio of wealth to income, causing a decrease in savings, which means an increase in the aggregate demand for consumption goods. Pigou's argument (which was formulated for a stationary state) thus had the far-reaching theoretical implication that even if the economy were caught in the 'liquidity trap', there existed a low enough wage rate that would generate a full-employment level of aggregate demand. In this way Pigou (1943, p. 351) reaffirmed the 'essential thesis of the classicals' that 'if wage-earners follow a competitive wage policy, the economic system must move ultimately to a full-employment stationary state'.

In his exposition and elaboration of Pigou's argument (which *inter alia* brought out the significance of the argument for dynamic stability analysis), Patinkin (1948) labelled the direct effect on consumption of an increase in the real value of money balances as the 'Pigou effect'. However, in subsequent recognition of the fact that this effect is actually an integral part of the quantity theory – as well as the fact that Pigou had been anticipated in drawing the implications of this effect for the Keynesian system by Haberler (1941, pp. 242, 389, and 403) and Scitovsky (1941, pp. 71–2) – Patinkin (1956, 1965) relabelled it the 'real-balance effect' and presented it as a component of the wealth effect.

In an immediate comment on Pigou's article, Kalecki (1944) pointed out that the definition of 'money' relevant for the real-balance effect is not the usual one of currency *plus* demand-deposits: for example, in the case of a price decline, the increase in the real value of the demand deposits has an offset in the corresponding increase in the real burden on borrowers of the loans they had received from the banking system. Thus (emphasized Kalecki) the monetary concept relevant for the real-balance effect in a gold-standard economy is only the gold reserve of the monetary system.

More generally, the relevant concept is 'outside money' (equivalent to the monetary base, sometimes also referred to as 'high-powered money'), which is part of the net wealth of the economy, as distinct from 'inside money', which consists of the demand deposits created by the banking system as a result of its lending operations and which accordingly is not part of net wealth (Gurley and Shaw, 1960). This distinction was subsequently challenged by Pesek and Saving (1967), who contended that banks regard only a small fraction of their deposits as debt, so that these deposits too should be included in net wealth. In criticism of this view, Patinkin (1969, 1972a) showed that if perfect competition prevails in the banking system, the present value of the costs of maintaining its demand deposits equals the value of these deposits, so that the latter cannot be considered as a component of net wealth. This is also the case if imperfect competition with free entry prevails in the system. On the other hand, if – because of restricted entry – the banking sector enjoys abnormal profits, then the present value of these profits should be included in net wealth for the purpose of measuring the real-balance effect.

There remains the question of whether – for the purpose of measuring the real-balance effect – one should include government interest-bearing debt, as contrasted with the non-interest-bearing debt (viz., government fiat money) which is a component of the monetary base. Clearly, in a world of infinitely lived individuals with perfect foresight, the former does not constitute net wealth and hence is not a component of the real-balance effect: for the discounted value of the tax payments which the representative individual must make in order to service and repay the debt obviously equals the discounted value of the payments on account of interest and principal that he will receive. Nor is the assumption of infinitely lived individuals an operationally meaningless one: for as Barro (1974) has elegantly shown, if in making his own consumption plans, the representative individual with perfect foresight is sufficiently concerned with the welfare of the next generation to the extent of leaving a bequest for it, he is acting as if he were infinitely lived.

More specifically, Barro's argument is as follows: assume that an individual of the present generation achieves his optimum position by consuming C_o during his lifetime and leaving a positive bequest of B_o for the next generation. Clearly, such an individual could have increased his consumption to $C_0 + \Delta C_0$ and reduced his bequest to $B_0 - \Delta C_0$ – but preferred not to do so. Assume now that the individual also holds government bonds payable by the next generation, and let the real value of these bonds increase as the result of a decline in the price level, expected to be permanent. The revealed preference of the present generation for the consumption-bequest combination C_o, B_o implies that this increase in the real value of its holdings of government interest-bearing debt will not cause it to increase its consumption at the expense of the next generation. In brief, government debt in this case is effectively not a component of wealth and hence of the real-balance effect.

Needless to say, the absence of perfect foresight, and the fact that individuals might not leave bequests (as is indeed assumed by the life-cycle theory of consumption) means that government interest-bearing debt should to a certain extent be taken account of in measuring the real-balance effect – or what in this context is more appropriately labelled the 'net-real-financial-asset effect' (Patinkin, 1965, pp. 288–94).

If we assume consumption to be a function of permanent income, and if we assume that the rate of interest which the individual uses to compute the permanent income flowing from his wealth to be 10 per cent and the marginal propensity to consume out of permanent income to be 0.80, then the marginal propensity to consume out of wealth (and out of real balances in particular) is the product of these two figures, or 0.08. However, in the case of consumers' durables (in the very broad sense that includes – besides household appliances – automobiles, housing, and the like), the operation of the acceleration principle implies an additional real-balance effect in the short run. In particular, assume that when the individual decides on the optimum composition of the portfolio of assets in which to hold his real wealth, W, he also considers the proportion, q, of these assets that he wishes to hold in the form of consumers durables, K_d, so that his demand for the *stock* of consumer-durable goods is $K_d = qW$. Assume now that wealth increases solely as a result of an increase in real balances, M/p. This leaves the representative individual with more money balances in relation to his other assets than he considers optimal. As a result he will attempt to shift out of money and into these other assets until he once again achieves an optimum portfolio. In the case of consumers' durables, this means that in addition to his preceding demand for new consumer-durable goods, he has a demand for

$$C_d = \Delta K_d = q[\Delta(M/p)] = q[(M/p)_t - (M/p)_{t-1}]$$

units, where $(M/p)_t$ represents real balances at time t. In general, the individual will plan to spread this additional demand over a few periods. In any event, once an optimally composed portfolio is again achieved, this additional effect disappears, so that the demand for new consumers' durables (which in the case of a stationary state is solely a replacement demand) will once again depend only on the ordinary real-balance effect as described at the beginning of this paragraph (Patinkin, 1967, pp. 156–62).

It is, of course, true that the process of portfolio adjustment generated by the monetary increase will cause a reduction in the respective rates of return on the other assets in the portfolio, so that the initial wealth effect of the monetary increase will be followed by substitution effects. Now, Keynes limited his analysis in the *General Theory* to portfolios consisting only of money and securities; hence (as indicated above) an increase in the quantity of money could increase the demand for goods only indirectly through the substitution effect created by the downward pressure on the rate of interest. But once one takes account of the broader spectrum of assets held by individuals, one must also take account of the direct real-balance effect on the purchase of these other assets as well.

Various empirical studies have shown that the real-balance effect as here defined (viz., as part of the wealth effect) is statistically significant (Patinkin, 1965, note M; Tanner, 1970). Other studies have demonstrated the statistical significance of yet another definition of this effect: namely, as the effect on the demand for commodities of an excess supply of money, defined as the excess of the existing stock of money over its 'desired' or 'long-run' level (Jonson, 1976; Laidler and Bentley, 1983; cf. also Mishan, 1958). It seems to me, however, that such a demand function is improperly specified: for though (as indicated above) the excess supply of money has a role to play in the consumption function (and particularly in that for consumers' durables), the complete exclusion of the real-balance effect *cum* wealth effect from the aforementioned demand function implies that in equilibrium there is no real-balance effect – an implication that is contradicted by the form of demand functions as derived from utility maximization subject to the budget constraint (Patinkin, 1965, pp. 433–8, 457–60; Fischer, 1981).

Granted the statistical significance of the real-balance effect, the question remains as to whether it is strong enough to offset the adverse expectations generated by a price decline – including those generated by the wave of bankruptcies that might well be caused by a severe decline. In brief, the question remains as to whether the real-balance effect is strong enough to assure the stability of the system: to assure that automatic market forces will restore the economy to a full-employment equilibrium position after an initial shock of a decrease in aggregate demand (Patinkin, 1948, part II; 1965, ch. 14: 1). On the assumption of adaptive expectations, Tobin (1975) has presented a Keynesian model with the real-balance effect which under certain circumstances is unstable. On the other hand, McCallum (1983) has shown that under the assumption of rational expectations, the model is generally stable.

In any event, no one has ever advocated dealing with the problem of unemployment by waiting for wages and prices to decline and thereby generate a positive real-balance effect that will increase aggregate demand. In particular, Pigou himself concluded his 1947 article with the statement that such a proposal had 'very little chance of ever being posed on the chequer board of actual life'. Thus the significance of the real-balance effect is in the realm of macroeconomic theory and not policy.

Correspondingly, recognition of the real-balance effect in no way controverts the central message of Keynes's *General Theory*. For this message – as expressed in the climax of that book, chapter 19 – is that the only way a general decline in money wages can increase employment is through its effect in increasing the real quantity of money, hence reducing the rate of interest, and hence stimulating investment expenditures; but that even if wages were downwardly flexible in the face of unemployment, this effect would be largely offset by the adverse expectations and bankruptcies generated by declining money wages and prices, so that the level of aggregate expenditures and hence employment would not increase within an acceptable period of time. In Keynes's words: 'the economic system cannot be made self-adjusting along these lines' (ibid., p. 267). And there is no reason to believe that Keynes would have modified this conclusion if he had also taken account of the real-balance effect of a price decline (Patinkin, 1948, part III; 1976, pp. 110–11).

The above discussion has considered only the real-balance effect on the demand for goods. In principle, this effect also operates on the supply of labour: for the greater the real balances and hence wealth of the individual, the greater his demand for leisure as well, which means the smaller his supply of labour. This influence, however, has received relatively little attention in the literature (but see Patinkin, 1965, p. 204; Phelps, 1972; Barro and Grossman, 1976, pp. 14–16).

Another limitation of the discussion is that it deals only with a closed economy. In the analysis of an open economy, the real-balance effect plays an important role in some of the formulations of the monetary approach to the balance of payments.

DON PATINKIN

See also MONEY ILLUSION; QUANTITY THEORY OF MONEY.

BIBLIOGRAPHY

American Economic Association. 1951. *Readings in Monetary Theory*. Philadelphia: Blakiston.

Barro, R.J. 1974. Are government bonds net wealth? *Journal of Political Economy* 82, November–December, 1095–117.

Barro, R.J. and Grossman, H.I. 1976. *Money, Employment and Inflation*. Cambridge: Cambridge University Press.

Fischer, S. 1981. Is there a real-balance effect in equilibrium? *Journal of Monetary Economics* 8, July, 25–39.

Gurley, J.G. and Shaw, E.S. 1960. *Money in a Theory of Finance*. Washington, DC: Brookings Institution.

Haberler, G. von. 1941. *Prosperity and Depression: A Theoretical Analysis of Cyclical Movements*. 3rd edn, Geneva: League of Nations.

Hicks, J.R. 1937. Mr Keynes and the 'classics': a suggested interpretation. *Econometrica* 5, April, 147–59. Reprinted in *Readings in the Theory of Income Distribution*, Philadelphia: Blakiston for the American Economic Association, 1946, 461–76.

Jonson, P.D. 1976. Money and economic activity in the open economy: the United Kingdom, 1880–1970. *Journal of Political Economy* 84, October, 979–1012.

Kalecki, M. 1944. Professor Pigou on 'The classical stationary state': a comment. *Economic Journal* 54, April, 131–2.

Keynes. J.M. 1923. *A Tract on Monetary Reform*. London: Macmillan

Keynes, J.M. 1930. *A Treatise on Money*. Vol. I: *The Pure Theory of Money*. London: Macmillan.

Keynes, J.M. 1936. *The General Theory of Employment, Interest and Money*. London: Macmillan.

Laidler, D. and Bentley, B. 1983. A small macro-model of the post-war United States. *Manchester School* 51, December, 317–40.

Leontief, W. 1936. The fundamental assumption of Mr Keynes' monetary theory of unemployment. *Quarterly Journal of Economics* 51, November, 192–7.

McCallum, B.T. 1983. The liquidity trap and the Pigou Effect: a dynamic analysis with rational expectations. *Economica* 50, November, 395–405.

Mishan, E.J. 1958. A fallacy in the interpretation of the cash balance effect. *Economica* 25, May, 106–18.

Modigliani, F. 1944. Liquidity preference and the theory of interest and money. *Econometrica* 12, January, 45–88. Reprinted in American Economic Association (1951), 186–240.

Patinkin, D. 1948. Price flexibility and full employment. *American Economic Review* 38, September, 543–64. Reprinted with revisions and additions in American Economic Association (1951), 252–83.

Patinkin, D. 1956. *Money, Interest, and Prices*. Evanston, Ill.: Row, Peterson.

Patinkin, D. 1965. *Money, Interest, and Prices*. 2nd edn, New York: Harper & Row.

Patinkin, D. 1967. *On the Nature of the Monetary Mechanism*. Stockholm: Almqvist and Wicksell. Reprinted in Patinkin (1972b), 143–67.

Patinkin, D. 1969. Money and wealth: a review article. *Journal of Economic Literature* 7, December, 1140–60.

Patinkin, D. 1972a. Money and wealth. In Patinkin (1972b), 168–94.

Patinkin, D. 1972b. *Studies in Monetary Economics*. New York: Harper & Row.

Patinkin, D. 1976. *Keynes' Monetary Thought: A Study of Its Development*. Durham, North Carolina: Duke University Press.

Pesek, B.P. and Saving, T.R. 1967. *Money, Wealth and Economic Theory*. New York: Macmillan.

Phelps, E.S. 1972. Money, public expenditure and labor supply. *Journal of Economic Theory* 5, August, 69–78.

Pigou, A.C. 1943. The classical stationary state. *Economic Journal* 53, December, 343–51.

Pigou, A.C. 1947. Economic progress in a stable environment. *Economica* 14, August, 180–88. Reprinted in American Economic Association (1951), 241–51.

Scitovsky, T. 1941. Capital accumulation, employment and price rigidity. *Review of Economic Studies* 8, February, 69–88.

Tanner, J.E. 1970. Empirical evidence on the short-run real balance effect in Canada. *Journal of Money, Credit and Banking* 2, November, 473–85.

Tobin, J. 1975. Keynesian models of recession and depression. *American Economic Review* 65, May, 195–202.

real bills doctrine. The 'real bills doctrine' has its origin in banking developments of the 17th and 18th centuries. It received its first authoritative exposition in Adam Smith's *Wealth of Nations*, was then repudiated by Thornton and Ricardo in the famous bullionist controversy, and was finally rehabilitated as the 'law of reflux' by Tooke and Fullarton in the currency–banking debate of the mid-19th century. Even now, echoes of the real bills doctrine reverberate in modern monetary theory.

The central proposition is that bank notes which are lent in exchange for 'real bills', i.e. titles to real value or value in the process of creation, cannot be issued in excess; and that, since the requirements of the non-bank public are given and finite, any superfluous notes would return automatically to the issuer, at least in the long run. The grounds for rejecting the real bills doctrine have been many and varied. The main counter-argument is that overissue is not merely possible but inevitable in the absence of any external principle of limitation; in this view, commercial wants are insatiable and excess notes would not return to the issuer but undergo depreciation in the exact proportion to their excess.

By the time the real bills doctrine appeared in the economic literature, fractional reserve banking was already well established, releasing unproductive hoards for trade and investment. This did not satisfy John Law, that 'reckless, and unbalanced but most fascinating genius' (Marshall, 1923, p. 41n.). He outlined a primitive real bills doctrine in the course of his proposal for a land bank, which would issue paper money on 'good security'. He imagined, however, that the need for a metallic reserve was superseded by the abolition of legal convertibility, and that *economic* convertibility would *always* be maintained by conformity with the real bills doctrine (Law, 1805, p. 89).

The problem was that, as a mercantilist, Law identified money with capital; he believed that creating paper money was equivalent to increasing wealth. It was his attempt to 'break through' the metallic barrier that gave him 'the pleasant character mixture of swindler and prophet' (Marx, 1894, p. 441). The spectacular collapse of Law's 'System' set off a negative reaction against financial innovation, which was reflected in Cantillon's 'anti-System' (Rist, 1940, p. 73) and in Hume's opposition to what he called 'counterfeit money' (1752, p. 168). A more positive effect was a shift in the focus of political economy itself to the production process. This shift was led by the Physiocrats and by Adam Smith, whose 'original and profound' (Marx, 1859, p. 168) analysis of money and banking was developed in the context of classical value theory.

A decade before the *Wealth of Nations*, Sir James Steuart had attempted to revive Law's ideas from a 'neo-mercantilist' viewpoint (1767, book IV, pt. 2). For Smith, by contrast, the role of bank credit was to increase not the quantity of capital but its *turnover* (1776, pp. 245-6; also Ricardo, *Works*, III, pp. 286-7). Output was fixed by the level of accumulation, which for all the classical economists included the speed of its turnover. Credit had the effect both of reducing the magnitude of reserve funds which economic agents needed to hold and of allowing the money material itself – treated as an element of circulating capital and an unproductive portion of the social wealth – to be displaced by paper, thus providing 'a sort of wagon-way through the air'.

Smith followed Law and Steuart, however, in arguing that an overissue of bank notes could not take place if they were advanced upon 'real' bills of exchange, i.e. those 'drawn by a real creditor upon a real debtor', as opposed to 'fictitious' bills, i.e. those 'for which there was properly no real creditor but the bank which discounted it, nor any real debtor but the projector who made use of the money' (1776, p. 239; also p. 231). When a banker discounted fictitious bills, the borrowers were clearly 'trading, not with any capital of their own, but with the capital which he advances to them'. When, on the other hand, real bills were discounted, bank notes were merely substituted for a substantial proportion of the gold and silver which would otherwise have been idle, and therefore available for circulation (p. 231). The quantity of notes was thus equivalent to the maximum value of the monetary metals that would circulate in their absence at a given level of economic activity (p. 227).

This development of the classical law of circulation applied to credit and fiduciary money alike, with the difference that in the latter case overissue in the 'short run' might result in a permanent depreciation of the paper. By contrast, credit-money, i.e. bank-notes, which were exchanged for real bills could never be in long-run excess:

> The coffers of the bank ... resemble a water-pond, from which, though a stream is continually running out, yet another is continually running in, fully equal to that which runs out; so that, without any further care or attention, the pond keeps always equally, or very near equally full (p. 231).

Only what Smith called 'over-trading' would upset this balance, by promoting excessive credit expansion and an accompanying drain of bullion.

Although the real bills doctrine was accepted by the Bank of England Directors as a guide to monetary management, it was challenged in the bullion controversy following the suspension of cash payments in 1797 as 'the source of all the errors of these practical men' (Ricardo, *Works*, III, p. 362; also Thornton, 1802, p. 244 and *passim*). In the view of the 'bullionists',

> The refusal to discount any bills but those for *bona fide* transactions would be as little effectual in limiting the circulation; because, though the Directors should have the means of distinguishing such bills, which can by no means be allowed, a greater proportion of paper currency might be called into circulation, not than the wants of commerce could employ but greater than what could remain in the channel of currency without depreciation (Ricardo, p. 219).

Indeed, there was no other limit to the depreciation, and corresponding rise in the price level, 'than the will of the issuers' (ibid., p. 226).

Nevertheless, the bullionist argument itself was open to challenge, because it confused money with credit. The inconvertible paper of the Bank Restriction was issued not as forced currency but on loan; it was therefore responsible not for increasing the money supply but simply altering its *composition*, by substituting one financial asset for another in the hands of the public. Only when cash payments were restored, however, was any further attempt made to rehabilitate the real bills doctrine, this time as the 'law of reflux': provided notes were lent on sufficient security, 'the reflux and the issue will, in the long run, always balance each other' (Fullarton, 1844, p. 64; Tooke, 1844, p. 60). The 'banking school' called this law 'the great regulating principle of the internal currency' (Fullarton, 1844, p. 68). Their opponents, the 'currency school' orthodoxy, 'never achieved better than this average measure of security'; and, after all, the average 'is not to be despised' (Marx, 1973, p. 131). The real bills doctrine made its next appearance in the Federal Reserve Act of 1913. In banking at least, discretion has always been the better part of valour.

ROY GREEN

See also BANKING SCHOOL, CURRENCY SCHOOL AND FREE BANKING SCHOOL.

BIBLIOGRAPHY

Cantillon, R. 1755. *Essai sur la nature du commerce en général*. Trans. H. Higgs, London: Macmillan, 1931.

Fullarton, J. 1844. *On the Regulation of Currencies*. London: John Murray.

Hume, D. 1752. *Essays, Literary, Moral and Political*. London: Ward, Lock & Co., n.d.

Law, J. 1705. *Money and Trade Considered*. Edinburgh: Anderson.

Marshall, A. 1923. *Money, Credit and Commerce*. London: Macmillan.

Marx, K. 1859. *A Contribution to the Critique of Political Economy*. Moscow: Progress Publishers, 1970.

Marx, K. 1894. *Capital*, Vol. III. Moscow: Progress Publishers, 1971.

Marx, K. 1973. *Grundrisse*. Harmondsworth: Penguin.

Ricardo, D. 1951–73. *The Works and Correspondence of David Ricardo*. Ed. P. Sraffa, Cambridge: Cambridge University Press.

Rist, C. 1940. *History of Monetary and Credit Theory from John Law to the Present Day*. London: Allen & Unwin.

Smith, A. 1776. *An Inquiry into the Nature and Causes of the Wealth of Nations*. London: Routledge, 1890.

Steuart, J. 1767. *An Inquiry into the Principles of Political Oeconomy*. Edinburgh: Oliver & Boyd, 1966.

Thornton, H. 1802. *An Enquiry into the Nature and Effects of the Paper Credit of Great Britain*. London: LSE Reprint Series, 1939.

Tooke, T. 1844. *An Inquiry into the Currency Principle*. London: LSE Reprint Series, 1959.

real cost doctrine. Real cost doctrine is the doctrine that the supply price of a good is the price required to overcome the disutility involved in producing it. The worker, in other words, produces output up to the point at which his (decreasing) marginal utility of income equals his (increasing) marginal disutility of labour. The real cost doctrine can be seen as a half-way house inhabited by economists who had adopted a subjective theory of value but stopped short of the 'alternative cost' doctrine whereby the supply price of a resource is equal to its potential earning in its next most productive use. Much of the discussion which took place between English and Austrian economists concerned whether, and to what extent, the two doctrines logically came to the same thing.

Jevons (1871) formulated the real cost doctrine in terms of the diagram in Figure 1. Jevons assumes here (no such assumption is strictly necessary) that the worker at the start of the day not only enjoys his work but that, for a while, his enjoyment increases as he warms up to it. But as the hours pass, the fatigue and boredom come to predominate over pleasure at an ever-increasing rate. The worker will maximize his surplus of utility over disutility by stopping at point *X* (*ab* = *bc*.)

The idea that subjective disutility of labour is central in determining output and price is, perhaps, Jevons's most unquestionably original idea. Not only is it absent from the work of Walras and Menger, but its prefigurations in the classical period are rare and rudimentary when compared with the pre-1871 analyses of marginal utility theory. (Jennings (1855) points out that marginal disutility of labour increases as the working day progresses but fails to build anything upon it.)

Marshall's theory of price determination, unveiled in his *Principles of Economics* (1890), differs little from Jevons's. Yet what looked radical in Jevons appears almost backward-looking in Marshall. This has something to do with the extension and dissemination of neoclassical principles in the intervening twenty years. But it also stems from a difference of presentation grounded in the contrast between Jevons's impatience with and Marshall's deference towards the Ricardian tradition. Much of Marshall's frequent praise for the English classical economists deftly sidesteps the question of how far they had actually been right. In the *Principles*, however, not only are cost and utility considerations given equal importance when determining price, but the fact that Marshall's conception of cost is ultimately a Jevonian 'subjective disutility' one is played down. It receives the strongest emphasis when Marshall argues that the capitalist as well as the worker undergoes real costs in the productive process, the capitalist's cost being that of 'waiting' rather than consuming his wealth immediately. (Nassau Senior had invoked Marx's sarcasm by speaking of capitalist 'abstinence' in the same context: Marshall tried both to circumvent the ridicule by renaming abstinence 'waiting' and to defend Senior from a neoclassical perspective, pointing out that *at the margin* of *aggregate* saving, considerable immediate sacrifice was undoubtedly involved.)

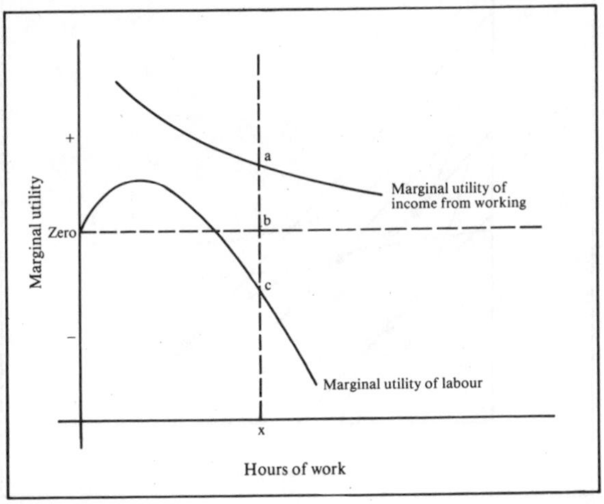

Figure 1

The rival doctrine, that of alternative cost, was espoused principally by the Austrians Wieser and Böhm-Bawerk and advertised in Britain by Wicksteed. All three denied the existence of any such thing as a supply curve, 'supply' simply being reverse demand. Böhm-Bawerk cited a horse fair: the buyer's utility from acquiring a horse and the seller's utility from keeping his horse played not just an equal but an identical role in determining price. Hence only a demand curve need be drawn; at the equilibrium price, it crosses the vertical line representing the fixed stock of horses. Both Marshallian and Austrian analysis predict the same price.

But, of course, the fixed stock of horses makes this a very simple case: we are ignoring the cost of producing them. Such considerations, however, were no problem to the Austrians, who proclaimed that the costs of factors of production and raw materials ultimately depended on utilities from alternative uses foregone. Thus, as regards the labour market, the wage in a particular industry was governed by the demand for labour in other industries. Each worker had to be paid enough to keep him out of his next best paid available job. The Jevonian notion of disutility of labour dropped out of the picture, Böhm-Bawerk (1894) arguing against it on the *empirical* ground that few workers had the chance to make fine adjustments to the length of their working day. To this Edgeworth retorted that the Austrian doctrine implied that individuals made the choice to work or not to work once and for all at the beginning of their careers – it could not handle variations in labour supply due to variations in the wage rate.

The debate as a whole thus seemed to imply that the choice between real cost and alternative cost depended on whether *flexible* labour supply at the *individual* level (assumed by Jevons) or *inflexible* labour supply at the *aggregate* level (implied by the Austrians) was the more objectionable violation of reality. Yet logically the two theories come to exactly the same thing, and are seen to do so as long as the two 'sides' make one clarification apiece.

Austrians must make it clear that 'foregone utility' includes not only foregone income but also foregone leisure (when you work at all) and foregone non-pecuniary benefits (when you choose a less pleasant but better-paid job in preference to a more pleasant but worse-paid one). Böhm-Bawerk (1894) did spell this out.

Real cost theorists must make it clear that when a baker ponders whether to work another hour, what matters is not the disutility of the work as compared with doing nothing, but the disutility of work as compared with what he would choose to do (it might still be nothing!) if he were not baking. Equally it is not the 'gross' marginal utility of income which matters but the marginal utility of the *additional* income gained from spending another hour at the bakery rather than doing something else (other paid work, some leisure activity, or nothing). Edgeworth (1894) *failed* to spell this out; had he done so, a number of economists might have realized sooner than they actually did that both theories ultimately come to the same thing. (See Hobson (1926) for an example of confusion persisting well into the present century.)

J. MALONEY

See also MARSHALL, ALFRED; OPPORTUNITY COST.

BIBLIOGRAPHY

Blaug, M. 1985. *Economic Theory in Retrospect*. 4th edn, Cambridge: Cambridge University Press.

Böhm-Bawerk, E. von. 1894. One word more on the ultimate standard of value. *Economic Journal* 4, December, 719–24.

Edgeworth, F.Y. 1894. Professor Böhm-Bawerk on the ultimate standard of value. *Economic Journal* 4, September, 518–21.

Hobson, J.A. 1926. *Free Thought in the Social Sciences*. London: G. Allen & Unwin.

Jennings, R. 1855. *Natural Elements of Political Economy*. London: Longman, Brown, Green, Longmans.

Jevons, W.S. 1871. *Theory of Political Economy*. Edited and with an introduction by R.D. Collison Black, Harmondsworth: Penguin, 1970.

Marshall, A. 1890. *Principles of Economics*. London: Macmillan.

Wicksteed, P.H. 1910. *The Common Sense of Political Economy*. London: Macmillan.

real income. Real income can be defined at two levels. As a statistic, it is money income corrected for changes in prices. If a person's income rose from \$20.000 in 1980 to \$25,000 in 1981, we say that the growth in his *money* income was 25 per cent, (25 − 20)/20 expressed as a percentage. However, if the price level rose from 100 in 1980 to 110 in 1981, we say that the growth in his *real* income was only 13.64 per cent [(25/110) − (20/100)]/(20/100). But statistics are not just manipulations of data, and real income is not completely defined until we identify the characteristic, property or aspect of the economy the statistic is intended to reflect. Real income must be defined as a concept as well as a statistic, to indicate what the statistic is for and to serve as a guide in choosing and manipulating the original data from which the statistic is compiled. In particular, the rules for constructing a price index to deflate money income into real income can only be established with reference to the information the statistic is designed to convey.

As a concept, real income is intrinsically comparative. It makes sense to say that real income is 3 per cent higher this year than last, or that the real income of one country is 30 per cent higher than the real income of another. It makes no sense to say that the real income of a country is such and such today, except as an implied comparison with another time or place. The concept of real income is usually, though not necessarily, applied to a country or a region rather than to a person or family.

What then is being compared? There are two standard answers to this question, giving rise to two distinct but related concepts of real income. Real income may be an indicator of welfare or of productive capacity. In both cases, real income is measured in dollars worth when quantities of goods are valued at an arbitrarily chosen set of prices, usually the market prices in some base year. When real income is looked upon as an indicator of welfare, an increase in real income signifies that the representative consumer, whose indifference curves are assumed to remain invariant, is becoming better off over time. To construct a time series of real income as an indicator of welfare, one would, ideally, require a complete set of indifference curves, a set of time series of all goods consumed, and a set of base year prices. One could then measure real income each year as the least amount of money required at base year prices to purchase a bundle of goods on the indifference curve attained with the bundle of goods that the representative consumer actually consumes in that year. When real income is looked upon as a measure of productive capacity, an increase in real income signifies that there has been an outward shift in the production possibility frontier for the economy as a whole. For any set of base year prices, real income each year is the maximum value at those prices of any bundle of goods on the production possibility frontier for that year. Both concepts of income give rise to a family of measures, each member of which corresponds to a different set of price weights.

The distinction between these concepts of real income is illustrated on Figure 1 for a comparison of two years, 0 and 1, in an economy with two goods, A and B. Outputs per head are measured on the horizontal and vertical axes. The dashed curves are indifference curves. The solid curves are production possibility frontiers in the years 0 and 1. Amounts produced and consumed are represented by the points q^0 and q^1. Relative prices may be represented as slopes of lines. Money income corresponding to any bundle of goods and any relative price may be represented as a distance on the vertical axis if we adhere to the convention, which is harmless in this context, that the money price of the good B is always equal to 1.0. The common slope of the parallel straight lines represents the relative price of the two goods in the year 0 which is the chosen base year. Money income in the year 0 is Y^0, the value of quantities produced in year 1 at prices in the year 0 is Y^1, real income in year 1 as a measure of welfare is Y^{1W} and real income as a measure of productive capacity is Y^{1P}. By construction, money income, real income as a measure of welfare and real income as a measure of productive capacity are all the same in the base year. Note that $Y^{1W} < Y^1 < Y^{1P}$ as long as indifference curves and the production possibility frontiers have their usual shapes. The corresponding rates of economic growth are $(Y^{1P}/Y^0 - 1)$ and $(Y^{1W}/Y^0 - 1)$. For each definition of real

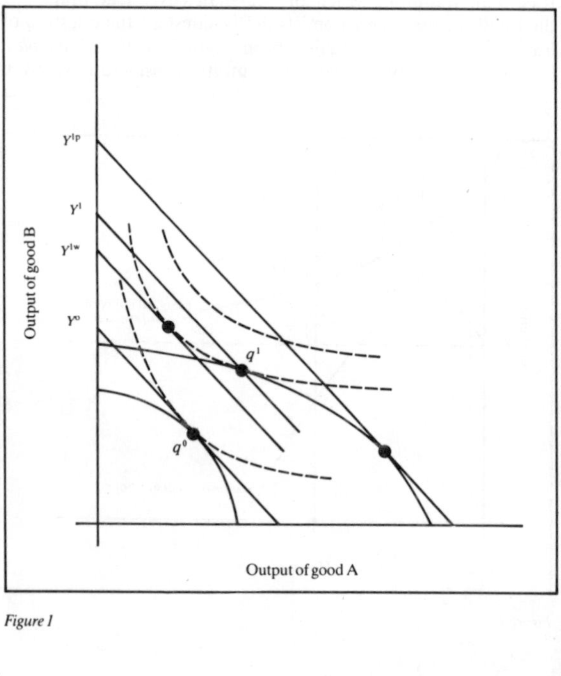

Figure 1

income and each choice of a base year, the appropriate price index may be constructed.

In practice, matters are at once simpler and more complex. They are simpler because the different measures of real income may not be too far apart and because users of the national accounts, impatient with the niceties of concepts, want an all-purpose measure of real income that gives a rough idea of what is happening to the economy. Matters are more complex because the world refuses to conform to the set of concepts within which income is defined: There are more than two goods. The decision to apportion the flow of income into amounts of a finite set of goods is somewhat arbitrary. The nature and quality of goods is changing over time, so that it is by no means certain how much the quantity of what the statistician calls a good has increased. Society consists of many people each with his own unique set of indifference curves. Even when people have the same indifference curves, their response to price changes is not independent of income. All that can be observed in practice are prices and quantities, not the underlying indifference curves or production possibility frontiers.

The welfare interpretation is better suited to the measurement of real consumption than to the measurement of real income because indifference curves are defined over consumption goods alone and items such as newly built factories or aircraft can only be accounted for as surrogates for the flow of consumption goods they will eventually bring forth. In practice, formulae appropriate for averaging prices of consumption goods are applied to prices of all goods, capital goods and consumption goods alike.

The productive capacity interpretation cannot be made to generate a time series of real income unless the production possibility frontier for each year in the series is a well-defined function of quantities of a set of goods that remains invariant over time. The frontiers in years 0 and 1 are comparable if actual and potential outputs in both years consist of certain amounts of apples and oranges. The frontiers are not comparable, and real income as a measure of productive capacity is ill-defined, if the economy produces only apples and oranges in year 0 and only grapes and lemons in year 1.

To measure real income, statisticians have to squeeze the flow of innumerable items each year into a set of quantities of a relatively small number of commodities, such that the nature of the commodities is assumed to remain the same over time. Each of the many different kinds of stereo sets must one way or another be represented as a definite amount of one homogeneous commodity. This may be done directly, or it may be done indirectly by deflating the value of stereo sets by a price index. The process by which time series of the supposedly homogeneous and invariant quantities of the different goods are forced into an index of aggregate quantity to reflect the chosen concept of real income as closely as possible (or, equivalently, time series of prices of different goods are forced into a price index to deflate money income) is described in the entry on Index Numbers.

D. Usher

See also HEDONIC FUNCTIONS AND HEDONIC INDEXES; INDEX NUMBERS.

BIBLIOGRAPHY

The distinction between the welfare and productive capacity interpretations of real income is due to John Hicks, 'The valuation of social income', *Economica* 7, 1940, 105–24.

For a survey of the concept of real income with an extensive bibliography see A.K. Sen, 'The welfare basis of real income comparisons', *Journal of Economic Literature*, 1979, 1–45.

On the measurement of prices in the presence of quality change, see George Stigler and James Kindahl, *The Behavior of Industrial Prices*, New York: Columbia University Press, 1970, and Zvi Griliches (ed.), *Price Indexes and Quality Change: Studies in New Methods of Measurement*, Cambridge, Mass.: Harvard University Press, 1971.

realization problem. The realization problem was first considered by classical economists such as Ricardo and Sismondi. Keynes's theory of effective demand has a bearing on it too. But it was Marx who gave it its most rounded – and controversial – treatment. At its simplest, the realization problem amounts to this: is there sufficient monetary demand for the commodities which have been produced to be sold, and sold at their value?

It is by no means obvious that there is really any problem at all. Why is the very act of production itself not enough to guarantee that there will be sufficient demand to ensure that all commodities will be sold? This was the view held strongly by Ricardo. His argument amounted to this: nobody produces except to sell and nobody sells except to buy something else. Marx showed that such arguments were wrong because they overlooked the specific nature of capitalist production (*see* CRISES).

The realization problem arises therefore because production under capitalism is but a phase within the circulation of capital, $M - C \ldots P \ldots - C' - M'$. Here, money is firstly converted into means of production and labour-power ($M - C$). Production then takes place ($C \ldots P \ldots C'$). The produced commodities must then be sold ($C' - M'$), they must be reconverted into money, their value must be realized (Marx, 1885, p. 709). This must happen if the circuit of capital is to be completed. That this must happen, and yet that it may not, is the realization problem.

Some of the features of the problem must be emphasized. The commodity has a value before it arrives on the market, this value being made up of the constant and variable capital consumed in its manufacture, along with the surplus value produced. By the time the question of realization arises, a certain level of output is presupposed, which depends particularly on the amount of capital thrown into production; and for the realization problem to be overcome, a certain level of monetary demand must be found in the sphere of circulation.

These aspects are derived from an analysis of the individual capital only. Whilst an investigation of the realization problem must take all of them into account, the problem can only fully be analysed in the context of the reproduction of the total social capital. This Marx did in his discussion of the reproduction schemes, in part three of Volume Two of *Capital*.

THE REPRODUCTION SCHEMES. The reproduction schemes can be viewed as abstract, two-sector models of the production and circulation of capital. Department one produces means of production. The value of its output is made up of $C_1 + V_1 + S_1$, where C_1 is the constant capital and V_1 the variable capital used up in production. S_1 is the surplus value produced. Department two produces means of consumption and the value of its product is likewise made up of $C_2 + V_2 + S_2$.

Marx considered two situations, simple and expanded reproduction. Simple reproduction is where capitalists devote all their surplus value to the purchase of consumption goods and seek only to produce in the next period at the same level as this. Expanded reproduction is where capitalists must accumulate some of their surplus value in order to obtain a larger stock of constant and variable capital, for use in the next period.

The point of the schemes was to investigate how the circulation must proceed in order for capital successfully to reproduce itself. This involves circulation both within and between the two departments. For example, simple reproduction requires that capitalists in department two acquire means of production to the value C_2 from department one in order to be able to produce again.

Two points should be noted. Firstly, when considering the reproduction of the total social capital, account must be taken of both value and use-value. This had not been necessary when considering the individual capital only. There, Marx had simply assumed that within the sphere of circulation would be found all the commodities necessary both to transform the capital value into new elements of production and commodities to satisfy workers' and capitalists' consumption (Marx, 1885, p. 470).

Secondly, the scheme for expanded reproduction requires capitalists to accumulate (rather than consume) value out of this year's surplus value. It is important to emphasize that the amount accumulated must be a sufficient value to cover the *entire* amount of extra capital needed, both the extra constant capital and the extra variable capital.

This means that in department one $(1-a_1)S_1$ must be equal in value to $dC_1 + dV_1$. Likewise, in department two $(1-a_2)S_2$ must be equal in value to $dC_2 + dV_2$. (a denotes the portion of surplus value devoted by capitalists to consumption whilst the prefix d denotes the additional capital required).

These, combined with the requirement that the supply of means of production must equal the demand for them:

$$C_1 + V_1 + S_1$$
$$= C_1 + C_2 \text{ (replacing what has been used up)}$$
$$+ dC_1 + dC_2 \text{ (the extra required for next year)}$$

are sufficient to construct workable examples of capitalist reproduction. (See, for example, the numerical examples given in Marx, 1885, pp. 586–91.)

Other relationships can be derived from these which must hold if reproduction is to proceed successfully. One such, the 'Bukharin condition' for expanded reproduction (Rosdolsky, 1968, p. 449) is:

$$C_2 + dC_2 = V_1 + dV_1 + a_1 S_1$$

In other words, what department two needs to buy from department one $(C_2 + dC_2)$ must equal what department one needs to buy from department two $(V_1 + dV_1 + a_1 S_1)$. In the case of simple reproduction this reduces to the more familiar expression: $C_2 = V_1 + S_1$.

INTERPRETATION OF THE REPRODUCTION SCHEMES. Analysis of the schemes shows that accumulation and the circulation of values and use-values can take place in such a way as to permit the successful resolution of the realization problem. The expansion of capital is shown to be possible. The theory must demonstrate this in view of the history of capitalist development. In so doing, Marx was refuting economists such as Sismondi who thought that expanded reproduction was impossible.

But one must be careful not to conclude too much from this result. The 'Austrian Marxists' for example concluded that the schemes showed that the reproduction cycle of capital need never break down. Hilferding went so far as to argue that the schemes proved that Marx had never been a supporter of the breakdown theory (cited in Rosdolsky, 1968, p. 451).

This view is mistaken. The schemes cannot just be interpreted as if they are a model of the 'real world'. They are at a particular level of abstraction and leave out of account, for example, not only technical progress but also any impact of changes in either the organic composition of capital or the rate of surplus value.

More importantly however, the fact that the simultaneous consideration of value, use-value and accumulation does not uncover insurmountable difficulties is by no means the same thing as proving that the circuit of capital need never be broken or that the realization problem is never going to manifest itself as a real difficulty.

What the schemes show – or more properly illustrate, for it is a result of the *method* of Marx's argument – is something rather different: the realization problem can be solved this year, but that solution creates anew all the conditions which will ensure that the problem arises again next year. To solve the problem this year, values must once more be tied-up as capital which must next year be put to use to produce surplus value. These values must subsequently be realized. This year's solution is the seed from which next year's problem springs.

THE REALIZATION PROBLEM AND GLUTS. The schemes also show the close connection between the realization problem and the potential, within the reproduction of capital, for general gluts of capital and commodities.

From the formulation of the reproduction schemes, it is easy to see that this year finishes up with a stock of means of production to be carried over to next year. This is not all that is carried over, however. For the value of output in department two $(C_2 + V_2 + S_2)$ exceeds the value of consumption out of this year's income, wages $(V_1 + V_2)$ plus capitalist consumption $(a_1 S_1 + a_2 S_2)$. The excess amounts to the value of the additional variable capital to be accumulated $(dV_1 + dV_2)$. This result is caused by the requirement that value be produced and accumulated to cover the *entire* amount of additional capital needed for production on an expanded scale, not just to cover the additional constant capital alone.

Thus both stocks of means of production and means of consumption are carried forward. Both grow in an orderly way if production grows smoothly and their value can be realized so long as this continues. But these stocks bear testimony to the fact that the process of reproduction contains the potential for a general glut, which in the first place can take the form of unused means of production and unsold consumption goods. This potential will not manifest itself so long as the realization problem is overcome. But the constant recurrence of the realization problem means that the potential of the general glut is constantly renewed.

THE REALIZATION PROBLEM AND THE THEORY OF EFFECTIVE DEMAND. Finally, what is the relationship between this analysis and Keynes's theory of effective demand? The schemes certainly include the result that the level of output at which all output can be sold is the one at which net investment equals that part of surplus value not devoted to capitalist consumption (assuming that workers do not save). This comes over clearly, for example in the discussion of the difficulties posed for simple reproduction by depreciation, that is, where capital is not fully exhausted within the one year (Marx, 1885, p. 528 et seq.).

There is, however, a significant difference between Marx and Keynes here. Whereas Keynes was investigating the 'theory of what determines the *actual employment* of the available resources (Keynes, 1936, p. 4), Marx was concerned with the "'theory" of what enables a given level and structure of output to be realized, to be sold, in order that production may begin anew'.

The theory of effective demand certainly sheds an interesting light on the realization problem. But Marx's investigation of the realization problem is part of a coherent whole. The fact that his analysis is firmly rooted in a theory of value shows this. In contrast, Keynes's theory was developed in opposition to the orthodox theory of value and output (which are of course one and the same theory). The theory of effective demand is beset with the difficulty of explaining *why* the monetary level of demand matters. Marx's analysis of the nature of capitalist production provides this (see Kenway, 1980).

An explanation of what determines the actual employment of the available resources is most pertinent, especially during a slump. But the investigation of how, why and whether capitalism can produce and reproduce itself is surely the more profound and more general question.

P. KENWAY

See also CRISES; MARX, KARL HEINRICH.

BIBLIOGRAPHY

Kenway, P. 1980. Marx, Keynes and the possibility of crisis. *Cambridge Journal of Economics* 4(1), March, 23–36.

Keynes, J.M. 1936. *The General Theory of Employment, Interest and Money*. London: Macmillan, 1973.

Marx, K. 1885. *Capital*, Vol. II. Harmondsworth: Penguin, 1978.

Rosdolsky, R. 1968. *The Making of Marx's 'Capital'*. London: Pluto, 1977.

real wages. *See* WAGES, REAL AND MONEY.

reciprocal demand. *See* OFFER CURVES.

recontracting. *See* TÂTONNEMENT AND RECONTRACTING.

recoupment period. *See* PAY-OFF PERIOD.

recreation. Problems of market failure and preferences for a wider distribution of recreational opportunities than might be provided by private market exchanges, have led to a large measure of public provision of parks and other recreational facilities in countries throughout the world. This non-market nature of recreation allocation has prompted most of the attention to recreation economics.

EXPENDITURES AND STANDARDS. The earliest interest in the economics of recreation centred on the impacts generated by expenditures on equipment, accommodation and travel associated with participation in recreational activities and the use of parks. Such expenditures have been seen to benefit local commercial interests and have been widely asserted to be appropriate measures of the economic value of recreation facilities and activities as well.

Consistent with the continuing interest in the impacts of such expenditure, most economic studies have been concerned with rural or resource-based recreation. Until recently, little attention was given to recreation taking place within urban areas, in spite of the far larger numbers of people and likely larger economic values involved. Most of the planning in cities and towns has been based on various standards of desired numbers of parks or other recreation facilities or the area of open space per unit of resident population, with little note of economic evaluations (Butler, 1959).

DEMAND AND SUPPLY. The more contemporary interest in the economics of recreation began in the late 1950s with an awareness of the rapidly increasing participation in recreation activities by large segments of populations, and a growing recognition of the appropriate economic claim of recreational use on scarce resources. The early writings of Clawson (e.g. 1959) and the report of the Outdoor Recreation Resources Review Commission (1962) in the US did much to focus attention on recreation in terms of demand and supply and to demonstrate the important impacts of the locations of recreation areas on people's participation in recreational activities. While the conclusions were initially based on US data, other studies confirmed similar patterns and problems of locational imbalances in other countries.

Largely because of planning and project justification requirements, much of the continuing interest in recreation demand has centred on the use and value of specific individual recreation sites rather than on more aggregate demand parameters. While many early studies considered individual sites in isolation, some dealt more formally with several determinants of site demand and with multiple sites (for example, Burt and Brewer, 1971). These studies have provided further insights into the demand for recreation, but their usefulness has been limited by their small number, the lack of much attention to factors other than population proximity, the poor specification of site characteristics, and the little attention given to such things as cross-elasticities between sites and types of facilities.

Useful progress on characterizing supply has been even more modest than on specifying demand. The lack of uniformity among recreation sites and facilities and the importance of location have proved to be severe impediments to incorporating supply into meaningful economic analyses. Much of the work has concentrated on classification of landscapes for potential recreation purposes and inventories of recreation resources.

In some studies, participation rates, which are a function of both the demand for facilities and their availability or supply, have often been taken to be due to demand alone – a difficulty somewhat akin to the identification problem. This confusion of use with demand has led to provision of more of what had already been supplied, and has added to spatial imbalances as observed use was taken as demand for similar facilities in the same areas.

VALUATION. The increased use of benefit cost analysis, particularly for water resource projects in the US, was largely responsible for the development of evaluation methods. An early, if incomplete, response to the requirement for explicit valuations was the use of an agreed-upon schedule of a specific value per site visit. This practice continues, but is widely regarded as largely arbitrary and to allow little discrimination in values to reflect relative scarcities of different resource attractions and facilities.

By far the most widely discussed improvement for valuing recreation is the so-called travel cost technique suggested by Clawson (1959) (a related technique was proposed by Hotelling, 1947). In this method, a demand curve is estimated from the observed relationship between travel costs and visit rates by calculating the decrease in the number of people that would be expected to visit from each origin as a result of varied increments of increased cost. The area under the resulting demand curve is normally taken as the measure of value.

The technique yields a meaningful economic measure of the recreation benefits provided by a site, but estimation problems remain in spite of many suggested improvements (for example, Mansfield, 1971; Smith, 1971; and Vickerman, 1974). Multiple destination trips provide further problems as does the poor ability to take account of the value of travel time and recreation occurring over broad areas rather than at single sites.

An alternative evaluation technique is the contingent valuation method, which derives values based on survey respondents' expressed preference between paying to have access to a recreation facility and not having it (Davis, 1964). Alternative question formats, such as open- and closed-ended questions and sequential bids, are used to overcome problems of bias and the reluctance of respondents to nominate a price.

The contingent valuation technique can be used in a much wider range of circumstances of non-pecuniary evaluations than can other techniques. For example, it can be used to evaluate recreation not associated with specific sites, and to assess the gain or loss of general environmental amenities. However, tests for biases and the effect of varying format remain incomplete.

Contingent valuation studies provided early evidence, confirmed later by experiments and studies involving real money exchanges, of an unexpected large disparity between alternative economic measures of a loss (Knetsch and Sinden, 1984). Contrary to the conventional assumption of near equivalence, differing only by a usually trivial amount due to an income or wealth effect, the empirical evidence from a wide range of studies indicates that the compensation demanded to give up an entitlement is very often far larger than the willingness to pay to keep the same entitlement. These findings suggest that many losses may be seriously understated when the willingness-to-pay measure is used instead of the more appropriate compensation-demanded measure. The inconsistency between the evidence and the traditional expectations remains unresolved, although data from a large body of psychological tests suggesting that people typically make evaluations on the basis of changes from a neutral reference point and value losses more than gains, offer at least a partial explanation (Kahneman and Tversky, 1979).

IMPACT OF ECONOMIC STUDIES. The direct impact of the considerable attention given to the development of techniques of economic analyses of recreation in terms of adoption and widespread use, has been very modest. Little direct use is yet being routinely made of demand and supply models or of the evaluation techniques. Evidence from economic studies is sometimes used by advocacy groups in support of particular interests, but such decisions typically still turn more on expenditure and employment claims than on more appropriate economic analyses.

Indirectly, the impact of recreation economics studies has no doubt been considerable and beneficial (Pigram, 1983). While seldom used to resolve specific issues, economic analyses have clearly demonstrated that recreation facilities may well have large economic value in many cases, and that recreation demands can have a commensurate economic claim on resources (Clawson and Knetsch, 1966).

JACK L. KNETSCH

See also ENVIRONMENTAL ECONOMICS.

BIBLIOGRAPHY

Burt, O.R. and Brewer, D. 1971. Evaluation of net social benefits from outdoor recreation. *Econometrica* 39, September, 813–27.

Butler, G.D. 1959. *Introduction to Community Recreation*. 3rd edn, New York: McGraw-Hill.

Clawson, M. 1959. *Methods of Measuring the Demand for and Value of Outdoor Recreation*. Reprint No. 10, Washington, DC: Resources for the Future.

Clawson, M. and Knetsch, J.L. 1966. *Economics of Outdoor Recreation*. Baltimore: Johns Hopkins Press.

Davis, R.K. 1964. The value of big game hunting in a private forest. In *Transactions of the 29th North America Wildlife and Natural Resources Conference*, Washington, DC: Wildlife Management Institute, 393-402.

Hotelling, H. 1947. Letter. In *The Economics of Public Recreation: An Economic Study of the Monetary Evaluation of Recreation in the National Parks*, ed. R.A. Prewitt, Washington, DC: US National Park Service.

Kahneman, D. and Tversky, A. 1979. Prospect theory: an analysis of decision under risk. *Econometrica* 47, 263–91.

Knetsch, J.L. and Sinden, J.A. 1984. Willingness to pay and compensation demanded: experimental evidence of an unexpected disparity in measures of value. *Quarterly Journal of Economics* 99, August, 507–21.

Mansfield, N.W. 1971. The estimation of benefits from recreation sites and the provision of a new recreation facility. *Regional Studies* 5, 55–69.

Outdoor Recreation Resources Review Commission. 1962. *Outdoor Recreation for America*. Washington, DC: Government Printing Office.

Pigram, J.J. 1983. *Outdoor Recreation and Resource Management*. London: Macmillan.

Smith, R.J. 1971. The evaluation of recreation benefits: the Clawson method in practice. *Urban Studies* 8, June, 89–102.

Vickerman, R.W. 1974. The evaluation of benefits from recreation projects. *Urban Studies* 11, October, 277–88.

Reddaway, William Brian (born 1913). Brian Reddaway was born in 1913 in Cambridge, England. He read economics at King's College, Cambridge (1932–4). Keynes supervised him at the time when he was writing the *General Theory*. Reddaway absorbed its message so well that he wrote one of the most perceptive reviews (1936) of the book. Reddaway has in recent years played a prominent role in defending Keynesian theory and policy against monetarist critics. Nevertheless, he is an open-minded eclectic, accepting ideas from any approach provided that they have an empirical foundation. In Australia, working with Giblin as a Research Fellow in Economics at the University of Melbourne, he so distinguished himself by his evidence (1937) on the Basic Wage to the Arbitration Court that the Wage itself in the year of his evidence (1937) became known as 'The Reddawage'.

In 1938 Reddaway returned to the United Kingdom to a Fellowship at Clare and also to a teaching post in the Faculty of Economics and Politics at Cambridge in 1939. He worked for the Board of Trade (1940–47). After the war, he 'settled down' to the life of a Cambridge don, first, as a Lecturer in the Faculty (1939–55), then as Director of the Department of Applied Economics (1955–70) and, finally, until his 'retirement' in 1980, as Professor of Political Economy (Marshall's chair) (1969–80).

Reddaway is a fine example of an applied economist in the tradition of Marshall and Keynes. He has one of the finest critical minds in the profession; he remorselessly reveals flaws in logic and ignorance of the nature and use of data alike. He is severely practical – the philosophical and speculative aspects of the discipline have little appeal for him and he has no use for theory for its own sake. Reddaway likes to be given questions – the effects of overseas investment on the UK economy (1967, 1968), the true incidence of SET (1970, 1973) – and he produces reports noted for their innovative approach and feel for orders of magnitude. He has also written a number of pioneering works, for example, his first book, on the Russian financial system (1935), his study of the economics of a declining population (1939), and his paper (1959) showing that job opportunities rather than relative wage movements were the main reason for the distribution of labour.

Reddaway's study of the Russian financial system includes an account of a tax system which will provide the appropriate price level to ensure the purchase of the residual production of consumption goods once the level of accumulation has been decided and given a socialist commitment to full employment of labour. While his analysis of the longer-run effects of a declining population is orthodoxly neoclassical – a higher standard of living emerges because of higher capital per person than otherwise would have been the case – his discussion of the relationship between population growth and the level of employment is an astute application of the then, very new Keynesian theory of employment. In addition the policy proposals of the concluding chapter read in a thoroughly modern manner.

Reddaway's work on the problems of developing nations is built up from first principles which are themselves founded in keen common-sense observations and empirical generalizations. The appendix to *The Development of the Indian Economy* (1962) on the importance of lags in the investment decision is one of his most significant insights. His policy recommendations are directed straight-forwardly to the problems in hand, always relevant if sometimes lacking a little in political nous.

Finally, no account of Reddaway's contributions would be complete without mention, first, of his regular column as 'academic investor' in the *Investors Chronicle* in which he reveals how both his college's and his own portfolios have fared; and, secondly, of the remarkable five years (1971–6) as joint editor of the *Economic Journal* with his lifelong friend from King's, David Champernowne.

G.C. Harcourt

SELECTED WORKS

1935. *The Russian Financial System*. London: Macmillan.

1936. 'General Theory of Employment, Interest and Money' (review). *Economic Record* 12(22), June, 28–36.

1939. *The Economics of a Declining Population*. London: George Allen & Unwin.

1959. Wage flexibility and the distribution of labour. *Lloyds Bank Review* 13(54), October, 32–48.

1962. *The Development of the Indian Economy*. London: George Allen & Unwin.

1967, 1986. *Effects of UK Direct Investment Overseas*. 2 vols. (Vol. 1 with J.O.N. Perkins, S.J. Potter and C.T. Taylor; Vol. 2. with D.R. Glynn, J.D. Sugden, P.M. Croxford, C.H. Fletcher and J.S. O'Donnell.) Cambridge: Cambridge University Press.

1970, 1973. *Effects of Selective Employment Tax*. 2 vols, Cambridge: Cambridge University Press; London: HMSO.

redistribution of income and wealth. The topic of redistribution is sometimes interpreted narrowly in rather dry terms: as the description and quantification of the simple fact of change in an income or wealth distribution. This can apply both to an actual change that takes place through time and also to the apparent alteration of the distribution at a point in time by taxes and transfers, and principally involves problems of measurement that are common to other fields of applied economics. However, redistribution can also be seen as a specific goal for economic policy-makers: as such it is a subject of special interest in its own right. Sections 1–4 below concentrate primarily on this second interpretation; some issues arising under the first interpretation are considered in section 5.

1. THE REASONS FOR WANTING TO REDISTRIBUTE. Perhaps the simplest and most direct reason for wishing to see a redistribution of income, consumption or wealth in the community is simple fellow feeling on the part of the citizens of the community. This can be incorporated into the utilitarian approach to welfare judgements within the tradition of Bentham and Mill, in two ways. One might suppose that judgements about distribution are made in a state of primordial ignorance about one's own position in the distribution: social aversion to inequality is thus rationalized as individual aversion to risk (Harsanyi, 1955). Secondly, it might be supposed that the poor are made to feel worse off in their plight by the very knowledge that the well-to-do are well-to-do, and the rich are made to feel uncomfortable by the low living standards of the poor – see Hochman and Rodgers (1969). Thus the problems of inequality are rationalized within individual utilities as 'externalities' in a manner similar to health hazards from pollution. A weakness of this approach is that it puts a heavy burden on the particular configuration of individual preferences that happen to be present within a given community at a given moment: should one *really* only redistribute if enough citizens happen to feel upset by it? And what if some citizens *like* knowing that the very poor are very poor?

An alternative approach is to take the motivation for redistribution as a direct moral imperative – see Tawney (1965), Rawls (1971); improvement in the well-being of the disadvantaged is perceived as a social objective in its own right, along with other apparently desirable goals such as civil liberties and growth in national income.

2. THE OBJECTIVES OF REDISTRIBUTION. Whatever the precise reasons for wishing to redistribute income or wealth may be, in *broad* terms the principal goals of redistribution policy can be stated very simply: the primary objectives are usually some goal of greater equity and of 'social insurance'; and as a secondary, though important, desideratum, one is usually also concerned with economic efficiency.

In order to examine these objectives in more detail two concepts need to be carefully distinguished: redistribution 'ex-ante' – the rearrangement of the structure of *income-earning opportunities* – and redistribution 'ex-post' – the reallocation of income or wealth that results from the economic processes of production and exchange, whatever individual opportunities may have been. In practice the two concepts may be difficult to disentangle since a policy measure that apparently just rearranges the prizes (such as an income-tax scheme) may also have repercussions on some people's *ex-ante* opportunities (by, for example, affecting market wages); but both are relevant to a discussion of the relationship between equity and other goals.

In a very simplified model of the distribution of income, 'equity' can be expressed fairly easily: if one considers that the cake has been cut very unequally, then one sets about trying to even up the slices. But in a dynamic view of the economy where people make economic choices which affect their future incomes, the slices-of-a-fixed-size-cake analogy can be misleading, and the position may be further complicated when those choices have to be made in the face of uncertainty. Obviously the size of the national cake to be 'shared out' is not, in practice, fixed: individual incomes (and hence the total income in the community) are determined by the choices people make as to how much they work, save, and take entrepreneurial risks, and again the total stock of wealth obviously also depends on the rate at which people save. So the elementary equity question of who ought to get what cannot be divorced in practice from the issue of how individual incomes and wealth holdings are generated: efficiency considerations have to be taken into account in the pursuit of greater equity. There is a second, more subtle, difficulty: because of incompetence, ignorance or plain 'bad luck' people who may have looked alike in terms of their original economic opportunities turn out to be very dissimilar in terms of outcomes once a few rounds have been played of the great economic game that determines how much everybody actually gets. Hence there is a good case for a government concerned with distributional equity to pay attention to both the ex-ante and the ex-post concepts of redistribution (Hammond, 1981).

For this reason an interest in social insurance is often taken to be a natural counterpart of a concern for equity. The public provision of protection against the slings and arrows of outrageous fortune is particularly important for those events for which conventional insurance markets are likely to give inadequate coverage, such as unemployment or ill health, for example – see Atkinson (1986). By filling such gaps social insurance may actually improve the efficient working of the economy. Besides this, social insurance can also apply to ex-post redistribution that is intended to circumvent the otherwise unsatisfactory workings of some markets. For example, the markets for private insurance and savings might, under ideal circumstances, allow people to look after themselves effectively; but in practice problems such as imperfect information and the consequent rationing of insurance or credit to those people who are perceived to be good risks will mean that coverage is far from complete (Arrow, 1985). Hence the provision of state pensions as a means of cushioning the possibly unfortunate effects of restrictions on savings by people of modest means.

3. WHAT SHOULD BE REDISTRIBUTED? Whether it is *income* (the flow of spending power during a given period) or *wealth* (the command over resources that a person may possess at a given point in time) that is to be redistributed depends to some extent on the precise definition of these terms (in particular the relevant period over which income is measured and the range of assets to be counted in as personal wealth) and also on the degree of importance that one attaches to ex-ante or ex-post concepts of redistribution. For example, some components of wealth (land, financial assets) may be regarded as part of the range of economic opportunities which results in the flow of spendable income. Again weekly money income might be more relevant than broader concepts of wealth or long-term income if one's primary concern is for redistribution to alleviate short-term need rather than to alter the structure of economic opportunities (Atkinson, 1983, ch. 3).

However, the issue of what one ought to use in order to achieve the objectives of redistribution cited above raises further questions. One of the most important of these is whether one ought to redistribute income itself (which yields purchasing power over consumption goods) or rather the consumption goods directly. The standard answer provided by economists is that cash is unquestionably more effective, since it allows individuals to be the judges of what is best for their welfare and to make substitutions between different goods under varying market conditions in pursuit of that welfare: money to buy soup is supposedly more effective than the provision of soup kitchens. However, this conclusion is strictly relevant only if one imposes a number of stringent conditions, for example, the assumption that everyone has access to perfect market opportunities and accurate information on which to base his judgement in the market. It is invalid in the presence of multiple market equilibria (Foldes, 1967). It ignores pressing requirements of crises such as war and famine: extreme circumstances may require direct intervention to act more swiftly and reliably to maintain living standards than the often capricious and sluggish movements of the 'invisible hand'.

4. THE AVAILABLE INSTRUMENTS. Among the more obvious instruments available for ex-post redistribution are taxes on income, wealth and the transfer of wealth via gifts and bequests, and transfer payments such as pensions and social-security benefits. However, it is not easy to draw a hard-and-fast line around the range of instruments that might be taken to be redistributive tools, particularly if one is concerned with description rather than prescription. There appears to be a good case in practice for including 'indirect' taxes (such as Value Added Tax), subsidies and also those benefits 'in kind' which are bestowed on *particular* households or persons, since the impact of these items on personal spending power is usually fairly clear. This may, for example, be extended to include such goods as state-provided education. However the precise distributional impact of publicly provided goods that are really consumed *jointly* by the community (in which category we might include items such as public sanitation, the police services, or even national defence) is less easy to determine, but should not be assumed to be negligible.

As an alternative to raising taxes and the public provision of goods and services, a government wishing to redistribute real spending power may choose to intervene directly in the market mechanism. The most obvious example of this policy is price control. This term applies not only to rationing and the regulation of prices paid by consumers for goods – which can be an effective method of intervention to achieve redistribution – in emergencies such as wartime, but also to the control of prices that individuals receive for services that they may supply (for example, minimum wage legislation) or assets that they possess (control of house-rents).

The instruments available for the purposes of ex-ante redistribution (i.e. the means of reorganizing the *opportunities* for creating income and accumulating wealth) are more disparate. One has the immediate problem that the range of policies considered to be available is strongly influenced by the economic philosophy which one considers to be relevant to the analysis and by the political and social system within the community. Take a prime example of this: education. There are many opinions on the potential for using this as a redistributional tool, some of which may be crudely summarized by the following three views: (a) it is a passport to higher positions on a ladder of economic opportunity whose rungs are pretty rigidly fixed, so that greater equality can be achieved simply by changing the method of issuing the passports; (b) it forms part of a complex of personal or family investment decisions, whereby intervention in the provision of education might upset the efficient allocation of the market mechanism without doing anything to alleviate the inequality of economic opportunity; (c) even if effective redistribution *could* be achieved in principle, substantial reorganization of educational opportunities is bound to be limited by what are seen as fundamental freedoms of choice. Note that the divergence of view concerns both the economic role of education and the extent to which one is free to use it as an instrument of public policy (Le Grand, 1982, ch. 4).

5. THE EFFECTIVENESS OF THE POLICY. Any attempt to quantify the effectiveness of redistribution policy has to surmount a number of extremely troublesome obstacles.

In the first place one has to confront the problem of 'unequal inequalities', which essentially arises from an attempt to compare intrinsically complex social states. Even if one puts this in elementary terms, whereby every person's welfare is accurately measured by his or her income, a fundamental difficulty remains: apart from special circumstances – for example, a comparison involving a hypothetical state of perfect equality – the question of which of two distributions is the more unequal does not generally have a clear-cut answer. In practice, even a very successful redistribution policy will have diminished rather than completely eliminated real income differences, so that an assessment of the policy's impact necessarily involves a comparison of the apparent change in inequality that has been achieved relative to the degree of inequality that would have obtained otherwise. There is no single method for measuring such inequality changes that commands universal support, and hence no generally agreed measuring rod to ascertain the extent of redistribution under all circumstances (Cowell, 1977; Foster, 1985). One of the practical difficulties to which this gives rise is that it is difficult to be dogmatic about labelling policy instruments in terms of degrees of 'progressivity' (Lambert, 1985). Moreover, in many cases redistribution may involve not just a narrowing (or indeed expansion) of income differentials, but also a *re-ranking* of income receivers within the pecking order so that, to quantify redistribution effectively, more is required than a simple measurement of the change in overall dispersion (Cowell, 1985).

The second problem follows directly from this: who is to say what *would* have happened otherwise and, therefore, what change in inequality has actually been achieved? If one is merely concerned with the documentation of trends in the perceived inequities of income distribution through time, this may not be too difficult. But if at any moment of history one attempts to draw the inference that 'according to our chosen inequality index, the inequality of disposable income would have been 20 per cent higher than it is now but for the high marginal tax rates on upper income groups', then one is making a much bolder assertion about how the underlying economic mechanisms are supposed to work. For the very presence of the instruments of redistribution policy will have influenced the choices people make about their jobs, business enterprises and savings, which in turn, can be expected to affect the resulting income distribution. The 'distribution before tax' – obtainable from a statistical office's published figures – cannot automatically be taken to be the same thing as the distribution *without* the tax – the income distribution that one might expect to see if the relevant redistribution instrument were to be abolished.

Some allowance for this problem is usually possible in the case of ex-post redistribution instruments – for example, it is possible to estimate the likely repercussion on the supply of different types of labour that will arise because of the supplementation of some people's incomes by public transfers and the reduction in other people's incomes through taxation (Hausman, 1985; Killingsworth, 1983), or the impact on private savings of the presence of state-provided pensions and social insurance schemes (Danziger et al., 1981; Kotlikoff, 1984). However, the allowance to be made for these feedback effects is usually quite sensitive to the particular model of household behaviour that is applied.

Despite these reservations, some broad conclusions are possible. Very narrowly based measures run the danger of the 'demarcation trap': for example, subsidizing particular commodities or taxing only certain forms of income or wealth may present some people with an incentive to change their behaviour, or even misrepresent their true status, so as to profit by the artificial distinctions drawn by the selective tax or subsidy scheme. The effectiveness of the measure may thereby be reduced and, even if this does not happen, the discrimination of the scheme may itself create substantial inequities by treating essentially similar people in different ways. On the other hand, very broadly based measures may scatter their shot so widely that much of it misses the target: blanket allowances or exceptions within income- or wealth-tax laws, and some broadly defined educational subsidies are often found to be regressive in their actual *ex-post* impact on income and wealth. Finally it is usually the case that *taxes*, taken as a whole, turn out not to be very progressive in terms of their *ex-post* impact whereas *transfers* usually are.

F.A. COWELL

See also INHERITANCE TAXES; NEGATIVE INCOME TAX; PROGRESSIVE AND REGRESSIVE TAXATION; TRANSFER PAYMENTS; SOCIAL SECURITY.

BIBLIOGRAPHY

Arrow, K.J. 1985. The economics of agency. In *Principals and Agents: The Structure of Business*, ed. J. Pratt and R. Zeckhauser, Cambridge, Mass: Harvard Business School Press.

Atkinson, A.B. 1983. *The Economics of Inequality*. 2nd edn, Oxford: Oxford University Press.

Atkinson, A.B. 1986. Income maintenance and social insurance: a survey. In *Handbook of Public Economics*, Vol. II, ed. A.J. Auerbach and M.S. Feldstein, Amsterdam: North-Holland.

Cowell, F.A. 1977. *Measuring Inequality*. Oxford: Philip Allan.

Cowell, F.A. 1985. Measures of distributional change: an axiomatic approach. *Review of Economic Studies* 52, 135–51.

Danziger, S., Haveman, R.H. and Plotnick, R. 1981. How income transfer programs affect work, savings and the income distribution: a critical review. *Journal of Economic Literature* 19, 975–1028.

Foldes, L.P. 1967. Income redistribution in money and in kind. *Economica* 34, February, 30–41.

Foster, J. 1985. Inequality measurement. In *Fair Allocation*, ed. H.P. Young, American Mathematical Society Proceedings of Symposia in Applied Mathematics 33.

Hammond, P.J. 1981. *Ex-ante* and *ex-post* welfare economics. *Economica* 48, 235–50.

Harsanyi, J.C. 1955. Cardinal welfare, individualist ethics and interpersonal comparisons of utility. *Journal of Political Economy* 63, 309–21.

Hausman, J.A. 1985. Taxation and labour supply. In *Handbook of Public Economics*, Vol. I, ed. A.J. Auerbach and M.S. Feldstein, Amsterdam: North-Holland.

Hochman, J.M. and Rodgers, J.D. 1969. Pareto optimal redistribution. *American Economic Review* 59, 542–57.

Killingsworth, M.R. 1983. *Labour Supply*. Cambridge: Cambridge University Press.

Kotlikoff, L.J. 1984. Taxation and savings: a neoclassical perspective. *Journal of Economic Literature* 22, 1576–629.

Lambert, P.J. 1985. Tax-progressivity: a survey of the literature. IFS Working Paper, London: Institute for Fiscal Studies.

Le Grand, J. 1982. *The Strategy of Equality*. London: Allen & Unwin.

Rawls, J. 1971. *A Theory of Justice*. Cambridge, Mass.: Harvard University Press.

Tawney, R.H. 1965. *Equality*. London: Allen & Unwin.

reforestation. *See* FORESTS.

regional development. Persisting and even increasing regional differentials in the course of national development are important economic phenomena that have continued to stimulate research. Most features of regional development analysis are related to these patterns of unequal progress, especially the studies and modelling of the regional location of particular types of industry, of urbanization and transportation systems, the interrelations of agricultural and industrial growth and interregional and intraregional migration. The grand and overall issue, however, continues to be that of unequal regional development. It is striking that research on this issue, which was in the mainstream of the early years of development economics, has, with only a few exceptions, retired to the regional science journals.

Early empirical work by Williamson (1965) established the perception that national economic growth has been accompanied by increasing regional income differentials for substantial periods of time, followed by a trend toward regional equality. While the first impressions and systematic research were based on the growth experience of advanced countries, subsequent research has confirmed that developing countries have been repeating the previously observed pattern.

Attempts to explain regional growth patterns analytically have always recognized both the potential contribution of international trade theory and its inadequacies. The implications of conventional trade theories applied to regional development are that there would be continual pressures for equalization of regional product prices and factor incomes. Unique mineral and land resources would receive differential rents but the migration of mobile factors to higher-income regions would equalize their returns. Practically speaking, it has been recognized that a substantial amount of time might be required for this theoretical prediction to work out. The long lifetimes and slow depreciation of immobile real capital, particularly buildings and civil works, would delay the movement of other factors which could use the capital.

Since standard trade theory cannot explain increasing regional inequality, alternative hypotheses have been generated outside that theory. One of the first of these argued that the existence of different export industries within regions would explain their differential development. Suppose that a new export industry, based on some regionally unique endowments, or the accident of a local improvement in production technology, expanded rapidly. Incomes in the newly exporting region would also expand faster than those in other regions. But persisting regional differences would require some additional conditions, however, or the differences would be eliminated by goods and factor mobility.

Another early hypothesis was that there are, in fact, regional differences in regional production functions, contrary to the assumptions of Hecksher–Ohlin–Samuelson trade theory, and also in the relative prices of non-traded goods. If one or more technologies used in producing goods and services in one region remain persistently inferior to those in other regions, that region would remain permanently poorer. It makes no difference whether or not the output is supplied to an export industry. The same result follows if, for any other reasons, the products produced in different regions make more or less effective use of their comparative advantage. Historically, differences in the levels and applications of technology have had a profound role in the explanation of regional incomes. Allocational inefficiencies arising from particular government policies have been widely recognized as retarding national growth and must have analogous implications for growth in particular regions, as their effects are not uniform (World Bank, 1983).

Such explanations can all be placed under the headline of 'structuralist' economic hypotheses: those which adduce non-economic influences or economic features outside the conventional characterizations to explain why predictions derived from the assumptions of perfect markets will be in error. Although for some economists a resort to explanations of this type is, virtually, 'the last refuge of a scoundrel', some of these explanations have become theoretically respectable when given the titles of 'adjustment costs', 'imperfect information', 'risk' and 'incomplete markets'.

It has often been alleged that regional biases in central government policy in taxing or supplying public services result in differences in regional economic development. This has, for example, been the most conventional explanation of the persisting economic retardation of the Italian Mezzogiorno after national unification and has been argued with respect to the US South after the Civil War, subjects that have attracted a relatively large amount of attention. Differences in regional savings rates or market structures can also work to the same end.

The idea that regional economic activity tends to concentrate in a '*pole de croissance*' is a relatively old one in the regional literature. It has a forerunner in Losch (1939) but was expressed most suggestively in Perroux (1955). The reasons advanced by Perroux included economies of scale in production and the clustering of technological innovations and investment. The descriptions of the process were suggestive but were not successfully embodied in a rigorous theory. Nonetheless, the idea became widely cited and used to justify methods which never became effective tools of regional economic policy, which is why 'growth pole theory' has been called one of the development literature's fads (Higgins, 1983).

The use of regional input–output tables as a means of determining the patterns of regional demands due to the expansion of a particular sector is one of the major features of 'growth pole' analysis. The criticism of the use of this tool, as not being able to capture the full range of nonlinear and dynamic interactions which occur in the process of development (Hansen, 1972), is really a criticism of the state of regional development theory. Nonetheless, regional input–output tables have helped in understanding some of the characteristic differences that exist and also in assessing the sources and consequences of industrial location decisions and population movements, that have been major preoccupations of the regional development field.

The hypothesis that increasing returns to scale play a major role in explaining diverging regional development is a 'purely' economic argument of long standing and, perhaps, the most powerful. The concept is intuitively appealing. Suppose there are initial differences in the levels of output in one or more sectors of different regions. If the output is produced with increasing returns to scale, that will mean that the sectors with a 'head start' will have lower costs and can effectively capture the entire market, unless constrained by regulation or private agreement. That would appear to lead to a 'cumulative and circular causation process' which favours the advanced region. Unless these are offsetting differences in savings rates or other structural characteristics, the poorer region could not catch up.

Nonetheless, the argument by itself is ultimately unsatisfactory as an explanation of regional differentials. There is nothing which localizes the benefits of increasing returns as long as all produced goods are traded. But, with the addition of another ingredient, the increasing returns to scale hypothesis does become a complete economic explanation of regional differentials. That ingredient, provided by Faini (1984), is the hypothesis that the increasing returns to scale occur in the production of non-traded intermediate inputs. That would mean that final product industries, using those nontraded inputs at falling prices, would have a continuing cost advantage, once an initial differential were created. The migration of capital toward the region with an initial advantage in producing a nontraded intermediate good would only increase the scale of that production and its cost advantage. As a result, the interregional migration of capital would not equalize its returns. Interregional labour mobility would equalize wages but not permit local labour to share in the rents in the nontraded goods sector created by the increasing returns to scale. That would leave the rents to capital in the nontraded goods sector as a permanent source of regional income differentials.

'Shift-share' analysis, which is another approach to regional development theory, is simply the use of an identity to divide total growth in employment in a region in separate parts: that due to growth in the aggregate of national employment, that part due to overall growth in the particular sectors in a region and that part due to the special comparative advantage of the region itself. The last source is the one of particular interest but 'shift-share' analysis has had relatively few new insights to offer on the subject (Andrikopoulos, 1980).

Grand theorizing about regional development has diminished in favour of studies of particular features of the process. The regional science journals provide much interesting reading which is distinguished by its empirical detail. These offer many insights into the processes of regional development, though they cannot be fitted together in an overall framework.

A continuing preoccupation with regional development theory reflects a worthy desire for an operational general theory. In principle, of course, that 'simply' requires an extension of existing economy-wide general equilibrium models or models of the world economy. The major obstacles are not mainly conceptual: most of the elements of a satisfactory theory are well known. The analytical problems are formidable, however, because of their high dimensionality. The addition of regional details to any model quickly makes it analytically cumbersome. International trade theory, for example, cannot easily manage more than two goods and two factors and two regions.

A computational approach to obtain both analytical and empirical insights is possible. Computable international trade models handle much more detail than the analytical models. Some of the sectorally detailed economy-wide computable models already distinguish rural and urban sectors and are embryonic regional models. Conceptually, it is a small step to full regional disaggregation. However, addition of the essential non-convexities of increasing returns to scale would now be a major barrier to computational solutions.

Nonetheless, the major and continuing obstacle to progress in developing overall regional analyses and policy is lack of detailed regional trade data. If that were available, modellers would be hard at work on their computers.

RICHARD S. ECKAUS

See also INEQUALITY BETWEEN NATIONS; POLES OF DEVELOPMENT; UNEVEN DEVELOPMENT.

BIBLIOGRAPHY

Andrikopoulos, A.A. 1980. A synthesis of the production function and the shift-share model. *Regional Science and Urban Economics* 10(4), November, 539–60.

Borts, G.H. 1960. The equalization of returns and regional economic growth. *Economic Journal* 70, 319–47.

Borts, G.H. and Stein, P. 1964. *Economic Growth in a Free Market.* New York: Columbia University Press.

Faini, R. 1984. Increasing returns, non-traded inputs and regional development. *Economic Journal* 94, 308–23.

Fukuchi, T. Growth and stability of multiregional economy. *International Economic Review* 14(1), 509–20.

Hansen, N. 1972. *Growth Centers in Regional Economic Development.* New York: Free Press; London: Collier–Macmillan.

Higgins, B. 1983. From growth poles to systems of interaction. *Growth and Change* 14(4), 3–13.

Lösch, A. 1939. *Die räumliche Ordnung der Wirtschaft.* Jena: Gustav Fischer Verlag. Translated as *The Economics of Location*, New Haven: Yale University Press, 1954.

North, D.C. 1955. Location theory and regional economic growth. *Journal of Political Economy* 63, 243–58.

Perroux, F. 1955. Note sur la notion de 'pôle de croissance'. *Cahiers de l'Institut de Science Economique Appliquée*, Series D No. 8.

Williamson, J.G. 1965. Regional inequality and the process of national development: a description of the patterns. *Economic Development and Cultural Change* 13(4), Pt 2, 1–84.

World Bank. 1983. *World Development Report.* Washington, DC: International Bank for Reconstruction and Development.

regional distribution of economic activity.

INTRODUCTION: REGIONS AND NATIONS. Our starting point for discussing the regional distribution of economic activity within nations is the recognition that economists interested in the emergence and persistence of economic disparities between regions have drawn heavily on theories relevant for understanding international economic relations between countries. There are, of course, important differences between regions and sovereign nation states, but they are often differences of degree rather than kind. Critically important for a region is its openness and interdependence with other regions. This arises because of the generally greater importance of trade to the region compared with the nation but also because of its greater dependence on investment brought in from other regions. Regions within a nation also share a common currency and this removes the possibility of currency adjustments. Inevitably this puts more weight on internal price flexibility and factor mobility between regions as means by which regions adjust to economic circumstances than is the case with nations. The mobility of labour and capital is greater between regions than countries and as we shall see this has been a major route by which regions adjust to change.

LIMITATIONS OF THE NEOCLASSICAL APPROACH. Perhaps the most influential of the theories of international trade which regional economists have used to explain the regional distribution of economic activity is that grounded in the neoclassical approach. A central conclusion of this theory is that each region will tend to specialize in producing what it is comparatively good at producing, even though it may be inferior (or superior) in producing *all* goods and services. This theory is based on a number of highly unrealistic assumptions, most notably the absence of factor mobility between regions and perfect internal mobility of resources; perfect markets – so that prices are perfectly flexible and markets clear; the absence of increasing returns to scale; perfect foresight on the part of economic agents. Not surprisingly, neoclassical theory has been severely criticized as a theoretical framework for understanding how regional economies function.

When applied to regions, the neoclassical approach is flawed for several reasons. Firstly inter-*regional* labour and capital mobility is a key feature of regional adjustment processes. This observation not only contradicts one of the underlying assumptions of the neoclassical approach, it implies that a region's growth is, to a significant extent, demand determined where factor supplies adjust to demand via inter-regional mobility.

Secondly, factor price flexibility within each region is a

necessary condition to ensure specialization of production and full employment in each region. The reason a region can specialize in the production of goods in which it has a comparative advantage, but not an absolute advantage, is that its real wages are much lower than in other regions. If real wages are not flexible and are at the same level in all regions then production will tend to concentrate in the high productivity regions. Workers in turn will either migrate from the low to high productivity regions in search of jobs or, in the absence of migration, unemployment will result in low productivity regions. In other words, real factor price flexibility is critical for the theory of comparative advantage as an explanation of the regional distribution of economic activity. Real factor returns must match the level of factor productivity region by region.

Perhaps a more fundamental criticism of the neoclassical approach to explaining regional economic activity is that it assumes instantaneous clearing of the labour market, or that wage adjustment and labour mobility are a feature of both the short and long run. Thus in the short run, regional wage flexibility clears the labour market which then induces inter-regional movements of labour and capital, until eventually (in the long run) a new equilibrium is reached. Unfortunately for the neoclassical approach, there is no guarantee that such a new equilibrium will be reached (Canning, 1985). The argument is quite simple. If real wages are flexible then they will fall in regions experiencing unemployment until full employment is reached. Low relative wages will attract firms from other regions and workers will seek jobs in other regions. The result is an excess demand for labour which eventually equalizes real wages. In other words the economy must be at over-full employment. However, over-full employment induces real wages to rise above their equilibrium level, relative to other regions, and as a result unemployment starts to rise again, eventually driving real wages down again. Thus when the dynamics of adjustment are examined no simple neoclassical answer to the question of regional growth emerges.

REAL WAGE RIGIDITIES AND ABSOLUTE ADVANTAGES. In most countries little evidence exists that real wages are sufficiently flexible to secure full employment or meet the conditions required for the theory of comparative advantage to provide an explanation of the regional distribution of economic activity. Quite apart from the role that labour unions play in setting national wage rates across all regions, the potential mobility of skilled labour will tend to equalize wages across regions (a point that Hicks made over half a century ago). Thus when internal labour markets are considered, firms are forced to pay the national (or even international) going wage to avoid losing their internal labour force. In those circumstances where real wages flexibility is small, the regional location of economic activity will be determined by the principle of absolute advantage rather than comparative advantage. Regions with an absolute advantage will grow relative to regions with an absolute disadvantage. Firms will move to areas with an absolute advantage and existing indigenous firms will expand as they exploit their absolute advantages and out-compete firms in other regions. If inter-regional migration is relatively easy, the workforce will also concentrate in these regions to satisfy their growing demand for labour. If inter-regional migration is difficult, perhaps because of housing constraints or union activity, the growth of the favoured region will be supply constrained and under-utilization of labour and other resources will persist in the disadvantaged region.

Absolute advantage may be enhanced if we admit the possibility of increasing returns to scale. In these circumstances, regions with small producers will face an increasingly uphill task in competing because their market penetration does not enable them to secure sufficient internal economies of scale.

THE COMPETITIVENESS OF A REGION'S EXPORT BASE. This analysis strongly suggests that the regional distribution of economic activity depends to a significant extent on the growth of demand that regions face rather than on the principle of comparative advantage implied by neoclassical theory. Neither is the growth of a region limited by labour or capital shortages since the availability of these two factors is constrained only insofar as there are barriers to inter-regional factor mobility. Of critical importance is the growth of demand that a region enjoys, particularly for the goods and services which it exports to other regions and to other nations. Regional economists have long recognized the importance of the traded goods sector in explaining regional growth. Manufacturing activity is traditionally regarded as the most important of the basic sectors but agriculture, mining, tourism and certain producer and financial services are also significant in the export sector of some regions. Other sectors such as construction, population-related services, transport and communications are largely dependent on income generated by the export sector.

The critical question therefore is 'what determines the growth of a region's export sector?'. Regions favourably endowed with climate and geological conditions will tend to specialize in the production of raw materials and commodities in which they have an absolute advantage. Once a region's specialization is established, the immobility of key factor inputs implies that changes in exports become important in determining the growth of demand for these outputs. The growth of output will however be constrained by the region's opportunities for increasing crop yields or mining productivity.

The role of manufacturing industry in the process of regional growth is more complex than the role of raw materials and agricultural output. In the first place, it is important to recognize that the export base depends on both the location decisions of manufacturing firms and the competitive performance of the indigenous sector (existing firms and newly spawned companies). With respect to existing firms, regional economists have pointed to the inherited structure of the region's industry in explaining regional differences in economic growth. Thus changes in the pattern of demand nationally and internationally, changes in production technology, and changes in the organizational structure of firms will influence different industries in quite diverse ways. How individual regions fare in this process of change will depend critically on which industries they possess and their importance to the region. In this sense it is difficult to deny that 'structural' factors must play some role in determining a region's economic performance. However, it is also clear that a region's growth might influence its structure. Structure and growth are interdependent.

Even when allowance is made for structural differences across regions at a relatively high level of disaggregation, significant differences in the regional growth performance persist. Differences in unit input costs between regions, combined with the locational flexibility permitted by improvements in transport and communications are one possible explanation. There are in many countries significant regional differences in operating costs, notably wages and transport costs. Such cost differences might be expected to lead to changes in a region's net export growth as well as to changes in location (investment) decisions in favour of relatively low cost regions.

There has also been a long term declining trend in the employment/floorspace ratio. This means that manufacturing firms located in urban centres which were established in earlier periods of industrialization, no longer find such locations appropriate or necessary. Expansion is often difficult in highly urbanized areas and non-manufacturing firms are willing to pay more for an urban location than manufacturing firms. As a result of this, regions dominated by urban concentrations of manufacturing are experiencing a relative decline as firms decentralize their activities to other more rural/small town regions where costs are lower and suitable industrial floorspace more easily and cheaply acquired.

This process of decentralization by manufacturing firms (observed in many advanced industrialized countries) is paralleled by population dispersal. It is difficult to judge the extent of cause and effect in this case, however, since there is evidence of a change in residential preferences in favour of small cities and towns, which in turn could influence the location decisions of firms. This is particularly so in the residential choices being made by professional and scientific workers. It is also clear that relocation decisions by firms provoke changes in the residential locations of households. Whatever the precise balance of cause and effect between population and employment dispersal from large cities, it is clear that regions are growing differentially, at least in part, as a result of their urban/rural structure.

Changes in the regional distribution of certain manufacturing industries have been influenced by the growth of large multi-regional, multinational corporations. A region's fortunes no longer depend merely on trends in its dominant sectors at the national and international level. Rather, companies are selecting locations according to the functional divisions of the company. Mass production and assembly activities will be drawn to regions with a surplus of unskilled or semi-skilled labour, where wages are relatively low and where female workers are more readily available. Control functions, product research and development are more typically located in or close to larger cities in the more favoured regions. Apart from the obvious implications for the spatial division of labour and regional growth it is important to recognize that large corporations are now able to organize their regional allocation of resources in a way that maximizes their advantages but at the cost of increasing uncertainty in the regions. In other words the process of industrial restructuring is now proving of critical importance to the emerging pattern of regional economic activity.

Closely related to the above notion of a regional functional division of labour is the concept of the product life-cycle whereby different regions are characterized by different points in the life-cycle. Initially, during the research and development phase, uncertainty requires good communications and flexibility in decision making afforded by proximity to key management personnel. Once the innovative monopoly advantage is exhausted and product development has largely ceased, cost advantages associated with internal economies of scale and the use of less skilled labour become more important. These advantages are to be found in regions with adequate space for high capital intensity or abundant supplies of low skilled labour. In this respect the product life-cycle process maps in closely with earlier observations on the significance of regionally differentiated input costs, the urban/rural shift of manufacturing activity and the functional division of labour across regions. Insofar as regions cannot maintain their competitive advantage at different stages in the product life-cycle they will suffer a loss of export markets, increased import penetration and relative economic decline. This pattern of events seems characteristic of many old industrialized regions in countries that industrialized early. Such regions often relied heavily on products such as steel, coal and textiles for their early economic development. These regions now face a major competitive threat from overseas, where low labour costs, higher productivity and greater economies of scale are securing significant price competitive advantages. Other industries such as engineering and motor vehicles are also increasingly vulnerable to such competitiveness as are the regions which depend on these industries to any significant extent.

CUMULATIVE REGIONAL GROWTH AND DECLINE. The discussion above points to a number of factors important in the changing net export performance of a region. Recent theories of cumulative causation, espoused initially by Myrdal (1959) and developed later by Kaldor (1971), attempt to provide a view of regional growth which emphasizes both the role of net export growth and the dynamic and interdependent processes of regional development. Of central importance to this view is the denial of comparative static models with their equilibriating tendencies resulting from the free play of market forces. Rather, cumulative causation models raise the possibility of increasing concentrations of economic intensity in favoured regions.

In cumulative causation models once growth becomes firmly established in a region, a virtuous circle is established whereby the participants enjoy the advantages of external economies associated with innovation, skill development, and an entrepreneurial culture which feeds on itself, generating yet greater externalities and dynamic economies of scale. At the same time the need for public infrastructure, public services and housing gives an added stimulus to the virtuous circle of growth. By contrast in declining areas the economic and social structure stagnates as population leaves and industries decline and wither away. Within this model export growth can provide the stimulus whereby faster output and productivity growth, greater product and process innovation and greater investment are secured. In particular Kaldor's (1966) incorporation of the Verdoorn relationship linking output growth and productivity growth is an important feature of the cumulative process whereby faster output growth gives rise to faster productivity growth, which in turn increases export competitiveness which feeds back into faster output growth and so on. Finally, although balance of payments disequilibrium is not manifest in terms of (for example) a growing deficit in a region's current account, it is manifest through a slower growth of real income and net emigration. The opposite occurs in regions enjoying cumulative growth.

Although much of the theoretical literature has emphasized the importance of net exports and private sector investment as sources of exogenous demand to a region, it is important to note that public expenditure has been of growing importance in the post-war period. There are several ways in which public expenditure supports economic activity differentially across a nation's regions. Firstly, there are net fiscal transfers to regions experiencing above average unemployment through unemployment benefits and lower tax revenues from regional expenditure and income. It is in this way that the implicit current account deficit of regions is often largely financed by surplus regions. Secondly, the provision of public sector infrastructure (including housing) may be important particularly in regions which are in the early stages of economic development. Thirdly, public sector procurement policies, related for example to a nation's defence expenditure, very often have pronounced regionally differentiated effects. The latter are also significant for regional development in that they will tend to encourage technology transfer between the public sector and private firms, thereby reinforcing the region's growth potential.

REGIONAL DIFFERENCES IN STRUCTURAL ADAPTATION. One important question which remains partly unanswered in our discussion so far is why structural adaptation of regions varies. Some regions are apparently able to adjust relatively easily to changing competitive conditions but others experience severe difficulties. Models which emphasize absolute advantage rely heavily on relative cost disadvantages as the major difficulty facing companies in satisfying export demand whilst non-cost factors operating on the supply side are largely ignored. The cumulative causation models include an endogenous supply response to demand but little is said about factors constraining the supply of inputs when the pattern of demand changes. In this respect there is evidence for regionally differentiated process and product innovation, with the latter of particular importance as a factor underpinning the success of the more rapidly growing regions. The rate of new firm formation is also important in securing a flexible supply response. The size structure of firms has been shown to be related to the rate of new firm formation, with regions dominated by small firms spawning new firms faster than regions dominated by larger firms.

THE CONTRIBUTION OF REGIONAL POLICY. Regional policy is designed to influence the geographical distribution of economic activity either by restraining economic development in fully employed regions and/or by encouraging expansion in problem regions through financial inducements to the private sector or a differentially high rate of public expenditure to improve the infrastructure. Such policies have been followed in the majority of OECD countries from the 1960s onwards.

The operation of such policies presented new challenges on how to disentangle their impact in promoting economic development in backward regions from all the other factors causing changes in the regional distribution of economic activity. Until this was possible the cost effectiveness of regional policies could not be properly assessed. Methods of evaluation based upon a variety of quantitative and qualitative techniques are gradually being developed.

The results of this work suggest that regional policy had a substantial influence on the regional distribution of economic activity, particularly in the 1960s and early 1970s, when the more advanced industrial economies were growing relatively quickly. The impact of policy declined, however, with the onset of slower growth and recession from the mid-1970s onwards. In the case of Britain, the most recent evaluation of policy suggested that it had contributed about half a million new jobs to the assisted areas during 1960–1981 – a very significant contribution.

In recent years, however, there has been growing dissatisfaction with regional policy and increasing pressure for reforms which would render policy more appropriate to the needs of backward regions and the economic conditions prevailing in the 1980s. Dissatisfaction arose in part from the seeming inability of policy to fully solve the economic problems of backward regions in which the policy-induced development fell far short of the needs of regions with large declining sectors. As the 1980s recession emerged, this gap between the needs of the problem regions and what policy could achieve became progressively wider.

The criticism was also expressed that regional policy had diverted too many branch plants into the problem regions, thus making those areas more vulnerable to subsequent closure in times of recession. In addition, such policies did not encourage decision-making in the region or enhance indigenous development which would lead to self-sustained growth from within the area. Branch plant economies, in addition to discouraging the development of entrepreneurship and the start-up of new small firms, also distorted the occupational structure towards lower skilled manual workers, leaving those with technical, professional and managerial skills to seek jobs in more prosperous regions.

A further point of contention raised by the critics of regional policy as pursued in the last two decades is that too much emphasis has been placed on attempting to influence the geographical distribution of manufacturing industries, which have been in decline or growing relatively slowly, and too little emphasis has been placed on attempting to encourage service industries to move to the depressed regions. This apparent imbalance in policy stance, which has only partially been rectified in recent years, was justified on two grounds. Firstly, most service industries depend on local income and population and therefore do not constitute part of the export base of a region. Secondly, those service industries which serve a wider regional, national or international market, such as financial and business services, are limited in their choice of location by the need for face to face contact with each other and with other national institutions and the need for instant information which can only be found in the larger capital cities.

Another issue concerning the efficacy of policy is the choice of regional policy inducements to private firms, between those which subsidize the use of labour and those which subsidize capital. Neoclassical theory suggests that labour subsidies should be favoured on the grounds that it is the use of the factor of production in excess supply which should be subsidized (i.e. labour) and not the factor of production which is in scarce supply (i.e. capital). Empirical work however suggests that capital subsidies are the more cost effective. Labour subsidies have to be applied continuously, year after year, to maintain jobs which have been created and they rely for their impact on marginal changes in costs and prices and the subsequent responses of those who purchase the region's output. Unless the labour subsidy is large and is passed on to the buyer in the form of lower prices, its impact on competitiveness and the volume of orders is limited. Capital subsidies, on the other hand, can influence company decisions at crucial times when large capital investment projects are being planned, and can influence their location in favour of high unemployment areas, thus capturing with one grant a relatively large number of new jobs for the entire length of the project's life which may be ten or twenty years.

Partly in response to such criticisms and partly in the search for improvements in the cost effectiveness of policy and the need to cut public expenditure, central governments have tended to reduce the priority afforded to regional policies in the 1980s, just at a time when the economic problems of backward regions have worsened. As a consequence, local authorities have become more active in the promotion of economic development in their areas, which encourages the 'leap-frogging' of financial inducements offered, leading to wasteful competition between authorities. The authorities with most natural advantages of location and environment tend to have most success.

Meanwhile the search continues for a regional policy which could be expected to meet the needs of problem regions more effectively. Regional Development Agencies form the basis of one set of proposals. Following the precedents of New Town Corporations and the Scottish and Welsh Development Agencies, such bodies can coordinate the activities of public and private sectors, raise funds from both public and private sources, assess local and regional needs more carefully and with more commitment, and generally act as a catalyst for indigenous growth and eventually self-sustaining development. The emphasis is thus shifting more towards increasing the amount of supply-side flexibility to improve a region's export competitiveness.

There have also been calls for improved monitoring of the role of the public sector in causing or reducing regional disparities through its own procurement and expenditure policies. But no type of regional policy will solve the problems of depressed areas effectively and efficiently unless the major industrialized economies return to an era of rapid growth and full employment.

BARRY MOORE AND JOHN RHODES

See also LOCATION OF ECONOMIC ACTIVITY; POLES OF DEVELOPMENT; SPATIAL ECONOMICS.

BIBLIOGRAPHY

Armstrong, H. and Taylor, J. 1978. *Regional Economic Policy*. Oxford: Philip Allan.

Borts, G. 1960. The equalization of returns and regional economic growth. *Economic Journal* 50, 319–47.

Canning, D. 1985. The dynamics of regional wage adjustment. Department of Applied Economics, Cambridge, Mimeo.

Dixon, R.J. and Thirlwall, A.P. 1975. A model of regional growth rate differentials along Kaldorian lines. *Oxford Economic Papers* 27(2), July, 201–14.

Isard, W. 1960. *Methods of Regional Analysis: An Introduction to Regional Science*. Cambridge, Mass.: MIT Press.

Kaldor, N. 1966. *The Causes of the Slow Rate of Economic Growth of the United Kingdom*. Cambridge: Cambridge University Press.

Kaldor, N. 1970. The case for regional policies. *Scottish Journal of Political Economy* 17(3), 337–48.

Moore, B., Rhodes, J. and Tyler, P. 1986. *The Effects of Government Regional Economic Policy*. London: HMSO.

Myrdal, G. 1957. *Economic Theory and Underdeveloped Regions*. London: Duckworth.

regional economics. The major problem of regional economics, which is to explain the location of production and population within a national economy, has often been approached as if it were not amenable to the usual tools of economic analysis. That regional economics is a distinct field can be seen by comparing the similarities and differences between a region and a nation. A region is like a nation in that goods are traded between it and the rest of the world. Locational differences in factor supplies lead to differences in goods produced among regions and hence to trade among regions, just as with nations. The similarities extend partly – but not wholly – to behaviour of the factors of production. Capital is a factor of production displaying mobility among nations and regions.

One of the most important differences between a nation and a region is with regard to another factor of production, labour. Labour is restricted from moving freely among nations, whereas the *sine qua non* of regions within a nation is that labour can move without restriction among regions. Beyond this crucial difference are differences in policy instruments. Unlike a nation, a region cannot undertake independent monetary and trade policies.

The differences make international trade and regional economics distinct from one another. In contrast to the nation, the demand for goods in a region depends on the endogenous number of people in the region. A determinant of demand as well as what is produced in the region is labour supply which is affected by degree of labour mobility, local goods demand and supply determined cost of living differences among regions, and amenities in the region. Regional economics is very much concerned with the resulting effects on the location of industry. The major policy concerns in regional economics are with effects of local taxation and expenditure policies and with efforts to influence the distribution of activities among regions. All this is in contrast to the concerns in international trade with tariffs, exchange rates and monetary policies not found in regional economics.

While regional economics has been relatively neglected, it has led other fields of economics in distinguishing between traded and nontraded goods, a distinction only recently of importance in international trade literature but long made in local area multiplier analysis. Furthermore, regional economics has recognized more fully than the rest of economics that the use of goods as intermediate inputs is fundamental to production, helping determine the location of economic activity. These and other strands of regional analysis are discussed below, followed by consideration of a comprehensive framework for analysing regions.

RECEIVED REGIONAL ANALYSIS

Early location theory. An early lasting contribution is Von Thünen's (1826) theory of agricultural land use around a city. Transport cost savings near a city lead to higher bids for land and thus more intensive land use. Formally this model is the same as used in the 20th century to explain land use within a city as a function of distance from the central business distinct. Von Thünen did not provide a theory of regions because the demand for agricultural products emanating from the city was not explained. However, he stressed competition for land in an area, an ingredient missing in most attempts to understand regions.

Weber (1929) attempted to explain the spatial location of industry as the choice of production location which minimizes input hauling costs. Weber did not explain how much production will occur at each location and ignored output price as an influence on location choice. Hoover (1937, 1948) modified the Weberian framework by allowing for a more complicated transportation cost structure, substitution of inputs and economies of scale in production. Isard (1956, 1975) added substitution between transportation and other inputs in production. Moses (1958) considered input substitutions more fully and showed that the optimum location is sensitive to the homogeneity characteristics of the production function. An unexplored implication of these analyses is that the value of certain locations is greater than others and that firms minimizing costs will compete with one another for a location leading to land rents as in the Von Thünen model which would be a further influence on location choice.

Losch (1940) extended industry location analysis to more than one industry, analysing sizes and types of cities with no resource differentials among regions, with population distributed uniformly, and with input goods available at all places in perfectly elastic supply. Spatial concentrations of production result from differences in scale economies and costs of transportation of finished goods. Mills and Lav (1964) showed that Losch's hexagon-shaped market areas are inappropriate and that free entry of firms need not result in market areas that completely exhaust all space.

Losch, like Von Thünen, Weber and Hoover did not recognize the effect of production on local labour demand and hence on the geographic distribution of population and the demand for output. Beckman's (1958) extension of Losch's work allows demands for local goods to influence city sizes in a hierarchy but is driven by uniformly distributed agricultural production and does not allow for serious analysis of production location.

Economic activity in a single region. North (1955) exemplifies the export base approach to regional analysis which is concerned with induced effects on a region deriving from the existence of so-called basic industries which export their output out of the region. The induced effects depend on additional employment attracted to the region due to the fact that demands of workers and firms in the basic industries can be partly satisfied by local production. The effects lead to a local employment multiplier. The reasons for the location, size and type of export industries to begin with are not explained in the export base approach, nor is the rule of prices considered. On the other hand, the approach provides a beginning for considering regional demand endogeneity not found in the industry location work discussed above.

The export base approach provides a rationale for a larger body of practically oriented work quantifying the regional effects of (unexplained) increases in exports out of a region, culminating in input–output models which adapt Leontief inter-industry analysis to regions as exemplified by Isard (1975).

More recent advances in regional analysis. Borts and Stein (1964) took a long step forward in considering flows of factors of production with analysis of labour, capital and labour–capital ratios applying tools from the mainstream of economics. Labour supply shifts are the major exogenous movers in their model stemming from an emphasis on high birth-rates and technological change in agriculture acting to eject labour from agriculture in different regions, particularly the South, during the decades just before and after World War II. The analysis does not bring in regional comparative advantage in production or amenities affecting where labour wishes to locate.

More recently, some urban models have recognized the fact that migration occurs between cities and have posited that what is truly exogenous to an area is the utility level necessary to induce people to locate in the region. Tolley (1974) developed a model of an area in which there is consumption and production of goods that are traded between cities, as well as non-traded goods for which area production equals area consumption. Differences in costs of production and demand for non-traded goods were shown to result in unequal money wages between areas even though utility is equalized. Henderson (1974) addressed the existence of cities and hierarchies of cities in view of economies of scale and population mobility, and Upton (1981) further analysed equilibrium city sizes. Tolley, Graves and Gardner (1979) examined the effects of externalities on city size, and Henderson and Ioannides (1981) applied similar principles to growth and change in systems of cities.

The strands in the contributions that have been cited provide the beginnings of a conceptual framework for investigating regional growth and decline phenomena, including the empirical issues brought up in Muth (1971), Engle and Hutchins (1978), Howland (1979), and Schmenner (1982), many of which are as of yet unresolved. In the next section we expand on these contributions in order to present a more comprehensive framework

INGREDIENTS OF A COMPREHENSIVE THEORY OF REGIONS

Production. Let the production of good i in a region be given by $x_i = F_i(\mathbf{X}_i, N_i, \mathbf{L}_i, \mathbf{A})$, where $\mathbf{X}_i$ is a vector of intermediate goods used in production of x_i, N_i is labour, $\mathbf{L}_i$ is location-specific capital including land, mineral deposits and port sites, and $\mathbf{A}$ is a vector of location-specific amenities. Amenities include climate characteristics and differ from region-specific capital in that they are public goods for all firms and households in the region. Non-region-specific capital, also an argument of the production function, is suppressed here with the idea that it exhibits little price variation among regions.

Given the vector of goods prices, $\mathbf{p}$, and the labour wage, W, the region supply curve of any x_i is given by

$$x_i^s = f_i^s(\mathbf{p}, W, \mathbf{A}) \tag{1}$$

where the entire vector of prices rather than simply own price, p_i, enters because of the use of goods as inputs whose prices affect the profitability of producing x_i. Accompanying the supply curve are demands for each good used in production of x_i

$$x_{i,j}^{dd} = f_{i,j}^{dd}(\mathbf{p}, W, \mathbf{A}) \tag{2}$$

and the demand for labour to produce x_i

$$N_i^d = N_i^d(\mathbf{p}, W, \mathbf{A}). \tag{3}$$

Equations (1), (2) and (3) represent the producer part of regional theory giving producer responses to prices, wage and regional amenities. Amenities will be taken here to be exogenous, though in extensions effects of output on pollution and congestion and effects of government on local services treated as public goods could be considered as making amenities endogenous. Given the amenities, prices $\mathbf{p}$ and the wage W are determined in an equilibrium depending not only on the producer behaviour conditions but also on product demand behaviour and labour supply behaviour, which are the other parts of the regional theory to be considered in later subsections.

The producer behaviour conditions have in common with regional input–output models that goods may be used as intermediate inputs. However, in input–output models the goods are used in fixed proportions, and the amount exported out of the region or some other concept of final demand is taken as exogenous. In contrast, a major purpose of the producer behaviour conditions here is to offer a price-theoretic explanation of how inputs and outputs are determined.

To derive equations (1), (2) and (3), multiply the marginal product of each input, obtained by partial differentiation of the production function, by output price p_i and set equal to input price which is an intermediate good price p_j, wage W, or price of location specific capital R depending on the input being considered. Together with the production function the result is $Q+1$ equations determining output x_i and the Q inputs used in its production. Total demand for each intermediate input is the sum of the demands in production of each x_i. Finally, a supply function may be posited for location-specific capital, $L_i = L(R_i)$, showing how its price is endogenous raised as more of it is demanded, adding one more equation to the system.

While the solutions for L_i and R_i are not shown, they influence equations (1), (2) and (3) since they are part of the same equation system. Consider, for example, the response of regional output of x_i in equation (1) to an increase in output price p_i. An increase in p_i would raise the marginal revenue product of all inputs leading to indefinite increase of output if all input prices remained the same. But, as region-specific capital L_i is expanded its price R_i rises leading to a rise in the marginal cost of producing x_i, stopping the increase in output when the rise in marginal cost has come to equal the increase in output price. A reason why supply curves of regional outputs slope upward is seen to be that there are upward sloping supply curves of location-specific capital, even though price and quantity of the region-specific capital have been substituted out in the solutions and thus do not explicitly appear in the regional producer behaviour conditions.

Some of the region-specific capital consists of land at various distances from production and consumption sites within the region. As demand for access to these sites grows people and firms will either have to locate more densely or locate further away from the sites. Rising access costs within the region are one of the regions for upward sloping supply curves for regional outputs. Access within an urban economy has been a subject of much urban economics analysis and is a feature linking urban and regional analysis.

Labour supply. If people can choose without restriction where within a nation to live, a tendency can be expected for labour to respond to any wage differentials among regions that would permit a bettering of well-being from moving. In equilibrium such differentials will be eliminated so that the wage in each region will equate utility of a marginal worker in the region to that attainable elsewhere. The nominal wage will be such that

$$\ln W = \ln W_0 + \mathbf{k}_x''[\ln(p/p_0)] - \mathbf{k}_A'(\mathbf{A}/\mathbf{A}_0) \quad (4)$$

where W_0 is the nominal wage available in the rest of the economy, $\mathbf{k}_x$ is a vector of expenditure shares on elements of $\mathbf{x}$, $\mathbf{p}_0$ is the vector of market good prices in the rest of the economy, $\mathbf{k}_A$ is a vector of the marginal evaluation of each amenity, and $\mathbf{A}_0$ is the set of amenity levels available in the rest of the economy. This specification indicates that the nominal wage differential between one region and any other depends on differences in the comprehensively defined cost of living consisting of the usual weighted sum of market or private goods prices plus the amounts of amenities or public goods weighted by marginal valuations attached to them.

Given W_0, p_0, and A_0, the wage W at which labour is supplied to a region is increased by higher market good prices contained in $\mathbf{p}$ and lower amounts of amenities contained in $\mathbf{A}$. This condition still holds if some degree of labour immobility is allowed for, introducing N on the right-hand side of the labour supply equation and not affecting the formal solution for region equilibrium.

Demand within the region. Turning to product demand in the region, a part of the demand for regional output already considered is the demand for goods as intermediate inputs in production as given by equation (2), to which must be added demands by households in the region.

The amount of each good demanded per household in the region, based on received consumer theory, is a function of the goods price vector $\mathbf{p}$, the wage W as a determinant of household income, and amenities $\mathbf{A}$ in view of their complementarity or substitutability with market goods. Multiplying per household demand by the number of households, demand for the ith good by households in the region is

$$x_i^d = d_i(\mathbf{p}, W, \mathbf{A}) * N \quad (5)$$

which presumes strict proportionality between employment and population and between the nominal wage and nominal earnings with no non-wage income influences on demand. Extensions could introduce behaviour determining fraction of the population in market employment and family size, as well as property income which is particularly important to where retirees and others not receiving wage income live.

Supply and demand from outside the region. The price of any good supplied from outside the region will be the price elsewhere in the economy plus the cost of transporting it into the region. Similarly the price received for a good exported to satisfy demands outside the region will equal the price elsewhere less the cost of transporting it to the destination outside the region. Possible values of each p_i are bounded below by the export price and above by the import price, since producers will send supplies of the good outside the region rather than sell below the export price and demanders will import rather than pay more than the import price.

Goods may be divided into two categories: (a) traded goods, whose prices are at one of the two bounds and hence are either exported or imported and (b) nontraded goods, whose prices are between the bounds.

Region equilibrium. For traded goods any difference between the amount demanded and supplied of a good is taken up by exports or imports. Equality between demand and supply within the region is not a condition of equilibrium. Moreover, the prices of traded goods may be treated as a first approximation as being exogenous. For nontraded goods, on the other hand, quantities demanded and supplied within the region must be equal. The prices of nontraded goods are thereby endogenously determined, occurring at the intersection of demand and supply within the region.

Let the price vector $\mathbf{p}$ be separated into two parts, one containing prices of traded goods and the other containing prices of nontraded goods. One subset of the system of equations determining regional equilibrium consists of the supply equations (1) pertaining to nontraded goods. Another subset consists of the demands for each nontraded good. The demand for a nontraded good is obtained by summing the demand for it as an intermediate input, which is to say summing equations (2) over all j, and adding to this sum the household demand for the good given by (5).

To the foregoing equations for supply and demand of nontraded goods are added two additional equations, one for the demand for labour consisting of the sum of the labour demands given by equation (3) over all traded and nontraded goods produced in the region and the other for the supply of labour which is given by (4). The result is a system of $2R + 2$ equations which is the basic regional system determining the prices and quantities of the R nontraded goods, the amount of labour employed in the region, N, and the region wage rate, W. Given the solution of these equations the resulting local goods prices may be used in the supply curves for traded goods to calculate the production of the traded goods.

Illustration: export trade-induced growth. As an illustration giving giving the flavour of adjustments implied by the framework, consider the response in a region to a rise in price of an export good. In addition to the initial expansion moving along the supply curve for the good as determined by equation (1) leading to induced demand increases because of the appearance of N in the household demand equations (5), costs and hence prices of other goods in the region using the exported good as an input would rise, leading to a decline in production of these other goods and an associated decline in employment partly offsetting the initial rise in employment, along with a rise in the wage because of the higher cost of living due to the higher prices. The rise in the wage would in turn affect the costs and hence prices of all goods produced in the region, leading to still further feedbacks. In the process, some goods could change as between being traded or nontraded. The example shows how the framework calls attention to market responses and leads to a great number of issues for empirical investigation.

CONCLUSION

Technical change broadly defined is at the heart of much regional change showing up as production function shifts within a region or changes in prices received or paid as a result of events in other regions. Historically the shift from water power to fossil and other fuel sources amounted to a pervasive lowering of costs of power sources in regions with little water power. As might be expected, transportation costs play a major role in regional change by altering prices paid and received. The coming of the railroad and then the automobile, followed by superhighways, have changed the regional distribution of activity directly and indirectly. Lower transportation costs have made it less costly to respond to climate and other regional amenities, helping explain differences between 19th- and 20th-century regional growth including shifts to the South and West in the United States.

Extension of the framework to a long-term dynamic version of regional theory is required to understand lagging regions and the failure to adjust instantaneously. These topics involve capital investment and intergenerational considerations in labour mobility as younger people move out of disadvantaged regions more readily then older people, with income disparities possibly exacerbated by induced effects on local government functions, cultural milieu and leadership including entrepreneurship.

Taxes, transfers between different levels of government and transportation measures are examples of policies that can be examined applying the framework. A stated purpose of some policies is to expand regional output, though even here the interest is in the more ultimate beneficiaries such as labour or capital in the region. Policies lead to regional expansion by acting on the profitability of firms or amenities to which labour supplies respond. To the extent policies are financed from within the region there are further taxation and price effects reducing profitability of firms already in the region and raising wages that must be paid. Inter-regional effects determine national consequences. A purpose of a comprehensive regional framework is to call attention to the parameters in the producer, household demand and labour supply behaviour relations determining policy effects.

RONALD J. KRUMM AND GEORGE S. TOLLEY

See also LOCATION OF ECONOMIC ACTIVITY; SPATIAL ECONOMICS.

BIBLIOGRAPHY

Beckmann, M.J. 1958. City hierarchies and the distribution of city size. *Economic Development and Cultural Change* 6, April, 243–8.

Borts, G.H. and Stein, J.L. 1964. *Economic Growth in a Free Market*. New York: Columbia University Press.

Engle, R. and Hutchins, A. 1978. Some evidence on the sources of Metropolitan growth. University of California, San Deigo Discussion Paper 78–16.

Henderson, J.V. 1974. The sizes and types of cites. *American Economic Review* 64(4), September, 640–56.

Henderson, J.V. and Ioannides, Y.M. 1981. Aspects of growth in a system of cities. *Journal of Urban Economics* 10(1), July, 117–39.

Hoover, E. 1937. *Location Theory and the Shoe and Leather Industry*. Cambridge, Mass.: Harvard University Press.

Hoover, E. 1948. *The Location of Economic Activity*. New York: McGraw-Hill.

Howland, M. 1979. The business cycle and long run regional growth. In *Interregional Movements and Regional Growth*, ed. W. Wheaton, Washington, D.C.: Urban Institute.

Isard, W. 1956. *Location and Space-Economy*. Cambridge, Mass. : MIT Press.

Isard, W. 1957. The value of the regional approach in economic analysis. In W. Isard, *Regional Income: Studies in Wealth and Income*, Princeton: Princeton University Press.

Isard, W. 1975. *Introduction to Regional Science*. Englewood Cliffs, NJ: Prentice-Hall.

Krumm, R.J. and Tolley, G. 1983. On the regional labor supply relation. In *The Urban Economy and Housing*, ed. R. Grieson, Lexington, Mass.: Lexington Books.

Lösch, A. 1940. *Die räumliche Ordnung der Wirtschaft*. Jena: Gustav Fischer. Trans. W.H. Woglom as *The Economics of Location*, New Haven: Yale University Press, 1954.

Mills, E. and Lav, M. 1964. A model of market areas with free entry. *Journal of Political Economy* 72, June, 278–88.

Moses, L. 1958. Location and the theory of production. *Quarterly Journal of Economics* 72, May, 259–72.

Muth, R.F. 1971. Migration: chicken or egg? *Southern Economic Journal* 37(3), January, 295–306.

North, D.C. 1955. Location theory and regional economic growth. *Journal of Political Economy* 63, June, 243–58.

Schmenner, R. 1982. *Making Business Location Decisions*. Englewood Cliffs, NJ: Prentice-Hall.

Tolley, G. 1974. The welfare economics of city bigness. *Journal of Urban Economics* 1(3), 324–45.

Tolley, G., Graves, P. and Gardner, J. 1979. *Urban Growth Policy in a Market Economy*. New York: Academic Press.

Upton, C. 1981. An equilibrium model of city size. *Journal of Urban Economics* 10(1), July, 15–36.

von Thünen, J.H. 1826. *The Isolated State*. Trans. C.M. Wartenburg, London: Pergamon Press, 1966.

Weber, A. 1929. *Theory of Location of Industries*. Trans. C. Friedrich, Chicago: University of Chicago Press.

regression and correlation analysis. Correlation is a tool for understanding the relationship between two quantities. Regression considers how one quantity is influenced by another. In correlation analysis the two quantities are considered symmetrically: in regression analysis one is supposed dependent on the other, in an unsymmetric way. Extensions to sets of quantities are important.

Suppose that for each value of a quantity x, another quantity y has a probability distribution $p(y|x)$, the probability of y, given x. The mean value of this distribution, alternatively called the expectation of y, given x, and written $E(y|x)$, is a function of x and is called the regression of y on x. The quantity x is often called the independent variable, though a better term is regressor variable: y is the dependent variable. The regression tells us something about how y depends on x. The simplest case is linear regression, where $E(y|x) = \alpha + \beta x$ for parameters α and β: the latter is called the regression coefficient (of y on x). Other features of the conditional distribution $p(y|x)$ are usually considered in addition to the mean. The variance (or standard deviation) measures the spread of the y – values, for fixed x. A common case is where this is constant over x: the regression is then said to be homoskedastic. A further common assumption is that $p(y|x)$ is normal, or Gaussian. Then y is normally distributed about $\alpha + \beta x$ with constant variance σ^2.

The regression concept of y on x does not involve a probability distribution for the regressor x. If it does have one, $p(x)$, then x and y have a joint distribution given by $p(x, y) = p(y|x)p(x)$. This joint distribution yields variances, σ_{xx} and σ_{yy}, for x and y, and a covariance σ_{xy}. The correlation between x and y is then defined as $\rho_{xy} = \sigma_{xy}/(\sigma_{xx}\sigma_{yy})^{1/2}$. It is the ratio of the covariance to the product of the standard deviations and is clearly unaffected by a change of scale in either x or y (and since the variances and covariance are unaffected, by a change in origin). It is easy to show that $-1 \leqslant \rho_{xy} \leqslant 1$, and if x and y are independent, ρ_{xy} is zero. When $\rho_{xy} = 0$, x and y are said to be uncorrelated. The correlation measures the association between x and y. If x and y have a joint distribution, then not only is there a regression of y on x, considered above, but also of x on y.

The linear, homoskedastic case is easily the most common one used in practice and has several important properties. We may write $y = \alpha + \beta x + \epsilon$, where ϵ has zero mean and variance σ^2. If x has a distribution, then the factorization $p(x, y) = p(y \mid x)p(x)$ shows ϵ is independent of x and therefore ϵ and x are uncorrelated. Averaging we have $\mu_y = \alpha + \beta\mu_x$, relating the means, μ_x and μ_y, of x and y. A change of origin enables both of these to be put equal to zero, when $\alpha = 0$ and $E(y \mid x) = \beta x$, or $y = \beta x + \epsilon$. Multiplying this last result by x and taking expectations, $\sigma_{xy} = \beta\sigma_{xx}$, as ϵ and x are uncorrelated. Consequently the regression coefficient of y on x equals σ_{xy}/σ_{xx}. Similarly the regression coefficient of x on y (if that regression is also linear homoskedastic) is σ_{xy}/σ_{yy} and the square of the correlation coefficient equals the product of the regression coefficients.

Returning to the relation $y = \beta x + \epsilon$ and considering the variances of both sides, we obtain $\sigma_{yy} = \beta^2\sigma_{xx} + \sigma^2$ (again using the lack of correlation between x and ϵ). Hence $\sigma^2 = \sigma_{yy} - \sigma_{xy}^2/\sigma_{xx}$, on using $\beta = \sigma_{xy}/\sigma_{xx}$, and we have the important relationship that $\sigma^2 = \sigma_{yy}(1 - \rho_{xy}^2)$, showing that the variance σ^2, of y about the regression, is a proportion $(1 - \rho_{xy}^2)$ of the total variance of y, σ_{yy}. In the form $\sigma_{yy} = \beta^2\sigma_{xx} + \sigma^2$, we have the result that the total variance of y is made up of two additive components, that due to x, $\beta^2\sigma_{xx}$, and that about the regression line. The former is called the component of variance ascribable to x: the latter is the residual variance and, as we have just seen, is a proportion $(1 - \rho_{xy}^2)$ of the total. That ascribable to x is a proportion ρ_{xy}^2. This decomposition of variance is at the heart of analysis of variance techniques.

The ideas of regression and correlation are due to Galton and Pearson. The classic example has x the height of a father and y that of his son. Both regressions are linear, homoskedastic and normal, having positive regression coefficients which are less than one. Galton noticed that tall (short) fathers have sons who are, on average, shorter (taller) than themselves. This follows since, centering the values at the mean, or average height, $E(y \mid x) = \beta x < x$ if $x > 0$ corresponding to tall fathers, $\beta x > x$ if $x < 0$ for short ones. This is the phenomenon of regression (of heights) towards the mean and is necessary if the variability in heights is not to increase from one generation to the next. An illustration from economics might have x as the price of an item and y the number sold. There β will be negative reflecting the average decrease in numbers sold as the price increases. Here x might not have a probability distribution but be at the control of the seller.

The modern tendency is to make increasing use of regression and less of correlation. Part of the explanation for this is the importance of dependency relations, instead of associations, between quantities. Another reason is that in so many examples (as item price) the regressor variable is not random, so that σ_{xx} and σ_{xy} are meaningless and correlation ideas are unavailable. A third consideration is that correlation can be misleading. As an illustration of this let x be a quantity, symmetrically and randomly distributed about zero. Let $y = x^2$. Then $\sigma_{xy} = E(xy) = E(x^3) = 0$ by the symmetry about zero. Hence the correlation is zero whilst y and x are highly associated, one being the square of the other. Correlation ideas work well when all variables are normally distributed but less well otherwise. (If $y = x^2$, y cannot be normal.)

The ideas and definitions extend to the case where there are several regressor variables $x_1, x_2, \ldots, x_m$. Write $\mathbf{x} = (x_1, x_2, \ldots x_m)$. Then $E(y \mid \mathbf{x})$ is the (multiple) regression of y on $\mathbf{x}$. In the linear case with means at zero, $E(y \mid \mathbf{x}) = \Sigma\beta_i x_i$ and β_i is the partial regression coefficient of y on x_i. The notation and nomenclature here are too brief and can be misleading, for β_i only measures the dependence of y on x_i in the presence of the other quantities in $\mathbf{x}$. Were, say x_m, to be omitted $\beta_i, i < m$, would typically change: indeed, the regression might not be linear. The cumbersome notation exemplified by $\beta_{2.134}$ ($i = 2, m = 4$) is sometimes used. In words, the coefficient of y on x_2, allowing for x_1, x_3 and x_4. The variance about the regression remains and the homoskedastic case, where this is constant, is the one usually considered.

In the linear case $E(y \mid \mathbf{x}) = \Sigma\beta_i x_i$ the x's can be functionally related. A common case is where $x_i = x^i$, the powers of a single quantity x. This is referred to as polynomial regression. It is usually more convenient to work with polynomials $P_i(x)$ of degree i in x which are orthogonal with respect to some measure. Then $E(y \mid \mathbf{x}) = \Sigma\beta_i P_i(x)$. Another possibility is where the x_i are periodic, say cos it. Notice that the linearity is in the terms $P_i(x)$ – or the coefficients β_i – not in x.

If the regressor variables have a joint distribution then the covariances σ_{yi}, between y and x_i, and σ_{ij} between x_i and x_j are available. With more than one regressor variable additional concepts can be introduced. For example, if all the x's are held fixed except for x_i there is a conditional joint distribution of y and x_i given all the x's except x_i. This has a correlation, defined as above as the ratio of the conditional covariance to the product of the conditional standard deviations, and is called the partial correlation between y and x_i. The notation is exemplified by $\rho_{y2.134}$. This will, in general, depend on the fixed values of the regressor variables but is normally only used when it is constant. This happens if the joint distribution of y and $\mathbf{x}$ is multivariate normal.

In the case of a single regressor variable we saw that $1 - \rho_{xy}^2 = \sigma^2/\sigma_{yy}$, where σ^2 is the residual variance of y, conditional on x. In the multiple case, continue to define σ^2 in this way conditional on all the quantities in $\mathbf{x}$. Then define R^2 by $(1 - R^2) = \sigma^2/\sigma_{yy}$, in analogy with the single variable case. The positive square root R is called the multiple correlation coefficient (of y on $\mathbf{x}$). As before, we may write $\sigma_{yy} = \sigma^2 + R^2\sigma_{yy}$, expressing the total variance of y additively in terms of the residual variance σ^2 and that due to the regression on $\mathbf{x}$. It is more common nowadays to work in terms of the variance components than R^2.

The mathematical theory of regression and correlation is now well understood. Centering at the means, all the concepts depend on the matrix of variances and covariances of y, the dependent variable, and $\mathbf{x}$, the set of regressor variables: σ_{yi} and σ_{ij}. The calculations are merely ways of rearranging these elements in convenient forms: correlations and components of variance in regression are just two possibilities. The real difficulty, and the real interest in regression lies in the interpretation of the results.

As an illustration consider the simple case of linear, homoskedastic regression of y on a single regressor variable x, written $y = \beta x + \epsilon$, with β as the regression coefficient and ϵ as the residual variation, with zero mean and variance σ^2. All this says is that for any fixed x, y has mean βx and variance σ^2: and it is only this aspect of the dependence of y on x that is described. Suppose a large amount of data consisting of pairs (x_i, y_i) is collected and the fit $y = 2x + \epsilon$ with $\sigma^2 = 2$ is established. (We discuss how this might be done below.) This shows a fairly close association between y and x. In order therefore to increase y it might be thought reasonable to set x to a high value. Suppose this is done, will this cause y necessarily to increase? Surprisingly, not so. Suppose there is another quantity z and the real relationships are that $y = -x + z + \epsilon_1$, and $x = \frac{1}{3}z + \epsilon_2$ so that z is the basic quantity determining the situation. This clearly yields $y = 2x + \epsilon$, with $\epsilon = \epsilon_1 - 3\epsilon_2$, the observed relation. If now x is controlled at a large value without affecting z which is, under natural conditions, the main determinant of x, the effect will be to decrease y through $y = -x + z + \epsilon_1$. Consequently a strong positive relationship between y and x need not imply an increase in y when x is increased. There can be an enormous difference between the association of y with x, when x is uncontrolled and allowed to vary freely, and the association when x is controlled. And the reason is the presence of another quantity z whose influence on x in the free system is disturbed by the control.

Whenever the regression of y on a set of quantities $\mathbf{x}$ is discussed, one has to beware of the possible presence of other, unobserved quantities $\mathbf{z}$ that could affect the relationship. A laboratory scientist, or even a social scientist doing a planned survey, can often guard against such hidden quantities by careful design or by appropriate randomization; but an economist, or anyone who has to rely on data from unplanned studies, has always to be on his guard against their effects. Another way of describing the difficulty is to distinguish carefully between association and causation. All regression and correlation analyses can do is study association: the underlying causal mechanism is not necessarily revealed. It is remarkable how little attention has been paid by statisticians to the meaning of causation, and to how it can be revealed by statistical analysis. Economists have had to rely on statistical analyses of randomly obtained data and some of the causal inferences they have drawn are totally unjustified by that data and the analyses.

We now consider the nature of these statistical analyses, confining ourselves predominantly to the case of homoskedastic, linear regression $y = \Sigma\beta_i x_i + \epsilon$, ϵ having mean zero and variance σ^2. There the means have been supposed zero. There is usually no difficulty over this as the mean of each variable can ordinarily be estimated by the sample means, $y_.$ and $x_{.i}$. The quantities being discussed here are, in terms of the original data, the deviations, $y - y_.$ and $x_i - x_{.i}$, from the sample means. The standard method of estimating the β's and σ^2 is least squares. This has been in use for two centuries and is still adopted by almost all data analysts. If that data is $(y_j, x_{ji}$: $i = 1, 2, \ldots m$; $j = 1, 2, \ldots n)$ consisting of n independent observations of y and the m regressor variables, then the least-squares estimates of β_i are provided by minimizing the sum of squares of residuals $y - \Sigma\beta_i x_i$ for each of the n observations: that is $\Sigma_j(y_j - \Sigma_i\beta_i x_{ji})^2$. Matrix notation is most convenient. Write $\mathbf{y} = (y_1, y_2, \ldots y_n)^T$, $\boldsymbol{\beta} = (\beta_1, \beta_2, \ldots \beta_m)^T$ and X as the matrix with elements x_{ji}, observation j on variable x_i. Then $\mathbf{y} = X\boldsymbol{\beta} +$ residual and the sum of squares to be minimized over $\boldsymbol{\beta}$ is $(\mathbf{y} - X\boldsymbol{\beta})^T(\mathbf{y} - X\boldsymbol{\beta})$ with minimum given by $\hat{\boldsymbol{\beta}} = (X^TX)^{-1}X^T\mathbf{y}$. The variance σ^2 is estimated by the sum of squares at $\hat{\boldsymbol{\beta}}$ divided by $(n - m)$. The $\hat{\beta}_i$ are called the least-squares estimates of β_i.

The method is deservedly popular because it is relatively easy to use and interpret, and many convenient computer programs are available. Its long and successful history testifies to its merits. Unfortunately it has been discovered that there can be very real difficulties when m, the number of variables is large. With the availability of fast computers capable of handling a lot of data, it is not uncommon to have 40 or more variables. The difficulties then become noticeable. Before the arrival of such computing power, least squares was only used with few variables and the difficulties are scarcely noticeable. It is easy to appreciate what could go wrong: it is not so easy to correct it. Consider the case where the sum of squares is $\Sigma_j(y_j - \beta_j)^2$. This apparently special and degenerate case is, in fact, a canonical form for least squares and any multiple regression situation can be transformed to it by linear transformations. (In so doing, the meanings of the y's and β's will change.) The minimization is trivial with estimate $\hat{\beta}_j = y_j$, and the minimum value is zero. But we know that y_j differs from its expectation, here β_j, but in general $\Sigma_i\beta_i x_{ji}$, by an amount which has variance σ^2, so the average of $\Sigma_j(y_j - \hat{\beta}_j)^2$ ought to be about σ^2, and indeed this is the usual estimate of σ^2 as mentioned above. But here this estimate is zero, which is absurd. This first, rigorous demonstration that least squares is unsatisfactory was given by Charles Stein. He showed that whenever the number of variables exceeds two, there is an estimate which is, for every value of the regression coefficients, better than least squares. Better here means having smaller mean-square error, though the statement remains true under many other meanings. The efficiency varies with the true values of the β's. The result just quoted says that it is always less than one. It can be as low as $2/m$: with $m = 40$ this gives only 5% efficiency, a rather serious loss.

It is surprising how little attention Stein's result has received outside of a small group, largely of theoreticians, yet its practical value could be enormous. Stein, and others, have produced estimates which improve on least squares but none has had much acceptance. Fairly early in the use of computers for regression analysis, it was appreciated that difficulties could arise when the matrix X^TX, which has to be inverted to obtain the least-squares estimates, is ill-conditioned, with determinant near zero. This is the matrix of sample variances and covariances of the regressor variables, a typical element being $\Sigma_r x_{ri}x_{rj}$ where the x's are deviations from their means, $x_{.i}$. It will be ill-conditioned if, in the data, there is a near linear relationship between the regressor variables. One suggestion was to put the matrix into correlation form, dividing each row and each column by the sample standard deviation of the variable corresponding to that row or column, so making all diagonal elements one and each off-diagonal element equal to a sample correlation coefficient between x_i and x_j, and then subtracting a constant λ from each unit diagonal element. This leads to ridge regression estimates and ways of choosing λ have been proposed. It often works well but can fail.

These ideas all lie within a frequentist school of inference. In principle, a solution is available with the Bayesian paradigm for inference. Here, in addition to the distribution of y, given $\mathbf{x}$, is included a probability distribution for the regression parameter $\boldsymbol{\beta} = (\beta_1, \beta_2, \ldots \beta_m)$. Inference is then made by calculating the revised probability distribution of $\boldsymbol{\beta}$ given the data. This procedure always avoids Stein's criticism provided the original distribution of $\boldsymbol{\beta}$ has total integral unity. (Least squares results from this procedure only if all the values of $\boldsymbol{\beta}$ are equally probable, a form which is not finitely integrable.) The practical difficulty is the choice of a distribution for $\boldsymbol{\beta}$. The ridge method can be produced for certain types of exchangeable distributions for $\boldsymbol{\beta}$. In the case of polynomial regression, a reasonable possibility is to suppose that the coefficients of the higher degree polynomials are likely to be smaller than those of lower degree. When the regressor variables refer to different quantities, a possibility is to suppose that few of them have an appreciable coefficient, and therefore influence y, but it is not known which are the determining ones.

This idea that only a few regressors matter has led to a lot of work on the choice of which to include in the regression. There are two broad ways to proceed. One can fit all the quantities available and then discard them one by one as long as the discarding has little effect. Or one can proceed in the reverse direction, introducing them one at a time only if they have an appreciable effect. In both of these methods it has to be decided how the effect is to be measured. The usual criterion is the change in the variance of y ascribable to $\mathbf{x}$; the quantity denoted above by $R^2\sigma_{yy}$. Alternatively expressed, this is the change in the multiple correlation coefficient. For example, in the method where the variables are discarded, R^2 will decrease when a variable is omitted from the regression. Only if this decrease is small will the omision be granted. There are two difficulties here. First, it is possible for two quantities, separately to have little effect, but jointly to be of considerable importance, so that tests of them one at a time may be misleading. (The possibility of computing all 2^m regressions is too extravagant.) Second, it is not clear what is meant by saying the change in R^2 is "small": how small? One possibility is to use an ordinary significance test, here a t-test. If significant the regressor causing the change can be included: if not, it is omitted. This is for some suitably chosen significance level. This has been thought to be unsatisfactory by some and other criteria have been proposed. It is here that the Bayesian and frequentist views part company. The usual Bayesian criterion for 'small' depends on the assumed distribution for the regression coefficients, but, in general, it seems to need more evidence to introduce a regressor when using the Bayesian approach than when employing a significance test. The former has been accused of favouring the hypothesis that the variable is not worth including. The Bayesian reply is that some 'significant' effects are spurious. Multiple regression techniques are so widely used today that one wonders how many effects of x_i on y reported in the literature are meaningful.

Regression concerns a relation, to take the linear, one variable form, $y = \beta x + \epsilon$ between y and x. This treats y and x asymmetrically and does not lead to $x = \beta^{-1}y + \epsilon'$ with ϵ' unrelated to y. There is, however, a symmetric form that is sometimes useful. Suppose two quantities, ξ and η, are exactly linearly related, $\eta = \beta\xi$, or equally $\xi = \beta^{-1}\eta$. Suppose that each is measured with error giving $y = \eta + \epsilon$, $x = \xi + \epsilon'$. Then the pair (x, y) may have linear regressions but the real interest lies in β, the coefficient of the exact relationship. This is often referred to as the case where both variables, independent and regressor, are subject to error. Ordinary least-squares techniques, even with a single regressor variable, require modification.

Linear multiple regression is part of the general theory of linear models in which, to use the notation above, $E(y|X) = X\boldsymbol{\beta}$, the linearity being in the parameter $\boldsymbol{\beta}$. Least squares and its Stein-type modifications are the standard techniques for analysis, together with the analysis of variance.

D. V. Lindley

See also BAYESIAN INFERENCE; ESTIMATION; HETEROSKEDASTICITY; LEAST SQUARES; MAXIMUM LIKELIHOOD; NON-LINEAR METHODS IN ECONOMETRICS; OUTLIERS; RESIDUALS; STATISTICAL INFERENCE.

BIBLIOGRAPHY

Efron, B. and Morris, C. 1975. Data analysis using Stein's estimator and its generalizations. *Journal of the American Statistical Association* 70, 311–19.

Hoerl, A.E. and Kennard, R.W. 1970. Ridge regression: biased estimation of non-orthogonal problems. *Technometrics* 12, 55–67.

Seber, G.A.F. 1977. *Linear Regression Analysis*. New York: Wiley.

Vinod, H.D. and Ullah, A. 1981. *Recent Advances in Regression Methods*. New York: Dekker.

Zellner, A. 1971. *An Introduction to Bayesian Inference in Econometrics*. New York: Wiley.

regressive taxation. *See* PROGRESSIVE AND REGRESSIVE TAXATION.

regular economies. General equilibrium theory describes those states of an economy in which the individual plans of many agents with partially conflicting interests are compatible with each other. Such a state is called an equilibrium. The concept of an equilibrium simply being based on a consistency requirement lends itself to the study of specific questions of quite different character. Indeed, equilibrium theory provides a unifying framework for the analysis of questions arising in various branches of economic theory. In our opinion it is fruitful to view equilibrium theory as a method of thinking applicable to a variety of problems of different origin.

Ideally one would like to have general principles which ensure that equilibria exist, that they are unique, and that, therefore, the equilibria resulting from different policy measures can unequivocally be compared. Moreover, one would like to know whether equilibria have some desirable properties when no single agent can exert an essential influence on the global outcome to his personal advantage. These welfare questions are particularly interesting because the concept of an equilibrium itself is not based on the well-being of the economic agents. Finally, although the concept of an equilibrium as described above is static in nature, one would like to have a dynamic theory according to which some equilibrium is approached in the course of time.

These and related questions such as the computability of equilibria have been studied in the past with different degrees of success. There are general principles which yield the existence of an equilibrium in an astonishingly large variety of cases. Furthermore, the welfare properties of equilibria are well understood. However, it is easy to construct examples of economies with an infinite number of equilibria and it appears to be very difficult to provide conditions which lead, without being artificial or ad hoc, to the uniqueness of an equilibrium. As a consequence, comparative statics does not have a basis which makes it generally a well-defined problem. Also, the difficulties encountered when studying the uniqueness issue present severe obstacles for the development of a dynamic theory.

The theory of regular economies may be viewed as an effort to advance general equilibrium theory in the absence of a satisfactory uniqueness result. The seminal paper is Debreu (1970). Debreu explicitly allows for the multiplicity of equilibria. However, he requires each equilibrium to be *locally* unique. Each equilibrium is well determined and robust in the sense that it is not destroyed by a small change in the parameters.

A regular economy is an economy with a certain, finite number of equilibria, all of which respond continuously to small parameter changes. Hence each of these equilibria can be traced for some while during a parameter change. Thus there is a basis for doing comparative statics locally, that is to say as long as the equilibrium under consideration stays robust. If, at a certain point, it ceases to be robust, a drastic change is to be expected, the size and direction of which are probably hardly predictable. The focus of the theory of regular equilibria is more on the continuous behaviour of robust equilibria than on drastic changes.

It is most remarkable that Debreu (1970), by using concepts and techniques developed in the mathematical field of differential topology, has introduced a new kind of thought into economic analysis. In the meantime this way of thinking has penetrated many areas of economic theory at different levels. One of the first applications has occurred in the technically advanced area of core theory, where the continuous dependence of the set of price equilibria on the characteristics of the agents, which is guaranteed in a regular economy, plays an important role. An application on a purely conceptual level in oligopoly theory is incorporated in the notion of a demand function which an oligopolist faces in the Cournot–Nash context. The graph of this function is considered as given by the equilibria of an exchange economy with initial endowments as varying parameters.

The dependence of the equilibria on initial endowments will be discussed in detail in the next section because this case is particularly suited to illustrate basic ideas of the theory of regular economies.

DEBREU'S THEOREM ON REGULAR EQUILIBRIA. The purpose of this section is to describe the kind of reasoning typical for the theory of regular economies in a prototypical situation. It is desirable to deal with parameter variations taking place in some Euclidean space because the mathematical structures to be used are most familiar in this case. We shall study exchange economies which differ by the allocation of initial endowments.

There are l commodities and m consumers. Individual initial endowments are supposed to be positive in each component. If we denote the strictly positive orthant in $\mathbb{R}^l$ by P, then an initial allocation is a vector $(e_1, \ldots, e_m) \in P^m$. Since the demand function f_i of each consumer i is considered as fixed, an economy E is fully specified by $(e_1, \ldots, e_m)$. The space of all economies under consideration can thus be identified with P^m, an extremely simple subset of a Euclidean space. We want to examine how the exchange equilibria of an economy – there may be several such equilibria – depend on the particular economy $E \in P^m$.

We assume that all goods are desired so that attention may be restricted to strictly positive relative prices. Price systems are normalized; to be specific we consider price systems in

$$S = \left\{ p = (p_1, \ldots, p_l) \gg 0 \mid \| p \| = \left(\sum_{h=1}^{l} p_h^2 \right)^{1/2} = 1 \right\}.$$

If consumer i initially possesses the commodity bundle e_i, his demand at the price system p is $f_i(p, p \cdot e_i) \in \mathbb{R}^l_+$, where $p \cdot e_i = w_i > 0$ is i's wealth. Hence the aggregate excess demand of the economy E, given by the initial allocation $(e_1, \ldots, e_m) \in P^m$, at p is

$$Z_E(p) = \sum_{i=1}^{m} [f_i(p, p \cdot e_i) - e_i].$$

We assume Walras' Law which states that the value $p \cdot Z_E(p)$ of the excess demand is identically equal to zero. Furthermore, every f_i is supposed to be continuous.

The desirability of all commodities will be captured in the following condition, which is always satisfied when consumers have strictly monotone preferences.

(D) If the price of at least one good approaches zero and the wealth $w_i > 0$ of every agent stays away from zero, then

$$\sum_{i=1}^{m} \| f_i(p, w_i) \|$$

tends to infinity.

An *equilibrium price system* of E is a price system $p \in S$ at which the consumption plans $f_i(p, p \cdot e_i)$ of all agents are consistent, i.e. a zero of the excess demand function Z_E. It is not difficult to show the following consequence of the desirability assumption (D) by a fixed point argument:

Every economy $E \in P^m$ has at least one equilibrium if (D) *holds.*

We would like to know how the equilibrium prices vary when the initial allocation is modified. Therefore we look at the graph Γ of the correspondence ('multi-valued function') Π which assigns to every economy $E \in P^m$ its set $\{p \in S \mid Z_E(p) = 0\}$ of equilibrium price systems. Defining $Z: P^m \times S \to \mathbb{R}^l$ by $Z(E, p) = Z_E(p)$ we get

$$\text{graph } (\Pi) = \Gamma = Z^{-1}(0).$$

Since Z is a continuous function, Γ is a closed set. It is well known that, in the case of a (single-valued) function, the closedness of the graph is intimately related to the continuity of the function. Here, where Π is a correspondence rather than a function, we obtain the following continuity result: *the graph Γ of the equilibrium price correspondence Π is upper hemi-continuous and compact-valued, if* (D) *holds.*

This is tantamount to the following explicit statement. If (E_n) is a sequence of economies in P^m converging to $E \in P^m$ and if $p_n \in \Pi\ (E_n)$ is an equilibrium price system of E_n for all n, then the sequence (p_n) has a subsequence which converges to an equilibrium price system of the limit economy E, provided (D) holds.

To improve our understanding of Γ, we assume that the demand functions f_i are continuously differentiable (C^1 for short) and we invoke the implicit function theorem in the following manner. Walras' Law allows us to disregard one market, say the lth, and to concentrate on

$$\hat{Z}: P^m \times S \to \mathbb{R}^{l-1}$$

which is obtained from Z by deleting the last component. Let p be an equilibrium price system of E, i.e. $\hat{Z}\ (E, p) = 0$. A simple calculation yields that the derivative $\mathrm{d}\hat{Z}\ (E, p)$ has maximal rank at (E, p). Therefore, the graph Γ is given by a smooth surface of dimension lm. That is to say each point in Γ has a neighbourhood in Γ which can be mapped onto an open subset of $\mathbb{R}^{lm}$ by a C^1 diffeomorphism, i.e. a C^1 map with a C^1 inverse. Such a locally Euclidean space is called a C^1 manifold, see Figure 1.

We have seen that *the graph Γ of the equilibrium price correspondence Π is a* C^1 *manifold*, but Figure 1 suggests more. In Figure 1, Γ is not only locally Euclidean, there is even a global diffeomorphism between Γ and $\mathbb{R}^{lm}$. Indeed, one can show that this global equivalence holds (see Balasko, 1975).

The equilibrium price correspondence is continuous except at two points, E_1 and E_2. If a parameter variation leads through E_1 (or E_2) the equilibrium may be forced to jump. The equilibrium reached after the jump, however, is robust in the sense that no sudden change must occur when one passes through E_1 (or E_2) again. One can imagine a situation such as in E_1 takes place when a slight reduction in the supply of an important raw material leads to a drastic increase in its price. If later on the supply begins to increase again prices perhaps vary but stay at their high level. A reversion of this phenomenon may occur when the supply has reached the much higher level corresponding to E_2.

In Figure 2 we have drawn a two-dimensional parameter space. The following remarkable phenomenon may happen here.

There are two paths, A and B, in the parameter space which have their starting point and endpoint in common. Following either path there is no need for the equilibrium to jump. However, the two equilibria reached at the end are quite

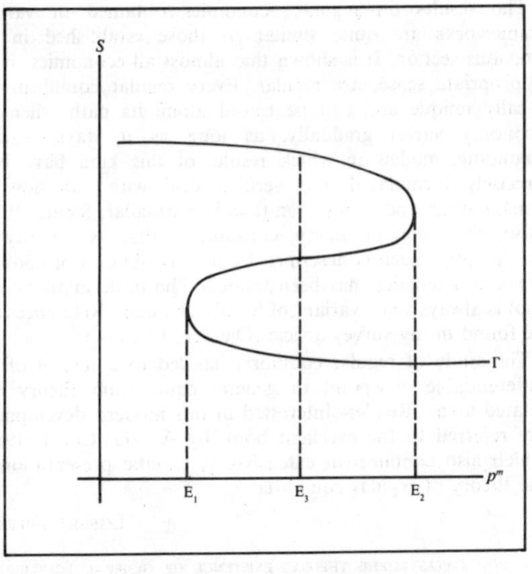

Figure 1

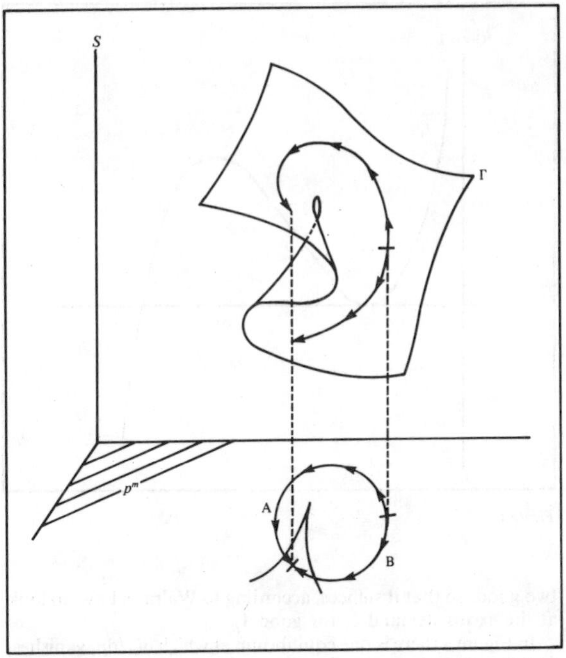

Figure 2

different equilibria of the same economy. In other words, if two or more policy variables are at one's disposal one must be aware of the possibility that the final outcome depends very well on the order in which the variables are utilized.

The economies E_1 and E_2 in Figure 1 are characterized by the fact that the graph Γ has a vertical tangent above E_1 and above E_2. Similarly, in Figure 2, Γ has vertical tangents above all points on the cusp drawn in the bottom plane, which represents P^m. Apparently qualitative changes of the equilibrium price set at an economy E are associated with vertical tangents of Γ above E. This motivates the following definitions. A *critical point* of the projection $\mathrm{pr}: \Gamma \rightarrow P^m$ is a point in Γ at which the derivative of pr has rank less than $\dim P^m = lm$. A *critical value* of $\mathrm{pr}: \Gamma \rightarrow P^m$ is the image of a critical point. A *regular value* of $\mathrm{pr}: \Gamma \rightarrow P^m$ is a point in P^m which is not a critical value. Figures 1 and 2 suggest that almost all points in P^m are regular values. Indeed, the concepts introduced above are defined in differential topology in a quite general context and Sard's theorem, an analytical tool of great importance, asserts that the critical values of a sufficiently differentiable mapping are rare. More precisely, *Sard's theorem* applied to our particular problem yields that the set of critical values of $\mathrm{pr}: \Gamma \rightarrow P^m$ is a (Lebesgue) null set.

Null sets are small in a probabilistic sense. At this point we make essential use of the space of economies P^m being part of a Euclidean space. If, for instance, consumers' demand functions or preferences are allowed to vary instead of consumers' endowments, it is not clear how null sets are to be defined. However, one can express quite easily when two demand functions or preference orderings are close to each other. That is to say metric structures are very often naturally given when there is no obvious way to define null sets. A set can then be defined to be small in a topological sense if its closure is nowhere dense.

Furthermore, if the concepts of smallness in the probabilistic and in the topological sense are both well-defined, as they are in the case of variable initial endowments, one has to be aware of the fact that the two variants of the intuitive notion of smallness apply to quite different sets. Defining a *critical economy* $E \in P^m$ as a critical value of $\mathrm{pr}: \Gamma \rightarrow P^m$ and *regular economy* as a regular value of pr we ask ourselves whether the null set of critical economies has a null closure. We know already that the desirability assumption (D) implies that the equilibrium price correspondence is upper hemi-continuous and compact-valued or, in more intuitive terms, that Γ has only finitely many layers above some compact ball B of economies in P^m. Hence the points in Γ which lie above B and have a vertical tangent form a compact set. Projecting this set down to B yields a compact set, the set of critical economies in B. Since this set is also null by Sard's theorem, it is nowhere dense. We obtain:

The set of critical economies in P^m is a closed null set if (D) *holds.*

Let $E \in P^m$ be a regular economy. Then E has a finite number of equilibria and this number is locally constant. If E has r equilibria, then there is a neighbourhood U of E and there are r C^1 functions $g_1, \ldots, g_r$ such that the set $\Pi(E')$ of equilibrium price systems of any economy $E' \in U$ is given by $\{g_1(E'), \ldots, g_r(E')\}$. In particular, *the equilibrium price correspondence Π is continuous in a neighbourhood of a regular economy.*

These results, with minor differences, have been obtained by G. Debreu (1970), whose proof, however, differs from the exposition given here.

EXTENSIONS

When one wants to extend the theory of regular equilibria to more general spaces of economies, it is often useful to employ a definition of a regular economy which focuses on the given economy and does not refer to the graph Γ or to the parameter space. To motivate the following definition we contrast figure 3, in which the excess demand of a critical economy such as E_1 or E_2 in Figure 1 is drawn, with Figure 4, which shows the graph of a regular economy such as E_3. It is assumed that there are

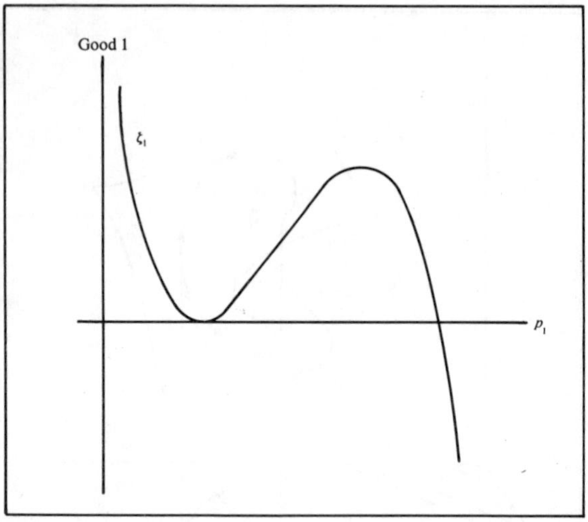

Figure 3

two goods so that it suffices, according to Walras's Law, to look at the excess demand ζ_1 for good 1.

In Figure 3 there is one equilibrium at which $d\zeta_1/dp_1$ vanishes. Shifting the graph of ζ_1 a little upwards destroys this equilibrium. In Figure 4, however, $d\zeta_1/dp_1$ does not vanish at any equilibrium and all equilibria are robust.

Let the excess demand function $\zeta : S \to \mathbb{R}^l$ of an economy E be C^1. A price system $p \in S$ is called a *regular equilibrium price system* if $\zeta(p) = 0$ and the matrix

$$\left[\frac{\partial \zeta_h}{\partial p_k}(p)\right]_{h,k=1,\ldots,l-1}$$

is regular. A *regular economy* is an economy all equilibrium price systems of which are regular. One can show that this definition, introduced by E. and H. Dierker (1972), is independent of the way in which goods are indexed and that it is consistent with the definition given above.

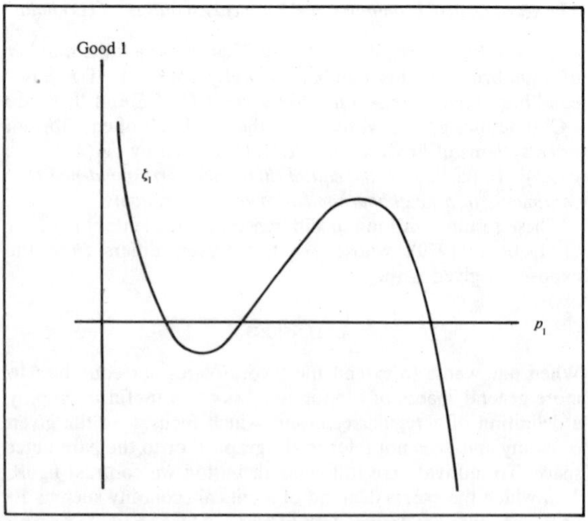

Figure 4

The results on regular economies obtained in various frameworks are quite similar to those established in the previous section. It is shown that almost all economies, in an appropriate sense, are regular. Every regular equilibrium is locally unique and can be traced along its path when the economy varies gradually, as long as it stays regular. Economic models in which results of this kind have been precisely formulated and verified deal with variations in consumption and production (see, in particular, Smale, 1974). Also the case of many consumers, that is to say of consumption sectors described by the distribution of consumers' characteristics, has been treated. The basic mathematical tool is always some variant of Sard's Theorem. References can be found in my survey article (Dierker, 1982).

The study of regular equilibria has led to a revival of the differentiable viewpoint in general equilibrium theory and related areas. Readers interested in this modern development are referred to the excellent book by A. Mas-Colell (1985), which also contains an extensive, systematic presentation of the theory of regular equilibria.

EGBERT DIERKER

See also CATASTROPHE THEORY; EXISTENCE OF GENERAL EQUILIBRIUM; GLOBAL ANALYSIS; MATHEMATICAL ECONOMICS.

BIBLIOGRAPHY

Balasko, Y. 1975. Some results on uniqueness and on stability of equilibrium in general equilibrium theory. *Journal of Mathematical Economics* 2, 95–118.

Debreu, G. 1970. Economies with a finite set of equilibria. *Econometrica* 38, 387–92.

Dierker, E. 1982. Regular economies. In *Handbook of Mathematical Economics*, ed. K. Arrow and M. Intriligator, Amsterdam: North-Holland, ch. 17, 795–830.

Dierker, E. and Dierker, H. 1972. The local uniqueness of equilibria. *Econometrica* 40, 867–81.

Mas-Colell, A. 1985. *The Theory of General Economic Equilibrium: A Differentiable Approach.* Econometric Society Monographs, Cambridge: Cambridge University Press.

Smale, S. 1974. Global analysis and economics IV: finiteness and stability of equilibria with general consumption sets and production. *Journal of Mathematical Economics* 1, 119–27.

régulation. During the debates of the 1980s, the term '*régulation*' suggested state intervention in the name of economic management though its opposite, '*dérégulation*', was more widely used. In the area of economic policy and in accordance with Keynesian precepts, regulation indicates the adjustment of macroeconomic activity by means of budgetary or monetary contracyclical interventions.

This term is also used in physics and biology, but with different meanings. In mechanics, a regulator is a means to stabilize the rotary speed of a machine. In biology, regulation corresponds to the reproduction of substances such as DNA. In general terms, the theory of systems involves the study of the role of a set of negative and positive feed-back loops in relation to the stability of a complex network of interactions.

Here, a third meaning of the term will be more thoroughly developed. While it is not completely disconnected from the preceding meanings, it is nevertheless distinct from them. Theories of *régulation* constitute an area of research which has focused on analysing long-term transformations in capitalist economies. Initially, this work was mainly French; but related studies can be found in various OECD as well as Third World countries (Hausmann, 1981; Ominami, 1985). These combine Marxian intuitions and Kaleckian or Keynesian macroeconomics in order to revive institutionalist or historicist studies.

At a primary level, a form of *régulation* denotes any *dynamic process of adaptation* of production and social demand resulting from a conjunction of economic adjustments linked to a given configuration of social relations, forms of organization and structures (Boyer, 1979 and 1986a). On a secondary, more ambitious level, this problematic aims at describing, and where possible at explaining, the transition from one mode of *régulation* to another in a long-term historical perspective (Aglietta, 1982; G.R.E.E.C., 1981). So the aim of this problematic is far-reaching and of a general character but its field is defined by three essential questions: How can we explain the *transition* from periods of high and relatively regular growth to periods of relative stagnation and instability? Why, *during the passage of time* do crises take different directions? Can one assume that growth and crises assume significantly different *national forms*?

Most economic theories – neoclassical, Keynesian, or even Marxist – emphasize the general invariables of eminently abstract systems, in which history serves merely as a confirmation, or failing that, as a perturbation. In contrast, the *régulation* approach seeks a broader interaction between history and theory, social structures, institutions and economic regularities (de Vroey, 1984).

As a starting point we consider the hypothesis of *the central role of accumulation* as the driving force of capitalist societies. This necessitates a clarification of factors that reduce or delay the conflicts and disequilibria inherent in the formation of capital, and which allow for an understanding of the *possibility* of periods of sustained growth (Boyer and Mistral, 1978). These factors are associated with particular regimes of accumulation, namely the form of articulation between the dynamics of the productive system and social demand, between the distribution of income between wages and profits on the one hand; and on the other hand the division between consumption and investment. It is then useful to explain the *organizational principles* which allow for a mediation between such contradictions as the extension of productive capacity under the stimulus of competition, and downward pressure on wages which inhibits the growth of demand. The notion of *institutional form* – defined as a set of fundamental social relations (Aglietta, 1982) – enables the transition between constraints associated with an accumulation regime and collective strategies; between economic dynamics and individual behaviour. A small number of key institutional forms, which are the result of past social struggles and the imperatives of the material reproduction of society, frame and channel a multitude of partial strategies which are decentralized and limited in terms of their temporal horizon. Research on the United States (Aglietta, 1982) and France (Boyer, 1979, 1986a) distinguish between five main institutional forms.

The forms of competition describe by what mechanisms the compatibility of a set of decentralized decisions is ensured. They are competitive while the ex post adjustment of prices and quantities ensure a balance; they are monopolist if the ex ante socialization of revenue is such that production and social demand evolve together (Lipietz, 1979). *The type of monetary constraint* explains the interrelations between credit and money creation: credit is narrowly limited in terms of movement of reserves when money is predominantly metallic; the causality is reversed when on the contrary the dynamics of credit conditions the money supply in systems where the external parity represents the only constraint weighing upon the national monetary system (Benassy et al., 1979). *The nature of institutionalized compromises* defines different configurations of relations between the State and the economy (Andre and Delorme, 1983): the State-as-Arbiter when only general conditions of commercial exchange are guaranteed; as the interfering State when a network of *régulations* and budgetary interventions codify the rights of different social groups. *Modes of support for the international regime* are also derived from a set of rules which organize relations between the Nation-State and the rest of the world in terms of commodity exchange, capital movements and monetary settlements. History goes beyond the traditional contrast between an open and a closed economy, free trade and protectionism; it makes apparent a variety of configurations spaced out between the hegemonic economy constituting the axis of the international system, and countries at the periphery of this system (Mistral, 1982; Lipietz, 1986a). Finally, *forms of wage relations* indicate different historical configurations of the relationship between Capital and Labour, i.e. the organization of the means of production, the nature of the social division of labour and work techniques, type of employment and the system of determination of wages, and finally, workers' way of life. If, in the first stages of industrialization, wage-earners are defined first of all as producers, during the second stage, they are simultaneously producers and consumers. Hence the contrast between 19th-century wage relations and the Fordist relations corresponding to the contemporary period (Coriat, 1978; Aglietta, Brender, 1984; Boyer, 1979 and 1987).

On the basis of these forms, one can analyse the logic of the behaviour of social groups and of individuals ensuring the relative coherence and stability of the current accumulation regime. At this point appears the notion of *régulation*, as a conjunction of mechanisms and principles of adjustment associated with a configuration of wage relations, competition, State interventions and hierarchization of the international economy. Finally, a distinction between *'small' and 'big' crises* is called for (Billaudot and Granou, 1985; Lorenzi et al., 1980; Boyer, 1986a; Mazier et al., 1984). The former, which are of a rather cyclical nature, are the very expression of *régulation* in reaction to the recurrent imbalances of accumulation. The latter are of a structural nature: the very process of accumulation throws into doubt the stability of institutional forms and the *régulation* which sustains it. The partial rupture in the functioning of the system paves the way to social struggles and political alternatives.

If the relevance of a theoretical model derives from the scope of its conclusions, it is imperative to point out some of the major findings in research pursued during the last decade. According to this problematic, in long-term dynamics as well as in short-term development *institutions are important*. Historical research confirms that sometimes institutional forms make an impression on the system in operation; at other times they register major changes in direction. At the end of a period which can be counted in decades, the very mode of development – i.e. the conjunction of the mode of *régulation* and the accumulation regime – is affected: there will be changes in the tendencies of long-term growth and eventually in inflation, specificities of cyclical processes (coexistence of recessions and deflations or marked stagflationist character) (CEPREMAP-CORDES, 1977).

So a periodization of advanced capitalist economies emerges which is not part of the traditional Marxist theory (Lorenzi et al., 1980). Despite the rise in monopoly, the interwar period is still marked by competitive regulation. After World War II an accumulation regime without precedent is instituted – that of intensive accumulation centred of mass consumption

(Bertrand, 1983) – known as *Fordist* and channelled through *monopolist* type regulation.

In fact, the alteration in wage relations – in particular the transition to Fordism (Coriat, 1978), i.e. the synchronization of mass production and wage-earners' access to the 'American way of life' – and in monetary management, i.e. transition to internally accepted credit money – seems to have played a greater role than the change in modes of competition or conjunctural stabilization policies *à la* Keynes (Aglietta, 1982; Aglietta and Orlean, 1982; Boyer, 1987).

Since the Sixties, we have allegedly been experiencing a big crisis without historical precedent; corresponding to an altogether original form of development (Boyer and Mistral, 1978; Mazier et al., 1984). This explains the absence, at least at the present, of cumulative depression and persistent, if more moderate, inflation (Lipietz, 1985).

In consequence, it is logical that former economic policies lose their efficacy (Boyer, 1986a). First, because the crisis is not cyclical but structural; this invalidates the policy of fine-tuning; second, because the structural changes which permitted the 1929 crisis to be overcome have become blocked (Lipietz, 1986b). They can therefore not be repeated in order to find a way out of the accumulated contradictions and imbalances.

There is no economic or technological determinism in the strictest sense. The multiplicity of past variants of Fordism and the diversity of strategies now deployed point to an opening, however partial, to ways out of crisis (Boyer, 1986b, 1986c). New problems are emerging which relate to an original articulation between industry and the service sector (Petit, 1986).

Moreover, research on social formations other than France, the United States and the old industrialized countries shows the extreme relativity of institutional forms, accumulation regimes and forms of regulation which cannot be reduced to a cardinal opposition between Taylorism and Fordism, competitive versus monopolist capitalism, etc. Rather than irrefutable results and a perfected theory, the regulation approach sets out general notions and a method of work. It is up to future research to turn these premises into a more complete theory.

ROBERT BOYER

BIBLIOGRAPHY

Aglietta, M. 1982. *Regulation and Crisis of Capitalism*. New York: Monthly Review Press.

Aglietta, M. and Brender, A. 1984. *Les métamorphoses de la société salariale*. Paris: Calmann-Levy.

Aglietta, M. and Orlean, A. 1982. *La violence de la monnaie*. Paris: PUF.

André, Ch. and Delorme, R. 1983. *L'état et l'économie*. Paris: Seuil.

Benassy, J.P., Boyer, R. and Gelpi, R.M. 1979. Régulation des économies capitalistes et inflation. *Revue économique* 30(3), May.

Bertrand, H. 1983. Accumulation, régulation, crise: un modèle sectionnel théorique et appliqué. *Revue économique* 34(6), March.

Billaudot, B. and Granou, A. 1985. *Croissance et crises*. 2nd edn, Paris: La Découverte.

Boyer, R. 1979. Wage formation in historical perspective: the French experience. *Cambridge Journal of Economics* 3, March, 99–118.

Boyer, R. 1986a. *Théorie de la régulation: une analyse critique*. Paris: La Découverte.

Boyer, R. 1986b. New technologies and employment in the Eighties. In *Barriers to Full Employment*, ed. J.A. Kregel, London: Macmillan.

Boyer, R. (ed.) 1986c. *Capitalismes fin de siècle*. Paris: PUF.

Boyer, R. (ed.) 1987. *Labour Flexibility in Europe*. Oxford: Oxford University Press.

Boyer, R. and Mistral, J. 1978. *Accumulation, inflation, crises*. Paris: PUF.

CEPREMAP-CORDES. 1977. Approches de l'inflation: l'exemple français. Convention de recherche No. 22, December.

Coriat, B. 1978. L'atelier et le chronomètre. Paris: C. Bourgois.

De Vroey, M. 1984. A regulation approach interpretation of the contemporary crisis. *Capital and Class* 23, Summer, 45–66.

G.R.E.E.C. 1981. *Crise et régulation*. Grenoble: PUG, DRUG.

Hausmann, R. 1981. State landed property, oil rent and accumulation in Venezuela: an analysis in terms of social relations. PhD Thesis, Cornell University, August.

Lipietz, A. 1979. *Crise et inflation, pourquoi?* Paris: Maspéro.

Lipietz, A. 1985. *The Magic World. From Value to Inflation*. London: Verso.

Lipietz, A. 1986a. New tendencies in the international division of labor: regimes of accumulation and mode of regulation. In *Production, Work, Territory*, ed. Scott and Storper, London: Allen & Unwin.

Lipietz, A. 1986b. Behind the crisis: the exhaustion of a regime of accumulation. A 'regulation school' perspective some French empirical works. *Review of Radical Political Economics* 18(1–2), Spring-Summer.

Lorenzi, J.H., Pastre, O. and Toledano, J. 1980. *La crise du XXè siècle*. Paris: Economica.

Mazier, J., Basle, M. and Vidal, J.F. 1984. *Quand les crises durent...* Paris: Economica.

Mistral, J. 1982. La diffusion internationale de l'accumulation intensive et sa crise. In *La recherche en économie internationale*, ed. J.L. Reiffers, Paris: Dunod, 205–37.

Mistral, J. 1986. Régime international et trajectoires nationales. In Boyer (1986c), 167–202.

Ominami, C. 1985. *Les transformations dans la crise des rapports nord–sud*. Paris: La Découverte.

Petit, P. 1986. *Slow Growth and the Service Economy*. London: Frances Pinter.

regulation and deregulation. Regulation, particularly in the United States, consists of governmental actions to control price, sale and production decisions of firms in an avowed effort to prevent private decision-making that would take inadequate account of the 'public interest'. The Federal Congress established the first national regulatory agency (the Interstate Commerce Commission) in 1887 to control railroad freight rates and passenger fares, and by 1910 had further directed that agency to set limits on charges for long-distance use of the telephone. Since then 14 Federal agencies and upwards of 100 state agencies have been given authority to regulate corporate activity (Domestic Council Review Group on Regulatory Reform, 1977).

The legal foundation for regulation consists of statutes allowing the government to grant or condition the right of a company to provide service. Certification or licensing of a common carrier or utility company by a regulatory agency was commonplace by the 1960s in the transportation, communication and energy distribution industries. By approving the tariffs of the licensed company, the regulatory bodies exercised control over almost all railroad, trucking, airline and telephone rates, they also set prices and conditions of sale for electricity and natural gas. Authority to offer service, further, was controlled in respect of commercial or savings banks and liquor distribution (in some states) and even dry cleaners (in Oklahoma; see Plott, 1965). But the regulatory mode for achieving public policy objectives in pricing has not been widely used in Europe and Asia; instead, most of these industries have been owned and operated by governmental authorities. Nonetheless, the rationale and the results of regulation in the United States can be used to a degree to gauge the performance of nationalized industry in Europe and Asia.

Federal certification has been extended over other, 'non-utility' industries. Companies that are issuers of securities and commodity contracts have been licensed ostensibly in order to protect depositors and investors. More recently, particularly since the 1970s, the federal government expanded the scope of regulation to encompass health, safety and the environment. It promulgated rules aimed at making safer automobiles, safer consumer products and a safer workplace. These rules often required firms to design their products or production processes to meet specified engineering standards. By 1975 federal regulation significantly controlled important product, price or process decisions by firms in industries accounting for about 24 per cent of gross national product (MacAvoy, 1979, p. 25).

These regulatory activities have involved an agency, board, or bureau that (i) contained a governmental bureaucracy and (ii) operated in an adversarial relation with private industry. The agency typically has exercised control by responding to a company request for a licence or tariff change with a decision based on an individual case adjudicatory proceeding or by comparing the request to its own standing rules.

This 'public/private' control relationship has advocates who view it as the method of economic control to be preferred over either the limited forces of competition found currently in private markets or the power in government ownership of enterprises. However, the results from analysis of firm behaviour under regulation do not establish such a preference. Both theoretical and empirical research question the extent to which regulation can achieve the goals for which it has been promulgated.

REASONS FOR REGULATION

Advocates of regulatory programmes assert many different reasons in support of them. Yet a small number of economic arguments are made as 'justification' for kinds of regulation. With market behaviour judged on the efficiency norm that prices equal full social costs at the margin, regulation is required to overcome one or more 'defects' that prevent corporations from operating according to the norm (see Lerner, 1964). The 'defects' that have most often led to policy proposals for regulation can be classified as follows.

1. The presence of monopoly power. When economies of firm scale in a particular market are so extensive as to create a significant cost advantage for a single enterprise, then this 'natural' monopolist can be expected to restrict output or directly set higher than marginal cost prices without concern for entry of a competitor (see Baumol and Bradford, 1970). Regulation of such a firm aims to provide cost-driven prices, but it cannot achieve 'efficiency', since to do so would require ending up with per-unit revenues below the level necessary for form survival (with marginal less than average costs, the natural monopolist cannot be required to set prices equal to marginal costs; see Lerner, 1964). And where the natural monopolist can discriminate among customers and on sales to a single customer, regulation is unnecessary because profit-maximizing prices on marginal sales will equal marginal costs. Thus the rationale for regulation of the natural monopolist has settled for less than the norm, such as constraining the monopolist to set average prices at average costs (see Kahn, 1970, vol. 1).

A variant of the argument has been used to regulate both monopolies and competitive industries. When and where 'rents' paid to scarce resources are unusually large in amount, and are the consequence of sharp, unexpected price increases of a widely used product, regulation has been sought to keep prices down. For example, the regulation of natural gas at the wellhead in the 1960s and of petroleum products at retail in the 1970s were for this purpose, without regard for the competitiveness of the market. But where there is competition, supply will fall short of demand; then regulation has to be justified on grounds that the shortage for a few does less harm than the good to come to the rest of the consumers from keeping prices down (see Kahn, 1960).

2. To account for spillover costs. Regulation has been proposed where a product's price does not reflect important costs inherent in the production process – costs that are imposed on neighbours or others in the economy. The price of electricity may not reflect the full cost of air pollution that results from using coal in power generation. If not, demand for electricity is greater than the norm of economic efficiency would dictate (since buyers do not pay the full marginal costs).

Of course, the harmful results of pollution derive both from the electricity generation process and the fact that people have moved into the area bordering the plant. In theory, electricity consumers and pollution sufferers would agree to share optimally the cost of anti-pollution devices if they could bargain efficiently among themselves (see Coase, 1980). Such bargaining typically has been found by legislatures to be impractical, however, as compared with direct regulation of emissions or discharges. Environmental regulation, as a way to constrain important spillovers, has attacked the pollution-generating process by setting engineering standards for equipment used in the production process – standards of which the aim is to reduce discharge.

The effectiveness of such regulatory controls has been much debated. To what extent they have been successful in taking account of 'spillover' costs in setting standards and in actually reducing pollution or increasing safety have been major issues in applied research. Local controls and penalties in the form of higher insurance charges, court damage awards, etc. existed before Federal environmental and auto safety regulation had been established. Some argue that strict engineering standards imposed through federal regulation have not done much better (see Lave, 1981; Crandall, 1983; MacAvoy, 1986; but see Freeman, 1982). Others agree, but state that taxes on pollution or unsafe cars or other incentive-based systems could be effective even if current methods were not (see Breyer, 1982; Stewart, 1985).

3. To compensate for inadequate information. Regulation sometimes aims at lowering the costs of obtaining information. In particular, government action has been called for when (i) suppliers profit from misleading consumers whose available legal remedies, such as private court actions, are more costly than regulation; (ii) consumers cannot readily evaluate the information available, and the costs of mistakes are high, such as on potential drug effectiveness or safety of a particular airline; and (iii) the market on the supply side fails for some reason to furnish the information as is demanded (at cost-based prices). Given the first and second reasons, the government has created special commissions to license 'safe' goods and services. For the last reason, the government may seek to provide more, if not better, information or to require producers to supply the information, as in the case of financial or securities disclosures. Most such approaches have been made without specific knowledge of markets for information or empirical studies on the 'failure' of current sources.

4. Other justifications. Of course, there are special-interest arguments for regulation. Price and entry regulation of airlines, trucking, and ocean shipping, for example, have been justified to control 'excessive' competition that allegedly would destroy all except one or two firms that would then set non-competitive prices. This argument is advanced by incumbent firms. The cost functions implicit in these depictions of behaviour are not widely found in these industries, however. Regulated firms have at times advanced a similar argument in an effort to extend regulation of entry to encompass the prices set by competitive, unregulated rivals. In the telephone industry, regulation of entry has been sought to prevent 'predatory' pricing on long-distance services in which the local service Bell Operating Company would allegedly set unregulated long-distance rates below variable costs to drive rivals out of that business, covering its own losses with high regulated returns on local service (see MacAvoy and Robinson, 1985; Brock, 1981). But unless regulation of local service itself is so defective as to allow 'padding' of regulated costs with losses on other services, firms cannot readily set such prices and profit from continually keeping others out of cross-subsidized markets. The argument is one in which ineffective regulation mandates regulation of another market.

A further justification in support of regulatory policy is that a source other than the consumer makes the purchasing decision, thus leading to inefficient increases in purchases. Medical care is often cited as an example, for it is the patient's insurance company or the government, not the patient, who pays the bill. And government regulation of medical service charges is sometimes advocated for this reason. This rationale may be viewed as a statement of belief that demand is more inelastic with respect to price than if there were only first-party purchases. For such price non-sensitivity to result in adverse market performance, suppliers would have to possess monopoly power, so that this is a version of the first (monopoly) rationale.

Unequal bargaining power sometimes is used as a rationale for regulation that would protect small firms, suppliers or customers from the power of the large firms or buyers with whom they must deal. State regulators, for example, prescribe standard forms for insurance contracts. This again is a monopoly rationale, stated from the viewpoint of the corporate purchaser of goods and services. The operationality of these arguments determines the worth of regulation. There has to be a direct relationship between rationale and results so as to establish a foundation for regulatory policy. Peltzman, whose work is based on earlier developments of G.J. Stigler, has established hypotheses which are based on the 'public interest' rationale, which can be tested against alternative hypotheses based on the claim that the regulatory agencies restrain market operations for those private interests willing to compensate such agencies for those services (Peltzman, 1976; Stigler, 1971). Thus, which is the 'true' rationale for a particular programme can be determined by examining regulatory methods and results.

METHODS OF REGULATION

As important as rationale are the means used for obtaining the desired results. Although all regulation involves a governmental bureaucracy that 'commands and controls' the individual actions of private firms, one can distinguish between different regulatory programmes according to the specific methods used to effectuate that 'control'. More to the point, certain regulatory methods have been used to attain specific regulatory ends. They include the following.

1. Cost of service ratemaking. This system has been commonly used to set prices in the electricity industry as well as for local and long-distance telephone service industries and for airlines, road transport companies and railways. In principle, the regulator determines a revenue requirement based upon the firm's accounting costs during a 'test year'. Income accounts at issue include operating costs, taxes, an allowance for depreciation and 'allowed returns' defined as a 'reasonable' rate of return times the 'rate base' including the undepreciated portion of investments relevant to regulated operations valued on a historical expenditure basis. Once the revenue requirement is determined, the regulator approves rates in a tariff designed to recover, during the foreseeable future until another proceeding, the amount of the revenue requirement.

A host of economic problems arise in transforming this practice into a set of bureaucratic procedures administerable through adversary hearings (see Kahn, 1970, vols 1 and 2). In principle, assuming market and accounting values of assets are the same, the process would set the 'allowed returns' rate equal to the firm's costs of capital, so that the level of prices would equal the firm's long-run average total costs of operation. The anti-monopoly rationale would be achieved, if only in the general sense that the monopoly could not set prices resulting in excessive returns. But this general rule cannot bring about prices equal to marginal costs, nor can it determine optimal departures of individual prices from the marginal costs of specific services (see Averch and Johnson, 1962; Baumol and Klevorick, 1970). And when applied with accounting data under economy-wide conditions if inflation and low growth of demands for regulated services, it can produce results that deviate widely from even the suboptimal goal inherent in average cost pricing (see Joskow, 1974; Joskow and Noll, 1981; MacAvoy, 1982).

2. Setting historically based price ceilings. This system, used during wartime rationing, has been adapted to controlling petroleum product prices, and it has been proposed for controlling hospital care fees (see Kalt, 1981; Joskow, 1981). It consists of holding prices at their level of a certain past date (e.g. 'last August 1') but then allowing increases above that level justified by changes in operating costs. Ceilings require continuous adjustment as administrators, for example, cope with new products, changing demand and the necessarily resulting shortages and deterioration of service quality.

3. Issuing permits. Agencies charged with allocating a commodity in scarce supply, such as television bandwidth or airline landing rights, have developed systems that allow them to choose among applicants after public hearings at which each sets forth qualifications. The system requires the agency first to define the precise commodity awarded, and then to apply standards that weed out those not qualified. Finally, the agency selects among competing applicants, subjectively deciding which will best serve the 'public interest' on the basis of their presentations.

This system could embody a process by which to achieve any of the goals in regulation. Indeed, by refusing to issue a permit, the agency can prevent an enterprise from operating as a monopoly or from causing spillover costs. The creative use of such operating authority has been advocated as the method for achieving the efficiency norms, without rate-base regulation (Demsetz, 1968; Bailey and Baumol, 1984). But in practice, licensing has not been an important substitute for price or spillover regulations. When applied to allocating such 'public goods' as bandwidth, it has often proved to be difficult or impossible to find any meaningful set of coherent criteria that will allow choice among qualified applicants. Instead, the system tends to spawn complex and extended hearings (all characteristics of applicants are treated as relevant), and the results have been open to charges of inconsistency or special-interest distortion (see Wilson, 1979).

4. Standard setting. Regulators set increasingly large numbers of standards forbidding, for example, methods or products that are unsafe or spread pollution. Standards typically require the regulator to obtain information from a wide range of interested parties: the industry, consumer groups, suppliers, customers, employees, other government bodies, and so forth. The regulator decides such questions as: (i) Should the standard directly control the relevant evil (such as pollution content) or control a surrogate discharge (such as smokestack or the sulphur content of coal?) (ii) How stringent should the standard be? (iii) To what extent should the standard embody a requirement for equipment performance rather than specification for a particular equipment design?

In practice, the agency considers standards proposed by firms before modifying and finally adopting them. It will receive comments from different parties and then 'negotiate' a final compromise among conflicting proposals, so as to reduce opposition by those regulated that could take the form of court suits or resistance to compliance which generates large enforcement costs.

Each of these four regulatory systems has proved to be controversial – with lengthy arguments about whether their application has costs that make the regulatory 'cure' worse than the 'disease' to be prevented. Operations under rate-base regulation are confounded by the fact that current costs seldom bear any relation to unregulated prices set on the basis of allowed returns on previous investments. The use of price ceilings can be worse, as last-period prices become more anachronistic. With permits and standards, the regulator must deal with the fact that tests for various potential results required for certification are often inconclusive and thus regulatory choices of operating conditions are random. As a result, the case for regulation has been embraced less enthusiastically in recent experience. Also, the results of regulation have cast doubt on how well this system has lined up to its 'public interest' rationale.

THE EFFECTS OF REGULATION

Enacting legislation to establish regulatory commissions is only the beginning. The impact of regulation is largely determined by the way an agency translates statutory goals into operating rules, so as to bring about changes in prices, sales and service quality from company adjustments to these rules. Most of the agencies regulating price and entry had their programmes in place by the 1960s, so that results can be documented.

The public utility and transportation industries showed little price-level effect from regulation before 1970 (see Moore, 1970; Jackson, 1969). During the 1970s, however, regulation had excessive price-reducing effects. The commission process became more constraining as companies with annual increases in 'justified' costs requested increases in rates that were denied by the regulatory agencies.

Telephone regulation, split between state and Federal commissions, experienced both a rate-level freeze and, as well, the tendency of commissions to shift any increases away from home consumers. Since significant portions of total costs were derived from the common operations of both local and long-distance systems, the agencies were able to assign more 'costs' to interstate long-distance services, thereby allowing the state regulators to hold down local residential charges (see the Federal Communications Commission Report, FCC Docket 20,003). But at the same time, long-distance rates were held constant while costs specific to this service fell, opening up a profit margin to cover the shift in joint costs (MacAvoy and Robinson, 1983).

Natural gas, not a monopoly industry, was regulated in the 1960s on the variant rationale of controlling 'rents' with the result that supply shortages had developed of as much as one quarter of total demands by the middle 1970s. The agency maintained wellhead prices at approximately the level that was realized in fixed markets before regulation began through ceiling which 'area rates' kept new contract prices at the level of average historical costs of production from in-ground reserves in any region. The system could not conceivably have worked to achieve price stability and sufficiency of supplies at the same time: gas demand increases, as a result of lower prices for gas relative to other fuels, exceeded the GNP and total energy consumption growth rates each year; commensurate supply increases were forthcoming only at marginal costs higher than average historical costs, which because controlled price ceilings were based on average costs, would not be undertaken (MacAvoy and Breyer, 1974; MacAvoy, 1983).

The airline industry showed the same results over the 1970s. In reaction to regulation and inflation, they reduced service quality significantly in the early part of the decade. Throughout this period the number of flights declined, and airline passengers were offered less convenient scheduling or more crowded flights. But the Civil Aeronautics Board also imposed fare structure rules that prevented selective cuts where demands were elastic and lower-than-average cost conditions would lead to expansion of service (Breyer, 1982). Airlines at the same time were offering service at rates which in respect of capacity were too low, and rates specifically which were too high (Breyer, 1982; Miller, 1977). The railroads realized somewhat the same results, but for slightly different reasons. In the presence of rising fuel, labour and capital costs, the Interstate Commerce Commission granted revenue increases that kept the rail rate index in line with average costs. But the commission did not allow reductions of service on lines experiencing greater-than-average cost increases. The railroads thus had to continue to provide for small shippers, those on short-distance lines and those seeking small-volume but frequent service, even though unit costs for these services increased more rapidly than revenues. To meet service requirements and still earn profits, rate-cost margins were increased in high-volume and long-distance markets were subject to incursions from competitive trucking suppliers. Thus railroads were faced with increasing the rate of market attrition to stay at an average price level covering costs (Coleman, 1977).

These results are the product of two distinct regulatory processes: (i) in the rate of return case loads created a regulatory lag that began to work against rather than for the unregulated companies; and (ii) the commissions, for political not efficiency reasons, kept down the size of current-dollar rate increases (in keeping with Peltzman hypotheses; see Peltzman, 1976). When costs began to rise in the late 1960s, regulatory lag penalized the firm – and the difference between historical and current costs widened as the increase in the number of case applications extended the amount of time required for case decisions. Thus the greater the inflation, and the longer the lag in deciding on increases in regulated prices, the greater the profit-reduction effect of controls on these industries. Further, beyond the clerical problems of regulatory lag, rate increases when granted were not enough to compensate for cost increases. Simply to avoid adverse public reaction, rate-setting agencies would not grant price increases that were very large in billions of dollars. The dollar sizes of proposed additional revenues so concerned regulators that they became reluctant to grant even those increases that were fully justified on the efficiency norm.

As the impact of the over-regulation was beginning to be felt by the public utilities and the transportation and communications industries in the late 1960s, the manufacturing industries were just beginning the new experiment with health, safety and environmental regulation. New agencies had been established to regulate company operations using the permit powers to force detailed equipment specifications. Because such standard setting has been litigious and prolonged, these regulations have proven to be extremely detailed and inflexible. They have forced substantial investments made to meet equipment specifications, which in turn have caused increases in production costs in the industries most subject to the new controls. Subsequent price increases in those industries were greater during the early years of health and safety regulation than in those industries not as subject to such regulation (the exceptions were the electricity utilities and the petroleum-refining industry, which were price-regulated through all or part of the period) (MacAvoy, 1982). Consumers in effect paid for the equipment outlays required by health and safety regulations.

These cost increases might have been compensated for by less pollution and fewer industrial and highway accidents. Analysts, however, have been unable to find significant reductions in the unhealthful conditions which were to be dealt with by the new regulatory activities. Research on worker safety regulation has indicated that there have not been widespread reductions in worker accident rates from agency activities (Smith, 1976; de Pietro, 1976; Viscusi, 1983; Nichols and Zeckhauser, 1977). Regulation of automobiles produced somewhat the same results. In its early years of operation, the Federal Highway Safety Agency directed its regulatory activities towards improving crash survivability, with a goal being to decrease the fatality rate per 100 million vehicle-miles by one-third (Second Annual Report on the Administration of the National Traffic and Motor Vehicle Safety Act of 1969). But recent highway accident rates have been better explained by (i) the cost of accident insurance, (ii) personal income levels, (iii) driving speed, (iv) driver age, (v) alcoholic intoxication, and (vi) a secular trend than by regulatory actions (Peltzman, 1975; Manne and Miller (eds), 1976). When the statistical equation for this relation in the pre-regulation period was used to generate predictions of accidents for the period after mandatory safety devices were introduced, it was found that projected highway fatality rates without regulation differed very little from actual rates under regulation.

The benefits of environmental regulation have not been substantially more important than those from the other major 'social control' initiatives. To be sure, environmental controls have realized positive results at certain locations – where the environmental agencies have invoked rules against pollution by a particular company. Certain rivers and air corridors have been made cleaner than they were five years ago because of such actions (Conservation Foundation, 1982). How widespread the improvement is, however, is debatable. Since standards for each industry and state have been different and have been enforced to widely differing degrees, it cannot be said that regulation has improved air and water quality nationwide. At the same time, industry-specific standards were being put in place after product and process improvements already underway were beginning to reduce pollution. Pollutants were being reduced because it was profitable, given new technology, to conserve inputs that had been previously discharged as waste (Crandall, 1983; Mills and White, 1978; see Mills and White, 1978, on automative emissions regulation). Thus, recent air- and water-quality changes may have been affected by changes in industrial activity, not simply by regulation.

On the whole, the health and safety regulatory systems have most likely increased prices and reduced GNP in the most regulated industries. Also, there are indications that because of drawing attention towards equipment and away from behaviour, the control system had not brought about improvements in health, safety and environmental quality that could have followed from use of other regulatory methods. In other words, these regulatory agencies have been generating substantial cost effects, but one cannot be certain they have brought about the benefits intended in the enabling legislation.

DEREGULATION

Beginning in the mid-1970s, public dissatisfaction with the burdens that regulation imposed, combined with economists' criticism of specific regulatory programmes, created a strong political movement bent upon ending many particular regulatory programmes. The first major programme to be dismantled was airline regulation. Economists had long criticized the regulatory regime imposed on airlines, claiming that the 'excessive competition' rationale was a chimera, without application to the structurally competitive airline industry. Since the elimination of the Civil Aeronautics Board in 1978, most of the facts have borne out the evaluation of regulation as operating a decade earlier. Regular fares have risen on regularly scheduled services but travellers have tended to fly on discount fares, and in such cases, where demands are elastic and costs lower than average, fares have fallen (Morrison and Winston, 1986; Meyer and Oster, 1984; Bailey, Graham and Kaplan, 1985). By most economic measures, the industry after deregulation has been operating more efficiently (Morrison and Winston, 1986). At the same time, even though some firms have faced the threat of bankruptcy, the average firm has increased profitability. The gains from service flexibility, in cost reduction, have allowed the more efficient airlines to offer more service between smaller and medium-sized cities resulting in consumer gains valued by Morrison and Winston at $6 billion.

On the heels of airline deregulation, other deregulatory legislation has followed. To a substantial degree, rate-of-return regulation has been eliminated or partially replaced by increased reliance upon competition as the determinant of prices and sales in trucking, railroads, stockbroking, long-distance telephone service and, to a somewhat lesser degree, banking. Each of these industries, however, satisfied (to a considerable degree) the structural economic preconditions for maintaining competition since their markets were usually large enough to support several competing firms of efficient size. The deregulatory movement has not advanced to the point of reducing the coverage of health, safety and the environment regulation given that the rationale for intervention is stronger and the market alternatives to classical regulation less obviously superior. In these latter areas, 'regulatory reform pressure' has taken the form of advocating, not total deregulation, but rather less restrictive or less burdensome methods of governmental intervention aimed at achieving the relevant regulatory end.

Most prominently, economists have proposed that the government create saleable rights to engage in limited undesirable conduct, such as polluting. With such rights, and a market for their sale, firms would find it costly to pollute. A system of marketable rights allows the firms and the regulatory agency to know in advance the amount of pollution (equal to the sum of unit rights issued), but not to know in advance the price of continuing to use a process that emits pollutants.

At the present time, significant progress has been made in 'deregulating' those industries where the economic case for controls has never been strong, and recent results from regulatory operations have caused significant declines in the quality of service. Whether 'reform' will go further to encompass 'less restrictive alternatives' to regulation is the theoretical and empirical research issue of the 1980s and 1990s. To date, however, the agenda in welfare economics for reform differs significantly from the political agenda to the point where regulation may be present for more than these decades.

STEPHEN BREYER AND PAUL W. MACAVOY

See also COMMUNICATIONS; ENERGY ECONOMICS; INDUSTRIAL ORGANIZATION; MARKET STRUCTURE.

BIBLIOGRAPHY

Ackerman, B. and Stewart, R. 1985. Reforming environmental law. *Stanford Law Review* 37, 301ff.

Averch, H. and Johnson, L.L. 1962. Behavior of the firm under regulatory constraint. *American Economic Review* 52, December, 1052–69.

Bailey, E.E. and Baumol, W.J. 1984. Deregulation and the theory of contestable markets. *Yale Journal on Regulation* 1(2), 111–38.

Bailey, E.E., Graham, D.R. and Kaplan, D.P. 1985. *Deregulating the Airlines*. Cambridge, Mass.: MIT Press.

Baumol, W.J. and Bradford, D.F. 1970. Optimal departures from marginal cost pricing. *American Economic Review* 60(3), June, 265–83.

Baumol, W.J. and Klevorick, A.K. 1970. Input choices in rate-of-return regulation: an overview of discussion. *Bell Journal of Economics* 1(2), Autumn, 162–90.

Breyer, S. 1982. *Regulation and Its Reform*. Cambridge, Mass.: Harvard University Press.

Brock, G.W. 1981. *The Telecommunications Industry: The Dynamics of Market Structure*. Cambridge, Mass.: Harvard University Press.

Coase, R.W. 1960. The problem of social cost. *Journal of Law and Economics* 3, October, 1–44.

Coleman, W.T., Jr. 1977. Time for corrective action. In *Railroad Revitalization and Regulatory Reform*, ed. P.W. MacAvoy and J.W. Snow, Ford Administration Papers on Regulatory Reform, American Enterprise Institute, Studies in Government Regulation, 63–70.

Conservation Foundation. 1982. *State of Our Environment*. Washington, D.C.: The Foundation.

Crandall, R. 1983. *Controlling Industrial Pollution: The Economics and Politics of Clean Air*. Washington, DC: Brookings Institution.

Demsetz, H. 1968. Why regulate utilities? *Journal of Law and Economics* 11, April, 55–65.

de Pietro, A. 1976. An analysis of the OSHA inspection program in manufacturing industries, 1972–1973. *Draft Technical Analysis Paper*, US Department of Labor.

Domestic Council Review Group on Regulatory Reform. 1977. *The Challenge of Regulatory Reform: A Report to the President*. Washington, DC: Government Printing Office.

Freeman, A.M. 1982. *Air and Water Pollution Control: A Benefit Cost Assessment*. New York: Wiley.

Harter, P. 1982. Negotiating regulations: a case for malaise. *Georgetown Law Journal* 71(1).

Jackson, R. 1969. Regulation on electric utility rate levels. *Financial Economics*, August, 370–76.

Joskow, P.L. 1974. Inflation and environmental concern: structural change in the process of public utility price regulation. *Journal of Law and Economics* 17(2), October, 291–311.

Joskow, P.L. 1981. *Controlling Hospital Costs: The Role of Government Regulation*. Cambridge, Mass.: MIT Press.

Joskow, P.L. and Noll, R. 1981. Regulation in theory and practice: an overview. In *Studies in Public Regulation*, ed. G. Fromm, Cambridge, Mass.: MIT Press, 1–65.

Kahn, A.E. 1960. Economic issues in regulating the field price of natural gas. *American Economic Review* 50, 507.

Kahn, A.E. 1970–71. *The Economics of Regulation*. 2 vols, New York: Wiley.

Kalt, J.E. 1981. *The Economics of Politics of Oil Price Regulation*. Cambridge, Mass.: MIT Press.

Lave, L. 1981. *The Strategy of Social Regulation*. Washington, DC: Brookings Institution.

Lerner, A.P. 1964. Conflicting principles of public utility rates. *Journal of Law and Economics* 7, October, 61–70.

MacAvoy, P.W. 1979. *The Regulated Industries and the Economy*. New York and London: W.W. Norton.

MacAvoy, P.W. 1982. *Energy Policy: An Economic Analysis*. New York: W.W. Norton.

MacAvoy, P.W. 1986. The record of the environmental protection agency in controlling industrial air pollution. In *Energy, Markets and Regulation: What Have We Learned?*, Cambridge, Mass.: MIT Press.

MacAvoy, P.W. and Breyer, S. 1974. *Energy Regulation by the Federal Power Commission*. Washington, DC: Brookings Institution.

MacAvoy, P.W. and Robinson, K. 1983. Winning by losing: the AT&T settlement and its impact on telecommunications. *Yale Journal on Regulation* 1(1), 1–42.

MacAvoy, P.W. and Robinson, K. 1985. Losing by judicial policymaking: the first year of the AT&T divestiture. *Yale Journal on Regulation* 2(2), 225–62.

Manne, H.G. and Miller, R.L. (eds) 1976. *Auto Safety Regulation: The Cure or the Problem?* Glenridge, NJ: Thomas Horton.

Meyer, J.R. and Oster, C.V. Jr. (eds) 1984. *Deregulation and the New Airline Entrepreneurs*. Cambridge, Mass.: MIT Press.

Miller, J.C., III. 1977. The effects of the administration's draft bill on air carrier finances. In *Regulation of Passenger Fares and Competition Among the Airlines*, ed. P.W. MacAvoy and J.W. Snow, Ford Administration Papers on Regulatory Reform, American Enterprise Institute for Public Policy Research: Studies in Government Regulation, 181–200.

Mills, E.S. and White, L. 1978. Government policies toward automotive emissions control. In *Approaches to Controlling Air Pollution*, ed. A.F. Friedlaender, Cambridge, Mass.: MIT Press, 348–409.

Moore, T.G. 1970. The effectiveness of regulation of electric utility prices. *Southern Economic Journal* 36(4), April, 365–75.

Morrison, S. and Winston, C. 1986. *The Economic Effects of Airline Deregulation*. Washington, DC: Brookings Institution.

National Highway Traffic Safety Administration. 1969. *Second Annual Report on the Administration of the National Traffic and Motor Vehicle Safety Act*. Washington, DC: Government Printing Office.

Nichols, A.L. and Zeckhauser, R. 1977. Government comes to the workplace: an assessment of OSHA. *The Public Interest* 49, Fall, 39–69.

Peltzman, S. 1975a. *Regulation of Automobile Safety*. Washington, DC: American Enterprise Institute for Public Policy Research.

Peltzman, S. 1975b. The effect of safety regulation. *Journal of Political Economy* 83(4), 667–725.

Peltzman, S. 1976. Toward a general theory of regulation. *Journal of Law and Economics* 19(2), August, 211–48.

Plott, C.R. 1965. Occupational self-regulation: a case study of the Oklahoma dry cleaners. *Journal of Law and Economics* 8, October, 195–222.

Smith, R.S. 1976. *The Occupational Safety and Health Act*. Washington, DC: American Enterprise Institute for Public Policy Research.

Stewart, R. 1985. Economics, environment and the limits of legal control. *Harvard Environmental Law Review* 9, 1.

Stigler, G.J. 1971. The theory of economic regulation. *Bell Journal of Economics* 2(1), Spring, 3–21.

Suskind, L. and McMahon, G.G. 1985. The theory and practice of negotiated rulemaking. *Yale Journal on Regulation* 3, 133.

US Senate Commission on the Juduciary, Subcommittee on Administrative Procedure. 1975. *Civil Aeronautics Board Producer and Procedures*, 94th Congress, 1st Session.

Viscusi, W.K. 1983. *Risk by Choice: Regulating Health and Safety in the Workplace*. Cambridge, Mass.: Harvard University Press.
Wilson, J.Q. (ed.) 1979. *The Politics of Regulation*. New York: Basic Books.

Reid, Margaret Gilpin (born 1896). Margaret Reid, a leading scholar in analysis of the economics of consumer behaviour, was made a distinguished fellow of the American Economic Association in 1980. She was Professor of Economics at Iowa State College (1930–43), the University of Illinois (1948–51), and the University of Chicago (1951–61).

A realistic theorist, Reid has always looked behind data to processes that generate structural relationships. Her 1934 book on household production anticipated by three decades analyses built on the allocation of time, and she was the first (1947) to use wage-equivalent time measures of household work.

Already in Iowa she had questioned attempts to improve resource allocations by farm women that disregarded the nature of income effects. She went on to criticize assessments of the war-time cost-of-living index that neglected effects of changing incomes on the quality of goods traded, and she became the 'directing' member of the technical committee responsible for a report to the President's Commission on the Cost of Living (1945). Later on she challenged conventional treatments of income elasticities of consumption in general and of housing expenditures in particular (1952, 1962).

The concepts of 'permanent' and 'transitory' income were early a part of Reid's thinking (1952, 1953). Friedman drew on Reid in his 1957 application of the permanent income hypothesis to short-term shifts in consumption and saving, and Modigliani built on her work in his treatment of 'life stages' (Modigliani and Ando, 1960 and subsequently). In Reid's hands the concepts of 'permanent' and 'transitory' income have evolved subtly and progressively in multiple facets of the analysis of consumer behaviour. Since her retirement she has been probing interactions between health and income both over life cycles and across cohorts.

MARY JEAN BOWMAN

SELECTED WORKS
1934. *Economics of Household Production*. New York: Wiley.
1943. *Food for People*. New York: Wiley.
1945. (With associates.) Appendix IV. Prices and the cost of living in wartime – an appraisal of the Bureau of Labor Statistics Index of the Cost of Living in 1941–44. In *Report of the President's Committee on the Cost of Living*, Washington, DC: Government Printing Office, 243–370.
1947. The economic contribution of homemakers. In *Women's Opportunities and Responsibilities*, ed. L.M. Young, Philadelphia: Annals of the American Academy of Political and Social Science, 61–9.
1952. Effect of income concept upon expenditure curves of farm families. In *Conference on Research in Income and Wealth, Studies* Vol. 15, Part IV, Philadelphia: National Bureau of Economic Research, 131–74
1953. Savings by family units in consecutive periods. In *Savings in the Modern Economy*, ed. W.W. Heller, F.M. Boddy and C.L. Nelson, Minneapolis: University of Minnesota Press, 218–19.
1955. Food, liquor and tobacco. In *America's Needs and Resources: A New Survey*, ed. J.F. Dewhurst and associates, New York: Twentieth Century Fund, 123–68.
1960. Comments on I. Friend and J. Crockett, a complete set of consumer demand relationships. In *Proceedings of the Conference on Consumption and Savings*, Vol. I, ed. I. Friend and R. Jones, Philadelphia: Wharton School of Finance and Commerce, University of Pennsylvania, 143–54.
1962. *Housing and Income*. Chicago: University of Chicago Press.

BIBLIOGRAPHY
Friedman, M. 1957. *A Theory of the Consumption Function*. Princeton: Princeton University Press.
Modigliani, F. and Ando, A. 1960. The 'permanent income' and the 'life cycle' hypothesis of saving behavior: comparisons and tests. In *Proceedings of the Conference on Consumption and Savings*, ed. I. Friend and R. Jones, Philadelphia: Wharton School of Finance and Commerce, University of Pennsylvania, 49–174.

relative income hypothesis. The relative income hypothesis as expressed by its foremost exponent was an effort to reconcile conflicting evidence revealed by consumption functions fitted to long and short-period time series, and budget data; to bring social psychology into consumer theory; and to restore virtue to the act of saving (Duesenberry, 1962). While proposed as a critique of the Keynesian consumption function, neither its formulation nor implications weakened the concept of deficient aggregate demand nor the grounds for stabilization policy. It was consequently well within the framework of the vast research programme stimulated by the *General Theory*.

Written twenty-five years after that book, Duesenberry's work gained widespread recognition. Twenty-five years later, it has fallen out of favour replaced by two new streams of research into saving, and consumption, behaviour: one based on a conception of the rational consumer dealing with the problem of consumption now or later by maximizing an intertemporal utility function in perfect or instantaneously cleared markets; and the other based on the consumer constrained on occasion by realized income generated in markets that do not clear – the familiar Keynesian consumption function now being placed on a rigorous micro-footing.

It is too soon to write an obituary for the relative income hypothesis and this survey is not so intended; the hypothesis provides a suggestive account of aspects of consumer behaviour and seems capable of further development and research stimulation. Limitations of the theory and difficulties in obtaining corroborative evidence, however, may hinder its return to prominence.

The fundamental psychological law to which Keynes appealed to give shape to his consumption function gave rise 'as a rule, to a greater proportion of income being saved as real income increases' (Keynes, 1935, p. 97). Increased saving that did not get absorbed by increased investment posed a threat as it led to inadequate effective demand, and output and employment below potential. Saving might be a superior good in this view, but hardly a superior social virtue. That the ratio of savings to income rose with income was consistent with budget data available at that time; but, the long-run time series data subsequently prepared by Kuznets did not reveal a change in that ratio (Kuznets, 1952, pp. 507–26). Contradictory evidence further accumulated in the postwar period as functions fitted to short and long-period data revealed different numerical results. Research hounds bayed after these hares.

In an innovative study utilizing four budget studies, Brady and Friedman compared family savings–income ratios to both absolute and relative income, the latter being the ratio of family income to the group mean. An improved fit was obtained in the latter case (Brady and Friedman, 1947, p. 261). Modigliani studied the procyclical movement of the savings rate and related it to the ratio of the aggregate current to highest previous income (Modigliani, 1949). The most comprehensive effort to devise an alternative hypothesis to encompass this evidence was made by the Duesenberry who wrote: 'that for any given relative income distribution, the percentage of income saved by a family will tend to be a unique, invariant, and increasing function of its percentile position in the income distribution' (Duesenberry, 1949, p. 3). On this foundation an aggregate saving or consumption function was erected that reconciled discrepancies in functions fitted to time series and budget data. An additional, and distinct, assertion that the savings, or consumption ratio, depends in the short run on the deflated, per capita ratio of current to prior peak income was required to reconcile functions fitted to long-run and cyclical time series data.

Why should the consumer unit's position in the income distribution matter? Our attention is first directed to the complex and differentiated package of services most commodities yield which consumers in our status-conscious society convert into a commodity quality hierarchy. The frequency of contact which consumers have with superior goods in the hierarchy is closely related to the comparisons they make between their consumption and that of others. This is the 'demonstration effect'.

Equally important is the drive, instilled in every individual's mind by the socialization process, toward a higher standard of living including the consumption of more and better quality goods and services. 'In view of these considerations it seems quite possible that after some minimum income is reached, the frequency and strength of impulses to increase expenditures for one individual depend entirely on the ratio of his expenditures to the expenditures of those with whom he associates' (Duesenberry, 1949, p. 32). Together with the demonstration effect, this drive toward emulation or the making of individious comparisons for which opportunities abound in our society, explain what makes the consumer tick.

In the light of this social psychological argument, the traditional assumption that the utility function of the individual is independent of the functions of others will not do. Duesenberry introduces an interdependent utility function whose arguments are divided by a weighted average of the consumption of other relevant individuals, the weights being those meaningful to the consumer. This system of individual utility functions must be solved simultaneously to obtain demand schedules which are made to depend on current income, current assets, future income, expected future interest rates, and most important, the current consumption of other people. The apparent contradiction between functions fitted to long-run and budget data may be reconciled by the following argument. If all incomes, now and expected, are increased by a factor k, the distribution of income being unchanged, the ratios in the consumption function both in range and domain are unchanged. In the new equilibrium the savings–income ratio is unchanged as everyone has just managed to keep up with the Jones's expenditures. The stagnationist's fear of an increasing savings–income ratio over the long run may be put to rest.

The idea of introducing interdependence into the utility function has not yet commanded general acceptance among economists, suggestive as the arguments are. It has proved difficult so far to deduce many implications from the function that could be subjected to testing. This compares unfavourably with the life cycle–permanent income hypothesis. The consumer unit is looking sidewards at the consumption of peers rather than toward the future, as in more recent research. A rigorous derivation of the implications of the budget constraint has yet to be carried out to reveal precisely how the consumer unit is to finance the invidious, apparently endless, and typically unsuccessful pursuit of material happiness.

There remain short run fluctuations in saving to be explained. A new element was introduced: it was a fundamental psychological postulate 'that it is harder for a family to reduce its expenditure from a high level than for a family to refrain from making high expenditures in the first place' (Duesenberry, 1949, p. 85). This postulate was given the following shape:

$$s/y = a(y/yo) + b$$

where the per capita real variables, in order, are current savings, current disposable income, and highest disposable income ever attained. This yields a changing but calculable multiplier in simple models, and an average greater than the marginal propensity to consume, solidly within the Keynesian tradition. The habitual standard of living appealed to in this saving function was further refined by a proposal to include the previous highest consumption rather than income (Brown, 1952). Lagged consumption has proved highly significant in a statistical sense in a variety of econometric studies; but, rather than habit it has been interpreted as embodying all the information available to the consumer at that time and representing, in a rational expectations point of view, the best forecast of the next period's consumption (Hall, 1978).

The pace and sophistication of quantitative and econometric studies of the relative income hypothesis and related ideas have been such that only a few highlights can be mentioned. The evidence is not conclusive, but has not been kind to the present formulation of the relative income hypothesis. Duesenberry found interesting evidence in Negro and white communities that apparent discrepancies in the saving behaviour by race can be reconciled by plotting the per cent saved against the family's position in the income distribution, instead of absolute income. Differences in group savings–income ratios, however, given comparable income distributions, are better explained in terms of differences in permanent income or life resources, or, more precisely, differences in the ratio of transitory or unexpected income to measured income.

The cyclical saving function when tested against limited data appeared to perform better than a simple function based solely on current income plus trend (Duesenberry, 1949 p. 51 and 82). Tobin compared the relative and absolute income hypotheses using both budget and time series data, however, and found that by modifying the latter with the introduction of a wealth or financial resource measures other than income, the latter did better or at least equalled the quantitative performance of the former (Tobin, 1951, pp. 135–56).

M. Friedman and F. Modigliani, both with associates, opened up a new horizon in consumption research by applying the pure theory of consumer behaviour in its traditional form (maximization of a utility function independent of the functions of others) to the problems of devising a long-run consumption plan. The former addressed the problem of the infinitely lived consumer who could be expected to consume a large proportion of permanent income, defined as the return on human and non-human wealth (Friedman, 1957). The latter addressed the problem of the finitely lived consumer who could be expected to consume at a relatively constant rate the life resources available to him or her (Modigliani, 1986). The implications of the permanent income and life cycle hypotheses have attracted the major share of research attention and their forward looking character has facilitated the application of rational expectations methodology to their development with a further accumulation of supporting evidence (Hall, 1978).

The relative income hypothesis remains as a contribution to

the development of knowledge of consumer behaviour so important for the advancement of macroeconomics. Whether the limitations in theoretical development – relatively few testable implications; difficulties in exploring the meaning of the budget constraint; the incorporation of expectations in an optimal way – can be overcome, constitute open questions.

RICHARD F. KOSOBUD

See also CONSUMPTION FUNCTION; LIFE CYCLE HYPOTHESIS.

BIBLIOGRAPHY

Brady, D.S. and Friedman, R.D. 1947. Savings and income distribution. In *Studies in Income and Wealth* No. 9, New York: National Bureau of Economic Research.

Brown, T.M. 1952. Habit persistence and lags in consumer behaviour. *Econometrica* 20, July, 355–71.

Duesenberry, J.S. 1949. *Income, Savings and the Theory of Consumer Behavior*. Cambridge, Mass.: Harvard University Press.

Friedman, M. 1957. *A Theory of the Consumption Function*. Princeton: Princeton University Press.

Hall, R.E. 1978. Stochastic implications of the life cycle–permanent income hypothesis: theory and evidence. *Journal of Political Economy* 86(6), December, 971–87.

Keynes, J.M. 1936. *The General Theory of Employment, Interest and Money*. London: Macmillan.

Kuznets, S. 1952. Proportion of capital formation to national product. *American Economic Review, Papers and Proceedings* 42, May, 507–26.

Modigliani, F. 1949. Fluctuations in the saving-income ratio: a problem in economic forecasting. In *Studies in Income and Wealth* No. 11, New York: National Bureau of Economic Research.

Modigliani, F. 1986. Life cycle, individual thrift, and the wealth of nations. *American Economic Review* 76(3), June, 297–313.

Tobin, J. 1951. Relative income, absolute income, and savings. In *Money, Trade, and Economic Growth, in Honor of John Henry Williams*, ed. H.L. Waitzman, New York: Macmillan.

relativity, principle of, in political economy. The principle that the economic doctrines true for any given epoch are relative to the particular circumstances of that epoch, and cannot be regarded as permanent or true for all times, is an essential element in the teaching of the historical school of economists. The idea of the relativity of economic doctrines follows easily from the conception of economic life as exhibiting continuous organic growth and development, and this conception is itself the natural outcome of historical study.

Richard Jones and Friedrich List are to be regarded as important forerunners of the historical movement rather than as themselves typical representatives of the movement itself. What is most characteristic, however, in their teaching is the insistence upon relativity in two particular spheres; and a brief reference to their views will serve to illustrate what is meant by the principle of relativity in general. Jones specially insisted on the limited applicability of the Ricardian theory of rent as regards both place and time. A theory based on the assumptions of individual ownership and freedom of competition could not, he pointed out, apply to oriental states of society in which joint ownership is the rule and rents are regulated by custom, nor even to those instances nearer home in which land is held on a customary tenure, as in the métayer system. Similarly, as regards limitation in time, he showed that the Ricardian law could not hold good in a condition of affairs such as existed in medieval economy, when land was to a great extent held in common, and the relations between the owners and the tillers of the soil were not controlled by free competition. Turning to List, we find that his defence of protective duties is based on the recognition of relativity in the conditions of economic productivity in a community. The foundation of the argument is the position that all civilized communities of the temperate zone pass through successive economic stages, of which the last three are the stage of agriculture pure and simple, the stage of agriculture combined with manufactures in a nascent and slowly developing condition, and then the stage in which agriculture, manufactures, and commerce have all reached a high and well-balanced development. In the purely agricultural stage free trade with richer and more developed countries is, in List's view, a necessary condition of advance, and in the last stage of all free trade is also advantageous. On the other hand, the training and development required for passing from the second stage to the third can be acquired only by means of a carefully arranged protective system; and in the second stage such a system is, therefore, necessary for progress. The solution of the problem of protection *versus* free trade is thus regarded as relative to each particular people, and the stage of development which they have reached.

The principle of relativity in the sphere of economics was expressed in a more general form by Wilhelm Roscher. Applying to economic phenomena ideas which writers on jurisprudence had already applied to legal institutions and conceptions, he insisted on the necessity of always taking into consideration the varying character of economic habits and conditions; and, in particular, he pointed out the fallacy of criticizing economic institutions, regardless of a people's history, and the stage of social and industrial development to which they had attained. Karl Knies affirmed still more definitely the relativity of economic doctrines in opposition to what he termed the *absolutism of theory*, that is, the claim – explicitly put forward by some of the older writers, and tacitly assumed by others – to offer something that is true unconditionally and in the same way for all times, lands, and nationalities.

> In opposition to the absolutism of theory, the historical conception of political economy rests [says Knies] upon the fundamental principle that the theory of political economy, in whatever form we find it, is, like economic life itself, a product of historical development; that it grows and develops, in living connection with the whole social organism, out of conditions of time, space, and nationality; that it has the source of its arguments in historical life, and ought to give to its results the character of historical solutions; that the laws of political economy should not be set forth otherwise than as historical explanations and progressive manifestations of the truth; that they represent at each stage the generalizations of truths known up to a certain point of development, and neither in substance nor in form can be declared unconditionally complete; and that the absolutism of theory – even when it gains recognition at a certain period of historical development – itself exists only as the offspring of the time, and marks but a stage in the historical development of political economy (*Die politische Ökonomie von geschichtlichen Standpunkte*, pp. 24, 25). This extract may be regarded as expressing the general view as to the relativity of economic doctrines taken by the historical school distinctively so-called.

The relativity of current political economy is affirmed no less definitely, but from quite a different point of view, by Walter Bagehot, who regards it of importance expressly to limit the science to one particular kind of society, namely, 'a society of grown-up competitive commerce', such as we find in the most highly civilized modern communities. Political economy is, in other words, limited to 'the theory of commerce, as commerce tends more and more to be when capital increases and competition grows'. It will be observed that whilst the object of the historical school is to concentrate attention on economic history and on the study of economic development as opposed to the study of economic relations in a given society, Bagehot's object is just the reverse. He wishes to concentrate attention on current economic phenomena, and to avoid the distraction that must result from turning aside to the superficially corresponding but yet essentially different phenomena of earlier epochs.

In endeavouring to form an estimate of the importance to be attached to the relativity of economic doctrines we shall do well to have regard (1) to the distinction between economic theorems and economic precepts, and (2) as regards economic theorems, to the distinction between abstract and concrete economics.

Roscher in his affirmation of relativity is thinking mainly of economic institutions and economic policy, and in this sphere the principle of relativity may be laid down with less qualification than when we are dealing with economic laws in the more strictly scientific sense, that is, with statements of uniformities as distinguished from recommendations as to what ought or ought not to be done in practice. It is only by the aid of abstraction that any claim to universality can be made good, and in formulating an economic policy, we cannot profitably carry abstraction very far. In theoretical investigations hypothesis and abstraction are often indispensible; but when we apply our theory with the object of laying down rules of practice, it is desirable to have recourse to hypothesis but sparingly. It is indeed doubtful how far, in the examination and criticism of economic institutions and policies, we can advantageously carry our abstraction even to the stage of neglecting social considerations of the purely non-economic character. Both the social and the economic bearings of a given line of action will, however, vary with the circumstances of different nations and different ages. Hence a given economic policy can in general be recommended only for nations having particular social and economic surroundings, and having reached a certain stage of economic development. It may be possible to formulate as having universal validity certain negative precepts, namely, that certain lines of action cannot under any circumstances be advisable; but on the whole the principle of relativity may be broadly accepted so far as economic precepts are concerned.

Passing from economic precepts to the body of positive doctrine which constitutes more distinctively the science of political economy, attention must be paid to the fact that economic doctrines vary in the degree of abstraction which they involve. Without professing to be able to draw any hard and fast line, we may adopt the suggestion made by W.S. Jevons, and distinguish broadly between two stages of economic doctrine, which may be called the abstract and the concrete stage respectively. Concrete economics is not content with merely hypothetical results, but avowedly takes into account special conditions of time, place, and circumstance; and it follows immediately that the conclusions already arrived at with regard to the relativity of economic precepts apply equally to concrete economic theorems. For the more fully we have regard to special conditions of time, place, and circumstance, the more limited must be the applicability of our results. Many of the circumstances which exert an important influence on economic phenomena vary widely with the legal form of society and with national character and institutions; and even when the same forces are in operation there may be variation to an almost indefinite extent in the relative influence which they exert. The contrasts presented by medieval and modern societies, and by contemporary oriental and European societies, considered in their economic aspects, are such as cannot possibly be overlooked. Many of the chief economic phenomena, such as rent, profit, exchange, have their counterparts on each side of the comparison, but are singularly unlike in many of their characteristics; and over and above this, as societies progress, new economic phenomena, practically novel is character, spring into existence. Consider, for example, modern problems of credit and of international trade; or again, the relations between the modern factory operative and the modern capitalist employer. Less striking contrasts, but contrasts that ought not to be neglected, are observable when we consider different modern communities of the European type in respect of particular economic phenomena, such as the tenure of land, the mobility of labour, and so forth. In every case the extent of the divergence can be ascertained only by direct observation and comparison; and it may be remarked in passing that as regards medieval and modern societies, whilst there was formerly danger of the differences being insufficiently emphasized, there is perhaps at the present time more danger of their being exaggerated. The notion, for example, that during the middle ages the forces of competition were entirely inoperative, is far from being borne out by the facts.

The relativity of concrete economic doctrines having been admitted, a claim for universality may still be put forward so far as the more abstract principles of the science are concerned. These principles do not profess to set forth the full empirical reality. They are admittedly based on hypothesis and abstraction. They require therefore to be constantly qualified and limited, sometimes in one direction, sometimes in another before they can serve for the interpretation and explanation of actual economic phenomena. At the same time, some at least of them are universal in the sense that they pervade all economic reasoning. The law of the variation of utility with quantity of commodity, and the principle that every man so far as he is free to choose will choose the greater apparent good, may be given as examples of fundamental economic principles, which, in the words of Jevons, 'are so widely true and applicable that they may be considered universally true as regards human nature'. There are many other principles, which, with due modifications, are applicable to economic phenomena under widely different conditions. Take, for instance, the law of substitution in the form that where different methods of production are available for obtaining a given result, the one that can do the work the most cheaply will in time supersede the others, or the doctrine that facilities of transport tend to level values in different places, while facilities of preservation tend to level values at different times. Compare, again, the Ricardian law of rent as ordinarily stated, with the principle of economic rent in its most abstract and generalized form. The Ricardian law, so far as it claims to determine the actual payments made by the cultivators of the soil, is a relative doctrine, that is to say, it is based on assumptions which, as regards both time and place, hold good over a limited range only. The theory of economic rent in its most generalized form, however, merely affirms that where different portions of the total amount of any commodity of uniform quality supplied to the same market are produced at different costs, those portions which are raised at the smaller costs will yield a differential profit; and there is now no similar limitation to its applicability. This principle may even be said to hold good in a socialistic community, for the differential profit does not cease to exist either by being ignored or by being municipalized or nationalized. To take a further illustration, there is a good deal of abstract reasoning in regard to the laws of supply and demand that has a very wide application indeed. These laws work themselves out differently under different conditions, and in particular there are differences in the rapidity with which they operate. Their operation may, however, be detected beneath the surface even in states of society where custom exerts the most rigid sway. In all these cases and others similar the principles involved and the modes of investigation employed have a significance and importance which it would be misleading to call merely relative; and hence as regards the more abstract portions of economic doctrine the principle of relativity cannot be accepted.

The relativity of concrete economic truths, together with the universality of fundamental economic principles, might be illustrated by reference to the writings of the classical English economists. The historical school have rightly taught us that the works of these economists can be fully understood and appreciated only if they are studied in close connection with the economic history of the times when they wrote. Frequently the assumptions on which their reasonings are based have a special relation to the actual circumstances of their time; or, even if this is not the case, the form in which their doctrines are cast, or the emphasis laid upon particular points, will often be found to be specially related to the economic conditions in the midst of which they wrote. It is, however, going much too far to regard their whole teaching as limited throughout by the character of relativity which belongs to some of it. Much of what they wrote will be valuable for all time, not merely because of the light which their doctrines throw on the phenomena of particular periods, but because the principles underlying their best work are not confined in their applicability to any narrow or limited sphere.

In connection with the general subject of relativity in political economy, a word or two may be added with regard to the relativity of economic definitions. Partly on account of the familiarity of much of its subject-matter, and partly for reasons connected with the growth of the science, political economy is for the most part limited in its nomenclature to terms already in common use. In different departments of economic enquiry, however, lines of distinction may need to be drawn at rather different points, and hence it is sometimes difficult to avoid the multiplication of technical terms, unless we are content to use the same terms in slightly varying senses in different connections. Thus, from the point of view of production it may be convenient to give a definition of wealth, not in all respects identical with the definition that is appropriate from the standpoint of distribution. Again, with special reference to its measurement, there may be advantages in defining wealth differently from the cosmopolitan, national, and individual points of view respectively. This procedure, that is to say, the frank adoption of the principle of relativity in framing economic definitions, has considerable weight of authority in its favour; but it is clear that, in so far as it is adopted, special precautions are necessary to avoid confusion. Further, economic definitions may be relative, not only to different points of view or different departments of study, but also to different stages of industrial development. Thus, in relation to the complex conditions of modern trade and industry, such terms as market and money may need different definitions from those that are appropriate in relation to more primitive conditions. Whilst, however, many economic definitions may be allowed to possess a relative or progressive character, this relativity cannot be extended to the ultimate analysis of the fundamental conceptions of the science. If these conceptions assume a some-what different character in different connections, we shall still find something generic or universal in each one of them. Hence in the case of economic definitions as well as in that of economic doctrines, the admission of the principle of relativity must not be absolute or unqualified.

[J.N. KEYNES]

Reprinted from *Palgrave's Dictionary of Political Economy.*

renewable resources. A resource stock may be termed 'renewable' if constant periodic removals from it can be indefinitely prolonged. A renewable resource may be further classified as depletable or nondepletable, according to whether or not its productivity is affected by the level of exploitation. Biological resources such as fish, bird and animal populations, forests, grasslands and agricultural soils, provide examples of the depletable type, while surface water resources, solar and geothermal energy may be classified as nondepletable.

ECONOMIC ANALYSIS. In spite of the absolute dependence of all economic systems upon renewable resources, no detailed economic analysis of the economics of renewal resources as such was attempted until the mid-20th century. Renewable resources were simply subsumed under the concept of economic rent of land, defined by Ricardo as 'that portion of the produce of the earth which is paid to the landlord for the use of the original and indestructible powers of the soil' (Ricardo, 1817). But expansion of human populations and technological development throughout the 19th century gradually resulted in the depletion, sometimes to the point of extinction, of once superabundant renewable resource stocks. (A famous example, the passenger pigeon of Eastern North America, once the New World's most abundant bird species and a resource of economic significance in colonial America, had passed into extinction by 1914.) Such development made it clear that the original powers of the soil were in fact far from indestructible. Popular concern with resource issues led to the 'conservation movement' of the early 20th century, resulting in legislation devoted toward the preservation of agricultural, forest and wildlife resources.

Theoretical analysis of the role of renewable resources in economics was hindered by the inevitable temporal dimension of resource exploitation, necessitating the use of dynamic models and the calculus of variations (see Hotelling, 1931). Works devoted to verbal analysis of 'the economics of conservation', such as those of Ciriacy-Wantrup (1952) and Scott (1955), set the stage for subsequent comprehensive theoretical treatment of resource economics by variational techniques. Finally by the 1970s, a major expansion of public interest in the 'environment', and in the 'limits to growth' (Meadows et al., 1972), combined with such resource-associated events as the OPEC cartelization of petroleum production and the collapse of major marine fisheries, led the economics profession to take a serious interest in resource and environmental issues – if merely in some instances to defuse the public hysteria. Theoretical developments in constrained dynamic optimization had meanwhile greatly improved the requisite mathematical techniques.

A generalized model of resource exploitation by private or public resource owners may be expressed as follows:

$$\frac{dx}{dt} = G(x) - h(t), \qquad t \geqslant 0 \tag{1}$$

$$x(0) = x_0, \qquad x(t) \geqslant 0, \qquad h(t) \geqslant 0 \tag{2}$$

$$\pi = \pi[x(t), h(t), t] \tag{3}$$

$$V(x_0) = \max_{[h(t)]} \int_0^\infty \alpha(t)\pi \, dt \tag{4}$$

in which $x(t)$ denotes the size ('state') of the resource stock at time t, $G(x)$ is the natural rate of replenishment, $h(t)$ is the rate of removals, or 'harvest', of the resource, π denotes the net flow of economic benefits at time t and $V(x_0)$ is the optimized present value of net benefits, relative to the discount factor

$$\alpha(t) = \exp\left[-\int_0^t r(s)\, ds\right] \tag{5}$$

where $r(s)$ is the instantaneous rate of discount at time s.

The specification $G(x) \equiv 0$ provides a general exhaustible resource model. A renewable resource model is obtained by allowing G to depend on the resource stock x, with $G(x)=0$ for some $\bar{x}>0$ and $G(x)>0$ for $0<x<\bar{x}$. For the case of a biological resource stock one would assume that $G(0)=0$: a nondepletable resource could be modelled (not very well) by assuming $G(0)>0$. For the latter two cases, $\bar{x}$ represents the natural, or environmental 'carrying capacity' for the given stock.

A popular, widely accepted objective of renewable resource management is the so-called 'maximum sustained yield' (MSY), characterized simply by the equation

$$h_{\text{MSY}} = \max_x G(x). \tag{6}$$

According to this principle, any renewable resource stock should be maintained at the level $x=x_{\text{MSY}}$ at which its exploitable productivity $G(x)$ is a maximum. Perpetuation of MSY has indeed been considered as the sacred and sole trust of many resource management agencies, seldom with any cognizance of the economic implications of such a policy. Not infrequently the resource industry itself seems to exhibit a preference for some quite different objective.

The solution of the optimization problem of equation (4) is characterized by the following necessary conditions:

$$\pi_h = \lambda(t) \tag{7}$$

$$G_x + \frac{\pi_x}{\pi_h} = r(t) - \frac{\dot{\lambda}(t)}{\lambda(t)} \tag{8}$$

where $\lambda(t)$ denotes the current 'shadow price' (formerly, user cost) of the resource stock, equal to the marginal value of the resource stock $x(t)$, and where subscripts designate partial derivatives and overdot the time derivative.

If π does not depend explicitly on time t, and if $r(t)=r$ is constant, equation (8) possesses an equilibrium solution $x=x^*$ determined by

$$G_x + \pi_x/\pi_h = r \tag{9}$$

$$h = G(x). \tag{10}$$

Equation (9) is recognizable as the standard marginal productivity rule of optimal capital accumulation, in which marginal productivity G_x is equated to the discount rate r. The correction term π_x/π_h arises from the fact that x and $G(x)$ are specified in physical units, rather than as asset and flow values, respectively (see Clark, 1976, ch. 3).

In the event that $\pi_x \equiv 0$ (costs and benefits independent of stock level x) and $r=0$, equation (9) becomes $G_x=0$, namely $x = x_{\text{MSY}}$, the MSY solution. In general, under the reasonable assumptions that $G_{xx}<0$ and $\pi_x>0$, $\pi_h>0$, we see from equation (9) that (i) discounting tends to decrease x^*, whereas (ii) the dependence of π on x tends to increase x^*, relative to the MSY solution. The numerical significance of these effects can only be assessed by estimating model parameters for particular cases.

The effects of discounting. A theme that runs through much of the conservation literature pertains to the effect of discounting, or time-preference, on the conservation of resource stocks. Pigou, for example, says that

> There is widespread agreement that the state should protect the interests of the future in some degree against the effects of irrational discounting, and of our preference for ourselves over our descendants. The whole movement for 'conservation' in the United States is based upon this conviction. (Pigou, 1920, p. 29, as quoted by Scott, 1955).

This raises the question of whether the social rate of time preference differs, or ought to differ, from the market rate.

For the case of renewable resources, equation (9) suggests that the effect of discounting will be large when G_x is small. Since G_x represents marginal growth rate of the resource stock, we conclude that discounting will be especially important for resource stocks having low growth rates (although the effect of π_x/π_h must also be considered).

Biological resources exhibit a wide range of growth rates. Some species, called '*r*-selected' by ecologists, are highly fecund: populations consisting of numerous small individuals expand rapidly to take advantage of environmental opportunities. At the opposite end of the growth spectrum are large, slow growing '*K*-selected' species, which are also often highly valued and easily exploited by modern techniques. The latter type, which includes whales and other marine mammals, forests, desert grazing lands, and the like, are particularly subject to severe over-exploitation, both under common-property conditions of exploitation and under private profit maximization by firms employing market rates of discount.

USER CONFLICTS. The paradigm, assumed above, of an isolated renewable resource stock exploited by a sole owner is seriously unrealistic for most actual renewable resource industries. Imperfection of ownership rights, multiple uses and users, and a wide variety of externalities, are the rule rather than the exception in fisheries, forestry, wildlife, water resources, and such like.

Most commercial fisheries, for example, are still exploited under common-property conditions, although the introduction of 200-mile fishing zones in the late 1970s has at least placed the majority of marine fishery resources under national jurisdiction. Wildlife, water, and recreational resources are often also utilized as common-property resources. The historical trend, however, is towards progressive allocation of resource-use rights to individuals, if not via outright sole ownership than vai user permits, quotas and fees. As a general rule, the delineation of resource sub-allocations can be expected to increase along with the economic importance of the resource, but the process is inevitably confounded by political and legislative components.

Over-exploitation of renewable resource stocks and over-expansion of harvest capacity are frequent occurrences in resource industries utilizing non-owned, or commonly owned resources. In the absence of property rights, each exploiter tends to ignore the effects that his own removals will have on the total resource stock and its future production. Thus in a common-property resource industry, the rate of harvest will increase (unless restricted by regulation) to a level at which the marginal exploiter receives zero net revenue:

$$\pi_h = 0. \tag{11}$$

The industry thus behaves as if the shadow price λ of the resource were zero [see equation (7)]. By imposing a removals tax $\tau=\lambda$ per unit of harvested resource, the management authority (should one exist) can in principle force the competitive exploiting industry to utilize the socially optimal rate of exploitation. Resource rents then accrue to the management authority, rather than being dissipated through over-exploitation or over-capacity.

Renewable resource industries impose a variety of externalities upon other resource users. Logging of forests may affect surface water retention and flow. Public demand for parks and wilderness areas may lead to conflicts with resource industries such as forestry, agriculture and hydroelectric power. Pesticides employed to protect forests or crops may damage fish and wildlife populations.

An important long-term externality resulting from the alteration or destruction of natural habitats by resource industries is the progressive loss of genetic material, which may ultimately limit the diversity of domestic crops and animals, and reduce the supply of naturally derived pharmaceutical and industrial compounds (Oldfield, 1984).

Most externalities of his kind increase in economic importance with the intensity of resource exploitation. Consequently the socially optimal exploitation policy will often involve less intensive exploitation than would be practised by private resource owners. Much of the rationale for the establishment of government management authorities doubtlessly stems from these considerations. The fact that the external costs of resource exploitation are often much longer lasting than the internal benefits adds to the need for timely government regulation.

RESOURCE MANAGEMENT. Numerous management agencies have been established to regulate the exploitation of renewable resources such as water supplies, marine and freshwater fish stocks, wildlife populations and forests. Such agencies face many difficulties, including particularly the allocation of a limited supply in the presence of excessive demand, enforcement of regulations, and the problem of dealing with major uncertainties regarding resource inventories, ecosystem dynamics and environmental factors. It is also becoming increasingly recognized that the traditional resource management objective of maximum sustained yield is often not adequate to deal with resource conflicts, multiple uses and externalities of resource use.

Both fiscal and quantitative instruments are frequently employed by resource management agencies. Fees and taxes levied on resource users reduce excess demand for the resource, while collecting resource rent for the public purse. In many localities where resource-based industries dominate the economy, such charges can constitute a major component of state revenue, although a dominant resource industry may have sufficient political influence to prevent the full capture of rents by government.

The degree to which resource taxes can be used in practice as proxies for shadow prices is severely limited by the complexity and uncertainty of both biological and economic systems. Consequently direct regulation is the usual rule, at least for resource industries based on publicly owned resource stocks. Regulation may ultimately pertain to almost evey aspect of exploitation, including time, place, amount and methods of harvest, as well as details of species, size, sex etc. permitted to be taken.

It might of course be argued that the need for such complex systems of regulation would be obtained if ownership were to be transferred entirely to private hands, but this may be neither feasible nor desirable in cases where resource stocks are not readily appropriated, or where significant externalities must be controlled. But it is certainly true that regulations can have perverse economic consequences. An example common by the 1970s was the tendency to regulate commercial fisheries by means of total annual catch quotas. Such non-allocated quotas force individual fishermen into a competitive 'scramble' wherein each attempts to catch as many fish as possible prior to the closure of the fishery. The consequences include unnecessary expansion of fishing capacity in terms of number, size and horsepower of vessels, reduction in the quality of fish and highly uneven rates of delivery of fish to processors and markets.

A potential method for overcoming these problems is the use of allocated quotas: if such quotas are transferable, the price of quotas will play a similar role to a tax on catches. Quota allocations are also of potential value for the regulation of other resources such as water resources and public grazing lands. Monitoring and enforcement are of course essential to the success of any allocated quota system. The quotas must also be flexible, to allow for natural fluctuations in resource abundance.

Fluctuations and uncertainties. Renewable resource industries face significant uncertainties regarding both supply and demand. Unpredictable environmental fluctuations can have large-scale effects on the production and availability of renewable resource stocks, which can in some cases have nationwide or worldwide economic consequences. Unexpected decreases in resource abundance become especially serious when exploitation has reached high levels, with industries or even entire segments of the economy dependent upon the resource. While developed nations may possess institutions to mollify the worst effects of such natural fluctuations, the less developed nations often face economic disaster in times of drought, flood, insect or crop pathogen plagues, or fishery collapses.

Temporary periods of low resource availability can be extremely unpleasant in themselves. But they can also result in severe over-exploitation as the dependent industry continues to harvest the resource in desperation. In extreme cases ultimate recovery may become impossible owing to irreversible destruction of breeding stocks, or of soil productivity. The more infrequent are the bad years, the more likely ultimate disaster may become, as communities grow to rely upon the resource and discount the possibility of a decline.

Resource managers face many kinds of uncertainty beyond that pertaining to the scope and timing of natural fluctuations (Mangel, 1985). The long-term response of depletable resource stocks to exploitation is often difficult if not impossible to predict quantitatively. Even current inventories of resource stocks such as marine populations may be highly uncertain – current estimates of whale stocks in the Antarctic, for example, range over two orders of magnitude. Discerning trends from such inaccurate data often borders on the impossible, but improving the accuracy of the data base is often unacceptably expensive.

In response to such gross levels of uncertainty the risk-averse public resource manager tends to prefer a conservative exploitation policy which minimizes the probability of depletion. The exploiting industry, however, often takes the opposite view, preferring certain current revenues to uncertain future benefits. Since uncertainty increases with the planning horizon, an additional bias towards depletion of renewable resource stocks is observed.

COLIN W. CLARK

See also BIOECONOMICS; EXHAUSTIBLE RESOURCES; FISHERIES; FORESTS.

BIBLIOGRAPHY

Ciriacy-Wantrup, S.V. 1952. *Resource Conservation: Economics and Policies*. Berkeley: Univesity of California Press. 3rd edn, 1968.

Clark, C.W. 1976. *Mathematical Bioeconomics: The Optimal Management of Renewable Resources*. New York: Wiley–Interscience.

Clark, C.W. 1985. *Bioeconomic Modelling and Fisheries Management*. New York: Wiley–Interscience.

Duerr, W.A. 1979. *Forest Resource Management*. Philadelphia: Saunders.

Hotelling, H. 1931. The economics of exhaustible resources. *Journal of Political Economy* 39, April, 137–75.

Mangel, M. 1985. *Decision and Control in Uncertain Resource Systems*. New York: Academic Press.

Meadows, D.H., Meadows, D.L., Randers, J. and Behrens, W.W. 1972. *The Limits to Growth*. New York: Universe Books.

Oldfield, M.L. 1984. *The Value of Conserving Genetic Resources*. Washington, DC: US Department of the Interior.

Pigou, A.C. 1920. *The Economics of Welfare*. London: Macmillan.

Ricardo, D. 1817. *Principles of Political Economy and Taxation*. Ed. R.M. Hartwell, Harmondsworth: Penguin, 1971.

Scott, A.D. 1955. *Natural Resources: The Economics of Conservation*. Toronto: University of Toronto Press. 2nd edn, Toronto: McClelland & Stewart, 1973.

rent. 'Rent' is the payment for use of a resource, whether it be land, labour, equipment, ideas, or even money. Typically the rent for labour is called 'wages'; the payment for land and equipment is often called 'rent'; the payment for use of an idea is called a 'royalty'; and the payment for use of money is called 'interest'. In economic theory, the payment for a resource where the availability of the resource is insensitive to the size of the payment received for its use is named 'economic rent' or 'quasi-rent' depending on whether the insensitivity to price is permanent or temporary.

To early economists, 'rent' meant payments for use of land; Ricardo, in particular, called it the payment for the 'uses of the original and indestructible powers of the soil' (Ricardo, 1821, p. 33). Subsequently, in recognition that a distinctive feature of what was called 'land' was its presumed indestructibility (i.e. insensitivity of amount supplied to its price), the adjective 'economic' was applied to the word 'rent' for any resource the supply of which is indestructible (maintainable for ever at no cost) and non-augmentable, and hence invariant to its price. In the jargon of economics, the quantity of present and future available supply is completely inelastic with respect to price, a situation graphically represented by a vertical supply line in the usual 'Marshallian' price-quantity graphs.

ECONOMIC RENT. The concept of 'economic rent' is graphically depicted by the standard demand and supply lines in Figure 1 with a vertical supply curve (quantity supplied invariant to price) at the amount X_r. At all prices the supply is constant. The entire return to the resource is an 'economic rent'. If the aggregate quantity of such resources may in the future be increased by production of more indestructible units of the resource in response to a higher price (but the amount available at any moment is fixed regardless of the rent for its services), the supply line at the current moment is vertical. The supply curve for future amounts slopes upward from the existing amount, as depicted by the line FF in Figure 1. The long run rent would be P_r and the equilibrium stock would be X_r: at that equilibrium stock the 'market supply' (in Marshall's terminology) would be a vertical line. Thus, the supply of

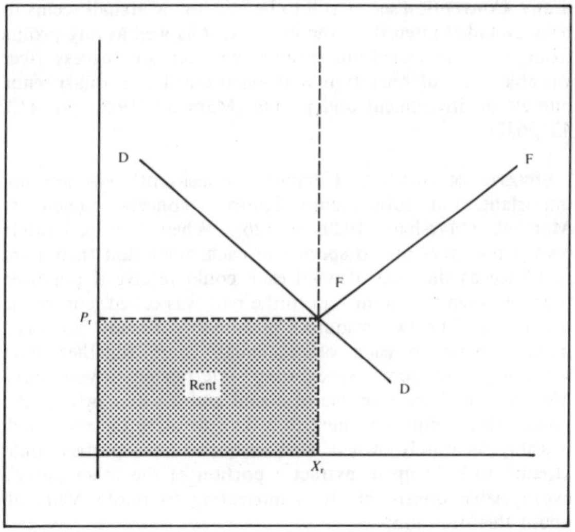

Figure 1

indestructible units would have depended on past anticipated prices about the present prices, but the supply of current units would be insensitive to the current price or rent. The return could be called 'economic rent', except that no convention has been developed with respect to the terminology for this situation of indestructible but augmentable resources.

QUASI-RENT. Closely related to 'economic rent' is 'quasi-rent', a term apparently initiated by Alfred Marshall (Marshall, 1920, pp. 74, 424–6). Because virtually every existing resource is unresponsive to a change in price for at least some very small length of time, the return to every resource is like an 'economic rent' for at least a short interval of time. In time, the supplied amount will be altered, either by production or non-replacement of current items. Yet, the fact that the amount available is not instantly affected by price led to the term 'quasi-rent', which denotes a return, variations in which do not affect the current amount supplied to the demander but do affect the supply in the future.

If a rental (payments) stream to an existing resource is not sufficient to recover the costs incurred in its production the durability of that existing resource will nevertheless enable the resource to continue to provide services, at least for some limited time. In other words, because of the resource's durability it will continue for some interval to yield services even at a rent insufficient to recover its cost of production, but sufficient for current costs of use including interest on its salvage value (which is its highest value in some other use). Any excess over those current costs is a 'quasi-rent'.

Quasi-rent resembles an 'economic rent' in that it exceeds the amount required for its current use, albeit temporarily – except that a flow of rents that did not cover all 'quasi-rent' would preserve it for only a finite future interval, after which the resource would be diminished until not worth more than its salvage value. If the resource received a payment exceeding all the initially anticipated and the realized costs of production and operation, it will have achieved a profit, that is, more than pure interest on the resource's investment cost. The question exists as to whether 'quasi-rent' means just that portion of the rent in excess of the minimum operating costs over the remaining life of the asset, or all the excess, including profits, if any. Convention seems still to be missing. Marshall seems to have excluded interest on the investment as well as any profits from what he called quasi-rents, so that any excess over variable costs of operation were partitioned into quasi-rents, interest on investment and profits (Marshall, 1920, pp. 412, 421, 622).

COMPOSITE QUASI-RENT. 'Composite quasi-rent' was another important, but subsequently ignored, concept coined by Marshall (Marshall, 1920, p. 626). When two separately owned resources are so specific to each other that their joint rent exceeds the sum of what each could receive if not used together, then that joint rent to the pair was called 'composite quasi-rent'. The two resources presumably already had been made specific to each other (worth more together than separately) by some specializing interrelated investments. Marshall cited the example of a mill and a water power site, presumably a mill built next to a dam to serve the mill, each possibly separately owned. One or both of the parties could attempt to hold up or extract a portion of the other party's expropriable quasi-rent. It is interesting to quote Marshall about this situation:

> The mill would probably not be put up till an agreement had been made for the supply of water power for a term of years; but at the end of that term similar difficulties would arise as to the division of the aggregate producer's surplus afforded by the water power and the site with the mill on it. For instance, at Pittsburg when manufacturers had just put up furnaces to be worked by natural gas instead of coal, the price of the gas was suddenly doubled. And the history of mines affords many instances of difficulties of this kind with neighbouring landowners as to rights of way, etc., and with the owners of neighbouring cottages, railways and docks (Marshall, 1920, p. 454).

A reason for attributing importance to the concept of 'composite quasi-rent' is now apparent. If it arises with resources that have been made specific to each other in the sense that the service value of each depends on the other's presence, the joint value of composite quasi-rent might become the object of attempted expropriation by one of the parties, especially by the one owning the resource with controllable flow of high alternative use value. To avoid or reduce the possibility of this behaviour, a variety of preventative arrangements, contractual or otherwise, can be used prior to making the investments in resources of which at least one will become specific to the other. These include, among a host of possibilities: joint ownership, creation of a firm to own both, hostages and bonding, reciprocal dealing, governmental regulation, and use of insurers to monitor uses of interspecific assets. This is not the place to discuss these arrangements, beyond asserting that without the concept of 'quasi-rent' and especially 'expropriable quasi-rent' – which Marshall called 'composite quasi-rent' – a vast variety of institutional arrangements would otherwise be inexplicable as a means of increasing the effectiveness of economic activity.

Though Marshall briefly mentioned similar problems between employers and employees, I have not found any subsequent exposition by him about the precautionary contractual arrangements and institutions that attempt to avoid this problem, which has become a focus of substantial important research on what is called, variously, 'opportunism, shirking, expropriable quasi-rents, principal–agent conflicts, monitoring, problems of measuring performance, asymmetric information, etc.'.

RICARDIAN RENT. The rents accruing to different units of some otherwise homogeneous resource may differ and result in differences of rent over the next most valued use, differences that are called 'Ricardian rents'. This occurs where the individual units, all regarded as of the same 'type' in other uses, are actually different with respect to some significant factor for its use *here*, though this factor, which is pertinent *here*, is irrelevant in any other uses. Examples of such factors can be location, special fertility, or talent that is disregarded in the other potential uses. For some questions, the inaccurate 'homogenization' can be a convenient simplification, but for explaining each unit's actual rents, it can lead to confusion and misunderstanding. The service value, hence rents, for the use of the services here may differ, though equal in every relevant respect elsewhere. Whether the specific use uniqueness is created by natural talent or sheer accident, the special differences in use value here imply differences in payments, often called 'Ricardian rents' to distinguish them from differences in rents (prices) obtained because of monopolizing or unnatural restrictions on any potential competitors, which may lead to higher rents, called 'monopoly rents' for the protected resources.

DIFFERENTIAL RENTS. 'Differential rents' are another category representing rent differences in a sort of reverse homogeneity. Units of resource that are equal with respect to their value in use *here* differ among themselves in their values of use elsewhere. This can be represented graphically as in Figure 2. The differential rents of successive units are represented by the differences between the price line and the curve RR, which arrays the units from those with the lowest alternative use values to the highest, a curve labelled RR. The arrayed units are not homogeneous for uses elsewhere, so even if identical for use here, calling them successive units of the same good is misleading. They are not totally homogeneous; if they were, each unit would have the same as any other unit's use value and rent elsewhere. A curve like RR is equivalent to Marshall's particular expenses curve, which arrayed units according to each individual unit's cost of production, or use value elsewhere, from lowest to highest (Marshall, 1920, p. 810n). The difference between price or rent here and the

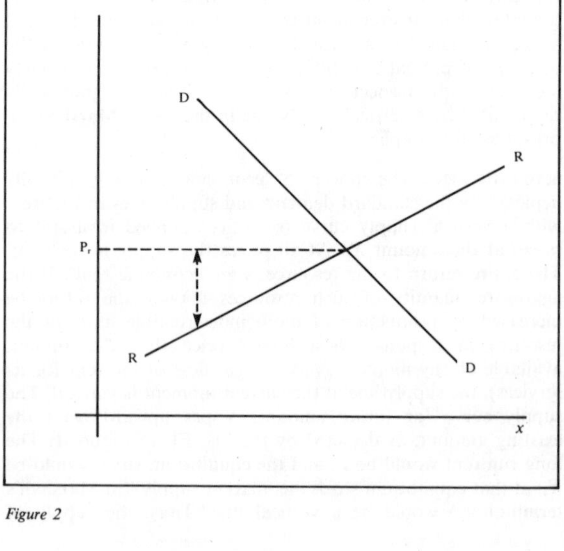

Figure 2

value on the RR curve is called 'producers' surplus' or 'differential rent'. In sum, 'Ricardian rents' indicate differences in rents to units that are equal in their best alternative use values, but different in their rent value here, while 'differential rents' are the premia to units that are the same value here but different in their best alternative use values.

It is worth digressing to note that an upward rising true supply curve, which reflects increasing marginal costs of production, is different from the RR curve. In the true supply curve the area between the supply curve and the price line does not represent any of the above mentioned rents nor 'producers' surplus' (as it does with the RR curve). It is the portion of earnings of the supplier that exceed the variable costs and are applicable to cover the costs (possibly past investment costs) that are invariant to the rate of output. That area does not represent any excess of rental or sale value of units produced over their full costs, since only the variable costs are under the marginal cost curve. It represents the classic distribution of income to capital, if, for example, labour is presumed to be a variable input and capital a fixed input.

HIGH RENTS A RESULT, NOT CAUSE, OF HIGH PRICES. An earlier unfortunate analytic confusion occurred in the common misimpression that high rents of land made its products more expensive. Thus the high rent of land in New York was and is still often believed to make the cost of living, or the cost of doing business, higher in New York. Or higher rent for some agricultural land is believed to increase the cost of growing corn on that land. Proper attention to the meaning of 'demand' and 'costs' would have helped avoid that confusion. Demand *here* for some unit for resource is the highest value use of that resource if used *here*. The cost of using it *here* is the highest valued forsaken alternative act elsewhere. For any resource the cost of its use *here* is its best value elsewhere, that is, its demand elsewhere. Land rent is high for 'this' use because the land's value in some other use is high. The reason the rent is high *here* and can be paid is that its use value *here* is bid by competitors for its use *here* into the offered rent and exceeds the value in some other use. The product of the land can get higher price *here*; that is why the rent is bid up so high, even though the particular winning bidder then believes a high price of the products must be obtained because the rent was high, rather than the reverse. As with every marketable resource, its highest value use *here* determines its rent, rather than the reverse. It was the implication of this kind of analysis that Marshall attempted to summarize in the famous aphorism, which he attributed to Ricardo (1817): 'Rent does not enter into [Money] Cost of production' (Marshall, 1890, p. 482).

Probably the source of the confusion in believing that high rents of land caused high prices for products produced on expensive land is that an individual user of that expensive resource has to be able to charge a higher price for the product, if the rent is to be covered. Bidders for that land compete for the right to the land that can yield a service worth so much – though to any individual successful bidder that rent has to be paid regardless of how well the successful bidder may be at actually achieving the highest valued use of the land. Hence it may appear to an individual bidder that the rent determines the price that must be charged, rather than, as is the correct interpretation, the achievable high valued use enables the high bid for the land for the person best able to detect and achieve that highest valued use.

FUNCTION OF RENT. Some people were aware of this bidding for the 'land' and concluded that the rent served no social purpose, since the land would exist anyway. But the high receipt resulting from competitive bidding for its uses serves a useful purpose. It reveals which uses are the highest valued and directs the land to that use. In principle, a 100 per cent tax on the land rent would not alter its supply (assuming initially that 'land' is the name of whatever has a fixed indestructible supply). This would be correct if in this case the 'owner' of the land had any incentive left to heed the highest bidder where the highest bid determines the rent. The assertion assumes that somehow the highest valued use can be known and that amount of tax be levied without genuine bona fide competitive bids for its use, a dubious if not plainly false proposition.

MONOPOLY RENT. Let the word 'monopoly' denote any seller whose wealth potential is increased by restrictions on other potential competitors, restrictions that are artificial or contrived in not being naturally inevitable. Laws prohibiting others from selling white wine, or opening restaurants, or engaging in legal practice are examples. It should be immediately emphasized that this does not imply nor is it to be inferred that all such restrictions are demonstrably undesirable. Nevertheless, the increased wealth potential is a 'monopoly rent'. Whether it is realized by the monopolist as an increase in wealth depends upon the costs of competing for the imposition of such restrictions. Competition for 'monopoly rents' may transfer them to, for example, politicians who impose the restrictions, and in turn may be dissipated by competition among politicians seeking to be in a position to grant such favours. The 'monopoly rents' may be dissipated (by what is often called 'rent-seeking' competition for such monopoly status of rights to grant it) into competitive payments for resources that enable people to achieve status to grant such restrictions. Those who initially successfully and cheaply obtained such 'monopoly' status may obtain a wealth increase, just as successful innovators obtain a profit stream before it is eliminated by competition from would-be imitators.

ARMEN A. ALCHIAN

See also ABSOLUTE RENT; ANDERSON, JAMES; EXTENSIVE AND INTENSIVE RENT; LAND RENT; MALTHUS, THOMAS ROBERT; MARSHALL, ALFRED; RICARDO, DAVID; SCARCITY; THÜNEN, JOHANN HEINRICH VON; WEST, EDWARD.

BIBLIOGRAPHY

Marshall, A. 1890. *Principles of Economics*. 1st edn, London: Macmillan.

Marshall, A. 1920. *Principles of Economics*. 8th edn, London: Macmillan; reprinted, 1946.

Ricardo, D. 1821. *Principles of Political Economy and Taxation*. 3rd edn, London: Dent Dutton, 1965.

rent control. Rent control, found the world over, is an arrangement under which a governmental agency prescribes the maximum rents private landlords may charge for accommodation, as the control is intended to benefit tenants. In Section I it is argued that rent control can help existing tenants, but only if it is accompanied by additional legal measures. Since the details of these legal measures change over time, and vary across areas, only examples can be provided to illustrate the argument. Yet, whatever these legal measures, rent control can not help *potential* tenants (except in unusual circumstances, e.g. when landlords expect it to be temporary). In Section II we examine why rent control leads to inefficiency.

I. Text-book treatments of price control in competitive markets stress that, for maximum price control to be effective, the ceiling price must be below the market clearing price. This condition is necessary, but not sufficient. Consider a government enacting a law which stipulates a ceiling rent for specified kinds of accommodation, unaccompanied by any other legal provisions. Assuming landlords do not expect a future tightening of the law, its effects would be short-lived. Tenants with unexpired leases would enjoy lower rents until their leases expired. What landlords did as leases expired would depend on other provisions of the law, for example, whether *all* tenancies, or only *existing ones*, for the class of accommodation defined were subject to the control. If the latter were the case, existing tenants could be offered new leases at market rents; if the former were the case, landlords would face a number of options, among them the sale of dwellings into owner occupation, the exercise of which would imply that rent control ceased to be effective. These examples suffice to show that the mere fixing of rent ceilings below the market clearing level cannot ensure the effectiveness of rent control. Additional measures are required.

The most obvious and usual measure is to accompany rent ceilings with security of tenure, i.e. with the tenants' right to remain in controlled dwellings for as long as rent control remains in force (a period inherently difficult to predict, for political reasons), provided they pay the ceiling rent. Security of tenure is an implicit form of rationing, which renders legally null and void the expiry dates of previously signed leases. If the purpose of rent control were only the protection of existing tenants, then this measure, accompanied by effective prevention of harassment (Cullingworth, 1979, p. 68), would be sufficient to protect them at the expense of their landlords (a qualification of this is noted below, Section II).

However, sometimes rent control legislation also provides security of tenure for new tenants, as, for example, in the 1965 Rent Act in the UK. If this is done, rent control is viewed, not merely as an emergency measure, but as a '...long-term ... policy for the privately rented sector' (Cullingworth, 1979, p. 67). It is important to consider what effects such a policy has, in additional to the effects just described. This can not be done in the absence of additional information about the law, in particular, about the legality of landlords charging premiums (key money) for new tenancies. If landlords are permitted to charge key money then rent control might not prevent market-clearing for new tenancies (assuming that landlords do not expect a retro-active tightening of the law, involving, e.g., a requirement to refund key money). If a market persisted, would the total rental cost be the same as that in an uncontrolled market? The answer sometimes suggested is that the cost would be the same, as key money would approximate '...the discounted present value of the difference between the expected market rent and the controlled rent over the relevant period' (Cheung, 1979, p. 28). This appears to ignore two differences between these alternative situations. First, prospective tenants would find borrowing for premiums difficult, since a tenancy is 'poor' collateral, and, if the landlord were the lender, he could not evict the tenant for non-repayment of the loan. Second, for any given premium, the cost to the tenant and the benefit to the landlord would decrease with the length of the tenant's stay. With security of tenure (see below) any agreement on the term of the tenancy would be unenforceable. Landlords would know that tenants have an incentive dishonestly to express an intention to stay for a short period. Tenants would know that, should they wish to stay less long than they had originally intended, they would face bargaining problems with their landlords on wishing to terminate the tenancy (see below, Section II). These strategic considerations suggest that some mutually advantageous bargains would be inhibited, and that the outcome would not approximate the situation in which the duration of leases can be freely negotiated. It has been suggested that 'statutory law is powerless to suppress...' the taking of key money, which can be easily 'disguised' (Cheung, 1979, p. 28). This cannot be true as a general statement unless it is qualified. U.K. statutory law (as consolidated in the Rent Act 1977, Section 126) appears to have suppressed exchanges of key money for residential tenancies, since otherwise the drying up of the supply of the latter – see below – would be difficult to explain, (assuming that, with key money, a market would exist).

In the absence of premiums landlords will be unwilling to offer new tenancies for the class of accommodation to which rent control applies. Text-book treatments (e.g. Le Grand and Robinson, 1984, pp. 96-99) do not stress the differential effects of rent control on existing, as against potential, tenants, and thus omit an indispensable element in the explanation of the drying up of the supply of new tenancies. That element is the legal status of security of tenure for statutory tenants (*Baxter* v. *Eckersley* [1950], 480 at 485). The kind of legislation which prevailed, e.g., in the UK from 1965–80, greatly increased the actual, and potential, number of statutory tenants. Under that kind of law a new tenant, who might be willing to pay a rent in excess of that stipulated by the legislation, and to forego security of tenure, has no legally enforceable means of assuring a landlord that he will do so, since the legislation affords tenants legally inalienable protection. Under these circumstances, if a landlord granted a tenancy, he would have to rely solely on the tenant's word. Thus, if, as was the case in the UK, the legal protection for new tenants is the same as that for existing ones, in general potential tenants will not be offered tenancies. It has been noted that 'had it been the long-term objective to kill off the private landlord, British housing policy has achieved a remarkable degree of success' (Cullingworth, 1979, p. 73). Moreover, neither existing tenants, nor the heirs who may inherit their tenancies, live for ever. When their dwellings become vacant landlords will not re-let them, but transfer them to other uses, e.g. owner occupation. In the 'long-run' (which, in the case of housing, may be long indeed) the dwellings subject to rent control tend to disappear. Then potential tenants are harmed rather than helped by rent control (Whitehead and Kleinman, 1986, ch. 6.).

An equity effect of rent control, and a constitutional aspect related to it, must be mentioned. It would be a sheer fluke if the wealth transfers resulting from effective rent control conformed to any reasonable criterion of equity (Friedman, 1985, p. 460). Moreover, they do not appear in the budget and are not explicitly considered by the legislature.

II. Apart from the redistributive effects stressed in Section I rent control also has efficiency effects. One of these follows from the analysis in the previous Section, i.e. the disappearance of a service to new buyers who would wish to buy it in the absence of rent control. The extent of the resulting welfare losses depends on how close are the substitutes which remain outside control, which, in turn, depends on how comprehensively rent control is applied. To give an example, in the UK, between 1965–1974, rent control with indefinite security of tenure applied to unfurnished accommodation only, so that furnished rented accommodation remained accessible to new tenants. In 1974 tenants of furnished accommodation were accorded the same protection as unfurnished tenants, with predictable results (Maclennan, 1978; Cullingworth, 1979, pp. 71–72). It may be surmized that welfare losses increased. The persistence of this inefficiency was explained in Section I.

Other inefficiencies commonly attributed to rent control can be exhaustively grouped under two headings; i) inefficiencies in the allocation of the existing housing, of which classic examples are the immobility of 'sitting' tenants and their excessive consumption of housing space (Olsen, 1972, pp. 1096–97); ii) inefficient maintenance, including reconstruction, of that stock. These claims about the effects of rent control are of long standing (e.g. *Rent Control*, 1975), but the concepts which might help to explain them have been systematically introduced into economics much more recently. These concepts concern the relationship between legislative enactments, such as rent control, and the resulting changes in property rights and transactions costs.

We saw in Section I that the introduction of rent control implies a capital levy on existing landlords and a capital subsidy to existing tenants. Why should such a windfall transfer cause the inefficiencies just listed, i.e. why should it prevent the full exploitation of subsequent potential gains from trade? For example, it has been calculated that the losses to landlords from rent control in New York City were twice as high as the gains to their tenants, but what prevented the elimination of this inefficiency is not explained (Olsen, 1972). Why do existing tenants not make arrangements to transfer their tenancies to other tenants, who value them more highly, or why do they not give them up, by making appropriate arrangements with their landlords, who could then transfer the dwellings to higher valued uses?

To answer this question one needs to consider the incentives which rent control with security of tenure offers to the potential parties to the exchange, which requires us to take account of the more detailed legal specifications of the rent control legislation (Cheung, 1974, 1975, 1979).

At first sight rent control would not seem to impede transfers of tenancies from existing to new tenants, the latter paying premiums to the former, as analysed in Section I. However, this presupposes that the law allows existing tenants to accept such premiums, which is not the case, e.g., in the UK (*Farrell* v. *Alexander* [1977]). It also presupposes that existing tentants have the right to assign tenancies without requiring their landlords' consent, which is rarely the case (Friedman, 1985, p. 460). Once the landlord's consent is required, the division of premiums is not market-determined, but is the outcome of bilateral bargaining, which raises the cost of reaching agreement between the parties. It may be noted that, *purely on grounds of efficiency*, it would be preferable if landlords could not refuse consent to the re-assignment of a tenancy – assuming tenants were allowed to accept premiums.

As regards transfers between tenants and landlords, the bargaining costs are the same as those just discussed, and whether there is a systematic bias in the direction of transfers would depend on legal influences on components of transactions costs other than bargaining. To illustrate: if security of tenure is legally inalienable a landlord cannot frame a contract which obliges the tenant to vacate the dwelling for a consideration; by contrast, if the landlord wishes to sell the property to the tenant, the transaction is an ordinary conveyance. However, landlords can offer tenants financial inducements to leave, the money being transferred to the tenant by a stake holder *after* the former has vacated the premises. These considerations do not yield any general conclusions, and it seems that the direction of transfers will depend on the circumstances of the case.

Turning to the second group of inefficiencies it is also appropriate to ask why rent control should generate them. As regards sub-optimal maintenance, one popular answer is that landlords 'cannot afford' to maintain rent-controlled properties, but this is not a satisfactory answer (Ricketts, 1981, p. 509). The appropriate answer is that landlords certainly have no incentive to maintain the quality of the property at a level above that for which the tenant is just willing to pay the controlled rent. Indeed, the landlord might find it profitable to allow the property to deteriorate so far that the tenant quits voluntarily, leaving the landlord free to sell to an owner-occupier, unless the landlord can be legally prevented from allowing that degree of deterioration (Ricketts, 1981, p. 511). But this does not explain why tenants should not undertake adequate maintenance, since, by assumption, this would make them better off. Once again, we need to invoke the fact that, with rent control and security of tenure, both tenants' and landlords' property rights are less clearly specified than in their absence, making tenants' investment in maintenance more risky than it would be for landlords in the absence of rent control. Hence the *possibility* that rent control may even make existing tenants worse off (Ricketts, 1981, pp. 507–510).

As regards rebuilding, it is conceivable that landlords, if legally obliged to house their protected tenants at a standard stipulated by the authorities, might find it less costly to rebuild than to repair properties. In practice, this does not appear to happen. Landlords rebuild if, by so doing, they can free the building from rent control (Cheung, 1975). The question is whether the legal provisions of the rent control legislation would affect landlords' decisions regarding rebuilding. We consider only two possible legal provisions: (a) if the landlord can prove that he will rebuild, he has the right to evict his rent-controlled tenants without compensation (as was the case in Hong Kong over a certain period, Cheung, 1975); (b) the landlord may not evict tenants to re-build his property, unless he offers them 'equivalent' accommodation (as has been the case for statutory tenants in the UK since 1965 – *Hill and Redman's*, 1976, pp. 824–827, 899). One might be tempted to conclude at once that, under (a), there would not only be more reconstruction than under (b), but that there would be excessive reconstruction. This conclusion is suggested by the consideration that the private return to the landlord exceeds the social return, since the former includes a recoupment of the transfer conferred on the tenant by rent control. However, the conclusion is not yet warranted, since it ignores the incentives tenants have to bribe landlords to forego excessive reconstruction. Nevertheless, taking these incentives into account does not vitiate qualitatively the initial, albeit unwarranted, conclusion, since, given the bargaining costs with tenants, the private returns to landlords from rebuilding are likely to exceed the social returns (Cheung, 1975). By contrast, under (b) the reverse seems likely, because of the costs imposed on landlords by having to establish that they are offering tenants equivalent accommodation.

KURT KLAPPHOLZ

BIBLIOGRAPHY

Baxter *v.* Eckersley. [1950] 1 KB 480.

Cheung, S.N.S. 1974. A theory of price control. *Journal of Law and Economics* 17, April, 53–71.

Cheung, S.N.S. 1975. Roofs or stars: the stated intents and actual effects of a rent ordinance. *Economic Inquiry*, April, 1–21.

Cheung, S.N.S. 1979. Rent control and housing reconstruction: the postwar experience of prewar premises in Hong Kong. *Journal of Law and Economics* 22, April, 27–53.

Cullingworth, J.B. 1979. *Essays on Housing Policy*. London: George Allen & Unwin.

Farrell *v.* Alexander. [1977] All E.R. 721, H.L. (E.).

Friedman, L.S. 1985. *Microeconomic Policy Analysis*. New York and London: McGraw-Hill.

Hill and Redman's Law of Landlord and Tenant. 16th edn, London: Butterworths, 1976.

Le Grand, J. and Robinson, R. 1984. *The Economics of Social Problems*. 2nd edn, London: Macmillan.
MaClennan, D. 1978. The 1974 Rent Act – some short run supply effects. *Economic Journal* 88, June, 331–40.
Olsen, E.O. 1972. An econometric analysis of rent control. *Journal of Political Economy* 80, November–December, 1081–100.
Rent Act 1977. London: HMSO.
Rent Control – A Popular Paradox. 1975. Ed. F.A. Hayek et al., Vancouver: Fraser Institute
Ricketts, M. 1981. Housing policy: towards a public choice perspective. *Journal of Public Policy*, October, 501–22.
Whitehead, C.M.E. and Kleinman, M.P. 1986. Private Rented Housing in the 1980s and 1990s. Cambridge, University of Cambridge Department of Land Economy, Occasional Paper 17.

rentier. An individual who lives on interest income (rent) received in compensation for the loan of property held in the form of money is called a *rentier*, not to be confused with landowners who receive rent paid for the loan of property in land. The original French word signifies the holder of *rentes*, a form of French government debt that was widely diffused in the 19th century. It served to distinguish this form of income from the definition of interest, used by some economists such as Walras (1926, p. 223), as payment made by the entrepreneur to the *capitaliste* for the use of his capital. Today the term refers generically to the owner of any debt obligation, public or private, paying periodic, annual or semi-annual, usually fixed amounts of interest over a long term.

As the origin of the word suggests, the emergence of rentiers accompanied the accumulation of the economic surplus in money form, and the finance of state expenditure (usually for bellicose purposes) by long-term debt. Modern securities markets originated in the sale and exchange of government 'stocks' in London and Amsterdam to merchants who could find no more remunerative employment for their capital in commercial activities. The rentier is therefore a typical feature of the money economy emerging from early capitalist development.

Thus Ricardo's (1821, p. 335) early 19th-century position that landlords' interests were inimical to industrial expansion was replaced in the 20th century by criticism of the rentier as a brake on the dynamics of capitalist accumulation. Individuals who derived income from neither labour nor productive capital investment were viewed as parasites living off the effort of the labourer and the entrepreneur-capitalist.

Economists' views of the rentier largely depend on their theory of interest. The rentier may be considered as enjoying the consumption he had postponed by saving out of income earned at an earlier time, or he may be considered as appropriating through interest the current output of labour and capital, thereby reducing the surplus available for expansion. For Schumpeter (1943, p. 175), rentiers could only exist if capitalist entrepreneurs were sufficiently dynamic to generate the profits required to pay interest, while for Marshall (1920, p. 232) investment was possible only when individuals were willing to 'wait' to consume their income and wealth.

Rentiers as a class have also been criticized for actively discouraging economic and social change in defence of their vested interests in private property rights and money contracts. As well as defending the right to interest income and accumulated wealth, the rentier has to defend the purchasing power of his interest income and the capital value of his wealth. Inflation is thus the first enemy of the rentier living on fixed interest payments, for it reduces the real purchasing power of current income. As a class, rentiers will thus favour conservative government policies to balance budgets and produce deflationary conditions, even at the expense of economic growth and high levels of employment. An example may be found in rentier support in the interwar years for re-establishing prewar gold parities in order to restore asset values decimated by the postwar inflations (Rolfe and Burtle, 1975). On the other hand, monetary policy to control inflation will be considered undesirable, for increasing interest rates reduces the current market value of fixed interest debt. Thus the rentier favours balanced budgets, and stable monetary policy and exchange rates to assure security of real income and capital value.

It may appear paradoxical that rentiers favour balanced government budgets, which would eliminate the creation of part of the assets which produce their incomes. However, this simply reflects different frameworks used to analyse the economic significance of the rentier. Ex post, existing rentiers who have already purchased debt and are receiving interest incomes which they seek to protect will have different interests from current savers who are seeking the highest possible future income and who thus look favourably on high interest rates and a plentiful supply of government debt produced by government deficits. A similar argument applies to the issue of private debt. This conflict between current holders and purchasers of debt reflects that between economists in favour of conservative and progressive government economic policies for growth and development.

This conflict of interests has had an important influence on both economic history and economic theory. Keynes, in his *Tract on Monetary Reform* (1923), had already noted the importance of the impact of monetary and fiscal policy on rentiers' standards of living for the political stability of the then emerging modern Europe. This is a theme which he also subsequently incorporated into his *General Theory* (1936, p. 376) in the guise of the concept of liquidity preference and his recommendation for the gradual 'euthanasia' of the rentier by means of expansionary fiscal policy and low rates of interest.

Keynes's theory did not rely on the earlier arguments concerning the inimical effects on growth and employment of the use made by rentiers of their income (for personal consumption) and wealth (to finance public consumption), but rather on the advantages that rentiers would find in holding liquid assets rather than in financing employment creating investment in periods when they felt threatened by uncertainty over the future value of their income and capital. In such conditions employment creating investment would have to compete with the rentiers' preference for liquidity, creating rates of interest far in excess of what entrepreneurs could pay from the expected earnings of productive investment. Further, rentier preferences might be so strong as to render the monetary authority powerless to reduce interest rates to stimulate activity. Keynes thus advocated a policy of direct intervention through the 'socialization of investment', accompanied by low, stable rates of interest which would eventually eliminate the power of rentiers to hinder policies for full employment.

In the 1950s and 1960s expansionary policies and low interest rates reduced the share of interest in total incomes; preservation of individual savings was secured by insurance companies, pension funds and investment trusts. In the 1970s, however, the oil crisis created large quantities of wealth for petroleum producers, many of whom were private individuals who behaved as typical rentiers in investing their funds. The use of restrictive monetary policy to combat the subsequent inflation led to sharply positive real rates of interest, an increase in the share of interest in total incomes and resuscitation of the rentier. Economists are also divided on the implications of this phenomenon, some relating it to the emergence of a new conservatism in economic policy, while others see it as having created the willingness to lend, upon which the investment necessary for the economic recovery and the reconstruction of the industrialized economies is thought to depend.

J.A. Kregel

See also INTEREST AND PROFIT; KEYNESIANISM.

BIBLIOGRAPHY

Keynes, J.M. 1923. *A Tract on Monetary Reform.* London: Macmillan.

Keynes, J.M. 1936. *The General Theory of Employment, Interest and Money.* London: Macmillan.

Marshall, A. 1920. *Principles of Economics.* 8th edn, London: Macmillan.

Ricardo, D. 1821. *On the Principles of Political Economy and Taxation.* Vol. I of *The Works and Correspondence of David Ricardo*, ed. P. Sraffa with M. Dobb, Cambridge: Cambridge University Press for the Royal Economic Society, 1951.

Rolfe, S.E. and Burtle, J.L. 1975. *The Great Wheel: The World Monetary System.* New York: McGraw-Hill.

Schumpeter, J. 1934. *The Theory of Economic Development.* New York: Oxford University Press, 1961.

Walras, L. 1926. *Elements of Pure Economics.* Trans. and ed. W. Jaffé, London: Allen & Unwin for the Royal Economic Society, 1954.

rent seeking. The term 'rent-seeking' was introduced by Ann O. Krueger (1974), but the relevant theory had already been developed by Gordon Tullock (1967). The basic and very simple idea is best explained by reference to Figure 1. On the horizontal axis we have as usual the quantity of some commodity sold, on the vertical axis its price. Under competitive conditions the cost would be the line labelled PP and that would also be its price. Given a demand curve, DD, quantity Q would be sold at that price. If a monopoly were organized, it would sell Q′ units at a price of P′.

The traditional theory of monopoly argued that the net loss to society is shown by the shaded triangle, which represents the consumer surplus that would have been derived from the purchase of those units between Q′ and Q, that are now neither purchased nor produced. The dotted rectangle, on the other hand, has traditionally been regarded simply as a transfer from the consumers to the monopolist. Since they are all members of the same society, there is no net social loss from this transfer.

This argument tends to annoy students of elementary economics (because they don't like monopolists), but until the development of the work on rent seeking it was nevertheless thought to be correct by most economists. Its basic problem, however, is that it assumes that the monopoly is created in a costless manner, perhaps by an act of God, whereas in fact real resources are used to create monopolies.

Most discussion of rent seeking has tended to concentrate on those monopolies that are government created or protected, probably because these are observed to be the commonest and strongest. It should be kept in mind, however, that purely private monopolies are possible – indeed, some actually exist. Concentration on government-created monopolies (or restrictions of various sorts that increase certain peoples' income) is probably reasonable, granted the contemporary frequency of such activities. Nevertheless, as we point out below there are certain significant areas where private rent seeking causes net social loss.

In the initial work both of Tullock and Krueger it was assumed that profit-seeking businessmen would be willing to use resources in an effort to obtain a monopoly, whether it was privately or government sponsored, up to the point where the last dollar so invested exactly counterbalanced the improved probability of obtaining the monopoly. From this it was deduced that the entire dotted rectangle (Figure 1) would be exhausted. Although this assumption is open to question (see Tullock, 1980), for the time being we will continue to assume that in effect there is no transfer from purchasers to the monopolist, but simply a social loss which comes from the fact that resources have been invested in unproductive activity, i.e. the negatively productive activity of creating a trade restriction of some sort. Theoretical reasons exist for believing that this assumption probably does not fit perfectly anywhere, but it is just as likely to overestimate as to underestimate the social cost; it will be discussed more thoroughly below.

To quote an aphorism frequently used in rent seeking: 'the activity of creating monopolies is a competitive industry.' For this reason it is anticipated that quite a number of people at any given time are putting at least some resources into an effort to secure a monopoly, only some of whom are successful. The situation is like a lottery, in which many people buy lottery tickets, a few win a very large amount of money and the rest lose, perhaps large or small amounts, depending on how much they have committed. In almost all existing lotteries, of course, the total investment of resources by the gamblers is considerably greater than the total payoff, whereas here it is still assumed that total resources committed to rent-seeking equal the total monopoly profits.

Thus the activity of creating monopolies could both absorb very large resources, particularly those resources that take the form of exceptionally talented individuals who devote their attention to this difficult and highly rewarded activity, and lead to considerable redistribution of wealth in the community. Suppose that ten different lobbyists go to Washington representing ten different associations, and each spends one million dollars over the course of a couple of years in the hope of influencing Congress to provide them with a monopoly. Only one of the lobbyists is successful and the monopoly turns out to have a present discounted value of ten million dollars. There is a substantial redistribution of resources from the unsuccessful lobbyists to the successful.

This substantial redistribution has occurred simultaneously with a considerable waste of resources in general, both because these highly intelligent people could otherwise be doing something of higher productivity and because the economy's use of resources has been further distorted by the creation of the monopoly. Further, although so far the discussion has been primarily about monopoly, actually very many possible interventions in the market process raise the same problem. A simple maximum or minimum price may have very large redistributive effects and the people who thus benefit may put considerable resources into receiving them. Of course there are many situations in which one lobbyist is pushing for a particular restriction and another lobbyist is pushing against it. The second activity is sometimes called 'rent avoidance', but it is costly and of course would not exist if there were not also rent seeking activity.

Another area is simple direct transfers. A tax on A for the purpose of paying B will lead to lobbying activity for the tax on the part of B and against it on the part of A. The total of these two lobbying activities could very well equal the total amount transferred (or prevented from being transferred), although one or other of these entrepreneurs will of course gain if his lobby is successful. Assume that A puts in \$50 for lobbying to get \$100 from B and B puts in \$50 lobbying against that. Regardless of the outcome, one party will gain \$50 from his lobbying. Society has lost \$100.

Of course it is not true that everyone in society is in an equally good position to seek rents. Some kinds of interest are more readily organized than others and we would anticipate that they would win. There are however very many such interests and anyone who spends any time in Washington quickly realizes that there is a major industry engaged in just this kind of activity.

Actual social cost however is clearly very much greater than the mere cost of the various lobbying organizations in Washington. In particular it is normally necessary for the rent-seeking group to undertake directly productive activities in a way that is markedly inefficient, because it is necessary to introduce a certain element of deception into the process. In 1937, when the US Civil Aeronautics Board was organized, it would not have been politically feasible to put a direct tax on purchasers of airline tickets and use it to pay off the stockholders of the airline companies. Regulation, which has a similar effect but at a very much higher cost to the users of airlines per dollar of profit to the owners, was however, politically possible. The necessity of using inefficient methods of transferring funds to the potential beneficiary, because the efficient methods would be just too open and above board, is often one of the major costs of rent seeking. The rent avoidance lobbyist would have had too easy a time if the proposal had been a tax on uses of airlines for the benefit of the stockholders.

Note that in this case the argument against rent seeking turns out also to be an argument against political corruption. Suppose you are in a society which has an exchange control system and that it is possible to buy foreign currency by bribing an official in the exchange control office. This is the kind of situation dealt with by Krueger (1974), who was able to obtain a measure of the total social cost in Turkey and India where the amounts of the necessary bribes were well known; the cost varied from 7–15 per cent of the total volume of transactions.

Traditionally economists have tended to view this kind of bribery as in itself desirable, because it gets around an undesirable regulation. However, it leads to rent seeking. In this case the rent seeking does not come from the users of the permits but from the competition to get into the position where you can receive the bribe. Throughout the underdeveloped world, large numbers of people take fairly elaborate educational programmes which have no real practical value for their future life and engage in long periods of complicated political manoeuvring in hope that they will be appointed, let us say, a customs inspect in Bombay. Since these young men have a free career choice presumably the expected returns from this career are the same as in any other. The difference is that a doctor, say, begins earning money immediately on completing medical school whereas the young man who has studied economics and is now trying to obtain appointment as customs inspector will have a considerable period of time in which he is not appointed at all. Indeed, there will probably be enough such candidates that he has only perhaps one chance in five of being so appointed. The total cost of the rent seeking is the inappropriate education and the political manoeuvring of the five people of whom only one is appointed.

So far we have assumed that the total cost of rent seeking is the present discounted value of the income stream represented by the dotted rectangle in Figure 1. This assumes a special

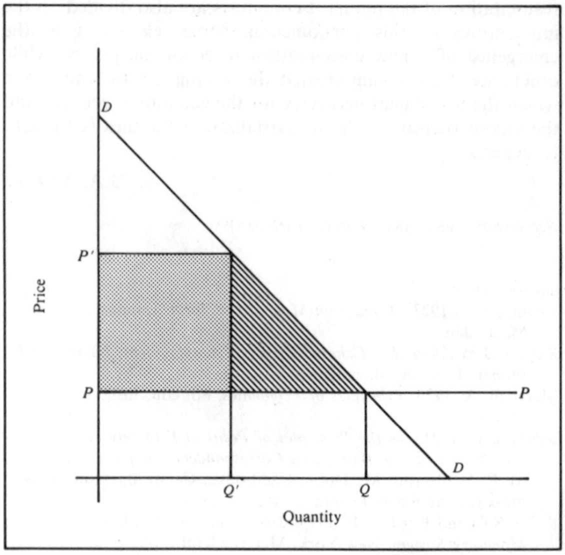

Figure 1

form for the function which 'produces' the monopoly or other privilege. It must be linear, with each dollar invested having exactly the same payoff in probability of achieving the monopoly as the previous dollar (Tullock, 1980). Most functions do not have this form, instead they are either increasing or decreasing cost functions.

If the organizing of private monopolies, or of influencing the government into giving you public monopolies, is subject to diseconomies of scale, then total investment in rent seeking will be less than the total value of the rents derived even if we assumed a completely competitive market with completely free entry. When there are economies of scale the situation is even more unusual. Either there is no equilibrium at all or there is a pseudo-equilibrium, in which total investment to obtain the rents is greater than the rents themselves. This is called a pseudo-equilibrium because although it meets all the mathematical requirements for an equilibrium, it is obviously absurd to assume that people would, to take a single example, pay \$75.00 for a 50–50 chance of \$100.

Obviously, what is needed is empirical research, and an effort to measure the production functions appropriate to rent seeking. So far, however, no one has been able to develop a very good way of making such measurements. It seems likely that it would be easier to measure the costs of generating political influence than of private monopolies, if only because many of the expenditures used to influence the government appear in accounts in various places. The costs of private monopolies on the other hand, tend to be much more readily concealed. This does not mean that they do not exist.

The reader has no doubt been wondering what is wrong with rents and why we concern ourselves deeply with rent seeking. The answer to this is that the term itself is an unfortunate one. Obviously, we have nothing against rents when they are generated by, let us say, discovering a cure for cancer and then patenting it. Nor do we object to popular entertainers like Michael Jackson earning immense rents on a rather unusual collection of natural attributes together with a lot of effort on his part to build up his human capital. On the other hand, we do object to the manufacturer of automobiles increasing the rent on his property, and his employees increasing the rent on their union memberships, by organizing a quota against imported cars. All of these things are economic rents, but strictly speaking the term 'rent seeking' applies only to the latter. Its meaning might be expanded to seeking rents from activities which are themselves detrimental. The man seeking a cure for cancer is engaged in an activity which clearly is not detrimental to society. Thus we may observe immediately that activities aimed at deriving rents cover a continuum, but that the term 'rent seeking' is only used for part of that continuum.

The analysis of 'rent seeking' has been one of the most stimulating fields of economic theory in recent years. The realization that the explanation of the social cost of monopoly which was contained in almost every elementary text in economics was wrong, or at the very least seriously incomplete, came as quite a surprise. Revision of a very large part of economic theory in order to take this error into account is necessary. And history also needs to be revised. That J.P. Morgan was an organizer of cartels and monopolies during most of his life is well known, as is the fact that he received very large fees for this, fees which were part of the rent seeking cost of generating these monopolies. It is possible to argue that as a stabilizing factor in the banking system, Morgan more than repaid to the United States the social cost of his monopolistic activities in industry. But that there was a very large rent seeking cost is obvious. This cost is in addition to the deadweight cost of the monopolies.

To date, research on rent seeking has to a considerable extent changed our way of looking at things. We now talk of a great deal of government activity as rent seeking on the part of somebody or other. It was known that special interest existed, but we have traditionally tended to underestimate its cost greatly because we looked only at the deadweight costs of the distortion introduced into the economy. The realization that the actual cost is much greater socially, that the large-scale lobbying industry is truthfully a major social cost, is new although presumably, at all times, anyone who thought about the matter must have realized that these highly talented people could produce more in some other activity.

GORDON TULLOCK

See also BRIBERY; DIRECTLY UNPRODUCTIVE PROFIT-SEEKING ACTIVITIES.

BIBLIOGRAPHY

Buchanan, J., Tollison, R. and Tullock, G. (eds) 1980. *Toward a Theory of the Rent-Seeking Society*. College Station, Texas: Texas A and M University Press.

Krueger, A.O. 1974. The political economy of the rent-seeking society. *American Economic Review* 64, 291–303.

Tullock, G. 1967. The welfare cost of tariffs, monopolies, and theft. *Western Economic Journal* (now *Economic Inquiry*) 5, 224–32.

Tullock, G. 1980. Efficient rent seeking. In Buchanan, Tollison and Tullock (eds), 91–112.

reparations. Reparations are payments, either in money or in kind, made by a nation which has lost a war, or injured some group of people. The transfer of territory from loser to winner is usually not called reparation, although there is no defensible distinction among money, land and goods. The word may seem to imply that the payer is at fault, but of course there is no reason to suppose, whether in general or in particular, that the balance of wrong-doing lies with the payer, or even that the payer has committed any wrong. In political and economic affairs the word is synonymous with 'indemnity', but it should not be confused with 'tribute': reparations or indemnities are in principle fixed in amount and/or limited in duration, and they involve no political subordination of vanquished to victor, although they may involve some foreign surveillance for a longer or shorter period; tributes involve indefinite payments by a subordinate nation to an overlord.

Reparations have been common in modern times. They have sometimes been justified either as a payment of the victor's war-costs, or as a recompense for damage to the victor's economy. Neither can be unambiguously defined or measured: are military pensions, for instance, part of the cost of a war? Thus even when it might be admitted that reparations ought to be paid, there will be endless disputation about the 'correct' amount. At the end of the Franco–Prussian War the victorious Prussians exacted 5000 million gold francs from the French. After the Boxer Rebellion the Imperial Chinese Government was obliged to pay reparations to the Western powers. These reparations payments were defined and paid in money, and there was little concern about the possible strain which their transfer might impose on the payer-economy, or on the international monetary system. Indeed, it does not appear that much strain resulted: France, a country whose current account was normally in surplus, had no difficulty in floating external loans and in servicing these; for China, a country with a much less healthy payments position, the burden of the indemnity loan was quickly submerged not only by other debt but by revolution and civil strife. World War I created problems of a very different order.

The Treaty of Versailles fixed the guilt for the war on Germany, obliging the nation to pay reparations but leaving the amount and the term of payment to be determined later. Commodity reparations soon began. In 1919 John Maynard Keynes, in *The Economic Consequences of the Peace*, observed that the punitive reparations would create impossible problems not only for Germany but for the whole world economy: the reparations, Keynes pointed out, could be transferred in 'real' terms only by the shipment of goods, and he doubted whether Germany could deliver goods on a sufficient scale, or whether the world would really welcome a reviving German economy with a very large export surplus. The warnings at first were without effect. In 1920 Germany's liability was fixed at 226,400 million gold marks – roughly 36 times what France had paid in the 1870s. Britain and most of the other powers quickly came to recognize that the transfers would be hard to make, and that the logical justification for reparation could and should be the war-debt payments that almost all the Allies had to make the United States – a protectionist state with a very large current-account surplus, which certainly would not take goods in settlement of the war debts. France, however, was anxious to receive reparations in excess of her war-debt obligations, and for most of the 1920s she succeeded in doing so. In 1921 the Allies ordered Germany to begin the transfer of reparations in cash according to a rising scale over a period of 42 years. It was far from clear that Germany could earn enough foreign exchange to make reparations payments in money: the Reich had run a current-account surplus before 1914, but the War had changed her payments position for the worse, and in the very rapid inflation of 1922–3, the situation was confused, nor was Germany anxious to pay, even though from time to time the German government did attempt to honour Allied demands.

In 1922 Germany was given a disguised moratorium, and early in 1923 France occupied the Ruhr so as to enforce payment; renewed international discussions resulted in 1924 in the Dawes Plan, which provided for an international loan and an initial moratorium, followed by the resumption of payments according to a scale which would rise to 2500 million reichsmarks annually by 1928–9. Neither the term of this payment, nor the total amount of reparations, was specified. The Plan provided for Allied supervision of German finances, and arranged that the reparations would actually be transferred only when the German payments position was sufficiently strong. In 1929 came the Young Plan, which fixed smaller annual payments over a 59-year period, and which also provided another international loan. It has been estimated that total German payments during the 1920s, whether in commodities or in goods, totalled 22.9 billion gold marks – less than one-tenth of the amount specified in 1920. The funds for cash transfers were coming partly from the special international Dawes and Young Plan Loans and partly from the large amounts that the German economy was borrowing under other headings and through other channels. The current account made no contribution, because Germany regularly ran current-account deficits from the stabilization of its currency late in 1923 until the onset of the Great Depression.

When foreign capital began to leave Germany the situation became first difficult and then impossible. In spring 1931 the German government announced that it could no longer make the Young Plan payments; the results were first an accelerated flight from the reichsmark, and then, in early summer 1931, exchange control for Germany. President Herbert Hoover of the USA quickly proposed a worldwide one-year moratorium not only on reparations but on war debts, which the Allies had been servicing from the proceeds of reparations. Over France's opposition the scheme was adopted, and in summer 1932, at Lausanne, the Allies proposed a final solution for the reparations problem: if America would be reasonable about war debts, they would settle for one final payment from Germany. The United States would not agree to the abolition of the war debts, but Germany ceased to pay reparations, and one by one the Allies defaulted on their debts to the United States, which collected little or nothing after the middle of 1933. In 1934, furthermore, Germany defaulted on the Dawes and Young Loans.

By the late 1920s specialists generally understood that the reparations were being paid not through a German commodity surplus but by American capital exports, which flowed across the Atlantic only to return in the service of war debts. In the 1930s it was widely believed, furthermore, that this situation contributed to the instability of the international economy, and to the onset of the Depression, or at least to its severity. Hence, well before the end of World War II the victorious United Nations were determined that they would not allow the whole absurd drama to be played a second time: there would be no monetary reparations, and no reparations from current production. Assets in the enemy lands, however, could be seized and dismantled. From the end of hostilities until the late 1940s the USSR imposed such exactions on occupied territories in Germany, Austria, Hungary, Rumania and Bulgaria. Britain and France did much the same thing in their occupation zones, and it might also be argued that the underpricing of Ruhr coal exports contained an element of reparation. The USSR, furthermore, collected some current output. However, with the coming of the Cold War and the Marshall Plan such exactions ceased, as both East and West became more interested in the reconstruction of the former enemy economies.

As economic recovery proceeded in Western Europe, West Germany began to pay reparations of a new sort – voluntary payments to Israel and to Jews as partial compensation for the Holocaust. When Japan began to extend development assistance in South-East Asia during the 1960s, from the Japanese point of view this aid contained an element of voluntary reparation. These Japanese and German payments imposed no strain on the world financial system in that they were transfers from countries possessing increasingly strong payments positions to countries whose current accounts were normally in deficit.

The interwar reparations phenomenon produced an explosion of scholarly analyses, differing with respect to assumptions, sophistication, and thoroughness. A 1949 bibliography on reparations and the transfer problem lists seventy-seven separate titles, and with respect to non-English materials it is certainly far from complete. Keynes, who may be said to have begun the discussion with his polemic of 1919, made a famous contribution in 1929, arguing that Germany would have to export more, and that to that end she would have to reduce her relative gold-costs of production – in particular, the relative gold-wages of German workers – through the deliberate creation of deflation and unemployment. A vigorous controversy at once ensued. Ohlin, for instance, argued that because the autonomous capital imports which had paid the reparations had also exerted an expansionary force on Germany economic activity, and thus on German imports, in the absence of capital imports a much stronger basic payments position would at once reveal itself; relative prices, furthermore, would then adjust in an accommodating way; an export surplus, therefore, might confidently be expected to appear, and sooner rather than later, if large capital imports were to cease.

Three years later Pigou analysed the effect of reparations on the ratio at which commodities would exchange for one another in international trade. He restricted himself to cases in which the reparation was sufficiently small, and where the relevant demand elasticities in the payee countries were sufficiently large, so that the payer country could raise the necessary foreign currency through exportation. While recognizing that these conditions might not always be met, Pigou believed that if gold reserves were sufficiently large in the payer country, there could not really be a problem: Germany would simply pay a quantity of gold to Britain, which would, in turn, spend it in Germany, so that at the end of each period the reparations would have been transferred in commodity terms, while the gold reserves of the several countries would be unchanged. Ten years later Metzler demonstrated that on 'Keynesian' fix-price and underemployment assumptions Pigou was incorrect: depending on the several marginal propensities to consume and to invest, a payment of reparation by means of a gold-shipment might or might not produce changes in imports and exports sufficient to transfer the equivalent amount in commodity terms. Metzler also showed that on certain arithmetic assumptions, perverse results were produced.

These and other analytical constructs may again become relevant in that although reparations of the 'Versailles' model will probably not be seen again, the end of reparations is not yet in sight. In the Iraq–Iran war which began in 1979, Iran proposed to exact reparations from Iraq, presumably in oil or in money raised by the export of oil. And if the 'Palestine problem' is ever solved, Israel may find herself making payments which the Palestinians and the Arab world will surely regard as reparations (it does not follow that they will be right to do so). Given the chronic weakness of the Israeli payments position, the world might then expect a re-run, *in parvo*, of the German reparations adventures. For how could such payments be transferred?

Ian M. Drummond

See also KEYNES, JOHN MAYNARD; OHLIN, BERTIL; TRANSFER PROBLEM; YOUNG, ALLYN ABBOTT.

BIBLIOGRAPHY

Keynes, J.M. 1919. *The Economic Consequences of the Peace*. London: Macmillan.

Keynes, J.M. 1929. The German transfer problem. Reprinted in American Economic Association, *Readings in the Theory of International Trade*, Philadelphia and Toronto: Blakiston.

Kindleberger, C.P. 1984. *A Financial History of Western Europe*. London: Allen & Unwin.

Mantoux, E. 1952. *The Carthaginian Peace*. New York: Scribners.

Metzler, L.A. 1949. The transfer problem reconsidered; and Classified Bibliography: IIIA. In American Economic Association, *Readings in the Theory of International Trade*, Philadelphia and Toronto: Blakiston.

Moulton, H.G. and Pasvolsky, L. 1932. *War Debts and World Prosperity*. Washington, DC: Brookings.

Ohlin, B. 1949. The reparation problem: a discussion. In American Economic Association, *Readings in the Theory of International Trade*, Philadelphia and Toronto: Blakiston.

Pigou, A.C. 1932. The effect of reparations on the ratio of international exchange. *Economic Journal* 42, December, 532–43.

repeated games. Repeated game is a generic name for any model where alternately players take simultaneous actions and then a lottery, depending on those actions and the current state of nature, selects jointly a new state of nature, and for each player a private signal and a current pay-off. Players are interested in some long term average of the pay-offs.

The 'repetitive' aspect will typically stem from an assumption of finiteness (or compactness ...) of the set of states of nature. The particular case where there is only one state of nature, and hence the same game is repeated over and over again, was originally named a supergame. We propose to keep that name, for the sake of precision in the vocabulary, and to reserve 'repeated game' for the above general model. Accordingly, we refer the reader to the entry on SUPERGAMES for that particular case, and will not treat it here.

To complete the above model, an initial state has to be specified, and the stipulation made that players remember all past information. The model is particularly flexible. For example, uncertainty about the initial state of nature (incomplete information) is modelled just by adding an initial state, in which the players' actions are immaterial, pay-offs zero, and an appropriate lottery selects the true initial state and initial information of the players. Information lags can be accommodated just by enlarging the state space, so as to keep in the current state all information about the past that still has to be transmitted. Similarly, all single stage games may in fact be extensive form games of varying duration – this too can be reduced to the above, etc. For the game to be well defined, the model must be such that, at every stage, players are at least informed of their current action set – but, by duplicating some actions, one can always assume each player has a single action set, independent of the state of nature.

Now the model is well defined. The long term average could be a limiting average, or a discounted average, or even an average over a fixed, large number of stages – note that the latter two can be reduced to the former, again by appropriately enlarging the state space. The signals may, but do not have to, inform players of their current pay-offs.

Such models apply to an enormous variety of situations – even outside economics: the original study of repeated games with incomplete information by Aumann and Maschler (1968) was (at least in part) motivated by arms control and disarmament negotiations. The first applications of information lags were to bomber–battleship duels; one could also consider, for example, negotiations over the release of hostages. Within economic theory the central importance of Harsanyi's model of games with incomplete information cannot be overstated; it now pervades most subfields – insurance, finance, labour economics, agency theory, industrial organization, and poses major questions for general equilibrium theory. 'Moral hazard' is the counterpart in the insurance literature of the fact that only some signals are observed, not the actions themselves (e.g. effort level) – just as in the same literature incomplete information is called adverse selection, because of its frequent effect of turning a market into a 'market for lemons' (Akerlof). More generally, this unobservability is referred to as 'imperfect monitoring' in the agency literature. The much more drastic unobservability of the actual outcome, and of the player's own pay-off as dependent on this outcome, constitutes the explanation for the enormous quality control literature and activity (and also probably in part for industrial standards, to make 'quality' more monitorable as well as more contractable).

Many situations require most features of the model at the same time, and in an essential way. Consider for instance a typical principal–agent relationship, such as that between a firm and a sub-contractor. Initially, the firm may have a high degree of uncertainty about the capabilities of the sub-contractor – and this explains a lot of signalling activity at that stage, as in Spence's analysis of the labour market or in Milgrom and Roberts's analysis of advertising. But the potentially long term nature of the relationship cannot be ignored, even at this stage: it will allow to monitor at least to some extent, if not capabilities, at least the final quality; and is the basic explanation for the signalling activity in Milgrom and Roberts: it is worthwhile for good-quality firms to engage in advertising in order to discriminate themselves from the others, since they may hope for a longer term, and so more profitable, relationship. During the repetition of the game, this initial uncertainty will continue to play a major strategic role, the high-capability subcontractor trying, for instance, to hide from the firm how low his costs in fact are. And not only can the actual costs or effort level of the subcontractor not be monitored, even the actual quality of output, which determines the firm's utility or objective function (e.g. some function of quality minus costs) will not be observable – except statistically, if the firm decides to take specific quality control steps; but those are costly, and part of the firm's strategic decision problem. In fact, in many such relationships those are one of the most essential parts of the relation. Furthermore, in many such situations there are essential state variables changing as a function of the players' actions. Think for instance of the subcontractor as a portfolio manager; the current value of the portfolio is the essential variable of the problem, and cannot be treated except as a state variable. It might be objected that, in this case at least, the state variable is monitorable through regular statements, but this leads us to the problem of information lags, which are of crucial importance in this business.

Analysis of repeated games has proceeded up to now in two main directions: (1) stochastic games, where the signals inform each player of at least the next state of nature and the last pay-off vector; and (2) repeated games with incomplete information, where all states but the initial state remain fixed forever. In (2), actions in the initial state are immaterial and the initial state is left immediately, in which case it is more convenient to remove the initial state from the model, to include the signals to the players which may arise from the initial lottery in the description of the states (thus expanding the state space), and to say that each player has a partition of the set of states, determined by his initial signals. An initial state is then selected with some probability distribution p on the set of states S, each player is informed of his corresponding partition element, and then players forever play the chosen game.

There is no room here to go into the history of (1) and (2), and we will briefly describe the current state of the art. A recent and much more thorough survey of the subject was given in a lecture by the present author at the International Congress of Mathematicians (1986) in Berkeley, and will appear in the *Proceedings* of that Congress. It also contains a fairly complete bibliography.

On stochastic games, fairly complete results are available by now. A recent result of Mertens and Parthasarathy (1986) shows the existence of equilibria (and a characterization) in the discounted case – or more generally, e.g. whenever there is a uniform (in initial state and in strategies) bound on the expected number of stages before the game stops (the discounted case can be interpreted as a uniform, fixed stopping probability). This allows for general state and action sets, with the usual measurability assumption in the state variables and continuity as a function of strategies. As for the infinite game, in the two-person zero-sum case, a value is known to exist (Mertens and Neyman, 1981) under essentially a somewhat strengthened convergence assumption on the values of the discounted games (those typically exist by the previously mentioned result – continuity assumptions can even be weakened). This assumption is always satisfied for finite state and action sets, by a previous result of Bewley and Kohlberg. It is also known (Mertens, 1982) that with finite state and action sets there exist stationary equilibria which are a semi-algebraic function of the discount factor, hence converge; but a result of Sorin (1986) shows that the ϵ-equilibria of the infinite game (for which no existence theorem is yet available) may be far away in pay-off space from those limits. It is not clear in his example which of the two solutions is more appropriate as a model for long games, and the result raises serious questions about any meaningful 'folk theorem' for stochastic games.

Games with incomplete information are systematically studied under finiteness assumptions on all sets (states and signals), which entails no conceptual loss of generality. We refer to the entry on supergames for the motivation of the study of the two-person zero-sum case. Under that assumption, three main cases are solved. The first is when one player is initially informed of everything, i.e. the true state of nature and the initial signal of the other players. In that case, Aumann, Maschler and Stearns proved the existence of the value and of optimal strategies (with easier strategies later by Kohlberg). The second is when the signals which the players receive after each state are independent of the state of nature. In this case, the limit v of V_n and of v was obtained by the author; later, Mertens and Zamir (1980) obtained maxmin and minmax of the infinite game, which are typically different, since the incentive to use one's information only after having obtained all possible information the opponent may reveal turns the game into a game like 'picking the largest integer'. The third is when both players always have the same information; here Forges (1982) proved existence of a value.

The non-zero sum case was studied only when one player is initially informed of everything, and the signals received by the players after each stage are the last pair of actions. A characterization of the set of Nash equilibria was obtained by Hart (1985), and further by Aumann and Hart (1986). A (generic) example by Forges (1984a) shows that the unbounded number of signalling stages required by the characterization is indeed necessary. This is even an example of a pure signalling games, where after the informed player has received his private information the players may exchange simultaneous messages in an arbitrarily large language for as long as they wish before the uninformed player takes a single action. Even in this case an unbounded (but finite) number of signalling stages – and in particular, of messages of the uninformed player – may be required to achieve pay-offs far superior to anything that can be achieved without.

Aumann's correlated equilibria (1974) and their extensive form relatives ('extensive form correlated equilibria' and 'communication equilibria') introduced in Forges (1986) were ($\pm$) characterized for the same model by Forges (1984b).

This body of work on incomplete information already provides many fundamental insights into the proper use of information in repetitive economic situations.

JEAN-FRANÇOIS MERTENS

See also EXCHANGE; GAME THEORY; NASH EQUILIBRIUM; PRISONER'S DILEMMA; SUPERGAMES.

BIBLIOGRAPHY

Akerlof, G. 1970. The market for 'lemons', qualitative uncertainty and the market mechanism. *Quarterly Journal of Economics* 84, 488–500.

Aumann, R.J. 1974. Subjectivity and correlation in randomized strategies. *Journal of Mathematical Economics* 1, 67–95.

Aumann, R.J. 1985. Repeated games. In *Issues in Contemporary Microeconomics and Welfare*, ed. G.R. Feiwel, London: Macmillan.

Aumann, R.J. and Hart, S. 1986. Bi-convexity and bi-martingales. *Israel Journal of Mathematics* 54, 159–80.

Aumann, R.J. and Maschler, M. 1968. Repeated games of incomplete information: the zero-sum extensive case. In *Mathematica* (Report to the US Arms Control and Disarmament Agency), ST–143, ch. III, 37–116 (prepared by Mathematica, Inc., Princeton).

Bewley, T. and Kohlberg, E. 1976a. The asymptotic theory of stochastic games. *Mathematics of Operations Research* 1, 197–208.

Bewley, T. and Kohlberg, E. 1976b. The asymptotic solution of a recursion equation occurring in the stochastic games. *Mathematics of Operations Research* 1, 321–36.

Bewley, T. and Kohlberg, E. 1978. On stochastic games with stationary optimal strategies. *Mathematics of Operations Research* 3, 104–25.

Forges, F. 1982. Infinitely repeated games of incomplete information: symmetric case with random signals. *International Journal of Game Theory* 11, 203–13.

Forges, F. 1984a. A note on Nash equilibria in repeated games with incomplete information. *International Journal of Game Theory* 13, 179–87.

Forges, F. 1984b. Communication equilibria in repeated games with incomplete information. CORE Discussion Papers 8406, 8411, 8412, Louvain-la-Neuve, Belgium.

Forges, F. 1986. An approach to communication equilibria. *Econometrica* 54(6), 1375–86.

Harsanyi, J.C. 1967–8. Games of incomplete information played by Bayesian players. *Management Science* 14, Pt I, 159–82; Pt II, 320–34; Pt III, 486–502.

Hart, S. 1985. Nonzero-sum two-person repeated games with incomplete information. *Mathematics of Operations Research* 10, 117–53.

Kohlberg, E. 1975. Optimal strategies in repeated games with incomplete information. *International Journal of Game Theory* 4, 7–24.

Mertens, J.-F. 1972. The value of two-person zero-sum repeated games: the extensive case. *International Journal of Game Theory* 1, 217–25.

Mertens, J.-F. 1982. Repeated games: an overview of the zero-sum case. In *Advances in Economic Theory*, ed. W. Hildenbrand, Cambridge: Cambridge University Press.
Mertens, J.-F. and Neyman, A. 1981. Stochastic games. *International Journal of Game Theory* 10(2), 53–6.
Mertens, J.-F. and Parthasarathy, T. 1986. Existence and characterisation of Nash equilibria for discounted stochastic games. CORE Discussion Paper, Louvain-la-Neuve, Belgium.
Mertens, J.-F. and Zamir, S. 1980. Minmax and maxmin of repeated games with incomplete information. *International Journal of Game Theory* 9, 201–15.
Milgrom, P. and Roberts, J. 1984. Price and advertising signals of product quality. Mimeo, Stanford University.
Sorin, S. 1986. Asymptotic properties of a non-zero sum stochastic game. *International Journal of Game Theory* 15, 101–7.
Spence, M. 1974. *Market Signalling*. Cambridge, Mass.: Harvard University Press.

replacement policy. Technological change, variable tastes and the consequent replacement of obsolete physical and human capital comprised the driving forces of the industrial revolution. They continue to be the most important dynamic elements of the modern fluctuating economy. The birth and death of firms and industries, the birth of job vacancies in new and expanding firms and industries, and the elimination of jobs in dying industries and bankrupt firms – these replacements are the essence of a modern capitalist economy. Critics of this system emphasize the mobility costs implied by this dynamism, whereas champions of the capitalist system marvel at the speed and efficiency of these adjustments. Our task is not to evaluate these positions or suggest optimal solutions to this grand replacement problem. We only mention it to remind the reader that 'replacement policy' when broadly construed is at the heart of any economic system and *that it includes both physical and human capital.* Our essay concentrates on the optimal replacement of stochastically failing equipment.

There are several fine books and surveys on capital theory beginning with I. Fisher (1930) and including Hirshleifer (1970), Jorgenson (1977) and Nickell (1978). Becker (1964) is the standard reference for human capital theory. A remarkable coincidence is the simultaneous appearance in 1930 of I. Fisher's *Theory of Interest* and R.A. Fisher's *The Genetical Theory of Natural Selection.* In the former we learn when a growing asset (a tree) should be cut; in the latter we are shown how to calculate the discounted value of future offspring of individuals of age x.

REPLACEMENT THEORY. Replacement theory resides at the centre of reliability theory, a vital area of applied probability that is a dynamic mechanism of microeconomics. The branch of applied probability that contains reliability is usually called operations research or management science. Inventory theory, queuing, and simulation are some of the other members of this discipline. Economists frequently cloak this vital discipline with an assortment of static 'production functions' thereby ignoring the very quick of the production process.

There are vast theoretical and applied literatures on both reliability theory and replacement policy. Fortunately, there are also several excellent surveys. The theory and statistical methods of reliability are surveyed in Thompson (1981), Bergman (1985), and Pierskalla and Voelker (1976) reviews the maintenance literature. The books, Barlow and Proschan (1965), Gnedenko et al. (1969), and Arrow et al. (1958, 1962) are classics.

From a probabilistic perspective replacement is a special topic in renewal theory. After a brief survey of renewal theory we turn to the economic problem – when should a piece of stochastically failing equipment be replaced. That is, at what point should the stochastic process be renewed. We use optimal stopping theory to answer this economic question. There are many versions of this problem. We consider three. A simple preventive maintenance model, a shock replacement policy, and an adaptive replacement policy. The concluding section observes that whereas economists sometimes overlook the dynamic stochastic aspects of production, engineers frequently tend to ignore incentive problems and miscalculate opportunity costs.

RENEWAL THEORY AND COUNTING PROCESSES. Let (T_i; $i = 1, 2, \ldots$) be a sequence of independent identically distributed random variables with distribution function F. The T's are non-negative and T_j denotes the time between the jth and $(j+1)$st event (failure or replacement). The mean time m between successive events i and $i+1$ is

$$m = E[T_i] = \int_0^\infty s\, dF(s)$$

with $0 < m \leqslant \infty$.

The time of the nth occurrence is denoted by Z_n, where

$$Z_0 = 0 \quad \text{and} \quad Z_n = \sum_{i=1}^{n} T_i, \quad n = 1, 2, \ldots$$

Finally, the number of occurrences $N(t)$ by time t is the largest n such that the time of the nth occurrence is less than or equal to t, that is,

$$N(t) = \sup\{n: Z_n \leqslant t\}.$$

The stochastic counting process $N(t)$ is called a *renewal process.*

The expected value of $N(t)$ is called the renewal function $\rho(t)$,

$$\rho(t) = \sum_{n=1}^{\infty} F^n(t),$$

where F^n is the n-fold convolution of F, that is, $F^n(t) = p\{T_1 + T_2 + \cdots + T_n \leqslant t\}$.

A SIMPLE PREVENTIVE MAINTENANCE MODEL. In a world of certainty one would never replace a piece of equipment until it was just about to fail (unless there were economies of scale in the very act of replacing a number of items at the same time). If the cost of replacement before failure is less than replacement after failure, replacements would be scheduled at the instant before failure. However, if failures occur stochastically, it may pay to replace well in advance of a failure even when the decision-maker is risk neutral.

Consider the optimal preventive maintenance policy for a single piece of equipment with a time-to-failure distribution characterized by an increasing failure rate. If the distribution of time-to-failure exhibits an increasing failure rate (IFR), then, by definition, the conditional probability $h(t)$ of failure at any specified instant t, given that the equipment has not failed prior to that specified instant t, is an increasing function of t. In this sense, the equipment can be said to be wearing out. The lifetime of the equipment is a random variable X with distribution function F. The failure rate function h, given by $h(t) = f(t)/[1 - F(t)]$ for $t > 0$, is assumed to be increasing. The equipment is continuously monitored and is replaced by a new item whenever it fails or reaches age N. A new item costs K (dollars). The marginal cost of replacement before (after) failure is $\alpha_1 (a_2)$, $\alpha_2 > \alpha_1$. Replacement is instantaneous, and the planning horizon is infinite. Because there (presumably) will be infinitely many replacements over the infinite future, the risk neutral agent may minimize either the expected cost per unit time or the expected discounted costs. To simplify the analysis, the average expected cost criterion is adopted.

The optimal replacement policy is periodic. The expected average cost $A(N)$ of 'policy N' is the ratio of the expected cost $C(N)$ of a cycle to the expected cycle length $L(N)$, where a cycle is the time between replacements (renewals). Thus,

$$A(N) = C(N)/L(N), \quad N > 0, \tag{1}$$

where

$$C(N) = K + \alpha_2 F(N) + \alpha_1[1 - F(N)] \tag{2}$$

and

$$L(N) = \int_0^N dF(t) + N[1 - F(N)]. \tag{3}$$

To find the optimal value of N, differentiate A:

$$A'(N) = \{(\alpha_2 - \alpha_1)f(N)L(N) - [1 - F(N)] \times [K + \alpha_1 + (\alpha_2 - \alpha_1)F(N)]\}/L(N)^2. \tag{4}$$

The solution, N^* is the optimal replacement interval. If $N^* = \infty$ and $\alpha_2 > \alpha_1$, the item must have a constant or a decreasing failure rate. Thus, the increasing failure rate *and* the larger in-service replacement cost justify preventive ($N^* < \infty$) maintenance.

A SHOCK MODEL OF PREVENTIVE MAINTENANCE. An equipment is bombarded by a random sequence of shocks. The amount of damage caused by each shock is also a random variable. Any shock can cause the equipment to fail, but the probability of failure by a shock at t is monotone increasing in the accumulated damage at t. Replacement is restricted to shock times. The accumulated damage is determined by a semi-Markov process, that is, the probability of moving from damage state i to damage state j is given by P_{ij}, $0 < i < j$, $i, j \in (1, 2, 3, \ldots)$ with F_{ij} the waiting time from i given that j is the next state.

The replacement decision can be formulated as an optimal stopping problem. The solution has the following '*control limit*' structure: there is a critical number ξ such that the optimal replacement policy is the optimal stopping time $N_\xi = \inf(n \in N: X_n \geqslant \xi)$, where X_n is the cumulative damage at n. This structure is identical to that of those search models possessing the '*reservation wage*' *property*. See Lippman and McCall, Volume 1 (1986).

ADAPTIVE REPLACEMENT POLICIES. The critical numbers characterizing an optimal replacement policy can be estimated when F is unknown. For moderate discount rates the policy designed by Fox (1965) is optimal, whereas for discount rules close to one stochastic approximation can be applied (Frees and Ruppert, 1985).

CONCLUSION. In this brief essay it is impossible to mention let alone exposit all the significant aspects of replacement policy. There are three of such paramount importance that their absence would eviscerate the essay. First, the incentive problem is manifest. The organization must be designed so that the 'true' opportunity costs of a replacement relative to a failure are correctly transmitted across all levels. For example, information about the state of an aircraft's components flows back and forth between the operations personnel and the maintenance crew. The repair activity may be hierarchical so that the information must cross several levels before it reaches the actual repair crew. Furthermore, maintenance is embedded in the overall production and repair activity that includes inventory control, production scheduling, queuing and transportation. The incentive structure must be such that management's assessment of the relative maintenance costs is reflected in the behaviour of the operations personnel, the information flow, and the work effort of the maintenance crew and its affiliated network.

The existence of this incentive problem reminds us that replacement is essentially a topic in the theory of insurance. Thus all of the difficulties attending the insurance activity and their practical resolution are pertinent. Finally, preventive medicine is one of the most important applications of replacement theory. Thus, while optimal replacement may appear to be a narrow and routine technical problem, it is in fact quite broad, ranging from extinction to the body's replacement of red blood cells, and its practical applications are riddled with complex incentive problems. The technical problems also are profound, entailing the basic physics of the deterioration process.

JOHN J. MCCALL

See also BIRTH-AND-DEATH PROCESSES; INVENTORY POLICY UNDER CERTAINTY.

BIBLIOGRAPHY

Arrow, K.J., Karlin, S. and Scarf, H. 1958. *Studies in the Mathematical Theory of Inventory and Production*. Stanford: Stanford University Press.

Arrow, K.J., Karlin, S. and Scarf, H. (eds) 1962. *Studies in Applied Probability and Management Science*. Stanford: Stanford University Press.

Barlow, R.E. and Proschan, F. 1965. *Mathematical Theory of Reliability*. New York: Wiley.

Barlow, R.E. and Proschan, F. 1975. *Statistical Theory of Reliability and Life Testing*. New York: Holt, Rinehart & Winston.

Becker, G.S. 1964. *Human Capital*. New York: Columbia University Press for the National Bureau of Economic Research.

Bergman, B. 1985. On reliability and its applications. *Scandinavian Journal of Statistics* 12, 1–42.

Derman, C. 1963. On optimal replacement rules when changes of state are Markovian. Ch. 9 in *Mathematical Optimization Techniques*, ed. R. Bellman, Berkeley and Los Angeles: University of California Press.

Derman, C. and Sacks, J. 1960. Replacement of periodically inspected equipment. *Naval Research Logistics Quarterly* 7, 597–607.

Fisher, I. 1930. *The Theory of Interest*. New York: Macmillan.

Fisher, R.A. 1930. *The Genetical Theory of Natural Selection*. Oxford: Oxford University Press.

Fox, B. 1965. *An Adaptive Age Replacement Policy*. Operations Research Center, Berkeley, Report No. 65–17(RR).

Gnedenko, B.V., Belyayev, Yu.K. and Solouyev, A.D. 1969. *Mathematical Methods of Reliability Theory*. New York: Academic Press.

Hirshleifer, J. 1970. *Investment, Interest, and Capital*. Englewood Cliffs, NJ: Prentice-Hall.

Jorgenson, D.W. 1971. Econometric studies of investment behavior: a survey. *Journal of Economic Literature* 9, 1111–47.

Jorgenson, D.W., McCall, J.J. and Radner, R. 1967. *Optimal Replacement Policy*. Amsterdam: North-Holland.

Lippman, S.A. and McCall, J.J. 1986. *The Economics of Search*. Vol 1, Oxford: Basil Blackwell.

Lotka, A.J. 1939. A contribution to the theory of self-renewing aggregates with special reference to industrial replacement. *Annals of Mathematical Statistics* 10, 1–25.

Nickell, S.J. 1978. *The Investment Decisions of Firms*. Cambridge: Cambridge University Press.

Pierskalla, W.P. and Voelker, J.A. 1976. A survey of maintenance models: the control and surveillance of deteriorating systems. *Naval Research Logistics Quarterly* 23, 353–88.

Smith, W.L. 1958. Renewal theory and its ramifications. *Journal of the Royal Statistical Society*, Series B 20, 243–302.
Thompson, W.A., Jr. 1981. On the foundations of reliability. *Technometrics* 23, 1–13.

representation of preferences. Three facets of subjective preferences have played central roles in economics. They are the qualitative structure of an agent's preferences, numerical representations of preferences, and the use of numerical representations or utility functions in economic analysis. We consider various representations and their ties to qualitative preference structures.

Preferences themselves are described by a binary relation $\succ$, *is preferred to*, on a non-empty set X. Axioms or assumptions about the behaviour of $\succ$ on X identify a qualitative preference structure. A representation provides a correspondence between this structure and properties of real valued functions based on X.

Elements in X are often viewed as decision alternatives or outcomes of choice. They may be arbitrary or have a prescribed structure, as when each x in X is a commodity bundle in some Euclidean space or a probability distribution (lottery) on wealth or on increments to current wealth.

Representations of preferences between lotteries date to Bernoulli (1738), who sought to explain why agents often prefer a sure level of wealth to a lottery with larger expected value than the sure level. Representations of preferences between commodity bundles were used by Jevons, Menger, Walras and Edgeworth in the late 19th century to examine the economic consequences of consumer behaviour within the theory of marginal analysis (Samuelson, 1947; Stigler, 1950). The commodity space and lottery contexts remain the preeminent structures for research in the representation of preferences.

Despite the early beginnings, detailed attention to qualitative preference structures for various representations is comparatively recent. Three examples are Frisch's axiomatization of comparable preference differences and Ramsey's theory of utility and subjective probability for decisions under uncertainty from the 1920s, and the axioms for expected utility of von Neumann and Morgenstern (1944). For general discussion of representations of various types, *see* MEASUREMENT, THEORY OF.

CLASSIFICATION. The structure of X and the degree of transitivity are two useful factors for classifying representations. The five most prominent structures are

S1 X is arbitrary except perhaps for cardinality or topological properties,
S2 $X = X_1 \times X_2 \times \cdots \times X_n$ or $X = X_1 \times X_2 \times \ldots$,
S3 X is a set of probability distributions,
S4 same as S3 except the outcomes are multidimensional as in S2,
S5 X is a set of mappings from a set S of states into an outcome set.

S2 includes commodity spaces and time streams, S3 is the setting for expected utility, and S5 is Savage's (1954) formulation for decisions under uncertainty. When S is countable, S2 can be used instead of S5 with X_i the possible outcomes for state i.

Our discussion is organized around S1 to S5 with transitivity as a subsidiary factor. It is assumed in all cases that $\succ$ is asymmetric, so $x \succ y$ precludes $y \succ x$. The agent's indifference relation $\sim$ and preference-or-indifference relation are defined by

$$x \sim y, \quad \text{if neither } x \succ y \text{ nor } y \succ x,$$
$$x \succsim y, \quad \text{if } x \succ y \text{ or } x \sim y.$$

Comparable preferences differences are discussed in the final section.

The preference relation $\succ$ is *transitive* if, for all x, y and z in X, $x \succ z$ whenever $x \succ y$ and $y \succ z$. Similar definitions pertain to $\sim$ and $\succsim$. Three levels of transitivity are

T1 both $\succ$ and $\sim$ are transitive,
T2 only $\succ$ is assumed to be transitive,
T3 neither $\succ$ nor $\sim$ is assumed to be transitive.

T1 is the usual assumption employed in economic analysis. T2 has little relevance before 1960 and T3 has little relevance before 1970.

T1 implies that $\succsim$ also is transitive. Under T1, $\succ$ is a 'weak order', and $\succsim$ is a 'weak order' or 'complete preorder'. T2 says that preferences are partially ordered; indifference need not be transitive. I include acyclic preferences–it is never true that $x_1 \succ x_2 \succ \cdots \succ x_k \succ x_1$–under T2. Unordered or non-transitive preferences fall under T3, which allows preference cycles such as $x \succ y, y \succ z$, and $z \succ x$, or $x \succ y \succ z \succ x$ for short.

Arbitrary sets: *S*1. The basic representation for weak orders is

$$x \succ y \Leftrightarrow u(x) > u(y), \tag{1}$$

where u is a real function on X. This and later expressions apply to all $x, y, \ldots$ in X. The function u in (1) is unique up to transformations that preserve order and is called an *ordinal* utility function.

T1 is necessary and sufficient for (1) when X is countable, but not otherwise. The general case also requires X to have a countable *order–dense* subset Y (Cantor, 1985) such that, whenever $x \succ z$ then $x \succsim y \succsim z$ for some y in Y. When (1) fails under T1 because no countable subset is order-dense in X, $\succ$ can be represented by vectors of utilities ordered lexicographically (Chipman, 1960; Fishburn, 1974). The finite-dimensional lexicographic representation is

$$x \succ y \Leftrightarrow [u_1(x), \ldots, u_n(x)] >_L [u_1(y), \ldots, u_n(y)], \tag{2}$$

where each u_i is real valued and $(a_1, \ldots, a_n) >_L (b_1, \ldots, b_n)$ if $a_i \neq b_i$ for some i and $a_i > b_i$ for the smallest such i.

Other conditions than order denseness can be used for (1) when X is a topological space. If X is connected and separable and T1 holds, there is a continuous u that satisfies (1) if, for each y in X, $\{x: x \succ y\}$ and $\{x: y \succ x\}$ are open sets in X's topology. This and related contributions on continuity appear in Debreu (1964) and Fishburn (1970a).

Under T2, (1) is replaced by the one-way representation

$$x \succ y \Rightarrow u(x) > u(y). \tag{3}$$

T2 is sufficient for (3) when X is countable, but not otherwise (Fishburn, 1970a, 1970b). For comments on continuity, see Sondermann (1980). Specialized partial orders use two functions for two-way representations. For example, if X is countable and $\{x \succ a, y \succ b\}$ implies $x \succ b$ or $y \succ a$, then there are real functions f and $\rho > 0$ on X such that

$$x \succ y \Leftrightarrow f(x) > f(y) + \rho(y).$$

Such an $(X, \succ)$ is called an *interval order*. The more specialized case in which ρ is a positive constant is known as a *semiorder*; see Fishburn (1985) for details.

Under T3, $(X, \succ)$ can be represented by a skew-symmetric $[\phi(y,x) = -\phi(x,y)]$ real function ϕ on $X \times X$ as

$$x \succ y \Leftrightarrow \phi(x,y) > 0. \quad (4)$$

This requires only asymmetry, and $\phi(x,y)$ can be set equal to 1, 0 or -1 when $x \succ y$, $x \sim y$ or $y \succ x$ respectively. We can view (1) as the specialization of (4) in which $\phi(x,y) = u(x) - u(y)$.

Product sets: *S2*. When $X = X_1 \times X_2 \times \cdots \times X_n$ with $x = (x_1, x_2, \ldots, x_n)$, (1) is

$$x \succ y \Leftrightarrow u(x_1, x_2, \ldots, x_n) > u(y_1, y_2, \ldots, y_n) \quad (1^*)$$

It is often assumed that each X_i is a real interval or a convex subset of a connected and separable topological space, and that u increases and is continuous in each component (Debreu, 1964; Fishburn, 1970a). When X is the positive orthant of n-dimensional Euclidean space, the indifference classes form a layered array of isoutility contours away from the origin. Isoutility contours that are convex to the origin are often presumed in the marginal analysis of consumption theory.

Houthakker (1961) provides a survey of consumption theory, including the fundamentals of demand as a function of prices and income, revealed preference, direct utility as a function of commodity bundles, and indirect utility. An example of the indirect approach, which expresses utility as a function of prices $p_1, \ldots, p_n$ and total expenditure $m > 0$, m is the indirect addilog function

$$v(p_1/m, \ldots, p_n/m) = \sum_{i=1}^{n} a_i (p_i/m)^{b_i}.$$

A related direct addilog function for quantities $q_i, \ldots, q_n$ is

$$u(q_1, \ldots, q_n) = \sum_{i=1}^{n} \alpha_i q_i^{\beta_i}.$$

These functions are special cases of the additive-utility specialization of (1), i.e.

$$x \succ y \Leftrightarrow u_1(x_1) + \cdots + u_n(x_n) > u_1(y_1) + \cdots + u_n(y_n), \quad (5)$$

where u_i is a real function on X_i. This presumes the *independence condition* which says that, whenever the n factors are partitioned into two parts, the preference order over one part conditioned on fixed values of the X_i in the other part is independent of the particular fixed values used. Other axioms are also needed for (5).

Necessary and sufficient conditions for (5) and its one-way counterpart under T2 when X is finite appear in Fishburn (1970a) and Krantz et al. (1971). Conditions sufficient for (5) with infinite X_i appear in Fishburn (1970a) and Krantz et al. (1971). The latter conditions imply that the u_i in (5) are unique up to similar positive linear transformations, so that $v_1, \ldots, v_n$ satisfy (5) in place of $u_1, \ldots, u_n$ if and only if there are numbers $\beta_1, \ldots, \beta_n$ and $\alpha > 0$ such that

$$v_i(x_i) = \alpha u_i(x_i) + \beta_i, \qquad \text{for all } i \text{ and all } x_i \text{ in } X_i.$$

Debreu and Koopmans (1982) study the conjunction of additive utilities and quasiconcavity of u when $u(x) = u_1(x_1) + \cdots + u_n(x_n)$.

The basic lexicographic representation for $X = X_1 \times X_2 \times \cdots$ (Chipman, 1960) with hierarchical importance ordering 1, 2, ... is

$$x \succ y \Leftrightarrow [u_1(x_1), u_2(x_2), \ldots] >_L [u_1(y_1), u_2(y_2), \ldots].$$

Luce (1978) combines the lexicographic and additive ideas in a two-factor model whose lexicographic part applies under significant differences in the dominant factor, and whose additive part applies otherwise.

One T3 representation is the additive-difference model in Tversky (1969) where

$$x \succ y \Leftrightarrow \sum_{i=1}^{n} f_i[u_i(x_i) - u_i(y_i)] > 0.$$

This is a special case of (4). Here f_i is an odd $[f_i(-a) = -f_i(a)]$, continuous and increasing real function. Fishburn (1980) combines the additive-difference and lexicographic notions.

Other T3 representations are implicit in Mas-Colell (1974) and elsewhere in a topological setting. A key axiom in this work is that $\{y: y \succ x\}$ is a convex subset of X for each x in X.

The homogeneous case $X = A^n$ or $X = A \times A \times \cdots$ provides a setting for time preference. Notions of persistence, impatience and stationarity for denumerable-period contexts are analysed by Koopmans (1960), Koopmans et al. (1964), and Fishburn and Rubinstein (1982). Fishburn (1970a) considers finite periods. One representation here is

$$x \succ y \Leftrightarrow \pi_1 u(x_1) + \pi_2 u(x_2) + \cdots > \pi_1 u(y_1) + \pi_2 u(y_2) + \ldots, \quad (6)$$

where $\pi_i \geqslant 0$ is an importance weight for period i. A particular case is $\pi_i = \sigma^{i-1}$, which obtains for the additive model (5) if preferences are 'stationary'.

Probability distributions: *S3*. This section and the next assume that X is a convex set of probability measures (distributions) on an outcome algebra $\mathscr{A}$. $x(A)$ is the probability that x yields an outcome in set A. When $0 \leqslant \lambda \leqslant 1$ and x and y are in X, $\lambda x + (1-\lambda)y$ denotes the linear convex combination of x and y that has $[\lambda x + (1-\lambda)y](A) = \lambda x(A) + (1-\lambda)y(A)$ for each A in $\mathscr{A}$. We say that $(X, \succ)$ is *linear* if $\lambda x + (1-\lambda)z \succ \lambda y + (1-\lambda)z$ whenever $x \succ y$, z is in X, and $0 < \lambda < 1$.

The von Neumann–Morgenstern theory (Fishburn, 1970a, 1982a) uses T1, linearity and a continuity condition to obtain a u on X that satisfies (1) and

$$u[\lambda x + (1-\lambda)y] = \lambda u(x) + (1-\lambda)u(y). \quad (7)$$

Such a u is unique up to an arbitrary positive linear transformation $[v(x) = \alpha u(x) + \beta, \alpha > 0]$ and is sometimes called a *cardinal utility function*. If the outcome set C is finite and $\mathscr{A}$ includes each singleton $\{c\}$ for c in C, then (7) yields the expected-utility form

$$u(x) = \sum_{C} x(c)u(c).$$

The extension of this to $u(x) = \int u(c)\,\mathrm{d}x(c)$ for infinite outcome sets is discussed in Fishburn (1970a, 1982a).

Generalizations of the von Neumann–Morgenstern theory that retain T1 but weaken the linearity axiom are discussed by Allais (1953), Kahneman and Tversky (1979), Machina (1982), Chew (1983), and Fishburn (1983). For example, Machina assumes a smooth preference field over X that is approximately linear locally, and Chew and Fishburn axiomatize the representation

$$x \succ y \Leftrightarrow u(x)w(y) > u(y)w(x), \quad (8)$$

in which each of u and w is linear, as in (7), and w is non-negative. When w is constant, (8) reduces to the von Neumann–Morgenstern case.

Generalizations that retain linearity but weaken T1 to T2 appear in Fishburn (1970a, 1982a). Other generalizations retain T1 and linearity but drop continuity to obtain lexicographic expected utility representations (Chipman, 1960; Fishburn, 1982a).

Axioms for unordered and nonlinear preferences over X are presented in Fishburn (1982b). Assumptions of continuity, convexity–such as $x \succ y$ and $z \succ y$ imply $\lambda x + (1-\lambda)z \succ y$, and symmetry are shown to be necessary and sufficient for the unordered representation (4) in which ϕ on $X \times X$ is skew-symmetric and *bilinear*, that is linear separately in each argument. Such a ϕ is unique up to an arbitrary similarity transformation of the form $\phi'(x, y) = \alpha\phi(x, y)$ with $\alpha > 0$. The von Neumann–Morgenstern model results when ϕ can be decomposed as $\phi(x, y) = u(x) - u(y)$, and (8) corresponds to $\phi(x, y) = u(x)w(y) - u(y)w(x)$.

Multiple attributes under risk: *S*4. Continuing with X as a set of probability distributions, we now assume that the outcome set C is a product set with $C = C_1 \times C_2 \times \cdots \times C_n$. We assume also that the basic expected utility axioms hold for $(X, \succ)$, so that, for all distributions x and y in X with finite supports,

$$x \succ y \Leftrightarrow \sum_C x(c_1, \ldots, c_n)u(c_1, \ldots, c_n) > \sum_C y(c_1, \ldots, c_n)u(c_1, \ldots, c_n). \quad (9)$$

A generalization of (9) is noted at the end of the section.

Representation (9) has several specializations involving decompositions of $u(c_1, \ldots, c_n)$. Many of these are reviewed in Keeney and Raiffa (1976), Fishburn (1977), and Farquhar (1978).

The additive decomposition is

$$u(c_1, \ldots, c_n) = u_1(c_1) + \cdots + u_n(c_n), \quad (10)$$

in which u_i is a real function on C_i and the u_i are unique up to similar positive linear transformations. When (10) holds, the sum in (9) simplifies to

$$\sum_C x(c_1, \ldots, c_n)u(c_1, \ldots, c_n) = \sum_{i=1}^{n} \sum_{C_i} x_i(c_i)u_i(c_i),$$

where x_i denotes the marginal distribution of x on C_i. Given (9), a necessary and sufficient condition for (10) is $x \sim y$ whenever $x_i = y_i$ for $i = 1, \ldots, n$. The same result holds (Fishburn, (1982a) when C is only assumed to be a subset of $C_1 \times \cdots \times C_n$, but in this case the preceding uniqueness property may fail.

Multiplicative decompositions of $u(c_1, \ldots, c_n)$ arise from independence conditions that are similar to the condition following (5). For any non-trivial two-part partition $\{I, J\}$ of $\{1, 2, \ldots, n\}$ we say that I is *utility independent* of J if the preference order over distributions on the product of the C_i for i in I, conditioned on fixed values of the C_j for all j in J, is independent of those fixed values. Moreover, I is *generalized utility independent* of J if any two such conditional preference orders are identical, duals, or one is empty. The importance of these notions is that if I is generalized utility independent of J then $u(c_I, c_J)$, where c_I is in the product of the C_i for $i \in I$ and similarly for c_J, decomposes as

$$u(c_I, c_J) = f(c_J) + g(c_J)h(c_I).$$

If I is utility independent of J, then g is a strictly positive function.

We mention one consequence of this two-part decomposition. If $\{1, \ldots i-1, i+1, \ldots, n\}$ is generalized utility independent of $\{i\}$ for each i in $\{1, \ldots n\}$, then there is a real function u_i on C_i for each i such that either (10) holds or there is a non-zero constant k such that, under a suitable rescaling of u,

$$ku(c_1, \ldots, c_n) + 1 = [ku_1(c_1) + 1] \cdots [ku_n(c_n) + 1].$$

Other types of independence among factors in the context of (9) are analysed by Farquhar (1975), Keeney and Raiffa (1976), and Fishburn and Farquhar (1982).

States of the world: *S*5. In our final setting, X is a set of functions from a set S of states of the world into a set C of outcomes or consequences. The set C may be unstructured or have one of the forms considered previously. For example, C could be a set of probability distributions defined on another set.

Following Savage (1954), we refer to each x in X as an *act* and to each subset of S as an *event*. It is presumed that exactly one state in S is the true state and that the agent is uncertain as to which state this is. Moreover, the true state, or state that 'obtains', is determined by circumstances beyond the agent's control. If the agent chooses act x and state s obtains, then $x(s)$ in C is the consequence that occurs as the result of the choice.

The best-known representation for $(X, \succ)$ is Savage's (1954) subjective expected utility model, which was inspired by Ramsey's earlier outline of a theory of preferences and beliefs under uncertainty, de Finetti's (1937) work in subjective probability, and the von Neumann–Morgenstern (1944) theory of expected utility. Savage's representation is

$$x \succ y \Leftrightarrow \int_S u[x(s)]\,\mathrm{d}P(s) > \int_S u[y(s)]\,\mathrm{d}P(s), \quad (11)$$

where u is a real function on C and P is a finitely-additive probability measure on the set of all events that is 'continuously divisible' in the sense that, for every event A and every $0 < \lambda < 1$ there is another event $B \subseteq A$ for which $P(B) = \lambda P(A)$. In addition, u is bounded (Fishburn, 1970a) and unique up to a positive linear transformation, and P is unique.

Savage's assumptions include strong structural conditions on X, T1, a few independence axioms, and a continuity condition that generates the form of P noted above. Criticisms of his conditions and alternative ways of conceptualizing decisions under uncertainty have stimulated a number of people to develop alternatives to Savage's theory with representations that are more or less similar to (11). The alternatives are reviewed in detail in Fishburn (1981).

Several authors (see Fishburn, 1981) derive Savage's representation for finite as well as infinite S by taking C as a set of probability distributions or lotteries. The same device is used extensively in Fishburn (1982a), which includes a one-way representation under T2. Schmeidler (1984) keeps T1 in the lottery approach but weakens independence to obtain a representation with monotonic but non-additive 'probabilities' that accommodates preference patterns that are inconsistent with Savage's theory (Ellsberg, 1961).

Loomes and Sugden (1982) propose a finite-state model for decision under uncertainty that allows non-transitive preferences and therefore falls in transitivity class T3. Their representation for n states is

$$x \succ y \Leftrightarrow \sum_{i=1}^{n} P(s_i)\phi[x(s_i), y(s_i)] > 0,$$

where $P(s_i)$ is the agent's subjective probability for states s_i and ϕ is skew-symmetric. Lottery-based axioms for this and other T3 models appear in Fishburn (1984).

Comparable preference differences. In contrast to preceding representations, we now consider representations based on a binary relation $\succ^*$ on $X \times X$. A common intuitive interpretation of $\succ^*$ is that $(x, y) \succ^* (z, w)$ signifies that the difference in preference between x and y exceeds the difference in preference between z and w, or that the intensity of preference for x over y exceeds the intensity of preference for z over w. When $\succ^*$ is used, $\succ$ is usually defined by $x \succ y$ if and only if $(x, y) \succ^* (y, y)$.

A basic representation in this setting is

$$(x, y) \succ^* (z, w) \Leftrightarrow u(x) - u(y) > u(z) - u(w). \quad (12)$$

This requires $\succ^*$ to be a weak order on $X \times X$ and entails other conditions like $(x, y) \succ^* (z, w) \Leftrightarrow (x, z) \succ^* (y, w)$ and $(x, y) \succ^* (z, y) \Leftrightarrow (x, w) \succ^* (z, w)$.

Early axiomatizations of (12) from the 1920s and 1930s are due to Frisch, Lange and Alt. Comments on these and more recent axiomatizations appear in Fishburn (1970a, chapter 6). The axioms for infinite X essentially use a bisection procedure to determine utility midpoints, as when $u(x) - u(z) = u(z) - u(y)$, or $u(z) = [u(x) + u(y)]/2$, and the resultant u is unique up to a positive linear transformation.

Specialized representations in the context of (12) arise when $X = X_1 \times \cdots \times X_n$. Dyer and Sarin (1979) and Kirkwood and Sarin (1980) consider decompositions of $u(x_1, \ldots, x_n)$ that are similar to ones mentioned under S4, and Fishburn (1970a) discusses the weighted additive form used in (6) when $X = A^n$.

PETER C. FISHBURN

See also PREFERENCES; SOCIAL CHOICE; UTILITY THEORY AND DECISION-MAKING.

BIBLIOGRAPHY

Allais, M. 1953. Le comportement de l'homme rationnel devant le risque: critique des postulats et axiomes de l'école Americaine. *Econometrica* 21, 503–46.

Bernoulli, D. 1738. Specimen theoriae novae de mensura sortis. *Commentarii Academiae Scientarium Imperialis Petropolitanae* 5, 175–92. Trans. L. Sommer, *Econometrica* 22, (1954), 23–36.

Cantor, G. 1895. Beiträge zur Begründung der Transfinite Mengenlehre. *Mathematische Annalen* 46, 481–512 and 49 (1897), 207–46. English translation: *Contributions to the Founding of the Theory of Transfinite Numbers*. New York: Dover, n.d.

Chew, S.H. 1983. A generalization of the quasilinear mean with applications to the measurement of income inequality and decision theory resolving the Allais paradox. *Econometrica* 51, 1065–92.

Chipman, J.S. 1960. The foundations of utility. *Econometrica* 28, 193–224.

Debreu, G. 1964. Continuity properties of Paretian utility. *International Economic Review* 5, 285–93.

Debreu, G. and Koopmans, T.C. 1982. Additively decomposed quasiconvex functions. *Mathematical Programming* 24, 1–38.

de Finetti, B. 1937. La prévision: ses logiques, ses sources subjectives. *Annales de l'Institut Henri Poincaré* 7, 1–68. Trans. by H.E. Kyburg in *Studies in Subjective Probability*, ed. H.E. Kyburg and H.E. Smokler, New York: Wiley, 1964, 93–158.

Dyer, J.S. and Sarin, R.K. 1979. Measurable multiattribute value functions. *Operations Research* 27, 810–22.

Ellsberg, D. 1961. Risk, ambiguity, and the Savage axioms. *Quarterly Journal of Economics* 75, 643–69.

Farquhar, P.H. 1975. A fractional hypercube decomposition theorem for multiattribute utility functions. *Operations Research* 23, 941–67.

Farquhar, P.H. 1978. Interdependent criteria in utility analysis. In *Multiple Criteria Problem Solving*, ed. S. Zionts, Berlin: Springer-Verlag, 131–80.

Fishburn, P.C. 1970a. *Utility Theory for Decision Making*. New York: Wiley.

Fishburn, P.C. 1970b. Intransitive indifference in preference theory: a survey. *Operations Research* 18, 207–28.

Fishburn, P.C. 1974. Lexicographic orders, utilities, and decision rules: a survey. *Management Science* 20, 1442–71.

Fishburn, P.C. 1977. Multiattribute utilities in expected utility theory. In *Conflicting Objectives in Decisions*, ed. D.E. Bell, R.L. Keeney and H. Raiffa, New York: Wiley, 172–94.

Fishburn, P.C. 1980. Lexicographic additive differences. *Journal of Mathematical Psychology* 21, 191–218.

Fishburn, P.C. 1981. Subjective expected utility: a review of normative theories. *Theory and Decision* 13, 139–99.

Fishburn, P.C. 1982a. *The Foundations of Expected Utility*. Dordrecht, Holland: Reidel.

Fishburn, P.C. 1982b. Nontransitive measurable utility. *Journal of Mathematical Psychology* 26, 31–67.

Fishburn, P.C. 1983. Transitive measurable utility. *Journal of Economic Theory* 31, 293–317.

Fishburn, P.C. 1984. SSB utility theory and decision-making under uncertainty. *Mathematical Social Sciences* 8, 253–85.

Fishburn, P.C. 1985. *Interval Orders and Interval Graphs*. New York: Wiley.

Fishburn, P.C. and Farquhar, P.H. 1982. Finite-degree utility independence. *Mathematics of Operations Research* 7, 348–53.

Fishburn, P.C. and Rubinstein, A. 1982. Time preference. *International Economic Review* 23, 677–94.

Houthakker, H.S. 1961. The present state of consumption theory. *Econometrica* 29, 704–40.

Kahneman, D. and Tversky, A. 1979. Prospect theory: an analysis of decision under risk. *Econometrica* 47, 263–91.

Keeney, R.L. and Raiffa, H. 1976. *Decisions with Multiple Objectives: Preferences and Value Tradeoffs*. New York: Wiley.

Kirkwood, C.W. and Sarin, R.K. 1980. Preference conditions for multiattribute value functions. *Operations Research* 28, 225–32.

Koopmans, T.C. 1960. Stationary ordinal utility and impatience. *Econometrica* 28, 287–309.

Koopmans, T.C., Diamond, P.A. and Williamson, R.E. 1964. Stationary utility and time perspective. *Econometrica* 32, 82–100.

Krantz, D.H., Luce, R.D., Suppes, P. and Tversky, A. 1971. *Foundations of Measurement. Volume I: Additive and Polynomial Representations*. New York: Academic Press.

Loomes, G. and Sugden, R. 1982. Regret theory: an alternative theory of rational choice under uncertainty. *Economic Journal* 92, 805–24.

Luce, R.D. 1978. Lexicographic tradeoff structures. *Theory and Decision* 9, 187–93.

Machina, M.J. 1982. 'Expected utility' analysis without the independence axiom, *Econometrica* 50, 277–323.

Mas-Colell, A. 1974. An equilibrium existence theorem without complete or transitive preferences. *Journal of Mathematical Economics* 1, 237–46.

Samuelson, P.A. 1947. *Foundations of Economic Analysis*. Cambridge, Mass.: Harvard University Press.

Savage, L.J. 1954. *The Foundations of Statistics*. New York: Wiley. 2nd rev. edn, Dover Publications, 1972.

Schmeidler, D. 1984. Subjective probability and expected utility without additivity. Preprint no.84, Institute for Mathematics and its Applications, University of Minnesota.

Sondermann, D. 1980. Utility representations for partial orders. *Journal of Economic Theory* 23, 183–8.

Stigler, G.J. 1950. The development of utility theory I, II. *Journal of Political Economy* 58, 307–27; 373–96.

Tversky, A. 1969. Intransitivity of preferences. *Psychological Review* 76, 31–48.

von Neumann, J. and Morgenstern, O. 1944. *Theory of Games and Economic Behavior*. Princeton: Princeton University Press; 2nd edn, 1947; 3rd edn, 1953.

reservation price and reservation demand. The simplest example of a reservation price is that price below which an owner will refuse to sell a particular object in an auction. Since the owner could always, in principle, enforce such a price by outbidding everyone else, this leads immediately to the more general concept of a reservation price as that price at which the owner of a fixed stock will choose to *retain* some given amount from that stock, rather than supply more, and of the amount retained as the owner's 'reservation demand' at the price in question. Considering alternative hypothetical prices, one sees that the owner's supply curve of the commodity can equally well be described as an 'own (reservation) demand' curve, where 'supply' and 'own demand' sum identically to the given stock. The same is naturally true of the market supply curve. Thus consider the standard example of the determination of the price of first-edition copies of a certain old book. A demand curve may be drawn up for those who at present own no copies. Taking account of each present owner's reservation price (or prices for those who possess more than one copy), we may also draw up a supply curve. (Of course 'supply' by present owners may be negative at low prices). Confrontation of the demand and supply curves will then show the market-clearing price. Equally, however, we could have drawn up the 'reservation demand' curve of present owners, summed it with the demand curve of non-owners and then confronted the 'total' demand curve with the given stock. Since 'supply' and 'reservation demand' sum identically to total stock, at every price, the alternative diagram inevitably shows the same market-clearing price as does the first; it does not show the number of books traded, however.

It will be clear that an agent's reservation price for any type of commodity can be expected to depend on one or more of the following considerations: the scope for direct 'own use' of the commodity; the agent's present need for liquidity; the agent's other resources; the perishability of the commodity and thus the various elements of storage costs (including interest costs); expectations about future prices, there being always a speculative element in the reservation price of any commodity which is not immediately perishable. These considerations all emerge in theories of 'factor supply', for example in the theory of household labour supply. Since 'labour time' is instantly perishable, there is no strictly speculative element to take into account (although someone seeking work may refuse a particular job offer because the wage offered is below a 'reservation wage' based on expectations as to the wage that can be obtained after further job searching). The conventional theory is, however, firmly based on viewing labour supply in terms of the 'reservation demand' for time not spent in market employment, and it is this that leads to the familiar argument that the income effect of a 'wage' change can both be large and contrary to the substitution effect, with the result that labour supply may be either positively or negatively related to the level of the 'wage'. Analogous arguments bear on the supply of land services by landowners who have an 'own use' for their land, on the supply of agricultural products etc. The reservation price concept is also useful in the context of privately owned natural resources, a context which introduces two further determinants of reservation price. The lowest price at which a natural resource owner will be prepared to extract the resource will naturally depend on extraction costs, both the present extraction costs and those expected in the future; it will also depend on the expected growth rate, if any, of the resource. It is to be noted that the 'neoclassical rule of free goods' would never have to be applied to primary inputs for which (a) there was a positive price below which supply would be zero, and (b) demand at a zero price would be positive (both conditions holding for all prices of other commodities); (*see* FREE GOODS).

It was noted above, in connection with the market for first-edition copies of a book, that the 'total' demand curve diagram gives the same information with respect to price, and less information with respect to quantity, than does the more conventional supply and demand diagram. How then could P.H. Wicksteed – whose name is so strongly associated with the concept of a supply curve's being merely a 'reversed demand curve' – have been so insistent that the former diagram is actually *superior* to the conventional one? (See Wicksteed, 1910, Book II, Ch. IV, and 1914). Because the 'total' demand curve diagram emphasizes the idea that essentially the *same* kind of forces underlie the conventional supply curve as underlie the usual demand curve, thus breaking down the idea that there is an asymmetry in market forces, with subjective factors being dominant on the 'demand side' and objective ones on the 'supply side'. The diagram in which a single demand curve (inclusive of reservation demand) confronts a fixed supply is at once congenial to any author both seeking to stress the subjective elements of the economic process and upholding the opportunity cost doctrine as against the real cost doctrine. While acknowledging that the demand and supply curves diagram illuminates the process through which the market clearing price is *discovered*, therefore, Wicksteed insisted that the other diagram brings out far more clearly the fundamental *determinants* of that price, namely subjective marginal valuations and given supplies. With reference to continuously produced commodities, as opposed to first-edition copies, maintenance of this viewpoint would presumably require that the 'given stocks' referred to should be those of primary inputs. Here it may be noted that, even in the course of denouncing the conventional supply curve, Wicksteed admitted that 'as we recede from the market and deal with long periods ... cases may arise in which something like a "supply curve" seems legitimate' and that nature does not have 'reserve prices in which she expresses her own demand!' (1914, p. 16, n.1).

IAN STEEDMAN

See also BIDDING; OFFER; WICKSTEED, PHILIP HENRY.

BIBLIOGRAPHY

Wicksteed, P.H. 1910. *The Common Sense of Political Economy, including a study of the human basis of economic law*. London: Macmillan.

Wicksteed, P.H. 1914. The scope and method of political economy in the light of the 'marginal' theory of value and distribution. *Economic Journal* 24, March, 1–23.

reserve army. *See* LABOUR SURPLUS ECONOMIES; MARX, KARL HEINRICH.

reserves, free. *See* CENTRAL BANKING; FINANCIAL INTERMEDIARIES.

reserves, international. *See* INTERNATIONAL LIQUIDITY.

residuals. Most commonly used statistical procedures, for analysis and interpretation of statistical data, rest on assumptions about the behaviour of the data. Quite often these assumptions can be adequately justified, and the procedures accepted as fair and reasonable. But that is not always so, and it behoves the analyst to check consistency of the data with the assumptions. Failure to do this may lead to a grossly misleading analysis and the drawing of wrong conclusions. Just how consistency can be checked depends on the complexity of the data. Often a step is calculation of *residuals*, which are measures of deviation between the observed values of a variable and the fitted (or estimated or predicted) values for that variable, calculated in accordance with the assumptions. The residuals, when found, are sometimes combined into a summary measure of goodness of fit, or sometimes they are displayed graphically, in various possible ways.

A very simple example of this kind of concern is afforded by the common practice of summarizing a single set of readings of a quantitative variable by the average of the readings and their standard deviation. Those two quantities would certainly form a good and convenient summary of the data, useful for a variety of purposes, if we knew that the readings were independent observations of a random variable following a normal (Gauss–Laplace) distribution, or something not very different from that. Usually in practice we do not have such knowledge. We can, however, check to see whether the distribution of the readings, shown perhaps by a histogram, is reasonably consistent with a normal distribution; and if the readings came to us arranged in some meaningful order we could look for evidence of serial dependence. If the readings contained one extreme outlier (a reading very far from all the others), the average and standard deviation calculated from all the readings could be quite different from those calculated from all the readings *except* that one outlier, and for most purposes the average and standard deviation of all the readings would be misleading.

The possibly devastating effect of outliers has suggested to some authorities that 'robust' measures of the centre and spread of a set of readings would be preferable to the traditional average and standard deviation – measures that rest on much weaker assumptions than a nearly normal distribution, measures that would be little affected by inclusion or exclusion of a few outliers if such occurred in the data. Instead of the average one could choose the median of the data, and instead of the standard deviation one could choose the median absolute deviation of readings from their median, or the interquartile range. Such robust measures cannot be said to rest on no assumptions at all – independence is assumed, for example – but they are safer to use if procedures must be used uncritically. A price is paid for the safety. The traditional assumptions permit a considerable body of simple inferential methods, that must be foregone or much modified when only the weaker assumptions for robust procedures are made. Thus in much statistical practice today, analytical procedures based on specific non-robust probabilistic assumptions are still often used, but checking conformity of the data with the assumptions is regarded as essential.

In the above discussion of summarizing a single set of readings of one variable, the word 'residual' has not been mentioned. Residuals could be defined as the differences between each of the readings and their average (or median or whatever central measure is adopted). The central measure is the 'fitted value', the same for all readings. An outlier is a reading whose residual is much larger in magnitude than nearly all the other residuals. In any graphical presentation of the data, the differences between individual readings and the common central value are easily seen, whether or not the residuals have been calculated; and therefore in this context it is hardly necessary to refer to residuals, even though it is just those differences that are of most interest.

The most widely used technique in the analysis of statistical data is linear regression, by which the association of a quantitative 'dependent' variable with one or more explanatory variables may be studied. Some of the considerations that arise concerning consistency of the data with the assumptions underlying linear regression can be seen in their simplest form if we consider linear regression of one dependent variable on just one explanatory variable.

For such simple linear regression, the standard least-squares calculation is based on the following theoretical description or 'model': the given number pairs (x_i, y_i) are related by

$$y_i = \beta_0 + \beta_1 x_i + \epsilon_i \qquad (i = 1, 2, \ldots, n), \tag{1}$$

where β_0 and β_0 are constants and the 'errors' $\{\epsilon_i\}$ are drawn independently from a normal probability distribution having zero mean and constant variance. The regression calculation leads to estimates b_0 and b_1 for β_0 and β_1, to the fitted values

$$\hat{y}_i = b_0 + b_1 x_i = \bar{y} + b_1(x_i - \bar{x}),$$

and to the residuals

$$e_i = y_i - \hat{y}_i.$$

The sum of squares of the latter, generally called the 'residual sum of squares', leads to an estimate of the variance of the distribution of errors. If the theoretical description were exactly correct (and all calculations were exact, without round-off error), these calculations would be entirely satisfactory, in the sense that b_0, b_1 and the residual sum of squares, together with the number of readings n and the first two moments of the x-values, would constitute sufficient statistics for the original data for all purposes with no loss of information. In practice, we do not know that the theoretical description is correct, we should generally suspect that it is not, and we cannot therefore heave a sigh of relief when the regression calculation has been made, knowing that statistical justice has been done.

Some of the possibilities for appropriateness or inappropriateness of the standard regression calculation are illustrated by the four artificial data sets given in Table 1. Each data set consists of eleven (x, y) pairs. For the first three data sets the x-values are the same, and they are listed only once. The four data sets have been constructed so as to yield the same

TABLE 1. Four artificial data sets, each consisting of eleven (x, y) pairs

Data set	1–3	1	2	3	4	4
Variable	x	y	y	y	x	y
Obs. no. 1:	10.0	8.04	9.14	7.46:	8.0	6.58
2:	8.0	6.95	8.14	6.77:	8.0	5.76
3:	13.0	7.58	8.74	12.74:	8.0	7.71
4:	9.0	8.81	8.77	7.11:	8.0	8.84
5:	11.0	8.33	9.26	7.81:	8.0	8.47
6:	14.0	9.96	8.10	8.84:	8.0	7.04
7:	6.0	7.24	6.13	6.08:	8.0	5.25
8:	4.0	4.26	3.10	5.39:	19.0	12.50
9:	12.0	10.84	9.13	8.15:	8.0	5.56
10:	7.0	4.82	7.26	6.42:	8.0	7.91
11:	5.0	5.68	4.74	5.73:	8.0	6.89

TABLE 2. The same standard output of a regression analysis of each of the data sets in Table 1

Number of observations $(n) = 11$
Mean of the x's $(\bar{x}) = 9.0$
Mean of the y's $(\bar{y}) = 7.5$
Regression coefficient (b_1) of y on $x = 0.5$
Equation of regression line: $y = 3 + 0.5x$
Sum of squares of $x - \bar{x} = 110.0$
Regression sum of squares $= 27.50$ (1 d.f.)
Residual sum of squares of $y = 13.75$ (9 d.f.)
Estimated standard error of $b_1 = 0.118$
Multiple $R^2 = 0.667$

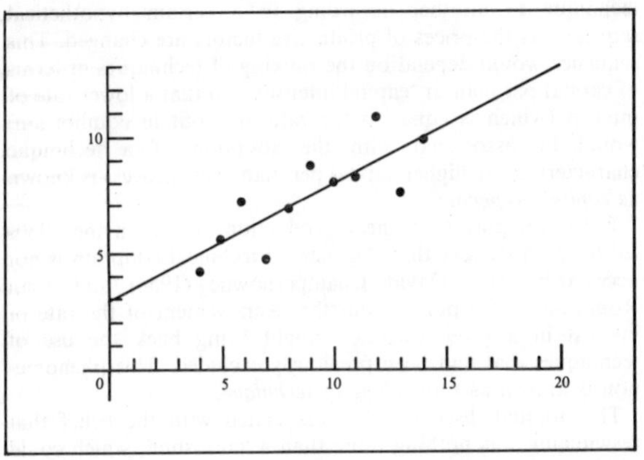

Figure 1

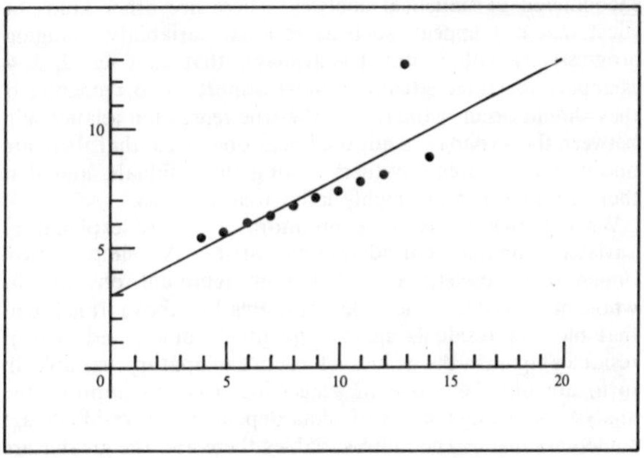

Figure 3

standard output from a typical regression programme, as shown in Table 2. Thus if equation (1) is a correct theoretical description of the data, all four data sets are equivalent – they mean the same thing.

Regression programmes often list the residuals, in the order in which the data were entered. Since in the present case the data have been entered in a random order, probably little would be seen if the eye were run down such a listing, especially if it were in abominable floating-point notation. Only if the residuals are presented graphically, or perhaps combined into one or more overall measures of goodness of fit, is the viewer likely to realize how very different in character these four data sets are, and therefore how inadequate the information in Table 2 is. The simplest kind of graphical presentation of the data sets is just a scatterplot of the given (x, y) pairs, together with the fitted regression line, as in Figures 1–4.

Figure 1, corresponding to data set 1, is the kind of thing most people would see in their mind's eye, if they were presented with the summary in Table 2. The theoretical description (1) seems to be perfectly appropriate here, and the summary fair and adequate. Figure 2 suggests forcefully that data set 2 does not conform with the theoretical description (1), but rather y has a smooth curved relation with x, possibly quadratic, and there is little residual variability. Figure 3 similarly suggests that (1) is not a good description for data set 3: all but one of the observations lie close to a straight line (not the one yielded by the standard regression calculation), namely

$$y = 4 + 0.346x;$$

and one observation is far from this line. Those are the essential facts that need to be understood and reported.

Figure 4, like Figure 1, shows data apparently conforming well with the theoretical description (1). If all observations are considered genuine and reliable, data set 4 is just as informative about the regression relation as data set 1; there is no reason to prefer either to the other. Yet in most circumstances we should feel that there was something unsatisfactory about data set 4. All the information about the slope of the regression line resides in one observation – if that observation were deleted the slope could not be estimated. Usually we are not quite sure that every observation is reliable. If any one observation were discredited and therefore deleted from data set 1, the remainder would tell much the same story. That is not so for data set 4. Thus the standard regression calculation ought to be accompanied by a warning that one observation has played a critical role. Of course, just one informative observation is much better than none. But we are usually happier about asserting a regression relation if the relation seems to permeate many of the observations and does not inhere mostly in one or two.

Each of the data sets 2, 3, 4 illustrates a peculiar effect in an extreme form. In less extreme forms such effects are often

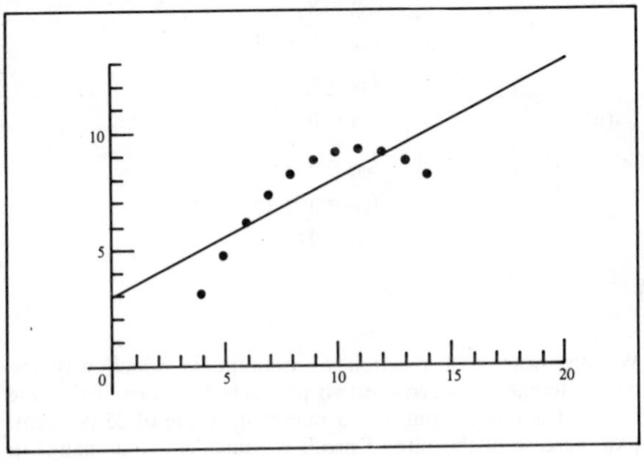

Figure 2

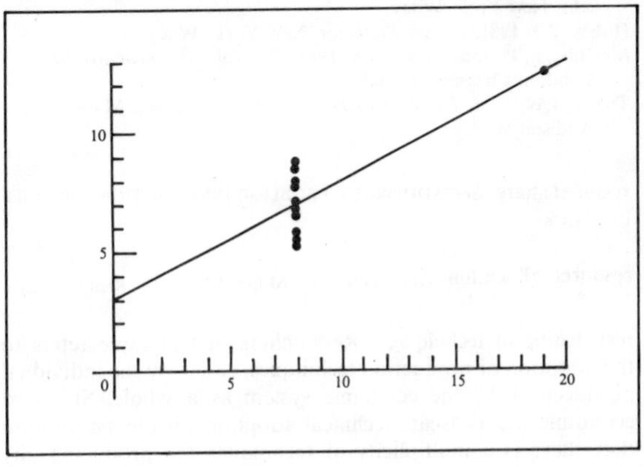

Figure 4

encountered in statistical analysis. There are other kinds of effect that can appear, such as residual variability changing progressively with x. But it is arguable that data sets 2, 3, 4 exemplify the three situations most important to recognize if they should occur, namely that the true regression relationship between the variables is not the linear one fitted, that there are one or more extreme outliers among the residuals, and that there are one or more highly influential x-values.

When regression is done on more than one explanatory variable, similar considerations arise. A simple two-dimensional scatterplot cannot now represent directly the whole of the data, in the style of Figures 1–4 above. It is found that plots of residuals against the fitted values, and also of residuals against the values of each explanatory variable in turn, are often effective in suggesting ways to improve the analysis; and other kinds of plots depending on residuals are sometimes made. The more variables there are, the greater are the possible complexities in the data, and the less sure we can be that all important effects will be perceived. That is the more reason for examining residuals carefully. Various specific test statistics can be formed from residuals and used to detect specific kinds of discrepancy between the data and the assumed theoretical description.

Examination of residuals has been most thoroughly developed for regression. But in many other cases when data are considered in light of a theoretical description, measures of difference between observed values and fitted values can be defined that behave like regression residuals and are similarly useful. Such residuals are, however, often not just simple differences between observed values and fitted values.

[Examination of residuals is discussed by Draper and Smith (1981), Cook and Weisberg (1982), Anscombe (1981), McCullagh and Nelder (1983), Cox and Snell (1968). The tables and figures given above are taken from Anscombe (1973). For robust methods see Tukey (1977) and Huber (1981).]

F.J. ANSCOMBE

See also OUTLIERS; RANDOM VARIABLES; REGRESSION AND CORRELATION ANALYSIS.

BIBLIOGRAPHY

Anscombe, F.J. 1973. *American Statistician* 27, 17–21.

Anscombe, F.J. 1981. *Computing in Statistical Science through APL.* New York: Springer-Verlag. (Especially Appendix 2.)

Cook, R.D. and Weisberg, S. 1982. *Residuals and Influence in Regression.* London: Chapman & Hall. (Especially Chapter 2.)

Cox, D.R. and Snell, E.J. 1968. *Journal of the Royal Statistical Society*, Series B 30, 248–75.

Draper, N.R. and Smith, H. 1981. *Applied Regression Analysis.* 2nd edn, New York: Wiley.

Huber, P.J. 1981. *Robust Statistics.* New York: Wiley.

McCullagh, P. and Nelder, J.A. 1983. *Generalized Linear Models.* London: Chapman & Hall.

Tukey, J.W. 1977. *Exploratory Data Analysis.* Reading, Mass.: Addison-Wesley.

residual share. *See* ADDING-UP PROBLEM; DISTRIBUTION THEORIES: CLASSICAL.

resource allocation. *See* EFFICIENT ALLOCATION OF RESOURCES.

reswitching of technique. Reswitching of technique refers to the adoption of production techniques, either by the individual producer or by the economic system as a whole. Standard economic theory treats technical adoption on the assumption that there is a multiplicity of techniques for producing any given good, and that the producer will switch from one technique to another according to a certain hypothetical sequence as the prices of productive factors are changed. This sequence would depend on the ranking of techniques in terms of capital per man or 'capital intensity', so that a lower rate of interest (which is equal to the rate of profit in equilibrium) would be associated with the adoption of a technique characterized by higher capital per man. This process is known as *capital deepening*.

The development of linear production models in the 1950s led to the discovery that this view of technical adoption is not necessarily true. David Champernowne (1954) and Joan Robinson (1956) pointed out that a movement of the rate of interest in a given direction might bring back the use of techniques that had been previously excluded. This phenomenon is known as *reswitching of technique*.

The original discovery was associated with the belief that reswitching was nothing more than a 'curiosum', which could not be excluded on grounds of pure logic but was nevertheless unlikely to happen. The discussion of this phenomenon by Piero Sraffa (1960) showed that reswitching is the normal outcome of a situation in which the various production processes are characterized by different proportions between 'direct' labour and the quantity of 'past' labour. (This latter is the quantity of labour that is indirectly required in a production process, being required in producing its intermediate inputs.) Sraffa's analysis also provides a clear insight into the reasons for technical reswitching. It is worthwhile considering his example in some detail.

THE 'PURE PRODUCTS' CASE. It is useful to start with the consideration of a special category of commodities, which we might call of the *pure product* type. These are commodities that are never used as productive inputs, so that their price reflects production cost, but cost is never influenced by the variation of their particular prices.

Let a and b be commodities of that type, and let them be produced with different proportions of direct labour to past labour. (This structure of labour requirements is representative of the differences in the proportions between labour and intermediate inputs in the production processes of the two commodities.)

Let a require more labour than b if we consider labour applied 8 years before the year in which the product is ready, whereas b requires more labour than a in the cases of labour applied in the current year and 25 years earlier. This situation may be represented as follows (n is the date at which labour is applied):

(i) $$n = 8$$
$$l_{a(8)} = v + 20$$
$$l_{b(8)} = v$$

(ii) $$n = 0$$
$$l_{a(0)} = x$$
$$l_{b(0)} = x + 19$$

(iii) $$n = 25$$
$$l_{a(25)} = y$$
$$l_{b(25)} = y + 1$$

We are now in a position to examine in which way the cost-difference between the two products may vary if the rate of profit is raised from 0 to a maximum value of 25 per cent. (An increase of the rate of profit is equivalent to a change in the weight of the different labour terms in each cost equation.)

The cost-difference is expressed by the following equation:

$$p_a - p_b = 20w(1+r)^8 - [19w + w(1+r)^{25}] \qquad (1)$$

Assuming that the wage rate (w) is inversely related to the rate of profit according to the following expression:

$$w = 1 - \frac{r}{25\%},$$

the cost–difference equation will be represented by the curve in Figure 1.

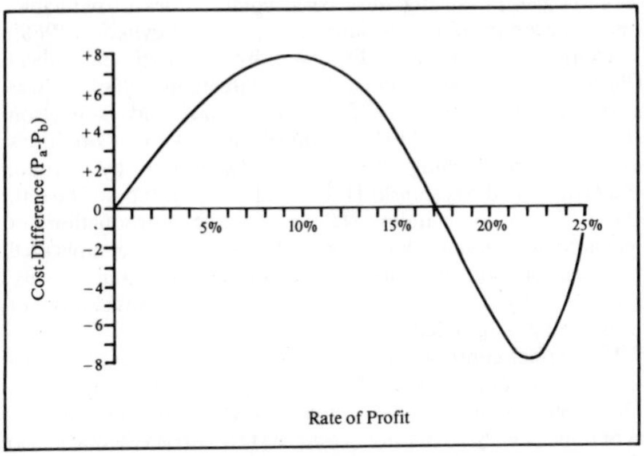

Figure 1

The cost of a rises relatively to b as r increases between 0 and 9%. The reason for this is that the change of r leaves the value of current labour unaffected, whereas the 'excess labour' of date 8 is much greater than the excess labour of date 25. The increase in the value of $l_{b\ (25)}$ is more than offset by the increase in the value of $l_{a\ (8)}$ and the compound effect of these two variations is an increase in the cost-difference. Beyond $r = 9\%$, the increasing weight of remote labour terms brings the cost–difference down. This reduction stops at $r = 22\%$, since at this particular level of the rate of profit the decline of the wage rate starts off-setting the increase in the value of remote labour terms due to a higher r.

The above argument has straightforward implications for technical choice in the case of commodities of the pure product type. For in this case we can take for granted that the price of each commodity reflects its cost of production, whereas this price has no influence at all on the cost. Under such conditions, equation (1) permits us to examine in which way the relative profitability of two techniques is varied as r goes from 0 to r (max). In fact, we may take equation (1) to illustrate the difference between the unit costs of production of the same commodity produced with two alternative techniques. (For reasons of symmetry with the previous argument we shall call such alternative techniques a and b respectively.) Figure 1 can be applied to this particular case. An immediate shortcoming would be that a change in the price of direct to 'dated' labour, as reflected in an increasing r, is associated with a positive excess of unit cost p_a over unit cost p_b until the curve intersects the horizontal axis for the first time. This involves that, over this interval, technique b is more profitable than technique a. A further increase of r (until r (max)) is associated with a negative difference ($p_a - p_b$), so that technique a is more profitable than technique b. However, the same figure shows that the *reduction* of the cost-difference stops at $r = 22\%$. For any r such that $22\% < r < r$ (max), the cost-difference is increasing once again. This increase stops at $r = 25\%$, when techniques a and b become equally profitable.

The movement of the cost-difference when r is increasing shows that the relative profitability of techniques a and b is subject to fluctuations which depend on the particular interval within which r is changed. The relative profitability of technique a with respect to technique b is initially decreasing, then increasing, finally decreasing again. These fluctuations show that the 'unevenness' of the input structure may bring about multiple switches between the two techniques as we consider a steadily increasing r: the same technique might be adopted at low and high rates of profit, with the alternative technique being adopted at intermediate levels of r.

THE 'INTERMEDIATE PRODUCTS' CASE. It might appear that the above picture gets greatly complicated when we consider the more general case of products that are used as productive inputs either of themselves or of other commodities. For in this new situation the price of a commodity reflects its production cost, but this cost might itself be influenced by that price. (Directly in the case of a product used in its own production, indirectly in the case of a product that is, at some stage, a necessary means of production for at least one of its inputs.)

An immediate consequence of the consideration of interdependence between production processes is that inspection of the cost-difference equation is no longer sufficient in order to assess the relative profitability of alternative techniques. The mutual influence between prices and production costs brings about the need of comparing systems of interrelated techniques (*production technologies*) rather than individual techniques. This requires consideration of the price system that will be associated with each technology at any given distribution of income between wages and profits.

The analysis of the 'intermediate products' case can be carried out by examining a simple model with two alternative two-good technologies A and B, in which all products are used as inputs of themselves and of the other commodity. We shall also assume that the two technologies differ only in the technique used to produce commodity 1.

The two price systems may be written as follows:

$$\begin{aligned} &(a_{11}p_1 + a_{21}p_2)(1+r) + l_1(a)w = p_1 \\ &(a_{12}p_1 + a_{22}p_2)(1+r) + l_2(a)w = p_2, \end{aligned} \qquad (2.1)$$

$$\begin{aligned} &(b_{11}p_1 + b_{21}p_2)(1+r) + l_1(b)w = p_1 \\ &(b_{12}p_1 + b_{22}p_2)(1+r) + l_2(b)w = p_2, \end{aligned} \qquad (2.2)$$

where $a_{ij}(i,j = 1,2)$ and $b_{ij}(i,j = 1,2)$ are the quantities of commodity i required to produce one unit of commodity j with technologies A and B respectively, $l_i(a)$ and $l_i(b)$ are the quantities of labour entering one unit of commodity i with technologies A and B respectively, p_i ($i = 1,2$) is the price of product i, w is the unit wage and r the rate of profit. The quantities a_{ij}, b_{ij}, $l_i(a)$ and $l_i(b)$ are known, whereas r, w, p_i are unknown.

Either product is common to both systems. We may thus choose either commodity 1 or 2 as the common standard of prices (*numéraire*) in both systems. If we put the price of commodity 1 equal to unity, commodity 1 becomes the common *numéraire* of price systems (2.1) and (2.2). At this stage, it is found convenient to assess the relative profitability of alternative technologies by considering the functional relationship between r and w for each technology.

The systems of equations (2.1) and (2.2) would each be associated with a particular relation between the rate of profit and the unit wage. The wage–profit relationships for the two systems would respectively be given by the following expressions:

$$w_A = \frac{1-(a_{22}+a_{11})(1+r)+(a_{11}a_{22}-a_{21}a_{12})(1+r)^2}{(1+r)[a_{21}l_2(a)-a_{22}l_1(a)]+l_1(a)} \quad (3.1)$$

$$w_B = \frac{1-(b_{22}+b_{11})(1+r)+(b_{11}b_{22}-b_{21}b_{12})(1+r)^2}{(1+r)[b_{21}l_2(b)-b_{22}l_1(b)]+l_1(b)} \quad (3.2)$$

It may be immediately noted that w is always a decreasing function of r, independently of the sign of the second order derivative (see also Morishima, 1966, p. 521). We may also note that the unit wage is expressed in terms of the same *numéraire* in (3.1) and (3.2). This suggests that the relationships between r and w (also known as *factor-price frontiers*) can be plotted as negatively sloped curves on the same diagram.

The intersections between the two curves occur at those levels of the rate of profit which are associated with the same unit wage in both technologies. The number of intersections can be obtained by equating w in equations (3.1) and (3.2) and solving for r. The resulting equation will generally have more than one positive solution (Bruno, Burmeister and Sheshinski, 1966, p. 534). In the case of technologies such that each product is a necessary input for all commodities including itself (all products are *basic commodities*), the maximum number of intersections is given by the number of distinct commodities in the two alternative systems of production (Bharadwaj, 1970). This implies that, in the two-good technologies of our example, there will be at most two intersections. Figure 2 represents a case in which there are two intersections in the positive quadrant.

Technologies A and B can now be compared, on grounds of profitability, by considering which technology yields the higher rate of profit for any given wage. (Or, alternatively, which technology yields the higher wage rate for any given rate of profit.)

Figure 2 makes clear that the relative profitability of the two technologies is subject to fluctuation as r increases from 0 to $r^*(B)$ (the maximum rate of profit with technology B). At a low level of the rate of profit ($r<r_1$), technology A is more profitable ('cheaper') than B. At $r=r_1$, A and B are equally profitable. At levels of r between r_1 and r_2, A is 'cheaper' than B. But at any rate of profit higher than r_2, B is again 'cheaper' than A.

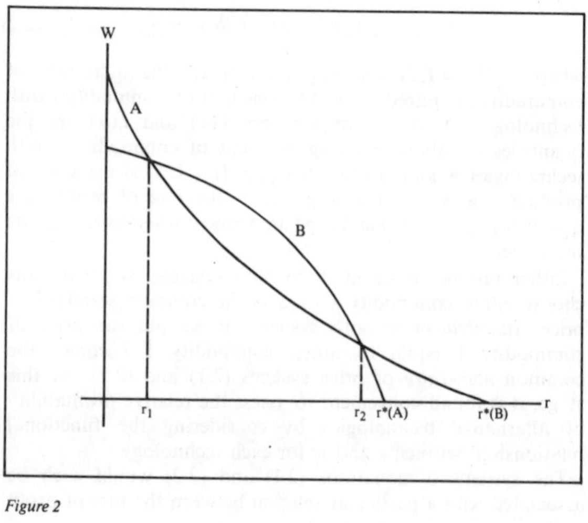

Figure 2

Reswitching of technique may be shown to be possible between complete production systems as well as between individual techniques. Shortly after the identification of the reswitching possibility by Champernowne (1954) and Robinson (1956), and its subsequent analysis by Sraffa (1960), Morishima (1964) and Hicks (1965), David Levhari proposed the argument that reswitching between production systems is only possible in the case of a 'reducible' or 'decomposable' technology matrix, so that reswitching would not occur with technologies producing only basic commodities ('irreducible' or 'indecomposable' technologies); see Levhari (1966). Levhari's argument was disproved by Pasinetti and others (Pasinetti, 1966; Morishima, 1966; Garegnani, 1966). It was also acknowledged to be false by Levhari and Samuelson (Levhari–Samuelson, 1966; Samuelson, 1966). Conditions excluding reswitching were then discovered by Bruno, Burmeister and Sheshinski (1966) and other authors (Starrett, 1969). Their outstanding feature is the introduction of technological assumptions that eliminate those 'complicated patterns of price-movement with several ups and downs' (Sraffa, 1960, p. 37) on which the very possibility of reswitching is founded.

The capital controversy of the 1960s has conclusively shown that the logical possibility of reswitching is of a general nature. Disagreement about the implications of reswitching for economic theory as a whole (*see* CAPITAL THEORY: PARADOXES) does not conceal the fact that a crucial discovery in the theory of production was made. In particular it was shown that technical choice is related to income distribution in a much more complex way than it was once thought to be, and that the rate of interest (or the rate of profit) cannot provide an unambiguous ranking of different technical alternatives as the distribution of income is varied.

R. SCAZZIERI

See also CAPITAL PERVERSITY; CAPITAL THEORY: PARADOXES; CAPITAL WIDENING AND CAPITAL DEEPENING; QUANTITY OF CAPITAL; REVERSE CAPITAL DEEPENING.

BIBLIOGRAPHY

Bharadwaj, K. 1970. On the maximum number of switches between two production systems. *Schweizerische Zeitschrift für Volkswirtschaft und Statistik* 106(4), December, pp. 409–29.

Bruno, M., Burmeister, E. and Sheshinski, E. 1966. The nature and implications of the reswitching of techniques. *Quarterly Journal of Economics* 80(4), November, 526–53.

Champernowne, D. 1954. The production function and the theory of capital: a comment. *Review of Economic Studies* 21(2), 112–35.

Garegnani, P. 1966. Switching of technique. *Quarterly Journal of Economics* 80(4), November, 554–67.

Hicks, J. 1965. *Capital and Growth*. Oxford: Clarendon Press.

Levhari, D. 1966. A nonsubstitution theorem and switching of techniques. *Quarterly Journal of Economics* 79(1), February, 98–105.

Levhari, D. and Samuelson, P. 1966. The nonswitching theorem is false. *Quarterly Journal of Economics* 80(4), November, 518–19.

Morishima, M. 1966. Refutation of the nonswitching theorem. *Quarterly Journal of Economics* 80(4), November, 520–25.

Pasinetti, L. 1966. Changes in the rate of profit and switches of techniques. *Quarterly Journal of Economics* 80(4), November, 503–17.

Robinson, J. 1956. *The Accumulation of Capital*. London: Macmillan.

Sraffa, P. 1960. *Production of Commodities by Means of Commodities*. Cambridge: Cambridge University Press.

Starrett, D. 1969. Switching and reswitching in a general production model. *Quarterly Journal of Economics* 80(4), November, 673–87.

retention ratio. The retention ratio of a corporation in any period may be defined as the ratio of retained earnings to the sum of retained earnings and dividend payments. The retention ratio is one factor in the decision concerning the optimal level of investment and the manner in which this investment is financed. The related variable, the dividend payout ratio, is defined as the proportion of available earnings paid out as dividends. In principle the sum of the retention ratio and the payout ratio should be unity. A major part of the economic debate concerning the retention ratio has mirrored the debate surrounding the debt-to-equity ratio chosen by a firm.

The subject of debate has been whether the market valuation of a firm is dependent upon its retention ratio. Miller and Modigliani (1961) conclude that, given the production and investment strategy of a firm, which determine its future earnings, the financing decision has no impact on its market value. First assume a world of perfect certainty and perfect capital markets in which all participants are price takers with costless access to all relevant information and in which there are no taxes or transactions costs. Under these conditions the choice of retention ratio will affect only the division of the return to the shareholder between dividend and capital gain and not the market valuation. When uncertainty is introduced, Lintner (1962) argues, different subjective assessments of a firm's prospects by investors will undermine the view that dividend policy is irrelevant. Furthermore, Gordon (1963) proposes that the discount rate will rise (and market value fall) with increases in the retention ratio due to the greater uncertainty of future returns. These attacks do not successfully undermine the argument in favour of the irrelevancy of dividend policy given the assumptions of perfect capital markets and the independence of the investment and financing decisions. However, the issue becomes more difficult to resolve when it is recognized that neither of these assumptions is likely to be true in reality.

Sources of capital market imperfections include transactions costs, taxes, lack of information and constraints on the supply of finance. Transactions costs include all charges concerned with the sale and purchase of shares and flotation of new shares. The existence of transactions costs limits the ability of the investor to create a 'home-made' payout ratio through dealing in shares. Taxation may influence retention ratios in a number of ways. In general, taxation of dividends is higher than that of capital gains. This will generally result in higher retentions being favoured, due to the lower rate of tax and tax deferral advantages of capital gains over dividends. However, different types of shareholders are affected in different ways, ranging from the charity or pension fund which is tax exempt to the wealthy private investor who may face a high marginal taxation of dividend income. This suggests that different types of shareholders will be attracted to different retention ratios. In equilibrium the range of retention ratios will reflect the range of shareholders, and no price advantage will be achieved by the firm through the choice of any particular retention ratio. Corporate taxation might itself be dependent upon the retention ratio, and a system which taxes dividends differentially will tend to reduce the payout ratio. Lack of information and risk aversion will tend to bias shareholders in favour of dividends. If there is a limited supply of finance, either in general or to specific companies, a higher retention ratio might result.

The residual theory of dividends suggests that the investment decision and the financing decision should be taken jointly. Providing the debt-to-equity ratio is optimal and given that taxes and transactions costs exist, the retention ratio will be determined by the availability and potential profitability of investment opportunities. Investment is taken to the point at which its prospective return is equal to the perceived opportunity cost to shareholders of dividends foregone. There are other equally important reasons for suggesting that the investment and financing decisions are not independent, which together imply that the market value may be influenced by the choice of retention ratio. Managerial models of the firm assume that management has discretion over the choice of business objectives and do not accord shareholder welfare-maximization a primary role in these objectives. In such models management may take investment beyond its optimal level financed by a higher retention ratio. This would generate a lower market valuation associated with a higher retention ratio. Less scrutiny by shareholders of investment financed by retentions would reinforce this effect. If cost-plus pricing is being employed and the margin is related to the firm's financial requirements, the retention ratio and the profitability (and market valuation) may be inversely related.

It might be hoped that empirical analysis would resolve the question of whether these multiple, and often conflicting, influences of dividend policy on market valuation yield a definite conclusion in practice. This is not the case. The evidence demonstrates that dividends are more stable then earnings and that efforts are made to avoid reductions in dividends. Dividends adapt to earnings changes over a period of time. This phenomenon means that there is an information content of dividends. Changes in dividends may provide the best guide to investors in a world of uncertainty to the future path of earnings. This results in considerable difficulty in distinguishing between the impact on share prices of changes in retention ratios themselves from the impact of the associated implications for future earnings and investment.

Therefore, the empirical evidence has not proved conclusive, but the observed dispersion of retention ratios across firms, even within the same industry, suggests that the market value is fairly insensitive to the choice of retention ratio. On the other hand, since different groups of shareholders may not be indifferent to the choice of retention ratio, and since changes in target retention ratios may be misinterpreted by shareholders, the analysis suggests that firms will not wish to change their target retention ratio.

A. COSH

See also DIVIDEND POLICY; FINANCE.

BIBLIOGRAPHY

Gordon, M. 1963. Optimal investment and financing policy. *Journal of Finance* 18, May, 264–72.

Lintner, J. 1962. Dividends, earnings, leverage, stock prices and the supply of capital to corporations. *Review of Economics and Statistics* 44, August, 243–69.

Miller, M.H. and Modigliani, F. 1961. Dividend policy, growth and the valuation of shares. *Journal of Business* 34, October, 411–33.

returns to scale. The technique of production of a commodity y may be characterized as a function of the required inputs x_i:

$$y = f(x_1, x_2, \ldots x_n)$$

If all inputs are multiplied by a positive scalar, t, and the consequent output represented as $t^s y$, then the value of s may be said to indicate the magnitude of returns to scale.

If $s=1$, then there are constant returns to scale: any proportionate change in all input results in an equiproportionate change in output. If $s>1$, there are increasing returns to scale. If $s<1$ (though not less than zero, given the possibility of free disposal) then there are decreasing returns to scale.

These mathematical definitions suggest a symmetry between the three classifications of returns to scale. This appearance of symmetry is entirely spurious.

The original arguments from which is derived the economic rationale underlying the various categories of returns to scale are to be found in the works of the classical economists. Yet there, as Sraffa (1925) pointed out, each category is derived from quite different economic phenomena. Increasing returns derived from the process of accumulation and technological change, associated as they were with the division of labour attendant upon the extension of the market. Decreasing returns were held to derive from the limited availability of land, and were an important component of the theory of income distribution, being the foundation of the theory of rent.

Yet it was from these disparate origins that Marshall (1890) attempted to formulate a unified, symmetric, analysis of returns to scale which would provide the rationale for the construction of the supply curve of a competitive industry, derived in turn from the equilibria of the firms within the industry. Marshall himself recognized the incompatibility of the assumption of competition and presence of increasing returns (1890, Appendix H). Piero Sraffa (1925, 1926) exposed the entire exercise as ill-founded by demonstrating that *neither* increasing nor *decreasing* returns to scale are compatible with the assumption of perfect competition in the theory of the firm or of the partial-equilibrium industry supply curve – a result which, although prominently published and debated, has apparently escaped the notice of those who still draw that bogus U-shaped cost curve whilst purporting to analyse the equilibrium of the competitive firm.

The difficulties identified by Sraffa rest upon the *economic* rationales for variable returns to scale.

The idea of constant returns to scale derives essentially from the proposition that a given set of production conditions may be replicated so long as all the requisite inputs may be varied in the same proportion. Indivisibilities in the production process may limit exact replication to particular levels of output. But the concept, though less precise, is not in any way diminished by the presence of indivisibilities, particularly if the optimal scale of operation of a given technique is small relative to the overall level of output.

The presence of decreasing returns *to scale* would suggest that replication is, for some reason, impossible. Yet if all inputs are correctly enumerated and all increased in the same proportion, then, barring indivisibilities, there can be no barrier to replication. Decreasing returns can derive only from a fixed input (or an input which cannot be increased in the same proportion as others) which prevents replication. In other words, there is no such thing as decreasing returns *to scale*. Decreasing returns derives from *substitution*, from the necessity of changing input proportions.

Whilst decreasing returns to scale do not exist, increasing returns to scale are typically based on propositions so general as to defy precise clarification.

There are some examples in which outputs are an increasing function of inputs for purely technical reasons. The capacity of a pipeline, for example, is defined by the area of its cross-section, πr^2, whereas the circumference of that cross-section is equal to $2\pi r$. If it were possible to increase capacity merely by increasing the circumference (if the walls of the pipe did not require strengthening), then a quadrupling of capacity could be achieved simply by doubling the material inputs.

There is one odd symmetry in this 'technical' case of increasing returns. Whereas decreasing returns can derive only from substitution and not from scale; increasing returns can derive only from scale, not from substitution! Choice of optimal proportions of inputs (with free disposal and no indivisibilities) will always ensure at *least* constant returns.

Such technical examples are not, however, the examples which typically come to mind in the discussion of increasing returns to scale. More typical are examples of mass production, of production lines, or, today, of production integrated by means of sophisticated information systems. Yet these examples, which are akin to Adam Smith's analysis of increasing returns, are associated more with technological change, and with the possibilities for change inherent in a larger, or more rapidly growing, market, than with a simple increase in the scale of identical inputs. Generalization of the concept to 'dynamic increasing returns' (Young, 1928; Kaldor, 1966) increasing returns associated with growth of output further distances the idea of increasing returns from the formal characteristics of scale.

These arguments suggest that the concept of 'returns to scale' is not merely a very limited means of characterizing technology, but it is also a very *limiting* concept. None of the interesting characteristics of the relationship between scale of production and method of production are captured by the idea of returns to scale. Indeed, the only really satisfactory formal characterization of returns to scale is that of constant returns – and this only because replication is formally a precise notion, however empty empirically.

JOHN EATWELL

See also ECONOMIES AND DISECONOMIES OF SCALE; INCREASING RETURNS.

BIBLIOGRAPHY

Kaldor, N. 1966. *Causes of the Slow Rate of Economic Growth in the United Kingdom*. Cambridge: Cambridge University Press.

Marshall, A. 1890. *Principles of Economics*. 9th (Variorum) edn, London: Macmillan, 1961.

Smith, A. 1776. *An Inquiry into the Nature and Causes of the Wealth of Nations*. London: Methuen, 1961.

Sraffa, P. 1925. Sulla relazioni fra costo e quantità prodotta. *Annali di Economia* 2, 277–328.

Sraffa, P. 1926. The laws of returns under competitive conditions. *Economic Journal* 36, December, 535–50.

Young, A.A. 1928. Increasing returns and economic progress. *Economic Journal* 38, December, 527–42.

revealed preference theory. Economists do not observe preferences. They may, however, observe demand behaviour – the choices made by consumers. Is there a way for economists to tell whether the observed behaviour is generated through the maximization of a preference relation or utility function? Since most economic theories are ultimately based on a consumer who maximizes a preference or utility, the question is clearly important for developing and testing theories.

Revealed preference theory answers this question by characterizing choice behaviour that is generated by preference or utility maximization. Relating choice behaviour and preference maximization is also a goal of integrability theory. What distinguishes the theories from each other, and from the other parts of rationality theory, is the special nature of their tools: integrability theory uses mathematical integration in its proofs, and usually states its hypotheses in differential form; revealed preference theory uses a variety of mathematical tools for its proofs, and its hypotheses are usually in a discrete 'revelation' form. The distinctions are not always sharp, however, and we shall see areas in which the theories overlap.

Samuelson invented revealed preference theory in 1938. The basic idea, much of the terminology, and some of the axioms are due to him. In the following outline, a useful paradigm is the one that guided the first three decades: a consumer with a finite-dimensional euclidean commodity space, facing 'competitive' budgets determined by fixed positive prices, and satisfying a budget equality constraint.

1. THE PROBLEM OF RATIONALITY

From the economist's point of view, unobservable preferences generate observable choices. Since many preference relations may generate the same choice correspondence, the map from preferences to choice correspondences is many-one: We cannot hope to find *the* preference generating choices, but only *some* preferences – a set of 'equivalent' preferences. For example:

It is well known in preference theory that a lexicographic preference on the plane does not admit a real-valued utility function (Debreu, 1954). A hasty conclusion might be that there is no hope of representing a lexicographic-maximizing consumer as a utility-maximizing consumer. Too hasty! For her behaviour clearly maximizes this function g on the non-negative plane (for positive prices):

$$g(x_1, x_2) = x_1 \tag{1}$$

Even if her 'intention' is to maximize a lexicographic preference, she acts *as if* her intention were to maximize g. In fact, even if the choices were made by a committee, a machine, or any other mindless decision maker, we can still say the actions are *as if* the intent were g-maximization.

This example shows the distinction between a typical question in utility and preference theory ('Does *this* preference have a utility function?'), and the basic question in revealed preference and integrability theories ('Is this demand generated by *some* preference?'). It also demonstrates the need for precise definitions. (Our notation will follow the glossaries of Richter, 1966, 1971.)

To describe choices, the theory requires an underlying set X and a family $\mathscr{B}$ of subsets $B \subset X$. (Often X is the non-negative orthant of n-space and each B is a 'competitive' budget determined by positive prices and income.) We call any $B \in \mathscr{B}$ a *budget*. A *choice* or *demand correspondence* h is a function assigning to each $B \in \mathscr{B}$ a subset $h(B) \subset B$, interpreted as the set of elements chosen from B. And any binary relation on X is called a *preference*. Rationality theory relates choices h on $(X, \mathscr{B})$ to preferences R on X in two ways.

(i) If we start with a preference relation R we can ask what kind of choice it generates. There are two obvious senses in which it could generate a choice h. First, we might have, for all $B \in \mathscr{B}$,

$$h(B) = \{x \in B : \forall y_{y \in B}\, xRy\}, \tag{2}$$

i.e., the set of elements chosen from B is the set of R-most preferred elements in B. Then we say that *R rationalizes h* (Richter, 1971).

Alternatively, we might have, for all $B \in \mathscr{B}$,

$$h(B) = \{x \in B : \forall y_{y \in B} \neg yRx\}, \tag{3}$$

i.e., the set of elements chosen from B is the set of elements in B for which nothing in B is R-more preferred. Then we say that *R motivates h* (Kim and Richter, 1986).

Definition (2) is appropriate if we think of R as a 'weak' (i.e. reflexive) relation, while (3) is appropriate if we think of R as a 'strict' (asymmetric) relation.

(ii) Conversely, if we start with a choice h we can ask whether any preference R generates, or 'explains' h. If there exists some R generating h in the sense of (2) (Richter, 1966, 1971), then we say that h is *rational.* Often we are interested in *reflexive*-rationality (rationalization by a reflexive preference), *transitive*-rationality (rationalization by a transitive preference), *regular*-rationality (rationalization by a reflexive, transitive, and total preference), etc. For example, *utility–rationality* requires the existence of a function $f: X \rightarrow R^1$ satisfying

$$h(B) = \{x \in B : \forall y_{y \in B} f(x) \geqq f(y)\} \tag{4}$$

for all $B \in \mathscr{B}$ – i.e., the set of elements chosen from B is the set of those elements in B with the highest utility.

If there exists some R generating h in the sense of (3), then we say that h is *motivated* (Kim and Richter, 1986). Again, we are often interested in *asymmetric*-motivation (motivation by an asymmetric preference), etc. In fact, h is rational if and only if it is motivated (Clark, 1985; Kim and Richter, 1986). Of course, the example (1) makes it clear that such a rationalizing or motivating R will not usually be unique: there will be a whole equivalence class of such relations generating the same choice (Kim and Richter, 1986).

It is important to note that rationality and motivation have been defined as properties of demand, not of preference. We do not say, for example, that a particular preference is rational or irrational. Instead, the definitions relate demand and preferences.

An economist who derives comparative statics results from preference maximization is answering questions of type (i). The issue arises – for both theoretical development and empirical testing – whether any further results can be derived, or whether all the (independent) consequences of preference maximization have been found. This is usually a much more difficult problem. A major task of both revealed preference and integrability theory is to address this issue, by answering questions of type (ii). The two questions are parts, then, of the fundamental Problem of Rationality: give necessary (i) and sufficient (ii) conditions for a demand to be rational (of a particular type), or motivated (of a particular type). Revealed preference theory solves the problem through axioms with a unique flavour.

2. REVEALED PREFERENCE SOLUTIONS

It is important to distinguish revealed preference definitions from revealed preference axioms, and these in turn from revealed preference theorems.

2.1. Revelation definitions. If consumer (i.e. choice) h selects alternative $x \in B$ from B – i.e., if $x \in h(B)$ – when alternative y could have been selected – i.e., if $y \in B$ – then we write xVy. And it is natural to say that x is *revealed as good as* y. If also $x \neq y$, then we write xSy, and it is natural to say that x is *revealed preferred to* y. This terminology of Samuelson's is very suggestive, because if $\succcurlyeq$ is any rationalization, then xVy implies $x \succcurlyeq y$, as does xSy. In fact, if $x \in h(B)$ & $y \in (B \backslash h(B))$ and if $\succcurlyeq$ is regular, then its asymmetric part $\succ$ also satisfies $x \succ y$. So an observer of h can deduce properties common to all rationalizations. But beware: xSy is a sttement about *choice*, not about a particular preference.

Unlike the psychologist, who may be able to present an individual with binary choices, and thereby uncover a total ordering, the economist will typically observe S as only a partial ordering. This is one of the challenging features of revealed preference theory. It is why, mathematically, revealed preference theory is a study of partial orders, in contrast to the classical theory of preference, which is a theory of total orders. It is also why there is generally more than one preference in the equivalence class of preferences that rationalize or motivate a given choice.

2.2. Revelation Axioms. We describe four revealed preference axioms. Samuelson proposed the *asymmetry* of S as a basic axiom of consumer theory: for all $x, y \in X$,

$$xSy \Rightarrow \neg ySx. \tag{5}$$

In other words, if x is revealed preferred to y (under some budget), then y is never (under any budget) revealed preferred to x. As Samuelson noted, this is a property of any single-valued demand function maximizing a regular preference. This is now called the *Weak Axiom of Revealed Preference*.

Houthakker noted other necessary consequences of regular-rationality, for single-valued demand functions: there can be no cycles of the form

$$xSy_1Sy_2S \ldots Sy_kSx. \tag{6}$$

In other words, x is never, even indirectly, revealed preferred to itself. Houthakker proposed this as a new axiom, now called the *Strong Axiom of Revealed Preference*. If we define xHy to mean that xSy or $xSv_1Sv_2S \ldots Sv_kSy$, then we can rephrase Houthakker's axiom as saying that H is asymmetric. In other words, if x is (even indirectly) revealed preferred to y, then y is never (even indirectly) revealed preferred to x.

Richter noted still another consequence of regular-rationality. For this it is convenient to define xWy to mean either xVy or $xVu_1V \ldots Vu_kVy$. Clearly regular-rationality implies: for all $x, y \in X$ & $B \in \mathscr{B}$,

$$x \in h(B) \;\&\; y \in B \;\&\; yWx \Rightarrow y \in h(B). \tag{7}$$

In other words, if x is chosen from B, and if y is also available in B and is revealed (even directly) as good as x, then y is also chosen from B. This is the *Congruence Axiom of Revealed Preference*. He also noted a behavioural consequence of any rationality: for all $x \in X$ & $B \in \mathscr{B}$,

$$x \in B \;\&\; \forall y_{y \in B}\, xVy \Rightarrow x \in h(B). \tag{8}$$

In other words, if x is in B and is revealed as good as everything in B, then x is chosen from B. This is the *V-Axiom*.

We will use these axioms to discuss the main solutions to the Problem of Rationality.

2.3. Revelation theorems. (a) *Weak Axiom.* Samuelson proposed the Weak Axiom in 1938, as a foundation for all consumer theory (1938 a,b). He did not name it, but he suggested that (for single-valued demand functions) it followed from maximizing a utility function (cf. also Samuelson (1955), pp. 110–11). In the opposite direction, his idea of founding consumer theory on it was implicitly a conjecture that it implied utility-rationality, or at least regular-rationality. Indeed, after preliminary work by I.M.D. Little, Samuelson succeeded in showing that, for two commodities and Lipschitz-continuous demand functions, the Weak Axiom implied regular-rationality (Samuelson, 1948).

(b) *Strong Axiom.* Then in 1950 Houthakker (1950) proposed the Strong Axiom (by a different name) as a basis for consumer theory, and showed that, for any number of commodities, it implied utility-rationality for Lipschitz-continuous demand functions. Samuelson (1950) then gave the Weak and Strong Axioms their modern names.

In 1959, Uzawa (1960, 1971) developed a more precise analogue of Houthakker's result, showing that the Strong Axiom and a Lipschitzian hypothesis on the demand implied irreflexive-transitive-monotone-convex-lower semi continuous-motivation. His proof was along the lines of the Samuelson–Little–Samuelson–Houthakker analytic methods.

Although the Strong Axiom implied the Weak, it was still not clear whether the Weak implied the Strong. Indeed, Rose (1958) showed that the Weak Axiom does imply the Strong Axiom, when there are only two commodities and prices are positive (needed!). Then Gale (1960) constructed an example with three commodities, showing that the Weak Axiom did not imply the Strong. And Kihlstrom, Mas-Colell, and Sonnenschein (1976) showed how to obtain very easily many examples, for any number of commodities greater than two. And Shafer (1977b), affirming a conjecture of Samuelson (1953), showed that the full strength of the Strong Axiom is needed: even for three goods, there is no upper bound on the length of S-cycles that must be ruled out. In the opposite direction, several authors have discussed special conditions under which the Weak Axiom does imply the Strong (Arrow, 1959; Uzawa, 1960, 1971).

Richter (1966) used set-theoretic methods – very different from the analytic methods of Samuelson, Little, Houthakker, and Uzawa – to simplify the proofs, eliminate extraneous assumptions, and strengthen the rationality results. In a framework of abstract budget spaces, and without the technical assumptions required by the earlier analytical approaches, he showed that the Strong Axiom is equivalent to regular-rationality for demand functions. Thus the Strong Axiom completely exhausts the theory of demand functions maximizing a regular preference.

Richter (1966) also showed that, if a competitive demand satisfies the Strong Axiom, then it is utility-rational if its range is well behaved, but it may not be utility-rational otherwise (Richter, 1971).

Extensions. There have been many extensions. Richter (1966) showed that the V-Axiom characterized rationality, and the Congruence Axiom characterized regular-rationality, for demand correspondences. (Hansson (1968) gave an alternative criterion for regular-rationality.) Other extensions have obtained stronger properties of the rationalization under special hypotheses (Hurwicz and Richter, 1971; Mas-Colell, 1978, Theorem 1; Richter, 1986; Matzkin and Richter, 1986); uniqueness of the rationalization within certain classes (Mas-Colell, 1977); revealed preference axioms characterizing more general rationality types (Richter, 1971; Kim and Richter, 1986; Kim, 1987); dual axioms (Sakai, 1977; Richter, 1979); and axioms for stochastic rationality (McFadden and Richter, 1970).

Applications. Several applications have supported Samuelson's original idea that revealed preference could provide an alternative to preference theory as a foundation for consumer theory. Revealed preference techniques have been applied to prove the existence of competitive equilibrium (Wald, 1936, 1951); to prove the stability of competitive equilibrium (Arrow and Hurwicz, 1958, 1960); to prove the Hicks Composite Commodity Theorem (Richter, 1970; Calsamiglia, 1978); to analyse and characterize aggregate excess demand functions (Debreu, 1974; McFadden et al., 1974); to prove aggregation properties for correspondences (Shafer, 1977a); to prove properties of measurable demand correspondences (Yamazaki, 1984); to prove theorems about social choice functions (Plott, 1973); etc.

3. REVEALED PREFERENCE AND INTEGRABILITY

With the same rationality goal as revealed preference theory, integrability theory uses axioms on the Slutsky or Antonelli matrices to characterize rational choice (cf. Hurwicz, 1971; see also INTERGBILITY OF DEMAND). Under some smoothness assumptions on the demand function, the basic theorems state that symmetry and negative semidefiniteness of these matrices is necessary and sufficient for (upper-semicontinuous-) regular-rationality.

Samuelson established a link between revealed preference theory and integrability theory by showing that his Weak Axiom implied negative semidefiniteness of the matrices (Samuelson, 1938b, 1955, pp. 111–14). Later Kihlstrom, Mass-Colell, and Sonnenschein (1976) demonstrated that negative semidefiniteness was equivalent to a Weak Weak Axiom.

This left open the question of finding a revealed preference axiom equivalent to the symmetry. The Strong Axiom was clearly too strong, since it already implied regular-rationality, and therefore both symmetry and negative-semidefiniteness. Then Hurwicz and Richter (1979a,b) showed that a differential axiom of Ville (1946, 1951) provided the exact strength needed. Although it does not even imply the Weak Axiom, it is similar in spirit to the Strong Axiom and can be given a revealed preference interpretation. It thus serves, like Kihlstrom, Mas-Colell and Sonnenschein's Weak Weak Axiom, as a bridge between the Revealed Preference and Integrability approaches to consumer rationality. Richter (1979) discussed these bridges from the viewpoint of duality.

4. OTHER NOTIONS OF RATIONALITY

Many economists have used notions of rationality different from Richter's notion (2).

Sometimes the term 'rational' has been applied to preference, rather than demand. (In such applications it is often a synonym for 'transitive'.) In Uzawa (1957) and Arrow (1959), on the other hand, it was applied to demand, but only in terms of axioms on demand behaviour. By contrast, (2) is applied to demand, but in terms that relate both demand and preferences.

Some economists have used weaker notions of rationality than (2), requiring only: for all $x, y \in X \,\&\, B \in \mathscr{B}$,

$$h(B) \subset \{x \in B : \forall y_{y \in B} xRy\}. \tag{9}$$

In other words, every element chosen from B is R-most preferred in B, but B may contain other R-most preferred elements that are not chosen. We will call this *subsemi-rationality*, although it has often been referred to as rationality.

A drawback of this concept is its loose linkage of preference and demand. Any constant function, for example, satisfies (9). On the other hand, if one interprets $h(B)$ as a set of incomplete observations, then one might wonder whether, with more observations of choices from B, the set $h(B)$ of chosen elements might grow. Then one might want to find a preference R satisfying just (9), rather than insisting (as does (2)) that R explain *precisely* the observed set $h(B)$.

Afriat (1967) gave conditions on a demand function, over a finite set of budgets, that are necessary and sufficient for it to be subsemi-rationalized by a continuous monotone concave function. His work was clarified by Diewert (1973) who gave a criterion for continuous-monotone-concave-subsemirationality in terms of a linear programming problem. Varian (1983) re-stated Afriat's finite-budgets result in terms of a Generalized Axiom of Revealed Preference – weaker than the Strong Axiom.

Matzkin and Richter (1986) obtained full rationality by replacing the Generalized Axiom with the Strong Axiom, which they proved was necessary and sufficient for continuous-monotone-strictly-concave-utility-rationality in the finite case. No revealed preference criterion for concave-regular-rationality is known for the not-necessarily-finite case.

MARCEL K. RICHTER

See also DEMAND THEORY; INTEGRABILITY OF DEMAND; PREFERENCES; SAMUELSON, PAUL ANTHONY.

BIBLIOGRAPHY

Afriat, S.N. 1967. The construction of utility functions from expenditure data. *International Economic Review* 8, 67–77.

Arrow, K.J. and Hurwicz, L. 1958. On the stability of competitive equilibrium, I. *Econometrica* 26, 522–52.

Arrow, K.J. 1959. Rational choice functions and orderings. *Economica,* N.S. 26, 121–7.

Arrow, K.J. and Hurwicz, L. 1960. Some remarks on the equilibria of economic systems. *Econometrica* 28, 640–46.

Calsamiglia, X. 1978. Composite goods and revealed preference. *International Economic Review* 19, 395–404.

Clark, S.A. 1985. A complementary approach to the strong and weak axioms of revealed preference. *Econometrica* 53, 1459–63.

Debreu, G. 1954. Representation of a preference ordering by a numbering function. In *Decision Processes*, ed. R.M. Thrall, C.H. Coombs and R.L. Davis, New York: Wiley, 159–65.

Debreu, G. 1974. Excess demand functions. *Journal of Mathematical Economics* 1, 15–21.

Diewert, W.E. 1973. Afriat and revealed preference theory. *Review of Economic Studies* 40, 419–25.

Gale, D. 1960. A note on revealed preference. *Economica*, NS 27, 348–54.

Hansson, B. 1968. Choice structures and preference relations. *Synthese* 18, 443–58.

Houthakker, H.S. 1950. Revealed preference and the utility function. *Economica*, NS 17, 159–74.

Hurwicz, L. 1971. On the problem of integrability of demand functions. In *Preferences, Utility and Demand*, ed. J.S. Chipman, L. Hurwicz, M.K. Richter, and H.F. Sonnenschein. New York: Harcourt, Brace, Jovanovich, ch. 9.

Hurwicz, L. and Richter, M.K. 1971. Revealed preference without demand continuity assumptions. In *Preferences, Utility and Demand*, ed. J.S. Chipman, L. Hurwicz, M.K. Richter, and H.F. Sonnenschein, New York: Harcourt, Brace, Jovanovich, ch. 3.

Hurwicz, L. and Richter, M.K. 1979a. An integrability condition with applications to utility theory and thermodynamics. *Journal of Mathematical Economics* 6, 7–14.

Hurwicz, L. and Richter, M.K. 1979b. Ville axioms and consumer theory. *Econometrica* 47, 603–19.

Kihlstrom, R., Mas-Colell, A. and Sonnenschein, H. 1976. The demand theory of the weak axiom of revealed preference. *Econometrica* 44, 971–8.

Kim, T. and Richter, M. 1986. Nontransitive-nontotal consumer theory. *Journal of Economic Theory* 38, 324–63.

Kim, T. 1987. Intransitive indifference and revealed preference. *Econometrica*.

Mas-Colell, A. 1977. The recoverability of consumers' preferences from market demand behavior. *Econometrica* 45, 1409–30.

Mas-Colell, A. 1978. On revealed preference analysis. *Review of Economic Studies* 45, 121–31.

Matzkin, R. and Richter, M.K. 1986. Testing concave rationality. Department of Economics, University of Minnesota, Minneapolis.

McFadden, D. and Richter, M.K. 1970. Stochastic rationality and revealed stochastic preference. Presented to the 1970 Winter Meetings of the Econometric Society.

McFadden, D. and Richter, M.K. 1988. Stochastic rationality and revealed stochastic preference. In *Uncertainty, Preferences and Optimality. Essays in Honor of Leonid Hurwicz*, ed. J.S. Chipman, D. McFadden, and M.K. Richter, New York.

McFadden, D., Mas-Colell, A., Mantel, R. and Richter, M.K. 1974. A characterization of community excess demand functions. *Journal of Economic Theory* 9, 361–74.

Plott, C.R. 1973. Path independence, rationality, and social choice. *Econometrica* 41, 1075–91.

Richter, M.K. 1966. Revealed preference theory. *Econometrica* 34, 635–45.
Richter, M.K. 1971. Rational Choice. In *Preferences, Utility, and Demand*, ed. J.S. Chipman, L. Hurwicz, M.K. Richter and H.F. Sonnenschein, New York: Harcourt, Brace, Jovanovich, ch. 2.
Richter, M.K. 1979. Duality and rationality. *Journal of Economic Theory* 20, 131–81.
Richter, M.K. 1986. Continuous demand functions. Department of Economics, University of Minnesota, Minneapolis.
Rose, H. 1958. Consistency of preference: the two-commodity case. *Review of Economic Studies* 25, 124–5.
Sakai, Y. 1977. Revealed favorability, indirect utility, and direct utility. *Journal of Economic Theory* 14, 113–29.
Samuelson, P.A. 1938a. A note on the pure theory of consumer's behaviour. *Economica*, NS 5, 61–71.
Samuelson, P.A. 1938b. A note on the pure theory of consumer's behaviour: an addendum. *Economica*, NS 5, 353–4.
Samuelson, P.A. 1948. Consumption theory in terms of revealed preference. *Economica*, NS 15, 243–53.
Samuelson, P.A. 1950. The problem of integrability in utility theory. *Economica*, NS 17, 355–85.
Samuelson, P.A. 1953. Consumption theorems in terms of overcompensation rather than indifference comparisons. *Economica*, NS 20, 1–9.
Samuelson, P.A. 1947. *Foundations of Economic Analysis*. Cambridge, Mass.: Harvard University Press.
Shafer, W.J. 1977a. Revealed preference and aggregation. *Econometrica* 45, 1173–82.
Shafer, W.J. 1977b. Revealed preference cycles and the Slutsky matrix. *Journal of Economic Theory* 16, 293–309.
Uzawa, H. 1957. Note on preference and axioms of choice. *Annals of the Institute of Statistical Mathematics* 8, 35–40.
Uzawa, H. 1960. Preference and rational choice in the theory of consumption. In *Mathematical Methods in the Social Sciences, 1959*, ed. K.J. Arrow, S. Karlin, and P. Suppes, Stanford: Stanford University Press, ch. 9.
Uzawa, H. 1971. Preference and rational choice in the theory of consumption. In *Preferences, Utility, and Demand*, ed. J.S. Chipman, L. Hurwicz, M.K. Richter and H.F. Sonnenschein, New York: Harcourt, Brace, Jovanovich, ch. 1.
Varian, H.R. 1983. Non-parametric tests of consumer behaviour. *Review of Economic Studies* 50, 99–110.
Ville, J. 1946. Sur les conditions d'existence d'une ophélimité totale et d'un indice du niveau des prix. *Annales de l'Université de Lyon* 9, Sec. A(3), 32–9.
Ville, J. 1951. The existence conditions of a total utility function. *Review of Economic Studies* 19, 123–8.
Wald, A. 1936. Über einige Gleichungssysteme der mathematischen ökonomie. *Zeitschrift für Nationalökonomie* 7, 637–70.
Wald, A. 1951. On some systems of equations of mathematical economics. *Econometrica* 19, 368–403.
Yamazaki, A. 1984. The critical set of a demand correspondence in the price space and the weak axiom of revealed preference. *Hitotsubashi Journal of Economics* 25, 137–44.

revelation of preferences. Competitive rational consumers reveal their preferences through their market behaviour as was made clear by Samuelson's (1947) revealed preference approach and by the literature on demand theory. Any bundle of commodities less costly than his chosen bundle must be less appreciated by a rational consumer than his chosen bundle.

However, in various circumstances collective decision processes must be used to mitigate market failures (public goods, externalities etc.). To what extent these processes can truthfully elicit agents' preferences, i.e., overcome the decentralization of information, is the issue raised here.

REVELATION. Consider an agent who has preferences, represented by a preordering parameterized by $\theta^i \in \Theta^i$, $R(\theta^i)$, over a set of social states A. It is not difficult to convince oneself that any mechanism, $x:\Theta^i \to A$, which induces truthful revelation by agent i is equivalent to giving to the agent a subset $B \subset A$ and letting him maximize over this set. The sufficiency is obvious; the necessity is shown by choosing

$$A = \bigcup_{\theta^i \in \Theta^i} x(\theta^i).$$

When I agents are present, a mechanism is a mapping $x\colon \Theta \equiv \Pi_{i=1}^{I}\Theta^i \to A$.

It is reasonable in most circumstances to assume that agent i does not know the characteristics θ^j of the other agents. The revelation of preferences is therefore imbedded necessarily in a game of imperfect information for which several solution concepts are possible. A game which induces truthful revelation of preferences is said to be incentive compatible.

IMPLEMENTATION. Consider a social choice function, i.e. a mapping $f:\Pi_{i=1}^{I} H^i \to A$. A social choice function f is said to be *implementable* if there exist message spaces M^i, $i = 1, \ldots, I$, and an outcome function $g:\Pi_{i=1}^{I} M^i \to A$ for which the equilibrium messages $m^i(\theta^i)i = 1, \ldots, I$ are such that:

$$g(m^1(\theta^1), \ldots, m^I(\theta^I)) = f(\theta) \qquad \forall \theta \in \Theta$$

The equilibrium messages depend on the chosen solution concept for the game of imperfect information. The strongest notion of implementation is implementation in dominant strategies. Then, $m^i(\theta^i)$ is the best message of agent i whatever the messages of the other agents, for any i. A weaker notion of implementation is Bayesian implementation. Consider common knowledge prior expectations $\Psi^i(\theta^{-i}/\theta^i)$ describing agent i's expectations about the other agents' characteristics

$$\theta^{-i} = (\theta^1, \ldots, \theta^{i-1}, \theta^{i+1}, \ldots, \theta^I), i = 1, \ldots, I.$$

For any $\theta^i \in \Theta^i$, $m^{*i}(\theta^i)$ is the best message for agent i in the sense of his expected utility computed by using his prior $\Psi^i(\theta^{-i}/\theta^i)$ and by assuming that the others are using the response functions $m^{*j}(\theta^j)$, $j \neq i$. Then f is implementable in Bayesian equilibrium if there exists a Bayesian equilibrium such that $f(\theta) = g(m^{*1}(\theta^1), \ldots, m^{*I}(\theta^I))$.

There are many other notions of implementation.

IMPLEMENTATION IN DOMINANT STRATEGY. The *revelation principle* says that any f which is implementable in a dominant strategy can be implemented by a mechanism in which messages are identified with characteristics spaces Θ^i – direct mechanisms – and truthful revelation is a dominant strategy equilibrium.

In other words, it is not useful to consider more complex mechanisms than revelation mechanisms. (This neglects problems due to multiple equilibria.) We will therefore concentrate in the sequel on direct revelation mechanisms.

A fundamental result due to Gibbard (1973) and Satterthwaite (1975) tells us that, for more than two states, when no a priori information is available about individuals' preorderings, the only deterministic social choice function implementable in dominant strategies are dictatorships. To obtain positive results we must either introduce a priori information or weaken the notion of incentive compatibility.

THE VICKREY AUCTION AND THE CLARKE–GROVES MECHANISMS. To fight non-competitive behaviour, Vickrey (1961) proposed an auction which has the remarkable property that each bidder should announce his true willingness to pay for the auctioned object as a dominant strategy. The auction gives the object to the agent who makes the highest bid, but the payment is only the second highest bid.

The solution to the Wicksell–Samuelson free rider problem of public goods provided by Clarke (1971) and Groves (1973) can be viewed as an adaptation of this result. Preferences for public goods are assumed to be restricted to the class of quasi-linear utility functions which permits to go away from the negative result of the Gibbard–Satterthwaite theorem.

Consider the simple case of a costless indivisible project ($d = 0$ or 1) and call v^i the willingness to pay of agent i, $i = 1, \ldots, I$. The Pareto optimal decision under perfect information is

$$d = 1 \Leftrightarrow \sum_{i=1}^{I} v^i \geqslant 0$$

The Clark mechanism chooses to realize the project if the sum of the answers $\Sigma_{i=1}^{I} w^i$ is positive and agent i must pay a transfer $\Sigma_{j \neq i} w^j$ if he is pivotal, i.e. his answer changes the sign of the sum. He must pay the cost he imposes on the rest of society, just as in the Vickrey auction, an agent must pay the cost he imposes on the society which is the second willingness to pay. Groves mechanisms are obtained by adding to the Clarke transfer of agent i an arbitrary function of the answers of the others.

The first best public project decision is implemented. However, the incentive compatible transfers do not sum to zero in general so that a Pareto optimal allocation is not achieved. This should not come as a surprise. The decentralization of information imposes a cost on allocation rules.

Preferences can be elicited but at the cost of some distortions in allocations rules.

LARGE NUMBERS. The problem of revelation of preferences for private goods is not a serious problem in large economies. Indeed, as a 'negligible' agent cannot affect prices he cannot affect his budget set and therefore the competitive equilibrium is incentive compatible in dominant strategies.

With public goods the problem becomes more and more severe with the number of agents since everyone can hope to have the others finance the public good. Despite the fact that, as the number of agents increases, the imbalance of transfers in the Groves mechanisms can be made negligible in various senses, the question of the strength of incentives must be raised in such circumstances.

HISTORICAL NOTE. The free rider problem was recognized by Wicksell (1896) and emphasized by Samuelson (1954). The positive results by Groves (1973) and Clarke (1971) and by Aspremont and Gerard-Varet (1979) using Bayesian equilibria have shown that positive results are achievable when prior information is available. These results have played a major role in opening new avenues in the economics of information. The reason is that generalizations of these mechanisms have provided a precise way of evaluating transaction costs due to asymmetric information. Industrial organization, macroeconomics, and public economics have been considerably renewed recently by the possibility of taking seriously into account the decentralization of information.

J.J. LAFFONT

See also BIDDING; INCENTIVE COMPATIBILITY; LINDAHL EQUILIBRIUM; ORGANIZATION THEORY; PUBLIC ECONOMICS; PUBLIC GOODS.

BIBLIOGRAPHY

d' Aspremont, C. and Gerard-Varet, L.A. 1979. Incentives and incomplete information. *Journal of Public Economics* 11, 25–45.

Clarke, E.H. 1971. Multipart pricing of public goods *Public Choice*, 19–33.

Gibbard, A. 1973. Manipulation of voting schemes. A general result. *Econometrica* 41, 487–601.

Groves, T. 1973. Incentives in teams. *Econometrica* 41, 617–31.

Samuelson, P.A. 1947. *Foundations of Economic Analysis*. Cambridge, Mass.: Harvard University Press.

Samuelson, P.A. 1954. The pure theory of public expenditure. *Review of Economics and Statistics* 37, 350–56.

Satterthwaite, M. 1975. Strategy-proofness and Arrow's conditions: existence and correspondence theorems for voting procedures and social welfare functions. *Journal of Economic Theory* 10, 187–217.

Vickrey, W. 1961. Counterspeculation, auctions and competitive sealed tenders. *Journal of Finance* 16, 1–17.

Wicksell, K. 1896. *Finanztheoretische Untersuchungen und das Steuerwesen*. Jena: Schweders.

revenue, gross and net. The term revenue was once used as equivalent to the modern 'income', which has now replaced it. Both the concept and the word came from France, where *revenu* is the past participle of *revenir*, to return.

Gross revenue is defined by Adam Smith as 'the whole annual produce of the land and labour' of a country. Net revenue is what the inhabitants are free to spend 'upon their subsistence, conveniences, and amusements' 'without encroaching upon their capital' (Smith, 1776, pp. 286–7). The ambiguities of this definition have generated a two centuries old discussion: should we consider the subsistence fund of the wage-earners as circulating capital, therefore excluding it from the net revenue, or as final consumption, and then as a part of it?

A clear-cut answer was offered by the 18th-century French predecessors of Smith. Having in mind a specific picture of the circular process of production, they defined net revenue (the physiocratic *produit net*) as the annually produced wealth (*reproduction totale*) minus the advances required to repeat the process on the same scale. Workers' subsistences, to which wages were strictly limited, were an obvious part of the advances, on the same footing as the feed for the cattle. Net revenue was then the value of the surplus product, which remained available to be – in the words of Nicolas Isnard (1781, p. 37), a civil engineer – 'nobly enjoyed by the proprietors'.

The clear-cutness faded away with Smith, and *pour cause*: he was trying to take into account workers' consumption (and the employment level) in assessing the prosperity of a nation. Therefore he was led sometimes to include wages in the net revenue and sometimes to consider gross (instead of net) revenue as the crucial indicator for the evaluation of prosperity.

Ricardo (1821, ch. XXVI) reverted unambiguously to the original meaning of net revenue, identifying it with the sum of rents and profits alone. He criticized Smith for his preferring 'a large gross, rather than a large net income'. The rationale of this attitude was that the power of a country 'of supporting fleets and armies, and all species of productive labour' is in proportion to its net income, from which taxes are paid (for a similar argument, see Quesnay, 1759). He also admitted, however, that if more than subsistence is allotted to wage-earners 'a part of the net produce of the country is received by the labourer'.

Marx followed the Ricardian definition, but stressed the importance of taking account of constant capital, that is of the value of raw materials and the depreciation of fixed capital, in evaluating the gross revenue.

In more recent times, the current notion of national income (inclusive of wages) definitely prevailed in applied economics; but the theoretical question remained unsettled. See, for instance: Edgeworth (1896), quoting Jevons's remark ('as the horse has to be clothed and stabled, so the productive labourer has to be clothed and housed') as an argument in favour of the exclusion of necessary consumption from the net income; Leontief (1941) who emphasized the arbitrary nature of the definition, depending on the type and level of aggregation of the input–output scheme (a completely consolidated table, reduced to a single box, would show no net revenue); and Sraffa (1960).

Piero Sraffa defines national income as the gross product minus the value of the commodities used up in all industries; while – à la Ricardo – the subsistences of the workers 'continue to appear with the fuel, etc., among the means of production' (§ 8). On the other hand, attention is focused on the movements of the 'surplus' part of the wage, which participates in net revenue.

GIORGIO GILIBERT

See also NET PRODUCT; PRODUIT NET.

BIBLIOGRAPHY

Edgeworth, F.Y. 1896. Income. In *Palgrave's Dictionary of Political Economy*, Vol. 2, London: Macmillan.

Isnard, A.N. 1781. *Traité des richesses*. Lausanne: Grasset.

Leontief, W. 1941. *The Structure of American Economy*. New York: Oxford University Press, 1951.

Quesnay, F. 1759. *Tableau économique*. Ed. M. Kuczynski and R. Meek, London: Macmillan, 1972.

Ricardo, D. 1821. *Principles of Political Economy*, 3rd edn. In *Works and Correspondence of David Ricardo*, Vol. I, ed. P. Sraffa, Cambridge: Cambridge University Press, 1951.

Smith, A. 1776. *An Inquiry into the Nature and Causes of the Wealth of Nations*. Ed. R.H. Campbell, A.S. Skinner and W.B. Todd, Oxford: Clarendon Press, 1976.

Sraffa, P. 1960. *Production of Commodities by Means of Commodities*. Cambridge: Cambridge University Press.

reverse capital deepening. It has long been taken for granted that there is an inverse monotonic relationship between the rate of interest (or the rate of profit) and the quantity of capital per man. This belief was founded on the principle of substitution, whereby 'cheaper' is substituted for 'more expensive' as the relative price of two inputs is changed.

In the field of capital theory, the principle of substitution persuaded many economists, such as E. von Böhm-Bawerk (1889), J.B. Clark (1899) and F.A. von Hayek (1941), that a lower rate of interest (which is equal to the rate of profit in equilibrium) is associated with the use of more 'capital intensive' techniques, and thus with the substitution of capital for other productive factors, such as labour or land. This process is called *capital deepening*.

Recent discussions have shown that this is not necessarily true, since a lower rate of interest might be associated with *lower*, rather than higher, capital per man. This phenomenon is called *reverse capital deepening*.

This discovery was made at the same time as it was realized that it is not generally possible to order 'efficient' techniques in such a way that technical choice becomes a monotonic function of the rate of interest (and of the rate of profit).

It can be shown that both reverse capital deepening and reswitching of technique are related to the same fundamental property of the economic system: the possibility (in fact, the near generality) of non-linear wage-profit relationships. To illustrate this proposition, it is useful to begin by considering the hypothetical case of linear wage–profit relationships (see Figure 1).

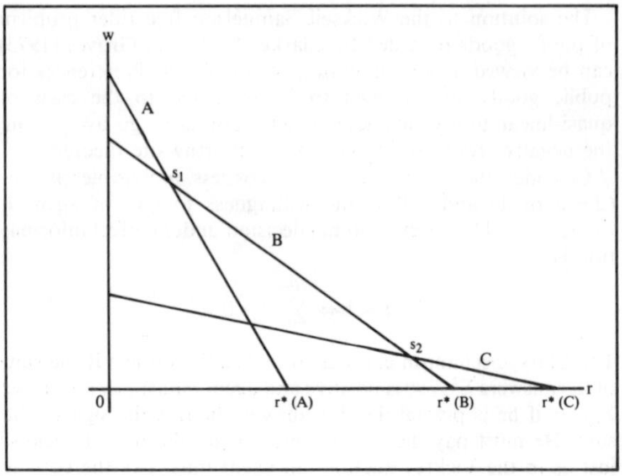

Figure 1

The linearity of the three wage-profit relationships makes reswitching impossible as r increases between 0 and $r^*(C)$ (which is the maximum rate of profit with technology C). The reason is that no wage–profit line can ever be crossed more than once by another wage–profit line. In this special case, there is an inverse monotonic relationship between the rate of profit and the quantity of capital per man. We can read the net final output per man on the w-axis of the figure at the point at which $r=0$. (At that point the net final output per man coincides with the maximum wage.) The net final output per man associated with technology A is higher than the net final output per man associated with technology B. The net final output per man associated with technology B is higher than the net final output per man associated with technology C. At switchpoints s_1 and s_2 the wage is the same for both technologies between which substitution takes place. It follows that, at switchpoint s_1, profit per man is higher with technology A than with technology B. Similarly, at switchpoint s_2, profit per man is higher with technology B than with technology C. Assuming that the rate of profit is uniform across technologies, we find that, at s_1, A is associated with higher capital per man than B. A higher rate of profit (or rate of interest) is thus associated with substitution of 'less capital' for 'more capital'. In this particular case, the traditional approach to capital theory would seem to be well founded.

However, these properties disappear altogether once we drop the assumption of linear wage–profit relationships. (It might be interesting to inquire into the economic meaning of straight wage–profit relationships, which are only possible in the case of a technology characterized by a uniform proportion between labour and intermediate inputs in all production processes: only in this case a change in the rate of profit leaves relative prices unaffected.)

But in general wage-profit relationships are of the non-linear type, which means that the proportion between labour and intermediate inputs is generally different from one production process to another. This feature of the wage-profit frontier makes it possible for wage-profit curves to intersect more than once thus bringing about the possibility of multiple switching. Under the same circumstances it can be shown that the relationship between the rate of profit and capital per man is no longer of the inverse monotonic type. This can be seen in the reswitching case (Figure 2), but it can also be seen in the case in which the wage-profit curves never intersect more than

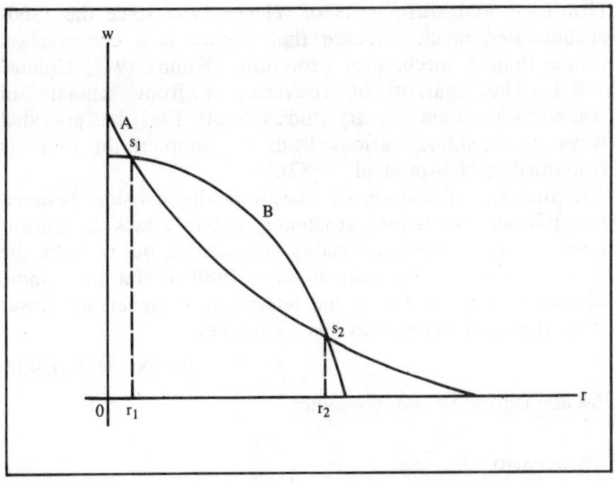

Figure 2

once on the efficiency frontier (Figure 3). (See also Pasinetti, 1966.)

In Figure 2, reswitching is associated with reverse capital deepening. Technology A is the more profitable at levels of the rate of profit lower than r_1, it is 'overtaken' by technology B at rates of profit between r_1 and r_2, it becomes again the more profitable at rates of profit higher than r_2. At the same time, switchpoint s_1 is associated with the substitution of the technology with lower value of capital per man (B) for the technology with the higher value of capital per man (A), whereas at switchpoint s_2 the opposite happens: the technology with higher capital per man (A) is substituted for the technology with lower capital per man (B), in spite of the fact that the rate of profit is higher (reverse capital deepening).

In Figure 3, there is no reswitching but we still have a reverse capital deepening. For no wage–profit curves cross one another more than once on the efficiency frontier, but at switchpoint s_2 an increasing rate of profit is associated with the substitution of a technology with higher capital per man (C) for a technology with lower capital per man (B).

Reverse capital deepening is associated with other phenomena which are not compatible with traditional beliefs about capital and capital accumulation. Simple inspection of Figure 2 or 3 shows that at a switchpoint associated with reverse capital deepening (s_2 in either figure) a technology with higher capital per man and higher net final product per man is substituted for a technology with lower capital per man and lower net final product per man. At such switchpoints a higher rate of profit (and rate of interest) could be associated with a higher ratio of capital per man to net final product per man, i.e. with a higher capital/output ratio.

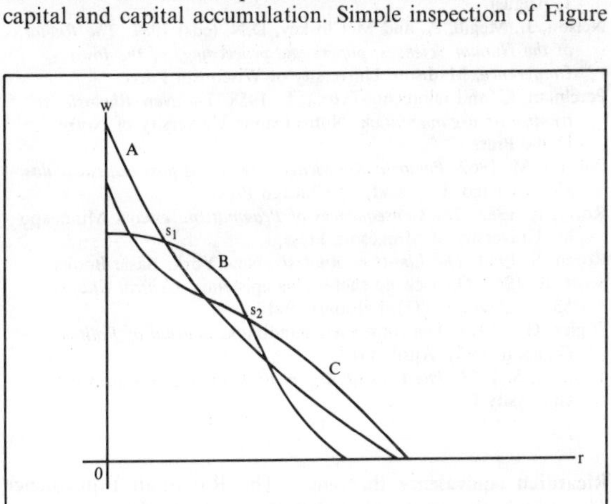

Figure 3

Figures 2 and 3 also alert us as to the possibility that a technology adopted at a high rate of interest is associated with higher maximum consumption per head than a technology adopted at a lower rate of interest. In addition, transition to a lower rate of interest may involve the switch to a lower maximum consumption per head. (This can be seen at switchpoint s_2 in either figure, where maximum consumption per head can be read on the w-axis at point $r=0$.) This behaviour of consumption per head in relation to the rate of interest is clearly incompatible with the view that a higher rate of interest brings about a special type of exchange, in which less consumption in the current period is substituted against higher consumption in the future. Reverse capital deepening alerts us as to the possibility that a higher rate of interest might be associated with greater current consumption per head than the consumption per head feasible with the technology adopted at a lower rate of interest (see Bruno, Burmeister and Sheshinski, 1966; Samuelson, 1966).

The relevance of reverse capital deepening is that the foundations of traditional capital theory are seriously questioned. In particular, the view that the rate of interest is the price of capital as a productive factor, and that interest may be explained by intertemporal preference, is shown to be untenable as soon as a more realistic model of productive systems is adopted.

R. SCAZZIERI

See also CAPITAL PERVERSITY; CAPITAL THEORY: PARADOXES; RESWITCHING OF TECHNIQUE.

BIBLIOGRAPHY

Böhm-Bawerk, E. von. 1889. *Positive Theorie des Kapitales.* Zweite Ableitung: *Kapital und Kapitalzins.* Trans. as *The Positive Theory of Capital*, London: Macmillan, 1891.

Bruno, M., Burmeister, E. and Sheshinski, E. 1966. The nature and implications of the reswitching of techniques. *Quarterly Journal of Economics* 80(4), November, 526–53.

Clark, J.B. 1899. *The Distribution of Wealth.* New York: Macmillan.

Hayek, F.A. von. 1941. *The Pure Theory of Capital.* London: Routledge.

Pasinetti, L.L. 1966. Changes in the rate of profit and switches of techniques. *Quarterly Journal of Economics* 80(4), November, 503–17.

Samuelson, P. 1966. A summing up. *Quarterly Journal of Economics* 80(4), November, 568–83.

rhetoric. Rhetoric is the study and practice of persuasive expression, an alternative since the Greeks to the philosophical programme of epistemology. The rhetoric of economics examines how economists persuade – not how they say they do, or how their official methodologies say they do, but how in fact they persuade colleagues and politicians and students to accept one economic assertion and reject another.

Some of their devices arise from bad motives, and bad rhetoric is what most people have in mind when they call a piece of writing 'rhetorical'. An irrelevant and inaccurate attack on Milton Friedman's politics while criticizing his economics would be an example, as would a pointless and confusing use of mathematics while arguing a point in labour economics. The badness does not reside in the techniques themselves (political commentary or mathematical argument) but in the person using them, since all techniques can be abused. Aristotle noted that 'if it be objected that one who uses such power of speech unjustly might do great harm, *that* is a charge which may be made in common against all good things except virtue itself'. Cato the Elder demanded that the user of analogy (or in our time the user of regression) be *vir bonus dicendi peritus*, the *good* man skilled at speaking. The protection against bad science is good scientists, not good methodology.

Rhetoric, then, can be good, offering good reasons for believing that the elasticity of substitution between capital and labour in American manufacturing, say, is about 1.0. The good reasons are not confined by syllogism and number. They include good analogy (production is *just like* a mathematical function), good authority (Knut Wicksell and Paul Douglas thought this way, too), good symmetry (if mining can be treated as a production function, so should manufacturing). Furthermore, the reasonings of syllogism and number are themselves rhetorical, that is, persuasive acts of human speech. An econometric test will depend on how apt is an analogy of the error term with drawings from an urn. A mathematical proof will depend on how convincing is an appeal to the authority of the Bourbaki style. 'The facts' and 'the logic' matter, of course; but they are part of the rhetoric, depending themselves on the giving of good reasons.

Consider, for example, the sentence in economics, 'The demand curve slopes down.' The official rhetoric says that economists believe this because of statistical evidence – negative coefficients in demand curves for pig iron or negative diagonal items in matrices of complete systems of demand – accumulating steadily in journal articles. These are the tests 'consistent with the hypothesis'. Yet most belief in the hypothesis comes from other sources: from introspection (what would I do?); from thought experiments (what would they do?); from uncontrolled cases in point (such as the oil crisis); from authority (Alfred Marshall believed it); from symmetry (a law of demand if there is a law of supply); from definition (a higher price leaves less for expenditure, including this one); and above all, from analogy (if the demand curve slopes down for chewing gum, why not for housing and love too?). As may be seen in the classroom and seminar, the range of argument in economics is wider than the official rhetoric allows.

The rhetoric of economics brings the traditions of rhetoric to the study of economic texts, whether mathematical or verbal texts. It is a literary criticism of economics, or a jurisprudence, and from literary critics like Wayne Booth (1974) and lawyers such as Chaim Perelman (1958) much can be learned. Although its precursors in economics are methodological criticisms of the field (such as Frank Knight, 1940), censorious joking (such as Stigler, 1977), and finger-wagging presidential addresses (such as Leontief, 1971, or Mayer, 1975), the main focus of the work has been the analysis of how economists seek to persuade, whether good or bad (Klamer, 1984; Henderson 1982; Kornai, 1983; McCloskey, 1986). Econometrics has its own rhetorical prehistory, more self-conscious than the rest (Leamer, 1978), reaching back to the founders of decision theory and Bayesian statistics.

The movement has parallels in other fields. Imre Lakatos (1976), Davis and Hersh (1981), and others have uncovered a rhetoric in mathematics; Rorty (1982), Toulmin (1958), and Rosen (1980) in technical philosophy; and numbers of scientists in their own fields (Polanyi, 1962; Medawar, 1964). Historians and sociologists of science have since the 1960s accumulated much evidence that science is a conversation rather than a mechanical procedure (Kuhn, 1977; Collins, 1985). The analysis of conversation from scholars in communication and literary studies (Scott, 1967) has provided ways of rereading various fields (a sampling of these is contained in Nelson et al., 1987).

A rhetoric of economics questions the division between scientific and humanistic reasoning, not to attack quantification or to introduce irrationality into science, but to make the scientific conversation more aware of itself. It is a programme of greater, not less rigour and relevance, of higher, not lower standards in the conversations of mankind.

DONALD N. MCCLOSKEY

See also PHILOSOPHY AND ECONOMICS.

BIBLIOGRAPHY

Booth, W. 1974. *Modern Dogma and the Rhetoric of Assent*. Chicago: University of Chicago Press.

Collins, H.M. 1985. *Changing Order: replication and induction in scientific practice*. London: Sage.

Davis, P.J. and Hersh, R. 1981. *The Mathematical Experience*. Boston: Houghton Mifflin.

Henderson, W. 1982. Metaphors in economics. *Economics* 18(4), No. 80, Winter, 147–53.

Klamer, A. 1984. *Conversations with Economists: new classical economists and opponents speak out on the current controversy in macroeconomics*. Totowa, NJ: Rowman and Allanheld.

Knight, F. 1940. 'What is truth' in economics? *Journal of Political Economy* 48, February, 1–32.

Kornai, J. 1983. The health of nations: reflections on the analogy between medical science and economics. *Kyklos* 36(2), June, 191–212.

Kuhn, T. 1977. *The Essential Tension: selected studies in scientific tradition and change*. Chicago: University of Chicago Press.

Lakatos, I. 1976. *Proofs and Refutations: the logic of mathematical discovery*. Cambridge: Cambridge University Press.

Leamer, E. 1978. *Specification Searches: ad hoc inferences with nonexperimental data*. New York: Wiley.

Leontief, W. 1971. Theoretical assumptions and nonobserved facts. *American Economic Review* 61(1), March, 1–7.

McCloskey, D.N. 1986. *The Rhetoric of Economics*. Madison: University of Wisconsin Press.

Mayer, T. 1980. Economics as a hard science: realistic goal or wishful thinking? *Economic Inquiry* 18(2), April, 165–78.

Medawar, P. 1964. Is the scientific paper fraudulent? *Saturday Review* 1, August.

Nelson, J., Megill, A. and McCloskey, D.N. (eds) 1987. *The Rhetoric of the Human Sciences: papers and proceedings of the Iowa Conference*. Madison: University of Wisconsin Press.

Perelman, C. and Olbrechts-Tyteca, L. 1958. *The New Rhetoric: a treatise on argumentation*. Notre Dame: University of Notre Dame Press.

Polyani, M. 1962. *Personal Knowledge: towards a post-critical philosophy*. Chicago: University of Chicago Press.

Rorty, R. 1982. *The Consequences of Pragmatism: essays*. Minneapolis: University of Minnesota Press.

Rosen, S. 1980. *The Limits of Analysis*. New York: Basic Books.

Scott, R. 1967. On viewing rhetoric as epistemic. *Central States Speech Journal* 18(1), February, 9–17.

Stigler, G.J. 1977. The conference handbook. *Journal of Political Economy* 85(2), April, 441–3.

Toulmin, S. 1958. *The Uses of Argument*. Cambridge: Cambridge University Press.

Ricardian equivalence theorem. The Ricardian Equivalence Theorem is the proposition that the method of financing any particular path of government expenditure is irrelevant. More precisely, the choice between levying lump-sum taxes and issuing government bonds to finance government spending does not affect the consumption of any household nor does it affect capital formation. The fundamental logic underlying this argument was presented by David Ricardo in Chapter XVII ('Taxes on Other Commodities than Raw Produce') of *The Principles of Political Economy and Taxation.* Although Ricardo clearly explained why government borrowing and taxes could be equivalent, he warned against accepting the argument on its face: 'From what I have said, it must not be inferred that I consider the system of borrowing as the best calculated to defray the extraordinary expenses of the state. It is a system which tends to make us less thrifty – to blind us to our real situation' (1960, pp. 162–3).

Another formulation of the question of debt vs. taxes arises in the determination of national income. The aggregate consumption function plays an important role in models of national income determination, and aggregate consumption is often specified to depend on contemporaneous aggregate disposable income and on aggregate wealth. The question is whether the public's holding of bonds issued by the government should be treated as part of aggregate wealth. If consumers recognize that these bonds, in the aggregate, represent future tax liabilities, then these bonds would not be part of aggregate wealth. If, on the other hand, consumers do not recognize, or for some reason do not care about, the implied future tax liabilities associated with these bonds, then they should be counted as part of aggregate wealth in an aggregate consumption function. Patinkin (1965, p. 289) recognized this question and specified that a fraction k of the stock of outstanding government bonds is to be treated as wealth. Under the Ricardian Equivalence view, k would be equal to zero; under the view that consumers ignore future tax liabilities, k would be equal to one. Bailey (1971) also examined the question of whether future tax liabilities affect aggregate consumption in a model of national income determination, though his formulation of the aggregate consumption function does not explicitly include aggregate wealth.

The question of whether government bonds are net wealth and the question of the effects of alternative means of financing a given amount of government expenditure are, in many contexts, basically the same question. For purposes of exposition, it is perhaps clearest to focus on one particular formulation of the question. Below the discussion will focus on the question of the choice between current taxation and debt finance.

The underlying logic of the Ricardian Equivalence Theorem is quite simple and can be displayed by considering a reduction in current (lump-sum) taxes of 100 dollars per capita. This reduction in government tax revenue is financed by the sale of government bonds on the open market in the amount of 100 dollars per capita. For simplicity, suppose that the bonds are one-year bonds with an interest rate of 5 per cent per year. In addition, suppose that the population is constant over time. In the year following the tax cut, the bonds are redeemed by the government. In order to pay the principal and interest on the bonds, taxes must be increased by 105 dollars per capita in the second year.

Now consider the response of households to this intertemporal rearrangement of their tax liabilities. Households can afford to maintain their originally planned current and future consumption by increasing their current saving by 100 dollars. In fact, the additional 100 dollars of saving could be held in the form of newly issued government bonds. In the second year, when the government increases taxes by 105 dollars to redeem the bonds, the household can pay the extra tax using the principal and interest on the bond. Thus, the originally planned path of consumption continues to be feasible after the tax change. In addition, since the originally planned path of consumption was chosen by the consumer before the tax change, it would continue to be chosen after the tax change since all relative prices remain unchanged. Therefore, household behaviour is invariant to the switch between tax finance and debt finance for a given amount of government spending.

The example above illustrates the fundamental insight that underlies the Ricardian Equivalence Theorem. Because the example is extremely simple, it is useful to point out which of the simplifying assumptions are fundamentally important for the result and which are merely for expositional clarity. In the example above, only lump-sum taxes were changed and it was assumed that the tax cut and the subsequent decrease fell equally on all consumers. Each of these assumptions is crucial for the result and will be discussed further below. The example made no explicit mention of the unpredictability of future taxes or future income, but the Ricardian Equivalence Theorem would hold in the above example even if future consumption is not known with certainty. It also would hold if the realized real interest rate on the government bonds is not perfectly predictable. Provided that in the first year the consumer adds 100 dollars of government bonds to his portfolio, he will be able to maintain precisely the same path of current and future consumption after the tax change as before the tax change.

In the basic example, the tax cut in the current year is financed by the issue of one-year government bonds. However, the invariance result continues to hold if the current tax cut is financed by the issue of N-year bonds. The argument is that once again each consumer uses the extra 100 dollars of disposable income in the first period to purchase 100 dollars of newly issued government bonds. If these government bonds pay interest in years before the bond is redeemed, then the government must increase lump-sum taxes in these years to service these bonds. Consumers who are holding the bonds and receive interest use the interest on their bonds to pay the increased taxes. Then, when the bonds mature after N years, each consumer uses the principal and final interest on these bonds to pay the higher taxes that are levied to redeem the debt. Once again, consumers can afford to maintain the originally planned path of current and future consumption and find it optimal to do so.

Having seen that the Ricardian Equivalence Theorem holds even if long-term bonds are issued to cover the current tax cut, it is natural to ask whether the invariance result continues to hold even if some or all of the currently living consumers die before the bonds are redeemed. The first answer to this question would appear to be that consumers who are alive during the tax cut, but who die before the newly issued bonds are retired, would have a reduction in the present value of their taxes and thus an increase in the present value of their disposable income. Equivalently, such consumers could afford to increase their current and future consumption. It is not necessary for these consumers to hold on to the extra bond which is issued in the first year because they will not have to use the bonds to pay for the future tax increase needed to redeem the bonds. Therefore, these consumers would tend to increase their current and future consumption, ceteris paribus.

If consumers are entirely self-interested, then escaping future taxes through death would invalidate the Ricardian Equivalence Theorem. However, Robert Barro (1974) presented an ingenious argument which extends the Ricardian Equivalence Theorem to cover the case in which consumers die before future taxes are increased to compensate for the current tax cut. Before discussing the substantive content of Barro's argument, it is interesting to observe that the term 'Ricardian Equivalence Theorem' apparently was first used by James Buchanan (1976) in a published comment on Barro's paper. Buchanan's comment begins by pointing out Barro's failure to credit Ricardo with the idea that debt and taxes may be equivalent and, indeed, the comment is titled, 'Barro on the Ricardian Equivalence Theorem'. Previously, Buchanan had referred to this result as the 'equivalence hypothesis' (1958, p. 118).

Barro postulated that consumers have bequest motives of a particular form which has been labelled 'altruistic'. An altruistic consumer obtains utility from his own consumption as well as from the utility of his children. Therefore, a consumer who is altruistic toward all of his children cares not only about his own consumption, but also indirectly about the consumption of all his children. Furthermore, if all of the altruistic consumer's children are also altruistic and care about the utility of their children, then the altruistic consumer cares indirectly about the consumption of all of his grandchildren. Provided that all consumers are altruistic, the argument can be extended ad infinitum with the important implication that an altruistic consumer cares, at least indirectly, about the entire path of current and future consumption of himself and all of his descendants.

Barro's insight that an intergenerationally altruistic consumer cares about the entire path of his family's consumption defuses the argument that consumers who escape future taxes through death will increase consumption in response to a current tax cut. For altruistic consumers, it does not matter whether they themselves, or their descendants, pay the higher taxes necessary to pay the principal and interest on the newly-issued bonds. In response to a 100 dollar tax cut in the current year, an altruistic consumer will not change his consumption but will hold an additional 100 dollars of government bonds. If the bonds are not redeemed until after the consumer dies, he will bequeath them to his children who can then use the bonds to pay the higher taxes in the year in which the bonds are redeemed, or else bequeath the bonds to their children if the bonds are not redeemed during their lifetimes.

It is important to note that the fact that a consumer leaves a bequest is not prima facie evidence that he is altruistic in the sense defined above. Bequests may arise as the accidental outcome of an untimely death or they may arise for motives other than pure altruism in the sense used by Barro. For instance, if the utility that a consumer obtains from leaving a bequest depends only on the size of the bequest, then he will not care about tax increases which may be levied on his children or his children's children. In this case the Ricardian Equivalence Theorem would not hold.

The argument that each current and future consumer in a family of intergenerationally altruistic consumers cares about his own consumption as well as the consumption of all of his descendants forever then raises the question of whether the government must ever pay off the newly-issued government bonds. If the government could roll over the principal and interest on this debt forever, so that it would never be necessary to increase future taxes, it would seem that a current tax cut financed by an issue of government bonds would reduce the present value of the taxes paid by the current and future members of the family and hence would lead to an increase in the family's consumption. The question of whether a current tax cut must be followed at some time by a tax increase depends on whether the interest rate is greater or less than the economy's growth rate. If the interest rate exceeds the growth rate, then it is impossible to roll over the principal and interest on the newly-issued bonds for ever. If the government attempted to do so by issuing new bonds, the stock of these bonds would grow in perpetuity at the rate of interest. If the rate of interest exceeds the economy's growth rate, then these bonds would not willingly be held in private portfolios. Alternatively, if the rate of interest falls short of the economy's growth rate – a condition which signals an inefficient over-accumulation to capital – then, as pointed out by Feldstein (1976), it is possible for the government to roll over the debt permanently. Carmichael (1982) has shown that in this case, the altruistic bequest motive will not be operative but that an altruistic gift motive from children to parents (which specifies that a consumer's utility depends on his own consumption and the utility of his parents) may be operative. If the gift motive is operative, then Carmichael argues that the Ricardian Equivalence Theorem will hold, despite the fact that government bonds may be regarded as net wealth.

Now that we have described a fairly general set of conditions under which the Ricardian Equivalence Theorem holds, it is useful to discuss several of the conditions that might lead to a violation of the Ricardian Equivalence Theorem. A clear overview of reasons why the Ricardian Equivalence Theorem may not provide an accurate description of the actual effects of debt finance vs. tax finance is provided by Tobin (1980).

The Ricardian Equivalence Theorem requires not only that consumers be intergenerationally altruistic, but that their bequest motives be operative in the sense that consumers can bequeath whatever amount they choose subject to their budget constraint. To be more precise, it is possible that an altruistic consumer may like to leave a negative bequest to his children, but he is constrained from leaving a bequest less than zero. The fact that a consumer may want to leave a negative bequest does not necessarily violate the assumption that the consumer is altruistic. It may be that the consumer's children will all be so much wealthier than the consumer that, even though the consumer cares about the utility of his children, he could achieve higher utility by taking some of his children's resources and consuming them himself. Formal conditions which imply that altruistic consumers would like to leave negative bequests have been presented by Drazen (1978) and Weil (1984). Under these conditions, if the consumer is constrained from leaving a negative bequest, he will instead leave a zero bequest. In such cases, a tax cut which is followed by a tax increase after the consumer's death will reduce the present value of the taxes paid by the consumer and he will increase his consumption. In effect, the current tax cut helps the consumer to effect the desired negative bequest by giving him current resources and taking resources away from his descendants.

Another reason for departure from the Ricardian Equivalence Theorem is that policy often redistributes resources among families and that families may have different marginal propensities to consume out of income or out of wealth. For instance, suppose that the tax cut in the current year affects only one half of the consumers. More precisely, suppose that one half of the consumers face a 200 dollar tax cut in the current year and the other half of the consumers have unchanged taxes in the current year. The government issues bonds in the amount of 100 dollars per capita and in the following period it redeems the bonds and pays the interest. For simplicity, suppose that the population is constant and that the interest rate on government bonds is 5 per cent per year. Then in the year following the tax cut, there is a tax increase of 105 dollars per consumer. Finally, suppose that this tax increase is levied on all consumers equally. In this case, the tax cut in the current year is clearly a redistribution of resources from the consumers whose taxes are unaffected to the consumers whose taxes are reduced in the current year. The recipients of the transfer will increase their consumption and the other consumers will reduce their current consumption. The re-allocation of consumption across consumers may be viewed as a violation of the Ricardian Equivalence Theorem. Whether aggregate consumption rises or falls depends on the marginal propensities to consume of the recipients of the transfer compared to the marginal propensities to consume of the other consumers. If all consumers have equal marginal propensities to consume, then there will be no effect on aggregate consumption or capital accumulation. However, if, for instance, the recipients of the transfers have a higher marginal propensity to consume than the other consumers, then aggregate consumption would increase. It should be pointed out that in some sense, this example does not represent a violation of the Ricardian Equivalence Theorem, because it ignores the possibility that there might exist an insurance market for individual tax liabilities. If there were such a market, then consumers could have insured themselves against the redistribution of taxes. Such markets do not generally exist, but whether the Ricardian Equivalence Theorem holds may depend on the reason why these markets do not exist.

Uncertainty about the length of an individual consumer's lifetime is not, by itself, sufficient to violate the Ricardian Equivalence Theorem, although there are situations in which it will lead to a violation. For simplicity, consider consumers who each contribute 1000 dollars to a social security fund during their working life. At the end of the working life, suppose that some of the consumers die and that some survive and live in retirement for a certain period of time. Although the number of consumers who die at retirement may be predictable, the identities of those who will die and those who will survive are not predictable. The surviving retired consumers each receive an equal share of the social security fund (with accrued interest) to which they contributed while they were working. Each survivor's social security income is greater than the 1000 dollars (plus interest) which he contributed, because the fund contains the contributions plus interest of his peers who died at the end of the working life.

Now the question arises as to whether the introduction of this type of social security system affects consumption and capital accumulation or whether the Ricardian Equivalence Theorem implies that consumption and capital accumulation will be unaffected. To answer this question, it is useful to observe that this stylized social security system has the characteristics of an actuarially fair annuity. That is, consumers pay a premium when young (the social security tax) and receive a payment if they survive to old age. Furthermore, if all consumers face the same probability of dying, the rate of return to the survivors is equal to the actuarially fair rate of return. If there were a competitive annuity market, it would also supply annuities offering the actuarially fair rate of return. In this case, the social security system would indeed have no effect on the consumption or capital accumulation of altruistic consumers. The reason is that workers who are taxed 1000 dollars are essentially forced to hold 1000 dollars of the publicly-provided actuarially fair annuity called social security; however, these consumers can afford to maintain their originally planned consumption and bequests by reducing their holdings of privately supplied annuities by 1000 dollars. This reduction in the holding of private annuities will be chosen by an individual consumer because it allows the consumer to re-establish his initial portfolio of annuities and other assets while maintaining his consumption unchanged. Thus, the Ricardian Equivalence Theorem holds in this example.

If the probability of surviving until retirement differs across consumers, and if individual consumers are better informed about their own survival probabilities than are insurance companies, then the funded social security system described above will have an effect on consumption and on capital accumulation. The reason is that if an insurance company offered annuities at a price that would be actuarially fair to the average consumer, it would suffer from what is known as 'adverse selection'. As a simple example, suppose that insurance companies know the average mortality probability but have no additional information about the mortality probabilities of individual consumers. If an insurance company offered annuities at a price that would be actuarially fair to the average consumer, then consumers who believe they are healthier than average would view these annuities as a bargain; consumers who believe they are less healthy (or engage in more dangerous activities) than average would view these annuities as overpriced because these consumers have a smaller chance of living to reap the rewards. As the healthy consumers would buy a disproportionately large share of annuities, they would, on average, inflict losses on the sellers of these annuities and would induce these sellers to charge a higher price for annuities. However, the social security system can supply its annuities at the actuarially fair price for the average consumer because a compulsory social security system is immune to adverse selection. That is, because the government can determine the amount of the publicly provided annuity held by each individual, it does not have to worry that a disproportionately large share of annuities are held by healthy consumers. Therefore, as shown in Abel (1986) the annuity offered by the social security system would yield a higher rate of return than private annuities, or equivalently, would be made available at a lower price to consumers. Because of the difference in the prices of the publicly provided and privately supplied annuities, consumers would not exactly offset the effects of social security by transacting in private annuity markets.

The basic argument underlying the Ricardian Equivalence Theorem is that it makes no difference whether the government issues debt in the amount of 100 dollars per capita or whether it collects taxes of 100 dollars per capita since in the latter case, consumers can borrow 100 dollars per capita to pay the higher taxes. In the former case, public borrowing is increased by 100 dollars per capita and in the latter case, private borrowing is increased by 100 dollars per capita. Under the appropriate conditions it makes no difference whether the borrowing is by the public sector or by the private sector. In order for the choice between debt finance and tax finance to have an effect, it must be the case that any changes in government borrowing cannot be fully offset by changes in private sector behaviour. Equivalently, there must be something that the government can do in credit markets that the private sector cannot do. For example, as shown above, if individual consumers would like to leave negative bequests, but are unable to do so, then a tax cut accompanied by an issue of government bonds allows at least some members of the current population to transfer resources from their heirs to themselves. This intergenerational transfer of resources permits some consumers to effect negative bequests which they were individually unable to effect. Another example of something the government can do that the private sector cannot do is provided by the discussion of adverse selection. Because of the compulsory nature of taxes, the government can avoid the adverse selection problem which private insurance companies would inevitably face.

The example in which adverse selection leads to violation of the Ricardian Equivalence Theorem was constructed to obey the strict set of rules demanded by strong adherents to the view that the choice between debt finance and tax finance is irrelevant. In particular, the following assumptions were maintained: (1) consumers have operative altruistic bequest motives so that they care about taxes after their death; (2) there is a complete set of competitive markets; and (3) only lump-sum taxes are changed. However, actual economies display several important departures from each of these assumptions. Violations of these assumptions are discussed below.

First, consumers may not have a bequest motive, either because they have no children or because they do not care about the welfare of anyone else. Even if consumers do have a bequest motive, it may not be operative as discussed above. Even if the bequest motive is operative, it may not be of the appropriate form for the Ricardian Equivalence Theorem to hold. If a consumer's utility depends directly on the size of the bequest he leaves rather than on the utility of his heirs, then a current tax cut followed by a tax increase on his heirs, would tend to raise the current consumption of the consumer. The reason is that he does not care about his heirs' utility per se. His bequest yields utility directly just as any other consumption good. As a result of the decrease in taxes he must pay over his lifetime, the consumer will have a higher level of lifetime income and can increase his own consumption and the bequest he leaves. If his own consumption and the bequest are both normal goods in his utility function, then he will choose to increase both of these.

Even if all consumers have operative altruistic bequest motives, a tax cut may increase current consumption. If all consumers have several children, but if each consumer cares about the utility of only one of his children, then there will be consumers in future generations whose utility is ignored by all current consumers. To the extent that future taxes are levied on these consumers, some part of future tax liabilities associated with a current tax cut will be ignored by current consumers. In this case, a tax cut would increase contemporaneous aggregate consumption.

A second type of departure from the strict set of assumptions is that there may not be a complete set of competitive markets. For instance, a young consumer with a high prospective income might like to borrow to increase his consumption when young with the intention of repaying the loan when his income is higher in the future. However, for a variety of reasons, it may simply not be possible for the young consumer to borrow the desired amount; if this is the case, the consumer is described as 'liquidity-constrained'. If the current tax is reduced, the liquidity-constrained consumer may choose to consume some portion, or even all, of the tax cut rather than save the entire tax cut. The reason is that the liquidity-constrained consumer would have liked to have borrowed to increase current consumption but was unable to do so. In effect, the current tax cut allows the consumer to borrow in order to increase current consumption. The current tax cut financed by an issue of government bonds can be viewed as the government borrowing on behalf of the consumer. Although this example makes it seem clear that a liquidity-constrained consumer would increase his current consumption in response to a current tax cut, some caution is required in interpreting this result. Unless the reason for the liquidity constraint is specified, one cannot determine what will be the effect of the tax cut. For example, suppose that a consumer is able to borrow some funds, but is liquidity-constrained in the sense that he would like to borrow even more funds. If his creditors determine how much they are willing to lend by looking at his ability to repay the loan, then, in response to the prospective tax increase accompanying the current tax cut, his lenders will reduce the amount they are willing to lend by the amount of the tax cut. In this case, the Ricardian Equivalence Theorem would continue to hold.

Another type of departure from complete competitive markets that could interfere with the Ricardian Equivalence Theorem is the absence of certain types of insurance markets. Chan (1983) and Barsky, Mankiw and Zeldes (1986) have recently argued that if there are no markets for insuring against unpredictable fluctuations in after-tax income, then a current tax cut could increase current consumption. The argument, which was outlined by Barro (1974, p. 1115) and Tobin (1980, p. 60) is that to the extent that individual tax liabilities are proportional to income, the tax system provides partial insurance against fluctuations in individual disposable income. Therefore, the increase in tax rates which follows a current tax cut will reduce the variability of future disposable income. The reduction in the riskiness of future disposable income reduces current precautionary saving which consumers undertake to guard against low future consumption. The counterpart of the reduction in precautionary saving is an increase in current consumption.

A third type of departure from the strict set of assumptions underlying the Ricardian Equivalence Theorem is that most taxes are not lump-sum taxes. Generally, taxes are levied on economic activities, and changes in these taxes provide incentives to alter the levels of these activities. Although the existence of distortionary taxes does not in all cases imply that the theorem is violated when applied to lump-sum tax changes, it does strain the interpretation of empirical tests of the Ricardian Equivalence Theorem that examine historical data on deficits and consumption.

As discussed above, there are many potential sources of departure from the Ricardian Equivalence Theorem, and ultimately the importance of these departures is an empirical question. The existing literature that attempts to test empirically whether the theorem holds has produced mixed results, some claiming to show that it holds, and others the opposite. In judging the empirical relevance of the Ricardian Equivalance Theorem, however, the important question from the viewpoint of fiscal policy formulation is not whether the theorem holds exactly but whether there are departures from it which are quantitatively substantial. Existing empirical work has not yet produced a consensus on this question.

ANDREW B. ABEL

See also GOVERNMENT BUDGET CONSTRAINT; PUBLIC DEBT; PUBLIC FINANCE.

BIBLIOGRAPHY

Abel, A.B. 1986. Capital accumulation and uncertain lifetimes with adverse selection. *Econometrica* 54(5), September, 1079–97.

Bailey, M.J. 1971. *National Income and the Price Level*. 2nd edn, New York: McGraw-Hill.

Barro, R.J. 1974. Are government bonds net wealth? *Journal of Political Economy* 82(6), November–December, 1095–117.

Barsky, R.B., Mankiw, G.N. and Zeldes, S.P. 1986. Ricardian consumers with Keynesian propensities. *American Economic Review* 76(4), September, 676–91.

Buchanan, J.M. 1958. *Public Principles of Public Debt*. Homewood, Ill.: Richard D. Irwin.

Buchanan, J.M. 1976. Barro on the Ricardian equivalence theorem. *Journal of Political Economy* 84(2), April, 337–42.

Carmichael, J. 1982. On Barro's theorem and debt neutrality: the irrelevance of net wealth. *American Economic Review* 72(1), March, 202–13.
Chan, L.K.C. 1983. Uncertainty and the neutrality of government financing policy. *Journal of Monetary Economics* 11, May, 351–72.
Drazen, A. 1978. Government debt, human capital and bequests in a lifecycle model. *Journal of Political Economy* 86, June, 337–42.
Feldstein, M.S. 1976. Perceived wealth in bonds and social security: a comment. *Journal of Political Economy* 84(2), April, 331–6.
Patinkin, D. 1965. *Money, Interest and Prices*. 2nd edn, New York: Harper & Row.
Ricardo, D. 1821. *The Principles of Political Economy and Taxation*. London: M. Dent & Sons, 1911. Reprinted, 1960.
Tobin, J. 1980. *Asset Accumulation and Economic Activity*. Chicago: University of Chicago Press.
Weil, P. 1984. 'Love thy children': reflections on the Barro debt neutrality theorem. Mimeo, Harvard University, October. Forthcoming in *Journal of Monetary Economics*.

Ricardian Socialists. The name 'Ricardian Socialists' was given currency by H.S. Foxwell. Introducing the English translation of a work by the Austrian jurist Anton Menger in 1899, he complained that 'the important work' of the Ricardian Socialists had been almost wholly ignored 'until the last few years'. Since that time the name has traditionally been used to refer to certain authors in England, especially between 1820 and 1830, and to a lesser extent in the decade following, who claimed that the workers had a right to the entire product of their labour. Starting from their observation of a contradiction, they developed a critique of existing distribution (with implications for development potentialities). On the one hand, it was admitted that labour was the sole source of value. On the other hand, they observed that much of the product of labour – that part which exceeds the 'necessary consumption' of the labourer – is taken, in the form of rent, profit and taxes, by the owning classes who contribute nothing to production.

Following M. Beer (1919), within this 'movement', whose members were in some respect very different from one another, we may distinguish two groups. On the one hand, there were the 'anti-capitalist economists', like T. Hodgskin, P. Ravenstone (pseudonym of Richard Puller) and some anonymous authors of pamphlets (such as *The Source and Remedy* etc., 1821). On the other hand, there were the 'cooperative socialists' close to Owen, such as W. Thompson, J. Gray and J.F. Bray. The distinction – with the further qualification that Bray's work can be viewed as a moment of synthesis between the two currents – is useful for tracing the broad outlines of the cultural and political background against which these authors stand. And it may also indicate that it is, above all, those belonging to the first group who are of greater interest from the point of view of economic analysis. With their greater interest in pursuing economic themes, these authors show a closer adherence to the mainstream of classical political economy, both as regards the structure of their analysis and its subject matter. This obviously holds true even when the motive behind their writings is frequently – as Foxwell (1899, p. lxxiii) also reminds us – that of opposition to the conclusions reached by Ricardo or other classical economists.

No consensus of opinion exists concerning the importance of these authors' contribution to economic analysis or the Ricardian (or at any rate 'classical') basis of their thought. Marx, among others, devoted several pages of his *Theories of Surplus-Value* to a careful analysis of the writings of the first of the two groups distinguished above (Marx, 1910, Part III, ch. XXI). Schumpeter, however, held that the writings of the group called Ricardian Socialists 'which of course is entitled to a great place in the history of socialist thought, offer but little that is relevant to a history of economic analysis' (Schumpeter, 1954, p. 479).

Introducing a discussion of these authors, Marx stated that their work derived entirely 'from the Ricardian form'. The link between Ricardo and the English proto-socialists was recognized by Foxwell but has, more recently, been denied by Hollander (1980) (but for hints in this direction see Lowenthal, 1911, p. 103; Blaug, 1958, p. 148; Hutchison, 1957, p. 89 and 1978, p. 242; in a very different context from these, Hunt, 1977, and 1979, p. 149). In the introduction from which we have quoted, Foxwell took the opportunity to unleash a fierce attack on Ricardo, employing the methodological critique of the German Historical School as well as the judgement of Jevons ('Ricardo's crude generalisations ... gave modern socialism its fancied scientific basis and provoked, if they did not justify, its revolutionary form'). If instead of being neglected for half a century the work of the Ricardian Socialists had been subjected to 'searching criticism by the best economists of the time' – he wrote – the 'elementary blunder in method' of Ricardo would have been more promptly rectified (Foxwell, 1899, pp. xl-xli). Hollander, however, in a study of the writings of Hodgskin, the most important and influential of the Ricardian Socialists, maintains that, on the one hand, the 'vehemence' of his critique of Ricardo, and on the other, his attachment to the so-called 'adding up theory' of value of Smith – which Ricardo rejected – make it impossible to rank Hodgskin in the Ricardian tradition.

1. Hodgskin and the other Ricardian socialists stand at an important crossroads in the development of British economic thought in the 19th century. Thus, aside from their intrinsic interest, their writings can also be studied for the support they lend to one or another of the three main interpretations that have been offered of that development, i.e. those of Marx, Jevons and Marshall. According to Marx (1873, vol. I, pp. 14–15), the end of classical political economy (which comes after Ricardo's death) and, parallel with this, the progressive search for and propagation of alternative theories of profit, must be traced back – together with the problems of analysis left unsolved by Ricardo – to the employment of the Ricardian theory 'as a weapon against bourgeois economy' used by the Labour writers. They had undermined the possibility of founding on the basis of that theory a 'harmonious' vision of capitalist society which would enable it to go on being considered as a 'definitive form' of social production. The anti-Ricardian reaction of the 1830s and 1840s – set against a background in which class struggles were becoming ever sharper and more extensive – must thus be seen, according to Marx, as a reaction to the '*unpleasant* side of classical political economy' (Marx, 1910, p. 502) which these authors had brought out.

Subsequently, Marx's interpretation has found support in Meek's (1950 and 1967) survey of the work of Read, Scrope and Longfield. According to Dobb (1973, p. 166), the 'anti-Ricardian reaction' of the 1830s and 1840s to some extent found its fulfilment in the analogous 'reaction' in the late 19th century associated with Jevons and his followers, among them Foxwell himself, which led to the 'rediscovery' of the Ricardian Socialists. Hollander's recent attempt to deny a Ricardian basis of Hodgskin's writings tends to suggest that after Ricardo's death not only would there have been no grounds for reacting against a 'dangerous' use of the Ricardian theory, but also that there was apparently no such reaction. In this view, Ricardo stands in a continuous line of development carrying the *entire* current of British economic thought from the first half of the 19th century up to Marshall and, more generally, to the marginalist theories of the last quarter of the 19th century.

2. If we except Thompson, who stands very close to Bentham's utilitarianism, even if in a contradictory way, all the other Ricardian Socialists argue from a premise of Natural Law that reflects the influence of Locke, Adam Smith and Godwin (and thus Rousseau). Whether dealing with the nature and origin of capital (Ravenstone and Hodgskin), the theory of value and distribution (Hodgskin) or the obstacles by which profit hinders accumulation (Hodgskin and some anonymous authors of *pamphlets*), the arguments start from very similar logical schemes. The necessary starting point is held to be 'first principles', the very first of which states that 'all wealth is the produce of labour'. On the basis of this principle (to which others are added, as in the case of Bray, 1839), a scheme is erected which is supposed to represent the workings of a 'natural society'. This is then contrasted with a representation of actual society. (The statistical foundation of this representation is often the 'Map of Civil Society' showing the distribution of income among 'different Classes' prepared by Colquhoun, 1814). The divergences of the second scheme from the first are explained by the presence of 'artificial' components, not intrinsically necessary and thus susceptible of modification, resulting from man-made institutions or contingent historical events. The contrast between 'nature' and 'artifice' is used by these writers to criticise both society and the economists who 'erected the results of their individual experience into general laws. Because a thing was, they thought it could not be otherwise' (Ravenstone, 1824, p. 6; see also Anon., 1821, pp. 7–8). Thus we have here not a 'positive' idea of Natural Right but, in the manner of Rousseau, a 'normative' one.

The contrast between 'nature' and 'artifice' finds an application in the idea, shared by many Ricardian Socialists, that in capitalist society the appropriation of the produce of labour takes place through a violation of the 'natural' principle of exchange, according to which each party should give and receive equal quantities of labour. However, there is an important difference between Gray, for instance, and Hodgskin (and Bray). (This difference is much fainter in popular proto-socialist literature of the 1830s.) In Gray's view, the violation emerges exclusively and directly from the comparison between a situation in which profit is absent and a capitalist situation. 'We have endeavoured to show that the real income of the country', Gray writes,' ... is taken from its producers, chiefly by the rent of land, by the rent of houses, by the interest of money, and by the profit *obtained by persons who buy their labour from them at one price and sell it at another*' (1825, p. 58, italics added). The conception of 'profit upon alienation', like that of the 'adding up theory', is, instead, lacking in Hodgskin. In the latter's conception the violation of the 'natural' principle of exchange does not derive directly from the presence of profit; it emerges from the comparison between exchanges effected *between capitalists*, on the one hand, and *between capitalist and labourer*, on the other. The former exchanges, according to the labour theory of value, are in agreement with the 'natural' principle of exchange; in the case of the latter exchanges, the violation is shown, as we shall see, by the difference between labour commanded and labour embodied.

3. As is well known, the theory of Natural Right has historically performed the function of justifying the application to the realm of history of the same conceptual tools that physicists had used to study the realm of nature. Reference to 'natural laws' was aimed not only at applying moral criteria but also reflected a search for phenomena endowed with 'universality and uniformity'. From the point of view of analysis, the theory of Natural Right, with all its limitations, fulfills the function of a 'counterfactual'; in other words, it enables the observer to stand back from existing society, a position which is in any case necessary in order to analyse the working of that society in depth.

In this connection, Hodgskin represents the most complex personality among the Ricardian Socialists. In his thought, the theory of Natural Right is grafted onto two very important cultural influences: on the one hand, that of the 'Scottish Historical School' (in his writings he quotes freely from Millar, Robertson and Lord Kames); on the other, that of Thomas Brown, an exponent of the Scottish philosophy of Common Sense (see in particular Hodgskin, 1827b, and Hodgskin, 1832). In Hodgskin these influences lead to a peculiar combination of a 'naturalistic optimism' and a philosophy of history based on materialism. Indeed Hodgskin holds that, in the long term, the 'material world' governs the formation of 'beliefs' since experience eventually leads to the correction of mistaken 'beliefs'. At the foundations of progress in knowledge and inventions, which, in turn, is the cause of a 'perpetual' productivity increase, lies a 'natural' phenomenon, the growth of population. 'Necessity is the mother of invention; and the continual existence of necessity can only be explained by the continual increase of people' (Hodgskin, 1827a, p. 86; see also Hodgskin in Halévy, 1903, p. 77; Ravenstone, 1821, p. 177). Since the growth of population, as Smith had argued, also leads to an extension of the division of labour, it ends by governing the development of society, independently of men's intentions and desires. The definition of 'natural' right of property accepted by Hodgskin comes from Locke. At one point in his *Two Treatises* (1690, Bk. II, ch. V, par. 27), Locke had stated that since each man owns his body, he also owns 'the *Labour* of his body' and 'the *Work* of his Hands'. The infringement of this law as of every other 'natural law' by 'artificial' institutions not only violates justice but also, by indirectly slowing down the growth of population, hinders the general progress of society.

As Halévy has noted (1903, p. 59), Hodgskin ascribes the same importance to population as does Malthus, but in a positive way. From the very outset he criticizes the *Malthusian elements* in the writings of Ricardo, expressing the hope that by getting rid of them one will be able to return to Adam Smith. As we shall see, the disagreement with Ricardo was not over his theory of value. As regards the theory of distribution, he argued that the current level of wages and the existence of an 'absolute' component in rent have an historical origin, to be sought in the 'power over labour' which landowners all over Europe have inherited from the previous state of slavery; he concluded that distribution depends 'entirely and exclusively on political regulations' (Hodgskin in Halévy, 1903, p. 78). Starting from a critique of the relevance of 'decreasing soil fertility', he proposes a different analysis of the relation between the growth of production (and population) and technical conditions in the production of necessaries. He studies firstly the effects of this relation on distribution, then its effects on development with a given distribution. The basic analytical tool used in this theoretical extension is no less than the Ricardian theory of value.

4. In Hodgskin's most widely read work, *Labour Defended* (1825), he re-expounds the Ricardian theory of wages, profits and differential rents, stating that the theory 'of that ingenious and profound writer' confirms that 'the exactions of the capitalist cause the poverty of the labourer' (Hodgskin, 1825, pp.

80–81). Yet in an important letter of May 1820 (first printed by Halévy in 1903), in setting out his opinions on value and distribution, Hodgskin had attacked Ricardo with criticisms of a fiercer and more explicit nature than can be found anywhere else in his work. Since in his subsequent writings his opinions remained substantially unaltered (except to give less attention to the problem of rent), a correct interpretation of that letter is crucial for defining Hodgskin's position. In 1820 he held that Ricardo, unlike Smith, had not made a clear distinction between 'natural' and 'artificial' circumstances. This had led him to mistake the latter for the former and to make incorrect forecasts. Consistent with his general conceptions, the main target of Hodgskin's critique is Ricardo's conclusion that, as population grows, profits tend to fall and development becomes stationary. Thus, on the basis of assumed 'natural laws', Ricardo is accused of having 'set bounds to our hopes for the future progress of mankind in a more definite manner' even than Malthus (Halévy, 1903, p. 67).

Hodgskin's most notable contribution (mentioned below) makes it idle to argue whether he should be labelled as 'Smithian' as opposed to 'Ricardian': he must be viewed as Ricardian reinterpreter of Smith and thus, more simply, as a 'classical political economist'. The contribution referred to is contained in his discussion of the difference of opinion between Smith and Ricardo on the subject of value. He holds that it lies not in the regulator principle of exchange – since both of them see value as determined by labour embodied – but in the different standards adopted for measuring prices. In asserting this Hodgskin clearly dissociates himself from Ricardo's interpretation of Smith, and thus also from the so-called 'adding up' theory.

According to Ricardo (1821, p. 13), Smith had confined the validity of the labour theory of value strictly to the 'early and rude state of society which precedes both the accumulation of stock and the appropriation of land'. But the entry of profit onto the scene necessitated that the theory be abandoned. In this situation, the natural price would be obtained as the sum of the 'component parts', at their respective natural rates, taken independently of one another. A corollary of this 'adding up' theory was that an increase in profit would determine a rise in prices without any corresponding fall in wages. Ricardo rejected this conclusion and asserted, on the basis of the labour theory of value, that relative prices were independent of variations in distribution: every increase in profits was offset by a fall in wages. Smith, in abandoning (according to Ricardo), the labour theory of value in favour of the 'adding up' theory, had simultaneously taken wages as the unit for measuring prices. This suggested to Ricardo the existence of a correspondence between the 'regulator principle of exchange' and the unit for measuring prices. (He may also have been led into this mistake by the experience with his own theory in the course of his search for an invariable measure of value: see Sraffa, 1951, p. xli, note 1.) Thus he charged Smith with contradicting the rule of exchange according to the labour embodied *because* he had adopted the labour commanded as the unit for the measurement of prices.

Actually Hodgskin rejects this since he reinterprets Smith's text on the basis of the inverse relation of wages to the rate of profit which Ricardo had derived from the labour theory of value. As the rate of profit increases – says Hodgskin (Halévy, 1903, p. 74) – price rises *in terms of wage units*, and therefore the labourer must perform a larger quantity of labour in order to purchase the same quantity of goods as before, because wages have fallen. To this fall in wages (rise in profit) he thus traces the divergence between labour embodied and labour commanded which Smith detected when the rate of profit is positive and accounted for, unlike Hodgskin, with the 'adding up' theory. (According to this theory, in any case, reductions in wages should lead to *reductions* in prices.) Hodgskin contrasts exchange between owners of the means of production, on the one hand, and, on the other, between commodities produced under capitalistic condition and labour. He accepts the hypothesis of uniformity in the ratio of profits (and rents) to wages in the price of each commodity (the hypothesis is set out explicitly in Hodgskin, 1827, p. 186, and implied in all his writings); this explains why in Hodgskin's view incomes other than wages 'do not enter' into the relative prices of commodities, whereas they do enter into the ratio of prices to wages, and indeed 'constitute the greatest part of it'.

In 1846, reviewing Ricardo's works, Hodgskin (1846, p. 1557), was to admit that Smith had made 'a verbal variation from his own principle' of 'labour paying all price', whereas Ricardo had maintained 'a technical adherence to it'. But he justified Smith as having tried to offer through the exchange of commodity and labour 'a truer representation of what actually occurs in society than Mr. Ricardo's'. (Hodgskin holds that Ricardo has focused his attention on a relatively minor problem, that of 'exchangeable variations in the value of commodities', instead of dealing, as Smith had tried to, with the 'important relations of the labourer to other classes'.) The result Hodgskin achieved by basing himself on the labour theory of value retains its validity – as Sraffa has demonstrated (1960, ch. VI) – within the framework of a rigorous theory of the prices of production. From his 'equations of reduction to dated quantities of labour' it can immediately be seen that when the rate of profit is zero, embodied labour and labour commanded coincide. When the rate of profit increases (i.e. when wages fall in terms of the price of products) the quantity of 'labour commanded' by each commodity increases and is greater than the quantity of 'labour embodied'. Since we are dealing with a 'price-relation between labour and the given product', Sraffa has remarked (1960, p. 40), this is independent of the 'medium' adopted as a measure of wages and prices.

5. Hodgskin holds that the measurement of prices in terms of labour commanded is important, among other things to show up the mistake in Ricardo's thesis on the 'natural' tendency of profits to fall as the growth of population requires the cultivation of less and less fertile land. He states that the direct and indirect application of 'machinery and ingenuity' to agricultural production has in actual fact *reduced* the quantity of labour embodied in each unit of production (defined as 'natural price'). What, on the contrary, has steadily grown, in the long run, is labour commanded. (Price measured in wage units is defined as 'exchange value' in *Labour Defended*, and as 'social price' in *Popular Political Economy*.) Ricardo has been deceived by the missing distinction between the two 'prices' into underestimating the long-term trend of technical progress, induced by the growth of population, to 'compensate for decreasing fertility'. This technical progress has led to an increase in the ratio between surplus and wages, and thus to an increase in labour commanded. In addition, Ricardo has drawn general conclusions on technology on the basis of the increase in the price of corn occurring in 'a short and single period' (after 1792). But this period, Hodgskin asserts, has been strongly affected by a series of exceptional circumstances and/or 'political regulations' (see Hodgskin, 1827a, pp. 226–31 and Hodgskin, 1848, p. 1228).

Though Hodgskin's disagreement with Ricardo on this point is important in several respects, it does not concern the theoretical structure of the theory of value and distribution.

Rather, it offers an instance of the flexibility injected into the analytic structure of the surplus theories by the separate determination of production, on the one hand, and distribution, on the other (see Garegnani, 1984, pp. 296–7). This separation enables various hypotheses about the shape of the relationship between levels of production and returns to be considered. In 1846, Hodgskin was to evince astonishment at Ricardo's disregard of the 'laws of production' especially in a period of rapid advance in output; in this disregard he found one of the reasons for the decline of the Ricardian theories. On the other hand, in a famous letter to Malthus of 9 October 1820, Ricardo had written: 'no law can be laid down respecting quantity, but a tolerably correct one can be laid down respecting proportions' (Ricardo, 1887, p. 278) – which may perhaps help to explain the meaning he attached to his acceptance of Say's principle.

6. In *Popular Political Economy*, Hodgskin states that the difference between 'natural price' and 'social price' is important not only 'to understand the natural laws which regulate the progress of nations', but also 'rightly to estimate the causes which retard it' (1827a, p. 220). He denies that redistribution in favour of profits and the very presence of profit itself promote development. First of all, that which enriches the individual capitalist, he writes, does not necessarily add to national wealth: not all the capital which brings profit to its owner 'assist production'. Moreover, the presence of profit requires a part of the product of labour be withdrawn from reproduction and handed over to 'unproductive idlers'. The capitalist neglects those investments that do not promise him sufficient profit, yet these same would provide labourers with a comfortable subsistence. Hodgskin does not deny that profits have a periodic tendency to shrink. In *Labour Defended* (1825, pp. 78–80) his explanation explicitly contradicts those of Smith and Ricardo. The fall in profits is ascribed to the need to balance, periodically, two contrasting forces. On the one hand, the need to obtain a rate of profit not less than the monetary rate of interest prompts capitalists to a continual reinvestment of profits, thus causing a continuous growth, at compound rate, of the bulk of profits (for a given labour force). The appropriation by capitalists of the fruits of technical progress may lead to an increase in the rate of profit which contributes to this growth. On the other hand, reinvestment is not concerned with 'gold or money, but food, clothing and instruments', and labour productivity can-increase continuously so as to satisfy 'the overwhelming demands of compound interest': there is thus a limit to the growth of profits. Hodgskin's thesis may be set alongside Marx's idea that the degree of exploitation of labour has unsurmountable limits bound up with the length of the working day. This idea led Marx to conclude that an increase in the rate of surplus-value could not in the long term determine a counter-tendency to the fall of the rate of profit. Hence Marx's simplifying hypothesis of the constancy of rate of surplus-value, so that his law of the tendency of the rate of profit to fall ultimately depends solely on the increase in the organic composition of capital (see Marx, 1910, pp. 298–311 and Marx, 1894, pp. 211–66).

7. A recurring theme in the writings of the Ricardian Socialists is the polemic against the thesis, originating with Lauderdale and Say – and partly accepted in revised versions by disciple of Ricardo – which casts capital in the role of an 'active agent' of production. According to these theories, capital is capable of increasing productivity and/or saving labour independently of the application of labour. *Labour Defended* (along with Ravenstone's book, 1821) appears to offer the most coherent and effective arguments, at the time, against such conceptions of 'economic fetishism'. In this work, circulating capital is traced back to 'coexisting labour', while fixed capital is identified with the knowledge and the skilled labour needed to construct and employ the instruments of production. Ultimately, capital for Hodgskin (and here we catch an echo of Smith) is 'a means of obtaining command over labour' (Hodgskin, 1825, p. 55). The arguments Hodgskin uses to demonstrate that capital enjoys no independent productivity are, however, mostly confined to the aspect of use-value. There are, moreover, two features which explain Hodgskin's tendency, noted by Marx, to 'underestimate somewhat the value which the labour of the past has for the labour of the present' (Marx, 1910, p. 276). On the one hand, the want of a clear distinction (this in common with other classical economists) between 'concrete labour' and labour as 'value magnitude' which, on the basis of the accepted theory of value, determines the exchange value. This also explains Hodgskin's reluctance to admit the influence of soil fertility on production, to the extent that he considers it 'a contradiction of Mr. Ricardo's own principle' that 'labour pays all cost' (Hodgskin, 1848, p. 1228). On the other hand, Hodgskin was attached to Smith's idea (restated by James Mill) that 'what is *annually* produced is *annually* consumed' (Hodgskin, 1825, p. 47). However, Marx's main objection to the Ricardian Socialists, reiterated against Lassalle in the *Critique of the Gotha Programme*, turns on the fact that by proposing a society governed by individual exchanges between independent producers, their critique of capitalism stopped short of discussing the market as a coordinating mechanism in the social division of labour. Some hints of criticism of competition do nevertheless occur in the writings of the Owenite current of Ricardian Socialists and, in particular, in the works of Thompson (1824 and 1827) and Gray (1825).

ANDREA GINZBURG

See also BRAY, JOHN FRANCIS; HODGSKIN, THOMAS; RAVENSTONE, PIERCY; THOMPSON, WILLIAM.

BIBLIOGRAPHY

Anon. 1821. *The Source and Remedy of the National Difficulties. A letter to John Russell.* London.

Beer, M. 1919. *A History of British Socialism.* London: Allen & Unwin.

Blaug, M. 1958. *Ricardian Economics.* New Haven: Yale University Press.

Bray, J.F. 1839. *Labour's Wrongs and Labour's Remedy.* Leeds. Reprints of Economic Classics, New York: A.M. Kelley, 1968.

Colquhoun, P. 1814. *A Treatise on the Wealth, Power and Resources of the British Empire.* London: J. Mawman.

Dobb, M.H. 1973. *Theories of Value and Distribution since Adam Smith.* Cambridge: Cambridge University Press.

Foxwell, H.S. 1899. Introduction to A. Menger (1886).

Garegnani, P. 1984. Value and distribution in the classical economists and Marx. *Oxford Economic Papers* 36(2), June, 291–325.

Gray, J. 1825. *A Lecture on Human Happiness.* London. Reprints of Economic Classics, New York: A.M. Kelley, 1971.

Halévy, E. 1903. *Thomas Hodgskin.* Edited in translation with an introduction by A.J. Taylor, London: E. Benn, 1956.

[Hodgskin, T.] 1825. *Labour Defended against the Claims of Capital,* by a Labourer. London. Reprints of Economic Classics, New York: A.M. Kelley, 1963.

Hodgskin, T. 1827a. *Popular Political Economy.* London. Reprints of Economic Classics, New York: A.M. Kelley, 1966.

Hodgskin, T. 1827b. *The Word BELIEF defined and explained.* London.

[Hodgskin, T.] 1832. *The Natural and Artificial Right of Property contrasted,* by the author of *Labour defended against the claims of capital.* London.

Hodgskin, T. 1846. Review of *The Works of David Ricardo,* (ed. J.R. McCulloch). *The Economist,* 28 November.

[Hodgskin, T.] 1848. Review of H.C. Carey, *The Past, the Present, and the Future. The Economist,* 28 October.

Hollander, S. 1980. The post-Ricardian dissension: a case study in economics and ideology. *Oxford Economic Papers* 32(3), November, 370–410.
Hunt, E.K. 1977. Value theory in the writings of the classical economists, Thomas Hodgskin and Karl Marx. *History of Political Economy* 9(3), Fall, 322–45.
Hunt, E.K. 1979. *History of Economic Thought: A Critical Perspective*. Belmont, California: Wadsworth.
Hutchison, T.W. 1957. Review of E. Halévy (1903), ed. A.J. Taylor. *Economica* 24, February, 88–9.
Hutchison, T.W. 1978. *On Revolutions and Progress in Economic Knowledge*. Cambridge: Cambridge University Press.
King, J.E. 1983. Utopian or scientific? A reconsideration of the Ricardian Socialists. *History of Political Economy* 15(3), Fall, 345–73.
Locke, J. 1690. *Two Treatises of Government*. Ed. P. Laslett, Cambridge: Cambridge University Press, 1967.
Lowenthal, E. 1911. *The Ricardian Socialists*. Reprints of Economic Classics, New York: A.M. Kelley, 1972.
Marx, K. 1873. Afterword to the 2nd German edn, in K. Marx, (1867) *Capital. A Critique of Political Economy*, Vol. I. New York: International Publishers, 1967.
Marx, K. 1894. *Capital. A Critique of Political Economy*, Vol. III. ed. F. Engels, New York: International Publishers, 1967.
Marx, K. 1910. *Theories of Surplus Value*, Part III. London: Lawrence & Wishart, 1972.
Meek, R.L. 1950. The decline of Ricardian economics in England. *Economica* 17, February, 43–62.
Meek, R.L. 1967. The decline of Ricardian economics in England. In R.L. Meek, *Economics and Ideology and Other Essays*, London: Chapman & Hall.
Menger, A. 1886. *The Right to the Whole Produce of Labour*. With an introduction and bibliography by H.S. Foxwell. London, 1899. Reprints of Economic Classics, New York: A.M. Kelley, 1962.
Ravenstone, P. 1821. *A Few Doubts ... on the subjects of Population and Political Economy*. London: Andrews. Reprints of Economic Classics, New York: A.M. Kelley, 1966.
Ravenstone, P. 1824. *Thoughts on the Funding System and its Effects*. London: Andrews.
Ricardo, D. 1821. *On the Principles of Political Economy and Taxation*. 3rd edn in *The Works and Correspondence of David Ricardo*, ed. P. Sraffa with the collaboration of M.H. Dobb, Vol. I, Cambridge: Cambridge University Press, 1951.
Ricardo, D. 1887. *Letters 1819-June 1821*. In *The Works and Correspondence of David Ricardo*, ed. P. Sraffa, Vol. VIII, Cambridge: Cambridge University Press, 1973.
Schumpeter, J.A. 1954. *History of Economic Analysis*. New York: Oxford University Press.
Sraffa, P. 1951. Introduction to *The Works and Correspondence of David Ricardo*, Vol. I. Cambridge: Cambridge University Press.
Sraffa, P. 1960. *Production of Commodities by Means of Commodities*. Cambridge: Cambridge University Press.
Stark, W. 1943. *The Ideal Foundations of Economic Thought*. London. Reprints of Economic Classics, Fairfield : A.M. Kelley, 1976.
Thompson, W. 1824. *An Inquiry into the Principles of the Distribution of Wealth most conducive to Human Happiness*. London. Reprints of Economic Classics, New York: A.M. Kelley, 1963.
[Thompson, W.] 1827. *Labour Rewarded. The claims of labour and capital conciliated, by One of the Idle Classes*. London. Reprints of Economic Classics, New York: A.M. Kelley, 1966.

Ricardo, David (1772–1823).

LIFE AND WORKS

Ricardo was born in the City of London on 18 April 1772 and died at his country seat of Gatcomb Park, Gloucestershire on 11 September 1823. Both his father, Abraham Israel Ricardo, and his mother, Abigail Delvalle, belonged to Sephardic Jewish families (to Ricardo's Semitic origin has often been ascribed his tendency to abstract deductive reasoning, as for instance by Marshall, who regarded him as un-English: 1890, p. 60n). Both the Ricardos and the Delvalles had strong religious commitments. Abraham Ricardo (at difference from his wife's family) had only recently settled in England, coming from Amsterdam. He was an affluent stockbroker; David was the third of his at least seventeen children.

The young Ricardo did not have a conventional schooling, and he himself later in life complained of his 'neglected education' (*Works*, VII, 190). However, the idea of Ricardo as an 'untutored genius' (Stigler, 1953, p. 326) is certainly a misconception. Indeed, he seems for instance to have attended from the age of eleven to the age of thirteen a Jewish school of high repute, in Amsterdam, with which also Spinoza seems to have had some relations. More generally, by the affluent conditions of his family, Ricardo 'was allowed any masters for private instruction whom he chose to have' (as his brother Moses wrote in a Memoir, now reprinted in X, 3–13). Given that, 'when young, [he] showed a taste for abstract and general reasoning' (X, 4), he would not have missed the opportunities allowed by his family's circumstances.

At the age of fourteen, he started his business career, working with his father. At the age of 21, a breach was caused with his family by his marriage to Priscilla Ann Wilkinson, a Quaker ('to the Sephardic Jew a son marrying outside of the faith was as one whose name passed out of the family circle and for whom the memorial prayer for the dead was recited': Hollander, 1910, pp. 33–4). Therefore he was thrown 'upon his own resources' – his brother tells us – but was in fact succoured by some of 'the most respectable members of the Stock exchange' (the banking firm of Lubbock, Forster, & Co., later absorbed by Coutts), and was thus allowed to pursue an independent career as a stockbroker, which was to be extremely successful. In a few years, he made a great fortune: at his death, his estate was worth something between £675,000 and £775,000, out of which he had been enjoying a yearly income of about £28,000 (X, 103).

By the age of 25, thanks to his 'lessened solicitude' for his business, he 'turned his attention to other subjects', chiefly mathematics, chemistry, mineralogy and geology (he was one of the early members of the Geological Society of London, like his friend and fellow economist William Blake). In 1799, at the age of 27, during a stay at Bath, he happened to borrow a copy of the *Wealth of Nations*, of which he soon became 'a great admirer' (VII, 246). His interest in political economy could not but be enhanced by the events of those years. Indeed, it was just towards the end of 1799 that the first effects of Britain's departure from a gold standard (decided in February 1797) started to be felt, with a fall of the Hamburg exchange and the appearance of a premium of gold upon paper money. As Bagehot put it, it was 'the peculiar circumstances of his time [which] conducted Ricardo to the task for which he was most fit. He did not go to political economy – political economy, so to say, came to him' (1888, p. 344).

Ricardo's life as an active economist only lasted fourteen years: his first publication, an article on 'The Price of Gold' in the *Morning Chronicle*, appeared 29 August 1809 (the article, as was then generally the case in newspapers and reviews, was anonymous). This article (which was followed by two letters defending it against some critics) had been prompted by the sharp rise in the paper price of gold and the corresponding fall in the external value of the pound which happened that summer, after some years of relative calm. (For the facts of the 1797–1819 suspension of the gold standard, see Hawtrey, 1930, ch. 18.)

While Ricardo's contributions in the *Morning Chronicle* did not apparently attract much notice (but Cobbett did notice them), this was not the case for his subsequent work, *The High Price of Bullion, a Proof of the Depreciation of Bank-Notes*, where he recast and developed the arguments put forward in the *Morning Chronicle* contributions. This pamphlet, published in the first days of 1810, had reached a fourth edition by April 1811. In fact, scarcely a month after its publication, Francis Horner moved in the Commons for 'an inquiry into the causes of the present high price of bullion, and the consequent effect upon the value of paper money' (Horner, 1853, II, p. 1), and this led to the celebrated Bullion Report (published August, 1810). The very phrasing of Horner's motion appears as a confirmation of the influence of Ricardo's pamphlet on the appointment of the Committee, and in fact Horner himself seems to have regarded Ricardo (together with Mushet) as the originator of the movement which led to the Report (Horner, 1853, II, p. 24). Thanks also to the fact that the Report shared most of Ricardo's positions (but he himself by no means agreed with the whole of it: III, 347ff.), he became one of the leading figures of the 'Bullion Controversy'. He defended the Report in three (anonymous) letters to the *Morning Chronicle* (in September 1810), and it was again he who, in January 1811, replied with a pamphlet to one of the most effective attacks on the Bullionist position, Bosanquet's *Practical Observations on the Report of the Bullion Committee*.

By this time, Ricardo had established his reputation as an economist, and felt confident enough to write to the Chancellor of the Exchequer (July 1811) and to one of the leaders of the Opposition (December 1811), suggesting the adoption of a plan for the resumption of cash payments (on this plan, see below).

Ricardo's participation in the Bullion Controversy led to his intimacy with James Mill (whom he had first met after the publication of Mill's *Commerce Defended* in 1808) and with T.R. Malthus, then the foremost British economist, who reviewed Ricardo's *High Price of Bullion* and *Reply to Bosanquet* in the February issue of the *Edinburgh Review*. (Ricardo answered Malthus's comments the following April with an Appendix to the fourth edition of *The High Price of Bullion*.)

The friendship with Mill was to be important for Ricardo on a practical plane, in helping him to attain his 'anxious desire to produce something worth publishing', which he himself 'unaffectedly fear[ed]' would not be in his power to do (VII, 88). Mill played the rôle of a 'schoolmaster' (VI, 321), setting tasks to Ricardo in order that he might improve his literary skills. He helped Ricardo in his moments of despondency about his capacity to write, sometimes even reproaching him, as becomes a schoolmaster ('I shall begin by and bye to think that your misgivings, and your faintness at heart, are apologies ingeniously contrived by you in defence of your idleness': VII, 59). Mill was also important in that he always pressed Ricardo to propagate what they sometimes indicate as 'the right faith' (VII, 36) with 'his tongue, as well as his pen' (VI, 138). As early as Autumn 1814 he was urging Ricardo to enter Parliament. Ricardo resisted these designs for some time, but in the end was convinced. In February 1819 he entered Parliament as the Member for Portarlington, an Irish rotten borough (with some twelve electors).

Ricardo's friendship with Malthus was instead mainly important for their economic discussions. Ricardo himself wrote:

> My discussions with Malthus have been innumerable, and in my eagerness to convince him that he was wrong, on some points on which we differed, I was led into a deeper consideration of many parts of the subject than I had before given them, and though I have failed to convince him, and may not have satisfied others, I have convinced myself; and think that I have a very consistent theory in my own mind (VII, 246).

(Ample records of these discussions have reached us, in the extensive correspondence between them, and in Ricardo's *Notes* on Malthus's *Principles*.)

After 1811, the monetary controversies before the general public subsided, and Ricardo did not publish anything else until 1815. His interest in political economy however did not lapse, and he continued to be engaged in private discussions on monetary points (especially with Malthus). In August 1813, however, their correspondence records a move from the 'old question' to one on the effects of the opening of new markets – in particular, its effects on the rate of profits. This was probably connected with the issue of the restrictions to the corn trade which had been raised before Parliament in the first months of 1813. The discussion caused Ricardo to go into the question of whether an increase of capital diminishes profits, and into the theory of distribution. By March 1814 he had written some 'papers on the profits of Capital' (which are not extant), and in February 1815, when 'the question of the Corn Laws came before Parliament for the third year in succession' (Smart, 1910, p. 445), Ricardo published his *Essay on the Influence of a Low Price of Corn on the Profits of Stock; Shewing the Inexpediency of Restrictions on Importation* (now generally known as *Essay on Profits*). The free trade party was however defeated, and a very restrictive Corn Law was passed by a large majority the following month.

By this time, Ricardo had decided to abandon his business in the Stock Exchange, and started to transfer his money into landed estates (he had already acquired his residence of Gatcomb Park, which he thought would allow him not to 'sigh after the Stock Exch.ge and its enjoyments': VI, 115).

The great profits that he made on the Government loan for which he had been one of the successful bidders just four days before Waterloo (18 June 1815), induced him to devote more time to political economy (which he now called his 'favourite subject'), and it was the theory of distribution which mainly engaged his attention. By 1817, with the publication of his *Principles*, he came to regard it as 'the principal problem in Political Economy' (I, 5).

In the period between the *Essay on Profits* and the *Principles*, consideration of monetary questions is generally not taken up at his initiative – as happened for instance in August 1815, when P. Grenfell, an influential speaker on financial questions, asked Ricardo to help him in his Parliamentary battle against what he regarded as the excessive profits of the Bank of England. Ricardo, who thought the Bank as 'an unnecessary establishment getting rich by those profits which fairly belong to the public' (VI, 268), responded positively and by September had written a pamphlet, *Proposals for an Economical and Secure Currency*, which was published in February 1816, shortly before the debate on Grenfell's motion on the Bank. This pamphlet contained a detailed account of his plan to make the Bank of England resume cash payments by making its notes convertible into gold ingots, instead of coins. This would have allowed Britain to go back to a gold standard, but to use paper as the actual means of payments. This plan Ricardo had first outlined in the Appendix to *The High Price of Bullion*, and submitted to both Government and Opposition (as mentioned above). It was to receive much attention in 1819, when the decision was taken to return to a gold standard, and it was in fact adopted, and implemented in 1821, when the resumption of cash payments actually took place (see below). It gave Ricardo a long-lasting fame: when in 1925 Britain returned to gold, 'Ricardo's Ingot Plan' was still referred to (see, e.g., Keynes, 1925, p. 357), and adopted.

In that same summer of 1815, when Ricardo wrote *Economical and Secure Currency*, Mill was already pushing him to prepare a new and enlarged edition of the *Essay on Profits*. (This in the end resulted in the writing of Ricardo's main work, *On the Principles of Political Economy, and Taxation*). By October 1815 Ricardo appears to have been convinced, and even desirous to write a book at last (VI, 314). He already conceives it as an inquiry upon 'the Principles of Rent, Profit and Wages':

> These principles are so linked and so connected with everything belonging to the science of Political Economy that I consider the just view of them as of the first importance. It is on this subject, where my opinions differ from the great authority of Adam Smith Malthus &c[a], that I should wish to concentrate all the talents I possess not only for the purpose of establishing what I think correct principles but of drawing important deductions from them (VI, 315–16).

This in fact he did in the book which was eventually published in April 1817.

It was particularly in the process of writing the *Principles* that Mill's encouragement and practical assistance proved very important to Ricardo. To this period belongs Ricardo's acquaintance with J.R. McCulloch, who was to become a 'tireless salesman of Ricardian economics' (Fetter, 1965, p. 424). In 1816 McCulloch introduced himself to Ricardo, sending him a complimentary copy of a pamphlet. In June 1818 he reviewed the *Principles* in the *Edinburgh Review*, bestowing undiluted praise upon it, though showing some misunderstandings (which Ricardo did not notice in the first place, but which were spotted by his friend H. Trower). The review was, however, very effective in boosting the sale of the book (to Malthus's not too well disguised disappointment). A few months later Murray, Ricardo's publisher, applied to him for permission to print a second edition (only 750 copies had been printed of the first). This second edition, with 'a few very trifling alterations', was published in February 1819. A third edition, with extensive changes especially in the first chapter, 'On Value', was published in May 1821.

Ricardo seems to have said that no more than twenty-five people in England could have understood his book (VIII, 376–7n.), but there is little doubt that by now he was quite famous, thanks also perhaps to the fact that political economy in those years had become very fashionable.

In 1818, Ricardo was asked to give evidence before the Commons Committee on the Usury Laws (he declared to be in favour of their repeal). In February 1819, as already mentioned, he entered Parliament, where a new bout of the controversy on the suspension of the cash payments had started, and both Houses had set up a Committee to consider the issue. Ricardo's plan for ingot payments was high on the agenda of these Committees. Ricardo himself was asked to give evidence before both of them, and he declared himself to be in favour of immediate resumption. One of his first speeches in the Commons was on the resolutions embodying the recommendations of the Committee. (A resumption by steps was decided, which in two years would have made pounds convertible into bullion at the pre-suspension price of £3.17.10$\frac{1}{2}$ per ounce; convertibility into coin would have ensued after a year). As the newspapers reported, Ricardo rose to give his speech 'amidst loud invitations' (V, 9n.).

In the four and a half years Ricardo was in Parliament, as indeed in virtually the whole of his adult life, the Tories were in office (Lord Liverpool was the Prime Minister from 1812 to 1827). Ricardo did not attach himself to any of the parties. On general questions he tended to side with the Opposition, as for instance on Reform of Parliament (he was a staunch advocate of a moderate reform, as 'the most efficacious preventative of Revolution'; VIII, 49), and on civil liberties (Peterloo happened just a few months after he had entered Parliament, and he voted against the 'Gagging Acts' which virtually suspended the Constitution). On monetary questions, however, he found himself increasingly on the Government's side.

Besides monetary questions, many of Ricardo's speeches were devoted to financial problems. The war had swelled the national debt, as well as taxation. Retrenchment after the war basically consisted in the abolition of the main direct tax (the income tax). In the Budget of 1819, the Chancellor of the Exchequer proposed a heavy increase of indirect taxation. Ricardo, who was 'an enemy to taxation altogether' (V, 26), in the debate on the Budget gave hints of a plan to repay the whole of the national debt in four or five years, by means of a tax on property. This proposal, which of course met with little favour, seems to have caused Ricardo's reputation in the House to change into that of 'a theorist' (Baring defined the proposal as that of 'a man who might calculate well and read deeply, but who had not studied mankind': V, 270). Ricardo had always resented 'the vulgar charge ... against theorists' (III, 160), and used to attack men who are 'all for fact and nothing for theory' ('Such men can hardly ever sift their facts. They are credulous, and necessarily so, because they have no standard of reference': III, 180). He often complained of the changed attitude of the House towards him.

In September 1819, Ricardo reluctantly accepted an invitation to write an article on the Sinking Fund for the Supplement to the Fourth, Fifth and Sixth Edition of the Encyclopaedia Britannica, edited by M. Napier. He was, of course, far from contrary in principle to the Sinking Fund, the object of which was (or ought to have been) the diminution of the national debt. But he wrote against the perversion of the Sinking Fund from its original purpose, which had happened in past experience (and, according to Ricardo, was bound to happen in the future). Part of the article dealt with the more general question of the mode of providing for public expenditure. The article met with the warm approval of both Mill and McCulloch. The latter insisted that it was not just an article on the Sinking Fund, but on the funding system in general. And with the title 'Funding System' it was actually published (September 1820).

The years 1821 and 1822 were a period of severe distress in agriculture, and in both years a Committee on Agriculture was appointed by the Commons. Ricardo served on both of them, and a by-product of this was a pamphlet on Protection to Agriculture (April 1822). The distress was mainly due to low prices (the price of corn in 1822 reached a historical minimum), and the increased real burden of taxation, again due to the fall of prices. The agriculturalists blamed the distress upon the deflationary policy linked to the return to gold. Ricardo, both in Parliament and in his pamphlet, claimed that the appreciation of the currency due to the resumption did not exceed ten per cent – half of which, he thought, was due to the conduct of the Bank directors, who, being 'ignorant of the principles of currency', had not followed his plan of bullion payments, and with their purchases of gold to be coined had caused an unnecessary rise in its value. Moreover, he maintained that the increased burden of taxation could not explain the crisis, which was peculiar to agriculture, because it affected all trades more or less in the same degree (though he reluctantly made some concession to the particular position of the landholder with respect to taxation).

Ricardo thought the distress was of a temporary nature, because according to him the cause of the fall in corn prices was excess of production. (Abundance of corn was not a curse to the country, but certainly to the producer of corn: 'If we lived in one of Mr. Owen's parallelograms, and enjoyed all our productions in common, then no one could suffer in consequence of abundance, but as long as society is constituted as it now is, abundance will often be injurious to producers, and scarcity beneficial to them': IV, 222). However, he did not miss this opportunity to attack the Corn Laws. They allowed corn to be grown at a much higher price in Britain than abroad, and this deprived the corn grower of one of the chief remedies to excessive production, namely exportation. Also, he blamed the absurd mechanism according to which no importation of corn was allowed until a certain (very high: 80 shillings per quarter) price was reached, but when it was reached, the ports were thrown open for three months, no matter what happened in this period to corn prices. To remedy these evils, Ricardo proposed a scheme which ought by steps to have replaced this mechanism with one of freedom of importation, coupled with a duty on importation to 'countervail the peculiar burthens to which the grower of corn is subject' in Britain (he generously fixed it at 10 shillings per quarter), and a parallel drawback on exportation (7 shillings per quarter). The proposal was duly rejected by the Commons (only twenty-five voted in favour).

The last of his works which Ricardo prepared for publication was a *Plan for the Establishment of a National Bank*, which he wrote in the Summer of 1823. It was published in February 1824, when Ricardo had been dead for about five months, and was seen through the press by his brother Moses. The plan (which Ricardo had already outlined in the *Principles*) consisted in taking the privilege of issuing paper money from the Bank of England, and entrusting it to a 'National Bank', which would have issued it on behalf of the Government. The Commissioners of this National Bank would have been granted total independence from the Government, and would have acted 'as the general banker to all the public departments, and only to them' (IV, 289). They would have not been allowed to lend money directly to the Government, but only to buy Government securities 'in the open market'. This scheme would, according to Ricardo, have made the issue of paper money more independent of the Government than it then was. The main effect of the plan would have been to deprive the Bank of England of the profits it derived from the issue of paper money, leaving it as an ordinary banking institution. This followed the conception, which Ricardo had entertained for a long time (see above), that the Bank of England was an unnecessary institution, making profits which 'fairly belong to the public'. No inconvenience would have been caused to the public, even in case the Bank of England, in consequence of the plan, went out of business altogether. (Ricardo's plan was to prove influential in 1844, when the separation of the Issue Department from the Banking Department of the Bank of England was decided with the new Bank Charter Act.)

Ricardo's attention during the last period of his life was however devoted rather to the theory of value than to money and banking. The problem of an invariable measure of value had haunted him since the publication of his *Principles*, and was very much at the centre of the discussions he had in this period with his economist friends. In particular, Malthus's *Measure of Value*, published in April 1823, had triggered a discussion not only with Malthus himself, but also with Mill and McCulloch, who on this subject strongly disagreed with Ricardo. As a result of these discussions, Ricardo, in the very last weeks of his life, wrote a paper, where he critically reviewed the measures and theories of value severally advanced by his opponents. The paper at Ricardo's death passed into the hands of Mill, who judged it not suitable for publication (as a matter of fact, Ricardo had only finished a rough version). It fell out of sight and of memory, until it was again brought to light with the Sraffa–Dobb edition of Ricardo's works.

Ricardo's death came quite suddenly on 11 September 1823, as a consequence of an ear infection. He was survived by his wife Priscilla, and seven of their eight children (a daughter, Fanny, had died in 1820). Ricardo's estate was divided between them, with a striking discrimination against his daughters ('the portion of a son being no less than eight times the value of that of a daughter': X, 104). His wife was granted an annuity and an additional bequest. Besides lesser bequests and annuities to other relatives, he also bequeathed a sum of money to his friends G. Basevi, Thomas Malthus, and James Mill. (For further details on Ricardo's life, see Part I of Hollander, 1910, and volume X of Ricardo's *Works*).

MONEY

There can be little doubt that Ricardo is to be numbered among the exponents of the quantity theory of money, and one of the most rigid at that. The bulk of his writings on money belong to the Bullion Controversy of the early 1810s; they are among the best known and most widely acclaimed of his works. There was little if no change in Ricardo's monetary thought in the later part of his life, as far as general principles are concerned. It is certainly true that, as noticed for instance by Viner (1937, p. 141), in his 1819 Parliamentary evidence on the resumption of cash payments Ricardo appears less rigid, and allows that the strict principles he had earlier advocated could be qualified, but this does not really depend upon a change in his theoretical positions, but rather reflects the very nature of that contribution: an oral argumentation with the members of the Committees. Moreover, the emphasis of the enquiry was rather on the practical than on the abstract aspects of monetary problems, and it is on practical matters that Ricardo appears to make concessions.

Although Ricardo's ideas on money did not themselves undergo major changes, this is not the case for the other parts of his theory, notably value theory. In the early 1810s, he entertained the notion that 'gold and silver, like all other commodities, have an intrinsic value, which ... is dependent on their scarcity, the quantity of labour bestowed in procuring them, and the value of the capital employed in the mines which produce them' (III, 52). This is very different from his later conception of scarcity as only influencing the value of *non reproducible* commodities ('a very small part of the mass of commodities daily exchanged in the market': I, 52). Ricardo's early idea that scarcity is a regulator of prices alongside cost of production, is (partly also thanks to its vagueness) much more in accordance with a quantity theory of money than his later labour theory of value, whose consistency with his monetary theory is problematic. These problems of consistency Ricardo failed to solve, and to a large extent even to consider. Our review of his theory in the present section will deal only with the monetary theory to which Ricardo adhered throughout. The problems which this basic framework later faced will be discussed below, in the section on foreign trade and international gold movements.

As becomes a quantity theorist, Ricardo formulates what is

now generally known as the equation of exchange: 'put the mass of commodities of all sorts on one side of the line, – and the amount of money multiplied by the rapidity of its circulation on the other. Is not this in all cases the regulator of prices?' (III, 311).

To interpret the equation of exchange in a causal way, as 'the regulator of prices', Ricardo has of course to deny that there is a functional relationship between the quantity of money and velocity of circulation, or output levels ('the mass of commodities'). As to the first point, he does not deny that the velocity of circulation can vary, but regards it as depending on the development of the credit system and the banking habits of the public, and could be therefore basically treated as an institutional datum. Where Ricardo's position appears weaker is in his denial that variations in the amount of money can generate changes in the level of output. He allows that changes in the quantity of money can have real effects through the changes in prices they would generate. For instance, he concedes that money wages are slow to adapt to changes in price levels, and therefore a rise in prices could cause a fall in real wages, and this, allowing more labourers to be employed (III, 302), could have positive effects on the levels of production (see also VI, 16). Ricardo, however, regards such effects of price changes as of only temporary nature and trifling importance, also because they were in his view countervailed by negative effects on savings, due to the parallel fall in the real incomes of the classes 'who are in possession of fixed monied rents and annuities', who have a high propensity to save (VI, 16). He therefore in general sticks to his view that 'money cannot call forth goods' (III, 301), the main justification of which seems to be that 'the funds for the maintenance of labour' are somehow given and fully utilized (see e.g. I, 143, 164; this partly foreshadows the wages-fund doctrine which the Ricardians later developed and rigidly adopted). Ricardo also seems to regard capacity as fully utilized (see e.g. V, 436, 438). That his argument is of this kind is also indirectly confirmed by the fact that he seems more inclined to accept that in the case of *falling* prices, significant changes in levels of production may take place (his argument would in fact be asymmetrical). No real discussion of the point is however to be found in his writings. It perhaps seemed so obvious to him as not to require much attention (perhaps also because he must have regarded the opposite view as based on a confusion of money with capital).

A crucial point in Ricardo's argument in favour of the quantity theory, is the demonstration that any amount of money would be absorbed by the system, and would not 'overflow'. His reasoning is the following. An increase in the quantity of money would in the first place lower the rate of interest. The rate of profits would not change, because it is determined by real factors (in the early 1810s, Ricardo entertained the vague notion of Smithian origin, that the rate of profits is determined by 'competition of capitals not consisting of circulating medium': III, 92; a view he later rejected, though retaining the point that the rate of profits is wholly determined in the real sphere). An indefinitely great amount of money will be applied for, because

> the applications to the Bank for money ... depend on the comparison between the rate of profits that may be made by the employment of it, and the rate at which they are willing to lend it. If they charge less than the market rate of interest, there is no amount of money which they might not lend (I, 364; see also III, 91).

This additional money 'would be sent into every market, and would every where raise the prices of commodities' (III, 91). What was initially an excess of money would therefore become necessary to circulate the commodities at these higher prices. Ceasing the excess of money, the rate of interest would rise back to the level of the rate of profits. The change in the amount of money in the end would affect only the level of prices.

The above reasoning is, according to Ricardo, applicable to paper money (both convertible and inconvertible), and to gold, so that the principle that 'circulation can never be over-full' (III, 91) always holds. But there are differences in the full effects of an increase in the quantity of money between the three cases.

In the case of a circulation consisting of gold, an increase in its quantity would raise all prices in terms of gold – i.e., it would lower the value of gold; being increased in quantity, gold is diminished in value, consistently with the notion that scarcity is a determinant of commodity values. (For money consisting of gold, the effect on prices of a change in its quantity can be direct, and does not necessarily require the mechanism outlined above). Gold therefore becomes 'the cheapest exportable commodity' in the country, say England. This causes England to have what is (wrongly, according to Ricardo) termed 'an unfavourable balance of trade' – an importation of commodities (other than gold) settled with gold exports ('the exportation of the coin is caused by its cheapness, and is not the effect, but the cause, of an unfavourable balance of trade': III, 61). The increase of gold therefore spreads over the rest of the world, and prices settle at a higher level not only in England (where their rise originated), but also in the other countries.

If the increase was one of an inconvertible paper money, all English prices would be raised, including that of gold. This would create an excess of imports over exports for this country, because 'the balance of payments ... [is] guided a great deal by the relative value of the currencies of the two countries' (V, 395) – i.e., by the relative price of English and say Dutch commodities. There would be an excess of bills on London over bills on Amsterdam, and therefore a bill on London which previously cost 100 florins would now cost say 90 florins (the pound value of bills on Amsterdam would correspondingly rise). This fall in the pound exchange (which acts on English trade as a duty on importation and a bounty on exportation, and conversely on Dutch trade) would only stop when the value of the pound had fallen enough to restore an equilibrium in the payments between the two countries. The new level of the exchange must be such as to make gold of nearly equal price (if expressed in the same currency) in the two countries (the percentage difference being within the percentage cost of sending gold from one country to the other).

If Bank of England paper had instead been convertible into gold at a fixed rate – the 'Mint price' of gold – the fall in the pound exchange could not have gone beyond the percentage cost of sending gold from England to Holland. At this level in fact it would be cheaper for an English importer to obtain gold from the Bank of England (at the Mint price) and send it to Holland, rather than settling his debt by buying a bill on Amsterdam. Once the gold export point ('the natural limit to the fall of the exchange') had been reached, any further increase of paper money would therefore cause a loss of gold to England. This could initially push things back towards the previous equilibrium, because the increase of gold abroad would raise prices there, while prices in England would not further rise, until paper money had replaced all the gold coin which might have been in circulation. If the issue of paper continued after this, the Bank of England would see its coffers progressively emptied of gold. It would therefore be forced to stop it, and restore the value of money by reducing its issues.

The above apparatus is put to work by Ricardo in the controversies on the English monetary system. His point of departure is the consideration that a change in the purchasing power of money is an unjust interference with the relations between the different classes of society. He therefore declares the best monetary system that which renders the value of money least variable. According to him, no invariable standard is available, but he thinks gold the best approximation to it (at one stage however he preferred silver). In any case, a variable standard is better than no standard, because 'without a standard [the currency] would be exposed to all the fluctuations to which the ignorance or the interests of the issuers might subject it' (IV, 59). He maintains that during the suspension of cash payments paper money had been issued in excess, as shown by the paper price of gold being above the Mint price, and by the fall in the exchange, which had gone much beyond the gold export point.

It is to be remembered that Ricardo *defined* money as being 'in excess' when the money price of gold was higher than the Mint price: it was in excess *with respect to the amount which would have ceteris paribus made them equal*. This was a bit of (no doubt involuntary) trickery: thanks to it Ricardo could consistently talk of money as being 'in excess' even when its amount had actually diminished, and the rise of prices was to be ascribed to the causes which in the definition are kept at bay by the *ceteris paribus*. It strongly suggested that the sound policy in case of a rise in prices always was the one he advocated: a reduction in the quantity of money. According to Ricardo, in fact, by whatever cause a change in the price of the standard (i.e. gold) might have been generated, it had to be countervailed by variations in the amount of money. (Ricardo maintained that paper money was depreciated and therefore, according to his definition, 'in excess', even if the rise in the paper price of gold had been caused by variations due to gold, and the paper prices of all commodities other than gold had not changed: V, 387: see also IV, 335; I, 149.)

The monetary system which Ricardo would have liked to see established in England was one where only paper money would be used, freely convertible into gold bullion at a fixed rate. This system would have approached nearest his definition of perfection: 'A currency may be considered as perfect, of which the standard is invariable, which always conforms to that standard, and in the use of which the utmost economy is practised' (IV, 55).

As is often the case with quantity theorists, Ricardo thought that the importance of money could be exaggerated (see, e.g., IX, 100). According to him, 'productions are always bought by productions, or by services; money is only the medium by which the exchange is effected' (I, 292) – an idea he had very early accepted, taking it from Mill's *Commerce Defended* of 1808, or from Say's *Traité* of 1804. Ricardo sees money only 'as an intermediary in the exchange of products' (as Marx writes: 1862–3, II, p. 501), and therefore he in fact equates a monetary and a barter economy. Thus he does not see the important point that will be made by J.S. Mill (and by Marx after him): 'in the case of barter, the selling and buying are simultaneously confounded in one operation; ... the effect of the employment of money ... is, that it enables this one act of interchange to be divided into two separate acts', and therefore to render crises ('periods of general excess') possible (Mill, 1844, p. 70; for Marx's views, see 1862–63, II, p. 492ff.). According to Ricardo, instead, 'to save is to spend' (II, 499), and 'a general glut of all commodities ... is evidently impossible' (III, 108). He kept to this so called 'Say's Law' with much more consistency than Say himself.

Parallel to the denial of the importance of money, runs the idea that the precious metals are commodities like any other, and have no peculiarity due to their being used as money: 'There does not appear to me to be any substantial difference between bullion and any other commodity, as far as regards the regulation of its value, and the laws which determine its exportation or importation' (VI, 24). The exportation of gold (an 'unfavourable balance of trade') is only caused by its being 'the cheapest exportable commodity'.

The shortcomings of Ricardo's position are made manifest in his criticism of Thornton, who had maintained that gold is partly different from other commodities, being 'that article by which a balance of trade is discharged, and not as itself constituting a commodity' (1802, p. 145). Thornton had accordingly maintained that harvest failures, and foreign expenditure of government for subsidies or war, could be *causes* of an unfavourable balance of trade, whereas Ricardo claimed that an 'unfavourable balance of trade' is always caused by redundancy of money.

According to Ricardo, the effect of a deficient harvest is a redundancy of money, because it diminishes the amount of commodities to be circulated. Gold therefore would have its value lowered in terms of commodities (Ricardo is of course referring to a case of metallic money), would become 'the cheapest exportable commodity', and be exported. There could be no other reasons for an exportation of gold: 'Mr Thornton has not explained to us, why any unwillingness should exist in the foreign country to receive our goods [rather than bullion] in exchange for their corn' (III, 61). On foreign expenditure, however, Ricardo was less firm, and was still struggling with this problem in 1823, as shown by his discussion of Blake's pamphlet on the effects of government expenditure (IV, 323ff.; cf. Marx, 1859, p. 179: 'Ricardo seems to have completely misunderstood the rôle which subsidies played in British gold export').

Ricardo came under attack on these points from Malthus (himself a bullionist), who observed that he overlooked that the precious metals are in the particular situation of 'having been constituted, by the universal consent of society, the general medium of exchange, and instrument of commerce' – or, in Huskisson's words, the 'universal equivalent' (Malthus, 1811, p. 345; he refers to Huskisson, 1810, p. 579). Therefore bullion 'will pay a debt of the largest amount at its nominal estimation', whereas there could be 'an unwillingness of the creditor nation to receive a great additional quantity of goods not wanted for immediate consumption, without being bribed to it by excessive cheapness' (Malthus, 1811, p. 345). Accordingly, Malthus maintains that in case of a deficient harvest, 'the exportation of bullion was the *effect of a balance of trade*, originating in causes which may exist without any relation whatever to redundancy or deficiency of currency', and not its cause (ibid., p. 342; see also VI, 21). Ricardo was apparently unable to see the point; he simply answers that his critics 'express the option they are endeavouring to controvert, viz. that when goods cannot be sent so advantageously as money, money will be exported' (III, 101). He accuses those who claim that the laws which regulate the export and import of bullion are different from those of other commodities, of sharing mercantilist prejudices – a weapon to which quantity theorists like to recur (Marshall for instance uses it, quoting Ricardo's reply to Malthus at length, in his evidence before the Gold and Silver Commission in 1887: pp. 117–18).

PROFITS

It has already been mentioned that Ricardo's attention turned towards the theory of distribution between the spring and the summer of 1813, when the question of the relation between an increase of capital and the rate of profits starts to appear in his correspondence with Malthus.

We know that Ricardo had in his 1809–11 writings on money subscribed to Smith's view that the rate of profits depends upon 'competition of capitals' (see above). By August 1813, however, we find him speaking of a theory of his own (VI, 95), that he opposes to Malthus's conception (very similar to Smith's) that the rate of profits depends 'upon the state of capital compared with the demand for it' (VI, 111) – or, more in general, that 'the *proportion* of *demand* to the *supply* ... is always the main point in question, as determining prices and profits' (VI, 117).

According to Ricardo, 'nothing ... can increase the profits permanently on trade, with the same or an increased Capital, but a really cheaper mode of obtaining food': 'in short it is the profits of the farmer which regulate the profits of all other trades' (VI, 104). Malthus instead maintains that 'the profits of the farmer no more regulate the profits of other trades, than the profits of other trades regulate the profits of the farmer' (ibid.). On this basis, Ricardo claims that restrictions to importation of corn, by causing worse conditions of production of corn, would render food more expensive, and therefore lower the rate of profits. Malthus instead maintains that restrictions to the importation of corn could raise the rate of profits.

As Sraffa has explained, Ricardo's position at this stage had as its 'rational foundation' the idea that 'in agriculture the same commodity, namely corn, forms both the capital (conceived as composed of the subsistence necessary for the workers) and the product' (I, xxxi). To the extent that this was true, the rate of profits in agriculture would be determined as a ratio between these two quantities of corn ('a material rate of produce', as Malthus referred to it: VI, 117), and therefore irrespective of the conditions of production of the other commodities, and their prices. It would only depend upon the conditions of production of corn, and the amount of corn given as wages to each labourer.

This 'corn-ratio' theory of profits (as Sraffa has called it: I, xxxiii) is at the centre of the debate between Ricardo and Malthus, in the period going from the summer of 1813, to the publication of Ricardo's *Essay on Profits* in February 1815, to the following summer. Malthus repeatedly objects to what he calls Ricardo's 'peculiar opinions', and in particular to the view that 'agriculture always takes the lead in the determination [of the rate of profits]' (VI, 153). Malthus accepts that Ricardo's theory is 'simple just and consistent as far as it goes', but writes that Ricardo is 'wrong in the application of it', in that he 'expect[s] similar results when the premises are essentially different' (VI, 216).

In fact, Malthus had rather early objected to Ricardo that his theory did not pay sufficient attention to prices (VI, 141), and in March 1815, shortly after the publication of Ricardo's *Essay*, he gets at the vital objection to Ricardo's argument: if one allows for non-corn elements in the capital employed in agriculture, the rise in the cost of production of corn, and therefore in its price, caused by a worsening in its conditions of production, would imply a diminished value (in corn) of those non-corn elements of the agricultural capital. This could (and, according to Malthus, would) 'occasion the whole mass of corn to be raised at a less corn expenditure; and consequently will leave a larger surplus', and allow a higher rate of profits. Malthus rightly stresses: 'This, if true, is a most important principle and deserves to be thoroughly considered' (VI, 191). Ricardo, of course, could not deny it ('Your statement is ... very ingenious': VI, 193).

The result of Malthus's 'ingenious statement' was to bring prices very much to the fore in the discussion. Ricardo very soon realizes that everything depends upon the magnitude of the variation in the prices of manufactured commodities relative to corn when the conditions of production of corn worsen. He is however rather unclear on what the rules are according to which this variation of prices would take place. Thus we find him sometimes supposing that prices would vary in proportion to the variation of wages, or in proportion to the variation in the amount of labour necessary to produce the commodities (VI, 193), or that they would not materially vary (VI, 213). Different rules of course yield different results. Ricardo seems baffled ('The whole appears to me a labyrinth of difficulties; one is no sooner got over than another presents itself'), and stresses the simplicity of his own solution ('my simple doctrine ... accounts for all the phenomena in an easy, natural manner': VI, 214).

Ricardo's 'corn-ratio' theory of profits also entailed a rule for the determination of the prices of manufactured commodities relative to corn: given the rate of profits of agriculture, the price of the product of any other trade had to be such, relative to its capital (corn), as to give the same rate of profits as that established in agriculture. But this simple rule (which is never spelled out in Ricardo's extant writings) stands or falls with the agricultural determination of the rate of profits. It is remarkable the extent to which Ricardo appears to be at a loss, once prices really enter the story. Indeed, prices are hardly ever considered by him (at least explicitly), before Malthus makes his 'ingenious statement'. This no doubt reflects the secondary role prices play in a 'corn-ratio' theory of profits.

It can safely be affirmed that it was to his 1813–15 discussions with Malthus on the theory of profits, that Ricardo was referring when he wrote of the importance of his discussions with Malthus, in leading him 'into a deeper consideration of many parts of the subject' (see above). Indeed, Ricardo was forced by these discussions to abandon his corn-ratio theory, and to give a stronger basis to his positions, i.e., to build a more general theory. As has been mentioned, his *Principles* was born out of an attempt to produce a second edition of the *Essay on Profits*.

The book *On the Principles of Political Economy, and Taxation*, as we already know (see above), was from the beginning conceived by Ricardo basically as a work on the theory of distribution. It consists of thirty-two chapters (thirty-one in the first two editions), but only the first seven constitute the *Principles of Political Economy* proper (see I, xv). The following eleven chapters deal with taxation, and chapters from nineteen to the end are a set of polemical dissertations on miscellaneous subjects. Six of the seven chapters on the principles of political economy are devoted to the theory of value and distribution (the seventh to foreign trade).

The main difficulty which Ricardo encountered, in the passage from the *Essay* to the *Principles* – and, correspondingly, the main novelty in this book – was of course the theory of value, which occupies the first (and by far the longest) chapter in the book. When starting to work on the *Principles* Ricardo wrote: 'I know I shall soon be stopped by the word price' (VI, 348).

The theory of profits of the *Principles* is essentially the same as that of the *Essay*. In the earlier version, Ricardo had maintained that '[t]he rate of profits ... must depend on the proportion of production to the consumption necessary to such production [i.e., wages]' (VI, 108), where these two magnitudes were seen as two quantities of corn (hence the 'material ratio'). In the later stage, the same principle is established by means of the labour theory of value – i.e., by the hypothesis that commodity values are proportional to the labour (directly and indirectly) necessary for their production. Ricardo still maintains that the rate of profits is determined by the proportion between product and wages, but these two magnitudes are now no longer two quantities of corn, but are measured in value, by the amount of labour they embody. Their proportion only depends upon the commodity wage, and the conditions of production of wage goods.

The *Principles*, even more explicitly than the *Essay*, is devoted to establish the basic point that 'profits depend on wages' (I, 143) – i.e., that 'profits would be high or low in proportion as wages were low or high' (I, 111). This inverse relation between wages and profits could easily be lost sight of, when viewing wages, profits, and product, in price terms: the price movements caused by say a rise in wages, could generate the delusion that such a rise could be paid out of higher prices, rather than diminished profits. Even Adam Smith had made this mistake, and had accordingly maintained that the effect of a rise in wages would simply have been a rise in all prices. (Ricardo himself had, before the *Essay on Profits*, subscribed to this view, which he later referred to as Smith's 'original error respecting value': VII, 100). The importance of the 'corn-ratio' theory had been just that, by allowing Ricardo to bypass the problem of value when determining distribution, it made that mistake impossible. With the labour theory of value, Ricardo achieved something very similar to a measurement of product and wages in terms of corn. According to the labour theory of value, in fact, prices do not change when distribution changes (as they only depend upon the labour embodied in the commodities). Therefore, as is the case with the 'corn-ratio' theory, no price movements could obscure the simple relationship between a rise of wages and a fall of profits. The only difference was that, as Sraffa writes,

> it was now labour, instead of corn, that appeared on both sides of the account ... the rate of profits was no longer determined by the ratio of the corn produced to the corn used up in production, but, instead, by the ratio of the total labour of the country [the value of the product] to the labour required to produce the necessaries for that labour [the value of wages] (I, xxxii).

To better understand Ricardo's position, it is important to remember that, as Marx noticed, 'in his observations on profits and wages, Ricardo ... treats the matter as though the entire capital were laid out directly in wages' (Marx, 1862–3, II, 373). This does not mean that Ricardo is not aware that non-wage capital was used in production: he even inserted a chapter 'On Machinery' in the third edition of the *Principles*. But he often reasons *as if* only wage capital were employed in production (a misconception originating in Smith). This implies that the amount of labour embodied in the wage rate is not only equal to its value, but is also equal to the proportion of the total labour necessary to reproduce the wages, and to the proportion of wages in the value of the product: if w is the amount of labour embodied in the wage rate, and L is the number of workers employed in producing the social product, the proportion of the total labour used to reproduce the wages is wL/L, which, for the labour theory of value, is also the proportion of the value of wages in the value of the product. This explains why Ricardo sometimes writes that the rate of profits depends upon the amount of labour embodied in the wage rate (e.g. VIII, 130), sometimes that it depends upon 'the proportion of the annual labour of the country devoted to the support of the labourers' (I, 49), sometimes that it depends on the proportion of the value of wages in the product (I, 125). The three statements are in fact equivalent.

Ricardo's proposition on the inverse wage–profit relation has been regarded as a 'truism' by a number of authors, ranging from Malthus (1820, p. 310) to Schumpeter (1954, p. 592) or Robbins (1952, p. 84). Now, it is a truism that, if something is divided in two shares, as one of them increases, the other must decrease. Thus it is obvious that, if wages and profits make up the value of the whole product, the shares of profits and wages must vary inversely with one another. Ricardo's interest was in the relation between the *rates*. But consider that, if one disregards non-wage capital, the ratio of the share of profits to the share of wages is equal to the rate of profits: (profits/product): (wages/product) = (profits/wages). This must of course fall with a rise in the share of wages. But the share, as we have just seen, is equal to the (labour value of the) rate of wages. The proposition that there is an inverse relation between the *rates* of wages and profits can therefore be 'translated' into the truism that there is an inverse relation between the *shares* of wages and profits. But this is only a way of proving that proposition, and of course does not render it a truism.

WAGES

Ricardo's interest in the theory of distribution, as has already been mentioned, arose with the problem of the determination of the rate of profits, and in a sense it was always on the rate of profits that he focussed. But in Ricardo's conception profits are '*the leaving of wages*' – according to a famous '*formula*' by the Ricardian de Quincey (1844, p. 257). To work out 'the Principles of Profit', he has therefore to deal with 'the Principles of Wages', with which they are so closely connected.

In the *Essay on Profits*, Ricardo deals only briefly with the theory of wages. He already has the two main points of the theory he will later develop in the *Principles*: that the rate of wages depends upon the proportion between capital and population, and that it will tend to be equal to 'that remuneration for labour, which is necessary to the actual subsistence of the labourer' (IV, 22). Thus he assumes the rate of wages to be constant, by means of the assumption that 'capital and population advance in the proper proportion' (IV, 12), but he does not really dwell on his conception – which, as Taussig (1896, p. 174n.) remarks, 'was an idea of Malthus's' (its main constituents, however, can be traced to the chapter on wages of the *Wealth of Nations*).

Chapter V of the *Principles* ('On Wages') starts with the distinction, which Ricardo makes for labour as for all commodities, between the 'natural price' and the 'market price'. In Ricardo's definition,

> The natural price of labour is that price which is necessary to enable the labourers, one with another, to subsist and perpetuate their race, without increase or diminution ... The market price of labour is the price which is really paid for it, from the natural operation of the proportion of the supply to the demand ... However much the market price of labour may deviate from its natural price, it has, like commodities, a tendency to conform to it (I, 93–4).

The conception of the mechanism through which wages wold be brought to their natural level is of course based on Malthus's population theory: any time wages were above the natural (subsistence) level, because the pace of capital accumulation has exceeded that of population, the latter would increase, and therefore cause wages to go down again. Conversely in the case where population had taken the lead over capital accumulation.

Ricardo remarks that

> it is not to be understood that the natural price of labour, estimated even in food and necessaries, is absolutely fixed and constant. It varies at different times in the same country, and very materially differs in different countries. It essentially depends on the habits and customs of the people (I, 96–7).

This point derives from Torrens's *Essay on the External Corn Trade* (which Ricardo had not known before writing the *Essay on Profits*). Ricardo explicitly avows Torrens's influence; he quotes a passage from his essay, on the importance of the 'habits of living' of the workers for the determination of natural wages, and adds: 'The whole of this subject is most ably illustrated by Colonel Torrens' (I, 97n.).

Notwithstanding the fact that Ricardo acknowledges the influence of *social* elements in the determination of the level of the workers' subsistence, his theory of the natural wage in the last analysis relies on a mechanical supply–demand equilibrium. Unlike the market-price natural-price mechanism for other commodities, in the case of labour the explanation of the reason why that particular level (subsistence) is stated to be the *natural* level of its price, appears to be *one and the same thing* with the mechanism which would have to bring the price to that level.

> The *value of labour* for Ricardo is ... determined by the *means of subsistence* which, in a given society, are traditionally necessary for the maintenance and reproduction of labourers. But why? By what law is the *value of labour* determined in this way? Ricardo has in fact no answer, other than the law of supply and demand reduces the average price of labour to the means of subsistence that are (physically or socially necessary in a given society) for the maintenance of the labourer. He determines *value* here, in one of the basic propositions of the whole system, by *demand and supply* – as Say notes with malicious pleasure (Marx, 1862–3, II, p. 400).

Ricardo has no notion that wages are kept at the 'natural' (subsistence) level by the historically determined imbalance in the forces of capital and labour (a point Smith for instance had very clearly made: 1789, I, pp 68–70). In Marx's words, Ricardo does not have the notion of capital as 'a *definite social relationship*'. He therefore in the end relies on supply and demand, inconsistently with his general position that 'natural price ... has nothing to do with demand and supply' (VIII, 207) (hence the 'malicious pleasure' of a supply and demand theorist like Say).

In addition to this, Ricardo's supply and demand mechanism was itself seriously defective, as again Marx notices:

> Before, in consequence of the rise of wages, any positive increase of the population really fit for work could occur, the time would have passed again and again, during which the industrial campaign must have been carried through, the battle fought and won ... What did the farmers do now [after the 1848–59 increases in agricultural wages in Britain]? Did they wait until, in consequence of this brilliant remuneration, the agricultural labourers had so increased and multiplied that their wages must fall again, as prescribed by the dogmatic economic brain? They introduced more machinery, and in a moment the labourers were redundant again in a proportion satisfactory even to the farmers (Marx, 1867, pp. 597–8).

The difficulty due to the long time that would be necessary for changes in population to affect the market price of labour, is after all recognized by Ricardo himself, who admits that 'notwithstanding the tendency of wages to conform to their natural rate, their market rate may, in an improving society, for an indefinite period, be constantly above it' (I, 94–5). But he had not realized the danger which this admission represented, given the importance that the *habits* of the workers had in his conception of the natural level of the wages: a 'market' rate of wages which for 'an indefinite period of time' is above the 'natural' level would in all probability change this 'natural' level. Thus it would be the natural level to adjust to the market level, rather than the other way round.

It is however worth noting that Ricardo's supply and demand mechanism is in any case entirely different from a marginalist one. Suffice here to say that Ricardo's mechanism works through changes in population – i.e., through changes in the endowment of labour – whereas the marginalist one works through changes *along* a supply curve of labour, derived from a *given* endowment of this 'factor of production' (as well as of the others).

RENT

Although in conventional accounts of the history of economic doctrine, the theory of the rent is generally associated with Ricardo's name, Ricardo himself tells us in the *Essay on Profits*:

> In all that I have said concerning the origin and progress of rent, I have briefly repeated, and endeavoured to elucidate the principles which Mr. Malthus has so ably laid down, on the same subject, in his 'Inquiry into the Nature and Progress of Rent' (IV, 15n).

Sraffa writes: 'When in February 1815 Malthus's pamphlets [*Inquiry* and *Grounds of an Opinion*] appeared, Ricardo was able to write within a few days his Essay ... , by using his already developed theory of profits, incorporating Malthus's theory of rent' (IV, 4). Indeed, 'the letters of Ricardo up to the time of the publication of Malthus's *Inquiry into Rent* contain no discussion of the subject of rent ... he had been working out his theory of profits without ever finding it necessary explicitly to mention rent' (IV, 7). Ricardo's interest in the theory of rent is, even more than in the case of wages, subordinated to his interest in the theory of profits. What he wants is simply to 'get rid' of rent, as he writes: 'By getting rid of rent,... the distribution between the capitalist and the labourer becomes a much more simple consideration' (VIII, 194).

The theory of rent which Ricardo actually adopts from Malthus (its real paternity however is often ascribed to Anderson, or to West; on this, see Cannan, 1917, pp. 216ff.) is based on the idea that as there are lands of different fertility, they are successively brought into cultivation, starting from those of which the degree of fertility is highest (Ricardo regards the order of fertility of different lands as given; but see Sraffa, 1960, ch. 11). Even if all the land is of the same degree of fertility, there will be lands which are worse, because they are farther from the market place, etc. On these lands, to produce the same amount of corn more capital is necessary – either for the actual production, or to bring the product to the market, etc. The idea is also to be found in Ricardo, that successive portions of capital expended on the same land could yield proportionately less (see e.g. IV, 14; I, 17). Given a uniform rate of wages, the rate of profits on lands of a worse quality must necessarily be less than the rate of profits obtainable on lands of the first quality. The competition of farmers to obtain these lands, will allow their owners to ask and get a rent for their use. Rent will settle at a level such as to leave farmers with the same rate of profits, no matter what kind of land they hire. It is only at this point that the convenience for them of bidding higher prices for the use of better lands will cease. (Rent therefore derives from the diminishing returns: 'If there had been no limits to fertility, if one capital after another had been equally productive, of produce, no rent could have been generated': II, 211).

Let us suppose, as Ricardo does in the *Essay* (IV, 17), that to produce three hundred quarters of corn on lands of the first quality, an outlay of two hundred quarters of corn is necessary. If these lands are sufficient to produce all the corn that is required, no landowner could get a rent for the use of it, and the whole of the surplus produce (one hundred quarters out of every three hundreds produced) would go to profits. The rate of profits will be 50 per cent. But if it was necessary also to grow corn on lands of a worse quality, where to obtain three hundred quarters, two hundreds and ten are necessary, the rate of profits will be, on the latter lands, only 43 per cent approximately. A rent will therefore arise on the better lands, which will be equal to fourteen quarters out of every three hundreds produced; only eighty-six quarters will be left for profits. At this point competition between farmers to hire the better lands will stop: their rate of profits will be 43 per cent, whether they employ lands of the first quality, paying fourteen quarters as rent (out of every three hundreds produced), or they employ the worse land, paying no rent.

If lands of a third quality start to be used, the rate of profits will go further down, a rent will arise also on the intermediate lands, and that on the best lands will accordingly rise. And so on.

Since, according to this conception, on the worst kind of land used in production there will be no rent, Ricardo could, by concentrating on this no-rent land, study 'the distribution between capitalist and labourer' in total separation from rent. The product of the worst land is in fact only divided between wages and profits.

In the *Essay*, Ricardo explicitly assumes that 'no improvements take place in agriculture' (IV, 12). From this it follows that

> by bringing successively land of a worse quality, or less favourably situated into cultivation, rent would rise on the land previously cultivated, and precisely in the same degree profits would fall; and if the smallness of profits do not check accumulation, there are hardly any limits to the rise of rent, and the fall of profit (IV, 14).

Hence the conception that there is a tendency to 'a stationary state', where profits be so low that accumulation ceases altogether. Also in the *Principles* Ricardo maintains that 'the natural tendency of profits ... is to fall' (I, 120). Here, however, he also writes that 'this tendency, this gravitation as it were of profits, is happily checked at repeated intervals by ... improvements' in agricultural techniques of production (ibid.), and repeatedly affirms that England is 'yet far distant' from the stationary state.

The theory of rent in the *Principles* does not materially differ from that of the *Essay*. The only important new point which Ricardo makes is of course related to the labour theory of value, and it is that the value of the agricultural produce is regulated by the quantity of labour necessary to produce it on the worst land used in its production – i.e., on the no-rent land. The value of the product obtained on better lands is therefore higher than the quantity of labour actually employed in its production, and on each kind of land this difference is of course equal to the value of the rent paid for it. Hence Ricardo's conception (famous for Marshall's misleading attempt to reconcile it with marginalist theory) that 'rent is not a component part of the price of commodities', and that accordingly it cannot be the *cause* of the high price of corn, but is rather its *effect* (I, 77–8; the last point however is already to be found in Smith: 1789, I, p. 147).

A GENERAL RULE OF VALUE AND ITS EXCEPTIONS

The adoption of the labour theory of value, i.e., of the principle that commodity prices are regulated by the quantity of labour directly and indirectly necessary to produce them, marks Ricardo's passage from the *Essay on Profits* to the *Principles*, as already mentioned. Of course, this theory was not an invention of Ricardo: it is often traced as far back as Thomas Aquinas. Ricardo's main point of reference was Adam Smith, who had confined the validity of the principle that commodities exchange in proportion to the labour necessary to produce them, to 'that early and rude state of society which precedes both the accumulation of stock and the appropriation of land' (1789, I, p. 49). Ricardo writes that Smith speaks

> as if, when profits and rent were to be paid, they would have some influence on the relative value of commodities, independent of the mere quantity of labour that was necessary to their production. Adam Smith, however, has nowhere analysed the effects of the accumulation of capital, and the appropriation of land, on relative value. It is of importance, therefore, to determine how far the effects which are avowedly produced on the exchangeable value of commodities, by the comparative quantity of labour bestowed on their production, are modified or altered by the accumulation of capital or the payment of rent (I, 23n.).

Here we have a clue to the whole position of Ricardo, on value. He claims that the 'general rule' of commodity value is that it is proportional to the quantity of labour embodied (the 'main ingredient' of value), but that there are 'exceptions' (or 'modifications') to this rule (see e.g. VIII, 193).

The chapter 'On Value' of the *Principles*, after starting with the statement (in the heading of Section I) that '*The value of a commodity ... depends on the relative quantity of labour which is necessary for its production*' (I, 11), goes on to state (in the heading of Section IV): '*The principle that the quantity of labour bestowed on the production of commodities regulates their exchangeable value,* [is] *considerably modified by the employment of machinery and other fixed and durable capital* (I, 30) – something which, as Cannan (1929, p. 176) remarks, appears to 'flatly contradict' the opening statement.

The 'modifications' to the 'general rule' of value are basically due to the fact that profits have different weights in the prices of different commodities. Let us write the (natural) price of commodity A, using Ricardo's device of reducing to labour its means of production (on this, see Sraffa, 1960, ch. VI). Let L_{1A} be the amount of labour used in the direct production of A, L_{2A} the amount of labour used in the direct production of the means of production of A, and so on; let r be the rate of profits, and w the (money) rate of wages; the (money) price of A will be:

$$p_A = wL_{1A}(1+r) + wL_{2A}(1+r)^2 + \cdots + wL_{NA}(1+r)^N + \cdots.$$

Analogously, the (money) price of a commodity B will be:

$$p_B = wL_{1B}(1+r) + wL_{2B}(1+r)^2 + \cdots + wL_{NB}(1+r)^N + \cdots.$$

It is only if the ratios L_{iA}/L_{iB} are equal for all *is* that p_A/p_B will be independent of r, and equal to those ratios, and therefore to the ratio of the total labours embodied in A and B ($\Sigma_i L_{iA}/\Sigma_i L_{iB}$). In this case, any change in the rate of profits would cause the same proportional change in the price of A and of B (and therefore no change in their ratio): profits would in fact be the same proportion of p_A as of P_B. It is only in this case that Ricardo's 'general rule' of value strictly holds. Otherwise, any change in distribution would cause a change in the relative price of the commodities (the relative price being equal to the ratio of embodied labours for $r = 0$). Ricardo accordingly concedes:

> my proposition that with few exceptions the quantity of labour employed on commodities determines the rate at which they will exchange for each other ... is not rigidly true, but I say that it is the nearest approximation to truth, as a rule for measuring relative value, of any I have ever heard (VIII, 279).

According to him, 'in the relative variation of commodities, any other cause, but that of the quantity of labour required for production, [is] comparatively of very slight effect' (II, 59). The other cause, of course, is a variation of distribution: given the amount of labour embodied, 'relative values may vary solely because the value of labour rises or falls' (i.e. the rate of profits falls or rises). Although not attaching much importance to this other cause, he writes, 'I cannot wholly shut my eyes to it' (IX, 178).

That commodities change in relative value when distribution changes, or that commodities which embody the same quantity of labour do not exchange one to one, are two different aspects of the same problem. Ricardo however generally looks at this problem from the point of view of the *change* in relative prices caused by changes in distribution (as it is the case in the passages just quoted). This is due to the fact that the problem of value does not interest Ricardo for its own sake, but essentially in connection with the theory of distribution, and, more specifically, with the problem of showing the inverse wage-profit relation. The 'modifications' to the labour theory of value are a disturbing element for Ricardo in so far as they imply that the value of the product to be distributed between profits and wages, changes when nothing but distribution changes. The simple picture made possible by the labour theory of value (or, for that matter, by a 'corn-ratio' theory), of a division between profits and wages of a product the size of which does not change when the size of the slices changes, is obfuscated by the 'modifications' to that theory, which endanger Ricardo's conclusion that if one slice is bigger, the other must be smaller.

When dealing with distribution, Ricardo reasons as if the labour theory of value admitted no qualifications at all. The whole chapter 'On Profits', for instance, is built upon the assumption that the value of the product to be shared between profits and wages is given. This was noticed by Malthus, who wrote that

> [Ricardo's] theory of profits depends entirely upon the circumstance of the mass of commodities remaining at the same price, ... whatever may be the variations in the price of labour. This uniformity in the value of wages and profits taken together is indeed assumed by Mr. Ricardo in all his calculations ... But if it be not true, the whole theory falls to the ground (1820, p. 326)

– and this was of course the case, according to Malthus.

The difficulty was a serious one for Ricardo, and he struggled with it until the very last days of his life. About a month before his death, he wrote to McCulloch: 'I cannot get over the difficulty of the wine which is kept in a cellar for 3 or 4 years, or that of the oak tree, which perhaps had not 2/- expended on it in the way of labour, and yet comes to be worth £100' (IX, 330–1). However, throughout he adheres to the view that the modifications to the labour theory of value are of a trifling importance. (This is of course linked with his inconsistencies in the treatment of non-wage capital: if only wage capital, i.e., direct labour, is employed in production, there are no 'modifications' to the exchange according to labour embodied, assuming yearly production cycles for all commodities.)

Ricardo attempts to solve the problem of the modifications to the labour theory of value by means of an 'invariable measure of value', or a measure of the 'absolute value', to which he devoted the very last of his writings.

There are two distinct though related problems which Ricardo groups under that of the search for an 'invariable measure of value'. The first is that of finding an invariable yardstick with which to measure the value of the commodities. When two commodities vary in relative value, it would be possible, by comparing them with such an invariable standard, to know which of them has really varied in value. This problem is not particularly Ricardian: it is for instance already to be found in Smith (Lauderdale had as early as 1804 condemned this search for an invariable measure as a search for the 'philosopher's stone': Lauderdale, 1804, p. 23). The question of an invariable yardstick was also present in Ricardo's writings on money during the suspension of cash payments, in connection with the problem of proving that the rise in the paper price of gold and the other commodities was due to depreciation of paper, not to a rise in the value of commodities. In these writings, Ricardo appears consistently to deny that an invariable standard could be found.

With the inception of the labour theory of value in Ricardo's thought, the question of finding an invariable yardstick seems nearer to a solution: if commodities exchange in proportion to labour embodied, a commodity produced with an unvarying quantity of labour would be an invariable yardstick. But it is at this point that the second (and more typically Ricardian) aspect of the search for an invariable measure of value comes out. Indeed, Ricardo admits that a commodity produced by an unvarying quantity of labour 'still ... would not be a perfect standard or invariable measure of value, because ... it would be subject to relative variations from a rise or fall of wages' (I, 44). Accordingly, the search for an invariable standard becomes that of a commodity invariable also in the latter respect, i.e., invariable with changes in distribution. Prices measured in terms of such a commodity would only reflect the main 'cause of value' (labour embodied), and would not depend upon the level of wages and profits. Ricardo apparently does not realize that if the prices of two commodities expressed in terms of a third, are not to one another as the labours embodied in them, to express these prices in terms of yet another standard cannot change their ratio, and render it equal to the ratio of embodied labours. Indeed, to change the standard simply means to divide the numerator and the denominator of the price ratio by the same number (the price of the new standard in terms of the previous one).

Ricardo's attempt to cancel the 'exceptions' to the labour theory of value by means of an invariable measure, was an 'attempt ... to square the circle' (Marx, 1862–3, I, p. 150). Marx was right in saying that the reson why Ricardo put himself on this 'blind alley' was that he basically saw the problem of the 'modifications' to the labour theory of value from the point of view of the *changes* to the value of commodities caused by changes in the level of wages, rather than from that of *differences* in the values of commodities produced by the same amount of labour (Marx, 1862–3, III, p. 71). Indeed, if one looks at it from the latter point, it is clear that no measure of value whatsoever can solve it. Contrary to what Ricardo tried hard to show, commodities which embody the same amount of labour will not in general exchange one to one: as Malthus put it, '[Ricardo's] rule may be considered as the exception, and the exceptions the rule' (1827, p. 27).

FOREIGN TRADE AND INTERNATIONAL GOLD MOVEMENTS

It has already been mentioned that as early as the 1813–15 debates on the Corn Laws, Ricardo came out as a strong supporter of free trade, and that his first published work which did not deal with money, the 1815 *Essay*, denounced *the Inexpediency of Restrictions on Importation* in its very (full) title (see above). It was however only in the 1817 edition of his *Principles* that Ricardo backed his position with a general theory of international trade, embodying the principle of comparative costs – which can perhaps be described as the most widely accepted of the 'truths' of political economy. (Marshall said of it: 'That doctrine ... established by Ricardo ... I do not know that any person has shaken it in the least; in fact, I do not myself believe that it has ever been seriously attacked by anyone who has taken the trouble to understand it': 1887, p. 65.)

The chapter 'On Foreign Trade' is the last of the seven chapters which constitute the *Principles of Political Economy* proper (see above). Ricardo argues first that foreign trade does not augment the value of the goods which the country has, because the value of the goods received is equal to that of the goods given in exchange for them (I, 128). Also, foreign trade *by itself* does not raise the rate of profits. It can only raise it if, by rendering wage goods cheaper, it diminishes the value of the (given) commodity wage – or, what is the same for Ricardo (see above), if it diminishes the proportion of wages in the value of the product. It would be the reduction of wages made possible by foreign trade, and not foreign trade itself, which would raise profits: 'the rate of profit can never be increased but by a fall in wages, and ... there can be no permanent fall of wages but in consequence of a fall of the necessaries on which wages are expended' (I, 132).

The effect of foreign trade is according to Ricardo to augment the riches of the trading countries. This he illustrates with a celebrated example (I, 135), which we shall reproduce, slightly changed. Let us suppose that the conditions of production of 'cloth' and 'wine' are the following: to produce one unit of cloth requires 50 labourers in England, and 25 in Portugal; to produce one unit of wine requires 200 labourers in England and 25 in Portugal. This country has therefore an (absolute) advantage in producing both goods. (This means that the English capitalists would get a higher rate of profits if English capital and labour were removed to Portugal, provided wages were not higher there: I, 136.) However, Portugal's advantage is greater in the production of wine, for which Portugal would require 25/200 of the labour required in England, than in that of cloth, where she would require 25/50. (Notice that in this conception the advantage only derives from differences in the technical conditions of production in the two countries.) If Portugal took say twenty-five workers from the production of cloth, and employed them in the production of wine, she would produce one unit of wine more, and one unit of cloth less. If at the same time England took one hundred workers from the production of wine, and employed them in that of cloth, she would obtain two units of cloth more, and half unit of wine less. As a whole, the amounts of commodities produced by the two countries would be augmented: there would be one unit of cloth and half unit of wine more than without any specialization. The greater the specialization the greater the gains. How they will be divided between the two countries depends upon the price at which the two products will be exchanged between them: if wine and cloth exchanged one to one, the whole advantage would be reaped by England; if one unit of wine exchanged for four units of cloth, the whole advantage would go to Portugal (the two limits are of course the labour values of the two commodities in the two countries). Any intermediate price would divide the benefits between the two countries (for each unit of labour embodied in the exported commodity, each country would receive an amount of the other commodity which would require more than one unit of labour to be produced at home).

According to Ricardo, 'the same rule which regulates the value of commodities in one country, *does not* regulate the relative value of the commodities exchanged between two or more countries' (I, 133, italics added). The cloth given by England would not necessarily exchange for the amount of wine produced in Portugal with the same amount of labour: 'The labour of 100 Englishmen cannot be given for that of 80 Englishmen, but the produce of the labour of 100 Englishmen may be given for the produce of the labour of 80 Portuguese' (I, 135; the reason for this is that within the same country, the same rates of wages and of profits must obtain, while this is not the case among different countries). Ricardo however does not apparently have a general rule for the determination of international prices.

The fact that it would be convenient for the two countries to specialize in consequence of a difference in the comparative costs of producing the two commodities, does not by itself ensure that the specialization will actually take place in the two (decentralized) economies: the price level of say England may be too high (in terms of bullion, which is 'the general medium of circulation'), and no cloth could therefore be sold to Portugal. English people will of course still be buying Portuguese wine. The exchanges will therefore turn against England. If this is not sufficient to stop the English purchases of wine (i.e. if Portuguese wine is cheap enough) the gold export point will be reached, and the English purchases of wine will be settled with gold. The loss of gold to Portugal will tend to lower the price level of England (relative prices remaining the same), and to raise that of Portugal, and will not cease until the point is reached that it is convenient for the Portuguese to buy English cloth. So the precious metals 'are, by the competition of commerce, distributed in such proportions amongst the different countries of the world, as to accommodate themselves to the natural traffic which would take place if no such metals existed, and the trade between countries were purely a trade of barter' (I, 137).

A change in the conditions of production might happen, so as actually to invert the comparative advantages. Let us suppose that it is the technique for producing wine in England which improves, and its price consequently falls lower than that at which Portuguese wine is obtainable there. The importation of wine would of course cease. The price of English cloth would be the same as before, Portugal would be buying cloth by means of bullion (according to the mechanism outlined in the preceding paragraph for England), and would thereby be raising the price level in England, and lowering her own. A new equilibrium will be reached, with England having a higher price level, and stock of gold, than before the improvement took place. Ricardo lays down the following principle: 'the improvement of a manufacture in any country ... tends to increase the quantity of commodities, at the same time that it raises general prices in the country where the improvement takes place' (I, 141).

From the foregoing discussion it very clearly appears that in the *Principles*, when Ricardo had already adopted the labour theory of value, and rejected his earlier conception of value as also determined by scarcity, he was still using the quantity theory of money, applying it to the precious metals (not simply to paper money), and by no means restricting it to temporary phenomena. There is no attempt, in his analysis of the specie flow mechanism and its effects on the levels of prices in the different countries, to reconcile it with the other notion, on which he lays much stress in the chapter 'On Currency and Banks' (and elsewhere), namely, that 'Gold and silver, like all other commodities, are valuable only in proportion to the quantity of labour necessary to produce them' (I, 352; notice the difference with the statement in *The High Price of Bullion*, quoted above).

The contradiction between a quantity and a labour (or a cost of production) theory of the value of money is obvious, and has often been discussed, as for instance by Marx, who deals with it in his critique of Ricardo's monetary theory in *A Contribution to the Critique of Political Economy* (Marx however overlooks the presence in the Ricardo of the early 1810s of a scarcity conception of value). As Marx writes, 'if the value of gold is given [by the labour embodied in it], the amount of money in circulation is determined by the prices of commodities' (1859, p. 171), and not the other way round. An abundance or scarcity of gold could only have temporary effects on its value, and would be made good by variations in its production – just as in the case of the movement of the market price of any commodity towards the natural price. But we have seen in the preceding examples that in Ricardo's theory of international gold movements, the cost of production of gold does not play any role – and in fact permanent changes of prices in terms of gold were taking place, totally unrelated to changes in the quantity of labour necessary to produce it.

There is no explicit attempt at reconciling the two conflicting views in Ricardo. In the chapter 'Taxes on Gold', however, he argues that gold, being money, has the peculiarity that there constantly is a stock of it in the economy, which would normally be large, with respect to its current production. This means that the market price of gold would only very slowly adapt to its natural price – as in the case of labour, the market price of which can, according to Ricardo, be different from its natural price 'for an indefinite period' (as we have seen above, in the section on wages) . This makes the link between cost of production and value much weaker for gold than for ordinary commodities.

Another reason why in the international specie flow mechanism the link with the cost of production of gold might have been obfuscated in Ricardo's mind, is the fact that he sees things from an English angle, and always tends to regard gold as an imported commodity. Therefore, at least within the country, the value of gold would not directly be dependent on its cost of production. But this of course does not mean that the value of gold is free to move in accordance only with changes in its quantity, without any reference to its cost in the producing country.

It is also to be remembered that the contradiction is only to be found in the *Principles*, and not in Ricardo's earlier works on monetary theory, where he does not yet have a labour theory of value (this is the case also for *Economical and Secure Currency*). But in the *Principles* Ricardo does not devote much attention to monetary theory as such. Actually, in the first two editions the chapter 'On Currency and Banks' opened with the following sentence: 'It is not my intention to detain the reader by any long dissertation on the subject of money. So much has already been written on currency, that ... none but the prejudiced are ignorant of its true principles' (I, 352 and n.). And after 1817 monetary theory was not again much in Ricardo's mind. When he devoted his attention to money, it was basically to *concrete* monetary problems, as in his 1819 Parliamentary evidence, or his posthumously published *Plan for the Establishment of a National Bank*. (On the contradiction between the quantity and the labour theory of the value of money in Ricardo, see also St. Clair, 1957, ch. 15.)

TAXATION AND PUBLIC DEBT

Besides international trade, the incidence of taxation is the main set of problems to which Ricardo applies the theory of value and distribution developed in the first chapters of the *Principles*. Although his treatment of taxation is generally regarded (together with that of Smith) as the foundation stone of the modern approach, there is truth in the remark that the part on taxation is 'the most defective portion of his book' (Patten, 1893, p. 156). Ricardo scatters his discussion in many (rather badly arranged) chapters, dealing with different kinds of taxes, and his exposition is very uneven, in some cases going deeply to trace the ultimate consequences of a tax, sometimes instead stopping at a rather initial stage. Moreover, Ricardo seldom gets at general principles, his results often depending for instance upon which assumptions are made on the spending behaviour of the people on whom the tax falls.

From the point of view of equity, Ricardo maintains that taxes ought to be equally divided among all the classes of society other than the working class. The main reason for this exclusion is that, on the basis of his subsistence theory of wages, Ricardo thinks that a direct tax on wages would cause a rise in nominal wages to the same amount (so as to leave real wages unaffected). The tax would not be borne by the workers, but by the capitalists, and would therefore be an unequal tax (if capitalists are already taxed *qua* capitalists). The same would happen if, instead of directly taxing wages, the government should lay a tax on a wage-good. Like every tax on produce, it would act as an increase of its cost of production, and therefore of its price. This would in turn cause a rise of money wages, so as to leave the commodity wage at the subsistence level (the only difference between a tax on wage goods and a direct tax on wages, would according to Ricardo be that 'the former will necessarily be accompanied by a rise in the price of necessaries, but the latter will not'; I, 215). For that part however in which the wage good was consumed by other classes, a tax on it 'might affect the consumers' generally, and to this extent would not be unequal (I, 159).

An important distinction which Ricardo draws at the very start of the first chapter on taxes, is of course that between taxes which fall upon income and taxes which fall upon capital (I, 151). He makes the general point that the ultimate incidence of taxation may be different from the apparent one: 'Taxes are not necessarily taxes on capital, because they are laid on capital; nor on income, because they are laid on income' (I, 152). To investigate whether a tax actually falls on income or on capital is of course of the utmost importance, because according to Ricardo taxes on capital 'must proportionably diminish that fund by whose extent the extent of the productive industry of the country must always be regulated'. He claims that 'there are no taxes which have not a tendency to lessen the power to accumulate', but allows that this is not the case if a tax falls on the revenue of people who are thereby induced to save its amount from their unproductive consumption (I, 152).

In general, Ricardo appears to regard public expenditure as unproductive, and he accordingly adopts 'the golden maxim of M. Say, "that the very best of all plans of finance is to spend little, and the best of all taxes is that which is the least in amount" ' (I, 242). He also considers the question of the effects of expenditure for public works (in 1817 and in 1818 the government decided to spend substantial amounts in relief works: see Smart, 1910, I, p. 543 and pp. 611–12). According to Ricardo, even when public expenditure is not for unproductive consumption, it cannot do any good: 'the raising of funds for the purpose of employing the poor ... diverts those funds from other employments which would be equally if not more productive to the community'. This capital 'cannot fail' to employ men somewhere else, and 'every interference is prejudicial' (VII, 116; see also IV, 356).

Ricardo had to reconcile his views with the undeniable fact that in 1817, 'notwithstanding the immense expenditure of the English government' during the years of war, 'the national capital ... has been greatly increased, and the annual revenue of the people, even after the payment of their taxes, is probably greater ... than at any other former period' (I, 151). This of course was not easy, especially after the forceful pamphlet in favour of government expenditure published in 1823 by Ricardo's friend William Blake – a pamphlet which engaged Ricardo's attention very much (see IV, 323ff.).

Blake had argued that, if public expenditure is simply 'a diversion of capital from a productive to an unproductive employment', the war could have only impoverished Britain, and left an enormous amount of people without 'any possibility of finding employment' for lack of what Ricardo usually calls 'the funds for the maintenance of labour' (Blake, 1823, pp. 51–3). Blake had touched a crucial point:

> It appears to me that the error lies in supposing, first, that the whole capital of the country is fully occupied; and, secondly, that there is immediate employment for successive accumulations of capital as it accrues from saving. I believe there are at all times some portions of capital ... lying wholly dormant

and therefore government expenditure can represent an addition to demand, 'without encroaching upon the existing capital' (pp. 54–5).

Ricardo allows that 'the only theory by which the actual phenomena of the last 25 years [i.e. the war] can be explained', is that 'simultaneously with the expenditure of Government' an amount of savings (from unproductive consumption) countervailing it accumulated (IV, 341; see also 339). And he apparently thinks that this is what must have taken place. (He does not see, however, that his 'theory' is still unable to explain the great increase in wealth recorded at the end of a war which had been accompanied by a huge increase of public expenditure and debt). His reaction to Blake's point about full employment of capital is that, even though there might be idle capital, 'these dormant portions never find their way into the hands of Government', because 'they consist of goods for which there is no market' (IV, 340).

While Ricardo *de facto* assumes full employment of capital, he nowhere appears to think in terms of full employment of labour. As a matter of fact, in the chapter 'On Machinery' (added in the third edition of the *Principles*) he accepts the idea that machinery could well create unemployment; he candidly declares (much to McCulloch's scandal) to have changed his mind on this question, and to think now that introduction of machinery may reduce the *gross* produce of the country (though increasing the net produce), in which case it 'will be injurious to the labouring classes, as some of their number will be thrown out of employment, and population will become redundant' (I, 390).

With respect to the policy of providing for public expenditure, the best course for Ricardo would be that of raising annually through taxes an amount equal to the annual expenditure. This, even in the event of an exceptional expenditure, like that due to a war (IV, 186). No debt had to be incurred, and, as mentioned above, in 1819 he put forward a plan to repay the whole national debt in four or five years. (He wrote that he had 'the firm conviction that nations will at last adopt the plan of defraying their expenses, ordinary and extraordinary, at the time they are incurred': IV, 190.) According to him, in fact, if a tax was laid on each individual of a nation so that the whole debt (and not only the interest on it) would be repaid, people might save this whole amount from their income. If instead the tax was only to raise the amount necessary for the payment of the interest on the debt, people would only save this lesser amount: 'the system of borrowing ... tends to make us less thrifty – to blind us from our real situation' (I, 247).

It is to be mentioned that Ricardo subscribes to Melon's view that 'the debts of a nation are debts due from the right hand to the left' (I, 244n.), and writes that the amount which is raised annually through taxes to pay the interest charges for the debt 'is merely transferred from those who pay it to those who receive it ... The real expense is the twenty millions [the amount of the debt], and not the interest which must be paid for it. Whether the interest be or be not paid, the country will neither be richer nor poorer' (I, 244). 'With a view to wealth only, it might be equally desirable' that a debtor (be it the nation or an individual) should or should not pay his debt. But Ricardo of course thinks that 'Justice and good faith demand that the interest of the national debt should continue to be paid, and that those who have advanced their capitals for the general benefit, should not be required to forego their equitable claims, on the plea of expediency' (I, 246).

RICARDO AND AFTER

J.H. Hollander, the famous Ricardo scholar, wrote in 1910 that there was 'an impressive unanimity' among economists, as to the great influence that, for good or evil, Ricardo has had on economic thought (Hollander, 1910, pp. 115–16). Today, there is not much reason to think otherwise.

Ricardo has had first of all a great influence in establishing that body of notions which form the groundwork of 'sound' economic policies. Say's Law, the quantity theory of money, and his theory of foreign trade, combined in Ricardo's hands to form a powerful machinery by which to get at clear-cut policy proposals. Although many recoiled from the extremes to which he would often push his arguments, only few were able successfully to contrast them. It is to this set of notions that Keynes must have been referring, when he wrote the famous sentence, that 'Ricardo conquered England as completely as the Holy Inquisition conquered Spain' (Keynes, 1936, p. 32). Indeed, it is sufficient only to mention a few of Ricardo's maxims, to realize how much they have contributed to shape the economists' mind: 'demand is only limited by production', 'to save is to spend', 'the raising of funds for the purpose of employing the poor ... diverts those funds from other employments', 'money cannot call forth goods', 'That which is wise in an individual, is wise also in a nation', 'Under a system of perfectly free commerce, each country devotes its capital and labour to such employments as are most beneficial to each'; and so on.

On these points, marginalists arrived much at the same conclusions as Ricardo. The paths through which they got at them were however generally different from those of Ricardo. Consider Say's Law. In Ricardo, the point that there cannot be an insufficiency of aggregate demand does not come so much from his theory, as from a *de facto* identification of saving and investment decisions. The same result is instead obtained by marginalists through an elaborate theoretical argument, involving the construction of 'well behaved' demand functions for each good and 'productive factor', including capital (of which saving and investment are of course the flow aspect).

In the case of comparative advantage theory, the difference is even greater, in that it is not the case (as one could argue it was with Say's Law) that marginalists simply provided Ricardo's conclusions with a theoretical basis which they otherwise lacked. Indeed, with comparative advantage there is the substitution of one theoretical construction for another. In marginalist theory, the trading countries are generally assumed to have the same technology, and the advantages of specialization derive from differences in the relative scarcities, and therefore in the prices, of the productive factors. Ricardo's argument instead assumes differences in the technologies of the trading countries, and the advantages of specialization derive from differences in the relative quantities of labour necessary to produce the commodities in the different countries. Therefore his argument, which is based on the labour theory of value, has nothing to do with the scarcities – or with the prices – of labour, land, or capital. A change in the rates of wages or profits would not touch the comparative advantages at all.

The point which did not really require much change, to fit into the scarcity approach of marginalism, was the quantity theory of money. But this theory, as we have seen above, was rather a misfit in Ricardo's system, and its consistency with the rest of it problematic.

It is also to be remembered that Ricardo was claimed by Marshall as a brilliant – if somewhat crude – forerunner of marginalist (or, according to this view, 'neo-classical') theory. Marshall, starting from the point that 'we must interpret him generously' (1920, p. 671), tried to divest Ricardo of the two points in his theory which basically conflicted with marginalism: the rate of wages given by the worker's subsistence, and the labour theory of value. The latter he reduced to the idea that value depends upon cost of production. As to the former, Marshall maintained that Ricardo had never seen wages as 'fixed', relying for this on passages where Ricardo had argued that the level of wages differs in different places and at different times. Indeed, given the rate of wages and productive techniques (and assuming no rent), the rate of profits would be wholly determined, and therefore the cost of production and the price of the product. No role would be left to play for the marginalist mechanism of supply and demand: the proportions in which goods are demanded become irrelevant to the determination of value and distribution, and there would not be any mechanism to bring the supply and demand of factors to equality.

Marshall claimed he could make a synthesis of Ricardo's cost of production and Jevons's utility: 'The "cost of production principle" and the "final utility" principle are undoubtedly component parts of the one all-ruling law of supply and demand; each may be compared to one blade of a pair of scissors' (1920, p. 675). On these grounds, he maintained that 'the foundations of the theory as they were left by Ricardo remain intact; ... much has been added to them, and ... very much has been built upon them, but ... little has been taken from them' (1920, p. 417). Notwithstanding the flimsy evidence on which the claim was based (see Ashley, 1891), 'so dominating was Marshall's authority that in Britain at any rate he was able to establish his view as the orthodox one' (Hutchison, 1952, p. 422).

The foregoing points can illustrate the links between Ricardo and mainstream economic thought. Ricardo is however with more foundation to be considered as a crucial influence on another important – if unorthodox – current of thought: that which passing through Marx gets at the modern revival of classical political economy, now generally associated with the name of Piero Sraffa, and often labelled with the slightly misleading name of 'Neo-Ricardianism'.

The importance of Ricardo's (and, more generally, classical) theory for Marx is such that Marx is often regarded as the last of the classical economists. Indeed, as M.H. Dobb wrote, Marx's

> criticism of Political Economy ... retains certain essential limbs of the classical structure, as representing important constituents of truth, at the same time as it emphasizes additional relationships which have the effect of remodelling the structure and revolutionizing the practical significance alike of the whole and of its several elements' (1940, p. 36).

The main element of the Ricardo–Marx connection is of course the labour theory of value. Ricardo had grouped the difficulties which this theory encountered under the heading 'exceptions' to the general rule of value, and had attempted to solve them by means of a measure of 'absolute value'. To these problems was devoted Marx's 'transformation of values into prices of production', and again to them is devoted Sraffa's 1960 book, with its solution to the problem of building a coherent wage–profit–price relationship.

Sraffa had the additional task of re-discovering classical political economy as a theoretical structure different from (and alternative to) marginalism, thus rescuing Ricardo from Marshall's interpretation. This Sraffa has done first of all in his edition of Ricardo's works (to which an important companion are the first three chapters of Dobb's *Political Economy and Capitalism*). Another important step towards this reappraisal of Ricardo's (and classical) theory is of course Sraffa's own book, with its solution to the difficulties which Ricardo and Marx had left unsolved in their theories of value and distribution. In providing this solution, Sraffa has also proved the impossibility of measuring the 'quantity of capital' as a single magnitude, independent of distribution. Thus, ironically, while solving the difficulties of classical theory, he has also proved the untenability of (among others) the theory which had been put forward by Böhm-Bawerk, the great marginalist critic of Marx, with his 'average period of production'. (On the Sraffa-based critique of orthodox capital theory, see Symposium, 1966.)

Sraffa's work has in two ways enhanced the importance of Ricardo's theory for a modern reader. On the one hand, because it has shown that this is a theory in its own right, different from marginalism (not simply a crude and incomplete version of it), and that it could be freed from the difficulties which had at least in part been the cause of its early demise. On the other hand, its forceful attack on the fundamentals of the received doctrine has shown that economics is far from being in a state of finality, and that it makes sense to work for an alternative to conventional wisdom.

G. DE VIVO

See also CLASSICAL ECONOMICS; CLASSICAL THEORY OF MONEY; COMPARATIVE ADVANTAGE; CORN MODEL; QUANTITY THEORY OF MONEY.

SELECTED WORKS

All references to Ricardo are to *The Works and Correspondence of David Ricardo*, edited by Piero Sraffa, with the collaboration of M.H. Dobb, Vols I–XI, Cambridge: Cambridge University Press, 1951–73; they are quoted with a Roman numeral for the volume, and an Arabic or a small Roman numeral, for the page.

BIBLIOGRAPHY

Ashley, W.J. 1891. The rehabilitation of Ricardo. *Economic Journal* 1, September, 474–89.

Bagehot, W. 1888. Ricardo. In *Economic Studies*, as reprinted in *The Collected Works of Walter Bagehot*, ed. N. St John-Stevas, Vol. XI, London: The Economist, 1978.

Blake, W. 1823. *Observations on the Effects Produced by the Expenditure of Government During the Restriction of Cash Payments*. London: Murray.

Cannan, E. 1917. *A History of the Theories of Production and Distribution in English Political Economy from 1776 to 1848*. 3rd edn, London: King.

Cannan, E. 1929. *A Review of Economic Theory*. London: King.

De Quincey, T. 1844. *The Logic of Political Economy*. As reprinted in *The Collected Writings of Thomas de Quincey*, ed. D. Masson, Vol. IX, Edinburgh: Black, 1890.

Dobb, M. 1940. *Political Economy and Capitalism. Some Essays in Economic Tradition*. 2nd edn, London: Routledge & Kegan Paul, 1980.

Fetter, F.W. 1965. Economic controversies in the *British Review*, 1802–1850. *Economica* 32, November, 424–37.

Hawtrey, R.G. 1930. *Currency and Credit*. 3rd edn, London: Longmans, Green & Co.

Hollander, J.H. 1910. *David Ricardo. A Centenary Estimate*. Reprinted, New York: Kelley, 1968.

Horner, L. 1853. *Memoirs and Correspondence of Francis Horner, M.P.*, edited by His Brother. 2nd edn, 2 vols, Boston: Little, Brown.

Huskisson, W. 1810. *The Question Concerning the Depreciation of Our Currency Stated and Examined*. As reprinted in *A Select Collection of Scarce and Valuable Tracts and Other Publications, on Paper Currency and Banking*, ed. J.R. McCulloch, privately printed, London, 1857.

Hutchison, T.W. 1952. Some questions about Ricardo. *Economica* 19, November, 415–32.

Keynes, J.M. 1925. The Gold Standard. *The Nation and Athenaeum*, 2 May. As reprinted in *The Collected Writings of John Maynard Keynes*, Vol. XIX, ed. D. Moggridge, London: Macmillan and Cambridge University Press, 1981.

Keynes, J.M. 1936. *The General Theory of Employment, Interest and Money*. London: Macmillan.

Lauderdale, L. 1804. *An Inquiry into the Nature and Origin of Public Wealth, and into the Means and Causes of Its Increase*. Reprinted, New York: Kelley, 1966.

Malthus, T.R. 1811. Depreciation of paper currency. *Edinburgh Review* 17, February, 340–72.

Malthus, T.R. 1820. *Principles of Political Economy Considered with a View to Their Practical Application*. London: Murray.

Malthus, T.R. 1827. *Definitions in Political Economy, Preceded by an Inquiry into the Rules Which Ought to Guide Political Economists in the Definition and Use of Their Terms; with Remarks on the Deviation from These Rules in Their Writings*. Reprinted, New York: Kelley, 1971.

Marshall, A. 1887. Evidence before the Gold and Silver Commission. As reprinted in *Official Papers by Alfred Marshall*, ed. J.M. Keynes, London: Macmillan, 1926.

Marshall, A. 1890. *Principles of Economics*. London: Macmillan.

Marshall, A. 1920. *Principles of Economics*. 8th edn, London: Macmillan, 1959.

Marx, K. 1859. *A Contribution to the Critique of Political Economy*. Moscow: Progress Publishers, 1970.

Marx, K. 1862–3. *Theories of Surplus Value*, Vols. I–III. London: Lawrence & Wishart, 1969–72.

Marx, K. 1867. *Capital. A Critique of Political Economy*, Vol. I. London: Lawrence & Wishart, 1977.

Mill, J.S. 1844. *Essays on Some Unsettled Questions of Political Economy*. Reprinted, London: London School of Economics and Political Science, 1948.

Patten, S.N. 1893. The interpretation of Ricardo. *Quarterly Journal of Economics*, April. As reprinted in S.N. Patten, *Essays in Economic Theory*, reprinted, Port Washington and London: Kennikat Press, 1971.

Robbins, L. 1952. *The Theory of Economic Policy in English Classical Political Economy*. London: Macmillan.

Schumpeter, J.A. 1954. *History of Economic Analysis*. London: Allen & Unwin.

Smart, W. 1910. *Economic Annals of the Nineteenth Century: 1801–1820*. 2 vols, reprinted, New York: Kelley, 1964.

Smith, A. 1789. *An Inquiry into the Nature and Causes of the Wealth of Nations*. 5th edn, 2 vols, ed. E. Cannan, London: Methuen 1922.

Sraffa, P. 1960. *Production of Commodities by Means of Commodities: Prelude to a Critique of Economic Theory*. Cambridge: Cambridge University Press.

St. Clair, O. 1957. *A Key to Ricardo*. London: Routledge & Kegan Paul.

Stigler, G.J. 1953. Sraffa's Ricardo. *American Economic Review* 43, September. As reprinted in G.J. Stigler, *Essays in the History of Economics*, Chicago: University of Chicago Press, 1965.

Symposium. 1966. Paradoxes in capital theory: a symposium. With contributions by L.L. Pasinetti, P.A. Samuelson, D. Levhari, M. Morishima, M. Bruno, E. Burmeister, E. Sheshinski, P. Garegnani. *Quarterly Journal of Economics* 80(4), November, 503–83.

Taussig, F.W. 1896. *Wages and Capital. An Examination of the Wages Fund Doctrine*. Reprinted, New York: Kelley, 1968.

Thornton, H. 1802. *An Enquiry into the Nature and Effects of the Paper Credit of Great Britain*. Ed. F.A. von Hayek, London: Allen & Unwin, 1939. Reprinted, New York: Kelley, 1978.

Viner, J. 1937. *Studies in the Theory of International Trade*. Reprinted, Clifton: Kelley, 1975

Ricardo–Hayek effect. Dwelling on the familiar Ricardian proposition (ch. I, section V, of the *Principles*) according to which a rise in wages will encourage capitalists to substitute machinery for labour and vice versa, F. von Hayek (1939) coined the expression 'Ricardo effect' for the assertion that a general change in wages relative to the prices of final goods will alter the relative profitability of the different methods of production employing labour and capital in different proportions. To be sure, Schumpeter (1939, pp. 345, 812) refers to the influence of factor prices on the introduction of a new method of production as the 'Hayek effect'. On the other hand, Hayek's Ricardo Effect is not to be confused with the celebrated Ricardo machinery effect: the latter concerns the employment *effects* of the introduction of a new method of production; the former deals with the *causes* of its introduction. To avoid misunderstandings, it is therefore proper to use the expression 'Ricardo–Hayek effect'.

In his 1939 paper, Hayek made use of the effect in order to show that a rise in the demand for consumer goods, with money wages and interest rates remaining unchanged, by causing an increase in prices of consumer goods and a decrement of real wages, will lead to a fall in the demand for capital goods thereby causing unemployment. So, contrary to Keynes, a rising level of consumption must, after a certain point, reduce rather than increase the rate of investment. This peculiar utilization of the effect within the realm of business cycle theory triggered more than one kind of criticism, the fiercest of which was Kaldor's (1939; 1942) who arrived to suggest that the real author of Professor Hayek's proposition is Wicksell and not Ricardo at all.

Responding to his critics, Hayek (1942) stressed that his Ricardo effect is a proposition of general character, whose validity and importance are quite independent from its special application to the problems of industrial fluctuations. Indeed, under the above mentioned assumptions, a fall of real wages, with a uniform rate of interest, will certainly change in the same proportion the costs of producing final goods by different methods, but this does not prevent the attractiveness of investing in different methods of production from being affected differently. Why this is so is due to the fact that the current distribution of the funds at the command of the firms between expenditures in wages (investment in circulating capital) and expenditures on machinery (investment in fixed capital) is determined by the circumstance that as long as the prices of final goods remain high relative to costs, the difference is a source of profit every time the capital is turned over, so that higher profits *per unit of time* will be made as the firm can turn over its capital more frequently.

The appropriate context in which to assess the validity and relevance of the Ricardo–Hayek effect is not – as Kaldor took it – the familiar comparative static exercise whereby an old and a new method of production are compared for their profitability, taking for granted that the equipment appropriate to the new method is already in existence or can be procured instantaneously. Rather the effect is to be couched in a dynamic context, since it deals with the transient phase before the new equipment becomes available during which the firms have to decide the relative rates at which they will spend their current outlay on renewing or adding to the two kinds (fixed and circulating) of capital assets. The essence of the Ricardo–Hayek effect is that 'profits will be higher on the method with the higher rate of turnover, *not* because they would accrue at a higher rate *after* the new equilibrium envisaged by Kaldor had been established ... but because the profits on the less capitalistic method will *begin to accrue* earlier than those on the more capitalistic method' (Hayek, 1942, p. 148). In other words, what Kaldor and others disregarded in their assessment of the effect is that – as shown in Zamagni (1984) – the new position which will be eventually achieved, if at all, is time dependent in the precise sense that it depends on the behaviour exhibited by the firms during the transition, a behaviour which, in turn, is affected by the profits accruing to them as the adjustment process goes on.

STEFANO ZAMAGNI

BIBLIOGRAPHY

Hayek, F. von. 1939. *Profits, Interest and Investment*. London: Routledge & Kegan Paul.

Hayek, F. von. 1942. The Ricardo Effect. *Economica* 9, May, 127–52.

Kaldor, N. 1939. Capital intensity and the trade cycle. *Economica* 6, February, 40–66.

Kaldor, N. 1942. Professor Hayek and the concertina-effect. *Economica* 9, November, 359–82.

Schumpeter, J. 1939. *Business Cycles*. New York: McGraw-Hill.

Zamagni, S. 1984. Ricardo and Hayek effects in a fixwage model of traverse. *Oxford Economic Papers* 36, November Supplement, 135–51.

Ricci, Umberto (1879–1946). Ricci was born in Chieti, Italy, and died in Cairo, Egypt. After an administrative career, his contributions to economic theory (he was an autodidact without academic training) won him a chair in economics (1912), after which he taught in various universities. A critic of the Fascist regime, an article (1928a) written in his humorous, ironic style was the occasion for the government to deprive him of his Rome chair. He then taught in the Universities of Cairo (1929–40) and Iştanbul (1942–6). He was a Fellow of the Econometric Society.

Ricci was a major theoretician in various fields: capital theory, demand and supply theory, public finance. He also wrote on economic policy, statistics, and the history of economic analysis. Although a follower of the Walras–Pareto general equilibrium approach, he upheld the usefulness of Marshall's partial equilibrium approach (1906, 1924). He stressed the importance of the elasticity concept and its connection with outlay (1931, 1932), and offered an original treatment of indivisible commodities (1935). Ricci is one of the independent originators of the cobweb theorem (1930) and among the first to realize the potentialities of the econometric approach to give empirical content to 'hypothetical experiments' (i.e. simulations) in economics (1928b, 1939). He coined the word 'polipolio' (polypoly) to denote a set of monopolies and theorized the extreme case of generalized corporativism as a polypolisitc system (1926). Also remarkable is his work in applied statistics as Director of the Statistical Service, International Institute of Agriculture, 1910–22 (1914). His posthumous book (1951), containing the lecture notes of his Istanbul courses, is a lucid treatment of microeconomics.

GIANCARLO GANDOLFO

SELECTED WORKS

1906. Curve piane di offerta dei prodotti. *Giornale degli economisti*, September.

1910. *Il capitale-Saggio di economia teoretica*. Turin: Bocca.

1914. *Les bases théoriques de la statistique agricole internationale*. Rome: Imprimerie de l'Institut International d'Agriculture.

1924. Pareto e l'economia pura. *Giornale degli economisti e rivista di statistica*, January-February. Trans. as 'Pareto and Pure Economics', *Review of Economic Studies* 1, October 1933, 3-21.

1926. *Dal protezionismo al sindacalismo*. Bari: Laterza.

1928a. La scienza e la vita. *Nuovi studi di diritto, economia e politica* 1(3), anno VI.

1928b. Il metodo in economia politica. In *Scritti della Facoltá giuridica di Roma in onore di A. Salandra*, Milan: Vallardi. Enlarged German version, Die Methode in der Nationalökonomie, *Zeitschrift für Nationalökonomie* 4(5), October 1933.

1930. Die 'Synthetische Ökonomie' von Henry Ludwell Moore. *Zeitschrift für Nationalökonomie* 1(5), 656.

1931. Courbes de la demande et courbes de la dépense. *L'Egypte contemporaine* 22, May, 556–8.

1932. The psychological foundation of the law of demand. *Journal of Political Economy* 40, April, 145–85.

1935. The modification of the utility curve for money in the cases of indivisible goods and goods of increasing utility. *Economica*NS 2, May, 168–97.

1939. Una nuova via aperta all'econometrica: la misura dei fatti ipotetici. *Rivista internazionale di scienze sociali* 10, January, 70–87.

1951. *Eléments d'économie politique pure – Théorie de la valeur*. Milan: Malfasi.

BIBLIOGRAPHY

A full bibliography of Ricci's works is published in his posthumous book (1951), which also contains obituaries by L. Einaudi and C. Bresciani-Turroni (the first of these is also published in English in *American Economic Review*, September 1946). For an evaluation of

Ricci's scientific contributions, see also L. Gangemi, In memoria di Umberto Ricci, *Studi Economici ed Aziendali*, April–June 1946 (with bibliography), and C. Grilli, Umberto Ricci e l'economia psichico matematica, *Studi Economici*, November–December 1951.

rising supply price. 'Rising supply price' is a name that partial equilibrium theorists give to their encounters with general equilibrium reasoning. Such encounters must have occurred ever since economics began but for us the story begins in 1912 with Pigou, who asserted that:

> in industries of increasing returns the supply price is greater than the marginal supply price; in industries of diminishing returns the supply price is less than the marginal supply price ... . It follows that, other things being equal, in industries of increasing returns the marginal net product of investment tends to exceed, and in industries of diminishing returns to fall short of, the marginal net product yielded in industries in general (1912, pp. 176–7).

These conclusions led him to argue that taxes should be placed on decreasing returns industries and bounties on increasing returns industries. Assuming, what Clapham (1922) seriously doubted, that actual industries can be sorted into such boxes, this is a policy recommendation that appears remarkably specific in content and general in application.

For Pigou, a decreasing returns industry is one in which the expenses of producing $x+\Delta x$ units exceed those of producing x units by more than the expenses attributable directly to the Δx units; this is what excess of 'marginal supply price' over supply price means. However, since the proposed tax-subsidy policy only makes sense for the long-run, replication of a plant of optimal size is always possible and at once rules out decreasing returns to scale in the physical sense. This makes it difficult to see how Pigovian decreasing returns industries can exist, unless the expansion in output from x to $x+\Delta x$ causes a rise in price of one or more of the resources used by the industry. Pigou was willing to admit this possibility.

But then, as Allyn Young gently pointed out in his review of Pigou's book, there is

> A more serious difficulty when we inquire as to the precise content of the 'resources' which are devoted to the work of production ... . Changes in the prices of product and of resources are the very essence of the situation. Increased prices for the use of land and the other factors in production do not represent an increased *using up* of resources in the work of production. They merely represent *transferences* of purchasing power (1913, p. 683, his italics).

Thus the rising supply price that accompanies expansion of the industry (as distinct from expansion of any one of its firms) is simply a consequence of increases in the rents of those resources that it uses relatively heavily. Barring net physical external diseconomies, it does not correspond to any increase in the use of real resources.

It took a long time for Young's fundamental point to sink in. In what was essentially the second, much enlarged and retitled, edition of his book, Pigou acknowledged that Young's criticism was 'very important' but defended himself with the feeble argument that 'each [industry] ... is supposed to make use of only a small part of the aggregate resources of the country' (1920, pp. 934–6). Thus Frank Knight, who had been Young's graduate student at Cornell when the latter's review of Pigou appeared, felt called upon to point out once more the nature of the errors that Pigou was making. So effective was the famous article in which he did this (1924) that it has been reprinted many times, which Young's prior contribution never was, not even by Young himself in his collection (1927).

But that was welfare economics. In positive economics, Clapham's article of 1922 set off a controversy over increasing returns and competition which exploded like a string of firecrackers in the pages of the *Economic Journal* over the next ten years, until the books on imperfect competition by Chamberlin and Joan Robinson in 1933 brought it sputtering to a close. The controversy inevitably touched upon problems of 'rising supply price', but nowhere did it do so effectively save in an article by Roy Harrod, written in 1928 but not accepted and published until 1930 ('An egoistic footnote' in 1951, p. 159, fn2, attributed the delay to an unfavourable referee's report by Frank Ramsey.) His argument went like this:

> Let us call the proportion in which the factors of production A,B,C ... are mixed in use at the margin in national industry as a whole a:b:c: ... if an industry using the factors in the proportion of a+x:b:c: ... expands, it can only get increasing quantities of A at an enhanced price in terms of B, C ... No doubt by the law of substitution x will be reduced in consequence of the expansion of this industry; but not to zero ... .
>
> ... it follows that every industry which uses an appreciable fraction of the factors of production, unless it be an industry using them at the margin in the proportions of a:b:c: . . . , obeys the law of increasing supply price. . . .
>
> This analysis seems to clear up the problem of the old classical distinction between agriculture and the manufacturing industries. If A is land, and a+x:b:c: ... the proportion in which the factors are mixed at the margin in agriculture as a whole, x/a is clearly large. Agriculture as a whole is thus markedly subject to increasing supply price (1930, pp. 240-41).

This is an explicit account of what Young merely sketched, though there is no evidence that Harrod had read Young's review. In the following year Viner (1931) published his much-reprinted codification of neoclassical partial equilibrium theory, in which without reference to either Harrod or Young he introduced the idea of 'pecuniary' economies and diseconomies, both internal and external. According to this classification what have been discussed here so far are 'net pecuniary external diseconomies', which at that time Viner did not emphasize. However, almost twenty years later Viner added a Supplementary Note to the 1950 reprint of (1931), in which he felt

> ... it incumbent upon me,... to avoid propagating serious error, to carry the analysis ... further ... by departing here from the traditional Marshallian pattern of assumptions to which the article adheres. The partial-equilibrium nature of the Marshallian assumptions leaves a wider range of possibilities to the long-run tendencies of costs for an expanding industry than is consistent with general-equilibrium analysis. I first saw this in 1938, and thereafter pointed it out to my students at the University of Chicago. But the first and, to my knowledge, still the only, analysis in print similar to what I have in mind is in Joan Robinson's excellent article, 'Rising Supply Price,' ... [1941] ... which has not attracted the attention which in my opinion it eminently deserves (Viner, 1951, p. 227).

In a further footnote, added to the 1951 reprint of the 1950 version, Viner also acknowledged Harrod's prior contribution in (1930). Joan Robinson's fine article is indeed the culmination of this whole line of reasoning, developing in much greater detail and in crystal-clear prose the mode of analysis that began with Harrod; but it is puzzling that Harrod (unlike Hicks, Marshall, Pigou, Robbins and Sraffa) is never mentioned, in spite of the striking similarities between the two analyses. An interesting sidelight is that, in a letter written soon after the appearance of her article and published in Robinson (1951, pp. 42–3), Keynes took a markedly general equilibrium approach to the problem.

Apart from relevant surveys of external economies by Ellis and Fellner (1943) and Chipman (1965, Section 2.8, pp. 736–49) there has been little further discussion of 'rising supply price', evidence perhaps that its nature is by now well understood. However, even as late as 1954, Scitovsky's well-received article with its Pigovian policy conclusions and remark that 'Pecuniary external economies clearly have no place in equilibrium theory' (1954, 149, 146), showed that confusion still existed. Maybe each generation of partial equilibrium theorists has to learn the lesson anew.

PETER NEWMAN

See also EXTERNAL ECONOMIES; GENERAL EQUILIBRIUM; PIGOU, ARTHUR CECIL; PECUNIARY AND NON-PECUNIARY ECONOMIES.

BIBLIOGRAPHY

Arrow, K.J. and Scitovsky, T. (eds) 1969. *Readings in Welfare Economics*. Homewood, Ill.: Richard D. Irwin. Reprints Knight (1924) and Scitovsky (1954).

Boulding, K.E. and Stigler, G.J. (eds) 1951. *Readings in Price Theory*. Homewood, Ill.: Richard D. Irwin. Reprints Clapham (1922), Ellis and Fellner (1943), Knight (1924), Robinson (1941) and Viner (1931).

Chipman, J.S. 1965. A survey of the theory of international trade. Part 2. The neo-classical theory. *Econometrica* 33, 685–760.

Clapham, J.H. 1922. Of empty economic boxes. *Economic Journal* 32, 305–14.

Clemence, R.V. (ed.) 1950. *Readings in Economic Analysis*. Vol. 2: *Prices and Production*. Cambridge, Mass.: Addison-Wesley. Reprints Viner (1931).

Harrod, R.F. 1930. Notes on supply. *Economic Journal* 40, 232–41.

Harrod, R.F. 1951. *The Life of John Maynard Keynes*. London: Macmillan.

Harrod, R.F. 1952. *Economic Essays*. London: Macmillan. Reprints Harrod (1930).

Knight, F.H. 1924. Some fallacies in the interpretation of social cost. *Quarterly Journal of Economics* 38, 582–606.

Knight, F.H. 1935. *The Ethics of Competition*. London: George Allen & Unwin. Reprints Knight (1924).

Pigou, A.C. 1912. *Wealth and Welfare*. London: Macmillan.

Pigou, A.C. 1920. *The Economics of Welfare*. London: Macmillan.

Robinson, J.V. 1941. Rising supply price. *Economica*, NS 8, 1–8.

Robinson, J.V. 1951. *Collected Economic Papers*. Oxford: Basil Blackwell. Reprints Robinson (1941).

Scitovsky, T. 1954. Two concepts of external economies. *Journal of Political Economy* 62, 143–51.

Viner, J. 1931. Cost curves and supply curves. *Zeitschrift für Nationalökonomie* 3, 23–46.

Viner, J. 1951. Reprint of (1931) in Boulding and Stigler (1951).

Young, A.A. 1913. Pigou's Wealth and Welfare. *Quarterly Journal of Economics* 27, 672–86.

Young, A.A. 1927. *Economic Problems New and Old*. Boston: Houghton Mifflin.

risk. The phenomenon of *risk* (or alternatively, *uncertainty* or *incomplete information*) plays a pervasive role in economic life. Without it, financial and capital markets would consist of the exchange of a single instrument each period, the communications industry would cease to exist, and the profession of investment banking would reduce to that of accounting. One need only consult the contents of any recent economics journal to see how the recognition of risk has influenced current research in economics. In this entry we present an overview of the modern economic theory of the characterization of risk and the modelling of economic agents' responses to it.

RISK VERSUS UNCERTAINTY. The most fundamental distinction in this branch of economic theory, due to Knight (1921), is that of risk versus uncertainty. A situation is said to involve *risk* if the randomness facing an economic agent can be expressed in terms of specific numerical probabilities (these probabilities may either be objectively specified, as with lottery tickets, or else reflect the individual's own subjective beliefs). On the other hand, situations where the agent cannot (or does not) assign actual probabilities to the alternative possible occurrences are said to involve *uncertainty*.

The standard approach to the modelling of preferences under uncertainty (as opposed to risk) has been the *state preference approach* (e.g. Arrow, 1964; Debreu, 1959. ch. 7; Hirshleifer, 1965, 1966; Karni, 1985; Yaari, 1969). Rather than using numerical probabilities, this approach represents the randomness facing the individual by a set of mutually exclusive and exhaustive *states of nature* or *states of the world* $S = \{s_1, \ldots, s_n\}$. Depending upon the particular application, this partition of all possible futures may either be very coarse, as with the pair of states {it snows here tomorrow, it does not snow here tomorrow} or else very fine, so that the description of a single state might read 'it snows more than three inches here tomorrow *and* the temperature in Paris at noon is 73° *and* the price of platinum in London is over $700.00 per ounce'. The objects of choice in this framework consist of *state-payoff bundles* of the form $(c_1, \ldots, c_n)$, which specify the payoff that the individual will receive in each of the respective states. As with regular commodity bundles, individuals are assumed to have preferences over state-payoff bundles which can be represented by indifference curves in the *state-payoff space* $\{(c_1, \ldots, c_n)\}$.

Although this approach has led to important advances in the analysis of choice under uncertainty (see for example the above references), the advantages of being able to draw on the modern theory of probability has led economists to concentrate on the analysis of risk, where the consequences of agents' actions are alternative well-defined probability distributions over the random variables they face. An important justification for the modelling of randomness via formal probability distributions are those joint axiomatizations of preferences and beliefs which provide consistency conditions on preferences over state-payoff bundles sufficient to imply that they can be generated by a well-defined probability distribution over states of nature and a von Neumann–Morgenstern utility function over payoffs of the type described in the following section (e.g. Savage, 1954; Anscombe and Aumann, 1963; Pratt, Raiffa and Schlaifer, 1964; and Raiffa, 1968, ch. 5).

CHOICE UNDER RISK – THE EXPECTED UTILITY MODEL. For reasons of expositional ease, we consider a world with a single commodity (e.g. wealth). An agent making a decision under risk can therefore be thought of as facing a choice set of alternative univariate probability distributions. In order to consider both discrete (e.g. finite outcome) distributions as well as distributions with density functions, we shall represent each such probability distribution by means of its cumulative distribution functions $F(\cdot)$, where $F(x) \equiv \text{prob}(\tilde{x} \leqslant x)$ for the random variable $\tilde{x}$.

In such a case we can model the agent's preferences over alternative probability distributions in a manner completely analogous to the approach of standard (i.e. non-stochastic) consumer theory: he or she is assumed to possess a ranking $\succcurlyeq$ over distributions which is complete, transitive and continuous (in an appropriate sense), and hence representable by a real-valued *preference function* $V(\cdot)$ over the set of cumulative distribution functions, in the sense that $F^*(\cdot) \succcurlyeq F(\cdot)$ (i.e. the distribution $F^*(\cdot)$ is weakly preferred to $F(\cdot)$) if and only if $V(F^*) \geqslant V(F)$.

Of course, as in the non-stochastic case, the above set of assumptions implies nothing about the functional form of the preference functional $V(\cdot)$. For reasons of both normative appeal and analytic convenience, economists typically assume that $V(\cdot)$ is a *linear functional* of the distribution $F(\cdot)$, and hence takes the form

$$V(F) \equiv \int U(x)\,\mathrm{d}F(x) \tag{1}$$

for some function $U(\cdot)$ over wealth levels x, where $U(\cdot)$ is referred to as the individual's *von Neumann–Morgenstern utility function.* (For readers unfamiliar with the *Riemann–Stieltjes integral* $\int U(x)\,\mathrm{d}F(x)$ it represents nothing more than the expected value of $U(\tilde{x})$, when $\tilde{x}$ possesses the cumulative distribution function $F(\cdot)$. Thus if $\tilde{x}$ took the values $x_1, \ldots, x_n$ with probabilities $p_1, \ldots, p_n$, $\int U(x)\,\mathrm{d}F(x)$ would equal $\Sigma\, U(x_i)p_i$, and if $\tilde{x}$ possessed the density function $f(\cdot) = F'(\cdot)$, $\int U(x)\,\mathrm{d}F(x)$ would equal $\int U(x) f(x)\,\mathrm{d}x$.

Since the right side of (1) may accordingly be thought of an the mathematical expectation of $U(\tilde{x})$, this specification is known as the *expected utility model* of preferences over random prospects (for a more complete statement of this model, see EXPECTED UTILITY HYPOTHESIS). Within this framework, an individual's attitudes toward risk are reflected in the shape of his or her utility function $U(\cdot)$. Thus, for example, an individual would always prefer shifting probability mass from lower to higher outcome levels if and only if $U(x)$ were an increasing function of x, a condition which we shall henceforth always assume. Such a shift of probability mass is known as a *first order stochastically dominating shift.*

RISK AVERSION. The representation of individuals' preferences over distributions by the shape of their von Neumann–Morgenstern utility functions provides the first step in the modern economic characterization of risk. After all, whatever the notion of riskier means, it is clear that bearing a random wealth $\tilde{x}$ is riskier than receiving a certain payment of $\bar{x} = E[\tilde{x}]$, i.e. the expected value of the random variable $\tilde{x}$. We therefore have from Jensen's inequality that an individual would be *risk averse*, i.e. always prefer a payment of $E[\tilde{x}]$ (and obtaining utility $U(E[\tilde{x}])$) to bearing the risk $\tilde{x}$ (and obtaining expected utility $E[U(\tilde{x})]$) if and only if his or her utility function were concave. This condition is illustrated in Figure 1, where the random variable $\tilde{x}$ is assumed to take on the values x' and x'' with respective probabilities 2/3 and 1/3.

Of course, not all individuals need be risk averse in the sense of the previous paragraph. Another type of individual is a *risk lover*. Such an individual would have a *convex* utility function, and would accordingly prefer receiving a random wealth $\tilde{x}$ to receiving its mean $E[\tilde{x}]$ with certainty. An example of such a utility function is given in Figure 2.

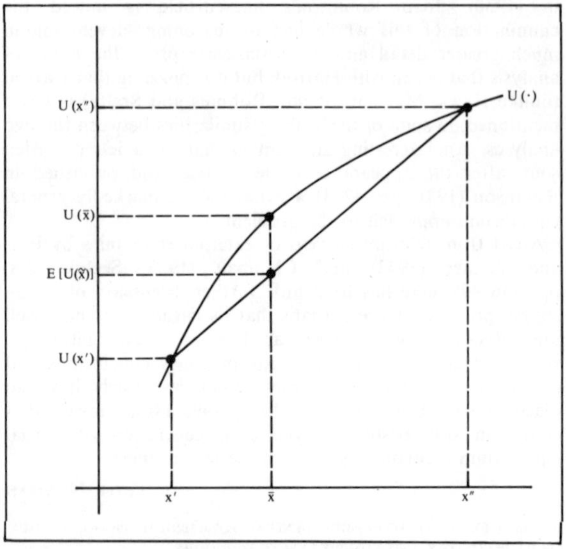

Figure 1 Von Neumann–Morgenstern Utility Function of a Risk Averse Individual

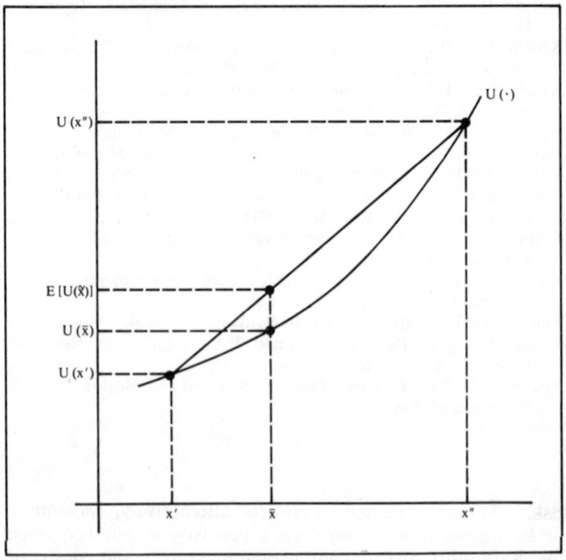

Figure 2 Von Neumann–Morgenstern Utility Function of a Risk Loving Individual

STANDARD DEVIATION AS A MEASURE OF RISK. While the above characterization of risk aversion (as well as its opposite) allows for the derivation of many results in the theory of behaviour under risk, it says nothing regarding which of a *pair* of non-degenerate random variables $\tilde{x}$ and $\tilde{y}$ is the most risky. Since real-world choices are almost never between risky and riskless situations but rather over alternative risky situations, such a means of comparison is necessary.

The earliest and best known univariate measure of the riskiness of a random variable $\tilde{x}$ is its *variance* $\sigma^2 = E[(\tilde{x} - \bar{x})^2]$ or alternatively its *standard deviation* $\sigma = \{E[(\tilde{x} - \bar{x}]^2\}^{1/2}$. The tractability of these measures as well as their well-known statistical properties led to the widespread use of *mean-standard deviation analysis* in the 1950s and 1960s, and in particular to the development of modern portfolio theory by Markowitz

(1952, 1959), Tobin (1958) and others. As an example of this, consider Figure 3. Points A and B correspond to the distributions of a riskless asset with (per dollar) gross return r_0 and a risky asset with random return $\tilde{r}$ with mean $\mu\tilde{r}$ and standard deviation $\sigma\tilde{r}$. An investor dividing a dollar between the two assets in proportions $\alpha:(1-\alpha)$ will possess a portfolio whose return has a mean of $\alpha \cdot r_0 + (1-\alpha)\cdot \mu\tilde{r}$ and standard deviation $(1-\alpha)\cdot\sigma_{\tilde{r}}$, so that the set of attainable (μ, σ) combinations consists of the line segment connecting the points A and B in the figure. It is straightforward to show that if the individual were also allowed to *borrow* at rate r_0 in order to finance purchase of the risky asset (i.e. could sell the riskless asset short), then the set of attainable (μ, σ) combinations would be the ray emanating from A and passing through B.

If we then represent the individual's risk preferences by means of indifference curves in this diagram, we obtain their optimal portfolio (the example in the figure implies an equal division of funds between the two assets). In the more general case of choice between a pair of risky assets, the set of (μ, σ) combinations generated by alternative divisions of wealth between them will trace out a locus such as the one between points C and D in the diagram, with the curvature of this locus determined by the degree of statistical dependence (i.e. covariance) between the two random returns.

As mentioned, the representation and analysis of risk and risk-taking by means of the variance or standard deviation of a distribution proved tremendously useful in the theory of finance, culminating in the mean-standard deviation based *capital asset pricing model* of Treynor (1961), Sharpe (1964), Lintner (1965) and Mossin (1966). However, by the late 1960s the mean-standard deviation approach was under attack for two reasons.

The first reason (known since the 1950s) was that the fact that an expected utility maximizer would evaluate all distributions solely on the basis of their means and standard deviations if and only if his or her von Neumann–Morgenstern utility function took the quadratic form $U(x) \equiv ax + bx^2$ for $b \lesseqgtr 0$. The sufficiency of this condition is established by noting that $E[U(\tilde{x})] = E[a\tilde{x} + b\tilde{x}^2] = a\bar{x} + b(\bar{x}^2 + \sigma^2)$. To prove necessity, note that the distributions which yield a 2/3:1/3 chance of the outcomes $x - \delta : x + 2\delta$ and a 1/3:2/3 chance of the outcomes $x - 2\delta : x + \delta$ both possess the same mean and variance for each x and δ, so that $(2/3)\cdot U(x-\delta) + (1/3)\cdot U(x+2\delta) \equiv (1/3)U(x-2\delta) + (2/3)U(x+\delta)$ for all x and δ. Differentiating with respect to δ and simplifying yields $U'(x+2\delta) + U'(x-2\delta) \equiv U'(x+\delta) + U'(x-\delta)$ for all x and δ. This implies that $U'(\cdot)$ must be linear and hence that $U(\cdot)$ must be quadratic.

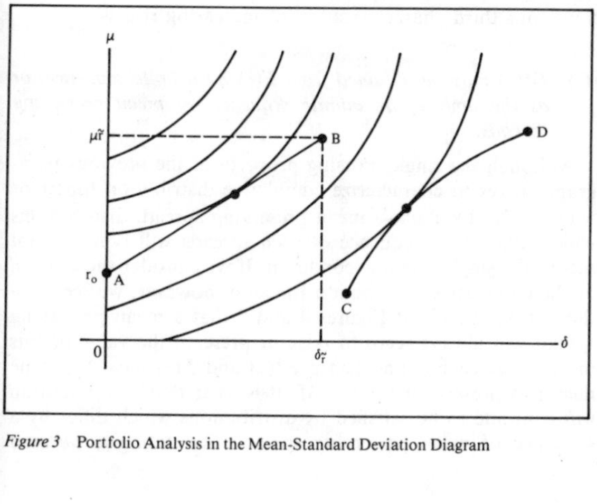

Figure 3 Portfolio Analysis in the Mean-Standard Deviation Diagram

The assumption of quadratic utility is objectionable. If an individual with such a utility function is risk averse (i.e. if $b < 0$), then (i) utility will decrease as wealth increases beyond $1/2b$, and (ii) the individual will be more averse to constant additive risks about high wealth levels than about low wealth levels – in contrast to the observation that those with greater wealth take greater risks (see for example Hicks (1962) or Pratt (1964)).

Borch (1969) struck the second and strongest blow to the mean-standard deviation approach. He showed that for any two points (μ_1, σ_1) and (μ_2, σ_2) in the (μ, σ) plane which a mean-standard deviation preference ordering would rank as indifferent, it is possible to find random variables $\tilde{x}_1$ and $\tilde{x}_2$ which possess these respective (μ, σ) values and where $\tilde{x}_2$ first order stochastically dominates $\tilde{x}_1$. However, *any* person with an increasing von Neumann–Morgenstern utility function would strictly prefer $\tilde{x}_2$ to $\tilde{x}_1$. In response to these arguments and the additional criticisms of Feldstein (1969), Samuelson (1967) and others, the use of mean-standard deviation analysis in economic theory waned. See, however, the recent work of Meyer (1987) for a partial rehabilitation of such two-moment models of preferences.

Besides the variance or standard deviation of a distribution, several other univariate measures of risk have been proposed. Examples include the *mean absolute deviation* $E[|\tilde{x} - \bar{x}|]$, the *interquartile range* $F^{-1}(0.75) - F^{-1}(0.25)$, and the classical statistical measures of *entropy* $\Sigma p_i \cdot \ln(p_i)$ or $\int f(x)\cdot \ln(f(x))\,dx$. Although they provide the analytical convenience of a single numerical index of riskiness, each of these measures are subject to problems of the sort encountered with the variance or standard deviation. In particular, the entropy measure can be particularly unresponsive to the values taken on by the random variable: the 50:50 gambles over the values \$50:\$51 and \$1:\$100 both possess the same entropy level.

INCREASING RISK. By the late 1960s, the failure to find a satisfactory univariate measure of risk led to another approach to this problem. Working independently, several researchers (Hadar and Russell, 1969; Hanoch and Levy, 1969; and Rothschild and Stiglitz, 1970, 1971) developed an alternative characterization of increasing risk. The appeal of this approach is twofold. First, it formalizes three different intuitive notions of increasing risk. Second, it allows for the straightforward derivation of comparative statics results in a wide variety of economic situations. Unlike the univariate measures described above, however, this approach provides only a partial ordering of random variables. In other words, not all pairs of random variables can be compared with respect to their riskiness.

We now state three alternative formalizations of the notion that a cumulative distribution function $F^*(\cdot)$ is riskier than another distribution $F(\cdot)$ with the same mean (in the following, all distributions are assumed to be over the interval $[0, M]$).

The first definition of increasing risk captures the notion that 'risk is what all risk averters hate'. Thus an increase in risk lowers the expected utility of all risk averters. Formally we may state this condition as:

(A) $F^*(\cdot)$ *and* $F(\cdot)$ *have the same mean and* $\int U(x)\,dF^*(x) \leq \int U(x)\,dF(x)$ *for all concave utility functions* $U(\cdot)$.

This criterion cannot be used to compare every pair of distributions with the same mean. However, if a pair of distributions

$F(\cdot)$ and $F^*(\cdot)$ do *not* satisfy condition (A) (in either direction), there must exist a risk averse (i.e. concave) utility function $U_a(\cdot)$ which prefers $F(\cdot)$ to $F^*(\cdot)$ and another risk averse function $U_b(\cdot)$ which prefers $F^*(\cdot)$ to $F(\cdot)$.

The second characterization of the notion that a random variable $\tilde{y}$ with distribution $F^*(\cdot)$ is riskier than a variable $\tilde{x}$ with distribution $F(\cdot)$ is that $\tilde{y}$ consists of the variable $\tilde{x}$ plus an additional noise term $\tilde{\varepsilon}$. One possible specification of this is that $\tilde{\varepsilon}$ be statistically independent of $\tilde{x}$. However, this condition is too strong in the sense that it does not allow the variance of $\tilde{\varepsilon}$ to depend upon the magnitude of $\tilde{x}$, as in the case of heteroskedastic noise. Instead, Rothschild and Stiglitz (1970) modelled the addition of noise by the condition:

(B) *$F(\cdot)$ and $F^*(\cdot)$ are the cumulative distribution functions of the random variables $\tilde{x}$ and $\tilde{x}+\tilde{\varepsilon}$, where $E[\tilde{\varepsilon}\,|\,x]\equiv 0$ for all x*

The third notion of increasing risk involves the concept (due to Rothschild and Stiglitz, 1970) of a *mean preserving spread.* Intuitively, such a spread consists of moving probability mass from the centre of a probability distribution to its tails in a manner which preserves the expected value of the distribution, as seen in the top panels of Figures 4 and 5. Formally we say

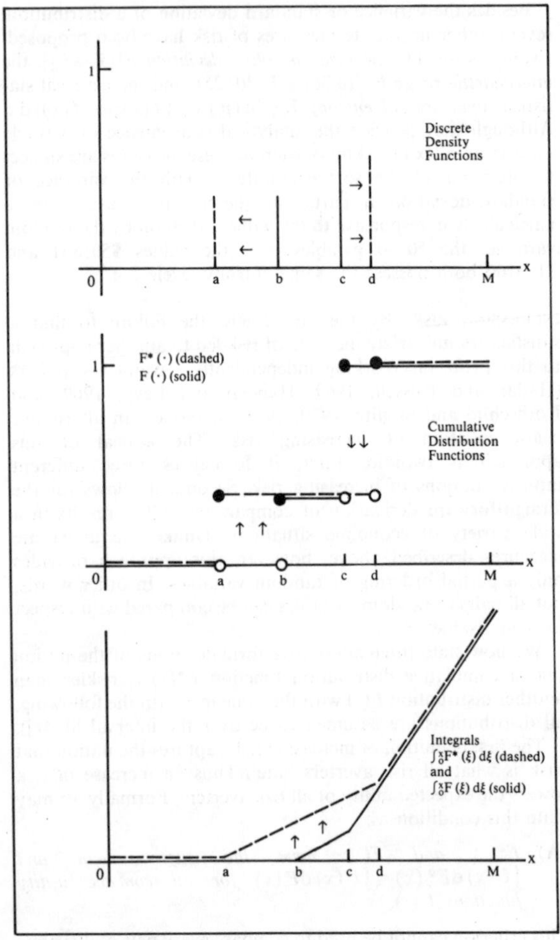

Figure 4 A Mean Preserving Spread of a Discrete Distribution

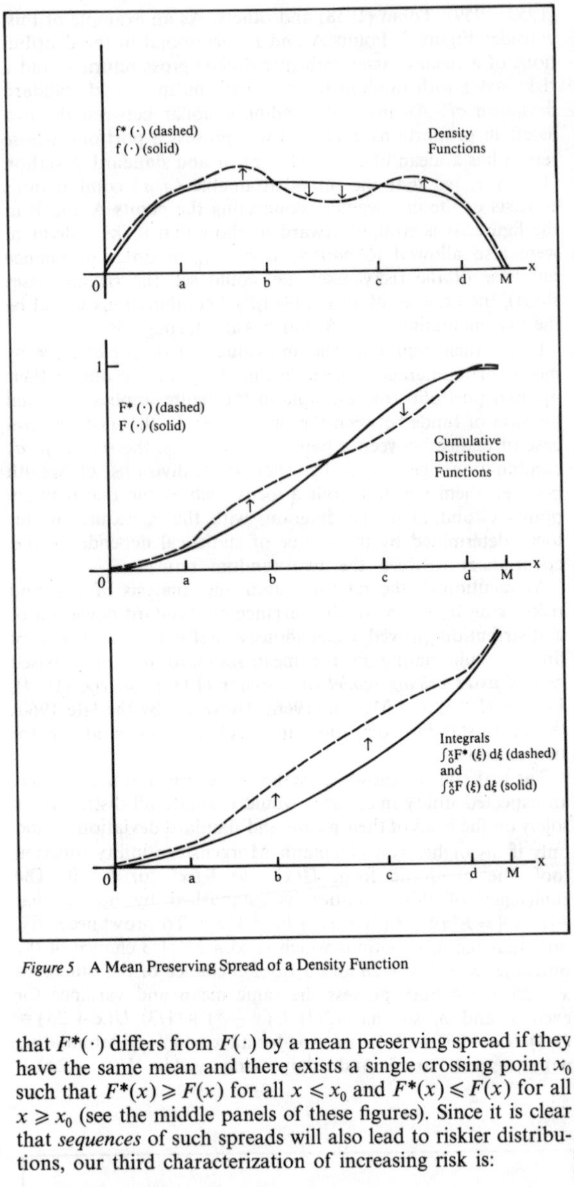

Figure 5 A Mean Preserving Spread of a Density Function

that $F^*(\cdot)$ differs from $F(\cdot)$ by a mean preserving spread if they have the same mean and there exists a single crossing point x_0 such that $F^*(x)\geqslant F(x)$ for all $x\leqslant x_0$ and $F^*(x)\leqslant F(x)$ for all $x\geqslant x_0$ (see the middle panels of these figures). Since it is clear that *sequences* of such spreads will also lead to riskier distributions, our third characterization of increasing risk is:

(C) *$F^*(\cdot)$ may be obtained from $F(\cdot)$ by a finite sequence, or as the limit of an infinite sequence, of mean preserving spreads.*

Although the single crossing property of the previous paragraph serves to characterize cumulative distribution functions which differ by a *single* mean preserving spread, distributions which differ by a sequence of such spreads will typically not satisfy the single crossing condition. If we consider the *integral* of the cumulative distribution function, however, we see from the bottom panels of Figures 4 and 5 that a mean preserving spread will always serve to raise or preserve the value of this integral for each x and (since $F^*(\cdot)$ and $F(\cdot)$ have the same mean) to preserve it for $x = M$. It is clear that this condition *will* continue to be satisfied by distributions which differ by a sequence of mean preserving spreads. Accordingly, we may rewrite condition (C) above by the analytically more convenient:

(C′) *The integral* $\int_0^x [F^*(\xi) - F(\xi)] \cdot d\xi$ *is non-negative for all* $x > 0$, *and is equal to* 0 *for* $x = M$.

Rothschild and Stiglitz (1970) showed that *these three concepts of increasing risk are the same* by proving that conditions (A), (B) and (C/C′) are equivalent. Thus, a single partial ordering of distribution functions corresponds simultaneously to the notion that risk is what risk averters hate, to the notion that adding noise to a random variable increases its risk, and to the notion that moving probability mass from the centre of a probability distribution to its tails increases the risk of that distribution.

This characterization of increasing risk permits the derivation of general and powerful comparative statics theorems concerning economic agents' response to increases in risk. The general framework for these results is that of an individual with a von Neumann–Morgenstern utility function $U(x, \alpha)$ which depends upon both the outcome of some random variable $\tilde{x}$ as well as a *control variable* α which the individual chooses so as to maximize expected utility $\int U(x, \alpha)\, dF(x; r)$, where the distribution function $F(\cdot\,; r)$ depends upon some exogenous parameter r (x for example might be the return on a risky asset, and α the amount invested in it). For convenience, we assume that $F(0; r) = \text{prob}(\tilde{x} \leqslant 0) = 0$ for all r. The first order condition for this problem is then:

$$\int U_\alpha(x, \alpha)\, dF(x; r) = 0 \qquad (2)$$

where $U_\alpha(x, \alpha) = \partial U(x, \alpha)/\partial\alpha$, and we assume that the second derivative $U_{\alpha\alpha}(x, \alpha) = \partial^2 U(x, \alpha)/\partial\alpha^2$ is always negative to ensure we have a maximum. Implicit differentiation of (2) then yields the comparative statics derivative:

$$\frac{d\alpha}{dr} = \frac{-\int U_\alpha(x, \alpha)\, dF_r(x; r)}{\int U_{\alpha\alpha}(x, \alpha)\, dF(x; r)} \qquad (3)$$

where $F_r(x; r) = \partial F(x; r)/\partial r$. Since the denominator of this expression is negative by assumption, the sign of $d\alpha/dr$ is given by the sign of the numerator $\int U_\alpha(x, \alpha)\, dF_r(x; r)$. Integrating by parts twice yields:

$$\begin{aligned}\int U_\alpha(x, \alpha)\, dF_r(x; r) &= \int U_{xx\alpha}(x, \alpha) \cdot \left[\int_0^x F_r(\xi, r)\, d\xi\right] dx \\ &= \int U_{xx\alpha}(x, \alpha) \cdot \left[\frac{d}{dr}\left(\int_0^x F(\xi, r)\, d\xi\right)\right] dx \qquad (4)\end{aligned}$$

Thus, if increases in the parameter r imply increases in the riskiness of the distribution $F(\cdot\,; r)$, it follows from condition (D) that the signs of the square bracketed terms in (4) will be non-negative, so that the effect of r upon α depends upon the sign of $U_{xx\alpha}(x, \alpha) = \partial^3 U(x, \alpha)/\partial^2 x \partial\alpha$. Thus if $U_{xx\alpha}(x, \alpha)$ is uniformly negative, a mean preserving increase in risk in the distribution of x will lead to a fall in the optimal value of the control variable α and vice versa. Another way to see this is to note that if $U_\alpha(x, \alpha)$ is concave in x then a mean preserving increase in risk will lower the left side of the first order condition (2), which (since $U_{\alpha\alpha}(x, \alpha) \leqslant 0$) will require a drop in α to re-establish the equality. Economists routinely use this technique when analysing models involving risk; see for example Rothschild and Stiglitz (1971).

RELATED TOPICS. The characterization of risk outlined in the previous section has been extended along several lines. Diamond and Stiglitz (1974), for example, have replaced the notion of a mean preserving spread with that of a mean *utility* preserving spread to obtain a general characterization of a *compensated increase in risk*. They related this notion to the well-known Arrow–Pratt characterization of comparative risk aversion (see EXPECTED UTILITY HYPOTHESIS).

In addition, researchers such as Ekern (1980), Fishburn (1982), Fishburn and Vickson (1978), Hansen, Holt, and Peled (1978), Tesfatsion (1976), and Whitmore (1970) have extended the above work to the development of a general theory of *stochastic dominance*, which provides a whole sequence of similarly characterized partial orders on distributions, each presenting a corresponding set of equivalent conditions involving algebraic conditions on the distributions, types of spreads, and classes of utility functions which prefer (or are averse) to such spreads, etc. The comparative statics analysis presented above may be similarly extended to such characterizations (e.g. Machina, 1987). An extensive bibliography of the stochastic dominance literature is given in Bawa (1982). Finally, various extensions of the notions of increasing risk and stochastic dominance to the case of multivariate distributions may be found in Epstein and Tanny (1980), Fishburn and Vickson (1978), Huang, Kira and Vertinsky (1978), Lehmann (1955), Levhari, Parousch and Peleg (1975), Levy and Parousch (1974), Russell and Seo (1978), Sherman (1951), and Strassen (1965) (see also the mathematical results in Marshall and Olkin, 1979).

MARK J. MACHINA AND MICHAEL ROTHSCHILD

[Portions of this material are from Machina (1987) and appear with the permission of Cambridge University Press.]

See also EXPECTED UTILITY HYPOTHESIS; UNCERTAINTY.

BIBLIOGRAPHY

Anscombe, F. and Aumann, R. 1963. A definition of subjective probability. *Annals of Mathematical Statistics* 34, 199–205.

Arrow, K. 1964. The role of securities in the optimal allocation of risk-bearing. *Review of Economic Studies* 31, 91–6.

Bawa, V. 1982. Stochastic dominance: a research bibliography. *Management Science* 28, 698–712.

Borch, K. 1969. A note on uncertainty and indifference curves. *Review of Economic Studies* 36, 1–4.

Debreu, G. 1959. *Theory of Value: An Axiomatic Analysis of General Equilibrium*. New Haven: Yale University Press.

Diamond, P. and Stiglitz, J. 1974. Increases in risk and in risk aversion. *Journal of Economic Theory* 8, 337–360.

Ekern, S. 1980. Increasing n'th degree risk. *Economic Letters* 6, 329–33.

Epstein, L. and Tanny, S. 1980. Increasing generalized correlation: a definition and some economic consequences. *Canadian Journal of Economics* 13, 16–34.

Feldstein, M. 1969. Mean-variance analysis in the theory of liquidity preference and portfolio selection. *Review of Economic Studies* 36, 5–12.

Fishburn, P. 1982. Simplest cases of n'th degree stochastic dominance. *Operations Research Letters* 1, 89–90.

Fishburn, P. and Vickson, 1978. Theoretical foundations of stochastic dominance. In Whitmore and Findlay (1978).

Hadar, J. and Russell, W. 1969. Rules for ordering uncertain prospects. *American Economic Review* 59, 25–34.

Hanoch, G. and Levy, H. 1969. The efficiency analysis of choices involving risk. *Review of Economic Studies* 36, 335–46.

Hansen, L., Holt, C. and Peled, D. 1978. A note on first degree stochastic dominance. *Economics Letters* 1, 315–19.

Hicks, J. 1962. Liquidity. *Economic Journal* 72, 787–802.

Hirshleifer, J. 1965. Investment decision under uncertainty: choice-theoretic approaches, *Quarterly Journal of Economics* 79, 509–536.

Hirshleifer, J. 1966. Investment decision under uncertainty: applications of the state-preference approach. *Quarterly Journal of Economics* 80, 252–77

Huang, C., Kira, D. and Vertinsky, I. 1978. Stochastic dominance for multi-attribute utility functions. *Review of Economic Studies* 45, 611–16.

Karni, E. 1985. *Decision Making Under Uncertainty: The Case of State Dependent Preferences.* Cambridge, Mass.: Harvard University Press.

Knight, F. 1921. *Risk, Uncertainty and Profit.* Boston: Houghton Mifflin Co.

Lehmann, E. 1955. Ordered families of distributions. *Annals of Mathematical Statistics* 26, 399–419.

Levhari, D., Parousch, J. and Peleg, B. 1975. Efficiency analysis for multivariate distributions. *Review of Economic Studies* 42, 87–91.

Levy, H. and Parousch, J. 1974. Toward multivariate efficiency criteria. *Journal of Economic Theory* 7, 129–42.

Lintner, J. 1965. The valuation of risk assets and the selection of risky investments in stock portfolios and capital budgets. *Review of Economics and Statistics* 44, 243–69.

Machina, M. 1987. *The Economic Theory of Individual Behavior Toward Risk: Theory, Evidence and New Directions.* Cambridge: Cambridge University Press.

Markowitz, H. 1952. Portfolio selection. *Journal of Finance* 7, 77–91.

Markowitz, H. 1959. *Portfolio Selection: Efficient Diversification of Investment.* New Haven: Yale University Press.

Marshall, A. and Olkin, I. 1979. *Inequalities: Theory of Majorization and Its Applications.* New York: Academic Press.

Meyer, J. 1987. Two moment decision models and expected utility maximization. *American Economic Review.*

Mossin, J. 1966. Equilibrium in a capital asset market. *Econometrica* 34, 768–83.

Pratt, J. 1964. Risk aversion in the small and in the large. *Econometrica* 32, 122–36.

Pratt, J., Raiffa, H. and Schlaifer, R. 1964. The foundations of decision under uncertainty: an elementary exposition. *Journal of the American Statistical Association* 59, 353–75.

Raiffa, H. 1968. *Decision Analysis: Introductory Lectures on Choice Under Uncertainty.* Reading, Mass.: Addison-Wesley.

Rothschild, M. and Stiglitz, J. 1970. Increasing risk: I. A definition. *Journal of Economic Theory* 2, 225–43. Reprinted in Diamond and Rothschild (1978).

Rothschild, M. and Stiglitz, J. 1971. Increasing risk: II. Its economic consequences. *Journal of Economic Theory* 3, 66–84.

Rothschild, M. and Stiglitz, J. 1972. Addendum to 'Increasing risk: I. A definition'. *Journal of Economic Theory* 5, 306.

Russell, W. and Seo, T. 1978. Ordering uncertain prospects: the multivariate utility functions case. *Review of Economic Studies* 45, 605–11.

Samuelson, P. 1967. General proof that diversification pays. *Journal of Financial and Quantitative Analysis* 2, 1–13.

Savage, L. 1954. *The Foundations of Statistics.* New York: John Wiley and Sons. Revised and enlarged edition, New York: Dover Publications, 1972.

Sharpe, W. 1964. Capital asset prices: a theory of market equilibrium under conditions of risk. *Journal of Finance* 19, 425–42.

Sherman, S. 1951. On a theorem of Hardy, Littlewood, Polya, and Blackwell. *Proceedings of the National Academy of Sciences* 37, 826–31. (See also 'Errata', *Proceedings of the National Academy of Sciences* 38, 382.)

Strassen, V. 1965. The existence of probability measures with given marginals. *Annals of Mathematical Statistics* 36, 423–39.

Tesfatsion, L. 1976. Stochastic dominance and the maximization of expected utility. *Review of Economic Studies* 43, 301–15.

Tobin, J. 1958. Liquidity preference as behavior toward risk. *Review of Economic Studies* 25, 65–86.

Whitmore, G. 1970. Third-degree stochastic dominance. *American Economic Review* 60, 457–9.

Whitmore, G. and Findlay, M. 1978. *Stochastic Dominance: An Approach to Decision Making Under Risk.* Lexington, Mass.: Heath.

Yaari, M. 1969. Some remarks on measures of risk aversion and on their uses. *Journal of Economic Theory* 1, 315–29.

Rist, Charles (1874–1955). Born at Prilly, Switzerland, 1874; died at Versailles, 1955. Professor at Montpellier (1899–1912) and Paris (1913–33), Rist was the most notable and influential thinker and actor in the field of money in France in the first half of the 20th century. As a member of the *Comité des experts* (1926) and as a vice-governor of the Bank of France (1926–8), he took an active part in monetary reconstruction in the Twenties. He supported the novel idea of stabilization with devaluation (1926–8). He was also involved as an expert in monetary reforms in Rumania (1928), Austria, Turkey and Spain. He was France's delegate at the London Economic Conference (1933).

Although Rist is most widely known for his *History of Economic Doctrines*, written in cooperation with Charles Gide, his lasting claim to fame rests on his profound and consistent interpretation of monetary history and thought as demonstrated in his masterwork, *History of Monetary and Credit Theory*. Based on his first-hand experience in times of great instability, Rist's critical analysis of monetary thought from a long-run viewpoint provides an impressive perspective on the evolution of money. By emphasizing the 'store of value' function of money, and by postulating the inability of the State to safeguard it, Rist is critical of authors who supported some form of non-metallic currency, such as John Law, Smith, Ricardo, Wicksell, Knapp and Keynes. He is in sympathy with Cantillon, Galiani, Turgot, Thornton, Tooke and Walras. What he describes as the confusion between money and credit is to be dispelled by drawing a distinction between money proper (gold), credit instruments (convertible banknotes and deposits) and inconvertible paper money. In strong opposition to Keynesianism, Rist is a sceptic in regard of managed currencies and international agreements of the Bretton Wood type. Rist provides the key to the understanding of the French position in monetary matters as opposed to the typical Anglo-American stance in the past 60 years.

ROGER DEHEM

See also GIDE, CHARLES.

SELECTED WORKS

1915. (With Ch. Gide.) *A History of Economic Doctrines.* London: G. Harrap. 2nd edn, 1948.

1924. *La déflation en pratique.* Paris: Giard.

1933. *Essais sur quelques problèmes économiques et monétaires.* Paris: Sirey.

1940. *History of Monetary and Credit Theory from John Law to the Present Day.* London: Allen and Unwin.

1961. *The Triumph of Gold.* New York: Philosophical Library.

Robbins, Lionel Charles (1898–1984). Lionel Robbins, who in 1961 became Baron Robbins of Clare Market, was one of the major academic economists of the interwar period. He remained active after World War II but never really regained the centre of the stage that he had occupied. He was also a great public servant for his country, serving it well and loyally in many aspects of social, political and cultural life. He was truly a 'renaissance man'.

Robbins was born in 1898 in Middlesex, the son of Rowland Richard Robbins – for many years President of the National Farmers' Union – and Rosa Marion Robbins. He spent one year reading for an Arts degree at University College London and then volunteered for war service with the Royal Artillery. He saw active service on the Western Front, was wounded and invalided back to England in 1918. He was an undergraduate at the London School of Economics and Political Science from

1920 to 1923, from which he graduated with a B.Sc. (Econ.) degree, choosing political ideas as his major field of study, and having had the left-wing Harold Laski as his tutor. Beveridge employed him as a research assistant for a year, after which Robbins was a tutor in economics at New College, Oxford. He returned to teach economics at LSE from 1925 to 1927, then back to New College as Fellow (1928–9) and finally, at the incredibly young age of 31, back to the Senior Professorship in Economics at LSE to succeed Allyn Young.

Apart from government service during World War II, Robbins remained at LSE as Head of the Economics Department until 1960 when, on accepting the Chairmanship of the *Financial Times*, the University of London forced him to resign his professorship – a move than brought Robbins great personal distress, although he retained his connection with LSE and taught courses there until a year or so of his death in 1984.

Outside academic and government advisory activity, Robbins had a distinguished record in arts administration, being connected with both the National Gallery and the Royal Opera House, but he may perhaps be best remembered, in such 'outside' activities, for his contribution to the structure of higher education in the United Kingdom. He chaired the Committee – commonly referred to as the Robbins Committee on Higher Education – that proposed the criterion that all qualified applicants should receive a place, and financial support, to read for a degree. The acceptance of the 'Robbins Principle' led to a vast expansion of degree courses, especially in the social sciences in the 1960s and early 1970s in the UK.

Robbins's contributions to economics may be considered under four headings; economic theory, methodology and philosophy of economics, the theory of economic policy, and the history of economic thought.

Those who only knew Robbins later in his life often forget that he made his initial mark in economics as a theorist. Three contributions here are worth noting; he launched a sustained attack on Marshall's concept of the Representative Firm which was apparently so successful that it drove the concept out of the pages of microeconomic texts. Robbins basically argued that neither the understanding of the equilibrium of the firm nor of the industry was aided by introducing the Representative Firm, hence it should be eliminated from analysis. More recent work has shown a greater sympathy towards Marshall's construct and it seems clear now that Robbins failed to understand the exact dynamic problem that Marshall was trying to cope with and why the Representative Firm was an important contribution to this problem.

Robbins also pioneered the micro-analysis of the labour supply function. Although he did not explicitly use the division of a wage change into an income and substitution effect, he showed clearly why the sign on the response of hours to a real wage rate change would be ambiguous.

In macroeconomics Robbins was a firm exponent of the Austrian theory of the trade cycle and here he was greatly influenced by Frederick von Hayek, who he brought to LSE from Vienna in 1928. The central feature of the Austrian analysis was that depression was due primarily to under-saving (or excess consumption) and these views, which Robbins expounded as an explanation of the 1930s depression in his book *The Great Depression*, led to a head-on collision between the senior LSE economists and the Cambridge school centred around Keynes. This rift was not finally healed until the wartime collaboration in Whitehall between Robbins and Keynes. After the war in the Marshall Lectures for 1946, published as *The Economic Problem in Peach and War*, Robbins announced his conversion to full employment policies via control of aggregate demand, although it is not clear that he became a Keynesian.

The second area where Robbins made a major contribution and where he wrote what is probably his best known work in economics, was that of the methodology and philosophy of economics. His *Nature and Significance of Economic Science* was one of the most cited, if not most read, books on the subject in the period 1932–60, and it influenced greatly economists' views about the nature of their discipline. There are several strands to the book, none original in themselves but Robbins put them together in beautifully clear prose and in a very persuasive manner. The major themes were; first, that economic science could be clearly demarcated from those discussions of economic issues that involved value judgements – by which latter term Robbins meant evaluative statements of the form 'better or worse' where inter-personal comparisons of utility were involved. He also argued that there was a clear demarcation between economic science and other branches of social enquiry such as social psychology, sociology, politics and so on.

The second major theme was that the subject matter of economic science was not a particular activity (for example, Cannan's view that economics was the science of wealth), but rather an aspect of all human conduct. This aspect was the 'fact' of economic scarcity – a manifestation of unlimited ends on the part of individuals and society and means of satisfying those ends that were limited in supply. In words so often quoted in economics texts Robbins defined economic science as 'that science that studies the relationship between ends and means that have alternative uses' – a definition that is more than reminiscent of Menger's exposition of the economizing process.

These two aspects of the *Nature and Significance* were widely accepted by the world of academic economists and are still propagated. But they have always had their critics; in particular, the view that there is a body of scientific economics 'free from value' is much disputed.

The third aspect of the book – Robbins's views on the procedures for checking the validity of economic theory – was less fortunate in its effect on the development of the subject. Robbins appeared to argue that the central propositions of economics were derived from very basic, and obvious, assumptions and a process of logical deduction from these assumptions. Moreover, these deductions gave essentially qualitative predictions. Robbins expressed great scepticism about the feasibility and meaningfulness of quantitative work in economics, and by the implication of his message inhibited the development of econometric testing in economics.

Robbins's contribution to discussions of economic policy were basically consistent throughout his career, although the purity of his earlier thoughts was muddled as he grew older. His major policy theme was his advocacy of, what may be loosely termed, economic liberalism. Robbins decreasingly argued this on the grounds of some alleged theoretical or *a priori* superiority of market solutions over collectivist or interventionist plans, but rather as an empirical point that the liberal solution seemed best to combine liberty and efficiency. In his earlier writings, for example *The Economic Causes of War* (1939a) and *The Economic Basis of Class Conflict* (1939b) he adopted an extreme free trade position and it was this stance as much as macro-theory debate that lead to his conflict with Keynes in the 1930s. His later work revealed a much greater readiness to allow *ad hoc* exceptions to strict economic liberalism – he espoused, among other measures, the Beveridge plan, grants for higher education, subsidies for the arts, control of the exports of works of art, overall macro-control for full employment. Probably the most rounded statement of his policy beliefs is to be found in his *Economic Problem in Peace and War*.

Finally, mention must be made of Lionel Robbins's contribution to the teaching and study of the history of economic thought. He, together with one or two other scholars of his generation – like his great friend, Jacob Viner – kept interest in the subject alive and flourishing when many economists regarded it, as they still do, as irrelevant to their studies. Much of his influence came via his masterly teaching of the subject and via the important theses that were produced under his supervision, as much as from his own specific contributions. He also aided the production of important series in the history of economic thought such as the LSE reprints and the collected works of Bentham and J.S. Mill.

Of his specific contributions, two are minor classics, his *Theory of Economic Policy in Classical Political Economy* (1952) and *Robert Torrens and the Evolution of Classical Economics* (1958). In the former work, Robbins argued very persuasively, if not entirely convincingly, that the British Classical economists did not adhere to the continental *laissez-faire* dogma but rather argued for freedom in economic relationships as a general principle with many *ad hoc* exceptions. He further tried to clear them of any anti-working class bias.

The book on Torrens is a perfect example of how to survey the collected works of a writer who, though not of the first rank of classical economists, is nonetheless a useful writer by whom to assess the general achievement of the classical school.

B.A. CORRY

See also VALUE JUDGEMENTS.

SELECTED WORKS

1932. *An Essay on the Nature and Significance of Economic Science*. London: Macmillan.
1934. *The Great Depression*. London: Macmillan.
1937. *Economic Planning and International Order*. London: Macmillan.
1939a. *The Economic Basis of Class Conflict*. London: Macmillan.
1939b. *The Economic Causes of War*. London: Jonathan Cape.
1947. *The Economic Problem in Peace and War*. London: Macmillan.
1952. *The Theory of Economic Policy in English Classical Political Economy*. London: Macmillan.
1958. *Robert Torrens and the Evolution of Classical Economics*. London: Macmillan.
1971. *Autobiography of an Economist*. London: Macmillan.

Robertson, Dennis (1890–1963). Dennis Robertson was born in 1890, the son of a clergyman and schoolmaster, and was educated at Eton and Trinity College, Cambridge. After taking a Part I in Classics and Part II in Economics he was elected a Fellow of Trinity College in 1914 and in 1930 became a Reader in the University of Cambridge. He left Cambridge in 1938 to become a Professor in the University of London but during most of his time in that post he was seconded to the Treasury on war-related work. Elected in 1944 to succeed Pigou in the Chair of Political Economy he returned to the University of Cambridge, holding that position until his retirement in 1957. He died in Cambridge in 1963.

Economics in Cambridge when Robertson commenced working at it was dominated by Marshall. Not by the man himself (although still alive he had retired in 1908) but by his analytical methods and by his *Principles of Economics*. It was quite natural that the topic selected by Robertson for his fellowship dissertation should involve a 'Marshallian' approach to a subject on which Marshall himself had written relatively little: the nature and causes of fluctuations in the general level of economic activity. As Robertson recorded in the introduction to the published version of this dissertation:

> In some of the more abstract portions of this essay I shall make use, without further explanation or apology, of the processes and terminology in common use among the school of economic thought associated in this country chiefly with the name of Dr Marshall. My reason is that after a study of many facts and theories I am deliberately of the opinion that one cause of the obscurity which still surrounds this problem is that in the attack upon it full and systematic use has never hitherto been made of the weapons supplied by this particular intellectual armoury (1915, p. 11).

Although Robertson did not suspect it then, the refinement and further development of the ideas about cycles and growth in economic activity presented in this study were to occupy him for the next twenty years. Two different sorts of factors led him in this direction. The first was the need to develop a framework for designing an organised policy response to the large-scale dislocation of economic life which had followed the end of World War I, while the second was a more specific, personal, influence. In the early 1920s Keynes commissioned him to write an introductory textbook (in the Cambridge Economic Handbook series) to be entitled, simply, 'Money'. The difficulties he encountered in attempting to provide an elementary account of monetary theory made Robertson particularly aware that, even in its more sophisticated variants, existing theoretical work provided an inadequate basis for dealing with the economic problems of the 1920s. The combined influence of these two resulted in a prolonged period of reflection and research, yielding a series of loosely related publications which recorded the development of a fairly comprehensive analytical scheme interrelating the problems of money, the trade cycle, economic growth, and the role of the state in promoting economic progress.

Robertson's approach to this analysis involved the development of successively more complicated, more 'realistic' models of economies each of which constituted a different, abstract, 'type'. All 'types' shared the characteristics that production was undertaken on the basis of 'rational' decision-making by competing producer 'groups', each making different products with a fixed labour force and a productive process involving fixed capital. Now although each type of economy was both a *production* and an *exchange* economy it was the possibility that these activities could be 'organized' in different ways that distinguished the different types. Production could be organized in two ways, cooperatively or non-cooperatively, while exchange could also be organized in two ways, direct exchange or monetary exchange. In total there were, then, four types of economies. The distinction between the two types of productive organization turned on the decision-making functions of the members of the groups: in a cooperative group decisions were *made* and *carried out* by the group members acting together, while in a non-cooperative group 'entrepreneurs' made decisions and 'workers' carried them out. In respect of the organisation of exchange it was on the existence and use of money that the distinction rested, in one case exchange was carried out by 'direct barter', while in the other, money supplied through a (potentially) government-controlled banking system provided the means of exchange.

Robertson's basic analytical building block was the 'cooperative non-monetary economy', an economy where each competing industrial group made its employment and, thus, output decision cooperatively, and exchanged its output without the use of money. Although in such an economy no distinction was made between the members of the group, a distinction was made between two different categories of producer groups, those providing consumer goods and those producing capital goods. The first group, consumer goods producers exchanged some of their output with the second group for capital goods, thereby providing consumption goods for capital goods producers. Now an economy of this type, Robertson argued, would experience cyclical fluctuations in aggregate output deriving from the effect of gestation lags on the time pattern of the supply of capital goods and of the durability of capital goods on the time-pattern of demand for their replacement.

A non-cooperative non-monetary economy would, though, experience fluctuations of even greater severity than those felt in an otherwise identical cooperative economy. This proposition derived directly from the fact that in a non-cooperative economy production decisions were taken by entrepreneurs who hired workers to carry them out, and workers and entrepreneurs had differing 'interests'. These divergent interests were reflected most importantly in the different utility attached to leisure by the two classes. An entrepreneur, for example, would wish to expand output further in the boom and contract it further in the slump than the workers in his group; and since entrepreneurs were in control, their interests prevailed. Although the degree of fluctuation in the non-cooperative economy was more pronounced than in the cooperative, Robertson adopted it as the benchmark which defined the 'appropriate' degree of fluctuation to be aimed at by policy-makers concerned with stabilization. He did so because he maintained that the failure to recognize that production was, in practice, organized non-cooperatively could lead to an attempt to reduce fluctuations too much. Such attempts, by altering the structure of incentives, could damage the longer-run growth possibilities of the economy.

The cooperative monetary economy construct was built directly on to the foundations provided by the cooperative non-monetary economy and this type of economy exhibited, therefore, a cyclical pattern in the production of fixed capital which generated cyclical fluctuations in output as a whole. Now the introduction of money also required a slight change of focus, since in the monetary case Robertson concentrated not on fixed capital but on the demand for circulating capital, essentially on the demand for consumption goods which were consumed by those engaged in the process of production. This concern with circulating capital was necessarily associated with the analysis of monetary economies because Robertson made the assumption (reflecting British banking practice) that it was with the finance of the acquisition of circulating capital that the banking system was concerned. His analysis then described the policies which, if adopted by the banking system, would lead to fluctuations being of no greater amplitude than in the corresponding non-monetary economy. A failure to implement such policies would lead to fluctuations in the price-level, and thus in output, of greater magnitude than was 'appropriate'.

The difference made by the substitution of cooperation in the monetary type turned principally on the effect on decision-making of changes in income distribution. In particular, it was assumed that only entrepreneurial incomes adjusted quickly to changes in the price-level, so that variations in the price-level over the cycle were an additional source of influence on production decisions. The nature of this influence led entrepreneurs to expand their activities further in the boom (as rising rices increased their profits) and contract them further in the slump (as falling prices reduced their profits) than would have been the case in the corresponding cooperative economy. But these changes in income distribution were not permanent. In the course of the boom workers managed to restore real wages to pre-recovery levels, the expansion of output would be slowed, and in the slump, as entrepreneurs restored profits to their pre-depression levels, the contraction of output would be slowed. The end of the boom and the slump, though, if an 'appropriate' monetary policy were adopted, would be dictated by the behaviour of the underlying non-cooperative non-monetary economy. So non-cooperation in the monetary case had additional effects only on the amplitude of cyclical fluctuations.

Robertson also developed a set of tools to analyse the process of cyclical change in monetary economies. He divided time up into a sequence of market periods (during each of which the supply of goods was fixed) and then focussed on the dynamics of the transfer of resources from current consumption by those already in employment to those newly employed to increase output during the expansion phase of the cycle. The mechanism generating this transfer was a price-level increase as the newly employed (whose wages had been borrowed from the banking system) outbid the existing employed on the goods market. Robertson's aim was to show how the magnitude of the price-level increase was determined and the nature of the monetary policies which could be adopted in order to minimize it. The rate of inflation was shown to depend upon the relationship between the rate at which the banking system made new loans to producers, and the rate at which this new money was absorbed into the money-holdings of the existing employed. The faster the new money was absorbed, that is the faster that the existing employed gave up their claims on current output, the smaller the rise in the price-level accompanying the transfer of resources from the public to the expanding producers. To the extent that this money was not immediately absorbed, the existing employed were *forced* to share current output with those producers by price-level changes. By minimizing these changes, then, the monetary authority through its control of the banking system would also be able to minimize the amount of 'forced' saving which accompanied the recovery. A similar approach was also applied to the non-cooperative case, but here policy design was more difficult because the inflation led to changes in the distribution of income between workers and entrepreneurs. Even so, monetary policy could play a useful role in reducing fluctuations to their 'irreducible' non-monetary amplitude.

The central concern of Robertson's analytical work was to provide an explanation of fluctuations in aggregate activity which was closely linked to a broader concern, that of remedying the adverse effects of such fluctuations. The identification of the use of capitalistic (though not necessarily capitalist) production methods as the source of fluctuations, though, left with a rather ambivalent attitude to possible remedies: capitalistic production methods always produced cycles, but also brought with them the possibility of economic progress. And he thought that there was a trade-off between these two, greater stability being associated with slower growth, less stability with faster growth:

> From some points of view the whole cycle of industrial change presents the appearance of a perpetual immolation of the present upon the altar of the future. During the boom sacrifices are made out of all proportion to the enjoyment over which they will ultimately give command: during the depression enjoyment is denied lest it should

> debar the possibility of making fresh sacrifices. Out of the welter of industrial dislocation the great permanent riches of the future are generated (1926, p. 254).

He concluded that the choice between these two conflicting goals was ultimately a question of: 'ethics, rather than economics'.

The theoretical framework sketched above had emerged by the early 1930s. But its further development was interrupted by the publication in 1936 of Keynes's *General Theory of Employment, Interest and Money*. Robertson's response to this book was to examine how the *General Theory* might affect his vision of how the world worked. The central issue for Robertson was Whether Keynes had provided a more satisfactory explanation than he had himself of the forces which determined the behaviour of the trend rate of growth of economic activity. The distinguishing feature of Keynes's approach identified by Robertson was in the treatment of the theory of the rate of interest. He interpreted as Keynes's central proposition the contention that there was an inherent tendency for the rate of interest to remain above the level consistent with the maintenance of full employment. And although Robertson was prepared to accept that an argument could, in principle, be made out along such lines he did not accept that Keynes had succeeded in doing so. In particular he maintained that while 'liquidity preference' might make the interest rate 'sticky' in the short period, with its downward movement resistent to monetary expansion, he rejected such an approach to the long period theory of interest rate determination, summarizing the argument in the following way:

> ... the rate of interest is what it is because it is expected to become other than it is; if it is not expected to become other than it is, there is nothing left to tell us why it is what it is. The organ which secretes it has been amputated, and yet it somehow still exists – a grin without a cat ('Mr Keynes and the Rate of Interest' in *Essays in Monetary Theory*, 1940, p. 36).

Keynes's theoretical argument was, therefore, flawed. And the associated case for stabilising the economy at a level other than that identified in Robertson's own analysis as 'appropriate' was consequently not proven.

The first repercussion of this reaction to the *General Theory* was an estrangement between Robertson and Keynes, virtually ending a close friendship which had lasted for more than twenty years (Robertson having been a student of Keynes, then a fellow teacher and collaborator in research). It then motivated Robertson's decision to leave Cambridge for London in 1938. Moreover, even after Keynes's death in 1946, strained and difficult relations with Keynes's disciples in Cambridge left him a somewhat isolated figure. The impact of Keynes's *General Theory* on Robertson's professional life was no less significant, the whole terrain of the area in which he worked was changed: from being on the creative frontier of the subject he felt himself forced into the role of commentator and critic. In the years after 1936 he wrote almost nothing new in what had been his specialist field. An explanation was provided in a letter to a friendly reviewer of one of his collections of essays who had called upon Robertson to prepare a monograph combining and extending his earlier analytical work, and to whom he wrote:

> ... I'm afraid there is no chance of my responding to your challenge and trying to produce a full length synthetic Theory of Money or Fluctuations or What-you-will. I'm too old and too lazy! But even if I were younger and less lazy, I think history had made it impossible. I believe that once Keynes had made up his mind to go the way he did it was my particular function to ... [elucidate and criticise the details of his work] ... and to go on pegging away at them (as is still necessary). It will not be easy for *anyone* for another twenty years to produce a positive and constructive work which is not in large measure a commentary on Keynes, – that is the measure of his triumph. For me, it would now be psychologically impossible, and the attempt is not worth making. (Private letter of D.H. Robertson to T.J. Wilson, 31 October 1953).

M. Anyadike Danes

SELECTED WORKS

1915. *A Study of Industrial Fluctuation*. London: P.S. King & Son. Reprinted with a new introduction, in Reprints of Scarce Works on Political Economy, London: London School of Economics and Political Science, 1948.

1922. *Money*. (Cambridge Economic Handbook). London: Bisbet & Co. Revised edn, 1924; new edn, 1948.

1923. *The Control of Industry*. (Cambridge Economic Handbook), London: Nisbet & Co. Revised edn, 1928; new edn (with S.R. Dennison), 1960.

1926. *Banking Policy and the Price Level*. London: P.S. King & Son. Reprinted, 1926; reprinted with revisions, 1932; reprinted in the United States of America with a new preface, New York: Augustus M. Kelley, 1949.

1931a. *Economic Fragments*. London: P.S. King & Son.

1931b. (With A.C. Pigou.) *Economic Essays and Addresses* London: P.S. King & Son.

1940. *Essays in Monetary Theory*. London: P.S. King & Son.

1950. *Utility and All That*. London: George Allen & Unwin.

1956. *Economic Commentaries*. London: Staples Press.

1957–9. *Lectures on Economic Principles*. 3 vols, London: Staples Press. Paperback edn in one volume, London: Fontana, 1963.

1960. *Growth, Wages, Money* (The Marshall Lectures at the University of Cambridge). London: Cambridge University Press.

Robinson, Abraham (1918–1974). A logician, mathematician and applied mathematician, Abraham Robinson was one of the foremost proponents of applying the methods and results of mathematical logic, in particular model theory to mathematics. This point of view led Abraham Robinson around 1960 to the creation of Non-standard Analysis.

Today, under the general term 'Non-standard Analysis' mathematicians understand the study of mathematical structures with the use of their non-standard models. Non-standard models of mathematical structures are proper extensions of such structures that are also models of the properties of the original structure which can be expressed in terms of formulas of a formal language chosen in advance.

Although in a formal sense non-standard models of a mathematical structure share the same properties with the given structure as far as they are expressible in terms of the formulas of a formal language. The main advantage of using them is that such models, being proper extensions, contain entities that may be considered as ideal mathematical objects of the given structure whose potential existence can only be predicted in the original structure. In this sense, non-standard analysis follows very closely the traditional philosophy and method of mathematics of creating new mathematical entities by means of extensions such as, for instance, the real numbers arise from the counting numbers via algebraic extensions.

In the calculus, non-standard models of the real number system are totally ordered field extensions of the field of real numbers of a special nature in that, in a precise formal sense, these field extensions also have the same properties as the real number system. Being proper extensions, however, they contain entities which can be viewed as playing the role of the intuitively introduced infinitely small numbers by the original founders of the calculus. This original discovery of Robinson around 1960 not only generated the development of the use of non-standard models in mathematics and applied mathematics but also solved the three-century-old problem of Gottfied Wilhelm Leibniz of providing a rigorous foundation of the calculus with the use of infinitely small as well as infinitely large numbers.

Abraham Robinson was born in Waldenburg, Lower Silesia, on 16 October 1918. He was the second son of Abraham Robinsohn and Hedwig Lotte Robinsohn, born Bähr. The father was an active zionist and private secretary to David Wolffsohn, leader of the Zionist World Organization, and the family lived in Cologne. He died very shortly before Abraham's birth upon which the family moved to Waldenburg in Lower Silesia to live with Mrs Robinsohn's family. The first seven years of his life were spent in Waldenburg.

In 1925 the Robinsohn family moved to Breslau where Abraham entered a private school headed by Rabbi Simonson. The only brother of his father, Dr Isaac Robinsohn – a prominent physician and head of the Rothschild Hospital in Vienna specializing in radiology, who served as the guardian of the two brothers – had a profound influence on the young Abraham.

After the national elections in Germany on 5 March 1933 which brought Hitler to power, Mrs Robinsohn made plans to leave for Palestine, where the family arrived at Haifa on 9 April of that year. The family settled in Tel-Aviv, where the two brothers entered high school. In 1936, Abraham took up his university studies at the Hebrew University in Jerusalem. The lectures of Abraham Fraenkel introduced him to mathematical logic and set theory. After a few years Fraenkel declared that there was nothing more he could teach his promising student. In 1939, Abraham won a scholarship to the Sorbonne and arrived in France at the start of World War II. In June 1940 he fled to England where he joined the Free French Air Force, after an attempt to join the British Forces, and left it in June 1942 to become a Scientific Officer in the Ministry of Aircraft Production, with an assignment to the Royal Aircraft Establishment at Farnborough.

All through the war years Abraham continued his research in logic and mathematics and published various papers. The work at Farnborough generated his interest in applied mathematics which led to a number of important and lasting contributions to aerodynamics. Also during these years he met his wife Renée Koppel, a refugee from Vienna.

His PhD thesis of 1949, written under the direction of Professor P. Dienes of Birkbeck College, London, was entitled 'The Metamathematics of Algebraic Systems' and constituted a major breakthrough in applying model theory to algebraic structures. In 1951, Robinson became Associate Professor of Applied Mathematics at the University of Toronto, and in 1958 was promoted to Professor and Chairman of the Department of Applied Mathematics. In these years he continued his research not only in aerodynamics but above all in his most cherished field of mathematical logic, model theory. In 1957 he became chairman of the Department of Mathematics of the Hebrew University in Jerusalem.

After five years in Jerusalem he moved to the University of California at Los Angeles, and in the fall of 1967 to Yale University, where he died prematurely at the age of 56 on 11 April 1974. He is buried on a hillside in Har Menuchot Cemetery near Jerusalem.

During his years at Yale, Robinson came into contact with mathematical economics. He discovered soon that the ideas of non-standard analysis could be fruitfully applied to various problems in mathematical economics. Jointly with Donald Brown, he successfully analysed large exchange economies and Edgeworth's conjecture with the use of non-standard analysis.

W.A.J. Luxemburg

SELECTED WORKS

1979. *Selected Papers of Abraham Robinson with a Biography by George B. Seligman*. Vol. 1: *Model Theory and Algebra*; Vol. 2: *Nonstandard Analysis and Philosophy*; Vol. 3: *Aeronautics*. Ed. H.J. Keisler, S. Körner, W.A.J. Luxemburg and A.D. Young, New Haven and London: Yale University Press.

Robinson, Edward Austin Gossage (born 1897). Austin Robinson was educated at Marlborough College and Christ's College, Cambridge. During World War I he served as a pilot in the RNAS and the RAF. After finishing his studies at Cambridge he became a Fellow of Corpus Christi College, from 1923 to 1926. In 1926 he married Joan, daughter of Major-General Sir Frederick Maurice and later to become the eminent economist. From 1926 to 1928 Robinson was tutor to the Maharaja of Gwalior. He returned to Cambridge as a university lecturer in economics in 1929, and from then on was an important figure on the Cambridge economics scene. He became Professor of Economics in 1950. He retired in 1965 (and it so happened that Joan Robinson was appointed to his chair). After his retirement, he continued to play a prominent role in Cambridge economics, as well as on the national and international scene.

Austin Robinson's first book, *The Structure of Competitive Industry* (1931), established his reputation as an economist. This seminal work drew on Alfred Marshall's writings on industry, and considered in detail the problems involved in determining the optimum size of firm. But although it emphasized the importance of scale, and inspired much of the later empirical work in this area, it also recognized that low British productivity in manufacturing industry was not primarily the consequence of scale, but of attitudes towards work and competition. All subsequent writing on this subject owed a considerable debt to Robinson. He followed up his work on competitive industry with a book on *Monopoly* (1941), as well as with a number of articles, including work on Africa. He was a member of the group surrounding Keynes when he was formulating the *General Theory*, and wrote a review of it in *The Economist*, insisting on signing it (against the traditions of the paper) because of the exceptionally controversial nature of the subject.

Robinson's long association with the *Economic Journal* began in 1934, as Assistant Editor to Keynes, and was later to be followed by much editorial work. Robinson did distinguished service during the war. He was a member of the Economic Section, War Cabinet Office, from 1939 to 1942, and from 1942 to 1945 was Economic Adviser and Head of Programmes Division, Ministry of Production. This was followed by a period as Economic Adviser to the Board of Trade. He returned to Cambridge in 1946, but served a further period in government on the Economic Planning Staff from 1945 to 1947. He was joint editor of the *Economic Journal* from 1944 to 1970, and played a leading role in the profession in other ways, holding a number of important posts, including that of managing editor of the Royal Economic Society's edition of Keynes's works. He was much involved in the work of the new International Economic Association: he was President from 1959 to 1962 and editor of its publications for many years. A good deal of his subsequent writing and editorial work, much of it on the problems of developing countries, was carried out in the context of the work of the IEA.

Austin Robinson's career has been a remarkable one. He has combined writing, teaching, editorial work and administration with advising governments in both the developed and developing world. He has played a leading role in the economics profession for an exceptionally long period, internationally as well as in Britain, and has done so throughout with much distinction.

Z.A. SILBERSTON

See also ROYAL ECONOMIC SOCIETY.

SELECTED WORKS

1931. *The Structure of Competitive Industry*. London: Nisbet & Co.; Cambridge: Cambridge University Press.

1941. *Monopoly*. London: Nisbet & Co.; Cambridge: Cambridge University Press.

Robinson, Joan Violet (1903–1983). Joan Robinson (née Maurice) was born at Camberley, Surrey, on 31 October 1903. She died in Cambridge on 5 August 1983.

She is the only woman (with the possible, but controversial, exception of Rosa Luxemburg) among the great economists. In 1975, which was proclaimed Woman's Year, most economists in the United States expected that she would naturally be chosen for the Nobel Memorial Prize in Economics for that year. She had received triumphant acclaim, as a Special Ely Lecturer, at the American Economic Association annual meeting three years earlier, in spite of the harsh hostility that her theories had always met in the United States. The American magazine *Business Week*, after sounding out the American economics profession, felt so sure of the choice as to anticipate the event by publishing a long article on her, presenting her explicitly as being 'on everyone's list for this year's Nobel Prize in Economics'. But the Swedish Royal Academy missed that opportunity (and alas, never regained it). Ever since, in shoptalk among economists all over the world, Joan Robinson has become the greatest Nobel Prize winner that never was.

BASIC BIOGRAPHY. Joan Robinson was the daughter of Major General Sir Frederick Maurice and of Helen Marsh (who was herself the daughter of a Professor of Surgery and Master of Downing College, Cambridge). Sir Frederick pursued a brilliant career in the British army, but in 1918 he found himself at the centre of a public debate, and he gave up his army career on a point of principle. This was very much in the family tradition. Sir Frederick's grandfather – Joan Robinson's great-grandfather – was Frederick Denison Maurice, the Christian Socialist who lost his chair of Theology at King's College, London, for his refusal to believe in eternal damnation.

Joan Robinson certainly had many of these traits: toughness and endurance of character, nonconformism and unorthodoxy of views, the absence of any reverential feeling or timidity, even in the face of the world's celebrities, a passionate longing for the new and the unknown.

She was educated at St Paul's Girls' School in London. (Curiously enough, Richard Kahn was educated in the boys' section of the same school.) In October 1922, she was admitted to the University of Cambridge, going up to Girton College, where she read economics at a time when the dominant figures in Cambridge were Marshall and Pigou. Marshall had retired (he died in 1924) but was extremely influential not only in Cambridge but in the whole of the British Isles. Pigou, his favourite pupil and chosen successor, was the Professor of Political Economy, at whose lectures Cambridge students absorbed the official *verbum* of Marshallian economics. Keynes was a sort of outsider, part-time in Cambridge and part-time in London, always involved with government policies, either at the Treasury or in public opposition. In those days he lectured on strictly orthodox monetary theory and policies. His lectures were not given regularly but were well attended.

The intellectual environment must have appeared solidly traditional. Joan graduated in 1925, as a good girl would: with second class honours.

In the following year (1926), she married E.A.G. Robinson (later Professor Sir Austin Robinson), who was six years her senior and at the time a junior Fellow of Corpus Christi College. Together they left Cambridge and set off for India, where they stayed for two years. Austin Robinson served as Tutor of the Maharajah of Gwalior. Joan was there as Austin's wife but did some teaching at the local school. When they returned, after their two-year Indian engagement, Austin Robinson took a permanent post as Lecturer in Economics at Cambridge, where they settled for life. They had two daughters.

It was on the return to Cambridge from India (summer 1928) that Joan Robinson began to do some College supervision of undergraduates, and then to do economics research in earnest. The Cambridge intellectual environment had changed dramatically. After Edgeworth's death (1926), Keynes became the sole editor of the *Economic Journal* and was engaged on his *Treatise on Money* (Keynes, 1930). Most of all, he had brought to Cambridge Piero Sraffa, the young Italian economist who had dared to launch a scathing attack on Marshallian economics (Sraffa, 1926). Moreover, some new stars were rising in the firmament of Keynes's *entourage* – Frank Ramsey, the brilliant mathematician; Ludwig Wittgenstein, the Austrian philosopher whom Keynes persuaded to come to Cambridge; and Richard Kahn, Keynes's favourite pupil. It was with Richard Kahn that Joan Robinson began an intense intellectual partnership that lasted for her whole life.

On a strictly academic level, Joan Robinson slowly ascended the academic ladder: Junior Assistant Lecturer in 1931, Full Lecturer in 1937, Reader in 1949. It was suggested in Cambridge that the fact that her husband was in the same faculty kept her back at all stages of her academic career. She became full professor only on Austin Robinson's retirement, in 1965. Her association with the Cambridge Colleges was more irregular. But she was, in succession, a Fellow of Girton College and of Newnham College. Yet whatever the formal position in the Faculty or in the Cambridge colleges, she was for years one of the major attractions in Cambridge for many generations of undergraduates, not only in economics. In the post-war period, she was certainly the best-known member of the Cambridge Economics Faculty abroad. An indefatigable traveller, she did not limit her foreign visits to universities; she also wanted to know local customs and local conditions of life, even far away from urban centres. Her strong constitution and temperamental toughness helped her enormously. A friend from Makerere University, who took her, when she was already in her seventies, on a month's travel in tribal Africa was amazed at how much she could endure in terms of living in most primitive conditions with raw food, lack of facilities and exposure to harsh tropical weather, day and night.

It would be impossible to list here all the places she visited or the talks, seminars and public lectures she gave all over the world. She rarely stayed in Cambridge during the summer or term vacations or during her sabbatical years, though punctually and punctiliously returning there on the eve of the terms of her teaching. Asia was her favourite continent (especially India and China). But hundreds of students in North and South America, Australia, Africa and Europe also knew her at first hand.

In Cambridge she rarely missed her classes, lectures and seminars and she was a regular attendant of other people's seminars, especially visitors', never avoiding discussion and confrontation. Professor Pigou – a well-known misogynist – had included her in his category of 'honorary men'.

She was extremely popular with the students – a clear, brilliant, stimulating teacher. She was a person who inspired strong feelings – of love and hate. Her opponents were frightened by her, and her friends really admired, almost worshipped her. Her nonconformism in everyday life and even in her clothing (most of which she bought in India) was renowned.

She retired from her professorship in Cambridge on 30 September 1971. On retirement she did not agree to continue lecturing in Cambridge. (Later on, in the late 1970s, she gave in partially, giving a course of lectures on 'the Cambridge tradition'.) But her writing and lecturing abroad, at the invitation of economics faculties and students all over the world, continued unabated.

When, in the late 1970s, King's College (Keynes's College) finally dropped the traditional anachronistic ban on women and became co-educational, Joan Robinson, upon an enthusiastic and unanimous proposal by all economists of the College, became the first woman to be made an Honorary Fellow of King's College. (She had earlier become an Honorary Fellow of Girton College and of Newnham College.)

Towards the end of her life, she became very concerned and disappointed with the direction in which economic theory had turned and with the ease with which the younger economists could bend their elegant models to suit the new conservative moods and the selfish economic policies of politicians and governments. Her friends also noticed a sort of stiffening rigidity in her views that had not appeared before. This was unfortunate, as it contributed to increasing the hostility of her opponents towards her.

She suffered a stroke in early February 1983, from which she never recovered. She lay for a few months in a Cambridge hospital, and died peacefully six months later.

DISTINCTIVE TRAITS OF HER INTELLECTUAL PERSONALITY. In order to understand better the nature of Joan Robinson's contributions to economic theory, it may be helpful to begin by considering explicitly a few characteristic traits of her intellectual personality.

Joan Robinson had a remarkable analytical ability. Since she did not normally use mathematics, this remarkable intellectual ability was of a nature that defies conventional description. In her early works she made use of geometrical representations, backed up by calculus (normally provided by Richard Kahn). In her mature works, her way of reasoning took up a more personal feature. Her style is difficult to imitate (as when she invites the readers to follow her in the construction of economic exercises) but very effective. The results are always impressive. Those who used to argue with her knew that she could grasp and keep in the back of her mind (to be brought out at the appropriate moment) a whole series of chain effects and interdependences which her interlocutors could hardly imagine.

She was not the type of person who could go on thinking in isolation. The way she could best express herself was by having somebody in constant confrontation. She could put her views best either in opposition or in support of somebody else's position. This made her extraordinarily open to concepts and contributions coming from the people she encountered. The accurate historian of economic ideas will probably find in her works traces of almost every person she met. It is therefore important, in considering Joan Robinson's contributions, to keep in mind at least the most important economists who influenced her. These include her teachers (Marshall through Pigou, Keynes, Shove), her contemporaries (Sraffa, Kaldor, and Kalecki, through whom she went back to Marx, but especially Richard Kahn, who read, criticized and improved every single one of her works) and also a whole series of other (younger) people – pupils and students.

This raises the question of her originality. The prefaces to her books are packed with acknowledgements, sometimes heavy acknowledgements – consider, for example, the following excerpt from the *Economics of Imperfect Competition*:

> ... this book contains some matter which I believe to be new. Of not all the new ideas, however, can I definitely say that 'this is my own invention'. I particularly have had the constant assistance of Mr R.F. Kahn ... many of the major problems ... were solved as much by him as by me (Robinson, 1933, p. v).

But one must remember what has been said above. In fact, Joan Robinson was a highly original thinker, but of a particular type. Besides the contributions to economic theory that are distinctly hers she had her own highly original way, even in small details, of presenting other authors' views, which she always did through a distinctly personal re-elaboration. Sometimes the re-elaboration is so personal as to sound parochial. But this trait is not exclusive to Joan Robinson. Cambridge parochialism is shared by almost all purely Cambridge-bred economists since Marshall (Keynes included). It sometimes creates unnecessary difficulties of communication with economists outside Cambridge (i.e. with the overwhelming majority!) or introduces a few odd notes into an otherwise impeccable performance.

One can clearly detect an evolution in Joan Robinson's approach to economics that with age strengthened her innovative tendencies. It looks as if she was very cautious in her early years, preoccupied at first with building up solid analytical foundations. But as soon as she felt sure of her analytical equipment, she began to venture more and more into the exciting field of innovation. In her mature works her typical style became established. A sort of mixture of educational, temperamental and intellectual factors made her one of the leading unorthodox economists of the 20th century. Always impatient with dogmas, constantly fighting for new unorthodox ideas, relentlessly attacking established beliefs, she acquired a sort of vocation to economic heresies (see Robinson, 1971). Her attitude reminds one of a dictum by Pietro Pomponazzi, the Italian Renaissance philosopher: 'It is better to be a heretic if one wishes to find the truth.'

Strongly related to this attitude is the social message that comes from her writings. Her 'box of tools' and her logical chain of arguments were not proposed for their own sake; they were always aimed at practical action, with a view to the world's most pressing problems – unemployment before the war, underdevelopment and the struggle of ex-colonial nations after the war (very noticeable is her special concern for Asia and her enthusiasm, at points rather naive, for Communist China). Consistently, she has been among the strongest assertors – second perhaps only to Gunnar Myrdal – of the non-neutrality of economic science and of the necessity of stating explicitly one's convictions and beliefs.

And yet, in spite of her bold attacks and her satirical mood, her literary style is surprisingly feminine – rich with fable-like parables, with down-to-earth examples from everyday life ('the price of a cup of tea ...') and with similes from scenes and examples taken from nature (the *Accumulation of Capital* begins with the economic life of the robin). Her sparkling prose and her entertaining asides make Joan Robinson one of the most brilliant writers among economists and certainly one of the most enjoyable and delightful to read.

HER SCIENTIFIC ACHIEVEMENTS. Joan Robinson wrote numerous books and an enormous number of articles, most of which have been collected in her *Collected Economic Papers* (1951–79).

They fall neatly into three broad groups, corresponding to the three basic phases of her intellectual development. A first group belongs to the phase of her by now classic *Economics of Imperfect Competition* (1933). A second group belongs to the phase of explanation, propagation and defence of Keynes's *General Theory*. Finally, a third group of writings grew around the major work of her maturity, *The Accumulation of Capital* (1956). Other books and articles have originated from miscellaneous or wider interests or from the desire to provide students with economics exercises or with a non-orthodox economics textbook (Robinson and Eatwell, 1973). Altogether, they make an impressive list. Even neglecting her articles (most of which are reprinted in the books), her bibliography contains no less than 24 books.

The most widely known of Joan Robinson's works is still the first, *The Economics of Imperfect Competition* (1933). It was the book of her youth, which placed her immediately in the forefront of the development of economic theory. It is a work conceived in Cambridge, at the end of a decade characterized by an intense controversy on cost curves and the laws of returns (see Sraffa, 1926, and the Symposium on the 'laws of returns' by Robertson, Sraffa and Shove, 1930). With this controversy in the background, Joan Robinson's book emerges in 1933 as a masterpiece in the traditional sense of the word. The restrictive conditions of perfect competition on which Marshall's theory was constructed are abandoned, and perfect competition is shown to be a very special case of what in general is a monopolistic situation. A whole new analysis of market behaviour is carried out on new, more general, assumptions; and yet the whole method of analysis, the whole approach – though refined and perfected – is still the traditional Marshallian one. Sraffa's criticism of the master is accepted, but is incorporated into the traditional fold by a generalization of Marshall's own theoretical framework. The outcome is extremely elegant and impressive. The whole matter of market competition is clarified. Marshall's ambiguities are eliminated, the various market conditions are rigorously defined, a whole technical apparatus (a 'box of analytical tools') is developed to deal with market situations in the general case (from demand and supply curves to marginal cost and marginal revenue curves). In a sense, therefore, rather than a radical critique, the *Economics of Imperfect Competition* might well be regarded as the completion and coronation of Marshallian analysis. This may help to explain why Joan Robinson herself came to like that book less and less, as her thought later developed on different lines. In 1969 she came to the point of writing a harsh eight-page criticism of it. Very courageously she published it, on the occasion of a reprint of the book, as a Preface to the second edition!

The book had appeared almost simultaneously with the *Theory of Monopolistic Competition* by Edward Chamberlin (1933); and the two books are normally bracketed together as indicating the decisive breakaway of economic theory from the assumptions of perfect competition. Chamberlin always complained about this association. For although the two books represent the simultaneous discovery of basically the, same thing, made quite independently by two different authors, they are in fact substantively different.

It may also be added that looked at in retrospect, fifty years later, these two books do not appear so conclusive a contribution to the theory of the firm as they apeared to be in the 1930s. The behaviour of firms in oligopolistic markets and the policies of the large corporations have turned out to require more complicated analysis. At the same time, the assumption of perfect competition, far from being completely dead, has recently come back in different guises in the works of many theoretical economists. Yet there is no doubt that the two books remain there to represent a definite turning-point in the development of the theory of the firm – so much so as to be referred to as representing the 'monopolistic competition revolution' (Samuelson, 1967). Very characteristically, Edward Chamberlin, after writing the *Theory of Monopolistic Competition*, spent the whole of his life in refining, completing and adding appendices to his masterpiece (no less than eight editions!). For Joan Robinson, the *Economics of Imperfect Competition* was only the first step on a very long way to a series of works in quite different and varied fields of economic theory.

It should be added that the *Economics of Imperfect Competition* was not Joan Robinson's only contribution to micro-economic theory in the 1930s. Her name appears again and again on the pages of the *avant-garde* economic journals of the time. From among her papers, explicit mention must be made at least of her remarkably lucid article on 'rising supply price' and of her contribution to clarifying the meaning of Euler's theorem as applied to marginal productivities, in the traditional theory of production (see her *Collected Papers*, I).

But something of extraordinary importance was happening in Cambridge in the 1930s. Keynes was in the process of producing his revolutionary work (Keynes, 1936). Joan Robinson abandoned the theory of the firm and threw herself selflessly and entirely into the new paths opened up by him. This was a really brave decision, if one thinks that her first book had gained her great reputation in the economic profession. Very rarely do we find someone who, after striking success and becoming a leading figure in a certain field, pulls out of it and puts him- or herself into the shadow of someone else, be this someone else even of the stature of Keynes. Joan Robinson did precisely that. She was one of the members – actually an important member, as is revealed by the recent publication of her correspondence with Keynes (see Keynes, 1973, 1979) – of that group of young economists known as the 'Cambridge Circus' (and including Kahn, Sraffa, Harrod, Meade, besides Austin and Joan Robinson) who regularly met for discussion, and played a crucial role in the evolving drafts of Keynes's *General Theory*.

It must be said that the new Keynes's ways were more congenial to her temperament. They were a break with tradition and this suited her nonconformist attitude; they dealt with the deep social problems of unemployment and this appealed to her social conscience. It is in this vein that she published her *Essays in the Theory of Employment* (1937a) and her *Introduction to the Theory of Employment* (1937b). These twin books were simply meant to be a help to the readers of Keynes's *General Theory*. In fact, they turned out to be much more than that. In particular, Joan Robinson contributes to the clarification of a major piece of Keynesian theory – the process through which investments determine savings – which had remained rather obscure from the *General Theory*. For her, this appeared important because it broke a crucial link in traditional theory, which presented the rate of interest as a compensation for the 'sacrifice' of supplying capital (i.e. for saving). Joan Robinson stresses the role of investment as an independent variable, while total saving is shown as being determined passively by investment through the operation of the multiplier; the conclusion being that the rate of interest cannot be remunerating anybody's 'sacrifice'. Even more so in depression times, when thrift – a 'private virtue' – becomes a 'public vice'. Other concepts, introduced by Joan Robinson at the time, that were to remain permanently in the following economic literature on the theory of employment are those concerning what she called 'beggar-my-neighbour' policies, 'disguised unemployment' and the generalization of the Marshall/Lerner conditions on international trade, in terms of 'the four elasticities'.

Towards the end of the 1930s, Joan Robinson met Kalecki, and discovered that quite independently of, and in fact earlier, than Keynes, he had come to the same conclusions. Kalecki had started from a Marxist background, against which Keynes was prejudiced. This led her to re-reading Marx and to re-thinking her own position *vis-à-vis* Marxian theory (Robinson, 1942).

Joan Robinson's flirtation with Marx is very curious. It has all the charm of a meeting and all the clamour of a clash. She is no doubt attracted by Marx's general conception of society. She finds in Marx much which she approves of. But she finds his scientific nucleus embedded in, and in need of being liberated from, ideology. To obtain this, she says, one must work hard. Her writings on Marx are specifically aimed at 'separating the wheat of science from the chaff of ideology'. Needless to say, this has caused her a lot of trouble with the Marxists. It should be kept in mind that in continental Europe discussions on Marx have a long and complex tradition of philological heaviness and ideological passion. Joan Robinson's discussion is short and simple. She is always looking at Marx as 'a serious economist'. Accordingly, she always tries to go straight to what she thinks is his economic analysis. Her insistence on the necessity of rescuing Marx, as a scholar and a first-rate analytical mind, has recently been vindicated, especially after the publication of Sraffa's book (1960; see also, for example, Samuelson, 1971).

But the postwar period was opening up new vistas. With Keynes's *General Theory* in the background, Joan Robinson saw a formidable task ahead, consisting in nothing less than a reconstruction of economic theory. This led, after a decade of intense work, to the publication of her second major contribution to economic theory – *The Accumulation of Capital* (1956), the work of her maturity and the one that expresses Joan Robinson's genius at her best. Here she has chosen to move on new and controversial ground. While in her first book the direction – once established – was clear and she had to fill in the details, here the direction itself is not entirely clear and has to be continually adjusted. The details acquire less importance and may well be abandoned altogether and replaced with others at a second attempt. As a consequence, a lot of re-writing had to be done.

The Rate of Interest and Other Essays (1952), with its central essay devoted to a 'Generalization of the *General Theory*' turned out to be a sort of preparation. *The Accumulation of Capital* represents the central nucleus of what she perceived as a new framework for economic theory. Then the *Exercises in Economic Analysis* (1960), the *Essays in the Theory of Economic Growth* (1962a) and a series of other articles fill in the gaps, clarify obscurities, and take the arguments further.

The 'Generalization of the *General Theory*' represents Joan Robinson's response to an interchange with Harrod, following Harrod's *Towards a Dynamic Economics* (1948) and also his earlier review of her *Essays in the Theory of Employment* (1937a). Joan Robinson breaks away from the limitations of the short run, but has not yet defined clearly her direction. Yet, once the process of 'generalization', i.e. 'dynamization', of the *General Theory* is started, the author is compelled to recast the Keynesian arguments in terms of the more fundamental categories of capital accumulation, labour supply, technical progress and natural resources. Through this recasting, it became inevitable that she should go to the earlier methodological approach (common to Ricardo and Marx) of stating the problems in terms of social aggregates. The evidence of her intense searching may be found at the end of the book in a chapter of 'acknowledgements and disclaimers', where she describes in succession the way she has been influenced by, or has reacted to, Marx, Marshall, Rosa Luxemburg, Kalecki and Harrod.

The years of transition from the *Rate of Interest and Other Essays* (1952) to the *Accumulation of Capital* (1956) had been marked by a series of intense discussions in Cambridge, especially with Kahn, Sraffa, Kaldor and Champernowne. In the end, Joan Robinson emerged centring her attention on the problem of capital accumulation as the basic process in the development of a capitalist economy. She began with a scathing attack on the traditional concept of 'production function' (in a well-known article, now in her *Collected Papers* II, which elicited a chain of angry responses: see, for example, Solow, 1955–6, and Swan, 1956). Then she patiently proceeded to a reconstruction. A crucial step was her own way of rediscovering the Swedish economist Knut Wicksell.

The Accumulation of Capital (1956) bears the same title as Rosa Luxemburg's book, to whose translation into English Joan Robinson wrote an introduction (Luxemburg, 1951). This was a great tribute to another woman economist. But we should not be misled. Joan Robinson's book belongs to an entirely different age and takes an entirely different approach. Set into a Keynesian framework extended to the long run, it takes its origin from a welding together of Harrod's economic dynamics and of Wicksell's capital theory. The main question Joan Robinson poses to herself is by now a typically classical one: what are the conditions for the achievement of a cumulative long-term growth of income and capital (what she characteristically christened a 'golden age'); and what is the outcome of this process, in terms of growth of gross and net output and of the distribution of income between wages and profits, given a certain evolution through time of the labour force and of technology? To answer these question Joan Robinson builds up a two-sector dynamic model with a finite number of techniques; and goes on to show the interactions of the relations between wages and profits, the stock of capital and the techniques of production, entrepreneurial expectations and the degree of competition in the economy, bringing in the effects of higher degrees of mechanization and both 'neutral' and 'biased' technical progress. The basic model and the basic answers are all worked out very quickly in the book. The rest is then devoted to relaxing the simplifying assumptions. The whole analysis is carried out *without* the use of mathematics. This is remarkable. Joan Robinson squeezes out of the model, one by one, all the answers that are needed. The non-use of mathematics has certain obvious disadvantages. Though the analysis need not necessarily be any less rigorous, in many passages it is not so easy to follow. It has, however, some advantages, which Joan Robinson is very ready and able to exploit. She succeeds, for example, in freeing herself from the symmetry that a mathematically formulated model normally imposes. In Joan Robinson's model, certain results are always more likely to happen than their symmetrical counterpart. Symmetry and formal elegance play no part; only relevance does, or at least it does in the way perceived by the author.

The overall result is, again, impressive. The oversimplified dynamic model of Harrod is enormously enriched by the introduction of the choice among a finite number of alternative techniques. At the same time the Wicksellian analysis of accumulation at a given technology is completed by the new analysis of a constant flow of inventions of various types. And this marriage of Harrod's model to Wicksellian analysis is made to fructify in a number of directions. So many and so rich are in fact these directions that Joan Robinson herself did not pursue all of them, as became evident from the abundant literature that followed.

To this literature, Joan Robinson contributed a whole series of essays and books (see her *Collected Papers* II, III, IV, V; and J. Robinson, 1960, 1962a), which represent clarifications and further elaborations. They also represent her way of recasting and adjusting her arguments in response to opposition from her critics and to comments, remarks and stimuli of any sort from her friends, as well as her way of coming to grips with results – not always or not entirely compatible with hers – coming from the works of other scholars, colleagues and pupils, who where broadly working on similar problems and with the same aims.

Meanwhile, proceeding on parallel lines, many other separate strands of thinking were emerging from her remarkable intellectual activity. At least a few must briefly be mentioned here.

First, a whole series of concepts and ideas were coming to fruition; which – though not belonging to her major fields of interest – came to complete her overall coverage of economic theory: writings on the theory of international trade (including her Professorial inaugural lecture at Cambridge on *The New Mercantilism* (1966a)), on Marxian economics (at various stages in her career), and on the theory of economic development and planning, reproducing her lectures delivered during her world travels or coming from calm reflection, once she had returned home (see her *Collected Papers*, and also J. Robinson, 1970b, 1979b).

Second, her deeply felt concern with economics students and economics teaching in general gave origin to books, such as Joan Robinson (1966b), (1971) and especially (with Eatwell) 1973, which contributed to giving substance to, and disseminating all over the world, her strongly felt conviction that an overall approach to economic reality, alternative to that of traditional economics, does exist and is viable.

Third, the ideas, reflections, rationalizations, accumulated in the course of her life took the form of books such as *Economic Philosophy* (1962b) and *Freedom and Necessity* (1970a), which were concerned with wider issues than economics itself, attempting to give an overall conception of the world and a whole philosophy of life. These writings contribute, not marginally, to place Joan Robinson among the influential thinkers of this century. At the same time, they may well be enjoyed, by the general reader, even more than her masterpieces. From a purely literary point of view, they make delightful reading.

It should be added that there are, moreover, many themes which, while not being exclusively connected with any specific work of Joan Robinson's, recur time and again in her writings, so as to have become characteristically associated with her approach. Here are a few: (a) the concept of 'entrepreneurs' animal spirits' – an expression picked up from Keynes and developed as an important element contributing to explain investment in capitalist economies; (b) the conviction that Marshall's notions of prices and rate of profit, with reference to industry, are much more akin to Ricardo's notions than to Walras's; (c) a sharp distinction between 'logical' time and 'historical' time, both of which have a place in economic analysis but with different roles. On this point Joan Robinson's characterization of the evolution of an economy in historical time as concerning decisions to be taken between 'an irrevocable past and an uncertain future' is well known; (d) an equally sharp distinction between *comparisons* of equilibrium–growth positions and *movements* from one equilibrium–growth position to another, in dynamic analysis; (e) a tendency, especially in the later part of her life, to shift nearer and nearer to the positions of Kalecki, as opposed to those of Keynes, in interpreting the over-all working of the institutions of capitalist economies, especially with reference to what she found as a more satisfactory integration in Kalecki, of the concept of effective demand with the process of price formation.

Finally, one must mention specifically an issue which may well continue to give rise to controversial evaluations. This concerns the role that may be assigned to Joan Robinson in the well-known controversy on capital theory that flared up between the two Cambridges in the 1960s (see Pasinetti et al., 1966). One view on this issue is that Joan Robinson had the merit of anticipating the controversy by her (already mentioned) attacks on the neoclassical production function in the mid-1950s (see Harcourt, 1972). Another view is that Joan Robinson, herself a victim of her emotional temperament, started her attacks on the traditional concepts too early and misplaced the whole criticism, by neglecting the really basic point (the phenomenon of re-switching of techniques; see Sraffa, 1960) that in the end delivered the fatal blow to the neoclassical notion of production function. What one can say for certain is that a hint at the re-switching phenomenon does appear in the *Accumulation of Capital*, but is relegated to the role of a *curiosum*, in an entirely secondary section. Perhaps, the phenomenon had been pointed out to her but she grossly underestimated its importance. What is curious is that she continued to underestimate it, even after it was brought to the foreground (see her 'Unimportance of Re-switching' in *Collected Papers* V).

But at this point the works of Joan Robinson merge into those of that remarkable group of Cambridge economists – notably, Piero Sraffa, Nicholas Kaldor and Richard Kahn, among others, besides Joan Robinson herself (on this, see the Preface to Pasinetti, 1981) – who happened to be concentrated in Cambridge in the postwar period and who took up, continued and expanded the challenge that Keynes had launched on orthodox economic theory. This remarkable group of economists started a stream of economic thought which is obviously far from complete. Its basic features, however, are clear enough; they embody a determined effort to shift the whole focus of economic theorizing away from the problems of optimum allocation of given resources, where it had remained for almost a century, and move it towards the fundamental factors responsible for the dynamics of industrial societies. This shift of focus inevitably brings into the foreground the once central themes of capital accumulation, population growth, production expansion, income distribution, and thus technical progress and structural change.

It is perhaps too early to try to evaluate the relative role played by Joan Robinson as a member of this remarkable group of economists. The single components of the group have made contributions which are sometimes complementary, at other times overlapping, and at yet other times even partly contradictory. To mention only one major problem, Piero Sraffa's book appeared too late for Joan Robinson to be able to incorporate it into her theoretical framework; and the brave efforts she later made to this effect are not always convincing. They actually reveal here and there a sort of ambivalent attitude. At the same time, her *Accumulation of Capital* ventures into fields of economic dynamics which Sraffa does not touch at all. Quite obviously, the common fundamental thrust behind post-Keynesian analysis does not presuppose complete identity of views or complete harmony of approach.

Future developments will clarify issues and will reveal which of the lines of approach proposed are the most useful, fruitful or fecund. There can be little doubt, however, that if this theoretical movement is going to prove successful, quite a lot of re-writing will have to be done in economic theory. If, and when, this re-writing occurs, Joan Robinson's contributions are going to take a major place.

LUIGI L. PASINETTI

See also ACCUMULATION OF CAPITAL.

SELECTED WORKS

1933. *The Economics of Imperfect Competition.* London: Macmillan. 2nd edn, 1969.
1937a. *Essays in the Theory of Employment.* London: Macmillan.
1937b. *Introduction to the Theory of Employment.* London: Macmillan.
1942. *An Essay on Marxian Economics.* London: Macmillan.
1951. *Collected Economic Papers*, Vol. I. Oxford: Basil Blackwell. (Vol. II, 1960a; Vol. III, 1965; Vol. IV, 1973a; V, Vol. 1979a.)
1952. *The Rate of Interest and Other Essays.* London: Macmillan.
1956. *The Accumulation of Capital.* London: Macmillan.
1960a. *Collected Economic Papers*, Vol. II. Oxford: Basil Blackwell.
1960b. *Exercises in Economic Analysis.* London: Macmillan.
1962a. *Essays in the Theory of Economic Growth.* London: Macmillan.
1962b. *Economic Philosophy.* London: C.A. Watts.
1965. *Collected Economic Papers*, Vol. III. Oxford: Basil Blackwell.
1966a. *The New Mercantilism – an Inaugural Lecture.* Cambridge Cambridge University Press.
1966b. *Economics – an Awkward Corner.* London: Allen & Unwin.
1970a. *Freedom and Necessity.* London: Allen & Unwin.
1970b. *The Cultural Revolution in China.* London: Penguin Books.
1971. *Economic Heresies: Some Old-fashioned Questions in Economic Theory.* London: Macmillan.
1973a. *Collected Economic Papers*, Vol. IV. Oxford: Basil Blackwell.
1973b. (ed.) *After Keynes.* Papers presented to Section F (economics) of the 1972 annual meeting of the British Association for Advancement of Science, Oxford: Basil Blackwell.
1973c. (With John Eatwell.) *An Introduction to Modern Economics.* New York: McGraw-Hill.
1978. *Contributions to Modern Economics.* Oxford: Basil Blackwell.
1979a. *Collected Economic Papers*, Vol. V. Oxford: Basil Blackwell.
1979b. *Aspects of Development and Underdevelopment.* Cambridge: Cambridge University Press.
1980. *Further Contributions to Modern Economics.* Oxford: Basil Blackwell.

BIBLIOGRAPHY

Chamberlin, E. 1933. *The Theory of Monopolistic Competition.* Cambridge, Mass.: Harvard University Press.

Harcourt, G. 1972. *Some Cambridge Controversies in the Theory of Capital.* Cambridge: Cambridge University Press.

Harrod, R.F. 1948. *Towards a Dynamic Economics.* London: Macmillan.

Keynes, J.M. 1930. *A Treatise on Money.* 2 vols, London: Macmillan.

Keynes, J.M. 1936. *The General Theory of Employment, Interest and Money.* London: Macmillan.

Keynes, J.M. 1973, 1979. *The Collected Writings of John Maynard Keynes*, Vols. XIII and XIV (1973) and XXIX (1979). Ed. D.C. Moggridge, London: Macmillan for the Royal Economic Society.

Luxemburg, R. 1913. *The Accumulation of Capital.* Trans. A. Schwarzschild, with an Introduction by Joan Robinson, London: Routledge & Kegan Paul, 1951.

Pasinetti, L.L. 1974. *Growth and Income Distribution: Essays in Economic Theory.* Cambridge: Cambridge University Press.

Pasinetti, L.L. 1981. *Structural Change and Economic Growth. A Theoretical Essay on the Dynamics of the Wealth of Nations.* Cambridge: Cambridge University Press.

Pasinetti, L.L., Levhari, D., Samuelson, P.A., Bruno, M., Burmeister, E., Sheshinski, E., Morishima, M. and Garegnani, P. 1966. Contributions to 'Paradoxes in capital theory – a symposium'. *Quarterly Journal of Economics* 80(4), 503–83.

Robertson, D.H., Sraffa, P. and Shove, G. 1930. Increasing returns and the representative firm: a symposium. *Economic Journal* 40, March, 76–116.

Samuelson, P.A. 1967. The monopolistic competition revolution. In *Monopolistic Competition: Studies in Impact*, ed. R.M. Kuenne, New York: Wiley & Sons.

Samuelson, P.A. 1971. Understanding the Marxian notion of exploitation: a summary of the so-called transformation problem between Marxian values and competitive prices. *Journal of Economic Literature* 9, 339–431.

Solow, R.M. 1955–6. The production function and the theory of capital. *Review of Economic Studies* 23(2), 101–8.

Sraffa, P. 1926. The laws of returns under competitive conditions. *Economic Journal* 36, December, 535–50.

Sraffa, P. 1960. *Production of Commodities by Means of Commodities: Prelude to a Critique of Economic Theory.* Cambridge: Cambridge University Press.

Swan, T.W. 1956. Economic growth and capital accumulation. *Economic Record* 32, 334–61.

Wicksell, K. 1901. *Lectures on Political Economy.* Vol. I, ed. L. Robbins, London: Routledge & Kegan Paul, 1934.

Robinson Crusoe. Written by Daniel Defoe, *Robinson Crusoe* was first published in 1719–20. By the end of the 19th century there were many references made to a Crusoe economy to illustrate the principles of supply and demand economic theory. Crusoe thus became a representative rational economic individual, allocating his available resources to obtain maximum satisfaction in the present or future.

The figure of Crusoe as the personification of supply and demand economic theory can be found in W.S. Jevons's *Theory* (1871), C. Menger's *Principles* (1871), P. Wicksteed's *Alphabet of Economic Science* (1888), E. Böhm-Bawerk's *Theory of Capital* (1890), A. Marshall's *Principles* (1891) and K. Wicksell's *Value, Capital and Rent* (1893). The principal uses of the device were to show how an isolated individual would allocate consumption items so as to maximize utility in a marginalist fashion and distribute labour effort between producing items for consumption or investment (creating 'capital'). Calculations were made according to the relative amounts of pleasure and pain immediately or ultimately involved in the various activities. Marshall also used Crusoe to illustrate producer and consumer surplus, while F.Y. Edgeworth's *Mathematical Psychics* (1881) introduced 'the black', Friday, when discussing issues in the theory of commodity exchange.

The role of a Crusoe economy was not simply to illustrate various components of supply and demand theory. It was also utilized to support the claim that the principles of rational behaviour, as defined by that theory, could be applied to any type of economy – from the isolated individual to 'modern civilization'. This point was made particularly clear in J.B. Clark's *The Distribution of Wealth* (1899). Similar references to a Crusoe economy can be found in textbooks today.

Two general characteristics of an economic Crusoe's actions are important to note. First, he must be able to calculate in a precise fashion making fine decisions between whether to work or rest, to consume or save/invest. Second, he has no resources other than those available in the island environment. Both characteristics mean the economic Crusoe bears no relation to the Crusoe in Defoe's novel. Defoe's Crusoe wastes time because he cannot calculate in a marginalist fashion; he cannot rationally allocate labour time because labour is as useful in one pursuit as another; and he would not have survived without items salvaged from the shipwreck. Other decisions, such as whether to consume or save, also preclude calculation on the basis of relative pleasure and pain (White, 1982). Moreover, the relation between Crusoe and Friday is not based on voluntary reciprocal exchanges, as in the supply and demand parable, but rather on power and violence (Hymer, 1980). The economic Crusoe could not, therefore, have been produced by relying on the letter of Defoe's text.

It is possible to find some references to Crusoe by English political economists during the 1830s, but these were sporadic and no attempts were made to utilize Crusoe in a systematic fashion. An economic Crusoe thus appears only after mid-century with references in F. Bastiat's *Economic Harmonies* (1850) and H. Gossen's *Entwickelung* (Gossen, 1854). These references owed a good deal to the rewriting of Defoe's text within the literary genre of the 'Robinsonade'.

The Robinsonade literature dates from the early 18th century (Gove, 1941) and includes voyage or shipwreck narratives, imaginary voyages to 'isolated lands' and more general discussions of colonial settlements which depicted various stages of societal development. The last group of Robinsonade texts bears some resemblance to the four-stage theory of societies produced during the Scottish Enlightenment, remnants of which can be found in the work of the classical political economists (Meek, 1976). One such remnant was the illustrative device, used by A. Smith and D. Ricardo, of hunters exchanging commodities according to the labour embodied in them. While Marx was critical of this device, he noted it made sense in the context of the previous century's Robinsonades. However he considered the later discussion of Crusoe by Bastiat for example, was 'twaddle' because it depicted an individual 'outside society' (Marx, 1857–8, pp. 83–5).

Bastiat's Crusoe relied on a different type of Robinsonade literature, particularly J.H. Campe's *Robinson the Younger* (1779/80). Campe rewrote Defoe's tale to show Crusoe's survival on the island was not dependent on the shipwreck items. Gossen also appealed to Campe's novel to illustrate his marginalist explanation of work and consumption decisions. By the mid-19th century, then, the 'individualist' Robinsonade was utilized by those theorists who conceptualized the economy as a series of voluntary exchanges, where the principles of economic activity were those of the individual writ large.

English supply and demand economists could also draw upon a discernible shift in the readings of Defoe's text by literary commentators after 1850. Earlier commentary had stressed the novel was useful for showing, especially to children and the 'working classes', the virtue of work and the need to accept the given social organization ordained by Divine Providence. Commentary after mid-century represented Crusoe more as an individual calculating costs and benefits in the manner of an English shop keeper. It was even argued Crusoe represented a 'national ideology' in that regard. The remarkable similarity between this Crusoe and the illustrative device of English supply and demand economic theory suggests the latter was able to appropriate the former as a recognizable referent.

The economic Crusoe served, in effect, as a useful defensive device against 'historical' critics of economic theory such as T.E. Cliffe Leslie and J.K. Ingram. Writing between the mid-1860s and early 1880s, the critics argued that there were no universal laws of economic behaviour since behaviour could change according to the type of society being considered. Supply and demand theorists, such as Jevons, rejected that criticism, claiming historical studies could only confirm the 'universal' laws of behaviour assumed in the theory (Jevons, 1876, pp. 196–7). In this context, the economic Crusoe provided an apparently tangible reference point when supply and demand theory began its analysis with the actions of an 'isolated' or representative individual. Indeed, Gossen had used Campe's Crusoe in precisely that fashion when criticizing the German 'National Economists' in 1854 (Gossen, 1854, pp. 45–7). The role of an economic Crusoe, as both illustrative and defensive device for supply and demand theory, was thus inscribed from its inception.

M.V. White

See also ECONOMIC MAN; RATIONAL BEHAVIOUR; SELF-INTEREST.

BIBLIOGRAPHY

Gossen, H.H. 1854. *Entwickelung der Gesetze des menschlichen Verkehrs und der daraus fliessenden Reglen für menschliches Handeln*. Brunswick: Vieweg.

Gove, P.B. 1941. *The Imaginary Voyage in Prose Fiction*. New York: Columbia University Press.

Hymer, S. 1980. Robinson Crusoe and the secret of primitive accumulation. In *Growth, Profits and Property*, ed. E.J. Nell, New York: Cambridge University Press.

Jevons, W.S. 1876. The future of political economy. In *The Principles of Economics and Other Papers*, ed. H. Higgs, London: Macmillan, 1905.

Marx, K. 1857–8. *Grundrisse*. Harmondsworth: Penguin, 1973.

Meek, R.L. 1976. *Social Science and the Ignoble Savage*. Cambridge: Cambridge University Press.

White, M.V. 1982. Reading and rewriting. The production of an economic Robinson Crusoe. *Southern Review* 15(2).

Rodbertus, Johann Karl (1805–1875). Rodbertus is chiefly remembered as a pioneer of the theory of state socialism. Born on 12 August 1805, at Griefswald on the Baltic, he came from a wealthy and intellectual background (his father was a professor). Rodbertus studied law at the universities of Göttingen and Berlin. After a period of service with the Russian Government he settled in 1836 at his country estate in Jagetzow in Pomerania and concentrated on the study of social and economic issues.

Rodbertus was strongly influenced by the writings of Sismondi and, like Sismondi, he was a distinguished historian. He drew analogies between modern capitalism and ancient serfdom, and he was the first continental writer to consider explicitly the grievances and claims of the working-classes. For Rodbertus, labour was the only true source of productive wealth. His fundamental proposition, taken from Ricardo, was that the working-classes would always receive only a subsistence wage: the 'iron law' of wages. Hence, any growth of national income would inevitably increase the share of rent and profits, whereas the proportion going to wage-earners would fall. This in turn would produce recurrent economic crises as consumption would fail to match output due to lack of demand. Rodbertus may thus be considered as a continental forerunner of underconsumptionist theorists.

Rodbertus considered that the permanent misery inflicted upon the working classes should be alleviated by the state. The state should ensure that the proportion of national wealth going to workers should rise alongside that going to capitalists; the state should fix minimum and maximum wages, fix the length of a normal working day, and determine the amount of work that could be done. Yet he was conservative in politics just as he was socialist in economics. He wished to maintain established laws of capital and land ownership, and to preserve the monarchy. He believed in gradualism, arguing that it might take five hundred years to educate the population for socialism, and he put his trust in the benevolence of existing state institutions. Indeed, he warned against the dangers of directing energies into movements for political liberalism, arguing that 'the tyranny of misery is felt much more deeply than the misery of tyranny'.

Rodbertus further refined his underconsumptionist approach to economic crises by relating such crises to imperialism. He suggested that falling home demand and glutted markets would lead capitalists to seek new markets in non-industrial countries. In turn the superior military strength of the industrial countries would threaten the independence of these new regions as capitalists sought to open them up to trade.

Despite Rodbertus' undoubted claims as a forerunner of theories of underconsumption, imperialism, and state socialism, he cannot be considered a major figure in the history of social and economic thought. Neither in terms of the intellectual force in his theories nor of his influence on others has his work been profound. He failed to link his underconsumptionist theories with any explanation of why capitalists' income should not create demand; he ignored the effect of continuing demand for labour or long-term real wages; and he had no explanation of why economic crises should recur periodically. Ferdinand Lassalle took up Rodbertus' 'iron law' of wages, but both Marx and Engels rejected his theories (with the consequence that Rodbertus has never found a favoured place in Marxist histories of socialism). Moreover Rodbertus had little influence outside Germany, and few of his works have been translated into other languages. According to Landauer, Rodbertus 'was one of the lost prophets who have been so frequent in the history of socialism'.

Rodbertus had a brief career in public life: he was elected to the Prussian National Assembly in 1848 and, for two weeks, became Minister of Worship and Education. But he retired from the Assembly in 1849 and returned to writing and study. He died in Jagetzow on 6 December 1875.

M. Falkus

SELECTED WORKS

1842. *Zur Erkenntnis unsurer Staatswirthschaftlichen Zustände*. Neubrandenburg.

1850–51. *Sociale Briefe an von Kirchmann.*

1872–85. *Zur Beleuchtung der Socialen Frage.*

1884. *Das Kapital* (unfinished).

BIBLIOGRAPHY

Dietzel, H. 1886–8. *Karl Rodbertus, Darstellung seines Lebens und seiner Lehre*. 2 vols, Jena: G. Fischer, 1923.

Gonner, E.C.K. 1890. *The Social Philosophy of Rodbertus*. London: Macmillan.

Plekhanov, G.V. 1923. Ekonomicheskaia teoriia Karla Rodbertusa – Iagetsova. *Sochinenii* I, Moscow.

Rogers, James Edwin Thorold (1823–1890). Rogers was educated at King's College, London, and Magdalen College, Oxford. From 1859 until his death he held the first Tooke Professorship of Statistics and Economic Science at King's College, London. In 1862 he was elected Drummond Professor of Political Economy in the University of Oxford, a post he lost in 1868 largely because of his outspoken radical views, but to which he was re-elected in 1888. He was ordained but abandoned the clerical profession. From 1880 to 1886 he served as a rather inconspicuous member of the House of Commons.

His chief work is his monumental *History of Agriculture and Prices*, where he did much to turn economic history into the field of distribution and attempted to use more exact methods in economic historical investigations on a large scale. His work is marred by his casual deductions. He argued for a high standard of living of the English labourer during the Middle Ages and explained the subsequent deterioration by legislative interference by the landowners controlling the government.

Politically, he was greatly influenced by his friend and brother-in-law Richard Cobden. He was firmly opposed to extensive government intervention. He did however support trade unions as providing the remedy for nearly all social ills. His advocacy of laissez-faire separates him from the rest of the English historical school, his allies in attacking theoretical economics in looking to economic history as a realistic foundation for the proper understanding and solution of contemporary social and economic problems.

O. Kurer

See also ENGLISH HISTORICAL SCHOOL.

SELECTED WORKS

1884. *Six Centuries of Work and Wages: The History of English Labour*. London: Swan Sonnenschein

1886–1902. *A History of Agriculture and Prices in England. From the Year After the Oxford Parliament (1259) to the Commencement of the Continental War (1793)*. 7 vols, Oxford: Clarendon.

1888. *The Economic Interpretation of History*. New York: Putnam.

1892. *The Industrial and Commercial History of England.* Ed. A.G.L. Rogers, New York: Putnam. Published posthumously.

BIBLIOGRAPHY

Ashley, W.J. 1889. James E. Thorold Rogers. *Political Science Quarterly* 4, 381–407.

De Marchi, N.B. 1976. On the early dangers of being too political an economist: Thorold Rogers and the 1868 election to the Drummond Professorship. *Oxford Economic Papers* 28, 364–80.

Hewins, W.A.S. 1897. James Edwin Thorold Rogers. In *Dictionary of National Biography*, Oxford: Oxford University Press.

Wood, J.C. 1983. *British Economists and the Empire, 1860–1914*. Beckenham, Kent: Croom Helm.

Roos, Charles Frederick (1901–1958). Born on 18 May 1901, in New Orleans, Roos completed his PhD in mathematics at Rice Institute in 1926. Influenced directly by his supervisor Evans (1922, 1924, 1930) and indirectly by Volterra, his main interests in graduate work were the calculus of variations, integral equations, and applications of those areas of mathematics to problems in dynamic economics.

Although he published several brilliant articles (Roos 1925, 1927a, 1927b, 1927c, 1928, 1930), Roos found no journal which would readily accept manuscripts in which he combined economics, mathematics and sometimes statistics at suitably advanced levels (cf. Roos, 1934, p. xiii). Spurred by similar frustrations, Frisch and Roos jointly took the initiative which led to creation of the Econometric Society in 1930 (of which Roos became President in 1948) and publication of its journal, *Econometrica*, from 1933 on.

In 1930 Roos set out to write a treatise on dynamic economics; he published an important book under that title in 1934. It was reviewed enthusiastically by Tintner (1936) and uncomprehendingly by Freeman (1935). *Dynamic Economics* (1934) is a brilliant combination of mathematical economic theory and applied econometrics. Roos's mathematical approach inspired Tintner to write a dozen articles on dynamic economic theory (e.g. Tintner, 1938).

Roos held a series of administrative positions during 1931–7 and published a major book on *NRA Economic Planning*. In 1938 he founded an econometric consulting firm in New York and directed it until his death. Examples of his later work are Roos and von Szeliski (1939a and b) and Roos (1955, 1957). He died in Milwaukee on 7 January 1958.

Hotelling (1958) describes Roos as 'a unique and outstanding figure', while Davis (1958) presents a complete list of his writings.

KARL A. FOX

SELECTED WORKS

1925. A mathematical theory of competition. *American Journal of Mathematics* 47, July, 163–75.

1927a. Dynamical economics. *Proceedings of the National Academy of Sciences* 13, 145–50.

1927b. A dynamical theory of economic equilibrium. *Proceedings of the National Academy of Sciences* 13, 280–85.

1927c. A dynamical theory of economics. *Journal of Political Economy* 35, October, 632–56.

1928. A mathematical theory of depreciation and replacement. *American Journal of Mathematics* 50, 147–57.

1930. A mathematical theory of price and production fluctuations and economic crises. *Journal of Political Economy* 38, October, 501–22.

1934. *Dynamic Economics: theoretical and statistical studies of demand, production and prices*. Cowles Commission Monograph No. 1, Bloomington, Indiana: Principia Press.

1937. *NRA Economic Planning*. Cowles Commission Monograph No. 2, Bloomington, Indiana: Principia Press.

1955. Survey of economic forecasting techniques. *Econometrica* 23(4), October, 363–95.

1957. *Dynamics of Economic Growth: the American Economy, 1957–1975*. New York: Econometric Institute.

1939a. (With V. von Szeliski.) *The Dynamics of Automobile Demand*. General Motors Corporation, Detroit, Michigan.

1939b. (With V. von Szeliski.) The concept of demand and price elasticity; the dynamics of automobile demand. *Journal of the American Statistical Association* 34, December, 652–66.

BIBLIOGRAPHY

Davis, H.T. 1958. Charles Frederick Roos. *Econometrica* 26(4), October, 580–89. Contains a complete bibliography of Roos's writings (91 items).

Evans, G.C. 1922. A simple theory of competition. *American Mathematical Monthly* 29, November–December, 371–80.

Evans, G.C. 1924. The dynamics of monopoly. *American Mathematical Monthly* 31, February, 77–83.

Evans, G.C. 1930. *Mathematical Introduction to Economics*. New York: McGraw-Hill.

Freeman, H.A. 1935. Review of C.F. Roos, *Dynamic Economics*. *American Economic Review* 25(3), September, 520.

Hotelling, H. 1958. C.F. Roos, econometrician and mathematician. *Science* 128(33), November, 1194–5.

Tintner, G. 1936. Review of *Dynamic Economics*. *Journal of Political Economy* 44(3), June, 404–9.

Tintner, G. 1938. The theoretical derivation of dynamic demand curves. *Econometrica* 6(4), 375–80.

Röpke, Wilhelm (1899–1966). German economist and social philosopher, a leading figure of German Neo-liberalism, Röpke was born on 10 October 1899 at Schwarmstedt (Hannover) and died on 12 February 1966 at Geneva. Obtaining the *Dr.rer.pol.* (1921) and *Habilitation* (1922) at the University of Marburg, he became professor of economics at Jena (1924), Graz (1928) and again Marburg (1929). A liberal adversary of National Socialism, Röpke was ousted from office for political reasons in 1933 and went into exile. He was professor at the University of Istanbul (1933–37) and at the Graduate Institute for International Studies, Geneva (1937–66).

Röpke's scholarly work was centred on applied economics, rather than pure theory, and on the economic order, including the political, social and philosophical foundations of the market economy. His numerous publications reflect the chronology of major problems in German and international economic policy. As a member of the Brauns Commission to advise the German government (1931) and in his 1932 book he advocated, at the right moment, a 'Keynesian' policy before Keynes: a government investment programme, financed by credit expansion, to provide the *Initialzündung* (initial ignition) for overcoming the depression. Röpke later became a critic of the inflationary bias in Keynesianism.

Rejecting laissez-faire no less than central planning, Röpke conceived an economic order that supposed government not only to set the rules of the game (*Ordnungspolitik*) but included also decentralization, deconcentration, environmental policy, and a 'liberal interventionism' backing up market forces by adjustment assistance and not interfering with the price mechanism ('market-conformity principle'). As one of the intellectual architects of the 'Social Market Economy' and an adviser to Minister Ludwig Erhard, Röpke exerted considerable influence on post-war German economic policy.

JOSEF MOLSBERGER

SELECTED WORKS

1929. Staatsinterventionismus. In *Handwörterbuch der Staatswissenschaften*, 4th edn, Supplementary volume, Jena: Gustav Fischer.

1931. Praktische Konjunkturpolitik: Die Arbeit der Brauns-Kommission. *Weltwirtschaftliches Archiv*, October.

1932. *Krise und Konjunktur*. Leipzig: Quelle & Meyer, Trans. as *Crises and Cycles*, London: W. Hodge, 1936.

1937. *Die Lehre von der Wirtschaft*. 12th edn, Bern and Stuttgart: Paul Haupt, 1979. Trans. as *Economics of the Free Society*, Chicago: Regnery, 1963.

1942a. *Die Gesellschaftskrisis der Gegenwart*. 6th edn, Bern and Stuttgart: Paul Haupt, 1979. Trans. as *The Social Crisis of Our Time*, Chicago: Regnery, 1950.

1942b. *International Economic Disintegration*. London.

1944. *Civitas Humana: Grundfragen der Gesellschafts- und Wirtschaftsreform*. 4th edn, Bern and Stuttgart: Paul Haupt, 1979. English trans. as *Civitas Humana*, London: W. Hodge, 1949.

1945a. *Internationale Ordnung*. Erlenbach-Zürich: Eugen Rentsch.

1945b. *Die deutsche Frage*, Erlenbach-Zürich: Eugen Rentsch. Trans. as *The German Question*, London: G. Allen & Unwin, 1946.

1947. Repressed inflation. *Kyklos* 1(3), 242–53.

1950a. *Ist die deutsche Wirtschaftspolitik richtig?* Stuttgart: Kohlhammer.

1950b. *Mass und Mitte*. 2nd edn, Bern and Stuttgart: Paul Haupt, 1979.

1954. *Internationale Ordnung – Heute*. 3rd edn, Bern and Stuttgart: Paul Haupt, 1979.
1958. *Jenseits von Angebot und Nachfrage*. 5th edn, Bern and Stuttgart: Paul Haupt, 1979.
1959. *Gegen die Brandung* (Collected articles). Ed. A. Hunold. Erlenbach-Zürich and Stuttgart: Eugen Rentsch. Trans. as *Against the Tide*, Chicago: Regnery, 1969.
1962. *Wirrnis und Wahrheit* (Collected articles). Erlenbach-Zürich and Stuttgart: Eugen Rentsch.
1979. *Ausgwählte Werke in sechs Bänden*. Ed. F.A. von Hayek, H. Sieber, E. Tuchtfeldt, H. Willgerodt, Bern and Stuttgart: Paul Haupt. (Comprising Röpke (1937), 12th edn; (1942a), 6th edn; (1944), 4th edn; (1954), 3rd edn; (1958), 5th edn; (1950b), 2nd edn.) Complete list of works 1920–1968 and bibliography in *In memoriam Wilhelm Röpke*, ed. E. Hoppmann, Marburg: N.G. Elwert, 1968.
Supplement 1967–1976 to list of works and bibliography in *Marburger Gelehrte in der ersten Hälfte des 20. Jahrhunderts*, ed. I. Schnack, Marburg: N.G. Elwert, 1977.

Roscher, Wilhelm Georg Friedrich (1817–1894). Roscher was born in Hannover into a well-established civil service family. He studied history and political science in Göttingen and Berlin. In 1840 he became lecturer in both subjects at Göttingen, in 1843 he was appointed extraordinary professor of political economy, and in the next year was promoted professor. In 1848 he transferred to Leipzig, where he taught for the rest of his life. Roscher had a protestant background and was deeply religious, adhering to a rather 'primitive form of religious belief' (Max Weber).

Roscher may be considered as one of the most important German economists of his time. He was one of the founders and the leading exponent of the German 'older' historical school. He did not develop any new theory: his main contribution to political economy lay in the field of method. He adhered to what he called the 'historical-physiological method', as opposed to the 'idealistic method' (1842; 1854–94, vol. 1, pp. 43–56). This inductive method intended to provide a description of the actual course of economic development and of real economic life. Thus, Roscher tried to analyse laws of economic development by comparing the history of different people and nations and showing analogies in stages of their development. The emphasis was on historical relativism: economic behaviour depended to a large extent on the specific national and historic conditions of the different people and nations. This implied that a nation had to be regarded as a whole, as an 'organic unity', and not as the mere sum of individuals.

This was opposed to what Roscher called the 'idealistic method', which intended to provide an ideal picture, logically derived from abstract principles, of the functioning of the economic system. An example of this was the classical economists' deduction of economic laws from a system of hypotheses. Although Roscher emphasized that in economic analysis there existed generally no definite causal relationships but reciprocal ones, he did not reject the existence of 'laws of motion' within economic life. However, these laws were distinct from laws of natural science in that they dealt with free human beings gifted with reason and hence with changing motives for action (1854–94, vol. 1, pp. 26–9). Roscher was closer to the theoretical system of the classics than the exponents of the 'younger' historical school. He tended to regard it as the appropriate system of analysis of the current stage of economic development. He only modified and supplemented it with a careful historical analysis, but he may still be regarded as being in the classical tradition.

The first volume of Roscher's main work, *System der Volkswirtschaft* (1854–94: 1854) still looked very much like a traditional textbook. It analysed essentially the same topics as the classical economists – production, distribution and prices. Roscher was already strongly influenced by supply and demand approaches, but still determined the exchange value of a commodity by its cost of production. His theory of rent was Ricardian and his thinking about population development followed Malthusian patterns. Differing from classical textbooks, Roscher supplemented the theoretical analysis with a historical description – the reader finds the history of rent, interest and wages, of population development, of the prices of necessary and luxury commodities, and of luxury in general. Roscher accepted the classical notion of individual self-interest as a central axiom of modern economic behaviour, but he did not follow the classical patterns in deriving his economic principles from this assumption. As a result of his religious beliefs, he included human conscience as a regulating mechanism into his analysis of the role of self-interest (1854–94, vol. 1, pp. 20–23).

The other four volumes of the *System der Volkswirtschaft* (1859, 1881, 1886 and 1894), which may be perceived as his main contribution to applied economics, were even more historically oriented and focused on agriculture, trade and industry, public finance, social policy and poor relief.

Roscher classified economic development into stages of maturity. The economic factors that govern the development of nations were land, labour and capital which subsequently dominated the different stages (1861, ch. 1). Later, Roscher presented a more detailed analysis of stages of political and societal development (1892) on the basis of a classification of the different forms of government during history: early patriarchal kingdom, aristocracy of knights and priests, absolute monarchy, democracy. The latter then degenerated into a plutocracy, which is followed by a military dictatorship Roscher called 'Caesarismus'. Roscher did not systematically attempt an integration of his theory of political development and the stages of economic evolution.

He wrote several contributions on the history of economic thought. His compendium on the history of political economy in Germany (1874) was his most outstanding work and has remained important. Roscher may be regarded as the most eminent historian of cameralism and early German political economy. His treatise on economic problems of the location of large towns (1871) was an original contribution to economic theory.

Roscher supported German imperialism. In order to secure raw materials and markets for German goods, as well as to relieve the national labour market and prevent social unrest, he advocated an expansive German colonial policy, especially towards Eastern Asia, where he saw Germany's colonial future (1885). He was a conservative but he remained all his life unaffiliated to any political party or group.

B. Schefold

See also GERMAN HISTORICAL SCHOOL.

SELECTED WORKS

1842. *Leben, Werk und Zeitalter des Thukydides*. Göttingen.
1854–94. *System der Volkswirtschaft*. Stuttgart: Cotta. Vol. 1: *Die Grundlagen der Nationalökonomie*, 1854. Trans. from 13th edn, by J.J. Lalor as *Principles of Political Economy*, 2 vols, New York, 1878. Vol. 2: *Nationalökonomik des Ackerbaues und der verwandten Urproduktionen*, 1859. Vol. 3: *Nationalökonomik des Handels und Gewerbefleißes*, 1881. Vol. 4: *System der Finanzwissenschaft*, 1886. Vol. 5: *System der Armenpflege und der Armenpolitik*, 1894.

1861. *Ansichten der Volkswirtschaft aus dem geschichtlichen Standpunkt*. Leipzig and Heidelberg: Winter.
1871. *Betrachtungen über die geographische Lage der grossen Städte*. Leipzig.
1874. *Geschichte der Nationalökonomik in Deutschland*. Munich: Oldenbourg.
1885. *Kolonien, Kolonialpolitik und Auswanderung*. Leipzig: Winter. Part II, ch. 1. Translated from 3rd edn by E.H. Baldwin and E.G. Bourne as *The Spanish Colonial System*, New York, 1904.
1892. *Politik: Geschichtliche Naturlehre der Monarchie, Aristokratie und Demokratie*. Stuttgart.

BIBLIOGRAPHY

Cunningham, W. 1894–5. Why had Roscher so little influence in England? *Annals of the American Academy of Political and Social Sciences* 5.

Weber, M. 1903–6. *Roscher und Knies und die logischen Probleme der Historischen Nationalökonomie*. Gesammelte Aufsätze zur Wissenschaftslehre, Tübingen, 1922.

Rosenstein-Rodan, Paul Narcyz (1902–1985). Rodan was one of the founders and first leaders of the field of development economics. His formative intellectual years were in the Austrian School of economics at the University of Vienna. He moved to the Department of Political Economy at University College, London, in 1931.

Rodan's early essays in economics show a preoccupation with themes which reappeared throughout his professional career: the interaction and complementarity of economic processes (1933) and their temporal patterns (1934). Rodan's seminal article on developing countries (1943) argued that complementarities and externalities in demand and production created a need for the programming of investment. The arguments were subsequently extended to justify the need for an across-the-board 'big push' for a successful start to the development process (1963). He was among the first to apply the concept of 'disguised unemployment', described by Joan Robinson (1936), to developing countries as a persisting rather than cyclical problem.

Rodan first became actively engaged in development policy during his tenure at the World Bank from 1947 to 1954. In 1954 he moved to the Department of Economics at the Massachusetts Institute of Technology, where he produced an influential article (1961) which demonstrated that feasible levels of assistance to developing countries would substantially improve their growth performance. After retirement from MIT in 1968 he moved to the University of Texas and then to Boston University in 1972, where he established and worked in the Center for Latin American Development Studies until his death. Rodan was an active policy adviser to international agencies and governments of many countries and served on the Panel of Experts, the 'Nine Wise Men' of the Alliance for Progress, from 1961 to 1966.

RICHARD S. ECKAUS

SELECTED WORKS

1933. La complementarita, prime delle tre fase del progresso della teoria economica pura. *Riforma Sociale* 44, 257–308.
1934. The role of time in economic theory. *Economica*, NS 1, 77–97.
1943. Problems of industrialization of Eastern and South-Eastern Europe. *Economic Journal* 53, 202–11.
1956. Disguised unemployment and underemployment in agriculture. *Monthly Bulletin of Agricultural Economics and Statistics* 6, 1957, 1–6.
1961. International aid for underdeveloped countries. *Review of Economics and Statistics* 43, 107–38.
1963. Notes on the theory of the 'Big Push' in economic development. In *Proceedings of a Conference of the International Economics Association*, ed. H.S. Ellis, London: Macmillan.

BIBLIOGRAPHY

Robinson, J. 1936. Disguised unemployment. *Economic Journal* 46, 225–37.

Rossi, Pellegrino Luigi Edoardo (1787–1848). Italian economist, jurist and statesman; born at Carrara in 1787, died at Rome in 1848. Rossi was a multi-national and a multi-talent. Expelled from his homeland for his zealous support of Italian unification, he emigrated to Switzerland, where he taught Roman history, championed constitutional reform, and became a naturalized citizen. After a major setback in his reform efforts he moved to France, and began lecturing on economics in 1827. In 1833 he succeeded J.B. Say in the chair of political economy at the Collège de France, winning the appointment over strong competition from Say's son-in-law, Charles Comte. The following year, Rossi became a naturalized French citizen. New honours followed quickly. In 1836 he was elected to the Académie des Sciences Morales et Politiques; he was elevated to the peerage in 1839; and in 1845, was named French Ambassador to Rome. The Revolution of 1848 cut him off from France, whereupon he became the semi-official adviser of Pope Pius IX, until an assassin's dagger took his life in the same year.

As an economist, Rossi was known for the effectiveness of his instruction and for his clearness of exposition. He made no great scientific discoveries, nor did he establish any doctrinal following. On the contrary, there is some evidence that politics diluted his economics. For example, he defended the artificial monopolies of the Paris stockbrokers, attorneys and central bankers, and he acquiesced in the sugar bounties. His *Cours d'économie politique*, mainly a pastiche of Ricardo and Say, nevertheless attained enough popularity to justify five editions over a span of almost half a century.

Schumpeter (1954, p. 382) contends that an appraisal of Rossi's performance in economics should not imply a like assessment of his person, an obvious concession to Rossi's catholic and peripatetic habits. Yet there is some substance to Schumpeter's (1954, p. 510) additional claim that the 'failures in his many political activities reveal more ability than do the successes of other people'.

R.F. HÉBERT

SELECTED WORKS

1840. *Cours d'économie politique*. Paris: Joubert. 5th edn, 1884.
1857. *Mélanges d'économie politique, d'histoire et de philosophie*. 2 vols, Paris: Guillaumin.

BIBLIOGRAPHY

Ledermann, L. 1929. *Pellegrino Rossi, l'homme et l'économiste, 1787–1848*. Paris: Librairie du Recueil Sirey.

Mignet, F.A.A. 1849. Notice historique sur la vie et les travaux de M. Rossi. *Institut National de France*. Paris: Firmin Didot.

Schumpeter, J.A. 1954. *History of Economic Analysis*. Ed. E.B. Schumpeter, New York: Oxford University Press.

Sforza, G. 1922. Fonti per la biografia di Pellegrino Rossi. *Risorgimento Italiano* 15, 1–24.

Rostas, Laslo (1909–1954). Rostas was born in Hungary in October 1909 and died in Cambridge, after prolonged illness, in October 1954 at the age of 45. He was educated at a grammar school, and at the University of Budapest. He was brought to England by Nicholas Kaldor in 1939. He collaborated with John and Ursula Hicks in the preparation of a book on *The Taxation of War Wealth*. He then collaborated with G. Findlay Shirras in the preparation of a book on *The Burden of British Taxation*.

His great pioneer work was in the comparison between different countries of productivity – especially the United Kingdom, United States and Germany. His results were published in a book and the articles set out in the Bibliography below.

He had become one of the country's leading authorities on industrial productivity. His important studies in this field led to his appointment at the Board of Trade, where Stafford Cripps had begun a campaign to promote higher productivity in industry. Rostas was recognized as a profound expert and his straightforward common sense made him a valuable member of a number of Committees.

In 1951 he was brought to Cambridge as a Research Officer in the Faculty of Economics. In the three years which remained before his death, he not only continued his work but exercised a marked influence on his colleagues. In his last illness his courageous refusal to let go of his intellectual interests was inspiring up to the last.

As his colleague at the Board of Trade, S.A.H. Dakin, wrote in the *Times* obituary (4 October 1954):

> The farewells to Rostas cannot be said without a word of appreciative recognition from someone who knew him in the Civil Service. My recollections are of an intense enthusiasm and belief in the importance to the country of these studies in which he was an acknowledged expert, of a mind always fertile and penetrating in analysis.

R.F. KAHN

SELECTED WORKS

1940. Capital levies in central Europe. *Review of Economic Studies* 8, October, 20–32.

1943. Industrial production, productivity and distribution in Britain, Germany and the United States. *Economic Journal* 53, April, 39–54. This paper was the subject of the Presidential Address of the Royal Statistical Society in March 1944 and of the discussion which followed.

1945. Productivity of labour in the cotton industry. *Economic Journal* 55, June–September, 192–205.

1955. *The Cost Structure of Selected British Industries*. Cambridge: Cambridge University Press.

Rothbarth, Erwin (1913–1944). Rothbarth was born on 16 December 1913 in Frankfurt am Main, and died on 25 November 1944 at Venraij. He emigrated to England in 1933, where he attained his BA(Econ.) at the London School of Economics in 1936. He became an assistant in Statistical Research in the Faculty of Economics in Cambridge from 1938 to 1940. From May to August 1940 he was interned as an enemy alien. After his release he returned to Cambridge to teach economic statistics. He then volunteered for active service in the British Army in 1944, and was killed in action in Holland.

In his short career Rothbarth made several interesting contributions (Kalecki, 1944–5). He updated for Keynes Colin Clark's national income estimates and may have been partly responsible for their presentation in accounting format (Keynes, 1940; Cuyvers, 1983). He applied index-number theory to the measurement of real income under rationing and to price grouping in demand analysis (Rothbarth, 1941, 1944). He contributed two valuable appendices on family income and saving to Madge (1943). His last paper, published posthumously, compares productivity in the US and the UK (Rothbarth, 1946).

J.R.N. STONE

See also RATIONING.

SELECTED WORKS

1940. Statistical contribution to J.M. Keynes, *How to Pay for the War*. London: Macmillan.

1941. The measurement of changes in real income under conditions of rationing. *Review of Economic Studies* 8, February, 100–107.

1943. Appendices IV and V to C. Madge, *Wartime Patterns of Saving and Spending*. National Institute of Economic and Social Research Occasional Paper IV, Cambridge: Cambridge University Press.

1944. A note on an index number problem. *Review of Economic Studies* 11(2), Summer, 91–8.

1946. Causes of the superior efficiency of U.S.A. industry as compared with British industry. *Economic Journal* 56, September, 383–90.

BIBLIOGRAPHY

Cuyvers, L. 1983. Keynes's collaboration with Erwin Rothbarth. *Economic Journal* 93(371), September, 629–36.

Kalecki, M. 1944–5. The work of Erwin Rothbarth. *Review of Economic Studies* 12(2), 121–2.

Rothschild, Kurt Wilhelm (born 1914). Rothschild was born in Vienna on 20 October 1914. He studied law in Vienna and, after emigration to England, economics in Glasgow. From 1940 to 1947 he was a lecturer in economics at the University of Glasgow. He returned to Vienna in 1947 and worked until 1966 in the Austrian Institute for Economic Research (AIER). From 1966 until his retirement in 1985 he was professor of economics at the University of Linz.

Rothschild has been both an empirical researcher and a gifted theoretician. As a leading member of the AIER he concentrated his research on labour market analysis and foreign trade. His field of interest in theory was wide. Best known are his book (1954) on the theory of wages, his paper (1947) on price theory and oligopoly and the readings on 'Power in Economics' edited by and provided with an introduction of Rothschild (1971). Other publications have dealt with economic growth in Austria, unemployment, income distribution, disarmament, disequilibrium theory, forecasting and methodological problems of economics.

Rothschild always tried to link pure theory with relevant practical investigations. Economic institutions, social classes and their political and economic power thus played an important role, especially in his analysis of income distribution and of prices. Another important feature of his theoretical work was a pragmatic and commonsense approach. He can hardly be classified as belonging to one school in economics. Influenced by the tradition of Marshallian microeconomics he was a leading representative of Keynesian macroeconomics in Austria, shared interest for neoclassical equilibrium with that for disequilibrium theory and, last but not least, combined a rather radical left 'Weltanschauung' and political activity with a luke-warm attitude towards the Marxian labour value theory and radical economics.

K. LASKI

SELECTED WORKS

1947. Prices theory and oligopoly. *Economic Journal* 57, September, 299–320.

1954. *The Theory of Wages*. Oxford: Basil Blackwell.
1957. Approaches to the theory of bargaining. In *The Theory of Wage Determination*, ed. J. Dunlop, London: Macmillan.
1971. (ed.) *Power in Economics*. Penguin Modern Economics Readings, Harmondsworth: Penguin Books.
1973a. Military expenditure, exports and growth. *Kyklos* 26(4), 804–14.
1973b. Distributive aspects of the Austrian theory. In *Carl Menger and the Austrian School of Economics*, ed. J.R. Hicks and W. Weber, London and New York: Oxford University Press.
1981. *Einführung in die Ungleichgewichtstheorie*. Berlin, Heidelber and New York: Springer-Verlag.
1985. Some notes on Weintraub's eclectic theory of income shares. *Journal of Post-Keynesian Economics* 7(4), Summer, 575–93.

roundabout methods of production. Methods of production are roundabout if they use produced means of production or the services of capital goods as well as those of land and labour, the latter being considered original or primary factors of production.

The concept of roundaboutness of production methods thus draws a distinction between 'rude' and more advanced methods of production, the latter capital good using, the former not. This, however, is not a distinction of much use as even in very primitive economies man-made tools are used. But the concept has been associated with the proposition that more roundabout methods of production yield more output per unit of input, but require more time because the capital goods they use have to be produced, too. This proposition in turn has been associated with the idea that the roundaboutness of production methods depends on the division of labour as well as on the fact that production takes time. The concept therefore plays an important role in those variants of capital theory like the 'Austrian' theory of Böhm-Bawerk (1889) which emphasize the time-consuming nature of production in an economy characterized by division of labour.

The proposition that production processes take time, and that their implementation therefore requires 'advances' in the form of wage goods as well as durable capital goods was fundamental to physiocratic theory as expounded by Quesnay (1759) and Turgot (1770). It also appears in such classical writers as Ricardo (1817, ch. 1, sect. iv, v). But from Adam Smith (1776) onwards, most classical economists followed Josiah Tucker (1774, p. 24) and linked the use of capital goods to the division of labour rather than the time-consuming nature of production. This can be seen as the consequence of a shift of emphasis from agricultural to industrial production processes. Time requirements in agricultural production are given by nature, and cannot be overcome by an appropriate organization of production processes. Industrial production processes, by contrast, can be, and often are, staggered in such a way that outputs are obtained continuously and the temporal structure of production processes does not matter.

Longfield (1834) combined both aspects by arguing that production takes time on account of the division of labour. Because an increasing division of labour requires more and more different capital goods, the production processes in which they are produced lengthen the overall or composite production process which links the original factors of production to the output obtained with their help as well as the help of intermediate produced means of production. Likewise, Rae (1834) argued that increased division of labour goes with increased durability of capital and hence longer periods of time required for production. Rae also emphasized that, at any time, entrepreneurs have a choice between industrial production processes of different degrees of roundaboutness, i.e. different productivity as well as associated time requirements. These ideas, however, remained outside the classical tradition, which remained wedded to the idea that the division of labour was the main reason for the use of roundabout methods of production. The time element in production was submerged in the conception of capital goods as 'stored-up' or 'congealed' labour (and land), and thus as the result of previous production processes, which had been advanced by Ricardo (1817, ch. 1, sect. iii) and James Mill (1821). On the basis of this conception Senior (1836, 57–8) introduced the distinction between land and labour as 'primary' and capital goods as 'secondary' requisites of production; this distinction was later converted into one between 'original' and 'derived' factors of production. Most authors, however, used these notions in a rather vague way in order to characterize the nature of capital goods, and to assert the advantages of their accumulation.

When formulating his temporal ('Austrian') theory of capital Böhm-Bawerk (1889) built upon this tradition. He went beyond it, however, when he posited the existence of a production function in which the level of output obtained per unit of input was made a function of the degree of roundaboutness of the production method employed which, he argued, was positive but subject to diminishing marginal returns. This required him to define formally the degree of roundaboutness. Considering only one original factor of production, say x, which is used in different stages x_t of the production process, and hence remains 'invested' in it for varying lengths of time s_t, Böhm-Bawerk defined the degree of roundaboutness as the average period of production S as

$$S = \sum_t x_t s_t \Big/ \sum_t x_t$$

Here $\Sigma_t x_t s_t$ is what Jevons (1871, ch. vii) had called the 'amount of investment of capital', while $\Sigma_t x_t$ is Jevons's 'amount of capital invested'.

Böhm-Bawerk used this definition in his proposition referred to above, and erected on it a theory of the role of capital goods in production which issued in a theory of distribution. This 'Austrian' theory of capital was elaborated by Wicksell (1893) and, in modern form, by Faber (1979). The gist of the argument is that more roundabout methods of production are both more capital intensive and more productive, such that the relative availability of capital determines the method of production used, the amount of output obtained per unit of original input, and, via marginal productivity conditions, factor prices.

This theory gave rise to a lengthy debate which ran for almost half a century; for partial summaries, see Kaldor (1937), Haavelmo (1960), and Reetz (1971). Much of it centred on Böhm-Bawerk's definition of the degree of roundaboutness.

When Böhm-Bawerk turned the rather vague notion of roundaboutness into the more precise concept of an average period of production, he tied it to a linear, unidirectional view of production in which original factors of production are turned into raw materials, these with the help of further original factors into capital goods, which in turn help to produce consumer goods with the help of still further original factors. However, the attempt to 'dissolve' in the classical manner all capital goods into various amounts of original factors of production that had helped to produce them was soon seen to involve an infinite historical regress (Steindl 1937). Similarly, if the problem is conceived, as Rae (1834) had done, as a planning problem (i.e. in a forward looking rather than a backward looking manner), taking into account all future effects on output of durable capital goods produced in the present leads to an infinite historical progress. In both cases, therefore, the time span involved is infinite. The answer to these conundrums, which stem from the fact that production processes which use capital goods are characterized by circularity as well as uni-directional linearity, was formulated as early as 1904 by Dmitriev. He demonstrated that in a well-integrated system of production processes the amount of original factors of production used directly and indirectly in the production of final outputs (i.e. consumer goods) could be calculated without resorting to the fiction of going backward or forward in time, and hence without any infinite regress or progress. Dmitriev also showed that the existence of more than one original factor of production does not pose a problem in this calculation. Yet his contribution remained unnoticed until Sraffa (1960) again drew attention to the issue of circularity and linearity in production processes.

Another major difficulty raised by the way in which Böhm-Bawerk concretized the notion of roundaboutness was that it seems superfluous for the analysis of an ongoing production process. As for example Clark (1899) argued, if production processes are appropriately staggered all one needs to observe, once the processes are in operation, are inflows of original inputs and outflows of outputs, without attempting to trace which outputs are due to which inputs, and thus without paying attention to the temporal structure of production processes. It can indeed be shown that in such circumstances Böhm-Bawerk's average period of production is equivalent to the capital–output ratio as used in modern growth theory (Dorfman, 1959). However, while correct, this argument applies to steady states only. In dynamic analyses, and particularly in transitions from one steady state to another (Hicks, 1973), or when starting more roundabout production processes, the temporal structure of production does play a role, and in these contexts the concept of a period of production may prove useful as a measure of the roundaboutness of production processes.

Yet another difficulty was pointed out by Samuelson (1966) and Steedman (1972): because Böhm-Bawerk's measure of roundaboutness has the nature of an average, there are necessarily various time profiles of original factors of production which give the same average period of production. If in addition a rate of interest is used when calculating the amount of investment of capital (as they argue one should do) before dividing by the amount of capital invested to obtain the average period of production, the latter turns into a function of the rate of interest which is not unique in the sense that it may exhibit reswitching.

Thus, if the concept of differing degrees of roundaboutness of production methods is to be given a precise meaning, it will have to be defined not as an average, but as an absolute measure relating to technical characteristics of the production processes involved. Moreover, it will have to be shown that more roundabout methods of production necessarily yield higher levels of output per unit of original input. These are the crucial assumptions. Without their validity being demonstrated, the notion of roundabout methods of production remains intuitively appealing but fruitless from an analytical point of view.

K.H. Hennings

See also BÖHM-BAWERK, EUGEN VON; FISHER, IRVING; PERIOD OF PRODUCTION; RAE, JOHN.

BIBLIOGRAPHY

Böhm-Bawerk, E. von. 1889. *Positive Theorie des Kapitales.* Innsbruck: Wagner. Trans. as *The Positive Theory of Capital*, London: Macmillan, 1891.

Clark, J.B. 1899. *The Distribution of Wealth.* New York: Macmillan.

Dmitriev, V.K. 1904. *Ekonomicheskie Ocherki.* Moscow: Richter. Trans. as *Economic Essays on Value, Competition and Utility*, Cambridge: Cambridge University Press, 1974.

Dorfman, R. 1959. Waiting and the period of production. *Quarterly Journal of Economics* 73, 351–72.

Faber, M. 1979. *Introduction to Modern Austrian Capital Theory.* Berlin: Springer.

Haavelmo, T. 1960. *A Study in the Theory of Investment.* Chicago: Chicago University Press.

Hicks, J.R. 1973. *Capital and Time.* Oxford: Clarendon Press.

Jevons, W.S. 1871. *The Theory of Political Economy.* London: Macmillan.

Kaldor, N. 1937. Annual survey of economic theory: the recent controversy on the theory of capital. *Econometrica* 5, 201–33.

Longfield, M. 1834. *Lectures on Political Economy.* Dublin: Milliken.

Mill, J. 1821. *Elements of Political Economy.* London: Baldwin, Craddock & Joy.

Quesnay, F. 1759. *Tableau économique.* Paris: Imprimerie Royale.

Rae, J. 1834. *Statement of Some New Principles on the Subject of Political Economy.* Boston: Hilliard Gray & Co.

Reetz, N. 1971. *Produktionsfunktion und Produktionsperiode.* Göttingen: Schwartz.

Ricardo, D. 1817. *On the Principles of Political Economy and Taxation.* London: Murray.

Samuelson, P.A. 1966. A summing up. *Quarterly Journal of Economics* 80, November, 568–83.

Senior, N.W. 1836. *Political Economy.* London: Griffin.

Smith, A. 1776. *An Inquiry into the Nature and Causes of the Wealth of Nations.* London: Strahan & Cadell.

Sraffa, P. 1960. *Production of Commodities by Means of Commodities.* Cambridge: Cambridge University Press.

Steedman, I. 1972. Jevons's theory of capital and interest. *Manchester School of Economic and Social Studies* 40, March, 31–52.

Steindl, J. 1937. Der historische Regress in der Theorie der Produktionsumwege. *Jahrbücher für Nationalökonomie und Statistik* 145, 143–57.

Tucker, J. 1774. *Four Tracts Together with Two Sermons on Political and Commercial Subjects* (written 1758). Gloucester and London: Raikes & Rivington.

Turgot, A.R.J. 1770. Réflexions sur la formation et la distribution des richesses. *Ephémérides du Citoyen.* Trans. as 'Reflections on the Formation and Distribution of Wealth (1766)', in *Turgot on Progress, Sociology, and Economics*, ed. R.L. Meek, Cambridge: Cambridge University Press, 1973.

Wicksell, K. 1893. *Über Wert, Kapital und Rente.* Jena: Fischer. Trans. as *Value, Capital and Rent*, London: George Allen & Unwin, 1954.

Rousseau, Jean Jacques (1712–1778). Political philosopher, moral reformer, citizen of Geneva. Rousseau's economic thought cannot readily be placed within the mainstream of the schools of 18th-century economic discourse. The entire thrust of his work, comprising a sustained argument against the luxury and conspicuous consumption of the rising European bourgeosie of new commerce, implied a sharp rejection of the practices as well as principles of the mercantilist. Rousseau's most explicit contribution to economic thought, a contribution to the *Encyclopédie* entitled 'Economie politique' (vol. v, 1755), significantly preceded publication of the earliest published statement of the Physiocrats, Quesnay's *Maximes générales du gouvernement économique d'un royaume agricole* (1758), and their positions on important issues of property and to a lesser extent taxation bear comparison but are by no means identical. For his position on the right of the State to tax its citizens and the inseparable relationship between justice and the sacred rights of property (see *Political Writings*, I, 234), 'Rousseau appears to have appealed to and hardly superseded Locke. Nonetheless, Rousseau influenced both contemporary and later proponents of economic as well as political reform through his single-minded opposition to economic inequality, his disbelief in the benign effects of unregulated laissez faire, and his attack on what he considered the trivialized conception of liberal public life which accepted the interactions of the market as an adequate substitute for a theory of social relations.

From the earliest writing to bring him public notoriety, a discourse on the question of whether the progress of the Arts and Sciences had tended to the purification or the corruption of morality (1751), Rousseau was certainly more than an economic opponent of nascent capitalism. His adversary was nothing less than the 'progress' of modern society, and the injury he believed men suffered when labour was socially divided and property distributed under conditions of radical inequality. Writing initially as a moral reformer, Rousseau's work attacked the social institutions and entrenched inequalities of a feudal society in transition which combined remnants of feudal personal dependence with a set of new bourgeois commercial values and individual self-serving relationships later characterized as 'the get ahead spirit' (Tocqueville, *Democracy in America*). Of the principal distinctions of inequality articulated by Rousseau – general wealth, nobility or rank, power and personal merit – he argued consistently that 'wealth is the last to which they are reduced in the end because, being the most immediately useful to well-being and the easiest to communicate, it is easily used to buy all the rest' (*l'Inégalité*, in *Political Writings*, I, 192). Thus the early aesthetic and moral critique of the *Discours sur les Sciences et les Arts*, that science and civilization served directly and indirectly to oppress rather than uplift man's well-being, was given an explicitly social and economic point in a second work, *Discours sur l'origine et les fondements de l'inégalité parmis les hommes* (1754).

> From the extreme inequality of conditions and fortunes, from the diversity of passions and talents, from useless arts, from pernicious arts, from frivolous sciences would come scores of prejudices equally contrary to reason, happiness, and virtue (*Political Writings* I, 193).

In the *Economie politique*, Rousseau does not confine himself to purely economic matters but, consonant with the intellectual style of the period, often blurs what are now distinctive disciplines to offer his tentative reflections on the proper construction of political society. The *Economie* discusses the relations between the family and the State and those differences necessarily separating familial regulation and political authority, the relationship of the individual to the State, and the power and importance of civic education and political law itself to create equal public citizens out of unequal private men. The discussions of both the family and the law would later reappear almost verbatim in Rousseau's more mature political statement, the *Contrat social* (1762). More importantly, the *Economie* also reproduces the essence of his earlier Lockean considerations on the right of property and a lengthy discussion, comprising more than a third of the entire essay, of the problem of taxation. It is these discussions of taxes and property rights that prove problematic for the coherence of Rousseau's economic thought.

With regard to taxes, Rousseau appears in agreement with the adage that in all but the ideal world, taxation, like death, is inevitable. Yet he offers no consistent position on the best type or method of taxation. In the *Economie*, he rejects on principle both a land and a corn tax in favour of a conditional capitation tax and heavy luxury taxes. In his last work, *Le Gouvernement de Pologne* (1772), his proposals are almost exactly the reverse (*Political Writings* I, 269–71; II, 482–4). By this work Rousseau had come to believe that education rather than sumptuary laws was more efficacious in directing the opinions of the citizens toward economic reform.

In regard to private property, it has been commonly noted that Rousseau's suggestion in the *Economie* of social ties (however rudimentary) and property relations predating the State and providing 'le vrai fondement de la société civile, et le vrai garant des engagements des citoyens' (*Political Writings*, I, 259), represents a lapse into an individualism sharply at odds with the organic and collectivist position of his most famous political concept, the General Will. On Rousseau's account, submission to the General Will means submission to a will which is so inflexible that no individual can escape and dominate others, and in which 'the [property] right exercized by each individual over his own particular share is always subordinate (*toujours subordonné*) to the right (*droit*) of the Community over everything (*à sur tous*)' (*Political Writings*, II, 39). Liberty is thus understood not as the removal of all 'chains' of obligation, but rather as the substitution of legitimate bonds of sovereign law for the personal dependence fostered by inequality of wealth.

The theory of government developed in the *Economie* and the later *Contrat social* expresses the sovereign law of the General Will, and is therefore legitimate, because its public policies eliminate the manipulation of political power by the wealthy. However, Rousseau did not expect government to eliminate all inequality. Although the author of *Contrat social* was interpreted by the leaders of the French Revolution, and most notably, Robespierre, as a proponent of a radical political egalitarianism, such a view sits uneasily within a general understanding of Rousseau's work. The fit is particularly poor with his final writing on Poland. There Rousseau is explicit in his claim that civil society is dependent upon rulers and that so long as rights and duties under the rule of law are respected and private citizens are unable to direct public affairs in the service of their private interests, inequality of authority is accepted. In this sense, Rousseau's own thought cannot be termed 'socialism', either economically or politically, though its overarching concern with the human and moral effects of extreme economic inequality has often supplied theoretical foundations to which later socialists have turned for support.

S.C. Stimson

Where applicable, my translations have been matched to the standard translation of Roger D. Masters and Judith R. Masters, *The First and Second Discourses*, New York: St Martins, 1964.

SELECTED WORKS

1915. *The Political Writings of Jean Jacques Rousseau.* 2 vols, ed. C.E. Vaughan, Cambridge: Cambridge University Press. Reprinted, Oxford: Basil Blackwell, 1962.

1964. *The First and Second Discourses.* Trans. R.D. and J.R. Masters, New York: St Martin's.

1964–80. *Oeuvres complètes.* 4 vols, published under the supervision of Bernard Gangnebin and Marcel Raymond, Paris: Gallimard, Bibliothèque de la Pléiade.

BIBLIOGRAPHY

Sklar, J.N. 1969. *Men and Citizens: A Study of Rousseau's Social Theory.* London: Cambridge University Press.

Roy, René François Joseph (1894–1977). René Roy was born in Paris on 21 May 1894. He entered the Ecole Polytechnique in 1914, and joined the army on 15 August 1914. He was seriously wounded on 14 April 1917 at the Chemin des Dames, as a result of which he was blinded at the early age of 23. This tragedy, which meant the collapse of all his youthful hope and dreams, brought him to the slough of despond, and exceptional spiritual strength alone enabled him eventually to accept the unacceptable with serenity and to undertake a double career as an engineer and economist that was to last 60 years.

He studied at the Ecole Polytechnique (from 1918 to 1920) graduating first in his year, and then at the Ecole Nationale des Ponts et Chaussées (1920–22). He entered the Ministry of Public Works and Transport as a state engineer in 1922, specializing in problems of local railway networks and urban transport until his retirement in 1964. He died in Paris in 1977.

In parallel with this activity, he became Professor of General Political Economy and Social Economy at the Ecole des Ponts et Chaussées in 1929, and Professor of Econometrics at the Statistical Institute of the University of Paris in 1931. In 1949 he taught econometrics at the Ecole d'Application de l'Institut National de la Statistique et des Etudes Economiques (School of Instruction of the National Institute of Statistics and Economic Studies). From 1947 he was in charge of an Econometrics Seminar at the National Centre of Scientific Research.

He was elected President of the Paris Statistical Society in 1949 and of the International Econometrics Society in 1953. He was also a fellow of the International Statistical Society (1949), a member of the Academy of Moral and Political Science (1951), and an honorary fellow of the Royal Statistical Society (1957). He received the degree of Doctor Honoris Causa from the University of Geneva in 1964.

René Roy's research was focused mainly on transport, demand functions, economic indices, fields of choice and their respective relationships. His main published works are *Le régime économique des voies ferrées d'intérêt local* (1925), his doctoral thesis; *La demande de biens de consommation directe* (1935); *De l'utilité – contribution à la théorie des choix* (1942); 'Les nombres indices' (*Journal de la Société de Statistique de Paris*, 1949); and *Eléments d'économétrie* (1970). In addition, in collaboration with François Divisia and Jean Dupin, he published in 1953–4 *A la recherche du franc perdu*, whose three volumes cover the movement of prices, production and wealth respectively in France from 1914 to 1950. Roy's analysis of the basic relationships of demand functions and price and quantity index numbers are contained in his 1949 publication.

René Roy's ability to analyse very difficult questions and constantly stay abreast of the main publications of his era was a truly remarkable achievement for a totally sightless person. He showed that accomplishment is possible in the face of an irremediable adversity by dint of unremitting energy associated with remarkable intelligence. His book *Vers la lumière* (1930) gives us his message as a blind man.

MAURICE ALLAIS

See also INDIRECT UTILITY FUNCTION.

SELECTED WORKS

1925. *Le régime économique des voies ferrées d'intérêt local*. Doctoral thesis.
1930. *Vers la lumière*. Paris: Bibliotheque-Charpentier.
1935. *Le demande de biens de consommation directe*. Paris: Hermann.
1942. *De l'utilité – contribution à la théorie des choix*. Paris: Hermann.
1949. Les nombres indices. *Journal de la Société de Statistique de Paris* (1–2), January–February, 15–34.
1953–4. (With F. Divisia and J. Dupin.) *A la recherche du franc perdu*. Paris: Société d'Editions Hommes et Mondes.
1970. *Eléments d'économétrie*. Paris: Presses Universitaires de France.

Royal Economic Society. Originally known as the British Economic Association (BEA), until it obtained a Privy Council charter and royal patronage in 1902, the Royal Economic Society (RES) was unquestionably the leading organization of professional economists in Britain until after World War II, when its hegemony was seriously threatened by the Association of University Teachers of Economics (AUTE), a body which had its modest beginnings in the late 1920s.

The inaugural meeting of the BEA in 1890 was preceded by a lengthy period of discussion and negotiation among its founder members, partly because of their uncertainty whether to establish a new body in addition to the Royal Statistical Society and Section F (Economics and Statistics) of the British Association For the Advancement of Science.

Although it was consciously modelled on the American Economic Association (AEA), which had been founded five years earlier, the BEA adopted a more cautious and restricted policy than its transatlantic counterpart. Some of the AEA's most prominent members had been vigorously engaged in public controversy over methodological and policy issues, and this may have led Alfred Marshall, the most influential British economist, to urge a more cautious procedure. In the event, the BEA refrained from organizing regular discussion meetings or conferences on theoretical or policy questions, partly for fear of exposing the substantial divisions within the ranks. Also unlike the AEA, the BEA's Council, in its early years, periodically selected as its President a prominent public figure, usually a senior politician or acknowledged statesman, rather than an academic personage.

Despite the presence of many non-academic persons among its members (who were designated as Fellows from 1902 to 1964, under the Royal Charter) and on its Executive Committee and Council right up to the present, the academics have always exercised the predominant influence over the RES's affairs. And, as might be expected given the British academic structure, Oxford and especially Cambridge men were effectively in control. The BEA's principal *raison d'être* was the inauguration of *The Economic Journal*, which soon became recognized as the leading British scholarly periodical in economics, although a rival publication, *The Economic Review*, had been launched a few months earlier in Oxford, by a group of economists with strong Christian Socialist leanings. Under a series of distinguished editors, including F.Y. Edgeworth, J.M. Keynes, R. Harrod, and E.A.G. Robinson, the *Journal* acquired a worldwide reputation, whereas *The Economic Review* ceased publication in 1914, and the AEA did not issue a regular periodical, *The American Economic Review*, until 1911. Another of the founder-members' aims, the issue of reprints of economic classics, was also successfully accomplished, albeit initially on a modest scale.

With the rapid post-1945 growth of economics in the provincial universities and at the London School of Economics, which had been a considerable force in the discipline since the 1920s, the balance of professional influence and authority inevitably shifted away from the older centres. New journals had been founded in the 1930s, and the growing desire for academic conferences and opportunities for professional discussion encouraged support for the AUTE, which did not rigidly restrict its membership to academic economists especially after the mid-1960s, when many of them were spending longer or shorter periods of employment in

Whitehall or in international agencies and other public bodies. These changes eventually had a marked impact on the RES's traditional organization and policies, especially after a severe financial crisis in the early 1970s. A more regular rotation of Council members had already been inaugurated in 1968 and a more open nomination procedure was introduced in 1975. A substantial Editorial Advisory Board was established for the *Economic Journal* in 1971. The editorship shifted decisively away from Cambridge in 1976, first to Oxford and Sussex, and then to York and Bath, and the Editorial Advisory Board was disbanded. Also the Society increasingly sponsored regular and occasional conferences either alone or with the AUTE and other bodies. Thus in its composition, management, and range of functions the RES now more closely resembles the AEA, its original model, than at any previous time in its history. Among its lasting contributions are the outstanding editions of the works of Edgeworth, Jevons, Keynes, Marshall, Overstone and Ricardo produced under RES sponsorship.

A.W. Coats

BIBLIOGRAPHY

Coats, A.W. 1967. Sociological aspects of British economic thought c. 1880 to 1930. *Journal of Political Economy* 75(5), October, 706–29.

Coats, A.W. 1968. The origins and early development of the Royal Economic Society. *Economic Journal* 78(2), June, 349–71.

Coats, A.W. (With S.E. Coats.) 1970. The social composition of the Royal Economic Society and the beginnings of the economics 'profession' 1890–1915. *British Journal of Sociology* 21(1), March, 75–85.

Coats, A.W. 1973. The changing social composition of the Royal Economic Society 1890–1960 and the professionalization of British economics. *British Journal of Sociology* 24(2), June, 165–87.

Maloney, J. 1985. *Marshall, Orthodoxy and the Professionalization of Economics*. Cambridge: Cambridge University Press.

Rueff, Jacques (1896–1978). Born in Paris, Rueff graduated from Ecole Polytechnique (1921), where he had been a pupil of Clément Colson. He lectured at the Institut de Statistique (1923–31) and held a chair at the Ecole libre des sciences politiques (1930–50). Rueff owes his reputation to his exceptional career in public administration and his persuasive talent. In Poincaré's monetary reform (1926–8), he was called to determine the new value of the franc. In 1930 he was posted to London, as financial attaché at the French Embassy. In 1934 he entered the Ministry of Finance, where as Director of Treasury (1936–9) he had to cope with the acute financial difficulties of the governments of the time. As Vice-Governor of the Bank of France (1939–40), he was in charge of exchange controls. He headed the Inter-Allied Agency for Reparations (1946–52). From 1952 to 1962 he was a Magistrate first at the Court of Justice of the ECSC and from 1958 on, at the Court of Justice of the European Communities. In 1958 Rueff played a leading role in the monetary reform that led to the convertibility and the stabilization of the franc. This was followed by his masterly contribution to the Armand–Rueff report on *The Obstacles to Economic Expansion* (1960).

As he argued in his first essay, *From the Physical to the Social Sciences* (1922), Rueff believed that the methodological principles of the natural sciences should also apply to the human sciences. This explains his imperturbable faith in the process of economic equilibrium. In the reparations controversy of the 1920s, Rueff saw the core of the problem in the budgetary difficulty of levying the reparations. In opposition to Keynes, Rueff (1929) held that the trade balance would adjust quickly and adequately. The persistent payments imbalances in the post-World War II period were also seen as the consequence of the reluctance to reduce internal demand in the deficit countries.

In the 1960s, Rueff became a vocal detractor of the gold exchange standard. As the adjustment mechanism in such a system can be seen as biased to the advantage of the key-currency country, Rueff's thesis obtained the official backing of President de Gaulle. The restoration of a symmetrical gold standard thus became the French alternative to proposals to extend the IMF prerogatives.

Besides his strong Ricardian-like monetary beliefs, Rueff had wider human concerns. Deeply impressed by the political consequences of the financial disorders and the gross interferences in the price mechanism since the Twenties, he heralded the dangers ahead in *L'ordre social* (1945), the French counterpart of Hayek's *Road to Serfdom*. Rueff's distinction between true and false claims (*vrais et faux droits*), that is, between those backed by real assets and those that are not, gives the clue to his distinction between civilizations based on the rule of law within a free market system, and those requiring compulsion to settle disorders resulting from defective markets. Government distribution and monetization of false claims, by leading to inflation, macro-imbalances and controls, are seen as the main threat to individual freedom.

Roger Dehem

SELECTED WORKS

1922. *Des sciences physiques aux sciences morales. Introduction à l'étude de la morale et de l'économie politique rationelles*. Paris: Alcan. Trans. by H. Green as *From the Physical to the Social Sciences. Introduction to a Study of Economic and Ethical Theory*, Baltimore: Johns Hopkins Press; London: H. Milford and Oxford University Press, 1929.

1925. *Sur une théorie de l'inflation*. Nancy and Paris: Berger-Levrault.

1927. *Théorie des phénomènes monétaires; statique*. Paris: Payot.

1929. *Une erreur économique: l'organisation des transferts*. Doin.

1935. *La crise du capitalisme*. Paris:Editions de la Revue Bleue.

1945. *L'ordre social*. Paris: Recueil Sirey.

1949. *Epître aux dirigistes*. Paris: Gallimard.

1953. *La régulation monétaire et le problème institutionnel de la monnaie*. Paris: Recueil Sirey.

1961. *Discours sur le crédit*. Paris: Editions du Collège Libre des Sciences Sociales et Économiques.

1964. *The Age of Inflation*. Chicago: H. Regnery.

1967. *Balance of Payments; proposals for the most pressing world economic problem of our time*. New York: Macmillan.

1971. *Le péché monétaire de l'Occident*. Paris: Plon.

1972. *Combats pour l'ordre financier; Mémoires et documents pour servir à l'histoire du dernier demi-siècle*. Paris: Plon.

1977. *Les fondements philosophiques des systèmes économiques. Textes de Jacques Rueff et essais rédigés en son honneur*. Paris: Payot.

rural economy. *See* DUAL ECONOMIES; PEASANTS.

Ruskin, John (1819–1900). Ruskin was born in London in 1819 and died at Brantwood, his house by Coniston Water in Cumberland, in 1900. In the 1840s and 1850s he rose to eminence in Victorian Britain as a critic of painting and architecture. A developing concern with the social relations of art and the influence of Thomas Carlyle led him to outspoken social criticism and from the 1860s he assumed a position as one of the most virulent opponents of 19th-century industrial capitalism. His lectures in Manchester in 1857 on *The Political Economy of Art* were followed by a series of works that castigated Victorian society in general and political economy in particular for sanctioning commercial immorality. Of these, the most important were *Unto This Last* (1862) – so controversial that its original publication as essays in the *Cornhill Magazine* in 1860 was stopped by the proprietor; a series of lectures and letters published in the mid-1860s including *Sesame and Lilies* (1865), *Ethics of the Dust* (1866), *Crown of Wild Olive* (1866) and *Time and Tide* (1867); *Munera Pulveris* (1872), which first appeared as four articles in *Fraser's Magazine* in 1862–3 and was to have formed the preface to a larger treatise on political economy that was never written; and the enigmatic and highly individual monthly letters 'to the workmen and labourers of Great Britain' issued by Ruskin between 1871–1884 as *Fors Clavigera*.

Much of Ruskin's writing on political economy originated in the attempt to refute specific economic doctrines as formulated by the discipline's more illustrious propagandists. He was not a systematic thinker but the most cogent exposition of his own economic ideas can be found in *Unto This Last* which was written to provide, as Ruskin explained in the preface, 'an accurate and stable definition of wealth' and to show that its acquisition was possible 'only under certain moral conditions of society'. These objects were at the heart of Ruskin's endeavours. He sought to redefine all the basic categories of political economy – not only wealth but value, labour and capital as well – as a prelude to the construction of harmonious social relations in an ideal, moral society to be characterized by cooperation, justice and hierarchic order rather than competition, avarice and flux. He launched an assault on the discipline of economics as an abstraction which deliberately excluded all questions of moral action, which caricatured human nature, and which spread doctrines that were inconsistent with Christianity. Political economy sanctioned speculation, the taking of interest on invested capital and the policy of laissez-faire: in practice it led to the intensification of social divisions and the dehumanization of work by divorcing mental from manual labour. To all of this Ruskin was implacably opposed.

His critique was by no means novel: Tory paternalists earlier in the century and the Christian Socialists who Ruskin met at the Working Men's College in London where he taught art from 1854 to 1860 had used similar arguments before him. But no other Victorian approached Ruskin's style of invective, his fluent fury and vehemence. Middle-class opinion ignored his 'windy hysterics' – *Unto This Last* sold only 900 copies in eleven years – and his challenge to orthodox economics came from too far outside accepted economic discourse to have troubled its practitioners. But Ruskin was an important influence on celebrated individuals including William Morris, Tolstoy, Gandhi and Proust, who translated *Sesame and Lilies* and *The Bible of Amiens* (1880–5) into French. And though personally hostile to socialism, Ruskin was read and revered throughout the emerging British labour movement at the turn of the century.

LAWRENCE GOLDMAN

SELECTED WORKS

1857. *The Political Economy of Art*. Later published as *A Joy for Ever*, London: Smith, Elder & Co., 1880. In *Works*, Vol. 16, 1904.

1862. *Unto This Last. Four Essays on the First Principles of Political Economy*. London: Smith, Elder & Co. In *Works*, Vol. 17, 1905. Also available in a good modern edition, ed. P.M. Yarker, London: Collins, 1970.

1871–84. *Fors Clavigera. Letters to the Workmen and Labourers of Great Britain*. London. In *Works*, Vols 27–9, 1907.

1872. *Munera Pulveris*. London. In *Works*, Vol. 17, 1905.

1893. *A Complete Bibliography of the Writings in Prose and Verse of John Ruskin, LL.D.* 2 vols, ed. T.J. Wise, London. Reprinted, London: Dawsons of Pall Mall, 1964.

1903–12. *The Works of John Ruskin*. 39 vols, ed. E.T. Cook and A. Wedderburn, London: George Allen. (This is still the standard collection of Ruskin's works.)

BIBLIOGRAPHY

J.A. Hobson's sympathetic biography (Hobson, 1898), which examines Ruskin's social and economic ideas in detail, is testimony to his influence over advanced liberals and socialists at the turn of the century. Other biographical studies include Leon (1949), Hunt (1982), and Hilton (1985). For modern studies of Ruskin's social and economic thought see Sherburne (1972) and Anthony (1983).

Anthony, P.D. 1983. *John Ruskin's Labour. A Study of Ruskin's Social Theory*. Cambridge: Cambridge University Press.

Hilton, T. 1985. *John Ruskin: The Early Years*. New Haven and London: Yale University Press.

Hobson, J.A. 1898. *John Ruskin, Social Reformer*. London: J. Nisbet & Co.

Hunt, J.D. 1982. *The Wider Sea: A Life of John Ruskin*. London: Dent.

Leon, D. 1949. *Ruskin, The Great Victorian*. London: Routledge & Kegan Paul.

Sherburne, J.S. 1972. *John Ruskin or the Ambiguities of Abundance*. Cambridge, Mass.: Harvard University Press.

Ryazanov, David (1870–1938). Ryazanov was born David Borisovich Goldendach on 10 March 1870, in Odessa. Because of his connections, first with the Narodniks, then with the budding social democracy, he spent several years in prison. In 1898, he joined the new Russian Social Democratic Party, belonging after 1903 to the Menshevik wing. Between 1900 and 1905, he did research abroad on the labour movement and contributed to Kautsky's *Neue Zeit*. He participated in the Revolution of 1905, and by 1907 was again in Germany, doing that research on Marx and Engels on which his fame is mainly based.

By this time Franz Mehring and others had started the publication of works of Marx and Engels hidden in archives, private collections and often obscure periodicals. Ryazanov contributed two volumes, *Gesammelte Schriften von K. Marx und F. Engels, 1852 bis 1862* (1920, published in Stuttgart and translated into German by Luise Kautsky), which contain among others the writings on the Crimean War and on Palmerston. The war intervened with a study on the First International, which was only published in 1926 as *Die Entstehung der Internationalen Arbeiter Assoziation* (Marx–Engels Archiv I, Frankfurt am Main).

The revolution of 1917 brought Ryazanov back to Russia, where he joined the Bolsheviks, who formed the Communist Party in 1918. He placed all his knowledge at the service of the Soviet State, and in 1920 became director of the new Marx–Engels Institute. His main purpose was the preparation of the collected works of Marx and Engels. To this end, Ryazanov went travelling abroad, collecting, copying, buying whatever he could find, including material from the rich archives of the German Social Democratic Party. The Institute bought up whole libraries on economic and labour conditions in various countries. Starting from scratch, the Institute in 1930 possessed 55,000 pages of photostats, 32,000 pamphlets, 450,000 books and periodicals, and was growing.

The Russian edition of the works of Marx and Engels came out between 1931 and 1951 in 28 volumes. The edition in the original languages included only seven volumes, containing works up to 1848. It is known as the MEGA, short for *Marx–Engels Gesamtausgabe* (published in Berlin, Moscow and Leningrad, 1927–35). It made available the *Deutsche Ideologie* and the *Economic–Philosophic Manuscripts of 1844*. The *Dialectics of Nature* came out in *Marx–Engels Archiv* II (1927, 117–395). The Institute also published many other works of marxist authors, such as Plekanov and Liebknecht.

Ryazanov's lectures on Marx and Engels, published in 1923 and 1928 in Russian, were published in English as *Karl Marx and Friedrich Engels* (1927) and republished with a new preface in 1973. His remarkable edition of *The Communist Manifesto* appeared in English in 1930.

Because of his involvement in Menshevik activity, Ryazanov lost his position in 1931, and was succeeded by V.V. Adoratskilz (1878–1945). He spent some time in Saratov and Leningrad, doing research. He died in Saratov in 1938.

D.J. STRUIK

SELECTED WORKS

1917. (ed.) *Gesammelte Schriften von Karl Marx und Friedrich Engels 1852 bis 1862*. 2 vols. Trans. L. Kautsky, Stuttgart: J.H.W. Dietz.

1926. (ed.) *Die Entstehung der Internationalen Arbeiter Assoziation. Marx–Engels Archiv* I, Frankfurt am Main.

1927a. (ed.) *Dialectics of Nature. Marx–Engels Archiv* II, 117–395.

1927b. *Karl Marx and Friedrich Engels*. New York: International Publishers. Republished with new preface by D.J. Struik, New York and London: Monthly Review Press, 1973.

1927–35. (ed.) *Marx–Engels Gesamtausgabe* (full title: *Karl Marx, Friedrich Engels, Historisch-Kritische Gesamtausgabe, Werke, Schrifte, Briefe*). 7 vols. Berlin and Moscow-Leningrad: Marx–Engels Institute.

1930. *The Communist Manifesto of Karl Marx and Friedrich Engels*. Introduction and explanatory note by D. Ryazanov. Trans. from the Russian edn of 1922. London: Martin Lawrence.

Rybczinski theorem. *See* HECKSCHER-OHLIN TRADE THEORY.

S

saddlepoints. The assumption that economic agents act as if they were maximizing some criterion function subject to feasibility constraints is central to much of modern economic theory. A typical static problem is

$$\max_x f(x) \qquad \text{subject to } g(x) \leq \alpha \tag{1}$$

where

$$x = (x_1, \ldots, x_n)$$
$$f(x) = f(x_1, \ldots, x_n)$$
$$g^i(x) = g^i(x_1, \ldots, x_n)$$
$$g(x) = [g^1(x), \ldots, g^m(x)]$$

and

$$\alpha = (\alpha_1, \ldots, \alpha_m).$$

The Lagrangian function for the constrained maximization problem (1) is

$$L(x, \lambda) = f(x) + \lambda[\alpha - g(x)]' \tag{2}$$

where the prime denotes the transpose operator and where

$$\lambda = (\lambda_1, \ldots, \lambda_m)$$

is a vector of Lagrangian multipliers.

A point (x^*, λ^*) is a *saddlepoint* if

$$L(x, \lambda^*) \leqslant L(x^*, \lambda^*) \leqslant L(x^*, \lambda) \tag{3}$$

for all finite x and all finite $\lambda \geqslant 0$. Equivalently, (x^*, λ^*) is a so-called max–min point of the function $L(x, \lambda)$ with

$$L(x^*, \lambda^*) = \max_x \min_\lambda L(x, \lambda).$$

The following theorem relating (1) and (3) is well known; see, for example, Intriligator (1971).

Theorem (a) x^* solves (1) if (x^*, λ^*) is a saddlepoint of $L(x, \lambda)$. (b) If (i) $f(x)$ is concave, (ii) $g(x)$ is convex, and (iii) there exists some vector x^0 such that $g(x^0) < \alpha$, then x^* is a solution to (1) only if (x^*, λ^*) is a saddlepoint of $L(x, \lambda)$ for some λ^*.

Suppose further that the constraints hold with equality, that is that $g(x) = \alpha$. It then can be proved that

$$\frac{\partial f(x^*)}{\partial \alpha} = \lambda^*. \tag{4}$$

That is, (4) implies that the Lagrangian multiplier λ_i^* measures the increase in the maximized value $f(x^*)$ if the constraint constant α_i is increased. A well-known example of this general result arises in consumption theory where an economic agent is assumed to maximize a concave utility function defined over consumption goods subject to a linear budget constraint with given consumption good prices and given income. For this standard problem the result that the associated Lagrangian multiplier is equal to the marginal utility of income is immediate from (4).

A typical dynamic maximization problem is of the form

$$\max_u \int_0^T f(x, u, t)\,\mathrm{d}t$$

subject to

$$\dot{x} = g(x, u, t), \quad x(0) = x_0, \quad x(T) = x_T \tag{5}$$

where $u = (u_1, \ldots, u_n)$ is a vector of control variables to be selected (often $u = \dot{x}$) and where f and g are concave functions. Analogous to (2), we may write

$$L[\{u(t)\}, \{\lambda(t)\}] = \int_0^T f(x, u, t)\,\mathrm{d}t + \int_0^T \lambda[g(x, u, t) - \dot{x}]'\,\mathrm{d}t \tag{6}$$

where $\{u(t)\}$ and $\{\lambda(t)\}$ denote paths from $t = 0$ to $t = T$. The paths solving (6) from $t = 0$ to $t = T$ are $\{u^*(t)\}$ and $\{\lambda^*(t)\}$, and these paths are a saddlepoint in function space with

$$L[\{u(t)\}, \{\lambda^*(t)\}] \leqslant L[\{u^*(t)\}, \{\lambda^*(t)\}] \leqslant L[\{u^*(t)\}, \{\lambda(t)\}]. \tag{7}$$

However, the situation is complex because there are *other* saddlepoints associated with the dynamic maximization problem (5), and we shall return to this observation subsequently; the reader interested in details is referred to Samuelson (1972) and the references there cited.

In game theory saddlepoints result from strategies which minimize the maximum loss. Similarly saddlepoints exist in problems where the objective is to maximize the minimum level of utility, either across agents or over time for a representative agent; see, for example, Burmeister and Hammond (1977). Finally, in many economic models saddlepoints are associated with the solutions to the differential equations which govern the motion of the system. Since the latter type of saddlepoints arise from (i) dynamic maximization problems similar to (5), (ii) many descriptive economic models, and (iii) most rational expectations models, a brief discussion to reveal the economic consequences of such dynamic saddlepoint equilibria is essential.

Consider an economy in which $x_1(t), \ldots, x_n(t)$ denote state variables (e.g. stocks of capital goods) at time t and $p_1(t), \ldots, p_n(t)$ denote corresponding dual variables (e.g. prices of capital goods) at time t. Let $x(t)$ and $p(t)$ be denoted by the vectors $[x_1(t), \ldots, x_n(t)]$ and $[p_1(t), \ldots, p_n(t)]$, respectively. Assume that the dynamics of the economy can be summarized by

$$\begin{bmatrix} \dot{x}(t) \\ \dot{p}(t) \end{bmatrix} = F[x(t), p(t)]. \tag{8}$$

Let (x^*, p^*) denote a rest point (dynamic equilibrium) of (8) for which

$$\begin{bmatrix} 0 \\ 0 \end{bmatrix} = F(x^*, p^*). \qquad (9)$$

The rest point (x^*, p^*) is called a *saddlepoint* when the system has certain stability properties to be discussed below.

Let the Jacobian matrix of (8) be

$$J(x, p) = \begin{bmatrix} \partial \dot{x}/\partial x & \partial \dot{x}/\partial p \\ \partial \dot{p}/\partial x & \partial \dot{p}/\partial p \end{bmatrix}. \qquad (10)$$

Assume that the matrix $J(x^*, p^*)$ is nonsingular and has distinct characteristic roots so that the local stability properties of the nonlinear system (8) are the same as the linear approximation to (8) in a neighbourhood of (x^*, p^*). In the discussion which follows it is assumed that the local stability properties of the rest point (x^*, p^*) also hold globally, thus excluding the possibility of either (i) cyclic behaviour around (x^*, p^*), or (ii) convergence to a different rest point. When the possibilities (i) and (ii) are not excluded, the subsequent analysis is valid only in a neighbourhood of (x^*, p^*).

The $n = 1$ case is easiest. Then J is a 2×2 matrix with characteristic roots λ_1 and λ_2, assumed distinct. In a neighbourhood of (x^*, p^*), the solution to the system (8) is (i) stable if the real parts of λ_1 and λ_2 are negative, (ii) unstable if the real parts of λ_1 and λ_2 are positive, and (iii) a *saddlepoint equilibrium* if λ_1 and λ_2 are of opposite signs (in the 2×2 case these roots are necessarily real).

A necessary and sufficient condition for case (iii) is $\det[J(x^*, p^*)] < 0$.

Suppose this saddlepoint case prevails. At any initial time, say $t = 0$, the state variable $x(0)$ is given. When will the system be stable in the sense that

$$\lim_{t \to \infty} [x(t), p(t)] = (x^*, p^*) \qquad (11)$$

starting from the initial condition with $x(0)$ given? The answer is that there exists one and only one initial value of the dual variable, say $\hat{p}(0)$, for which (11) holds. For all other initial values $p(0) \neq \hat{p}(0)$, the system (8) diverges away from (x^*, p^*).

Additional possibilities arise when $n > 1$. A rest point (x^*, p^*) of (8) for which the Jacobian matrix $J(x^*, p^*)$ has k characteristic roots with negative real parts and $2n - k$ characteristic roots with positive real parts is termed a *stationary point of type k* or a *k-saddle*; see El'sgol'c (1964). Thus a stationary point of type $2n$ is stable, a stationary point of type 0 is unstable, and all other stationary points are saddlepoints. A k-saddle is said to have a *convergent manifold of dimension k* in the $2n$-dimensional (x, p) space.

Saddlepoints always imply that (8) will converge for some *but not all* initial conditions $[x(0), p(0)]$. In economic applications the initial state vector $x(0)$ is fixed, so in effect stability depends upon 'choosing' the appropriate $p(0)$ vector.

In optimal growth or other optimizing models similar to (5) above with $\lambda = p$, normally the rest point (x^*, p^*) is a saddlepoint of type n or a *regular saddlepoint*. In such cases there exists a *unique* initial price vector $\hat{p}(0)$ which solves the optimization problem. It follows that the optimizing solution path is unique and stable.

However, in other economic models more complex cases can arise. If, for example, $k < n$, then convergence is impossible no matter what the initial condition $p(0)$. The interesting economic examples are featured by $n < k < 2n$. Burmeister et al. (1973) have constructed a model with two capital goods for which $n = 2$ and $k = 3$. That is, given the fixed initial conditions $x_1(0)$ and $x_2(0)$, there exists a whole set $\{p_1(0), p_2(0)\}$ for which (11) holds. In this case the convergent manifold in 4-dimensional space has dimension 3: given arbitrary (economically feasible) $x_1(0)$, $x_2(0)$, and one of $p_1(0)$ or $p_2(0)$, there exists a unique initial value of the other price such that (11) holds. Taylor (1977) has studied macroeconomic models which exhibit the same kind of stability properties.

Most rational expectation models have saddlepoints of type n. A unique equilibrium can then be determined if (11) is assumed to hold, or if some other condition implies (11). In other words, in rational expectations models having a saddlepoint equilibrium of type n, the stability condition (11) suffices to determine the initial price vector $p(0)$ uniquely; the dynamic evolution of the model is then uniquely determined by the 'laws of motion' (8). However, when $n < k < 2n$, there are many initial price vectors for which (11) holds; thus in general the stability condition (11) alone is not sufficient to determine a unique evolution of the economic system. Some of these issues are elaborated in Burmeister (1980, 1985).

Analogous results to those discussed above hold in the discrete-time case where (8) is replaced by a first-order difference equation.

EDWIN BURMEISTER

See also DUALITY; OPTIMAL CONTROL AND ECONOMIC DYNAMICS; STABILITY.

BIBLIOGRAPHY

Burmeister, E. 1980. On some conceptual issues in rational expectations modeling. *Journal of Money, Credit and Banking* 12(4), November, 800–16.

Burmeister, E. 1985. On the assumption of convergent rational expectations. In *Issues in Contemporary Macroeconomics and Distribution*, ed. G.R. Feiwel. London: Macmillan.

Burmeister, E. and Hammond, P.J. 1977. Maximin paths of heterogeneous capital accumulation and the instability of paradoxical steady states. *Econometrica* 45(4), May, 853–70.

Burmeister, E., Caton, C., Dobell, A.R. and Ross, S. 1973. The 'saddlepoint property' and the structure of dynamic heterogeneous capital good models. *Econometrica* 41(1), January, 79–95.

El'sgol'c, L.E. 1964. *Qualitative Methods in Mathematical Analysis.* AMS Translation of Mathematical Monographs, Vol. 12, Providence, RI: American Mathematical Society.

Intriligator, M.D. 1971. *Mathematical Optimization and Economic Theory*. Englewood Cliffs, NJ: Prentice-Hall.

Samuelson, P.A. 1972. The general saddlepoint property of optimal-control motions. *Journal of Economic Theory* 5(1), August, 102–20.

Taylor, J.B. 1977. Conditions for unique solutions in stochastic macroeconomic models with rational expectations. *Econometrica* 45(6), September, 1377–85.

Saint-Simon, Claude-Henri de Rouvroy (1760–1825). Born in 1760 into a noble family, Saint-Simon spent the first forty years of his life as a soldier and speculator before devoting himself to the study of science and society. Commissioned in 1778, he served with the French forces in the Caribbean and in America, taking part in the Battle of Yorktown (1781). In 1787 he left the army and became associated with a Spanish project for a canal linking Madrid to the Atlantic, in which project he intended to direct the workforce of 6000 men. The outbreak of the French Revolution prompted his return to France, where he became President of the Municipal Assembly in Falvy, near Péronne. His ambitions for social improvement led him into the purchase of aristocratic and church property from the government, and a financial partnership he formed to this end met with great success. A period of imprisonment in 1793–4 ended with the fall of Robespierre, and in the ensuing period his business interests expanded rapidly. On the proceeds of his financial successes he founded a salon and became a patron of the sciences. During the peace of 1801–2 he travelled to England, and then to Genèva to visit Madame de Stäel. While in Geneva he published his first text of any significance on the reform of society, *Lettre d'un habitant de Genève à l'humanité* (1802). Returning to Paris via Germany, he published further pieces on social reorganization, though his writing was interrupted by the collapse of his personal fortune in 1806. With the support of a former servant, Saint-Simon found time for full-time study and in 1807 was able to publish an introduction to the scientific tasks of the 19th century. In 1814 he was joined in his work by the historian Augustin Thierry, and with his aid assumed the role of a leading publicist for liberal interests. This found its most direct expression in the editing of a series of journals: *L'Industrie* (1816–18); *Le Politique* (1819); and *L'Organisateur* (1819–20). This last brought him some recognition in France and abroad, and led him to the publication of a series of pieces in 1821 under the title *Du Système industriel*, one of his most important works. Despite this success, he felt that his work failed to gain appropriate recognition, and he attempted suicide in 1823. Nursed back to health by a loyal band of followers, he continued writing and studying, his final years being marked increasingly by his interest in religious sentiment as a means of social change. He died in May 1825.

The work of Saint-Simon has been variously described as corporatist, totalitarian and even anarchist. Some care is needed in such characterizations, for the work of Saint-Simon must be distinguished from that of his followers like Comte or Halévy who contributed to the formation of 'Saint-Simonianism'; and it is also necessary to treat with care the accounts of Saint-Simon to be found in the work of those heavily influenced by him, such as Proudhon or Durkheim. Saint-Simon's own writing was not presented in a systematic manner, nor did he pay much regard to scholarly niceties when developing his ideas. Nevertheless, his name is associated with a number of important ideas which have marked the development of social thought.

Saint-Simon believed that the study of society should be conducted on a scientific basis; that a positive, empirical science of society was both necessary and possible. Society, he argued, was like an organism governed by natural laws; and a 'healthy' society was one which is well-organized. Proper recognition of this fact would make possible the reconstruction of society on sound foundations – utopia would become constructible through the application of science to society.

Future society would be *industrial* society, in which 'general directors' would ensure that useful work was unhindered and government would therefore administer things, not people. Politics would become the 'science of production' – the link to 19th-century socialist thought is here quite evident. 'Industry' embraced all kinds of productive activity, and so 'industrial society' is one of productive activity in general, not a vision of a technological or manufacturing future. Accordingly, society is primarily arranged into 'industrious' and 'idle' classes. The future society was not to be a classless one: differences between groups would continue to exist, but would not be a source of social antagonism.

In later life the teachings of Saint-Simon assumed an ever more spiritual cast, a development that was promoted after his death by the group of followers that he had gathered. In the early 1830s the sect had a large number of influential adherents, although a formal organization in the shape of a 'Church' soon collapsed. Napoleon III was an open admirer of Saint-Simon's ideas, and the creation of the Crédit Mobilier investment bank, a model commercial bank involved in economic and financial developments, owed much to Saint-Simon's ideas.

K. Tribe

SELECTED WORKS

Oeuvres de Claude-Henri de Saint-Simon. 6 vols, Paris: Editions Anthropos, 1966.

Social Organization, The Science of Man and other writings. Ed. F.M.H. Markham, New York: Harper & Row, 1964.

Henri Saint-Simon (1760–1825), Selected Writings on Science, Industry and Social Organisation. Ed. K. Taylor, London: Croom Helm, 1975.

St Petersburg paradox. *See* EXPECTED UTILITY HYPOTHESIS; EXPECTED UTILITY AND MATHEMATICAL EXPECTATION.

Salin, Edgar (1892–1974). Salin was born in Frankfurt am Main of Jewish origin. He studied in Heidelberg with Max and Adolf Weber, Eberhard Gothein and others. He became a university lecturer in Heidelberg in 1919, and in 1927 he was appointed professor of political economy at the University of Basle (Switzerland).

Salin's main work was his history of economic ideas from Plato to the present (1923). It provided a very broad overview about economic reasoning and may be perceived rather as a history of the relationship between political and economic thought, than as a mere history of economic analysis. It was also extremely provocative: at a time when the historical school still dominated the German economics profession, Salin criticized its anti-theoretical approach. Twenty-one years later, when historicism had practically disappeared, he was still discussing it at length in the revised third edition of this book, while he treated the postwar neoclassicals and Keynesians on a few pages as 'descendants and precursors' for their lack of a new social theory.

Salin himself always put the emphasis on economic history, and was sceptical of the use of mathematical methods. He was interested in many questions of applied economics and economic policy, such as regional, transport and development economics, technological development, monetary theory and policy, and problems of European integration, which he strongly supported. Salin did not identify with the German 'Ordoliberalismus', and advocated an active technology policy and other interventionist measures. In the debates of the Verein für Sozialpolitik in 1960 he advocated industrial concentration in order to increase German competitiveness and realize the advantages of European integration. He admired Keynes but was sceptical with regard to the possibility of stabilizing the business cycle.

Salin was an enlightened and liberal conservative. He was long-time executive secretary of the List Society, which he had refounded after World War II. He was founder of *Kyklos*, the international review for social sciences, and of Prognos, a well-known Swiss forecasting institute. Apart from being a versatile economist, he was also a brilliant *homme de lettres.* He wrote a book on the poet Stefan George and his personal and literary influence, and another on the encounter of Friedrich Nietzsche and Jakob Burckhardt and their later intellectual exchanges, and he translated four volumes of Plato.

B. Schefold

SELECTED WORKS

1923. *Geschichte der Volkswirtschaftslehre.* Berlin: Julius Springer, 1923. 3rd enlarged edn, Bern: A. Francke, 1944.

1963. *Lynkeus. Gestalten und Probleme aus Wirtschaft und Politik.* Tübingen: J.C.B. Mohr.

Salter, Wilfred Edward Graham (1929–1963). When Salter died in Pakistan at the very early age of 35 he had already established himself as an authority on technical progress and productivity change, both theoretically and empirically. A graduate of the University of Western Australia, and Clare College, Cambridge (where he won the much-coveted Stevenson Prize), his PhD thesis was to become his most cited work – *Productivity and Technical Change* (1960).

Techniques of production change through time for two, sometimes interacting reasons – improving technical knowledge and changing factor prices. But new techniques in firms will coexist beside old, change towards the most new taking place as extant plant reaches the limit of its economic life. These sustained technique changes Salter analyses through their impacts on prices, costs, investment and productivity using methods that are Marshallian in character relating to comparative performances of industries in the medium term. He then examines some of the implications against British and American industry data. The observation that above average increases in productivity are not reflected in earnings but are distributed to consumers through relative price reductions retains its relevance.

Further work on capital took him into the critical capital debates of the 1950s. He also wrote an innovative paper depicting the complex relationships between price and expenditure effects in reconciling full employment with balance of payments policy. After a period at Johns Hopkins University and the Australian National University, he served in the Prime Minister's Department from which he was seconded to assist the Pakistan Government in economic planning, the task he was absorbed in at his death.

MALCOLM R. FISHER

SELECTED WORKS

1954. *The Measurement of Australian Production*. Perth: University of Western Australia Press.

1958. L'expansion de la main-d'oeuvre Australienne. *Revue de la Société Belge d'études et d'expansion*, July.

1959a. The production function and the durability of capital. *Economic Record* 35, April, 47–66.

1959b. Internal and external balance: the role of price and expenditure effects. *Economic Record* 35, August, 226–38,

1960. *Productivity and Technical Change*. Cambridge: Cambridge University Press.

1962. Marginal labour and investment coefficients of Australian manufacturing industry. *Economic Record* 38(82), June, 137–55.

1965. Productivity growth and accumulation as historical process. In *Problems in Economic Development*, ed. E.A.G. Robinson, London: Macmillan.

Samuelson, Paul Anthony (born 1915). Paul Anthony Samuelson (born in Gary, Indiana, in 1915) has made fundamental contributions to nearly all branches of economic theory. Besides the specific analytic contributions, Samuelson more than anyone else brought economics from its pre-1930s verbal and diagrammatic mode of analysis to the quantitative mathematical style and methods of reasoning that have dominated for the last three decades. Beyond that, his *Economics* (McGraw Hill, first edition, 1948, now in its twelfth edition, the first with a co-author, William D. Nordhaus) has educated millions of students, teaching that economics, however dismal, need not be dull.

Ten eminent economists describe and evaluate his work in their respective fields in Brown and Solow (1983). Arrow (1967) and Lindbeck (1970) provide useful overall reviews. (See also the papers in Feiwel, 1982.)

Samuelson's work consists of *Foundations of Economic Analysis* (1947, reprinted in an enlarged edition in 1983), *Economics, Linear Programming and Economic Analysis* (1958, joint with Robert Dorfman and Robert M. Solow) and his *Collected Scientific Papers* (Volumes I and II, 1966; Volume III, 1972, Volume IV, 1977, and Volume V, 1986). The five volumes of the *Collected Papers* include 388 articles, most of them indeed scientific.

Bliss in his 1967 review of the first two volumes of the *Collected Scientific Papers* comments on the impossibility for anyone other than Samuelson of reviewing his work. The task has not been made any easier by the publication of another two volumes of collected papers, and by the 144-page summary of developments in economic theory since the *Foundations* in the 1983 enlarged edition. Rather than try to be comprehensive, I will describe the major analytic contributions in several areas, ending with macroeconomics where I also discuss Samuelson's views and advice on economic policy. I conclude with a description of his role at and through MIT.

Although the topic-by-topic approach is unavoidable, the man and the economist is more than the sum of his contributions in several areas. The verve and sparkle of his style, the breadth of his economic and general knowledge, the mastery of the historical setting and the generosity of his hyphenated freight-train allusions to predecessors, are unique. Samuelson's presidential address to the American Economic Association (1961: II, ch. 113) is a good sampler. (References to the *Collected Scientific Papers* (*CSP*) will give year of publication of the original article where needed, followed by volume number, and chapter and/or page number as needed.)

I. BACKGROUND

Samuelson has provided fragments of his autobiography in 'Economics in a Golden Age: A Personal Memoir' (1972: IV, ch. 278), and in biographical articles on contemporaries and teachers. He attended fourteen schools, in Gary, Indiana, on the North Side of Chicago, in Florida, and then at Hyde Park High in Chicago. From Hyde Park High he entered the University of Chicago in January 1932, taking his first economics course from Aaron Director. 'It was as if I was made for economics' (1972: IV, p. 885). Milton Friedman and George Stigler were Chicago graduate students at the time. Jacob Viner's famous course in economic theory provided the sound non-mathematical microeconomics that any economist needs to truly understand the field (1972: IV, ch. 282; see also Bronfenbrenner, 1982).

In 1935 he moved to graduate school at Harvard, propelled by a fellowship that required him to leave Chicago and attracted, he claims, by the ivy and the monopolistic competition revolution. Samuelson spent five years at Harvard, the last three as a Junior Fellow. It was the time of both the Keynesian and monopolistic competition revolutions, and 'Harvard was precisely the right place to be' (1972: IV, p. 889). The teachers he mentions most are Hansen, Leontief, Schumpeter and E.B. Wilson, the mathematical physicist and mathematical economist.

His fellow students make up the larger part of the honour roll of early post-World War II United States economics (1972: IV, p. 889). Among them was his wife of forty years, Marion Crawford (1915–1978), author of a well-known 1939 article on the tariff. Abram Bergson (particularly his 1938 article on the social welfare function) and Lloyd Metzler are most mentioned among his other fellow students. Samuelson was the dominant presence among the students: Cary Brown in conversation describes the excitement as his papers were analysed and absorbed by the graduate students; James Tobin in correspondence says that the students loved the seminars, where Samuelson could be counted on to put down his seniors with brash brilliance.

The Keynesian revolution and Alvin Hansen had a greater impact on Samuelson's work and attitudes than the monopolistic competition revolution and Chamberlin. Chamberlin is barely mentioned in his reminiscences of Harvard and his only monopolistic competition article appeared in 1967 in the Chamberlin *festschrift* (III, ch. 131). Much of Samuelson's work assumes perfect competition, but none of his macroeconomics or his policy advice gives any credence to the view that the macro-economy is better left alone than treated by active policy (except perhaps his views on flexible exchange rates).

His first published article 'A Note on the Measurement of Utility' (1937: I, ch. 20) appeared when he was a twenty-one-year-old graduate student. By 1938 the flow was up to five articles a year, a rate of production that has been maintained with perturbations for half a century. And of course, since 1948 he has produced a new edition of *Economics* almost every three years.

Samuelson moved to MIT as an Assistant Professor in 1940 and has remained there since. Harvard's failure to match MIT's offer at that time has been the subject of much speculation. Samuelson himself has been eager to find excuses for Harvard (1972: IV, ch. 278, footnote 11, p. 896). His is not the best position from which to judge or to write freely; he has noted that academic life, and by implication the chairman of the Economics Department, Burbank, one of the few of whom Samuelson speaks harshly in print, were not innocent of antisemitism in that pre-World War II era. Burbank was a political power in the Department and University. His attitude to mathematical economics can be gauged by the fact that indifference curves were outlawed in the introductory course he supervised.

It is hard to believe that even the Harvard of 1940 would have been unable to find room for an economist of Samuelson's already recognized stature unless a non-academic reason or reasons stood in the way. Among those reasons were antisemitism, his then brashness, and his brilliance: indeed Schumpeter is rumoured to have told his colleagues that it would have been easier to forgive their vote if it had been based on antisemitism rather than on the fact that Samuelson was smarter than they were.

Samuelson has been at MIT since 1940, virtually without a break. Except for a few months away on a Guggenheim, he has taken time off only in Cambridge, Mass. He proudly claims that he has never been in Washington for as long as a week – though he was a major adviser to President Kennedy. His only departure from academic economics came in 1944–5, when he worked at MIT's Radiation Laboratory. He became one of twelve MIT Institute Professors in 1966.

He has gathered all the honours the profession can offer: the first John Bates Clark medal (1947); the second Nobel Memorial Prize in Economics (1970); he has been President of the American Economic Association (1961), the Econometric Society (1951), and the International Economic Association (1965–68); and he has been awarded numerous other prizes and honorary degrees.

Although many graduate students have passed through his classes and been profoundly affected by him, there is no Samuelson school of economics, no overarching grand design for either economics or the world that is uniquely his. It is for that reason that his contributions have to be discussed field by field. The nearest that he has come to proclaiming a vision is in the *Foundations*.

II. FOUNDATIONS OF ECONOMIC ANALYSIS

Foundations, published in 1947, is based on Samuelson's 1941 David Wells prize-winning dissertation, *Foundations of Analytic Economics*, subtitled 'The Observational Significance of Economic Theory'. Its themes are partially described by the subtitle and by the motto from J. Willard Gibbs, 'Mathematics is a language'. The thesis, dated 1940, is very close in content to the *Foundations*.

The *Foundations* in places claims to be an attempt to derive empirically meaningful comparative equilibrium results from two general principles, that of maximization, and Samuelson's *correspondence principle*. The correspondence principle states that the hypothesis of dynamic stability of a system yields restrictions that make it possible to answer comparative equilibrium questions.

The maximizing theme recurs in Samuelson's 1970 Nobel Prize lecture, 'Maximum Principles in Analytic Economics' (III, ch. 130). The point is not the now common view that only models in which everyone is relentlessly maximizing are worth considering. Rather it is that the properties of the maximum (for instance, second order conditions) usually imply the comparative static properties of the system. Samuelson also invokes the generalized Le Chatelier principle, which loosely interpreted states that elasticities are larger the fewer constraints are imposed on a system. Analogies from physics (and biology) figure prominently in Samuelson's analytic methods and explanations of his results.

The correspondence principle was intended to do for market or macroeconomic comparative statics what maximization did for the comparative statics of the individual or firm. The principle can be useful when the analyst knows something about the dynamic behaviour of a system, but as noted by Tobin (1983), is ambiguous in that different dynamics may be consistent with the same steady state behaviour.

The simplest example of the ambiguity can be seen in a demand–supply diagram where the supply curve is negatively sloped. Whether a tax on the good will increase or reduce price depends on which curve is more steeply sloped. Whether the market is stable or not depends on the same fact and whether quantity or price rises in response to excess demand – that is, whether dynamics are Marshallian or Walrasian.

In the introduction to the 1983 enlarged edition, Samuelson records correctly that the *Foundations* was better off for not sticking to its narrow themes. Substance keeps breaking in on the methodology. The treatment of the theory of the consumer and firm, developed in detail, does not differ in essence from that of Hicks in *Value and Capital*. But where Hicks hides the mathematics in appendices, Samuelson flaunts his in the text. Nonetheless Samuelson takes pains to provide economic insight, including interpretations of Lagrange multipliers as shadow prices. These portions of the *Foundations* apparently existed in 1937–8 and were written independently of *Value and Capital* (Bronfenbrenner, 1982, p. 349), though not of course of Hicks and Allen (I, ch. 1, p. 4).

The theory of revealed preference (see below) receives prominence, as do two chapters on welfare economics, and in Part II chapters on the stability of general equilibrium. A few pages on money in the utility function (pp. 117–24) remain authoritative. The mathematical appendices on maximization and difference equations have been useful despite an elliptical style that leaves many steps to be filled in by the user.

Samuelson's thesis is dated 1940: *Foundations* is the work of a 25-year-old. There are signs of youth in the eagerness to proselytize for the new mathematical faith and its overreaching in trying to impose an entirely coherent theme on the material.

But the book bears the unmistakable mark of the master, in command of the economics of his material, at home with technique, and most remarkably for a young man in a hurry, thoroughly familiar and patient with the literature. It is, as Schumpeter no doubt remarked, a remarkable performance.

III. CONSUMER THEORY AND WELFARE ECONOMICS

Samuelson's first published paper (1937: I, ch. 20) set up a finite horizon continuous time intertemporal optimization model of a consumer with additively separable utility function and exponential discounting, and derived the result that the profile of consumption is determined by the relation between the interest rate and rate of time preference. The focus is however the measurability of utility.

The theory of revealed preference, his major achievement in consumer theory, made its unnamed appearance in 1938 in 'A note on the pure theory of consumer's behaviour' in *Economica* (I, ch. 1; see also Houthakker, 1983, and Mas-Colell, 1982, for exceptionally lucid accounts). The purpose was to develop the entire theory of the consumer free of 'any vestigial traces of the utility concept' (I, p. 13). Rather than postulate a utility function or, as Hicks and Allen had done, a preference ordering, Samuelson imposed conditions directly on the choices made by individuals – their preferences as revealed by their choices. The key condition was the weak axiom of revealed preference, applying to choices made in two situations, say zero and one. With prices and quantities of goods j, $j = 1, \ldots, n$ in situation i given by p_j^i and x_j^i, the axiom is

$$\sum_j p_j^0(x_j^1 - x_j^0) \leqslant 0 \quad \text{implies} \quad \sum_j p_j^1(x_j^1 - x_j^0) \leqslant 0$$

In words, if the individual chooses consumption bundle zero when he could have chosen the bundle one, he will not choose one when zero is available.

This minimal condition of consistency is shown to imply most of the conditions on demand implied by utility theory. But the symmetry and negative definitiveness of the Slutsky matrix could not be established using the weak axiom. Equivalently, the issue was the so-called integrability of demand functions, with the question being whether the preference map could be recovered given enough observations on the individual's choices. Houthakker (1950) solved the problem, by proposing the strong axiom of revealed preference, namely that for any finite string of choices in which B is revealed preferred to A, C is revealed preferred to B,..., and Z is revealed preferred to Y, then A is *not* revealed preferred to Z. In this case, and given appropriate continuity conditions on demand, the demand functions are integrable and an entire preference map, satisfying the Slutsky conditions, can be recovered from the individual's choices.

The full equivalence between the properties of the demand functions of an individual and the preference ordering is the leading example of Samuelson's definition of the operational or observational significance of economic theory. Samuelson regards a theory as meaningful if it is potentially refutable by data. A single consumer could make a succession of choices that contradict the strong axiom. But the theory is not operational in the sense that a modern econometrician would want it to be: it does not apply to aggregate data, nor, in the form in which Samuelson left it, does it apply to choices that are made in chronological time.

Revealed preference links the theory of demand, index numbers, and parts of welfare economics. The link between demand and index number theory comes in the *Foundations*' (pp. 147–8) recognition that the fundamental index number problem is to deduce from price and quantity information alone whether an individual is better off. Using the weak axiom, Samuelson demonstrates the conditions under which, in a comparison of two situations, it is possible to say whether an individual is better off in one (*Foundations*, pp. 156–63). He argues that index numbers add no information on the essential question and indeed may be positively misleading in tempting the observer to attach significance to the numerical scale of measurement.

A similar concern no doubt motivates Samuelson's long-standing hostility to the use of consumer surplus measures. He has frequently argued that there is no need for the concept. He asserts in *Foundations* (p. 197) that there is no need for consumer's surplus in answering, for example, the question of whether Robinson Crusoe, a socialist state, or a capitalist one, should build a particular bridge. That view may have been moderated over the decades: the 1985 Samuelson–Nordhaus *Economics* (p. 418) states that the concept 'is extremely useful in making many decisions about public goods – it has been employed in decisions about airports, roads, dams, subways, and parks' (bridges are conspicuously absent).

The revealed preference axiom comes into play too in Samuelson's 'Evaluation of Real National Income' (1950: II, ch. 77), a largely negative report on the then new welfare economics that attempted to deduce from aggregate data criteria that would make it possible to say whether society was better off in one situation than another. Taking, as he has since 1938, the viewpoint that a Bergsonian social welfare function is the best way of understanding social welfare issues, Samuelson showed that no index-number type national income comparison between situations A and B could reveal whether society's feasible utility possibility frontier (a useful Samuelson innovation, apparently simultaneously invented by Allais) in A lies uniformly outside that of B. And, he argued, we could claim situation A is better than B only if that is the case.

In the *Foundations* (chapter 8) Samuelson draws extensively on the Bergsonian social welfare function to elucidate definitively the notion of Pareto optimality and the 'germ of truth in Adam Smith's doctrine of the Invisible Hand' (*Foundations*, 1983 edn, p. xxiv). Arrow (1967) is critical of Samuelson's failure to look behind the social welfare function, and of his failure to link it to actual policy decisions. Similar sentiments are conveyed along with a more complete evaluation of Samuelson's welfare economics in Arrow (1983). Samuelson (1967: III, ch. 167) asserts that the Bergson Social Welfare Function and the Arrow Constitution Function are distinct concepts, though the argument is difficult to follow.

The expected utility theorem shows Samuelson wrestling for decades with his doubts over the independence axiom (I: ch. 12, 1950; ch. 13, 1952; ch. 14, 1952; *Foundations*, 1983, pp. 503–18). Despite his tentative 1983 acceptance of the expected utility formulation, he notes with approval Machina's 1982 development of expected utility without the independence axiom. Of course, these doubts have not kept him from making creative use of the expected utility approach in models of portfolio choice and finance.

IV. CAPITAL THEORY

The theory of capital and growth sections of the first four volumes of *CSP* account for 38 papers, the largest single category. Although capital theory is the branch of economics most vulnerable to Samuelson's comparative technical advantage, and although both his earliest papers are placed in that category in *CSP* (1937: I, ch. 17, ch. 20) the output in this area is concentrated in *CSP* III, covering the years from 1965 to 1970. Solow (1983) provides a fine review of this part of Samuelson's research, some of which he co-authored.

Among the early papers, the 1943 Schumpeter *festschrift* contribution 'Dynamics, Statics, and the Stationary State' (I, ch. 19) discusses the economics of the steady state and the possibility of a zero interest rate. Samuelson argues that a steady state with a zero real interest rate is possible if the rate of time preference of the infinitely lived individuals is zero; he has in mind a situation in which the marginal product of capital can be driven to zero. In this article (I, p. 210), as in his first paper (I, p. 216), Samuelson makes highly favourable reference to Ramsey, in contrast to the famous unflattering 1946 remark (II, p. 1528). The well-known argument that a zero rate of interest is impossible because income generating assets would have an infinite value is rejected, on the ground that an infinite value is not a problem since assets could trade against each other at finite price ratios. Some second thoughts are presented in a 1971 paper (IV, ch. 217); curiously, Samuelson discusses the Schumpeter issue entirely in a model with infinite horizon maximizers rather than in an overlapping generations framework.

The modern contributions in *CSP* I include the famous 1958 consumption loans model, which will be examined in the macroeconomics section, and the surrogate production function (1962: I, ch. 28). As Solow (1983) notes, much of the capital theory in *CSP* is related to developments in Dorfman, Samuelson and Solow (1958), which itself grew out of a 1949 Samuelson three-part memorandum for the Rand Corporation.

Notable among the contributions is a variety of turnpike theorems. A turnpike theorem is conjectured in the 1949 Samuelson memorandum, and fully worked out in the 1958 volume. The theorem states that for any accumulation programme, starting from an initial vector of capital goods, and with specified terminal conditions, as the horizon lengthens the optimal programme spends an increasing proportion of its time near the von Neumann ray; more generally in problems with intermediate consumption, the economy spends time near the modified golden rule. Several of the papers in the capital and growth section of *CSP* III contain turnpike theorems. A periodic turnpike result is reported in 1976 (IV, ch. 224).

The surrogate production function was an attempt to justify the aggregate production function as being consistent with an underlying model with heterogeneous capital goods and production techniques, and one type of labour. The article names and uses the factor price frontier, noting that it had been used earlier by others, including himself (in 1957: I, ch. 29). Samuelson shows that a downward sloping factor price frontier is traced out in a competitive multi-capital goods multi-technique economy, with higher steady state wages accompanying a lower steady state interest rate. Further, this frontier has the same properties as in the one-sector model, with the slope of the factor price frontier equal to the capital labour ratio. The theorem is correct, but as noted by Solow (1983), the conditions for it to obtain are special.

Under more general conditions, the famous reswitching result may occur in which a given technique of production that had been used at a low interest rate comes back into use again at a high interest rate (see the November 1966 *Quarterly Journal of Economics*). Reswitching implies that the one-sector neoclassical production function cannot be viewed as a general 'as if' construct that describes the behaviour of economies with several techniques of production. Cambridge (England) critics of neoclassical capital theory viewed reswitching as a confirmation of the view that marginal productivity had nothing to do with distribution, since the same techniques of production might be used with two (or many) different distributions of income. Various criticisms are offered by Robinson (1975) and responded to with forebearance in *CSP* (1975: IV, ch. 216).

Samuelson started the surrogate production function article by denying the need for any concept of aggregate capital. That position would be strengthened by the reswitching result. However, as with so many useful constructs in economics, the concept of aggregate capital has survived the demonstration that its validity may be limited. Neither Samuelson nor other neoclassics have been constrained by reswitching from using one-sector production functions or marginal productivity factor-pricing conditions.

The property that the slope of the factor price frontier is equal to the capital–labour ratio is one example of the duality between price and quantity that Samuelson began to emphasize in the *Foundations* and has used repeatedly since. *Foundations* (p. 68) contains the Roy's Identity envelope condition that the derivative of the minimized cost function of the firm with respect to the wage of factor i is the demand for factor i. It also provides shadow price interpretations of Lagrange multipliers. Samuelson has used duality in optimal growth and linear programming problems ('Market mechanisms and maximization', 1949 (I, ch. 33) is a gem) and in *CSP* (1965: III, ch. 134).

V. DYNAMICS AND GENERAL EQUILIBRIUM

Chapters IX through XI of *Foundations* cover stability analysis and dynamics, in both individual markets and the economy at large. The basic assumption of this dynamics is the 'law of supply and demand' that price rises in response to excess demand.

The impetus for the multi-market analysis came partly from Hicks's *Value and Capital* discussion of stability, in which there is no explicit dynamical system. The Samuelson approach is general equilibrium, though it does not start from the primitives of endowments. As Hahn (1983) notes, the underlying microeconomics is not specified. Samuelson nonetheless set the agenda of the next fifteen years for the study of dynamics in a more explicitly general equilibrium framework, and most important, in a framework in which the issue of stability is precisely posed.

Explicit use of the law of supply and demand in theoretical work has fallen out of favour, though the Phillips curve can be interpreted as using that approach. The monopolistic competition wing of macroeconomics prefers to model price setting by firms and workers explicitly rather than rely on an auctioneer, and the equilibrium approach assumes prices are continuously at market-clearing levels. The older approach is used in disequilibrium macroeconomics, but is typically regarded as suspect.

Samuelson has not been a general equilibrium theorist in the sense of one striving for maximum generality. He has been general equilibrium in the sense opposed to partial equilibrium: he frequently works with models of the whole economy, in growth and capital theory, in trade and macroeconomics, and in his excursions into the history of thought.

The most micro-oriented of these general equilibrium contributions are the non-substitution theorem (1951: I, ch. 36) and factor–price equalization. The non-substitution theorem was presented at a 1949 conference, and was obtained independently by Samuelson and Georgescu-Roegen (I,

p. 521). Consider an economy where labour is the only primary factor, and where goods are used either for consumption or as input into the production of other goods. Suppose the production function for each good is neoclassical, permitting substitution among factors of production, but there is no joint production.

The theorem is that relative prices in this economy are independent of demand, that is, are determined on the supply side alone. There is a single least cost way of producing each good, where cost is determined by direct and indirect labour requirements. Hahn (1983) provides a clear account of the theorem, and generalizations to dynamic systems with capital (1961: I, ch. 37). The question in the system with capital is whether, given the interest rate, the relative price structure is unique. Conditions for uniqueness are discussed in Hahn. The link with the surrogate production function, published at about the same time, is clear. The nonsubstitution theorem is used also in Samuelson's discussions of Ricardo (1959: I, chs 31, 32).

VI. INTERNATIONAL TRADE

'Our subject puts its best foot forward when it speaks out on international trade' (1969: III, p. 683), and some of Samuelson's best-known contributions are undoubtedly in this field. Jones's 1983 article describes Samuelson's considerable impact on trade theory: on the gains from trade; the transfer problem; the Ricardian model; the Heckscher–Ohlin–Samuelson model; and the Viner–Ricardo model.

Earliest among the well-known contributions is the 1941 Stolper–Samuelson result (II, ch. 66) which uses the two-sector, two-country Heckscher–Ohlin model with identical production functions in the two countries to analyse the effects of the opening of trade, or the imposition of a tariff, on the wage. The result is that protection will benefit the factor that is relatively (to the other country) scarce. Or, the opening of trade benefits the relatively plentiful factor. But the paper contains more than that result. As Jones (1983) notes, it introduces the basic elements of Heckscher–Ohlin theory for small-scale trade models – and those models were the analytic core of real trade theory for decades.

Stolper–Samuelson flags the issue of factor–price equalization, the question of whether trade in goods alone can produce the factor price equalization that would obtain if factors were freely mobile. Ohlin claimed that trade would cause a necessarily incomplete tendency to equalization. Samuelson (1948 and 1949: II, ch. 67, 68) showed in the Heckscher–Ohlin context conditions under which equalization would be complete: identical production functions in the two countries, no factor-intensity reversals, and similarity of the ratio of endowments (so that countries are not specialized in production). The paper was remarkable and surprising, and did not suffer from the happy coincidence that a 1933 Abba Lerner contribution rediscovered by Lionel Robbins had independently reached the same conclusions in a similar model.

Factor price equalization in more generality is considered in the famous 1953 paper 'Prices of factors and goods in general equilibrium' (II, ch. 70), which caused a substantial literature including Gale–Nikaido (1965). It is striking that many of Samuelson's famous papers led to prolonged discussion of the exact conditions needed for his particular results to obtain: he opened more doors in economics than he closed.

The transfer problem is an old issue in the literature that arose in the twenties, after World War II, and arises again in contemplation of the world debt crisis. Samuelson's 1952 and 1954 papers (II, chs 74, 75) are classics in this extensive literature, on the issue of whether a transfer from one country to another (such as German reparations) is likely also to worsen the terms of trade of the country making the transfer, which Samuelson describes as the orthodox presumption. In the modern context the orthodox presumption would be that the developing countries will have to suffer a terms of trade loss to run current account surpluses to reduce their indebtedness. Samuelson typically argues that there is no presumption about the terms of trade shift, though the orthodox presumption is more likely to hold where there are non-traded goods or impediments to trade (1971: III, ch. 163).

Samuelson's contributions to trade theory are classics: the contributions are basic, the models are tractable and fecund, the problems come from the real world as well as the literature, the articles continue to reward the reader. And they continue to be read.

VII. FINANCE

Despite his long-time personal interest in capital markets, Samuelson's contributions to finance theory started only as he turned fifty. These papers are concentrated in *CSP* III and IV; the earlier ones are self-reviewed in 'Mathematics of speculative price' (1972: IV, ch. 240). Merton (1983) describes and evaluates six of Samuelson's favourite papers in finance, broadly defined to include his 1952 paper on expected utility and the independence axiom (I, ch. 14).

The two most important papers are 'Proof that properly anticipated prices fluctuate randomly' (1965: III, ch. 198) and 'Rational theory of warrant pricing', (1965: III, ch. 199). 'Proof ...' provides a first precise formulation of the consequences for speculative prices of market efficiency. The theorem describes the behaviour of the current price of a commodity for delivery at a given future date, e.g. June 1990 wheat. Assuming that speculators do not have to put up any money to enter the contract, the result is that the market price should be the expectation at each date of the June 1990 wheat price. Given rational expectations, there is no serial correlation in the changes in price. Hence 'properly anticipated prices fluctuate randomly'.

Samuelson says of this theorem, that is now entirely basic: 'This theorem is so general that I must confess to having oscillated over the years between regarding it as trivially obvious (and almost trivially vacuous) and regarding it as remarkably sweeping. Such perhaps is characteristic of basic results' (III, p. 186).

Note what the theorem does not say, using the exchange rate as the example. The theorem is not that the exchange rate fluctuates randomly; predictable inflation or predictable business cycle fluctuations can cause predictable movements in the exchange rate. Rather it is the current price of foreign exchange at a *given* future date that fluctuates randomly. The notion that efficiency produces random motion is itself fascinating. But far more important is the restriction on empirical behaviour implied by efficiency that Samuelson derives in a well-defined context. Testing for efficiency of speculative markets has become a major industry.

'Rational theory of warrant pricing' missed its target, but it is as Merton (1983) remarks, a near miss. Samuelson had pursued option pricing for well over a decade. He supervised Kruizenga's 1956 MIT dissertation on the topic, and was familiar with Bachelier's 1900 continuous time stochastic calculus calculation of rational option prices. Samuelson derived a partial differential equation for the option price that depends, among other variables, on the expected return on the stock and the required return on the option. The remarkable feature of the Black–Scholes solution to the problem is that the rational price of the warrant does not depend on the expected return on the stock, but rather on the risk-free rate. Nonetheless, the Samuelson differential equation can be specialized to the correct Black–Scholes equation.

Other contributions to finance theory include papers on diversification (1967: III, ch. 201), and on conditions under which mean-variance analysis can be justified (1970: III, ch. 203) – with continuous time models providing the best argument for the procedure.

VIII. MACROECONOMICS

All the Samuelson contributions described to this point are firmly neoclassical. His work in macroeconomics presents a more mixed picture. I take up in turn the early multiplier–accelerator model, which is not at all price-theory oriented, the neoclassical synthesis, Samuelson the policy adviser and commentator, and the entirely neoclassical consumption loans model.

The Multiplier–Accelerator Model. In a 1959 note (II, ch. 84) on the multiplier–accelerator model, Samuelson describes his contribution as being the algebraic generalization of a numerical example of Alvin Hansen's. The model (1939: II, ch 82, 83) is a simple one in which current consumption is proportional to lagged output and investment is determined by the difference between current and lagged consumption (the accelerator). This implies a second order difference equation, which can generate asymptotic or oscillatory damped approaches to equilibrium, or oscillatory or non-oscillatory explosive paths for output. Although Frisch and Slutsky had already written on the ability of stochastic difference equations to mimic cycle-like behaviour, Samuelson does not – except for a quotation from J.M. Clark that receives little emphasis – link his second order equation with a stochastic forcing term.

Samuelson (1939: II, p. 1111), while emphasizing the simplicity of the algebraic analysis, argues for the empirical importance of the accelerator. This judgment has held up over time as flexible accelerator effects continue to feature strongly in modern estimated investment functions. From the theoretical point of view, the multiplier–accelerator model is interesting for the lack of concern over microfoundations. Where a 1980s macroeconomist might agonize over the microfoundations of the consumption function, over the accelerator, or over the impact of rational expectations of future output on investment, Samuelson proceeds constructively with a simple implicitly fix-price model. The famous 45-degree diagram popularized in *Economics* – and for several editions on the cover – forcefully emphasizes Samuelson's view that aggregate demand is the key determinant of output.

In the 1940 'Theory of pump-priming reexamined' (II, ch. 85) he stipulates

> the basic features of the private economy forming the environment within which governmental action must take place ... – (1) The economic system is not perfect and frictionless so that there exists the possibility of unemployment and under-utilization of productive resources ...

This view pervades Samuelson's macroeconomics. Indeed, when asked recently his view of the causes of wage and price stickiness, he replied that he decided forty years ago that wages and prices were sticky, that he could understand the behaviour of the economy and give policy advice on that basis, that he had seen nothing since then to lead him to change his view on the issue – and that he had not seen a payoff to researching the question.

He was of course aware of the issues. An abstract of a paper presented at the 1940 meetings of the Econometric Society (II, ch. 88) describes a totally modern discussion of the question of whether general involuntary unemployment is impossible in a world of price flexibility. His penetrating 1941 review of Pigou's *Employment and Equilibrium* (II, ch. 89) outlines a simple classical model in which price flexibility through its effects on aggregate demand produces full employment even with a constant real wage. This is not however Pigou's model; according to Samuelson, Pigou adopts a model in which money wage flexibility is an alternative to active monetary policy. Samuelson never regarded the Pigou effect as being of real world significance (1963: II, ch. 115).

The Neoclassical Synthesis. Tobin (1983, p. 197) describes the neoclassical synthesis as Samuelson's greatest contribution to macroeconomics. The synthesis is outlined in articles in the early Fifties (1951: II, ch. 98; 1953: II, ch. 99; 1955: II, ch. 100) and developed in successive editions of *Economics*. It argues that monetary and fiscal policy can be used to keep the economy close to full employment, and the monetary–fiscal mix can be used to determine the rate of investment.

The synthesis represents the views of mainstream macroeconomics in the Fifties and Sixties, and perhaps in the Seventies and even the Eighties. Its activist spirit was evident in the Kennedy administration. Its acceptance must have been helped by the widespread use of Samuelson's *Economics* and by the many clones that preached its message.

Perhaps the most notorious component of the neoclassical synthesis is the 1960 Samuelson–Solow 'Analytic aspects of anti-inflation policy' (II, ch. 102), which presents a United States Phillips curve. This article is frequently cited as containing the view that the Phillips curve presents society's long-run tradeoffs between inflation and unemployment.

It does not. The paper starts by discussing the difficulties of distinguishing cost–push from demand–pull inflation. Samuelson and Solow then plot the scatter of percentage changes in average hourly earnings in manufacturing against the unemployment rate (the years plotted are not specified, but include the Thirties). The discussion that follows considers alternative points on the Phillips curve as policy choices for the next few years. But the authors warn explicitly that the discussion is short-term, and that it would be wrong to think that the menu of choices represented by the Phillips curve 'will maintain its same shape in the longer run. ... [I]t might be that ... low-pressure demand would so act upon wage and other expectations as to shift the curve downward in the longer run ...' (II, p. 1352). This is though hardly a clear demonstration of the vertical long-run Phillips curve – for Samuelson–Solow suggest that low demand might also cause the Phillips curve to shift up (a notion that many in Europe now find entirely believable) – but it is clear evidence that the authors were not guilty of believing the Phillips curve would stay put no matter what. In conversation, Samuelson has said that he was always the Kennedy administration pessimist about the long-run Phillips curve tradeoff.

The policy adviser and commentator. Samuelson has long taken an active part in economic policy debates, through Congressional testimony, as consultant to the Treasury and the Fed, in his *Newsweek* column that ran every three weeks from 1966 to 1981, in other newspaper columns, public addresses, advice to candidates and Presidents, and in contributions at academic conferences and in symposia.

His views reflect the neoclassical synthesis, a disdain for rules rather than discretion in determining policy, and an almost shameless eclecticism. He knows the macroeconomic numbers and can speak the language of policy discussions. He is a cautious forecaster, rarely committing numbers to print, preferring to decide on which side of the consensus to place his bets. His 1941 consumption function remains his only econometric work (II, ch. 87); he has said that the major disappointment in economics in the last forty years has been the failure of econometric evidence to settle disputes.

Macroeconomics is Samuelson's primary applied economics field, with finance the second. He keeps up with the current state of the macroeconomy, drawing on forecasts and empirical work of others. He is sceptical of individual forecasts though a law of averages permits him to put some trust in the mean or median forecast. His eclecticism makes his policy views less exciting than those of economists with a strong view of the way the world works – but he has never sought to be interesting rather than right. (This despite his 1962 (II, ch. 113, p. 1509) comment on John Stuart Mill: 'It is almost fatal to be flexible, eclectic, and prolific if you want your name to go down in the history books ....')

Nonetheless, Samuelson's implied attitude to the applications of economics gives pause. As Arrow (1967) notes, his work reveals ambivalence about the relevance of neoclassical price theory. He shows no great faith that his microeconomics can be applied to the real world. No doubt comparative advantage plays a role in that attitude. But the theoretical sophistication he brings from microeconomics does not distinguish his macroeconomic policy advice and forecasting from that of the pack; his neoclassical training is not seriously used in Samuelson's applied macroeconomics. *Economics* may be evidence however that he values simple microeconomics.

The Consumption Loans Model. In the classroom Samuelson has confessed that among his many offspring the consumption loans model (I, ch. 21) is his favourite. The affection is amply rewarded: within macroeconomics the two-period lived overlapping generations structure of the model has been used in countless papers in which a tractable framework with an explicit time structure is needed. The original consumption loans model examined the role of money or bonds as institutions for making Pareto-improving trades feasible; the structure has been used subsequently to examine the dynamics of capital accumulation, the burden of the debt, Ricardian equivalence, social security, the role of money, the effects of open market operations, intertemporal substitution of leisure, labour contracts, government financial intermediation, and more.

The set-up for the original model is one in which people live two periods, with utility functions defined over consumption in the two periods. Each young person receives an endowment of one nonstorable chocolate in period 1. In the absence of trade each person could consume only in period 1. Trades are possible in which the current young give part of their chocolate to the current old in return for chocolate to be received next period from the then young. But there is no double coincidence of wants, no direct way of making the bilateral trades.

Now comes the ostensible point of the model: the social contrivance of money makes trade possible, and its introduction is a Pareto-improving change given the pattern of endowments. The consumption loans model has been much criticized as a model of money, because it implies the velocity of circulation is one per generation. Equivalently, the criticism is that the model describes money as effectuating integenerational transactions whereas in practice other assets, such as bonds, serve that role. (Patinkin 1983 discusses the consumption loans model as a basis for monetary theory and also Samuelson's excursions into the history of monetary thought.)

This is certainly correct. But the significance of the consumption loans model is not its rationale for the existence of money. Rather the model has been so influential and popular because it provides a simple *tractable* general equilibrium structure for modelling intertemporal problems with life-cycle maximizing individuals. The earlier examples prove how easily the general structure can be adapted. It can also be adapted to more periods of life (in the original article Samuelson extended lifetimes to three periods), with fifty period lifetime models being easily solvable on computers. Its strength lies in the elegance and robustness with which it captures the essential point that finite lived individuals exist in an infinitely lived economy (we are each but not all dead in the long run).

Nearly thirty years after the consumption loans model was first published, Malinvaud (1987) drew attention to the little-noticed earlier discovery and extended development of the overlapping generations model by Allais (1947). No doubt Samuelson's eminence and location in the United States, as well as publication in *Journal of Political Economy* rather than a book, had much to do with his independent discovery providing the impetus for the exploitation of this extraordinarily useful model – though even so, it took several years before the overlapping generations structure found its way into common use.

IX. SAMUELSON AND MIT

MIT had famous economists before Samuelson: Francis A. Walker, third president of MIT (1881–99) and first president of the American Economic Association (1886–92), and Davis R. Dewey, president of the AEA (1909) and editor of the *American Economic Review* (1911–40). But the modern era, in which the Department of Economics has risen to world-wide prominence within the profession begins with the arrival of Samuelson in 1940. Brown and Solow (1983) describe the MIT Department of the Thirties, and the transformation that nearly began in 1941 after Samuelson arrived and the first PhD class, including Lawrence Klein and George P. Shultz, was about to get under way. World War II intervened, and it was only in the late Forties and early Fifties that the faculty and the PhD programme reached full strength.

The MIT department and PhD programme have been consistently among the best in the world since the early Sixties. The names of the faculty members are well known. Equally remarkable is the collection of eminent economists who are MIT PhDs, whose names are legion but whom it would only be invidious to begin to list.

Samuelson's role in this success was pivotal but not domineering. His research habits (including sheer hard work), the open-door policy for students (a lesser burden for someone of whom the students were in awe than for others) and fellow faculty, his absolute refusal to use authority instead of reason in faculty meetings, his zest for conversation about economics, economists, and all else, made him a role model for a department where cooperation and friendliness have been extraordinary. He helped shape the department but he did not dictate its shape; he told one of his young co-authors that as a young man he decided that at age forty he would stop taking initiatives in the department, at fifty he would venture an opinion only when asked, and at sixty would stop attending faculty meetings. Within the margin of error allowed to economists, he held to that resolution.

Samuelson the teacher played a lesser role. His world-wide fame (and that of other faculty members) doubtless was a major reason many of the outstanding students were there. But, at least in the last two decades, he supervised relatively few theses. His method of supervision was ideally suited to better students, for he would ask broad questions and give general guidance rather than involve himself in details.

His classroom lectures in the period 1966–9 when I heard them were not a model of organization. His advanced theory lectures were given in the first class of the day and it was always possible to tell whether the traffic had been bad that day by whether his hand-written mimeographed lecture notes were available at the beginning of the lecture or only later. The time until the notes arrived was taken up by stories setting the historical background for the problem, and anecdotes about the protagonists. The day he lectured en route to deliver his contribution to the Irving Fisher *festschrift* (1967: III, ch. 184) was especially memorable, though word filtered back from New Haven that his Yale audience was less than enchanted by the stories. His students were not surprised to find in his Nobel lecture (1970: III, ch. 130) both that he had been warned that the lecture was to be serious, and that he started a less than serious story with that warning.

His lectures were simply not designed for the novice. But they were superb for those with some background. He explained finer points, threw out open questions, made unexpected connections between topics, and communicated the zest with which he approaches economics.

X. CONCLUDING COMMENTS

Among the missing from this list of Samuelson's contributions are his work in the history of thought (where he has been more interested in clarifying analysis than in evaluating contributions), his methodological articles, the famous public goods theorem, the recent work on mathematical biology, the informative and entertaining biographies of contemporaries, the frank self-evaluations, and *Economics*.

The extraordinary success of *Economics* is something of a mystery, for the book is not easy – as witness the fact that simpler texts that follow Samuelson's structure have found a large market. *Economics* is a multi-level book that in its appendices, footnotes, and allusions goes far beyond elementary economics. Depending on what students retain from their economics courses, *Economics* may have done much to raise the level of public discourse about economic policy.

Samuelson's self-evaluations, as in 'Economics in a Golden Age' (1972: IV, ch. 278), must have shocked many readers. The typical self-effacing scientist does not include stories of Newton and Gauss in his intellectual autobiography. Reflection leads to a different perspective: it would have been easy for Samuelson not to 'tell the truth and shame the devil' (1972: IV, p. 881). But how much more interesting it is to have the account of how Samuelson views his own achievements.

Samuelson was described in 1967 as 'knocking on the door ... of the pantheon of the greats ...' (Seligman, p. 160). He may have been let in by now. But the final word has to be left to Franco Modigliani, who, after the speeches at the 1983 party at which Samuelson was presented with the Brown–Solow *festschrift*, walked over to the seated Samuelson, wagged his finger at him, and said 'You', and after a pause 'You have enriched our lives.'

STANLEY FISCHER

SELECTED WORKS

1947. *Foundations of Economic Analysis*. Cambridge, Mass.: Harvard University Press. Enlarged edn, 1983.

1948. *Economics, an Introductory Analysis*. 12th edn, co-author William Nordhaus, New York: McGraw-Hill, 1985.

1958. (With R. Dorfman and R.M. Solow) *Linear Programming and Economic Analysis*. New York: McGraw-Hill.

1966–86. *The Collected Scientific Papers of Paul A. Samuelson*, Vols I–V. Vols I and II, ed. J.E. Stiglitz, Cambridge, Mass: MIT Press, 1966; Vol. III, ed. R.C. Merton, Cambridge, Mass. and London: MIT Press, 1970; Vol. IV, ed. H. Nagatani and K. Crowley, Cambridge, Mass. and London: MIT Press, 1977; Vol. V, ed. K. Crowley, Cambridge, Mass. and London: MIT Press, 1986.

BIBLIOGRAPHY

Allais, M. 1947. *Economie et intérêt*. Paris: Imprimerie Nationale.

Arrow, K.J. 1967. Samuelson collected. *Journal of Political Economy* 75(5), October, 730–37.

Arrow, K.J. 1983. Contributions to welfare economics. In Brown and Solow (1983).

Bachelier, L. 1900. Théorie de la speculation. Trans. by A.J. Boness and ed. P. Cootner, as *The Random Character of Stock Market-Prices*, Cambridge, Mass.: MIT Press, 1967.

Bliss, C.J. 1967. Review of *Collected Scientific Papers of Paul A. Samuelson*, 2 vols. *Economic Journal* 77(306), June, 338–45.

Bronfenbrenner, M. 1982. On the superlative in Samuelson. In Feiwel (1982).

Brown, E.C. and Solow, R.M. (eds) 1983. *Paul Samuelson and Modern Economic Theory*. New York: McGraw-Hill.

Feiwel, G. (ed.) 1982. *Samuelson and Neoclassical Economics*. Boston: Kluwer-Nijhoff.

Gale, D. and Nikaido, H. 1965. The Jacobian matrix and the global univalence of mappings. *Mathematische Annalen* 159(2), 81–93.

Hahn, F.H. 1983. On general equilibrium and stability. In Brown and Solow (1983).

Hicks, J.R. 1939. *Value and Capital*. Oxford: Oxford University Press.

Houthakker, H. 1950. Revealed preference and the utility function. *Economica* 17, May, 159–74.

Houthakker, H. 1983. On consumption theory. In Brown and Solow (1983).

Jones, R.W. 1983. International trade theory. In Brown and Solow (1983).

Lindbeck, A. 1970. Paul Samuelson's contribution to economics. *Swedish Journal of Economics* 72, 341–54.

Machina, M.J. 1982. 'Expected utility' analysis without the independence axiom. *Econometrica* 50(2), March, 277–324.

Malinvaud, E. 1987. The overlapping generations model in 1947. *Journal of Economic Literature*.

Mas-Colell, A. 1982. Revealed preference after Samuelson. In Feiwel (1982).

Merton, R.C. 1983. Financial economics. In Brown and Solow (1983).

Patinkin, D. 1983. Monetary economics. In Brown and Solow (1983).

Robinson, J. 1975. The unimportance of reswitching. *Quarterly Journal of Economics* 89(1), February, 32–9.

Samuelson, M.C. 1939. The Australian case for protection re-examined. *Quarterly Journal of Economics* 54, November, 143–9.

Seligman, B.B. 1967. On the question of operationalism. *American Economic Review* 57(1), March, 146–61.

Solow R.M. 1983. Modern capital theory. In Brown and Solow (1983).

Tobin, J. 1983. Macroeconomics and fiscal policy. In Brown and Solow (1983).

sanctions. *See* ECONOMIC WAR.

Sanger, Charles Percy (1871–1930). A barrister with extraordinarily varied interests, a contributor to the original *Palgrave*, Sanger was born at Brighton on 7 December 1871 and died in London on 9 February 1930. He was educated at Winchester and Trinity College, Cambridge, and was Second

Wrangler in the Mathematical Tripos of 1893. He then turned to economics, coming under Alfred Marshall's influence. Called to the Bar in 1896, he thereafter practised law in London, meanwhile pursuing intellectual avocations which ranged from economics and statistics to philosophy and literature. He lectured part-time for many years on mathematical economics and statistics, first at University College, London, and then at the London School of Economics, and was active in the Royal Statistical Society.

His economic publications were small in number, diverse in character, and restricted to the years 1894 to 1903 – although he continued for many years to review copiously for the *Economic Journal*. His most important theoretical work was probably his first, a pioneering joint contribution to the mathematical theory of demand (Johnson and Sanger, 1894), but his masterful survey of Italian contributions to mathematical economics (1895a) stood for many years as the high water mark of technical sophistication in the *Economic Journal*. Sanger's statistical and legal interests reveal themselves more clearly in his applied work, such as Sanger (1895b), (1896) and (1903).

Sanger was highly regarded in the legal profession and established himself as an authority on wills, publishing a manual on the subject (Sanger, 1914). But he dissipated his enormous talents too widely to achieve fame. Election as an undergraduate to the exclusive Society of Apostles provided the entrée to distinguished philosophical and literary circles and led to many lifelong associations. His wide and admiring circle of friends included Maynard Keynes, Bertrand Russell and Lytton Strachey. See Fry (1930), Hawtrey (1930), Keynes (1930) and Russell (1967) for further details.

J.K. WHITAKER

SELECTED WORKS

1894. (With W.E. Johnson.) On certain questions connected with demand. Text of a paper presented to the Cambridge Economic Club, Cambridge, privately printed. Reprinted in W.J. Baumol and S.M. Goldfeld, *Precursors in Mathematical Economics*, London: London School of Economics, 1968.

1895a. Recent contributions to mathematical economics. *Economic Journal* 5, March, 113–28.

1895b. The fair number of apprentices in a trade. *Economic Journal* 5, December, 616–36.

1896. *The Place of Compensation in Temperance Reform*. LSE Studies in Economic and Political Science No. 8, London: London School of Economics.

1903. The legal view of profits. *Economic Journal* 13, June, 177–85.

1914. *The Rules of Law and Administration Relating to Wills and Intestacies*. London: Sweet & Maxwell.

BIBLIOGRAPHY

Fry, R. 1930. Appreciation of C.P. Sanger. *The Times*, London, February 22.

Hawtrey, R.G. 1930. Obituary: Charles Percy Sanger. *Journal of the Royal Statistical Society* 93, Part 2, 316.

Keynes, J.M. 1930. Obituary: Charles Percy Sanger. *Economic Journal* 40, March, 154–55. Reprinted in *The Collected Writings of John Maynard Keynes*, Vol. X: *Essays in Biography*, London: Macmillan, 1972.

Russell, B. 1967. *The Autobiography of Bertrand Russell, 1872–1914*. London: Allen & Unwin.

satellite models. Business and government forecasting and policy simulation frequently call for models with a high level of detail hence, the model of the industry, the region, the commodity market, and the firm. Satellite modelling places the smaller unit into the framework of a model of the national or world economy.

A cascade is a good way to view the relation between the national economy and the smaller economic unit (Adams, 1986). Such a linkage between the national economic model and models of industry and firms is shown in figure 1. On the top, the macro model describes the environment in which the industry operates. At the next level, the industry satellite models describe the operation of the market in which firms, shown at the bottom, develop their business strategy. The solid lines between the blocks of Figure 1 show the top down direction of influence. The satellite model system assumes a unidirectional flow scheme, the industry and the firm models depend on the aggregate economy, but there is no feedback. This is often a useful simplification. The impact of national developments on a particular industry and firm may be large, but the influence back from the particular enterprise or industry to the national scene is likely in many cases to be small. This justifies the satellite relationship. Sometimes a feedback to recognized (as shown in the dashed lines in Figure 1).

The macro model must be designed to provide the many data inputs needed in the satellite models. One of the advantages of a complex macro model is the consistent detailed forecast of the economy which can be fed into models at lower stages of aggregation.

External inputs affect the economy at each level. The influence of the international economy and of fiscal and monetary policy operate primarily at the national economy level. At the industry satellite level, the business cycle situation of the macroeconomy dominates the movement of demand for specific products over the short and medium term. Exogenous factors operating at the satellite model level include foreign competition, industrial policy incentives, regulatory policy, and prices of material and supplies. Over the longer run, technological developments affecting the product or the production process may have significant impact at the industry level.

Firms operate as satellites within the constraints of the industry. They are affected by the situation of the industry in general and by firm specific exogenous developments. In turn, the industry is affected (note the dashed lines). Decisions at the level of the firm, about capacity, the introduction of new technology, or new products often influence – and sometimes revolutionize – the entire industry. Business strategy by a specific firm and its competitors is the most important consideration at the firm level (note the reaction relationship implied by the two-headed arrow connecting each firm).

The range of satellite models is very large, as large as the potentials for disaggregating the economy into industries, commodity markets, financial markets, regions and firms (Labys, 1975). Whereas the model of the macro economy falls into a fairly standard pattern determined by macroeconomic theory, the satellite model must reflect the characteristics of the micro unit which it seeks to describe. This means that satellite models use theoretical concepts of microeconomics; that they are based on industry statistics and describe technological, institutional, and commercial behaviour. Often they draw on the eclectic techniques of systems analysis and simulation modelling. Sometimes they embody maximization algorithms. The distinctions between the typical industry model and the commodity market model offer some characteristic examples. The industry model is a model of an industrial process (Adams, 1986). Firms adjust production schedules for manufactured products directly in line with orders for the product. Production function relationships determine requirements for labour, materials and energy. Price determination is through cost-markup subject to the con-

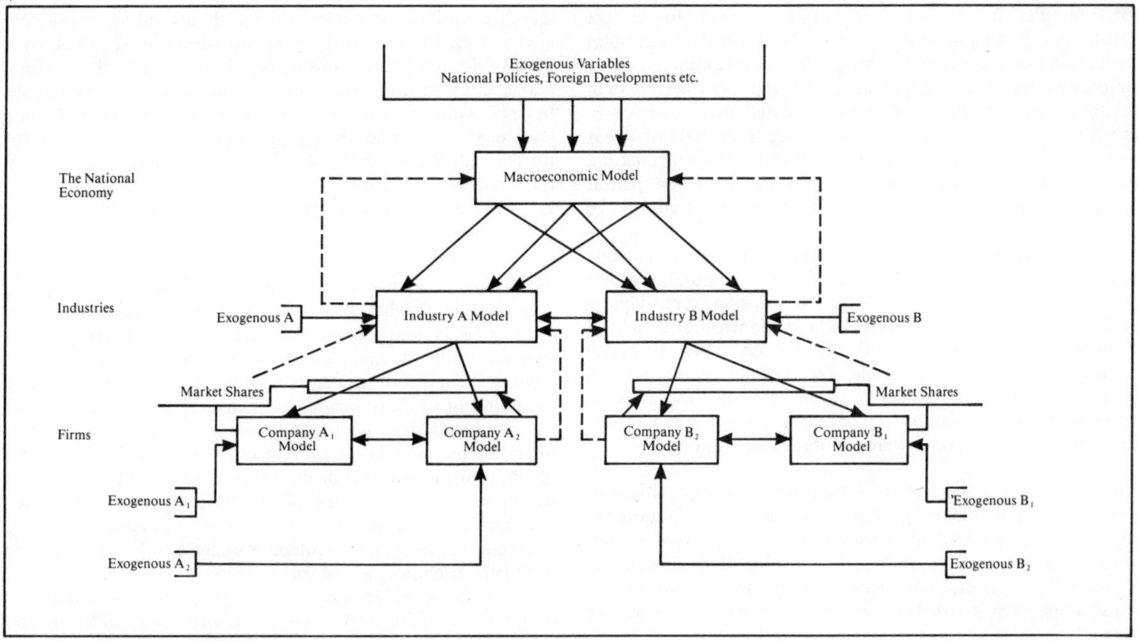

Figure 1 A Cascade of Satellite Models
Nation, Industry and Firm

straints of capacity utilization and competition from foreign sources.

In sharp contrast, the model of the commodity market model (Labys and Pollak, 1984) visualizes a world of many producers participating in a worldwide market for a standardized commodity – coffee, cocoa, tin, copper, etc. On the demand side, consumers respond to income and to product price. On the supply side, producers respond to product price relative to production cost. Price determination is through the equilibrium of demand and supply (in many cases with particular emphasis on inventory holding). The commodity market model functions as a satellite to a global world macro model system which determines economic activity in the consuming countries.

Regional models are another very characteristic form of satellite (Adams and Glickman, 1980). The regional economy is seen as dependent on the national economy through the flows of goods and services sold in the national market place. Using the concept of the 'economic base', the 'regional export' industries generate a flow of income which feeds back into the economy to support 'local' activities such as services. The competitiveness of the 'exporting' industries with respect to those in other regions, is a principal determinant of regional development.

APPLICATIONS. Satellite models are an effective way to disaggregate the economy without requiring a complex and complete disaggregation of the entire model system. They are useful for a wide range of forecasting and simulation activities.

The question has been posed: if one were to build satellite models for all the regions of an economy, would the sum total result of the regional models correspond to the result of the national model? One can ask the same question with respect to aggregation of industry models. In most cases the sum of the detailed satellite models will not be the same as the result of the aggregate model. Feedbacks are omitted in the satellite model system whereas in turn the structure of the economy may have been treated in less detail in the aggregate national model. But consistency is not the primary objective of satellite models. They are intended to provide a less costly and more manageable way to model detailed sub-elements of the national and world economy.

F. GERARD ADAMS

See also MACROECONOMETRIC MODELS.

BIBLIOGRAPHY

Adams, F.G. 1986. *The Business Forecasting Revolution: Nation-Industry-Firm*. New York: Oxford University Press.

Adams, F.G. and Glickman, N.J. 1980. *Modeling the Multiregional Economic System*. Lexington, Mass.: D.C. Heath.

Labys, W.C. 1975. *Quantitative Models of Commodity Markets*. Cambridge, Mass.: Ballinger.

Labys, W.C. and Pollak, P.K. 1984. *Commodity Models for Forecasting and Policy Analysis*. New York: Nichols.

satiation. *See* DEMAND THEORY; FREE GOODS.

satisficing. A decision maker who chooses the best available alternative according to some criterion is said to optimize; one who chooses an alternative that meets or exceeds specified criteria, but that is not guaranteed to be either unique or in any sense the best, is said to satisfice. The term 'satisfice', which appears in the *Oxford English Dictionary* as a Northumbrian synonym for 'satisfy', was borrowed for this new use by H.A. Simon (1956), in 'Rational Choice and the Structure of the Environment'.

OPTIMIZATION AND ITS PROBLEMS. In the literature of economics and statistical decision theory, rationality has usually been defined in such a way as to imply some form of optimization, for example, maximization of utility subject to budget constraints. In simple situations, like the illustrative examples used in economics textbooks, computing a maximum may be a simple process, requiring, perhaps, nothing more onerous than taking a first derivative and setting it equal to zero. Even in much more complex situations, involving thousands of linear equalities and inequalities but also a linear criterion function, the powerful methods of linear programming often permit optimal choices to be found with tolerable amounts of computing effort.

In many (most?) real-world situations, however, genuine optima (maxima or minima) are simply not computable within feasible limits of effort (*see* BOUNDED RATIONALITY). This is especially true when decisions must be made without benefit of computer, but it is frequently true even when powerful computing facilities are available. The complexity of the world is not limited to thousands or even tens of thousands of variables and constraints, nor does it always preserve the linearities and convexities that facilitate computation.

THE SATISFICING ALTERNATIVE. Faced with a choice situation where it is impossible to optimize, or where the computational cost of doing so seems burdensome, the decision maker may look for a satisfactory, rather than an optimal alternative. Frequently, a course of action satisfying a number of constraints, even a sizeable number, is far easier to discover than a course of action maximizing some function.

The example has been given of searching for a needle in a haystack. Given a probability density distribution of needles of varying degrees of sharpness throughout the haystack, searching for the sharpest needle may require effort proportional to the size of the haystack. The task of searching for a needle sharp enough to sew with requires an effort that depends only on the density of needles of the requisite sharpness, and not at all on the size of the stack. The attractiveness of the satisficing criterion derives from this independence of search cost from the size and complexity of the choice situation.

In a formal sense, a process of satisficing could always be converted into a process of optimizing by taking into account the cost of search, and only searching up to the point where the expected gain derivable from another minute of search is just equal to the opportunity cost of that minute (Simon, 1955; Stigler, 1961). However, this conversion imposes a new, possibly heavy, informational and computational burden upon the chooser: the burden of estimating the expected marginal return of search and the opportunity cost. Solving these estimation problems may be as difficult as making the original choice, or even more difficult. An alternative is to search until a satisfactory alternative is found.

Conversely, most of the so-called optimization models of operations research and management science can more profitably be viewed as satisficing models. In the application of OR optimization techniques, some highly simplified approximation to a real-world situation is reduced to a formal model (e.g. a linear programming or integer programming model), and an optimum is then calculated for this approximation with respect to a similarly approximate criterion function. The resulting 'optimal' decision will often provide a satisfactory decision for the real-world situation, but without guarantee that it will be better than a decision arrived at by some alternative satisficing technique.

How may the satisficer set the level of the criteria that define 'satisfactory'? Psychology proposes the mechanism of aspiration levels: if it turns out to be very easy to find alternatives that meet the criteria, the standards are gradually raised; if search continues for a long while without finding satisfactory alternatives, the standards are gradually lowered. Thus, by a kind of feedback mechanism, or 'tâtonnement', the decision maker converges toward a set of criteria that are attainable, but not without effort. The difference between the aspiration level mechanism and the optimization procedure is that the former calls for much simpler computations than the latter. It is somewhat analogous to the difference between adaptive and rational expectations, respectively, in the theory of choice under uncertainty.

INCOMMENSURABILITY OF GOALS AND OUTCOMES. Satisficing can also provide another kind of computational advantage over optimizing. Human decision makers often find it very difficult to make trade-offs among aspects or dimensions of value that seem to them incommensurable. Of course, it is the function of the utility function to insure commensurability in all cases, but we may not wish to postulate in advance that such a function exists, or may not know how to characterize it. Three classes of situations into which incommensurability is especially likely to intrude are: (1) cases of uncertainty, where, for each alternative, a bad outcome under one contingency must be balanced against a good outcome under another; (2) cases of multiperson choice, where one person's gain is another's loss; and (3) cases where each choice involves gain along one dimension of value and loss along another very different one.

It has been observed empirically that in circumstances of these kinds, and especially when each outcome entails unpleasant as well as pleasant consequences, decision makers do not proceed promptly to a choice, but instead seek to avoid the necessity for comparison. One common reaction, for example, is to refuse to choose among the given set of alternatives, and instead, to initiate a search for a new alternative that: in case (1), will ensure at least a minimally satisfactory outcome under all contingencies; in case (2), will ensure all participants a satisfactory outcome; and in case (3), will ensure an outcome that is at least minimally satisfactory along all dimensions. The acceptance of such alternatives comes within our definition of satisficing (Hogarth, 1980).

CONSEQUENCES FOR ECONOMIC THEORY. It is easier to reconcile a satisficing than an optimizing theory of economic decision making with what is known empirically of actual choice behaviour and of the computational limits of the human mind. On the other hand, a great deal is given up by the substitution of the former for the latter – given up in terms of the strength and variety of theorems that can be derived from the postulate of rationality in the two cases. To make predictions about behaviour on the basis of a satisficing theory requires much more empirical data about, for example, aspiration levels and their adaptivity, than does prediction on the basis of the optimizing theory. The magnitude of the difference becomes less, however, when we recognize that the optimizing theory says nothing about the shape or content of the utility function. It simply postulates a consistency of behaviour over time that may not be found if the decision maker is satisficing instead of optimizing.

In the last analysis, a choice between the two kinds of postulates will have to be made in terms of their relative effectiveness and accuracy in predicting and explaining economic behaviour, at both micro and macro levels. There is still little consensus in the economics profession as to the circumstances under which one postulate or the other will be the more advantageous.

HERBERT A. SIMON

See also BEHAVIOURAL ECONOMICS; BOUNDED RATIONALITY; ECONOMIC MAN.

BIBLIOGRAPHY

Hogarth, R.M. 1980. *Judgment and Choice: The Psychology of Decision.* New York: Wiley.

Radner, R. 1975. Satisficing. *Journal of Mathematical Economics* 2, 253–62.

Simon, H.A. 1955. A behavioral model of rational choice. *Quarterly Journal of Economics* 69, 99–118. Reprinted in Simon (1982), ch. 7.2.

Simon, H.A. 1956. Rational choice and the structure of the environment. *Psychological Review* 63, 129–38. Reprinted in Simon (1982), ch. 7.3.

Simon, H.A. 1982. *Models of Bounded Rationality.* Cambridge, Mass.: MIT Press.

Stigler, G.J. 1961. The economics of information. *Journal of Political Economy* 69, 213–25.

Winter, S.G. 1971. Satisficing, selection and the innovating remnant. *Quarterly Journal of Economics* 85, 237–61.

Sauvy, Alfred (born 1898). Sauvy was born 31 October 1898, in Villeneuve-de-la-Raho, France. He graduated from the Ecole Polytechnique, and is known as a demographer, economist, statistician and sociologist. He was an adviser to Jean Monnet and Paul Reynaud 1938–1940, a member of the Population Commission of the United Nations from 1947 to 1974, and he occupied a chair in social demography at the College of France from 1959 to 1969. He founded the Institut National d'Etudes Démographiques, one of the world's leading centres of demographic research, which he directed from 1945 to 1962. He was president of the International Union for the Scientific Study of Population from 1961 to 1963. A prolific author, his works include 45 books and many articles, on a broad range of topics from French economic history since World War I to the effect of technological change on employment and the history of thought in demography. But he is best known among demographers and economists for his two-volume treatise *Théorie générale de la population* (1966), published in English in 1969 as *The General Theory of Population.*

The General Theory of Population attempts both theoretical and substantive generality and is largely independent of the English-language literature on the subject. Thus one finds no references to or integration of the English literature on the economics of fertility or the consequences of population change or optimum population theory. Rather, the treatise presents a highly individual view of the subject. The book is full of briefly presented but penetrating insights on a wide variety of topics, often illustrated with descriptive data. For an economist, however, the main interest of the book is in its more rigorous development and extension of the concepts of economic–demographic equilibrium, and of maximum, minimum and optimum population. The analysis is entirely comparative statics, based on the assumption of first increasing, then decreasing returns to labour and population. At the minimum population and again at the maximum, the average product of labour equals the subsistence level; in between these population sizes there remains an economic surplus after subsistence needs are met. Per capita product is of course maximized when the marginal product equals the average; more interestingly, total surplus is maximized when the marginal product of labour equals subsistence, at what is termed the 'power optimum' population – with the notion that a costly collective social goal can best be met at this size. The military optimum will be at a point between the power optimum and the maximum, since it requires both soldiers and surplus output. The implications of inequalities in income distribution are also discussed; the labour intensity of the consumption goods demanded by the rich will influence the size of the equilibrium population. Sauvy's theories, particularly of the determinants of the equilibrium population, have had an important influence on the thinking of economic demographers and social historians on the subject of homeostasis in human populations.

RONALD LEE

SELECTED WORKS

1966. *Théorie générale de la population.* Paris: Presses Universitaires de France. Trans. by C. Campos as *The General Theory of Population*, New York: Basic Books, 1969.

Savage, Leonard J. (Jimmie) (1917–1971). L.J. (Jimmie) Savage, né Leonard Ogashevitz, was born in Detroit on 20 November 1917 and died in New Haven on 1 November 1971. His interests were encyclopedic: as a youth he immersed himself in the *Book of Knowledge*, and at the time of his death he was preparing for the Peabody Museum a demonstration-exhibit on animal odorants. The dominant theme of Savage's professional work was the mathematical analysis of normative behaviour.

He received a BS (1938) and PhD (1941) from the University of Michigan. In the early 1940s he obtained a broad post-doctoral exposure to pure and applied mathematics at the Institute for Advanced Study in Princeton, at Cornell, Brown, the Statistical Research Group of Columbia, the Courant Institute at New York University, and at Woods Hole Marine Biological Laboratory. From 1946 to 1960 he was at the University of Chicago, where he was central to the development of the statistics programme. Subsequently, he held professorships at Michigan and at Yale. Always, he was intellectually generous with students, colleagues, visitors and correspondents.

Savage's basic views and results on normative behaviour appear in his *Foundations* (1954). His essential theme, still being elaborated, is the relation between a person's probability for an event and his utility for the event. In particular, his probabilities and utilities must be consistent with the principle of maximizing his expected utility. These results flow from compelling axioms of coherent behaviour and they recommend specific strategies for applied statistics, such as the use of Bayesian statistics and the likelihood principle.

Savage's axioms imply that all probabilities reflect individual experience so that there is no reason for two people to have the same probability for a particular event. His theory conflicts with traditional views that hold probabilities to be basic constants of nature. At first Savage thought this conflict would not be significant in applying statistical theory but he remarked in the preface to the second edition of the *Foundations* (1972) that he was not successful in bringing the theories of statistics together at the applied level. He recognized the long process from elegant theory to serious applications. His paper on elicitation of probabilities (1971) develops methods to implement his theory of personal probability. And Savage (1977) warns against holding theoretical foundations as adequate to cover all aspects of applied statistics.

Savage's work on the foundations of statistics had major antecedents in Frank Ramsey and B. de Finetti, whose work was developed, polished and taught to a generation of scholars by Savage himself. Hewitt and Savage (1955) is both elegant mathematics and an extension of a basic result of de Finetti in the foundations of statistics. Dubins and Savage (1965) stems from a normative problem and bears mathematical fruit. Exposition of the basic ideas of applied Bayesian statistics combined with the new theory of stable estimation appears in Edwards, Lindman and Savage (1963). Additional biographical and critical analysis as well as most of Savage's published papers appear in Ericson et al. (1981).

I. RICHARD SAVAGE

See also BAYESIAN INFERENCE; EXPECTED UTILITY AND MATHEMATICAL EXPECTATION.

SELECTED WORKS

1948. (With M. Friedman.) The utility analysis of choices involving risk. *Journal of Political Economy* 56, 279–304.

1954. *The Foundations of Statistics*. New York: John Wiley & Sons. 2nd revised edn, New York: Dover Publications, 1972.

1955. (With E. Hewitt.) Symmetric measures on Cartesian products. *Transactions of the American Mathematical Society* 80, 470–501.

1963. (With W. Edwards and H. Lindman.) Bayesian statistical inference for psychological research. *Psychological Review* 70, 192–242.

1965. (With L.E. Dubins.) *How to Gamble If You Must: Inequalities for Stochastic Processes*. New York: McGraw-Hill. Reprinted with a new Bibliographic Supplement and Preface by L.E. Dubins as *Inequalities for Stochastic Processes (How to Gamble If You Must)*, New York: Dover Publications, 1976.

1971. Elicitation of personal probabilities and expectations. *Journal of the American Statistical Association* 66, 783–801.

1977. The shifting foundations of statistics. In *Logic, Laws and Life: Some Philosophical Complications*, ed. R.G. Colodny, Pittsburgh: University of Pittsburgh Press.

1981. *The Writings of Leonard Jimmie Savage – A Memorial Selection* Prepared by a Committee (W.H. DuMouchel, W.A. Ericson (chair), B. Margolin, R.A. Olshen, H.V. Roberts, I.R. Savage and A. Zellner) for the American Statistical Association and the Institute of Mathematical Statistics, Washington, DC.

saving. *See* FINANCE AND SAVING; FORCED SAVING; LIFE-CYCLE HYPOTHESIS.

saving equals investment. For the best part of the last two centuries, this equality (and the ways by which it comes to be established) has been at the heart of long and protracted debates. Indeed, two of the most fruitful periods in the history of economic thought were entirely devoted to this riddle which, still today, is far from being satisfactorily solved. For all the participants in the 'general glut controversy' as well as for Keynes and all the leading economists of the interwar period, the saving–investment problem was the key to macroeconomic stability.

The earliest saving–investment discussion between Ricardo, Malthus, Say and Sismondi exhibits similarities with that between Keynes and other economists like Robertson, Hawtrey, Hayek and Pigou. Broadly speaking (and like Keynes), Malthus and Sismondi recognized the possibility that demand could set a limit to aggregate production, whereas Ricardo and Say (along lines similar to Keynes's opponents) denied that possibility. However, the similarities in the question discussed should not obscure the rather different analytical apparatus used. As is well known, and taking over that argument from Smith, both Ricardo and Malthus in England and Say and Sismondi on the Continent *always identified decisions to save with decisions to invest*. Since they all considered as a fact that 'what is annually saved is as regularly consumed as what is annually spent, and nearly in the same time too' (Smith, 1776, vol. I, pp. 337–8), the question of a possible divergence between saving and investment was never asked. With the possible exception of Sismondi (who never pushed this kind of analysis very far), none of these authors suggested a short-run analysis of the time-lags that might elapse between the acts of saving and investment; such an approach would have forced them to admit the possibility of divergences between planned savings and investment, and thus brought them to reject Say's Law. Even their surprisingly sophisticated monetary theory did not draw their attention to the consequences 'forced saving' could (temporarily) have on the saving–investment equality and capital accumulation in the course of the adjustment process.

Ricardo's theory of profit is the key to the understanding of the paradox that was to dominate economic theory for the next 70 years. Since, in the long run, wages are determined by the level of subsistence, the rate of profit can fall in the process of accumulation only as a result of a diminished productivity of labour on progressively less fertile lands. No room is thus left for any permanent influence of demand on profits. Hence, since Ricardo identified decisions to save with decisions to invest, to recognize a connection between production and income amounted to admitting Say's principle that 'demand is only limited by production' (or to use Say's own terminology that '*l'offre crée sa propre demande*'). In other words, in the Classical framework, Say's Law is not the result of an analysis of the saving–investment process but rather the result of the lack of such an analysis.

The advent of the marginal revolution coincided with the first attempt to provide Say's principle with a firm theoretical basis. Here the market for capital (in its stock as well as in its flow versions) is no exception to the general theory of prices based on the twin concepts of marginal utility and marginal productivity. On the one hand, an interest-elastic investment demand function establishes an inverse relation between the volume of planned investment and the rate of interest and, on the other, this interest rate is seen to be sensitive enough to divergences between investment decisions and full employment savings to ensure its equilibrating role.

In this context, the obvious need to account for cycles forced the whole weight of the explanation to rest on the second premise; the rate of interest might after all not be sufficiently sensitive to divergences between planned investment and planned savings to ensure permanently the full employment of both labour and capital. The reasons for this were to be found in obstacles which postponed or retarded the action of the underlying forces described by the pure theory of interest. These obstacles were usually attributed to the presence of money. The analysis of the fluctuations of the level of economic activity came thus to be part of a theory of money separate from the theory of prices and distribution. In fact, working within a theoretical construction in which money has (in the long run) no role to play, marginalist economists had paradoxically to resort to monetary factors to build a plausible stability analysis.

Although some authors put less emphasis on formal analysis than others, most theorists followed the path exemplified by Wicksell's cumulative process. The discontinuous nature of technical progress (or alternatively Marshall's change in the entrepreneur's expectations) results in fluctuations of the profitability of investment. The term structure of interest rates on money loans fails to adjust immediately causing variations of prices and temporary changes in the level of activity. Fundamental to either Marshall's or Wicksell's theory is the relationship between the expected return on 'newly created capital' (which will tend under normal circumstances to equal the 'natural' or 'real' interest rate) and the rate at which money can be borrowed on the market for loans. Since the banks can accommodate any variations in the demand for loans without changing their interest rate, they can sever the link between the market rate and the 'natural' rate which would have otherwise operated through demand and supply on the loan market. Merging with this analysis the income approach to the quantity theory of money taken over from Tooke, Wicksell concludes that the cumulative process of inflation (or deflation) set up by banks failing to adjust their money rate to the new 'natural' rate (and opening thus a temporary gap between savings and investment) will eventually compel them to raise (or lower) the market rate towards its 'equilibrium' level, the only level at which there is price stability. Hence, this cumulative process is not explosive and, clearly, the influence of monetary factors in the loan market can only temporarily endanger the claimed tendency to the full employment of all factors of production. If the elasticity of the demand for capital with respect to the rate of interest may temporarily fail to adjust savings to investment following monetary disturbances, this very elasticity would nevertheless suffice to re-establish equilibrium (and price stability) in the face of variations of aggregate demand due to inequality between savings and investment. Ultimately, in the long run, variations of monetary expenditure are seen to have effects on the price level but not on the levels of production and employment.

The interwar period marks the apogee of this type of analysis and witnessed an orgy of debates between the leading theorists of the day. English economists (centred at Cambridge), followers of Wicksell in Sweden and a few Austrian theorists (soon to emigrate to England and the United States) built endless variations on this basic theme.

For some, cycles are of purely monetary nature; for others, though money and the banking system are crucial in disrupting the relationship between 'real' magnitudes, underconsumption, over-investment, 'forced' saving, capital shortage, hoarding and a large variety of other causes inherent to any dynamic monetary economy could also be at the origin of macro-disequilibria between savings and investment. However, if these authors sometimes disagreed very strongly on how this gap between savings and investment comes into existence, they certainly did not disagree on the meaning of this gap itself and how it would come to be closed through variations in the rate of interest. As Schumpeter put it, the gap between the 'natural' and the market rates of interest (the corollary of a gap between saving and investment) is 'a kind of *coefficient of tension in the system*, which expresses the degree of disequilibrium present in the latter' (1939, vol. 2, p. 126). In the short run, planned savings and desired investments need not coincide; rigidities and frictions may interfere with the long-run tendency to equality between these two magnitudes, but, in the end, variations in the rate of interest would tend to make good of these temporary deviations from full employment. This type of saving–investment analysis was brought to its ultimate stage by Keynes in his *Treatise on Money* (1930).

In the *General Theory* (1936), Keynes offered his principle of effective demand as a radically different theory of how 'the demand for investment and the willingness to save [are brought] into equilibrium with one another' (1936, p. 175). The central argument which distinguishes the *General Theory* is straightforward and revolves around the crucial role that it assigns to *changes in the level of income as the equilibrating force between saving and investment*: 'it is not the rate of interest but the level of income which ensures equality between saving and investment' (1937, p. 212). Accordingly, Keynes thought he had proved that the economic system would generally find itself in a position where planned investment is equal to saving without there being any guarantee that the level of employment is full. In this theory, furthermore, 'saving equals investment' simply because investment induces savings to a like amount. Accordingly, saving is a 'passive' variable of no causal significance, and the theory of capital has therefore to be tackled without relying on the traditional intertemporal preference argument (Keynes, 1936, p. 243). Unfortunately, Keynes's 'alternative' theory of interest and his investment theory based on the marginal efficiency of capital paved the way for a return to traditional thinking about saving and investment. Indeed, these two elements left within the *General Theory* the possibility of the establishment of a (natural) rate of interest that would bring investment into equality with savings compatible with full employment output. The relevance of Keynes's principle of effective demand was eventually reduced to nothing more than an interesting addition to short-run adjustment processes between full-employment equilibria.

Following the publication of the *General Theory*, some twenty years of IS–LM exercises failed to improve this ambiguous result: with various degrees of sophistication, the saving-investment analysis ended up bogged down in the neoclassical synthesis. Since in the long run saving and investment have to do with the allocation of output (but nothing to do with the determination of output or the price level) in the short run some exogeneous fixity had to be brought in to support Keynes's explanation of unemployment. Thanks notably to its sweeping endorsement of the real-balance effect, the economics profession for a long time failed to address again the fundamental insight on the instability of decentralized economies Keynes had raised with his principle of effective demand. Inevitably, dissatisfaction was soon to emerge from such an analytical framework. Working within its limits and by submitting to critical discussions the various ad hoc Keynesian rigidities/elasticities, Monetarist theorists were rapidly in a position to reassert boldly that in the long run the interest rate can be relied upon to coordinate saving and investment; or, as Friedman put it, that 'there is no fundamental "flaw in the price system" that makes unemployment the natural outcome of a fully operative market mechanism' (1971, p. 16). Using the same standard Walrasian general equilibrium model, Rational Expectations theorists even managed to bring this argument one step further away from any analysis in terms of savings and investment: pre-Keynesian trade cycle theorists as well as the postwar neoclassical synthesis and the Monetarist School were all clearly concerned with the problem of pushing the economy to its natural rate of interest (even if they obviously disagreed about how savings could be best brought in line with investment) and not to describe, like Rational Expectations economists, an economy that is there already.

From very different angles, and with diametrically opposed time-spans in mind, two important streams of economic theorizing have however taken up Keynes's challenge. Though with very different objectives in mind, both the powerful modern non-Walrasian temporary equilibrium approach and the neo-Ricardian School are sharing Keynes's doubts about the stability of decentralized economies. In particular, they both consider that the interest rate is not the obvious mechanism by which intertemporal decisions between savings and investment can be coordinated.

The former – dropping the traditional short run/long run

method – attempts to analyse *short-period* positions of a decentralized economy *in sequences over time*; the time-honoured idea of a centre of gravity around which the system is seen to oscillate disappears completely from this analytical picture. The latter – rejecting the entire marginalist framework on the grounds of the inconsistencies revealed by the capital controversies of the 1960s – attempts to graft Keynes's principle of effective demand (his theory of production) onto a Ricardian–Sraffian theory of value and distribution. If both approaches are still in their infancy, they are however alone today in carrying on under admittedly very different guises the crucial and century-old problem associated with the savings–investment analysis.

P. BRIDEL

See also EFFECTIVE DEMAND; FINANCE AND SAVING; KEYNES, JOHN MAYNARD.

BIBLIOGRAPHY

Bridel, P. 1987. *Cambridge Monetary Thought. The Development of Saving–Investment Analysis from Marshall to Keynes*. London: Macmillan.

Friedman, M. 1971. *A Theoretical Framework for Monetary Analysis*. New York: National Bureau of Economic Research.

Keynes, J.M. 1930. *A Treatise on Money*. Reprinted in *The Collected Writings of John Maynard Keynes*, Vols V and VI, London: Macmillan, 1971.

Keynes, J.M. 1936. *The General Theory of Employment, Interest and Money*. Reprinted in *The Collected Writings of John Maynard Keynes*, Vol. VII, London: Macmillan, 1973.

Keynes, J.M. 1937. Alternative theories of the rate of interest. *Economic Journal* 47, 241–52. Reprinted in *The Collected Writings of John Maynard Keynes*, Vol. 14. London: Macmillan, 1973.

Schumpeter, J. 1939. *Business Cycles*. 2 vols, New York: McGraw-Hill.

Smith, A. 1776. *An Inquiry into the Nature and Causes of the Wealth of Nations*. 2 vols, Oxford: Clarendon Press, 1976.

Sax, Emil (1845–1927). Sax was born in Jauernig (then, Austrian-Silesia; today, Javornik in Czechoslovakia). He studied in Vienna, where he became an university lecturer. After some practical activity (among other things in the railway organization), he became, in 1879, professor of political economy at the University of Prague. From 1879 to 1885 he was a member of the Vienna Chamber of Deputies. In 1893 he abandoned his Prague professorship and retired to Abbazia, Istria (then, Italy; today, Opatija in Yugoslavia), where he died in 1927.

Sax holds a peculiar place within the older Austrian school. He shared its basic idea according to which 'value' virtually opens the way to the explanation of all economic problems. However, in methodological matters, in the conception of economics, and in the interpretation of the value phenomenon itself, he went his own way. For Sax 'value' is not the rationally perceived significance of a commodity for the welfare of a person, but an emotional relationship between the person and the world of goods. His conception of economics is based on the distinction between individualism and collectivism. Behaviour is individualistic if it results (self-determined) from the individual personality; behaviour is collectivistic if the individual is motivated only as a member of a (larger and stable) group and in relation to this group. According to Sax, these two fundamental forces shape all economic and social phenomena in a characteristic way: the simple feeling of value becomes, individualistically, the exchangeable value; collectivistically, the complicated determination of value within a group. In relation to the social environment, these two fundamental forces can appear egoistic, altruistic and (as a mixture of both) mutualistic. Sax believed he had overcome the psychological one-sidedness of the classical school, and therefore he considered the findings of his theoretical work as exact results of inductive research.

According to Sax, the distinction between individualism and collectivism corresponds to the (value based) theories of private and public economy. The absolute tax level (today called tax–GNP ratio) is determined by evaluations of such individuals in whom the fundamental force of collectivism is effective; they take care of the fact that the levels of the private and the public sphere are balanced. The relative tax level (today called tax apportionment to individuals) is deduced by Sax from the 'equivalence of value' of the individual tax liabilities; this results in the application of the equal sacrifice theory. For Sax, compulsion in taxation merely substitutes for a lack of correct insight. The 'statemindedness of those governing' and the 'resistance of those governed' prevent the abuse of power.

Besides fiscal theory problems, Sax paid particular attention to the then young science of transport economics. His statements on transport policy (1878–79) are founded on a theoretically analysed historical experience, although the theoretical sections do not reach up to the abstract (mathematical) level such as Launhardt's treatment of transport problems. Despite the fact that much of Sax's writings on transport economics, have since become obsolete, the book remains an excellent piece of applied economics.

K. SCHMIDT

SELECTED WORKS

1878–9. *Die Verkehrsmittel in Volks- und Staatswirthschaft*. 2nd edn. 3 vols, Berlin: Springer, 1918–22.

1884. *Das Wesen und die Aufgaben der Nationalökonomie, Ein Beitrag zu den Grundproblemen dieser Wissenschaft*. Vienna: Hölder.

1887. *Grundlegung der theoretischen Staatswirthschaft*. Vienna: Hölder.

1924. Die Wertungstheorie der Steuer. *Zeitschrift für Volkswirtschaft und Sozialpolitik*, NS 4, Vienna and Leipzig: Deuticke.

BIBLIOGRAPHY

Beckerath, E. von. 1930. Emil Sax, ein Nachruf. *Zeitschrift für Nationalökonomie* 1, Vienna: Springer.

Beckerath, E. von. 1956. Sax, Emil. *Handwörterbuch der Sozialwissenschaften*, Vol. 9. Stuttgart: Fischer; Tübingen: Mohr; Gottingen: Vandenhoeck & Ruprecht.

Say, Horace Emile (1794–1860). French businessman and economist, H.E. Say was born at Noisy in 1794, and died in Paris in 1860. He was the eldest son of Jean-Baptiste Say, the famous economist. In his youth he was sent to study at Geneva, where a branch of the Say family had emigrated after the Edict of Nantes. Afterwards, he travelled extensively in North and South America, establishing connections in Brazil that later served his business interests. Back in Paris, Say founded a firm in 1818 for trading with South America, and some time later married the daughter of a rich industrialist, thus assuring his financial security and freeing him to indulge his other interests.

Say published his *Histoire des relations commerciales entre la France et le Brésil* in 1839, but thereafter devoted himself to administrative and commercial interests closer to home. He advanced to the position of Director of the Paris Chamber of Commerce, served as Councillor of State from 1849 to 1851, and was elected to the Académie des Sciences Morales et Politiques in 1857.

Say was a devoted follower of his father's economic doctrines and a faithful editor of his literary works. Although he added nothing new to economic theory, he contributed to the popularization of economic literature by helping Guillaumin found his publishing firm in the 1830s. He was also a founder of the Société d'Economie Politique and the *Journal des Economistes*.

R.F. HÉBERT

SELECTED WORKS

1839. *Histoire des relations commerciales entre la France et le Brésil*. Paris: Guillaumin.

1846. *Etudes sur l'administration de la ville de Paris et du département de la Seine*. Paris: Guillaumin.

Say, Jean-Baptiste (1767–1832). Although Jean-Baptiste Say is remembered primarily for Say's Law, one of the cornerstones of classical economics, he was also an early proponent of the utility theory of value, and was therefore very much at odds with his classical contemporaries, to whom labour was the source of value. Say's best-known work, his *Traité d'économie politique* (published in five editions, from 1803 to 1826) was intended as a shorter and more systematic presentation of economics than Adam Smith's *Wealth of Nations*. The success of this book made Say the best-known expositor of Smith in Europe and America, and he became in 1815 France's first professor of political economy. Translations of the *Traité* were used as textbooks at universities on both sides of the Atlantic.

Say was not, however, a mere uncritical expositor of Smith. The central importance of labour in Smith's discussions of value was replaced by Say's concern to show utility as the ultimate foundation of value. Production itself was defined as the production of utility, not of physical output. He noted in the first chapter of his *Traité* that this was subjective utility, which the economist must take as given data, however much moralists might attempt to change people's valuations. Businessmen also played a much more important and honourable role in Say than in Smith – Say having been a businessman himself and descended from a mercantile family. The *Traité d'économie politique* also went beyond Smith in developing what Say called 'one of the most important truths of political economy' – that supply creates its own demand, the doctrine ultimately named Say's Law.

Much controversy has surrounded the question of Say's originality in developing this principle, or rather, related series of principles. Claims have been made for James Mill as the real author of Say's Law. However, Mill's earliest published discussion of issues involving aggregate supply and demand came in an 1804 review in *The Literary Journal* of a book by Lauderdale – one year after the first edition of Say's *Traité* was published. While the chapter ('Des Débouchés') in which Say's Law was first set forth was very brief in the first edition, there was further discussion of the same principle in that same edition, notably in chapter 5 of the second volume. Later editions brought these scattered discussions together in an enlarged chapter on aggregate supply and demand, but much of the substance was there from the beginning. Mill was only the first of many to reformulate and elaborate what Say had done.

Say was concerned with the methodology as well as the substantive propositions of economics. He advocated systematic analysis rather than naive empiricism, but was also highly critical of the abstract deductive method of Ricardo and his followers. According to Say, Ricardo 'pushes his reasonings to their remotest consequences, without comparing their results with those of actual experience'. During a friendly correspondence with Ricardo, Say pointed out that facts 'are the masters of us all'. In the introduction to his *Traité d'économie politique*, Say also expressed his fear of 'our always being misled in political economy, whenever we have subjected its phenomena to mathematical calculation'.

Say was in touch with the leading economists of his day, by mail and in person. He never resolved his differences with Ricardo as to whether value was based on labour or utility, but in attempting to clarify his position in 1822, Say spoke of 'the last quantity of useful things' as being crucial – a suggestion of the missing *marginal* concept essential to the utility theory of value. In his correspondence with Sismondi and Malthus, he came ultimately to reconcile Say's Law with their theories of aggregate disequilibrium. The fifth edition of his *Traité d'économie politique* in 1826 incorporated some of Sismondi's reasoning at the end of his chapter on Say's Law of markets (unfortunately, the English translation is from the previous edition) and called this to Malthus's attention as an admitted 'restriction' on this doctrine. A later textbook by Say, *Cours complet d'économie politique*, published in 1828–9, followed the chapter on Say's Law with one entitled 'Limits of Production', a phrase from Sismondi along with Sismondian analysis in the chapter.

Say was a policy-oriented economist rather than a model-builder like Ricardo. In his introduction to the new restrictions added to his chapter on the law of markets, Say remarked: 'Now, we are studying practical political economy here.' To Malthus he wrote: 'It is better to stick to facts and their consequences than to syllogisms.'

THOMAS SOWELL

See also CLASSICAL ECONOMICS.

Say's Law. Say's Law, the apparently simple proposition that supply creates its own demand, has had many different meanings, and many sets of reasoning underlying each meaning – not all of these by Jean-Baptiste Say. Historically, Say's Law emerged in the wake of the industrial revolution, when the two striking new economic phenomena of vastly increased output and the economy's cyclical inability to maintain sales and employment led some to fear that there was some inherent limit to the growth of production – some point beyond which there would be no means of purchasing it all. At the very least, some feared, there would not naturally or automatically be generated sufficient purchasing power to absorb the ever-growing output of the industrial economy, unless special policy arrangements were made to insure that income would be large enough to purchase output. Robert Owen and Karl Rodbertus exemplified these views, which were not those of any school of economists.

Say's Law attempted to answer such concerns by pointing out that the production of output tends of itself to generate purchasing power equal to the value of that output: supply creates its own demand. But Say's Law did not spring forth, full blown, like Minerva from the head of Zeus. It emerged piecemeal over a span of years, enveloped in controversies that ultimately involved nearly every noted economist of the early 19th century, and as its elaboration proceeded its definitions shifted under polemical stress. Moreover, the basic terms of discourse in economics were themselves in a process of evolution. The words 'supply' and 'demand' had different meanings for those economists like Sismondi and Malthus, groping toward the schedule or functional meanings of today, from those in the writings of David Ricardo or John Stuart Mill, who rigidly defined the terms as quantity supplied and quantity demanded. They repeatedly argued past each other.

The central meaning of Say's Law was implied by J.B. Say's rhetorical question, 'how could it be possible that there should now be bought and sold in France five or six times as many commodities as in the miserable reign of Charles VI?' This dramatized his main point, that there was no long-run limit to the growth of output, or of the demand for it. This did not deny that a *short run* derangement of the economy could take place, but Say described this as 'an evil which can only be passing'. Moreover, he attributed these short-run phenomena to a wrong mixture of output, compared to consumer demand, rather than to aggregate overproduction. This was an *ad hoc* addendum, not logically implied by the principle of supply creating its own demand. Say thus created a subsidiary meaning of Say's Law – a denial that there was such a thing, even in the short-run, as aggregate overproduction – which is to say, that there was no such thing as an equilibrium aggregate output. There could be a 'partial glut' of particular commodities produced in excess of demand but there could be no 'general glut' of commodities in the aggregate. It was this vulnerable subsidiary argument which Sismondi and Malthus attacked in the 19th century and Keynes in the 20th.

The first edition of Say's *Traité d'économie politique* in 1803 contained the crucial propositions of Say's Law, though not all in his chapter on markets ('Des Débouchés'). The quantity of products demanded was 'without a doubt' determined by the quantity of products created, according to Say. 'The demand for products in general is therefore always equal to the sum of the products', he said. The distinction between secular stagnation and short-run downturns, and between partial and general gluts, was also present from the first edition of Say's *Traité*. These ideas all reappeared in James Mill's writings shortly afterward, but Say's priority is clear, both from the dates of the publications and from Mill's citation of Say in his own early writings, depriving him of even subjective originality.

The elder Mill did, however, make a significant contribution to the evolution of Say's Law. Where Say had asserted the inherent sufficiency of demand to purchase supply in terms of half the goods being essentially bartered for the other half, or in terms of saved money being spent as investment, Mill added the behavioural theory that people produced only because of, and only to the extent of, their demand for other goods. Each individual's supply equalled his demand *ex ante*; therefore society's supply must equal society's demand *ex ante*. Unfortunately, Mill also cited the *ex post* identity of supply and demand as evidence, as did J.R. McCulloch, Robert Torrens and John Stuart Mill.

While Say's priority over James Mill is readily established, the notion that in the long run aggregate demand 'has no known limits' was stated by the Physiocrat Mercier de la Rivière in the year of Say's birth. Nor was this a passing remark. His book, *L'Ordre naturel et essential des sociétés politique* (1767), especially Chapter 36, contained both the concept of a circular flow of money and of goods, and discussions of the conditions under which the existing level of aggregate output would be reproduced in subsequent time periods, as well as the conditions in which it would fall because receipts failed to cover the supply price of inputs. Yet it was not through Mercier de la Rivière but through Say that Say's Law entered the mainstream of economics. Ironically, both Say and Mill attacked Mercier de la Rivière. While his statement that aggregate demand is unlimited anticipated both of them, his concept of aggregate equilibrium and disequilibrium was anathema to the subsidiary version of Say's Law that was an integral part of the doctrine during the early 19th century.

Adam Smith also anticipated Say when he asserted in *The Wealth of Nations* (p. 407) that 'a particular merchant' could have a glut of goods but that a whole nation could not. Moreover, Smith's doctrine that savings rather than consumption promoted growth provided yet another dimension to Say's Law and the controversies surrounding it. One possible meaning of Smith's statement was that a shift in the savings function – a willingness to save and invest more at a given rate of return – would tend to increase future output. But another interpretation, equally permissible in the absence of functional concepts, was that an increased quantity saved would promote future growth. Lord Lauderdale interpreted Smith in the latter sense, and attacked this proposition on grounds that there was some equilibrium level of savings and investment which, if exceeded, would reduce rates of return to a point that would cause the existing levels of savings to decline in subsequent time periods. In short, Lauderdale argued that there could be a general glut of capital, just one step from saying that there could be a general glut of aggregate output.

The leading critics of Say's Law during the classical era – Sismondi, Malthus and Lauderdale – all asserted short-run disequilibrium, not long-run stagnation, but the long-run comparative-statics approach of the Ricardians made it especially difficult for them to understand what the critics were saying in short-run dynamic terms. While Say himself ultimately came to understand – and reproduce in his later writings – the aggregate equilibrium theories which he now reconciled with the central meaning of Say's Law, more than twenty years later John Stuart Mill was still representing Lauderdale, Sismondi and Malthus as stagnationists. However, after completely misinterpreting their positions, J.S. Mill also set forth the most sophisticated analysis of the issues in classical economics in the second of his *Essays on Some Unsettled Questions in Political Economy* (1844).

After denouncing the 'mistakes', the 'completely erroneous' ideas and 'palpable absurdities' of those who emphasized the need for adequate aggregate demand, J.S. Mill nevertheless conceded that there could be 'general excess' in the sense that when money was not immediately respent, a seller 'does not therefore necessarily add to the *immediate* demand for one commodity when he adds to the supply of another'. Thus there may be 'a superabundance of all commodities relative to money'. Both the previous classical economists and such critics as Sismondi and Malthus had analysed the issue of aggregate output in essentially barter terms, despite incidental references to money. The theory of equilibrium aggregate output in Sismondi and Malthus was based on a balance of the utility of output and the disutility of the efforts required to produce it – a balance which could be temporarily unbalanced in their short-run dynamic models, though not in the long-run comparative statics model of James Mill.

John Stuart Mill's model, in which the role of money was important, was a different dimension, though not unique – Robert Torrens having expressed similar ideas more than two decades earlier. However, on the crucial issue of an aggregate equilibrium output in a non-monetary model, J.S. Mill remained adamant that there could be only internal disproportionality, not aggregate overproduction. Output, 'if distributed without miscalculation among all kinds of produce in the proportion which private interest would dictate, creates, or rather constitutes, its own demand'. The issue remained to J.S. Mill one of internal 'proportions', not aggregate amounts.

Discussions of Say's Law virtually disappeared from economics for at least a generation after John Stuart Mill wrote on it in the 1840s. Even the sweeping challenges of neoclassical economics to classical orthodoxy, beginning in the 1870s, largely by-passed the issue of Say's Law. Isolated criticisms came from beyond the pale – from Marx, Hobson and assorted cranks. Within the economics profession, Say's Law was one of those things simply assumed and ignored. Early in the 20th century, Knut Wicksell explored the relationship between the quantity theory of money and Say's Law. The classical assumption that money is demanded only for transactions during the current period is incompatible with the price level being determined by the quantity of money, for a change in the price level requires that, at some point in the process, there must be either an excess or deficient money demand for goods in the aggregate, causing the general price level to go up or down in response. However, Wicksell's own belated recognition by the English-speaking world meant that Say's Law did not become a major concern again until the appearance of John Maynard Keynes's *General Theory of Employment, Interest and Money* in 1936.

Modern, and especially Post-Keynesian, discussions of Say's Law have revealed it to be not one, but a number of related, propositions. The most general of these propositions is that the aggregate value of goods suppled (including money) equals the aggregate value of goods demanded (including money). Thus an excess supply of goods is the same as an excess demand for money. This proposition has been christened 'Walras' Law'. Where there is assumed to be no excess demand for money, as in James Mill, for example, then aggregate supply is identically equal to aggregate demand. This proposition has been christened 'Say's Identity'. When the equality of aggregate supply and demand is stated as an equilibrium condition – a sense in which equilibrium output theorists like Sismondi and Malthus could subscribe to it – then it merely states that both equilibrium and disequilibrium levels of output may exist. This proposition has been christened 'Say's Equality'. This Ricardo, James Mill, and initially Say, all denied.

The Keynesian revolution not only produced a more sophisticated theory of aggregate equilibrium, but also contributed to the distortion of Say's Law, which Keynes reduced to Say's Identity. According to Keynes, Say's Law 'is equivalent to the proposition that there is no obstacle to full employment'. Only the cruder statements of the Ricardians said that.

Say's Law has been an important proposition in many ways. By indicating that the possibility of purchasing output from the income generated during its production is ultimately not limited by the mere size of output, Say's Law exposed the fallacy of recurrent popular fears that economic growth must collide with some impassable limit. The modern post-Keynesian delineations of the different senses of Say's Law (Walras' Law, Say's Identity, Say's Equality) more precisely specify the conditions of aggregate equilibrium and disequilibrium, and indicate the theories of economic behaviour behind them. Finally, the long history of controversies over Say's Law sheds light on the enormous difficulties involved when even intelligent thinkers with honesty and goodwill try to understand each other's theories without clearly defined terms and without a clear sense of the conceptual framework of the opposing views. In short, its implications reach beyond economics to intellectual history in general.

THOMAS SOWELL

See also DÉBOUCHÉS, THÉORIE DES.

BIBLIOGRAPHY

Becker, G. and Baumol, W.J. 1960. The classical monetary theory: the outcome of the discussion. In *Essays in Economic Thought*, ed. J.J. Spengler and W.R. Allen, Chicago: Rand McNally.

Malthus, T.R. 1820. *Principles of Political Economy*. New York: Augustus M. Kelley, 1951.

Mill, J. 1803. *Commerce Defended*. London: C. and R. Bladwin, ch. VI.

Say, J.-B. 1803. *Traité d'économie politique*, Vol. I. Paris: Chez Rapilly, 1826, ch. XV.

Sismondi, J.C.L. de. 1827. *Nouveaux principes d'économie politique*. Paris: Delaunay, Libraire, Vol. I, Books 1, 4; Vol. II, Appendix.

Sowell, T. 1972. *Say's Law: An Historical Analysis*. Princeton: Princeton University Press.

Sowell, T. 1974. *Classical Economics Reconsidered*. Princeton: Princeton University Press.

Spengler, J.J. 1960. The physiocrats and Say's law of markets. In *Essays in Economic Thought*, ed. J.J. Spengler and W.R. Allen, Chicago: Rand McNally.

Say, (Jean-Baptiste) Léon (1826–1896). French statesman, financier and economist, born in Paris in 1826; died there on 22 April 1896. He was the son of Horace Emile Say, the grandson of Jean-Baptiste Say, the nephew of Louis Auguste Say and Charles Comte. Léon Say became one of the most prominent statesmen of the French Third Republic. He served as Finance Minister from 1872 to 1879, and again in 1882, overseeing the largest financial operation of the century – payment of war reparations in Germany. His financial policies were directed toward a decrease in public expenditures and the removal of barriers to internal trade. A brilliant speaker and debater, he railed against socialism from the left and protectionism from the right. With Gambetta and Freycinet, he launched the ambitious programme of public works that bears the latter's name. Upon leaving the Cabinet, Say returned to his seat in parliament, assuming the leadership of the free trade party. He was at one time considered for the presidency of the republic, but was gradually set apart from his constituency by a rising tide of radicalism.

As an economist, Say's talents fall somewhere between the modest gifts of his father and the more imposing skills of his grandfather. He left no large work nor did he create any school of thought. Like his father, he was faithful to the doctrines of his namesake, and was a competent editor of his grandfather's works. In his youth he associated briefly with Léon Walras in a scheme to promote cooperative associations of production. He later became a frequent contributer to the *Journal des Economistes*, mostly on economic policy, and a lecturer at the Ecole des Sciences Politiques, which was the prototype of the London School of Economics and Political Science. Say had a broad knowledge of history and theory, and he was capable of sustained exposition at a high level. As an example, his *Solutions démocratiques de l'impôt* was directed against the idea of using taxation as a means of social equalization. He argued, instead, that the basis of taxation should always be real (based on property), never personal.

A curious parallel exists in the careers of Say and Turgot, whose name Say declared he could not even pronounce without emotion. They shared a body of ideas and a similar destiny. Both achieved eminence as finance ministers in the French government, only to be turned out upon losing public favour. Say however, helped to immortalize his predecessor by writing one of the earliest biographies of Turgot.

R.F. HÉBERT

SELECTED WORKS
1886. *Les solutions démocratiques de la question des impôts*. 2 vols, Paris: Guillaumin.
1888. *Turgot*. Trans. M.B. Anderson, Chicago: A.C. McClurg & Co.
1891. *Economie sociale*. Paris: Guillaumin.
1891–2. *Nouveau dictionaire d'économie politique*. 2 vols, Paris: Guillaumin.
1896. *Finances publiques, liberté du commerce*. Paris: Guillaumin.
1898–1901. *Les Finances de la France sous la Troisième République*. 4 vols, Paris: C. Levy.

BIBLIOGRAPHY
Michel, G. 1900. *Léon Say, sa vie, ses oeuvres*. 2nd edn, Paris: Calmann Levy.
Picot, G.M.R. 1907. Léon Say. In *Etudes d'histoire contemporaine. Notices historiques*, Paris: Hachette, Vol. II, 1–53.

Say, Louis Auguste (1774–1840). A brother of J.B. Say, and founder of two great sugar refineries at Nantes and Paris.

He wrote several works on economics: *Considérations sur l'industrie et la législation* (1822); *Études sur la richesse des Nations et Réfutation des principales erreurs en Économie Politique* (1836); *Principales causes de la richesse des peuples et des particuliers* (1818); *Traité élémentaire de la richesse individuelle et de la richesse publique* (1827).

A severe and uncompromising critic, he insists on the necessity, 'if one wants to be clear and well understood, to call each thing by its name', and inveighs against the looseness and fluctuation of the terminology of Adam Smith and Ricardo. He also accuses the former of exclusively prizing things 'after the fashion of merchants' who only care about the price at which an article can be sold. 'His book contains highly interesting parts and a great deal of valuable information, but his theory of value has done much harm to the progress of theory.' Louis Say considers his brother's book as 'having above all previous works presented in the best way the greatest number of useful truths'; still he reproaches him with having too often forgotten the leading principle 'that there can be no production of wealth without a creation or increase of utility'. He steadily and repeatedly states that 'a thing is only wealth in proportion to its degree of utility'; the question of its *value in exchange* is quite a secondary matter.

[E. Castelot]

Reprinted from *Palgrave's Dictionary of Political Economy*.

SELECTED WORKS
1818. *Principales causes de la richesse des peuples et des particuliers*. Paris.
1822. *Considérations sur l'industrie et la législation*. Paris.
1827. *Traité élémentaire de la richesse individuelle et de la richesse publique*. Paris.
1836. *Études sur la richesse des nations et réfutation des principales erreurs en économie politique*. Paris.

Sayers, Richard Stanley (born 1908). Born at Bury St Edmunds into a large poor family, Sayers was to become the doyen of English monetary economists/historians in the decades following 1950. He read economics at Cambridge, where Sraffa's lectures began 'in time for me to learn enough of the "continentals" to free me from the shadow of Marshall' (personal communication to the present author). In the 1930s he taught at the London School of Economics – where with P. Barrett Whale he formed a minority backing Keynes's *Treatise on Money* against the prevailing Robbins/Hayek orthodoxies – and then at Oxford, where in two summer months of 1937 he wrote what became the first of seven editions of his *Modern Banking* (1938), on which generations of English students were to be reared. After war service in the Ministry of Supply and the Cabinet Office, and struggle against ill-health, in 1947 he succeeded D.H. Robertson in the Cassel Chair at LSE, where he remained for twenty years. Retiring from his chair at sixty, he devoted several years to updating Clapham's celebrated two-volume history on the Bank of England, and to editing and introducing the economic volumes (IX–XI) of *The Collected Works of Walter Bagehot* (1978).

These latter volumes represent only a small part of the extraordinarily rich and varied corpus of writings on monetary history that constitute the most enduring memorial to Richard Sayers's career. He first achieved widespread recognition in 1936, with *Bank of England Operations 1890–1914*. His reputation as a financial historian was firmly consolidated by a stream of contributions that included the official history of *Financial Policy 1939–1945* (1956) and *Lloyds Bank in the History of English Banking* (1957). He had earlier edited (with T.S. Ashton, 1953) *Papers in English Monetary History*, and in 1957 issued a volume of his own papers on historical and contemporary monetary issues under the title *Central Banking after Bagehot*. At the end of his tenure of the Cassel Chair came the centenary volume *Gilletts in the London Money Market 1867–1967* (1968). This prolific output was accompanied not only by vigorous development at LSE of monetary studies with historical emphasis, but also by many visits to lecture at home and foreign universities, frequently on historical topics.

But R.S. Sayers's work was by no means confined to monetary history. It included, though very importantly *not* in a 'separate compartment', work on public policy issues. For example, he served from 1952 to 1957 on the Colonial Economic Research Committee organized by the Colonial Office. In 1968 he participated in the enquiry into UK banking practices by the Monopolies Commission. But undoubtedly his major contribution in this area was connected with his membership, in 1957–9, of the Committee on the Working of the Monetary System (the Radcliffe Committee), of whose report he is widely acknowledged to be the major architect. To this investigation he brought mastery of monetary theory as well as historical perspective, though he believed in what he called 'Adam Smith's tradition of economic theory in plain language'. This blend of skills (which, if not unique to Sayers, he certainly possessed in virtually unrivalled degree) is exhibited not only in the Radcliffe Report itself, but also in easily accessible – and still highly relevant – form in his presidential address to Section F of the British Association for the Advancement of Science, reprinted in the *Economic Journal* December 1960.

In this address, Sayers set out Radcliffian doctrine with superb clarity. Neither monetary theory nor monetary policy could be crisply formalized on account of real-world complexity. Even in periods of relative stability of institutions and practices, the elasticity of substitution between various classes of (more or less) liquid asset was too high for the attempt to distinguish operationally between 'monetary' and 'non-monetary' assets to succeed. Aggregate demand might be influenced by the economy's stock of liquidity, but the paths of influence were too subtle and complex to be charted and measured; liquidity and demand might, however, be inversely related to general interest rate movements on a scale that policy could make use of (the 'availability doctrine'). Times of institutional change would so disturb the underlying relationships as to further complicate monetary policy's already formidable task. Governments would be well advised to make fiscal policy the main tool of stabilization efforts.

A.B. Cramp

SELECTED WORKS
1936. *Bank of England Operations 1890–1914*. London: P.S. King.
1938. *Modern Banking*. Oxford: Oxford University Press. 7th edn, 1967.
1952. (ed.) *Banking in the British Commonwealth*. Oxford: Oxford University Press.
1956. *Financial Policy 1939–45*. London: HMSO.
1957. *Lloyds Bank in the History of English Banking*. Oxford: Oxford University Press.
1962. (ed.) *Banking in Western Europe*. Oxford: Oxford University Press.
1968. *Gilletts in the London Money Market*. Oxford: Oxford University Press.
1976. *The Bank of England 1891–1944*. Cambridge: Cambridge University Press.

scarcity. The notion of scarcity plays a central role in economic theory. Indeed, some economists consider it essential for a proper definition of economics itself. The best example is perhaps Walras' definition of social wealth, i.e. economic goods. 'By *social wealth*', says Walras, 'I mean all things, material or immaterial (it does not matter which in this context), that are *scarce*, that is to say, on the one hand, *useful* to us and, on the other hand, only available to us in *limited quantity*' (1926, p. 65).

Walras explains that by 'useful' he means a thing 'capable of satisfying a want' and by 'in limited quantity' all things which 'exist in such quantities that each of us can find at hand enough, completely to satisfy his desires', i.e. air, water etc. These things, which everyone can take as he wishes, are not social wealth. Only when they become scarce can they be considered as part of social wealth.

Walras points out three important consequences which follow from the existence of scarcity, and usefulness. (1) 'Useful things limited in quantity are *appropriable*', a consideration which is very important for the theory of property, which economics studies in common with law. (2) 'Useful things limited in quantity are *valuable and exchangeable*', i.e. all things which can be appropriated can be exchanged with other things belonging to other individuals at a certain rate of exchange, called price. Therefore, economics deals typically with the problem of the determination of prices on the market. (3) 'Useful things limited in quantity are *things that can be produced and multiplied by industry*. In other words, they are reproducible'. Therefore economics must consider production of commodities, or industry, as one of the main subjects to be studied.

That concept of scarcity was widely accepted by all economists of the time and it was adopted by Robbins, too, in his well-known definition of economics. Robbins, who was well aware of Weber's methodological lesson, rejected the 'materialist' definition of economics adopted by Marshall and other economists, which held that economics is the science which studies the causes of material welfare. But since it is possible to obtain revenue for work not producing anything material at all (like music, literature etc.) there are many 'economic' activities which are left out of this definition of economics. Labour is 'productive', contrary to what Adam Smith says, even when it does not produce material goods. 'Whatever Economics is concerned with', Robbins concludes, 'it is *not* concerned with the causes of material welfare as such' (1932, p. 9).

Therefore Robbins turns towards the 'scarcity' definition of economics. He points out that every economic problem is characterized by a multiplicity of ends and by the scarcity of means. But a multiplicity of ends is not enough to define a problem as 'economic'. When a particular good is redundant, no particular problem arises over its use, even if the ends are quite different. Nor is the limitation of means sufficient to raise an economic problem, if there is no possibility of alternative uses. But when it is possible to choose alternative ends and the means are scarce, then we are faced with an economic problem. 'Economics', says Robbins, 'is the science which studies human behaviour as a relationship between ends and scarce means which have alternative uses' (1932, p. 16).

This definition gave rise to great number of comments and critiques which cannot be taken into consideration here. Nevertheless, nobody seriously objected to the concept of scarcity as an essential element entering the definition of economics, until the recent restatement of the classical approach to the problem of value and distribution by Piero Sraffa based on a modern analytical framework (Sraffa, 1960). Within this theoretical framework it is possible to put forward a radical critique of the notion of the 'scarcity' of production factors, a notion which plays an essential role in the traditional marginalist theory of value and distribution. The level of the rate of profits, for instance, does not depend on the relative quantity of capital in relation to the labour employed in a certain economic system (Garegnani, 1970). Even more clearly, the marginalist concept of scarcity is challenged as far as a scarce natural resource, like land, is considered. A certain land can become 'scarce' or 'redundant' because of a change in the income distributed between profits and wages, but without changes in the quantities produced (Montani, 1975). In a more general way, we can say that the shares of the net product going to wages, profits and rents do not depend on the relative size of the production factors employed.

But the meaning of scarcity within the marginalist theory of distribution is very peculiar: it concerns only the *relative* quantities of the factors employed in production. We may say that a factor is *scarce* when increasing quantities of it applied to a given quantity of the other gives rise to decreasing returns. The meaning of scarcity is very different when referred to economic goods. Here we may say, as Walras has clearly stated, that a good is scarce when its quantity is limited in relation to its capacity to satisfy needs. It is this general meaning that is interesting when evaluating the significance of Sraffa's approach. In other words, are the commodities considered by Sraffa 'scarce' in a different meaning as compared to the economic goods considered by Walras?

To answer this question it may be useful to consider the idea of 'economic goods' in classical political economy, especially in Ricardo, who is quite explicit on this point and in Marx, who can be considered the closest follower of Ricardo as far as the theory of value is concerned.

According to Ricardo, 'Possessing utility, commodities derive their exchangeable value from two sources: from their scarcity, and from the quantity of labour required to obtain them' (Ricardo, 1821, p. 12). We can, therefore, distinguish two fundamental categories of economic goods. The first, such as pictures, scarce books and coins, etc., are those whose value is determined 'by their scarcity alone'. For these categories of goods the price is independent of the labour employed in their production. Their value 'varies with the varying wealth and inclinations of those who are desirous to possess them'.

A second category of goods, specifically called commodities, is on the contrary produced by entrepreneurs and brought to the market for sale at the end of the production cycle. The commodities, which represent nearly all the wealth of a country, can be multiplied or reproduced, according to Ricardo, 'almost without any assignable limit', provided that labour and the other means of production are disposable. Therefore Ricardo affirms that he considers in his analysis only the value or, more simply, the price of those commodities which 'can be increased in quantity by the exertion of human industry, and on the production of which competition operates without restraint'.

Marx's classification is more complex. In the first chapter of *Capital*, Marx put forward the distinction between use-value and exchange-value.

> The utility of a thing makes it a use-value. ... This property of a commodity is independent of the amount of labour required to appropriate its useful qualities ... Use-values become a reality only by use or consumption (Marx, 1867, p. 44).

Exchange-value, i.e. what we call price, is on the contrary a quantitative relationship, it is 'the proportion in which values in use of one sort are exchanged for those of another sort'.

Of course, there is a relationship between use-value and exchange-value: exchange-value presupposes use-value. Two commodities can be exchanged-and therefore have an exchange-value-if the buyer and the seller attach a use-value to them. It may happen, therefore, as Marx points out, that a certain good has a use-value without having an exchange-value. We can imagine two circumstances which give rise to such a case. The first concerns goods which are useful, but not scarce, when they are not produced by labour. 'A thing can be a use-value, without having value. This is the case whenever its utility to man is not due to labour. Such are air, virgin soil, mineral meadows, etc.' (Marx, 1867, p. 48). The second case regards a good produced with labour, but without any social utility, i.e. subjectively useful but not exchangeable on the market: 'A thing can be useful, and the product of human labour, without being a commodity. Whoever directly satisfies his wants with the produce of his own labour, creates, indeed, use-values, but not commodities.'

The principles used in Marx's classification are, therefore, the following: utility, scarcity and labour. On the whole, in the first chapter of *Capital*, he takes into consideration four cases. (a) Goods which are useful and scarce, produced by labour. These goods are proper commodities and their exchange-value is peculiarly of interest for economic analysis. (b) Goods which are useful, but not scarce and not produced by labour. Their exchange-value is zero and they can be ignored by the economist. (c) Goods produced by labour, but socially useless. These goods cannot properly be considered as scarce, because there is no demand for them on the market, (d) 'Lastly nothing can have value, without being an object of utility. If a thing is useless, so is the labour contained in it; the labour does not count as labour, and therefore creates no value.' This is the case of goods useless from a subjective point of view too.

In addition to these four categories of commodities, a fifth one exists, which should be considered if we wish to understand the relationship between Marx's and Ricardo's classification. There are commodities which are useful, scarce and not produced by labour, or produced by labour but without the quantity employed having any necessary relationship with its exchange-value. This is the case of works of art or scarce coins and rare books recalled by Ricardo.

We can summarize Ricardo's and Marx's position saying that there is a given category of goods, which we may call 'economic goods', whose characteristic is to have a use-value, not a subjective but a social use-value; they can be exchanged with other goods. Among this very general category of economic goods we can single out so-called 'commodities', i.e all goods reproducible by human labour, given a certain technological knowledge, in the quantities required by the market.

There is, therefore, no substantial difference between the classical notion of 'economic goods' and that of Walras or Robbins. Every good which is scarce and useful is taken into consideration by the economist. But, of course, commodities reproducible by labour are of special interest, because the wealth of modern societies consists in 'an immense accumulation of commodities' (Marx, 1867, p. 43). Sraffa's analysis concerns only the 'production of commodities', i.e. the most important categories of 'economic goods'. Works of art, scarce coins and rare books are excluded from Sraffa's theoretical framework, exactly as they are in Ricardo. The extension of the field considered is important inasmuch as we want to explain prices and the distribution of income: we cannot explain the price of an antique book by means of Sraffa's production equations. And yet we cannot say that the explanation of this particular kind of price is of no interest for the economist.

GUIDO MONTANI

See also GOODS AND COMMODITIES.

BIBLIOGRAPHY

Garegnani, P. 1970. Heterogeneous capital, the production function and the theory of distribution. *Review of Economic Studies* 37, 407–36.

Marx, K. 1867. *Capital*. London: Lawrence and Wishart, 1954.

Montani, G. 1975. Scarce natural resources and income distribution. *Metroeconomica* 27, 68–101.

Montani, G. 1979. *Valore e prezzo. Saggio su Sraffa e sulla scienza economica*. Pavia: GJES.

Ricardo, D. 1821. *On the Principles of Political Economy and Taxation*. In *The Works and Correspondence of David Ricardo*, Vol. I, ed. P. Sraffa, Cambridge: Cambridge University Press, 1951.

Robbins, L. 1932. *An Essay on the Nature and Significance of Economic Science*. London: Macmillan, 1952.

Sraffa, P. 1960. *Production of Commodities by Means of Commodities*. Cambridge: Cambridge University Press.

Walras, L. 1926. *Elements of Pure Economics, or the Theory of Social Wealth*. Trans. W. Jaffé, London: George Allen & Unwin, 1954. Reprinted, Fairfield: A.M. Kelley, 1977.

Schacht, Horace Greeley Hjalmar (1877–1970). Raised in an atmosphere of open-minded, liberal thinking in his family and of national patriotism among the general public, Schacht studied history of literature, German language and finally economics. Besides this he gained an education as a journalist. The theme of his doctoral thesis, 'Der theoretische Gehalt des englischen Merkantelismus', forced him to deepen his knowledge of finance, credit systems and foreign trade policy, which was relevant for his work in the years that followed. In 1903 he became an employee of the Dresdner Bank and in 1916 a member of the board of directors of the National Bank, which after its fusion with the Darmstädter Bank was one of the biggest banks in Germany.

Appointed to the Reichsbank Presidency in December 1923, Schacht was instrumental in stabilizing the German mark after the great inflation. In 1924 he was appointed as an expert to the Dawes Committee, which elaborated a plan for German reparation payments. The economic revival, which was vital if these payments were to be made, was to be stimulated by foreign loans. Schacht consistently argued for the channelling of these loans into profitable economic activities – in contrast to many politicians – rather than using them for reparation payments and social services.

As chief of the German delegation on the Young Committee of 1929, he made every effort to replace the Dawes Plan with a settlement more beneficial to Germany. His ultimate aim was to terminate German reparation payments (Schacht, 1931). When he recognized that the German government would not follow his strategy he resigned the presidency of the Reichsbank in March 1930. Once a member of the liberal German Democratic Party (from 1918 to 1926), he shifted more and more to the right, supported the Harzburger Front, an assembly of extreme right politicians including leaders of the Nazis (among them Hitler), and finally called for the formation of a nationalist government with Hitler as Chancellor.

Schacht saw the reasons for the economic depression in Germany as discrimination against German exports by the former enemy powers; excessively high costs of production as a result of excessive taxes, social insurance contributions and wages; abuses of financial resources by public bodies, and a mistaken monetary policy (Schacht, 1932). As a representative of German big business, especially heavy industry, his main objective was to rebuild a powerful German economy on the basis of orthodox capitalism. This entailed, for him, the conquest of colonies as a source of raw materials. Therefore two preconditions had to be met: first, suppression of working-class organizations; second, the forced rearmament of Germany. Both could be managed only by an authoritarian conservative government, which he and many leaders of heavy industry began to demand in the early Thirties. In January 1933 Hitler became Chancellor and in March Schacht was again appointed Reichsbank President. In addition, he was Minister of Economics from 1934 until 1937 and Plenipotentiary General of War Economy from 1935 until 1937. He was therefore one of the most powerful persons in the realm of economic policy during the early years of the Third Reich. Although he generally thought in categories of orthodox economic theory, he practised a quite unorthodox economic policy. His most well-known official acts were the creation of a system to finance work-providing measures (which had been partially introduced by previous governments), and, above all, rearmament and his foreign trade policy (the 'New Plan'). He instituted a state-controlled supply of credit by means of the so-called 'Mefo'-bills whereby government contractors drew bills on the 'Metall-Forschungsanstalt', a fictitious company founded for this purpose, all of whose debts where guaranteed by the Reich. The bills were always discountable at the Reichsbank and could be prolonged maximally for five years. They thus functioned as a sort of 'Keynesian' deficit spending, in particular for rearmament, by which economic growth was induced.

In 1934 Germany experienced a serious crisis of foreign exchange: the economic revival since 1933 and the beginnings of rearmament led from 1933 to 1934 to higher imports. Simultaneously German exports decreased as a result of the general protectionism of the time. Moreover, Germany had to repay foreign debts, so that the German funds of gold and foreign exchange dwindled away. That was the background of Schacht's New Plan, which showed signs of a mercantilistic foreign trade policy. It consisted of a total bilaterization of German foreign trade, a limitation of German imports to economically necessary commodities, especially in respect to rearmament, a complicated system of export promotions, and dubious behaviour with regard to the repayment of foreign debts of the Reich (Mühlen, 1939). Ultimately the entire foreign trade of Germany was controlled by the state.

When full employment was nearly achieved in 1936–7, Schacht wanted to stop a further expansion of credit to avoid inflationary pressures and consolidate economic successes so far. That would have meant, in consequence, the limitation of rearmament to the given capacities of the economy. His attitude contradicted the war aims of the Nazi leaders. Instead of reducing rearmament they desired to accelerate it. The ensuing conflict between the Nazi leaders on the one side and Schacht and some leaders of big industry on the other, was the personification of the rivalry between politics and economics for predominance in the Third Reich. Schacht lost this conflict. Step by step he was dismissed from his posts, finally from the Reichsbank presidency in 1939. In connection with the attempted assassination of July 1944 he was imprisoned in a concentration camp. At the Nuremberg Trials he was cleared of charges as a war criminal. In 1952 he became owner of a bank in West Germany.

WOLFGANG-DIETER CLASSEN

SELECTED WORKS

1927. *Die Stabilisierung der Mark*. Stuttgart: Deutsche Verlagsanstalt.
1931. *Das Ende der Reparationen*. Oldenburg: Gerhard Stalling.
1932. *Grundsätze deutscher Wirtschaftspolitik*. Berlin: Druckerei der Reichsbank.
1935. *Deutschland und die Weltwirtschaft*. Berlin: Druckerei der Reichsbank.
1936. *Why Germany Requires Colonies*. Berlin: Druckerei der Reichsbank.
1948. *Abrechnung mit Hitler*. Berlin: Rowohlt Verlag.
1955. *My First Seventy-Six Years. The Autobiography of Hjalmar Schacht*. Trans. D. Pyke, London: Allan Wingate.
1969. *1933: Wie eine Demokratie stirbt*. Düsseldorf: Econ Verlag.

BIBLIOGRAPHY

Beck, R. 1955. *Verdict on Schacht: A Study in the Problem of Political 'Guilt'*. Tallahassee: Florida State University.
Erbe, R. 1958. *Die nationalsozialistische Wirtschaftspolitik 1933–1939 im Lichte der modernen Theorie*. Zurich: Polygraph-Verlag.
Kroll, G. 1958. *Von der Wirtschaftskrise zur Staatskonjunktur*. Berlin: Duncker & Humblot.
Mühlen, N. 1939. *Schacht: Hitler's Magician. The Life and Loans of Dr. Hjalmar Schacht*. Trans. E.W. Dickes, New York: Alliance.
Pentzlin, H. 1980. *Hjalmar Schacht. Leben und Wirken einer umstrittenen Persönlichkeit*. Berlin, Frankfuram Main and Vienna: Ullstein.
Peterson, E.N. 1954. *Hjalmar Schacht: For and Against Hitler. A Political Economic Study of Germany 1923–1945*. Boston: Christopher Publishing House.
Simpson, A.E. 1969. *Hjalmar Schacht in Perspective*. The Hague and Paris: Mouton.

Schäffle, Albert Eberhard Friedrich (1831–1903). Originally destined for a theological career, Schäffle changed to economics during his studies, which he did not complete. After serving as editor of the *Schwäbischer Merkur* he became Professor of Economics at the University of Tübingen in 1860. Along with his academic activities he was engaged in politics as a member of the second Chamber of Württemberg (Württembergischen Kammer) (1861–5) and in the Customs Parliament (Zollparlament) (1868). In 1868 the busy and eloquent Swabian obtained a professorship at the university of Vienna and in 1871 he was appointed Austrian Minister of Trade (Handelsminister). In the same year the ministry was dissolved and Schäffle returned to Stuttgart, where he worked as an economist and published much popular literature during the next thirty years.

Schäffle's original achievements might be seen to lie in extending von Thünen's regional or space theory, i.e. the agrarian model, to the mining industry and to industrial production. But he did not recognize Thünen's marginalism and his model of general equilibrium in terms of realistic econometric parameters. Like Dietzel he invested considerable yet fruitless efforts in value theory. He attempted to integrate exchange or objective value and use-value or subjective value. Schäffle's influence as theorist and teacher of economics was in his own day rather limited. It seems to be of little importance for our time.

H.C. RECKTENWALD

SELECTED WORKS

1861. *Die Nationalökonomie oder allgemeine Wirtschaftslehre*. 2 vols, Tübingen and Leipzig: Spamer. 2nd and 3rd edns published as *Das gesellschaftliche System der menschlichen Wirtschaft*, Tübingen, 1873.

1895–7. *Die Steuern*. 2 vols, Leipzig: Hirschfeld.

1905. *Aus meinem Leben* (posthumous). Berlin: Hofmann.

1919. *Die Quintessenz des Sozialismus*. 16th edn, Gotha: Perthes. Trans. into English (London, 1889), Italian (Geneva, 1891), French (Brussels, 1886; Paris, 1904), Spanish (Madrid, 1885).

BIBLIOGRAPHY

Recktenwald, H.C. 1983. *Lexikon der Staats- und Geldwirtschaft: Ein Lehr- und Nachschlagewerk*. Munich: Vahlen. See particularly the introduction.

Recktenwald, H.C. and Samuelson, P.A. 1986. *Über Thünens 'Der isolierte Staat'*. Darmstadt–Düsseldorf: Wirtschaft und Finanzen.

Schlesinger Karl (1889–1938). Karl Schlesinger was born in Budapest; in 1919, after Béla Kun's communist revolution in Hungary, he moved to Vienna, where he committed suicide when Hitler occupied Austria in March 1938. As early as 1914 he had published his important work on monetary theory, *Theorie der Geld- und Kreditwirtschaft*, which went, however, more or less unnoticed at that time because it used mathematical tools and was written in German – a forbidding combination at a time when the only German-speaking economists interested in theory, the Austrians, were rather adverse to mathematical economics. Schlesinger was also an exceptional figure in so far as he was not a university teacher but a banker and influential member of the financial community. Nevertheless, he became a respected member of the Vienna Economic Society and, in the 1930s, one of the most active participants in Karl Menger's mathematical colloquium.

As an economic theorist, Schlesinger was a Walrasian, in fact the only Walrasian (with the exception, perhaps, of Wicksell) who significantly advanced Walras' theory of the demand for money balances and of equilibrium in the money market. In his 1914 book, Schlesinger clearly distinguished between payments the magnitudes and future dates of which are fixed, and those whose time profile is subject to uncertainty. While the first type of payment streams offers no choice but generates a money 'demand' equal to the maximum cumulative payments deficit for a given period (though Schlesinger correctly points to the possibility of modifying the payment stream by investing and disinvesting temporary cash surpluses), the second type, which lies at the centre of Schlesinger's analysis, gives rise to a choice between higher and lower cash reserves held as an insurance against illiquidity losses. Schlesinger determines the individual demand for theses precautionary balances from the equality between the marginal utilities respectively of interest income lost due to holding a cash reserve and of the insurance service provided by this reserve. He also demonstrated the economies of scale from an increase in the number (but not in the nominal magnitudes) of transactions. Finally, Schlesinger derives an aggregate money demand function, additively separable in transactions and precautionary demand, virtually identical to the one set up by Keynes much later, and determines the partial equilibrium money rate of interest as that which equalizes aggregate demand and stock supply of money. Schlesinger also addressed himself to problems of international monetary economics: in a publication of 1916 he advocated and gave a clear exposition of the purchasing power parity theory. In 1931, in the context of a book review, Schlesinger developed a rigorous and detailed mathematical analysis of money creation on the level of individual banks and for the financial system as a whole.

Apart from his writings on money, Schlesinger made another original and remarkable contribution to economic theory, viz. to the mathematical theory of Walrasian general economic equilibrium described by n zero-profit conditions (equating commodity prices which are given functions of quantities produced with the respective sums of products of factor input coefficients and factor prices) and m factor market equilibrium conditions (equating factor supplies with the respective sums of products of factor input coefficients and quantities of goods produced). At the beginning of the 1930s it came to be recognized that such a system of equations need not have a solution, at least not an economically meaningful solution (in non-negative output and factor prices). In 1934 Schlesinger suggested, in Menger's colloquium, to introduce non-negative slack variables on the demand side of the factor market equations and to enlarge the system of $n+m$ equations by additional m equations setting the respective products of slack variables and factor prices equal to zero. Schlesinger had arrived at this ingenious idea independently of an identical proposal made by Zeuthen in 1932. Going definitely beyond Zeuthen however, he also raised the conjecture that this procedure would solve the existence problem. Schlesinger's conjecture was proved to hold true by A. Wald, with whom Schlesinger had taken lessons in mathematics.

G. SCHWÖDIAUER

SELECTED WORKS

1914. *Theorie der Geld- und Kreditwirtschaft*. Munich: Duncker & Humblot. Partial English translation as 'Basic principles of the money economy', *International Economic Papers* 9, 1959, 20–38.

1916. *Die Veränderungen des Geldwertes im Kriege*. Vienna: Manz.

1931. Bankpolitik, von F. Somary [book review]. *Archiv für Sozialwissenschaft und Sozialpolitik* 66, 1–35.

1934. Über die Produktionsgleichungen der ökonomischen Wertlehre. *Ergebnisse eines mathematischen Kolloquiums* 6, 10–11.

BIBLIOGRAPHY

Menger, K. 1973. Austrian marginalism and mathematical economics. In *Carl Menger and the Austrian School of Economics*, ed. J.R. Hicks and W. Weber, Oxford: Oxford University Press.

Morgenstern, O. 1968. Schlesinger, Karl. In *International Encyclopedia of the Social Sciences*, New York: Macmillan and Free Press, Vol. 14.

Nagatani, K. 1978. *Monetary Theory*. Amsterdam: North-Holland.

Patinkin, D. 1965. *Money, Interest and Prices*. 2nd edn, New York: Harper & Row, Supplementary Note D, 573–80.

Schmoller, Gustav von (1838–1917). Schmoller was born in Heilbronn, the son of a Württemberg civil servant. He studied Staatswissenschaften (a combination of economics, history and administrative science) in Tübingen. After a short period in the financial department of the Württemberg civil service, which he had to quit because of his pro-Prussian views, be became Professor in Halle (1864–72), Strassburg (1872–82), and Berlin (1882–1913).

Schmoller was the leading economist of Imperial Germany. He was the leader of the 'Kathedersozialisten' (socialists of the chair), and founder and long-time chairman of the Verein für Socialpolitik. He was editor or co-editor of several publications such as *Staats- und sozialwissenschaftliche Forschung* and *Jahrbuch für Gesetzgebung, Verwaltung und Volkswirtschaft im Deutschen Reich* – later known simply as *Schmollers Jahrbuch*; he was named official historian of Brandenburg and Prussia, and supervised the publication of the *Acta Borussica* and the *Forschungen zur brandenburgischen und preussischen Geschichte*. Thus Schmoller was one of the major organizers of research in the social sciences. He is said to have controlled almost every important academic appointment in economics in the German Reich.

As the outspoken leader of the 'younger' historical school, Schmoller was against the abstract axiomatic–deductive approach of the classicals and neoclassicals (1893; 1900, pp.1–124). When Menger, the Austrian marginal utility theorist, attacked Schmoller's point of view and asserted the necessity of applying the exact methods of natural sciences and abstract logical reasoning to political economy, the Methodenstreit (struggle over methods) began, which was by and large a dispute between the inductive and the deductive method. It occupied two generations of German-speaking economists, produced a vast literature and was perceived essentially as 'a history of wasted energies' (Schumpeter) by theoretical economists of the next generation. However, it may also be viewed as the expression of the endeavour to preserve seminal insights into the historical and changing nature of economic and social phenomena against simplified and mechanistic views of the laws of 'rational' behaviour, and as such it had important consequences for the development of neighbouring disciplines, especially sociology.

Although Schmoller put the emphasis on the inductive method, he was not excluding deduction from economic reasoning. In his opinion, it was of the utmost importance for the application of deductive methods and for economic theory formation in general to be based on the knowledge of sufficient historical facts and material. He advocated a somewhat interdisciplinary approach that would also take into account the psychological, sociological and philosophical aspects of the problems. Through detailed and monographic historical research he intended to free political economy from 'false abstractions' (1904, p. vi), and to put it on a solid empirical foundation. His most important historical studies were his works on the history of the weavers guild of Strassburg (1879), on the guilds in 17th and 18th-century Brandenburg and Prussia, on the Prussian silk industry in the 18th century, on the history of Prussian financial policy (1898a) and on the history of German towns in general and Strassburg in particular (1922). He was also interested in the history and formation of social classes and the historical development of class struggle (1900, Book II; 1904, pp. 496–577; 1918). He further made some important contributions to the study of mercantilism (1898a, ch. 1; 1904, pp. 580–605), which he regarded essentially as the process of the formation of the national state and the national economy. The adoption of mercantilist policies was of special significance for Germany, whose backwardness in the 17th and 18th century Schmoller ascribed to the absence of a centralized national state and the consequent domination of particularist regional and local interests. Schmoller perceived the enlightened and despotic sovereigns – especially the Prussian kings – as the only power that would implement a policy aimed at the breaking-up of these particularist tendencies and at the establishment of large and unified economic territories. An important step in that direction was the abolition of town autonomy after 1713 under Friedrich Wilhelm I (1922, pp. 231–428).

This glorification of the Prussian state and its rulers was probably the most characteristic feature of Schmoller's work. He regarded the Prussian monarchy with its corps of loyal civil servants, which he perceived as standing above the social classes and their egoistic interests, as the central achievement of German history. Only this type of government had been able to overcome the earlier feudal corporate state and the class rule of the Junker (1898a, p. 302), and was at present capable of implementing social reforms.

Social reform and social justice were central to Schmoller's thinking. We may regard him as a conservative in the specific German or, better, Prussian sense of the word. He rejected Marxism, Manchester Liberalism and also reactionary, anti-reformist views such as those of the historian Heinrich von Treitschke, with whom he had a famous polemic on the notion of social reform (1874–5; Small, 1924–5).

Schmoller advocated a paternalistic social policy to raise the material and cultural standard of the working classes as the only means to prevent revolution, integrate the workers into the monarchic state, and keep the traditions of Prussia alive. He even envisaged an alliance between the monarchy and the working classes (1918, p.648).

It is nowadays generally agreed that Schmoller's influence on the development of the economic sciences in Germany was rather unfortunate: it contributed to the neglect of economic theory in Germany for a full half century. Neither Schmoller nor his pupils achieved their goal of building a new theory based on the historical material they collected, however valuable it was. Schmoller's main work, the *Grundrisse* (1900; 1904) remained rather traditional in its theoretical part – the treatment of value and prices was not too far away from mainstream neoclassical economics – and constituted all in all a rather incoherent analysis. Perhaps this was the main reason why Schmoller's work and with it the whole historical school was to fall into oblivion in Germany soon after his death.

B. Schefold

See also GERMAN HISTORICAL SCHOOL.

SELECTED WORKS

1870. *Zur Geschichte der deutschen Kleingewerbe im 19. Jahrhundert: Statistische und nationalökonomische Untersuchungen.* Halle: Waisenhaus.

1879. *Die Strassburger Tucher- und Weberzunft; Urkunden und Darstellungen nebst Regesten und Glossar. Ein Beitrag zur Geschichte der deutschen Weberei und des deutschen Gewerberechts vom XIII.–XVII. Jahrhundert.* Strassburg: Trübner.

1888. *Zur Litteraturgeschichte der Staats- und Sozialwissenschaften.* Leipzig: Duncker & Humblot.

1898a. *Umrisse und Untersuchungen zur Verfassungs-, Verwaltungs- und Wirtschaftsgeschichte besonders des preussischen Staates im 17. und 18. Jahrhundert.* Leipzig: Duncker & Humblot.

1898b. *Über einige Grundfragen der Sozialpolitik und der Volkswirtschaftslehre.* Leipzig: Duncker & Humblot. It contains the works *Über einige Grundfragen des Rechts und der Volkswirtschaft* (1874–5), *Die Volkswirtschaft, die Volkswirtschaftslehre und ihre Methode* (1893), and *Wechselnde Theorien und feststehende Wahrheiten im Gebiete der Staats- und Sozialwissenschaften und die heutige deutsche Volkswirtschaftslehre* (1897).

1900–1904. *Grundriss der allgemeinen Volkswirtschaftslehre.* Vol. I, 1900; Vol. II, 1904. Munich and Leipzig: Duncker & Humblot.

1918. *Die soziale Frage: Klassenbildung, Arbeiterfrage, Klassenkampf.* Ed. L. Schmoller, Munich und Leipzig: Duncker & Humblot.
1922. *Deutsches Städtewesen in älterer Zeit.* Bonner Staatswissenschaftliche Untersuchungen, Bonn and Leipzig: Schröder.

BIBLIOGRAPHY
Brinkmann, C. 1937. *Gustav Schmoller und die Volkswirtschaftslehre.* Stuttgart: Kohlhammer.
Small, A.W. 1924–5. The Schmoller–Treitschke controversy. *American Journal of Sociology* 30, 49–86.

Schmookler, Jacob (1918–1967). Schmookler was born in Woodstown, New Jersey, in 1918 and died in Minneapolis, Minnesota, in 1967. In 1951 he received his PhD in economics from the University of Pennsylvania, where he was a student of Simon Kuznets. He subsequently held teaching positions at Michigan State University and the University of Minnesota.

Schmookler's work helped to establish the importance of technological change as a contributor to economic growth. His article 'The Changing Efficiency of the American Economy, 1869 to 1938' appeared in 1952 (Schmookler, 1972, pp. 3–36), several years before the seminal papers of Abramovitz and Solow. However, in his later work he also analysed the specific economic mechanisms that determined the allocation of resources among different categories of invention. By an extremely careful and original use of patent data, Schmookler demonstrated the decisive role played by changes in demand in shaping the pattern of inventive activity. In his most important work, *Invention and Economic Growth* (1966), he showed how changes in demand have accounted for variations in inventive activity in a specific industry (such as railroad equipment, petroleum refining and building) over time, as well as different rates of inventive activity among different industries at a given moment of time.

Schmookler's writing showed that technological change need not be treated as an exogenous variable. On the contrary, he showed that the changing direction of inventive activity could be accounted for by readily identifiable economic variables, most especially changes in the pattern of demand that determine the size of the prospective market, and hence potential profitability, for particular classes of inventions. Thus, inventions are significant not only because they influence the growth rate of an economy but also because they constitute forms of economic activity in their own right.

N. Rosenberg

SELECTED WORKS
1966. *Invention and Economic Growth.* Cambridge, Mass.: Harvard University Press.
1972. *Patents, Invention and Economic Change.* Ed. Z. Griliches and L. Hurwicz, Cambridge, Mass.: Harvard University Press. (This volume contains the patent data which formed the basis for Schmookler's research. It also contains a complete bibliography of his writings.)

Schneider, Erich (1900–1970). When Erich Schneider died unexpectedly a few days before his 70th birthday, he left part of his work unfinished, in particular his *History of Economic Thought*. His *Introduction to Economic Theory*, comprising three volumes, reflected in its latest edition the state of microeconomics and macroeconomics up to the mid-1960s and was translated into several foreign languages. Above all other textbooks, this work was instrumental in narrowing the wide margin by which German economics had fallen below international standards during the Hitler era, but also even before that due to the dominance of the Historical School. The impact of Schneider's personality and work reached well beyond the academic domain. He advocated the use of circular flow concepts and sound empirical foundations, promoting econometrics as well as the rapid development of modern national income accounting. By this, he turned not only against the Historical School, but also against those advocates of the social market economy who feared that the new instruments would lead back to a planned economy. Schneider always favoured the market economy and minimal state intervention, though without adhering to a dogmatic concept of 'free competition'. As for competition he preferred to aim at pragmatic solutions.

Erich Schneider was born in Siegen, Westphalia, on 14 December 1900. He received his Doctorate *rer. pol.* in 1922 after studying economics at the universities of Frankfurt, Göttingen and Münster. Disappointed by the Historical School, he found encouragement with the important business economists in Frankfurt. To gain his own access to Walras and to modern economics, he subsequently studied mathematics. From 1925 until 1936 he made a living as a school teacher in mathematics, which enabled him to keep in close contact with Joseph Schumpeter in Bonn during economically hard times. He earned his habilitation in 1932, under Schumpeter's supervision, with work on monopolistic and oligopolistic competition. This continued to be his favourite area of research, ranking him among the important pioneers of the theory of imperfect competition. Using Frisch's concept of conjectural elasticities, he later developed a dynamic theory of oligopoly.

In 1936, Schneider was appointed professor of managerial economics at the University of Aarhus, Denmark, where he stayed until 1945. It was in this period that he wrote his important contributions to the theory of production, investment and corporate planning which anticipated many later developments. With microeconomic problems as a point of departure, he found his way to J.M. Keynes who, together with Marshall, was to influence him much more than his mentor Schumpeter. Important work on fiscal theory was also completed in Denmark.

In 1946, Schneider moved to the University of Kiel and stayed there for the rest of his life, except for lecture tours throughout the world. He taught microeconomics and macroeconomics in masterly fashion, and occasionally taught statistics. He never ceased to believe in the neoclassical synthesis. The posthumous 12th edition of the 3rd volume of his *Introduction* contains a brilliant attack against monetarism. However, this was written before the acceleration of inflation, which was unacceptable to Schneider. He disagreed with the then popular hypothesis that moderate inflation fosters growth. Since he considered full employment the most important goal, he recommended wage controls.

As a director of the Kiel Institute of World Economics (1961–9), Schneider was particularly concerned with the issues of international trade, exchange rate formation and international monetary reform. He regularly commented on policy issues in newspaper articles, but he was never actively involved in politics. He won international recognition early on and became an honorary member of numerous associations and academies. Seven universities awarded him an honorary doctorate. On 5 December 1970, he died while speaking at a symposium, 'on the open stage' as he had always wished.

Gottfried Bombach

SELECTED WORKS
1934. *Theorie der Produktion*. Vienna: J. Springer.
1939. *Einführung in die Grundfragen des industriellen Rechnungswesens*. Copenhagen.
1944. *Investering og Rente*. Copenhagen: A. Busck.
1968. *Zahlungsbilanz und Wechselkurs*. Tübingen: Mohr. All important articles are included in E. Schneider, *Volkswirtschaft und Betriebswirtschaft*, Tübingen: Mohr, 1964. Japanese and Spanish translations, 1968.

scholastic economic thought. Scholastic economic thought, which flourished during the Middle Ages, differs in many respects from the economic thought of our own time. It was not positive or hypothetical but normative, directing the faithful to do certain things and abstain from doing others. Human weakness or wickedness would account for gaps between the norm and its fulfilment. Furthermore, scholastic economic thought did not generate rules that were uniformly applicable to *homo oeconomicus*; instead there was a division among its addressees between the select few capable of abiding by the counsel of perfection and the general run of humanity that required a less exacting rule. Moreover, scholastic economic thought was not presented in systematic form but arose sporadically and incidentally in conjunction with other matters treating, perhaps, of sales, fraud or usury. It was not shaped by professional economists but by theologians and lawyers. It did not form an autonomous discipline but relied on precepts derived from theology, philosophy and law. A number of social ideals that are characteristic of modern times were alien to it, chiefly the ideal of progress; instead, stratified medieval society, which was organized more on the principle of status than of contract, looked for a golden age that was located in the past rather than the future. Scholastic economic thought was the thought of an age of faith whose overriding concern was the salvation of souls in the next world rather than this-worldly concern with reforms that might produce an earthly paradise. With man fallen and tainted by original sin, perfection was not of this world.

What scholastic economic thought had in common with modern and indeed with all economic thought was its function to cope with the central economic problem of scarcity. It did this in its own way, different from the way it was done at other times. The Greek philosophers counselled moderation that would reduce the demand for goods as the principal means to resolve the economic problem of scarcity. Modern economic thought attempts to resolve this problem by increasing the supply of goods. As for the medievalists, a case may be made to the effect that their way to cope with the problem of scarcity was to impress upon the faithful the need to maximize charity and minimize sin.

Scholastic economic thought had its principal sources in the Bible, the writings of the Fathers of the Church, in Roman, canon and civil law, in the evolving theological tradition and, at a relatively late stage, in the writings of Aristotle, whose authority was high and who was referred to as 'the philosopher'. The scholastics typically employed a method of analysis in which a question was raised, a possible answer to the question discussed in detail, and after the reader was almost convinced, another answer discussed, again in detail and all with copious citations of authorities. The last answer provided was the one chosen by the writer in question.

A medieval theologian might set forth views about economics in a comprehensive *Summa* that covered the entire field of theology, or in a monograph devoted to a special topic. Of the highest authority were the *Summa* and other writings of Saint Thomas Aquinas (*c*1224–74), whose teachings were at first considered controversial but were eventually endorsed by the papacy to become the official Catholic doctrine.

Scholastic economic thought, though it was generated in a number of different countries, did not reflect national diversity but the universalism of a civilization integrated by the common faith. Thus, for instance, Saint Thomas left his native Italy to be educated at Paris and Cologne and teach at the University of Paris, then the centre of theological studies, just as the University of Bologna was the centre of legal studies. Scholastic economic thought also had a time dimension. As it grew and developed over a period of a thousand years, certain features came to the foreground while others receded into the background.

The scholastics were no egalitarians, but the practice of private charity, to which the faithful were exhorted and which they generously carried out, brought a levelling tendency into the medieval distribution of income and wealth. It did not, however, place an unduly heavy burden on the faithful, because they were under no duty to allow charitable donations to endanger their position in the hierarchically ordered society. Thus, while charity was highly commendable, no one had to impoverish himself on account of it. Austerity and asceticism were counsels of perfection addressed to the select few. Contrariwise, the wealthy were exhorted to practice not only charity but also liberality and munificence, that is, to use their riches generously and for some great and noble purpose.

At the end of the Middle Ages, with the coming of the reformers, the role of private charity declined because of the reformers' emphasis on faith rather than good works. The passing of the Elizabethan Poor Law in 1601 marks this change. It made poor relief a function of public authorities.

If the property owner is under a religious duty to practise charity, liberality and munificence, a sort of spiritual mortgage is placed on his property. The stewardship of wealth with which he is entrusted detracts from the absolute character of property rights such as prevailed in Roman Law. The medievalists distinguished between property and the use of property; they recognized private property as not being in violation of natural law but did not go so far as to consider it required by natural law. The latter interpretation would have done violence to the patristic tradition of the early Church, which had extolled the virtues of communal ownership. It was in effect a concession to this tradition that required a use of private property that would be conducive to the common good. Communal ownership was advised as a counsel of perfection to the spiritual elite.

Tradition, as embodied in the Bible, Greek thought and the teachings of the Fathers of the Church, also took a dim view of money making and trading. As time went on, attitudes became more permissive and reference was made to a distinction in the writings of Saint Augustine, who held that the trader must not be confused with trade, that is, that trading itself is morally neutral but may be corrupted by a sinful trader. It became recognized that the trader served a useful purpose, especially if he transformed or transported goods, stored them or took care of them. He was allowed a return that would cover his labour and expenses, including a premium for risk. Even pure profit could be legitimized by the trader's intention, that is, if he intended to use the profit for self-support or charity, or if he was motivated by the desire to perform business as a service to the public.

The enforcement of the charity requirement and of business ethics in general took place mainly in the agent's conscience rather than before a court of law. This was different in the case of the just price, another important concept in scholastic economics. Here there was the Roman Law tradition of *laesio enormis*, excessive violation, which originally had applied only to transactions in land at unduly low prices. Medieval practice expanded the rule to apply to any transaction where the buyer had been overcharged by more than 50 per cent of the just price, or where the seller had obtained less than 50 per cent of it. In cases involving these matters, recourse could be had to a court of law, civil or ecclesiastical, rather than only to the internal forum of the agent's conscience.

The just price was the market price prevailing at a certain place at a certain time, as estimated by a fair-minded person. The estimate might be expressed in the form of a range of prices rather than as a fixed amount. If the actual price deviated 'considerably' from the just price, restitution was owed. The just-price rule thus was stricter than the *laesio enormis*, reflecting, it was held, the greater strictness of divine law as compared with civil law. Justification for the just-price doctrine was found in the golden rule – do to others as you want them to do to you – as well as in the requirement of justice in exchange as set forth by Aristotle.

Some scholastic writers interpreted the just price as one covering labour and expenses. To others, a just price reflected a good's usefulness or its capacity to satisfy human wants. These interpretations have made it possible for later schools of thought to claim the scholastics as their forerunners. To some, the scholastics were exponents of a labour theory of value such as was held by the classical economists and Karl Marx. Others argued that the scholastics anticipated the utility approach to the theory of value that came into vogue late in the 19th century. Still others found the germ of a demand-and-supply theory in the just-price doctrine. Again others interpreted the just price as a competitive one. It may be noted that the scholastics were not familiar with the concept of competition and had no word for it, the English word and its French counterpart, *concurrence*, making their appearance only in the 17th century. The scholastics were familiar, however, with monopoly, both the word and the concept, and condemned it in no uncertain terms. The word 'monopoly' can indeed be traced back to Aristotle, who uses it in the first book of his *Politics*, chapter 8. The scholastics were familiar also with monopolistic combinations, but had no word for oligopoly, a term that was introduced by Saint Thomas More in his *Utopia* of 1518 but which did not come into common usage until some four hundred years later.

If a price was regulated by a public authority, as was often the case, the regulated price was considered the just one. At times, the regulated price constituted a ceiling; at other times it served as a floor. Depending upon the circumstances, the regulated price either strengthened or weakened the conservative tendency of the medieval price system.

If the just price was meant to cover the labour and expenses of the seller, it would bring into the medieval price system a conservative tendency that resisted changes in the allocation of productive resources. In the modern market economy changing prices act as guide-posts that draw productive resources from certain employments and channel them into others. A price system that legitimizes only a price that covers the cost of production will tend to preserve the prevailing allocation of productive resources.

In the centre of scholastic economic thought stood the usury doctrine. During the Middle Ages, usury as an object of the Church's condemnation played a role comparable to such later targets as socialism in the 19th century and abortion and birth control in the 20th century. It was a matter of profound concern that occupied clerics and lawyers alike and gave rise to a voluminous literature. 'Usury', at that time, referred to the lender's intention to receive in return more than the principal of the loan, so that any interest was considered usurious. In modern usage, only exorbitant interest is called usurious.

The usury doctrine was compatible with the primitive economic conditions that prevailed in the early Middle Ages, when the typical loan was a consumption loan. Later on, the flourishing economies of the emerging cities and the requirements of commerce were accommodated by a number of exceptions from the strict usury doctrine which allowed interest or its equivalent on the strength of so-called extrinsic titles. One of the most important of these was the compensation granted to the lender on account of escaped gain. Such a compensation was legitimized only hesitatingly, but once it was established any businessman who employed productive capital funds in his enterprise could in good conscience claim interest on money he had lent out.

In the usury doctrine money is considered a measure with a fixed and stable value. If a lender received more money than he had given to the borrower, a different measure would prevail, an ostensibly obvious inequity. By the same token, a debasement of money would yield a different measure resulting from an action of the monetary authority – the prince – that was as damnable as usury itself. Throughout the Middle Ages, the debasement of the coin constituted indeed an ever-recurring problem that absorbed much of the attention of writers on monetary matters, comparable to the problem of inflation in modern times. Everybody was against it, but it was practised on a large scale.

A notable contribution to the theory of money was made by Jean Buridan, the 14th-century philosopher still famous for his conundrum of the ass that would starve between two equal bales of hay. In its terseness and conciseness Buridan's analysis of the nature of money in terms of the four causes of Aristotle's logic is a masterpiece that illustrates scholastic economic thought at its best. In his discussion of the *Ethics* of Aristotle, printed posthumously in Paris in 1489, Buridan has this to say: The material cause of money, from which it is made, is a rare commodity. Its efficient cause, which produces money, is the government. Its formal cause, which transforms the rare commodity into money, is the symbol of value that is inscribed on the coin. Its final cause, or purpose, is to be of service to man by serving as a medium of exchange.

The late scholastics also made significant contributions to the theory of prices. The quantity theory of money was a multiple discovery to which a number of writers contributed. While Jean Bodin is usually credited with a full-fledged statement of the quantity theory, the nucleus of the theory can be found in a manual on moral theology, with an appendix devoted to a discussion of usury, written by Martin de Azpilcueta, also known as Navarrus, who taught canon law at Toulouse and Salamanca. This manual was published in 1556, twelve years ahead of Bodin's *Reply to the Paradoxes of M. Malestroit*. The context within which Navarrus develops the quantity theory is a discussion of the legitimacy of profit earned as a result of disparities of the value of money in different countries. These disparities in the purchasing power of money reflect the relative scarcity of the two moneys. Money, according to Navarrus, is worth more where it is scarce than where it is plentiful. Where money is scarce, goods and services fetch low prices; prices are high where it is plentiful, as it is in Spain as a result of the inflow of precious metals from the New World.

The teaching of the scholastics forms the background of Max Weber's thesis of the Protestant or Puritan origin of capitalism, which has provoked a lively discussion since the beginning of this century. Weber's thesis, like Tawney's similar argument, fails to account for the flourishing economic life in the Italian cities, whose residents adhered to the old faith. As far as these are concerned, an idea recently advanced by the French economic historian Jacques Le Goff may be more to the point. In *The Birth of Purgatory* (1984) Le Goff develops the idea that Purgatory, a third place between Heaven and Hell, the notion of which was instilled in the minds of the faithful between 1150 and 1200, contributed to the birth of capitalism by making the salvation of the usurer possible (p. 305). Others have pointed out that what are known as Puritan attitudes can be found in earlier periods as well. For example, reference is made to the rule of Saint Benedict with its insistence on an austere way of life, discipline, clockwork regularity, hard work and poverty, which may have invited imitation (Hallam, 1976, pp. 28–49). Again others elucidate the complex relationships that connect the mendicant friars of the Middle Ages with the rise of an urban ideology favouring the commercial society (Little, 1978).

In North America, scholastic economic thought lingered on in the business ethics of the Puritan divines. An illustration is provided by the case of Robert Keayne, a Boston merchant who was castigated from the pulpit of the First Church in 1639 by the Puritan clergyman, John Cotton, for overcharging and other sharp practices. In his sermon, Cotton established the requirements of a just price and listed a number of other rules of proper business behaviour similar to the rules of the scholastics (see Hosmer, 1908, vol. 1, pp. 315–18). The just price continues to play a role in our own time in connection with such concepts as fair return and reasonable value, which are determined by regulatory commissions.

HENRY W. SPIEGEL

BIBLIOGRAPHY

For treatments of the period by outstanding economists see Joseph A. Schumpeter (1954, ch. 2) and Jacob Viner (1978, ch. 2), the latter being chapters of an unfinished work published posthumously and also available in book form. For a survey that treats not only the scholastics but Roman and canon law as well see Gordon (1975, pp. 122–272). For a textbook treatment with ample bibliography see Spiegel (1983, chs 3 and 4). For a collection of articles by the outstanding specialist of his time dealing with such topics as scholastic economics, the scholastic attitude towards trade and entrepreneurship, and monopoly theory, see de Roover (1976, 1958, 1967). For a work by an historian on the same subject see Baldwin (1959). On usury see Noonan (1957) and Nelson (1969), the first the work of a legal historian, the second that of a sociologist, and both based on original sources. About Navarrus and other Spanish writers see Grice-Hutchinson (1978). For an English translation of a manual on business ethics see Nieder (1966), originally published in Latin in 1468 and authored by a lesser-known scholastic. See also Monroe (1924, chs 3 and 4) for translations from Saint Thomas Aquinas and Nicole Oresme.

Baldwin, J.W. 1959. The medieval theories of the just price. *Transactions of the American Philosophical Society*, NS 49(4), 15–92.

de Roover, R. 1958. The concept of the just price. *Journal of Economic History* 18, December, 418–34.

de Roover, R. 1967. *San Bernadino of Siena and Sant'Antonio of Florence: The Two Great Economic Thinkers of the Middle Ages.* Publication No. 19 of the Kress Library of Business and Economics, Boston: Baker Library, Harvard Graduate School of Business Administration.

de Roover, R. 1976. *Business, Banking and Economic Thought in Late Medieval and Early Modern Europe.* Chicago: University of Chicago Press.

Gordon, B. 1975. *Economic Analysis before Adam Smith.* London: Macmillan.

Grice-Hutchinson, M. 1978. *Early Economic Thought in Spain, 1177–1740.* London: Allen & Unwin.

Hallam, H.E. 1976. The medieval mind. In *Feudalism, Capitalism and Beyond*, ed. E. Kamenka and R.S. Neale, New York: St Martin's Press.

Hosmer, J.K. (ed.) 1908. *Governor John Winthrop's Journal*, Vol. 1. New York: Scribner's.

Le Goff, J. 1984. *The Birth of Purgatory.* Chicago: University of Chicago Press.

Little, L.K. 1978. *Religious Poverty and the Profit Economy in Medieval Europe.* Ithaca: Cornell University Press.

Monroe, A.E. 1924. *Early Economic Thought.* Cambridge, Mass.: Harvard University Press.

Nelson, B.N. 1969. *The Idea of Usury.* 2nd edn, enlarged, Chicago: University of Chicago Press.

Nieder, J. 1966. *On the Contracts of Merchants.* Trans. C. H. Reeves, ed. R.B. Schuman, Norman: University of Oklahoma Press.

Noonan, J.T., Jr. 1957. *The Scholastic Analysis of Usury.* Cambridge, Mass.: Harvard University Press.

Schumpeter, J.A. 1954. *History of Economic Analysis.* New York: Oxford University Press.

Spiegel, H.W. 1983. *The Growth of Economic Thought.* Revised and expanded edn, Durham, North Carolina: Duke University Press.

Viner, J. 1978. Religious thought and economic society. *History of Political Economy* 10(1), Spring, 9–189. Published as *Religious Thought and Economic Society: Four Chapters of an Unfinished Work by Jacob Viner*, ed. J. Melitz and D. Winch, Durham, North Carolina: Duke University Press.

schoolmen. *See* SCHOLASTIC ECONOMIC THOUGHT.

Schultz, Henry (1893–1938). Schultz was one of a small group of pioneering econometricians who, in the 1920s and 1930s, laid the groundwork for the phenomenal development of mathematical economics and econometrics that occurred after World War II. His graduate courses in mathematical economics and statistics inspired students to address themselves to economic problems in quantitative terms, to reformulate economic theory in empirically testable form, and to test theories by means of diligent search for relevant statistical information and careful application of appropriate statistical analysis. His own research, culminating in his magnum opus, *The Theory and Measurement of Demand* (1938), could well serve as a model for a proper approach to economic analysis today, nearly 50 years after its publication. Schultz devoted all his professional life to the integration of pure economic theory with empirical analysis. Unlike considerable econometric work today, which is often empirical without much grounding in economic theory, his statistical analysis is solidly based on mathematical economic theory, as well as on the statistical theory of correlation and curve-fitting. Elegant summaries of both fields, based in large part upon his lecture notes and his research work, appear in the book, along with the empirical studies of demand for a large number of agricultural commodities for which the theories served as the basic foundation. The student wishing to get a good introduction to mathematical economics as formulated by Cournot, Walras and Pareto, and to the fundamentals of Gaussian curve-fitting analysis, will find clear and lucid presentations of these subjects in Schultz's book. At the same time he will not fail to be impressed by the extraordinary concern for statistical accuracy and precision demonstrated in the empirical analysis throughout the book.

Schultz, who was born in Russian Poland on 4 September 1893, was brought by his parents to the United States in 1907, as part of the large wave of migration of Russian Jews after the Russo-Japanese War of 1905. Despite the family's poverty, Schultz's drive and determination enabled him to enter college and even to pursue a graduate education – no small feat in those days for the oldest child of an immigrant family. After receiving his AB from City College in 1916, Schultz entered Columbia University, where he came under the lasting influence of one of the world's leading econometricians, Professor Henry L. Moore. Schultz felt so indebted to him that in 1938, when he was himself internationally recognized as an outstanding authority in econometrics, he dedicated his major work to 'Professor Henry Ludwell Moore, trail blazer in the statistical study of demand'.

Schultz's studies were interrupted by World War I, during which he was wounded in the Meuse–Argonne offensive. In the spring and summer of 1919, an Army scholarship enabled him to study at the London School of Economics and at the Galton Laboratory of University College, London, under two leading statisticians, A.L. Bowley and Karl Pearson. After returning to the United States in 1920, he served with several agencies of the United States Government and became Director of Statistical Research of the Children's Bureau of the Department of Labor. At the same time he continued his academic work, receiving the PhD degree from Columbia University in 1925. His dissertation on 'The Statistical Law of Demand as Illustrated by the Demand for Sugar' was published the same year in the *Journal of Political Economy*.

The following year Schultz received his appointment at the University of Chicago. His courses in mathematical economics and statistics were highly organized and presented his students with a clear and systematic exposition both of the classic texts and of the most important up-to-date journal articles from the English, French, Italian and Russian literature. He was a voracious reader of economic and statistical literature, and enriched his courses by examination of related material in the fields of biology, physics and psychology.

It was the research laboratory, however, that absorbed most of his energies. Almost from the time he came to the University of Chicago, he embarked on an ambitious research project intended to harness theory and empirical analysis for the purpose of filling some of the 'empty boxes' in the theory of exchange. At first his interest focused on determining the coefficients of elasticity of demand as well as the magnitudes of the average shifts in demand over time. At a later stage be became interested in testing the consistency of demand coefficients for a set of commodities whose demands were interrelated. The work was so thoroughly organized, documented and proof-checked, and the calculations were so systematically set out, with automatic sum-checks at every appropriate point, that research assistants picking up a worksheet prepared by others even a decade earlier had no difficulty tracing the sources and checking the accuracy of every figure on the sheet.

Shortly after his book was published, Schultz was killed, together with his wife and two daughters, on 26 November 1938, in a car accident in California, where he had gone to teach on sabbatical leave from the University of Chicago. Paul Douglas wrote of Schultz:

> All in all, he was about the finest man it has ever been my privilege to know in academic life. The world of scholarship and of science (for I may so use the term in connection with him) was the richer for his fruitful life. We are much the poorer for his death at the full height of his powers.

JACOB L. MOSAK

SELECTED WORKS

1925. The statistical law of demand as illustrated by the demand for sugar. *Journal of Political Economy*, Part I, October, 481–504; Part II, December, 577–637.

1938. *The Theory and Measurement of Demand*. Chicago: University of Chicago Press.

Schultz, Theodore Wilhain (born 1902). A scholar, research entrepreneur, and intellectual catalyst, Schultz has been motivated through a long and active life by a drive to deepen economic understanding and to foster enlightened policies in the furtherance of human welfare. Although he has served as adviser to agencies of the United States, the United Nations, other governments and many non-profit organizations, Schultz has always maintained independence. He has received many honours, including the Walker award (the highest given by the American Economic Association) and a Nobel prize for contributions to development economics.

Growing up on a farm in South Dakota, Schultz never attended secondary school, but as a young man he tested for entrance to South Dakota State College where he obtained an MS degree (1928), going on to an economics PhD from the University of Wisconsin (1930). For most of his professional life Schultz has been at the University of Chicago, to which he came from Iowa State College in 1943.

Initially Schultz focused on problems faced by agriculture in the United States during the 1930s and the war years. A vital young department head, he brought together a lively group of colleagues, stimulating them and students to explore strategies for dealing with the impact of economic fluctuations and of the vagaries of weather on farmers and farming. As important as his 1945 book on *Agriculture in an Unstable Economy* was his active involvement in dissemination to both lay and professional audiences, reflected in the bibliography attached to my essay on Schultz in the *Scandinavian Journal of Economics* (1980). Two themes that recur both in this and in later work are distortions of incentives and dealing with change and uncertainty.

With his increasing interest in economic development around the world, and in less developed countries in particular, Schultz came increasingly to consider the importance of agricultural development for general economic growth. His understanding of what rural poverty can mean, his respect for the shrewdness of unschooled practical men, and his appreciation of the value of education were joined in *Transforming Traditional Agriculture* (1964). This book challenged the 'zero marginal product' hypothesis in agriculture and proposed that ultimately farmers' education could be a low-cost investment in acquiring a 'permanent income stream'.

Though his roots are in agricultural economics, in the late 1950s Schultz began his pursuit of human capital theory on a broad front, gleaning fresh insights (as he often does) from the wisdom of great predecessors (Marshall, Knight, Irving Fisher). His contributions to the economics of education have been distinctive in their dynamic emphasis, in contrast to most of the technical econometric studies that proliferated following early contributions of Gary Becker and Jacob Mincer. Thus Schultz has stressed the importance of enhanced 'ability to deal with disequilibria' as an essential component in economic progress, and more recently he has given particular attention to innovative behaviour in his continuing pursuit of a dynamic approach to the present and the future. Schultz has never stood still, but a continuity of emphasis on incentives, on change and uncertainty, and on human potentials is ever present in his work.

MARY JEAN BOWMAN

SELECTED WORKS

1932. Diminishing returns in view of progress in agricultural production. *Journal of Farm Economics* 14(4), October, 640–49.

1934. Trade and tariff problems related to agriculture. In *Report of the Committee of Inquiry into National Policy in International Economic Relations*, Minneapolis: University of Minnesota Press.

1940. Capital rationing, uncertainty, and farm tenancy reform. *Journal of Political Economy* 48, June, 309–24.
1941. Economic effects of agricultural programs. *American Economic Review* 30, February, 127–54.
1944. Two conditions necessary for economic progress in agriculture. *Canadian Journal of Economics and Political Science* 10, August, 298–311.
1945a. *Agriculture in an Unstable Economy*. New York: McGraw-Hill.
1945b. Food and agriculture in a developing economy. In *Food for the World*, ed. T.W. Schultz, Chicago: University of Chicago Press. Reprinted, New York: Arno Press, 1976, in the 'World Food Supply' Series.
1950. Reflections on poverty within agriculture. *Journal of Political Economy* 43, February, 1–15.
1951. Declining economic importance of agricultural land. *Economic Journal* 61, December, 725–40.
1953. *The Economic Organization of Agriculture*. New York: McGraw-Hill. (Translated into Spanish, Portuguese, French, Japanese, Italian.)
1956. The role of the government in promoting economic growth. In *The State of the Social Sciences*, ed. L.D. White, Chicago: University of Chicago Press. 372–83.
1960. Capital formation by education. *Journal of Political Economy* 68, December, 571–83. (Translated into Spanish.)
1961. Investment in human capital. *American Economic Review* 51, March, 1–17. (Presidential address: Reprinted at least 20 times, and translated into Slovak, Spanish, Portuguese, Hungarian, Italian, French and Japanese.)
1963. *The Economic Value of Education*. New York: Columbia University Press. (Translated into Spanish, Portuguese, Japanese, Greek.)
1964. *Transforming Traditional Agriculture*. New Haven: Yale University Press. (Translated into Japanese, Korean, Portuguese, Spanish.) Reprinted, 1976, New York: Arno Press.
1965. Investing in poor people: an economist's view. *American Economic Review* 45, May, 510–20.
1968. Institutions and the rising economic value of man. *American Journal of Agricultural Economics* 50, December, 1113–22.
1971. *Investment in Human Capital: The Role of Education and Research*. New York: Free Press and Macmillan. (Translated into 9 other languages.)
1975. The value of the ability to deal with disequilibria. *Journal of Economic Literature* 13(3), 827–46.
1980. *Investing in People; The Economics of Population Quality*. San Francisco: University of California Press. (Translated into 9 other languages.)

Schumacher, E.F. (Fritz) (1911–1977). Economist, journalist, industrial adviser and eventually 'guru' with a world wide following, Schumacher was born a German citizen in 1911 and died a British citizen in 1977. One of the first German Rhodes scholars at Oxford University after World War I, he spent much of the 1930s studying and working in Britain and United States. When World War II came he cast his lot with Britain. Interned as an 'enemy alien', he was released to work as a farm labourer and then allowed to return to Oxford. His credentials as an economist were quickly established in a memorandum (1943a) on a multilateral clearing union for postwar international payments, similar to the famous 'Keynes Plan' put forward by the British at Bretton Woods. Another paper, written jointly with Michal Kalecki (1943b), proposed an International Investment Board as a means to inject liquidity into the international economy, an idea revived twenty years later as the 'Link'. He was also one of a group of economists working out policies for full employment.

Schumacher had early shown a desire to grapple with big questions, and to participate in great events. He became economic adviser to the British Control Commission in Germany, and then became adviser to the British coal industry, which had been nationalized after the war. Notwithstanding the glut of Middle East oil in the 1950s and 1960s, he stood for maintaining the output of British coal, albeit with an emphasis on conservation. Nuclear energy he rejected on the grounds that it would create an environmental and ecological problem of waste disposal 'of monstrous magnitude'. A visit to Burma in 1955 aroused his interest in developing countries, and for economists the most striking outcome was his idea of 'intermediate technology'. In developing countries the indigenous technology required little equipment for each worker, but the outcome was low productivity and low standards of living. With only limited amounts of capital, poor countries adopting advanced technology might achieve much higher output but would gain little in employment. What was needed was an intermediate technology adapted to the special needs of a developing country. This idea unquestionably changed the direction of thought about economic development, although its practical implementation has proved far from easy, since it runs against the grain of large-scale multinational capitalist enterprise.

While in Burma, Schumacher became a Buddhist (he was later to become a Roman Catholic) and this coloured his subsequent attitude to conventional Western economics. Capitalism, he argued, might bring higher living standards through competition and efficiency, but only at the cost of debasing human culture. Bigness, whether of industrial firms or cities was anathema. The planet's resources were finite and should be conserved. These ideas were brought together in a set of essays with the brilliantly evocative title *Small is Beautiful*, whose publication in 1973 marked the transformation of an economic programme into something like a religious movement.

G.D.N. Worswick

SELECTED WORKS

1943a. Multilateral clearing. *Economica* 10, May, 150–65.
1943b. (With M. Kalecki.) International clearing and long-term lending. *Oxford University Institute of Statistics Bulletin* 5, Supplement 6, August, 29–33.
1971. Industrialisation through 'intermediate technology'. In *Developing the Third World: The Experience of the Nineteen-Sixties*, ed. R. Robinson, Cambridge Commonwealth Series, New York and London: Cambridge University Press.
1972. The work of the intermediate technology development group in Africa. *International Labour Review* 106(1), July, 75–92.
1973. *Small is Beautiful. A study of economics as if people mattered.* London: Blond & Briggs.

Schumpeter, Joseph Alois (1883–1950). Economist and social scientist of Austrian origin, Schumpeter was born in Triesch, Moravia, in 1883, the son of the owner of a textile factory, and died in Taconic, Connecticut, in 1950. Schumpeter attended an academic high school in Vienna and studied law and economics at the University of Vienna. In 1908 he published an important book on the nature and content of economic theory, which established his fame as the ablest among the younger group of Austrian economists. Schumpeter had F. von Wieser and E. von Böhm-Bawerk as his teachers. After being nominated at the University of Czernowitz, he became professor of economics at the University of Graz in 1911. His famous book on the theory of economic development was published in 1912. Much of his later work on business cycles and the evolution of capitalism into socialism is to a certain extent an elaboration and improvement of the ideas and analysis presented in his book on economic development.

From 1925 to 1932 Schumpeter was a professor at the University of Bonn and in 1932 he became a permanent professor of economics at the Harvard University, a post he held until 1950. His impressive work on *Business Cycles* appeared in 1939, and in 1942 he published *Capitalism, Socialism and Democracy*, in which he predicted the gradual decay of capitalism. On the basis of his numerous works, one would be inclined to think that Schumpeter devoted his whole life to teaching, writing and theorizing. In fact his life has been even more colourful. From spring 1919 up to October of the same year he held the position of Austrian Minister of Finance in Renner's cabinet. During his term he was in favour of sound finance and a capital levy; he even started as a strong defender of massive socialization. He changed his mind, however, partly because he acknowledged the necessity to import capital and gradually his attitude caused tensions with his socialist colleagues in the cabinet, which finally led to his downfall. Between his professorships in Graz and Bonn, Schumpeter accepted the presidency of a Viennese private bank, the Biedermann Bank. Around 1926 the bank went bankrupt and Schumpeter was left with huge debts, probably due to speculations with borrowed money. Schumpeter was married three times, for the first time in 1907 to an English woman, a marriage that ended in divorce in 1920. In 1925 he married a Viennese, twenty-one years his junior, who died in 1926 in childbirth. In 1937 Schumpeter married Elizabeth Boody, who, after his death in 1950, edited his monumental work, the *History of Economic Analysis*.

In Schumpeter's interpretation of capitalism, the entrepreneur, who applies new combinations of factors of production, plays a central role. He is the innovator, and the agent of economic change and development. Centred around the role of the Schumpeterian entrepreneur, is the rise and decay of capitalism. The gifted few, pioneering in the field of new technologies, new products and new markets, carry out innovations and, joined some time later by many imitators, they are at the heart of the short and long cycles observed in economic life. The importance Schumpeter assigns to the creation of money and overexpansion of credit in his early work foreshadows his later work. He argues that since in static analysis there is no room for (a) new combinations of factors of production; (b) the entrepreneur (in the Schumpeterian sense); and (c) profit, there is no need for the further creation of money. He also questions whether in a static context one can speak of economic development at all. Here he is not questioning that economic phenomena and magnitudes change, but he is suggesting that the causes of change may not lie in economic factors. In modern economic theory, this would be expressed by asking whether economic development is due to endogenous or exogenous factors. In the case of exogenous factors, Schumpeter would not speak of economic development at all, for he regards factors such as population growth, consumer preferences, technical development and social organization as non-economic factors. On the other hand, he argues that changes in human nature and social organization can in fact be attributed to economic causes, which can then be regarded as endogenous factors.

The somewhat ambiguous terminology Schumpeter uses in order to describe and explain the development of the economic process is repeated in his book on economic development. Saving is no longer regarded as a factor leading to economic development in the sense of entrepreneurial innovations. Capital formation and the increase of population determine the growth rate in the stationary economy. The terms 'development' and 'economic development' are not used to describe the actual course of economic events but to distinguish between changes caused in the economic process by endogenous factors and other changes.

Not all endogenous factors lead to economic development, and Schumpeter explicitly excludes continuous endogenous changes. His theory of economic development is reduced to the treatment of spontaneous and discontinuous changes in the economic cycle. The endogenous changes Schumpeter has in mind are not found on the demand side of the economic process, but on the supply side. Economic development consists of the discontinuous introduction of new combinations of products and means of production. The five examples mentioned by Schumpeter show that the term 'new combination' must be taken in a very broad sense; it comprises a new product, a new method of production, the opening-up of a new market, the utilization of new raw materials, and the reorganization of sectors of the economy.

He restricts the meaning of the word 'enterprise' to the creation of new combinations, and the meaning of the word 'entrepreneurs' to those economic figures who introduce new combinations. Schumpeter's entrepreneur operates in an uncertain world, has the courage to start up new ventures, and must be strong enough to swim against the tide of society. In Schumpeter's view, new combinations can be financed only if a successful appeal can be made to the banking system to create money.

According to Schumpeter, ups and downs in economic development can be explained quite simply by the fact that new combinations or innovations appear, if at all, discontinuously in groups or swarms. The appearance of entrepreneurs in 'bursts' is due exclusively to the fact that the appearance of one or a few entrepreneurs facilitates the appearance of others. This is the only reason for an upswing in the business cycle. The downturn sets in as a result of smaller profit margins due to imitation and a new equilibrium will be reached after the diffusion process is completed.

In his book on business cycles, Schumpeter sharpened his analytical tools. He introduced the concept of the production function, which – in his words – tells us all we need to know about the technological aspects of production. Schumpeter regards the setting up of a new production function as the introduction of new combinations. The changes caused by innovations are no longer regarded as economic development but as economic evolution. He uses the term 'technical development' only for innovations that involve the introduction of new methods of production. Innovations must be distinguished from inventions. The application of new combinations by entrepreneurs is possible without inventions, while inventions as such need not necessarily lead to innovations and need not have any economic consequences. Innovation itself is the independent endogenous factor that causes economic life to go through a number of cycles.

Innovations lead to cyclical fluctuations whose length is determined by both the character and the period of implementation of the innovations. Schumpeter applies this general explanation to the forty-month Kitchin, the ten-year Juglar and the sixty-year Kondratieff cycles. The combination of the use of the innovations, overinvestment and of credit expansion going too far, brings the upswing to an end. The recession, which in Schumpeter's view is a healthy phase of restructuring, sets in, paving the way for a new burst of future innovations. Schumpeter's prediction of the decay of capitalism is based on the vision that it is not economic failure, but rather the economic success of capitalism that causes the march into socialism. Social rather than economic factors are according to Schumpeter responsible for the structural change in the organization of society.

Typical of this economic scene is the process of creative destruction. In Schumpeter's view it is the essential fact about capitalism. The process of creative destruction concerns the implementation of new combinations that incessantly modifies the economic structure from within. The competitive character of capitalism is mainly determined by creative destruction and far less by the case of textbook competition, in which prices play such a dominant role. This process of creative destruction must be judged by its long-term results. Schumpeter has the highest possible opinion of the dynamic character and productive capability of capitalism. In weighing up the static optimal allocation of resources in case of perfect competition, and dynamic efficiency of monopolistic structures, in particular with regard to innovative activities, he has an outspoken preference for monopoly and oligopoly and a disdain for free competition. Schumpeter did not adhere to the theory that vanishing investment opportunities and a slowdown of technical change would lead to stagnation and in the end to a breakdown of capitalism.

The rate of growth of production is not reduced because the technical possibilities are exhausted, but because capitalism suffers from a change in the behaviour of entrepreneurs. On the one hand, it is now easier than before to do things that lie outside familiar routine – innovation itself is being reduced to routine. Technological progress is increasingly becoming the business of teams of trained specialists who make technical change a predictable process. On the other hand, characteristics such as personality, will-power and a dynamic attitude count less in environments which have become accustomed to economic and social change.

Economic development thus becomes more and more impersonal and mechanical. The success of the capitalist mode of production makes capitalism itself redundant: capitalism undermines the social institutions which protect it. These institutions are the remnants of the feudal system and the existence of many small businesses and farmers. The disappearance of these social forms weakens the political position of the bourgeoisie. The elimination of the socio-economic function of the entrepreneur, especially in large corporations where technical change is a matter of routine and management is bureaucratized, reinforced by the growing influence of the public sector, further undermines the bourgeoisie. Above all, however, capitalism produces an army of critical and frustrated intellectuals who by their negative attitude contribute to the decline of capitalism and help to establish an atmosphere in which private property and bourgeois values are daily subjected to heavy criticism (for example, in newspapers). In short, capitalism's economic success leads to its political failure.

Schumpeter's thoughts on the effects of monopolistic and oligopolistic markets on technical change and on the influence of technology on the emergence of big business have given a great impetus to the study of the relationship between technical change and market structure. His sharp distinction between innovations and inventions has triggered off several reactions, and both theoretical analysis and empirical research have been directed to the question whether innovations are really as independent of inventions as Schumpeter supposed. A critical evaluation of Schumpeter's theory has led to a discussion of the nature of technical change, the time-lag between invention and application, the significance of patents and the diffusion process of technical change. Schumpeter's predictions about the decay of capitalism have not come about. He seems to have underestimated the dynamic character of capitalism, the importance of which he himself emphasized so eloquently. He did not realize that a new generation of entrepreneurs might come to the fore, prepared to apply new technology and start a new wave of innovations. There is much more room for Schumpeterian entrepreneurial activity, especially on a small-scale basis, than Schumpeter foresaw.

It can be admitted that in large firms in particular the emergence of new technical knowledge is to a certain extent mechanized and that the decision-making process about its application, both in the sphere of production and marketing, is often hampered by bureaucratic features, threatening the static and dynamic efficiency of the firm and therefore the level of output. But these decisions still take place in a world of uncertainty and financial risk. These latter aspects of the decision-making process come more to the fore as the size of the firm becomes smaller. Within these firms, individuals who take final and major decisions and bear the responsibility of profits and losses do still exist. If, due to a lack of such individuals, Schumpeterian developments arise, the result will often be a new dynamic leadership. Many small firms still exist or come into being in order to gain a place in the market. Their managers take initiatives and often have to overcome resistance of consumers to achieve their market goals. It may be true that nowadays nearly everybody is confronted with change and new developments at a very high rate, but this does not imply that everybody accepts this state of affairs. So, on the whole, there are traces of a Schumpeterian development in Western economies, but mechanization and routinization of the entrepreneurial function are by no means the general picture. Economic life is still a melting-pot of conflicting tendencies, ups and downs, major risks and minor certainties. In short, it is the dynamic, ever-changing scene for entrepreneurs who have to be innovative and sensitive to new opportunities. Those entrepreneurs who follow the Schumpeterian line will be punished by the market, that is by competitors who are prepared to take risks and to bear losses.

On balance, it seems that innovation as a process of development, application and diffusion of new technical possibilities has not been reduced to routine. Nor have people become so reconciled to change that personal characteristics such as will-power and perseverance are no longer needed to break traditional patterns. However, even this kind of modification of Schumpeter's views, does not mean that over some much longer run he may still not turn out to have been right. It therefore seems appropriate to look more carefully at the empirical evidence about the entrepreneurial function and about the acceptability of the level of output as the sole yardstick for economic performance. This may enable us to look into the future of capitalism, as well.

Is the essence of the entrepreneurial function really the exploitation of new technical possibilities and of new opportunities in general? On the basis of Schumpeter's distinction between inventions and innovations, it is natural to identify entrepreneurial activity with innovative activity. But in the no-man's-land between invention and innovation there is a missing link; a link which according to Kirzner comprises three essential entrepreneurial components in human action: (a) the alertness to information; (b) the awareness of new existing opportunities, waiting to be noticed; and (c) the response to possibilities offered by the market system. Although in many cases those who are on the look-out for new opportunities are the same men and women who exploit them, Kirzner's refinement of Schumpeter's characterization of entrepreneurship is of the utmost importance – particularly if this view is combined with the idea of the market as an ongoing process of creative discovery. It may be argued that certain stages of the application and execution of new ideas can be routinized. However, the property of being alert to marketable applications of what already exists, but is currently overlooked by others, is still an individualistic characteristic, not one for being automatized. Even if we comprehend in the definition of the entrepreneurial function the application and implementation of new combinations, it is still true that first of all one has to be alert to what may be applied. In this sense entrepreneurship never was and never will be a matter of routine.

With regard to the level of output as a yardstick for economic performance, it may be observed that other aspects of welfare are taken into account as well. The operational meaning of welfare, in the broad sense of the level of the satisfaction of wants in so far as this depends on the allocation of scarce resources, comes more and more to the fore. The level of output is no longer the only thing that matters; the quality of growth, job satisfaction and other immaterial aspects of welfare are becoming more and more important. They are often the source for new methods of production and products, which give new impetus to capitalism. As an Austrian, Schumpeter would certainly welcome the broadening of the economic dimension to the formal and subjective concept of welfare.

Furthermore, socialism as an alternative to capitalism seems to be less and less attractive as a system able to take care of aspirations and heterogeneous preferences of individuals. Since the beginning of the 1980s the economic recovery seems to have inspired the reinforcement of the market, especially on the supply-side of the economy. Against this background a revival of Schumpeter's ideas in economic theory seems possible. While Keynes dominated economic thinking during a large part of the present century, there are indications that Schumpeter will be a major source of inspiration during the rest of this century. His concern with permanent and endogenous changes in economic life show up the limited significance of static equilibrium theory and paved the way for a neo-Austrian emphasis on the importance of the market mechanism as a vehicle for the discovery of new products and new methods of production, in short of the market as a dynamic institution.

Within the realm of social theory, Schumpeter's distinction between political and methodological individualism should also be mentioned. In particular, the concept of methodological individualism has proved to be very important for the analysis of social phenomena, outside the sphere of the market mechanism. As a method of analysis, methodological individualism prescribes starting from the economic behaviour of the individual in order to build a theory about the structure and working of the political process and about the behaviour of groups. In this sense, Schumpeter's thinking is the opposite of Marx's analysis in terms of the class struggle. The modern theory of public choice, in which the maximization of individual welfare of politicians and bureaucrats plays an essential role, in order to describe their social behaviour as part of the government, is a direct application of methodological individualism. Related to this development is the economic theory of democracy, of which Schumpeter is a forerunner. In his view, the democratic method is that institutional arrangement for arriving at political decisions in which individuals acquire the power to decide by means of a competitive struggle for the people's vote. In other words, Schumpeter introduces the idea that democracy is a type of horizontal coordination in the public sector that can be compared to the role of the market mechanism in the private sector of the economy. The political process is regarded as a market process in which the voters are the demanders and politicians and bureaucrats are the suppliers.

This idea appears to be very fruitful in both theory and practice and contributes to Schumpeter's fame as a social and economic thinker of lasting significance.

Schumpeter's view of society is based on the integration of historical facts, philosophical considerations and sociological visions. While Marx predicted the breakdown of capitalism as an inevitable consequence of the objective inner structure of the system, determined in its development by technical change, Schumpeter, although also pointing out structural changes from within, leaves room for the role of individuals, who by their behaviour can turn the tide. His message on the march into socialism is not meant to be defeatist; it would only be so if all differences between individuals disappeared and, in particular, leadership vanished.

Schumpeter will always be referred to for his impressive contributions to the history of economic thought. His *Economic Doctrine and Method*, originally published in German in 1914, is an early expression of his interest. His book *Ten Great Economists* provides further evidence, and his monumental work, the *History of Economic Analysis*, is a lasting culmination. It illustrates his detailed knowledge of the vast literature on economic theory since the days of the Greeks and Romans.

On the whole his discussion of the theoretical contributions of numerous economists is fair, generous and well-balanced. There are, however, a few notable exceptions. He ranks Cournot higher than Ricardo, and although we find both economists in modern economic theory, it seems fair to conclude that Ricardo's contributions to economics leave a broader scope and impact. Furthermore he considers Walras the greatest economist of all time, greater than, for example, Marshall. His great appreciation for two mathematical economists is in contrast with his own non-mathematical treatment of economics, although he even became a founder and first president of the Econometric Society.

Reading Schumpeter, one realizes that his lasting significance stems from historical description and non-mathematical theoretical analysis. His inability to put his ideas about the development of economic life into a mathematical form may eventually change our assessment of him. But whatever the final evaluation of Schumpeter may be, it cannot be denied that he gave new direction to the development of economic science by posing some entirely new questions. Schumpeter's preoccupation with the dynamics of economic life broke the spell of the static approach to economic problems.

Throughout his life Schumpeter was an *enfant terrible*, who was always ready to take extreme positions for the sake of argument, and often seized the chance to irritate people. But he was also a giant on whose shoulders many later scholars contributing to economic science stood. As an economist he is no longer in the shadow of Keynes, but in the centre of the economic scene, both in the theoretical and empirical sense.

ARNOLD HEERTJE

See also CREATIVE DESTRUCTION.

SELECTED WORKS

1912. *The Theory of Economic Development*. Leipzig: Duncker & Humblot. Trans. R. Opie, Cambridge, Mass.: Harvard University Press, 1934. Reprinted, New York: Oxford University Press, 1961.
1914. *Economic Doctrine and Method*. Trans. R. Aris, London: George Allen & Unwin, 1954.
1939. *Business Cycles*. 2 vols, New York: McGraw-Hill.
1942. *Capitalism, Socialism and Democracy*. New York: Harper & Brothers. London: George Allen & Unwin, 1943. 5th edn, London: George Allen & Unwin, 1976.
1951. *Ten Great Economists*. New York: Oxford University Press.

1954. *History of Economic Analysis*. Ed. E. Boody, New York: Oxford University Press; London: George Allen & Unwin.
1986. *Aufsätze zur Wirtschaftspolitik*. Tübingen: J.C.B. Mohr.

BIBLIOGRAPHY
Bös, D. and Stolper, W. (eds) 1984. *Schumpeter oder Keynes*. Berlin: Springe-Verlag.
Frisch, H. (ed.) 1982. *Schumpeterian Economics*. New York: Praeger.
Harris, S.E. (ed.) 1951. *Schumpeter, Social Scientist*. Cambridge, Mass.: Harvard University Press.
Heertje, A. (ed.) 1981. *Schumpeter's Vision*. New York: Praeger.
Kirzner, I.M. 1986. *Discovery and the Capitalist Process*. Chicago: University of Chicago Press.
März, E. 1983. *Joseph Alois Schumpeter*. Vienna: Verlag for Geschichte und Politik.
Seidl, C. (ed.) 1984. *Lectures on Schumpeterian Economics*. Berlin: Springer-Verlag.
Wolff, J. 1982. Schumpeter. In J. Wolff, *Les grandes oeuvres économiques*, Paris: Editions Cujas.

Schwartz, Anna Jacobson (born 1915). Born in New York, Anna Schwartz received her education at Barnard College and the Graduate Faculties of Columbia University. Aside from a few years of research at Columbia University, she has been associated throughout her career with the National Bureau of Economic Research. She was also the Staff Director of the US Commission on the Role of Gold in the Domestic and International Monetary Systems in 1981–2.

Dr Schwartz is most widely known for collaborations with Milton Friedman that resulted in three monumental books and several articles on monetary economics. (Friedman and Schwartz, 1963a, 1963b, 1969, 1970, 1982a, 1982b and 1982c). She has also made major contributions to quantitative economic history. These began with the study of the British economy in 1790–1850 (Gayer, Rostow and Schwartz, 1953), mainly written in the late 1930s, and have continued through a dozen or so articles on monetary and financial history, including Schwartz (1947a, 1947b, 1960, 1975, 1979, 1981a, 1981b and 1984a) and Bordo and Schwartz (1977, 1979, 1980 and 1981). Since the late 1960s, Dr Schwartz has also published articles on current monetary and policy issues, including Schwartz (1969a, 1969b), Cagan and Schwartz (1975a and 1975b), and Bordo and Schwartz (1983), as well as a large part of the US Gold Commission Report (US 1982). More recently, Dr Schwartz has written also on international financial problems (1983, 1984b).

Both in the historical research and in the analyses of current events, Dr Schwartz has been a major force in the revival of monetarism and particularly of emphasis on the role of the quantity of money, and her research has provided much of the empirical evidence for these theories. Beyond that, she has become a leading historian of monetary developments and an unequalled expert on the statistics of the monetary and banking systems of the United States and the United Kingdom. In all these fields, her work has been characterized by thoroughness in the understanding of the data and their deficiencies and by meticulous care in their use.

ROBERT LIPSEY

SELECTED WORKS
1947a. The beginning of competitive banking in Philadelphia, 1782–1809. *Journal of Political Economy* 55, October, 417–31.
1947b. An attempt at synthesis in American banking history. *Journal of Economic History* 7, November, 208–17.
1953. (With A.D. Gayer and W.W. Rostow.) *The Growth and Fluctuation of the British Economy, 1790–1850*. 2 vols, Oxford: Clarendon Press. 2nd edn, Brighton, Sussex: Harvester Press, 1975.
1960. Gross dividend and interest payments by corporations at selected dates in the 19th century, In *Trends in the American Economy in the Nineteenth Century*. Studies in Income and Wealth, Vol. 24, Princeton: National Bureau of Economic Research.
1963a. (With M. Friedman.) Money and business cycles. *Review of Economics and Statistics* 45(1), February Supplement, 32–64.
1963b. (With M. Friedman.) *A Monetary History of the United States, 1867–1960*. Princeton: Princeton University Press for the National Bureau of Economic Research.
1969a. (With M. Friedman.) The definition of money: net wealth and neutrality as criteria. *Journal of Money, Credit and Banking* 1(1), February, 1–15.
1969b. Short-term targets of some foreign central banks. In *Targets and Indicators of Monetary Policy*, ed. Karl Brunner, San Francisco: Chandler.
1969c. Why money matters. *Lloyds Bank Review* 94, October, 1–16.
1970. (With M. Friedman.) *Monetary Statistics of the United States*. National Bureau of Economic Research, New York: Columbia University Press.
1975. Monetary trends in the United States and the United Kingdom, 1878–1970: selected findings. *Journal of Economic History* 35(1), March, 138–59.
1975a. (With P. Cagan.) How feasible is a flexible monetary policy? In *Capitalism and Freedom: Problems and Prospects*, ed. R.T. Selden, University Press of Virginia.
1975b. (With P. Cagan.) Has the growth of money substitutes hindered monetary policy? *Journal of Money, Credit and Banking* 1(2), May, 137–59.
1977. (With M.D. Bordo.) Issues in monetary economics and their impact on research in economic history. In *Research in Economic History*, ed. R.E. Gallman, Greenwich, Conn.: Johnson Associates.
1979. The banking reforms of the 1930's. In *Regulatory Change in an Atmosphere of Crisis: The Current Implications of the Roosevelt Years*, ed. G.M. Walton, New York: Academic Press.
1979. (With M.D. Bordo.) Clark Warburton: pioneer monetarist. *Journal of Monetary Economics* 5(1), January, 43–65.
1980. (With M.D. Bordo.) Money and prices in the nineteenth century: an old debate rejoined. *Journal of Economic History* 40(1), March, 61–7.
1981a. Understanding 1929–1933. In *The Great Depression Revisited*, ed. K. Brunner, The Hague: Martinus Nijhoff.
1981b. *A Century of British Market Interest Rates, 1874–1975*. The Henry Thornton Lecture, January, London: The City University, Centre for Banking and International Finance.
1981. (With M.D. Bordo.) Money and prices in the nineteenth century: was Thomas Tooke right? *Explorations in Economic History* 18(2), January, 97–127.
1982a. Commission on the role of gold in the domestic and international monetary systems. *Report to the Congress*. March, Vol. 1.
1982b. (With M. Friedman.) The effect of the term structure of interest rates on the demand for money in the United States. *Journal of Political Economy* 90(1), February, 201–12.
1982c. (With M. Friedman.) Interrelations between the United States and the United Kingdom, 1873–1975. *Journal of International Monetary Economics* 1, April.
1982d. (With M. Friedman.) *Monetary Trends in the United States and the United Kingdom: Their Relation to Income, Prices, and Interest Rates, 1867–1975*. Chicago: University of Chicago Press for the National Bureau of Economic Research.
1983. The postwar institutional evolution of the international monetary system. In *The International Transmission of Inflation*, ed. M. Darby et al., Chicago: University of Chicago Press for the National Bureau of Economic Research.
1983. (With M.D. Bordo.) The importance of stable money: theory and evidence. *Cato Journal* 3(1), Spring, 63–82.
1984a. Introduction to *A Retrospective on the Classical Gold Standard, 1821–1931*. Chicago: University of Chicago Press for the National Bureau of Economic Research.
1984b. International lending and the economic environment. *Cato Journal* 4(1), Fall, 205–9.

Schwartz, Nancy Lou (1939–1981). Nancy L. Schwartz was educated at Oberlin College (Phi Beta Kappa, AB 1960) and Purdue University (MS 1962, PhD 1964). She taught at Carnegie-Mellon University from 1964 to 1970, and Northwestern University from 1970, where she was appointed Morrison Professor of Managerial Economics and Decision Sciences in 1981. She served as director of Graduate Studies of the Kellogg Graduate School of Management, and as chair of the Department of Managerial Economics and Decision Sciences from 1977 to 1979. She served on the Council of The Institute of Management Sciences (1974–6), on the Board of Editors of the *American Economic Review* from 1981, and was an Associate Editor of *Econometrica* from 1981. Her dissertation research dealt with a problem of determining the routing and timing of movements of barges and towboats to carry out given freight movements between pairs of ports at minimal cost. She developed a linear discrete programming problem of this dynamic optimization problem, and was able to solve it for moderate problems. Her later research was mainly in two related areas: methods of dynamic optimization, with particular focus on application, and the effect of industry structure on technological innovation. She also published on other topics; her work includes more than forty published papers, including a fundamental paper on limit pricing under certainty with M.I. Kamien, which appeared in *Econometrica* in 1971, and two books. Her work in the field of control theory, or dynamic optimization, is contained in the book *Dynamic Optimization* (1981, with M.I. Kamien). Her contributions to the subject of technological innovation are contained in numerous journal articles culminating in a book, *Market Structure and Innovation* (1982, with M.I. Kamien). She had a preference for problems related to application, and for hard (as opposed to soft) analysis, for which she had a considerable talent. Her work and personality had a strong effect on her students, many of whom are active contributors to research in Economics and Management Science.

STANLEY REITER

SELECTED WORKS

1971. (With M.I. Kamien.) Limit pricing and uncertain entry. *Econometrica* 39(3), May, 441–54.

1981. (With M.I. Kamien.) *Dynamic Optimization: the calculus of variations and optimal control in economics and management.* Westport, Conn. and London: Greenwood Press.

1982. (With M.I. Kamien.) *Market Structure and Innovation.* Cambridge: Cambridge University Press.

scientific management. *See* TAYLORISM.

Scitovsky, Tibor (born 1910). Tibor Scitovsky was born in Budapest. He received a degree in Law from the University of Budapest and a degree in Economics from the London School of Economics. He migrated to the United States in 1939 and served in the US Army during World War II. He taught at Stanford, the University of California at Berkeley, Yale, Harvard, and the London School of Economics. He also worked at the OECD from 1966 to 1968.

His writings are brilliant, original, succinct, lucid, and full of subtlety. They always enlighten and move the debate forward. He has made fundamental and lasting contributions to a large number of subjects: welfare economics, international trade, economic development, and microeconomics. One can discern a unifying theme to these varied contributions; it is to indicate ways in which neoclassical equilibrium analysis fails to capture important aspects of economic reality and, therefore, leads to misleading policy implications from efficiency, stability, or welfare points of view. He stresses dynamics, and interdependence among the utilities of consumers and decision-outcomes of producers, as the major sources of divergence of social optima from market equilibria of perfectly competitive economies.

His work in welfare economics points to the impossibility of purging policy analysis from value judgements concerning the optimality of the initial and final distributions of income. This is true whether the initial and final situations are efficient or inefficient, in static terms, or whether or not the possibility for compensation of losers by winners exists. (Compensation restores the original distribution and therefore implies the judgement that the original distribution was optimal.) Rather than abandon the possibilities for policy recommendations entirely, economists should make explicit the value judgements that underlie their policy advice.

His contributions to economic development make the capturing of external economies the cornerstone of development strategy. His classic paper, 'Two Concepts of External Economies', distinguishes between technological and pecuniary external economies. In developing countries, the existence of pecuniary externalities argues for the planning of coordinated investment decisions since market prices provide imperfect signals when those decisions are interdependent. He also argues for economic integration and export-led growth in economies too small to secure the advantages of both economies of large-scale production and pecuniary economies of balanced growth.

In trade theory, his 'Reconsideration of the Theory of Tariffs' points to the parallelism between tariffs and the monopolist's markup (or monopsonist's markdown) for exploiting his trading partners and argues that market forces could never approximate free trade, which would have to be imposed and enforced by international agreement or by a dominant large power against each nation's selfish preferences.

His most controversial but most original book, *The Joyless Economy*, tries to introduce into consumption theory the psychologist's classification of satisfactions into comfort, stimulation and pleasure, with emphasis on the psychological trade-off between them. The second part of the book explores the implications of the consumer's ignorance of that psychological trade-off on the rationality of his choice behavior, using American lifestyles as an illustration.

Reading his writings, one is made painfully aware of how much has been lost by the modern trend to mathematize and computerize. By comparison, modern economics appears mechanical and myopic, lacking in subtlety and sweep. Many of the themes raised in his writings appear as fresh today as they were when they were first written. And there are many points still worth following up almost half a century after they were first made. His recent integration of microeconomics with macroeconomics, contained in his analysis of the real side of inflation, which builds on the price-maker price-taker distinction first introduced by him in his book on Welfare and Competition, is a case in point.

IRMA ADELMAN

SELECTED WORKS

1952. *Welfare and Competition: The Economics of a Fully Employed Society*. London: Allen & Unwin.

1954. Two concepts of external economies. *Journal of Political Economy* 62, 70–82.

1958. *Economic Theory and Western European Integration*. London: Allen & Unwin.

1964. *Papers on Welfare and Growth*. London: Allen & Unwin.

1969. *Money and the Balance of Payments*. Chicago: Rand McNally.

1970. (With I.M.D. Little and M.F. Scott.) *Industry and Trade in Some Developing Countries*. Oxford: Oxford University Press.
1976. *The Joyless Economy*. Oxford: Oxford University Press.
1986. *Human Desire and Economic Satisfaction*. Brighton: Wheatsheaf; New York: New York University Press.

Scott, William Robert (1868–1940). W.R. Scott ('the chief' as A.L. Macfie used to describe him) was born in Armagh on 31 August 1868, the eldest son of Charles and Margaret Scott. He was educated at Canon Stewart's Preparatory School and then St Columba's College, Rathfarnham. Scott went to Trinity College Dublin in 1885, graduating BA in 1889 and MA two years later. 1891 saw his first major publication, *An Introduction to Cudworth's Treatise Concerning Eternal and Immutable Morality*. Scott's philosophical interests were also marked by his *Simple History of Ancient Philosophy* (1894).

In 1896 Scott took up the post of assistant to the Professor of Moral Philosophy in the University of St. Andrews, and three years later became the University's first Lecturer in Political Economy. Scott was responsible for planning the teaching of economics until 1915 when he was translated to the Adam Smith Chair of Political Economy in Glasgow, in succession to William Smart. Scott died in Glasgow on 3 April 1940, after a brief illness.

Scott was extremely active as examiner, teacher, researcher, and adviser to government with a marked interest in contemporary, as well as historical, issues. There are three identifiable strands to his work.

The first was through his interest in contemporary economic and social problems, encouraged by his chairmanship for many years of his family's firm of millers in Tyrone. It led to an active involvement in public affairs, in days when economists were less consulted than subsequently. Apart from his membership and chairmanship of committees, national and regional, especially in the 1920s, Scott's name became attached to several departmental and other reports, even when he was not the sole or main author.

He was appointed by the Secretary for Scotland to examine home industries in the North. The ensuing Report was published in 1914. He subsequently addressed the *Economic Problems of Peace after War* (1917, 1918), and later worked (with James Cunnison) on *Industries of the Clyde Valley during the War* (1924) as part of a Carnegie Series.

A second stream is represented by his pioneering work in economic history. Scott published an edition of *The Records of a Scottish Cloth Manufactory at New Mills, Haddingtonshire 1681–1703* (1905). This was followed by one of his best known studies, the definitive, three volume, *Constitution and Finance of English, Scottish and Irish Joint Stock Companies to 1720* (1910–1912). He was president of the Economic History Society from 1928 until his death.

A third contribution is represented by Scott's work as an historian of ideas. His book on *Francis Hutcheson* (1900) is the work of a philosopher well versed in economics and is still a classic. Scott also dramatically advanced contemporary knowledge of Hutcheson's most famous pupil with the publication of *Adam Smith as Student and Professor* (1937) which featured his discovery of important Smith papers in the Buccleuch MSS. Scott's ability to find records was impressive. Some criticism of his handling of them is possible but many of the difficulties which impeded his work have been reduced for later scholars by the discovery and cataloguing of many relevant records of economic and intellectual history which he helped to bring about.

At the time of his death Scott was working on a bibliography, which was published under the auspices of the British Academy, and edited by his successor in Glasgow, Alec Lawrence Macfie.

As his obituarist noted in the *Glasgow Herald* (4 April 1940),

> If one today were to seek the model of his famous and beloved predecessor (Adam Smith) it would be impossible to find a closer re-incarnation than William Robert Scott. He had the same temper, controlled, wide-eyed impartiality of mind allied with an absorbing fire of enthusiasm for reasoned practice and disinterested policy. This is the tribute he would most have appreciated, and it is one which all his friends and students would endorse as the most appropriate.

The British Academy published an appreciation by Sir John Clapham, *William Robert Scott 1868–1940* (London, 1940).

ANDREW SKINNER

SELECTED WORKS

1891. *An Introduction to Cudworth's Treatise concerning Eternal and Immutable Morality, with Life of Cudworth and a few critical Notes*. London: Longmans.
1893. *Geography of Ptolemy Elucidated*. Ed. T.G. Rylands, Dublin: Ponsonby & Weldrick.
1894. *A Simple History of Ancient Philosophy*. London: E. Stock.
1900. *Frances Hutcheson: His Life, Teaching, and Position in the History of Philosophy*. Cambridge: Cambridge University Press.
1903. Free Trade in relation to the future of Britain and the Colonies: a plea for an Imperial Policy: a lecture. St Andrews: W.C. Henderson & Son.
1903-4. The fiscal policy of Scotland before the Union. *Scottish Historical Review* 1, 173.
1903-5. Scottish industrial undertakings before the Union. *Scottish Historical Review* 1 (1903–4), 407; 2 (1905), 53, 287, 406; 3 (1906), 71.
1905. *Records of a Scottish Cloth Manufactory at New Mills, Haddingtonshire, 1681–1703*. Edinburgh: Scottish History Society.
1907. Scottish industry before the Union; Scottish industry after the Union. In *The Union of 1707*, ed. P. Hume Brown, Glasgow, 93 and 102.
1910-12. *The Constitution and Finance of English, Scottish and Irish Joint Stock Companies to 1720*. 3 vols, Cambridge: Cambridge University Press.
1911a. Is increasing utility possible? In *Celebration of the Five-Hundredth Anniversary of the Foundation of St. Andrews*, Glasgow.
1911b. *Scottish Economic Literature: A List of Authorities*. Scottish Exhibition of History, Art and Industry, Glasgow.
1913. The trade of Orkney at the end of the eighteenth century. *Scottish Historical Review* 10, 360.
1917. Mercantile shipping in the Napoleonic wars. *Scottish Historical Review* 14, 272.
1917–18. *Economic Problems of Peace after War*. The W. Stanley Jevons Lectures at University College, London, Cambridge: Cambridge University Press.
1920. William Cunningham, 1849–1919. *Proceedings of the British Academy* 9, 465–74.
1921. (ed.) Adam Smith, *An Inquiry into the Nature and Causes of the Wealth of Nations*. 2 vols, London: Bohn's Standard Library.
1923. Books as links of Empire: *The Wealth of Nations*. *Empire Review*.
1924a. (With James Cunnison) *The Industries of the Clyde Valley during the War*. Oxford: Clarendon Press.
1924b. Adam Smith. *Proceedings of the British Academy*, London.
1924c. Adam Smith and the City of Glasgow. In *Proceedings of the Royal Philosophical Society of Glasgow* 52.
1926a. Alfred Marshall, 1842–1924. *Proceedings of the British Academy*, London.

1926b. Scottish land settlement. In *Scotland During the War*, in *Economic and Social History of the World War*, ed. R.D. Jones et al., London: Humphrey Milford.
1928. Joseph Shield Nicholson, 1850–1927. *Proceedings of the British Academy*, London.
1929-30. Economic resiliency. *Economic History Review* 2, 291.
1931. The manuscript of Adam Smith's Glasgow lectures. *Economic History Review* 3, 91–2.
1934. Adam Smith and the Glasgow merchants. *Economic Journal* 44, 506–8.
1935a. Adam Smith at Downing Street, 1766–67. *Economic History Review* 6, 79–89.
1935b. The manuscript of an early draft of part of *The Wealth of Nations*. *Economic Journal* 45, 427–38.
1936. New light on Adam Smith. *Economic Journal* 46, 401–11.
1937. *Adam Smith as Student and Professor, with Unpublished Documents*. Glasgow: Jackson.
1938a. A manuscript criticism of the *Wealth of Nations* in 1776 by Hugh Blair. *Economic History* 4, 47–53.
1938b. *Adam Smith: An Oration*. Glasgow: Jackson.
1939. *Greek Influence on Adam Smith*. Athens: Pyros Press.
1940. Studies relating to Adam Smith during the last fifty years. In *Proceedings of the British Academy*, ed. A.L. Macfie, London.

Scottish Enlightenment. Between 1740 and 1790 Scotland provided one of the most distinguished branches of the European Enlightenment. David Hume and Adam Smith were the pre-eminent figures in this burst of intellectual activity; and around them clustered a galaxy of major thinkers, including Francis Hutcheson, Lord Kames, Adam Ferguson, William Robertson, Thomas Reid, Sir James Steuart and John Millar. The interests of individual thinkers ranged from metaphysics to the natural sciences; but the distinctive achievements of the Scottish Enlightenment as a whole lay in those fields associated with the enquiry into 'the progress of society' – history, moral and political philosophy and, not least, political economy.

In the European context, Scotland's was a characteristically 'provincial' Enlightenment. Conscious of their membership of a wider movement, the Scottish thinkers cultivated connections with Paris, the Enlightenment's acknowledged metropolitan centre. But the Scottish Enlightenment is perhaps best understood when it is compared with the Enlightenment in France's provinces, or in the provincial states of Italy and Germany. The concern with economic improvement and its moral and political conditions and consequences was as urgent, for instance, in the distant Kingdom of Naples as in Scotland; and political economy was equally absorbing to the Neapolitan philosopher-reformers Genovesi and Galiani.

At the same time, the experience of Scotland in the 18th century was distinctive in a number of respects, which offered a particular stimulus to Scottish thinkers. First of all, there was the actual achievement of economic growth. Slow in coming, but increasingly perceptible, it gave Scottish thinkers an unusually direct acquaintance with the phenomena of development. Political change was also significant. The Union of 1707 with England was in no simple sense the cause of Scotland's economic growth (or the precondition of its Enlightenment). But the sacrifice of the nation's independent parliament for the opportunity of free trade with England and its empire highlighted the problem of the institutional conditions of economic development. Most dramatic of all were the changes in religion and culture. The fierce, covenanting presbyterianism of the 17th century was dissipated, as the 'Moderate' group of clergy rose to power in the Kirk. The four universities of Edinburgh, Glasgow, Aberdeen and St Andrews were reformed, allowing professorial specialization; and around the universities flourished a vigorous informal culture of voluntary clubs, most famous of which was the Select Society of Edinburgh. Together these changes secured for Scottish thinkers unprecedented intellectual freedom and social support; and they provided an object lesson in the importance of the moral and cultural as well as the material dimensions of progress.

Nothing in Scotland's comparatively successful provincial experience, moreover, inclined its Enlightenment in a very radical direction. It was not that the Scottish thinkers were complacent: on particular issues they were anxious to influence the leaders of Scottish society. But where in backward provinces like Naples, Enlightenment thinking was programmatic, even utopian, the thought of the Scottish Enlightenment was characterized by a relatively detached, analytic interest in the underlying mechanisms of society's development.

Against the background of Scotland's particular provincial experience, it was natural for the Scottish thinkers to study economic phenomena in the framework of a wider enquiry. There were three principal dimensions to that enquiry: the historical, the moral and the institutional.

The historical theory of the Scottish Enlightenment developed a line of argument from later 17th-century natural jurisprudence, a tradition made familiar to the Scots by its incorporation in the moral philosophy curriculum of the reformed universities. Discarding the older jurisprudential thesis of the contractual foundations of society and government, the Scots focused on the new insights of Pufendorf and Locke into the origin and development of property. According to Pufendorf, there had never been an original state of common ownership of land and goods; from the first, property was the result of individual appropriation. As increasing numbers made goods scarce, individual property became the norm, and systems of justice and government were established to secure it. What the Scots added to this argument was a scheme of specific stages of social development, the hunting, the pastoral, the agricultural and the commercial. At each of these four stages the extent of property ownership was related to the society's means of subsistence, and both shaped the nature and sophistication of the society's government. Different versions of the theory were offered by Adam Ferguson in his *Essay on the History of Civil Society* (1767) and by John Millar in his *Origin of the Distinction of Ranks* (1770), and underlay Lord Kames's investigations into legal history and William Robertson's historical narratives. The *locus classicus* of the theory, however, was Adam Smith's *Lectures on Jurisprudence*, delivered to his students in Glasgow in the early 1760s.

As Smith's exposition makes particularly clear, the stages theory of social development provided the historical premises for political economy. An explicitly conjectural theory – a model of society's 'natural' progress – it provided a framework for a comparably theoretical treatment of economic development as 'the natural progress of opulence'. By positing the systematic interrelation of economic activity, property and government, with consequences which could be neither foreseen nor controlled by individuals, the theory also established the essential irreversibility of the development process. Short of a natural catastrophe, it demonstrated, the advent of commercial society was unavoidable.

The moral thought of the Scottish Enlightenment was closely related to the historical, sharing a common origin in 17th-century natural jurisprudence. Here the inspiration was the jurisprudential thinkers' increasingly sophisticated treatment of needs. These, it was recognized, could no longer be thought of primarily in relation to subsistence; with the progress of society, needs must be understood to cover a much wider range of scarce goods, luxuries as well as necessities. The potential of this insight was seen by every Scottish moral philosopher, but again it was Smith who exploited it to the full, in the *Theory of Moral Sentiments* (1759). Beyond the most basic necessities, Smith acknowledged, men's needs were always relative, a matter of status and emulation, of bettering one's individual condition. But it was precisely the vain desires of the rich and the envy of others which served, by 'an invisible hand', to stimulate men's industry and hence to increase the stock of goods available for all ranks.

Such an argument, however, had to overcome two of the most deeply entrenched convictions of European moral thought: the Aristotelian view that the distribution of goods was a matter for justice, and the classical or civic humanist view that luxury led to corruption and the loss of moral virtue. The Scots answered the first more confidently (but perhaps less satisfactorily) than the second. Following Grotius, Hobbes and Pufendorf, they defined justice in exclusively corrective terms, setting aside questions of distribution. On the issue of corruption, they were divided. Hume, who ridiculed fears of luxury, was the most confident; Ferguson, who defiantly reasserted the ideal of virtue, the least. Smith was closer to Hume in preferring propriety to virtue, at least for the great majority; but he showed that he shared Ferguson's doubts when he added, at the end of his life, that the disposition to admire the rich and the great did tend to corrupt moral sentiments. At a fundamental level, however, there was general agreement. As a consequence of the progress of society, the multiplication of needs was not only irreversible; it was the essential characteristic of a 'cultivated' or 'civilized' as distinct from a 'barbarian' society. And civilization, however morally ambiguous, was preferable to barbarism. With consensus on this, the moral premises of political economy were secure.

The definition of justice in simple corrective terms provided the starting-point for the institutional dimension of the Scottish enquiry. The priority of any government, the Scots believed, must be the security of life and property, ensuring every individual liberty under the law. This, as Smith put it, was freedom 'in our present sense of the word'; and there was a general confidence that it was tolerably secure under the governments of modern Europe, including the absolute monarchies. In principle, individual liberty was a condition of a fully commercial society: its provision, therefore, was the institutional premise of political economy.

Few of the Scots took institutional analysis beyond this relatively simple, if vital, point; the theory of the modern commercial state was not a Scottish achievement. But Hume and Smith did get further than the rest, identifying and exploring a two-fold problem in the government of commercial society. Most urgently, they argued that it was necessary to limit the opportunities for governmental aggrandizement at the expense of 'productive' society, by confining government to the minimum necessary provision of justice, defence and public works. In the longer run, as the lower ranks of society acquired material and moral independence, it would also be necessary to satisfy their demands for an extension of citizenship and enlargement of political liberty. It was the responsibility of legislators, Hume and Smith believed, gradually to adapt institutions to meet these needs. Both outlined models by which legislators might proceed, Hume reworking the institutional concepts of the classical, civic tradition in his 'Idea of a perfect Commonwealth', Smith elaborating the principles of parliamentary sovereignty in his exemplary vision of British–American imperial union.

A large part of the originality of the Scottish Enlightenment's conception of political economy lay in this exploration of the historical, moral and institutional framework of economic activity. But of course the Scots also engaged directly in economic analysis; and one such work of analysis, Adam Smith's *Wealth of Nations* (1776), so outshone all others that it seemed to establish political economy as a science in its own right.

The Scots' attention naturally focused on growth. In contemporary terms, the issue was the means by which a poor country (such as Scotland) could best hope to catch up on a rich country (such as England). The alternatives, canvassed afresh by Hume in his *Political Discourses* (1752), were those aired in the Scottish debate before the Union, fifty years earlier: free trade to take advantage of the poor country's lower wages, or protection and credit creation to assist its manufactures. An optimist, Hume favoured the free trade alternative. Sir James Steuart countered in his *Principles of Political Economy* (1767) that rich nations would not permit free trade to their disadvantage, and that protection and credit creation were therefore essential. Unfortunately for Steuart, his arguments were simply ignored in the *Wealth of Nations*. Smith was agnostic about the prospects for poor countries; but he was unequivocal about free trade. The uninhibited expansion of the market was necessary, he explained, to achieve the maximum extension of the division of labour and the optimum allocation of capital, the twin motors of growth.

Smith's confidence in the powers of the market was the cornerstone of more than his explanation of growth. It shaped his entire presentation of political economy. In writing the *Wealth of Nations*, Smith consciously set himself to achieve the standards of simplicity, coherence and comprehensiveness which he associated with successful philosophical systems, and with the Newtonian philosophy in particular. What gravity was to Newton's astronomy, the market was to Smith's political economy. For the market was not simply the matrix of growth. It was also, he believed, the mechanism by which the fruits of growth were distributed, so that the unprecedented inequality of commercial society was offset by an equally unprecedented increase in the standard of living of even the lowest and poorest ranks. (As a means of improving the condition of the poor, in other words, the market was far more effective than any previous arrangement guided by the notion of distributive justice. It was the 'invisible hand' through which the vain desires of the rich were transformed into an increased stock of goods for all). In addition, the market could help to check the growth of unproductive government, since in Smith's view most institutions could be subjected to some degree to its disciplines. The market, in short, was cast in the *Wealth of Nations* as the hub of a complete, virtually self-sustaining economic system.

It was the systematic and comprehensive analysis which this faith in the market made possible, rather than simply the account of growth, which set the *Wealth of Nations* above any other work of Enlightenment political economy, Scottish or European. To be systematic and comprehensive had earlier been the ambition, at least, of Quesnay's *Tableau Economique* (1758–9), Genovesi's *Lezioni di Commercio* (1765) and Steuart's *Principles*; but the *Wealth of Nations* eclipsed them all. Its success, moreover, was such as to suggest that political economy had an identity all of its own. Smith himself did not admit such an implication, continuing to insist that political economy was but 'a branch of the science of a statesman or legislator': his own work in jurisprudence and moral philosophy left him disinclined to drop the wider intellectual framework in which political economy had been conceived.

But when the single concept of the market made possible an analysis at once so extensive and so self-contained, it was at least plausible to suppose that what was being presented in the *Wealth of Nations* was a distinct, autonomous science of political economy.

Smith's death in 1790 coincided with the end of the Scottish Enlightenment. In Scotland as throughout Europe, the French Revolution transformed the conditions and assumptions of intellectual life, while political economy had to come to terms with machinery. Within Scotland Dugald Stewart set himself to adapt the Enlightenment conception of political economy to these new circumstances; but his expansive, didactic approach had few imitators. Another Scot, Thomas Chalmers, took the lead in attaching political economy to newly urgent theological concerns, while in England Ricardo and his followers simply took a narrower view of the subject. Even so, it would be a mistake to see 19th-century classical political economy as a new departure. As the philosophical analysis of Hegel (who learnt much from Steuart) and the radical critiques of Marx and the early socialists pointed out, the historical, moral and institutional premises on which political economy rested were still those elucidated by the Scots. In any case, it was the Scottish Enlightenment, and specifically the *Wealth of Nations*, which had first shown how political economy might be presented as an independent science.

JOHN ROBERTSON

BIBLIOGRAPHY

Bryson, G. 1945. *Man and Society: the Scottish Enquiry of the Eighteenth Century*. Princeton: Princeton University Press.

Campbell, R.H. and Skinner, A.S. 1982. *The Origins and Nature of the Scottish Enlightenment*. Edinburgh: John Donald.

Hont, I. and Ignatieff, M. (eds) 1983. *Wealth and Virtue. The Shaping of Political Economy in the Scottish Enlightenment*. Cambridge: Cambridge University Press.

Medick, H. 1973. *Naturzustand und Naturgeschichte der bürgerlichen Gesellschaft*. Göttingen: Vandenhoeck and Ruprecht.

Phillipson, N.T. 1981. The Scottish Enlightenment. In *The Enlightenment in National Context*, ed. R. Porter and M. Teich, Cambridge: Cambridge University Press.

Sher, R.B. 1985. *Church and University in the Scottish Enlightenment*. Princeton and Edinburgh: Princeton: Princeton University Press; Edinburgh: Edinburgh University Press.

Scrope, George Poulett (1797–1876). George Poulett Scrope was one of the most prolific contributors to the literature of political economy in the mid-19th century. He was also one of the more able critics of features of the Ricardian economic orthodoxy which came to dominate that literature. Scrope is at his best as an economist in the series of articles he contributed when chief economics reviewer for the *Quarterly Review* (1831–3). His *Principles of Political Economy* (1833c) is disappointing by comparison.

After education at Harrow, Scrope entered Pembroke College, Oxford in 1815. During the following year he moved to St John's College, Cambridge where he graduated in 1821. He married the heiress Emma Phipps Scrope, altering his surname (which had been 'Thomson') to that of his wife, and establishing himself as one of the leading gentlemen of the County of Wiltshire. Scrope was appointed a magistrate of the County in 1823.

Research in geology was an early and enduring involvement. Scrope's distinguished work in this field led to his election to the Geological Society (1824). Two years later, he became a Fellow of the Royal Society, and he continued to publish papers on geological subjects until shortly before his death.

Scrope entered Parliament, and he remained Member for Stroud from 1833 to 1867. During his first twenty years in the Commons he spoke frequently and was a member of numerous parliamentary committees. His contributions in the legislature distinguish him as a 'man with a philosophic and inquiring mind, trying to explain the upheavals in economic relations, and also to guide policy on behalf of interests that went beyond his own personal gain' (Fetter, 1980). In debate, Scrope found himself in alliance at times with doctrinaire Ricardians such as Joseph Hume. Scrope supported repeal of the Corn Laws and the Navigation Acts. he was also in favour of parliamentary reform. On a variety of issues, however, he was decidedly 'unorthodox'. Those issues included: the nature of the currency and the structure of the banking system; the public funding of education; the maintenance of outdoor relief for the unemployed; and, closer government regulation of working conditions in factories. The problems of Ireland were among his special concerns, and he was a leading advocate of the extension of poor law provisions to that country.

The interventions of Scrope within Parliament were supplemented by his publication of numerous pamphlets on current policy issues. In addition, he contributed periodical articles in which he assailed the economic theories of the followers of David Ricardo, and the population doctrine of Thomas Robert Malthus. Scrope rejects a theory of value based on cost of production and he argues for recognition of a relationship between value-in-use and value-in-exchange. He finds the reasoning of Richard Jones on rent much superior to that of Ricardo. Noting the absence of any account of a basis for profit in Ricardian theory, he constructs an abstinence theory of interest and allies this to a risk-effort theory of profit which incorporates the concept of quasi-rent. Scrope is also concerned with the possibilities of over-saving and of a general glut of markets. In this latter respect, his ideas are akin to those of Malthus. However, Scrope is a persistent and incisive critic of Malthusian population theory and the policy implications which his contemporaries drew from it.

BARRY GORDON

SELECTED WORKS

Scrope's bibliography (Sturges, 1984) contains 175 items on economic, geological, and local history topics. The following is a list of some of the more notable publications dealing with economic issues.

1830a. *The Currency Question Freed from Mystery*. London.

1830b. *On Credit – Currency and its Superiority to Coin*. London.

1831a. The political economists. *Quarterly Review* 44, January, 1–51.

1831b. Malthus and Sadler – population and emigration. *Quarterly Review* 45, April, 97–245.

1832. The rights of industry and the banking system. *Quarterly Review* 47, July, 407–55.

1833a. Martineau's monthly novels. *Quarterly Review* 49, April, 136–51.

1833b. *An Examination of the Bank Charter Question*. London: John Murray.

1833c. *Principles of Political Economy*. London: Longman. Reprinted, New York: Kelley, 1969. Italian trans., 1855. 2nd edn, published as *Political Economy for Plain People*, 1873.

1848. Irish clearances and improvement of waste lands. *Westminster and Foreign Quarterly Review* 50, October, 163–87.

BIBLIOGRAPHY

Fetter, F.W. 1958. The economic articles in the Quarterly Review and their authors, 1809–1852. *Journal of Political Economy* 66, Pt I, February, 47–64; Pt II, April, 154–70.

Fetter, F.W. 1980. *The Economist in Parliament: 1780–1868*. Durham, North Carolina: Duke University Press.

Gordon, B. 1965. Say's Law, effective demand and the contemporary British periodicals, 1820–1850. *Economica* 32(128), November, 438–46.

Gordon, B. 1969. Criticism of Ricardian views on value and distribution in the British periodicals, 1820–1850. *History of Political Economy* 1(2), Fall, 390–87.
Opie, R. 1928. A neglected English economist: George Poulett Scrope. *Quarterly Journal of Economics* 44, November, 101–37.
Rashid, S. 1981. Political economy and geology in the early nineteenth century: similarities and contrasts. *History of Political Economy* 13(4), Winter, 726–44.
Rudwick, M.S. 1974. Poulett Scrope on the volcanoes of Auvergne: Lyellian time and political economy. *British Journal for the History of Science* 7(3), 205–42.
Sturges, P. 1984. *A Bibliography of George Poulett Scrope: Geologist, Economist and Local Historian.* Kress Library Publication No. 24, Boston, Mass.: Harvard Business School.

search theory. Walrasian analysis presumes that resource allocation can be adequately modelled using the assumption of instantaneous and costless coordination of trade. In contrast, Search Theory is the analysis of resource allocation with specified, imperfect technologies for informing agents of their trading opportunities and for bringing together potential traders. The modelling advantages of assuming a frictionless coordination mechanism, plus years of hard work, permit Walrasian analysis to work with very general specifications of individual preferences and production technologies. In contrast, search theorists have explored a variety of special allocation mechanisms together with very simple preferences and production technologies. Lacking more general theories, we examine the catalogue of analyses that have been completed.

Paralleling the Walrasian framework, we first examine individual choice and then equilibrium. There are a large number of variations on the basic search – theoretic choice problem. We explore one set-up in detail, while mentioning some of the variations that have been developed. Coordination of trade involves two separate steps: information gathering about opportunities, and arrangement of individual trades. One simple case is where information gathering is limited to visiting stores sequentially, combining the costs of collecting goods and of gathering information. Alternatively, there can be an information gathering mechanism which is independent of the process of ordering and receiving the good. We begin with models where the only information gathering is associated with visiting stores and then look at the changes that come from additional devices for information spread.

Once two potential traders have met there are several ways of determining whether they trade and the terms of trade if they do. Among these are price setting on a take-it-or-leave-it basis, idealized negotiations where any mutually advantageous trade occurs at a price satisfying some bargaining solution, and more realistic negotiation processes that recognize the time and cost of negotiation, the possibility of a negotiating impasse, and the possible arrival of alternatives for one or the other of the trading partners. We explore the first two mechanisms.

One final distinction in the literature is between one-time purchases of commodities and on-going trade relations. Infrequently purchased consumer goods are the classic example of the former, while the employment relationship is the classic example of the latter. Introducing on-going relationships permits the exploration of delayed learning of the quality of a match and associated rearrangements through quits and firings. Intermediate between these two cases is a situation such as that of frequently purchased consumer goods, where past trades facilitate future trades but do not bring about the closeness of an employment relationship. We discuss mainly the one-shot purchase. The discussion of individual choice and partial equilibrium will be given in terms of a consumer purchase. The parallel discussion of labour markets is only briefly mentioned.

I INDIVIDUAL CHOICE

Consider a consumer in a store who is deciding whether to make a purchase or to visit another store with an unknown price. Denote by $U(p, 1)$ the utility that the consumer receives (net of purchase costs) if the purchase is made in the first store at a price equal to p. This assumes an ability to purchase the optimal number of units at a constant per unit price of p. If the purchase is made at the second store at price p, utility is $U(p, 2)$. This utility is less than $U(p, 1)$ because of the cost and the time delay from visiting a second store. We assume that the entire purchase is made at a single store, that it is impossible to return to the first store, and that there are no other stores that can be visited. Ignoring the possibility of making no purchase and no further searches, the alternative to purchasing in store 1 at price p, is a single visit to store 2 where the price will be drawn from a (known) distribution which we denote $F(p)$. The purchase should be made in store 1 if the utility of purchase there is at least as large as the expected utility of purchase in store 2:

$$U(p_1, 1) \geqslant \int U(p, 2)\, \mathrm{d}F(p). \tag{I–1}$$

As long as the consumer views the distribution of prices in store 2 as independent of the price in the first store, the rule in (I–1) yields a cut-off price, p^*, given by (I–2):

$$U(p^*, 1) = \int U(p, 2)\, \mathrm{d}F(p). \tag{I–2}$$

For prices above p^*, optimal behaviour calls for visiting the second store, while for prices below p^*, optimal behaviour calls for making a purchase in the first store. Thus p^* is the cut-off price. Implicit in this formulation is the assumption that it is not desirable to make some purchase in store 1 and the remaining purchase in store 2. While this assumption is true for many consumer goods it is certainly not true for all of them. Without this assumption the decision resembles portfolio choice and has not been explored in the literature. A similar analysis applies to the search for high quality.

If the consumer does not know with certainty the distribution of prices in the second store, the consumer's beliefs about those prices may depend upon the price observed in the first store. We write the subjective distribution of prices in the second store, conditional on an observed price of p_1 in the first store as $F(p; p_1)$. The purchase should be made in the first store if p_1 satisfies the inequality:

$$U(p_1, 1) \geqslant \int U(p, 2)\, \mathrm{d}F(p; p_1). \tag{I–3}$$

With no restriction on the beliefs of the consumer as to the structure of prices found in both stores, the set of prices resulting in a purchase in store 1 does not necessarily satisfy a cut-off price rule. For example, if either a high or a low observed price implies the same price in both stores, while an intermediate price in store 1 implies a low price in store 2, then the consumer should purchase in store 1 at the high and low prices but not at an intermediate price. Thus, the intermediate price might signal a price war. If the information content of the price found in store 1 is a greater likelihood of similar prices in store 2, the optimality of a cut-off price rule is restored (Rothschild, 1974). For the remainder of this entry we restrict analysis to the case of known distributions. The caveats implicit in this counter example should be kept in mind.

Returning to the set-up with a known distribution, we can increase the options of the shopper by adding the possibility of returning to the first store after observing the price in the second store. Denote by $U(p, 3)$ the utility that is realized if this option is followed. The utility function $U(p, 3)$ is less than $U(p, 2)$, which, in turn, is less than $U(p, 1)$. Once in the second store, the choice is between buying there and returning to the first store with both prices known. Therefore it pays to purchase in the first store in the first period if the price there, p_1, satisfies the inequality:

$$U(p_1, 1) \geqslant \int \max[U(p, 2), U(p_1, 3)]\, \mathrm{d}F(p). \qquad \text{(I–4)}$$

That is, the purchase should be made in store 1 if utility there is higher than expected utility with optimal behaviour in choosing between the second store and returning to the first store. This is a particularly simple example of the backwards induction that can be used to solve the finite horizon sequential shopping problem. Behaviour in the first store, (I-4), again satisfies a cut-off price rule if the utility function has constant search costs and discount rate.

We now specialize the example by assuming additive, constant search costs c and utility discounting with a discount factor R. That is, $U(p, 2)$ equals $RU(p, 1) - c$, with $R \leqslant 1$. Returning to the choice problem without a return to store 1, we denote by $V(p_1)$ expected utility on observing the price p_1 in store 1, given optimal behaviour:

$$V(p_1) = \max\left[U(p_1), -c + R \int U(p)\, \mathrm{d}F(p) \right]. \qquad \text{(I–5)}$$

The value of being in a store that has price p_1 is the larger of (i) the utility from making the optimal purchase at that price, and (ii) the expected utility if the search cost c is paid and the purchase is made in the second store. Using this function V, we can describe choice in the first period of a new three period search problem with no return to previous stores. The optimal rule is to purchase if

$$U(p_1) \geqslant -c + R \int V(p)\, \mathrm{d}F(p). \qquad \text{(I–6)}$$

That is, purchase is made in the first period if the achievable utility there is at least as large as that achievable with optimal behaviour, beginning with a visit to a randomly selected second store. The latter utility is the discounted expected optimized utility minus the search costs of the visit, recognizing that the second period choice is again a choice between a purchase and a search in the following period. By having $F(p)$ independent of p_1, we are sampling with replacement rather than sampling without replacement from the known distribution of prices. The choice rule given in (I-6) again shows cut-off price behaviour for period one choice. However, the cut-off price is higher in the second period than in the first because of the reduction in options as the end of the search process comes closer. Denoting the cut-off prices in the two periods by p_1^* and p_2^*, they satisfy the two equations:

$$U(p_1^*) = -c + R \int V(p)\, \mathrm{d}F(p) \qquad \text{(I–7a)}$$

$$U(p_2^*) = -c + R \int U(p)\, \mathrm{d}F(p) \qquad \text{(I–7b)}$$

$V(p)$ is at least as large as $U(p)$ since it represents the choice between purchase and searching again. Thus $p_1^* \leqslant p_2^*$, with a strict inequality in problems where the search cost and discount rate are not so large as to always imply a purchase in the current store.

There are additional reasons for cut-off prices to rise over time or equivalently, in a job search setting, for reservation wages to fall over time. In many settings, search costs rise over time. The utility of a purchase or of finding a job can fall over time. In the job setting, these can arise from declining wealth being used to finance consumption while searching for a job and from the shortening period over which any job might be held.

A known finite horizon for the end of search is incorrect in many settings. In addition, with many periods, the backwards induction optimization process is a cumbersome description of individual choice. Fortunately, the infinite horizon stationary case is easy to analyse. In this setting, a parallel analysis to that in (I.7) is a straightforward application of dynamic programming principles. With the assumption of a stationary environment the cut-off price is the same period after period. Denote by p^* the cut-off price and by V the optimized expected value of utility after paying the search cost to enter a store but before observing its price. Then V equals the utility of purchase if a purchase is made plus the probability of not making a purchase times the discounted optimized utility from facing the same problem one period later after paying search cost c:

$$V = \int_0^{p^*} U(p)\, \mathrm{d}F(p) + [1 - F(p^*)][-c + RV]. \qquad \text{(I–8)}$$

Solving (I–8) for V we have:

$$V = \frac{\int_0^{p^*} U(p)\, \mathrm{d}F(p) - c[1 - F(p^*)]}{1 - R[1 - F(p^*)]}. \qquad \text{(I–9)}$$

The optimal p^* maximizes V and can be calculated by differentiation. More intuitively, we note that a purchase just worth making will give the same utility as will waiting to search again:

$$U(p^*) = -c + RV. \qquad \text{(I–10)}$$

Rearranging terms, we can write the implicit equation for p^*:

$$(1 - R)U(p^*) = -c + R \int_0^{p^*} [U(p) - U(p^*)]\, \mathrm{d}F(p). \qquad \text{(I–11)}$$

Using this first order condition we can analyse the comparative statics of optimal search behaviour. Naturally, the cut-off price increases if the search cost increases or if the discount factor becomes smaller. Interestingly, an increase in the riskiness of the distribution of prices (holding constant mean utility from a randomly selected price, $\int U(p)\mathrm{d}F$) makes search more valuable and so lowers the cut-off price. This result follows from the structure of optimal choice – decreases in low prices make search more attractive while increases in high prices are irrelevant since no purchase is made at high prices. Analysis of the relationship between the expected number of searches and the distribution of prices is complicated since it depends on the shape of that distribution.

Thus far we have assumed that all stores are ex ante identical; that is, that a choice to search is a choice to draw from the distribution $F(p)$. In many problems one can choose where to search. In that case, one is choosing which distribution $F(p)$ to sample from or, if there are limited draws allowed from a particular distribution, the sequence of distributions from which prices should be sampled. Interestingly, the reservation prices which tell whether to purchase or to sample again from a given distribution also serve to rank distributions.

In the choice problem analysed so far we have used discrete time, with the arrival of one offer in each time period. There are two straightforward generalizations. First, one might have the opportunity to receive more than one offer in any period, with the number of offers received being a function of the chosen level of search costs. In this way one can model the choice of search intensity. Second, the process of attempting to locate stores might have a stochastic rather than a determinate time structure. The simplest such model has the arrival of purchase opportunities satisfying the Poisson distribution law. That is, at any moment of time there is a constant flow probability of an offer arriving, any such offer being an independent draw from the distribution of available prices. Let us denote by a, the arrival rate of these offers; and by c, the constant search cost from being available to receive these offers. Utility is discounted at the constant (exponential) rate r. One can derive the optimal cut-off price and the optimized level of expected utility by analysing the discrete time process as above and passing to the limit. As a more intuitive alternative, let us think of the opportunity to purchase as an asset, where V now represents the value of that asset. The utility discount rate plays the role of an interest rate in asset theory. The asset is priced properly when the rate of discount times the value of the asset equals the expected flow of benefits from holding that asset. The expected flow of benefits is the gain that will come from making a purchase at a price below the cut-off price rather than continuing to search, adjusted for the probability of such an event, less search costs. Thus asset value satisfies

$$rV = a\int_0^{p^*} [U(p) - V]\,\mathrm{d}F(p) - c. \qquad \text{(I–12)}$$

It is worthwhile to make any purchase with a higher utility than that from continued search. Thus the cut-off price satisfies

$$rU(p^*) = a\int_0^{p^*} [U(p) - U(p^*)]\,\mathrm{d}F(p) - c. \qquad \text{(I–13)}$$

Again one can introduce search intensity by having the Poisson arrival rate be a function of the search cost. In the equilibrium discussions below we will use the choice problem in the form (I-13).

So far we have ignored events after a purchase. In the labour setting this is equivalent to the assumption that taking a job is the end of search. In practice individuals frequently shift from job to job with no intervening period of unemployment. One can model job choice recognizing the possibility of continued search while working. Such an analysis must consider the rules that cover compensation between the parties in the event of a quit or firing, with no compensation and compensatory and liquidated damages being the situations analysed in the literature. The search for a better job is only one aspect of turnover. Also, one can model learning about the quality of match in a particular job as a function of the time on the job and the stochastic realization of experience. With a shadow value for quitting to search for a new job, one then has a second aspect of the theory of turnover.

The formulation of job taking given above has been combined with data on individual experience to examine empirically the determinants of the distribution of spells of unemployment. Since this essay focuses on equilibrium and the empirical literature has not examined the determinants of the distribution of opportunities, we do not explore this sizeable and interesting literature, nor the estimates of the effect of unemployment compensation on the distribution of unemployment spells. For an example, see Kiefer and Neumann (1979).

In the model above we have assumed that no additional information is received during the search process. In practice, individuals are simultaneously searching for many different consumer goods and often for jobs and investment opportunities as well. The relations among search processes coming from the arrival of information and the random positions with simultaneous search for many different goods have not been explored in the literature. Focusing on search for a single good, we have added several new factors to the theory of demand, particularly the cost of attempting to purchase elsewhere and the knowledge and beliefs of shoppers about opportunities elsewhere. In practice, these are important determinants of demand.

II EQUILIBRIUM WITH BARGAINING

The theory of choice above is a simple version of the complex problem people face when making decisions about information gathering and purchases over time. That simplicity yields a choice theory that can be embedded in an equilibrium model. To complete an equilibrium model, we need to model the determination of two endogenous variables: the arrival rate of purchase opportunities and the distribution of their prices. In this section, we consider prices that satisfy the bargaining condition of equal division of the gains from trade. In the next section, we consider take-it-or-leave-it prices set by suppliers. In both cases we assume that there are no reputations either of soft bargaining or low price setting that affect the arrival rate of potential customers. We begin by assuming that all buyers are identical and all sellers are identical. This case brings out the role of search in determining the level of prices. Below we consider determinants of the distribution of prices.

Axiomatic bargaining theory relates the terms of trade to the threat points of the two bargainers and the shapes of their utility functions. To avoid complications from the latter, we assume that a single unit is purchased and utility from purchase equals a constant, u_d, minus the price paid. We also assume that each seller has a single unit to sell. The utility from a sale is the price received less the cost of the good, u_s. One might think of this as a homogeneous used car market. To divide equally the gains from trade, the differences between the utility position with the trade and the utility position without it are equalized for the two parties. The value of purchasing at price p is $u_d - p$; expected utility without a trade is V_d, the optimized expected utility from continued search. We restrict ourselves to an economic environment where all trades take place at the same price. With a degenerate distribution of prices, we can rewrite the value equation (I-12) as

$$rV_d = a_d(u_d - p - V_d) - c_d. \qquad \text{(II–1)}$$

For suppliers, the utility from a sale is $p - u_s$. The gain from selling now rather than later is $p - u_s$ less the value of having a car for sale, V_s. The carrying cost of having a car available for sale can be incorporated in the search cost. The value equation for suppliers is

$$rV_s = a_s(p - u_s - V_s) - c_s. \qquad \text{(II–2)}$$

We ignore the sufficient conditions for search to be worthwhile ($V_d, V_s \geqslant 0$).

Equal division of the gains from trade implies

$$u_d - p - V_d = \frac{r(u_d - p) + c_d}{r + a_d}$$

$$= \frac{r(p - u_s) + c_s}{r + a_s} = p - u_s - V_s. \qquad \text{(II–3)}$$

We have assumed the same utility discount rate for both parties. Thus we have a relationship between the equilibrium price, the arrival rates of trading opportunities, the search costs, and the utility from ownership. Solving (II–3) for the equilibrium price, we have:

$$p = \frac{(r + a_s)(ru_d + c_d) + (r + a_d)(ru_s - c_s)}{r(2r + a_s + a_d)}. \qquad \text{(II–4)}$$

Without direct search costs ($c_d = c_s = 0$), the position of the price between the seller's reservation price of u_s and the demander's reservation price u_d depends on the relative ease of finding alternative trading partners. As it becomes very easy to find buyers (a_s becomes infinite), the price goes to u_d. Alternatively, as it becomes very easy to find suppliers (a_d becomes infinite), the price goes to u_s. Furthermore, an increase in one's search cost pushes the price in an unfavourable direction. In this extremely simplified setting, (II-4) brings out the new element that search theory brings to equilibrium analysis, namely the dependence of equilibrium prices on the abilities of traders to find alternatives. Implicit in Walrasian theory is the idea that a perfectly substitutable trade can be found costlessly and instantaneously. In this restricted sense, there is no consumer surplus in a Walrasian equilibrium.

To complete the theory we need to determine the two endogenous arrival rates of trading partners. Assuming a search process without history, these depend on the underlying technology for bringing together buyers and sellers and the stocks of buyers (N_d) and sellers (N_s). We write the arrival rates as $a_d(N_d, N_s)$ and $a_s(N_d, N_s)$. The two arrival rate functions satisfy the accounting identity between the numbers of purchases and of sales:

$$a_d(N_d, N_s)N_d = a_s(N_d, N_s)N_s. \qquad \text{(II–5)}$$

Next, we must examine the determinants of the stocks of buyers and sellers. This theory can be based on the stocks of traders or the flows of new traders. One extreme example is that the steady state stocks of buyers and sellers are exogenous. One then inserts the functions a_d and a_s in the price equation (II–4).

An alternative extreme to perfect inelasticity is the assumption of perfectly elastic supplies of buyers and sellers at given reservation values for search, $\bar{V}_s$ and $\bar{V}_d$. Assuming reservation values that are consistent with the existence of equilibrium with positive trade, the equality of gains from trade (II-3) implies

$$p = \frac{u_d + u_s + \bar{V}_s - \bar{V}_d}{2}. \qquad \text{(II–6)}$$

The numbers of traders actively searching adapts to give this simple formula. Substituting from (II-6) in (II-1) and (II-2) we have the necessary values of a_d and a_s and so two equations for N_s and N_d.

For a market with professional suppliers one can consider the case of inelastic demand ($\bar{N}_d$) and a perfectly elastic supply ($\bar{V}_s$). If we assume further that demanders visit suppliers at a rate and cost independent of the number of suppliers, then a_d and c_d are parameters. Solving (II–3) for p in terms of the exogenous variables we now have

$$p = \frac{(r + a_d)(u_s + \bar{V}_s) + ru_d + c_d}{2r + a_d}. \qquad \text{(II–7)}$$

In this case the response of price to an increase in the cost of the good or the reservation utility of suppliers is $(r + a_d)/(2r + a_d)$, which is less than one. The speed of the search process relative to the interest rate determines the extent to which search equilibrium is different from Walrasian equilibrium. In a labour setting, an analogue to (II-7) shows how unemployment compensation affects wages by changing search costs.

Efficiency. There are two decisions implicit in the model above – whether to enter the search market and whether to accept a particular trade opportunity. The decision to enter a search market, like the choice of search intensity, affects the ease of trade of others. There is nothing in the process that determines prices which reflects the externalities arising from the impact of changed numbers on the opportunities to trade. Thus, in general, equilibrium will not be efficient and one has the possibility of both too much entry and too little entry.

In order to explore the efficiency of the choice of acceptable trades, we need a reason for waiting for a better deal in the future. This can be done by introducing differences in traders or differences in matches between preferences of demanders and goods on sale. However formulated, we have the proposition that the marginally acceptable trade generates no surplus to the two agents making that trade, yet the marginal trade changes the search environment of others. This involves externalities of the same kind as the entry decision already discussed. Again, in general, equilibrium is not efficient.

Individual differences. There are many patterns of differences among demanders in their evaluations of different goods. We explore two simple cases which have been dubbed quality differences and variety differences. With quality differences, all demanders have the same utility evaluation of goods. One asks how the price of a good varies with the quality of the good. With variety differences, all demanders have the same distribution of utility evaluations of the set of goods in the market, but demanders disagree as to which is better. There is then an issue of 'matching' preferences with goods. One asks how the price in a transaction varies with the quality of the match.

We use q as the index of universally agreed on quality, and denote by $p(q)$ the price paid in a transaction for a good of quality q. By suppressing all other differences, we have the same price in all the purchases of a good of any quality. We denote by $V_s(q)$ the optimized net value to a supplier of having a unit of quality q for sale. Paralleling (II-2), we can calculate the net gain to a supplier of selling his unit. This gain, $p(q) - u_s(q) - V_s(q)$, satisfies

$$p(q) - u_s(q) - V_s(q) = \frac{r[p(q) - u_s(q)] + c_s}{r + a_s}. \qquad \text{(II–8)}$$

For the demander, we denote by V_d the value of entering the search market to make a purchase, and by $u_d(q)$ the utility, gross of purchase price, of purchasing a unit of quality q. Paralleling (I-12), the utility discount rate times the value of being a demander is equal to the net flow of gains from search. The gross flow of gains equals the arrival rate of purchase opportunities times the expected gain from a purchase. The expected gain is the utility of buying the good less the price that has to be paid for the good less the shadow value of being a searcher. Denoting the distribution of qualities in a randomly selected trade encounter by $F(q)$, the value of being a demander satisfies

$$rV_d = a_d \int [u_d(q) - p(q) - V_d]\,\mathrm{d}F(q) - c_d. \qquad \text{(II–9)}$$

A full equilibrium analysis of this model would require determination of the distribution $F(q)$ as well as the arrival rates a_d and a_s. $V_s(q)$ would play an important role in determining $F(q)$. Such a model could consider investment in human capital with a search labour market. We will not carry out such an analysis, but focus merely on the relative prices $p(q)$, given a non-degenerate distribution $F(q)$. This problem is kept simple by the uniformity of product evaluations, which results in consumers' purchasing the first unit encountered, just as in the homogeneous case above. In any trade, the gains are shared equally between buyer and seller. Using (II–8) and (II–9) to eliminate V_d and $V_s(q)$ in the equal gain condition (II–3), we have the equilibrium price function

$$(2r + a_s)p(q) = (r + a_s)u_d(q) + ru_s(q) - c_s + (r + a_s) \times \left\{c_d - a_d \int [u_d(z) - p(z)]\,\mathrm{d}F(z)\right\} \Big/ (r + a_d). \qquad \text{(II–10)}$$

This generalization of the homogeneous case, (II–4), shows a price that rises with quality assuming that cost does.

$$p'(q) = \frac{(r + a_s)u_d'(q) + ru_s'(q)}{2r + a_s}. \qquad \text{(II–11)}$$

The speed of search relative to the interest rate determines the magnitude of deviation from the Walrasian result that with identical demanders all transactions give the same utility level $[p'(q) = u_d'(q)]$.

With pure quality differences, all consumers have the same expected utility from search, while suppliers have expected utilities which vary with the quality of goods for sale. In a symmetric variety model, both demanders and suppliers have the same expected utility from search. The variable q now represents the quality determined by the particular match of demander and good. We view the distribution of these qualities, $F(q)$, as given and the same for all demanders and all goods. Implicitly we are assuming random matching between demanders and different goods. It is now the case that a sufficiently poor match will not result in a trade. We denote by $u_d(q)$ the utility evaluation, gross of purchase price, of buying a good, by $u_s(q)$ the cost of supplying a good, and by $p(q)$ the price when the quality of a match is q. The value of search for a supplier satisfies

$$rV_s = a_s \int_{q_1}^{q_2} [p(q) - u_s(q) - V_s]\,\mathrm{d}F(q) - c_s \qquad \text{(II–12)}$$

where q_1 is the lower bound of match qualities at which it is mutually advantageous to carry out a trade. At the lowest acceptable quality, q_1, $p(q_1)$ is equal to $u_s(q_1) + V_s$. The value of search for a demander continues to satisfy (II–9). The assumption that all mutually advantageous trades are taken implies that q_1 also equates the gain from a purchase $u_d(q_1) - p(q_1)$ with the utility from search V_d. Equating the gains from trade for buyer and seller and solving for the price we have

$$2p(q) = u_d(q) + u_s(q) - V_d + V_s. \qquad \text{(II–13)}$$

Price increases with match quality to reflect the changed cost of supply, $u_s'(q)$, plus half the change in surplus, $[u_d'(q) - u_s'(q)]/2$.

Recapitulating our analysis of search equilibrium with bargaining, we have seen two themes. The first is how the search for trading partners introduces an additional element in the determination of trading prices: namely, the relative ease of the two potential trading partners in finding alternative trades. Secondly, the presence of a costly trade coordination mechanism is naturally replete with externalities as the availability of traders affects the trading opportunities of others.

In the model used in this section negotiation is instantaneous while search is slow. A fascinating recent literature explores equilibrium in models where the negotiation process is an explicit game of exchanging bids that can be interrupted by the arrival of an alternative trading partner (cf. Rubinstein and Wolinsky, 1985).

III EQUILIBRIUM WITH PRICE SETTING

In contrast to the bargaining theory used above, we now assume that prices are set on a take-it-or-leave-it basis by suppliers. This rule of (not) bargaining over prices gives the supplier a potential for monopoly power. The search for alternatives limits this monopoly power. The fundamental question is how much. We begin with the assumption that the only source of price information is visiting randomly chosen suppliers sequentially one at a time. We assume many identical suppliers, implying equal profitability of different pricing strategies used in equilibrium. If all buyers have identical positive search costs and identical demand curves that yield a unique profit maximizing price, then the unique equilibrium is the price that would be set by a monopolist. This result assumes a sufficient number of suppliers that buyers will not search for a single low price. This extreme result comes from the uniformity of trading opportunities. The best a buyer can do is wait to make exactly the same deal in the future. Therefore a buyer is always willing to pay a little bit more today than he has to pay in the future. Thus the demand curve for an individual seller coincides with the underlying demand curve in the neighbourhood of the equilibrium price. Even though this result is limited to unrealistic cases, it is interesting that the price is independent of the cost and speed of search, as long as search is not costless and instantaneous.

Given the pervasive reality of price distributions in retail markets, it has been natural for the literature to concentrate on generating equilibria without uniform prices. With differences in demanders, either from differences in underlying characteristics or from differences in their history of past purchases, the equilibrium can involve a distribution of prices and the structure of that distribution will depend upon search costs. In this case, consumers care about the characteristics of other consumers since these characteristics affect price setting behaviour. Similarly, with differences among suppliers the equilibrium price distribution varies with search costs.

Information gathering. When visiting a store is the only way to learn its price, price quotations are gathered one at a time. Separating the gathering of price information from going to stores does not necessarily change the model. If price quotations are still gathered one at a time, the cost of going to purchase the good can be deducted from the utility of acquiring it, leaving the model unchanged. However, the separation of the gathering of information from the collection of goods opens up the possibility of sometimes receiving price quotations one at a time and sometimes two or more at a time. This possibility destroys the single price equilibrium in the model of identical buyers and sellers. To see this result, note that profit per sale is continuous in price but, with uniform prices, the number of sales is discontinuous in price since a slight decrease in price wins all sales when a firm's price is one of two that are learned simultaneously. With positive profit made on each sale it would always pay to decrease price slightly below the uniform price of all other suppliers. With constant costs the competitive price is not a possible equilibrium either since a price increase gains profits when one is the only price quote while losing zero profit sales when one is not the only price quote. Thus there is necessarily a distribution of prices in equilibrium. Without price reputations, a store can choose any price it wants without affecting the flow of information about that store. Therefore, with identical firms the equilibrium will satisfy an equal profit condition. There will be low price high volume stores and high price low volume stores. One way to complete this model is to allow purchasers a choice of intensity of search which stochastically generates varying numbers of price quotations per period. We examine three additional models – price guides, advertising, and word of mouth.

Price guide. In this extension of the model we continue to have consumers seek price information one price at a time. In addition, consumers can purchase a guide to lowest cost shopping, with the purchase cost varying across consumers. A consumer who purchases such a guide is directed to one of the lowest price stores; a consumer who does not, follows the search procedure described above. Assuming free entry of identical firms with U-shaped costs and an equilibrium where some consumers purchase the price guide and some do not but otherwise consumers are identical, we have a two-price equilibrium. Some of the stores set the price at the competitive equilibrium level. These stores sell to all consumers who purchase price information and those sequential shoppers who are lucky enough to find one of these stores on their first shopping visit. The remaining stores have higher prices, equal to the cut-off price for searching consumers or the profit maximizing price for selling to such a consumer, whichever is lower. The fraction of stores of the two kinds and the aggregate quantity of stores per consumer are determined by the zero profit condition for the two pricing strategies. When more consumers purchase the price guide, there will be more stores setting the competitive price and a drop in the cut-off price of searching consumers. This external benefit to searching consumers implies the inefficiency of the original equilibrium. A very slight subsidization of the cost of the price guide involves a second order efficiency cost to the purchase of guides, no effect on firms (which have zero profits), and a first order gain to searching consumers.

Advertising. It is obviously counterfactual to have all the information flows resulting from actions by shoppers. Advertising is a pervasive modern phenomenon. We continue to assume that stores have no price reputations. If the form of advertising is direct communication of prices to individual consumers, we can construct a model that again results in a distribution of prices. Stochastic communication from stores to consumers naturally generates a distribution of the number of price quotes that consumers receive. Any specific model of the stochastic structure of attempted communication will generate a distribution of numbers of price quotes learned by consumers. Free entry then implies a particular equilibrium distribution of prices provided some consumers receive a single price quotation and others receive more than one.

Word-of-mouth. It is natural to model both the seeking of price information and the spreading of price information as costly activities. However, some price information passes between consumers as a costless activity, part of the pleasure of discussing life. The presence of word-of-mouth communication in addition to sequential shopping alters equilibrium. The natural way to model word-of-mouth price communication brings price reputations into the model, since the prices set in one period affect communications about stores in future periods when their prices might be different. In order to isolate the effect of word-of-mouth we consider a very artificial model. Stores set prices which must hold for two periods. Consumers shop in the first or second period but are otherwise identical. In the first period, there is only sequential search, visiting stores one at a time as modelled above. Between the first and second periods there are random contacts between first period shoppers and second period shoppers. In this way, each second period shopper receives information about the price in some positive number of stores. We assume that some people hear of only one store, while others hear of at least two. Then there will be a distribution of prices, with the structure of the distribution depending on the details of the word-of-mouth process. This analysis can be extended by having shoppers tell not only of the prices they paid, but also of prices they have heard from others. Both types of communication require a model of memory. The density of stores has different effects on equilibrium prices for different models of memory. This approach has been used in a setting of search for quality rather than low price to argue that doctors' fees can be higher where there are more doctors per capita (Satterthwaite, 1979).

Recapitulating the analysis of search equilibrium with price setting but not price reputation, we have seen two themes. One is the tendency for even low cost search to generate sizeable amounts of monopoly power because of similar incentives for all suppliers. The second is a tendency for equilibrium to have a distribution of prices. Since price distributions are a widespread phenomena in decentralized economies, it is reassuring that the theory produces such distributions.

IV ADDITIONAL ISSUES

We have considered the search analogue to competitive equilibrium. It was assumed that there were many small firms, whose behaviour was adequately approximated while ignoring their impacts on certain aspects of equilibrium. Search theory has also examined equilibria with small numbers of firms. It may pay a monopolist to have a distribution of prices across his outlets rather than a single price as a method of discriminating among consumers with different search costs, even though the need to search for a low price adds to the cost of purchase of the good (Salop, 1977). In a duopoly or oligopoly setting, it is natural to consider randomized pricing strategies which again give rise to a distribution of prices (Shilony, 1977). This may be one of the many factors that go into the empirical fact of sales by retail outlets.

The technology of shopping in the models above is extremely simple. Little has been done to marry the underlying search issues with some of the realities of the geographic distributions of consumers and firms and the normal travels of shoppers. Similarly, little has been done to model the search basis for the role of intermediaries.

Price reputations. All the models mentioned above omit or severely limit the intertemporal links in profitability that arise from price reputations. This is a major hole in the existing literature. Probably significant progress in this area will have to await the discrimination of cases in which optimal strategies (whether determinate or stochastic) are stationary, from those in which optimal strategies involve building up a reputation which is then run down. In such a setting analysis will be very sensitive to the assumptions made about consumer knowledge both of existing prices and of price strategies followed by firms. It would be nice to have both an empirical evaluation of the level of consumer ignorance about opportunities, and a theoretical structure capable of examining the relationship between equilibrium and the extent to which consumers are accurately informed.

CONCLUSION

Walrasian theory assumes that consumers are perfectly informed about the prices of all commodities in the economy. This assumption is central for the law of one price, that a homogeneous commodity sells at the same price in all transactions in a given market. This assumption is also central for a variety of inequalities on prices, limiting price differences to be less than transportation costs. These inequalities are consequences of the absence of opportunities for arbitrage profits. In order to make a rigorous arbitrage argument, there must be simultaneous purchase and sale of the same commodity at different prices net of transportation costs. If the purchase and sale are at different times, there is likely to be risk for the would-be arbitrageur. Similarly, a proper arbitrage arguments requires homogeneous commodities. It is improper to apply arbitrage arguments to labour markets for example, although migration arguments may lead to similar conclusions. In search theory with a known distribution of prices, there is a cost to finding any trading partner and possibly a large cost to finding one willing to trade at some particular price. This idea captures one aspect of the limitations on the extent of arbitrage arguments.

Realistically, one must recognize that infrequent traders are often ill-informed about the distribution of prices in the market. This introduces two important changes in the basic theory. One is that gathering information changes beliefs about the distribution of prices, as well as revealing the location of possible transactions. The second is the incentive created for sellers to find consumers whose beliefs make them willing to transact at high prices. The differences between the search for suckers and the hunt for the highest value use of resources has not been clearly drawn in the literature, yet this distinction is valid and important for evaluating the functioning of some markets. Search-based theory and empirical work have a long way to go until we have satisfactory answers to a number of allocation questions that are totally ignored in a Walrasian setting. Nevertheless, the theory has already shown how informational realities can seriously alter the conclusions of Walrasian theory.

It would have been highly duplicative to have reviewed search theory of the labour market as well as that of the retail market. For a survey of labour search theory and a partial guide to the literature, see Mortensen (1984). Individual patterns of unemployment spells are the key empirical fact requiring revision of the Walrasian paradigm.

The failure of the profession, thus far, to produce a satisfactory integration of micro and macroeconomics based on the Walrasian paradigm (with or without price stickiness) raises the thought that such an integration might come out of search theory. For a presentation of this view and discussion of some applications of search ideas to macro unemployment issues, see Diamond (1984).

P. DIAMOND

See also ECONOMIC ORGANIZATION AND TRANSACTION COSTS; EXCHANGE.

BIBLIOGRAPHY

Diamond, P. 1984. *A Search-Equilibrium Approach to the Micro Foundations of Macroeconomics.* Cambridge, Mass.: MIT Press.

Kiefer, N. and Neumann, G. 1979. An empirical job search model with a test of the constant reservation wage hypothesis. *Journal of Political Economy* 87, 69–82.

Mortensen, D. 1984. Job search and labor market analysis. In *Handbook of Labour Economics*, ed. R. Layard and O. Ashenfelter, Amsterdam: North-Holland.

Rothschild, M. 1974. Searching for the lowest price when the distribution is not known. *Journal of Political Economy* 82, 689–711.

Rubinstein, A. and Wolinsky, A. 1985. Equilibrium in a market with sequential bargaining. *Econometrica* 53, 1133–50.

Salop, S. 1977. The noisy monopolist: imperfect information, price dispersion and price discrimination. *Review of Economic Studies* 44, 393–406.

Satterthwaite, M. 1979. Consumer information, equilibrium industry price, and the number of sellers. *Bell Journal of Economics* 10(2), 483–502.

Shilony, Y. 1977. Mixed pricing in oligopoly. *Journal of Economic Theory* 14, 373–88.

seasonal variation. When observations are taken at regular intervals within a year (by month or by quarter), most economic time series are likely to exhibit some degree of seasonal variation. An obvious example, known to everyone, is the existence of a 'high' and 'low' season for air transportation and other recreational activities. Perhaps less obvious, but equally important, is the presence of a seasonal pattern in most economic aggregates such as the index of production, price indices, the unemployment rate and so on.

In order to appraise the economic situation and take appropriate action, it is extremely important to be able to 'isolate' or 'extract' the seasonal component from an economic time series. Take, for instance, the case of an increase of one-half of a percentage point in the unemployment rate between two successive quarters. Does not mean that the conditions in the labour market are deteriorating? Not necessarily, if typically between those two quarters of the year the economy experiences a rise in seasonal unemployment. Conversely, the situation may be more alarming than that indicated by the mere increase of one-half of a percentage point if the past record shows a declining rate between the two quarters.

The main difficulty in assessing the seasonal pattern is that an economic time series is the aggregate outcome of many different forces and not simply the result of a pure seasonal movement. Traditionally, in time series analysis, one thinks of an economic time series (E) as being composed of three elements: a seasonal component (S), a trend-cycle component (T) and a residual component (R). The two widely adopted specifications are the linearly additive one ($E = S + T + R$) and the multiplicative one ($E + S \cdot T \cdot R$). In both cases, the seasonal component is intimately tangled with the others and the task of eliminating it from the series (known as the problem of seasonal adjustment) is a delicate one.

Related to the seasonal adjustment problem is the question of how one should estimate an economic relationship in the presence of seasonal data. These two aspects of seasonality are briefly addressed below.

SEASONAL ADJUSTMENT. A seasonally adjusted series is one from which the seasonal component has been removed ($E - S$ and E/S for the additive and multiplicative cases respectively). Two characteristics common to practically all seasonal adjustment procedures may be stressed. Firstly, they all belong to the class of univariate methods, in the sense that each series is adjusted individually. Secondly, they do not offer any real explanation of seasonality, as it is implicitly assumed that the seasonal movement is intrinsic phenomenon governed by the rhythms of nature.

The two most commonly used procedures are the moving average method and the regression method.

THE MOVING AVERAGE METHOD. It is the official method used by most government agencies. The best known variant is the programme X-11 of the US Bureau of Census. In brief (neglecting the complications arising from the treatment of extreme points) it consists of three main steps: (1) a preliminary estimation of the seasonal component; (2) the estimation of the trend-cycle component from the preliminary deseasonalized series; and (3) the final estimation of the seasonal component from the original series from which the trend-cycle has been removed.

In spite of its technical complexity, the moving average method is easy to use (as computer programmes are readily available) and has the great advantage of being able to handle, in an effective way, a changing seasonal pattern. Its major drawback is that, as in the case of all moving average procedures, the results tend to be less reliable at each end of the time series and consequently the most recent data are subject to frequent revisions. To eliminate (or at least attenuate) this adverse effect, it has been proposed to extend the original series at each end by one year by means of an autoregressive moving average process prior to deseasonalizing the series (as in the programme X-11 ARMMI developed by Dagum; see Dagum, 1978).

THE REGRESSION METHOD. Contrary to the moving average method, in which all the three components are implicitly assumed to be stochastic, the regression method is based on the assumption that the seasonal component and the trend component can be represented by deterministic functions of time, the stochastic element being confined to the residual term.

By far the simplest way to model the seasonal component is to use dummy variables. In the case of quarterly data, and neglecting the trend-cycle for the moment, the proper specification reads

$$E_t = a_1 S_{1t} + a_2 S_{2t} + a_3 S_{3t} + a_4 S_{4t} + u_i$$

where s_{it}, $i = 1, \ldots, 4$, are the four dummies, one for each season and u_t represents the residual. The seasonal coefficients a_i are estimated by the least squares method. The above specification implies a constant seasonal pattern, but more complex items of seasonal variation can be contemplated. Furthermore, to account for the trend-cycle, we can easily add to the above equation to the term bt (where t represents time) or a higher polynomial expression in t.

The regression method does have some appeal to economists because it satisfies some simply consistency requirements that might reasonably be expected from a seasonal adjustment procedure (sum preserving, orthogonality and idempotency, see Lovell, 1963). In addition, it is extremely easy to implement.

ESTIMATION OF ECONOMIC RELATIONSHIPS WITH SEASONAL DATA. Two options are available to the econometrician interested in the estimation of economic relations in the presence of seasonal data: the use of seasonally adjusted series for all the relevant variables or, alternatively, the use of the original series accompanied by the explicit inclusion in the relation of a time function representing the seasonal pattern (such as seasonal dummy variables).

Although there is still lack of consensus concerning the most suitable technique for handling seasonal movements, many economists prefer the second alternative on the ground that the seasonal adjustment procedure applied individually to each variable eliminates too much variability from the underlying economic phenomena. However, when seasonal adjustment is performed by regression methods, the above two alternatives produce exactly the same results (Lovell, 1963).

PIETRO BALESTRA

BIBLIOGRAPHY

Dagum, E.B. 1978. Modelling, forecasting and seasonally adjusting economic time series with the X-11-ARIMA method. *The Statistician* 27 (3,4) 203–16.

Lovell, M.C. 1963. Seasonal adjustment of economic time series and multiple regression analysis. *Journal of the American Statistical Association* 58(304), 993–1010.

second best. One of the passages most often quoted in the literature on economic policy is the following from a seminal paper by R.G. Lipsey and K. Lancaster (1956, p. 11):

> The general theorem for the second best optimum states that if there is introduced into a general equilibrium system a constraint which prevents the attainment of one of the Paretian conditions, the other Paretian conditions, although still attainable, are, in general, no longer desirable.

The implication of this theorem was that most of the simple and general guidelines for policy provided by welfare economics – e.g. the 'Paretian conditions' stating that price should equal marginal cost – would not be relevant for real-world economies which are likely to be subject to constraints on policy. The Lipsey–Lancaster article seems to have come as a shock to economists in general and has since had a significant impact on the theory, and practice, of economic policy. Apparently, until the publication of this article, the conventional wisdom was that it was desirable to pursue a 'piecemeal policy', here and there fulfilling the 'Paretian conditions' – which, if applied everywhere, would lead to a Pareto optimum – regardless of whether these conditions actually were attained elsewhere.

This state of affairs in 1956 was somewhat puzzling considering that the Lipsey–Lancaster conclusion was not entirely novel. As early as 1909, V. Pareto himself had argued that free trade (which in modern terminology may be interpreted as fulfillment, as far as possible, of the 'Paretian conditions') may not be preferable to protection and that individuals may not end up in a better position if one of several distortions to resource allocation were eliminated. Both of these arguments are in line with the general theory of second best. Even closer to the Lipsey–Lancaster result was the statement by Paul Samuelson in his *Foundations* (1947, p. 252) that a 'given divergence in a subset of the optimum conditions necessitates alterations in the remaining ones'.

Second best reasoning had also been prevalent in various areas of applied welfare economics. (For reviews using different perspectives, see Lipsey and Lancaster, 1956; Negishi, 1972; and McKee and West, 1981.) Thus, concerning *optimal pricing* in the presence of monopolies and other forms of imperfect competition, Hicks (1940) had argued that price equal to marginal cost in an industry A is not compatible with efficiency if other industries B are not competitive. As marginal inputs in A at the expense of B are then worth more than is reflected by input prices, the marginal cost confronting A is less than the true social marginal cost and therefore unsuitable as a benchmark for the price in this industry.

Early 'second best results' had also been obtained in *public finance*. For example, given that leisure is untaxable, ordinary income taxation cannot be considered more efficient than indirect taxation of one commodity, as in both cases at least one 'Paretian condition' (that between commodities and leisure vs. that between the commodity subject to an indirect tax and the other commodities, respectively) is violated. Hence, it is an open question which tax system is the better of these two imperfect alternatives (Little, 1951). Somewhat later, it was shown that a 'second best optimal' way of raising a given amount of government revenue, barring the use of lump-sum taxes, was a set of unequal indirect taxes with low tax rates on commodities which are substitutes for leisure and high tax rates on commodities complementary to leisure (Corlett and Hague, 1953). In fact, a similar result had already been obtained by Ramsey in 1927. These cases clearly illustrate that when all 'Paretian conditions' cannot be met, it may not be efficient to fulfil some of them.

The field of *trade policy* had been especially rich in providing examples of second best reasoning. Viner (1950) showed that in a world of trade protection, a reduction of some trade barriers or introduction of a customs union for some of the trading countries – both of which constitute steps towards free trade and the fulfillment of some of the 'Paretian conditions' – will not necessarily increase efficiency in world production. In the customs union case, the explanation is that the positive welfare effect of trade creation within the union may be outweighed by the negative welfare effect of trade diversion between member countries and the rest of the world.

Meade (1955a, 1955b) dealt with a number of trade policy problems as well as some domestic policy problems where it would not be possible to reach a Pareto optimum – or Utopian optimum, as he tellingly called it. Assuming the existence of several market imperfections and efficiency-distorting policy interventions, he analysed the effect of reducing or eliminating one of them and tried to determine what policy rule would perform better. Meade coined the term 'theory of second best' for this type of policy analyses whose real-world relevance and basic similarities were elucidated especially in his *Trade and Welfare* (1955a).

In retrospect, it may be argued that the catalogue of separate but similar policy issues in distorted economies provided by Meade goes as far as the theory of second best has reached. But Lipsey and Lancaster were the ones who put second best problems on the map of the average economist. This was accomplished by their attempt to present a general theory of second best, covering the main characteristics of the particular cases dealt with by Meade and others up to that point. Although their 1956 article contained a number of comments on these particular cases as well as reservations on their general theory, it was their concise version of this theory that gained most of the attention.

The Lipsey–Lancaster General Theorem of the Second Best departs from 'the typical choice situation in economic analysis' where an objective function $F(x_1, \ldots, x_n)$ is to be maximized or minimized subject to a constraint $\Phi(x_1, \ldots, x_n) = 0$. Lipsey and Lancaster called the solution to this problem the Paretian optimum. To make the problem explicitly harmonize with what is generally meant by a Paretian optimum, we may interpret $x_1, \ldots, x_n$ as the elements of the consumption vectors of all individuals in the economy in some given order (x_1 being Alpha's consumption of commodity I, x_2 Alpha's consumption of commodity II, etc., up to x_n, the last individual's consumption of the last commodity). As in most of the literature on the subject, we assume for simplicity that the objective function reveals an interest in efficiency alone (i.e. attaining any Pareto optimum) and not in distribution (i.e. one particular Pareto optimum).

Optimizing $F(\ )$ subject to $\Phi(\ ) = 0$, where Φ can be seen as the transformation function specifying the constraint given by available technology and initial resources, we get the following necessary optimum conditons (assuming that all functions are well behaved):

$$F_i/F_n = \Phi_i/\Phi_n \qquad i = 1, \ldots, n-1 \tag{1}$$

These 'Paretian conditions' – or first best Pareto optimum conditions as they are now commonly called – may be interpreted as requiring equality between the marginal rates of substitution and the marginal rates of transformation. The purpose of deriving these conditions in the present context, it should be stated explicitly, is (a) to check whether they are fulfilled in a particular situation and, if they are not, (b) to provide guidelines for policy.

Lipsey and Lancaster then tried to formulate an additional constraint which would cover most of what the literature had observed as obstacles to achieving a first best Pareto optimum. They attempted to accomplish this about as generally as when the function Φ is taken to represent the production constraint of the economy. They argued that, if for some reason monopoly elements, externalities or other so-called imperfections were 'out of bounds' for policy intervention, one of the conditions (1) could not be fulfilled due to a constraint

$$F_1/F_n = k\Phi_i/\Phi_n \tag{2}$$

with $k \neq 1$ and k – 'for simplicity' – assumed to be constant. The resulting problem amounts to the optimization of the Lagrangean function

$$F - \lambda\Phi - \mu(F_1/F_n - k\Phi_1/\Phi_n) \tag{3}$$

where λ and μ are Lagrangean multipliers. A solution to this problem, it should be noted, is also a Pareto optimum as it does not allow anyone to become better off without making someone else worse off, given the two constraints now in force. The necessary optimum conditions can be written

$$\frac{F_i}{F_n} = \frac{\Phi_i + (\mu/\lambda)(Q_i - kR_i)}{\Phi_n + (\mu/\lambda)(Q_n - kR_n)}, \qquad i = 2, \ldots, n-1 \tag{4}$$

where

$$Q_i = (F_n F_{1i} - F_1 F_{ni})/F_n^2 \quad \text{and} \quad R_i = (\Phi_n \Phi_{1i} - \Phi_1 \Phi_{ni})/\Phi_n^2.$$

Aside from some special cases (see below), this means that, in second best optimum, $F_i/F_n \neq \Phi_i/\Phi_n$, from which follows the theorem quoted in the introduction.

These second best optimum conditions are obviously quite complicated – in fact, so complicated that in many cases a great deal of detailed information would be required even to determine the signs of the second derivatives F_{ni}, Φ_{ni}, etc. Hence, it would often be impossible to know whether in second best optimum $F_i/F_n > \Phi_i/\Phi_n$ or the opposite. Moreover, it is no longer possible to translate the second best optimum conditions into intuitively simple relationships between price and marginal cost, which was true for (some of) the first best optimum conditions (Eq. 1).

The great impact of this result on economists in general must be attributed to the simplicity of the theorem itself, given that, in essence, the same thing had been said on earlier occasions. A large part of the ensuing debate concerned whether this simplicity was warranted by real-world conditions. In particular, (a) the origin and form of the additional constraint were questioned. A second dominating issue in the debate concerned (b) the complexity of the rules for second best policy and attempts at identifying important cases where simple first best optimum conditions are still valid in second best situations. We deal with these two issues in turn.

THE NATURE OF THE ADDITIONAL CONSTRAINT. In regard to the alleged generality of the formulation of the Lipsey–Lancaster theory, the question was asked: What exactly does this constraint (2) stand for? Clearly, the optimization problem in the 'second best literature' refers to a national government *or* an independent unit of government (such as a public monopoly) which operates as if it tried to optimize function F. Obviously, the government-unit perspective (represented for example, by, the work of Davis and Whinston (1965, 1967) and developed by McFadden (1969)) could allow a number of constraints like (2) concerning variables that are out of reach for this unit. But, what about additional constraints imposed on the overall allocation problem confronting the *national government*? Here, two interpretations have been considered in the literature.

First, for an initial state of the economy in which one of the conditions (1) is violated, it may be *technically* impossible for the government to have this condition fulfilled along with all the others. For example, markets for certain commodities such as specific kinds of insurance may not be possible to introduce or may be too costly to administer. Or it may be impossible or prohibitively expensive to correct for certain externalities or instances of imperfect competition. Likewise, when the government, in an attempt to attain a feasible Pareto optimum, needs to raise money for subsidies or for the production of public goods, there may not be any nondistortive taxation scheme available (note e.g. the 'impossibility' of taxing leisure assumed above).

It should be noted that constraints of this technical type are irremovable, in the same way that the constraint imposed by the transformation function is irremovable. Thus, if a market economy does not by itself reach a first best Pareto optimum, the government could not reach one either when policy constraints of this type are strictly binding. Then, a Lipsey–Lancaster Paretian optimum does not exist and the only optimum conceivable is in fact what has here been called a second best optimum (see, e.g., McKee and West, 1981).

Second, the constraint (2) can be interpreted as a *behavioural* constraint on policy, reflecting the fact that certain measures, although technically speaking feasible and in principle capable of removing the restraint, are not at the government's disposal or just not believed to be so. For example, tha law may prohibit or delimit the use of a specific policy instrument. Or the government may have other and hierarchically higher goals than Pareto optimality: it may for example, simply dislike nationalization of certain industries. Or the government may want to avoid the use of a policy for 'political reasons', believing, for example, that it would lose the next election if this policy was used. Traditions, idiosyncrasies etc. could play a similar role. Economists who have paid attention to the origin of constraints like (2) seem to have adhered primarily to this 'behavioural' interpretation.

Obviously, the 'behavioural' type of constraint need not be such that all policies with the same effects on the objective function are restrained to the same extent. (For a different perspective which holds that constraints are or should be, in some narrow sense, 'rational', see Faith and Thompson (1981).) For example, assume that there are two policy instruments, say, a tax and a regulation, each of which, if unconstrained, would have attained the first best, as k could then be made equal to one, but that policy now is constrained so that just one of them is ruled out. If so, a constraint of type (2) would not exist. This means that, in general, it is not possible to presume what constraints on policy instruments imply in terms of the relations between endogenous variables such as the marginal rates of transformation and substitution in (2). (Actually, the literature has not been able to present any great number of cases where policy constraints yield an expression like (2) with k constant and not equal to one.) Instead, to obtain a solution to the allocation problem, it must be specified exactly what the actual constraints on policy instruments are, i.e., to what domain or what combinations with other instruments or variables each policy instrument is restricted.

Specifying the policy constraints in this way has some important implications for a general theory of second best (McManus, 1959, 1967; Bohm, 1967).

First, it cannot be known beforehand whether policy constraints prevent the attainment of a first best optimum or not.

Second, the actual impact of policy constraints, including now also the technical ones mentioned earlier, will depend on the actual behavioural properties of the agents operating in the market economy. Thus, actual rules of market behaviour would, at least in principle, have to be added as constraints on the objective function along with the constraints on policy.

Third, the many possible forms of the policy constraints imply that there cannot be any *general* second best optimum conditions in the sense that there exist general first best optimum conditions (when no policy constraints exist) in terms of a specific relationship between marginal rates of substitution and marginal rates of transformation. In fact, constraints on policy instruments will require that the optimum-feasible solution be derived directly in terms of optimum-feasible values for the policy instruments. Thus, there would not even be any role for policy guidelines in the form of second best conditions such as (4). This, of course, does not preclude the existence of special cases, which *ex post* turn out to coincide with the Lipsey–Lancaster formulation. These are the cases where the constraint on policy happened to affect only the relationship between one marginal rate of substitution and one marginal rate of transformation exactly in the way specified by (2), with no impact whatsoever on the use of policy instruments that could influence other such rates in the economy.

Given that additional constraints on the allocation problem can have any shape – with (2) being a possible *ex post* formulation of one of many special cases – the use of the term 'second best' becomes somewhat unclear: Should a *second best problem* be defined as an allocation problem with constraints on policy regardless of whether a first best optimum will turn out to be impossible? Or should it be reserved for such problems where analysis will eventually show that a first best optimum cannot be reached? Although the second alternative is in line with the intended problem formulation in Lipsey–Lancaster, it is obviously inconvenient as it cannot be used until after the problem has been solved. The term *second best optimum*, on the other hand, is predominantly used for a constrained optimum not equal to a first best optimum and is not likely to cause much of a problem. Hence, a practical, and nowadays probably the dominant, terminology is to distinguish between first best and second best problems according to the first-mentioned definition, where a second best problem may have a first best *or* a second best optimum solution.

FIRST BEST RULES FOR SECOND BEST PROBLEMS. To deal with the second issue prominent in the literature on second best, we return to the problem as it was formulated by Lipsey and Lancaster. They had argued that second best conditions, in contrast to first best ones, were so complicated and required so much information that, on this account, the conditions could not be used for practical policy. This spurred a number of economists to undertake a rescue operation, in which they tried to show that in many instances the simple first best conditions would still be relevant for the controllable part of the economy. To the extent this was true, it would restore at least part of the relevance of piecemeal policy, i.e., policy guided by principles which are unaffected by the exact nature of the circumstances in the uncontrollable part of the economy.

First, it has been pointed out that first best rules may be optimal even with the particular Lipsey–Lancaster formulation of the second best problem, e.g. when $Q_i - kR_i = Q_j - kR_j = 0$; $i, j = 2, \ldots, n$; $i \neq j$ (see Santoni and Church, 1972; Dusansky and Walsh, 1976; Rapanos, 1980). Similar special cases may be found for other forms of additional constraints on the objective function (Mishan, 1962).

Second, and of more general interest for practical policy, it was pointed out that if the additional constraints affect only a limited set of markets in the economy, the relation between this sector and the remaining 'perfectly controllable' sector may be such that first best conditions are optimal in the latter sector even when they turn out to be unattainable in the former sector. This must be true, of course, if the two sectors are completely independent of each other with different primary inputs, no input deliveries between the sectors and different final consumers. Approximately the same results hold if interdependence between sectors is negligible, for example due to one of the sectors being relatively small (Mishan, 1962).

Other attempts at identifying similar cases of separability have been made without much success in terms of general and easily applicable principles for ascertaining when the first best optimum conditions that are still attainable should in fact be attained. Moreover, the very idea of identifying two sectors, one of which is imperfectly controllable, has appeared to be less and less attractive as a description of the real world. Instead, in most countries, income taxes, distorting institutional rules and regulations, etc. emerge as irremovable constraints affecting the economy as a whole. Moreover, as the typical allocation problems confronting real-world governments are beset with a multitude of policy constraints – technical as well as behavioural – it is only by pure chance that optimum conditions for the irrelevant first best problem can be found to be a priori relevant. This does not mean, of course, that first best optimum conditions never will *turn out* to be valid in second best optimum or that information may not be so inadequate that these conditions appear to be acceptable as a rule of thumb (see Ng, 1977).

Thus, the outcome of the literature on general second best theory up to this point is disillusioning in several respects. There do not seem to be any *general* second best problems of the type formalized by Lipsey and Lancaster, much less any general second best optimum *conditions*. Granted that there remains some disagreement on the purpose of second best theory, what has emerged from the literature by way of a general description of second best problems can be summarized as follows:

All economies – even real-world centrally planned economies – have at least some (most often, a very large number of) given behaviour functions which contribute to determining the outcome of any policy 'intervention'. Hence, these functions must be observed in the formulation of the allocation problem; or, which is the same thing, they must be included as constraints on the optimization of the objective function. 'At the same time, the authorities have at their command a set of policy instruments which enter these functions as arguments. The optimum is then found by [optimizing the objective function] subject to all the constraints over the domain of these instruments. Indeed the whole problem has little practical interest without some such explicit policy formulation' (McManus, 1967, p. 321). The fact that this is a highly demanding analytical task in actual practice requires simplifications and approximations of the models to be used, but it cannot justify an oversimplification of the actual problem to be tackled.

This in effect may seem to take us back to the case-by-case approach of applied welfare economics that was used by Meade and others in the beginning of the 1950s (represented in later and technically more elaborate studies by e.g. Boiteux, 1956; Rees, 1968; and Guesnerie, 1975). However, matters have changed in one important respect since then. Much more empirical knowledge is now available concerning behaviour of individual markets which in itself improves the outlook for practical second best policy.

This is not to say that attempts to construct a general theory of second best have not made a significant contribution to economic theory and policy. Should one result be highlighted, it may quite likely be the general theorem of second best as quoted in the introduction. If nothing else, this theorem has probably made economists more careful when providing governments with policy prescriptions.

PETER BOHM

See also MARGINAL COST PRICING; OPTIMAL TARIFFS; PARETO EFFICIENCY.

BIBLIOGRAPHY

Allingham, M. and Archibald, G.C. 1975. Second best and decentralisation. *Journal of Economic Theory* 10(2), April, 157–73.

Boadway, T.J. and Harris, R. 1977. A characterisation of piecemeal second best policy. *Journal of Public Economics* 8(2), October, 169–90.

Bohm, P. 1967. On the theory of 'second best'. *Review of Economic Studies* 34, July, 301–14.

Boiteux, M. 1956. Sur le gestion des monopoles publics astreints à l'équilibre budgetaire. *Econometrica*. Translated into English as: On the management of public monopolies subject to budgetary constraints, *Journal of Economic Theory* 3(3), September 1971, 219–40.

Corlett, W.J. and Hague, D.C. 1953. Complementarity and the excess burden of taxation. *Review of Economic Studies* 21(1), 21–30.

Davis, O.A. and Whinston, A.B. 1965. Welfare economics and the theory of second best. *Review of Economic Studies* 32, January, 1–14.

Davis, O.A. and Whinston, A.B. 1967. Piecemeal policy in the theory of second best. *Review of Economic Studies* 34, July, 323–31.

Dusansky, R. and Walsh, J. 1976. Separability, welfare economics, and the theory of second best. *Review of Economic Studies* 43(1), February, 49–51.

Faith, R. and Thompson, E. 1981. A paradox in the theory of second best. *Economic Enquiry* 19(2), April, 235–44.

Guesnerie, R. 1975. Production of the public sector and taxation in a simple second best model. *Journal of Economic theory* 10(2), April, 127–56.

Hatta, T. 1977. A theory of piecemeal policy recommendations. *Review of Economic Studies* 44(1), February, 1–21.

Hicks, J.R. 1940. The rehabilitation of consumers' surplus. *Review of Economic Studies* 8, February, 108–16.

Kawamata, K. 1977. Price distortion and the second best optimum. *Review of Economic Studies* 44(1), February, 23–29.

Lipsey, R.G. and Lancaster, K. 1956. The general theory of second best. *Review of Economic Studies* 24(1), October, 11–32.
Little, I.M.D. 1951. Direct versus indirect taxes. *Economic Journal* 61, September, 577–84.
McFadden, D. 1969. A simple remark on the second best Pareto optimality of market equilibria. *Journal of Economic Theory* 1(1), June, 26–38.
McKee, M. and West, E.G. 1981. The theory of second best: a solution in search of a problem. *Economic Inquiry* 19(3), July, 436–48.
McManus, M. 1959. Comments on the general theory of second best. *Review of Economic Studies* 26, June, 209–24.
McManus, M. 1967. Private and social costs in the theory of second best. *Review of Economic Studies* 34, July, 317–21.
Meade, J.E. 1955a. *Trade and Welfare, [including the] Mathematical Supplement*. London, New York: Oxford University Press.
Meade, J.E. 1955b. *The Theory of Customs Unions*. Amsterdam: North-Holland.
Mishan, E.J. 1962. Second thoughts on second best. *Oxford Economic Papers* 14, October, 205–17.
Negishi, T. 1972. *General Equilibrium and International Trade*. Amsterdam, North-Holland.
Ng, Y.K. 1977. Towards a theory of third-best. *Public Finance* 32(1), 1–15.
Pareto, V. 1909. *Manuel d'Economie Politique*. Paris: Girard et Brière.
Ramsey, F.P. 1927. A contribution to the theory of taxation. *Economic Journal* 37, March, 47–61.
Rapanos, V.T. 1980. A comment on the theory of second best. *Review of Economic Studies* 47(4), 817–19.
Rees, R. 1968. Second-best rules for public enterprise pricing. *Economica* 35, August, 260–73.
Samuelson, P.A. 1947. *Foundations of Economic Analysis*. Cambridge, Mass.: Harvard University Press.
Santoni, G. and Church, A. 1972. A comment on the general theorem of second best. *Review of Economic Studies* 39(4), October, 527–30.
Sontheimer, K.C. 1971. An existence theorem for the second best. *Journal of Economic Theory* 3(1), March, 1–22.
Viner, J. 1950. *The Customs Union Issue*. New York: Carnegie Endowment for International Peace; London: Stevens & Sons.

Secrétan, Charles (1815–1895). Secrétan was professor of philosophy in the university of Lausanne, and as a philosopher was held in high repute. His great work, *La Philosophie de la Liberté* (1849), seeks to reconcile reason and religious faith, by showing that the fundamental dogmas of Christianity are the best philosophic explanation of the origin and destiny of man.

As he grew older Secrétan turned his attention to social problems, and devoted himself wholly to these; the reference to him in these pages is taken only from this point of view.

Of his writings on this subject *Civilisation et Croyance* (1887) was the earliest. This treated the question from the side of philosophy. It was followed by more works in a more popular style in rapid succession. *Les droits de l'humanité* (1890); *Études sociales* (1891); *Mon Utopie* (1892). Secrétan was an advocate of liberty and opposed to Collectivism, but he did not rank himself as one of the adherents of the Manchester School. While he held that, in principle, liberty should be the only solution of the social question; he also held that in practice this is impossible, because the economic order now existing *is not the product of liberty*. He considered the land as a usurped possession, and that this usurpation – justified as it was in some respects by the advantage resulting to the community – still required as just compensation the recognition of the right of the needy for assistance. He regarded property and the system of labourers' working for hire, etc., as institutions which drew their historical origin from the abuse of the right of the strongest. Hence these cannot be considered as the ultimate stage in human progress, and it becomes necessary to modify the social organization from its base to bring it into conformity with justice. As Secrétan would not permit, even in order to attain these ends, that anything contradictory to justice should be employed, because 'good that is obtained by coercion is no longer good', there are no other means but free association, cooperation, and profit-sharing.

This shows that the doctrines which Secrétan held were very close to those of the Christian Socialists, who, during the 19th century, had so large a share in the cooperative movement in England, and of those who at the present time advocate the nationalization of the land. Secrétan, however, gave this theory a more original and a more solid character by basing it on solidarity and by showing that solidarity is the real basis of Christianity. Even allowing for the apologetic character of this doctrine, it has none the less exercised a considerable influence over the younger school of economists who take solidarity for their motto.

[C. GIDE]

Reprinted from *Palgrave's Dictionary of Political Economy*.

security, national. *See* ARMS RACES; DEFENCE, ECONOMICS OF.

Seers, Dudley (1920–1983). Seers was educated at Rugby and Pembroke College, Cambridge, and served in the Royal Navy during World War II. Once the war was over he joined the Prime Minister's Office in New Zealand, but by 1946 had moved to Oxford. He became a leading economist in the field of development studies, moving from his early work in statistics and national income to a wide range of topics in development and an extraordinary diversity of country studies. In his later work he turned back to the problems of developed countries, in two major edited volumes on the European Economic Community. His claim was one that increasingly finds echo: the study of the underdeveloped world provides much insight into the structural problems of the developed countries.

Perhaps his outstanding characteristic as an economist, apart from exceptional professional competence, was his passionate concern that the subject should deal with people and real issues, fearlessly crossing discipline boundaries if necessary. His instinctive ability to see the subject in the terms of people is apparent in his first book, written while at the Institute of Statistics, Oxford, in the 1940s. Discussing the difficulty of assessing shifts in income distribution, he wrote:

> one may find a wage-earner with a large family in a council house who was unemployed before the war and has enjoyed a great rise in living standard. His brother may be an engine driver and vegetarian, who has been forced to rent furnished rooms and can afford much less pipe tobacco than he could in 1939 (Seers 1949, p. 3).

These interests led him naturally to the 'structuralist' school when he worked at the UN and in 1957–61 for the UN Economic Commission for Latin America. In 1962 he published what was to become a seminal article in the structuralist view of inflation: an eloquent and precise presentation of the view that inflation results not from monetary expansion but from rigidities inherent in the economic, social and political system (Seers, 1962). As the structuralists became more radical, and the 'dependency' school emerged, Seers was a sympathetic critic, insisting in his edited volume in 1981 that its insights were real and important: it 'raises the right questions – much more relevant ones than those derived from neo-classical economics' (Seers, 1981).

This preoccupation with 'the right questions' runs through his writing, and led to his best-known articles: those on methodology and the development of the discipline. Although not a writer where it is easy to identify 'seminal contributions', his role as *agent provocateur* was truly original and of great value. In this way the same personality trait that led him to list his recreation in *Who's Who*, as 'teasing bureaucrats' led him to provoke and stimulate also at a professional level. In 'The Limitations of the Special Case' in 1963, he argued that the corpus of economic theory is in fact based on the special case; the few highly industrialized economies comprising a small minority of the world population. His analysis of 'the typical case', the unindustrialized economy, although dated by now, remains a prophetic statement of the need for a different 'text book economics' more helpful to teachers, students and practitioners in LDCs. The challenge is unmet more than twenty years later.

In addition to his stimulating role as a persistent questioner, he was also a careful empirical economist, as witnessed in the thoroughness of his many country studies, including his book on Cuba, edited in 1964 with Richard Jolly and for some years the only serious and accessible study in English of the Cuban economy, and the ILO report on employment in Colombia, of which he was the chief author.

His desire to link academic thinking and the real world led him to become also an institution builder – first at the new Ministry of Overseas Development established in 1964 where with Barbara Castle as Minister and Andrew Cohen as Permanent Secretary he shaped the new Ministry's work, and subsequently as the first Director of the Sussex Institute of Development Studies. He was Director 1967–72 and a Fellow till his death. He played a major role in establishing the international reputation of the IDS and in leading the effort to link academics and policy advice.

The willingness to step into 'real life' was reflected also in his work as Chairman of the World University Service Awards for Chile (1974–8), following the collapse of Allende's government and the ensuing wave of refugees to the UK.

Dudley Seers died in 1983 at the age of 62, in the midst of continued productive work: he had just arrived in Washington to edit for the World Bank a series of papers by 'pioneers' in development thinking.

ROSEMARY THORP

SELECTED WORKS

1949. *The Levelling of Incomes since 1938*. Oxford: Basil Blackwell.

1962. Inflation and growth: a summary of experience in Latin America. UNECLA, *Economic Bulletin for Latin America* 7, February 23–51.

1963. The limitations of the special case. *Bulletin of the Oxford University Institute of Economics and Statistics* 25(2), May, 77–98.

1981. *Dependency Theory: a Critical Reassessment*. London: Frances Pinter.

segmented labour markets. Segmented labour markets may refer to descriptive features of labour markets or to theoretical models of the processes and outcomes of labour market behaviour. This entry emphasizes the latter, but the two aspects of the term are not neatly separable. In its descriptive uses segmentation may refer to industries, geographic areas, or to such demographic characteristics of workers as gender or race.

The term 'segment' may be usefully viewed as resting somewhere between the neutral 'separate' and the more highly charged 'stratified'. Neoclassical economists (a term used in this entry as a convenient synonym for 'conventional' or 'orthodox' economists) often discuss separate labour markets, as when they describe or analyse the market for college-trained workers and the market for unskilled labour. Stratification is a term in contemporary sociology, but when it refers to occupations it coincides with usage in economics, and the sociological concept of class stratification in industrialized societies is derived from the classical economists' three groups of the factors of production: workers, capitalist-entrepreneurs, and landowners. In modern usage in economics, the concept of segmented labour markets is imbued with more theoretical content when it moves closer to stratification and takes on political and sociological connotations.

No single theory and no single taxonomy of descriptive classification dominates the literature dealing with segmented labour markets (see Note on the Bibliography at the end of the entry). The widely used term 'dual labour market' has been referred to as a metaphor for unnumbered (but few) segments by Michael J. Piore, one of its principal advocates (Berger and Piore, 1980, pp. 2, 142), and such terms as tripartite, hierarchical, tiers, cores, peripheries, and radical abound. The only pervasive theoretical posture is that of dissent from neoclassical theories of the labour market, and segmented labour market theories are sometimes a part of radical or Marxian economics, which is a broader alternative to neoclassical economic analysis.

The first and second editions of *Palgrave's Dictionary of Political Economy* (1894–7 and 1926) contain no entries for such terms as segmented, radical, dual, or internal labour markets. *The International Encyclopedia of the Social Sciences* (1967 edition) has an entry for just one of these terms, 'dual economy' (Werthheim, 1967), and this refers solely to preindustrialized economies that fail to achieve sustained economic growth because of stagnation in a dominant peasant (or traditional) sector. Segmented labour market theories continue to play a role in the field of development economics, but they usually apply to the industrialized or urban sectors of high-income economies.

Are there, then, new ideas in the theories of segmented labour markets? It is no disservice to their contemporary advocates to claim that there are not, and that the original editions of *Palgrave* address the major problems posed in the literature on segmented labour markets. There is merit in giving old ideas fresh and insightful applications in new settings.

Inequality is the dominant problem that motivates the analysis and policy prescriptions in the literature on segmented labour markets; specifically, inequality in wages and working conditions among various occupational, industrial, and demographic groups. To understand the segmentationists' approach to this problem, it is useful to consider the modern neoclassical restatement of the five sources of wage inequality that were originally advanced by the classical economists.

1. Compensating differentials, the theory of which is found in Chapter 10 of Adam Smith's *Wealth of Nations*, and which allow for non-pecuniary aspects of work as equilibrating sources of wage differences.

2. Human capital investments, which, although recognized already by Smith, have become increasingly important and can explain how wage differentials that are associated with different age-earnings profiles among workers can coexist with identical lifetime present values of the workers' earnings.

3. Barriers to entry in certain protected, high-paying

occupations, wherein the barriers may be well-defined labour market institutions – such as trade unions or governmental regulation and licensing – or in the form of the amorphous barriers of, historically, class distinctions and class deprivation, and of, in modern times, racial, ethnic, and gender discrimination in labour markets (discussed below).

4. Transitory differentials that reflect chance factors, lags in mobility, and temporary gains or losses because of seasonal and cyclical variation in demand conditions, often associated with temporary unemployment.

5. Real differences that are in accordance with differences in preferences and abilities among workers.

John Stuart Mill ([1848], 1900, pp. 369–77) and also his follower, John E. Cairnes (1874, pp. 65–8), who coined the term 'noncompeting groups', dismissed item 1 in criticizing Smith, remarking that allowances for non-pecuniary aspects of employment would increase overall inequality in the labour market, even though the principle of compensating differentials was valid within narrow strata of skill levels. They stressed, as do the segmentation theorists, item 3, barriers to mobility. Both neoclassical and segmentation economists give attention to the institutional barriers created by certain practices of trade unions and by various laws that regulate entry and conditions of work in certain industries and occupations. The segmentationists generally have a different political and ideological interpretation of these practices, viewing them as manifestations of an employer-dominated political system that seeks to pit one group of workers against another.

Class stratification was emphasized by Mill, Cairnes, and Alfred Marshall as a deeply rooted barrier to mobility and as a source of intergenerational transmission of poverty. Marshall spoke of the inability of the poorer classes to invest 'capital in the rearing and early training' of their children because of the parents' limitations in 'resources ..., power of forecasting the future, and ... willingness to sacrifice themselves for the sake of their children' (Marshall [1890], 1959, pp. 467–8). Nevertheless, Marshall was characteristically optimistic about the uplifting and egalitarian results from publicly supported education and technological progress – the latter which would not only raise total wealth and reduce drudgery but facilitate the mobility of workers among industries and occupations (Marshall [1890], 1959, pp. 176–82, 214–19, 476).

Economists from all schools of thought recognize that the class stratifications producing much of today's inequality are often based on ethnic divisions and associated historical circumstances, such as the legacy of slavery among blacks in the United States or the lower economic status of immigrant groups, particularly coloured immigrants, throughout Western Europe. In addition, the unequal status of men and women in the labour market is a contemporary concern and controversy.

There is little dispute about the descriptive facts of differential wages and earnings between men and women, white and coloured groups, and certain other ethnic groups. However, the analysis of labour market discrimination, which has been abundant by both neoclassical and segmentation economists, epitomizes the latter's dissenting theories. Using a research methodology that draws primarily upon historical, institutional, and case-study materials, the segmentation economists emphasize the roles of technology, the shaping of attitudes and preferences, and certain features of bureaucratic organization – aspects of labour markets that neoclassical economists tend to place in the background.

Technology is viewed as an instrument of employers to dilute or make obsolete the skills of workers, thereby diminishing the workers' bargaining power (Braverman, 1974). This Marxian view derives consequences for inequality that are obviously the reverse of Marshall's. A second and less sinister role of technology is to necessitate within-firm, 'internal' labour markets. The complexity of modern technology and the large size of firms require firm-specific on-the-job training, internal promotion ladders, and a stable and loyal work-force. Wage rates are higher in these large and technologically advanced firms, initially to ensure a large pool of applicants and eventually as a reflection of training, tenure, and promotions. The wage rates, which tend to be rigid, are attached to jobs, not to workers.

On the supply side of the market, workers form queues for these jobs in the 'primary sector' and are selected on the basis of their trainability and future loyalty. The employers will tend to choose (discriminate) in favour of men, who are viewed as traditional career-committed workers, and in favour of workers with similar ethnic or cultural backgrounds as those of the managerial class. The rejected applicants (or non-applicants) obtain jobs in the 'secondary' or 'informal' sector, to use terms that refer to the dual labour market.

Each of the two sectors influences the worker's preferences, attitudes, and habits in ways that reinforce and shape the long-run progress, or lack thereof, of the worker's career. In the secondary sector, low wages, the lack of upward mobility, and instability in tenure – exacerbated by enervating periods of unemployment – have negative feedback effects on the worker's attitudes towards work and training. Preferences are, therefore, endogenous. The contrast with the typical neoclassical paradigm is evident, and the issue is important. Consider the problem of determining whether unemployment, or the receipt of public assistance (the 'dole'), or an initial experience of working in a 'dead-end job' has an important effect on a worker's future earnings. A change in the worker's attitudes and habits is one of several possible explanations for such an effect. Whether this explanation is admissible in neoclassical theories of labour market behaviour is less important than the formidable empirical task of ascertaining causality in these chains of events.

A dynamic model of mutual causation between tastes and labour market outcomes is unusual, but it is not a new idea. It was proposed by Gunnar Myrdal in his analysis of economic discrimination against blacks in the United States (1944, pp. 75–8, 1065–70). Two problems with its application may be responsible for its subsequent neglect. The model's dynamic properties appear to lead to explosive results which are not observed empirically. A second, related objection is that the model appears to offer implausibly easy solutions, in the form of positive interventions that set in motion the dynamics of continual progress.

Attention to institutional features of employer–employee relations and the internal labour markets of firms have also appeared in the neoclassical literature. In *Human Capital* (1964), Gary S. Becker developed theoretical models of general and firm-specific on-the-job training that provided a rigorous neoclassical explanation for internal labour markets. Becker's work shows, incidentally, that a variety of shapes of age-earnings profiles – flat to steeply rising – are perfectly consistent with neoclassical models of the investment in human capital. The flat profile is not a challenge to neoclassical theory, as some segmentationists imply, but Mill's challenge of 140 years ago remains: reconciling neoclassical models of competitive markets with persistent differences in the present values of career earnings among workers of comparable abilities and preferences.

The firm as an internalizing agent for various externalities in workers' cooperation, mutual training, and tenure longevity is another old idea in economics. A recent neoclassical application, with abundant citations, is that of Oliver E. Williamson (1975), who argues that such institutional devices as implicit contracts, collective bargaining, internal promotion ladders, and seniority rights are economically efficient when jobs and workers are heterogeneous and idiosyncratic.

A fixed structure of wages for jobs, which is emphasized by segmentation economists, is descriptively accurate and useful for analysing short-run behaviour, but even in the short run a human capital model of supply-side productivity traits can explain the match of workers to a hierarchy of wage-fixed jobs. In the long run the human capital model can explain changes in workers' productivity traits, and neoclassical models generally would predict changes in the structure of both jobs and wages.

A discussion of empirical work and policy issues concerning segmented labour markets is beyond the scope of this entry (see the bibliography below). It should be stated, however, that the sometime claim that the neoclassical economists ignore the demand side of the market in policy discussions is unfounded.

That labour market outcomes and processes are complex and controversial is evident in the intellectual legacy of the above-listed five sources of inequality. The criticisms and empirical work of the segmented labour market economists have added to this legacy, but they, like the earlier dissenters, the Marxists and the Institutionalists, remain on the bank of the mainstream.

GLEN G. CAIN

BIBLIOGRAPHY

The literature on segmented labour markets is extensive and diversified, and there are disputes about who are the leading theorists and which are the landmark articles. These characteristics make it difficult to provide a brief bibliography. In addition to the items cited in the text, several survey articles and books contain lengthy bibliographies: Taubman and Wachter (1986); Gordon, Edwards and Reich (1982); Wilkinson (1981); Cain (1976). The application of segmented labour market theories to development economics is not, however, covered in these sources, and the author is unaware of any survey or bibliographic sources for this application.

Becker, G.S. 1964. *Human Capital*. New York: Columbia University Press for the National Bureau of Economic Research.

Berger, S. and Piore, M.J. 1980. *Dualism and Discontinuity in Industrial Societies*. Cambridge: Cambridge University Press.

Braverman, H. 1974. *Labor and Monopoly Capital*. New York: Monthly Review Press.

Cain, G. 1976. The challenge of segmented labor market theories to orthodox theory: a survey. *Journal of Economic Literature* 14(4), December, 1215–57.

Cairnes, J.E. 1874. *Some Leading Principles of Political Economy*. New York: Harper & Brothers.

Gordon, D.M., Edwards, R.C. and Reich, M.S. 1982. *Segmented Work, Divided Workers: The Historical Transformation of Labor in the United States*. Cambridge: Cambridge University Press.

Marshall, A. [1890] 1959. *Principles of Economics*. 8th edn, London: Macmillan.

Mill, J.S. [1848] 1900. *The Principles of Political Economy*, Vol. 1. Revised edn, The World's Greatest Classics, New York: Colonial Press.

Myrdal, G. 1944. *An American Dilemma*. New York: Harper & Row.

Taubman, P. and Wachter, M.L. 1986. Segmented labor markets. In *Handbook of Labor Economics*, ed. O. Ashenfelter and R. Layard, Amsterdam: Elsevier Science Publishers.

Werthheim, W.F. 1967. Economy, dual. In *International Encyclopedia of the Social Sciences*, Vol. 4, New York: Macmillan and Free Press, 495–500.

Wilkinson, F. (ed.) 1981. *The Dynamics of Labor Market Segmentation*. New York: Academic Press.

Williamson, O.E. 1975. *Markets and Hierarchies: Analysis and Antitrust Implications*. New York: Free Press.

seigniorage. Full-bodied monies such as gold coin contain metal approximately equal in value to the face value of the coin. Under the gold standard, metal could be brought to the mint and freely coined into gold, less a small *seigniorage* charge for the privilege. Subsidiary or token coin and paper money by contrast cost much less to produce than their face value. The excess of the face value over the cost of production of currency is also called *seigniorage*, because it accrued to the *seigneur* or ruler who issued the currency, in early times.

The use of paper money instead of full-bodied coin by modern governments generates a very large social saving in the use of the resources that would otherwise have to be expended in mining and smelting large quantities of metal. The value of this seigniorage can be measured by considering the aggregate demand curve for currency, as a function of the rate of interest. The area under this demand curve represents the aggregate flow of social benefits from holding currency, under certain assumptions. The social cost of holding currency is measured by the opportunity cost of the resources it takes to produce the currency. If gold were used for currency, its opportunity cost would be measured by the rate of interest that could be earned on those resources if transferred to some other use. Thus the area under the demand curve between the market rate of interest and the cost of providing paper currency represents the flow of seigniorage or social saving that accrues from the use of paper currency instead of gold.

In the international monetary system, gold remains a very large fraction of total holdings of international reserves (about 45 per cent of total reserves valued at market prices at the end of March 1985). Substitution of fiduciary reserve assets such as Special Drawing Rights created by the International Monetary Fund or United States dollars for gold would generate a substantial social gain in the form of seigniorage equal to the excess of the opportunity cost of capital over the costs of providing the fiduciary asset. If interest is paid to the holders of the reserve asset, the seigniorage is split between the issuer and the holder.

The existence of these large seigniorage gains is what led to the development of the gold exchange standard, under which first British sterling, before World War II, and since then United States dollars and other currencies have substituted for gold in international reserve holdings. As interest rates paid on these reserve assets have risen, more of the seigniorage has accrued to holders of reserve assets.

Further substitution of fiduciary reserve assets for gold in the international monetary system has frequently been suggested, and the Second Amendment to the Charter of the International Monetary Fund adopted in 1978 proposed such a goal. Little progress has been made, however, since the underlying issue is one of trust in the financial probity of the issuer and its continued political stability, as well as its continued willingness to convert reserve assets into usable currencies over long periods of time.

S. BLACK

selection. *See* COMPETITION AND SELECTION.

selection bias and self-selection. The problem of selection bias in economic and social statistics arises when a rule other than simple random sampling is used to sample the underlying population that is the object of interest. The distorted representation of a true population as a consequence of a sampling rule is the essence of the selection problem. Distorting selection rules may be the outcome of decisions of sample survey statisticians, self-selection decisions by the agents being studied or both.

A random sample of a population produces a description of the population distribution of characteristics that has many desirable properties. One attractive feature of a random sample generated by the *known rule* that all individuals are equally likely to be sampled is that it produces a description of the population distribution of characteristics that becomes increasingly accurate as sample size expands.

A sample selected by any rule not equivalent to random sampling produces a description of the population distribution of characteristics that does not accurately describe the true population distribution of characteristics no matter how big the sample size. Unless the rule by which the sample is selected is known or can be recovered from the data, the selected sample cannot be used to produce an accurate description of the underlying population. For certain sampling rules, even knowledge of the rule generating the sample does not suffice to recover the population distribution from the sampled distribution.

This entry defines the problem of selection bias and presents conditions required to solve the problem. Examples of various types of commonly encountered sampling frames are given and specific economic selection mechanisms are presented. Assumptions required to use selected samples to determine features of the population distribution are discussed.

The analytical framework developed to understand the inferential problems raised by selection bias is also fruitful in understanding the economics of self-selection. The prototypical choice theoretic model of self-selection is that of Roy (1951). In his model, agents choose among a variety of discrete 'occupational' opportunities. Agents can pursue only one 'occupation' at a time. While every person can, in principle, do the work in each 'occupation', at least at some level of competence, self-interest drives individuals to choose that 'occupation' which produces the highest income (utility) for them. As in the statistical selection bias problem, there is a latent population (of skills). Observed (utilized) skill distributions are the outcome of a selection rule by agents. The relationship between observed and latent skill distributions is of considerable interest and underlies recent work on worker hierarchies (see Willis and Rosen, 1979). The 'occupations' can be: (a) market work or non-market work (b) unemployed and searching or working at the offered wage (c) working in one province or working in another, or (d) any choice among a set of mutually exclusive opportunities.

Because the insights in the Roy model underly much recent research, we present a brief exposition of it and demonstrate how it can be or has been fruitfully extended to a variety of settings. An important issue, closely linked to the problem of identifying population parameters from selected sample distributions, is the empirical content of economic models of self-selection and worker hierarchies. Are they artefacts of distributional assumptions for unobservable skills or are they genuine behavioural hypotheses?

1. A DEFINITION AND SOME EXAMPLES OF SELECTION BIAS

Any selection bias model can be described by the following set-up. Let $\mathbf{Y}$ be a vector of outcomes of interest and let $\mathbf{X}$ be a vector of 'control' or 'explanatory' variables. The population distribution of $(\mathbf{Y}, \mathbf{X})$ is $F(\mathbf{y}, \mathbf{x})$. To simplify the exposition we assume that the density is well defined and write it as $f(\mathbf{y}, \mathbf{x})$.

Any sampling rule can be interpreted as producing a non-negative weighting function $\omega(\mathbf{y}, \mathbf{x})$ that alters the population density. Let $(\mathbf{Y}^*, \mathbf{X}^*)$ denote the sampled random variables. The density of the sampled data $g(\mathbf{y}^*, \mathbf{x}^*)$ may be written as

$$g(\mathbf{y}^*, \mathbf{x}^*) = \omega(\mathbf{y}^*, \mathbf{x}^*)\mathbf{f}(\mathbf{y}^*, \mathbf{x}^*) / \int \omega(\mathbf{y}^*, \mathbf{x}^*) f(\mathbf{y}^*, \mathbf{x}^*)\, \mathrm{d}\mathbf{y}^*\, \mathrm{d}\mathbf{x}^* \quad (1.1)$$

where the denominator of the expression is introduced to make the density $g(\mathbf{y}^*, \mathbf{x}^*)$ integrate to one as is required for proper densities.

Alternatively, the weight may be defined as

$$\omega^*(\mathbf{y}^*, \mathbf{x}^*) = \frac{\omega(\mathbf{y}^*, \mathbf{x}^*)}{\int \omega(\mathbf{y}^*, \mathbf{x}^*)\mathbf{f}(\mathbf{y}^*, \mathbf{x}^*)\, \mathrm{d}\mathbf{y}^*\, \mathrm{d}\mathbf{x}^*}$$

so that

$$g(\mathbf{y}^*, \mathbf{x}^*) = \omega^*(\mathbf{y}^*, \mathbf{x}^*) f(\mathbf{y}^*, \mathbf{x}^*). \quad (1.2)$$

Sampling schemes for which $\omega(\mathbf{y}, \mathbf{x}) = 0$ for some values of $(\mathbf{Y}, \mathbf{X})$ create special problems. For such schemes, not all values of $(\mathbf{Y}, \mathbf{X})$ are sampled. Let indicator variable $i(\mathbf{x}, \mathbf{y}) = 0$ if a potential observation at values $\mathbf{y}, \mathbf{x}$ cannot be sampled and let $i(\mathbf{y}, \mathbf{x}) = 1$ otherwise. Let $\Delta = 1$ record the occurrence of the event 'a potential observation is sampled, i.e. the value of $\mathbf{y}, \mathbf{x}$ is observed' and let $\Delta = 0$ if it is not. In the population, the proportion that is sampled is

$$\Pr(\Delta = 1) = \int i(\mathbf{y}, \mathbf{x}) f(\mathbf{y}, \mathbf{x})\, \mathrm{d}\mathbf{y}\, \mathrm{d}\mathbf{x}. \quad (1.3)$$

while

$$\Pr(\Delta = 0) = 1 - \Pr(\Delta = 1).$$

For samples in which $\omega(\mathbf{y}, \mathbf{x}) = 0$ for a non-negligible proportion of the population $(\Pr(\Delta = 0) > 0)$, it is clarifying to consider two cases. A *truncated sample* is one for which $\Pr(\Delta = 1)$ is not known and cannot be consistently estimated. For such a sample, (1.1) is the density of all of the sampled $\mathbf{Y}$ and $\mathbf{X}$ values. A *censored sample* is one for which $\Pr(\Delta = 1)$ is known or can be consistently estimated. The sampling rule in this case is such that values of $\mathbf{y}, \mathbf{x}$ for which $\omega(\mathbf{y}, \mathbf{x}) = 0$ are not known but it is known whether or not $i(\mathbf{y}, \mathbf{x}) = 0$ for all values of $\mathbf{Y}, \mathbf{X}$. In this case it is notationally convenient to define $(\mathbf{Y}^*, \mathbf{X}^*) = (\mathbf{0}, \mathbf{0})$ for values of $\mathbf{y}, \mathbf{x}$ such that $\omega(\mathbf{y}, \mathbf{x}) = i(\mathbf{y}, \mathbf{x}) = 0$. Such a definition is innocuous provided that in the population there is no point mass (concentration of probability mass) at $(\mathbf{0}, \mathbf{0})$. (Any value other than $(\mathbf{0}, \mathbf{0})$ can be selected provided that there is no point mass at that value). Given $\Delta = 0$, the distribution of $\mathbf{Y}^*, \mathbf{X}^*$ is

$$G(\mathbf{y}^*, \mathbf{x}^*) = 1 \quad \text{for} \quad \Delta = 0$$

at

$$\mathbf{Y}^* = \mathbf{0} \quad \text{and} \quad \mathbf{X}^* = \mathbf{0}.$$

The joint density of $\mathbf{Y}^*, \mathbf{X}^*, \Delta$ for the case of a censored sample is obtained by combining (1.1) and (1.3). Thus

$$g(\mathbf{y}^*, \mathbf{x}^*, \delta) = \left[\frac{\omega(\mathbf{y}^*, \mathbf{x}^*) f(\mathbf{y}^*, \mathbf{x}^*)}{\int \omega(\mathbf{y}^*, \mathbf{x}^*) f(\mathbf{y}^*, \mathbf{x}^*)\, \mathrm{d}\mathbf{y}^*\, \mathrm{d}\mathbf{x}^*}\right]^{\delta} \times \left[\int i(\mathbf{y}, \mathbf{x}) f(\mathbf{y}, \mathbf{x})\, \mathrm{d}\mathbf{y}\, \mathrm{d}\mathbf{x}\right]^{\delta} \times [1]^{1-\delta} \left[\int (1 - i(\mathbf{y}, \mathbf{x})) f(\mathbf{y}, \mathbf{x})\, \mathrm{d}\mathbf{y}\, \mathrm{d}\mathbf{x}\right]^{1-\delta}. \quad (1.4)$$

The first term on the right-hand side of (1.4) is the conditional density of $\mathbf{Y}^*, \mathbf{X}^*$ given $\Delta = 1$. The second term is the probability that $\Delta = 1$. The third term is the conditional density of $\mathbf{Y}^*, \mathbf{X}^*$ given $\Delta = 0$. This density assigns unit mass to $\mathbf{y}^* = 0, \mathbf{x}^* = \mathbf{0}$ when $\Delta = 0$. The fourth term is the probability that $\Delta = 0$. Notice that in the case in which $\omega(\mathbf{y}, \mathbf{x}) > 0$ for all $\mathbf{y}, \mathbf{x}, \Delta = 1$ and (1.4) is identical to (1.1).

In a random sample $\omega(\mathbf{y}^*, \mathbf{x}^*) = 1$ (and so $\omega^*(\mathbf{y}^*, \mathbf{x}^*) = 1$). In a selected sample, the sampling rule weights the data differently. Values of $(\mathbf{Y}, \mathbf{X})$ are over-sampled or under-sampled relative to their occurrence in the population. In the case of truncated samples, the weight is zero for certain values of the outcome.

In many problems in economics, attention focuses on $f(\mathbf{y}|\mathbf{x})$, the conditional density of $\mathbf{Y}$ given $\mathbf{X} = \mathbf{x}$. In such problems knowledge of the population distribution of $\mathbf{X}$ is of no direct interest. If samples are selected solely on the $\mathbf{x}$ variables ('selection on the exogenous variables'), $\omega(\mathbf{y}, \mathbf{x}) = \omega(\mathbf{x})$ and there is no problem about using selected samples to make valid inference about the population conditional density. This is so because in the case of selection on the exogenous variables

$$g(\mathbf{y}^*, \mathbf{x}^*) = f(\mathbf{y}^*|\mathbf{x}^*)\frac{\omega(\mathbf{x}^*)f(\mathbf{x}^*)}{\int \omega(\mathbf{x}^*)f(\mathbf{x}^*)\,\mathrm{d}\mathbf{x}}$$

and

$$g(\mathbf{x}^*) = \frac{\omega(\mathbf{x}^*)f(\mathbf{x}^*)}{\int \omega(\mathbf{x}^*)f(\mathbf{x}^*)\,\mathrm{d}\mathbf{x}^*}.$$

Thus

$$g(\mathbf{y}^*|\mathbf{x}^*) = \frac{g(\mathbf{y}^*, \mathbf{x}^*)}{g(\mathbf{x}^*)} = f(\mathbf{y}^*|\mathbf{x}^*).$$

For such problems, sample selection distorts inference only if selection occurs on $\mathbf{y}$ (or $\mathbf{y}$ and $\mathbf{x}$). Sampling on both $\mathbf{y}$ and $\mathbf{x}$ is termed *general stratified sampling*.

From a sample of data, it is not possible to recover the true density $f(\mathbf{y}, \mathbf{x})$ without knowledge of the weighting rule. On the other hand, if the weighting rule is known $(\omega(\mathbf{y}^*, \mathbf{x}^*))$, the density of the sampled data is known $(g(\mathbf{y}^*, \mathbf{x}^*))$, the support of $(\mathbf{y}, \mathbf{x})$ is known and $\omega(\mathbf{y}, \mathbf{x})$ is nonzero, then $f(\mathbf{y}, \mathbf{x})$ can always be recovered because

$$\frac{g(\mathbf{y}^*, \mathbf{x}^*)}{\omega(\mathbf{y}^*, \mathbf{x}^*)} = \frac{f(\mathbf{y}^*, \mathbf{x}^*)}{\int \omega(\mathbf{y}^*, \mathbf{x}^*)f(\mathbf{y}^*, \mathbf{x}^*)\,\mathrm{d}\mathbf{y}^*\,\mathrm{d}\mathbf{x}^*} \qquad (1.5)$$

and by hypothesis both the numerator and denominator of the left-hand side are known. From the requirement that $(\mathbf{y}^*, \mathbf{x}^*)$ has a well defined density

$$\int f(\mathbf{y}^*, \mathbf{x}^*)\,\mathrm{d}\mathbf{y}^*\,\mathrm{d}\mathbf{x}^* = 1.$$

Integrating the left-hand side of (1.5) it is possible to determine $\int \omega(\mathbf{y}^*, \mathbf{x}^*)f(\mathbf{y}^*, \mathbf{x}^*)\,\mathrm{d}\mathbf{y}^*\,\mathrm{d}\mathbf{x}^*$ and hence to use (1.5) to recover the population density of the data.

The requirements that (a) the support of $(\mathbf{y}, \mathbf{x})$ is known and (b) $\omega(\mathbf{y}, \mathbf{x})$ is nonzero are not innocuous. In many important problems in economics requirement (b) is not satisfied: the sampling rule excludes observations for certain values of $\mathbf{y}, \mathbf{x}$ and hence it is impossible without invoking further assumptions to determine the population distribution of $(\mathbf{Y}, \mathbf{X})$ at those values. If neither the support nor the weight is known, it is impossible, without invoking strong assumptions, to determine whether the fact that data are missing at certain $\mathbf{y}, \mathbf{x}$ values is due to the sampling plan or that the population density has no suport at those values. We now turn to some specific sampling plans of interest in economics.

Example 1. Data are collected on incomes of individuals whose income Y exceeds a certain value c (for cutoff value). The rule is to observe Y if $Y > c$. Thus $\omega(y) = 1$ if $y > c$ and $\omega(y) = 0$ if $y \leqslant c$. Because the weight is zero for some values of y, we know that knowledge of the sampling rule does *not* suffice to recover the population distribution. From a random sample of the entire population, the social scientist knows or can consistently estimate (a) the sample distribution of Y above c and (b) the proportion of the original random sample with income below c ($F(c)$ where F is the distribution function of Y). The social scientist does not observe values of Y below c.

In this example, observed income is a *truncated random variable*. The point of truncation is c. The *sample* of observed income is said to be *censored*. If the proportion of the original random sample with income below c is not known and cannot be consistently estimated, the *sample* is *truncated*. In a truncated sample, nothing is known about the proportion of the underlying population that can appear in the sample. A sample is truncated only if $\omega(\mathbf{y}) = 0$ for some intervals of $\mathbf{y}$ (for $\mathbf{y}$ continuous) or if $\omega(\mathbf{y}) = 0$ at values of $\mathbf{y}$ at which there is finite probability mass. In a censored sample, the proportion of the underlying population that can appear in the sample is known, at least to an arbitrarily high degree of approximation, as sample size increases.

Let $Y^* = Y$ if $Y > c$. Define $Y^* = 0$ otherwise (the choice of the value for Y^* when Y is not observed is inessential and any value can be used in place of 0 provided that the true distribution places no mass at the selected value). Define an indicator variable $\Delta = 1$ if $Y > c$. $\Delta = 0$ otherwise. Then the distribution of Y^* is

$$G(y^*|Y > 0) = F(y^*|Y > c) = F(y^*|\delta = 1)$$
$$= \frac{F(y^*)}{1 - F(c)}, y^* > c. \qquad (1.6a)$$

$$G(y^*|Y^* > 0) = 1 \quad \text{for} \quad Y^* = 0\,(\Delta = 0). \qquad (1.6b)$$

Observe that (1.6a) is obtained from (1.1) by setting $\omega(y^*) = 1$ if $y > c$, and $\omega(y^*) = 0$ otherwise, and integrating up with respect to y^*. The distribution of Δ is

$$\mathrm{pr}(\Delta) = [1 - F(c)]^{\delta}[F(c)]^{1-\delta}.$$

The joint distribution of (Y^*, Δ) is

$$F(y^*, \delta) = F(y^*|\delta)\Pr(\delta)$$
$$= \left\{\frac{F(y^*)}{(1 - F(c))}\right\}^{\delta}[1 - F(c)]^{\delta}(1)^{1-\delta}[F(c)]^{1-\delta}$$
$$= [F(y^*)]^{\delta}[F(c)]^{1-\delta}. \qquad (1.7)$$

Note that (1.7) is obtained from (1.4) by setting $\omega(y) = 0, y < c, \omega(y) = 1$ otherwise, by setting $i(y) = \omega(y)$, and by integrating up with respect to y^*. For normally distributed Y, (1.7) is the 'Tobit' distribution.

The difference between the information in a truncated sample and the information in a censored sample is encapsulated in the contrast between (1.6a) and (1.7). Clearly there is more information in a censored sample than in a truncated sample because one can obtain (1.6a) from (1.7) (by conditioning on $\Delta = 1$) but not vice versa.

Inferences about the population distribution based on assuming that $F(y^*|Y > c)$ closely approximates $F(y)$ are potentially very misleading. A description of population income inequality based on a subsample of high income people may convey no information about the true population distribution.

Without further information about F and its support, it is not possible to recover F from $G(y^*)$ from either a censored or a truncated sample. Access to a censored sample enables the analyst to recover $F(y)$ for $y > c$ but obviously does not provide any information on the shape of the true distribution for values of $y \leqslant c$.

This problem is routinely 'solved' by assuming that F is of a known functional form. This solution strategy does not always work. If F is normal, then it can be recovered from a censored or truncated sample (Pearson, 1901). If F is Pareto, F cannot be recovered from either a truncated or a censored sample (see Flinn and Heckman, 1982). If F is real analytic (i.e. possesses derivatives of all order) and the support of Y is known, then F can be recovered (Heckman and Singer, 1985).

Example 2. Expand the discussion in the previous example to a linear regression setting. Let

$$Y = \mathbf{X}\boldsymbol{\beta} + U \tag{1.8}$$

be the population earnings function where Y is earnings, $\mathbf{X}$ is a regressor vector assumed to be distributed independently of mean zero disturbance U. '$\boldsymbol{\beta}$' is a suitably dimensioned parameter vector. Conventional assumptions are invoked to ensure that ordinary least squares applied to a random sample of earnings data consistently estimates $\boldsymbol{\beta}$.

Data are collected on incomes of persons for whom Y exceeds c. Again the weight depends solely on y, i.e. $\omega(y, \mathbf{x}) = 0, y \leqslant c, \omega(y, \mathbf{x}) = 1, y > c$. The social scientist knows or can consistently estimate (a) the sample distribution of Y above c (b) the sample distribution of the $\mathbf{X}$ for Y above c and (c) the proportion of the original random sample with income below c. The social scientist does not observe values of Y below c.

As before, let $Y^* = Y$ if $Y > c$. Define $Y^* = 0$ otherwise. $\Delta = 1$ if $Y > c, \Delta = 0$ otherwise. The probability of the event $\Delta = 1$ given $\mathbf{X} = \mathbf{x}$ is

$$\begin{aligned}\Pr(\Delta = 1 \mid \mathbf{X} = \mathbf{x}) &= \Pr(Y > c \mid \mathbf{X} = \mathbf{x}) \\ &= \Pr(Y > c - \mathbf{x}\boldsymbol{\beta} \mid \mathbf{X} = \mathbf{x}).\end{aligned}$$

Invoking independence between U and $\mathbf{X}$ and letting F_u denote the distribution of U,

$$\Pr(\Delta = 1 \mid \mathbf{X} = \mathbf{x}) = 1 - F_u(c - \mathbf{x}\boldsymbol{\beta}) \tag{1.9a}$$

and

$$\Pr(\Delta = 0 \mid \mathbf{X} = \mathbf{x}) = F_u(c - \mathbf{x}\boldsymbol{\beta}). \tag{1.9b}$$

The distribution of Y^* conditional on $\mathbf{X}$ is

$$\begin{aligned}G(y^* \mid Y > \mathbf{0}, \mathbf{X} = \mathbf{x}) &= F(y^* \mid X = x, Y > c) \\ &= F(y^* \mid \mathbf{X} = \mathbf{x}, \Delta = 1) \\ &= \frac{F_u(y^* - \mathbf{x}\boldsymbol{\beta})}{1 - F_u(c - \mathbf{x}\boldsymbol{\beta})}, \quad y^* > c.\end{aligned} \tag{1.10a}$$

$$G(y^* \mid Y \leqslant 0) = 1 \quad \text{for} \quad Y^* = 0\ (\Delta = 0). \tag{1.10b}$$

The joint distribution of (Y^*, Δ) given $\mathbf{X} = \mathbf{x}$ is

$$\begin{aligned}F(y^*, \delta \mid \mathbf{X} = \mathbf{x}) &= F(y^* \mid \delta, \mathbf{x}) \Pr(\delta \mid \mathbf{x}) \\ &= \{F_u(y^* - \mathbf{x}\boldsymbol{\beta})\}^{\delta} \{F_u(c - \mathbf{x}\boldsymbol{\beta})\}^{1-\delta}.\end{aligned} \tag{1.11}$$

In particular,

$$\begin{aligned}E(Y^* \mid \mathbf{X} = \mathbf{x}, \Delta = 1) &= \mathbf{x}\boldsymbol{\beta} + E(U \mid \mathbf{X} = \mathbf{x}, \delta = 1) \\ &= \mathbf{x}\boldsymbol{\beta} + \int_{c - \mathbf{x}\boldsymbol{\beta}}^{\infty} \frac{z \, \mathrm{d}F_u(z)}{(1. - F_u(c - \mathbf{x}\boldsymbol{\beta}))}\end{aligned} \tag{1.12}$$

where z is a dummy variable of integration. In contrast, the population mean regression function is

$$E(Y \mid \mathbf{X} = \mathbf{x}) = \mathbf{x}\boldsymbol{\beta}. \tag{1.13}$$

The contrast between (1.12) and (1.13) is illuminating. Many behavioural theories in social science produce empirical counterparts of (1.8) with population conditional expectations like (1.13). Such theories sometimes restrict the signs, permissible values and other relationships among the coefficients in $\boldsymbol{\beta}$. When the theoretical model is estimated on a selected sample ($\Delta = 1$), the true conditional expectation is (1.12) not (1.13). The conditional mean of U depends on $\mathbf{x}$. In terms of conventional omitted variable analysis, $E(U \mid \mathbf{X} = \mathbf{x}, \Delta = 1)$ is omitted from the regression. Since this term is a function of $\mathbf{x}$ it is likely to be correlated with $\mathbf{x}$. Least squares estimates of $\boldsymbol{\beta}$ obtained on selected samples which do not account for selection are biased and inconsistent.

To illustrate the nature of the bias, it is useful to draw on the work of Cain and Watts (1973). Suppose that X is a scalar random variable (e.g. education) and that its associated coefficient is positive ($\beta > 0$). Under conventional assumptions about U (e.g. mean zero, independently and identically distributed and distributed independently of X), the population regression of Y on X is a straight line. The scatter about the regression line and the regression line are given in Figure 1. When $Y > c$ is imposed as a sample inclusion requirement, lower population values of U are excluded from the sample in a way that systematically depends on x. ($Y > c$ or $U > c - x\beta$). As x increases, the conditional mean of $U[E(U \mid X = x, \Delta = 1)]$ decreases. Regression estimates of β that do not correct for sample selection (i.e. include $E(U \mid X = x, \Delta = 1)$ as a regressor) are downward biased because of the negative correlation between x and $E(U \mid X = x, \Delta = 1)$. See the flattened regression line for the selected sample in Figure 1.

In models with more than one regressor, no sharp result on the sign of the bias in the regression estimate that results from ignoring the selected nature of the sample is available except when the $\mathbf{X}$ variables are from certain distributions (e.g. normal, see Goldberger, 1983). None the less, the key result – that conventional least squares estimates of $\boldsymbol{\beta}$ obtained from selected samples are biased and inconsistent remains true.

As in example 1, it is fruitful to distinguish between the case of a truncated sample and the case of a censored sample. In the truncated sample case, no information is available about the fraction of the population that would be allocated to the truncated sample [$\Pr(\Delta = 1)$]. In the censored sample case, this

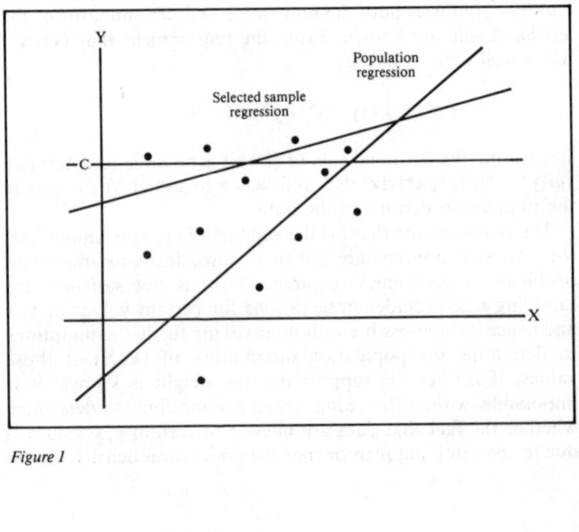

Figure 1

fraction is known or can be consistently estimated. In the censored sample case it is fruitful to distinguish two further cases: (a) the case in which $\mathbf{X}$ is not observed when $\Delta = 0$ and (b) the case in which it is. Case (b) is the one most fully developed in the literature (Heckman and MaCurdy, 1981).

Note that the conditional mean $E(U|\mathbf{X} = \mathbf{x}, \Delta = 1)$ is a function of $c - \mathbf{x}\boldsymbol{\beta}$ solely through $\Pr(\Delta = 1|\mathbf{x})$. Since $\Pr(\Delta = 1|\mathbf{x})$ is monotonic in $c - \mathbf{x}\boldsymbol{\beta}$, the conditional mean depends solely on $\Pr(\Delta = 1|\mathbf{x})$ and the parameters F_u i.e. since

$$F_u^{-1}(1 - \Pr(\Delta = 1|\mathbf{x})) = c - \mathbf{x}\boldsymbol{\beta},$$

$$E(U|\mathbf{X} = \mathbf{x}, \Delta = 1) = \int_{F_U^{-1}[1-\Pr(\Delta = 1|\mathbf{x})]}^{\infty} \frac{z \, \mathrm{d}F_u(z)}{\Pr(\Delta = 1|\mathbf{x})}.$$

This relationship demonstrates that the conditional mean is a function of the probability of selection. As the probability of selection goes to 1, the conditional mean goes to zero. For samples chosen so that the values of $\mathbf{x}$ are such that the observations are certain to be included in the sample, there is no problem in using ordinary least squares on selected samples to estimate $\boldsymbol{\beta}$. Thus in Figure 1, ordinary least squares regressions fit on samples selected to have large $\mathbf{x}$ values closely approximate the true regression function and become arbitrarily close as $\mathbf{x}$ becomes large. The condition mean in (1.12) is a surrogate for $\Pr(\Delta = 1|\mathbf{x})$. As this probability goes to one, the problem of sample selection in regression analysis becomes negligibly small.

Heckman (1976) demonstrates that $\boldsymbol{\beta}$ and F_u are identified if U is normally distributed and standard conditions invoked in regression analysis are satisfied. Gallant and Nychka (1984) and Cosslett (1984) establish conditions for identification for non-normal U. In their analyses, F_u is consistently non-parametrically estimated.

Example 3. The next example considers *censored random variables*. This concept extends the notion of a truncated random variable by letting a more general rule than truncation on the outcome of interest generate the selected sample. Because the sample generating rule may be different from a simple truncation of the outcome being studied, the concept of a censored random variable in general requires at least two distinct random variables.

Let Y_1 be the outcome of interest. Let Y_2 be another random variable. Denote observed Y_1 by Y_1^*. If $Y_2 < c$, Y_1 is observed. Otherwise Y_1 is not observed and we can set $Y_1^* = 0$ or any other convenient value (assuming that Y_1 has no point mass at $Y_1 = 0$ or at the alternative convenient value). In terms of the weighting function ω, $\omega(y_1, y_2) = 0$ if $y_2 > c$, $\omega(y_1, y_2) = 1$ if $y_2 \leqslant c$.

Selection rule $Y_2 < c$ does not necessarily restrict the range of Y_1. Thus Y_1^* is not in general a truncated random variable. Define $\Delta = 1$ if $Y_2 < c$; $\Delta = 0$ otherwise. If $F(y_1, y_2)$ is the population distribution of (Y_1, Y_2), the distribution of Δ is

$$\Pr(\Delta = \delta) = [1 - F_2(c)]^{1-\delta}[F_2(c)]^{\delta}, \quad \delta = 0, 1,$$

where F_2 is the marginal distribution of Y_2. The distribution of Y_1^* is

$$G(y_1^*) = F(y_1^*|\delta = 1) = \frac{F(y_1^*, c)}{F_2(c)}, \qquad \Delta = 1, \tag{1.14a}$$

$$G(y_1^* = 0) = 1, \qquad \Delta = 0. \tag{1.14b}$$

Note that (1.14a) is the distribution function corresponding to the density in (1.1) when $\omega(y_1, y_2) = 1$ if $y_2 \leqslant c$ and $\omega(y_1, y_2) = 0$ otherwise.

The joint distribution of (Y_1^*, Δ) is

$$G(y_1^*, \delta) = [F(y_1^*, c)]^{\delta}[1 - F_2(c)]^{1-\delta}. \tag{1.15}$$

This is the distribution function corresponding to density (1.4) for the special weighting rule of this example. In a censored sample, under general conditions it is possible to consistently estimate $\Pr(\Delta = \delta)$ and $G(y_1^*)$. In a truncated sample, only conditional distribution (1.14a) can be estimated. A degenerate version of this model has $Y_1 \equiv Y_2$. In that case, censored random variable Y_1 is also a truncated random variable. Note that a censored random variable may be defined for a truncated or censored sample.

Example 3 and variants of it have wide applicability in economics. Let Y_1 be the wage of a woman. Wages of women are observed only if women work. Let Y_2 be an index of a woman's propensity to work. In Gronau (1974) and Heckman (1974), Y_2 is postulated as the difference between reservation wages (the value of time at home determined from household preference functions) and potential market wages Y_1. Then if $Y_2 < 0$, the woman works. Otherwise, she does not. $Y_1^* = Y_1$ if $Y_2 < 0$ is the observed wage.

If Y_1 is the offered wage of an unemployed worker, and Y_2 is the difference between reservation wages (the return to searching) and offered market wages, $Y_1^* = Y_1$ if $Y_2 < 0$ is the accepted wage for an unemployed worker (see Flinn and Heckman, 1982). If Y_1 is the potential output of a firm and Y_2 is its profitability, $Y_1^* = Y_1$ if $Y_2 > 0$. If Y_1 is the potential income in occupation one and Y_2 is the potential income in occupation two, $Y_1^* = Y_1$ if $Y_1 - Y_2 < 0$ while $Y_1^* = Y_2$ if $Y_1 - Y_2 \geqslant 0$. We develop this example at length in section 2 where we consider explicit economic models of self-selection. There we discuss the identifiability of this model.

Example 4. This example builds on example 3 by introducing regressors. This produces the *censored regression model* (Heckman, 1976; 1979). In example 3 set

$$Y_1 = \mathbf{X}_1\boldsymbol{\beta}_1 + U_1 \tag{1.16a}$$

$$Y_2 = \mathbf{X}_2\boldsymbol{\beta}_2 + U_2 \tag{1.16b}$$

where $(\mathbf{X}_1, \mathbf{X}_2)$ are distributed independently of (U_1, U_2), a mean zero, finite variance random vector. Conventional assumptions are invoked to ensure that if Y_1 and Y_2 can be observed, least squares applied to a random sample of data on $(Y_1, Y_2, \mathbf{X}_1, \mathbf{X}_2)$ would consistently estimate $\boldsymbol{\beta}_1$ and $\boldsymbol{\beta}_2$. $Y_1^* = Y_1$ if $Y_2 < 0$. If $Y_2 < 0, \Delta = 1$. Then the regression function for the selected sample is

$$E(Y_1^*|\mathbf{X}_1 = \mathbf{x}_1, Y_2 < 0) = E(Y_1^*|\mathbf{X}_1 = \mathbf{x}_1, \Delta = 1)$$

$$= \mathbf{X}_1\boldsymbol{\beta}_1 + E(U_1|\mathbf{X}_1 = \mathbf{x}_1, \Delta = 1) \tag{1.17}$$

and the regression function for the population is

$$E(Y_1|\mathbf{X}_1 = \mathbf{x}_1) = \mathbf{X}_1\boldsymbol{\beta}_1. \tag{1.18}$$

As in the regression analysis of truncated random variables, there is an illuminating contrast between the conditional expectation for the selected sample (1.17) and the population regression function (1.18). The two functions differ by the conditional mean of $U_1[E(U_1|\mathbf{X}_1 = \mathbf{x}_1, \Delta = 1)]$. In the regression analysis of truncated random variables, ordinary least squares estimates of $\boldsymbol{\beta}$ (in equation (1.14)) are biased and inconsistent because the conditional mean is improperly omitted from the selected sample regression. The same analysis applies to the regression analysis of censored random variables. The conditional mean is a surrogate for the probability of selection $[\Pr(\Delta = 1|\mathbf{x}_2)]$. As $\Pr(\Delta = 1|\mathbf{x}_2)$ goes to one, the problem of sample selection bias becomes negligible. However, in the censored regression case, a new phenomenon appears. If there are variables in $\mathbf{X}_2$ not in $\mathbf{X}_1$, such variables may appear to be statistically important determinants of Y_1 when ordinary least squares is applied to data generated from censored samples.

As an example, suppose that survey statisticians use some extraneous (to $\mathbf{X}_1$) variables to determine sample enrolment. Such variables may appear to be important determinants of Y_1 when in fact they are not. They are important determinants of Y_1^*. In an analysis of self-selection, let Y_1 be the wage that a potential worker could earn were he to accept a market offer. Let Y_2 be the difference between the best non-market opportunity available to the potential worker and Y_1. If $Y_2 < 0$, the agent works. The conditional expectation of observed wages ($Y_1^* = Y_1$ if $Y_2 < 0$) given $\mathbf{x}_1$ and $\mathbf{x}_2$ will be a non-trivial function of $\mathbf{x}_2$. Thus variables determining non-market opportunities will determine Y_1^*, even though they do not determine Y_1. For example, the number of children less than six may appear to be significant determinants of Y_1 when inadequate account is taken of sample selection, even though the market does not place any value or penalty on small children in generating wage offers for potential workers.

Heckman (1976) develops the analysis of this model when (U_1, U_2) is normally distributed. Gallant and Nychka (1984) and Cosslett (1984) demonstrate that under mild restrictions on $F(u_1, u_2)$, if there is one continuous valued variable in $\mathbf{X}_2$ not in $\mathbf{X}_1$ (so that there is no exact linear dependence between $\mathbf{X}_2$ and $\mathbf{X}_1$), $\boldsymbol{\beta}_1, \boldsymbol{\beta}_2$ and $F(u_1, u_2)$ can be consistently non-parametrically estimated. Heckman and MaCurdy (1986) develop this class of models at length.

Example 5. This example demonstrates how self-selection bias affects the interpretation placed on estimated consumer demand functions when there is self-selection. We postulate a population of consumers with a quasi-concave utility function $U(\mathbf{Z}, E)$ which depends on the consumption of goods and preference shock E which represents heterogeneity in preferences among consumers. The support of E is $\mathbf{E}$. For price vector $\mathbf{P}$ and endowment income M, the consumer's problem is to

$$\operatorname{Max} U(\mathbf{Z}, E) \quad \text{subject to} \quad \mathbf{P}'\mathbf{Z} \leqslant M.$$

In the population $\mathbf{P}$ and M are distributed independently of E. First order conditions for this problem are

$$\frac{\partial U(\mathbf{Z}, E)}{\partial \mathbf{Z}} \leqslant \lambda \mathbf{P}, \tag{1.19}$$

where λ is the Lagrange multiplier associated with the budget constraint. Focusing on the demand for the first good, Z_1, none of it is purchased if at zero consumption of Z_1

$$\left.\frac{\partial U(\mathbf{Z}, E)}{\partial Z_1}\right|_{Z_1=0} \leqslant \lambda P_1 \tag{1.20}$$

i.e. marginal valuation is less than marginal cost in utility terms. Conventional interior solution demand functions for Z_1 are defined for a given $\mathbf{P}, M$ only for values of E such that

$$\left.\frac{\partial U(\mathbf{Z}, E)}{\partial Z_1}\right|_{Z_1=0} \geqslant \lambda P_1. \tag{1.21}$$

Let the set of E for which conventional interior solution consumer demand functions for Z_1 are defined be denoted by $\underline{\underline{E}}$. Then

$$\underline{\underline{E}} = \left\{ E \,\middle\|\, \left.\frac{\partial U(\mathbf{Z}, E)}{\partial Z_1}\right|_{Z_1=0} \geqslant \lambda P_1 \quad \text{for given} \quad \mathbf{P}, M \right\}.$$

Let $\Delta_1 = 0$ if the consumer does not purchase Z_1. Let $\Delta_1 = 1$ otherwise. If $F(\epsilon)$ is the population distribution of E, the proportion purchasing none of good Z_1 given $\mathbf{P}, M$ is

$$\Pr(\Delta_1 = 0 \mid \mathbf{P}, M) = 1 - \int_{\underline{\underline{E}}} \mathrm{d}F(\epsilon).$$

Provided inequality (1.21) is satisfied, $\Delta_1 = 1$ and interior solution demand function

$$Z_1 = Z_1(\mathbf{P}, M, E) \tag{1.22}$$

is well defined and $Z_1 = Z_1^*$. When $\Delta_1 = 0$, observed $Z_1 = Z_1^* = 0$.

Equation (1.22) is the conventional object of interest in consumer theory. Partial derivatives of that function *holding E and the other arguments constant* have well defined economic interpretations. Suppose that some non-negligible proportion of the population buys none of good Z_1. Regression estimates of the parameters of (1.22) using Z_1^* approximate the conditional expectation

$$E(Z_1 \mid \Delta_1 = 1, \mathbf{P}, M) = \int_{\underline{\underline{E}}} Z_1(\mathbf{P}, M, \epsilon)\, \mathrm{d}F(\epsilon). \tag{1.23}$$

The derivatives of (1.23) are different from the derivatives of (1.22). In order to define these derivatives, it is helpful to define $I_{\underline{\underline{E}}}(E)$ as an indicator function for set $\underline{\underline{E}}$ which equals one if $E \in \underline{\underline{E}}$ and equals zero otherwise. When prices or income change, the set of values of E that satisfy inequality (1.21) changes. Let $\underline{\underline{E}} + \Delta \underline{\underline{E}}_{\mathbf{P}}$ be the set of E values that satisfy (1.21) when there is a finite price change $\Delta\mathbf{P}$. $I_{\underline{\underline{E}} + \Delta \underline{\underline{E}}_{\mathbf{P}}}(E)$ is an indicator function which equals one when $E \in \underline{\underline{E}} + \Delta \underline{\underline{E}}_{\mathbf{P}}$. Then the derivatives of (1.23) are, for the jth price

$$\frac{\partial E(Z_1 \mid \Delta = 1, \mathbf{P}, M)}{\partial P_j} = \int_{\underline{\underline{E}}} \frac{\partial Z_1(\mathbf{P}, M, \epsilon)}{\partial P_j}\, \mathrm{d}F(\epsilon)$$

$$+ \lim_{\Delta P_j \to 0} \int_{\underline{\underline{E}}} \frac{[(I_{\underline{\underline{E}} + \Delta \underline{\underline{E}}_{P_j}}(\epsilon) - I_{\underline{\underline{E}}}(\epsilon)] Z(\mathbf{P}, M, \epsilon)}{\Delta P_j}\, \mathrm{d}F(\epsilon). \tag{1.24}$$

When the limit in the second term does not exist, the derivative does not exist. We assume for expositional convenience that the limit is well defined.

The first expression on the right-hand side of (1.24) is the *average effect* of price change on commodity demand. The second term on the right-hand side of (1.24) arises from the change in sample composition of E as the proportion of non-purchasers changes in response to price change. This term generates the selection bias.

Neither term is the same as the price derivative of (1.22) for an arbitrary value of $E = \epsilon$ although the first term on the right-hand side of (1.24) approximates the price derivative of (1.22) for some value of $E = \epsilon$.

A similar decomposition of the derivatives of the conditional demand function can be performed if it is defined solely for a sample of non-zero purchasers (see Heckman and MaCurdy, 1981, 1986).

Just as in the statistical sample selection bias problem, there is a population of interest. In this case, the population parameters of interest are the distribution of E and the parameters of $U(\mathbf{Z}, E)$. Those who buy Z_1 are a self-selected sample of the population. Estimates of population parameters estimated on self-selected samples are biased and inconsistent. There is a population distribution of $Z_1(\mathbf{P}, M, E)$ generated by the distribution of E. Observations of Z_1 are obtained only if $E \in \underline{\underline{E}}$ ($\omega(E) = 1$ if $E \in \underline{\underline{E}}$, $\omega(E) = 0$ otherwise). Alternatively one can express the inclusion criteria in terms of the latent population distribution of Z_1 induced by E (given $\mathbf{P}$ and M) *and write* $\omega(z_1) = 1$ if $z_1 > 0$, $\omega(z_1) = 0$ if $z_1 \leqslant 0$.

Heckman (1974) and Heckman and MaCurdy (1981) provide further discussion of this type of model which is widely used in applied economics and consider issues of identifiability for such models.

Example 6. Length biased sampling. Let T be the duration of an event such as a completed unemployment spell or a completed duration of a job with an employer. The population distribution of T is $F(t)$ with density $f(t)$. The sampling rule is such that *individuals* are sampled at random. Data are recorded on a completed spell *provided that at the time of the interview the individual is experiencing the event*. Such sampling rules are in wide use in many national surveys of employment and unemployment.

In order to have a sampled completed spell, a person must be in the state at the time of the interview. Let '0' be the date of the survey. Decompose any completed spell T into a component that occurs before the survey T_b and a component that occurs after the survey T_a. Then $T = T_a + T_b$. For a person to be sampled, $T_b > 0$. The density of T given $T_b = t_b$ is

$$f(t \mid t_b) = \frac{f(t)}{1 - F(t_b)}, \quad t \geqslant t_b. \tag{1.25}$$

Suppose that the environment is stationary. The population entry rate into the state at each instant of time is k. From each vintage of entrants into the state distinguished by their distance from the survey date t_b, only $1 - F(t_b) = \Pr(T > t_b)$ survive. Aggregating over all cohorts of entrants, the population proportion in the state at the date of the interview is P where

$$P = \int_0^\infty k(1 - F(t_b))\,\mathrm{d}t_b \tag{1.26}$$

which is assumed to exist. The density of T_b^*, sampled pre-survey duration, is

$$g(t_b^* \mid t_b^* > 0) = \frac{k(1 - F(t_b^*))}{P}. \tag{1.27}$$

The density of sampled completed durations is thus

$$\begin{aligned} g(t^*) &= \int_0^{t^*} f(t^* \mid t_b^*) g(t_b^* \mid t_b^* > 0)\,\mathrm{d}t_b^* \\ &= k \frac{f(t^*)}{1 - F(t_b^*)} \frac{1 - F(t_b^*)}{P} \int_0^{t^*} \mathrm{d}t_b^* \\ &= k \frac{t^* f(t^*)}{P}. \end{aligned}$$

Observe from (1.26) that by a standard integration by parts argument

$$P = k \int_0^\infty (1 - F(z))\,\mathrm{d}z = k \int_0^\infty z\,\mathrm{d}F(z) = kE(T).$$

Note that

$$g(t^*) = \frac{t^* f(t^*)}{E(T)}. \tag{1.28}$$

In this form (1.28) is equivalent to (1.1) with $\omega(t) = t$. Hence the term 'length biased sampling'. Intuitively, longer spells are oversampled when the requirement is imposed that a spell be in progress at the time the survey is conducted ($T_b > 0$). Suppose, instead, that individuals are randomly sampled and data are recorded on the *next* spell of the event (after the survey date). As long as successive spells are independent, such a sampling frame does not distort the sampled distribution because no requirement is imposed that the sampled spell be in progress at the date of the interview. It is important to notice that the source of the bias is the requirement that $T_b > 0$, not that only a fraction of the population experiences the event ($P < 1$).

The simple length weight ($\omega(t) = t$) that produces (1.28) is an artefact of the stationarity assumption. Heckman and Singer (1985) consider the consequences of non-stationarity and unobservables when there is selection on the event that a person be in the state at the time of the inverview. The also demonstrate the bias that results from estimating parametric models on samples generated by length biased sampling rules when inadequate account is taken of the sampling plan. Vardi (1983, 1985) and Gill and Wellner (1985) consider nonparametric identification and estimation of models with densities of the form (1.28).

It is unfortunate that the lessons of length biased sampling are not adequately appreciated in economics. Two widely cited studies by Clark and Summers (1979) and Hall (1982) use length biased data to prove, respectively, that unemployment and employment spells are 'surprisingly long'. Whether their findings are artefacts of sampling plans remains to be determined.

Example 7. Choice based sampling. Let D be a discrete valued random variable which assumes a finite number of values I. $D = i, i = 1, \ldots, I$ corresponds to the occurrence of state i. States are mutually exclusive. In the literature the states may be modes of transportation choice for communters (Domencich and McFadden, 1975), occupations, migration destinations, financial solvency status of firms, schooling choices of students, etc. Interest centres on estimating a population choice model

$$\Pr(D = i \mid \mathbf{X} = \mathbf{x}), \quad i = 1, \ldots, I. \tag{1.29}$$

The population density of $(D, \mathbf{X})$ is

$$f(d, \mathbf{x}) = \Pr(D = d \mid \mathbf{X} = \mathbf{x}) h(\mathbf{x}) \tag{1.30}$$

where $h(\mathbf{x})$ is the density of the data.

In many problems, plentiful data are available on certain outcomes while data are scarce for other outcomes. For example, interviews about transportation preferences conducted at train stations tend to over-sample train riders and under-sample bus riders. Interviews about occupational choice preferences conducted at leading universities over-sample those who select professional occupations.

In choice based sampling, selection occurs solely on the D coordinate of $(D, \mathbf{X})$. In terms of (1.1) (extended to allow for discrete random variables), $\omega(d, \mathbf{X}) = \omega(d)$. Then sampled $(D^*, \mathbf{X}^*)$ has density

$$g(d^*, \mathbf{x}^*) = \frac{\omega(d^*) f(d^*, \mathbf{x}^*)}{\sum_{i=1}^{I} \int \omega(i) f(i, x^*)\,\mathrm{d}x^*} \tag{1.31}$$

Notice that the denominator can be simplified to

$$\sum_{i=1}^{I} \omega(i) f(i)$$

where $f(d^*)$ is the marginal distribution of D^* so that

$$g(d^*, \mathbf{x}^*) = \frac{\omega(d^*) f(d^*, \mathbf{x}^*)}{\sum_{i=1}^{I} \omega(i) f(i)} \tag{1.32}$$

Also, integrating (1.31) with respect to $\mathbf{x}$ using (1.32) we obtain

$$g(d^*) = \frac{\omega(d^*) f(d^*)}{\sum_{i=1}^{I} \omega(i) f(i)} \tag{1.33}$$

which makes transparent how the sampling rule causes the sampled proportions to deviate from the population proportions. Note further that as a consequence of sampling only on D, the population conditional density

$$h(\mathbf{x}^*|d^*) = \frac{f(d^*, x^*)}{f(d^*)} \tag{1.34}$$

can be recovered from the choice based sample. The density of $\mathbf{x}$ in the sample is thus

$$g(\mathbf{x}^*) = \sum_{i=1}^{I} h(x^*|i)g(i). \tag{1.35}$$

Then using (1.32)–(1.35) we reach

$$g(d^*|\mathbf{x}^*) = f(d^*|\mathbf{x}^*) \times \left\{ \left[\frac{\omega(d^*)}{\sum_{i=1}^{I} \omega(i)f(i)} \right] \left[\frac{1}{\sum_{i=1}^{I} f(i|\mathbf{x}^*)\frac{g(i)}{f(i)}} \right] \right\}. \tag{1.36}$$

The bias that results from using choice based samples to make inference about $f(d^*|x^*)$ is a consequence of neglecting the terms in braces on the right-hand side of (1.36). Notice that if the data are generated by a random sampling rule, $\omega(d^*) = 1, g(d^*) = f(d^*)$ and the term in braces is one.

Manski and Lerman (1977), Manski and McFadden (1981) and Cosslett (1981) provide illuminating discussions of choice based sampling.

Example 8. Size biased sampling. Let N be the number of children in a family. $f(N)$ is the density of discrete random variable N. Suppose that family size is recorded only when at least one child is interviewed. Suppose further that each child has an independent and identical chance β of being interviewed. The probability of sampled family size of $N^* = n^*$ is

$$g(n^*) = \frac{\omega(n^*)f(n^*)}{E[\omega(N^*)]} \tag{1.37}$$

where $\omega(n^*) = 1 - (1-\beta)^{n^*}$ (the probability that at least one child from a family of size n^* will be sampled) and

$$\mathrm{E}[\omega(N^*)] = \sum_{n^*} (1 - (1-\beta)^{n^*})f(n^*)$$

is the probability of observing a family. In a large population $\beta \to 0$ with increasing population size. Using l'Hospital's rule, and assuming that passage to the limit under the summation sign is valid

$$\lim_{\beta \to 0} g(n^*) = \frac{n^* f(n^*)}{E(N^*)} \tag{1.38}$$

Thus the limit form of (1.37) is identical to (1.28). Larger families tend to be oversampled and hence a misleading estimate of family size will be produced from such samples. Since the model is formally equivalent to the length biased sampling model, all references and statements about identification given in example 6 apply with full force to this example. See the discussion in Rao (1965).

2. ECONOMIC MODELS OF SELF-SELECTION

We begin our analysis by expositing the Roy model of self-selection for workers with heterogeneous skills. The statistical framework for this model has been outlined in examples 3 and 4. Following Roy, we assume that there are two market sectors in which income-maximizing agents can work. Agents are free to enter the sector that gives them the highest income. However, they can work in only one sector at a time.

Each sector requires a unique sector-specific task. Each agent has two skills, T_1 and T_2 which he cannot use simultaneously. The model is short run in that aggregate skill distributions are assumed to be given. There are no costs of changing sectors, and investment is ignored. Because of this assumption, the model presented here applies to environments with certain or uncertain prices for sector-specific tasks. For simplicity and without any loss of generality (given the preceding assumptions), we assume an environment of perfect certainty.

Let T_i be the amount of sector i specific task a worker can perform. The price of task i is π_i. An agent works in sector 1 if his income is higher there, that is

$$\pi_1 T_1 > \pi_2 T_2 \tag{2.1}$$

Indifference between sectors is a negligible probability event if the $T_i = 1, 2$ are assumed to be continuous nondegenerate random variables. Throughout we assume that prices are positive ($\pi_i > 0$).

The log wage in task i of an individual with endowment T_i is

$$\ln W_i = \ln \pi_i + \ln \ T_i \tag{2.2}$$

The proportion of the population working at task i is the proportion of the population for whom

$$T_1 > \frac{\pi_2}{\pi_1} T_2.$$

Roy assumes that $(\ln T_1, \ln T_2)$ is normally distributed with mean (μ_1, μ_2) and covariance matrix Σ. Letting (U_1, U_2) be a mean zero normal vector, agents in the Roy model choose between two possible wages:

$$\ln W_1 = \ln \pi_1 + \mu_1 + U_1$$

or

$$\ln W_2 = \ln \pi_2 + \mu_2 + U_2.$$

Workers enter sector 1 if $\ln W_1 > \ln W_2$. Otherwise they enter sector 2.

Letting

$$\sigma^* = \sqrt{\mathrm{var}(U_1 - U_2)}$$

and

$$c_i = (\ln(\pi_i/\pi_j) + \mu_i - \mu_j)/\sigma^*, \quad i \neq j,$$

$$\Pr(i) = P(\ln W_i > \ln W_j) = \Phi(c_i), \quad i \neq j, \quad i,j = 1, 2$$

where $\Phi(\ )$ is the cumulative distribution function of a standard normal variable. When standard sample selection bias formulae are used (see, e.g. Heckman 1976), the mean of log wages observed in sector i is

$$E(\ln W_i|\ln W_i > \ln W_j) = \ln \pi_i + \mu_i + \frac{\sigma_{ii} - \sigma_{ij}}{\sigma^*} \lambda(c_i), \quad i,j = 1, 2, \quad i \neq j, \tag{2.3}$$

where

$$\lambda(c) = \frac{\frac{1}{\sqrt{2\pi}} \exp(-\frac{1}{2}c^2)}{\Phi(c)}$$

is a convex monotone decreasing function of c with $\lambda(c) \geqslant 0$, and

$$\lim_{c \to \infty} \lambda(c) = 0, \quad \lim_{c \to -\infty} \lambda(c) = \infty.$$

Convexity is proved in Heckman and Honoré (1986).

The variance of log wages observed in sector i

$$\text{var}(\ln W_i | \ln W_i > \ln W_j) = \sigma_{ii}\{\rho_i^2[1 - c_i\lambda(c_i) - \lambda^2(c_i)] + (1-\rho_i^2)\}, \quad i \neq j \quad (2.4)$$

where $\rho_i = \text{correl}(U_i, U_i - U_j), i \neq j = 1, 2$. The variance of the log of observed wages never exceeds σ_{ii}, the population variance, because the term in braces in (2.4) is never greater than unity. In general, sectoral variances decrease with increased selection. For example, if ρ_1 and ρ_2 do not equal zero, as π_1 increases with π_2 held fixed so that people shift from sector 2 to sector 1, the variance in the log of wages in sector 1 increases while the variance in the log of wages in sector 2 decreases.

Using the fact that $W_i = \pi_i T_i$, we may use (2.3) to write

$$E(\ln T_1 | \ln W_1 > \ln W_2) = \mu_1 + \frac{\sigma_{11} - \sigma_{12}}{\sigma^*}\lambda(c_1), \quad (2.5a)$$

$$E(\ln T_2 | \ln W_1) > \ln W_2) = \mu_2 + \frac{\sigma_{22} - \sigma_{12}}{\sigma^*}\lambda(c_2). \quad (2.5b)$$

Focusing on (2.5a) and noting that λ is positive for all values of c_1 (except $c_1 = \infty$), the mean of log task 1 used in sector 1 exceeds, equal, or falls short of the population mean endowment of log task 1 as $\sigma_{11} - \sigma_{12}$ is greater than, equal to, or less than zero. If endowments of tasks are uncorrelated ($\sigma_{12} = 0$), self-selection always causes the mean of $\ln T_1$ employed in sector 1 to be above the population mean μ_1. The opposite case occurs when $\sigma_{11} - \sigma_{12}$ is negative. This case can arise only when values of $\ln T_1$ and $\ln T_2$ are sufficiently positively correlated. If this occurs, the mean of log task 1 used in sector 1 falls below the population mean μ_1. Since covariance matrices must be positive semidefinite, $\sigma_{11} + \sigma_{22} - 2\sigma_{12} \geqslant 0$. Thus if $\sigma_{11} - \sigma_{12} < 0, \sigma_{22} - \sigma_{12} > 0$ so the mean of log task 2 employed in sector 2 necessarily lies above the population mean μ_2. In the Roy model the unusual case can arise in at most one sector. Notice from (2.5) that only if $\sigma_{11} - \sigma_{12} = 0$ (so $\rho_1^2 = 0$) is the variance of log task 1 employed in sector 1 identical to the variance of log task 1 in the population. Otherwise, the sectoral variance of observed log task 1 is less than the population variance of log task 1.

To gain further insight into the effect of self-selection on the distribution of earnings for workers in sector 1, it is helpful to draw on some results from normal regression theory. The regression equation for $\ln T_2$ conditional on $\ln T_1$ is

$$\ln T_2 = \mu_2 + \frac{\sigma_{12}}{\sigma_{12}}(\ln T_1 - \mu_1) + \epsilon_2, \quad (2.6)$$

where $E(\epsilon_2) = 0$ and $\text{var}(\epsilon_2) = \sigma_{22}[1 - (\sigma_{12}^2/\sigma_{11}\sigma_{22})]$.

Figure 2 plots regression function (2.6) for the case $\sigma_{12} = \sigma_{11}$ and $\mu_2 > \mu_1 > 0$. For each value of $\ln T_1$, the population values of $\ln T_2$ are normally distributed around the regression line. Individuals with high values of $\ln T_1$ also tend to have a high value of $\ln T_2$. Assuming $\pi_1 = \pi_2$, individuals with ($\ln T_1, \ln T_2$) endowments above the 45° line of equal income shown in Figure 1 choose to work in sector 2, while those individuals with endowments below this line work in sector 1. Because $\sigma_{12} = \sigma_{11}$, the regression function is parallel to the line of equal income.

The distribution of ϵ_2 about the regression line is the same for all values of $\ln T_1$. When individuals are classified on the basis of their $\ln T_1$ values the same proportion of individuals work in sector 1 at all values of $\ln T_1$. For this reason the distribution of $\ln T_1$ employed in sector 1 is the same as the latent population distribution. If π_1 is raised (or π_2 is lowered) so that the 45° equal income line is shifted upward, the same proportion of people enter sector 1 at each value of $T_1 = t_1$. Figure 3 plots regression function (2.6) for the case $\sigma_{12} > \sigma_{11}$ and $\mu_2 > \mu_1 > 0$.

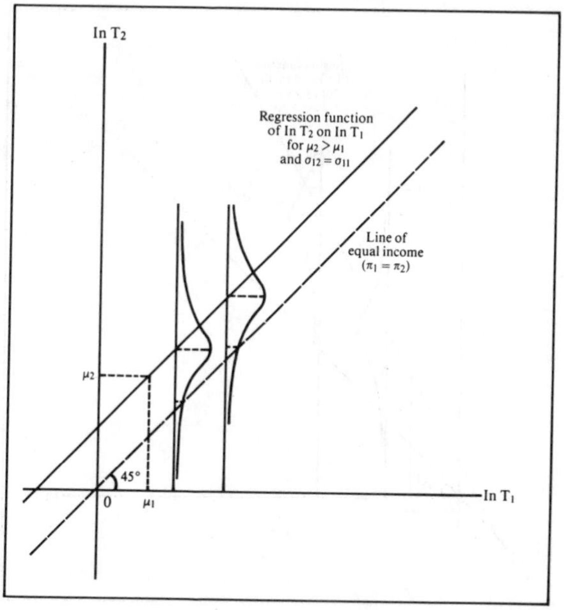

Figure 2

As before we set $\pi_1 = \pi_2$. Individuals with endowments above the 45° line choose to work in sector 2, while those with endowments below this line work in sector 1. When individuals are classified on the basis of their T_1 values, the fraction of people working in sector 1 decreases the higher the value of T_1. Self-selection causes the mean of log task 1 employed in sector 1 to be less than the mean of log task 1 in the total population. People with high values of T_1 are under-represented in sector 1 and low T_1 values are over-represented. In the extreme, when $\ln T_1$ and $\ln T_2$ are perfectly positively correlated, all high-income individuals are in sector 2, while all the low-income individuals are in sector 1. The highest-paid sector 1 worker earns the same as the lowest-paid sector 2 worker (Roy, 1951; Willis and Rosen, 1979). In this case there is really only one skill dimension and individuals can be unambiguously ranked along this scale.

If π_1 is raised (or π_2 is lowered) so that the line of equal income is shifted upward, the mean of $\ln T_1$ employed in sector 1 must rise. The only place left to get T_1 is from the high end of the T_1 distribution. Unlike the case of $\sigma_{12} = \sigma_{11}$, in which a 10 per cent increase in π_1 results in a 10 per cent increase in measured average earnings in sector 1, when $\sigma_{12} > \sigma_{11}$, a 10 per cent increase in π_1 results in a greater than 10 per cent increase in the measured average earnings in sector 1 as the average quality of the sector 1 work-force increases. The variance of log wages in sector 1 increases.

If $\sigma_{11} < \sigma_{12}$, than $\sigma_{12} < \sigma_{22}$ in order for Σ to be a covariance matrix. In the population, log task 2 must have greater variability than log task 1. Individuals with high T_1 values tend to have high T_2 values. But the population distribution of log task 2 has more mass in the tails. The higher an agent's value of T_1, the more likely it is that he will be able to get higher income in sector 2. At the lower end of the distribution, the process works in reverse: lower T_1 individuals on average have poor T_2 values. Self-selection causes the $\ln T_1$ distribution in sector 1 to have an evacuated right tail, an exaggerate left tail, and a lower mean than the population mean of $\ln T_1$.

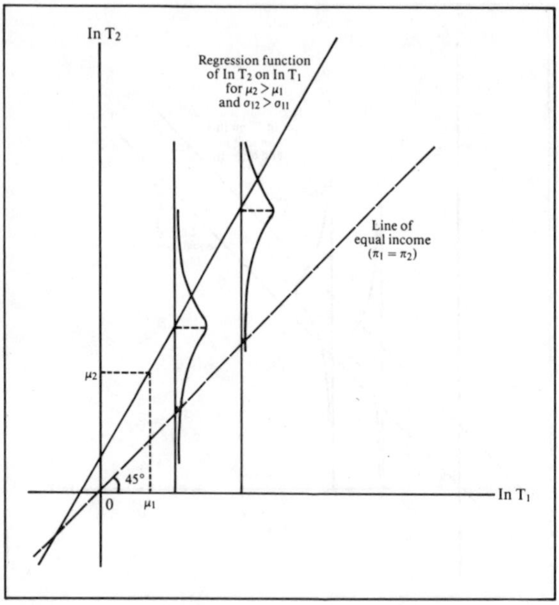

Figure 3

If $\sigma_{12} < \sigma_{11}$ (a case not depicted graphically), the proportion of each T_1 group working in sector 1 increases, the higher the value of T_1. The mean of the log task employed in sector 1 exceeds μ_1. A 10 per cent increase in π_1 produces an increase of less than 10 per cent in the average earnings of workers in sector 1 as the mean of $\ln T_1$ employed in sector 1 declines. In fact if $\sigma_{12} > \sigma_{22}$ it is possible for an increase in π_1 to cause measured sector 1 wages to decline. Thus through a selection phenomenon it is possible for the average wage of people working in sector 1 to decline even though the price per unit skill increases there.

How robust are these conclusions if the normality assumption is relaxed? Heckman and Sedlacek (1985) show that many propositions derived from assumed normality of skills do not hold up for more general distributions. For example, increasing selection need not decrease sectoral variances. The effects of selection on mean employed skill levels are ambiguous. Heckman and Honoré (1986) demonstrate that in a single cross-section of data, it is possible to identify all of the parameters of the model from the data if the normality asumption is invoked. However, in a single cross-section many other models can explain the data equally well. In particular, intuitive notions about the degree of correlation or dependence among skills have no empirical content and so models of skill 'hierarchies' based on the extent of such dependence have no content for single cross-sections of data with all individuals facing common prices.

To show this, write the density of skills as $f(t_1, t_2)$. Let

$$Z = \begin{cases} T_1 & \text{if} \quad T_1 > T_2 \\ 0 & \text{otherwise} \end{cases}$$

$$Z_2 = \begin{cases} T_2 & \text{if} \quad T_2 > T_1 \\ 0 & \text{otherwise} \end{cases}$$

Prices are normalized to unity ($\pi_1 = \pi_2 = 1$). Then the density of Z_1 is

$$Q_1'(z_1) = \int_{\{t_2 | t_2 < z_1\}} f(z_1, t_2)\,dt_2 = \int_0^{z_1} f(z_1, t_2)\,dt_2.$$

The density of z_2 is

$$Q_2'(z_2) = \int_0^{z_2} f(t_1, z_2)\,dt_1.$$

Note that $Q_1'(n)$ and $Q_2'(n)$ summarize all of the available data on observed earnings.

Now if T_1, T_2 are independent with cdf's F_1^* and F_2^* respectively

$$Q_1'(n) = f_1^*(n) F_2^*(n)$$
$$Q_2'(n) = F_1^*(n) f_2^*(n).$$

Define

$$\bar{Q}(n) = \int_0^n [Q_1'(l) + Q_2'(l)]\,dl = F_1^*(n) F_2^*(n).$$

Then

$$\int_\phi^\infty \frac{Q_1'(n)}{\bar{Q}(n)}\,dn = \int_\phi^\infty \frac{f_1^*(n)}{F_1^*(n)}\,dn = -\ln F_1^*(\phi).$$

Thus we can write

$$F_i^*(\phi) = \exp - \left(\int_\phi^\infty \left[\frac{Q_i'(n)}{\bar{Q}(n)} \right] dn \right) \qquad i = 1, 2$$

so that we can always rationalize the data on wages in a single cross-section by a model of skill independence, and economic models of skill hierarchies have no empirical content for a single cross-section of data.

Suppose, however, that the observing economist has access to data on skill distributions in different market settings i.e. settings in which relative skill prices vary. To take an extreme case, suppose that we observe a continuum of values of π_1/π_2 ranging from zero to infinity. Then it is possible to identify $F(t_1, t_2)$ and it is possible to give empirical content to models based on the degrees of dependence among latent skills.

This point is made most simply in a situation in which Z is observed but the analyst does not know Z_1 or Z_2 (i.e. which occupation is chosen). When $\pi_1/\pi_2 = 0$, everyone works in occupation two. Thus we can observe the marginal density of t_2. When $\pi_1/\pi_2 = \infty$, everyone works in occupation one. As π_1/π_2 pivots from zero to infinity it is thus possible to trace out the full joint distribution of (T_1, T_2).

To establish the general result, set $\sigma = \pi_2/\pi_1$. Let $F(t_1, t_2)$ be the distribution function of T_1, T_2. Then

$$\Pr(Z \leqslant n) = \Pr(\max(T_1, \sigma T_2) \leqslant n) = \Pr\left(T_1 \leqslant n, T_2 \leqslant \frac{1}{\sigma} n \right) = F\left(n, \frac{n}{\sigma} \right).$$

As σ varies between 0 and ∞, the entire distribution can be recovered since N is observed for all values in $(0, \infty)$. Note that it is not necessary to know which sector the agent selects.

This proposition establishes the benefit of having access to data from more than one market. Heckman and Honoré (1986) show how access to data from various market settings and information about the choices of agents aids in the identification of the latent skill distributions.

The Roy model is the prototype for many models of self-selection in economics. If T_1 is potential market productivity and T_2 is non-market productivity (or the reservation wage) for housewives or unemployed individuals, precisely the same model can be used to explore the effects of self-selection on measured productivity. In such a model, T_2 is never observed. This creates certain problems of identification discussed in Heckman and Honoré (1986). The model has been extended to allow for more general choice mechanisms. In particular, selection may occur as a function of variables other than or in addition to T_1 and T_2. Applications of the Roy model include studies of the union–non-union wage differential (Lee, 1978), the returns to schooling (Willis and Rosen, 1979), and the returns to training (Bjorklund and Moffitt, 1986) and Heckman and Robb (1985). Amemiya (1984) and Heckman and Honoré (1986) present comprehensive surveys of empirical studies based on the Roy model and its extensions.

JAMES J. HECKMAN

BIBLIOGRAPHY

Amemiya, T. 1984. Tobit models: a survey. *Journal of Econometrics* 24, 3–61.

Bjorklund, A. and Moffitt, R. 1986. Estimation of wage gains and welfare gains from self selection models. *Review of Economics and Statistics* 24, 1–63.

Cain, G. and Watts, H. 1973. Toward a summary and synthesis of the evidence. In *Income Maintenance and Labor Supply*, ed. G. Cain and H. Watts, Madison: University of Wisconsin Press.

Clark, K. and Summers, L. 1979. Labor market dynamics and unemployment: a reconsideration. *Brookings Papers on Economic Activity*, 13–60.

Cosslett, S. 1981. Maximum likelihood estimation from choice based samples. *Econometrica.*

Cosslett, S. 1984. Distribution free estimator of regression model with sample selectivity. Unpublished manuscript, University of Florida.

Domencich, T. and McFadden, D. 1975. *Urban Travel Demand.* Amsterdam: North-Holland.

Flinn, C. and Heckman, J. 1982. New methods for analyzing structural models of labor force dynamics. *Journal of Econometrics* 18, 5–168.

Gallant, R. and Nychka, R. 1984. Consistent estimation of the censored regression model. Unpublished manuscript, North Carolina State.

Gill, R. and Wellner, J. 1985. Large sample theory of empirical distributions in biased sampling models. Unpublished manuscript, University of Washington.

Goldberger, A. 1983. Abnormal selection bias. In *Studies in Econometrics, Time Series and Multivariate Statistics*, ed. S. Karlin, T. Amemiya and L. Goodman, Wiley, NY

Gronau, R. 1974. Wage comparisons-a selectivity bias. *Journal of Political Economy* 82, (6), 1119–1144.

Hall, R. 1982. The importance of lifetime jobs in the U.S. economy. *American Economic Review* 72, September, 716–724.

Heckman, J. 1974. Shadow prices, market wages and labor supply. *Econometrica* 42(4), 679–94.

Heckman, J. 1976. The common structure of statistical models of truncation, sample selection and limited dependent variables and a simple estimator for such models. *Annals of Economic and Social Measurement* 5(4), 475–92.

Heckman, J. 1977. Sample selection bias as a specification error. *Econometrica* 47(1), 153–62.

Heckman, J. and Honoré, B. 1986. The empirical content of the Roy model. Unpublished manuscript, University of Chicago.

Heckman, J. and MaCurdy, T. 1981. New methods for estimating labor supply functions. In *Research in Labor Economics*, Vol. 4, ed. R. Ehrenberg, Greenwich, Conn.: JAI Press.

Heckman, J. and Robb, R. 1985. Alternative methods for evaluating the effect of training on earnings. In *Longitudinal Analysis of Labor Market Data*, ed. J. Heckman and B. Singer. Cambridge: Cambridge University Press.

Heckman, J. and Sedlacek, G. 1985. Heterogeneity, aggregation and market wage functions. *Journal of Political Economy* 93, December, 1077–125.

Heckman, J. and Singer, B. 1985. Econometric analysis of longitudinal data. In *Handbook of Econometrics*, Vol. III, ed. Z. Griliches and M. Intriligator, Amsterdam: North-Holland.

Lee, L. F. 1978. Unionism and wage rates: a simultaneous equations model with qualitative and limited dependent variables. *International Economic Review* 19, 415–33.

Manski, C. and Lerman, S. 1977. The estimation of choice probabilities from choice based samples. *Econometrica* 45, 1977–88.

Manski, C. and McFadden, D. 1981. Alternative estimates and sample designs for discrete choice analysis. In *Structural Analysis of Discrete Data with Econometric Applications*, ed. C. Manski and D. McFadden, Cambridge: MIT Press.

Pearson, K. 1901. Mathematical contributions to the theory of evolution. *Philosophical Transactions*, 195, 1–47.

Rao, C. R. 1965. On discrete distributions arising out of methods of ascertainment. In *Classical and Contagious Distributions*, ed. G. Patil, Calcutta: Pergamon Press.

Roy, A. D. 1951. Some thoughts on the distribution of earnings. *Oxford Economic Papers*, 3, 135–46.

Vardi, Y. 1983. Nonparametric estimation in the presence of length bias. *Annals of Statistics* 10, 616–20.

Vardi, Y. 1985. Empirical distributions in selection bias models. *Annals of Statistics*, 13, 178–203.

Willis, R. and Rosen, S. 1979. Education and self selection. *Journal of Political Economy* 87, S7-S36.

self-interest. Two of the basic questions with which moral philosophers have been concerned are: (a) what are the fundamental principles of morality? (b) why should we obey them? One tempting answer to the second question is: because obeying them is in your own interest. Tempting, because any other answer simply invites a further 'why?'. For example, 'why bother about helping others to get what they want?' clearly demands an answer. But 'why bother about getting what *you* want?', though of course it can be *asked*, hardly makes sense.

Self-interest as the answer to the second question, however, implies a similar answer to the first. Self-interest can only be a reason for obeying moral principles if those principles do always benefit us as individuals, so that the fundamental one becomes: Do whatever will enable you to satisfy your own desires. And this seems perverse, since most moralists tell us to consider others rather than ourselves. Self-sacrifice, we are told, is noble, and self-seeking base.

Thomas Hobbes answers this objection by pointing out that, while human desires are diverse, so that there is no common end, there is a single means common to all ends. They all require the cooperation of other people, or at least their non-interference. Everyone has an interest in maintaining a peaceful and harmonious society. Moral principles are simply the rules which everyone must follow in order to obtain such a society. We should obey them because obeying them makes for peace and security, and without peace and security no one has much chance of satisfying *any* desires. If morality requires us to consider others and not ourselves, it is for our own sakes in the long run.

To suppose that men imposed moral restraints on themselves for this reason might suggest a far-sightedness greater than most of us are capable of. Bernard Mandeville suggested that men are motivated less by this consideration than by vanity. Morality, he conjectured, came about through the artifice of a relatively few far-sighted men who, in order to make men useful to their fellows, spread the myth that man is somehow different from the other animals and shows his superiority by being able to conquer his desires. 'Moral Virtues', he says, 'are the Political Offspring which Flattery begot upon Pride' (Mandeville, 1724, vol. 1, p. 51). Part of Mandeville's purpose is to satirize the doctrine that no action is virtuous unless it involves self-denial. If that is true, he argues, then virtue does not exist, since all actions aim at some gratification, if only an increase in self-esteem. Civilization did not come about through self-denial, but through what moralists regard as moral weaknesses: avarice, vanity, luxuriousness, ambition and the rest. Hence his famous paradox: 'Private Vices, Publick Benefits.' In developing it he gives an example which has often been quoted: the many materials garnered from all over the world, and the toil and hardship endured by a multitude of workmen, in order to produce a scarlet coat. Even a tyrant, Mandeville says, would be ashamed 'to exact such terrible Services from his Innocent Slaves' merely for 'the satisfaction a Man receives from having a Garment made of Scarlet or Crimson Cloth'. Yet in pursuit of their own private ends men perform feats of endurance which neither their own benevolence nor the tyranny of others would drive them to (Mandeville, 1724, vol. 1, pp. 357–8). This passage has often been used to illustrate the efficiency and smooth working of a market economy; but, looked at in a slightly different way, it would really fit just as well into the first book of Marx's *Das Kapital*, which is full of atrocity stories about the sufferings of workers under capitalism.

Mandeville distinguishes between virtue and goodness. Virtue, in the sense of complete self-denial, is an illusion, since all actions spring from self-interest. It is not possible to subdue the passions, but only to set one passion against another. No action is completely virtuous, but (he seems to imply) it may be good, if it is useful to others. Mandeville, then, agrees with Hobbes that self-interest is the ultimate motive for all actions, but probably does not agree with his other thesis, that self-interest, as distinct from the general happiness, is ultimately the sole good.

The first of these two theses is ambiguous, because 'self-interest' is ambiguous, in more ways than one. If the thesis is that every action springs from some desire or other, including disinterested desires for the welfare of others, then it is probably a truism and in any case of very little interest. If it means that in every action the agent is aiming at his own greatest happiness in the long run ('enlightened self-interest' or 'cool self-love'), then it is significant but false. Actually Hobbes seems to mean something else again: that there are no altruistic or disinterested desires. Apparent altruism turns out on examination to be selfish or interested in the ordinary sense of those words, aiming perhaps at public acclaim or enhanced self-esteem.

It was argued against Hobbes that benevolence, the disinterested desire for the welfare of others, is as basic a part of human nature as self-interest. But, if there are two basic human instincts instead of one, which should we follow when they conflict? The stronger? But it would be rash to claim that benevolence is a stronger feature of human nature than selfishness. Shaftesbury and Hutcheson detected a third instinct, an innate moral sense which requires us to prefer benevolence to self-interest when they conflict. But why should we prefer *that* instinct? As an answer to the question 'why be moral?' this is hardly more satisfactory than to say (with other philosophers) that it is an eternal and immutable truth, known by intuition, that we should allow benevolence to prevail over self-interest.

David Hume and Adam Smith, while agreeing with Hutcheson in the main, try to make his position more plausible by going more deeply into the psychological sources of benevolence. An important one, they say, is sympathy, the tendency to enter into the joys and sorrows of others. Mandeville had regarded pity as a weakness, because it is a passion, though an amiable one: a self-indulgent desire to rid ourselves of a particular kind of uneasiness. Adam Smith insists that sympathy is disinterested, and suggests that 'that whole account of human nature ... which deduces all sentiments and affections from self-love ... seems to me to have arisen from some confused misapprehension of the system of sympathy' (Smith, 1759, p. 317).

Smith called attention to another tendency in human nature: the aesthetic delight in 'the fitness of any system or machine to produce the end for which it was intended', leading, very often, to the means being valued for its own sake, quite apart from the original end. (Smith would have understood the secretary of a home for unmarried mothers who said in an annual report: 'It would be a great pity if, after so much devoted work by so many people, this home had to close for lack of girls needing help'.) Although he regards this tendency as distinct from both self-interest and benevolence, consideration of it leads Smith to conclusions curiously like Mandeville's. One manifestation of it, he says, is the heaping up of riches far beyond the needs of the rich themselves:

> The rich only select from the heap what is most precious and agreeable. They consume little more than the poor, and in spite of their natural selfishness and rapacity, though they mean only their own conveniency, though the sole end which they propose from the labours of all the thousands which they employ be the gratification of their own vain and insatiable desires, they divide with the poor the produce of all their improvements. They are led by an invisible hand to make nearly the same distribution of the necessaries of life which would have been made had the earth been divided into equal portions among all its inhabitants; and thus, without intending it, without knowing it, advance the interest of the society, and afford means to the multiplication of the species (Smith, 1759, pp. 184–5).

It is clear from this that Smith, like Mandeville, sees that the actual consequences of actions may be quite different from those intended. The bees in Mandeville's fable intended merely to lead virtuous and abstemious lives; they did not foresee that this would lead to the ruin of dressmakers, milliners, lawyers, turnkeys, footmen, courtiers, cooks and many others, and eventually to the economic collapse of the hive. Mandeville concludes that public benefits flow from public vices; but obviously the practitioners of those vices are not thinking of the public benefit, but solely of their own gratification.

Adam Smith, in his other reference to the invisible hand, says that most individuals, in their economic transactions, neither intend to promote the public interest nor realise that they are doing so. 'He intends only his own gain, and he is in this, as in many other cases, led by an invisible hand to promote an end which was no part of his intention'. He adds that this is on the whole a good thing. 'By pursuing his own interest he frequently promotes that of the society more effectually than when he really intends to promote it. I have never known much good done by those who affected to trade for the publick good. It is an affectation, indeed, not very common among merchants, and very few words need be employed in dissuading them from it' (Smith, 1776, p. 456).

Nor is that all. It is not only that the pursuit of wealth or power leads the ambitious to promote the public interest while seeking only their own; the aesthetic tendency to value a means for its own sake causes them to have false notions about where their own real interests lie. The pleasures of wealth and greatness, which do not really add much to happiness,

> strike the imagination as something grand, and beautiful, and noble, of which the attainment is well worth all the toil and anxiety which we are so apt to bestow on it. And it is well that nature imposes upon us in this manner. It is this deception which rouses and keeps in continual motion the industry of mankind (Smith, 1759, p. 183).

But perhaps the most optimistic version of the theory of the invisible hand is put forward by T.H. Green. The actions of bad men, he says (at least when they are also powerful) are 'overruled for good'. There is, he tells us, nothing supernatural about this; it is simply one of the beneficent effects of living in society, and particularly in a nation state. He gives Napoleon as an example:

> With all his egotism, his individuality was so far governed by the national spirit in and upon him, that he could only glorify himself in the greatness of France; and though the national spirit expressed itself in an effort after greatness which was in many ways of a mischievous and delusive kind, yet it again had so much of what may be called the spirit of humanity in it, that it required satisfaction in the belief that it was serving humanity. Hence the aggrandisement of France, in which Napoleon's passion for glory satisfied itself, had to take at least the semblance of a deliverance of oppressed peoples, and in taking the semblance it to a great extent performed the reality ... (Green, 1882, p. 134).

One may doubt whether the world's experience of dictators would yield much evidence of such overruling.

For Hobbes, moral principles ('laws of nature') are sociological laws about how men may cooperate peacefully. For Hume and Smith they are rather psychological truths about what men have come to approve, given their peculiar amalgam of dispositions (of which self-interest is merely one) and also the social need (which Hobbes had stressed) for some fixed standards of behaviour.

The psychological approach was also taken by the early Utilitarians. They were, however, less unwilling to found morality on self-interest, because the alternatives, 'intuition', 'the moral sense', 'natural law' and the rest, seemed to them to be merely an excuse for deifying one's own prejudices. 'Nature', Bentham said, 'has placed mankind under the governance of two sovereign masters, pain and pleasure. It is for them to point out what we ought to do, as well as to determine what we shall do' (Bentham, 1789, p. 11). These masters might have been expected to order each individual to pursue his own greatest happiness. But, according to Bentham, they set a different goal, the happiness of *everybody*. Bentham does not explain this transition.

Mill attempts to explain it, in a brief and much-criticized argument. Like Adam Smith, he appeals to the tendency for a means to become an end in itself. Virtue, he says, the desire to promote the general happiness, originally cultivated as a means to one's own happiness, comes to be aimed at for its own sake. From being a means to happiness, it has become a part of that happiness. G.E. Moore dismisses this contemptuously as a blatant failure to distinguish two very different things, a part and a means. Mill's argument may, however, be more subtle than that (Moore, 1903, pp. 71–2).

According to Hobbes, moral rules state the way men must behave if society is to be possible. Needing society, the individual accepts as his aim, not self-interest merely, but a compromise between his own interests and those of everybody else. He accepts the compromise because half a loaf is better than no bread. Consequently he feels obliged to subordinate his own interests to the compromise when they conflict. But he obeys moral rules only as a means, in order to induce others to obey them too. Having others obey them is his reward; obeying them himself is the price he pays. But it may be objected that we do not think of morality like that. We want to do the right thing for the sake of doing it. It would seem to follow from Hobbes's account that it would be more rational to be a successful hypocrite than a genuinely good person.

Consider, however, what happens once the compromise is accepted. Since society depends on that acceptance, society will take pains to inculcate in each new generation the importance of accepting it. To anyone so trained, the compromise will not be thought of *as* a compromise, but simply as the right thing to do. Moreover, he will feel uneasy at the prospect of attaining his personal ends in a way that could run counter to the compromise. In Mill's words, he comes to think of himself as a being who *of course* pays regard to others (Mill, 1863, p. 232). Conformity with morality, aiming at the general happiness, has become part of his private happiness and not just a means to it.

Mill's answer to the question, what is the fundamental moral principle? is: do whatever makes for the greatest happiness all round. His answer to the other question (why obey it?) is: because you have been socially conditioned to associate your own happiness with that of other people. If you had not been so conditioned, there would be no stable society, and your life would be miserable. Moreover (and Mill learned this from David Hartley rather than Hobbes) greater satisfaction is to be derived from our socially conditioned desires than from our primary or biological ones.

Later Utilitarians have not usually followed Mill in this. Henry Sidgwick, indeed, in spite of Bentham, founded the greatest happiness principle on a rational, self-evident intuition. Moral philosophers of other persuasions have either accepted some form of intuitionism or have argued (unconvincingly) that 'why be moral?' is a nonsensical question.

D.H. Monro

See also ECONOMIC MAN; ENTITLEMENTS; HEDONISM.

BIBLIOGRAPHY

Bentham, J. 1789. *An Introduction to the Principles of Morals and Legislation*. Ed. J.H. Burns and H.L.A. Hart, London: Athlone Press, 1970.

Green, T.H. 1886. *Lectures on the Principles of Political Obligation*. London: Longmans, 1941.

Hobbes, T. 1651. *Leviathan, or The Matter, Forme & Power of a Commonwealth, Ecclesiasticall and Civill*. Oxford: Clarendon Press, 1909.

Hume, D. 1739. *A Treatise of Human Nature*. Ed. L.A. Selby-Bigge, Oxford: Clarendon Press, 1896.

Hume, D. 1751. *Enquiries Concerning the Human Understanding and Concerning the Principles of Morals*. Ed. L.A. Selby-Bigge, Oxford: Clarendon Press, 1902.

Hutcheson, F. 1728. *An Essay on the Nature and Conduct of the Passions, with Illustrations upon the Moral Sense*. Facsimile edn prepared by B. Fabian, Hildesheim: G. Olms, 1971.

Mandeville, B. 1724. *The Fable of the Bees, or Private Vices, Publick Benefits*. Ed. F.B. Kaye, Oxford: Clarendon Press, 1924.

Mill, J.S. 1863. *Utilitarianism.* In *Essays on Ethics, Religion and Society*, ed. J.M. Robson, Toronto: University of Toronto Press; London: Routledge & Kegan Paul, 1969.

Moore, G.E. 1903. *Principia Ethica.* Cambridge: Cambridge University Press.

Shaftesbury [A.A. Cooper], 3rd Earl. 1699. *An Inquiry Concerning Virtue or Merit.* Ed. D. Walford, Manchester: Manchester University Press, 1977.

Sidgwick, H. 1907. *The Methods of Ethics.* 7th edn, ed. E.E.C. Jones, London: Macmillan, 1962.

Smith, A. 1759. *The Theory of Moral Sentiments.* Ed. A.L. Macfie and D.D. Raphael, Oxford: Clarendon Press, 1974.

Smith, A. 1776. *An Inquiry into the Nature and Causes of the Wealth of Nations.* Ed. R.H. Campbell, A.S. Skinner and W.B. Todd, Oxford: Clarendon Press, 1976.

self-selection. *See* SELECTION BIAS AND SELF-SELECTION.

Seligman, Edwin Robert Anderson (1861–1939). Seligman was born in New York City on 25 April 1861 and died on 18 July 1939 at Lake Placid, New York. An economist of unusual erudition, energy and wide-ranging interests, Seligman successfully combined a life of distinguished scholarship with philanthropy and active participation and leadership in a variety of reform causes. Raised in a talented and wealthy New York Jewish business family, Seligman studied privately under Horatio Alger Jr. and at Columbia Grammar School before graduating from Columbia in 1879. After three years' study in Berlin, Heidelberg (under Karl Knies), Geneva and Paris he returned to Columbia obtaining MA and LLB degrees in 1884, the PhD cum laude in 1885 and a full professorship in political economy at age 30, a post he held until retirement in 1931. Dignified, wise and balanced in outlook, Seligman personified the best in late 19th-century efforts to blend orthodox classical and German historical economics. His original studies of neglected British and American economists, and his compilation of perhaps the world's greatest library of economic works, reveal his lifetime devotion to doctrinal history, while his widely read and durable *Economic Interpretation of History* (1902) testifies to the breadth and sensitivity of his historical knowledge. Like Henry Carter Adams, with whom he created the field of public finance in America, Seligman was influenced by Adolph Wagner. But he was more of a theorist than Adams, and his concepts of 'faculty' or ability to pay, and benefit, were the first systematic modern efforts to develop theoretical criteria of taxation. A severe critic of Henry George, Seligman nevertheless favoured taxes on land values and progressive inheritance taxes, and advocated proportional income taxes as early as 1894. Sympathetic to labour unions, federal railroad legislation, effective central banking measures and other moderate reform proposals, including deficit finance and public works during the depression of the 1930s, Seligman also advocated US aid to Europe after 1918 and the cancellation of their debts.

Seligman served on innumerable public bodies as a taxation and financial specialist, and as a social reformer, for example as Chairman of the Bureau of Municipal Research and with the National Civic Federation. A founder, first Treasurer and later President (1902–4) of the American Economic Association, he was an outstanding champion of academic freedom and co-founder of the American Association of University Professors, of which he was President 1919–20. His success as fund-raiser and Editor in Chief of the *Encyclopaedia of the Social Sciences* 1927–35 was a fitting culmination of an outstanding career of scholarly and public service.

A.W. COATS

SELECTED WORKS

1892. *On the Shifting and Incidence of Taxation.* Baltimore: American Economic Association. 5th edn, revised, New York: Columbia University Press, 1927.

1894. *Progressive Taxation in Theory and Practice.* Baltimore: American Economic Association. 2nd edn, revised and enlarged, Princeton: American Economic Association, 1908.

1895. *Essays in Taxation.* New York and London: Macmillan. 10th edn, 1925.

1902. *The Economic Interpretation of History.* New York: Columbia University Press. 2nd edn, revised, 1924.

1905. *The Principles of Economics, with Special Reference to American Conditions.* New York: Longmans Green & Co. 12th edn, revised, 1929.

1911. *The Income Tax: A Study of the History, Theory, and Practice of Income Taxation at Home and Abroad.* New York: Macmillan 2nd edn, revised and enlarged, 1914.

1925a. *Essays in Economics.* New York: Macmillan.

1925b. *Studies in Public Finance.* New York: Macmillan.

selling costs. Exchanging goods and services through a market permits great increases in the efficiency of productive activity. Yet markets are not costless. Appreciable costs must be incurred to bring buyer and seller together and to inform their transactions. When borne by the seller, these are conventionally called selling costs.

The magnitude of selling costs varies widely with the nature of the transaction. Such costs are modest on organized exchanges in which middlemen routinely link the buyers and sellers of standardized commodities, such as securities and grain, without producing or taking an inventory position. Thus, the commission of a 'no frills' New York Stock Exchange broker in 1985 was 1.7 per cent on a \$4000 common stock transaction and 0.4 per cent on a \$40,000 transaction. For more specialized goods, brokerage fees rise. Sotheby Parke Bernet, renowned auctioneers of antiques and *objets d'art*, charged sellers a standard commission of 10 per cent on lots selling at \$5000 or more, and up to 20 per cent on smaller lots, plus the cost of catalogue photographs. In addition, buyers paid a 10 per cent commission. Goods manufacturers often undertake extensive selling activities, including technical advisory service, personalized sales representation, the distribution of samples, providing point-of-sale displays, offering promotional devices such as sales coupons, and advertising. US Federal Trade Commission survey data for 1975 reveal that in consumer goods industries, manufacturers' media advertising outlays were 3.6 per cent of sales on average (with a maximum of 20 per cent for over-the-counter drug makers). 'Other' selling costs (including sales administration) averaged 9.8 per cent of sales. For producer goods (e.g. machinery) and intermediate materials industries, manufacturers' advertising and other selling costs averaged 0.6 and 6.1 per cent of sales respectively (see Weiss, Pascoe and Martin, 1983).

Additional costs are incurred to make goods conveniently available to consumers at the retail level. In the United States, 17 per cent of all employed persons worked in retailing during 1982. Socialist 'command' economies characteristically provide fewer services at this stage than their market-oriented counterparts. Then buyers, not sellers, must bear extra costs of searching out desired products and queuing to purchase them. In a comparison of data for ten quite diverse nations, Pryor (1977) found that these costs roughly balance, other things (such as per capita consumption levels) held equal. That is, the labour effort saved by command economy wholesale and retail establishments was approximately offset by longer consumer shopping hours.

Particularly high selling costs may arise in introducing new products to the market. Marshall (1920, pp. 305–6) records how the typewriter's acceptance was hastened when trained demonstrators were dispatched far and wide to show how much quicker the new way of writing was. For modern consumer goods, advertising is used as a primary instrument for directing attention to new products. A 1970 rule-of-thumb in the US cigarette industry held that launching a new product required an advertising blitz costing $10 million. When television advertising of cigarettes was outlawed in 1971, less powerful media were substituted, more reliance was placed on distributing free samples, and average product launch costs escalated to some $50 million.

The first economist to assign selling costs a central role in microeconomic theory was Chamberlin (1933). He defined selling costs as 'those which alter the demand curve for [a product]'. Chamberlin raised many fundamental questions that still crowd economists' research agenda: for example, whether more expenditure on selling costs reduces prices to the consumer (by permitting greater exploitation of production and retailing scale economies) or raises them, how consumer welfare is affected by the way advertising alters knowledge and product 'images', and how business strategy in non-atomistic markets is influenced by having selling costs as an additional instrument of rivalry.

An important theoretical contribution of Dorfman and Steiner (1954) demonstrated how the monopolistically competitive firm's optimal level of selling costs is determined simultaneously with price. Assuming diminishing marginal returns in the demand-shifting effect of selling outlays S, their profit-maximizing level in relation to sales PQ (price times quantity) can be derived as:

$$\left(\frac{S}{PQ}\right)^* = e_s\left(\frac{P - MC}{P}\right),$$

where e_s is the elasticity of the quantity sold with respect to selling outlays [i.e. $(\partial Q/\partial S) \times (S/Q)$]. Thus, a higher fraction of sales revenue will be devoted to selling costs, the more elastic is the response of consumers to incremental sales effort and the higher is the price–cost margin $(0 - MC)/P$ on each additional unit of output sold as a consequence of the effort.

How much stimulus high price–cost margins provide to selling effort depends in part upon whether the effort renders demand less elastic, permitting higher prices to be charged, and upon other factors (such as market structure) affecting the intensity of price competition. Price–cost margins are likely to be higher under monopoly and oligopoly than under atomistic competition. Market structure may also influence the level of selling costs in another way. Advertising and other demand-stimulating activities may benefit all sellers in a product market, so the benefit appropriated by any given firm incurring the cost will be larger, the greater is the firm's market share, with pure monopoly as the limit. On the other hand, selling costs are a non-price weapon by which oligopolists strive to take business away from one another. What balance of selling cost incentives will result from price–cost margins, appropriability, and inter-firm non-price rivalry under particular structural conditions is difficult to determine theoretically. In an ambitious empirical study, Lambin (1976) has shown that for some products, oligopolistic rivalry led to advertising outlays well above the levels that would have maximized sellers' collective profits.

Manufacturers' sales and profitability may also depend upon the level of selling costs incurred by their retailers. There too incentive problems can intrude. The provision of pre-sale demonstration services and reputational advertising is costly, and the benefits may not be fully appropriable by the cost-absorbing retailer. Other retailers may 'free-ride' on those efforts, drawing sales away from the providers by offering a lower price consistent with their lower level of selling costs. To encourage their retailers to incur desired selling costs, manufacturers have often insulated them from some price competition by conferring exclusive franchises upon them or by specifying minimum resale prices. With higher price–cost margins ensuing, retailers are motivated under the Dorfman–Steiner theorem or some variant to increase their selling efforts (and costs). However, too high a price–cost margin may stimulate excessive and duplicative selling outlays as oligopolistic retailers vie for patronage, and too rigid a price policy may stifle marketing channel innovation. On these dilemmas, arising when the 'invisible hand' conveys erroneous signals on non-price dimensions, considerable new theoretical and empirical research continues. No definitive synthesis has yet emerged.

F.M. SCHERER

See also ADVERTISING; CHAMBERLIN, EDWARD HASTINGS; MONOPOLISTIC COMPETITION; PRODUCT DIFFERENTIATION.

BIBLIOGRAPHY

Chamberlin, E.H. 1933. *The Theory of Monopolistic Competition.* Cambridge, Mass.: Harvard University Press.

Dorfman, R. and Steiner, P.O. 1954. Optimal advertising and optimal quality. *American Economic Review* 44, December, 826–36.

Lambin, J.-J. 1976. *Advertising, Competition, and Market Conduct in Oligopoly over Time.* Amsterdam: North-Holland.

Marshall, A. 1920. *Industry and Trade.* 3rd edn, London: Macmillan.

Pryor, F.L. 1977. Some costs and benefits of markets: an empirical study. *Quarterly Journal of Economics* 91(1), February, 81–102.

Weiss, L.W., Pascoe, G. and Martin, S. 1983. The size of selling costs. *Review of Economics and Statistics* 65(4), November, 668–72.

semiparametric estimation. A structural econometric model typically has the form $y = f(x, u, \theta)$, where y is a set of observed dependent variables; x a set of observed explanatory variables; u represents some unobserved variables, often called 'error' terms or stochastic terms; and θ is a parameter vector which is to be estimated. The main focus of econometric modelling is on specification of the function f. But estimation and inference also require assumptions about the statistical properties of u. Very little may be known about those variables, so one should be cautious of estimators that rely on a specific distribution function for them.

This applies particularly to a large class of non-linear econometric models that are commonly estimated by maximum likelihood (ML) under the assumption of normally distributed error terms. Examples are discrete choice models, censored and truncated regression models, and some disequilibrium models (see Maddala, 1983). In particular, let $y^* = v(x, \theta) + u$ be an unobserved (latent) variable and let y be the observed dependent variable: then $y = 1[y^* > 0]$ defines the binary choice model; $y = y^* \cdot 1[y^* > 0]$ defines the simplest version of the censored regression model; and in the truncated regression model neither y^* nor x is observed unless y^* is positive. (The indicator function $1[\cdot]$ equals one if its argument is true, and equals zero otherwise.) The sample $(x_i, y_i), i = 1, \ldots, n$, is assumed to be a cross-section with independent errors u_i.

The model can generally be rewritten in regression form as $y = g(x, \theta; F) + \epsilon$ with $E[\epsilon] = 0$, where F is the distribution function of u. A special case is the *single-index* model where $g(x, \theta; F) = h(v(x, \theta); F)$ for some given index function v – for example, the models given above with partially observed y^*.

Semiparametric (also called *distribution-free*) methods estimate θ consistently when F is unknown but f (or g) is specified. Some of the methods described below can handle more general kinds of unknown functional dependence, and border on the separate topic of non-parametric regression. If, on the other hand, g does not depend on F, one has the *nonlinear regression* model: while least squares and method of moments estimators are, strictly speaking, semiparametric estimators, that is also a separate topic (see, for example, Amemiya, 1983). For an account of adaptive estimation of nonlinear regression models (i.e., semiparametric estimation with the same large-sample efficiency as if F were known), see Manski (1984).

The following headings cover some of the main directions of semiparametric estimation in econometrics.

LEAST ABSOLUTE DEVIATIONS AND RELATED METHODS

One can rewrite the model as $y = \mu(x, \theta; F) + \epsilon$ where now median $[\epsilon] = 0$ (instead of $E[\epsilon] = 0$). If μ does not depend on F, and suitable regularity conditions hold, then θ is consistently estimated by minimizing the sum of absolute deviations $\Sigma_i |y_i - \mu_i|$ with respect to θ, where $\mu_i = \text{median}[f(x_i, u_i, \theta)]$. This applies to the censored regression model (Powell, 1984), and to the binary choice model, where the method reduces to the maximum score estimator (Manski, 1974 and 1985). An important feature of this approach is that the errors u_i need not be identically distributed.

Unlike many semiparametric estimators, Powell's least absolute deviations (LAD) estimator has a known asymptotic distribution: under the assumption of independent identically distributed (i.i.d.) errors, $\hat{\theta}$ converges at the rate $n^{-1/2}$ to a normal distribution with an explicit expression for the asymptotic variance (Powell, 1984). The asymptotic distribution of the maximum score estimator is not yet known; preliminary investigations indicate an $n^{-1/3}$ rate of convergence.

Manski's maximum score method is more than a special case of LAD, because it can be applied to the random utility model with any number of discrete choices, although only under the following condition. Let $u_{i,j}$ be the stochastic component of the utility function for case i and choice j; then the $u_{i,j}$ must be i.i.d. across choices for each case. This is quite restrictive. The only other practicable semiparametric method for polychotomous choice models is Gallant's semi-nonparametric approach (see below).

If the error distribution is known to be *symmetric*, then Powell's LAD method can be applied also to the truncated regression model by 'symmetric trimming': in effect, large positive residuals are trimmed to compensate for observations with large negative residuals having been dropped from the sample. Symmetry may be thought a rather artificial assumption. But if it holds, then symmetric trimming can be applied also to least squares estimation of both the censored and the truncated regression models (Powell, 1986), with considerable savings in computation when compared with LAD estimation.

NONPARAMETRIC MAXIMUM LIKELIHOOD ESTIMATION OF F

If θ were known, the error terms ϵ would be observable and would allow nonparametric maximum likelihood (NPML) estimation of F, say $\hat{F}(\cdot|\theta)$. Tractable NPML estimators are available for several cases, the best known being the Kaplan–Meier estimator for a censored distribution (Kaplan and Meier, 1958); there is a similar estimator in the truncated case (Lynden-Bell, 1971). In fact θ must also be estimated, for which two approaches have been developed.

Semiparametric maximum likelihood. Semiparametric maximum likelihood (SPML) estimation is possible if the likelihood function can be maximized over both θ and F. This is a theoretically attractive approach but is practical in only a few cases. The following examples are special in that the ML estimator exists without any prior smoothness assumptions on F.

A method for implementing the SPML estimator of the binary choice model is given by Cosslett (1983). Here F is the distribution function of the error term in the underlying regression model for y^*: a normal distribution would give the probit model, a logistic distribution the logit model. Both θ and F are consistently estimated, but the asymptotic distribution is not known.

Heckman and Singer (1984) give an algorithm for the SPML estimator of a mixture model of duration data (specifically, unemployment duration). The distribution function of durations for an individual, $G(t|u,x,\theta)$, depends on an unobserved characteristic u, so the distribution of observed durations is $\int G(t|u, x, \theta)\,\mathrm{d}F(u)$. Heckman and Singer investigate the case where F is unknown but G is a given parametric function (the Weibull model). The classical parametric ML estimator is sensitive to misspecification of F. The SPML estimator of θ and F is shown to be consistent, but also in this case the asymptotic distribution is unknown.

Bias-corrected regression. Consider again a limited dependent variable model with the underlying regression equation $y^* = v(x,\theta) + u$ and the observed dependent variable y. Let $\eta(y, v(x, \theta); F)$ be an exogenous correction term such that $E[\eta] = E[y - y^*]$. Then, if F were known, θ could be consistently estimated from the regression $y = v(x,\theta) + \eta(y, v(x, \theta); F) + \epsilon$. When F is normal, this is the basis of Heckman's two-stage estimator (see Maddala, 1983, ch. 8).

In fact F is unknown, but one can replace it by its NPML estimator (suitably trimmed if necessary to avoid instability at large values of residuals) and estimate

$$y = v(x,\theta) + \eta[y, v(x,\theta); \hat{F}(\cdot|\theta)] + \epsilon$$

by least squares or method of moments. This is computationally awkward because the dependence of $\hat{F}$ on θ is not explicit: the most practical approach seems to be the EM algorithm, an iterative scheme where one alternately estimates F and θ.

Several authors have taken this approach, and we mention in particular the truncated regression estimator of Buckley and James (1979) (see also Miller and Halpern, 1982). Despite much research effort, a definitive proof of consistency of $\hat{\theta}$ has not yet been published.

SEMI-NONPARAMETRIC ESTIMATION

A straightforward response to misspecification of a distribution is to make it a member of a larger parametric family. If the number of parameters is allowed to grow with sample size, it may be possible to find an estimate $\hat{F}$ that converges to the true distribution. This has been formalized by Gallant, who coined the term 'semi-nonparametric' and established conditions under which the resulting least squares or maximum likelihood estimators of θ and F are strongly consistent (see Gallant and Nychka, 1987). The Phillips ERA (Phillips, 1983) can be used as a parametric representation of an unknown distribution function. A convenient special case of this is the Hermite expansion used by Gallant and Nychka, who investigate the nonlinear regression model with sample selection. (The method also works for more general classes of unknown functions.)

The dimensionality $k(n)$ of the parametric family containing $\hat{F}$ may be fixed *a priori* or may be data based. Once $k(n)$ is determined, existing parametric estimation methods can be used. The question of an operational data-based rule for $k(n)$ remains, and it is not known under exactly what circumstances the 'traditional' method is valid (add parameters as long as they are statistically significant). It also remains to be seen whether conventional statistical tests, which treat $k(n)$ as fixed, are asymptotically valid for any data-based selection rule.

INSTRUMENTAL VARIABLES

If the semiparametric model has the single-index form with a linear index function, i.e., $y = h(x \cdot \theta; F) + \epsilon$, then integration by parts gives

$$\theta_j E[\partial h/\partial v] = -E[y \partial \ln p(x)/\partial x_j],$$

where $p(x)$ is the density of x. This of course assumes the existence of $\partial p(x)/\partial x_j$, so it does not hold for the coefficients of discrete explanatory variables or for the constant term. The term $E[\partial h/\partial v]$ depends on F and so is unknown, but the right-hand side can be consistently estimated by the covariance between y and the instrumental variable $\partial \ln p/\partial x_j$. Thus the coefficients θ_j of the continuous components of x can be estimated up to an overall scale factor (Stoker, 1986).

The problem of the unknown distribution of u has been replaced by that of the unknown distribution of x. Logically this is a simpler problem, because x is an observed variable and estimation of $\partial \ln p/\partial x$ does not involve the econometric model at all. The higher the dimensionality of x, the more difficult it will be to get adequate estimates of $\partial \ln p/\partial x$ from data sets of realistic size. Several standard methods available for nonparametric density estimation can also be used to estimate $\partial \ln p/\partial x$, including the semi-nonparametric approach of Gallant.

STEPHEN R. COSSLETT

BIBLIOGRAPHY

Amemiya, T. 1983. Nonlinear regression models. In *Handbook of Econometrics*, Vol. 1, ed. Z. Griliches and M.D. Intriligator, Amsterdam: North-Holland,

Buckley, J. and James, I. 1979. Linear regression with censored data. *Biometrika* 66, 429–36.

Cosslett, S.R. 1983. Distribution-free maximum likelihood estimator of the binary choice model. *Econometrica* 51, 765–82.

Gallant, A.R. and Nychka, D.W. 1987. Semi-nonparametric maximum likelihood estimation. *Econometrica* 55.

Heckman, J. and Singer, B. 1984. A method for minimizing the impact of distributional assumptions in econometric models for duration data. *Econometrica* 52, 271–320.

Kaplan, E.L. and Meier, P. 1958. Nonparametric estimation from incomplete observations. *Journal of the American Statistical Association* 53, 457–81.

Lynden-Bell, D. 1971. A method of allowing for known observational selection in small samples applied to 3CR quasars. *Monthly Notices of the Royal Astronomical Society* 155, 95–118.

Maddala, G.S. 1983. *Limited Dependent and Qualitative Variables in Econometrics*. Cambridge: Cambridge University Press.

Manski, C.F. 1974. Maximum score estimation of the stochastic utility model of choice. *Journal of Econometrics* 3, 205–28.

Manski, C.F. 1984. Adaptive estimation of non-linear regression models. *Econometric Reviews* 3, 145–94.

Manski, C.F. 1985. Semiparametric analysis of discrete response: asymptotic properties of the maximum score estimator. *Journal of Econometrics* 27, 303–33.

Miller, R. and Halpern, J. 1982. Regression with censored data. *Biometrika* 69, 521–31.

Phillips, P.C.B. 1983. ERA's: a new approach to small sample theory. *Econometrica* 51, 1505–25.

Powell, J.L. 1984. Least absolute deviations estimation for the censored regression model. *Journal of Econometrics* 25, 303–25.

Powell, J.L. 1986. Symmetrically trimmed least squares estimation for tobit models. *Econometrica* 54, 1435–60.

Stoker, T.M. 1986. Consistent estimation of scaled coefficients. *Econometrica* 54, 1461–81.

Senior, Nassau William (1790–1864). Born at Compton Beauchamp in Berkshire, the eldest son of John Raven Senior, Vicar of Durnford, Nassau Senior studied for the Bar in London, was the first Drummond Professor of Political Economy at Oxford, 1825–30, and was elected to a second term, 1847–52. In 1831 he was appointed Professor of Political Economy at King's College, London, but was soon forced to resign over his controversial recommendation that some of the revenues of the Established Church in Ireland be turned over to the Roman Catholics. Senior became a respected adviser: he served on the Commission for inquiring into the Administration and Operation of the Poor Laws (1832–4), being mainly responsible for the writing of its report, and was consulted by Lord John Russell on Irish Poor Law Reform in 1836. In 1841 Senior drew up the Report of the Commission on the condition of the Unemployed Hand-loom Weavers (on this see Stigler, 1949, Lecture 3). Two years after it was founded in 1821 Senior was elected to membership of the Political Economy Club and remained a member, except for the years 1848–53, until his death.

Senior first came to the notice of those conversant with political economy through an article on the Corn Laws in the *Quarterly Review* (1821), and he was a regular contributor to the *Edinburgh Review* from 1841 to 1855. He was at home in both literary and political circles in London and cultivated an interest in continental affairs via frequent travels and the company of men of influence, among whom were Guizot and De Tocqueville. Conversations with such men in France and Italy and in Ireland were assiduously recorded (and checked for accuracy) and, together with a traveller's observations on these and other countries, filled many journals. Several of these were published, including conversations with De Tocqueville spanning the years 1834–59.

It was Senior's intention to publish a systematic account of political economy, collecting the ideas that were largely scattered in periodicals, lectures, official reports and pamphlets into a major treatise. The plan was not fulfilled and his main printed legacy is his 1836 *Outline of the Science of Political Economy*, plus a collection of pamphlets and public letters published by Augustus Kelley, entitled *Selected Writings on Economics* (1966) and his *Three Lectures on the Rate of Wages* (1830a). S. Leon Levy undertook the work Senior never brought to fruition, in a volume entitled *Industrial Efficiency and Social Economy* (1928). This is a composite, organized by a plan of the editor's own making, and comprising selections from periodical articles, reports and – mainly – manuscript lectures from Senior's second term as Drummond Professor. The work is supposed to represent Senior's 'mature' thoughts, but the manner of its composition makes it of very limited value from a scholarly point of view.

Senior belonged to the band of eminent political economists of the second quarter of the 19th century who may be called respectful dissenters from Ricardo's doctrines. He did not dissent on methodological grounds, as did Whewell and Richard Jones (de Marchi and Sturges, 1973; Hollander, 1985, vol. 1, chs 1–3), but on value and distribution he followed Smith and Say more closely than Ricardo. Thus 'value' to Senior meant value in exchange rather than cost of production or labour cost (1836, pp. 13–14). And distribution he preferred to treat as a question of factor incomes rather than of functional shares. The expression 'high wages', for example, Senior used to stand for high nominal or real wages rather than for a large share of labour's product actually received by labour (1830a, pp. 2–3). This is not to say that he anticipated the marginal productivity theory of distribution, although at least as far as labour and capital are concerned he liked to think of the incomes attributable to each as payment for services rendered or, even more especially, as a 'reward ... [for] conduct' (1836, p. 89).

Senior's approach to distribution displays tensions that are unavoidable in trying to combine a Ricardian concern with macro-issues such as capital and population growth and the time-path of wages with a Smithian predilection to treat value and distribution as the outcome of voluntary exchanges entered into by individuals. To illustrate: Senior retained the Ricardian theory of rent, whereby rent is an intra-marginal surplus. This surplus accrues to ownership. Where, however, there is competitive access to the powers of nature, the price of the product equals the sum of wages, a reward for labour services, and profit, a return for waiting or 'abstinence' (ibid.). This falls short of an integrated theory of distribution, reflecting as it does the institutional fact of appropriation, on the one hand, and economic conduct by free agents, on the other. Similarly, in discussing the time-path of wages, Senior reverted to a wages-fund approach: given labour productivity, 'the rate of wages depends on the extent of the fund for the maintenance of labourers, compared with the number of labourers to be maintained' (1830a, p. xii). This refers to the average wage; but we are not told how individual contracts struck between worker and employer upon the value of labour services relate to this average. The problem is familiar to modern theorists wanting to make explicit the micro-foundations of macro-economics; though the major difficulty, changing relative wages, Senior neatly sidestepped by following Smith in the conviction that, once established, relative wage scales remained fixed (1830b, p. 15).

Senior's Ricardianism is perhaps most evident in his views on trade and on the international aspects of money. In *Three Lectures on the Transmission of the Precious Metals*, delivered at Oxford in June 1827 and printed the following year, which issue he felt to be 'next to the Reformation, next to the question of free religion, the most momentous that has ever been submitted to human decision' (1828, p. 88), Senior employed Hume's doctrine (and Ricardo's) to show that no country can have a permanently favourable or unfavourable balance of trade or exchange rate; then used this against the mercantilist view. His main concern is the efficient allocation of labour, and this leads him to the Ricardian conclusion that if a domestic tax on one industry hurts its international competitiveness then a 'countervailing duty' on the competing import is 'not a departure from the principles of free trade but an application of them' (p. 70; compare Ricardo 1822, vol. IV, p. 217). In another set of three lectures, this time *On the Cost of Obtaining Money* (1830b), Senior addressed the question of international comparisons of wages and argued that the productivity of labour measured in the goods required to import precious metals (in a non-mining country), determines whether wages are high or low. In both sets of lectures Senior discusses paper money and reaches the basic Ricardian conclusion that variations in the amount of the currency, whether metal or paper, may cause sudden disturbances but these will be transitory.

It is worth stressing that the Stoic tradition so evident in Smith's writings – self-respect issuing from prudent behaviour, most notably self-restraint – also infuses Senior's discussions of distribution and related social issues. Senior takes it as given that men tend to be myopic and to prefer taking their ease to working (Senior 1827, p. 8; 1836, pp. 26 ff.). He therefore considered the supply of goods to be a result of prudential exertions to overcome these obstacles (1836, pp. 15–16). There is no such exertion attached to mere ownership. Hence the income of a landlord is a transfer and categorically distinct from wages and profits, which are properly considered rewards. They are like the good which results from confronting and overcoming unavoidable evil (pain). Although Senior is properly extolled for having glimpsed marginal utility, his contribution on the side of supply and the overcoming of obstacles is at least as interesting.

Marx, it need hardly be added, saw Senior as 'a mere apologist of the existing order' (Marx, 1905–10, vol. 3, p. 353). This in part refers to Senior's view that profit is the reward of 'abstinence'. Senior's sacrifice-reward approach to the sharing out of the price of product at the margin, however, was adopted fully by the later Ricardians, John Stuart Mill (1848, p. 400) and John Elliott Cairnes (1874, p. 74).

Senior's views on method too are indistinguishable in all but two details from John Stuart Mill's. One reasons in political economy from true premises known by introspection (the desire for wealth, subject to a preference for least effort and present enjoyment) or from observation (the laws of return and of population). Being true these premises will, upon correct reasoning, yield true principles. In the *science* of political economy, therefore, there resides as much certainty as in any science outside axiomatic logic (Senior, 1827, p. 11). Nonetheless, the psychological drives for wealth, leisure and present satisfaction produce counteracting conduct, so that it is difficult to assign motives (causes) to or predict behaviour (p. 9).

Mill tended to bundle the three psychological motives together and make the wealth motive do most of the work. He also chose to reason hypothetically, as if the desire for wealth were the sole motivation of an individual. This meant that his results could be true only in the abstract, or to the degree to which that assumption was in fact true. In later years Senior, despite his early warning that counteracting motives could not readily be disentangled (1827, p. 9), argued against Mill's simplifying approach. His *Four Introductory Lectures* from the second period of his tenure of the Drummond Professorship (1847–52) lamented the slow progress made in political economy. He found reason in the Millian manner of dealing with the science. Hypothetical reasoning, in Senior's view, rendered the subject unattractive, because unrealistic; and laid the reasoner open to error, either from forgetting some relevant additional cause or from forgetting that the reasoning itself was based on arbitrary assumptions and was not directly transferable to real world situations (Senior, 1852, pp. 63–5). In more recent discussion, T.W. Hutchison has kept Senior's objections alive, protesting in particular a tendency to confuse tautological with empirical propositions, and to leap straight from abstract models to policy conclusions (Hutchison, 1938). While Senior's concern is understandable, to the extent to which his earlier judgement was well-founded – 'that we are liable to the greatest mistakes when we endeavour to assign motives [causes] to ... conduct' (1827, p. 9) – it is not clear that the gains anything by his later modified approach, and there is in that case less practical difference between his position and Mill's than some modern commentators have made out (Bowley, 1937, pp. 59–62).

Both Senior and Mill cautioned against applying the principles of political economy without the utmost care and a broad and detailed knowledge of the facts applying to any case in question. Senior, however, nonetheless confidently offered advice on the great issues of the 1830s and 1840s: Poor Law reform; the Factory Act (Ten Hours Bill); agricultural unrest, overpopulation and emigration; free trade and the role of banks in commercial crises. In few of the views he expressed is there anything very remarkable – an exception is noted below in connection with the Ten Hours Bills – but he had a striking ability to cut through to the heart of complex issues, and he had a persuasive pen. To illustrate, his overriding criterion for judging all schemes of relief to the able-bodied poor was whether they destroyed incentives by separating effort from reward (1830a, preface; 1834, pp. 126 ff.). In a particular argument against reducing factory hours, he held that if capital replenishment is, say, 11/12ths of gross turnover, then interest plus profits depend essentially on the last hour of a twelve-hour day. A ten-hour day, therefore, would spell ruin (1837, pp. 12–13). This not only presupposed constant returns to hours worked, but confused stocks and flows in the calculation of returns (Johnson, 1969).

N. DE MARCHI

SELECTED WORKS

1827. *An Introductory Lecture on Political Economy*. In *Selected Writings on Economics. A Volume of Pamphlets 1827–1852*, New York: Kelley Reprint, 1965.

1828. *Three Lectures on the Transmission of the Precious Metals*. In *Selected Writings*.

1830a. *Three Lectures on the Rate of Wages*. London: Murray.

1830b. *Three Lectures on the Cost of Obtaining Money*. In *Selected Writings*.

1834. *Report from his Majesty's Commissioners on the Administration and Practical Operation of the Poor Laws*. British Parliamentary Papers.

1836. *An Outline of the Science of Political Economy*. New York: Kelley Reprint, 1965.

1837. *Two Letters on the Factory Acts*. In *Selected Writings*.

1852. *Four Introductory Lectures on Political Economy*. In *Selected Writings*.

1872. *Correspondence and Conversations of Alexis De Toqueville with Nassau William Senior from 1834 to 1859*. 2 vols, ed. M.C.M. Simpson, 2nd edn, London: Henry S. King.

BIBLIOGRAPHY

Bowley, M. 1937. *Nassau Senior and Classical Economics*. London: Allen & Unwin.

Cairnes, J.E. 1874. *Some Leading Principles of Political Economy Newly Expounded*. London: Macmillan.

De Marchi, N. and Sturges, R.P. 1973. Malthus' and Ricardo's inductivist critics: four letters to William Whewell. *Economica* 40(160), November, 379–93.

Hollander, S. 1985. *The Economics of John Stuart Mill*. 2 vols, Oxford: Blackwell.

Hutchison, T.W. 1938. *The Significance and Basic Postulates of Economic Theory*. London: Macmillan.

Johnson, O. 1969. The 'last hour' of Senior and Marx. *History of Political Economy* 1(2), Fall, 359–69.

Levy, S. L. (ed.) 1928. *Industrial Efficiency and Social Economy* by Nassau W. Senior. 2 vols, New York: Henry Holt & Co.

Marx, K. 1905–10. *Theories of Surplus Value*, 3 vols, London: Lawrence & Wishart, 1969, 1972.

Mill, J.S. 1848. *Principles of Political Economy with some of their Applications to Social Philosophy*. In *Collected Works of John Stuart Mill*, ed. J.M. Robson, Vols II, III, Toronto: University of Toronto Press, 1965.

Ricardo, D. 1822. On protection to agriculture. In *The Works and Correspondence of David Ricardo*, ed. P. Sraffa with the collaboration of M.H. Dobb, Vol. IV, Cambridge: Cambridge University Press for the Royal Economic Society, 1951.

Stigler, G.J. 1949. The classical economists: an alternative view. In G.J. Stigler, *Five Lectures on Economic Problems*, London: Longmans, Green for the London School of Economics and Political Science.

separability. Suppose you were interested in the demand for tomatoes in Ireland. A few words with traders, producers, agricultural scientists, official statisticians and anthropologists would provide a mass of 'facts' about that particular market, the data available, and the role of tomatoes in Irish culture, which would never occur to pure-minded economists. We commonly neglect such matters, assembling our models from stock components which may be incapable of catching what may, after all, be the essence of the problem we believe ourselves to be investigating.

To proceed differently we would need to be able to tailor models for particular problems and particular data. That is where separability, duality, and the idea of characteristics common to different phenomena, for instance, come in.

Separability is about the structure we are to impose on our model: what to investigate in detail, what can be sketched in with broad strokes without violence to the facts. Perfect competition and the absence of external economies, which allow us to examine the behaviour of individual firms in isolation; constant returns, permitting us to discuss the structure of a firm's production plans without knowing its size; Samuelson's independence axiom which says that how we use our resources when it shines is independent of how we would have had it rained; and Bergson's Social Welfare Function, based on the sovereignty of self-regarding households; all embodying separability assumptions, whose function is to allow us to examine one aspect of a problem in at least relative isolation from the others, given that we have posed it in terms of appropriate independent variables.

However, the classical locus of the idea is in the theory of demand and the classical treatment in Leontief's two papers (1947a, 1947b) on functional structure; the first including a proof that addition is, in essence, the only really well behaved associative operation; the second, a diagram showing that he realized the full implications of that fact as spelled out below, in 1947.

Say that the vector x is *separable* in the utility function $f(\cdot)$ if $u = f(x, y) = F(\phi(x), y)$, say, where all the functions are *well behaved* – that is to say scalar valued, strictly increasing in their functional arguments, and continuous. Such an assumption might be appropriate were the goods X – in an obvious notation – closely related. In that case the Y might be broad aggregates, whose effect on the X needs to be sketched in.

Suppose that each of the vectors x_t, or better, of the *sectors* $t \in T$, is separable in $f(\cdot)$, then and only then

$$u = f(x, y) = F(v, y), \tag{1}$$

either locally or globally according to the nature of the domain, where

$$x = (x_t)_{t \in T}, \quad v = (v_t)_{t \in T}, \quad v_t = f^t(x_t), \tag{2}$$

and the functions are well behaved, so that the sectors are

jointly separable. Say that the *function* $f(\cdot)$ is weakly separable, whenever (1)–(2) hold, and *separable* when y is the null vector so that $u = f(x) = F(v)$.

One reason for postulating separability, first advanced by Strotz in 1958, is that households may budget in two stages, first deciding how much, m_t, to allocate to each of the broad groups, leaving the final choice

$$x_i = \psi^t(p_t, m_t), \qquad \text{each } i \in t, \tag{3}$$

of how to spend it until the 'appropriate' prices $p_t = (p_i)_{i\in t}$, are known. Given that the right m_t were chosen at the first stage, a separable utility function would clearly lead to demands like (3), which in turn effectively implies separability. Everything therefore turns on the likelihood of the m_t being chosen well, and hence on the information needed to do so.

Strotz was formally wrong in assuming that we only need to know a single set of price indices, but essentially right. Should a household have converged on the correct m_t at some stage, perhaps in a period of stable prices, it would be able to update its budget continuously from then on, using two sets of differential indices of the form $\mathrm{d}P_t/P_t = \Sigma_{i\in t} w_i \,\mathrm{d}p_i/p_i$, one, a Divisia Index with the weights $w_i = p_i x_i/m_t$, to deflate the money expenditures m_t, the other, using the corresponding marginal expenditure pattern $w_i = p_i \partial x_i/\partial m_t$, to allow for substitution between goods. To budget in real terms, then, only the second set is needed. This is because (3), coupled with their symmetry, implies that the substitution effects

$$\begin{aligned}\sigma_{ij} = \delta x_i/\delta p_j &= \lambda_{rs}\partial x_i/\partial m_r, \partial x_j/\partial m_s \\ &= \mu_{rs}\partial x_i/\partial m . \partial x_j/\partial m, \text{ say,}\end{aligned} \tag{4}$$

each $i \in r$, $j \in s \neq r$, where the δ's denote compensated derivatives, as Pearce showed in 1961. The λ's and μ's are symmetrical, the former being intergroup substitution effects.

If households do budget in two stages, it is probably to save hassle, even at the cost of mistakes – so that (4) would hold only approximately. Given the quantity and quality of our data it would be well worth imposing nevertheless to save degrees of freedom. Unfortunately it does not save enough in practice, so that Stone, Theil, and their colleagues in Cambridge and Rotterdam followed Frisch and his in Oslo in assuming *additive* utility

$$u = f(x) = \sum f^t(x_t), \tag{5}$$

where $f(\cdot)$, and each $f^t(\cdot)$, is well behaved, in an appropriate normalization, as had the early utilitarians Bentham and Paley in their really rather sophisticated discussions, not to speak of Bernouilli, Ramsey, von Neumann and Savage. Indeed, they commonly imposed *complete additivity*, with the x_t scalars, not just *group-wise additivity*. In either case, each set of sectors is clearly separable, so that

$$\mu_{rs} = \mu_{r,-r} = \mu_{-s,s} = \mu, \text{ say,} \tag{6}$$

where $-r = \{t \in T \mid t \neq r\}$, in (4).

The substitution effects as measured in these early studies were commonly very small – so small indeed that gross complementarity was the norm. If correct this would have had important implications for economic policy. Suspecting that this might reflect the approximate proportionality between own price and income elasticities, pointed out by Pigou in 1910, and commonly implied by (6), Deaton ran straightforward regressions in 1974, finding no such tendency towards proportionality and much more substitution. Since then demand analysts, following Deaton and Muellbauer (1980), have tended to forgo additivity, except over time, and use composite commodities, a generalization of quasi-homothetic separability as defined below, instead.

Slutsky had shown in his classic article that the marginal utility of at most one good increases near a chosen point in the case of complete additivity. If one does, all the other goods are inferior, which is frequently unacceptable, so that we can commonly assume each $f^t(\cdot)$ concave, implying that all the goods are normal and substitutes for each other, points of importance in both theoretical and empirical work.

Since additivity plays such a large role in the theoretical analyses of choice over time, under uncertainty, and by benevolent governments, it is worth discussing further. Equation (6) suggests that it will hold if each set of sectors is separable, as Debreu proved in 1959 for rather general product spaces, beyond which it can readily be extended. Indeed it looks as if it should be enough that each set $-t$ were separable, a particular case of a general result that we need only a few sets to be separable for all to be if they overlap enough. This follows from the fact that addition is, in effect, the only strictly increasing continuous operation, so that $f(x, y, z) = G(g(x, y), z) = H(x, h(y, z))$, implies that it can be written as $F(a(x) + b(y) + c(z))$, where each function is well-behaved. Because of this it is frequently easy to dream up plausible, easily understood, assumptions to justify additivity in an appropriate normalization.

Consider, for example, a benevolent government, facing uncertainty, interested only in the welfare of its self-centred citizens. Let x_{is} be the consumption vector for individual i in state s. The rows of the corresponding grid are separable, and so are the columns if it satisfies a weak form of Samuelson's independence axiom, which many would say is a minimal condition for rationality. These overlap a great deal more than needed to imply

$$W = f(x) = \sum_{is} f^{is}(x_{is}) = \sum_i v_i = \sum_s w_s, \text{ say,} \tag{7}$$

in an appropriate normalization, where $v_i = \Sigma_s f^{is}(x_{is})$, is i's welfare, ex ante, and $w_s = \Sigma_i f^{is}(x_{is})$, society's, ex post in state s: Savage and Bentham at a blow, if you like, with state-dependent preferences, too.

This does not say that individual utility functions are additive, but that the government cannot act rationally – in the sense of the weak independence axiom – on the basis of a Bergson Social Welfare Function, if they are not. Even if we applied that axiom to the individuals, it would imply only separability, not additivity. This paradox is not unduly worrying here, because a stronger form of Samuelson's axiom which is also widely accepted, would imply additivity if applied to individual utility functions.

Look therefore at another case. The future is separable in a utility function iff it can be written $u_t = f^t(x_t, u_{t+1})$, $t = 0, 1, \ldots$. Apply this to the social welfarc function instead, and we get (7) once again, though there is no obvious justification for additivity over time in the case of individuals.

That a set of axioms implies additivity is as likely to be evidence against them as for it.

Separability is often used in the analysis of market choices, for which prices are the natural independent variables. It is therefore useful that additivity is readily specified in the dual. Appropriately generalized, Slutsky's result implies that any reasonable additive quasiconcave utility $f(\cdot)$ is concave, so that its component functions $f^t(\cdot)$ are too. It can therefore be represented by its profit function

$$g(p, q) = \sup\{qf(x) - p, x\} = \sum_t g^t(p_t, q),$$

where $g^t(\cdot)$ is that corresponding to $f^t(\cdot)$, and q, the shadow price of utility, is the inverse of the marginal utility of expenditure. Moreover

$$x_i = -g_i(p, q) = -g_i^t(p_t, q), \qquad \text{each } i/\epsilon t,$$

$$u = g_0(p, q) = \sum_t g_0^t(p_t, q), \tag{8}$$

under strict quasiconcavity, where subscripts stand for derivatives, and 0 corresponds to q.

The only disadvantage with completely additive utility, then, is that it does not fit the facts. Can it be adapted to do so? Under it

$$f'^i(x_i) = \lambda p_i = \mu r_i, \tag{9i}$$

$$x_i = -g_i^i(p_i, q) = -h'^i(\mu r_i), \tag{9ii}$$

by (5), (8) and homogeneity, where λ is the marginal utility of expenditure, $\mu = \lambda m = \mu(r)$, $r_i = p_i/m$, $h^i(z) = g^i(z, 1)$, and the prime denotes differentiation.

Pollak (1972) defined *generalized additive separability* as yielding demand curves of the form

$$x_i = \alpha^i(r_i, \rho(r)); \qquad \text{that is, } r_i = \beta^i(x_i, \xi(x)), \text{ say.} \tag{10}$$

The Slutsky conditions yield a complicated set of partial differential equations here, because the compensating change in m alters each of the r's. Not surprisingly, therefore, it yields several distinct classes of solution. However, the largest and most interesting has utility functions

$$u = \sum f^i(\xi x_i) - \phi(\xi) = \sum h^i(\rho r_i) - \theta(\rho). \tag{11}$$

ξ, then, is costly to produce, in terms of utility, but increases the *effective quantity* of each good from x_i to $x_i^* = \xi x_i = \xi(x)x_i$ while its *effective price* becomes $r_i^* = \rho r_i = \rho(r)r_i$. One might expect that $\rho\xi = 1$, were it not for (9ii) which suggests $\rho\xi = \mu$ instead. This is correct; utility not money income, is the appropriate numeraire here. The corresponding quantities demanded and 'price' offered are $x_i^* = \xi(x)x_i = -h'^i(\rho(r)r_i) = -h'^i(r_i^*)$; $r_i^* = \rho(r)r_i = f'^i(\xi(x)x_i) = f'^i(x_i^*)$ which is satisfying and is paralleled by $\xi = -\theta'(\rho)$, $\rho = \phi'(\xi)$ in a trivial normalization.

I have not seen this system tried, which is a pity, since it is easily understood, is related to a leading theoretical model, and would be very useful should it fit. μ, too, is dimension free, given the utility function, as is $r_j x_j$ – a further advantage of this formulation.

Pollak suggests corresponding generalizations of group-wide additivity and straightforward separability, which can also be interpreted in terms of decentralization, reminiscent of two-stage budgeting.

We have already seen that additive utility does not stand up in empirical demand analysis, and it is easily shown that separable utility cannot in general be simply represented in the dual, unless the *component functions* $f^t(\cdot)$ are *quasi-homothetic*, that is to say have cost functions which may be written

$$m_t = g^t(p_t, v_t) = a^t(p_t)v_t + b^t(p_t), \text{ say,} \tag{12}$$

in an appropriate normalization. Say that $f(\cdot)$ is *quasi-homothetically separable* in such cases. Its cost function $g(p, u) = G(a(p), u) + b(p)$, say, where $G(., u)$ is that corresponding to $F(\cdot)$, $a(p) = (a^t(p_t))_{t\in T}$, because $a^t(p_t)$ is the marginal cost, or shadow price, of V_t, and $b(p) = \Sigma_{t\in T} b^t(p_t)$.

This is a useful result for three reasons. First, given strict quasiconcavity, it implies that

$$x_i = G_t a_i^t(p_t) + b_i^t(p_t) = v_t a_i^t(p_t) + b_i^t(p_t),$$

each $i \in t$, where $G_t = \partial G/\partial a^t$, by which (12) yields

$$x_i = (m_t - b^t(p_t))a_i^t(p_t))a^t(p_t) + b_i^t(p_t), \tag{13}$$

so that both stages in the decision process are easily carried out, and analysed; secondly because (12) may be taken as a Taylor approximation around a 'typical' value of v_t to a general cost function; and thirdly because it not only implies that the Engel curves are straight lines as in (13) but is implied by it, so that separable quasi-homothetic functions are quasi-homothetically separable.

Turn now to production theory, and let u be the firm's output. Businessmen, accountants, operations research workers and statisticians who work in the field all talk of overhead, and variable costs, fixed per unit of output up to near capacity – that is quasi-homothetic production functions; if these are separable then, they are quasi-homothetically separable.

Return again to utility theory. Long ago Hicks interpreted the $f^t(\cdot)$ in (1)–(2) as production functions for intermediate goods V_t, 'produced' in the household, or human body, from the physical goods we buy, and themselves yielding utility. If these are anything like the businessman's production functions, the utility function will be quasi-homothetically separable, or nearly so.

Quasi-homotheticity is at once empirically plausible, at least as an approximation, analytically tractable, at least for those who can handle the dual, and apt to turn up in the solution of puzzles. Here accordingly is a little more about its interpretation.

Clearly $b^t(p_t) = g^t(p_t, 0)$ in (12), and so may be regarded as representing overhead costs, just as $a^t(p_t)$ does variable or prime costs per unit of 'output'. As a cost function $b^t(\cdot)$ is closed concave *conical* – that is, positively homogeneous of degree one. Suppose v_t is unbounded above; then $a^t(\cdot)$ is closed concave conical too. It may therefore be interpreted as a unit cost function corresponding to an *activity* yielding constant returns and running at the level v_t. Call the conical production functions corresponding to these unit cost functions $\alpha^t(\cdot)$, $\beta^t(\cdot)$. Then $v_t = f^t(x_t) = \sup\{\alpha^t(y_t) | \beta^t(z_t) \geqslant 1, y_t + z_t \leqslant x_t\}$, so that it is in itself separable in a slightly generalized sense. Moreover $\alpha^t(\cdot)$, $\beta^t(\cdot)$, being conical, may certainly be regarded as the quantities of composite goods, A_t, B_t, an interpretation which I will often use below, and one which underlies much modern demand analysis. Strictly, of course, it is available only when $a^t(\cdot)$ is concave. Equally well, it is only needed because most of us continue to think more naturally in the primal. The important thing about $\alpha^t(\cdot)$ is that it generates an expenditure pattern $a'^t(p) = (a_i^t(p))$ at the margin, whether or not $\alpha^t(\cdot)$ is concave.

So far I have only discussed the extreme cases of separability – that in which none of the separable sets overlap or even intersect, and that in which they overlap as much as possible. What if we are given a general collection of separable sets $A \subseteq T$?

It yields a utility tree, each node being either weakly separable, as in (1)–(2), or additive, as in (5), so that a knowledge of these two polar cases is in fact all that we need. Note that, since a quasi-homothetic separable function is quasi-homothetically separable, quasi-homotheticity is inherited from any function in this tree to its component functions and hence to their components, and so on. If, therefore, the top node is quasi-homothetically separable, so is very node, and the dual representation follows immediately from the primal.

Businessmen talk of overheads and variable costs, economists of constant returns. That is, we neglect the overheads. This is partly because overheads raise difficulties for perfect competition, and partly because they cannot easily be represented in the primal. Despite apparent unreality, constant returns are historically important; they also emerge as the solution to various theoretical puzzles. The corresponding concept here is *homothetic separability* – the special case of quasi-homothetic separability in which we can take each $b^t(p_t) = 0$, or equivalently, each $f^t(\cdot)$ conical. Everything I said about quasi-homothetic separability holds for homothetic separability. The Engel curves in question are, of course linear – straight lines through the origin – rather than merely affine, so that the income elasticity of demand for each good in the same sector is the same. If we think of these as being closely related goods, that is commonly unacceptable in utility theory, where different models of the 'same' good correspond roughly to different income levels.

If some postulates turn out to imply homothetically separable utility, check carefully before accepting them.

Another way of bringing duality and separability to bear on the same problem is to work with the distance function $h(x, u) = k$ if $u = f(x/k)$, introduced into economics by Malmquist as a measure of the standard of living compared with a norm u, but also underlying Debreu's coefficient of resource utilization. It is clearly conical, and so may be called the *conical representation* of preferences. It is concave iff $f(\cdot)$ is quasiconcave, and is then easily shown to be the full dual of the cost function $g(p, u)$, so that

$$g(p, u) = \inf\{p \cdot x \,|\, h(x, u) \geqslant 1\},$$
$$h(x, u) = \inf\{x \cdot p \,|\, g(p, u) \geqslant 1\}, \qquad (14)$$

for instance. The corresponding separability concept is *quasi-separability* which holds when

$$h(x, u) = H(v, u); \quad v = (v_t)_{t \in T}; \quad v_t = h^t(x_t, u), \qquad (15)$$

are well-behaved in which case the cost function $g(p, u) = G(w, u)$, where $w = (w_t)_{t \in T}$, $w_t = g^t(p_t, u)$, and $G(\cdot)$, $H(\cdot)$, and each pair $g^t(\cdot)$, $h^t(\cdot)$, are duals, so that

$$x_i = g_i(p, u) = G_t g_i^t(p_t, u) = v_t g_i^t(p_t, u), \qquad (16)$$

each $i \in t$, in the obvious notation, and a compensated change in the price of a good causes the demand for each good in any other group to change in the same proportion, as with homothetic separability, and for the same reason, but less objectionably because real income u has remained constant, so that there is no immediate difficulty about luxuries, conventional necessities, and inferior goods being in the same group. Nevertheless, quasi-separable tastes seem to me somewhat unlikely. They do, however, emerge as the solution of various technical problems. I stumbled upon them myself, for instance, when discussing a problem in decentralization.

Note that (16) yields an analogue of (4): the substitution effect

$$\sigma_{ij} = \delta x_i / \delta p_j = \mu_{rs} x_i x_j \qquad \text{when } i \in r, \quad j \in s \neq r, \quad (17)$$

where

$$\mu_{rs} v_r v_s = G_{rs} = \delta v_r / \delta w_s = \delta v_s / \delta w_r, \quad r \neq s. \qquad (18)$$

is the intergroup substitution effect. Note that (4) and (17) are equivalent iff tastes are homothetically separable.

So far u has been a scalar. This is quite unnecessary. Consider, for example, a short-run technology $S(u)$, where u is a vector of fixed inputs. Its *conical representation* $h(x, u) = \inf\{k \,|\, x \in kS(u)\}$, is indeed conical in x, defines $S(u)$ exactly if it is closed, and is concave in x iff $S(u)$ is convex, under normal assumptions. Equations (14)–(18) go through just as before. Indeed, u might contain a complete description of the firm and its endowment, or, in the case of a household, of all its relevant characteristics – including for instance its composition – as well as the utility level, or the levels for the different individuals in it.

So far we have considered concepts of separability of preferences related to two modes of specification: the utility and distance functions. Many others of the form $k(x, u) = 1$, are possible, to each such there corresponds a separability concept

$$k(x, u) = K(v, u); \quad v = (v_t)_{t \in T}; \quad v_t = k^t(x_t, u), \qquad (19)$$

where the functions are well behaved. Most are uninteresting, largely because they do not relate easily to the dual, except in a special case which bears much the same relation to quasi-homothetic separability as quasi-separability does to homothetic. Another relates to the representation, $y = -k(x, u)$, which is sometimes convenient, particularly if Y is in some sense a natural numeraire and we have reduced the economy to two sectors, its advantage being that the price $p_i = k_i(x, u)$, each i. The separability concept (19) with this $k(\cdot)$ sometimes turns up in theoretical investigations, for instance in the theory of taxation.

Another possibility is to start from the indirect utility function, considered either as a function of $r = p/m$, as by Pollak above, or of (p, m).

Separability, then, is an organizing idea, to be deployed in a form appropriate to the problem under discussion. To do that effectively, one has to have played about with it enough to be able to guess where a particular concept may lead when combined with other assumptions, and how to get there. Now most economic series deal with aggregates, commonly taken to be over independent agents acting competitively. It is to separability in that context that I will now turn.

Here the classical problem is the measurement of the quantity, $v = k(u)$, of Capital in an economy, where $u = (u_f)_{f \in F}$, $x = \Sigma_{f \in F} x_f$, give the *endowments of fixed inputs*, and *net outputs of current goods* in the economy, F, as a whole; u_f, x_f, in firm f.

I will sketch the basic arguments in this context, and in the remarkably similar problem of measuring the quantity of Labour, though they can be deployed much more widely to yield similar results, suggesting natural generalizations of *classical separability* as used above, until it effectively becomes equivalent to the use of composite goods, as in modern demand analysis.

To state the problem of measuring Capital formally in terms of classical separability, say that v is a *perfect measure* of it if the equation of the production frontier may be written

$$\Phi(x, v) = 1, \qquad \text{where } v = k(u), \qquad (20)$$

where $\Phi(\cdot)$ and $k(\cdot)$ are well behaved, and $k(\cdot)$ is strictly increasing, though this last is unnecessarily strong.

Now bring to bear the fact that F is made up of perfectly competing firms. I will require that there are no external effects, though that can be weakened to allow, for example, for public fixed inputs. Hence the *short-run technology* for the economy F as a whole $S(u) = \Sigma S^f(u_f)$, where $S^f(u_f)$ is that for f. This simple additive structure is best exploited here by using the *gross profit functions* $h(p, v) = g(p, u) = \Sigma g^f(p, u_f)$, which have the advantage of being scalar rather than set valued. Sometimes it is better to use the *net supply functions* which add up in the same way. That they are vector valued leads to difficulties with the inversion below, which sometimes implies that the results are only local in p, but it does allow us to deal with more complicated problems.

The crucial point in each case is that current goods are represented by their prices rather than their quantities. That is what is to be expected: it is by having common shadow prices that the individual firms are kept in line, and total output kept on the production frontier; and, by holding prices constant we can observe the effects of changing the endowments of one firm in isolation. This suggests that some sort of separability in a dual may emerge as the basic notion, as indeed it will.

I will now show that there exist perfect Capital measures $v_f = k^f(u_f)$, such that $v = \Sigma v_f$, in an appropriate normalization, in terms of which the gross profit functions may be written

$$g^f(p, u_f) = a(p)v_f + b^f(p), \quad g(p, u) = a(p)v + b(p), \qquad (21)$$

where $b(p) = \Sigma b^f(p)$. If we take v^f as a measure at the *scale* of which f operates, and $-b^f(p)$ of its overheads, this is reminiscent of what businessmen say. That is agreeable, as is the fact that the quantities, v_f, of Capital in the individual firms, add up to that, v, in the economy as a whole. At first glance the fact that the shadow price $a(p)$ of Capital is automatically the same in each firm is also agreeable. At the second, not so. Give any firm enough extra equipment to raise its profits by \$M, and it will produce exactly $a_i(p)/a(p)$ more of good i, so that each has the same marginal production plan: about as unrealistic an assumption as one could imagine for a natural economy.

'What would you expect', Mrs Robinson would have asked, 'if you attempt anything so absurd as measuring Capital?' Unfortunately, precisely the same problem arises if one tries to measure Labour, or for that matter, the production of Food, or Plastic goods. This is less surprising when we realize that (20) can be solved for $v = \phi(x)$, say, and the corresponding equation for firm f for $v_f = \phi^f(x_f)$, so that

$$k^f(u_f) = v_f = \phi^f(x_f), \quad k(u) = v = \phi(x), \qquad (22)$$

and v_f, v may just as well be taken as a measure of Production as of Capital. Indeed, it is in that role that (21) is equivalent to quasi-homothetic separability. Think of V as an intermediate good, produced from fixed inputs and itself defining the scale of current production. Given appropriate convexity, indeed, $a(\cdot)$ is the unit profit function of an activity which runs at level v_f in f.

Next for the 'proof'. It consists of four stages, of which only the third leads to problems in more complicated cases.

(a) Take a *base endowment vector* $\bar{u} = (\bar{u}_f)_{f \in F}$, define *base profits* $b^f(p) = g^f(p, \bar{u}_f)$, $b(p) = \Sigma b^f(p) = g(p, \bar{u})$, and the *quasi-rents*

$$r^f(p, u_f) = g^f(p, u_f) - b^f(p);$$
$$s(p, v) = h(p, v) - b(p), \qquad (23)$$

to get

$$s(p, v) = \sum r^f(p, u_f), \ = r^f(p, u_f) \quad \text{when } u_{-f} = \bar{u}_{-f}, \qquad (24)$$

so that this trick has allowed us to bring the existence of an economy-wide measure of Capital to bear on the individual firms.

(b) Define the quasi-rents,

$$v^*: \ = s(\bar{p}, v) = \sum r^f(\bar{p}, u^f) =: \sum v_f^*, \qquad (25)$$

earned at standard prices $\bar{p}$, as tentative measures of the quantities of Capital.

(c) Invert (25) to get $v = \theta(v^*) = \theta(\Sigma v_f^*)$, say, and substitute into (24) to get

$$s(p, v) = s^*\left(p, \sum v_f^*\right) = \sum r'^f(p, u_f) = \sum s^*(p, v_f^*), \text{ say}, \qquad (26)$$

by (25).

(d) Equation (26) is Cauchy's equation. $s^*(p, .)$ is both continuous and strictly increasing. Either would imply that its solution is $s^*(p, v^*) = a(p)v^*$, say. Substituting this into (23), using (24), and dropping the stars we get (21) as required.

Now Cauchy's functional equation yields linearity when v is a vector, too. It is therefore unsurprising that there exist perfect measures, $v_{ft} = k^{ft}(u_{ft})$, such that $v_t = \Sigma_f v_{ft}$, is an appropriate normalization, for each firm, if $v = (v_t)_{t \in T}$ in a vector of perfect measures of Land, Structures and Equipment, for instance, so that (20) holds with $v_t = k^t(u_t)$, all in an obvious notation, and that this happens iff $g^f(p, u_f) = \Sigma_t a^t(p)v_{ft} + b^f(p)$, which lends itself to the same interpretation as (22), and is just as unrealistic, for the same reasons, unless we chose separate classes for fixed inputs for every industry, or process, which defeats the purpose of such aggregates in most cases.

Turn now to aggregates $v_t = k^t(x_t)$, for classes $t \in T$ of current goods: say Labour, Plastic goods, Services, ... Here one works with the supply functions instead of the gross profit functions. Since I will deal with labour, I will use the input demand function instead. Hold prices constant throughout the argument as before. First give a particular firm f enough additional fixed inputs to persuade it to spend an extra \$M on labour, called t. It will increase its demand for the various types of labour by a vector Δx_{ft}. Now go back to square one. Give firm $g \neq f$ fixed inputs leading to it spending an extra \$M on labour instead. It would change its demand by Δx_{gt}. The economy wide demand for labour, x_t, has changed by the same amount, Δx_t in each case. Hence $\Delta x_{gt} = \Delta x_t = \Delta x_{ft}$ – exactly what worried us earlier. However, we can go further. Keeping all the other firms in their original positions, but leaving g with its gift, give it a further such, leading to a further increase $\Delta' x_{gt}$, say, in its demand vector for labour. This is the same increase as would have occurred if f had had a corresponding gift. But f is in the same position as it was initially, hence its change would once again be Δx_{ft}. Hence, $\Delta' x_{gt} = \Delta x_{ft} = \Delta x_{gt}$, so that the Engel curves for labour, for instance, are straight lines. Measuring quantities as net supplies again, we get

$$g_i^f(p, u_f) = a_i^t(p_t)v_{ft} + b_i^f(p), \qquad \text{each } i \in t, \qquad (27)$$

easily, as one would expect. Integrating yields

$$g^f(p, u_f) = R^f(a(p), u_f) + b^f(p), \text{ say},$$

where $a(p) = (a^t)p_t))_{t \in T}$. We can clearly normalize so that $b^f(p) = g^f(p, \bar{u}_f)$, the gross profits available at the base endowments $\bar{u}_f$, as in the case of capital, so that $R^f(a(p), u_f) = r^f(p, u_f)$, the quasi-rents due to having u_f instead of $\bar{u}_f$. Multiplying (27) by p_i, adding and using the fact that the a's and b's are conical, we get $R^f(a(p), u_f) = \Sigma_t a^t(p_t)v_{ft}$, so that $v_{ft} = R_t^f(a(p), u_f) = \partial R^f / \partial a^t$, $= 0$ when $u_f = \bar{u}_f$, which is highly agreeable, a^t being the common shadow price of V_t. However, we do not have $v_{ft} = k^{ft}(x_{ft})$, in the obvious notation, in general, though we do if returns are constant in the long run, or if $g^f(p, u_f) = 0$ for some u_f in its domain.

Two points emerge: that measuring Labour is quite as unrealistic as measuring Capital under these assumptions; and that the appropriate separability concept may be that of the quasi-rent function, as, indeed, it often is.

Household behaviour can be analysed in the same way, where u_h will commonly be a vector of h's characteristics, and the conclusion, that each behaves in the same way at the relevant margin, is comparably unreasonable.

Separability as we have defined it so far, then, is not well adapted to the aggregative data with which we commonly have to work. What if each variable were allowed to enter into the basic model through several channels, rather than just one?

Once again, I will begin with Capital theory and suppose that the endowment u of fixed inputs affects the short-run production possibilities $S(u)$ through a vector $v = (v_t)_{t \in T}$ of intermediate variables. There are two main cases

$$v_t = k^t(u); \qquad (28i)$$

$$v_t = k^t(u, p). \qquad (28ii)$$

Think of v as not just intermediate variables, but quantities of intermediate goods. In each case then $v \in S^*(u)$, say, the *upstream technology*. In (i), v is determined once u is known – a case of generalized fixed coefficients if you like. In (ii), it may be chosen from $S^*(u)$ in the light of the prices p of the ultimate products. In each case we deal with an appropriate set of £T net supply equations. Commonly those can only be inverted locally, but the rest of the argument (a)–(d) above goes through as before since Cauchy's equation yields linearity for vector valued functions too. We therefore get that corresponding intermediate variables v_{ft} exist for each firm, with corresponding shadow prices $a^t(p)$, $\Sigma_f v_{ft} = v_t$ in an appropriate normalization, and the quasi-rent functions

$$r^f(p, u_f) = \sum_t a^t(p) v_{ft}; \quad v_{ft} = k^{ft}(u_f), \text{ say} \tag{29i}$$

$$r^f(p, u_f) = R^f(a(p), u_f) = \sum_t a^t(p) v_{ft}, \tag{29ii}$$

since $v_{ft} = R_t^f(a(p), u_f)$. Note now that the vector $v_f = (v_{ft})_{t \in T}$ can be interpreted either as giving several measures of Capital; or as the levels at which the corresponding activities $a^t(\cdot)$ are run: measures either for Capital or Current goods, as in the initial scalar case (22).

Equations (29) look very like our previous results. Nevertheless they are, on the face of it, far less obviously unrealistic, because a gift of a piece of equipment will lead to a change $\Sigma_t \Delta v_{ft} a''(p)$ in f's net output vector x_f, which depends on how it affects the individual v_{ft}, and so may be quite different in different firms.

Equation (28i) was applied to Sri Lankan households by Deaton in 1980 with considerable success. Since we cannot observe utility levels, household income, m_h, is one of the components of its characteristic vector u_h. Since it is the only characteristic which interests us at the moment, incorporate the others into the label h. Then there exist functions $v_{ht} = k^{ht}(m_h)$ for each household for which the household demand functions are of the form $x_{hi} = \Sigma_t v_{ht} a^{hti}(p) + b^{hi}(p)$. That these should be homogeneous of degree zero in (p, m_h) already implies a lot; Slutsky a lot more. Indeed, it almost turns out that the indirect utility function is of the form

$$\alpha(p) + \beta(p)/[1 - (m/\gamma(p))^\theta] \tag{30}$$

where θ is either real or a pure imaginary, $\alpha(\cdot)$, $\beta(\cdot)$ are homogeneous of degree zero, and $\gamma(\cdot)$ of degree one, with log z replacing z^θ when $\theta = 0$, as in Deaton's application, where the budget shares are quadratic in log m. The surprising point is that it was on survey – i.e. micro-data – that it proved itself, not on the macro-data for which it was designed, though it would obviously permit the use of both in investigating the same demand system.

Equation (30) makes no mention of the households other characteristics. θ might even differ from one block of households to another. However, the natural case is that in which it does not, and we take $\alpha^h(p) = \alpha(p)$, $\beta^h(p) = b_h \beta(p)$, $\gamma^h(p) = c_h \gamma(p)$, where b_h, c_h are the effective characteristics of h. These enter into the households weighting system. That said, the corresponding aggregates v_t are appropriate averages of m_h, $m_h^{1-\theta}$ and $m_h^{1+\theta}$, or m_h, $m_h \log m_h$, and $m_h(\log m_h)^2$, respectively. $\theta = 1$ corresponds to demand functions quadratic in income, and appropriate averages of m_h and m_h^2. In other words, we are dealing in appropriate moments of the income distribution.

Equation (28ii) finds its obvious application in organization theory, where we may imagine a businessman building up an empire which he can rule by setting a relatively small £T of targets, and then letting the serfs get on with it. He would presumably do so by buying up this, and selling off that, until he had a viable organization. If so, the prices would have quasi-rent functions $R^f(a(p), u_f)$; his effective controls would not be the targets $v = (v_t)$, but a knowledge of the likely marginal profitabilities, or shadow prices, $a^t(p)$ of the various activities. These he, in the central office, would pass on to the factory managers, who would calculate the $v_{ft} = R_t^f(a(p), u_f)$, in the light of their detailed knowledge of their factory's plant, u_f. The specialist activity managers would be told these levels v_{ft} at which they should run their activities, and choose the net supply vectors $v_{ft} a''(p)$ in the light of their up to date knowledge of the appropriate prices in p. Given appropriate convexity, each stage would be a profit centre. Given time, the businessman would learn a good deal about the $R^f(., u_f)$, and hence where to direct his investment. Note the similarity with two-stage budgeting.

Many of these arguments were driven by varying the fixed inputs parametrically. In the long run there are none. As long as we confine ourselves to classical separability – scalar aggregates corresponding to different classes of goods – we can vary appropriate prices instead to get the same results as before, except in one anomalous case, from only slightly stronger assumptions. They are quite as unacceptable here, as you might argue, as is the assumption of perfect competition, or something very like it, which underlies much of this analysis, and which sits badly with the stress I put on overheads – hence my concentration on demand analysis, and the efficient organization of a firm.

Another weakness in this resumé is the requirement of strict monotonicity. The maximum, or the minimum, of a pair of elements, is a continuous, increasing function of them. Each is a limiting case of additivity, but not additivity itself; Bliss in his book on Capital, and, more recently, Mak have done valuable work here.

Yet another is that I have confined myself to functional separability – though some of the functions are vector valued. If you reread my third paragraph, you will see that this is a distinctly special case. Even here, I have neglected homogeneity in the main, and uniformity over time entirely as well as Barten's work on nearly additive utility, Diewert's on flexible functional forms, Jorgenson's on translog functions, and, above all, that of Nataf – e.g. Fourgeaud and Nataf (1959) – on demand and aggregation. More importantly, I have had nothing to say about separability in complete models, where, incidentally, the aggregates appropriate to one sector very rarely are to others; or, like Fisher, and more recently, Mak, about approximate separability. Nor have I taken account of possible statistical regularities, as Theil did admirably in the 1950s, and Stoker in the 1980s.

Should you want to go into functional separability more deeply, Blackorby, Primont and Russell (1978) and, on the demand side, Deaton and Muellbauer's *Economics and Consumer Behaviour* have full bibliographies as well as being well worth reading for their own sakes.

W.M. Gorman

A FEW KEY REFERENCES

Blackorby, C., Primont, D. and Russell, R.R. 1978. *Duality, Separability, and Functional Structure*. Amsterdam: North-Holland.

Deaton, A. and Muellbauer, J. 1980. An almost ideal demand system. *American Economic Review* 70, 312–26.

Fourgéaud, C. and Nataf, A. 1959. Consommation en prix et revenu réels et théorie des choix. *Econometrica* 27, 329–54.

Leontief, W.W. 1947a. A note on the interrelation of subsets of independent variables of a continuous function with continuous

first derivatives. *Bulletin of the American Mathematical Society* 53, 343–56.
Leontief, W.W. 1974b. Introduction to a theory of the internal structure of functional relationships. *Econometrica* 15, 361–73.
Pollak, R.A. 1972. Generalized separability. *Econometrica* 40, 431–53.

sequence economies. A *sequence economy* is a general equilibrium model in discrete time including specific provision for the availability of markets at a sequence of dates (Radner, 1972). Markets reopen over time, and at each date firms and households act so that plans and prospects for actions on markets available in the future significantly affect their current actions.

This model is in contrast with the Arrow–Debreu model with a full set of futures markets (Debreu, 1959). There, all exchanges for current and future goods (including contingent commodities, futures contracts contingent on the realization of uncertain events) are transacted on a market at a single point in time. In the Arrow–Debreu model, there is no need for markets to reopen in the future; economic activity in the future consists simply of the execution of the contracted plans. The Arrow–Debreu model with a full set of futures markets appears unsatisfactory in that it denies commonplace observation: futures markets for goods and Arrow securities (contingent contracts payable in money) are not generally available for most dates or a sufficiently varied array of uncertain events; markets do reopen over time. The sequence economy model is an alternative that allows formalization and explanation of these observations.

The sequence economy model is particularly suitable for study of the store-of-value function of money. It is precisely because markets reopen over time that agents may find it desirable to carry abstract purchasing power from one date to succeeding date. Typically, this will take the form of transactions on spot markets at a succession of dates with money or other financial assets held over time to reflect the (net) excess value of prior sales over purchases. This may occur simply because the model does not provide for futures markets or because futures markets, though available in principle, are in practice inactive. Endogenously determined inactivity of futures markets is the result of transactions costs which tend to make the use of futures markets disproportionately costly compared with spot markets.

There are three principal reasons for the excess cost of futures markets:

(i) The necessarily greater complexity of futures contracts over time may simply imply use of more resources (e.g. for record keeping or enforcement) than spot markets;

(ii) The transactions costs of a futures contract are incurred (partly) at the transactions date, those of an equivalent spot transaction are incurred in the future. The present discounted value of the spot transactions costs incurred in the distant future may be lower than the futures market transaction cost incurred in the present, simply because of time-discounting;

(iii) Use of a full set of futures markets under uncertainty implies that most contracts transacted become otiose and are left unfulfilled as their effective dates pass and the events on which they were contingent do not occur. There is a corresponding saving in transaction costs associated with reducing the number of transactions required by use of a single spot transaction instead of many contingent commodity contracts, though this reduction may imply a different and inferior allocation of risk-bearing.

We now present a formal pure exchange sequence economy model with transactions costs (Kurz, 1974; Heller and Starr, 1976).

Commodity i for delivery at date τ may be bought spot at date τ or futures at any date t, $1 \leqslant t < \tau$. The complete system of spot and futures markets is available at each date (although some markets may be inactive). The time horizon is date K; each of H households is alive at time 1 and cares nothing about consumption after K. There are n commodities deliverable at each date; in the monetary interpretation of the model spot money is one of the goods. At each date and for each commodity, the household has available the current spot market, and futures markets for deliveries at all future dates. Spot and futures markets will also be available at dates in the future and prices on the markets taking place in the future are currently known. Thus in making his purchase and sale decisions, the household considers without price uncertainty whether to transact on current markets or to postpone transactions to markets available at future dates. There is a sequence of budget constraints, one for the market at each date. That is, for every date, the household faces a budget constraint on the spot and futures transactions taking place at that date, (4) below. The value of its sales to the market at each date (including delivery of money) must balance its purchases at that date.

In addition to a budget constraint, the agent's actions are restricted by a transactions technology. This technology specifies for each complex of purchases and sales at date t, what resources will be consumed by the process of transaction. It is because transactions costs may differ between spot and futures markets for the same good that we consider the reopening of markets allowed by the sequence economy model. Specific provision for transaction cost is introduced to allow an endogenous determination of the activity or inactivity of markets. In the special case where all transactions costs are nil, the model is unnecessarily complex; there is no need for the reopening of markets, and the equilibrium allocations are identical to those of the Arrow–Debreu model. Conversely, in the case where some futures markets are prohibitively costly to operate and others are costless, then there is an incomplete array of spot and futures markets and the model is an example of that of Radner (1972).

All of the n-dimensional vectors below are restricted to be non-negative.

$x^h_\tau(t)$ = vector of purchases for any purpose at date t by household h for delivery at date τ.
$y^h_\tau(t)$ = vector of sales analogously defined.
$z^h_\tau(t)$ = vector of inputs necessary to transactions undertaken at time t. The index τ again refers to date at which these inputs are actually delivered.
$\omega^h(t)$ = vector of endowments at t for household h.
$s^h(t)$ = vector of goods coming out of storage at date t.
$r^h(t)$ = vector of goods put into storage at date t.
$p_\tau(t)$ = price vector on market at date t for goods deliverable at date τ.

With this notation, $p_{it}(t)$ is the spot price of good i at date t, and $p_{i\tau}(t)$ for $\tau > t$ is the futures price (for delivery at τ) of good i at date t.

The (non-negative) consumption vector for household h is

$$c^h(t) = \omega^h(t) + \sum_{\tau=1}^{t} [x^h_t(\tau) - y^h_t(\tau) - z^h_t(\tau)] + s^h(t) - r^h(t) \geqq 0, \qquad (t = 1, \ldots, K). \quad (1)$$

That is, consumption at date t is the sum of endowments plus all purchases past and present with delivery date t minus all sales for delivery at t minus transactions inputs with date t (including those previously committed) plus what comes out of storage at t minus what goes into storage. We suppose that households care only about consumption and not about which market consumption comes from. Thus, households maximize $U^h(c^h)$, where c^h is a vector of the $c^h(t)$'s, subject to constraint.

The household is constrained by its transaction technology, T^h, which specifies, for example, how much leisure time and shoeleather must be used to carry out any transaction. Let $x^h(t)$ denote the vector of $x^h_\tau(t)$'s [and similarly for $y^h(t)$ and $z^h(t)$]. We insist

$$[x^h(t), y^h(t), z^h(t)] \in T^h(t), \qquad (t = 1, \ldots, K). \qquad (2)$$

Naturally, storage input and output vectors must be feasible, so

$$[r^h(t), s^h(t+1)] \in S^h(t), \qquad (t = 1, \ldots, K-1). \qquad (3)$$

The budget constraints for household h are then:

$$p(t)\cdot x^h(t) \leqslant p(t)\cdot y^h(t), \qquad (t = 1, \ldots, K). \qquad (4)$$

Households may transfer purchasing power forward in time by using futures markets and by storage of goods that will be valuable in the future. Purchasing power may be carried backward by using futures markets. But these may be very costly transactions. In a monetary interpretation of the model, where money and promissory notes are present, the household can either hold money as a store of wealth, or it can buy or sell notes.

Let $a^h(t) \equiv [x^h(t), y^h(t), z^h(t), r^h(t), s^h(t)]$, let a^h be a vector of the $a^h(t)$'s, and define x^h, y^h, z^h, r^h and s^h similarly. Define $B^h(p)$ as the set of a^h's which satisfy constraints (1)–(4). The household maximizes $U^h(c^h)$ over $B^h(p)$. Denote the demand correspondence (i.e. the set of maximizing a^h's) by $\gamma^h(p)$.

The model can be interpreted as monetary or non-monetary. We think of money as simply a 0th good that does not enter household preferences. Futures contracts in money are discounted promissory notes. $x^h_{0t}(t)$ is h's monetary receipts at t, $x^h_{0\tau}(t)$ is h's note purchase at t due at τ. Money is not treated as numeraire – positivity of its value cannot be assumed – it has a price $p_{0t}(t)$.

The correspondences $\gamma^h_t(p)$ are always homogeneous of degree zero in $p(t)$, as is seen from the definition of $B^h(p)$. We can therefore restrict the price space to the simplex. Let S^t denote the unit simplex of dimensionality, $n(T-t+1)$. Let $P = \mathsf{X}^T_{t=1} S^t$.

An *equilibrium* of the economy is a price vector $p^* \in P$ and an allocation a^{h*}, for each h, so that $a^{h*} \in \gamma^h(p^*)$ for all h and

$$\sum_{h=1}^{H} x^{h*} \leqslant \sum_{h=1}^{H} y^{h*} \qquad (5)$$

(the inequality holds coordinate-wise), where for any good i, t, τ such that the strict inequality holds in (5) it follows that $p^*_{i\tau}(t) = 0$. The equilibrium of a monetary economy is said to be *non-trivial* (that is, the economy is really monetary) if $p^*_{0t}(t) \neq 0$ for all t. Sufficient conditions for existence of equilibrium are continuity and convexity requirements typical of an Arrow–Debreu model appropriately extended. Transactions costs are often thought to be non-convex, leading to approximate equilibrium rather than full equilibrium results (Heller and Starr, 1976). Existence of non-trivial monetary equilibrium requires additional restrictions designed to maintain positivity of the price of money (boundedness of the price level expressed in monetary terms). Monetary trade is actively used in non-trivial equilibrium in the case where transactions costs and storage losses of monetary trade are small relative to other means of intertemporal transfer of purchasing power.

In contrast to the Arrow–Debreu economy, an equilibrium allocation is not generally Pareto efficient. This is not due simply to the presence of transactions costs; transactions costs technically necessary to a reallocation must be incurred, and they represent no inefficiency. The Arrow–Debreu model, however, uses a lifetime budget constraint. The corresponding constraint here is the sequence of constraints in (4). Transfer of purchasing power intertemporally – costless in the Arrow–Debreu model – is here a resource using activity; it requires purchase and sale of assets with resultant transactions cost. But the intertemporal transfer of purchasing power, unlike reallocation of goods among households, is needed not to satisfy technical or consumption requirements but rather to satisfy the administrative requirements of the market embodied in (4). Hence technically feasible Pareto-improving reallocations may be prevented in equilibrium by prohibitive transactions costs which would have to be incurred to satisfy the purely administrative requirements of crediting and debiting agents' budgets intertemporally (Hahn, 1971). If trade in monetary instruments is costless, however, then an equilibrium allocation is Pareto efficient (Starrett, 1973). Hence the sequence economy model provides a formal framework for the store-of-value role of money.

Ross M. Starr

See also GENERAL EQUILIBRIUM; MULTISECTOR GROWTH MODELS; MYOPIC DECISION RULES.

BIBLIOGRAPHY

Debreu, G. 1959. *Theory of Value*. New York: Wiley

Hahn, F.H. 1971. Equilibrium with transaction costs. *Econometrica* 39(3), 417–39.

Heller, W.P. and Starr, R.M. 1976. Equilibrium with non-convex transactions costs: monetary and non-monetary economies. *Review of Economic Studies* 43(2), 195–215.

Kurz, M. 1974. Equilibrium in a finite sequence of markets with transactions cost. *Econometrica* 42(1), 1–20.

Radner, R. 1972. Existence of equilibrium of plans, prices, and price expectations in a sequence of markets. *Econometrica* 40(2), 289–303.

Starrett, D.A. 1973. Inefficiency and the demand for 'money' in a sequence economy. *Review of Economic Studies* 40, 437–48.

sequential analysis. Statistical experiments are of either fixed sample or sequential design. A *fixed sample size* experiment is one in which the sample size taken for experimentation is predetermined, while a *sequential* experiment involves monitoring incoming data to help determine an appropriate time to stop experimentation.

To formalize these notions, suppose the data can be observed one-at-a-time; let $X_1, X_2, \ldots$ denote this possible stream of data. Examples include a series of products coming off an assembly line, a series of missiles being tested for accuracy, and a series of patients participating in a clinical trial.

A key concept is that of a *stopping rule*, R, which is a description of the manner in which the data stream will be used to determine cessation of the experiment.

Example 1. Consider the stopping rule R_1: stop experimentation after n observations have been taken. This stopping rule effectively defines what we earlier called a fixed sample size experiment, since we will take precisely n observations.

Example 2. Consider the stopping rules (where $\bar{X}_j = \Sigma^j_{i=1} X_i/j$) R_2: stop experimentation if $\bar{X}_{50} > 0.62$, or (failing that) when $n = 100$; R_3: after each new observation, X_j, check whether or not $\bar{X}_j \geqslant 0.5 + 0.823/\sqrt{j}$; if so, stop experimentation and otherwise take the next observation. Note that R_2 allows experimentation to stop only after 50 or 100 observations have been taken, while R_3 gives rise to the possibility of stopping after any observation.

To see why stopping rules such as R_2 and R_3 can be desirable, consider a clinical trial investigating a new treatment in which, for the jth participating patient, the observation is a Bernoulli (θ) random variable, X_i, which can assume the values 1 (denoting treatment success) or 0 (denoting treatment failure). Thus θ is the probability of the treatment being successful. Suppose that the standard (old) treatment is known to have a success probability of $\frac{1}{2}$, so it is desired to test the hypothesis (H_0) that $\theta \leqslant \frac{1}{2}$ (the old treatment is better) versus the hypothesis (H_a) that $\theta > \frac{1}{2}$ (the new treatment is better).

A typical fixed sample size test of these hypotheses would proceed by choosing a sample size, say $n = 100$, observing $X_1, \ldots, X_{100}$ from $n = 100$ independent patients, and then rejecting H_0 if $\bar{X}_{100} \geqslant 0.582$. This is an $\alpha = 0.05$ level test. (We make no judgement here concerning the appropriateness of formulating this problem as a statistical hypothesis test.)

Suppose now that the experimenters happen to look at the data after 50 patients have participated in the trial, and observe that, for all 50, the treatment proved successful. This would appear to be overwhelming evidence that the new treatment is better, and would lead reasonable people to stop the clinical trial and recommend adoption of the new treatment. It is a rather surprising fact that this conclusion would be *forbidden* by classical statistics, because the original design called for a sample of size 100. (Classical analyses do not allow deviation from original experimental protocol.) It would have been possible, however, to plan for such a possible eventuality by adopting a sequential design, whereby after every observation (or every few observations) the possibility of stopping is allowed. Indeed, R_2 and R_3 are two such stopping rules, and had either been employed, the above-mentioned clinical trial would certainly have stopped by the time the overwhelming evidence had accumulated.

As indicated in the above example, the advantage of a sequential experimental design is that it allows one to stop the experiment precisely when sufficient evidence has accumulated. The disadvantages of a sequential design are that it can be more expensive (often it is cheaper per observation if the data is collected all at once or in large batches), and that it is harder to analyse from the classical perspective. This last point has to do with the fact that the stopping rule can significantly affect classical statistical measures.

Example 2 (continued). Suppose the stopping rule R_2 had been employed in the clinical trial (i.e., an *interim analysis* at the halfway point in the trial had been performed). Also, suppose that, if one did stop after 50 observations (i.e., if $\bar{X}_{50} > 0.62$), then H_0 would be rejected, and that, if the trial lasted for all 100 observations (i.e, if $\bar{X}_{50} \leqslant 0.62$ so that the experiment did not stop at the halfway point), then H_0 would be rejected when $\bar{C}_{100} > 0.582$. It can be shown that, for a *fixed* sample of 50 observations, rejecting H_0 when $\bar{X}_{50} > 0.62$ is an $\alpha = 0.05$ level test, as is rejecting H_0 if $\bar{X}_{100} > 0.582$ for a *fixed* sample size experiment with $n = 100$. For the experiment using R_2, however, it can be shown that the level is $\alpha = 0.083$. (One obtains an error probability larger than each of the separate $\alpha = 0.05$, because use of R_2 gives 'two chances' to reject H_0.) Thus, if R_1 had been used and $\bar{X}_{100} = 0.582$ had been observed, one could claim significant evidence against H_0 at the $\alpha = 0.05$ level, while if R_2 had been used, one could not claim significance at the $\alpha = 0.05$ level.

It should be mentioned that there is considerable controversy over the issue of whether use of stopping rules should affect statistical conclusions. When classical measures are used, there is no denying a substantial effect. But, interestingly, for certain other statistical measures, such as Bayesian measures, the stopping rule has *no* effect. Thus, employment of the Bayesian approach to statistics allows one to collect data without having to prespecify a rigid initial stopping rule, greatly increasing the flexibility of experimentation. For discussion of this issue, and support for the Bayesian viewpoint, see Berger and Wolpert (1984) and Berger (1985).

The founder of sequential analysis is generally acknowledged to be Abraham Wald, with Milton Friedman and W. Allen Wallis providing substantial motivational and collaborative support. Early history of sequential analysis is given in Wald (1947), which developed the basic formulation of the problem in terms of stopping rules and analysed a number of basic situations, such as the Sequential Probability Ratio Test (for testing between two simple hypotheses). Most of the subsequent work in sequential analysis has focused on either (i) evaluating classical measures, such as error probabilities, for special stopping rules (see Siegmund, 1985); or (ii) determining optimal stopping rules. This last problem is very difficult, and can be rephrased as the problem of deciding if enough information is already available to reach a decision, or if another (or several) observations should be taken. The mathematics of this problem is essentially that of Dynamic Programming. For general reviews of sequential analysis, see DeGroot (1970), Ghosh (1970), Govindarajulu (1981), Berger (1985), and Siegmund (1985).

JAMES O. BERGER

BIBLIOGRAPHY

Berger, J. 1985. *Statistical Decision Theory and Bayesian Analysis*. New York: Springer-Verlag.

Berger, J. and Wolpert, R. 1984. *The Likelihood Principle*. Institute of Mathematical Statistics Monograph Series, Hayward, California.

DeGroot, M.H. 1970. *Optimal Statistical Decisions*. New York: McGraw-Hill.

Ghosh, B.K. 1970. *Sequential Tests of Statistical Hypotheses*. Reading, Mass.: Addison-Wesley.

Govindarajulu, Z. 1981. *The Sequential Statistical Analysis of Hypothesis Testing, Point and Interval Estimation, and Decision Theory*. Columbus: American Science Press.

Siegmund, D. 1985. *Sequential Analysis: Tests and Confidence Intervals*. New York: Springer-Verlag.

Wald, A. 1947. *Sequential Analysis*. New York: Wiley.

serfdom. *See* FEUDALISM; PEASANTS.

Serra, Antonio (*fl.* 1613). Italian economist of the late 16th and early 17th century, and author of an important treatise, *Breve trattato delle cause che possono far abbondare li regni d'oro et d'argento, dove non sono miniere con applicazione al Regno di Napoli*, published in 1613. Little else is known of his life apart from the fact that he was born in Cosenza, Calabria, had studied theology and law, and was imprisoned for ten years in Naples, probably on a charge of coining.

Although Serra's treatise had as its ultimate objective opposition to the popular contemporary view that the scarcity of coin in the Kingdom of Naples was due to the high rate of exchange, this argument is preceded by a general introductory part dealing with the factors influencing money supply in a nation. Abundance of gold and silver in a kingdom is ascribed by Serra to particular and to common factors. The first are exclusive properties of a nation, such as the advantage of having a surplus of a particular product, or a location very suitable for the carrying trade (Venice). The common factors are subdivided into the extent of manufactures and trade, quality of the workforce and influence of government. These factors are interdependent, as Serra demonstrates in his explanation of the superior wealth of Venice, where trade causes the increase of manufactures and this, in turn, expands trade. Although Serra's work has generally been noted for its early exposition of the balance of trade including invisibles. Schumpeter (1954, p. 354) correctly points out that his monetary analysis of the effects of the balance of trade is supported by a real analysis of commodity production interconnecting the common factors of industrial and commercial development, resource availability and effectiveness of government. 'In this scheme monetary phenomena are consequences rather than cause [because] if the economic process as a whole functions properly, the balance of trade will look after itself.' The quality of this real analysis is illustrated by the hint at increasing returns in Serra's explanation of the productive potential of manufactures relative to agriculture, because 'they can be multiplied ... two-hundred fold, and with proportionately less expense' (Serra, 1613, p. 147). The second part of his treatise applies this general analysis to the special situation of Naples.

PETER GROENEWEGEN

SELECTED WORKS

1613. *Breve trattato delle cause che possono far abbondare li regni d'oro e d'argento dove non sono miniere*. In *Scrittori classici Italiani di economia politica*, parte antica, Vol. 1, ed. P. Custodi, Milan: G.G. Destefanis, 1803. Extracts translated as *A Brief Treatise on the Causes which can make Gold and Silver plentiful in Kingdoms where there are no Mines*, in *Early Economic Thought*, ed. A.E. Monroe, Cambridge, Mass.: Harvard University Press, 1924.

BIBLIOGRAPHY

Schumpeter, J.A. 1954. *History of Economic Analysis*. London: Allen & Unwin, 1959.

services. In everyday language, we make a clear distinction between goods and services. When we refer to services, we tend to think of services rendered to people (classic examples are Fourastie's much cherished hairdresser, Baumol's singer and Pigou's valet). A more recent use of 'services', namely business services, refers to the process of externalizing parts of R&D or management functions. Services are commonly seen as extending to activities like retailing, banking, insurance and non-market activities linked to public and private administration. It is, moreover, current practice to include transport and telecommunications within this already vast set of activities. If we consider this heterogeneous whole covering all services, we note that the building industry is excluded (an exception can be found in Clark, 1940).

What *is* striking is the contrast between the relative simplicity of current usage and the difficulties encountered in defining services within an economic analysis.

For here we find ourselves close to the fringe of the sphere of exchange, on which early economic theory focused. For Adam Smith (1776), it is the perishable characteristic of tertiary production which is the real problem: '[they] perish in the very instant of their performance.' This non-material aspect allows for neither storage nor further transaction. Hence, for classical economists, services do not contribute to an increase in the volume of exchange. Services are in this sense unproductive. Simultaneity of act of production and consumption nullifies the value of work dispensed: '[services] seldom leave any trace or value behind them' (Smith, 1776).

Marx continued this distinction between productive and unproductive labour. But he placed it in the context of an analysis of the circuit of value in which the worker's labour power, and not his service, determined value.

The theoretical concept of unproductive labour was often identified with an evaluation of the social utility of service activities. John Stuart Mill (1848) pointed out that educational and medical provision had a favourable effect upon producers and thus indirectly upon production. The duration of this effect seemed more important to him than the non-material aspect of services.

On a different level, in the national accounts of socialist countries where distinction is made between material and non-material production, services that contribute directly to production (transport, trade etc.) are classified under activities related to the production of goods. So the distinction advocated by the classical economists does not appear clear-cut.

This does, however, not imply that the neoclassical approach, which attaches little theoretical importance to the distinction between goods and services, is satisfactory. The Walrasian model of exchange presupposes a clear distinction between prices and quantities of merchandise. Here transactions can be located and potentially reversed since they are subject to property rights. Excess supply is supposed to lead to an accumulation of stocks. Characteristics of products and agents are clearly identifiable and are not affected by transactions.

All these propositions are difficult to extend to the case of services. A pragmatic definition of services allows for a closer understanding of the different interpretations. According to Hill (1977), a service represents a transformation of the user in the case of services to persons) or the user's goods (in the case of services involving goods) as a result of the voluntary intervention by the producer of services. Service utilization therefore does not involve any transferable acquisition but a modification to the characteristics of the agents or their goods. A consequence of this approach is that products and agents are diversified indefinitely.

GROWTH AND DEVELOPMENT OF THE SERVICE SECTOR. The theory of the three stages of economic growth – primary, secondary and tertiary – was initially formulated by G.B. Fisher (1939), then developed by Clark (1940) and Fourastie (1949), and finally reformulated in a different form by Rostow (1953). The theory is based on two straightforward assumptions on production and consumption in order to link economic growth to the development of a service economy. As far as production is concerned, productivity gains (production or added value per head) are assumed to be higher in industry than in the service sector. As for consumption, the income elasticity of demand for services has to be greater than that of demand for goods.

These propositions explain the forms rather than the causes of economic growth. From the experience of the developed economies in the period 1970–1980 we can conclude that a slowdown in growth has no effect upon the development of the service sector. The rise in service economies can therefore not be identified with an affluent society blessed with full employment. A critique of the propositions underlying the standard model can aid in the identification of positive and negative aspects of service sector development, both in terms of growth and in terms of quality of life.

The assumption of productivity growth differentials is hampered by two obstacles; first, by the difficulty of measuring productivity in the service sector; secondly, by links between growth processes in industry and services.

The measurement of productivity presupposes knowledge of the quantities produced. In practice, the measurement of productivity in services is sometimes based on very limited production indicators (i.e. the number of processed cheques, the number of telephone calls), but more often it is based on input volumes, or *ad hoc* assumptions (in retailing the margin in volume is defined as equal to that observed in value). Other equally plausible propositions would thoroughly modify the standard results by inverting the hierarchy of sectoral rates of growth (Smith, 1972).

To these indeterminacies must be added the existence of interrelations between productivity gains in the service and industry sectors. This is most apparent in the very long term, in the benefits the labour force derives from an efficient health service and education.

On the same level, services contributing to economic integration (transport, telecommunications, business, banks, insurance) constitute the logistic base for the internal organization of companies (Williamson, 1975). First, the internal division of labour within the enterprise (research, personnel, production) favours the development of oligopolies. Secondly, a reorganization of these oligopolistic structures by product division facilitates the use of external services. According to Stigler (1951), this second stage of external division of labour (at work in the United States in the 1930s and in Europe in the 1960s) corresponds to the development of business services, activities which were missing in Fisher's (1906) scheme. These service activities constituted 8.5 per cent of GDP in the USA in 1977 and played a major role in gains in industrial productivity.

Propositions relating to the final demand for services encounter well-known limits. Engel's Law, on which these propositions are based, emphasizes the fact that their income elasticity of demand for services is greater than one, which does not imply anything about changes in volume. However, all empirical studies from Fuchs (1968) to Gershuny and Miles (1983) deny a more rapid growth in the volume of final demand for services. To be more precise, in an analysis of consumption by purpose, note there is a rapid increase of expenditure (in constant prices) on leisure, education, housing and health. But within each purpose, purchase of goods grows faster than purchase of services. This indicates a trend towards goods being substituted for services – a trend which lies at the root of the material development of our societies.

So the standard model of the relationship between services and development becomes rather patchy. In order to assess the efficiency of the manufacturing sector it is necessary to consider service activities. But the global performances of these latter are difficult to assess. Moreover, the rapid growth of expenditure in certain areas induces substitution and complementarity movements between goods and services.

The development toward a 'service economy' increases uncertainty about the forms of development of advanced industrial economies.

The existence of some latitude in the organization of service production (job time-sharing, choice of techniques) as in their pricing (local monopolies) lends support to fears of downgrading in wages and conditions of work, the normalization of which had stabilized demand and facilitated the expansion of production during the postwar period. The fall in growth on a global scale, which led to unemployment and a re-evaluation of systems of social security, in turn sets off a real risk of deterioration in wages and working conditions in countries where service sector activities represent nearly two-thirds of total employment. The growing differentiation in the modes of consumption – which is implied by the limits to service standardization – increases the risk of marked social discrimination. Moreover, during a period of slow growth, a service economy can buttress the development of a dual society (see Petit, 1986).

Pascal Petit

BIBLIOGRAPHY

Clark, C. 1940. *The Conditions of Economic Progress*. London: Macmillan. Revised edn, 1957.

Fisher, A.G.B. 1939. Production, primary, secondary and tertiary. *Economic Record* 15, June, 24–38.

Fisher, I. 1906. *The Nature of Capital and Income*. New York: Macmillan. Reprinted, 1965.

Fourastie, J. 1949. *Le grand espoir du XXème siècle*. Paris: PUF. 4th edn, 1958.

Fuchs, V.R. 1968. *The Service Economy*. New York: National Bureau of Economic Research.

Gershuny, J. and Miles, I. 1983. *The New Services Economy*. London: Frances Pinter.

Hill, T.P. 1977. On goods and services. *Review of Income and Wealth* 23(4), December, 315–38.

Katz, A.J. 1983. Valuing the services of consumer durables. *Review of Income and Wealth* 29(4), December, 405–27.

Mill, J.S. 1848. *Principles of Political Economy*. Ed. W. Ashley. Reprinted, New York: Kelley, 1965.

Petit, P. 1986. *Slow Growth and the Service Economy*. London: Frances Pinter.

Rostow, W.W. 1953. *The Process of Economic Growth*. Oxford: Oxford University Press.

Smith, A. 1776. *An Inquiry into the Nature and Causes of the Wealth of Nations*. Harmondsworth: Penguin, 1979.

Smith, A.D. 1972. The measurement and interpretation of service output changes. National Economic Development Office (NEDO), London.

Stigler, G.J. 1951. The division of labor is limited by the extent of the market. *Journal of Political Economy* 59, June, 185–93.

Williamson, O. 1975. *Markets and Hierarchies*. New York: Free Press.

settlement. *See* CONFLICT AND SETTLEMENT.

Shackle, George Lennox Sharman (born 1903). Shackle was born in Cambridge. Financial circumstances compelled him to take an external degree while working first as a bank clerk and then as a schoolmaster; it was only in 1935 that he was able to study under Hayek at the London School of Economics. This was an exciting time to be starting out and later, in one of his best-loved books, *The Years of High Theory* (1967), Shackle was to look back at the problem-solving activities responsible for the interwar theoretical breakthroughs. Within two years, and very much influenced by the latest work of Myrdal and Keynes, he completed his first doctorate (published as Shackle, 1938). By 1940 he was employed in wartime official service, having completed a second thesis that drew on material from his work as assistant to E.H. Phelps Brown at Oxford. Despite the demands of official work, he produced a series of articles on uncertain, crucial choices, whose outcomes may define, for good or bad, the chooser's future possibilities (see especially Shackle, 1942, 1943). These were reworked into his (1949) book and he rose rapidly, after returning to academia as Reader in Economics at Leeds University in 1950, to become Brunner Professor of Economic Science in the University of Liverpool in 1951. His retirement from Liverpool in 1969 saw no easing in his industry or in his desire to see economists deal with knowledge-problems as analytical rudiments rather than refinements (see Shackle, 1972).

Although Shackle's (1949) analysis of crucial choices attracted immediate attention, it won few adherents. In this book, as in many of his subsequent works, Shackle argued that probabilistic notions are questionable if choice experiments can destroy any possibility of their own replication. (Post-Keynesians have extended his view in criticizing the Rational Expectations Hypothesis.) Shackle suggested that, in such situations, choosers would come to focus on particularly attention-arresting pairs of *possibilities* (one pair for each scheme of action). A possibility is not something which a chooser would expect to happen, given enough tries, with a particular frequency, but something whose taking place looks *ex ante* surprising (unsurprising) because potentially fatal obstacles to it can (cannot) be envisaged. Shackle insisted that possibility is not in general distributive: thoughts about a possible outcome not previously imagined need not affect assignments of potential surprise to its rivals, since potential surprise ratings do not sum to any fixed, bounded value. Despite this, many theorists found his 'potential surprise curves' difficult to distinguish from inverted probability distributions; they also took issue with his view that it is not rational for choosers to weigh together values for possibilities that are mutually exclusive. Behaviouralists were ill-disposed to the large role played by indifference surfaces in his analysis of how ascendant gain/loss pairings were focused upon and then ranked; whereas orthodox theorists (e.g. Ford, 1983) argued that it would be irrational for choosers to focus in the way he proposed, and that his selection device – the 'gambler preferences' map – produced the questionable result that an investor will choose a portfolio consisting of no more than two types of financial asset.

Much of his noteworthy retirement output (especially his 1974 book) seeks to make economists recognize that the incompatibility of speculators' expectations, and changes in the 'state of the news', will make the relative demands for durable assets prone to kaleidoscopic instability. To many orthodox model-builders, his kaleidic conception of economic systems has unacceptably nihilistic implications, but it has led some Post-Keynesians to examine how institutions and policies might be designed to constrain explosive and implosive forces whose precise timings and strengths may be impossible to anticipate.

PETER EARL

SELECTED WORKS

1938. *Expectations, Investment and Income*. Oxford: Oxford University Press.

1942. A theory of investment-decisions. *Oxford Economic Papers*, NS 6, April, 77–94.

1943. The expectational dynamics of the individual. *Economica*, NS 10, May, 99–129.

1949. *Expectation in Economics*. Cambridge: Cambridge University Press.

1967. *The Years of High Theory: Invention and Tradition in Economic Thought 1926–1939*. Cambridge: Cambridge University Press.

1972. *Epistemics and Economics*. Cambridge: Cambridge University Press.

1974. *Keynesian Kaleidics*. Edinburgh: Edinburgh University Press.

BIBLIOGRAPHY

Ford, J.L. 1983. *Choice, Expectation and Uncertainty*. Oxford: Martin Robertson.

shadow pricing. When a businessman evaluates a project, he does it with a view to calculating the prospective profit from it. These calculations can be seen as taking place in two steps. At the first step, all the physical consequences of relevance to the businessman – the inputs to and outputs from the project – are assessed. At the second stage, these inputs and outputs are converted into costs and revenues, using *market prices*. It is natural that a private businessman should use the ruling market prices for costing inputs and for valuing sales, since these are the prices at which transactions take place and hence profit generated.

Consider now the evaluation of a project by a government. Such evaluation will differ at each of the two steps referred to above. At the first step, the government will be interested in *all* of the repercussions of the project, however indirect. This is because it is the government rather than a private businessman concerned with his own narrowly defined activities. At the second step, the government will wish to use not the ruling market prices but prices which reflect social costs and social benefits, in order to calculate what might be termed social profit. These prices are referred to as *shadow prices*, or accounting prices (see Little and Mirrlees, 1974), and the name suggests that they are to be used in lieu of the actual market prices.

Market prices are what they are. But how are shadow prices to be calculated? Clearly they depend on the government's objective function and on the constraints it faces. The shadow prices should be such that the social profit from the project is positive if and only if the project increases the value of the government's objective function. In a general competitive equilibrium, if the government's objective is economic efficiency, then it can be argued that for a small project the shadow prices do in fact coincide with market prices. If the government's objective includes the pursuance of equity, but it has lump sum instruments to carry this out, then shadow prices still coincide with market prices. Basically the government should use redistributive lump sum taxation to pursue equity and the project to pursue increases in aggregate economic welfare.

But if the government does not have a sufficient range of instruments to pursue effective redistribution without distortion it may be the case that, even with a full competitive equilibrium, shadow prices may differ from market prices. In addition to this, if the economy is not in a full competitive equilibrium, then the case for using shadow prices different from market prices can be argued strongly.

In programming terms, shadow prices are simply dual to the changes in the government's objective function. One justification for their use is the benefits of decentralization: local project evaluators are better equipped to analyse the physical consequences of a project, and this localized knowledge should be used in conjunction with centrally determined shadow prices to evaluate the social profitability of projects. But the real difficulties arise in specifying the objectives of the government and in specifying its constraints, and this is in turn related to who is thought of as doing the project evaluation.

The standard assumption is one of a unitary government with a given social welfare function – a benevolent dictator. But the reality is one where the project evaluator is either part of a government which is a coalition of interests, or the project evaluation is being done by an international agency which faces a government made up of conflicting and competing objectives. The logical procedure for an international agency should be clear – in evaluating a project it should incorporate a model of the political process to clarify the responses of various government instruments to the project. Sen (1972) gives an illuminating discussion of a project which requires importing an input on which there is already a quota – so that the border price of the input is very different from its domestic scarcity value. The Little and Mirrlees (1974) method of using border prices is predicated on the assumption that it is these prices which represent the transformation possibilities for the economy as a whole. But if the assessment of the political realities is such that this quota will not be removed by the government – because of the overriding influence of interest groups that benefit from the rents generated by the quota – then the domestic scarcity value should be used in costing the input.

Similarly, any project which alters significantly the distribution of income will have repercussions on the political process – and there will be attempts by groups who are adversely affected to restore their standard of living. Project evaluation in general, and shadow pricing in particular, should take these into account. Consider, for example, the shadow cost of labour. If the labour used on the project comes from the agricultural sector, and if this labour is a constraint on output, then agricultural output will fall. If government revenue depends on taxation of this output, this will fall too. If, in turn, government expenditure is a major source of non-agricultural (urban) incomes, then at constant fiscal deficit urban incomes will fall. This change in the distribution of income will be an important element in the shadow cost of labour. But suppose now that the political processes are such as to not allow a decline in urban living standards. Rather, government expenditure remains constant and the fiscal deficit increases. Now it is the increased burden on future generations which has to be taken into account. Either way, it should be clear that a model of the political process is crucial in specifying shadow prices even if the project evaluator (be it an international agency or a project evaluation unit within the government) is clear about what the objectives are. Braverman and Kanbur (1985) have provided a prototype analysis of how such constraints might be taken into account, in the specific context of projects in West Africa.

RAVI KANBUR

See also PROJECT EVALUATION.

BIBLIOGRAPHY

Braverman, A. and Kanbur, S.M.R. 1985. Urban bias, present bias, and the shadow cost of labour for agricultural projects: the West African context. The World Bank, Mimeo.

Little, I.M.D. and Mirrlees, J.A. 1974. *Project Appraisal and Planning for Developing Countries*. London: Heinemann.

Sen, A.K. 1972. Control areas and accounting prices: an approach to economic evaluation. *Economic Journal* 82, Supplement, 486–501.

Shapley–Folkman theorem. The Shapley–Folkman theorem places an upper bound on the size of the non-convexities (loosely speaking, openings or holes) in a sum of non-convex sets in Euclidean N-dimensional space, R^N, as a function of the size of non-convexities in the sets summed and the dimension of the space. When the number of sets is large, the bound is independent of the number of sets summed, depending rather on N, the dimension of the space. Hence the size of the non-convexity in the sum becomes small as a proportion of the number of sets summed; the non-convexity per summand goes to zero as the number of summands becomes large. The theorem is used to demonstrate the existence of approximate equilibrium in large finite economies with non-convex preferences (increasing marginal rate of substitution), or non-convex technology (increasing returns) and to demonstrate the convergence of the core to the set of competitive equilibria (Arrow–Hahn, 1972). It may also be used to characterize the solution of non-convex programming problems (Aubin–Ekeland, 1976).

For $S \subset R^N$, S compact, we define rad(S), the radius of S, as a measure of the size of S, $r(S)$, the inner radius of S, and $\rho(S)$, inner distance of S, as measures of the non-convexity (size of holes) of S. Let con$S$ denote the closed convex hull of S (smallest closed convex set containing S as a subset).

$$\text{rad}(S) \equiv \inf_{x \in R^N} \sup_{y \in S} |x - y|;$$

$$r(S) \equiv \sup_{x \in \text{con}S} \inf_{\{T \subset S \mid T \text{ spans } x\}} \text{rad}(T);$$

$$\rho(S) \equiv \sup_{x \in \text{con}S} \inf_{y \in S} |x - y|.$$

$r(S)$ is the smallest radius of a ball centred in the convex hull of S, so that the ball is certain to contain a set of points of S that span the ball's centre. A set of points T is said to span a point x, if x can be expressed as a convex combination (weighted average) of elements of T. Hence $r(S)$ represents a measure of breadth of non-convexities in S. $\rho(S)$ is the maximum distance from a point in con$S$ to (the nearest point of) S. Hence it represents the smaller of breadth or depth of non-convexities of S.

Let $S_1, S_2, \ldots, S_m$ be a (finite) family of m compact subsets of R^N. The vector sum of $S_1, S_2, \ldots, S_m$, denoted W is a set composed of representative elements of $S_1, S_2, \ldots, S_m$ summed together. W is defined as

$$W \equiv \sum_{i=1}^{m} S_i \equiv \left\{ w \mid w = \sum_{i=1}^{m} x^i, x^i \in S^i \right\}$$

where the sum in the brackets is taken over one element of each S_i.

Theorem (Shapley–Folkman): Let $S_1, \ldots, S_m$ be a family of m compact subsets of R^N; $W = \Sigma S_i$. Let $L \geqslant \text{rad}(S_i)$ for all S_i; let $n = \min(N, m)$. Then for any $x \in \text{con } W$

(i) $x = \Sigma_{i=1}^m x^i$, where $x^i \in \text{con } S_i$, and with at most N exceptions, $x^i \in S_i$;

(ii) there is $y \in W$ so that $|x - y| \leqslant L\sqrt{n}$.

Corollary (Starr): Let $S_1, \ldots, S_m$ be a finite family of compact subsets of R^N. $W = \Sigma_{i=1}^m S_i$. Let $L \geqslant r(S_i)$ for all S_i, $n = \min(m, N)$. Then for any $x \in \text{con } W$ there is $y \in W$ so that

$$|x - y| \leqslant L\sqrt{n}.$$

Corollary (Heller): Let $S_1, \ldots, S_m$ be a finite family of compact subsets of R^N; $W = \Sigma_{i=1}^m S_i$. Let $L \geqslant \rho(S_i)$ for all S_i, $n = \min(m, N)$. Then for any $x \in \text{con } W$ there is $y \in W$ so that

$$|x - y| \leqslant Ln.$$

Statements and proofs of the theorem and corollaries along with applications are available in Arrow–Hahn (1972), and Green–Heller (1981). Development of the theorem is due to L. S. Shapley and J. H. Folkman (private correspondence) with publication in Starr (1969). Extensions, alternative proofs, and applications appear in the other references.

ROSS M. STARR

See also PERFECT COMPETITION.

BIBLIOGRAPHY

Arrow, K.J. and Hahn, F.H. 1972. *General Competitive Analysis*. San Francisco: Holden-Day.

Artstein, Z. 1980. Discrete and continuous bang-bang and facial spaces or: look for the extreme points. *SIAM Review* 22(2), 172–85.

Aubin, J.-P. and Ekeland, I. 1976. Estimation of the duality gap in nonconvex optimization. *Mathematics of Operations Research* 1(3), 225–45.

Cassels, J.W.S. 1975. Measure of the non-convexity of sets and the Shapley–Folkman–Starr theorem. *Mathematical Proceedings of the Cambridge Philosophical Society* 78, 433–6.

Ekeland, I. and Temam, R. 1976. *Convex Analysis and Variational Problems*. Amsterdam: North-Holland.

Green, J. and Heller, W.P. 1981. Mathematical analysis and convexity with applications to economics. In *Handbook of Mathematical Economics*, vol. 1, Amsterdam: North-Holland.

Howe, R. 1979. On the tendency toward convexity of the vector sum of sets. Cowles Foundation Discussion Paper No. 538, Yale University, November.

Mas-Colell, A. 1978. A note on the core equivalence theorem: how many blocking coalitions are there? *Journal of Mathematical Economics* 5, December, 207–16.

Starr, R.M. 1969. Quasi-equilibria in markets with non-convex preferences. *Econometrica* 37, 25–38.

Starr, R.M. 1981. Approximation of points of the convex hull of a sum of sets by points of the sum: an elementary approach. *Journal of Economic Theory* 25(2), 314–17.

Shapley value. The *value* of an uncertain outcome (a 'gamble', 'lottery', etc.) to a participant is an evaluation, in the participant's utility scale, of the prospective outcomes: It is an a priori measure of what he expects to obtain (this is the subject of 'utility theory'). In a similar way, one is interested in evaluating a *game*; that is, measuring the *value* of each player in the game.

Such an approach was originally developed by Lloyd S. Shapley (1951, 1953a). The framework was that of *n-person games in coalitional form with side-payments*. Such a game is given by a finite set N together with a function v that associates to every subset S of N a real number $v(S)$. Here, N is the set of 'players', v is the 'characteristic function' and $v(S)$ is the 'worth' of the 'coalition' S: the maximal total payoff the members of S can obtain. This model presumes the following: (i) There are finitely many players. (ii) Agreements between players are possible and enforceable (the game is 'cooperative'). (iii) There exists a medium of exchange ('money') that is freely transferable in unlimited amounts between the players, and moreover every player's utility is additive with respect to it (i.e. a transfer of x units from one player to another decreases the first one's utility by x units and increases the second one's utility by x units; the total payoff of a coalition can thus be meaningfully defined as the sum of the payoffs of its members). This assumption is known as existence of 'side-payments' or 'transferable utility'. (iv) The game is adequately described by its characteristic function (i.e. the worth $v(S)$ of each coalition S is well defined, and the abstraction from the extensive structure of the game to its characteristic function leads to no essential loss; the game is then called a 'c-game'). It should be noted that these underlying assumptions may be interpreted in a broader and more abstract sense. For example, in a voting situation, a 'winning coalition' is assigned worth 1, and a 'losing' coalition – worth 0. The important feature is that, for each coalition, its prospects may well be summarized by one real number.

The *Shapley value* of such a game is a unique payoff vector for the game (i.e. a payoff to each player). It is determined by the following four axioms (this differs from Shapley's original approach only unessentially). (1) *Symmetry* or *equal treatment*: If two players in a game are substitutes (i.e. the worth of no coalition changes when replacing one of the two players by the other one), then their values are equal. (2) *Null* or *dummy player*: If a player in a game is such that the worth of a coalition never changes when he joins it, then his value is zero. (3) *Efficiency* or *Pareto optimality*: The sum of the values of all players equals $v(N)$, the worth of the grand coalition of all players (in a superadditive game $v(N)$ is the maximal amount that the players can jointly get; note that this axiom actually combines feasibility with efficiency). (4) *Additivity*: The value of the sum of two games is the sum of the values of the two games (an equivalent requirement is that the value of a probabilistic combination of two games is the same as the probabilistic combination of the values of the two games; this is analogous to the 'expected utility' postulate). The result of Shapley is that these axioms uniquely determine one payoff vector for each game.

Remarkably, the Shapley value of a player i in a game v turns out to be exactly the *expected marginal contribution of player i to a random coalition S*. For a coalition S not containing i, the marginal contribution of i to S is the change in the worth when i joins S, i.e. $v(S \cup \{i\}) - v(S)$. A random coalition S not containing i is obtained by arranging all n players in line (e.g. 1, 2,..., n), and then putting in S all those that precede i; it is assumed that all $n!$ orders are equally likely. This formula is remarkable, first, since it is a consequence of the very simple and basic axioms above and, second, since the idea of marginal contribution is so fundamental in much of economic analysis.

It should be emphasized that the value of a game is an *a priori* measure – before the game is actually played. Unlike other solution concepts (e.g. the core, von Neumann–Morgenstern solutions, bargaining sets, etc.), it need not yield a 'stable' outcome (the probable final result when the game is played). These final stable outcomes are in general not well determined; the value – which is uniquely specified – may be thought of as their *expectation* or average. Another interpretation of the value axioms regards them as rules for 'fair' division, guiding an impartial 'referee' or 'arbitrator'. Moreover, as suggested above, the Shapley value may be understood as the utility of playing the game (Shapley, 1953a; for a formalization, see Roth, 1977).

In view of both its strong intuitive appeal and its mathematical tractability, the Shapley value has been the focus of much research and applications. Some of these will be briefly mentioned here (an excellent survey is Aumann, 1978).

CHANGING THE DOMAIN. Following Shapley's pioneering approach, the concept of *value* has been extended to additional classes of games, dispensing with (part of) the assumptions (i) – (iv) above.

'Large games' – where the number of players is infinite – have been extensively studied. This includes games with countably many players (Shapley, 1962; Artstein, 1971; Berbee, 1981); non-atomic games (a continuum of small players who are individually insignificant; the monumental book of Aumann and Shapley, 1974; Kannai, 1966; Neyman and Tauman, 1976; Hart, 1977a; Neyman, 1977, 1981; Tauman, 1977; Mertens, 1980); 'oceanic games' (a continuum of small players together with finitely many large players; Shapiro and Shapley, 1960; Milnor and Shapley, 1961; Hart, 1973; Fogelman and Quinzii, 1980; Neyman, 1986). The study of large games, which involves the solution of deep mathematical problems, has led to very valuable insights. One example is the so-called 'diagonal principle': the value is determined by those coalitions S which are close in composition to the whole population (i.e. the proportion of each type of player in S is almost the same as in the grand coalition N of all players).

When the game is not necessarily a 'c-game e (iv) above; this is the case when, for example, threats by tne complement $T=N-S$ of the coalition S are costly to T), Harsanyi (1959) has suggested using a 'modified characteristic function' and applying to it the Shapley value (see also Selten, 1964).

Another class of much interest consists of games 'without side-payments', or 'with non-transferable utility' ('NTU-games', for short); here, assumption (iii) on the existence of a medium of utility exchange is not necessarily satisfied. The simplest such games – two-person pure bargaining – were originally studied by Nash (1950): a unique solution is determined by a set of simple axioms. A value for general NTU-games, which coincides with the Shapley value in the side-payments case, and with the Nash solution in the two-person case, was proposed by Harsanyi (1959, 1963). Another value (with the same properties) was introduced by Shapley (1969). The latter has been widely studied, in particular in large economic models (see below).

Other extensions include games with communication graphs (Myerson, 1977), coalition structures (Aumann and Drèze, 1974; Owen, 1977; Hart and Kurz, 1983), and so on.

CHANGING THE AXIOMS. The four axioms (1) to (4) have been in turn replaced by alternative axioms or even completely dropped. This has led to new foundations for the Shapley value, as well as to the introduction of various generalizations.

If, in addition to the characteristic function, the data of the game include (relative) weights between the players, then a *weighted Shapley value* may be defined (Shapley, 1953b). In the unanimity game, for example, the values of the players are no longer equal but, rather, proportional to the weights; the usual (symmetric) Shapley value results if all the weights are equal. This model is useful when players are of unequal 'size' (e.g. a player may represent a 'group', a 'department', and so on).

Abandoning the efficiency axiom leads to the class of *semi-values* (Dubey, Neyman and Weber, 1981). An interesting semi-value is the *Banzhaf-Coleman index* (Banzhaf, 1965; Dubey and Shapley, 1979); it has been proposed originally as a measure of power in voting games. It can be computed in the same way as the Shapley value: expected marginal contribution, but assuming that all coalitions not containing player i are equally likely.

Another approach to the value uses the following 'consistency' or 'reduced game' property: Given a solution concept (that associates payoff vectors to games), assume that a group of players in a game has already agreed to it, and they are paid off accordingly; consider the reduced game among the remaining players. If the solution of the reduced game is always the same as that of the original game, then the solution is said to be *consistent*. It turns out that consistency, together with some simple requirements for two-player games, characterizes the Shapley value (Hart and Mas-Colell, 1985).

ECONOMIC APPLICATIONS. The model of an *exchange economy* has been the focus of much study in economic theory. The main solution concept there is the *competitive equilibrium*, where prices are determined in such a way that total supply equals total demand. The cooperative game obtained by allowing each coalition to exchange freely the commodities they own among themselves, is called a *market game*. One can then find the value of the corresponding market game. The following result (known as the 'value equivalence principle') has been obtained in various models of this kind (in particular, both when utility is transferable and when it is not): In a *large* exchange economy (where traders are individually insignificant), all value allocations are competitive; moreover, if the utilities are smooth, then all competitive allocations are also value allocations. (It should be noted that in the NTU case there may be more than one value allocation.) This remarkable result joins together two very different approaches: on the one hand, competitive prices which arise from supply and demand; on the other hand, marginal contributions of the economic agents (Shapley, 1964; Shapley and Shubik, 1969; Aumann and Shapley, 1974; Aumann, 1975; Champsaur, 1975; Hart, 1977b; Mas-Colell, 1977; note moreover that for large markets, the set of competitive equilibria coincides with the core).

Other applications of the value to economic theory include models of taxation, where a political power structure is superimposed on the exchange or production economy (Aumann and Kurz, 1977). Further references on economic applications can be found in Aumann (1985).

Next, consider the problem of allocating joint costs in a 'fair' manner. It turns out that the axioms determining the Shapley value are easily translated into postulates suitable for this kind of problem (e.g. the efficiency axiom becomes total cost sharing). The various 'tasks' (or 'projects', 'departments', etc.) become the players, and $v(S)$ is the total cost of the set S of tasks (Shubik, 1962). Two notable applications are airport landing fees (a task here is an aircraft landing; Littlechild and Owen, 1973) and telephone billing (each time unit of a phone call is a player; the resulting cost allocation scheme is in actual use at Cornell University; Billera, Heath and Raanan, 1978). Further research in this direction can be found in Shapley (1981a; the use of weighted Shapley values is proposed there); Billera and Heath (1982); Mirman and Tauman (1982); and the book edited by Young (1985).

POLITICAL APPLICATIONS. The Shapley value has been widely applied to the study of power in voting and other political systems. A trivial observation – although not always remembered in practice – is that the political power need not be proportional to the number of votes (the Board of Supervisors in the Nassau County, N.Y. is a good example; Shapley, 1981b). It is therefore important to find an objective method of measuring power in such situations. The Shapley value (known in this setup as the *Shapley–Shubik index*; Shapley and Shubik, 1954) is, by its definition, a very good candidate. Indeed, consider a simple political game; it is described by specifying for each coalition whether it is 'winning' or 'losing'. The Shapley value of a player i is then the probability that i is a 'pivot'; namely, that in a random order of all players, those preceding i are losing, whereas together with i they are winning. For example, in a simple majority voting situation (half of the votes are needed to win), assume there is one large party having $\frac{1}{3}$ of the votes, and the rest of the votes are divided among many small parties; the value of the large party is then approximately $\frac{1}{2}$ – much higher than its share of the votes. In comparison, when there are two large parties each having $\frac{1}{3}$ of the votes (the rest being again divided among a large number of small parties), the value of each large party is close to $\frac{1}{4}$ – less than its voting weight (this phenomenon may be explained by the competition – or lack of it – for the 'favours' of the small parties).

The Shapley value has also been used in more complex models, where 'ideologies' and 'issues' are taken into account (thus, not all arrangements of the voters are equally likely; an 'extremist' party, for example, is less likely to be the pivot than a 'middle-of-the road' one; Owen, 1971; Shapley, 1977). References on political applications of the Shapley value may be found in Shapley (1981b); these include various parliaments (USA, France, Israel), United Nations Security Council and others.

SERGIU HART

See also COOPERATIVE GAMES; GAME THEORY.

BIBLIOGRAPHY

The following list is by no means complete; it contains some of the original contributions to the study of value as well as surveys and pointers to further references.

Artstein, Z. 1971. Values of games with denumerably many players. *International Journal of Game Theory* 1, 27–37.

Aumann, R.J. 1975. Values of markets with a continuum of traders. *Econometrica* 43, 611–46.

Aumann, R.J. 1978. Recent developments in the theory of the Shapley Value. *Proceedings of the International Congress of Mathematicians*, Helsinki, 995–1003.

Aumann, R.J. 1985. On the non-transferable utility value: a comment on the Roth–Shafer examples. *Econometrica* 53, 667–78.

Aumann, R.J. and Drèze, J.H. 1974. Cooperative games with coalition structures. *International Journal of Game Theory* 3, 217–37.

Aumann, R.J. and Kurz, M. 1977. Power and taxes. *Econometrica* 45, 1137–61.

Aumann, R.J. and Shapley, L.S. 1974. *Values of Non-atomic Games.* Princeton: Princeton University Press.

Banzhaf, J.F. 1965. Weighted voting doesn't work: a mathematical analysis. *Rutgers Law Review* 19, 317–43.

Berbee, H. 1981. On covering single points by randomly ordered intervals. *Annals of Probability* 9, 520–28.

Billera, L.J. and Heath, D.C. 1982. Allocation of shared costs: a set of axioms yielding a unique procedure. *Mathematics of Operations Research* 7, 32–9.

Billera, L.J., Heath, D.C. and Raanan, J. 1978. Internal telephone billing rates: a novel application of non-atomic game theory. *Operations Research* 26, 956–65.

Champsaur, P. 1975. Cooperation versus competition. *Journal of Economic Theory* 11, 393–417.

Dubey, P. and Shapley, L.S. 1979. Mathematical properties of the Banzhaf Power Index. *Mathematics of Operations Research* 4, 99–131.

Dubey, P., Neyman, A. and Weber, R.J. 1981. Value theory without efficiency. *Mathematics of Operations Research* 6, 122–8.

Fogelman, F. and Quinzii, M. 1980. Asymptotic value of mixed games. *Mathematics of Operations Research* 5, 86–93.

Harsanyi, J.C. 1959. A bargaining model for the cooperative n-person game. In *Contributions to the Theory of Games*, Vol. 4, ed. A.W. Tucker and D.R. Luce, Princeton: Princeton University Press, 324–56.

Harsanyi, J.C. 1963. A simplified bargaining model for the n-person cooperative game. *International Economic Review* 4, 194–220.

Hart, S. 1973. Values of mixed games. *International Journal of Game Theory* 2, 69–85.

Hart, S. 1977a. Asymptotic value of games with a continuum of players. *Journal of Mathematical Economics* 4, 57–80.

Hart, S. 1977b. Values of non-differentiable markets with a continuum of traders. *Journal of Mathematical Economics* 4, 103–16.

Hart, S. and Kurz, M. 1983. Endogenous formation of coalitions. *Econometrica* 51, 1047–64.

Hart, S. and Mas-Colell, A. 1985. The potential: a new approach to the value in multi-person allocation problems. Harvard University Discussion Paper 1157.

Kannai, Y. 1956. Values of games with a continuum of players. *Israel Journal of Mathematics* 4, 54–8.

Littlechild, S.C. and Owen, G. 1973. A simple expression for the Shapley value in a special case. *Management Science* 20, 370–72.

Mas-Colell, A. 1977. Competitive and value allocations of large exchange economies. *Journal of Economic Theory* 14, 419–38.

Mertens, J.-F. 1980. Values and derivatives. *Mathematics of Operations Research* 5, 523–52.

Milnor, J.W. and Shapley, L.S. 1961. Values of large games II: oceanic games. RAND RM 2649. Also in *Mathematics of Operations Research* 3, 1978, 290–307.

Mirman, L.J. and Tauman, Y. 1982. Demand compatible equitable cost-sharing prices. *Mathematics of Operations Research* 7, 40–56.

Myerson, R.B. 1977. Graphs and cooperation in games. *Mathematics of Operations Research* 2, 225–9.

Nash, J.F. 1950. The bargaining problem. *Econometrica* 18, 155–62.

Neyman, A. 1977. Continuous values are diagonal. *Mathematics of Operations Research* 2, 338–42.

Neyman, A. 1981. Singular games have asymptotic values. *Mathematics of Operations Research* 6, 205–12.

Neyman, A. 1986. Weighted majority games have asymptotic values. The Hebrew University, Jerusalem, RM 69.

Neyman, A. and Tauman, Y. 1976. The existence of non-diagonal axiomatic values. *Mathematics of Operations Research* 1, 246–50.

Owen, G. 1971. Political games. *Naval Research Logistics Quarterly* 18, 345–55.

Owen, G. 1977. Values of games with a priori unions. In *Essays in Mathematical Economics and Game Theory*, ed. R. Henn and O. Moeschlin, New York: Springer-Verlag, 76–88.

Roth, A.E. 1977. The Shapley value as a von Neumann–Morgenstern utility. *Econometrica* 45, 657–64.

Selten, R. 1964. Valuation of n-person games. In *Advances in Game Theory*, ed. M. Dresher, L.S. Shapley and A.W. Tucker, Princeton: Princeton University Press, 577–626.

Shapiro, N.Z. and Shapley, L.S. 1960. Values of large games I: a limit theorem. RAND RM 2648. Also in *Mathematics of Operations Research* 3, 1978, 1–9.

Shapley, L.S. 1951. Notes on the n-person game II: the value of an n-person game. RAND RM 670.

Shapley, L.S. 1953a. A value for n-person games. In *Contributions to the Theory of Games*, Vol. II, ed. H.W. Kuhn and A.W. Tucker, Princeton: Princeton University Press, 307–17.

Shapley, L.S. 1953b. Additive and non-additive set functions. PhD thesis, Princeton University.

Shapley, L.S. 1962. Values of games with infinitely many players. In *Recent Advances in Game Theory*, Princeton University Conferences, 113–18.

Shapley, L.S. 1964. Values of large games VII: a general exchange economy with money. RAND RM 4248-PR.

Shapley, L.S. 1969. Utility comparison and the theory of games. In *La Décision: agrégation et dynamique des ordres de préférence*, Paris: Editions du CNRS, 251–63.

Shapley, L.S. 1977. A comparison of power indices and a nonsymmetric generalization. RAND P–5872.

Shapley, L.S. 1981a. Comments on R.D. Banker's 'Equity considerations in traditional full cost allocation practices: an axiomatic perspective'. In *Joint Cost Allocations*, ed. S. Moriarity, Norman, OK: University of Oklahoma, 131–6.

Shapley, L.S. 1981b. Measurement of power in political systems. *Game Theory and its Applications*, Proceedings of Symposia in Applied Mathematics, Vol. 24, American Mathematical Society, 69–81.

Shapley, L.S. and Shubik, M. 1954. A method for evaluating the distribution of power in a committee system. *American Political Science Review* 48, 787–92.

Shapley, L.S. and Shubik, M. 1969. Pure competition, coalitional power, and fair division. *International Economic Review* 10, 337–62.

Shubik, M. 1962. Incentives, decentralized control, the assignment of joint costs and internal pricing. *Management Science* 8, 325–43.

Tauman, Y. 1977. A non-diagonal value on a reproducing space. *Mathematics of Operations Research* 2, 331–7.

Young, H.P. (ed.) 1985. *Cost Allocation: Methods, Principles, Applications.* New York: Elsevier Science.

sharecropping. Sharecropping is a form of land tenancy, in which the landlord allows the tenant to use his land, in return for a stipulated fraction of the output (the 'share'). It is an institutional arrangement which has prevailed in many parts of the world. Though today sharecropping is most commonly found in l.d.c.'s, sharecropping arrangements exist even in more advanced countries (such as the United States).

The sharecropping relationship may take on a variety of forms. The landlord may share in the costs (other than labour), or may bear none of the costs or all of the costs. If he shares in the cost, the fraction of the costs he bears may or may not be equal to the fraction of output which he receives. A variety of restrictions may be imposed on the tenant (e.g.

concerning what crops to be grown, how much non-labour inputs have to be supplied, etc.).

Since the early 1970s there has been a resurgence of interest in sharecropping, for two reasons. First, sharecropping *appears* to be an inefficient institutional arrangement, since workers receive less than their marginal product. The question naturally arises, how could such an inefficient system seem to flourish in so many places and over such a long duration? The New Institutional Economics begins with the presumption that one should not simply take the institutional structure of the economy as given, but should attempt to explain it, to identify the economic rationale for the observed features of the economy. (This is not to say that inefficient economic institutions might not persist, but one must explain why that is the case.) Thus, researchers in the theory of rural organization have attempted to explain not only the persistence of sharecropping, but also the particular features which it exhibits.

Secondly, it has increasingly become clear that the share-cropping relationship is, in fact, quite similar to a number of other economic relationships, found in both developed and less developed countries. For instance, capitalists often let others use their capital, in return for a fixed share in the profits; thus understanding sharecropping may provide insights into understanding modern capital markets (stock markets). Thus, the sharecropping model has served as the basic paradigm for a wider class of relationships known as principal–agent relationships (*see* PRINCIPAL AND AGENT, ii). This basic similarity was noted in Stiglitz (1974); this entry draws heavily upon that paper.

Views on the reasons for, and efficiency of, sharecropping relationships have gone through several stages. The earlier view that depicted sharecropping as simply an inefficient institutional arrangement was followed by a view that it represented an efficient institutional arrangement for risk-sharing, in an environment where other forms of insurance were not available; the landlord and the tenant shared in the risks associated with the fluctuations in output caused by weather, disease, etc. as well as those associated with the vicissitudes in the prices of marketed commodities. Sharecropping contracts had the distinct advantage over rental contracts in that the landlord, who because of his higher wealth, was in a better position to bear risks, bore a larger fraction of those risks than he did under the rental agreement (where the worker bore all the risks). Cheung (1969) went so far as to suggest that there were not, in fact, any efficiency losses, provided that the sharecropping contract specified the labour required of the worker.

Three objections were raised to these conclusions. First, if sharecropping were just a risk-sharing institution, why did not the landlord bear still more of the risk? Secondly, it was shown that *the same risk-sharing opportunities could be provided without sharecropping, simply by having workers mix wage contracts and rental contracts.* Thirdly, if sharecropping was primarily a risk sharing contract, then the terms (shares) should vary according to the riskiness of the crops grown and the differences in wealth between the landlord and the tenant. Though terms did vary from place to place, the variations did not appear to be of the magnitude that the risk-sharing theory would have suggested.

Moreover, it seemed implausible that the landlord could perfectly monitor the worker, so that a contract which specified precisely the labour to be applied would not be enforceable.

Thus Stiglitz (1974) argued that sharecropping was an institutional arrangement designed both to share risks and to provide incentives, in a situation where monitoring effort (labour supply) was costly. Sharecropping represented a *compromise*: while rental contracts provided (in the absence of bankruptcy) perfect incentives (since the individual kept all of the value of his marginal product), it provided no risk sharing; on the other hand, wage contracts shifted all of the risk on to landlords, who were in the best position to bear it, but provided no incentives. To ensure that workers did not shirk, the landlord would have to spend resources monitoring the workers.

In this approach, it appears as if the sharecropping contract has certain optimality properties: indeed, the contract is usually represented as maximizing the welfare of the worker, subject to the landlord obtaining a particular value of expected rents from his land. (Even the inefficiency associated with the worker receiving less than the value of his marginal product may be mitigated with long-term contracts; workers who fail to produce a sufficiently high level of output over a long enough period may find their tenancy contract terminated.)

This general approach could be used to explain not only the persistence of sharecropping, but also some of its important features:

(a) The landlord had an incentive to encourage the tenant to use inputs (such as fertilizer) which raised the workers' marginal product, and which therefore resulted in the workers working harder. This explains why the landlord might bear a fraction of the costs of inputs that exceeded the fraction of the output that he received.

(b) Important externalities might arise between land markets and credit markets; these externalities can explain the interlinking between credit and land markets that is frequently observed in l.d.c.'s (i.e. the landlord is also the lender). An increase in the amount of outstanding debt affects both workers' efforts and their choice of technique (risk). These, in turn, affect the return to the landlord. Conversely, a change in the terms of the sharecropping contract will in general affect the probability of default, and hence the return to the lender. See Braverman and Stiglitz (1982).

This analysis leaves three questions outstanding:

(1) To implement a cost sharing contract, costs have to be observable. If costs are observable, then the contract could, in principle, specify the level of inputs; no 'moral hazard' problem need arise. Why then are cost sharing contracts so widespread? Again, the answer lies in an information asymmetry: the worker often is more informed than the landlord about what the appropriate level of inputs are. Thus, the contract should provide the worker with an incentive to use his superior information; and this the cost sharing contract does.

(2) The theory predicts a wider variation in the terms of the contract than is in fact observed. Shares of between $\frac{1}{2}$ and $\frac{2}{3}$ are observed in widely varying circumstances. Allen (1985) provides an interesting explanation of this phenomenon. He argues that unless the worker is provided adequate incentives (a large enough share) he will have an incentive to abscond with the entire output. Assume, for instance, that if a worker were to do so, he would remain unemployed for one period, and then obtain land (at similar terms) in another village. If his output is Q, the present discounted value of his absconding is

$$Q + \alpha Q/(1+r)r$$

where α is the share the worker receives, and r is the rate of interest; if he does not abscond, the present discounted value of his income is

$$(1+r)\alpha Q/r.$$

Hence, if he is not to abscond,

$$\alpha > (1+r)/(2+r)$$

If r is not too great, this is approximately 0.5. Thus, if this constraint is binding, changes in economic circumstances will have little effect on the terms of the contract.

(3) Economic theory predicts that, in general, the share received by different farmers would differ. Then there would be opportunities for arbitrage.
would be a constant is that, if it were not, the effective price received by different farmers would differ. Then would there be opportunities for arbitrage?

There may be a simpler explanation: the gains to the use of non-linear contracts are not worth the additional costs of implementing them. In particular, the exact form of the 'optimal non-linear contract' (to be described below) may be sensitive to details concerning the probability distribution of the random variables affecting output, the nature of the technology, and the utility function of workers. Much more limited information is required to implement the optimal linear sharecropping contract. Indeed, in the standard specifications of the optimal contract, the share contracts should be random, under quite general conditions. The fact that they are not suggests that something important is left out of the analysis.

Current views on sharecropping suggest that while it may not have the deleterious consequences suggested by the earlier views, it may not have the optimality properties associated with the 'principal-agent' view. First, though the contracts are 'locally efficient' (that is, they maximize the expected utility of the worker, given the expected rents to be received by the landlord), they are not 'general equilibrium efficient', that is, there exist, in general, taxes and subsidies which could lead to Pareto improvements.

Secondly, for a variety of reasons, one may be concerned with the level of production in the economy; and sharecropping may have a deleterious effect on this. A sharecropping contract with a 50 per cent share has the same effects that a tax on output of 50 per cent would have; there is a presumption that such a tax might significantly decrease output, unless the labour supply schedule was backward bending. If this is the case, then a land reform, in which workers receive the land which they formally worked as sharecroppers, may increase agricultural productivity significantly.

There has also been some concern that the contractual form may affect the adoption of innovations. It undoubtedly does: innovations which increase output (at any level of input of labour), but which decrease the marginal product of labour (and hence reduce workers' incentives to work) will be resisted by landlords (they may impose restrictions on the use of such technologies). But these innovations would, at the same time, have reduced agricultural productivity.

DETERMINATION OF THE EQUILIBRIUM CONTRACT. The analysis of sharecropping contracts depends critically on the set of admissible contracts. Three sets of contracts have been investigated: (a) fixed shares; (b) linear contracts; and (c) non-linear contracts.

In the case where the share is fixed (by convention, say), then the problem of the landlord is a simple one. The 'competitive' landlord takes the opportunity cost of a worker as given, represented by his reservation utility level U^*; he must offer a contract which generates at least that level of utility. For simplicity, we assume all workers and all land are identical.

Output per acre is assumed to be a function of a random variable (S) and labour input per unit land, which in turn is a function of the effort level of workers (e) and the number of workers per acre (a):

$$q = f(S, ea)$$

We simplify by using the multiplicative form,

$$q = Sf(ea).$$

The worker chooses his effort level to maximize his expected utility, given his outside wage opportunities and the terms of the contract. For simplicity, for the moment we ignore the outside opportunities. His utility is a function of his effort and his income, y; y in turn depends simply on the share and the amount of land he has, i.e.

$$y = \alpha q/a,$$

where α is the share (q is the output per acre, and $1/a$ is the number of acres the representative tenant worker has). He then maximizes

$$EU(\alpha q/a, e).$$

The solution yields effort, and his output, as a function of the contract terms a and α:

$$y = y(a, \alpha).$$

We denote the maximized value of expected utility by $V(\alpha, a)$. The landlord thus

$$\underset{\{\alpha,a\}}{\text{maximizes}}\ E(1-\alpha)q$$

subject to the constraint that

$$V(\alpha, a) \geqslant U^*.$$

In the case where α is dictated by custom, there are two possible patterns of equilibrium.

(a) Increasing the density (reducing the amount of land per worker) has two effects; it reduces his welfare, and this income effect induces him to work harder; and it reduces the marginal return to his effort, and this induces him to work less hard. If the individual has outside opportunities, he may spend more of his energies on these outside activities. It is thus possible that reducing acreage per worker below a certain level actually reduces output per acre. There may thus exist an interior solution to the unconstrained problem,

$$\max_{\{a\}} Eq.$$

Denote the solution by a^*. Denote the available worker/land ratio by a'. If

$$a^* < a',$$

then some individuals will get land, with plot sizes $1/a^*$; there will be unemployed individuals (or individuals who work in non-agricultural occupations, at a lower expected utility); but they cannot persuade any landlords to give them land.

On the other hand, if

$$a^* > a',$$

then in equilibrium everyone will get land, with plot size $1/a'$.
(b) By the same token, if there is no interior solution, then the equilibrium plot size will be simply determined by the available land/laborer ratio.

The analysis when the share can be determined endogenously follows along parallel lines. We now need to solve again the unconstrained problem. (The optimal share in the unconstrained problem will be between zero and one; at $\alpha = 0$, the worker has no incentive to work; and at $\alpha = 1$, the landlord receives mothing.) Thus, at the optimal value of $\{\alpha, a\}$, if $a^* < a'$, then some individuals will not be successful in obtaining the use of land.

Linear contracts. The next most complicated set of sharecropping contracts involves a fixed payment (either to or from the landlord) plus a share. Many contractual relations may have an implicit or explicit provision calling for such fixed payments; payments from the landlord to the worker to finance stipulated inputs, like fertilizer, can be interpreted this way. Now, the income of the worker can be written

$$y = \alpha q/a + \beta.$$

The mathematical formulation follows exactly along the lines of the previous case. This formulation has the advantage that it can generate, as limiting cases, a pure rental contract (where $\alpha = 1$, $\beta < 0$) and a pure wage contract ($\alpha = 0$, $\beta > 0$). Not surprisingly, the exact form of the contract depends both on the properties of U and f, as well as the magnitude of the uncertainty. If, for instance, workers were risk neutral, a pure rental contract will be used; the greater the risk aversion and the greater the risk, the closer the optimal contract approximates a pure wage contract. Moreover, the greater the (compensated) labour supply elasticity, i.e. the more sensitive the worker is to incentive, the greater α, i.e. the closer to a rental contract. (If the worker supplied labour inelastically, again a wage contract would be efficient.) (For detailed formulae, see Stiglitz, 1974.)

Non-linear contracts. In the formulations presented thus far, it makes little difference whether workers supply their effort before or after S is known (though the contract must be signed before S is known). (Most of the sharecropping literature focuses on the case where the effort decision is made before S is known.) This is no longer true when non-linear contracts are employed.

The simplest case is that where effort must be applied before S is known, and there are unbounded penalties (no restrictions on the set of admissible contracts). In the case where there is a finite range to S, the landlord calculates what the first-best optimal level of effort would be, i.e.

$$\max_e U(\bar{y} + \beta, e)$$

(where $-\beta$ is his rent and $\bar{y} = Ey$). Denote this by e^{**}. He then calculates the minimum output associated with this

$$\min_{\{S\}} \{f(S, e^{**}a')\}.$$

The worker gets a fixed wage, regardless of output, provided output per acre exceeds this level; and he gets an infinite punishment if it falls short (being thrown off the land may suffice, if alternative opportunities are unavailable).

Thus, in this case, optimal contracting will never entail sharecropping, but will always involve a wage contract, with a severe penalty for deficient performance. Though the landlord may be able to detect deficient performances only in extreme cases, the severe punishment in those situations is enough to provide the worker with the requisite incentives. (This result does not, however, appear to be robust to changes in information structure.)

The other situation is that where effort is applied after S is known. Consider the simplest case where there are only two states of nature, S_1 and S_2. The landlord will, ex post, be able to distinguish which of the two states has occurred by observing the output (one can show that this will always be the case with optimally chosen incentive structures).

An incentive structure provides a relationship between output and what the worker gets, i.e. assuming for simplicity that everyone has one unit of land, it specifies

$$y = \tilde{y}(q).$$

For each incentive function, we could calculate the levels of effort and output in the two states and hence the landlord's expected income; if the two states are equally likely, his expected income is

$$R = 1/2\{q_1 - y_1 + q_2 - y_2\}.$$

We then look for that function $\tilde{y}$ which maximizes this, subject to the workers' reservation utility constraint. It is easier, however, if we simply ask, what are the values of $\{q_i, y_i\}$ which maximize rents, subject to the reservation utility constraint, and subject to the 'self-selection constraints' which enable us to differentiate among the two states (that is, the self-selection constraint ensure that, when the state is state 1, the individual undertakes the action which we intended in state 1, and similarly for state 2). Formally, then, the optimal sharecropping contract is that set of $\{y_i, q_i\}$ which

$$\max R$$

subject to

$V(y_i, q_i, S_i) > V(y_j, q_j, S_i)$ $i \neq j$ (the self-selection constraint)

and subject to

$$\Sigma V(y_i, q_i, S_i)p_i > U^*,$$

where u^* is the reservation utility constraint, p_i is the probability of state i, and where

$$V(y, q, S) = U[y, l(q, S)],$$

the utility in state S when output is q and income is y; where $l(q, S)$ is the labour (effort) required to produce output q in state S.

JOSEPH E. STIGLITZ

See also ASYMMETRIC INFORMATION; INCENTIVE CONTRACTS; PEASANT ECONOMY; PRINCIPAL AND AGENT.

BIBLIOGRAPHY

Allen, F. 1985. On the fixed nature of sharecropping contracts. *Economic Journal*, March, 30–48.

Braverman, A. and Stiglitz, J.E. 1982. Sharecropping and the interlinking of agrarian markets. *American Economic Review* 72(4), September, 695–715.

Cheung,S. 1969. *The Theory of Share Tenancy*. Chicago: University of Chicago Press.

Stiglitz, J.E. 1974. Incentives and risk sharing in sharecropping. *Review of Economic Studies*, April, 219–55.

Shaw, George Bernard (1856–1950). Shaw's interest in economics belongs to the 1880s. Wandering into a Henry George lecture in London in 1882 he was so impressed that he immediately read *Progress and Poverty* and thence converted to socialism. This vaccination by George seems to have prevented him from becoming a true marxist, even though 'I never took up a book that proved better worth reading than "Capital" ' (1887c; 1930, p. 168). His first venture into economics was a letter on marxian value theory entitled 'Who is the Thief?', which appeared in the weekly *Justice* (1884; 1930, pp. 1–8) under one of his many facetious pseudonyms, G.B.S. Larking. Criticizing Volume I of *Capital*, he asked why competition did not drive down surplus value and so leave the consumer as the exploiter, a reasonable enough question if marxian value is confused with price.

The next foray of this 'clever dilettante' (Stigler, 1965, p. 286) ensued upon Wicksteed's own debut in economics (1884; 1930; 1933), which made use of Jevonian final utility in a sympathetic but penetrating criticism of marxian value theory. Wicksteed's article appeared in *To-Day*, the magazine of the Social Democratic Federation, and was so sharp that it cried out for rebuttal. But who was to do it?

> Hyndman ... would not waste time in squelching the presumptuous insect Wicksteed; and finally R.P.B. Frost, then one of the proprietors of ... [*To-Day*] ..., assured me as we stood among the tombs within the consecrated precinct of St Paul's Cathedral, that if I did not do it he (Frost) must do it himself. The threat prevailed; and I undertook to write 'a comment' ... the survival of Wicksteed in robust health came to pass in due course (1889a; 1930, pp. 177–8).

By his own account (1887b; 1930, pp. 138–9n) Shaw's comment on Wicksteed 'proved nothing but his own incompetence' in Jevonian utility theory. Moreover, his rashness in poking fun at mathematics for its apparent ability to demonstrate that $1=2$ provoked a crushing reply from Wicksteed:

> Mr Shaw arrived at the sapient conclusion that there was 'a screw loose somewhere' – not in his own reasoning powers, but – 'in the algebraic art'; and thenceforth renounced mathematical reasoning in favour of the literary method which enables a clever man to follow equally fallacious arguments to equally absurd conclusions *without seeing that they are absurd* (1885; 1930; pp. 96–7, original italics).

Irrepressible as ever, Shaw carried the battle to the cliffs of North London. At the Hampstead Historic Society (formerly, the Karl Marx Club);

> F.Y. Edgeworth as a Jevonian and Sidney Webb as a Stuart Millite, fought the Marxian theory tooth and nail; whilst Belfort Bax and I, in a spirit of transcendent Marxism, held the fort recklessly, and ... I suffered many a bruise in defence of an untenable position (1889a; 1930, pp. 178–9).

But 'Wicksteed's attack on *Capital* ... had shaken Shaw, and his doubts were intensified by his experience in yet another group (later to become the British Economic Association) which met regularly in Hampstead at the house of the stockbroker Henry R. Beeton' (MacKenzie, 1977, p. 64).

Like so much else in the 1880s this last group, known as the Economic Circle, was of Georgeite origin (see Howey, 1960, ch. 13). Beeton himself became a member in March 1884 and by October was its host, his fortnightly meetings alternating with those of the Historic Society. When Shaw joined in 1885 its membership included Foxwell and Wicksteed as well as Edgeworth and Webb, and the group stayed together for the next five years. Shaw could not have had better tutors in marginalist theory but his block in mathematics apparently precluded full understanding. Listen to him describe to Graham Wallas (also a member) what was obviously an embryonic version of Wicksteed (1894):

> At Beeton's Wicksteed turned up. He had been working out the fact that if a man undertakes productive operations which require a great many tools, they will not be productive at all if he has not tools enough. With a few simple curves he managed to extract from this position a degree of mental confusion that bids fair to last us the whole season (Laurence, 1965, p. 237; letter dated 21 January 1890).

This economic education left Shaw with an odd but for him serviceable amalgam of George, Jevons and Marx, which is on display in his Fabian Essay on the Economic Basis of Socialism (1889b). Thereafter he made no substantive progress in economics but went on to the many other things for which he is known and admired. His debates on value theory in the 1880s were just an episode in the life of a great man, but they show him to advantage as a witty, courteous and ferocious opponent; not a bad act to follow.

PETER NEWMAN

See also WICKSTEED, PHILIP HENRY.

SELECTED WORKS

Apart from (1889b) all the articles by Shaw listed below are reprinted in the elegant limited edition (1930), as are Wicksteed (1884), (1885). These two as well as Shaw (1885) may also be found in Wicksteed (1933, Vol. II).

1884. Who is the thief? *Justice* (9), 15 March.
1885. The Jevonian criticism of Marx. *To-Day*, January.
1887a,b,c. Karl Marx and 'Das Kapital': First Notice, Second Notice, Third Notice. *National Reformer*, 7, 14 and 21 August respectively.
1889a. Bluffing the value theory. *To-Day*, May.
1889b. The basis of socialism; economic. In *Fabian Essays in Socialism*, ed. G.B. Shaw, London: Walter Scott.
1930. *Bernard Shaw and Karl Marx. A Symposium, 1884–1889*. New York; printed for Random House by Richard W. Ellis: The Georgian Press.

BIBLIOGRAPHY

Howey, R.S. 1960. *The Rise of the Marginal Utility School 1870–1889*. Lawrence: University of Kansas Press.
Laurence, D. 1965. *Bernard Shaw. Collected Letters 1874–1897*. New York: Dodd, Mead & Co.
MacKenzie, N. and J. 1977. *The Fabians*. New York: Simon & Schuster.
Stigler, G.J. 1965. Bernard Shaw, Sidney Webb, and the theory of Fabian Socialism. Chapter 9 in G.J. Stigler, *Essays in the History of Economics*, Chicago: University of Chicago Press. Reprinted from *Proceedings of the American Philosophical Society* 103, June 1959.
Wicksteed, P.H. 1884. Das Kapital; a criticism. *To-Day*, October.
Wicksteed, P.H. 1885. The Jevonian criticism of Marx: a rejoinder. *To-Day*, April.
Wicksteed, P.H. 1894. *An Essay on the Co-ordination of the Laws of Distribution*. London: Macmillan.
Wicksteed, P.H. 1933. *The Common Sense of Political Economy*. 2 vols, ed. L. Robbins, London: Routledge.

Shephard, Ronald William (1912–1982). Shephard was born in Portland, Oregon, or 22 November 1912 and died in Berkeley, California, on 22 July 1982.

He received his BA in Mathematics and Economics in 1935 and his PhD in Mathematics and Statistics in 1940 at the University of California at Berkeley.

During the years 1943–6 he was a statistical consultant at the Bell aircraft corporation. In the years 1949–51 he worked under the direction of Oskar Morgenstern of Princeton University, producing his path-breaking work, *Cost and Production Functions*. During 1950–52, he was a senior economist at the RAND Corporation and during 1952–6 he was the manager of the systems analysis department at the Sandia Corporation. From 1957 to 1980 he was a Professor of Industrial Engineering and Operations Research at the university of California at Berkeley.

Shephard made several fundamental contributions to economics. He was the first to rigorously derive a duality between cost and production functions; i.e. given a knowledge of either function, the other may be derived from it. He also introduced the distance function to the economics literature in the course of establishing his duality theorems; the distance function is used to define a theoretical index number concept due to Malmquist. Shephard was also the first to derive the derivative property of the cost function (or Shephard's Lemma) starting from the cost function (the derivations by Hicks and Samuelson started from the production or utility function). Shephard also appreciated the econometric implications of Shephard's Lemma.

Shephard also defined the concept of a homothetic production or utility function: a function is homothetic if it is a monotonic transform of a linearly homogeneous function. He also deduced the implications of a homothetic function for its dual cost function.

Shephard also realized the importance of the assumption of homogeneous weak separability for index number and aggregation theory.

Finally, Shephard postulated an ingenious system of axioms or properties for a production function and then was able to deduce the classical law of diminishing returns to a subset of the factors as a theorem.

W.E. DIEWERT

See also COST FUNCTIONS; GAUGE FUNCTIONS.

SELECTED WORKS

1953. *Cost and Production Functions.* Princeton: Princeton University Press.

1970a. *Theory of Cost and Production Functions.* Princeton: Princeton University Press.

1970b. Proof of the law of diminishing returns. *Zeitschrift für Nationalökonomie* 30, 7–34.

Shibata, Kei (1902–1986). Educated at the Commercial College of Yamaguchi, Kei Shibata proceeded to the Imperial University of Kyoto to carry out postgraduate studies. He became a lecturer in economics at the University in 1929, and a professor in 1939. Ten papers he wrote in English for the *Kyoto University Economic Review* were well received both inside and outside Japan, and in 1939 he was awarded a doctorate by the University for his book *Riron Keizaigaku* (Theoretical Economics), published in two volumes in 1935. In 1936–7 he was sent abroad for further studies at Harvard.

Shibata set out to reconcile Marxian political economy and Lausanne economics. While studying *Das Kapital* under Kawakami Hajime, the leading Marxist economist in Japan, he became fascinated by the elegant system of Walrasian general equilibrium equations, which he came across under the guidance of Takata Yasuma, the pioneer of modern economics in Japan, who had succeeded to Kawakami's chair. Shibata's first paper for the solution of this problem was written in 1933, and this paper strongly influenced Lange and led him to publish his famous article, 'Marxian economics and modern economic theory' (*Review of Economic Studies*, 1935).

Shibata's method was to link the simplified Walrasian system of equations with the subdivided Marxian reproduction scheme. He discussed the problem not in terms of dimension of value and surplus value but rather in terms of price and profit, and through this approach he examined the so-called transformation problem and the law of declining rate of profit. Two papers that arose from this study (1934, 1939) aroused the attention of Dobb and Sweezy.

Shibata's study of Marxism extended beyond economic theory to a materialistic view of humanity and history. He pointed out two conflicting views of labour in Marx. One is that labour is the means by which we live, that is, to live is the aim and labour is merely the means to that end, or, in other words, emancipation and the realm of freedom lie beyond productive labour. The other view is that labour is the essence of human life. The young Marx adopted the latter approach, while in later life Marx turned to the first view. Like the young Marx, Shibata hoped that the road to a new society would be opened by cooperation between entrepreneurs and labourers, both of whom recognize that useful life lies not in consumption but in production (1956).

SHIRO SUGIHARA

SELECTED WORKS

1933. Marx's analysis of capitalism and the general equilibrium theory of the Lausanne School. *Kyoto University Economic Review* 8(1), July, 107–26.

1934. On the law of decline in the rate of profit. *Kyoto University Economic Review* 9(1), July, 61–75.

1935. *Riron Keizaigaku* (Theoretical Economics). 2 vols, Tokyo.

1937. Some questions on Mr Keynes' *General Theory of Employment, Interest and Money. Kyoto University Economic Review* 12(1), July, 83–96.

1939. On the general profit rate. *Kyoto University Economic Review* 14(1), January, 40–66.

1956. Ningenteki Kaiho Ron (On human emancipation of labour). *Yamaguchi Keizaigaku Zasshi* (Economic Review of Yamaguchi University) 6(7–8).

1977. *Beyond Keynesian Economics.* Minerva Press.

Shonfield, Andrew Akiba (1917–1981). Andrew Shonfield was educated at St. Paul's School and at Magdalen College, Oxford. His career evolved from journalism to research in political economy. During four years, at the turn of the 1950s he was economic editor of *The Observer*. He then moved to the Royal Institute of International Affairs (Chatham House) to be in charge of its research and became the Institute's Director in 1972. From 1978 until his death in 1981, he was professor of economics at the European University Institute in Florence, responsible for the economic research programme of this Institute. Shonfield's public activities included membership of the Royal Commission on Trade Unions (1965–68) and of the FCO Review Committee on Overseas Representation (1968–69). From 1969 to 1971 he chaired the Social Science Research Council. He was knighted in 1978.

There is a unifying theme in most of his writings: a vigorous and convincing advocacy of cooperative behaviour between private and public powers as well as within each of them. This conviction was anchored in his detailed knowledge of economic history, economics, the workings and sociology of institutions. Two empirical questions were at the centre of his research programme: (i) What are the distinctive features which gave to *Modern Capitalism* – itself the title of his well-known book (1965) – the capacity to achieve such outstanding success during the period 1945–1965? (ii) Are these very features responsible for the twilight of interventionism in the late 1970s?

The balance of public and private power – the mixed economy – was the answer to the first question. But here the mixed economy does not carry the usual meaning of the 'welfare state'. It is, rather, a set of institutions through which the incompatible claims of diverse groups are made consistent.

French planning is an explicit example. But there are many others, though implicit: *dirigisme* is also alive and well in Germany, even if hidden by the doctrinal discourse of the politicians. In *Modern Capitalism*, Andrew Shonfield made this point at length, building on his detailed knowledge of history and institutions. There is little doubt that the demonstration was convincing, even though at that time some critics argued that he did not demonstrate his points analytically. But the insights gained through his sociology of institutions were much more forceful than would have been the conclusions of any (macro)model of the business cycle.

The answer to the second question is much more difficult, in that not only are there many candidates, but also most of them would contradict the answer to the first question. Is not the problem due to 'too much' state, too many interventions? At least this would be the European answer, which lead to the political economy of austerity of the eighties. Andrew Shonfield was prompt to disentangle appearances from reality, but he died before being able to give a fully articulated answer to this query. Nonetheless two posthumous books edited by his widow Zuzanna Shonfield and whose titles are self-explanatory – *The Use of Public Power* (1982) and *In Defence of the Mixed Economy* (1984) – contain his last thought on the subject. The institutional framework which accounted for the years of triumphant Keynesianism should not be ruled out. The main problem does not lay with the buoyant state becoming an inefficient monster, but with the weakening of political consensus and with the growth of interdependency which restrict the room for manoeuvre for national decisions.

Andrew Shonfield was a Keynesian in a particular sense. All his writings – and there are many more than have been cited here – constitute a coherent whole, a significant contribution to the political economy of capitalism, not as an abstract system, but as a dynamic process in which the design of institutions plays an essential role. In that sense his work fills an important gap in Keynesian theory since it illuminates the political processes of government in the management of the economy. The missing theory of the state in Keynesianism was to be found in the qualitative behavioural properties of the 'social framework' rather than in an optimizing principle.

J.P. Fitoussi

SELECTED WORKS

1965. *Modern Capitalism. The changing balance of public and private power*. London: Oxford University Press.

1982. *The Use of Public Power*. Ed. Z. Shonfield, Oxford: Oxford University Press.

1984. *In Defence of the Mixed Economy*. Ed. Z. Shonfield, Oxford: Oxford University Press.

short run. *See* LONG RUN AND SHORT RUN.

Shoup, Carl Sumner (born 1902). Carl Shoup was born 26 October 1902 in San Jose, California, son of Paul Shoup, an officer of the Southern Pacific Railroad. After a BA from Stanford in 1924 he shook the golden dust of California from his feet and obtained a PhD in 1930 at Columbia, which remained his home base until his retirement in 1971. During this tenure he was closely associated first with E.R.A. Seligman and Robert Murray Haig, then with William Warren, William Vickrey, Robert Anthoine and Lowell Harriss, and served as chairman of the Economics Department from 1961 to 1964. From 1971 to 1974 he served as interregional advisor on tax reform planning for the United Nations Center for Development Programs Planning and Policy. Since his formal retirement he has continued an active participation in public finance matters from his home in Sandwich, New Hampshire.

One of his outstanding lines of activity has been the study of and recommendations for the improvement of public finance systems in many countries around the world, beginning with a study with Seligman of the revenue system of Cuba published in 1932 followed by a further study with Haig in 1939. In the summers of 1949 and 1950 he headed study teams producing two reports setting forth a programme for the fundamental revision of the tax system of Japan, for which work he was decorated with the Order of Sacred Treasure. In spite of the subsequent watering down of many of the main proposals by subsequent action of the Diet, this remains one of the most successful broad tax reform studies of modern times, in part due to the extraordinary cooperation that Shoup was able to elicit on all sides.

Later studies of national fiscal systems directed by him include one for Venezuela in 1959, and for the Federal district (Caracas) in 1960; for Brazil, in 1965; for Liberia, in 1970; and briefer studies in a number of countries while working for the UN from 1971 to 1974. As a team leader Shoup proved to be extraordinarily effective as a hard but scrupulously fair driver, coupled with a genuine concern for the welfare of his team members that brought out the best in their work.

His more narrowly focused work includes early work on sales and poll taxes, later followed up in studies of fiscal harmonization and value added taxes at the time of the formation of the European Common market. During the depression of the 1930s, in a period before deliberate Keynesian deficit-financing became respectable, he conducted a study of possibilities for dealing with the mounting US deficits by heavier income taxes. This was soon followed by studies of how to deal by taxation with the problem of wartime inflation, and in a related field by a salient contribution to the then growing field of national income analysis.

His *Public Finance*, published in 1969, gathers together his contributions in the field of government finances, among the outstanding features of which are a searching examination of the criteria by which public finance measures are to be judged, an examination of the principles behind public expenditure determinations, and integration of these matters with macroeconomic considerations, particularly in relation to a deeper analysis of the incidence of taxes.

William Vickrey

SELECTED WORKS

1930. *The Sales Tax in France*. New York: Columbia University Press.

1932. (With E.R.A. Seligman) *A Report on the Revenue System of Cuba*. Havana: Tallares Tipograficos de Carasa y Cia.

1937a. (With R.M. Haig) *The Sales Tax in the American States*. New York: Twentieth Century Fund.

1937b. (With R. Bough and M. Newcomer) *Facing the Tax Problem*. New York: Twentieth Century Fund.

1940. Capitalization and the shifting of the property tax. In Tax Policy League, *Property Taxes*, New York: Tax Policy League.

1940–41. The taxation of excess profits. *Political Science Quarterly* 60, December 1940, 535–55; 61, March 1941, 84–106; 61, June 1941, 226–49.

1941. *Federal Finances in the Coming Decade*. New York: Columbia University Press.

1943a. Three plans for post-war taxation. *American Economic Review* 34, March, 74–97.

1943b. (With M. Friedman and R. Mack) *Taxing to Prevent Inflation*. New York: Columbia University Press.

1947. *Principles of National Income Analysis*. Cambridge, Mass.: Riverside Press.

1948. Development and use of national income data. In *A Survey of Contemporary Economics*, ed. H.S. Ellis, Philadelphia: Blakiston, Vol. I.
1949. (Director) *Report on Japanese Taxation*. Tokyo: General Headquarters, Supreme Commander for the Allied Powers.
1950. (Co-author) *Second Report on Japanese Taxation*. Tokyo: Japan Tax Association.
1951. Some considerations on the incidence of the corporation income tax. *Journal of Finance* 6, June, 187–96.
1952. (With R.M. Haig and L.C. Fitch) *The Financial Problem of the City of New York*. New York: Mayor's Committee on Management Survey.
1956. Theory and background of the value-added tax. *Proceedings of the 48th National Tax Conference, 1955*, Sacramento: National Tax Association.
1957. Some distinguishing characteristics of the British, French, and United States public finance systems. *American Economic Review, Papers and Proceedings* 47(2), May, 187–97.
1959a. (With R.A. Musgrave, eds) *Readings in the Economics of Taxation*. Homewood, Ill.: Richard D. Irwin.
1959b. (Director) *The Fiscal System of Venezuela: A Report*. Baltimore: Johns Hopkins Press.
1960. *Ricardo on Taxation*. New York: Columbia University Press.
1961. Tax tension and the British fiscal system. *National Tax Journal* 14, March, 1–40.
1962a. Tax problems of a Common Market in Latin America. *Tax Policy* 24(11), November, 3–7. Reprinted in *Readings on Taxation in Developing Countries*, ed. R.M. Bird and O. Oldman, Baltimore: Johns Hopkins Press, 1964.
1962b. Debt financing and future generations. *Economic Journal* 72, December, 887–98. Reprinted in *Public Debt and Future Generations*, ed. J.E. Ferguson, Chapel Hill: University of North Carolina Press, 1964; and in *Public Finance*, ed. R.W. Houghton, Harmondsworth: Penguin Books, 1969.
1963. Linear programming in public finance. *Finanzarchiv* 22(3), August, 464–83.
1965a. Public goods and joint production. *Rivista internazionale di scienze economiche e commerciale* 12, 254–64. Also in *Essays in Honour of Marco Fanno*, ed. T. Bagiotti, University of Padua and the *Giornale degli Economisti*, 1966.
1965b. Production from consumption. *Public Finance* No. 2, 173–202.
1967. (ed.) *Fiscal Harmonization in Common Markets*. 2 vols, New York: Columbia University Press.
1968a. Federal grants to cities, direct and indirect. In *Revenue Sharing and the City*, ed. H.S. Perloff and R.P. Nathan, Baltimore: Resources for the Future and Johns Hopkins Press.
1968b. Consumption tax, wages tax, and the value-added tax, consumption-type. *National Tax Journal* 21, June, 153–61.
1969. *Public Finance*. Chicago: Aldine.
1970. Tax reform. In *Theorie und Praxis des finanzpolitischen Interventionismus*, ed. H. Haller et al., Tübingen: J.C.B. Mohr.
1972a. The economic theory of subsidy payments. In *The Economics of Federal Subsidy Payments. Part I: General Study Papers*. (A Compendium of papers submitted to the Joint Economic Committee, U.S. Congress. Printed for the Use of the Committee.) Washington, DC: Government Printing Office.
1972b. (With Jerry Jasinowski.) *The Economics of Federal Subsidy Programs*. (Printed for the use of the Joint Economic Committee.) Washington, DC: Government Printing Office.
1972c. Risk as a dimension in measuring level of service. In *Uncertainty and Expectations in Economics: Essays in Honour of G.L.S. Shackle*, ed. C.F. Carter and J.L. Ford, Oxford: Basil Blackwell.
1972d. *Public Expenditures and Taxation*. National Bureau of Economic Research: Prospect and Retrospect IV. New York: Columbia University Press.
1973. Factors bearing on an assumed choice between a Federal Retail Sales Tax and a Federal Value-Added Tax. In *Broad-based Taxes: New Options and Sources*, ed. R.A. Musgrave, A Supporting Paper for the Committee for Economic Development, Baltimore and London: Johns Hopkins University Press, 215–16.
1974. Non-zero marginal cost per consumer with non-excludability. In *Public Finance and Stabilization Policy: Essays in Honor of Richard A. Musgrave*, ed. W.L. Smith and J.M. Culbertson, New York: Elsevier.
1975a. Economic aspects of tax administration. In *Readings on Taxation in Developing Countries*, 3rd edn, ed. R.M. Bird and O. Oldman, edn, Baltimore: Johns Hopkins University Press.
1975b. Surrey's pathways to tax reform: a review article. *Journal of Finance* 30(5), December, 1329–41.
1976. Collective consumption and the relative size of the government sector. In *Public and Urban Economics: Essays in Honor of William S. Vickrey*, ed. R.E. Grieson, Lexington, Mass., Toronto, and London: Lexington-Heath, 191–212.
1977a. Development of fiscal economics during the decade 1975–85. In *The Organization and Retrieval of Economic Knowledge: Proceedings of a Conference held by the International Economic Association at Kiel, W. Germany*, ed. M. Perlman, London: Macmillan; Boulder: Westview.
1977b. Modernization of direct and indirect taxation – experiences of developed and developing countries. In *Tax Losses in Turkey and Preventive Measures*, Istanbul: Economic and Social Studies Conference Board, English Supplement, 13–26.
1970. (With John G. Head) Excess burden: the Corner Case vs. Ballantine and McClure. *Quarterly Economic Review* 68(1), March, 235–6.
1979. Envoi: the National Energy Act of 1978. *Growth and Change* 12(1), January, 90–91.

Shove, Gerald Frank (1888–1947). Shove was born in Brighton and died prematurely in Cambridge at the early age of 59. A shy, studious boy, he was educated at Uppingham School. In December 1906 he won a Scholarship at King's College, Cambridge. Among his many friends were Lytton Strachey, Arthur Waley, Rupert Brooke, Philip Baker and Hugh Dalton. He was a member of the select society of Apostles, of which Keynes was one of the leading members.

He was deprived of his scholarship by the College Council, with unusual severity, as a result of being placed only in the Second Class in Part I of the Classical Tripos. Shove then deviated to Economics. Keynes recognized his promise. At no time in his life was Shove a ready writer. Although he produced only a few answers in each paper, they were of such outstanding merit that he was placed in the First Class of Part II of the Economics Tripos.

For a College Fellowship he had to wait for years, although he submitted two Dissertations, of which Keynes thought well – one on the application to political theory of the ethics of Moore, the great Cambridge philosopher, the other on local taxation. He was a convinced and deeply anxious pacifist, with the result that the years of World War I were inevitably burdensome. He had thought of the Bar as a career, but following an intuition that his best work would be done in studying and teaching economics, as a means to social justice, he resolved to live in Cambridge and to take his chances as a freelance coach. It was a brave decision, providing at best poor pay, hard work and scanty recognition. However he was elected a University Lecturer in 1923 and in 1926 Keynes was at last successful in urging his claims to a Fellowship. At that time he was delivering five lectures a week and giving individual tuition to about fifty people.

His fastidious self-criticism explains why he rarely published his results and never wrote a book, but it was generally recognized that behind his greatness as a teacher lay originality as a dauntless thinker.

He wrote much but published little. It is a great misfortune that in his Will he left instructions that all his manuscripts were to be destroyed. His determination not to publish anything until it seemed to say exactly what he meant – just that, and not another thing – sprang ultimately from a deep, indeed religious, fealty to truth. That, and the modest human kindness which went with it, is the explanation of the influence which he had exercised on the thought and writings of his colleagues, not at Cambridge only, but on the pupils whom he would serve with all his strength. One of his most distinguished pupils wrote: 'Shove was in many ways the best *teacher* that I ever had. He took pains always to discuss our written work in detail and to make us talk about it. He talked easily and, almost more important, he was easy to talk to.' Another pupil wrote that Shove's clarity of exposition, his gift of communicating to an audience his own precision of thought gave a delightful sense that all were following a complicated argument with ease. Another wrote: 'He was more concerned that your answer was internally consistent than that it should jump with every orthodoxy ... he had the knack of making you see the thing for yourself, as if for the first time. He did not expound, he led you into understanding.'

Among the pupils on whom he exercised a most fruitful influence were Kenneth Berrill, Robin Marris and Richard Kahn. Indeed, although the name Richard Kahn is associated with that of Keynes, it was to Shove's encouragement that Kahn owes his career as an economist. Kahn's performance in Part II of the National Sciences Tripos in Physics, in 1927, was disappointing – he was placed only in the Second Class. Encouraged by his father he felt a desire to try his hand at a fourth year on Economics, aiming at Part II of the Economics Tripos. The College Tutor was most discouraging – 'It is about time that you gave financial help to the father of seven children rather than be a further financial burden on him which he can ill afford.' But Shove was most encouraging and won the day. While Kahn in his fourth year owed much to Keynes, he owed far more to Shove, as a teacher; his successful Fellowship Dissertation owed much to Shove (and also to Piero Sraffa), little to Keynes.

The period was one of great intellectual excitement among Cambridge economists, both university teachers and the leading undergraduates. This activity took three forms, in one of which – the Keynesian Revolution – Shove did not take more than a natural interest. The second arose from the fact that while Professor Pigou, together with Keynes and Dennis Robertson, was the outstanding economist of his day, the successive editions of his *Economics of Welfare* resulted in great confusion over the subject of increasing and diminishing returns, involving distinction between internal and external economies, a confusion resulting in part from Pigou's loyalty to Marshall. The other cause of excitement was growing emphasis on the unreality of the assumption of perfect competition.

Piero Sraffa, brought to Cambridge by Keynes in the middle Twenties, was a great pioneer on both these controversial issues. In his great article on the 'Laws of returns under competitive conditions' (*Economic Journal*, December 1926) he dealt in masterful fashion with both issues. It was a draft of this article which led Keynes (editor of the *Economic Journal*) to bring Sraffa to Cambridge. In this article Sraffa introduced his path-breaking emphasis on imperfection of competition as the factor which explains the possibility of equilibrium for an industry in which the average cost curves of individual firms fall with an increase of their output.

Marshall had fudged the problem by his famous analogy, with the 'trees in the forest', by the 'fear of spoiling the market', and by the 'representative firm'. Pigou exacerbated the confusion.

Apart from an article on 'Varying Costs and Marginal Net Products' (1928), a few reviews, including one on Joan Robinson's 'Marxian Economics' (1944), Shove's great written contribution was made in collaboration with Dennis Robertson and Piero Sraffa in the Symposium on 'Increasing Returns and the Representative Firm' (1930). Shove looked more closely than was customary at the distinction between the 'internal' and 'external' economies of large-scale production. He wrote that 'Marshall (intentionally no doubt) left his definitions of these terms a little vague'. He asked the question whether

> we do not need a terminology which distinguishes between
> (a) the effect which the expansion of *an industry as a whole* has upon the productive capacity of the resources employed in it and
> (b) changes in the efficiency of an industrial firm consequent upon an increase in its own output while that of the industry as a whole remains unchanged?

Thus Shove drew a fundamental distinction between 'internal' and 'external' economies. In the course of fifteen pages he threw out a host of path-breaking ideas, which have exercised a deep influence on the development of economic thought in this field.

R.F. KAHN

SELECTED WORKS

1928. Varying costs and marginal net products. *Economic Journal* 38, June, 258–66.

1930. (With P. Sraffa and D.H. Robertson) Increasing returns and the representative firm. A symposium. *Economic Journal* 40, March, 79–116.

1944. Mrs Robinson on Marxian economics. *Economic Journal* 54, April, 47–61.

Sidgwick, Henry (1838–1900). Henry Sidgwick, one of the two founding fathers of the Cambridge School of Economics (the other being Alfred Marshall) was born in Skipton, Yorkshire, in 1838 into a highly respectable middle class family which had made its modest fortune in the cotton-spinning boom of the post-Napoleonic war era. At the time of his birth his father (a graduate in 1829 of Trinity College, Cambridge, who had taken Holy Orders) was headmaster of the local grammar school. Young Henry went on to Rugby School and thence to his father's college where, after taking a brilliant double first in classics and mathematics, he was appointed a classical Fellow at the age of 21.

His family and friends expected him to follow again in his father's footsteps by being ordained; but Sidgwick, who in his undergraduate years became deeply absorbed in the most influential of Cambridge intellectual communities – the Society of the Apostles – took his first open step away from the traditional academic groove by deciding against ordination. That was in 1861, two years after Charles Darwin had launched the great 19th-century debate on science and religion by publishing *The Origin of Species*. Many years later, in an autobiographical memoir dictated from his death-bed, Sidgwick was to say of the Apostles: 'Absolute candour was the only duty that the tradition of the society enforced. No consistency was demanded with options previously held – truth as we saw it then and there was what we had to embrace and maintain, and there were no propositions so well established that an Apostle had not the right to deny or question, if he did so sincerely and not from mere love of paradox.' Thus, in his early twenties, Sidgwick had (in his own words) 'taken service with reason' and begun the earnest search for scientific truth. During his first ten years as a fellow of Trinity he continued to teach classics and study theology (and also to take an interest in psychical research), but his intellectual interests became increasingly focused on areas embraced by the Moral Sciences Tripos (moral philosophy, ethics, political theory, political economy and scientific method) all areas in which J.S. Mill was the contemporary mastermind. Then in 1869, after much mental struggle, for he had what he called a 'hunger for orthodoxy', he took the dramatic and decisive step of resigning his Trinity fellowship because he could no longer subscribe fully to the doctrine of the Thirty-Nine Articles to which he had sworn adherence on appointment. It was at once a sign of the new spirit of the age, and of Sidgwick's moral and intellectual authority in the university, that Trinity did not cast him adrift, but kept him as its lecturer in moral sciences, a post which he held until he was elected the Professor of Moral Philosophy. Significantly, religious tests were abolished by the university and colleges in 1871.

Sidgwick published three major textbooks, the first on ethics in 1874, the next on political economy in 1883 and the last on politics in 1891. The first of these was his most famous and original work, while the third attracted relatively little attention. The most distinctive feature of each reflected an inexorable determination to approach the problems of the moral and social sciences from an objective scientific standpoint, an attitude of mind which had more impact on current thinking (at least as far as his fellow economists were concerned) than the substantive content of the volumes. For his texts were generally distinguished more by the careful clarity of his exposition and the evenhandedness with which he weighed the pros and cons of every debate and his conscientious scepticism, than by innovative ideas or stimulating rhetoric. It was in letters to friends, and to some extent in his 1885 presidential address to Section F of the British Association for the Advancement of Science (though not, it would seem, in his lectures) that he expressed himself in more colourful terms.

The Methods of Ethics, for example, was a pioneering attempt to apply a scientific methodology to a wide range of philosophical topics; 'I conceive the one important lesson that Philosophy and Theology have to learn from the progress of science', he asserted characteristically, 'is the vague lesson of patience and hope.' Often labelled the last of the Utilitarians, Sidgwick displayed a more cautious utilitarianism than Mill's – in particular, for example, in modifying the greatest happiness formula so as to include equal distribution of happiness as a requirement ranking with its maximization.

The Principles of Political Economy was the book which he least enjoyed writing. In a letter written two years before it was ready for the press he said, for example: 'I am labouring slowly at my Political Economy. But the greatest event that has occurred to me is that my interest in Spiritualism has revived.' The book was well reviewed and the first edition sold out in three years, but he regarded it as a failure – as indeed it was in the sense that it was already being overtaken by the marginal revolution in economic theory. The fact is that the *Principles* owed more to the classical tradition of J.S. Mill than to what contemporaries were then calling the 'new political economy' of Jevons and Marshall. Again, however, it was the methodological message that went home to his fellow economists. Sidgwick made careful distinction, for example, between normative and positive reasoning processes and was insistent on the need to insulate empirical or theoretical economic analysis from contamination by moral or political doctrine. In his 1885 presidential address to the British Association he made the crucial point thus: 'The English Economist in giving an explanation of the manner in which prices, wages, profits, etc. are determined is not attempting to justify the result.'

Several of Sidgwick's distinguished contemporaries have testified to his moral and intellectual stature and to his immense personal influence on pupils and colleagues. Marshall, for example, described him as his 'spiritual father and mother', which was not altogether inconsistent with the fact that he quarrelled with him furiously and continuously as a tyrannical Chairman of the Board of Moral Sciences. Most of those who were genuinely impressed with the quality of Sidgwick's mind, the range of his scholarship and his unrelenting honesty found his candidly critical comments on their own work more than a little galling at times. It has to be said, however, that for all his studied impartiality, he was an active agent in the cause of academic liberalism and not merely an advocate. Mill and other educated liberals, for example, had enthusiastically defended the case for women's education. It was Sidgwick who set the seed for what was to become Newnham College by personally renting and furnishing a house in the town centre, appointing a suitable principal and arranging courses for the five young women who constituted the first group of resident females to take regular instruction from senior members of the University; and it was Sidgwick who fought fiercely and successfully to get women the privilege of taking Tripos examinations – though not until 1948 did they obtain the title of full members or graduates of the University of Cambridge.

PHYLLIS DEANE

See also EDGEWORTH, FRANCIS YSIDRO.

SELECTED WORKS

1874. *The Methods of Ethics*. London: Macmillan

1883. *Principles of Political Economy*. London: Macmillan.

1891. *The Elements of Politics*. London: Macmillan.

BIBLIOGRAPHY

Schneewind, J.B. 1977. *Sidgwick's Ethics and Victorian Moral Philosophy*. Oxford: Clarendon Press.

Sidgwick, A. and E.M. 1906. *Henry Sidgwick, A Memoir by A.S. and E.M.S.* London: Macmillan.

Sidrauski, Miguel (1939–1968). Sidrauski was born and educated in Buenos Aires. He entered the University of Chicago PhD programme in 1963, completed his dissertation in 1966, and accepted an assistant professor appointment at MIT. He died of cancer in September 1968, leaving his wife, Martha, and two-month old daughter, Carmela.

Sidrauski is best known in economics for his 1966 article 'Rational Choice and Patterns of Growth in a Monetary Economy', based on his dissertation written under the supervision of Hirofumi Uzawa and Milton Friedman. The model is one of an economy with a representative intertemporally maximizing household, which derives instantaneous utility from both consumption and the holding of real balances. The thesis contains a careful discussion of the device of putting money in the utility function. The household can hold capital as well as money. Sidrauski derives necessary conditions for a maximum, and then studies the dynamics and steady states of inflation and capital accumulation in the model.

The key result is that steady state capital intensity is invariant to the rate of monetary expansion, and thus that money is superneutral between steady states. Sidrauski indicates in his thesis, which extends the paper in several directions, that the superneutrality result changes if money is given a productive role in the economy. In the dynamic analysis he assumes that expectations of inflation are adaptive.

In a non-maximizing money-and-growth model (1967) Sidrauski confirms the Tobin result that an increase in the growth rate of money increases steady state capital intensity. This is based on the effects of an increase in the growth rate of money in reducing consumption. Sidrauski shows also in this paper that, with adaptive expectations, an increase in the growth rate of money first causes capital accumulation to fall and only later to increase, taking capital intensity above its initial level.

He published four other articles, including one on exchange rate determination, and a book, *Monetary and Fiscal Policy in a Growing Economy*. The book, written jointly with Duncan Foley and published posthumously in 1970 develops a three-asset (money, bonds and capital) two-sector Tobinesque growth model. The two sector structure gives a key role in the investment process to the relative price of capital, p_k, which is Tobin's q. The authors succeed in making the model answer questions about the effects on growth and inflation of policy changes such as fiscal expansion, increases in the growth rate of all outside assets, and open market operations. The model has not been widely used despite its usefulness and versatility; this may be because the full employment assumption makes it unattractive for use as a cyclical model and the absence of explicit maximizing assumptions makes it unattractive to many who study long-term growth.

In his two years at MIT Sidrauski established himself as an excellent teacher and adviser, and as an economist of outstanding promise. Milton Friedman's eulogy (1969) speaks not only of his technical skill and promise, but also of his personal warmth and generosity. It concludes:

> The death of this young man is a grievous loss to our profession and to the world. Here was a man who would have pushed out the frontiers of our subject, would have changed and added to economic analysis, would have enlightened and informed generations of students – struck down at the very beginning of his career, full of promise but as yet almost bereft of fulfillment.

STANLEY FISCHER

SELECTED WORKS

1967a. Rational choice and patterns of growth in a monetary economy. *American Economic Review, Papers and Proceedings* 57(2), May, 534–44.

1967b. Inflation and economic growth. *Journal of Political Economy* 75, 796–810.

1970. (With Duncan K. Foley) *Monetary and Fiscal Policy in a Growing Economy*. London: Macmillan.

BIBLIOGRAPHY

Friedman, F. 1969. Miguel Sidrauski. *Journal of Money, Credit and Banking* 1, May, 129–30.

Sieber, N.I. *See* ZIBER, NIKOLAI IVANOVITCH.

signalling. If product quality of individual units cannot be observed at the time of purchase, but buyers do eventually learn average quality, goods will be traded at a price which reflects buyers' beliefs about this average. The price will then adjust until buyers' beliefs about average quality are confirmed ex post.

Such a market has two highly undesirable features. First, to the extent that a seller can lower costs by lowering the quality of his product, he has an incentive to do so. Secondly, even when such hidden actions are not possible, if a seller of a product of above average quality has a high opportunity cost, he may be better off withdrawing from the market. Average quality thus falls below that in a world of complete information, and *adverse selection* occurs.

As Akerlof (1970) showed, this process of withdrawal from the market might even continue until only the very worst 'lemons' would actually be traded.

It was Spence (1973) who provided a striking new insight into how the potential gains to trade might still be realized despite the problems created by informational asymmetry. His essential point was that if a seller of a higher quality product could find some activity that was less costly for him than for a seller of a lower quality product, it might pay him to undertake this activity as a *signal* of high quality. On the other side of the market, even if buyers were not aware of the underlying differences in the cost of the activity, they would learn that the signal was associated with higher quality and thus be willing to pay a premium price.

Going beyond the special case of either signalling or not signalling, Spence argued that, as long as the *marginal cost* of some activity was lower for sellers of higher quality, an equilibrium would emerge in which quality could be perfectly inferred by buyers from the level of signalling undertaken by the seller.

In Spence's own work and in most of the ensuing literature it is assumed that there are many buyers and many sellers of the product. It is therefore natural to focus on this case here. I also follow most of the literature in ignoring possible opportunities for sellers to change product quality without being observed, that is, I shall abstract from problems of *moral hazard*.

Perhaps the most widely analysed application of signalling theory is to insurance markets. In this case risky outcomes are 'sold' by individuals to insurance companies. As Rothschild and Stiglitz (1976) first argued, an individual with a preferred risk is more willing to co-insure since his loss probability is lower. The level of co-insurance is thus a potential signal of risk quality.

A second major application of signalling theory has been to issues in finance. In this case a manager (Ross, 1977) with superior knowledge about a high quality investment opportunity can signal to potential investors by his choice of financing or dividend policy. More recently, Titman and Trueman (1986) have also argued that an entrepreneur can signal project quality by his choice of an independent auditor. Here it is the favourable estimate of actual quality which makes an entrepreneur more willing to spend funds on a high-cost, high-reputation auditor whose report, he anticipates, is likely to be confirming.

Spence's own focus was primarily on the use of education as a signal of productivity. He argues that an individual of higher ability is able to accumulate educational credentials at lower cost. Education thus not only enhances human capital but also has a valuable informational role for higher ability workers.

The basic insight that agents can signal quality via observable actions is intuitively plausible. However, upon closer inspection, the precise characterization of a 'competitive' signalling equilibrium turns out to be subtle. Indeed, a decade after the early challenges posed by Riley (1975), Rothschild and Stiglitz (1976) and Wilson (1977), the issue remains controversial. My goal here is to lay out the central themes of the on-going debate by means of a bare-bones labour market example.

To make the exposition as simple as possible, suppose that marginal productivity in some industry is unaffected by the level of education s. It will be convenient to refer to an individual with productivity θ as being of type θ. Suppose also that the cost of education level s, for a type θ worker is given by

$$C_\theta(s) = s/\theta. \tag{1}$$

Higher quality workers thus have a lower marginal cost of signalling.

If type θ accepts the offer (s, w), that is, a wage w for an education level of at least s, his net payoff is

$$U_\theta(s, w) = w - C_\theta(s) \tag{2}$$

Suppose that there are just two types, θ_1 with productivity 1 and θ_2 with productivity 5. Finally suppose that there is another industry (industry R) which pays a wage $w_R = 2$ to all workers.

At the heart of Spence's analysis is the following description of an equilibrium.

Definition: Signalling Equilibrium (*Spence*) 'A signalling equilibrium in the market is a set of conditional probabilistic beliefs for the employer which, when translated into offered wages, employee investment responses and new market data, are confirmed by the new market data relating educational levels to productivity.'

For our simple example, suppose workers who do not signal are offered a wage of 1 and workers who signal at level $s = 5$ are offered a wage of 5. A worker of type θ has a net payoff, if he signals, of

$$U_\theta(5, 5) = 5 - 5/\theta = \begin{cases} 0, & \text{if } \theta = 1 \\ 4, & \text{if } \theta = 5 \end{cases}.$$

Low quality workers thus choose to work in industry R and earn a wage of 2. High quality workers, however, are better off signalling.

This equilibrium is depicted in Figure 1 as the pair of offers

$$\{E_1^*, E_2\} = \{(0, 2), (5, 5)\}.$$

Given our assumptions (see (1) and (2) above), indifference curves for each type are linear. Type 1 workers, with their steeper indifference curves, prefer E_1^* to E_2. Type 2 workers, however, with their flatter (dashed) indifference curves prefer E_2 to E_1^*. The intial beliefs of firms that only high quality workers will choose to signal are thus confirmed by the market.

To complete the description of the equilibrium it is necessary to introduce beliefs about the productivity of a worker who chooses a signal other than $s_2 = 5$. Clearly the equilibrium is sustained by the belief that anyone who chooses a level of s below 5 has low productivity. However, in Spence's world firms (buyers) never test such beliefs.

This is the heart of the critiques by Riley (1975) and Rothschild and Stiglitz (1976). Firms can readily test their beliefs by offering lower wages for slightly lower levels of the signal. Consider Figure 1. With other firms making offers of E_1^* and E_2 a firm offering (s_0, w_0) finds that no workers are attracted. However as long as the firm recognizes that higher quality workers have lower costs of signalling it knows that by raising the wage it will eventually attract high quality workers. The point (s_0, w_{00}) is one such offer. Since it is strictly profitable, the belief that a worker choosing s_0 would be of low quality is disconfirmed by market data.

This same argument holds for any Spencian equilibrium in which low quality workers are strictly better off not signalling. Therefore the only candidate pair of 'competitive' equilibrium offers is the pair $\{E_1^*, E_2^*\}$ depicted in Figure 1. (We ignore here the purely technical issue of what a seller does when indifferent between offers, and simply assume that he will always choose the one involving the smallest amount of signalling.)

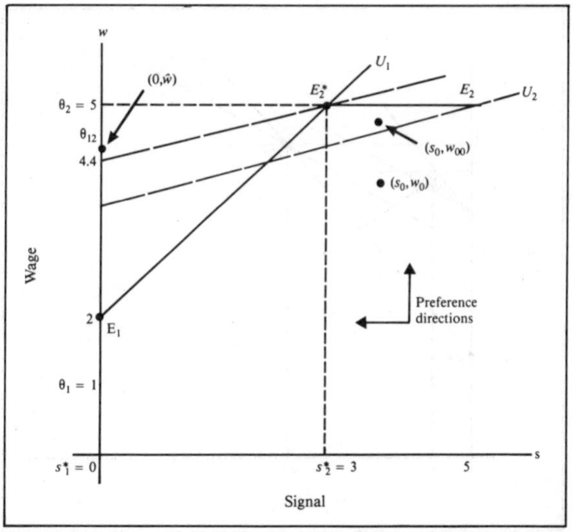

Figure 1 Signalling with two types

Experimenting with offers in the neighborhood of E_2^* is not profitable since any wage offer below 5 which is attractive to type 2 workers is also attractive to type 1 workers. However, the market also provides information about the proportion of high quality workers. If this is less than 0.25 so that $\bar{\theta}_{12}$, the average productivity of the two types, is less than $w_R = 2$ it is clear that $\{E_1^*, E_2^*\}$ is a competitive equilibrium set of offers. On the other hand, suppose the proportion of high quality workers is sufficiently high that $\bar{\theta}_{12}$ is above the point where type 2's indifference curve through E_2^* intersects the vertical axis. Then, as depicted, there are alternative offers such as $(0, \hat{w})$ which attract both types and are profitable. In this latter case all the signalling equilibria are potentially subject to destabilizing competition.

This suggests that an equilibrium must involve pooling of different types. However, as Rothschild and Stiglitz emphasized, whenever a pool of heterogeneous types chooses the same offer, a buyer can always "skim the cream" by exploiting the fact that the highest quality workers in the pool have the lowest marginal cost of signalling.

This is illustrated in Figure 2. Suppose that the best offer currently available for both types is D. Since the two types are pooled, the wage w_D must be strictly less than θ_2, the value of a high quality worker. Then there is always an offer such as T which is attractive only to the high quality workers and which is strictly profitable.

We conclude then that, in general, there is no equilibrium which is "competitive" in the usual sense. Equivalently, in the language of game theory, there is no Nash equilibrium in pure strategies.

Despite this, in Riley (1985) it is argued that, for certain applications of the theory including cases in which there is a continuum of types, the conditions for equilibrium are likely to be met. The point can be simply made using Figure 1. For any particular distribution of types there is some average productivity $\bar{\theta}_{12}$. The pair of offers $\{E_1^*, E_2^*\}$ is not subject to destabilizing competition if the indifference curve for type θ_2 through E_2^* cuts the vertical axis at a point above $\bar{\theta}_{12}$. For then any offer which attracts high quality workers must pay a wage in excess of average productivity. But this will be the case if the indifference curve for type θ_2 through E^* is sufficiently less steep

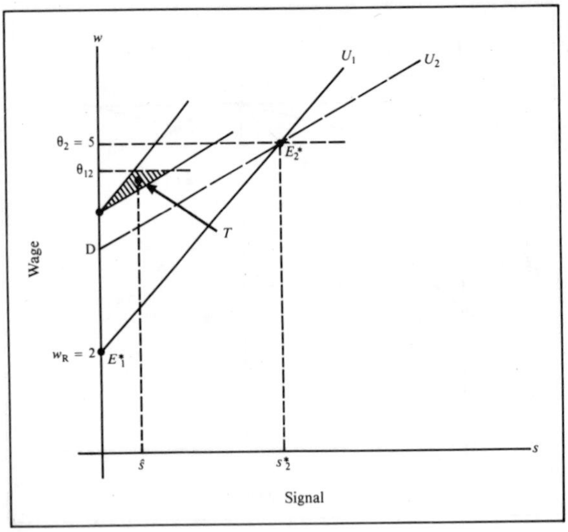

Figure 2 Reactive equilibrium

than the corresponding indifference curve for type 1. That is, the ratio of marginal costs

$$\frac{\partial C_2(s)/\partial s}{\partial C_1(s)/\partial s}$$

is sufficiently small. Thus it is the *rate* at which the marginal cost of signalling declines with productivity which is critical. As long as the proportional rate of decline is sufficiently large, $\{E_1^*, E_2^*\}$ is a competitive equilibrium set of offers.

This still leaves unreasolved the theoretically important issue of how competitive markets perform when there is informational asymmetry and the sufficient conditons are not satisfied. One way out of the dilemma has been suggested by Wilson (1977) and further examined by Miyazaki (1977) and Riley (1979). The key idea is that, when competitive behavior of the type described above does not result in convergence to an equilibrium, agents will begin to learn that certain actions result in predictable responses by others. In particular, certain offers which are profitable, *ceteris paribus*, result in losses when other buyers react.

To illustrate, the essential features of the two type example have been reproduced in Figure 2. Since average productivity, $\bar{\theta}_{12}$, is close to θ_2, there are offers such as D which attract both types away from $\{E_1^*, E_2^*\}$ and which are strictly profitable. But such a 'defection' creates its own profitable opportunities. Any firm reacting with the offer T depicted in the figure succeeds in skimming the cream from the pool and hence garnering additional profits. As a result the initial defector attracts only low quality types and hence loses money.

Note also that, since the reactor makes money on every worker who accepts, the worst that can happen is that other firms introduce preferred reactions so there are no takers for T. The profit of the reactor is thus bounded from below by zero. Since such opportunities to react arise for every defection it seems reasonable to conclude that, if reactions are known to be rapid, firms will be deterred from introducing a new offer such as D. The pair $\{E_1^*, E_2^*\}$ is thus a 'Reactive Equilibrium'.

Formally we have the following definition.

Definition: Reactive Equilibrium. A set of offers $E = \{E_1, E_2, \ldots\}$ is a reactive equilibrium if, for any additional set D which is profitable when $D \cup E$ is offered, there is a further set T such that, when $T \cup D \cup E$ is offered, D generates losses and each offer in T is strictly profitable.

As argued in Riley (1979) and, under weaker assumptions, by Engers and Fernandez (1986), there exists a unique reactive equilibrium as long as the signalling activity has a lower marginal cost for higher quality sellers.

To this point I have focused on an environment in which the uninformed buyers (firms) must first commit themselves to offers. Recently, as part of the new literature on entry deterrence, theorists have become interested in modelling signalling when it is the informed sellers (workers) who must first commit themselves to a level of the signal (Stiglitz and Weiss, 1983; Cho and Kreps, 1987). In this literature it is argued that switching the order in which agents move results in a multitude of equilibrium rather than a problem of existence.

The point is easily made using our simple labour market example. Consider Figure 1 once more. Workers believe that they will be treated as low quality types unless they signal at level $s_2 = 5$. Given such beliefs, low quality workers choose $s = 0$ and high quality workers $s = s_2$.

If firms know that workers have these beliefs they will bid wages up to 1 and 5 respectively. As a result the pair $\{E_1^*, E_2\}$ is an equilibrium *relative to workers' beliefs*.

But the particular beliefs assumed are not consistent with the underlying model. Suppose a seller were to choose $s = s_0$ rather than s_2. Note that low quality workers are strictly better off at E_1^* than choosing $s = s_0$ even if by doing the latter they would be paid the high wage. Thus if all other workers were to choose $s = 0$ or $s = s_2$, it is rational for firms to believe that a worker choosing s_0 is of high quality.

Arguing along these lines Kreps concludes that the Pareto dominating pair of offers $\{E_1^*, E_2^*\}$ is the only "stable" equilibrium. But taking this argument one step further, suppose a worker were to choose some level $\hat{s}$ between zero and s_2^* as depicted in Figure 2. With $\bar{\theta}_{12}$ so close to θ_2 it would be rational for a firm to believe that this worker is a random drawn from the population. For, given these beliefs, the wage the worker would be paid, $\bar{\theta}_{12}$, is attractive to both high and low quality workers. But then we are forced to conclude that there is no static competitive equilibrium with rational beliefs.

Comparing this with the earlier argument it should be clear that the non-existence problem arises under exactly the same conditions as when the uninformed firms must make the first moves. Once again, however, if an offer cannot be quickly withdrawn there are reactions which seem likely to operate as an effective deterrent. If one firm responds to a signal level $\hat{s}$ with an offer of $\hat{w} \leqslant \bar{\theta}_{12}$, a high quality worker has an incentive to raise his signal above $\hat{s}$ in the expectation that a second firm will "skim the cream" just as argued above.

To conclude, Spence's initial insight that information could be conveyed by endogenous signalling activity in a competitive environment is theoretically valid. However, the conditions under which signalling equilibria are free of potential dynamic instability are rather more restrictive than he supposed. His assumption that the potential signalling activity should have a lower marginal cost for high quality workers is necessary but not sufficient. None the less it is sufficient that the proportional rate of decline in the marginal cost of signalling with respect to product quality be sufficiently large.

The issue of what happens when this condition fails remains open. It seems to me that it will only be resolved when theorists take up the challenge of modelling dynamics as a process in which agents react with very incomplete information, rather than attempting to build ever more subtle 'rational' beliefs into essentially static models. My conjecture is that the eventual resolution will hinge critically on the length of time for which agents are committed to announced strategies. For environments where it is not possible to withdraw an offer quickly once it is made, I believe that Wilson's insight into the deterrent effect of potential reactions will prove to be correct. However, for environments where agents are not committed to strategies I believe we will have to accept that there may be no stable equilibrium. Instead market behaviour will have to be modelled as intrinsically uncertain, within prescribable bounds.

JOHN G. RILEY

See also INCENTIVE COMPATIBILITY; INCENTIVE CONTRACTS; MORAL HAZARD; REVELATION OF PREFERENCES.

BIBLIOGRAPHY

Akerlof, G.A. 1970. The market for 'lemons': qualitative uncertainty and the market mechanism. *Quarterly Journal of Economics* 84, August, 488–500.

Bhattacharya, S. 1980. Nondissipative signalling structures and dividend policy. *Quarterly Journal of Economics* 95, August, 1–24.

Cho, I.-K. and Kreps, D.M. 1987. Signalling games and stable equilibria. *Quarterly Journal of Economics* 102, May, 179–222.

Engers, M. and Fernandez, L. 1986. On the existence and uniqueness of signalling equilibria. *Econometrica* 54.

Leland, H.E. and Pyle, D.H. 1977. Informational asymmetries, financial structure, and financial intermediation. *Journal of Finance* 32, May, 381–7.

Miyazaki, H. 1977. The rat race and internal markets. *Bell Journal of Economics* 8, Autumn, 394–418.

Riley, J.G. 1975. Competitive signalling. *Journal of Economic Theory* 10, April, 174–86.

Riley, J.G. 1979. Informational equilibrium. *Econometrica* 47, March, 331–60.

Riley, J.G. 1985. Competition with hidden knowledge. *Journal of Political Economy* 93, October, 958–76.

Ross, S. 1977. The determinants of financial structure: the incentive signalling approach. *Bell Journal of Economics* 8, Spring, 23–40.

Rothschild, M. and Stiglitz, J.E. 1976. Equilibrium in competitive insurance markets: an essay on the economics of imperfect information. *Quarterly Journal of Economics* 80, November, 629–49.

Spence, A.M. 1973. *Market Signalling: Information Transfer in Hiring and Related Processes.* Cambridge, Mass.: Harvard University Press.

Stiglitz, J.E. and Weiss, A. 1983. Alternative approaches to analyzing markets with asymmetric information: reply. *American Economic Review* 73, March, 246–9.

Titman, S. and Trueman, B. 1986. Information quality and the value of new issues. *Journal of Accounting and Economics* 8.

Wilson, C.A. 1977. A model of insurance markets with incomplete information. *Journal of Economic Theory* 16, December, 167–207.

Simmel, Georg (1858–1918). Simmel was born in Berlin. He became a lecturer in the University of Berlin in 1885 but was not promoted beyond the position of Extraordinary Professor. This was mainly because of his Jewish ancestry. Reluctantly he finally accepted a call from Strassburg to become Professor of Philosophy.

Simmel was a brilliant and much admired teacher who attracted large audiences. He was been described by Spykman (1925) as 'the philosopher of European culture'; he was also a pioneer of modern sociology.

Simmel's seminal work, *Die Philosophie des Geldes* (1900) has received more recognition from other social scientists than from economists, as is shown in the comprehensive Introduction, by Tom Bottomore and David Frisby, to the first English translation, *The Philosophy of Money* (1978). The late appearance of an English translation contributed to its unfortunate neglect by English-speaking economists.

Simmel's philosophy tried always to find in single appearances or instances of life, the meaning of the whole. As one of these he selected money. He saw it in functional relativistic terms: the symbol of the spirit, forms and thought of modern civilization. He viewed money not in mechanical terms but as a conflict between our abstract conceptions of money and the social trust on which it is based. He elucidated the moral basis of the monetary order and warned that it might be subverted through our tendency to think of money in purely abstract terms.

If it was through John Maynard Keynes that the revolt against the predominant 19th-century view of money was made respectable, it was Simmel who had laid bare the causes of that revolt. He was pessimistic about the survival of the free monetary order, fearing that it might not prove possible to make it work in terms of specific goals for experimental measures.

The fact that money grew out of the process of exchange is to Simmel of prime importance: curtailment of individual freedom to express values in money reduces correspondingly the full functioning of money. Without this freedom, money loses its *raison d'être* as the medium for expressing, incorporating and symbolizing contractual relationships – past, present or future. In the development of ever higher levels of abstraction Simmel finds some of the most intractable problems of modern money. Forms survive the conditions that produce them, whether in the field of religion, law, culture or art. They endure even when conditions have changed, so it is with money. It develops ever more sophisticated forms. Finally, and wrongly, it comes to be regarded as incorporating the purest form of potentiality – of political power itself. He cautioned that because money was inevitably a symbolic image through which we express economic relationships, it could not be divorced from the circumstances which gave rise to them.

Simmel was above all concerned with the hidden dichotomy within the money economies of Europe and beyond. That dichotomy had been obscured by the growing prosperity during the 19th century. It was then assumed that the monetary trust on which that prosperity was based would continue. 'Simmel was not sure that it would. There were destructive irrational forces at work which were, to Europe's peril, generally and dangerously ignored' (Frankel, 1977, p. 16).

S. HERBERT FRANKEL

SELECTED WORKS

1900. *Die Philosophie des Geldes.* Leipzig: Duncker & Humblot. Trans. T. Bottomore and D. Frisby as *The Philosophy of Money*, London: Routledge & Kegan Paul, 1978.

BIBLIOGRAPHY

Coser, L. (ed.) 1965. *Georg Simmel.* Englewood Cliffs, NJ: Prentice-Hall.

Frankel, S.H. 1977. *Money: Two Philosophies. The Conflict of Trust and Authority.* Oxford: Basil Blackwell; New York: St Martin's Press, under the title *Two Philosophies of Money.*

Levine, D.N. 1971. *Georg Simmel on Individuality and Social Forms.* Chicago: University of Chicago Press.

Spykman, N.J. 1925. *The Social Theory of Georg Simmel.* Reissued, New York: Russell & Russell, 1964.

Weingartner, R.H. 1962. *Experience and Culture: The Philosophy of Georg Simmel.* Middletown: Wesleyan University Press.

Simons, Henry Calvert (1899–1946). Simons was born in Virden, Illinois, and died in Chicago. An economist at the

University of Chicago from 1927 to 1946, he was the first Professor of Economics at the University of Chicago Law School. A leader of the 'Chicago School', he had an important influence on American thinking about economic policy.

Simons's central theme was stated in the title of his first writing to attract attention, a 1934 pamphlet: 'A Positive Program for Laissez Faire: Some Proposals for a Liberal Economic Policy'. The conjunction of the words 'positive' and 'laissez faire' set him apart from both the conventional conservatives of his time and the conventional liberals (in the American sense of interventionists). Simons visualized a division of labour between the government and the market. The market would determine what gets produced, how and for whom. The government would be responsible for maintaining overall stability, for keeping the market competitive and for avoiding extremes in the distribution of income. This system would preserve liberty by preventing concentration of power, and liberty is the primary virtue, followed closely by equality.

Simons's work was the response of a free society liberal – or, as he preferred, 'libertarian' – to the rise of totalitarianism in Europe, to the worldwide depression and to the attempt in the democracies, including the United States, to cope with the depression in ways that Simons regarded as threats to freedom. Simons's close friend, Professor Aaron Director, later said that Simons acted as if the end of the world was at hand. During the period of Simons's work, if not the end of the world at least the end of the free society could realistically be considered a serious possibility. Simons undertook to help to prevent that, by showing that the free society had not failed but that the government had failed to discharge its role in the free society.

The 1934 pamphlet contained the elements of a policy for a free economy that he was to restate and refine for the next 12 years, with some changes of emphasis. As he put it in 1934:

> The main elements in a sound liberal program may be defined in terms of five proposals or objectives (in a descending scale of relative importance):
>
> I. Elimination of private monopoly in all its forms ... . II. Establishment of more definite and adequate 'rules of the game' with respect to money ... . III. Drastic change in our whole tax system, with regard primarily for the effects of taxation upon the distribution of wealth and income ... . IV. Gradual withdrawal of the enormous differential subsidies implicit in our present tariff system ... . V. Limitation upon the squandering of our resources in advertising and selling activities (1934, p. 57).

In later years the fifth of these items fell from the list.

The first proposal, 'elimination of private monopoly in all its forms', was substantially altered later. In 1934 Simons had said, 'The case for a liberal-conservative policy must stand or fall on the first proposal, abolition of private monopoly; for it is the *sine qua non* of any such policy' (p. 57). His measures for achieving this included limitation on the absolute size of corporations and on their relative size in their industries. He suggested, for example, that 'in major industries no ownership unit should produce or control more than 5 per cent of the total output' (p. 319).

By 1945 he was saying 'Industrial monopolies are not yet a serious evil' (1945, p. 35). Simons's concern about private monopoly had always been about its interaction with the state. He feared that government would support private monpolies and then have to become more powerful to control the warring monopolies it had created. The 1934 pamphlet was written at the time of Roosevelt's National Recovery Administration, which was promoting the universal cartelization of business under government aegis. But in 1945 all that was past and the political influence of business seemed too small to be a danger.

In 1945 what he had said about business monopoly he now said about labour unions. In 1934 Simons had expressed concern about labour monopolies, but in a rather subdued way. In the decade after the 1934 pamphlet, labour union membership quadrupled, and this growth showed no sign of diminishing. In his final credo (1945) Simons said 'the hard monopoly problem is labour organization'. For this problem he could offer no 'specific', only a rather uncertain question about 'the capability of democracy to protect the common interest' (1945, pp. 35–6).

As World War II drew to an end, the preservation of free international trade received more of Simons's attention. Peace was essential for all the goals he cherished. Even the fear of war would require a centralization of power in government that would be incompatible with personal freedom. Simons believed that economic nationalism would be the greatest threat to peace after World War II. Therefore, he devoted much of his work in the mid-1940s to arguing for a liberal international economic order.

While the emphasis of some points in Simons's initial policy agenda shifted, two items remained of major importance and constituted Simons's chief contribution aside from the general idea of conjoining 'positive program' with 'laissez faire'. These were the need for monetary certainty and stability and the need to finance government primarily by progressive taxation of 'income' defined in a comprehensive way.

His analysis of the monetary problem and proposals for its solution, already outlined in the 1934 pamphlet, were elaborated in a 1936 essay whose title defined the issue for years to come, 'Rules versus Authorities in Monetary Policy' (1936). Simons believed that economic instability was due largely to the instability of the financial system. The system rested excessively on private debt, mainly short-term debt. Variations in the quantity and quality of this debt caused destabilizing variations in the quantity of money, in the quantity of 'near-money', and thereby of velocity, and in the financial requirements of business. The monetary authority, the central bank, was unreliable in discharging its responsibility to counter these devastating tendencies.

Simons's remedy for this condition was a radical reform of the financial structure and the establishment of a rule to govern the conduct of monetary policy. He regarded as an 'approximately ideal solution' one in which all property was held in equity form. Failing that, he would have preferred that all debt be in the form of perpetuities, or at least of very long maturities. He did not, however, expect to achieve even that much. But he was specific in recommending the insulation of the banking system and government finance from the malignancy of short-term debt. Banks would be required to hold reserves in currency and Federal Reserve deposits against 100 per cent of their deposits. The government would have only two kinds of debt: currency and consols.

This arrangement would give the government effective control of the quantity of money, a control that it would exercise by fiscal means – by altering the size of its own debt or the division of the debt between currency and controls. This control would be exercised 'under simple, definite rules laid down in legislation', to provide the private sector with the maximum certainty.

Simons wrestled continuously with the question of what the rules should be. His indecision appeared at the beginning, in 1934, when he referred to controlling 'the quantity, (or through quantity, the value) of effective money' (1934, p. 57).

He debated with himself on this issue in the 'Rules versus Authorities' and elsewhere. He recognized that a rule aimed at the price level (or the value of money) would necessarily leave the authority with discretion to decide what quantity of money would achieve the goal. But he also feared that with the existing financial situation the velocity of money would be so variable that a quantity rule would yield great price-level instability. His solution to this dilemma was to opt for the price-level rule until reform of the financial system would reduce the quantity of near moneys and the instability of the debt structure, after which stabilizing the quantity of money would be the preferred rule.

Simons's only two books were on taxation. The first, *Personal Income Taxation* was his doctoral dissertation, written in the early 1930s and published in 1938. The second, *Federal Tax Reform*, was commissioned by the Committee for Economic Development, an organization of businessmen, mainly written in 1943 and published posthumously in 1950. A few main elements ran through all of his work on taxation. The nearly exclusive source of revenue should be taxation of personal income, meaning what has come to be called the Haig–Simons definition of income as the sum of the value of the taxpayers' consumption plus the addition to his net assets. (The reference is to Robert M. Haig, 'The Concept of Income', in *The Federal Income Tax*, ed. R.M. Haig, New York, 1921.) This definition should be applied as comprehensively as possible, for the sake of equity and economic efficiency. Simons fully explored the implication of that for the treatment of capital gains, gifts, income in kind and corporate profits. Finally, he emphasized the use of the progressive income tax as a means of reducing inequality both because reducing inequality was important and because the progressive income tax was a way of reducing inequality that was much more compatible with a free economy than other measures commonly proposed for that purpose.

Simons was a leading member of what became known in the 1930s as the 'Chicago School'. Other members at the time were Frank H. Knight, Lloyd W. Mints and Aaron Director; Jacob Viner shared many of their views but did not consider himself a member. Simons more than the others translated their general attitudes into specific policy proposals, which he advanced forcefully in his own writing and defended in a series of strong reviews of the writings of the opposition.

Simons's great attraction for his colleagues, students and sympathetic readers was a matter of personal and literary style as well as of substance. His writing was polished, ironical, free of technical jargon, statistics or mathematics, rising above 'mere' economic analysis to grand pronouncements on eternal subjects. It was not very difficult but difficult enough to leave the reader with a sense of accomplishment at having recognized its merits. He gave his readers and students a feeling of being initiated into a select club that had great insights that politicians, businessmen and most economists were intellectually, morally and ethically incapable of appreciating.

After World War II, and after his death in 1946, national discussion and, to some extent, policy turned in Simons's direction. There was no possibility of reverting to the negative conservativism of the prewar years. But with a greatly enlarged Federal budget and debt, and with the experience of inflation, the naive expansionism of Keynes's American disciples was no longer an acceptable policy. In this gap, Simons's ideas filled a need. A 'modern conservativism' emerged that accepted government responsibility for overall economic stability, was strongly anti-inflationary, sought a rule to govern stabilization policy, relied on tax changes rather than expenditure changes when positive fiscal measures were needed, opposed protectionism, sought to weaken the power of labour unions and accepted the progressive personal income tax as the main source of Federal revenue. Simons's work contributed to this development. By the 1950s some of his principal concepts had become common currency in policy discussion – the combination of positive measures with laissez faire, the rules-versus-authority issue and the Haig–Simons definition of the tax base. Many of his colleagues and students came into positions from which they could influence public opinion and policy.

By 1960 a new-generation Chicago School had come into prominence. Typified by Milton Friedman and George Stigler, they had been profoundly influenced by Simons as students but were departing substantially from his policy positions. Monetary history convinced them that Simons was wrong in opting for a price-level rule rather than a quantity-of-money rule for monetary policy. They concluded that anti-trust activity, on which he had once placed so much emphasis, was on the whole destructive of competition. Whereas Simons never contemplated a peacetime Federal budget exceeding 10 per cent of the national income, they were living with one exceeding 20 per cent, and that changed their views of many things. They came to doubt Simons's reliance on rational discussion as a way to improve government policy in a democracy; this led them, in the case of Friedman, to a search for constitutional amendments that would limit the political process or, in the case of Stigler, to concentrating on explaining rather than influencing the process. But still, they all retained the Simons vision of the good free society with a division of responsibility between the government and the market, and through them his voice was still heard 40 years after his death.

HERBERT STEIN

See also CHICAGO SCHOOL; TAXATION OF INCOME.

SELECTED WORKS

1934. A positive program for laissez-faire: some proposals for a liberal economic policy. First published as 'Public Policy Pamphlet' No. 15, ed. H.D. Gideonse, Chicago: University of Chicago Press. Reprinted in (1948).

1936. Rules versus authorities in monetary policy. *Journal of Political Economy* 54(1), February, 1–30. Reprinted in (1948).

1938. *Personal Income Taxation.* Chicago: University of Chicago Press.

1945. Introduction: a political credo. First published in (1948).

1948. *Economic Policy for a Free Society.* Chicago: University of Chicago Press. Contains 12 previously published and one previously unpublished article, a prefatory note by Aaron Director and a complete bibliography of Simons's writings.

1950. *Federal Tax Reform.* Chicago: University of Chicago Press. With a prefatory note by Aaron Director.

simple and extended reproduction. The schemes for Simple Reproduction and for Extended Reproduction refer to Marx's pioneering formulation of a two-sector general equilibrium growth model. Quesnay's *Tableau économique* is their forerunner; Leontief's Input–Output model and the Fel'dman–Mahalanobis planning model could be claimed among their progeny.

The two sectors (Departments) reproduce capital goods (Dept I) and consumption goods (Dept II). Marx's accounts are written in terms of labour values, i.e. after physical inputs and outputs have been converted into the direct and indirect labour time required for their production. Total value produced are divided into value of capital goods used up (constant capital), the value of the wage goods purchased by the workers who spend their entire wage bill on them (variable capital) and surplus value.

Thus for the two Departments we have

$$c_1+v_1+s_1=Y_1$$

$$c_2+v_2+s_2=Y_2$$

$$C+V+S=Y$$

where c_i is the input of constant capital, v_i variable capital and s_i surplus value in the *i*th Dept. Now in simple reproduction, we assume zero growth. This requires $Y_1=C$, i.e. output of constant capital, to equal the inputs required to sustain the given level of total output Y. Then the consumption goods output must satisfy the condition $V+S=Y_2$. These two conditions together imply an intersectoral balance of trade requirements

$$c_2=v_1+s_1$$

i.e. the demand for capital goods input by Dept II (and hence implicitly its projected output level given linear technology) must match the wage bill and capitalists' consumption requirement in Dept I.

In chapter XX of *Capital* Vol. 2, where Marx formulates simple reproduction, much attention is devoted to the problem of accounting for constant capital, which is consumed within the production process. Marx was groping here for a distinction between gross output and net output and the relation between income and output. Thus V and S represent incomes received respectively by workers and capitalists. To this corresponds as net output Y_2. But what, Marx puzzled, happens to the payments corresponding to C, the constant capital? The national income and accounting categories implicit in simple reproduction were brought out by Shigeto Tsuru in an appendix to Sweezy (1942).

It was the scheme for a growing economy – for extended reproduction–that was the origin of a long debate and could also be said to have encouraged the formulation of business cycle theory. In this case, the formal scheme was as above but it was allowed that $Y_1>C$, i.e. more capital goods were produced than were required for reproduction of output at the level Y. Let us denote each production period by subscript t. So we have $Y_{1t}>C_t$ and by implication $Y_{2t}<V_t+S_t$. To allow continued reproduction of the economy without causing excess supply of capital goods or excess demand for consumption goods, there had to be some diversion of demand away from Y_2 towards Y_1. This of course implies net investment. Marx proposed that capitalists of Dept I would accumulate one half of the surplus value they received and spend the other half on consumption goods. The capitalists of Dept II would then absorb the remaining capital goods so as to clear the market for Y_1. This automatically clears the market for Y_2.

Despite such seemingly arbitrary rules for accumulation behaviour, i.e. a fixed proportion of surplus value to be invested by Dept I capitalists, the passive adaptive behaviour of Dept II capitalists, no flow of investment across Departments etc., Marx was able to arrive at a remarkable result. Starting from seemingly arbitrary numerical values, the economy would settle down to balanced growth between the two Departments by the second period. Morishima (1973) has characterized this as the fastest converging two-sector growth model in the economic literature.

The result given in *Capital* 2/XXI aroused a long debate among Marxists. How could one reconcile this picture of an economy in perpetual balanced growth with Marx's prediction elsewhere in his work of a capitalist economy riddled with crises and liable to breakdown as a result of increasing contradictions including a falling rate of profit despite growth and accumulation? Was Marx portraying the improbability of this outcome in absence of a planning mechanism that could order capitalists to invest a given proportion? Was this another example of a glaring inconsistency between different parts of *Capital*, as had been argued in the case of the value–price relationship by Böhm-Bawerk?

In the long debate that followed the publication of *Capital* Vol. 2, many attempts were made to alter the numerical magnitudes of Marx's example to generate business cycles. The notion that disproportionality in the investment in and/or growth of the two sectors could cause cycles was developed by Tugan-Baranovsky. The centrality of Dept I investment decision, although arbitrarily imposed by Marx, led to development of theories of business cycle emphasizing the capital goods industries as the source of these fluctuations (Aftalion, Spiethoff). But the most searching critical analysis of Marx's scheme came from Rosa Luxemburg. *The Accumulation of Capital* offers both a survey of the pre-1914 debate in this area and an attempt to probe the reasons for the puzzle of a balanced growth equilibrium in a Marxian model.

Luxemburg raises questions about the reasons for capitalists to invest in absence of any strong demand signals. Could investment be indefinitely sustained by capitalists buying from each other? Should there not be some examination of the markets for the products of the two Departments? In this respect, Luxemburg proposed that such a model should be put in the context of a world economy with exports to 'less developed' areas playing a crucial role in providing markets especially for capital goods. This export relation could be part of an imperial relation between the developed country at the core and the periphery but need not be so. Another source for products of Dept I could be state expenditure on armaments.

As far as Dept II was concerned, Luxemburg saw that perpetual balanced growth required unlimited supplies of labour or some other condition to guarantee the constancy of real wages. If not, the expansion in Dept II would slow down, thus disrupting the balanced growth equilibrium. Here again the role of the less developed sectors in the economy (agriculture, small business) and of the less developed countries in the periphery as sources of reserve labour and of supplies of cheap foodstuffs were articulated by her.

Despite her insights, Luxemburg cannot be said to have integrated growth and cycles in a Marxian framework. There was a tension in such an enterprise for a Marxist, since a cyclical economy could perpetuate itself. It was thought necessary for a Marxist to demonstrate not only that cycles occurred but that they got increasingly severe and led eventually to a breakdown of capitalism. Subsequent discussion of schemes for expanded reproduction became involved with the breakdown controversy (surveyed in Sweezy, 1942; see also Brewer, 1980).

The analytical problem of the likely coexistence of growth and cycle within the schemes of extended reproduction was not tackled till Morishima (1973). He formulates the schemes of extended reproduction as a matrix difference equation and considerably generalizes the assumptions. Thus he assumes a constant propensity to save on part of all capitalists and allows for capitalists to invest in either Department. He shows that under such conditions growth is accompanied by oscillations of increasing amplitude if Dept II has a higher organic composition of capital ($c_i(c_i+v_i)$) than Dept I. Otherwise growth is explosive without oscillations. Note that this contrasts strongly with Uzawa's two-sector growth model where the relatively higher capital labour intensity of the consumption goods sector is required for stability. This Morishima's result would indicate that by allowing unequal propensities to save (and invest) in the two Departments and restricting capitalists to invest within the Department, Marx was able to obtain a balanced growth outcome. This may lead to a conclusion that restrictions in capitalists' investment behaviour may be necessary to stabilize an otherwise unstable economy.

The schemes of extended reproduction can be further reduced to a single nonlinear difference equation in which the differential in the growth rates between the two sectors $\Delta \ln(y_1/y_2)$ depends on the proportion of output levels (y_1/y_2). This is done while retaining all the original assumptions in schemes of extended reproduction. For a suitable choice of the propensity to save of Department I capitalists, convergence to balanced growth can be immediate, i.e. even faster than in the original (Desai, 1979).

An offshoot of the schemes of extended reproduction has been their influence on the Soviet planning practice. Fel'dman used the extended reproduction scheme framework to tackle the question of investment priorities for the Soviet First Five Year Plan. The priority accorded in Soviet planning to Dept I can be said to have some roots in the Marx-Fel'dman extended reproduction scheme. Independently of Fel'dman, Mahalanobis used a similar two sector model for India's Second Five Year Plan (see Desai, 1979, for detailed references).

The intimate connection required between profits (surplus value) and investment to clear markets and sustain growth in an economy that the extended reproduction scheme illustrates could also be said to have influenced Kalecki's formulation of the macroeconomic model, which he arrived at independently of Keynes.

Thus the reproduction schemes have usefulness both in the understanding of static macroeconomic equilibrium and of multisectoral growth equilibrium. The fruitfulness of extended reproduction schemes for a theory of growth cycles could be said to be underexplored even today.

MEGHNAD DESAI

See also MARXISM; MODES OF PRODUCTION.

BIBLIOGRAPHY

Brewer, A. 1980. *Marxist Theories of Imperialism*. London: Macmillan.

Desai, M. 1979. *Marxian Economics*. Oxford: Basil Blackwell.

Luxemburg, R. 1913. *Die Akkumulation des Kapitals. Ein Beitrag zur ökonomischen Erklärung des Imperialismus*. Berlin: Vereinigung Internationaler, Verlags-Austalten, 1922. Trans. by A. Schwarzschild as *The Accumulation of Capital*, London: Routledge & Kegan Paul, 1951.

Marx, K. 1885. *Das Kapital*, Vol. II. Ed. F. Engels, Hamburg: Otto Meisner.

Morishima, M. 1973. *Marx's Economics: A Dual Theory of Value and Growth*. Cambridge: Cambridge University Press.

Sweezy, P.M. 1942. *The Theory of Capitalist Development*. New York: Monthly Review Press.

simplex method for solving linear programs. The data for the linear programming problem (LP) is stated below in standard form:

FIND Min $z, x_j \geqslant 0$:

$$
\begin{array}{ll}
 & a_{11}x_1 + \cdots + a_{1s}x_s + \cdots + a_{1n}x_n = b_1 \\
 & \cdots\cdots\cdots\cdots \\
 & a_{r1}x_1 + \cdots + a_{rs}x_s + \cdots + a_{rn}x_n = b_r \\
 & \cdots\cdots\cdots\cdots \\
 & a_{m1}x_1 + \cdots + a_{ms}x_s + \cdots + a_{mn}x_n = b_m \\
\text{obj:} & c_1x_1 + \cdots + c_sx_s + \cdots + c_nx_n = z - b_0
\end{array} \qquad (1)
$$

Obj is the objective or cost equation defining z. In economic applications, the coefficient a_{ij}, depending on sign, is the input or output of item i per unit level of activity j and x_j is the level of activity j to be determined.

Any particular set of values $x^0 = (x_1^0, \ldots, x_n^0)$ that satisfies the first m equations of (1) is called a solution; if in addition $x_j^0 \geqslant 0$ for all j then x^0 is a feasible solution; if upon substitution into the obj equation of (1), x^0 yields a value of $z = \text{Min } z$, then x^0 is an optimal feasible solution.

The LP, however, could have been given in one of several other ways which, from a mathematical point of view, are all equivalent. Suppose the LP were originally stated as – minimize a linear form subject to a system of linear inequalities – it is easily converted to (1). For example, the relation $2u + 3v \leqslant 4$ can be replaced by the equation $2(x_1 - x_2) + 3(x_3 - x_4) + x_5 = 4$ where $x_j > 0$ by setting u and v each equal to the difference of two non-negative variables $u = x_1 - x_2$, $v = x_3 - x_4$, and introducing a non-negative *slack* variable x_5.

Commercial software for LP usually allows the user to specify which variables are unrestricted in sign and whether the relation is an equation or an inequality. The software program does not make the above substitutions but uses a modified form of the simplex algorithm designed to handle the mixed case of signed/unsigned variables and equation/inequality relations.

PIVOTING DEFINED. The simplex method consists of a sequence of $t = 0, 1, 2 \ldots$ pivot steps (iterations) performed on system (1) which transforms it on each step to a new, mathematically equivalent, system of equations. Any solution of (1) is also a solution for the system of iteration t, and conversely. Thus feasible and optimal feasible solutions remain feasible and optimal after pivoting and so remain for all t. Since the generated systems all have the same solution set as (1), it is not necessary to store in the memory of the computer a record of all the intermediate steps.

We will use the same symbols a_{ij}, c_j, b_i to denote the updated system after pivoting as before. When necessary to distinguish as to which iteration t they pertain, we will use a superscript a_{ij}^t, c_j^t, b_i^t.

To perform a pivot step on system (1) iteration $t = 0$ or a subsequent iteration t, select any term $a_{rs}x_s$ where $a_{rs} \neq 0$, called the *pivot term*. Replace equation r by dividing it through by a_{rs}, then replace each equation $i \neq r$ by subtracting from it the new rth equation multiplied by a_{is}. Do the same thing with the objective equation by subtracting from it the rth equation multiplied by c_s. This eliminates the variable x_s from all equations except the rth. During a pivot step, the current solution x^t is also updated to a new solution x^{t+1} by some rule.

A number of different methods are used to solve LPs all based on pivoting from one iteration to the next which are variants of the simplex method such as the dual simplex method; the primal-dual method; and the symmetric method. They differ only in the rules used for choosing the pivot term or the way the current solution is updated.

The simplex method to be described was first proposed in 1947; it can be stated in twenty or so instructions for a computer. Commercial codes based on the simplex method, however, usually involve thousands of instructions which are there to take advantage of sparsity (most coefficients of practical problems are zero), to make it easy to start from solutions to variants of the same problem, and to guarantee numerical accuracy of the solution for large-scale systems.

Outline of the procedure. The simplex method consists of phase I which finds a feasible solution if one exists, and phase II which finds an optimal one if one exists. Thus the method can terminate with (a) no feasible solution, (b) an optimal feasible solution, or (c) a class of feasible solutions whose values for the objective $z \to -\infty$. Each phase applies a special subroutine called the simplex algorithm to a related but different LP problem. We begin by describing this algorithm.

SIMPLEX ALGORITHM. This algorithm requires the system to be given in canonical form with the right-hand side constants $b_i \geq 0$. The system is said to be in canonical form if we can permute the order of the variables of the first m equations so that coefficients of the first m variables form an identity matrix, i.e., a square array of all zeros except for a diagonal of all ones. We also require their corresponding terms in the obj equation be zero. We illustrate with an $m = 2$, $n = 5$ example.

FIND Min z, $(x_1, \ldots, x_5) \geq 0$:

$$\begin{aligned} &2x_1 \quad + 1x_3 + a_{14}x_4 + 1x_5 = 8 \\ &-3x_1 + 1x_2 \quad - 7x_4 + 1x_5 = 6 \\ &\quad \cdots\cdots\cdots\cdots \\ \text{obj:}\quad &4x_1 \quad + c_4x_4 + 1x_5 = z - 3. \end{aligned} \tag{2}$$

By choosing the constants $c_4 = +5$ or -5 and $a_{14} = -2$ or $+1$, we have, in fact, four different examples. System (2) is in canonical form because we can reorder the variables so that x_3, x_2 come before the rest. When we do so the matrix of coefficients of x_3, x_2 in the first two equations is the 2×2 identity matrix:

$$\begin{bmatrix} 1 & 0 \\ 0 & 1 \end{bmatrix}. \tag{3}$$

The *ordered* set of m indices giving rise to the identity matrix, in the example $\{3, 2\}$, is called the basic set; its corresponding variables are called the basic variables; its set of coefficients is called the basis. Each iteration t will give rise to varying basic sets of m indices.

Termination. The simplex algorithm terminates with an optimal solution when a canonical system is generated on some iteration t with $c_j \geq 0$ for all j. This is the case in the example if $c_4 = +5$. Note $c_1 = 4$, $c_2 = c_3 = 0$, $c_4 = 5$, $c_5 = 1$. Phase I will always terminate in this way. Phase II can also terminate with a class of feasible solutions in which $z \to -\infty$. This happens when a canonical system is generated on some iteration t with some variable x_s whose $c_s < 0$ and all its other coefficients $a_{is} \leq 0$. In the example if $c_4 = -5$ and $a_{14} = -2$, then for variable x_4 this termination condition holds, namely: $c_4 = -5$, $a_{14} = -2$, $a_{24} = -7$.

Basic feasible solutions. The solution obtained by setting the values of all non-basic (independent) variables equal to zero and solving for the basic (dependent) variables is called a basic solution. Since the canonical form for each iteration t satisfies $b_i \geq 0$ for all i, the basic feasible solution is simply $x_j = 0$ for j non-basic and $x_{j_i} = b_i$ where $j_1, j_2, \ldots, j_m$ are the basic set of indices in the order that their coefficients form an identity matrix. In the example, $\{j_1, j_2\} = \{3, 2\}$; the basic feasible solution is $x_3 = 8$, $x_2 = 2$, $x_1 = x_4 = x_5 = 0$. Substituting this solution into the obj equation, we obtain $z = 3$.

Proof of optimality. To prove that the basic feasible solution yields Min $z = b_0$ when $c_j \geq 0$ for all j, we observe for our example with $c_4 = +5$ that the objective equation states that $z = 3 + 4x_1 + 5x_4 + x_5$. Therefore the value of $z \geq 3$ because $4x_1 + 5x_4 + x_5 \geq 0$ for all $x_j \geq 0$ and its lower bound $z = 3$ is attained for the basic feasible solution. Therefore $z = 3$ is minimum.

In general, the value of z for the basic feasible solution for iteration t is clearly $z = b_0$ and the obj equation can be rewritten $z = b_0 + \Sigma c_j x_j$. Therefore if $c_j \geq 0$ and $x_j \geq 0$, then $z \geq b_0$. Since the lower bound $z = b_0$ is attained for the basic feasible solution, this implies Min $z = b_0$.

Proof that $z \to -\infty$. We wish to show z has no lower bound when for some x_s, $c_s < 0$ and $a_{is} \leq 0$, for all i. In the example let $c_4 = -5$ and $a_{14} = -2$, then for x_4, $c_4 = -5$, $a_{14} = -2$, $a_{24} = -7$ which satisfies the termination condition. Setting all non-basic variables $= 0$ *except* x_4 and solving for the basic variables and z in terms of x_4, we have:

$$\begin{aligned} x_3 &= 8 + 2x_4, \qquad x_1 = x_5 = 0, \\ x_2 &= 6 + 7x_4, \\ z &= 3 - 5x_4. \end{aligned} \tag{4}$$

As $x_4 \to +\infty$, a class of feasible solutions is generated in which $z \to -\infty$.

In general, setting all non-basic variables $x_j = 0$ except x_s, and solving for basic x_j and z in terms of x_s, we have:

$$\begin{aligned} x_j &= b_i - a_{is}x_s \qquad \text{for } j_i \text{ basic} \\ z &= b_0 + c_s x_s. \end{aligned} \tag{5}$$

Again we see for $a_{is} \leq 0$, $c_s < 0$, that a class of feasible solutions $x_j \geq 0$ is generated in which $z \to -\infty$.

Improving a basic feasible solution. Let s be such that $c_s =$ Min c_j. If $c_s \geq 0$ the algorithm terminates with an optimal basic-feasible solution. If $c_s \leq 0$, then clearly setting all non-basic $x_j = 0$ except x_s and allowing x_s to increase causes $z = b_0 + c_s x_s$ to decrease towards $-\infty$; hence the more we can decrease x_s the better. However, the values of the basic variables in terms of x_s is $x_{j_i} = b_i - a_{is}x_s$ and therefore the maximum increase allowable for x_s in order to keep all x_j non-negative is $x_s = x_s^*$ where

$$x_s^* = \operatorname*{Min}_i (b_i / a_{is}) \tag{6}$$

where Min_i is restricted to i such that $a_{is} > 0$. If there are no $a_{is} > 0$, then we have the termination case already discussed of $z \to -\infty$. Otherwise the minimum occurs at some $i = r$ and $x_s^* = b_r / a_{rs}$. The value of x_{j_r} when $x_s = x_s^*$ is $x_{j_r} = b_r - a_{rs}(b_r / a_{rs}) = 0$. This suggests that the variable x_s replace x_{j_r} as rth basic variable by pivoting on $a_{rs}x_s$.

We illustrate this for our example with $c_4 = -5$ and $a_{14} = 1$. Since $c_4 =$ Min c_j and $c_4 < 0$, we have $s = 4$. Accordingly we set all non-basic $x_j = 0$ except x_4 and solve for the values of basic variables in terms of x_4. Thus:

$$\begin{aligned} x_3 &= 8 - 1x_4, \qquad x_1 = x_5 = 0, \\ x_2 &= 6 + 7x_4 \\ z &= 3 - 5x_4. \end{aligned} \tag{7}$$

We are blocked from increasing x_4 indefinitely because x_3 would become negative if $x_4 > 8$ and our class of generated solutions would no longer remain feasible. At $x_4 = 8$ we have two variables positive, $x_4 = 8$ and $x_2 = 62$, and all the rest $x_1 = x_3 = x_5 = 0$. Therefore we drop $j = 3$ from our basic set and replace it by $j=4$ by pivoting on $a_{14}x_4$. Thus we have:

Iteration $t=0$

$$\begin{aligned} 2x_1 \quad\quad + 1x_3 + \boxed{1x_4} + 1x_5 &= 8 \\ -3x_1 + 1x_2 \quad\quad - 7x_4 + 1x_5 &= 6 \\ \cdots \\ \text{obj:}\quad 4x_1 \quad\quad - 5x_4 + 1x_5 &= z-3. \end{aligned} \tag{8}$$

Iteration $t=1$ (after pivoting using $\boxed{1x_4}$ as pivot term).

$$\begin{aligned} 2x_1 \quad + 1x_3 + 1x_4 + 1x_5 &= 8 \\ 11x_1 + x_2 + 7x_3 \quad + 8x_4 &= 62 \\ \cdots \\ \text{obj:}\quad 14x_1 \quad + 5x_3 \quad + 6x_5 &= z+37. \end{aligned} \tag{9}$$

We conclude that the basic feasible solution for iteration 1, namely $x_4=8$, $x_2=62$, $x_1=x_3=x_5=0$ and $z=-37$ is the optimal feasible solution. If the obj equation for iteration $t=1$ had some $c_j<0$, we would have continued the algorithm.

PHASE I. To initiate phase I, multiply by -1 all equations of (1) with $b_i<0$, $i\neq 0$, so that (1) after modification $b_i\geqslant 0$. Next adjoin auxiliary variables, called artificials, $x_{n+1},\ldots,x_{n+m}$ as shown below.

Phase I Problem, Iteration $t=0$.

FIND Min w, $x_j\geqslant 0$:

$$\begin{aligned} a_{11}x_1+\cdots+a_{1s}x_s+\cdots+a_{1n}x_n+x_{n+1} &= b_1 \\ \cdots \\ a_{r1}x_1+\cdots+a_{rs}x_s+\cdots+a_{rn}x_n+x_{n+r} &= b_r \\ \cdots \\ a_{m1}x_1+\cdots+a_{ms}x_s+\cdots+a_{mn}x_n+x_{n+m} &= b_m \\ \text{obj:}\quad d_1x_1+\cdots+d_sx_s+\cdots+d_nx_n &= w-d_0 \end{aligned} \tag{10}$$

The obj equation has been replaced by a phase I obj defined by

$$d_j=-\Sigma_i a_{ij} \quad\text{and}\quad d_0=+\Sigma_i b_i. \tag{11}$$

Note the system is in canonical form with $b_i\geqslant 0$, so that we are all set to apply the simplex algorithm.

Special rule. Once an artificial variable x_{n+i} is pivoted out of the set of basic variables on some iteration t and becomes non-basic, it is discarded (i.e., all terms involving x_{n+i} are dropped from the canonical form). Hence the pivot term $a_{rs}x_s$ will be one from among the first m rows and n columns of (10).

If we add the first m equations of (10) to the obj equation, we obtain by (11) that:

$$x_{n+1}+x_{n+2}+\cdots+x_{n+m}=w. \tag{12}$$

Thus the phase I objective is equivalent to minimizing the sum of the artificial variables. If a feasible solution to (1) exists, then a feasible solution to (10) exists in which all $x_{n+i}=0$ and therefore a feasible solution to (10) exists in which $w=0$. Since $x_{n+i}\geqslant 0$, it follows for all feasible solutions to the phase I problem, $w\geqslant 0$ and Min $w\geqslant 0$. It is therefore impossible in phase I to find a class of solutions in which $w\to-\infty$. If the optimal solution yields Min $w>0$, the simplex method is terminated with the statement that no feasible solution to (1) exists. If phase I terminates with $w=0$, then we set up the phase II problem.

TRANSITION TO PHASE II. At the end of phase I if Min $w=0$, then all artificial variables have value 0 in the basic solution. Usually there are no longer any artificial variables left among the basic ones in the canonical form. When this is the case, we replace the obj equation of phase I by the original one given as input data (1). Next we eliminate from the obj all terms c_jx_j corresponding to $j=j_i$ in the basic set. This is done by subtracting from the obj equation the ith equation of the canonical form multiplied by c_{j_i}. The phase II problem is now in canonical form ready to apply the simplex algorithm to find Min z.

For example, suppose at the end of phase I we have:

FIND Min z. $(x_1,\ldots,x_4)\geqslant 0$:

$$\begin{aligned} 2x_1 \quad\quad + 1x_3 + a_{14}x_4 + 1x_5 &= 8 \\ -3x_1 + 1x_2 \quad\quad - 7x_4 + 1x_5 &= 6 \\ \text{obj:}\quad c_1x_1+c_2x_2+c_3x_3+c_4x_4+c_5x_5 &= z-3. \end{aligned} \tag{13}$$

The basic set is $\{j_1,j_2\}=\{3,2\}$. Multiplying the first equation by c_3 and the second by c_2 and subtracting from obj, we eliminate the basic variables x_3,x_2 from the obj equation obtaining an obj equation of the form:

$$\text{obj:}\quad c_1x_1+c_4x_4+c_5x_5=z-b_0. \tag{14}$$

It can happen, however, at the end of Phase I for some iteration t that Min $w=0$ and some artificial variable, say x_{n+r}, still is basic. Its basic solution value is $x_{n+r}=b_r=0$. x_{n+r} is gotten rid of by pivoting on any term $a_{rs}x_s$ of the canonical form where $a_{rs}\neq 0$ and $s\leqslant n$. The new basic solution will have as rth basic variable $x_s=0$ and x_{n+r}, now non-basic, is then discarded. This process is continued until all artificials are dropped.

There still remains the possibility that a pivot term for some r cannot be found because all $a_{rj}=0$ for $j=1,2,\ldots,n$. In this case it is easy to prove that the rth equation of the original problem is *redundant* and the rth equation of the canonical form of the phase I problem can be discarded or, alternatively, x_{n+r} can be reclassified as belonging among the *true* variables – it will do no harm to include it because in all subsequent iterations its basic solution value will remain zero. Once the artificials are made non-basic and removed, we complete the transition as outlined in the paragraph above.

Upon termination of the simplex algorithm applied to the Phase II problem, the software program is directed to print out a statement about the type of termination. In the case of an optimum solution, this is followed by the list of indices of the obj, the basic variables, and alongside them the values of the corresponding b_0 and b_i.

In the case z is unbounded below, the list printed is

obj	b_0	$+c_s$
j_i	b_i	$-a_{is}$
s	0	1

for $i=1,\ldots,m$. (15)

This information permits one to generate z and a feasible solution for any choice of $x_s\geqslant 0$.

Proof of convergence. It is not difficult to show that if any basic set of indices were to be repeated in some subsequent iteration, the entire canonical form would be repeated including the value of z in the basic solution. In the example (8), the value of z in the basic solution is $z=3$. After pivoting, see (9), the value of $z=-37$. We see that its value decreased from 3 to -37.

In general, if there is a *positive* decrease in the value of z in the basic solution from one iteration to the next, the canonical form cannot be repeated since the value of z is lower. On the other hand, the iterative process must stop sometime because there is only a finite number of canonical forms. But the only way it could have stopped is via one of the two termination conditions. Hence the iterative process is finite when there is a positive decrease on each iteration. This should not be interpreted, however, as meaning the algorithm is efficient because the number of ways to pick m objects out of n grows exponentially with increasing m and n.

Degeneracy. Should the pivot term occur on a row r whose $b_r = 0$, then the updated value of z in the basic solution is $z = b_0 - b_r(c_s/a_{rs}) = b_0$, i.e., the change in value of z is zero and the proof of convergence given above is no longer applicable. In this case, one or more of the values of the basic variables in a basic solution are zero and the basic solution is said to be *degenerate*. There are examples of canonical forms with degenerate basic solutions, which after a number of pivots return to the original canonical form.

To avoid this possibility of cycling, special rules have been invented that are easy to implement but are not found in commercial codes. Almost all practical problems are degenerate. Failure to provide a rule has never (or almost never) caused the algorithm to cycle in practice. From a theoretical point of view, however, devices that prevent cycling are important because the simplex method is used as a powerful analytic tool for proving theorems like the duality theorem.

ECONOMIC INTERPRETATIONS. *Feasible*. In planning, a feasible solution is a plan or policy that is physically implementable. The plan may be feasible but not necessarily an optimal one.

Prices. Associated with a basic solution is a set of prices $(\pi_1, \pi_2, \ldots, \pi_m)$, also called Lagrange Multipliers, which are defined so that if we 'price out' the inputs and outputs of activities associated with basic variables, they *break even*. By this is meant for each j in the basic set:

$$c_j^0 - \Sigma_i \pi_i a_{ij}^0 = 0, \qquad j = \{j_1, \ldots, j_m\}. \tag{16}$$

where a_{ij}^0, c_j^0 refer to a_{ij}, c_j of iteration $t = 0$.

The value of c_j of iteration t is denoted by c_j^t. It is easy to show that c_j^t can be obtained directly from the data of iteration $t = 0$ by 'pricing out' any activity j:

$$c_j^t = c_j^0 - \Sigma_i \pi_i a_{ij}^0, \qquad j = 1, \ldots, n. \tag{17}$$

If $c_j^t < 0$ for any activity $j = j^*$, it pays to replace one of the activities of the basic set by activity j^*. The simplex method chooses among the activities j in the non-basic set $j^* = j_s$ that shows the greatest profitability per unit change of activity level x_j, namely s such that $c_s = \text{Min } c_j$ and $c_s < 0$.

DUALITY. The dual of the LP (1) iteration $t = 0$ is defined by:

FIND Max $\mathbf{z}$, $(\pi, \pi_2, \ldots, \pi_m)$, and $(y_1, \ldots, y_n) \geqslant 0$:

$$y_j = c_j - \Sigma_i \pi_i a_{ij}, \qquad j = 1, \ldots, n.$$

$$\mathbf{z} = b_0 + \Sigma_i \pi_i b_i \tag{18}$$

It is easy to show that $\mathbf{z} \leqslant z$ for all feasible solutions to the original primal system (1) and feasible solutions to the dual system (18). This implies when feasible solutions to both the primal and dual systems exist that z has a finite lower bound and $\mathbf{z}$ has a finite upper bound. We have shown in this case that an optimal feasible solution exists to the primal system. Moreover for the optimal canonical form of some iteration t that π_i defined by (16), satisfies $c_j^t \geqslant 0$ in (17). Setting $y_j = c_j^t \geqslant 0$ for all j, we see that π_i and $y_j \geqslant 0$ satisfy (18). It is easy to show that z of this basic feasible solution satisfies Min $z = b_0^0 + \Sigma_i \pi_i b_i^0$ so that $\mathbf{z} = z$. It follows therefore that Max $\mathbf{z}$ = Min z. This is called the *strong* duality theorem; note that we have proved it using the properties of the simplex algorithm.

Computational experience. Since 1947 the simplex method and its variants have successfully solved each day thousands of large and small scale practical problems. New methods for solving LPs are constantly cropping up. Many LPs have special structures and special algorithms have been developed to solve them. For example there is considerable research on how to efficiently solve large-scale dynamic economic models under uncertainty. One approach makes use of parallel computers, random sampling, methods of decomposing the problem into many subproblems which are solved using the simplex method as a subroutine.

GEORGE B. DANTZIG

simulation models. To clarify the concept of simulation requires placing simulation models in the context of available modelling approaches. One can distinguish models by their structure, size, complexity, purpose, solution technique and probabilistic specification. Generally, the purpose for which a model is specified, the state of knowledge in the area, and the relative importance of indirect effects should guide model specification (Robinson, 1987).

Analytic models aim at capturing some key feature(s) of the economy and then doing some comparative statics by differentiating key structural or reduced form relationships with respect to key parameters or variables. Their use is in qualitative economics, to 'sign' some effects, or to compare orders of magnitude.

Stylized numerical models, in which the parameters are specified numerically and parametrized, are used for strategic analysis of policy postures (e.g. import substitution vs. export-led growth) since they highlight some specific casual mechanisms. Numerical models can be more complex than analytic models, may require the use of computers for solution, and incorporate more structural features of the economy. They generally tend to be deterministic and static and stay rather close to analytic models in their transparency.

Applied models are used for policy analysis. They aim at realism. They are institutionally and situationally more specific and more disaggregated in terms of factors and activities. They are usually dynamic and may be stochastic. They may or may not be optimizing. They are numerical and solved by computer. The analytic structure of applied models is not transparent, since they usually incorporate many countervailing processes, but stylized versions of analytic models, which capture some of their essential features, can sometimes be formulated. The stylized versions are either analytic models or numerical models. Applied models are solved numerically under various policy-regime scenarios to derive specific policy recommendations for managers or policymakers.

Applied models are simulation models. Stylized numerical models that are stochastic and require computers for their solution are also generally referred to as simulation models. Policy analysis thus always requires simulation models; strategic analysis sometimes does.

Following Naylor et al. (1966), we define model A to be a simulator of real system B if: (1) A is a close representation of

B; (2) A is used to perform 'experiments' that are intended to represent how B would react under the experimental conditions applied to A; and (3) digital or analog computers are used to perform the experiments. The condition that A represents B only in its stochastic distribution is usually added to the theoretical definition of simulation models, but, in practice, many simulation models are treated as deterministic. (General discussions of simulation models are given in Adelman, 1982; Balderston and Hoggatt, 1963; Orcutt et al., 1961; and Naylor et al., 1966).

Simulation models are fully accepted in engineering, where they are used for design purposes, in management, where they are used for corporate decision making, and in economic planning, where they are used in plan formulation. But simulation models are only partially accepted in economics proper as a tool for understanding the properties of an 'economy' that is too complex, either mathematically or structurally, for analytic solution. The closer a given model is to a numerical model, the more acceptable it is to economists. Nevertheless, simulation models are in wide use in practice. For example, four out of six articles in the Fall, 1985 issue of the *Journal of Policy Modelling* contained simulation models.

The formulation of a simulation model involves the following steps: (1) Specification and estimation of applied model A; (2) writing of a computer program that solves for the endogenous variables of A under particular stochastic specifications of the distributions of the exogenous variables; (3) validation of the model; (4) design of the experiments to be performed with the model; and (5) analysis of the results of the experiments. Step 1 is common to both simulation and numerical models. It requires defining the objectives of the analysis (what questions must be answered, what hypotheses tested, what effects estimated), formulating the model, estimating its parameters and forecasting its exogenous variables. Particularly critical questions in choosing a model specification are: How situation-specific should the model be, how realistic, and how transparent in structure? Answers to these questions will require compromise among conflicting criteria, as well as insights into system B and into the phenomena relevant to the objectives of the analysis.

While steps (3)–(5) are not specific to simulation models, the amount of output generated requires that one pay more attention to these steps in simulation models than with other model types. Model validation (step 3) is particularly important, since it tests the assertion that A is a close representation of B. Usually, the validation is based on the comparison of some quantitative and qualitative aspect of the simulated record with the historical record. The procedure is also central to the validation of econometric models, but it has methodological problems which stem from the fact that the information used to estimate the model is reused to test it. Comparisons involve qualitative tests: Are the dynamic features of A – turning points, amplitudes, timing and duration – similar to those of system B (Adelman and Adelman, 1959)? Does a graphic representation of the simulated output of A over the historical period look like that of B (Cyert and March, 1963)? Do the multipliers of A look sensible? Statistical tests of goodness of fit are also useful in model validation. These include regressions of simulated on historical time series, analysis of variance techniques, multiple ranking procedures, and nonparametric tests.

The design of experiments to be performed with the simulation models (step 4) poses difficulties which arise from the virtually infinite number of experiments which could be performed. One can narrow down the number of actual experiments by using the statistical principles of experimental design. This entails equating the 'factors' or 'treatments' in experimental design to the exogenous, controlled or uncontrolled, variables of A and setting the 'responses' in factorial design equal to the endogenous, target or irrelevant variables of A. The multiplicity of such experiments usually limits the investigator to 'main effects' or to a few combinations of treatments, called scenarios. One can also use regression techniques to estimate the functional relationships between the response variables and the exogenous variables to generate a 'response surface'. Optimal experimental designs for the fitting of response surfaces have been suggested by Box (1954).

Analysis of the results of experiments (step 5) can be of two types: (1) Summarizing the 'story' told by the experiment by tracing through the causal chains giving rise to a set of simulation results. At this point resort to smaller numerical models or analytic models may be helpful. (2) Analysing the results statistically, by methods similar to those used in step 3.

Simulation has had wide application in economics. The earliest applications were to business cycle analysis and used both analog and digital computers (Phillips, 1957; Adelman and Adelman, 1959; Duesenberry et al., 1960) to study the cyclical characteristics of economic systems. Microsimulations of macroeconomic systems have been important in tax and social security analysis (Orcutt et al., 1861; Pechman and Okner, 1974) and in forecasting (Bergmann, 1974; Fair, 1974–6). The major current uses are in business management and in economic planning. In business, simulation models are used to aid corporate decision making and to study corporate behaviour (Balderston and Hoggatt, 1963; Bonini, 1963; Cyert and March, 1963). In economy-wide planning, simulation models are used by planning agencies and international organizations to analyse issues such as what development strategy is optimal for a given country during a particular period (Dervis, de Melo and Robinson, 1982), how one might increase economic equality and reduce poverty in a particular country (Adelman and Robinson, 1978), what effects changes in population growth might have (Rodgers, Hopkins and Wery, 1978), or how best to adjust to heavy foreign indebtedness burdens.

The construction of a 'good' simulation model is an art. It requires striking appropriate compromises between realism, on the one hand, and the generality of the conclusions and the transparency of the model, on the other. As far as possible, the behavioural descriptions and the choice of variables and functional forms should be anchored in theory and estimated econometrically. This is especially important for specifications that drive the results of a given model (for example, the coupling of exponential resource exhaustion with arithmetic growth in technology in Forrester (1973), for which there is almost no empirical justification). Where theory is lacking, however, the only alternative to ad hoc specification based on descriptive information is to omit a potentially important factor, building block, or interaction altogether – in itself a misspecification. Finally, a good simulation model is one that replicates history well and whose major results can be explained *ex post*, though not divined *ex ante*, in terms which are consistent with available theory and relevant stylized facts.

IRMA ADELMAN

See also MONTE CARLO METHODS.

BIBLIOGRAPHY

Adelman, I. 1982. Simulation of economic processes. In *International Encyclopaedia of Statistics*, London: Macmillan.

Adelman, I. and Adelman, F.L. 1959. The dynamic properties of the Klein-Goldberger Model. *Econometrica* 27, 596–625.

Adelman, I. and Robinson, S. 1978. *Income Distribution Policy in Developing Countries*. Stanford: Stanford University Press.
Balderston, F.E. and Hoggatt, A. 1963. *Symposium on Simulation Models*. Cincinnati: Southwest Publishing.
Bergmann, B. 1974. A microsimulation of the macroeconomy with explicitly represented money flows. *Annals of Economic and Social Measurement* 3, 457–89.
Bonini, C.P. 1963. *Simulation of Information and Decision Systems in the Firm*. Englewood Cliffs, NJ: Prentice-Hall.
Box, G.E.P. 1954. The exploration and exploitation of response surfaces. *Biometrics* 10, 16–60.
Cyert, R.M. and March, J.G. 1963. *A Behavioral Theory of the Firm*. Englewood Cliffs, NJ: Prentice-Hall.
Dervis, K., de Melo, J. and Robinson, S. 1982. *General Equilibrium Models for Development Planning*. Cambridge: Cambridge University Press.
Duesenberry, J.S., Eckstein, O. and Fromm, G. 1960. A simulation model of the United States economy in recession. *Econometrica* 28, 749–809.
Fair, R.C. 1974–6. *A Model of Macroeconomic Activity*. 2 vols, Cambridge, Mass.: Ballinger.
Forrester, J.W. 1973. *World Dynamics*. 2nd edn, Cambridge, Mass.: Wright Allen.
Naylor, T.H., Balinfy, J.L., Burdick, D.S. and Chu, K. 1966. *Computer Simulation Techniques*. New York: Wiley.
Orcutt, G.H. et al. 1961. *Microanalysis of Socioeconomic Systems: a Simulation Study*. New York: Harper.
Pechman, J.A. and Okner, B.A. 1974. *Who Bears the Tax Burden?* Washington, DC.: Brookings.
Phillips, A.W. 1957. Mechanical models in economic dynamics. *Economica*, NS 17, 283–305.
Robinson, S. 1987. Multisectoral models of developing countries. In *Handbook of Development Economics*, ed. H.B. Chenery and T.N. Srinivasan, Amsterdam: North-Holland.
Rodgers, G.B. and Hopkins, M.J.D. and Wery, R. 1978. *Population, Employment and Inequality, Bachue-Philippines*. Farnborough: Saxon House.

simulation of microanalytic systems. To simulate is both to develop a process model which can be operated and to actually run the model. A running model is a simulation and a model run provides a specific solution of the model.

The focus of this paper is the simulation of socioeconomic systems, such as national economies, and sectors of such systems, such as household sectors, social security systems, or tax and transfer systems. Microanalytic system simulation is system modelling largely in terms of the behaviour and interaction of microentities. The microentities modelled may be thought of as persons imbedded within families and labour market areas; plants imbedded within firms, industries and geographical areas; or local, state and national governments associated with geographical areas.

COMPETING APPROACHES TO SYSTEM MODELLING. There are literally hundreds of quantitatively estimated models of socioeconomic systems. However, all of these models can be grouped according to which of four approaches to system modelling was used in their development. These four approaches are: the macroeconometric, the inter-industry, the cell frequency-transitional matrix, and the microanalytic. The macroeconometric approach dates back to the pathbreaking work of Tinbergen (1937, 1939). The inter-industry approach stems from Leontief's highly important work (1941, 1953). Stone (1966) is most closely identified with the fruitful development of the cell frequency-transitional matrix approach. The microanalytic approach was conceived by Orcutt (1957) and first implemented by Orcutt, Greenberger, Korbel and Rivlin (1961).

Each of these four approaches has been used in the development of quantitatively estimated system models for policy analysis. Each approach is distinguished by the particular entities given centre stage, the consequent data needed for implementation and testing, and the varying conceptualizations of the interactions between entities to be modelled.

The advantages and associated difficulties of the microanalytic system simulation approach stem from the fact that it explicitly recognizes individual micro-entity decision-making units, such as persons, families, enterprises, and state and local political entities and undertakes to model their behaviour and interaction.

References to much of the literature relating to microanalytic economic system simulation may be found in volumes written or edited by Bennett and Bergmann (1986); Bergmann, Eliasson and Orcutt (1980); Haveman and Hollenbeck (vols 1 and 2, 1980); Orcutt, Caldwell, Wertheimer et al. (1976); Orcutt, Merz and Quinke (1986); and US Department of Health, Education and Welfare (1973).

THE NEED FOR MICROANALYTIC MODELLING. The following considerations indicate the need for and some of the advantages of microanalytic modelling for theoretical and policy purposes.

(a) Much of the theory and output of current research cannot be appropriately applied in models restricted to macrocomponents and macrorelationships. Social science theory and research often relate to the behaviour of microentities. For instance, consumption theory is based on the behaviour of individuals, not the household sector. While it is generally a simple matter to aggregate outputs of microentity behaviour, such as the amount individuals spend in a given period of time, there is no satisfactory way to aggregate microentity behavioural relationships, such as the consumption function, except when the relationships are linear and there are no feedbacks (see Orcutt et al., 1961, pp. 11–12). In microanalytic simulation, behavioural relationships are estimated and used at appropriate levels of aggregation. Needed aggregates are obtained by summing the outcomes of microentity simulated behaviour, rather than by aggregating microentity behavioural relationships.

(b) Many relationships that are treated as simultaneous at the macro level, such as the consumption–income relationship, are not simultaneous at the micro level. A person's spending has a negligible effect on his or her own income within the same time period.

(c) Satisfactory estimation and testing of the theory underlying highly aggregative models cannot be achieved since there is only one of each type of entity and there are relatively few macro time series observations available for testing the implications of such models against actual developments. Multicollinearity, autocorrelation, feedbacks, and errors of observation serve to complicate and worsen what is already a precarious situation as far as satisfactory testing is concerned. With the use of microsimulation, the information available for estimation and testing can be enormously increased by the appropriate use of data relating to microcomponents (Orcutt, 1968; Orcutt, Watts and Edwards, 1968; Orcutt and Edwards, 1969).

(d) Models that are solely based upon the interaction of major sectors cannot yield many important kinds of predictions. For example, not only is it important to predict how the unemployment rate or national income would be affected by alternative policies, but it is also important to predict how unemployment and income would be *distributed* among individuals and families according to characteristics such as previous unemployment, age, sex, race and family size.

(e) Since tax and transfers laws and regulations relate to microentities and typically involve substantial nonlinearities, they cannot be represented by relationships among macrovariables. However, they can be given a literal representative in microanalytic modelling.

THE STRUCTURE AND SOLUTION OF MICROANALYTIC MODELS. The previous section presents reasons favouring development of observationally based, microanalytic models. But in the middle 1950s, when my ideas on this subject were developing, there was no known way of solving such models without the use of very strong and, to many of us, totally unbelievable assumptions. Enthralment with the neoclassical conception of an economy composed of millions of microentities interacting through markets was tempered for us by the belief that model solvability was purchased by use of dubious assumptions designated as axioms. But theory not grounded on observation or modified in the face of empirical evidence risks becoming sheer dogma, bereft of any relevance for policy guidance. The hope in the development of microsimulation system simulation has been to find ways by which the solvability of microanalytic system models could be enormously enhanced without the use of assumptions having little, if any, foundation in systematic observation and measurement.

The distinctive feature of a microanalytic system model is that it will contain a microentity-specific representation of one or more populations of microentities. It is this feature which could make possible the realization of the potential advantages of microanalytic modelling set forth in the last Section. It is also a feature which seemed to make model solution impossible if nonlinearities and feedbacks are involved. The structure of microanalytic system models and macroeconometric models are similar in that process rather than equilibrium representation characterizes both types. Also, models of both types may be probabilistic in conception, be expressed as systems of equations, and may use previous values of dependent variables as part of what is treated as given.

A distinctive feature of the way I have sought to conceptualize microentity modelling is to represent structural elements as joint conditional probability functions that are intended to be autonomous characterizations of the within-period behaviour of individual microentities. These joint conditional probability functions may be described by sets of simultaneous equations and many other ways, but the most advantageous way of expressing them is as recursive sets of equations. It is important to note that it is an equation set which is to be regarded as a structural characteristic rather than an individual equation, as is frequently the case in macroeconometric modelling (Orcutt, 1986).

In 1956, a Carnegie Fellowship permitted me to spend two months with the University of Michigan Survey Research Center. While there, a rather simple understanding came to me which suggested a simulation approach for solution of microanalytic models of almost any desired specification. In essence, this amounted to the realization that any real or hypothetical population of microentities, or of microentity histories, may be represented by a probabilistic sample drawn from it. Statistics of such a sample will be suitable estimates of the corresponding parameters of the populations being modelled, particularly with entity sample sizes of 10,000 to 100,000, which are easily accommodated with modern computers.

Full accuracy of representation of the status of individual microentities can thus be retained, making it possible to develop and use behavioural relationships with unaggregated microentity variables as inputs and outputs. Not only does this avoid aggregation bias, but it makes it possible to use the vast amount of information available in microentity specific data for improved estimation and testing.

Initial samples for use in computer runs can be sample representations of populations of any size. Updated samples can be regarded as samples of implicitly updated populations. Histories, associated with using a microanalytic model to guide the movement through time of a sample representation of a theoretically implied population, can be regarded as drawing from populations of histories, implied by a theoretical representation of a real process involving interacting populations of microentities. Of course, the conception of a solution process is far from its fruitful realization, but Orcutt, Greenberger, Korbel and Rivlin (1961) demonstrated, using a computer of that vintage, a complex microanalytic monthly model of family formation and dissolution, and a sample size of about 16,000 persons embedded in families, that an otherwise unsolvable model could be run and made to yield explicit solutions.

CONCLUDING REMARKS. Microanalytic system simulation was initially developed during the 1950s to facilitate the use of results from microentity focused research. The ongoing computer revolution and the growing availability of microentity data have aided the development of microanalytic system simulation and will continue to ease its use in research and policy-making. However, it is evident that a vastly increased volume of high quality, microentity focussed research, based on an improved and appropriately extended data base, is needed if economics is to emerge as a true science that is socially useful in giving policymakers guidance about consequences of actions that might be taken. To the extent that needed data can be collected and team research efforts organized and financed, the securing of improved understanding of microentity behaviour and interactions is to be expected. Microanalytic system simulation is an effective means of using such understanding for policy analysis.

GUY H. ORCUTT

BIBLIOGRAPHY

Bennett, R. and Bergmann, B. 1986. *A Microsimulated Transactions Model of the United States Economy*. Baltimore and London: Johns Hopkins University Press.

Bergmann, B., Eliasson, G. and Orcutt, G. (eds) 1980. *Micro Simulation Models, Methods and Applications. Stockholm:* The Industrial Institute for Economic and Social Research; distributed by Almqvist and Wiksell International.

Haveman, R. and Hollenbeck, K. (eds) 1980. *Microeconomic Simulation Models for Public Policy Analysis*. Vols 1 and 2, New York: Academic Press.

Leontief, W. 1941. *The Structure of American Economy, 1919–1929*. Cambridge, Mass.: Harvard University Press.

Leontief, W. 1953. Static and dynamic theory. In W. Leontief, *Studies in the Structure of the American Economy*, New York: Oxford University Press.

Orcutt, G. 1957. A new type of socio-economic system. *Review of Economics and Statistics* 39, May, 116–23.

Orcutt, G. 1967. Microeconomic analyses for production of national accounts. In H. Wold et al., *Forecasting on a Scientific Basis*, Lisbon: Centro de Economia Finansas.

Orcutt, G. 1968. Research strategy in modeling economic systems. In *The Future of Statistics*, ed. D.G. Watts, New York: Academic Press.

Orcutt, G. 1986. Joint conditional probability functions for modeling national economies. In *Specification Analysis in the Linear Model*, ed. D. Giles and M. King, London: Routledge & Kegan Paul.

Orcutt, G., Greenberger, M., Korbel, J. and Rivlin, A. 1961. *Microanalysis of Socio-Economic Systems: A Simulation Study*. New York: Harper & Row.

Orcutt, G., Watts, H. and Edwards, J. 1968. Data aggregation and information loss. *American Economic Review* 58, September, 773–87.

Orcutt, G. and Edwards, J.B. 1969. Should aggregation prior to estimation be the rule. *Review of Economics and Statistics* 51(4), November, 409–20.

Orcutt, G., Caldwell, S., Wertheimer II, R., Franklin, S., Hendricks, G., Peabody, G., Smith, J. and Zedlewski, S. 1976. *Policy Exploration through Microanalytic Simulation*. Washington, DC: Urban Institute.

Orcutt, G., Merz, J. and Quinke, H. (eds) 1986. *Microanalytic Simulation Models to Support Social and Financial Policy*. Amsterdam: North-Holland.

Stone, R. 1966. *Mathematics in the Social Sciences and Other Essays*. London: Chapman & Hall.

Tinbergen, J. 1937. *An Econometric Approach to Business Cycle Problems*. Paris: Hermann et cie.

Tinbergen, J. 1939. *Statistical Testing of Business Cycle Theories. Vol. II: Business Cycles in the United States of America, 1912–1932*. Geneva: League of Nations.

US Department of Health, Education and Welfare. 1973. *User's Manual for Popsim*. Rockfille, Maryland: National Center for Health Statistics, DHEW Publication No. (HSM) 73–1216.

simultaneous equations models. Models that attempt to explain the workings of the economy typically are written as interdependent systems of equations describing some hypothesized technological and behavioural relationships among economic variables. Supply and demand models, Walrasian general equilibrium models, and Keynesian macromodels are common examples. A large part of econometrics is concerned with specifying, testing, and estimating the parameters of such systems. Despite their common use, simultaneous equations models still generate controversy. In practice there is often considerable disagreement over their proper use and interpretation.

In building models economists distinguish between *endogenous* variables which are determined by the system being postulated and *exogenous* variables which are determined outside the system. Movements in the exogenous variables are viewed as autonomous, unexplained causes of movements in the endogenous variables. In the simplest systems, each of the endogenous variables is expressed as a function of the exogenous variables. These so-called 'reduced-form' equations are often interpreted as causal, stimulus-response relations. A hypothetical experimental is envisaged where conditions are set and an outcome occurs. As the conditions are varied, the outcome also varies. If the outcome is described by the scalar endogenous variable y and the conditions by the vector of exogenous variables x, then the rule describing the causal mechanism can be written as $y = f(x)$. If there are many outcomes of the experiment, y and f are interpreted as vectors; the rule describing how the ith outcome is determined can be written as $y_i = f_i(x)$.

Most equations arising in competitive equilibrium theory are motivated by hypothetical stimulus-response experiments. Demand curves, for example, represent the quantity people will purchase when put in a price-taking market situation. The conditions of the experiment are, in addition to price, all the other determinants of demand. In any given application, most of these determinants are viewed as fixed as the experiment is repeated; attention is directed at the handful of exogenous variables whose effects are being analysed. In an n good world, there are n such equations, each determining the demand for one of the goods as a function of the exogenous variables.

Reduced-form models where each equation contains only one endogenous variable are rather special. Typically, economists propose interdependent systems where at least some of the equations contain two or more endogenous variables. Such models have a more complex causal interpretation since each endogenous variable is determined not by a single equation but *simultaneously* by the entire system. Moreover, in the presence of simultaneity, the usual least-squares techniques for estimating parameters often turn out to have poor statistical properties.

WHY SIMULTANEITY? Given the obvious asymmetry between cause and effect, it would at first thought appear unnatural to specify a behavioural economic model as an interdependent, simultaneous system. Although equations with more than one endogenous variable can always be produced artificially by algebraic manipulation of a reduced-form system, such equations have no independent interpretation and are unlikely to be interesting. It turns out, however, that there are many situations where equations containing more than one endogenous variable arise quite naturally in the process of modelling economic behaviour. These so-called 'structural' equations have interesting causal interpretations and form the basis for policy analysis. Four general classes of examples can be distinguished.

1. Suppose two experiments are performed, the outcome of the first being one of the conditions of the second. This might be represented by the two equations $y_1 = f_1(x)$ and $y_2 = f_2(x, y_1)$. In this two-step causal chain, both equations have simple stimulus-response interpretations. Implicit, of course, is the assumption that the experiment described by the first equation takes place before the experiment described by the second equation. Sequential models where, for example, people choose levels of schooling and later the market responds by offering a wage are of this type. Such *recursive* models are only trivially simultaneous and raise no conceptual problems although they may lead to estimation difficulties.

2. Nontrivial simultaneous equations systems commonly arise in multi-agent models where each individual equation represents a separate hypothetical stimulus-response relation for some group of agents, but the outcomes are constrained by equilibrium conditions. The simple competitive supply-demand model illustrates this case. Each consumer and producer behaves as though it has no influence over price or over the behaviour of other agents. Market demand is the sum of each consumer's demand and market supply is the sum of each producer's supply, with all agents facing the same price. Although the market supply and demand functions taken separately represent hypothetical stimulus-response situations where quantity is endogenous and price is exogenous, in the combined equilibrium model both price and quantity are endogenous and determined so that supply equals demand.

Most competitive equilibrium models can be viewed as (possibly very complicated) variants of this supply–demand example. The individual equations, when considered in isolation, have straightforward causal interpretations. Groups of agents respond to changes in their environment. Simultaneity results from market clearing equilibrium conditions that make the environments endogenous. Keynesian macromodels have a similar structure. The consumption function, for example, represents consumers' response to their (seemingly) exogenous wage income – income that in fact is determined by the condition that aggregate demand equal aggregate supply.

3. Models describing optimizing behaviour constitute a third class of examples. Suppose an economic agent is faced with the problem of choosing some vector y in order to maximize the

function $F(y, x)$, where x is a vector of exogenous variables outside the agent's control. The optimum value, denoted by y^*, will depend on x. If there are G choice variables, the solution can be written as a system of G equations, $y^* = g(x)$. If F is differentiable and globally concave in y, the solution can be obtained from the first-order conditions $f(y^*, x) = 0$, where f is the G-dimensional vector of partial derivatives of F with respect to y. The two sets of equations are equivalent representations of the causal mechanism. The first is a reduced-form system with each endogenous variable expressed as a function of exogenous variables alone. The second representation conists of a system of simultaneous equations in the endogenous variables. These latter equations often have simple economic interpretations such as, for example, setting marginal product equal to real input price.

4. Models obtained by simplifying a larger reduced-form system are a fourth source of simultaneous equations. The Marshallian long-run supply curve, for example, is often thought of as the locus of price–quantity pairs that are consistent with the marginal firm having zero excess profit. Both price and quantity are outcomes of a complex dynamic process involving the entry and exit of firms in response to profitable opportunities. If, for the data at hand, entry and exit are in approximate balance, the reduced-form dynamic model may well be replaced by a static interdependent equilibrium model.

This last example suggests a possible re-interpretation of the equilibrium systems given earlier. It can be argued (see, for example, Wold, 1954) that multi-agent models are necessarily recursive rather than simultaneous because it takes time for agents to respond to their environments. From this point of view, the usual supply–demand model is a simplification of a considerably more complex dynamic process. Demand and supply in fact depend on *lagged* prices; hence current price need not actually clear markets. However, the existence of excess supply or demand will result in price movement which in turn results in a change in consumer and producer behaviour next period. When time is explicitly introduced into the model, simultaneity disappears and the equations have simple causal interpretations. But, if response time is short and the available data are averages over a long period, excess demand may be close to zero for the available data. The static model with its simultaneity may be viewed as a limiting case, approximating a considerably more complex dynamic world. This interpretation of simultaneity as a limiting approximation is implicit in much of the applied literature and is developed formally in Strotz (1960).

THE NEED FOR STRUCTURAL ANALYSIS. These examples suggest that systems of simultaneous equations appear quite naturally when constructing economic models. Before discussing further their logic and interpretation, it will be useful to develop some notation. Let y be a vector of G endogenous variables describing the outcome of some economic process; let x be a vector of K 'predetermined' variables describing the conditions that determine those outcomes. (In dynamic models, lagged endogenous variables as well as the exogenous variables will be considered as conditions and included in x.) By a simultaneous equations model we mean a system of m equations relating y and x:

$$g_i(y, x) = 0 \qquad (i = 1, \ldots, m).$$

In the important special case where the functions are linear, the system can be written as the vector equation

$$By + \Gamma x = 0, \tag{1}$$

where B is an $m \times G$ matrix of coefficients, Γ is an $m \times K$ matrix of coefficients, and 0 is an m-dimensional vector of zeros. (The intercepts can be captured in the matrix Γ if we follow the convention that the first component of x is a 'variable' that always takes the value one.) A complete system occurs when $m = G$ and B is non-singular. Then the vector of outcome variables can be expressed as a linear function of the condition variables.

$$y = -B^{-1}\Gamma x = \Pi x. \tag{2}$$

Although the logic of the analysis applies for arbitrary models, the main issues can most easily be illustrated in this case of a complete linear system.

If both sides of the vector equation (1) are premultiplied by any $G \times G$ nonsingular matrix F, a new representation of the model is obtained, say

$$B^*y + \Gamma^*x = 0 \tag{3}$$

where $B^* = FB$ and $\Gamma^* = F\Gamma$. If F is not the identity matrix, the systems (1) and (3) are not identical. Yet if one representation is 'true' (that is, the real world observations satisfy the equation system) then the other is also 'true'. Which of the infinity of possible representations should we select? The obvious answer is that it does not matter. Any linear combination of equations is another valid equation. Any nonsingular transformation is as good as any other. For simplicity, one might as well choose the solved reduced form given by equation (2).

In practice, however, we are not indifferent between the various equivalent representations. There are a number of reasons for that. First, it may be that some representations are easier to interpret or easier to estimate. The first-order conditions for a profit maximizing firm facing fixed prices may, depending on the production function, be much simpler than the reduced form. Secondly, if we contemplate using the model to help analyse a changed regime, it is useful to have a representation in which the postulated changes are easily described. This latter concern leads to the concept of the degree of *autonomy* of an equation.

In the supply–demand model, it is easy to contemplate changes in the behaviour of consumers that leave the supply curve unchanged. For example, a shift in tastes may modify demand elasticities but have no effect on the cost conditions of firms. In that case, the supply curve is said to be autonomous with respect to this intervention in the causal mechanism. Equations that combine supply and demand factors (like the reduced form relating quantity traded to the exogenous variables) are not autonomous. The analysis of policy change is greatly simplified in models where the equations possess considerable autonomy. If policy changes one equation and leaves the other equations unchanged, its effects on the endogenous variables are easily worked out. Comparative static analysis as elucidated, for example, by Samuelson (1947) is based on this idea. Indeed, the power of the general equilibrium approach to economic analysis lies largely in its separation of the behaviour of numerous economic agents into autonomous equations.

As emphasized by the pioneers in the development of econometrics, it is not enough to construct models that fit a given body of facts. The task of the economist is to find models that successfully predict how the facts will change under specified new conditions. This requires knowing which relationships will remain stable after the intervention and which will not. It requires the model builder to express for every equation postulated the class of situations under which it will remain valid. The concept of autonomy and its importance in econometric model construction is emphasized in the classic paper by Haavelmo (1944) and in the expository paper by Marschak (1953). Sadly, it seems often to be ignored in applied work.

The autonomy of the equations appearing in commonly proposed models is often questionable. Lucas (1976) raises some important issues in his critique of traditional Keynesian macromodels. These simultaneous equations systems typically contain distributed lag relations which are interpreted as proxies for expectations. Suppose, for example, consumption really depends on expected future income. If people forecast the future based on the past, the unobserved expectation variable can be replaced by some function of past incomes. However, since income is endogenous, the actual time path of income depends on all the equations of the model. Under rational expectations, any change in the behaviour of other agents or in technology that affects the time path of income will also change the way people forecast and hence the distributed lag. Thus it can be argued that the traditional consumption function is not an autonomous relation with respect to most interesting policy interventions. Sims (1980) pursues this type of argument further, finding other reasons for doubting the autonomy of the equations in traditional macroeconomic models and concluding that policy analysis based on such models is highly suspect. Although one may perhaps disagree with Sims's conclusion, the methodological questions he raises cannot be ignored.

Even if one accepts the view that structural equations actually proposed in practice often possess limited autonomy and are not likely to be invariant to many interesting interventions, it may still be the case that these equations are useful. A typical reduced-form equation contains all the predetermined variables in the system. Given the existence of feedback, it is hard to argue a priori about the numerical values of the various elements of Π. It may be much easier to think about orders of magnitude for the structural coefficients. Our intuition about the behaviour of individual sectors of the economy is likely to be considerably better than our intuition about the general equilibrium solution. As long as there are no substantial structural changes, specification in term of structural equations may be appropriate even if some of the equations lack autonomy.

SOME ECONOMETRIC ISSUES. The discussion up to now has been in terms of exact relationships among economic variables. Of course, actual data do not lie on smooth monotonic curves of the type used in our theories. This is partially due to the fact that the experiments we have in the back of our mind when we postulate an economic model do not correspond exactly to any experiment actually performed in the world. Changing price, but holding everything else constant, is hypothetical and never observed in practice. Other factors, which we choose not to model, do in fact vary across our sample observations. Furthermore, we rarely pretend to know the true equations that relate the variables and instead postulate some approximate parametric family. In practice we work with models of the form

$$g_i(x, y, \theta, u_i) = 0 \qquad (i = 1, \ldots, m)$$

where the g's are known functions, θ is a vector of unknown parameters, and the u's are unobserved error terms reflecting the omitted variables and the misspecification of functional form. In the special case where the functions are linear in x and y with an additive error, the system can be written as

$$By + \Gamma x = u, \tag{4}$$

where u is a m-dimensional vector of errors. If B is non-singular, the reduced form is also linear and can be written as

$$y = -B^{-1}\Gamma x + B^{-1}u = \Pi x + v. \tag{5}$$

Equation system (4) as it stands is empty of content since, for any value of x and y, there always exists a value of u producing equality. Some restrictions on the error term are needed to make the system interesting. One common approach is to treat the errors as though they were draws from a probability distribution centred at the origin and unrelated to the predetermined variables. Suppose we have T observations on each of the $G + K$ variables, say, from T time periods or from T firms. We postulate that, for each observation, the data satisfy equation (4) where the parameters B and Γ are constant but the n error vectors $u_1, \ldots, u_T$ are independent random variables with zero means. Furthermore, we assume that the conditional distribution of u_t given the predetermined variables x_t for observation t is independent of x_i. A least-squares regression of each endogenous variable on the set of predetermined variables should then give good estimates of Π if the sample size is large and there is sufficient variability in the regressors. However, unless the inverse of B contains blocks of zeros, equation (5) implies that each of the endogenous variables is a function of all the components of u. In general, every element of y will be correlated with all the endogenous variables, if the correlation is small compared with the sample variation in those variables. able will result in biased parameter estimates.

The conclusion that structural parameters in interdependent systems can not be well estimated using least squares is widely believed by econometric theorists and widely ignored by empirical workers. There are probably two reasons for this discrepancy. First, although the logic of interdependent systems suggests that structural errors are likely to be correlated with all the endogenous variation, if the correlation is small compared with the sample variable in those variables, least squares bias will also be small. Given all the other problems facing the applied econometrician, this bias may be of little concern. Secondly, alternative estimation methods that have been developed often produce terrible estimates. Sometimes the only practical alternative to least squares is no estimate at all – a solution that is rarely chosen.

In some applications, the reduced form parameters Π are of primary concern. The structural parameters B and Γ are of interest only to the extent they help us learn about Π. For example, in a supply–demand model, we may wish to know the effect on price of changes in the weather. Price elasticities of supply and demand are not needed to answer that question. On the other hand, if we wish to know the effect of a sales tax on quantity produced, knowledge of the price elasticities might be essential. Although least squares is generally available for reduced form estimation (at least if the sample is large), it is not obvious that, without further assumptions, good structural estimates are ever attainable. The key assumption of the model is that the G structural errors are uncorrelated with the K predetermined variables. These GK orthogonality assumptions are just enough to determine (say by equating sample moments to population moments) the GK parameters in Π. But the structural coefficient matrices B and Γ contain $G^2 + GK$ elements. Even with G normalization rules that set the units in which the parameters of each equation will be measured, there are more coefficients than orthogonality conditions. It turns out that structural estimation is possible only if additional assumptions (e.g., that some elements of B and Γ are known a priori) are made. These considerations lead to three general classes of questions that have been addressed by theoretical econometricians: (1) When, in principle, can good structural estimates be found? (2) What are the best ways of actually estimating the structural parameters, given that it is possible? (3) Are there better ways of estimating the reduced-form parameters than by least squares?

These questions are studied in depth in standard econometrics textbooks and will not be examined here. The answers, however, do have a common thread. If each structural equation has more than K unknown parameters, structural estimation is generally impossible and least squares applied to the reduced form is optimal in large samples. If, on the other hand, each structural equation has fewer than K unknown coefficients, structural estimation generally is possible and least squares applied to the reduced form is no longer optimal. In this latter situation, various estimation procedures are available, some requiring little computational effort. However, the sample size may need to be quite large before these procedures are likely to give good estimates.

The assumption that the errors are independent from trial to trial is obviously very strong and quite implausible in time-series analysis. If the nature of the error dependence can be modelled and if the lag structure of the dynamic behavioural equations is correctly specified, most of the estimation results that follow under independence carry over. Unfortunately, with small samples, it is usually necessary to make crude (and rather arbitrary) specifications that may result in very poor estimates. Despite the fact that simultaneous equations analysis in practice is mostly applied to time series data, it can be argued that the statistical basis is much more convincing for cross-section analysis where samples are large and dependency across observations minimal. Even there, the assumption that the errors are unrelated to the predetermined variables must be justified before simultaneous equations estimation techniques can be applied.

THE ROLE OF SIMULTANEOUS EQUATIONS. Many applied economists seem to view the simultaneous equations model as having limited applicability, appropriate only for a very small subset of the problems actually met in practice. This is probably unwise. Estimated regression coefficients are commonly used to explain how an intervention which changes one explanatory variable will affect the dependent variable. Except for very special cases, this interpretation requires us to believe that the proposed intervention will not affect any of the other explanatory variables and that, in the sample, the errors were unrelated to the variation in the regressors. That is, the mechanism that determines the explanatory variables must be unrelated to the causal mechanism described by the equation under consideration. Unless the explanatory variables were in fact set in a carefully designed controlled experiment, viewing the explanatory variables as endogenous and possibly determined simultaneously with the dependent variable is a natural way to start thinking about the plausibility of the required assumptions.

In a sense, the simultaneous equations model is an attempt by economists to come to grips with the old truism that correlation is not the same as causation. In complex processes involving many decision-makers and many decision variables, we wish to discover stable relations that will persist over time and in response to changes in economic policy. We need to distinguish those equations that are autonomous with respect to the interventions we have in mind and those that are not. The methodology of the simultaneous equations model forces us to think about the experimental conditions that are envisaged when we write down an equation. It will not necessarily lead us to good parameter estimates, but it may help us to avoid errors.

THOMAS J. ROTHENBERG

See also ECONOMETRICS; ESTIMATION; MACROECONOMETRIC MODELS; MAXIMUM LIKELIHOOD.

BIBLIOGRAPHY

Haavelmo, T. 1944. The probability approach in econometrics. *Econometrica* 12, Supplement, July, 1–115.

Lucas, R. 1976. Econometric policy evaluation: a critique. In *The Phillips Curve and Labor Markets*, ed. K. Brunner and A. Meltzer, Carnegie-Rochester Conference Series on Public Policy No. 1, Amsterdam: North-Holland.

Marschak, J. 1953. Economic measurement for policy and prediction. In *Studies in Econometric Method*, ed. W. Hood and T. Koopmans, New York: Wiley.

Samuelson, P. 1947. *Foundations of Economic Analysis*. Cambridge, Mass.: Harvard University Press.

Sims, C. 1980. Macroeconomics and reality. *Econometrica* 48(1), January, 1–48.

Strotz, R. 1960. Interdependence as a specification error. *Econometrica* 28, April, 428–42.

Wold, H. 1954. Causality and econometrics. *Econometrica* 22, April, 162–77.

single tax. Single Tax is a generic label for the programme of Henry George and others to socialize land rent by substituting one heavy tax on land value for most other taxes. It is not an adequate descriptor but a slogan that caught on. 'Land Value Taxation' is more used today, especially for a limited tax by a local authority. In Scotland and England 'taxation of ground values' and 'site-value rating' are used.

Specifically, the 'Single Tax' slogan marked a shift in the movement after 1887 as George swung towards the Centre after purging the Marxists from his United Labour Party, losing Powderley and Gompers, and demurring to the quixotic demands of Fr. Edward McGlynn. He was losing Irish-American support from the hostility of Parnell and the Catholic hierarchy.

Thomas Shearman, a corporate lawyer, coined 'Single Tax' to differentiate George's free-market, pro-capitalist programme from those of others who had coalesced around him in the radical and protest awakening of 1879–87. Soon it also served to differentiate Georgism from Bellamy nationalism and Bryan inflationism. In Britain it distinguished Georgists from Wallace's land nationalizers, Hyndman's Marxists, Webb's Fabians, and Parnell's and Chamberlain's movements for peasant proprietorship.

A change of emphasis followed. George had originally striven for rent socialization, redistribution and augmented social spending. Critics on the Right saw too much taxation and levelling. The Single Tax slogan emphasized the counterpart benefits of relief from other taxes. Single Taxers would remove state and local property taxes from buildings and movable capital, and lower most transit and utility rates, often to zero, meeting deficits from the rent-fund (anticipating the marginal-cost pricing policies elaborated by Hotelling and Vickrey). Critics on the Left now saw too limited a revenue; so did machine Democrats, militarists, public contractors, and of course landholders seeking developmental public works at the general expense.

The heavy national taxes in America were tariffs. With *Protection or Free Trade*? (1886) George attacked them, invoking Quesnay, Ricardo, Cobden and Bright. Two million copies were printed, equalling his earlier *Progress and Poverty*. He supported Grover Cleveland in 1888 and 1892, hoping that free trade would force Congress to turn to land for revenues. Single Taxers in Congress succeeded in having the Income Tax Act of 1894 include land rent and unearned increments in the base, even though that was likely to be the grounds for its being held unconstitutional, and was. Single Tax began to connote tax limitation.

In *Protection or Free Trade?* George had restated the Physiocratic doctrine of tax incidence, while broadening it to include urban land, which most Physiocrats (except Turgot) had oddly excluded. There is only so much taxable surplus to tap under any system, and most of it lodges in land rent. Single Tax was simply the way to tax this surplus without what is now called the excess burden of indirect taxation. This might refute the charge of inadequacy, but the point has not been widely understood, and some still question revenue adequacy.

Shearman invited more such questions when he went another step from the Left with his 'Single Tax Limited', the upper limit being 2/3 of economic rent. To some adherents Single Tax is a tax limitation device. George remained a 'Single Taxer, Unlimited'. He held that taxation is only a means to Justice; Justice means every infant has an equal right to the Earth, its use and its rents. He remained a populist who supported Bryan in 1896, even though cold to the free silver panacea.

In Scotland and England George was active and well received by the radical wing of the Liberal Party. But Single Tax continued to mean an extreme position which moderates shunned, even when the Liberal Party put a land tax plank in its platform after Gladstone retired in 1895. Liberals under Asquith and Lloyd George introduced a token land tax in their 1909 budget. The Single Tax bogey frightened the Conservative members of the House of Lords into an intransigent obstructionism that alienated the voters and was used to consolidate the power of the Commons, the Liberals and Lloyd George, who then temporized away the land tax. Labour re-introduced a land tax in 1931 under MacDonald and Snowden, but Neville Chamberlain scuttled it finally in 1934. Postwar Labour Governments abandoned Single Tax as being too market-oriented.

Henry George died in 1897. Single Tax remained a power for another generation. Leaders like Shearman and Louis Post sought to professionalize the movement and reconcile it with middle-class values, a timely adaptation to the ethos of progress under scientific management. Somers, Pollock and Zangerle professionalized land assessment. Lawson Purdy helped found the National Tax Association. The Progressive and New Freedom movements absorbed many Single Taxers and reflected some of their ideals.

A century earlier at the court of Louis XV, François Quesnay and his Physiocrats had advanced the '*impôt unique*', an even more limited single tax restricted to farm land, and one-third the rent. Like Shearman, Quesnay argued efficiency and laissez-faire, not redistribution: it was the age of enlightened despotism, not of populism. They (and later their disciple Walras) called it 'co-proprietorship of land by the state'.

But there is a touch of class-levelling inherent in any proposal to tax land directly, however sugar-coated with the doctrine that landholders gain from removing other taxes; however limited by the safeguard of 'co-proprietorship'. Physiocracy could beguile a despot dreaming of energizing a decadent gentry, and liberating his people from tax farmers and a jumble of enervating excises that weakened France's economy. It was the fate of Quesnay, and of France, that the privileged gentry proved more sensitive to Physiocracy's threat than others were to its benefits.

Quesnay was closer than he knew to an age of populism; he might better have addressed the new constituency. Indirectly he did through his influence on Jefferson, transmitted through his disciples Pierre Samuel Du Pont and Destutt de Tracy; and through his influence on Smith, Ricardo and Mill, whose special treatment of land rent set the stage for George's Single Tax.

MASON GAFFNEY

See also GEORGE, HENRY.

BIBLIOGRAPHY

Brown, H.G. 1932. *The Economic Basis of Tax Reform*. Columbia, Missouri: Lucas Bros.

Douglas, R. 1976. *Land, People and Politics*. London: Allison & Busby.

Geiger, G.R. 1936. *The Theory of the Land Question*. New York: Macmillan.

Groenewegen, P.D. (ed. and trans.) 1977. *The Economics of A.R.J. Turgot*. The Hague: Martinus Nijhoff.

Holland, D.M. (ed.) 1970. *The Assessment of Land Value*. Madison: University of Wisconsin Press.

Howe, F.C. 1925. *Confessions of a Reformer*. New York: Chares Scribner's Sons.

Lindholm, R.W. and Lynn, A.D., Jr. (eds) 1981. *Land Value Taxation in Thought and Practise*. Madison: University of Wisconsin Press.

Lissner, W. (ed.) 1941–. *The American Journal of Economics and Sociology*. New York: Robert Schalkenbach Foundation.

Miller, J.D. (ed.) 1917. *Single Tax Yearbook*. New York: Single Tax Review Publishing Co.

Scott, A. (ed.) *Natural Resource Revenues: a Test of Federalism*. Vancouver: University of British Columbia Press.

Shearman, T. 1888. *Natural Taxation*. 2nd edn, New York: Doubleday, 1911.

Skouras, A. 1977. *Land and its Taxation in Recent Economic Theory*. Athens: Papazissis Publishers.

Young, A.N. 1916. *History of the Single Tax Movement in the United States*. Princeton: Princeton University Press.

Sismondi, Jean Charles Leonard Simonde de (1773–1842). A number of concepts and theories that later became important in the history of economics first appeared in the writings of the Swiss economist J.C.L. Simonde de Sismondi. Whether or not these can be considered as his 'contributions' to economics is a question not unlike that as to whether a tree that falls in a deserted forest makes a sound. Sismondi developed the first aggregate equilibrium income theory and the first algebraic growth model. Yet both concepts had to be rediscovered and redeveloped by others before they entered the mainstream of economics, long after Sismondi's time. The fact that Sismondi wrote in French may have been part of the reason why his work made so little impact at a time when the development of classical economics was largely the work of British economists. However, the fame achieved by his French contemporary, Jean-Baptiste Say, suggests that language differences alone cannot explain the neglect of Sismondi. His economic writings were neglected in France and Switzerland as well.

When he was born in Geneva in 1773, his name was Jean Charles Leonard Simonde. After an exile in Italy, during which he determined that he was descended from a noble Italian family named Sismondi, he returned to Geneva in 1800 with his new surname, Simonde de Sismondi. However, he was sufficiently tentative about it to use his original name on his first book in economics, *De la richesse commerciale, in* 1803. Sismondi also wrote extensively on history, including a 16-volume history of Italy. All his writings were pervaded by considerations of public policy in general, and the interests of the less fortunate in particular.

Sismondi was born into a prosperous bourgeois family, which was despoiled of much of its wealth during Swiss political upheavals reflecting the contemporary revolution in France. Shifting political fortunes led not only to Sismondi's exile but to two imprisonments as well. After the turmoil subsided, Sismondi worked at a variety of occupations, including gentleman farmer and professor of philosophy.

Sismondi's first venture into economics, the two-volume *De la richesse commerciale*, was intended as a systematic exposition of the ideas of Adam Smith. Yet in it Sismondi also pointed out that he was presenting an 'absolutely new' way of looking at aggregate output changes. Crude arithmetic examples depicted output during a given year as a function of investment during a previous year, and showed how a closed economy differed from an economy with international trade, and how the latter differed when there was an export surplus and an import surplus. Algebraic formulas in his footnotes repeated the same arguments presented arithmetically in the text. But the book was little noticed, and so Sismondi's original efforts produced no contribution to the development of economics.

In the wake of the post-Napoleonic War depression, Sismondi turned his attention once more to economics and to issues of aggregate income equilibrium. In 1814, he produced a long article entitled 'Political Economy', written in English for the *Edinburgh Encyclopaedia.* In the midst of a summary presentation of classical economics appeared an early version of Sismondi's own theory of aggregate equilibrium income. Four years later, this theory was elaborated in Sismondi's main economic work, the two-volume *Nouveaux principes d'économie politique*. With this work he entered the controversy over Say's Law and general gluts.

According to Sismondi, the utility of output was balanced against the disutility of work, whether by Robinson Crusoe on an island or by a complex society. But, with different people doing partial balancing in isolation from one another in a complex economy, the aggregate balance was not always continuously assured. Whenever the disutility of labour exceeded the utility of output in a given time period, subsequent time periods would see a decline in aggregate output until the balance was restored. Conversely, when the utility of output exceeded that of labour, output would tend to rise.

The germ of this reasoning had already appeared in *L'Ordre naturel* by the Physiocrat Mercier de la Rivière in 1767. Sismondi elaborated it into a theory of equilibrium income, with which he challenged the reigning view, expressed in Say's Law, that there were no limits to production.

Say's Law, then as later, had many meanings. But one of the contemporary meanings was that there was no such thing as an equilibrium level of aggregate output. Whatever level of output was supplied could always find a demand, and where this did not happen, it was because the assortment of goods did not match consumer preferences, not because the total output was at an unsustainable level. Sismondi rejected this reasoning, arguing that the demand for leisure would at some point outweigh the demand for other goods, and that when production went beyond the point at which this happened, it would be unsaleable at cost-covering prices and so fail to be reproduced in subsequent time periods.

Sismondi understood the full implications of what he was saying and how it contradicted prevailing views. The balance of aggregate supply and demand he considered the most important question in economics, and especially so during the depression following the Napoleonic wars. J.B. Say and the Ricardians maintained that the unsaleability of some goods showed only that insufficient other goods had been produced to exchange with them – that output had the wrong internal proportions, not an excess in the aggregate, and that the proper proportions could be restored at a still higher level of aggregate production. In this view, there could be a partial glut of particular commodities but not a *general* glut of commodities.

Sismondi argued that there could be a general glut of commodities because one of the goods desired was leisure – that is, exemption from the production of commodities. He did not believe that this occurred in the normal course of free market competition but because government policy sometimes artificially fostered production at an unsustainable level. Like the orthodox economists of his time, Sismondi regarded money as an unessential factor, a 'veil' obscuring but not fundamentally changing the behaviour of economic aggregates. His disagreements with the classical economists had nothing to do with monetary controversies such as those in 20th-century macroeconomics.

When Sismondi's *Nouveaux principes* appeared in 1819, it was immediately attacked in the *Edinburgh Review* in October of that year, in the midst of a discussion of Robert Owen. Its reasoning was declared a 'fallacy' and once more 'proportions' – not aggregates – were declared to be the only prerequisites for markets to be cleared and increased output sustained. A glut was there defined as 'an increase in the supply of a particular class of commodities, unaccompanied by a corresponding increase in the supply of those other commodities which should serve as their equivalents'. In short, there were partial gluts but no general gluts and a still higher level of output was sustainable if properly proportioned internally. The basis of this reasoning was explicitly attributed to 'the celebrated M. Say', with a 'most clear and conclusive' treatment of the subject added by James Mill.

The appearance of T.R. Malthus's *Principles of Political Economy* the following year added fuel to the debate, for he too challenged Say's Law in the same way. Marx later characterized Malthus's book as simply the 'English translation' of Sismondi, but in fact it represented views which Malthus had long expressed in correspondence with Ricardo. Replies to both authors began to appear in both French and English publications during the 1820s, provoking rejoinders in books and articles. Their controversy over general gluts persisted for more than a decade, involving not only the leading economists of the time – Say, Ricardo, Malthus, Sismondi, Torrens, McCulloch and both Mills – but also Samuel Bailey, William Blake, Thomas Chalmers, and others either forgotten or little remembered in the history of economics. These published controversies were supplemented by correspondence between Sismondi and Say, Sismondi and Ricardo, Malthus and Say, and Malthus and Ricardo. Only Say seems to have acknowledged that the theory of aggregate equilibrium income had relevance to one version of Say's Law that was current at the time. In the fifth edition of his *Traité d'économie politique* in 1826 he added three paragraphs to his chapter on the law of markets, discussing 'the limit to a growing production' and repeating (without citation) Sismondi's argument that when output's 'utility is not worth what it cost', such output is unsustainable. A year later he admitted in a letter to Malthus that his law of markets was 'subject to some restrictions' which he had included in the most recent edition of his book. (Unfortunately, the English translation of Say's *Traité* is from the previous edition.) Finally, in a textbook published in 1828–9, Say followed the chapter on his law of markets with a chapter entitled, 'Limits to Production' – a phrase from Sismondi.

No such impact or even acknowledgement occurred in British economic writings. There Sismondi and Malthus were answered as if they were arguing for secular stagnation instead of temporary aggregate disequilibrium. John Stuart Mill enshrined this misunderstanding of Sismondi and Malthus in his classic *Principles of Political Economy* in 1848. Thus things stood for nearly a century, until John Maynard Keynes resurrected Malthus, but not Sismondi, as his predecessor in aggregate equilibrium theory.

Sismondi's anticipations of later economic theory were not limited to aggregate income theory. In the course of dealing with that large topic he also proposed a theory of destabilizing responses to overproduction, which would initially take the economy further from equilibrium, though it would ultimately return to equilibrium 'after a frightful suffering'. He also dealt with the issue of the short-run shut down point of a firm, which he argued would produce even below cost-covering prices if much of its cost was fixed rather than variable. Sismondi also argued against the reigning Malthusian population theory, pointing out fatal ambiguities in the word 'tendency' as Malthus used it and using empirical evidence to show that the *historical* tendency was for food supply to grow faster than population.

In many ways Sismondi also anticipated Marx. Sismondi's emphasis on 'the proletarians', on an increasing concentration of capital, recurring business cycles, technological unemployment and economic dynamics in general all reappeared (without credit) in Marx's writings.

None of these pioneering efforts by Sismondi received either contemporary acknowledgement or later recognition by the profession. His loose and sometimes inconsistent writings and his emotional assertions made it easy to dismiss him and throw away his insights along with his errors. He left no disciples and his eclecticism provided no dogma around which a school could crystallize.

THOMAS SOWELL

SELECTED WORKS

1814. *Political Economy*. New York: Augustus M. Kelley, 1966.
1819. *Nouveaux principes d'économie politique*. Paris: Delaunay, 1827.

BIBLIOGRAPHY

Rappard, W.E. 1966. *Economistes Genèvois du XIXe siècle*. Geneva: Libraire Droz, 1966, 330–54.
Salis, R. de. 1932. *Sismondi, 1775–1842*. Paris: Libraire Ancienne Honoré Champion.
Sowell, T. 1968. Sismondi: a neglected pioneer. *History of Political Economy* 1, Spring, 62–88.

slavery. Slavery entails the ownership of one person by another. As a form of labour organization it has existed throughout history, in a large number of different societies. Indeed, while today we regard slavery as 'the peculiar institution', by historical standards it is wage-labour markets that are 'unusual'. Given slavery's long and varied history a precise definition is not always agreed upon, but there are certain general characteristics found in most societies. The status of slave is generally applied to outsiders – individuals not belonging to the dominant nation, religion, or race – although the definition of exactly who is an outsider has varied; Orlando Patterson (1982) considers the basic characteristic of slavery to be 'social death', with a loss of honour as well as legal rights by the enslaved. So widespread and acceptable was slavery that in Europe and the Americas no movement developed to attack slavery as a system until the late 18th century. In Western thought slavery had long been regarded as a necessity or as a 'necessary evil'. The pre-19th-century discussions of slavery often pointed to the desirability (on grounds of religion and morality) of ameliorating the conditions of the enslaved or of facilitating the liberation of individual slaves, but it was only in the late 18th century that widespread thought was given to abolishing the institution itself (see Davis, 1966; 1975; 1984).

THE ECONOMIC BASIS OF SLAVERY. In some societies, particularly at low levels of income, slavery was entered into voluntarily as a means of obtaining a minimum level of living. Slavery generally played a quite different role in such cases than in the major slave societies of Greece, Rome, Brazil, the United States South and the West Indies (see Finley, 1980), where slave labour was used on large-scale agricultural units and in mines to produce goods to be sold in foreign or urban markets. These major slave societies were marked by an extensive external trade in slaves – war captives, kidnapped or otherwise acquired.

The economic basis of slavery seems quite straightforward (see, however, Pryor, 1977). While slavery existed in some parts of the world to provide prestige to owners or for purposes of lineage needs, slavery as an economic institution generally persisted because it provided slaveowners with an ability to capture a surplus of the value of production above the costs of the slave's subsistence. In 1900 the Dutch ethnographer H.J. Nieboer presented a detailed comparative study of slavery throughout the world. He argued that at relatively primitive stages of production, among hunters and fishers and in pastoral societies, slavery was generally nonexistent. It was only with the development of settled agriculture in areas with productive land still available, that slavery became widespread. The role of 'open resources' – free land – has been more formally presented by Evsey Domar (1970), who argues that only two of the following three conditions can hold simultaneously: free land, free peasants and non-working landowners. The basic argument is that if it were possible for workers to produce more than their subsistence, with unrestricted mobility they would move to freely available land; it is only with a form of labour coercion (serfdom or slavery) that landowners can obtain an income. The benefit of coerced labour to the slaveowner involves a redistribution of that part of the income above subsistence that would go to a free worker. Thus if everything (e.g. crops grown, slave and free productivity, etc.) were equal, slavery would provide a means of redistributing the excess above subsistence from the labourer to the landed slaveowner.

While this model of forced redistribution points to the need for slave output to exceed subsistence to make the system desirable to slaveowners, it is incomplete as an explanation for most large-scale slave economies. The critical point has been that free labourers have avoided certain types of labour – producing certain crops, or working in certain locations, as well as limiting their labour force participation. Thus slavery expanded the available labour supply, and was particularly important to the production of certain outputs – from mines and in large-scale agricultural units – for which labour would have been available only at very high prices needed to offset non-pecuniary aspects of the labour process (Barzel, 1977). It is the existence of crops such as sugar, for which free labour cannot easily be attracted, that explains the development of New World slavery and accounts for the fact that where slavery has been economically important the slaves have performed functions quite different from those of free labourers.

The Domar–Nieboer argument, by itself, explains neither the existence of slavery as a form of coerced labour nor even the actual existence of coerced labour. The theoretical point is consistent with any form of coerced labour– slavery as well as serfdom – with the general pattern being that slavery dominated where it was necessary to move more labour into an area. The availability of free land by itself can have a quite opposite impact, as Adam Smith (1776) and others argued was the case for the northern states of the United States. There, free land (and labour mobility) meant a wider distribution of property and a more egalitarian society. The conditions for a successful cartel of slaveowners require methods of restricting the movement of the labour force, measures precluding direct bargaining between labourers and potential owners, and means of identifying and returning those slaves who attempt to leave the system. Why such restrictions would not be enforced against Europeans was no doubt the outcome of various cultural, religious and racial forces, so that the availability of free land provided quite different outcomes in the northern and in the southern states. Importantly, different technologies of crop production – the larger optimum scale for cotton, sugar, rice and tobacco, in comparison with the family farm for grains – meant that some form of coerced labour was needed to attract workers onto the southern plantations, while the prices of slaves became too high to permit large numbers of slave imports into the north.

Between the ending of Roman slavery and the origins of large-scale slavery in the New World settlements of the European powers, slavery persisted throughout Europe, but the relative absence of a large trading sector and the limited need to attract a larger population to new areas of settlement meant that slavery was generally economically unimportant and serfdom was a more frequent form of labour organization.

THE TRANSATLANTIC SLAVE TRADE. The slave trade westward from Africa began with the movement of African slaves to the offshore islands by Portuguese traders in the middle of the 15th century. From that year until the last slave was landed in Cuba in the late 1860s, more than 10 million Africans landed in the New World. Allowing for death in the 'Middle Passage' about 12 million slaves left Africa (Curtin, 1969; Lovejoy, 1983). Higher numbers for the impact of the slave trade on Africa have been presented, allowing for deaths between enslavement and shipment, as well as for estimates of the deaths due to military actions which led to enslavement. While the transatlantic slave trade was most intense in terms of numbers carried per year, it has been estimated that the trans-Saharan slave trade to Arabia and the Middle East may have carried a comparable number over a longer time span. It appears, however, that except for some small areas, the slave trade did not lead to depopulation within Africa. And, although slavery had long existed in Africa, many believe that it was the European contact that transformed African slavery into a harsher institution.

Most countries of Western Europe were involved in the Atlantic slave trade, and slaves were sent to all parts of the Americas. Although the high-risk nature meant that some voyages could be very profitable, recent work has cast doubt on the argument that the slave trade provided abnormal profits to European traders, given the African control of the inland traffic and competition among shippers. The first attacks upon slavery were aimed at restricting the transatlantic shipments of Africans. The British, after initial regulatory legislation beginning in 1788, and the United States, as a result of a constitutional compromise permitting its outlawing, ended the slave trade in 1808. Denmark, a minor carrier, had ended the slave trade in 1802. Due to British pressures other countries ended their slave trades, although the 'illegal' slave trade to Cuba and Brazil did not end until after mid-century (Eltis, 1987).

The slave trade was linked to European overseas expansion and played an important part in the settlement of the Caribbean colonies. Because of its early start and late ending Brazil was the largest of the New World recipients of slaves. Large numbers were sent to the British and the French West Indian colonies, whose populations soon became 80 to 90 per cent enslaved blacks. The United States, which was to become the largest slaveholding nation in the 19th century, received only a small part of the African slave trade, its large population being due to the unusually rapid rate of natural increase of the slave population. Cuba rose to dominance as a sugar producer in the 19th century but, unlike the other major sugar-producing Caribbean islands, its population was only about one-third slave, a ratio similar to that in Brazil and in the United States at that time.

The major use of slave labour during the period of the slave trade was in the production of sugar (see Deerr, 1949–50; Klein, 1986). In the case of mainland North America, although slavery existed in every colony, the major uses of slave labour in the 18th century were for tobacco production in the Chesapeake and rice and indigo production in South Carolina. Cotton was grown in the West Indies and Brazil and, after the invention of the cotton gin in 1793, it became the most important crop produced by slave labour in the United States. These and other slave-grown crops in the Americas, such as coffee and cocoa, were grown on units larger than the family farm.

SLAVERY IN THE AMERICAS. In the Americas, after some initial attempts at the enslavement of the native Americans, the condition of slave became limited to Africans and their descendants. The black–white ratio was generally highest in the Caribbean, declining as one moved north and south. There were pronounced differences in the demographic performance of slave populations in the Americas, as reflected in differences between the total number of slaves imported and the number of blacks in various areas. The most dramatic and widely noted differences were seen between the United States and the West Indies. In the West Indies, with few exceptions, the slave population was unable to maintain its numbers, and there was a continued need for new slaves brought from Africa. In the British Caribbean, for example, it is estimated that the approximately two million Africans received before 1808 left a population of only about 780,000 blacks at the time of emancipation (1834). The United States provided a quite different case – unique for a slave population and unusual for any population. There an estimated 600,000 slaves imported resulted in black population of over 2.3 million in 1830, rising to about 4.4 million in 1860. The relatively high death rates during the period euphemistically known as 'seasoning' (the initial period of exposure to the new disease environment) accounts for some of the correlation between imports and mortality. Despite claims at the time there seems little evidence that planters systematically either worked slaves to death or deliberately engaged in the breeding of slaves.

There was both a considerably higher birth rate for slaves in the United States than in the West Indies (a rate about equal to that of United States whites, about 50 per cent above that in Europe and the West Indies), as well as a lower death rate. The higher birth rate was due in part to an earlier onset of menarche in the United States (due to better nutrition), a shorter child-spacing interval (reflecting differences in lactation practices) and a higher frequency of childbearers among adult women (due perhaps to differences in working conditions as well as in nutrition and health care) (see Steckel, 1985). The lower death rate reflected, in part, the differences between the location and work routines of tropical sugar plantations and the major uses of slave labour in the United States – tobacco and cotton (see Higman, 1984).

Recent studies of the New World slave economies indicate that, despite arguments of contemporaries and subsequent scholars, slavery was expanding throughout its period of existence and that there were no signs that slavery was becoming unprofitable and non-viable on economic grounds. Slave prices in Brazil, Cuba and the United States peaked around 1860 (Moreno Fraginals, Klein and Engerman, 1983). The United States Civil War ended slavery there, and while prices in Brazil and Cuba declined somewhat from peak levels, they remained higher than they had been before mid-century, until there were clear signals that the system was soon to be ended legislatively. The basic importance of labour coercion in sugar production can also be seen in the drive to import contract labour from India, China and Africa, in the West Indies after the ending of slavery – in some cases (most importantly Cuba) even while slavery still existed.

Whatever alternatives may be argued to have been ultimately in their self-interest, throughout the 19th century (and earlier) slavery was profitable to planters. Rather than facing economic difficulties, planters were benefiting from the increased European demands for sugar, cotton, coffee and other plantation commodities. Despite the theoretical logic of the arguments by Cairnes (1862) and others about the ultimate limits to slavery's profitability, for the major slave powers of the New World emancipation required political or military action to overcome a profitable slave economy in which few planters anticipated an immediate collapse in the productive value of their principal assets.

EMANCIPATION AND ITS ECONOMIC EFFECTS. Several states of the northern United States ended slavery by judicial or legislative measures between the Revolutionary War and the early 19th-century, as did several of the formerly Spanish colonies after their independence was achieved in the first part of the 19th century, but these were areas where slavery was relatively unimportant. The major sugar-producing area of Saint Domingue (now Haiti) ended slavery, as the result of a major slave revolt, by the start of the 19th century, and after violently opposing attempts by its new leaders to reintroduce a plantation economy to produce sugar, it became an area devoted to small-scale peasant production.

The first major area to end slavery after the Haitian Revolution was the British West Indies in 1834. The legislation passed in 1833 in response to a decade of pressure by the antislavery movement, provided for (1) a cash payment to owners and slaves of £20 million based on (but less than one-half of) the 1823–30 market values; and (2) an 'apprenticeship' of from four to six years, depending upon the slave's occupation. It is estimated that the value of the monetary compensation, plus the labour dictated by apprenticeship, would be nearly equal to the average 1823–30 value of slaves although, as the slaveowners pointed out, the loss in the value of land due to emancipation was not compensated (Fogel and Engerman, 1974b). The period of apprenticeship was terminated in 1838.

Metropolitan legislations ended slavery, with compensation, in the French West Indies and in the Danish West Indies in 1848, and in the Dutch colonies in 1863. The American Civil War provided an uncompensated end to United States slavery with the passage of the Thirteenth Amendment. The Moret Law of 1870 provided that all those born to slave mothers in Cuba and Puerto Rico (which then ended slavery, with compensation to masters, in 1873) were considered free, subject to a period of compelled labour. The Rio Branco Law of 1871 in Brazil included a similar provision – a 'law of the free womb' – with a period of controlled labour. In Cuba slavery was ended in 1880, subject to a proposed eight-year period of *patronato*, which was terminated in 1886. In Brazil slavery was ended without compensation in 1888.

The causes of this century-long process of emancipation have become a major historical controversy, with particular attention given to the movements in England and the United States. For England, the view that emancipation was the outcome of disinterested humanitarianism came under attack with the economic interpretation of Eric Williams (1944), which related the timing of the ending of the slave trade and of slave emancipation to the British industrial revolution. While the specific groups and mechanisms remain debated, the linkage now stresses the rise of individualism, the 'free labour ideology' and 'modernization', all of which meant that slavery was considered an unacceptable arrangement. Similarly for the United States the link between the 'free labour ideology' and anti-slavery has become central to the interpretation of various political issues of the 1850s which culminated in the Civil War.

The economic effects of slavery upon production can be seen clearly in the general patterns of output that developed after the emancipation of the slaves in most areas. With few exceptions, emancipation led to initial declines in the level of output, with particularly sharp declines in the production of the staple export commodities (Engerman, 1982). There was a movement of ex-slaves away from the plantation sector into small-scale agriculture. The ending of slavery thus demonstrated anew why most New World slavery had developed – people, given free choice, preferred not to work on plantations producing staple crops for exports, since landowners would (or could) not provide sufficient wages to provide an adequate voluntary plantation force from the local population.

There were, however, several notable exceptions. In Barbados the end of slavery did not end the plantation system nor did it lead to declines in sugar production. Rather the labour-to-land ratio was already so high that land for the ex-slaves to move to was unavailable. Barbados thus maintained its plantation sector, while serving as an area for labour outflow to other parts of the Caribbean through the 19th and 20th centuries. Another important exception was Cuba. By the time of emancipation the rise of the large central mill utilizing cane from smaller farms permitted an alternative there which offset the impact of declines in the plantation labour force, and so the output of sugar did not decline after slavery ended.

The two largest slave economies, the United States and Brazil, were nations where slave labour did not reach the proportionate dominance that it did in most of the Caribbean and they had rather different problems. United States sugar, rice, cotton and tobacco production declined with emancipation, with output recovering pre-Civil War levels subsequently, at speeds that were in inverse relation to the optimum scale of plantation production – tobacco and cotton recovering fastest, and sugar and rice least rapidly. Dramatic regional shifts occurred, with prolonged declines in the older tobacco areas of Virginia and the ultimate transfer of rice production from its antebellum base in South Carolina and Georgia to Louisiana. Cotton production expanded quickly after the post-emancipation decline, recovering antebellum peaks within a decade and the United States regained its dominance in world markets by 1880. Yet plantation production declined, and there emerged a system of small-scale farms, often sharecropped, which were less productive than were antebellum plantations; and while most blacks remained within the cotton sector, increased numbers of whites became involved in the cotton economy. Unlike most other ex-slave societies, with this expansion of cotton production the South was exporting a higher proportion of its agricultural output than before emancipation.

In Brazil, the emancipation of slaves had a sharp initial impact upon the expanding coffee industry. Recovery occurred with a decline in the importance of plantations and a shift in the nature of the labour force, with the attraction of immigrants from southern Europe (mainly Italy) to produce on small units. A move to smaller farms producing sugar for central mills also permitted recovery in the production of sugar, with limited numbers of ex-slaves remaining in sugar production.

This general pattern of ex-slave withdrawal from plantation work was a characteristic of the post-emancipation period throughout the Americas. Important in some parts of the Caribbean after slave emancipation was the attraction of a new labour force from overseas, through indentured labour transported under contract to work on plantations for specified periods of time. The areas of the British Caribbean expanding in the late slave period – Trinidad and British Guiana – regained pre-emancipation levels of sugar output within a plantation-based economy. The labour force on the plantations was not primarily ex-slave, but rather indentured labour brought in from Africa, Madeira, China and India, the latter being the predominant group. This system of contract labour had been employed initially in the British Indian Ocean colony of Mauritius. Called 'a new system of slavery', contract labour was a widely discussed and regulated form of labour movement by metropolitan powers as well as in areas of outflow and inflow until its abolition in 1917. The importance of the problem of maintaining a labour force on a continuous basis on sugar plantations is seen also in the expansion of contract labour from foreign areas to the newly emerging sugar-producing regions, such as Fiji, Hawaii, Natal and Australia, in the late 19th century. As late as 1880, the production of most cane sugar that entered export markets took place in areas where the predominant plantation labour force was based either on slavery or indentured labour (Engerman, 1983).

SLAVERY IN ECONOMIC THOUGHT. The consideration of slavery in the literature of economics has helped shape subsequent interpretations of the slave economy. Adam Smith (1776) has been the most frequently quoted economist against slavery, his arguments featuring in contemporary debates as well as historical writings. To Smith slavery was an inefficient system: the slave lacked incentives to work as well as to innovate in technological change. Smith explained the existence of slavery in the production of such crops as sugar and tobacco as indicative that these were so profitable that they could afford to utilize slave labour, something not possible with less profitable crops such as corn. Smith drew upon existing arguments, his proposition on relative incentives having a long history going back to the classical world; but Smith's reputation as a political economist served to make his arguments a central component in the emerging anti-slavery argument. Recent views on Smith stress less that he was presenting an empirical proposition than that his remarks on slavery should be regarded as a basic ideological statement.

Several of the classical economists, for example McCulloch (1825) and Mill (1848), agreed with Smith's contention as to the relative effectiveness of slave and free labour when both were undertaking the same type of work, but they stressed that slavery seemed essential for production in areas and in conditions where free labour could not be obtained, particularly in tropical areas for the production of plantation crops. These, however, they regarded either as special cases (where a different economics applied) or else a transient stage (of undefined duration) along the road to free labour.

The most systematic writer on the economics of slavery was John Elliot Cairnes, whose *The Slave Power* (1862) focused on the United States and combined a theoretical analysis of slave labour with a propagandistic attempt to influence British opinion during the Civil War. He argued that slave labour was inefficient – it is given reluctantly; it is unskillful; it is wanting in versatility – and that it precluded southern economic development because of its negative effects upon technology and upon the attitudes of the free white population towards labour. Cairnes did allow that slavery could survive under certain unusual or temporary conditions – the availability of new lands which would offset the retarding effects of the land exhausted by slave labour. This statement, one of theoretical tendencies, was consistent with arguments that expansion was economically necessary for the southern economy. The role of the increasing ratio of labour-to-land in ending slavery's profitability in the long run was also a theme of various American writers of the early 19th century, and the same point re-emerged in the historiography of United States slavery in the 1920s, with arguments about the natural limits of slavery's expansion, the imminent unprofitability of slavery and the 'needless' Civil War.

Discussions of the economic role of slavery and the causes of its ending were often presented in the 19th and 20th centuries. Yet because of the ideological views of many writers and the emotive implications of slavery it was often difficult to secure entirely accurate descriptions. To the Marxist, slavery is an inefficient economic system, incapable of high levels of productivity and of technical innovation – a system which, however necessary in its time, is incapable of generating sustained economic development. The decline of Roman slavery was thus attributed to its inability to innovate and adapt, and the re-emerged slavery of the modern world was similarly doomed to defeat in economic competition with the capitalistic order. (The relation of slavery and capitalism has itself become a debated subject, even among Marxists.) So, in the examination of the slave economies of the Americas, a perhaps surprising consistency of opinion between those coming from the classical, laissez-faire tradition and those coming from a Marxist perspective meant that a view of slavery as a backward, inefficient economic system had come to dominate the economic and historical literature on slavery.

ECONOMIC HISTORY AND THE ECONOMICS OF SLAVERY. In the mid-20th century, work of a detailed empirical nature on slavery in the British Caribbean and in the United States was expanded. This has provided more detailed information as well as having led to new questions and issues being studied. Perhaps the dominant figure in the historiography of the British West Indies has been Eric Williams, the late Prime Minister of Trinidad and Tobago, whose most famous work *Capitalism and Slavery* (1944) dealt with three topics of importance: (1) the link of slavery and racism; (2) the role of slavery and the slave trade in the British Industrial Revolution; and (3) the impact of a declining West Indian economy upon the British abolition of the slave trade and the emancipation of slaves. Williams argued that it was the need for a cheap labour force that led to slavery, and that the justification for enslavement of Africans led to the development of racist beliefs about blacks – a view which remains the subject of a major historical controversy. Using arguments provided by contemporaries justifying the slave trade, Williams traced an important role in financing and in providing markets for British industrial development to the slave economies of the West Indies and the slave trade with Africa. Williams's last two propositions have formed the basis of much of the recent work on slavery in West Indian economic history. Recent writings point to a more limited role for slavery and the slave trade in the British industrialization than that advanced by Williams. Even more attention has been devoted to the question of the conditions for the abolition of slavery and its link to a possible decline of the economies of the British West Indies. The thesis of decline has come under strong attack, particularly by Seymour Drescher (1977), who argues that the politically mandated end of the slave trade led to declining West Indian economic fortunes, and not vice versa. The issue of the specifics of the movement to end the slave trade, and the relative contributions of ideological, class and economic forces has become a central historical issue (see Drescher, 1986; Solow and Engerman, 1987).

In the United States there has been a more specific concern by economists and economic historians with issues related to the economics of slavery. A key breakthrough in the new approach to the economics of slavery was an article by Conrad and Meyer (1958) which dealt with the profitability of antebellum slavery. This article was concerned with a major historical issue – was slavery economically unprofitable in the late antebellum period? – and was also intended more generally to demonstrate the value of an economic approach to historical problems. By framing the issue as one of the rate of return on investment, and using available data on interest rates, slave prices, life expectation, costs of consumption by slaves and of their supervision, and crop production and prices, they argued that a planter purchasing a slave at the market price in the late antebellum period would have earned a return equal to that upon alternative assets. The response to this article – both positive and negative, in regard to substance as well as method – has been enormous, and the economics of slavery became one of the most heated and widely discussed topics in American history. It was seen, however, that profitability, as measured by 'normal' profits on an existing asset, did not really adequately answer the question of the possible economic ending of slavery in the absence of the Civil War, since the comparison had been based on market price, and not on the cost of 'producing' a slave.

An analysis by Yasukichi Yasuba (1961) pointed out that, given the illegality of slave imports and the constraints on the demographic expansion of the slave population, the market price of slaves could exceed the costs of rearing slaves, yielding a rent to the slaveowning class (see also Evans, 1962). Yasuba showed that the surplus above rearing costs for slaves was rising in the late antebellum period, peaking just before the onset of the Civil War. Thus far from being on the verge of economic collapse, slavery was becoming more profitable to the slaveowning class, who did not foresee an economic end to their system in the immediate future. The linking of Easterlin's regional income estimates with Gallman's GNP estimates for 1840 to 1860, indicated that the South was growing about as rapidly in terms of per capita income as was the North, and in 1860 had reached a level of per capita income above that of the agrarian Midwest and most of the rest of the world (Fogel and Engerman, 1971, 1974a). While these estimates cover only a limited time span, they did help to provide a different view of the dynamics of the southern slave economy.

Questions of profitability, viability, and rates of growth of income were not seen, however, as of central historical interest by historians such as Eugene Genovese (1965), who argued that the important questions concerned rather the development and potential for industrialization in the slave economy, reflected particularly in the differences in economic structure in comparison with that of the northern states, as well as the political issues posed by the differing class structures of the two societies. It is argued that the antebellum expansion of the South was due to the demand for one major crop, cotton, leading to a less diversified and industrialized economy than in the North – a growth that could not be sustained. At debate remain the causes and consequences of the southern specialization in agriculture rather than the development of a larger manufacturing sector, and the implications of the limited industrialization, urbanization, and expansion of education (in comparison with the North).

An extensive debate on the efficiency of slavery in United States agriculture was generated by the application of total factor productivity estimates by Fogel and Engerman (1974a). The question was an old one – frequent comparisons of slave versus free labour had been made by contemporaries as part of the anti-slavery argument. In their analysis Fogel and Engerman used a sample of over 5000 farms in cotton-producing counties, drawn by William Parker and Robert Gallman from the census manuscript schedules. The specific contention that in 1860 southern agriculture was more efficient than northern, in the sense of getting more output per unit of input, became widely discussed and criticized (see David et al., 1976; Wright, 1978). The extensive debate included discussion of alternative measures of factor inputs and adjustments for variations in crop-mix, as well as arguments about the emotive content of the term 'efficiency'. Nevertheless, this debate did lead to changes in depictions of the slave economy. More attention was paid to the flexibility of the economy, in terms of shifting patterns of production and location in response to economic stimuli as well as in the use of various mechanisms, in addition to the whip, to elicit work effort from the slaves. More attention was also given to the standard of living provided for the slaves and to their actual work experiences.

Much of the writing on United States slavery in the 1970s, coming from a variety of backgrounds and using different sources, also led to reinterpretations of the nature of slavery and the slave experience. Attention was given to the slave culture, affected, but not destroyed, by the controls of the master. While there remain disagreements about the frequency of the sales of slaves and the extent to which they separated spouses as well as young children, much work has established the strength of the slave family. Descriptions of slave religion, slave culture and the slave family all pointed to the capacity of the slaves to resist being reduced to Sambos – a point with obvious implications for the behaviour of masters as well. Slavery has come to be seen as a system which, with its initial imbalance of power, permitted a range of give-and-take between master and slave (see Genovese, 1974), with the power of the former not as complete, and the impact on the latter not as destructive, as earlier argued.

S.L. ENGERMAN

BIBLIOGRAPHY

Barzel, Y. 1977. An economic analysis of slavery. *Journal of Law and Economics* 20(1), April, 87–110.

Cairnes, J.E. 1862. *The Slave Power*. London: Parker, son & Bourn.

Conrad, A.H. and Meyer, J.R. 1958. The economics of slavery in the antebellum south. *Journal of Political Economy* 66, April, 95–130.

Curtin, P.D, 1969. *The Atlantic Slave Trade*. Madison: University of Wisconsin Press.

David, P.A. et al. 1976. *Reckoning with Slavery*. New York: Oxford University Press.

Davis, D.B. 1966. *The Problem of Slavery in Western Culture*. Ithaca: Cornell University Press.

Davis, D.B. 1975. *The Problem of Slavery in the Age of Revolution 1770–1823*. Ithaca: Cornell University Press.

Davis, D.B. 1984. *Slavery and Human Progress*. New York: Oxford University Press.

Deerr, N. 1949–50. *The History of Sugar*. 2 vols, London: Chapman & Hall.

Domar, E. 1970. The causes of slavery or serfdom: a hypothesis. *Journal of Economic History* 30(1), March, 18–32.

Drescher, S. 1977. *Econocide*. Pittsburgh: University of Pittsburgh Press.

Drescher, S. 1986. *Capitalism and Antislavery*. London: Macmillan.

Eltis, D. 1987. *Economic Growth and the Ending of the Translatlantic Slave Trade*. New York: Oxford University Press.

Engerman, S.L. 1982. Economic adjustments to emancipation in the United States and British West Indies. *Journal of Interdisciplinary History* 13(2), Autumn, 191–220.

Engerman, S.L. 1983. Contract labour, sugar, and technology in the nineteenth century. *Journal of Economic History* 43(3), September, 635–59.

Evans, R., Jr. 1962. The economics of American Negro slavery. In Universities National Bureau Committee for Economic Research, *Aspects of Labor Economics*, Princeton: Princeton University Press.

Finley, M.I. 1980. *Ancient Slavery and Modern Ideology*. New York: Viking Press.

Fogel, R.W. and Engerman, S.L. 1971. The economics of slavery. In *The Reinterpretation of American Economic History*, ed. R.W. Fogel and S.L. Engerman, New York: Harper & Row.

Fogel, R.W. and Engerman, S.L. 1974a. *Time on the Cross*. 2 vols. 1: *The economics of American Negro slavery*; 2: *Evidence and methods*. Boston: Little, Brown.

Fogel, R.W. and Engerman, S.L. 1974b. Philanthropy at bargain prices: notes on the economics of gradual emancipation. *Journal of Legal Studies* 3(2), June, 377–401.

Genovese, E.D. 1965. *The Political Economy of Slavery*. New York: Pantheon.

Genovese, E.D. 1974. *Roll, Jordan, Roll*. New York: Pantheon.

Higman, B.W. 1984. *Slave Populations of the British Caribbean, 1807–1834*. Baltimore: Johns Hopkins University Press.

Klein, H.S. 1986. *African Slavery in Latin America and the Caribbean*. New York: Oxford University Press.

Lovejoy, P.E. 1983. *Transformations in Slavery*. Cambridge: Cambridge University Press.

McCulloch, J.R. 1825. *The Principles of Political Economy*. Edinburgh: W. & C. Tait.

Mill, J.S. 1848. *Principles of Political Economy*. 2 vols, London: J.W. Parker.

Moreno Fraginals, M., Klein, H.S. and Engerman, S.L. 1983. The level and structure of slave prices on Cuban plantations in the mid-nineteenth century: some comparative perspectives. *American Historical Review* 88(5), December, 201–18.

Nieboer, H.J. 1900. *Slavery as an Industrial System*. The Hague: M. Nijhoff.

Patterson, H.O. 1982. *Slavery and Social Death*. Cambridge, Mass.: Harvard University Press.

Pryor, F.L. 1977. *The Origins of the Economy*. New York: Academic Press.

Solow, B.L. and Engerman, S.L. (eds) 1987. *Caribbean Slavery and British Capitalism*. Cambridge: Cambridge University Press.

Smith, A. 1776. *An Inquiry into the Nature and Causes of the Wealth of Nations*. Ed. E. Cannan. New York: Modern Library, 1937.

Steckel, R.H. 1985. *The Economics of US Slave and Southern White Fertility*. New York: Garland Publishing.

Williams, E. 1944. *Capitalism and Slavery*. Chapel Hill: University of North Carolina Press.

Wright, G. 1978. *The Political Economy of the Cotton South*. New York: W.W. Norton.

Yasuba, Y. 1961. The profitability and viability of plantation slavery in the United States. *Economic Studies Quarterly* 12, September, 60–67. Reprinted in *The Reinterpretation of American Economic History*, ed. R.W. Fogel and S.L. Engerman, New York: Harper & Row.

Slichter, Sumner Huber (1892–1959). Slichter was both a wide-ranging general economist and a scholar in industrial relations, regarding the two disciplines as parts of a seamless whole. He wrote an introductory economics textbook (1931) and was probably the most widely read economist by the general public of his day. He was a highly respected economic forecaster, Paul Samuelson calling him 'our best economic forecaster for the period 1935–55', and served as president of the American Economic Association, 1940–41. In industrial relations his two large classics (1941 and 1960) grew out of extended field work.

Slichter took his undergraduate degree in 1913 at the University of Wisconsin (where his father was professor of mathematics), did graduate work there with John R. Commons and completed his doctorate (1918) at the University of Chicago with H.A. Millis. He taught at Cornell for a decade, moved to Harvard Graduate School of Business Administration in 1930 and joined the Department of Economics in 1935. In 1940 he was appointed the first university professor at Harvard.

Among the themes that Slichter stressed were that the American economy was not in danger of stagnation; that World War II would not be followed by a depression but rather a boom; that America was becoming a 'laboristic' economy in which value judgements of the community reflect those of employees; that the challenges that unions have presented to managements have created superior and better-balanced managements; and that a vigorous and healthy economy is associated with an upward creep in prices that results from strong demand for goods and services and a slow climb in labour costs.

JOHN T. DUNLOP

SELECTED WORKS

1919. *The Turnover of Factory Labor*. New York: D. Appleton.

1931. *Modern Economic Society*. New York: Henry Holt.

1941. *Union Policies and Industrial Management*. Washington, DC: Brookings.

1943. *Present Savings and Postwar Markets*. New York: McGraw-Hill.

1947. *Trade Unions in a Free Society*. Cambridge, Mass.: Harvard University Press.

1948. *The American Economy: Its Problems and Prospects*. New York: Knopf.

1951. *What's Ahead for American Business?* Boston: Little, Brown.

1960. (With James J. Healy and E. Roberts Livernash) *The Impact of Collective Bargaining on Management*. Washington, DC: Brookings.

1961. *Potentials of the American Economy: Selected Essays of Sumner H. Slichter*. Ed. J.T. Dunlop, Cambridge, Mass.: Harvard University Press. A full bibliography appears on pp. 435–56.

slumps. *See* DEPRESSIONS.

Slutsky, Eugen (1880–1948). Born in the Yaroslav province of Russia, Slutsky had troubled years as a student: he enrolled in the department of physics and mathematics at Kiev University, was expelled for taking part in student revolts, went abroad to the Munich Institute of Technology to study engineering and finally graduated in the department of law in 1911 back at Kiev University. He became a member of the faculty at Kiev Institute of Commerce in 1913 and full professor there in 1920. In 1926 he moved to Moscow as a staff member of the Conjuncture Institute; in 1934 he became a staff member of the Mathematical Institute of the University of Moscow and in 1936 a member of the Mathematical Institute of the Academy of Sciences, Moscow, a post which he held until his death.

Slutsky was a mathematician, statistician and economist. His fame as an economist rests mainly on one single contribution (1915), which went unnoticed until the 1930s, when it was discovered independently by Dominedò (1933, p. 790), Schultz (1935, pp. 439ff), and Allen (1936), and subsequently influenced the further development of consumer theory. Hicks – who, together with Allen (Hicks and Allen, 1934), had independently arrived at Slutsky's results – writes: 'The theory to be set out in this chapter and the two following is essentially Slutsky's ... The present volume is the first systematic exploration of the territory which Slutsky opened up' (Hicks, 1939, p. 19). Building on earlier work by Pareto (who had already derived the formulae which express the change in the consumer's demand when any one of its arguments changes, but without seeing their implications), Slutsky showed that the effect of a price change on the quantity demanded can be divided into two effects. One is the effect of a *compensated variation* of price; if a price increases and the consumer is given an income increase so as to make possible the purchase of the same quantities of all the goods previously purchased, the individual – though being in the position to purchase the preceding bundle of goods – will no longer consider it preferable to any other, and there will take place some kind of *residual variation* of demand. This is called the *residual variability* by Slutsky (the substitution effect in Hicks's terminology). It should be noted that the compensated variation of price can also be defined in terms of the income change which leaves the consumer's *real* income unchanged, that is which causes the consumer to remain on the *same* indifference curve (this is the concept used by Hicks, 1939, in the text, while in the mathematical appendix he gives the same definition as Slutsky). Although the two definitions are equivalent for infinitesimal changes (as was first shown by Mosak, 1942), Slutsky's is preferable from the operational point of view since it does not require knowledge of the consumer's indifference map. The other effect is the *income effect*, which gives the change in the consumer's purchases when his money income changes at unchanged prices. The two effects turn out to be independent and additive and their algebraic sum gives the *price effect*: this is, in Hicks' terminology, the 'Fundamental Equation of Value Theory', also called the Slutsky Equation.

Slutsky proved the complete properties of the various effects and of the demand curves. The income effect may be either normal (demand increases as income increases: 'relatively indispensable goods' in Slutsky's terminology) or abnormal ('relatively dispensable' goods). The 'own' substitution effect is always negative ('The residual variability of a good in the case of a compensated variation of its price, is always negative', [1915] 1953, p. 42) and the cross substitution effect is symmetric ('The residual variability of the j-th good in the case of a compensated variation of the price p_i is equal to the residual variability of the i-th good in the case of a compensated variation of the price p_j', [1915] 1953, p. 43). The 'own' price effect, therefore, is necessarily normal in the case of relatively indispensable goods. Slutsky also proved the relation which implies that the individual demand functions are homogeneous of degree zero. He gave a definition of complementary and competing goods, and made an important methodological point which is usually overlooked in his contribution: he stressed the need for *experiment* in order to obtain all the values of the relevant magnitudes (which cannot be obtained by observation of existing budgets) which enter into the definition. This emphasis on the need for experimental verification of economic laws, which concludes his contribution, is worthy of note and obviously arises from his statistical background.

Slutsky did no other noticeable work in economics but made important contributions to mathematical statistics and probability theory.

In (1914) he suggested the use of a χ^2 variate to test the goodness of fit of a regression line ('line' is taken in the broad sense, i.e. including both straight lines and curves); as a logical consequence, he introduced the concept of *minimum chi-square estimator* ('the most probable values of the coefficients will be those which bring our χ^2 to a minimum', 1914, p. 83) as a general method of fitting regressions. This paper was written several years before R.A. Fisher's work on the subject.

Slutsky was one of the originators of the theory of stochastic processes and time-series analysis. In his renowned (1927) paper he proved several important theorems. One is that the summation of random causes may be the source of cyclic or undulatory processes, and that these waves will show an approximate regularity in the sense that they can be approximated quite well by a relatively small number of terms (sine curves) of the Fourier series. Another is the sinusoidal limit theorem, which states that under certain conditions the summation of random causes will tend to give rise to a specific sine wave. For example, if one takes a moving average (of two terms) of a random series n times and then takes the mth difference of the result, and lets $n \to \infty$ so that m/n tends to a constant c between zero and one, it follows that the series will tend to a sine wave with wavelength arc cos $(1-c)/(1+c)$. A corollary of these theorems is the famous Slutsky-Yule Effect (so named because it was also independently discovered by Yule): if a moving average of a random series is taken (for example to determine trend), this may *generate* an oscillatory movement in the series where none existed in the original data.

Slutsky also worked in the theory of probability, where he studied the concept of asymptotic convergence in probability (e.g. 1925, 1928, 1929). He spent the last years of his life in preparing tables for the computation of the incomplete gamma-function and the chi-square probability distribution (1950).

GIANCARLO GANDOLFO

SELECTED WORKS

A bibliography (1912–46) is contained in the memorial article (in Russian) by A.N. Kolmogorov, in *Uspekhi Matematicheskikh Nauk*, Vol. 3, No. 4, 1948. This bibliography is reproduced in Allen (1950). A collection of selected papers was published posthumously in Russian (1960). On Slutsky's life and works see also the memorial article (in Russian) by N. Smirnov, in *Izvestiia Akademiia Nauk SSSR*, Mathematical Series, Vol. 12, 1948, and Allen (1950).

1914. On the criterion of goodness of fit of the regression lines and on the best method of fitting them to the data. *Journal of the Royal Statistical Society* 77, Pt I, December, 78–84.

1915. Sulla teoria del bilancio del consumatore. *Giornale degli Economisti e Rivista di Statistica* 51, July, 1–26. Trans. as 'On the

theory of the budget of the consumer' in *Readings in Price Theory*, ed. K.E. Boulding and G.J. Stigler, London: Allen & Unwin, 1953, 26–56.
1925. Über stochastische Asymptoten und Grenzwerte. *Metron* 5, December, 3–89.
1927. The summation of random causes as the source of cyclic processes. (In Russian.) *Problems of Economic Conditions*, The Conjuncture Institute, Moscow, Vol. 3, No. 1. Revised English version in *Econometrica* 5, April 1937, 105–46.
1928. Sur un critérium de la convergence stochastique des ensembles de valeurs éventuelles. *Comptes rendu des séances de l'Académie des Sciences* 187, Paris, 17 July to 13 August.
1929. Quelques propositions sur les limites stochastiques éventuelles. *Compte rendu des séances de l'Académie des Sciences* 189, Paris, 2 September.
1950. *Tables for the computation of the incomplete Gamma-function and the Chi-square probability distribution.* (In Russian.) Ed. A.N. Kolmogorov, Moscow: Akademiia Nauk SSSR (posthumous).
1960. *Selected Works.* (In Russian.) Moscow: Akademiia Nauk SSSR (posthumous).

BIBLIOGRAPHY
Allen, R.G.D. 1936. Professor Slutsky's theory of consumers' choice. *Review of Economic Studies* 3, February, 120–29.
Allen, R.G.D. 1950. The work on Eugen Slutsky. *Econometrica* 18, July, 209–16.
Dominedò, V. 1933. Considerazioni intorno alla teoria della domanda, II-Le principali premesse e caratteristiche delle curve statiche. *Giornale degli Economisti e Rivista di Statistica* 48, November, 765–807.
Hicks, J.R. and Allen, R.G.D. 1934. A reconsideration of the theory of value. *Economica* 1, Pt I, February, 52–76; Pt II, May, 196–219.
Hicks, J.R. 1939. *Value and Capital.* Oxford: Clarendon Press. 2nd edn, 1946.
Mosak, J. 1942. On the interpretation of the fundamental equation of value theory. In *Studies in Mathematical Economics and Econometrics in Memory of Henry Schultz*, ed. O. Lange, F. McIntyre and T.O. Yntema, Chicago: University of Chicago Press, 69–74.
Samuelson, P.A. 1947. *Foundations of Economic Analysis*. Cambridge, Mass.: Harvard University Press. Enlarged edn, 1983.
Schultz, H. 1935. Interrelations of demand, price, and income. *Journal of Political Economy* 43, August, 433–81.

Smart, William (1853–1915). William Smart was an entrepreneur turned academic economist. Born at Barrhead in Renfrewshire on 10 April 1853 he was educated at the University of Glasgow, where he was later to occupy the (newly created) Adam Smith Chair of Political Economy from 1896 until his death on 19 March 1915. However, his transition from student to professor was interrupted by a successful career in industry which began in the early 1870s and terminated in 1884 when the firm in which he was a partner was sold to the considerable financial advantage of its principals.

Smart's main contribution to economics probably remains his translations into English of the work of Böhm-Bawerk (1890 and 1891a), and his edition of von Wieser (1893). In certain circles, Smart is felt to have been primarily responsible for introducing the work of the Austrian school to English readers (but see the entry on James Bonar in this Dictionary). As well as making available the originals, Smart published in 1891 his own account of Austrian economics under the title *Introduction to the Theory of Value* – a book which went through three editions during Smart's lifetime. Smart's other work includes a book (1895) dealing principally with wages, consumption and currency. It seems that Smart's advocacy of a bimetallic standard had made his election to the Adam Smith Chair at Glasgow in 1896 more problematic than it might have been. He also wrote on the distribution of income (1899), the single tax (1900), and tariff reform (1904); the last two being essentially contributions to popular debates of the day.

As a young man, and while still a practising businessman, Smart was a Ruskinite. He was a member of the Guild of St George and his first publication was his inaugural address as president of the Ruskin Society of Glasgow (1880). Smart's own account of these intellectual influences on his early development can be found in his *Second Thoughts of an Economist*.

Separate mention should be made of Smart's *Economic Annals of the Nineteenth Century* (1910–17), which he began as a result of the difficulties he had experienced in gathering information in his role as member of the Poor Law Commission in 1905. The simple rationale was to render more accessible official material related to actual economic conditions and debates of the period. Although Smart only saw through to completion two volumes of the *Annals* before he died (which cover less than one third of the 19th century), a glance at the material assembled in the extant volumes is sufficient to confirm their value.

MURRAY MILGATE

SELECTED WORKS
1880. *John Ruskin: His Life and Work*. Manchester: A. Heywood & Sons.
1883. *A Disciple of Plato*. Glasgow: Wilson & McCormick.
1890. (trans.) E.v. Böhm-Bawerk, *Capital and Interest*. London and New York: Macmillan & Co.
1891a. (trans.) E.v. Böhm-Bawerk, *Positive Theory of Capital*. London and New York: Macmillan & Co.
1891b. *Introduction to the Theory of Value on the Lines of Menger, Wieser and Böhm-Bawerk*. London: Macmillan. 2nd edn 1910; 3rd edn 1914.
1893. (ed.) F.v. Wieser, *Natural Value*. Trans. C.A. Malloch, London and New York: Macmillan & Co.
1895. *Studies in Economics*. London: Macmillan & Co.
1899. *The Distribution of Income*. London: Macmillan & Co.
1900. *The Taxation of Land Values and the Single Tax*. Glasgow: J. MacLehose & Sons.
1904. *The Return to Protection*. London: Macmillan & Co.
1910–17. *Economic Annals of the Nineteenth Century*. 2 vols, London: Macmillan & Co.
1916. *Second Thoughts of an Economist*. London: Macmillan & Co.

Smith, Adam (1723–1790). Adam Smith was born in Kirkcaldy, on the east coast of Scotland, and baptized on 5 June, 1723. He was the son of Adam Smith, Clerk to the Court Martial and Comptroller of Customs in the town (who died before his son was born) and of Margaret Douglas of Strathendry.

Smith attended the High School in Kirkcaldy, and then proceeded to Glasgow University. He first matriculated in 1737, at the not uncommon age of fourteen. At this time the university, or more strictly the college, was small. It housed only twelve professors who had in effect replaced the less specialized system of regents by 1727. Of the professoriate, Smith was most influenced by the 'never-to-be-forgotten' Francis Hutcheson (Corr., letter 274, dated 16 November 1787). Hutcheson had succeeded Gerschom Carmichael, the distinguished editor of Pufendorf's *De Officio Hominis et Civis*, as Professor of Moral Philosophy.

Smith left Glasgow in 1740 as a Snell Exhibitioner at Balliol College to begin a stay of six years. The atmosphere of the college at this time was Jacobite and 'anti-Scotch'. Smith was also to complain: 'In the university of Oxford, the greater part of the publick professors have, for these many years, given up altogether even the pretence of teaching' (WN, V. i. f. 8). But there were benefits, most notably ease of access to excellent libraries, which in turn enabled Smith to acquire an extensive knowledge of English and French literature, which was to prove invaluable.

Smith left Oxford in 1746 and returned to Kirkcaldy without a fixed plan. But in 1748 he was invited to give a series of public lectures in Edinburgh, with the support of three men – the Lord Advocate, Henry Home; Lord Kames; and a childhood friend, James Oswald of Dunnikier.

The lectures, which are thought to have been primarily concerned with rhetoric and belles lettres, brought Smith £100 a year (Corr., letter 25, dated 8 June 1758). They also seem to have been wide-ranging.

Smith's reputation as a lecturer brought its reward. In 1751 he was elected to the Chair of Logic in Glasgow University, again with the support of Lord Kames. According to John Millar, Smith's most distinguished pupil, he devoted the bulk of his time to the delivery of a system of rhetoric and belles lettres, which was based on the conviction that the best way of

> explaining and illustrating the various powers of the human mind, the most useful part of metaphysics, arises from an examination of the several ways of communicating our thoughts by speech, and from an attention to the principles of those literary compositions which contribute to persuasion or entertainment (Stewart, I. 16).

Smith continued to teach the main part of his lecture course on logic after he had been translated to the Chair of Moral Philosophy in 1752. A set of lecture notes, discovered by J.M. Lothian in 1958, relate to the session 1762/3. The notes correspond closely to Millar's description of the course given more than a decade earlier, in that they are concerned with such problems as the development of language, style and the organization of forms of discourse which include the oratorical, narrative and didactical. Smith was primarily concerned with the study of human nature and with the analysis of the means and forms of communication. He no doubt continued to lecture on these subjects to students of moral philosophy because he rightly believed them to be important (see J.M. Lothian, 1963; W.S. Howell, 1975).

Smith's lectures on language were published in expanded form as *Considerations Concerning the First Formation of Language*, in the *Philological Miscellany* for 1761. They were reprinted in the third edition of the *Theory of Moral Sentiments* in 1767.

Smith's teaching from the Chair of Moral Philosophy fell into four parts and in effect set the scene for the major published works which were to follow. Again on the authority of John Millar, it is known that Smith lectured on natural theology, ethics, jurisprudence and 'expediency', or economics, *in that order*. The lectures on natural theology (a sensitive subject at the time) have not yet been found. But Millar made it clear that the lectures on ethics form the basis for the *Theory of Moral Sentiments* and that the subjects covered in the last part of the course were to be further developed in the *Wealth of Nations* (Stewart, I. 20). As to the third part, on jurisprudence, Millar noted that:

> Upon this subject he followed the plan that seems to be suggested by Montesquieu; endeavouring to trace the gradual progress of jurisprudence, both public and private, from the rudest to the most refined ages, and to point out the effects of those arts which contribute to subsistence, and to the accumulation of property, in producing correspondent improvements or alterations in law and government (Stewart, I. 19).

Illustration and confirmation of this claim proved impossible until 1896 when Edwin Cannan published an edition of the *Lectures on Jurisprudence*. The notes edited by Cannan are dated 1766, although they were taken in the session 1763/4. This was Smith's last session in Glasgow, so that these lectures, where 'public' (broadly constitutional law) precedes 'private' jurisprudence (concerning man's rights as a citizen), *may* reflect a preferred order. A second set of notes, this time relating to the previous session, were also found by J.M. Lothian as recently as 1958 and are here styled LJ (A).

Academically, the major event for Smith was the publication of the *Theory of Moral Sentiments* in 1759. The book was well received by both the public and Smith's friends. In a delightful letter Hume reminded Smith of the futility of fame and public approbation, and having encouraged him to be a philosopher in practice as well as profession, continued:

> Supposing therefore, that you have duely prepared yourself for the worst by these Reflections; I proceed to tell you the Melancholy News, that your Book has been most unfortunate: For the Public seem disposed to applaud it extremely (Corr., letter 31, dated 12 April 1759).

The book was to establish Smith's reputation. There was a second revised edition in 1761 and further editions in 1767, 1774, 1781 and 1790.

Charles Townshend was among those to whom Hume had sent a copy of Smith's treatise. Townshend had married the widowed Countess of Dalkeith in 1755 and was sufficiently impressed by Smith's work as to arrange for his appointment as tutor to her son, the young Duke of Buccleuch. The position brought financial security (£300 sterling p.a. for the rest of his life), and Smith duly accepted, formally resigning his chair early in 1764.

Smith and his party left almost immediately for France to begin a sojourn of some two years. At the outset, the visit was unsuccessful, causing Smith to write to Hume, with some humour, that 'I have begun to write a book in order to pass away the time. You may believe I have very little to do' (Corr., letter 82, date 5 July 1764, Toulouse).

But matters improved with Smith's increasing familiarity with the language and the success of a series of short tours. In 1765 Smith, the Duke, and the Duke's younger brother Hew Scott, reached Geneva, giving Smith an opportunity to meet Voltaire, whom he genuinely admired as 'the most universal genius perhaps which France has ever produced' (Letter, 17). The party arrived in Paris in mid-February 1766, where Smith's fame, together with the efforts of David Hume, secured him a ready entré to the leading *salons* and, in turn, introductions to *philosophes* such as d'Alembert, Holbach and Helvetius.

During this period Smith met François Quesnay, the founder, with the Marquis de Mirabeau, of the Physiocratic School of economics (Meek, 1962). By the time Smith met Quesnay, the latter's model of the economic system as embodied in the *Tableau Economique* ([1757], trans. in Meek, 1962) had already been through a number of editions. Quesnay was then working on the *Analyse* (trans. in Meek, 1962), while it is also known that A.R.J. Turgot was currently engaged on his *Reflections on the Formation and Distribution of Riches* (trans. in Meek, 1973).

Smith, who had already developed an interest in political economy, had arrived in Paris at the very point in time that the French School had reached the zenith of its influence and output. The contents of Smith's library amply confirm his interest in this work (Mizuta, 1967).

Smith's stay in Paris had been enjoyable both socially and in academic terms. But it was marred by the developing quarrel between Hume and Rousseau and sadly terminated by the death of Hew Scott. Smith returned to London on 1 November 1766.

Smith spent the winter in London, where he was consulted by Townshend and engaged in corrections for the third edition of the *Theory of Moral Sentiments*. By the spring of 1767 (the year in which Sir James Steuart published his *Principles of Political Oeconomy*) Smith was back in Kirkcaldy to begin a study of some six years. It was during this period that he struggled with the *Wealth of Nations*. Correspondence of the time amply confirms the mental strain involved. But by 1773 Smith was ready to return to London, leaving his friends, notably David Hume, under the impression that completion was imminent. As matters turned out, it took Smith almost three more years to finish his book; a delay which may have been due in part to his increasing concern with the American War of Independence and with the wider issue of the relationship between the colonies and the 'mother country' (WN, IV. vii).

An Inquiry into the Nature and Causes of the Wealth of Nations was published by Strahan and Cadell on 9 March 1776, and elicited once more a warm response from Hume:

> Dear Mr. Smith: I am much pleas'd with your Performance, and the Perusal of it has taken me from a State of great Anxiety. It was a Work of so much Expectation, by yourself, by your Friends, and by the Public, that I trembled for its Appearance; but am now much relieved. Not but the Reading of it necessarily requires so much Attention, and the Public is disposed to give so little, that I shall still doubt for some time of its being at first very popular (Corr., letter 150, dated I April 1776).

In fact, the book sold well, with subsequent editions in 1778, 1784, 1786 and 1789.

1776 was marred for Smith by the death of David Hume, after a long illness, and by his concern over the future of the latter's *Dialogues Concerning Natural Religion*. This work, together with Hume's account of 'My Own Life' had been left in the care of William Strahan, to whom Smith wrote expressing the hope that the *Dialogues* should remain unpublished, although Hume himself had determined otherwise.

But Smith proposed to 'add to his life a very well authenticated account' of Hume's formidable courage during his last illness (Corr., letter 172, dated 5 September 1776). The letter was published in 1777, and as Smith wrote later to Andreas Holt, 'brought upon me ten times more abuse than the very violent attack I had made upon the whole commercial system of Great Britain' (Corr., letter 208, dated October 1780).

In 1778 Smith was appointed Commissioner of Customs, due in part to the efforts of the Duke of Buccleuch. The office brought an income of £600, in addition to the pension of £300 which the Duke refused to discontinue (Corr., letter 208). Smith settled in Edinburgh, where he was joined by his mother and a cousin, Janet Douglas.

During 1778 Alexander Wedderburn sought Smith's advice on the future conduct of affairs in America. Smith's 'Thoughts on the State of the Contest with America' were written in the aftermath of the battle of Saratoga. The Memorandum was first published by G.H. Guttridge in the *American Historical Review* (vol. 38, 1932/3).

In this document, Smith rehearsed a number of arguments which he had already stated in WN (IV. vii. c). He advocated the extension of British taxes to Ireland and to America, provided that representatives from both countries were admitted to Parliament at Westminster in conformity with accepted constitutional practice. Smith noted that 'Without a union with Great Britain, the inhabitants of Ireland are not likely for many ages to consider themselves as one people' (WN, V. iii. 89). With respect to America, he observed that her progress had been so rapid that 'in the course of little more than a century, perhaps, the produce of American might exceed that of British taxation. The seat of the empire would then naturally remove itself to that part of the empire which contributed most to the general defence and support of the whole' (WN, IV. vii. c. 79).

But Smith also repeated a point already made in WN; namely, that the opportunity for union had been lost, and proceeded to review the bleak options, now all too familiar, which were actually open to the British Government. Military victory was increasingly unlikely (WN, V. i. a. 27) and military government, even in the event of victory, unworkable (Corr., 383). Voluntary withdrawal from the conflict was a rational but politically impracticable course, given the probable impact on domestic and world opinion (ibid.). The most likely outcome, in Smith's view, was the loss of the thirteen united colonies and the successful retention of Canada – the worst possible solution since it was also the most expensive in terms of defence (Corr., 385).

Smith worked hard as a Commissioner, and to an extent which, as he admitted, affected his literary pursuits (Corr., letter 208). But in this period he completed the third edition of WN (1784), incorporating major developments which were separately published as 'Additions and Corrections'. The third edition also features an index and a long concluding chapter to Book IV entitled 'Conclusion of the Mercantile System'.

After 1784 Smith must have devoted most of his attention to the revision of TMS. The sixth edition of 1790 features an entirely new Part VI which includes a further elaboration of the role of conscience, and the most complete statement which Smith offered as to the complex *social* psychology which lies behind man's broadly economic aspirations.

In addition to the essay on the 'Imitative Arts', which is mentioned in his letter to Andreas Holt (Corr., letter 208), Smith observed that 'I have likewise two other great works upon the anvil; the one is a sort of Philosophical History of all the different branches of Literature, of Philosophy, Poetry and Eloquence; the other is a sort of theory and History of Law and Government' (Corr., letter 248 dated 1 November 1785, addressed to the Duc de la Rochefoucauld).

Smith's literary ambitions also feature in the Advertisement to the 1790 edition of TMS, where he drew attention to the concluding sentences of the first edition of 1759. In these passages Smith makes it clear that TMS and WN are parts of a single plan which he hoped to complete with a published account of 'the general principles of law and government, and of the different revolutions which they had undergone in the different ages and periods of society'. Smith's 'present occupations' and 'very advanced age' prevented him from completing this great work, although the approach is illustrated by LJ (A) and LJ (B), and by those passages in WN which can now be recognized as being derived from them (most notably WN, III and V. i. a, b).

Smith died on 17 July 1790, having first instructed his executors, Joseph Black and James Hutton, to burn his papers, excepting those which were published in *Essays on Philosophical Subjects* (1795).

In what follows, Smith's system will be expounded in terms of the order of argument which he is known to have employed as a lecturer; namely, ethics, jurisprudence and economics. Each separate area of analysis may be represented as highly systematic: all are interdependent, forming in effect the component sections of a greater whole.

THE THEORY OF MORAL SENTIMENTS

The Theory of Moral Sentiments shows clear evidence of a model, and of a form of argument which is in part designed to explain how so self-regarding a creature as man succeeds in erecting barriers against his own passions.

In Part VII of TMS, Smith reviewed different approaches to the questions confronting the philosopher in this field, basically as a means of differentiating his own contribution from them.

In Smith's view there were two main questions to be answered: 'First, wherein does virtue consist', and secondly, 'by what means does it come to pass, that the mind prefers one tenour of conduct to another'? (TMS, VII. i. 2). In dealing with the first question, Smith described all classical and modern theories in terms of the emphasis given to the qualities of propriety, prudence and benevolence. In each case, he argued that the identification of a particular quality was appropriate, but rejected what he took to be undue emphasis on any one. He criticized those who found virtue in propriety, on the ground that this approach emphasized the importance of self-command at the expense of 'softer' virtues, such as sensibility. He rejected others who found virtue in prudence because of the emphasis given to qualities which are useful, thus echoing his criticism of David Hume in TMS, Part IV. In a similar way, while he admired benevolence, Smith argued that proponents of this approach (notably Francis Hutcheson) had neglected virtues such as prudence.

Smith's criticism of Hutcheson's teaching is remarkable for the emphasis which he gave to self-interest and his denial of Hutcheson's proposition that self-love 'was a principle which could never be virtuous in any degree or in any direction' (TMS, VII, ii. 3.12). Smith also rejected the argument of Mandeville, whose fallacy it was 'to represent every passion as wholly vicious, which is so in any degree' (TMS, VII. ii. 4.12). Smith contended that 'The condition of human nature were peculiarly hard, if these affections, which, by the very nature of our being, ought frequently to influence our conduct, could upon no occasion appear virtuous, or deserve esteem and commendation from anybody' (TMS, VII, ii. 3.18).

A further distinctive element in Smith's approach emerges in his treatment of the second question. He accepted Hutcheson's argument that the perception of right and wrong rests not upon reason but 'immediate sense and feeling' (TMS, VII. iii. 2.9). But Smith rejected Hutcheson's emphasis on a special sense, the moral sense, which was treated as being analogous to 'external' senses, such as sight or touch. But in so doing Smith in effect elaborated on the argument of his teacher, who had already presented moral judgements as being disinterested and as based upon sympathy or fellow-feeling. Smith also enlarged on the role of the *spectator*, which had been a feature of the work done by Hutcheson and Hume.

Smith argued that the spectator may form a judgement with respect to the activities of another person by visualizing how he would have behaved or felt in similar circumstances. It is this capacity for acts of imaginative sympathy which permits the spectator to form a judgement as to the propriety or impropriety of the conduct observed, and as to the 'suitableness or unsuitableness, the proportion or disproportion which the affection seems to bear to the cause or object which excites it' (TMS, I. i. 3.6).

Since we can 'enter into' the feelings of another person only to a limited degree, Smith was able to identify the 'amiable' virtue of sensibility with the quality of imagination, and that of self-command with a capacity to control expressions or feeling to such an extent as to permit the spectator to comprehend, and thus to 'sympathize', with them.

The argument was extended to take account of those actions which have consequences for other people, in suggesting that in such cases the spectator may seek to form a judgement as to the propriety of the *action* taken and of the *reaction* to it. The sense of *merit* 'seems to be a compounded sentiment, and to be made up of two distinct emotions; a direct sympathy with the sentiments of the agent, and an indirect sympathy with the gratitude of those who receive the benefit of his actions' (TMS, II. i. 5.2). Conversely, a sense of *demerit* is compounded of 'antipathy to the affections and motives of the agent' and 'an indirect sympathy with the resentment of the sufferer' (TMS, II. i. 5.4).

Smith further contended that 'Nature, when she formed man for society, endowed him with an original desire to please, and an original aversion to offend his brethren' (TMS, III. 2.6).

But this general disposition is not of itself sufficient to ensure an adequate degree of control. The first problem which Smith confronted is that of *information*, a problem which arises from the fact that the actual spectator of the conduct of another person is unlikely to be familiar with his *motives*.

Smith solved this problem by arguing that we tend to judge our own conduct by trying to visualize the reaction of an imagined or 'ideal spectator' to it; that is, by seeking to visualize the reaction of a spectator, who is necessarily fully informed, with regard to our own motives. Smith gave more and more attention to the role of the ideal spectator in successive editions as an important source of control; that is, to the voice of 'reason, principle, conscience ... the great judge and arbiter of our conduct' (TMS, III. 3.4). Looked at in this way, the argument depends on man's desire not merely for praise, but praiseworthiness (TMS, III. 2. 32).

The second problem arises from the fact that Smith, following Hume, presents man as an active, self-regarding being, whose legitimate pursuit of the objects of ambition, notably wealth, can on some occasions have hurtful consequences for others. The difficulty here is that of *partiality* of view, even where we have the information which is needed to arrive at accurate judgements. When we are about to act, 'the eagerness of passion will seldom allow us to consider what we are doing with the candour of an indifferent person', while after we have acted, we often 'turn away our view from those circumstances which might render ... judgement unfavourable' (TMS, III. 4.3–4). The solution to this particular problem is found in man's capacity for generalization on the basis of particular experience:

> It is thus that the general rules of morality are formed. They are ultimately founded upon experience of what, in particular instances, our moral faculties, our natural sense of merit and propriety, approve, or disapprove of. ... The general rule ... is formed, by finding from experience, that all actions of a certain kind, or circumstanced in a certain manner, are approved or disapproved of (TMS, III. 4.8).

It is these rules that provide the yardstick against which man can judge his actions in all circumstances; rules which command respect by virtue of the desire to be praiseworthy and which are further supported by the fear of God (TMS, III. 5. 12).

Smith thus offered an explanation of the way in which men were fitted for society, arguing in effect that they typically erect a series of barriers to the exercise of their own (self-regarding) passions, which culminate in the emergence of generally accepted rules of behaviour.

The rules themselves vary in character. Those which relate to justice 'may be compared to the rules of grammar; the rules of the other virtues, to the rules which critics lay down for the attainment of what is sublime and elegant in composition. The one, are precise, accurate and indispensable. The other, are loose, vague, and indeterminate' (TMS, III. 6.11).

But Smith was in no doubt that the rules of justice were indispensable. Justice 'is the main pillar that upholds the whole edifice' (TMS, II. ii. 3.4). Smith added that the final precondition of social order was a system of positive law, embodying current conceptions of the rules of justice and administered by some system of magistracy:

> As the violation of justice is what men will never submit to from one another, the public magistrate is under the necessity of employing the power of the commonwealth to enforce the practice of this virtue. Without this precaution, civil society would become a scene of bloodshed and disorder, every man revenging himself at his own hand whenever he fancied he was injured (TMS, VII. iv. 36).

Smith's ethical argument forms an integral part of his treatment of jurisprudence precisely because it is concerned to show how particular rules of behaviour emerge. In LJ the focus is narrower than in TMS, but it is still the spectator that is of critical importance whether Smith is discussing accepted standards of punishment or of law. Attention has also been drawn to the role of the magistrate in this connection (Bagolini, 1975) and of the Legislator (Haakonssen, 1981).

Smith's emphasis in TMS is interesting. He chose to concentrate on the means by which the mind forms judgements as to what is fit and proper to be done or to be avoided, as distinct from trying to formulate specific rules of behaviour. He had recognized that while the *processes* of judgement might claim universal validity, *specific* judgements must be related to experience.

No one living in the age of Montesquieu could fail to be aware of variations in standards of accepted behaviour in different societies at the same point in time, and in the same societies over time. The point at issue seems to have been grasped by Edmund Burke in writing to Smith: 'A theory like yours founded on the Nature of man, which is always the same, will last, when those that are founded upon his opinions, which are always changing, will and must be forgotten' (Corr., letter 38, dated 10 September 1759).

But Smith did not deny that common elements could be found on the basis of experience. Although he did not complete his intended account of the 'general principles' involved (TMS, VII. iv. 37), Smith did provide an argument which related the discussion of private and public jurisprudence to four broad types of socio-economic *environment*, the stages of hunting, pasture, farming and commerce. The importance of the argument in the present context is that it was designed in part to explain the origin of government, thus solving a problem which was only noted in TMS. At the same time the historical dimension throws light on the causes of change in accepted rules of behaviour. As part of the same exercise, Smith supplied a successful account of the emergence of the stage of commerce, the stage with which he, as an economist, was primarily concerned.

THE HISTORY OF CIVIL SOCIETY

The first stage of society was represented as the 'lowest and rudest', such 'as we find it among the native tribes of North America' (WN, V. i. a. 2). In this case life is supported by gathering the fruits of the earth, by hunting and fishing. As a result, Smith suggested that such communities would be small and characterized by a high degree of personal liberty. He also noted that disputes between different members of the community would be limited in the absence of private property, and that 'there is seldom any established magistrate or any regular administration of justice' (WN, V. i. b. 2) in this situation.

The second stage, that of pasture, is represented as a 'more advanced state of society, such as we find it among the Tartars and Arabs' (WN, V. i. a. 3). Here the use of cattle is the dominant economic activity, indicating that communities would be larger in size and nomadic in character. But the key feature of the second stage was found in the emergence of a form of property which could be accumulated and transmitted from one generation to another. It is property which 'necessarily requires the establishment of civil government' (WN, V. i. b. 2). Elsewhere he noted that 'Civil government, so far as it is instituted for the security of property, is in reality instituted for the defence of the rich against the poor' (WN, V. i. b. 12). In another passage where Smith associated the emergence of government with the stage of pasture, he drew the attention of his auditors to the proposition that 'Laws and government may be considered in this and indeed in every case as a combination of the rich to oppress the poor' (LJ (A), iv. 22–3).

At the same time, Smith noted that the prevailing form of economic organization must lead to a high degree of dependence, since those who do not own the means of subsistence have no way of earning it save through personal service:

> The second period of society, that of shepherds, admits of very great inequalities of fortune, and there is no period in which the superiority of fortune gives so great an authority to those who possess it. There is no period accordingly in which authority and subordination are more perfectly established (WN, V. i. b. 7).

In effect, Smith used *contemporary* evidence regarding the Arabs, Tartars and North American Indians to illustrate the socio-economic stages through which the nations which overran the Western (Roman) Empire had probably passed. It is in this and in this sense only that the term 'conjectural history' accurately reflects Smith's purpose (Stewart, II. 48).

The German and Scythian nations had already attained what is in effect a higher form of the second stage, with some idea of agriculture and property in *land*. Smith argued that these nations would naturally use existing institutions in their new situation, and that their first act would be a division of the conquered territories (WN, III. ii. 1). In this way, Smith traced the movement from the second to the third stage, that of agriculture. Here property in land is the source of power and distinction, although the basic pattern of subordination remains the same.

But the feature on which Smith concentrated most attention was that of *political* instability: 'In those disorderly times, every great landlord was a sort of petty prince. His tenants were his subjects. He was their judge, and in some respects their legislator in peace, and their leader in war' (WN, III. ii. 3). The first historical response to this situation led to the emergence of the feudal system, which Smith represents as involving a complex of agreements for mutual service and protection. But even here: 'The authority of government still continued to be, as before, too weak in the head and too strong in the inferior members, and the excessive strength of the inferior members was the cause of the weakness of the head' (WN, III. iv. 9).

The second response was the most critical and is illustrated by the support given by monarchs to cities, partly as a means of enabling their inhabitants to protect themselves, but largely with a view to forming a new tactical alliance (WN, III. iii) which could offset the power of the aristocracy. Cities emerged as 'a sort of independent republicks' with important powers of self-government which brought 'along with them the liberty and security of individuals' (WN, III. iii. 8, 12).

The institution of the self-governing city was to satisfy a basic precondition of economic growth (as it had done in classical Greece), especially where it was supported by ease of access to the sea. Growth was based on foreign trade, and Smith proceeded to trace a general pattern which was based upon particular examples, such as Venice, Genoa and Pisa. This pattern initially involved the importation of foreign manufactures in exchange for limited surpluses in primary products, to be followed by the development of domestic manufactures based on foreign materials, and then by a process of refinement of those 'coarse and rude' products which were domestic in origin. Such developments, Smith continued, made it quite possible for the city to 'grow up to great wealth and splendor, while not only the country in its neighbourhood, but all those to which it traded, were in poverty and wretchedness' (WN, III. iii. 13).

But in the next part of the analysis, Smith outlined the way in which the pattern of economic growth based on the city would impinge on the agrarian sector. He argued that economies based upon manufacture and trade inevitably provided the great proprietors of land with a means of expending their surpluses, thus giving an incentive to maximize them (WN, III. iv. 10). This led to the gradual dismissal of retainers and to a process of modification in the pattern of leaseholding; a process which witnessed a move away from the use of slave labour to the metayer system, and eventually to the appearance of farmers properly so called, 'who cultivated the land with their own stock, paying a rent certain to the landlord' (WN, III. ii. 14).

As a result of these two trends, the great proprietors slowly lost their authority, until a situation was reached where 'they became as insignificant as any substantial burgher or tradesman in a city' (WN, III. iv. 15). Smith was able to conclude:

> commerce and manufactures gradually introduced order and good government, and with them, the liberty and security of individuals, among the inhabitants of the country, who had before lived almost in a continual state of war with their neighbours, and of servile dependency upon their superiors. This, though it has been the least observed, is by far the most important of all their effects. Mr. Hume is the only writer who, so far as I know, has hitherto taken notice of it (WN, III. iv. 4).

The argument as a whole provides one of the most dramatic examples of Smith's doctrine of unintended social outcomes (WN, III. iv. 17). The *historical* analysis of the third book of WN is highly polished in part because Smith perceived that it could be presented as a model and in part because the argument had been rehearsed over many years. But the lectures add a further dimension. The treatment of 'public jurisprudence' sets out to provide a philosophical or scientific account of developments which began in Athens and end in modern Europe. But within this broad sweep, more and more attention is given to what was in effect a 'Historical View of the English Government' – significantly, the title of John Millar's major work, first published in 1786.

Attention was drawn to the nature of the English constitution and the claims to liberty, an argument which is conveniently summarized in LJ (A) (iv. 165 – v. 15). Smith drew on this analysis in WN when giving attention to the 'admirable' structure of the courts in England, and to the importance of a separation of powers:

> In order to make every individual feel himself perfectly secure in the possession of every right which belongs to him, it is not only necessary that the judicial should be separated from the executive power, but that it should be rendered as much as possible independent of that power (WN, V. i. b. 25).

In the same way, Smith drew attention to the need for, and dangers of, a standing army, while indicating that in England a solution close to the ideal had been found where: 'the military force is placed under the command of those who have the greatest interest in the support of the civil authority' (WN, V. i. a. 41).

Equally important was the gradual shift in the balance of power which had elevated the House of Commons to a superior degree of influence as 'an assembly of the representatives of the people who claim the sole right of imposing taxes' (WN, IV. vii.b. 51). This was the system which had been 'perfected by the revolution' (WN, IV. v. b. 43), and which could only be fully understood by reference to underlying economic trends. Yet Smith insisted that England alone had escaped from absolutism (LJ (A), iv. 168), a circumstance which he attributed to the fact that a solution had been found to the Scottish problem, to the natural fertility of the soil, and to Britain's position as an island. Smith added to this list the peculiarities of sovereigns, such as Elizabeth I, who, being childless, sold off crown lands and thus weakened the position of her successors (LJ (A), iv. 171). He also drew attention to the character of the Stuart kings, a family which 'were set aside for excellent reasons' at the time of the Revolution (LJ (B), 82).

But Smith was aware of the fact that England was not unique, that her institutions had been deliberately exported to the American colonies in a more republican form, thus short-circuiting the historical process and contributing to a rapid rate of economic development (WN, IV. vii. b. 51) in the West.

Expediency (Economics). As Smith moved to the last section of his course, his students would be well aware of the relevance of the materials just considered. His treatment of the stage of commerce makes it clear that the usual features of dependence and subordination would be found in this, as in all other, types of social organization. But here wealth only commands respect and thus deference (TMS, I. iii. 2.3), while dependence relates to the forces of the market rather than to individuals. In this context: 'Each tradesman or artificer derives his subsistence from the employment, not of one, but of a hundred or a thousand different customers. Though in some measure obliged to them all, he is not absolutely dependent upon any one of them' (WN, III. iv. 12). The stage of commerce is one where goods and services command a price, and where the 'great commerce of every civilised society, is that carried on between the inhabitants of the town and those of the country' (WN, III. i. 1).

Smith's students would also be aware that many of the psychological judgements which Smith deployed in TMS were peculiarly relevant to a situation where the institutional impediments to economic growth had been largely removed. It was in this context that he drew attention to the deception involved in the pursuit of wealth; a deception which 'rouses and keeps in continual motion the industry of mankind' (TMS, IV. 1. 10). In another notable passage, which draws upon the analogy of the Invisible Hand, Smith drew attention to the fact the 'rich', in expending their surpluses, contribute 'to make nearly the same distribution of the necessaries of life, which would have been made, had the earth been divided into equal portions among all its inhabitants' (TMS, IV. 1. 10).

But perhaps the most striking passages are those in which the reader is reminded of the proposition that self-interested actions, including economic actions, have a 'social' reference. From whence, Smith enquired, 'arises that emulation which runs through all the different ranks of men, and what are the advantages which we propose by that great purpose of human life which we call bettering our condition?' He answered: 'To be observed, to be attended to, to be taken notice of with sympathy, complacency, and approbation' (TMS, I. iii. 2. 1). Smith went further in suggesting that a person 'appears mean-spirited' who does not pursue the 'more extraordinary and important objects of self-interest', contrasting the 'man of dull regularity' with the 'man of enterprise' (TMS, III. 6. 7).

Later in the argument Smith stated that men tend to approve of the *means* adopted to attain the *ends* of ambition. Hence 'that eminent esteem with which all men naturally regard a steady perseverance in the practice of frugality, industry and application, though directed to no other purpose than the acquisition of fortune'. In a further passage Smith was to argue that it 'is the consciousness of this merited approbation and esteem which is alone capable of supporting the agent in this tenour of conduct', since normally the 'pleasure which we are to enjoy ten years hence interests us so little in comparison with that which we may enjoy today' (TMS, IV. i. 2. 8).

ECONOMIC THEORY

Smith's writings on economics (apart from two fragments on the division of labour (styled FA and FB in the Glasgow edition) are contained in the lecture notes for 1762/3 and 1763/4 together with the document first discovered by W.R. Scott and described by him as an '*Early Draft*' of WN (Scott, 1937). The first set of lectures is less complete than the second, and omits the discussion of Law's Bank, interest, exchange and the causes of the slow progress of opulence. On the other hand, those topics which *are* covered in LJ (A), and which correspond to sections 1–12 of Part 2 in Cannan's edition of LJ (B) are typically handled with much more elaboration. LJ (B) is not only more complete, at least in terms of coverage, but also more highly finished.

Each version of Smith's early analysis shows an interest in major themes, which are developed in an order which owe much to Hutcheson (Scott, 1900, ch. 11), most notably the discussion of the division of labour and its implications, and the treatment of price and allocation. Smith departs from Hutcheson, and discloses a debt to Hume, in developing a third topic; namely, the critique of the mercantile 'fallacy' (Stewart, IV. 24).

But the later work reveals a smooth, progressive, analytical development, as compared to LJ. In WN the treatment of the division of labour assumes its most elaborate form, while the theory of price features for the first time a clear distinction between factors of production (land, labour, capital) and categories of return (rent, wages, profit). These distinctions enabled Smith to give new meaning to his earlier grasp of the general interdependence of economic phenomena and to proceed to an account of a macroeconomic model which owed much to the teaching of Quesnay. Although some commentators have suggested that Smith's treatment of physiocratic teaching in WN (IV. ix) was slighting, the fact remains that his assessment of the contribution of the school accurately reflects its purpose and provides details of the more sophisticated model associated with 'revisionists' such as Turgot (Meek, 1962). There is no reason to doubt the truth of Dugald Stewart's assertion that 'the intimacy in which he lived with some of the leaders of that sect, could not fail to assist him in methodizing and digesting his speculations' (Stewart, III. 5). Stewart also noted that 'If he had not been prevented by Quesnay's death, Mr. Smith once had an intention (as he told me himself) to have inscribed to him his 'Wealth of Nations ' (Stewart, III. 12). Stewart also recorded that the division between rent, wages and profit may have originally been suggested to Smith by his old friend James Oswald (Works, 1856, ix. 6).

Division of labour. Although Smith's model, in its post-physiocratic form, has several distinct elements, the feature on which he continued to place most emphasis was the *division of labour*. In terms of the content of the model outlined in the previous section, a division of labour is of course implied in the existence of distinct *sectors* or types of productive activity. But Smith also emphasized the fact that there was specialization by types of employment, and even within each employment. To illustrate the basic point, Smith chose the celebrated example of the pin, a very 'trifling manufacture' which none the less required some eighteen distinct processes for its completion.

Smith was at pains to point out that the division of labour (by process) helped to explain the relatively high productivity of labour in modern times – a phenomenon which he ascribed to the increase in 'dexterity' which inevitably results from making a single, relatively simple operation 'the sole employment of the labourer'; to the saving of time which would otherwise be lost 'in passing from one species of work to another'; and to the associated use of machines which 'facilitate and abridge labour, and enable one man to do the work of many' (WN, I. i. 6–8). Although Smith was later to claim that agriculture was the most productive area for investment, he pointed out that the scope for the division of labour was more limited in this field than in manufactures (WN, I. i. 4; see below, p.lines 1230–33).

Four important points followed. First, Smith associated the division of labour with the process of *invention* (technical change);

> A great part of the machines made use of in those manufactures in which labour is most subdivided, were originally the inventions of common workmen, who, being each of them employed in some very simple operation, naturally turned their thoughts towards finding out easier and readier methods of performing it (WN, I. i. 8).

He also drew attention to the contribution of the 'makers of machines', and to the work of

> those who are called philosophers or men of speculation, whose trade it is, not to do any thing, but to observe every thing; and who, upon that account, are often capable of combining together the powers of the most distant and dissimilar objects. In the progress of society, philosophy or speculation becomes, like every other employment, the principal or sole trade and occupation of a particular class of citizens (WN, I. i. 9).

Secondly, Smith argued that the division of labour is limited only by the extent of the market (WN, I. iii), drawing attention in this context to the importance of the means of communications, such as good roads, and of access both to the sea and to navigable rivers. The latter point bears directly on Smith's historical analysis (see above, p. lines 458); the former was taken up in his treatment of public works (see below, p. lines 1445–5). The same argument was to be developed in terms of Smith's plea for freedom of trade (see below, p. lines 1305) and serves as a reminder that the division of labour would both contribute to, and be sustained by, the process of economic growth (which is analysed in WN, II). Thirdly, Smith contended that the institution of the division of labour helped to explain not only the enormous increase in the productivity of labour in modern times, but also an improvement in the level of material welfare of such an order that the accommodation of the 'frugal peasant' now 'exceeds that of many an African king, the absolute master of the lives and liberties of ten thousand naked savages' (WN, I. i. 11). Smith also observed that the consumer who purchases a single commodity acquires, in effect, the separate outputs of a 'great variety of labour' (WN, I. i. 11). 'The woollen coat, for example, which covers the day labourer, as coarse and rough as it may appear, is the produce of the joint labour of a great multitude of workmen' (WN, I. i. 11).

However, the aspect of this discussion which is most immediately relevant is the light it throws on the necessity of *exchange*. As Smith observed, once the division of labour is established, our own labour can supply us with only a very small part of our wants. He thus noted that even in the barter economy the individual can best satisfy the whole range of his needs by exchanging the surplus part of his own production, receiving in return the products of others. Where the division of labour is *thoroughly* established, it is then to be expected that each individual is in a sense dependent on his fellows, and that 'Every man thus lives by exchanging, or becomes in some measure a merchant' (WN, I. iv. 1).

Smith argued, indeed, that:

> As it is by treaty, by barter, and by purchase, that we obtain from one another the greater part of those mutual good offices which we stand in need of, so it is this same trucking disposition which originally gives occasion to the division of labour (WN, I. ii. 3).

Value. These observations brought Smith directly to the problem of *value*, and it is noteworthy that in order to simplify the analysis he used the *analytical* (as distinct from the *historical*) device of the barter economy.

In dealing with the *rate* of exchange, Smith argued that 'the proportion between the quantities of labour necessary for acquiring different objects seems to be the only circumstance which can afford any rule for exchanging them for one another' (WN, I. vi. 1). Thus he suggested that if it takes twice the labour to kill a beaver than it does to kill a deer, then 'one beaver should naturally exchange for or be worth two deer'. This is one way of looking at the problem of exchange value, but Smith seems to have treated it, not as an end in itself, but as a means of elucidating those factors which govern the value of *the whole stock of goods* which the individual creates, and which it is proposed to use in exchange.

Looking at the problem in *this way*, Smith went on to argue that:

> The value of any commodity ... to the person who possesses it, and who means not to use or consume it himself, but to exchange it for other commodities, is equal to the quantity of labour which it enables him to purchase or command. Labour, therefore, is the real measure of the exchangeable value of all commodities (WN, I. v. 1).

Smith's meaning becomes clear when he remarks that the exchangeable value of a *stock* of goods must always be in proportion to

> the quantity ... of other men's labour, *or, what is the same thing, of the produce* of other men's labour, which it enables him to purchase or command. The exchangeable value of everything must always be precisely equal to the extent of this power (WN, I. v. 3; italics supplied).

In other words, Smith is here arguing that the real value of the goods which the workman has to dispose of (in effect, his income) must be measured by the quantity of goods which he receives once the whole volume of (separate) exchanges has taken place.

Now, if, as Smith suggested, the *rate* of exchange between goods is always equal to the ratio of the labour *embodied* in them, then it follows that the labour embodied in the stock of goods used in exchange must be equal to the labour embodied in the goods received. The argument has two important features. First, Smith suggests that in the barter economy, the labour which the individual expends, and which is embodied in the goods *he* creates, must exchange for, or command, an equal quantity. In short, labour embodied equals labour commanded. But it is also evident, in the modern economy, that labour is no longer the sole factor of production, and that in 'this state of things, the whole produce of labour does not always belong to the labourer' (WN, I. vi. 7). The equality between labour embodied and labour commanded appears to be relevant to the barter economy and to no other.

A clear difference between the barter and modern economies is to be found in the fact that, while in the former, goods are exchanged for goods, in the latter, goods are exchanged for a sum of money, which may then be expended in purchasing other goods. Under such circumstances the individual, as Smith saw, tends to estimate the value of his receipts (received in return for undergoing the 'fatigues' of labour) in terms of money rather than in terms of the quantity of goods he can acquire by virtue of his expenditure. But Smith was at some pains to insist that the real measure of our ability to satisfy our wants is to be found in 'the money's worth' rather than the money, where the former is determined by the quantity of products (labour 'commanded') which either individuals or groups can purchase. Smith went on to distinguish between the nominal and the real value of income, pointing out that if the three original sources of revenue in modern times are wages, rent and profit, then the real *value* of each must ultimately be measured 'by the quantity of labour which they can, each of them, purchase or command' (WN, I. vi. 9).

The determinants of price. Smith's emphasis on exchange also focused attention on the issue of demand, which had already been elaborated in TMS, most notably in Part IV ('Of the beauty which the appearance of UTILITY bestows upon all the productions of Art'.) In LJ Smith contrasted the demand for commodities of immediate use, such as those related to subsistence and shelter, with a desire for refinement which was based on the 'delicacy' of body and the 'much greater delicacy' of mind (LJ (B), 208; cf. LJ (A), iv. 1–30). In this connection, he drew attention to man's 'taste of beauty, which consists chiefly in the three following particulars, proper variety, easy connection and simple order', before going on to note that 'These qualities, which are the ground of preference and which give occasion to pleasure and pain, are the cause of the many insignificant demands which we by no means stand in need of' (LJ (B), 209).

The argument is given further point by Smith's handling of the famous paradox; namely, that the 'things which have the greatest value in use (e.g. water) have frequently little or no value in exchange; and, on the contrary, those which have the greatest value in exchange (e.g. diamonds) have frequently little or no value in use' (WN, I. iv. 13).

Smith's handling of the first part of the problem is based on his recognition that both goods are considered to be 'useful'. In the former case (water) a value is placed upon the good because it can be used in a practical way, while in the latter case (diamonds) the good appeals to our 'senses', an appeal which, as Smith observed, constitutes a ground 'of preference', 'merit' or 'source of pleasure'. He concluded: 'The demand for the precious stones arises altogether from their beauty, they are of no use, but as ornaments' (WN, I. xi. c. 32).

At the same time, Smith appreciated that merit (value) is a function of scarcity: 'the merit of an object which is in any degree either useful or beautiful, is greatly enhanced by its scarcity' (WN, I. xi. c. 31). Even more specifically, he remarked: 'Cheapness is in fact the same thing with plenty. It is only on account of the plenty of water that it is so cheap as to be got for the lifting, and on account of the scarcity of diamonds (for their real use seems not yet to be discovered) that they are so dear' (LJ (B), 205–6). The argument can be extended to the problem of particular commodities in a way which is consistent with the negatively sloped demand curve, which his formal analysis of the determinants of price effectively employs.

On the supply side, Smith assumes the existence of given 'ordinary' or 'average' rates of wages, profit and rent; rates which may be said to prevail within any given society or neighbourhood, during any given (time) period (WN, I. vii. 1). The assumption is important for three reasons: first, it indicates that in dealing with the problem of price, Smith may be seen to have used the analytical device of a static system. Secondly, it should be noted that these rates determine the supply price of commodities and establish in effect the *position* of the (horizontal) supply curve. Thirdly, the argument suggests that the price of commodities may be established by 'adding up' the component parts of wages, profit and rent.

With these three points forming Smith's major premises, he proceeded to examine the determinants of price and may be seen to have produced a discussion which involves two distinct but related problems. First, he set out to illustrate those forces which determine the prices of particular commodities (Blaug, 1962, p. 42). Secondly, he appears to have used the analysis as a means of elucidating the phenomenon of *general interdependence* already hinted at in the *Lectures* (Hollander, 1973, p. 114).

In dealing with the first aspect of the problem, Smith examined the case of a commodity manufactured by a number of sellers, opening the analysis by confirming the distinction between 'natural' and 'market price' already established in LJ. *Natural price* is now defined as that amount which is 'neither more nor less than what is sufficient to pay the rent of the land, the wages of the labour, and the profits of the stock ... according to their natural rates' (WN, I. vii. 4). Where the natural price prevails, the seller is just able to cover his costs of production, including a margin for 'ordinary or average' profit. By contrast, *market price* is defined as that price which may prevail at any given point in time, being regulated 'by the proportion between the quantity which is actually brought to market, and the demand of those who are willing to pay the natural price of the commodity' (the 'effectual demanders'; WN, I. vii. 8). The two 'prices' are interrelated, the essential point being that while, in the short run, market and natural price may diverge, in the long run they will tend to coincide. Natural price thus emerges as an *equilibrium* price, which will obtain when the commodity in question is sold at its cost of production. The latter point may be illustrated by examining the consequences of a divergence between the two prices. For example, if the quantity offered by the seller was less than that which the consumers were prepared to take at a particular (natural) price, the consequence would be a competition among consumers to procure some of a relatively limited stock. Under such circumstances, Smith argued that the 'market' will rise above the 'natural' price, the extent of the divergence being determined by 'the greatness of the deficiency' and varying 'according as the acquisition of the commodity happens to be of more or less importance' to the buyer (WN, I. vii. 9). In making the latter point, Smith took note of the fact that where a relative shortage occurs of goods which are 'necessaries' of life, the extent of the divergence between the two prices (in effect the demand and supply prices) would be greater than that which would occur in other cases (for example, luxuries).

Under such circumstances, the price received by the seller must exceed the natural price (cost of production), with the result that rates of return accruing to factors in this employment (notably wages and profit) also rise above their 'ordinary' level. The consequence of such a divergence between the returns paid in a particular employment and the 'natural' rates prevailing must then be an inflow of resources to this relatively profitable field, leading to an expansion in the supply of the commodity, and a return to that position where it is sold at its natural price. Given a relative shortage of the commodity in the market, Smith concluded: 'The quantity brought thither will soon be sufficient to supply the effectual demand. All the different parts of its price will soon sink to their natural rate, and the whole price to its natural price' (WN, I. vii. 14). In short, the 'natural price' emerges as the equilibrium or 'central' price 'to which the prices of all commodities are continually gravitating' (WN, I. vii. 15).

The first stage of the discussion establishes that in the case of any one commodity, equilibrium will be attained where the good is sold at its natural price, and where each of the (relevant) factors is paid for at its natural rate. It is evident that if this process, and this result, holds good for all commodities taken separately, it must also apply to all commodities 'taken complexly', at least where a competitive situation prevails. *Over the whole economy*, a position of equilibrium would be attained where each different type of good is sold at its natural price, and where each factor in each employment is paid at its natural rate. The economy can then be said to be in a position of 'balance', since where the above conditions are satisfied there can be no tendency to move resources within or between employments. Where a position of 'balance' is disturbed (for example, as a result of changes in tastes) it will naturally tend to be re-established as a result of (simultaneous) adjustments in the factor and commodity markets. Departure from, and reattainment of, a position of equilibrium depends upon the essentially self-interested actions and reactions of consumers *and* producers. Smith's treatment of price and allocation thus provides one of the best examples of his emphasis on 'interdependence' and a further example of his thesis of the Invisible Hand.

THE NATURAL RATES OF FACTOR PAYMENT

Smith's theory of price was built upon the assumption of given rates of factor payment. His next task was to elucidate the forces which determine the *level* of ('ordinary or average') rates of return during any given time period, or over time. He applied the simple 'demand and supply' type of analysis just considered, while taking pains to differentiate between different types of factor payment (WN, I. vi).

Wages constitute payment for the use of the factor labour. The payment is made by those classes who require the factor (undertakers, farmers) and accrues to those who effectively sell their labour power. The process of wage determination may then be viewed as a kind of bargain or contract (WN, I. viii. 11) where the balance of advantage generally lies with the 'masters'; the reason being that while contemporary legislation permitted their 'combinations', it prevented those of the workers. But Smith also pointed out that the bargaining strength of the two parties would itself be affected by demand and supply relationships, irrespective of legal privileges (WN, I. viii. 17).

Wage rates may be relatively high or low, depending on the available supply of labour and the size of the fund (or capital stock) available for its purchase. Smith did not in fact set out to define some upper limit for wages, but he did suggest that the lowest limit, in the long term, must be determined by the needs of *subsistence* (WN, I. viii. 15). The importance of the 'subsistence wage' lies in the fact that it constitutes the long-run supply price of labour, the argument being in effect that over time labour may be produced at constant cost, leading to the conclusion that the subsistence wage could be regarded as a kind of 'natural' or equilibrium rate. Smith made use of three cases to illustrate an argument which is analogous to the previous treatment of equilibrium price.

In a position of long-run equilibrium the demand for, and supply of, labour must be such that the workforce is in receipt of a subsistence wage. Under such circumstances, a position of equilibrium is established in the sense that there can be no tendency for population to increase or diminish, a condition which will obtain so long as there is no change in the size of the wages fund. This is Smith's example of the stationary state, as illustrated by the experience of China (WN, I. viii. 24). Secondly, Smith examined a case where there is a fall in the demand for labour either in any one year or continuously over a number of years. Under such circumstances the actual wage rate must fall below the subsistence rate, resulting in a fall in population until the level is such as to permit subsistence wages to be paid. This example represents Smith's 'declining' state, the cases cited being Bengal and certain East Indian colonies; areas where the decline in the wages fund had led to want, 'famine and mortality', until 'the number of inhabitants ... was reduced to what could easily be maintained by the revenue and stock which remained' (WN, I. viii. 26).

In the 'advancing state' an increase, or series of (annual) increases, in the size of the wages fund causes rates in excess of the subsistence level to be paid at least for as long as it takes to increase the level of population; an increase which would inevitably follow from the higher standard of living involved (WN, I. viii. 40). Smith also pointed out that the feature of the 'advancing state' would be a continuous improvement in the demand for labour, thus making it possible for high wage rates to be paid over a number of years, and at least for as long as the *rate* of increase in the demand for labour exceeded the rate of increase in supply. Smith considered the case of North America to be a good example of the trend, but also that many European countries, including Great Britain, showed the same tendency, albeit to a lesser degree (WN, I. viii. 22). All three cases illustrate the same basic principle; namely, that the demand for men, 'like that for any other commodity, necessarily regulates the production of men' (WN, I. viii. 40).

Profit was not considered by Smith to be the reward payable for undertaking the managerial function of 'inspection and direction' but rather as the compensation for the trouble taken, and the risks incurred, in combining the factors of production (WN, I. vi. 5). The profits which accrue to individual producers will be affected by the selling price of the commodity and its cost of production. Profits are thus likely to be particularly sensitive to changes in the direction of demand, together with the 'good or bad fortune' of rivals and customers; facts which make it difficult to speak of an 'ordinary or average' rate of return (WN, I. ix. 3). However, Smith did suggest that the rate of *interest* would provide a reasonably accurate index of profit levels at any one time and over time, basically on the ground that the rate payable for borrowed funds would reflect the profits to be gained from their use: 'It may be laid down as a maxim, that wherever a great deal can be made by the use of money, a great deal will commonly be given for the use of it; and that wherever little can be made by it, less will commonly be given for it' (WN, I. ix. 4).

At least as a broad generalization, Smith felt able to suggest that the rate of profit accruing at any one point in time (other things remaining equal, and with wage rates given) would be determined by the quantity of stock (capital) available, taken in conjunction with the volume of business to be transacted by it, or the extent of the outlets for profitable investment. It thus followed that over time the rate of profit will tend to fall, partly in consequence of the gradual increase of stock, and partly because of the increasing difficulty of finding 'a profitable method of employing any new capital'. The 'diminution of profit is the natural effect of ... prosperity' (WN, I. ix. 10), although, as Smith pointed out, in advancing states the tendency for profits to fall might be reversed or halted, due to the acquisition of new investment outlets or of new territories (WN, I. ix. 12).

The basic points are clear: in the long term the tendency is for profits (like wages) to fall. At any one point in time (say, a single year), the 'ordinary or average' rate of profit prevailing must be a function of the quantity of stock and the 'proportion of business' to which it can be applied. Smith made an important qualification to the latter point when he indicated that even where the quantity of stock remains the same (say, in two different time periods), other things remaining equal, the rate of profit will also be related to the prevailing wage rate. If labour is relatively abundant in relation to a given capital stock (that is, the wages fund), the rate of profit will be higher, and wage rates lower, than they would be where labour was relatively scarce.

In the following chapter Smith added a further important dimension to his treatment of wages and profits. The point follows directly from his recognition (following Hutcheson) of the fact that employments differ qualitatively. As Smith put it, 'certain circumstances in the employments themselves ... either really, or at least in the imaginations of men, make up for a small pecuniary gain in some, and counter-balance a great one in others' (WN, I. x. a. 2). He noted, for example, that wage rates would tend to vary between different types of employment according to the difficulty of learning the trade, the constancy of employment and the degree of trust involved. Similarly, he observed that both wages and profits would vary with differences in the agreeableness of the work, and with the probability of success in particular fields. He concluded that in a competitive environment, 'The whole of the advantages and disadvantages of the different employments of labour and stock must, in the same neighbourhood, be either perfectly equal or continually tending to equality' (WN, I. x. 1).

Rent is defined as the 'price paid for the use of land' (WN, I. xi. a. 1), a price paid because land is of itself productive, part of the property of individuals and (presumably) scarce. Smith argued that rent constitutes a pure surplus; the proprietors of land emerge as 'the only one of the three orders whose revenue costs them neither labour nor care, but comes to them, as it were, of its own accord' (WN, I. xi. p. 8). Moreover, Smith suggested that rent payments are somewhat akin to a 'monopoly price' at least in the broad sense that they are generally the highest which can be got in the 'actual circumstances of the land' (WN, I. xi. a. 1). Smith recognized that rent payments would vary with both the fertility and the situation of the land involved.

Smith generally took the view that land used for the production of human food would always yield a rent, and indeed computed that rent would be of the order of one-third of the gross produce. Moreover, he suggested that in the long term, rent payments would tend to increase, at least absolutely, due to the increased use of the available stock (of land) which the growth of population inevitably involves. 'The extension of improvement and cultivation tends to raise it directly. The landlord's share of the produce necessarily increases with the increase of the produce' (WN, I. xi. p. 2). He added that the real value of the landlord's receipts would also tend to increase over time, since all 'those improvements in the productive powers of labour, which tend directly to reduce the real price of manufactures, tend indirectly to raise the real rent of land' (WN, I. xi. p. 4).

Two aspects of Smith's argument are of particular importance in the present context. First, the analysis serves to suggest that at any point in time, or during any given annual period, rent payments will be a function of the proportion (of the fixed stock of land) used, where the latter is in turn a function of the level of population. Secondly, Smith's argument indicates that during any given annual period rent payments will be related not only to the fertility of the soil but also to the prevailing rates of wages and profit (WN, I. xi. a. 8).

A MACROECONOMIC MODEL

It is apparent that there is a 'static' element in Smith's treatment of distribution, linking it to the theory of price. There is also a dynamic element, in the sense that Smith was partly concerned with long-run trends in rates of return, treating factors as flows rather than stocks.

The first theme was to be continued in terms of Smith's treatment of period analysis in the physiocratic manner; the second is relevant in the context of the discussion of growth.

Period analysis. Smith's analysis of the 'circular flow' may be seen as a direct development of results already stated in connection with the theory of price. Costs of production are incurred by those who create commodities, thus providing individuals with the means of exchange. It follows that if the price of each good (in a position of equilibrium) comprehends payments made for rent, wages and profit, according to their natural rates, then 'it must be so with regard to all the commodities which compose the whole annual produce of the land and labour of every country, taken complexly' (WN, II. ii. 2). Smith concluded: 'The whole price or exchangeable value of that annual produce, must resolve itself into the same three parts, and be parcelled out among the different inhabitants' (ibid.). Smith thus established that there must be a relationship between aggregate output and aggregate income: 'The gross revenue of all the inhabitants of a great country, comprehends the whole annual produce of their land and labour' (WN, II. ii. 5).

The three major socio-economic groups have distinctive and particular roles. The proprietors of land are typically associated with habits of expense and conspicuous consumption, while wage labour as a group faces the problem of meeting more basic levels of need. It is the 'undertakers' who are normally linked with the 'principle which prompts to save' (WN, II. iii. 28) and with a willingness to invest in both fixed and circulating capital; categories which are reminiscent of physiocratic teaching.

Fixed capital is defined as that portion of savings used to purchase 'useful machines' or to improve, for example, the productive powers of land, the characteristic feature being that goods are created, and profits ultimately acquired, by using and *retaining* possession of the investment goods involved. *Circulating capital* is that portion of savings used to purchase investment goods other than 'fixed' implements, such as labour power or raw materials, the characteristic feature being that goods are produced through temporarily 'parting with' the funds so used. Smith also noted that different trades would use different proportions of fixed and circulating capital, and that no fixed capital 'can yield any revenue but by means of a circulating capital' (WN, II, i. 25).

The system which Smith described featured the production and use of both investment and consumption goods, but also a demand for *services* which do not *directly* contribute to the (annual) output of commodities (in physical terms) and which thus cannot be said to contribute to that level of income associated with it. Smith formally described such labour as 'unproductive', but did not deny that services of this kind were useful. He pointed out that the services of 'players, buffoons, opera singers, and musicians' have a certain *value* because they represent sources of satisfaction to those who pay for them. He also observed that the services provided by governments, such as justice and defence, which are paid for out of taxes, have a value, the reason being that society could not subsist without them. However, all such services are by definition unproductive:

> The sovereign ... with all the officers both of justice and war who serve under him, the whole army and navy, are unproductive labourers. They are the servants of the publick, and are maintained by a part of the annual produce of the industry of other people (WN, II. iii. 2).

Smith then proceeded to develop a model of the 'circular flow' which owed much to physiocratic analysis, while giving his account a distinctive style by dividing the stock of *society* into a number of components. These are, first, that part of total stock which is reserved for immediate consumption, and which is held by *all* consumers (undertakers, labour and proprietors). The characteristic feature of this part of the total stock is that it affords no revenue to its possessors since it consists in 'the stock of food, cloathes, household furniture, etc. which have been purchased by their proper consumers, but which are not yet entirely consumed' (WN, II. i. 12).

Secondly, there is that part of the total stock which may be described as 'fixed capital' and which will again be distributed between the various groups in society. This part of the stock, Smith suggested, is composed of the 'useful machines' purchased in preceding periods and held by the undertakers engaged in manufacture, and the quantity of useful buildings and of 'improved land' in the possession of the 'capitalist' farmers and the proprietors, together with the 'acquired and useful abilities' of all the inhabitants (WN, i. 13–17), that is, human capital.

Thirdly, there is that part of the total stock which may be described as 'circulating capital' and which again has several components. These include the quantity of money necessary to carry on the process of circulation (WN, II. iii. 23); the stock of provisions and other agricultural products which are available for sale during the current period, but which are still in the hands of either the farmers or merchants; the stock of raw materials and work in process, which is held by merchants, undertakers or those capitalists (i.e. undertakers) engaged in the agricultural sector (including mining etc.). Finally, there is the stock of manufactured goods (consumption and investment) created during a previous period, but which remain in the hands of undertakers and merchants at the beginning of the period examined (WN. II. i. 19–22).

The logic of the process can best be represented by distinguishing between the activities involved. Suppose, at the beginning of the time period in question, that the major capitalist groups possess the total net receipts earned from the sale of products in the previous period, and that the undertakers engaged in agriculture open by transmitting the total rent due to the proprietors of land, for the use of that factor. The income thus provided enables the proprietors to make necessary purchases of consumption goods in the current period, thus contributing to reduce the stocks of such goods available for sale. The undertakers (capitalists) engaged in both sectors, together with the merchant groups, transmit to wage labour the content of the wages fund, thus providing this socio-economic class with an income which can be used in the current period. The undertakers (or entrepreneurs) engaged in agriculture and manufactures purchase consumption and investment goods from each other (through the medium of retail and wholesale merchants), thus generating a series of expenditures which *link* the two sectors. The process of circulation may be seen to be completed by the purchases made by individual undertakers *within* their own sectors. These purchases will include consumption and investment goods, thus contributing still further to reduce the stocks of commodities which formed part of the circulating capital of the society at the beginning of the period (i.e. year).

Given these points, the working of the system can be represented in terms of a series of *flows* whereby money (accruing in the form of rent, wages and profit) is exchanged for commodities. The consumption goods withdrawn from the existing stock may be entirely exhausted during the current period, used to *increase* the stock 'reserved for immediate consumption', or to replace more durable goods which had reached the end of their lives in the course of the same period. Similarly, undertakers may *add* to their stocks of raw materials and of fixed capital, or *replace* machines which had finally worn out in the current period, together with the materials which had been exhausted. Looked at in this way, the 'circular flow' may be seen to involve purchases which *withdraw* goods from the circulating capital of *society*, a process which is matched by a simultaneous process of *replacement* by virtue of current production of materials and other commodities.

Two additional matters should be noted before going further. In discussing the working of the 'flow', Smith had in effect introduced a treatment 'Of the Different Employment of Capital'. As he noted, in a passage reminiscent of Turgot's *Reflections* (sect. LXXXIII), capitals may be employed in agriculture, manufacture or in the wholesale and retail trades: 'Each of those four methods of employing a capital is essentially necessary either to the existence or extension of the other three, or to the general conveniency of the society' (WN, II. v. 3).

Secondly, he noted that profit levels in each area must be seen to be interrelated, with due allowance made for the advantages and disadvantages which attend the different employments of capital (WN, III. i. 3; cf. I. x. a). Smith also pointed out that profits in the different employments of stock would tend to equality as a result of the movement of resources between fields. In a passage which recalls the earlier treatment of allocation, Smith noted that 'The consideration of his own private profit, is the sole motive which determines the owner of any capital to employ it either in agriculture, in manufactures, or in some particular branch of the wholesale or retail trade' (WN, II. v. 37).

Dynamics. In choosing to examine the working of the economy during a given time period such as a year, Smith gave his model a broadly short-run character, albeit one which *includes* a time dimension. But he did not seek to formulate *equilibrium* conditions for the model as Quesnay had done in the *Analyse*, at least in the sense that he did not try to develop an argument which used specific assumptions of a quantitative kind. Smith's lack of concern with 'macro-static' *equilibrium* was to some extent announced by the fact that he made allowance for the problem of the different *rates* at which goods may be used up.

Nor did Smith suggest that the level of output attained during any given period would be exactly sufficient to replace the goods which had been exhausted during its course. On the contrary, he argued that levels of output attained in any time period could well *exceed* previous values. Smith's main concern was with economic growth:

> The annual produce of the land and labour of any nation can be increased in its value by no other means, but by increasing either the number of its productive labourers, or the productive power of those labourers who had before been employed (WN, II. iii. 32).

Both sources of increased output required 'additional capital' devoted either to increasing the size of the wages fund or to the purchase of 'machines and instruments which facilitate and abridge labour' (ibid.), *Net* savings are the key to the process:

> Parsimony, by increasing the fund which is destined for the maintenance of productive hands, tends to increase the number of those hands whose labour adds to the value of the subject upon which it is bestowed. It tends therefore to increase the exchangeable value of the annual produce of the land and labour of the country. It puts into motion an additional quantity of industry, which gives an additional value to the annual produce (WN, II. iii. 17).

Net savings, where used for 'productive' purposes, are likely to generate an increase in the level of output and income in subsequent periods. Where there are opportunities for investment, the process of capital accumulation and economic growth can be seen to be self-generating, indicating that Smith's version of the 'flow' is to be regarded not as a 'circle' but as a spiral of constantly expanding dimensions. It was in this connection that Smith advanced a proposition that was to figure prominently in the formulation of the classical system later to be associated with J.B. Say and James Mill; namely, that what is 'annually saved is as regularly consumed as what is annually spent, and nearly in the same time too; but it is consumed by a different set of people' (WN, II. iii. 18). This echoes an earlier statement: 'A man must be perfectly crazy who, where there is tolerable security does not employ all the stock which he commands' (WN, II. i. 30).

The treatment of growth was further supported by reference to the division of labour, which suggested that technical change was endogenous and continuous (see above, p. lines

638–652 ff). While Smith in effect made the point that the economic process is likely to be subject to increasing returns, it is doubtful if he fully appreciated the rate of technical change currently taking place. But he also expressed interest in other elements which could affect the *rate* of growth, all of which relate to the argument so far.

Smith noted the importance of the level of resources needed to maintain a fixed capital (WN, II. ii. 7) and drew attention to the effect of commercial failure, which always tends 'to diminish the funds destined for the maintenance of productive labour' (WN, II. iii. 26). The size of the government sector was also important, since the 'whole, or almost the whole publick revenue, is in most countries employed in maintaining unproductive hands' (II. iii. 30).

In the same vein, he drew attention to the significance of 'the enormous debts which at present oppress, and will in the long run probably ruin, all the great nations of Europe' (WN, V. iii. 10). Smith noted that the debt in Britain had reached #130 million by 1775 and that some £124 million of the total was funded (WN, V. iii. 46). Quite apart from the associated problem of taxation, Smith was concerned to point out that the practice of funding in effect meant that 'a certain portion of the annual produce' was 'turned away from serving in the function of a capital, to serve in that of a revenue' (WN, V. iii. 47). The point was a variant on Smith's basic thesis that the rate of growth must be determined by the extent to which resources are used to support productive as distinct from unproductive labour (WN, II. iii. 3).

Smith further elaborated on the basic point at issue in contending that the rate of growth would be affected by the area of investment to which specific injections of capital were applied. He contended that the main fields of investment which were mentioned in the account of the 'flow' would support, directly or indirectly, different quantities of productive labour. The *retailer* replaces the stock of the merchant from whom he purchases goods, thus supporting a certain quantity of labour even though the retailer himself is the only productive labourer directly employed. The *wholesaler* replaces the capitals of the farmers and merchants with whom he deals and from 'whom he purchases the rude and manufactured produce which he deals in, and thereby enables them to continue their respective trades' (WN, II. v. 10). Both indirectly and directly the merchant supports a larger number of productive hands than the retailer. If the wholesale trade was preferred to the retail, *manufactures* emerge as still more important since investment in this area would indirectly support a relatively large amount of productive labour by replacing the capitals of those who supply machinery and materials, while at the same time tending directly to employ a relatively significant number of people. But undoubtedly Smith's preference was for agriculture, a point already established in LJ: 'No equal capital puts into motion a greater quantity of productive labour than that of the farmer' – leading to the conclusion that 'Of all the ways in which a capital can be employed, it is by far the most advantageous to the society' (WN, II. v. 12).

Smith advanced two additional propositions which *seem* to follow from the argument just stated. First, he asserted that where the total stock available is insufficient for the purpose of agriculture, manufacture and trade, the rate of growth will be maximized by first concentrating on the former. He believed as a matter of fact that the rate of growth in Europe was lower than it might be and that 'agriculture ... is almost every where capable of absorbing a much greater capital than has ever yet been employed in it' (WN, II. v. 37). Secondly, he argued that there is a natural *sequence* of investment: 'According to the natural course of things ... the greater part of the capital of every growing society is, first, directed to agriculture, afterwards to manufactures, and last of all to foreign commerce' (WN, III. i. 8).

Smith's theory of accumulation is the dominant theme of the second book and helps to complete the logic of the earlier exposition by clarifying the source of long-run trends in factor payments. Smith's preoccupation with the long run also helps to explain the focus of WN, I. v., where he was chiefly concerned to establish a measure of value in the context of the discussion of economic welfare. The argument was intended to illustrate the point that the real value of income can only be measured in terms of the quantity of goods or the quantity of labour' (labour *embodied*) which it enables the individual 'to purchase or command' (WN, I. v. 1). Smith also sought to provide a means of measuring the extent to which individuals were better (or worse) off over long periods of time, associating improvements in welfare with 'a reduction in the sacrifices required to obtain a slab of real income' (Blaug, 1962, p. 49).

Yet 'complete' as it is, there are a number of areas of 'tension' in the work, three of which may be mentioned here. Having advanced the thesis regarding the 'natural progress of opulence', Smith went on to assert that 'this natural order of things' has:

> in all the modern states of Europe, been, in many respects, entirely inverted. The foreign commerce of some of their cities has introduced all their finer manufactures ... and manufactures and foreign commerce, together, have given birth to the principal improvements of agriculture (WN, III. i. 9).

These passages preface the analysis of Book III, which traces the emergence of the stage of commerce and have the remarkable effect of presenting the historical *record* which had been featured in LJ as being in some sense *un*natural.

Similar difficulties surround Smith's ranking of areas of investment in Book II, a ranking which is employed in the analysis of the relationship with America in order to 'demonstrate' that the rate of growth would diverge from that of the mother country. The nature of the relationship with America, Smith contended, had the effect of confining the colonists to the development of primary products (WN, IV. vii. c. 51), while in contrast, the colonial trade of Great Britain had drawn capital from a near market (Europe) and diverted it to a distant market, while forcing a certain amount of capital from a direct to an indirect foreign trade – all with consequent effects on the rate of return, the employment of productive labour and therefore on the rate of economic growth.

Governor Pownall was the first to observe that Smith had not led *empirical* evidence in support of his case (1776, Corr., 369). In recognizing Smith's reliance on the different productivities of investment, Pownall also noted that 'propositions' which had been advanced in Book II were used 'in the second part of your work [Book IV] as data; whence you endeavour to prove, that the monopoly of the colony trade is a disadvantageous commercial institution' (Corr., 354). Smith acknowledged Pownall's perceptive analysis (letter 182, dated London, 1777) and later wrote to Andreas Holt (Corr., letter 208, dated October 1780) that he had met the Governor's objections in the second edition of WN. Far from so doing, Smith added a passage to the third edition of 1783, the year of peace with America, which suggests that it is unnecessary to 'say any thing further, in order to expose the folly of a system, which fatal experience has now sufficiently exposed' (WN, IV. viii. 15).

A third area of criticism is revealed in David Ricardo's *Principles of Political Economy and Taxation* (1817). Ricardo sought to generalize the labour *embodied* theory of value, which Smith had confined to the primitive state where labour is the only factor of production (WN, I. vi. 7), combining this with a clear statement of a theory of differential rent, which effectively removed the ambiguities in Smith's treatment. It is now well known that he also deployed these areas of analysis together with Smith's population mechanism in producing a formal account of the progression from the 'advancing' to the 'stationary' state, at which Smith had also hinted.

POLICY

Smith's analytical apparatus, allied to his judgement with respect to the probable trends of the economy, led him to advance the claims of economic liberty; claims which had already featured in LJ and which date back to his days in Edinburgh (Stewart, IV. 25). The argument is repeated in WN, where Smith called upon the sovereign to discharge himself from a duty:

> in the attempting to perform which he must always be exposed to innumerable delusions, and for the proper performance of which no human wisdom or knowledge could ever be sufficient; the duty of superintending the industry of private people, and of directing it towards the employments most suitable to the interests of the society (WN, IV. ix. 51).

The statement is familiar, yet conceals a point of great significance; namely, that while the institutions of the exchange economy are consistent with the emergence of personal freedom (for example, under the law), they are not of themselves sufficient to establish what Smith described as the 'system of natural liberty' (ibid.). In fact, one of the most important functions of government is that of *identifying* and *removing* impediments to the effective working of the economy. Smith drew attention, for example, to the adverse effects of the statute of apprenticeship, and of corporate privileges. Regulations of this kind were criticized on the ground that they were both impolitic and unjust: unjust in that controls over qualification for entry to a trade were a violation 'of this most sacred property which every man has in his own labour' (WN, I. x. c. 12) and impolitic in that such regulations are not of themselves sufficient to guarantee competence. But Smith particularly emphasized that the regulations in question would adversely affect the working of the market mechanism. The 'statute of apprenticeship obstructs the free circulation of labour from one employment to another, even in the same place. The exclusive privileges of corporations obstruct it from one place to another, even in the same employment' (WN, I. x. c. 42). He also commented on the problems presented by the Poor Laws and the Laws of Settlement (WN, IV. ii. 42), which further restricted the free movement of labour from one geographical location to another.

Smith objected to positions of privilege, such as monopoly power, which he regarded as creations of the civil law. The institution was again represented as impolitic and unjust: unjust in that a monopoly position is one of privilege and advantage, and therefore 'contrary to that justice and equality of treatment which the sovereign owes to all the different orders of his subjects'; impolitic in that the prices at which goods so controlled are sold are 'upon even occasion the highest that can be got' (WN, I. vii. 27). He added that monopoly is 'a great enemy to good management' (WN, I. xi. b. 5) and that the institution had the additional defect of restricting the flow of capital to the trades affected as a result of the legal barriers to entry which were involved.

It is useful to distinguish Smith's objection to monopoly from his criticism of one expression of it; namely, the mercantile system of regulation which he described as the 'modern system' of policy, best understood 'in our own country and in our own times' (WN, IV. 2). Smith asserted that mercantile policy aimed to secure a positive balance of trade through the control of exports and imports, a policy whose 'logic' was best expressed in terms of the Regulating Acts of Trade and Navigation, which currently determined the pattern of trade between Great Britain and her colonies and which were designed to create in effect a self-sufficient Atlantic Economic Community.

Smith objected to current policies of the type described on the ground that they artificially restricted the market and thus damaged opportunities for economic growth. It was Smith's contention that such policies were liable to that general objection which may be made to all the different expedients of the mercantile system, 'the objection of forcing some part of the industry of the country into a channel less advantageous than that in which it would run of its own accord' (WN, IV. v. a. 24). In WN Smith placed more emphasis on interference with the allocative mechanism than he had done in LJ, where greater attention had been given to the inconsistency which was involved in seeking a positive balance of trade, an argument which relied heavily on Hume's analysis of the Specie Flow.

While it is difficult to judge the extent to which the claim for economic liberty explains the contemporary reception of WN, it may have been a major factor, at least in Britain (Schumpeter, 1954, p. 185). There can be no doubt that later generations found Smith's argument (and rhetoric) attractive. The celebrations to mark the fiftieth anniversary of the book showed a wide and continuing acceptance of the doctrines of free trade. In 1876, at a dinner held by the Political Economy Club to mark the centenary of WN, one speaker identified free trade as the most important consequence of the work done by 'this simple Glasgow professor', and predicted that

> 'there will be what may be called a large negative development of Political Economy tending to produce an important beneficial effect; and that is, such a development of Political Economy as will reduce the functions of government within a smaller and smaller compass' (Black, 1976, p. 51).

This view still commands wide contemporary support.

There can be no argument with Jacob Viner's contention that 'Smith in general believed that there was, to say the least, a strong presumption against government activity' (Viner, 1928, p. 140). But as Viner also reminded his auditors during the course of the Chicago conference which celebrated the 150th anniversary of the publication of WN, 'Adam Smith was not a doctrinaire advocate of laissez-faire. He saw a wide and elastic range of activity for government' (pp. 153–4). A number of examples, all identified by Viner in a classic article, may briefly be reviewed here.

First, Smith was prepared to justify specific policies to meet particular needs as these arose; the principle of intervention *ad hoc*. He defended the use of stamps on plate and linen as the most effectual guarantee of quality (WN, I. x. c. 13), the compulsory regulation of mortgages (WN, V. ii. h. 17), the legal enforcement of contracts (WN, I. ix. 16) and government control of the coinage. In addition, he supported the granting of temporary monopolies to mercantile groups, to the inventors of new machines and, not surprisingly, to the authors of new books (WN, V. i. e. 30). He further advised governments that where they were faced with taxes imposed by their competitors, retaliation could be in order, especially if such action had the effect of ensuring the 'repeal of the high duties or prohibitions complained of. The recovery of a great foreign market will generally more than compensate the transitory inconveniency of paying dearer during a short time for some sorts of goods' (WN, IV. ii. 39).

Secondly, Smith advocated the use of taxation, not as a means of raising revenue but as a source of social reform, and as a means of compensating for what would now be described as a defective telescopic faculty. In the name of the *public* interest, Smith supported taxes on the retail sale of liquor in order to discourage the multiplication of alehouses (WN, V. ii. g. 4) and differential rates on ale and spirits in order to reduce the sale of the latter (WN, V. ii. k. 50). He advocated taxes on those proprietors of land who demanded rents in kind, and on those leases which prescribed a certain form of cultivation. In the same way, Smith argued that the practice of selling a future, for the sake of present, revenue should be discouraged on the ground that it reduced the working capital of the tenant and at the same time transferred a capital sum to those who would use it for the purposes of consumption (WN, V. ii. c. 12) rather than investment which would directly support productive labour.

Smith was well aware, to take a third example, that the modern version of the 'circular flow' depended on paper money and on credit; in effect, a system of 'dual circulation' involving a complex of transactions linking producers and merchants, and dealers and consumers (WN, II. ii. 88). It is in this context that he advocated control over the rate of interest, to be set in such a way as to ensure that 'sober people are universally preferred, as borrowers, to prodigals and projectors' (WN, II. iv. 15). He was also willing to regulate the small note issue in the interests of a stable banking system. To those who objected to such a proposal Smith replied that the interests of the community required it, and concluded that 'the obligation of building party walls, in order to prevent the communication of fire, is a violation of natural liberty, exactly of the same kind [as] the regulations of the banking trade which are here proposed' (WN, II. ii. 94). Although Smith's monetary analysis is not regarded as amongst the strongest of his contributions, it should be remembered that as a witness of the collapse of the Ayr Bank, he was acutely aware of the problems generated by a sophisticated credit structure, and that it was in this context that he articulated a very general principle; namely, that 'those exertions of the natural liberty of a few individuals, which might endanger the security of the whole society, are, and ought to be, restrained by the laws of all governments; of the most free, as well as of the most despotical' (WN, II. ii. 94).

Fourthly, emphasis should be given to Smith's contention that a major responsibility of government must be the provision of certain public works and institutions for facilitating the commerce of the society which were 'of such a nature, that the profit could never repay the expence to any individual or small number of individuals, and which it, therefore, cannot be expected that any individual or small number of individuals should erect or maintain' (WN, V. i. c. 1). The examples of public works which he provided include roads, bridges, canals and harbours – all thoroughly in keeping with the conditions of the time and with Smith's emphasis on the importance of transport as a contribution to the effective operation of the market and to the process of economic growth. But although the list is short by modern standards, the discussion is of interest for two main reasons. First, Smith contended that public works or services should only be provided where market forces have failed to do so; secondly, he insisted that attention should be given to the requirements of efficiency and equity.

As Nathan Rosenberg (1960) has pointed out in an important article, Smith did not argue that governments should *directly* provide relevant services; rather, they should establish institutional arrangements so structured as to engage the motives and interests of those concerned. Smith tirelessly emphasized the point that in every trade and profession 'the exertion of the greater part of those who exercise it, is always in proportion to the necessity they are under of making that exertion' (WN, V. i. f. 4); teachers, judges, professors, civil servants and administrators alike.

With regard to equity, Smith argued that public works such as highways, bridges and canals should be paid for by those who use them and in proportion to the wear and tear occasioned – an expression of the general principle that the beneficiary should pay. He also defended direct payment on the ground of efficiency since only by this means would it be possible to ensure that necessary services would be provided where there was an identifiable need (WN, V. i. d. 6).

Yet Smith recognized that it would not always be possible to fund or to maintain public services without recourse to general taxation. In this case he argued that 'local or provincial expenses of which the benefit is local or provincial' ought to be no burden on general taxation since 'It is unjust that the whole society should contribute towards an expence of which the benefit is confined to a part of society' (WN, V. i. i. 3). However, he did agree that a general contribution would be appropriate in cases where public works benefit the whole society and cannot be maintained by the contribution 'of such particular members of the society as are most immediately benefited by them' (WN, V. i. i. 6).

But here again, the main features of the system of liberty are relevant in that they affect the way in which taxation should be imposed. Smith pointed out on welfare grounds that taxes should be levied in accordance with the canons of equality, certainty, convenience and economy (WN, V. ii. b), and insisted that they should not be raised in ways which infringed the liberty of the subject – for example, through the odious visits and examinations of the tax-gatherer. Similarly, he argued that taxes ought not to interfere with the allocative mechanism (as, for example, taxes on necessities or particular employments) or constitute important disincentives to the individual effort on which the effective operation of the whole system depended (for example, taxes on profits or on the produce of land).

ETHICS AND HISTORY

The policy views which have just been considered are closely related to Smith's economic analysis. Others are only to be fully appreciated when seen against the background of his work on ethics and jurisprudence.

It will be recalled that for Smith moral judgement depends on a capacity for acts of imaginative sympathy, and that such acts can only take place within the context of some social group (TMS, III. i. 3). However, Smith also observed that the mechanism of the impartial spectator might well break down in the context of the modern economy, due in part to the size of the manufacturing units and of the cities which housed them.

Smith observed that in the actual circumstances of modern society, the poor man could find himself in a situation where the 'mirror' of society (TMS, III. i. 3) was ineffective. The 'man of rank and fortune is by his station the distinguished member of a great society, who attend to every part of his conduct, and who thereby oblige him to attend to every part of it himself'. But the 'man of low condition', while 'his conduct may be attended to' so long as he is a member of a country village, 'as soon as he comes into a great city, he is sunk in obscurity and darkness. His conduct is observed and attended to by nobody, and he is therefore very likely to neglect it himself, and to abandon himself to every sort of low profligacy and vice' (WN, V. i. g. 12).

In the modern context, Smith suggests that the individual thus placed would naturally seek some kind of compensation, often finding it not merely in religion but in religious *sects*; that is, small social groups within which he can acquire 'a degree of consideration which he never had before' (WN, V. i. g. 12). Smith noted that the morals of such sects were often disagreeably 'rigorous and unsocial', recommending two policies to offset this.

The first of these is learning, on the ground that science is 'the great antidote to the poison of enthusiasm and superstition'. Smith suggested that government should institute 'some sort of probation, even in the higher and more difficult sciences, to be undergone by every person before he was permitted to exercise any liberal profession, or before he could be received as a candidate for any honourable office of trust or profit' (WN, V. i. g. 14). The second remedy was through the encouragement given to those who might expose or dissipate the folly of sectarian bitterness by encouraging an interest in painting, music, dancing, drama – and satire (WN, V. i. g. 15).

If the problems of solitude and isolation consequent on the growth of cities explain Smith's first group of points, a related trend in the shape of the division of labour helps to account for the second. In the earlier part of the argument, Smith had emphasized the gain to society at large which arose from improved productivity. But he noted later that this important source of economic benefit could also involve social costs:

> In the progress of the division of labour, the employment of the far greater part of those who live by labour, that is, of the great body of the people, comes to be confined to a few very simple operations; frequently to one or two. But the understandings of the greater part of men are necessarily formed by their ordinary employments. The man whose life is spent in performing a few simple operations, of which the effects too are, perhaps, always the same, or very nearly the same, has no occasion to exert his understanding, or to exercise his invention in finding out expedients for removing difficulties which never occur (WN, V. i. f. 50).

Smith went on to point out that despite a dramatic increase in the level of *real income*, the modern worker could be relatively worse off than the poor savage, since in such primitive societies the varied occupations of all men – economic, political and military – preserve their minds from that 'drowsy stupidity, which, in a civilized society, seems to benumb the understanding of almost all the inferior ranks of people' (WN, V. i. f. 51). It is the fact that the 'labouring poor, that is the great body of the people' will fall into the state outlined that makes it necessary for government to intervene.

Smith's justification for intervention is, as before, market failure, in that the labouring poor, unlike those of rank and fortune, lack the leisure, means or (by virtue of their occupation) the inclination to provide education for their children (WN, V. i. f. 53). In view of the nature of the problem, Smith's programme seems rather limited, based as it is on the premise that 'the common people cannot, in any civilized society, be so well instructed as people of some rank and fortune' (WN, V. i. f. 54). However, he did argue that they could all be taught 'the most essential parts of education ... to read, write, and account' together with the 'elementary parts of geometry and mechanicks' (WN, V. i. f. 54, 55). Smith added:

> The publick can *impose* upon almost the whole body of the people the necessity of acquiring those most essential parts of education, by obliging every man to undergo an examination or probation in them before he can obtain the freedom in any corporation, or be allowed to set up any trade either in a village or town corporate (WN, V. i. f. 57; italics supplied).

Distinct from the above, although connected with it, is Smith's concern with the decline of martial spirit, which is the consequence of the nature of the fourth, or commercial, stage. He concluded that:

> Even though the martial spirit of the people were of no use towards the defence of the society, yet to prevent that sort of mental mutilation, deformity and wretchedness, which cowardice necessarily involves in it, from spreading themselves through the great body of the people would still deserve the most serious attention of government (WN, V. i. f. 60).

Smith went on to liken the control of cowardice to the prevention of 'a leprosy or any other loathsome and offensive disease' – thus moving Jacob Viner to add public health to Smith's already lengthy list of governmental functions (Viner, 1928, p. 150). Such concerns have enabled Winch (1978) to find in Smith evidence of the *language* of an older, classical, concern with the problem of citizenship. Others (e.g. see contributions in Hont and Ignatieff, 1983) have located Smith more firmly in the tradition of civic humanism.

The historical dimension of Smith's work also affects the treatment of policy, noting as he did that in every society subject to a process of transition, 'Laws frequently continue in force long after the circumstances, which first gave occasion to them, and which could also render them reasonable, are no more' (WN, III. ii. 4). In such cases Smith suggested that arrangements which were once appropriate but are now no longer so should be removed, citing as examples the laws of succession and entail; laws which had been appropriate in the feudal period but which now had the effect of limiting the sale and improvement of land. The continuous scrutiny of the *relevance* of particular laws is an important function of the 'legislator' (Haakonssen, 1981).

In a similar way, the treatment of justice and defence, both central services to be organized by the government, are clearly related to the discussion of the stages of history, an important part of the argument in the latter case being that a gradual change in the economic and social structure had necessitated the formal provision of an army (WN, V. i. a, b).

But perhaps the most striking and interesting features emerge when it is recalled that for Smith the fourth economic stage could be seen to be associated with a particular form of social and political structure which determines the *outline of government* and the context within which it must function. It may be recalled in this connection that Smith associated the fourth economic stage with the elimination of the relation of direct dependence which had been a characteristic of the feudal agrarian period. Politically, the significant and associated development appeared to be the diffusion of power consequent on the emergence of new forms of wealth which, *at least in the peculiar circumstances of England*, had been reflected in the increased significance of the House of Commons.

Smith recognized that in this context government was a complex instrument, that the pursuit of office was itself a 'dazzling object of ambition' – a competitive game with as its object the attainment of 'the great prizes which sometimes come from the wheel of the great state lottery of British politicks' (WN, IV. vii. c. 75).

Yet for Smith the most important point was that the same economic forces which had served to elevate the House of Commons to a superior degree of influence had also served to make it an important focal point for sectional interests – a development which could seriously affect the legislation which was passed and thus affect that extensive view of the common good which ought ideally to direct the activities of Parliament.

It is recognized in the *Wealth of Nations* that the landed, moneyed, manufacturing and mercantile groups all constitute special interests which could impinge on the working of government. Smith referred frequently to their 'clamourous importunity', and went so far as to suggest that the power possessed by employers generally could seriously disadvantage other classes in the society (WN, I. x. c. 61; cf. I. viii. 12, 13). Smith insisted that any legislative proposals emanating from this class:

> ought always to be listened to with great precaution, and ought never to be adopted till after having been long and carefully examined, not only with the most scrupulous, but with the most suspicious attention. It comes from an order of men, whose interest is never exactly the same with that of the publick, who have generally an interest to deceive and even to oppress the publick, and who accordingly have, upon many occasions, both deceived and oppressed it (WN, I. xi. p. 10).

He was also aware of the dangers of manipulation arising from deployment of the civil list (LJ, (A), iv. 175–6).

It is equally interesting to note how often Smith referred to the constraints presented by the 'confirmed habits and prejudices' of the people, and to the necessity of adjusting legislation to what 'the interests, prejudices, and temper of the times would admit of' (WN, IV. v. b. 40, 53, and V. i. g. 8; cf. TMS, VI. ii. 2. 16). Such passages add further meaning to the discussion of education. An educated people, Smith argued, would be more likely to see through the interested complaints of faction and sedition. He added a warning and a promise in remarking that:

> In free countries, where the safety of government depends very much on the favourable judgment which the people may form of its conduct, it must surely be of the highest importance that they should not be disposed to judge rashly or capriciously concerning it (WN, V. i. f. 61).

THE LITERATURE OF SCIENCE

In contrast to the modern reader, students of Smith's course in Glasgow would more readily perceive that the different parts into which it fell were important of themselves, and also that they display a certain pattern of interdependence. The ethical argument clearly indicates the manner in which general rules of conduct, including those of *justice*, emerge and postulates the need for some system of government or magistracy. The treatment of jurisprudence shows the manner in which government emerged and developed through time, while throwing some light on the actual content of the rules of behaviour which were manifested in different societies.

It would also be evident to Smith's students that the treatment of economics was based upon psychological judgements (such as the desire for status) which are only explained in the ethics, and that this branch of Smith's argument takes as given that particular socio-economic structure which is appropriate to the fourth economic stage, that of commerce. This kind of perspective can only be attained by examining the logical progression of ideas as outlined in the lectures on ethics, jurisprudence and economics as they unfolded in the order in which they are now known to have been delivered. Equally, the treatment of public policy in WN is transformed in its meaning when seen not merely as a development of the earlier treatment of economics but also in terms of the appropriate ethical and jurisprudential setting.

But it should also be recalled that each separate component of the system represents scientific work in the style of Newton, contributing to a greater whole which was conceived in the same image. Smith's scientific aspirations were real, as was his consciousness of the methodological tensions which may arise in the course of such work. Such facts make it appropriate to conclude this account by reference to Smith's awareness, and treatment, of the literature of science.

Smith's interest in mathematics dates from his time as a student in Glasgow (Stewart, I. 7). He also appears to have maintained a general interest in the natural and biological sciences, facts which are attested by his purchases for the University Library (Scott, 1937. p. 182) and for his own collection (Mizuta, 1967). Smith's 'Letter to the Authors of the *Edinburgh Review*' (1756), where he warned against any undue preoccupation with Scottish literature, affords evidence of wide reading in the physical sciences, and also contains references to contemporary work in the French *Encyclopédie* as well as to the productions of Buffon, Daubenton and Reaumur. D.D. Raphael has argued that the Letter owes much to Hume (TMS, *10, 11*; cf. Bryce, EPS, 248, n. 13).

The essay on astronomy, which dates from the same period (it is known to have been written before 1758), indicates that Smith was familiar with classical as well as with more modern sources, such as Galileo, Kepler and Tycho Brahe, a salutary reminder that an 18th-century philosopher could work close to the frontiers of knowledge in a number of fields.

But Smith was also interested in science as a form of communication, arguing in the LRBL that the way in which this type of discourse is organized should reflect its purpose as well as a judgement as to the psychological characteristics of the audience to be addressed.

In a lecture delivered on 24 January 1763 Smith noted that didactic or scientific writing could have one of two aims: either to 'lay down a proposition and prove this, by the different arguments that lead to that conclusion' or to deliver a system in any science. In the latter case Smith advocated what he called the Newtonian method, whereby we 'lay down certain principles known or proved in the beginning, from whence we account for the several phenomena, connecting all together by the same Chain' (LRBL, ii. 133). Two points are to be noted. First, Smith makes it clear that Descartes rather than Newton was the first to use this method of *exposition*, even although the former was now perceived to be the author of 'one of the most entertaining Romances that have ever been wrote' (LRBL, ii. 134; cf. Letter 5). Secondly, his reference to the pleasure to be derived from the 'Newtonian method' (LRBL, ii. 134) draws attention to the problem of scientific *motivation*, a theme which was to be developed in the 'Astronomy', where Smith considered those principles 'which lead and direct philosophical enquiry'.

The 'Astronomy' takes as given certain results which had already been established in the lectures on language and in the

Considerations; namely, that men have a capacity for acts of 'arrangement or classing, or comparison, and of abstraction' (LRBL, ii. 207; cf. Corr., letter 69, dated 7 February 1763).

But the essay on astronomy approaches the matter in hand in a different way by arguing that a mind thus equipped derives a certain pleasure from the contemplation of relation, similarity or order – or as Hume would have put it, from a certain association of ideas. Smith struck a more original note in arguing that when the mind confronts a new phenomenon which does not fit into an already established classification, or where we confront an unexpected association of ideas, we feel the sentiment of surprise, and then that of wonder (Astronomy, II. 9). This is typically followed by an attempt at explanation with a view to returning the 'imagination' to a state of tranquillity (Astronomy, II. 6).

Looked at in this way, the task of explanation is related to a perceived need, which can only be met if the account offered is coherent and conducted in terms which are capable of accounting for observed appearances in terms of 'familiar' principles. It was Smith's contention that the philosopher or scientist would react in the same way as the casual observer, and that nature as a whole 'seems to abound with events which appear solitary and incoherent', thus disturbing 'the easy movement of the imagination' (Astronomy, II. 12). But he also observed that philosophers pursue scientific study 'for its own sake, as an original pleasure or good in itself' (Astronomy, III. 3).

The bulk of the essay is concerned to illustrate the extent to which the four great systems of thought which he identified were actually able to 'soothe the imagination', these being the systems of Concentric and Eccentric Spheres, together with the theories of Copernicus and Newton. But Smith added a further dimension to the argument by seeking to expose the dynamics of the process; arguing that each thought-system was subject to a process of modification as new observations were made. Smith suggested that each system was subjected to a process of development which eventually resulted in unacceptable degrees of complexity, thus paving the way for the generation of an alternative explanation of the same phenomena, but one which was better suited to meet the needs of the imagination by offering a simpler account (Astronomy, IV. 18, 28). In Smith's eyes, the work of Sir Isaac Newton thus marked the apparent culmination of a long historical process (Astronomy, IV. 76).

The argument as a whole also contains some radical conclusions. There is nothing in the analysis which suggests that the Newtonian (or Smithian) system embodies some final truth. At the same time, Smith seems to have given emphasis to what is now known as the problem of 'subjectivity' in science in arguing that scientific thought often represents a reaction to a perceived psychological need. He also likened the pleasure to be derived from great productions of the scientific intellect to that acquired when listening to a 'well composed concerto of instrumental music' (Imitative Arts, II. 30). Elsewhere he referred to a propensity, natural to all men, 'to account for all appearances from as few principles as possible' (TMS, VII. ii. 2. 14) and commented further on the ease with which the 'learned give up the evidence of their senses to preserve the coherence of the ideas of their imagination' (Astronomy, IV. 35). Smith also emphasized the role of the prejudices of sense and education in discussing the reception of new ideas (Astronomy, IV. 35).

He drew attention to the importance of analogy in suggesting that philosophers often attempt to explain the unusual by reference to knowledge gained in unrelated fields, noting that in some cases the analogy chosen could become not just a source of 'ingenious similitude' but 'the great hinge upon which everything turned' (Astronomy, II. 12).

Smith made extensive use of mechanistic analogies, derived from Newton, seeing in the universe 'a great machine' wherein we may observe 'means adjusted with the nicest artifice to the ends which they are intended to produce' (TMS, II. ii. 3. 5). In the same way he noted that 'Human society, when we contemplate it in a certain abstract and philosophical light, appears like a great, an immense machine' (TMS, VII. ii. 1. 2), a position which leads quite naturally to a distinction between efficient and final causes (TMS, II. ii. 3. 5), which is not inconsistent with the form of Deism associated with Newton himself. It is also striking that so systematic a thinker as Smith should have extended the mechanistic analogy to systems of thought:

> Systems in many respects resemble machines. A machine is a little system, created to perform, as well as to connect together, in reality, those different movements and effects which the artist has occasion for. A system is an imaginary machine invented to connect together in the fancy those different movements and effects which are already in reality performed (Astronomy, IV. 19).

Each part of Smith's contribution is in effect an 'imaginary' machine which conforms closely to his own stated rules for the organization of scientific discourse. All disclose Smith's perception of the 'beauty of a systematical arrangement of different observations connected by a few common principles' (WN, V. i. f. 25). The whole reveals much as to Smith's drives as a thinker, and throws an important light on his own marked (subjective) preference for system, coherence and order.

Andrew S. Skinner

See also CLASSICAL ECONOMICS.

SELECTED WORKS

Editions and Abbreviations. An excellent edition of the *Lectures on Jurisprudence* was brought out by Edwin Cannan in 1896. Cannan also prepared a valuable edition of the *Wealth of Nations* in 1904. J.M. Lothian edited the *Lectures on Rhetoric* in 1963.

Subsequent references are to the Glasgow edition of the *Works and Correspondence of Adam Smith* (Oxford: Clarendon Press, 1976–83) and follow the usages of that edition. The edition consists of:

I *The Theory of Moral Sentiments* (TMS). Edited by D.D. Raphael and A.L. Macfie (1976).

II *An Inquiry into the Nature and Causes of the Wealth of Nations* (WN). Ed. R.H. Campbell, A.S. Skinner and W.B. Todd (1976).

III *Essays on Philosophical Subjects* (EPS). Ed. D.D. Raphael and A.S. Skinner (1980).

This volume includes:

(i) 'The History of the Ancient Logics and Metaphysics' (Ancient Logics)

(ii) 'The History of the Ancient Physics' (Ancient Physics)

(iii) 'The History of Astronomy' (Astronomy)

(iv) 'Of the Affinity between Certain English and Italian Verses' (English and Italian Verses)

(v) 'Of the External Senses' (External Senses)

(vi) 'Of the Nature of the Imitation which takes place in what are called the Imitative Arts' (Imitative Arts)

(vii) 'Of the Affinity between Music, Dancing and Poetry' Items (i) to (vii), above, were prepared by W.P.D. Wightman.

(viii) 'Of the Affinity between Certain English and Italian Verses'

(ix) Contributions to the *Edinburgh Review* (1755–6):

(a) Review of Johnson's Dictionary

(b) A Letter to the Authors of the *Edinburgh Review* (Letter).

(x) Preface to William Hamilton's *Poems on General Occasions*. Items (viii) to (x), above, were prepared by J.C. Bryce.

(xi) Dugald Stewart, 'Account of the Life and Writings of Adam Smith LL.D.' (Stewart)

Edited by I.S. Ross.

IV *Lectures on Rhetoric and Belles Lettres* (LRBL) Edited by J.C. Bryce; general editor, A.S. Skinner (1983).

This volume includes:

'Considerations Concerning the First Formation of Languages' (Considerations)

V *Lectures on Jurisprudence* (LJ)

Edited by R.L. Meek, P.G. Stein and D.D. Raphael (1978). This volume includes:

(i) Student notes for the session 1762–3 (LJA)

(ii) Student notes for the session 1763–4 but dated 1766 (LJB)

(iii) The 'Early Draft' of the *Wealth of Nations* (ED)

(iv) Two Fragments on the Division of Labour (FA) and (FB)

VI *Correspondence of Adam Smith* (Corr.). Edited by E.C. Mossner and I.S. Ross (1977). This volume includes:

(i) 'A Letter from Governor Pownall to Adam Smith (1776)'

(ii) 'Smith's Thoughts on the State of the Contest with America, February 1778'. Edited by D. Stevens.

(iii) Jeremy Bentham's 'Letters' to Adam smith (1787, 1790).

Associated volume

Essays on Adam Smith (EAS). Edited by A.S. Skinner and T. Wilson (1975).

References to Corr. give letter number and date. References to LJ and LRBL give volume and page number from the MS. All other references provide section, chapter and paragraph number in order to facilitate the use of different editions. For example: Astronomy, II. 4 = 'History of Astronomy', section II, para. 4 Stewart, I. 12 = Dugald Stewart, 'Account', section I, para. 12 TMS, I. i. 5. 5 = TMS, Part I, section i, chapter 5, para. 5. WN, V. i. f. 26 = WN, Book V, chapter i, section 6, para. 26.

BIBLIOGRAPHY

Bagolini, L. 1975. The topicality of Adam Smith's notion of sympathy and judicial evaluation. In *Essays on Adam Smith*, ed. T. Wilson and A.S. Skinner, Oxford: Clarendon Press, 100–13.

Black, R.D.C. 1975. Smith's contribution in historical perspective. In *Essays on Adam Smith*, ed. T. Wilson and A. Skinner, Oxford: Clarendon Press, 42–63.

Blaug, M. 1962. *Economic Theory in Retrospect*. London: Heinemann.

Campbell, R.H. and Skinner, A.S. 1982. *Adam Smith*. London: Croom Helm.

Campbell, T.D. 1971. *Adam Smith's Science of Morals*. London: Allen & Unwin.

Haakonssen, K. 1981. *The Science of a Legislator: The Natural Jurisprudence of David Hume and Adam Smith*. Cambridge: Cambridge University Press.

Hollander, S. 1973. *The Economics of Adam Smith*. Toronto: University of Toronto Press.

Hont, I. and Ignatieff, M. 1983. *Wealth and Virtue: The Shaping of Political Economy in the Scottish Enlightenment*. Cambridge: Cambridge University Press.

Howell, W.S. 1975. Adam Smith's lectures on rhetoric: an historical assessment. EAS, 11–43.

Koebner, R. 1961. *Empire*. Cambridge: Cambridge University Press.

Lindgren, J.R. 1973. *The Social Philosophy of Adam Smith*. The Hague: Martinus Nijhoff.

Macfie, A.L. 1967. *The Individual in Society: Papers on Adam Smith*. London: Allen & Unwin.

Meek, R.L. 1962. *The Economics of Physiocracy: Essays and Translations*. London: Allen & Unwin.

Meek, R.L. 1973. *Turgot on Progress, Sociology and Economics*. Cambridge: Cambridge University Press.

Meek, R.L. 1976. *Social Science and the Ignoble Savage*. Cambridge: Cambridge University Press.

Mizuta, H. 1967. *Adam Smith's Library*. Cambridge: Cambridge University Press.

O'Brien, D.P. 1975. *The Classical Economists*. Oxford: Oxford University Press.

Rae, J. 1895. *Life of Adam Smith*. London: Macmillan.

Raphael, D.D. 1985. *Adam Smith*. Oxford: Oxford University Press.

Rosenberg, N. 1960. Some institutional aspects of the *Wealth of Nations*. *Journal of Political Economy* 68, 557–70.

Schumpeter, J.A. 1954. *History of Economic Analysis*. London: Allen & Unwin.

Scott, W.R. 1900. *Francis Hutcheson*. Cambridge: Cambridge University Press.

Scott, W.R. 1937. *Adam Smith as Student and Professor*. Glasgow: Jackson.

Skinner, A.S. 1979. *A System of Social Science: Papers Relating to Adam Smith*. Oxford: Oxford University Press.

Taylor, W.L. 1965. *Francis Hutcheson and David Hume as Predecessors of Adam Smith*. Durham, North Carolina: Duke University Press.

Viner, J. 1928. Adam Smith and laissez faire. In *Adam Smith, 1776–1926*, Chicago: Chicago University Press.

Winch, D. 1978. *Adam Smith's Politics: An Essay in Historiographic Revision*. Cambridge: Cambridge University Press.

Wood, J.C. 1984. *Adam Smith: Critical Assessments*. 4 vols, London: Croom Helm.

Smithies, Arthur (1907–1981). Smithies was born in Tasmania in 1907. He studied law at the University of Tasmania, read Politics, Philosophy and Economics as a Rhodes Scholar at Oxford (1930–32) followed by a PhD at Harvard (1932–5). He taught at the University of Michigan (1934–43), then became a government servant at the Bureau of the Budget until he returned to academic life in 1948 in the economics department at Harvard. He was editor of the *Quarterly Journal of Economics* (1957–65) and a founder of the *Journal of Economic Abstracts* (1962), which later became the prestigious and useful *Journal of Economic Literature*. He died after a typically vigorous rowing session on the Charles at the age of 73.

Smithies was widely known and respected as a staunch advocate of Keynesian theories and policies, especially their relationship to budgetary policy. Yet this was only a small part of his contributions. His publications range over the whole spectrum of economic theory and its applications, from the more obscure aspects of capital theory – his first publication (1935a) was on the Austrian theory of capital – through duopoly theory (1940) and spatial competition (1941a, 1941b) to the problems of trend and cycle and the longer-run aspects of the consumption function (1957). (His best-known doctoral student, James Duesenberry, explicitly acknowledged Smithies' influence on the development of his own relative income hypothesis and the ratchet effect.) Thus Smithies was a great all rounder, if something of a loner in that his methods were often idiosyncratic. Yet he was as much at home in setting out a wages policy for the depression in Australia (1935b) as with examining the relationship between trend and cycle in a theory of growth (1957) or with putting content into the concept of profit maximization when demand and cost curves change over time (1939). He was good at both synthesizing different approaches to issues and reconciling opposing approaches. Thus, in his 1942 *Econometrica* paper on 'Process analysis and equilibrium analysis', he bridged the gulf between those who concentrated on equilibrium positions but neglected to examine whether they could be reached from arbitary starting points and those who concentrated on processes but neglected to ask whether they would eventually end in equilibria. In his 1957 *Econometrica* paper on 'Economic fluctuations and growth', he examined trends and cycles as endogenous, interelated processes as well as cycles without trends and trends without cycles. In later years he became interested in the problems of developing countries, especially in the South Vietnamese government's budgetary and production problems in a period of war.

Evidently Smithies was regarded as a great teacher 'with a breezy manner and an ability to stimulate debate that delighted students'. Certainly Arthur Smithies, through his active and useful life, brought more lustre if not quite as much fame to his native Tasmania than did his cousin, Errol Flynn.

G.C. Harcourt

SELECTED WORKS

1935a. The Austrian theory of capital in relation to partial equilibrium theory. *Quarterly Journal of Economics* 50, November, 117–50.

1935b. Wages policy in the depression. *Economic Record* 11, December, 249–68.

1939. The maximization of profits over time with changing cost and demand functions. *Econometrica* 7, October, 312–18.

1940. (With L.J. Savage) A dynamic problem in duopoly. *Econometrica* 8, April, 130–43.

1941a. Monopolistic price policy in a spatial market. *Econometrica* 9, January, 63–73.

1941b. Optimum location in spatial competition. *Journal of Political Economy* 49, June, 423–39.

1942. Process analysis and equilibrium analysis. *Econometrica* 10, January, 26–38.

1957. Economic fluctuations and growth. *Econometrica* 25, January, 1–52.

smuggling. Smuggling, or illegal trade, has traditionally been consigned to a peripheral role in the theoretical analysis of international trade. The phenomenon was noted but not integrated into formal analysis, except for exotic, early efforts such as Beccaria's (1764–5) which would surface after the demise of this neglect.

The growth of empirical and analytical studies, in the 1960s and later, of the trade policies of the underdeveloped countries did much to focus the analysis of trade theorists on the phenomenon of illegal trade. For, in these countries, it is foolish to disregard leakages from tariffs and quotas on trade transactions, and the theorist who advises on policy needs to incorporate smuggling in an essential way into his modelling.

Of particular interest among the early empirical studies were two that addressed different ways in which smuggling occurs: first, through normal entry points, via faking of invoices that falsify the nature and value of what is being traded; and second, through unregulated loading and offloading locations. The former was the subject of the examination of Turkish imports by Bhagwati (1964) where the partner-country trade-data-comparison technique was introduced to detect underinvoicing (so as to avoid tariff duties), with subsequent extension of this technique to detect capital flight from 28 underdeveloped countries by Bhagwati, Krueger and Wibulswasdi (1974). The latter was the subject of the analysis by Cooper (1974) of the smuggling of exports, from several islands that provide innumerable illegal exit points, from Indonesia (to avoid paying export taxes).

The theoretical analysis of smuggling was initiated by Bhagwati and Hansen (1973). They extended the conventional Marshall–Edgeworth trade-theoretic model to incorporate illegal trade into the main corpus of general-equilibrium theory. Illegal trade was modelled by postulating that it involved transformation of exports into imports at a (socially) less favourable rate than legal trade (i.e. a terms-of-trade loss): in illegal trade, there would be higher real costs of packaging, loss in transit, use of expensive clandestine routes of entry and exit, etc. Privately, however, such trade would be profitable as the illegal trade escaped the tariff. As such, their model yielded results analogous to those for the theory of trade-diverting customs unions where trade is diverted to the partner country in the union which supplies at higher cost but which does not have to pay the tariff. Thus, for example, illegal trade (like trade diversion) could improve welfare despite its higher cost, by bringing prices to consumers and producers closer to the 'true' world prices. Again, if illegal and legal trade coexisted, the domestic price-ratio would remain unchanged from the level without smuggling, and therefore any finite level of illegal trade would necessarily immiserize the country since it would carry the inherent terms-of-trade loss without any offsetting production and consumption gains.

While the Bhagwati–Hansen analysis was extended to the analysis of the optimal and maximal-revenue tariffs in the presence of smuggling in Johnson (1972), Bhagwati and Srinivasan (1973) and Kemp (1976), and to optimal intervention in the presence of non-economic objectives by Ray (1978), the shift in theoretical models (rather than in the problems analysed) was undertaken by Sheikh (1974) and Pitt (1981). Sheikh (1974) modelled smuggling as withdrawing resources from production, while introducing risk in illegal trade into the model explicitly. The former departure enabled him to argue that, even if legal and illegal trade coexisted, welfare improvement could result in his model, though not in the Bhagwati–Hansen model, since waste of resources from a protection-distorted equilibrium could be enriching rather than immiserizing (an insight from the generalized theory of immiserizing growth, as developed in Bhagwati, 1968).

More importantly, Pitt (1981) developed a model which, unlike the Bhagwati-Hansen and Sheikh analyses, could explain a phenomenon that Cooper (1974) had noticed: that legally traded goods often carried a loss in the presence of smuggling but were traded anyway. Thus for smuggled imports, the domestic price was less than the tariff-inclusive price, whereas for smuggled exports the foreign price was below the export-duty-inclusive price. Pitt called this the 'price disparity' phenomenon. His model built in this 'price disparity' and essentially explained it by arguing that legal trade was required to make illegal trade possible or less risky and that the marginal loss from the legal trade would equal the marginal gain from the illegal trade it facilitated. The question has been further examined in Bhagwati (1981), and the theoretical analysis extended by Martin and Panagariya (1984).

Finally, the normative theory of smuggling has been integrated into the general theory of directly-unproductive profit-seeking (DUP) activities in Bhagwati (1982).

Jagdish Bhagwati

See also DIRECTLY UNPRODUCTIVE PROFIT-SEEKING ACTIVITIES; IMMISERIZING GROWTH.

BIBLIOGRAPHY

Beccaria, C. 1764–5. *Tentativo analitico sui contrabbandi. Estratto dal foglio periodico intitolato: Il Caffè*. Vol. 1, Brescia. Reprinted in *Scrittori classici italiani di economia politica, parte moderna*, Vol. XII, Milan, 1804, 235–41.

Bhagwati, J.N. 1964. On the underinvoicing of imports. *Bulletin of the Oxford University Institute of Economics and Statistics* 26. Reprinted in Bhagwati (1974), 138–47.

Bhagwati, J.N. 1968. Distortions and immiserizing growth: a generalization. *Review of Economic Studies* 35(104), 481–5.

Bhagwati, J.N. (ed.) 1974. *Illegal Transactions in International Trade: Theory and Measurement*. Amsterdam: North-Holland.

Bhagwati, J.N. 1981. Alternative theories of illegal trade: economic consequences and statistical detection. *Weltwirtschaftliches Archiv* 117(3), 409–26.

Bhagwati, J.N. 1982. Directly unproductive profit-seeking (DUP) activities. *Journal of Political Economy* 90(5), October, 988–1002.
Bhagwati, J. and Hansen, B. 1973. A theoretical analysis of smuggling. *Quarterly Journal of Economics* 87, May, 172–87.
Bhagwati, J. and Srinivasan, T.N. 1973. Smuggling and trade policy. *Journal of Public Economics* 2, 377–89.
Bhagwati, J., Krueger, A. and Wibulswasdi, C. 1974. Capital flight from LDCs: a statistical analysis. In Bhagwati (1974), 148–54.
Cooper, R.N. 1974. Tariffs and smuggling in Indonesia. In Bhagwati (1974), 183–92.
Falvey, R.E. 1978. A note on preferential and illegal trade under quantitative restrictions. *Quarterly Journal of Economics* 92, February, 175–8.
Johnson, H.G. 1972. Notes on the economic theory of smuggling. *Malaysian Economic Review*, 17, April, 1–7. Reprinted in Bhagwati (1974).
Kemp, M.C. 1976. Smuggling and optimal commercial policy. *Journal of Public Economics* 5, April–May, 381–4.
Martin, L.C. and Panagariya, A. 1984. Smuggling, trade and price disparity: a crime-theoretic approach. *Journal of International Economics* 17, August, 201–17.
Pitt, M. 1981. Smuggling and price disparity. *Journal of International Economics* 11, November, 447–58.
Ray, A. 1978. Smuggling, import objectives, and optimum tax structure. *Quarterly Journal of Economics* 92(3), August, 509–14.
Sheikh, M. 1974. Smuggling and welfare. *Journal of International Economics* 4, November, 355–64.

Snyder, Carl (1869–1943). Snyder was born in 1869 in Cedar Falls, Iowa: he died in Santa Barbara, California, in 1943. In 1920 he joined the Federal Reserve Bank of New York, where he remained until his retirement in 1935.

Early in his career at the New York Fed, Snyder began to assemble statistical data on long-term trends in output, the volume of payments, and prices that would permit empirical confirmation of the equation of exchange. He verified that over the course of the cycle, the velocity of circulation, V, and the volume of transactions, T, moved in unison. Thus, during the cycle the ratio V/T was approximately a constant, and the price level moved in proportion to prior changes in the money supply. Secularly, however, he perceived that the ratio V/T moved downward due to the trend growth of T, which he estimated to be about 4 per cent a year. Hence, he anticipated modern monetarist policy views by proposing that the money supply should increase by 4 per cent annually in order to attain long-term price stability (Tavlas, 1982).

Snyder's statistical work so convinced him of the short-run proportionate relation between movements in V and T, that he viewed velocity in mechanical terms. Thus, his approach to the quantity theory was one of measurement without theory. While his statistical work at the Fed was pathbreaking in some areas – particularly in constructing series dealing with business cycles (Garvy, 1978) – his approach to the quantity theory was inflexible and devoid of a viable policy prescription for combating depressions.

George S. Tavlas

SELECTED WORKS

1923. A new index of the volume of trade. *Journal of the American Statistical Association* 18, December, 949–63.
1924. New measures in the equation of exchange. *American Economic Review* 14, December, 699–713.
1927. *Business Cycles and Business Measurements: Studies in Quantitative Economics.* New York: Macmillan.
1930. New measures of the relations of credit and trade. *Proceedings of the Academy of Political Science* 13(4), January, 468–86.

BIBLIOGRAPHY

Garvy, G. 1978. Carl Snyder, pioneer economic statistician and monetarist. *History of Political Economy* 10(3), Fall, 454–90.
Tavlas, G.S. 1982. Notes on Garvy, Snyder, and the doctrinal foundations of monetarism. *History of Political Economy* 14(1), Spring, 89–100.

social accounting. Social accounting, or national accounting as it is usually termed today, broadly refers to the body of data that portrays a nation's economic activity in terms of the output produced and incomes created, the stocks of capital goods and other inputs required, and the financial pathways and instruments used. More narrowly, the national accounts are the system of double-entry accounts in which this information is displayed, together with the more detailed data underlying them.

HISTORY AND DEVELOPMENT

Interest in measuring the income of a nation's inhabitants goes back a long way. (For an excellent history, see Studenski, 1958.) Early estimates – in England from the 17th century – were often made in order to estimate potential tax revenues. Typically, early estimators divided the population into broad social groups and assigned an average income to each on the basis of whatever information was available to them. Over time, data sources improved and methods became more sophisticated, but the basic principles for estimating what came to be called 'national income' remained much the same. It was recognized at an early stage by theorists such as the French Physiocrats that the same total would be obtained by adding up all of the outputs produced – 'national product' – but statistical implementation of estimates of output or product required more extensive and more sophisticated data, and it came much later. By the early 1900s, however, estimates of both national income and national product had been made in a number of countries.

The great depression of the 1930s led to the next major step. In response to pressing policy needs and taking advantage of the concurrent developments in economic theory, statisticians began to convert the aggregate national income time-series into a system of national income statistics, where the components – consumption, investment and saving, on the one hand; wages and profits, on the other – were looked upon as necessary ingredients in explaining the behaviour of the whole, and of as much interest as the aggregate figures. The statistical developments in some cases preceded the theoretical – Kuznets's first data came well before Keynes's theory – but both reflected the same need, and they reinforced and stimulated each other.

World War II, with its policy need to focus simultaneously on production and finance, pushed the statistical and theoretical development into the next phase, which culminated at the war's end in the first true national accounts. The name of Richard Stone is pre-eminently associated with this achievement; he, with Keynes's advice, was largely responsible for the British White Papers on national accounts that appeared at intervals through the war period, and later he headed the work of the international committees that developed the United Nations standards in this area. But similar developments were taking place in other countries, among them Norway, Denmark, the Netherlands, France, Canada and Australia. In the United States, the first formal national accounts were published in 1947.

In 1952 the United Nations published international standards for national accounts, *A System of National Accounts and Supporting Tables* (UN/SNA), and in the next 10 or 15 years scores of countries began to supply national accounting data. By the mid-1960s it had become clear that both statistical capabilities and analytic needs were outrunning the existing standards, and a revised and greatly expanded UN/SNA was published in 1968. This remains the international standard today, and it is used, with minor adaptations, by upwards of 150 countries. A review of the UN/SNA is now under way, however, and a new version is anticipated in about 1990.

NATIONAL ACCOUNTS TODAY

The characteristic of national accounts, as distinguished from a collection of national income time-series, is that they show the relationships among the activities taking place in the economy. The economic system functions through a complex of transactions, which are engaged in by numerous transactors. The national accounts provide a way to record those transactions sorted into homogeneous and analytically useful groups, just as business accounts sort the transactions of a business to provide an analytically useful record of its activities. Like business accounts, the national accounts include both flow accounts showing what has happened over a given period of time (such as a year) and balance sheets showing the status at a given point of time (such as a year-end).

The transactors of the system. The transactors of the economic system may be grouped in various ways, and into larger or smaller groups. Two principles of classification are commonly employed. In the main accounts, transactors are grouped into sectors on the basis of their institutional character, as enterprises, households, governmental units and the rest of the world. Each of these groups, in turn, may be further subdivided. Enterprises are often divided into corporate and unincorporated; public and private; or financial and non-financial. Governments are classified by level, into national, state or provincial, and local. In the accounts relating to production, however, an alternative classification of transactors is also used, which assigns each transactor to the industry in which it is chiefly engaged.

The flow accounts. The transactions in which these transactors engage are arranged into accounts that closely resemble the accounts of a business firm. In the UN/SNA, four types of flow account are presented: (1) the production account, which shows the value of production and its associated costs; (2) the income and outlay account, which shows income derived from productive activity and other sources, and the outlays for which that income is used; (3) the capital accumulation account, which shows additions to the capital stock and the sources of their finance, and (4) the capital finance account, which shows changes in financial assets and liabilities. Other national accounting systems may either subdivide some of these accounts (as does ESA, the European System of Accounts used by the European Common Market), or combine some of them (as do the United States National Income and Product Accounts, NIPA).

Such a set of accounts for a set of institutional sectors form a double-entry accounting system that shows the flow of income and expenditure through the economy and displays the interrelations among its various parts. Each kind of transaction appears twice, once in the accounts of the transactor making the payment and once in the accounts of the recipient. Thus wages appear as an outlay in the production account of enterprises and also as a receipt in the income and outlay account of households. Household expenditures on consumption appear as an outlay on the household income and outlay account and as a receipt on the production account of enterprises. Income taxes appear as outlays on the income and outlay accounts of the payers and as receipts on the income and outlay account of the government. Purchases of plant and machinery by enterprises appear as sales receipts on the production account of the selling enterprise, and as outlays on the capital accumulation account of the purchasing enterprise.

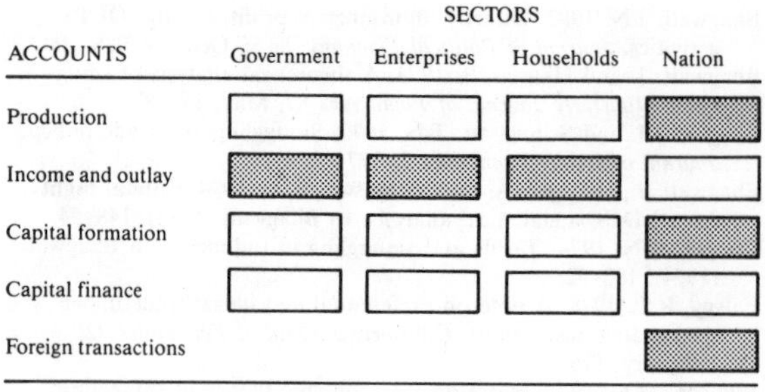

Figure 1 Scheme of sector flow accounts in the UN/SNA

Figure 1 shows the scheme of sector flow accounts for which data are collected and published annually by the United Nations, in its *Yearbook of National Accounts Statistics*. In addition to accounts for the three major sectors (government, enterprises and households), the scheme includes a total column, which refers to the nation as a whole.

The UN *Yearbook* also presents a condensed set of accounts that meet the needs of most general users. This condensed set is composed of the shaded boxes in Figure 1. It contains the accounts for the nation as a whole for production, capital formation and foreign transactions, together with sector income and outlay accounts. The production account for the nation as a whole adds up to gross domestic product (GDP), the value of the total output produced in the nation during a given period of account such as a year. (An alternative total measure, gross national product (GNP), is used by some countries including the United States. It differs from GDP in that it refers to the nation's residents rather than its geographic territory, and so it includes any net income received by residents from abroad.) The household income and outlay account adds up to household income, which is very close to what is called 'personal income' in the US accounts. It shows the composition of household income and of household outlays and saving. The government income and outlay account reflects the government budget – the sources of its receipts and the uses to which they are put. The capital formation account shows gross capital formation – the additions to the nation's capital stock of plant, machinery, transportation equipment, housing – and how it was financed. The foreign transactions account shows exports and imports and the balance between them. This set of condensed accounts closely resembles the US National Income and Product Accounts (NIPA), except that NIPA combines the enterprise income and outlay account with the production account. The condensed accounts still form a balancing double-entry set, but they show much less detail than the full set. Table 1 presents skeleton condensed accounts for the United States for 1980; the UN *Yearbook* presentation is slightly more detailed than what is shown here.

These accounts are useful for exploring many broad questions, such as the impact of changes in taxes or government expenditures of various types, changes in exports or imports, or changes in household income and its

TABLE 1. Condensed National Accounts, US 1980 (billions of dollars)

			Production account		
Compensation of employees		1600	Household consumption expenditure		1668
Indirect taxes		213	Govt. consumption expenditure		527
Less: subsidies		−6	Gross capital formation		487
Consumption of fixed capital		367	Government	85	
Government	74		Enterprises	402	
Enterprises	293		Exports		264
Net operating surplus		486	*Less:* imports		−286
GROSS DOMESTIC PRODUCT		2660	GROSS DOMESTIC PRODUCT		2660
			Government income and outlay account		
Consumption expenditures		527	Indirect tax receipts		213
Interest paid to residents		22	Direct taxes from households		540
Interest paid to abroad		12	Direct taxes from enterprises		85
Subsidies		6			
Transfer payments to households		286			
Net transfer payments to abroad		5			
Surplus or deficit		−20			
GOVERNMENT OUTLAYS AND SAVING		838	GOVERNMENT RECEIPTS		838
			Enterprise income and outlay account		
Property income paid		472	Net operating surplus		486
Direct taxes		85	Consumer debt interest		50
Transfers to persons		12	Government debt interest		22
Net saving		34	Net factor income from abroad		45
ENTERPRISE OUTLAY AND SAVING		603	ENTERPRISE INCOME		603
			Household income and outlay account		
Consumption expenditures		1668	Compensation of employees		1600
Consumer debt interest		50	Property income received		472
Direct taxes paid		540	Transfers received from government		286
Net transfers paid to abroad		1	Transfers received from enterprises		12
Household saving		111			
HOUSEHOLD OUTLAYS AND SAVING		2370	HOUSEHOLD INCOME		2370
			Capital formation account		
Gross domestic capital formation		487	Consumption of fixed capital		367
Government	85		Government	74	
Enterprises	402		Enterprises	293	
			Enterprise net saving		34
			Government net saving		−20
			Household saving		111
			Net foreign balance		−5
GROSS DOMESTIC CAPITAL FORMATION		487	GROSS SAVING		487
			Foreign transactions account		
Exports		264	Imports		286
Net factor income from abroad		45	Government interest paid to abroad		12
Net foreign balance		−5	Net transfers from households		1
			Net transfers from government		5
RECEIPTS FROM ABROAD AND BALANCE		304	PAYMENTS TO ABROAD		304

Source: Integrated economic accounts for the United States, 1947–80. *Survey of Current Business*, May 1982.

composition. In analysing any such question, it is necessary to look at both accounts in which the affected item appears, and to consider the further repercussions of any changes.

For example, consider the impact of an increase in household direct (income) taxes. This will appear in both the household and government income and outlay accounts, and both sectors will have to make adjustments to maintain the balance of the accounts. If households, for example, compensate for the increased taxes by reducing the level of their consumption, this will reduce consumption expenditures in the production account. This, in turn, will reduce expenditures for GDP, and some of the flows on the cost side of the production account will have to fall correspondingly in order to maintain the balance of that account. It is likely that indirect taxes (which are mainly sales taxes) will fall somewhat, since they are related to consumer sales, and this will partially offset the increase in personal income tax receipts in the government account. And it is also likely that wages and other income flows to households will fall as GDP shrinks, which in turn will further reduce consumption expenditures and further decrease the yield of the tax increase. Thus the net increase in government revenue may be substantially less than would at first appear. Whatever net impact there is, however, needs to be traced through the government account. If the government uses the revenue increase to reduce its deficit, there will be an impact on the capital formation account. There, the decline in the government deficit may be partially offset by a decline in household saving (resulting both from the initial tax increase and from the subsequent decline in household income) or by a decline in enterprise net saving (resulting from reduced profits following the decline in GDP). It may also be partially offset by an increase in the net foreign balance if the decline in GDP results in favourable export price developments while reducing the demand for imports. It might also, in accounting terms, be offset by an increase in gross domestic investment, but that is an unlikely accompaniment to falling consumer expenditures.

A proper analysis of most macroeconomic questions requires much more detailed data than the simplified headings shown in Table 1. Macroeconomic models frequently use very detailed data and large numbers of relationships. But the principles involved are those illustrated in the preceding paragraph.

Flow of funds and the capital finance account. The flow accounts shown in Table 1 show the output produced and the income generated during a given period of account, but they throw very little light on the financial mechanisms and pathways through which the results shown are achieved. It is the function of the capital finance account (UN/SNA terminology) or flow-of-funds accounts (US terminology) to fill this gap. What the capital finance account for each sector shows are the changes in each type of its financial assets and liabilities (both fixed claims and equities) during the period of account. Flow-of-funds accounts, as presented by the US Federal Reserve Board, are somewhat more comprehensive; they encompass not only changes in financial assets and liabilities but also summary national income and product accounts, so that they reflect changes in nonfinancial as well as financial assets and liabilities.

Balance sheets. It is increasingly being recognized that, for nations as for individual businesses, flow accounts are not enough. Balance sheets, which show the stocks of tangible and financial assets and liabilities held by each of the sectors at the beginning and end of the reporting period, are necessary to complete the accounts and essential to their analytic use.

For each sector, the balance sheet shows ownership of land and other natural resources; reproducible tangible assets like buildings, transport equipment and machinery; financial assets, including fixed-claim assets like currency and deposits, loans and bonds, and equities like corporate stock and pension fund reserves; and financial liabilities owed to other sectors. The difference between a sector's assets and its liabilities is its net worth. Both enterprises and households will normally have a positive net worth, although it will shrink in periods of acute economic crisis. In countries where land and natural resources are primarily in private hands, the government often has a negative net worth; that is, the government debt exceeds its assets. But in countries where the government has retained ownership of subsoil assets such as petroleum, or where it holds amounts of land (as in the US), government net worth will also be positive.

For the nation as a whole, financial assets will by definition equal financial liabilities, except for the amounts owed to or by foreigners. Eliminating these internal obligations, it is possible to calculate what is called 'national wealth': the sum of all tangible assets in the country, plus the net balance of foreign assets less foreign liabilities.

Revaluations. The accounts discussed so far do not show all of the elements entering into the difference between a beginning and ending balance sheet. This is mainly because prices change, so that an asset in the ending balance sheet – a share of corporate stock or a house, for example – may have a value different from that of the same asset in the beginning balance sheet. To account for these revaluations, the complete system of national accounts requires one more type of account, which in the UN/SNA is called the reconciliation account. It provides a place for all the changes between one balance sheet and the next that are not already accounted for in one of the flow accounts.

Capital finance or flow-of-funds accounts are becoming quite widespread, and several countries have compiled balance sheets. Very few countries, however, have yet taken the step of providing reconciliation accounts on an official basis, although some private researchers have made the necessary estimates.

Table 2 displays these additional accounts for the US in 1980. Its columns show, successively, the opening balance sheet, a combined capital accumulation and capital finance account, the reconciliation account and the closing balance sheet. Its rows show the various kinds of tangible and financial assets, financial liabilities and net worth. Although this table relates to the nation as a whole, the net worth figures are broken down by sector in order to show the wealth holdings of each sector. National wealth is the sum of the net worth of all sectors except the rest of the world. It is, of course, possible to compile the complete table on a sectorial basis.

Input–output tables. The final component of the standard national accounts today (as reflected in the UN/SNA) is a further detailing of the production account, in what is called in the terminology of its originator (Wassily Leontief) an input–output table. This table is in the form of a matrix which shows, for each industry or type of product, in the columns, what products are used in its production and/or which industries supply them (the sources of its inputs), and in the rows, what becomes of its products in terms of the industries or final users which purchase them (the disposition of its outputs).

Countries have produced input–output tables in a wide variety of sizes, ranging from as few as three or four industries or products to as many as 500. There seems, however, to be a developing consensus that tables containing about 40 to 50 industries or product categories represent the optimum balance of cost and analytic usefulness. The construction of an input–output table is an expensive undertaking, and most countries do not attempt it on an annual basis. An industrial census is almost essential as a data source, and these are often taken (as in the US) at intervals of about five years.

FUTURE DIRECTIONS FOR NATIONAL ACCOUNTS

The national accounts are not, and by their very nature never can be, a finished product. They are meant to portray the nature of the economic system in ways that are useful for analysing current economic problems. Over time, economic systems change. New institutions and new industries grow up, and old ones fade. Private pension systems, home ownership and government-financed health care are examples of institutions whose importance has greatly increased since the

TABLE 2. Capital Accounts for the Nation, US 1980 (billions of dollars)

ASSETS	Beginning of year value	Capital transactions account	Reconciliation account	End of year value
Land	2,270	—	302	2,572
Reproducible assets	7,929	186	817	8,931
Residential structures	2,279	43	20	2,527
Non-residential structures	2,497	47	283	2,826
Equipment and durables	2,128	79	236	2,443
Inventories	1,025	17	93	1,136
Gold and foreign exchange	14	−1	1	14
Fixed-claim assets	7,055	710	—	7,765
Currency and deposits	1,800	195	—	1,995
Credit market instruments	4,354	401	—	4,755
US government securities	894	122	—	1,016
State and local obligations	309	27	—	336
Corporate and foreign bonds	465	38	—	504
Mortgages	1,327	121	—	1,448
Consumer credit	383	2	—	385
Other	857	106	—	963
Trade credit	495	43	—	538
Other fixed claims	416	72	—	478
Equities held	3,934	64	708	4,706
Corporate stock (market value)	1,229	21	386	1,636
Noncorporate nonfarm	974	−4	150	1,120
Farm	617	−14	69	672
Pension reserves, trusts and other	1,114	61	103	1,278
TOTAL ASSETS	17,268	895	1,119	9,282
LIABILITIES AND NET WORTH				
Fixed-claim liabilities	7,055	710	—	7,765
Equities owed	3,934	64	708	4,706
Net worth	10,213	185	1,119	11,517
Of which:				
Enterprises (residual)	1,958	96	—	2,054
Households	6,745	174	870	7,789
Tangible assets	3,326	85	348	3,760
Net fixed-claim assets	652	96	—	748
Corporate stock (market value)	746	−1	251	996
Pensions, insurance (cash value)	200	12	3	215
Other equities	1,821	−18	268	2,071
Government	1,541	−38	248	1,751
Rest of world and discrepancy	−31	−47		−78
TOTAL LIABILITIES AND NET WORTH	17,268	895	1,119	19,282

Source: Integrated economic accounts for the United States, 1947–80. *Survey of Current Business*, May 1982.

last revision of either the UN/SNA or US/NIPA; computers and nuclear energy are new industries not adequately accounted for in the current standards. The national accounts require periodic updating in order to take these new developments into account.

The problems that are the chief focus of policy attention also change. In the 1940s and 1950s, when the original UN/SNA and the US/NIPA were constructed, the main concerns were with the short-term management of the economy in order to avoid recessions and maintain full employment, and these national accounting systems reflected the needs of this type of analysis. In the early 1960s, long-term development planning became important, and the revised UN/SNA contained much expanded information on production, including input–output tables. In the later 1960s, distributional questions came to the fore, and statistics on income distribution were added to the system along with a new interest in the relation between the economic accounts and social, demographic and environmental data. The 1970s saw both widespread inflation and a renewed incidence of relatively severe recession, and this in turn led to an increased interest in the financial accounts.

The review of the international standards for national accounts now under way is considering both the changes in the institutional structure of the economy and the kinds of policy questions that have arisen since the present standards were formulated in the late 1960s. It is too early to discern the precise form of the modifications that will be adopted, but is seems likely that they will not change the basic structure of the system. Rather, they will move towards enhancing the system by adding more detail, more supplementary information and more underlying microdata.

NANCY D. RUGGLES

BIBLIOGRAPHY

Keynes, J.M. 1936. *The General Theory of Employment, Interest and Money*. London: Macmillan.

Kuznets, S. 1934. *National Income 1929–1932*, US Congress, S. Doc. 124, 73rd Congress, 2nd session.

Ruggles, R. and Ruggles, N. 1982. Integrated economic accounts for the United States, 1947–1980. US Department of Commerce, *Survey of Current Busines* s62, May, 1–53.

Studenski, P. 1958. *The Income of Nations*. New York: New York University Press.

United Nations Statistical Office (New York):

Series F, No. 2. A system of national accounts and supporting tables. 1952.

Series F, No. 2, rev. 3. A system of national accounts. 1968.

Series F, No. 14, rev. 1. Input–output tables and analysis. 1973.

Series M, No. 60. Provisional international guidelines on the national and sectoral balance-sheet and reconciliation accounts of the system of national accounts.

Series M, No. 61. Provisional guidelines on statistics of the distribution of income, consumption and accumulation of households.

social choice. Social choice theory, pioneered in its modern form by Arrow (1951), is concerned with the relation between individuals and the society. In particular, it deals with the aggregation of individual interests, or judgements, or well-beings, into some aggregate notion of social welfare, social judgement or social choice. It should be obvious that the aggregation exercise can take very different forms depending on exactly what is being aggregated (e.g., the personal interests of different people, or their moral or political judgements) and what is to be derived on that basis (e.g., a measure of social welfare, or public decisions regarding what is to be done or what outcomes are to be accepted). The formal similarities between these exercises in the analytical format of aggregation should not make us overlook the diversities in the nature of the exercises performed (see Sen, 1977a, 1986). In fact, the axioms chosen for different exercises are often quite divergent, and the general conception of aggregation in social choice theory permits such variation.

1. WELFARE ECONOMICS AND SOCIAL CHOICE. Although the origins of social choice theory – in one form or another – can be traced back at least two hundred years (Borda, 1781; Condorcet, 1785; Bentham, 1789), the formal theory of social choice was initiated by Kenneth Arrow (1951) less than four decades ago. Arrow drew on some existing notions of welfare economics. One concept of a *social welfare function* had been introduced by Bergson (1938). This was defined in a very general form indeed: as a real-value function W(.), determining social welfare, 'the value of which is understood to depend on all the variables that might be considered as affecting welfare' (p. 417). Such a social welfare function – *swf* for short – might be thought to be a real-valued function defined on X, the set of alternative social states. It is a bit more permissive to see a Bergson social welfare function as an *ordering* R of X (more permissive because not all orderings can be numerically represented).

Various uses to which a *swf* can be put in welfare economics were investigated, particularly by Samuelson (1947). His exercises made use of several criteria that a *swf* may be required to satisfy, including the Pareto criterion, demanding that unanimous individual preference over any pair of states should yield the corresponding social preference over that pair.

None of the conditions that Samuelson imposed on a *swf* for his exercises required any general specification of how the social ordering might change if *different* sets (strictly, n-tuples) of individual orderings were considered. If any n-tuple of individual preference orderings is called a 'profile', then Samuelson's exercises – and those considered by Bergson – were all 'single-profile' problems, without additional requirements of *inter-profile* consistency.

Arrow (1951) defined a social welfare function – henceforth *SWF* (to be distinguished from a Bergson–Samuelson *swf*) – as a functional relation specifying one social ordering R for any given n-tuple of individual orderings (R_i), with one ordering R_i for each person i: $R = f(R_i)$).

Note that if a Bergson–Samuelson *swf* is defined as a social ordering R (rather than as a real-valued function $W(\cdot)$), then an Arrow *SWF* is a function the value of which would be a Bergson–Samuelson *swf*. Arrow's exercise, in this sense, is concerned with the way of arriving at a Bergson–Samuelson *swf*.

Arrow proceeded to impose a few conditions that any reasonable *SWF* could be expected to satisfy. His 'impossibility theorem' (more formally called 'the General Possibility Theorem') shows that no *SWF* can satisfy all these conditions together. One of the conditions deals specifically with the multiple-profile characteristics of a *SWF*, viz., the independence of irrelevant alternatives (condition I). This requires that the chosen alternatives from any subset of social states must remain unaltered as long as the individual preferences over this subset remain unaltered, even though the individual preferences may have been revised over other subsets. Another condition is a weak version of the Pareto principle (condition P) which requires that unanimous *strict* preference over a pair must be reflected in the same strict preference for the society. Another requirement is that of unrestricted domain (condition U), which demands that the domain of the *SWF* must include all logically possible n-tuples of individual orderings, that is, the *SWF* should be able to specify a social ordering R no matter what the individual orderings happen to be. Finally, there is a condition of non-dictatorship (condition D), which demands that there is no individual such that if he or she prefers any x to any y, then x is socially preferred to y, no matter what the other individuals prefer.

One version of the 'impossibility theorem' of Arrow establishes that if the set of individuals is finite and the number of distinct social states is at least three, then there is no social welfare function (*SWF*), satisfying conditions U, I, P, and D.

This result has been the starting point of much of modern social choice theory. Even though the focus has somewhat shifted in recent years from impossibility results to other issues, there is no question at all that Arrow's formulation of the social choice problem in presenting his 'impossibility theorem' laid the foundations of social choice theory as it has evolved.

Two *interpretational* issues may be sorted out first before formal social choice theory is considered for a general examination. The first issue concerns the interpretation of 'social preference'. As has already been remarked, the nature of the social choice exercise can vary in many different ways, and one source of variation is the nature of the end-point that is sought (in particular the interpretation of R). Consider the relation of strict social preference xPy. It can be given different interpretations depending on the nature of the exercise. For example, xPy can stand for the judgement that society is better off in state x than in state y. Such a judgement can be the view of a particular individual (in his or her capacity as an aggregating judge), or the mechanical outcome of some institutional process of aggregating judgements (e.g., the result of a voting procedure). Or, alternatively, xPy can stand for the statement that in the choice exactly over the pair (x, y), x alone must be chosen. A further alternative is to interpret xPy as the requirement that y must not be chosen from any set which contains x (whether or not it contains any other alternative). These and other interpretations give different views of 'social preference', and careful attention has to be paid to the nature of the exercise depending on the interpretation given. Although Arrow's 'impossibility theorem' and similar results apply to *all* the interpretations (and here there is a genuine economy in the general axiomatic method), extensive variations in the relevance of the results to different types of problems must be recognized.

Second, a different source of variation relates to the interpretation of the individual preference orderings. The individual ordering can stand for the ranking of personal well-being, and if so, the exercise is one of *well-being aggregation*. An example may be found in arriving at overall judgements of the well-being of the community based on rankings of individual well-beings. To take a very different type of example, in making a committee decision, the different judgements of the members of the committee may be aggregated together in an overall judgement or an overall decision, and that exercise is one of *judgement aggregation*. This is not to deny that the judgements of members of the committee may, in fact, be influenced by their individual interests, but the nature of the exercise is primarily that of aggregating the possibly divergent judgements of the members of a committee to arrive at an over-all committee view. In some other exercises, for example, in electing a candidate or a member of Parliament or a Mayor, the individual votes may well reflect a clear-cut mixture of individual interests and political beliefs, so that the exercise may have features of interest aggregation as well as judgement aggregation. Once again, it is worth emphasizing that while the formal results such as Arrow's 'impossibility theorem' apply to each of the interpretations, the exact substantive content of the result would depend on the particular interpretation chosen.

The specific context of Arrow's exercise was that of supplementing the work of Bergson and Samuelson in deriving social welfare functions for welfare-economic studies. If the individual orderings are interpreted as utility rankings of individuals, and social preferences interpreted as a judgement of social welfare, the Arrow theorem asserted that there is no way of combining individual utility orderings into an overall social welfare judgement satisfying the four specified conditions. The result can be easily translated into a choice-theoretic framework by adopting a choice-based notion of 'social preference', e.g., the 'base' relation or the 'revealed preference' relation of social choice. On this interpretation, it would appear that there is no way of arriving at a social choice procedure specifying what is to be chosen (over pairs, or over larger subsets), satisfying the appropriately interpreted (i.e., in terms of choice) conditions specified by Arrow (see Blair, Bordes, Kelly and Suzumura, 1976; and Sen, 1977a, 1982).

This is, of course, a negative result. A great deal of social choice theory, at least in the early stage, consisted of trying to deal with this result, suggesting different interpretations, different extensions, different ways of 'resolution', and other responses to the 'impossibility' identified by Arrow.

The main lines of response to Arrow's result will be examined presently. It is, however, worth emphasizing that the 'impossibility theorem' must not be seen as primarily a 'negative' achievement. The axiomatic method, as used here, can take a set of axioms which look reasonable enough and then derive some joint implications of these axioms. If the implications are unacceptable, the axioms can be re-examined. Interpreted thus, the axiomatic method is a procedure for assessing a set of principles reflected in the axiom structure, and it persistently invites attention to the content and acceptability of the axioms chosen.

Arrow's impossibility result brought out the unviability of the welfare-economic structure that had emerged in the discussion preceding the birth of modern social choice theory. After the rejection of 'interpersonal comparisons' of well-being (on this see Robbins, 1932, 1938), it was increasingly accepted that social choices or social judgements would have to be based on individual utility orderings without interpersonal comparisons. The four axioms chosen by Arrow make a good deal of sense in that context, and had indeed been used – formally or informally – in the pre-existing literature. What Arrow's theorem demonstrates is the unviability of that structure. The primary impact of Arrow's initial result was to demand that the entire question of the basis of social welfare judgement be re-examined. While this is, in one sense, a negative result, in another sense it opened up various ways of reformulating the social choice problem as a result of the demonstrated unviability of the pre-existing approach. The later literature in social choice theory bears testimony to the fact that many of these ways have been found to be both feasible *and* useful. Several of these approaches will be examined later on in this note, but the positive contribution of the negative impossibility result presented by Arrow has to be kept in view to see these advances in their appropriate perspective.

2. VARIATIONS AND EXTENSIONS OF ARROW'S IMPOSSIBILITY RESULT. The literature of social choice theory contains a large number of theorems that take the form of presenting variations of the type of impossibility identified by Arrow. In fact, Arrow himself has presented several distinct versions. The one presented in 1951 contained a formulational error, which was identified and corrected by Blau (1957). A later version, which was the one cited in the last section, is presented in Arrow (1963). Various other variations can be found in the literature, modifying one condition or another, and presenting impossibility results based on conditions that are more demanding in some respects and less demanding in others (see particularly Blau, 1957; Murakami, 1968; Pattanaik, 1971; Fishburn, 1973, 1974; Hansson, 1976; Brams, 1976; Plott, 1976; Kelly, 1978; Monjardet, 1979; Roberts, 1980b; Chichilnisky, 1982; McManus, 1982; Suzumura, 1983; Hurley, 1985; Nitzan and Paroush, 1985, among many others). Each of Arrow's conditions has been modified in one way or another in these different variants.

One particular variation, which is both illuminating and simple, relates to results presented by Wilson (1972) and Binmore (1976). This shows that given unrestricted domain and independence, all permissible social welfare functions will either have social rankings 'imposed' irrespective of individual preferences, or have a dictator, or have a 'reverse dictator' (a person such that whenever he prefers x to y, society prefers y to x). Arrow's impossibility theorem can be seen as a corollary of this when the Pareto principle is also demanded, since Pareto will eliminate both 'imposition' and 'reverse dictatorship', leaving dictatorship as the only remaining possibility.

One line of variation that has been very extensively investigated is that of weakening the demand of 'collective rationality', i.e., relaxing the requirement that social choice must be based on a social *ordering* (complete, reflexive and transitive). The 'range' of the social welfare function is supposed to include only social orderings, and the proposed relaxation weakens that demand. It can be shown that if the transitivity of only *strict* social preference is demanded (without also demanding the transitivity of social indifference), then all of Arrow's conditions can be simultaneously satisfied and there is no impossibility (see Sen, 1969, 1970; see also Schick, 1969).

This condition of transitivity of strict preference, formally called 'quasi-transitivity', when imposed on social preferences, for a social welfare function satisfying unrestricted domain, independence and the Pareto principle, has the effect of confining social choice procedures to 'oligarchies' (this result was first presented in an unpublished paper by Gibbard, and reported in Sen, 1970). An oligarchic group consists of a set of individuals such that if any one of them prefers any x to any y, then x must be taken to be socially preferred to or indifferent to y, and if all the individuals in that group unanimously prefer x to y, then x must be taken to be socially strictly preferred to y. One extreme case of oligarchic is that of a one-person oligarchy, which corresponds to Arrow's dictatorship. The other extreme makes the oligarchy group include every individual in the community. In this latter case, the fact that all of them taken together happen to be decisive is not remarkable (it follows in fact immediately from the Pareto principle). But it also gives every member of the community 'veto' power in the sense that whenever anyone prefers any x to any y, this precludes the possibility of y being socially strictly preferred to x, and this has the effect of producing lots of social indifferences all around (see Sen, 1969).

This 'veto' result can be obtained even without demanding quasi-transitivity of social preference, by supplementing the weaker demand of 'acyclicity' (i.e. the absence of strict preference cycles) with some other conditions, as has been investigated by Mas-Colell and Sonnenschein, 1972; Schwartz, 1972, 1986; Guha, 1972; Brown, 1974, 1975; Blau, 1976; Blau and Deb, 1977; Monjardet, 1979, and others. Partial 'veto' results have been established with still weaker conditions (see Blair and Pollak, 1982; Kelsey, 1984).

On a somewhat different line of investigation, it has been possible to somewhat weaken the condition of full transitivity of social preference and still retain exactly the impossibility identified by Arrow, i.e., dictatorship following from conditions U, I and P. This is easily done by replacing the requirement of ordering by that of having 'semi-orders', but it can be relaxed further (see Blair and Pollak, 1979; Blau, 1979).

These investigations of relaxation of collective rationality have not been confined only to the weakening of transitivity of social preference. It is possible to drop the requirement of completeness of social preference, permitting the possibility that many pairs of states x and y may be not socially rankable vis-à-vis each other, and still the impossibility result may survive if the Arrow conditions are correspondingly redefined to cover this case with sufficient richness of social ranking, in line with Arrow's original motivation (see Barthelemy, 1983; Weymark, 1983).

Yet another line of investigation consists of relaxing the requirement that social choice must be 'binary' in nature, in the sense of the choice function being representable by a binary relation (whether or not that binary relation R is called social preference). Some positive possibility results were obtained by Schwartz (1970, 1972), Fishburn (1973), Plott (1973), Bordes (1976), and Campbell (1976), by demanding consistency conditions on choice functions that are weaker than the requirement of binary choice.

One way of doing this is to convert preference cycles into indifference classes. For example, take the case of the so-called 'paradox of voting' in which person 1 prefers x to y, and y to z, person 2 prefers y to z, and z to x, and person 3 prefers z to x, and x to y. In this case the majority rule yields x being socially preferred to y, y being socially preferred to z, and z being socially preferred to x, producing a strict preference cycle, with no alternative that is not beaten by another alternative. If, in this case, all the three alternatives are declared socially indifferent, by converting the cycle into an indifference class, then much of Arrow's requirements can be retained. However, one type of consistency will certainly be violated by this formulation of social choice, to with, relating social choice over the pair (x, y) to that over the triple (x, y, z). Due to the majority preference for x over y, and the demand of the 'independence' condition (I) that individual preferences only over (x, y) be considered when choosing over this pair only, x must be chosen and y rejected in the choice over the pair (x, y). But in the choice over the triple (x, y, z), even state y can be selected as a member of the indifference class, when the majority cycle is converted into indifference. The choosability of y from the larger set (x, y, z), and its non-choosability from the smaller set (x, y) contained in the larger set, does violate a standard condition of consistency of choice, variously called Property α, or the 'Chernoff condition', or standard 'contraction consistency'. In the absence of this consistency, the choice function cannot possibly be represented in a binary form, i.e., through a binary relation R such that the choices correspond to the R-maximal elements (with R being derived from the internal properties of choice, e.g., $x\text{R}y$ when x is chosen in the presence of y). But this condition (Property α) is, in fact, much weaker than the requirement that the choice function be binary.

Since binariness may not in itself be a compelling requirement, the plausibility of this line of resolution of Arrow's impossibility depends on the value of the consistency conditions that these 'solutions' may actually satisfy. By imposing some relatively appealing consistency conditions, it can be shown that the dictatorship result of Arrow, and the other related results regarding oligarchy, veto power, etc., derived in the binary framework can reappear easily enough in non-binary choice as well (see Blair, Bordes, Kelly and Suzumura, 1976; Sen, 1977a). It can also be pointed out that even when the social choice procedures do not satisfy binariness in the sense of being *representable* by a binary relation, there would, of course, be binary relations that are *generated* by the choice function. For example, the 'revealed preference' relation (xRy if x is chosen in the presence of y) will be defined by any choice function, since the choice of any alternative (say, x) from any set containing another alternative (say, y), will yield the deduction $x\text{R}y$. The issue of binariness arises when it is further demanded that is what is chosen from each subset consists exactly of the R-maximal elements of that set, according to that binary relation R. It can be shown that binariness in this form demands much the same thing whether we concentrate on the 'revealed preference' relation, or the 'base relation' (the latter being defined as: $x\text{R}y$ if and only if x is chosen specifically from the pair x, y). Binariness according to the 'revealed preference' relation is equivalent to that according to the 'base' relation (see Herzberger, 1973).

Although the demands of binariness provide one way of re-establishing Arrow's 'impossibility' results, a different way is not to demand binariness at all, but to translate all of Arrow's demands to one specific binary relation generated by social choice, e.g., the 'revealed preference', or the 'base' relation. The Arrow theorem will hold exactly in the same way for each such interpretation of R, provided the Arrow conditions are correspondingly reinterpreted. In this sense binariness is not a central issue in the inescapability of the 'impossibility' result of Arrow (on this see Sen, 1977a, 1982; on related matters, see Grether and Plott, 1982; Suzumura, 1983; and Matsumoto, 1985).

One general conclusion that seems to emerge from these investigations of relaxation of 'collective rationality' properties is the durability and robustness of Arrow's 'impossibility' result. The tension between different types of principles seems to survive various ways of relaxing these principles, and the particular 'impossibility theorem' of Arrow is a centre piece of a much broader picture. Demands on consistency of social choice can be dramatically changed without the 'impossibility' features disappearing.

3. DOMAIN RESTRICTIONS. When presenting his impossibility result, Arrow had suggested the possibility that a resolution might be found in terms of restricting the domain of the social welfare function (no longer requiring that it works no matter what the individual preferences happen to be). It is, of course, clear that there are many preference combinations for which such procedures as the method of majority decision will yield perfectly consistent social choice. Arrow (1951) himself had explored a particular type of restriction of individual preferences called 'single-peaked preferences' (earlier discussed by Black, 1948). This corresponds to the case in which the alternatives can be so arranged on a line that everyone's intensity of preference has one peak only, i.e., the preference drops monotonically as we move from left to right, or rises monotonically, or it rises to a peak and then falls. Arrow showed that if individual preferences are single-peaked and the number of voters is odd, then majority decision will yield transitive social preference.

The positive possibility result for single-peaked preferences can be generalized in many different ways. It can be shown that individual preferences being single-peaked in every triple of alternatives is equivalent to the condition that in every triple there is one state such that no one regards it to be 'worst'. It can be shown that a similar agreement on some alternative being regarded as not 'best' would do, and so would an agreement on some alternative being not 'medium'. Altogether, this sufficiency condition is called 'value restriction', and the particular type of agreement (whether 'not best', or 'not worst', or 'not medium') may vary from triple to triple (see Sen, 1966). Also the requirement of oddness of the number of voters can be eliminated if the demand is not for full transitivity of social preference, but only the absence of preference cycles and the existence of a majority winner (Sen, 1969). In this general line of investigation, necessary and sufficient conditions for transitivity as well as acyclicity of majority decisions (i.e., for the existence of a majority winner) have been identified by Inada (1969, 1970) and Sen and Pattanaik (1969). The former requirement is called 'extremal restriction'. The relationships among these and other related conditions are discussed in Inada (1969), Sen (1970), Pattanaik (1971), Fishburn (1973), Salles (1976), Slutsky (1977), Kelly (1978), Monjardet (1979), Blair and Muller (1983), Larsson (1983), Suzumura (1983), Dummett (1984), Arrow and Raynaud (1986), Jain (1986) among many others.

On a different line of analysis, domain conditions can be specified not only in terms of general qualitative correspondence of individual preferences, but also in terms of number-specific requirements on the distribution of voters over the different preferences (see particularly Plott, 1967; Tullock, 1967, 1969; Saposnik, 1975; Slutsky, 1977; Gaertner and Heinecke, 1978; Grandmont, 1978; Dummett, 1984).

These domain conditions all deal specifically with the method of majority decision, but the problem can be investigated more generally. Domain conditions for other voting rules have been investigated (see, for example, Pattanaik, 1971). More recently, the necessary and sufficient domain conditions for the existence of any social welfare function satisfying all of Arrow's other conditions (whether or not based on counting majority) have been investigated (see Kalai and Muller, 1977, and Maskin, 1976; see also Dasgupta, Hammond and Maskin, 1979; Kalai and Ritz, 1980, and Chichilnisky and Heal, 1983).

These domain restrictions are indeed very demanding, and counterexamples can be found without any loss of plausibility in terms of real-life situations (see particularly Kramer, 1973). But if these restrictions are not fulfilled, then there is no general 'solution' to be found in opting for the majority rule, or some other rule like that. Indeed, it can be shown for the majority rule that the cycles that may be generated may well be extremely extensive, yielding 'total cycles' involving all social states (see Schofield, 1978; McKelvey, 1979). This line of investigation too, like the one on collective rationality (discussed in the last section), yields rather discouraging results. No general solution of impossibility theorems of the type presented by Arrow can be easily found by opting for a rule like the majority decision, hoping that the domain conditions will be somehow satisfied.

In many economic decisions, it is quite straightforward to see that these conditions will indeed be all violated. However, when the number of alternatives happen to be small, and when there are complex balancing of conflicting considerations, as in many political contexts (elections, committee decisions over rival proposals, etc.), there might possibly be some room for optimism. If cycles or other types of intransitivities turn out to be rather rare in these cases, then the approach of domain restriction may well offer some help. In contrast, in welfare-economic problems, that hope is very limited.

Indeed, if we take such a simple social-welfare problem as the division of a given cake between three or more individuals, with each person voting according to his or her own share of the cake, it can be easily shown that there will indeed be majority cycles. But it is worth noting in this context that the method of majority decision is not particularly appropriate for such economic problems anyway. Any distribution of the given cake can be improved by choosing one of the persons (even the poorest one) and dividing a part of his or her share for the benefit of all others, thereby producing an 'improvement' according to the majority rule. Indeed, we can go on 'improving' the distribution in this way, following the majority ranking procedure, making the worst-off individual more and more worse off all the time. As a criterion for welfare-economic judgement, majority rule is, in fact, a non-starter. The recognition of this fact makes it less tragic that majority cycles will tend to arise easily enough in many economic problems involving distributional variations. The majority rule would not have offered any 'real solution' to the task of making social welfare judgements in this type of economic problems even if it had been fully consistent. It is more in the context of political decisions involving a few diverse alternatives (rather than welfare-economic judgements in general) that majority rule and related decision procedures have some *prima facie* plausibility. It is, thus, of some interest that it is in the context of these problems that the domain conditions investigated by the social choice literature are of direct relevance and offer some hope.

4. MANIPULABILITY AND IMPLEMENTATION. A different type of problem for voting procedures arises from the possibility of 'manipulation' of the decision mechanism by the voters voting 'dishonestly'. A voting procedure is 'manipulable' when it is in the interest of some voter for some set of individual

preferences to vote differently from his or her sincere preference.

The ubiquity of the possibility of manipulation had been conjectured for a long time, but it was established only recently in a remarkable theorem first presented by Gibbard (1973), and then by Satterthwaite (1975). A similar result, and a pointer to positive possibility if the conditions are relaxed, was presented by Pattanaik (1973.) The Gibbard–Satterthwaite manipulation theorem establishes that every non-dictatorial voting scheme with at least three distinct outcomes must be manipulable.

Gibbard established this theorem as a corollary of another one dealing with 'game forms' in general, of which voting schemes happen to be special cases. A game form does not restrict the strategies to be chosen by the individuals to the orderings of social states (i.e., to 'ballots'), and each person's strategy set can be any set of signals. Gibbard established that no non-dictatorial game form with at least three possible outcomes can be 'straightforward' (a concept first used by Farquharson, 1956), in the sense that each person would have a *dominant* strategy (i.e., a best strategy with respect to his ordering of the outcomes, irrespective of what the strategies of others might be). Thus for every non-dictatorial game form of this type, there is at least one person who does not have a dominant strategy for some preference ordering of outcomes. From this the manipulability theorem follows immediately. If a voting scheme were *non*-manipulable, then everyone would have had a dominant strategy, viz., recording his or her *true* preference irrespective of what others do. Since the existence of dominant strategies is disestablished, so is the existence of *honest* dominant strategies.

Various variations of this discouraging result and some avenues of escape have been investigated in the literature, which is quite vast (but excellent discussions can be found in Barbera, 1977; Pattanaik, 1978; Laffont, 1979; Peleg, 1984; Brams and Fishburn, 1983; Moulin, 1983; and Jain, 1986).

The focus on 'honest' revelation of preferences has gradually given way to discussions of equilibrium and of implementation (for an early pointer in this direction, see Dummett and Farquharson, 1961). If the object of the exercise is effectiveness in the sense of getting an appropriate outcome (rather than seeking honesty as such), then the thing to investigate is indeed the existence of an effective mechanism rather than a 'strategy-proof' one. If, for example, a non-strategy-proof mechanism yields an equilibrium of dishonest behaviour that produces the same outcome as honest revelation of preferences would, then that mechanism could well be regarded as successful in terms of effectiveness.

The shift in attention towards equilibrium and implementation has opened up new lines of investigation, which are being explored (see particularly Dutta and Pattanaik, 1978; Dasgupta, Hammond and Maskin, 1979; Sengupta and Dutta, 1979; Peleg, 1984; Moulin, 1983). The implementation literature also links up with more standard problems of public economics, in which it has received attention in a somewhat different but related form (see, particularly, Groves and Ledyard, 1977; Green and Laffont, 1979; Laffont, 1979).

5. INFORMATION: UTILITY, COMPENSATIONS AND FAIRNESS. The alleged impossibility of interpersonal comparisons of utility was entirely accepted in the early works on social choice theory. Arrow's (1951) format gave no room to interpersonally comparable utility information, and indeed took utility information in the form of non-comparable ordinal utility rankings. This was entirely in line with the dominant position of welfare economics at that time. Even though there were formats for interpersonal comparisons of utility suggested in some contributions to welfare economics (see particularly Vickrey, 1945, and Harsanyi, 1955), these suggestions were not followed up in the formal social-choice-theoretic literature until much later.

There had been earlier attempts to by-pass the need for utility comparisons by using the notion of compensation tests (e.g., whether the gainers *could* compensate the losers), and this had led to the identification of problems of internal consistency as well as of cogency (see Kaldor, 1939; Hicks, 1939; Scitovsky, 1941; Little, 1950; Samuelson, 1950; Baumol, 1952; Gorman, 1953; Graaff, 1957). The problem of cogency is perhaps deeper, in some ways, than that of consistency. To make sure that gainers have gained so much that they can compensate the loser does, of course, have some immediate plausibility as a requirement. However, the relevance of the compensation tests suffers from the following limitation. If compensations are not paid, then it is not clear in what way the situation can be taken to be an improvement (since those who have lost may well be a great deal poorer, needier or more deserving – whatever our criteria for such judgements might be – than the gainers). And if compensations *are* in fact paid, then *after* the compensation what we observe is a Pareto improvement, so that no compensation tests are in fact needed. Thus, the compensation approach suffers from having to face a choice between being unconvincing or being irrelevant.

Another approach that by-passes the need for interpersonal comparisons proper is that of 'fairness', presented first by Foley (1967). Here a person's advantage is judged by comparing his bundle of goods with those enjoyed by others, and a situation is called 'equitable' if no individual prefers the bundle of goods enjoyed by another person to his own. If an allocation is both Pareto optimal and equitable then it is called 'fair'. (There is some non-uniformity of language in the literature, and sometimes the term 'fair' has been defined simply as 'equitable', e.g., in Feldman and Kirman, 1974 and Pazner and Schmeidler, 1974.) This approach has been pursued by a number of authors (such as Kolm, 1969; Schmeidler and Vind, 1972; Varian, 1974, 1975; Goldman and Sussangkarn, 1978; Archibald and Donaldson, 1979; Crawford, 1979; Crawford and Heller, 1979; Svensson, 1980; Champsaur and Laroque, 1981; Suzumura, 1983, and others). There are interesting problems of the *existence* of fair allocations and of the *consistency* of fairness with other principles.

It should be noted that the comparisons involved in the calculus of 'fairness' are not interpersonal ones, but in fact comparisons of different positions that the same individual might occupy (e.g., having commodity bundles), as it is evaluated by the given person. The criterion of 'non-envy' does clearly have some appeal, even though it can be argued that our deprivations may be related not only to other people's commodity bundles but also to *non-commodity* features of their advantage. For example, a person with a disability may well prefer to be in somebody else's position without that disability, but that is not the same thing as envying that other person's commodity bundle. As such, it could be argued, that the informational base of the fairness calculus is fundamentally limited.

Another difference between the 'fairness' approach and the standard social-choice-theoretic procedures relates to the more limited aim of the former. As Varian (1974) puts it, the fairness criterion in fact limits itself to answering the question as to whether there is a 'good' allocation (pp. 64–5). It is certainly true that social choice theory has been abundantly more ambitious, perhaps unrealistically so. On the other hand, it can be argued, that even the features of 'goodness' identified by the approach of fairness (e.g., equitability with efficiency) may often fail to be satisfied by any feasible allocation at all, so that the question of ranking the 'non-good' allocations is not really avoidable. In addition, it can be argued that insofar as the foundation of the 'fairness' approach is based only on comparing the commodity bundles of different persons without going further into the relative advantages enjoyed by the persons (taking everything into account), the criterion of 'goodness' used in the 'fairness' literature is itself rather a limited one. It is perhaps for these reasons that the use of interpersonal comparisons of well-being in social choice theory (in the literature on social welfare functionals, to be discussed presently) has tended to aim at going a great deal further than the 'fairness' literature was programmed to achieve.

6. SOCIAL WELFARE FUNCTIONALS AND INTERPERSONAL COMPARISONS. The empirical problem of obtaining information on interpersonal comparisons of utility has to be distinguished from the formal problem of accommodating such information within the structure of social choice theory. The format of social welfare functions used by Arrow, and the related formats of collected choice rules (involving such various forms as social decision functions, social choice functions, etc.), make no provision for any utility information finer than that of non-comparable individual orderings. One way of extending that framework is to permit the use of more utility information, through what have been called 'social welfare functionals' (SWFL): $R = F(\{U_i\})$. For each set (strictly, n-tuple) of utility functions $U_i, \ldots, U_n$ (one function per person), the social welfare functional F determines exactly one social ordering R. However, since utility functions can be nominally varied through alternative presentations without involving any 'real' change (e.g., doubling all the utility numbers), any social welfare functional has to be combined with some 'invariance' requirement. If two utility n-tubles (U_i) and (U_i^*) are judged to be informationally equivalent, differing from each other only in representation, then $F\{U_i\}) = F(\{U_i^*\})$. The assumed structure of measurability and interpersonal comparability of utilities can be incorporated through specifying these invariance requirements (see Sen, 1970, 1977b; d'Aspremont and Gevers, 1977; Roberts, 1980a; Blackorby, Donaldson and Weymark, 1984).

Arrow's social welfare function is a special case of a social welfare functional with the invariance requirement corresponding to ordinal non-comparability (i.e., if one n-tuple of utility functions is replaced by another obtained from the first by taking positive, monotonic transformations of each utility function – not necessarily the same for all – then the social ordering R determined by the first n-tuple will also be yielded by the second). It is obvious that Arrow's 'impossibility theorem' can be translated in the format of social welfare functionals with *ordinal non-comparability*. More interestingly, this result can be generalized to the case of *cardinal non-comparability* also. When individual utilities can be cardinally measured but not in any way interpersonally compared, the same impossibility result continues to hold (see Sen, 1970). On the other hand, introducing interpersonal comparability without cardinality (i.e., using ordinal comparability only) does resolve the Arrow dilemma, and various possible SWFLs exist fulfilling all of Arrow's conditions in this case. An example is provided by Rawls's maximin rule (or the lexicographic version of it), defining these exercises in terms of utility comparison, rather than that of indices of 'primary goods', as in Rawls's own framework.

Richer utility information can be systematically used to admit various social choice procedures not admissible in Arrow's framework. The use of various axioms to characterize particular rules utilizing richer utility information can be found in an influential and important contribution by Suppes (1966). In the recent years the more formal frameworks of social choice theory (in particular, that of SWFLs) have been extensively used to derive axiomatically a number of standard aggregation procedures, such as the Rawlsian lexicographic maximin, utilitarianism, and some others (see particularly Hammond, 1976, 1977, 1979; Strasnick, 1976; d'Aspremont and Gevers, 1977; Arrow, 1977; Sen, 1977b; Deschamps and Gevers, 1978, 1979; Maskin, 1978; Gevers, 1979; Roberts, 1980a; Blackorby, Donaldson and Weymark, 1984; d'Aspremont, 1985). While these results are formal and do not address the question of the empirical content of interpersonal comparisons of utility (though this too is discussed by Hammond, 1977), the axiom structures have been related to various empirical insights thrown up by the substantive literature on interpersonal comparisons.

One format that has also been investigated relates to the intermediate possibility of making *partial* interpersonal comparisons of utilities. Various formal structures of partial comparability and partial cardinality have, in fact, been investigated in the social-choice-theoretic literature (see Sen, 1970; Blackorby, 1975; Fine, 1975; Basu, 1979; Bezembinder and van Acker, 1979). This is a less ambitious approach, admitting that not all types of interpersonal comparisons may be possible, and such comparability may be at best partial, with many undecided cases. Nevertheless *some* definite results can be obtained even on the basis of the incomplete structures.

Various other informational frameworks involving richer utility data can be and have been investigated, and some of them lend themselves to fruitful social-choice-theoretic use. One of the structures that need further investigation is the problem of combining n-tuples of 'extended orderings' reflecting each person's interpersonal comparisons. These are ordinal structures, but instead of there being one interpersonal comparison covering all the individuals in the different possible positions, this starts with the set of interpersonal comparisons made by different individuals (one 'extended ordering' per person), and addresses the problem of aggregation in that framework. Some interesting results in this area have been obtained (see Hammond, 1976; Kelly, 1978; Suzumura, 1983; Gaertner, 1983). The task, however, is rather a difficult one, since the information to marshall is extremely extensive, and progress in this area has tended to be rather slow. On the other hand, since social choice theory has to be concerned with the problem of combining different persons' possibly divergent views, that 'extended' problem certainly has a good deal of relevance and potential importance.

7. LIBERTY AND RIGHTS. The informational limitations of the early social-choice-theoretic structures have led to responses in the later literature not only in the form of enriching the utility information (by the use of such structures as social welfare functionals SWFL), but also that of making more systematic use of *non-utility* information. One of the areas that has been investigated in this context is that of rights in general and of liberty in particular. Liberty can be an important consideration in matters of social choice, but it cannot be adequately captured in terms of utility information, however rich it might be. If it is asserted that a person should be free to do what he or she likes in certain purely personal matters, that assertion is based on the non-utility characteristics of the 'personal nature' of these choices, and not primarily on utility considerations. As John Stuart Mill (1859) had argued, even if others might be

offended by someone's personal behaviour in such matters as religious practice, it would not be appropriate to count the disutility of the offended in the same way as the utility of the person whose freedom of religious practice is under consideration. Various notions of 'protected spheres', 'personal domains', etc., have been formalized in the social-choice-theoretic literature in specifying domains of personal liberty.

One of the results obtained in this field that has led to a great deal of controversy concerns the conflict between the Pareto principle and certain minimal conditions of liberty when imposed on a social choice framework with unrestricted (or a fairly wide) domain. The 'impossibility of the Paretian liberal', presented in Sen (1970), has led to a variety of responses, including extensions, disputations, and suggestions of different ways of 'resolving' the conflict (see Ng, 1971; Batra and Pattanaik, 1972; Gibbard, 1974; Blau, 1975; Seidl, 1975; Campbell, 1976; Kelly, 1976, 1978; Aldrich, 1977; Breyer, 1977; Ferejohn, 1978; Karni, 1978; Suzumura, 1978, 1983; Mueller, 1979; Barnes, 1980; Bernholz, 1980; Breyer and Gardner, 1980; Breyer and Gigliotti, 1980; Fountain, 1980; Gardner, 1980; McLean, 1980; Weale, 1980; Baigent, 1981; Gaertner and Krüger, 1981; Gärdenfors, 1981; Hammond, 1981; Schwartz, 1970, 1972, 1986; Sugden, 1981, 1985; Austen-Smith, 1982; Levi, 1982; Krüger and Gaertner, 1983; Basu, 1984; Kelsey, 1985; Wriglesworth, 1985; Coughlin, 1986; Elster and Hylland, 1986; Gaertner, 1986; Riley, 1986; Webster, 1986, among others). The literature is vast, and covers issues of political compatibility, moral cogency and strategic consistency; it has been critically surveyed and assessed by Suzumura (1983) and Wriglesworth (1985). Various alternative formulations of liberty, in terms of social judgements, social decisions and social institutions can be shown to yield corresponding impossibility results (see Sen, 1983).

It is not really surprising that conditions of liberty or rights which make essential use of non-utility information may clash with exclusively utility-based principles, such as the Pareto principle. Non-utility considerations cannot be immovable objects if utility considerations, even in a rather limited context (as in the Pareto principle), are made into an irresistable force. One role of this type of impossibility result lies in pointing to the possibility that utility data may not be informationally adequate for social judgement or social choice, even when the utility information comes in the most articulate and complete form. Other lessons have also been suggested, and each interpretation has also been substantively disputed.

While impossibility results like this have received good deal of attention, relatively little effort has so far been spent on investigating the positive implications of various theories of rights, liberties and freedom, in the general area of social choice. The need for caution in formulating the demands of liberty because of problems of internal consistency has in fact been investigated. But the more general question of developing a fruitful and positive theory of rights and liberty within the general structure of social choice theory has not yet been much investigated.

8. INDEPENDENCE AND NEUTRALITY. The independence of irrelevant alternatives, used by Arrow, plays a major part in the social choice formats in the Arrovian tradition. It is also crucial for Arrow's impossibility theorem. The nature, implications and acceptability of the independence condition have been subjected to a good deal of critical examination in the literature (see particularly Gärdenfors, 1973; Hansson, 1973; Ray, 1973; Fine and Fine, 1974; Fishburn, 1974; Mayston, 1974; Young, 1974a, 1974b; Binmore, 1976; Kelly, 1978; Pattanaik, 1978; Moulin, 1983; Suzumura, 1983; Peleg, 1984; Hurley, 1985; Schwartz, 1986).

One of the objections that was originally raised about the relevance of Arrow's impossibility theorem related to the acceptability of the independence condition. Some authors (in particular Little, 1950 and Samuelson, 1967) argued that seeking inter-profile consistency in any form (including Arrow's 'independence' condition) is largely gratuitous. It was also argued that traditional welfare economics had never sought such a condition, and because of the crucial use of condition I, 'Arrow's work has no relevance to the traditional theory of welfare economics, which culminates in the Bergson–Samuelson formulations' (Little, 1950, pp. 423–5). 'For Bergson,' argued Samuelson (1967), 'one and only one of the ... possible patterns of individuals' orderings is needed' (pp. 48–9), and the question of inter-profile consistency does not arise.

In response to this line of objection, several 'single-profile impossibility theorems' in the spirit of Arrow's original theorem have been derived and discussed (see particularly Parks, 1976; Kemp and Ng, 1976; Pollak, 1979; Roberts, 1980b; Rubinstein, 1981; Hurley, 1985). These results depend on dropping inter-profile consistency in favour of rather strong intra-profile requirements, typically including some condition of single-profile neutrality, requiring that whatever combination of individual orderings be decisive for establishing xRy should be sufficient for establishing aRb if each individual ranking over (x, y) is the same as that over (a, b) in that given profile. the nature of the alternatives – whether x and y, *or* a and b – is, thus, not to make any difference, in relating individual preferences over particular pairs to social preference over those pairs, for any given profile of individual preferences.

These results are interesting, but it must be noted that the requirements on which they are based (e.g., of single-profile neutrality) are rather strong. Also the dictatorial result that follows from the other conditions is that of single-profile dictatorship, which might not be thought to be as objectionable as the existence of one inter-profile dictator who wins for *every* possible preference profile (as in Arrow's theorem).

No matter what one thinks of these single-profile impossibility results, it can certainly be argued that the original objection raised by Little and Samuelson about the relevance of inter-profile conditions for social choice theory is hard to sustain. Given the motivation underlying demands for consistency in the relation between individual preferences and social choice, it is not at all clear why such consistency requirements should be thought to be applicable only for a given profile and not between different profiles of individual preferences (no matter how close these profiles are in relevant respects).

It could, of course, be argued that utility orderings (or preferences) are not adequate informational base anyway for social choice, and if that position were taken, then the very idea of a social welfare function would have to be rejected in favour of some richer informational formulation, such as a social welfare functional SWFL. If, on the other hand, the motivation underlying the use of a social welfare function is accepted, and it is agreed that for a given preference n-tuple (i.e., a given profile), there is only one social ordering, then it is not clear why it would be thought to be perfectly okay that social preferences might change over a given pair when there is a change of individual preferences over some pair of alternatives quite unconnected with this particular one. The need for some interprofile consistency is hard to deny altogether. It could, of course, be argued that Arrow's particular inter-profile condition is not the appropriate one to use for inter-profile consistency, but that would not be an objection to inter-profile conditions as such, only to the particular formulation of Arrow's condition I. It should also be noted that there are other inter-profile conditions that can be used in order to generate impossibility results like Arrow's, without any use of condition I (see in particular Chichilnisky, 1982).

If Arrow's condition I is dropped, a number of alternative possibilities do, in fact, open up for social choice procedures. For one thing, 'positional' information can be used to rank alternative social states and to arrive at social choice. In fact, in an early contribution to social choice theory, Borda (1781) had used a decision procedure that violates condition I in arriving at overall rankings based on rank-order weights. This method – often called the Borda rule – is a special case of a general class of 'positional' rules. The general properties of 'positional' rules have been fruitfully investigated by Gärdenfors (1973) and Fine and Fine (1974), among others. The Borda ruling in particular has also received attention, and various particular rules have been investigated, critically examined and axiomatized (see Young, 1974a; Fishburn and Gehrlein, 1976; Hansson and Sahlquist, 1976; Gardner, 1977; Farkas and Nitzan, 1979; and Nitzan and Rubinstein, 1981, among others).

Positional rules take note of the fact that an alternative *x* preferred to another alternative *y* may be proximate to each other in a person's preference ordering without any other alternative in between, or may be separated by the existence of one or more other alternatives intermediate between the two. The rationale of positional rules relates to attaching importance to the placing of intermediate alternatives in individual preferences, which can be taken as suggesting that the gap between the two must be, other things given, larger. This argument is not entirely convincing. Many intermediate alternatives can be placed in a small interval, while large intervals may happen to be empty because of the contingent fact that there happens to be no other alternative that fits in just there. On the other hand, if information is thought to be extremely hard to get in social choice (a view that was certainly taken by Borda, 1781), then it is not entirely unreasonable to attach some significance to the fact that the placing of intermediate alternatives might be indicative of something. With some implicit assumption of uniformity of distribution of alternatives over the preference line (or some other suitable belief), the positional rules may have some clear rationale, and the Borda rule in particular might be particulary handy and useful.

It is possible to use positional information also in the context of richer informational base, e.g., when interpersonal comparisons of utilities are permissible. Indeed 'interpersonal positional rules' may have some distinct advantage both (1) over rules that make non-positional use of interpersonally comparable individual orderings, and (2) over non-comparable positional rules. Such interpersonal positional rules may also be demonstrably more reasonable, in some contexts, than voting procedures like the majority rule which use neither interpersonal comparisons nor positional information (on this see Sen, 1977b; Gaertner, 1983).

9. CONCLUDING REMARKS. In understanding the literature of social choice theory it is important to bear in mind that while there are considerable analytical similarities between different problems tackled in this vast literature, the interpretations of the results and of their implications must take note of the particular nature of each of the substantively different problems. The axiomatic method, which has been so extensively used in the literature, offers enormous scope for efficient economy, but that economy will be self-defeating if the substantive differences are not carefully taken into account in interpreting exactly the content of the theorems derived. For example, the classic 'impossibility' result of Arrow may impose informational constraints that are much more reasonable in aggregating political preferences of different individuals over a small set of alternative proposals (or candidates) than in arriving at aggregative judgements of social justice taking note of conflicting individual interests over possible distributions of commodity vectors.

There is sometimes a temptation to see social choice theory as providing a particular 'method' of dealing with problems of aggregation. There is some truth in this diagnosis, in the sense that the discipline of axiomatic procedures has some exacting demands. On the other hand, the axioms can vary a great deal, and the interpretation of the axioms also will vary with the nature of the problems considered. The monolithic view of something called 'the social-choice-theoretic approach', which is often referred to both by those who wish to use it and those who wish to criticize it, may be deeply misleading. For some arguments on different sides on this question, see Elster and Hylland (1986).

There are, in fact, two different ways of seeing social choice theory. First, it is a field, and in this field there is scope for having different approaches. There are many problems of interpersonal aggregation, and in the broader sense, social choice theory is a field in which such aggregation – of different types – is studied. Second, social choice theory also provides a method of analysis, in which the insistence on the explicitness of axioms and on the clarity of assumptions imposes exacting formulational demands. Indeed, some of the more notable achievements of social choice theory have come from this insistence on explicitness and clarity (e.g., Arrow's own demonstration of the impossibility of combining a set of assumptions that were being implicitly invoked in the literature of the welfare economics of that period, including eschewing interpersonal comparisons of utility). While the second interpretation is a narrower one than the first, it is nevertheless broad enough to permit different types of axioms to be used, and different political, economic and social beliefs to be incorporated in the axiom structure. Neither interpretation would give any cogency to the search for 'the social-choice-theoretic approach'.

One reason why social choice theory has received as much attention as it has in the last few decades relates to the importance of the field with which that theory has been concerned (and which characterizes that theory in the *broader* sense). Another reason has been the fruitfulness of making implicit ideas explicit, and of following their implications consistently and clearly. As a methodological discipline, social choice theory has contributed a great deal to clarifying problems that had been obscure earlier. While insistence on clarity at all costs has also some limitations (sometimes the narrowness of the axiom structure used in social choice theory has indeed been seen as a limitation), social choice theory has undoubtedly been a creative tradition among other methodological traditions that can be used to analyse economic, social and political problems involving group aggregation. The vast literature surveyed in this article can be ultimately judged by what has been achieved in terms of clarifying the obscure and illuminating the unclear. Perhaps the successes have been rather mixed, but that fact is not surprising.

AMARTYA SEN

See also ARROW'S THEOREM; CONSTITUTIONAL ECONOMICS; PUBLIC CHOICE; SOCIAL WELFARE FUNCTION; VOTING.

BIBLIOGRAPHY

Aldrich, J. 1977. The dilemma of a Paretian liberal: Some consequences of Sen's theorem. *Public Choice* 30, 1–21.

Archibald, G.C. and Donaldson, D. 1979. Notes on economic equality. *Journal of Public Economics* 12, 205–14.

Arrow, K.J. 1951. *Social Choice and Individual Values.* New York: Wiley.

Arrow, K.J. 1963. *Social Choice and Individual Values.* 2nd edn, New York: Wiley.

Arrow, K.J. 1977. Extended sympathy and the possibility of social choice. *American Economic Review* 67, 219–25.

Arrow, K.J. and Raynaud, H. 1986. *Social Choice and Multicriterion Decision-Making.* Cambridge, Mass.: MIT Press.

Austen-Smith, D. 1982. Restricted Pareto and rights. *Journal of Economic Theory* 26, 89–99.

Baigent, N. 1981. Decomposition of minimal libertarianism. *Economic Letters* 7, 29–32.

Barbera, S. 1977. Manipulation of social decision functions. *Journal of Economic Theory* 15, 226–78.

Barnes, 1980. Freedom, rationality and paradox. *Canadian Journal of Philosophy* 10.

Barthelemy, J.P. 1983. Arrow's theorem: Unusual domains and extended codomains. In Pattanaik and Salles (1983).

Basu, K. 1979. *Revealed Preference of Governments.* Cambridge: Cambridge University Press.

Basu, K. 1984. The right to give up rights. *Economica* 51, 413–22.

Batra, R.M. and Pattanaik, P.K. 1972. On some suggestions for having non-binary social choice functions. *Theory and Decision* 3, 1–11.

Baumol, W.J. 1952. *Welfare Economics and the Theory of the State.* Cambridge, Mass.: Harvard University Press.

Bentham, J. 1789. *An Introduction to the Principles of Morals and Legislation.* London: Payne. Reprinted, Oxford: Clarendon Press, 1907.

Bergson, A. 1938. A reformulation of certain aspects of welfare economics. *Quarterly Journal of Economics* 52, 310–34.

Bernholz, P. 1980. A general social dilemma: Profitable exchange and intransitive group preference. *Zeitschrift für Nationalökonomie* 40, 1–23.

Bezembinder, Th. and van Acker, P. 1979. A note on Sen's partial comparability model. Department of Psychology, Katholieke Universiteit, Nijmegen, The Netherlands.

Binmore, K. 1976. Social choice and parties. *Review of Economic Studies* 43, 459–64.

Black, D. 1948. On the rationale of group decision making. *Journal of Political Economy* 56, 23–34.

Black, D. 1958. *The Theory of Committees and Elections.* London: Cambridge University Press.

Blackorby, C. 1975. Degrees of cardinality and aggregate partial orderings. *Econometrica* 43, 845–52.

Blackorby, C., Donaldson, D. and Weymark, J.A. 1984. Social choice with interpersonal utility comparisons. *International Economic Review* 25, 327–56.

Blair, D.H., Bordes, G., Kelly, J.S. and Suzumura, K. 1976. Impossibility theorems without collective rationality. *Journal of Economic Theory* 13, 361–79.

Blair, D.H. and Muller, E. 1983. Essential aggregation procedures on restricted domains of preferences. *Journal of Economic Theory* 30, 34–53.

Blair, D.H. and Pollak, R.A. 1979. Collective rationality and dictatorship: The scope of the Arrow theorem. *Journal of Economic Theory* 21, 186–94.

Blair, D.H. and Pollak, R.A. 1982. Acyclic collective choice rules. *Econometrica* 50, 931–43.

Blau, J.H. 1957. The existence of a social welfare function. *Econometrica* 25, 302–13.

Blau, J.H. 1975. Liberal values and independence. *Review of Economic Studies* 42, 413–20.

Blau, J.H. 1976. Neutrality, monotonicity and the right of veto: a comment. *Econometrica* 44, 603.

Blau, J.H. 1979. Semiorders and collective choice. *Journal of Economic Theory* 21, 195–206.

Blau, J.H. and Deb, R. 1977. Social decision functions and veto. *Econometrica* 45, 871–9.

Bonner, J. 1986. *Politics, Economics and Welfare.* Brighton: Wheatsheaf.

Borda, J.C. 1781. Memoire sur les élections au scrutin. *Mémoires de l'Académie Royale des Sciences*; English translation by A. de Grazia, *Isis* 44 (1953).

Bordes, G. 1976. Consistency, rationality and collective choice. *Review of Economic Studies* 43, 447–57.

Bose, A. 1975. *Marxian and Post-Marxian Political Economy.* Harmondsworth: Penguin Books.

Brams, S.J. 1975. *Game Theory and Politics.* New York: Free Press.

Brams, S.J. 1976. *Paradoxes in Politics.* New York: Free Press.

Brams, S.J. and Fishburn, P.C. 1983. *Approval Voting.* Boston: Birkhäuser.

Breyer, F. 1977. The liberal paradox, decisiveness over issues, and domain restrictions. *Zeitschrift für Nationalökonomie* 37, 45–60.

Breyer, F. and Gardner, R. 1980. Liberal paradox, game equilibrium and Gibbard optimum. *Public Choice* 35, 469–81.

Breyer, F. and Gigliotti, G.A. 1980. Empathy and respect for the right of others. *Zeitschrift für Nationalökonomie* 40, 59–64.

Brown, D.J. 1974. An approximate solution to Arrow's problem. *Journal of Economic Theory* 9, 375–83.

Brown, D.J. 1975. Aggregation of preferences. *Journal of Economics* 89, 456–69.

Buchanan, J.M. and Tullock, G. 1962. *The Calculus of Consent.* Ann Arbor: University of Michigan Press.

Camacho, A. 1974. Societies and social decision functions. In Leinfellner and Kohler (1974).

Campbell, D.E. 1976. Democratic preference functions. *Journal of Economic Theory* 12, 259–72.

Campbell, D.E. 1980. Algorithms for social choice functions. *Review of Economic Studies* 47, 617–27.

Champsaur, P. and Laroque, G. 1982. Strategic behavior in decentralized planning procedures. *Econometrica* 50, 325–44.

Chichilnisky, G. 1982. Social aggregation rules and continuity. *Quarterly Journal of Economics* 96, 337–52.

Chichilnisky, G. and Heal, G. 1983. Necessary and sufficient conditions for a resolution of the social choice paradox. *Journal of Economic Theory* 31, 68–87.

Condorcet, M. de. 1785. *Essai sur l'Application de l'Analyse à la Probabilité des Décisions Rendues à le Pluralité des Voix.* Paris.

Çoughlin, P.J. 1986. Rights and the private Pareto principle. *Economica* 53.

Crawford, V.P. 1979. A procedure for generating Pareto-efficient egalitarian-equivalent allocations. *Econometrica* 47, 49–60.

Crawford, V.P. and Heller, W.P. 1979. Fair division with indivisible commodities. *Journal of Economic Theory* 21, 10–27.

Dasgupta, P., Hammond, P. and Maskin, E. 1979. The implementation of social choice rules: Some general results on incentive compatibility. *Review of Economic Studies* 46, 185–216.

Dasgupta, P. and Heal, G. 1979. *Economic Theory and Exhaustible Resources.* London: James Nisbet, and Cambridge: Cambridge University Press.

d'Aspremont, C. and Gevers, L. 1977. Equity and informational basis of collective choice. *Review of Economic Studies* 46, 199–210.

d'Aspremont, D. 1985. Axioms for social welfare orderings in Hurwicz, Schmeidler and Sonnenschein 1985.

Davis, O.A., De Groot, M.H. and Hinich, M.J. 1972. Social preference orderings and majority rule. *Econometrica* 40, 147–57.

Deb, R. 1976. On Schwartz's rule. *Journal of Economic Theory* 16, 103–10.

Deschamps and Gevers, L. 1978. Leximin and utilitarian rules: a joint characterisation. *Journal of Economic Theory* 17, 143–163.

Deschamps and Gevers, L. 1979. Separability, risk-taking and social welfare judgements. In Laffont (1979).

Dummett, M. 1984. *Voting Procedures.* Oxford: Clarendon Press.

Dummett, M. and Farquharson, R. 1961. Stability in voting. *Econometrica* 29, 133–43.

Dutta, B. 1980. On the possibility of consistent voting procedures. *Review of Economic Studies* 47, 603–16.

Dutta, B. and Pattanaik, P.K. 1978. On nicely consistent voting systems. *Econometrica* 46, 163–70.

Elster, J. and Hylland, A. (eds) 1986. *Foundations of Social Choice Theory*. Cambridge: Cambridge University Press.

Farkas, D. and Nitzan, S. 1979. The Borda rule and Pareto stability: A comment. *Econometrica* 47, 1305–6.

Farquharson, R. 1956. Straightforwardness in voting paradoxes. *Oxford Economic Papers* 8, 80–9.

Farrell, M.J. 1976. Liberalism in the theory of social choice. *Review of Economic Studies* 43, 3–10.

Feldman, A. and Kirman, A. 1974. Fairness and envy. *American Economic Review* 64, 995–1005.

Ferejohn, J.A. 1978. The distribution of rights in society. In Gottinger and Leinfellner 1978.

Fine, B.J. 1975. A note on interpersonal aggregation and partial comparability. *Econometrica* 43, 173–4.

Fine, B.J. and Fine, K. 1974. Social choice and individual ranking. *Review of Economic Studies* 41, 303–22, 459–75.

Fishburn, P.C. 1973. *The Theory of Social Choice*. Princeton: Princeton University Press.

Fishburn, P.C. 1974. On collective rationality and a generalized impossibility theorem. *Review of Economic Studies* 41, 445–59.

Fishburn, P.C. and Gehrlein, W.V. 1976. Borda's rule, positional voting, and Condorcet's simple majority principle. *Public Choice* 28, 79–88.

Foley, D. 1967. Resource allocation in the public sector. *Yale Economic Essays* 7, 73–6.

Fountain, J. 1980. Bowley's analysis of bilateral monopoly and Sen's liberal paradox in collective choice theory: A note. *Quarterly Journal of Economics* 95.

Gaertner, W. 1983. Equity- and inequity-type Borda rules. *Mathematical Social Sciences* 4, 137–54.

Gaertner, W. 1986. Pareto, independent rights exercising and strategic behaviour. *Journal of Economics: Zeitschrift für Nationalökonomie* 46.

Gaertner, W. and Heinecke, A. 1978. Cyclically mixed preferences: A necessary and sufficient condition for transitivity of the social preference relation. In Gottinger and Leinfellner 1978.

Gaertner, W. and Krüger, L. 1981. Self-supporting preferences and individual rights: The possibility of Paretian libertarianism. *Economica* 48, 17–28.

Gaertner, W. and Krüger, L. 1983. Alternative libertarian claims and Sen's paradox. *Theory and Decision* 15, 211–30.

Gärdenfors, P. 1973. Positional voting functions. *Theory and Decision* 4, 1–24.

Gärdenfors, P. 1981. Rights, games and social choice. *Nous* 15.

Gardner, R. 1977. The Borda game. *Public Choice* 30, 43–50.

Gardner, R. 1980. The strategic inconsistency of Paretian liberalism. *Public Choice* 35, 241–52.

Gevers, L. 1979. On interpersonal comparability and social welfare orderings. *Econometrica* 47, 75–90.

Gibbard, A. 1973. Manipulation of voting schemes: A general result. *Econometrica* 41, 587–601.

Gibbard, A. 1974. A Pareto-consistent libertarian claim. *Journal of Economic Theory* 7, 338–410.

Goldman, S.M. and Sussangkarn, C. 1978. On the concept of fairness. *Journal of Economic Theory* 19, 210–16.

Gorman, W.M. 1953. Community preference fields. *Econometrica* 21, 63–80.

Gottinger, H.W. and Leinfellner, W. 1978. *Decision Theory and Social Ethics: Issues in Social Choice*. Dordrecht: Reidel.

Graaff, J. der. 1957. *Theoretical Welfare Economics*. Cambridge: Cambridge University Press.

Grandmont, J.M. 1978. Intermediate preferences and majority rule. *Econometrica* 46, 317–30.

Green, J. and Laffont, J.-J. 1979. *Incentives in Public Decision Making*. Amsterdam: North-Holland.

Grether, D.M. and Plott, C.R. 1982. Nonbinary social choice: An impossibility theorem. *Review of Economic Studies* 49, 143–9.

Groves, T. and Ledyard, J. 1977. Optimal allocation of public goods: A solution to the 'free rider' problem. *Econometrica* 45, 783–810.

Guha, A.S. 1972. Neutrality, monotonicity and the right of veto. *Econometrica* 40, 821–6.

Hammond, P.J. 1976. Equity, Arrow's conditions and Rawls' difference principle. *Econometrica* 44, 793–804.

Hammond, P.J. 1977. Dual interpersonal comparisons of utility and the welfare economics of income distribution. *Journal of Public Economics* 6, 51–71.

Hammond, P.J. 1979. Equity in two person situation: some consequences. *Econometrica* 47, 1127–36.

Hammond, P.J. 1981. Liberalism, independent rights, and the Pareto principle. In L.J. Cohen, et. al., *Logic, Methodology and Philosophy of Sciences*, Amsterdam: North-Holland.

Hansson, B. 1973. The independence condition in the theory of social choice. *Theory and Decision* 4.

Hansson, B. 1976. The existence of group preferences. *Public Choice* 28, 89–98.

Hansson, B. and Sahlquist, H. 1976. A proof technique for social choice with variable electorate. *Journal of Economic Theory* 13, 193–200.

Harsanyi, J.C. 1955. Cardinal welfare, individualistic ethics, and interpersonal comparisons of utility. *Journal of Political Economy* 63, 309–21.

Harsanyi, J.C. 1979. Bayesian decision theory, rule utilitarianism and Arrow's impossibility theorem. *Theory and Decision* 11, 289–318.

Herzberger, H.G. 1973. Ordinal preference and rational choice. *Econometrica* 41, 187.

Hicks, J.R. 1939. *Value and Capital*. Oxford: Clarendon Press.

Hurley, S. 1985. Supervenience and the possibility of coherence. *Mind* 94, 501–26.

Hurwicz, L., Schmeidler, D. and Sonnenschein, H. (eds) 1985. *Social Goals and Social Organization: Essays in Memory of Elisha Pazner*. Cambridge: Cambridge University Press.

Inada, K. 1984. On the economic welfare function. *Econometrica* 32, 316–38.

Inada, K. 1964. A note on the simple majority decision rule. *Econometrica* 37, 490–506.

Inada, K. 1969. On the simple majority decision rule. *Econometrica* 32, 525–31.

Inada, K. 1970. Majority rule and rationality. *Journal of Economic Theory* 2, 27–40.

Kalai, E. and Muller, E. 1977. Characterization of domains admitting non-dictatorial social welfare functions and nonmanipulable voting procedures. *Journal of Economic Theory* 16, 457–69.

Jain, S. 1986. Special majority rules: a necessary and sufficient condition for quasi-transitivity with quasi-transitive individual preferences. *Social Choice and Welfare* 3, 99–106.

Kalai, E. and Ritz, Z. 1980. Characterization of private alternative domains admitting Arrow social welfare functions. *Journal of Economic Theory* 22, 23–36.

Kaldor, N. 1939. Welfare propositions in economics. *Economic Journal* 49, 549–52.

Karni, E. 1978. Collective rationality, unanimity and liberal ethics. *Review of Economic Studies* 45, 571–4.

Kelly, J.S. 1976. The impossibility of a just liberal. *Economica* 43, 67–75.

Kelly, J.S. 1978. *Arrow Impossibility Theorems*. New York: Academic Press.

Kelsey, D. 1984. Acyclic choice without the Pareto principle. *Review of Economic Studies* 51, 693–9.

Kelsey, D. 1985. The liberal paradox: A generalization. *Social Choice and Welfare* 1, 245–50.

Kemp, M.C. and Ng, Y.K. 1976. On the existence of social welfare functions, social orderings and social decision functions. *Economica* 43, 59–66.

Kolm, S.Ch. 1969. The optimum production of social justice. In *Public Economics*, ed. J. Margolis and H. Guitton, London: Macmillan.

Kramer, G.H. 1973. On a class of equilibrium conditions for majority rule. *Econometrica* 41, 285–97.

Kramer, G.H. 1978. A dynamic model of political equilibrium. *Journal of Economic Theory* 16, 310–34.

Krüger, L. and Gaertner, W. 1983. Alternative libertarian claims and Sen's paradox. *Theory and Decision* 15.

Laffont, J.J. (ed.) 1979. *Aggregation and Revelation of Preferences*. Amsterdam: North-Holland.

Larsson, B. 1983. *Basic Properties of the Majority Rule*. Lund: University of Lund.

Leinfellner, W. and Kohler, E., eds. 1974. *Developments in the Methodology of Social Sciences*. Dordrecht: Reidel.

Levi, I. 1982. Liberty and Welfare. In Sen and Williams (1982).

Little, I.M.D. 1950. *A Critique of Welfare Economics*. Oxford: Clarendon Press. 2nd edn, 1957.

Machina, M. and Parks, R. 1981. On path independent randomized choices. *Econometrica* 49, 1345–7.

Mas-Colell, A. and Sonnenschein, H.F. 1972. General possibility theorems for group decisions. *Review of Economic Studies* 39, 185–92.

Maskin, E. 1976. Social welfare functions on restricted domain. Mimeographed; forthcoming in *Review of Economic Studies*.

Maskin, E. 1978. A theorem on utilitarianism. *Review of Economic Studies* 45, 93–6.

Matsumoto, Y. 1985. Non-binary social choice: Revealed preferential interpretation. *Economica* 52, 185–94.

Mayston, D.J. 1974. *The Idea of Social Choice*. London: Macmillan.

McKelvey, R.D. 1979. General conditions for global intransitivities in formal voting models. *Econometrica* 47, 1085–112.

McLean, I.S. 1980. Liberty, equality and the Pareto principle: a comment on Weale. *Analysis* 40.

McManus, M. 1982. Some properties of topological social choice functions. *Review of Economic Studies* 49, 447–60.

Mill, J.S. 1859. *On Liberty*. Reprinted, Harmondsworth: Penguin Books, 1974.

Monjardet, B. 1979. Duality in the theory of social choice. In Laffont (1979).

Moulin, H. 1983. *The Strategy of Social Choice*. Amsterdam: North-Holland.

Mueller, D.C. 1979. *Public Choice*. Cambridge: Cambridge University Press.

Murakami, Y. 1968. *Logic and Social Choice*. New York: Dover.

Myerson, R.B. 1983. Utilitarianism, egalitarianism, and the timing effect in social choice problems. *Econometrica* 49, 883–97.

Ng, Y.K. 1971. The possibility of a Paretian liberal: Impossibility theorems and cardinal utility. *Journal of Political Economy* 79, 1397–402.

Ng, Y.K. 1979. *Welfare Economics*. London: Macmillan.

Nitzan, S. and Rubinstein, A. 1981. A further characterization of the Borda Ranking Methods. *Public Choice* 36, 153–8.

Nitzan, S. and Paroush, J. 1985. *Collective Decision Making: An Economic Outlook*. Cambridge: Cambridge University Press.

Nozick, R. 1974. *Anarchy, State and Utopia*. Oxford: Blackwell.

Parks, R.P. 1975. An impossibility theorem for fixed preferences: A dictatorial Bergson-Samuelson social welfare function. *Review of Economic Studies* 43, 447–450.

Pattanaik, P.K. 1971. *Voting and Collective Choice*. Cambridge: Cambridge University Press.

Pattanaik, P.K. 1973. On the stability of sincere voting situations. *Journal of Economic Theory* 6, 558–74.

Pattanaik, P.K. 1978. *Strategy and Group Choice*. Amsterdam: North-Holland.

Pattanaik, P.K. and Salles, M. (eds) 1983. *Social Choice and Welfare*. Amsterdam: North-Holland.

Pazner, E.A. and Schmeidler, D. 1974. A difficulty in the concept of fairness. *Review of Economic Studies* 41, 441–3.

Peleg, B. 1978. Consistent voting systems. *Econometrica* 46, 153–62.

Peleg, B. 1984. *Game Theoretic Analysis of Voting in Committees*. Cambridge: Cambridge University Press.

Plott, C.R. 1967. A notion of equilibrium and its possibility under majority rule. *American Economic Review* 57, 788–806.

Plott, C.R. 1973. Path independence, rationality and social choice. *Econometrica* 41, 1075–91.

Plott, C.R. 1976. Axiomatic Social Choice Theory: An Overview and Interpretation. *American Journal of Political Science* 20, 511–96.

Pollak, R.A. 1979. Bergson-Samuelson social welfare functions and the theory of social choice. *Quarterly Journal of Economics* 93, 73–90.

Ray, P. 1973. Independence of irrelevant alternatives. *Econometrica* 41, 987–91.

Riley, J. 1986. *Liberal Utilitarianism: Social choice theory and J.S. Mill's philosophy*. Cambridge: Cambridge University Press.

Robbins, L. 1932. *An Essay on the Nature and Significance of Economic Science*. London: Macmillan.

Robbins, L. 1938. Interpersonal companions of utility. *Economic Journal* 48, 635–41.

Roberts, K.W.S. 1980a. Interpersonal comparability and social choice theory. *Review of Economic Studies* 47, 421–39.

Roberts, K.W.S. 1980b. Social choice theory: The single and multiple-profile approaches. *Review of Economic Studies* 47, 441–50.

Rubinstein, A. 1981. The single profile analogues to multiple profile theorems: mathematical logic's approach. Murray Hill: Bell Laboratories.

Salles, M. 1976. Characterization of transitive individual preferences for quasi–transitive collective preferences under simple games. *International Economic Review* 17, 308–18.

Samuelson, P.A. 1947. *Foundations of Economic Analysis*. Cambridge, Mass.: Harvard University Press.

Samuelson, P.A. 1950. Evaluation of real national income. *Oxford Economic Papers* 2, 1–19.

Saposnik, R. 1975. On transitivity of the social preference relation under simple majority rule. *Journal of Economic Theory* 10, 1–7.

Schick, F. 1969. Arrow's proof and the logic of preference. *Journal of Philosophy* 36, 127–44.

Satterthwaite, M. 1975. Strategy-proofness and Arrow's conditions: existence and correspondence theorems for voting procedures and social welfare functions. *Journal of Economic Theory* 10, 187–217.

Schmeidler, D. and Sonnenschein, H. 1978. Two proofs of the Gibbard–Satterthwaite theorem on the possibility of a strategy-proof social choice function. In Gottinger and Leinfellner 1978.

Schmeidler, D. and Vind, K. 1972. Fair net trades. *Econometrica* 40, 637–42.

Schofield, N. 1978. Instability of simple dynamic games. *Review of Economic Studies* 40, 575–94.

Schofield, N. 1983. Generic instability of majority rule. *Review of Economic Studies* 50, 695–705.

Schwartz, T. 1970. On the possibility of rational policy evaluation. *Theory and Decision* 1, 89–106.

Schwartz, T. 1972. Rationality and the myth of the maximum. *Nous* 6, 97–117.

Schwartz, T. 1986. *The Logic of Collective Choice*. New York: Columbia University Press.

Scitovsky, T. 1941. A note on welfare propositions in economics. *Review of Economic Studies* 9, 77–88.

Seidl, C. 1975. On liberal values. *Zeitschrift für Nationalökonomie* 35, 257–92.

Sen, A.K. 1966. A possibility theorem on majority decisions. *Econometrica* 34, 75–9.

Sen, A.K. 1969. Quasi-transivity, rational choice and collective decisions. *Review of Economic Studies* 36, 381–93.

Sen, A.K. 1970. *Collective Choice and Social Welfare*. San Francisco: Holden-Day; Edinburgh: Oliver & Boyd. Republished, Amsterdam: North-Holland.

Sen, A.K. 1977a. Social choice theory: A re-examination. *Econometrica* 45, 58–89.

Sen, A.K. 1977b. On weights and measures: Informational constraints in social welfare analysis. *Econometrica* 45, 1539–72.

Sen, A.K. 1982. *Choice, Welfare and Measurement*. Oxford: Blackwell, and Cambridge, MIT Press.

Sen, A.K. 1983. Liberty and social choice. *Journal of Philosophy* 80, 5–28.

Sen, A.K. 1986. Social choice theory. In *Handbook of Mathematical Economics* Vol III, ed. K.J. Arrow and M. Intriligator, Amsterdam: North-Holland.

Sen, A.K. and Pattanaik, P.K. 1969. Necessary and sufficient conditions for rational choice under majority decision. *Journal of Economic Theory* 1, 178–202.

Sen, A.K. and Williams, B. 1982. *Utilitarianism and Beyond*. Cambridge: Cambridge University Press.

Sengupta, M. 1980. The knowledge assumption in the theory of strategic voting. *Econometrica* 49, 1301–4.

Sengupta, M. and Dutta, B. 1979. A condition for Nash stability under binary and democratic group decision functions. *Theory and Decision* 10, 293–310.

Slutsky, S. 1977. A characterization of societies with consistent majority decision. *Review of Economic Studies* 44, 211–26.
Strasnick, S. 1976. Social choice theory and the derivation of Rawls' difference principle. *Journal of Philosophy* 73, 85–99.
Sugden, R. 1981. *The Political Economy of Public Choice*. Oxford: Martin Robertson.
Sugden, R. 1985. Liberty, preference and choice. *Economics and Philosophy* 1, 213–30.
Suppes, P. 1966. Some formal models of grading principles. *Synthese* 6, 284–306.
Suzumura, K. 1978. On the consistency of libertarian claims. *Review of Economic Studies* 45, 329–42. A correction, 46, (1979), 743.
Suzumura, K. 1980. Liberal paradox and the voluntary exchange of rights-exercising. *Journal of Economic Theory* 22, 407–42.
Suzumura, K. 1983. *Rational Choice, Collective Decisions and Social Welfare*. Cambridge: Cambridge University Press.
Svensson, L.G. 1980. Equity among generations. *Econometrica* 48, 1251–6.
Tullock, G. 1967. The general irrelevance of the general possibility theorem. *Quarterly Journal of Economics* 81, 256–70.
Tullock, G. 1969. *Toward a Mathematics of Politics*. Ann Arbor: University of Michigan Press.
Varian, H. 1974. Equity, envy and efficiency. *Journal of Economic Theory* 9, 63–91.
Varian, H. 1975. Distributive justice, welfare economics and the theory of fairness. *Philosophy and Public Affairs* 4, 223–47.
Vickrey, W. 1945. Measuring marginal utility by reactions to risk. *Econometrica* 13, 319–33.
Vickrey, W. 1960. Utility, strategy and social decision rules. *Quarterly Journal of Economics* 75, 507–25.
Ward, B. 1965. Majority voting and alternative forms of public enterprise. In *The Public Economy of Urban Communities*, ed. J. Margolis, Baltimore: Johns Hopkins Press.
Weale, A. 1980. The impossibility of a liberal egalitarianism. *Analysis* 40.
Webster, N. 1986. Liberals and information. *Theory and Decision* 20, 41–52.
Weymark, J.A. 1983. Arrow's theorem with social quasi-orderings. *Public Choice* 42, 235–46.
Wilson, R.B. 1972. Social choice theory without the Pareto principle. *Journal of Economic Theory* 5, 478–86.
Wilson, R.B. 1975. On the theory of aggregation. *Journal of Economic Theory* 10, 89–99.
Wriglesworth, J. 1985. *Libertarian Conflicts in Social Choice*. Cambridge: Cambridge University Press.
Young, H.P. 1974a. An axiomatization of the Borda's rule. *Journal of Economic Theory* 9, 43–52.
Young, H.P. 1974b. A note on preference aggregation. *Econometrica* 42, 1129–31.

social contract. *See* ROUSSEAU, JEAN JACQUES.

social cost. The idea underlying the notion of social cost is a very simple one. A man initiating an action does not necessarily bear all the costs (or reap all the benefits) himself. Those that he does bear are *private* costs; those he does not are *external* costs. The sum of the two constitutes the *social* cost.

Behind this apparently straightforward statement lies a host of difficulties of definition, valuation and aggregation. They are considered in Section I. Section II discusses very briefly certain contexts in which, despite the ambiguities, the concept is often used.

I. PROBLEMS OF DEFINITION

Private cost is usually defined in opportunity-cost terms as the highest valued (or most preferred) option necessarily forgone. In practice this usually means no more than that the private cost of an object is the money paid for it. The definition works because the individual (or firm) is assumed to be optimizing. Every choice entails a sacrifice. There is always an option 'necessarily forgone'.

The external costs imposed on others by the initiator of an action are imposed on optimizing agents, so the definition works for them too. But it does not work for social cost because there is no reason to suppose that society is optimizing. Society may, without giving up leisure or anything else, be able to get more guns *and* more butter. Technically, this will be possible whenever it is operating 'within' (rather than 'on') its social production frontier – a situation as likely to be the norm as the exception. These would, in these circumstances, be no option forgone and therefore no cost.

If society does happen to be 'on' its production frontier, there is at least a cost. But is significance may depend on who bears it. Is butter forgone by A (who is rich) as important as that forgone by B (who is poor)? Can the two amounts simply be added together to get the cost to society?

The definition of social cost as the sum of private and external costs avoids the difficulty that society may not be optimizing but not the one that costs borne by different people have to be added together. Nor does it avoid certain other difficulties. We shall discuss these under separate headings, starting with the least troublesome.

(1) *Scope of society*. If I build a house that obstructs my neighbour's view, but affects no one else, it is fairly clear that the external cost I impose on him is the only one to be added to my own in determining the cost of my action to society. He will suffer an immediate loss of amenity, which may or may not be easy to value, and a decline in the resale value of his property which, if the market functions as it should, will be a reasonable estimate to the loss of his successors in title.

In other situations the position may not be so simple. Pollution of the atmosphere, or of a common waterway, may affect several nations. Are we interested in the cost to *our* society, or to the world community? What of activities that may affect unborn generations? How is the cost to them to be estimated? If one is dealing with questions such as the social cost of nuclear energy, these matters may be very relevant.

We must be clear about the scope, in time and space, of the society in which we are interested before talking about social cost. When we are, we can proceed to the other difficulties.

(2) *Costs and benefits*. The external costs imposed on others by the initiator of some action need not all be positive. Some may be negative costs, or benefits. (If I paint my house bright yellow it may horrify Jones, but delight Smith.) It is largely a matter of convention whether we reckon these negative costs separately, and call them benefits, or set them off against the positive ones immediately, to arrive at a figure for *net* cost.

In Cost Benefit Analysis the usual practice is to deal with the two categories separately, and then to weigh the one against the other. But in other branches of the subject it is common to reckon costs net of benefits. An example is the proposition, advanced in many standard texts, that *social cost excludes rent*. What is meant is that the increased rents earned by factors whose prices have risen in the face of increased demand for their services represent mere transfers of wealth, not costs to society.

If a project creates a demand for labour and other factors that results in higher wages and prices, these of course mean higher private costs for the entrepreneur who initiates it. But they are offset by negative external costs in the form of benefits to the factors (or their owners). The two balance out, so that when private and external costs are summed there is not net contribution to social cost. The increased rents enter into both private and external costs (with opposite signs), and – as the proposition says – not into the cost to society.

When costs borne by individuals are not costs to society it is often proper to call them *losses*, and their counterpart *gains*. If I own a shop next to yours and take away your trade by cutting prices, you will suffer a loss that is counterbalanced by the gain to consumers and my profit (if there is any) on the extra sales. Gains and losses due to price changes are not costs to society.

Implicit in the assertion that price changes do not give rise to social costs is the assumption that we are dealing with a closed economy. In an open economy a movement in the international terms of trade may either impose real costs on nationals or enable them to earn rents at the expense of foreigners. Also implicit in the assertion is the assumption that the problems of measurement and aggregation have been solved.

(3) *Short and long run costs.* When measuring costs it is essential to state the time period under consideration. There is a tendency for most to be lower in the long run than in the short, and this applies with especial force to external ones. Injured parties are at first taken by surprise, but then will try to reduce costs imposed on them by adjusting their operations to the new circumstances. If the laws of society are such that they have a claim against the initiator of the activity that precipitated the external costs, the victims may succeed in getting him to modify it in a way that reduces them still further. Of course the *sum* of private and external costs (i.e. the social cost) may not reduce to the same extent – but that is another matter.

An old example (Pigou, 1932, p. 134) can be adapted to illustrate the point. If sparks from a railway engine increase the probability of fire damage to crops planted by a farmer whose land the line traverses, a sudden doubling of the number of trains will impose additional external costs on him. Over time he may be able to mitigate these by planting evergreens near the line, or leaving a strip of land fallow. If the law allows, he may be able to sue the railway company for any damage actually caused, or claim compensation for loss of profit on land put to inferior use. This may eventually persuade the company to fit spark suppressors to the locomotives or reduce the number of trains. These factors all combine to make it probable that external costs will decrease with time.

In an example such as this, where only two parties are involved, negotiation might be expected to be a real alternative to legal action. The division of the gains would of course depend on the bargaining strength of the negotiators, which would in part be determined by their rights, but the outcome would be much the same: a reduction in the sum of private and external costs until a further reduction would bring about a greater reduction in benefits. As negotiation is always time-consuming, one would again expect the result to be a social cost that was lower in the long run than the short.

(4) *Aggregation.* When we add external costs to private costs to get social cost we are adding costs borne by different people. In the last resort this amounts to saying that, all else being equal, a cost of \$10 borne by A represents a greater cost to society than one of \$9 borne by B, no matter who A and B might be. There are really only two possible justifications for this procedure.

The first is along *utilitarian* lines, with full interpersonal comparability and an assumption that the marginal utility of money is the same to everyone. Lower social cost then represents a lower loss of aggregate satisfaction.

The second is in terms of *compensation tests* (Graaff, 1957, chap 5). Very briefly, these tests use as a criterion of social desirability the possibility of those who benefit from some change being able to compensate those who lose by it, without themselves becoming losers. Obviously, the lower the sum of private and external costs, the greater the possibility of being able to compensate those who bear them.

Neither justification is entirely satisfactory. Utilitarianism still has its adherents, but few among them would lightly assume that the marginal utility of money was the same to rich and poor. And the *possibility* of compensation means very little unless the compensation is actually carried out. (What does it help to say that, although several men will starve, the cost to society is low, because they *could* be given sufficient food to prevent their starving?). If, on the other hand, the compensation is paid, price changes can lead to *reversals* of the sort analysed by Scitovsky (1941). The social cost of A may then be lower than that of B before compensation, higher after it. Choosing the activity with the lower cost entails a prior choice between two distributions of wealth. Otherwise we go round in circles.

II APPLICATIONS

The principal application of the notion of social cost is in the field of *Cost Benefit Analysis.* Valuation problems abound. How, for instance, does one value the cost of a human life, if the probability is that an extra one will be sacrificed when savings are made on safety or design specifications for a new highway? And how does one value other goods for which there are no markets? (In practice one uses prices in related markets; but these are what they are precisely because there are no prices for the goods one is trying to value!) Cost Benefit analysts handle these matters with great skill, and if they were the only problems they had to contend with, would emerge with great credit.

But the theory also has to face the aggregation problems just mentioned. The utilitarian approach tends to use 'distributional weights' to indicate the analyst's rough assessment of differences in the marginal utility of money to different people. In this way \$1 borne by a poor man can be made to contribute more to social cost than \$2 borne by someone rich. It is almost fair to say that social cost then becomes what the analyst wants it to be.

Those who use the compensation-test approach tend to hope that price changes following hypothetical compensation would not be large enough to bring about embarrassing reversals. The matter cannot be disposed of that easily. Comparing social costs with social benefits to determine social choice is an exercise subject to all the impossibility theorems of Social Choice Theory. Reversals that give rise to intransitive choices can be expected unless our assumptions are rich enough to exclude them. Utilitarians recognize this when they boldly allocate distributional weights. Without a similar boldness those who base their analysis on the possibility of compensation leave the significance of the costs they calculate in considerable doubt.

Social cost theory has also been used in the analysis of *market failure.* Without too much regard for the niceties of definition, the older theory (Pigou, 1932) went something like this. Maximization of the national dividend requires the equality of marginal social costs and benefits. Optimizing behaviour in markets secures the equality of marginal private cost and benefits. Unless the two sets of cost and benefits coincide, market behaviour will not maximize the national dividend. Divergences between private and social costs (and benefits) are the cause of failure. Various measures are available to correct these divergences. (Some are discussed under TAXES AND SUBSIDIES).

A more modern statement would be that a market fails when it clears without all mutually advantageous bargains having been struck. This is most likely to happen when a transaction affects parties other than those directly involved in its negotiation. The existence of these external costs and benefits entails a divergence between private and social costs and benefits. (This follows directly from the definition.)

The more modern version brings out the central problem. *Why* are the 'other parties' not directly involved in the negotiations? Even if they have no legal standing (which, if property rights are clearly defined, they may well have), they can never be worse off negotiating. The answer, of course, lies in *transaction costs*. Bargaining is a costly and time-consuming procedure, especially when large numbers of people are involved. In addition, to get full benefit from deals struck, it may be necessary to take expensive steps to exclude freeloaders. (I may make it worth my neighbour's while not to park in front of my house, but unless I can stop others using the vacant space it will help me very little.) Any analysis of market failure that does not explicitly recognize the role played by the costs of bargaining is severely flawed.

If bargaining were costless and without legal impediment, optimising behaviour by market participants would automatically imply that all mutually advantageous bargains were struck. With zero transaction costs, market failure is impossible. This result, often attributed to Coase (1960), has been described as the Say's Law of Welfare Economics (Calabresi, 1968). But it might be fairer to reserve that accolade for the version of it that says that, if a bargain is not struct, it can only be because optimizing agents, in their wisdom, have decided that the transaction cost would exceed the benefit. It would be nice if the world were really like that.

A treatment of social cost that deals adequately with the costs of bargaining has not yet been developed. That, and the unsolved problems of aggregation, should make us wary of using the concept without the necessary circumspection.

J. DE V. GRAAFF

BIBLIOGRAPHY

Calabresi, G. 1968. Transaction costs, resource allocation and liability rules: a comment. *Journal of Law and Economics* 11, April, 67–73.

Coase, R.H. 1960. The problem of social cost. *Journal of Law and Economics* 3, October, 1–44.

Graaff, J. de V. 1957. *Theoretical Welfare Economics*. Cambridge: Cambridge University Press.

Pigou, A.C. 1932. *The Economics of Welfare*. 4th edn, London: Macmillan.

Scitovsky, T. 1941. A note on welfare propositions in economics. *Review of Economic Studies* 9(1), 77–88.

social democracy. Social democracy is a concept with multiple meanings – since its coinage in the latter half of the 19th century it has been applied to an array of theoretical and actual political and economic arrangements. It is noteworthy that the first edition of this Dictionary did not contain a separate reference to this concept.

The term 'social democracy' is generally considered to include both a commitment to the democratic institutions of public discussion (including an extensive franchise, party competition for votes, and parliamentarianism) and a commitment to socialism. Socialism on this understanding generally denotes a wide measure of control and planning of the economy. Democracy is then instrumental in the transformation of capitalism into socialism. However, when interpreted in this way, the question remains very much alive as to whether commitments to socialism and to democracy in this sense can be consistently maintained. It is a question participants in the early social democratic movement, such as Karl Kautsky and Eduard Bernstein in Germany, Jean Jaurès in France, and Harold Laski in England, asked and attempted to answer for themselves. This should come as little surprise. While the terms 'democracy' and 'socialism' both suggest a concern for the equality of the individual, each has its own history of discrete usage prior to the 19th century such that there would seem no necessary reason to assume that there should be basic conceptual congruence between *them*. Indeed, there are reasons to suggest an inherent conceptual tension.

The origins of social democracy may be understood in part as a critical reaction to the failure of the liberal democratic programme to achieve its own twin commitments to the values of economic liberty and political equality. It has been argued that during the period between 1776 and 1848 (that is to say the period between the date marking both the publication of the *Wealth of Nations* and the onset of the American revolution, and that marking the publication of the *Communist Manifesto* and the massacre of the Paris proletariat by the army of the newly elected French Republic) the liberal democratic movement exhausted its promise to all but the few.

Philosophers concerned with social equality, most notably Rousseau (1754), had developed an earlier, unrelenting critique of the corrupted quality of modern life and nascent capitalism, berating its human costs of extreme economic inequality, the trivialized conception of public life and social relations on the analogue of the market, and the destructive effects of laissez-faire. Nearly three-quarters of a century later a much better friend of liberal democracy, Alexis de Tocqueville, still found it necessary to remark on the devastating effects of unregulated industrial production on the life of the common citizens of Manchester:

> Look up and all around this place you will see the huge palaces of industry. You will hear the noise of furnaces, the whistle of steam. These vast structures keep air and light out of the human habitations which they dominate; they envelop them in perpetual fog; here is the slave, there the master; there the wealth of some, here the poverty of most; there the organized effort of thousands produce, to the profit of one man, what society has not yet learnt to give. Here the weakness of the individual seems more feeble and helpless even than in the middle of a wilderness; here the effects, there the causes (1835, p. 107).

The dichotomy between the condition of life of workers and that of owners, and that between the liberal commitment to freedom and the undeniable misery of the conditions of that freedom, brought about a resurgence of an older democratic fervour, though now on a new social basis.

What has been called the decisive event in the history of modern socialism – the meeting of the First International Working Man's Association of 1864 – might more accurately be described as a gathering of English and Continental leaders of an international labour movement organized on democratic principles. The International purportedly obtained its first public notoriety when one of its organizers, Karl Marx, drafted a address congratulating President Abraham Lincoln on his re-election in 1864. In fact, when the platform and workings of the International are examined, it might even be said that Marx's association with the International represents perhaps his only direct involvement in the early expression of the principles of social democracy, rather than with socialism as he understood it. The programme of the International – which Marx ostensibly wrote with an eye to satisfying the diverse demands of the five affiliated national labour groups participating (English, French, Italian, German and Polish) – stands in marked contrast to his own theory of the process of arriving at socialism. It is a rather tepid document, expressing routine political commitments to parliamentary reform, the extension of the franchise to workers, expanded trade unionism, and even to the practical efficacy of 'working men's experiments' such as Robert Owen's New Lanark.

Of course, Marx's vision of socialism is not the same as this social democratic vision. The principles underlying his own discussions of universal suffrage and of political action in such early works as *On the Jewish Question*, or *The Civil War in France* – his pamphlet delivered to the General Council of the First International – are not consonant with the 'reformist' tradition of Social Democracy. In those works, as well as in the later *Manifesto*, Marx consistently argued that socialism lies at the end of politics, or more accurately just beyond it. Socialism's achievement comes when the political state has been *aufgeheben*.

SOCIAL DEMOCRACY IN EUROPE. It is precisely along these lines of cleavage – between gradual, evolutionary reform and revolutionary change – that the founders of the German social democratic movement such as Eduard Bernstein sought to revise Marx. Bernstein's major work, *Evolutionary Socialism* (1899), outlines his basic agreement with Marx's evolutionary explanation of modern society in the *Manifesto*. Nevertheless, Bernstein disagreed fundamentally with Marx's timetable for revolutionary change. Their disagreement sprang from divergent diagnoses of capitalism's malady as well as prescriptions for its cure. On Bernstein's account, Marx's basic optimism that the internal contradictions of capitalist production would produce a final catastrophe any time in the near future failed to fit the facts: 'trade statistics show an extraordinarily elaborated graduation of enterprises in regard to size. No run of the ladder is disappearing from it' (1899). What is more, Bernstein actually feared the possibility of such a disruptive general collapse of capitalism, believing instead that 'a greater security for lasting success lies in a steady advance than in the possibilities offered by a catastrophic crash' (p. xiv). Bernstein concluded that 'It is impossible to leap beyond the state: we can only hope to change it' (1922, p. 90). His economic position with regard to capitalism suggests an equally revisionary claim that progress toward socialism depended indefinitely on capitalist prosperity. The enemy of the proletariat was not capitalism itself, but rather those few private interests who refused to give attention to the common welfare. The very instrument to break the grip of the greedy few was political democracy. For these reasons, Bernstein's philosophy of social democracy prefers to build explicitly on the perceived democratic political gains of liberalism: 'as far as liberalism as a world historical movement is concerned, Socialism is not only temporally, but spiritually its legitimate heir.' Social Democracy's task became that of 'organizing liberalism'.

Karl Kautsky, later to figure as the principle opponent of Bernstein's theory of rising equity in the distribution of wealth, initially characterized *Evolutionary Socialism* as 'the first sensational piece of writing produced in the literature of German Social Democracy' (Kautsky, 1899). Indeed, Bernstein's revisionism fits well in practical terms with the non-revolutionary component of Kautsky's 'Erfurt' programme. Rudolf Hilferding added – only to retract later – the threat of general strike to the parliamentary tactics of 'Erfurt': 'Behind universal suffrage must stand the will to the general strike' (1930). However, Bernstein's revisionism rejected the move from suffrage to the threat of direct action, just as he rejected in principle that part of Kautsky's programme which drew inspiration from the *Manifesto* and made its political aim the complete and revolutionary transformation of society. It was left to Rosa Luxemburg to attempt the reconciliation of Bernstein and Kautsky, or rather to close the significant rift between the evolutionary and revolutionary programmes. Luxemburg's solution as developed in *Mass Strike, The Party and The Trade-Unions* (1905–6) was to argue that the function of both parliamentary and trade union activity – doomed as they were to eventual failure – was to prepare the proletariat for a 'spontaneous' revolution (Schorske, 1955).

If the judgement of history is to be trusted, none of these solutions provided the programme for German social democracy or counterparts elsewhere in Europe during the first half of the 20th century. The sweeping defeat of the German Social Democratic Party in the Reichstag elections of 1907 (over an issue of foreign rather than domestic policy) left the party internally divided and largely impotent as a force for significant social or political reform. While mass strikes undertaken to support the demand for universal suffrage proved of use to the Social Democratic parties in Belgium and Sweden, industrial action in the name of economic goals resulted in disastrous defeats, followed closely by decimated trade-union membership and repressive legislation, not only in Belgium (1902) and Sweden (1909), but also in France (1920), Norway (1921) and Britain (1926).

That the character of social democracy as understood by Bernstein, or by Jean Jaurès in France, demonstrates a fundamental preoccupation with an older liberal position seems clear enough. Jaurès could claim that 'the triumph of socialism will not be a break with the French Revolution but the fulfilment of [it] in new economic conditions.' Bernstein's commitment to democratic political participation as both a means *and* an end is not unlike the position developed by the later John Stuart Mill. Bernstein believed that democracy was not simply a condition for the realization of socialism but the very substance of socialism; that 'the right to vote in a democracy makes its members virtually partners in a community and this virtual partnership must in the end lead to real partnership' (1899). Bernstein's philosophy bears comparison with the later Mill as well in its generally ambivalent attitude toward the expansion of the state. While remaining optimistic about the potential achievement of a future social democratic state, what could be managed best privately should not with reason be given over to state control. Bernstein's proposed economic reforms, including nationalization, various forms of social insurance, a national distribution of food and housing, were intended to promote the proximate aims of improving the material conditions for greater social and political equality and thus rendering possible citizenship for all. In this regard, his programme might be compared with that which T.H. Marshall would later claim had been followed in England, thereby indefinitely suspending the relevance of Marxism to that country.

SOCIAL DEMOCRACY IN BRITAIN. If later German social democracy seems to spring from ideological revisionism and a conscious repudiation of Marx, only to offer a different though equally optimistic theoretical argument for evolution over revolution, the origins of British social democracy were very different. It has been remarked that the origins of British socialism are to be discovered less in Marx (or his revision) than in a homespun amalgam of historical experience – of distant memories of Chartism, infiltrations of Owenism, radical Benthamism, and the teachings and preachings of Christian Socialists. Added to this domestic content was the influence of the American economist Henry George. George's widely read *Progress and Poverty* offered a simple economic reform philosophy. George's programme transformed the Ricardian law of rent into a redistributive formula for state taxation in which land values provide the sole source of tax revenue, and the state would appropriate all rent by taxation. George's attack on the unearned increment of landed wealth found a welcome home in the gradualist socialism of the Fabians. Alexander Gray's account of the *The Socialist Tradition* portrays the Fabians as essentially pragmatic in their socialist perspective; as immersed in 'sewage, gas, and the municipal politics of pawnshops and slaughterhouses', yet not without a sense of the otherwordly, ethical, even mystical origins of their task. They were above all masters of detail rather than architects of theory. Gray notes: 'the transition from the Rights of Man to the Tenant's Sanitary Cathechism is, in its way, symbolical of what Fabianism achieved' (p. 396).

Collectivism most accurately captures Fabian social democratic economic and political aims. Their programmatic belief entailed that everything organized as a trust is ripe for appropriation by the community. Not unlike the German revisionists, the early Fabian programme of nationalization was quite general and unspecific. The Fabian society pledged to work for 'the extinction of private property in Land and of the consequent individual appropriation in the form of Rent, of the price paid for permission to use the earth ... for the transfer to the community of the administration of such industrial Capital as can conveniently be managed socially' (*Fabian Tracts*, No. 7, 1908). Public ownership of the railways had been purposed as early as 1881, while mines, factories and workshops were thought to require only state supervision. Thus Sidney and Beatrice Webb, whom Tawney correctly perceived as the movement's ideological leaders, came to believe that the peaceful transition to a municipal socialism was well underway, insisting in 1889 that 'unconscious' progress toward socialism and the democratic ideal had been made as 'step by step the political power and political organization of the country have been used for industrial ends', and 'almost every conceivable trade is, somewhere or other, carried on by parish, municipality, or the National Government itself without the intervention of any middleman or capitalist' (*Fabian Essays*, p. 44).

In this way, Fabian social reform came to be identified with an indefinite extension of state control if not exactly with nationalization. It expressed a preference for a society organized on 'scientific' principles and administered by an elite of civil servants with superior knowledge and experience. In retrospect, they would seem to have preferred authoritative direction from above over the cultivation of democracy or individuality, believing as Sidney Webb did that individualism could not survive the advent of the masses to political power. Yet, their commitment to a through-going socialist economic programme was limited by a desire to remain indefinitely within the constitutional constraints of the existing Parliamentary form – a position evident in Shaw's preface to the 1931 edition of the *Fabian Essays*. For this reason, despite their later flirtations with Soviet-style state power and planning, Fabians such as the Webbs fit more comfortably within the loose conceptual framework of social democracy than within that of proper socialism. They were thus satisfied to take advantage, as Shaw notes in a 1947 postscript to these same *Essays*, 'of every legislative step towards Collectivism no matter what quarter it came from, nor how little its promoters dreamt that they were advocating an instalment of Socialism' (p. 211).

What was left to write was a plan for the conscious and democratic socialism of industrial life. This chapter was first written in England by E.F.M. Durbin. In *The Politics of Democratic Socialism* (1940), Durbin revised the Fabians' gradualist perspective of capitalism in transition. His theory suggested an inseparable relationship between socialism, understood generally as a limited extension of public ownership and control, and democracy, characterized by responsible government and legal opposition. This compatibility of aims was made not only possible, but made necessary, Durbin recognized, by two developments. First, the transformation of capitalism from pure 'laissez-faire' to a society characterized by substantial ameliorative measures such as welfare services for the ill, the unemployed, the old and the uneducated, established the characteristics of a political community upon which the realization of socialism no longer required the complete supplanting of capitalism. Yet Durbin did not understand this transformation – as did the early Fabians – in fact to *be* socialism. Rather, it meant that the fundamentalist doctrine of a common ownership of land and capital through unilateral nationalization (identified with Bevanism) could be replaced by more creative and politically less disruptive solutions.

Second, and perhaps as influential when developed in greater detail by C.A.R. Crosland, was Durbin's hostile portrait of nationalization as creating a society out of reach of popular control and in the hands of a new 'managerial class'. On this view, democracy was necessary to realize 'socialism without statism'. This understanding of social democracy – as market socialism – was explicitly shared by the New Fabians of the 1950s such as R.H.S. Crossman and Hugh Gaitskell. Public ownership was not to be completely forgone in sectors providing public goods such as utilities, transportation and communication, or in activities unprofitable for private investment but necessary for the economy as a whole, such as the construction of roads or the training of labour. However, in the postwar period, this new vision of the democratic control of market socialism was to be undertaken less by an electorate traditionally organized through political parties than by the political participation of organized bodies of producers and consumers representing the principal interests groups of the managed economy as well as the welfare state. Characterized by Samuel Beer as 'the new group politics', democracy came to be understood as a perpetual series of bargains between government, groups of producers such as trade unions, trade associations and professional organizations, and consumer groups. As a result, by the later sixties 'what had previously appeared as the common ground of a new social and economic order began to look like a swamp of pluralistic stagnation' (Beer, 1969, p. 17). 'Butskellism', as it was termed, proved satisfactory neither to socialist nor to democratic aims.

The continuing aim of the proponents of social democracy has been to establish congruence between the ideals of socialism in the economic sphere and those of democracy in the polity at large. Although never proven to be incompatible at an abstract level, the historical record of social democracy suggests that democratic advances towards socialism can be just as easily reversed at the ballot box. The tensions between satisfying the socialist goals of organizing the production and distribution of goods within society, and securing the democratic commitments to a decentralized and participatory politics, it would seem still remain to be overcome.

S.C. Stimson

BIBLIOGRAPHY

Beer, S. 1969. *British Politics in the Collectivist Age*. New York: Vintage Books.

Beer, S. 1982. *Britain Against Itself: the Political Contradictions of Collectivism*. London: Faber; New York: Norton.

Bernstein, E. 1899. *Die Voraussetzungen des Sozialismus und die Aufgeben der Sozialdemokraite*. Stuttgart. Trans. by E.C. Harvey as *Evolutionary Socialism*, London: Schocken, 1961.

Crossman, R.H.S. (ed.) 1952. *New Fabian Essays*. London: Turnstile Press.

Durbin, E.M.F. 1940. *The Politics of Democratic Socialism*. London: G. Routledge & Sons. *Fabian Tracts*, Nos 1–142. London: G. Routledge & Sons. The Fabian Office, 1884–1909.

Gay, P. 1952. *The Dilemma of Democratic Socialism*. New York: Columbia University Press.

George, H. 1879. *Progress and Poverty*. San Francisco: W.M. Hinton & Co.

Gray, A. 1944. *The Socialist Tradition, Moses to Lenin*. London: Longmans, Green & Co.

Greenleaf, W.H. 1983. *The British Political Tradition*. 2 vols, London: Methuen.

Jaurès, J. 1894–1914. *L'esprit du socialisme: six études et discours*. Paris: Bibliothèque Mèditations, 1964.

Kautsky, K. 1899. *Bernstein und das sozialdemokratische Programm*. Stuttgart: J.H. Dietz.

Landauer, C. 1959. *European Socialism*. Vol. 1, Berkeley: University of California Press.

Lichtheim, G. 1970. *A Short History of Socialism*. New York: Praeger.

Miliband, R. 1961. *Parliamentary Socialism*. London: Allen & Unwin. 2nd edn, London: Merlin, 1972.

Marshall, T.H. 1977. *Class, Citizenship and Social Development*. Chicago: University of Chicago Press.

Pimlott, B. (ed.) 1984. *Fabian Essays in Socialist Thought*. London: Heinemann.

Shaw, G.B. (ed.) 1889. *Fabian Essays*. London: Fabian Society.

Schorske, C.E. 1955. *German Social Democracy 1905–1917*. Cambridge: Cambridge University Press.

Schumpeter, J.A. 1942. *Capitalism, Socialism and Democracy*. New York: Harper & Bros.

Tocqueville, A. 1835. *Journeys to England and Ireland: 1833–35*. New York: Arno Press, 1979.

socialism. It is said that the word 'socialism' was first used by Pierre Leroux, a supporter of Saint-Simon, in 1832, and was quickly taken up by Robert Owen. The word has meant so many different things to different people. It has been used as a synonym for communism, i.e. as a bright vision of a future in which there are neither rich nor poor, neither exploiters nor exploited, in which, to use an expression borrowed from Charles Taylor, 'generic man is harmoniously united in the face of nature'. It is by definition the solution of most if not all economic problems, the end of 'alienation'. As such it has religious overtones: Man was at one time in harmony with society, and will become so once again. For others, these utopian-sounding aims are either meaningless or a vague ideal, the higher stage of communism. 'Socialism' is, so to speak, here on earth, and can be seen (according both to Soviet doctrine and to right-wing critics) in the 'really existing socialism' of countries in the Soviet sphere, who claim to be on the way towards a communist future. Still others criticize this 'really existing socialism' from the left, declaring it not to be socialism at all; their criteria for what constitutes socialism are not always very clear, some using the marxist vision as their point of departure, others laying stress on the lack of democracy, the hierarchical nature of society, and other departures from what, in their view, ought to be. The term 'socialism' is also used, or misused, to describe the aims and programme of the British Labour party, or the state of affairs actually achieved under a series of social-democratic governments in Sweden. The term at one time had an appeal to moderates. Thus the moderate-reforming party of the Third Republic in France chose to call itself Radical-Socialist, though its leaders, such as Edouard Herriot, had no aims which could qualify as socialist. Then, at the extreme right of the political spectrum, Hitler's party was self-described as national-*socialist*.

So one should proceed at an early stage to a definition, or rather to exclusions. Not Hitler, obviously. Nor Herriot either. If one were to adopt a definition which corresponds with Marx's vision of socialism (of which much more below), there is the evident danger of adopting an impossibly rigid criterion by which to judge any real-world society: thus, whatever reasons there may be to criticize or condemn today's USSR, it would be rather pointless to 'accuse' it of not having ensured the withering away of the state, or not having 'surmounted' (*aufgehoben*) the division of labour. Let us provisionally accept the following as a definition of socialism: a society may be seen to be a socialist one if the major part of the means of production of goods and services are not in private hands, but are in some sense socially owned and operated, by state, socialized or cooperative enterprises. 'The major part' is enough. Just as any non-dogmatic socialist would accept that most 'capitalist' countries contain sizeable state and cooperative sectors but still deserve the label 'capitalist'. This leaves three big questions unanswered:

(1) What are the relationships between management and workforce *within* the enterprise?

(2) How do the production units interrelate? (i.e. by plan, by contractual or market relations, or some combination of both).

(3) If the state or other public bodies own and operate any part of the economy, who controls the state, and how. One remembers the remark attributed to Engels, that if state ownership is the criterion of socialism, the first socialist institution was the regimental tailor.

If the world 'socialist' was coined in 1832, the idea of socialism long preceded it. Among the first to put forward principles which contain strong socialist elements was Gerard Winstanley, representing the Levellers of Cromwell's time. They believed in equality, wished property to be held in common, opposed concentrations of private wealth. During the French revolution Babeuf denounced inequalities of wealth and advocated the overthrow of the government, which he saw as representing property-owners. Robert Owen could be described as a paternalist, in that he believed in good treatment of his employees (as can be seen even today in the housing he built for his workers in New Lanark), but he also envisaged what would now be called producers' cooperatives. As essentially a practical man, he can be distinguished from those 'utopian socialists' who, before Marx have painted a series of pictures of imaginary socialist-type societies. Leszek Kolakowski (1981) analyses the ideas of men like Fourier, Saint-Simon, Proudhon, and notes certain elements of similarity with those of Marx, and also some essential differences. They have in common, inter alia, a hate for the 'bourgeois' order, a society based upon greed, profit, the mercantile spirit. The French revolution substituted plutocracy for aristocracy. Unlike Marx, they did not consider this to be a progressive stage in the history of mankind, but, like Marx, they stressed the ugly features of capitalist industrialism and wished to do away with it, substituting a new harmony, cooperation, the reassertion of the true rights of Man. They rejected Adam Smith's basic idea that common good is generally attained through the competitive profit-making process. As, for instance, was asserted by Saint-Simon, the basic cause of human misery is free competition and the anarchy of the market. The so-called utopians varied in their approach to the issue of equality: thus in Fourier's 'phalansteries' the means of production were held in common, children were to be brought up together, the family would dissolve, there would be provision of subsistence for all, but Fourier would encourage individual enrichment through work (though not the inheritance of riches or unearned incomes). Some advocated violent revolution to achieve their objectives, others hated violence and hoped to persuade their fellow-citizens to adopt freely the ideas of the good and just society of their imagination.

As will be argued later, Marx differed from his predecessors not because he conceived of a realistic alternative to capitalism: there was much that was utopian in his ideas too. However, *firstly* he did not go into detail as to how a future society would function; nothing in Marx is similar to such notions as phalansteries, or radiant cities of 1800 persons with 810 different human characteristics, or the idea that dirty work that needs doing will be done by boys, who, as everyone knows, like dirt; Marx favoured the emancipation of women, but he did not follow Fourier in drawing up a 'table des termes de l'alternat amoureux'.

Secondly, and more important, he provided a set of powerfully argued historical reasons as to why the desired state of affairs must come to pass. As Engels said at his graveside: 'Just as Darwin discovered the law of development of organic nature, so Marx discovered the law of development of human history.' The class struggle, the growth of monopoly capitalism, the proletarianization of the petty bourgeoisie (peasants, shopkeepers, small business men of all kinds), the growing misery of the masses, the growth of class-consciousness, the logic and consequences of large-scale industry, the belief that, having spectacularly developed the forms of production, the bourgeois-capitalist relations of production act as fetters on the further development of productive forces, all these things will lead inexorably towards socialism. Ever-deepening crises, the falling rate of profit, the refusal of the poverty-stricken masses to accept their lot, i.e. the accumulation of capitalist contradictions, will bring the system down. The proletariat, having overthrown the bourgeoisie, would inaugurate the classless society. In the marxist tradition there are various interpretations of the relative importance of historic necessity (i.e. inevitableness, a march towards a predestined goal) and voluntariness (deliberate human action designed to achieve the goal). These two principles coexist uneasily, and they can be seen as mutually inconsistent, but they can be reconciled. To take two examples, it *is* meaningful to assert that, should a professional soccer team play a school side, the professionals would 'inevitably' win. The same would be (was) true of a conflict between the Germans and say the Luxemburg army. However, the outcome requires human action, on the part of the footballers and the German soldiers respectively.

This calls for two kinds of comments. One relates to the interpretation of history, the other to the utopian elements of so-called scientific socialism.

It hardly needs stressing that capitalism has not evolved in the manner foreseen by Marx. He himself stressed, in a famous passage, that no mode of production passes from the historical scene before its productive potential is exhausted. He believed that capitalism was reaching exhaustion already when he was writing *Das Kapital*. Over a hundred years later it is still not exhausted, and ever-new technological revolutions, while certainly presenting new problems and dilemmas of which we shall speak, continue to enlarge the productive potential of capitalist society. It is also clear that the concept of 'proletarianization' was wide of the mark. Yes, great concentrations of 'monopoly-capital' do exist, but so do very large numbers of small businesses and a far larger number of 'professionals' of all sorts and grades who are, or consider themselves to be, middle class. This fact has given rise to much debate among marxists, typified by the argument between Poulantzas and Erik Wright (see for example, Wright, 1979). We need not go into this argument, which turns on who could or could not be considered to be working class. The political and social fact remains that a large and growing proportion of the citizenry of developed countries do not own the means of production and are emphatically not class-conscious proletarians.

Furthermore, the development of the forces of production has made possible a substantial improvement in the living standards even of those who in any definition are workers. Clearly, they do not have 'nothing to lose but their chains'. It is neither original nor amusing to say that men who have 'nothing to lose' except a three-bedroomed house, a car, a video-tape machine and a holiday in Spain are not very likely to be revolutionaries, or indeed particularly interested in socialism. It is true none the less. Marx himself, and some of his followers, when willing to recognize that living standards could rise, insisted that this does not remove the essential antagonism between labour and capital, the existence of exploitation and alienation. In a sense this is so, though one must avoid an oversimplified zero-sum-game approach; situations arise in which both profits and wages can rise together, as they have done in successful capitalist countries in the twenty-five years that followed the last war. Nor is there any necessary correlation between the depth of human misery and the spirit of revolt. None the less, the lack of support for the socialist alternative in developed countries cannot be treated as merely a temporary aberration. It is also true that revolutions, whatever their merits or necessities, impose grave hardship upon people, notably the masses. The association of the word 'socialism' with revolution is therefore an important reason for many 'proletarians' *not* to support the socialist idea, at least in developed countries. 'Underdeveloped socialism' is a different question, to be tackled later.

Now to the utopian nature of Marx's 'scientific socialism'. The key points to make are:

1. *Abundance*. Here Marx reflects the optimism of his century, yet natural resources are not inexhaustible. Human needs and wants increase – as indeed Marx himself recognized. Conservationist and ecological socialism can be strongly defended, but this is precisely because resources (even the air we breathe, the water we drink) are finite. It is not the case that the problem of production has been 'solved', and that socialists will not require to take seriously the question of the allocation of scarce resources. I define 'abundance' as a sufficiency for all reasonable requirements at zero price.

2. *The non-acquisitive 'new man'*. His (and her) appearance surely presupposes abundance. Marx himself was perfectly clear that a share-poverty 'socialism' would reproduce 'the old rubbish'. Men do not become good by being so persuaded, or by reading good books. If there is enough for everyone, then there is no need to strive to keep things for oneself, one's

family, one's locality, one's institution. If there is scarcity, therefore opportunity cost, therefore a situation in which there are mutually exclusive alternatives, then conflict on priorities of resource allocation is inevitable. This does not in fact require any assumption about individual egoism. Even unselfish persons tend to identify the needs they know with the common good. Indeed, in a complex modern society there is no generally accepted and objectively based criterion as to what 'the common good' is. Nor can any individual apprehend the multitude of alternative uses potentially available for the resources he or she desires, either for him/her self or for the given township, library, orchestra, football team, industry or whatever.

3. *The political assumptions*. These are linked with (1) and (2), above. The state withers away, not only because it is assumed that its 'essential' repressive functions are not needed when no ruling class imposes its will on the masses, but also because, to re-cite Charles Taylor, Marx assumed a 'generic man harmoniously united in the face of nature'. Consequently there would be no need for legal institutions, coercive powers, police, indeed any politics as we know them. Civil society and individuals will have merged, the task of the 'administration of things' would not be undertaken by political institutions, would be merely technical. There *is* no marxist *political* theory of socialism.

4. *The economic assumptions*. (a) *Value theory and economic calculation*. The suppression of the market, of commodity production, of money, seems to involve the 'withering away' of the law of value. What is to replace it? Presumably it will continue to be important to use resources economically to provide the goods and services desired by society. How are calculations to be made? On this Marx is almost totally silent. Engels, in *Anti-Dühring*, speaks of assessing use-values and relating them to the labour-time required to provide for them. This runs at once into several rather evident problems. First is the theoretical one that Marx most emphatically (at the very beginning of the first volume of *Das Kapital*) asserted that different use-values were not comparable, so could not be added up or subtracted. A pen, a cup, a book, a skirt, a light-bulb (to take a few examples at random) satisfy different needs. The one thing they have in common, apart from satisfying various needs, is that they are the products of labour. How, in any case, are Engels's use-values to be computed, by whom, on the basis of what criteria? In a book wholly devoted to marxian use-value (*valeur d'usage*), G. Roland (1985) goes at length into the basically unsatisfactory treatment by Marx of use-value, due apparently to his anxiety to distance himself from subjective value theory. This has created some awkward problems for Soviet pricing theory, or at the very least does nothing to help. The dogmatists insist that Marxian labour-values ought to underlie Soviet prices, or alternatively that these be modified into the equivalence of 'prices of production', but both of these share the characteristic of being based on effort, on cost. This not only fails to give due weight to utility (or user preferences), but also runs into yet another problem, or rather two interlinked problems; measuring labour inputs, and the failure to take into account other scarcities. A few brief remarks are appropriate on each of these points.

Can one actually identify the labour content, including the labour embodied in machine and materials, and the 'share' in joint overheads, of hundreds of thousands or even millions of different goods and services? This is a hugely difficult if not impossible task, even if one calculated only in hours of labour. But then what of skilled labour? How is it to be 'reduced' to simple labour? Marx does not handle this 'reduction' satisfactorily in discussing value in capitalist society, and in the end one is left with actual wage ratios as the only usable criterion, which is unhelpfully circular. And then can one treat labour as the only scarce factor? What of land, oil, timber, what of time (not labour-time, but, say, delay in construction)? Novozhilov remarked that the most modern equipment would be scarce even under full communism unless it be assumed that technical progress ceases.

Space forbids further remarks about other deficiencies of the labour-theory inherited from Marx. (Thus demand or price must affect labour-content if there are economies or diseconomies of scale, or if relative prices influence choice of techniques.) And if the purist retorts that Marxian value theory is not supposed to apply to socialist economies at all, then he or she must be asked: 'What is your alternative?'. This has (so far) usually taken the form of some surrogate labour-theory (such as hours of human effort), with all the deficiencies of such an approach.

(b) '*Simplicity*'. The lack of interest – until comparatively recently – of Marx and marxists in the question of economic calculation under socialism is explicable by a grave misunderstanding, i.e. by the belief that the complexities of modern industrial society are a consequence of commodity production and 'commodity fetishism', which conceal relations which, as Marx said, were inherently 'clear and transparent'. 'Everything will be quite simple without this so-called value', said Engels. Planning under socialism 'will be child's play', said Bebel. 'To organize the entire economy on the lines of the postal service,... under the leadership of the armed proletariat, this is immediate [*sic*] task' (Lenin, in 1917), and so on. But evidently in a modern industrial society with hundreds of millions of people, hundreds of thousands of productive units, millions of products and services (if disaggregated down to specific items, there *are* millions), it is a hugely complex task to discover exactly who needs what, and to identify the most effective means of providing for needs, especially if one bears in mind that any output requires the acquisition (or allocation) of dozens or more of inputs. Barone (in his path-breaking 'Ministry of production in a collectivist state') pointed this out in 1908, but failed to get a hearing from the socialists of his time. It is nonsense to talk of labour under socialism being 'directly social', in the sense of being applied with advance knowledge of needs – contrasting with *ex post* validation through the market under capitalism. This can only be so if perfect knowledge and foresight were assumed, and the need to test *ex post* for possible error assumed to be unnecessary. All socialists (rightly!) reject theories which assume perfect foresight, perfect markets, perfect competition, when put forward by neoclassical model-builders. So, apart from problems of value theory, there is the sheer complexity of marketless, quantitative planning, the formidable obstacles in the way of identifying requirements and providing for their satisfaction.

(c) *Political-social implications*. Lest the above be seen as 'merely technical', and so remediable by computers, the objective requirements of marketless planning in a complex industrial economy are centralizing (who but the centre can identify need and ensure the allocation of means of production?), hierarchical, bureaucratic, and concentrate immense power over both people and things in the hands of the state apparatus. The importance of political democracy is undeniable, but the officials (who else?) who plan the output and allocation of sheet steel, sulphuric acid and flour are taking decisions unconnected with democratic voting – save in the sense that such voting should affect broad priorities. There were moments when Marx, Engels, Lenin, showed that they understood the inevitability of hierarchy: thus Lenin saw the socialist economy as a sort of 'single office, a single factory', with 'a single will linking all the sub-units together' to ensure the parts of the economy fitted together 'like clockwork' (Lenin, 1962, pp. 157). But whereas clockwork functions automatically (i.e. is not unlike the 'hidden hand', or maybe the hidden pendulum), in a marketless economy the parts have to be moved by human beings charged with the purpose. The contrast between 'the administration of man' and 'the administration of things' (a phrase borrowed by Marx from Saint-Simon) is a false contrast: I am quite unable to 'administer' this piece of paper, but I can persuade a secretary to type it, a postman to deliver it to the publisher, and (hopefully!) the publisher decides to tell the printers to print it! All Soviet experience underlines the political and social consequences of the high concentration of hierarchically-organized economic power.

5. *Division of labour and 'alienation'*. There is, and must surely be, a division of labour between productive units (those that produce sulphuric acid, steel or hairdressing services are unlikely also to be making hats, computer software or music). Marx's notion of a universal man, who fishes, looks after sheep and writes literary criticism, without being a professional fisherman, shepherd or critic, makes no sense, other than in the (sensible but weaker) form of aiming at a greater degree of job interchangeability. Thus the author of these lines was once a soldier, then a bureaucrat, then a university teacher, but could not be all of these at once. The vertical division of labour (e.g. between management and those managed) could also be modified by some system of rotation or election, but management is also a skill, and human intelligence is not of itself a guarantee of tolerable administrative ability: we all know of good specialists who could not (and would not wish to) administer anything well. One is then struck by the inherent unreality of such books as by I. Mészáros (1972). Mészáros fully and correctly sets out Marx's view, and he does state that 'the political road to the supersession of alienation and reification' is a long one and success is not guaranteed. But he still sees the 'transcendence of alienation' as a meaningful goal, as if separation of Man from his product, his subordination to outside forces, the division of labour, can be overcome through the elimination of private ownership. And Kolakowski (1981, p. 172) is surely right when he notes that for Marx 'the fundamental premise of alienation is already present as soon as goods become commodities', and that 'the division of labour leads necessarily to commerce'. So alienation appears to be the inescapable consequence of an inescapable division of labour, so how can it be *aufgehoben*? Private ownership represents a particular manifestation of 'outside' control, and it is an important part of any socialist programme to give to labour a greater influence over the work process. But what can one make of Bettelheim (1968), when he criticizes Yugoslav-type self-management enterprises for what is surely the wrong reason: that they are controlled not by the workforce but by the market. It ought to be clear that production is for use, and that *what* is produced ought in the last analysis to conform to user needs, i.e. to be controlled by a force outside the production unit itself. This could be the market, in which bargaining takes place between producer and user. It could be a planning agency, who informs the production unit what is should be doing. *Tertium non datur*.

6. *Labour, wages, 'the proleteriat'*. Several distinct points need to be made.

(a) *The end of the wages system*. This is not what real workers want. Money wages give freedom of choice, including the choice of hiring the services of each other (to repair the roof, baby-mind, drive to work or what ever). Marx's idea of tokens denominated in hours of labour ('which are not money and do not circulate') makes very little sense, and not surprisingly has not been applied. If goods are distributed free, this usually limits consumer choice: you take what you are *given*.

(b) *Labour direction* is the sole known alternative to material incentives or other forms of inequality. This was understood by Kautsky, Trotsky and Bukharin, when they discussed this question. The term 'labour market' has an opprobrious sound, reminiscent perhaps of a slave market. Yet workers are freer, have greater choice, more possibility to bargain, than under direction of labour, necessarily exercised by officials with power over persons.

(c) *The proletariat as redemptor humanis* is essentially a religious concept, unrelated to the qualities and desires of the real working class. Eloquent words on this subject have been written by Andre Gorz: 'No empirical observation or actual experience of struggle can lead to the discovery of the historic mission of the proletariat which, according to Marx, is the constituent of its class being' (Gorz, 1980, p. 22). Rudolf Bahro wrote that 'the proletariat, the collective subject of general emancipation, remains a philosophical hypothesis in which is concentrated the utopian element of marxism', and he added, rightly, that 'the immediate objectives of subordinate classes and strata are always conservative' (*sind immer Konservativ*) (1977, p. 174). But if one accepts these and other similar arguments, if follows that, as Lenin said, the working class left to itself will limit itself to 'trade union' types of demands, and so it is the task of the revolutionary intelligentsia to provide the revolutionary theory. This in turn leads to what has been called 'substitutionism', i.e. a party dominated at the top by non-workers, which in its turn dominates society, an outcome prophesied by Bakunin well over a hundred years ago. It is clearly not the case that, to cite Marx's letter to Weydemeyer in 1852, 'the class struggle leads necessarily to the dictatorship of the proletariat', which 'is but a transition to the withering away of classes' (letter dated 5 March 1852, Marx, 1962, p. 427).

Marxists may now be impatiently protesting that the above analysis is a vision of full communism, that no one, certainly not Marx himself, expected this to be realized quickly, or even certainly. The much-used words 'socialisme ou barbarie' show a recognition that barbarism can be an outcome if the socialist idea fails. Trotsky spoke often of a 'transitional epoch' during which money, markets, commodity production, are indeed indispensables. Soviet discussions refer to the indeterminate length of time required to move from 'socialism' (i.e. Soviet reality, which they define as socialism) to full communism. For example, a book devoted to the subject and published for the fiftieth anniversary of the revolution duly lists the characteristics of communism (abundance; from each according to his ability, to each according to needs; the elimination of commodity money relations, and so on), but goes on to stress that communism must be preceded by the lower 'socialist' phase, and that to try to overleap that phase is 'a harmful utopia' (Gatovski, et al (eds), 1967, p. 9, p. 43).

Marx himself used 'socialism' and 'communism' almost as interchangeable terms. Whether 'really existing socialism' should be seen as a transitional society or as socialist is to some extent just a terminological question. In either case it is supposed to be evolving towards fully-fledged socialism or communism. But does it? Should it? What are the signs by which such an evolution can be identified?

Bettelheim has good evidence for his view that, for Marx and

Engels, when the workers acquire the means of production, 'there will be in socialist society, even at the beginning, no commodities, no value, no money, and consequently no prices and no wages' Bettelheim, 1968, p. 32. Equally strongly, the French critic Cornelius Castoriadis roundly asserts that 'Marx knew nothing of transitional societies infinitely contained within each other like Russian dolls or Chinese boxes, which Trotskyists later invented' (Castoriadis, 1979, p. 299). Marx did specifically say, in the *Grundrisse*, that 'nothing is more absurd than to imagine that the associated producers' would choose to interrelate via commodity production, exchange, markets. We have already noted that, in his *Critique of the Gotha Programme*, Marx envisaged an immediate conversion of wages into tokens denominated in hours of labour, not despite but *because* society will still bear the stigmata of pre-socialist attitudes. In the 1920s in the Soviet Union it seemed obvious to the party comrades that reducing the area of market relations was in some sense the equivalent of an advance towards socialism. Indeed those who forced 25 million peasant households to join so-called collective farms thought that this was part of the class struggle, though the effect was to turn independent 'petty-bourgeois' households, who did to a considerable degree control their own means of production and their product, into something akin to a new sort of state serfdom. If socialism is to do with the liberation of the 'direct producers', then surely this was a march in the wrong direction.

Similarly, can we say that the Hungarian or Soviet reformers of today are wrong in advocating an extension of 'commodity-money relations'? And if the point is made that such a judgment would be premature, but that communism is still an aim to pursue when circumstances are propitious, it is legitimate to ask: what circumstances can be imagined in which communism/socialism in Marx's sense *could* come about? No wonder the Soviet orthodoxy of today is to speak of 'mature socialism' as a long-term stage, with communism seen as a remote objective of no short-term operational significance.

There were also socialist alternatives to Marx, during and since his lifetime. William Morris combined some ideas derived from Marx with ethical socialism and devotion to arts and crafts. Others further developed Christian socialism of various kinds, and indeed much could be made of the contrast between Christian ideals and the mercantile spirit, the 'dark satanic mills' ('and we will build Jerusalem in England's green and pleasant land'). The British Labour party in its origins and for many decades afterwards was heavily influenced by Christian beliefs, especially those based on Methodist and other nonconformist creeds (thereby attracting some contemptuous remarks from Lenin). The Fabian society (Shaw, the Webbs and others) by contrast, preached non-religious (and non-violent) socialism, opposed extremes of inequality, and advocated industrial democracy. However, though they too influenced the Labour party, the Society remained a small intellectual group, with a tendency to believe that an elite (themselves), or even a strong dictator, would show the way. It is perhaps no accident that both Shaw and the Webbs lived to express an admiration for Stalin – even though they themselves would recoil from cruelty and killing. Mention must also be made of G.D.H. Cole and 'guild socialism', with decentralized decision-making by producers' associations.

On the continent, social-democracy nominally retained its allegiance to Marxism. However already in 1899 Edward Bernstein advocated a non-revolutionary revision of many of Marx's theories. While the leaders of German social-democracy, men like Bebel and Kautsky, rejected Bernstein's 'revisionism', it was in fact rooted in the considerable improvement of the workers' living standards, the weakening of revolutionary spirit. In the end, while retaining marxism as their nominal creed, German and other continental social-democrats (notably the 'Austro-marxists', such as Otto Bauer) adopted a non-revolutionary position which differed little from Bernstein's and became a party of moderate reform within capitalist society.

In Russia, side by side with the growth of marxism (initially preached by men such as Plekhanov and Zieber) there arose other and non-marxist socialist currents, sometimes labelled 'populist'. They believed that a Russian road to some form of socialism could be found, perhaps based on traditional communal institutions, which would enable capitalism to be by-passed. These ideas came from men such as Mikhailovsky and Vorontsov. As we shall see, Marx himself did not reject this possibility. There were also some influential anarchist socialists, owing inspiration to Bakunin, of which Prince Peter Kropotkin was a colourful example.

Since 1945 European social-democrats have tended to abandon their already tenuous allegiance to Marx and Marxism, and it may be hard to discern the extent of commitment to socialism of any sort in the programme and policies of the German and French parties. By contrast, the recent evolution of the Italian *communist* party has put it close to a social-democratic, evolutionist position. Opinions vary within the British and the Scandinavian Labour parties. Further change may well depend greatly on what happens to contemporary capitalism.

Of course the future may reserve surprises for us all. While material resources may be finite, the scientific-technical revolution may enable us to economise labour on a big scale. The resulting high level of unemployment may be a chronic disease. True, by freeing factory and office labour, we could, in a more rational society, greatly enlarge labour-intensive forms of providing a higher quality of life. But precisely this is opposed, and successfully so, by the New Right, by the 'Chicago' ideology, which is vehemently against public expenditures. Yet we may already be reaching a stage in which the *profitable* (privately-profitable) use of labour can cover only a portion of those available for work. A possible reading of Marx places emphasis on equating the realm of freedom with freedom *from* work (i.e. from necessity), with a much shorter working week, and Gorz too sees freedom as a situation where one can undertake handicrafts and other hobbies. This would be a paradoxical reversal of the view that the one scarce factor of production is labour, since then it would be the abundant factor, the problem being how to share it out. This would not be the era of abundance. To cite an example, fish could be caught by modern trawlers using fewer fishermen, but dangers of over-fishing would compel a strict limitation on numbers caught. This brings one back to the idea of an environment-preserving, ecologically-conscious, employment-sharing socialism as an attractive alternative to capitalism. But this was not Marx's alternative.

A case for socialism can be made, not only along the 'ecological' lines mentioned above. In the developed world, massive resources are devoted to persuading people to buy trivia, to keep up with the Joneses. Unemployment is a scourge which is a threat to public order. External diseconomies (and external economies too) frequently cause the pursuit of private micro-profit to conflict with more general interest. The 'quality of life' may not be readily quantifiable, but several economists (for instance Kuznets, Tobin) have noted that conventional measures of economic growth by GNP can conceal real losses, or indeed count real *costs* of urban living as a net addition to welfare. The inequalities of income and property-ownership have all too often no visible connection with the contribution to society or to production of the individuals concerned. Schumpeter (cited in Brus, 1980) rightly pointed out that no social system 'can function which is based exclusively on free contracts ... and in which everyone is guided only by personal short-term interest'. Furthermore, fanatics of the New Right are engaged in reducing essential public services, disintegrating where possible the welfare state, cutting back public transport, pursuing dogmatic monetarism, in the naive belief that primitive laissez-faire is the best of all possible worlds. It may turn out that that the grave-diggers of capitalism will be those ultra-'liberal' ideologists who fail to understand how modern capitalism really works, that the so-called imperfections (price and wage stickiness, administered prices, oligopoly and so on) are preconditions for the functioning of the system. On the assumption of perfect competition, perfect markets, perfect foresight, there is no role for the entrepreneur, no reason for firms to exist, and logically enough profits tend to zero in equilibrium. The idea that rational investment decisions are possible when we face so many inflationary uncertainties (what will the rate of the dollar, or the rate of interest, be in a year's time?) is somewhat far-fetched, to put it mildly, and inconsistent with meaningful 'rational expectations'. The belief that all markets clear, that unemployment is 'voluntary leisure preference', curable by freeing the labour market, will sound very odd to future generations.

No socialist should deny the need for economic calculations. With no price mechanism it is not possible to calculate or compare cost, or to measure the intensity of wants. Microdemand cannot be derived from voting or from clamour, nor should there be 'dictatorship over needs', to cite the title of a critique of East European socialism (Feher et al., 1983). There really is no alternative to allowing choice, i.e. to 'voting' with money. Choice necessarily involves competition between actual and potential suppliers. Yet the limitations of the price mechanism also require to be clearly seen. As the Hungarian economist Janos Kornai (1971) has pointed out, major decisions are not and cannot be taken on the basis of price information alone. The currently fashionable 'methodological individualism' goes far to deny the very existence of the general interest, distinct from that of individuals composing the society, confining 'public goods' to defence and lighthouses. (Yet it is not even true that the interests of a *firm* are only the sum total of that of the individuals composing it!)

Socialism as an idea lays stress on the general interest, but has not always avoided overstressing this at the expense of the individuals, for otherwise the dangers of totalitarianism (albeit of a paternalist kind) may loom ahead. The notion that Man is at the mercy of blind forces he cannot control, or of mighty and remote corporations (faceless, *societés anonymes*, or worse still, inhuman computers) sets up a search for a 'socialist' alternative, more human, fairer, and not necessarily less 'efficient' in terms of human welfare. Acquisitiveness and competitiveness may be unavoidable, must indeed be utilized, but do not require to be encouraged. Individualist profit-seeking as the dominant purpose in life, can be regarded by socialists as inhuman and ultimately destructive of society. A greater – not exclusive, but a greater – emphasis on caring for others may be a precondition for survival. More directly destructive would be nuclear war. There was a long-standing attachment of the idea of socialism with that of peace. This can be less confidently argued today, alas (when Chinese and Vietnamese soldiers shot at each other, could they both be 'socialist'?). Experience does show that states aiming to be socialist can commit aggressive acts, and accumulate immense stores of destructive weapons. None the less, the autonomous role of the arms lobby and of hate-propaganda may be particularly associated with militant capitalism.

Socialist ideas in the Third World raise some specific problems. While it is dangerous to generalize about so heterogenous a group of countries, in many of them the logic and spirit of capitalism is rejected. There too, to re-quote Bahro, ordinary people are 'immer konservativ', and it is capitalism which is new, which threatens traditional ties and attitudes. The effect may or may not be to provide mass support for socialist slogans: we have had such phenomena as Khomeini and Moslem fundamentalism by way of reaction. But socialist ideas do attract many, in places as far apart and as different as Chile, India, Egypt, Zimbabwe. Of course many blunders have been committed in the name of pursuing socialist policies, not least in relations with the peasantry. But there are many examples which demonstrate that there are countries where free-market capitalism, far from being associated with free and democratic institutions, requires repressive police-state measures. Pinochet's Chile is but one such example.

The relationship between socialism and economic development is a subject in itself, on which volumes could be written. It has often been pointed out that, paradoxically, marxist-inspired revolutions have occurred in relatively backward countries. Indeed, the Russian Empire in 1917 was in no sense 'ripe' for socialism. The preconditions were absent, and the Mensheviks considered themselves to be orthodox marxists when they denounced the Bolsheviks for trying to overleap the predestined historical stages. Lenin, on the contrary, believed that it was possible, indeed essential, to seize power when opportunity offered and *then* to create the preconditions, with (he hoped) the help of revolutions in developed industrial countries. Some of the less agreeable features of the Soviet system can be ascribed to isolation in a hostile world, or to 'socialism in one country', though it would be wrong, in the light of later experience (such as the evolution of the relations between the USSR and China) to regard this one factor as decisive. But, true enough, backward countries seeking to introduce 'socialism' introduce backward 'socialism'. It becomes an industrializing ideology, mobilizing the masses and imposing sacrifices for the goal of modernization, of industrialization, with a substantial admixture of nationalism. Whatever may have been their conscious aim, a strong case can be made for the proposition that Lenin and Mao re-established their respective empires, after a period of breakdown and disintegration, which in China's case lasted almost a century.

Marx's attitude to the socialist transformation of backward countries was by no means clear-cut. While his basic model did point to a socialist revolution occurring in highly industrialized capitalist countries, his correspondence with Vera Zasulich showed that he had great difficulty in applying his ideas to Russia. Theodor Shanin has edited a lively and (in the best sense of the word) provocative volume (Shanin, 1984), which does show Marx's perplexity, his partial recognition that there would perhaps be a road which by-passes capitalism. This was far from the view of Russian marxists, and the correspondence with Zasulich remained unpublished until 1924. However, on other occasions Marx took a different view, as when he regarded British rule in India as progressive, in the sense of introducing capitalist relations into a traditionalist society.

Any analysis of 'really existing socialism' would have to take account of the major role of nationalism, though this at least would have astonished Marx. It influences Soviet internal and foreign policies, it surely played a key role in the split between Russia and China, it may be seen in the treatment of the Hungarian minority by the Romanians. The Soviet author Vasili Grossman, in his major novel *Life and Fate*, put into the mouth of one of his characters the thought that the battle of Stalingrad completed the process of transforming Bolshevism into National-Bolshevism (needless to say, the book was not published in the Soviet Union). We are very far from the idea that 'the workers have no fatherland', and the proper translation of the Soviet official doctrine of 'proletarian internationalism' is 'acceptance of the leadership of Moscow on all important questions'.

There is one aspect of 'backward socialism' which has profound political and social significance. In the USSR, in China, and in many Third World countries, the peasantry formed a large part of the population and there was a sizeable petty bourgeoisie. Far from having exhausted its potentialities, the 'marketization' of the economy was still in its early stages. In Marx's model the bulk of the petty bourgeoisie has been eliminated by monopoly-capital. But in these countries, in the name of the class struggle, it was destroyed by coercive state policies, i.e. by police measure. Indeed, the police has to be ever-watchful in case the banned private activities are reborn. This is one reason, among others, for there being socialist police states, which have only a remote connection with Marx's 'dictatorship of the proletariat'.

Much could be said about socialist analyses of underdevelopment, and such names as André Gunder Frank, Samir Amin and Arrighi Emmanuel come to mind. How far was underdevelopment due to capitalism and to links with the world capitalist market? Do socialist remedies require a break with that market? Is the poverty of the Third World due to 'unequal exchange' and exploitation? Is there any operational meaning in the so-called transfer of values? Thus if (say) Zaire buys a machine from the United States and a precisely similar machine at the same price from India, are 'values transferred' in the one case and not in the other?

If Amin is to be believed, such a deal would actually impoverish Zaire if the purchase is from the United States, for presumably the machine would contain much less labour than the similar machine bought from India, or than whatever Zaire exports to America in exchange for it. Yet frankly this is nonsense. Which by no means excludes the possibility, or even the likelihood, of unequal *gains* from trade.

It is of interest, in the light of some socialist theories of development, to compare the experience of various countries which follow widely different models. In doing so it is evidently important not to select countries which suit a prearranged *roman à thèse*. Thus Cuba's record on literacy, health, the poor, compares favourably with (say) Guatemala, its economic performance is outshone by South Korea and Singapore, but it would be far-fetched to imagine that Cuba under another Batista would have equalled such countries as these; many factors are involved other than the economic system. More to the point would be to compare South Korea with North Korea: same people, same historical experience until 1945. In this instance South Korea undoubtedly out-performs the North. In Africa the free-market orientated Côte d'Ivoire has done better, even for its poor, than those of its neighbours who have opted for socialist-type solutions, but again, some African countries have achieved an appalling mess for reasons very far removed from socialism: Ghana and Uganda can serve as examples.

Those who assign to capitalism, or the links with the world market, the responsibility for income inequality, unemployment regional underdevelopment, etc. should be made to study China. China also illustrates the correctness of the idea advanced by Arthur Lewis: the general level of wages in a given country depends not on the relative productivity of specific workers: thus an Indian or Chinese driver of a five-ton truck is probably as 'productive' as his American or British equivalent. It is determined by what he called opportunity-cost, notably (in predominantly peasant countries) the very low productivity and rewards available in agriculture. Thus wages in Shanghai, even in the modern industrial sector, are very low indeed. Were China a capitalist country, this would be the effect of the enormous 'reserve army of labour' constituted by 800 million peasants, whose income is much lower than that of Shanghai workers. In China it is a matter of public policy that urban wages be not too excessively far above the levels in rural areas. The effect is not dissimilar.

True enough, any comparison between China and India must note the great inequalities of income in India, and also the fact that the lowest strata of the poor in India are very poor indeed, compared with China. However, as was pointed out by Amartya Sen, India since independence has found it politically indispensable to avoid mass famine, while China suffered acutely from the politically imposed effects of the Great Leap Forward: millions died.

Nor should one ignore the big regional disparities in China, or the very considerable inequalities which existed even before Deng's reform policy was adopted. Also Yugoslavia's regional inequalities persist. Of course in both these instances there are historical and geographic explanations. All that can be said is that these matters resist speedy solutions under all systems.

To return to the developed world, the Soviet model has come to serve as a negative factor, and Western socialists, and indeed Eurocommunists, have tried to distance themselves from it.

The negative influence of the Soviet example is partly due to the revelations about the Stalin terror and Gulag. But, paradoxically, it was the Stalin period which, with all its horrors, did show a high degree of dynamism, high growth rates, evoking some enthusiasm and commitment from many Soviet citizens as well as foreign observers. It was brutal, it was crude, but they were forcing through a huge industrialization programme, preparing for war, fighting it, eventually winning it. There is, unfortunately, some Stalin-nostalgia in the Soviet Union today, analysed vividly by the emigré Viktov Zaslavsky (1982). 'Really existing socialism' has become grey, dull, undramatic, inefficient, more than a little corrupt. The ruling stratum under Stalin was young and faced sizeable risks of purge and execution. People could find little to enthuse about under the Brezhnev gerontocracy; the privileged abused their privileges without fear of punishment, shortages and poor quality contrasted with official claims of successes. Of course, under Stalin, things were in fact much worse. There were indeed horrors, but they were little understood outside the Soviet Union. (Thus the brutalities of collectivization and the famine that followed it were fairly successfully concealed from view.) The result was that the Soviet Union and the 'socialism' it represented became for a time a pole of attraction for millions. 'I have seen the future, and it works', 'Soviet communism – a new civilization', to cite two contemporary judgements. Today the Soviet model no longer impresses or convinces. It is not in chaos, it is not about to fall apart, but it is no beacon, can inspire nobody either in or out of the Soviet Union. And this despite the fact that much has gone wrong in the capitalist West. We will see if the new generation of leaders can restore the lost dynamism.

A few left-wing intellectuals transferred their allegiance to

Mao. As was the case with some Western admirers of Stalin's Russia of the Thirties, this allegiance or admiration was based on misunderstanding, on ignorance. The 'Maoists' simply did not know about the real Great Leap Forward and its millions of victims, or just what the 'Great Proletarian Cultural Revolution' was really about. The post-Mao reaction brought them to their senses. The Yugoslav self-management model too has had its admirers, and indeed its principles are attractive, and will be looked at below. However, grave economic problems have hit Yugoslavia. By no means all of them are connected with the self-management model, but the fact remains that the negative aspects now tend to predominate in observers' minds. Then there was Poland. The 'Solidarność' story, in the present context, is one which not only highlights governmental economic ineptitude, but more important, makes spectacular nonsense of the communist claims to represent the workers, or to be the advance-guard of the proletariat.

So, to summarize, socialism is not, at present, a politically attractive slogan, and this despite the quite vigorous efforts of the New Right to destroy 'consensus-capitalism'. Worse, the immediate political programme of (for instance) Labour's left in Great Britain may be a sure recipe for trouble, reminiscent of the tragic errors of the Allende regime in Chile (which I had the sad experience of witnessing: price control, import controls, large wage increases, the disruption of the normal functioning of the market with no coherent idea of how to replace it).

Democratic socialism, however defined, can come only if the majority of the people are convinced that the old order has outlived itself, that major changes in a socialist direction are urgently needed. In a percipient analysis, S.C. Kolm has noted a repeated tendency: a left-wing government is elected, and its economic policies begin to hurt those middle strata (or middle-class, or left-centre parties) whose votes brought this government to power. The result is a rightward shift of opinion, and either the loss of the parliamentary majority (as in France, in 1937–8, for example) or a successful right-wing coup, as in Chile. Some draw far-reaching conclusions about there not being any democratic road to socialism (although, for example, in Chile there was no left-wing majority in Congress, Allende having been elected on a 'reformist' programme and with some support from left-wing Christian Democrats). Whatever may be the actual or anticipated resistance of the powers-that-be, one can only repeat that democratic socialism requires the support over a prolonged period of the democratic majority – and right now this is not available – *except* for Swedish-style welfare state social-democracy (which has again won an election in Sweden on a welfare-state programme).

Perhaps Sweden is in fact the model we should study, if what we seek is a programme which a moderate, non-revolutionary, democratic-socialist party ought to 'sell' to the electorate. Yes, it is a high-tax solution, but one which the electorate, at least in Sweden, can be persuaded to prefer to any Swedish translation of Thatcherism. In my book on *Feasible Socialism* (Nove, 1983), I rejected the notion that Sweden is a socialist republic ('and not only because it is a monarchy'), and of course there is a large 'capitalist' sector. But there is no serious current of opinion in Sweden which would support a policy of nationalizing the privately owned enterprises, or other drastic changes of existing arrangements. So if this is in fact the practical policy recipe of moderate-socialism or social-democratic parties in Western Europe, then this might be seen as a medium-term objective. Leaving the term 'socialist' as a distant perspective, just as the official Soviet propaganda now views full communism. Just as the Soviet government does not tell people that they actually intend at any particular date to abolish wages and prices, so a Western socialist party should not be committed to 'the introduction of socialism' as a policy for today. But there should be a longer-term objective. What objective?

For reasons already examined at length, it cannot be the socialism/communism foretold by Marx. Then what can it be? Let us examine this subject, bearing in mind the three points made earlier: what relationship between management and workforce; how do productive units interrelate; and what sort of state can be envisaged – bearing in mind that a state there would and must be, with important functions to perform.

So let us look at self-management. Why has its Yugoslav version lost much of its attractiveness? As already suggested, some of the reasons have little to do with the self-management model as such: centrifugal tendencies in a multi-national state with a relatively weak central authority; unwise policies on interest rates (which have been negative in real terms) and on foreign exchange; lack of any effective control over bank credits, to cite some examples. However, certain lessons can none the less be drawn.

One is that self-management is not necessarily desired by the workforce, in the sense that many wish to spend long hours sitting in committee-rooms or studying the firm's accounts. However, the formal responsibility of management to the workforce is an important principle, as is the right of participation, which can be exercised when something goes wrong or feelings run high.

A second point relates to the lack of interest of much of the workforce in the longer term. This is a consequence of that fact that the capital assets do not belong to them, and when they leave they have no saleable asset to dispose of. Their only interest is in the income they can earn. This inclines them to a short-term view, to a desire to increase current income rather than invest in the future. One effect is to increase inflationary pressure.

Thirdly, neither the workforce nor the management has any real responsibility for investment decisions, past or present. Suppose they prove disastrous, who is to blame? If indeed the initial investment decision (to set up the firm) was mistaken, and it was taken before there could be a workers' council or the election (appointment) of a manager, why should management or labour be penalized? This is one aspect of a wider problem: that of how to cope with failure under socialism (other than be assuming that it will not occur!).

Fourthly, by making the workforce's incomes dependent on the given enterprise's financial results (subject, to be sure, to a legal minimum), one ensures unequal pay for equal work, and thus a chronic source of tension and discontent. Thus suppose citizen A and citizen B both drive five-ton lorries from Zagreb to Split, but A works for a more successful enterprise than B; they may well receive very different pay. The resultant pressure for higher pay in the financially less successful enterprises is yet another source of inflationary pressure.

Fifthly, Yugoslavia suffers from unemployment. Yet material incentives based upon dividing net revenues among the existing labour force builds in a reluctance to employ extra labour, whenever such employment would diminish the sum represented by net (distributable) revenue per head. In choosing between investment variants, there is for the same reason a tendency to choose the more capital-intensive variant, in comparison with the profit-orientated capitalist or the 'plan-fulfilling' Soviet manager.

For what should be obvious reasons, self-management requires a market. The self-managed units decide what to produce by reference to market criteria, and purchase their inputs by freely negotiating contracts with suppliers. Charles Bettelheim was quite right when he wrote that 'commodity production' (i.e. for exchange) must exist so long as units of production are autonomous and not wholly integrated into the plan. Yet he criticizes Yugoslav-type self-management: the workers do not really control their means of production and the product – the market does. This presupposes the existence of some unrealizable alternative, in which what is done and the acquisition of means to do it are controlled by no outside force at all. Yet needs have to be conveyed somehow, if not through negotiating contracts then via instructions from a superior authority.

Another significant moral to draw from Yugoslav experience relates to regional questions. In a country which, for historical and geographical reasons, has a relatively highly developed north and a backward south, measures to correct these disparities have had little success. Experience elsewhere shows that such matters defy solution in very different systems (for instance, compare Italy's *mezzogiorno*, or the megalopolis problem in such countries as Mexico and Brazil). However, the combination of autonomous 'self-managed' units and centrifugal forces, with the centre in a relatively weak position, tends to perpetuate or even reinforce regional inequalities. Indeed – and Soviet experience with *sovnarkhozy* (regional economic councils) points in the same direction – one might conclude that regional power over enterprises is very likely to result in irrationalities. The reason is clear: a local authority has information about the needs of its locality and, unless prevented, will tend to give them priority to the detrimnent of other localities, with duplication of investments as yet another undesirable consequence. In other words, if one were to imagine a modern industrial society with complex inter-regional links, there are two possible logical solutions: central control or enterprise autonomy (the 'enterprise' could, in some circumstances, be large or even, in such cases as electricity supply, a centrally controlled monopoly). If power over resources were given to an authority covering one area, it would divert resources for its own purposes, with potentially disruptive effects.

Finally, one must refer to the very considerable literature, of which Ward's fascinating excursion into 'Illyria' is the original example (Ward, 1958), which appears to prove that self-managed enterprises, in which the workforce's income depends on that enterprise's net revenue, are of their nature inefficient. Some of the conclusions are irrelevant to the real world. Thus Ward's model shows that it would 'pay' the firm to reduce output if prices rose, but this would only be so under the assumption of so-called 'perfect competition', in which such considerations as real competition do not enter. For example, in real competition one is concerned not to lose customers to one's competitors, who might not be regained if prices fall, as in future they might. Nor are self-managed enterprises likely to dismiss fellow-workers without some extremely strong reasons. None the less, as already noted, they may choose labour-saving, capital-intensive investment variants even when unemployment is a major social problem. It may be necessary (and it surely is possible) to devise fiscal means to counteract this tendency. As for efficiency, this depends (inter alia) on the attitude of the workforce. Would the sense of participation increase commitment and loyalty, and so the quality of the work effort? These considerations seldom figure in economic analysis (with Albert O. Hirschman an honourable exception). Some unimaginative model-builders would doubtless also conclude that the reluctance of Japanese firms to shed labour is 'inefficient', yet any loss can be counterbalanced by the sense of 'belonging' that goes with security of employment. A recent study of Israeli *kibbutzim* noted that one finds no resistance there to labour-saving innovations, which can be encountered in private firms, because such innovations do not threaten loss of jobs.

There are lessons to be learnt from the experience of the Mondragon cooperatives in northern Spain. Unlike the Yugoslav enterprises, they pay wages, so that there is an identifiable profit. They also ensure that the workforce has shares in the business (if necessary lending them the money to acquire them), and this also gives them a longer-term stake in its prosperity. It is, however, worth recalling that the Mondragon enterprises function in an area of strong local loyalties, just as the *kibbutz* members are committed volunteers. The outcome may be different with different human material.

Socialists must be aware that there are bound to be problems connected with property ownership and long-term responsibility, involving also risk-taking and the consequences of failure. Where uncertainty exists – i.e. in any conceivable situation – there must be the possibility of failure. A capitalist can go bankrupt, but what of 'socialist bankruptcy'? One cannot 'solve' this question simply by assuming either perfect foresight or perfect planning. The existence of genuine autonomy of decision-making is surely an aim desirable in itself, and freedom necessarily involves both uncertainty and freedom to err, to act in ways not necessarily consistent with the general interest or the national plan.

What, then, could a 'feasible socialism' be like? Should the word be redefined? Surely a non-utopian definition of socialist values should be counterposed to the crude laissez-faire ideology of the New Right. Some of the traditional slogans associated with socialism have become deservedly unpopular. There are good reasons to associate nationalization with bureaucracy, satisfying neither the workforce nor the customers. It is in a review in *Radical Philosophy* (Spring 1985) that one can read: 'A regime devoted to equality in its literal sense would have to be authoritarian, ready to crush inequalities whenever they reasserted themselves, as they inevitably and constantly would.' The New Right's view of 'liberty' may be distasteful, but one must recognize that the aims of equality and freedom can conflict with one another. Socialism cannot be happy with a purely acquisitive society. Indeed such a society would fall apart, for why should civil servants, judges, police officers, not be crude income-maximizers, i.e. behave as most doctors seem to do in America? Yet acquisitiveness is not a value to be disparaged, the vast majority of citizens do have material aspirations. Thus a conscientious doctor does his best for his patients, even if they cannot pay an economic fee, but he or she is also not averse to acquire a country cottage and go on holiday to Greece. Furthermore, at least since the days of Adam Smith it has been rightly noted that there are worse ambitions than making money: the men who, in the process of competing for power, sent their comrades to be shot in cellars were not seeking to maximize profits. What is to be sought is a balance between (enlightened) self-interest and a sense of social responsibility. Inevitably this differs as between individuals.

Individuals also differ greatly in what might be called 'producers' preferences'. Some like to be independent innovators, others prefer routine. Some gladly take responsibility, others prefer to avoid it. Some opt for life in a commune or *kibbutz*, others would be very unhappy there. While Marx's vision of a universal Man is a fantasy, it is not at all a fantasy to provide both for variety and for the opportunity to change one's specialization if the spirit so moves one. A socialism based on one economic model might be a sort of procrustean bed for a sizeable part of the population. (Imagine, for example, *compulsory* communal living!) Hence it seems desirable to redefine 'socialism' as a mixed economy: enterprises large and small, many if not most self-managed or cooperative, with some private enterprises too. If the private sector does not play a dominant role, its existence should be consistent with a sensibly defined socialism; otherwise its suppression would be the constant task of a 'socialist' police (unless, of course, it proves not to be needed, in which case 'privateers' no more require to be banned than to outlaw private water-carriers when everyone has tap water). A major objective would be not only to ensure variety of choice of occupations, but also work for all, when unemployment is in danger of becoming a major social curse. Only in ideological textbooks of economics do labour markets automatically clear. One must anticipate the need to take job-creating action. One must also anticipate that freedom to organize involves freedom to form not only political parties but also interest groups which will press for additional resources. Since money will undoubtedly continue to exist, it would be possible to issue too much of it in the face of pressures, so inflation (and some species of monetarism) will not just go away. Freedom of choice implies both a market and competition, both in consumers' goods and producers' goods and services, though there must also be some large-scale natural monopolies (such as electricity, water, public transport), where responsibility of management to the users is as important as its responsibility to its workforce.

Mises, Hayek, and later on also Friedman, have argued that efficiency in resource allocation is impossible under socialism. At a formal level they were answered by Lange, Lerner, Dickinson, but there were and are major practical obstacles in realizing their socialist models, which are anchored (as are so many of the neoclassicals') in static equilibrium assumptions, and it is unclear why either the central planning board or the managers in Lange's model should act out their parts in the prescribed manner. It should be admitted that the absence of (or severe limits on) a real capital market can cause inefficiencies, that rewards for risk-taking and innovation may well sit uneasily with social or state ownership of capital assets. Nor is this all. Kornai, in his Dublin lecture (Kornai, 1985) pointed to contradictions between the requirements of efficiency and socialist ethics. But the world is full of contradictions, and one usually arrives at some species of compromise; 'maximization' in terms of just one objective function can seldom be encountered in really existing societies (a fully-fledged and devoted 'profit maximizer' would probably suffer a nervous breakdown, if not already dead of cardiac arrest). Mises and company are right to insist that economically meaningful prices are needed, wrong to assert that socialist prices cannot be meaningful (though today's Soviet prices are indeed irrational, reflecting neither use-value nor relative scarcity). But it must be emphasized how far the contemporary Western system is from the free-market model of the textbooks. Thus in his challenging 'Profits without production', Seymour Mellman notes and deplores the narrow concentration on short-term profits, by executives who have no long-term commitment to their corporation (on average they move to another one within five years or so). Current uncertainties about prices, interest rates, inflation, are hardly conducive to 'rational' long-term investment decisions. Too often critics of socialist economics (with its imperfections) implicitly compare it with a Chicago utopia, which is in its own way as unreal as a marxist one. Perfect markets and perfect plans are equally utopian.

But in the end much will depend on the ability of contemporary capitalism to surmount its many problems, not least that of mass unemployment and ecological decline (acid rain, deforestation, over-fishing, etc.). The masses will not opt for a different system unless faced with the bankruptcy of the existing one. To repeat, it was Marx who wrote that no mode of production passes from the scene unless and until its productive potential is exhausted. With Soviet-type socialism seen as obsolete, in contradiction with the forces of production, it offers no alternative model. A great deal remains to be done to revive socialism as an aim worthy of effort and sacrifice.

ALEC NOVE

See also COMMAND ECONOMY; ECONOMIC CALCULATION IN SOCIALIST ECONOMIES; ENGELS, FRIEDRICH; MARKET SOCIALISM; MARX, KARL HEINRICH; MATERIAL BALANCES; PLANNED ECONOMY; PRICES AND QUANTITIES.

BIBLIOGRAPHY

Bahro, R. 1977. *Die Alternative: zur Kritik des real existierenden Sozialismus*. Cologne: Europäische Verlaganstalt.

Bettelheim, C. 1968. *La transition vers l'économie socialiste*. Paris: F. Maspero.

Brus, W. 1980. Political system and economic efficiency – the East European context. *Journal of Comparative Economics* 4(1), 40–55.

Castoridis, C. 1979. *Les carrefours du labyrinthe*. Paris: Editions du Seuil. Trans. K. Soper and M.H. Ryle as *Crossroads in the Labyrinth*, Brighton: Harvester, 1984.

Feher, F., Heiler, A. and Markus, G. 1983. *Dictatorship Over Needs*. Oxford: Basil Blackwell.

Gatovsky, L. (ed.) 1967. *Zakonomernosti i puti sozdaniia materialno-tekhnicheskoi bazy kommunizma* (On legality and the means of creating a material-technical base for communism). Moscow: Akademii Nauk SSSR.

Goroz, A. 1980. *Adieux au prolétariat*. Paris: Editions Galilée.

Grossman, V. 1985. *Life and Fate*. Trans. from the Russian by R. Chandler, London: Collins Harvill.

Kolakowski, L. 1976. *Main Currents of Marxism: its rise, growth and dissolution*. Vol. 1, trans. from the Polish by P.S. Falla, Oxford: Clarendon Pres, 1978.

Kornai, J. 1971. *Anti-Equilibrium. On economic systems theory and tasks of research*. Amsterdam and London: North-Holland.

Kornai, J. 1985. The dilemmas of the socialist economy. Geary Lecture, Dublin, 1979. In J. Kornai, *Contradictions and Dilemmas*, Corvina: Kner Printing House.

Kuznets, S. 1941. *National Income and its Composition, 1919–1938*. New York: National Bureau of Economic Research.

Lenin, V.I. 1962. *Sochineniia* (Works). 5th edn, Vol. 36, Moscow.

Marx, K. 1962. *Marx–Engels Works* (Russian). Vol. XXVIII, Moscow.

Mészáros, I. 1972. *Marx's Theory of Alienation*. 3rd edn, London: Merlin Press.

Nove, A. 1983. *The Economics of Feasible Socialism*. London: Allen & Unwin.

Roland, G. 1985. *Valeur d'usage chez Karl Marx*. Brussels.

Schumpeter, J. 1976. *Capitalism, Socialism and Democracy*. 5th edn, London: Allen & Unwin.

Shanin, T. 1984. *Late Marx and the Russian Road*. London: Routledge & Kegan Paul.

Ward, B. 1958. The firm in Illyria: market syndicalism. *American Economic Review* 48, September, 566–89.

Wright, E.O. 1979. *Class Structure and Income Determination*. New York: Academic Press.

Zaslavsky, V. 1982. *The Neo-Stalinist State: class, ethnicity, and consensus in Soviet society*. New York: Sharpe; Brighton: Harvester.

socialist economies. One way to introduce the theoretical arguments made for socialism by economists is to consider the weaknesses of market systems. In theory, socialism offers the potential to overcome these deficiencies of market capitalism. In practice, these problems have been attenuated but not overcome and many new problems have been created by socialist economies. The effort to confront these problems has led to the development of new socialist models, hybridization of these models in practice, and ongoing attempts at piecemeal reforms in the socialist countries.

Market shortcomings are generally well-known and can be outlined cursorily. First, market capitalism engenders exploitation. Exploitation has several dimensions and meanings. To a neoclassical economist, a worker is exploited when he or she is paid less than his or her marginal revenue product, as occurs, for instance, under conditions of monopsony. To a Marxian economist, a worker is exploited when paid less than the average revenue product, after accounting for payments to embodied labour. In the latter case, it may be noted, exploitation is endemic to capitalism; in the former, it is an exception in the model of perfectly competitive markets. For a Marxist, among others, exploitation has many other dimensions. Exploited workers are also alienated from the means of production and from the production decision-making process. This condition, in turn, often leads to de-humanization and deskilling of the production process, in both static and dynamic senses.

Finally, exploitation also implies a larger degree of inequality in the distribution of income. Inequality, many have argued, undermines or at least diminishes the value of consumer sovereignty. That is, the democratic principle of one person, one vote is violated in the marketplace where people with more dollars or pounds are given more votes in the determination of resource allocations. Some consumers are more sovereign than others.

Second, there are various types of market failure. Markets register private, not social costs. Hence, there is an overproduction (more than socially optimal level) of goods yielding negative externalities, underproduction of goods yielding positive externalities, an absence of public good production, an excess of unemployment. These results, of course, obtain in pure, unregulated markets, and there is much room for debate about the optimal approach to rectifying the misallocation of resources they imply. Further, non-competitive market structures which render resource allocation suboptimal are not only possible in theory but seemingly ubiquitous in practice.

From a comparative static and dynamic perspective, cobwebs and uncertainty are additional sources of possible market failure. Cobwebs, wherein production decisions for the next period are based on present period prices, result in explosive markets when the supply elasticity exceeds the demand elasticity; that is, movement is away from rather than toward equilibrium over time. Market uncertainty results not only from intertemporal choice but from lack of knowledge about market conditions and competitor behaviour. Uncertainty may engender higher rates of discount, less productive investment, duplicative research and development, excess production and other forms of waste.

Each of the above market weaknesses results from micro considerations. Markets are also associated with a lack of coordination and consequent instability at the macro level. Perhaps the most heralded macro-imbalance results from the inequality of ex ante investment and ex ante savings, rendering aggregate demand and supply unequal. Such macro-imbalances lead to, inter alia, unemployment, inflation, greater market uncertainty and a variety of socio-political problems.

One final critique of the market has been made by economic historians. Most notably, Karl Polanyi has argued that historically the introduction of the market tended to disembed, or separate out, the economic sphere from the social sphere and make the former, with its attendant values of profit maximization, efficiency, materialism and individualism, dominant. The resulting disruption of the socio-cultural fabric is seen as unintended and deplorable.

It is fair to say that socialist economies have been perceived to be the appropriate antidote, depending on the writer, to some or all of these weaknesses of market capitalism. We shall now turn to a discussion of how economists have modelled the various incarnations of the socialist economy. This will be followed by a brief analysis of the weaknesses and strengths of the socialist economy in practice and, then, a conclusion on the economic lessons of the socialist experience.

MODELS OF SOCIALIST ECONOMIES

Although socialism is primarily seen as means of righting the wrongs of market capitalism, there is no agreement on how the socialist economy should correct these wrongs. Three principal variants of socialism have existed in the 20th century in the Soviet Union, Hungary and China, and Yugoslavia: the centrally planned economy, market socialism, and worker-managed socialism. Economists have developed models of these three types of socialism, and we now turn to these models to identify the differences in assumptions about the nature of the material world and about human nature that underlie the different versions of socialism.

The centrally planned economy. The first state to establish socialism on a major and lasting basis was the Soviet Union. Centrally planned socialism is historically associated with the system of planning in the Soviet Union from 1928 onward. Derived from the analysis of centrally planned socialism in the Soviet Union and from the theoretical structure of the Leontief input-output framework, economists now have a model of the centrally planned economy (CPE).

In the CPE, as in all models of socialism considered here, individuals work for money income and spend their money in markets for final goods. The CPE model assumes that planners will know what the consumers want. Under certain conditions, this assumption seems warranted. For example, a simple survey of the income elasticities of consumers' preferences will provide the necessary information if, as in the case of the Leontief input–output matrix, there is one scarce factor of production and one technique for each product and constant returns to scale. Under those conditions, there are constant costs of production for all goods, so that the opportunity costs do not change as a function of the quantities demanded. Thus, the prices at which they are offered for sale to consumers can remain constant, independent of the quantities purchased. In this case, the only consumer information required is the income elasticity of demand for all products which, combined with estimates of the increases in income in each time period, generates the vector of final demand. Under these same conditions, the technical information required is simple, because there is only one technique of production for each good. The only production possibility information missing is the supply of the single scarce factor, labour, which can be estimated from demographic data, since social policy requires all able adults to work.

Under the circumstances described, optimal allocation can be attained with minimal information. If, however, there are multiple factors of production and multiple techniques of production, or non-constant returns to scale, the opportunity costs will not be constant. In that case, much more information is required about both production possibilities and consumer preferences in order to plan production so that the socially optimal bill of goods is produced. This raises questions about the ability of the planners to collect and to process the large amounts of data required to solve this problem.

Even if the socially optimal mix of goods to be produced can be determined, can the central planners implement the plan? Under the same conditions described above, the input–output matrix yields the gross activity level of all sectors. Orders can be issued to the agents managing the producing units at the periphery. If these orders are followed, the right amounts of all intermediate goods will be forthcoming to sustain the desired vector of final output.

In addition to assuming that the central planners can know the consumers' preferences and the production possibilities frontier and can implement the plan, the CPE model assumes that the central planners are efficient and disinterested, that is, that they have no interests of their own, no other 'agenda'. The plant managers are assumed to follow faithfully the orders given them by the central planners.

As we shall see in the section on the institutional development of socialism, the Soviet system of centrally planned socialism suggests that not all of these assumptions are warranted. It is far from clear that the central planners are disinterested, or that planning carried out in the manner prescribed produces either consistency or efficiency.

Lange's market socialism. In the 1930s, while Soviet central planning was just being established, the Polish economist Oskar Lange developed a model of market socialism. Three decades later this model is used by economists to analyse the economic reforms of the type taking place in Hungary and China.

The principal contrast to the assumptions of the centrally planned economy is that Lange assumes multiple inputs and multiple techniques of production and, thus, opportunity costs that are not independent of demand. To ascertain centrally the optimal bill of goods and to issue directives to producers would require more information than the centre could possibly collect. Lange, therefore, sees the task as one of designing a game between the centre and the plant managers to induce the plant managers, who have this vital information, to act on it themselves in such a way that efficient allocation of resources occurs without the information being collected in any single place.

The key players in this game are the central planners, the industry managers and the plant managers. Workers, as such, play no explicit role in solving the problem Lange formulated. The central planners determine the distribution policy, set the rate of investment, operate as a Walrasian auctioneer to set the prices for intermediate goods, and make adjustments in prices to deal with externalities. The adjustment to a change in final demand cannot be instantaneous. The short-term response is handled by a change in the prices of final goods, which leads to adjustments in the utilization of current capacities. This is the task of the enterprise managers, who operate existing plants according to the two rules, 'determine the lowest possible cost method of producing any given output', and 'set output so that marginal cost equals price'. Profits or losses revert to the state. The long term response is handled by industry managers, who adjust the industry capacity according to the rule that long run marginal cost equals long run price. The decision to expand or contract capacity must be taken from the industry-wide, not the plant, point of view, so as to avoid the decision errors that would arise due to lack of knowledge of what the other decision-makers are doing.

As in the case of the CPE, the central planners in Lange's market socialism are assumed to be efficient and disinterested. The industry managers and plant managers are assumed to follow orders, in this case not specific production orders but specified rules. The game provides the managers with the information necessary to make correct decisions. The rules the managers follow, set marginal cost equal to price and minimize the average cost of production for any output, are simply the logically appropriate rules for maximizing the use value of output and, if followed, they logically assure the achievement of that result.

Worker-managed socialism. In contrast to the two versions of socialism considered above, where the key decisions are made by the central planners and the plant and industry managers who are assumed to be efficient and disinterested, and where the workers have no explicit decision-making role, in worker-managed socialism control of the factories by the workers is central. Yugoslavia is the principal national economy that has, to date, replaced or significantly modified the role of the central planners to make place for workers' control.

The version of worker-managed socialism implemented in Yugoslavia in the 1960s starts from the ideas that every member of society should be assured an equal access to social capital and that workers should run their own factories, participating equally in making decisions within the enterprise. If the worker managers exchange their products on competitive markets, the resulting rewards to workers are fair returns to the effort put forth. The notion of workers exchanging their products on competitive markets is supplemented by the central place given to the role of entrepreneurship. The problem of attaching appropriate rewards and penalties to the use of social capital is an important one in socialism. On the one hand, there can be too little risk-bearing in socialism if the penalties for absence of innovation are very weak; on the other hand, there can be an excessive appetite for social capital if there are virtually no penalities for poor entrepreneurial judgement. In this Yugoslav view of worker-managed socialism, cost minimization, responses to changes in demand and supply, and development of new technology are assumed to be primarily questions involving entrepreneurial judgement, not questions involving coordinating the responses of many participants. In this view, the key to efficient management of firms and, thus, the economy, lies in the way risk-bearing is handled in a world with uncertainty. In the Yugoslav worker-managed market socialist model, the workers function as the collective entrepreneurs. They have no rights to deplete existing capital, but their incomes are paid out of the variable profits that reflect the soundness of their judgement. The focus of this version of worker-managed socialism on exchange on competitive markets and on the central role of entrepreneurship is complemented by the very limited role given to planning at the central level.

In the version of worker management that became influential in Yugoslavia in the 1970s, if not fully implemented, the role ascribed to the market was reduced and a mechanism for planning in the key sectors was established. Each factory was to send delegates to industrial and regional councils which, in turn, send delegates to national councils where the national economic plan for key sectors was to be prepared. This plan was then to be disaggregated back to the individual factories which ratify the plan by signing binding contracts concerning their own individual responsibilities. This form of worker-management may be regarded as planning from below, in contrast to the planning from above of the centrally planned economy and Lange's market socialism, and the virtual absence of planning in the market-oriented version of worker-managed socialism.

The underlying concerns of both models of worker-managed socialism are how to give the workers an appropriate say about running both the factory and the socialist economy. Unlike the centrally planned economy and Lange's market socialism, workers, managers and central planners are all viewed as complex human beings. Workers are assumed to have legitimate concerns about the organization of the workplace that must be resolved in the factory itself. Thus, worker-managed socialism pays specific attention to the workplace quality of life issues including hours worked, pace of work, degree of mechanization of work, methods of reaching decisions. Workers have different interests in their capacities as workers, consumers, and taxpayers, which must be resolved. Unlike the centrally planned economy and Lange's market socialism, worker-managed socialism does not make automatically benign assumptions about the possibilities of aggregating the preferences of the workers into a social welfare function or about the motives of the planners and managers and their relationship to the workers. Further, it considers explicitly the possibility that central planners and plant managers can become part of some 'new' class over the workers.

THE HISTORICAL DEVELOPMENT AND ACCOMPLISHMENTS OF SOCIALISM

Each of the socialist models discussed above has exhibited weaknesses and strengths in practice. The weaknesses account for the ongoing experimentation and reform efforts in all of the socialist economies. The strengths help to account, along with political factors, for the durability of many of socialism's key economic institutions.

Centrally planned socialism has performed superlatively in some areas and reasonably well in others. With few exceptions, today's CPEs have maintained full employment along with very high labour force participation rates. They have also experienced marked success in the realm of equity. Income distribution figures reveal a strong underlying equality with decile ratios varying between 4 and 7 to 1. Of course, there are perquisites and privileged access to goods and services for the top Party leaders, but the effects of these benefits on income distribution are largely, if not entirely, offset by free services such as health and education and by heavily subsidized basic goods.

The growth record of the CPEs has been creditable. Central planning seems to offer greater advantages for growth during earlier stages of development and fewer advantages during later stages. During early stages, central planning can put to effective use its ability: to mobilize resources quickly for needed projects; to nurture, finance and protect infant industry; to be a surrogate for the fledgling or non-existent entrepreneurial class; to coordinate investment projects and reduce uncertainty; to develop human capital and employ labour resources fully, etc. During later stages, the growing complexity of the economy, the approach to the technological frontier in many industries, the poor innovative potential, among other things, seem to encumber the already centralized and overburdened structures of central planning. It should be stressed, however, that centrally planned economies are not homogeneous either in their structures or in their performance. Some developed CPEs, such as the German Democratic Republic, have very strong growth records superior to those of their capitalist counterparts over certain periods. Due to different national income accounting systems, different price systems, different currencies and fixed exchange rates, however, it is an extremely complicated task to measure comparative growth rates and even more difficult to gauge comparative living standards. There is still much discussion and disagreement about comparative growth performance.

There is less disagreement, however, about the nature of the problems engendered by central planning. It would appear to be an uncontestable virtue of the market that its demands for the central collection and processing of information are practically nil. Producers and consumers interface directly and communicate through price signals. Eliminate the market and all the information must be centrally processed. In the Soviet economy there are over 12 million commodities, thousands of technologies, millions of supply contracts with input specifications and dates, over 12 million prices to be set, thousands of investment projects, etc. To balance, let alone allocate efficiently all of these resources requires comprehensive, accurate and timely information. This information must then be processed and converted into an operative economic plan.

These informational requirements for a balanced plan are many magnitudes too great to be achieved. Planners, instead, must take short-cuts. The more short-cuts are taken, however, the greater the margin for error in the plan and the greater the possibility for imbalances. Moreover, since supply contracts among producers and consumer goods production are centrally planned, without direct contact between the seller and buyer, there is always a greater likelihood that what is produced (even if it is produced in the right quantity at the right time) will not be exactly what the consumer wants. If the good is unusable and there is nowhere else to obtain the good, then shortages develop. If the good in question happens to be an input to another producing enterprise then that enterprise will not be able to meet its supply contracts to other enterprises. Bottlenecks can, thus, routinely spread throughout the economy. If the good in question is a consumer good, then the frustrated consumer will over time learn that there is a greater payoff to leaving work early to be the first in line for scarce goods than there is to working harder and earning more income when there is an insufficient supply of desirable goods to be bought.

In the absence of universal altruism, planners must also find a means to motivate producers. This problem has several dimensions. First, since the centre cannot possibly know all the production technologies, the inventory levels, the personnel issues, and so on at the enterprise level, it must rely on enterprises sharing accurate information on these things in order to plan production. Enterprise managers, however, are rewarded with bonuses or better jobs for meeting the output targets in the central plan. They are judged by the industrial ministry to which they are subordinated and the ministry, in turn, is judged according to the industry-wide target by the central planning board. At each level the communication is vertical, not horizontal. The effort is to satisfy someone above you in the planning hierarchy instead of the consumer of your product. The easiest way to meet the plan is to overstate your need for inputs and to understate your potential for output. Elicitation schemes to induce accurate information from production units have been devised but they have foundered.

Second, once the target is set, the problem becomes getting the enterprise to meet its target on time, with the correct output mix and desired quality. But if the enterprise finds some products easier to produce than others or, due to a problematic and often inconsistent price system, more profitable than others and it is worried about input shortages, then it is likely to take whatever short-cuts are necessary to meet the most important indicators of the plan. When an enterprise takes short-cuts, such as reducing quality, it is natural for the centre to specify new success indicators, such as quality standards. The enterprise counters by finding new short-cuts in a manner perhaps analogous to tax shelter abusers in the West. Eventually, an enterprise may find itself with literally hundreds of success indicators. Under these circumstances, there must obviously be a ranking or prioritization of the indicators. The indicator that inevitably gains priority is the physical output target. The reason for this is simple: it is upon this indicator that the balance in the national plan is based.

Exhortations for greater efficiency and profitability run up against the same constraint. Furthermore, since worker job rights have to date been an inalienable part of the political bargain, enterprises have not been allowed to fail. Hence, incurring losses means much less to a CPE executive than to the market economy executive. The profitability criterion applies a weak brake at most to input hoarding in the face of supply uncertainty. Put differently, financial targets play a distant secondary role to physical targets.

Third, assuming workers' objective functions are more complex than simply wanting to maximize the common weal, there is the problem of motivating the direct producers. Financial incentives, however, for reasons noted above, are insufficient at best. Given this, it would seem desirable to give workers a greater voice in enterprise and extra-enterprise decision-making. Among other things, if workers were to participate effectively in setting enterprise and national economic goals (as well as in implementing these goals), it is more likely that they would identify with these goals and be, to a greater extent, self-motivated. Although only scanty information is available on the degree of worker involvement in management in today's CPEs, the information we do have suggests that this involvement, with some uneveness across countries, has been rather limited.

Limited worker participation suggests little progress toward reducing worker alienation. Nevertheless, it should be emphasized that the maintenance of full employment along with socialist ideology gives the socialist worker de facto power not present in the typical capitalist factory. This power can be used variously to shirk, leave work early, to be absent or, generally, reduce the intensity of labour. That is, the worker in a CPE appears to have greater flexibility to identify the optimal point in his or her work–leisure trade-off.

There does, however, seem to be a new recognition of the economic and political value of worker participation in the socialist economies. Since 1980 in many countries there have been new statutes expanding the scope of worker decision-making powers and establishing production brigades, which are sub-units of industrial enterprises and state farms. These production brigades are intended (a) to make the decision-making process more immediate and relevant to the workers; and (b) to connect more directly a worker's pay to his or her effort through brigade-level, in contrast to enterprise-level, incentives. Early indications are that the brigades have had some success, particularly in agriculture.

It is also far from apparent that social classes have been eliminated in today's CPEs. Many have argued that the socialist leaders are a ruling class, making all the important economic and political decisions for the country and even appropriating surplus enabling them to live very comfortably, if not luxuriously. Finally, it does not appear that CPEs have outperformed the developed market economies regarding pollution. Obsession with physical output targets causes the same environmental abuse as does obsession with profit.

The problems of CPEs denote inefficiency and waste, but they do not denote catastrophe. If they did, the CPEs would not have shown the resilience and durability they have. Put simply, the industrialized CPEs have exhibited less efficiency but more equity than the advanced market capitalist economies.

As the possibilities for extensive growth have eroded and growth rates for most CPEs have slowed since the early 1970s, there has been an ongoing quest to improve the economic mechanisms of planning. The most substantial reforms have occurred in Hungary and China. Both have been dubbed experiments in market socialism. The reform experience in Hungary is longer and, it appears, more stable and systematic than that in China.

The underlying approach of the 1968 Hungarian reform has been to decentralize by introducing (a) direct material supply contracting between enterprises; (b) the market mechanism and free or bounded prices wherever feasible; and (c) limited private production of goods and services under a watchful eye. In essence, the Hungarian approach recognizes that it is impossible to centrally plan an entire economy and that the more planners attempt to control everything, the less actual control planners have over the important parts of the economy. Instead, the Hungarians have retained control of important investments and key industries and gradually allowed more and more of economic activity to be regulated by the market within those limits.

This effort has encountered many setbacks, and some basic tensions as well as tradeoffs inherent to the market mechanism have become manifest. For instance, to expect enterprises to make decentralized decisions about production implies reliance upon price signals. Prices must reflect the underlying conditions of supply and demand if they are to promote efficient resource use and market equilibrium. Market pricing, however, opens up the possibility for inflation as well as uncertainty, speculation and monopoly prices. Further, if the price signals are truly to allocate resources in certain markets, then enterprises producing financial losses must be allowed to fail. This implies job instability and short-run unemployment, at least. Neither have been acceptable political outcomes to date. On the other side, some enterprises and private small businesses will succeed, generating higher incomes for some and greater overall inequality – also politically troublesome outcomes.

Moreover, as free markets and private production come to coexist with regulated markets and state production, there is the danger that resources will find their way through semi-legal and illegal channels to the private sector. It is also likely that workers will reserve effort from state production for their private production or marketing activities. In short, the existence of a substantial private sector can challenge the predominance of the public sector.

All this is not to say that mixed economies are impossible. It is rather to acknowledge the complexity of reform efforts and to suggest that such efforts must be, first, carefully planned and prepared and, then, flexibly and gradually administered. The actual process is likely to be fraught with social tensions and political struggles. The preparation for a substantive, decentralizing reform, then, requires not only a modicum of prior economic balance but also a high degree of political stability and Party unity.

Another variant of reform away from central planning began

in the early 1950s in Yugoslavia. This reform was prompted as much by political forces as by the economic problems of central planning. Through 1976 the Yugoslavs gradually substituted the market for central planning, until only a system of loose indicative planning prevailed. What distinguished the Yugoslav experiment most, however, was its system of worker self-management or workers' councils in the enterprises, with legal rights for workers to appoint, control and remove management. By 1974, the Yugoslavs could boast of a good growth record but they were also experiencing significant economic instability with high unemployment and inflation. Furthermore, the Yugoslav leadership began to see the market as disrupting the socialist fabric of society, substituting managerialism for worker participation in the enterprises, materialism and individualism for collectivism, and so on. The 1974 Constitution sought to replace the market as the coordination mechanism with bottom-up planning. Although the full record is not yet in, it appears that this new system has fallen far short of its goals.

CONCLUSION. The foregoing sketch of the socialist economic experience suggests that the model of pure central planning is impracticable. The information, coordination and motivational barriers to this model are insuperable.

Thus, to improve upon economic performance or to approximate better the socioeconomic goals of socialism, reform is necessary. The paths to reform are through administrative or market decentralization and/or greater democracy in the management and political spheres. To varying degrees, subject to the prevailing cultural and political constraints, each socialist economy has experimented with one or more of these reform paths.

At the February 1986 Soviet Party Congress, General Secretary Mikhail Gorbachev outlined a long-term strategy for reforming the Soviet economy. He envisions weakening the power of the Ministries, strengthening the power of the enterprises and reducing the scope of what is centrally planned. This vision is not dissimilar in its economic content to that of the 1960s reform movements in Czechoslovakia and Hungary. As yet, few concrete steps have been taken to suggest that Gorbachev's vision will become a reality, and Gorbachev has scarely broached the issue of meaningful price reform. The political obstacles in the Soviet Union to serious reform are formidable. Yet there is more open and far-ranging discussion of the need for decentralization to rejuvenate the Soviet economy now than at any time since the Industrialization Debate of the 1920s. Whether or not this debate affects policy in the USSR, it is likely to legitimate further and to fuel reform efforts elsewhere in the Soviet bloc.

DEBORAH DUFF MILENKOVITCH AND ANDREW ZIMBALIST

See also COMMAND ECONOMY; ECONOMIC CALCULATION IN SOCIALIST ECONOMIES; ENGELS, FRIEDRICH; LANGE-LERNER MECHANISM; MARKET SOCIALISM; MARX, KARL HEINRICH; MATERIAL BALANCES; PLANNED ECONOMY; PRICES AND QUANTITIES.

BIBLIOGRAPHY

Brus, W. 1972. *The Market in a Socialist Economy*. London: Routledge & Kegan Paul.

Comisso, E. 1979. *Workers' Control under Plan and Market*. New Haven: Yale University Press.

Connor, W.D. 1979. *Socialism, Politics and Equality: Hierarchy and Change in Eastern Europe and the USSR*. New York: Columbia University Press.

Dobb, M.H. 1955. *Economic Theory and Socialism*. New York: International Publishers.

Ellman, M. 1979. *Socialist Planning*. Cambridge: Cambridge University Press.

Granick, D. 1954. *Management of the Industrial Firm in the USSR*. New York: Columbia University Press.

Haraszti, M. 1977. *Worker in a Worker's State*. Harmondsworth: Penguin Books.

Hare, P., Radice, H. and Swain, N. (eds) 1981. *Hungary: A Decade of Economic Reform*. London: George Allen & Unwin.

Horvat, B. 1982. *The Political Economy of Socialism*. Armonk, NY: M.E. Sharpe.

Kornai, J. 1980a. *The Economics of Shortage*. Amsterdam: North-Holland.

Kornai, J. 1980b. The dilemmas of a socialist economy. *Cambridge Journal of Economics* 4(2), 147–57.

Lane, D.S. 1971. *The End of Inequality? Stratification under State Socialism*. Harmondsworth: Penguin Books.

Lange, O. and Taylor, F.M. 1964. *On the Economic Theory of Socialism*. New York: McGraw-Hill.

Milenkovitch, D. 1983. Is market socialism efficient? In *Comparative Economic Systems: An Assessment of Knowledge, Method, and Theory*, ed. A. Zimbalist, Boston: Kluwer-Nijhoff.

Mises, L. von. 1922. *Socialism: An Economic and Sociological Analysis*. 2nd edn, New Haven: Yale University Press, 1951.

Nove, A. 1980. *The Soviet Economic System*. London: George Allen & Unwin. 2nd edn, 1980.

Nove, A. 1983. *The Economics of Feasible Socialism*. London: George Allen & Unwin.

Polanyi, K. 1957. *The Great Transformation*. Boston: Beacon Press.

Riskin, C. 1985. *Political Economy of Chinese Development since 1949*. Oxford: Oxford University Press.

Schrenk, M. et al. 1979. *Yugoslavia: Self-Management Socialism*. Baltimore: Johns Hopkins University Press.

Triska, J. and Gati, C. (eds) 1981. *Blue Collar Workers in Eastern Europe*. Cambridge: Cambridge University Press.

Yanowitch, M. (ed.) 1979. *Soviet Work Attitudes: The Issue of Participation in Management*. White Plains, NY: M.E. Sharpe.

socialists of the chair. *Kathedersozialisten* (socialists of the chair, i.e. the professorial chair) was the nickname given by the liberal journalist, H.B. Oppenheim, in 1872, to a number of the younger German professors of political economy, and quoted by one of the most influential of them, Professor Gustav Schmoller, of Strasburg, in his opening speech at the Eisenach congress of economists held in the same year. The group of teachers thus characterized agreed in believing that there were grave social questions to which it was their duty to call attention, and that these could not be solved, as the Manchester School, then dominant in the German press, and organized in the *Volkswirthschaftliche Kongress*, believed, by a mere resort to laissez faire. On the other hand they differed from the social democrats in that they disbelieved in the possibility or desirability of violent revolutionary changes: and they rejected as inaccurate the 'scientific' formulae both of Lassalle and Marx – the 'iron law' and the doctrine of 'surplus value'. Among themselves, opinions ranged all the way from a disposition to think well of trade unions to an eagerness for state intervention in industry in all directions. But most of them were moderate in their expectations and cautious in their proposals. From Hegel and the philosophers on the one side, and from the bureaucratic traditions of the Prussian monarchy on the other, they had learned a high doctrine of the state; but they were guided in their application of it by their firm hold on the principle of relativity which had been inculcated by Roscher and the creators of the historical school. The whole group may be described as the historical school become militant – under the stress of new industrial conditions, the stimulus of the social democratic movement, and with the confidence engendered by the establishment of the German empire. They did much to promote factory legislation, and to prepare the way for the system of compulsory insurance which may be regarded as the most notable outcome of their activity. The term 'socialists of the chair', after playing a considerable part in the controversies of a decade, chiefly in the mouths of their critics, seemed to have passed out of current use. Marked divergences had made themselves apparent among those who once bore that name – as in practical politics between Professors Brentano and Schmoller, and with regard to scientific method, between Professors Schmoller and Wagner; while the Liberal and *Fortschritt* parties had begun to manifest a greater interest in social reform. Thus the apparent unity and distinctness of the group of 1872 – then chiefly the unity of protest – had largely disappeared; though most German economists were still dominated by the leading principles of the Eisenach congress. But in 1896–7 in the attack in the German Reichstag, led by the Freiherr von Stumm, upon Professors Schmoller and Wagner, and most of the other teachers of political economy in the country, the use of the term 'Katheder-sozialisten' was once more resorted to as indicating the dangerous character of their teaching, and many explanations were again given of its origin and significance.

[W.J. ASHLEY]

Reprinted from *Palgrave's Dictionary of Political Economy*.

BIBLIOGRAPHY

The best general accounts of the movement are given in the chapters under that head in Emile de Laveleye, *Le socialisme contemporain* (2nd edn, 1883), and John Rae, *Contemporary socialism* (2nd edn, 1891).

The most characteristic writings of the period are perhaps Adolf Wagner, *Rede über die soziale Frage* (1871); Gustav Schmoller, *Ueberei-nige Grundfragen des Rechts und der Volkswirthschaft* (1875), in reply to the attack of the historian Von Treitschke in a pamphlet, *Der Sozialismus und seine Gönner*; and Lujo Brentano, *Das Arbeiterverhältniss gemäss dem heutigen Recht* (1877).

Among the fugitive writings concerning the more recent discussions, may be singled out the article by Professor Hasbach in *Die Zukunft* for 14 August 1897.

Brentano, L. 1877. *Das Arbetierverhältniss gemäss dem heutigen Recht*. Leipzig (Altenburg).

Hasbach, 1897. Article in *Die Zukunft*. 14 August.

Laveleye, E.L. Baron de 1881. *Le socialisme contemporian*. Paris. Trans. G.H. Orpen, London, 1885.

Rae, J. 1891. *Contemporary Socialism*. 2nd edn, London: Sonnenschein.

Schmoller, G. 1875. *Uebereinige Grandfragen des Rechts und der Volkswirthschaft*. Jena: F. Mauke.

Treitschte, H.G. von. 1875. *Der Sozialismus und Gönner*. Berlin: G. Reimer.

Wagner, A. 1871. *Rede über die Soziale Frage*.

socially necessary technique. The typical representation of the problem of choice of technique involves the selection of a desired combination of production methods from a 'book of blue-prints' which contains the set of all available methods. In a competitive economy the cost-minimizing combination of techniques is chosen, and it is this 'efficient' set of techniques which is relevant to the analysis of price determination.

The representation does not accord with the manner in which techniques are invented and introduced. Typically, the entrepreneur does not face a wide range of technological options (and certainly not an indefinitely large range of input combinations). And changes in the method of production most typically incorporate innovations – in other words, rather than turning the pages of the book of blue-prints, new pages are added.

Marx (1867) attempted to capture these processes of technological innovation inherent in technical choice in his concept of the 'socially necessary technique'. The socially necessary technique or 'dominant' technique is that which is used by those producers whose activities constitute the determination of 'normal' costs-of-production and hence, normal prices, which producers and so which technique this might be will differ according to market structure which may in turn be affected by the relationship between technology, entry and competition. In a highly competitive sector in which entry is easy and techniques easily acquired, then most producers will use the socially necessary technique and most pay the same cost of production and receive the same price. In more concentrated sectors, in which entry is limited and access of techniques is difficult or even restricted, then a small group of dominant firms will tend to be price leaders, and it is technique used by these firms which is relevant in analysing the determination of normal cost and normal price.

The technique which is 'dominant' in the determination of prices is not necessarily dominant technologically. A superior technique may be used by a limited number of producers, yielding them 'super-profits', yet be insufficiently generalized in use to affect current price determination.

Conversely, some 'fossils', embodying out-of-date methods, are also used. These are not reproduced since they would yield a rate of return on their supply price lower than the general rate of profits, but they nonetheless yield positive quasi-rents, and are worth retaining so long as there is demand for their services.

Neither 'superior' techniques nor 'fossils' are relevant to the determination of value and distribution.

The idea of socially necessary technique, 'the conditions of production normal for a given society' (Marx, 1867, p. 129) is thus not a technological, but economic concept. It must be related to conditions of competition and accumulation. And in a changing economy it is inevitably imprecise. Nonetheless, Marx's discussion should alert us against a too facile representation of technology, and of the relationship between conditions of production and normal cost of production.

JOHN EATWELL

See also MARXIAN VALUE ANALYSIS.

BIBLIOGRAPHY

Marx, K. 1867. *Capital*, Vol. I. Harmondsworth: Penguin Books, 1976.

social security. Since Bismarck's introduction of social security in Germany in 1891 a large number of countries have adopted social security systems. The growth of social security in the postwar period has been particularly rapid. In some countries, such as the United States, social security has become a major, if not the major fiscal institution. Because of its scale, method of finance, and role in providing insurance, social security may be greatly influencing the performance of a number of economies, particularly with respect to their rates of saving and employment.

This brief description of social security begins by considering its principal functions, rationale, method of finance, and sensitivity to recessions and demographics. This is followed by a discussion of social security's potential impact on savings, labour supply and economic efficiency, and risk sharing. The savings discussion also includes an examination of the relationship of unfunded social security to traditional deficit finance.

PRINCIPAL FUNCTIONS. Social security is primarily involved with financing the period of retirement. Benefit payments are provided to the elderly, typically in the form of annuities which continue until the death of the recipient. In addition to old age annuities, social security systems often provide benefits to the disabled and to surviving spouses and children. These benefits are also typically paid in the form of annuities. The levels of the various social security benefits are often based on both the recipient's need and the amount previously contributed by the recipient to social security.

After old age income support, social security's most important function is the provision of insurance. In some countries, social security's disability and survivor benefits represent the public's primary source of disability and life insurance. By providing benefits in the form of annuities social security also insures against uncertain longevity; relative to receiving benefits in a one-time lump sum, receiving an annuity hedges both the risk of dying prior to spending one's lump-sum benefits as well as the risk of dying after exhausting one's lump-sum benefits.

RATIONALE FOR SOCIAL SECURITY. There are a number of possible explanations for the emergence of social security. One is simply a desire to transfer resources to a particularly needy generation of elderly, albeit at the potential expense of subsequent generations. A second rationale is paternalistic concern by the government that, left to their own devices, households will inadequately save and insure. A third rationale for social security is that the problem of adverse selection precludes the provision of certain types of insurance, particularly annuity and disability insurance, by the private market. A fourth rationale is that social security permits certain intergenerational exchanges and risk sharing arrangements that may be Pareto improving.

While determining whether social security represents a Pareto improvement is quite difficult, one can find evidence, at least in the United States, supporting each of the first three explanations. Social security was initiated in the United States during the Great Depression when the elderly were particularly hard hit by financial reverses; and the postwar dramatic United States reduction in the rate of poverty among the elderly appears largely due to the growth of social security. The paternalistic rationale for social security is supported by evidence of inadequate private saving (Diamond, 1977) and inadequate private purchase of life insurance (Auerbach and Kotlikoff, 1986). And the adverse selection problems in annuity and disability insurance markets are suggested both by theory (Rothschild and Stiglitz, 1976) and by the fact that outside of employer-provided disability insurance and old age pensions there is essentially no private United States market in these important types of insurance.

METHOD OF FINANCE. Social security is generally financed through taxes levied on workers' earnings, part of which may be collected from the employer and the rest from the worker. Social security payroll tax rates currently range from 10 to 25 per cent in most Western economies. In some countries, such as the United States, most workers pay more in social security taxes than they do in federal income taxes and other federal taxes. Since social security benefits received are often only loosely linked to taxes paid, social security also plays a role in redistributing resources. This redistribution is both across generations, intergenerational, as well as within generations, intragenerational.

Redistribution under social security is associated with its method of finance. If social security were financed on a fully funded, individually actuarially fair basis, then each dollar contributed by a worker would be allocated by the government to provide the worker with a dollar's worth of old age annuity and other insurance benefits. In this case the government would have, at any point in time, a trust fund that would be just sufficient to meet all its future insurance obligations arising from the past contributions of all currently living workers and retirees. Dropping the requirement that workers receive back (on an actuarially fair basis) what they pay in, raises the possibility for inter- and intragenerational redistribution and also eliminates the requirement that the trust fund be of the size required for full funding.

Underfunded, rather than fully funded social security systems appear to be the rule in most countries. In the United States, for example, social security is currently essentially unfunded with the Old Age Income, Survivors, and Disability Trust Funds sufficient to cover only a few months of benefits. In contrast, a fully funded trust fund would have assets equal to roughly 30 times annual benefit payments. Rather than pay for current benefits from the principal and investment income of past contributions, unfunded social security systems use current tax contributions to pay for current benefits. The 'pay as you go' method of finance greatly benefits those 'start up' generations of the elderly who are old at social security's initiation. These 'start up' elderly receive old age social security benefits despite having paid little or no social security taxes when young. Initial young and future generations, however, do not receive the same treatment. They pay taxes to social security during their working years and receive benefits in exchange in old age. The present expected value of their tax contributions is likely to be less than the present expected value of their benefits. The reason is that a mature unfunded social security system can only pay, on average, a return on contributions equal to the rate of population plus productivity growth (plus a term of second order). If this return is less than the economy's interest rate, workers contributing to social security will receive a smaller return on their contributions than if they had been allowed to save these contributions and invest them in the economy.

To understand why social security's steady state rate of return equals the sum of the rates of population growth, denoted by m, and productivity growth, denoted by g, consider a two-period model in which individuals work in their first period when young and are retired in their second period. Suppose workers at time t in the economy's steady state contribute a fixed percentage, θ, of their labour earnings, W_t, to social security. When the worker is old he or she will receive benefits at time $t+1$ equal to $\theta W_t(1+m)(1+g)$ in social security benefits, since there are $(1+m)$ workers for every beneficiary in period $t+1$ and the earnings of each worker in period $t+1$ are $(1+g)$ times larger than they were at time t. Note that if the worker in period t had been permitted to save the amount θW_t, the principal plus interest in period $t+1$ on this saving would have been $\theta W_t(1+r)$, where r is the steady state interest rate. Hence, if r exceeds $m+g+mg$ the worker is worse off under social security. This discussion has so far concentrated on social security's redistribution in partial equilibrium and has ignored the possible general equilibrium effects of social security on factor rewards, particularly the wage rate and the interest rate. If unfunded social security depresses long-run savings and capital formation as suggested by Feldstein (1974), it will make capital relatively scarce in comparison with labour and reduce the wage earned by workers and raise the interest rate. This means a further reduction in the welfare of future generations because of social security. Ignoring issues of economic distortions, one can show that if economic losses to young and future generations do arise from unfunded social security, these losses will equal, in present value, the economic gains to initial elderly start up generations. This is not to suggest that social security necessarily makes future generations worse off in improving the lot of the start up elderly. If $m+g+mg$ exceeds r, the introduction of an unfunded social security system can be Pareto improving (Samuelson, 1958), i.e., all generations can benefit from this 'chain letter' system that involves each new generation passing resources to the previous generation.

Unlike a chain letter or Ponzi scheme with a finite number of participants in which the last participants are made worse off, unfunded social security, when $m+g+mg$ exceeds r, can make all participants better off because there are an infinite number of participants, namely all future generations. As long as $m+g+mg$ exceeds r the growth in the number and earnings capacity of the new chain letter participants exceeds the cost of waiting for them to arrive on the scene. Of course, if capital formation is reduced by social security the interest rate will begin to rise. Once r equals $m+g+mg$, further increases in social security are no longer Pareto improving.

SENSITIVITY OF UNFUNDED SOCIAL SECURITY TO RECESSIONS AND DEMOGRAPHICS. As mentioned, under an unfunded social security system current benefits are financed by current tax contributions. Hence, any increase in the number of beneficiaries relative to the number of workers or any decline in the earnings and, thus, tax contributions of workers requires either a reduction in benefit levels or an increase in contribution rates. The adjustments required of social security to changing demographics and economic conditions can be substantial. For example, in the United States the fraction of adults over age 64 is projected to rise from a value of about one-fifth in the 1980s to a value of two-fifths by 2040. To avoid a doubling or more of social security tax rates by the early part of the 21st century, legislation was enacted in 1983 to raise gradually social security's normal age of retirement from 65 to 67 and to accumulate over the period 1985–2010 a huge trust fund that would be available to finance benefits after 2010.

SOCIAL SECURITY AND SAVINGS

A. Savings effects in the Keynesian and Barro models. The impact of social security on savings is quite sensitive to one's theoretical model of saving. In the simplest Keynesian model in which each household consumes the same fraction of its disposable income, transfers from young to old households under social security have no effect on aggregate consumption and aggregate saving (assuming no social security induced changes in aggregate labour earnings).

Another saving model in which social security is not predicted to reduce savings is Barro's (1974) model of intergenerational altruism. In this neoclassical model each household is altruistically linked to all its future descendants. Interestingly, this altruistic linkage to future descendants can arise even if households do not directly care about their future descendants, but simply care about their own children. The fact that their children care in turn about their own children and the grandchildren care about the great grandchildren, etc., is sufficient to establish altruistic linkages to all future descendants. In making current consumption decisions such intergenerationally altruistic households consider the welfare as well as the economic resources of all of their descendants. Indeed, current households effectively act as if they were going to live forever and were maximizing an infinite horizon utility function of the consumption of themselves and all their progeny. The budget constraint in this maximization problem is that the present value of current and future consumption of the household and its descendants (1) equals the household's current net worth, plus (2) the sum of their own and their descendant's human wealth, less (3) the sum of their own and their descendant's present value of tax payments net of transfers made to the government.

Note that if the government redistributes intergenerationally between the current household and its descendants, the infinite horizon budget constraint is unaffected since the present value change in the current household's net taxes will exactly equal minus the present value change in the net taxes of the household's descendants; since the budget constraint involves the sum of the present values of net taxes of the current household and its descendants, the budget constraint is unaltered, and, pari passu, the household's current consumption is unaltered. Thus in the Barro model, unfunded social security's intergenerational redistribution has no affect on current household consumption (ignoring any associated redistribution between different infinite horizon Barro families).

B. Savings effects in the life cycle model. In the life cycle model of saving developed by Modigliani and Brumberg (1954) and Ando and Modigliani (1963), unfunded social security is predicted to reduce savings and, in a closed economy, the capital stock. Simulation studies (Kotlikoff, 1979; Auerbach and Kotlikoff, 1987) suggest that unfunded social security systems of the scale observed in the 1980s in many developed economies could reduce the long-run capital stock of these economies by 20 to 30 per cent, assuming, of course, that these economies adhere to the life cycle model. To date, the results of numerous empirical analyses of social security's impact on savings have been mixed (e.g. Feldstein, 1974; Barro, 1978).

Since the life cycle model has such strong predictions concerning unfunded social security it is worth illustrating this model in some detail. Consider, for simplicity, a two period model in which both the utility and production functions are Cobb–Douglas:

$$U_t = C_{yt}^{\beta} C_{ot+1}^{1-\beta} \tag{1}$$

$$Y_t = K_t^{\alpha} L_t^{1-\alpha} \tag{2}$$

Equation (1) expresses the lifetime utility of a member of generation t as a function of consumption when young, C_{yt}, and consumption when old, C_{ot+1}. The economy's production function relates output per young worker, Y_t, to capital per young worker, K_t, labour per young worker, L_t. L_t is exogenously supplied by each young worker and is measured in units such that $L_t = 1$. We ignore productivity growth here and assume that the population grows at rate n Equation (3) gives the lifetime budget constraint of an individual who is young at time t.

$$C_{yt} + C_{ot+1}/(1 + r_{t+1}) = W_t(1 - \theta_t) + B_{t+1}/(1 + r_{t+1}) \tag{3}$$

where W_t is the wage earned in period t, θ_t is the social security tax rate at time t, B_{t+1} is the social security benefit paid at $t + 1$, and r_{t+1} is the period $t + 1$ return on savings. Equation (3) states that the present value of consumption equals the present value of labour earnings. It can also be expressed as:

$$C_{ot+1} = A_{t+1}(1 + r_{t+1}) + B_{t+1}, \tag{3'}$$

where A_{t+1}, the assets (net wealth) of the old at time $t + 1$, equals the saving done by these elderly when they were young, $W_t(1-\theta_t) - C_{yt}$. Maximization of (1) subject to (3) yields consumption demands. In particular, $C_{yt} = \beta[w_t(1-\theta_t) + B_{t+1}/(1+r_{t+1})$, and the supply of capital by the household sector, A_{t+1}, can be written as:

$$A_{t+1} = W_t(1-\theta_t) - \beta[W_t(1-\theta_t) + B_{t+1}/(1+r_{t+1})] \quad (4)$$

Since the social security system is assumed to be financed on a 'pay as you go' bais, social security revenues per young worker must equal benefit payments per young worker:

$$B_t = \theta_t W_t(1+n) \quad (5)$$

Using (5), rewrite (4) as:

$$A_{t+1} = W_t(1-\theta_t) - \beta[W_t(1-\theta_t) + \theta_{t+1} W_{t+1} \times (1+n)/(1+r_{t+1})] \quad (4')$$

Profit maximization by representative firms in the economy implies the following expressions relating factor demands to factor returns:

$$W_t = (1-\alpha)K_t^{\alpha} \quad (6)$$

$$r_t = \alpha K_t^{\alpha-1} \quad (7)$$

The condition for equilibrium in the market for capital is given by:

$$K_t = A_t/(1+n), \quad (8)$$

where (8) reflects the fact that K_t is capital per young worker and A_t is assets per old retiree.

Substituting for W_t, r_t, and A_{t+1} in (4′) from (6), (7), and (8) yields a nonlinear first order difference equation in K_t. This equation determines the transition path of the economy's capital stock and, via (6) and (7), the general equilibrium changes in the wage and interest rate. Denoting steady state values by ˆ , the steady state value of $\hat{K}$ is implicitly defined by:

$$(1+n)\hat{K} = \hat{W}(1-\hat{\theta}) - \beta\left[\hat{W} - \frac{(\hat{r}-n)\hat{\theta}\hat{W}}{1+\hat{r}}\right], \text{ or:} \quad (9)$$

$$(1+n)\hat{K}^{1-\alpha} = (1-\alpha)\left[(1-\hat{\theta}) - \beta\right.$$

$$(1+n)\hat{K} = \hat{W}(1-\hat{\theta}) - \beta\left[\hat{W} - \frac{(\hat{r}-n)\hat{\theta}\hat{W}}{1+\hat{r}}\right], \text{ or:} \quad (9)$$

Differentiating (9′) at $\hat{\theta} = 0$ yields:

$$(1+n)\frac{\partial \hat{K}^{1-\alpha}}{\partial \theta} = -(1-\alpha)\left[1 + \beta\frac{(n-\alpha\hat{K}^{\alpha-1})}{1+\alpha\hat{K}^{\alpha-1}}\right] \quad (10)$$

i.e., introducing unfunded social security reduces ('cowds out') the steady state capital stock.

The intuitive explanation for this crowding out of savings and the capital stock is as follows: If, starting at time t, B_t is raised from zero to a positive value $\bar{B}$, the consumption of the elderly at time t, $C_{0,t}$, rises by $\bar{B}$ since the marginal consumption propensity of the elderly is unity. Ignoring for the moment changes through time in benefit levels, tax rates, and factor rewards, the present value loss to the initial young from this policy is $\bar{B}(r-n)/(1+r)$, since they pay $\bar{B}$ when young, but receive $\bar{B}(1+n)$ when old. The young, whose marginal propensity to consume is less than unity, will reduce their consumption by a fraction of this present value loss. Hence, in the initial period in which social security is introduced each elderly individual increases his or her consumption, measured per young person, by $\bar{B}/(1+n)$, while each young person reduces his or her consumption by a fraction of $\bar{B}(r-n)/(1+r)$. Total private consumption in the initial period therefore increases, and saving is crowded out.

While each future generation suffers a loss in present value of $\bar{B}(r-n)/(1+r)$, at any point in time there will always be future generations who have yet to arrive on the scene and experience this resource loss. Thus, at any point in time the initial period increase in private consumption will not yet have been fully offset by reduced consumption of future generations. This explains why the economy ends up in a new steady state with a permanently lower stock of savings.

Adding general equilibrium effects to this partial equilibrium story only reinforces the intergenerational transfer away from future generations. As the capital stock is crowded out the wage falls and the interest rate rises. Those generations who are elderly when interest rates rise benefit from the greater return on their savings, while the corresponding young and future generations are worse off because the concomitant fall in their wages is more detrimental to their economic welfare than the reduced price of old age consumption reflected in the higher interest rate. In the case of a two-period model in which the social security tax rate is levied at time t at a given rate and kept constant thereafter, the first generation of young workers benefits from the general equilibrium changes in factor returns; since the crowding out takes one period to get under way, the interest rate is high when they are old, but the wage received by this first set of young workers is unaffected by the introduction of social security. In contrast, generations born after the first generation, while benefiting from higher interest rates, receive lower wages during their initial working period.

C. The relationship of unfunded social security to traditional deficit finance. The 'crowding out' of capital has often been associated with deficit finance. It is worthwhile, therefore, in the context of this simple model to point out that unfunded social security could easily be run as an explicit government debt policy. Suppose that at the initiation of social security the government chooses to label its initial benefit payments as transfer payments, but labels its initial and subsequent social security receipts from young workers as 'borrowing' from young workers rather than as 'taxes'. In addition, the government labels benefit payments, with the exception of those made in the initial period, as 'principal plus interest payments' on the government's borrowing. Let the government also levy a special tax (possibly transfer) on each elderly generation reflecting the fact that social security benefits do not correspond precisely to tax payments when young plus interest.

With the new language exactly the same model, after the initial period, can be described in the following five equations:

$$C_{o,t} = A_t(1+r_t) - T_t \quad (11)$$

$$C_{y,t} + C_{o,t+1}/(1+r_{t+1}) = W_t - T_{t+1}/(1+r_{t+1}) \quad (12)$$

$$K_{t+1} = [(W_t - C_{y,t}) - D_t]/(1+n) \quad (13)$$

$$T_t = \Theta_t W_t(1+r_{t+1}) - \Theta_{t+1} W_{t+1}(1+n) \quad (14)$$

$$D_t = \Theta_t W_t \quad (15)$$

where T_t is the special old age tax, and D_t is the stock of official government debt owed to the public by the social security system. A_t is still private assets, but A_t now equals $W_{t-1} - C_{y,t-1}$ rather than $W_{t-1}(1-\Theta_{t-1}) - C_{y,t-1}$, and capital per retiree equals assets per retiree, A_t, less debt per retiree, D_t. Comparison of the above five equations with equations (3), (3′), (4), (5), and (8) shows that the economy's real behaviour is not altered by the relabelling. However, the relabelling makes explicit the debt policy associated with running unfunded social security; i.e., the relabelling increases from zero to D_t the level of officially reported debt in period t.

For the United States such a change in the labelling of social security taxes and benefits would have enormous implications for the level of government debt reported to the public. In this case, the amount of additional government debt that would show up on the United States books equals the sum over all cohorts of the accumulated (at historic interest rates) amount of social security taxes paid less benefits received. Formulae presented by Kotlikoff (1979) suggest that this number for 1986 could be as large as \$8 trillion (30 × social security tax revenues), which is more than 4.5 times larger than the 1986 official stock of United States debt. Calculations of this kind should make one wary of relying on official government debt numbers as indicators of the government's true policy with respect to intergenerational redistribution.

SOCIAL SECURITY, LABOUR SUPPLY AND ECONOMIC EFFICIENCY. Social security can influence labour supply both through income and substitution effects. The transfers to start up generations represent potentially large windfalls that could induce early retirement, assuming that leisure is a normal good, i.e., leisure increases with income. In addition, social security's payroll tax may reduce work incentives leading individuals to substitute more leisure for consumption especially if future social security benefits are not linked at the margin to tax contributions. A third potential inducement to leisure is the earnings testing of social security benefits that occurs in some countries. Earnings testing refers to the fact that social security benefits may be reduced if recipients earn too much. In the United States social security recipients have often been permitted only to earn small amounts, beyond which they lose as much as 50 cents in benefits for every dollar they earn, until their benefits are exhausted. This earnings test effectively constitutes a 50 per cent marginal tax rate which, when combined with federal and state income and sales taxes, may leave many recipients in very high effective marginal tax brackets.

The postwar period in the United States saw a very considerable acceleration of the trend towards early retirement. For example, between 1950 and 1985 the labour force participation rate of males 65 and older declined from 45 per cent to 16 per cent. A number of studies (e.g. Boskin and Hurd, 1984) suggest that the United States social security system is in large part responsible for this decline in the labour supply of the elderly. The size of effective marginal labour taxation arising from social security is critically important for determining potential economic inefficiencies caused by social security. As is well known the degree of economic inefficiency associated with the distortions from taxation rises with the square of the tax rate (ignoring second best considerations). Thus if social security's effective marginal tax on labour supply is 10 per cent and the effective marginal tax from other forms of taxation is 30 per cent, social security may be almost doubling the excess burden (economic inefficiency) arising from taxing labour. The extent to which social security's payroll tax raises effective labour taxes depends on the linkage between tax payments and benefits received and how that linkage is perceived by workers. In some countries there is a strong link between marginal benefits and marginal taxes, but the formulae determining this linkage are so complex that workers are not likely to understand the degree of linkage and may simply assume it is zero.

Even if marginal linkage were correctly understood there would still be considerable labour supply distortion in many instances. For example the United States in the postwar period has permitted wives (husbands) to receive dependent and survivor benefits based on their husbands' (wives') social security contributions if such benefits exceed what the wife (husband) could receive based on her (his) own history of contributions. This means that spouses who will elect to collect benefits as dependents or survivors receive nothing back at the margin for their own contributions to social security. For such spouses their effective marginal tax on labour earnings includes the entire social security payroll tax. For primary married earners the failure in many cases of social security to require additional contributions to pay for survivor and dependent benefits means that such earners may face negative effective taxes from social security at the margin since their additional contributions mean additional benefits both to themselves, their spouse, and often their children. Parenthetically, the fact that social security often provides dependent and survivor benefits to spouses and children without requiring additional contributions from the worker means that married couples with only one working spouse may fare much better under social security than either two earner couples or single individuals. In the United States the difference in lifetime treatment of one earner and two earner couples by social security has often been of the order of a year's earnings; i.e., social security's intragenerational redistribution has often been quite substantial.

SOCIAL SECURITY AND RISK SHARING. Social security's improvement in risk sharing may make the introduction of a funded and possibly even an unfunded social security system Pareto efficient. In addition to potentially improving annuity and disability insurance arrangements, social security may play a role in pooling the risk of the return on human as well as non-human capital across generations. Finally, social security may be pooling economic risks, such as the risks of recession, across generations in ways that are not available to private markets. Social security's improvement in insurance may not only affect the efficiency of risk pooling, but it may also have implications for saving. In the absence of such insurance precautionary savings might be considerably larger (Kotlikoff, Shoven and Spivak, 1986).

The risks associated with uncertain longevity which are hedged with annuities can be quite substantial. Kotlikoff and Spivak (1981) suggest that risk averse older individuals with no other source of annuity insurance might be willing to give up as much as a third to one half of their economic resources in order to gain access to an actuarially fair annuity market. While risk sharing within families may be providing a considerable amount of implicit annuity insurance, social security has undoubtedly improved annuity insurance considerably.

Insurance for disability appears particularly difficult for the private market to insure since certain types of medical conditions, such as back pain and fatigue, associated with ageing cannot be objectively identified. The government can insure disability without subjecting itself to widespread fraudulent claims by earnings testing disability benefits. Such earnings testing may be quite difficult for private insurance companies since private companies, unlike the government, do not have access to earnings information. Hence, the government may be the most efficient provider of disability insurance, and social security's earnings tests may be viewed as the deductible for this type of insurance (Diamond and Mirrlees, 1978).

Under pay as you go social security unexpected declines (increases) in labour earnings and social security tax revenues may lead to reductions in benefits. In this case retirees will share some of the human capital risk of younger workers. In addition, other elements of the tax structure may spread the riskiness of retirees' returns to their savings to workers. Thus if there is a consumption tax in place, reduced capital income means less revenues from retirees and higher required revenues from young workers. Merton (1983) has shown that by appropriately structuring social security and other elements of the tax structure, the government can potentially efficiently diversify human and non-human capital risk across young workers and old retirees.

Another aspect of social security's insurance provision is the pooling of risks across generations. One interpretation of the growth of unfunded social security in the United States in the postwar period is that the government elected to redistribute to a generation that had suffered from the depression in the 1930s and had made significant contributions to the nation during World War II. As described above, the burden for paying for these transfers is likely to fall on future generations both in the form of receiving a lower than market return on their social security contributions and in the form of receiving lower wages in their working years because of the crowding out of the capital stock. Clearly, the sharing of risks of wars and recessions across generations cannot be accomplished by the private insurance market if only for the simple reason that future generations are not yet alive to sign private insurance contracts.

LAURENCE J. KOTLIKOFF

See also AGEING POPULATIONS; INTERGENERATIONAL MODELS; LIFE-CYCLE HYPOTHESIS; PAYROLL TAXES, TRANSFER PAYMENTS.

BIBLIOGRAPHY

Ando, A. and Modigliani, F. 1963. The 'life cycle' hypothesis of saving: aggregate implications and tests. *American Economic Review* 53, March, 55–84.

Auerbach, A.J. and Kotlikoff, L.G. 1986. Life insurance of the elderly: adequacy and determinants. In *Work, Health, and Income Among the Elderly*, ed. Gary Burtless.

Auerbach, A.J. and Kotlikoff, L.J. 1987. *Dynamic Fiscal Policy*. Cambridge: Cambridge University Press.

Barro, R.J. 1974. Are government bonds net wealth? *Journal of Political Economy* 82(6), November/December, 1095–118.

Barro, R.J. 1978. Social security and private saving – evidence from the U.S. time series. In *Studies in Social Security and Retirement Policy*. Washington, DC: American Enterprise Institute.

Boskin, J.M. and Hurd, M. 1984. The effects of social security on retirement in the early 1970s. *Quarterly Journal of Economics* 99(4), November, 767–90.

Diamond, P.A. 1977. A framework for social security 'analysis'. *Journal of Public Economics* 8, 275–98.

Diamond, P.A. and Mirrlees, J.A. 1978. A model of social insurance with variable retirement. *Journal of Public Economics* 10(3), 295–336.

Feldstein, M. 1974. Social security, induced retirement, and aggregate capital accumulation. *Journal of Political Economy* 82(5), Part 2, September/October, 905–26.

Kotlikoff, L.J. 1979. Social security and equilibrium capital intensity. *Quarterly Journal of Economics* 93(2), May, 233–54.

Kotlikoff, L.J., Shoven, J.B. and Spivak, A. 1986. The effect of annuity insurance on savings and inequality. *Journal of Labor Economics* 4(3), Part 2, July, 183–207.

Kotlikoff, L.J. and Spivak, A. 1981. The family as an incomplete annuities market. *Journal of Political Economy* 89(2), April, 372–91.

Merton, R.C. 1983. On the role of social security as a means for efficient risk-bearing in an economy where human capital is not tradeable. In *Financial Aspects of the U.S. Pension System*, ed. Z. Bodie and J.B. Shoven, Chicago: University of Chicago Press.

Modigliani, F. and Brumberg, R. 1954. Utility analysis and the consumption function: an interpretation of cross-section data. In *Post-Keynesian Economics*, ed. K.K. Kurihara, New Brunswick, NJ: Rutgers University Press.

Rothschild, M. and Stiglitz, J. 1976. Equilibrium in competitive insurance markets: an essay on the economics of imperfect information. *Quarterly Journal of Economics* 90(4), November, 630–49.

Samuelson, P.A. 1958. An exact consumption-loan model of interest with or without the social contrivance of money. *Journal of Political Economy* 66(6), December, 467–82.

social welfare function. 1. The old welfare economics originated by Pigou (1920) was constructed on the supposition of interpersonally comparable and cardinal welfares and was meant to help improve human well-being by prescribing rational economic policy. Therefore it was natural (if not of necessity) to aim at maximizing the Benthamite sum of individual welfares in pursuit of socially optimal resource allocation. In the 1930s, harsh ordinalist criticism against the epistemological basis of Pigovian welfare economics was raised by Robbins (1932). Serious doubts were cast on the scientific possibility of verifying, for example, whether the welfare Mr A obtained from a state x was more (or less) than the welfare Mr B obtained from a state y. Likewise, doubts were raised whether an economist *qua* economist had any qualification in judging aggregate welfare improvement or detriment.

The immediate response to this criticism (other than a few lame rebuttals) was to reformulate welfare economics on the basis of ordinal as well as interpersonally non-comparable information only. This step, which was followed, for example, by Lerner (1934) and Hicks (1939), brought about a resurgence of Pareto's (1913) earlier contribution, namely, the characterization and pursuit of Pareto optimal resource allocation. Needless to say, this was a useful preliminary step. But the real problem was how far we could go with this ordinalist Paretian basis in resuming Pigou's agenda, that is, to design economic policy in quest of improvement in human well-being.

Note that, behind the concept of Pareto optimality, there lies what one may call the Pareto principle, to the effect that a change from a state x to a state y is socially good if at least one individual is thereby made better off and that nobody is made worse off in exchange. Note also that *every* economic policy would inevitably favour some individuals at the cost of disfavouring others with a result that there would be virtually *no* real situation of substance where the Pareto principle *per se* could be directly applied. Left to themselves, therefore, the Pareto principle and Pareto optimality constitute only a small step in guiding actual economic policy.

Two distinct attempts were made in order to rectify this unsatisfactory status of welfare economics. The first was the introduction of *compensation criteria* by Kaldor (1939), Hicks (1940), Scitovsky (1941), Samuelson (1950) and Little (1950). The gist of this approach was to expand the applicability of the Pareto principle by introducing hypothetical compensation payments between gainers and losers. (See, e.g., Suzumura (1980) for analytical details.) Another was the introduction of the *social welfare function* by Bergson (1938) and Samuelson (1947). It started from a belief that to examine the logical consequences of various value judgements, to say nothing of whose ethical belief they represented, whether or not they were shared by economists, or how they were generated, was a legitimate and important exercise of economic analysis. A function which characterized some ethical belief, which was required only to be *rational* in the sense of enabling complete and transitive welfare judgements over alternative social states, was introduced and christened a social welfare function. In particular, a social welfare function which judges in concordance with the Pareto principle if the latter does judge may be called a Paretian (or individualistic) social welfare function.

2. To make matters more transparent and precise, let us consider a society consisting of $n(\geqslant 2)$ individuals. Let R_i denote the preference ordering of individual $i \in N := \{1, 2, \ldots, n\}$, viz., a complete and transitive binary relation on the set X of all social states such that xR_iy for $x, y \in X$ implies that individual i regards x to be at least as good as y. Let $P(R_i)$ denote the asymmetric part of R_i, which is defined by $xP(R_i)y$ if and only if (xR_iy and not yR_ix) for all $x, y \in X$.

Let R denote a rational ethical belief, the logical implication of which an economist would like to analyse, such that xRy if and only if x is judged to be at least as good for society as y is. A social welfare function is nothing other than a numerical representation u of R, viz., $u(x) \geqslant u(y)$ if and only if xRy, where $x, y \in X$. Clearly, a social welfare function is an ordinal concept in that any positive transformation of u is a social welfare function if u is.

R is said to be Paretian (or individualistic) if

(1) xR_iy for all $i \in N$ implies xRy and

(2) xR_iy for all $i \in N$ and $xP(R_i)y$ for some $i \in N$ implies $xP(R)y$, where $P(R)$ denotes the asymmetric part of R. A Paretian social welfare function is a numerical representation of a Paretian R.

3. Concerning the logical basis of the Bergson-Samuelson social welfare function, there are three subtle problems:

(a) Given an ethical ordering R, does there exist a social welfare function representing it?

(b) Given a profile of individual preference orderings $(R_1, R_2, \ldots, R_n)$, does there exist an ethical ordering R which satisfies (1) and (2)?

(c) Does there exist a reasonable process or rule through which an ethical ordering R is formed from a profile of individual preference orderings $(R_1, R_2, \ldots, R_n)$?

The problem (a) may be answered affirmatively. We only refer the reader to, for example, Debreu (1959), as the problem (a) does not seem to be of crucial importance from the welfare-theoretic viewpoint.

The problem (b) may also be answered affirmatively along the line suggested by Suzumura (1976) and Arrow (1983). Let R_N be defined by xR_Ny if and only if xR_iy for all $i \in N$, where $x, y \in X$, viz., $R_N := \bigcap_{i \in N} R_i$. Let $P(R_N)$ denote the asymmetric part of R_N. Then the requirements (a) and (b) boil down to (a^*) $R_N \subset R$, and (b^*) $P(R_N) \subset P(R)$. R_i being an ordering for each $i \in N$, R_N is a quasi-ordering, viz., transitive. Therefore there exists an ordering R satisfying (a^*) and (b^*) by virtue of Szpilrajn's (1930) extension theorem.

It was Arrow (1951) who first posed the problem (c). The negative answer he gave, which has been called Arrow's general impossibility theorem, initiated a long (and somewhat confused) controversy among welfare economists, as exemplified by Little (1952), Kemp and Asimakopulos (1952), Bergson (1954), Arrow (1963), Samuelson (1967), Kemp and Ng (1976), Pollak (1979), Samuelson (1981) and Arrow (1983).

4. In essence, what Arrow (1951) has established is the following. Let F be a function which maps each profile of individual preference orderings $(R_1, R_2, \ldots, R_n)$ into a social ethical ordering. In words, F is a process or rule, through which individual preferences are amalgamated into a social ethical ordering. In order for this rule to be reasonable, F should satisfy several conditions.

Firstly, it is desirable that F be robust enough to accommodate all logically possible variations of individual preference orderings (*Universal Applicability*).

Secondly, it is desirable that F be parsimonious in informational requirements. Otherwise the preference aggregation mechanism might require each individual to submit unnecessarily detailed private information, viz., it might infringe upon individual privacy. One way to formalize this desideratum is as follows. Let S be a subset of X. In order to make social ethical judgements on S, it is indispensable to collect information about individual preferences over S unless one wishes to neglect individual wishes altogether. If only this much information collection is needed in order to arrive at social ethical judgements on S through F, we say that F economizes informational input, maximally at that. Formally we require the following (*Independence of Irrelevant Alternatives*): Let $(R_1, R_2, \ldots, R_n)$ and $(R'_1, R'_2, \ldots, R'_n)$ be two profiles such that $R_i \cap (S \times S) = R'_i \cap (S \times S)$ for all $i \in N$. Then $R \cap (S \times S) = R' \cap (S \times S)$, where $R = F(R_1, R_2, \ldots, R_n)$ and $R' = F(R'_1, R'_2, \ldots, R'_n)$.

Thirdly, it is desirable that F respect the *(Weak) Pareto Principle*: For each profile of individual preference orderings $(R_1, R_2, \ldots, R_n)$, $\bigcap_{i \in N} P(R_i) \subset P(R)$, where $R = F(R_1, R_2, \ldots, R_n)$.

Arrow's general impossibility theorem asserts that every F which satisfies Universal Applicability, Independence of Irrelevant Alternatives and Weak Pareto Principle must admit a *dictator*, i.e., an individual whose strict preferences are always complied with by society. See Arrow (1963) and Sen (1970) for more details.

5. From this it should be clear that Arrow's F is a quite different animal from a social welfare function à la Bergson and Samuelson. Not a little confusion ensued, however, partly because Arrow (1951) christened his F a social welfare function. To get rid of this terminological intricacy, let us follow Kemp and Asimakopulos (1952) and call F a *constitution*.

What is the substantial impact of Arrow's negative result on Paretian welfare economics? Little (1952), Bergson (1954), Samuelson (1967; 1981) and others repeatedly contended that Arrow's theorem has nothing to do with Paretian welfare economics. Instead they exported Arrow from economics to politics and regarded his impossibility theorem on the existence of a constitution as the first fundamental contribution to mathematical politics. The alleged watershed between welfare economics and mathematical politics was identified in between the *fixed profile approach* à la Bergson and Samuelson and the *multiple profile approach* à la Arrow and his followers: In welfare economics individuals are identified as the possessors of the given preferences, whereas mathematical politics is concerned with the workability of alternative constitutions in the face of diversified opinions which individuals may possibly hold.

This clear-cut separation between welfare economics and mathematical politics (and the concomitant export of Arrovian social choice theory from the former to the latter) would conclude a rather futile controversy unless it could be shown that there were fixed profile analogues of Arrow's impossibility theorem. Kemp and Ng (1976), Pollak (1979) and others proved that, even if there exists only one profile of individual preference orderings, its aggregation into a social ethical ordering is possible only by admitting the existence of a dictator, provided that several conditions – literally translating Arrow's conditions into the fixed profile framework – are imposed.

One condition for this fixed-profile impossibility theorem, corresponding to the Independence of Irrelevant Alternatives, seems as Samuelson (1981) pointed out to be quite insidious. Called *Independence + Neutrality** by Pollak (1979) it requires that: if xRy[resp. $xP(R)y$] and $\{(zR_iw$ if and only if $xR_iy)$ and $(wR_iz$ if and only if $yR_ix)\}$ for all $i \in N$, then zRw[resp. $zP(R)w$]. To extract an unpalatable implication of this condition, let there be two selfish chocolate-lovers and 100 chocolates. Consider three alternative distributions $x = (100, 0)$, $y = (99, 1)$ and $z = (0, 100)$ in an obvious notation. Clearly, we have $xP(R_1)y$, $yP(R_1)z$, $xP(R_1)z$, $z(P_2)y$, $yP(R_2)x$ and $zP(R_2)x$. If, in this case, we somehow believe that $yP(R)x$ should be the case, then we are forced by the condition in question to accept that $zP(R)y$ and $zP(R)x$, which is indeed hard to swallow.

Despite the formal validity of the single-profile impossibility theorem, therefore, the status of the Bergson–Samuelson social welfare function seems to be logically impeccable.

6. Two concluding remarks are appropriate. First, the genesis of the social welfare function is sometimes traced as far back as to Pareto (1913) by, for example, Chipman (1975). True enough Pareto was remarkably ahead of his time, and sympathetic eyes may well catch the glimpse of social welfare function in Pareto (1913). Nevertheless it would be fair to say that, without Bergson (1938) and Samuelson (1947), the concept would not have become the central piece of modern welfare economics. (See also Samuelson, 1981 and Bergson, 1983.) Secondly, the informational basis of social welfare function may be strengthened with an interesting restriction on the admissible forms of social welfare function. Interested readers are referred to Harsanyi (1955) and Pattanaik (1968), who discussed a justification of the Benthamite social welfare function along this line.

KOTARO SUZUMURA

See also ARROW'S THEOREM; SOCIAL CHOICE; WELFARE ECONOMICS.

BIBLIOGRAPHY

Arrow, K.J. 1951. *Social Choice and Individual Values*. Cowles Commission Monograph No. 12; 2nd edn, New York: Wiley, 1963.

Arrow, K.J. 1983. Contributions to welfare economics. In *Paul Samuelson and Modern Economic Theory*, ed. E.C. Brown and R.M. Solow, New York: McGraw-Hill.

Barone, E. 1908. Il Ministro della Produzione nello stato collectivista. *Giornale degli economisti*, September. Trans. as 'The ministry of production in the collectivist state' in *Collectivist Economic Planning*, ed. F.A. von Hayek, London: Routledge, 1935.

Bergson, A. 1938. A reformulation of certain aspects of welfare economics. *Quarterly Journal of Economics* 52(2), February, 310–34.

Bergson, A. 1954. On the concept of social welfare. *Quarterly Journal of Economics* 68, May, 233–52.

Bergson, A. 1983. Pareto on social welfare. *Journal of Economic Literature* 21(1), March, 40–46.

Chipman, J.S. 1975. The Paretian heritage. *Cahiers Vilfredo Pareto: Revue européene des sciences sociales* 14, June, 65–171.

Debreu, G. 1959 *Theory of Value: an axiomatic analysis of economic equilibrium*. Cowles Foundation Monograph No. 17, New York: Wiley.

Harsanyi, J.C. 1955. Cardinal welfare, individualistic ethics, and interpersonal comparisons of utility. *Journal of Political Economy* 63, August, 309–21.

Hicks, J.R. 1939. The foundations of welfare economics. *Economic Journal* 49, December, 696–712.

Hicks, J.R. 1940. The valuation of social income. *Economica* 7, May, 105–24.

Kaldor, N. 1939. Welfare propositions in economics and interpersonal comparisons of utility. *Economic Journal* 49, September, 549–52.

Kemp, M.C. and Asimakopulos, A. 1952. A note on 'social welfare functions' and cardinal utility. *Canadian Journal of Economics and Political Science* 18, May, 195–200.

Kemp, M.C. and Ng, Y.K. 1976. On the existence of social welfare functions, social orderings and social decision functions. *Economica* 43, February, 59–66.

Lange, O. 1942. The foundations of welfare economics. *Econometrica* 10(3–4), July–October, 215–28.

Lerner, A.P. 1934. The concept of monopoly and the measurement of monopoly power. *Review of Economic Studies* 1, June, 157–75.

Little, I.M.D. 1950. *A Critique of Welfare Economics*. 2nd edn, London: Oxford University Press, 1957.

Little, I.M.D. 1952. Social choice and individual values. *Journal of Political Economy* 60, October, 422–32.

Pareto, V. 1913. Il massimo di utilità per una collettivita in Sociologia. *Giornale degli economisti e rivista di statistica*, April.

Pattanaik, P.K. 1968. Risk, impersonality and the social welfare function. *Journal of Political Economy* 75, November–December, 1152–69.

Pigou, A.C. 1920. *The Economics of Welfare*. London: Macmillan.

Pollak, R.A. 1979. Bergson–Samuelson social welfare functions and the theory of social choice. *Quarterly Journal of Economics* 93(1), February, 73–90.

Robbins, L. 1932. *An Essay on the Nature and Significance of Economic Science*. 2nd edn, London: Macmillan, 1935.

Samuelson, P.A. 1947. *Foundations of Economic Analysis*. Cambridge, Mass.: Harvard University Press.

Samuelson, P.A. 1950. Evaluation of real national income. *Oxford Economic Papers* 2(7), January, 1–29.

Samuelson, P.A. 1967. Arrow's mathematical politics. In *Human Values and Economic Policy*, ed. S. Hook, New York: New York University Press.

Samuelson, P.A. 1981. Bergsonian welfare economics. In *Economic Welfare and the Economics of Soviet Socialism*, ed. S. Rosefielde, New York: Cambridge University Press.

Scitovsky, T. 1941. A note on welfare propositions in economics. *Review of Economic Studies* 9, November, 77–88.

Sen, A.K. 1970. *Collective Choice and Social Welfare*. San Francisco: Holden-Day.

Suzumura, K. 1976. Remarks on the theory of collective choice. *Economica* 43, November, 381–90.

Suzumura, K. 1980. On distributional value judgements and piecemeal welfare criteria. *Economica* 47, May, 125–39.

Szpilrajn, E. 1930. Sur l'extension de l'ordre partiel. *Fundamenta mathematicae*.

Sohmen, Egon (1930–1977). Born in Linz, Austria, on 1 June 1930 and died in Heidelberg, Federal Republic of Germany, on 8 March 1977. He was educated at the Universities of Vienna, Kansas and Tübingen, and at the Massachusetts Institute of Technology, from which he received a doctorate in economics in 1958. He taught economics at Yale University from 1958 to 1961, at the University of Saarlandes in Saarbrücken from 1961 to 1969, and at Heidelberg University from 1969 to his death. Sabbatical leaves were spent at the University of Minnesota in 1963–4, and at the Smithsonian Institution in Washington, DC, in the spring of 1975.

Sohmen played a significant part in the 1960s in making the case for flexible exchange rates respectable. He wrote widely on the subject, attacking the Bretton Woods system and insisting that free floating would produce exchange rates that approached equilibrium continuously, as opposed to fixed-rate systems with their encouragement of speculation, wide departures from equilibrium and ultimate necessities for parity changes. With the adoption of floating rates in 1973, he turned his attention to other problems in economic theory with emphasis on competitive markets.

CHARLES P. KINDLEBERGER

SELECTED WORKS

A complete bibliography of Sohmen's work is contained in a volume of essays in his memory, edited by J.S. Chipman and C.P. Kindleberger, *Flexible Exchange Rates and the Balance of Payments* (Amsterdam: North-Holland, 1980). The chief items are:

1961. *Flexible Exchange Rates*. Chicago: University of Chicago Press. Revised edn, 1969.

1964. *International Monetary Problems and the Foreign Exchanges*. Special Papers in International Economics, Princeton: International Finance Section.

1966. *The Theory of Forward Exchange*. Princeton Studies in International Finance, Princeton: International Finance Section.

1976. *Allokationstheorie und Wirtschaftspolitik*. Tübingen: J.C. Mohr (Paul Siebeck).

solidarity. The word solidarity expresses the relations of mutual dependence existing between the individual members of one and the same whole. Thus, in biology we speak of the solidarity between the organs of the same body, – between the functions of the brain, for instance, and those of the heart. Thus also in jurisprudence there is said to be solidarity between persons responsible for the same debt. Solidarity may exist not only in the order of co-existence, but in the order of succession; thus, in history there is solidarity between the present and the past generation.

This theory of solidarity has for some years held an important place in sociology, economics, and philosophy – it has even become the motto of a new school which has gathered its adherents, by a rare coincidence, both among Christian socialists and positivist and evolutionist socialists. Auguste Comte exemplified the subject as 'the connection of each to all others under many different aspects, so as to render the feeling of social solidarity extending to all time and in all places instinctively familiar' (*Discours sur l'esprit positif*). But long before him St Paul, addressing not only the church but the whole human race, had uttered the noble sentence, 'We all are members of one body' – a speech in itself the noblest illustration of the solidarity of the race of man.

The discovery by science of order, under very different aspects, has given examples how far these declarations are founded on fact, for instance, in political economy in the question of the division of labour. It is obvious, also, that the larger part of the great recent inventions – railways, telegraphs, telephones, and, above all, of modern journalism, tend to increase continually 'these relations of mutual dependence' which exist between men, and make them vibrate throughout the universe in the community of the same emotions, causing economic and political crises to be as contagious as epidemics.

The 'school of solidarity' believes that this growing interdependence of individuals and peoples is a harmonic law, and that the solution of the social question must be sought in the continual development of this solidarity, especially in cooperation in all its forms, since cooperation, with its motto 'Each for all, and all for each', is only the practical application of solidarity. Some objections, however, may be made to this doctrine. At first it seems that solidarity appears as a simple *fact*, devoid of all moral value and often even opposed to our ideas of justice. For instance, nothing can appear more unjust than that solidarity which makes the innocent suffer for the guilty, and visits the sins of the fathers on the children, or that which binds the destiny of the bee to that of the drone, of the industrious to that of the parasite; and almost justifies the severe remark, 'the only solidarity discoverable in the world is that of mutual exploitation'. The reply to this is that, even as a simple fact, solidarity testifies to the unity of the human species, its common origin and its common destiny, and compels our attention to all that happens to our fellow-creatures, whether fortunate or not, since all that concerns them concerns us. Thus, the certainty of contagious disease obliges the rich to interest themselves in the question of dwellings for the poor, to construct workmen's houses, to impose laws with regard to unhealthy dwellings, etc. Again, the feeling of the solidarity of nations, from the point of view of their economic interests, is the principal check on war.

But solidarity will gain a high moral value when it is understood, accepted, and desired by men, when it becomes the basis of *duty*, and when men, instead of resigning themselves to it as to a fatality, endeavour to realize freely that 'Moral good will then be the desire to be and to behave as members of a common humanity. Moral evil will then be the desire to isolate ourselves and to keep separate from the body of which we all are members' (C. Secrétan, *Civilisation et Croyance*). Now this is exactly the course of evolution; history shows us solidarity becoming free and voluntary, gradually separating itself from the 'drift of circumstance'. In primitive society solidarity reigns – a solidarity imposed by the accidents of nature or of birth. For example, all the members of the Roman *Gens*, or of the clan, were responsible for all offences committed or all debts contracted by one of them, and the inheritance of this was obligatory on the heir. The necessity of contending with the Nile floods compels all the inhabitants to Egypt of solidarity in labour and cultivation. The struggle against natural forces obliges weak individuals to combine – 'Nature commands either solidarity or death' (Metchnikoff, *Les Grands Fleuves Historiques*). But little by little, and in proportion as men become more powerful, the individuals incline to separate from the primitive collectivism: in fact, as regards offences, each one now answers only for himself. Men would proceed rapidly to absolute individualism if the feeling of human solidarity did not fortunately stop this dispersion by bringing them back by means of the thousand forms of association and insurance under a bond of a voluntary solidarity similar in a degree to primitive solidarity, but as superior to it as liberty is superior to fatalism.

At this point this theory closely approaches that of Herbert Spencer, which consists in the progressive substitution of an industrial system resting on free contract for a military system depending on coercion, in other words, the substitution of spontaneous cooperation for obligatory cooperation. This school, however, differs from that of Herbert Spencer in the sense that it does not reject all state interference, but, on the contrary, regards the state as the highest form of social solidarity. It is true it has the defect of being coercive, but it can and ought to serve to develop in the people the feeling of solidarity, which remedies the defect and prepares the means for its realization – for instance, the system of obligatory assurance in Germany. Also it is almost needless to add that the school of solidarity, in opposition to the individualism of Spencer, or of the Manchester school, does not favour competition, but raises the device, 'union for existence', against the phrase, 'struggle for existence'; and 'each for all' – against 'everyone for himself'.

[C. GIDE]

Reprinted from *Palgrave's Dictionary of Political Economy*.

Sombart, Werner (1863–1941). Sombart was born in Ermsleben (Germany), the son of a well-to-do National Liberal member of the Prussian Diet. He studied economics, history, philosophy and law in Berlin, Pisa and Rome. In 1888 he received his PhD from the University of Berlin and became an officer of the Bremen chamber of commerce. Two years later he was appointed extraordinary professor of political economy at the University of Breslau; in 1906 he became full professor at the Handelshochschule in Berlin and in 1917 transferred to the University of Berlin.

Sombart started his career as a left-wing advocate of social reform, influenced by Marxian theory. This was the reason why for a long time he could hold only second-rate positions within the German university system.

His dissertation on the economic and social conditions of the Roman campagna (1888) was brilliant and much less controversial than his later works.

An important work was his description of the German economy in the 19th century (1903). His outstanding study on the historical genesis of modern capitalism from its medieval origins to modern times (1902) may be considered Sombart's magnum opus. The really important edition was the second, published between 1919 and 1927, which differed completely from the first. Its three volumes treated three stages of capitalist development: early capitalism (Frühkapitalismus), high capitalism (Hochkapitalismus) – beginning with the industrial revolution in the 1760s – and late capitalism (Spätkapitalismus), starting with World War I. The scope of this study was extremely broad. The reader is confronted with an amazing richness of facts. However, the data that Sombart presented were mostly second-hand and contained many speculative notions. Still, this work of 'unsubstantial brilliance' was 'highly stimulating even in its errors' (Schumpeter).

In the course of his research on *Der moderne Kapitalismus* Sombart published several special studies on the psychology and spirit of capitalism, on the Jews, on war and on luxury. In an outstanding study of the bourgeois individual in general and the entrepreneur in particular he analysed the emergence of a certain economically oriented mentality and psychology, the 'Wirtschaftsgeist' (economic spirit), for the development of capitalism (1913a).

In a voluminous work on the role of the Jews in economic life (1911) he described the Jews much along the lines of Max Weber's analysis of puritanism, as the most dynamic part of the population, introducing 'capitalist spirit' into commerce and industry. At this time, Sombart was *not* antisemitic: on the contrary, he perceived the Jews' contribution to the rise of capitalism positively, regarded them as one of the most valuable 'species' of mankind (1912, p. 56) and was in favour of Zionism as the national renaissance of the Jewish people. However, the foundations for his later antisemitic turn were laid: his description of the characteristics of the Jews treating them as a 'species' was full of prejudices and exaggerations and included a discussion of their 'race' and 'blood' peculiarities.

Sombart further analysed the development of luxury consumption, which he connected in a very original way with the erotic, and its economic importance as a creator of new markets and industries (1913b, vol. 1). In a similar way Sombart treated war as a creator of new markets due to the services and goods required by the military (1913b, vol. 2). Two years later, during World War I, Sombart wrote a chauvinistic, strongly anti-English book, which glorified war and militarism (1915).

The best way to observe his political views is to follow his discussion of Marx: Sombart was never a Marxist. But when the third volume of *Capital* appeared, he praised Marx as an outstanding thinker and described his theory in a very positive way (1894), which in turn was warmly welcomed by Engels. Also, in the first edition of his famous work on socialism and social movements (1896), he discussed Marx from a sympathetic point of view. Its tenth edition, now titled *Der proletarische Sozialismus (Marxismus)* (1924), was violently antisocialist and full of hatred and personal insults against Marx. However, this did not hinder Sombart from stating three years later that his *Der moderne Kapitalismus* was written in the Marxian spirit and that he regarded it in a certain way as the conclusion of Marx's work ([1902], 1927, p. XIX).

What had occurred was an evolution in Sombart's assessment of capitalist development. While he still appreciated Marx as a historian of capitalism, he now disliked the latter's optimistic view of the future, his regard for capitalism as the creator of the better world to come ([1902], 1927, p. xx). Marx had been an admirer of technical progress and of the historical forces which fostered it. Sombart no longer believed that industrial development was automatically beneficial and he realized its destructive potential. He contrasted the uniformity and ugliness of modern civilization with the cultural variety of the pre-industrial past.

This enmity towards industrial development and what he called the 'economic age' was the reason why Sombart sought to ally himself with right-wing anticapitalism and temporarily turned to fascism. When the Nazis came to power he made a contribution towards a programme of German (National) Socialism (1934). Contrary to proletarian socialism, which accepted the industrial society and only intended to redistribute its surplus, Sombart perceived German socialism as rejecting the industrial age (1934, pp. 160–68). Beside the corporative state, the Führerprinzip (leader principle), a state interventionist regulation of the German economy, autarky and a partial reagrarianization of Germany, he advocated state planning and, as a key idea, control of technological development based on what would now be called technology assessment (1934, pp. 263–7). However, his proposals were not welcomed by the Nazis, who, as Sombart was later to realize, intended to use the most advanced technologies available in order to win political hegemony.

It is not easy to regard Sombart as member of an economic school. He first rejected and then accepted the deductive method. Although he claimed that *Der moderne Kapitalismus* bridged the gap between the abstract-theoretical and the empirical-historical method ([1902], 1927, p. xvi), there is no doubt that this book lacked an analytical framework and, though not without theory, was mainly a historical description of a large mass of facts. Sombart even 'out-Schmollered Schmoller' (Schumpeter) and had to be regarded as belonging to the younger, or, as Schumpeter called it, the 'youngest' historical school. Sombart himself, however, would certainly not have admitted that. He distinguished between three kinds of political economy (1930): the 'richtende Nationalökonomie' (judging economics), which was intended to decide what was right and wrong, and whose scientific character Sombart denied; the 'ordnende Nationalökonomie' (ordering or systematizing economics) that tried to apply quantitative exact methods, and, finally, the 'verstehende Nationalökonomie' (understanding or interpretative economics), which should be a 'Geistwissenschaft' (science of social mind) and was both theoretical and historical and tried to grasp the motives of economic life. It goes without saying that Sombart regarded his own work as being in the tradition of the latter.

Sombart extended his claims to being a theorist beyond economics. He also perceived sociology as a

'Geistwissenschaft' and developed a new type of sociology, which he called 'Noo-Soziologie', which was supposed to be a general theory of culture (1936).

He remains one of the most brilliant and interesting personalities of the German economics profession, being a gifted writer with profound historical insights. While many works of the historical school are boring collections of facts, the best of Sombart's books are sparkling and still make fascinating reading.

B. SCHEFOLD

See also GERMAN HISTORICAL SCHOOL.

SELECTED WORKS

1888. Über Pacht- und Lohnverhältnisse in der römischen Campagna. PhD dissertation, Berlin.

1894. Zur Kritik des ökonomischen Systems von Karl Marx. *Archiv für soziale Gesetzgebung und Statistik* 7, 555–94.

1896. *Sozialismus und soziale Bewegungen im 19. Jahrhundert*. Jena: Gustav Fischer. Trans. as *Socialism and the Social Movement*, London: Dent; New York, Dutton, 1909. 10th edn published as *Der Proletarische Sozialismus (Marxismus)*, 1924.

1902. *Der moderne Kapitalismus: Historisch-systematische Darstellung des gesamteuropäischen Wirtschaftslebens von seinen Anfängen bis zur Gegenwart*. 2 vols, Leipzig. 2nd edn, 3 vols, Munich and Leipzig: Duncker & Humblot, 1916–27.

1903. *Die deutsche Volkswirtschaft im neunzehnten Jahrhundert*. Berlin: Georg Bondi.

1909. *Das Lebenswerk von Karl Marx*. Jena: Gustav Fischer.

1911. *Die Juden und das Wirtschaftsleben*. Leipzig: Duncker & Humblot. Trans. as *The Jews and Modern Capitalism*, London: T.F. Unwin, 1913.

1912. *Die Zukunft der Juden*. Leipzig: Duncker & Humblot.

1913a. *Der Bourgeois: Zur Geistesgeschichte des modernen Wirtschaftsmenschen*. Munich and Leipzig: Duncker & Humblot. Trans. and ed. M. Epstein as *The Quintessence of Capitalism: A Study of the History and Psychology of the Modern Business Man*, New York: Dutton, 1915.

1913b. *Studien zur Entwicklungsgeschichte des modernen Kapitalismus*. Munich and Leipzig: Duncker & Humblot. Vol. I: *Luxus und Kapitalismus*. Trans. into English as a report under the auspices of the Works Progress Administration and the Department of Social Science, Columbia University, Project number 465–97–3–81. Vol. II: *Krieg und Kapitalismus*.

1915. *Händler und Helden. Patriotische Besinnungen*. Munich and Leipzig: Duncker & Humblot.

1930. *Die drei Nationalökonomien*. Munich and Leipzig: Duncker & Humblot.

1934. *Deutscher Sozialismus*. Berlin: Buchholz & Weisswange. Trans and ed. K.F. Geiser as *A New Social Philosophy*, Princeton: Princeton University Press; Oxford: Oxford University Press, 1937.

1936. *Soziologie: Was sie ist und was sie sein soll*. Berlin: Sitzungsberichte der Preussischen Akademie der Wissenschaften, Berlin.

BIBLIOGRAPHY

Crosser, P.K. 1941. Werner Sombart's philosophy of National-Socialism. *Journal of Social Philosophy* 6, 263–70.

Mitchell, W.C. 1929. Sombart's Hochkapitalismus. *Quarterly Journal of Economics* 43, February, 303–23.

Sonnenfels, Joseph von (1733–1817). Sonnenfels was born of Jewish parents who shortly afterwards converted to Catholicism; the family moved in 1744 from Moravia to Vienna, where the father taught oriental languages. Joseph first served in the army from 1749 to 1754, when he began to study law and literature at Vienna University. A prominent member of the Enlightenment literati, he was in late 1763 appointed to the newly founded chair in 'Police and Cameralistic Sciences' at the University of Vienna. Until his death he was prominent in constitutional reform, also engaging in a campaign for the abolition of torture and of usury. The textbook which he wrote for his own teaching, the *Grundsätze der Polizei Handlungs- und Finanzwissenschaft*, (1765, 1769, 1776) remained the official text in the Austrian Empire until 1848, running to eight editions and several abbreviated teaching editions.

The *Grundsätze* devotes a volume each to police, commerce and finance. The leading idea running through all three is the importance of a large population gainfully employed for the general welfare of the state. Coupled with this is a conception of the accumulation of wealth as the 'multiplication of means of subsistence', governed however by the necessity of maintaining equilibrium in the society, which is the task of police. The functioning of police is therefore tied less directly to economic welfare than is the case with Justi, to whom Sonnenfels makes reference. The treatment of commerce owes a great deal to Forbonnais' *Elémens du commerce*, who also laid emphasis on the advantages of a large population and the need for proportion within it. But while Sonnenfels takes much from Forbonnais, he remains more concerned with general political order than the economic structure of an advancing society.

K. TRIBE

SELECTED WORKS

1765, 1769, 1776. *Grundsätze der Polizei, Handlungs- und Finanzwissenschaft*. 3 vols, Vienna: Camensina. 8th and final edn, 1818–22.

sound money. Curiously enough, this is not an established term of art in economic debate (it rarely appears in the indexes of monetary treatises), but it certainly stands for an enduring idea, frequently also described by some such term as stable money or monetary stability. As these latter labels more obviously imply, the general doctrine underlying the idea is that the monetary system should be prevented from acting as an independent source, or from magnifying non-monetary sources, of instability in the economy. Numerous specific criteria of stability, however, have been proposed. Most commonly, perhaps, writers have focused upon stability in the value of the currency unit – but it is necessary to divide such approaches into those emphasizing, respectively, the *external* value (the command over some specific quantum of precious metal(s), or of foreign currency), and the *internal* value (the reciprocal of some general domestic price level). At particular periods, the focus has commonly shifted to the prevention of liquidity crises, calling for an adequate degree of 'elasticity of the currency', that is to say an elastic supply of legal tender, implying typically some course of central bank action resulting, if not in stability of interest rates, at least in markedly reduced *in*stability of short-term rates. Keynesian economics tended to shift the focus still further from stability in the money unit towards stability in the economy, notably to levels of activity and employment. In this, however, it had been substantially anticipated over a century earlier by the 'real bills doctrine' which had implied the possibility for the supply of credit adequately to be limited to meeting what were then called 'the needs of trade'.

Mention of the real bills doctrine enables us to pick up the story during the Napoleonic Wars, when it was formulated in a manner that typifies the 'practical' orientation of this whole topic – to deal with the issue of how the temporarily inconvertible 'paper pound' could be protected against the observable tendency to depreciation of its external value. The doctrine proposed that banks could safely discount bills of exchange for the finance of genuine trade transactions, i.e. those giving rise to 'real' bills as opposed to bills drawn to provide funds for speculative financial transactions. Aside from the practical difficulty of distinguishing real from un-real bills, the argument presupposed that only the bank funds (notes and/or deposits) created by discounting represented 'money' needing safeguard against over-issue. It is thus somewhat paradoxical that it was espoused by adherents of what was in due course to become the Banking School, with its contention that the monetary character of bills of exchange themselves would undermine the effects of restriction of the fiduciary issue of Bank of England notes (for which the opposing Currency School contended, and which was enshrined in the 1844 Bank Charter Act).

Banking School teaching thus conceded that in the real bills doctrine there resided no defence against inflationary expansion of money and credit, and against depreciation of the external value of the currency. By that stage, of course, convertibility into gold had been restored, and the long 19th-century test had begun of the theoretical proposition that maintenance of a currency's external value would activate mechanisms (traceable back at least to David Hume), resulting in adequate stability of its internal value (as well as in rapid adjustment of the balance of payments on current account). The secular depression of 1873–96, with its sagging levels of prices, notably in agriculture, was to cause many to judge that the test had been failed, and that traders had been 'crucified on the cross of gold'. Others however argued that the problem was due to a more or less fortuitous inadequacy of gold supplies (the period lay between the Californian and the South African gold discoveries), and that a policy of 'bimetallism' – a joint gold and silver standard – would provide an acceptable solution by expanding the stock of monetary metal.

This pre-1914 period was one in which academic economists were fertile with schemes for improved, or ideal, monetary standards that would guarantee sound/stable money. Alfred Marshall, for example, proposed a specific form of bimetallism called symmetallism, based on ingots comprising gold and silver in proportions fixed by weight. More adventurously, Léon Walras proposed that gold should remain the standard monetary metal and be coined without limit for private parties, but that a supplementary token silver coinage should be so varied in amount as to stabilize price levels. Irving Fisher, however, believed that a system based on gold alone could be made to function satisfactorily, and proposed a scheme for what he called the Compensated Dollar, combining a gold-exchange standard with a device for so varying the gold content of the monetary unit according to an official price index that the dollar would represent, not a constant quantity of gold, but a constant quantity of purchasing power.

This intellectual fertility bore little practical fruit, perhaps because practitioners were instinctively conscious of what emerged only gradually from slow-moving academic debate, namely that the bewitching simplicity of abstract schemes for sound and stable money was wholly deceptive, a lesson that has been driven home yet again by later 20th-century experiment with monetarist anti-inflation policies. Once contemplate the practical implementation of such schemes as those of Walras and Fisher, and difficult questions proliferate, even with regard to the precise definition of objectives.

For example, when we focus on the internal objective, should the goal be price stability, or should it be the neutrality of money? The goals are not the same, for the former focuses on the *general* price level, the latter on the structure of *relative* prices. On some arguments, price movements matter little if they are truly general, i.e. the structure of relative prices emerging from microeconomic market forces is undisturbed. On other arguments, truly sound money requires stability in the general price level, and so in the purchasing power of the unit of currency, facilitating business calculation and ensuring justice between debtors and creditors. But even were this latter agreed, questions remain. Do we really want absolute price stability, or would gently rising prices not desirably favour business expansion? – a question that foreshadows again Keynesian preoccupation with aggregate demand and employment levels. Or, would not (gently) *falling* prices permit the fruits of economic growth to be realized in rising real incomes? – implying stability of money wages and, as some would have it, a labour standard of value under which the currency unit commands a stable quantity of labour. Few have backed this last alternative strongly, because of awareness both of the effect of falling prices on entrepreneurial calculations, and of the predilection of trade union leaders for rising wage-levels, in money as well as in real terms.

But those who have backed stable or rising prices still need to specify whether the index to which attention is directed should relate to the whole range of prices, or to some subset such as the prices of capital or – more commonly supported – consumer goods. It will be noted that these arguments about how to achieve monetary stability are reflected in later discussion and experiment concerning the indexation of prices to deal with inflationary breakdown of stability.

Behind these broad general questions about precise definition of the goal(s) implied by the ideal of sound money, there lurk technical complications, of which space and relevance permit only an illustrative example to be cited. Suppose that it were decided, as was frequently recommended, to seek stabilization of the level of prices of consumer goods. There would then have to be faced, on the one hand, the usual 'index number problems' – of definition, of responding appropriately to innovation and obsolescence of goods, of base- or current-weighted indices, of possible manipulation for political purposes, and so on. On the other hand, it would need to be recognized that to stabilize product prices, in periods when rising productivity tended to reduce unit production costs, would imply artificial inflation of profit margins. Such inflation might, for reasons already touched upon, be regarded as desirable, but it would represent money-induced 'distortion' of relative prices. Sound or stable money, again, would be different from neutral money; managed monetary stability would imply, not replication of some notionally 'ideal' price-structure that would rule under barter and laissez faire, but 'distortion' of relative prices.

It was doubtless in part the recognition of such technical complications, inevitable if managed money (even if managed on some quasi-automatic rule) were to offer escape from crucifixion, which induced willingness in Keynesian circles to depart even more radically from the old ways, and to orient monetary policy towards broadly conceived stabilization goals focusing upon intrinsic rather than instrumental desiderata, notably the volume of employment. The implicit recognition of serious cyclical instability in modern market economies undermined the old attractions of Quantity Theory reasoning, and shifted emphasis in discussion of monetary policy from ensuring reasonable stability or appropriate adaptation in the quantity of money, towards ensuring reasonable stability or appropriate adaptation in levels of interest rates; if liquidity/money preference schedules were recognized or argued to be unstable in significant degree, the two types of criteria were by no means to be identified. Stabilization of interest rates, even of the modest form that counselled central bank 'leaning into the wind', implied possibly vigorous official security purchases to prevent rising interest rates from prematurely choking off expansion of real investment in the upswing, and thus to some extent coalesced with older concerns that there be sufficient elasticity in the currency to prevent dramatic increases in interest rates in liquidity crises at the peak of the boom.

Keynes, of course, was well aware that such policies posed inflationary dangers if pressed too far. The excessive ambition of so-called Keynesian economists in the postwar period – notably the American advisers who aspired in the early 1960s to fine-tune the economy to perpetual boom conditions – combined with unwise growth in the general level of government spending, eventually undermined pursuit in the postwar period of non-inflationary economic stability, that is, of full employment combined with sound money. Revulsion against inflation and its associated problems has caused revival in some quarters (notably in the USA) of support for the gold standard, or of basically fixed exchange rates on the Bretton Woods model, or of regional arrangements of more or less equivalent effect such as the European Monetary Union.

These proposals for returning to an externally oriented basis for sound money are seen by many as having the basic virtue of restraining the inflationary proclivities of individual governments tempted to follow quasi-Keynesian policies against unemployment. But each proposal, by this juncture, has recognized defects which have stimulated resumption of the search, in the manner of Marshall, Walras and Fisher, for some (more or less) ideal standard that would guard against repetition of old problems. One such modern scheme, associated with the names of E.F. Fama, R.L. Greenfield, R.E. Hall and L.B. Yeager, has become known as the plywood standard. In part it follows Marshall's approach in guarding against variations in the value of the commodity base, in this case by proposing to use four commodities (ammonium nitrate, copper, aluminium and plywood) chosen because their combined price index has tended to reflect closely movements in the general price index. To avoid incurring real resource costs, it is proposed that the standard be a 'tabular' one, based on the prices of defined quantities of the commodities cited, but not using them for transactions purposes nor holding them as backing for money. Indeed, in what is the truly novel feature of the proposal, specific exchange media would be deregulated out of existence. The tabular resource unit would function as a unit of account, ostensibly analogous to physical units of, for example, volume or weight, with rapid electronic transfer of assets of all kinds facilitating settlement of debts. Soundness of money would have been ensured in effect by converting virtually all assets into money, effectively returning to the barter basis of trade – which is to say by abolishing money as a separate, identifiable category of asset.

Ingenious, but arguably too clever by half. Intermediaries would probably be tempted to offer claims in the form of bearer units whose price was fixed in terms of the resource unit of account. Such units would be highly attractive in reducing the uncertainties of barter. Money would be reinvented, with all its problems. There is no *monetary* mid-course between on the one hand (international) automaticity with crucifixion potential, and on the other (national) discretionary management with proneness to human and political frailty. In this writer's view, only renewed search for (localized) stability in production arrangements offers real hope of escape from the occasionally widespread and devastating effects of adopting either pole of past orthodoxies.

A.B. CRAMP

See also DEAR MONEY; TIGHT MONEY.

Spann, Othmar (1878–1950). Spann was born in Altmannsdorf (Austria). He studied social sciences, economics and philosophy in Vienna, Zurich, Berne and Tübingen, became professor at the Technische Hochschule Brünn (Moravia) and transferred after World War I to the University of Vienna.

In the interwar period Spann was one of the most popular economics professors in Germany and Austria.

He opposed individualism, liberalism, Marxism and materialism. Contrary to the non-theoretical approach of the historical school, he intended to provide a solid theoretical framework for economic analysis. His theory of 'universalism' had a strong philosophical orientation. Spann regarded society as being an organic unity, a totality (Ganzheit) which had to be perceived as being more than the mere sum of individuals. It is a higher order of reality, beyond and above the individuals who exist only as components of the organic whole. We may view this totality as realized in partial wholes, such as philosophy, religion, arts and sciences. He found precursors of his views in economists of the Romantic period such as Adam Müller.

In the 'Fundament der Volkswirtschaftslehre', his most important economic work Spann tried to develop a universalist economic theory. He rejected the application of the causality principle for the analysis of social phenomena and stressed the importance of functionality: it is according to its consequences for society that individual behaviour has to be regarded. The determinant of the economic activities of individuals is their integration into the societal whole, and not individual motives such as self-interest and striving for profits, however important they may be.

Spann advocated a decentralized corporative state, where the various professional groups of workers and capitalists should be organized in a hierarchy of guilds with far-reaching political powers. Within this concept there was no room for political parties and democratic structures. In fact, Spann sympathized with fascism in its various forms. His theories were particularly influential among the Austro-fascists. The Nazis deeply distrusted the universalist concepts in general and Spann's rejection of racial antisemitism in particular. After the Nazi occupation of Austria they arrested him for a short time. He subsequently retired to the countryside and never resumed his teaching activities.

B. SCHEFOLD

SELECTED WORKS

1967–74. *Gesamtausgabe*. Ed. W. Heinrich et al., 21 vols, Graz: Akademische Druck- und Verlagsanstalt.

BIBLIOGRAPHY

Landheer, B. 1931. Othmar Spann's social theories. *Journal of Political Economy* 39, April, 239–48.

spatial competition. Imperfect competition has been an important branch of economic theory, at least since Cournot's (1838) model of duopoly. A more recent development is spatial competition, which serves as a foundation for models of imperfect competition. The concept of space as the groundwork for imperfect competition provides many useful insights into price determination and resource allocation. Our goal is to illustrate these insights. In pursuing this track, we ignore many traditional issues in location theory including issues revolving around the shape of market ares. We also bypass questions about the existence of equilibrium in spatial models, which are discussed along with many of the locational issues in a recent lengthy survey by Gabszewicz and Thisse (1984).

The major early work on imperfect competition was Cournot's duopoly model, in which firms adjust their output based on expectations of other firms' output; the market clears at a price greater than marginal cost.

This model was criticized by Bertrand (1883) and others on the grounds that firms have an incentive to pursue a price rather than quantity strategy. By slightly undercutting its opponent's price a firm can capture the entire market. The potential instability implied by price undercutting led to the seminal paper by Hotelling (1929), which contains many of the important insights from spatial models.

Hotelling provides a model of imperfect competition (duopoly), which does not suffer from instability due to chronic undercutting. In his model buyers are continuously distributed along a line segment with firms located at specific points because of scale economies. Firms charge a mill price (f.o.b.) and households pay transportation costs which are proportional to distance to the store. As a result households at different locations face different delivered prices. Transportation costs provide stability because as a firm lowers its price below its competitor's price it captures only the customers near the boundary between firms – not the entire market. Customers close to the competitor still find the competitor's delivered price lower even though the mill price is higher.

Hence, space and transport costs imply a generally continuous relationship between market area and price. The nature of the response depends on rivals' conjectured responses, a matter of some controversy which we consider below. None the less, the fundamental insight of Hotelling carries over into a wide range of more recent models. Once we introduce space into models we cannot in general *derive* perfect competition; rather it is a limiting case when transportation costs or fixed costs go to zero rather than when the number of firms becomes very large as in Cournot models. Imperfect competitive models can lead to stable solutions based on sound micro-foundations.

These foundations can be interpreted in terms of Chamberlin's (1933) model of monopolistic competition. Space is a device which can be used to derive the demand curve faced by the monopolistic firm as distinct from individual or market demand curves. It can also be used to determine the different elasticities of these curves. Furthermore, as Hotelling himself suggested, the notion of space can be generalized beyond physical space to include 'position' in characteristics space as detailed in Lancaster (1979). In this generalization, the scale economies needed for dispersed production originate in set up or advertising costs, and transport costs are the disutility consumers experience from being away from their preferred bundle of characteristics.

We will proceed with a very simple generic model of spatial competition which illustrates the major points of research on this topic. The model is intended to show how the degree of competition can be derived from tastes and technology and whether, given these tastes and technology, markets allocate resources efficiently.

THE BASIC SPATIAL MODEL

Assumptions. (A1) *The industry.* A single commodity is produced by firms with the same cost function (i.e. ubiquitous resources and technology). (A2) *Demand.* Identical consumers are located along an infinitely long line at uniform density, D. Each consumer purchases a units of output or none at all from the supplier with the lowest delivered price. That is,

$$x_i = a \quad \text{if} \quad p + tr \leqslant p_0$$
$$0 \quad \text{if} \quad p + tr > p_0$$

where x_i is demand of identical i, p is the f.o.b. or mill price, t is transport cost per unit distance, and r is the distance to the nearest supplier. (A3) *Transportation.* Transport cost per mile, t, is constant between all points in the linear market. (A4) *Production cost.* For every firm costs, C, are linear in output X. We write

$$C = f + cX$$

where c is marginal cost and f is fixed cost. We assume that fixed costs are not so large that no firm can produce profitably. (A5) *Long-run equilibrium.* Firms enter the industry until profits are driven to zero for all firms (free entry). (A6) *Conjectures.* Firms conjecture that competitors will not change their prices or locations (zero conjectural variation).

Solution. In general, the solution of spatial models makes use of the zero profits assumption and profit maximization conditions to obtain two equations which can be solved for equilibrium price and market area. That is, zero profits implies that profits, Y, will be

$$Y = Y(p, R) = 0. \tag{1}$$

Profit maximization implies

$$\mathrm{d}Y/\mathrm{d}p = Y_p + Y_R \mathrm{d}R/\mathrm{d}p = 0 \tag{2}$$

where subscripts denote partial derivatives. Equations (1) and (2) can usually be solved for the equilibrium levels of p and R.

For example, under the assumptions outlined above, in a market of half length (radius) R, total demand observed by a firm will be (from (A2))

$$X = 2aRD$$

Profits, Y, will be (from (A4))

$$Y = pX - C$$
$$= 2aDR(p - c) - f$$

Making use of (A5) gives the zero profit condition

$$p = c + f/(2aDR) \tag{1a}$$

Maximizing profits gives

$$2aDR + (p - c)2aD(\mathrm{d}R/\mathrm{d}p) = 0$$

and

$$p = c - R/(\mathrm{d}R/\mathrm{d}p) \tag{2a}$$

If a neighbouring firm charging price p_i is U miles distance, the boundary between them will occur when (from (A2)) delivered prices are equal

$$p_i + tR = p + t(U - R)$$

That is, when

$$R = U/2 - (1/2t)(p_i - p)$$

so that

$$\mathrm{d}R/\mathrm{d}p = -1/2t(\mathrm{d}p_i/\mathrm{d}p - 1) \tag{3}$$

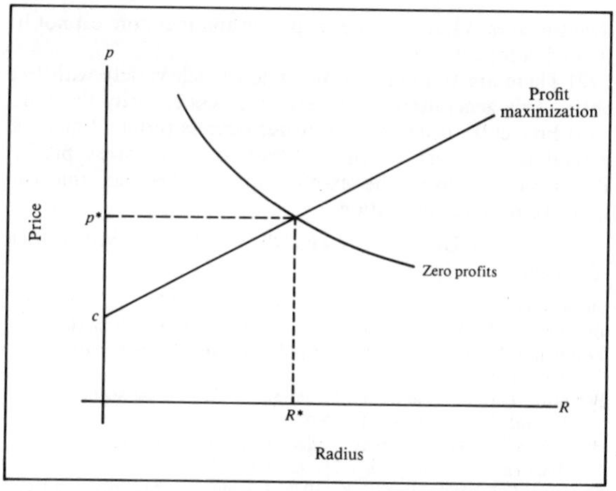

Figure 1 Equilibrium in a spatial market

and with zero price conjectures (from (A6))

$$dR/dp = -1/2t$$

Now we are able to solve (1a) and (2a) to obtain the equilibrium values p^*, R^*

$$p^* = c + (tf/aD)^{1/2}$$
$$R^* = (f/4aDt)^{1/2} \quad (4a)$$

Figure 1 illustrates. The upward sloping profit maximization curve, equation (2a), and the downward sloping zero profits curve, equation (1a), intersect at p^*, R^*.

Comparative statics. The comparative statics in the above model are 'normal' in the sense that they replicate the usual results from non-spatial models. Reading immediately from equations (3a) we can see that increases in costs whether marginal, c, transport, t, or fixed, f, all have a positive effect on price. Increases in demand density from either higher demand per person, a, or from an increased density of customers, D, will result in lower prices.

However, 'perverse' comparative statics can arise in spatial models. For example, higher costs may result in lower prices. These situations are more likely to arise when the price conjecture is large or when market areas are close to maximum size. They will not arise when the demand curve is sufficiently convex (Capozza and Van Order, 1978; Ohta, 1981).

Perfect competition as a limiting case. The unique features of spatial competition are transportation costs and indivisibilities. Transport costs give the spatial competitor some monopoly power over nearby customers and weaken the impact of distant competitors. Indivisibilities, captured here by fixed costs and a downward sloping average cost curve, force production to concentrate at specific locations. In the limit, however, the spatial model should reduce to the perfectly competitive model. This can be seen from equations (4a). As transport costs, t, approach zero, price is driven to marginal cost as all firms become equal competitors at every location. As fixed costs fall to zero, concentrated production is less essential and price again falls to the perfectly competitive marginal cost price (Capozza and Van Order, 1978; Eaton and Wooders, 1985).

Efficiency and the excess capacity theorem. The excess capacity theorem of monopolistic competition carries over into spatial models. Too many firms enter the market and sell their output at too high a price for efficient resource allocation.

In the above model, with all or nothing demand, the efficient allocation simply minimizes the average total costs. Average total costs (transport plus production) are

$$\text{ATC} = aDtR^2/4 + 2aDR + f/(2aDR)$$

These are minimized when

$$R^e = [2f/(aDt)]^{1/2}$$

The ratio of the efficient radius to the equilibrium (from (2a)) is

$$R^e/R^* = 2\sqrt{2}$$

The efficient radius is more than twice as large as the equilibrium radius. Firms charge too high a price and operate with excess capacity. In terms of product characteristics there is too much variety.

Other conjectural variations. Other price conjectural variations ranging from -1 (Greenhut and Ohta, 1973) to $+1$ (Mills and Lav, 1964) are often found in spatial models. It is easy to see from equations (2a) and (3) that higher conjectures result in higher equilibrium prices since increasing the conjecture increases the slope of the profit maximization curve. In some models the conjecture is crucial in determining the 'perverse' comparative statics (see Capozza and Van Order, 1978).

One way to derive the conjecture instead of assuming it is to introduce 'consistent' conjectures (Bresnahan, 1981; Capozza and Van Order, 1980b; Decanio, 1985; Perry, 1982) where firms anticipate the optimal reaction of competitors. Since firms are identical, this implies that in equilibrium what they believe about others is true of themselves as well.

The consistent conjecture is found by differentiating equation (2) with respect to a competitor's price change to find the optimal reaction. In full equilibrium with identical firms all reactions must be identical. This provides a third equation in p, R, and the conjecture which along with equations (1) and (2) determines the equilibrium values. In the simple model above, the 'consistent conjecture' is 1/3. In models with more realistic demand curves the consistent conjecture is even closer to zero, suggesting that the Nash zero conjecture is a reasonable simplification.

The principle of minimum differentiation. The principle of minimum differentiation extends from Hotelling's original model where he concluded, 'Buyers are confronted everywhere with an excessive sameness.' The conclusion derives from his spatial model which is identical to the model above with the exception of the topology of the market. The Hotelling market is bounded and only large enough for two firms. The two firms must decide where to locate along the bounded line segment. It is easy to see that if the two firms locate initially at the first and third quartiles of the line segment, there will be an incentive for both to gravitate toward the centre. By moving closer to the centre, a firm captures customers from the competitor at the boundary between them but does not lose customers from the opposite flank because there is no competitor on the opposite side. In equilibrium both firms are located at the centre of the interval, i.e. minimally differentiated. This minimum differentiation result contrasts with the excessive variety result above when the market is infinitely long. The conditions under which this result holds have been explored extensively (Smithies, 1941; Eaton and Lipsey, 1975; de Palma et al., 1985).

Free entry and positive profits. In models of monopolistic competition, the free entry assumption (A5) underlies the result that in long-run equilibrium firms earn zero profits. A number of authors since at least Kaldor (1935) have questioned the consistency of free entry with zero profits. The missing links between free entry and zero profits are two additional strong assumptions. For free entry to yield the zero profit result the market must be infinitely long and firms (capital) must be perfectly mobile.

In a spatial context it is easy to see why both these additional assumptions are necessary. Suppose capital is mobile but the market is finite in length. If each firm requires a market of length $2R$ to break even, zero profits will arise only if the total market length is an integer multiple of $2R$. In all other cases each firm has a market slightly larger than that needed to break even and earns positive profits.

If the market is infinitely long but capital is not mobile, new entrants will break even only if existing firms are serving a market that is twice the break-even size. A new firm will enter half-way between the existing firms and serve a market half as large as existing firms since with immobile capital the existing firms cannot move away. As a result firms earn excess profits until their market areas are twice the break-even level and new entrants can at least break even (Eaton and Lipsey, 1978).

Notice that immobile capital also gives rise to non-uniqueness of equilibrium. Market areas between the break-even size and twice the break-even size are all consistent with equilibrium. As a result history matters.

One paradoxical result arises when there is immobile capital. The immobile capital acts as a barrier to entry and provides positive profits for firms. But since there are too many firms in zero profits equilibrium, the barrier to entry can actually improve efficiency (Eaton and Lipsey, 1977, 1978; Capozza and Van Order, 1980a; Gabszewicz and Thisse, 1984).

Price discrimination. Spatial models lead naturally into price discrimination because each customer faces a different delivered price. If individual demand curves are linear, setting marginal revenue equal to marginal cost at each location means that the spatial firm absorbs half the cost of transportation (see Singer, 1937; Beckmann, 1968; Holahan, 1975; Norman, 1981). Nearby customers whose demand is relatively less elastic are charged relatively more in relation to cost than distant customers.

Most forms of price discrimination are illegal but space provides legal ways to separate customers. Firms can target rebate coupons to specific locations in its market area, use delivered pricing (e.g. free delivery), or target advertising at those customers with more elastic demand.

CONCLUSIONS

The purpose of spatial theory is not to provide models that are entirely 'realistic'. Spatial models are for the most part extremely simple and capture only the barest of stylized facts. To date, there has been very little empirical work done based on these models (Capozza and Attaran, 1976; Hwang, 1979; Greenhut, Greenhut, and Li, 1980; Greenhut, 1981).

It is more fruitful to view spatial models as illuminating counterexamples, which question the standard notions of perfect competition and free entry. Some important points demonstrated by spatial models are:

(1) Perfect competition is only a limiting case when fixed or transport costs go to zero or demand density becomes infinite. Perfect competition cannot be salvaged by defining goods at each location as different industries and proceeding with the usual competitive analysis. Space implies that suppliers at each location *always* have monopoly power and therefore cannot be treated competitively.

(2) There are too many firms or too much variety with free entry. This generalizes Chamberlin's excess capacity theorem.

(3) Free entry need not lead to zero excess profits. Immobile capital is a barrier which can lead to large excess profits. Paradoxically, given the excess capacity theorem, this can improve resource allocation.

DENNIS R. CAPOZZA AND ROBERT VAN ORDER

BIBLIOGRAPHY

Beckmann, M. 1968. *Location Theory*. New York: Random House.

Beckmann, M. 1976. Spatial price policies revisited. *Bell Journal of Economics* 7, 619–30.

Bertrand, J. 1883. Théorie mathématique de la richesse sociale. *Journal des savants* 48, 499–508.

Bresnahan, T. 1981. Duopoly models with consistent conjectures. *America Economic Review* 71, 934–45.

Capozza, D.R. and Attaran, K. 1976. Pricing in urban areas under free entry. *Journal of Regional Science* 16, 167–82.

Capozza, D.R. and Van Order, R. 1978. A generalized model of spatial competition. *American Economic Review* 68, 896–908.

Capozza, D.R. and Van Order, R. 1980a. Unique equilibria, pure profits, and efficiency in location models. *American Economic Review* 70, 1046–53.

Capozza, D.R. and Van Order, R. 1980b. On competitive reactions in spatial monopolistic competition. Working Paper No. 6, Urban Land Economics Division, University of British Columbia.

Chamberlin, E.H. 1933. *The Theory of Monopolistic Competition*. Cambridge, Mass.: Harvard University Press.

Cournot, A. 1838. *Researches into the Mathematical Principles of Wealth*. Trans. N.T. Bacon, London: Macmillan, 1897.

Decanio, S. 1985. Delivered pricing and multiple basing point equilibria: a reevaluation. *Quarterly Journal of Economics* 99, 329–49.

de Palma, A., Ginsburgh, V., Papageorgiou, Y.Y. and Thisse, J. 1985. The principle of minimum differentiation holds under sufficient heterogeneity. *Econometrica* 53, 767–81.

Eaton, B.C. and Lipsey, R. 1975. The principle of minimum differentiation reconsidered: some new developments in the theory of spatial competition. *Review of Economic Studies* 42, 27–49.

Eaton, B.C. and Lipsey, R. 1977. The introduction of space into the neo-classical model of value theory. In *Studies in Modern Economic Analysis; the Proceedings of the Association of University Teachers of Economics Edinburgh 1976*, ed. M.J. Artis and A.R. Nobay. Oxford: Basil Blackwell, 59–96.

Eaton, B.C. and Lipsey, R. 1978. Freedom of entry and the existence of pure profit. *Economic Journal* 88, 455–69.

Eaton, B.C. and Wooders, M.H. 1985. Sophisticated entry in a model of spatial competition. *Bell Journal of Economics* 16, 282–97.

Gabszewicz, J. and Thisse, J. 1984. Spatial competition and the location of firms. *Encyclopedia of Economics*.

Greenhut, M. 1981. Spatial pricing in the US, West Germany and Japan. *Economica* 48, 79–86.

Greenhut, J., Greenhut, M. and Li, S. 1980. Spatial pricing patterns in the United States. *Quarterly Journal of Economics* 95, 329–50.

Greenhut, M. and Ohta, H. 1973. Spatial configurations and competitive equilibrium. *Weltwirtschaftliches Archiv* 109, 87–104.

Holahan, W. 1975. The welfare effects of spatial price discrimination. *American Economic Review* 65, 498–503.

Hotelling, H. 1929. Stability in competition. *Economic Journal* 339, 41–57.

Hwang, M. 1979. A model of spatial price discrimination for the pricing schedule of coal. *Journal of Regional Science* 19, 231–43.

Kaldor, N. 1935. Market imperfection and excess capacity. *Economica* 2, 33–50.

Lancaster, K. 1979. *Variety, Equity, and Efficiency*. Oxford: Basil Blackwell.

Lösch, A. 1954. *The Economics of Location*. New Haven: Yale University Press.

Mills, E.S. and Lav, M. 1964. A model of market areas with free entry. *Journal of Political Economy* 72, 278–88.

Norman, G. 1981. Spatial competition and spatial price discrimination. *Review of Economic Studies* 48, 91–111.
Ohta, H. 1981. The price effects of spatial competition. *Review of Economic Studies* 48, 317–25.
Perry, M. 1982. Oligopoly and consistent conjectural variation. *Bell Journal of Economics* 13, 197–205.
Salop, S. 1979. Monopolistic competition with outside goods. *Bell Journal of Economics* 10, 141–56.
Singer, H. 1937. A Note on spatial price discrimination. *Review of Economic Studies* 5, 75–7.
Smithies, A. 1941. Optimum location in spatial competition. *Journal of Political Economy* 49, 423–39.

spatial economics. Spatial economics is concerned with the allocation of resources over space and the location of economic activity. While location theory has had a long history and a number of distinguished contributions which have drawn on general developments in economics, it is fair to say that space, unlike time, has not yet been successfully integrated into the main corpus of economic theory. The main reason for this is that the two essential features of spatial economies are transport costs (a form of transactions costs) and increasing returns in production and consumption (e.g. local public goods) both of which are assumed away in the standard Arrow–Debreu model of general equilibrium. To see why transport costs and increasing returns to scale are essential, consider how economic activity would be located without them in a spatially homogeneous economy without externalities. With constant returns to scale and no transport costs, both the scale and location of economic activity would be indeterminate; with either constant returns to scale plus transport costs, or decreasing returns, everyone would produce his requirements in his backyard; with increasing returns to scale and no transport costs, all economic activity would occur at a point in space; and with variable returns to scale and no transport costs, all economic activity would operate at locally constant returns to scale – the scale of economic activity would be determinate but not the movement of factors and commodities over space. Only if there are transport costs and variable or increasing returns to scale is there the possibility of an empirically interesting locational equilibrium. Spatial inhomogeneities and externalities complicate the picture, but the fact remains that it is the tradeoff between increased transport costs and decreased production costs which occurs when economic activity is more spatially concentrated that is the heart of spatial economics. Locational equilibrium obtains when the forces of deglomeration balance those of agglomeration.

NON-STRATEGIC LOCATION THEORY. In the last half century, it has come to be recognized that the friction of space confers market power on producers and as a result causes them to behave strategically. Classical location theory, however, ignores this.

Not surprisingly, location theory was originally developed to explain where different agricultural goods were produced. Two complementary theories were put forward, by Ricardo (1821) who developed a theory of agricultural rent based on relative fertility while ignoring transport costs, and by von Thünen (1826) who formulated a theory of agricultural rent and location which treated transport costs but assumed that land was homogeneous.

Ricardo's theory has been extended to other economic activities and to other exogenous spatial inhomogeneities such as natural resource endowments and topography. It produces a theory of location based on comparative advantage. Since such 'Ricardian' differences in land can be incorporated into the Arrow–Debreu model without difficulty, while practically important, they are of little interest in the context of spatial economic theory *per se*, and so will be ignored for the rest of the discussion.

It is von Thünen's theory that has formed the basis for modern, non-strategic location theory. In his theory, a group of price-taking farmers of different agricultural products who sell at the same central market bid rents for land at different distances from the market equal to gross revenues less factor payments less transport costs. Land goes to that use which bids the most, and rent equals this use's bid-rent. The locational equilibrium entails a set of use-specific concentric rings around the central market. A more complete account of his work may be found in the entry under his name. His simple model has been extended in a number of directions. First, agricultural and transport prices can be made endogeneous and a general equilibrium theory of agricultural land rent and land use developed. Secondly, and more significant, the model has been adapted to treat urban land use. The pioneer in this adaptation is Alonso (1964). Urban business land use is determined in essentially the same way as in von Thünen, with the central business district replacing the central market and different businesses replacing different agricultural products. Alonso's extension to treat urban residential land use was more innovative, and has spawned a large literature; for a discussion, *see* MONOCENTRIC MODELS IN URBAN ECONOMICS. More recently, with explicit modelling of the forces of agglomeration, the theory has been extended to treat the endogenous formation of centres and subcentres. The stage is set to extend further the theory to treat systems of cities and regional locational equilibrium.

Another strand of non-strategic location theory is the location of plants. Weber (1909) solved the problem of locating a plant so as to minimize the sum of its production and input and output transport costs. Using programming techniques, the theory has been extended in many ways, among others to determine the optimal location of public facilities.

STRATEGIC LOCATION THEORY. The friction of space generates non-competitive behaviour. An example is the corner store which faces a downward-sloping demand curve because some customers are willing to pay a higher price to avoid walking an extra few blocks to the next corner store. When firms have some control over their prices, each firm in deciding where to locate and what price to charge will try to anticipate the reactions of its rivals to any change it introduces – strategic or game-theoretic considerations therefore become important.

The basic model in strategic location theory is called the 'ice-cream sellers' problem' and derives from Hotelling (1929), though he did not employ this particular example. There are two ice-cream sellers on a beach of bounded length. The bathers are uniformly distributed along the beach. Each inelastically demands a single ice cream and walks to the nearer seller to buy it. If the price of ice creams is for some reason fixed, where will the two ice-cream sellers locate? This is termed the Hotelling location game. It is assumed that each ice-cream seller has zero locational conjectural variations, i.e. he chooses his location assuming that the other seller will not alter his. As a result, each seller will locate next to the other, on the long side of the market. This process will continue until both sellers are located at the centre of the market – the well-known principle of minimum differentiation.

The ice-cream sellers' problem has been extended in numerous directions. The price game, the simultaneous price-location game, the sequential price-location game (in which the pair of sellers first compete over prices, locations fixed, and then compete over locations, with prices at their equilibrium levels conditional on the firms' locations), and the sequential location-price game, have been analysed. Elastic demands, a variety of transport and production functions, different strategies, an unbounded market, many sellers, entry and exit, firms with multiple plants, adjustment costs, uncertainty, and firms bearing transport costs, have all been considered in a huge variety of combinations.

The two general results of the literature are negative: (i) in many models equilibrium fails to exist; and (ii) if equilibrium exists, its characteristics are very sensitive to the assumptions made.

Non-existence arises as a result of discontinuities in firms' reaction functions. The simplest example of non-existence is in the simultaneous price-location game in the Hotelling model, with zero conjectural variations in both price and location. Suppose that ice-cream seller 1 locates at x_1 and sets price p_1, which is significantly above marginal cost, and that ice-cream seller 2 finds it most profitable to locate right next to ice-cream seller 1 and undercut him slightly, just enough to gain the whole market. This process, if it were to continue indefinitely, would result in both firms eventually setting price equal to marginal cost (corresponding to the Bertrand–Nash equilibrium of non-spatial duopoly theory). But this cannot be an equilibrium here since, with price equal to marginal cost, each seller has an incentive to move away; he will lose most of the market by doing so, but will make a profit on that part of the market he serves. When one seller moves away and raises his price, the other seller will locate next to him and undercut him. This 'cycle' will continue, and no equilibrium exists.

Some economists consider that non-existence in a model is evidence that it is not well-posed and should be modified to restore existence; in this context, existence has been restored by modifying strategies (e.g., introducing mixed strategies, ruling out undercutting), and introducing noise and product heterogeneity.

If equilibrium exists, its characteristics are sensitive to the assumptions made concerning strategies, the transport technology, the characteristics of demand functions, etc. Two approaches might be taken to restrict the set of acceptable game-theoretic equilibria. First, it seems reasonable to require that, through experience, firms learn to predict their rivals' reactions; unfortunately, no agreement has been reached on what constitutes rational behaviour in strategic settings. Secondly, experimentation and empirical analysis, to determine how players actually behave, may prove insightful.

Given the current state of knowledge, strategic location theory can explain a lot, but, because of the multiplicity of possible equilibria, has little predictive content.

SPACE IN GENERAL EQUILIBRIUM. Spatial economics has remained outside the mainstream of microeconomics primarily because space cannot be fitted neatly into competitive general equilibrium models of the Arrow–Debreu type. Competitive equilibrium, if it exists, is inconsistent with economies of scale. But a non-trivial locational equilibrium necessarily entails economies of scale. Hence, a non-trivial locational equilibrium cannot be an Arrow–Debreu-type competitive equilibrium (see Starrett, 1974).

There have been several responses to this result. One is that spatial concentrations of economic activity can be explained in terms of Ricardian differences in land, broadly interpreted. Debreu provides such an explanation in *Theory of Value*. He treats space by spatially indexing commodities, each of which has a separate equilibrium price. Good i at location j is transformed into good i at location j' via a convex production technology that has good i at location j and transport services as inputs. This treatment of space is deficient in several respects. First, it is inconsistent with empirical observation, since one does observe spatial agglomeration even on homogeneous plains. Secondly, transport technology is typically not convex; there are usually decreasing costs to volume transported. And thirdly, the Debreu characterization of space breaks down as soon as consumer mobility is admitted. The journey to work costs the same however many units of labour the consumer supplies; similarly, the transport costs associated with a shopping trip do not increase proportionally with the quantity and variety of goods purchased. Fourthly, and relatedly, when residential location choice is allowed, the Debreu model predicts that, because of convexity of preferences, each consumer will purchase land and housing at a variety of locations. But because of the costs of travelling between locations, consumers typically purchase only at one location; as a result, a consumer's consumption set over land at different locations is essentially nonconvex.

A second response to the impossibility result is that economies of scale are agglomerative (e.g. Kanemoto, 1980) – scale economies are present but are external to the individual firm. In this case, a price-taking equilibrium exists, but it is not competitive in the Arrow–Debreu sense. Moreover, it is not Pareto-efficient because firms ignore the positive externality associated with expanding output. This response has proved useful since it has permitted the characterization of non-strategic equilibria in spatial economies where agglomeration occurs because of the tradeoff between increasing returns in production and decreasing returns due to transportation. Nevertheless, the response is incomplete since there is nothing in these models which precludes an entrepreneur from buying up all existing firms and the hinterland, thereby making a profit by internalizing the externality. If there were competition among such entrepreneurs, each spatial unit of replication would operate at minimum total cost, a point of locally constant returns to scale and therefore zero profits – the losses in production from marginal-cost pricing with increasing returns would be just offset by land rents collected. The characteristics of this equilibrium are, however, unrealistic.

A third response is to argue that in a spatial economy firms have market power, and as a result strategic behaviour must be considered. This is a reasonable position, but, given the possibility of non-existence of equilibrium and the multiplicity of equilibrium concepts in strategic location theory, not very attractive to the positive economist who wants a predictive theory.

It is commonly asserted that, with variable returns to scale and no externalities, the general equilibrium of a spatial economy with transport costs should approach a competitive economy of the Arrow–Debreu type as transport costs tend to zero. This intuition has not, however, been formalized, and indeed may be incorrect since with an elastic demand for space, a fall in unit transport costs can lead to an increase in aggregate transport costs. Thus, it remains an open question whether mainstream economics ignores something essential in neglecting space.

Due to the limitations of space, this essay has ignored many strands of the literature, including: (i) the insightful but incomplete attempts of economists in the European tradition to develop general spatial economic theories (e.g. Lösch, 1940; and Isard, 1956), usefully reviewed in Beckmann (1968) and Ponsard (1983); (ii) the programming/activity analysis literature deriving from Samuelson (1952) which treats space as a set of points; and (iii) the relevant literatures in transport economics, spatial housing economics, spatial externalities, and local public goods.

RICHARD ARNOTT

See also LOCATION OF ECONOMIC ACTIVITY; MONOCENTRIC MODELS; URBAN ECONOMICS.

BIBLIOGRAPHY

Alonso, W. 1964. *Location and Land Use*. Cambridge, Mass.: Harvard University Press.

Beckmann, M. 1968. *Location Theory*. New York: Random House.

Christaller, W. 1966. *Central Places in Southern Germany*. Englewood Cliffs, NJ: Prentice-Hall.

Debreu, G. 1959. *Theory of Value*. New Haven: Yale University Press.

Hotelling, H. 1929. Stability in competition. *Economic Journal* 39, March, 41–57.

Isard, W. 1956. *Location and Space-Economy*. Cambridge, Mass.: MIT Press.

Kanemoto, Y. 1980. *Theories of Urban Externalities*. Amsterdam: North-Holland.

Lösch, A. 1940. *The Economics of Location*. New Haven: Yale University Press, 1954.

Ponsard, C. 1983. *History of Spatial Economic Theory*. Berlin: Springer-Verlag.

Ricardo, D. 1821. *The Principles of Political Economy*. 3rd edn, Homewood, Ill.: Irwin, 1963.

Samuelson, P.A. 1952. Spatial price equilibrium and linear programming. *American Economic Review* 42, June, 283–303.

Starrett, D. 1974. Principles of optimal location in a large homogeneous area. *Journal of Economic Theory* 9(4), 418–48.

Thünen, J.H. von. 1826. *Der isolierte Staat in Beziehung auf Landwirtschaft und Nationalökonomie* . 3rd edn, Stuttgart: Gustav Fischer, 1966.

Weber, A. 1909. *Alfred Weber's Theory of Location of Industries*. Trans. C.J. Friedrich, Chicago: University of Chicago Press, 1929.

specie-flow mechanism. The 'specie-flow mechanism' is an analytic version of automatic, or market, adjustment of the balance of international payments. In competitive markets with specie-standard institutions, behaviour will lead to national price levels and income flows consistent with equilibrium in the international accounts, commonly interpreted in this context to mean zero trade balances.

The classic exposition of the mechanism, for the better part of two centuries all but universally accepted, at least as a first approximation, was provided by David Hume in a 1752 essay, 'Of the Balance of Trade'. While it is appropriate to associate the essence of the model with Hume, all the ingredients of Hume's argument had long been available. There were even notable prior attempts to fit the analytic pieces into a self-contained model. Further, even if we give to Hume all the considerable credit due to his systematic, compact statement, his version is not the whole of the specie-flow mechanism; and the specie-flow mechanism is not the whole analysis of balance of payments adjustment.

Hume's presentation is a simple application of the quantity theory of money in a setting of international trade and its financing. With a pure 100 per cent reserve gold standard, and beginning with balance in the international accounts, a decrease in the money stock of country A results in a directly proportionate fall in its price level, which is also a decrease relative to the initially unaffected price levels of other countries; as country A's price level falls, consumer response, in Hume's account, will reduce A's imports and increase its exports; when the exchange rate is bid to the gold point, the export trade balance will be financed by gold inflow, which will raise prices in A and lower prices abroad until the international price differentials and net trade flows are eliminated. The line of causation runs from changes in money to changes in prices to changes in net trade flows to international movements of gold that eliminate the earlier price differentials and thereby correct the trade imbalance and stop the shipment of gold. In equilibrium, the distribution of gold among countries (and regions within countries) yields national (and regional) price levels consistent with zero trade balances.

This theory of trade equilibration links with the Ricardian theory of production specialization. In a comparative advantage model of two countries, two commodities, and labour input, country A has absolute advantages of different degrees in both goods. To have two-way trade, the wage rate of country A must be greater than that abroad, within the wage-ratio range specified by the proportions of A's productive superiority in the two goods. Gold will flow until the international wage ratio-yields domestic prices that equate total import and export values.

The conclusion that trade imbalances, and thus gold flows, cannot long obtain was in fundamental contrast to the mercantilistic emphasis on persistent promotion of an export balance and indefinite accumulation of gold. Still, the mercantilists decidedly associated gold inflows with export surpluses of goods and services; a good many writers had posited a direct relation between the money stock and the price level; similarly, it had been indicated that relative national price level changes would affect trade flows. However, while we should bow to such predecessors of Hume as Isaac Gervaise (1720) and Richard Cantillon (1734) and perhaps nod to Gerard de Malynes (1601) for attempts to construct adjustment models, Hume put the elements together with unmatched elegance and awareness of implication – and influence.

Hume's version was specifically a *price*-specie-flow mechanism, with the prices being national price levels (and exchange rates). Even as a price mechanism, the model has problems.

While it is reasonable to presume that price levels will move in the same directions (even if not in the same proportions) as the huge changes in the money stock envisioned by Hume, there remain questions of the impact on import and export expenditures. Vertical demand schedules in country A for imports and in other countries for A's exports would leave the physical amounts of imports and exports unresponsive to price changes. If, following Hume, we upset the initial equilibrium by a large decrease in money and thus in prices in country A, foreign expenditure on A's goods will fall proportionately with the fall in A's prices. The import balance of A will be financed with gold outflow, resulting in a further fall in A's prices and export value and an increase in prices abroad and in A's import expenditure. The gold flow, rather than correcting the trade flow, will increase the import trade balance of A when demand elasticities are zero (or sufficiently small). The import and export demand (and supply) elasticity conditions required for price (including exchange rate) changes to be equilibrating – conditions which are empirically realistic – came much later to be summarized in the 'Marshall–Lerner condition'. Under the most unfavourable circumstances of infinite supply elasticities and initially balanced trade, all that is required for stability is that the arithmetic sum of the elasticities of foreign demand for A's exports and of A's demand for imports be greater than unity.

Aside from the nicety of specifying elasticity conditions for stability, is it appropriate to couch the model in terms of diverging national price levels or of changes in a country's import prices compared to its export prices? Suppose country A has a commodity export balance, resulting perhaps from a shift in international demands reflecting changed preferences in favour of A's goods or imposition of a tariff by A or a foreign crop failure. As gold flows in, A's expenditures expand and prices are expected to rise. Prices of A's *domestic* goods (which do not enter foreign trade) do rise; but prices of *internationally* traded goods are affected little, if at all, for the increase in A's demand for such goods is countered by decrease in demand for them in gold-losing countries. Consumers in A, facing the domestic–international price divergence, shift to now relatively cheapened international goods (imports and A-exportables) from more expensive domestic goods, thus increasing import volume and value and also absorption of exportables. Producers in A shift out of international goods into domestic, thus reducing exports and expanding imports. Corresponding, but opposite, substitutions and shifts are diffused among the other countries. These respective domestic adjustments in consumption and production would continue until the gold flow ceases and the trade imbalance is corrected.

Substantial modern empirical research, however, is more supportive of Hume's changes in the terms of trade or of transitory divergences in relative prices of traded and non-traded goods than of the assumed invariant applicability of the equilibrium 'law of one price' commonly adopted in the modern 'monetary approach' to the balance of payments.

When gold flows into country A, portfolio equilibria of individuals and firms are upset, with cash balances now in excess. People try to spend away redundant balances. Expenditure rises and money income becomes larger. With greater income, demands for goods – including foreign goods – increase: at any given commodity price, quantity demanded has become larger. Import quantities and values rise. Changes in money give rise abroad to opposite portofolio adjustments and changes of income, thereby decreasing A's exports. In all this, there are some changes (upward in A and downward abroad) in prices of domestic goods and production factors, but the adjustment process entails income changes as well as price changes.

Some such role of changes in money income and demand schedules was noted – in different contexts and with different degrees of clarity and emphasis – by many writers in the 19th and early 20th centuries. But single-minded emphasis on income, with little or no explicit role for the money stock and prices, came only with application to balance of payments adjustment of the national income theory of J.M. Keynes. However, such application – with its regalia of marginal propensities and secondary, supplemental repercussions of multipliers – is not contingent on, or uniquely associated with, an international gold standard. Further, neglect of money in the foreign-trade multiplier analysis is a grievous omission. Equilibrium in the income model is characterized by equating of the flows of income leakages (saving, tax payments, imports) and income injections (investment, government expenditure, exports). But such equality of totai leakages and injections permits a continuing trade imbalance. And a trade imbalance financed by a gold flow – or accompanied by money change generally – leads to further change in income; that is, income had not reached a genuine equilibrium.

The actual world, even with the classical gold standard in the generation prior to World War I, has not conformed well in institutions and processes with the construct of Hume. A world generally of irredeemable paper money and universally of demand deposits along with fractional-reserve banking and discretionary money policy – a world including the International Monetary Fund arrangement of indefinitely pegged exchange rates – has relied on selected adjustment procedures more than on automatic adjustment mechanisms. So Hume's model in its own terms is inadequate and in important empirical respects is even inappropriate. But it provided analytical coherency and expositional emphasis in an early stage of a discussion which continues to evolve.

William R. Allen

BIBLIOGRAPHY

Blaug, M. 1985. *Economic Theory in Retrospect*. Cambridge: Cambridge University Press.

Darby, M. and Lothian, J. 1983. *The International Transmission of Inflation*. Chicago: University of Chicago Press.

Fausten, D. 1979. The Humean origin of the contemporary monetary approach to the balance of payments. *Quarterly Journal of Economics* 93, November, 655–73.

Rotwein, E. (ed.) 1970. *David Hume: Writings on Economics*. Madison: University of Wisconsin Press.

Yeager, L. 1976. *International Monetary Relations: Theory, History, and Policy*. 2nd edn, New York: Harper & Row.

specification problems in econometrics. A lengthy list of implicit and explicit assumptions is required to draw inferences from a data set. Substantial doubt about these assumptions is a characteristic of the analysis of non-experimental data and much experimental data as well. If this doubt is left unattended, it can cause serious doubt about the corresponding inferences.

The set of assumptions used to draw inferences from a data set is called a 'specification'. The treatment of doubt about the specification is called 'specification analysis'. The research strategy of trying many different specifications is called a 'specification search'.

When an inference is suspected to depend crucially on a doubtful assumption, two kinds of actions can be taken to alleviate the consequent doubt about the inferences. Both require a list of alternative assumptions. The first approach is statistical estimation which uses the data to select from the list of alternative assumptions and then makes suitable adjustments to the inferences to allow for doubt about the assumptions. The second approach is a sensitivity analysis that uses the alternative assumptions one at a time, thereby demonstrating either that all the alternatives lead to essentially the same inferences or that minor changes in the assumptions make major changes in the inferences. For example, a doubtful variable can simply be included in the equation (estimation), or two different equations can be estimated, one with and one without the doubtful variable (sensitivity analysis).

The borderline between the techniques of estimation and sensitivity analysis is not always clear since a specification search can be either a method of estimation of a general model or a method of studying the sensitivity of an inference to choice of model. Stepwise regression, for example, which involves the sequential deletion of 'insignificant' variables and insertion of 'significant' variables is best thought to be a method of estimation of a general model rather than a study of the sensitivity of estimates to choice of variables, since no attempt is generally made to communicate how the results change as different subsets of variables are included.

When the data evidence is very informative, estimation is the preferred approach. But parameter spaces can always be enlarged beyond the point where data can be helpful in distinguishing alternatives. In fact, parameter spaces in economics are typically large enough to overwhelm our data sets, and when abbreviated parameter spaces appear to be used, there usually lurks behind the scene a much larger space of assumptions that ought to be explored. If this larger space has been explored through a pretesting procedure and if the data are sufficiently informative that estimation is the preferred approach, then adjustments to the inferences are in order to account for the pretesting bias. If the data are not adequately informative about the parameters of the larger space, we need to have answers to the sensitivity question whether ambiguity about the best method of estimation implies consequential ambiguity about the inferences. A data analysis should therefore combine estimation with sensitivity analysis, and only those inferences that are clearly favoured by the data or are sturdy enough to withstand minor changes in the assumptions should be retained.

Estimation and sensitivity analyses are two phases of a data analysis. Simplification is a third. The intent of simplification is to find a simple model that works well for a class of decisions. A specification search can be used for simplification, as well as for estimation and sensitivity analysis. The very prevalent confusion among these three kinds of searches ought to be eliminated since the rules for a search and measures of its success will properly depend on its intent.

The function of econometric theory is to plan responses to data. A response may be an action (e.g. the choice of an hypothesis) or a feeling (e.g. a confidence interval). In settings in which the theory and the method of measurement are clear, responses can be conveniently planned in advance. In practice, however, most analysers of economic data have very low levels of commitment to whatever plans they may have formulated before reviewing the data. Even when planning is extensive, most analysts reserve the right to alter the plans if the data are judged 'unusual'. A review of the planned responses to the data after the data are actually observed can be called criticism, the function of which is either to detect deficiencies in the original family of models that ought to be remedied by enhancements of the parameter space or to detect inaccuracies in the original approximation of prior information. When either the model or the prior information is revised, the planned responses are discarded in favour of what at the time seem to be better responses.

The form that criticism should take is not clear cut. Much of what appears to be criticism is in fact a step in a process of estimation, since the enhancement of the model is completely predictable. An example of an estimation method masquerading as criticism is a t-test to determine if a specific variable should be added to the regression. In this case the response to the data is planned in advance and undergoes no revision once the data are observed.

Criticism and the prospect of the revision of planned responses create a crippling dilemma for classical inference since, according to that theory, the choice of response should be based entirely on sampling properties, which are impossible to compute unless the response to every conceivable data set is planned and fully committed. When a criticism is successful, that is to say when the family of models is enhanced or the prior distribution is altered in response to anomalies in the data, there is a severe double counting problem if estimation then proceeds as if the model and prior distribution were not data-instigated. Even if criticism is not successful, the prospect of successful criticism makes the inferences from the data weaker than conventionally reported because the commitment to the model and the prior is weaker than is admitted.

CHOICE OF VARIABLES FOR LINEAR REGRESSION. Specification problems are not limited to but are often discussed within the context of the linear regression model, probably because the most common problem facing analysers of economic data is doubt about the exact list of explanatory variables. The first results in this literature addressed the effect of excluding variables that belong in the equation, and including variables that do not. Let y represent the dependent variable, x an included explanatory variable, and z a doubtful explanatory variable. Assume that:

$$E(y \mid x, z) = \alpha + x\beta + z\theta.$$
$$\mathrm{Var}(y \mid x) = \sigma^2,$$
$$E(z \mid x) = c + xr$$
$$\mathrm{Var}(z \mid x) = s^2$$

where α, β, θ, c, r, σ^2, and s^2 are unknown parameters, and y, x, and z are observable vectors. Then β can be estimated with z included in the equation:

$$b_{.z} = (x'M_z x)^{-1}(x'M_z y),$$

or with z excluded:

$$b = (x'x)^{-1}x'y,$$

where

$$M_z = I - z(z'z)^{-1}z'.$$

The first two moments of these estimators are straightforwardly computed:

$$E(b_{.z}) = \beta, \qquad E(b) = \beta + r\theta$$
$$\mathrm{Bias}(b_{.z}) = 0 \qquad \mathrm{Bias}(b) = r\theta$$
$$\mathrm{Var}(b_{.z}) = \sigma^2(x'M_z x)^{-1} \qquad \mathrm{Var}(b) = \sigma^2(x'x)^{-1}$$

where

$$\mathrm{Bias}(b) = E(b) - \beta.$$

A bit of algebra reveals that $\mathrm{Var}(b_{.z}) \geqslant \mathrm{Var}(b)$. These moments form two basic results in 'specification analysis' made popular by Theil (1957): (1) If a relevant variable is excluded ($\theta \neq 0$), the estimator is biased by an amount that is the product of the coefficient of the excluded variable times the regression coefficient from the regression of the included on the excluded variable. (2) If an irrelevant variable is included ($\theta = 0$), the estimator remains unbiased, but has an inflated variance.

This bias result can be useful when the variable z is unobservable and information is available on the probable values of θ and r, since then the bias in b can be corrected. But if both x and z are observable, these results are not useful by themselves because they do not unambiguously select between the estimators, one doing well in terms of bias but the other doing well in terms of variance. The choice will obviously depend on information about the value of $r\theta$, since a small value of $r\theta$ implies a small value for the bias of b. The choice will also depend on the loss function that determines the tradeoff between bias and variance.

For mathematical convenience, the loss function is usually assumed to be quadratic:

$$L(\beta^*, \beta) = (\beta^* - \beta)^2,$$

where β^* is an estimator of β. The expected value of this loss function is known as the mean squared error of the estimator, which can be written as the variance plus the square of the bias:

$$\mathrm{MSE}(b_{.z}, \beta) - \mathrm{MSE}(b, \beta) = r(\mathrm{Var}(\theta^*_{.x}) - \theta\theta')r'$$

where $\theta^*_{.x}$ is the least squares estimator of θ controlling for x, and where the notation allows x and z to represent collections of variables as well as singlets. By inspection of this formula we can derive the fundamental result in this literature. The estimator based on the restricted model is better in the mean squared error sense than the unrestricted estimator if and only if θ is small enough that $\mathrm{Var}(\theta^*_{.x}) - \theta\theta'$ is positive definite. If θ is a scalar, this condition can be described as 'a true t less than one', $\theta^2/\mathrm{Var}(\theta^*_{.x}) < 1$.

This result is also of limited use since its answer to the question 'Which estimator is better?' is another question 'How big is θ?' A clever suggestion is to let the data provide the answer, and to omit z if its estimated t value is less than one. Unfortunately, because the estimated t is not exactly equal to the true t, this two-step procedure does not yield an estimator that guarantees a lower mean squared error than unconstrained least squares. Thus the question remains: how big is θ? For more discussion consult Judge and Bock (1983).

A Bayesian analysis allows the construction of estimators that make explicit use of information about θ. It is convenient to assume that the information about θ takes the form of a preliminary data set in which the estimate of θ is zero (or some other number, if you prefer). Then the Bayes estimate of β is a weighted average of the constrained and unconstrained estimators:

$$b_{\mathrm{B}} = (v^{-1} + v'^{-1})^{-1}(v^{-1}b_{.z} + v'^{-1}b)$$

where v' is the prior variance for h, and v is the sampling variance for $\theta^*_{.x}$. Instinct might suggest that this compromise between the two estimators would depend on the variances of $b_{.z}$ and b, but the correct weights are inversely proportional to prior variance and the sample variances for θ.

A card-carrying Bayesian regards this to be the solution to the problem. Others will have a different reaction. What the Bayesian has done is only to enlarge the family of estimators. The two extremes are still possible since we may have $v' = 0$ or $v' \to \infty$, but in addition there are the intermediate values $v' > 0$. Thus the Bayesian answer to the question is another question: 'What is the value of v'?'

SENSITIVITY ANALYSIS. At this point we have to switch from the estimation mode to the sensitivity mode, since precise values of v' will be hard to come by on a purely *a priori* basis and since the data usually will be of little help in selecting v' with great accuracy. A sensitivity analysis can be done from a classical point of view simply by contrasting the two extreme estimates, $b_{.z}$ and b, corresponding to the extreme values of v'. A Bayesian approach allows a much richer set of sensitivity studies. A mathematically convenient analysis begins with a hypothetical value for v', say v'_0, which is selected to represent as accurately as possible the prior information that may be available. A neighbourhood around this point is selected to reflect the accuracy with which v'_0 can be chosen. For example, v' might be restricted to lie in the interval

$$v'_0/(1+c) < v' < v'_0(1+c),$$

where c measures the accuracy of v'_0. The corresponding interval of Bayes' estimates b_{B} is

$$1/(v'_0(1+c)+v) < (b_{\mathrm{B}} - b_{.z})/v(b - b_{.z}) < (1+c)/(v'_0 + v(1+c)),$$

where it is assumed that $(b - b_{.z}) > 0$. If this interval is large for small values of c, then the estimate is very sensitive to the definition of the prior information. For example, suppose that interest focuses on the sign of β. Issues of standard errors aside, if $b_{.z}$ and b are the same sign, then the inference can be said to be sturdy since no value of c can change the sign of the estimate b_{B}. But if $b > 0 > b_{.z}$, then the values of c in excess of the following will cause the interval of estimates to overlap the origin:

$$c^* = \max[u - 1, u^{-1} - 1],$$

where $u = -(v/v'_0)(b/b_{.z})$. Thus if u is close to one, the inference is fragile. This occurs if differences in the absolute size of the two estimates are offset by differences in the variances applicable to the coefficient of the doubtful variable. Measures like these can be found in Leamer (1978, 1982, 1983b).

ROBUSTNESS. When a set of acceptable assumptions does not map into a specific decision, the inference is said to be fragile. A decision can then sensibly be based on a minimax criterion that selects a 'robust' procedure that works well regardless of the assumption. The literature on 'robustness' such as that reviewed by Krasker et al. (1983) has concentrated on issues relating to the choice of sampling distribution, but could be extended to choice of prior distribution.

SIMPLIFICATION, PROXY SELECTION AND DATA SELECTION. A specification search involving the estimation of many different models can be a method of estimation or a method of sensitivity analysis. Simplification searches are also common, the goal of which is to find a simple quantitative facsimile that can be used as a decision-making tool. For example, a model with a high R^2 can be expected to provide accurate forecasts in a stable environment, whether or not the coefficients can be given a causal interpretation. In particular, if two explanatory variables are highly correlated, then one can be excluded from the equation without greatly reducing the overall fit since the included variable will take over the role of the excluded variable. No causal significance necessarily attaches to the coefficient of the retained variable.

A specification search can also be used to select the best from a set of alternative proxy variables, or to select a data subset. These problems can be dealt with by enlarging the parameter space to allow for multiple proxy variables or unusual data points. Once the space is properly enlarged, the problems that remain are exactly the same as the problems encountered when the parameters are coefficients in a linear regression, namely estimation and sensitivity analysis.

DATA-INSTIGATED MODELS. The subjects of estimation, sensitivity analysis and simplification deal with concerns that arise during the planning phase of a statistical analysis when alternative responses to hypothetical data sets are under consideration. A distinctly different kind of specification search occurs when anomalies in the actual data suggest a revision in a planned response, for example, the inclusion of a variable that was not originally identified. This is implicitly disallowed by formal statistical theories which presuppose the existence of a response to the data that is planned and fully committed. I like to refer to a search for anomalies as 'Sherlock Holmes inference', since when asked who might have committed the crime, Holmes replied, 'No data yet.... It is a capital mistake to theorize before you have all the evidence. It biases the judgements'. This contrasts with the typical advice of theoretical econometricans: 'No theory yet. It is a capital mistake to look at the data before you have identified all the theories'.

Holmes is properly concerned that an excessive degree of theorizing will make it psychologically difficult to see anomalies in the data that might, if recognized, point sharply to a theory that was not originally identified. On the other hand, the econometrician is worried that data evidence may be double counted, once in the Holmesian mode to instigate models that seem favoured by the data and again in the estimation mode to select the instigated models over original models. Holmes is properly unconcerned about the double counting problem, since he has the ultimate extra bit of data: the confession. We do not have the luxury of running additional experiments and the closest that we can come to the Holmesian procedure is to set aside a part of the data set in hopes of squeezing a confession after we have finished identifying a set of models with a Holmesian analysis of the first part of the data. Unfortunately, our data sets never do confess, and the ambiguity of the inferences that is clearly present after the Holmesian phase lingers on with very little attenuation after the estimation phase. Thus we are forced to find a solution to the Holmesian conundrum of how properly to characterize the data evidence when models are instigated by the data, that is to say, how to avoid the double counting problem. Clearly, what is required is some kind of penalty that discourages but does not preclude Holmesian discoveries. Leamer (1978) proposes one penalty that rests on the assumption that Holmesian analysis mimics the solution to a formal presimplification problem in which models are explicitly simplified before the data are observed in order to avoid observation and processing costs that are associated with the larger model. Anomalies in the data set can then suggest a revision of this decision. Of course real Holmesian analysis cannot actually solve this sequential decision problem since in order to solve it one has to identify the complete structure that is simplified before observation. But we can nonetheless act as if we were solving this problem, since by doing so we can compute a very sensible kind of penalty for Holmesian discoveries (Leamer, 1978).

CRITICISM. Estimation and sensitivity analysis are two important phases of a data analysis. The third is criticism. The function of criticism is to highlight anomalies in a data set that might lead to Holmesian revisions in the model. Criticism and data instigated models are not as frequent as they may appear. As remarked before,. much of what is said to be criticism is only a step in a method of estimation, and many models that seem to be data-instigated are in fact explicitly identified in advance of the data analysis. For example, forward stepwise regression, which adds statistically significant variables to a regression equation, cannot be said to be producing data-instigated models because the set of alternative models is explicitly identified before the data analysis commences and the response to the data is fully planned in advance. Stepwise regression is thus only a method of estimation of a general model. Likewise, various diagnostic tests which lead necessarily to a particular enhancement of the model, such as a Durbin–Watson test for first order autocorrelation, select but do not instigate a model.

'Goodness of fit' tests which do not have explicit alternatives are sometimes used to criticize a model. However, the Holmesian question is not whether the data appear to be anomalous with respect to a given model but rather whether there is a plausible alternative that makes them appear less anomalous. In large samples, all models have large goodness of fit statistics, and the size of the statistic is no guarantee, or even a strong suggestion, that there exists a plausible alternative model that is substantially better than the one being used. Still, I admit that there are examples in which a goodness-of-fit statistic can be suggestive, probably because the set of alternative hypotheses, though not explicitly stated, is nonetheless 'intuitive'.

Unexpected parameter estimates are probably the most effective criticisms of a model. A Durbin–Watson statistic that indicates a substantial amount of autocorrelation can be used legitimately to signal the existence of left-out variables in settings in which there is strong prior information that the residuals are white noise. Aside from unexpected estimates, graphical displays and the study of influential data points may stimulate thinking about the inadequacies in a model.

EDWARD E. LEAMER

See also BAYESIAN INFERENCE; ECONOMETRICS; STATISTICAL INFERENCE.

BIBLIOGRAPHY

Box, G.E.P. 1980. Sampling and Bayes' inference in scientific modelling and robustness. *Journal of the Royal Statistical Society*, Series A, Pt 4, 383–430.

Judge, G.G. and Bock, M.E. 1983. Biased estimation. In *Handbook of Econometrics*, Vol. 1, ed. Z. Griliches and M. Intriligator, Amsterdam: North-Holland.

Krasker, W.S., Kuh, E. and Welsch, R.E. 1983. Estimation for dirty data and flawed models. In *Handbook of Econometrics*, Vol. 1, ed. Z. Griliches and M. Intriligator, Amsterdam: North-Holland.

Leamer, E.E. 1978. *Specification Searches*. New York: Wiley.

Leamer, E.E. 1982. Sets of posterior means with bounded variance priors. *Econometrica* 50, May, 725–36.

Leamer, E.E. 1983a. Let's take the con out of econometrics. *American Economic Review* 73, March, 31–43.

Leamer, E.E. 1983b. Model choice and specification analysis. In *Handbook of Econometrics*, Vol. 1, ed. Z. Griliches and M. Intriligator, Amsterdam: North Holland.

Theil, H. 1957. Specification errors and the estimation of economic relationships. *Review of the International Statistical Institute* 25, 41–51.

spectral analysis. A univariate discrete time-series x_t is said to be second-order stationary if its mean, variance and autocovariances $\mu_r = \operatorname{cov}(x_t, x_{t-r})$ are all time invariant. If x_t has no strictly cyclical or deterministic components and is stationary, there are two mathematical relationships with important interpretations, the Cramer representation

$$x_t = \int_{-\pi}^{\pi} \mathrm{e}^{it\omega}\,\mathrm{d}z(\omega) \tag{1}$$

where

$$E[\mathrm{d}z(\omega)\,\overline{\mathrm{d}z(\lambda)}] = 0, \quad \omega \neq \lambda \\ = f(\omega)\,\mathrm{d}w, \quad \omega = \lambda \tag{2}$$

and the spectral representation of the autocovariances

$$\mu_r = \int_{-\pi}^{\pi} \mathrm{e}^{ir\omega} f(\omega)\,\mathrm{d}w. \tag{3}$$

Each relationship is a Fourier representation of the sequence on the left-hand side. The interpretation of (1) is that a stationary series can be thought of as a (non-countably infinite) sum of uncorrelated components. As x_t is a random sequence, so the components are random and each is associated with a particular frequency in the range from zero to π. As frequency is proportional to the inverse of period, a component with frequency near π corresponds to the quickly changing oscillations in the data, that is the 'short-run', and those with low frequencies correspond to the slowly-changing components of the data, the 'long-run'. These components will be uncorrelated for different pairs of frequencies and the component with frequency ω will have a variance proportional to the value of the function $f(\omega)$ at ω, as shown in (2). These components, denoted by $\mathrm{d}z(\omega)$ in (1), are complex for technical reasons. Because the components are uncorrelated, the variance of x_t, denoted by μ_0, will be the sum (actually the integral) of the variances of the components, as seen in (3) by putting $r=0$. Thus, the relative importance of components can be measured in terms of their contribution to the variance of x_t, which is seen directly from the plot of $f(\omega)$ against ω. $f(\omega)$, known as the spectral density function, has the property that it is non-negative and is symmetric about $\omega=0$, so that $f(-\omega)=f(\omega)$. Once $f(\omega)$ is known, all the autocovariances are uniquely determined from it by (3). There is also a reverse relationship, so that if the sequence μ_r is known, then $f(\omega)$ is determined. There is thus a one-to-one relationship between the sequence μ_r and the spectral function $f(\omega)$.

There are basically two forms of analysis of a single stationary series. The so-called time-domain analysis involves estimation and interpretation of the autocovariances μ_r and then building a model that generates data giving this particular sequence μ_r. The frequency-domain or spectral analysis concentrates on the function $f(\omega)$. Because of the one-to-one relationship, each analysis provides exactly the same information about the series, at least in theory. In practice, certain types of analysis are easier in one domain than the other, and so familiarity with both is convenient.

If x_t is a stationary series with spectrum $f_z(\omega)$ and z_t is a series derived from it by a filter, such as

$$z_t=\sum c_j x_{t-j}$$

then z_t has spectrum $f_z(\omega)$ given by

$$f_z(\omega)=|c(z)|^2 f_z(\omega)$$

where $c(z)=\Sigma c_j z^j$ and $z=e^{iw}$.

The spectrum of an uncorrelated, or 'white noise', series ϵ_t is flat, taking the form

$$f(\omega)=\frac{\operatorname{var}(\epsilon)}{2\pi},\qquad -\pi\leqslant\omega\leqslant\pi.$$

It follows that the spectrum of any stationary autoregressive or moving average model can be derived immediately, as these are filtered versions of white noise. Any series that has a spectrum highest at low frequencies will be smooth, but if the higher frequencies dominate the spectral shape, the series will be very unsmooth.

The theory can be extended to the case when the series contains a cycle, or near cycle, as then the spectrum will have a strong peak at the frequency of the cycle. For example, if a monthly series contains a seasonal, it will have spectral peaks at frequencies $2\pi k/12, k=1,\ldots,6$.

When analysing a single series, the estimated spectral shape is useful for detecting cycles in the data and for determining the relative importance of different frequency components, such as the long-run versus short-run components. If a theory suggests a particular temporal structure, such as white noise for changes of prices from an efficient market, this can be tested from the shape of the estimated spectrum. Experience shows that many macroeconomic series have a typical spectral shape, with a peak at zero frequency, often seasonal peaks and a smooth, generally declining background shape. This typical shape, which is by no means inevitable, does not necessarily coincide with a finite-variance, stationary model; but rather with a series known as integrated of order one. A series is so called if it needs to be differenced once to produce a series with spectrum which is everywhere positive but without a distinct peak or zero frequency. Using the filter result above, the spectrum of an integrated of order one series takes the form $f_x(\omega)=(1-\cos\omega)^{-2}f_{\Delta x}(\omega)$ where $f_{\Delta x}(\omega)$ is the spectrum of the differenced series and does not have the typical shape. Other generalizations of the stationarity condition have been considered by Priestley (1981) for time-varying spectra and by Hatanaka and Suzuki (1967) for a variety of trending series.

Care has to be taken in estimating the spectrum as it seems that it is impossible to have an unbiased and consistent estimate. A variety of methods of estimation is available and several are discussed in the Proceedings of the IEEE, September 1982, *Special Issue on Spectral Estimation*, and in Koopmans (1974).

The usefulness of spectral techniques is increased when several series are considered. If x_t, y_t are both stationary, zero-mean series with no cycles, and they are also second-order jointly stationary so that the cross-covariances $\mu_r^{xy}=E[x_t y_{t-r}]$ are not functions of time, then expanding the notation of (1) in an obvious way, the bivariate version of (2) is

$$\begin{aligned}E[dz_x(\omega)\,\overline{dz_y(\lambda)}]&=0, &\omega\neq\lambda\\ &=\operatorname{cr}(\omega)\,dw, &\omega=\lambda\end{aligned}$$

where $\operatorname{cr}(\omega)$ is the cross-spectrum. Equation (3) becomes

$$\mu_r^{xy}=\int e^{ir\omega}\operatorname{cr}(\omega)\,dw.$$

As $\mu_r^{xy}\neq\mu_{-r}^{xy}$ in general, $\operatorname{cr}(\omega)$ will not be a real function of frequency. A more convenient pair of functions is the coherence, defined by

$$C(\omega)=\frac{|\operatorname{cr}(\omega)|^2}{f_z(\omega)f_y(\omega)}$$

and the phase defined by

$$\Phi(\omega)=\tan^{-1}\left[\frac{\text{Imaginary part of cr}(\omega)}{\text{Real part of cr}(\omega)}\right].$$

If x_t, y_t are jointly stationary, they can be considered as sums of uncorrelated components where their components at different frequencies are also uncorrelated across series. Thus, the series are related only through corresponding frequency components, and the coherence measures the squared correlations of these components, so that essentially

$$C(\omega)=[\operatorname{corr}(dz_x(\omega), dz_y(\omega))]^2.$$

It is thus possible to find that a pair of series are highly related at low frequency (the long run) but little related at other frequencies. The phase diagram is generally less useful, but in a few simple cases can help determine a time-lag between the series. If $x_t=ay_{t-k}+z_t$, where y_t, z_t are independent stationary series, then $\Phi(\omega)=k\omega$ and so the lag k can be detected as the slope of a trend in $\Phi(\omega)$ plotted against ω. In this analysis k need not be an integer. However, for more complicated lagged relationships between x_t and y_t the phase diagram becomes very difficult to interpret.

For more than two series, spectra can be defined from partial autocorrelations, but a more and useful approach is that of band-pass regression discussed and applied by Engle (1974, 1980). Suppose that $x_t(\omega)$ represents the component of x_t consisting of frequencies around ω. Theoretically, such a series might be obtained by application of special filters. Similarly, if there are a number of explanatory series, $y_{jt}, j=,\ldots,N$, each will have corresponding components $y_{jt}(\omega)$. If the series are jointly stationary, then $x_t(\omega)$ should be explained just by the $y_j(\omega)$, as only similar frequency components are potentially correlated. This suggests a regression of the form

$$x_t(\omega)=\sum_j \beta_j(\omega)y_{jt}(\omega)+\text{residual}.$$

Economists might expect the β's to change with frequency, as long-run components may be explained in a differently way than are seasonal or short-run components. The $\beta_j(\omega)$ can be estimated directly from the spectra and cross-spectra and although they can be complex, they are generally easy to interpret. In an application, Engle considered the consumption function to determine whether the marginal propensity to consume an additional dollar of income appeared to be different for high and low frequencies. Interpreting high frequencies as the transitory component and low frequencies as the permanent component of income, the permanent income hypothesis would suggest a substantial difference, but none was observed. These methods can also be used as a test for correct specification of a model.

In another multivariate situation, spectral techniques have been used to identify and interpret common factors in a group of series. Considering a group of interest rates, Singleton (1980) investigated how many independent noise sources there were acting as common factors, and found evidence for just two.

Although time domain modelling techniques are certainly more useful for forecasting and possibly for some policy selection situations, the frequency domain methods are helpful as complementary methods of analysis and for testing various types of economic theories. An early reference is Granger and Hatanaka (1964) which emphasizes interpretation, the more recent book by Koopmans (1974) being more comprehensive. A history of the use of spectral techniques in economics has been given by Granger and Engle (1984).

C.W.J. GRANGER

BIBLIOGRAPHY

Engle, R.F. 1974. Band spectrum regression. *International Economic Review* 15, 1–11.

Engle, R.F. 1980. Exact maximum likelihood methods for dynamic regressions and band spectrum regressions. *International Economic Review* 21, 391–407.

Granger, C.W.J. and Engle, R.F. 1984. Applications of spectral analysis in econometrics. Ch. 5 in *The Handbook of Statistics*, Vol. 3: *Time Series in the Frequency Domain*, ed. D.R. Brillinger and P.R. Krishnaiah, Amsterdam: North-Holland.

Granger, C.W.J. and Hatanaka, M. 1964. *Spectral Analysis of Economic Time Series*. Princeton: Princeton University Press.

Hatanaka, M. and Suzuki, M. 1967. The theory of the pseudospectrum and its application to non-stationary dynamic econometric models. Ch. 23 in *Essays in Mathematical Economics, in Honor of Oskar Morgenstern*, ed. M. Shubik, Princeton: Princeton University Press.

IEEE. *Proceedings*, September 1982.

Koopmans, L.H. 1974. *The Spectral Analysis of Time Series*. New York: Academic Press.

Priestley, M. 1981. *Spectral Analysis and Time Series*. New York: Academic Press.

Singleton, K.J. 1980. A latent time-series model of the cyclical behavior of interest rates. *International Economic Review* 21, 559–76.

Spencer, Herbert (1820–1903). Though largely ignored today, Herbert Spencer was one of the most influential scientists and philosophers of the late 19th century. He was born at Derby to a family of Dissenters, and educated at home. As a young man he worked on the London & Birmingham Railway, acquiring considerable practical knowledge of civil engineering and, through his observation of railway cuts, expertise in geology. He had no university training, but read extremely widely in an array of fields.

He was an early and enthusiastic partisan of Darwin and of evolutionist ideas. In 1860 he published a prospectus for a 'system of synthetic philosophy', a general compendium of knowledge, which was to occupy him for much of the rest of his life. He set out to survey, from the 'evolutionary point of view', the fields of biology, psychology, sociology and ethics, publishing in turn *First Principles* (1862); *Principles of Biology* (2 vols, 1864–7); *Principles of Psychology* (2nd edn, 2 vols, 1870–72); *Principles of Sociology* (3 vols, 1876–96) and *Principles of Ethics* (2 vols, 1879–93).

His most important work bearing on social policy was the polemical *The Man versus the State* (1884). Spencer was a highly vocal champion of Social Darwinism, applying the principle he termed 'survival of the fittest' to a broad variety of struggles, including economic competition. He conceived society by analogy to an organism, arguing that it developed according to immanent processes of growth, and hence that the positive actions and interventions of politicians were likely to be harmful or superfluous.

M. DONNELLY

SELECTED WORKS

1862. *First Principles*. London.

1864–7. *The Principles of Biology*. 2 vols, London: Williams & Norgate.

1870–72. *The Principles of Psychology*. 2 vols, 2nd edn, London: Williams & Norgate. (First published 1855.)

1876–96. *Principles of Sociology*. 3 vols, London: Williams & Norgate.

1879–93. *The Principles of Ethics*. 2 vols, London: Williams & Norgate.

Spengler, Joseph John (born 1902). American demographer and historian of economic thought. Born in Ohio and educated at Ohio State University, he taught at Duke University from 1932 until his retirement. Under his influence Duke became a centre for studies devoted to the history of economics, a development that culminated in the publication (begun 1969 and at Duke) of the specialized journal, *History of Political Economy*.

Spengler has given special attention to French demography and the history of French economic thought. Two of his books, *France Faces Depopulation* (1938) and *French Predecessors of Malthus* (1942), testify to this interest. Much of Spengler's work is in periodical articles, some of which were reprinted under the title *Population Economics: Selected Essays* in 1972.

Spengler is virtually the only economist of note who has taken an interest in ancient non-Western economic thought. He published a book on *Indian Economic Thought* (1971) and another one on *Origins of Economic Thought and Justice* (1980), which treats of ancient economic thought in Mesopotamia, India, China and Greece.

Spengler's work is informed by wide reading, yielding references that are comprehensive and include elusive sources. He would, to given an example, trace the origin of the phrase 'invisible hand' and find it in the writings of a 17th-century theologian who commented on mechanical interrelations in the physical world that are hidden to the senses. The reader who follows Spengler's references then comes across another 17th-century writer who interprets the same phenomenon in terms of hidden stage machinery in the theatre, an observation that shows the old phrase in a new light and demonstrates the virtue of Spengler's approach.

HENRY W. SPIEGEL

SELECTED WORKS

For a bibliography of Spengler's publications from 1929 to 1971 see Spengler (1972), 515–28.

1938 *France Faces Depopulation*. Durham, North Carolina: Duke University Publications.
1942. *French Predecessors of Malthus. A study in eighteenth-century wage and population theory*. Durham, North Carolina: Duke University Publications.
1950. Evolutionism in American economics 1800–1946. In *Evolutionary Thought in America*, ed. S. Persons, New Haven: Yale University Press, 201–66.
1961 (With R. Braibanti) *Tradition, Values, and Socio-Economic Development*. Durham, North Carolina: Duke University Press; London: Cambridge University Press.
1963. (With R. Braibanti, eds) *Administration and Economic Development in India*. Durham, North Carolina: Duke University Press; London: Cambridge University Press.
1971. *Indian Economic Thought; a preface to its history*. Durham, North Carolina: Duke University Press.
1972. *Population Economics: Selected Essays of Joseph J. Spengler*. Compiled by R.S. Smith et al., Durham, North Carolina: Duke University Press.
1980a. *Origins of Economic Thought and Justice*. Carbondale: Southern Illinois University Press.
1980b. (With R.L. Clark.) *The Economics of Individual and Population Aging*. Cambridge: Cambridge University Press.

BIBLIOGRAPHY
Sobel, I. 1983. Joseph J. Spengler: the institutional approach to the history of economics. In *Research in the History of Economic Thought and Methodology*, Vol. 1, ed. W.J. Samuels, Greenwich: JAI Press.

Spiegel, Henry William (born 1911). Spiegel was born in Germany, where he received his early education in the classics and law. The rise of the Nazi regime and a fellowship offer from Cornell brought him to the United States in 1936. In 1939 he received his PhD from Wisconsin. After brief sojourns at Duquesne University and in the US Army, he visited Brazil on a Guggenheim Fellowship. In 1947 he accepted a position at the Catholic University in Washington, DC, his permanent base until his retirement in 1977.

Initially his research was in Land Economics, but with the outbreak of World War II he became concerned with the economics of war, publishing a textbook on that subject in 1942. Following the war and another trip to Brazil he turned to the then new sub-discipline, economic development. In 1949 he published *The Brazilian Economy*, one of the early case studies in economic development focusing on the interaction between inflation and industrialization. His research then shifted to the history of economic thought, culminating in the widely read books, *The Development of Economic Thought* (1954) and *The Growth of Economic Thought* (1971). In between, he published *The Rise of American Economic Thought* (1960). Since 1974 he has been a member of the Advisory Board of the *History of Political Economy*.

W.O. Thweatt

SELECTED WORKS
1942. *The Economics of Total War*. New York: D. Appleton–Century.
1949. *The Brazilian Economy*. Philadelphia: Blakiston.
1952. *The Development of Economic Thought*. New York: John Wiley & Sons.
1960. *The Rise of American Economic Thought*. Philadelphia: Chilton.
1971. *The Growth of Economic Thought*. Englewood Cliffs, NJ: Prentice-Hall.

BIBLIOGRAPHY
[Anon.] 1959. Henry William Spiegel. *Social Science* 34(1), January, 46–8.

Spiethoff, Arthur August Kaspar (1873–1957). Spiethoff was born on 13 May 1873 in Düsseldorf and died on 4 April 1957 in Tübingen. He was a student of Adolph Wagner and research assistant to Gustav Schmoller. In 1908 he was appointed professor at Prague University and from 1918 held a chair of political economy at Bonn University until his retirement in 1939. He was the long-time editor of *Schmollers Jahrbuch* and (with Edgar Salin) of *Hand- und Lehrbücher aus dem Gebiet der Sozialwissenschaften*.

Spiethoff is best known for his path-breaking research into business cycles, as well as for his studies on methodology, culminating in his concept of 'economic style' (*Wirtschaftsstil*). In his methodological studies Spiethoff, strongly influenced by the German Historical School, sought for a solution to the antinomy of history and theory: the quest for generalizing statements about an ever-changing reality. He stressed the distinction between two methods of inquiry: pure economic theory (brought to perfection by Quesnay, Ricardo, Thünen, Menger, Jevons and Pareto) and 'observational' (*anschauliche*) or 'economic Gestalt theory' (in the tradition of the mercantilists, List, Sombart and Schmoller). Pure economic theory, whether or not it exclusively deals with time-less phenomena, such as those common to all forms of economic life, abstracts and isolates arbitrarily, depending on the particular purpose in view. 'Observational theory', on the other hand, takes its time-conditioned data from the real world and abstracts only from their historical uniqueness to isolate the regular and essential features. It thus yields an 'explanatory description' – that is, an effigy, or replica, of reality – 'purged of historical accidents' (Spiethoff, 1953b, p. 76). With its findings derived from time-conditioned data, 'economic Gestalt theory' is a 'historical' theory, the validity and applicability of its generalizations dependent on the existence and dominance of a certain 'economic style', representing uniformities of economic life in a certain historical epoch (e.g. the 'economic styles' of medieval town economy, of free market capitalism or of interventionism). Spiethoff's ultimate aim was an all-embracing general economic theory that would include as many different 'historical' theories as there are 'economic styles', together with the pure theory of time-less phenomena.

The foremost field of application of Spiethoff's methodological approach has always been his research on business cycles. In his writings (see Schweitzer, 1941, for a comprehensive bibliography), starting from the work of Clément Juglar, he emphasized three points: first, the necessity not to focus exclusively on crisis or overproduction, but instead to visualize the phenomenon of cyclical fluctuations as an entity; second, the strategic role to be ascribed to capital investment in the explanation of business cycles; and third, the fact that booms and depressions should not be considered as merely an accidental and insignificant concomitant of economic activity but must be understood as the essential form of capitalist life itself. This basic perception made him one of the founding fathers of modern business cycle research.

In keeping with this notion of 'time-conditioned' theory, Spiethoff considered his findings to be valid only for a certain 'economic style', representing an age marked by the prevalence of a highly developed capitalist economy and a free-market system. This era lasted from 1820 to 1913, with the capitalist economy not yet fully developed in earlier periods, while increasingly becoming subject to manipulation, planning and management in later times. Spiethoff's striving for 'historical' generalization took the form of distilling a 'typical cycle' to give account of the recurrent and essential features of all historically known business cycles. This 'typical cycle', now generally accepted, consists of three 'cyclical stages' (upswing, crisis and downswing), two of which may be subdivided into five 'cyclical phases': the downswing comprises the recession phase with investment declining and a 'first revival' during which the decline in investment is halted, while the upswing includes the 'second revival' with rapidly increasing investment, the boom phase characterized by rising interest rates and, finally, 'capital scarcity' with declining investment paving the way for the next downturn.

With his observation of 'cyclical periods', during which years of either boom or depression preponderate, Spiethoff in fact anticipated what later would become known as the Kondratieff cycle or 'long wave'.

INGO BARENS

SELECTED WORKS

1933. Overproduction. In *Encyclopaedia of the Social Sciences*, New York: Macmillan, Vol. 11.

1952. The 'historical' character of economic theories. *Journal of Economic History* 12, 131–9.

1953a. Pure theory and economic Gestalt theory: ideal types and real types. In *Enterprise and Secular Change: Readings in Economic History*, ed. F.C. Lane and J.C. Riemersma, London: George Allen & Unwin, 444–63.

1953b. Business cycles. *International Economic Papers* 3, 75–171. Originally published in German as 'Krisen', in *Handwörterbuch der Staatswissenschaften*, Vol. 6, Jena: G. Fischer, 1923, 8–91.

1955. *Die wirtschaftlichen Wechsellagen: Aufschwung, Stockung, Krise.* 2 vols, Zurich: Polygraph.

BIBLIOGRAPHY

Clausing, G. (ed.) 1933. *Der Stand und die nächste Zukunft der Konjunkturforschung. Festschrift für Arthur Spiethoff.* Berlin: Duncker & Humblot.

Clausing, G. 1958. Arthur Spiethoffs wissenschaftliches Lebenswerk. *Schmollers Jahrbuch für Gesetzgebung, Verwaltung und Volkswirtschaft* 78, 257–90.

Lane, F.C. 1956. Some heirs of Gustav von Schmoller. In *Architects and Craftsmen in History: Festschrift für Abbott Payson Usher*, ed. J.T. Lombie, Tübingen: Mohr.

Lane, F.C. and Riemersma, J.C. 1958. Introduction to Arthur Spiethoff. In *Enterprise and Secular Change: Readings in Economic History*, ed. F.C. Lane and J.C. Riemersma, London: George Allen & Unwin, 431–43.

Schweitzer, A. 1941. *Spiethoff's Theory of the Business Cycle.* Laromie: University of Wyoming Publications, Vol. 8, 1–30 (contains an extensive bibliography).

spline functions. In the everyday use of the word, a *spline* is a flexible strip of material used by draftsmen in the same manner as French curves to draw a smooth curve between specified points. The mathematical *spline function* is similar to the draftsman's spline in that its graph resembles the curve drawn by a mechanical spline. More formally, a spline function is a piecewise continuous function with a specified degree of continuity imposed on its derivatives. Usually the pieces are polynomials. The abscissa values which define the segments are referred to as *knots* or *joint points*, and the set of knots is referred to as the *mesh*. Examples of spline functions in economics are discussed below.

Although spline functions are a fairly simple mathematical concept, the development of spline functions is relatively new. The terminology and impetus for most contemporary work can be traced to the seminal work of I.J. Schoenberg (1946), although the basic idea can be found in the writings of E. T. Whittaker (1923), and in Schoenberg's (1946, p.68) own modest opinion, in the earlier work of Laplace. Today the literature on spline functions comprises an integral part of modern approximation theory; see Schumaker (1981) for an accessible introduction and historical review. Furthermore, the many important contributions of Grace Wahba in the 1970s and 1980s (see Wegman and Wright, 1983, for references) have served to unite the approximation theory and statistics literatures.

The importance of spline functions in approximation theory can in large part be explained by the following best approximation property. Consider the data points (x_i, y_i) $(i = 1, 2, \ldots, n)$ and suppose without loss of generality that $0 < x_1 < x_2 < \cdots < x_n < 1$. Let $\lambda > 0$ and consider the optimization problem

$$\min_{f(\cdot)} \sum_{i=1}^{n} [y_i - f(x_i)]^2 + \lambda \int_0^1 [D^m f(x)]^2 \, \mathrm{d}x, \qquad (1)$$

where D^m denotes the differentiation operator of degree m and $f(\cdot)$ is a function defined on [0, 1] such that $D^j f$, $j \leqslant m-1$, is absolutely continuous and $D^m f$ is in the set of measurable square integrable functions on [0, 1]. The first term in (1) comprises the familiar least squares measure of fit and the second term comprises a measure of the smoothness in $f(\cdot)$. The parameter λ measures the tradeoff between fit and smoothness. The solution to (1) is a polynomial spline of degree $2m-1$ with possible knots at all the data points. As $\lambda \to 0$, the solution is referred to as an *interpolating spline* and it fits the data exactly. The choice of λ is obviously crucial and the method of cross-validation is a popular method for choosing λ. The most popular choice for m is $m = 2$ yielding a *cubic spline* as the solution to (1).

While spline functions have proved to be valuable approximation tools, they also arise naturally in their own right in economics. Standard income tax functions with increasing marginal tax rates constitute a *linear spline* as do familiar 'kinked' demand curves and 'kinked' budget sets. *Quadratic splines* serve as useful ways of generating asymmetric loss functions for use in decision theory. Spline functions are also useful tools for capturing structural change. For example, a researcher may believe the relationship between two variables y and x to be locally a polynomial, but that at precise points in terms of x the relationship 'changes', not in a discontinuous fashion. Common choices for such x variables are time, age, education or income to name a few, with a nearly unlimited number of choices of candidates for y variables. An extensive reference source for the use of spline functions in economics, especially in models of structural change, is Poirier (1976).

In econometrics spline functions are most often employed to parametrize a regression function. This usage may reflect an attempt to permit structural change, or simply reflect the flexibility and good approximation properties of splines. In distributed lag analysis, spline functions have been used as natural generalizations of Almon polynomial lags. *Periodic* cubic splines have also proved useful in seasonal adjustment and in analysis of electricity load curves. In all such settings the number of knots is significantly less than the number of data points. The attractiveness of spline functions in these applications is in part due to the fact that given the knots they can be expressed as linear functions of unknown parameters, hence facilitating statistical estimation. Estimation of the knots themselves, however, is a difficult task due both to numerical and statistical complications.

In statistics spline functions are also used in many additional areas. Examples include non-parametric regression, multidimensional splines, histogram smoothing, spectral density estimation, isotonic regression and interpolation of distribution functions for which there is no closed-form analytic representation. The survey by Wegman and Wright (1983) serves as an excellent reference source for the many uses of splines in statistics.

DALE J. POIRIER

See also ESTIMATION; LEAST SQUARES; NON-LINEAR METHODS IN ECONOMETRICS.

BIBLIOGRAPHY

Poirier, D.J. 1976. *The Econometrics of Structural Change with Special Emphasis on Spline Functions*. Amsterdam: North-Holland.

Schoenberg, I.J. 1946. Contributions to the problem of approximation of equidistant data by analytic functions: Parts I and II. *Quarterly Journal of Applied Mathematics* 4, 45–99; 112–41.

Schumaker, L.L. 1981. *Spline Functions: Basic Theory*. New York: Wiley.

Wegman, E.J. and Wright, I.W. 1983. Splines in statistics. *Journal of the American Statistical Association* 78, June, 351–65.

Whittaker, E.T. 1923. On a new method of graduation. *Proceedings of the Edinburgh Mathematical Society* 41, 63–75.

sports. Professional team sports leagues and amateur sports associations typically operate as cartels in input and output markets. While details differ from sport to sport, most professional leagues follow the pattern of baseball, whose institutional structure was first described in the seminal paper by Rottenberg (1956). There have also been studies of the National Football League (Neale, 1964), the Professional Golfers Association (Cottle, 1981), cricket (Schofield, 1982), English soccer (Bird, 1982; Sloane, 1971; Wiseman, 1977), the National Hockey League (Jones, 1969), Scottish soccer (Vamplew, 1982) and Australian football (Dabschek, 1975). The literature on amateur sports is less extensive, but includes some interesting work on US college athletics (Koch, 1973). Basic sources of background information include several Congressional studies (US Congress, 1952a, 1952b, 1957, 1972) and a Brookings volume (Noll, 1974a).

There is of course a widespread and growing public interest in sports (see Horowitz, 1974), which helps to account for the attraction of economists to studies of the industry, and especially of economists concerned with cartel behaviour. Moreover, professional sports leagues are among the few cartels for which detailed current and historical information on cartel rules and decision making is publicly available, along with a wealth of data on inputs, outputs, and financial measures such as attendance, ticket prices, television and radio revenues, and sales prices of franchises. The ambiguous antitrust status of sports leagues has led to a long history of court cases in which even more information about the workings of the leagues has been made public.

Organized baseball in the United States was the first organization to develop a detailed set of rules governing the economic operations of a sports league, and subsequent organizations in football, hockey, basketball, soccer and other sports have simply adapted the baseball rules to their own situations. Cartel rules in each of these sports have evolved over time in response to competition from other leagues, the emergence of player unions, changes in legislation relating to the league, court cases and cheating by cartel members. There have been changes as well in response to technological innovations from within a league such as the invention of the farm system by Branch Rickey, and Bill Veeck's discovery of tax sheltering from team ownership; or innovations from without such as radio and commercial and pay television. Davis (1974) presents a history of the evolution of cartel rules in baseball in response to such factors.

Following the lead of organized baseball, in all professional sports leagues restrictions on input and output markets include the granting of monopoly rights to teams to present league games within designated geographic areas, and the adoption of gate-sharing rules and the sharing of television and radio receipts. There are also rules that regulate the entry of new teams into a league and govern the sale of existing teams or the transfer of a team from one geographic location to another. Of particular importance are the restrictions on player mobility through the so-called 'reserve clause' or 'option clause' ('retain and transfer' in English soccer) in player contracts, combined with waiver rules governing the disposition of veteran players and drafting rules governing rights to new players. As the reserve clause was interpreted in baseball for almost a century, a player signing his first contract with a team was bound to that team for the remainder of his playing career or until the contract was sold, in which case he was bound to the team buying the contract. Other sports placed a less stringent interpretation on the clause. Under pressure from competitive leagues, player unions and the courts, the restrictions on player mobility were weakened substantially from about 1975 on.

These league rules reduced the bargaining power of players in wage negotiations, created local monopolies, limited entry into the industry and redistributed the income of the cartel among the cartel members. Estimates of the monopsony effects of the reserve clause in baseball range from those by Scully (1974b), who found that player salaries in the late 1960s averaged only between 10 and 20 per cent of their net marginal revenue products, to Medoff's (1976) estimate that salaries during the same period were approximately 50 per cent of net marginal revenue products. These estimates were constructed from theoretical models relating player performance to team revenues, and can be compared with later data on the effects of the introduction of free agency on player salaries. Average salaries in baseball rose from $51,000 in 1976 to $76,000 in 1977, the first year under free agency (Hill and Spellman, 1983), and to $100,000 in 1978 (Lehn, 1982). During negotiations preceding the one-day baseball strike of 1985, it was reported in the press that the average salary for the 1985 season was $340,000.

Most if not all of the rules of sports leagues would be violations of the antitrust laws if adopted by other industries, but baseball has the benefit of an exemption from those laws through a Supreme Court decision (*Federal Baseball Club* v. *National League*, 1922), reaffirmed in *Curtis C. Flood* v. *Bowie K. Kuhn* (1972), while for other sports there have been exemptions for certain specific actions through Congressional legislation (e.g. AFL–NFL merger, 1966; joint negotiations over television contracts, 1961). When sports leagues have been attacked in the courts or Congress or in the public press because of such rules (or actions taken under the rules), the leagues' argument has been that in the absence of such restrictions on economic competition, rich teams or big-city teams would acquire a disproportionate share of the best players, resulting in an imbalance of competition on the playing field that would ultimately destroy the league. The validity of this argument has been a central topic in the literature on the economics of sports.

Rottenberg was the first to show its invalidity under the assumption of profit-maximizing owners, arguing that big-city team owners would have economic incentives to limit the quality of their teams (and so help to maintain a degree of competitive balance within the league) even if players were free to sell their services to the highest bidder in a competitive labour market. El Hodiri and Quirk (1971, 1974) presented a formal model of a sports league in which the profit-maximization assumption was used to prove: that, so long as player contracts can be freely bought and sold among team owners, the distribution of playing strengths in a league is the same under the 'reserve clause' as it would be under free competition for players; that big-city teams on average will be stronger than small-city teams; that the distribution of playing strengths is independent of the gate-sharing rules; and that the distribution is one that maximizes total profits for the league. Combined with rules for the drafting of new players according to reverse order of finish, the 'reserve clause' was shown to redistribute income from players to owners, and to redistribute income from big-city to small-city teams. Certain of the El Hodiri–Quirk results can be viewed as applications of the Coase Theorem.

The profit-maximization assumption was challenged by Davenport (1969), who argued that team owners also obtain utility from winning *per se*. Dabschek (1975), Schofield (1982), Sloane (1971) and Vamplew (1982) presented rather convincing evidence that the profit-maximization assumption does not hold in cricket or in British soccer or in Australian football, where few if any teams operate at a profit, instead being financed through contributions by their owners and supporters. (Since teams can always costlessly withdraw from a league rather than operate at a loss, survival of a team that loses money contradicts the profit-maximization assumption.) While this evidence weakens the economists' argument that the reserve clause is not needed to maintain competition on the playing field, the same studies also showed that leagues in these sports have survived over long periods despite a dominance by a few big-city teams that is even more pronounced than in US sports leagues. Taking a different tack, Canes (1974) showed that one of the beneficial effects of the reserve clause is that it restricts the level of team quality, which, from an allocative standpoint, would be excessive if a free market in labour services operated.

Empirical studies of the demand for sports contests indicate that certain sports – baseball (Noll, 1974b), English soccer (Bird, 1982) – are inferior goods, and that price-inelastic demands for sports contests are also observed. Estimation of the demand function for sports contests is subject to the two facts that the marginal cost of presenting a game is close to zero and that teams operate with fixed stadium capacities. Ignoring stochastic elements, these two facts argue for an observed elasticity of demand of unity, except for sold-out games. It is also clear that even when a sports league maintains a monopoly in its sport (historically the most common situation, providing some evidence for Neale's claim that sports leagues are natural monopolies), it is still subject to competition from leagues in other sports and from suppliers of other recreational services. Noll, among others, argues that this makes the price elasticity of demand for league contests higher in big-city than in small-city markets, thus limiting the monopoly power of big-city owners and increasing their incentives to field winning teams.

Because production relations are relatively simple in sports and data on inputs and outputs are readily available, a number of studies have been done on the relation between pay and performance in the various sports leagues, on managerial efficiency, and related matters. (see Fort and Noll, 1984; Porter and Scully, 1982). Likewise, because of the same factors, questions relating to the existence of racial discrimination are somewhat easier to formulate and resolve in this industry than in others. The pioneering work in this field was the study on racial discrimination in baseball by Pascal and Rapping (1972), followed by work also on baseball by Scully (1974a) and later work on basketball (Vining and Kerrigan, 1978). This work provides rather strong evidence for the presence of discrimination in baseball, with the case less clear in basketball; on the other hand, those baseball owners who were the first to employ blacks benefited from this decision (Gwartney and Haworth, 1974).

Sports has proved to be a fertile field for other applied economic studies as well. Cassing and Douglas (1980) claimed to find evidence of a 'winner's curse' resulting from the free agency auction mechanism that operates in baseball. De Brock and Roth (1981) used the Nash bargaining model to explain the economic rationale underlying the union and management strategies in the baseball strike of 1980, one in which the management had strike insurance that paid $1 million per day for 50 days of a strike, following a two-week grace period. The strike was settled just as the insurance benefits were being exhausted. Lehn (1982) looked at the pattern of contracts that were signed under free agency in the context of the principal–agent model and the allocation of risk as between players and owners. As the principal-agent model would predict, a change from the reserve clause to the long-term contracts signed under free agency has led to a marked (25 to 33 per cent) increase in the time spent on the disability list by players under long-term contracts.

Koch's (1973) work on college athletics provides an almost textbook example of the problems which beset a cartel (the NCAA) with a large and diverse group of members, limited resources for policing and enforcing its regulations (which cover the recruiting, support and maintenance of academic standards of student athletes), and subject to outside competition from organizations such as the Amateur Athletic Union (AAU) and the US Olympic committee. He argues that in amateur athletics as in professional team sports, the economic theory of cartels provides a predictive as well as an explanatory framework for analysing the behaviour of the governing organization.

JAMES QUIRK

BIBLIOGRAPHY

Bird, P. 1982. The demand for league football. *Applied Economics* 14, 637–49.

Canes, M. 1974. The social benefits of restrictions on team quality. In *Government and the Sports Business*, ed. R. Noll, Washington, DC: Brookings.

Cassing, J. and Douglas, R. 1980. Implications of the auction mechanism in baseball's free agent draft. *Southern Economic Journal* 48(1), 110–21.

Cottle, P. 1981. Economics of the PGA Tour. *Social Science Quarterly* 62(4), 721–34.

Dabschek, B. 1975. The wage determination process for sportsmen. *Economic Record* 51, 52–64.

Davenport, D. 1969. Collusive competition in major league baseball: its theory and institutional development. *American Economist* 13(2), 6–30.

Davis, L. 1974. Self regulation in baseball, 1909–71. In Noll, (1974a).

De Brock, L. and Roth, A. 1981. Strike two: labor–management negotiations in major league baseball. *Bell Journal of Economics* 12(2), 413–25.

El Hodiri, M. and Quirk, J. 1971. An economic model of a professional sports league. *Journal of Political Economy* 79, 1302–19.

El Hodiri, M. and Quirk, J. 1974. The economic theory of a professional sports league. In Noll (1974a).

Fort, R. and Noll, R. 1984. Pay and performance in baseball: modeling regulars, reserves and expansion. SS Working Paper, Caltech.

Gwartney, J. and Haworth, C. 1974. Employer costs and discrimination: the case of baseball. *Journal of Political Economy* 82(4), 873–81.
Hill, J. and Spellman, W. 1983. Professional baseball: the reserve clause and salary structure. *Industrial Relations* 22(1), 1–19.
Horowitz, I. 1974. Sports broadcasting. In Noll (1974a).
Jones, J. 1969. The economics of the National Hockey League. *Canadian Journal of Economics* 2, February, 1–20.
Koch, J. 1973. A troubled cartel: the NCAA. *Law and Contemporary Problems* 38(1), 135–50.
Lehn, K. 1982. Property rights, risk sharing, and player disability in major league baseball. *Journal of Law and Economics* 45, 343–66.
Medoff, M. 1976. On monopsonistic exploitation in professional baseball. *Quarterly Journal of Economics and Business* 16(2), 113–21.
Neale, W. 1964. The peculiar economics of professional sports. *Quarterly Journal of Economics* 78(1), 1–14.
Noll, R. (ed.) 1974a. *Government and the Sports Business*. Washington, DC: Brookings.
Noll, R. 1974b. Attendance and price setting. In Noll (1974a).
Pascal, A. and Rapping, L. 1972. The economics of racial discrimination in organized baseball. In *Racial Discrimination in Economic Life*, ed. A. Pascal, Lexington, Mass.: Heath.
Porter, P. and Scully, G. 1982. Measuring managerial efficiency: the case of baseball. *Southern Economic Journal* 48(3), 642–50.
Rottenberg, S. 1956. The baseball players' labor market. *Journal of Political Economy* 64, 242–58.
Schofield, J. 1982. The development of first class cricket in England: an economic analysis. *Journal of Industrial Economics* 30(4), 337–60.
Scully, G. 1974a. Discrimination: the case of baseball. In Noll (1974a).
Scully, G. 1974b. Pay and performance in major league baseball. *American Economic Review* 64(6), 915–30.
Sloane, P. 1971. The economics of professional football: football club as utility maximizer. *Scottish Journal of Political Economy* 18, 121–45.
US Congress. 1952a. House Committee on the Judiciary. Subcommittee on Study of Monopoly Power. Study of Monopoly Power, Pt 6, Organized Baseball. Hearings. 82 Cong. 1 sess. Washington: Government Printing Office.
US Congress. 1952b. Organized Baseball. Report of the Subcommittee on Study of Monopoly Power. House Report 2002. 82 Cong. 2 sess. Washington: Government Printing Office.
US Congress. 1957. Antitrust Subcommittee. Organized Professional Team Sports. Hearings. 85 Cong. 1 sess. Washington: Government Printing Office.
US Congress. 1972. Professional Basketball. Hearing. 92 Cong. 1 sess. (Pt 1) and 2 sess. (Pt 2). Washington: Government Printing Office.
Vamplew, W. 1982. The economics of a sports industry: Scottish gate money football, 1890–1914. *Economic History Review* 48(3), 549–67.
Vining, R., Jr. and Kerrigan, J.F. 1978. An application of the Lexis Ratio to the detection of racial quotas in professional sports: a note. *American Economist* 22(2), Fall, 71–5.
Wiseman, N.C. 1977. The economics of football. *Lloyds Bank Review* 123, January, 29–43.

spot and forward markets. The foreign-exchange market is the market in which currencies of different countries are traded. The market performs two major functions: it facilitates the foreign-exchange needs of exporters and importers, and it enables individuals, corporations and governments to obtain a desired currency mix of their portfolios, both in terms of assets and liabilities.

The great majority of foreign-exchange trading takes place in the interbank market between traders or market makers who represent large commercial banks or other financial institutions. The interbank market is worldwide, with 24-hour trading. There is no national or international agency that is charged with monitoring foreign-exchange market practices, which therefore depend on self-regulation and competitive pressures.

The primary actors in the market are brokers and traders. Brokers match orders between buyers and sellers and do not hold inventories exposed to foreign-exchange risk. Traders transact for their own account and assume the risk of exchange-rate changes (Kubarych, 1983).

The foreign-exchange market facilitates transactions that include *spot* and *forward* contracts. The former refers to contracts for an *immediate* delivery and the latter refers to contracts for a *future* delivery. In practice, the trading conventions specify that spot contracts are delivered within one or two business days. A forward contract is an agreement made on a given date that carries with it the obligation to deliver a specified amount of foreign exchange at a future date. The standard maturities for which forward contracts are available are 1, 2, 3, 6 and 12 months; more recently maturities up to 5 years have also become available for some currencies. Typically, forward contracts do not entail explicit margin requirement. This should be contrasted with the conventions in currency *futures* markets (such as the International Monetary Market of the Chicago Mercantile Exchange), which require an explicit commitment of funds.

The prices applicable to spot and forward transactions are the spot and the forward exchange rates. For the subsequent discussion, exchange rates are expressed in units of domestic currency per one unit of foreign exchange.

THE DETERMINATION OF SPOT AND FORWARD EXCHANGE RATES. The two major functions performed by the foreign-exchange market have underlain the development of alternative approaches to modelling exchange-rate determination. One approach – the flow approach – emphasizes the use of the foreign-exchange market by exporters and importers in carrying out current transactions. It views the equilibrium exchange rate as the price that equilibrates the demand for and the supply of foreign exchange arising from imports and exports. Another approach – the asset (stock) approach – emphasizes the use of the foreign-exchange market by asset-holders. It views the equilibrium exchange rate as the price that brings about the desired composition of assets and liabilities of different currency denominations.

In modelling exchange-rate determination the various assets in the world economy have typically been classified into two main groups: money and securities. The perspective underlying the asset approach has been embedded in several models which emphasize the role of alternative assets in determining exchange rates. Among such models is the monetary approach to exchange-rate determination, which highlights the conditions of money-market equilibria in the various countries as the proximate determinants of equilibrium exchange rates, while de-emphasizing the role of other assets. Another model – the portfolio-balance model – focuses on the relative quantities of the various assets as important determinants of the equilibrium exchange rate; the assumption underlying this approach is that there is a limited degree of substitutability among alternative assets. A common feature of the several variants of the asset approach is that expectations concerning future policies and events play a critical role in determining the current spot exchange rate (Frenkel and Mussa, 1985).

Models of forward exchange-rate determination incorporate the notion that the exchange rate is an anticipatory variable. Accordingly, a key factor governing the current equilibrium forward exchange rate is the expectation regarding the future value of the spot rate at the date of maturity. Another factor allows for a discrepancy between the current forward rate and the expected value of the future spot rate resulting from risk considerations. Accordingly, the equilibrium forward rate reflects both expectations of the future spot rate and a risk premium (Fama and Farber, 1979).

THE BEHAVIOUR OF SPOT AND FORWARD EXCHANGE RATES. Empirical research of the behaviour of spot and forward exchange rates during flexible exchange-rate regimes has uncovered several regularities. First, both spot and forward exchange rates tend to be highly volatile. For example, the average absolute change of the exchange rates for the major currencies since the beginning of generalized floating in the early 1970s has exceeded 2 per cent per month. In comparison, the absolute monthly percentage change for wholesale and consumer-price indices and for the ratios of national price levels were only about half that of the exchange rates. Hence, short-run changes in exchange rates have been associated with significant divergences from purchasing-power parity. Second, the data indicate that exchange-rate changes are largely unpredictable. If the forward premium on foreign exchange (i.e. the percentage discrepancy between the current forward and spot exchange rates) is regarded as a measure of the market's prediction of the future change in the exchange rate, then the comparison between actual percentage exchange-rate changes and the forward premium indicates that predicted changes account for a very small fraction of actual changes. Frequently the variances of monthly percentage changes in exchange rates exceed the variances of the monthly forward premia by a factor larger than 20. Third, contemporaneous spot and forward exchange rates tend to move together, and typically they exhibit high positive correlation (Frenkel, 1981).

These empirical regularities concerning the behaviour of spot and forward exchange rates are best interpreted in terms of the asset-market approach to exchange-rate determination. The volatility and the unpredictability of price changes are key characteristics of auction and organized asset markets like the foreign-exchange market. In such markets, current prices reflect expectations concerning the future course of events, and new information which induces changes in expectations is immediately reflected in changes in prices, thus precluding unexploited profit opportunities. The strong dependence of asset prices on expectations implies that periods dominated by significant 'news' that alters expectations are likely to be characterized by large changes in asset prices. Exchange rates (spot and forward) are viewed as asset prices, and therefore they will display large volatility during such periods. Since by definition the 'news' cannot be predicted on the basis of past information, it follows that, by and large, exchange-rate fluctuations must be unpredictable. This unpredictability of exchange-rate movements is also reflected in the fact that, as an empirical matter, exchange rates of the major currencies have followed approximately a random-walk process. The third empirical regularity concerning the high correlation between spot and forward exchange rates (as well as between changes in these rates) reflects the fact that both exchange rates depend on expectations concerning the future and both respond at the same time to the flow of new information. In general, however, the details of the relation between the spot and forward exchange rates depend on the time-series properties of the 'fundamentals' relevant for exchange-rate determination (e.g. monetary policy and the like), and in particular on whether the new information is viewed as permanent or transitory.

The links between spot and forward exchange rates have also been examined in the context of studies of the *efficiency* of the foreign-exchange market. In general, tests of foreign-exchange-market efficiency have focused on (1) the statistical properties of forward rates as predictors of future spot rates, (2) the time-series properties of exchange rates and of deviations of exchange rates from past forward rates, (3) the ability to improve on market forecasts of future exchange rates by using past spot and forward exchange rates and other publicly available information, and (4) the capacity to make extraordinary profits by employing various trading rules. Tests of these questions have been applied to different exchange rates in different time periods (Levich, 1985). These tests have not reached unanimous consensus concerning the narrow technical hypothesis of market efficiency, but the broader perspective of foreign-exchange markets as asset markets has received considerable empirical support. Within this broader perspective, the poor forecastability of exchange rates, as measured by the fact that only a small fraction of the variability of exchange-rate changes can be accounted for in terms of variability of the forward premia, does not indicate a failure of theory or market inefficiency. In fact, as already indicated, when the prime cause of fluctuations is new information, one may expect that lagged forward exchange rates (which are based on past information) are imprecise (even though possibly the best unbiased) forecasts of future rates.

SPOT AND FORWARD EXCHANGE RATES AND OTHER ASSET RETURNS. Spot and forward exchange rates are also linked to the rates of return on other financial assets. These linkages are illustrated by the *covered* and the *uncovered* interest-rate parities. First, the covered interest-rate parity theory maintains that in equilibrium the premium (or discount) on a forward contract for foreign exchange is related to the interest differential according to $[F(t) - S(t)]/S(t) = (i - i^*)/(1 + i^*)$, where $F(t)$ and $S(t)$ are, respectively, the forward and spot exchange rates at time t, i is the domestic rate of interest on a particular class of securities with the same maturity as the forward contract, and i^* is the corresponding foreign rate of interest. The pair of domestic and foreign securities should be identical in all respects (e.g. maturity, risk class, etc.) except for the currency of denomination. When the interest-rate parity relationship does not hold, it may be possible to undertake a set of transactions (known as *covered interest arbitrage*) to take advantage of risk-free profit opportunities.

Research on the empirical performance of the covered interest-rate parity theory reveals that when account is taken of the costs of making transactions in the various markets, the predictions of the theory are confirmed (Frenkel and Levich, 1977). Thus, as an empirical matter, covered-interest arbitrage seems to eliminate unexploited profit opportunities.

The *uncovered interest-rate parity* links the interest-rate differential to the expected percentage change in the spot exchange rate. This formulation of the interest-rate parity condition states that

$$[E_t S(t+1) - S(t)]/S(t) = (i - i^*)/(1 + i^*),$$

where $E_t S(t+1)$ denotes the *expected* future spot exchange rate for period $t+1$ (the same as the maturities of the securities) and where the expectations operator, E_t, indicates that the expectation of the future exchange rate (for period $t+1$) is formed on the basis of the information available in the current period (period t). Since expectations are unobservable, a practice in empirical research has been to replace the actual (*ex-post*) exchange rate, $S(t+1)$ for the (*ex-ante*) expectation thereof, $E_t S(t+1)$. Hence, an empirical formulation of the uncovered interest parity relation is

$$[S(t+1)-S(t)]/S(t)=(i-i^*)/(1+i^*).$$

As is evident, the difference between the covered and the uncovered formulations of the interest-rate parities is that the former relates the interest differential to the forward premium on foreign exchange, $[F(t)-S(t)]/S(t)$, whereas the latter relates the interest differential to the percentage change in the spot exchange rate $[S(t+1)-S(t)]/S(t)$. The two formulations are equivalent if the current forward exchange rate $F(t)$ equals the expected future spot exchange rate $E_tS(t+1)$ and if the latter equals the realized future spot exchange rate $S(t+1)$. If the future were known with certainty, it would be clear that indeed $F(t)=E_tS(t+1)=S(t+1)$. In this case the forward exchange rate would be an unbiased predictor of the future spot exchange rate, and the interest differential would correspond to the expected (and realized) percentage change in the spot exchange rate. In reality, when uncertainty is present and the future is unknown, expectations may not be realized, and investors may incorporate a (possibly time varying) *risk premium*, RP(t), into the pricing of the forward contract so that $F(t)=E_tS(t+1)+\text{RP}(t)$. Under such circumstances the forward exchange rate becomes a biased predictor of the future spot rate. Speculative transactions that keep the interest differential in line with the expected change in the spot exchange rate are referred to as *uncovered interest arbitrage*.

Research on the empirical validity of the uncovered interest-rate parity relation has been less supportive of the theory than the corresponding research on the performance of the covered interest-rate parity theory. This poor performance has been rationalized by reference to the possible existence of a time-varying risk premium (Hansen and Hodrick, 1983). It is relevant to note, however, that studies of the determinants of the risk premium have failed to provide a satisfactory account of the factors governing the magnitude and the behaviour of the risk premium (Frankel, 1982).

JACOB A. FRENKEL AND RICHARD M. LEVICH

BIBLIOGRAPHY

Fama, E.F. and Farber, A. 1979. Money, bonds and foreign exchange. *American Economic Review* 69(4), September, 639–49.

Frankel, J.A. 1982. The search of the exchange rate premium: a six-currency test assuming mean-variance optimization. *Journal of International Money and Finance* 1, December, 255–74.

Frenkel, J.A. 1981. Flexible exchange rates, prices and the role of 'news': lessons from the 1970s. *Journal of Political Economy* 89(4), August, 665–705.

Frenkel, J.A. and Levich, R.M. 1977. Transaction costs and interest arbitrage: tranquil versus turbulent periods. *Journal of Political Economy* 85(6), December, 1209–26.

Frenkel, J.A. and Mussa, M.L. 1985. Asset markets, exchange rates and the balance of payments. In *Handbook of International Economics*, Vol. II, ed. R.W. Jones and P.B. Kenen, New York: Elsevier Science Publishers.

Hansen, L.P. and Hodrick, R.S. 1983. Risk averse speculation in the forward exchange market: an econometric analysis of linear models. In *Exchange Rates and International Macroeconomics*, ed. J.A. Frenkel, Chicago: University of Chicago Press.

Kubarych, R.M. 1983. *Foreign Exchange Markets in the United States*. New York: Federal Reserve Bank of New York.

Levich, R.M. 1985. Empirical studies of exchange rates: price behavior, rate determination and market efficiency. In *Handbook of International Economics*, Vol. II, ed. R.W. Jones and P.B. Kenen, New York: Elsevier Science Publishers.

spurious regression. If a theory suggests that there is a linear relationship between a pair of random variables X and Y, then an obvious way to test the theory is to estimate a regression equation of form

$$Y=\alpha+\beta X+e$$

Estimation could be by least-squares and the standard diagnostic statistics would be a t-statistic on β, the R^2 value and possibly the Durbin–Watson statistic d. With such a procedure there is always the possibility of a type II error, that is accepting the relationship as significant when, in fact, X and Y are uncorrelated. This possibility increases if the error term e is autocorrelated, as first pointed out by Yule (1926). As the autocorrelation structure of e is the same as that or Y, when the true $\beta=0$, this problem of 'nonsense correlations' or 'spurious regressions' is most likely to occur when testing relationships between highly autocorrelated series.

If X_t, Y_t are a pair of independent non-drifting random walks given by

$$X_t-X_{t-1}=\epsilon_{1t}$$
$$Y_t-Y_{t-1}=\epsilon_{2t}$$

where ϵ_{1t}, ϵ_{2t} are independent zero-mean white-noise (uncorrelated) series, then it was shown by Granger and Newbold (1974) by simulation that high R^2 values can occur together with apparently significant t-values. For example, using samples of length 50, 100 simulations produced 87 t-values greater than 2 in magnitude, including 53 greater than 4 and 27 greater than 6. Thus, the majority of these regressions between a pair of independent series would have produced relationships that appear to be significant under the standard classical test. The problem, of course, is that the t-statistic does not have the standard distribution if the error term in the regression is not white noise, and this problem is particularly important when the error-term is strongly autocorrelated. Thus, a high value for t or for R^2, when combined with a low d-value is no indication of a true relationship. That this finding is not just a small-sample problem has been proved by some asymptotic theory results of Phillips (1985). He found that when non-drifting random walks are regressed using a least-squares procedure, then asymptotically the distribution of R^2 is non-degenerate so that a positive R^2 value can occur, d tends to zero in probability and the t-statistic when divided by the square root of the sample size tends to a non-degenerate, finite variance distribution, but not the t-distribution. He further finds that the estimate of α has variance proportional to the sample size, so that this estimate divided by the square root of sample size tends to a random variable with finite variance.

These results, plus simulations by Granger and Newbold (1974), suggest that similar problems will occur if any pair of independent series that are integrated of order one are analysed by a simple least-squares regression. (A series is said to be integrated of order one (I(1)) if the differenced series is stationary with positive spectrum at zero frequency.) This result is of some practical importance because many macroeconomic series appear to be I(1), and so spurious regressions can easily occur if care is not taken in the model specification. It is, in fact, rather easy to find examples in early applied economic literature of regressions with large R^2 values but low d-values. Sometimes, when the regression is repeated using changes of the variables, a very low R^2 value is achieved, but a satisfactory d-value, suggesting that the regression in levels was probably spurious.

If more than two independent I(1) series are used in a regression, the possibility of a spurious relationship increases further. For example, a simulation by Granger and Newbold (1974) where one random walk was 'explained' by five other independent random walks found in 100 cases that a t-value of 2 or more in magnitude occurred in 96 occasions, with an average corrected R^2 of 0.59, and with 37 corrected R^2 values over 0.7 and an average d-value of 0.88. When the same regression was run on changes, only six t-values were over 2 in size, the average corrected R^2 was 0.012 with none over 0.7 and the average d-value was 1.99.

The possibility of a spurious relationship also increases further if the random walks contain drift, and if no trend term is included in the regression. A simulation by Newbold and Davies (1975) found that a Cochran–Orcutt correction to the estimation procedure did not completely remove the problem if residuals are not actually autoregressive of order one.

The obvious difficulty with the likelihood of spurious regression is to know when a regression is spurious or not. A simple cure with I(1) series is to perform the regression on differenced series, but this is not completely recommended as important parts of the potential relationship can be lost. A better approach is to embed the relationship being investigated within a sufficiently complex dynamic specification, including lagged dependent and independent variables, so that the truth might be discovered. An obvious objective is to make the residuals stationary, as discussed, for example, by Hendry et al. (1985).

C.W.J. GRANGER

See also ESTIMATION.

BIBLIOGRAPHY

Granger, C.W.J. and Newbold, P. 1974. Spurious regressions in econometrics. *Journal of Econometrics* 2(2), July, 111–20.

Hendry, D.F., Pagan, A. and Sargan, J.D. 1985. Dynamic specification. In *Handbook of Econometrics*, Vol. 2, ed. Z. Griliches and M.D. Intriligator, Amsterdam: North-Holland.

Newbold, P. and Davies, N. 1975. Error mis-specification and spurious regressions. Department of Mathematics, University of Nottingham.

Phillips, P.C.B. 1985. Understanding spurious regressions in econometrics. Working paper, Cowles Foundation, Yale University.

Yule, G.U. 1926. Why do we sometimes get nonsense correlations between time-series? *Journal of the Royal Statistical Society* 89, 1–64.

Sraffa, Piero (1898–1983). In the history of economics, Piero Sraffa is an enigma. His reputation as a major economic theorist rests on but three works: the *Economic Journal* article of 1926, the Introduction to his edition of Ricardo's *Principles* (the first of the 11 volumes of the complete *Works and Correspondence* of *David Ricardo*, which established Sraffa as the finest scholar to have edited a major work in the literature of economics), and the 99 pages of *Production of Commodities by Means of Commodities*, a sparse, terse collection of logical propositions, the significance of which is a matter of often heated debate.

A reclusive figure, of great personal warmth and puckish humour, Sraffa spent most of his life in Cambridge. Yet his influence extended far beyond academic economics.

Throughout the Thirties he spent every Thursday afternoon and evening, during term, with Ludwig Wittgenstein. It was Sraffa who forced Wittgenstein to accept that the theory of language advanced in the *Tractatus Philosophicus* was logically inadequate, paving the way for the recognition of the social content of signs and language presented in *Philosophical Investigations*. In the preface of the latter, Wittgenstein acknowledged the importance of Sraffa's criticism of his arguments over many years, and added 'I am indebted to *this* stimulus for the most consequential ideas of this book.' He later commented that after discussion with Sraffa he felt 'like a tree stripped of all its branches', but that a consequence of this drastic pruning was healthier growth.

Of perhaps wider significance was Sraffa's close friendship with Antonio Gramsci. After Gramsci's imprisonment, Sraffa led the effort to ameliorate the harsh conditions in which he was held, and to secure his release. The essential contents of Gramsci's letters from prison, written to his sister-in-law Tatiana, were channelled through Sraffa in Cambridge to the exiled Italian Communist Party. And it was Sraffa who ensured, by establishing an account with unlimited credit at a Milanese bookshop, that Gramsci was supplied with the materials he needed to work on his *Prison Notebooks*.

The philosophical debates with Wittgenstein, and his political and intellectual commitment to socialism, point to important elements in Sraffa's intellectual make-up. His economics, always rigorous, became in the 1930s increasingly formal, to the extent that the search for logically precise and unambiguous expression inhibited his writing. His socialism demanded an economics that was concrete; that, however abstract, was appropriate to the interpretation of real economic institutions and phenomena.

The compelling empiricism of marxian socialist thought, and the rejection of the use of subjective concepts, are themes running throughout Sraffa's economics. Economics should be constructed from variables and relationships which are, at least in principle, observable and measurable. The classical analysis of value and distribution is constructed on just such 'empirical' foundations, whilst neoclassical theory, based as it is on unverifiable hypotheses concerning individual choice, evidently is not.

But although Sraffa's contribution to economic theory may have been motivated by these methodological concerns, its substance involves the logic of theoretical argument, in particular the demonstration of the logical consistency of the classical analysis of value and distribution, and, as a corollary, the logical deficiencies of neoclassical theory.

LIFE AND WORKS

Piero Sraffa was born in Turin on 5 August 1898. His father was Angelo Sraffa, a professor of commercial law who later became Chancellor of the Bocconi University in Milan. The Piazza Sraffa in Milan is named for Angelo, not Piero. Piero's mother was Irma Tivoli.

Sraffa was educated at the Liceo d'Azeglio in Turin, where he was greatly influenced by Umberto Cosmo, who introduced him to socialist ideas and, in 1919, to Antonio Gramsci. Sraffa's studies at the University of Turin, from 1916 to 1920, were interrupted by military service, which he spent as both a ski instructor and an engineer, blowing up bridges to stem the Austrian advance. He attended relatively few lectures. Nonetheless his honours thesis, 'Monetary inflation in Italy during and after the War', was considered by his supervisor, Luigi Einaudi, to be quite brilliant. It was published in 1920.

After graduation, Sraffa worked for a few weeks in a bank to learn some banking 'from the inside'. He then went to the London School of Economics (1921–2) where he attended lectures by Cannan, Foxwell and Gregory.

During his stay in London, Sraffa visited Cambridge, bearing a letter of introduction to Keynes from Mary Berenson, a friend of Sraffa's family who, ten years earlier, had entertained Keynes and other young Cambridge graduates in her villa near Florence. Keynes was at the time engaged in the debate on the reconstruction of the international monetary system, and had agreed to be editor of a weekly supplement to the *Manchester Guardian*, dealing with the monetary and financial problems of Europe. Keynes asked Sraffa to contribute an article on the Italian banking system, which was at the time experiencing a severe crisis. The article proved to be too long for the newspaper, and was published in the *Economic Journal* instead, a shorter version appearing in the *Manchester Guardian*.

These two articles were also published in Italian, and caused the Fascist regime considerable irritation. Now back in Italy, Sraffa was accused by Mussolini of 'banking defeatism' and 'sabotage of Italian finance'. Keynes invited Sraffa to return to England until things had calmed down. However, on 23 January 1923 Sraffa was detained at Dover, and after being questioned for three hours was informed that he had been refused permission to land by order of the Home Secretary. The reason for the denial of entry is still not clear. Keynes secured the removal of Sraffa's name from the list of 'undesirables' in 1924.

Fortunately the situation in Italy was less severe than had been expected, though Sraffa resigned the job he had obtained as Director of the Bureau of Labour Statistics of the Province of Milan. The Bureau had been established by the socialist provincial administration in 1922, and was experiencing difficulties with the Fascist government. A few months later he was appointed to a lectureship in Political Economy and Public Finance at the University of Perugia.

The preparation of his lectures at Perugia stimulated him to write 'Sulle relazioni fra costo e quantita prodotta' (1925). As a result of this article Sraffa was appointed to a Professorship in Political Economy at the University of Cagliari, a post he held *in absentia* to the end of his life, donating his salary to the support of the library. Edgeworth's high opinion of the article led to an invitation to submit a version to the *Economic Journal* (1926). This, in turn, led to Sraffa's being offered the lectureship in Cambridge which he took up in October 1927.

Before leaving Italy, Sraffa had pursued his interest in monetary problems by translating Keynes's *Tract on Monetary Reform* into Italian, and writing several short reviews of books on money and banking for the *Giornale degli Economisti* (1925b, 1926b, 1926c, 1927b).

In 1919, Sraffa had joined the Socialist Students' Group at the University of Turin and had participated actively in the political life developing around *Ordine Nuovo*, the magazine founded in 1919 by Gramsci, Tasca, Terracini and Togliatti, the group who were to play the crucial role in the split from the Socialist Party at the Congress of Livorno in 1921 and the foundation of the Italian Communist Party.

Whilst in London Sraffa wrote three articles for *Ordine Nuovo* on the condition of the working class in England and the role of trade unions. In 1924 he published an open letter to Gramsci in *Ordine Nuovo* criticizing the Communist Party for its dogmatic refusal to contemplate an alliance with other democratic groups against Fascism. A few years later Gramsci, now imprisoned, accepted Sraffa's argument.

Sraffa also opposed the orthodox Party line in two letters to *Stato Operaio* in 1927. In a discussion of the devaluation of the Italian lira, he criticized the prevalent view that policy decisions are always mechanically and '*directly* dictated by the *immediate* interests of the banks and the big industrialists' (1927a, p. 180). He advanced instead the view that political bodies such as the Fascist Party have their own interests which can enter into the dynamics of the decision process.

In October 1927 Sraffa began his lectures in Cambridge, presenting courses on the theory of value and on the relationship between banks and industry in continental Europe. He was to lecture for only three years, finding the very process increasingly difficult. Joan Robinson, who attended the lectures on her return from India, recalled them vividly, not least because Sraffa liked to develop a dialogue with his class – a procedure unknown in Cambridge. In 1930 Sraffa was appointed Marshall Librarian, and also placed in charge of graduate studies. He gave up lecturing for good.

Shortly after arriving in Cambridge, Sraffa had shown Keynes the set of propositions (derived from Marx's reproduction schemes) which were to grow into *Production of Commodities*. But this work was somewhat overwhelmed both by the intense debate in Cambridge surrounding Keynes's *Treatise on Money* and, later, *The General Theory* (it was Sraffa who organized the famous 'circus' which discussed the *Treatise* in 1931), and by Sraffa assuming in 1930 the editorship of the Royal Economic Society edition of *The Works and Correspondence of David Ricardo*. Sraffa's work on the theory of value, and his interest in monetary theory, coalesced in a critical review of Hayek's *Prices and Production* (Sraffa, 1932a, 1932b).

Sraffa's participation in political debate was necessarily limited after his arrival in Cambridge. He maintained contact with the leadership of the Italian Communist Party in Paris, and in 1927 wrote to the *Manchester Guardian* denouncing the ill treatment of the imprisoned Gramsci. He visited Gramsci and attempted, to no avail, to use the influence of his uncle, an eminent judge, to secure Gramsci's release. Following Gramsci's death in 1937, it was Sraffa who conveyed to Togliatti Gramsci's wishes concerning the editing of the *Quaderni dal Carcere*.

In another service to a friend, Sraffa travelled to Austria following the *Anschluss* to inform Wittgenstein's family that Ludwig had renounced his Austrian citizenship.

In 1939 Sraffa was elected to a Fellowship of Trinity College (he had previously held dining rights at King's), a post he took up shortly after the outbreak of war. When Italy entered the war in June 1940, Sraffa was interned as an enemy alien on the Isle of Man. Keynes managed to extricate him by the end of the summer. Sraffa never gave up his Italian citizenship.

By the late 1940s, the publication of the edition of Ricardo had been long delayed. This was partly due to the reorganization required when in 1943, after six volumes were already in the press, Ricardo's letters to Mill and, amongst other writings, the papers on Absolute and Exchangeable Value, were discovered. But delay was also caused by the difficulty Sraffa was having in writing the introductions to the volumes, particularly the introduction to the *Principles*. The second problem was solved after 1948 with the assistance of Maurice Dobb. Dobb and Sraffa would discuss each paragraph in detail. Dobb would write it up. Sraffa would revise what Dobb had written. Dobb would rewrite. And so on, until the job was done. The first four volumes of the *Works and Correspondence of David Ricardo* were published in 1951, the next five volumes in 1952, a bibliographical miscellany formed the tenth volume published in 1955, and, after a number of false starts by others, a general index, compiled by Sraffa himself, was published as the eleventh volume of the set in 1971.

The edition is widely acknowledged to be a scholarly masterpiece. George Stigler (1953) commented,

> Ricardo was a fortunate man. He lived in a period – then drawing to a close – when an untutored genius could still remake economic science... . And now, 130 years after his death, he is as fortunate as ever: he has been befriended by Sraffa – who has been befriended by Dobb.

Keynes told us, in 1933, that Sraffa, 'from whom nothing is hid', would give us the full works of Ricardo within the year. The truth of the first part of the statement had as its cost the falsification of the second, and it has been a splendid bargain. For Sraffa's *Ricardo* is a work of rare scholarship. The meticulous care, the constant good sense, and the erudition make this a permanent model for such work; and the host of new materials seem to suggest that Providence meets half-way the deserving scholar.

The *Ricardo* completed, Sraffa could return to the work he had done on the theory of value and distribution in the Thirties and early Forties. Old notes were reassembled, including a proof of the Perron-Frobenius theorem on non-negative square matrices, which the Trinity mathematician Besicovitch (an analyst with no prior knowledge of the theorem) had provided on a postcard delivered on Christmas Day 1944. The result of assembling these old notes was *Production of Commodities by Means of Commodities* (1960).

This book was greeted with almost universal puzzlement. It seemed to present, in odd, formal terms, propositions which had become familiar with the development of linear models in the 1940s and 1950s. Had Sraffa's brilliant insights of thirty years before been overtaken by events in mainstream theory? Of the earlier reviewers only Dobb (1961), Meek (1961) and Newman (1962) grasped the fact that this was a work of profound significance, with implications for the logical foundations of both classical and neoclassical theories of value and distribution.

Sraffa spent the rest of his life in Cambridge though up to 1973 he visited Italy in every vacation, staying in his apartment in Rapallo, and going to Rome to attend meetings of the economic section of the Academia dei Lincei. Other than economics and politics, Sraffa's great interest was the collection of books. He assembled a magnificent collection of economics books and pamphlets, including a first edition of *Kapital* inscribed by Marx himself (which he later presented to the Istituto Gramsci) and a copy of the *Wealth of Nations* containing Adam Smith's bookplate. He shared this enthusiasm with Keynes. Together they discovered, identified, and wrote an introduction to an edition of David Hume's *An Abstract of a Treatise on Human Nature* (1938). When he died, on 3 September 1983, Sraffa left his collection to Trinity College.

CONTRIBUTIONS TO ECONOMIC THEORY

The early years. Sraffa's dissertation (1920) dealt with central *practical* issues occupying writers on monetary matters at the end of World War I – the causes and consequences of inflation, the stabilization of internal prices and exchange rates within an unstable international monetary system, the argument for restoring the gold standard and revaluing the currency to the pre-war gold parity.

Sraffa argued that since the abandonment of the gold standard at the beginning of the war had been followed by halving of the purchasing power of gold, then a return to the gold standard would require a rise in the value of the metal, forcing countries which fixed parity either to devalue, or to bear the consequences of deflation. Since, in these circumstances, the monetary authorities could not achieve stability of both prices and the rate of exchange, it was better to opt for the former. There is no law which forced the authorities to stabilize the currency at the pre-war level. The *normal* value of the currency is completely 'conventional', i.e. it can be at *any* level that common opinion expects it to be (Sraffa, 1920, p. 42). Sraffa, in opposition to Einaudi, and in common with the position which Cassel, Hawtrey and Keynes were to urge on the Genoa Economic Conference in April 1922, favoured a 'managed currency'.

Sraffa's 'practical' case embodied an implicit theoretical argument. He stressed the role of the State, moulded by the pressure of the major economic classes, in determining the distribution of income. Monetary policy was thus considered in terms of its impact on the real wage. Sraffa, like Keynes in *A Tract on Monetary Reform*, accepted a version of the quantity theory. But whereas Keynes's views on the determination of the distribution of income were essentially neoclassical, Sraffa's position was more akin to that of the classical economists and Marx. Keynes argued that social forces and monetary factors have only temporary effects on the distribution of income, influencing only the disequilibrium real wage rate. Unless, that is, they were able to effect the real factors which determined the equilibrium distribution (Keynes, 1923, p. 27). Sraffa, however, argued that monetary policies, and hence inflation and deflation, are aspects of the social conflicts that directly regulate the equilibrium or normal real wage rate (Sraffa, pp. 25, 40–42).

A similar view of the role of economic institutions in social conflict was spelt out in the *Economic Journal* and *Manchester Guardian* articles. The articles focused on the financial needs of newly developing Italian industry, and on the evolution of the links between industry and the banks. His study of the formation of large groups or 'concentrations' of financial and industrial power is similar to that in Hilferding's *Finance Capital.* He stressed the enormous economic and political power which such groups can acquire and outlined the way in which conflicts within the groups might affect economic policy. He also revealed the accounting tricks which had been used by two major banks to disguise their financial difficulties, and showed how the authorities had evaded legal restrictions in order to favour some major financial groups (Sraffa, 1922b, p. 676). No wonder Mussolini was so upset.

Laws of Returns. Sraffa's early writings, although imbued with a certain critical radicalism, provided no hint of the theoretical *tour de force* that was to come. It is true that he had emphasized the role of social classes and institutions in the normal (as opposed to disequilibrium) operation of the economy, but in Sraffa's examination of the neoclassical (predominantly Marshallian) theory of cost (1925, 1926) these concerns with the 'objective' characteristics of economic activity were transformed into a penetrating critique of the logical foundations of the theory of the equilibrium of the competitive firm and of the supply curve.

Sraffa's starting point in the *Annali di Economia* was a distinction between an analysis in which the relationship between cost and quantity produced was determined by 'objective' factors, such as the ordering of different qualities of land, and a relationship which was based on 'subjective' factors, namely the marginal disutility which accompanies the offer of increased quantities of factor services. The former relation is, as Wicksteed had argued (1914), essentially descriptive; it is the latter which is, in neoclassical theory, analytic. The supply curve is simply the demand curve 'reversed' (Wicksteed, 1914, p. xxx).

In the *Economic Journal* Sraffa made the same point in a rather different way. In classical economics, he argued, the 'laws of returns' did not derive from a unified analysis of cost. Quite the contrary. The discussion of increasing returns was associated with the analysis of accumulation, most notably Adam Smith's examination of the relationship between the extent of the market and the division of labour. Diminishing returns, on the other hand, were the distinctive component of the theory of rent. The suggested symmetry of increasing and diminishing returns is a quite different construction, characteristic of the neoclassical supply curve.

But if cost is subjective disutility, how does a phenomenon which is defined by personal psyche manifest its influence in the determination of the equilibrium of the competitive firm, and in the determination of the supply curve of the industry? The apparent similarity between the determination of equilibrium in individual choices, and the equilibrium of the firm, is quite spurious. For whereas all the determinants of individual choice – preferences and endowments – are peculiar to the individual, the determinants of the equilibrium in production in a competitive economy – the technical conditions of production and the supply of factor services – are external to the firm.

Sraffa then demonstrated that neither increasing *nor* diminishing returns are compatible with the assumption of perfect competition in the determination of the supply curve of an industry, except in the peculiar case in which economies or diseconomies of scale are external to the firm but internal to the industry.

Diminishing returns are incompatible with perfect competition, since the presumption of price taking precludes any impact of the output of individual firms, or, in Marshall's *ceteris paribus* world, the output of individual industries, on prices, unless it is assumed that endowments are fixed in individual firms, or are peculiar to individual industries.

Increasing returns are also incompatible with assumption of perfect competition – other than those which are external to the firm, but internal to the industry.

Only the assumption of constant returns to scale is compatible with the assumption of perfect competition:

> In normal cases the cost of production of commodities produced competitively ... must be regarded as constant in respect of small variations in the quantity produced. And so, as a simple way of approaching the problem of competitive value, the old and now obsolete theory which makes it dependent on the cost of production alone appears to hold its ground as the best available (Sraffa, 1926, pp. 186–7).

There were two ways out of the conundrum, either to adopt the general equilibrium reasoning which Sraffa had deployed so effectively against the notion of the supply curve, or to abandon the assumption of perfect competition. Marshall's theory must be abandoned (Sraffa, 1930a, 1930b).

The first course was ruled out on the grounds that examination of 'the conditions of simultaneous equilibrium in numerous industries', though a well-known approach, is far too complex; 'the present state of out knowledge ... does not permit of even much simpler schemata being applied to the study of real conditions' (1926, p. 187).

The second course recognizes both the 'everyday experience ... that a very large number of undertakings – and the majority of those which produce manufactured consumers' goods – work under conditions of individual diminishing costs', and that

> the chief obstacle against which they have to contend when they want gradually to increase their production does not lie in the cost of production ... but in the difficulty of selling the larger quantity of goods without reducing the price, or without having to face increased marketing expenses. This ... is only an aspect of the usual descending demand curve, with the difference that instead of concerning the whole of a commodity, whatever its origin, it relates only to the goods produced by a particular firm ... (1926, p. 189).

Sraffa's second option launched the Cambridge analysis of imperfect competition, first in Richard Kahn's fellowship dissertation (1931) at King's, then in Joan Robinson's *Economics of Imperfect Competition.*

Apart from his contribution in the *Economic Journal* symposium on increasing returns, Sraffa did not participate further in the debate on the Marshallian theory of cost. The reasons are not hard to seek.

First, imperfect competition theory, instead of providing a new, more concrete approach to the analysis of value and distribution, was simply absorbed into neoclassical theory. The fact that imperfectly competitive models do not provide a foundation for a theory of value, seemed to enhance the status of partial equilibrium analysis, rather than hasten its rejection; with the competitive theory of value still holding sway at the level of general equilibrium (a neat rationale is provided by Hicks, 1946, pp. 83–4). The survival of the 'U' shaped cost curve as an analytical tool, constructed from the presumption of increasing, then diminishing returns, is in no small part attributable to the longevity provided by models of the imperfectly competitive firm. Nonetheless, the appearance of the 'U' shaped curve in models of the competitive firm, more than 60 years after Sraffa clearly demonstrated the illegitimacy of the construction, is an indication of just how intellectually disreputable theoretical economics can be.

Second, Sraffa's implicit identification of classical and Marxian theory with the notion that competitive value is 'dependent on the cost of production' is clearly wrong, as examination of neoclassical models which take account of 'simultaneous equilibrium in numerous industries' readily demonstrates. Sraffa had deployed general equilibrium reasoning to demolish the theory of the competitive firm and the industry supply curve. Further criticism of neoclassical theory would require consideration of general equilibrium models of value and distribution. And a constructive rehabilitation of classical theory would require a general analysis too. It would require, that is, an analysis of 'the process of diffusion of profits throughout the various stages of production and of the process of forming a normal level of profits throughout all the industries of a country' – the problem Sraffa acknowledged was 'beyond the scope of this article' (1926, p. 197).

Monetary theory. There was no sign of Sraffa's emerging critique of neoclassical theory in his review of Hayek's *Prices and Production* (1932a, 1932b). Instead, the review displays some similarities between Sraffa's position and that held by Keynes soon after the publication of the *Treatise*.

Sraffa argued that Hayek had failed to identify the essential properties of money by neglecting the fact that

> money is not only a medium of exchange, but also a store of value and the standard in terms of which debts, and other legal obligations, habits, opinions, conventions, in short all kinds of relations between men, are more or less rigidly fixed (Sraffa, 1932a, p. 43).

The absence of any conception of wage agreements and debts fixed in money terms prevented Hayek from analysing correctly the effects on the distribution of income of a general fall or rise in prices. Since money had been thoroughly 'neutralized' it could not effect the distribution of income or the rate of accumulation. Hence Hayek could characterize 'forced saving' as a disequilibrium phenomenon, with no permanent effects.

Sraffa argued that this conclusion was contrary to a 'common sense' view of the economy. During a period of inflation

> one class has, for a time, robbed another class of a part of their incomes; and has saved the plunder. When the robbery comes to an end, it is clear that their victims cannot possibly consume the capital which is now well out of their reach (Sraffa, 1932a, p. 48; see also 1932b, p. 249).

Sraffa's view that class conflict determines the *normal* real wage, and that monetary policy may be part of that conflict, is an echo of Sraffa's earlier position, yet nothing is said on the theory of distribution as such.

The most enduring construction in the article is Sraffa's invention of the concept of the own rate of return. Sraffa utilized the idea to elucidate the concept of equilibrium underpinning much of Hayek's discussion. In particular he demonstrates that whilst in disequilibrium there may be as many 'natural' rates of interest (i.e. own rates of return) as there are commodities, competition will tend to equalize these natural rates just as competition eliminates any divergence between market prices and normal prices – indeed these are two aspects of the same process.

Yet Sraffa does not consider how the equilibrium rate of interest is determined. Nor does he criticize Hayek's association of the rate of interest with the length of the production process.

Ricardo. Sraffa's edition of *The Works and Correspondence of David Ricardo* proved to be more than a great scholarly achievement. For in his introduction to *The Principles of Political Economy and Taxation* Sraffa presented an entirely new interpretation of Ricardo's theory of value and distribution. Sraffa's interpretation established a new, theoretically consistent version of the surplus approach to the analysis of distribution in the *Essay on Profits*. Further, he demonstrated that this approach was sustained in the *Principles* by Ricardo's use of the labour theory of value, and that, contrary to the accepted view of Ricardo's analysis presented by Jacob Hollander (1904), Ricardo did not retreat from his use of the labour theory of value in successive versions of the *Principles*.

In the *Essay on Profits* Ricardo stated that it is the rate of profit in agriculture which determines the rate of profit in the economy as a whole. Sraffa argued that

> The rational foundation of the principle of the determining role of the profits of agriculture, which is never explicitly stated by Ricardo, is that in agriculture the same commodity, namely corn, forms both the capital (conceived as composed of the subsistence necessary for workers) and the product; so that the determination of profit by the difference between total product and capital advanced, and also the determination of the ratio of this profit to the capital, is done directly between quantities of corn without any question of valuation (Sraffa, 1951, p. xxxi).

The beautiful simplicity of this interpretation – the rate of profit being determined in the agricultural sector as a ratio of quantities of corn, and in the other sectors as a ratio of values, with the price ratio between corn and other commodities adjusting so as to equalize the rate of profit (corn, being the wage good, is part of the capital in all sectors) – suggested itself in the preparation of *Production of Commodities by Means of Commodities*. If there is but one 'basic' commodity in the economy (i.e. but one commodity which enters directly or indirectly the production of all others), then not only must all the inputs to that commodity consist of itself, but the general rate of profit must be determined by the ratio of surplus of the commodity produced to its means of production.

This powerful result, in which the rate of profit is clearly determined as the ratio of surplus to means of production was sustained in the *Principles*, where it was generalized to incorporate the fact that surplus and means of production will consist of heterogeneous 'bundles' of commodities. The homogeneity necessary to find the ratio of surplus to means of production was achieved by evaluating the two bundles in terms of the labour embodied directly and indirectly in their production.

As is well known, this generalization foundered on the fact that commodities do not exchange at their labour values, and hence that the ratio, evaluated in terms of labour values, does not measure the rate of profit. As Sraffa pointed out, Ricardo's persistent struggle with this difficulty was expressed as the fact that prices might change due to a change in ditribution when labour values (dependent upon conditions of production) were unchanged. Hence he sought an 'invariable standard of value' which would tie movements in price to movements in labour values alone:

> Ricardo was not interested for its own sake in the problem of why two commodities produced by the same quantities of labour are not of the same exchangeable value. He was concerned with it only in so far as thereby relative values are affected by changes in wages. The two points of view of difference and of change are closely linked together; yet the search for an invariable measure of value, which is so much at the centre of Ricardo's system, arises exclusively from the second and would have no counterpart in an investigation of the first (Sraffa, 1951, p. xlix).

Sraffa was able to demonstrate that Ricardo had continued the search for an invariable standard to the end of his life, sustaining thereby the exposition of his theory of distribution in terms of the labour theory of value. The conclusive proof of Sraffa's argument was found in Ricardo's papers on *Absolute and Exchangeable Value* discovered together with other papers and letters in 1943, their existence having been previously unknown.

Sraffa's interpretation of Ricardo had a considerable impact at the time of its publication, not least because there was great interest in the analysis of growth at the time. The analysis of distribution plays a central role in the classical theory of growth (accumulation by the capitalists is determined by their share of the product). The problems in the theory of the rate of profit posed by the neoclassical analysis of growth, and in some versions of Keynesian growth theory, excited interest in Ricardo's approach.

However, the real importance of Sraffa's new interpretation was for the understanding of Marx's analysis of value and distribution, which is based on Ricardo's theory, and for the general rehabilitation of the surplus approach to value and distribution, which had, for so long, been regarded as logically deficient.

Production of Commodities by Means of Commodities. The subtitle of Sraffa's book (1960) is *Prelude to a Critique of Economic Theory*, and in the Preface he suggested that 'If the foundation holds, the critique may be attempted later, either by the writer or by someone younger and better equipped for the task' (Sraffa, 1960, p. vi), echoing Ricardo's comment in the Preface to his *Principles* (1817, p. 6).

Production of Commodities is a peculiarly sparse book. The argument has been pared to the absolute minimum to sustain the propositions which Sraffa wishes to advance. Yet, the precision and logical elegance of the argument are 'the work of an artist working in the medium of economic theory' (Newman, 1962).

The theoretical essence of the book may be distilled from the argument of Part 1 in which Sraffa deals with single-product industries and circulating capital. There Sraffa demonstrates that the approach to the analysis of value and distribution adopted by Ricardo and by Marx is logically consistent. Taking as data the size and composition of output, the conditions of reproduction, and the real wage it may be shown that (1) in an economy which is capable only of reproducing itself, relative prices are determined by the conditions of production; and (2) that in an economy which is capable of producing a physical surplus over and above the needs of reproduction, relative prices are determined by the conditions of production of basic commodities, and the manner in which the surplus is distributed. If, in the latter case, the surplus is distributed as a rate of profit, then the data determine relative prices and that rate of profit. The economically meaningful solution – that with non-negative prices – is unique. (The prices of non-basics depend upon their own conditions of production and the prices of basics, but the prices of basics are not affected by the prices of non-basics.) These propositions had already been advanced by Dmitriev (1898), though they were not well known.

Sraffa then drops the assumption that the real wage is given. The degree of freedom thus introduced into the analysis is expressed in the locus of the rates of profit associated with any particular values of the wage (in terms of the *numéraire*). For any given value of the wage there is a unique rate of profit (and associated prices), and *vice versa*. There is a maximum wage, when the rate of profit is equal to zero; and a maximum rate of profit when the wage is equal to zero. Closure of the model requires either that the real wage be given (i.e. determined outside the determination of the rate of profit and normal prices) as in classical theory; or that the rate of profit be given.

Sraffa's suggestion that the rate of profit is 'susceptible of being determined from outside the system of production, in particular by the level of the money rates of interest' (1960, p. 33), is essentially symmetrical with the classical approach in which the real wage is 'given'. For the classical economist the real wage is determined by social and historical forces, circumstances which may be analysed quite separately from the determination of relative prices and the rate of profit. Likewise, it may be argued that the money rate of interest, to which, in a competitive economy, the rate of profit must conform, is determined by the normal operations of monetary institutions, especially the state. This position is reminiscent of Sraffa's earlier work in monetary theory, and of Keynes's remark that 'the rate of interest is a highly conventional, rather than a highly psychological, phenomenon' (Keynes, 1936, p. 203).

While the 'data' of Sraffa's analysis of value and distribution are identical with the data of the analyses advanced by Ricardo and by Marx (other than in his not taking the real wage as given), and hence his results are a validation of their arguments, his method of solution is different. Whereas Ricardo and Marx sought to determine the rate of profit as a ratio of aggregates, Sraffa solves for the rate of profit and prices simultaneously. Indeed, his argument demonstrates the necessity of doing so. Yet in his construction of the standard commodity, Sraffa seeks to recreate the clarity of the classical derivation of the rate of profit from the ratio between surplus and means of production.

Sraffa first constructs from the given conditions of production a 'standard system', an hypothetical economy in which the composition of means of production and net product (wages and profits) are the same. If the wage is expressed as a proportion of standard net product, w, then the proportion of net product accruing to profits is $(1-w)$. If the ratio of total net product to surplus is R – a ratio which may be evaluated because the composition of inputs and net output is the same – then the rate of profit will be equal to $R(1-w)$.

The standard system is therefore a direct descendant of the agricultural sector in the *Essay on Profits*, the rate of profit is expressed as a ratio between two physical quantities.

Sraffa then demonstrates that if the standard net product is adopted as *numéraire*, and hence as the measure in terms of which the wage is expressed, then the rate of profit will be equal to $R(1-w)$, exactly as in the standard system in which the relationship between the wage and the rate of profit is expressed in purely physical terms.

The purpose of this construction is, Sraffa tells us, to 'give transparency to a system and render visible what was hidden' (1960, p. 23). The rate of profit is seen to be determined by the magnitude of surplus. yet the use of the standard commodity must be distinguished from Ricardo's use of the 'corn sector', or the use of the labour theory of value by Ricardo and Marx. In Sraffa's case, the rate of profit is *determined* by the solution of the simultaneous equations, the standard commodity is a purely auxiliary construction. In the case of Ricardo and Marx, the rate of profit is determined (albeit imperfectly) by calculating ratio of surplus to mean of production by means of the labour theory of value.

It cannot be said that the standard commodity is entirely successful as a means of rendering visible what might otherwise be hid. It is, perhaps, too complex, lacking the simple force of the labour theory. It has the virtue, however, of being analytically correct.

Considerable puzzlement was engendered by Sraffa's statement in the Preface of his book that 'The investigation is concerned exclusively with such properties of an economic system as do not depend on changes in the scale of production ...' (1960, p. v). The absence of any reference to demand led unsuspecting readers to equate his results with the non-substitution theorem, and hence with the assumption of constant returns to scale. However, a careful reading of Sraffa's analysis reveals that no knowledge of any relationship between *changes* in outputs and *changes* in inputs, or between price and quantity is *necessary* for the solution of the equations, and hence for the determination of the rate of profit and prices (given the wage). This contrasts with neoclassical theory, in which the determination of prices is dependent upon knowledge of functional relationships between supply and demand. If, in Sraffa's analysis, quantities should change, then any consequential change in conditions of production will result in changes in prices.

In Part II of his book, Sraffa extends his analysis to multi-product industries and fixed capital, and to the analysis of economies with more than one non-reproducible input. As might be expected, the analysis is considerably more complex, and in some cases the results less clearcut (the solution of the system may not, for example, be unique, and the definition of basics and non-basics is more abstract than is the case with single-product industries). Yet the basic structure of classical analysis is preserved – the prices, the rate of profit, and other distributive variables (say, land rents), are determined by the conditions of production, given the wage.

Sraffa's analysis is a triumphant restatement of the classical analysis of value and distribution. It is therefore somewhat misleading to refer to a 'Sraffa-based critique of Marx', a phrase which implies, perhaps unintentionally, that Sraffa has developed a method of analysis which is conceptually different from that advanced by his predecessors in the theory of surplus value. This is not the case.

The label 'neo-Ricardian' which is often attached to Sraffa's work (a term which he himself vehemently rejected) is also unfortunate, implying as it does that the argument of *Production of Commodities* is in some way a solution to problems posed by Ricardo, but not encountered by Marx, or by other surplus theorists. The confusion may have derived from simplistically identifying Sraffa with Ricardo, given his edition of Ricardo's works, or from a confusion of the standard commodity with Ricardo's invariable standard of value (even though the latter cannot exist). It may also derive from a fear that any weakening of 'commitment' to the labour theory of value implies a rejection of surplus theory. This is to confuse a tool which is used to solve an analytical problem, with the data of the problem. The labour theory of value is not a datum in surplus theory (if it were, Quesnay would not be a surplus theorist), it is a means of demonstrating that the rate of profit is determined by the magnitude of surplus (less rent).

Almost as a by-product of his examination of the fundamentals of classical theory, Sraffa produced a decisive critique of the neoclassical theory of the rate of profit (and hence of the neoclassical theory of long-run normal prices). An examination of the relationship between the changes in the distribution of income and the consequent changes in relative prices leads to the conclusion that such changes 'cannot be reconciled with *any* notion of capital as a measurable quantity independent of distribution and prices' (1960, p. 38). In Part 3 of *Production of Commodities* Sraffa extended his examination of changes in distribution and prices to the case in which changes in distribution lead to changes in the technique of production. He demonstrates that as distribution is varied switches between methods of production, according to which is cheapest, do not follow any particular pattern. Indeed, a technique which is cheapest when the rate of profit is low, may be superseded by another technique at a higher rate of profit, and at a yet higher rate of profit the first technique may again prove to be cheapest and so supersede the second technique. In other words, competitive choice of technique does not result in any particular ordering of techniques. Most notably, the capital intensity of production is *not* an inverse function of the rate of profit, as is implied by the concept of the marginal productivity of capital.

The discussion of 'reswitching' (see Symposium, 1966; Garegnani, 1970) following Levharil's failed attempt (1965) to demonstrate that Sraffa's result was confined to decomposable systems, blossomed into a general critique of the logical foundations of the neoclassical theory of the rate of profit. The conclusion of the debate may be stated as:

> it is not possible, using the data of neoclassical theory – the preferences of individuals, the technology, and the size and distribution of the endowment – to determine the normal long-run rate of profit and the associated prices.

Neoclassical models of competitive value which are consistent in their own terms (say, the model presented in Debreu's *Theory of Value*, 1959) do not determine a long-run equilibrium, in which stocks of produced means of production are adjusted to the demand for them and, in consequence, there is a uniform rate of profit. The definition of equilibrium used in such models is different from the traditional long-run equilibrium (Garegnani, 1976; Milgate, 1979). If the model in Debreu (1959) were constrained to yield a uniform rate of profit, it would be over-determined to degree $k-1$, where k is the number of reproducible means of production. Paradoxically, this latter result is derivable from Hahn's (1982) attempt to refute the above conclusion.

CONCLUSION

Piero Sraffa's consistently critical approach to the neoclassical theory of value and distribution was motivated by a distaste for 'subjective' models, but was conducted in purely logical terms, at least in his later works.

His admiration for the 'objective' structure of classical theory, and for the 'openness' of that structure which permits the incorporation of concrete institutional factors into the formal analysis, led him to attempt to establish that theory on logically more rigorous grounds than had hitherto been available.

The critical debate set off by *Production of Commodities* has been somewhat blunted by the change in the notion of equilibrium used in general equilibrium theory (the implications of this change for the operational content of economic theory, i.e. for the relationship between the theory and the competitive market economy it purports to analyse, have not as yet been satisfactorily analysed).

The well-known propensity of economists to ignore uncomfortable results has also led to the critique being viewed as an esoteric debate in capital theory, with little general significance. This view is clearly wrong. Any critique of the neoclassical theory of value and distribution is a critique of the entire corpus of neoclassical analysis, for the theory of price formation is central to all neoclassical results. (See, for example, Eatwell and Milgate, 1984, on the relevance of these results for the theory of output and employment.)

But it was the revival of the classical (and Marxian) approach to value and distribution, with all the consequences that has for the study of employment, accumulation, technical change, and so on, which was Sraffa's central concern. *Production of Commodities* was designed to lay the groundwork for that revival.

JOHN EATWELL AND CARLO PANICO

See also BASICS AND NON-BASICS; CAPITAL THEORY: PARADOXES; DMITRIEV, VLADIMIR KARPOVITCH; JOINT PRODUCTION IN LINEAR MODELS; LAND RENT; QUANTITY OF CAPITAL; OWN RATES OF INTEREST; RESWITCHING OF TECHNIQUE; STANDARD COMMODITY; SURPLUS APPROACH TO VALUE AND DISTRIBUTION

SELECTED WORKS

1920. *L'Inflazione Monetaria in Italia.* Milan: Primiata Scuola Tipografica Salesiana.

1921a. Open shop drive. *L'Ordine Nuovo*, 5 July, 3.

1921b. Industriali e governo inglese contr i lavoratori. *L'Ordine Nuovo*, 24 July, 3.

1921c. Labur leaders. *L'Ordine Nuovo*, 4 August, 1–2.

1922a. The bank crisis in Italty. *Economic Journal*, 32, *June*, 179–97.

1922b. Italian banking to-day. *The Manchester Guardian Commercial, Reconstruction in Europe, Supplement*, 7 December, 675–6.

1924a. Problemi di oggi e di domani. *L'Ordine Nuovo*, 1–15 April, 4.

1924b. Obituary – Maffeo Panteloni, *Economic Journal*, 34, 648–53.

1925a. Sulle relazioni tra costi e quantità prodotta. *Annali di Economia II*, 277–328.

1925b. A short review of Hastings, H.B., *Cost and Profit: their relation to business cycles*, Boston: Houghton Mifflin, 1923. *Giornale degli Economisti* 66, July, 389–90.

1926a. The laws of return under competitive conditions. *Economic Journal* 36, 535–50.
1926b. A short review of Lehfeldt, R.A., *Money*, London, Oxford University Press, 1926. *Giornale degli Economisti* 67, April, 230.
1926c. A short review of Segre, M., *Le banche nell'ultimo decennio, con particolare riguardo al loro sviluppo patologico nel dopo guerra*, Milano, La Stampa Commercial, 1926. *Giornale degli Economisti* 67, April, 230.
1927a. Il vero significato della 'quoto 90', two letters to A Tasca with a reply. *Stato Operaio*, Vol. 1, November–December 1927, 1089–1095. Reprinted in *Capitalismo Italiano del novecento*, Bari: Laterza, 1972, 180–91.
1927b. A short review of Phillips, H.W., Modern foreign exchange and foreign banking, London, Macdonald and Evans, 1926. *Giornale degli Economisti* 68, October, 610.
1927c. The methods of Facscism. The case of Antonio Gramsci. *Manchester Guardian*, 24 October.
1930a. Symposium on 'Increasing returns and the representative firm', A criticism. *Economic Journal* 50, 89–92.
1930b. Symposium on 'Increasing returns and the representative firm', Rejoinder. *Economic Journal* 50, 93.
1930c. An alleged correction of Ricardo. *Quarterly Journal of Economics* 44, 539–44.
1932a. Dr. Hayek on money and capital. *Economic Journal* 42, March, 42–53.
1932b. Money and capital: a rejoinder. *Economic Journal* 42, June, 249–51.
1938. D. Hume: *An Abstract of a Treatise on Human Nature* (1740). Cambridge: Cambridge University Press. (Introduction with J.M. Keynes.)
1951–73. *The Works and Correspondence of David Ricardo*. 11 vols, Cambridge: Cambridge University Press.
1960. *Production of Commodities by Means of Commodities*. Cambridge: Cambridge University Press.
1962. Production of Commodities. A comment. *Economic Journal* 72, 477–9.

BIBLIOGRAPHY

Dobb, M. 1961. Review of Production of Commodities by Means of Commodities. *De Economist*. Reprinted in *A Critique of Economic Theory*, ed. E.K. Hunt and J.G. Schwartz, Harmondsworth: Penguin.
Eatwell, J. 1975. Mr Sraffa's standard commodity and the rate of exploitation. *Quarterly Journal of Economics* 89(4), November, 543–55.
Eatwell, J. and Milgate, M. (eds) 1984. *Keynes's Economics and the Theory of Value and Distribution*. London: Duckworth.
Garegnani, P. 1970. Heterogeneous capital, the production function and the theory of distribution. *Review of Economic Studies* 37, 407–36.
Garegnani, P. 1976. On a change in the notion of equilibrium in recent work on value and distribution. In *Essays in Modern Capital Theory*, ed. M. Brown, K. Sato and P. Zarembka, Amsterdam: North Holland.
Garegnani, P. 1978. Sraffa's revival or Marxist economic theory. *New Left Review*, No. 112, 71–5.
Hahn, F. 1982. The neo-Ricardians. *Cambridge Journal of Economics* 6, 353–74.
Hicks, J. 1946. *Value and Capital*. 2nd edn, Oxford: Clarendon Press.
Hollander, J. 1904. The development of Ricardo's theory of value. *Quarterly Journal of Economics* 18, August.
Keynes, J.M. 1923. *A Tract on Monetary Reform*. London: Macmillan.
Keynes, J.M. 1936. *The General Theory of Employment, Interest and Money*. London: Macmillan.
Levhari, D. 1965. A non-substitution theorem and reswitching of techniques. *Quarterly Journal of Economics* 79, February, 98–105.
Meek, R.L. 1961. Mr Sraffa's rehabilitation of classical economics. *Scottish Journal of Political Economy* 8, 119–36.
Milgate, M. 1979. On the origin of the notion of 'intertemporal equilibrium'. *Economica* 46, February, 1–10.
Newman, P. 1962. Production of Commodities by Means of Commodities. *Schweizerische Zeitschrift fur Volkwirtschaft und Statistik* 98, 58–75.
Pasinetti, L.L. 1985. In memoria di Piero Sraffa: economista italiano a Cambridge. *Economica politica*.
Ricardo, D. 1817. *On the Principles of Political Economy and Taxation*. London: Murray.
Roncaglia, A. 1978. *Sraffa and the Theory of Prices*. London: Wiley.
Roncaglia, A. 1983. Piero Sraffa: una bibliografia ragionata. *Studi Economici* 21, 137–61.
Roncaglia, A. 1984. Sraffa e le banche. *Rivista Milanese di Economia* 10, April–June, 104–12.
Stigler, G.J. 1953. Sraffa's Ricardo. *American Economic Review* 43, September, 586–99.
Symposium. 1966. Symposium on paradoxes in capital theory. *Quarterly Journal of Economics*.
Wicksteed, P. 1914. The scope and method of political economy in the light of the 'marginal' theory of value and distribution. *Economic Journal* 24, March, 1–23.

Sraffian economics. Piero Sraffa, born in 1898 at Turin as the son of a well-off professor of law, lived from the twenties to his death in 1983 the quet bachelor life of a don at King's and Trinity Colleges, Cambridge. Though his published and unpublished works are few, Sraffa has four claims to fame in the science of economics and the history of ideas.

(i) His 1926 article, 'The Laws of Returns Under Competitive Conditions', was a seminal progenitor of the monopolistic competition revolution. It alone could have justified a lifetime appointment.

(ii) An intimate of Keynes and Wittgenstein, Sraffa is said to have speeded Wittgenstein on his second philosophical road to Damascus by a rail station query, 'What then is the meaning of this [Sicilian] gesture?' The young Sraffa provided books and pin money to the marxist Antonio Gramsci jailed by Mussolini, and he remained quietly interested in leftist matters. Sraffa was an organizer of the famous 1931–5 Cambridge 'Circus' which included Joan and Austin Robinson, Roy Harrod, James Meade and many others. Using Richard Kahn as messenger Gabriel, Maynard Keynes derived much benefit for his nascent *General Theory* from their brilliant group. Except for the chapter 17 discussion of *own* rates of interest, where Keynes must have benefited from Sraffa's 1932 polemic with Friedrich Hayek, there are few signs of a Sraffian interest in the macroeconomics of effective demand. Sharing with Keynes an antiquarian's preoccupation with rare books, Sraffa and Keynes jointly discovered, identified, and edited the valuable *Abstract of A Treatise on Human Nature* that David Hume had published anonymously as a puff for his great initial work on philosophy.

(iii) Sraffa's editing of *The Works and Correspondence of David Ricardo*, a lone-wolf effort over a quarter of a century (aided much toward the end by Maurice Dobb) is one of the great scholarly achievements of all time, ranking in its perfections with the team efforts of the editors of Horace Walpole and James Boswell.

(iv) Finally, in the seventh decade of his life, Piero Sraffa published a classic in capital theory, *The Production of Commodities by Means of Commodities* (1960). As with Mozart if not Mendelssohn, Sraffa's death leaves posterity wistful that his full potential never came into print: what would we not give the good fairies, if somewhere in the attic of a country house there should be discovered a manuscript presenting Sraffa's planned critique of marginalism?

A fresh survey of Sraffa requires the reverse of a chronological order. First comes his 1960 book, which has spawned an extensive literature but still needs – if the technology is to be adequately handled – to have Sraffa's special equalities embedded in the general inequalities – equalities of the 1937 von

Neumann model. The essentially completed Sraffa–Leontief circulating capital model provides by itself a prism with which to diffract the paradigms of Marx, Ricardo, and various brands of neoclassicism; and, self-reflexively, it can serve to help judge Ricardo's editor. The unity in Sraffa's scientific vision, from before 1926 until death at age 85, then becomes visible.

TRULY GENERAL TIME PHASING. The polemics of Böhm-Bawerk, Knight, and other capital theorists are illuminated, and seen through, by the 1937 von Neumann general model once that is made explicitly *time-phased* and open-ended, to allow (a) for *primary* factors (labour, land, ...) not necessarily producible within the system, and (b) for *net consumptions* of outputs not necessarily ploughed back into the system for self-propelled growth.

We can summarize the n outputs produced by J activities, where each jth activity uses as inputs a vector of M primary factors and a vector of commodity-inputs, while producing a vector of joint products:

$$q_i^{t+1} = \sum_{j=1}^{J} b_{ij} \min [Q_{1j}^t/a_{2j}, \ldots, Q_{nj}^t/a_{nj}; L_{1j}^t/l_{1j}, \ldots, L_{Mj}^t/l_{Mj}] \quad (1)$$

$$= Q_{i1}^{t+1} + \cdots + Q_{iJ}^{t+1} + C_i^{t+1},$$

$$i = 1, \ldots, n \gtreqless J, \quad Q_{ij}^t \geqq 0, \quad C_i^{t+1} \geqq 0, \quad L_{mj}^t \geqq 0 \quad (2)$$

$$a = [a_{ij}] = \begin{bmatrix} a_{11} & \cdots & a_{1J} \\ \vdots & & \vdots \\ a_{n1} & \cdots & a_{nJ} \end{bmatrix} \geqq 0;$$

$$b = [b_{ij}] = \begin{bmatrix} b_{11} & \cdots & b_{1J} \\ \vdots & & \vdots \\ b_{n1} & \cdots & b_{nJ} \end{bmatrix} \geqslant 0 \quad (3)$$

$$= [l_{mj}] = \begin{bmatrix} l_{11} & \cdots & l_{1J} \\ \vdots & & \vdots \\ l_{M1} & \cdots & l_{MJ} \end{bmatrix} \geqslant 0; \quad J \gtreqless M \gtreqless n$$

The a's are input/output coefficients; l's are Walrasian factor coefficients; b's are joint-product proportions (as with 1 bu. wool and 2 pounds mutton per sheep). We use standard notation: for a matrix or vector z, $z > 0$ means all its elements are positive; $z = 0$ means all elements zero; $z \geqq 0$ means no element negative, with all possibly zero; $z \geqslant 0$ means no element negative, but at least one being strictly positive; z' is the transpose of z: thus, $[1 \cdots 1]'$ is a column vector of ones. I is the identity matrix, with 1's in the main diagonal and zero elsewhere:

$$I = [\delta_{ij}], \text{ as in } I = [1], \; I = \left[\begin{smallmatrix} 1 & 0 \\ 0 & 1 \end{smallmatrix}\right], \ldots, \text{etc.}$$

For systems in a *stationary* state, regardless of the variable we have $z^{t+1} = z^t = z$. An important case is where supplies of primary factors are specified to be positive constants:

$$\sum_{1}^{J} L_{mj} = L_m, \quad m = 1, \ldots, M.$$

Remark: the circulating capital models occupying most pages in Sraffa (1960) are a special case of (3) where each column of (b_{ij}) can be written to contain a single 'one' with the remaining elements zero. In general, any or all a_{ij}'s could be assumed by a mathematician to be zero; but, to be interesting, every b must have at least one positive element in each of its rows and its columns, so that every good is produced somewhere and every activity produces at least one good. An activity might not require any *direct* primary input; but, if we are not to be in the Land of Cockaigne, where lollipops grow freely on trees and don't even require picking, indirectly or directly every good must require some primary factor(s).

GENERAL HAWKINS–SIMON CONDITIONS. For a circulating-capital system to be 'productive', in the sense of providing positive net consumptions, a must satisfy simple Hawkins–Simon conditions, such as that powers of a, a^k go to zero as $k \to \infty$. When b involves joint products, matters are more complex and the literature needs the equivalent of the following two constructive tests:

Axiom 1 (No Land of Cockaigne). The following standard linear programming problem must have a solution of zero:

Subject to

$$lx \leqq 0, \quad x \geqq 0$$

$$[b - a]x \geqq 0,$$

$$\max_x [1 \cdots 1][b - a]x = Z^* = 0$$

Axiom 2 (Generalized Hawkins–Simon). The following standard LP problem will have a *positive* solution if, and only if, the system is "productive."

Subject to

$$lx \leqq [L_1 \cdots L_M] > 0, \quad x \geqq 0$$

$$[b - a]x \geqq C \geqq 0$$

$$C \geqq (c \cdots c)' \geqq C$$

$$\max_{x,C} c = c^* > 0$$

Example: Suppose, as in the joint-production passages of Sraffa (1960), that $(b - a)$ is $n \times n$, with $J = n$. It will then be *sufficient* that $b - a$ have row sums positive for the productiveness axiom to be satisfied. (Contrary to what seems to be suggested by the mathematician C. F. Manara (1979), these row-sum conditions are *not* necessary—as $b - a$ with diagonal elements near to 1's and off-diagonals of -10 and -0.01 demonstrates.)

COMPETITIVE PRICING RELATIONS. In the absence of any uncertainty, or restrictions on entry and knowledge, perfect competition will be led in (1) by Darwinian arbitrage to equality of the profit rate in all processes positively operated. In matrix terms, with P a non-negative row vector of n goods prices, W a non-negative row vector of M primary-factor prices, and r the common profit or interest rate, we have the general dynamic equalities–inequalities:

$$P^{t+1}b \leqq (P^t a + W^t l)(1 + r^t), \quad (P^t, P^{t+1}, W^t, r^t) \geqslant 0 \quad (4)$$

$$P^{t+1}q^{t+1} = [P^t a x^{t+1} + W^t l x^{t+1}](1 + r^t)$$

$$= [P^t a q^t + W^t L^t](1 + r^t) \quad (4')$$

where x^{t+1} is the column-vector of the J 'intensities' at which the respective activities are carried on:

$$0 \leqq x_j^{t+1} \leqq L_{mj}^t/l_{mj}, \qquad m = 1, \ldots, M; \; j = 1, \ldots, J$$

$$\leqq Q_{ij}/a_{ij}, \qquad i = 1, \ldots, n$$

$$\geqq q_i^{t+1}/b_{ij} \quad (4'')$$

The convention is understood in (4″) and (1) that when a denominator vanishes, the term in which it appears is ignorable. In (4) P's and W's are measured in any numeraire and equality of r's in all processes used does not imply equality of different goods' *own* rates of interest when P^{t+1} is not proportional to P^t.

Wherever a strong inequality holds in (4), that activity must cease to operate, in accordance with the perfect-competition *duality* conditions:

$$0 = x_j^{t+1}\left[\sum_{i=1}^{n} P_i^{t+1} b_{ij} - \sum_{i=1}^{n} P_i^t a_{ij}(1+r^t) - \sum_{m=1}^{M} W_m^t l_{mj}(1+r^t)\right] \quad j = 1, \ldots, J \qquad (4''')$$

In stationary equilibrium, $(P^t, W^t, r^t) = (P, W, r)$, and all time scripts can be omitted. All *own* rates of interest are then the same.

Then (4) becomes

$$Pb \leqslant (Pa + Wl)(1 + r) \qquad (5a)$$

$$Pbx = (Pax + Wlx)(1 + r) \qquad (5b)$$

These equality-of-profit-rate conditions are not merely competitive arbitrage conditions. Taken together with the steady-state version of (1)–(2), namely with

$$(b - a)x \geqslant C \geqslant 0, \quad lx \leqslant L > 0 \qquad (5c)$$

(5a)–(5b) are the necessary and sufficient conditions for *intertemporal* production efficiency (or intertemporal Pareto efficiency on the allocation side). Unless there exists, at the observed steady state, an existent (P, W, uniform r), the society must be planning wastefully. So aside from Marx's 1867 innovation being a backward step in positivistic realism, it was a bad (avoidable) blunder from the standpoint of social planning and efficiency – a point never glimpsed by Marx or his admiring editor Engels. Because Sraffa's brief text never grapples with the *intertemporal* relations implied by *his* steady states, his readers are left unaware of this technocratic property of dualistic competitive pricing.

Sraffa (1960) considers for the most part very special cases of (5), and of (1)–(2), cases for which n happens to equal J with $b - a$ square and of rank n and with all equalities holding in (4). Save for the brief chapter on land, he mostly works with labour as the only primary factor and seems to presuppose that $[l_{11} \cdots l_{1n}][b - a(1 + r)]^{-1}$ happens to be positive in an open neighbourhood above r equal to zero. (*Remark*: in many technologies, even when J greatly exceeds n, the number of activities operated at a *positive* level will be equal to n; this endogenous fact should not obscure the more general truth, that changes in demand will generically alter the choice of n viable activities – so that, as will be seen, von Neumann's rectangular matrices cannot be sidestepped.)

PROPERTIES OF COMPETITIVE EQUILIBRIUM. The following twenty properties of Sraffian steady-state systems are straightforwardly verifiable:

1. When goods require more than one primary input, as for example labour and land, a shift in demand away from a land-intensive good and toward a labour-intensive good, will at each ruling profit rate raise the price ratio of the latter relative to the former; and it will tend to raise labour's distributive share at the expense of land's. *The labour theory of value*, even in the absence of the complication of time-phasing and interest, *thus generally fails and the theory of distribution cannot be separated from the complications of value theory* (of supply–demand pricing theory).

2. Even when labour is the only primary factor, time-phasing means that Smith's bipartite formula of wage-*plus*-interest is indeed a necessary statement of price and of national income. Save in singular cases where all goods happen to have exactly the same percentage of direct-wage cost to total cost – what Marx called the case of 'equal organic compositions of capital' – *a change in the interest rate must alter relative commodity prices* – again vitiating the simple labour theory of value.

3. Suppose there are no joint products, all raw materials being used up in a single employment. It follows from the last paragraph that competitive prices in time-phased systems must generally at positive interest rates differ from the 'marked-up values' of Marx's *Capital* (1967, Volume I, ch. IX) which replace a uniform industry-by-industry rate of profit by a uniform rate of surplus value: the 1867 marked up values mark up the direct wage costs only, with allegedly no mark up earned on raw-materials outlays for produced goods (for 'constant' capitals). Ratios of these peculiar 'marked-up values' agree with ratios of zero-profit-rate prices, and do so no matter how great the capitalists' surplus! So, in consequence of paragraph numbered 2 above, the 1867 Marxian constructs do systematically depart from realistic competitive prices and need to be 'transformed' into correct Sraffian competitive prices *by abandoning them* – as L. von Bortkiewicz had demonstrated in 1907.

4. Staying with the assumption of no joint products, we can deduce the existence of a *factor-price tradeoff frontier*: at any specified Sraffian interest rate, there is defined a convex tradeoff frontier between the maximal real wage rate of labour and real rent rate of land (where *any* good is the numeraire for measuring such real factor prices); a rise in the interest rate must shift inward the convex contour relating real factor prices (but equal upward increments of r can induce inward shifts in the frontier that both accelerate and decelerate). Though Sraffa does not use this name for the frontier, for the case where labour is the sole primary factor, he recognizes the properties of this basic frontier.

5. The amount of *net consumptions* produced in the stationary state will be *maximal* when the competitive system chooses those golden-rule techniques that are supported by a zero rate of interest. (If all primary factors grow at a Harrod natural rate of $[1 + g]^t$, the maximal *per capita net consumptions* will be realized only when competition mandates use of the golden-rule techniques supportable by an interest rate of g: $1 + r = 1 + g$.) This paragraph states something different from the earlier remarks around equations (5) concerning *intertemporal* Pareto efficiency.

6. At any interest rate r, prevailing in Sraffa's time-phased system, the competitively viable techniques observed can be verified from (5) to achieve *intertemporal Pareto optimality*. By contrast, consider the 1867 Marxian techniques that maximize the rate of surplus value for a specified vector of relative primary-factor prices. Not only are these techniques unrealistic describers of the positive facts about the laws of motion of capitalism. In addition they would achieve a Planner's nightmare, in general producing permanently in the steady state less of goods than the system is capable of and involving more of society's scarce primary factors than is technologically needed. When Sraffa's readers begin to worry about consumption preferences over different time periods, they will additionally have to revert back from 1867 Marxian values to (5)'s dualistic competitive pricing to restore *intertemporal* Pareto efficiency of consumption.

HOW DEMAND-TASTES AFFECT PRICING AND DISTRIBUTION. The above half-dozen rules of a Sraffian system are valid either for *his* von Neumann technologies or for *all* versions of neoclassical technologies (involving convexity and first-degree homogeneity). Although Sraffa reserved judgement for half a century on whether he wanted to assume constant returns to scale, experiments with returns laws that depart from that property will be found to rob his algebra of *any* interesting economic applications, as the paucity of results on this point in the literature of the last quarter of a century attests. (Thus, specify for the coal and iron example of the opening page of Sraffa (1960) that in the iron industry doubling inputs quadruples output, while in the wheat industry tripling inputs doubles output. Then none of the pricing relations have other than empty definitional content!) The Perron input/output matrices don't define *existent* prices of production.

Further properties of steady-state competitive systems are the following.

7. Prior to Sraffa (1960), the Leontief literature had established and generalized the 1949 Non-Substitution Theorem. *When labour is the only primary factor and there are no joint products, at any observed profit rate the competitive prices at which all goods are positively produced must be independent of the composition of steady-state demand: even when alternative techniques could be reasonably substituted, changes in demand can never mandate their new use.* Also, with labour the only primary factor, a shift in demand toward goods that involve a high relative fraction of direct-wage cost must be at the observed profit rate raise the wage-profit share. As already indicated, when labour must cooperate with land, shifts in demand toward or away from goods that are relatively labour-rather-than-land-intensive must at the observed competitive profit rate raise or lower their relative prices and presumptively alter the distribution of income between workers and landlords. The Ricardian dream of ridding distribution theory from the complications of (consumer-demand) value theory is seen to be, in general, a pipe dream – as Ricardo realized in his occasional lapses into good sense (as for example, when recognizing that Napoleonic-war shift of demand toward labour-intensive soldiering would raise the wage share prior to a repopulating of the countryside). At a given interest rate, in the absence of technical innovation and non-labour primary factors, a rise in the money wage rate cannot force a permanent substitution of machines for labour since machines' steady-state costs then rise proportionally with the wage rate.

SOME JOINT-PRODUCT PHENOMENA. The following properties of joint-product systems are also common to Sraffian technologies of the von Neumann type and to *all* versions of neoclassical technologies.

8. When joint products are admitted – surely the realistic case – the classical economists' hope to deduce steady-state price ratios from technology and supply alone is *generally* frustrated. When one species of sheep produces wool and mutton in joint proportions – or when one roundtrip of a ship supplies east and west transportation jointly – each alteration in tastes and demands for the joint products alters their steady-state price ratio and does so even under perfect Arrow–Debreu certainty.

Sraffa's favourite case of joint products would involve as many independent activities used as there are goods: $J = n$. For a simple example, consider 2 sheep species, each producing 2 products: say, species 1 produces 2 of wool and 1 of mutton, while species 2 produces 1 of wool and 2 of mutton; for simplicity let both sheep require the same inputs and cost, which might as well be labour only.

So long as consumer's demand involves relative expenditures on the two goods not too unequal – no good ever attracting more than two-thirds of consumers' dollars – Sraffa is correct in expecting cost-technology alone to determine competitive pricing of $P_{\text{mutton}}/P_{\text{wool}} = 1.0$. But, as soon as people want to spend more than two-thirds of their incomes on mutton, Sraffa loses his equality of number of goods and number of positively used activities: only the meat-intensive species is competitively viable; consumer demand functions are then price determining.

Let us add a third sheep species, producible like the others but yielding 1.75 of wool and 1.75 of mutton. Now $J = 3 > 2 = n$. When people singularly spend exactly half their incomes on wool and mutton, only the species 3 is viable and $P_m/P_w = 1.0$ as set by demand. When people spend a bit more on mutton than wool, less than $J = 3$ activities are positively viable, namely $2 = n < J = 3$, as species 3 and species 2 alone survive. For a range of demands, $P_m/P_w = 1/3$, a numerical value that can be calculated from Sraffa's 2 cost-prices of production relations. However, as the demand for mutton relative to that of wool runs the gamut of possible ratios, we reach the limit of each Sraffian horizontal step and must traverse the staircase's vertical risers with market price being consumer-demand determined. In realistic cases, J is large relative to n; and there are many different n-by-n square submatrices that consumer-demand functions will endogenously select out of the rectangular n-by-J matrix of technology.

In sum, *globally* demand generally helps determine relative prices of Sraffa's joint products between zero and infinity, doing so along a staircase's vertical risers and (*locally* horizontal) step segments.

This general rule of global dependence on demand of joint-products' price ratios does admit of an exceptional case where an aspect of a Non-Substitution theorem does obtain. Let us, so to speak, introduce so weak a degree of jointness of production that we are still in a close neighbourhood of indecomposable non-joint-production. This will occur when a positive *net* amount of each good is available only from a single process, and where each process does produce one such positive amount net. Under this stipulation the square matrix $(b_{ij} - a_{ij})$, after feasible renumbering of the goods and of the processes, will be specified to have positive elements in its diagonal and negative off-diagonal elements. Its general Hawkins–Simon conditions will also require that the inverse $[b - a]^{-1}$ exists and is positive. Under these strong stipulations, as is well known, the same Non-Substitution theorem that holds for circulating-capital and exponential-depreciation models will hold for joint production.

Otherwise, however, demand conditions can in general have an essential effect on relative prices; and can do so even when we grant Sraffa special indulgences (such as equality of J and n, non-singularity of $b - a$, and labour the only primary factor). Thus, often, even when $(l_{1j})(b - a)^{-1}$ is positive, some elements of $(b - a)^{-1}$ will be negative—with the result that for some ratios of consumptions, $(b - a)^{-1}\ C$ will not define positive feasible gross outputs, and price ratios will have to be influenceable by demand-tastes.

SRAFFIAN ARTIFACTS: STANDARD COMMODITY BASKETS. The following properties are special and hold only for singular subsets of von Neumann technologies or for singular subsets of neoclassical technologies.

9. Postulate no joint products, no primary factors other than labour, no alternative techniques for producing goods, and that all goods considered are *basics* in the sense that a is indecomposable so that every good requires for its production

something directly or indirectly of every good as input. Then, Sraffa (1960) deduces the existence of a market basket of goods or *standard commodity*, with unique positive weights $(Q_1^*, \ldots, Q_n^*)'$, such that the *real wage expressed in terms of the standard commodity* and paid to the workers postfactum (at the *end* of the period when they work at the beginning of the period) is a declining *linear* relation:

$$w = 1 - (r/r^*) \tag{6a}$$

where r^* is the maximum positive profit rate the system can pay, with the column vector (Q_i^*) uniquely definable by the eigenvector relation:

$$a(1+r^*)[Q_i^*] = [Q_i^*] > 0$$
$$[l_{11} \cdots l_{1n}][I-a]^{-1}Q^* = 1 \tag{6b}$$

Some real prices rise faster with the profit rate than the standard commodity's price does; some rise less fast. When the real *standard*-basket wage rate is half its zero-profit-rate level, the postfactum wage share of the basket's cost is also one half; and similarly for any other fraction.

Sraffa, for reasons not easy to understand, thought that (6)'s truth somehow provided Ricardo with a defence for his labour theory of value. Even in the restricted case where (6) does validly obtain, one perceives no successful resurrection of Ricardo's desired labour theory of value or absolute standard of value that is provided by Sraffa's demonstration of the existence of this standard commodity: price ratios are still not equal to zero-profit-rate price ratios as the crude labour theory of value wants them to be.

10. It is by now understood that a Sraffian Standard Commodity often fails to exist, for a variety of reasons:

(i) In circulating-capital and exponentially depreciating models, as soon as competition mandates a switch in technology when interest rates or relative primary factor prices change, there will then generally not be any market-basket weights that entail a *linear* tradeoff frontier between the real wage and the profit rate.

(ii) In these same models, realistic decomposabilities can negate the existence of *positive* weights that yield linearity.

(iii) In still other cases, as shown by Takahiro Miyao in 1977, for various vectors of direct-labour coefficients, there can be an infinity of positive weights that produce the same normalized linearity as the Sraffian standard.

(iv) In joint-product cases, as C. F. Manara (1979) instanced. $(b - a[1+r])$ may have only *complex* eigenvalues and eigenvectors. Again, no Sraffian standard validity obtains. (For such Manara cases, at some feasible interest rates certain processes cease to be competitively viable; so Ricardo can never find his middling composite, which is neither too time-consuming nor too time-economizing, to provide him with the chimera of an absolute standard of value for making comparisons across time and space.)

(v) There exist many joint-product cases in which Sraffa's eigenvector of $(b - a[1+r])$ is real, but involves some *negative* elements. Playing the game of defining market baskets with negative weights cannot, by some analogy with foreign-trade exports and imports or debtor-creditor ownings and owings, make economic sense useful to a Ricardian critical of Adam Smith or of J. B. Clark.

(vi) There are many joint-product cases in which Sraffa's eigenvector for $(b - a[1+r])$ is all positive. But still there may be no standard market basket that yields a *linear* factor-price frontier validity applicable over the *whole* interval of feasible profit rates. (On one side of some critical r, all of Sraffa's $J(=n)$ processes are competitively viable. On the other side of that r, less than n processes can earn the competitive profit rate. The *true* market cost of Sraffa's nominated market basket there ceases to obey the linear law that allegedly Ricardo's value theory could benefit from.)

(vii) Instead of abandoning the hunt for a chimera, some Sraffians sought comfort in the belief that the important joint-product cases are not those of the wool-mutton type but rather are those of the new-machine-old-machine type or are of the permanently-durable-land type; and nursed a hope that for these important cases, the 'pathologies' of non-existent standard commodities might be absent.

If anyone ever believed this, it was an illusion. Under (i) above, we saw land–labour models in which induced changes in a_{ij} coefficients take place, which induce violation of the Sraffian desired linearity. A locus linear *piecewise* is *not* linear.

Also, a model where the only jointness is of the durable-good type may well not admit of a standard commodity defined over the whole interval of feasible profit rates. The following counterexample settles the issue of possible non-existence:

$$b = \begin{bmatrix} 1 & 1 \\ 7/8 & 0 \end{bmatrix}, \quad a = \begin{bmatrix} 7/8 & 0 \\ 0 & 1/2 \end{bmatrix}, \quad [l_{11} l_{12}] = [1 \quad 9] \tag{7}$$

Here is its story. Good 1 can be consumed directly or be used as a new machine to produce, in cooperation with labour, Good 1 itself along with the joint product of an old machine. The used machine, called Good 2, can be used with labour to produce Good 1 and worthless scrap. (Later, we'll recognize that Good 2 might be an object of final utility for its own sake, distinct from Good 1's marginal and total utility.)

This example's numbers involve the need in Process 2 for (relatively) much labour and little of the old machine to produce 1 of Good 1. Process 1, by contrast, produces 1 of Good 1 with relatively little labour and a fair amount of new machines: for Process 1, labour with 7/8 of a new machine, produces 1 of a new machine and 7/8 of an old machine; for Process 2, 9 of direct labour, with 1/2 of an old machine, produces 1 of a new machine and scrap.

Calculation shows that competition must then work out as follows:

At very low profit rates, the used machine is so consuming of high-wage direct labour that it (and Process 2) cannot be used in production under viable competition. The price ratio P_2/P_1 will then be set completely by utility tastes for Goods 1 and 2: with enough yen for Good 2, P_2/P_1 can be anything from zero to infinity at low profit rates.

Between the critical profit rates of 1.59%, and 109.67% both processes *could* be used competitively. If both are useable throughout that interval, then over that interval (and only it) Sraffa will get his desired *linear* standard commodity; but it must fail him at the lower interval of profit rates. Worse still, even in the higher interval where algebra does yield him a linear function, economics can veto the relevance of Sraffa's standard function: as soon as people have strong enough marginal utility for Good 2, *all* of it is bid away from production uses! Process 2 becomes competitively unviable and Sraffian cost-prices lose relevance; demand becomes decisive, frustrating the primitive classicist's yearning to determine prices from supply considerations alone. The 1960 purported defence of Ricardo's absolute standard has collapsed.

MORAL. The Walrasian paradigms are in general unavoidable

in the most unrestricted von Neumann paradigm. What began as a classicist-inspired critique of 'marginalism' ends up as a demonstration that the classical-economics paradigm does need to be broadened into the post-1870 mainstream economics – even when smooth Clarkian marginal products are scrupulously avoided! Where a critique succeeds, and is needed, is in exposing how special are the one-sector, homogeneous-scalar-capital paradigms of Clark.

The genuine Fisher, von Neumann, Arrow–Debreu structure of time-phased general equilibrium stands confirmed by the Sraffa–Leontief probings.

1960 LIGHT ON CLARKIAN OVERSIMPLIFICATIONS. Heroic works clarifying faults of neoclassical parables have been done by Joan Robinson, Luigi Pasinetti, Pierangelo Garegnani, Bertram Schefold, J. S. Metcalfe and I. Steedman, C. F. Manara, V. K. Dimitriev, and many others.

11. Before she knew of Sraffa's 1960 model, Joan Robinson had usefully debunked the notion that some aggregate Platonic Kapital, $K = \Sigma P_j k_j$, enters into real-world production functions and defines (aggregate) *marginal net product* of Kapital, $\partial[K(t+1) - K(t)]/\partial K(t)$, to give the real-world interest or profit rate. Sraffa's model showed once and for all the falsity of the following neoclassical apologetics:

> Roundabout ['mechanized'] methods are productive and the interest rate measures the incremental social product obtainable by extending the degree of roundaboutness through the effective action of *saving* (by the exercise of painful 'waiting' and 'abstinence').

Sraffa showed this: As soon as there are more capital goods than 1, it is impossible to say of every pair of techniques which one is the more roundabout, time-intensive, or mechanized. Increases in the interest rate above zero can first raise various P_2/P_1 ratios and then later lower them. So above a critical high interest rate, competition may revert back to a technique that had been viable only at very low interest rates.

> Sraffian *reswitching* thus implies: Lowering the interest rate may result in lower steady-state consumption levels, prior to its ultimately raising them to the maximal golden-rule level.

Oskar Lange once wrote, sardonically but seriously, that Ludwig von Mises, the enemy of socialism, deserved a statue in the socialist Hall of Fame for compelling Abba Lerner and Lange (to say nothing of earlier Pareto, Barone and Fred Taylor) to work out how socialists might devise efficient decentralizing-pricing planning algorithms. One can insist, seriously, that a neoclassical Hall of Fame deserves Sraffa's statue.

12. Actually all of Sraffa's findings about the impossibility of defining 'more roundaboutness' and 'less roundaboutness' apply precisely to smoothly differentiable *vector*-capital Clarkian models. Neoclassicists should reproach themselves, and thank Robinson and Sraffa, for belated recognition that the locus of (stationary-state consumption, interest rate) need not be a one-way tradeoff. This recognition is achievable quite apart from the dramatic case of *double-switching*.

Example. Let $[L, K_1, K_2, C_1, C_2, \dot{K}_1 = \mathrm{d}K_1/\mathrm{d}t, \dot{K}_2]$ depict, for a 2-sector neoclassical economy in which marginal products are *not* illusory, its labour, its 2 heterogeneous capital good's stocks, its 2 consumptions, and its net investments. Its production function and steady-state profit-rate are given by

$$L = F[K_1, K_2;\; C_1 + \dot{K}_1, C_2 + \dot{K}_2] \tag{8a}$$

$$r = -(\partial F/\partial K_i)/(\partial F/\partial \dot{K}_i),\; i = 1,2 \tag{8b}$$

where F is a first-degree-homogeneous, smooth, convex function. Set L by convention at a plateau of unity, and for simplicity specify C_2/C_1 always to be unity; and, as a condition of stationarity, make all $\dot{K}_i$ vanish. Then the above pair of relations permit us to determine the level of consumption as a function of the profit rate: $C_1 = f(r)$. What neoclassicals insufficiently realized before 1960, away from $r = 0$ there is no necessity for C_1 to fall as r rises. This valid Sraffa–Robinson point does not score against 'marginalism'. Their razor cuts as deeply against the discrete-activity technology!

'Marginalism' per se is not what deserves the razor of Sraffa's critique. As already said, whatever Clarkian marginalism can display for good or ill is already capable of being displayed by a von Neumann discrete-activities technology.

Space permits only a few further mentions of paradoxical neoclassical phenomena that can result from *positive* profit rates in time-phased models. A critique to reveal them, as shown by several valuable works of Metcalfe and Steedman, cuts as much within von Neumann-*activities* models as within smooth *marginalist* models of the marginal-product type.

13. The Non-Substitution Theorem, which makes relative costs and prices, at each interest rate, independent of the composition of final demands when only one primary factor is present, is common to *discrete* and *marginalist* models. When more than one primary factor is present, the Non-Substitution Theorem becomes a Substitution Theorem – again, generally both for discrete and marginalist models.

14. Both for discrete and marginalist no-joint-product models, for each interest rate there is a convex tradeoff between various real factor returns (expressed in terms of *any* good as numeraire). For both models, it is *not* necessarily true that the tradeoff relation between the interest rate itself and real factor returns is convex. (Point 14 has a considerable overlap with Point 4.)

15. For both models, the substitutions of technique that win out under competition are Pareto efficient. For both models, any technique observed to be viable under competition is a golden-rule technique for that Harrod-growth rate which is equal to the observed interest rate!

16. For both models, when the real wage rises relative to the real land-rent (independently of the good used as numeraire), any mandated technical substitution must (if anything) involve a shift to lower embodied-dated-labour contents of each good and to higher embodied-dated-land contents. This is as true for a positive interest rate as for a zero one, since we deal exclusively with golden-rule technologies. (The difference, when r is zero, is that there is then no need for *dating* of the direct-and-indirect labour and land contents.)

17. As shown by Metcalfe and Steedman, Pasinetti, Samuelson, and others, in both models one must guard against a tempting fallacy.

In both models, when r is zero, the change in technique induced by a rise in the Wage/Rent ratio must economize on the *actual* Labour/Land ratios observed to be used in the various industries in the stationary state. Something like this remains true for very low interest rates. (For economy of space, explanatory qualifications are omitted.) However, for large enough r, what are called embodied-dated-labour contents and embodied-dated-land contents can be substantially different from synchronized-stationary-state labour and land actually observed to be used. So beware of believing that observed $(\Delta W_m)(\Delta L_m)$ must be negative when r is positive.

This has implications for the correct Heckscher–Ohlin and Stolper–Samuelson trade theorems under time-phasing.

18. Related to the above is the following observation. At $r = 0$, the competitive system is out on its true *stationary-state production-possibility-frontier*. At positive r, although the system moves to a new *steady*-state (not stationary-state!) golden-rule set of techniques, what it can produce and does produce in the *stationary* state is generally *not* out on the stationary-state production-possibility frontier – but rather is inside that frontier. As demand changes, what we observe inside that frontier need not trace out well-behaved *concave* loci.

Some Marxians, bemused by notions of 'unequal exchange', think that the above phenomena are Pareto inefficient: the system and the world get less product than is producible in the zero-interest-rate golden-rule state. Yes, of course. But that is unavoidable in any scenario where the economic system could only obtain the produced inputs needed for Schumpeter's golden-rule zero-interest rate utopia by doing current 'waiting' and sacrificing of current consumptions. The curse of the poor societies is their poverty – even when *intertemporal* Pareto efficiency is always obtaining. Again, all this is as true of *discrete* as of *marginalist* technologies.

SRAFFIAN REFUTATION OF MARXISM. On the basis of this elaborate description of findings about Sraffian time-phased systems, one can apply the results to appraise and correct (1) neoclassical economics, (2) Marxian economics, (3) Ricardian and classical economics. Its thrust on neoclassical economics was sampled in the previous section.

20. Sraffian economics, as earlier passages make clear, devastatingly repudiates that central part of Marx's economics, *Capital*, Volume I (1867) which proposed a new paradigm involving an *equal* 'rate of surplus value' by industries or departments. Sraffa and Darwinian arbitrage require an *equal* 'rate of profit' by industries or departments. Under exploitative capitalism, Marx misidentifies what is out there to be observed in the competitive market, for the reason that Marx has the capitalists garnering too little in the industries using much capital goods and garnering too much in those using relatively little capital goods. It is a gratuitous error, and a sterile one, since Marx's paradigm does not help predict the laws of motion of competitive capitalism, or help understand the average magnitude of the profit level around which Marx's errors spread. Equal profit rates are not a capitalist shibboleth; dual to the primal variables of the von Neumann technology is an equalized profit rate.

Ian Steedman, a scholar sympathetic to the *Weltanschauung* of Marx and of economic reform, has documented the Sraffian rejection of 1867 Marxian rate of surplus value in his book, *Marx After Sraffa* (1981). So here it need only be said: In the end, from the posthumous publication of *Capital*, volume III (1894), one can recognize that the 'transformation' from Marx's 1867 [marked-up] 'values' to bourgeois 'prices' involves *abandoning* the 1867 relations and *returning* to the pre-Marx and post-Marx cost-profit relations of the Sraffian model.

One cannot leave it quite at that. Karl Marx does deserve a statue in the Sraffian Hall of Fame. Not, of course, for his sterile detour into the rate of surplus value. As documented by Samuelson in the 1974 Lloyd Metzler *Festschrift*, Marx was the first scholar after Quesnay to grapple explicitly with input/output capital models. Implicitly, Marx was the first to use (a_{ij}) coefficients. Moreover, in his Tableaus of Steady Reproduction and of Expanded Reproduction, *Capital*, volume II (1885), Karl Marx was the first to present coherent row-and-column arrays of steady-state equilibrium. This is Marx's imperishable contribution to analytical economics, and it is impervious to the deflating of hyperbole concerning Marx as allegedly a great *mathematical* economist.

1926 RECONSIDERED FROM 1960. There were two main parts to Sraffa's celebrated 1926 paper. The first part, which today we realize was by far the more important one, dealt with the phenomena of *increasing returns to scale*. So long as demand is insufficiently large to take a firm beyond such an initial phase of increasing returns or decreasing costs, the firm cannot find a maximum-profit equilibrium while still remaining a perfect competitor. Cournot knew this in 1838, and it was not new doctrine even then. The turn of the century literature on trusts and industrial organization, in America and Germany, was never in doubt on this. By 1926 the whole issue would have been old hat save for Alfred Marshall's tergiversations on the compatibility of *increasing* (internal, statical and reversible) *returns* and perfection of competition. Marshall, at the time of his death in 1924, was at the height of his prestige, with the greatest capacity for good and for potential confusion. Therefore, it was important for Piero Sraffa to restate elegantly that real-life firms, with localized and segmented markets, were in imperfect-competition equilibrium with falling marginal production costs that were offset by selling and transport costs and by price declines inducible by expansion of their own outputs and sales. Independently, E.H. Chamberlin and J.M. Clark were saying much the same thing at the time in America. But the ruling establishment of Cambridge, understandably, could learn something best from one of its own publishing in the *Economic Journal*. The 1960 book has no relation to this part of Sraffa's early work.

Within the mid-1920s, Sraffa's other thesis generated a disproportionate amount of interest. Not only was the familiar downward-sloping Marshallian supply curve to be ruled out as incompatible with perfection of competition; the young Sraffa was newly arguing that upward-sloping supply curves were also of vacuous importance for Marshallian partial equilibrium. All that Sraffa left his reader, then, was a horizontal, *constant-cost* competitive supply curve.

This is plain wrong. Sraffa's 1960 book demonstrates that when primary factors other than a single homogeneous labour exist, rightward shifting Marshallian and Walrasian demand curves will generally trace *rising* price intersections on the relevant supply curves. Joan Robinson's famous 1941 *Economic Journal* article on rising supply price was the first East Anglian recognition of the formal comparative statics of general equilibrium. I doubt that she or Piero ever noticed the incompatibility with 1926 Sraffa; or the incompatibility of Heckscher–Ohlin and Stolper–Samuelson in the foreign-trade literature with Sraffa's thesis of *constant* costs and implied *linear* production-possibility frontiers. The pre- and post-Ricardian classical literature is full of examples of wine grown on special vineyard lands: for generations students have followed Viner's 1931 example of calling this 'the pure Ricardian case' – while the modern teachers of the young know this as the Jones–Samuelson–Haberler specific-factors model.

Students of rhetoric should be interested to analyse the elements of style that enable the erudite author of a faulty thesis to persuade himself and several generations of thinkers of its truth and importance. Because Sraffa wrote so little, and wrote so rarely on the mainstream topics of contemporary scholarship, his skills as a writer have perhaps been insufficiently noticed.

Knowing what we now know – that it is a mistake to believe that constant-cost cases exhaust the categories of admissible competitive price – we are in a position to study the young

Sraffa's extra-scientific motivations. Why does a sophisticated intelligence make *this* mistake? Just as inside a fat man is a thin man trying to get out, so outside the Sraffa of the post-World War I heyday of Walras–Marshall neoclassicism, there was already in 1925 an atavistic classical economist trying to get back in. This is why one can say that, from before 1925 to after 1960, there is a discernible consistency in Piero Sraffa's thought and ideology. An objective reader will want to be alert to this tendency.

1960 VERDICTS ON 1817 RICARDIANISM. Sraffa's models, we have by now seen, tellingly reject the following Ricardian stereotypes:

(a) Prices are determinable by the labour theory of value.

(b) Land and rent can be ignored by concentrating on external-marginal land with zero rent (or on internal margins in every positive-rent acre).

(c) The complication for pricing of time and the interest rate can somehow be avoided or ameliorated by defining an intermediate standard commodity or workbasket, which is less time consuming and interest-rate-inflated than the most time consuming goods (old wine and tall trees) and is more time consuming and interest-rate inflated than the most directly produced goods (shrimp picked up by labour on the seashore).

(d) One can correctly understand the distribution of income among workers, landowners, and capitalists independently of the complications of demand theory (consumers' demand functions, marginal utility, revealed preferences, etc.).

(e) It is superficial to base goods' and factors' pricings on mere supply and demand.

(f) Adam Smith committed some grave errors in decomposing price and national income eclectically into wage-plus-rent-plus-profit components, and in enunciating his notion of 'labour command'.

Enough has been given of current misunderstandings related to Ricardo for the present exegesis. What does a close rereading of Smith and Ricardo reveal under the light of the post-1960 analysis?

Most of both scholars' actual inferences about the real world are compatible with the post-1960 findings. Smith's scorecard is certainly not inferior to Ricardo's, even after we make allowances for the latter's tendency to proclaim as being universal what is only likely.

Ricardo began to write on microeconomics because he thought he discerned basic *logical* flaws in Smith's system. Just as Steedman showed, in the Ronald Meek *Festschrift*, that Marx's criticisms of Ricardo could not stand up to modern examination, Robert L. Bishop (1985) has shown that Ricardo's criticisms of Smith similarly cannot stand up.

Both Smith and Ricardo tried to compare, by one scalar parameter, the diverse price vector of two times and places: $[P_i/P_1, P_i/W_1, W_m/W_1; r]$ for China and Scotland, or for the Englands of 1780 and 1688. *We* know that just cannot be done: then, now, or ever. Smith's 'labour command' notions merely proceeded from the prosaic observation that people always have about two-thirds of a 24-hour day available to them: $\Sigma P_j C_j/W$ is the hours people have to work for what they consume; because per capita C's tend to rise only with long-term productivity, the above ratio tends to decline only slowly as people enjoy more leisure.

Ricardo never supplanted this imperfect measure by a better one, for all his palaver about absolute standards of value. Worse: gratuitously he attributed to Adam Smith *unwarranted* deviations from the labour theory of value by virtue of Smith's labour command passages. Actually, there is no valid connection. Smith only introduces deviations between what $[P_i/P_j, P_i/W]$ are and what they would be under a labour theory of value when these deviations are warranted by (1) scarcities of needed lands and natural resources, and (2) time-phasing of production that involves produced goods as inputs and which takes place when the competitive market displays positive interest and profit rates.

For all of Ricardo's scolding of Smith as a recanter from the labour theory of value, Ricardo up to his dying month admitted the cogency of the point (2) – that goods of the same content but involving manifestly different time involvements and relative profits would have prices that systematically fail to be proportional to their embodied labour contents. And on point (1), as we have already seen, Smith was right; and Ricardo was wrong in his belief that he could get rid of the complication of rent by use of external (or internal) margins. George Stigler's Pickwickian 1958 defence of 'Ricardo's 93% labour theory of value' on the positivistic grounds that his labour theory of value allegedly averages out in practice to errors of only about 7 per cent makes one wonder what scientists would think of a defence of Lamarck as being 49.99% right; or of the stone-fire-air-and water paradigm as offering a theory of matter that is at least 0.001% as accurate as Mendelev's 93-element periodic table. For some comparisons a 7% error becomes a 70% or a 700% error.

Ricardo does seem to make two major advances on Smith. Paradoxically for Sraffa's hero, *Ricardo made a giant step beyond Smith toward marginalism.* His ubiquitous numerical examples presuppose almost a *continuum* of alternative doses of labour-and-produced-goods applied to the same acre(s) of land. Inside Ricardo there is a von Thünen and a J.B. Clark striving to be born!

A second Ricardian advance is not so important or clear-cut. You must read Smith closely to perceive his understanding that the rent of inelastically supplied land is price determined rather than price-determining. In Ricardo the point is made crystal clear; in the chapter on land in Sraffa (1960), you must read with sophistication to perceive the point.

Also, Ricardo stresses, indeed overstresses, the point that the profit rate would not have to decline – as saving brings into existence new capital stocks and enlarged populations – if new lands were ever available in unlimited and redundant supply. A good point, even if readers of his expositions might be forgiven for misunderstanding him to imply that the only reason for a drop in interest and profit rates is a rise in rent: actually, as Smith knew, a persistent excess in the growth rate of capitals relative to population must in many realistic technologies raise the real wage and lower profit rates *even in the presence of superabundant lands.*

The post-1960 Sraffian analysts who grade Ricardo's blue books must often mark down his submissions. It is time therefore to study how Ricardo's 1951 editor dealt with these issues.

1960 LIGHT ON THE 1951 EDITOR OF RICARDO. The history of humane letters involves only history. Samuel Johnson's mistakes may be more interesting than his correct observations. To the antiquarian, antiquarianism is all there is to the history of the humanities.

The history of scientific thought is a two-fold matter. We are interested in Newton's alchemy and biblical prophecy because we are interested in Newton the man and scientist. At the same time his stepsister's theology is likely to elicit a yawn from even the most besotted antiquarian. How Newton discerned that a homogeneous sphere of non-zero radius attracts as if all its mass were at its center point, that is part of the history of cumulative science. Say that this attitude involves an element of

Whig history if you will, but remember that working scientists have some contempt for those historians and philosophers of science who regard efforts in the past that failed as being on a par with those that succeeded, success being measurable by latest-day scientific juries who want to utilize hindsight and ex post knowledge.

Economics is in between *belles lettres* and cold science. Serious economists below the age of 60 will judge Sraffa's edition of Ricardo both for its antiquarian and its scientific interests and insights. How then will they judge it?

From an antiquarian view the work is a jewel of perfection. Reviewers' enthusiasm has been unbounded. By luck and Sraffa's energetic skills, virtually every scrap written by David Ricardo has been made available to the interested reader. This is a boon to scholars who lack the slightest interest in the history of thought for its own sake: Baconian scientific observation of Ricardo's economics has now been made possible by Sraffa's labours.

Editorial emendations have also been done in the new edition with skill and brevity. You might almost say that the editor has for the most part stayed chastely out of the act, letting David and his friends speak their pieces without an accompaniment of Greek Chorus expressions of approval or disapproval.

From the scientific viewpoint, and now a minority viewpoint is being expressed here, there is something anticlimactic about the great Sraffa edition of Ricardo. It is not just that we see, as if imprisoned in amber, the backward and forward gropings of a scholar who from his 1814 entrance into microeconomics until his death in 1823 makes almost no progress in resolving his self-created ambiguities and problematics. Somehow one had hoped that the whole picture would be a prettier scientific picture, so that the editor's Herculean framings would be for a more worthwhile object.

There is, however, no point in lamenting that Ricardo was only what he was. It is the 'road not taken' by the editor that occasions a twinge of regret. From the scientist's rather than the antiquarians' viewpoint, we appreciate from an editor and commentator what Jacob Viner gave economists in his magnificent 1937 *Studies in the Theory of International Trade* and what Eli Heckscher supplied in his *Mercantilism*. It is what Clifford Truesdell's lengthy introductions to the collected works of Euler provide, and what Abraham Pais succeeds in bringing off in his 1984 survey of the scientific physics of Albert Einstein. Admittedly old Edwin Cannan carried to excess his patronizing reviews of past economic giants, not only faulting them for their sins in failing to believe what Cannan believed in 1928 but also managing to convict them of the crime of not being so smart as himself. Surely, there is a golden mean somewhere between Cannan's dominating the act and Sraffa's avoiding getting into it?

Fortunately, in his Introduction to Ricardo's *Principles* (written late in the day, with the help of Maurice Dobb), Piero Sraffa does let himself go a little bit. Thus, he conjectures that Ricardo, in a lost 1814 manuscript or letter or conversation, may have worked out a model in which the profit rate is determined within agriculture, as a ratio of so to speak corn to corn; and, Sraffa all but says, in such a model distribution theory is successfully emancipated from value theory. Unlike Viner and Cannan, who can be very hard indeed on the guinea pigs they are judging, one reads Sraffa in his Introduction as being quite indulgent of Ricardo. When he quotes Ricardo as purporting to get rid of the complication of rent by concentrating on the external margin, Sraffa never seems tempted to add that this is a *non sequitur*. When Ricardo tries to overdifferentiate his product from Smith's, Sraffa never writes: 'Of course, when Smith made the emergence of positive interest cause a divergence of price from labour contents, he was doing what Ricardo often admits must be done – namely formulating a two-factor rather than a one-factor model of pricing.' The critique of mainstream twentieth century that Sraffa never lived to articulate was evidently festering inside the editor of Ricardo during the 1930–1951 period and serving to soften his critical judgments.

SALUTATIONS. Did any scholar have so great an impact on economic science as Piero Sraffa did in so few writings? One doubts it. And there cannot be many scholars in any field whose greatest works were published exclusively in their second half century of life.

Piero Sraffa was much respected and much loved. With each passing year, economists perceive new grounds for admiring his genius.

PAUL A. SAMUELSON

BIBLIOGRAPHY

Bishop, R.L. 1985. Competitive value when only labor is scarce. *Quarterly Journal of Economics* 100, November, 1257–92.

Bortkiewicz, L. von. 1907. On the correction of Marx's fundamental theoretical construction in the third volume of *Capital*. Trans. in *Karl Marx and the Close of his System*, ed. P.M. Sweezy, New York: August M. Kelley, 1949.

Garegnani, P. 1970. Heterogeneous capital, the production function and the theory of distribution. *Review of Economic Studies* 37, 407–36.

Garegnani, P. 1984. Value and distribution in the classical economists and Marx. *Oxford Economic Papers* 36(2), 291–325.

Manara, C.F. 1979. Sraffa's model for the joint production of commodities by means of commodities. In *Essays on the Theory of Joint Production*, ed. L.L. Pasinetti, New York: Columbia University Press.

Marx, K. 1867, 1885, 1894. *Capital*, Vols. I, II, III. English translations in C.H. Kerr (ed.), Chicago: Chicago University Press, or other editions.

Metcalfe, J.S. and Steedman, I. 1972. Reswitching and primary input use. *Economic Journal* 82, March, 140–57.

Miyao, T. 1977. A generalization of Sraffa's standard commodity and its complete characterization. *International Economic Review* 18, February, 151–62.

Neumann, J. von. 1945. A model of general economic equilibrium. *Review of Economic Studies* 13, 1–9. Trans. of an article in *Ergebnisse eines mathematischen Kolloquiums*, Vol. 8, ed. K. Menger, Leipzig, 1937.

Pasinetti, L.L. 1977. *Lectures on the Theory of Production*. New York: Columbia University Press.

Robinson, J. 1956. *The Accumulation of Capital*. London: Macmillan.

Samuelson, P.A. 1975. Marx as mathematical economist: steady-state and exponential growth equilibrium. In *Trade, Stability, and Macroeconomic, Essays in Honor of Lloyd A. Metzler*, ed. G. Horwich and P. Samuelson, New York: Academic Press, 269–307. Also ch. 225 in *The Collected Scientific Papers of Paul A. Samuelson*, Vol. III, Cambridge, Mass.: MIT Press, 1972.

Samuelson, P.A. 1975. Trade pattern reversals in time-phased Ricardian systems and intertemporal efficiency. *Journal of International Economics* 5, November, 309–63. Also ch. 251 in *The Collected Scientific Papers of Paul A. Samuelson*, Vol. IV, Cambridge, Mass.: MIT Press, 1977.

Samuelson, P.A. 1983. Thünen at two hundred. *Journal of Economic Literature* 21, December, 1468–88.

Schefold, B. 1971. *Theorie der Kuppelproduktion (Mr. Sraffa on Joint Production)*. Privately printed, Basel.

Seton, F. 1957. The transformation problem. *Review of Economic Studies* 25, 149–60.

Sraffa, P. 1926. The laws of returns under competitive conditions. *Economic Journal* 36, December, 535–50.

Sraffa, P. (ed.) 1951–73. *The Works and Correspondence of David Ricardo*. Cambridge: Cambridge University Press, for the Royal Economic Society; with editorial collaboration by M.H. Dobb.

Sraffa, P. 1960. *Production of Commodities by Means of Commodities: Prelude to a Critique of Economic Theory*. Cambridge: Cambridge University Press.

Steedman, I. 1977. *Marx After Sraffa*. London: New Left Books. Reprinted, London: Verso, 1981.

Steedman, I. 1982. Marx on Ricardo. In *Classical and Marxian Political Economy: Essays in Honour of Ronald L. Meek*, ed. I. Bradley and M. Howard, London: Macmillan.

Stigler, G.J. 1958. Ricardo and the 93% labor theory of value. *American Economic Review* 48, June, 357–67.

stability.

> Positions of unstable equilibrium, even if they exist, are transient, nonpersistent states, and hence on the crudest probability calculation would be observed less frequently than stable states. How many times has the reader seen an egg standing upon its end? (Samuelson, 1947, p. 5; see also Marshall, 1890, pp. 424–5n, subsequently – since the 5th edition – in Appendix H, §2, n. 1).

> From a physical point of view only equilibria that are 'stable' are of interest. A pendulum balanced upright is in equilibrium, but this is very unlikely to occur; moreover, the slightest disturbance will completely alter the pendulum's behavior. Such an equilibrium is unstable. [...] An equilibrium point ... must satisfy a certain stability criterion in order to be very significant physically ... Since in applications of dynamical systems one cannot pinpoint a state exactly, but only approximately, an equilibrium must be stable to be physically meaningful (Hirsch and Smale, 1974, pp. 145 and 185).

The central place of the concept of equilibrium in economic theory justifies the interest of economists in stability (a concept they employ in the same sense as mathematicians and physicists, as the quotations show). In fact, an equilibrium which (supposing that it has been hit upon by chance) is such that the slightest disturbance starts a movement away from it – i.e., an unstable equilibrium – is usually considered unmeaningful from an economic point of view. Besides, the comparative static and/or comparative dynamic analysis of an equilibrium, which are among the main tools of the trade, become useless if the equilibrium is unstable. The concern over stability, which dates back at least to Marshall (1879) and Walras (1874; for a discussion of the priority problem see Jaffé's note 5 to lesson 7, pp. 502–3 in his translation of Walras's *Elements*), has led economists either to *assume* that equilibrium is stable (this involves the study of the necessary stability conditions and their use in comparative statics) or to search for 'plausible' conditions which *ensure* stability; these are usually *sufficient* stability conditions only (this is, for example, the approach taken in the study of the stability of general competitive equilibrium). However, in some cases, the presence of *instability* is an essential feature as, for example, in Hicks's trade cycle model (1950). Therefore the epistemological question arises of whether stability is a good ontologically (and instability an evil) or not. This problem will be discussed in the last section.

Besides stable and unstable equilibria there are also *neutral* equilibria: an equilibrium is neutral if a (small) disturbance leads to a new situation which does not change unless there is a further disturbance.

BASIC CONCEPTS AND DEFINITIONS. The idea of stability that economists usually have in mind corresponds to what mathematicians call '*asymptotic stability*'. Therefore some definitions are in order, which we shall give by appealing to intuition rather than mathematical rigour (for rigorous definitions the reader is referred to Andronov *et al.*, 1966; Bellman, 1953; Coddington and Levinson, 1955; Hirsch and Smale, 1974; Kalman and Bertram, 1960; Krasovskii, 1963; LaSalle and Lefschetz, 1961; Minorsky, 1962; Sansone and Conti, 1964).

Stability. A system is *stable* if, when perturbed slightly from its equilibrium state, all subsequent motions remain in a correspondingly small neighbourhood of the equilibrium. If, in addition to being stable, every motion starting sufficiently near the equilibrium point converges to it as $t \rightarrow \infty$, then the equilibrium is *asymptotically stable*. These are *local* concepts (also called 'in the small'); if stability is independent of the distance of the initial state from the equilibrium point, we have (*asymptotic*) *stability in the large* (or *global*).

It may sometimes happen that an equilibrium point is stable or unstable according to the initial position of the system (one-sided stability–instability in Samuelson's terminology (1947) or, more briefly, *semi-stability*).

These definitions are sometimes taken to imply that the equilibrium point is unique, but this is true only for global stability (henceforth we shall omit the adjective 'asymptotic', on the understanding that it is implicitly present unless otherwise stated), because if there are multiple equilibria none of them can be globally stable; on the contrary, there can be locally stable multiple equilibria (but usually they will be alternatively stable and unstable). The not infrequent occurrence of multiple equilibria in economics has led mathematical economists to introduce the concepts of global stability of an *adjustment process* and of quasi-stability. An adjustment process is said to be globally stable if, for any initial state, there is an equilibrium point to which the system converges (this point need not be the same for all initial conditions). The concept of *quasi-stability* is more complicated and involves the construction of a sequence of points (from any initial point) corresponding to a sequence of times. If any such sequence of points converges to a point when the sequence of times tends to infinity, and if all these limit points are equilibrium points, then the process is called quasi-stable. This has important applications in the theory of the stability of general competitive equilibrium.

A related problem that worries economists is that of *path-dependent* equilibrium and stability. This was noted long ago (e.g. Marshall, 1879a, ch. II, § 7; 1879b, ch. I, § 7; Edgeworth [1881] 1967, pp. 19–20; Kaldor [1934] 1960, pp. 17ff) and was called the problem of the indeterminateness of equilibrium (for a recent treatment see Fisher, 1983). It is due to the fact that the movement of the system when it is out of equilibrium may change the data on which the static equations which define the equilibrium are based, so that these equations will change and determine a *different* equilibrium and so on and so forth. In other words, the (set of) equilibrium point(s) is *not* independent of the dynamic movement of the system, that is, this set is path-dependent. This problem is particularly important in general competitive equilibrium. If path-dependence occurs, it is logically mistaken to study (the existence of) equilibrium without simultaneously studying its stability, unless the path-dependence is in some sense 'small' (how 'small' it should be is an open question, but we believe that a fruitful line of investigation lies in the study of structural stability, on which see below) and/or the convergence to equilibrium is almost instantaneous (or at least very fast, so that, as it were, the equilibrium point is 'reached' before any appreciable change in the data can occur).

This leads us to two considerations. The first is that the study of the *rapidity of convergence* becomes essential; it should be noted that this study is important in any case, since the knowledge that the system tends to equilibrium as $t \to \infty$ is not very interesting if (due to the slowness of the motion) a great deal of time is required for the system to get reasonably near to equilibrium. This study requires either the assignment of 'plausible' numerical values to the parameters involved (see, e.g., the references quoted by Gandolfo, 1980, p. 207) or more sophisticated econometric analyses in continuous time (Gandolfo, 1981; Gandolfo and Padoan, 1984). The second is the importance of the study of *structural stability*, which is yet another concept of stability. The problem of structural stability arose in mathematical physics precisely because none of the factors taken as given can remain absolutely constant during the motion of the system, so that when one hypothesizes that certain parameters are constant one is really assuming that small variations in these parameters do not significantly alter the character of the motion. Systems which are such as not to vary in their essential features for a small variation of the form of the differential equations are called 'coarse' or structurally stable systems, and are often considered to be the only ones of physical interest, i.e. capable of serving as useful theoretical models of real physical systems (Andronov et al., 1966, pp. xxix, 374 ff; a similar view is held by Thom [1972] 1975, e.g. p. 14, as regards all natural 'forms'). One could then perhaps also qualify the economists' interest in stability by suggesting that in economics, just as in physics and morphogenesis, one should look for *structurally* stable (not merely stable) models as the only ones which can serve as useful theoretical models of real economic systems. The problem, however, is open (see the last section).

A distinction used in economics is that between *static* and *dynamic* stability. Static stability only tells us whether the economic forces that act on the system tend to make it move towards the equilibrium point, but does not tell us anything about the actual path of the system nor whether the system converges over time to the equilibrium point. Therefore, the study of static stability is not sufficient, and it is necessary to study dynamic stability: the latter, being based on functional equations, can solve the problems left unsolved by the former. As a matter of fact, after the debate between Hicks (1939, 1946) and Samuelson (1947), it is now generally accepted that the 'true' concept of stability in economics is the dynamic one (for a summing up of the debate see Gandolfo, 1980 pp. 286–99).

A final observation: stability can be investigated not only with respect to a point, but also with respect to a path. If, for example, the system possesses a periodic motion (*limit cycle*) which all nearby paths approach from both sides, then the limit cycle is said to be *orbitally stable*.

METHODS. Methods currently used to analyse stability are based on differential equations and difference equations, which embody the dynamics assumed by the economist. The choice between these two types of functional equations is related to whether economic phenomena are considered to occur continuously in time or discretely (mixed differential–difference equations, which can account for both aspects, are usually too difficult to handle analytically and are rarely used). This is a moot problem, which we cannot deal with here (see, e.g., Gandolfo, 1980, *passim*; 1981, ch. 1); therefore in what follows we shall refer to differential equations, although what we are going to say in this section can equally well refer to difference equations. Also note that for simplicity we shall deal with single equations, but the extension to systems of differential equations is straightforward (the references to the mathematical literature are the same as in the previous section).

A first useful distinction is that between '*quantitative*' and '*qualitative*' (or '*topological*') methods. The former consist in trying to find the explicit solution of the differential equation or to approximate it by using power series and other methods; it is then easy to check whether the time path of the variable involved converges to the equilibrium point. The latter consist in the analysis of the properties of the solution of a differential equation without actually knowing the solution itself or trying to approximate it; this is based on phase diagrams, Lyapunov's second method, etc.

A second useful distinction, partially overlapping with the previous one, is that between the study of *local* and *global* stability. The former involves the *linear approximation* (by expanding in Taylor's series and neglecting all terms of order higher than the first) of the original non-linear dynamic equation at the equilibrium point. A linear differential equation with constant coefficients is thus obtained, which can be examined by 'quantitative' methods. If this equation is stable, then the original non-linear system is locally stable. It should be noted that the legitimacy of this procedure rests on the fulfilment of the conditions of the Lyapunov–Perron–Poincaré theorem (Gandolfo, 1980, p. 397), that economists usually neglect to check; fortunately, these are automatically fulfilled when the original equation is autonomous. To study global stability no linear approximation can be performed, so that – unless the original differential equation is linear by itself or belongs to those types of non-linear equations which can be solved explicitly (e.g. a Bernoulli equation) – only qualitative methods can be used. These are also indispensable (in most cases) if one wishes to preserve the richness of motions (e.g. limit cycles, strange attractors, etc.) which a non-linear differential equation can give rise to and which is lost as a consequence of the linearization.

A third useful distinction – which concerns the economic nature of the problem, not the mathematical methods – is that between what we call 'built-in' and 'superimposed' dynamic stability analysis. A model can be built from the very start in such a way that the dynamic equation to be studied for the analysis of stability is intrinsic to the model: this is the case, for example, of business cycle models and of growth models (in the latter a further distinction could be made between equilibrium and disequilibrium dynamics). A different case arises when one has a model whose solution only determines the equilibrium and wishes to examine its stability (a case is that of demand-and-supply equilibrium). Here one must 'superimpose' a disequilibrium dynamics on the model, in the sense that one has to make *assumptions about the behaviour* of the relevant variables out of equilibrium, which – duly formalized – give rise to the dynamic equation to be studied. Since, in principle, it is usually possible to make different, and equally plausible, such assumptions, there follows the *relativity of stability conditions*, since in some cases a given equilibrium may be stable or unstable according to the different assumptions made.

We conclude this section by mentioning Samuelson's *correspondence principle* between comparative statics and dynamic stability. This principle suggests that the ambiguity of certain expressions which appear in the solution of a comparative static system can be removed by *assuming* that the equilibrium is stable and using the dynamic stability conditions.

IS STABILITY A GOOD ONTOLOGICALLY? We now briefly deal with

the question posed at the beginning. A first case in which stability is not necessarily a desirable feature is found in business cycle analysis. If a business cycle model gives rise to a motion which converges towards an equilibrium point, this means that the business cycle will die out, unless it is kept alive by exogenous shocks; thus if one wants a self-sustaining endogenous cycle, convergence must be excluded, and one must consider models in which a constant-amplitude oscillation takes place. But one might object that such a motion, though not asymptotically stable, is stable or perhaps orbitally stable in the sense defined in the second section. However, there are models where the *instability* of equilibrium is essential to give rise to the cycle, as in Hicks (1950), where a divergent movement from the trend is intrinsically present, but is kept in check by an upper and a lower limit (the 'ceiling' and the 'floor'): it is the unstable nature of the motion, coupled with these limits, that gives rise to a permanent cyclical motion. This is an intrinsically non-linear model and brings out the importance of non-linear dynamics in business cycle models (for many types of non-linear dynamic models which possess unstable equilibrium points and give rise to limit cycles see Goodwin, 1982). The features illustrated are essentially related to non-linearity and do not hold for truly linear systems (in these systems, instability of equilibrium implies that the initial deviation grows larger and larger). Thus one might suggest that, in general, stability is a good (and instability an evil) in linear models, whilst this need not be the case in non-linear ones.

Some writers take a still more radical position and deny that stability, in particular structural stability, is necessarily desirable. One reason for this could be that (structural) stability may prevent the attainment of a better position. Suppose that a system has two stable equilibria, 1 and 2, the former of which is in some sense better. If the system is in equilibrium 2, it will be unable to attain equilibrium 1. In such a case *instability* of equilibrium 2 would be preferable. But since equilibrium 1 would have to be stable, it is clear that one cannot maintain that instability is generally desirable: it all depends. For further considerations on the significance of instability see Lotka ([1925] 1956, pp. 294ff), Vercelli (1982) and Blatt (1983, chs 7 and 8).

It is also worthwhile mentioning the idea that instability is sometimes the *deus ex machina* which enables a system to change from its old structure to a new structure (e.g. phase transitions in the physical sciences) through a mechanism which involves the 'slaying' of the stable 'modes' by the unstable ones; the latter serve as 'order parameters' which determine the macroscopic behaviour of the system. This idea is at the basis of the approach of *synergetics* (Haken, 1983a, 1983b), which – though discussed mainly in physics, chemistry and biology – seems to offer fruitful insights also for economists (see, e.g., Gandolfo and Padoan, 1984; Medio, 1984; Silverberg, 1984). But this lies in the area of possible future research.

The conclusion seems to be that, although a strong bias in favour of the stability of equilibrium still exists and is often justified, stability cannot be considered a good *ontologically*.

GIANCARLO GANDOLFO

BIBLIOGRAPHY

Andronov, A.A., Vitt, A.A. and Khaikin, S.E. 1966. *Theory of Oscillators*. London: Pergamon Press.
Bellman, R. 1953. *Stability Theory of Differential Equations*. New York: McGraw-Hill.
Blatt, J.M. 1983. *Dynamic Economic Systems – A Post Keynesian Approach*. Armonk, New York: Sharpe.
Coddington, E.A. and Levinson, N. 1955. *Theory of Ordinary Differential Equations*. New York: McGraw-Hill.
Dore, M.H.I. 1985. On the concept of equilibrium. *Journal of Post Keynesian Economics* 7(2), Winter, 1984–5, 193–206.
Edgeworth, F.Y. 1881. *Mathematical Psychics*. London: Kegan Paul. Reprinted, A.M. Kelley: New York, 1967.
Fisher, F.M. 1983. *Disequilibrium Foundations of Equilibrium Economics*. Cambridge: Cambridge University Press.
Frisch, R. 1936. On the notion of equilibrium and disequilibrium. *Review of Economic Studies* 3, February, 100–105.
Gandolfo, G. 1980. *Economic Dynamics: Methods and Models*. Amsterdam: North-Holland.
Gandolfo, G. 1981. *Qualitative Analysis and Econometric Estimation of Continuous Time Dynamic Models*. Amsterdam: North-Holland.
Gandolfo, G. and Padoan, P.C. 1980. *A Disequilibrium Model of Real and Financial Accumulation in an Open Economy*. Berlin, Heidelberg, New York and Tokyo: Springer-Verlag.
Goodwin, R.M. 1982. *Essays in Economic Dynamics*. London: Macmillan.
Hahn, F.A. 1982. Stability. In *Handbook of Mathematical Economics*, ed. K.J. Arrow and M.D. Intriligator, Amsterdam: North-Holland, Vol. II.
Haken, H. 1983a. *Synergetics – An Introduction*. 3rd edn, Berlin, Heidelberg, New York and Tokyo: Springer-Verlag.
Haken, H. 1983b. *Advanced Synergetics*. Berlin, Heidelberg, New York and Tokyo: Springer-Verlag.
Hicks, J.R. 1939. *Value and Capital*. Oxford: Oxford University Press. 2nd edn, 1946.
Hicks, J.R. 1950. *A Contribution to the Theory of the Trade Cycle*. Oxford: Oxford University Press.
Hirsch, M.W. and Smale, S. 1974. *Differential Equations, Dynamical Systems, and Linear Algebra*. New York: Academic Press.
Kaldor, N. 1934. A classificatory note on the determinateness of equilibrium. *Review of Economic Studies* 1, February, 122–36. Reprinted as 'Determinateness of static equilibrium', in N. Kaldor, *Essays on Value and Distribution*, London: G.Duckworth, 1960.
Kalman, R.E. and Bertram, J.E. 1960. Control system analysis and design via the 'second method' of Lyapunov, Part I. *Journal of Basic Engineering*, Transactions of the ASME, Series D 82(2), June, 371–93.
Krasovskii, N.N. 1963. *Stability of Motion – Applications of Lyapunov's Second Method to Differential Systems and Equations with Delay*. Stanford: Stanford University Press.
LaSalle, J.P. and Lefschetz, S. 1961. *Stability by Liapunov's Direct Method with Applications*. New York: Academic Press.
Lotka, A.J. 1925. *Elements of Physical Biology*. Baltimore: Williams & Wilkins. Reprinted as *Elements of Mathematical Biology*, New York: Dover, 1956.
Marshall, A. 1879a. *The Pure Theory of Foreign Trade*. Privately published. 1879b. *The Pure Theory of Domestic Values*. Privately printed and circulated. Reprinted with Marshall (1879a) in one vol. in the London School of Economics Series, Reprints of Scarce Tracts in Economic and Political Science, No. 1, London: London School of Economics and Political Science, 1930.
Marshall, A. 1890. *Principles of Economics*. London: Macmillan. 8th edn, 1920. 9th (Variorum) edn, ed. C.W. Guillebaud, 1961.
Medio, A. 1984. Synergetics and dynamic economic models. In *Non-linear Models of Fluctuating Growth*, ed. R.M. Goodwin, M. Krüger and A. Vercelli, Berlin, Heidelberg, New York and Tokyo: Springer-Verlag.
Minorsky, N. 1962. *Nonlinear Oscillations*. New York: Van Nostrand.
Newman, P. 1961. Approaches to stability analysis. *Economica* 28, February, 12–29.
Samuelson, P.A. 1947. *Foundations of Economic Analysis*. Cambridge, Mass.: Harvard University Press. Enlarged edn, 1983.
Sansone, G. and Conti, R. 1964. *Non-linear Differential Equations*. London: Pergamon Press.
Silverberg, G. 1984. Embodied technical progress in a dynamic model: the self-organization paradigm. In *Nonlinear Models of Fluctuating Growth*, ed. R.M. Goodwin, M. Krüger and A. Vercelli, Berlin, Heidelberg, New York and Tokyo: Springer-Verlag.
Thom, R. 1972. *Stabilité structurelle et morphogénèse*. Trans. as

Structural Stability and Morphogenesis, Reading, Mass.: Benjamin, 1975.
Varian, H.R. 1981. Dynamical systems with applications to economics. In *Handbook of Mathematical Economics*, ed. K.J. Arrow and M.D. Intriligator, Amsterdam: North-Holland, Vol. I.
Vercelli, A. 1982. Is instability enough to discredit a model? *Economic Notes* No. 3, 173–90.
Walras, L. 1874. *Eléments d'économie politique pure*. Lausanne: Corbaz et Cie. Definitive edn, Paris: Pichon et Durand Auzias, 1926. Trans. with notes and collation of editions by W. Jaffé as *Elements of Pure Economics*, London: Allen & Unwin, 1954.

stabilization policy. The term 'stabilization policy' normally refers to deliberate changes in government policy instruments in response to changing macroeconomic conditions, in order to stabilize the economy. It is often used to refer to the Keynesian policies which stemmed from Keynes's *General Theory*: the new commitment of many Western governments after World War II to use policy to pursue high and stable employment. (An example is the UK White Paper on Employment Policy (Minister of Reconstruction, 1944).) But other types of stabilization policies had been known previously (such as the return to the Gold Standard in the UK in 1925 in order to stabilize currency values (Moggridge, 1986) and have been known since (such as the policy of monetary restraint carried out in the United Kingdom in the late 1970s and early 1980s in order to stabilize inflation). In fact stabilization policy cannot easily be distinguished from macroeconomic policy in general.

Debate about the theory of stabilization policy operates at two levels. At one level there are discussions about the kind of policy which a government ought to pursue: the policy objectives and the policy instruments which it should use (for example 'Keynesian' versus 'Monetarist' policy). At another level there are discussions about the technical details of a government's chosen kind of policy (for example about whether instruments should be assigned to targets, and about how policy can be prevented from actually amplifying economic fluctuations). These issues are interrelated, as we shall see.

Keynesian stabilization policy saw governments assume simultaneous responsibility for the objectives of full employment, economic growth, and the balance of payments, using the instruments of fiscal, monetary, and exchange rate policy. Two technical aspects of the design of these policies were important. Initially it was thought that the policy instruments could be assigned as follows: fiscal policy to full employment, monetary policy (through the setting of a low interest rate) to economic growth, and exchange rate policy (and commercial policy) to the balance of payments. But Tinbergen (1952), Meade (1951), Swan (1960) and others pointed out that difficulties could arise if all the interrelationships between targets and instruments were not considered, in that the pursuit of one target could drive another off course. An example is the balance of payments difficulties which resulted from the pursuit of full employment in the UK, and which led to a 'stop-go' conduct of fiscal policy: expansion to promote employment followed by contraction to protect the balance of payments. Furthermore, it was recognized that without care, policy could actually magnify economic fluctuations. Even the simple case of a fiscal expansion embarked upon to deal with unemployment, for example, might be carried out with such a lag that it coincided with the economy's in-built recovery, causing an excessive boom and excessive employment growth (Friedman, 1953; Phillips, 1954, 1957). The need to design Keynesian policies so as to avoid these two difficulties led to the growth of the use of econometric models in the design of policy.

The fundamental problem with Keynesian stabilization policies – much more important than the above two technical difficulties – is that they are unable to deal with the problem of inflation. This is because the commitment to full employment removes any threat of unemployment resulting from high wage settlements, and it is upon this threat that wage stability in part depends. Keynesian economists recognized this difficulty (Kalecki, 1944) but had no clear remedy. The resort to incomes policy (compulsory or voluntary) has – in many countries including Britain – proved unequal to the task. Apart from administrative difficulties, incomes policies face a prisoner's dilemma: given the commitment to full employment it is in the interests of each group of wage setters to break the incomes policy themselves whilst relying upon other groups to adhere to it.

More conservative economists used this difficulty as a basis on which to erect an entire monetarist counter-revolution to Keynesian policies (Friedman, 1968). Friedman argued first that, instead of the pursuit of full employment, stabilization policy ought to be devoted to stabilizing the growth of money incomes, and second that this policy ought to be carried out by monetary means. His third claim was that these monetary means ought to involve the pursuit of a constant rate of growth of the money supply.

The first of Friedman's proposals is a natural response to the fundamental difficulty in the Keynesian position. By stabilizing the growth of money incomes, policy replaces the commitment to full employment with a commitment that inflation will not be passively accommodated. It does, it is true, leave the private sector free to determine the split in money incomes between low prices and high employment or high prices and low employment, but it ensures that inflation, or accelerating inflation, will be met by contractionary policies, thereby creating a threat of potential unemployment which helps to inculcate wage stability (and at least partly to internalize the prisoner's dilemma externality which groups of wage setters create when pressing for high wages at the expense of other groups.) Many who are not monetarists now support this proposal of Friedman's (Meade, 1982; Tobin, 1980). But the optimism, engendered by those who developed Friedman's ideas into 'rational expectation monetarism' – that inflation can be controlled by stabilizing the growth of money incomes, without generating the difficulties of high levels of unemployment – has proved completely unfounded. Not only may it take years of high unemployment to reduce inflation, but it also seems that permanently high levels of unemployment are required to keep inflation stable. Thus Meade, for example, argues that the stabilization of money incomes has to be combined with a large number of measures – profit sharing, arbitration of pay settlements, a wage inflation tax, employment subsidies – to exert further downward influences on wage costs, so as to ensure a higher level of output and a lower level of prices consistent with any particular level of money income.

The second of Friedman's recommendations is about the assignment of instruments to objectives. It has, in the judgement of many, been responsible for another set of difficulties. The control of money income growth by the instrument of a tight monetary policy makes the burden of the control of inflation fall on investment rather than on consumption, since it is primarily investment which is reduced in the face of tight monetary conditions and high interest rates. This makes it very difficult for economies to add to their productive potential as a way of meeting inflationary pressure. In an open economy high interest rates also cause an excessive appreciation of the exchange rate (Dornbusch, 1976), for example the overvaluation of both sterling and the dollar in the 1980s. This has seriously affected the international monetary system. Furthermore it has also damaged the manufacturing industries in the UK and the US which participate in international trade. In the US this led to the protectionist pressures which were so strong that, for a time in 1985, they threatened to engulf the entire international trading system as well. A better outcome could be achieved if monetary policy were not alone assigned to the control of money income growth, but if the instruments of fiscal and monetary policy were together used to control money income growth.

Friedman's third proposal (a constant rate of growth of the money supply) appears equally misguided. It ignores the practical difficulties of controlling the money supply (although these are more difficult in Britain than, say, in the US). More importantly it ignores the volatility of the demand for money which would disturb the level of money income in an economy with a fixed money supply (Poole, 1970). And, especially, it relies too heavily on the supposed ability of the private sector economy to dampen economic fluctuations automatically. If real expenditures fall so that the growth of nominal income falls, wages and prices are supposed to fall so that the growth in the demand for money falls, and interest rates fall. This is supposed to stimulate expenditures and so to rekindle the growth of nominal income as required (and vice versa). But it is an enduring contribution of Keynesian economics to have shown that the ability of the private sector to dampen fluctuations in this way is entirely problematic (Tobin, 1975): as wages and prices fall, expectations of further falls may lead real expenditures to fall still further, rather than to recover. Herein lies an irony. As noted above, Friedman (1953) argued that Keynesian policies were likely to magnify economic fluctuations. But if Friedman's proposal for a fixed rate of growth of the money supply were adopted, then this might have a similar effect. It thus seems that even if Friedman's first two proposals were to be accepted, monetary policy would still need to be actively manipulated so as to ensure the damping of fluctuations. (There is a famous 'proof' that any such active monetary policy would, if it was fully understood, be *entirely* ineffective. But that demonstration rests on the assumption that the private sector's supposed automatic mechanism for damping fluctuations is *instantaneous*; see Maddock and Carter, 1982.)

What kind of stabilization policy will emerge after monetarism? It will need to draw the lesson from the monetarist counter-revolution that policy cannot give a commitment to full employment independently of inflationary developments. But it will have to recognize that measures like those proposed by Meade are essential if less expansionary policies are not to cause unemployment, that fiscal policies need to play a part in the stabilization policy (so that fiscal and monetary imbalance does not damage investment and cause exchange rate fluctuations) and that this stabilization policy needs to be activist to some degree (see Vines, 1986).

What technical methods will be available for the design of these policies? First, the assignment of instruments to targets (two unfortunate examples of which have been mentioned above) will need to give way to the simultaneous use of policy instruments to simultaneously achieve the desired outcome for a number of policy objectives, unless there are very good reasons to the contrary. Methods of 'optimal control theory' will be useful in the search for these policies using econometric models; these methods view the problem as one of minimizing a cost function expressed in terms of deviations of both targets and instruments from their desired values, and examine the trade-offs between more closely achieving the desired value for one target and less closely achieving the desired values for the instruments and for the other targets (See Preston and Pagan, 1982). Second, 'classical control theory' will be important (Vines, Maciejowski and Meade, 1983, Part 4) in allowing economists to examine in detail the extent to which their policies are likely to dampen fluctuations. Control engineers have much of value to offer economists from their experience with these methods in feedback systems design, for example in the design of automatic pilots for aeroplanes. These methods view the economy as a set of differential equations, and feedback policies are designed to influence the solution of these equations, so that the fluctuations in them die out quickly. (In continuous time this means ensuring that the roots of the equations have negative real parts and large absolute value.) Third, economists will need to recognize that economic agents are intelligent – in the way that aeroplanes are not – so that the design of policies will need to allow for the fact that participants in the economy change their behaviour as a result of the policies which are applied (Lucas, 1976). The 'rational expectations revolution' has so far shown us what to do about this if the policies are fully understood. Policies can now be designed using an econometric model, on the assumption that people understand these policies very well, so well in fact that they base their actions exactly upon the predictions of the model about the effects of both present *and* future policies. But this is not really satisfactory. Finding ways to design policies which work well and are robust, when these policies are not fully comprehended and yet do cause changes in behaviour, is now the major technical challenge of policy design (Currie, 1985).

DAVID VINES

See also BUILT-IN STABILIZERS; FINE TUNING; PUBLIC WORKS.

BIBLIOGRAPHY

Currie, D. 1985. Macroeconomic policy design and control theory – a failed partnership? *Economic Journal* 95, 285–306.

Dornbusch, R. 1976. Expectations and exchange rate dynamics. *Journal of Political Economy* 84(6), December, 11 61–76.

Friedman, M. 1953. The effects of a full employment policy on economic stability: a formal analysis. In M. Friedman, *Essays in Positive Economics*, Chicago: Chicago University Press.

Friedman, M. 1968. The role of monetary policy. *American Economic Review* 58, 1–17.

Kalecki, M. 1944. The White Paper on employment policy. *Bulletin of the Oxford Institute of Economics and Statistics* 67, 131–5.

Lucas, R.E. 1976. Econometric policy evaluation: a critique. *Journal of Monetary Economics*, Supplement, Carnegie-Rochester Conference Series on Public Policy 1, 19–46.

Maddock, R. and Carter, M. 1982. A child's guide to rational expectations. *Journal of Economic Literature* 20, 39–51.

Meade, J.E. 1951. *The Balance of Payments*. London: Oxford University Press.

Meade, J.E. 1982. *Stagflation*, Vol. I: *Wage Fixing*. London: George Allen & Unwin.

Minister of Reconstruction 1944. *Employment Policy*, cmd. 6527, presented by the Minister of Reconstruction to Parliament. London: HMSO.

Moggridge, D.E. 1986. Keynes and the international monetary system, 1909–46. In *International Monetary Problems and Supply-Side Economics*, ed. J.S. Cohen and G.C. Harcourt, London: Macmillan.

Phillips, A.W. 1954. Stabilization policy in a closed economy. *Economic Journal* 64, 290–323.

Phillips, A.W. 1957. Stabilization policy and the time-forms of lagged responses. *Economic Journal* 67, 265–77.
Poole, W. 1970. Optimal choice of monetary policy instruments in a simple stochastic macro model. *Quarterly Journal of Economics* 84, 197–216.
Preston, A.J. and Pagan, A.R. 1982. *The Theory of Economic Policy, Statics and Dynamics*. Cambridge: Cambridge University Press.
Swan, T.W. 1960. Economic control in a dependent economy. *Economic Record* 36, 51–66.
Tinbergen, J. 1952. *On the Theory of Economic Policy*. Amsterdam: North-Holland.
Tobin, J. 1975. Keynesian models of recession and depression. *American Economic Review Papers and Proceedings* 65, 195–202.
Tobin, J. 1980. Stabilization policy ten years after. *Brookings Papers on Economic Activity* No. 1 (10th Anniversary Issue), 19–71.
Vines, D. 1986. Macroeconomic policy after monetarism. *Royal Bank of Scotland Review*, December.
Vines, D., Maciejowski, J.M. and Meade, J.E. 1983. *Stagflation* Vol. II: *Demand Management*. London: George Allen & Unwin.

stable population theory. Many years ago A.J. Lotka (1911) proved that a population (of one sex; for simplicity this discussion will be restricted to females) not gaining or losing by migration, and subject to an unchanging age-schedule of death rates and rates of childbearing, has an age distribution, birth rate, death rate, and rate of increase that do not change. All of these fixed characteristics are determined by the mortality and fertility schedules to which the population is subject. Lotka called such a population stable, using the term in a technical sense borrowed from physics; if the population is perturbed by a momentary change in fertility or mortality, 'stability' implies that it returns after a while to its equilibrium state of constant birth rate, death rate, and age structure.

Lotka's proof of stability implies that a closed population experiencing fixed mortality and fertility schedules arrives at a fixed and determinate age structure, no matter what arbitrary and irregular age distribution and population had at an early point. This property of converging to a fixed form was labelled 'strong ergodicity' by John Hajnal (1958). Strong ergodicity means that when fixed rates have long prevailed, the unchanging age structure of the stable population is independent of its form at any much earlier time; figuratively, it can be said that a stable population forgets its past.

More than forty years later, Coale (1957) made the conjecture that all human populations forget their past. Obviously, when fertility and mortality schedules constantly change, the age structure of the population constantly changes. The changing age structure is nevertheless independent of the remote past. The age distribution of France is no longer much affected by excess mortality and reduced numbers of births during the Napoleonic wars, and the age distribution of Greece is no longer affected at all by the Peloponnesian Wars. The independence of a changing age distribution from long past influences is called 'weak ergodicity'. Any population, whether or not stable, has forgotten the remote past; the stable population, in addition to forgetting the past, has a fixed form, and fixed birth and death rates. A mathematical proof of the weak ergodicity of human population was provided by Alvaro Lopez (1961).

BASIC EQUATIONS OF THE STABLE POPULATION. A proof of weak ergodicity when population density is treated as a continuous function of age and time (Lopez, 1967) provides a convenient background for the equations that characterize a stable population.

In any closed population, the number of persons at age a at time t is

$$N(a,t) = B(t-a)p(a,t), \qquad (1)$$

when $B(t)$ is the number of births at time t, and $p(a,t)$ is the proportion surviving from birth to age a of those born at time $t-a$. The number of births, in turn is determined as follows:

$$B(t) = \int_{\alpha}^{\beta} N(a,t)m(a,t)\,\mathrm{d}a, \qquad (2)$$

where $m(a,t)$ is the proportion of women at age a at time t bearing a female child, and α and β are the lower and upper limits of the age-span in which childbearing occurs.

Lopez proved that age structure is independent of the remote past by showing that the birth sequences in two populations subject to the same succession of mortality and fertility schedules approach a constant ratio one to the other, no matter how different the two populations may be at some initial moment. In other terms, the ratio $B_1(t)/B_2(t)$ approaches a constant K as populations 1 and 2 remain subject to the same changing sequences of fertility and mortality schedules.

Let $\gamma(t) = B_1(t)/B_2(t)$. It follows from equations (1) and (2) that

$$B_1(t) = \int_{\alpha}^{\beta} B_1(t-a)p(a,t)m(a,t)\,\mathrm{d}a, \qquad (3)$$

and that $B_2(t)$ conforms to the same equation with a change only in subscript. But $B_1(t-a) = \gamma(t-a)B_2(t-a)$; hence

$$B_1(t) = \int_{\alpha}^{\beta} \gamma(t-a)B_2(t-a)p(a,t)m(a,t)\,\mathrm{d}a. \qquad (4)$$

Since $B_1(t)/B_2(t)$ is $\gamma(t)$,

$$\gamma(t) = \int_{\alpha}^{\beta} \gamma(t-a)\{B_2(t-a)p(a,t)m(a,t)/B_2(t)\}\,\mathrm{d}a. \qquad (5)$$

The expression in brackets in equation (5) is the proportionate distribution by age of mother, $B_2(t)$, of the births at time t in the second population. Thus the expression in brackets is a frequency distribution, $f(a,t)$, summing to 1.0 when added over ages α to β. Hence equation (5) can be rewritten as

$$\gamma(t) = \int_{\alpha}^{\beta} \gamma(t-a)f(a,t)\,\mathrm{d}a. \qquad (6)$$

The ratio of $B_1(t)$ to $B_2(t)$ is the weighted average of the sequence of ratios of $B_1(t)$ to $B_2(t)$ α and β years in the past. Continued application of such averaging over many generations ultimately brings the ratio $B_1(t)/B_2(t)$ to a constant. When the ratio has been constant for ω years (ω the highest age attained) and mortality in the two populations is the same, the ratio $N_1(a,t)/N_2(a,t)$ is also the same at all ages; the populations differ in size, but have the same proportionate age composition. If two populations with arbitrarily different initial conditions come to have the same age distribution when subject to the same sequence of fertility and mortality schedules, they may be said to have forgotten the past. The full proof (not repeated here) of weak ergodicity includes a formal demonstration of the intuitively appealing proposition that repeated averaging by a continuous weighting function with positive values over a finite range leads to a constant value of the ratio. The essential feature, then, of human fertility that leads to weak ergodicity is the prevalence in all large populations of positive fertility rates in an extended span of ages. If, on the contrary, fertility were concentrated at a single age, there would be no averaging, no convergence of $B_1(t)/B_2(t)$ to a constant, and no 'forgetting' of the remote past.

Strong ergodicity is an immediate corollary of weak ergodicity. If a population experiences unchanging fertility and mortality schedules for a long time, this year's history is the same as last year's. Two populations with the same history of fertility and mortality have the same age distribution. It follows that unchanging fertility and mortality produce an unchanging age distribution – the age distribution of a stable population.

Let $c(a)da$ be the proportion of the stable population in the age interval a to $a + da$; then $c(a) = N(a)/\int_0^\omega N(a)da$, where ω is the highest age attained. In any female population, the birth-rate is $b = \int_0^\omega c(a)m(a)da$, and the death-rate is $d = \int_0^\omega c(a)\mu(a)da$, where $\mu(a)$ is the death-rate at age a. Since the age distribution in a population with fixed fertility and mortality schedules is unchanging, it follows that the birth-rate and death-rate do not change. Hence the rate of increase r (which equals $b - d$) is fixed.

An exact expression for the unchanging age distribution of a stable population is implied by the mortality and fertility schedules to which it is subject. The formula for the age distribution of a stable age distribution is derived as follows. The proportion at age $a, c(a)$, is defined as $N(a,t)/N_T(t)$, where $N_T(t)$ is the total population at time t. But $N(a,t) = B(t-a)p(a,t)$, and $B(t-a) = b \cdot N_T(t-a)$. Moreover, $N_T(t-a) = N_T(t)e^{-ra}$; hence $c(a) = bN_T(t)e^{-ra}p(a)/N_T(t)$, or

$$c(a) = b\,e^{-ra}p(a). \qquad (7)$$

Since $\int_0^\omega c(a)\,da = 1.0$, it follows that

$$b = 1\bigg/\int_0^\omega e^{-ra}p(a)\,da. \qquad (8)$$

There remains the determination of r. In any female population the birth rate is determined by the age distribution and the age schedule of bearing female children; that is, $b = \int_\alpha^\beta c(a)m(a)\,da$. Thus $b = b\int_\alpha^\beta e^{-ra}p(a)m(a)\,da$, from which it follows that

$$\int_\alpha^\beta e^{-ra}p(a)m(a)\,da = 1.0. \qquad (9)$$

Equation (9) provides the means for calculating the rate of increase r in the stable population by successive approximation, given the maternity schedule, $m(a)$, and the mortality schedule, $\mu(a)$. [The proportion surviving, $p(a)$ equals $\int_0^a e^{-\mu(x)}\,dx$.] The numerical value of the integral in equation (9) is a monotonically decreasing function of r; the integral for any specified value of r can be determined by standard numerical methods; and trial and error can quickly find the value of r that causes the integral to equal 1.0. When r is known, b can be calculated from equation (8), $c(a)$ from equation (7).

The description to this point of stable population theory is expressed in terms of fertility and mortality schedules and age distributions that are continuous functions of age. The theory has alternatively been formulated with distributions and schedules expressed as discrete variables. A population distributed in discrete age intervals at a given moment can be considered a vector that is transformed into the ensuing population vector through multiplication by a transition matrix, the Leslie matrix (Leslie, 1945). The terms 'weak' and 'strong' ergodicity were first applied to finite Markov chains (Hajnal, 1958); weak ergodicity as a property of populations was first proved by employing matrix algebra and discrete age distributions (Lopez, 1961).

USE OF STABLE POPULATED CONCEPTS AND RELATIONS BEFORE LOTKA. Mathematicians, actuaries and demographers made use of the characteristics of a stable population long before Lotka's discovery of what Hajnal called strong ergodicity.

A century and a half earlier Leonard Euler (1760) worked out many of the relations that characterize stable populations. He postulated a population subject to two hypotheses; the hypothesis of mortality, by which Euler meant a fixed life table [or $p(a)$ in the terminology employed here), and the hypothesis of multiplication (or constant value of r]. He noted that the hypothesis of mortality is an assumption that the regime of mortality remains ever the same, and that the hypothesis of multiplication is equivalent to an assumption of a constant birth-rate. Euler's equations treat age and time as discrete variables, with one-year intervals, rather than as continuous variables. Translated into continuous notation, one of his equations is $N = B\int_0^\omega e^{-ra}p(a)$, where N is the total population, and B the number of births in a given year. This equation is equivalent to equation (8) above. Euler notes that if the life table is known, the growth rate can be calculated from the birth-rate, or the birth-rate from the growth rate. He also shows that $N(a) = B\,e^{-ra}p(a)$ [equivalent to equation (7)], and derives a number of other equations, including an expression for the distribution of deaths by age in a population described by his two hypotheses.

Euler's work seems to have been little noted in subsequent years except by actuaries, one of whom, Joshua Milne (1815), cited Euler and developed himself a full set of equations for a constantly growing population with a fixed life table. Like Euler, Milne used integral values of age and time, and expressed growth over x years at the rate r as $(1+r)^x$, but explained in a footnote that a 'logarithmic expression' would be more precise. Milne is of special interest to demographers because he made calculations to help Malthus in Malthus's preparation of an essay entitled *Population*, published in 1824 in the Supplement to the Fourth Edition of the *Encyclopaedia Britannica*. In this essay Malthus (with Milne's help) constructed a stable population from a life table borrowed from Sweden and Finland and a rate of increase that causes the populations to double every 25 years. He showed that the age distribution of this stable population closely matched the distribution recorded in the United States in 1800, 1910 and 1820; and supported his hypothesis that by natural increase alone the American population was growing at such a rapid rate (Coale, 1979).

ANALYTICAL USES OF STABLE POPULATIONS. In a single-volume summary of his contributions to the mathematics of population, Lotka (1939) devoted many pages to the analysis of constantly growing populations with a fixed schedule of mortality. Only in later chapters did he introduce the relations (including stability) that incorporate a schedule of fertility rates by age of mother. Apparently unaware of the earlier work by Euler and Milne, he designated populations that are subject to an unchanging life table and grow at a constant rate *Malthusian populations*; not, evidently, because he knew of the use of the mathematics of such populations in Malthus's last essay on population, but rather because of Malthus's well-known belief that populations tend to grow at a geometric rate unless checked.

The incorporation of a schedule of rates of childbearing in addition to a mortality schedule into the mathematical analysis of population has been quite useful, not merely because it permits the proof of stability (strong ergodicity). A fundamental and analytically useful feature of stable population theory is that the combination of any schedule of fertility with any schedule of mortality connotes a population with a specific age structure, birth rate, death rate, and rate of natural increase. The implied population may never exist but it nevertheless is implied in full calculable detail.

For example, equations (7) to (9) can be used to determine the characteristics of the population that would be generated by a combination of the highest observed (or highest imaginable) fertility in a human population with the lowest observed (or lowest imaginable) mortality rates. Some highly fertile populations have recorded rates of childbearing that would yield 8.0 to 8.5 children ever born by women who reach age 50 subject to these rates. Other populations have recently attained female expectations of life approaching 80 years. The stable population generated by a combination of this high fertility and this low mortality would have a rate of increase of 49.5 per thousand. If all women survived to age 100, the rate of increase would be very slightly higher (49.7 per thousand), the birth rate would be 50.0 per thousand, and the death rate 0.3 per thousand. Higher fertility than in the above example has been observed among married women in some populations. If marriage were universal by age 15, if the widowed remarried immediately, and if married women experienced these very high marital fertility rates, the mean number of children born by age 50 would be about 12. With an expectation of life at birth of 80 years, this still higher fertility would yield a stable population with a birth rate 65.9 per thousand, a death rate of 1.1 per thousand, and a rate of increase of 64.8 per thousand. Again, a mortality schedule with no deaths below age 100 would generate a stable population with a slightly higher rate of increase (65.0 per thousand).

Another application of the stable population inherent in a combination of a fertility schedule and a mortality schedule is the comparison of the characteristics of such a stable population with the characteristics of the actual population that experiences the fertility and mortality in question. The age distribution of the actual population is determined by its past experience. Its age distribution in combination with its current fertility and mortality schedules, determines its birth and death rates. A comparison of actual characteristics with stable population characteristics shows how different the population would be if shaped by current birth and death experience rather than by its past.

Table 1 illustrates this use of stable analysis.
In 1941 the observed birth-rate was higher, and the observed death-rate lower, than actual rates, because history had created an age distribution with a higher proportion in the reproductive ages, and a lower proportion in the old ages, where mortality is higher, than in the stable. Note the negative rate of increase, high proportion over 65, and high mean age ultimately implied by the low fertility of 1941. In 1963 the contrasts between actual and stable population are the opposite.

SOME PRACTICAL USES OF STABLE POPULATION MATHEMATICS. The constant fertility and constant mortality that would establish a stable population are certainly not universal features of the history of actual populations. By the middle of the 20th century, the mortality of most populations had fallen; in the more industrialized countries, at least, fertility was much reduced from earlier levels. Nevertheless, the equations relating fertility, mortality, growth, and age composition in stable populations have proven highly useful in estimating the true characteristics of some populations for which accurate and complete data are lacking.

The usefulness of stable population theory in making good estimates from faulty data originates in a phenomenon called 'quasi-stability'. A quasi-stable population is one in which fertility has in recent years been approximately constant, but mortality has steadily declined for one or two decades, or more. Such a population has an age distribution little different from the stable distribution implicit in current fertility and mortality schedules. It could be said, metaphorically, that trends in mortality are almost completely forgotten as they occur (Bourgeois-Pichat, 1958; Coale, 1962). Because of the resemblance of the age distribution of a quasi-stable population to the currently implied stable age distribution, the equations of stable population mathematics can be used to obtain approximate values of the birth-rate and other measures of fertility, and of the death-rate and other measures of mortality, from a recorded age distribution and an estimated rate of increase. A history of constant fertility and recently declining mortality was characteristic of many less developed countries in the 1950s and 1960s. Such application of stable population analysis occupies all of a report written by Bourgeois-Pichat for the United Nations (1968b), and is a major theme in two other manuals on estimation published by the United Nations (*Manual IV*, 1968, and *Manual X*, 1983).

In recent years it has been shown (Bennett and Horiuchi, 1981; Preston and Coale, 1982; Arthur and Vaupel, 1984) that the question relating the age distribution of a stable population to its constant rate of increase and to the fixed mortality schedule to which it is subject can be modified slightly to apply to any population, in particular to a closed population in which fertility and mortality have recently varied rather than remaining unchanged. The equation for the age distribution of a stable population

$$c(a) = b^{-ra}p(a)$$

is modified to

$$c(a) = b\,\exp\left[-\int_0^a r(x)\,\mathrm{d}x\right]p(a),$$

where $p(a)$ is now an expression of the proportion that would survive to age a according to the mortality schedule at the moment (or during the period) for which $c(a)$ is the proportion at age a. The exponential factor now incorporates the sum of the growth rates, $[r(x)]$, that vary with age (rather than a times

TABLE 1. Vital Rates and Age Distribution of Actual and Stable Female Populations Compared, England and Wales, 1941 and 1963

	Rates per thousand persons						Percent in age interval					
	Birth		Death		Natural increase		0–14		65+		Mean age	
Year	O	S	O	S	O	S	O	S	O	S	O	S
1941	13.1	10.3	11.8	20.5	1.3	−10.2	19.6	15.5	10.3	19.9	35.9	42.4
1963	17.2	20.0	11.6	9.2	5.6	10.8	21.4	27.1	14.1	11.0	37.7	33.2

'O' means Observed population; 'S' the Stable.
Source: Keyfitz, N. and Flieger, W. (1968).

a fixed rate r) over the range from 0 to a. This extension provides a much more flexible basis for estimation, and doubtless will replace stable population analysis in most such uses.

Progenitors of stable population theory existed at least 150 years before the concept of stability was invented, and its validity proven. The theory promises to have descendants for many years in the future, non-stable descendants that will doubtless have as much abstract and practical value as the stable theory itself.

ANSLEY J. COALE

BIBLIOGRAPHY

Arthur, W.B. and Vaupel, J.W. 1984. Some general relationships in population dynamics. *Population Index* 50(2), Summer, 214–26.

Bennett, N. and Horiuchi, S. 1981. Estimating the completeness of death registration in a closed population. *Population Index* 47(2), Summer, 207–21.

Bourgeois-Pichat, J. 1958. Utilisation de la notion de population stable pour mesurer la mortalité et la fecondité des populations des pays sous-développés. *Bulletin de l'Institut International de Statistique* 36(2), 94–121.

Coale, A. 1957. How the distribution of human population is determined. *Cold Spring Harbor Symposium on Quantitative Biology*, Vol. 22, 83–9.

Coale, A. 1962. Estimates of various population measures through the quasi-stable age distribution. *Annual Conference of the Milbank Memorial Fund.*

Coale, A. 1979. The use of modern analytical demography by T.R. Malthus. *Population Studies* 33(2), July, 329–32.

Euler, L. 1760. Recherches générales sur la mortalité et la multiplication du genre humain. *Histoire de l'Académie royale des Sciences et Belles Lettres.* Belgium. Partial translation with interpretive introduction, by Keyfitz, N., and Keyfitz, B., 1970, *Theoretical Population Biology* 1(3), November, 307–14.

Hajnal, J. 1985. Weak ergodicity in non-homogeneous Markov chains. *Proceedings of the Cambridge Philosophical Society* 54, Pt 2, April, 233–46.

Keyfitz, N. and Flieger, W. 1968. *World Population. An Analysis of Vital Data.* Chicago: University of Chicago Press.

Leslie, P.H. 1945. On the use of matrices in certain population mathematics. *Biometrika* 33, 183–212.

Lopez, A.J. 1961. *Some Problems in Stable Population Theory.* Princeton: Office of Population Research.

Lopez, A. 1967. Asymptotic properties of a human age distribution under a continuous net maternity function. *Demography* 4(2), 680–87.

Lotka, A.J. 1939. *Théorie analytique des associations biologiques.* Paris: Hermann et Cie.

Lotka, A.J. and Sharpe, F.R. 1911. A problem in age distribution. *Philosophical Magazine* 21(124), April, 435–8.

Milne, J. 1815. *A Treatise on the Valuation of Annuities and Assurances; on the Construction of Tables of Mortality; and on the Probabilities and Expectations of Life.* 2 vols, London:

Preston, S. and Coale, A. 1982. Age structure, growth, attrition, and accession: a new synthesis. *Population Index* 48(2), Summer, 217–59.

United Nations. 1968a. *Manual IV. Methods of Estimating Basic Demographic Measures from Incomplete Data* (written by A. Coale and P. Demeny). New York: United Nations.

United Nations. 1968b. *The Concept of a Stable Population. Application to the Study of Countries with Incomplete Demographic Statistics* (written by Bourgeois-Pichat). New York: United Nations.

United Nations. 1983. *Manual X. Indirect Techniques for Demographic Estimation.* New York: United Nations.

Stackelberg, Heinrich von (1905–1946). Heinrich von Stackelberg was born on 31 October 1905, in Kudinowo, near Moscow, where his father was the director of a factory. The homeland of the family was the Baltic state of Estonia, although his mother was born in Argentina of Spanish descent. The family escaped the Russian revolution, retiring first to Yalta in the Crimea, and afterwards to Germany. They initially settled in Ratibor, Silesia but moved to Cologne in 1923. He completed his high school education in Cologne, studied economics at the University of Cologne, obtaining his 'Diplomvolkswirt' (master of economics) in 1927, 'Dr. rer.pol.' in 1930, and his habilitation in 1935.

He began his scientific career in 1928 as an assistant professor at the University of Cologne (1928–35). From 1935 until 1941 he was 'Dozent' and 'ausserordentlicher Professor' (associate professor) at the University of Berlin, and from 1941 until 1944 full professor at the University of Bonn. During World War II he was for some time drafted to military service. In 1944 and 1945 he held a guest professorship at the University of Madrid. He died at the early age of 41 in Madrid on 12 October 1946.

Stackelberg was the most gifted theoretical economist in Germany during his time. His habilitation thesis *Marktform und Gleichgewicht* (1934) has had a lasting influence on price theory. 'Stackelberg asymmetric duopoly' is known all over the world. His contributions to Austrian capital theory are the basis for all modern extensions of this theory. His textbook *Grundzüge der theoretischen Volkswirtschaftslehre* (1943) was the first 'modern' introduction to economics in the sense that it is based on a coherent theory of household and firm behaviour. Moreover, Stackelberg contributed to several other fields: cost theory, exchange rate theory, saving theory and others. In Germany he was one of the few leading economists who introduced mathematics into economics and took up the Anglo-Saxon approach in price and cost theory (Edgeworth, Marshall, Hicks, Harrod, Chamberlin and others).

The difficulty of oligopoly theory consists in the fact that the oligopolists are in a game theoretic situation which, in general, cannot be put into the form of a pure maximum problem. Stackelberg's seminal idea was that this can nevertheless be done if – in the case of a duopoly – one firm takes a 'dependent' position (i.e. takes the actual price or production of the other firm as given) and the other an 'independent one (i.e. knows this behaviour and fixes its price or production accordingly so that it maximizes its profits or other utility indices). If both firms wish to be in the 'dependent' position, a Cournot-type equilibrium results; on the other hand if both firms wish to be in the 'independent' position, a contradiction arises since each firm assumes a behaviour of the other which is incompatible with its actual behaviour. If they nevertheless fix their prices (or production) at that level, a 'Bowley'-type oligopoly solution, as Stackelberg calls it, would emerge. Since it is unclear which position the firms will take, Stackelberg considered the oligopoly as a market form without equilibrium. *Marktform und Gleichgewicht* (1934) is comparable with Chamberlin's *The Theory of Monopolistic Competition* (1933) and Joan Robinson's *The Economics of Imperfect Competition* (1933), but goes further in the analysis and in mathematical rigour.

Stackelberg accepted Austrian capital theory, which emphasizes the time structure of production ('zeitlicher Aufbau der Produktion'). The main drawback of this theory is that one of its basic concepts, namely the average gestation period, could not be well defined and measured for a modern interdependent economy. In 'Kapital und Zins in der stationären Verkehrswirtschaft' (1941) Stackelberg suggests the following solution. In a simple economy where the original factor input takes place in period O and the product ripens by nature (such as in the production of wood), the subsistence fund S, the yearly income (= harvest) Y, the interest factor $q=1+r$, where r=rate of interest, and the gestation period T satisfy the relation $S=Y/q^T$. Stackelberg defines an economy as equivalent to this simple economy, if they correspond with respect to S, Y and r, where S is identified with labour income L. Thus the average gestation period may be calculated by $T=(\log Y-\text{Log } L)/\log q$.

In the article 'Beitrag zur Theorie des individuellen Sparens' (1939), Stackelberg deals with the problem: why does a household save? What are the effects of interest rate expectations on household saving? He took up the conceptual framework of Hicks and Allen (1934) and applied it to the allocation of expenditures in the time space. He derived Böhm-Bawerk's law of under-evaluation of future commodities from the law of declining marginal rates of substitution and showed how the optimal allocation of expenditure in time depends on it.

Stackelberg was a neoclassical economist. In his opinion, Keynes really added nothing new to available economic knowledge. He also considered Keynes's interest rate theory as a special case of Böhm-Bawerk's theory of exchange of present against future commodities (see 'Zins und Liquidität', 1947).

Stackelberg kept intimate relations with that group of German economists (Walter Eucken, Erwin v. Beckerath and others) who during the war prepared the transition of the German economy to a free enterprise system. In spite of his untimely death, his influence especially on economic theory in Germany was most important in the sense that he initiated the reorientation of German economic thinking to the Anglo-Saxon approach. His very original contributions to economic theory have had a lasting effect.

WILHELM KRELLE

SELECTED WORKS

1932. *Grundlagen einer reinen Kostentheorie*. Vienna: Julius Springer.

1934. *Marktform und Gleichgewicht*. Vienna and Berlin: Julius Springer.

1938a. Probleme der unvollkommenen Konkurrenz. *Weltwirtschaftliches Archiv*, 95–141.

1938b. Arbeitszeit und Volkswirtschaft. *Jahrbuch des Arbeitswissenschaftlichen Instituts*, Berlin, 61–86.

1938c. Das Brechungsgesetz des Verkehrs. *Jahrbücher für Nationalökonomie und Statistik*, 680–96.

1939a. Beitrag zur Theorie des individuellen Sparens. *Zeitschrift für Nationalökonomie*, 167–200.

1939b. Theorie der Vertriebspolitik und Qualitätsvariation. *Schmollers Jahrbuch für Gesetzgebung, Verwaltung und Volkswirtschaft im Deutschen Reich*, 43–85.

1940. Die Grundlagen der Nationalökonomie, Bemerkungen zu dem gleichnamigen Buch von Walter Eucken. *Weltwirtschaftliches Archiv* 41, 245–85.

1941. Kapital und Zins in der stationären Verkehrswirtschaft. *Zeitschrift für Nationalökonomie*, 25–61.

1941a. Elemente einer dynamischen Theorie des Kapitals. *Archiv für mathematische Wirtschafts- und Sozialforschung*, 8–29, 70–93.

1943. *Grundzüge der theoretischen Volkswirtschaftslehre*. Stuttgart and Berlin; Kohlhammer.

1944. Theorie des Wechselkurses bei vollständiger Konkurrenz. *Jahrbücher für Nationalökonomie und Statistik*, 1–65.

1947. Zins und Liquidität. Eine Auseinandersetzung mit Keynes. *Schweizerische Zeitschrift für Volkswirtschaft und Statistik*, 311–28.

1951. *Grundlagen der theoretischen Volkswirtschaftslehre*. Tübingen and Zurich: J.C.B. Mohr and Polygraphischer Verlag.

BIBLIOGRAPHY

Chamberlin, E. 1933. *The Theory of Monopolistic Competition*. Cambridge, Mass.: Harvard University Press.

Hicks, J.R. and Allen, R.G.D. 1934. A reconsideration of the theory of value. *Economica*, NS 1, 196–219.

Robinson, J. 1933. *The Economics of Imperfect Competition*. London: Macmillan.

Staehle, Hans (1903–1961). Statistician and applied economist, whose work on the theory and application of index numbers to the problem of cost of living comparisons and on the theoretical and empirical study of cost functions is likely to be that by which he will remain best known, Staehle spent most of his professional career in research for international organizations. Between 1930 and 1939 he was an economist for the International Labour Office at Geneva, 1946–7 he was with the IMF, he then returned to Geneva to take up the post of director of statistical research for the UN Economic Commission for Europe (1947–53), and thereafter he led the Trade Intelligence Division of GATT until his death in January 1961. During the second world war he taught economics in the USA, mainly in the capacity of visiting lecturer at Harvard.

Staehle's work on index numbers seems to have begun at the ILO where in 1932 he was responsible for research into the comparative cost of living of similar groups of workers in Europe and the United States. These early inquiries developed into two more theoretically oriented papers that appeared in the *Review of Economic Studies* in 1935 and 1947. The first of these concentrated on cost of living comparisons under the assumption of identical tastes in different price regimes, the second extended the exercise to situations where both prices and tastes differed. These exercises are among the first to attempt to apply the results which were then beginning to emerge in consumer theory to the more practical problem of cost of living comparisons: Hicks–Slutsky compensation questions lie at the centre of Staehle's approach to this issue.

Staehle's article on the empirical study of cost functions appeared in the *American Economic Review* for June 1942. It is of interest not only because of the originality of its attempt to bring together the results of a field of study then only just beginning, but also because of the concern it shows for the historical development of the subject. Two examples may serve to highlight this aspect. The first consists in his discussion of the work of an obscure Austrian economist, Wilhelm von Nördling, who published in 1886 in the *Annales des Ponts et Chaussées* an article on the cost of production of transportation by rail. According to Staehle, von Nördling must be credited with having been first actually to publish the formula for elasticity ($x/y \cdot dy/dx$). The second is his remark, following hard upon a passage from Cournot's *Théorie des richesses*, to the effect that 'it can never be idle to read and quote Cournot' (p. 322).

MURRAY MILGATE

See also INDEX NUMBERS.

SELECTED WORKS

1935. A development of the economic theory of price index numbers. *Review of Economic Studies* 2, June, 163–88.

1937. A general method for the comparison of the price of living. *Review of Economic Studies* 4, June, 205–14.

1940. Elasticity of demand and social welfare. *Quarterly Journal of Economics* 50, February, 217-31.

1942. Statistical cost functions: appraisal of recent contributions. *American Economic Review 32*, June, 321–33.

stagflation.

UNEMPLOYMENT, INFLATION AND PRODUCTIVITY GROWTH. Until the early 1970s it was widely believed among economists that rates of unemployment and inflation were inversely related. The higher the rates of unemployment and excess capacity, the lower the rates of wage and price inflation. And since low levels of economic activity generated low rates of profit as well as excess capacity, low rates of investment and productivity growth would be associated with low rates of inflation. The downward sloping Phillips curve was meant to capture much of this.

Events of the early 1970s throughout the capitalist world undermined the belief that there existed a negative association between the rate of unemployment on the one hand, and rates of productivity growth and inflation on the other. Beginning roughly in 1974 rising rates of unemployment were accompanied by higher if not accelerating rates of inflation, while productivity growth declined sharply.

Table 1 brings out some of the relevant facts. Rates of growth of productivity and inflation for the seven largest OECD economies are given for the periods 1963–73 and 1974–9 along with average rates of unemployment during the two periods. In every country there is an increase in unemployment and inflation rates and a decrease in rates of growth of productivity from the decade preceding the advent of worldwide decline to the five-year period preceding the second oil shock. The simultaneous occurrence of accelerating inflation and rising unemployment and declining productivity growth, i.e. stagnation, brought a new term into popularity in economics, 'stagflation'.

KEYNES REBORN. Events during the 1970s were responsible for a re-evaluation of what had come to be known as Keynesian economics. The advent of stagflation gave rise to a view that in some (often vague) sense 'Keynesianism had been proven wrong'. Basically, this view held that Keynesian aggregate demand policies were proven ineffective by events of the 1970s. Supposedly, if government spending increases or tax decreases could have stimulative effects on output and employment when there were unutilized resources, restrictive aggregate demand policies should have a noticeable impact on rates of inflation. Yet while country after country pursued restrictive policies beginning in 1974, inflation rates were only mildly affected, if at all.

Table 1. Annual Average Rates of Productivity Growth ($\dot{\rho}$), Consumer Prices ($\dot{p}$) and Unemployment (U) for the Seven Largest OECD Economies 1963–73 and 1974–79

	$\dot{\rho}$	$\dot{p}$	U*
Canada			
1963–73	2.4%	4.6%	4.8%
1974–79	0.1	9.2	7.2
France			
1963–73	4.6	4.7	2.0
1974–79	2.7	10.7	4.5
Italy			
1963–73	5.4	4.0	5.2
1974–79	1.4	16.1	6.6
Japan			
1963–73	8.7	6.2	1.2
1974–79	3.3	10.2	1.9
UK			
1963–73	3.0	5.3	3.0
1974–79	0.8	15.7	5.3
USA			
1963–73	1.9	3.6	4.5
1974–79	−0.1	8.6	6.7
West Germany			
1963–73	4.6	3.6	0.8
1974–79	2.9	4.7	3.2

*1965–73.

Sources: OECD, *Economic Outlook*, Paris, various issues.

An alternative view held that stagflation could be understood quite well in 'Keynesian' terms provided it was acknowledged that certain ideas embodied in the *General Theory* were incomplete. Thus, increases in aggregate demand, as Keynes predicted, lead to increases in output and employment whenever there are involuntarily unemployed resources, while decreases in aggregate demand lead to declines in output and employment. The output and employment effects of aggregate demand policies are symmetrical under these circumstances, a belief strongly supported by events of the 1970s and 1980s.

What needed to be augmented, according to the alternative view, was another important idea found in the *General Theory*, namely the asymmetrical response of wages and prices to changes in their determinants. Specifically, Keynes had argued that increases in aggregate demand lead to increases in wages and prices because markets were 'flexprice' upwards, while decreases in aggregate demand lead not be declines in wages but to declines in employment. Labour markets at least were 'fixprice' downwards.

Since the *General Theory* economists have generalized the notion of wage asymmetries in at least two ways. First, it has been allowed that prices as well as wages may respond in an asymmetric way to increases and decreases in demand. Second, it has been argued that with the increased power of labour in the postwar period, wage and price movements came to be dominated by forces other than shifting demand and supply curves (Brown, 1968; Lewis, 1978; Scitovsky, 1978). These forces were responsible for additional asymmetries in wage and price movements and also for the increased importance of cost–push influences, both wage–price and wage–wage, in the inflationary process (Cornwall, 1983, ch. 6). Only the second expansion need be considered.

Wage–price inflation is based on 'fixprice' markets in which changes in wages and prices no longer reflect shifting demand and supply curves. Rather price changes reflect changes in average (normalized) costs while wage changes reflect changes in the cost of living. Wage–wage inflation arises in economies in which collective bargaining is decentralized, inducing labour groups to demand wage increases that are very much related to wage settlements in other labour markets. Hopefully the resulting settlements will increase their relative position in the wage structure.

INFLATION OVER THE CYCLE. Both wage–price and wage–wage inflationary pressures intensify when unemployment rates fall. Tighter labour markets mean more aggressive labour and more compliant management. Higher wage settlements then feed through to prices which feed back to higher wages, etc. They also increase the likelihood that the wage structure will be disturbed, setting in motion a leapfrogging process, i.e. wage–wage inflation.

However, the response of wages to changes in the level of economic activity is asymmetrical in the sense that decreases in unemployment rates lead to stronger upward pressures on wages than increases in unemployment rates attenuate such pressures. This follows for two reasons.

A relatively large increase in the cost of living, the kind associated with the boom, will induce a large increase in wage demands because labour has everything to lose if it fails to demand and obtain wage increases that protect its real wages. However, a relatively small increase in the cost of living, one characteristic of a recession, cannot be expected to induce a proportionately smaller increase because labour groups, acting in their own self-interest, have nothing to gain by wage restraint.

A similar asymmetry applies to disturbances to the wage structure. A large settlement in some market during the boom will set off stronger wage–wage forces and with more likelihood than will an abnormally small wage increase in some market during the slump lessen these pressures. Individual labour groups have everything to lose in the former case by unaggressive behaviour and nothing to gain by holding back in the latter case.

The relevance of the notion of price and wage asymmetries (in contrast to output and employment symmetries) for explaining stagflation in Keynesian terms follows directly. Consider a situation in which aggregate demand pressures lead to a sustained boom in the economy. This is naturally accompanied by falling unemployment rates but also by an intensification of wage–price and wage–wage inflationary pressures.

Suppose that the boom then comes to an end as the authorities introduce a strong restrictive policy out of a fear that inflation has got out of hand. As unemployment rates begin to rise, the increased looseness in labour markets can be expected to lead to some reduction of the rate of price and wage inflation. For example, prices in international commodity markets can be expected to respond to decreases in demand which will feed through to the consumer price index eventually in the form of a lower rate of price inflation. In addition wage settlements in individual labour markets may begin to reflect looser labour markets leading to a reduction in the force of wage–wage inflation.

However, given the asymmetrical response of wages to its 'cost' determinants, a decline in economic activity of some given magnitude will not generate the decline in rates of wage inflation of comparable magnitude to the increase in the rate of inflation caused by a comparable increase in economic activity. As a result from one cycle to the next inflation rates ratchet upwards.

Furthermore, if just prior to the downturn an abnormal increase in the cost of living occurred or if during the course of the previous boom powerful labour groups fell behind in the wage structure, the behaviour of wage (and price) inflation in the early stages to the downswing may even be decidely upward (Wachter, 1970). For additional measure expectational variables can be added leading to a period of rising unemployment and zero growth at the same time as rising unemployment, i.e. stagflation.

STAGNATION. Events of the 1970s lend support to this explanation of stagflation and a slight extension of the analysis allows a better understanding of events of the 1980s, a period of stagnation. Thus while inflation rates eventually came down towards the second half of the 1970s they remained high compared to the experience prior to the late 1960s. However, following the rapid rise in unemployment rates in the 1980s, inflation rates fell dramatically almost everywhere. What this reveals is that the negative relation between unemployment rates on the one hand and rates of inflation and productivity growth on the other is re-established following an inflationary period if unemployment rates are increased far enough and for long enough. But once accelerating rates of inflation get into a system it is hard and costly to get them out. Economies may have to go through a period of stagflation before this happens.

JOHN CORNWALL

See also SUPPLY SHOCKS IN MACROECONOMICS.

BIBLIOGRAPHY

Brown, E. 1968. *A Century of Pay*. London: George Allen & Unwin.

Cornwall, J. 1983. *The Conditions for Economic Recovery: A Post-Keynesian Analysis*. Oxford: Blackwell.

Lewis, W. 1978. *Growth and Fluctuations: 1870–1913*. London: George Allen & Unwin.

Scitovsky, T. 1978. Market power and inflation. *Economica* 45(179), August, 221–33.

Wachter, M.L. 1970. Cyclical variations in the interindustry wage structure. *American Economic Review* 60(1), March, 75–84.

stagnation. As far as modern experience is concerned, stagnation is linked to the decade of the 1930s when accumulation in the US practically ceased. The concept of stagnation as the inevitable fate of capitalism, however, is as old as classical economics; only its motivation has not always been the same. The source or inspiration of the idea may be traced to various lines of thought. They are, first, historical: it is known that a number of civilizations stagnated, decayed and perished. Some philosophers, among them Oswald Spengler (1923), believed in a general pattern of creative phase followed by decadence in all civilizations. The knowledge that, in the past, civilizations have decayed must have had an influence on speculation about the future of our society. The second source is biological: in analogy to the organic world, societies are seen to age. Growth is followed by stagnation and finally decay. This underlies the term 'maturity' (Hansen 1938), used for a society which has reached the end of its growth phase. There are two different interpretations of the process of ageing. One refers to the gradual exhaustion of natural resources. This covers the ideas of the classics who anticipated a scarcity of land in relation to the growing population as well as the modern ideas about the limits of growth determined by the exhaustion of fossile resources of energy or of the healthy environment. The alternative interpretation of ageing is social. With the evolution of capitalism it is seen to pass from its competitive to its monopolistic (and imperialistic) phase. The pioneers of this outlook have been Hilferding (1910) and Luxemburg (1913) with their affirmation of the existence of a new phase of capitalism, characterized by monopoly elements and by imperialism. The elaboration of a theory of stagnation on this basis has been possible only after Kalecki and Keynes had provided the analytical tools in the form of a consistent theory of effective demand.

The third inspiration of stagnation may be called dogmatic. It was the conviction of Karl Marx that all class systems sooner or later must decay and die on account of inner contradictions. Actually the approach just described, which is based on monopoly capitalism, might be regarded as filling in this Marxian programme with a concrete and consistent theory. For Marx himself it was not possible to develop such a theory because he did not anticipate the stage of monopoly capitalism. Instead, we find in Marx quite a different theory which in fact does not fit into the above programme of decay arising from inner social contradictions at all: it is the theory of the declining rate of profit, based on nothing but a supposed technological law (increasing organic composition of capital) which acts from the outside, as it were, like a *deus ex machina*, on the development of capitalist society. This is, in spite of its authorship, a very un-Marxian theory. In a somewhat modified form it is this theory, in essence, which has been used by H. Grossmann (1929) to demonstrate the necessity of breakdown of capitalism. It should be noted here that breakdown and stagnation are not the same thing. Stagnation involves breakdown if it is assumed (a) that the capitalist system cannot exist without growth, and (b) that it is impossible, in the long run, to overcome stagnation by adequate economic policies. Many Keynesians will readily accept the truth of the first condition, but the second cannot so easily be demonstrated on purely economic grounds, and discussion of it tends to shift to the political and sociological plane.

In opposition to the stagnation theories, Schumpeter (1939) appealed to the concept of long waves to explain the great depression of the 1930s. It was so exceptionally severe, he maintained, because the trough of the trade cycle coincided with the trough of the Kondratieff cycle. This leaves some open questions. The empirical evidence for long cycles is limited and refers mainly to price rather than volume series. There is little theory behind the long wave. A. Hansen (1938) linked it to dominant innovations (railway, motorcar). More recently Freeman, Clark and Soete (1982) interpreted it as a succession of product innovations and process innovations, the one resulting from the other.

In what follows, a number of authors will be reviewed whose ideas on stagnation are closely related. They were all influenced by Keynes or Kalecki. In fact, there are occasional glimpses of stagnation in the *General Theory* and more so in Harrod's and Joan Robinson's work.

A. Hansen (1938, 1941) starts from a contemplation of the long secular growth process in the US which reached from the civil war to the great depression. There was, he explains, extensive growth in the form of an increase of population and an expansion of the economy into undeveloped territory in the west of the US; in addition, the capital-intensive infrastructure of the economy (transport, communications, power), was built up during this time. All this involved high rates of investment with the consequence that the economy was proceeding at full steam.

The extensive growth also facilitated intensive growth, by which he means growth of consumption per head involving innovation, new industries, growing productivity and cheapening of consumption goods. The extensive growth had also favoured competition whereas for a stagnating industry it is difficult to tolerate competition. The consequence of the decline in competition was less innovation and a price policy of corporations not favourable to the expansion of the market. The decisive reason why the economy had become 'mature' lay in the cessation of extensive growth and the completion of the capital-intensive infrastructure. From this and the difficulty of replacing extensive by intensive growth followed the decline of investment opportunities. The resulting gap in investment could only be filled, according to Hansen, by public investment, the provision of 'utility creating assets'. The characteristic feature of Sweezy's (1942) work is a mixture of Marxian and Keynesian elements. A long-run tendency to underconsumption is deduced from the following assumptions: the share of wages and of capitalists' consumption in the total output decreases in the long run while the share of investment increases; the ratio of the capital stock to output remains constant. It follows that there must be a long-run tendency for consumption to decline while the capacity of production rises. The question why capitalism has not been ruined a long time ago by this tendency to underconsumption is answered as follows: there have been counteracting tendencies but they have become weaker in the course of time so that the underlying depressive tendency had become visible in the 1930s. The offsetting tendencies include building up of new industries, population increase, unproductive consumption (personal and commercial services) and government spending.

Monopoly is given due attention in connection with its effect on profits and its tendency to retard innovation. Under competition, innovations are made by new entrants who need not care about the ruin they inflict on the older capital of the others, whereas under oligopolistic conditions the innovator will render his own existing equipment obsolescent. Sweezy makes it clear that he does not favour the concept of breakdown. All that can be shown are tendencies which impair the working of the system, especially the accumulation process. He strongly believes, however, that the counteracting tendencies will ultimately not prevail. The work of Baran (1957) and Baran and Sweezy (1966), written during the postwar period of prosperity, dealt extensively with the counteracting factors. They stressed in particular the importance of selling cost and of public spending but played down the effect of innovations on investment.

Starting from a similar mixture of strands, but more specifically from Kaleckian economics, Steindl (1952) asked what consequences the shift of capitalism from competition to oligopoly near the turn of the century might have had. He chose the US because it seemed more nearly a closed and private system. Steindl saw the function of competition in the elimination or prevention of excess capacity. Excess capacity had two effects: it discouraged investment; and it increased competitive pressure since everybody wanted to gain room at the expense of his competitors. This could succeed only in the long run by squeezing some of the capacity out of the market. The procedure involved a simultaneous squeezing of the profit margin (measured at normal utilization of capacity). Restoration of a normal degree of utilization had to go hand in hand with restoration of a normal profit margin.

Here a link between distribution and the process of investment was established which so far had been missing. In Kalecki's system the utilization of capacity played a purely passive role, while here it was regarded as an important determinant of investment, independently of its influence on profits, so that in two cases with the same rate of profit but with different utilization the investment would be larger with the higher utilization.

The distribution theory implied in this mechanism of competition supposes that profits are adjusted to the needs of the accumulation process: if they are higher than the rate of accumulation (which is somehow determined by the past development and by exogenous influences) warrants, then excess capacity will appear and will, *via* competition, bring about a corrective squeezing of the margins.

It is only plausible that the momentous structural change of the economy which led to the dominance of oligopolies would fatally weaken the mechanism just described. Oligopolies would tend to increase profit margins (for example by failing to pass on cost reductions to prices), but owing to the great risk of a struggle between giants and the difficulty of a new entry there would be no sufficient corrective action of competition. In consequence effective demand would be depressed.

An alternative version of this stagnation theory assumes that the oligopolistic concerns anticipate the effects of declining competition on excess capacity. They become more cautious in their investment decisions even before excess capacity actually appears. Thus a weakening of the investment incentive occurs as a direct consequence of the economy's shift from a competitive to an oligopolistic regime.

The above theories were intended to explain the decline in the rate of growth of accumulation in the US which was shown by Kuznets's data to have taken place between the 1880s and the beginning of World War II. In a modern economy the existence of large government budgets will to a greater or lesser extent attenuate the effects of inadequate private investment on effective demand and employment. The role of finance (stock markets) and debt is also treated extensively in the above work.

Sylos-Labini (1956) also regarded the replacement of competitive by oligopolistic structures as the source of depressive and stagnationist tendencies. He concentrated in particular on the effects which oligopolistic structures have on technical progress and innovation. Under the oligopolistic regime the chances of new entries are small. Innovations are therefore not made by new entrants who would undertake new investment, but by the existing large concerns. They will have a strong bias in favour of process innovations (which are less favourable to employment). In addition, they will finance their innovations to a large extent out of depreciation. They space out their innovations in such a way as to avoid premature obsolescence. Sylos-Labini concludes that under oligopoly the forces generating unemployment are stronger than those absorbing it. A basic reason for this is the price policies prevailing in a concentrated industry, where cost reductions due to technical progress are less likely to be passed on to the consumer than under a competitive regime. The oligopolistic profits of concentrated industries yield more disposable funds than are required for self-financing; in other words there is a drain on effective demand.

Stagnation had passed out of sight for some time when at the very end of the 1960s a new element appeared on the scene: the environmental problems which at that time started to command official attention (National Environmental Policy Act 1969). With the publication a short time later of *Limits to Growth* (Meadows, 1972), stagnation for the first time appeared as a desirable policy to be pursued and not as a threat to the functioning of our society. The threat of exhaustion of resources and destruction of environment was used as the motive for a proposed no-growth policy.

With the weakening of growth and the appearance of mass unemployment in the 1970s, the old stagnation theory again received some attention. Interest now shifted, however, to structural changes: the decline of the basic or smoke-stack industries, the appearance of distressed regions all over the world, the decline of manufacturing, the crisis of large concerns with their bureaucratic and hierarchical organization and their tendency to switch from production to finance and speculation. The crisis of the large concern involves retardation of innovation and investment and therefore links up naturally with the stagnation theories based on oligopoly and concentration of industry. On the face of it the interests of environment and employment are opposed to each other and there are repeated clashes between the two. In spite of this manifest conflict there are, however, close parallels between the ecologist's problems and certain problems of economic structure. Thus the depressed regions have an analogy in the local ecological catastrophes such as the 'death' of a river or a lake. Again, the new cottage industries of Charles Sabel (1982) and the rural industrialization of central Italy, which represent alternatives to the concentrated large-scale industry of the big concerns, are closely related to the 'alternative technologies' desired by ecologists. There is a common element of dissatisfaction and criticism of existing institutions which unites the environmentalists and those who are concerned with unemployment.

It thus appears that thinking about stagnation is not a closed chapter of the history of doctrines but is actually very much in a state of flux.

JOSEF STEINDL

See also DECLINING POPULATIONS; STRUCTURAL DYNAMICS.

BIBLIOGRAPHY

Baran, P.A. 1957. *The Political Economy of Growth*. New York: Monthly Review Press.

Baran, P.A. and Sweezy, P.M. 1966. *Monopoly Capital*. New York: Monthly Review Press.

Freeman, C., Clark, J. and Soete, L. 1982. *Unemployment and Technological Innovation: a Study of Long Waves and Economic Development*. London: Frances Pinter.

Grossmann, H. 1929. *Das Akkumulations- und Zusammerbruchsgesetz des kapitalistischen Systems*. Leipzig: C.L. Hirschfeld.

Hansen, A.H. 1938. *Full Recovery or Stagnation?* New York: W.W. Norton.

Hansen, A.H. 1941. *Fiscal Policy and Business Cycles*. New York: W.W. Norton.

Hilferding, R. 1910. *Das Finanzkapital*. Vienna: Ignaz Brand & Co. Trans. as *Finance Capital*, ed. T. Bottomore, London: Routledge, 1981.

Kalecki, M. 1954. *Theory of Economic Dynamics*. London: Allen & Unwin; New York: Monthly Review Press, 1965.

Lenin, V.I. 1917. *Imperialism: The Newest Stage of Capitalism*. New York: International Publishers Company, 1933.

Luxemburg, R. 1913. *Die Akkumulation des Kapitals*. Berlin: P. Singer. Trans. by A. Schwarzschild as *The Accumulation of Capital*, London: Routledge & Kegan Paul, 1951.

Meadows, D.H. et al. 1972. *The Limits to Growth*. New York: Universe.

Piore, M.J. and Sabel, Ch.F. 1984. *The Second Industrial Divide: Possibilities for Prosperity*. New York: Basic Books.

Sabel, Ch.F. 1982. *Work and Politics: The Division of Labour in Industry*. Cambridge: Cambridge University Press.

Schumpeter, J.A. 1939. *Business Cycles*. New York: McGraw-Hill.

Spengler, O. 1923. *Der Untergang des Abendlandes*. Munich: C.H. Beck. Trans. as *The Decline of the West*, 2 vols, New York: Knopf, 1926–8.

Steindl, J. 1952. *Maturity and Stagnation in American Capitalism*. Oxford: Basil Blackwell. Reprinted New York: Monthly Review Press, 1976.

Steindl, J. 1979. Stagnation theory and stagnation policy. *Cambridge Journal of Economics* 3(1), March, 1–14.

Steindl, J. 1985. Distribution and growth. *Political Economy Studies in the Surplus Approach* 1(1), April.

Sweezy, P.M. 1942. *The Theory of Capitalist Development*. New York: Monthly Review Press, 1956.

Sylos-Labini, P. 1956. *Oligopolio e progresso tecnico*. Milan: Giuffrè. Trans. as *Oligopoly and Technical Progress*, Cambridge, Mass.: Harvard University Press, 1962.

Stalin, Josif Vissarionovich (original name Djugashvili) (1879–1953). Stalin was ruler of the USSR (1929–53), leader of the international Communist movement (1929–53) and an important theoretician of Marxism-Leninism. A russified Georgian, his parents were born in serfdom. He was a professional revolutionary from the end of the 19th century, a Central Committee member from 1912, and General Secretary of the Central Committee from 1922. After Lenin's third stroke (March 1923) he was one of the triumvirate which succeeded to supreme power in party and state. He defeated the other triumvirs in 1925, Trotsky in 1927 and Bukharin in 1928. He organized mass collectivization in 1929–32 (and hence caused, directly and via the subsequent famine, several million deaths) and mass arrests and mass expansion of the concentration camp system in 1937–39 (and hence was responsible for a large number of additional deaths prior to the outbreak of the war). He led the USSR in the Great Patriotic War (the Soviet-German war, 1941–45) and hence was responsible both for the early defeats and also for the subsequent victories. He imposed Soviet-style socialism on Eastern Europe after World War II. His plans for a new wave of arrests and intensified terror were prevented by his death (March 1953). He established leader worship, unconditional obedience to Moscow, intellectual sterility and anti-Americanism throughout the international Communist movement. At the twentieth congress of the Communist Party of the Soviet Union (1956) his theoretical legacy was publicly criticized and in a closed session his liquidation of loyal party leaders in the 1930s, and poor military leadership at the beginning of the Great Patriotic War, were severely criticized. In 1961 his policies were severely criticized at the twenty-second congress of the Soviet Communist Party. He was publicly revered in China under Mao.

Stalin's significance for economics relates to economic policy, the model of the functioning of a socialist economy, and the political economy of socialism. He implemented an economic policy based on the general use of coercion to attain a high proportion of investment in the national income, high rates of growth, rapid industrialization and the rapid development of strategic industries. Living standards were depressed and held at a low level. Everyday life was marked by shortages and fear. Food shortages, inequality, piecework, state-directed Taylorism, the rapid expansion of education, rapid social mobility, the rapid expansion of urban employment opportunities and high participation rates were characteristic of Stalinist economic policy. Trade unions functioned primarily as agencies of the state to raise labour productivity. State and collective farms were assessed primarily by their ability to meet the state procurement plans. Foreign trade was mainly valued for its *import* possibilities, for the raw materials, machinery and foreign technology, the import of which it made possible.

Stalin created, maintained and disseminated the statist model of socialism. In the statist model, private ownership of the means of production is replaced by state ownership, and the whole national economy is administered as if it were one giant firm according to the Marxist 'one nation – one factory' model. The only exception is the collective farms, which formally are cooperatives and not managed by the state. In fact in the USSR under Stalin their management was appointed by organs of the state but the state did not accept any responsibility to pay them wages or provide them with social security. The course of economic development in the USSR and the people's democracies in the Stalinist period was supposed to be planned, by means of annual, five-year and long-term plans. In fact the five-year and long-term plans had little operational significance being primarily used for public mobilization and propaganda. The behavioural regularities generated by the statist model and exogenous factors, were of great importance in determining the actual course of economic development. Within the state sector, the role of prices and indirect levers of control in the statist model is small and reliance is placed on direct methods of economic management (i.e. normal bureaucratic processes plus political and police measures). As far as consumption goods are concerned, in the statist model individual choice in the market is not abolished, but reduced in importance by administrative allocation and rationing. The labour market is not entirely abolished either in the statist model, but reduced in importance by forced labour camps, the internal passport system, the abolition of the right to resign without good reasons (e.g. the USSR 1940–56) and criminal sanctions for lateness, absenteeism and damage. In *Economic Problems of Socialism in the USSR* (1952) Stalin took it for granted that in the future financial relations between state enterprises would be abolished and replaced by direct product exchange, i.e. the exchange of goods without the intermediation of money. Informed public or professional discussion of economic policy in a country implementing the statist model is impossible because reliable statistics are not published, extensive use is made of misleading statistics and there is a comprehensive pre-publication censorship. Public discussion is dominated by 'the propaganda of success', that is, the suppression of 'negative' facts and publication only of 'positive' facts and also of purely imaginary achievements. By the end of Stalin's lifetime, it was a trivial orthodoxy of the international Communist movement, and widely accepted outside it, that the statist model (usually referred to as 'socialist planning') was a rational and equitable form of economic organization and represented a higher mode of production than capitalism.

On the theoretical level, his main achievement was to develop and apply to the USSR the theory of 'socialism in one country'. According to Lenin, and all Bolsheviks prior to 1924, the successful building of socialism in only one country was impossible because socialism was international in its very essence. Furthermore, the complete building of socialism in Russia in particular was impossible because of the ever-present danger of imperialist attack and also because of the economic backwardness of the country. According to the theory of socialism in one country, first formulated by Stalin in the winter of 1924/25, the economic backwardness of Russia did not prevent the successful building of socialism in Russia. While the successful completion of the socialist project in Russia could not be guaranteed (because of the danger of imperialist aggression) Bolsheviks should bend all their efforts to the task of building socialism in the USSR, i.e. to the rapid industrialization of the USSR. In this way it would be possible to build up a mighty socialist industry in the USSR and hence weaken capitalism on a global scale. The theory of socialism in one country both provided an explanation of how the maintenance of Soviet power in Russia was possible in the absence of a revolution in the West and also provided a general theoretical orientation for Soviet economic policy. It also provided a theoretical basis for the merging of Marxist Bolshevism and Russian patriotism into the powerful sentiments of Soviet Patriotism. In addition it provided the theoretical basis for Stalin's defeat of the other party leaders and his emergence as the sole party leader in the 1920s.

One of the most important, influential and controversial figures of the 20th century, Stalin played by far the most important role in maintaining and spreading 'real socialism'.

MICHAEL ELLMAN

SELECTED WORKS

1952–56. *Works*. 12 vols. Moscow: Foreign Languages Publishing House.

1952. *Economic Problems of Socialism in the USSR*. Moscow: Foreign Languages Publishing House.

1957. *Correspondence between the Chairman of the Council of Ministers of the USSR and the President of the USA and the Prime Minister of Great Britain during the Great Patriotic War of 1941–1945*. Moscow: Foreign Languages Publishing House, 2 vols. Also published as *Stalin's correspondence with Churchill, Attlee, Roosevelt and Truman*, London: Lawrence & Wishart, 1958.

BIBLIOGRAPHY
Brus, W. 1975. *Socialist Ownership and Political Systems.* London: Routledge & Kegan Paul.
Carr, E.H. 1958. *Socialism in One Country 1924–1926.* Part I. London: Macmillan.
Davies, R.W. 1980–. *The Industrialisation of Soviet Russia.* London: Macmillan.
Fitzpatrick, S. 1979. Stalin and the making of a new elite, 1928–1939. *Slavic Review* 38(3), September, 377–402.
Harrison, M. 1985. *Soviet Planning in Peace and War 1938–1945.* Cambridge: Cambridge University Press. *History of the AUCP(b) (short course).* 1939. Moscow.
Kantorovich, L.V. 1965. *The Best Use of Economic Resources.* Oxford: Pergamon Press.
Kornai, J. 1959. *Overcentralization in Economic Administration.* Trans. John Knapp, London: Oxford University Press.
Mao Tsetung. 1977. *A Critique of Soviet Economics.* Trans. Moss Roberts, New York: Monthly Review Press.
Medvedev, R.A. 1979. *On Stalin and Stalinism.* Oxford: Oxford University Press.
Nove, A. 1969. *An Economic History of the USSR.* London: Allen Lane, The Penguin Press.
Tucker, R.C. (ed.) 1977. *Stalinism.* New York: W.W. Norton.
Xue Muqiao. 1981. *China's Socialist Economy.* Beijing: China Books.

Stamp, Josiah Charles (1880–1941). Stamp was born on 21 June 1880 in London, and was killed in an air raid on 16 April 1941. He was knighted in 1920, and given the title Baron Stamp of Shortlands, in 1938. In 1926 he was made a Fellow of the British Academy. He entered the Civil Service as a clerk in 1896, and spent most of the next 23 years in the Department of Inland Revenue, rising to Assistant Secretary in 1916. While he was there, he taught himself economics, obtaining in 1911 a first-class external BSc from London University, and in 1916, under the supervision of A.L. Bowley, a DSc from the London School of Economics with his thesis on *British Incomes and Property* (Stamp, 1916). He left the Civil Service in 1919, becoming Secretary and Director of Nobel Industries (later ICI). He was Chairman of the London Midland and Scottish Railway from 1926 to 1941, and from 1928 he was Director of the Bank of England.

His other principal activities included being a member of the Royal Commission on Income Tax from 1919, and of the Dawes and Young Committees on German war reparations in 1924 and 1929. From 1924 to 1927 he was a member of the Committee on National Debt and Taxation, and from 1930 onwards the Economic Advisory Council. He was Adviser on Economic Coordination from 1938 to 1941. He was elected President of the Royal Statistical Society from 1930 to 1932, the British Association for the Advancement of Science in 1936, and the National Institute of Economic and Social Research (NIESR) from 1938 to 1941.

As an economist, Stamp made a major contribution to the economics of taxation and to the understanding of tax returns as a statistical source. His interest in political economy dated from his early school days and he worked in the Inland Revenue in the spirit not of a bureaucrat but of a scientific researcher. His doctoral thesis (Stamp 1916), which remains his most important work, exhibited immense knowledge of the changing law and conventions relating to British income tax and succeeded in charting the innumerable pitfalls which lay beneath the surface of published income-tax statistics, thereby laying sure foundations for their interpretation. He also wrote authoritatively about the effect of taxation on income and wealth (Stamp, 1921, 1922), about industrial profits (Stamp, 1918, 1932), about the national capital (Stamp, 1931), and joined with Bowley in estimating the British national income (Bowley and Stamp, 1927).

In addition to his direct contributions to economics, Stamp rendered many indirect services to it. To mention three: he was an active and helpful vice-chairman and chairman of the Court of Governors of the London School of Economics from 1925 until his death; he was one of the prime movers in the establishment of the NIESR in 1938; and during World War II it was at his instigation, as Adviser on Economic Coordination in charge of surveying the economic and financial plans of government departments, that work was undertaken on the estimates of national income and expenditure which were first published in the Budget White Paper of 1941 and were to become a regular feature of British official statistics.

As a public figure Stamp showed acumen, geniality, sympathy, adaptability and resourcefulness, characteristics of the ideal negotiator. It is not often that the academic and practical qualities he possessed in such high degree are to be found in one man.

J.R.N. Stone

SELECTED WORKS
1916. *British Incomes and Property.* London: P.S. King. Reissued with supplementary tables, 1920.
1918. The effect of trade fluctuations upon profits before the war. *Journal of the Royal Statistical Society,* 81(4), July, 563–600. Reprinted in *The National Capital and Other Statistical Studies,* London: P.S. King, 1937.
1921. *The Fundamental Principles of Taxation in the Light of Modern Developments.* London: Macmillan. New edition, 1936.
1922. *Wealth and Taxable Capacity.* London: P.S. King. Reprinted, 1930.
1927. (With A.L. Bowley.) *The National Income 1924.* Oxford: Clarendon Press.
1931. The national capital. *Journal of the Royal Statistical Society* 94(1), 1–25. Reprinted in J.C. Stamp, *The National Capital and Other Statistical Studies,* London: P.S. King, 1937.
1932. Industrial profits in the past twenty years: a new index number. *Journal of the Royal Statistical Society,* 95(4), 658–83. Reprinted in J.C. Stamp, *The National Capital and Other Statistical Studies,* London: P.S. King, 1937.

BIBLIOGRAPHY
Beveridge, W. 1959. Stamp, Josiah Charles. In *Dictionary of National Biography 1941–1950,* ed. L.G. Wickham Legg and E.T. Willliams, Oxford: Oxford University Press.
Bowley, A.L. 1941. Lord Stamp, GCB, GBE, FBA, DSc, LLD. *Journal of the Royal Statistical Society* 104(2), 193–6.
Henderson, H.D. 1941. Josiah Charles Stamp, Baron Stamp of Shortlands. *Economic Journal* 51, June–September, 338–47.
Jones, J.H. 1964. *Josiah Stamp, Public Servant: the Life of the First Baron Stamp of Shortlands.* New York and London: Pitman.
Mogey, J. 1968. Stamp, Josiah Charles. In *International Encyclopedia of the Social Services,* Vol. 15, London: Macmillan and New York: Free Press.

standard commodity. Piero Sraffa developed the device of a 'standard commodity' subsequent to the formulation of the basic propositions presented in his *Production of Commodities by Means of Commodities.* The device is not used to *prove* that the relationship between prices and distribution may be determined from the classical data of size and composition of output, conditions of reproduction and an exogeneously given distributive variable (the real wage or the rate of profit), but rather to illustrate and clarify the form of that relationship. It is therefore an ancilliary device, a *hilfskonstruktion,* designed to 'reveal what otherwise might be hidden'.

The interest that classical economists displayed in the problem of distribution arose from their conception of the economic roles of social classes. Workers worked, and all their earnings were devoted to the needs of consumption and survival; capitalists accumulated, and landlords' extravagant consumption was regarded as a deduction from the fund available for accumulation. The distribution of income between these classes was, therefore, seen as the causal antecedent to the dynamic behaviour of the economy.

Net social product was regarded as a given bundle of commodities, the division of which depended on the relative economic power with which social classes are endowed in a market economy, which is determined by their ownership of the means of production. Abstracting from problems of rent, the distribution of the commodities comprising net product between wages and profits in a simple model without joint production, may be characterized by the expression,

$$s = [x - A'x] - ba'x, \tag{1}$$

where s, b and x are vectors of the commodities comprising total profits, the wage per worker and gross output bundles, respectively, A and a represent the matrix of commodity input coefficients and the vector of labour input coefficients, A' = transpose A.

If variations (of both size and composition) in the heterogeneous commodity bundles s and b are to reflect accurately the command over resources, including labour power, acquired by the capitalists, the components of these bundles must be weighted by the proportions at which, in reality, they exchange. Normal exchange ratios are determined by the level of wages and the rate of profit in the familiar relation,

$$Ap(1+\pi)+a_0w=p, \tag{2}$$

where p is the vector of prices, $p_1 = 1$, w (a scalar) $=p'b$, and π is the rate of profit.

The rate of profit π is the amount of profits s divided by the produced means of production used in the production process $A'x$, the two heterogeneous bundles being reduced to a homogeneous measure by valuation at natural prices,

$$\pi = \frac{p'[I - A']x - p'ba_0'x}{p'A'x} \tag{3}$$

The argument appears to be in danger of circularity since (3) is merely a rearrangement of (2). But if b is given, and the value of the produced means of production in terms of the numeraire is a known function of π, (3) is soluble for unique values of p and π (by Frobenius' theorem on non-negative square matrices).

Nonetheless, it is clear from examination of (2) and (3) that the dependence of the values of the commodity bundles, $p'[I - A']x$, $p'ba_0'x$, and $p'A'x$ on π, will obscure the simple 'physical' trade-off between wages and profits implied in (1). Similarly, no simple proportional relationship can be found between wages and the rate of profit as would be the case if the ratio of net product less wages to produced means of production were expressed in 'physical' terms. These problems apply a fortiori in the case of joint production.

A measure of value independent of π would penetrate the complexity of the price relations, a complexity that derives from the functional dependence on π of all prices, including that of any arbitrary numeraire. Such a measure would reveal the origin of a value surplus, analogous to the commodity surplus of (1).

Problems of measurement of this type were circumvented by Ricardo in his *Essay on Profits*, when he defined corn as the only commodity entering the production of all other commodities, yet requiring no other commodities for its own reproduction. This procedure elevated the distributional relations of the corn sector to the position of a *physical analogue* of the distributional relations of the system as a whole.

But Ricardo's device is clearly of very limited value, for all sectors require direct or indirect inputs of many commodities. Thus, any physical analogue used to describe the distributional relations of a complex system must include all the appropriate commodities used as means of production and appearing as outputs.

A commodity which takes account of the complexity of the economy and yet the production of which possesses the characteristics of a physical analogue, would be a commodity for which the ratio of the value of its output to the value of its means of production was invariant under distributional changes. Such a commodity would exhibit a simple one-to-one relationship in the division of the value added in its production between wages (expressed in terms of units of this commodity) and profits.

As Sraffa has pointed out, this can only be the case when a 'commodity' is the sole input to its own production, and thus when proportions of labour to means of production are 'balanced' (are the same), at all 'layers' of the production process. But

> It is not likely that an individual commodity could be found which possessed even approximately the necessary requisites. A mixture of commodities, however, or a 'composite commodity' would do equally well.... We should, however, not get very far with the attempt to concoct such a mixture before realizing that the perfect composite commodity of this type, in which the requirements are fulfilled to the letter, is one which consists of the same commodities (combined in the same proportions) as does the aggregate of its own means of production... (Sraffa, 1960, pp. 18–19).

A composite commodity with the requisite characteristics may always be found for any particular technology denoted by A (where A is non-negative and indecomposable – in Sraffa's terms all non-basics have been eliminated from the system).

By Frobenius' theorem there exists a unique non-negative eigenvalue of A, λ^*, with which a non-negative eigenvector x^* may be associated. The components of $A'x^*$ bear the same proportionate relationship to each other as the component of $[I - A']x^*$, i.e. in the production system the proportions of inputs are the same as the proportions of outputs.

Let the rate of physical surplus of each commodity be Q_i. Since the proportions of input to output are the same for all commodities, $Q_i = Q$, all i. If the excess of output over input is c_i, then $Q_i = c_i/(x_i - c_i)$. Since

$$A'x + c = x, \quad A'x(1+Q) = x \quad \text{and} \quad [A' - I\lambda]x = 0, \tag{4}$$

where $\lambda = 1/(1+Q)$. The minimum eigenvalue associated with a non-negative eigenvector is λ^*. The associated eigenvector is x^*.

The proportionate composition of x^* is that of Sraffa's Standard Commodity. The scale of standard net product $[I - A']x^*$ is defined such that $1 = a_0'x^* = a_0'x = L$, where x is the vector of actual gross outputs and L the total number of man hours worked in the actual system.

If the actual system is such that outputs and inputs are in the same proportions as the components of x^*, i.e. the actual system is the *Standard System*, the physical ratio of net product to means of production $[I - A']x^*: A'x^* = Q = R$, the maximum rate of profit found by solution of the equations $Ap(1+R) = p$, even though Q is a physical ratio and R is a ratio of values. Q may be defined without reduction of the physical bundle of commodities to a common standard (value), only because numerator and denominator consist of the same proportions of heterogeneous commodities. Q remains the same whatever prices may be. Fractions of Q may be similarly expressed as physical ratios. Thus, if $Q = 20$ per cent and three-quarters of the net product $A'x^*Q$ goes to wages, one quarter goes to profits, and the rate of profit is $1/4Q$, i.e. 5 percent. 'The rate of profits in the Standard system thus appears as a ratio between quantities of commodities irrespective of their prices' (Sraffa, 1960, p. 22). Thus,

$$\pi = Q(1 - w^*) = R(1 - w^*), \tag{5}$$

where w^* represents wages expressed as a proportion of standard net product. In a more general system, with p_1 used as numeraire ($p_1 = 1$), and the wage in terms of p_1, the linear relation (5) between π and w does not hold. But if a unit of standard net product is used as numeraire, $p'[I - A']x^* = 1$, then $w/p'[I - A']x^* = w^*$, the wage measured in units of standard net product. In consequence, the relation (5) holds *whatever* the proportions of outputs to inputs may be, and *whatever* the combination of commodities on which wages are actually spent. In terms of our notation it can be shown as follows:

$$Ap(1+\pi) + a_0 w^* = p \tag{6}$$

$$A'x^*(1+R) = x^* \tag{7}$$

$$a_0'x^* = a_0'x = 1 \tag{8}$$

$$p'[I - A']x^* = 1 \tag{9}$$

From (6), (8) and (9) $\qquad x^{*\prime}Ap\pi = 1 - w^* \qquad$ (10)

From (7) and (9) $\qquad p'A'x^*R = 1 \qquad$ (11)

Multiplying the left-hand side of (10) by 1, and the right-hand side of $p'A'x^*R$, we have immediately

$$\pi = R(1 - w^*).$$

Slightly different proofs are provided by Newman (1962), and Schefold (1971, pp. xxvi–xxvii).

The implications of this result are quite striking. For any technology A there exists a standard commodity x^*, which, when standard net product is used as *numéraire*, yields a relationship between wages and profits identical to that found independently of prices. This is consistent with the classical view that the determination of the distribution of income between wages and profits is logically *prior to*, and independent, of prices. Furthermore, it reveals the origin of surplus, in a manner freed from the ambiguities engendered by price calculations. This result does not depend on any assumption concerning the fixity of the components of A. Even if the components of A are different as between time periods, due to variable returns to scale or technical progress, at every moment of time there will exist a unique x^*, which, when used to express the relevant magnitudes, will define the relationships between w, π, and total profits in the form of a physical analogue.

JOHN EATWELL

See also SRAFFA, PIERO; SRAFFIAN ECONOMICS; CLASSICAL ECONOMIES.

BIBLIOGRAPHY

Garegnani, P. 1960. *Il Capitale nelle teorie della distribuzione*. Milan: Giuffrè.

Newman, P. 1962. Production of commodities by means of commodities. *Schweizerische Zeitschrift für Volkswirtschaft und Statistik* 98, 58–75.

Schefold, B. 1971. *Theorie der Kuppelproduktion*. PhD, Basel, privately printed.

Sraffa, P. 1960. *Production of Commodities by Means of Commodities: Prelude to a Critique of Economic Theory*. Cambridge: Cambridge University Press.

state. *See* ECONOMIC THEORY OF THE STATE.

state-dependent preferences. It is commonplace to formulate theories of individual decision-making under uncertainty using three sets: the set of *states of nature*, S, the set of *consequences*, C, and the set of *acts*, L. Following Savage (1954) we define nature as the object of concern to the decision-maker and a state of nature is a portrayal of nature leaving no relevant aspect undescribed. A consequence is anything that may happen to a person. An act is a course of action. Each combination of an act $f \in L$ and a state of nature $s \in S$ determines a unique consequence denoted $c(f, s)$ in C. In addition, the theory postulates the existence of a preference relation, $\succcurlyeq$, on acts. For our purposes preference relations are taken to be complete and transitive binary relations on L, with the symbol $\succcurlyeq$ being interpreted as 'preferred or indifferent'.

Loosely speaking a preference relation is state-dependent when the prevailing state of nature is of direct concern to the decision-maker. To define this notion formally we let f, f', g, g' be acts in L. Then given $\succcurlyeq$ and $s \in S$, we define *preferences over acts conditional on* s, $\succcurlyeq_s$, by $f \succcurlyeq_s f'$ if $g \succcurlyeq g'$ whenever $c(f, s) = c(g, s)$, $c(f', s) = c(g', s)$ and $c(g, s') = c(g', s')$ for all $s' \in S \backslash \{s\}$. Since $c: L \times S \rightarrow C$ is defined uniquely, $\succcurlyeq_s$, defines a preference relation on C conditional on $s \in S$. We denote this preference relation by $\succcurlyeq_s$.

A state $s \in S$ is said to be *null* if $f \succcurlyeq_s f'$ for all f, f' in L. Finally, we say that $\succcurlyeq_s$ and $\succcurlyeq_{s'}$ *agree* if for all $c, c' \in C$, $c \succcurlyeq_s c'$ if and only if $c \succcurlyeq_{s'} c'$ that is, $\succcurlyeq_s$ and $\succcurlyeq_{s'}$ are the same preference ordering on C.

Definition: A preference relation $\succcurlyeq$ on L is said to be *evidently state dependent* if $\succcurlyeq_s$ and $\succcurlyeq_{s'}$ do not agree for some non-null s, s' in S.

Notice that if s is null and s' is non-null then, by definition, $\succcurlyeq_s$ and $\succcurlyeq_{s'}$ do not agree. This, however, does not imply that the preference relation is state-dependent since s may be null as a result of the decision-maker's belief that s being the true state is virtually impossible. Notice also that even if $\succcurlyeq_s$ and $\succcurlyeq_t$ agree for all non-null s and t in S, the preference relation is not necessarily state-independent since $s' \in S$ may be null as a result of all the consequences being equally preferred if s' is the true state. Thus, a preference relation may be state-dependent but not evidently state-dependent.

Circumstances in which the dependence of the decision-maker's preferences on the state of nature constitute an indispensable feature of the decision-problem include the choice of health insurance coverage (see Arrow, 1974; Karni, 1985); the choice of air travel insurance coverage (see Eisner and Strotz, 1961); the choice of optimal consumption and life-insurance plans in the face of uncertain life-time (see Yaari, 1965; Karni and Zilcha, 1985); and the provision of collective protection (see Cook and Graham, 1977).

REPRESENTATION. Preferences among acts are a matter of personal judgement, presumably combining the decision-maker's evaluation of the consequences with his beliefs regarding the likely realization of alternative states of nature. Expected utility theory postulates preference structures that permit the numerical representation of preference relations over acts separating in a unique way, tastes, which are represented by a utility function, from beliefs, which are represented by subjective probability distribution over states of nature. Under the usual assumptions of expected utility theory when the preference relation is state-dependent a unique separation along these lines is impossible and additional structure is called for.

To convey the issues involved in obtaining an expected utility representation of state-dependent preferences we present in some detail the theory developed in Karni, Schmeidler and Vind (1983), followed by brief comments on the alternative theories.

Following Anscombe and Aumann (1963) let the space of consequences be lotteries with objectively known probabilities over finite, non-empty sets of prices. Let $X(s)$ be the set of prizes available in state s, and let $Y(s)$ be the set of lotteries in s that have elements of $X(s)$ as prizes, that is, the set of probability distributions on $X(s)$. Denote by $|X(s)|$ the cardinality of $X(s)$ and by l the cardinality of the space of prizes, $\Sigma_{s\in S}|X(s)|$. The set of acts is $L=\{f\in R^l | f(s)\in Y(s) \text{ for } s\in S\}$. Decision-makers are assumed to have preference relations $\succcurlyeq$ on L that satisfy the von Neumann–Morgenstern axioms of weak order (completeness and transitivity), continuity and independence. Under these conditions a version of the classic von Neumann–Morgenstern theorem holds, namely, that for each $s\in S$ there exists a real valued function $w(s,\cdot)$: $X(s)\rightarrow R$ such that for all $f, g\in L$:

$$f\succcurlyeq g \Leftrightarrow \sum_{s\in S} w(s)f(s) \geqq \sum_{s\in S} w(s)g(s),$$

where $w(s)$ is a von Neumann–Morgenstern utility function associated with s, and $w(s)f(s)$ is the inner product $\Sigma_{x\in X(s)} w(s,x)f(s,x)$ in $R^{|X(s)|}$. Furthermore, if some other utility $w'\in R^l$ represents $\succcurlyeq$ on L then there exist $b>0$ and real numbers $a(s)$ one for each state such that $w'(s)=bw(s)+a(s)$ for all $s\in S$. We say that $w=(w(s))\in R^l$ is unique up to cardinal unit comparable transformation.

The representation of $\succcurlyeq$ by w in this manner does not imply a unique subjective probability distribution on S. Indeed, *any* list of positive numbers $p(s)$, $s\in S$ that sum to 1 is consistent with $\succcurlyeq$, provided that $p(s)u(s)=w(s)$. To obtain a unique subjective probability distribution on S we need to restrict $\succcurlyeq$ further. One way of doing so is to postulate the existence of a preference relation on acts compatible with a hypothetical, strictly positive, probability distribution p' on S that satisfies the von Neumann–Morgenstern axioms, and to assume that the hypothetical preference relation is consistent with $\succcurlyeq$. To grasp the significance of consistency let $L_{p'}=\{f'\in R^l_+ |$ for all $s\in S$: $\Sigma_{x\in X(s)} f'(s,x)=p'(s)\}$, and denote by $\succcurlyeq'$ a hypothetical preference relation on $L_{p'}$. The restriction on $\succcurlyeq$ is then the condition that $\succcurlyeq$ and $\succcurlyeq'$ are consistent in the sense that they are induced by the same utilities and the difference between them is fully explained by the difference in the underlying probabilities. The preference relation $\succcurlyeq'$ captures the decision-maker's evaluation of acts if he has reason to believe that the probability distribution p' reflects the likely realization of alternative states. The consistency condition attributes the difference between the hypothetical preference relation $\succcurlyeq'$ and the actual preference relation $\succcurlyeq$ to the difference between the hypothetical and actual probability beliefs, respectively.

To present these ideas formally, define an injective mapping H: $L_{p'}\rightarrow L$ as follows: For all $f'\in L_{p'}$, $H(f'(s))=f'(s)/p'(s)$. Using this notation we define a state $s\in S$ to be *evidently null* with respect to $\succcurlyeq'$ if $f\succcurlyeq_s g$ for all $f, g\in L$ and not $f'\succcurlyeq_s g'$ for all f', g' in $L_{p'}$. A state $s\in S$ is *evidently non-null* if not $f\succcurlyeq_s g$ for all $f, g\in L$.

Weak Consistency Axiom For all $s\in S$ and $f', g'\in L_{p'}$, if f' agrees with g' outside s and $H(f')\succ H(g')$ then $f'\succ' g'$. Moreover, if s is evidently non-null then if f' agrees with g' outside s, $f'\succ' g'$ implies $H(f')\succ H(g')$.

Finally, a preference relation $\succcurlyeq$ is non-trivial if not $f\succcurlyeq g$ for all $f, g\in L$.

Theorem: (Karni, Schmeidler and Vind, 1983) Suppose that two binary relations are given: a nontrivial relation $\succcurlyeq$ on L and $\succcurlyeq'$ on $L_{p'}$ for some strictly positive p'. Assume that each of the two relations satisfies the von Neumann–Morgenstern axioms of Weak Order, Continuity and Independence and that jointly they satisfy the Weak Consistency axiom. Then:

(a) There exists a real valued function on $\{(s,x)|s\in S, x\in X(s)\}$ and a probability distribution p on S such that for all $f, g\in L$

$$f\succcurlyeq g \Leftrightarrow \sum_{s\in S} p(s)u(s)[f(s)-g(s)]\geqq 0,$$

where

$$u(s)\in R^{|X(s)|} \quad \text{for all} \quad s\in S, \quad \text{and for all} \quad f', g'\in L_{p'}$$

$$f'\succcurlyeq' g' \Leftrightarrow \sum_{s\in S} u(s)[f'(s)-g'(s)]\geqq 0.$$

(b) The u of part (a) is unique up to a cardinal unit comparable transformation.

(c) For s evidently null $p(s)=0$ and for s evidently non-null $p(s)>0$. Furthermore, the probability p restricted to the event of all evidently non-null states is unique.

Wakker (1985) has adapted the theory presented above to the case where the set of consequences is a connected topological space. This permits the derivation of unique subjective probabilities without the use of objective lotteries. However, foregoing the linearity of the utility functions, which is implied by the Anscombe and Aumann framework, requires the replacement of the weak consistency axiom by a stronger 'cardinal consistency' condition. Loosely speaking this condition requires that the intensity of preferences of the hypothetical and actual preference relations are never contradictory.

ALTERNATIVE THEORIES. The first axiomatic treatment of expected utility theory with subjective probabilities appears in Ramsey (1931). Ramsey's method of defining subjective probabilities does not rule out state-dependent preferences. It does require, however, that there be at least two states ('propositions' in Ramsey's terminology) that are 'ethically neutral', that is two states in which preferences over consequences are identical. Ramsey did not elaborate on this point.

Drèze (1961, 1985) presents a theory of individual decision-making under uncertainty with moral hazard and state-dependent preferences. Departing from the theory of Savage (1954), which requires that the occurrence of events lies beyond the control of the decision-maker, Drèze exploits the fact that in many circumstances the decision-maker does exercise some control over events by adapting his behaviour. He then shows that if there are as many behavioural modes yielding linearly independent probability distributions as there are states of nature then, under additional assumptions, it is possible to obtain a unique separation of state-dependent utilities from behaviourally dependent probability distributions over the set of states of nature.

According to Drèze's theory, the elicitation of subjective probabilities can be accomplished in principle with exclusive reliance upon observed choices among acts. In this respect Drèze's theory enjoys a methodological advantage over theories that must, to obtain the same objective, rely on comparisons of hypothetical acts using direct questions. Its shortcoming is the restriction that it imposes on the decision problems. One restriction is the need for a large degree of freedom in the manipulation of probabilities, which is not always available. The second is the requirement that there exist at least two acts that yield constant utility. The latter requirement may be irreconcilable with some applications of the theory (e.g. the choice of life insurance coverage).

Fishburn (1973) presents a theory based on preference relations over the set of acts conditional on events (non-empty subsets of S). These preference relations are assumed to satisfy axioms analogous to those of von Neumann and Morgenstern and several additional structural restrictions. In particular, Fishburn requires that for every two disjoint events not all the consequences conditioned upon one event are preferred to all the consequences conditioned upon the other. This restriction renders the theory inapplicable to important decision problems involving state-dependent preferences, such as the choice of life and some health insurance coverage.

THE MEASUREMENT OF RISK AVERSION AND OF RISK. As with state-independent preferences, the economic analysis of many decision problems involving state-dependent preferences requires measures of risk aversion and of risk. Such measures are developed in Karni (1985). The key notion required for comparability of attitudes towards risk and for the definition of increasing risk is the reference set, defined as the optimal allocation of wealth across states that would obtain under fair insurance. For classes of preferences that are comparable in the sense of inducing identical reference sets the Arrow (1965) and Pratt (1964) measures of risk aversion and the Rothschild and Stiglitz (1970) definition of increasing risk apply with some modifications. Unlike the case of state-independent preferences, however, in the case of state-dependent preferences not all preference relations are comparable in this sense. Despite its limited applicability expected utility theory with state-dependent preferences is a generalization of the same theory with state-independent preferences.

EDI KARNI

See also PREFERENCES; REPRESENTATION OF PREFERENCES.

BIBLIOGRAPHY

Anscombe, F.J. and Aumann, R.J. 1963. A definition of subjective probability. *Annals of Mathematical Statistics* 34(1), March, 199–205.

Arrow, K.J. 1965. The theory of risk aversion. In *Aspects of the Theory of Risk Bearing*, Helsinki: Yrjö Jahnsson Foundation.

Arrow, K.J. 1974. Optimal insurance and generalized deductibles. *Scandinavian Actuarial Journal.*

Cook, P.J. and Graham, D.A. 1977. The demand for insurance and protection: the case of irreplaceable commodities. *Quarterly Journal of Economics* 91(1), February, 143–56.

Drèze, J.H. 1961. Les fondements logique de l'utilité cardinale et de la probabilité subjective. *La Décision.* Colloques Internationaux du CNRS.

Drèze, J.H. 1985. Decision theory with moral hazard and state-dependent preferences. In *Essays on Economic Decision under Uncertainty*, Cambridge: Cambridge University Press.

Eisner, R. and Strotz, R.H. 1961. Flight insurance and the theory of choice. *Journal of Political Economy* 69(4), August, 355–68.

Fishburn, P.C. 1973. A mixture-set axiomatization of conditional subjective expected utility. *Econometrica* 41(1), January, 1–25.

Karni, E. 1985. *Decision Making under Uncertainty: The Case of State-Dependent Preferences.* Boston: Harvard University Press.

Karni, E., Schmeidler, D. and Vind, K. 1983. On state-dependent preferences and subjective probabilities. *Econometrica* 51(4), July, 1021–31.

Zilcha, I. 1985. Uncertain lifetime, risk aversion and life insurance. *Scandinavian Actuarial Journal.*

Pratt, J.W. 1964. Risk aversion in the small and in the large. *Econometrica* 32(1-2), January–April, 122–36.

Ramsey, F.P. 1931. Truth and Probability. In *The Foundation of Mathematics and Other Logical Essays*, ed. R.B. Braithwaite, London: Kegan Paul, Trench, Trubner and Co.

Rothschild, M. and Stiglitz, J.E. 1970. Increasing risk I: a definition. *Journal of Economic Theory* 2(3), September, 225–43.

Savage, L.J. 1954. *The Foundations of Statistics.* New York: John Wiley.

Wakker, P. 1985. Subjective probabilities for state-dependent continuous utility. Report 8506, Department of Mathematics, Catholic University, Nijmegen, The Netherlands.

Yaari, M.E. 1965. Uncertain lifetime, life insurance and the theory of the consumer. *Review of Economic Studies* 32, 137–50.

state preference approach. Under certainty, with commodities $i \in I$, individual preferences are defined over commodity bundles $c = (c_i: i \in I)$, which are the objects of choice of individuals. Under uncertainty, production possibilities and individual and aggregate endowments, for instance, may vary with the realization of random states of nature $s \in S$. It is then necessary to define individual preferences over plans $\tilde{c} = (c(s); s \in S)$ which assign to each state of nature a commodity bundle.

Rationality, under certainty, is identified with the assumption that an individual's preference relation over commodity bundles is complete and transitive. Under regularity conditions it is then possible to show that a continuous utility function $u(c)$ represents this preference relation. Furthermore, it is a common additional assumption that the preference relation is convex; equivalently, that a utility function which represents it is quasi-concave: if the individual is indifferent between two commodity bundles c_1 and c_2: $u(c_1) = u(c_2)$, he finds any convex combination $c_\lambda = \lambda c_1 + (1 - \lambda)c_2, 0 \leqslant \lambda \leqslant 1$, at least as good: $u(c_\lambda) \geqslant u(c_1) = u(c_2)$. Note that quasi-concavity of the utility function is not an aspect of rationality but rather a qualitative assumption. The stronger assumption of concavity, according to which $u(c_\lambda) \geqslant \lambda u(c_1) + (1 - \lambda)u(c_2)$ for any two commodity bundles c_1 and c_2, is not well taken: unlike quasi-concavity, concavity is not preserved by monotonically increasing transformations and thus does not derive from the underlying preference relation. The utility function $u(c)$ is ordinal.

It is possible to maintain that, beyond completeness and transitivity, rationality imposes no further restrictions on an individual's preference over plans. The *state preference approach* to choice under uncertainty then obtains. With the set of commodities extended from I under certainty to $I \times S$ under uncertainty, individual and aggregate behaviour remain unaffected.

The state preference approach, as exposited, for example, in Debreu (1959, ch. 7) reduces analytically uncertainty to certainty. It poses, however, a dilemma. It is often of interest to associate with a utility function $u(\tilde{c})$ over plans a utility function $v(c; s)$ over consumption bundles conditional on the realization of the state of nature. This is necessary, for instance, in order to answer the question whether the individuals find it desirable to revise their choices after the uncertainty has been resolved, and the related question of ex-ante versus ex-post optimality. The state preference approach either is agnostic on this issue or it adopts the following solution: Given a plan

$$\vec{c}^*, v(c; s) = u(\vec{c}), \quad \text{where } c(s) = c$$

and

$$c(s') = c^*(s'), \quad \text{for } s' \neq s$$

That is, individuals behave as if the states of nature which failed to occur did occur and their plan conditional on those states was carried out. This is analytically consistent, but it is contrived.

Alternatively, rationality under uncertainty can be argued to extend beyond completeness and transitivity. A series of postulates, most definitively developed by Savage (1954), implies that the utility function $u(\vec{c})$ over plans has an expected utility representation $u(\vec{c}) = E_p v(c)$ for some probability measure p over the set of states of nature S. Note that well defined probability beliefs are derived from the postulates which characterize rationality and are not taken for granted. The function $v(c)$ over consumption bundles is the individual's cardinal utility index; it is unique up to monotonically increasing, linear transformations.

Two of the postulates which yield the expected utility representation have been most consistently criticized. The 'sure thing principle', which corresponds to the 'strong independence axiom' when the state probabilities are given, asserts that the preference between two plans $\vec{c}_1$ and $\vec{c}_2$ does not depend on the commodity bundles they assign to states of nature on which they coincide. This postulate yields the additive separability of the utility function over state contingent commodity bundles; Machina (1982) has argued that it can be understood as an approximation. Note that, with the sure thing principle conditional, preferences are well defined: conditional on an event B, a subset of the set of states of nature, a plan $\vec{c}_1|B = (c_1(s): s \in B)$ is at least as good as another $\vec{c}_2|B = (c_2(s): s \in B)$ if and only if there exist extensions $\vec{c}_1$ and $\vec{c}_2$ to S of $\vec{c}_1|B$ and $\vec{c}_2|B$ respectively, which coincide on $\sim B = S/B$ and $\vec{c}_1$ is at least as good as $\vec{c}_2$. (An event B is said to be null if, conditional on B, any plan $\vec{c}_1$, is at least as good as any other, $\vec{c}_2$).

Consider two plans $\vec{c}_1$ and $\vec{c}_2$, both of which are constant; that is, $c_1(s) = c_1(s')$ and $c_2(s) = c_2(s')$ for any states of nature s, s'. It is then postulated that if c_1 is unconditionally preferred to c_2 it is also preferred conditional on any non-null event B. Thus state-dependent preferences are excluded and the cardinal utility index takes the form $v(c)$, as opposed to the state dependent form $v(c; s)$. For this postulate to be tenable it is necessary to keep clear the distinction between states of nature (or plans) and commodities. State dependence can be introduced in a formal sense, by introducing the state of nature as an additional argument in the commodity bundle: $c^* = (c_i: i \in I, s)$; of course this obliges the individual to contemplate plans which assign to, say, state s the bundle $c^* = (c, s')$, while s and s' are mutually exclusive! This notwithstanding, state dependent cardinal utility indices are indeed employed, and the term *state preference approach* often refers to state dependence. Note that this is a different use of the term from the one outlined earlier. Both are, however, generalizations of the (state-independent), expected utility approach to choice under uncertainty.

When individual preferences have an expected utility representation, the cardinal utility index is often assumed to be concave. This is a qualitative property. Note that in this context concavity does reflect a property of the underlying preference relation since the latter determines the cardinal utility index up to monotonically increasing; linear transformations which do preserve concavity. It is a straightforward argument to show that concavity of the cardinal utility index implies that the individual is risk-averse (Arrow, 1965; Pratt, 1964). The characterization of risk averse behaviour for the state preference approach was developed, among others, by Yaari (1969); roughly, risk aversion follows from the quasi-concavity of the individual's utility function over plans.

We have considered only static choice under uncertainty. If choice occurs at more than one time period and uncertainty is resolved sequentially, the state preference approach is more problematic. We already mentioned the difficulties it presents in obtaining from a given utility function prior to the resolution of uncertainty an objective function after the uncertainty has been (partly) resolved.

H.M. Polemarchakis

BIBLIOGRAPHY

Arrow, K.J. 1965. *Aspects of the Theory of Risk-Bearing*. Helsinki: Yrjö Jahnsson Foundation.

Debreu, G. 1959. *Theory of Value*. New Haven: Yale University Press.

Machina, M. 1982. 'Expected utility' analysis without the independence axiom. *Econometrica* 55(2), 277–323.

Pratt, J. 1964. Risk aversion in the small and in the large. *Econometrica* 32(1), 122–36.

Savage, L.J. 1954. *The Foundations of Statistics*. New York: John Wiley & Sons.

Yaari, M. 1969. Some measures of risk aversion and their uses. *Journal of Economic Theory* 1(2), 315–29.

state provision of medical services.

WHAT IS THE PROBLEM? Many countries have responded to the problem of market failure in the provision of medical services by going beyond regulation and the provision of state insurance schemes to the full-scale 'nationalization' of all their personal health services, i.e. state ownership of the plant and equipment (hospitals, etc.) and making all health service personnel employees of the state. The reasons for doing this are many and complex, and vary according to the particular history and culture of each country, but there is one common feature which is fundamental, namely the decision that willingness and ability to pay shall not be the primary criterion for determining access to medical care. There is invariably a strong egalitarian ethic present in such countries, but because this gets tempered by other objectives, actual performance seldom matches the system's ethical pretensions. It is nevertheless useful for analytical purposes to sharpen up the issues by following through the logic of such a system to see where it leads, and what problems such a system would face if it did pursue the egalitarian ethic singlemindedly.

In order that this does not become too abstract and disembodied, the British National Health Service might be borne in mind as an exemplar of such a system, though it is not really a full-blown state system as defined above, since a (small) private sector exists alongside it, and in the primary care sector most of the personnel are not state employees, but independent subcontractors. Nevertheless, it fits the ideal type quite well, in that it is almost entirely financed from central taxation, all citizens have equal entitlements, charges at the point of consumption are both very limited in scope and nominal in amount, and (apart from accident and emergency work) access to the expensive part of the system (hospital care) is channelled through the primary care doctors, who act as 'gatekeepers', charged with the task of filtering cases according to 'need', not according to willingness or ability to pay.

NEED VERSUS DEMAND. The meaning of 'need' (as opposed to 'willingness and ability to pay') is thus at the heart of the matter, and it is therefore worth reflecting on what its content and implications are, or might be. Economists are used to working with the concept of 'demand' rather than 'need', and have spent a fair amount of time and energy clarifying the distinction between, on the one hand, 'want' or 'desire' (which refer to the situations in which the individual believes that he or she would be better off with the good in question than without it) and, on the other hand, 'demand' (which requires, in addition, that the individual is willing to sacrifice something he or she already has in order to get it). To fit 'need' distinctively into this categorization I believe it has to convey the information that some 'expert' believes that the individual would be better off with the good in question, i.e. it is a judgement made by some other than the individual her- or him-self. Thus individuals may 'want' something without 'demanding' it, yet be regarded as 'needing' it, or conversely may 'want' *and* 'demand' something which they do not 'need'. They may even neither 'want' nor 'demand' something which they nevertheless 'need'! Such are the semantics of needology!

This problem is a salient feature of health care (public or private) because of the peculiar role of the doctor acting both on the demand side as an agent of the consumer and on the supply side as one of the producers. Thus the sharp division economists typically draw between 'demand' considerations and 'supply' considerations gets very blurred here. It also creates great ethical tensions for doctors in a private system motivated by profit and responding to willingness and ability to pay, and different, but no less acute, ethical tensions for doctors in a state system motivated by a desire to use the limited capacity of the system to maximize the overall health of the community, whilst trying at individual level to do the best they can for each and every patient whom they judge to 'need' health care.

Thus even the concept of 'need', as defined above, is not sufficient to cope with the 'gatekeeping' role of doctors in a state system, because so long as there is anyone capable of benefitting from medical care (no matter by how little), then there will be 'unmet need' (which will show up to some extent in waiting lists), and some method of *establishing priorities amongst those 'in need'* will be required, and it must be a method which does not depend on willingness or ability to pay. So our next task is to consider what such a prioritizing system might be.

OBJECTIVES. Suppose that the general objective of state provision of medical services is to maximize some index of the level of health of the community, subject to some resource constraint. We would then need to specify an appropriate (operational) index of health, determine the nature (and level) of the resource constraint, and find some way of designing a management system which ensures that all of the significant decisionmakers are motivated to act appropriately. These are the problems that will be addressed in the remainder of this essay. This concentration on the contribution of medical services to health should not be taken to imply that such services are the only, or indeed the most important, determinants of people's health. Obviously diet, exercise, smoking, occupational and environmental hazards are also important, as are public health measures (considered elsewhere). It is simply that here it is personal health services that are the focus of attention.

WHAT IS HEALTH? To construct a useful index of health for use in this context requires the identification of the key *characteristics* of health that people value, a set of relative valuations reflecting the rate at which people are willing to trade-off one good characteristic against another at the margin, and a means of aggregating individual valuations to achieve a composite index for the whole community. Moreover, throughout this process, willingness and ability to pay must be rigorously excluded from playing any role whatsoever.

In general the characteristics of health which people value may be divided into two broad dimensions, length of life and quality of life. The first may simply be measured by life-expectancy, but the second is more difficult, since it embraces many sub-dimensions from which a selection has to be made if the enterprise is to remain feasible. The two characteristics which appear to dominate quality of life for people who are seriously ill are the degrees of disability and distress they are suffering. By disability is meant both physical immobility (e.g. being bedridden or chairbound) and incapacity to care for oneself in the activities of daily living (e.g. washing, dressing, feeding, etc.). By distress is meant experiencing pain, anxiety, depression, emotional disturbance, etc. Other dimensions, such as capacity to play normal social roles, are often added, and the only limits to this process are those of practicality of measurement and valuation.

HOW IS IT TO BE VALUED? The valuation problem can be tackled by simulating the derivation of an indifference map across these characteristics, initially to condense all the quality-of-life characteristics into a single ordinal index (the 'equivalence' method). But this is not enough, for we also need to know the trade-off between length and quality of life, and this can be approached by eliciting how much time in one health state (i.e. on one 'quality-of-life' indifference curve) is equivalent to some stated length of time in some other ('numeraire') health state. Since being healthy (i.e. being free of disability and distress and able to play all normal social roles) is one such health state (and being dead is another!) it could be used as the numeraire, and if its value were set at 1 (and being dead at 0) a cardinal index could be derived in which most unhealthy states would be valued between zero and one, though some really bad ones are usually rated less than zero (i.e. worse than being dead) by many respondents participating in the psychometric experiments that have been conducted along these lines.

Supposing we now have a cardinal index of this kind for each relevant individual (all citizens?) we *either* need some aggregation principle *or* some way of selecting a 'representative' consumer (the median voter?). Since the latter solution is essentially a political matter, it seems more fruitful to concentrate here on the former, since it is a rather familiar economic problem, namely the selection of the appropriate weights to use in an index of performance. Here it concerns the weight to be given to one person's views about the relative value of different degrees of (ill) health versus another person's views on that same matter. This has to be an ethical statement (either explicitly or implicitly), and since the starting point of the exercise was a strong social preference for equality, it would have to reflect that preference. One obvious possibility is to say that one year of healthy life expectancy is to be considered as of equal value to everybody (and being dead is also the same for everybody!), so that we could treat 'being healthy = 1' as not only a convention to elicit *individual* valuations of non-healthy states, but also as the definition of a *common* unit of value. It would imply that the society is indifferent as to *who* gets each additional year of healthy life expectancy which the provision of medical services might make possible. A more complex aggregation method would be necessary if the society believed that *one* year of healthy life expectancy was to be regarded as more valuable if offered to (say) a young woman with small children than to a very old man with no dependents. But the fundamental point is that the aggregation method must be seen as essentially an operationalization of the dominant social ethic of the society as regards distributive justice in access to health, from which there will follow important consequences for the determination of priorities in organizing access to medical services.

Note that in this process no attempt has been made to place a money value on life or on health, and the non-monetary unit of value we have been describing has come to be known as the quality-adjusted-life-year, or QALY for short. Crudely it says that you can 'score' +1 on the performance index (a) by giving someone an extra year of *healthy* life expectancy or (b) by giving that person two years of extra life expectancy, each of which is rated at only .5, or (c) by giving two people each one extra year of life expectancy in that same .5 rated unhealthy state, and so on. It is this index which is then to be maximized as a matter of policy, and which is to be used in cost-effectiveness studies of particular activities within the field of medical provision as the measure of 'effectiveness'.

RESOURCE CONSTRAINTS. In a system where the state provides medical services, the decision as to how much medical care gets provided has to be made by the state too. If by 'the state' we mean the national government, this typically means that the elected representatives who form the government determine the amount of tax revenue to be allocated to the national health service each year, and the service is then expected to work within that predetermined budget. The national government may of course go further, and determine the geographical distribution of the budget between different regions or districts within the country, and/or it may specify separate budgets for capital and current expenditure, and possibly break each of these broad categories down further into, say, buildings and equipment, and different categories to staff, drugs, catering, etc. Thus the complexity of the resource constraints facing decisionmakers, within what has to be a decentralized system, will vary with the complexity of the budget system.

Most systems depart from this simple case in rather significant ways, e.g. by operating systems whereby subsystems face not a fixed budget but a price per unit of work done. If 'work done' meant 'QALYs produced' that would be fine within a system such as we are analysing, but usually it bears only a tenuous relationship to QALY production, and hence generates unhelpful incentives. A somewhat different problem arises where central allocations, distributed according to some egalitarian principle across the whole nation, are replaced or supplemented with locally generated funds on an optional basis, for then any egalitarian preference could only be effected within the locality, not between localities. There may be a further class of problems concerning the modelling of (and appropriate reaction to) resource constraints when some of them are financial, and some 'real' (e.g. constraints over levels of manpower), generating the likelihood that some will prove to be 'slack' and some 'binding', and it will not be clear in advance, from period to period or place to place, which are going to be which. Finally, it may be that different parts of the system are subjected to different budgeting regimes (e.g. capital developments may be centrally controlled in real terms, current expenditures on hospital care subject to overall cash limits but with selective manpower constraints, whilst primary care works on a fee per item of service) so that each subsystem suboptimizes within its own peculiar resource constraints with little likelihood that the outcome will even approximate to what the system's overall optimum might be.

COSTS PER QALY. In principle the way out of this morass is clear. First of all, all constituent activities need to be placed in ascending order of marginal cost per QALY, since it is the activities with low costs per QALY that offer the largest health benefits per unit of expenditure. Then a decision has to be made as to what fraction of the nation's real resources should be devoted to medical care, and command of that volume of resources is then to be distributed to the different activities, until some cut off point is reached. The cost-per-QALY of the marginal activity is then the implied value of a year of healthy life expectancy, and if the society regards that as too high, it should decrease the proportion of its resources that it devotes to health care. If too low, it should increase that proportion. Within the health care system, each activity should be expanded or contracted to the point where the cost of a marginal QALY was equal to this cut-off value. Some activities would be squeezed out altogether (cost per QALY too high) but these might nevertheless be continued outside the main therapeutic budget of the health service, as research or development activities financed from a separate research and development fund, subject to the usual scientific protocols and competing with other *prospectively* cost-effective activities.

The problem in practice in implementing such a system is that surprisingly little is known even about the contribution of most 'proven' medical practices in terms of costs per QALY, and when it comes to clinical support services (e.g. diagnostic activities), nursing, remedial and rehabilitative activities, things are even worse, and by the time one gets to catering, cleaning, laundry, finance and administrative functions the imagination boggles at the enormity of the task involved in establishing cost per QALY ratings for each of them. Consequently most of the system has to operate at a much lower level of aspiration.

INCENTIVES. This highlights the problem of incentives in a complex organization in which the profit motive can have little role. Even salaried staff can be motivated by the knowledge that their 'fixed' remuneration will rise faster from year to year if they do a good job, take on more challenging tasks, etc., so financial incentives are not to be entirely ruled out. But in the medical care system there are typically a high proportion of people who are motivated by a desire to do a good job, to help their suffering fellows as much as possible, and who will respond to incentives which place in their control additional resources which enable them to do so, even though they cannot convert such a resources into personal income.

Thus the most promising lines of experiment in the drive for improved performance in the state provision of medical services have been concerned with participative forms of management in which decisions about priorities (based vaguely on cost-per-QALY), workload, and resources are made jointly by doctors, nurses, and managers at unit level (i.e. at the level of a speciality within a hospital) with improved efficiency rewarded by 'sharing' the saved resources between the system as a whole (for redeployment elsewhere) and those who generated the savings (for development of their own service). The latter element may, of course, distort the preferred development of the whole system, but it is the price to be paid for gaining entry to otherwise impenetrable parts of what has perforce to be a strongly decentralized set-up.

CONCLUSION. Thus the switch from 'demand-led' privately provided medical services to 'need-led' state provision is no easy option. In practice most countries exhibit 'hybrid' systems, i.e. there is a dominant 'demand-led' system with a subsidiary 'need-led' system to act as a safety net for the poor or otherwise inadequately covered sections of the population, whilst in other places there is a dominant 'need-led' system with a subsidiary 'demand-led' system to act as a safety valve for those people who are willing and able to spend more on health care than the state system is willing and able to offer them. Each system has its own logic and its attendant difficulties. The choice between them is a matter of how well each performs according to the particular principle for controlling access which people think is right.

ALAN WILLIAMS

See also HEALTH ECONOMICS; PUBLIC HEALTH.

BIBLIOGRAPHY

Arrow, K.J. 1963. Uncertainty and the welfare economics of medical care. *American Economic Review* 53(5), 941–73.

Buchanan, J.M. 1965. *The Inconsistencies of the National Health Service*. London: Institute of Economic Affairs.

Culyer, A.J. 1976. *Need and the National Health Service*. London: Martin Robertson.

Culyer, A.J., Maynard, A.K. and Williams, A. 1981. Alternative systems of health care provision: an essay on motes and beams. In *A New Approach to the Economics of Health Care*, ed. M. Olson, Washington, DC: American Enterprise Institute.

Kind, P., Rosser, R. and Williams, A. 1982. Valuation of quality of life: some psychometric evidence. In *The Value of Life and Safety*, ed. M.W. Jones-Lee, Amsterdam: North-Holland.

McLachlan, G. and Maynard, A.K. 1982. *The Public/Private Mix for Health*. London: Nuffield Provincial Hospitals Trust.

Torrance, G.W. 1986. Measurements of health state utilities for economic appraisal: a review. *Journal of Health Economics* 5(1), 1–30.

Williams, A. 1985a. The nature, meaning and measurement of health and illness: an economic viewpoint. *Social Science and Medicine* 20(10), 1023–7.

Williams, A. 1985b. The economics of coronary artery bypass grafting. *British Medical Journal* 291, 326–9.

stationary state. Adam Smith mentioned the 'stationary state', describing it as the state in which a country had 'that full complement of riches which the nature of its laws and institutions permits it to acquire' (*Wealth of Nations*, book i, ch. viii; in bk. i, ch. ix the 'full complement' is said to be determined by 'the nature of its soil and climate'). China is several times referred to as being in the stationary state; Holland is really stationary; Bengal is even 'decaying'. In the stationary state, as described by Adam Smith, wages are low; it is only in countries which progress rapidly that wages are high. Profits also are low. Adam Smith said nothing as to rent in the stationary state, but it was an easy step for his followers to proceed to say that rent was high. James Mill simply followed the hints in the *Wealth of Nations*, when in *Commerce Defended* (1808) he remarked that in a stationary country wages are at 'the lowest rate which is consistent with common humanity' (ch. vi, p. 87).

Ricardo, while he did not mention the stationary state in so many words, yet made the conception more definite. The stationary state virtually is that in which profits are just high enough to make the 'trouble' and 'risk' of 'accumulation' worthwhile. Wages in any case are fixed, being the natural or necessary wages which habit and custom fix for the labourers. With the progress of society and the resort to poorer soils, profits fall and rents rise until profits are at the minimum which just suffices to maintain accumulation. But when 'the very low rate of profits will have arrested all accumulation' (Ricardo's *Works*, p. 67), 'almost the whole produce of the country, after paying the labourers', will go the landowners. This was certainly considered by Ricardo a deplorable situation, and was expressly so described by his contemporaries, and especially by M'cCulloch. For writers of the school of M'cCulloch wages were 'naturally' low, and high profits were 'the real barometer, the true and infallible criterion of national prosperity'; hence any approach to a stationary state in which profits were at the minimum was an evil. Some protest against this point of view was raised by Chalmers (*Political Economy*, vol. i, p. 43; vol. ii, p. 133), who pointed out that wages might be kept high 'by the moral preventive check' even in 'the ultimate stages of the wealth of a country'.

J.S. Mill finally protested eloquently against the notion that the stationary state was to be looked forward to with aversion (*Political Economy*, bk. iv, ch. vi). Indeed, he wished the progress of society to relax before the utmost limit had been approached, pleading in noble language for the enjoyment of solitude and of the beauties of nature, for mental culture, and for moral and social progress.

With later writers, the discussion of a stationary state has ceased. The assumptions of an inevitably low, or at least fixed, rate of natural wages, and of a stage when accumulation would cease, which dominated the reasoning of the followers of Ricardo, have been shaken by the experience of a gradual and steady advance in wages, and by an extraordinary and uninterrupted accumulation of capital; while the rapid progress of the arts has lessened the likelihood of any approach to a really stationary state. Hence the topic hardly appears in recent books on political economy. A writer like Roscher, imbued with the historical spirit, refers to 'flourishing' and 'declining' states of society (thus with reference to wages, to population, to luxury; *Politische Oekonomie*, §§ 171, 225, 244); but a clearly-defined stationary state is not deemed worth mention, even in a historical sketch of population. Professor Marshall, again, uses the conception of a stationary state, not as indicating a stage which society will certainly or even probably reach, but as a means of reasoning hypothetically on permanent tendencies in the distribution of wealth.

> The hypothesis of a stationary state is useful to illustrate many points in economics; but it is the nature of such hypotheses to be treacherous guides if pursued far away from their starting-points (*Principles of Economy*, bk. v, ch. xi, § 2, 2nd edn; cf. 5th edn, book v, ch. v, §§ 2–4).

In one sense, France may be said to present the case of a country that has in fact reached the stationary state. The population of France, after having advanced at a fairly steady though gradually slackening rate through the greater part of the 19th century (setting aside changes from gain or loss of territory), has become practically stationary since 1886. The census figures for the population of France were 38,218,903 in 1886; 38,342,948 in 1891; 39,252,245 in 1906. But industrial progress has continued in France; wealth has augmented, capital has increased, wages have tended to rise, cities have gained in numbers, the country districts have lost, so that the stationary state, in the sense in which the older economists understood it, has not been reached.

[F.W. TAUSSIG]

Reprinted from *Palgrave's Dictionary of Political Economy*.

See also CLASSICAL ECONOMICS; MILL, JOHN STUART, AS AN ECONOMIC THEORIST.

BIBLIOGRAPHY
Chalmers, T. 1832. *On Political Economy*. Glasgow: William Collins.
Marshall, A. 1890. *Principles of Political Economy*. London: Macmillan. 2nd edn, 1891; 3rd edn, 1895; 5th edn, 1907.
Mill, J. 1808. *Commerce Defended*. London: C. and R. Baldwin.
Mill, J.S. 1848. *Principles of Political Economy*. London: J.W. Parker.
Ricardo, D. 1846. *Works*. London: J. Murray.
Smith, A. 1776. *An Inquiry into the Nature and Causes of the Wealth of Nations*. London: W. Strahan & T. Cadell.

stationary time series. The concept of a stationary time series was, apparently, formalized by Khintchine in 1932. An infinite sequence $y(t), t = 0, \pm 1, \ldots,$ of random variables is called stationary if the joint probability law of $y(t_1), y(t_2), \ldots, y(t_n)$ is the same as that of $y(t_1 + t), \ldots, y(t_n + t)$ for any integers, $t_1, t_2, \ldots, t_n, t$ and any n. Thus the stochastic mechanism generating the sequence is not changing. In the natural sciences approximately stationary phenomena abound, but the continuing social evolution of man makes such phenomena rarer in social science. Nevertheless, stationary time series models have been widely used in econometrics since they may fit the data well over periods of time that are not too long and thus may provide a basis for short term predictions. The notions of trend, cycle, seasonal are closely related to a frequency decomposition of a series, with the trend corresponding to very low frequencies, and the spectral decomposition of a stationary series [see (2) below] is therefore of interest to economists. Finally, models have also been used where the observed series is regarded as the output of an evolving mechanism whose input is stationary.

If $\{y(t)\}$ is stationary then $E\{y(s)y(t)\}$ depends only on $t - s$. A sequence for which this is so is called weakly stationary but it is the (strict) concept of stationarity that is physically important. Khintchine (1934) obtained the Wiener–Khintchine relation (from theorems due to von Neumann and Wintner), for weakly stationary series,

$$E\{y(s)y(s+t)\} = \int_{-\pi}^{\pi} e^{it\omega}\, dF(\omega). \qquad (1)$$

Here $F(\omega)$ is a distribution function (and an odd function) that distributes the total variance, $E\{y(t)^2\}$, over the frequencies $\omega \in [-\pi, \pi]$. (The frequency in oscillations per time unit is $\omega/2\pi$.) Strictly, Khintchine considered continuous time functions and Wold (1934) translated the theory into discrete time. About the same time, and independently, Wiener essentially constructed (1) from a (suitable) time function. Loosely his theory could be taken as constructing (1) from a single realization (history) of the random process, $y(t)$ when that is ergodic (see below). Corresponding to (1) there is a representation (Cramér, 1942):

$$y(t) = \int_0^{\pi} \{\cos t\omega \cdot d\xi(\omega) + \sin t\omega \cdot d\eta(\omega)\} \qquad (2)$$

where $\xi(\omega)$, $\eta(\omega)$ are random functions of ω with 'orthogonal increments', so that changes in these functions over non-overlapping intervals are uncorrelated. Also

$$E\{\xi(\omega_1)\eta(\omega_2)\} \equiv 0$$

and

$$E\{d\xi(\omega)^2\} = E\{d\eta(\omega)^2\}$$
$$= 2dF(\omega), \omega \neq 0, \pi,$$
$$E\{d\xi(0)^2\} = dF(0), E\{d\xi(\pi)^2\} = dF(\pi).$$

Thus $y(t)$is represented as a linear superposition of sinusoidal oscillations with randomly determined amplitude and phase. This chaotic uncorrelated, behaviour of the 'Fourier transform'. $[\zeta(\omega), \eta(\omega)]$, of $y(t)$ is characteristic of stationary time series. If $F(\omega)$ jumps at ω_0 then $y(t)$ contains a periodic component at that frequency (e.g. a seasonal component) but the most relevant case is that where $F(\omega)$ is absolutely continuous (a.c.) so that $dF(\omega)$ may be replaced by $f(\omega)\, d\omega$ in (1). Then each frequency contributes only infinitesimally to (2). It is this case that is considered below.

Let $z(0)$ be some (measurable) function of the sequence $y(t)$ and $z(s)$ be the value of the function when the sequence is translated through s time units. If $E\{|z(0)|\} < \infty$, Birkhoff (1931) established the (pointwise) ergodic theorem, namely that for all such $z(t)$ the mean, $T^{-1}\Sigma_1^T z(t)$, converges almost surely. The limit will be $E\{z(0)\}$ for all such $z(0)$ if and only if $z(t) \equiv z(0)$ a.s. implies that $z(0)$ is a constant. The process is then said to be ergodic. In that case the whole stochastic structure of $y(t)$ can be discovered from one, indefinitely long, realization. If only one realization is available (the standard case) then ergodicity cannot be verified or disproved and to assert that $y(t)$ is ergodic is merely to assert that all aspects of the structure that are constant over any one realization shall be treated as constants.

Kolmogoroff (1939) developed the theory for the prediction of a stationary time series, linearly from its infinite past, and Wiener also, shortly after and independently, developed much of the same theory (see Wiener, 1942), p. 59, footnote.) In this connection Wold (1934) showed that:

$$y(t) = \sum_0^{\infty} \kappa(j)\epsilon(t-j) + v(t), \qquad \kappa(0) = 1,$$
$$\sum \kappa(j)^2 < \infty, \qquad E\{\epsilon(s)\epsilon(t)\} = \delta_{st}\sigma^2. \qquad (3)$$

The $\epsilon(t)$ are the linear innovations (or one step prediction errors) and $v(t)$ is purely deterministic, i.e. can be exactly predicted from its own past. Also

$$\sigma^2 = \exp\left\{(2\pi)^{-1}\int_{-\pi}^{\pi} \log 2\pi f(\omega)\, d\omega\right\},$$

a remarkable formula due initially to Szego. If $\sigma^2 > 0$, that is $\log f(\omega)$ is integrable, then

$$f(\omega) = (\sigma^2/2\pi)\left|\sum_0^{\infty} \kappa(j)\, e^{ij\omega}\right|^2,$$

$$k(z) = \sum_0^{\infty} \kappa(j) z^j \neq 0, \qquad |z| < 1, \qquad (4)$$

and the spectrum is said to be 'factored'. The function $k(z)$ is said to be 'outer' and is uniquely determined. This theory is important for an understanding of structure but, since the infinite past will not be available, has to be replaced by a constructive theory for practical purposes. Any $y(t)$ for $\sigma^2 > 0$, in the a.c. case [when $v(t)$ in (3) is null], may be represented as:

$$y(t) = Cx(t) + \epsilon(t), \qquad x(t+1) = Ax(t) + B\epsilon(t) \qquad (5)$$

where $x(t)$ is an unobserved 'state' vector. If A may be taken as finite, and only then, $k(z)$ [see (4)] is a rational function of z. Then Kalman (1960) showed how the best linear predictor of $y(t+1)$, from $y(t), y(t-1), \ldots, y(1)$, could be calculated by a recursion on t, a construction that has come to be called the 'Kalman filter'.

Though for $y(t)$ ergodic the whole structure may be known from an indefinitely long realization, the statistical problem of constructing estimates of (or approximations to) aspects of that structure remains. Work as early as the 18th century is still of some relevance here. Early work was mainly concerned to represent $y(t)$ by means of finitely many sinusoids, plus a 'white noise' error term (that is a sequence whose $f(\omega)$ is constant). The central technique is the calculation of

$$w(\omega) = T^{-1/2}\sum_{1}^{T}\{y(t)\exp it\omega\},$$

nowadays usually for $\omega_j = 2\pi j/T$, $j = 0, 1, \ldots, [T/2]$. However, for computational reasons this was initially computed at equal intervals of the period, $2\pi/\omega$. Thus $I(\omega) = |w(\omega)|^2$ was called the periodogram by Schuster (1851–1934). For T even [subtract $w(\pi)\cos t\pi$ when T is odd],

$$y(t) = \omega(0) + 2\sum_{1}^{T/2}\{\cos t\omega_j \mathscr{R}[w(\omega_j)] + \sin t\omega_j \mathscr{I}[w(\omega_j)]\}. \quad (6)$$

A comparison of (6) with (2) shows the close relation of $w(\omega)$ to $\xi(\omega), \eta(\omega)$. In 1965 computationally cheap methods for computing $w(\omega_j)$ were rediscovered (fast Fourier transform algorithm). Direct estimation of $f(\omega)$ through the averaging of a few values of $I(\omega_j)$ for ω_j near to ω is thus computationally feasible and has largely replaced methods based on the use of autocovariances,

$$c(j) = T^{-1}\sum_{j+1}^{T} y(t)y(t-j)$$

(see Blackman and Tukey, 1958).

A second main stream of ideas centres on directly estimating $k(z)$. Here an important class of autoregressive (AR) models was introduced by Yule (1927), namely

$$\sum_{0}^{p}\alpha(j)y(t-j) = \epsilon(t), \qquad \alpha(0) = 0,$$
$$\sum\alpha(j)z^j \neq 0, \qquad |z| \leq 1, \quad (7)$$

that puts $k(z) = [\Sigma\alpha(j)z^j]^{-1}$. Yule also introduced the equations of estimation (Yule–Walker equations)

$$\sum_{0}^{p}\hat{\alpha}_p(j)c(j-k) = \delta_{0k}\hat{\sigma}_p^2, \qquad k = 0, 1, \ldots, p. \quad (8)$$

A recursion on p, due initially to Levinson (see an appendix to Wiener, 1942) enables this to be cheaply computed for a succession of p values. However, (8) is not ideal and other, closely related procedures have been introduced; for a discussion of such 'lattice' methods see Friedlander (1982). Akaike (1969) suggested that p might be chosen to minimize $\text{AIC}(p) = \log\hat{\sigma}_p^2 + 2p/T$, which completes the estimation method. Box and Jenkins (1971) emphasized the case where $k(z)$ is a rational function, hoping thereby to reduce the number of parameters needed for a good approximation, as compared with (7). If A in (5) has minimal dimension p (the 'McMillan degree') then

$$\sum_{0}^{p}\alpha(j)y(t-j) = \sum_{0}^{p}\beta(j)\epsilon(t-j),$$
$$\sum\alpha(j)z^j \neq 0, \qquad |z| \leq 1,$$
$$\sum\beta(j)z^j \neq 0, \qquad |z| < 1. \quad (9)$$

It is this ARMA (autoregressive-moving average) representation that Box and Jenkins used for estimation purposes. The estimation equations are non-linear and are obtained via a Gaussian likelihood for $y(t)$, $t = 1, \ldots, T$. Again p may be chosen by $\text{AIC}(p)$, which now is $\log\hat{\sigma}_p^2 + 2p/T$, $\hat{\sigma}_p^2$ being the estimate of $\sigma^2 = E\{\epsilon(t)^2\}$ in (9). In practice the maximum lag on the right side in (9) might be taken as different from p so as possibly to reduce further the number of parameters needed. If $\hat{\alpha}(j), \hat{\beta}(j)$ are the estimated parameters then $\hat{k}(z) = \Sigma\hat{\beta}(j)z^j/\Sigma\hat{\alpha}(j)z^j$, whence an estimate of $f(\omega)$ results [see (4)].

In a more general situation $y(t)$ might be a vector and regarded as the output of a stationary system (endogeneous variables) for which a vector input of exogenous variables is also observed. The analogue of (3) would now be

$$y(t) = \sum_{0}^{\infty}K(j)\epsilon(t-j) + \sum_{0}^{\infty}L(j)u(t-j)$$

from which an analogue of (5) would follow, namely:

$$y(t) = Cx(t) + Du(t) + \epsilon(t),$$
$$x(t+1) = Ax(t) + Gu(t) + B\epsilon(t), \quad (10)$$

where again $x(t)$ is an observed state vector and now $E\{\epsilon(s)\epsilon(t)\} = \delta_{st}\Omega, \Omega > 0$. If and only if $k(z) = \Sigma K(j)z^j$, $l(z) = \Sigma L(j)z^j$ are rational, may A be chosen finite and its minimal dimension will be the maximum lag in an ARMAX (ARMA plus exogenous variables) model of the form of (9), but with $u(t-j), j = 1, \ldots, p$, also occurring. The problem of a unique specification of (10), or of the ARMAX representation, is the identification problem. This was considered in an econometric context in Hannan (1971) but the decisive contributions came from systems engineers who recognized the importance of the McMillan degree and constructed coordinate systems that 'name' equivalence classes of structures for systems of given degree. Some account of these ideas as well as of methods for estimating (10) are given in Hannan and Kavalieris (1984).

Many of the statistical methods begin from a Gaùssian likelihood or from an approximation to it of the form (Whittle, 1951):

$$-2T^{-1}.\log \text{likelihood}$$
$$= \Sigma\{\log[2\pi f(\omega_j)] + I(\omega_j)/[2\pi f(\omega_j)]\}. \quad (11)$$

The validity of the methods is much wider and extends to the case where the best linear predictor for $y(t)$ is actually the best predictor, that is, $\epsilon(t)$ is a sequence of stationary martingale differences. However modification of this theory is commencing, both to introduce methods that are more robust then those based on a Gaussian likelihood and to deal with truly non-linear phenomena.

E.J. HANNAN

See also ERGODIC THEORY; MARTINGALES; TIME SERIES ANALYSIS.

BIBLIOGRAPHY

A good general reference for the structure theory of stationary time series is Rozananov (1967). General treatments of this theory and of the statistical methods are in Priestley (1981). There is historical material in Wold (1934) and Doob (1953). For recent material, for example on robust methods and non-linear models, see Brillinger and Krishnaiah (1983) and Hannan, Krishnaiah and Rao (1985).

Akaike, H. 1969. Fitting autoregressive models for prediction. *Annals of the Institute of Statistical Mathematics* 21, 243–7.

Birkhoff, G.D. 1931. Proof of the ergodic theorem. *Proceedings of the Nationnal Accademy of Sciences of the United States of America* 17, December, 556–600.

Blackman, R.B. and Turkey, J.W. 1958. *The Measurement of Power Spectra.* New York: Dover.

Box, G.E.P. and Jenkins, G.M. 1971. *Time Series Analysis, Forecasting and Control.* San Francisco: Holden-Day.

Brillinger, D.R. and Krishnaiah, P.R. (eds) 1983. *Handbook of Statistics 3, Time Series in the Frequency Domain.* New York: North-Holland.

Cramer, H. 1942. On harmonic analysis in certain functional spaces. *Arkiv för Matematik, Astronomi och Fysik* 28B, no. 12.

Doob, J.L. 1953. *Stochastic Processes.* New York: Wiley.

Friedlander, B. 1982. Lattice filters for adaptive processing. *Proceedings I.E.E.E.* 70, August, 830–67.

Hannan, E.J. 1971. The identification problem for multiple equation systems with moving average errors. *Econometrica* 39, September, 751–66.
Hannan, E.J. and Kalvalieris, L. 1984. Multivariate linear time series models. *Advances in Applied Probability* 16, September, 492–561.
Hannan, E.J. and Krishnaiah, P.R. and Rao, M.M. 1985. *Time Series in the Time Domain.* New York: North Holland.
Kalman, R.E. 1960. A new approach to linear filtering and prediction problems. *Transactions of the American Society of Mechanical Engineers. Journal of Basic Engineering, Series D* 82, March, 35–45.
Khintchine, A. 1934. Korrelationstheorie de stationären stochastiischen Prozesse. *Mathematische Annalen* 109, 604–15.
Kolmogoroff, A.N. 1939. Sur l'interpolation et extrapolation des suites stationnaires. *Comptes Rendus. Académie des Sciences (Paris)* 208, June, 2043–5.
Priestley, M.B. 1981. *Spectral Analysis and Time Series.* New York: Academic Press.
Rozanov, Yu.A. 1967. *Stationary Random Processes.* San Francisco: Holden-Day.
Whittle, P. 1951. *Hypothesis Testing in Time Series Analysis.* Uppsala: Almqvist and Wiksell.
Wiener, N. 1945. *Extrapolation, Interpolation and Smoothing of Stationary Time Series.* New York: Wiley.
Wold, H. 1934. *A Study in the Analysis of Stationary Time Series.* Stockholm: Almqvist and Wiksell.
Yule, G.U. 1927. On a method of investigating periodicities in disturbed series with special reference to Woolfer's sunspot numbers. *Philosophical Transactions of the Royal Society of London. Series A* 226, 267–98.

statistical decision theory. Decision theory is the science of making optimal decisions in the face of uncertainty. Statistical decision theory is concerned with the making of decisions when in the presence of statistical knowledge (data) which sheds light on some of the uncertainties involved in the decision problem. The generality of these definitions is such that decision theory (dropping the qualifier 'statistical' for convenience) formally encompasses an enormous range of problems and disciplines. Any attempt at a general review of decision theory is thus doomed; all that can be done is to present a description of some of the underlying ideas.

Decision theory operates by breaking a problem down into specific components, which can be mathematically or probabilistically modelled and combined with a suitable optimality principle to determine the best decision. Section 1 describes the most useful breakdown of a decision problem – that into actions, a utility function, prior information and data. Section 2 considers the most important optimality principle for reaching a decision – the Bayes Principle. The frequentist approach to decision theory is discussed in section 3, with the Minimax Principle mentioned as a special case. Section 4 compares the various approaches.

The history of decision theory is difficult to pin down, because virtually any historical mathematically formulated decision problem could be called an example of decision theory. Also, it can be difficult to distinguish between true decision theory and formally related mathematical devices such as least squares estimation. The person who was mainly responsible for establishing decision theory as a clearly formulated science was Abraham Wald, whose work in the 1940s, culminating in his book *Statistical Decision Functions* (1950), provided the foundation of the subject. (The book does discuss some of the earlier history of decision theory.) General introductions to decision theory can be found, at an advanced level, in Blackwell and Girshick (1954) and Savage (1954); at an intermediate level in Raiffa and Schlaifer (1961), Ferguson (1967), De Groot (1970), and Berger (1985); and at a basic level in Raiffa (1968) and Winkler (1972).

1 ELEMENTS OF A DECISION PROBLEM

In a decision problem, the most basic concept is that of an action a. The set of all possible actions that can be taken will be denoted by A. Any decision problem will typically involve an unknown quantity or quantities; this unknown element will be denoted by θ.

Example 1. A company receives a shipment of parts from a supplier, and must decide whether to accept the shipment or to reject the shipment (and return it to the supplier as unsatisfactory). The two possible actions being contemplated are:

$$a_1\text{: accept the shipment,} \qquad a_2\text{: reject the shipment.}$$

Thus $A = \{a_1, a_2\}$. The uncertain quantity which is crucial to a correct decision is:

$$\theta = \text{the proportion of defective parts in the shipment.}$$

Clearly action a_1 is desirable when θ is small enough, while a_2 is desirable otherwise.

The key idea in decision theory is to attempt a quantification of the gain or loss in taking possible actions. Since the gain or loss will usually depend upon θ as well as the action a taken, it is typically represented as a function of both variables. In economics this function is generally called the *utility function* and is denoted by $U(\theta, a)$. It is to be understood as the gain achieved if action a is taken and θ obtains. (The scale for measuring 'gain' will be discussed later.) In the statistical literature it is customary to talk in terms of loss instead of gain, with typical notation $L(\theta, a)$ for the loss function. Loss is just negative gain, so defining $L(\theta, a) = -U(\theta, a)$ results in effective equivalence between the two formulations (whatever maximizes utility will minimize loss).

Example 1 (cont.). The company determines its utility function to be given by:

$$U(\theta, a_1) = 1 - 10\,\theta, \qquad U(\theta, a_2) = -0.1$$

To understand how these might be developed, note that if a_2 is chosen the shipment will be returned to the supplier and a new shipment sent out. This new shipment must then be processed, all of which takes time and money. The overall cost of this eventuality is determined to be 0.1 (on the scale being used). The associated utility is -0.1 (a loss is a negative gain). Note that this cost is fixed: that is, it does not depend on θ.

When a_1 is chosen, quite different considerations arise. The parts will be utilized with, say, gain of 1 if none are defective. Each defective part will cause a reduction in income by a certain amount, however, so that the true overall gain will be 1 reduced by a linear function of the proportion of defectives. $U(\theta, a_1)$ is precisely of this form. The various constants in $U(\theta, a_1)$ and $U(\theta, a_2)$ are chosen to reflect the various importance of the associated costs.

The scale chosen for a utility function turns out to be essentially unimportant, so that any convenient choice can be made. If the gain or loss is monetary, a suitable monetary unit often can provide a natural scale. Note, however, that utility functions can be defined for any type of gain or loss, not just monetary. Thus, in example 1, the use of defective parts could lead to faulty final products from the company, and affect the overall quality image or prestige of the company. Such considerations are not easily stated in monetary terms, yet can be important to include in the overall construction of the utility function. (For more general discussion of the construction of utility functions, see Berger, 1985.)

The other important component of a decision problem is the information available about θ. This information will often arise from several sources, substantially complicating the job of mathematical modelling. We content ourselves here with consideration of the standard statistical scenario where there are available (i) *data*, X, from a statistical experiment relating to θ; and (ii) background or *prior* information about θ, to be denoted by $\pi(\theta)$. Note that either of these components could be absent.

The data, X, is typically modelled as arising from some *probability density* $p_\theta(X)$. This, of course, is to be interpreted as the probability of the particular data value when θ obtains.

Example 1 (cont.). It is typically too expensive (or impossible) to test all parts in a shipment for defects, so that a statistical sampling plan is employed instead. This generally consists of selecting, say, n random parts from the shipment, and testing only these for defects. If X is used to denote the number of defective parts found in the tested sample, and if n is fairly small compared with the total shipment size, then it is well known that $p_\theta(X)$ is approximately the binomial density:

$$p_\theta(X)=\frac{n!}{X!(n-X)!}\theta^X(1-\theta)^{n-X}.$$

The *prior* information about θ is typically also described by a probability density $\pi(\theta)$. This density is the probability (or mass) given to each possible value of θ in the light of beliefs as to which values of θ are most likely.

Example 1 (cont.). The company has been receiving a steady stream of shipments from this supplier and has recorded estimates of the proportion of defectives for each shipment. The records show that 30 per cent of the shipments had θ between 0.0 and 0.025, 22 per cent of the shipments had θ between 0.025 and 0.05, 15 per cent had θ between 0.05 and 0.075, 11 per cent had θ between 0.075 and 0.10, 13 per cent had θ between 0.10 and 0.15, and the remaining 9 per cent had θ bigger than 0.15. Treating the varying θ as random, a probability density which provides a good fit to these percentages is the beta (1,14) density given (for $0\leqslant\theta\leqslant1$) by:

$$\pi(\theta)=14(1-\theta)^{13}.$$

(E.g. the probability that a random θ from this density is between 0.0 and 0.025 can be calculated to be 0.30, agreeing exactly with the observed 30 per cent.) It is very reasonable to treat θ for the current shipment as a random variable from this density, which we will thus take as the prior density.

2 BAYESIAN DECISION THEORY

When θ is known, it is a trivial matter to find the optimal action; simply maximize the gain by maximizing $U(\theta,a)$ over a. When θ is unknown, the natural generalization is to first 'average' $U(\theta,a)$ over θ, and then maximize over a. The correct method of 'averaging over θ' is to determine the overall probability density of θ, to be denoted $\pi^*(\theta)$ (and to be described shortly), and then consider the *Bayesian expected* utility:

$$U^*(a)=E^{\pi^*}[U(\theta,a)]$$
$$=\int U(\theta,a)\pi^*(\theta)\,\mathrm{d}\theta.$$

(This last expression assumes that θ is a continuous variable taking values in an interval of numbers. If it can assume only one of a discrete set of values, then this integral should be replaced by a sum over the possible values.) Maximizing $U^*(a)$ over a will yield the optimal *Bayes action*, to be denoted by a^*.

Example 1 (cont.). Initially, assume that no data, X, are available from a sampling inspection of the current shipment. Then the only information about θ is that contained in the prior $\pi(\theta)$; $\pi^*(\theta)$ will thus be identified with $\pi(\theta)=14(1-\theta)^{13}$ Calculation yields:

$$U^*(a_1)=\int_0^1(1-10\theta)14(1-\theta)^{13}\,\mathrm{d}\theta=0.33,$$

$$U^*(a_2)=\int_0^1(-0.1)14(1-\theta)^{13}\,\mathrm{d}\theta=-0.1.$$

Since $U^*(a_1)>U^*(a_2)$, the Bayes action is a_1, to accept the shipment.

When data, X, are available, in addition to the prior information, the overall probability density π^* for θ must combine the two sources of information. This is done by *Bayes's Theorem* (from Bayes, 1763), which gives the overall density, usually called the *posterior density*, as:

$$\pi^*(\theta)=p_\theta(X)\cdot\pi(\theta)/m(X),$$

where:

$$m(X)=\int p_\theta(X)\pi(\theta)\,\mathrm{d}\theta$$

(or a summation over θ if θ assumes only a discrete set of values), and $p_\theta(X)$ is the probability density for the experiment with the observed values of the data X inserted.

Example 1 (cont.). Suppose a sample of $n=20$ items is tested, out of which $X=3$ defectives are observed. Calculation gives that the posterior density of θ is:

$$\pi^*(\theta)=p_\theta(3)\cdot\pi(\theta)/m(3)$$
$$=\left[\frac{20!}{3!17!}\theta^3(1-\theta)^{17}\right]\cdot[14(1-\theta)^{13}]/m(3)$$
$$=(185{,}504)\theta^3(1-\theta)^{30},$$

which can be recognized as the beta (4, 31) density. This density describes the location of θ in the light of all available information. The Bayesian expected utilities of a_1 and a_2 are thus:

$$U^*(a_1)=\int_0^1(1\text{–}10\theta)\pi^*(\theta)\,\mathrm{d}\theta$$
$$=\int_0^1(1-10\theta)(185{,}504)\theta^3(1-\theta)^{30}\,\mathrm{d}\theta=-0.14,$$

and

$$U^*(a_2)=\int_0^1(-0.1)\pi^*(\theta)\,\mathrm{d}\theta=-0.1.$$

Clearly a_2 has the largest expected utility, and should be the action chosen.

3 FREQUENTIST DECISION THEORY

An alternative approach to statistical decision theory arises from taking a 'long run' perspective. The idea is to imagine repeating the decision problem a large number of times, and to develop a decision strategy which will be optimal in terms of some long-run criterion. This is called the *frequentist* approach, and is essentially due to Neyman, Pearson and Wald (see Neyman and Pearson, 1933; Neyman, 1977; Wald, 1950).

To formalize the above idea, let $d(X)$ denote a *decision strategy* or *decision rule*. The notation reflects the fact that we are imagining repetitions of the decision problem which will yield possibly different data X, and must therefore specify the action to be taken for any possible X. The utility of using $d(X)$ when θ obtains is thus $U[\theta,d(X)]$. The statistical literature almost exclusively works with loss functions instead of utility functions; for consistency with this literature we will thus use the loss function $L(\theta, d) = -U(\theta, d)$. (Of course, we want to minimize loss.)

The first step in a frequentist evaluation is to compute the *risk function* (expected loss over X) of d, given by:

$$R(\theta, d) = E_\theta\{L[\theta, d(X)]\}$$
$$= \int L[\theta, d(X)]p_\theta(X)\,\mathrm{d}X.$$

(Again, this integral should be a summation if X is discrete valued.) For a fixed θ this risk indicates how well $d(X)$ would perform if utilized repeatedly for data arising from the probability density $p_\theta(X)$. For various common choices of L this yields familiar statistical quantities. For instance, when L is 0 or 1, according to whether or not a correct decision is made in a two action hypothesis testing problem, the risk becomes the 'probabilities of type I or type II error'. When L is 0 or 1, according to whether or not an interval $d(X)$ contains θ, the risk is 1 minus the 'coverage probability function' for the confidence procedure $d(X)$. When $d(X)$ is an estimate of θ and $L(\theta, d) = (\theta - d)^2$, the risk is the 'mean squared error' commonly considered in many econometric studies. (If the estimator $d(X)$ is unbiased, then this mean squared error is also the variance function for d.)

Example 2. Example 1, involving acceptance or rejection of the shipment, is somewhat too complicated to handle here from the frequentist perspective; we thus consider the simpler problem of merely estimating θ (the proportion of defective parts in the shipment). Assume that loss in estimation is measured by *squared error*; that is:

$$L[\theta, d(X)] = [\theta - d(X)]^2.$$

A natural estimate of θ, based on X (the number of defectives from a sample of size n), is the sample proportion of defectives $d_1(X) = X/n$. For this decision rule (or *estimator*), the risk function when X has the binomial distribution discussed earlier (so that X takes only the discrete values $0, 1, 2, \ldots, n$) is given by:

$$R(\theta, d) = \sum_{X=0}^{n}\left(\theta - \frac{X}{n}\right)^2 p_\theta(X) = \theta(1-\theta)/n.$$

The second step of a frequentist analysis is to select some criterion for defining optimal risk functions (and hence optimal decision rules). One of the most common criteria is the *Minimax Principle*, which is based on consideration of the maximum possible risk:

$$R^*(d) = \max_\theta R(\theta, d).$$

This indicates the worst possible performance of $d(X)$ in repeated use, and hence has some appeal as a criterion based on a cautious attitude. Using this criterion, an optimal decision rule is, of course, defined to be one which minimizes $R^*(d)$, and is called a *minimax decision rule*.

Example 2 (cont.). It is easy to see that:

$$R^*(d_1) = \max_\theta R(\theta, d_1) = \max_\theta \frac{\theta(1-\theta)}{n} = \frac{1}{4n}.$$

However, d_1 is not the minimax decision rule. Indeed, the minimax decision rule turns out to be:

$$d_2(X) = (X + \sqrt{n}/2)/(n + \sqrt{n}),$$

which has $R^*(d_2) = 1/[4(1+\sqrt{n})^2]$ (cf. Berger, 1985, p. 354). The minimax criterion here is essentially the same as the minimax criterion in game theory. Indeed, the frequentist decision problem can be considered to be a zero-sum two-person game with the statistician as player II (choosing $d(X)$), an inimical 'nature' as player I (choosing θ), and payoff (to player I) of $R(\theta, d)$. (Of course, it is rather unnatural to assume that nature is inimical in its choice of θ.) (For further discussion of this relationship, see Berger, 1985, ch. 5.)

Minimax optimality is but one of several criteria that are used in frequentist decision theory. Another common criterion is the Invariance Principle, which calls for finding the best decision rule in the class of rules which are 'invariant' under certain mathematical transformations of the decision problem. (See Berger, 1985, ch. 6, for discussion.)

There also exist very general and elegant theorems which characterize the class of acceptable decision rules. The formal term used is 'admissible'; a decision rule, d, is *admissible* if there is no decision rule, d^*, with $R(\theta, d^*) \leqslant R(\theta, d)$, the inequality being strict for some θ. If such a d^* exists, then d is said to be *inadmissible*, and one has obvious cause to question its use. Very common decision rules, such as the least squares estimator in three or more dimensional normal estimation problems (with sum of squares error loss), can turn out rather astonishingly to be inadmissible, so this avenue of investigation has had a substantial impact on decision theory. A general discussion, with references, can be found in Berger (1985).

4 COMPARISON OF APPROACHES

For solving a real decision problem, there is little doubt that the Bayesian approach is best. It incorporates all the available information (including the prior information, $\pi(\theta)$, which the frequentist approach ignores), and it tends to be easier than the frequentist approach by an order of magnitude. Maximizing $U^*(a)$ over all actions is generally much easier than minimizing something like $R^*(d)$ over all decision rules; the point is that, in some sense, the frequentist approach needlessly complicates the issue by forcing consideration of the right thing to do for each possible X, while the Bayesian worries only about what to do for the actual data X that are observed. There are also fundamental axiomatic developments (see, Ramsey, 1931; Savage, 1954; and Fishburn, 1981, for a general review) which show that only the Bayesian approach is consistent with plausible axioms of rational behaviour. Basically, the arguments are that situations can be constructed in which the follower of any non-Bayesian approach, say the minimax analyst, will be assured of inferior results.

Sometimes, however, decision theory is used as a formal framework for investigating the performance of statistical procedures, and then the situation is less clear. In Example 2, for instance, we used decision theory mainly as a method to formulate rigorously the problem of estimating a binomial proportion θ. If one is developing a statistical rule, $d(X)$, to be used for binomial estimation problems in general, then its repeated performance for varying X is certainly of interest. Furthermore, so the argument goes, prior information may be unavailable or inaccessible in problems where routine statistical analyses (such as estimating a binomial proportion θ) are to be performed, precluding use of the Bayesian approach.

The Bayesian reply to these arguments is that (i) optimal performance for each X alone will guarantee good performance in repeated use, negating the need to consider frequentist measures explicitly; and (ii) even when prior information is unavailable or cannot be used, a Bayesian analysis can still be performed with what are called 'non-informative' prior densities.

Example 2 (cont.). If no prior information about θ is available, one might well say that choosing $\pi(\theta) = 1$ reflects this lack of knowledge about θ. A Bayesian analysis (calculating the posterior density and choosing the action with smallest Bayesian expected squared error loss) yields, as the optimal estimate for θ when X is observed:

$$d_3(X) = (X+1)/(n+2).$$

This estimate is considerably more attractive than, say, the minimax rule $d_2(X)$ (see Berger, 1985, p. 375).

In practical applications of decision theory, it is the Bayesian approach which is dominant, yet the frequentist approach retains considerable appeal among theoreticians. A general consensus on the controversy appears quite remote at this time. This author sides with the Bayesian approach in the above debate, while recognizing that there are some situations in which the frequentist approach might be useful. For an extensive discussion of these issues, see Berger (1985).

JAMES O. BERGER

See also BAYESIAN INFERENCE.

BIBLIOGRAPHY

Bayes, T. 1763. An essay towards solving a problem in the doctrine of chances. *Philosophical Transactions of the Royal Society*, London 53, 370–418.

Berger, J. 1985. *Statistical Decision Theory and Bayesian Analysis*. New York: Springer-Verlag.

Blackwell, D. and Girshick, M.A. 1954. *Theory of Games and Statistical Decisions*. New York: Wiley.

De Groot, M.H. 1970. *Optimal Statistical Decisions*. New York: McGraw-Hill.

Ferguson, T.S. 1967. *Mathematical Statistics: A Decision Theoretic Approach*. New York: Academic Press.

Fishburn, P.C. 1981. Subjective expected utility: a review of normative theories. *Theory and Decision* 13, 139–99.

Neyman, J. 1977. Frequentist probability and frequentist statistics. *Synthese* 36, 97–131.

Neyman, J. and Pearson, E.S. 1933. On the problem of the most efficient tests of statistical hypotheses. *Philosophical Transactions of the Royal Society*, London, 231, 289–337.

Raiffa, H. 1968. *Decision Analysis: Introductory Lectures on Choices under Uncertainty*. Reading, Mass.: Addison-Wesley.

Raiffa, H. and Schlaifer, R. 1961. *Applied Statistical Decision Theory*. Boston: Division of Research, Graduate School of Business Administration, Harvard University.

Ramsey, F.P. 1931. Truth and probability. In *The Foundations of Mathematics and Other Logical Essays*, London: Kegan, Paul, Trench and Trubner. Reprinted in *Studies in Subjective Probability*, ed. H. Kyburg and H. Smokler, New York: Wiley, 1964, 61–92.

Savage, L.J. 1954. *The Foundations of Statistics*. New York: Wiley.

Wald, A. 1950. *Statistical Decision Functions*. New York: Wiley.

Winkler, R.L. 1972. *An Introduction to Bayesian Inference and Decision*. New York: Holt, Rinehart & Winston.

statistical inference. Deduction is the process whereby we pass from a general statement to a particular case: the reverse procedure, from the particular to the general, is variously called induction, or inference. Statistical inference is ordinarily understood to involve repetition or averaging, as when an inference is made about a population on the basis of a sample drawn from it. Economic facts are typically established by means of statistical inference. Economists construct a model of the world and deduce from it implications for the real world. These are checked against the available data, leading to some degree of support for the model. Statistical inference is concerned with how this support should be calculated.

Statistical inference incorporates a parameter θ which describes the model. In the simplest cases θ is a real number but in many models it is a set of numbers or even a function. The other basic element is the data x being observations made on the actual economic system. So θ corresponds to the general element and x to the particular. The model describes how the data follow from the parameter value. This is usually in the form of a probability distribution $p(x|\theta)$: the probability of x, given the value of θ. The problem of statistical inference is to make some statement about θ given the value of x. A simple example is provided by a model that says one variable y has linear regression on another z, the regression line having equation $y = \alpha + \beta z$ and the parameter being the pair $(\alpha, \beta) = \theta$. Data may then be collected for several pairs (y_i, z_i), $i = 1, 2, \ldots, n$ and an inference made about θ. The probability specification will ordinarily be that, for any z, y is normally distributed about $\alpha + \beta z$ with constant variance σ^2. If σ^2 is unknown then it will need to be included with α and β in θ.

Two types of inference statement are ordinarily made about θ: estimation and testing. The main distinction being that in testing some values of θ are singled out for special consideration, whereas in estimation all values of θ are treated equally. In the regression example, the hypothesis may be made that z does not affect y in the sense that $\beta = 0$. It would then be usual to test the hypothesis $\beta = 0$. In estimation, on the other hand, $\beta = 0$ plays no special role and the reasonable values of β on the basis of x are required. Estimation takes two forms, point and interval. In the former θ is estimated by a single number, the point estimate; or in the multidimensional case by a set of numbers. In the latter an interval, or region, of values of θ which are reasonably supported by the data is given. In the regression example

$$b = \sum (y_i - y_.)(z_i - z_.) \Big/ \sum (z_i - z_.)^2$$

is the least-squares point estimate of β, $y_.$ and $z_.$ being the means of the y- and z-values respectively. An interval estimate would be of the form $b \pm ts$, where s is the standard deviation evaluated from the data and t is the value obtained from Student's t-distribution. Point estimates are usually inadequate because they do not include any expression of the uncertainty that exists about the parameter: interval estimates are much to be preferred and usually, as in the regression case, start with the point estimate b and construct the interval about it. Interval estimates and tests are often related by the fact that the interval contains those parameter values which would not be judged significant were a test of that value to be carried out.

There is no general agreement on how statistical inference should be performed though, in some common situations, there is good agreement about the numerical results. It is possible to recognize three main schools named after Fisher; Neyman, Pearson and Wald (NPW); and Bayes.

The Fisherian school is the least formalized and is the one most favoured by scientists, especially those on the biological side, in medicine and agriculture. Because of its lack of a strict mathematical structure it is the hardest to describe succinctly, yet, because of this it is often the easiest to use. The name is entirely apposite since it is essentially the creation of one man, R.A. Fisher (1925, 1935). Estimation is based on the log-likelihood function $L(\theta) = \log p(x|\theta)$. Here $p(x|\theta)$, the probability of data x given parameter θ, is considered as a function of θ for the observed values of the data, now considered as fixed. A point estimate of θ is provided by the maximum likelihood value $\hat{\theta}$, that maximizes, over θ, $L(\theta)$. The precision of $\hat{\theta}$ can be found using minus the second derivative of $L(\theta)$ at $\hat{\theta}$. An interval estimate is then of the form $\hat{\theta} \pm s$, where s depends on the measure of precision. Extensions to the multidimensional case are readily available and, although cases are known where the method is unsatisfactory, it often works extremely well and is deservedly popular. In the case of normal means, maximum likelihood and least-squares estimates agree. A Fisherian test of the hypothesis that θ is equal to a specified value θ_0 is found by constructing a statistic $t(x)$ from the data x and calculating the probability, were $\theta = \theta_0$, of getting the value of $t(x)$ observed, or more extreme. This probability is called the significance level: the smaller it is, the more doubt is cast on θ having the value θ_0. The best-known example is the F-test for the equality of means in an analysis of variance. It is typical of the Fisherian approach that few rules are available for the choice of the statistic $t(x)$. His genius was enough to produce reasonable answers in important cases. Often $t(x)$ is based on a point estimate of θ.

In some ways NPW is a formalized version of Fisher's approach. It has been much developed in the United States, though even there much applied work is Fisherian and it is the theoreticians who espouse NPW. There are many good expositions: for example, Lehmann (1959, 1983). Statistical inferences are thought of as decisions about θ and the merit of a decision is expressed in terms of a loss function measuring how bad the decision is when the true value is θ. If $t(x)$ is a point estimate of the real parameter θ, squared error $\{t(x)-\theta\}^2$ is the loss function ordinarily used, the loss diminishing the nearer the estimate is to the true value. In testing, the decisions are to reject or to accept the null value θ_0 being tested. The simplest loss function is zero for a correct decision and some constant, positive value for each incorrect one. The probability of rejection of $\theta=\theta_0$ when in fact it is true is typically the significance level in Fisher's approach. Having the concept of a decision and a loss function, it becomes possible to ask the question, what is the best decision (estimate or test)? The criterion used to answer this is the expected loss, the expectation being over the data values according to the probability specification $p(x\,|\,\theta)$. Thus, for point estimate $t(x)$, the expected loss is $\int\{t(x)-\theta\}^2 p(x\,|\,\theta)\,\mathrm{d}x$. The problem then is to choose $t(x)$ to minimize this function. There is a substantial difficulty in that this expected loss depends on θ, which is unknown. Consequently additional criteria have to be used in order to select the optimum decision. For example, the decisions may be restrained in some way, as when a point estimate is restricted to be unbiased. A basic result is that the only sensible decisions are those which arise from the following procedure. Select a probability distribution $p(\theta)$ for θ and minimize the expected loss obtained by averaging over both x and θ – in the point estimation case, $\iint\{t(x)-\theta\}^2 p(x\,|\,\theta)p(\theta)\,\mathrm{d}x\,\mathrm{d}\theta$. This expectation being a number, the minimization is usually possible without ambiguity. However, the choice of $p(\theta)$ remains to be made. It is important to notice that in NPW theory the distribution of θ is merely introduced as a device for producing a reasonable decision (the technical term is 'admissible') and is not necessarily held to express opinions about θ.

The third system of inference is named, quite inappropriately, after the discoverer of Bayes' theorem. Laplace was the first significant user. Inference is a passage from the special x to the general θ on the basis of a model $p(x\,|\,\theta)$ going in the opposite direction, from θ to x. In the Bayesian view, inference is similarly accomplished by a probability distribution $p(\theta\,|\,x)$ of θ, given x. The two distributions are related by Bayes' theorem, $p(\theta\,|\,x)\propto p(x\,|\,\theta)p(\theta)$, where $p(\theta)$ is a distribution for θ. NPW and Bayes are similar in their introduction of probabilities for θ. A basic difference is that the Bayesian approach recognizes $p(\theta)$ as a statement of belief about θ, and not, as does NPW, just as a technical device. With this strong statement about $p(\theta)$ both x and θ have probabilities attached and the full force of the probability calculus can be employed: in particular, to make the inference $p(\theta\,|\,x)$. Now the inference is couched, not in terms of estimates or tests, but by means of a probability distribution. If $p(\theta\,|\,x)$ is centred around $t(x)$, say as its mean, then $t(x)$ may be conveniently thought of as a point estimate of θ. If θ_0 is of special interest $p(\theta_0|x)$ may be used as a test of the hypothesis that $\theta=\theta_0$. But the full inference is the distribution $p(\theta\,|\,x)$. Consequently, once the big step of introducing $p(\theta)$ has been made, the inference problem is solved by use of the probability calculus: no other considerations are needed. For example, typically θ is multi-dimensional $\theta=(\theta_1,\theta_2,\ldots,\theta_m)$ and only a few parameters are of interest, the remainder are called nuisance parameters. If only θ_1 matters, inferences about it are easily made by the marginal distribution $p(\theta_1|x)$ found by integrating out the nuisance parameters from $p(\theta\,|\,x)$. The regression example above for slope β(α and σ^2 being nuisance) provides an illustration.

Until World War I, Bayesian and non-Bayesian views had alternated in popularity, but the work of R.A. Fisher was so influential that it led to an almost complete suppression of the Bayesian view, which was reinforced by the work of Neyman, Pearson and Wald. Savage (1954) renewed interest in the Bayesian approach by providing it with its axiomatic structure, following Ramsey (1931) whose original ideas had lain unappreciated. Savage was much influenced by the work of de Finetti (his most accessible work is 1974/5) who provided a new view of probability that has had considerable impact upon subsequent thinking. Today the three disciplines lie uneasily together.

The Bayesian approach is the most formalized of the three inferential methods because everything is expressed within the single framework of the probability calculus, which is itself very well formalized. It has been relatively little used largely because of the perceived difficulty of assigning a distribution to θ. An important property of this method is that it is easily extended to include decision-making. As with NPW theory, a class of decisions d is introduced together with a loss function $\ell(d,\theta)$ expressing the loss in selecting d when θ obtains, and choosing that decision d that minimizes the expected (over θ) loss $\int\ell(d,\theta)p(\theta\,|\,x)\,\mathrm{d}\theta$, using the inference $p(\theta\,|\,x)$. (This is in contrast to the NPW approach, using the expectation over x.)

There are two basic differences between the Bayesian paradigm and the other two. These concern the logical structure, and the likelihood principle. Both the Fisherian and NPW paradigms tackle an inference problem by thinking of several, apparently sensible procedures, investigating their properties and choosing that procedure which overall has the best properties. Fisher's work on maximum likelihood and its demonstrated superiority to the method of moments provides an example. In neither of these approaches are there general procedures: for example, there is no way known of constructing an interval estimate. Within NPW, Wald did introduce the minimax principle but it is generally unsatisfactory in the inference context and has not been used in practice. Against this, the techniques that are available, like maximum likelihood and analysis of variance, are easy to use and interpret (though the interpretation is often wrong: see equations (1) and (2) below). The lack of a formal structure has enabled statisticians to extemporize and come up with valuable concepts and techniques that are of substantial practical value though sometimes with weak justifications. The Bayesian paradigm proceeds differently. It begins by laying down reasonable, elementary properties to be demanded of an inference and then, by deduction, discovers which procedures have these properties. In that sense it is the complete opposite of the Fisherian and NPW views that start with the procedures. It is the method used in other branches of mathematics where the basic properties provide the axioms for the subsequent, logical development. Though there are important variants, all the axiom systems proposed lead to the result that the only inference procedures satisfying them are those that use probability: that the only sensible inference for θ, given x, is a probability statement about θ, given x. The Bayesian position is therefore a deduction from simple requirements about our inferences. NPW comes near to recognizing this in its technical introduction of $p(\theta)$. The Fisherian view never addresses the problem.

The second difference between the Bayesian and other views involves the likelihood principle. The model provides $p(x\,|\,\theta)$ which, for fixed θ, is a probability for x. Considered as a function of θ for fixed x, it is called the likelihood for θ (given x). It was an important contribution of Fisher's to emphasize the distinction between the probability and likelihood aspects, and to show us, for example, in the maximum likelihood estimate, the importance of the likelihood function. However, Fisher did not consider the likelihood to be the only tool for inference. In a significance test, based on a statistic $t(x)$, he used the significance level, which is an integral over values of x giving more extreme values to t than that observed, for the tested value θ_0. Clearly this cannot be calculated from the likelihood function which holds x fixed and varies θ. NPW uses the expected (over x) loss and therefore does not use the likelihood function. On the other hand, the only feature of the data used in a Bayesian procedure is the likelihood, supplementing it with the distribution for θ. The likelihood principle says that if two data sets, x and y, have the same likelihood, then the inferences from x and y should be the same. Most statistical procedures in common use today violate the principle, but Bayesian procedures do not. The latter part of that statement is clearly true from Bayes' theorem which, in order to calculate the inference, uses only the likelihood. Here is an example of its violation when an unbiased estimate is used.

Given θ, x is a random sample from a population in which each value is either 1 or 0 with probabilities θ and $1-\theta$. In one case the sample is selected to be of size n and r of the values are found to be 1. In the second case, r is chosen and the population sampled until r 1's have been observed, the total sample being of size n. In each case the likelihood is $\theta^r(1-\theta)^{n-r}$ and so, by the likelihood principle, the inferences should be the same. However, in the first case the unbiased estimate of θ based on (r, n) is the familiar r/n: in the second case it is $(r-1)/(n-1)$. Significance tests of $\theta=\frac{1}{2}$ say are different in the two cases because 'more extreme' in one case means more extreme values of r for fixed n, and in the other more extreme values of n for fixed r. There are many impressive arguments in favour of the likelihood principle, even outside the Bayesian paradigm, yet it is not accepted by most statisticians and almost all inferential procedures used today violate it: maximum likelihood estimation is the obvious exception.

There is another interesting consequence of the axiomatic, Bayesian approach leading to the probabilistic form of inference, and that is that any non-probabilistic inference will somewhere violate the basic properties set out in the axioms. Indeed, it is true that every non-Bayesian procedure has a counter-example where it behaves in an absurd fashion. In illustration let $(l(x), u(x))$ be a confidence interval for θ at level α based on data x. The precise meaning of this is that

$$p(l(x)<\theta<u(x)\,|\,\theta)=\alpha, \qquad \text{for all } \theta. \tag{1}$$

Notice that this is a probability statement about x, given θ, based on $p(x\,|\,\theta)$. In words, the probability that the random interval $(l(x), u(x))$ contains θ is α, for all given θ. It is easy to produce examples for x in which the interval is the whole line; $l(x)=-\infty$, $u(x)=+\infty$, and $\alpha=0.95$. Here we are 95 per cent confident that θ is real. This is absurd in the case of the observed x, although it is true that for 95 per cent of x's the statement will be true. Contrast this with the Bayesian statement that

$$p(l(x)<\theta<u(x)\,|\,x)=\alpha, \qquad \text{for all } x, \tag{2}$$

based on $p(\theta|x)$. This is about θ, given x: in words, the probability is α that θ lies between $l(x)$ and $u(x)$. Clearly, with $\alpha<1$, it could never happen that the interval is the whole real line.

A key ingredient in any form of inference is clearly probability, whose laws are well understood. But there is considerable dispute over the interpretation of probability: disputes which have practical consequences. There are two broad groups: subjective and frequentist views. In the subjective view, a probability is an expression of the subject's belief. Thus (2) expresses a belief that θ lies between the numbers $l(x)$ and $u(x)$. In the frequentist view, probabilities are related to observed frequencies. Thus (1) says that the frequency with which the interval contains θ is α. The latter are objective, in the sense that the frequencies can be objectively observed by all subjects. The great majority of statisticians today adopt the frequency view, claiming an objectivity for their methods. Most Bayesians hold to the subjective approach, claiming that economists have to express beliefs about the system they are discussing. It is undoubtably true that many users of statistics think of the frequency statements, like (1), as belief statements, like (2). It had been thought that the two views were opposites but de Finetti showed that the frequentist view of probability is a special case of the subjective view, namely when the data are believed to be exchangeable. The values $x_1, x_2, \ldots, x_n$ are exchangeable if their probability distribution is invariant under permutation of the x's. A random sample from a population would ordinarily be judged to possess this invariance. The case mentioned earlier where each x_i is either 1 or 0, with probabilities θ and $1-\theta$ respectively, is the standard example. Here θ is a frequency probability, or chance, about which there are beliefs $p(\theta)$ changed by the data x to new beliefs $p(\theta\,|\,x)$.

Resistance to the Bayesian approach and subjective probability has centred around the genuine difficulty of assessing beliefs, especially when there is little knowledge of the parameter. Rather than face the formidable, and perhaps impossible, task of measuring belief, statisticians have concentrated on frequentist methods, sometimes ignoring their defects. A related difficulty with the subjective approach is the lack of objectivity in the sense that two subjects may, on the basis of the same data, have different beliefs. The Bayesian response is that this reflects reality and if each economist were to express all his beliefs probabilistically, we would have a clearer appreciation of the situation; and, in any case, different beliefs come together with increasing amounts of data. This is why observational studies are so important. Economics is predominantly frequentist but does have a substantial school, particularly in econometrics, of the Bayesian persuasion. The close connection between that view and decision-making makes it more attractive to the economist than to the laboratory scientist who sees himself as acquiring knowledge, not making decisions.

Inference that is statistical, involving repetition, is naturally allied to the frequency view: whereas inference, in general, has no frequency basis. But de Finetti's observation connecting exchangeability (which is essentially a finite, frequentist property) with subjectivity shows that the Bayesian view

Steindl, Josef (born 1912). Steindl was born in Vienna on 14 April 1912. He studied economics in Vienna and received his PhD working under Richard Strigl. He worked in the Austrian Institute for Economic Research (AIER) from 1935 to 1938, the year of his emigration to England. He was a lecturer at Balliol College, Oxford, from 1938 to 1941, and then a research worker at the Oxford Institute of Statistics. He worked there with Michal Kalecki, who left a lasting mark on his theoretical work. He returned to Austria in 1950. He was barred from teaching at the University of Vienna for ideological reasons and resumed his job at AIER, where he worked until his retirement in 1978. In 1970, however, the University of Vienna bestowed upon him a honorary professorship. He was visiting professor at Stanford University in 1974/5.

Steindl dealt with the economic problems of the size of firms (1945) and of the distribution of firms according to size (1965a). He explained the pattern of size distribution of firms by means of random processes (birth and death processes). Other fields of interest were education (1965b) and technology (e.g. 1980).

However, the research which secured him a permanent place in economics has been his work on the development and the present phase of capitalist economies. His main work (1952) deals with the tendency to stagnation of the mature capitalist economy. His point of departure was that oligopoly leads to increased profit margins and consequently to a fall in effective demand. The ensuing decline in the degree of capacity utilization causes *ceteris paribus* a lower level of investment and a decline in the rate of growth in mature capitalist economies. The slowing down of capital growth reduces further the utilization of capacity and leads to a cumulative process of declining growth. Steindl thus treats the utilization parameter differently from Kalecki, for whom it is a purely passive variable. Another difference consists in the explanation of the growth trend of the capitalist economy without having recourse to exogenous factors like innovations.

Maturity and Stagnation in American Capitalism was largely ignored during the period of high employment and intensive growth. Only in recent times, when the old weaknesses of unemployment and stagnation have reappeared, has the book aroused wider interest and proved its lasting significance. The evolution of his ideas is shown in the introduction to (1976) and in the penetrating analysis both of present economic trends (e.g. 1979, 1985a and 1985b) and of the present state of economics (1984).

K. Laski

See also STAGNATION.

SELECTED WORKS

1945. *Small and Big Business: Economic Problems of the Size of Firms*. Oxford: Basil Blackwell.

1952. *Maturity and Stagnation in American Capitalism*. Oxford: Basil Blackwell. Republished, New York: Monthly Review Press, 1976.

1965a. *Random Processes and the Growth of Firms: A Study of the Pareto Law*. London: Griffin.

1965b. The role of manpower requirement in the educational planning experience of the Austrian EIP. In *Manpower Forecasting in Educational Planning*, Paris: OECD.

1979. Stagnation theory and stagnation policy. *Cambridge Journal of Economics* 3(1), March, 1–14.

1980. Technical progress and evolution. In *Research, Development and Technological Innovation*, ed. D. Sahal, Lexington, Mass.: Lexington Books.

1981. Ideas and concepts of long run growth. *Banca Nazionale del Lavoro Quarterly Review* 136, March, 35–48.

1982. The role of household savings in the modern economy. *Banca Nazionale del Lavoro Quarterly Review* 140, March, 69–88.

1984. Reflections on the present state of economics. *Banca Nazionale del Lavoro Quarterly Review* 148, March, 3–14.

1985a. Distribution and accumulation. *Political Economy Studies in the Surplus Approach* 1(1), April.

1985b. Structural problems in the present crisis. *Banca Nazionale del Lavoro Quarterly Review* 154, September, 223–32.

Stephen, Leslie. (1832–1904). Stephen was born in London on 28 November 1832 and died there on 21 February 1904. He was educated at Eton, King's College London, and Trinity Hall, Cambridge, where he graduated as twentieth Wrangler in 1854. After holding a Fellowship at Trinity Hall from 1854 to 1867, he worked in London as a literary journalist and freelance man of letters. He edited the *Cornhill Magazine* from 1871 to 1882, and was the first editor of the *Dictionary of National Biography* from 1882 to 1891.

Though he published no substantial work on the theory of political economy, it was a subject in which he took an enduring interest, beginning with his undergraduate days when he and his close friend Henry Fawcett thoroughly absorbed Mill's *Principles*, and continuing through his membership of the Political Economy Club. An orthodox Millian conception of the discipline is evident in his political journalism of the 1860s and 1870s, and his one extended essay on the subject ('The Sphere of Political Economy', first given as a popular lecture and published in a collection of such lectures in 1896) reaffirmed his commitment to what was by then a distinctly old-fashioned position, particularly in its assumption that the premises of political economy consisted of descriptive laws of universal human behaviour, as well as in its conviction that sound economic reasoning issued in a narrowly individualist conclusion about the role of the state. The so-called 'marginalist revolution' of the 1870s and the arguments of the Historical School and of the Socialists in the 1880s and 1890s seem to have left little impression on his conception of the subject.

Stephen's most significant contribution was his historical account of the place of classical political economy in the Utilitarian tradition. His *Life of Henry Fawcett* (1885) contains a particularly revealing exploration of the beliefs and sensibilities underlying the economic views of his generation of Mill's disciples at Cambridge. Above all, his classic study of *The English Utilitarians* (1900), in which he discussed the economic theories of Ricardo, the Mills and several other early 19th-century political economists, was particularly influential in propagating the idea of an intrinsic, and not merely historically contingent, relation between classical political economy and the moral and political theory of Utilitarianism.

Stefan Collini

SELECTED WORKS

1885. *The Life of Henry Fawcett*. London: Smith, Elder & Co.

1896. The sphere of political economy. In *Social Rights and Duties*, 2 vols, London: Swan Sonnenschein.

1900. *The English Utilitarians*. 3 vols, London: Duckworth & Co.

Steuart, Sir James (1713–1780). James Steuart, the Scottish political economist, was born in Edinburgh on 10 October 1713. He was the only son of Sir James Steuart, Bart., Solicitor General of Scotland and a Member of the London Parliament after the Union.

Steuart succeeded to his father's title in 1727 and after travels on the Continent between 1735 and 1740, where he

Steindl, Josef (born 1912). Steindl was born in Vienna on 14 April 1912. He studied economics in Vienna and received his PhD working under Richard Strigl. He worked in the Austrian Institute for Economic Research (AIER) from 1935 to 1938, the year of his emigration to England. He was a lecturer at Balliol College, Oxford, from 1938 to 1941, and then a research worker at the Oxford Institute of Statistics. He worked there with Michal Kalecki, who left a lasting mark on his theoretical work. He returned to Austria in 1950. He was barred from teaching at the University of Vienna for ideological reasons and resumed his job at AIER, where he worked until his retirement in 1978. In 1970, however, the University of Vienna bestowed upon him a honorary professorship. He was visiting professor at Stanford University in 1974/5.

Steindl dealt with the economic problems of the size of firms (1945) and of the distribution of firms according to size (1965a). He explained the pattern of size distribution of firms by means of random processes (birth and death processes). Other fields of interest were education (1967) and technology (e.g. 1980).

However, the research which secured him a permanent place in economics has been his work on the development and the present phase of capitalist economies. His main work (1952) deals with the tendency to stagnation of the mature capitalist economy. His point of departure was that oligopoly leads to increased profit margins and consequently to a fall in effective demand. The ensuing decline in the degree of capacity utilization causes *ceteris paribus* a lower level of investment and a decline in the rate of growth in mature capitalist economies. The slowing down of capital growth reduces further the utilization of capacity and leads to a cumulative process of declining growth. Steindl thus treats the utilization parameter differently from Kalecki, for whom it is a purely passive variable. Another difference consists in the explanation of the growth trend of the capitalist economy without having recourse to exogenous factors like innovations.

Maturity and Stagnation in American Capitalism was largely ignored during the period of high employment and intensive growth. Only in recent times, when the old weaknesses of unemployment and stagnation have reappeared, has the book aroused wider interest and proved its lasting significance. The evolution of his ideas is shown in the introduction to (1976) and in the penetrating analysis both of present economic trends (e.g. 1979, 1985a and 1985b) and of the present state of economics (1984).

K. Laski

See also STAGNATION.

SELECTED WORKS

1945. *Small and Big Business: Economic Problems of the Size of Firms.* Oxford: Basil Blackwell.

1952. *Maturity and Stagnation in American Capitalism.* Oxford: Basil Blackwell. Republished, New York: Monthly Review Press, 1976.

1965a. *Random Processes and the Growth of Firms: A Study of the Pareto Law.* London: Griffin.

1965b. The role of manpower requirement in the educational planning experience of the Austrian EIP. In *Manpower Forecasting in Educational Planning*, Paris: OECD.

1979. Stagnation theory and stagnation policy. *Cambridge Journal of Economics* 3(1), March, 1–14.

1980. Technical progress and evolution. In *Research, Development and Technological Innovation*, ed. D. Sahal, Lexington, Mass.: Lexington Books.

1981. Ideas and concepts of long run growth. *Banca Nazionale del Lavoro Quarterly Review* 136, March, 35–48.

1982. The role of household savings in the modern economy. *Banca Nazionale del Lavoro Quarterly Review* 140, March, 69–88.

1984. Reflections on the present state of economics. *Banca Nazionale del Lavoro Quarterly Review* 148, March, 3–14.

1985a. Distribution and accumulation. *Political Economy Studies in the Surplus Approach* 1(1), April.

1985b. Structural problems in the present crisis. *Banca Nazionale del Lavoro Quarterly Review* 154, September, 223–32.

Stephen, Leslie. (1832–1904). Stephen was born in London on 28 November 1832 and died there on 21 February 1904. He was educated at Eton, King's College London, and Trinity Hall, Cambridge, where he graduated as twentieth Wrangler in 1854. After holding a Fellowship at Trinity Hall from 1854 to 1867, he worked in London as a literary journalist and freelance man of letters. He edited the *Cornhill Magazine* from 1871 to 1882, and was the first editor of the *Dictionary of National Biography* from 1882 to 1891.

Though he published no substantial work on the theory of political economy, it was a subject in which he took an enduring interest, beginning with his undergraduate days when he and his close friend Henry Fawcett thoroughly absorbed Mill's *Principles*, and continuing through his membership of the Political Economy Club. An orthodox Millian conception of the discipline is evident in his political journalism of the 1860s and 1870s, and his one extended essay on the subject ('The Sphere of Political Economy', first given as a popular lecture and published in a collection of such lectures in 1896) reaffirmed his commitment to what was by then a distinctly old-fashioned position, particularly in its assumption that the premises of political economy consisted of descriptive laws of universal human behaviour, as well as in its conviction that sound economic reasoning issued in a narrowly individualist conclusion about the role of the state. The so-called 'marginalist revolution' of the 1870s and the arguments of the Historical School and of the Socialists in the 1880s and 1890s seem to have left little impression on his conception of the subject.

Stephen's most significant contribution was his historical account of the place of classical political economy in the Utilitarian tradition. His *Life of Henry Fawcett* (1885) contains a particularly revealing exploration of the beliefs and sensibilities underlying the economic views of his generation of Mill's disciples at Cambridge. Above all, his classic study of *The English Utilitarians* (1900), in which he discussed the economic theories of Ricardo, the Mills and several other early 19th-century political economists, was particularly influential in propagating the idea of an intrinsic, and not merely historically contingent, relation between classical political economy and the moral and political theory of Utilitarianism.

Stefan Collini

SELECTED WORKS

1885. *The Life of Henry Fawcett.* London: Smith, Elder & Co.

1896. The sphere of political economy. In *Social Rights and Duties*, 2 vols, London: Swan Sonnenschein.

1900. *The English Utilitarians.* 3 vols, London: Duckworth & Co.

Steuart, Sir James (1713–1780). James Steuart, the Scottish political economist, was born in Edinburgh on 10 October 1713. He was the only son of Sir James Steuart, Bart., Solicitor General of Scotland and a Member of the London Parliament after the Union.

Steuart succeeded to his father's title in 1727 and after travels on the Continent between 1735 and 1740, where he met the Stuart Pretenders to the English throne, he became a leading advocate of a Jacobite Restoration, and a contemporary has even suggested that he might have become 'the first man in the State' if this had succeeded. He helped to draft Prince Charles Edward's manifestos in 1745, 'had a hand in everything', and was a Member of his Council. He was sent to Paris just before the Pretender's abortive march to Derby with a brief to negotiate full-scale assistance from the French. After the destruction of the Stuart army at Culloden, he was obliged to live abroad until 1763. Shortly after his return from exile, he published his two-volume, 1300-page *An Inquiry into the Principles of Political Oeconomy* (1767) on which his reputation as a political economist rests.

His role in the 1745 Rebellion was finally pardoned (with the assistance of Lord Bute) in 1771. This allowed him to be presented at Court in 1772, and to become an adviser to the East India Company, for whom he wrote *The Principles of Money Applied to the State of the Coin in Bengal* (1772). He inherited further estates in 1773 on condition that he add Denham to his name, with the result that his entry in the *Dictionary of National Biography* and in several library catalogues is as Denham, Sir James Steuart, or else as, Denham-Steuart, Sir James, which is how he signed himself after 1773. He died on 26 November 1780.

To economists he has always been Sir James Steuart, because that is how he appears on the title page of his 1767 book. This is subtitled, *An Essay on the Science of Domestic Policy in Free Nations, in which are particularly considered, Population, Agriculture, Trade Industry, Money, Coin, Interest, Circulation, Banks, Exchange, Public Credit and Taxes*. It offers a detailed, comprehensive and often original account of the application of economic argument to this enormous range of questions.

The population theory with which the book opens anticipates much that Malthus went on to say, and Marx even suggested in the first volume of *Capital* that, 'admirers of Malthus do not even know that the first edition of the latter's work on population contains, except in the purely declamatory part, very little but excerpts from Steuart' (Marx [1867], 1974, p. 333).

His analysis of the balance of payments has also been much admired. He went considerably further than Hume by incorporating a detailed analysis of the capital account, and this led him to the conclusion (among several where he differs from Hume) that a country with a persistent capital account deficit will be unable to find an equilibrium price level at which specie flows cease.

Steuart's travels on the Continent during his 18 years of exile from 1745 to 1763 acquainted him with monetary developments in Paris and Amsterdam, and this enriched his theoretical and empirical chapters on money and banking. But it is his analysis of economic policy which has attracted most 20th-century attention. The contrast between his analysis and Smith's in *The Wealth of Nations* published just nine years later is especially marked. Steuart's years of exile had given him a detailed knowledge of economic and financial policy on the Continent, and in particular in France, Germany and Holland, and he advocated a degree of state intervention into every aspect of economic life, which contrasted sharply with the principles that Smith enunciated. Skinner (1981) has suggested that it was precisely Steuart's long years of residence on the Continent that led him to evolve a 'system' which was so much more dirigiste than that of his great Scottish contemporary.

In his book, Steuart offers extensive and detailed advice to an idealized statesman, who is assumed to possess unlimited knowledge and whose 'inclinations are always to be virtuous and benevolent' (1966, p. 333) Steuart believed that markets do not clear, and this was especially the case with the labour market, where there was always liable to be an imbalance between 'demand' and the supply of 'work'. Manufacturers, merchants and workers sought to 'consolidate' any high living standards they temporarily achieved into permanently higher incomes, and they often achieved this by restricting competition. Once prices and wages were consolidated at high levels, employment necessarily suffered as soon as foreign manufacturers began to produce more cheaply. With these assumptions about the behaviour of workers and entrepreneurs, and the impotence or non-existence of corrective market forces, there was an extensive range of policies through which state intervention could be expected to increase wealth, welfare and employment.

As soon as domestic production became overpriced, imports would undermine domestic employment and the creation of wealth, and Steuart therefore proposed that 'a branch of trade should be cut off' where the Statesman shall find, 'upon examining the whole chain of consequences,... the nation's wealth not at all increased, nor her trade encouraged, in proportion to the damage at first incurred by the importation' (1966. p. 293).

In addition to protecting industry against imports, Steuart advocated export subsidies, because he saw the alternative to, for instance, subsidizing exports of fish by £250,000 so that what cost £1,000,000 could be sold overseas for £750,000, as the total loss of the £750,000 of potential domestic output. Without the subsidy,

> those employed in the fishery will starve; ... the fish taken will either remain upon hand, or be sold by the proprietors at a great loss; they will be undone, and the nation for the future will lose the acquisition of £750,000 a year (1966, pp. 256–7).

Steuart was also concerned that as industry and population grew, the price of subsistence would rise as the population forced farming onto inferior land, where 'the progress of agriculture demands an additional expence'. In order to 'preserve the intrinsic value of goods at the same standard as formerly; [the Statesman] must assist agriculture with his purse, in order that exportation may not be discouraged' (1966, p. 200).

As well as seeking to avert the influence of agricultural diminishing returns by subsidizing agriculture in order to keep export costs down, Steuart actually proposed the setting up of a 'policy of grain' in 'the Common Markets of England', where the government would buy up all the grain that farmers were prepared to produce at 'the minimum price expedient for the farmers', and sell all that could be marketed at 'the maximum price expedient for the wage-earners', and store any excess in state granaries. Steuart actually drafted this anticipation of the European Economic Community's agricultural policies of the 1970s and the 1980s in 1759 while he was in exile in Tübingen.

Steuart also anticipated post-World War II industrial policies, for he argued that a Statesman should not hesitate to intervene directly in the finance and management of any new undertaking where he saw economic potential, and should

> inquire into the capacity of those at the head of it; order their projects to be laid before him; and when he finds them reasonable and well planned, he ought to take unforeseen losses upon himself ... the more care and expence he is at in setting the undertaking on foot, the more he has a right to direct the prosecution of it towards the general good (1966, p. 391).

Steuart was a powerful advocate of public works to create employment whenever there was an excess supply of labour. The government should always finance the employment of 'the deserving and the poor', and they should be employed to extend a nation's social and economic infrastructure rather than for unproductive purposes:

> If a thousand pounds are bestowed upon making a firework, a number of people are thereby employed, and gain a temporary livelihood. If the same sum is bestowed for making a canal for watering the fields of a province, a like number of people may reap the same benefit, and hitherto accounts stand even; but the firework played off, what remains, but the smoke and stink of the powder? Whereas the consequence of the canal is a perpetual fertility to a formerly barren soil (1767, vol. I, p. 519).

All these interventionist policies needed to be financed, and Steuart actually welcomed the high taxation this would entail. He argued that taxes redistribute income and wealth and create employment, for they, 'advance the public good, by drawing from the rich, a fund sufficient to employ both the *deserving* and the *poor* in the service of the state' (1767, vol. I, pp. 512–3). They also increase the power and prestige of the Statesman, for 'By taxes the Statesman is enriched, and by means of his wealth, he is enabled to keep his subjects in awe, and to preserve his dignity and consideration' (1966, p. 304). Economists who believe in the efficacy of market forces have often been concerned that high taxation may have adverse supply-side effects, but Steuart actually believed that taxation would often have *favourable* supply-side effects. High taxes 'may discourage idleness; and idleness will not be totally rooted out, until people be forced, in one way or other, to give up superfluity and days of recreation ... When the hands employed are not diligent, the best expedient is to raise the price of their subsistence by taxing it' (1966, 691–5). Steuart was aware that this analysis of the social and economic benefits from high taxation would not be popular with his contemporaries, and that 'the politics of my closet is very different from those of the century in which I live', but he comforted himself with the though that 'reason is reason', and that in another century these startling opinions would be acknowledged as correct (1767, vol. I, p. 514).

Steuart's industrial policies amount (as Eltis (1986) has suggested) to the setting up of a corporate state with a social contract between producers who are protected against foreign competition and whose employment is guaranteed, and the state to whom they pay high taxes. Some of these are then returned to inefficient producers, while the rest furthers the state's social and political objectives.

In addition to welcoming high taxation as a tool for the finance of industrial policies, Steuart was an advocate of state banks which would issue paper money. By making money less scarce, he believed that they would reduce interest rates and so benefit industry and commerce. He argued that John Law's Mississippi Scheme could have been successful in France with only a few minor modifications in the manner it was set up and administered, and that this could have established the long-term rate of interest at 2 per cent in France.

The many kinds of government expenditure Steuart so strongly advocated could also be financed through borrowing, and here again Steuart was ahead of his time. He believed that in the limit, whatever a government could raise from taxation could be devoted to the payment of interest on public debt so that at a 5 per cent rate of interest, governments could borrow 20 times their tax revenues:

> If no check be put on the augmentation of public debts, if they be allowed constantly to accumulate, and if the spirit of a nation can patiently submit to the natural consequences of such a plan, it must end in this, that all property, that is income, will be swallowed up in taxes; and these will be transferred to the creditors.

But even that state of affairs where all property income is paid as interest to those who have lent to the government does not represent the limit of the state's power to borrow. It can go on to tax the recipients of debt interest and so provide the wherewithall to finance still further borrowing, for these taxes 'may be mortgaged again to a new set of men, who will retain the denomination of creditors' (1767, vol. II, pp. 633–4). Some may doubt that governments can at the same time continue to borrow, and defraud those from whom they borrowed in the past by taxing away their interest so that this provides the finance for still further borrowing. Won't there be a refusal to go on lending to such governments? No, opines Steuart, because 'The prospect of a second revolution of the same kind with the first would be very distant; and in matters of credit, which are constantly exposed to risk, such events being beyond the reach of calculation, are never taken into any man's account who has money to lend' (1966, p. 647). Hence Steuart was perceptive enough to appreciate that sovereigns (and sovereign governments) can continually defraud their creditors, while new lenders will still queue up to be defrauded because the prospect of this will be so distant and problematical that it has a negligible influence on the immediate willingness to lend.

Steuart's book was well received at first, but Smith, who believed that economies would make full use of their labour and capital in the complete absence of government-inspired employment policies, and at the same time wholly distrusted the omniscience and benevolence of governments, greatly weakened Steuart's reputation as a serious economist by totally ignoring the existence of his book in *The Wealth of Nations*. Four years before its publication, he wrote that 'Without once mentioning [Steuart's book], I flatter myself, that every false principle in it, will meet with a clear and distinct confutation in mine' (1977, p. 164).

In the 19th century Marx gave Steuart his due, and there are 13 references to him in the first volume of *Capital*. Several 19th-century German economists have compared Steuart's historical and institutional approach to political economy favourably with Smith's deductive methodology, but most accolades to the richness and originality of Steuart's contribution only emerged after the Keynesian revolution.

His monetary and employment theory have been much praised, most comprehensively by Vickers (1959), though Hutchison (1978) and Schumpeter (1954) have also recognized his Keynesian anticipations. Steuart's monetary theory has much more in common with Keynes than the mere proposition that sufficient monetary expansion will reduce interest rates to 2 per cent. In Steuart's argument, money expenditure is not closely linked to the money supply, for idle balances will often be freely held, and the price level depends upon

> demand and competition ... Let the specie of a country,... be augmented or diminished, in ever so great a proportion, commodities will still rise and fall according to the principles of demand and competition... Let the quantity of coin be ever so much increased, it is the desire of spending it alone which will raise prices (1966, 344–5).

But Steuart's monetary and employment theory describe only

one element of his thought which has anticipated modern developments. S.R. Sen, the distinguished Indian economic planner who published an important book on Steuart in 1957, commended him as 'the first Economic Adviser to the Government of India', praised his case for detailed intervention into every aspect of economic life and suggested that 'it would not be any great exaggeration to say that A.P. Lerner's chapter on functional finance seems almost a paraphrase of Steuart' (Sen, 1957, p. 122). Twenty years later, Akhtar (1979), of the New York Federal Reserve Bank restated Steuart in thirty equations, and compared his growth theory favourably with Smith's.

The classical counter-revolution of the 1980s has, of course, challenged the case for detailed state intervention which became so fashionable after the Keynesian revolution, and Steuart's dirigisme has been criticized by Anderson and Tollison (1984). It will be evident that there has been a more extensive response to the interventionist political economy of Sir James Steuart in the 20th century than there was in his own time.

WALTER ELTIS

SELECTED WORKS

1767. *An Inquiry into the Principles of Political Oeconomy: being an Essay on the Science of Domestic Policy in Free Nations*. 2 vols. London.

1805. *Works, Political, Metaphysical and Chronological*. 6 vols, ed. General Sir James Steuart. London.

1842. Memoir of St James Steuart-Denham, Bart., of Coltness and Westfield, MDCCXIII–MDCCLXXX, Compiled for the Lady Frances Steuart, His Disconsolate Widow. *The Coltness Collections*. Printed for the Maitland Club.

1966. *An Inquiry into the Principles of Political Oeconomy*. (Abbreviated) 2 vols. Edited with an introduction by Andrew S. Skinner, Edinburgh: Oliver & Boyd for the The Scottish Economic Society.

BIBLIOGRAPHY

Akhtar, M.A. 1978. Steuart on Growth. *Scottish Journal of Political Economy* 25, February, 57–74.

Akhtar, M.A. 1979. An analytical outline of Sir James Steuart's macroeconomic model. *Oxford Economic Papers* 31, July, 283–302.

Anderson, G.M. and Tollison, R.B. 1984. Sir James Steuart as the apotheosis of mercantilism and his relation to Adam Smith. *Southern Economic Journal* 51, October, 456–68.

Chamley, P. 1965. *Documents relatifs à Sir James Steuart*. Paris: Dalloz.

Eltis, W. 1986. Sir James Steuart's corporate state. In *Ideas in Economics* (The Proceedings of the 1985 Meeting of Section F of the British Association), ed. R.D.C. Black, London: Macmillan.

Hutchison, T.W. 1978. *On Revolutions and Progress in Economic Knowledge*. Cambridge: Cambridge University Press.

Marx, K. 1867. *Capital*. Moscow: Progress Publishers for Lawrence & Wishart, 1974.

Schumpeter, J.A. 1954. *History of Economic Analysis*. New York: Oxford University Press.

Sen, S.R. 1957. *The Economics of Sir James Steuart*. London: Bell.

Skinner, A.S. 1966a. Biographical Sketch. In Steuart (1966).

Skinner, A.S. 1966b. Analytical Introduction. In Steuart (1966).

Skinner, A.S. 1981. Sir James Steuart: author of a system. *Scottish Journal of Political Economy* 28, 20–42.

Smith, Adam. 1977. *The Correspondence of Adam Smith*. Ed. E.C. Mossner and I.S. Ross, Oxford: Oxford University Press.

Vickers, D. 1959. *Studies in the Theory of Money 1690–1776*. Philadelphia: Chilton.

Stewart, Dugald (1753–1828). Stewart was the most important early commentator on Adam Smith's work. He was born in Edinburgh in 1753 and died there in 1828. He was the brilliant and well-connected son of an Edinburgh professor and was destined for an academic career from the earliest age. Educated at Edinburgh and Glasgow Universities, Stewart was taught by Adam Ferguson and Thomas Reid and became a close acquaintance of Adam Smith. He was appointed to the Edinburgh Chair of Moral Philosophy on Ferguson's retirement in 1785 and held it until 1810, when ill-health forced his retirement. A charismatic and influential teacher, his vast erudition and synthetic skill was shaped by an acute sensitivity to the ideological responsibilities of the pedagogue. He was a prolific writer whose contemporary reputation was built on the first volume of his *Elements of the Philosophy of the Human Mind* (Vol. I, 1792; Vol. 2, 1815; Vol. 3, 1826) and its companion text book *Outlines of Moral Philosophy* (1793). These works circulated widely in the universities of Britain, America and the continent in the early 19th century and did much to establish Scottish Common Sense Philosophy as the most influential vehicle of elite education in the age of the American, French and Industrial Revolutions. Stewart's collected works were published posthumously in 1854–60.

Stewart's *Account of the Life and Writings of Adam Smith LL.D* (1793) was frequently republished, often as an introduction to Smith's works. He discussed the *Wealth of Nations* in relation to the *Theory of Moral Sentiments* and both in relation to Smith's abortive plan for publishing a theory of jurisprudence. At Edinburgh he lectured on the principles of government and political economy in 1800–1808 to an influential group of students who were to do much to form Whig and Tory opinion in the early 19th century. These lectures were intended for publication but the manuscript was accidentally destroyed and never rewritten. Their substance can, however, by inferred from a posthumous text which was compiled from his notes and published with his collected works.

Stewart was the first academic to detach the study of political economy from that of the theory of government and to treat each as a distinct branch of political science and it is in this methodological innovation rather than for any particular economic theory that his importance for political economy lies. His lectures were addressed to those 'who study Political Economy with a view to the improvement of the theory of legislation' (Stewart, vol. ix, p. 255). He defined political economy as the sum of 'all those speculations which have for their object the happiness and improvement of Political Society'. This, not 'the mistaken notions concerning Political Liberty which have been so widely disseminated in Europe by the writing of Mr Locke' was the only proper foundation on which a true science of government could be raised (Stewart, vol. viii, pp. 10, 23). In general, Stewart's lectures offered an intelligent, critical presentation of the arguments of the *Wealth of Nations* illuminated by occasional information about Smith's last thoughts, by a sustained and sympathetic reappraisal of the physiocrats and by a persistent preoccupation with perfectibility, progress, and the gradual improvement of the British Constitution.

NICHOLAS PHILLIPSON

SELECTED WORKS

1854–60 *The Collected Works of Dugald Stewart*. 10 vols, ed. Sir William Hamilton, Edinburgh: Thomas Constable & Co.

BIBLIOGRAPHY

Collini, S., Winch, D. and Burrow, J. 1893. *That Noble Science of Politics: a Study in Nineteenth-century Intellectual History*. Cambridge: Cambridge University Press.

Phillipson, N.T. 1983. Dugald Stewart and the pursuit of virtue in Scottish university education; Dugald Stewart and Scottish moral philosophy in the Enlightenment. In *Universities, Society and the Future*, ed. N. Phillipson, Edinburgh: Edinburgh University Press.

Stigler, George Joseph (born 1911). Born in Seattle to European immigrants (his father from Bavaria, his mother from Austro-Hungary), George Stigler attended schools there and graduated from the University of Washington in 1931. After a year at Northwestern he moved to the University of Chicago, from which he received the PhD in 1938 with his celebrated thesis on the history of neoclassical theories of production and distribution. At Chicago he was strongly influenced by three central figures of the Chicago School – Knight (his thesis supervisor), Simons and Viner – and equally so by his fellow students Milton Friedman and Allen Wallis.

His teaching career began in 1936 at Iowa State College, as it then was, where Theodore Schultz was department chairman. After two years he moved to the University of Minnesota, taking leave during the Second World War to work with the famous Statistical Research Group at Columbia, among whose members were Friedman, Wallis and Wald. From Minnesota he moved to Brown, thence in 1947 to Columbia. Finally, in 1958 he moved back to Chicago, where he has remained ever since. Professor Stigler was awarded the Nobel Memorial Prize in Economic Science in 1982.

PETER NEWMAN

Stigler as an historian of economic thought. George J. Stigler's work in the history of economic thought can be divided into five broad categories: (1) analyses of the theories of particular economists, such as Ricardo, J.S. Mill, or Stanley Jevons; (2) analysis of particular concepts, such as perfect competition or the Giffen paradox; (3) analyses of trends in the economics profession, such as the emergence of professional journals and the changing emphases of their contents; (4) considerations of the influence of economic theories on events, and vice-versa; and (5) methodological considerations, such as the meaning and role of originality, or the canons of textual exegesis. The versatility of his work in these areas has been matched by its depth and insight – and unmatched by any other historian of economic thought.

For a scholar who has written no broad, general historical survey of economics like Schumpeter's *History of Economic Analysis*, Stigler nevertheless has covered a very wide range of economists in the course of his career. His first book, *Production and Distribution Theories*, covered the formative period of neoclassical economics. His journal articles on Ricardo are landmark analyses of that special and difficult system of thought. However, it is not only the acknowledged giants of the profession who have received Stigler's attention. Stuart Wood and Henry L. Moore were also subjects of Stigler's articles, as were the Fabian socialists. Contemporary economists such as E.H. Chamberlin and John Kenneth Galbraith have also received a modest amount of Stigler's attention, though quite possibly more than they wished.

Stigler's contributions to the history of economic thought do not consist, however, in who or what he 'covered', but rather in the penetration and clarity of his analysis, and the originality of his thinking – though this originality is not announced to a blare of trumpets or a clutter of newly coined phrases. 'If we cannot associate a catchword with the man, we are inclined to deny him originality', he wrote of John Stuart Mill, who he thought deserved much more credit on this score. Finally, there is the scrupulous accuracy of his scholarship – which might be taken for granted as a matter of course, but only by those who have not done investigative reporting on footnotes.

It would be an exercise in futility to attempt to summarize Stigler's already terse analyses of the theories of particular economists, or even of such concepts as perfect competition. But his broader themes on the history of economic thought may be usefully brought together.

Originality is as good a place as any from which to start. Stigler argued that the question of originality was not a simple, naive question as to who first stated a particular proposition but, rather, who first made the idea important intellectually. With this conception of originality, Stigler implicitly disclaims the petty one-upsmanship of those who discover from a passing remark or an obscure footnote the 'real' originator of an idea developed by Adam Smith, J.M. Keynes, or others.

At the same time, Stigler does not grant originality to the first economist to make a big noise about ideas already in use, nor does he regard as more original those who called more attention to their innovations. John Stuart Mill smoothly blended his new ideas into the existing classical theories, but Stigler considered him one of the most original economists in the history of the profession, on the basis of such concepts as non-competing groups, joint products, and alternative costs.

For Stigler, it is no accident that great discoveries have many obscure 'anticipations'. It is precisely the ability to evolve a new concept out of currently familiar notions – and to get it accepted by the profession – which marks the great economist, in Stigler's view. A totally new idea would simply have little chance of being accepted, and so would remain like Gray's 'gem of purest ray serene', buried deep in the ocean. Only after the profession has evolved to the point of being ready for such an idea would someone become its historic 'originator' and any earlier economist an 'anticipator'. Cournot was perhaps the classic anticipator in this sense.

It is not clear just where and how Stigler would limit this conception of originality. At one extreme, it forces us to recognize that Newton was not the first man to see an apple fall. On the other hand, Stigler's conception would presumably imply that a very pig-headed profession would have a higher ratio of 'anticipators' to 'discoverers', since it would take many efforts to break down resistance to a new idea. And what if an 'anticipator' did not merely suggest a certain innovation but developed it more fully than its ultimate 'discoverer'? Stigler's discussion, however, seems more intended to be suggestive than definitive.

The impact of economists on events and of events on economists is another broad theme of Stigler's. The once-fashionable view that external events generally shape the development of economic theory – conditions during the Napoleonic wars giving rise to rent theories, for example, or the Great Depression to Keynesian economics – has been decisively rejected by Stigler. At the height of the industrial revolution, he noted, classical economics treated the state of technology as given. When leading economists took opposite positions on the wages-fund doctrine, both sides could not be mere reflections of surrounding conditions. The marginal utility revolution, according to Stigler, reflected no discernible environmental change.

What Stigler saw as a growing insulation of the evolution of economic analysis from surrounding events he attributed to the metamorphosis of economics from a subject pursued by isolated individuals to a cohesive profession. After economics became a full-time occupation and life-long career for many, its fundamental development reflected inward-looking concerns for logical consistency and the further improvement of a shared analytical apparatus. What is important from this disciplinary perspective need not coincide with what is important in terms of the events of the world at large. According to Stigler: 'A war may ravage a continent or destroy a generation without posing new theoretical questions.'

Just as Stigler treats the impact of immediate events on economics as exaggerated, so too he regards the impact of economists on immediate events as exaggerated. The economic purist can expect to have little effect on current policy, according to Stigler, while the more 'statesmanlike' economist, attuned to the political realities, may have a marginal influence. But, in being statesmanlike, Stigler argues, the economist surrenders his comparative advantage to others, who are at least equally attuned to those realities. It is the purist, who fights on his own ground and unfurls an unsullied banner, who has the *long-run* prospect of attracting disciples who may ultimately prevail in a changed climate of opinion. The repeal of the Corn Laws long after Ricardo's death is an example.

While Stigler's books and articles are justly renowned, there is a lesser-known genre in which he has also excelled: book reviews. Like the rest of his writings, his book reviews reflect thorough work and serious analysis – which is not to say, without humour. One review of a history of economic thought text began with a paragraph written in the same rambling and convoluted style as the book itself, and the second paragraph began: 'If the reader can wade through 508 pages of this style of writing ...'. But Stigler's reviews do not sacrifice balance to wit, and high praise is at least as common in some as devastating dismissals are in others.

Stigler's review of Schumpeter's *History of Economic Analysis* began with a salute to the author's performance of his task, followed by a question as to why anyone should undertake such a monumental task in one book. The result, according to Stigler, was such brief treatment of so many complex theories as to constitute a largely bibliographic survey of many centuries of economic thinking. Stigler's own approach was just the opposite – to take on more limited and more manageable tasks *seriatim*, building over the years a body of thorough work of wide scope and the highest quality.

THOMAS SOWELL

Stigler's contributions to microeconomics and industrial organization. George Stigler has adapted and enhanced microeconomic theory so that it can be used to analyse a wide range of real phenomena. He has been concerned as much with testing the implications of theory as with developing elegant new models. Stigler has made important substantive contributions and demonstrated the power of microeconomic theory, without making heavy use of advanced mathematical technique. He has an extraordinary ability to pose important questions clearly and to address them with exceptional economic insight and ingenuity. His prose is clear and incisive, and his wit justly famous.

In the realm of pure theory, Stigler (1939) introduced the notion that firms could decide how much flexibility to build into short-run cost functions. His formulation of the problem of minimizing the cost of obtaining a balanced diet (1945) played an important role in the early history of linear programming. His seminal essay on 'The Economics of Information' (1961) made obvious the point that information is generally imperfect because it is expensive to produce. He derived a number of implications from this insight, stressing the role of search when the prices of individual sellers are unknown. This paper has inspired a large literature on labour market search and its macroeconomic consequences, and has led to a reassessment of advertising as a source of information and the development of a large number of models of markets in which actors have imperfect information.

Stigler's contributions to industrial organization showed by example that classic polar case models of competition and monopoly could be imaginatively and rigorously applied to yield important insights into real market processes. In pursuing this approach he stood against those who believed that 'realistic' models (with few definite predictions) were required for the analysis of modern economies and helped pave the way for the large-scale invasion of industrial organization by formal microeconomic theory that began in the 1970s.

In his 1947 paper, 'The kinky oligopoly demand curve and rigid prices', Stigler exposed the theoretical incompleteness and predictive failures of the kinked demand curve model of oligopoly. (All the essays mentioned in this paragraph and the next two are collected, along with other significant contributions, in Stigler, 1968.) He stressed the frequency of price changes in oligopolistic markets, a point he later made even more forcefully in a major empirical study of transaction price movements (Stigler and Kindahl, 1970).

Stigler's 1951 essay, 'The division of labour is limited by the extent of the market', was a pioneering analysis of the determinants of the structures and boundaries of firms. His 1958 essay on 'The economies of scale' proposed the 'survivor principle', according to which scale economies can be assessed by observing the sizes of plants that survive the prosper in the marketplace. This approach is still an important item in industrial economists' tool kits. In a brief analysis of the *Loews* case, Stigler laid the foundations for the recent literature on commodity bundling. His similarly brief analysis of the US Steel consolidation provided what has become the standard picture of the decline of market dominance.

Stigler's 1964 paper, 'A theory of oligopoly', applied classic (but then neglected) cartel theory to the analysis of markets with 'few' sellers. He argued that the stability of collusive behaviour depends on the possibility of detecting and punishing departures from tacit or overt agreements to restrict output. His formal analysis of the detection problem led to a new information-based interpretation of the significance of seller concentration, and his discussion of punishment raised issues of credible threats, deterrence, and commitment that are at the heart of much of the most interesting theoretical work in industrial organization today. This important paper did much to shake economists' faith in the ubiquity of tacit collusion in oligopolies and has provided useful tools for the analysis of individual markets.

Stigler's first seminal paper on the economics of regulation (Stigler and Friedland, 1962) concluded that early state regulation of electric utilities in the US had no effect on electricity prices. Though one can argue that the evidence presented does not strongly support the null hypothesis of *no* effect, that evidence does suggest a much weaker effect than one might have expected from young, vigorous agencies pursuing the public interest by protecting the public from monopolists. This essay stimulated a great deal of important empirical work on public regulation in the US. It also posed a basic problem: if regulation does not generally achieve its stated objectives, why have so many agencies been established and kept in existence?

In 'The theory of economic regulation' (1971), Stigler attempted to answer this question by extending the assumption of wealth maximization to the political arena. He argued that regulation generally has its origins in the self-interested political activity of the regulated, so that it should be no surprise that it usually serves their interests by sheltering them from market forces. This seminal essay has stimulated a basic re-examination of the origins and effects of regulatory institutions in the United States. Though most scholars now feel that Stigler's basic model of the political process must be enriched, his approach and insights have endured. Economists simply do not look at regulatory policy, or indeed at many other government policies, as they did before he wrote.

RICHARD SCHMALENSEE

See also CHICAGO SCHOOL; INCREASING RETURNS; INDUSTRIAL ORGANIZATION; MARKET STRUCTURE.

SELECTED WORKS

1939. Production and distribution in the short run. *Journal of Political Economy* 47(3), June, 305–27.

1941. *Production and Distribution Theories*. New York: Macmillan.

1945. The cost of subsistence. *Journal of Farm Economics* 2, May, 303–14.

1950. *Five Lectures on Economic Problems*. New York: Macmillan.

1961. The economics of information. *Journal of Political Economy* 69(3), June, 213–25.

1965. *Essays in the History of Economics*. Chicago: University of Chicago Press.

1968. *The Organization of Industry*. Homewood, Ill.: Irwin.

1971. The theory of economic regulation. *Bell Journal of Economics* 2(1), Spring, 3–21.

1962. (With C. Friedland.) What can regulators regulate? *Journal of Law and Economics* 5, October, 1–16.

1970. (With J. Kindahl.) *The Behaviour of Industrial Prices*. New York: Columbia University Press.

1972. The adoption of the marginal utility theory. *History of Political Economy* 4(2), Fall, 571–86.

Stirner, Max (1806–1856). Max Stirner, born at Bayreuth, is the name by which Caspar Schmidt, the philosophic individualist anarchist, is most generally known in Germany. After studying philosophy and theology, he became a master at the Gymnasium in Berlin, and was also a teacher in a girls' school. He published, in 1845, his chief work, *Der Einzige und sein Eigenthum*. This had a brilliant but transitory success. He also wrote a *History of the Reaction after 1848*, and published translations of Adam Smith and other English economists. His life was spent in humble circumstances, and he died in poverty. His position was that of an individualist anarchist of the most extreme and uncompromising kind, preaching the cultus of the *ego* of the individual almost as a religion. He maintained in his *Einzige und sein Eigenthum* the crudest form of the doctrine 'might is right', deriving every right and moral sanction from the individual alone. His views on property are best expressed in his own words which form a remarkable contrast to Proudhon's view that 'property is theft'. 'What is my property?' asks Stirner, and answers at once, 'Nothing but that which is in my power: to what property am I entitled? to any to which I entitle myself. I myself give myself the right to property by taking property.' He accepts the principle that in labour-questions each should look out for himself, and will have no organization and no division of goods among the community. He would let all struggle for existence, and fare as best they can. The only form of community he would admit is that of a 'free union of egoists', which should only last as long as any one member of the union pleased. Stirner, in fact, is the philosophic exponent of the extremest form of laissez faire and individualism in society and economics, and as such has had considerable influence over the modern school of anarchists in Germany and Russia.

[H. DE B. GIBBINS]

Reprinted from *Palgrave's Dictionary of Political Economy*.

stochastic dominance. The notion of stochastic dominance is quite old (see, for example, Blackwell, 1953). Although it was (in various forms) used in statistical or economic theory, it was for some reason not developed until 1969–70, when four papers were published by Hadar and Russell (1969), Hanoch and Levy (1969), Rothschild and Stiglitz (1970) and Whitmore (1970). Since then almost 400 papers have been written on this topic; for a good survey article see Kroll and Levy (1980) and for a good bibliography see Bawa (1982).

The stochastic dominance criteria have been developed in three main directions: (a) Further theoretical development, for example, the ordering of uncertain options for specific distributions or for more restricted classes of utility functions, the effect on the stochastic dominance rules of including a riskless asset, and partial ordering in the multi-period case. (b) Application of stochastic dominance rules to empirical data: various algorithms have been developed to this end. (c) Application of stochastic dominance rules to other economic and financial issues, for example, optimum financial leverage with bankruptcy, the analysis and definition of risk, and optimality of diversification.

THE CRITERIA. Given two risky options with cumulative distribution functions F and G, we seek to determine if an order of preference can be established between F and G. Obviously, if one has full information on the investor's utility, for example, $u(X) = \log X$, then one has simply to calculate the expected utility $E_F(\log X)$ and $E_G(\log X)$, and the option with the highest expected value is preferable. The importance of stochastic dominance rules is that they enable us to compare options even when there is only partial information on the investor's preference, for example $u' > 0, u'' < 0$, etc.

Stochastic dominance rules deal mainly with three classes of utility functions $U_i (i = 1, 2, 3)$, where $u \in U_1$ if $u' \geqslant 0$; $u \in U_2$ if $u' \geqslant 0$, and $u'' \leqslant 0$; and $u \in U_3$ if $u' \geqslant 0, u'' \leqslant 0$, and $u''' \geqslant 0$.

The decision rules appropriate for the classes $U_i (i = 1, 2, 3)$ are called First, Second and Third degree stochastic dominance (FSD, SSD, and TSD respectively).

Theorem 1. Let F and G be the cumulative distribution of two distinct uncertain options. Then F dominates G (FDG) by FSD, SSD, and TSD, if and only if:

(1) $F(x) \leqslant G(x)$, for all x FSD

(2) $$\int_{-\infty}^{X} [G(t) - F(t)]\,dt \geqslant 0,$$ for all x SSD

(3) $$\int_{-\infty}^{x}\int_{-\infty}^{v} [G(t) - F(t)]\,dt\,dv \geqslant 0,$$ for all x and $E_F(x) \geqslant E_G(x)$. TSD

(Obviously we need also a strict inequality for at least one value x.)

STOCHASTIC DOMINANCE WITH A RISKLESS ASSET. Levy and Kroll (1979) applied the *quantile approach* to develop stochastic dominance criteria with a riskless asset (SDR criteria). According to this approach, the FSD, SSD, and TSD criteria can be reformulated in terms of the inverse function of the cumulative probability function; that is, they can be restated in terms of $Q_F(P)$, where P is the probability of obtaining values lower than or equal to $Q_F(P)$ under distribution F. According to this formulation F dominates G by FSD if and only if $Q_F(P) \geqslant Q_G(P)$ for all P, with a strict inequality for at least one P; F dominates G by SSD if and only if

$$\int_0^P Q_P(t)\,\mathrm{d}t \geqslant \int_0^P Q_G(t)\,\mathrm{d}t$$

for all P, with a strict inequality for at least one P; and F dominates G by TSD if and only if

$$\int_0^P \int_0^t Q_F(t)\,\mathrm{d}z\,\mathrm{d}t \geqslant \int_0^P \int_0^t Q_G(t)\,\mathrm{d}z\,\mathrm{d}t$$

with a strict inequality for at least one P and in addition

$$\int_0^1 Q_F(t)\,\mathrm{d}t \geqslant \int_0^1 Q_G(t)\,\mathrm{d}t.$$

Employing the quantile approach, and allowing riskless lending and borrowing, Levy and Kroll (1979) established stochastic dominance rules which allows us to establish preference in a case where the criteria given in Theorem 1 fail.

The SDR criteria have some interesting properties. First, recall that F dominates G by stochastic dominance only if $E_F \geqslant E_G$. Such a requirement is not necessary for dominance by FSDR, SSDR, or TSDR (when R is added to indicate the existence of a riskless asset) since we can always change the mean of the risky portfolio by changing the proportion of the riskless asset in the mixed portfolio. Second, the stochastic dominance and SDR criteria are related as follows:

$$\begin{array}{ccccc} \text{FSD} & \rightarrow & \text{SSD} & \rightarrow & \text{TSD} \\ \downarrow & & \downarrow & & \downarrow \\ \text{FSDR} & \rightarrow & \text{SSDR} & \rightarrow & \text{TSDR} \end{array}$$

Since these are all transitive relations, it is obvious that FSD implies TSDR as well as SSDR, and SSD implies TSDR. Thus, the TSDR-efficient set must be a subset of all other efficient sets derived by either stochastic dominance or SDR criteria.

EMPIRICAL STUDIES. Most of the empirical work attempts to give answers to questions such as the relative effectiveness of the criteria, or differences in the contents of the efficient sets produced by the alternative criteria.

The main results are as follows: (1) FSD is, in most cases, a totally ineffective criterion. (2) The SSD criterion is about as effective as the Mean Variance (M-V) criterion. This means that by using SSD instead of M-V one can avoid the restrictive assumptions on the probability distribution or on the utility function) without cost since the size of the efficient set does not change significantly. (3) The assumption of borrowing and lending at a risk-free interest rate (SDR rules) leads to an impressive reduction of the size of the efficient sets for risk averters. However, FSDR remains relatively ineffective. (4) The SSDR and TSDR efficient sets contain only 1–3 risky asset; namely, almost an 'empirical separation' exists. That is, SSDR and TSDR are very effective in yielding small efficient sets. For example, Levy and Kroll (1979) in a study of mutual fund found about 3 per cent of the feasible set remained in the efficient set using SSDR and TSDR.

HAIM LEVY

BIBLIOGRAPHY

Bawa, V.S. 1982. Stochastic dominance: a research bibliography. *Management Science* 28(6), June, 698–712.
Bawa, V.S. 1975. Optimal rules for ordering uncertain prospects. *Journal of Financial Economics* 2(1), March, 95–121.
Blackwell, D. 1953. Equivalent comparisons of experiments. *Annals of Mathematical Statistics* 24, 265–72.
Hadar, J. and Russell, W.R. 1969. Rules for ordering uncertain prospects. *American Economic Review* 59(1), March, 25–34.
Hanoch, G. and Levy, H. 1969. Efficiency analysis of choices involving risk. *Review of Economic Studies* 36(3), July, 335–46.
Kroll, Y. and Levy, H. 1980. Stochastic dominance: a review and some new evidence. *Research in Finance* 2, 163–227.
Levy, H. and Hanoch, G. 1970. Relative effectiveness of efficiency criteria for portfolio selection. *Journal of Financial and Quantitative Analysis* 5(1), March, 63–76.
Levy, H. and Kroll, Y. 1978. Ordering uncertain options with borrowing and lending. *Journal of Finance* 33(2), May, 553–74.
Levy, H. and Kroll, Y. 1979. Efficiency analysis with borrowing and lending: criteria and their effectiveness. *Review of Economics and Statistics* 61(1), February, 125–40.
Quirk, J.P. and Saposnik, R. 1962. Admissibility and measurable utility functions. *Review of Economic Studies* 29, February, 140–46.
Rothschild, M. and Stiglitz, J.E. 1970. Increasing risk I: a definition. *Journal of Economic Theory* 2(3), September, 225–43.
Rothschild, M. and Stiglitz, J.E. 1971. Increasing risk II: its economic consequences. *Journal of Economic Theory* 3(1), March, 66–84.
Whitmore, G.A. 1970. Third-degree stochastic dominance. *American Economic Review* 60(3), June, 457–9.

stochastic models. *See* CONTINUOUS-TIME STOCHASTIC MODELS.

stochastic optimal control. In the long history of mathematics, stochastic optimal control is a rather recent development. Using Bellman's Principle of Optimality along with measure-theoretic and functional-analytic methods, several mathematicians such as H. Kushner, W. Fleming, R. Rishel, W.M. Wonham and J.M. Bismut, among many others, made important contributions to this new area of mathematical research during the 1960s and early 1970s. For a complete mathematical exposition of the continuous time case see Fleming and Rishel (1975) and for the discrete time case see Bertsekas and Shreve (1978).

The assimilation of the mathematical methods of stochastic optimal control by economists was very rapid. Several economic papers started to appear in the early 1970s among which we mention Merton (1971) on consumption and portfolio rules using continuous time methodology and Brock and Mirman (1972) on optimal economic growth under uncertainty using discrete time techniques. Since then, stochastic optimal control methods have been applied in most major areas of economics such as price theory, macroeconomics, monetary economics and financial economics.

In this entry we (1) state the stochastic optimal control problem, (2) explain how it differs from deterministic optimal control and why that difference is crucial in economic problems, (3) present intuitively the methodology of optimal stochastic control and, finally, (4) give an illustration from optimal stochastic economic growth.

Consider the problem:

$$J[k(t), t, \infty] = \max E_t \int_t^\infty \mathrm{e}^{-\rho s} u[k(s), v(s)]\,\mathrm{d}s \qquad (1)$$

subject to the conditions

$$\mathrm{d}k(t) = T[k(t), v(t)]\,\mathrm{d}t + \sigma[k(t), v(t)]\,\mathrm{d}Z(t), \qquad k(t) \text{ given.} \quad (2)$$

Here $v = v(t) = v(t, \omega)$ is the control random variable, $k = k(t) = k(t, \omega)$ is the state random variable, $\rho \geqslant 0$ is the discount on future utility, u denotes a utility function, T is the drift component of technology, σ is the diffusion component, dZ is a Wiener process and E_t denotes expectation conditioned on $k(t)$ and $v(t)$.

We note immediately that (1) and (2) generalize the deterministic optimal control by incorporating *uncertainty*. The modelling of economic uncertainty is achieved by allowing both the control and state variables to be random and more importantly by postulating that condition (2) is described by a stochastic differential equation of the Itô type.

In the problem described by (1) and (2), if $\sigma(k, v) = 0$ and if k and v are assumed to be real variables instead of random then (1) and (2) reduce to the special case of deterministic optimal control. Thus, the stochastic optimal control problem differs from the deterministic optimal control in the sense that the former generalizes the latter, or equivalently, in the sense that the latter is a special case of the former. This is crucial mathematical difference.

For the economist, the generalization achieved from stochastic optimal control means that the analysis of dynamic economic models becomes more realistic. The economic theorist who uses stochastic optimal control in positive or in welfare economics, in free market or centrally planned economies allows for randomness. Measurement errors, omission of important variables, non-exact relationships, incomplete theories and other methodological complexities are modelled in stochastic optimal control by allowing the control and state variables to be random, and also, by incorporating *pure randomness* through the white noise factor $dZ(t)$. The random variable $dZ(t)$ describes increments in the Wiener process $\{Z(t), t \geqslant 0\}$ that are independent and normally distributed with mean, $E[dZ(t)] = 0$ and variance $\mathrm{Var}[dZ(t)] = dt$.

In particular, equation (2) is a significant economic generalization of the analogous equation in deterministic control. The reader may recall that in deterministic control the constraint is given by $\dot{k} \equiv dk(t)/dt = T[k(t), v(t)]$. Because $dk(t)$ in (2) is a random variable we can compute its mean and variance. They are given by

$$E[dk(t)] = T[k(t), v(t)]; \quad \mathrm{Var}[dk(t)] = \sigma^2[k(t), v(t)]\, dt.$$

Thus (2) is a meaningful generalization of its counterpart in deterministic control because it involves means, standard deviations and pure randomness in capturing the complexities of economic reality. A comprehensive analysis of Itô equations, such as (2), is given in Malliaris and Brock (1982).

The problem in (1) and (2) is a stochastic analogue of the deterministic one studied in Arrow and Kurz (1970, pp. 27–51). A standard technique for our problem, as in the case of Arrow and Kurz, is Bellman's (1957, p. 83) *Principle of Optimality* according to which 'an optimal policy has the property that, whatever the initial state and control are, the remaining decisions must constitute an optimal policy with regard to the state resulting from the first decision'. The problem in equations (1) and (2) is studied here for the undiscounted, finite horizon case, i.e. for $\rho = 0$ and $N < \infty$.

Using Bellman's technique for dynamic programming, equations (1) and (2) can be analysed as follows:

$$\begin{aligned}
&J[k(t), t, N] \\
&= \max E_t \int_t^N u(k, v)\, ds \\
&= \max E_t \int_t^{t+\Delta t} u(k, v)\, ds + \max E_{t+\Delta t} \int_{t+\Delta t}^N u(k, v)\, ds \\
&= \max E_t \int_t^{t+\Delta t} u(k, v)\, ds + J[k(t+\Delta t), t+\Delta t, N] \\
&= \max E_t \left\{ \int_t^{t+\Delta t} u(k, v)\, ds + J[k(t+\Delta t), t+\Delta t, N] \right\} \\
&= \max E_t \{ u[k(t), v(t)]\Delta t + J[k(t), t, N] \\
&\quad + J_k \Delta k + J_t \Delta t + \tfrac{1}{2} J_{kk} (\Delta k)^2 \\
&\quad + J_{kt} (\Delta k)(\Delta t) + \tfrac{1}{2} J_{tt} (\Delta t)^2 + o(\Delta t) \}. \qquad (3)
\end{aligned}$$

Observe that Taylor's theorem is used to obtain (3) and therefore it is assumed that J has continuous partial derivatives of all orders less than 3 in some open set containing the line segment connecting the two points $[k(t), t]$ and $[k(t+\Delta t), t+\Delta t]$. Let (2) be approximated and write

$$\Delta k = T(k, v)\Delta t + \sigma(k, v)\Delta Z + o(\Delta t). \qquad (4)$$

Insert (4) into (3) and use the multiplication rules

$$(\Delta Z) \times (\Delta t) = 0, \quad (\Delta t) \times (\Delta t) = 0 \quad \text{and} \quad (\Delta Z) \times (\Delta Z) = \Delta t$$

to get

$$\begin{aligned}
0 = \max E_t[u(k, v)\Delta t + (J_k T + J_t + \tfrac{1}{2} J_{kk} \sigma^2)\Delta t \\
+ J_k \sigma \Delta Z + o(\Delta t)]. \qquad (5)
\end{aligned}$$

For notational convenience let

$$\Delta J = [J_t + J_k T + \tfrac{1}{2} J_{kk} \sigma^2]\Delta t + J_k \sigma \Delta Z. \qquad (6)$$

Using (6), equation (5) becomes

$$0 = \max E_t[u(k, v)\Delta t + \Delta J + o(\Delta t)]. \qquad (7)$$

This is a partial differential equation with boundary condition $[(\partial J)/\partial k][k(N), N, N] = 0$. Pass E_t through the parentheses of (7) and after dividing both sides by Δt, let $\Delta t \to 0$ to conclude

$$0 = \max[u(k, v) + J_t + J_k T(k, v) + \tfrac{1}{2} J_{kk} \sigma^2(k, v)]. \qquad (8)$$

This last equation is usually written as

$$-J_t = \max[u(k, v) + J_k T(k, v) + \tfrac{1}{2} J_{kk} \sigma^2(k, v)] \qquad (9)$$

and is known as the *Hamilton–Jacobi–Bellman equation* of stochastic control theory.

Next, we define the costate variable $p(t)$ as

$$p(t) = J_k[k(t), t, N]$$

from which it follows that its partial derivative with respect to k is

$$p_k = \partial p/\partial k = J_{kk}. \qquad (10)$$

Therefore, we may rewrite (9) as

$$-J_t = \max H(k, v, p, \partial p/\partial k), \qquad (11)$$

where H is the functional notation of the expression inside the brackets of (9). Assume next that a function v exists that solves the maximization problem of (11) and denote such a function by

$$v^0 = v^0(k, p, \partial p/\partial k). \qquad (12)$$

Note that v^0 is a function of $k(t)$ and t alone, along the optimum path, because J_k is a function of $k(t)$ and t alone. In the applied control literature, and more specifically in economic applications, v^0 is called a *policy function*. Assuming then that a policy function v^0 exists, (11) may be rewritten as

$$\begin{aligned}
-J_t &= \max H(k, v, p, \partial p/\partial k) \\
&= H[k, v^0(k, p, \partial p/\partial k), p, \partial p/\partial k] \\
&= H^0(k, p, \partial p/\partial k). \qquad (13)
\end{aligned}$$

This last equation is again a functional notation of the right-hand side expression of (9) under the assumption of the existence of an optimum control v^0, that is,

$$H^0(k, p, \partial p/\partial k) = u(k, v^0) + pT(k, v^0) + \frac{1}{2}\frac{\partial p}{\partial k}\sigma^2(k, v^0). \quad (14)$$

Equipped with the above analysis we can now state

Proposition 1 (Pontryagin Stochastic Maximum Principle). Suppose that $k(t)$ and $v^0(t)$ solve for $t \in [0, N]$ the problem:

$$\max E_0 \int_0^N u(k, v)\,dt$$

subject to the conditions

$$dk = T(k, v)\,dt + \sigma(k, v)\,dZ, \qquad k(t) \text{ given.}$$

Then, there exists a costate variable $p(t)$ such that for each t, $t \in [0, N]$:

(1) v^0 maximizes $H(k, v, p, \partial p/\partial k)$ where

$$H(k, v, p, \partial p/\partial k) = u(k, v) + pT(k, v) + \frac{1}{2}\frac{\partial p}{\partial k}\sigma^2;$$

(2) the costate function $p(t)$ satisfies the stochastic differential equation $dp = -H_k^0\,dt + \sigma(k, v^0)J_{kk}\,dZ$; and

(3) the transversality condition holds

$$p[k(N), N] = \frac{\partial J}{\partial k}[k(N), N, N] = 0,$$

$$p(N)k(N) = 0.$$

Finally, we briefly illustrate the stochastic optimal control technique to the stochastic Ramsey problem studied in Merton (1975). The problem is to find an optimal saving policy s^0 to

$$\text{maximize } E_0 \int_0^T u(c)\,dt \quad (15)$$

subject to

$$dk = [sf(k) - (n - \sigma^2)k]\,dt - \sigma k\,dZ \quad (16)$$

and $k(t) \geq 0$ for each t. Here, u is a strictly concave, von Neumann–Morgenstern utility function of per capita consumption c for the representative consumer and $f(k)$ is a well-behaved production function. Note that $c = (1 - s)f(k)$ and that equation (16) generalizes Solow's equation of neoclassical economic growth. Uncertainty enters (16) via randomness in the rate of growth of the labour force. Let

$$J[k(t), t, T] = \max_s E_t \int_t^T u[(1 - s)f(k)]\,dt.$$

The Hamilton–Jacobi–Bellman equation is given by

$$0 = \max\{u[(1 - s)f(k)] + J_t + J_k[sf(k) - (n - \sigma^2)k] + \tfrac{1}{2}J_{kk}\sigma^2k^2\} \quad (17)$$

which yields

$$\frac{du}{dc}[(1 - s^0)f(k)] = J_k. \quad (18)$$

To solve for s^0, in principle, one solves (18) for s^0 as a function of k, $T - t$ and J_K, and then substitutes this solution into (17) which becomes a *partial differential equation for J*. Once (17) is solved, then its solution is substituted back into (18) to determine s^0 as a function of k and $T - t$. The nonlinearity of the Hamilton–Jacobi–Bellman equation causes difficulties in finding a closed form solution for the optimal saving function. However, if we let $\sigma = 0$ in (17) one obtains the classical Ramsey rule of the certainty case.

From the fact that numerous economic questions involve uncertainty and can be formulated as stochastic optimal control problems, one may conclude that economic interest is likely to be lively in this area for some time to come.

A.G. Malliaris

See also DYNAMIC PROGRAMMING AND MARKOV PROCESSES; OPTIMAL CONTROL AND ECONOMIC DYNAMICS; WIENER PROCESS.

BIBLIOGRAPHY

Arrow, K.J. and Kurz, M. 1970. *Public Investment, the Rate of Return, and Optimal Fiscal Policy*. Baltimore: Johns Hopkins Press.

Bellman, R. 1957. *Dynamic Programming*. Princeton: Princeton University Press.

Bertsekas, D.P. and Shreve, S.E. 1978. *Stochastic Optimal Control: the Discrete Time Case*. New York: Academic Press.

Brock, W.A. and Mirman, L. 1972. Optimal economic growth and uncertainty: the discounted case. *Journal of Economic Theory* 4, 479–513.

Fleming, W.H. and Rishel, R.W. 1975. *Deterministic and Stochastic Optimal Control*. New York: Springer-Verlag.

Malliaris, A.G. and Brock, W.A. 1982. *Stochastic Methods in Economics and Finance*. Amsterdam: North-Holland.

Merton, R.C. 1971. Optimal consumption and portfolio rules in a continuous-time model. *Journal of Economic Theory* 3, 373–413.

Merton, R.C. 1975. An asymptotic theory of growth under uncertainty. *Review of Economic Studies* 42, 375–93.

stochastic processes. *See* CONTINUOUS-TIME STOCHASTIC PROCESSES.

Stockholm School. The Stockholm School existed between the years 1927 and 1937 as a separate and distinctive school of economics. The School was given its name by Ohlin in his review of the *General Theory* (cf Ohlin, 1937). A 'School' is here defined as an interrelated development of a common theme among its members, who included Myrdal, Lindahl, Hammarskjöld, Ohlin and Lundberg. The common theme is the development of *dynamic methods*, which refer to notions such as temporary equilibrium and intertemporal equilibrium.

The development of dynamic methods is an original contribution. There is no evidence that the members were influenced in any significant way by other contemporary economists. After 1937 there are clear indications that the Swedish economists took up ideas from Hicks and Samuelson (cf. Hansen, 1951). The Stockholm School generally applied their concepts to macroeconomic problems and there are similarities to Keynes's *General Theory*, but they did not construct the principle of effective demand (Hansson, 1982; Landgren, 1960; Patinkin, 1982; Steiger, 1971).

EQUILIBRIUM APPROACHES. The first contribution to the development of dynamic method is Myrdal's dissertation from 1927, *Prisbildningsproblemet och föränderligheten* (The problem of price formation and change). His method includes anticipations i.e. among the data or the immediate determinants of relative prices. The direct stimulus to this idea seemed to have come from what Myrdal considered to be Cassel's incomplete handling of the dynamic problem.

The inclusion of anticipations implies that future anticipated changes have effects on the economic process long before they actually take place. The theoretical determination of an equilibrium has therefore to include the anticipated consequences of probable changes. Myrdal's method of putting the anticipated effects alongside the other data has been called 'the method of expectation', which means the inclusion of expectations as explicit variables in a formal equilibrium theory (cf. Hicks, 1973, p. 143 n.11).

Lindahl's construction of intertemporal and temporary equilibrium are both examples of an *equilibrium approach*, which means that for each individual and commodity the anticipated price achieves a balance of demand and supply and all expectations are therefore fulfilled. Lindahl also considered the assumption of perfect foresight a necessary condition for the determination of a price situation as a state of equilibrium.

Lindahl's aim in the article 'The place of capital in the theory of price' (1929) was to analyse the effects of including capital goods in the determination of a static equilibrium. Intertemporal equilibrium emerges from the shortcomings of comparative statics in handling some of the problems related to this analysis and it is not aimed at solving macrotheoretical problems. Hayek had already constructed intertemporal equilibrium in 1928 but there is no evidence that Lindahl at this time was aware of Hayek's contribution.

Intertemporal equilibrium can analyse dynamic conditions, since there is a movement in the system. However, the mathematical formulation shows that there is no 'movement' in any meaningful sense, since it is a simultaneous determination of prices, quantities and interest rates for all periods under the assumption of equilibrium within each period. Lindahl's development of temporary equilibrium grew out of this inadequacy of intertemporal equilibrium. He looked for a method which should include the analysis both of relative prices in each period and of the price relations between different periods, and temporary equilibrium was meant to solve this problem.

The notion of a period plays an important role both in intertemporal and temporal equilibrium as methods to analyse dynamic conditions. The principal difference between dynamic and stationary conditions is that in the former case the factors determining the prices – the data – are constantly changing. The dynamic case implies practically continuous changes in data but Lindahl assumed for analytical reasons that:

> In order to analyse such a dynamic process, we imagine it to be subdivided into periods of time to short that the factors *directly* affecting prices, and therefore also the prices themselves, can be regarded as *unchanged in each period*. All such changes are therefore assumed to take place at the transition points between periods. The development of prices can then be expressed as a series of successive price situations (Lindahl, 1930, p. 158).

To divide the dynamic process into periods was in the beginning just introduced as an heuristic device, but later on Hammarskjöld gave it an analytical base.

The application of temporary equilibrium implies that for each period the prices are in equilibrium states in the sense that there will be equality between supply and demand during the period; the determination of prices is expressed as a system of equations for each period. The dynamic process is then analysed as a series of temporary equilibria. It shows that temporary equilibrium was developed before the publication of Hicks's *Value and Capital* (1939).

Lindahl's analysis was almost immediately criticized by both Lundberg and Myrdal. Lundberg's criticism relates only to intertemporal equilibrium but his critique is also valid for temporary equilibrium. The main weakness is that the accommodations to the disturbances are unexplained and outside the model, and the successive sequence of equilibria is therefore not explained (cf. Lundberg, 1930, p. 157; Myrdal, 1939, p. 122). The missing element is an analysis of the accommodation process, that is to say to explain the 'link' between consecutive periods. In fact, Lindahl himself later described his method as introducing 'dynamical problems within the static framework' (Lindahl, 1939a, p. 10), since this method could employ the entire static apparatus for the analysis of a dynamic sequence.

DISEQUILIBRIUM APPROACHES. In *Monetary Equilibrium* (1931) Myrdal attempted a critical reconstruction of Wicksell's normal rate of interest; the starting-point was Lindahl's analysis in *The Rate of Interest and the Price Level*. However, the most important contribution to the School is the construction of the famous *ex ante*/*ex post* calculus. The *ex ante* anticipations are the driving force in the dynamic process, but the *ex post* results do still play a role since they are a basis for the forthcoming *ex ante* calculations.

The method is constructed in such a way that there is always an *ex post* balance. But the interesting problem is to analyse the changes during the period which are required to bring about the *ex post* balance. These changes must be the result of inconsistent anticipations or due to exogenous changes during the period. It was precisely Lindahl's insufficient analysis of the balancing changes that was criticized by Myrdal and by Lundberg: the intervening changes could not be explained because time is divided into a number of short equilibrium periods during which no changes occur. However, with the application of *ex ante* and *ex post*, which makes a proper analysis of the intervening changes, it is possible to be released from the straitjacket of the equilibrium approach implied by temporary equilibrium.

Hammarskjöld was the first within the Stockholm School to give an explicit explanation of the means by which two periods may be connected in a disequilibrium approach. Both Lindahl and Myrdal held, with greater or lesser clarity, that unexpected changes in the price level and the concomitant income changes would keep the process going, but their equations have no formal connections with plans in subsequent periods. Before Hammarskjöld nobody within the Stockholm School had shown that there was a relation between fixed plans and the length of the period, but after his contribution it was generally assumed that the duration of unchanged plans determines the length of the unit period.

Like the other members of the Stockholm School, Ohlin was interested in explaining changes in the price level, but he also wanted to give the most general analysis of the driving force behind price movements. His explanation is a restatement of an old Wicksellian idea. An explanation of price changes must look at the factors influencing the demand and supply of both consumption goods and investment goods. It is therefore not surprising that Ohlin found the idea of the disequilibrium in the capital market as representing the driving force – the hallmark of the Wicksellian approach – as a too narrow explanation. In particular, since he could construct examples where a disequilibrium in the consumer goods market was the main factor behind a price movement.

Ohlin's specific extension of Wicksellian macro-theory was his explicit treatment of *autonomous* changes in consumption, which seemed to have been Ohlin's own evaluation of his contribution to the Stockholm School (cp. Steiger, 1976, p. 356 n.22). But he made no significant contribution to the dynamic method.

SEQUENCE ANALYSIS. Lindahl's 'Note on the dynamic pricing problem', a short (four pages) and privately circulated paper from 1934, lays the foundation of sequence analysis. His unpublished manuscript 'Introduction to the theory of price movements in a closed community' (1935) gives his idea on a general dynamic approach, which should be the basis for all theories, and most of these ideas were later reproduced in 'The dynamic approach to economic theory' (1939).

To define a determinate sequence it is necessary to prove that certain human actions will necessarily follow from a definite situation at a given point of time. However, human actions or the results of human actions are not deterministic and can not be explained in the same way as events in the physical world, but this is only a problem for the empirical relevance of the theory and it does not show that the theory is inconsistent. The construction of a dynamic theory 'solves' the problem. To develop his general dynamic approach Lindahl had to postulate that individual actions represent the fulfilment of certain plans, which at the beginning of the period are determined according to explicit principles. It obviously takes a certain amount of time to realize these actions and a period of time is resolved. As far as changes in plans are concerned, Lindahl assumed that these take place at the transition point between two consecutive periods. It is implied that a period is defined by unchanged plans, which was already hinted at by Hammarskjöld. The notion of plan had played a central role within the Stockholm School almost from its beginning, but now it is explicitly stated as the pivot for the dynamic method.

To develop sequence analysis Lindahl assumed: at an arbitrary point in time (t) the plans for production and consumption are given for a certain period of time (t to $t+1$), which means that if the prices are known then the individual actions are determined for the period; the supply prices are given during the period and all changes in prices and plans take place at the transition point between two consecutive periods, i.e. a *fixprice* method. The problem to be solved is then the following:

> the analysis of what happens during the said period, that is, the determination of the situation at the point $t+1$ as it *results* from the situation at the point t. When this problem is solved, the situation at the point $t+2$ can in the same manner be explained as it results from the situation at the point $t+1$, and so on. The solution of this problem implies, therefore, [...], the solution of the whole dynamic problem. (Lindahl, 1934, p. 204).

This solution contributes to the 'whole dynamic problem' in the sense that the same method could be employed for the period ($t+1$ to $t+2$) at point $t+1$. This is an example of a *single-period analysis*, which shows that is going to happen during one single period; how certain *ex ante* plans at the beginning of the period lead to determinate *ex post* results at the end of the period. But it does not determine the whole dynamic process (from t to $t+1$ and onwards) at point t. It is also necessary to have a *continuation analysis* to show the effects of the *ex post* results in the current period on the plans for the subsequent period. It is obvious that both parts are necessary components in a sequence analysis which is supposed to determine a process spanning several consecutive periods.

To solve the single-period analysis Lindahl assumed that the spending plans are assumed to be realized as far as quantities are concerned; it is implied that there are enough unemployed factors of production and sufficient stocks of goods and therefore all adjustments during a period can take place via changes in stocks. The role of this assumption is to show that the actions during the period can be directly deduced from the plans once the prices are given at the beginning of the period. Hence, the result of the period is a necessary outcome of the *ex ante* plans for the current period.

To determine the *ex post* results from the given *ex ante* plans at time t does not imply that the ongoing process after time $t+1$ can be determined at t without further assumptions. The crucial assumption of the continuation analysis concerns the relation between *ex ante* plans for the forthcoming period and the *ex post* results for the current period. Lindahl now assumed: if the plans are fulfilled, and there are no changes in the exterior events, then it is possible to postulate a simple functional relation between the *ex ante* plans for the next period and the *ex post* results of the current period. The application of this assumption for several periods gives as a result that the whole dynamic process can be deduced from the data given at the beginning of the first period. Thus, in Lindahl's analysis each single period is in equilibrium and this type of sequence analysis can be interpreted as a sort of moving equilibrium. Lundberg left out the postulate that the plans have to be fulfilled within each period, which is the difference between equilibrium and disequilibrium sequence analysis.

Lundberg's development of sequence analysis, in *Studies in the Theory of Economic Expansion* (1937) used a disequilibrium approach but at the same time it is an equilibrium process. It is this two-sided character of disequilibrium and equilibrium in Lundberg's sequence analysis which is important to understand.

Lundberg criticized static equilibrium but such equilibrium notions might still be useful to explain the development of aggregate relations. In fact, if a sequence analysis should be possible then some equilibrium relations must hold even out of equilibrium, and equilibrium constructions play therefore a fundamental role in sequence analysis. The question is to what an extent equilibrium constructions may be used in a sequence analysis which starts with aggregate categories. Lundberg's analysis is a *disequilibrium sequence analysis*, while Lindahl in 1934 pursued an *equilibrium sequence analysis*. In Lundberg's analysis the equilibrium notion is represented by the fixed response functions – an expectation function of a constant form – which is presupposed for the existence of equilibrium through time (cf. Hahn, 1952, p. 804). Sequence analysis belongs therefore to the class of equilibrium processes, since constant expectation functions imply that behaviour is invariant over a certain period of time which is a crucial aspect of a general notion of equilibrium. Hence, disequilibrium sequence analysis is an equilibrium process, but, at the same time, it is a disequilibrium approach since expectations are not fulfilled within each period.

ASSESSMENT.

After the late 1930s there was almost no contribution to the development of dynamic method from the original members of the School. Most of them had also left the world of pure academics: Myrdal worked on the problem of black people in the United States in the early 1940s and was later minister for trade in the social democratic government; Hammarskjöld was already in the mid-1930s a prominent civil servant; Ohlin became leader of the liberal party in the early 1940s; Lundberg was in 1937 appointed as the first director of the Swedish Business Cycle Research Institute; Lindahl was the only one who pursued a pure academic career and now and then he would dwell on his original ideas, but there was no further development.

BJÖRN HANSSON

See also LINDAHL, ERIK ROBERT; MONETARY EQUILIBRIUM; MYRDAL, GUNNAR; OHLIN, BERTIL; WICKSELL, JOHN GUSTAF KNUT.

BIBLIOGRAPHY

Hammarskjöld, D. 1933. *Konjunkturspridningen*. Stockholm: P.A. Norstedt.

Hansen, B. 1951. *A Study in the Theory of Inflation*. London: George Allen & Unwin.

Hansson, B.A. 1982. *The Stockholm School and the Development of Dynamic Method*. London: Croom Helm.

Hicks, J.R. 1973. Recollections and documents. *Economica* 40, 2–11. As reprinted in J.R. Hicks, *Economic Perspectives*, Oxford: Clarendon Press, 1977.

Landgren, K.-G. 1957. *Den 'nya ekonomien' i Sverige*. Stockholm Almqvist & Wiksell.

Lindahl, E. 1929. Prisbildningsproblemets uppläggning från kapitalteoretisk synpunkt. *Ekonomisk Tidskrift* . 2. Translated as 'The place of capital in the theory of price', in Lindahl (1939a).

Lindahl, E. 1930. *Penningpolitikens medel*. Malmö: Förlagsaktiebolaget. Translated as 'The rate of interest and the price level', in Lindahl (1939a).

Lindahl, E. 1934. A note on the dynamic pricing problem. Stencil, Gothenburg, 23 October 1934. As reprinted in Steiger (1971).

Lindahl, E. 1935. Introduction to the theory of price movements in a closed community. Chapter 1 (the only surviving) of the planned book *Monetary Policy and its Theoretical Basis*. Unpublished manuscript from the beginning of 1935.

Lindahl, E. 1939a. *Studies in the Theory of Money and Capital*. London: George Allen & Unwin.

Lindahl, E. 1939b. The dynamic approach to economic theory. Part I of Lindahl (1939).

Lundberg, E. 1930. Om begreppet ekonomisk jämvikt. *Ekonomisk Tidskrift* 32(4), 133–60.

Lundberg, E. 1937. *Studies in the Theory of Economic Expansion*. Reprinted, New York: Kelley & Millman, 1955.

Myrdal, G. 1927. *Prisbildningsproblemet och föränderligheten*. Uppsala and Stockholm: Almqvist & Wiksell.

Myrdal, G. 1939. *Monetary Equilibrium*. A translation and extended version of the German edition of 1933, which is a translation and an extension of an article in *Ekonomisk Tidskrift* (1931). Reprinted, New York: Kelley, 1965.

Ohlin, B. 1933. Till frågan om penningteoriens uppläggning. *Ekonomisk Tidskrift*. Translated as 'On the formulation of monetary theory', *History of Political Economy*, 1978.

Ohlin, B. 1937. Some notes on the Stockholm theory of savings and investment. *Economic Journal* 47, Part I, March, 53–69; Part II, June, 221–40.

Patinkin, D. 1982. *Anticipations of the General Theory?* Oxford: Basil Blackwell.

Steiger, O. 1971. *Studien zur Enstehung der neuen Wirtschaftslehre in Schweden*. Berlin: Duncker & Humblot.

Steiger, O. 1976. Bertil Ohlin and the origins of the Keynesian revolution. *History of Political Economy* 8(3), Fall, 341–66.

stocks and flows. The essence of stock–flow analyses of individual or market behaviour is an explicit recognition of the interdependence of current production, consumption and asset-holding plans. The term 'stock–flow analysis' is used here generically to refer to any theories dealing simultaneously with the economic activities of production, consumption and asset-holding. At a market level this implies a distinction between plans to purchase a good in the current period in order to consume it during the current period (flow demand) and for the purpose of holding it at the end of the current period as an asset (stock demand), and an analogous distinction between plans to supply the good from current production (flow supply) and past production (inventories, or stock supply). In this essay we review the nature of the distinction between stocks and flows and then illustrate the importance of the distinction for alternative theories of market price determination. Detailed references to the folklore of the stock–flow literature may be found in Burstein (1982), Bushaw and Clower (1957), Clower (1968) and Harrison (1980). We focus here on markets: see Archibald and Lipsey (1958), Clower (1963), Clower and Burstein (1960), Hadar (1965; 1971, ch. 11) and Johnson (1971) for important contributions to theories of individual behaviour in a stock-flow environment.

Whether acknowledged or not, there are three respects in which stocks and flows are commonly distinguished. We shall refer to these, for convenience, as the dimensional, behavioural and heuristic distinctions. It is crucial to keep these conceptually separate. For purposes of exposition we shall discuss the analytical characterization of the trading and exchange processes pertaining to a market period of given length. For convenience and familiarity presume that market-price determination occurs instantaneously at discrete points of time spaced equally apart in calendar time. Hicks (1946; ch. 9) chose to visualize this point at the beginning of each 'week'. Providing we do explicitly identify some such reference date, there is no reason to visualize it at any particular point during the week. For the sake of tradition we follow Hicks's vision of traders coming together at the beginning of the week. Their trading plans, which we shall characterize precisely in a moment, are presumed to be coordinated in some fashion by the activities of an auctioneer in setting a particular price vector that is to prevail until the next meeting at the Bourse (the beginning of the week). For present purposes we shall assume that prices are set so as to satisfy the Hicksian temporary equilibrium condition that planned purchases equal planned sales.

By viewing what happens at the Bourse as happening at a point in time we are led to characterize trading plans, for whatever purpose, *dimensionally* as stocks. At a given price a trader plans to buy or sell a particular quantity of a good; when the auctioneer cries out a particular price for a particular good, the traders each respond with no more than a positive or negative number (positive for purchase offers and negative for sales offers, let us presume). The auctioneer is not in the least interested in what the trader plans to do with the bottle of whisky he bid for – for all he cares, the trader may sip it continuously for the ensuing week, gulp it down completely at some instant during the week, or just add it to his stockpile. It is only his *trading* plans that are relevant for the price determination that occurs at the Bourse, and they are unambiguously measured at the instant the Bourse is open. Thus we have the first stock–flow distinction – trading plans are dimensionally stocks (measured at some reference date) and not flows (measured per some market period).

The illustration of the opening of the Bourse is just one of many possible characterizations. Such a conception permits us to focus on the important implications of a behavioural stock-flow distinction implicit in many writings. Referring to his own temporary equilibrium condition, Hicks argues (1965; p. 85) that:

> As long as we hold to the principle of price determination by 'equilibrium of demand and supply', on which that theory is based, we have no call to attend to anything but transactions. We do not need to distinguish between stocks and flows; for stocks and flows enter into the determination of equilibrium in exactly the same way.
>
> There can, in competitive conditions, be no more than one price for the same commodity at the same time; and even in conditions that are only partially competitive, it does not have one price at stock and another as flow. The supply and demand that are equated, in the single period of Temporary Equilibrium theory, may (and probably will) contain stock elements as well as flow elements. Supply comes partly from stock carried over, partly from new production; demand is partly a demand for carry-forward. Expectations of futures prices affect both elements; interest affects both elements. The analysis does not require that stock and flow should be separated into compartments. It is not the case that there is one stock equilibrium and one flow equilibrium. There is one 'stock–flow' equilibrium of the single period; and that is all.

The stock–flow distinction implicit in Hicks's discussion is the behavioural one that calls the activities of current period production and consumption 'flow activities' and the activity of asset-holding a 'stock activity'. It cannot be emphasized too strongly that the terms stock and flow are in this respect merely euphemisms for asset-holding and production/consumption behaviour, respectively. Thus we shall distinguish those trading plans related to asset-holding plans from those trading plans related to current production and/or consumption plans. We may refer to the former as excess stock demand and the latter as excess flow demand.

There are two important reasons for wanting to make such a behavioural distinction. The first concerns the alternative ways in which we may then choose to characterize trading plans as being 'coordinated'. In terms of the Hicksian temporary equilibrium condition, market price is set such that at that price excess market demand (the sum of excess stock and excess flow demand) is zero. In terms of the Marshallian temporary equilibrium condition, market price is set such that excess stock demand is zero. Indeed, a failure to recognize the behavioural stock–flow distinction has led some authors to fail to see that these (and other) price determination conditions are alternatives; these implications of the behavioural stock–flow distinction are taken up below.

The second reason for making the behavioural distinction is that it raises the important difference between *temporary* (current period) market equilibrium and *full* (stock–flow, stationary, long-run static) market equilibrium. Clower (1968) argues that this may be the only reason for adopting a stock–flow analysis of market behaviour. This point may be put more accurately by saying that a recognition of stock and flow trading plans leads to a non-trivial explicit dynamic model of market behaviour from period to period. The overwhelming majority of received theory is written in terms of stock *or* flow trading plans; in such cases, a Hicksian temporary equilibrium in any period is, ceteris paribus, a full equilibrium. To account for observed non-stationary time series of market prices and/or inventories, recourse in such cases must be had either to persistent exogenous shocks to the system and/or 'ad hoc' adjustment lags in production or expectations formation.

We now highlight the point of separating the dimensional and behavioural stock–flow distinctions. When describing the Hicksian temporary equilibrium condition, we shall talk about flow trading plans rather than production and consumption plans. The reason for doing so is that we may wish to visualize the latter plans as being dimensionally flows. Similarly, we may wish to visualize asset-holding plans as being dimensionally stocks – we may accordingly choose to reference-date stock demand as planned holdings as at the end of the period and stock supply as existing inventory at the beginning of the period. The point is that '... we have no call to attend to anything but transactions', and all trading plans are dimensionally comparable, obviously leaving the theorist great scope in terms of the 'real' economic processes he may wish to discuss in terms of this scenario of market price determination. This scope is, however, often restricted by a third heuristic stock–flow distinction in common use.

The heuristic distinction asserts that current production and consumption are economic activities occuring in 'real time', while portfolio formation plans are not. It is often an implicit presumption, based intuitively but not necessarily on the behavioural stock–flow distinction. The rate at which whisky may be currently consumed at some price is, let us say, fixed in terms of calendar time units by taste considerations. Hence, it is argued, the number representing flow demand trading plans at that price varies directly with the market period length adopted. At all prices I, for example, like to sip one bottle of whisky a day; if the market opens once a week my (perfectly inelastic) flow demand is seven; if it opens daily, it is one. In each case my planned purchases remain dimensionally a stock. With respect to asset–holding behaviour it is argued conversely that the number representing (end of market period) stock demand is invariant to the market period length adopted. One thinks perhaps of speculators who are only concerned with inter-period price changes. It makes no difference to them, so it is argued, if the price changes daily or weekly (storage costs aside). The argument is far less plausible in the case of whisky retailers, however. The heuristic stock–flow distinction involves, in Patinkin's words,

> implicitly defining a 'flow' not as a quantity whose dimensions are 1/T, but as a quantity whose magnitude is directly proportionate to h [the length of the market/planning period]; similarly, the implicit definition of a 'stock' is that a quantity whose magnitude is independent of h. Clearly such 'stocks' and 'flows' can be added together (Patinkin, 1965, p. 521).

We might just add at the end of this quote: '... for a period of given, fixed length with respect to the conceptual experiments underlying these relations'. An obvious extension to this received presumption is to consider the factors influencing the cost of adjustment of portfolios in real time (cf. Clower and Howitt, 1978). With respect to production, consumption and portfolio formation, we may think of transaction costs (as distinct from learning by doing and indigestion) as common to all three activities. This extension implies, for the time being, an elaboration rather than refinement of the basic price theory under discussion here. It does clarify, however, the basis (such as it is) of a stock–flow dichotomy in the literature, focusing on price determination *at an instant* (for example, the approach of Tobin (1969) may be viewed as an application of the Marshallian temporary equilibrium condition along with the explicit assumption of a perfectly elastic flow supply schedule). Knowing this, one would hardly wish to make this received presumption an article of modelling faith.

We now consider the importance of the behavioural stock–flow distinction for alternative theories of market price determination. For expository purposes consider an isolated market model for some good which is, with respect to the market period length adopted, capable of being produced, consumed and held as an asset. Such a good is referred to as a stock–flow good. A perishable good which may only be currently produced and currently consumed is called a pure flow good and a non-augmentable durable a pure stock good. Define the following notation with respect to any market period t: D_t : planned stock demand to hold the good at the end of the current period; S_t : existing stock supply of inventory of the good at the beginning of the current period; d_t: planned flow demand to consume the good over the current period; s_t: planned flow supply of current period production of the good; p_t: money-price of one unit of the good in the current market period; x_t: excess flow demand $\equiv d_t - s_t$; and X_t: excess stock demand $\equiv D_t - S_t$. Stock supply in period t is defined as the accumulated sum of past excess flow supply: $S_t \equiv s_0 - x_{t-1} - x_{t-2} - \cdots - x_0$.

The alternative temporary equilibrium conditions introduced earlier are defined as follows:

$$\text{Hicksian: } x_t + X_t = 0;$$

and

$$\text{Marshallian: } X_t = 0.$$

It is clear from these specifications of the two temporary equilibrium conditions that they do not in general predict that the current market price will be the same value. Moreover, the periodic rate of accumulation of inventory also depends on the theory employed. This accumulation process feeds back on the market price in period $t+1$, due to an induced shift of the excess stock demand schedule. The properties of the first-order difference equations implied by the alternative theories are well known: Bushaw and Clower (1957 chs 3 and 4) discuss the Hicksian condition, and Clower (1954a) the Marshallian condition.

A full (or stationary, or stock flow) equilibrium sequence in this market is characterized not only by a stationary market price from period to period, but also by zero accumulation of inventory holdings from period to period. The three conditions defining such a static equilibrium sequence (only two of which are independent) are

$$x_t + X_t = 0$$
$$X_t = 0$$
$$x_t = 0.$$

These conditions define the static equilibrium for both Hicksian and Marshallian theories of market behaviour.

Presuming linear functional forms for the basic trading relations, the alternative theories are illustrated in Figures 1 and 2, and their common static equilibrium in Figure 3. Note that S_{t+1} in Figures 1 and 2 will be located to the right of S_t by the amount of net new production shown. The market supply schedule $S_{t+1}+s_{t+1}$ correspondingly shifts to the right implying, ceteris paribus, a new temporary equilibrium price p_{t+1} and further net new production. In Figures 1 and 2 current period excess flow supply is shown by the amount $q_1 - q_2$. In Figure 3, S^* and p^* denote static equilibrium values of these endogenous variables.

Taken at face value, these stock–flow models may be used to generate sequences of non-stationary temporary equilibria that eventually converge on some full equilibrium (presuming the system to be stable). Indeed Clower (1954a, 1954b) and Bushaw and Clower (1957; pp. 63–75) illustrate these deterministic paths at length. What of the dynamic behaviour

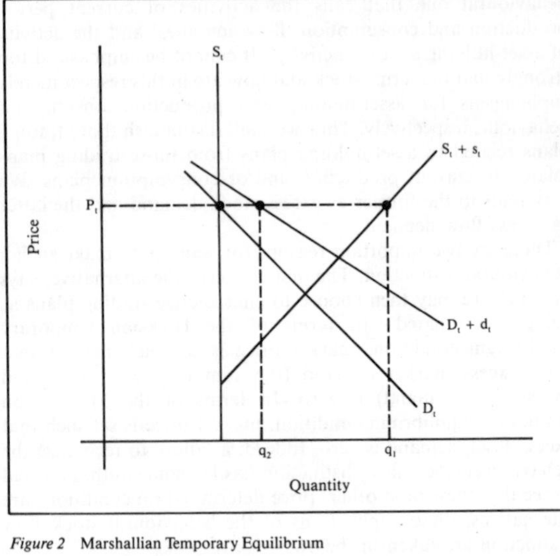

Figure 2 Marshallian Temporary Equilibrium

of the basic stock-flow model, however, when economic agents have some form of Rational Expectations (RE) about the future course of the system?

Muth (1961; pp. 321–9) presented a model of an isolated market with certain stock–flow characteristics. If we amend that model to include flow supply as a function of the current period price, it can be shown that Muth's derivation of the RE equilibrium remains essentially valid. Using our notation, the system is:

$$d_t = -\beta p_1$$
$$D_t = \alpha[E(p_{t+1}) - p_t]$$
$$s_t = \gamma p_t + \epsilon_t$$
$$D_t + d_t = S_t + s_t,$$

where $E(p_{t+1})$ denotes the price expected in period t to prevail in period $t+1$, this expectation based on all information about

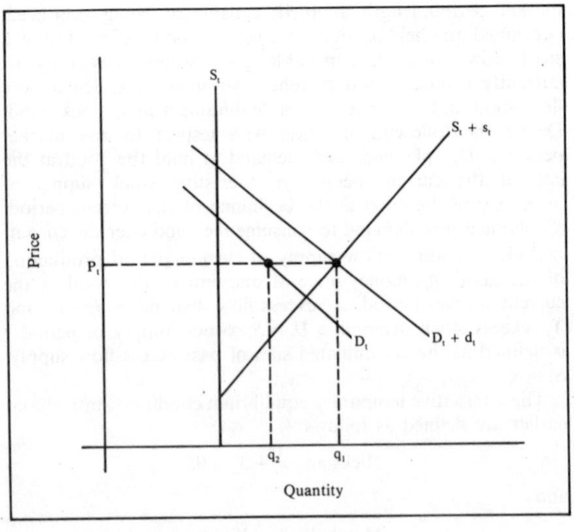

Figure 1 Hicksian Temporary Equilibrium

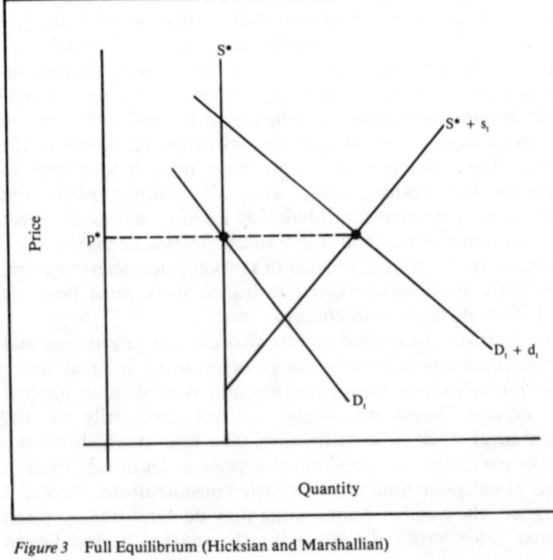

Figure 3 Full Equilibrium (Hicksian and Marshallian)

the history of this system up to and including period t. The first three equations refer to the deviations of endogenous variables from their *full equilibrium* values in the absence of any stochastic influences (following Muth). The form of this stock demand equation may be rationalized along several lines (e.g. the 'supply of storage' literature uses a similar relation to explain spot/futures differentials); for current purposes we need not pursue these. It can be shown that, if we accept the RE hypothesis that $E(p_{t+1}) = E(p_{t+1}|\epsilon_t, \epsilon_{t-1}, \epsilon_{t-2}, \ldots)$ and we assume that the stochastic disturbances ϵ_t are independent, the expected price is given by $E(p_{t+1}) = \lambda p_t$. The parameter λ in this case depends on the coefficients of flow demand, flow supply, and stock demand in a very specific way (see McCallum, 1972). It can also be shown that the use of RE in the simple stock-flow model leads to more robust dynamic market behaviour when compared to alternative expectations schemes.

These results, however, are not intuitively appealing. Stock–flow analysis emphasizes the distinction between temporary and full equilibrium, and the study of the stability (or otherwise) of sequences of temporary equilibria. The notion of rational expectations postulates that agents know the nature of the market they operate in, and pattern their current behaviour on expectations based on that knowledge. Why, then, do agents in Muth (1961, section 4) only consider the current *temporary* equilibrium of their market? It would seem more logical for *speculators* to be concerned with expectations of the *full* equilibrium of the market (note that the first model introduced by Muth (1961, p. 317) is a pure flow market with a one-period supply lag; in this case it may seem more appropriate to focus on the expected price next period, given that producers are facing a point-input point-output decision problem). Burstein (1982) recognizes this point, arguing correctly that

> under rational expectations, transactors, knowing the structure of the economy and the structure of the sub-economies in which they operate, will optimize relative to 'best estimates' of future data; under characteristic formulations of stock-flow disequilibrium, transactors do not optimize even relative to data-sequences ground out by deterministic models; in the non-stochastic world of standard stock-flow theory, 'rational' transactors would achieve an equilibrium at the onset of the process – one spanning the *phase space* of the system. The upshot would support the basic insights of earlier stock–flow analysts but would require a quite different paradigm of market behavior.

In the amended stock–flow model with RE, a similar derivation with the added *full equilibrium* condition leads to the result $E(p_{t+1}) = 0$. Recall that we are specifying the basic structural model in deviation form (thus a zero here implies that expected price is equal to the expected full equilibrium price). There are many ways to relax this result formally, as evidenced in recent literature on exchange rate dynamics. One major determinant of dynamics in stock-flow models is therefore the assumed 'term-structure' of expectations (rational or otherwise).

GLENN W. HARRISON

BIBLIOGRAPHY

Archibald, G.C. and Lipsey, R.G. 1958. Monetary and value theory: a critique of Patinkin. *Review of Economic Studies* 26, 1–22.

Burstein, M.L. 1982. Stock-flow analysis. In *McGraw-Hill Encylopedia of Economics*, New York: McGraw-Hill.

Bushaw, D.W. and Clower, R.W. 1957. *Introduction to Mathematical Economics*. Homewood, Ill.: Irwin.

Clower, R.W. 1954a. An investigation into the dynamics of investment. *American Economic Review* 44, 64–81.

Clower, R.W. 1954b. Productivity, thrift, and the rate of interest. *Economic Journal* 64, 107–15.

Clower, R.W. 1963. Permanent income and transitory balances: Hahn's paradox. *Oxford Economic Papers* 15, 177–90.

Clower, R.W. 1968. Stock–flow analysis. In *International Encylopedia of the Social Sciences*, New York: Macmillan and Free Press, Vol. 12.

Clower, R.W. and Burstein, M.L. 1960. On the invariance of demand for cash and other assets. *Review of Economic Studies* 28, 32–6.

Clower, R.W. and Howitt, P.W. 1978. The transactions theory of the demand for money: a reconsideration. *Journal of Political Economy* 86, 445–66.

Hadar, J. 1965. Comparative statics of stock–flow equilibrium. *Journal of Political Economy* 73, 304–9.

Hadar, J. 1971. *Mathematical Theory of Economic Behavior*. Reading, Mass.: Addison-Wesley. 1980.

Harrison, G.W. 1980. The stock–flow distinction: a suggested interpretation. *Journal of Macroeconomics* 2, 111–28.

Hicks, J.R. 1946. *Value and Capital*. 2nd edn, Oxford: Clarendon Press.

Hicks, J.R. 1965. *Capital and Growth*. Oxford: Clarendon Press.

Johnson, M.B. 1971. *Household Behaviour: Consumption, Income and Wealth*. Harmondsworth: Penguin.

McCallum, B.T. 1972. Inventory holdings, rational expectations, and the law of supply and demand. *Journal of Political Economy* 80, 386–93.

Muth, J.F. 1961. Rational expectations and the theory of price movements *Econometrica* 29, 315–35.

Patinkin, D. 1965. *Money, Interest and Prices*. 2nd edn, New York: Harper & Row.

Tobin, J. 1969. A general equilibrium approach to monetary theory. *Journal of Money, Credit and Banking* 1, 15–29.

Stolper–Samuelson theorem. *See* HECKSCHER-OHLIN TRADE THEORY.

Stone, John Richard Nicholas (born 1913). Sir Richard Stone, knighted in 1978 and Nobel Laureate in Economics in 1984, is the outstanding figure in postwar British applied econometrics. His work in social accounting has had a profound influence on the way that measurement is carried out in economics, and his econometric model building has changed the way that economists analyse those measurements. In contrast to most economists of his time, he is a scientist and scholar whose command of methodology and theory has always been at the command of the interpretation and measurement of the evidence. He is the inheritor of the British empiricist tradition in economics that saw its first flowering among the 'political arithmeticians' of the English Restoration, men such as William Petty, Gregory King and Charles Davenant. To a large extent, he has abstained from the short-term policy advice that many of his contemporaries were so anxious to proffer, preferring to concentrate on the advancement of his science. But his contributions have had an incalculable effect on economic policy and his career provides eloquent testimony to the long-run social value of scientific scholarship in economics and a contrast to the unenviable record of those economists who have involved themselves in the day-to-day conduct of British economic policy.

Richard Stone was born in 1913, attended Westminster School, and set out to follow his father's profession by reading law at Gonville and Caius College, Cambridge. He moved to economics midway through his undergraduate career, and came under the influence of Colin Clark, who was then lecturing in statistics to the economists and who was himself deeply involved in the measurement of national income (see particularly Clark, 1937). Stone's interest in modelling, in measurement and in estimation was immediate. During the long vacation prior to his graduation from Cambridge, he set out to estimate a two-factor Cobb–Douglas production function, a pioneering effort the results of which excited little interest in the eyes of his professors, perhaps the first evidence of a Cambridge attitude to econometrics that was later to be reinforced by Maynard Keynes's reactions to Tinbergen's work (Keynes, 1939) and was to be maintained long after similar perceptions had died out elsewhere. After a brief spell in the City, during which he devoted his spare time to producing a monthly bulletin of current economic trends, Stone moved at the outset of World War II to Whitehall, where eventually he came to work, along with James Meade, on the construction of wartime national accounts. At Keynes's instigation, their results were published in the 1941 Government White Paper, *An analysis of the sources of war finance and an estimate of the national income and expenditure in 1938 and 1940*. In 1945, and again under Keynes's stimulus, the Cambridge Department of Applied Economics was founded and Richard Stone was appointed its first Director with an indefinite tenure in the position. Stone brought enormous distinction and worldwide recognition to the department until he was manoeuvred out of the directorship by the Cambridge 'Keynesians' in the mid-1950s. Since then, he has remained in Cambridge; until his retirement in 1980 he held the P.D. Leake Chair of Finance and Accounting. The 1984 Nobel Prize in Economics is perhaps the greatest of many professional honours bestowed on Sir Richard. He has been a Fellow of King's College, Cambridge, since 1945 and of the Econometric Society since 1946. He was president of the Econometric Society in 1955 and President of the Royal Economic Society from 1978-80.

The work for which Stone received the 1984 Nobel Prize in Economics was his 'fundamental contributions to the development of national accounts' that 'greatly improved the basis for empirical economic analysis'. The full history of the development of modern national income accounting remains to be written, and any attempt is well beyond the scope of an article such as this. It is of course not true that Stone was responsible for the basic concepts of national product, consumption, investment and so on, nor that he provided the first estimates of these magnitudes for the United Kingdom or anywhere else (see for example Stone's brief history of the subject in his Nobel Memorial Lecture: Stone, 1984). What Stone should be credited with is the vision of an interlocking *system* of balanced national accounts, and the implementation of that system on a worldwide basis. Stone's system of national accounts, the SNA, published by the United Nations Statistical Office in 1953 with several subsequent revisions, is not simply a set of tables containing the national income magnitudes, but a set of interlocking accounts in which the principles of double-entry bookkeeping are scrupulously maintained. Each outlay for each agent must be matched somewhere else by an inflow for some other agent, so that each entry in each account must appear somewhere else in some other account. Of course, this is only of value because each account, whether for production, accumulation, consumption, or international trade, is independently filled in so that in the end the whole system provides its own complete set of internal consistency checks. Of course, there are always errors and omissions, and some magnitudes cannot be independently measured from both sides of the account, but the credibility and usefulness of each of the numbers hinges on the systematic framework in which they are set. It was Richard Stone, in the first place with James Meade in the Cabinet Office in London, and later on the world stage at the United Nations and the Organization for European Cooperation and Development, who was largely responsible for the way in which national accounts are collected and presented throughout the world (Stone, 1947; OEEC, 1952).

Stone has always favoured the presentation of his national accounts in a matrix format, so that each account appears as the row (incomings) and column (outgoings) of a single matrix. In this social accounting matrix (SAM), the standard magnitudes such as national product, consumption or the balance of trade all have their place, but the detailed entries provide a rich picture of the structure and functioning of the economy. For example, the Leontief input–output matrix of inter-industry transactions is the submatrix corresponding to the detail of the production accounts. Demand patterns of households appear in the submatrix with industries in the rows and households in the columns, while the incomes generated in production flow into households through the value added submatrix. Such social accounting matrices can be disaggregated to show any amount of data, and they can be supplemented by balance sheet data (the opening and closing stocks corresponding to the national income flows); and they can be related to socio-demographic variables in a set of demographic accounts. For a typically elegant and lucid account of this with simple examples, see again Stone (1985). One of the most important features of such 'tableaux économiques' is that it is almost impossible to look at them for long without being led into attempts to model the behaviour that they reveal. For some cases, the SAM is close to *being* a model; the input–output matrix can be thought of both as a record of transactions, and as a succinct description of the technology of production. Similarly, the links between production, accumulation and consumption lead naturally to models of the allocation of household income between saving and the purchases of goods and services. Together with his first wife, Stone had published one of the very first empirical papers on the marginal propensity to consume (Stone and Stone, 1938), and his work on modelling, particularly of consumer behaviour, continued along with his work on national accounts through the late 1940s and 1950s.

In my view, Stone's greatest work lies in his empirical analysis of consumer behaviour and the contributions to econometric methodology that came with it. In a series of papers (Stone, 1945, 1948, 1951; Stone and Prais, 1953) that culminated in 1954 in a book, *The Measurement of Consumers' Expenditure and Behaviour in the United Kingdom, 1920–38*, which to this day remains one of the classics of applied econometrics, Stone presented models that analysed the determination of consumers' expenditures. The book contains a dazzling display of all of the elements of the econometrician's art as of the mid-1950s, and there is very much that can be learned from it even today. There is a great deal of very careful and painstaking description of the data, not tucked away where the details cannot be seen, but proudly and prominently displayed for readers to see and quarrel with should they choose. There is a masterly exposition of the theory of demand and of revealed preference, and there is a chapter on econometric methodology that reads like a text until one realizes that this is where the texts originated. The standard matrix algebra formulation of the general linear model $y = X\beta + u$ appears in its modern form, together with such now standard diagnostics as the Durbin–Watson test, then just invented in the Department of Applied Economics by two young statisticians.

For each of the commodities that he analyses, Stone begins with a loglinear formulation in which the logarithm of the quantity of the good is related to the logarithm of income and the logarithms of other prices, together with a number of other factors that vary from commodity to commodity. For example, the demand for beer is influenced by the average strength of beer. Stone's major practical problem is lack of degrees of freedom; with only nineteen annual observations, disentangling the separate effects of prices, income, and other influences requires generous application of theory and or of prior information. Stone uses both. In the first place, he uses the Slutsky decomposition to absorb the income effects of prices into the income term, thus converting the latter into real rather than money income. Second, he uses zero degree homogeneity to convert prices to relative prices, saving one degree of freedom. Third, he uses elasticities estimated from Engel curve analysis on cross-sectional household budget data to estimate the income elasticities so that, with these imposed, the time-series data are liberated to estimate as many price effects as precisely as possible. Fourth, Stone recognizes the difficulties presented by strong positive autocorrelation in the residuals and to counteract them takes first differences of model and data prior to estimation. The problems that non-stationary time-series pose for econometrics is very much a current research topic, and Stone's procedure, though less than perfect, is much superior to and much less misleading than the ignoring of the problem that characterized most applied work for the quarter of a century after Stone's book. His general procedure set up, Stone then goes on to analyse commodities one by one, reporting results and testing alternative specifications with a care and conviction that has been a model for generations of those of us who have tried to follow him.

The other work of Stone's that I should like to discuss briefly is his paper on the linear expenditure system that appeared in the *Economic Journal* in 1954, the same year that the book appeared. The transition from the models of the book to the model in the paper is in some respects one of the most important transitions in modern applied econometrics, and the methodological issues that are involved are still far from settled. In Stone's book, the influence of the theory of demand is pervasive throughout the discussion of specification and interpretation, but the functional form of the demand equations is essentially *ad hoc*, the double logarithmic form having been widely adopted because of its convenient parametrization of the elasticities which are routinely used to describe demand behaviour. The consequences of using such an equation, and of treating demand equations one by one, is that certain aspects of the theory cannot be used nor easily tested. In particular, the symmetry of the compensated substitution elasticities could not be imposed within the analysis of the book, much as it would have been desirable to do so to gain degrees of freedom and precision of estimation. In the *EJ* paper, Stone comes up with a solution. Starting from a *system* of expenditure equations that are linear in prices and total expenditure, the theoretical requirements of adding-up, homogeneity, and symmetry are imposed algebraically to yield a set of estimating equations, the linear expenditure system, that is fully consistent with demand theory. Although the model cannot be estimated by linear methods, Stone invents an iterative procedure that allows him to obtain estimates for a small system using the interwar data. There are many things to admire in this paper, and many things that can be criticized, especially with the benefit of hindsight. The linear expenditure system is a rather primitive model, and Stone's estimation technique was a poor one; similar things could no doubt be said about the first wheel and its first uses. It is also true that Stone did not solve out for the linear expenditure system utility function, even though the theory of the model had been fully analysed some years before in papers by Klein and Rubin (1947), Samuelson (1947–8), and Geary (1950–51). The real originality and importance of the paper lie elsewhere. Nowhere is the previous literature had anyone ever had the extraordinary idea that it might be possible to use economic theory to confront the data so directly; demand equations had been estimated before, but no one had ever attempted to estimate the parameters of a *utility* function. Economic theory might be used as a general guide as to what to look for, but not to yield estimating equations directly. Today, when every graduate course teaches that this is the way econometrics should be done, and when even macroeconomists routinely estimate their models by fitting data to the Euler conditions of stochastic intertemporal maximization problems, it is easy to forget that 'taking theory to the data' is a relatively young methodology. I believe that Stone's linear expenditure system is a major landmark along the route that leads to where we are now.

In an article of this length it is impossible to give any detail on more than a tiny fraction of Stone's contributions to economics. In addition to his work on the detail of commodity expenditures, there are a set of important papers on savings behaviour (Stone and Rowe, 1962; Stone, 1964, 1966, 1973) and on the development of the stock-adjustment model for explaining the dynamic demands for durable goods (Stone and Rowe, 1957, 1958, 1960). A fuller appreciation of this work and other papers on demand analysis can be found in Johansen (1985) and in Houthakker (1985). Stone has published important work on the theory of price indexes (1956), on seasonal adjustment (1970), and on methods of handling errors of measurement in national accounts (Champernowne, Stone and Meade, 1942; Stone, 1984). Over many years, he supervised the construction of the Cambridge Growth Model, in which social accounting matrices and behavioural equations for demand and production were integrated so as to provide a tool for planning and policy evaluation (see in particular Stone and Brown, 1952, and Stone 1964). More recently, he has extended his work on economic accounting to incorporate demographic accounts (Stone, 1971, 1975; Stone and Weale, 1986).

There is another very great contribution that Stone has made to economics and econometrics that is not reflected in his own published work, but in that of those who have been associated with him over the years. Stone is not, and never really was a teacher in the conventional way. He is a reluctant lecturer, especially to students, and he participated very little in the routine of Cambridge instruction over more than thirty years of formal attachment to the faculty. However, his personal influence has been extraordinarily strong, partly because of the compelling lucidity of his writings, but also by the example he set to the stream of economists and statisticians who spent time in the Department of Applied Economics with him. That stream is still flowing, but there is no doubt that the outstanding years were at the beginning, in the late 1940s and early 1950s, when Stone himself was working on demand and on the econometric techniques of estimating demands. I have no complete list of those who passed through, but a partial list would include Brumberg working on life-cycle models, Houthakker working on revealed preference and applied demand analysis, Prais working on family budgets, and Tobin working on demand analysis and on rationing. On the more statistical side, Durbin, Watson, Cochrane, Orcutt and Anderson spent time in the Department working on autocorrelation in economic time-series, early visitors included Tintner and Duesenberry, Klein, Leontief, Samuelson, Koopmans, Wold, Frisch, Ruggles and Hoffman. Farrell began his academic life in Stone's department and did fine empirical work on dynamic demands and on aggregation theory. Prest worked on demand analysis and on time-series problems. Alan Brown worked on Engel curves and wrote a distinguished book with Aitchison on the uses of lognormal distribution. Afriat began his work on price indexes in the Department. Not only did all of this work owe much to Stone's presence and to the existence of the Department of Applied Economics, but the joint output of all of these people represents an explosion of econometric and economic knowledge that has never been exceeded in the history of the subject and has perhaps only been equalled by the work of the Cowles Commission.

ANGUS DEATON

SELECTED WORKS

1938. (With W.M. Stone.) The marginal propensity to consume and the multiplier. *Review of Economic Studies* 6, 1–24.

1942. (With D.G. Champernowne and J.E. Meade.) The precision of national accounts estimates. *Review of Economic Studies* 9, 111–25.

1945. The analysis of market demand. *Journal of the Royal Statistical Society* 108, 1–98.

1948. The analysis of market demand: an outline of methods and results. *Review of the International Statistical Institute* 16, 23–35.

1951. The demand for food in the United Kingdom before the war. *Metroeconomica* 3, 8–27.

1952. (With S.J. Prais.) Forecasting from econometric equations: a further note on derationing. *Economic Journal* 62, 565–83.

1954a. Linear expenditure systems and demand analysis: an application to the pattern of British demand. *Economic Journal* 64, 511–27.

1954b. (With D.A. Rowe et al.) *The Measurement of Consumers' Expenditure and Behaviour in the United Kingdom, 1920–1938*, Vol. 1, Cambridge: Cambridge University Press.

1956. *Quantity and Price Indexes in National Accounts*. Paris: OECD.

1957. (With D.A. Rowe.) The market demand for durable goods. *Econometrica* 25, 423–43.

1958. (With D.A. Rowe.) Dynamic demand functions: some econometric results. *Economic Journal* 68, 256–70.

1960. (With D.A. Rowe.) The durability of consumers durable goods. *Econometrica* 28, 407–16.

1962. (With D.A. Rowe.) A post-war expenditure function. *Manchester School of Economic and Social Studies* 30, 187–201.

1964a. Private saving in Britain, past, present and future. *Manchester School of Economic and Social Studies* 32, 79–112.

1964b. *The Model in its Environment*. Number 5 in *A Programme for Growth*, London: Chapman & Hall.

1966. Spending and saving in relation to income and wealth. *L'industria* No. 3, 350–61.

1970. *Mathematical Models of the Economy and Other Essays*. London: Chapman & Hall.

1971. *Demographic Accounting and Model Building*. Paris: OECD.

1973. Personal spending and saving in post-war Britain. In *Economic Structure and Development: Essays in honour of Jan Tinbergen*, Amsterdam: North-Holland.

1984. Balancing the national accounts: the adjustment of initial estimates. In *Demand, Equilibrium and Trade*, ed. A. Ingham and A.M. Ulph, London: Macmillan.

1985. The accounts of society. Nobel Memorial Lecture in *Les Prix Nobel 1984*, Stockholm: Almqvist and Wicksell. Reprinted in *Journal of Applied Economics* 1, 1986, 5–28.

BIBLIOGRAPHY

Geary, R.C. 1950–51. A note on 'A constant utility index of the cost of living'. *Review of Economic Studies* 18, 65–6.

Houthakker, H.S. 1985. Richard Stone and the analysis of consumer demand. Cambridge, Mass.: Harvard Institute of Economic Research, Processed.

Johansen, L. 1985. Richard Stone's contribution to economics. *Scandinavian Journal of Economics* 87, 4–32.

Keynes, J.M. 1939. Professor Tinbergen's method. *Economic Journal* 49, 306–18.

Keynes, J.M. 1940. On a method of statistical business-cycle research: comment. *Economic Journal* 50, 154.

Klein, L.R. and Rubin, H. 1947–8. A constant utility index of the cost of living. *Review of Economic Studies* 15, 84–7.

OECC. 1952. *A Standardised System of National Accounting*. Paris: OECC.

Samuelson, P.A. 1947–8. Some implications of linearity. *Review of Economic Studies* 15, 88–90.

Storch, Heinrich Friedrich von (1766–1835). Storch was born in Riga, Russia, of German parents, and in later life wrote fluently in both German and French. After studying at the universities of Jena and Heidelberg, he entered the Russian government service in 1789 and launched a massive historical-statistical description of the Russian Empire, which earned him a membership in the Russian academy of sciences. Hired to tutor the sons of Tsar Alexander I in political economy, he published his *Cours d'economie politique* (1815) in six volumes, followed in 1824 by *Considerations sur la nature du revenu national*. Neither work is particularly distinguished, but the *Cours* does contain a vigorous critique of Smith's distinction between productive and unproductive labour and a theory of stages of economic development similar to that of List's later *National System of Political Economy* (1841). It is difficult to improve on Schumpeter's (1954, p. 502) judgement of Storch's work as a series of glosses on *The Wealth of Nations*: 'his bases and conceptual apparatus are substantially Smithian but Storch disagreed with both Smith and Say on a number of important points. Particularly as regards income analysis, Storch has some claim to being listed, along with Lauderdale, Malthus, and Sismondi, as a forerunner of Keynesianism and of similar tendencies that asserted themselves, on and off, later on'. But to link Storch's name with those of Lauderdale, Malthus and Sismondi is perhaps misleading. Storch was a 'forerunner of Keynesianism' not in the sense of giving credence to one or another version of underconsumptionism, for which he in fact had little sympathy, but rather because of the attention he gave to the concept of national income: although he doubted that it could be calculated with any accuracy, he discussed the problem of making such calculations at considerable length (Studenski, 1961, pp. 20, 87, 138).

MARK BLAUG

BIBLIOGRAPHY

Schumpeter, J.A. 1954. *History of Economics Analysis*. New York: Oxford University Press.

Studenski, P. 1961. *The Income of Nations*. New York: New York University Press.

Strachey, John (1901–1963). A popularizer of political and economic theory, expositor of marxism, and Labour politician. His early political career (cf. Strachey, 1925) was dominated by the influence of the underconsumptionist analyses (especially J.A. Hobson) then highly popular on the Labour left, and by the currency theory of the early Keynes – an association of some precocity. Strachey was the theoretical influence behind the 'Mosley Memorandum' of early 1931, which proffered a solution to the crisis based upon 'national planning', a public works programme and Empire Protectionism.

He soon afterwards rejected this approach altogether, and went on to become probably the best-known British marxist of the decade. His *The Coming Struggle for Power* (1932) was extraordinarily influential amongst the university-educated young. His major work of marxian economics was *The Nature of Capitalist Crisis* (1935), which counterposed the underconsumptionist and neoclassical (in fact Hayekian) accounts of crisis, arguing that they comprised the horns of the dilemma of capitalist accumulation. The book reasserted the classical marxian analyses of value and of the tendency of the rate of profit to fall as fundamental explanations of the causes underlying the slump – an approach then somewhat heterodox in the Communist movement (cf. Eugen Varga). *A Programme for Progress* (1940), by contrast, was an ill-starred attempt to combine an immediate programme for a potential Popular Front government with an understanding of Keynes's *General Theory*.

After the war he served as a minister in the Attlee government, and in the 1950s became a prime intellectual influence on the 'revisionist' wing of the Labour Party. *Contemporary Capitalism* (1956) exorcised his marxist past, aiming to supplant the limitations of the labour theory of value with a Keynesian post-value solution to the 'problem of accumulation', and to provide the analytical framework for stabilising a gradual transition to socialism. Other, diverse, influences at this time included Michal Kalecki and J.K. Galbraith.

He died a very moderate social-democratic theorist, on the eve of a promised Cabinet post in the Wilson government.

DAVID BURCHELL

SELECTED WORKS

1925. *Revolution by Reason*. London: Leonard Parsons.
1932. *The Coming Struggle for Power*. London: Victor Gollancz.
1935. *The Nature of Capitalist Crisis*. London: Victor Gollancz.
1936. *The Theory and Practice of Socialism*. London: Victor Gollancz.
1940. *A Programme for Progress*. London: Victor Gollancz.
1956. *Contemporary Capitalism*. London: Victor Gollancz.
1959. *The End of Empire*. London: Victor Gollancz.

BIBLIOGRAPHY

Thomas, H. 1973. *John Strachey*. London: Eyre Methuen.

strategic behaviour and market structure. Since Bain (1959) the predominant framework for analysis in industrial organization has been the structure-conduct-performance approach. As described in Scherer (1980), this starts with the premise that market structure is determined by basic conditions in an industry, like technology and demand elasticity. Market structure then affects the behaviour of firms which determines economic performance. Traditionally, research in industrial organization has taken market structure as being exogenously determined and has analysed the effects of market structure on firms' conduct and economic performance.

A major area of recent theoretical work in industrial organization has been to investigate a 'reverse' causality – running from firms' behaviour to market structure. Research has centred on the strategic use of price, advertising, capacity and other instruments by firms in order to affect future market structure. In their review of the literature, Encaoua, Geroski and Jacquemin (1986) refer to such work as dynamic extensions of the structure-conduct-performance approach and observe that 'current conduct can become embedded in future market structure through strategic investments made by firms to bar entry and reduce intra-industry mobility' (p. 55). Kreps and Spence (1985) view research which analyses the impact of strategic behaviour on market structure as part of an agenda concerned with having history play a significant role in understanding mature industries:

> The behaviour and performance of a mature industry depend crucially on the history of that industry. Missing from the structure-conduct-performance trichotomy is an explicit consideration of the history of the industry. Every mature industry was once immature, and both its structure and conduct at maturity are influenced by the sort of youth it enjoyed (p. 341).

The motivating force behind strategic behaviour to affect market structure is a desire by firms to maximize discounted profits by increasing their role in the market. This can be achieved by reducing the number of active firms through the strategic deterrence of entry and/or the promotion of exit by rival firms. An alternative approach which does not entail changing the number of competitors is for a firm to gain a relatively large share of some tangible or intangible asset which results in market share being skewed in its favour. At the heart of research on strategic competition is then a concern with understanding how dominant firms arise and whether dominance can be sustained over time (see Geroski and Jacquemin, 1984).

This essay will concentrate on assessing the method of analysis used by researchers in investigating strategic competition, the mechanisms and instruments available to firms for strategically influencing market structure, and the types of results which have been derived. Prior to this, a preliminary task is to attempt to define the concept of 'strategic behaviour'.

The natural place to start is Schelling (1960): 'a strategic move is one that influences the other person's choice, in a manner favorable to one's self, by affecting the other person's expectations on how one's self will behave' (p. 160). Certainly, much of the behaviour we will analyse will meet this definition. For example, the limit-pricing literature is based on the premise that an incumbent firm can affect the entry decision of a potential entrant through its pre-entry output choice because it constrains its post-entry output decision. Of specific interest is the case where the incumbent firm can commit itself to a high post-entry output rate in order to make entry unprofitable. However, strategic competition may also entail behaviour designed to constrain the other player rather than one's self. For example, Salop and Scheffman (1983) analyse how a firm can favourably influence market structure by increasing the cost faced by competitors. If the other firms use a more labour-intensive technology, this could be achieved by pushing for an industry-wide union contract with higher wages.

In order to encompass the wide array of firms' behaviour which has arisen in the literature on strategic competition, we will offer a more general definition which builds on that of Schelling. An agent is said to act strategically when in choosing an action it takes into account the dependence of the other agents' actions on its behaviour. As an example, consider the two-agent situation of an incumbent firm and a potential entrant. Suppose the decision to enter depends on the pre-entry action of the incumbent firm. An incumbent firm is acting strategically if it recognizes this dependence and acts to influence the decision of the potential entrant. The essential element is that the incumbent firm takes as fixed the entry rule of the potential entrant, which may be dependent on the incumbent firm's pre-entry choice, and not the decision to enter or not enter. Taking the latter as fixed implies that the incumbent firm is ignoring the effect its action has on the decision of the potential entrant.

Given the role of strategic behaviour, it is natural that non-cooperative game theory should be the predominant mode of analysis. The appeal of the game-theoretic approach is that it provides a framework in which strategies are well defined and equilibrium concepts that require a player to take into account the strategies (i.e. the proposed behaviour) of the other players in choosing his strategy. The particular game form which is most well suited is the extensive form because it describes explicitly the sequence of moves of players and the information a player possesses when it is his turn to move.

A common property of all the noncooperative games which have been used to analyse strategic competition is that they are multi-stage, so that there is a sequential nature to the moves of players. In order for there to be an opportunity for one player to influence the actions of other players, he must move first, and the other players must have information on that move when they choose their actions. A simultaneous-move game is thus inappropriate for analysing the incentives for firms to act strategically in order to influence market structure. Of course, whether it is reasonable for players to move sequentially depends on the particular economic situation.

Having formulated a noncooperative game to describe some economic setting, the final critical step for a researcher is the choice of a solution concept. The most widely used solution concept in the literature on strategic behaviour and market structure is subgame perfect equilibrium (Selten, 1975). To form a subgame perfect equilibrium, the strategies of the players must form a Nash equilibrium for every subgame. This then requires that a player's strategy be a best reply to the strategies of the other players, no matter where he is in the game. Subgame perfect equilibrium would seem to be the appropriate solution concept if all players are assumed to be strategic-minded since it eliminates Nash equilibria which are based on incredible threats. That is, a Nash equilibrium may entail one player threatening to perform some action in response to another player's action even though it would not be in his own best interest to go through with the threat. If all players are believed to be equally strategic-minded, an equilibrium based upon an incredible threat seems unreasonable. Such a Nash equilibrium is not subgame perfect, because the strategies of the players do not form a Nash equilibrium in the subgame in which the player is forced to go through with his threat. It is this property that makes subgame perfect equilibrium an appealing solution concept for analysing the incentives for strategic competition.

Having discussed general methods of analysis, let us consider a particular model which is an adaptation of the work of Dixit (1980) and Ware (1984). In a three-stage game an incumbent firm and a potential entrant interact. In stage 1, the incumbent firm chooses a level of capital, K_1, where the cost of producing output rate q_1 is $C(q_1; K_1) = f(K_1)q_1 + rK_1$ and $f'(K_1) < 0$ and $f(0) = \infty$. Given knowledge of K_1, the potential entrant makes an entry decision in stage 2. If entry is chosen, the potential entrant incurs a cost of γ and then chooses a value for K_2 (it faces the same cost function). Finally, the stage 3 game involves the active firms simultaneously choosing output. If entry occurred, subgame perfection then requires the two firms to achieve a Nash equilibrium in the stage 3 game given the capital levels (K_1, K_2). Let the equilibrium profit rate for firm i be denoted $\hat{\pi}_i(K_1, K_2)$.

Given the conjectured outcome of the stage 3 game, the potential entrant will enter if and only if $\hat{\pi}[K_1, \psi(K_1)] - \gamma > 0$ where $\psi(K_1)$ is defined by

$$\hat{\pi}_2[K_1, \psi(K_1)] = \max_{K_2} \hat{\pi}_2(K_1, K_2).$$

Thus, it figures out what equilibrium profits would be if it entered. Since $f'(K_1) < 0$ then the incumbent firm's post-entry output rate will be increasing in K_1. It is then reasonable to assume there exists a value for K_1, $\bar{K}$, such that

$$\hat{\pi}_2[K_1, \psi(K_1)] - \gamma \gtreqless 0 \quad \text{as} \quad K_1 \lesseqgtr \bar{K}$$

In equilibrium, the potential entrant will enter if and only if $K_1 < \bar{K}$.

To complete the derivation of the subgame perfect equilibrium, we need to solve for the optimal strategy of the incumbent firm in stage 1. Define K' by

$$\hat{\pi}_1(K', 0) = \max_{K_1} \hat{\pi}_1(K_1, 0).$$

If there was no other active firm, the incumbent firm would set $K_1 = K'$. If $K' \geqslant \bar{K}$ then entry is naturally deterred. Assume for the remainder of the analysis that $K' < \bar{K}$. One strategy option is for the incumbent firm to set $K_1 = \bar{K}$, deter entry, and earn $\hat{\pi}_1(\bar{K}, 0)$. The alternative option is to set $K_1 < \bar{K}$, induce entry but maximize post-entry profits by acting as a Stackelberg leader. The optimal value of K_1, in that case is $\tilde{K}$ where

$$\hat{\pi}_1[\tilde{K}, \psi(\tilde{K})] = \max_{K_1} \hat{\pi}_1[K_1, \psi(K_1)].$$

Subgame perfect equilibrium behaviour then has entry being naturally deterred if $K' \geqslant \bar{K}$. If $K' < \bar{K}$ and $\hat{\pi}_1(\bar{K}, 0) > \pi_1[\tilde{K}, \psi(\tilde{K})]$ then entry is strategically deterred, while if $\hat{\pi}_1[\tilde{K}, \psi(\tilde{K})] > \pi_1(\bar{K}, 0)$ then entry occurs in equilibrium. It is important to note that an asymmetric solution occurs in all three cases. This is obvious in the first two cases as the incumbent firm is the only active firm. However, even when entry occurs the incumbent firm will have a larger market share. By choosing capital first, it can ensure itself a relatively large share of capital. The incumbent firm is then dominant in the industry even when entry occurs.

Much of the literature on strategic behaviour and market structure has focused on the first-mover advantage possessed by incumbent firms. Of particular concern is how it can be used to influence entry decisions and whether it results in a long-run effect on market structure. It is significant to note, however, that having the opportunity to move first is by no means sufficient for a firm to affect market structure strategically. Since future market structure is endogenously determined in equilibrium, a firm's current decision must affect future cost or demand conditions in order to alter the equilibrium path of the industry. The decision variable available to an incumbent firm must then be durable, that is, its effects are felt over time. When firms have imperfect information on cost or demand functions, strategic behaviour can also influence market structure by conveying information and thus changing firms' expectations on the equilibrium path. In that case the variable need not be durable.

In order for a firm to affect market structure strategically, there must then exist an intertemporal interdependence between some current decision variable and the future equilibrium path of the industry. From a game-theoretic perspective, this is interpreted as current behaviour changing the initial conditions to the future equilibrium path. In our example, the stage 3 equilibrium was defined by the initial condition (K_1, K_2). Thus the incumbent firm influenced the future path of the industry by its choice of capital, K_1. The key element is to credibly commit the industry to pursue a particular path. Since firms expect the industry to be in equilibrium (so that idle threats play no role), this can be achieved only by affecting real cost or demand conditions or firms' beliefs over those conditions.

An implicit assumption here is that firms are certain about the future oligopoly solution; that is, how firms will behave given cost and demand functions. An opportunity for strategic behaviour can arise even when cost and demand functions are atemporal and known, provided some firms have private information on future conduct. A natural setting for such an information asymmetry to exist is between incumbent firms and potential entrants. A potential entrant is apt to be uncertain about the ability of firms to collude once it enters. Incumbent firms have private information on that event since they know whether they are currently able to collude. In such a setting, Harrington (1984) shows that a cartel may be able to deter entry strategically by acting noncooperatively. Noncooperation signals that the post-entry solution is unlikely to entail collusion and therefore that entry is unprofitable.

While the literature on strategic behaviour and market structure covers a vast array of models, a common element is that each focuses on a single strategic instrument. The three most popular decision variables are price (or output), durable capital and the timing of lumpy investment. The most widely investigated instrument is price, which began with research on limit pricing and predatory pricing. Limit pricing is the use of pre-entry price to prevent entry, while predatory pricing is the use of price to promote exit (though it may be for the purpose of deterring future entry). A significant part of the research in this area examines the use of price as a signal to influence entry or exit decisions. Milgrom and Roberts (1982a) show that when a potential entrant is uncertain of the incumbent firm's cost function the incumbent firm can prevent entry by setting a low pre-entry price. This credibly signals that it is a low-cost firm, which implies that entry is unprofitable. Kreps and Wilson (1982) and Milgrom and Roberts (1982b) investigate how predatory behaviour can be used to build a reputation for toughness under imperfect information. Such a reputation will prevent entry and lead to a dominant position for an incumbent firm.

An incumbent firm's initial output rate has also been shown to affect market structure by changing the future cost function it faces when there are costs to adjusting output over time. Flaherty (1980) shows that an incumbent firm can credibly commit itself to a high output path in the future by producing at a high rate today. Even if such behaviour does not prevent entry, market share will be skewed in the incumbent firm's favour. It is interesting to note, however, that dominance cannot be sustained over time, as the only stable steady-states are symmetric. Other mechanisms which allow output to be used as a strategic weapon include learning curve effects (Fudenberg and Tirole, 1983) and brand loyalty (Schmalensee, 1982). In contrast to adjustment costs and the learning curve, which work through the cost function, brand loyalty takes the form of positive inertia for the incumbent firms' demand functions.

A considerable amount of research has also investigated the use of capital to commit the industry to pursuing a particular equilibrium path. As shown in our example, it is the durability of capital which allows firms to change future market structure. The classics of this literature are Dixit (1980), which concentrates on capacity and how it affects marginal cost, and Spence (1979). In a continuous-time framework, Spence shows that a firm with a head-start in investing could create a dominant position for itself by investing at a very fast rate. In contrast to Flaherty (1980), Spence finds that this dominance can be sustained in the long run. There has also been a growing amount of research which investigates the use of advertising as an instrument to affect market structure (e.g. Schmalensee, 1983). By investing in goodwill, an incumbent firm can increase the future demand for its product and lead to an asymmetric equilibrium path.

A third instrument for influencing market structure is the timing of lumpy investment. The types of lumpy investments which have been analysed include the location of a plant (Eaton and Lipsey, 1979), the introduction of a new product (Schmalensee, 1978) and the discovery and patenting of an innovation (Gilbert and Newbery, 1982). The main result of this literature is that if it is profitable for a new firm to make such an investment at time t, then it is always profitable for the incumbent firm to pre-empt the new firm by making the investment just before t. As an example, consider the introduction of a new product which will be an imperfect substitute for the existing products of the incumbent firms. Suppose an anticipated increase in demand at time t' yields a positive profit rate for a new product. Introduction of the product prior to t' results in a negative profit rate. In anticipation of this demand increase, potential entrants will compete by trying to pre-empt one another. There exists a time t'' ($< t'$) such that introduction of a new product at that time yields normal discounted profits. If a new firm introduces this product, it will of course compete with existing firms and earn less than monopoly profits. However, if an existing firm introduces the new product, it can coordinate its pricing policy with that for its other products and yield higher profits than a new firm would earn. Thus an incumbent firm would find it profitable to introduce the new product just before t'' and pre-empt entry.

A related literature which has elements in common with those outlined above is that on research and development (R&D). Models in this area analyse how firms compete for innovations through expenditure on R&D. While strategic behaviour does not play a major role, the R&D literature does focus on firms' investment which will change future market structure by altering basic conditions in the industry, like the production technology. We mention this research in light of the difficulty in defining the boundaries to the literature on strategic behaviour and market structure.

Finally, we observe that merger activity is a very straightforward way to change market structure. Of particular interest is to determine whether merger may result in a firm which is bigger than the sum of its parts. Unfortunately, research in this area is still attempting to show the profitability of horizontal mergers and has not yet begun to show how it can be used to create a dominant firm. Since merger activity is widely observed in the real world, this would seem to be a promising task.

JOSEPH E. HARRINGTON, JR.

BIBLIOGRAPHY

Bain, J. 1959. *Industrial Organization*. New York: John Wiley.

Caves, R. and Porter, M. 1977. From entry barriers: conjectural decisions and contrived deterrence to new competition. *Quarterly Journal of Economics* 91, 241–61.

Dixit, A. 1980. The role of investment in entry deterrence. *Economic Journal* 90, 95–106.

Eaton, B.C. and Lipsey, R. 1979. The theory of market pre-emption: the persistence of excess capacity and monopoly in growing spatial markets. *Economica* 46, 149–58.

Encaoua, D., Geroski, P. and Jacquemin, A. 1986. Strategic competition and the persistence of dominant firms: a survey. In *New Developments in the Analysis of Market Structure*, ed. J.E. Stiglitz and G.F. Mathewson, Cambridge, Mass.: MIT Press.

Flaherty, M.T. 1980. Dynamic limit pricing, barriers to entry, and rational firms. *Journal of Economic Theory* 23, 160–82.
Fudenberg, D. and Tirole, J. 1983. Learning-by-doing and market performance. *Bell Journal of Economics* 14, 522–30.
Geroski, P. and Jacquemin, A. 1984. Dominant firms and their alleged decline. *International Journal of Industrial Organization* 2, 1–27.
Gilbert, R. and Newbery, D. 1982. Preemptive patenting and the persistence of monopoly. *American Economic Review* 72, 514–26.
Harrington, J. 1984. Noncooperative behavior by a cartel as an entry-deterring signal. *Rand Journal of Economics* 15, 426–33.
Kreps, D. and Spence, A.M. 1985. Modelling the role of history in industrial organization and competition. In *Issues in Contemporary Microeconomics and Welfare*, ed. G.R. Feiwel, Albany: State University of New York Press.
Kreps, D. and Wilson, R. 1982. Reputation and imperfect information. *Journal of Economic Theory* 27, 253–79.
Milgrom, P. and Roberts, D.J. 1982a. Limit pricing and entry under incomplete information: an equilibrium analysis. *Econometrica* 50, 443–59.
Milgrom, P. and Roberts, D.J. 1982b. Predation, reputation, and entry deterrence. *Journal of Economic Theory* 27, 280–312.
Salop, S. 1979. Strategic entry deterrence. *American Economic Review* 69, 335–8.
Salop, S. and Scheffman, D. 1983. Raising rivals' costs. *American Economic Review* 73, 267–71.
Schelling, T. 1960. *The Strategy of Conflict*. Cambridge, Mass.: Harvard University Press.
Scherer, F. 1980. *Industrial Market Structure and Economic Performance*. 2nd edn, Chicago: Rand-McNally.
Schmalensee, R. 1978. Entry deterrence in the ready-to-eat breakfast cereals industry. *Bell Journal of Economics* 9, 305–27.
Schmalensee, R. 1982. Product differentiation advantages of pioneering brands. *American Economic Review* 72, 349–65.
Schmalensee, R. 1983. Advertising and entry deterrence: an exploratory model. *Journal of Political Economy* 91, 636–53.
Selten, R. 1975. Re-examination of the perfectness concept for equilibrium points in extensive games. *International Journal of Game Theory* 4, 25–55.
Spence, A.M. 1979. Investment strategy and growth in a new market. *Bell Journal of Economics* 10, 1–19.
Ware, R. 1984. Sunk costs and strategic commitment: a proposed three-stage equilibrium. *Economic Journal* 94, 370–8.
Waterson, M. 1984. *Economic Theory of the Industry*. Cambridge: Cambridge University Press.

strategic reallocation of endowments. In the framework of pure exchange economies it might well happen that economic agents will find it advantageous to change their endowment holdings and by this increase their utility. Such an increase is achieved by acting competitively with the new endowments and comparing the new equilibrium allocation with the one that would have been achieved without the change.

When such a phenomenon happens we say that a *strategic reallocation of endowments* has occurred. Examples of such strategic behaviour can easily be found in reality. For example, farmers sometimes destroy part of their crops in order to raise their selling price; oil companies give false reports on their reserves for the same reason and insured agents, partially for that reason, report to the insurer on less levels of wealth than they really have.

Such strategic behaviour by single economic agents contradicts the fundamental competitive assumption that agents cannot influence market prices. Mathematically, this assumption is equivalent to single agents being negligible relative to the whole economy. For that reason strategic behaviour of single economic agents is strongly connected to the finiteness of the economy. Strategic behaviour of groups of agents, however, can very well be effective in continuum economies. Thus the phenomenon of strategic reallocation of endowments, although more probable in finite economies, is surely not limited to the finite cases.

Strategic change in endowments, sometimes called *manipulation via endowments*, is closely related to the subject called manipulation of preferences, which deals with strategic behaviour that concerns the second parameter of economic agents – their preferences (utility functions). In fact, it can be shown that every manipulation via endowments can be considered as a manipulation of preferences. This relation, however, does not prove to be very valuable in answering questions concerning the existence of strategic reallocation of endowments or the existence of Nash equilibrium in the resulting game (see below). For that reason, results from manipulation of preferences cannot be directly applied here.

We now turn to definitions of pure exchange economies and to the notions that are needed for the definition of strategic reallocation of endowments. Then we define four kinds of manipulation via endowments. Finally, we give some important results concerning this phenomenon. In stating the results we choose to put more emphasis on group manipulations and to explain the other results more briefly.

DEFINITIONS

Assume a pure exchange economy with $l \geqslant 2$ commodities that consists of $m \geqslant 2$ consumers (the economic agents). All consumers have the same consumption set X, which is a subset of the l-dimensional Euclidean space R^l. Consumer i has a vector of initial endowment ω_i in X and a quasi-concave surjective and smooth utility function $u_i: R^l \to R$ such that (i) u_i has a strictly positive gradient; (ii) $u_i^{-1}(t)$ has non-zero Gaussian curvature and (iii) $u_i^{-1}(t, \infty)$ is bounded from below, for all t in R. These assumptions ensure that consumer i has a smooth demand function f_i: $S \times R \to X$ where

$$S = \{p \in R^l_{++} \mid p^l = 1\}$$

is the set of price vectors (where the lth commodity serves as the numeraire) and R represents the possible range for ω_i – consumer i's income (which, in this case, is equal to $p\omega_i$, the scalar product of the price and the initial endowment vectors). The function Z_i: $S \times R \to R^l$ defined by $Z_i = f_i - \omega_i$ is consumer i's excess demand function.

A vector p in S is an *equilibrium price vector* for the initial allocation $\omega = (\omega_1, \ldots, \omega_m)$ in X^m if

$$Z(p, \omega) = \sum_{i=1}^{m} Z_i(p, p\omega_i) = 0,$$

that is, if total demand is equal to total supply. The pair (p, ω) is called an *equilibrium* and the allocation $f(p, \omega) = [f_1(p, p\omega_1), \ldots, f_m(p, p\omega_m)]$ is called an *equilibrium allocation*. We denote by E the set of all possible equilibrium pairs (p, ω) in $S \times X^m$.

It is known that, generically, every initial allocation has an odd number of isolated equilibrium price vectors. Since this number can be greater than one we define for every equilibrium (p, ω) a function $P: X^m \to S$ by

$$P(\omega'; p, \omega) = \arg\min \| p' - p \| \quad \text{s.t. } Z(p', \omega') = 0.$$

The function P gives the equilibrium price vector p' of ω' which is closest to the equilibrium price vector p(of ω). If (p, ω) is regular (which means that the Jacobian matrix of Z at (p, ω) is of full rank, and generically this is the situation) then P is really a function that describes the smooth selection of E that passes through (p, ω).

We can now formally define the concepts of strategic reallocations of endowments. For this let (p, ω) be in E and assume that ω' in the following definition is close enough to ω so that P is well defined.

Definition: (i) A coalition D of consumers can *C-manipulate* in (p, ω) if there exist ω' in X^m and $p' = P(\omega'; p, \omega)$ such that

$$\omega'_i = \omega_i \quad \text{for } i \notin D, \qquad \sum_{i \in D} \omega'_i = \sum_{i \in D} \omega_i$$

and

$$u_i[f_i(p', p'\omega'_i)] > u_i[f_i(p, p\omega_i)], \qquad \text{for all } i \in D.$$

(ii) Consumer i can *W-manipulate* in (p, ω) if there exist ω' in X^m and $p' = P(\omega'; p, \omega)$ such that

$$\omega'_i < \omega_i, \quad \omega'_j = \omega_j, \qquad \text{for } j \neq i$$

and

$$u_i[f_i(p', p'\omega'_i) + \omega_i - \omega'_i) > u_i[f_i(p, p\omega_i)].$$

(iii) Consumer i can *G-manipulate* in (p, ω) if there exist $j \neq i$, ω' in X^m and $p' = P(\omega'; p, \omega)$ such that

($t > 0$ is in R^l)

$$\omega'_i = \omega_i - t, \quad \omega'_j = \omega_j + t, \quad \omega'_h = \omega_h \qquad \text{for } h \neq i, j$$

and

$$u_i[f_i(p', p'\omega'_i)] > u_i[f_i(p, p\omega_i)].$$

(iv) Consumer i can *D-manipulate* in (p, ω) if there exist ω' in X^m and $p' = P(\omega'; p, \omega)$ such that:

$$\omega'_i < \omega_i, \quad \omega'_j = \omega_j, \qquad \text{for } j \neq i$$

and

$$u_i[f_i(p', p'\omega'_i)] > u_i[f_i(p, p\omega_i)].$$

The definition of C-manipulation (C for coalition) captures the main idea of strategic reallocations of endowments. The coalition C-manipulates in (p, ω) if its participants can reallocate their resources (this is the change from ω to ω') and by this achieve a new equilibrium allocation $[f(p', \omega')]$ which gives each one of them a higher utility level than in the original equilibrium allocation $f(p, \omega)$. By doing so, the coalition D exploits its ability to influence the equilibrium prices and does it to its advantage.

The definition of W-manipulation (W for withholding) is also a kind of strategic reallocation of endowments, except that here the reallocation is done by a unique consumer (i in the definition) and it deals with the partition of his initial endowment vector ω_i into two parts: the first is the part that is declared as his new endowment (ω'_i) and enters the market; the second is the part of the endowment that is withheld from the market. At the end of the trade the W-manipulating consumer adds the withheld part $(\omega_i - \omega'_i)$ to his new equilibrium vector $f_i(p', p'\omega'_i)$ and his utility is thus computed at the vector that is the sum of these two vectors. To summarize, by changing the allocation of his initial endowment ω_i from 'ω_i to the market and 0 to withholding' to 'ω'_i to the market and $\omega_i - \omega'_i$ to withholding' the final utility of consumer i may increase. If this is the case then we say that consumer i can W-manipulate in (p, ω).

The third part of the definition refers to G-manipulation (G for gift). In such a manipulation a gift (the vector t) is given by consumer i to consumer j such that in the new resulting equilibrium allocation $f(p', \omega')$ the utility level of i is higher than his utility level of the original equilibrium allocation. In this case the reallocation is made among consumers i and j. Note that a conceptual shortcoming of this reallocation is that consumer j has to agree to accept this gift, and he would do so only if his utility will also rise. In such a case we are back in the C-manipulation situation. However, since this kind of manipulation attracted a lot of interest in the theory of international trade (under the name of *the transfer paradox*) we decided to define it separately.

The last part of the definition deals with manipulation of endowments that is done by destroying part of them (D is for destroying). In this case a consumer might find it advantageous simply to destroy part of his endowments and by this achieve a better equilibrium allocation. Again, some kind of reallocation of consumer i's endowments is done here: part of his endowments is taken away from the market and transferred to the 'non-existing' phase.

RESULTS

C-manipulation. The first example of an economy where C-manipulation exists was given by Gabszewicz and Dreze (1971). In that example the economy had a continuum of consumers. Examples of finite exchange economies were given by Gale (1974) for non-smooth utilities and then by Aumann and Peleg (1974) for the smooth case. The existence of those examples was very nicely generalized by Guesnerie and Laffont (1978) who proved that any set of consumers in which at least two have different vectors of income effects can be embedded in an infinite number of economies where it can C-manipulate.

The vector of income effects of consumer i is simply the vector of the partial derivatives of the demand function f_i with respect to i's income; that is, the vector $(\partial f^1_i/\partial w_i, \ldots, \partial f^l_i/\partial w_i)$. Their result thus implies not only that examples exist where C-manipulation occurs, but that indeed there is an infinite number of such examples. Moreover, almost every set of consumers (the condition of their result is generic) can be that coalition that can C-manipulate, and again, in an infinite number of economies.

Guesnerie and Laffont's result, although saying that many examples of C-manipulation exist, says nothing about the size of the set of economies where this phenomenon happens. It might still be the case that such economies are very exceptional. Some results that shed more light on the structure of the set of C-manipulable economies (and that of its complement) were given by Safra (1983). In that work the number of consumers, their utilities and the sum of the economy's resources are given; the main results are the following.

First, if every initial allocation has a unique (and fixed) price equilibrium, then no equilibrium is C-manipulable. This case is very exceptional. Secondly, in all other cases the set of C-manipulable equilibria has a non-empty interior, it 'spreads' over all the equilibrium set E and, generically, it contains every non-regular equilibrium. This result clearly implies that C-manipulation is very common. The last part of the result is very intuitive since a necessary condition for C-manipulation is that the change in prices will be large enough to compensate each coalition's members for possible losses of wealth. Thirdly, the complement of the set of C-manipulable equilibrium contains an open set which includes the equilibria of the Pareto-optimal allocations and finally, a given coalition can *C*-manipulate if, and only if, a condition similar to that of Guesnerie and Laffont is satisfied.

Another result concerning C-manipulation (as well as G-manipulation and D-manipulation) is that of Polterovich and Spivak (1983). They have shown that if the demand correspondence (it need not be a function) satisfies gross substitutability and responds positively to changes in income, then no coalition of consumers can C-manipulate.

Postlewaite (1979) was concerned with manipulating more general resource allocating mechanisms. His result concerning C-manipulation states that *every* individually rational and Pareto optimal mechanism (including the competitive mechanism) can be C-manipulated in the sense that there exists at least one economy where such a mechanism can be C-manipulated.

W-manipulation. An example for the occurrence of W-manipulation was given by Postlewaite (1979) who also showed (as mentioned above) that a whole class of mechanisms are W-manipulable. In fact, the occurrence of W-manipulation for the competitive mechanism is much more common than one might surmise from the above example; as claimed by Thomson (1979), almost every economy is W-manipulable.

In view of these negative results interest has shifted to questions of second-best type, concerning the degree of W-manipulability of the competitive mechanism. For measurement of that degree one looks at the Nash equilibria of the W-manipulation game, (where the strategies of the consumers are the W-manipulations available to them) and measures the distance between these Nash equilibria and the equilibrium allocation. An important work was that of Thomson (1979) who defined and characterized those Nash-equilibria (although no proof of their existence was given) and gave specific examples showing that no specific relation exists between those equilibria and the equilibrium allocation. The existence question was addressed by Safra (1985) for (finite) large enough economies, which also showed that under some regularity conditions every sequence of such Nash equilibria converges (as the economy becomes large) to an equilibrium allocation.

G-manipulation. As mentioned above, this kind of strategic reallocation of endowments is closely related to what is called the *transfer paradox* in the theory of international trade. The first example of this phenomenon was given by Leontief (1936) and the main interest in that literature has been the relation between that phenomenon and (Walrasian) instability of the price equilibrium. Many researchers have been working on this and it is now known that with more than three consumers G-manipulability can very well occur at stable equilibria.

Other results concerning G-manipulability can easily be deduced from results concerning C-manipulability.

D-manipulation. The last kind of strategic reallocation of endowments is also related to the theory of international trade where its mirror image was discussed under the name of *immiserizing growth.* The phenomenon of immiserizing growth occurs when a consumer's resources increase and his utility in the new resulting equilibrium decreases. It can be seen that under very mild conditions D-manipulation occurs if and only if immiserizing growth occurs.

The first discussion of this phenomenon is that of Bhagwati (1958), while an example can also be found in Aumann and Peleg's paper (1974). Bhagwati, and later Mas-Colell (1976) and Mantel (1982) gave conditions which preclude this phenomenon, and Hatta (1983) showed some similaries among these various conditions. Relating to gross substitutability and normality also appear in Polterovich and Spivak (1983).

The last result to be mentioned is that of Postlewaite (1979) and concerns general mechanisms. This time, contrary to the above cases, there exist mechanisms that are immune to D-manipulability and which yield Pareto optimal and individually rational allocations.

Zvi Safra

See also IMMISERIZING GROWTH; TERMS OF TRADE.

BIBLIOGRAPHY

Aumann, R. and Peleg, B. 1974. A note on Gale's example. *Journal of Mathematical Economics* 1, 209–11.

Bhagwati, J.N. 1958. Immiserizing growth: a geometrical note. *Review of Economic Studies* 25, June, 201–5.

Gabszewicz, J.J. and Dreze, J.H. 1971. Syndicates of traders in an economy, In *Differential Games and Related Topics*, ed. H.W. Kuhn and G. Szego, Amsterdam: North-Holland.

Gale, D. 1974. Exchange equilibrium and coalitions: an example. *Journal of Mathematical Economics* 1, 63–6.

Guesnerie, R. and Laffont, J.J. 1978. Advantageous reallocation of initial resources. *Econometrica* 46(4), July, 835–41.

Hatta, T. 1983. Immiserizing growth in a many commodity setting. Working Paper, The Johns Hopkins University, September.

Leontief, W. 1936. Note on the pure theory of capital transfer. In *Explorations in Economics*, Taussig Festschrift, New York: McGraw-Hill.

Mantel, R. 1982. Substitutability and the welfare effects of endowment increases. Paper presented at the Econometric Society Meeting in Mexico.

Mas-Colell, A. 1976. En torno a una propiedad poco atractiva del equilibrio competitivo. *Moneda y Credito* [Madrid], no. 136, 11–27.

Polterovich, V.M. and Spivak, V.A. 1983. Gross substitutability of point-to-set correspondences. *Journal of Mathematical Economics* 11(2), April, 117–40.

Postlewaite, A. 1979. Manipulation via endowments. *Review of Economic Studies* 46(2), April, 255–62.

Safra, Z. 1983. Manipulation by reallocating initial endowments. *Journal of Mathematical Economics* 12(1), September, 1–17.

Safra, Z. 1985. Existence of equilibrium for Walrasian endowment games. *Journal of Economic Theory* 37(2), December, 366–78.

Thomson, W. 1979. The equilibrium allocations of Walras and Lindahl manipulation games. Discussion Paper, University of Minnesota, Center of Economic Research, No. 111.

strategy-proof allocation mechanisms. In abstract form an allocation mechanism may be thought of as a function mapping agents' preferences into final allocations. For example, the competitive allocation mechanism calculates market-clearing prices to select a feasible, Pareto optimal, final allocation that varies with agents' preferences. This simple view, however, of the mechanism being only a map from preferences to final allocation is inadequate because it fails to satisfy the basic tenet of microeconomic theory: agents, within the rules of the mechanism, maximize their utility subject to technological and informational constraints.

The problem is this. An agent's preferences may be private to himself and unverifiable except through circumstantial interference. Therefore, whenever they are private, the competitive mechanism must in fact depend on each agents' report of what his preferences are, not on his actual preferences. That is, agents can lie about their preferences. Provided that the number of agents in the economy is finite, then each individual agent can affect the market-clearing prices by strategically misreporting his preferences.

If he knows what other agents are likely to report as their preferences, then through misrepresentation he can affect prices so that he secures a final allocation that he prefers over the final allocation that he would have received if he had reported his preferences truthfully. Consequently, the competitive mechanism, for finite collections of agents, is in fact a mapping from preferences and each agent's information about other agents' preferences and information. Inclusion of agents' information about other agents enormously complicates the analysis of allocation mechanisms. Game theoretic methods become necessary.

These observations are not new. Black (1958, p. 182) reports that J.-C. Borda, 18th-century French inventor of the 'Borda count' rule for making committee decisions, exclaimed that 'My scheme is only intended for honest men' when he was confronted with the possibilities of strategic misrepresentation. Careful analyses of the competitive mechanism have generally skirted the problem by proceeding under cover of the assumption that the numbers of buyers and sellers in each market are so large that no individual agent can affect price strategically. Arrow (1951, p. 7), in his classic study of social-welfare functions, recognized that agents may have an incentive to misrepresent. Vickrey (1960) evaluated several committee voting procedures using vulnerability to strategic misrepresentation as one of his criteria.

The study of strategy-proof allocation mechanisms is an effort to circumvent the complications that strategic misrepresentation creates. Roughly speaking, an allocation mechanism is strategy-proof if every agent's utility-maximizing choice of what preferences to report depends only on his own preferences and not on his expectations concerning the preferences that other agents will report. If the mechanism is strategy-proof, then each agent can disregard his expectations concerning other agents' reports and straightforwardly report the preference ordering that uniformly maximizes his utility. That is, each agent always has a dominant strategy if the mechanism is strategy-proof. Understanding the strategic choices of agents when the allocation mechanism is strategy-proof is trivial; they always play their dominant strategies. Thus, for example, if the Borda count were a strategy-proof mechanism, Borda would not have needed to wish for honest men only to utilize his mechanism. He could have settled for maximizing men, an easier order to fill.

Strategy-proof mechanisms are desirable, but do they exist? This is the central question of this essay and has been the central question in the study of strategy-proof allocation mechanisms. That some voting procedures and the competitive mechanism fail strategy-proofness suggests the conjecture that all other attractive allocation mechanisms also fail strategy-proofness. This conjecture, which Dummett and Farquharson (1961) first made, turns out to be true. An impossibility theorem due to Gibbard (1973) and Satterthwaite (1975) shows that no strategy-proof allocation mechanism exists that satisfies minimal requirements of responsiveness to individual agents' preferences.

Precise statement of this fundamental result requires the introduction of some notation. Let $I = \{1, 2, \ldots, n\}$ be a fixed set of n agents who must select a single alternative from a set $X = \{x, y, z, \ldots\}$ of $|X|$ distinct, conceivable final allocations. Each agent $i \in I$ has asymmetric, transitive preferences P_i over the allocations X. Let P_i represent strict preference. Thus for each $x, y \in X$ and each $i \in I$, only three possibilities exist: xP_iy (agent i strictly prefers x over y), yP_ix (agent i strictly prefers y over x), or neither xP_iy nor yP_ix (agent i is indifferent between x and y). Not every asymmetric, transitive ordering X is necessarily admissible as a preference ordering P_i. For example, for a particular $x, y \in X$, xP_iy might be the only admissible ordering because allocation x dominates allocation y in terms of the usual non-satiation axiom of consumer demand theory. Therefore let Σ represent all possible asymmetric, transitive preference orderings over X and let $\Omega \subset \Sigma$ represent the set of all asymmetric, transitive preference orderings over X that are admissible. Thus P_i is an admissible ordering for agent i only if $P_i \in \Omega$. Let $\Omega^n = \Omega \times \Omega \times \cdots \times \Omega$ be the n-fold Cartesian product of Ω. If every asymmetric, transitive ordering is admissible, then preferences are said to be unrestricted and $\Omega = \Sigma$. Let the triple $\langle I, X, \Omega \rangle$ be called the environment.

An n-tuple $P = (P_1, \ldots, P_n) \in \Omega^n$ is called a preference profile, and a subset $W \subset X$ is called a feasible set. Let Δ be the set of subsets of X. An allocation mechanism is then a function $f: \Omega^n \times \Delta \to X$. That is, an allocation function maps a preference profile and feasible set into the feasible set: $f(P \mid W) \in W$. Agent i can manipulate allocation function f at profile $P \in \Omega^n$ and feasible set $W \subset X$ if an admissible ordering $P_i' \in \Omega$ exists such that:

$$f(P_1, \ldots, P_{i-1}, P_i', P_{i+1}, \ldots, P_n \mid W)\, P_i f(P \mid W). \quad (1)$$

The interpretation of (1) is this. Preference ordering P_i is agent i's true preferences. The other agents report preference orderings $P_{-i} = (P_1, \ldots, P_{i-1}, P_{i+1}, \ldots, P_n)$. If agent i reports his preferences truthfully, then the outcome is $f(P_i, P_{-i} \mid W) \equiv f(P \mid W)$. If he misrepresents his preferences to be P_i', then the outcome is $f(P_i', P_{-i} \mid W) \equiv f(P_1, \ldots, P_{i-1}, P_i', P_{i+1}, \ldots, P_n \mid W)$. Relation (1) states that agent i prefers $f(P_i', P_{-i} \mid W)$ to $f(P_i, P_{-i} \mid W)$. Therefore agent i has an incentive to manipulate f at profile P by misrepresenting his preferences to be P_i' rather than P_i.

An allocation mechanism f is strategy-proof if no admissible profile $P \in \Omega^n$ and subset $W \subset X$ exists at which f is manipulable. This means that even if, for example, agent i has perfect foresight about the preferences the other $n - 1$ agents will report, agent i can never do better than to report his true preferences P_i. Truth is always every agent's dominant strategy. Presumably this is sufficient to induce every agent always to report his preferences truthfully. Gibbard (1973) and Satterthwaite (1975) showed that strategy-proof allocation mechanisms generally do not exist.

Theorem. If admissible preferences are unrestricted ($\Omega^n = \Sigma^n$) and at least three possible allocations exist ($|X| \geqslant 3$), then no strategy-proof allocation mechanism f exists that is non-dictatorial and Pareto optimal.

An allocation mechanism is dictatorial if, for some feasible set $W \subset X$ ($|W| \geqslant 2$) and all profiles $P \in \Omega^n$, an agent i exists such that $f(P \mid W) \in \max_W P_i$ where $\max_W P_i = \{x \colon x \in W$ and, for all $y \in W$, not $yP_ix\}$. That is, a dictatorial mechanism always gives the dictator one of the feasible alternatives that he most prefers. A non-dictatorial mechanism is a mechanism that is not dictatorial. A mechanism satisfies Pareto optimality if and only if, for any profile $P \in \Omega^n$, any feasible set $W \subset X$, and any $x, y \in W$, xP_iy for all $i \in I$ implies $f(P \mid W) \neq y$. Pareto optimality in this context means that if unanimity exists among the agents that an allocation x is the most preferred feasible allocation, then the mechanism picks x.

The theorem can be provided either by appeal to Arrow's impossibility theorem for social-welfare functions (Gibbard, 1973) or through a self-contained, constructive argument (Satterthwaite, 1975). Schmeidler and Sonnenschein (1978) present short proofs of both types.

Gibbard and Satterthwaite's theorem is a non-existence theorem for a strategy-proof allocation mechanisms because mechanisms that violate either non-dictatorship or Pareto optimality are unattractive. If the environment is $\langle I, X, \Sigma \rangle$ where $|X| = 2$, then majority rule is an attractive, non-dictatorial, Pareto optimal and strategy-proof mechanism. But as soon as $|X|$ increases beyond two, if $\Omega = \Sigma$, then non-dictatorship, Pareto optimality and strategy-proofness become incompatible. Normally $|X| > 2$ for economic environments. Therefore the theorem implies that existence can be obtained (if at all) only for environments $\langle I, X, \Omega\rangle$ where admissible preferences Ω are restricted to a strict subset of Σ.

Strategy-proof allocation mechanisms are – almost – formally equivalent to social welfare functions of the type Arrow (1951) analysed. A social welfare function, for a given environment $\langle I, X, \Omega\rangle$ is a mapping $g: \Omega^n \rightarrow \Omega$. Thus a social welfare function g has as its argument an admissible preference profile and as its image an admissible ordering of X. The ordering $g(P)$ is interpreted to be the social ordering of X given that individual preferences $P = (P_1, \ldots, P_n)$. Arrow's impossibility theorem states that if $|X| \geqslant 3$ and admissible preferences are unrestricted, then no non-dictatorial social welfare function exists that satisfies the conditions of Pareto optimality, independence of irrelevant alternatives, and monotonicity.

An allocation mechanism f is called rational if and only if a social welfare function g exists such that, for all $P \in \Omega^n$ and all $W \subset X, f(P|W) \in \max_W g(P)$. That is $f(P|W)$ is rational if a social ordering $g(P)$ exists that rationalizes its choices. Kalai and Muller (1977) showed that, for a given environment $\langle I, X, \Omega\rangle$, a non-dictatorial, rational, strategy-proof allocation mechanism f satisfying Pareto optimality can be constructed if and only if a non-dictatorial social welfare function satisfying Pareto optimality, monotonicity, and independence of irrelevant alternatives can be constructed. In other words, if one limits consideration to rational allocation mechanisms, reasonable strategy-proof mechanisms exist for an environment if and only if reasonable (in Arrow's sense) social welfare functions exist for the environment.

A great deal of research has been done to identify environments on which non-dictatorial, Pareto optimal, strategy-proof allocation mechanisms exist. Two main approaches have been taken. First, authors have characterized sets of admissible preferences Ω for which rational, Pareto optimal, non-dictatorial, strategy-proof allocation mechanism exists on $\langle I, X, \Omega\rangle$ for $|X| > 2$. Second, for specific sets of restricted preferences Ω authors have investigated if reasonable strategy-proof allocation mechanisms exist on $\langle I, X, \Omega\rangle$ for $|X| > 2$. The results of both approaches have been uniformly discouraging. Generally, in order to get existence, Ω must be restricted to an extent that is greater than can be justified within economic contexts. Gibbard and Satterthwaite's theorem seems to apply to a much wider class of environments than just $\langle I, X, \Sigma\rangle$ with its unrestricted preferences. Muller and Satterthwaite (1985) review this literature.

There appear to be only two exceptions to this generalization that Gibbard and Satterthwaite's impossibility result is robust to restrictions on Ω. First, if Ω has the property that all admissible preferences are linear in money, then Groves mechanisms are strategy-proof in an attractive way. Groves mechanisms do, however, violate Pareto optimality (see Groves and Loeb, 1975; Green and Laffont, 1979). Second, if Ω has the property that all admissible preferences are single-peaked, then generalizations of majority rule are strategy-proof and Pareto optimal (see Blin and Satterthwaite, 1976; Border and Jordan, 1983).

This discussion, as is the case for most of the literature on strategy-proofness, uses the social-choice-theory model of requiring agents to report their preference orderings as the allocation rule's input. This seems restrictive because most economic allocation mechanisms do not require agents to report their full preference orderings. Gibbard (1973), however, showed that in fact this model is not restrictive at all. The insight is this. The essence of strategy-proofness is that each agent's optimal strategy depends only on his own preferences and is invariant with other agents' choices of strategies. That is, if an allocation mechanism is strategy-proof, then each agent always has a dominant strategy. Gibbard called such allocation mechanisms, for which each agent always has a dominant strategy, straightforward game forms. Gibbard showed that if a straightforward game form requires agents to select among an arbitrary set of admissible strategies that are not necessarily orderings of X, then the game form is equivalent to a strategy-proof allocation mechanism. Thus, if a non-dictatorial, Pareto optimal, strategy-proof allocation mechanism does not exist for an environment $\langle I, X, \Omega\rangle$, then neither does a non-dictatorial, Pareto optimal, straightforward game form.

The implication of Gibbard's observation concerning straightforward game forms is that if an economic situation is such that agent's preferences are not *a priori* known with certainty, then the situation is not strategy-proof (or, equivalently, straightforward). That is, each agent's optimal strategy depends on his own preferences, his expectations concerning other agents' strategies and, by backward induction, his expectations concerning the other agents' preferences and their expectations concerning agents' strategies and preferences, etc. The resulting game is formally a game of incomplete information and should be analysed using techniques appropriate for such games. Thus, to summarize, for economic theory the main implication of Gibbard and Satterthwaite's impossibility theorem for strategy-proof allocation mechanisms is that whenever agents' preferences are *a priori* uncertain to other agents, then the agents are engaged in a game of incomplete information.

MARK A. SATTERTHWAITE

BIBLIOGRAPHY

Arrow, K. 1951. *Social Choice and Individual Values*. New York: Wiley.

Black, D. 1958. *The Theory of Committees and Elections*. Cambridge: Cambridge University Press.

Blin, J.-M. and Satterthwaite, M. 1976. Strategy-proofness and single-peakedness. *Public Choice* 26, 51–8.

Border, K. and Jordan, J. 1983. Straightforward elections, unanimity and phantom voters. *Review of Economic Studies* 50, 153–70.

Dummett, M. and Farquharson, R. 1961. Stability in voting. *Econometrica* 29, 33–44.

Gibbard, A. 1973. Manipulation of voting schemes: a general result. *Econometrica* 41, 587–602.

Green, J. and Laffont, J.-J. 1979. *Incentives in Public Decision-making*. Studies in Public Economics, vol. I. Amsterdam: North-Holland.

Groves, T. and Loeb, M. 1975. Incentives and public inputs. *Journal of Public Economics* 4, 211–26.

Kalai, E. and Muller, E. 1977. Characterization of domains admitting non-dictatorial social welfare functions and non-manipulable voting procedures. *Journal of Economic Theory* 16, 457–69.

Muller, E. and Satterthwaite, M. 1985. Strategy-proofness: the existence of dominant-strategy mechanisms. In *Social Goals and Social Organization: Essays in Memory of Elisha Pazner*, ed. L. Hurwicz, D. Schmeidler and H. Sonnenschein, Cambridge: Cambridge University Press, 131–71.

Satterthwaite, M. 1975. Strategy-proofness and Arrow's conditions: existence and correspondence theorems for voting procedures and social welfare functions. *Journal of Economic Theory* 10, 187–217.

Schmeidler, D. and Sonnenschein, H. 1978. Two proofs of the Gibbard–Satterthwaite theorem on the possibility of a strategy-proof social choice function. In *Decision Theory and Social Ethics: Issues in Social Choice*, ed. H. Gottinger and W. Leinfellner, Dordrecht, Holland: Reidel, 227–34.

Vickrey, W. 1960. Utility, strategy and social decision rules. *Quarterly Journal of Economics* 74, 507–35.

Strigl, Richard von (1891–1942). Strigl was born on 7 February 1891 at Rokytzan (Moravia) and died on 11 November 1942 in Vienna. He studied at the University of Vienna, where he became Privatdozent (1923) and titular extraordinary professor (1928). He also held a leading position in the social administration (labour exchange office).

Strigl's first book (1923) was a methodological study of economics which anticipated the work of L. Robbins (1932). He regarded the pure logic of choice as the only proper subject of economic theory. Although the philosophical nature of the contents of this economic theory remains puzzling (it does not depend on experience yet conclusions about policy are drawn from it), this restrictive view of the subject is perhaps no more than an extreme formulation of a position common to many neoclassicists.

Like Mises, Strigl was a pupil of Böhm-Bawerk, whose influence is shown in his *Applied Wage Theory* (1926), where he argues that trade union power is incapable of improving the position of the working class as a whole. Another work, *Capital and Production* (1934), starts from Böhm-Bawerk's capital theory in an explanation of cyclical crises which, as with Mises and Hayek, are conceived as the result of a preceding over-accumulation of capital: an excessive investment in the boom locks up capital in long-term investments which cannot be unfrozen so as to provide the subsistence for the workers, who must then remain unemployed.

Strigl was an excellent and inspiring teacher, even for those who could not accept his opinions. He was able to show students accustomed to descriptive economics the usefulness of theoretical analysis in dealing with economic policy questions of the day. The importance of his teaching has to be judged against the background of the romantic-nationalist and thoroughly anti-rational trends of thought which prevailed in Austrian universities in the interwar period.

JOSEF STEINDL

SELECTED WORKS

1923. *Die Ökonomischen Kategorien und die Organisation der Wirtschaft*. Jena: Gustav Fischer.

1926. *Angewandte Lohntheorie. Untersuchungen über die wirtschaftlichen Grundlagen der Sozialpolitik*. Leipzig and Vienna: Deuticke.

1934. *Kapital und Produktion*. Vienna: Julius Springer.

BIBLIOGRAPHY

Robbins, L. 1932. *An Essay on the Nature and Significance of Economic Science*. London: Macmillan. Reprinted, 1984.

strikes. The term 'strike' is applied to a wide variety of acts of collective work stoppage, ranging from brief political demonstrations to economic struggles over terms of a collective agreement that last for several months. It is unlikely that any one model will be appropriate for all strike events. Until the past decade, the study of strikes consisted of socio-historical descriptions of individual events and statistical summaries of various strikes characteristics such as length, frequency of occurrence and number of workers involved. Intertemporal changes in these characteristics, and/or differences across industries, countries, demographic subgroups, etc. were studied as reflections of changes or differences in worker and, less frequently, employer attitudes; for example, militancy, dissatisfaction, alienation. Whether done by sociologists or economists, these studies contained no attempt to treat strike events as one possible outcome of rational decision-making by bargainers with limited information.

In what follows, 'strike' covers both strikes and lock-outs. For brevity, it is assumed that strikes may occur only at the time of a contract expiration; that is, the large number of short strikes, usually involving small numbers of workers, that occur during the life of a contract will be neglected. For a similar reason, we will also neglect organizing strikes, and strikes that occur in the early stages of a bargaining relationship when learning (how to bargain efficiently) is of major importance.

It is convenient to regard the start of the economic analysis of strikes as being marked by Hicks's observation that

> Under a system of collective bargaining, some strikes are more or less inevitable ... but nevertheless the majority of actual strikes are doubtless the result of faulty negotiation ... Under such circumstances, a deadlock is inevitable and a strike will ensue; but it arises from the divergence of estimates, and from no other cause ... adequate knowledge will always make a settlement possible (Hicks, 1932, pp. 146–7).

However, although the remark was never ignored, until the onset of 'Rational Expectations' (circa 1970) its implications were not in keeping with prevailing modes of economic analysis and it was not fully appreciated. The point at which Hicks was driving was that, as of the conclusion of a strike, the participants can perceive that both would have been better off had they reached the strike-terminating contract without having engaged in a strike. Thus, failure to avoid a strike implies either irrationality or miscalculation (by one or both parties) as to the response of the other bargainer to his behaviour.

For brevity, I dismiss the possibilities of irrationality and/or of 'a positive utility of conflict' (striking) and concentrate upon miscalculation. Since contract negotiations with the accompanying possibility of a strike are recurrent events, presumably rational bargainers will learn to calculate better as their (bargaining) experience accumulates. This suggests that expected losses to a given bargaining couple on account of strikes will diminish with their bargaining experience. Whether, given sufficient experience of the bargaining parties, strikes will vanish depends on the costs of deriving and applying information from the bargaining process. Where learning is difficult (costly) and/or strikes relatively inexpensive, it may be rational for bargainers to proceed in a manner that implies acceptance of the risk that some strikes will occur rather than strain further to reduce their probability of occurrence and/or expected duration. Put differently, in situations where bargaining is recurrent, bargainers who are both experienced and rational will behave so as to equate the marginal cost of learning how to avoid strikes with the marginal gain from a reduction in strike activity.

Absent estimates of the cost of engaging in strike activity, and of avoiding it, this implication of joint rationality tells us very little. Thus far, the only available estimates of strike cost to participants are for US manufacturing industries (Neumann and Reder, 1984). These rough pioneer estimates suggest that, contrary to appearances, the cost of a man-day of strike activity is 'low'. One important reason for this is the tendency of struck producers to substitute output through time; that is, to accumulate and/or rebuild inventories before and after strikes to offset output and wages lost while they are in progress.

But while the expected cost of a strike (at least in manufacturing) may be far less than a reader of journalistic accounts might think, it is not zero. Moreover, it is hard to believe that the expected cost of a strike does not exceed that of setting the contract terms by binding arbitration.

Nevertheless, agreements to accept binding arbitration of disputes over the terms of new contracts – as distinguished from arbitration of grievances – are very infrequent in the US, UK and EEC countries. Why this should be the case is an important unsolved puzzle for students of the subject.

There is a number of ways in which students of strike phenomena can bypass this puzzle: (1) abandon the assumption of rationality for either or both bargainers so that strikes may be interpreted as reflections of anger or as expressions of sentiment rather than as calculated attempts of the participants to advance their interests; (2) posit an extra cost – loss of efficiency – of operating under a contract imposed by an arbitrator (or otherwise) rather than under one negotiated by the parties (e.g., grievances may be more frequent and pursued more vigorously under an imposed contract); (3) frequent changes of bargaining environment and or personnel may effectively prevent accumulation of the experience required for avoidance of impasses and strikes.

Each of these bypasses might, under appropriate circumstances, provide an acceptable rationalization of why bargainers fail to avoid (some) strikes. There may be circumstances in which yet other explanations of why strikes sometimes occur might be applicable. However, the entire topic (i.e. why strikes have not been precluded by compulsory arbitration) has failed to become a focal point of strike research. Typically, empirical researchers have assumed that – for whatever reason – strikes do occur and then proceeded to analyse their quantitative characteristics.

This research, well summarized by Kennan (1986), has been scattered and inconclusive. One reason for this is inadequacy of the data, but conceptual shortcomings are at least of equal importance. One theme, prominent in the recent literature (Fudenberg et al., 1983; Hayes, 1984; Morton, 1983) is that strikes result from the fact that some critical information is private to one bargainer or the other, with the result that it may be rational for one party, A, to reject terms offered by the other, B (thereby causing a strike), which he (A) would have accepted if only he could have shared the information possessed by B. While such stories can account for the occurrence of strikes, and have some plausibility in the context of bargaining between strangers, they are not very convincing when applied to a well established relationship. Once it is perceived that the total cost of negotiating contracts (to both parties combined) could be appreciably reduced by disclosing information (e.g. about future orders, cash flow, worker attitudes), it is not easy to see what would inhibit the transmission of such information. In any event, the empirical aspects of the question are almost completely unexplored.

However, it is plausible to suppose that the smaller the expected total loss (to both parties) from a strike, the more likely it is that fear of losing a competitive advantage from disclosing information (about orders or costs) might inhibit employers from aborting potential strikes by making such disclosures. This is in keeping with the conjecture made by Reder and Neumann (1980) and by Kennan (1980) that the greater the expected cost of a strike (to both parties combined) the greater will be the effort of the parties to avoid it, and the lower its probability of occurrence. It is also in the spirit of the finding that the probability of a strike, conditional on a contract expiration, varies pro-cyclically (is greater in prosperity than in depression) but that the mean duration of strikes varies counter-cyclically (Kennan, 1986).

The cyclical pattern of strike activity may be rationalized by considering that both strikes and lawsuits are usually, though not always, analysed as though they were two-person games. In the small literature on the economics of lawsuits (including prosecutions), it is usually found – or assumed – that going to trial is, like striking, a rare event (Gould, 1973; Landes, 1971; Posner, 1973; Priest, 1984). Typically, a suit is settled out of court to avoid the cost of a trial, implying that the greater the expected cost, the smaller will be the number of trials resulting from a given population of suits. The suits that go to trial are, disproportionately, those where the stake is unusually high and/or the uncertainty of the outcome is unusually large.

The 'size of stake' effect may be interpreted as follows: assume that each party believes that his own probability of winning at trial is higher than the other party believes it to be; that the expected cost of a trial, and its division between the parties, is more or less invariant with respect to the size of the stake; and that the difference between the parties' estimates of the probability of success (in the event of a trial) is roughly independent of the size of the stake. On these assumptions, it is likely that only suits with a large stake will generate a sufficient expectation of gain from trial (as compared with pretrial settlement) to either party as to motivate refusal to settle without trial.

To apply the lawsuit model to strikes, make the (plausible) assumption that (at least in manufacturing), strikes are likely to be less costly to participants in prosperity than in depression. This is because often, in a depressed product market, non-struck firms with heavy inventories and/or under-utilized capacity will be able promptly to supply customers of struck firms with resulting loss of wages and quasi-rents to those engaged in striking. In a strong product market heavy inventories and idle capacity will be less frequent, so that strikers and their employers will be more likely to recoup lost sales and wages (through greater production before and after the strike) than in a depressed market. Hence strikes will be less costly to those participating when product markets are strong than when they are depressed and, accordingly, are more likely to be allowed (by the bargainers) to occur.

In depressed markets, to avoid the high cost of a strike, bargainers tend to compromise all but very large differences (i.e. big stakes). Very often, such differences arise in situations where the survival of one or both parties is at issue, and concessions are made only after the struggle has altered their relative strength. Typically, this requires passage of time which implies strikes of long duration. Hence, such strikes as do occur during depressions tend to be long.

To unify the insights and evidence of the largely disjoint literatures of legal contests, strikes and yet other forms of confrontational interaction such as wars, it will be necessary to develop a general theory of confrontational interaction in which different types of conflicts, distinguished by configurations of critical parameters, are nested. Such a theory would exploit the differentiating characteristics of (say) actions at law and collective bargains to derive 'conflict specific' implications concerning the incidence and magnitude of trials and strikes.

While the treatment of both strikes and lawsuits as a two-person game simplifies the argument, it obscures important aspects of the negotiating process, especially in the case of strikes. For example: in almost any union, heterogeneity of age-seniority status, job, location, ethnicity, etc. creates the potential for conflicts of interest among the members. Depending upon the distribution of voting strength, a union leader may require the support of several groups to maintain a winning coalition.

At any given contract negotiation, each of these groups may have a set of 'minimum demands', the sum of whose cost would exceed what the employer would pay without a long strike, if at all. Yet failure *credibly* to endorse each group's minimum demands would result in destruction of the winning coalition. Hence, the leader may refuse to initiate appreciable concessions, but will hold firm until the cost of further prolonging a strike becomes sufficiently onerous to induce the various groups to develop a menu of joint concessions adequate to end the strike. The critical point is that, as a condition of survival, the leader must function as a mediator among the groups and avoid the appearance of seeking to impose concessions upon any one of them.

The implication of this argument for strike behaviour is that, at least for some strikes, duration is determined by the time (and accumulation of lost wages) necessary to induce various groups within the union to reconcile the sum of their demands to what the employer will concede. This is much in the spirit of the argument of Ashenfelter and Johnson (1969). However, there is an important difference: Ashenfelter and Johnson posit an homogeneous group of workers who, despite repeated bargaining encounters, persist in overestimating the employer's willingness to concede wage (and fringe) demands even though their leader does not share in this error. This assumption of persisting asymmetrical error is difficult to accept without evidence to support it.

By contrast, in the argument offered above, leaders (may) convey their knowledge of the employer's position and what it entails in *total* concessions from all union members, but for reasons of electoral survival refuse to suggest a *division* of the concession pie among the members, and wait for them to 'bargain it out'. It would seem far more plausible to suppose that the interdependent concession functions of various groups within a union should remain unknown, and/or unstable through time, than that an employer's concession function, assumed known to a union leader, should remain unknown to its members.

For the near future, empirical and theoretical research on strikes will proceed on parallel tracks, the latter dominated by game theory and the former by econometric attempts to find regularities in the still scarce stock of data. Although the two research communities are becoming increasingly aware of one another, we are still far from an empirically implemented theory of strikes.

MELVIN W. REDER

See also ARBITRATION; COLLECTIVE BARGAINING; TRADE UNIONS.

BIBLIOGRAPHY

Ashenfelter, O. and Johnson, G.E. 1969. Bargaining theory, trade unions and industrial strike activity. *American Economic Review* 59, March, 35–49.

Fudenberg, D., Levine, D. and Ruud, P. 1983. Strike activity and wage settlements. NBER Conference on the Economics of Trade Unions, May.

Gould, J.P. 1973. The economics of legal conflicts. *Journal of Legal Studies* 2, 279–300.

Hayes, B. 1984. Unions and strikes with asymmetric information. *Journal of Labour Economics* 2(1), January, 57–83.

Hicks, J.R. 1932. *The Theory of Wages*. London: Macmillan.

Kennan, J. 1980. Pareto optimality and the economics of strike duration. *Journal of Labour Research* 1, Spring, 77–94.

Kennan, J. 1986. The economics of strikes. In *Handbook of Labour Economics*, ed. O. Ashenfelter and R. Layard, Amsterdam: North-Holland.

Landes, W.M. 1971. An economic analysis of the courts. *Journal of Law and Economics* 14, 61–107.

Morton, S. 1983. The optimality of strikes in labour negotiations. Discussion Paper No. 83/7. New Orleans: Tulane University.

Neumann, G.R. and Reder, M.W. 1984. Output and strike activity in US manufacturing: how large are the losses? *Industrial and Labour Relations Review* 37(2), January, 197–211.

Posner, R.A. 1973. An economic approach to legal procedure and judicial administration. *Journal of Legal Studies* 2, 399 et seq.

Priest, G.L. and Klein, B. 1984. The selection of disputes for litigation. *Journal of Legal Studies* 13(1), 1–55.

Reder, M.W. and Neumann, G.R. 1980. Conflict and contract: the case of strikes. *Journal of Political Economy* 88(5), October, 867–86.

structural change. Structural change is defined as a change in the relative weight of significant components of the aggregative indicators of the economy, such as national product and expenditure, exports and imports, and population and the labour force. It is a complex phenomenon involving, for example, differential effects upon the happiness of the people in different strata, changes in the society's value system and even impacts on international relations. However, we confine ourselves with the processes in which economic growth brings about the above structural change in various types and either directly or indirectly through organizational and institutional changes.

Broadly speaking, two different approaches exist in the literature on structural change.

The first approach seeks to identify statistically certain universal relationships between economic growth and structural change, using intercountry cross-section data or time-series data of selected countries. Contributions of Fisher (1939), Clark (1940), Kuznets (1957–64) and Chenery and Syrquin (1975) are noteworthy. In particular, Chenery–Syrquin's work succeeded in describing as 'stylized facts' multi-sided patterns of structural change that some hundred countries commonly experienced along with economic growth. Their studies might be regarded, though, as ultimately aiming at constructing a general theory of structural change. Chenery–Syrquin also tries to identify some alternative patterns of structural change among countries with different initial conditions and development strategies. But the results are yet preliminary.

The second approach concentrates, from the beginning, on a study of historical experiences of a group of countries under similar initial conditions and economic systems and explores particular theories by which the process of structural changes that occurred can best be explained. Examples of such partial theories are W.A. Lewis's theory (1954) of industrialization through 'unlimited supplies' of labour from the overpopulated subsistence sector to the capitalist sector; Myint's 'Vent for Surplus' theory (1958) which describes the process by which sparsely populated lands, under the pressure of external demand for the products of those lands, are opened and developed as monoculture export economies; a Staple Theory (Watkins, 1963) of successful development through skillful switching of staple exports in response to changing external demand; and Todaro's model of two-step labour-migration from agriculture to industry (Todaro, 1969).

Although these theories are not very formal and sometimes even merely descriptive, they provide useful insights and frameworks of reference when we investigate economic growth of countries with similar initial conditions. The benefit of this second approach may be greater, in particular for policy-makers, if (1) some review of the existing theories in this approach is attempted with the aim of rendering the theories capable of responding to contemporary developmental problems, and if (2) further endeavours to develop similar theories are made for groups of countries for which such theories are yet nonexistent. From the view point of (1), examples may be given such as the desirability of marrying

Lewis's theory with such discussions as the process of increase in agricultural productivity (Hayami and Ruttan, 1985; Ishikawa, 1967 and 1982). The challenge to the Vent-for-Surplus theory is to develop an additional analytical framework to consider the further course of development after all the surplus lands disappear. Either the course of 'export substitution' proposed by Myint himself (1972) or the course of joint venture manufacturing with multinational companies whose behaviour is described for example by Vernon's Product Cycle Theory (1966) might be a candidate.

The above two approaches, though seemingly unrelated, may become complementary with the progress of studies on both sides, especially if the studies of the first approach on the alternative patterns of structural change were continued.

NEW FRONTIERS TO BE EXPLORED. The structural change discussed above relates to productive forces in various aspects. It takes place in close relationship with changes in organizational and institutional (mainly systemic) structure. Explorations of these relationships are currently becoming new frontiers to be explored.

First, as to organizational change. It tends to promote specialization of production units and strengthen cooperation among them, thus creating both internal and external economies in Marshall's sense (1920). In countries of an earlier development stage, however, situations where the deficiency of organization prevents economic growth and transformation are the immediate issue. McKinnon (1973) discovered that in such countries governmental policy of extending to the organized sector deliberately low-rate interest credits has resulted in already fragmented capital markets becoming further fragmented, hence enhancing self-financing. Aside from such policy-imposed organizational deficiencies, others are formed spontaneously. For example, in a small, labour surplus economy, specialization of export production of labour-intensive and skill-saving manufactured goods is usually regarded, on the basis of the comparative advantage doctrine, as best for growth and transformation. But as Myint (1984) argued, this is not actually so if the economy suffers from organizational deficiency such that the movement of both commodities and the labour force are constrained. Therefore, the economy is prevented from benefiting from the existing abundant unskilled labour. As for the spontaneously formed organizational deficiencies, however, systematic studies are available only on a partial basis.

In historical terms, J.R. Hicks (1969) presented a classical analysis of the rise and development of the market economy. Gurley and Shaw (1967) developed a stage theory of 'financial development', starting from a stage of self-financing. Concerning the labour market, a dualism based on the supply of unskilled labour from family-based agriculture to the organized industry has been studied as a phenomenon transitional to the phase of equal marginal labour productivities (Lewis, 1954; Fei and Ranis, 1964; and Sen, 1975). Another kind of dualism emerged, also transitionally, in a different context in the form of differential wages among modern firms of different sizes (Shinohara, 1962; Ohkawa and Rosovsky, 1973). Overall, however, a taxonomy has to be attempted first with regard to the underdeveloped and developed market economies and their transition. For each of them significant characteristics should be identified concerning product and factor markets and, for each kind of market, concerning transaction rules, the things transacted, production and management units and their organizations (Ishikawa, 1982). Useful agenda for exploring new theories must follow it.

The taxonomic study, however, will also indicate that organizational change is often not realized without prior structural change. For example, specialization of commodities into parts and processes does not come into being without sufficient development of inter-industry relations. Commercialization of the product does not arise without the development of infra-structure for the product market, such as transportation and communication networks (Ishikawa, 1982 and 1985).

As for systemic change: although in the above discussion of organizational change, we assumed the prevalence of the market economy, the economic system usually also contains other types of economic institutions that are each based on a particular resource allocation principle – most notably the market economy, the customary economy and the command (or state) economy, to use Hicks's phrases. The systemic change is almost equivalent to the change in the nature of the combination of these constituent institutions. Why does such a mixed system arise, and how does it change?

When the economy is in a low-income stage and the economic as well as organizational structures are correspondingly at low levels, the resource-allocation function of the market economy is weak. This is defined as the state in which, in most market transactions, transaction costs are high enough to more than counterbalance the gains obtainable from participating in them: the gains from specialization, competitive pressure and so on. Among the various items of transaction costs, costs to insure the market participants against the risk of loss of the subsistence income (either by falling into unemployment or by incurring financial loss) are distinctive. In such a case, the weak allocation function of the market economy is possibly supplemented and reinforced by the command and especially the customary economies. In particular, people want to rely on the customary economy to obtain the security of job and subsistence income.

An example of the working of the customary economy to supplement the weakness of the market economy is village-community practices of work- and income-sharing and joint operations among villagers that were and are widely observable in Asia, including Japan (Epstein, 1962; Geertz, 1970; Strout, 1975; Hayami and Kikuchi, 1981; Ishikawa, 1982). Although the customary economy would in the long-run be replaced by the market economy, the former has often played at least temporarily the role of making possible a better allocation of labour, a greater mobilization of savings and even a wider diffusion of new agricultural technologies. Thus, it promotes economic growth and transformation.

On the other hand, for achieving the targeted industrialization, contemporary developing countries may have relied too much upon the command economy to supplement the weak allocation function of the market economy. A centralized planning system like that of China and a regulated economy system of that of India (through manipulation of licensing systems) are extreme examples. Although they seem to have worked well in an earlier period, after greater sophistication of the economic structure, these systems came to suppress rather than supplement the market economy, thus leading to overall inefficiency.

In both these countries, economic reform is currently being tried to increase the role of the market economy. If successful, the reform will contribute to economizing transaction costs, particularly for acquiring economic information for planning and regulation and for infusing competitive pressure into the economy, thus overcoming the thwarted structural change. However, while reform would proceed smoothly as far as it is effected by removal of the policy-imposed inefficiency, further progress would be possible only to the extent that changes in the spontaneously formed organization and economic structure can be effected (Ishikawa, 1985).

SHIGERU ISHIKAWA

See also MARKET STRUCTURE AND INNOVATION; TECHNICAL CHANGE.

BIBLIOGRAPHY

Chenery, H. and Syrquin, M. 1975. *Patterns of Development, 1957–1970*. London: Oxford University Press.

Clark, C. 1940. *The Conditions of Economic Progress*. New York: St Martin's.

Epstein, T.S. 1962. *Economic Development and Social Change in South India*. Manchester: Manchester University Press.

Feik, J.C.H. and Ranis, G. 1964. *Development of the Labor Surplus Economy: Theory and Policy*, Homewood, Ill.: Richard D. Irwin.

Fisher, A.G.B. 1939. Primary, secondary and tertiary production. *Economic Record* 15, June, 24–38.

Geertz, C. 1963. *Agricultural Involution: The Process of Ecological Change in Indonesia*. Berkeley: University of California Press.

Gurley, J.G. and Shaw, E.S. 1967. Financial structure and economic development. *Economic Development and Cultural Change* 15, April, 257–68.

Hayami, Y. and Kikuchi, M. 1981. *Asian Village Economy at the Crossroads: an Economic Approach to Institutional Change*. Tokyo: University Press of Tokyo.

Hayami, Y. and Ruttan, V.W. 1985. *Agricultural Development: an International Perspective*. Baltimore: Johns Hopkins University Press.

Hicks, J.R. 1969. *A Theory of Economic History*. Oxford: Clarendon Press.

Ishikawa, S. 1967. *Economic Development in Asian Perspective*. Tokyo: Kinokuniya Co.

Ishikawa, S. 1982. *Essays on Technology, Employment and Institutions in Economic Development: Comparative Asian Experience*. Tokyo: Kinokuniya Co.

Ishikawa, S. 1985. Sozialistische Wirtschaft und die Erfahrungen Chinas – Gedanken zur ökonomischen Reform. *Journal für Entwicklungs Politik* 3.

Kuznets, S.S. 1957–64. *Population Redistribution and Economic Growth: United States, 1870–1950*. 3 vols, Philadelphia: American Philosophical Society.

Kuznets, S.S. 1971. *Economic Growth of Nations: Total Output and Production Structure*. Cambridge, Mass.: Belknap Press of Harvard University Press.

Lewis, W.A. 1954. Economic development with unlimited supplies of labour. *Manchester School of Economics and Social Studies* 22, May, 139–91.

Marshall, A. 1920. *Principles of Economics*. 8th edn, London: Macmillan.

McKinnon, R. 1973. *Money and Capital in Economic Development*. Washington, DC: The Brookings Institution.

Myint, H. 1958. The 'classical theory' of international trade and the underdeveloped countries. *Economic Journal* 68, June, 317–37.

Myint, H. 1972. *Southeast Asia's Economy: Development Policies in the 1970s*. A study sponsored by the Asian Development Bank, London: Penguin Books.

Myint, H. 1984. Comparative analysis of Taiwan's economic development with other countries. *Academic Economic Papers* (Academic Sinica, Taiwan), March.

Ohkawa, K. and Rosovsky, H. 1973. *Japanese Economic Growth. Trend Acceleration in the Twentieth Century*. Stanford: Stanford University Press.

Sen, A. 1975. *Employment, Technology and Development*. Oxford: Clarendon Press.

Shinohara, M. 1962. *Growth and Cycles in the Japanese Economy*. Tokyo: Kinokuniya Co.

Strout, A.M. 1975. Agricultural involution and the green revolution on Java. Agro-Economic Survey, Research Note No. 01/75/Rn.mim.

Todaro, M.P. 1969. A model of labor migration and urban unemployment in less developed countries. *American Economic Review* 59(1), March, 138–48.

Vernon, R. 1966. International investment and international trade in the product cycle. *Quarterly Journal of Economics* 80, May, 190–207.

Watkins, M. 1963. A staple theory of economic growth. *Canadian Journal of Economics and Political Science* 29(2), May, 141–58.

structural economic dynamics. The dynamics of modern economic systems since the Industrial Revolution show that permanent changes in the absolute levels of some basic magnitudes (such as gross national product, total consumption, total investments, total employment, etc.) are inherently associated with changes in their *composition*; that is, with *structural change*.

In the short run, it is not always easy to distinguish between genuine structural changes (i.e. changes in composition that are permanent and irreversible) and purely transitory and reversible changes (reflecting adjustments to temporary scarcities or to various temporary exogeneous shocks). But, as time goes on, transitory changes in either direction cancel out and long-run tendencies emerge more clearly. It thereby becomes possible to single out the interrelations between the cumulative movements of certain magnitudes and the changes that take place in their structure.

HISTORICAL EVOLUTION OF THE BASIC CONCEPTS. The problems of medium- and short-term economic dynamics – already considered by certain Classical economists, such as Ricardo (1817) and Malthus (1820), as well as by Marx (1867–94) – have been analysed at length in the literature on business cycles. By contrast, the problems of long-run structural dynamics have been studied far less frequently, in spite of the interest in the topic shown by Adam Smith and Ricardo. The former, in his enquiry into the conditions for the growth of the national wealth, pointed out that a continuous process of expansion presupposes changes in the structure of employment, with the increase in the share of 'productive' (versus 'unproductive') labour (Adam Smith, 1776, II, ch. 3). The latter, starting from the assumption that land and other natural resources are limited and scarce, noted that total production cannot increase beyond a certain level, unless there also is a continuous process of change in the relative sizes of the various branches of an economy (Ricardo, 1817, ch. 2, 5, 6). Some interest in long-term structural dynamics can also be found in Marx. In Marxian terminology, the tendency towards an increase in the ratio of 'constant' to 'total' capital (i.e. an increase in the 'organic composition of capital') presupposes a series of changes in the proportions among commodity outputs (Marx, 1867–94).

It is something of a paradox that those parts of Classical economic theory which have been more fertile from an analytical viewpoint have also been those that have required the most restrictive assumptions on the structure of the economic system (examples are the assumption of a uniform organic composition of capital in Marx, and that of uniform proportions between capital and labour in Ricardo's labour-theory of value). This feature of Classical economic theory clearly did not encourage research on structural dynamics.

The decline of Classical political economy and the subsequent emergence, since the 1870s, of the marginalist theory were accompanied by a gradual loss of interest in the dynamics of the 'wealth of nations', while the problems concerning the allocation of already existing resources moved into the foreground.

The relationships between economic growth and structural change came once again to the fore in the business-cycle literature of the 1920s, when the distinction was advanced between 'merely temporary influences' and changes producing permanent alterations in the fundamental relationships of the economic system, or 'structural changes' (Harms, 1926). Interest in the concept of 'economic structure' led to applied and theoretical work in the 1930s by economists such as Leontief (1936, 1941) and Perroux (1939); and again later by Tinbergen (1952). In particular, Perroux defined economic structure as those 'proportions and relationships that characterize ... an economic setting in space and in time' (1939, vol. I, p. 194). It was this definition that happened to be taken up subsequently by a number of other writers, and became particularly influential amongst a group of economists in Latin America, who called themselves 'structuralist' and channelled their elaborations into a descriptive–historical–institutional approach (see Furtado, 1967). The development of these ideas in the strict field of economic theory, however, on which we shall concentrate in this survey, were much slower to emerge.

In the period between the two world wars, the revival of interest in economic growth did not lead immediately to a revival of interest in the economic theory of *structural* dynamics. This can be seen by considering the two most important dynamic theories formulated in this period: that of von Neumann and that of Harrod. Von Neumann (1937) studied the dynamic properties of a multisectoral economic system which undergoes a *proportional* expansion of all the sectors of the economy (thus maintaining an unchanged structure). For his part Harrod (1939) and, after him Evsey Domar (1946), studied the relationships among certain *macroeconomic* magnitudes (investments, savings, employment, national income), as well as the relationships among their rates of change. They did admit that economic growth might take place through a periodic succession of booms and depressions; but they remained unable to deal with the problems of change in the *composition* of macroeconomic magnitudes.

This aspect of the literature on long-term economic dynamics is openly at variance with the historical development of all actual economic systems, which exhibit profound changes in composition. Inevitably, the problems of structural change were therefore bound to emerge.

In the recent economic literature, attempts to formulate a theory of the structural dynamics of an economic system in the long run were made in the 1960s (Pasinetti, 1962 and 1965; Leon, 1967). These works insist on a link between structural change and (1) the increases of labour productivity in the technological sphere and (2) the increase of average incomes which consumers can spend on goods and services – a link which is established by making use of an empirical generalization known as Engel's Law (Engel, 1857), according to which the share of personal income which an average consumer allocates to the purchase of any given good is continually changing, as his or her income is increasing. The causal chain is very simple. The growth of per capita disposable income brought about by technical progress affects the composition of global demand, and this causes adjustments in the composition of total production. One may add that technical progress is not uniform throughout the various branches of an economy either quantitatively or qualitatively, and that this also brings about a series of structural changes in the price system.

All the above-mentioned structural changes, concerning Engel's Law, technical progress, non-uniform productivity increases and changes in the consumption structure, have recently been brought together in a general theory of the structural dynamics of an economic system, to which we may now turn.

POPULATION, PRODUCTIVITY AND EVOLUTION OF CONSUMER'S DEMAND. Consider an industrial economy in which the division and specialization of labour is well advanced. The economy is supposed to produce a wide range of different goods and services. As time goes on, three basic sources of economic change may be seen to be at work.

A first source of change is population growth (either by natural growth or by migration), accompanied by variations in the ratio of the working to total population.

A second source of change is represented by the application to productive processes of scientific research and technical progress, which causes increases of productivity in each industrial branch; that is, increases in the quantity of outputs per unit of inputs 'absorbed'. For the sake of simplicity, we shall consider the economic system as a set of vertically integrated sectors. In each vertically integrated sector only one final consumption good is produced, while all means of production will be considered as consolidated into one global factor of production, which we shall call 'labour'. This simplification does not affect the conclusions following from our analysis of the structural dynamics of the economic system. At the same time, the process of vertical integration permits us to consider not only all straight quantitative changes but also the quantitative aspects of the qualitative changes in production methods. The changes in the quantity of each final output per unit of 'labour' absorbed will normally be positive, though some changes might be negative. In any case, all changes will generally be different from sector to sector. If we denote by $1, 2, \ldots, m$, the different productive sectors, and therefore the corresponding goods and services, we may say that productivity is increasing in sector 1 at the annual percentage growth rate ρ_1 (e.g. 20 per cent per year), in sector 2 at the annual percentage rate $\rho_2, \ldots,$ in sector m at the annual percentage rate ρ_m. Suppose that productive sectors have been numbered in a decreasing order of productivity so that $\rho_1 > \rho_2 > \cdots \rho_m$. Since we are supposing, for the sake of simplicity, that each productive sector produces only a single good or service, there is a one-to-one correspondence between productive sectors and goods or services.

There is a third source of economic changes, which is a straightforward consequence of Engel's Law. Technical progress brings about a continuous increase in average *per capita* real incomes, and thus it brings about increases in the demand for the various goods and services. Such demand increases will generally be different for different goods and services, and, as a consequence, also for different sectors. We shall denote by r_1 the annual percentage growth rate of *per capita* demand for good 1, by r_2 the annual percentage growth rate of *per capita* demand for good 2, and so on, until r_m. Obviously, there is no reason whatsoever why one should expect a particular order in the sequence $r_1, r_2, \ldots, r_m$. The growth rate r's will generally be positive, as a consequence of increasing real *per capita* incomes, even though some r's might be negative (in the case of 'inferior' goods, demand for which is declining as real income is rising).

It should be noted that all the above changes are characteristic of industrial systems as such, independently of their institutional set-ups. In other words, the movements of working population, the increases of productivity and the evolution of consumption demand are all consequences of industrial growth as such, independently of whether it takes place in a market (or 'capitalist') economy, or in a centrally planned (or 'socialist') economy.

It is with reference to these fundamental relationships which are common to all types of institutional set-ups that it has been possible to derive a pretty complete picture of the structural dynamics of an industrial economy. On the other hand, with reference to specific institutions, the economic analysis is still at the initial and preliminary stages, even though important results have already been achieved. In the following two sections, a series of arguments will be presented that refer to both types of investigations.

THE STRUCTURAL DYNAMICS OF PRODUCTION, PRICES AND EMPLOYMENT. As a starting point, it is necessary to define what might be called a 'satisfactory' state of economic growth. It seems reasonable to consider as 'satisfactory' a state of economic growth in which the evolution of the economic system is taking place by maintaining both an approximately full employment of the labour force and an approximately full utilization of the productive capacities in the various branches of the economy. If this definition is accepted, then some constraints are immediately imposed on the growth of the economic system. It is possible to show that, in each productive sector, there is a relationship between the rate of increase in sectoral demand, the technical capital–output ratio and the amount of new investments to be undertaken. It is also possible to show that there is a macroeconomic relationship (i.e. a relationship connecting all the sectors of the economy), that defines the level at which the overall effective demand should be maintained.

When these constraints are satisfied, it is possible to sketch out a path that may be termed 'satisfactory' for the structural dynamics of the relevant magnitudes of an economic system.

In each sector $i (i = 1, 2, \ldots, m)$, the physical output will grow each year at the percentage rate $(r_1 + g)$, where g is the percentage annual rate of population growth and r_1 is the percentage annual rate of increase in the *per capita* demand of good (or service) i, as defined above. Since all the r's are different from one another, a *structural dynamics of production* becomes inevitable.

Moreover, in each sector i, the annual percentage growth rate of productivity ρ_1 generates a decrease in the unit cost of production. Under certain ideal conditions, this will also cause a decrease, at the same percentage rate ρ_1, of the corresponding equilibrium price for given rewards to the factors of production. This would imply a distribution of the gains of technical progress through price reductions. There is, however, an alternative way of distributing the gains of productivity increases, which has become more common in industrial economies. This way consists in maintaining unchanged the commodity price (the price of the ith good or service, in our example) while at the same time letting the reward of productive factors (of labour, particularly) increase. It is clear that, if all sectors behave in this way, wages and salaries would increase at a different rate from sector to sector. But if, as is reasonable to expect, the growth of the wages and salaries is roughly uniform across sectors, then there will be a series of differentiated changes in the equilibrium prices of the various commodities. This means a *structural dynamics of the system of prices*.

It is to be noted that, in an industrial economy, exactly the same structural dynamics of prices may be associated with *different* movements of the general price level. To begin with, on the basis of what has been said so far, price stability, in the sense of a constancy of *all* prices, would represent an inefficient and thus undesirable state of affairs, if productivity is increasing at different rates in different sectors. However, one might aim at stability of prices *on the average*; that is, with reference to the general price level. Such a target implies decreases of prices in those sectors where the rate of growth of productivity is above average, and increases of prices in those sectors where the rate of growth of productivity is below average. At the same time (barring changes in income distribution among the factors of production), wages and salaries could increase at a percentage rate equal to the average percentage rate of growth of productivity in the economic system as a whole.

But, of course, in modern economic systems, where the monetary unit of account is purely conventional (i.e. no longer pegged to a physical quantity of gold, as it was in the monetary systems of the past), there is no objective constraint on the rate of increase of nominal wages and salaries. So that, whenever nominal wages and salaries increase at a percentage rate that is higher than the average percentage rate of growth of productivity, this will entail an increase of the general price level (i.e. *inflation*). As a matter of purely logical implication, for any given structural dynamics of prices, the general price level will grow at a rate equal to the difference between the percentage rate of increase of nominal wages and salaries and the average percentage rate of increase of productivity.

A further important consequence may immediately be derived. As time goes on, the various productive sectors are undergoing a structural dynamics of both their outputs and their costs (and thus prices). What follows is a well-defined evolution of the sectoral demands for the factors of production in general, and in particular for labour. If we consider labour services only, and assume a constant total population, it is clear that, if labour productivity increases at percentage rate ρ_i in sector i, and the demand for commodity i increases at percentage rate r_i, the demand for labour services in sector i will remain constant through time only if $\rho_i = r_i$. If, on the other hand, $r_i > \rho_i$, the ith sector will need additions to its labour force, whereas if $r_i < \rho_i$, this sector will find itself compelled to dismiss workers (or not to recruit new personnel, as workers retire). As a result, there will be relative changes in the quantity of labour services needed in the different productive sectors, thus determining a *structural dynamics of employment*.

Some of the most serious troubles characterizing industrial economies arise precisely from the structural dynamics of employment; for it is impossible to separate the labour services from the individuals offering such services. Each individual worker possesses a specific range of skills and is seldom indifferent between working in a familiar environment and working in an unfamiliar place, or according to rules that may conflict with his (or her) attitudes, customs and goals.

APPLICATIONS OF THE THEORY OF STRUCTURAL ECONOMIC DYNAMICS. The analytical framework outlined in the above discussion is open to numerous applications, both in the field of economic theory and in the investigation of the actual working of economic systems. A few examples will be given here.

To begin with, the analysis of the structural evolution of economic systems through time provides a clear explanation of a preoccupying phenomenon which has emerged as a characteristic of industrial societies since the beginning of the Industrial Revolution; namely the co-existence of declining and expanding industries in a process of economic growth. Within the foregoing theoretical framework, it is easy to show that the declining industries are the logical counterpart of the expanding industries, when technical progress is continuously taking place. When certain productive branches enjoy increases of labour productivity due to the introduction of machinery, and, at the same time, their possibilities of finding outlets do not increase at the same rate, or have saturated, the possibilities of employing labour in such branches will inevitably shrink. This does not necessarily entail overall unemployment, but it does mean that a satisfactory level of overall employment will be maintained only on the condition of an adequate degree of labour mobility between productive branches, or a reduction in the working week (an increase of leisure time), or an appropriate mixture of these changes.

Moreover, within the above theoretical framework, it has become easier to understand why and how, in the industrial economies, the long-run tendency to the growth of the national income and employment is accompanied by short-run difficulties of various kinds, causing interruptions of growth and economic depressions. Short-run difficulties are explained as a consequence of the same phenomena that produce the long-run expansion of the economic system. For the structural dynamics needed by an economic system that is expanding through time, while maintaining full employment and full utilization of productive capacity, can seldom be achieved without delays and discontinuities. There is a fundamental contrast between the non-steady character of the expansion of demand for any given good and service (as emerges from the Engel curves analysis mentioned earlier) and the steadier expansion that would be required, for organizational reasons, by an efficient growth of the production units. Instantaneous adjustments are not always possible, particularly in those cases in which it is necessary for each product to use 'specialized' productive resources (such as machinery of a special type, or workers of a particular skill). This characteristic of a growing economy helps to explain booms and depressions and their periodic recurrence through time – and also (which is even more interesting) both in the case of market economies and in the case of centrally planned economies.

Another phenomenon which it has been possible to shed light on is the tendency to the increase in the general level of prices (inflation) that has become so characteristic of many industrial economies of our time. Without going into too many details, suffice it to refer back to the previous remark that a necessary condition for a stable average level of prices is to have price *reductions* for those goods that are produced in sectors where productivity increases above average. (This is because the prices of goods in those sectors where productivity grows below average will have to increase anyway.) But if there are institutional or organizational rigidities that prevent prices from being reduced, a necessary condition for keeping an efficient structure of prices is an even stronger increase of those prices that should increase anyway. The consequence will be an upward increase in the general level of prices.

We may finally consider briefly international economic relations. Traditional economic theory has never been able to explain in a satisfactory way the growing inequalities among the various economies on the world scene. Long-run movements provide a shocking evidence of such a phenomenon, as it is shown by a comparison of the average *per capita* incomes of the various countries. (They range at present from an order of magnitude of $10,000 in the United States to an order of magnitude of little more than $100 in the poorest countries of South-East Asia). It is possible to show that the benefits deriving from productivity increases remain in the countries that have obtained them, and are not leaked by international trade to the remaining countries of the world. At the same time, the poorest countries are compelled, by the very structural characteristics of their internal demand, to concentrate their production in sectors with very low, or even zero, rates of growth of productivity. The very same principles also help to explain phenomena to which development economists have paid so much attention, such as the declining trend in the terms of trade between the countries producing primary products and the countries producing manufactured commodities (see Prebisch, 1959) as well as many other phenomena that characterize the contemporary world economic scene.

LUIGI L. PASINETTI AND ROBERTO SCAZZIERI

See also CUMULATIVE CAUSATION.

BIBLIOGRAPHY

Domar, E. 1946. Capital expansion, rate of growth and employment. *Econometrica* 14, 137–47.

Engel, E. 1857. Die Productions- und Consumptionsverhältnisse des Königreichs Sachsen. *Zeitschrift der Statistischen Büreaus des Königlich Sächsischen Ministerium des Innern* No. 8–9. Republished in *Bulletin de l'Institut International de Statistique* 9, 1895.

Furtado, C. 1967. *Teoria e politica do desenvolvimento económico*. São Paulo: Companhia Editora Nacional.

Harms, B. 1926. Strukturwandlungen der deutschen Volkswirtschaft. *Welwirtschaftliches Archiv* 24, 259–73.

Harrod, R.F. 1939. An essay in dynamic theory. *Economic Journal* 49, 14–33.

Leon, P. 1967. *Structural Change and Growth in Capitalism*. Baltimore: Johns Hopkins University Press.

Leontief, W.W. 1936. Quantitative input–output relations in the economic system of the United States. *Review of Economics and Statistics* 18, 105–25.

Leontief, W.W. 1941. *The Structure of American Economy, 1919–1929*. New York: Oxford University Press, 1951.

Malthus, T.R. 1820. *Principles of Political Economy*. London: J. Murray, and subsequent editions.

Marx, K. 1867–94. *Das Kapital*. Hamburg: O. Meissner. Vols I–III, and subsequent editions and translations.

Pasinetti, L.L. 1962. A multisectoral model of economic growth. PhD dissertation, Cambridge University.

Pasinetti, L.L. 1965. A new theoretical approach to the problems of economic growth. *Pontificiae Academiae Scientiarum Scripta Varia* 28, Vatican City.

Pasinetti, L.L. 1981. *Structural Change and Economic Growth: a Theoretical Essay on the Dynamics of the Wealth of Nations*. Cambridge: Cambridge University Press.

Perroux, F. 1939. *Cours d'économie politique*. 2nd edn, Paris: Domat-Montchretien.

Prebisch, R. 1959. Commercial policy in the underdeveloped countries. *American Economic Review, Papers and Proceedings* 49, 251–73.

Ricardo, D. 1817. *Principles of Political Economy and Taxation*. London: J. Murray.

Smith, A. 1776. *An Inquiry into the Nature and Causes of the Wealth of Nations*. London: W. Strahan & T. Cadell.

Tinbergen, J. 1952. De quelques problèmes posés par le concept de structure économique. *Revue d'économie politique* 1, 27–46.

Von Neumann, J. 1937. Über ein ökonomisches Gleichungssystem und eine Verallgemeinerung des Brouwerschen Fixpunktsatzes. *Ergebnisse eines mathematischen Kolloquiums* 8. Trans. as 'A model of general economic equilibrium', *Review of Economic Studies* 13, 1945, 1–9.

structuralism. Structuralism is basically a method of enquiry which challenges the assumptions of empiricism and positivism. This method is found in literary criticism, linguistics, aesthetics and social sciences both Marxist and non-Marxist.

The principal characteristic of structuralism is that it takes as its object of investigation a 'system', that is, the reciprocal relations among parts of a whole, rather than the study of the different parts in isolation. In a more specific sense this concept is used by those theories that hold that there are a set of social and economic structures that are unobservable but which generate observable social and economic phenomena.

In anthropology, structuralism is particularly associated with Lévi-Strauss and Godelier. The main structuralist current in Marxist thought has its origins in Althusser and stands in opposition to the version of Marxist theory developed by Lukacs, Gramsci and the Frankfurt School. While structuralism seeks to explain social phenomena by reference to the underlying structure of the mode of production (hence, trying not to be 'humanistic' or 'historicist' in a teleological sense), the second group of Marxist theories stress the role of human consciousness and action in social life, with a concept of history in which (arguably) some idea of 'progress' is either implicit or explicit.

In economics structuralism is primarily associated with the school of thought originated in ECLA (United Nations' Economic Commission for Latin America), and in particular with the work of its first Director, Raul Prebisch.

The key to the internal unity of ECLA thought lies in its early postulation of the original ideas and hypotheses around which its subsequent contributions would be organized. The starting point was the idea that the world economy was composed of two poles, the 'centre' and the 'periphery', and that the *structure of production* in each differed substantially. That of the centre was seen as homogeneous and diversified, that of the periphery, in contrast, as heterogeneous and specialized; heterogeneous because economic activities with significant differences as to productivity existed side by side, with the two extremes provided by an export sector with relatively high productivity of labour, and a subsistence agriculture in which it was particularly low; specialized because the export sector would tend to be concentrated upon a few primary products, with production characteristically confined to an 'enclave' within the peripheral economic structure, or, in other words, having very limited backward and forward linkage effects with the rest of the economy. It was this structural difference between the two types of economy which lay behind the different function of each pole in the international division of labour, and this in turn had the effect of reinforcing the structural difference between the two.

Thus the two poles were closely bound together, and were mutually and reciprocally conditioning. Therefore, the structural difference between centre and periphery could not be defined or understood in static terms, as the transformation of either pole would be conditioned by the interaction between them. Centre and periphery formed a single system, dynamic by its very nature.

The nucleus of ECLA analysis was the critique of the conventional theory of international trade (as expressed in the Heckscher–Ohlin–Samuelson version of Ricardo's theory of comparative advantages); it aimed to show that the international division of labour which conventional theory claimed was 'naturally' produced by world trade was of much greater benefit to the centre (where manufacturing production is concentrated) than to the periphery (which was destined mainly to produce primary products, be they agricultural or mineral). The analysis of ECLA has a unity and an internal coherence which is not always perceptible at first sight, as its component parts are scattered through numerous documents published over a period of years (mainly in the 1950s and 1960s). Several contributions had their origins in the examination of specific problems, around which a series of theoretical arguments were articulated, in an attempt to isolate their causes and to justify the economic policy measures recommended to resolve them.

The ECLA analysis turns on three tendencies which are considered inherent to the development of the periphery: unemployment of the labour force, external disequilibrium, and the tendency to deterioration of the terms of trade (see Rodriguez, 1980).

(i) *Structural heterogeneity and unemployment*. The problem of employment in the periphery has two facets: the absorption of additions to the active population, and the re-absorption of the labour force of the most backward areas into economic activities in which productivity is higher. As the ECLA analysis assumes that demand for labour is proportionate to the level of investment (its rate of growth is directly related to the rate of capital accumulation), and this takes place almost exclusively in the modern sector, full employment of the labour force at adequate levels of productivity can only be achieved if the rate of capital accumulation in the export sector and in import-substituting manufacturing activities is sufficient not only to absorb the growth in the whole of the active population, but also to reabsorb labour from the traditional sector. Thus the level of employment depends on the balance between the growth of the active population and the rhythm of the expulsion of labour from the traditional sector, and on the level of capital accumulation in the modern sector. It is from the heavy burden on the modern sector to provide full employment in the economy at an adequate level of productivity that the structural tendency towards unemployment in the peripheral economies is deduced.

(ii) *Specialization in production and external disequilibrium*. The structure of production in the periphery is specialized in a double sense: mainly primary products are exported, and the economies are in general poorly integrated. From this it follows that a significant proportion of the demand for manufactured products is oriented towards imports, and given that their income elasticity is greater than unity, imports tend to grow faster than the level of real income. The opposite is the case in the centre, as imports from the periphery consist essentially of primary products, for which income elasticity is usually less than unity; hence they grow less rapidly than real income.

Thus for a given rate of growth of real income in the centre, the disparity between the income elasticities of imports at each pole will impose a limit upon the rate of growth of real income in the periphery (unless the latter is able to diversify its productive structure). This will not only tend to be less than that of the centre, but to be less in proportion to the degree of the disparity between the respective income elasticities of demand for imports. If the periphery attempts to surpass this limit, it will expose itself to successive deficits in its balance of trade; the only long term alternative will be an increased effort to satisfy the highly income-elastic demand for manufactured products with internal production, and to diversify its export trade towards income elastic products. Only a process of industrialization, given these assumptions, can allow that and enable the periphery to enjoy a rate of growth of real income higher than that determined by the rate of growth in the centre and the disparity between income elasticities of demand for imports.

As this process of industrialization also generates a need for imports which can exceed the availability of foreign currency deriving from the slow expansion of primary exports, ECLA argues in its documents that there is a role for foreign capital in the first stages of the process, both to remedy the shortage of foreign currency, and to complement internal savings.

(iii) *Specialization, heterogeneity, and the tendency to deterioration of the terms of trade*. The explanation for the phenomena of the tendency to deteriorating terms of trade and the disparity in incomes which it brings with it are, in the thought of ECLA, a logical analytical deduction from the phenomena of specialization and heterogeneity. (It is not, as it is usually assumed, the starting point of ECLA thought, but – given its assumptions and hypotheses – a natural analytical deduction.)

There are, basically, a demand and a supply element behind this tendency to deterioration of the terms of trade of the periphery (see R. Prebisch for a more detailed analysis of this point). The basic problem is the effect of economic growth on the terms of trade. From a demand point of view – given the problem of specialization and the differences in income elasticities for imports between the centre and periphery – the 'consumption path' of the periphery is biased towards trade (i.e. as incomes grow the proportion of importables in total consumption increases). From the point of view of supply – given the effect of heterogeneity on technological change and the differences in price elasticity of supply of exports between the centre and the periphery – the 'production path' of the periphery is also biased towards trade (i.e. as output grows the proportion of exportables in domestic production increases). The combined effect would be a tendency towards an increased demand for imports of manufacturing goods and an increased supply of primary products from the periphery. If left to the 'invisible hand' of international markets, this would tend to push up prices of imports and push down prices of exports of these countries as a whole; thus the tendency towards deterioration of the terms of trade of the periphery.

According to ECLA, it is possible to escape from this vicious circle through a process of transformation of the economic structure of the periphery capable, ideally, of providing those economies with a rapid and sustained rate of growth, and avoiding unemployment, external disequilibrium, and the deterioration of the terms of trade. The central element in this structural transformation is the process of industrialization, which could provide those highly income-elastic importables and eventually also produce more price-elastic exportables; thus Prebisch, in a recently published article, summarizes ECLA's task as having been that of 'showing that industrialization was an unavoidable prerequisite for development' (1980, p. viii). Furthermore, the article in question appears at times to use the concepts 'industrialization' and 'development' as synonyms.

In other words, to achieve accelerated and sustained economic growth in the periphery a necessary condition (and, some ECLA writings seemed to suggest, a sufficient one) was the development of a process of industrialization. But this process could not be expected to take place spontaneously, for it would be inhibited by the international division of labour which the centre would attempt to impose, and by a series of structural obstacles internal to the peripheral economies. Consequently, a series of measures was proposed, intended to promote a process of deliberate or 'forced' industrialization; these included state intervention in the economy both in the formulation of economic policies oriented towards these ends and as a direct productive agent. Among the economic policies suggested were those of 'healthy' protectionism, exchange controls, the attraction of foreign capital into manufacturing industry, and the stimulation and orientation of domestic investment. The intervention of the state in directly productive activities was recommended in those areas where large amounts of slow-maturing investment were needed, and particularly where this need coincided with the production of essential goods or services.

The dimensions of the thought of ECLA are based then not only upon its breadth and internal unity, but also upon its structuralist nature. The three most important characteristics of the development of the economy in the periphery – unemployment, external disequilibrium, and the tendency to deterioration of the terms of trade – are derived directly from the characteristics of the structure of production in the periphery, thus the possibility of tackling them is seen in terms of an ideal pattern of transformation, which indicates the conditions of proportionality which must hold if those features are to be avoided. This leads to the formulation, tacitly or explicitly, of the law of proportionality in the transformation, which will avoid heterogeneity and will thus allow full employment at adequate levels of productivity, avoid specialization and thus permit the escape from external disequilibria, and thus counteract the tendency towards deterioration of the terms of trade.

Nevertheless, it is also in this very structuralist nature that the limitations of ECLA thought lie; at this level of analysis no consideration is given to the social relations of production which are at the base of the process of import-substituting industrialization, and of the transformation in other structures of society that this brings in its wake.

ECLA proposes an ideal model of sectoral growth – and hence of global growth – designed in such a way that the three tendencies peculiar to economic development of the periphery are not produced; from this are derived the necessary conditions of accumulation which will allow the proportionality required in the transformation of the different sectors of material production. Nevertheless, even when pushed to the limits of its potential internal coherence, the structural approach is inadequate for the analysis of the evolution in the long term of the economic system as a whole, as it clearly involves more than the transformation of the structure of production alone. The theories of ECLA describe and examine certain aspects of the development of the forces of production (to the extent that they deal with the productivity of labour and the degree of diversification and homogeneity of the structures of production), but do not touch on relations of production, nor, as a result, on the manner in which the two interact.

Furthermore, the analysis of the inequalities of development cannot be carried out solely in terms of the patterns of accumulation necessary to avoid the creation of certain disproportions between the different sectors of material production, as inequalities of development are clearly linked to the possibility of saving and accumulation in each pole. That is to say, the requirements as far as accumulation is concerned are derived from those disproportions, but their feasibility depends more upon the general conditions in which accumulation occurs at world level than upon those disproportions. In other words, if the intention is to analyse the bipolarity of the centre–periphery system, it is not enough to postulate the inequality of development of the forces of production; it is necessary also to bear in mind that those forces of production develop in the framework of a process of generation, appropriation and utilization of the economic surplus, and that process, and the relations of exploitation upon which it is based, are not produced purely within each pole, but also between the two poles of the world economy.

It is not particularly surprising that ECLA should have attracted its share of criticism, particularly as it went beyond theoretical pronouncements to offer packages of policy recommendations. It was criticized from sectors of the left for failing to denounce sufficiently the mechanisms of exploitation within the capitalist system, and for criticizing the conventional theory of international trade only from 'within' (see for example Frank, 1967 and Caputo and Pizarro, 1974). On the other hand, from the right the reaction was immediate and at times ferocious: ECLA's policy recommendations were totally heretical from the point of view of conventional theory, and threatened the political interests of significant sectors. A leading critic in academic circles was Haberler (1961), who accused ECLA of failing to take due account of economic cycles, and argued that single factorial terms of trade would be a better indicator than the simple relationship between the prices of exports and imports (see also Baldwin, 1955).

On the political front, the right accused ECLA of being the 'Trojan horse of Marxism', on the strength of the degree of coincidence between both analyses. In both cases the principal obstacle was located overseas (international division of labour imposed by the centre), and both share the conviction that without a strenuous effort to remove the internal obstacles to development (the traditional sectors) the process of industrialization would be greatly impeded.

Furthermore, the coincidence between crucial elements in the analysis of the two respective lines of thought is made more evident by the fact that the processes of reformulation in each occurred simultaneously. Thus when it became evident that capitalist development in Latin America was taking a path different from that expected, a number of ECLA members began a process of reformulation of the traditional thought of that institution, just at the time that an important sector of the Latin American left was breaking with the traditional Marxist view that capitalist development was both necessary and possible in Latin America, but hindered by the 'feudal-imperialist' alliance. Moreover, both reformulations had one extremely important element in common: *pessimism* regarding the possibility of capitalist development in the periphery (see DEPENDENCY).

Some of the ECLA analysis reemerged in the 1980s in some North American academic circles (see especially Taylor, 1983), but in a way more as conventional economic analysis attempting to integrate some of the assumptions and hypotheses of the traditional ECLA analysis, or as an attempt to formalize classical ECLA thought – which has, nevertheless, proved to be an important contribution (and a much needed one) to mainstream economics – rather than an attempt to use structuralism as a new method of enquiry into economic analysis.

J.G. PALMA

See also NATIONALISM; NORTH–SOUTH ECONOMIC RELATIONS; PERIPHERY.

BIBLIOGRAPHY

Bacha, E.L. 1978. An interpretation of unequal exchange from Prebisch to Emmanuel. *Journal of Development Economics* 5, 319–30.

Baer, W. 1962. The economics of Prebisch and ECLA. *Economic Development and Cultural Change* 10, 169–82.

Baldwin, R.E. 1955. Secular movements in the terms of trade. *American Economic Review, Papers and Proceedings* 45, 259–69.

Bhagwati, Y. 1960. A skeptical note on the adverse secular trend in the terms of trade of underdeveloped countries. *Pakistan Economic Journal* 8, 235–48.

Cardoso, F.H. 1977. The originality of the copy: CEPAL and the idea of development. *CEPAL Review* 4, 7–40.

Caputo, O. and Pizarro, A. 1974. *Dependencia y relaciones internacionales*. Costa Rica: EDUCA.

Di Marco, L.E. (ed.) 1972. *International Economics and Development: Essays in Honour of Raul Prebisch*. New York and London: Academic Press.

ECLA. 1963. *El desarrollo social de América Latina en la post-guerra*. Buenos Aires: E. Solar-Hachette.

ECLA. 1964. *El desarrollo económico de América Latina en la post-guerra*. Santiago: UN (CEPAL).

ECLA. 1965. *El financiamiento externo de América Latina*. Santiago: UN (CEPAL).

ECLA. 1966. *El proceso de industrialización de América Latina*. Santiago: UN (CEPAL).

ECLA. 1969. *El pensamiento de la CEPAL*. Santiago: Editorial Universitaria.

ECLA. 1973. *Bibliografía de la CEPAL. 1948–1972*. Santiago: UN (CEPAL).

Ellsworth, P.T. 1956. The terms of trade between primary producing and industrial countries. *Interamerican Economic Affairs*, Summer.

Flanders, F.J. 1964. Prebisch on protectionism: an evaluation. *Economic Journal* 74, 305–26.

Frank, A.G. 1967. *Capitalism and Underdevelopment in Latin America: Historical Studies of Chile and Brazil*. New York: Monthly Review Press.

Johnson, H.G. 1972. *Economic Policies Towards Less Developed Countries*. New York: Brookings.

Haberler, G. 1961. Terms of trade and economic development. In *Economic Development of Latin America*, ed. H.S. Ellis, New York: St. Martin's Press, 275–97.

Hirschman, A. 1961. Ideologies of economic development. Reprinted in A. Hirschman, *A Bias for Hope*, New Haven: Yale University Press, 1971.

Kindleberger, C.P. 1956. *The Terms of Trade: a European Case Study*. New York: The Technology Press of MIT and J. Wiley & Son.

Mynt, M. 1954. The gains from international trade and the backward countries. *Review of Economic Studies* 22(2), 234–51.

Palma, J.G. 1981. Dependency and development: a critical overview. In *Dependency Theory: a Critical Reassessment*, ed. D. Seers, London: Francis Pinter.

Pinto, A. 1965. La concentración del progreso técnico y de sus frutos en el desarrollo. *El Trimestre Económico* 25, 3–69.

Pinto, A. 1973. *Inflación: raices estructurales*. Mexico: Fondo de Cultura Económico.

Pinto, A. 1974. Heterogeneidad estructural y el modelo de desarrollo reciente. In *Desarrollo Latinoamericano, ensayos críticos*, ed. J. Serra, Mexico: Fondo de Cultura Económico.

Pinto, A. and Knakel, J. 1973. The centre–periphery system twenty years later. *Social and Economic Studies*, March, 34–89.

Prebisch, R. 1980. Prologo. In Rodriguez (1980).

Rodriguez, O. 1980. *La teoría del subdesarrollo de la CEPAL*. Mexico: Siglo XXI Editores.

Taylor, L. 1983. *Structuralist Macroeconomics*. New York: Basic Books.

UNESCO. 1949. *Postwar Price Relations Between Under-developed and Industrialized Countries*. New York: UN.

Viner, J. 1953. *International Trade and Economic Development*. Oxford: Clarendon Press.

structural unemployment. Economists have generally distinguished between various types of unemployment, both in terms of their characteristic features and their underlying causal mechanisms. Some of these distinctions are non-controversial and relatively straightforward both in their definition and in their measurement. Thus, for example, there is not too much disagreement about the scale and nature of 'seasonal unemployment' or about the need for 'seasonal adjustments' to the regular monthly series of unemployment statistics published in all industrial countries.

However, when it comes to such categories as 'structural' unemployment and 'cyclical' unemployment, and even more in the case of 'voluntary' unemployment, 'natural' unemployment or 'technological' unemployment, there is intense disagreement not only with respect to their importance but even with respect to their very existence. In the case of structural unemployment, there is agreement that such a phenomenon does indeed exist, but there is a wide area of disagreement about its extent and even more about its causes.

The distinction between 'frictional' and 'structural' unemployment has never been a precise and unambiguous one. Nevertheless, there is general agreement that whereas *frictional* unemployment is a transitory and very short-lived form of unemployment based on minor imperfections in the labour market, *structural* unemployment is a more intractable and persistent phenomenon. Some frictional unemployment is generally regarded as an inevitable accompaniment of a dynamic economy, since there will probably always be imperfections in the available information about job opportunities, in the speed of response and in mobility. However, such frictional unemployment can be reduced to a very low level (i.e. less than half of one per cent) of the aggregate labour force, as the experience of many countries showed in the high boom period after World War II.

Structural unemployment could in principle be caused by a variety of forms of 'mis-match' in the labour market with more persistent characteristics. The 'mis-match' might, for example, be caused by *regional* disparities in the availability of new employment opportunities, and in the decline of older industries. The persistence of high unemployment levels in southern Italy over prolonged periods, when there were labour shortages in northern and in central Italy, is one instance of this type of structural disequilibrium in regional development, which exists to a greater or lesser degree in most industrialized countries.

Another form of 'mis-match' relates to the *skill* profile of the labour force. Whereas the concept of 'frictional' unemployment presupposes a rapid process of re-training or learning-by-doing, (or none at all), in practice the skill requirements for new job opportunities may differ very substantially from the skills of those in search of work. The degree of mis-match may be so great and so deeply rooted in educational and cultural aspects of society, that it is necessary to analyse 'segmented' labour markets, each with their own specific characteristics. If mobility between 'segments' is very low then it is possible to explain the persistence of, for example, very high levels of unemployment among young, black, unskilled workers in the big cities of the United States, side by side with labour shortages in other segments of the market associated with high professional and skill requirements, and lower levels of general unemployment (Doeringer and Piore, 1971; Edwards, Reich and Gordon, 1975).

Whereas almost all economists would agree that such problems as change in skill requirements and the uneven development of different regions of a country may give rise to problems of structural adjustment, they have differed greatly in their views about the severity of such problems, about their underlying causes and about the appropriate policy prescriptions. They have differed in particular about the feasibility of substitution between labour and capital and the time lags involved.

Ricardo (1821) provoked an intense and continuing debate amongst economists with his famous remark that 'The opinion entertained by the labouring class that the employment of machinery is frequently detrimental to their interests, is not founded on prejudice or error, but is conformable to the correct principles of political economy' (Ricardo, 1821, p. 387).

Although controversy still continues about the interpretation of his remarks and he himself revised some of his earlier formulations because they were misunderstood, it is nevertheless clear that Ricardo was drawing attention to the fact that rapid technical change in the form of mechanisation of existing processes of production, could in principle give rise to serious unemployment problems for the labour force, at least in specific industries and regions. Although he certainly acknowledged that what would now be called 'compensation mechanisms' could ultimately lead to the growth of new employment, both in the machine-building industries and elsewhere in the system, he was pointing out that there could be substantial time lags in the adjustment of the capital stock and the mobility of the labour force. In today's terminology he was emphasizing that rapid process innovation could lead to structural unemployment.

This conclusion has never been a comfortable one for neoclassical economics, which has generally sought to minimize the severity and complexity of these problems, and to put the emphasis almost exclusively on wage flexibility. One of the reasons for this was the neoclassical 'principle of substitution' between capital and labour which, provided wages and interest rates are flexible, should in theory assure that there cannot be more than short-term disequilibrium in the labour market. Since entrepreneurs are assumed to be free to make a rational choice between a wide spectrum of alternative combinations of labour and capital, they will substitute labour for capital in the event of a surplus of labour and an appropriate fall in wage rates and vice-versa in the case of a shortage of labour. This means that a self-regulating mechanism will always tend to clear the labour market.

Indeed in the period before World War I, when neoclassical theories were first established, it was often assumed that structural unemployment could not and would not be a serious problem, and that the problem of 'technological unemployment' simply did not exist (Gourvich, 1940). The remaining problems of imperfect information, imperfect mobility and re-training could be handled through such institutional innovations as 'labour exchanges' (Beveridge, 1909).

The relative neglect of the issue of unemployment by most mainstream neoclassical theory led Keynes (1936) to complain when he came to write his *General Theory of Employment, Interest and Money* that he could not find any adequate statement of a theory of employment in the classical tradition. The somewhat myopic way in which Say's Law was invoked to rule out the possibility of persistent high levels of unemployment was one reason for the severity of Keynes's onslaught on the classical tradition.

The rather complacent mainstream view was shattered by the deep depression of the 1930s, and even before that by high levels of unemployment in many countries already in the 1920s. Although traditional theorists continued to emphasise the issue of wage flexibility, most professional economists in the 1930s and 1940s ultimately followed Keynes in recognizing that there were other fundamental problems in maintaining a high level of employment. The Keynesian school can probably best be distinguished from the neoclassical school by its rejection of the notion that equilibrium necessarily implies full employment. Keynes (1936) denied both to wages and to interest rates the self-regulating equilibrating functions which neoclassical theory had assumed. Thus, within a Keynesian framework of analysis there is far more scope for positive structural adjustment policies designed to deal with the problems of regional disequilibrium, skill mis-match and technical change. The problem of structural unemployment is by no means assumed out of existence, but is tackled within an overall framework, emphasizing the cardinal importance of aggregate demand. Beveridge (1944) suggested that given a strong commitment to 'full employment' policies on the part of central government, structural unemployment could be reduced to a relatively low figure, perhaps one per cent of the labour force.

An alternative critique of the neoclassical general equilibrium theory of employment came from Schumpeter (1939) and from other economists, who, for want of a better description, might be designated as 'structuralists'. In his theory of economic development, Schumpeter stressed in particular the role of major technical innovations as a disequilibriating phenomenon. Such revolutionary new technologies could give rise to 'creative gales of destruction' in which old industries, technologies, crafts and employment were decimated by the rise of investment in new products and processes and the opening up of new markets.

Schumpeter (1939) regarded the process of technical change as inherently uneven and disequilibrating, giving rise to cyclical behaviour in the system:

> Economists have a habit of distinguishing between, and contrasting cyclical and technological unemployment. But it follows from our model that, basically, cyclical unemployment is technological unemployment. ... We have seen, in fact, in our historical survey, that periods of prolonged supernormal unemployment, coincide with the periods in which the results of inventions are spreading over the system ... (Volume 2, p. 515).

Schumpeter (1952) criticized the Keynesian model for its neglect of technical change and for its concentration on the short-term business cycle:

> ... it limits applicability of the analysis to a few years at most – perhaps the duration of the '40 months' cycle' – and in terms of phenomena to the factors that would govern the greater or the smaller utilisation of an industrial apparatus *if* the latter remains unchanged. All the phenomena incident to the creation and change in the apparatus, that is to say the phenomena that dominate the capitalist process are thus excluded from consideration (p. 480).

In Schumpeter's view the most important problems were associated with long-term processes or Kondratiev cycles. Thus, in his analysis, periods of 'supernormal. Unemployment' occurred approximately every half century or so, i.e. in the 1820s, in the 1880s and in the 1930s, when problems of structural adjustment to technical change were particularly severe. Lederer (1911) had already pointed out that severe structural unemployment could arise from the problems of adjustment in the capital stock. The shift of capital investment from 'static' branches to the innovative sectors would be hampered by the inertia and rigidity of the existing pattern of investment; 'capital shortage' unemployment could be a serious problem side by side with surplus capacity in declining branches of the economy. Thus capital mis-match may give rise to structural unemployment as well as skill mis-match, since the 'principle of substitution' does not in fact operate in the simple and instantaneous manner postulated in neoclassical models.

In the prolonged boom after World War II Keynesian ideas predominated both in academic economics and in the policy advice offered to governments. Unemployment fell to historically low levels in most industrial OECD countries; female participation rates rose to much higher levels, and in many countries there was substantial net immigration. In these circumstances there was again some tendency to assume that the problems of structural unemployment had been largely resolved, this time through a combination of aggregate demand management policies and active labour market and regional policies. In such countries as Sweden, the German Federal Republic and Austria in particular, active labour market policies were followed which laid great stress on the training and re-training of the labour force to cope with changing skill requirements, and these did indeed help to minimize structural unemployment problems. In the 1970s and 1980s, however, there came renewed recognition that the problem had still not completely disappeared and with general unemployment rates in the OECD area often two or three times as high as in the 1960s, and a rising proportion of long-term unemployed within the total, structural problems of adjustment once more moved to the centre of the stage.

The increasing seriousness of structural mis-match unemployment within the OECD area was shown by 'Okun curve' analysis in papers presented to the OECD Conference on employment and structural change (Soete and Freeman, OECD, 1985b) and in the OECD's own publications (OECD, 1985a). This evidence showed that the problem was no longer just a cyclical one since the level of unemployment associated with any particular degree of capacity utilisation had tended upwards in the 1970s and 1980s, most notably in Europe, but also in the USA and even in Japan. The Secretary-General of the OECD, M. Paye (1985) used the results of this analysis to emphasize the magnitude of the problems of structural adjustment confronting all the OECD countries, and to point to major problems of 'mis-match' both in relation to the skill composition of the work force and in relation to the capital stock.

This marked some degree of consensus within the economics profession that the wave of new technology associated with computerization and microelectronics did indeed raise important problems of structural adjustment. The mis-match of skill requirements was very widely recognized and almost all countries initiated special training and re-training programmes to cope with this problem. It was also increasingly recognized that mis-match in the capital stock could give rise to problems of capital shortage unemployment, particularly in countries which had experienced structural rigidity in adapting to new technology. The severe international disequilibria arising from differential rates of technical change once again aroused anxiety over those problems of international structural adjustment which had so much concerned both Ricardo and Keynes.

However, opinions continue to diverge about the relative significance of wage flexibility, incomes policies, interest rates, national and international monetary and demand policies, industry and technology policies in overcoming the structural unemployment problems. Both neoclassical economists and Keynesians continued to insist on the crucial importance, on the one hand of wage rigidity and on the other hand of aggregate demand in explaining the persistence of high unemployment and indicating the appropriate remedies (Layard and Nickell, 1985).

C. FREEMAN

See also UNEMPLOYMENT.

BIBLIOGRAPHY

Beveridge, W.H. 1909. *Unemployment: a Problem of Industry*. London: Longmans, Green.

Beveridge, W.H. 1944. *Full Employment in a Free Society*. London: George Allen & Unwin.

Doeringer, P.B. and Piore, M. 1971. *Internal Labor Markets and Manpower Analysis*. Lexington, Mass.: D.C. Heath.

Edwards, R.C., Reich, M. and Gordon, D.M. (eds) 1975. *Labor Market Segmentation*. Lexington, Mass.: D.C. Heath.

Freeman, C. and Soete, L.L.G. 1987. *Technical Change and Full Employment*. Oxford: Blackwell.
Gourvich, A. 1940. *Survey of Economic Theory on Technological Change and Employment*. Reprinted, New York: A.M. Kelley.
Keynes, J.M. 1936. *General Theory of Employment, Interest and Money*. London: Macmillan; New York: Harcourt, Brace.
Layard, R. and Nickell, S. 1985. The causes of British unemployment. *National Institute Economic Review*, February, 62–85.
Lederer, E. 1938. *Technischer Fortschritt und Arbeitslosigkeit*, Tubingen. Trans. as *Technical Progress and Unemployment*, Geneva: ILO, 1938.
OECD. 1985a. *Economic Outlook*. Paris, June, 26–34.
OECD. 1985b. *Employment Growth and Structural Change*. Paris.
Ricardo, D. 1821. *Principles of Political Economy and Taxation*. 3rd edn, *The Works and Correspondence of David Ricardo*, ed. P. Sraffa, Vol. 1, Cambridge: Cambridge University Press, 1951.
Schumpeter, J.A. 1939. *Business Cycles: A Theoretical, Historical, and Statistical Analysis of the Capitalist Process*. 2 vols, New York: McGraw-Hill.
Schumpeter, J.A. 1952. *Ten Great Economists*. London: Allen & Unwin.
Soete, L.L.G. and Freeman, C. 1985. New technologies, investment and employment growth. In OECD (1985b).

Strumilin, Stanislav Gustavovich (1877–1974). Born Strumillo-Petrashkevich, of Polish descent, in Dashkovtsy, Russia, on 29 January 1877, Strumilin died in Moscow on 25 January 1974. He studied at the St Petersburg Polytechnical Institute under P.B. Struve and M.I. Tugan-Baranovsky and was twice sentenced to internal exile before the 1917 Revolutions. A Menshevik delegate to the Stockholm (1906) and London (1907) Party Congresses, he did not formally join the Bolshevik side until 1923. Apart from a break in 1937–43, when as an ex-Menshevik he was banished to the Urals in the Great Purge, he was on the staff of the State Planning Committee from 1921 (nominated by Lenin personally) to 1951; then aged 74, he moved to the Party's Academy of Social Sciences. An Academician from 1931, he received a Stalin Prize in 1942 for work on the wartime development of the Urals.

The expedient marshalling of economics to salvage politically determined measures, which characterized his considerable output (180 publications), was exemplified during the earliest phase of the Soviet system, 'War Communism'. To the Supreme Economic Council's committee which in 1920 considered replacing money (the rouble already being depreciated by hyper-inflation) by 'labour units', Strumilin proposed a rational price mechanism by defining (in terms of work-days of unskilled manpower) a single good as numeraire, each other good being related by the logarithm of its labour content (a surrogate for declining marginal utilities), corrected by differences in productivity and in the intensity of need (Malle, 1985; Sutela, 1984). The 'labour unit' scheme was abandoned when Lenin reintroduced a market and sound money under his New Economic Policy; Strumilin returned to his pre-revolutionary research on labour economics. Strumilin (1924) is pioneering in its sampling of wage differentials associated with educational input, measured by the cost of teaching and (for those of working age) income forgone. Invited many years later by UNESCO to update his analysis, Strumilin (1962) changed his approach from the microeconomic to a macroeconomic Cobb–Douglas-type function (without apparent acquaintance with the original) to indicate the share of the national income increment attributable to improvement in the qualifications of the labour force. Econometrically not robust, the exercise was nevertheless a *tour de force* for a man of 85 and illustrated how, as Soviet economics was released from Stalinist shackles, it was the old who led the way; his concern to widen the perspectives of the post-Stalin generation was heightened by comparison with the intellectual freedom of his own youth, as Davies (1960) perceives from Strumilin's autobiography (1957).

Strumilin (1913) is officially credited with the first 'balance method' – branch availabilities and disposals in physical quantities (*Ekonomicheskaya entsiklopediya*, 1980), as Davies (1960), also documents – but Strumilin's claim (*Selected Works*, vol. 2, p. 180) to priority for macroeconomic input–output in money terms has rightly been disputed in favour of his Planning Committee subordinate, V.G. Groman (Wheatcroft and Davies, 1985, p. 46; Jasny, 1972, p. 104). N.A. Voznessensky brought Strumilin back to the Committee as soon as he resumed the chairmanship, coincidentally with Stalin's signal that formal analysis of the Soviet economy could recommence. He took up the theory of capital efficiency – to which he had been one of the last earlier Soviet contributors (Strumilin, 1929) – by proposing an ideologically acceptable discount rate in the form of productivity change (Strumilin, 1946).

M.C. Kaser

SELECTED WORKS

1924. The economic significance of national education. Trans. by B. Jeffrey in *The Economics of Education*, ed. E.A.G. Robinson and J.E. Vaizey, London: Macmillan, 1966, from *Ekonomika truda* (The Economics of Labour), Moscow, 1925. Reprinted in *Selected Works*, Vol. 3, 101–31, from *Planovoe khoziastvo* (Planned Economy), No. 9–10, 1924.
1929. K problem effektivnosti kapital'nykh zatrat' (On the problem of the efficiency of capital expenditure). *Planovoe khoziastvo* (Planned Economy), No. 7. In Selected Works, Vol. 2, 417–30.
1946. The time factor in capital investment projects. *International Economic Papers* No. 1, London: Macmillan, 1951 Trans. from *Izvestiia Akademii Nauk SSSR. Otdelenie ekonomiki i prava* (News of the USSR Academy of Sciences. Division of Economics and Law), No. 3. Reprinted in Selected Works, Vol. 4, 213–31.
1957. *Iz perezhitogo 1897–1917 gg.* (Out of my past 1897–1917). Moscow: Gospolitizdat.
1962. The economics of education in the USSR. *International Social Science Journal* 14(4). Reprinted in Selected Works, Vol. 5, 265–77, from *Ekonomicheskaia gazeta* (Economics Gazette), 2 April 1962.
1963–5. *Izbrannye proizvedeniia* (Selected Works). 5 vols, Moscow: Izdatel'stvo Nauka.

BIBLIOGRAPHY

Davies, R.W. 1960. Some Soviet economic controllers. *Soviet Studies* 11(3).
Ekonomicheskaia entsiklopediia: Politicheskaia ekonomiia. 1980. Vol. 4. Moscow: Izdatel'stvo sovetskaia entsiklopediia.
Jasny, N. 1972. *Soviet Economists of the Twenties. Names to be Remembered*. Cambridge: Cambridge University Press.
Malle, S. 1985. *The Economic Organization of War Communism, 1918–1921*. Cambridge: Cambridge University Press.
Sutela, P. 1984. *Socialism, Planning and Optimality. A Study in Soviet Economic Thought*. Commentationes Scientiarum Socialium No. 25, Helsinki: Societas Scientiarum Fennica.
Wheatcroft, S.G. and Davies, R.W. (eds) 1985. *Materials for a Balance of the Soviet National Economy, 1928–1930*. Cambridge: Cambridge University Press.

Struve, Pyotr Berngardovich (1870–1944). The son of the Provincial Governor in Perm', Russia, Struve was born on 26 January 1870 and died in Paris on 26 February 1944. He was born in the year that A.I. Herzen died and his biographer (Pipes, 1970, 1980) and editor of his *Collected Works*, 1970, quoted Struve's words on Herzen as applicable 'with equal justice to himself ... "he was repelled by the subtlest, most spiritual form of despotism – dogmatism" '. Struve's formal training in economics was limited to Hildebrand's course at Graz University but he was one of the most prominent and certainly the most prolific (160 publications) of marxist economists in Tsarist Russia, and helped to create the country's first modern faculty of economics. While a marxist (he was the editor of marxism's first legally published journal in Russia), Struve in (1900) integrated 'Ricardo's careful realism' and the Austrian's School's utility within 'the grandiose framework of Marx's sociological generalizations'. As his marxism waned (in his autobiography (1934), Struve saw himself as the first 'revisionist'), he criticized value as a valid economic concept and insisted that price was the only scientifically acceptable relevant unit of measurement. In later writings (Struve, 1913; 1916) he so defined price as to deny any Walrasian *tâtonnement* by maintaining that bid and offer are comprised within a price.

As historian (in pioneering work on the economics of serfdom) and observer of the current economy, he criticized Marx's formularies when they appeared counter to empirical evidence. Thus he contested the explanation of unemployment as solely 'the reserve army of capitalism' by demonstrating its cyclical, seasonal, structural and wage-bargaining elements; he opposed marxist historical determinism in accepting that human ideals existed independently of economic and social realities and was convinced that socialism could be introduced by a peaceful transition from capitalism, without violent revolution. The 'legal marxism' which he embraced soon brought a clash with Lenin, with whom he was nevertheless at one both in contesting 'utopian' socialism and populism (Struve, 1894) and in believing that 'the working class is the only revolutionary class in Russia' (Struve, 1897). Like Lenin, he also contended that the path for the scarcely monetized Russian peasant economy (serfdom had been abolished only in 1861) lay through capitalist farming. His break with Lenin (paradoxically while following him in banishment and then exile) was over the advocacy of overthrow force. A Soviet assessment is that 'he became an opponent of revolutionary marxism, in particular on the concept of socialist revolution and the dictatorship of the proletariat'(*Bol'shaya sovetskaya entsiklopediya*, 1976): as a Constitutional Democratic deputy to the Second Duma he vigorously advocated parliamentary government in contrast to both the autocracy of the Tsar and the 'democratic centralism' of Lenin.

Kindersley (1962, ch. 5) and Pipes (1980, ch. 3) trace his path – parallel with that of Tugan-Baranovsky in the final four years of the century – to rupture with the labour theory. His fundamental divergence was to contend that surplus value was generated by both constant and variable capital and could be attributable to either one: 'the proportions in which the whole produce is divided between landlords, capitalists and labour is not essentially connected with the doctrine of value' (Struve, 1900). Moreover, as the Soviet *Istoriya russkoy ekonomicheskoy mysli*, 1960, correctly discerns in Struve, factor price ratios change as capital productivity, rising with technical progress, depresses *ceteris paritus* labour productivity.

M.C. Kaser

SELECTED WORKS

1894. Kriticheskie zametki k voprosu ob ekonomicheskom razvitii Rossi (Critical remarks on the question of the economic development of Russia). St Petersburg: 15 in *Collected Works*.

1897. Po povodu S. Peterburgskoi stachki (On the St Petersburg strikes). *Rabotnik* 3–4: 60 in *Collected Works*.

1900. Osnovnaya antinomiya teorii trudovoy tsennosti Marksa (The fundamental antinomy in Marx's theory of value). *Zhizn'* 2: 89 in *Collected Works*.

1913, 1916. *Khozyaistvo i tsena* (Economy and Price), Vols I and II. St Petersburg and Moscow (446 in *Collected Works*).

1934. My contacts with Rodichev; My contacts and conflicts with Lenin. *Slavonic Review* 12 and 13 (625, 626 and 626a in *Collected Works*).

1970. *Collected Works*. Ed. R. Pipes (with 'Introduction' to each volume), 15 vols, Ann Arbor: University of Michigan Press.

BIBLIOGRAPHY

Bezman, R.R. and Shukhov, N.S. 1960. The Legal Marxists. In *Istoriya russkoy ekonomicheskoy mysli* (History of Russian Economic Thought) ed. A.I. Pashkov and N.A. Tsagolov, Moscow: Izdatelstvo sotsial'no-ekonomicheskoy literatury.

Bol'shaya sovetskaya entsiklopediya (Great Soviet Encyclopedia). 1976. 3rd edn, vol. 24, book I, Moscow: Izdatel'stvo Sovetskaya entsiklopediya.

Kindersley, R. 1962. *The First Russian Revisionists. A Study of 'Legal Marxism' in Russia*. Oxford: Clarendon Press.

Pipes, R. 1970, 1980. *Struve*. Vol. 1: *Liberal on the Left*, 1870–1905; Vol. 2: *Liberal on the Right*, 1905–1944. Cambridge, Mass.: Harvard University Press.

stylized facts. The concept of 'stylized facts' is usually attributed to Nicholas Kaldor, who discussed this concept in a well-known 1958 conference paper on capital accumulation and economic growth. While the term 'stylized facts' is widely used today in many varied contexts, Kaldor had a specific use in mind.

Kaldor noted that everyone agrees 'that the basic requirement of any model is that it should be capable of explaining the characteristic features of the economic process as we find them in reality'. But how are we to explain results of a theoretical model which are contrary to what we observe in reality? Too often, Kaldor complains, the contrary results are explained away by simply noting that the assumptions of the model did not account for changes in such things as knowledge or merely assumed away uncertainty and technological progress. For Kaldor, such a method of explaining away discrepancies between the results of the theoretical model and the facts of the world we see outside of our window is of very little 'interpretive value'.

The problem that Kaldor is concerned with is not the simplistic view that recognizes that assumptions of models and theories 'must necessarily be based on abstractions'. Rather it is the more difficult one of being careful to choose a type of abstraction that is 'appropriate to the characteristic features of the economic process as recorded by experience.' In Kaldor's view, when choosing between competing theoretical approaches we 'ought to start off with a summary of the facts' which we regard as relevant to the task at hand.

Since Kaldor wished to focus our attention on the difficult problem of choosing an appropriate type of abstraction for the economic world we hope to explain, he wanted to avoid unproductive debate over details of historical accuracy. He said that we should be free to start off with a 'stylized' view of the facts to be explained. Specifically, we should be free to concentrate on broad tendencies, ignoring individual detail, and proceed on what he calls the 'as if' method. His use of an 'as if' method is different from the common neoclassical use of an 'as if' method. Unlike neoclassical economists who employ simplistic *assumptions* 'as if' they are true, Kaldor would have us explain 'stylized' facts as if they truly represented the reality we want to explain. As long as we can come to an agreement regarding the 'stylized' facts, the comparative appropriateness of competing explanatory abstractions can be brought into clear and decisive focus.

In the construction of any theoretical model of economic growth and capital accumulation, Kaldor suggested six 'stylized' facts as a starting point. These included such things as a steady rate of growth of production and productivity of labour, a growing capital to labour ratio, a steady rate of profit on capital, steady capital-output ratios over long periods, high correlation between the share of profits in income and the share of investment in output while allowing that there are differences in the rate of growth of labour productivity and of total output between societies.

To emphasize that the critical issue involves choosing between competing theoretical assumptions with respect to a set of given 'stylized facts', Kaldor compares his Keynesian–classical model with one he attributes to neoclassical economists. Kaldor claims that none of his suggested 'stylized facts' can be plausibly 'explained' by the assumptions of neoclassical models while the alternative model of income distribution and capital accumulation which he presents is capable of explaining some if not all of his 'stylized facts'.

Economists today who claim to explain 'stylized facts' usually are not fully aware that Kaldor used the term only in the context of a theoretical comparison. Today most neoclassical model-builders who claim to be explaining only stylized facts do so merely as a convenient simplification of the model-building process. If these model-builders think they are following Kaldor's lead, they are clearly mistaken. To be following Kaldor's meaning of stylized facts they would have to show that their chosen model has a comparative advantage over other possible models that might be used to explain the stylized facts. The purpose of using stylized facts is both to emphasize the comparative advantage of the chosen model and to preclude unproductive arguing at cross purposes.

The primary methodological reason for Kaldor's stressing the use of 'stylized facts' for the purpose of comparing models and theoretical abstractions is that 'facts, as recorded by statisticians, are always subject to snags and qualifications, and for that reason are incapable of being accurately summarized'. Whenever facts are stylized for purposes other than establishing a basis for model or theory comparison, it is much too easy for a critic of that model to claim that the theorist's use of stylized facts was 'ad hoc' – that is, invoked solely to avoid obvious empirical refutations (see Boland, 1982, 1986). Evading this methodological criticism will always be difficult. Clearly, unless one follows Kaldor by comparing one's chosen abstraction with the ability of one or more alternative types of abstraction to explain the stylized facts in question, the choice of one's type of abstraction will remain open to a charge of useless 'ad hocery'.

In discussing Kaldor's 'stylized facts', Robert Solow said that 'there was no doubt that they are stylized' and that 'it is possible to question whether they are facts'. It would seem that without an agreement about which 'stylized facts' are acceptable, it is questionable whether Kaldor's strategy of theory comparison will always be fruitful. Nevertheless, Kaldor is to be admired for insisting that we identify our facts to be explained in advance of any argument between competing explanatory models.

LAWRENCE A. BOLAND

See also MODELS AND THEORY.

BIBLIOGRAPHY

Boland, L. 1982. *The Foundations of Economic Method.* London: George Allen & Unwin.

Boland, L. 1986. *Methodology for a New Microeconomics: the Critical Foundations.* Boston: Allen & Unwin.

Kaldor, N. 1963. Capital accumulation and economic growth. In *The Theory of Capital*, ed. F. Lutz, London: Macmillan.

Solow, R. 1970. *Growth Theory: an Exposition.* Oxford: Clarendon Press.

subadditivity. In the economics literature 'subadditivity' is a mathematical representation of the concept of natural monopoly. An industry is a natural monopoly if total output can be produced at lower cost by a single firm than by any collection of two or more firms. If all potentially active firms in the industry have access to the same technology, which is represented by a cost function c, then at aggregate output x, the industry is a natural monopoly if $c(x) \leqslant c(x^1) + \cdots + c(x^t)$ for any set of outputs $x^1, \ldots, x^t$ such that

$$\sum_{i=1}^{t} x^i = x.$$

A cost function c is globally subadditive if for any non-negative output vectors x and y,

$$c(x_1 + y_1, \ldots, x_n + y_n) \leqslant c(x_1, \ldots, x_n) + c(y_1, \ldots, y_n).$$

In the production of a set $N = \{1, \ldots, n\}$ of indivisible objects the cost function is subadditive if $c(S \cup T) \leqslant c(S) + c(T)$ for any disjoint subsets S and R. While this 'economic' definition of subadditivity is intuitively appealing, it is generally not obvious whether or not a particular cost function is subadditive. It is therefore of interest to determine both necessary and sufficient conditions for subadditivity in order to formulate empirical tests for natural monopoly. Subadditivity is closely associated with the concepts of 'economies of scale' and 'economies of scope'. A cost function exhibits economies of scale if $c(\lambda x) \leqslant \lambda c(x)$ for $1 \leqslant \lambda \leqslant 1 + \epsilon$, for small positive ϵ. A cost function exhibits economies of scope if the subadditivity condition is applied only for orthogonal output vectors. For example, the cost function $c(x_1, x_2) = 1 + (x_1 + x_2)^2 + (x_1 x_2)^{1/2}$ exhibits economies of scale whenever $x_1 + x_2 \leqslant 1$, economies of scope whenever $x_1 x_2 \leqslant 1/4$, and is subadditive whenever $x_1 + x_2 \leqslant 2$ and $x_1 x_2 \leqslant 1/4$. While economies of scope are clearly necessary for subadditivity, economies of scale are neither necessary nor sufficient for subadditivity of a function of two or more variables. Therefore a valid empirical test for multiproduct natural monopoly, based on subadditivity, should not depend entirely on a test for economies of scale.

Subadditivity of a function f is equivalent to superadditivity of $-f$. Many of the known properties of subadditive functions are based on the equivalent properties of superadditive characteristic functions in the theory of cooperative games. For example, a firm producing n discrete outputs with a subadditive cost function, c, is said to choose 'subsidy free' prices, p, if $\Sigma_{i \in S} p_i \leqslant c(S)$ for all subsets S of N. If the firm is also subject to a break-even constraint then the subsidy free prices correspond exactly to the core of a cooperative game defined by N and $-c$. For general cost functions the core concept is captured in the definition of 'supportable cost functions'. A cost function c is supportable at x if there exists a price vector p such that $\Sigma_{i=1}^{n} p_i x_i = c(x)$ and $\Sigma_{i=1}^{n} {}^z p_i x_i \leqslant c(x')$ for all $x' \leqslant x$. Also closely related is the concept of 'sustainable prices'.

Supportability of a function is a sufficient condition for subadditivity. Similarly, if a function satisfies the core property on a set N then the subadditivity conditions hold for all subsets S and T such that $S \cup T = N$. A stronger sufficient condition for subadditivity is based on the definition of a 'convex game'. The corresponding property, known as cost complementarity, is the condition that

$$c(S)+c(T) \leqslant c(S \cup T)+c(S \cap T).$$

For general cost functions which are differentiable, global cost complementarity holds if all second partial derivatives are non-positive. In some applications only the cross-partial derivatives need be non-positive. For non-differentiable functions a closely related property known as submodularity, which is also sufficient for subadditivity, may be defined (Sharkey, 1982).

W.W. SHARKEY

See also NATURAL MONOPOLY.

BIBLIOGRAPHY
Sharkey, W.W. 1982. *The Theory of Natural Monopoly.* Cambridge: Cambridge University Press.

subjective probability.

1. KINDS OF PROBABILITY. The usual meaning of 'probable' in ordinary conversation is closely related to its derivation from a Latin word meaning provable or capable of being made convincing. The concept is even clearer in the derivation of the German word *Wahrscheinlichkeit*, 'having the appearance of truth'. In fact, when we say an event is probable we usually mean that we would not be surprised (or we ought not to be) if it occurred, or that we *would* be somewhat surprised (or ought to be) if did not occur. Since 'surprise' refers to a personal or subjective experience it seems clear that the ordinary concept of probability is subjectivistic (or else in some sense logical). Also a probability, in this subjective or logical sense, can be more or less large so it can be interpreted as a degree of belief or a rational degree of belief or intensity of conviction. A subjective probability is usually regarded as somewhat more than just a degree of belief – it is a degree of belief that belongs to a body of beliefs from which the worst inconsistencies have been removed by means of detached judgements. In short, the degree of belief should be more or less rational.

To appreciate better the meaning of a subjective probability it is necessary to consider other kinds or interpretations of probability. We begin by contrasting subjective probability with what is often called *physical probability* by considering an example.

Suppose you are given a solid cube that appears superficially symmetrical and you are asked to paint the numbers 1 to 6 on its six faces so that the cube becomes a die (the singular of 'dice'). What is the probability that you will obtain the 6 uppermost on the first throw of the die? Because of the symmetry of the information available to you it seems that your probability, at least for betting purposes, *ought* to be equal to or close to 1/6. (Irrational gamblers, when they say 'When you're hot you're hot' seem to believe that dice have memories.) But, for all you know, the die might not be symmetrical inside, it might be a loaded die, and the intrinsic or material or physical probability or propensity to come up 6 might be far from 1/6. Thus your betting or subjective or personal probability need not be equal to the physical probability. I shall use the term 'subjective' to avoid being too personal.

That there are two kinds of probability was perhaps first emphasized by Poisson (1837, p. 31). He used the French (or English) word 'chance' for physical probability, and

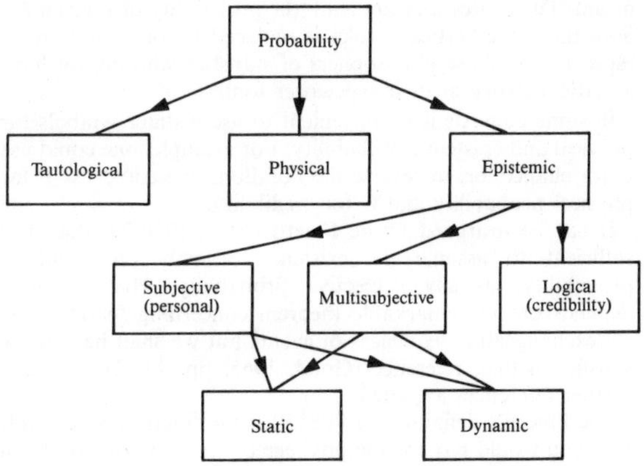

Figure 1 A dendroidal classification of kinds of probability or usages of the term.

'probabilité' for something close to subjective probability. I say 'close' because Poisson did not make it clear whether his use of 'probabilité' was intended to denote subjective probability, or, on the other hand, the only rational probability, or objective degree of belief, on the evidence available. This latter kind of probability, the existence of which is controversial, has been called a *credibility* (for example by F.Y. Edgeworth and Bertrand Russell) or a *logical probability*. A probability that is either subjective or logical, or something intermediate, is conveniently called an *epistemic probability* although some writers use the term 'subjective' to mean 'epistemic' in order to avoid sounding too philosophical. A probability agreed upon by a group of people is sometimes called *multisubjective* or multipersonal. The subject whose subjective probability is under discussion is often called 'You'. This has the merit of being ambiguously singular or plural.

For a dendroidal classification of kinds of probability see Figure 1 (based on Good, 1966). This classification mentions 'tautological probability' which is a probability occurring in a mathematical theory without an interpretation outside the mathematics.

Your probability that a die will come up 6 depends on the information available to you; for example, if you have thrown it 6000 times and it has come up 6 exactly 500 times then your subjective probability on the next throw would presumably be close to 500/6000 or 1/12. Furthermore, I think you will agree that if you throw the die an exceedingly large number of times, but not so many that the die or you get worn out, then the credibility is close to 1 that your subjective probability *should* become close to the physical probability (if you are rational and if the die is thrown properly). This assumes of course that the die is of durable material and not made of soft clay. If it is made of soft clay the physical probability presumably exists but is more difficult or impossible to measure by long-run relative frequency.

This example makes it entirely clear that a subjective probability should depend on the available information just as a physical probability depends on the 'set-up'. To capture this fact symbolically it is customary in modern books on statistics or mathematical probability to write $P(E|F)$ or $Pr(E|F)$ or $Prob(E|F)$ or $p(E|F)$, etc., for the probability of E given F. Here E and F might denote events, hypotheses, or propositions and the notation is often used whatever kind of probability is meant. The expressions are read 'the probability of E given F'. Sometimes the vertical stroke is replaced by other notations, especially by those philosophers of statistics who do not have a vertical stroke in their typewriter fonts.

In some contexts it is convenient to use distinct symbols for physical and epistemic probability. For example, one could use C for chance, or, to reverse the notation, one could use P for physical probability and C for credibility.

It has been argued by de Finetti (1937, 1968/70) that it is sufficient to assume the existence of only one kind of probability, namely subjective probability. His argument depends on his remarkable theorem concerning 'permutable' or 'exchangeable' sequences of events but we shall have to be satisfied with a reference (Good, 1965, pp. 13, 21–3) where further references are cited.

De Finetti's definition of $P(E|F)$ is the fraction of a rouble that you would pay for the privilege of receiving one rouble if the event E obtains, the whole set being cancelled if F does not obtain.

2. A THEORY OF SUBJECTIVE PROBABILITY. Except when it is folly to be wise most of us would like our probabilities to be in some sense rational or approximately so. For example, if $P(E_1|F_1)$, though not necessarily numerical, in some sense 'exceeds' $P(E_2|F_2)$ and the latter exceeds $P(E_3|F_3)$ then we would want $P(E_1|F_1)$ to exceed $P(E_3|F_3)$, for the sake of rationality. This property is known as 'transitivity'. (Condorcet's paradox of voting is *not* a serious objection to the assumption of transitivity but only shows that a familiar voting procedure is faulty.) For example, probabilities might be only 'partially ordered', that is, we might not always be able to state whether $P(E_1|F_1)$ exceeds, 'subceeds', or equals $P(E_2|F_2)$. The concept that logical probabilities are only partially ordered was emphasized by Keynes (1921) and Koopman (1940a, 1940b), while the partial ordering of *subjective* probabilities has been emphasized by the present author in countless publications beginning in Good (1950).

The purpose of a theory of subjective probability is *to make your subjective probabilities more objective*. We all have subjective probabilities but those libertines without a theory are free to be as subjective and irrational as they like. They call themselves objectivists! In nearly all theories of subjective probability there is a set of axioms resembling the following set (Good, 1950, p. 19). These axioms contain equality signs, but a theory of partially ordered probabilities can nevertheless be based on them as will be explained below.

(A1) *Numerical probability*. $P(E|H)$ is a non-negative real number.

(A2) *The addition law*. If $P(E\&F|H)=0$, then $P(E \vee F|H) = P(E|H)+P(F|H)$, where the symbol $\vee$ denotes the (inclusive) 'or'.

(A3) *The product law*. $P(E\&F|H)=P(E|H)\cdot P(F|E\&H)$.

(A4) *Equivalence*. If E and F logically imply one another, given H, then $P(E|H)=P(F|H)$ and $P(H|E)=P(H|F)$.

(A5) $P(H^*|H^*)\neq 0$, where H^* is logically true. (One can deduce that $P(H^*|H^*)=1$.)

(A6) $P(E^*|H^*)=0$ for some proposition E^*.

For attempts to justify some such set of axioms, based on one's intuitive understanding of language, without introducing bets, see, for example, Jeffreys (1939, Ch. 1), Cox (1946, 1961), Schroedinger (1947), and Good (1950, pp. 1–20, 33, and 105–106). For attempts based on your behaviour (choice of actions), which many people find more convincing because actions speak louder than words, see Ramsey (1926/31), de Finetti (1937), and Savage (1954). (Indeed the mathematical theory of probability arose out of gambling problems.) The implication of these writers is that if your behaviour, including your linguistic behaviour, satisfies certain seemingly compelling desiderata for rationality then you will behave *as if* you had subjective probabilities and 'utilities' (values), satisfying a familiar set of axioms, and that you appear to be trying to maximize your mathematical expectation of the utility. Of course 'utility' is not necessarily monetary value, in fact anyone who equated utility with money in all circumstances would be extremely irrational. Your calculations need not be done at a conscious level: nice people are not 'calculating'. It is not even obvious whether animals are less rational than humans according to this interpretation of rationality, for language can lead to irrationality as well as to rationality.

In Savage's book a main desideratum is the 'sure-thing' principle, that if action A is to be preferred if E occurs and also if E does not occur, then A is to be preferred period. Some people have questioned the sure-thing principle by reference to the *amalgamation paradox* or Pearson–Yule paradox (Pearson, 1899; Yule, 1903), sometimes incorrectly attributed to Simpson. The amalgamation paradox is exemplified by the fact that a drug can be beneficial for men and also for women, but, when the samples (2-by-2 contingency tables) are amalgamated, can appear to be harmful to the mixed population. The appearance is of course deceptive so the amalgamation paradox is not a genuine objection to the sure-thing principle.

From the axioms we can deduce non-trivial probabilities only from other probabilities, so we have to begin with some judgemental ones.

Axioms expressed explicitly in terms of partially-ordered probabilities have been derived in various ways by Koopman (1940a, b), Good (1960/62), and Smith (1961).

As mentioned above, a theory of partially-ordered probability can be based on numerical axioms. This can be done by introducing the notion of a 'black box' or 'abstract theory'. A collection of non-numerical inequality *judgements* of the kind '$P'(E_1|H_1)$ exceeds $P'(E_2|H_2)$' are plugged into the black box where P' refers to a degree of belief, not necessarily numerical. Such a judgement is interpreted by the black box as $P(E_1|H_1) > P(E_2|H_2)$, where the probabilities are now treated as numbers. The abstract or mathematical theory, based on the numerical axioms, is then used to produce new inequalities such as $P(E_3|H_3) > P(E_4|H_4)$, which are reinterpreted as *discernments*, such as $P'(E_3|H_3)$ *exceeds* $P'(E_4|H_4)$, at the output of the black box, and are fed back into the 'body of beliefs'. The input and output specifications are not axioms, but are *rules of application* of the abstract theory. (See Figure 2.)

Because 'landmark probabilities' can be introduced by imagining perfectly shuffled packs of cards, or rotating pointers, a partially-ordered theory is equivalent to a theory of interval-valued probabilities, or upper and lower probabilities, denoted

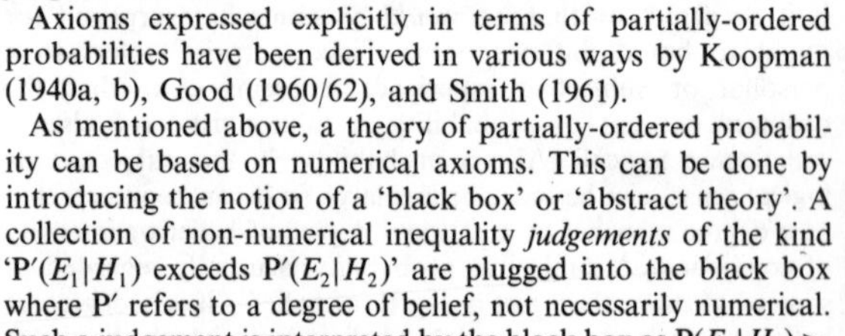

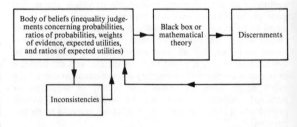

Figure 2 The black-box theory of subjective probabilities. The discernments are fed back into the body of beliefs. This enables you to enlarge the body of beliefs and to check it for consistency. Observed inconsistencies encourage more mature judgement.

by P* and P$_*$. (In practice, however, even P* and P$_*$ are fuzzy.) From the black-box theory one can deduce axioms satisfied by the upper and lower probabilities, such as

$$P^*(E\&F|H)/P_*(F|E\&H) \geqslant P^*(E|H).$$

This approach was used by Good (1960/62), whereas the independent approach by Smith (1961) was based on betting behaviour and resembled the behavioural method used by Savage (1954) for sharp numerical probabilities.

Even if you support the theory of partially-ordered, or upper and lower probabilities, you might often work with a theory of sharp probabilities for the sake of simplicity, and especially for simplicity of exposition. You will then find that axiom (A4) is only an ideal, not always attainable. For example, you might be asked to bet whether the billionth digit of π, after the decimal point, is a 7. (Good, 1950, p. 49, considered the millionth digit, but that digit is now known.) Your betting probability is presumably 1/10, but if you could complete the calculations the probability would become 1 or 0. Thus a subjective probability can be changed by calculation or by pure thought, as in the analysis of a chess position, without any change of empirical evidence. Such probabilities have been called 'evolving' or, better, *dynamic* and the topic is reviewed by Good (1977). To allow for dynamic probabilities one can replace (A4) by

(A4′) If you have *seen* or proved that E and F are logically equivalent given H then

$$P(E|H) = P(F|H) \quad \text{and} \quad P(H|E) = P(H|F)$$

(Good, 1950, p. 49).

Dynamic probabilities have an important application in the philosophy of science (Good, 1968, p. 129; 1983a, p. 223; 1985b): it is there pointed out that the philosophy of explanation definitely requires the concept of dynamic probability when an explanation, like the inverse square law of gravitation, does not involve any new empirical observations.

3. 'SUGGESTIONS'. In practice a theory that deals with judgements needs more than axioms and rules of application; it also needs suggestions or hints for forming and adjusting judgements. There are apt to be an almost unlimited supply of possible suggestions because they relate largely to your psychology. Experiments on the psychology of probability judgements have been reviewed by Hogarth (1975). You can use the results to help you to avoid pitfalls when making your own judgements.

Let us now consider a few suggestions.

(i) *The device of imaginary results* (Good, 1983, indexes). A theory of subjective probability is basically a theory of consistency of judgements, a point made by Ramsey (1926/31). (When dynamic probability, or axiom (A4′), is incorporated, the consistency can be intended only at a given time or *in a given report*.) Hence, when formulating our judgements we can usefully imagine possible outcomes of experiments and use these to help us to form judgements. This suggestion will be made clearer after we discuss Bayes' theorem in Section 4. An example of the device of imaginary results is sensitivity analysis where we vary our initial model and see whether the conclusions are affected too much (in our judgement).

(ii) *Surprise indexes.* Shackle (1949) suggested that entrepreneurs rely on the concept of potential surprise and not on subjective probability. Since there are surprise indexes formulated in terms of subjective probability (Good, 1953/57 who cites Weaver, 1948; Good, 1986b), one can in my opinion express Shackle's views in terms of subjective probability (although Shackle has opposed this opinion). In this manner you can hope to play off your judgements about surprise and about probabilities to achieve improvements in both. This use of potential surprise can be regarded as a special case of the device of imaginary results.

(iii) *The use of computer programs.* Novick and Jackson (1974) have described computer programs that can help you to deduce consequences interactively and rapidly from your probability judgements thus carrying out the purpose of a black-box theory as described above, almost as if the computer were the black box. To make rapid deductions is clearly an advantage because, if you have the facilities, it enables you to make deductions from your judgements that you otherwise might not have had the time or energy to make.

4. BAYES' THEOREM AND WEIGHTS OF EVIDENCE. Suppose that we are interested in discriminating between two or more hypotheses $H_1, H_2, \ldots, H_n$ ($n \geqslant 2$), and we have evidence E in addition to background information B. The probabilities $P(H_i|B)$ ($i = 1, 2, \ldots, n$) are known as prior or initial probabilities (prior to the taking of E into account, but not necessarily chronologically prior to the occurrence of E), and the $P(H_i|B\&E)$ are known as posterior or final probabilities. Then, leaving aside the possibility of zero probabilities, it follows very quickly from the axioms that

$$P(H_i|E) = \frac{P(E|H_i)P(H_i)}{\sum_j P(E|H_j)P(H_j)} \tag{1}$$

and this is known as Bayes' theorem though he did not use the modern notation. It is interesting that so simple a theorem can have far-reaching consequences. Bayes' work was published posthumously having been found among his papers by Price who made contributions to the publication (Bayes, 1763/65). The fact that Bayes did not publish the theorem during his lifetime has several possible explanations one being that he was perhaps not satisfied with the part of the work dealing with the values of the prior probabilities.

$P(E|H_i)$, or $\lambda P(E|H_i)$, where λ does not depend on i, is called the likelihood of H_i given E, so Bayes' theorem can be expressed in the form 'the posterior probability of H_i is proportional to its prior probability times its likelihood' (Jeffreys, 1939, p. 29).

When subjective probabilites are used in statistics, in conjunction with Bayes' theorem, the approach is called *Bayesian* or *neo-Bayesian*. (There are, however, at least 6^6 possible shades of meaning: see Good, 1983a, Ch. 3, or twice this number if allowance is made for dynamic versus static probabilities. One of the 2×6^6 is known as Doogian: see Berger, 1984.) Non-Bayesian methods of statistical inference are exemplified by the use of tail-area probabilities ('Fisherian') and confidence intervals ('Neyman–Pearsonian'). Non-Bayesian methods are also called *frequentist* or *sampling-theory* methods. The Bayesian would claim that these methods, when they can be justified at all, can be justified only by means of informal or formal Bayesian arguments. One example will be given in Section 5.

The case $n = 2$ of Bayes' theorem is especially interesting. It leads very easily to the further simple identity (almost as important as Bayes' theorem itself),

$$\frac{O(H|E\&B)}{O(H|B)} = \frac{P(E|B\&H)}{P(E|B\&-H)} \tag{2}$$

where $-H$ denotes the negation of H and O denotes *odds*. (The odds corresponding to a probability p are defined as $p/(1-p)$.) The ratio of the posterior to the prior odds of H is now known as the *Bayes factor* in favour of H provided by E (given B all along) although Bayes never mentioned it. Its logarithm is sometimes called the *weight of evidence in favour of H provided by E given B*, and can be denoted by $W(H:E|B)$. The base of the logarithms merely defines the unit in terms of which the weight of evidence is measured. The expression 'weight of evidence' was seemingly first proposed in this sense by Peirce (1878) for the special case in which the initial probability of H was 1/2 (Good, 1983c) but the expression in this technical sense dropped out of use until the publication of Good (1950). (Peirce proposed but did not *use* the expression for he was a non-Bayesian.) The expression was temporarily called 'support' by Jeffreys (1936) and the concept, though not the name, was introduced into the cryptanalysis of the Enigma by A.M. Turing during World War II. (He never mentioned Jeffreys, 1936, and probably had not seen that publication.) When the base was 10 Turing called the unit a ban, one-tenth of which he called a deciban. The deciban is about the smallest unit of weight of evidence that the human mind can apprehend and is analogous to the decibel in acoustics. For the Enigma publication a weight of evidence was called a 'score' or a 'decibannage'.

To justify the expression 'weight of evidence' in this technical sense, imagine that H represents the guilt of an accused man and its negation his innocence, and let E denote the evidence presented in court. Let $W_1(H:E)$ denote the weight of evidence in favour of guilt *provided by the evidence E alone* (though *given* the background information), where here 'weight of evidence' is to be interpreted in its intuitive and ordinary sense of the *balance* of the evidence (*not* as the sum of the favourable and unfavourable pieces of evidence). The background information B can be included in the notation by writing $W_1(H:E|B)$ but we omit B to simplify the exposition. The following desiderata seem natural:

(i) $W_1(H:E)$ should depend only on $P(E|H)$ and $P(E|-H)$;

(ii) $P(H|E)$ should depend only on $W_1(H:E)$ and on the initial probability $P(H)$.

It can then be proved that $W_1(H:E)$ must be a function of $W(H:E)$ (Good, 1984). We may as well take $W_1 = W$ because we have the desirable additive property

$$W[H:(E\&F)] = W(H:E) + W(H:F|E). \qquad (3)$$

Bayes factors have a corresponding multiplicative property, but, when talking about 'weights', additivity is more appropriate. A survey of properties of weights of evidence is given by Good (1985a).

It is necessary that magistrates, jurymen, and doctors doing differential diagnoses, should have at least implicit judgements of final probabilities of the form $P(H|E)$, the probability of a hypothesis when evidence E is provided. A 'suggestion', that can be appended to those listed in Section 3, is that such judgements would be aided by introducing semi-quantitative judgements of weights of evidence or of inequalities between them. (They can be used as inputs to the Black Box.) This would be especially valuable when there are approximately independent pieces of evidence such as evidence from reliable witnesses, fingerprints, motivation, behaviour of the accused in court, previous convictions (!), and previous convictions of the unreliable witnesses!

Bayes' theorem, and especially the concept of a Bayes factor or of a weight of evidence, can be combined with the device of imaginary results to work backwards from a final probability (based on an imagined outcome) to an initial probability. The words 'prior' (or 'initial') and 'posterior' (or 'final') have repeatedly misled people into overlooking this possibility although it has been recognized since at least 1950. Note too that what is called 'prior' might often be better called 'intermediate'.

The use of Bayes' theorem in reverse exemplifies that neo-Bayesianism is basically a theory of (approximate) consistency of judgements.

An important part of statistics is not primarily inferential, namely descriptive statistics and exploratory data analysis both of which consist of techniques for presenting salient features or interesting patterns or 'clues' in data to the eye-brain system. Exploratory data analysis leans a little further towards scientific discovery than does descriptive statistics. A case is made by Good (1983b) that there is an implicit Bayesian component even in these seemingly non-inferential activities. The reason is that you need to judge whether a pattern is a mere 'kinkus', that is, probably has no physical cause. Cranks take kinkera seriously. A *scientifically interesting* pattern is one that probably has a cause even if the cause is unknown. When you conjecture *specific* causes you have begun doing science rather than statistics.

5. BAYES/NON-BAYES OR BAYES-FREQUENTIST COMPROMISES. If a statistic X takes a value x for which the tail-area probability or P-value, $P = P(X \geqslant x|H)$, is 'small', the Fisherian will regard this as evidence against the null hypothesis H, whereas the Bayesian will measure the evidence by $W = W(-H:X = x)$, the weight of evidence against H provided by the knowledge that X took the value x. In other words the Bayesian requires that the Bayes factor $P(X = x|H)/P(X = x|-H)$ should be 'large'; but the non-Bayesian will usually regard the expression $P(X = x|-H)$ as meaningless when $-H$ is not a 'simple statistical hypothesis'. In many cases there is some very rough mathematical anticorrelation between the P-value and W. When this is so one has a rough informal justification of the use of P-values, but when it is not so the Bayesian will regard the use of the P-value as misleading. I have often found that a 'single-tailed' P-value of precisely 0.05 corresponds to a Bayes factor of only about 3 or 4, and as such it is only weak evidence against the null hypothesis. Indeed, if the null hypothesis had prior odds of more than 4 to 1 on, then it might very well be 'odds on' after suffering from a P-value of 0.05. Note, however, that an intelligent and honest Fisherian who, because, being human (and not merely a statistician) is also a covert or informal Bayesian in his heart, happens to regard the prior odds of H as more than 4 to 1 on, then he will perhaps choose the rejection threshold for P as say 0.01 or lower. (He might of course report a P-value without either accepting or rejecting the null hypothesis.)

Note too that when a Fisherian makes the choice between single-tail and double-tail probabilities he is allowing for the class of non-null hypotheses that are of interest to him. This too is consistent with a Bayesian outlook.

When a sample size N is large enough a P-value of 0.05 can be strong *support* for the null hypothesis (see, for example, Good, 1983d, where this is made abundantly clear). Good (1982b) suggests that any P-value should be 'standardized' to a fixed sample size, say 100, like adjusting to 'constant dollars' to allow for inflation. The proposed formula is $\min[\frac{1}{2}, P(N/100)^{1/2}]$. For other examples of Bayes/non-Bayes (or Bayes-frequentist) compromises see Good (1983a, Indexes; 1986a).

6. INDUCTION. The concept of epistemic probability is necessary for any constructive theory of scientific induction. Induction is usually defined as arguing from the the particular to the general. For example, if all of many swans you have seen in the past have been white then it would be natural to conjecture that all swans are white, at least under similar circumstances. When circumstances are different in some way

judged to be important, for example, if the observation is carried out in Australia, the inference seems less probable (and in fact is false).

We can regard an inference about the next case as another form of induction because it is so similar to induction yet does not argue from the particular directly to the general. It may be called *induction to the next case*. The earliest formula proposed for induction to the next case is known as *Laplace's Law of Succession*. It relates to Bernoulli trials or binomial sampling. For example, we might throw a drawing-pin (thumb-tack) on the table and define a 'success' as each occasion that it comes to rest pointing upwards. Let the physical probability of a success be denoted by p. Initially, if you are a 'sharp' Bayesian (one with sharp probability estimates), you have a prior subjective probability density concerning the value of p. Laplace assumed that this 'prior' was uniform, that is, that the subjective or logical probability density of the physical probability p is the same (and therefore equal to 1) at each value of p. This assumption is called a *Bayes postulate*. Then, if we have had n successes in n throws, the probability of a success in the next trial is found to be

$$(n+1)/(n+2). \tag{4}$$

This is Laplace's Law of Succession. It is by no means a perfect estimate, and has even been called 'notorious', but it is much better than the maximum-likelihood estimate which is unity and absurd in this application.

Laplace's Law of Succession can be applied to the case of the US Space Shuttle disaster of February 1986. There had been 24 successful launchings of the Shuttle so Laplace's Law of Succession would lead to an estimated probability of 1/26 for a failure on the 25th attempt. But conditions were different in an important manner, for the temperature on the 25th occasion was far below that on any previous occasion, so, having no inside information, your subjective probability of a disaster could well have been much larger than 1/26. (Apart from the temperature there had been other engineering concerns.)

We now return to general discussion of Laplace's Law of Succession. It follows from this 'law' that the probability of successes on each of the next m trials (after the original n) is equal to

$$\frac{n+1}{n+2}\cdot\frac{n+2}{n+3}\cdots\frac{n+m}{n+m+1}, \tag{5}$$

because, for example, after the $(n+1)$th success the probability of a success on the $(n+2)$th trial is $(n+2)/(n+3)$ (by a second application of Laplace's Law of Succession) and so on. The product (5) reduces at once to

$$(n+1)/(n+m+1), \tag{6}$$

a formula with interesting implications. It suggests, for example, by taking $m = n+1$, that, putting it roughly, what has gone on for a certain length of time will, with subjective probability $\frac{1}{2}$, continue for about the same length of time again—which has been somewhat facetiously called the first law of meteorology. In the meteorological application the length of time must not exceed about one month because we all have background knowledge about seasons. But in other contexts we might let $m \to \infty$ and infer that the probability of a general law is zero. Jeffreys (1957, p. 51) attributed this conclusion to Karl Pearson and inferred that the Bayes postulate needed amendment. Haldane (1931) and Jeffreys (1939, p. 114) proposed that non-zero epistemic positive probabilities q_0 and q_1 should be assumed at $p = 0$ and $p = 1$ in the prior, the remaining probability being (perhaps) uniformly spread. This observation is also fairly explicit in Pearson (1892/1937, p. 125). It comes to the same thing as assuming two null hypotheses, each with positive prior probability, the Bayes postulate being assumed conditional on the falsity of both null hypotheses. (Other 'null hypotheses', with positive prior probabilities, might be natural such as the hypothesis that $p = \frac{1}{2}$.) Such modifications of Bayes' postulate permit induction to a general law. Under these assumptions, the 'likelihoods' of the three hypotheses $p = 0$, $p = 1$, and $p \neq 0$ or 1, after n successes in n trials, are 0, 1, and $1/(n+1)$ so, by Bayes' theorem, the final odds of the 'general law' $p = 1$ are

$$(n+1)q_1/(1-q_0-q_1) \tag{7}$$

which tends to infinity with n. In particular, if $q_0 = 0$ and $q_1 = \frac{1}{2}$, the final probability that $p = 1$ is $(n+1)/(n+2)$ (Jeffreys, 1957, p. 53). This just happens to equal formula (4), but its meaning is different.

When we have substantial background knowledge these results break down for a variety of reasons. For example, when tossing a coin for the first time the prior probability density of p is (if you are sensible) sharply peaked at $p = \frac{1}{2}$. The Bayes postulate is often generalized to a 'beta' prior for p whose density is proportional to $p^{a-1}(1-p)^{b-1} (a > 0, b > 0)$ (Hardy, 1889). This is flexible enough on most occasions of binomial sampling and has the merit of being a 'conjugate prior'; that is, after r successes and s failures, the posterior density of p belongs to the same (beta) family and is obtained by adding r to a and s to b. One way to judge the values of a and b is to judge the lower and upper quartiles of the prior.

Closely related is a paper by W.E. Johnson (1932) in which he introduced some assumptions related to multiple or multinomial sampling. His argument was incorrect for the special case of binomial sampling: see Good (1965, p. 26), but for the sake of simplicity I consider the binomial case here. Johnson's work anticipated the basic idea of the 'continuum of inductive methods' (Carnap, 1952) in which Laplace's formula is replaced by $(n+k)/(n+2k)$ $(k>0)$. (For each value of k there is a distinct 'inductive method'.) Good (1965) proposed putting a 'hyperprior' on k, the method being a special case of what is now called the *hierarchical Bayesian* method. For a review of this method as applied especially to multinomials and contingency tables see Good (1979/81, 1981/83). The latter paper again indicates that induction to the next case (or to the next several cases) is much more convincingly attainable than induction to a general law. Fortunately, in many practical situations, induction to the next several cases is more important than induction to a general law. For example, we would like to be able to say with confidence that our next 100 aircraft flights will probably be successful, but we are not concerned with eternally safe flights.

Similarly, in general applications of Bayesian methods in statistics, prediction to the next several cases is usually more important than the estimation of parameters as such. In recent years the Bayesian predictivist point of view has been especially emphasized by de Finetti and, for numerous applications, by Geisser: see, for example, de Finetti (1968/70) and Geisser (1983/85). The over-preoccupation with parameters, which are usually denoted by Greek letters, has been called the worship of Greek gods. Nevertheless the religion of parameters and even of hyperparameters (parameters in priors) is at least psychologically useful.

7. DECISION THEORY

We have already mentioned the close relationship of the theory of subjective probability to decision theory. The black box theory extends in a straightforward manner to this theory (Good, 1952). We have to append to the axioms the principle of rationality, *maximize the mathematical expectation of the utility*, and input judgements need to be extended to include preferences. It is often necessary to allow for the costs of calculation and thought and when you do so you can be regarded as applying a principle of rationality of 'type 2'. It is unlikely that this principle can be fully formalized but it cannot be avoided in practice.

The large influence of Bayesianism (the explicit use of epistemic probability) on statistics is typified by the opinion that is sometimes held that the whole of inferential statistics should be regarded as an application of Bayesian decision theory. Historically, Bayesianism received a set-back in the second quarter of the 20th century under R.A. Fisher's influence. He was a great practitioner but a mediocre philosopher. But statistics needed an adequate philosophical background and the pendulum swung back a long way in the third quarter of the century. In the writer's opinion, the swings will soon be damped and a Bayes/non-Bayes compromise will emerge as the majority position among statisticians for the next hundred years (Good, 1983a, p. 95).

I.J. GOOD

See also SAVAGE, LEONARD JIMMIE; PROBABILITY; RAMSEY, FRANK PLUMPTON; STATISTICAL INFERENCE.

BIBLIOGRAPHY

For an article covering somewhat similar ground to the present one see Good (1982a). On some points it says more and on some less.

For books giving applications of subjective or logical probability in statistics see, for example, Jeffreys (1939–61), Lindley (1965), Zellner (1971, 1980), De Groot (1970), Box and Tiao (1973), Rosenkratz (1977), Good (1965, 1983a), and Berger (1985).

Bayes, T. 1763. An essay toward solving a problem in the doctrine of chances (with discussion and a foreword by Richard Price). *Philosophical Transactions of the Royal Society* 53, 370–418; 54, 295–325. Reprinted by the Graduate School, US Department of Agriculture, Washington, DC (1940); and in *Biometrika* 45 (1958), 293–315.

Berger, J.O. 1984. The robust Bayesian viewpoint. In *Robustness of Bayesian Analysis*, ed. J.B. Kadane, Amsterdam: North-Holland, 64–144.

Berger, J.O. 1985. *Statistical Decision Theory and Bayesian Analysis.* 2nd edn, New York: Springer-Verlag.

Bernardo, J.M., De Groot, M.H., Lindley, D.V. and Smith, A.F.M. (eds) 1983–85. *Bayesian Statistics 2: Proceedings of the Second Valencia International Meeting September 6–10, 1983.* Amsterdam: North-Holland.

Box, G.E.P. and Tiao, G.C. 1973. *Bayesian Inference in Statistical Analysis.* Reading, Mass.: Addison-Wesley.

Carnap, R. 1952. *The Continuum of Inductive Methods.* Chicago: University of Chicago Press.

Cox, R.T. 1946. Probability, frequency and reasonable expectation. *American Journal of Physics* 14, 1–13.

Cox, R.T. 1961. *The Algebra of Probable Inference.* Baltimore: Johns Hopkins University Press.

de Finetti, B. 1937. La prévision: ses lois logiques, ses sources subjectives. *Annales de l'Institut Henri Poincaré* 7, 1–68. Translated in Kyburg and Smokler (1980).

de Finetti, B. 1968–70. Initial probabilities: a prerequisite for any valid induction. *Synthese* 20, 1969, 2–24 (with discussion). Also in *Induction, Physics and Ethics: Proceedings and Discussions of the 1968 Salzburg Colloquium in the Philosophy of Science*, ed. P. Weingartner and G. Zechs, Dordrecht, Holland: D. Reidel, 1970.

De Groot, M.H. 1970. *Optimal Statistical Decisions.* New York: McGraw-Hill.

Geisser, S. 1983–85. On the prediction of observables: a selective update, in Bernardo *et al.* (1983–85), 203–29 (with discussion).

Good, I.J. 1950. *Probability and the Weighing of Evidence.* London: Charles Griffin; New York: Hafners.

Good, I.J. 1952. Rational decisions. *Journal of the Royal Statistical Society B*, 14, 107–114. Reprinted in Good (1983a).

Good, I.J. 1953–57. The appropriate mathematical tools for describing and measuring uncertainty. In *Uncertainty and Business Decisions*, ed. C.F. Carter, G.P. Meredith, and G.L.S. Shackle, Liverpool: Liverpool University Press, 20–36. Partly reprinted in Good (1983a).

Good, I.J. 1960–62. Subjective probability as the measure of a non-measurable set. In *Logic, Methodology, and Philosophy of Science*, ed. E. Nagel, P. Suppes and A. Tarski, Stanford: Stanford University Press, pp. 319–29. Reprinted in Kyburg and Smokler (1980) and in Good (1983a).

Good, I.J. 1965. *The Estimation of Probabilities: An Essay on Modern Bayesian Methods.* Cambridge, Mass.: MIT Press.

Good, I.J. 1966. How to estimate probabilities. *Journal of the Institute of Mathematics and its Applications* 2, 364–83.

Good, I.J. 1968. Corroboration, explanation, evolving probability, simplicity, and a sharpened razor. *British Journal for the Philosophy of Science* 19, 123–43.

Good, I.J. 1977. Dynamic probability, computer chess, and the measurement of knowledge. In *Machine Intelligence* 8, ed. E.W. Elcock and D. Michie, Chichester: Ellis Horwood, 139–150. Reprinted in Good (1983a).

Good, I.J. 1979–81. Some history of the hierarchical Bayesian methodology, *Bayesian Statistics: Proceedings of the First International Meeting held in Valencia (Spain), May 28 to June 2, 1979*, ed. J.M. Bernardo, M.H. De Groot, D.V. Lindley, and A.F.M. Smith, University of Valencia, 1981, 489–510 and 512–19 (with discussion).

Good, I.J. 1981–83. The robustness of a hierarchical model for multinomials and contingency tables. In *Scientific Inference, Data Analysis, and Robustness*, ed. G.E.P. Box, Tom Leonard, and Chien-Fu Wu, New York: Academic Press.

Good, I.J. 1982a. Degrees of belief. In *Encyclopedia of Statistical Sciences*, Vol. 2, ed. S. Kotz and N.L. Johnson, New York: Wiley, 287–93.

Good, I.J. 1982b. Standardized tail-area probabilities. C140 in *Journal of Statistical Computation and Simulation* 16, 65–6.

Good, I.J. 1983a. *Good Thinking: The Foundations of Probability and its Applications.* Minneapolis: University of Minnesota Press.

Good, I.J. 1983b. The philosophy of exploratory data analysis. *Philosophy of Science* 50, 283–95.

Good, I.J. 1983c. A correction concerning my interpretation of Peirce, and the Bayesian interpretation of Neyman–Pearson 'hypothesis determination', C165 in *Journal of Statistical Computation and Simulation* 18, 71–4.

Good, I.J. 1983d. The diminishing significance of a fixed P-value as the sample size increases: a discrete model. C144 in *Journal of Statistical Computation and Simulation* 16, 312–14.

Good, I.J. 1984. The best explicatum for weight of evidence. C197 in *Journal of Statistical Computation and Simulation* 19, 294–9.

Good, I.J. 1985a. Weight of evidence: a brief survey. In Bernardo et al. 1983–85, 249–69 (with discussion).

Good, I.J. 1985b. A historical comment concerning novel confirmation. *British Journal for the Philosophy of Science* 36, 184–5.

Good, I.J. 1986a. Statistical evidence. In *Encyclopedia of Statistical Sciences*, Vol. 8, ed. S. Kotz, N.L. Johnson and C. Read, New York: Wiley.

Good, I.J. 1986b. Surprise index. In *Encyclopedia of Statistical Sciences*, Vol. 9, ed. S. Kotz, N.L. Johnson and C. Read, New York: Wiley.

Haldane, J.B.S. 1931. A note on inverse probability. *Proceedings of the Cambridge Philosophical Society* 28, 55–61.

Hardy, G.F. 1889. In correspondence in *Insurance Record*, reprinted in *Transactions of the Faculty of Actuaries* 8, (1920), 174–82, esp. 181.

Hogarth, R.M. 1975. Cognitive processes and the assessment of subjective probability distributions. *Journal of the American Statistical Association* 70, 271–94.

Jeffreys, H. 1926. Further significance tests. *Proceedings of the Cambridge Philosophical Society* 32, 416–45.

Jeffreys, H. 1957. *Scientific Inference*. 2nd edn, Cambridge: Cambridge University Press.
Jeffreys, H. 1961. *Theory of Probability*. Oxford: Clarendon Press.
Johnson, W.E. 1932. Appendix (ed. R.B. Braithwaite) to 'Probability: deductive and inductive problems'. *Mind* 41, 421–3.
Keynes, J.M. 1921. *A Treatise on Probability*. London: Macmillan.
Koopman, B.O. 1940a. The basis of probability. *Bulletin of the American Mathematical Society* 46, 763–74.
Koopman, B.O. 1940b. The axioms and algebra of intuitive probability. *Annals of Mathematics* 41, 269–92.
Kyburg, H.E. and Smokler, H.E. (eds) 1980. *Studies in Subjective Probability*. 2nd edn, Huntington: New York, Robert E. Krieger. (1st edn New York: John Wiley, 1964.)
Lindley, D.V. 1965. *Introduction to Probability and Statistics*, Vol. 2. Cambridge: Cambridge University Press.
Novick, M.R. and Jackson, P.H. 1974. *Statistical Methods for Educational and Psychological Research*. New York: McGraw-Hill.
Pearson, K. 1892. *The Grammar of Science*. Reprinted, London: J.M. Dent & Sons, 1937.
Pearson, K. 1899. Theory of genetic (reproductive) selection. *Philosophical Transactions of the Royal Society of London (A)* 192, 260–78, esp. 277–8, 'On the spurious correlation produced by forming a mixture of heterogeneous but uncorrelated materials'.
Peirce, C.S. 1878. The probability of induction. *Popular Science Monthly;* reprinted in *The World of Mathematics* 2, ed. James R. Newman, New York: Simon & Schuster, 1956, 1341–54.
Poisson, S.-D. 1837. *Recherches sur la probabilité des jugements en matière criminelle et en matière civile*. Paris: Bachelier.
Ramsey, F.P. 1926. Truth and probability. In *The Foundations of Mathematics and Other Logical Essays*, London: Kegan Paul; New York: Harcourt, Brace & Co. Reprinted in Kyburg and Smokler (1980).
Rosenkrantz, R.D. 1977. *Inference, Method and Decision*. Dordrecht, Holland: Reidel.
Savage, L.J. 1954. *The Foundations of Statistics*. New York: John Wiley.
Schroedinger, E. 1947. The foundation of probability. *Proceedings of the Royal Irish Academy* 51A, 51-66 and 141–6.
Shackle, G.L.S. 1949. *Expectation in Economics*. Cambridge: Cambridge University Press.
Smith, C.A.B. 1961. Consistency in statistical inference and decision. *Journal of the Royal Statistical Society, Series B*, 23, 1–37 (with discussion).
Weaver, W. 1948. Probability, rarity, interest and surprise. *Scientific Monthly* 67, 390–92.
Yule, G.U. 1903. Notes on the theory of association of attributes in statistics. *Biometrika* 2, 121–34. Reprinted in *Statistical Papers of George Udny Yule*, ed. A. Stuart and M.G. Kendall, London: Griffin, 1971, 71–84.
Zellner, A. 1971. *An Introduction to Bayesian Inference in Econometrics*. New York: John Wiley.
Zellner, A. (ed.) 1980. *Bayesian Analysis in Econometrics and Statistics: Essays in Honor of Harold Jeffreys*. Amsterdam: North-Holland.

subsidies. *See* TAXES AND SUBSIDIES.

subsistence. In ancient economies where slave labour was the predominant form of labour, and for a long time after, when the material conditions of the labourer were not much better, the earnings of labour were viewed as not very different from the feed of horses. There were no 'theories' of wages but it was automatically supposed that they receive subsistence, certain fixed quantities of the necessaries of life. As working horses need to be maintained in adequate supply, the worker or the slave would be so provisioned as to be enabled to work and reproduce.

During the second half of the 17th and early 18th century with the rapid rise of commercial capitalism, intensification of competition among trading nations seeking new markets and sources of supply in Europe, discussions arose on management of labour and of wages – in particular, the advantages of maintaining cheap labour. In pursuance of mercantilist ideas, cheap labour was considered a favourable factor in competition. 'National Wealth', wrote Mandeville 'consists not in money' but in a 'multitude of laborious poor'. It was also believed that hard work could be compelled out of the poor only by extreme need and want. 'Men have nothing to stir them up to be serviceable but their wants which it is Prudence to relieve but Folly to cure' (Mandeville, 1714, p. 194). It was believed that low wages not only spur productivity but also yield commercial advantage since cheap labour meant cheap produce. Thus the mercantilist policy sought to encourage population and selective migration to keep prices of necessaries high through taxes, if necessary, and set wages at a low subsistence level. 'An increase of people in the country to such a degree as may make things necessary to life dear and thereby force general industry from each member of the family' seemed a statesman's maxim (William Temple, 1693, p. 116). Discussions on wages were, at this stage, an issue of labour policy and the idea of fixed subsistence rested on the extant conditions, as observed. No attempt either to explain the level or the mechanisms stabilizing or restoring that level were discussed. However, it was already recognized, as a practical premise, that taxes on necessaries of subsistence were likely to be accompanied by a rise in money wages (cf. among others, Thomas Mun, 1664, and John Locke, 1692).

It is in William Petty, rightly considered by Marx as among the founders of political economy, that a theoretical role was assigned to the norm of subsistence and the difference between the labourer's subsistence and his produce brought to the fore. Petty was also concerned with quantitative relations within production and with evolving a measure of value.

> The most important consideration in Political Oeconomics [is], viz how to make a Par and Equation between lands and labour, so as to express the value of anything by either alone ... wherefore the days food of an adult man ... and not the days labour, is the common measure of value ... (Petty, 1691, p. 181).

Thus subsistence became a constant measure of value. Defining the value of a commodity in terms of the quantity of food necessary for the day's payment for an adult, he extended the same measure for valuation of different types of labourers. The unit of food was thus a standard of commodity wage.

Already by Petty's time the legislative fixation of wages and actual compliance to it were being violated. Attention was gradually drawn to the observed stable level of subsistence, not as an axiom or as a statutory fixation but as an economic condition. The mechanisms that tend to keep wages down were thus explored. John Locke (1692) attempted to explain its existence in terms of psychological inertia among the poor induced by the lowness of wage itself. While active struggle occurred between the land owners and merchants,

> the labourer's share, being seldom more than a bare subsistence, never allows that body of men time or opportunity to raise their thoughts above that unless when some common and great distress, uniting them in one universal ferment, makes them forget respect and emboldens them to carve to their wants with armed force; and then sometimes they break it upon the rich, and sweep all like a deluge (Locke, 1692, p. 57).

The phenomenon of wages gained importance with the gradual breakdown of guilds, spread of commercial capital and 'labour' becoming a commodity. The role played by migration of labour to level wages down to a subsistence level appeared prominently in the writings of Josiah Child who highlighted the effects of national and international migration and brought to the fore also the possibility that higher wage levels may go along with national riches. In contrast to the English emphasis on migration, in France, Boisguillebert and Cantillon took up the question of variations in wages and their effect on accumulation. They, too, while not explaining the *level* of the wage, took it as a datum to draw out the implications of an increase in wage on agricultural surplus and accumulation. The hypothesis of wage as a necessary part of productive consumption led them to consider the net product and the circular process of reproduction. Boisguillebert argued that a higher wage, cutting into the revenues of the landlord, would inhibit further expansion of agriculture and, in turn, diminish the demand for labour, thus putting a downward pressure on wages to revert to their subsistence level. Agriculture was, for him, the branch of the economy which conditioned the national economy – a position that continued with the physiocrats – and wage rises in agriculture and its adverse effects on accumulation would spread to other spheres of the national economy. However Boisguillebert did not discuss the possibility of wages getting depressed below subsistence or analyse its implications. Cantillon (1755) who also developed the important role of the agricultural surpluses in forming and shaping the effective demand for products and, in turn, demand for various categories of labour, emphasized the mechanism by which the number of farmers, artisans and labourers adjust their supplies of labour to match the level and pattern of demands. He emphasized the role of territorial migration, intra-occupational mobility and also the population mechanism through which supplies of labour adjusted themselves to needs.

This however did not explain the *level* of the wage norm but only the tendencies towards uniformity. While accepting as given the limitation of wages of the unskilled labourer to the amounts necessary for subsistence, he discussed the wage differentials among various occupations arising from 'varying conditions and circumstances' – such as

> the number of tradesmen in a given branch of industry, the period of time necessary for learning the trade, the skill and the quality of the labour, the risks and dangers connected with it and finally, the degree of responsibility required of the person entrusted with the performance of a given task (1755, pp. 25–7).

(An echo of these, we find in Adam Smith's discussion of the natural differences in wages of different labourers.) Unlike his predecessors, Cantillon did give some thought to the content of the subsistence wage and, on certain assumptions (that, half the children born die before 17, one-third under one year and that the labour of the wife, on account of her necessary attendance on the children is no more than sufficient to provide for herself), he worked out that a worker, to maintain himself and the family, must have double what he requires for his own subsistence, which may be 'somewhat exceeding that of a slave'.

With the physiocrats, the assumption of the *given* necessary wage, constituting part of 'productive consumption', being 'advanced', played an important role in the theory of production and accumulation. Quesnay argued that a tax on necessaries would inevitably be shifted to entrepreneurs. Further, a 'high price of bread' was advantageous, not only to the agriculturists but also to the workers (whose money wages would rise sympathetically). 'It would', he argued, 'encourage agriculture, increase the revenue of the nation, increase the wages of the worker and insure a life of comfort, plenty and convenience which would attract people to the land and keep them where they partake all the advantages'. Contrary effects would follow with constraints on exports or a fall in the price of bread. Quesnay, unlike Boisguillebert, did not stress forces preventing the rise of wages above subsistence. He was concerned, it would seem, more with establishing the harmony of interests among the workers and the agriculturists.

It was, however, Turgot who offered a more complete theoretical treatment of subsistence wages:

> The exchange value of food products, profits, the level of wages, and the population are phenomena which are mutually inter-connected and interdependent. The balance among them is established in accordance with a peculiar natural proportion and the proportion is constantly maintained if trade and competition are completely free (1844, pp. 437–8).

The interaction was visualized as follows: A higher wage (above the natural) increases costs of production, reduces net product, decreases profits. On the other hand, a reduction below the proper level reduces efficiency of labour and also reduces consumption demand, leading eventually to a fall in prices of the produce. A high wage may encourage growth of population or lead to immigration and then, competition among the labourers would tend to lower wages again. Thus for the continued and harmonious economic reproduction, wages and profits must bear a 'natural proportion'. Thus Turgot attempted to combine, in a complementary fashion, the analysis of Boisguillebert (effect of wage changes on the price of the product, prosperity of entrepreneurs and their demand for labour) and that of Sir Josiah Child (effects of wage changes on migration of labour and its effect on competition).

Somewhat as a reaction to the physiocratic notion of the 'natural order' the writing of Jacques Necker (1775) reflected the political unease of the impending revolution in France. He attributed the tendency of wages to fall to the subsistence minimum to 'social forces', particularly to the highly inequitable relationship of power and need that bound the owners 'who force others to serve them and the propertyless who serve the owners'. The price of labour could adjust to the price of bread only after a time, worsening the state of the worker in the meanwhile. He thus foresaw a 'dark struggle' between the owners and the workers. The numerousness of the property-less, their consequent immediate need and acute competition, rendered their bargaining power hopelessly weak, while the growing concentration of property, accentuated further by technical innovations, enhancing productivity of labour but not wages, widened the gap relentlessly. He also pointed out that the accumulation of luxuries at the cost of means of production was leading to a decline in demand for labour. Many of Necker's ideas were to find an echo in Adam Smith.

Steuart (1767) whose approach to wages was more from the point of view of establishing a norm of subsistence for a suitable wage policy beneficial to the development of industry, offered many interesting observations on the process of 'primitive accumulation'. An interesting contribution on the discussion of subsistence was his distinction between the needs, 'physically necessary' and 'politically necessary'; the former, being 'ample subsistence where no superfluity is implied' and the latter, 'proceeding from the affections of his mind, are formed by habit and education, and when once regularly established create another kind of necessity' (Steuart, 1767, p. 312). Already the subsistence as strict physiological necessity was being modified with 'custom', 'habit', 'rank-based conventions' playing an important part.

With Adam Smith, Ricardo and Marx, a more integrated view of distribution emerged, along with a distinction between natural wage and market wage. While the forces that tend to put down wages were recognized, the assumption of a fixed wage was replaced by a 'given' wage, determined by a complex of historical and economic factors.

The physiocratic notion of capital as 'wages advanced' and the idea that the demand for labour was limited by the provision of subsistence, developed in later classical theory into the concept of wage fund and to an explanation of wage determined by the 'proportion of capital to labour'. In an entirely different theoretical framework, Böhm-Bawerk used also the notion of subsistence fund to represent given endowments of 'capital'. In both, the explanation of wage was different from that of the 'natural wage'.

KRISHNA BHARADWAJ

BIBLIOGRAPHY

Boisguillebert, P. 1707. *Traité de la nature, culture, commerce et intérêt des grains*. In *Economistes et financiers du xviiie siècle*, ed. E.D. Daire, Paris: Guillaumin, 1851.

Cantillon, R. 1755. *Essai sur la nature du commerce en général. Traduit de l'anglais*. London: F. Gyles. Trans. H. Higgs, London: Macmillan, 1931.

Child, Sir J. 1690. *A New Discourse of Trade*. London.

Locke, J. 1692. *Some Considerations of the Consequences of the Lowering of Interest and Raising the Value of Money*. London.

Mandeville, B. de. 1714. *Fable of the Bees or Knaves Turned Honest*. Oxford: Clarendon Press, 1924.

Mun, T. 1664. *England's Treasure by Foreign Trade*. London. Ed. W.J. Ashley, London: Macmillan, 1894.

Necker, J. 1775. *De la législation et du commerce des grains*. Paris.

Petty, W. 1691. *Political Anatomy of Ireland*. Reprinted in *Economic Writings of Sir William Petty*, ed. C.H. Hull, Cambridge: Cambridge University Press.

Ricardo, D. 1817. *Principles of Political Economy and Taxation*. In *The Works and Correspondence of David Ricardo*, Vol. I, ed. P. Sraffa and M.H. Dobb, Cambridge: Cambridge University Press, 1951.

Smith, A. 1776. *An Inquiry into the Nature and Causes of the Wealth of Nations*. Ed. E. Cannan, New York: Modern Library, 1937.

Steuart, Sir J. 1767. *An Inquiry into the Principles of Political Economy*. London: Oliver & Boyd.

Temple, Sir W. 1673. *An Essay Upon the Advancement of Trade in Ireland*. London.

Turgot, A.R.J. 1844. *Observations sur le mémoire de M. Graslin*. In *Oeuvres de Turgot*, ed. E. Daire and H. Dussard, Paris.

substitutes and complements. Economists have found it surprisingly hard to nail down the obvious intuition that in some rough unspecified way tea and coffee are substitutes, and bacon and eggs complements. Not that they can't do it. Quite the opposite, they have all too many ways of doing it, so much so that even if their less attractive inventions are discarded still an abundance is left, each with its own usefulness and charm. Yet because complementarity and income effects are the two chief impediments to sharp results in microeconomic theory, this question of appropriate definition cannot be shrugged off. Neither does it help that what 'appropriate' means tends to vary from problem to problem.

Two important examples exhibit briefly and in turn the fair face of substitutability and the ugly mug of complementarity. In the theory of Walrasian adjustment processes for multiple markets, a famous result traceable in its origins to Metzler (1945) is that if all commodities are (gross) market substitutes then equilibrium is reached from any initial position, i.e. the system is *globally stable* (see Negishi, 1962). Secondly, in capital theory Hatta (1976) has shown that in order for the output/labour ratio to fall as the interest rate falls, i.e. in order for *capital perversities* to appear, it is *necessary* that at least one input pair be (net) complements, which in turn implies that there must be at least three inputs in total.

Despite these examples and purely for reasons of space, this essay will concentrate entirely on substitution and complementarity in the theory of consumer's demand, to the neglect of production. In doing this it differs only in degree rather than kind from the literature of the subject, of which surveys may be found in Schultz (1938, pp. 22–4, and chs 18 and 19, written with the help of Milton Friedman), Stigler (1950, section VI; reprinted in 1965), Georgescu-Roegen (1952) and Samuelson (1974).

Two further disclaimers are in order. Neither the important role in the Austrian theory of value played by what Menger called complementary goods (e.g. 1950, ch. I.3), nor the question of the relations between complementarity and changes in tastes or endowments (begun by Lange, 1940, and analysed by Hicks, 1956, pp. 161–8) is discussed here.

I. THE AUSPITZ–LIEBEN DEFINITIONS

Passing recognition that certain pairs of goods can be called substitutes and other pairs complements must have occurred ever since economics became a serious subject. However, that is far from developing formal definitions and results. A clear though crude attempt to derive explicit comparative static propositions for substitutes and 'co-elements' may be found in chapter IX of Donisthorpe (1876) but a more adequate theory had to await formulation of utility functions in general form, i.e. $u(x, y, \ldots)$, rather than in the additively separable form $u^1(x) + u^2(y) + \cdots$ employed for example by Jevons.

So it is not unexpected that the first hint of a definition is to be found in *Mathematical Psychics* (1881, p. 34). Edgeworth was concerned to prove that his newly-minted indifference curves between 'sacrifice objectively measured' x, and 'objectively measured remuneration' y, were convex. Writing $u_x, u_{xx}, \ldots$ for $\partial u(\,.\,,.)/\partial x$, $\partial^2 u(\,.\,,.)/\partial x^2$, etc., Edgeworth's five assumptions may be expressed: $u_x < 0$, $u_y > 0$, and u_{xx}, u_{yy}, and u_{xy} all 'continually *negative*. (Attention is solicited to the interpretation of the third condition.)' Maddeningly, he stopped right there. Here, the invited attention will be delayed for two paragraphs.

At various times Fisher (1892, Part II), Edgeworth (1897, p. 21; 1925, Vol. 1, p. 117 n.1), and Pareto (e.g. 1927, pp. 268–9, 575–6) have each been said to have introduced the first formal definitions of substitutes and complements. However, Stigler (1950; 1965, p. 131) pointed out that in fact the credit belongs to Auspitz and Lieben (1889, p. 482; 1914, Texte, pp. 318–19), for whom two commodities x and y were *complements*, *independent*, or *competitive* according as

$$u_{xy} > 0; \qquad u_{xy} = 0; \qquad u_{xy} < 0;$$

These A–L definitions (as they will be called here) have three important virtues and one fatal flaw. First, they are intuitively appealing. It seems commonsensical to say that y is a complement of x if an increase in the latter raises the marginal utility of the former, and so on. Secondly, for sufficiently smooth utility functions Young's Theorem implies that always $u_{xy} = u_{yx}$, so that the A–L definitions are symmetrical; if (and only if) x is a substitute for y then y is a substitute for x. Finally, the relations between any pair of commodities involve only that pair alone and the individual agent. In particular, they do not 'depend upon the incidents of a comparatively advanced regime, such as the distribution of money among different purchases' (Edgeworth, 1925, Vol. II, p. 465), i.e. they do not depend upon market phenomena. For positivistically inclined economists like Slutsky ([1915] 1951, pp. 52–56) this last property appeared more vice than virtue.

However, the flaw truly is (as Bertrand would say) 'une objection peremptoire'. Suppose that u is transformed to $v = F(u)$, where $F' > 0$. Then u_x is transformed to $v_x = F'u_x$ and u_{xx} to $v_{xx} = F'u_{xx} + F''u_x^2$ and similarly for u_y and u_{yy}, respectively; in particular, u_{xy} is changed to $v_{xy} = F'u_{xy} + F''u_x u_y$. So by cunning choice of F the sign of u_{xy} can be changed. For example, F can be taken to be very convex by making F'' positive and large, in this way changing a negative u_{xy} into a positive v_{xy}. Substitutes can be made complements, or complements substitutes, all without any change occurring in the agent's tastes. The A–L definitions are therefore meaningless in any theory of demand that abandons cardinal utility.

Now to interpret Edgeworth's assumption $u_{xy} < 0$. According to the A–L definitions, $u_{xy} < 0$ means that sacrifice x is a substitute for remuneration y; increasing the amount of labour supplied, for example, lowers the marginal utility of the commodity received, so that leisure (non-labour) is then a complement for y (c.f. Stigler, 1965, p. 99, fn 84). While the argument of the last paragraph would seem to imply that this A–L interpretation is obviously meaningless, as so often with Edgeworth matters are actually rather more subtle. His sufficient condition C for strict convexity of indifference curves, given in (1881, pp. 35–6), is indeed the same as the modern strong quasiconcavity condition on the bordered Hessian of u, as given by Hicks (1939, p. 306). Hence C is invariant under strictly monotonic transformations F, and so one cannot pick F merely to change from $u_{xy} < 0$ to $v_{xy} > 0$. The F chosen to do this trick must also simultaneously transform u_x, u_y, u_{xx}, and u_{yy} in such a way as to preserve C as well.

II. JOHNSON AND AFTER

Pareto himself, so vehement against cardinal utility, seems never to have seen the inconsistency between that epistemological position and his continued use of the A–L definitions, and in this he was followed by Zawadzki (1914, pp. 171–4). But not by Slutsky, who was quite explicit that the A–L definitions were meaningless in his radically new theory of demand ([1915] 1951, pp. 54–5). However, unlike Hicks and Allen (1934) he did not see the possibilities, opened up by the new theory, of defining substitutes and complements in a way free of dependence on cardinally measurable utility.

One reason for this omission may have been Slutsky's apparent unawareness of the work of the logician W.E. Johnson (1913; 1968) who, from the partial-equilibrium isolation of Cambridge and without specific reference to anybody else, had already offered definitions not dependent on a particular utility index. Let $V = u_x/u_y$ and $W = V^{-1}$, so that in Hicks–Allen language V is the *marginal rate of substitution of y for x*. Then Johnson (1968, 108) defined x and y to be complementary if both $\partial V/\partial x$ and $\partial W/\partial y$ are negative, while they are competitive if either $\partial V/\partial x$ or (disjunctively) $\partial W/\partial y$ is positive. He shows later (p. 114) that, at least in the case of two goods, x and y are complementary if and only if (iff) each of them is normal (i.e. has a positive income elasticity), whereas $\partial V/\partial x > 0$ ($\partial W/\partial y > 0$) holds iff x is normal (inferior) and y inferior (normal).

These definitions are clearly invariant to permissible transforms of u, and equally obviously symmetrical; moreover, they are at least formally independent of market phenomena. The main difficulties in accepting them are their lack of intuitive appeal (which Johnson did nothing to mitigate) and their excessively stringent implications. An *ex post facto* rationalization of the definition of complements can however be given, using arguments couched in the language of cardinally measurable utility (a similar account can be given of his substitutes). Thus an increase in x has two effects: (a) If y is a complement of x in the rough everyday sense, then as in the A–L case we would expect u_y to rise, and hence the rate of compensation for the loss of x by this now more highly valued y to fall; and (b) By the law of diminishing marginal utility u_x is lowered, and so again this reduces the necessary rate of compensation by y for the loss of x.

The implication that if both goods are normal they must be Johnsonian complements seems unacceptably restrictive, though perhaps little more so than the conclusion that if there are only two goods they must be Hicks–Allen substitutes. The latter result has of course been familiar and broadly accepted for over half a century, though not without serious criticism (see e.g. Pearce, 1958, pp. 136ff).

The textbook definitions of substitutes and complements used today first appeared in Hicks and Allen (1934), although recent versions are much simpler and more transparent than the original. Given that their work was in large part a response to the lack of invariance of the A–L definitions (Hicks, 1981, p. 27, fn42), it is not surprising that substitution and complementarity played so prominent (to modern eyes, too prominent) a role in both parts of their paper. Moreover, Hicks' 'literary' expositions of this topic, not only in (1934) but also in (1939, ch. 3) and (1956, ch. 16), seem overly complex and unrelated to his mathematical expositions, to such a degree that Samuelson (1947, pp. 183–9) was led to allege actual inconsistencies between them, a criticism that he later formally withdrew (1950, p. 379, fn1; 1974, p. 1286).

One reason why it is hard to understand Hicks's analysis is that he works always with a numéraire commodity ('money'), which itself enters into the agent's preferences. Thus in considering Hicks–Allen substitutability between a pair of goods x and y, for example, he has to consider the effect of a change in the 'money' price of x on the compensated demand for y, which necessarily involves three goods, x, y and 'money', not two. It is simpler and clearer to treat all goods symmetrically, by normalizing their prices not by use of a numéraire but by income or total expenditure, assumed always to be positive. Such a normalization will be used throughout the next section, even though that prevents any direct comparison of its analysis with much of the earlier literature on the subject, especially that influenced by Hicks.

III. SOME MODERN DEFINITIONS

Assume that the representative agent (trader, consumer) has preferences $\succsim$ defined over the commodity space R^n, and focus attention on his (or her) "target" bundle $z' = (x', y', \ldots)$, assumed for present purposes to be given exogenously. Then his "better set" B' is $\{z : z \in R^n,\ z \succsim z'\}$, which will be assumed always to be convex, closed and such that if z is in it then so is λz for all $\lambda \geqslant 1$. If preferences are incomplete a utility function will not exist, but in any case those preferences can be represented by an *s-gauge* function for B', defined as follows (see the entry on GAUGE FUNCTIONS):

$$j(z \mid z') = \sup\{\mu > 0 : z \in \mu B'\} \quad \text{if } z \neq O$$
$$= 0 \quad \text{if } z = O \qquad (1)$$

where O denotes the origin. This function $j(\cdot \mid z')$ is a generalization of the so-called distance function, discussed for example in Deaton (1979) and Deaton and Muellbauer (1980, pp. 53–7). It is easy to show that it is concave and positively homogeneous of degree 1 (phd1) in z. Next, assume that the agent faces a vector of prices $p = (p_x, p_y, \ldots)$ determined on competitive markets, and give him the following problem of cost-minimization for the target z^t:

Find $z \in R^n$ that achieves $\inf\langle z, p\rangle$ subject to $z \in B^t$ where $\langle .,. \rangle$ denotes the inner product of z and p. The value of any solution to this problem is functionally dependent on its parameters p and z^t, a fact summarized by writing down the expenditure function $e(p\,|\,z^t)$. Assume now and always that $e(p\,|\,z^t)$ is positive and divide each market price by this amount, thus arriving at a vector of normalized (indeed personalized) prices $w = (w_x, w_y, \ldots)$. Following this normalization, the function $e(\cdot|z^t)$ becomes the *cost function* $c(\cdot|z^t)$, where $c(w\,|\,z^t) = 1$, a pure number. This function is concave and phd1 in w, and is actually the (concave) support function of B^t.

So defined, the s-gauge and cost functions are dual to each other, in the sense that under general conditions $c(\cdot|z^t)$ is the s-gauge function of the set B^{t*} in the (normalized) price space that is polar to B^t; and dually, under similar conditions $j(\cdot|z^t)$ is the concave support function of B^{t*}.

We can now expeditiously set out various modern definitions of substitutes and complements. For this purpose I will assume where necessary and without blushing that each function concerned is as differentiable as desired.

A. HICKS–ALLEN. By the well-known Shephard's Lemma, the compensated or Hicksian demand function h_i for the ith commodity is given by

$$\forall i \quad h_i(w\,|\,z^t) = \partial c(w\,|\,z^t)/\partial w_i \tag{2}$$

Then good x is a *substitute* (*net* or *Hicks-Allen* substitute) for good y if

$$\partial h_x(w\,|\,z^t)/\partial w_y > 0 \tag{3}$$

i.e. increasing the price of y leads the agent to buy more x, all the time keeping to the better set B^t and minimizing the cost of doing so (as Marshall would say, obeying the Law of Substitution). Similarly, x is a *complement* (*net* or *Hicks–Allen* complement) if the inequality in (3) is reversed; otherwise, x is *independent* of y.

It follows from (2) and (3) that it is equivalent to say that x is a substitute for y if

$$\partial^2 c(w\,|\,z^t)/\partial w_y \partial w_x > 0 \tag{4}$$

For sufficiently smooth $c(\cdot|z^t)$, the left-hand-side (LHS) of (4) is the same as $\partial^2 c(w\,|\,z^t)/\partial w_x \partial w_y$, from which it follows that if x is a substitute (complement, independent) of y, then y is a substitute (complement, independent) of x. The Hicks-Allen definitions are symmetrical.

Since $c(\cdot|z^t)$ is phd1 it follows from (2) that $h_i(\cdot|z^t)$ is phd0, and thence from Euler's Theorem that

$$\forall i \quad \langle w, \nabla h_i(w\,|\,z^t)\rangle = 0 \tag{5}$$

Because $c(\cdot|z^t)$ is concave, $\partial^2 c(w\,|\,z^t)\partial w_i^2 \geqslant 0$ for every i. So it follows from this and (5) that, taking the summation over all $j = 1, 2, \ldots, n-1$ for $j \neq i$,

$$\forall i \quad \textstyle\sum w_j \partial h_i(w\,|\,z^t)/\partial w_j \geqslant 0 \tag{6}$$

Hence, while all goods can be substitutes for each other, it cannot happen that all goods are complements, for that would imply the negation of the inequality in (6). It is in this sense that, in a Hicks-Allen world, substitution predominates. Moreover, in the two good (x, y) case (6) implies that $\partial h_x(w\,|\,z^t)/\partial w_y \geqslant 0$, so that x and y cannot ever be complements. An extension of this reasoning shows that in the three good case, at most one pair of goods can be complements; and so on.

B. HICKS–DEATON. By design, the s-gauge function $j(\cdot|z^t)$ has just the same mathematical properties as its polar transform $c(\cdot|z^t)$. So the following result is polar to Shephard's Lemma and is obtained in precisely the same way (cf Deaton, 1979, 394):

$$\forall i \quad w_i = \partial j(z\,|\,z^t)/\partial z_i \tag{7}$$

The interpretation of (7) is that it yields the compensated or Hicksian *inverse* demand functions. Roughly speaking, these show how the "marginal valuation" of (or the "marginal-willingness-to-pay" for) good i varies, as one moves around the lower boundary of B^t (see Hicks, 1956, ch. 16, which uses a numéraire, and Deaton, 1979, which does not). Note the similarities to and contrasts with the definitions of Johnson, which did not involve movements around this lower boundary but, instead, movements away from it.

Denote these inverse Hicksian functions by H_i, so that from (7)

$$\forall i \quad H_i(z\,|\,z^t) = \partial j(z\,|\,z^t)/\partial z_i \tag{8}$$

If x and y are complements in the rough everyday sense, one would expect that as one has more y one would be willing to pay more for a marginal unit of x, while if they are substitutes one would be willing to pay less. This is the intuitive basis for the following Hicks–Deaton definitions. A good x is a *q-substitute* for y if $\partial H_x(z\,|\,z^t)/\partial y < 0$, and a *q-complement* if this inequality is reversed; otherwise, x and y are *q-independent* (the language, though not the precise definitions, is due to Hicks, 1956, ch. 16). From (7) and (8) these definitions are symmetrical.

Since $j(\cdot|z^t)$ is phd1 each $H_i(\cdot|z^t)$ is phd0. From this and the fact that $j(\cdot|z^t)$ is concave, analogues to (5) and (6) are readily derived and imply, for example, that in the Hicks–Deaton world q-complements predominate, and that in a two-good world there cannot be q-substitutes. It obviously follows that it is *not* true in general that if x and y are Hicks–Allen substitutes then they are q-substitutes, and similarly for the two definitions of complements.

Note that the gradient mappings $\nabla j(\cdot|z^t)$ and $\nabla c(\cdot|z^t)$ are inverse to each other, a property which persists even when compensated demand functions (direct and inverse) are generalized to compensated demand correspondences (see Theorem 9 in the entry on GAUGE FUNCTIONS).

C. SAMUELSON'S MONEY-METRIC DEFINITIONS. Samuelson (1974, pp. 1272–3) proposed the following 'local measure of money-metric complementarity'. The good x is a substitute for, independent of, or a complement of y, according as $\partial^2 c(w\,|\,z^t)/\partial x \partial y$ is negative, zero, or positive, i.e. the test criterion is the behaviour of (minimized) cost as the target bundle z^t is varied. The original paper should be consulted for Samuelson's rationale of this measure, which does not appear to have become popular.

IV. GROSS SUBSTITUTES AND COMPLEMENTS

Stigler (1950; 1965, pp. 134–5) argued that once the intuitively appealing A–L definitions have succumbed to the ordinalist critique, there is no point in stopping at such halfway non-intuitive houses as the Johnson or the Hicks–Allen definitions. Instead, one should go the whole way to 'simple criteria such as the cross-elasticity of demand', moving completely from psychological to market data.

For individual ordinary (Marshallian) demand functions $z_i = f_i(p, \omega)$, $i = 1, 2, \ldots, n$, where w is the individual's wealth and prices are normalized by a numeraire, these criteria in essence reduce to the following definitions, given originally by Mosak (1944, p. 45): A good x is a *gross substitute* for y if $\partial f_x(p, \omega)/\partial p_y$ is positive, a *gross complement* if it is negative, and *independent* of y otherwise. Actually, in Mosak's original definitions these three situations corresponded not to x being a gross substitute for y, etc., but to y being a gross substitute for x, etc. Subsequent literature has continued this ambiguity, which is by no means trivial, for the chief problem with these 'simple criteria' is that they are not symmetrical. Hence x can be a gross complement for y, and y simultaneously a gross substitute for x, a highly non-intuitive state of affairs.

The proof of such possible non-symmetry is standard textbook fare and so is only quickly sketched here. The standard Hicks decomposition of the effect on the (ordinary) demand for a good x of a simple price change in a good y, utility level τ^* and chosen bundle $z^* = (x^*, y^*, \ldots)$ is,

$$\partial f_x(p, \omega)/\partial p_y = \partial h_x(p, \tau^*)/\partial p_y - y^* \partial f_x(p, \omega)/\partial \omega \qquad (9)$$

Suppose x is a gross substitute for y, so that the LHS of (9) is positive. Suppose also that x is a Hicks–Allen substitute for y, so that the first term on the RHS is also positive (h_x being the compensated demand function for x). Consider now the similar Hicks decomposition for good y. By the symmetry of Hicks–Allen substitutes the first term on its RHS will be the same as the corresponding term of (9), and so positive. But if y is a normal good and x^* sufficiently large, then the whole RHS might be negative, and so y a gross complement for x. If on the other hand x is a Hicks–Allen complement for y the first term on the RHS of the decomposition for y will be negative, and so if it is a normal good, again it will be a gross complement for x.

Given a fixed distribution of endowments the individual ordinary demand functions for each good may be aggregated to a market demand function (or an excess demand function) for that good, and gross substitutes and complements then defined in terms of these market functions, as done for example by Metzler (1945). Mosak (1944, pp. 46–7) inverted such market functions and defined 'gross complementarity [and substitutability] in the inverse sense', which differs from ordinary gross complementarity in very roughly the same way that q-complements differ from Hicks–Allen complements.

PETER NEWMAN

BIBLIOGRAPHY

Auspitz, R. and Lieben, R. 1889. *Untersuchungen über die Theorie des Preises*. Leipzig: Duncker & Humblot. French translation published in two volumes (Texte et Album), Paris: Giard, 1914.

Baumol, W.J. and Goldfeld, S.M. 1968. *Precursors in Mathematical Economics. An Anthology*. Reprints of Scarce Works in Political Economy No. 19, London: London School of Economics.

Boulding, K.E. and Stigler, G.J. 1951. *Readings in Price Theory*. London: George Allen & Unwin Ltd.

Deaton, A. 1979. The distance function in consumer behaviour with applications to index numbers and optimal taxation. *Review of Economic Studies* 46, 391–406.

Deaton, A. and Muellbauer, J. 1980. *Economics and Consumer Behaviour*. Cambridge: Cambridge University Press.

Donisthorpe, W. 1876. *Principles of Plutology*. London: Williams and Norgate.

Edgeworth, F.Y. 1881. *Mathematical Psychics*. London: Kegan Paul.

Edgeworth, F.Y. 1897. Teoria pura del monopolio. *Giornale degli Economisti* 33. Translated in Edgeworth (1925), Vol. I, 111–42.

Edgeworth, F.Y. 1925. *Papers Relating to Political Economy*. 3 vols, London: Macmillan.

Fisher, I. 1892. Mathematical investigations in the theory of value and prices. *Transactions of the Connecticut Academy*, IX. Republished, New Haven: Yale University Press, 1925.

Georgescu-Roegen, N. 1952. A diagrammatic analysis of complementarity. *Southern Economic Journal* 19, 1-20.

Hatta, T. 1976. The paradox in capital theory and complementarity of inputs. *Review of Economic Studies* 43, 127–42.

Hicks, J.R. 1939. *Value and Capital*. Oxford: Clarendon Press.

Hicks, J.R. 1956. *A Revision of Demand Theory*. Oxford: Clarendon Press.

Hicks, J.R. 1981. *Wealth and Welfare*. Cambridge, Mass.: Harvard University Press.

Hicks, J.R. and Allen, R.G.D. 1934. A reconsideration of the theory of value. *Economica*, N.S.1, 52–76, 196–219. Reprinted in Hicks (1981), 3–55.

Johnson, W.E. 1913. The pure theory of utility curves. *Economic Journal* 23, 483–513. Reprinted in Baumol and Goldfeld (1968), 97–124.

Lange, O. 1940. Complementarity and interrelations of shifts in demand. *Review of Economic Studies* 8, 58–63.

Menger, C. 1871. *Grundsätze der Volkswirtschaftslehre*. Trans. by J. Dingwall and B. Hoselitz as *Principles of Economics*, Glencoe, Ill: Free Press, 1950.

Metzler, L.A. 1945. Stability of multiple markets: the Hicks conditions. *Econometrica* 13, 277–92.

Mosak, J.L. 1944. *General Equilibrium Theory in International Trade*. Cowles Commission Monograph No. 7, Bloomington: Principia Press.

Negishi, T. 1962. The stability of a competitive economy: a survey article. *Econometrica* 30, 635–69.

Pareto, V. 1909. *Manuel d'économie politique*. Paris: Giard. 2nd edn, 1927.

Pearce, I.F. 1964. *A Contribution to Demand Analysis*. Oxford: Clarendon Press.

Samuelson, P.A. 1947. *Foundations of Economic Analysis*. Cambridge, Mass.: Harvard University Press.

Samuelson, P.A. 1950. The problem of integrability in utility theory. *Economica*, N.S. 17, 355–85.

Samuelson, P.A. 1974. Complementarity – an essay on the 40th anniversary of the Hicks–Allen revolution in demand theory. *Journal of Economic Literature* 12, 1255–89.

Schultz, H. 1938. *The Theory and Measurement of Demand*. Chicago: University of Chicago Press.

Slutsky, E. 1915. Sulla teoria del bilancio del consumatore. *Giornale degli Economisti* 51. Trans. in Boulding and Stigler (1951), 27–56.

Stigler, G.J. 1950. The development of utility theory. *Journal of Political Economy* 58, 307–27, 373–96. Reprinted in Stigler (1965), 66–155.

Stigler, G.J. 1965. *Essays in the History of Economics*. Chicago: University of Chicago Press.

Zawadzki, W.L. 1914. *Les mathematiques appliquées a l'économie politique*. Paris: Rivière. Reprinted New York: Burt Franklin Research & Source Works Series No. 93, n.d.

Sumner, William Graham (1840–1910). Sumner was born on 30 October 1840 in Paterson, New Jersey and died 12 April 1910 in Englewood, New Jersey. After graduating from Yale in 1863, he studied in Geneva, Gottingen and Oxford. Ordained an Episcopal clergyman in 1869, he engaged in a church career until 1872, when he was appointed by Yale University to a chair as professor of political and social science, having had a tutorship there in 1866. He was the second president of the American Sociological Association, 1909–10.

In political theory, Sumner analysed the limits of state action as a mode of change. In economics, he did important work on the history of monetary and banking institutions, American war finance and American protectionism. In sociology, he was the first major theorist of the evolutionary origin, nature, function and persistence of group habits, belief systems and institutions generally; that is, of social norms (the folkways and the mores) in social, political and economic life.

Best known for his articulate Social Darwinist elitist individualism and his uncompromising laissez faire, his economic individualism and determinism were combined with an emphasis on the social and cultural: free individuals were also social products. Moreover, his conservative Darwinism masked a deep relativism in matters of economics, ethics and social organization.

WARREN J. SAMUELS

SELECTED WORKS

1874. *A History of American Currency*. New York: Holt.
1883. *What Social Classes Owe to Each Other*. New York: Harper.
1884. *Lectures on the History of Protection in the US*. New York: Putnam's Sons.
1885a. *Protectionism*. New York: Holt.
1885b. *Collected Essays on Political and Social Science*. New York: Holt.
1891. *The Financier and the Finances of the American Revolution*. New York: Dodd, Mead.
1896. (With others.) *A History of Banking in All Leading Nations*. New York: Journal of Commerce and Commercial Bulletin.
1907. *Folkways*. Boston: Ginn.
1927–8. (With A.G. Keller.) *The Science of Society*. 4 vols, New Haven: Yale University Press.
1934. *Essays*. Ed. A.G. Keller and M.R. Davie, New Haven: Yale University Press.

sunspot equilibrium. How does one explain the randomness which we see in the economy? Part of it can be traced to the randomness in the physical world which is transmitted through the economic fundamentals (such as endowments, technology and preferences). The weather provides an example. The randomness in rainfall causes randomness in crop yields which in turn generates randomness in agricultural outputs and agricultural prices. Since rainfall affects the economic fundamentals (in particular, it affects agricultural technology), it is said to be an intrinsic variable. Hence, uncertainty about rainfall is also an example of *intrinsic uncertainty* (see Cass and Shell, 1983, p. 194). The classic Arrow–Debreu extension of the general-equilibrium model to include uncertainty has long been the basis for analysing intrinsic uncertainty (see, e.g., Debreu, 1959, ch. 7).

Not all economic randomness can be explained in this way. Even if the fundamental parameters were non-random, economic outcomes would generally be random. This is because the economy is a social system composed of individual economic actors who are uncertain about each other's behaviour. In seeking to optimize his own actions, each participant in the market economy must attempt to predict the actions of the other participants. It is a complicated matter. Mr. A, in forecasting the market strategy of Mr. B, must forecast Mr. B's forecasts of the forecasts of others including that of Mr. A himself. And so on. Since market participants are not certain about the actions of others, they are uncertain about economic outcomes. Businessmen, for example, do not know what others will bid for their products, they do not know whether potential rivals will decide to enter or decide to hold back, they are uncertain about the inflation rate, and so forth.

Uncertainty of this sort is referred to as *market uncertainty* (see Peck and Shell, 1985). It is either created by the market economy or it is adopted from outside the economy as a means of coordinating the plans of the individual market participants. Market uncertainty is not transmitted through the fundamentals. It is, therefore, an instance of *extrinsic uncertainty*.

The interdependence of beliefs, even of 'rational' beliefs, is a central theme in the *General Theory*; see Keynes (1936, ch. 12). Keynes postulates that it is possible to encounter self-justifying expectations, beliefs which are individually rational but which may lead to socially irrational outcomes. The possible interdependence of individually rational beliefs is the central theme of the Townsend (1983) paper and the Frydman–Phelps (1983) volume. Nevertheless, it is fair to say that the formal modelling of market uncertainty has until recently lagged behind the modelling of uncertainty which is transmitted to the economy through its fundamental parameters. The recent work on 'Sunspot Equilibrium' introduced by Cass and Shell, reported in Shell (1977) and Cass–Shell (1983), is meant to provide a rigorous basis for the theory of market uncertainty. The Cass–Shell 'sunspots' are highly stylized. Contrary to fact and contrary to Jevons (1884), it is assumed that the sunspots represent purely extrinsic uncertainty: the economic fundamentals are assumed to be unaffected by the level of sunsport activity.

Can the level of sunspot activity affect the allocation of resources in a market economy? It has been known for some time that if probability beliefs (about sunspot activity) differ across individuals, then sunspots can matter. Consider the two-consumer, two-state, one-good, competitive exchange economy. Draw the usual Edgeworth box. Measure good consumption in state α on the horizontal. Measure good consumption in state β on the vertical. Because uncertainty is purely extrinsic, the box is a square: aggregate resources are independent of the state of nature. Also, because uncertainty is purely extrinsic, the endowment vector lies on the diagonal: individual endowments are independent of the state of nature. Assume that the consumers possess von Neumann–Morgenstern utility functions. Competitive equilibrium always exists. There are two cases: (1) The consumers have the same probability beliefs about the occurrence of states α and β. Indifference curve tangency, and hence contingent claims competitive equilibrium, occurs only on the diagonal. Sunspots do not matter. (2) The consumers have differing beliefs about the probabilities of α and β. Indifference curves will not be tangent on the diagonal. A contingent-claims competitive equilibrium will exist off the diagonal. Sunspots must matter.

There is a sense, however, in which the above sunspot equilibrium is unstable. Assume that the differences in probability beliefs are solely because of differences in information: the consumers share common prior beliefs, but because of differing information they have different posterior beliefs. The contingent-claims prices, however, reveal information. Indeed, in this example, the only competitive equilibrium in which individuals do not revise their beliefs from market information is based on common probability beliefs. Hence, we are especially interested in the special case where beliefs are commonly held. This might be thought of as the strong rational-expectations case.

Indeed, the original research on sunspot equilibrium was inspired by and in reaction to the rational-expectations macroeconomics literature as exemplified by Robert Lucas's (1972) classic paper in the *Journal of Economic Theory*. The Lucas paper was well received in some circles, while it was heavily criticized in others. Most of the critics took issue with the assumptions of individual rationality and perfect markets. Others, rather few in number at the time, were willing to ask whether or not the conclusions of the rational-expectations school follow from the assumptions. Does it follow that passive or simple 'monetary' rules are necessarily best? More generally, if individuals are rational and the government is nonerratic, will the social outcome be nonerratic?

Lucas gave us a formal model to shoot at. His model is based on the overlapping-generations model of Samuelson

(1958), in which time is treated seriously and there is room for government debt (see Cass–Shell, 1980). In my Malinvaud lectures (Shell, 1977), I present an example of an overlapping-generations economy in which sunspots affect the allocation of resources solely because individuals believe that sunspot activity affects the price level. Their beliefs are rational: any single individual believing otherwise would be worse off. In the particular example, the best government policy is perpetually active and exhibits high variance. There is a continuum of perfect-foresight (nonsunspot) equilibria parametrized by the initial price of money and a vast multiplicity of sunspot equilibria partly parametrized by beliefs about the effects of sunspots. (The Shell (1977) model is in at least one way borderline: utility functions are linear. However, David Cass and I had presented similar results based on a non-linear overlapping-generations model at a Mathematical Social Science Board seminar in 1975.)

What features of this model allow for the existence of sunspot equilibria? The Shell (1977) model includes many of the salient features of decentralized, dynamic economies: Government debt is denominated in nominal (i.e. money) units. The time horizon is infinite. Market participation is restricted by natural lifetimes; that is, individuals cannot trade in markets which meet when they are not alive. Too much is included in the dynamic model of Shell (1977) to permit one to isolate 'the' source of sunspot equilibria.

Cass and Shell (1983) focus on only one of these aspects, the natural restrictions imposed on market participation. The model is finite. There is no government debt. Some individuals ('the old') can insure against the effects of sunspots; some individuals ('the young') cannot. If there were no restricted individuals ('no young'), there would be no sunspot equilibria. If there were no unrestricted individuals, a sunspot equilibrium would only be a randomization over nonsunspot equilibria. Otherwise, the typical sunspot equilibrium is not a mere lottery over nonsunspot equilibria. The set of equilibria has been expanded in a fundamental way: the classical Walrasian (nonsunspot) equilibria are only a subset of the set of equilibria. The new equilibria, the sunspot equilibria are never Pareto-optimal.

Cass and Shell (1983, Appendix) provide an example in which there is only one nonsunspot equilibrium but in which there is at least one sunspot equilibrium. The sunspot equilibrium cannot in this case be a randomization over nonsunspot equilibria, since there is only one nonsunspot equilibrium. What goes on in this simple example? Of course, the restricted consumers cannot transfer income across states of nature. The unrestricted consumers believe that relative prices will differ from one state to another. The unrestricted consumers have tastes which differ: in particular, intrastate indifference curves differ and rates of risk aversion differ. Hence the unrestricted consumers may find it advantageous to transfer income across states of nature. Consequently, when conditions are right consumer beliefs in a sunspot equilibrium outcome are validated.

I showed in my overlapping-generations paper (Shell, 1971) that the set of perfect-foresight equilibria is unaffected by the natural restrictions on market participation. (In particular, the possible inoptimality of perfect-foresight competitive equilibria in the overlapping-generations model is *not* due to restricted participation. It is due to the 'double-infinity' of (dated) commodities and (dated) consumers.) Hence, the restriction on market participation which naturally arises in dynamic economies, while not a source of the inoptimality of some nonsunspot equilibria (the 'Samuelson' cases), is *a* source of the existence of sunspot equilibria, which are always Pareto inoptimal. Is restricted market participation the only source of sunspot equilibria in rational-expectations economies? The answer is no! Indeed, absence of sunspot equilibria seems to be the exception rather than the rule. If Pareto optimality is assured, then strong rational-expectations equilibria (based on shared beliefs) are not affected by sunspots. The so-called Philadelphia Pholk 'Theorem' is the assertion: in each 'class' of models in which Pareto-optimal allocations are not guaranteed, one can find an example of sunspot equilibrium. The 'proof' is based on several examples put together by Cass and me and our co-authors. We deviate from the preconditions for Pareto-optimality in only one aspect per example. Tested deviations giving rise to the existence of sunspot equilibria are: incomplete markets, externalities, imperfect competition, and the double-infinity of consumers and commodities (but with imagined unrestricted market participation). In this last case, sunspots can be a partial substitute for money. Sunspots offer the possibility of improved (but never Pareto-optimal) coordination. In general, sunspot equilibria are at best optimal in only a weak sense in which consumers are labelled in the conventional way but are also differentiated by the history of the prenatal states of nature (see Cass–Shell, 1983, pp. 215–18).

It is fair to say that the existence (indeed the prevalence) of proper sunspot outcomes came as a big surprise to many rational-expectations equilibrium theorists. Game theorists, on the other hand, long ago accepted the naturalness of stochastic solutions to nonstochastic games. Consider the well-known notion of mixed strategy or Aumann's (1974, 1985) generalization, correlated strategy. Mixed-strategy equilibria and, more generally, correlated equilibria are examples in which extrinsic uncertainty matters to the outcomes and payoffs of games. The possibility of asymmetric information is what makes correlated equilibrium an interesting generalization of Nash equilibrium.

Peck and Shell (1985) analyse market uncertainty in an imperfect-competition model. The particular model chosen is that of the *market game* due to Shapley and Shubik (1977). Any other model of imperfect competition might have served as well for analysing market uncertainty. The market-game model is, however, a perfect stage for comparing sunspot equilibrium (originally applied to competitive *market* models) and correlated equilibrium (originally applied to matrix *games*).

Peck and Shell establish the following: In the market game, there exists a proper (non-degenerate) correlated equilibrium if and only if the endowments are not Pareto-optimal. For correlated equilibrium the uncertainty device is outside the rules of the game. If the device becomes part of the rules of the game, we create from the market game the 'securities game', an imperfect-competition analogue of the Arrow (1964) securities model. Every correlated equilibrium allocation to the market game is also a pure-strategy Nash equilibrium allocation to the securities game. Proper correlated equilibria to the market game are sunspot equilibria to the securities game. Because the securities game allows for across-state transfers, some sunspot equilibrium allocations are not correlated equilibrium allocations (see Peck and Shell, 1985). Assuming common priors and common knowledge, we know that the set of correlated equilibrium allocations is equivalent to the set of Bayes-rational equilibrium allocations (see Peck and Shell, 1985, which follows Aumann, 1985).

Here, a subset of the sunspot equilibria arise as sophisticated solutions to simple games. The observed uncertainty is the rational consequence of the uncertainty that one player has about the moves of the others. All sunspot equilibria could be considered as simple solutions to sophisticated games. In the sophisticated games, securities are traded. These securities are intended to insure against disturbances caused by randomness in the natural world, even though the effect of this randomness on economic fundamentals is negligible. For examples of correlated equilibria and related sunspot equilibria, see Maskin and Tirole (1985), Aumann, Peck and Shell (1985) and Peck and Shell (1985).

The original impetus for sunspot equilibrium comes from intertemporal economics (cf. Shell, 1977). While the importance of the sunspot-equilibrium notion and related notions of market uncertainty – such as correlated equilibrium, Bayes-rational equilibrium and speculative bubbles (see Tirole, 1985) – are quite general, much of the development of the sunspot model itself has been closely related to economic dynamics. Azariadis (1981) and Azariadis and Guesnerie (1986) go back to the simplest overlapping-generations model from macroeconomics with a stationary environment. Azariadis (1981) provides sufficient conditions for the existence of *stationary* stochastic business cycles based on sunspot activity. Azariadis and Guesnerie (1986) related the conditions for stationary sunspot cycles to the conditions for deterministic cycles. Spear (1985) challenges the view that the stationary sunspot cycles are 'likely' to be encountered when there is more than one commodity per period. Peck (1985) shows, however, that in simple overlapping generations models the existence of a continuum of nonsunspot equilibria (as 'often' arises in economies with taxes and transfers denominated in money units) implies the existence of (possibly nonstationary) sunspot equilibria. Peck's results do not depend on stationarity of the environment. Sunspot equilibria are not 'flukes'.

The connection between endogenous nonstochastic cycles and stationary sunspot equilibria is currently receiving substantial attention. It is too early to review this promising field. The interested reader should turn to the *Journal of Economic Theory* symposium issue (October 1986) on 'Nonlinear Economic Dynamics' edited by Jean-Michel Grandmont. There is a fair sampling of papers on these topics and related topics. The symposium issue also contains several references.

Sunspot equilibrium represents an example of the more general phenomenon, symmetry-breaking, in which symmetric problems have asymmetric solutions. See Balasko (1983) but expect to hear more from him on the subject of symmetry-breaking in economics.

KARL SHELL

BIBLIOGRAPHY

Arrow, K.J. 1964. The role of securities in the optimal allocation of risk-bearing. *Review of Economic Studies* 31, April, 91–6.

Aumann, R.J. 1974. Subjectivity and correlation in randomized strategies. *Journal of Mathematical Economics* 1(1), March, 67–96.

Aumann, R.J. 1987. Correlated equilibrium as an expression of Bayesian rationality. *Econometrica* 55(1), January, 1–18.

Aumann, R.J., Peck, J. and Shell, K. 1985. Correlated equilibrium in a market game an example which is not based on perfectly correlated signals nor on uncorrelated signals. Mimeo, Center for Advanced Study in the Behavioral Sciences, Stanford, California, July.

Azariadis, C. 1981. Self-fulfilling prophecies. *Journal of Economic Theory* 25(3), December, 380–96.

Azariadis, C. and Guesnerie, R. 1986. Sunspots and cycles. *Review of Economic Studies* 53(5), October, 725–38.

Balasko, Y. 1983. Extrinsic uncertainty revisited. *Journal of Economic Theory* 31(2), December, 203–10.

Cass, D. and Shell, K. 1980. In defense of a basic approach. In *Models of Monetary Economies*, ed. J. Kareken and N. Wallace, Minneapolis: Federal Reserve Bank of Minneapolis, 25–60.

Cass, D. and Shell, K. 1983. Do sunspots matter? *Journal of Political Economy* 91(2), April, 193–227.

Debreu, G. 1959. *Theory of Value*. New York: Wiley.

Frydman, R. and Phelps, E.S. (eds) 1983. *Individual Forecasting and Aggregate Outcomes*. Cambridge: Cambridge University Press.

Jevons, W.S. 1884. *Investigations in Currency and Finance*. London: Macmillan. (The paper on 'The Periodicity of Commercial Crises and its Physical Explanation', read at the Meeting of the British Association, 19 August 1878.)

Keynes, J.M. 1936. *The General Theory of Employment, Interest and Money*. London: Macmillan.

Lucas, R.E. 1972. Expectations and the neutrality of money. *Journal of Economic Theory* 4(2), April, 103–24.

Maskin, E. and Tirole, J. 1985. Imperfectly correlated equilibria: a note. Mimeo, Harvard University and MIT, May.

Peck, J. 1986. On the existence of sunspot equilibria in an overlapping-generations model. Mimeo, MEDS, Northwestern, April 1984. Revised 1986. Forthcoming in *Journal of Economic Theory*.

Peck, J. and Shell, K. 1985. Market uncertainty: sunspot equilibria in imperfectly competitive economies. CARESS Working Paper No. 85–21, July.

Samuelson, P.A. 1958. An exact consumption loan model of interest with or without the social contrivance of money. *Journal of Political Economy* 66(6), December, 467–82.

Shapley, L. and Shubik, M. 1977. Trade using one commodity as a means of payment. *Journal of Political Economy* 85(5), October, 937–68.

Shell, K. 1971. Notes on the economics of infinity. *Journal of Political Economy* 79(5), September–October, 1002–11.

Shell, K. 1977. Monnaie et allocation intertemporelle. Communication to Roy–Malinvaud seminar. Mimeo, Paris, November. (Title and abstract in French, text in English.)

Spear, S. 1985. Rational expectations in the overlapping generations model. *Journal of Economic Theory* 35(2), April, 251–75.

Tirole, J. 1985. Asset bubbles and overlapping generations. *Econometrica* 53(5), September, 1071–100.

Townsend, R.M. 1983. Equilibrium theory with learning and disparate expectations: some issues and methods. Ch. 9 in Frydman and Phelps (1983, eds), 169–97.

supergames. 'Supergame' is the original name for situations where the same game is played repetitively, and players are interested in their long run average pay-off. Repeated game is used for more general models, and we refer the reader to that article for those. For the supergame to be well defined, one has to specify the information players receive after each stage: it is assumed that a lottery, depending on the pure strategy choices of all players in the last stage, will select for each player his pay-off and a signal. The lottery stands for the compound effect of all moves of nature in the extensive form of the game, while the signals stand for a new datum – an information partition for each player on the terminal nodes of this extensive form. It is assumed that this information partition describes all information available to the player at the end of the game – in particular, he is not informed (except possibly through the signal) of his own pay-off. The motivation for this degree of generality in the model is discussed in the entry on REPEATED GAMES. The present article is quite brief; a more thorough survey may be found in a lecture by the author at the International Congress of Mathematicians (1986) in Berkeley, which will appear in the *Proceedings* of that Congress, under the title 'Repeated Games', together with a bibliography.

For the supergame to be completely defined, a pay-off function still has to be specified. The 'long run average' could be the limiting average, or the average over a fixed number of periods, or a discounted average – and in the latter two cases, one is basically interested in the asymptotic behaviour of the solutions, as the number of periods grows to infinity or the discount factor tends to zero. In the former case, additional care is needed in the definitions. Everything in the literature concerns the non-zero-sum case: in the zero-sum case, players just repeat period after period their optimal strategies in the single period game.

The study of supergames was initially – and still is to a large extent – motivated by the theme that 'repetition enables cooperation'. This theme has far-reaching implications in economic theory, far exceeding its obvious implications in industrial organization and anti-trust policy. It is best illustrated by the Prisoners' Dilemma. This is the game where, simultaneously, each of both players can ask the referee *either* to give \$2 to his opponent, *or* to give \$1 to himself. Clearly, in equilibrium, each will ask for the latter. But in the supergame they can reach, in equilibrium, the pay-off (2,2), by always asking the referee to give 2 to the opponent (until this one no longer does – from that time on, take always 1 for yourself). Clearly, this is an equilibrium; nobody has any advantage in deviating from his strategy if the opponent adheres to his. This argument proves more generally that, when the signals are the opponents' last actions, the equilibrium pay-offs of the supergame are the feasible, individually rational points of the game: this is the 'folk theorem' of game theory. Feasible pay-offs are those in the convex hull of the pay-off vectors appearing in the normal form – they are achieved in the supergame by alternating in a fixed, prescribed order between pure strategy choices, such that the limiting frequency yields the appropriate point in the convex hull. Individual rationality of a player's pay-off means that he can be prevented by his opponents from achieving more in the game. The 'folk theorem' can thus be interpreted as saying that any cooperatively feasible point of the game can be achieved in equilibrium in the supergame (and vice versa). Experimental evidence is amply documented in Axelrod (1984).

Starting from this paradigm, interest has fanned out in a number of directions. The first, by Aumann, consisted in showing that other cooperative solution concepts of the game, like the core, could also be 'justified' as a set of appropriate equilibrium points ('strong equilibrium points') of the supergame.

The equilibrium of the supergame we exhibited for the folk theorem has the obvious defect in relying on threats which are suboptimal when carried out. A modified equilibrium concept, like perfect equilibrium, would not have this defect. Aumann, Rubinstein and Shapley showed that the folk theorem still holds even with perfect equilibria. The investigation of finite and discounted games brought another surprise: in any finite repetition of the prisoners' dilemma, there is still a unique equilibrium, (1,1): we have a discontinuity in the limit. It was shown, however, by Benoît and Krishna (1985), that (generically), as soon as the game had, for any player, a (perfect) equilibrium giving him more than his individually rational level, then the set of (perfect) equilibria of the finitely repeated games would converge to that of the infinite game. For the equilibria of the discounted games, convergence does hold generically (Sorin), but not always (Forges, Mertens and Neyman, 1986).

Even for the prisoners' dilemma, Kreps, Milgrom, Roberts and Wilson (1982) showed that, if only one player assigned initially an ϵ-probability to his opponent being in fact a 'tit-for-tat' player (start with '2', next repeat always your opponents' previous move), then the perfect equilibria of the finitely repeated games would converge to (2,2): repetition even forces cooperation. The high expectations generated by this conclusion were, however, soon quashed by Fudenberg and Maskin (1986), who showed that in a generic class of games, if one assigned for each player an ϵ-probability to his having a different pay-off function, then the limits of perfect equilibria of the finite games would cover the whole equilibrium set of the supergame when the different payoff functions vary: the 'folk theorem' was restored. The four authors' work had, however, a major impact in the recognition of reputation effects (as related to signalling): a very small number of deviations of a player from a hypothetical equilibrium strategy towards the tit-for-tat strategy will be sufficient to change his opponent's probability of his being the tit-for-tat player from ϵ to a very substantial number; his reputation as a tit-for-tat player thus established, the opponent will follow suit, with result (2,2). The same authors have amply documented the importance of such reputation effects in a number of economic situations – like potential entry in a monopolistic market. Despite this result of Fudenberg and Maskin, Aumann and Sorin succeeded recently in restoring some plausibility to the theme that repetition forces cooperation.

Finally, in the last few years, there has been considerable interest in extending the analysis to the more general information pattern described in the beginning of this article, in order to allow the study of economic phenomena like long term insurance relationships or principal–agent relationships, where imperfect monitoring is essential. Radner, Rubinstein, Yaari and others have studied a number of examples. Lehrer has recently obtained a characterization of the equilibrium pay-offs of the supergame in the two player case, where the signals inform each player of his own utility. This is a very significant extension of the folk theorem, in that it shows in particular that all efficient individually rational points can be achieved as equilibria of the supergame.

JEAN-FRANÇOIS MERTENS

See also GAME THEORY; NASH EQUILIBRIUM; REPEATED GAMES.

BIBLIOGRAPHY

Aumann, R.J. 1959. Acceptable points in general cooperative n-person games. In *Contributions to the Theory of Games*, Vol. IV, ed. A.W. Tucker and R.D. Luce, Annals of Mathematics Studies 40, Princeton: Princeton University Press, 287–324.

Aumann, R.J. 1960. Acceptable points in games of perfect information. *Pacific Journal of Mathematics* 10, 381–7.

Aumann, R.J. 1961. The core of a cooperative game without side payments. *Transactions of the American Mathematical Society* 98, 539–52.

Axelrod, R. 1984. *The Evolution of Cooperation*. New York: Basic Books.

Benoit, J.-P. and Krishna, V. 1985. Finitely repeated games. *Econometrica* 53, 905–22.

Forges, F., Mertens, J.-F. and Neyman, A. 1986. A counterexample to the folk-theorem with discounting. *Economic Letters* 20, 7.

Fudenberg, D. and Maskin, E. 1986. The folk theorem in repeated games with non-observable actions. The Hebrew University, Jerusalem, CRIME and GT, RM 72.

Kreps, D., Milgrom, F., Roberts, J. and Wilson, R. 1982. Rational cooperation in the finitely-repeated prisoners' dilemma. *Journal of Economic Theory* 27, 245–52.

Kreps, D. and Wilson, R. 1982a. Reputation and imperfect information. *Journal of Economic Theory* 27, 253–79.

Lehrer, E. 1986. Lower equilibrium payoffs in two-players repeated games with non-observable actions. The Hebrew University, Jerusalem, CRIME and GT, R.M. 72.

Mertens, J.-F. 1980. A note on the characteristic function of supergames. *International Journal of Game Theory* 9, 189–90.

Milgrom, P. and Roberts, J. 1982. Predation, reputation and entry deterrence. *Journal of Economic Theory* 27, 280–312.

Radner, R. 1980. Collusive behavior in non-cooperative epsilon-equilibria in oligopolies with long but finite lives. *Journal of Economic Theory* 22, 136–54.

Radner, R. 1986. Optimal equilibria in a class of repeated partnership games with imperfect monitoring. *Review of Economic Studies* 53, 43–58.
Rubinstein, A. 1977. Equilibrium in supergames. The Hebrew University, Jerusalem, CRIME and GT, RM 25.
Rubinstein, A. 1980. Strong perfect equilibrium in supergames. *International Journal of Game Theory* 9, 1–12.
Rubinstein, A. and Yaari, M. 1983. Repeated insurance contracts and moral hazard. *Journal of Economic Theory* 30, 74–97.
Sorin, S. 1986. On repeated games with complete information. *Mathematics of Operations Research* 11, 147–60.

'supply and demand'. Although the notion of supply and demand in the context of market price determination potentially goes back to the economic writings of the Greek philosophers, the terminology itself is of more recent origin. It was not given any prominence in a chapter title or table of contents until well into the second decade of the 19th century (see Groenewegen, 1973), though during the previous two decades the phrase was used in the literature with increasing frequency. Its first use in English writings appears to have occurred in 1767 (see Thweatt, 1983). The discussion here is confined to English usage: French, Italian and German developments are omitted. This unfortunately means ignoring the interesting distinction made in German by Marx between 'Zufuhr und Nachfrage' (supply and demand) and 'Angebot und Nachfrage' (offer and demand) with its analytical connotations for more modern developments in economics (see Schefold, 1981).

It is certain that by the end of the 17th century the expression 'supply and demand' was not in use by English economic writers. For example, Locke (1691, pp. 45–6, 59, 61), despite the importance of the concept for his general argument, followed the contemporary practice and expressed the notion either in terms of the 'proportion of the number of Buyers and Sellers' or, more novel, the 'quantity in proportion to [the] vent'. This terminology was explicitly criticized by John Law (1705, p. 5) who stated, 'The Prices of Goods are not according to the quantity in proportion to the Vent, but in proportion to the Demand.' By the end of the 1730s the demand part of the phrase was being used by prominent authorities like Erasmus Phillips, Jacob Vanderlint and Bishop Berkeley and during the 1730s and 1740s was partially transformed by Francis Hutcheson (1755, II, pp. 53–4) into the argument that 'prices of goods depend on these two jointly, the *Demand* ... and the *Difficulty* of acquiring ...'.

Another Scottish writer, Sir James Steuart, has the distinction of combining supply and demand together on a number of occasions in the context of price determination and competitive analysis and thereby originating the first major use of the phrase. For example, in his chapter 'Of Demand', Steuart (1767, p. 153) argues, 'The nature of demand is to encourage industry; and when it is regularly made, the effect of it is, that the supply for the most part is found to be in proportion to it, and then the demand is simple.' Steuart (e.g. 1767, p. 184) used the phrase on a number of other occasions and presumably it is from this source that it spread to authors like Adam Smith, Malthus, Thornton, James Mill, Horner, Brougham, Lauderdale and others, whose practice in this respect has been documented by Thweatt (1983). Some other aspects of the adoption in economics of the phrase 'supply and demand' may be mentioned. By the middle of the second decade of the 19th century usage of the phrase was still relatively rare. Only a few examples of more than twenty uses in a single work have been identified, no more than a dozen works use it more than ten times and most of the works Thweatt (1983) examined used the phrase only sparingly. Secondly, Scottish use of the new terminology was decisive with Steuart as the pioneer, Smith as a considerable influence and the *Edinburgh Review* circle as most important disseminator of the new terminology. This is not to say that English sources were unimportant. Malthus, for example, used it no less than twenty times in his influential second edition of the *Essay on Population* (1802); Torrens used it 29 times in his *The Economists Refuted* (1808) and over seventy times in his *Essay on Money and Paper Currency* (1812). However, the phrase 'supply and demand' did not really gain prominence until 1817 when Ricardo (1817, p. 382) used it in a chapter heading, while in the previous year, Mrs Marcet (1816, p. 296) had used it in the summary table of contents at the start of her Conversation XV on value and price.

Three further observations can be made on the etymology of the phrase 'supply and demand'. First, the very slow adoption of the word 'supply' in conjunction with the much earlier use of 'demand' may be explained by the distinct usages associated with that word in expressions like 'granting supply' used in the language of public finance and its associated military connotations of supply troops. Secondly, the predominance of Scottish usage of the new terminology combined with their undisputed role in originating its usage in English economic discourse suggests the adaptation of the word from the French *suppliéer*, a verb with a less restricted meaning than English usage of the verb 'to supply'. Thirdly, and most importantly, up to the 1830s either term was rarely used in its modern sense, that is, as a function of price. English pioneers in this modern usage appear to have included West (1826), Whewell (1930) and Longfield (1833) but systematic exposition of the practice had to await the work of Cournot (1838) and to a lesser extent that of John Stuart Mill (1848), and was of course especially developed by Marshall.

PETER GROENEWEGEN

BIBLIOGRAPHY

Cournot, A.A. 1838. *The Mathematical Principles of the Theory of Wealth*. Trans. N.T. Bacon with notes of Irving Fisher, London: Macmillan, 1897. Reprinted Homewood: Irwin Economic Classics, 1963.
Groenewegen, P.D. 1973. A note on the origin of the phrase, supply and demand. *Economic Journal* 83(2), June, 505–9.
Hutcheson, F. 1755. *A System of Moral Philosophy*. Glasgow: Robert and Andrew Foulis.
Law, J. 1705. *Money and Trade Consider'd, with a Proposal for Supplying the Nation with Money*. Edinburgh: Anderson.
Locke, J. 1691. *Some Considerations of the Consequences of the Lowering of Interest and Raising the Value of Money*. 2nd edn, London, 1696.
Longfield, M. 1833. *Lectures on Political Economy, Delivered in Trinity and Michaelmas Terms, 1833*. Dublin: Milliken, 1834.
Marcet, J. 1816. *Conversations on Political Economy*. 5th edn, London, 1824.
Malthus, T.R. 1803. *Essay on the Principle of Population*. 2nd edn, London: J. Johnson.
Mill, J.S. 1848. *Principles of Political Economy*. London: Parker.
Ricardo, D. 1817. *Principles of Political Economy and Taxation*. In *Works and Correspondence of David Ricardo*, Vol. 1, ed. P. Sraffa and M.H. Dobb, Cambridge: Cambridge University Press.
Schefold, B. 1981. Nachfrage und Zufuhr in der klassischen Ökonomie. In *Studien zur Entwickelung der ökonomischen Theorie*, Vol. 1, ed. F. Neumark, Berlin.
Steuart, Sir J. 1767. *An Inquiry into the Principles of Political Oeconomy*. Reprinted, ed. A.S. Skinner, Edinburgh and London: Oliver & Boyd for the Scottish Economic Society, 1966.
Thweatt, W.O. 1983. Origins of the terminology, supply and demand. *Scottish Journal of Political Economy* 30(3), November, 287–94.
Torrens, R. 1808. *The Economists Refuted*. London and Dublin.
Torrens, R. 1812. *Essay on Money and Paper Currency*. London.

West, E. 1826. *Price of Corn and Wages of Labour*. London.
Whewell, W. 1830. Mathematical exposition of some doctrines of political economy. In *Transactions of the Cambridge Philosophical Society*. Reprinted New York: A.M. Kelley, 1971.

supply functions. Think of an economy with consumers, firms and markets. Consumers sell resources (factors) to firms and use the incomes they receive to purchase final goods. Firms sell outputs to consumers and firms, and use the revenue so obtained to hire inputs, also from consumers and firms. All goods and payments for them flow through markets in which consumers and firms participate as buyers (demanders) and sellers (suppliers).

To model such an economy, assume that consumers have preferences among various baskets of final goods and resources, and that these preferences are represented by utility functions exhibiting appropriate properties to be described subsequently. Each consumer also possesses a fixed initial endowment of resources. Suppose that upon specification of prices by the markets, consumers demand goods and supply resources so as to maximize utility subject to their budget constraints. As market prices vary, repeated maximization associates quantities of resources supplied (along with, of course, quantities of final goods demanded) to each collection of prices. This procedure defines individual consumer resource supply functions. Summing over all suppliers in any resource market gives that market's supply function.

Assume that firms, on the other hand, face fixed technologies in the form of single-output production functions. The latter functions are taken to have certain properties also indicated below. For the time being, focus attention on the short-run situation in which some (but not all) inputs employed by firms are fixed. Given market prices, suppose that firms determine the inputs they demand (hire) and the outputs they supply (produce) according to profit maximization. Again, with changing market prices, repeated maximization associates quantities of output supplied (and inputs demanded) to all possible combinations of price values. As before, individual firm output supply functions are defined, and summing over the suppliers in an output market secures the market supply function for that good.

In all of the above, markets are usually assumed to be perfectly competitive and operate to equate market demand with market supply.

Supply functions, then, may be classified according to the source from which they come: consumers or firms. Each type of supply function is now considered in turn. In so doing, the following notational conventions are employed: There are I produced goods, each defining a single industry, and J factors. The indices $i = 1, \ldots, I$ and $j = 1, \ldots, J$ run, respectively, over produced goods (industries) and factors. Let n index all goods by first listing produced goods and then factors so that $n = 1, \ldots, I, I+1, \ldots, I+J$. The number of firms in industry i is written L_i, and these firms are indexed by $l = 1, \ldots, L_i$. There are K consumers enumerated as $k = 1, \ldots, K$.

Let the variable y_{I+jk} denote quantities of factor j consumed (demanded) by person k, and take this person's initial endowment of factors to be $(\bar{y}_{I+1k}, \ldots, \bar{y}_{I+Jk})$. When $y_{I+jk} < \bar{y}_{I+jk}$, person k is a supplier of factor j; with the inequality reversed he is a demander. In the former cases $s_{jk} = \bar{y}_{I+jk} - y_{I+jk} > 0$ represents quantity supplied. In the latter $s_{jk} < 0$ is net demand. Write person k's (ordinal) utility function as

$$u^k(x_{1k}, \ldots, x_{Ik}, y_{I+1k}, \ldots, y_{I+Jk}), \tag{1}$$

where x_{ik} ranges over final good i consumed by person k, and u^k is the symbolic name of the function. Assume that u^k is continuous everywhere on its domain (the non-negative orthant of Euclidean $I+J$-space) and that it is also increasing and strictly quasi-concave. Set

$$x_k = (x_{1k}, \ldots, x_{Ik}) \quad \text{and} \quad y_k = (y_{I+1k}, \ldots, y_{I+Jk}).$$

Let p_i and r_j represent respective prices for output i and input j. Let π_{il} be the profit accruing to firm l in industry i, and take b_{il} to be this firm's fixed cost (i.e., the cost of the firm's fixed inputs). Suppose that all profit and fixed cost are returned to consumers in given proportions θ_{kjl}, where θ_{kil} is the fraction of $\pi_{il} + b_{il}$ received by person k from firm l in industry i. (Of course, $\Sigma_{k=1}^{K} \theta_{kil} = 1$ for all i and l). Then the budget constraint faced by person k is

$$\sum_{i=1}^{I} p_i x_{ik} + \sum_{j=1}^{J} r_j(y_{I+jk} - \bar{y}_{I+jk}) = \sum_{i=1}^{I} \sum_{l=1}^{L_i} \theta_{kil}(\pi_{il} + b_{il}). \tag{2}$$

Write $p = (p_1, \ldots, p_I)$ and $r = (r_1, \ldots, r_J)$. As indicated later on, the π_{il} may be thought of as functions of (p, r).

Maximization of the utility function (1) subject to the budget constraint (2) defines the function $h^k = (h^{1k}, \ldots, h^{I+Jk})$ in the sense that for all $p > 0$ and $r > 0$, $(x_k, y_k) = h^k(p, r)$ if and only if (x_k, y_k) uniquely maximizes (1) subject to (2). (All parameters $\bar{y}_{I+jk}$, θ_{kil} and b_{il} are subsumed in the functional symbol h^k.) The resource supply functions of person k are then

$$s_{jk} = S^{jk}(p, r), \qquad j = 1, \ldots, J,$$

where

$$S^{jk}(p, r) = \bar{y}_{I+jk} - h^{I+jk}(p, r),$$

for all $(p, r) > 0$. Appropriately modified to fit the present context, the usual properties of functions derived from utility maximization apply. Thus, for example, each S^{jk} is continuous and homogeneous of degree zero. Moreover, supply curves or graphs of equations such as

$$s_{jk} = S^{jk}(\bar{p}, \bar{r}_1, \ldots, \bar{r}_{j-1}, r_j, \bar{r}_{j+1}, \ldots, \bar{r}_J),$$

where all prices but the jth are fixed, may slope either upward or downward at any $r_j > 0$, provided that such slopes exist.

The slope (assuming it exists) of any supply curve at a point may be split up into two parts, one relating to the substitution effect and the other to the income effect. The former is the limit of the change in resource supply per change in its price, assuming all other prices remain fixed and the individual's endowment or profit-plus-fixed-cost income is adjusted so that he remains on his original indifference surface. The latter is approached by the change in resource supply per change in its price when the price of the resource is set at the new level, the other prices continue to be constant, and the above income or endowment adjustment is reversed. This measure of the substitution effect is always positive while that of the income effect may be either positive or negative. Since the slope of the supply curve at any point is the sum of the two, the supply curve slopes upwards provided that, at the point in question, the measure of the income effect is not negative enough to offset the measure of the substitution effect. But if the individual's preferences at the point are such that a larger, say, profit-plus-fixed-cost income or endowment causes him to use more of the resource himself and release less on the market, and if this effect is sufficiently large, then the resource supply curve would slope downward.

The market supply function for factor j is

$$s_j = S^j(p, r),$$

where

$$s_j = \sum_{k=1}^{K} s_{jk} \quad \text{and} \quad S^j(p, r) = \sum_{k=1}^{K} S^{jk}(p, r),$$

for all $(p,r)>0$. Some, but not all, of the properties of individual supply functions carry over to market supply functions without requiring additional assumptions. Thus the S^j are continuous and homogeneous of degree zero, and the signs of the slopes of the market supply curves are indeterminate.

Turning to the individual firm, let the production function, f^{il}, of firm l in industry i be

$$x_{il}=f^{il}(x_{il1},\ldots,x_{ilI},y_{ilI+1},\ldots,y_{ilI+J}), \tag{3}$$

where x_{iln} and y_{iln} describe, respectively, varying quantities of produced good and factor n hired by firm il. (The variable x_{ili} represents that part of the gross output x_{il} used by firm il in production. All fixed inputs are subsumed in the functional symbol f^{il} and are not included among the x_{iln} and y_{iln}). Assume f^{il} is such that no input yields no output and non-negative input provides non-negative output, that it is continuous everywhere and twice continuously differentiable in the interior of its domain (the non-negative orthant of Euclidean $I+J$-space), that its first-order partial derivatives f^{il}_n are positive and take on all positive real numbers as function values over every expansion path, and that it is strictly concave. Suppose further that both bordered and unbordered Hessian determinants of f^{il} are never zero, and that to obtain positive output, a positive quantity of every input has to be used. (Alternative assumptions are considered subsequently.) The profit of firm il is given by

$$\pi_{il}=p_i f^{il}(x_{il1},\ldots,x_{ilI},y_{ilI+1},\ldots,y_{ilI+J}) - \sum_{n=1}^{I} p_n x_{iln} - \sum_{n=I+1}^{I+J} r_n y_{iln} - b_{il}. \tag{4}$$

Having the firm choose inputs and output so as to maximize profit determines output supply (and input demand) as a function of p and r. One method of explicitly deriving the output supply function of firm il is to first find those inputs which, at (p,r), minimize the firm's total cost for each level of output. This permits the expression of total cost as a function of firm output, $\mathrm{TC}^{il}(x_{il})$. Total revenue also depends on the same output, that is, $\mathrm{TR}^{il}(x_{il})=p_i x_{il}$. Thus the profit equation (4) simplifies to

$$\pi_{il}=\mathrm{TR}^{il}(x_{il})-\mathrm{TC}^{il}(x_{il}). \tag{5}$$

Letting s_{il} represent output supplied, the supply function of firm il may now be defined as $s_{il}=S^{il}(p,r)$, where $(x_{il}=)s_{il}$ maximizes (5) for each $p>0$ and $r>0$. A second (equivalent) way of obtaining S^{il} is to first select inputs $(x_{il1},\ldots,y_{ilI+J})$ which maximize (4) and then place them into the production function (3). In any case, since the profit-maximizing values of x_{il}, the x_{iln} and the y_{iln} all depend on input and output prices, substitution of the former as functions of p and r into (4) exhibits π_{il} as the function of (p,r) needed in the derivation of consumer resource supply functions presented earlier.

Not only do the previous properties imposed on f^{il} guarantee that a profit-maximixing output x_{il} exists uniquely for all $(p,r)>0$, but they also force S^{il} to display certain characteristics of its own. In particular, S^{il} is continuously differentiable, homogeneous of degree zero, and $S^{il}(p,r)>0$, for all $(p,r)>0$; and the supply curve, that is the graph of

$$s_{il}=S^{il}(\bar{p}_1,\ldots,\bar{p}_{i-1},p_i,\bar{p}_{i+1},\ldots,\bar{p}_I,\bar{r}),$$

where all prices but p_i are fixed, is positively sloped at each $p_i>0$. Indeed, under present assumptions, the supply curve is identical to the firm's marginal cost curve given $\bar{p}_1,\ldots,\bar{p}_{i-1},\bar{p}_{i+1},\ldots,\bar{p}_I$ and $\bar{r}$.

As before, the market supply function for output i is

$$s_i=S^i(p,r), \tag{6}$$

where

$$s_i=\sum_{l=1}^{L_i} s_{il} \quad \text{and} \quad S^i(p,r)=\sum_{l=1}^{L_i} S^{il}(p,r).$$

All of the properties described above for the individual firm supply functions apply to the market supply functions S^i as well.

The assumptions upon which this construction of supply functions rests may be modified to fit a variety of circumstances. To begin with, the properties imposed on production functions might be altered. For example, constant returns to scale could be permitted, in which case, if profit maximization at a nonzero output is possible at all, then it necessarily occurs at all levels of output. Hence, when f^{il} is of the constant returns to scale variety, $s_{il}=0$ or $s_{il}=\infty$ for most $(p,r)>0$, while for those particular $(p^0,r^0)>0$ at which profit may be maximized, $S^{il}(p^0,r^0)$ is multivalued – its value set consisting of all outputs $x_{il}\geqslant 0$. Alternatively the production function f^{il} could be allowed to exhibit properties that yield U-shaped average cost curves. Here, although identically zero for all $(p,r)>0$ such that p_i is less than the minimum average variable cost as determined by r, and although continuous for all $(p,r)>0$ that are associated with a positive output, supply functions are, nevertheless, discontinuous as (p,r) varies from one of these (p,r)-categories to the other. For (p,r) in the category identified with positive output, any supply curve obtained from S^{il} is identical to the firm's marginal cost curve (given the appropriate r) only above minimum average variable cost.

Shifting from the short-run to the long-run context imposes a second form of assumption modification. This requires the elimination of all fixed inputs so that each $b_{il}=0$, and the inclusion of the long-run equilibrium condition $\pi_{il}=0$ for every firm. Unfortunately, however, the addition of these extra conditions to the original assumptions forces all $x_{il}=0$. Thus in long-run models, the original production functions are often replaced by those which generate U-shaped average cost curves. For such situations output price is always fixed at minimum long-run average cost and hence can no longer appear as a variable in the output supply functions. Input prices set the location of minimum long-run average cost, and are therefore the sole determinant of long-run output price and quantity.

A third possibility for assumption modification is the introduction of imperfectly competitive elements that give firms some influence over the prices they charge for their outputs. In such cases, if output supply functions are defined at all, output price once again is eliminated as an argument since the profit-maximizing output determines output price in conjunction with the (inverse) demand function facing the firm.

Now return to the short-run model with the original assumptions intact. For the particular situation in which the quantities of all factors supplied by consumers are thought of as fixed independently of prices (a circumstance which is not encompassed by the earlier discussion of consumer resource supply functions), the same market output supplies of (6) may also be derived in relation to the economy-wide transformation function

$$x_I=t(x_1,\ldots,x_{I-1}), \tag{7}$$

where $x_i=\Sigma_{l=1}^{L_i}x_{il}$ for each i, and $t(x_1,\ldots,x_{I-1})$ is taken to be the maximum output obtainable in industry I, when outputs in the remaining industries are $x_1,\ldots,x_{I-1}$ and no more than the given amounts of the fixed factor supplies available are employed in production. If individual firm production functions can be aggregated into industry production functions that are strictly concave, then t is also strictly concave and, when t

is differentiable, its first-order partial derivatives are always negative.

Suppose further that t is twice continuously differentiable on the interior of its domain and that its Hessian determinant is nonzero there. Then the alternative market output supply functions, S^{*i}, may be defined for all $p > 0$ by $s_i = S^{*i}(p)$, where $i = 1, \ldots, I$, if and only if $(x_1 =)s_1, \ldots, (x_I =)s_I$ maximize the value of output. $\Sigma_{i=1}^{I} p_i x_i$, subject to the transformation function (7). Under previous assumptions, such a maximum always exists uniquely. Furthermore, the supply functions $S^{*1}, \ldots, S^{*I}$ are non-negative, continuously differentiable, homogeneous of degree zero, and any $I - 1 \times I - 1$ submatrix of the matrix of their first-order partial derivatives is symmetric and positive definite at prices p whose corresponding market outputs $S^{*1}(p), \ldots, S^{*I}(p)$ are all positive.

These two sets of supply functions, $\{S^i\}$ and $\{S^*\}$, are closely related. With $(p, r) > 0$ given, if all firms hire inputs so as to minimize the cost of producing each level of output (which is necessary for profit maximization), and if the fixed factor supplies are used to the fullest extent possible, then the vector of market outputs supplied must satisfy the transformation function (7). If, in addition, these inputs hired and outputs produced also maximize firm profit, then the vector of market outputs supplied also maximizes $\Sigma_{i=1}^{I} p_i x_i$ subject to (7). Hence

$$S^i(p, r) = S^{*i}(p),$$

for $i = 1, \ldots, I$ and all $(p, r) > 0$. It does not matter that input prices r do not appear as functional arguments of the S^{*i}. However, in many fixed-factor-supply cases r can be calculated anyway once p is specified.

It should be noted that models similar to those described above may also be used as the basis for deriving output supply functions for multiproduct firms. As an illustration, consider a perfectly competitive case in which firm l employs a single (scalar) input y_l to produce I outputs x_{il}, where $i = 1, \ldots, I$. The firm's 'production function' may be written as, say,

$$y_l = \xi^l(x_{1l}, \ldots, x_{Il}),$$

where, in a reverse analogy with (3), ξ^l indicates the minimum quantity of input needed to produce $(x_{1l}, \ldots, x_{Il})$. Sometimes ξ^l may be solved for x_{Il}:

$$x_{Il} = \tau^l(x_{1l}, \ldots, x_{I-1l}, y_l).$$

In this 'transformation function' form, τ^l indicates (in parallel to (7)) the maximum output of good I obtainable when the remaining outputs are $(x_{1l}, \ldots, x_{I-1l})$ and the factor employed is fixed at y_l. Regardless, the profit of firm l is given by

$$\pi_l = \sum_{i=1}^{I} p_i x_{il} - r\xi^l(x_{1l}, \ldots, x_{Il}),$$

where r is the (scalar) input price. Supply functions for each of the firm's outputs are now secured by choosing $(x_{1l}, \ldots, x_{Il})$ so as to maximize π_l for all $(p_1, \ldots, p_I, r) > 0$. As before, market supply functions are the sum of individual supply functions over l.

Historically, Walras (1874) was probably the first to express quantity supplied mathematically as a function of more than one price. However, all of his supply functions grew out of constrained utility maximization on the part of persons and hence would be classified here as consumer resource supply functions. An explicit formulation of output supply functions derived from profit maximization and constrained value of output maximization had to wait for Hicks (1939).

DONALD W. KATZNER

See also COST AND SUPPLY CURVES; COST FUNCTIONS; DUALITY.

BIBLIOGRAPHY

Hicks, J.R. 1939. *Value and Capital*. Oxford: Clarendon Press, Mathematical Appendix.

Katzner, D.W. 1968. A general approach to the theory of supply. *Economic Studies Quarterly* 19(2), July, 32–45.

Katzner, D.W. 1988. *Walrasian Microeconomics: An Introduction to the Economic Theory of Market Behaviour*. Reading, Mass.: Addison-Wesley.

Walras, L. 1874–7. *Eléments d'économie politique pure*. Lausanne: Corbaz. Trans. W. Jaffé as *Elements of Pure Economics*, Homewood, Ill.: Richard D. Irwin, 1954.

supply shocks in macroeconomics. The decade of the 1970s saw a resurgence of interest in the influence of the supply side on macroeconomic phenomena. The new attention paid to the supply side was driven by two major factors. First, the world economy faced a series of major supply-side shocks. These shocks lead to a breakdown of major relationships embodied in macroeconomic models. Second, the new classical macroeconomics brought about a reconsideration of the Keynesian emphasis on the demand side. The breakdown of the relationships in the Keynesian models would have been predicted by the new classical economists. These relationships were often based on historical correlations that could shift when the nature of the underlying shocks facing the economy changed. Keynes emphasized the role of effective demand in business cycle fluctuations. Following Keynes, much macroeconomic analysis neglected the role of the supply side. In periods when shocks to supply are minimal doing so will provide an adequate, if incomplete, understanding of economic fluctuations. The emphasis on effective demand proved inadequate for forecasting, analysis, and policy prescription in the face of supply shocks of the 1970s.

OUTPUT, THE PRICE LEVEL, AND AGGREGATE SUPPLY. If prices and wages are less than fully flexible, changes in the cost of production will have important effects on both the aggregate price level and aggregate output. Shocks to the cost of production yield very different business cycle correlations of prices and output than do the shocks to effective demand. It is convenient to study these movements in terms of the aggregate supply and aggregate demand schedules in price–output space. The aggregate demand curve traces out the negative relation between aggregate demand and output which holds as long as the interest elasticity of demand for goods and for real balances are both negative. The aggregate demand curve defines the set of equilibria in the goods market and asset market for a fixed price level. Along the aggregate demand curve, output increases as price decreases because real balances increase. An aggregate demand curve (DD) is drawn in Figure 1. Stimulative shocks to demand such as a tax cut or a monetary expansion will raise aggregate demand given price. To close the model, the price level is determined by the intersection of aggregate supply and aggregate demand. The aggregate supply curve is determined by the productive capacity of the economy and the market forces determining factor cost. In the strict, neoclassical case, aggregate supply will be fixed for all levels of the general price level. More generally, if frictions in markets for factors of production, especially the labour market, prevent instantaneous adjustment of prices to shocks, then there will be a positive relation between the general price level and aggregate supply. That is, if firms see their prices increasing due to an aggregate demand shock, but do not expect or perceive that their costs may (eventually) increase proportionally, they will supply more output. In the long run, these changes in cost will be fully realized, so there is no long run positive relationship between

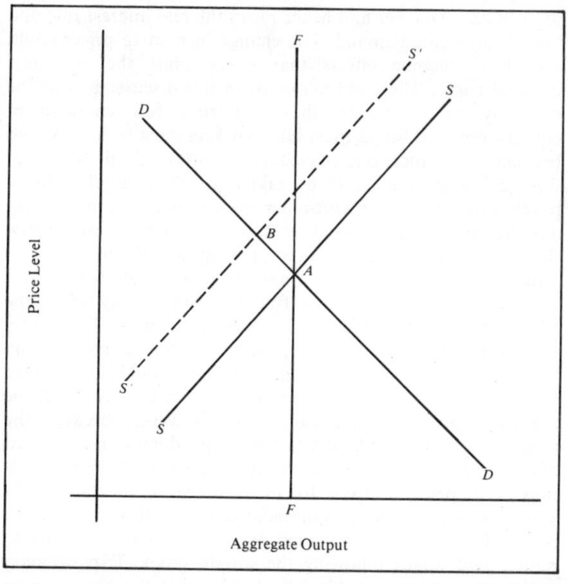

Figure 1 Aggregate Supply and Aggregate Demand

the aggregate price level and supply. An aggregate supply curve (SS) is drawn in Figure 1. The point A, the intersection of the aggregate supply and demand schedules indicates equilibrium output. The long run aggregate supply curve is defined by FF. In the long run the level of output is invariant to the general price level. The point A is a long run as well as a short run equilibrium.

The positive slope of the aggregate supply curve can be rationalized by a variety of models. If firms set their prices as constant mark ups over their costs and if these costs – especially labour costs – react slowly to changes in demand there will be a positive relation between the aggregate price level and output. (See Dornbusch and Fischer, 1984, for a Keynesian treatment of aggregate supply.) The derivation of the positive aggregate supply relation between price and quantity does not depend, however, on Keynesian price stickiness. If firms have imperfect knowledge of the prices facing other agents in the economy, they will not know exactly the relative prices of their outputs and inputs. If, as the general price level increases, the firm first perceives the increase in the price of its output, it will increase output, at least temporarily, when the general price level increases (see Lucas, 1981). It is difficult to distinguish in the data these two sources of the positive slope of the aggregate supply schedule. Misperceptions of the general price level should be short-lived, but costs of adjustment and other rigidities could make the consequences of a transitory misperception long-lived.

The observed correlations of aggregate output and the aggregate price level will depend on the shape of the aggregate supply and demand curves and on the nature and magnitude of the shocks shifting them. Different types of shocks will be more or less important at different times, so the output–price correlation will change accordingly. Supply shocks will shift the aggregate supply curve. Specifically, an adverse supply shock will lower aggregate supply given the aggregate price level. Examples of adverse shocks include declines in productivity and increases in crude materials prices. In order to accommodate such shocks at full employment, the real wage must fall. If nominal wages are sticky, some of this decline will be accomplished through an increase in the general price level. As costs increase due to increases in crude materials prices or declines in productivity, firms raise prices for a given level of output.

Consider the correlation of aggregate output and prices when the economy is subject to both aggregate supply and demand shocks. If the Keynesian view that demand factors are the major determinants of output fluctuations at business cycle frequencies is correct, then one would expect to see a positive correlation of price and quantity in the aggregate data. Business cycles would be fluctuations of demand which would trace out a relatively stable aggregate supply relationship. This positive correlation of price and output is related to, but not identical to the positive correlation of inflation and output (or negative correlation of inflation and unemployment) known as the Phillips curve. With lags of adjustment and data alignment it is difficult, however, to distinguish the relationship in levels and differences. No attempt is made here to sort out these lags.

Suppose, on the other hand, that fluctuations in aggregate supply are relatively more important over the business cycle. That is, that fluctuations in the cost of production trace out a relatively stable aggregate demand relationship. An adverse aggregate supply shock will shift the aggregate supply schedule upward from SS to S′S′. At any level of real economic activity, the price level is higher. The observed correlation between price and output caused by supply shocks will be negative in the aggregate data. Examination of this correlation, if done in the context of a structurally invariant model, can provide evidence as to the nature of the shocks.

SUPPLY SHOCKS AND STAGFLATION. The 1970s saw a distinct shift in the output-price correlation. In the 1960s, the correlation was strongly negative. In the 1970s, the correlation became positive. Hence, although in the 1960s, there appeared to be a trade-off between prices and output, the 1970s witnessed the combination of stagnant real economic and increasing prices that became known as stagflation. (See Federal Reserve Bank of Boston (1978), Blinder (1979), and Bruno and Sachs (1985) for extensive discussion of these events and their ramifications for economic theory.) During the 1970s, there was a series of supply shocks that can explain the changing correlation of output and prices and that caused substantial output loss as world economies adjusted to the shocks. In the early seventies, there were a series of bad harvests that raised agricultural prices. These occurred after a policy in the US of depleting grain reserves. The low stockpiles exacerbated the price increases. The price of oil rose dramatically during the 1973/74 Organization of Petroleum Exporting Organization's (OPEC) embargo and again in 1979/80 following the fall of the Shah of Iran. Each of these shocks has the effect of increasing goods price relative to wages and hence requires an increase in the general price level unless nominal wages fall. Consequently, the aggregate supply curve shifts upwards. The direct effect of the energy and food price increases is illustrated in Table 1. The first column gives the annual inflation rate of consumer prices in the US. The next two columns give the inflation rates for energy and food. These rose dramatically in 1973. Energy prices again begin to rise dramatically in 1979. The last column gives the inflation for all items excluding food and energy. The direct impact of increases in food and energy prices accounted for almost all the acceleration in inflation in 1973 and a high fraction of it in the later episode.

The decade of the 1970s also witnessed a dramatic slowdown in the rate or productivity growth in industrialized nations. Measured by per capita real gross national product,

TABLE 1. Consumer price inflation in the United States: all items, energy, and food

	All items	Energy	Food	Excluding food and energy
1970	5.9	2.7	5.6	6.3
1971	4.2	3.9	3.0	4.7
1972	3.3	2.7	4.4	3.0
1973	6.2	8.1	14.4	3.5
1974	11.0	29.3	14.4	8.3
1975	9.2	10.6	8.5	9.2
1976	5.7	7.2	3.1	6.5
1977	6.5	9.5	6.3	6.3
1978	7.6	6.4	10.0	7.3
1979	11.3	25.2	10.9	9.7
1980	13.5	30.8	8.6	12.4
1981	10.4	13.5	7.8	10.5
1982	6.2	1.5	4.0	7.4
1983	3.2	0.7	2.1	3.9
1984	4.3	1.0	3.9	5.0
1985	3.5	0.7	2.2	4.4

Data are annual per cent changes in the United States Consumer Price Index.

Source: United States Bureau of Labor Statistics.

productivity in the U.S. grew at 2.8 per cent per year from 1964 to 1973. In the European Organization for Economic Cooperation and Development (OECD) countries it grew 3.7 per cent over the same period. From 1973 to 1981, these rates fell to 1.3 per cent in the U.S. and 1.5 per cent in Europe. (See Organization for Economic Cooperation and Development, *Historical Statistics, 1952–1982* (Paris, 1984), p. 86, for these statistics.) A decline in productivity growth directly reduces the rate of output growth. It also has an indirect effect through the aggregate supply-aggregate demand mechanism. Lower productivity means higher costs of production for firms. This shifts the aggregate supply schedule up. Consequently, output falls, at least in the short run, by more than the amount due directly to the productivity shock.

This list of supply shocks – those due to OPEC, poor harvests, and slow productivity growth – is clearly motivated by the experience of recent history. It is by no means definitive. Shocks could include exogenous changes in any commodity price, natural disasters such as earthquakes, floods and droughts, and man-made disasters such as wars or nuclear accidents. Of course, the shocks need not be adverse. Specifically, technological improvement has been the key to economic growth in the West since the Renaissance.

To see how a supply shock propagates in an economy with less than perfectly flexible prices, consider in detail the effect of an increase in the price of imported oil. Firms will immediately attempt to raise prices to pass through the higher cost of oil used as an input. As long as non-commodity prices are less than perfectly flexible in the short run, the increase in the price of oil with increase with aggregate price level. If the oil price increase took place instantaneously and the cost increase were reflected in final goods prices instantaneously, the price level would rise once and for all. Because of lags in adjustment and reporting, prices will rise only slowly. The slow adjustment of the price level will appear in the data, and perhaps be perceived by households, firms, and policy makers, as an increase in the inflation rate. In terms of Figure 1, the aggregate supply curve has shifted up. Holding government policy constant, output will be lower as the economy moves up the aggregate demand curve. The increase in the price level reduces real balances and hence raises the real interest rate and lowers aggregate demand. The change in relative prices could also have income effects that would shift the aggregate demand curve. These are neglected in this discussion. For the economy to return to the long run, full employment equilibrium, real wages must fall. Workers must be less well off because of the increased payments for imported oil. Note that this real wage cut must be taken in the face of reduced purchasing power for consumer goods that require a large amount of energy to produce or to maintain. Consequently, there is the danger that a wage–price spiral will ensue.

In the absence of government policy intervention, a protracted period of less than full employment may follow the supply shock during which real wages are reduced. The supply shocks may be attenuated by government policy intervention. Wage–price controls or incomes policies could be used to combat the inflationary pressure from the cost increase. These are likely to be counter-productive, however, because the relative prices of goods and factors of production must adjust after a supply shock. Since the relative price of some goods must rise, price controls are likely to cause shortages. The supply shock can be accommodated by fiscal and monetary policy. Recall that a protracted recession may be necessary to reduce real wages following the supply shock. Expansionary policy can ameliorate this fall in output at the cost of even higher prices. While any expansionary policy will raise demand, cutting excise taxes would have the compound benefit of producing a favourable supply shock by lowering costs of production. The extra inflation from expansionary policy may be a relatively painless way of accomplishing the reduction in real wages necessary to achieve long run equilibrium. On the other hand, contractionary policy to combat the incipient inflation from the supply shock will be particularly costly because it will add to the recessionary pressures from the supply shock itself.

It is instructive to consider briefly actual policy experience in light of the supply shocks of the 1970s. In the US, the Nixon price freeze and controls and the Carter guidelines were ineffective in containing price increases. Moreover, price controls on gasoline created long lines in both 1973 and 1979. Monetary policy became contractionary following the oil price increases of 1973–4 rather than accommodative and produced what was then the largest recession since the Great Depression. (See Blinder (1979) and Solow (1980) on the neo-Keynesian model of supply shocks, the shocks of the 1970s, and the policy experience in the United States.)

In Europe, unlike the United States, there was virtually no recovery between the first and second oil price shocks. Consequently, unemployment was high in Europe throughout the 1970s. In the US, there have been recoveries punctuated by increases in oil prices. In Europe, real wages appear to be more rigid than in the United States. Centralized, synchronized wage negotiations allow unions to take into account the effect of the wage bargains on the price level. Hence, achieving real wage cuts is difficult. Moreover, unions appear to have preferred to reduce employment rather than the wages of employed wokers. Consequently, the adjustment to accommodate the higher oil price was costly in terms of forgone employment and output.

SUPPLY SHOCKS WITHOUT PRICE STICKINESS. Simultaneously with the collapse of the Phillips curve correlation between price and output there was an attack on the theoretical underpinnings of the neo-Keynesian model. In particular, the belief that there was an exploitable trade off between output and inflation was called into question. The theoretical revolution, called rational expectations or the new classical macroeconomics, denied the role of Keynesian effective demand by reintroducing price flexibility into macroeconomics. The Keynesian macroeconomics models were criticized for treating reduce form correlations such as the negative correlation between output and inflation as structurally invariant. Specifically, the models were criticized for the fact that the correlations embodied in them would change when economic policy was exercised. (See Lucas and Sargent in Federal Reserve Bank of Boston (1978) and Lucas (1981)).

This critique can be broadened to encompass the case where the changes in the reduced form correlations do not arise from attempts by policy makers to exploit them but rather from changes in the nature of the shocks facing the economy. As discussed above, such a change occurred in thee decade of the 1970s when supply shocks were more important than they had been in the past. The development of new classical macroeconomics was certainly driven by theoretical considerations, but its wide acceptance was probably abetted by its explanation of the collapse of the neo-Keynesian models of the 1960s.

Supply shocks can have an important role in economies not characterized by price stickiness. Indeed, since the new classical economics discarded effective demand as a source of fluctuations in output, it is natural that the supply side features prominently in its analyses of business cycles. In most textbook treatments of macroeconomic fluctuations, the business cycle is treated as a cyclical deviation of output from a path determined by factors relating to long-term growth. These factors – growth in population and labour supply, technological progress, and increases in the capital–labour ratio – are assumed to evolve independently of fluctuations at business cycle frequencies. Hence, whether they are deterministic or random, macroeconomic phenomena could be analysed by abstracting from long run growth in the economy. This dichotomy is especially appealing given the view of the business cycle fluctuations as demand driven deviations from supply determined trend.

Emphasis on supply factors, especially productivity shocks, in business cycles vitiates the dichotomy. If factors affecting long-term growth are also important at business cycle frequencies then, in both theoretical and empirical studies, business cycle fluctuations cannot be divorced from long-term growth. Moreover, statistical tests suggest that it is difficult to reject the hypothesis that current shocks to aggregate output have a permanent component. (In the language of statistical time series analysis, it is difficult to reject the hypothesis that output has a unit root.) The persistence of output shocks does not guarantee, however, that productivity shocks are important in the short run. Demand shocks, especially in an imperfectly competitive economy, may be very persistent.

Consider the macroeconomic effects of a shock to productivity. The effects will depend on whether the shock is temporary (from the weather, for example) or permanent (a technological innovation, for example). A temporary shock will affect output directly, but should not affect the technology or level of factor input in the long run. A permanent shock will affect output in the short run, but the entire response of output should not take place immediately. Because capital is costly to adjust and investment entails delivery lags, the response of the capital stock to a productivity shock will take time. Hence, output may appear to be leading investment despite the fact that they are each responding to the same, underlying productivity shock.

If productivity shocks are an important determinant of output at business cycle frequencies, two long-standing empirical puzzles are resolved. Real wages are acyclical or slightly pro-cyclical. Both Keynesian sticky wage theory and neoclassical marginal product theory suggest that real wages should vary counter-cyclically. If productivity shocks are important at business cycle frequencies, wages will be procyclical. Productivity shocks can also account for the short run increasing returns to labour. The estimated short-run elasticity of output with respect to labour equals or exceeds one, which is inconsistent with a neoclassical, constant returns to scale production function. Such a correlation would be expected, however, if productivity shocks were jointly moving output and labour demand. Short run increasing returns to labour, is, however, also consistent with labour hoarding in response to a demand shock.

There are difficulties, however, with attributing too much of the business cycle variance in output to productivity shocks. It seems unlikely that technology moves enough on a quarter basis to account for all of the variability of observed output. Because it is unlikely that technological regress can be an importance source of fluctuations in modern economies, that output falls in recessions might be taken as evidence that demand as well as supply factors account for fluctuations. Hence, to attribute a high fraction of output variance at the business-cycle frequencies to technological shocks, it is necessary to postulate frictions or costs of adjustments of either Keynesian or classical character that magnify the effects of the shocks. Examples of such frictions include the cost to workers of changing jobs or locations in response to technological change and the difficulty of adapting old capital to new techniques.

FISCAL AND MONETARY POLICY AND THE SUPPLY SIDE. Although fiscal and monetary policy are usually thought to work primarily through aggregate demand, they have important supply side effects. Certain supply shocks can be said to be induced by policy decisions. Tax rules that reduce the cost of capital by investment tax credits and accelerated deductions for depreciation expenses have been an important supply side component of fiscal policy in the United States since 1962. (See the *Economic Report of the President* (1962) for a discussion of these investment incentives in particular and for an early treatment of the supply-side effects of macroeconomic, demand-management policies.) Tight fiscal policy will encourage investment (for a given level of aggregate demand) by increasing the supply of saving and hence reducing interest rates.

Monetary policy can also have important consequences for the supply side. Monetary tightening will increase the required rate of return for holding commodities or the domestic currency. As the interest rate increases, the opportunity cost of holding these assets increases. Hence, a monetary contraction will reduce commodity prices and appreciate the currency. Such relative price changes work just as uncontrollable supply shocks by changing the cost of production and hence shifting the aggregate supply schedule. This supply-side channel for monetary policy thus creates a supply shock that amplifies the demand-side deflationary pressure from a monetary contraction.

MATTHEW D. SHAPIRO

See also BUSINESS CYCLES; INFLATIONARY EXPECTATIONS.

BIBLIOGRAPHY

Blinder, A.S. 1979. *Economic Policy and the Great Stagflation*. New York: Academic Press.

Bruno, M. and Sachs, J.D. 1985. *The Economics of Worldwide Stagflation*. Cambridge, Mass.: Harvard University Press.
Dornbusch, R. and Fischer, S. 1984. *Macroeconomics*. 3rd edn, New York: McGraw-Hill.
Economic Report of the President. 1962. Washington, DC: U.S. Government Printing Office.
Federal Reserve Bank of Boston. 1978. *After the Phillips Curve: Persistence of High Inflation and High Unemployment*. Boston.
Lucas, R.E., Jr. 1981. *Studies in Business Cycle Theory*. Cambridge, Mass.: MIT Press.
Solow, R.M. 1980. What to do (macroeconomically) when OPEC comes. In *Rational Expectations and Econometric Practice*, ed. S. Fischer, Chicago: University of Chicago Press.

surplus approach to value and distribution.

1. INTRODUCTION. When we look back over two centuries of economic analysis we find that we can distinguish two successive approaches to the theory of distribution and relative prices. The modern approach was preceded by one which had at its centre a notion of 'social surplus'. This earlier 'classical' or 'surplus' approach, as it has been called, had its beginnings with writers like William Petty and Richard Cantillon, found its first systematic expression in Quesnay's *Tableau Economique* of 1758, became dominant with the classical economists from Adam Smith to Ricardo, and was then taken over and developed by Marx at a time when the main stream of economic analysis was already moving in a different direction.

The purpose of this essay will be to present the basic elements of this approach and consider its central analytical part concerned with the determination of relative prices and the rate of return on capital. Here, the surplus approach will not be examined only from the angle of the history of economic thought, but also from that of the possibilities it may open for contemporary theorizing. Thus we shall also concern ourselves with the resumption of the surplus approach at the hands of Sraffa and of other authors in recent years – in parallel with the emergence of difficulties within the dominant demand-and-supply approach.

Part I of this essay examines the premises that characterize the surplus approach (section I) and then proceeds (section II) to compare the analytic structure of that approach with that of later theory. Finally, the third section will deal with the influence of demand conditions on prices in the classical as distinct from the 'neoclassical' approach – which we shall refer to as the 'marginal' or 'marginalist' approach. This qualification appears in fact to be more appropriate, given the basic role which substitutability between goods and factors, and hence 'margins', plays in it, and its profound difference from the classical approach (the reader who so prefers can however safely replace 'marginal' or 'marginalist' with 'neoclassical' whenever he finds the former adjectives in the present essay; on the origin of the expression 'neoclassical' economics and its shortcomings, see the entry 'NEOCLASSICAL').

Part II, on the other hand, examines the difficulties which the development of the classical approach has raised in connection with the determination of the rate of profits and of relative prices – difficulties which, as will be seen, proved easy to overcome in later years, but at the time played an important part in the progressive obfuscation and abandonment of the approach. Thus the first of these (section IV) deals with the role of the labour theory of value in the development of the classical approach and with the problems that theory left unsolved. The two remaining sections deal with the solution to those difficulties provided in the context of the contemporary resumption of the classical approach. In particular, section V shows how Sraffa's solution in terms of the system of price equations directly follows from the development of Marx's theory of prices of production. Section VI examines the solutions which can be provided by the 'surplus equation method' founded on the integrated wage-goods sector, or else, under Sraffa's partially different hypotheses about the wage rate, on the Standard system.

PART I: THE ANALYTICAL STRUCTURE OF THE CLASSICAL THEORIES

SECTION I. WAGES AND THE SURPLUS.

2. *The concept of surplus*. The concept of social surplus characteristic of the classical theories can perhaps be seen in its simplest form in Quesnay's *Tableau Economique*. Quesnay saw that if the social product – which he considered to consist entirely of agricultural commodities – was to reproduce itself year after year without increase or diminution, a part of it had to be put back into production. Besides the necessary replacement of the means of production, this part included the subsistence of the agricultural labourers. What remained of the annual product after deducting this part constituted a 'surplus', or '*produit net*', of which society could dispose without impairing the conditions of its survival.

The fact that the subsistence of workers was considered necessary for reproduction established a direct link between this analysis of reproduction and that of the division of the product among the classes into which society is divided. Thus Quesnay linked the surplus with the landowners' share of the social product. And when Smith extended Quesnay's notion of surplus by showing that surplus originated from production in general and not from agricultural production alone, profits emerged as a second component of the surplus alongside the rent of land, thus providing the basis for the theory of distribution of the classical economists down to Ricardo.

The determination of the size of the social surplus was accordingly the centre around which these theories revolved. In principle this way of determining the non-wage incomes is simple. Three sets of circumstances are assumed to be known prior to this determination (on this choice of data, see, in particular, Garegnani, 1960, Part I, ch. 1; Eatwell, 1977, p. 62):

(i) the real wage: that is, the quantities of the several commodities constituting the wage rate (for the possibility of assuming a single 'normal' wage, and thus homogeneous labour, see the assumption by these authors of a sufficient persistence of the ratios between the normal wages for labour of different qualities: Ricardo, 1951–73, I, pp. 20–38; Smith, 1776 vol. I, Bk. I, ch. x, p. 130; on this issue see also Garegnani, 1984, p. 293, n.5);

(ii) the social product: that is, the output of the commodities produced in the year;

(iii) the technical conditions of production.

On the other hand a known social product and known technical conditions imply a known number of labourers employed. (For simplicity, we are here assuming that each commodity can be produced by means of one method only, but alternative methods of production could easily be introduced. Keeping to a given physical social product one could let the employment of labour in Figure 1 depend on the wage rate; on the assumption of given outputs in the face of changes in wages and employment, cf. par. 9 below). By multiplying the number of labourers employed by the known physical wage, we obtain the share of the product that goes to

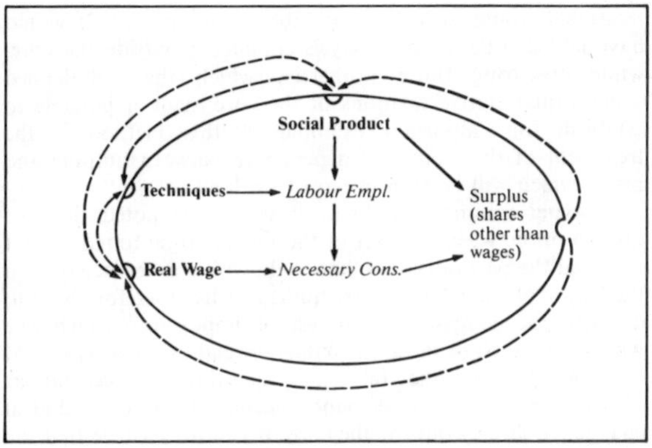

Figure 1 A diagram of the 'core' in the surplus theories. Bold-face distinguishes circumstances determined outside the core. Continuous arrows point to dependencies studied inside the core; discontinuous arrows indicate influences studied outside the core.

the labourers and which, for brevity, we may call 'necessary consumption' (Ricardo, 1951–73, VI, p. 108).

The surplus, that is, the share of the product that goes to classes of society other than labourers, is then determined as the residual obtained by subtracting the necessary consumption from the social product (taken here, for simplicity, net of the replacement of means of production). We have therefore:

$$\text{Social product} - \text{Necessary consumption} = \text{Shares other than wages (Surplus)} \quad (1)$$

an equation where 'shares other than wages' is the only unknown (cf. also Figure 1), and which encloses the underlying logic of the theory, whatever the mathematical form the determination of the 'shares other than wages' may then take: the 'simultaneous price equations' of Sraffa or, the 'surplus equation' of Ricardo, Marx, or those we shall see in section VI below.

Thus the peculiar feature of these theories, the determination of the shares of the product other than wages as a residual or 'surplus' – has its logical basis in the consideration of real wage and social product as being determinable *prior to those shares*. It is to the determination of the real wage and the social product, therefore, that we must turn however briefly for an understanding of the *substance* of these theories, as distinct from the *formal aspect* concerning the choice of independent variables in equation (1).

3. The determination of real wage and social product. Ricardo and Quesnay envisaged the wage as determined by 'subsistence' – the level, that is, that will ensure the reproduction of workers and the repetition of the social process of production. In assessing their views in this respect it is however important to notice that they considered this subsistence to be determined by historical, rather than physiological conditions.

Adam Smith's position regarding the average, or 'natural' wage, on the other hand, was more complex and in some respects more interesting than that of Ricardo. He did not directly explain the tendency of wages to a historical subsistence level by some tendency of the population to grow in excess of the possibility of employment offered by accumulation. He explained that tendency by the advantage which 'the masters' have in disputes over wages. Thus, for example, Smith noted how the 'masters' could 'hold out' much longer than the workers in all wage disputes, since the master's 'necessity' for the workman is not so 'immediate' as the workman's for his master (Smith, 1776, Bk. I, ch. viii, pp. 58–64).

Marx, for his part, was also far from adhering to a simple theory of wages based on subsistence. He asserted that the 'regulating average wage' is given by a historically determined level of subsistence, but the tendency to this 'average wage' was the result of a complex interaction between the actual wage and the size of the 'industrial reserve army' of umemployed labour. This mechanism gave considerable flexibility to his position on the long-term evolution of the 'average' wage. So, for example, in *Capital* (1867, vol. I, ch. xxv, p. 580), Marx states that the real wage can rise in the long run to the extent in which the corresponding 'diminution of the unpaid labour ... would [not] threaten the [capitalist] system itself'.

Thus, it appears that what all these authors had in common was not, as is often held, the idea of a wage determined by subsistence (cf. e.g. Samuelson, 1971, pp. 414, 423). It was the more general notion of a real wage governed by conditions (often of a conventional or institutional kind) that are *distinct* from those affecting the social product and the other shares in it, and are therefore best studied *separately* from them. This separation between the determination of the wage and that of the social product is evident when, as in Quesnay or Ricardo, the wage is explained in terms of a customary subsistence. But the same separation between the two questions emerges in Smith and Marx who admitted a greater influence of current economic phenomena on the real wage. It is this separate determination of the real wage that entails the treatment of the latter as a known magnitude when the determination of the other shares of the product is approached (cf. e.g. Marx, 1905–10, vol. I, p. 45: on the different interpretation of the classical theory of distribution indicated as the 'canonical classical model' cf. Hicks and Hollander, 1977; Samuelson, 1978; Casarosa, 1978; for a critical comment on that interpretation, cf. Garegnani, 1983, p. 311).

As for the physical social product, the circumstances that were seen to determine it were also such that it was natural to suppose the product to be known prior to its division among the classes. In fact, if we attempt to reduce analyses as different as those of Quesnay, Smith, Malthus, Ricardo or Marx to their common basic elements, what we find is the view that the *volume* of the social product depends on:

(i) the stage reached by accumulation, which governs the number of 'productive' labourers employed (where the process of accumulation was seen by some classical authors like Malthus and Marx not to be independent of aggregate demand);

(ii) the technical conditions of production which regulate the physical product per labourer and depend in turn on the stage reached by accumulation (see Smith, 1776, vol. I, pp. 1–2).

The *commodity composition* of the social product, on the other hand, was studied mainly from the angle of the needs of reproduction (see, for example, Quesnay's *Tableau Economique* or Marx's reproduction schemes in chapters xx–xxi of vol. II of *Capital*).

These views on the forces determining wages and outputs are what led to their separate determination and thus to reckoning the non-wage shares as the residual of equation (1) – that is, as the difference between (net) social product and necessary consumption.

SECTION II: SHORT CHAINS OF DEDUCTIVE REASONING.

4. The 'core' of classical theories. It is important to notice now how that *separate* determination of the real wage and social product entails a structuring of the analysis which is radically different from that of the theories which were to become dominant later. The surplus theories have, so to speak, a *core* which is isolated from the rest of the analysis because the wage, the social product and the technical conditions of production appear there as already determined. It is in that 'core' that we find the determination of the shares other than wages as a residual – a determination which, as we shall see in Part II, will also entail the determination of the relative prices of commodities. There we shall find, more generally, an analysis of the relations between, on the one hand, the real wage, the social product and the technical conditions of production (treated as the *independent* variables) and, on the other hand, the 'shares other than wages', constituting the surplus, and the relative prices (treated as the *dependent* variables).

However, this treatment of real wages, social product and technical conditions of production as independent variables in the 'core' in no way entailed a denial of the existence of influences of any single one of these three sets of 'independent' variables upon the other two, nor did it imply the denial of influences which prices and the shares other than wages could have upon any of the three 'independent' variables of the core. This treatment only implied a study of these influences which was *separate* from, and not simultaneous with, the examination of the relationships characteristic of the 'core'.

Let us look at this basic point in some greater detail. The interaction between the three independent variables of the 'core' was freely admitted by the classical economists and by Marx. An example is Marx's discussion of the 'realization' of surplus value, in which the real wage played a key role in the determination of the size of the social product (cf. e.g. Marx, 1905–10, vol. II, pp. 492–4). Another example is the influence which a greater speed of growth of the social product was seen by all classical economists to have in raising the real wage. Likewise admitted were reactions of the surplus (profits and rents) and of relative prices upon one or other of the above three independent variables. For example, the classical economists generally admitted the influence of the rate of profits on the real wage, via the speed of accumulation, as just mentioned. Marx went further by considering how a fall of the rate of profits, consequent upon a rise of the wage rate, would check accumulation and cause technical change, thus re-creating a level of labour unemployment sufficient to reverse the initial wage rise. And the examples could easily be multiplied.

What the structure of classical analysis did imply was something different from ignoring all those relations. It was that – like the action of any other factor that determine wages, social product and available techniques – these interactions and reactions were left to be studied outside the 'core' just described. This separate study was the natural result of what was seen as the multiplicity of these influences and their variability according to circumstances. In fact this multiplicity and variability prevented the generalizations about them from assuming the form of quantitative relations of known general properties like those, studied in the core, which the assumption of competitive uniform rates of wages, profits or rents made it possible to establish between these rates and between them and the relative prices of commodities. This heterogeneity between the relationships examined in the 'core' and those considered outside it was in fact such that, in order to be sufficiently general, a simultaneous quantitative treatment of the two would have had to refer to mathematical functions of largely indefinite properties. As a result any simultaneous quantitative treatment would have been of little or no content. It would have added little to the analysis conducted outside the core, while obscuring those properties which the well-defined general quantitative relations of the core made it possible to establish (an important example of this method is the treatment of the reciprocal dependence between outputs and prices which will be seen in para.10 below).

To avoid misunderstandings, it should be noted that the distinction between the part of the theory to be found in that core and the part outside it, has to do with a difference only in the *nature* of the relationships studied. It has therefore little to do with the comparative interest or importance which one wished to attach to those two kinds of relationships, as should be evident from the fact that questions as central as distribution, aggregate demand, accumulation or technical change fell largely outside the core. It is however true that the relationships studied in the core had been found to provide the necessary basis for dealing with just those questions. An interesting instance of this is Ricardo's need to deal with relative prices in the course of the preparation of that second edition of his *Essay on Profits*, which became the *Principles of Political Economy* (cf. Sraffa, 1951, pp. xxxii–xxxiii).

5. A comparison with later theory. This structure of classical analysis and in particular its distinction in separate logical stages contrasts sharply with what we find in modern theory. Distribution is there seen to result from the interaction between 'demand and supply functions' for the services of the factors of production, based on their reciprocal substitution, and this imposes on the theory an entirely different analytic structure.

That substitutability between factors is in fact supposed to result from two kinds of choice: that of the entrepreneurs and that of the consumers. Taking the latter first let us assume, for simplicity, an economy with two consumer goods, 'corn' and 'cloth', each producible by a single method, and such that cloth requires more 'capital' per worker than corn, and for both goods 'capital' consists exclusively of corn. Any fall in the rate of interest would lower the price of cloth relative to corn and the analysis of consumer preferences would lead us to conclude that a higher proportion of the available labour would generally have to be employed in producing cloth – with a consequent increase in the quantity of corn-capital demanded in the economy as a whole.

This effect is of course enhanced when we introduce the other kind of choice mentioned above and therefore the switch in both industries to methods which require more corn-capital per worker and which have become cheaper with the fall of the interest rate. (The 'demand functions' for factors we are here referring to are those implicit in a *general* equilibrium system: for a definition see Garegnani, 1970, p. 423.)

Three consequences follow from this demand-and-supply explanation of distribution. The first is that two of the former independent variables of the classical core, the real wages and the social product, can no longer be determined separately from each other, but have to be determined *simultaneously*. This is evident from the fact that because of both the technical and the consumer substitutability mentioned above, at each point of the demand function for labour there will correspond a different level of the product per head in each industry and a different commodity composition of the social product: size and composition of the social product will therefore only be determinable simultaneously with the wage.

The second consequence is that those two independent variables of the classical authors have to be now determined *simultaneously* with the former *dependent* variables of the classical 'core'. In fact the real wages, and the social product, can no longer be determined before, and independently of, the other rates of renumeration and of relative prices. Each distributive variable is determined by a strictly analogous demand and supply mechanism. Each point on the demand function of labour implies a price for the service of any of the other factors, just as it implies a level of their employment equal to the supply forthcoming at those prices. Thus the equilibrium in the market for labour (more generally in the market for any of the factors) also defines the equilibrium in the markets of all the other factors. The classical authors' *asymmetry* between the determination of wages and that of the other shares in the product – which showed in the asymmetric treatment of the wage as an independent variable and of the other distributive variables as a dependent residual – gives way to a *symmetric* determination of all distributive variables.

As the real wage cannot any longer be treated as an independent variable when determining the shares other than wages, two new sets of data have to make their appearance to determine it. These are the two necessary elements of the marginalist demand-and-supply mechanism: the tastes of the consumers and the endowment of factors. Thus, in these theories, distribution, outputs and the relative values of commodities are all determined simultaneously, taking as data the tastes of consumers, the endowments of factors of production and the technical conditions of production. The determination of *these* three sets of data is then seen as falling largely outside the domain of economics (the main exception being the size of the capital stock, dependent on savings). This in turn entails a third more general difference from classical theory, in addition to simultaneous determination of the wage and social product and the symmetry in the theory of distribution. In marginal theory the determination of relative prices and of the distributive variables other than wages – which we may describe as 'the theory of value' – becomes almost co-extensive with economics itself, instead of constituting the limited 'core' of economic analysis that it was in the classical economists.

6. Short versus long 'chains of deduction': social and historical factors in economic theory. We may note how this more limited scope which the theory of value has in the classical theories gives them the greater flexibility which seems required by a discipline like economics. (An example of the greater flexibility may be provided by the analysis of possible deficiencies of aggregate demand. Because of it separation from the analysis of outputs, the classical analysis of distribution is open, 'in the sense that it neither provides premises capable of justifying the tendency of investment to adjust to saving, nor is it dependent on the existence of any such tendency', contrary to what is true for modern theory (Garegnani, 1978–9, II, p. 340).)

The above limitation of the theory of value in the classical authors appears to have been the result of an instinctive methodological adaptation to the requirements of economics, where, because of the impossibility of experiment and of the complexity and variability of the material, 'the function of analysis and deduction ... is not to forge a few long chains of reasoning, but to forge rightly many short chains'; the limited scope of the theory of value and the analysis by separate stages, are a way of keeping the 'chains of reasoning' short as Marshall realised to be necessary (Marshall, 1949, App. C, 3, p. 638. The success of Marshall's attempt to preserve short chains of reasoning within a marginalist context by means of his method of 'partial analysis' is open to doubt to the extent in which we have to resort to the long chain of reasoning of the general equilibrium system in order to ascertain the legitimacy of that method, and the degree of approximation of the results obtained in each particular case).

In fact the flexibility resulting from the classical reasoning 'by stages' and the recognition it implies of the multiplicity and variability of the relations examined outside the 'core', appear to be a more or less conscious recognition of the role which broader social, institutional and political factors, in a word historical factors, play in economic phenomena, particularly in the spheres of distribution, accumulation and technical change. The absence of this recognition from later economic theory has often been lamented.

7. Production versus exchange? We may also comment at this point on the frequent characterization of classical theories as concentrated on reproducible commodities and hence 'production', as opposed to the concentration on commodities of the 'scarcity type', and hence 'exchange', which would be the hallmark of marginal theories. According to this characterization the two kinds of theory would deal with two distinct series of problems, with an opposite practical relevance in relation to time, the classical theory becoming relevant for the long run, just when marginal theory becomes irrelevant (cf. e.g. Pasinetti 1965, pp. 573–4; cf. also Hicks, 1976, p. 216).

Whereas this distinction may help to describe some differences between the two approaches, it does not seem to go to the roots of such differences, which lie rather in the way in which *both* 'production' *and* 'exchange' are treated in each approach. Thus, with respect to exchange, the classical determination of the real wage on the basis of the kind of forces discussed above, leads to the determination of profits as a surplus, and hence to the view of relative prices as no more than a way of distributing that surplus between sectors and firms. This implies that the problems of exchange themselves cannot be viewed as problems of 'scarcity' – whether in the short or in the long run. Equally, the determination of distribution by the substitutability between factors of production and their relative scarcity, implies that the problems of production themselves have to be viewed as problems of 'scarcity' in the long run no less than in the short run, and it is only to the extent in which production is so viewed that exchange itself can emerge as a problem of scarcity (on this question, cf. also Roncaglia, 1978, pp. 125–6).

SECTION III. DEMAND CONDITIONS AND RELATIVE PRICES IN THE CLASSICAL THEORIES.

8. Relative prices independent of consumer preferences. What we have seen in Section I prepares the ground for understanding the feature of the surplus theories which is perhaps most striking for people used to modern theory: namely, the fact that (as implied in par. 4 above, and as we shall see in more detail in Part II of this essay) relative prices are determined without any appeal to consumer preferences (for a typical reaction to this feature, see Harrod 1961; see also Sraffa's reply, 1961).

The essential terms of this question are simple. As had to be rediscovered in comparatively recent years under the form of a 'non-substitution theorem' (cf. e.g. Samuelson, 1961; cf. also par. 15 and 17 below), the system of relative prices is determined independently of demand conditions and consumers' preferences, once the real wage – or the rate of profit (interest) – is given, and constant returns to scale to labour and means of production are assumed together with single product industries, (two assumptions that we shall retain for the moment). We saw how the classical economists could take the real wage as given when approaching the determination of relative prices. The two things together mean:

(a) that demand conditions and consumer preferences are

irrelevant for the determination of relative prices in the classical theories where the wages are in fact given in approaching that determination;

(b) that their irrelevance is due to the different theory of distribution allowing that treatment of wages.

Indeed let us look at the modern demand and supply functions for an individual product, which may have fostered the impression that the influence of consumer preferences on the prices of products has to do with the marginalist analysis of the market of the product and not with the general marginal theory of distribution. The non-horizontality of the supply curve necessary for that influence – in particular, under constant returns to scale, its upward slope – is simply an expression of the rise in the relative price of the services which are required in a higher proportion in the production of that commodity (cf. Garegnani, 1983, p. 310). Thus the relevance of consumer preferences for the price of an individual product is but an expression of the dependence of distribution upon the output of the commodity in question.

The 'non-substitution theorem' is of course generally known. What has engendered misunderstandings has been a failure to appreciate that what in modern theory is a purely hypothetical proposition, constitutes on the contrary an essential aspect of the classical theory of relative prices. The theorem is a purely hypothetical proposition in modern theory because the real wage (interest rate) is *not* known independently of demand conditions and consumer tastes. The relevance of the theorem lies therefore in indicating that demand conditions and consumer preferences can affect prices *only to the extent to which they affect distribution* – which those conditions and preferences do of course affect, because they underlie the demand functions for the factors of production. The position is entirely different in classical theory where the separate determination of distribution allows the wage to be taken as given when determining prices.

As a result of this, the assumption of constant returns to scale will be irrelevant to the question of the determination of prices that we find in the classical surplus theories (and in Sraffa). Constant returns to scale would *not* prevent demand conditions from being relevant, were it not for the underlying theory of distribution, which is different from the modern one. The different classical theory of distribution, on the other hand, makes it possible to determine prices without introducing demand functions and this is so even when returns to scale are variable, as we shall now see.

9. The theory of the outputs of individual commodities. Of course, when the hypothesis of constant returns to scale to labour and means of production is abandoned – as it must be in order to deal, for example, with the rent of land – outputs become relevant for determining prices in classical theory. However, the different theory of distribution will be found to entail a determination of outputs which in turn involves their treatment as independent variables in the determination of prices (above, par. 3) – that is, a treatment of them incompatible with the demand functions of modern theory.

The levels of the individual outputs will generally depend, in the first place, on:

(a) the level of aggregate income governing the level of the general purchasing power;

(b) the technical conditions of production (governing, among other things, the outputs of means of production);

(c) the distribution of the social product among the different classes (which will generally use their income in different ways), expressed by the level of the independent distributive variable.

As we saw, in the classical theories the above three sets of circumstances are data when determining the relative prices and the dependent distributive variables. Therefore, insofar as the levels of output depend on these circumstances, they can also be taken as given for the purpose of that determination.

However, and here we get closer to the point in dispute, outputs also depend on individual choices, that is on what modern theory describes as consumer preferences. With respect to this *fourth* determinant it is essential to start by distinguishing between two aspects of 'consumer preferences'. The first aspect is what we may describe as the *content* of these preferences – the fact, that is, that at given relative prices, say 1:1 an individual may consume 1 of commodity A and 9 of B, and another individual 9 of A and 1 of B. The second aspect is the *formal property* for which, as the relative price of any commodity falls, its quantity consumed will generally increase (we refer to this as a 'formal property', because it is supposed to hold irrespective of the *content* of tastes). In the terms of modern theory, we may associate the content of preferences with the 'position' of the demand curve, and their formal property with the 'slope' of the curve.

It seems evident that what is primarily relevant for determining outputs is the content of consumer tastes. But, this content is just what modern theorists leave to the analysis of psychologists or sociologists, and take as a *datum* when conducting their analysis of demand – which is exclusively concerned with the second aspect above and with the slope of the demand function. It is then difficult to see why the same procedure (to take the 'content' of tastes as given) should be objectionable in the classical theories. The paradox is in fact that, unlike their modern counterparts, classical theorists generally considered the analysis of the 'content' of preferences to be an important part of economics (as shown for example, by the analysis of the cultural elements affecting workers' 'necessaries').

10. The dependence of outputs on prices. However, it could be objected at this point that, though it would be readily agreed that the content of consumers' preferences can be taken as given when determining prices, the need for a *simultaneous* determination of prices and outputs does arise in classical theory also, because of the *dependence of outputs on prices* – that is, exactly because of the above formal property on which marginalist theorists have concentrated. For example – it could be insisted – if we consider a change in the real wage, how can we determine the new outputs, before, and independently of, the new prices since, plausibly enough, the new outputs will *to some extent* also depend on the new prices? Will it not again be necessary to introduce demand functions expressing this dependence? Will we not arrive then, in the case of variable returns to scale, at a simultaneous determination of prices and quantities in the classical theory of relative prices, just as in modern theory, and this in spite of the two different theories of distribution?

The reply to this objection will here proceed in two steps: we shall first notice how the dependence of outputs on prices can be dealt with by means *other* than demand functions; we shall then indicate why this alternative treatment appears to be the more appropriate one.

The first step centres on an important instance of the classical reasoning by separate logical stages. When relevant, the dependence of outputs on prices can indeed be dealt with in two successive stages:

(i) the effect on prices and on the dependent distributive variable of the change in the independent variable is conducted while assuming that outputs remain constant – or undergo the specified change when the changing independent variable is some output level (as, e.g., in Ricardo's case of the increased cultivation of 'corn');

(ii) the possible effect (or further effect) on outputs of that change in prices and the dependent distributive variables – together with any *direct* effects on outputs of the changed independent variable (e.g. the change in the output of the means of production which a technical change may have introduced, or rendered obsolete, or the change in the output of wage goods which a change in the real wage will entail) – are then examined in a second stage of reasoning in accordance with the circumstances of the case under consideration. In that same second stage of reasoning, it will be possible to consider any effects which those changes in outputs are likely to have on relative prices and on the dependent distributive variables, when the returns to scale are not assumed constant (together with any further converging secondary changes in outputs and prices).

This two-stage method which can take care of any dependence of prices on normal outputs resulting from variable returns to scale, can also take care, it seems, of the similar dependence which exists in the case of jointly produced commodities, even when constant returns to scale are assumed. The relative scarcity of jointly produced commodities will generally find an objective expression in the co-existence of different processes producing the same commodities (cf. Sraffa, 1960, p. 43n, and Schefold, 1985, pp. 23–6). Therefore a change in the proportions in which the jointly produced commodities are demanded (cf. the concept of 'effectual demand', para. 12 below), resulting either directly from the changes in the independent variables, or from their effects on prices, will generally bring about changes in processes of production in order to adjust to the new proportions, and therefore further changes in prices. Moreover, changes in distribution may render convenient at the existing prices of products some alternative processes of production which will here be associated with different proportions of the jointly produced commodities and, therefore, conceivably, even the appearance or disappearance of scarce commodities. These effects can be taken into account by the above reasoning by stages.

This procedure by stages, which might at first sight appear less satisfactory than the modern *simultaneous* determination of prices and outputs, appears to be the only possible one when we take two further elements into account – and here we come to the second step of the reply to the question raised at the beginning of this section.

Any demand function clearly depends on individual incomes. Now, in marginal theories, the conditions relating to the equilibrium in the market for factors (or other equivalent conditions in the case, e.g., of 'disequilibrium' theories) ensure that, as the demand price varies, the associated constancy or variation in individual incomes can be simultaneously determined together with its influence on the quantity demanded. However, as we abandon marginal theory, we no longer find any such condition relating to factor markets. More generally, it does not seem possible to postulate functional relations of known properties – and, at the same time, of a generality sufficient to render the procedure meaningful – by which to determine the individual incomes and the quantity demanded associated with different prices of the product (cf. the second field of analysis mentioned at para. 4 above). It therefore seems natural to proceed by *separate* logical stages. (To avoid misunderstanding it should be stressed that the above discussion refers to the marginalist *general* relations between the quantity demanded of a commodity and its *price*, and does not relate to the possibility or appropriateness of referring in some cases, to functional relations chosen in accordance with the case in hand and involving the quantities demanded as variables.)

This first consideration is corroborated when we examine a second element. When the dependence on prices of the normal quantity demanded is likely to be appreciable enough to need consideration, it will often be found that the effect has to be considered as an *irreversible change* in the habits of the consumers (e.g., think of the increase in the demand for cars in the US in the 1920s, as technical developments led to an appreciable fall in their price). Even in marginalist theory any such change could not be treated as a movement along a demand function, but as a change in 'tastes', to be examined, if at all, in a separate stage of analysis, where the data themselves are being discussed.

11. Demand functions and classical theory: some conclusions. If we now try to summarize the main conclusions of our discussion concerning demand functions in classical theory, we find:

(a) That in a classical context the formal properties of consumer tastes lose their importance for the theory of distribution because no attempt is there made to explain distribution by means of the substitutability between 'factors of production'. Consequently they lose their former relevance for the determination of relative prices.

(b) That with the former importance of consumers' tastes, there disappears also the need for a simultaneous determination of outputs and prices: outputs can be studied separately from prices, and can therefore be taken as data when determining the latter.

(c) That, on the other hand, important dependencies of outputs on prices can be taken into account by the two-stage procedure described above.

(d) That, as a result of this and contrary to what is at times held, the assumption of constant returns to scale is not only not essential to the determinations of relative prices in the classical economist (as shown e.g. by Ricardo's treatment of agricultural outputs) but would add little to the significance of their 'natural prices' or 'prices of production'.

12. The classical economists' conception of 'demand and supply'. What we have seen concerning the absence of demand functions in the classical economists should not of course be taken to imply that the 'natural prices' or 'prices of production' to which they referred did not entail an equality between quantity demanded and quantity supplied. The absence of demand functions only implied a treatment of 'demand and supply' which was just as different from that of marginalist authors, as the treatments of distribution and outputs were.

In fact the different determination of distribution and individual outputs allowed the classical economists to envisage demand as a single definite point in the price–quantity diagram, and not as the curve of later theory. This single point was that of 'effectual demand' (Smith, 1776, Bk. I, ch. viii, p. 49), giving the quantity demanded at the 'natural price', or 'price of production'. This conception of demand as a single point, to be compared with the quantity supplied ('actually brought to market': Smith, ibid.) in each given situation is what underlies the expression 'proportion' between demand and supply generally used by the classical economists, which shows clearly how demand and supply were not conceived as curves or functions (the term 'proportion' was indeed criticized when the latter conception began to emerge: cf. Bharadwaj, 1978, pp. 256–7). Apart from that single demand point the classical economists needed only the assumption that a shortage of the quantity supplied, relative to the 'effectual demand', will entail an actual or 'market' price higher than the 'natural' or normal price, and that the opposite will be true when the quantity supplied exceeds the 'effectual demand'. Thus, in the classical economists the interplay of 'demand and supply' only explains the oscillations of *actual* prices and outputs around the *normal* relative prices and the normal outputs, equal to the 'effectual demands', where these normal levels are known independently of any such interplay. As Marx aptly put it 'if supply and demand balance one another, they cease to explain anything' (1894, p. 189).

The case is entirely different in marginal theory, where distribution is functionally connected to the relative demand and supply for products, and accordingly the *normal* price of products cannot be known independently of the interplay of 'demand and supply'. There, the demand cannot conceivably be defined by the single definite point corresponding to a normal price, which is unknown. Accordingly it has to be defined in terms of a function or curve (for the difference between the classical and marginalist treatment of demand and supply, cf. Garegnani, 1983).

[It follows that, contrary to what has sometimes been held, the outputs to which the 'natural' prices, or 'prices of production' of the classical economists, or of Sraffa (1960, cf. e.g. p. 9) refer, are not *actual* outputs at one instant of time, taken as in 'a photograph' (Roncaglia, 1978, p. 21 and *passim*). They are *normal* outputs, no less than those determined by the intersection between the demand and supply functions we find in marginalist theory: only, these normal outputs are determined in the different way we have attempted to describe above. The above view of outputs is sometimes associated with that view according to which the treatment of the real wage (or profit rate, cf. par. 22 below) and of the outputs as independent variables results from the purely analytical interest of examining as 'in a vacuum' the relationships between these variables, the prices, and the residual distributive variables (cf. Roncaglia 1978, p. 21 and passim: for a seemingly similar position cf. also Sen, 1978, p. 180). This purely analytical interest would then be compatible with any explanation of those variables. This view likewise seems disputable. In Sraffa that choice of independent variables appears to be the rigorous expression of the procedure we find in the classical economists and, therefore an expression of the kind of explanation those economists gave of such phenomena. Sraffa not only refers to the classical economists for his procedure (1960, pp. v, 9, 93–5), but with respect to the rate of profits he explicitly indicates how his treatment of it as an independent variable expresses the view taken of the forces determining it (1960, p. 33).]

PART II: THE CLASSICAL DETERMINATION OF PROFITS AND PRICES

SECTION IV: THE 'MEASUREMENT' OF VALUE.

13. Ricardo and the labour theory of value. In the remainder of this essay we shall be exclusively concerned with problems that arise in the 'core' of the classical theories and, more particularly, with the problems raised by the analysis of the relationship between the real wage, the rate of profits and the system of relative prices.

The conception of social surplus we saw in Section I is the basis from which Ricardo starts his determination of the rate of profits. Since we are concerned with aspects of the classical problem of value which are independent of the rent of land, we may assume that fertile land abounds and rent can be ignored. Thus, on the right hand side of equation (1) we shall find aggregate profits. Since in Ricardo, as in other classical economists, a yearly production cycle is implicitly assumed, and wages are supposed to be advanced at the beginning of the cycle, wages are a part of capital. Moreover, because of an error (which Marx was later to correct), Ricardo sees the *rate* of profit r as depending exclusively on the division of the product between wages and profits and, therefore, as if the entire social capital consisted of the wages advanced at the beginning of the yearly production cycle (cf. e.g. Ricardo 1951–73, vol. 1, p. 298, also 289–92; and Garegnani, 1984, p. 4). Then we have the equation

$$r = (P - N)/N \qquad (2)$$

where for the reasons already seen for equation (1), r should constitute the only unknown.

It is here that a basic problem arises in these theories of distribution. Since the rate of profits r is the ratio between the *value* of the social surplus and the *value* of the necessary consumption, and since these magnitudes in general will be physically heterogeneous, the quantities P and N of equation (2) must be expressed in value terms. But as we have just seen, P and N are taken to be known *as physical aggregates of commodities*; will they remain known magnitudes when they are expressed as *value magnitudes*?

In dealing with the question Ricardo – after his earlier attempt to refer to the agricultural rate of profits, with P and N measurable as quantities of corn (cf. Sraffa 1951, pp. xxxi–xxxii) – has to face the problem of exchange value. His point of departure is Adam Smith's notion of 'natural price': that is, the sum of the wages and profits calculated at their 'natural' or 'average' rates, that must be paid in order to produce the commodity.

In order to overcome the difficulty that arises out of the variability of the value of money, Smith had suggested a 'real' measure of value, consisting of 'the labour which a commodity can command' (e.g., if one kilogram of bread is worth 50 pence, and one hour of labour 500 pence, the 'real' value of the bread will be 0.10 labour hours).

However, when this measurement of the natural prices is adopted in equation (2), we find that the social product, though known in physical terms, is *not* known in value terms. In fact, let us suppose an economy with 3 million workers (assisted, we may assume, by means of production so simple that they can be ignored). By definition the yearly necessary consumption will 'command' 3 million labour years and its value will accordingly be $N = 3$m. The 'natural value' of the social product resulting from those wages plus the profits on them will however be $P = 3.3$ m, if $r = 10\%$, but $P = 6.6$ if $r = 120\%$, although the physical social product is exactly the same in the two cases. The attempt to determine the rate of profits by means of equation (2) seems to involve us in circular reasoning; in order to determine r, it is necessary to know P which, however, is only known when r is known.

This variability of P as r varies means in fact that the constraint by which the real wage cannot rise without profits falling (so obvious if we could think of the division of the social product in physical terms) is no longer immediately visible. An 'illusion', as Marx was to put it, is engendered by which prices seem capable of accommodating the increase of wages without any decrease of the rate of profits. Let us indeed suppose that the real wage increases: what will happen to the rate of profits? If the 'real' value of P was 3.3, might it not have remained the same, thus ensuring the constancy of $r = 10\%$, or, possibly, have even increased to 3.6, giving $r = 20\%$? Thus, Smith often lost sight of the constraint binding wages and profits, and envisaged the wage and the profit rate as determined 'independently and separately' (Marx [1905–10], 1969, p. 217) – the level of the rate of profits being explained in ch. ix of the *Wealth of Nations* (1776, I, p. 78) by the 'competition' of capitalists.(It may incidentally be noted here how the 'adding-up theory or prices' (Sraffa, 1951, p. xxxv), which resulted from this confusion of Smith has been often construed as anticipating the demand-and-supply explanation of value and distribution of the later marginalist theories, in contrast with the explanation of these phenomena which was to be provided by Ricardo: cf. Schumpeter, 1954, p. 189. However, behind Smith's vague references to the rate of profit as determined by the 'competition' of capitalists, there appears to lie only the inconsistency mentioned above. The demand and supply forces of the modern theories, founded on the substitutability between 'factors of production', are in fact as absent in Smith as they are in Ricardo.)

Ricardo's great merit was to see through this circularity, or 'illusion'. This he did by means of a bold hypothesis. Let us suppose that commodities exchange according to the quantity of labour embodied in them: the ratio between the *value* of the surplus product (the physical surplus) and that of the necessary consumption in equation (2) – i.e. *the exchange value of the former, a composite commodity, relative to the latter, a second composite commodity* – will then be equal to the ratio between the respective quantities of embodied labour, like *any* other exchange value. (Should the necessary consumption advanced at the beginning of the year not be replaced in kind, so that we cannot find a physical surplus product, the rate of profits $r=(P/N)-1$ would still be determined by an analogous exchange value, that of social product relative to the necessary consumption P/N.) The values of the two aggregates in equation (2) can therefore be 'measured' in terms of embodied labour (cf. Sraffa 1951, p. xxxii). In our example above, if the yearly wage of a worker requires 0.5 labour years to produce, we shall have besides $P=3\text{m}$, $N=1.5\text{m}$ and hence $r=(3-1.5)$ $1.5=100\%$. If however the wage increase to 2/3rds of a labour year, we shall have $N=2\text{m}$ and r will fall to $(3-2)/2=50\%$. There is no circularity in equation (2), and no 'illusion' any more that in the given technical conditions, wages might increase without profits decreasing. (The constancy in labour employment at 3m is not essential to the argument; the rate of profits only depends on the ratio P/N.)

14. The 'prices of production'. Marx extended this analysis by developing the instrument that had made it possible in Ricardo: the labour theory of value. He distinguishes between a 'constant capital' consisting of means of production, and a 'variable capital' consisting of wages, thus avoiding Ricardo's failure to recognise the proportion between the two kinds of capital as a determinant of the rate of profits. Accordingly, Ricardo's equation (2) can be replaced by

$$r=s/(c+v) \tag{3}$$

where c, the labour necessary to produce the means of production (here assumed to consist of circulating capital only, that is of capital used up entirely during the year) appears alongside the 'variable capital' v (Ricardo's N), and the 'surplus value' s (Ricardo's $P-N$).

What chiefly interests us here, however, is a second advance of Marx with respect to Ricardo: his theory of the 'prices of production'. Commodities do not exchange according to the quantities of labour embodied, but Ricardo's analysis had in fact remained confined to that hypothesis (see, however, Sraffa 1951, pp. xi–xix for Ricardo's attempt to develop an 'average commodity' in terms of which P and N would remain constant in spite of changes in relative prices). It was left for Marx to develop a more general treatment, which came within a single step of the correct solution to the problem.

The idea which guides Marx is that the cause of the deviation of the exchange ratios of the commodities ('prices of production') from the ratios of the quantities of embodied labour ('values') is the need to *redistribute* the social surplus value s among the several industries with capital of a different 'organic composition' c/v in order to realize the uniform competitive rate of profits. But if a *redistribution* of surplus value among industries is what is involved, it would seem that the resulting *general* rate of profits must necessarily be the ratio of aggregate surplus value to aggregate capital and, accordingly, that it will remain that of equation (3), as if commodities exchanged according to embodied labour (cf. Garegnani, 1984, pp. 306–7). The 'prices of production' of the commodities could then be obtained by applying that rate of profits on the capital employed for their production. In an economy with two commodities only, corn and steel, we would have the two price equations

$$p_c=(1+r)(c_c+v_c)$$
$$p_s=(1+r)(c_s+v_s) \tag{4}$$

which should determine p_c and p_s, the level of r being determined by equation (3) (the prices would be determined in terms of the natural product since the sum of prices would be equal to the sum of values).

However, Marx's argument was not correct. This can be seen immediately, if we remember that (see para. 13 above) the rate of profits is *a value in exchange* – that of the 'surplus product' relative to social capital: if commodities in general do not exchange according to embodied labour, there is no reason to expect this to be the case for those two particular (composite) commodities. The rate of profits r will not, therefore, be generally determined by equation (3), nor, consequently, will the prices of production be those of equations (4). Marx's intuitive argument about prices resulting from a redistribution of surplus value in proportion to capital overlooked the fact that the former changes relative to the latter while it is being distributed. (It may, however, be of interest to note that the argument would be true if referred to the *wage goods sector* we shall see below in Section VI.)

Marx had a glimpse of the error, though from a different angle. He noticed that in equations (4) the variable and constant capital should have been expressed in terms of 'prices of production' and not in terms of embodied labour (Marx, 1894, p. 164): evidently competition can only equalize the rate of profits on what capitalists pay for capital goods, that is, on their prices of production. Let us introduce the correction into our simple example and see where it leads. If we suppose the variable capital to consist of corn and the constant capital to consist of steel, and the prices p_c, p_s to refer to the quantities of each commodity embodying one labour year, we shall obtain:

$$p_c=(1+r)(c_c p_s+v_c p_c)$$
$$p_s=(1+r)(c_s p_s+v_s p_c) \tag{5}$$

It is sufficient to divide both equations by p_c in order to see that they in fact contain *one* unknown only, the relative price p_s/p_c, and that they contradict one another when a profit rate determined in accordance with equation (3) is introduced into them. To overcome this contradiction the profit rate must be left to be determined by equations (5) themselves. Again, equation (3) turns out to be incorrect.

There is, however, a sense in which Marx's error was productive. He treated as integral parts of a *single* method for the determination of the rate of profits and the prices what are in fact, when consistently developed, two *alternative and equivalent methods*, each of which is sufficient to determine that rate and hence also relative prices. The first, which we may call the 'price-equations method' is exemplified by equations (5) and determines the rate of profits – or, more generally, the relation between the wage and the profit rate – *simultaneously* with relative prices. However, the basic idea of profits (the non-wage share) as a *surplus product*, which they can be seen to be whenever the economy is in a self-replacing state, inevitably leads one on to look for some simpler method. The second method, which we may here call the 'surplus-equation method', is exemplified by equation (2) or (3), for the case in which commodities exchange according to labour embodied. Essentially, this method depends on the possibility of expressing both the surplus and the capital that appear in the equation in terms which are proportionate to their values, but do not contain the unknown price, so that we have one equation in which the rate of profits is the only unknown. As Part III below indicates, this second method is also available for sufficiently general hypotheses and as we shall see, it exhibits notable advantages of simplicity and transparency with regard to the underlying properties of the system.

15. The labour theory of value in Ricardo and Marx. Before proceeding to the solution which can be provided for Ricardo and Marx's problem along the lines of the two methods just mentioned, we may note how what we saw concerning the role of Ricardo's labour theory of value in overcoming the error implicit in Smith's 'adding up' theory of prices, brings us to question a view of that theory which is still widely accepted. The view is that according to which the labour theory of value in Marx – and in Ricardo – was an analytically unnecessary 'detour', undertaken mainly under the influence of ethical or ideological preoccupations (cf. e.g. Myrdal, 1929, p. 63; Samuelson, 1971, p. 69; cf. also Sen, 1978, pp. 177–9, where any 'predictive' meaning is denied to Marx's use of the theory; Morishima, 1973, e.g. pp. 85–6; Meek, 1977, p. 121, etc.). However, if what we contend is correct, it was owing to the labour theory of value that Ricardo and Marx reached the conclusion that the rate of profit (interest) is determined once the real wage is given. Now, a few decades ago this proposition was still new enough to constitute the crux of a 'non-substitution theorem' (Samuelson, 1961; cf. par. 8 above). A theory like the labour theory of value which made it possible to arrive at it nearly 150 years earlier, would seem to have been more a drastic analytical advance than an 'analytical detour'.

This purely analytical role of the labour theory of value is in fact confirmed by a closer consideration of Marx's double distinction between the 'apparent' relations of production of 'bourgeois society' and its inner or 'intrinsic' relations or connections, on the one hand, and between 'vulgar' and 'classical' forms of political economy on the other.

According to Marx, the 'apparent' relations are those which are perceived by the unsystematic observer. We still find them in Adam Smith's 'adding up' theory of prices, when 'instead of resolving exchange-value into wages, profit and rent, Smith constructs the exchange-value of the commodity from the value of wages, profit and rent, which are determined independently and separately' (Marx, 1905–10, II, p. 217). In such an inconsistent representation of the economic system 'the contradictory character of capital is totally concealed and effaced ... no contradiction to labour is evident' (Marx, 1905–10, III, p. 467).

There are, on the other hand, the real relations constituting the 'intrinsic', or 'inner' connections of the bourgeois system. These are the relations which had been progressively brought to light by the systematic 'scientific' analysis, carried out by 'classical' political economy (Marx, 1867, p. 85; 1905–10, vol. II, p. 165), including the naive, still contradictory stage represented by Smith. These relations centre on the constraints (or 'inner' connections) that bind changes in wages to changes in profits and rents (on this double distinction of Marx cf. also Garegnani, 1984, pp. 303–4).

Now, in order to arrive at those true relations it appeared necessary to measure the product – that is, for the reasons we saw above, the *value* of the product – *independently* of its division between the three classes, so that this value could be shown to 'resolve' itself into wages, profits and rent. Hence the role of Ricardo's measurement of values in a labour embodied standard, in terms of which, in Marx's own words, the value of the commodity 'does not depend upon its division into wages, profits and rents' and constitutes instead 'the *limit* ... for the dividends which the labourers, capitalist and landlord will be able to draw from this value in the form of wages, profits and rents' (Marx, 1894, p. 854, and 1905–10, II, p. 219).

If what has been argued above is correct, it will also appear difficult to accept the distinction between a 'labour theory of value' and a 'cost of production theory of value' which would alone be attributable to Ricardo (Stigler, 1958, p. 357), insofar as 'analytical statements' are concerned (ibid. p. 366). Indeed it seems that neither Ricardo nor Marx ever held what is there called a 'pure labour theory of value' and that, in a sense, both authors held a 'cost of production theory of value'. The problems to which the labour theory of value is an answer are neither an approximate estimation of relative prices for their own sake, nor some *a priori* considerations on the nature of society. Rather they lie in how the rate of profit appearing in a 'cost of production theory' can be correctly determined. (If the distinction, also drawn in Stigler, 1958 p. 366, between an 'empirical' labour theory of value based on 'costs of productions' held by Ricardo, and an *a priori* one, held by Marx, thus appears questionable, no less questionable seems the similar view sometimes advanced according to which there would be a 'Ricardo approach' to the problem of value which, contrary to that of Marx, would be founded on the simultaneous determination of both the general rate of profits and the prices of production (cf. Garegnani, 1984, p. 305 n.25.)

SECTION V. THE 'PRICE-EQUATIONS METHOD' OF DETERMINING PROFITS.

16. The price equations. The 'price-equations method' arises from the generalization of equations (5). In these equations we assumed that constant capital consists of one commodity only. When that assumption is abandoned, the constant capital of each industry has to be distinguished into as many quantities of embodied labour as there are different means of production. This is required in order to apply the price appropriate to each kind. Of course, to each additional *unknown price* so introduced in the equations, there will correspond an additional *price equation*. Matters are even simpler for the variable capital: the assumption of a uniform real wage ensures that, in all industries, variable capital consists of the same composite 'wage commodity' and that we may apply to it the single price obtainable from the prices of its constituent commodities.

We may now write the price equations obtained by generalizing equations (5) for the case of any number k of commodities $a, b, \ldots, k$.

Let a be produced during the year by L_a labourers assisted by the quantities of constant capitals $A_a, B_a, \ldots, K_a$, (some of which may be zero) consisting respectively of commodities $a, b, \ldots, k$; so that the quantity of commodity a produced in the year requires a total quantity of labour (direct and indirect) given by $A = L_a + A_a + B_a + \cdots + K_a$ of direct and indirect labour; $L_b, A_b, B_b, \ldots, K_b, B; \ldots; L_k, A_k, B_k, \ldots, K_k, K_k$, being the analogous quantities in the production of commodities $b, \ldots, k$; w being the quantity of labour necessary to produce the given real wage; $\lambda_a, \lambda_b, \ldots, \lambda_g$ (such that $\lambda_a + \lambda_b + \cdots + \lambda_g = 1$) being the quantities of labour embodied in the wage goods (g in number) constituting a unit of the 'wage commodity' λ, which is chosen as the numéraire.

We shall then have:

$$[(A_a p_a + B_a p_b + \cdots K_a p_k) + L_a w](1 + r) = A p_a$$
$$[(A_b p_a + B_b p_b + \cdots K_b p_k) + L_b w](1 + r) = B p_b$$
$$\cdots$$
$$\cdots$$
$$[(A_k p_a + B_k p_b + \cdots + K_k p_k) + L_k w](1 + r) = K p_k$$
$$\lambda_a p_a + \lambda_b p_b + \cdots \lambda_g p_g = 1. \qquad (6)$$

Equations (6) are $(k + 1)$ in number and contain the same number of unknowns: the rate of profit r and the k prices of production $p_a, p_b, \ldots, p_k$. (For the existence and properties of the solution cf. Garegnani, 1973, pp. 332–40; cf. also par. 22 below.)

It can now easily be seen that the need to distinguish the constant capital of an industry, say a, into the quantities $A_a, B_a, \ldots, K_a$ makes it no longer essential to measure them in terms of labour embodied. The prices of production $p_a, p_b, \ldots, p_k$ may be applied directly to the physical inputs of $a, b, \ldots, k$. The same applies to the variable capital $(L_a w), (L_b w), \ldots$, consisting of the composite 'wage commodity' (which being our numéraire, has a unit price of production). These physical quantities are generally preferable, because they depend only on the method of production *of the commodity concerned*, and not, in addition, on the methods of the commodity's direct and indirect means of production, as is the case for the corresponding quantities of labour embodied. Equation (6) can therefore also be read with the quantities $w, A_a, \ldots, B_a$, etc., taken as physical quantities. Henceforth, we shall adopt this alternative reading of equations (6).

17. The price equations from Marx to Sraffa. Equations (6) are in fact those we find in Sraffa's *Production of Commodities by Means of Commodities* (cf. e.g. 1960, p. 6, where the equations only differ from the above because the wages are included, commodity by commodity, among the means of production). Indeed Sraffa's own symbols were chosen for equations (6), so as to bring out how his equations are the same as Marx's equations (3) and (4), once the latter are modified by applying the price of production to variable and constant capital. The fact that such a modification had been suggested by Marx himself does not however prevent this procedure from changing his equation (3) and (4) beyond *easy recognition*. The essential point, however, is that equations (6) provide a general solution to precisely the same problem which Ricardo and Marx had faced by means of the labour theory of value. The characteristic premises of the surplus approach, for which the real wage and the social product are given when determining the rate of profit and relative prices have remained unaffected. Therefore, the notion of profits as a residual and the view of the forces determining distribution associated with it have remained equally unaffected (cf. below on the meaning, in this respect, of ch. 1 of Sraffa, 1960).

However, equations (6) are less transparent about the forces governing the rate of profits than were Ricardo's equations (2) and Marx's (3). The basic asymmetry between a wage independently determined and profits resulting *as a residual* is obscured. In equations (6), to envisage profits as a *difference* between the value of the product and that of the wages and means of production seemingly makes less sense than the reverse idea of the price of the product, an unknown of the equations, resulting from adding profits to the wages and to the value of the means of production. These 'appearances' are the very ones which, as we saw (par. 13), had misled Smith and the 'vulgar' political economists into thinking that profits and wages could be determined independently of one another – the same appearances that were overcome by Ricardo and Marx's measurement of value in terms of embodied labour. They have their source in the difficulty of grasping the interdependence of prices and can today be dispelled by the consideration of the *system* of price equations as distinct from the indeterminate individual price equation. (It was long after the times of Smith and Ricardo, or even of Marx, that it became possible for economists to think of the *system* of price equations and for the latter to reveal their implications for the constraint linking the real wage and the rate of profit.) Thus equations (6) reveal that once the real wage is given, the rate of profits is determined and that the two cannot change independently of one another.

But a reasoning that relies on theorems which abstract from the content of the problems analysed, cannot fully overcome the difficulty of grasping the effects of the interdependence of $(k+1)$ unknowns, and cannot therefore have the transparency of surplus equations like (3). Thus, e.g., the nature of profits as a residual had to be clarified by Sraffa in the first chapter of (1960) by showing how prices just sufficient to repay the wages and to replace the means of production, which are possible when no surplus product exists, *become contradictory* when that surplus is present: a point that would have been evident in equations (2) or (3), or the corresponding more general equations (8) or (10) below. A further, and perhaps more striking example of this lack of transparency is the sense of novelty which greeted the 'non-substitution theorem' already mentioned above (para. 8 and 15), the proposition, that is, that, in an economy like that of equations (6), the real wage is given irrespective of consumer's demand, when the rate of profits (rate of interest) is given – a proposition obvious from equations (2), (3), (8) or (10).

The transparency of surplus equations like (2) or (3) was ultimately due to what we referred to above as the 'surplus equations method' (para. 14). The surplus equation provides a 'picture': that of a *known* product to be divided between wages and profits; with the rate of profits originating from the distribution of the surplus of this product over wages, in proportion to the amount of capital. This 'picture' allowed a concrete mental representation of a highly abstract analysis: so that the dependence of the rate of profit on real wages could be *seen* 'at a glance', and the properties of the economic system associated with this basic relationship were under a correspondingly better grasp. Of course social product, necessary consumption and social capital are, in themselves, highly abstract notions. The mind can, however, fit them into a 'picture' and proceed to operate with them (as the mind of a child can with an abacus), as if they were concrete objects connected by the simple relations of the part and the whole.

The importance of this 'picture' should of course not be

confused with that of a mere didactic device, which could always be obtained by means of simplifying assumptions. This importance has to do with the command it allows the mind to obtain over purely abstract relations. It has therefore, ultimately to do with the possibility of advancing our knowledge and of achieving new results (cf. Garegnani, 1984, p. 312, n.38).

Naturally, reality need not be simple, and need not allow for a 'surplus equation', like (2) or (3), beyond the hypotheses necessary to validate the exchange of commodities according to the quantity of labour required for their production. In the next section we shall however indicate how, under our present assumptions regarding the wage rate, a determination of the rate of profits along the lines of the 'surplus equation method' becomes possible, provided we focus our attention on the 'integrated wage goods sector' of the economy, where the general rate of profit is in fact determined. We shall then see how an even simpler 'picture' becomes possible – in the shape of Sraffa's standard system – when, with him, we come to envisage the possibility that the rate of profits should become the independent variable of the system, to the extent to which, as we shall see in para. 23 below, wages are allowed to share in the surplus.

SECTION VI. THE SURPLUS-EQUATION METHOD: 'INTEGRATED WAGE-GOODS SECTOR' AND 'STANDARD SYSTEM'.

18. The determining role of the commodities entering the wage. Let us single out in system (6) the price equations of commodities $a, b, \ldots, h$, consisting of the wage goods $a, b, \ldots, g$, and of their direct and indirect means of production $(g+1), \ldots, h$. The definition of these commodities, h in number (where $h \leqslant k$), implies that, in the corresponding h price-equations, we shall find as unknowns only their h prices, plus the rate of profits r. It follows that these h equations, together with the last equation in system (6), defining the 'wage commodity' as the numéraire, will be sufficient to determine the rate of profits and the h prices independently of the remaining k–h price equations. It results therefore that once the level of the real wage is given, the general rate of profit will depend exclusively upon the technical conditions of production *of the wage goods and of their direct and indirect means of production* (on the origin of this result, cf. Garegnani, 1984, p. 313, n. 39).

19. The integrated wage-goods sector. Let us now look more closely at the particular part of the productive system which consists of those h industries taken in the particular proportions required in order directly and indirectly to reproduce the aggregate wages advanced to the workers for the year together with the means of production directly or indirectly required for that purpose. This part of the economy constitutes what may be called the 'vertically integrated sector of the wage-goods' or *integrated wage-goods sector* for short.

Let us express both the net yearly product of this sector and the wages paid in it in terms of Smith's 'labour commanded' standard, that is in terms of the quantity of labour which those aggregates of commodities can buy. In terms of this measure both product and wages will be known *before* the rate of profits and the individual relative prices are known. In fact the net product, being the yearly wages of the known number L of labourers employed in the economy will evidently 'command' L labour years. The wages paid in the sector, on the other hand, will command L_v labour years, L_v being the number of labourers required for the direct and indirect production of the 'necessary consumption' – also a known quantity since the real wage and the technical conditions of the direct and indirect

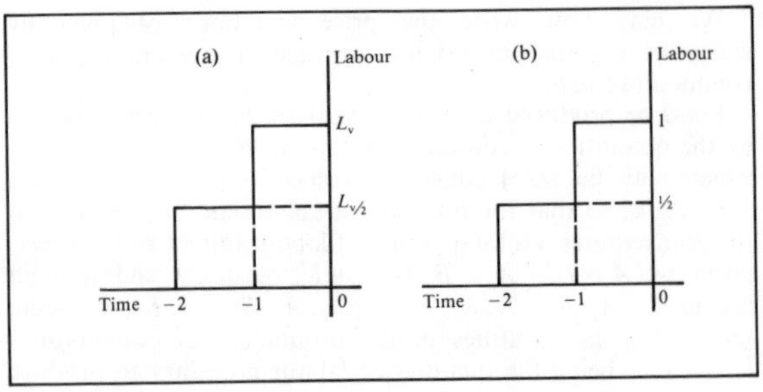

Figure 2 The quantities of 'dated labour' required for the production of the yearly aggregate of wage goods (section a) and the proportional distribution of labour overtime in the production of the wage commodity (section b).

production of its constituents are known (cf. the assumption of a single method of production discussed above, par. 3).

It follows that in the integrated wage-goods sector, the amount of profits in terms of 'commanded labour' constitutes what may be called a *surplus value* $(L - L_v)$ which is also known before the rate of profits and the relative prices are determined. Interestingly enough, this surplus value coincides numerically with Marx's own social surplus value s (since $L = v + s$ and $L_v = v$), though it differs from the latter because: (i) it is the surplus value of the wage-goods sector, and not that of the entire economy; (ii) it is expressed in terms of labour commanded, and not of labour embodied.

20. The rate of profits. When we proceed, as we must, from the *amount* of profits to the *rate* of profits, the obstacle we meet is that unlike the value of the product and the wages, the value of the means of production in the wage-goods sector, expressed in commanded labour, is not known independently of the rate of profits and of the individual relative prices. We might therefore seem unable to obtain a 'surplus equation' where the rate of profits is the only unknown (para. 17 above). The obstacle can however be overcome by the device of reducing the means of production to 'dated labour'.

A simple example will show how this view of capital can be applied to the means of production of the integrated wage-goods sector in order to obtain a 'surplus equation' determining the rate of profits. Consider an economy where wages consist exclusively of 'corn'. Corn is produced with one 'plough' per worker. The 'plough', which is entirely consumed during the year, is in turn produced by one unassisted worker. The L workers employed in the integrated wage-goods sector will accordingly have to be distributed half in (directly) producing the 'corn', and half in reproducing the 'plough'. The capital advanced for the direct production of corn during the year will consist of the wages of the agricultural workers *and* of the ploughs.

If we now consider that ploughs must have been produced during the year before the one in which corn is being produced, the capital used in the production of corn emerges as the wages of the two quantities of 'dated labour' shown in Figure 2a: $L_v/2$ labour years applied at moment (-2) for producing the 'ploughs', which are then used in the successive 'stage' of corn production, together with a further $L_v/2$ labour years applied at moment (-1) (we are assuming labour to be applied in the moment in which the wages for it are paid). Expressed in 'commanded labour' the wages, to which the entire capital of the integrated wage-goods sector has thus been reduced, will equal the corresponding quantities of dated labour, that is $L_v/2$ advanced at moment (-2) and $L_v/2$ advanced at moment (-1).

The rate of profits can then been seen to emerge from the distribution of the surplus value $L - L_v$, in proportion *both* to the wages advanced, and to the time for which they have been so advanced, account being taken of compound profits, that is

$$L - L_v = r\frac{L_v}{2} + 2r\frac{L_v}{2} + r^2\frac{L_v}{2} \qquad (7)$$

where the term $rL_v/2$ indicates the share of surplus value allotted to the capitalists advancing the wages paid at time (-1); and the term $2rL_v/2$, together with the compound profit term $r^2L_v/2$, indicates the share alloted to those paying the wages at time (-2). The rate of profits is the only unknown in (7). (For a general discussion of this representation of capital, cf. Garegnani, 1960, pp. 25–30.)

It is convenient at this point to divide both sides of equation (7) by L_r obtaining

$$\frac{L - L_v}{L_v} = r\frac{I}{2} + 2r\frac{I}{2} + r^2\frac{I}{2}. \qquad (8)$$

On the left of the equality sign we find, expressed in commanded labour, the amount of surplus value per worker in the integrated wage-goods sector. This amount is identical to Marx's rate of surplus value s/v. On the right of the equality sign we find instead a function expressing the amount of profits per worker, also expressed in commanded labour, which would be necessary in the sector in order to pay a rate of profits r. This function, which we may call the 'profits function' for short, depends purely on the *proportional* time distribution of the labour necessary to produce the wage commodity (see Figure 2b). It does not therefore depend on the *level* of the real wage: it depends only on the physical *composition* of the real wage and on the methods for the direct and indirect production of the wage-goods.

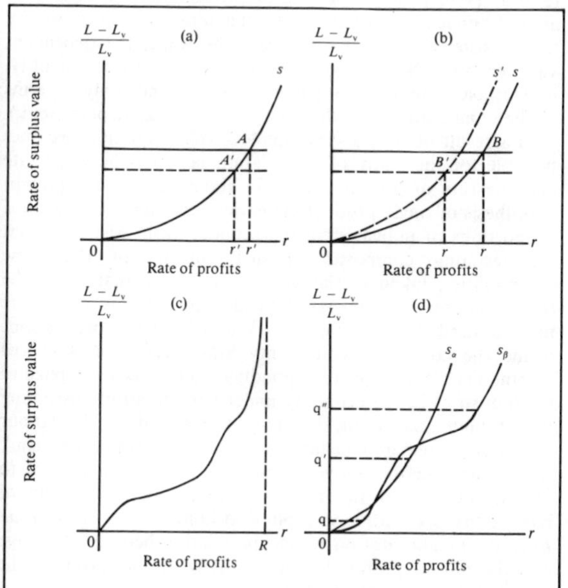

Figure 3 Determination of the rate of profits by means of the amount or rate of 'surplus value' and of the 'profits function' in the integrated wage goods sector. Section (a) considers the rise of a real wage of unchanged physical composition; section (b) the rise of a real wage of changed composition. Section (c) considers the shape of the 'profits function' when production is 'circular'; section (d) shows the possible shape of the 'profits function' corresponding to two different wage commodities α and β.

The 'profits function' has an important property which can be shown to hold with any kind of circulating capital, and also with fixed capital of constant efficiency (cf. Garegnani, 1984, p. 317, n. 45). It is zero when $r=0$ and it rises monotonically with r.

The solution of the 'surplus equation' can now be represented in the diagram of Figure 3a, where r is measured horizontally and the rate of surplus value is measured vertically. There we have the curve 0s representing the 'profits function', which rises monotonically from the origin. Furthermore, in the case of our example, where the reduction to labour can be completed in a finite number of steps, the 'profits curve' rises indefinitely *as r rises indefinitely*, as represented in Figure 3a. It will however more generally be the case that either a wage good or one of its direct and indirect means of production requires directly or indirectly itself in order to be produced and, accordingly, the reduction to labour cannot be completed in any finite number of steps. In this case, which may be called of 'circular production', the 'profits curve' rises indefinitely as the rate of profits approaches a 'maximum rate of profit' R, as in Figure 3c (cf. Garegnani 1973, p. 335–6). The rate of surplus value $(L - L_v)/L_v$ can on the other hand always be represented by a horizontal line. The level of the rate of profits which solves the equation will be that for which the 'profits curve' 0s cuts the surplus value line.

The fact that the 'profits curve' is rising monotonically ensures that the solution will be unique and positive for any positive rate of surplus value – that is, for any level of the real wage less than the product per head in the integrated wage-goods sector. Figure 3a makes it clear that this single positive rate of profit depends exclusively on two circumstances: (i) the rate of surplus value, and (ii) the proportional time-distribution of the labour necessary to produce the wage commodity, which determines the shape of the 'profits function' (taking the place of Marx's 'organic composition of capital', cf. para. 22 below).

The fact that the 'profits function' is an increasing function also clarifies a second set of properties of the system, pertaining to the relation between the wage and the rate of profits. A rise in the wage that leaves its commodity composition unchanged will decrease the rate of profits. This will be so because L_v will rise in the same proportion as the real wage rises and the rate of surplus value $(L/L_v) - 1$ will accordingly have to decrease. Its line will then intersect the unchanged 'profits function' for a lower rate of profits (cf. the shift from A to A' and from r to r' in Figure 3a).

The same conclusion can be seen to apply if the real wage changes in composition, but in such a way that it increases in one or more of its components with no decrease in any of the others. However, in order to see why the conclusion applies, it is convenient to shift our attention from Figure 3a, which relates to *rates* of surplus value $(L - L_v)L_v$, to Figure 3b, which refers instead to *total* surplus values $(L - L_v)$ in the integrated wage-goods sector as a whole. No point of the 'total profits curve' of Figure 3b will be shifted downwards, indeed all its points (except that for $r = 0$) will generally be shifted upwards because of the amount of profits to be paid on the wages for the labour required to produce the additional items of the aggregate real wages (the new 'total profits curve 0s could only remain unaffected in the unlikely case that the labour required for the additional items were all paid at the moment the production of such wage goods is completed). On the other hand, the aggregate surplus value $(L - L_v)$ will fall, because of the increase in L_v: the rate of profits will therefore fall, as shown by the shift from B to B' and from r to r' in Figure 3b.

However, when the composition of the real wage changes in

such a way that the quantity of some components rises while that of others falls, then the profits curve can change in any way whatever. In that case the rate of profits may also change in a direction opposite to that in which the rate of surplus value has changed, in line with what Marx saw as possible when the organic composition of social capital changes together with the real wage (cf. e.g. Marx, 1974b, p. 869). However, contrary to what Marx thought, it will not be possible independently of the rate of profits to order the different physical compositions of the social product, or of the wage commodity, according to the organic composition of the capital required and, therefore, according to their effect on the rate of profits, whatever the rate of surplus value. As Figure 3d shows, a composite wage commodity α, giving the profits curve $0s_\alpha$ would yield a higher rate of profits than the wage commodity β giving the profits curve $0s_\beta$ at the low rate of surplus value q, but a lower rate at the higher rate of surplus value q' and a higher one at the still higher rate of surplus value q'' (cf. para. 22 below).

21. Physical measurements also possible in the wage-goods sector. It may be noted at this stage that a measurement independent of the rate of profits alternative to labour commanded is also available for the magnitudes of the integrated wage-goods sector. The net output of the integrated wage-goods sector is physically homogeneous with the wages paid there, since both consist of the same composite wage-commodity. The amount of profits in the sector could therefore be obtained as the difference between two *physical* quantities of the wage commodity, and the rate of profit could be seen to arise from the distribution of this *surplus product* over the capital of the wage-goods sector, reduced to wages in the manner we have considered above and consisting of the same wage commodity.

The 'commanded labour' standard has however the advantage that in terms of it the product of the integrated wage-goods sector can continue to be expressed in the same units, and remains constant, when the real wage changes either in level or composition, in the way we saw above.

22. The determinants of the rate of profits. These properties of the wage-profits relation, made easily visible by surplus equations (7) and (8), are thus closer than we might perhaps have expected to Marx's conclusions on the matter. In particular, it is confirmed that the rate of profits depends on two circumstances, and two alone; the rate of surplus value s/v, and the proportion between means of production and labour. However, the correction of the error implicit in equation (3), modifies Marx's own specification of the second circumstance as the 'organic composition' of social capital, in two important respects.

In the first place the proportion of labour to means of production on which the rate of profits depends, is that of the integrated wage-goods sector, and not that of the whole economy, as Marx thought. This in turn implies that he was mistaken in believing that changes in the relative outputs of commodities could affect the rate of profits through variations in the proportion of labour to means of production in the economy as a whole, independently of any change in the real wage (cf. e.g. Marx 1894 p. 162: it may be noted here, how this flaw in Marx's analysis is repeated in recent works: cf. e.g. Mandel, 1975, p. v; Rowthorn, 1976, pp. 62–3). The same general deficiency implies that Marx was incorrect when he implied that changes in the technical conditions of production of 'luxuries', or of their specific means of production, could affect the rate of profits because of the connected variations in the organic composition of social capital.

In the second place, the proportion of labour to means of production (whether in an individual sector or in the economy as a whole) cannot be expressed by the ratio c/v and must instead be expressed by the proportionate distribution over time of the labour necessary to produce the wage commodity or, of course, by the physical quantities of the several constituents of capital. We have seen above (para. 20) one consequence of this in the different sign which the effect on r of a given change in the physical composition of the wage commodity will have at different levels of the rate of surplus value. This is of course a consequence of the fact that it is impossible to measure capital by a single magnitude independent of distribution, a fact which, as is well known, deeply affects the validity of the dominant theories.

23. Sraffa's standard system. Sraffa's 'standard system' provides a similar 'surplus equation method' for analysing the relations between wages and the rate of profits, under hypotheses regarding the determination of distribution which are partly different from those we have considered here.

The classical authors (in particular, Smith and Marx) had admitted or implied that normal wages could include an element of surplus, when the surplus is conceived as the entire excess of the product over the *subsistence* of workers. However, it was also implied that the circumstances determining the *division of the surplus* between wages and profits would act, so to speak, from the side of wages (as e.g. in the case of trade unions managing to bargain for a real wage above subsistence), and would therefore require no modification in the treatment of real wage (including its surplus element) as a datum or independent variable in the 'core' of the theory. Instead, Sraffa suggests that the division of the surplus might be influenced by circumstances acting from the side of the rate of profits: he suggests that the rate of profits is susceptible of being determined by the money rate of interest (Sraffa, 1960, p. 33). The rate of profits can then appear as an independent variable, up to the maximum limit set by the subsistence wage. In that case the wage, the dependent variable, may be envisaged as an abstract value quantity, measurable in terms of any commodity and not only in terms of the commodities on which wages are actually spent (ibid.).

As a result of this, a very simple surplus equation becomes possible for the study of the relation between the wage rate and the rate of profits. As Sraffa shows, under our present hypothesis of single-product industries, a unique set of positive proportions of industries in the economy will exist such that the resulting composite product consists of the same commodities, taken in the same proportions, that are to be found among the means of production of this composite product itself (Sraffa, 1960, chs IV and V). These proportions define the composite commodity Sraffa calls the 'standard commodity'. When the corresponding multipliers are applied to the industries in the economy under consideration – assuming the absolute size of the latter as represented by the labour employed to remain constant – we have the 'standard system'. If we then use the above freedom acquired with respect to wages, by measuring them in terms of the standard commodity, we shall have a physical homogeneity between *all three* the magnitudes on which the relation between the wage and the rate of profits depends, namely the net product, the wages and the means of production.

Let us now choose as the unit for expressing the physical quantities of the standard commodity, the *net product* of the standard system. Let us also choose the labour employed in the economy, and therefore in the standard system, as our unit of labour, so that the wage rate w, assumed to be paid *post-factum*, coincides with total wages. We may then write

$$w = 1 - rM \quad (9)$$

where M is the amount of standard commodity used as means of production in the standard system. The quantity of M is however the reciprocal of R, Sraffa's standard ratio: the ratio, that is, between the net product (our physical unit for the standard commodity) and the means of production of the standard system. As a result, equation (9) can be written as

$$w = 1 - r/R. \quad (10)$$

This linear relation between r and w will apply to the real economy with its actual outputs as soon as wages are measured in terms of the standard commodity. (Indeed the price equations of the real system will then differ from those of the standard system only because of the different proportions in which the equations are taken. What the Standard system thus does, is to provide a 'surplus equation method' of arriving at that relation, with a corresponding 'picture' of the relations of distribution (para. 15 above). In Sraffa's own words, the purpose of the standard system is 'to give transparency to the system and render visible what was hidden' (1960, p. 23).

24. CONCLUSIONS. In this essay we have been concerned with introducing the basic elements of the approach to distribution and relative prices which had been developing for about two centuries from William Petty to Adam Smith, Ricardo and Marx. A characteristic phenomenon which has not perhaps yet been studied sufficiently is indeed the way in which this approach has been 'submerged and forgotten' (Sraffa, 1960, p. v), rather than criticized and shown to be deficient. Its abandonment came as a slow process which occupied the half century following the death of Ricardo and was largely one of progressive obfuscation. Later, this process was clinched, so to speak, by interpretations of the work of the classical economists as a primitive, incomplete version of the later marginalist theories. The failure to draw the distinction we saw in section III above, between the classical conception of a 'proportion' between supply and demand, and the later conception of demand-and-supply functions helped in this direction (cf. e.g. Bharadwaj, 1978, pp. 264–5 and Garegnani, 1983, pp. 312–13; also cf. the 'canonical classical model mentioned in par. 3 above).

Our purpose, which was confined to providing an introduction to this approach, has led us to focus on three main issues. The first concerned the analytic structure of the theory and the 'short chains of deductive reasoning' which deeply differentiate it from later theory. The second concerned the problem of the 'measurement' of aggregates of commodities, which is peculiar to this approach and explains the role which Ricardo and Marx's labour theory of value has played in it. (This point acquires some additional interest when we remember that the marginalist criticism of the classical approach, in so far as it occurred at all, was focused on that value theory, and on the fact that commodities do not exchange according to the quantity of labour embodied as if Ricardo or Marx had ignored it: a leader of this kind of criticism was Böhm-Bawerk, 1889, pp. 353–62; 367–8.) The third and final issue concerned the continuity between the work of the classical economists and the contemporary work of Sraffa and other authors working along the same lines.

Thus, the introductory purpose of this essay explains why it concentrates on the analytic structure of the theory and on the problem of relative prices to the exclusion of the problems of distribution proper (except for what we saw in Part I), accumulation and aggregate demand together with their links with monetary theory. The same purpose explains the simplifications which we have used for our discussion, such as the hypothesis that only one method exists for the production of each commodity (cf. however para. 2 above) and, for most of the essay, the assumptions of circulating capital, no joint production and free natural resources. For these questions the reader may turn to the classical authors themselves and to the already extensive recent literature associated with the resumption of the classical approach.

PIERANGELO GAREGNANI

See also QUANTITY OF CAPITAL.

BIBLIOGRAPHY

Besides the references given in the essay, a useful first bibliography will be found in Roncaglia (1978), 151–71.

Bharadwaj, K. 1978. The subversion of classical analysis: Alfred Marshall's early writing on value. *Cambridge Journal of Economics* 2, September 253–71.

Böhm-Bawerk, E. von. 1884. *Kapital und Kapitalzins. Trans as Capital and Interest.* Reprinted New York: Kelley, 1962.

Casarosa, C. 1978. A new formulation of the Ricardian system. *Oxford Economic Papers* 30(1), March, 38–63.

Eatwell, J. 1977. The irrelevance of returns to scale in Sraffa's analysis. *Journal of Economic Literature* 15(1), March, 61–8.

Garegnani, P. 1960. *Il capitale nelle teorie della distribuzione*. Milan: Giuffrè.

Garegnani, P. 1970. Heterogeneous capital, the production function and the theory of distribution. *Review of Economic Studies* 37(3), July, 407–36.

Garegnani, P. 1973. 'Nota matematica' for 'Beni capitali eterogeni, la funzione della produzione e la teoria della distribuzione'. In *Prezzi relativi e distribuzione del reddito*, ed. P. Sylos-Labini, Turin: Boringhieri, 1973. (This 'Mathematical Note' is also available in English in the Marshall Library of the Economics of the University of Cambridge.)

Garegnani, P. 1978–9. Notes on consumption, investment and effective demand. *Cambridge Journal of Economics*, Pt I, 2(4), December 1978, 335–53; Pt II, 3(1), March 1979 63–82.

Garegnani, P. 1983. The classical theory of wages and the role of demand schedules in the determination of relative prices. *American Economic Review Papers and Proceedings* 73, May, 309–13.

Garegnani, P. 1984. Value and distribution in the classical economists and Marx. *Oxford Economic Papers* 36(2), May, 291–325.

Harrod, R.F. 1961. Review of P. Sraffa, *Production of Commodities by Means of Commodities. Economic Journal.*

Hicks, J.R. 1976. Revolutions in economics. In *Method and Appraisal in Economics*, ed. J.S. Latsis, Cambridge: Cambridge University Press.

Hicks, J.R. and Hollander, S. 1977. Mr. Ricardo and the moderns. *Quarterly Journal of Economics* 91(3), August, 351–69.

Mandel, E. 1975. *Late Capitalism.* London: New Left Books.

Marshall, A. 1920. *Principles of Economics*. 8th edn. Reprinted London: Macmillan, 1949.

Marx, K. 1867. *Capital*, Vol. I. London: Lawrence & Wishart, 1954.

Marx, K. 1894. *Capital*, Vol. III. London: Lawrence & Wishart, 1974.

Marx, K. 1905–10. *Theories of Surplus Value*. 3 vols, London: Lawrence & Wishart, 1969, 72.

Meek, R.L. 1977. *Smith, Marx and After*. London: Chapman & Hall.

Morishima, M. 1973. *Marx's Economics: A Dual Theory of Value and Growth*. Cambridge: Cambridge University Press.

Myrdal, G. 1932. *The Political Element in the Development of Economic Theory*. Trans. London: Routledge, 1953.

Pasinetti, L.L. 1965. A new theoretical approach to the problems of economic growth. In *Semaine d'étude sur le rôle de l'analyse économétrique dans la formation de plans de developement*, Rome: Ex Aedibus Academicis in Civitate Vaticana.

Ricardo, D. 1951–73. *The Works and Correspondence of David Ricardo*. Ed. P. Sraffa with the collaboration of M.H. Dobb, Cambridge: Cambridge University Press for the Royal Economic Society.

Roncaglia, A. 1978. *Sraffa and the Theory of Prices*. New York: Wiley.

Rowthorn, B. 1976. Late capitalism. *New Left Review* 98, August.

Samuelson, P.A. 1961. A new theorem on non-substitution. In *Money, Growth and Methodology and Other Essays in Economics; In Honor of Johan Akerman*, ed. V. Hegeland, Lund: CWK Gleerup. Reprinted in P.A. Samuelson, *Collected Scientific Papers*, Vol. I, Cambridge, Mass.: MIT Press, 1966.

Samuelson, P.A. 1971. Understanding the Marxian notion of exploitation: a summary of the so-called transformation problem between Marxian values and competitive prices. *Journal of Economic Literature* 9, 339–431.

Samuelson, P.A. 1978. The canonical classical model of political economy. *Journal of Economic Literature* 16(4), December 1415–34.

Schefold, B. 1985. Sraffa and applied economics. *Political Economy – Studies in the Surplus Approach* 1(1), 17–40.

Schumpeter, J.A. 1954. *History of Economic Analysis*. New York: Oxford University Press.

Sen, A.K. 1978. On the labour theory of value: some methodological issues. *Cambridge Journal of Economics*, June, 175–180.

Smith, A. 1776. *An Inquiry into the Nature and Causes of the Wealth of Nations*. Vol. 1. London: Dent & Sons, 1950.

Sraffa, P. 1951. Introduction to *The Works and Correspondence of David Ricardo*, Vol. I. Cambridge: Cambridge University Press.

Sraffa, P. 1960. *Production of Commodities by Means of Commodities*. Cambridge: Cambridge University Press.

Sraffa, P. 1961. Production of commodities: a comment. *Economic Journal*.

Stigler, G.J. 1958. Ricardo and the 93% labour theory of value. *American Economic Review*, June.

surplus value. Profitability regulates the health of capitalist society. In this regard, Marx identifies *two* distinct sources of profit: profit on transfer (or even forcible appropriation) of wealth, which dominates the Mercantilist period; and profit on production of surplus value, which comes into prominence under Industrial Capital. Since trading activities can be linked to either source or profit, it is useful to begin with trading profits.

Individual trading profit arises whenever a commodity is re-sold at a profit. To the merchant who acquires a commodity for £100 and resells it for £200, it is his entrepeneurial ability to 'buy cheap and sell dear' which determines his gain (which covers trading costs and profit). But from the perspective of the system as a whole, the chain of transactions from initial to final sale simply serves to share out the total selling price among the various transactors, including the merchant. This holds true whether or not the transactions are fair or unfair, free or forced.

The merchant's gain is his 'balance of trade surplus'. But it is crucial to distinguish between a situation in which the overall 'balance of trade' is zero because the merchant's surplus is offset by a corresponding deficit somewhere else in the chain; and one in which the total balance is positive because the merchant's gain is merely his particular share in some overall surplus *whose origin therefore lies outside of trading activities themselves*. The former case corresponds to profit on the transfer of wealth, and the latter to profit on the production of surplus value. We will consider each in turn.

PROFIT ON TRANSFER OF WEALTH. A system-wide profit on the transfer of wealth appears mysterious because the surplus of the merchant does not seem to be counterbalanced by any corresponding deficit. Suppose merchant capitalists barter goods costing them £100 for those of a non-capitalist community or tribe, which they then resell for £200. This swap leaves the combined wealth of the participants unchanged. Yet it gives rise to a profit on the capitalist side without any corresponding loss on the non-capitalist side, so that a net profit appears *for the system as a whole*. How is that possible?

The tribe's participation in trade may be motivated by fear, by ceremonial considerations, or by the hope of gaining objects which are socially more desirable. In all cases, it is a social assessment which stands behind the trade. But for the merchants, the important thing is that the tribal objects they acquire can be resold for a monetary gain. In Marx's terminology, the tribe is operating within the simple commodity circuit C–C', in which one set of use-values C is exchanged for another useful set C'; while the merchants are operating within the capital circuit M–C–C'–M', where a sum of money $M = £100$ is ultimately transformed into a larger sum $M' = £200$, through the exchange of one set of use-values C for a more valuable set C'.

The above circuits form the two poles of the transaction. However, because only one of these poles is assessed in monetary terms, any monetary gain recorded there has no counterpart at the other pole. A net monetary gain can thus appear for the system as a whole. Note that this would not be the case if both poles were treated in the *same* terms. If the tribe's goods were valued at their final selling price of £200, it would be obvious that the tribe had exchanged a set of commodities worth £200 for another worth only £100, thereby losing in monetary value exactly as much as the merchants gain. In the end, it is *inequality of exchange* which underlies profit on transfer of wealth (profit on alienation) (Marx, 1863, ch. 1).

Interestingly, enough, neoclassical economics tends to treat profit as simply profit on alienation. This is why the analysis of 'pure exchange' occupies so prominent a position within the theory. For instance, a classic illustration depicts a prisoner-of-war camp in which all prisoners receive equal (Red Cross) packages of commodities. An entrepreneur among the prisoners then mediates a more desirable distribution of the total mass of commodities, a part of which he pockets as his own reward. Since the other prisoners all gain in terms of their respective subjective (and hence non-comparable) utilities, that portion of their collective endowment which is gained by the entrepreneur is not treated as their loss. On the other hand, for the entrepreneur it is precisely this transferred wealth which is counted as his profit. With one pole of the transaction in subjective utility and the other in material gain, profit seems to be created out of thin air. Instead of attempting to dissolve this false appearance, neoclassical economics concentrates on presenting profit as the just reward of the capitalist class (Alchian and Allen, 1969, chs. 1–4).

PROFIT ON PRODUCTION OF SURPLUS VALUE. With the rise of industrial capital, it became increasingly clear that industrial profit was quite different from profit on alienation. The latter was dependent on trade and unequal exchange, while the former was tied to production, wage labour, and apparently equal exchange (Meek, 1956, Ch. 1). It is exactly in order to locate the fundamental difference between the two that Marx insists on explaining industrial profit even when all exchanges are essentially equal (Marx, 1867, Ch. 5).

Marx begins by noting that every society must somehow direct the labour time at its disposal toward the production of the goods and services necessary to sustain and reproduce itself. In the case of class societies, the reproduction of the ruling class requires that it be able to extract a surplus product from the subordinate classes. This means that every ruling class must somehow get the subordinate classes to work beyond the time necessary to produce their own means of consumption, for it is this *surplus labour time* which creates the requisite surplus product (*see* EXPLOITATION).

The same basic process operates in capitalist society, but it is hidden under the surface of exchange relations and money magnitudes. To show this, Marx starts by assuming that the money price of each commodity is proportional to the total abstract labour time socially necessary for its production (its labour value). In the case of wage-labour, this means that money wages are proportional to the number of hours (v) workers must put in a given day in order to produce their collective daily means of consumption. Under the above circumstances, all commodities, including labour power (the capacity to work), exchange in proportion to the labour time socially necessary for their reproduction. All exchanges are therefore equal in a fundamental social sense, so that (for the moment) profit on alienation is ruled out of consideration.

During the production process a particular quantity of means of production (raw materials and machines) is used up each day. The abstract labour time (c) which was previously required to reproduce them is thereby transferred to the product. If we add to this the labour time worked by workers in a given day (l), the resultant sum ($c + l$) represents the total abstract labour time socially necessary to produce the daily product.

If exchange is proportional to labour times, then the price of the total social product is proportional to $c+l$. But the corresponding money cost of producing this product is proportional to $c+v$, since c represents the abstract labour cost of the means of production used up and v represents the corresponding costs of the workers employed. It follows from this that aggregate profits will exist only if $c+l>c+v$, which implies $l>v$. In other words, when prices are proportional to labour values (equal exchange), profit is the direct monetary expression of surplus labour time $s=l-v>0$. This surplus labour time, performed by workers who produce commodities for capitalists (i.e. who produce commodity-capital), is what Marx calls *surplus value*.

Even when exchange is no longer proportional to labour value, the connection between profit and surplus value continues to hold, but in a more complex manner. In effect, when prices deviate from proportionality with labour values, this can give rise to transfers of value from one set of transactors to another. Now total profits can depart from proportionality with total surplus value – even though in the aggregate the gains and losses due to transfers of value exactly cancel out! This apparent paradox, which has long bedevilled the extensive literature on the so-called Transformation Problem, is easily resolved once one recognizes that the profit is a measure which only picks up a portion of the overall transfers of value involved. By definition, aggregate profit is simply the difference between the price of aggregate output and the price of that portion of this output which corresponds to the *flows* of commodities used up as 'inputs' into production, either directly as means of production or indirectly as wage goods. Thus, insofar as value is transferred between total output and these particular inputs, what capitalist producers' as a whole may gain in revenues through a higher selling price is at the same time what they thereby lose through higher input costs. Total profits are therefore unchanged, because feedback between the price of outputs and the prices of these particular inputs prevents any overall transfer of surplus value. But the same cannot be said for those transfers involving the remaining portions of aggregate output, which enter respectively into the capital stock of the firm (as inventories, plant and equipment) or into the possession of the capitalists themselves as consumption goods. In the former case, any transfers are reflected in the balance sheets of the firms and are at best only partially transmitted to costs; whereas in the latter case, any gain in profits through a higher selling price of capitalist consumption goods is reflected in a corresponding loss in the personal accounts of the capitalists themselves, rather than in increases in business costs. Because the measure of profit only picks up a subset of the value transfers, total profit can end up departing from proportionality with surplus value – within strict limits. *This is merely the same principle which underlies mercantilist profit*. It was well known to Marx himself (Shaikh, 1984).

FURTHER ISSUES. First of all, it is important to note that only at an abstract level of analysis is money profit (with or without the equalization of the rate of profit) the sole expression of surplus value. At a more concrete level, surplus value appears as producers' profits, gross trading margins, rents, interest, taxes, and dividends. Similarly, one can develop the analysis to account for profits across industries, across firms within industries, across regions, and across nations. Contained within this movement from the abstract to the concrete is a subtle and powerful theory of competition and pricing, on whose basis this analysis can be developed (*see* MARKET VALUE).

Secondly, our earlier discussion of profit on alienation should alert us to the fact that surplus value is not the only source of profit. This understanding is one of the great strengths of Marx's analysis of the determinants of profit. It is also an important historical and empirical issue in its own right. Even in the modern capitalist world, where surplus value is clearly the dominant basis for profit, one must be careful to account for transfers of wealth and value from non-capitalist spheres (petty commodity and non-commodity production) to capitalist ones – particularly in analysing the so-called Third World.

Thirdly, it should be noted that the very concept of the *transfer* of wealth and value is predicated on a distinction between those activities which produce the goods and services (use-values) comprising the annual wealth, and those which serve to transfer this wealth from one set of hands to another. This distinction is in turn merely part of a more general one between production and non-production activities. In the latter camp we find not only the familiar category of personal consumption activities, but also the classical notion of *social consumption* activities such as those involved in the exchanging of goods, services and money; general administrative activities in both the private and public sectors; and various other social activities such as defence, etc. Production uses up use-values in order to produce more use-values. Personal and social consumptions use up use-values in order to achieve some other desired end. As such, the distinction between them has nothing to do, *per se*, with other distinctions such as those between necessary/unnecessary, desirable/undesirable, and basic/non-basic activities. More importantly, the distinction between production and non-production activities has profound implications for the manner in which the wealth of capitalist nations is measured and analyzed (Shaikh, 1978, section IV.C).

Fourthly, within the general category of production activities, a further difference arises between those which produce surplus value (i.e. produce surplus labour for a capitalist employer), and those which either produce value (petty commodity producers) or produce use-values for direct use (households, non-commodity producing communities). Though all these labours are productive of social wealth, only the first is directly productive of surplus value. This is why Marx singles out this particular form of labour as that labour which is productive-of-capital – i.e. which is 'productive labour' from the point of view of capital. As a corollary to the above, it is then necessary to distinguish between the rate of exploitation (which applies to all workers employed by capital) and the rate of surplus value (which is the rate of exploitation of only 'productive labour', since it alone produces surplus value), (Marx, 1867, Appendix, part II).

Lastly, it is important to recognize that the preceding categories interact in complex ways. For example, surplus value is simply the difference between the length of the working day (l) of productive workers, and that portion of it (v) which is required to produce the commodities they and their families consume. But the quantity of social labour time represented by v is not at all the same as the total social labour time required to reproduce productive workers, because the latter generally includes household and community labour involved in the reproduction of labour-power. To the extent that these non-capitalist labours are responsible for the bulk of the use-values consumed by productive workers, only a small amount of *commodities* will be involved. But since capitalists need only pay workers just enough to acquire the commodity portion of their standard of living, v will be low and s correspondingly high. Then, as capitalist production erodes village and/or household production, commodities will begin to comprise an ever greater portion of the standard of living of workers even as this overall standard may itself decline. To the capitalists, workers will be getting progressively more 'expensive' as their commodity requirements rise. Yet the workers themselves may be getting ever poorer if their overall standard of living is declining. Over certain periods, a rising real wage is perfectly compatible with a falling standard of living – as the history of many a developing capitalist country demonstrates. All this goes to show that no analysis of a concrete social formation can afford to ignore the *interrelationships* between profit on transfer of wealth and profit on production of surplus value, between production and non-production activities, and between capitalist and non-capitalist labour.

ANWAR SHAIKH

See also MARX, KARL HEINRICH; ORGANIC COMPOSITION OF CAPITAL.

BIBLIOGRAPHY

Alchian A.A. and Allen, W.A. 1969. *Exchange and Production Theory in Use*. Belmont, California: Wadsworth.

Marx, K. 1863. *Theories of Surplus Value*, Part I. Moscow: Progress Publishers.

Marx, K. 1867. *Capital*, Vol. I. London: Penguin, 1976.

Meek, R.L. 1956. *Studies in the Labour Theory of Value*. New York: Monthly Review Press.

Shaikh, A. 1978. An introduction to the history of crisis theories. In *U.S. Capitalism in Crisis*. New York: Union for Radical Politcal Economics.

Shaikh, A. 1984. The transformation from Marx to Sraffa. In *Ricardo, Marx, Sraffa*, ed. E. Mandel, London: Verso.

survey research. Getting facts, expectations, reasons or attitudes by interviewing people has a long history, but scientific survey research required three innovations which only came in the 20th century – scientific probability sampling, controlled question stimuli and answer categorization, and multivariate analysis of the rich resulting data sets. Textbooks abound (Moser and Kalton, 1971; Lansing and Morgan, 1971; Sonquist and Dunkelberg, 1977; Rossi et al., 1983).

Interview surveys were conducted in Germany in the last century on such things as the attitudes of workers in factories (Oberschall, 1964). But political concerns overwhelmed scientific interests, and objectivity was soon lost. Later, mostly early in this century, surveys in England and France documented the plight of the poor, usually those in urban slums as a result of the industrial revolution. Soon after that, surveys of income and expenditures started appearing, and by 1935 it was possible to produce an annotated list of 1500 family living studies in 52 countries (Williams and Zimmerman, 1935). Starting in the 1940s a rapid expansion of surveys was driven by concerns about measuring unemployment, establishing weights for cost-of-living indexes, estimating income elasticities for various expenditure types, studying saving and wealth, and investigating markets for consumer goods (International Labour Office, 1961; Glock, 1967).

SAMPLING. Inferring anything about some population requires some kind of unbiased sampling, not necessarily random, but surely with a known probability of selection for every eligible unit. Since people do not stay in one spot, and there are seldom complete lists that can serve as a 'sampling frame', the innovation that allowed progress was the notion of sampling geography – occupied dwellings – and trying to associate everyone with some place where he or she lived during most of the interviewing period. Since it is expensive to travel, or even get detailed sampling materials for every place, clustering of samples reduced the information per interview, but increased it per dollar. Clustering usually means multi-stage selection of increasingly smaller chunks of space, ending with a dwelling where all occupying families may be included (Kish, 1965). But areas are not selected at random. One can do better than random by arranging areas at each stage in systematic order and using a random start and an interval – a process called stratification, which gains precision at no cost and with no bias. A final sophistication and improvement involves controls beyond simple stratification which can further reduce the probability of inadvertent concentrations.

Even the use of telephone for sampling involves innovation. Random digit dialling allows the inclusion of unlisted numbers, but requires stepwise procedures for avoiding ranges of numbers with few or no operating telephones in private households. And adjustments for or separate inclusion of those without telephones may be called for. There is less final clustering at the block level, but otherwise clustering and stratification is possible.

INTERVIEWING. The second breakthrough after sampling was careful, reproducible procedures for uniform stimuli (questions and introductions) and controlled categorization of responses (Kahn and Cannell, 1965; Oppenheim, 1966; Turner and Martin, 1984). The development of fixed questions, asked word for word, and central office coding of verbatim answers allows potentially reproducible results, and studies of change unsullied by changes in categorization procedures. (One can recode a sample of the earlier protocols with the new coding staff to be sure.) Of course, this requires careful pre-testing and development, and there is an extensive body of research literature on the differences in responses one gets with different question wording, question order, interviewer training or even different survey organizations. Furthermore, once questions have been tested and used, and codes established, it is tempting, particularly with the more factual items, to allow the interviewer or respondent to check boxes. With mail questionnaires the pressure to use precoded categories and check boxes is ever greater. The cost is, of course, lack of control over the coding process, since it is being done by many different interviewers or still more varied respondents, with no chance to review or re-do it. A quality-control process for check coding is customary in survey organizations, even for check boxes where it only picks up mechanical errors (Zarkovich, 1966).

COMPUTERS. The third and final crucial breakthrough was of course the computer, which allows the rich complex matrix of information elicited in an interview to be analysed. Parallel with the explosion of computer capability has been development of statistical analysis procedures to take advantage of the many more degrees of freedom with thousands of interviews rather than a few years of a time series (O'Muircheartaigh and Payne, 1977). There was a relatively rapid movement from tables to multiple regression to recursive path models (though little use of structural equation systems). Categorical predictors were handled without elaborate scaling analysis by the use of dichotomous (dummy) variables, and categorical dependent variables by log linear analysis. The basic impossibility of separating the effects of age, year of birth and year of history for their effects led to various (imperfect) 'solutions'. The need to estimate things when not all the relevant group was measured (selection bias) led to (again imperfect) adjustments for (and estimates of) the selection bias.

The computer also allowed improvements in processing and even in interviewing. Direct data entry allows checking for inconsistencies and wild codes immediately, reduces transcription errors and allows long records immediately without merging decks of IBM cards. Computer-assisted telephone interviewing goes even further and helps the interviewer to move properly through complex sequences and can also catch inconsistencies and wild codes instantly. It opens up possibilities for complex interactive interviews which can cycle back when necessary, or introduce information or insights to elicit reactions to them.

Computer data files are also increasingly transferrable and usable by researchers for secondary analysis. The Interuniversity Consortium for Political and Social Research at the University of Michigan distributes free to its member institutions a vast archive of survey data in the social sciences, and the Census has vastly expanded its facilities for distributing data from its collections. The Roper Collection at Williams is largely attitudinal surveys. Procedures for transferring data files and dictionaries from one software to another are appearing; for example, between SPSS and OSIRIS.

PROGRESS AND PROBLEMS IN ANALYSIS. Survey data by age groups (and hence birth cohorts), repeated in later surveys, and even enriched by panels following the same individuals as they aged, did not solve the problem of disentangling the effects of age, year of birth and period of history, since any one is a linear function of the other two. Better data plus some assumptions helped, but the results proved sensitive to which assumptions, and the solution probably lies in direct measurement of the various things thought to be represented by age, or year of birth, or year of history.

Another analysis problem was generically called 'selection bias'. Any sampling statistician knows that if a sample uses different probabilities of selection for different people, unweighted estimates can have bias except when a model happens to be perfectly specified. If the probabilities are known, that bias can be eliminated simply and for all problems by weighting each case by the inverse of its probability of falling into the sample. If some individuals have no chance of inclusion, then in principle they would have infinite weights (we can say nothing about them). But in intermediate cases where there is some stochastic selection process, various methods have been proposed for estimating the probability of inclusion and (with proper attention to distributions of the errors) introducing it into the model, both to reduce bias and to test for the significance of the selection bias (Chamberlain, 1978; Heckman, 1979).

The problem, of course, is to find predictors of inclusion in the sample that are not also the variables in the explanatory model. And if the selection bias adjustments are small and insignificant, that may only mean that we were not able to model the selection process well. Sometimes selection is clearly endogenous, as when some women, presumably different from others, decide not to work for pay.

A third and perhaps most crucial problem of all arose, interestingly enough, only when we had dynamic panel data and sought to untangle causal effects across time. It seemed tempting to think that looking at change over time for each individual would allow us to eliminate many interpersonal differences that plagued cross-section analysis. We could then ask what the effect of events or conditions at one point in time was on subsequent changes, events or conditions.

The introduction of panel (reinterview) data seemed to open up vast new possibilities for analysis, reducing the amount of interpersonal difference to be accounted for, but it did not really allow clean and simple estimation of effects across time. As soon as we pooled observations in order to estimate effects for populations, we found that persistent interpersonal differences confounded our interpretation of the effects.

Relations between a state or event at one time and a state or event at a later time could occur in four ways: 1. Negatively, but with no causal implications, if there were measurement errors or random shocks. 2. Positively, also without causal inference, if there were persistent interpersonal differences. Moving is correlated with moving again later, because some people just like to move, and just adjusting for age doesn't account for all the differences in propensity to move. 3. Negatively, with causal implications, if an adaptive act reduced the need for further action. A better job may reduce the likelihood of changing again. 4. Positively, showing real effects, if scarring of unemployment or seniority in job tenure made the same state (unemployed or employed) more likely later on.

Sophisticated procedures for attempting to sort out the reasons behind intertemporal relations have been proposed by Heckman and by Chamberlain, both methods requiring multiple waves of data. (Heckman, 1981; Chamberlain, 1984).

Elsewhere you can read about selection bias, about state-dependence and heterogeneity (true and false autocorrelation), about log-linear models and path analysis and age–period–cohort problems. A combination of computer power to make estimates iteratively when there is no analytic solution, and of models which call for the simultaneous combination of multiple measures (confirmatory factor analysis) with estimation of relationships and of error components has led to increasingly complex models and directed attention to issues of robustness and to the importance of better data.

SUBSTANTIVE CONTRIBUTIONS. What are surveys good for substantively, and why not just use available micro data from files and records?

Records tend to be narrow, limited, often inaccessible. Only an individual can provide a coherent picture of the various connections with other individuals, employers, financial institutions, a dwelling and its environment, as well as interpretations of the past, expectations about the future and reasons (however biased or defensive) for decisions. People can move in and out of records, so that longer-term analysis of change using records is often difficult. Even Social Security records omit some income, deal with individuals not their families and provide little related information. Much of the early development of surveys was by sociologists and involved an extensive concern with attitudes and perceptions. Economists, with a much larger set of data from other sources, were slower to come to the conviction that better data would be worth the cost.

Economic surveys tend to focus on what appear at first to be hard data, but soon turn out to have many of the same conceptual and measurement problems. For example, an early driving concern as the United States was going through the great depression of the 1930s and its aftermath, was the measurement of unemployment. But this turned out to require measuring just who was really in the labour force, and deciding what to do about people on temporary layoff, or who wanted more work than they could get, or who, like teachers, had the summer off. It also led to a complex sample design with overlapping reinterviews which eliminated or at least averaged out a curious tendency for people on subsequent reinterviews to be less and less likely to call themselves unemployed. The Census uses a very narrow and explicit set of questions about employment status in order to minimize the measurement error.

Even such apparently simple facts as home ownership turn out to be frequently ambiguous, with titles tied up in probate, mixed with a cooperative or condominium arrangement, owned by a temporarily absent family member.

Survey data are used in the first instance for descriptive purposes, then to estimate static relationships, but finally to attempt to estimate more dynamic relationships starting with initial state-subsequent change relations. The ultimate payoff from the availability of such data would appear to be from using them in simulation models to spell out the system-dynamics of socio-economic systems. So far the quantity and quality of behavioural data and of the funding and development of simulation capacities have restricted this development. But it seems likely that ultimately a coherent and cooperative programme will develop in which the needs of the system analysts will help set the agenda for empirical survey research on behaviour, and the kinds of analysis done on those data, while the data people will advise on revisions of the system models.

SOME HISTORY. National sample surveys in economics got their first impetus, funding and concerns with accuracy from issues of unemployment and inflation. The range of uncertainty before World War II about the percentage unemployed was substantial. Inflation raises questions of proper weighting of the different prices, in proportion to the fraction of family incomes spent on each item, and hence calls for expenditure surveys. And economists have always been interested in saving because it can reduce inflation and encourage investment and progress. It was partly concern over what people would do with their accumulated war bonds after World War II that led to the annual surveys of consumer finances, conducted by The Institute for Social Research at the University of Michigan for the Board of Governors of the Federal Reserve System. Surveys made it quite clear that there would be no mass attempt to cash the bonds when the war was over.

Repeated cross-sections can reveal trends and change, but with higher sampling variances than the more dynamic micro data available from retrospective (memory) or from reinterviews and panel studies. Measurement of saving adequately probably requires reinterviews. Some reinterviews were built into the Surveys of Consumer Finances. The Current Population Surveys have a pattern of overlapping reinterviews, used not to produce change data for individuals but to reduce the sampling variances of estimates of change without the need to follow movers.

Starting around 1968, however, a number of panel studies following people for extended periods, were started. The Longitudinal Retirement History Study of the Social Security Administration interviewed a cohort of people close to retirement age six times over ten years. The National Longitudinal Surveys started with three cohorts; young men and women expected to make the transition from school to work, middle-aged women expected to re-enter the labour market and mature men expected to retire. Later two new cohorts of young men and of young women were added. The Panel Study of Income Dynamics started in 1968 with a combined sample – a low-income, heavily minority sample subselected from the Survey of Economic Opportunity (Census for Office of Economic Opportunity) and a fresh cross-section sample from the Institute for Social Research national sample frame. Weights allow proper merging of the two samples and allowance for the widely different sampling fractions. More recently, out of a concern both for more precise information about income and its short-run fluctuations, and about the impact of government programmes, the Survey of Income and Program Participation (Census) was started, with overlapping panels each interviewed three times a year over a two-and-a-half-year period.

Panels similar to the Panel Study of Income Dynamics have been started in West Germany, Sweden, the Netherlands, Luxemburg and Belgium, and attempts are being made to increase the comparability of these data sets in order to facilitate international comparisons not just of overall measures but of relationships and dynamics.

Starting right after World War II there were repeated surveys of expectations and intentions of both businessmen and consumers. In the case of consumers there was a theoretical base provided by George Katona which affected the nature of the data collected and made them useful both for short-term forecasting and for studying the impact of national events on consumer optimism and confidence and thereby on their willingness to spend and make commitments to future standards of living (and repayments), (Katona, 1975).

There are, of course, many other data collections, some involving reinterviews, some involving repeated cross-sections but with enough consistency to facilitate studies of change in subgroups. The annual Housing Survey and the various health surveys are examples. Numerous Presidential Commissions have in the course of their short lives managed to commission surveys on such things as pensions, impact of minimum-wage laws on employers, and bankruptcy. Finally, the occasional large-scale consumer expenditure survey has been replaced by more regular ongoing expenditure surveys combining diaries for small frequent items with interviews to cover the larger less frequent ones.

The Commission on National Statistics of the National Research Council, National Academy of Sciences, has, among others, been concerned with the quality of survey data and problems of proper revelation of essential procedures. We have mentioned the Interuniversity Consortium for Political and Social Research at the University of Michigan, which documents, archives and distributes to its member universities and other organizations a wide range of survey and other data and has vastly improved the access to survey data for secondary analysis.

FUTURE PROMISE. While survey data, particularly panel data, have vastly expanded the possibilities for studying behaviour and testing theories about behavioural responses, particulary to policy-relevant variables, there are still untapped possibilities both for analysis and use of existing survey data and for specifying better data tailored to the important issues. Little has been done with the data to study lagged responses to exogenous changes nor untangle joint-decision processes. Nor, as we have said, has there been an adequate effort to have the data collected, analysed and used in simulation models to spell out the aggregate dynamic implications in socio-economic systems of the behavioural responses. Much of what is called simulation is static use of survey data to spell out the impact of proposed new taxes or subsidies on various subsets of the population. Dynamic microsimulation is both more difficult and more promising.

More promising still is the specification of data that would allow bypassing presently difficult or intractable problems. One can disentangle age, period and cohort effects by imposing constraints, such as assuming that one of them has only a linear effect, but the results are highly sensitive to the particular constraint chosen. Collecting more information about the specific things that are supposed to be affected by age, year or year of birth would appear more promising. Joint and related decisions cannot really be untangled by looking at sequence, nor easily inferred statistically, but people might well be able to provide direct evidence about what was related to what and how one choice influenced or was influenced by or was made jointly with some other choice. Persistent interpersonal differences which pollute attempts to estimate effects across time, or the differences associated with selection biases, might be investigated directly. Even the rational expectations or the implicit contracts so favoured in economic theory might be asked about in interviews in various indirect or direct ways.

The ultimate coherent development of economics might be seen as cooperative efforts in three related domains: designing and collecting information about human behaviour, analysing survey and other data to estimate dynamic behavioural responses, particularly responses to crucial policy parameters (manipulable?) and using those estimates in simulation models to spell out the aggregate dynamic implications, the sensitivity of the system to changes in rules or behaviour, and the impact of changes on subgroups in society. Such an articulated programme would allow the modellers to specify which behavioural parameters are needed with the most precision and the statistical analysts to specify what survey data they need for making such estimates. The influence might also go the other way, with empirical survey researchers helping make the models more realistic and more parsimonious, omitting relationships known to be trivial or weak. The result should be a unified science of economics that was both behavioural and analytical, micro and macro, equilibrium and dynamic.

JAMES N. MORGAN

See also KATONA, GEORGE.

BIBLIOGRAPHY

Chamberlain, G. 1978. Omitted variable bias in panel data: estimating the returns to schooling. In *The Econometrics of Panel Data* Colloque International ce CNRS, *Annales de l'INSEE*, 50–82.

Chamberlain, G. 1984. Heterogeneity, omitted variable bias and duration dependence. In *Longitudinal Analyses of Labor Market Data*, ed. J. Heckman and B. Singer, New York: Academic Press.

Federal Reserve System, Board of Governors. 1950–60. Surveys of consumer finances. In various issues of the *Federal Reserve Bulletin*.

Glock, C.Y. 1967. *Survey Research in the Social Sciences*. New York: Russell Sage.

Heckman, J.J. 1979. Sample selection bias as a specification error. *Econometrica* 47(1), 153–61.

Heckman, J. 1981. Heterogeneity and state dependence. In *Studies in Labor Markets*, ed. S. Rosen, Chicago: University of Chicago Press.

Heckman, J. and Borjas, J. 1980. Does unemployment cause future unemployment? Definitions, questions and answers from a continuous time model of heterogeneity and state dependence. *Economica* 47, August, 247–83.

International Labour Office. 1961. *Family Living Studies: A Symposium*. Geneva: ILO.

Kahn, R. and Cannell, C. 1965. *Dynamics of Interviewing*. New York: Wiley.

Kalton, G. 1983. *Introduction to Survey Sampling*. Beverly Hills: Sage.

Katona, G. 1975. *Psychological Economics*. New York: Elsevier.

Kish, L. 1965. *Survey Sampling*. New York: Wiley.

Lansing, J.D. and Morgan, J.N. 1971. *Economic Survey Methods*. Ann Arbor: Institute for Social Research.

Moser, C.A. and Kalton, G. 1971. *Survey Methods in Social Investigation*. London: Basic Books.

Oberschall, A. 1964. *Empirical Social Research In Germany*. Paris: Mouton & Co.

O'Muircheartaigh, C.A. and Payne, C. 1977. *The Analysis of Survey Data*. Vol. I, *Exploring Data Structures*; Vol. II, *Model Fitting*. London: Wiley.

Oppenheim, A.N. 1966. *Questionnaire Design and Attitude Measurement*. New York: Basic Books.

Rossi, P.A., Wright, J.D. and Anderson, A.B. 1983. *Handbook of Survey Research*. New York: Academic Press.

Sonquist, J.A. and Dunkelberg, W.C. 1977. *Survey and Opinion Research*. Englewood Cliffs, NJ: Prentice-Hall.

Sudman, S. 1976. *Applied Sampling*. New York: Academic Press.

Turner, C.F. and Martin, E. (eds) 1984. *Surveying Subjective Phenomena*. 2 vols, New York: Russell Sage.

Williams, F.M. and Zimmerman, C.C. 1935. *Studies of Family Living in the United States and Other Countries: An Analysis of Materials and Method*. USDA Miscellaneous Publication 223, Washington, DC: USGPO.

Zarkovich, S.S. 1966. *Quality of Statistical Data*. Rome: Food and Agriculture Organization of the United Nations.

survival. *See* COST MINIMIZATION AND UTILITY MAXIMIZATION; SUBSISTENCE.

Svennilson, Ingvar (1908–1972). Svennilson was born and died in Stockholm. A PhD in economics (1938) at the University of Stockholm, he was co-editor of *Ekonomisk Tidskrift* (1939–56); Professor in Economics at the University of Stockholm (1947–72) and Vice-president of the University of Stockholm (1958–66). His dissertation (Svennilson, 1938) tackled the problem of 'planning in an unplanned world' and is a theoretical analysis of the investment decisions taken by individual firms under risk and uncertainty. Plans are based on uncertain future events, which implies a choice of strategy in a multiperiod model. The strategy embodies the idea of alternative planning, which means that the firms have plans how to adapt their actions periodically in accordance with the realized events. The ideas and the concepts used in the dissertation are developed of earlier Swedish works on sequence analysis, e.g. Lindahl's *The Rate of Interest and the Price Level* (1930).

Throughout his career Svennilson published many empirical and theoretical works on the problem of structural transformation and technical change. In Svennilson (1954) structural maladjustment plays the major role in the lagging and unstable growth of the European economy during the interwar period. He always tried to incorporate technical change in the analysis of capital formation, as in Svennilson (1956). In Svennilson (1964) he made an attempt to give a systematic understanding of 'the residual factor' in the production function, and the equilibrium is shown to be determined by the growth rate as well as the functional distribution of income.

Svennilson was for twenty years (1947–67) chairman and expert to the Long-Term Planning Commission and he obviously had a significant influence on these documents, which are published almost every fifth year as a Swedish Government Official Report; the reports play an important role in the debates on economic policy. From 1942 to 1952 he was director of the Industrial Institute for Economic and Social Research, which is funded by private industry. This organizational and intellectual background explains why Svennilson always encouraged closer cooperation between government and private research and planning.

BJORN HANSSON

SELECTED WORKS

1933. (With G. Bagge and E. Bagge Lundberg.) *Wages, Cost of Living and National Income in Sweden 1860–1930*. London: P.S. King & Son.
1938. *Ekonomisk Planering. Teoretiska Studier* . Uppsala: Almqvist & Wiksell.
1954. *Growth and Stagnation in the European Economy*. Geneva: UN Economic Commission for Europe.
1956. Capital accumulation and national wealth in an expanding economy. In *25 Essays in Honour of Erik Lindahl*, Stockholm: Svenska Tryckeribolaget.
1964. Economic growth and technical progress: an essay in sequence analysis. In *The Residual Factor and Economic Growth*, Paris: OECD.

BIBLIOGRAPHY

Lundberg, E. 1972. Ingvar Svennilson: a note on his scientific achievements and a bibliography of his contributions to economics. *Scandinavian Journal of Economics* 74, 313–28.

Swedish school. *See* STOCKHOLM SCHOOL.

Sweezy, Paul Malor (born 1910). One of the leading figures in Western Marxism and co-editor (with Harry Magdoff) of *Monthly Review*, Sweezy is known both for his contributions to economics and his influence on the development of socialist thought. Born on 10 April 1910 in New York, the son of an officer of the First National Bank of New York, he obtained his early education at Exeter and Harvard University, from which he received his BA in 1931. In 1932 he left Cambridge, Massachusetts for a year of graduate study at the London School of Economics. Awakened by the Great Depression, and responding to the intellectual ferment in Britain during what was to be a turning point in world history, Sweezy quickly gained sympathy for the Marxist perspective to which he was introduced for the first time. Returning to the US in 1933 to do graduate studies at Harvard, he found the academic climate much changed, with Marxism becoming a topic of intense interest in some of the larger universities. As he recalled many years later,

> It was under these circumstances that I acquired a mission in life, not all at once and self-consciously but gradually and through a practice that had a logic of its own. That mission was to do what I could to make Marxism an integral and respected part of the intellectual life of the country, or, put in other terms, to take part in establishing a serious and authentic North American brand of Marxism (Sweezy, 1981a, p. 13).

In pursuing this goal at Harvard, Sweezy received much direct help and indirect inspiration from the great conservative economist Joseph Schumpeter, whose analysis of the origins, development and imminent decline of capitalism revealed a complex, critical appreciation of the Marxian schema. Sweezy's 1943 essay on 'Professor Schumpeter's Theory of Innovation', which compared Schumpeter's analysis of entrepreneurial development to Marx's theory of accumulation, was to be one of the pathbreaking studies in this area.

Receiving his PhD in 1937, Sweezy assumed a position as instructor at Harvard until 1939, when he rose to the rank of assistant professor. During these years he played a central role in two of the major areas of debate in economics: (1) the theory of imperfect competition, and (2) the issue of secular stagnation. Sweezy's interest in the monopoly question began early in his career, as shown by his first book (winner of the David A. Wells prize), *Monopoly and Competition in the English Coal Trade, 1550–1850* (1938). His 1939 article, 'Demand Under Conditions of Oligopoly', in which he presented the kinked demand curve analysis of oligopolistic pricing, remains one of the classic essays in modern price theory. Along with a small group of Harvard and Tufts economists, Sweezy was one of the authors and signatories of the influential Keynesian tract, *An Economic Program for American Democracy* (1938), which provided a convincing rationale for a sustained increase in public spending during the final years of the New Deal. While continuing to carry out his teaching responsibilities at Harvard, Sweezy worked for various New Deal agencies (including the National Resources Committee and the Temporary National Economic Committee) investigating the concentration of economic power. His study, 'Interest Groups in the American Economy', published as an appendix to the NRC's well-known report, *The Structure of the American Economy* (1939), was to be an important guide to later research.

From the lecture notes to his Harvard course on the economics of socialism, Sweezy produced his seminal work, *The Theory of Capitalist Development* (1942). Containing a comprehensive review of Marxian economics up until the time of World War II, this study also did much to determine the character of later Marxian theory through its advocacy of Laudislau von Bortkiewitz's solution to the 'transformation problem', its presentation of a logically acceptable 'underconsumptionist' model of accumulation and crisis, and its elaboration of Marxian views on monopoly capitalism. Rapidly translated into several languages, *The Theory of Capitalist Development* soon established Sweezy's reputation as the foremost Marxian economist of his generation.

During World War II Sweezy served in the Office of Strategic Services (OSS) and was assigned to the monitoring of British plans for postwar economic development. With a number of years still remaining in his Harvard contract when the war ended, he opted to resign his position rather than resume teaching, recognizing that his political and intellectual stance would hinder his receiving tenure. In this period, Sweezy authored numerous articles on the history of political economy and socialism, some of which were reprinted in his book, *The Present as History* (1953), and edited a volume containing three classic works on the 'transformation problem': *Karl Marx and the Close of His System* by Eugene Böhm-Bawerk, *Böhm-Bawerk's Criticism of Marx* by Rudolf Hilferding, and 'On the Correction of Marx's Fundamental

Theoretical Construction in the Third Volume of *Capital*' by Bortkiewicz (which Sweezy translated into English). His 1950 critique of Maurice Dobb's *Studies in the Development of Capitalism*, in which Sweezy, following his interpretation of Marx, emphasized the role of the world market in the decline of feudalism, launched the famous debate over the transition from feudalism to capitalism which has played a key role in Marxian historiography ever since.

With the financial backing of literary critic F.O. Matthieson, Sweezy and the Marxist historian Leo Huberman founded *Monthly Review* (subtitled 'An Independent Socialist Magazine') in 1949 as an intellectual resource for an American left threatened by anti-Communist hysteria. Two years later they began publishing books under the imprint of Monthly Review Press, when it came to their attention that in the repressive climate of the times even such celebrated authors as I.F. Stone and Harvey O'Conner were unable to find publishers for their book manuscripts.

In 1953, at the height of the McCarthyite period in the US, the state of New Hampshire conferred wide-ranging powers on its attorney general to investigate 'subversive activities'. On this basis, Sweezy was summoned to appear before the state attorney general on two occasions in 1954. Adopting a principled opposition to the proceedings, he refused to answer questions regarding: (1) the membership and activities of the Progressive Party, (2) the contents of a guest lecture delivered at the University of New Hampshire, and (3) whether or not he believed in Communism. As a result, he was declared in contempt of court and consigned to the county jail until purged of contempt by the Superior Court of Merimack County, New Hampshire. On appeal, this decision was upheld by the New Hampshire Supreme Court. In response to a further appeal, the US Supreme Court overturned the verdict of the state court in 1957, on the grounds that there was no legal evidence that the New Hampshire legislators actually wanted the attorney general to obtain answers to these questions; and that the obvious violation of Sweezy's constitutional liberties could not be justified on the basis of political activities only 'remotely connected to actual subversion' (US Supreme Court, *US Reports*, Vol. 354, October Term, 1956).

Despite the adverse ideological climate, Sweezy continued to author articles on all aspects of Marxian theory, adding up to hundreds of essays by the 1980s. The publication of Paul Baran's book, *The Political Economy of Growth* (1957), marked the beginning of Marxian dependency theory and helped to established *Monthly Review's* primary identity as a backer of third world liberation struggles. Visiting Cuba shortly after the revolution, Huberman and Sweezy co-authored two influential works on the transformation of Cuban economic society: *Cuba: Anatomy of a Revolution* (1960) and *Socialism in Cuba* (1969).

The appearance in 1966 of *Monopoly Capital* by Baran and Sweezy (published two years after Baran's death) represented a turning point in Marxian economics. Although described by the authors themselves as a mere 'essay-sketch', it rapidly gained widespread recognition as the most important attempt thus far to bring Marx's *Capital* up to date, as well as providing a formidable critique of prevailing Keynesian orthodoxy.

Where Sweezy himself was concerned, *Monopoly Capital* reflected dissatisfaction with the analysis of accumulation and crisis advanced in *The Theory of Capitalist Development*. His earlier study had been written when mainstream economics was undergoing rapid change due to the Keynesian 'revolution' and the rise of imperfect competition theory. Thus, he had provided a detailed elaboration of both Marx's theory of realization crisis (or demand-side constraints in the accumulation process), and of work by Marx and later Marxian theorists on the concentration and centralization of capital. As with mainstream theory, however, these two aspects of Sweezy's analysis remained separate; and hence he failed to develop an adequate explanation of the concrete factors conditioning investment demand in an economic regime dominated by the modern large enterprise. It was essentially this critique of Sweezy's early efforts that was provided by Josef Steindl in *Maturity and Stagnation in American Capitalism* (1952: 243–46); who went on to show how a more unified theory could 'be organically developed out of the underconsumptionist approach of Marx' based on Michal Kalecki's model of capitalist dynamics, which had connected the phenomenon of realization crisis to the increasing 'degree of monopoly' in the economy as a whole.

In fact, it was out of this argument, as outlined by Steindl, that the underlying framework for Baran and Sweezy's own contribution in *Monopoly Capital* was derived. Thus, they suggested that Marx's fundamental 'law of the tendency of the rate of profit to fall' associated with accumulation in the era of free competition, had been replaced, in the more restrictive competitive environment of monopoly capitalism, by a law of the tendency of the surplus to rise (defining surplus as the gap, at any given level of production, between output and socially necessary costs of production). Under these circumstances, the critical economic problem was one of surplus absorption. Capitalist consumption tended to account for a decreasing share of capitalist demand as income grew, while investment was hindered by the fact that it took the form of new productive capacity, which could not be expanded for long periods of time independently of final, wage-based demand. Despite the fact that there was always the possibility of new 'epoch-making innovations' emerging that would help absorb the potential economic surplus, all such innovations – resembling the steam engine, the railroad and the automobile in their overall effect – were few and far between. Hence, Baran and Sweezy concluded that the system had a powerful tendency toward stagnation, largely countered thus far through the promotion of economic waste by means of 'the sales effort' (including its penetration into the production process) and military expenditures, and through the expansion of the financial sector. All such 'countervailing influences' were, however, of a self-limiting character and could be expected to lead to a doubling-over of contradictions in the not too distant future.

The publication of *Monopoly Capital* coincided with the rise of the New Left, largely in response to the Vietnam War. The work of Baran and Sweezy thus constituted the initial theoretical common ground for a younger generation of radical economists in the US who formed the Union for Radical Political Economics in 1968. In 1971, Sweezy delivered the Marshall Lecture at Cambridge University. Some of his most influential writings during this period were reprinted in *Modern Capitalism and Other Essays* (1972). From 1974 to 1976 he served on the executive of the American Economic Association, and in 1983 was granted an honorary doctorate of literature from Jawaharlal Nehru University in India.

Together with Harry Magdoff (who replaced Huberman as co-editor of *Monthly Review* after the latter's death in 1968), Sweezy has continued to strengthen the analysis of *Monopoly Capital* in the decades following its publication, utilizing the original framework to explain the reemergence of stagnation and the rise of financial instability, in such works as *The Dynamics of US Capitalism* (1970), *The End of Prosperity*

(1977), *The Deepening Crisis of US Capitalism* (1979) and *Four Lectures on Marxism* (1981).

With the demise of detente and the appearance of a new cold war, Sweezy has grappled increasingly with the question of 'actually existing socialism' in Eastern Europe – emphasizing the class-exploitative character of these societies, as well as their advances over capitalist states at similar levels of development, and their largely defensive international posture – in such works as *Post-Revolutionary Society* (1981).

JOHN BELLAMY FOSTER

See also MONOPOLY CAPITALISM.

SELECTED WORKS

1938. *Monopoly and Competition in the English Coal Trade, 1550–1850.* Cambridge, Mass.: Harvard University Press.
1939a. Demand under conditions of oligopoly. *Journal of Political Economy* 47, August, 568–73.
1939b. Interest groups in the American economy. In US National Resources Committee, *The Structure of the American Economy*, Pt I, Washington, DC: US Government Printing Office.
1942. *The Theory of Capitalist Development: Principles of Marxian Political Economy*. New York: Monthly Review Press.
1943. Professor Schumpeter's theory of innovation. *Review of Economics and Statistics* 25, February, 93–96.
1949. (ed.) *Karl Marx and the Close of His System by Eugen Böhm-Bawerk and Böhm-Bawerk's Criticism of Marx by Rudolf Hilferding*. Reprinted, London: Merlin Press, 1976.
1960. (With L. Huberman.) *Cuba: Anatomy of a Revolution*. New York: Monthly Review Press.
1966. (With P.A. Baran.) *Monopoly Capital: an Essay on the American Economic and Social Order*. New York: Monthly Review Press.
1969. (With L. Huberman.) *Socialism in Cuba*. New York: Monthly Review Press.
1970. (With H. Magdoff.) *The Dynamics of US Capitalism*. New York: Monthly Review Press.
1972. *Modern Capitalism and Other Essays*. New York: Monthly Review Press.
1976. (With others.) *The Transition from Feudalism to Capitalism*. London: New Left Books.
1977. (With H. Magdoff.) *The End of Prosperity*. New York: Monthly Review Press.
1981a. *Four Lectures on Marxism*. New York: Monthly Review Press.
1981b. *Post-Revolutionary Society*. New York: Monthly Review Press.

BIBLIOGRAPHY

Foster, J.B. 1986. *The Theory of Monopoly Capitalism*. New York: Monthly Review Press.
Gilbert, R. et al. 1938. *An Economic Program for American Democracy*. New York: Vanguard.
Steindl, J. 1952. *Maturity and Stagnation in American Capitalism*. Oxford: Blackwell. Reprinted, New York: Monthly Review Press, 1976.
US Supreme Court 1957. Sweezy *v*. New Hampshire. *US Reports*. October Term, 1956.

Swift, Jonathan (1667–1745). Dean of St Patrick's Dublin, the austere Rabelais, the party pamphleteer from whom Rousseau learnt to detest politics and society, the high churchman from whom Voltaire and Lessing learnt their religion, the author of *Gulliver's Travels*, Swift is a writer to whose economic views critics are often unjust. *The Humble Petition of the Colliers, Cooks, Cook-maids*, etc., against the use of focused rays by a supposed company instead of fires, represents that this 'will utterly ruin ... your petitioners ... and trades on them depending, there being nothing left to them after the said invention but warming of cellars and dressing of suppers in the wintertime'. And 'whereas the said' company 'talk of making use of the moon by night as of the sun by day, they will utterly ruin the numerous body of tallow chandlers', and so the tallow tax will fail. The fame of Bastiat is chiefly based on his expansion of this parable in the seventh of his *Sophismes Economiques* (1846), of which his admirers still say 'nothing is more brilliant, nothing more French'.

Swift's *Maxims controuled in Ireland*, suggested perhaps by Sir William Temple (*Works*, 1814 edn, vol. i. p. 177), exposes, after the manner of Bastiat, popular economic fallacies which deceived Temple, Locke, and Child, whom he had studied; e.g. that a large population, high prices for land, dear provisions, and big towns (cf. Barbon) *must* imply wealth, and that low interest *must* be due to much money. For 'must', he says, you should write 'may'; thus, in trading countries like Holland and England, low interest and high capital values for land were effects of the causes alleged, but in Ireland of the absence of trade, and therefore of a demand for loans. He perceived 'that in the arithmetic of the customs two and two, instead of making four, make sometimes only one' (Smith, *Wealth of Nations*, book v, ch. ii).

Otherwise Swift belongs to his age. Thus the king of Brobdingnag's belief that 'whoever could make two ears of corn or two blades of grass to grow ... where only one grew before would deserve better of mankind ... than the whole race of politicians', and the echo of this belief at the end of the last of the Drapier's Letters resembles Molesworth's ideas (1723), and afterwards became a favourite motto with Arthur Young. He thinks with Locke that traces fall mainly upon land, which, like Harrington, he overrates (*Works*, 1824 edn, vol. iii, p. 518); and his anger against ploughlands being turned into sheep-runs makes him akin to Latimer, Boulter (*Letters*, 24 February 1727), and, as he himself said, to Ajax. He pillories the trading spirit in his abuse of the Dutch; and wishes a weavers' corporation to regulate prices and qualities, and to punish offenders by 'warnings' (*Works*, vol. vii, pp. 49, 50, 137). He denounces 'the restriction' and urges Irishmen to raise by way of reply what Berkeley called 'a wall of brass a thousand cubits high' round Ireland; and thinks that this could be done by a resolution to consume home-made goods instead of 'unwholesome drugs and unnecessary finery' imported from India and elsewhere (*Proposal for the universal use of Irish Manufacture*). His sumptuary mercantilism is the same as that of Sir William Temple, Polexfen and Berkeley.

For the rest he advocated national education and beggars' badges, and adopted Temple's fallacy that high rents caused high prices, Prior's facts and fallacies on absentees, and Molesworth's views on rack-rents; he deplored with Temple the destruction of timber, and opposed Boulter's lowering of the gold coin, and Berkeley's proposal for a bank; and like Prior, Berkeley, James King, Simon, and others, he advocated an Irish mint in his Drapier's Letters (1723–4). In these Swift's economic objection to Wood's copper – if stripped of its figures, which Swift meant to be figures of speech – was that the coin being hammered and not milled was easily forged, was base, excessive, and not convertible by the patentee; further, the patent did not make it legal tender, so that when this was known it would at once lose its mint value unless it should, by an abuse of the royal prerogative, be made full legal tender, in which case it would drive out gold and then depreciate. Swift did not, nor could any writer at that time, analyse the latter process, and he omitted a third possibility, that it might be made limited legal tender.

If this omission was uncandid what shall we say of his critics Leslie Stephen (*Swift*, pp. 153ff.) and Moriarty (*Swift*, 1893, p. 211), who assume that the coin was legal tender up to 5½d.? Further, token coins, if redundant and difficult to convert, are open to these objections, so that the omission weakens but does not vitiate the argument. Lastly, facts and dates indicate that there was a likelihood that these coins would be made legal tender either to an unlimited or to a dangerously high extent. Wood boasted, 9 February 1722, that his coins were or would be made legal tender (Coxe, *Walpole*, ii. 371); and from Lady-day 1722, when his coining rights began, to 16 September 1723, the terms were unknown even in Dublin Castle; had the whole amount, £108,000, been floated in the dark, the hands of ministers must have been forced and most of Swift's fears realized. Again, the crown rent was £100, and Walpole's report valued it at £800; under the Armstrong–Knox patent of 1680 the copper need not be quite so good, and was only limited legal tender, but the rent was only £16. Further, there was virtually no silver in Ireland (Sir John Browne, *Scheme*, 1729; British Museum, Add. MSS 34358, pp. 74, 79); and every one was either bimetallic or silver-monometallic; and only thirty-three years before James II had substituted full legal tender brass for silver. Further, the customs officers were practically ordered (Coxe, p. 393) to receive these coins without limit, and in the efforts referred to in Coxe (pp. 346–438) and Monck Mason (Appendix, note *c*) to dissuade ministers from making them legal tender, no limit is mentioned. Lastly, it was clear ever since the first letter that the patent would always be onerous; yet when it was revoked, 14 August 1725, the treasury paid Wood instead of Wood paying the treasury; a compact with Wood to make the coins legal tender would explain this. Ruding cites against these arguments Walpole's *Report of the Privy Council*, 24 July 1724, which disclaimed any intention to make the coins legal tender; and argues that because danger was averted it was not real. Yes, but Swift's first *Letter* was published November (?) 1723, and doubtless caused the report, just as the second letter doubtless caused its publication, and the third letter criticized it. (Faulkner's reprint (1725) misprints 'four' for 'three' in the third paragraph of the first letter, and so makes the date autumn 1724. A similar sentence occurs in the seventh letter (vol. vii, p. 52) where 'four' is correct; the seventh is therefore a year later than the first letter, and its date is the end of October 1724. Lord Midleton probably refers to the first letter as written but not yet published, 1 November 1723 (Coxe, vol. ii, p. 372).) In the next two letters the storm centre shifts from economics to politics; the next is retrospective, the last prospective. Or it will be said 'how absurd to think that Walpole would do what James II did and in the same way!' Of course the patent was a mere blunder; if the coin were private it ought to have been, like promissory notes, convertible into legal tender coin by the issuer; if public, it ought to have been legal tender; and it was neither. But blunders often have the same effect as crimes. To conclude, Swift described, with popular but not misleading rhetoric, a grave economic peril which he more than anyone averted.

[J.D. Rogers]

Reprinted from *Palgrave's Dictionary of Political Economy*.

With regard to Swift's contributions to economic thought, it might be added that his unmatched gifts for satire tower in general import over his undoubtedly sincere proposals for actual reform. This disparity can be seen, for example, by comparing his 'Modest Proposal' with the seventh of the *Drapier's Letters*, which Swift entitled 'An Humble Address to Both Houses of Parliament' (1724). Somewhat less than half of the latter is given over to the larger project of slinging arrows at those who tolerated the Englishman Wood's monopoly in the issue of 'Hogsheads' (copper halfpennies). The remainder is taken up with Swift's concrete proposals for the economic restoration of Ireland – proposals which indicate the extent of its economic subjection to England. These proposals include: creation of a national mint, reform of the structure of rent paid to absentee landlords and salaries paid to absentee governmental placeholders, cessation of the forced importation of English goods, and cessation of the devastating practice of deforesting and depopulating the Irish countryside for the creation of pastureland. The last of these reforms was particularly urgent. For, if the 'Hogshead' symbolized Ireland's political subjugation and economic dependence on England, Swift was quite aware that the vista of its countryside populated by sheep rather than men signalled something yet more sinister. However, in style, these 'humbly' formulated and half-plaintive proposals for reform clearly lack the bite and moral outrage of Swift's direct attacks on Wood. By comparison, the satirical 'A Modest Proposal For Preventing The Children Of Ireland From Being a Burden To Their Parents Or Country' (1729) far more effectively ridicules the extent of England's exploitation of Ireland through the image of cannibalism. If England's economic policy toward Ireland is to remain the same, then the 'modest proposal' of creating a market for the raising and consumption of Irish children, reveals more starkly both its aims and absurd destructiveness than do the more sober proposals of the Drapier's letters. One may wonder whether in writing this 'modest proposal' Swift presumed correctly that the English, like the ministers of Yahoodom, feared far more the sting of having their policies proven foolish than of having them shown to be unjust.

S.C. Stimson

T

tabular standard. *See* INDEX NUMBERS.

Tarbell, Ida Minerva (1857–1944). In a profession where women have been denied the liberties of expression otherwise permitted to men of lesser quality, Ida M. Tarbell made her mark as an economic journalist. She had a keen sense of ethical issues, but regrettably, her blend of reformism and conservatism was sometimes bewildering.

Born in 1857 in Erie County, Pennsylvania, Tarbell is best known for her *History of the Standard Oil Company* (1904), a two-volume attack on the ruthlessness of the oil monopolies (her father was ruined by them). As a muckraker, Tarbell could be expected to favour state intervention in wages setting, then a hotly debated issue. But ironically, whereas the progenitor of marginal productivity theory, J.B. Clark, edged towards arbitration to reduce labour strife, Tarbell embraced Taylorism, whose logic of work atomization builds on the marginalist principle. From 1912 to 1915 Tarbell toured factories she handpicked to study industrial conditions. Favourably struck with Fordism, she wrote a contemporary equivalent of the 'excellently managed corporation' entitled *New Ideals in Business* (1916). The ideals were scientific management, humanistic labour relations and a belief in the fundamental goodness of entrepreneurs.

In her feminist outpourings, Tarbell is better remembered for the way she lived than by what she wrote. Unusual for a woman at the time, Tarbell moved to Paris after college to study women in the French Revolution, was praised by Woodrow Wilson for her 'common sense' views on the tariff (which she opposed), attended the Paris Peace Conference, corresponded with notables, including Richard T. Ely, interviewed Mussolini, and shunned marriage for a career. The same Tarbell, however, fought against woman's suffrage and in *The Business of Being a Woman* (1912) advised members of her sex to stay at home.

ALICE H. AMSDEN

SELECTED WORKS

1904. *The History of the Standard Oil Company*. New York: McClure, Phillips.

1911. *The Tariff in Our Times*. New York: Macmillan.

1912. *The Business of Being a Woman*. New York: Macmillan.

1915. *The Ways of Woman*. New York: Macmillan.

1916. *New Ideal in Business: An Account of Their Practice and Their Effects Upon Men and Profits*. New York: Macmillan.

1926. *The Life of Elbert H Gray: the Story of Steel*. New York: D. Appleton.

1936. *The Nationalizing of Business, 1878–1898*. New York: Macmillan.

targets and instruments. These are two concepts used in the theory of economic policy. Although the subject of economic policy as one of the forms of applied economic theory is as old as economic science itself, the more systematic treatment meant by the phrase 'theory of economic policy' started much more recently, in close connection with the development of econometrics. Econometrics, as the combination of theory and observation in the area of intersection of economics, statistics and mathematics, introduced the possibility of dealing with economic policy not only qualitatively, but also quantitatively. This enables economists to formulate policy recommendations in the most concrete form conceivable, as they are needed by policy-makers – government, parliament and representatives of social groups. It seems appropriate to consider as the starting document of the theory of economic policy in this sense, Ragnar Frisch's document (1949), written for the United Nations' short-lived Employment Commission, 'A memorandum of price–wage–tax–subsidy policies as instruments in maintaining optimal employment'.

The term 'targets and instruments' refer to economic variables in a special case of a more flexible version of the theory of economic policy, where the more general terms 'aims and means of a policy' are used, which may be qualitative as well as quantitative. An aim may then be the maximization (under possible restrictions) of social welfare, and among the means a reform may appear. Targets are numerical values of variables appearing in a social-welfare function and are supposed a priori to be the values that maximize social welfare. Instruments are quantitative values of means controllable by the policy-maker (cf. Preston and Pagan, 1982).

Examples of target variables are employment, current balance-of-payment surplus, current government surplus, income, the rate of inflation, and others. Examples of instrument variables are direct and indirect tax rates, interest, total or specific public expenditures, working hours per week, working weeks per year, age of retirement, wage rates, and so on.

Problems of economic science may be subdivided into two categories: explanatory or analytical problems, and normative or policy problems. The complete mathematical formulation and solution of these problems require the introduction of two more categories of variables, to be called 'exogenous' (or 'data') variables and 'other' (or 'irrelevant') variables. In what follows, the four categories will sometimes be indicated by x (irrelevant), y (target), z (instrument) and u (data) variables. In addition, the mathematical formulation of the two types of problems requires the fulfilment of a number I of equations or relations, numbered $i\ (=1, 2, \ldots, I)$, a number of J of variables x_j, a number K of variables y_k, a number L of variables z_l, and I variables u_i.

The equations will be assumed to be linear, which for small variations is no restriction, but for large variations constitutes a limitation. They will be written:

$$\sum_j a_{ij}x_j + \sum_k b_{ik}y_k + \sum_l c_{il}z_l = u_i, \qquad i = 1, 2, \ldots, I. \qquad (1)$$

Examples of relations are definitions, technical or legal relations, balance equations and behavioural relations such as demand or supply equations for either goods or factors of production (labour types, capital, etc.). The group of I equations (1) describes, in a simplified way, the operation of the economy studied and is called a 'model' of that economy, more particularly when all coefficients a, b and c have been given numerical values obtained from a series of values for all x, y, z and u over some observation period.

The mathematical-statistical (or econometric) methods of estimation will not be discussed here, but the choice of, in particular, the variables x and u will be such as to obtain reliable values of the coefficients. This implies that the coefficients of determination R^2, corrected for the number of degrees of freedom (and then written $\bar{R}^2$) as well as the so-called t-values satisfy certain conditions, usually $\bar{R}$ should be not far below 1 and $ts > 3$, but this ideal is rarely attained.

A problem (and this applies to both types of problem mentioned) can be solved only if the number of unknowns N equals the number of equations' I – this being a necessary but not a sufficient condition. The unknowns for each time unit are, for the explanatory problem, the target variables and the 'other' variables. So we must have:

$$K+J=N \tag{2}$$

For the political problem the unknowns are the instrument and the 'other' variable, and we must have:

$$L+J=N \tag{3}$$

From (2) and (3) we deduce that $K=L$ must apply for the problems to be solvable; that is, *the number of instruments must equal the number of target variables*. Later we will discuss some exceptions to this thesis, but as a general rule our conclusion stands.

For a more concise treatment of our problems it is sometimes preferable to formulate the model in a simplified form by eliminating the irrelevant variables x. This elimination requires J equations and so we are left with $N-J=K=L$ equations, in which only the y, z and u appear. In order to avoid confusion we will now use capital letters for the coefficients:

$$\sum_k B_k y_k + \sum_l C_l z_l = u_i \qquad i = 1, 2, \ldots, I \tag{4}$$

For simplicity's sake we will discuss examples where $K = L = 4$. The explanatory problem's solution is obtained by solving (4) for the target variables y:

$$y_k = \sum_l p_{kl} z_l + \sum_i s_{ki} u_i \qquad k = 1, 2, \ldots, K \tag{5}$$

The policy problem's solution is found from solving (4) for the instrument variables z:

$$z_l = \sum_k q_{lk} y_k + \sum_i t_{li} u_i \qquad l = 1, 2, \ldots, L \tag{6}$$

By use of matrix notation these equations might have been written more elegantly, but we shall refrain from doing so. It seems desirable, though, to express verbally the meaning of the coefficients used. Evidently p_{kl} constitutes the change in y_k caused by a unit change in z_l and no change in the other zs or any u. If normalized variables had been used (i.e. variables with a mean equal to 0 and a standard deviation equal to 1, as is customary in sociologists' path analysis) p_{kl} becomes the partial elasticity of y_k with respect of z_l. In both cases p constitutes a measure for the impact of instrument variable z_l on target variable y_k, all other z and all u assumed constant. Inversely and similarly q_{lk} measure the impact of a unit change in target y_k on instrument z_l, all other y and all data u assumed unchanged.

As previously observed the conditions so far mentioned are necessary but not sufficient. Other conditions which must be fulfilled are that equations (4) be neither incompatible nor dependent nor overdetermined. Simple illustrations are the following. If of four unknowns three appear in only two of the equations and the fourth in the other two equations, then the first two equations are overdetermined and the other two are either incompatible or dependent. Overdetermination implies that there is not just one solution but an infinity of them. Incompatibility means that the solution of one of the two equations does not satisfy the other. Dependency of equations means that one equation can be deduced from the other. In that case they do have the same solution, and so the occurrence of one unknown in both equations does no harm, but the solution for the three other unknowns from the two remaining equations is impossible.

An example of a system of equations suffering from non-fulfilment of the conditions just discussed can be found in Tinbergen (1956), Problem 161, using Model 16. As a counter-example without this difficulty, Problem 162 has been added. In these examples the irrelevant variables had not been eliminated first and the complete model containing 17 variables is shown.

Some politicians think that the normal situation is that there is a one-to-one correspondence between particular targets and particular instruments, for example that a tax rate is used to equilibrate the government budget, an exchange rate to equilibrate the balance of payments, and a wage rate to create enough employment. As a rule this is not correct, for such a situation would imply that only one z_l appears in each of the four equations (5) and only one y_k in each of the four equations (6), implying in turn that equations (5) and (6) could be arranged so that only the diagonal elements of the matrices P and Q could be non-zero. The normal situation is that not all elements off the diagonal vanish.

There are however some elements equal to zero in most models. An interesting case is that where the equations can be ordered so that all elements above the diagonal are nought, or where blocks of elements are equal to zero. Connected with such coefficient matrices is H.A. Simon's concept of the 'order' of an unknown, which in a policy problem corresponds to the instruments and the irrelevant variables. The concept indicates that the unknowns can be solved in a predetermined order only; the one with order 1 depends on one coefficient only, or if a group of unknowns has order 1, they depend on as many coefficients as appear in the group of equations in which these unknowns only appear. A next unknown or group of unknowns depends on the coefficients appearing in the equations containing groups 1 and 2 of the unknowns, and so on. Evidently an ordered system may be organized in a simpler way, because some decision-makers (say, government ministers) can decide quite independently of other decision-makers without deviating from the optimal policy.

Further deviations from the standard case discussed in illustrating equations (5) and (6) will occur if some instrument variables are subject to restrictions, such as the impossibility of negative values or of values less than a previous value. A large number of economic variables (for instance, production and consumption as well as prices) cannot be negative. In today's industrial countries a reduction in nominal wages is almost impossible. If without such a restriction an impossible value of some instrument would be part of the solution, the restriction becomes active; that is, it becomes an equation instead of an inequality. Since the number of unknowns is then less than the number of equations, we have either to add an unknown (an additional instrument) or to omit one equation. A possible example is that a foreign loan may be introduced as an instrument in order to keep the balance of payments in equilibrium.

The introduction of several restrictions (non-negativity of several unknowns) may leave us, after using all the equations to eliminate unknowns, with, say, two unknowns and three restrictions, still permitting any point within a triangle. The latter is called the 'admissible' or 'feasible' area and the remainder of the policy problem may be presented as a problem of linear programming. A choice among the points within this feasible area is now possible by adding the condition that some function of the remaining two unknowns be maximized. The substitution of equations by inequalities need not be used only to express the necessity that a variable be non-negative; a production function may also be interpreted as yielding the maximum quantity of product obtainable from given inputs, any deviation from that maximum then representing waste or 'X-inefficiency'.

Finally, a few words may be said about the use of target and instrument variables in interactive planning (J.A. Hartog, P. Nijkamp, J. Spronk). Frisch and his school built their policy-planning on a social-welfare function obtained by interviewing policy-makers on a universe of local trade-off rates between the variables that determined, in their opinion, the population's level of satisfaction. If *n* such variables are thought to exist, hypersurfaces of *n* dimensions would be the hypersurfaces of constant satisfaction. The interaction planning school doubts whether the average policy-maker is able to describe such hypersurfaces. The method they propose is that the policy-planner starts with a given situation and subsequently shows the policy-maker what change in the targets is obtained by an assumed first set of changes in instruments, asking him whether that change in the targets constitutes an improvement. The policy-maker may propose a further change in the instruments and the planner will inform him on the consequences for the targets. Thus, step by step, in this dialogue, planner and policy-maker will approach a situation which does not admit any improvement as a consequence of changes in instruments to be proposed by the policy-maker. In this dialogue the policy-maker will have to compare a limited number of sets of instruments and targets, presumably a much lower number than was needed by the interview method (cf. also Hughes Hallett and Rees, 1983).

JAN TINBERGEN

See also CONTROL AND COORDINATION OF ECONOMIC ACTIVITY.

BIBLIOGRAPHY

Frisch, R. 1949. A memorandum of price–wage–tax–subsidy policies as instruments in maintaining optimal employment. United Nations Employment Commission. E/CN.1/Sub 2/13, April.

Hughes Hallett, A. and Rees, H. 1983. *Quantitative Economic Policies and Interactive Planning*. Cambridge: Cambridge University Press.

Preston, A.J. and Pagan, A.R. 1982. *The Theory of Economic Policy, Statics and Dynamics*. Cambridge: Cambridge University Press.

Tinbergen, J. 1956. *Economic Policy: Principles and Design*. Amsterdam: North-Holland.

tariffs. Tariffs are taxes levied on foreign trade: on the importation and, less often, the exportation of goods as they cross the border of a country or other geographical area. Since they are easy to enforce and collect and seem to be (and partly are) paid by foreigners, tariffs have been an important and popular source of government revenue from the earliest times. In early days, the ostensible purpose of tariffs was to pay the government levying them for the protection it afforded to foreign traders on its territory. In modern times, arguments for and against tariffs as well as the determination of their level focus on their impact or supposed impact on the economy.

Tariffs nowadays are paid in money and specified either as so much money per unit of merchandise (specific tariffs) or as a given percentage of its value (ad valorem tariffs). With demand a diminishing function of price, tariffs reduce the quantity of dutiable goods imported or exported; and, with the price elasticity of demand also a diminishing function of price, Government's revenue from the tariff (i.e. the product of its level and the quantity on which it is levied) first increases then diminishes as the tariff rate is raised. Accordingly, there is a rate of tariff that maximizes tariff revenue; but the proper criterion for judging the desirability of tariffs and determining their level is not the amount of revenue they yield but their impact on the whole economy, which is usually discussed under two headings: the protection they provide to domestic producers and their effect on the terms of trade.

PROTECTIVE TARIFFS. Tariffs on imports raise their domestic prices, thereby shifting demand from imports to their domestic substitutes and increasing the profitability of the latter's production. Import duties also lower the purchasing power of income over imports and import substitutes (collectively known as importables) but add to the money incomes of producers of imports substitutes, their employees and suppliers. Accordingly, the tariff-imposing country's real national income may be raised or lowered, depending on whether the sum of the Government's tariff revenue and the additional incomes generated exceeds or falls short of the loss of purchasing power over importables. That, however, is still only a small part of a full cost-benefit calculation, which must also take into account other costs and benefits of the tariff.

By far the most important among the costs is the danger of retaliation by the foreign countries whose export industries are hurt, or believed to be hurt by the first country's import duties. That cost is especially great when the trade restrictions other countries impose in retaliation to the first country's tariff lead, in their turn, to further retaliations, and so to a general overall reduction in the volume of trade and its gains.

For the impact of import duties is to discourage the imports on which they are levied. It is true that they also stimulate domestic activity and domestic income generation, which, in the long run, may well counteract their restrictive effect on imports, at least to the extent of more or less offsetting the reduction in *overall* imports. But the combined influence of the restrictive short- and expansionary long-run effects of tariffs would have to keep unchanged not only the overall value of total imports but also their structure by country of origin in order to eliminate the economic justification and pressure for retaliation; whereas even the commodity composition of imports would have to remain unchanged in order to eliminate the political pressure for retaliation as well. Needless to say, those conditions necessary to obviate retaliation are not likely to be fulfilled.

The benefits of import duties include increased employment, an improved balance of trade, the enhanced stability of a more diversified economy, the political and economic advantages of greater self-sufficiency, and the increased efficiency of protected industries when their comparative disadvantages are remediable and can be remedied through learning by doing. Some of those advantages, however, are mutually exclusive. Tariffs, for example, that greatly stimulate the domestic economy are unlikely to improve the balance of trade – a fact that was strikingly brought home to many of the developing countries that engaged in import-substitution policies.

Of the benefits listed, by far the most important is the last-mentioned, which is a permanent benefit secured by temporary tariff protection. It has also received the most attention in the professional literature under the name of the infant industry argument. Trade restriction to nurture budding industries was well known and much practised already during the mercantilist period; but after the advent of economic liberalism, the argument in its favour needed to be reasserted. Its best known and most influential statements in modern times are those of Alexander Hamilton and Friedrich List. Hamilton's celebrated 'Report on Manufactures' to the US Congress (1791) had a great influence on american tariff policy, and its prediction of the hoped-for consequences of protection turned out to be a remarkably accurate forecast of the country's subsequent economic development. List's similar argument half a century later (List, 1841) had even more influence on both US and German foreign-trade policy.

The US and German protective tariffs of the 19th century, however, which seem to have been so successful in promoting those countries' economic development, were very much more moderate then the mid-20th-century import barriers behind which India, Pakistan and the Latin-American and other developing countries pursued their not very successful import-substitution policies (Little et al., 1970). That raises the question of what level and structure of protective tariffs are the most conducive to a country's economic development. We cannot answer here that much-debated and highly controversial question; but something must be said about effective tariffs, a statistical tool designed to help the search for an answer.

EFFECTIVE TARIFFS. The height of a tariff levied on imports of a good (also known as the nominal tariff) is not a good measure of the degree of encouragement of its domestic manufacture. For one thing, a manufacturer almost never creates a whole good, only a greater or lesser contribution to it, which is called his value added or effective price; and a given percentage tariff on imports, which enables domestic manufacturers of its substitutes to raise their prices by a like amount, makes a greater, often very much greater *percentage* addition to their value added, in a proportion that is the inverse of the ratio in which their value added stands to price. For example, if the value added in cloth manufacture is 40 per cent of price, then a 20 per cent nominal tariff on imported cloth enables domestic cloth manufacturers to increase their value added by 50 per cent.

For another thing, tariffs are often levied on final, intermediate and primary goods alike; and an import duty on a primary or intermediate good, while encouraging its domestic production, also *dis*courages the domestic manufacture of all those other goods that use it as an input. An import duty on yarn, for example, discourages domestic cloth manufacture by reducing the value added cloth manufacturers can earn.

The concept of effective tariff (ET) is designed to measure the degree of encouragement provided to given productive activities by the combined effect of the nominal tariffs imposed on their outputs *and* inputs. A simple formula for the effective tariff protection on the manufacture of good j is:

$$\mathrm{ET}_j = \frac{t_j}{1-\Sigma a_{ij}} - \frac{\Sigma a_{ij} t_i}{1-\Sigma a_{ij}},$$

where t_j is the nominal ad valorem tariff on good j, t_i are the nominal tariffs on its several inputs, and the a_{ij} show the share of the cost of input i in the price of good j at free trade prices. Note that the two terms show the contributions of the two factors discussed in the text, note also that the denominator represents value added as a proportion of price.

THE TERMS-OF-TRADE EFFECT OF TARIFFS. In contrast to all the attention economists, politicians and the general public have paid to the protection that tariffs provide to domestic industry, the tendency of tariffs to improve the terms on which a country trades its exports for imports, and thereby to increase its share in the gains from international specialization, have been very much neglected. The subject has attracted some attention at the end of the last and the beginning of this century, but mainly as a theoretician's intellectual exercise and an economic curiosum.

While protection results from import duties' raising the *domestic* price that *domestic* buyers have to pay for importables, they improve the terms on which the duty-imposing country trades its exports for imports, provided that they lower the *foreign* price that the *foreign* producers of it receive for them. Similarly, an export duty will also improve a country's terms of trade if it raises the *foreign* price that *foreign* buyers of its exports have to pay for them. Accordingly, tariffs improve a country's terms of trade if the foreign supply of its imports or the foreign demand for its exports is less than perfectly elastic; and a given tariff has the greater impact on the terms of trade, the lower are those elasticities (Bickerdike, 1906; Kaldor, 1940).

The advantage of a tariff that improves the terms of trade can be given two interpretations. First, when a tariff changes the foreign price of imports and/or exports to the foreigners' disadvantage, it causes *them* to pay part of the tariff – a clear and obvious gain for the tariff-imposing country. Secondly, the same gain can also be looked upon as a monopoly or monopsony profit extracted from foreigners by the tariff, which in turn closely resembles the profit margin a monopolist adds on to marginal cost, or a monopsonist subtracts from marginal worth, when he sets his profit-maximizing price. Indeed, when perfect competition among a country's export producers causes them to equate prices to marginal costs and causes its importers to equate the marginal value product of imports to their prices, then export and import duties coincide exactly with a monopolist's and monopsonist's profit margins.

Such a situation resembles a cartel agreement among domestic competitors with respect to their foreign transactions, except that the monopoly or monopsony profits generated accrue to the State in the form of tariff revenue and that the private producers and traders are made worse off than they would be under free trade, because the tariff reduces the volume of their business. From the point of view of the country's national welfare, however, tariffs can be beneficial, in the sense of increasing the sum of the country's private and public real income, just as monopolistic or monopsonistic pricing can increase the monopolist's or monopsonist's profit. Indeed, there are optimum tariffs, which maximize a country's gain from trade, and whose level depends on the price elasticities of the foreign supply of imports and the foreigners' demand for exports, just as the monopolist's profit maximizing profit margin depends on the price elasticity of demand he faces (Scitovsky, 1942).

Tariffs, like monopoly pricing, redistribute income in favour of those imposing them in a way that inflicts a greater loss on those hurt than the gain they secure for those favoured. For that reason, it is important to prevent competitive tariff impositions and increases, whereby each country retaliates in self-defence to the tariffs imposed by others, and so contributes to a general impoverishment of all or almost all, due to the all-round reduction of international specialization and of the gain it generates. Yet, that happened during the 1930s depression; and it can easily happen when each country believes itself to have a small enough share in world trade to erect or raise tariffs unpunished and retaliation is effective or believed to be effective in recapturing some of the lost gain of the retaliating country. Free trade therefore is not a stable situation, unless imposed by a dominant country, such as Great Britain in the 19th century or the United States during the period following World War II (Scitovsky, 1942; Kahn, 1947). What happens when free trade is not enforced, which countries gain, which lose from tariffs and retaliatory tariffs, and what is the nature of the path and final outcome of competitive trade restrictions has received considerable attention in the theoretical literature (Kaldor, 1940; Scitovsky, 1942; Graaff, 1949–50; Johnson, 1953–4; Gorman, 1957–8), but is too complex to summarize here.

Also, the subject has remained a theoretical exercise and faded into the background. Yet, it has two aspects that, though largely overlooked in the literature, deserve mention here. One is that tariffs can exploit a country's monopoly or monopsony position in world markets *only* if that is not already exploited by private firms within the country. The other is that an import duty can be used as countervailing power to prevent a country's being exploited by a foreign exporter's use of *his* monopoly power.

A country's only large producer of an exportable product or its single importer of a foreign product enjoys, of course, the same monopoly or monopsony position in world markets as does the country as a whole. Accordingly, he can, and usually does, exploit that position to his own – as well as to his country's – advantage by setting the profit-maximizing monopoly or monopsony price. The same is approximately true also if, instead of a single monopolist, a few large firms act in open or tacit oligopolistic collusion in setting monopoly prices. When they do that, tariffs for the purpose of exploiting the country's bargaining position in world markets are not only redundant but harmful, because, added to a producer's monopoly (or subtracted from an importer's monopsony) price, they are liable to push the foreign price beyond its profit-maximizing level, thereby inflicting a loss on domestic exporters or importers that exceeds the government's tariff revenue. In short, tariffs and monopolistic profit margins can substitute one for another, complement each other, but cannot be used to exploit the same monopoly or monopsony position twice over.

That explains, for example, why export tariffs and other export restrictions have been imposed almost exclusively on primary products and only in countries where those are grown by many small growers under competitive conditions. Export duties on coffee and the Ghanaian State monopoly for the export of cocoa are the obvious examples. The industrial countries, which export manufactures, have no need for export duties to exploit their monopoly position in world markets, because the large manufacturers of their exportables are usually able to charge monopoly prices on their own, thus making export duties redundant.

The same argument also explains why Britain practised and preached free trade up to the end of the 19th century. Her heavy manufactures were produced and exported by large, monopolistic firms, her light manufactures (textiles), though produced competitively, were exported by large wholesale merchants, and some of her primary-product imports were also handled by large British firms, most of them able to set prices that exploited their foreign and domestic monopoly positions alike and rendered tariffs superfluous.

We come now to the use of an import duty to offset a foreign exporter's monopoly and diminish or eliminate his monopoly profits. Ross Shepherd has shown (Shepherd, 1978) that a variable import duty which varies, and is *expected to vary*, directly with the foreign price of an imported good, raises the country's apparent price elasticity of demand for that import and correspondingly reduces its manufacturer's monopoly power and with it his profit maximizing price. Indeed, under constant cost conditions, a suitable duty will leave unchanged both the volume imported and the domestic price paid for it by domestic consumers, while expropriating the foreign exporter's monopoly profit. Abba Lerner, who seems to have arrived at the same conclusion independently, advocated imposing such a variable duty (which he called 'extortion tax') on oil imports, thereby creating an incentive for OPEC's members to break ranks by reducing price (Lerner, 1980).

In closing, it is worth noting some similarities and differences between the imposition of tariffs and devaluation. A uniform ad valorem duty on all imports combined with a uniform ad valorem subsidy (negative duty) of the same magnitude on all exports is identical to a devaluation of that magnitude in its effects on the balance of trade but leaves unchanged all other international transactions and financial obligations. For that reason, countries anxious not to increase the burden on domestic debtors of foreign debt denominated in foreign currencies have used such and similar policies as means of improving their balance of trade in preference to devaluation. Also, since devaluation worsens a country's terms of trade when the foreign demand for some of its exports is very inelastic, it may be combined with a duty or other restraint on those of its exports (usually primary products), thereby to prevent the deterioration of its terms of trade, or import restriction may be substituted for devaluation.

TIBOR SCITOVSKY

See also EFFECTIVE PROTECTION; INTERNATIONAL TRADE; OPTIMAL TARIFFS; TRADE SUBSIDIES.

BIBLIOGRAPHY

Bickerdike, C.F. 1906. The theory of incipient taxes. *Economic Journal* 16, December, 529–35.

Gorman, W.M. 1958. Tariffs, retaliation, and the elasticity of demand for imports. *Review of Economic Studies* 25, June, 133–62.

Graaff, J. de V. 1949. On optimum tariff structures. *Review of Economic Studies* 17, 47–59.

Johnson, H.G. 1954. Optimum tariffs and retaliation. *Review of Economic Studies* 21, 142–53.

Kahn, R.F. 1947. Tariffs and the terms of trade. *Review of Economic Studies* 15, February, 14–19.

Kaldor, N. 1940. A note on tariffs and the terms of trade. *Economica*, N.S. 7, November, 377–80.

Lerner, A.P. 1980. OPEC – a plan – if you can't beat them, join them. *Atlantic Economic Journal*, September, 1–3.

List, F. 1841. *The National System of Political Economy*. Trans. S.S. Lloyd, London: Longmans, Green & Co., 1885.

Little, I.M.D., Scitovsky, T. and Scott, M.F. 1970. *Industry and Trade in Some Developing Countries: A Comparative Study*. London: Oxford University Press.

Scitovsky, T. 1942. A reconsideration of the theory of tariffs. *Review of Economic Studies* 9, Summer, 89–110.

Shepherd, A.R. 1978. *International Economics: A Micro-Macro Approach*. Columbus: Charles E. Merrill.

Tarshis, Lorie (born 1911). Tarshis was born in Toronto, Canada on 22 March 1911. After a commerce degree at the

University of Toronto, he went to Trinity College, Cambridge, where he took a BA in 1934 and a PhD in 1939. His years in Cambridge, 1932–6, which coincided with the emergence of Keynes's *General Theory*, shaped much of his subsequent professional life. His notes for Keynes's annual series of eight lectures on his work in progress for the years 1932–5 have become an important source for those interested in tracing the evolution of Keynes's views. The two Cambridge revolutions of the 1930s, Keynes's and imperfect competition, focused the analysis of his PhD dissertation, 'The Distribution of Labour Income'. From this came two classic articles in 1938 and 1939 which, along with a contemporaneous piece by John Dunlop (1938), forced Keynes to reconsider his generalization that real and money wages moved inversely over the trade cycle and its implications for the assumption of perfect competition that underlay the analysis of the book (Keynes, 1939).

By then Tarshis had moved to the United States, first to Tufts University (1936–9, 1942–6) and subsequently to Stanford (1946–71). While at Tufts, along with his Cambridge classmate R.B. Bryce, he played a significant role in spreading Keynes's ideas among the Harvard community of economists. Then in 1938 he participated with several other economists in the manifesto *An Economic Program for American Democracy*. Only seven of them eventually signed it – R.V. Gilbert, G.H. Hildebrand Jr., A.W. Stuart, M.Y. and P.M. Sweezy, Tarshis and J.D. Wilson – the government or other connections of the rest preventing them from doing so. The *Program* was 'Keynesian in analysis, stagnationist in diagnosis and all-out in prescription', and was 'instrumental' in driving home to New Deal Washington the need for more spending to overcome the fatal flaw of contemporary capitalism, underinvestment (Stein, 1969, pp. 165–7). His move to Stanford coincided with another effort at Keynesian persuasion, *The Elements of Economics*, the first unashamedly Keynesian introductory textbook. Dogged by controversy over its supposed 'left wing' views, it was much less successful than the slightly later competing text of Paul Samuelson.

During the subsequent forty years, despite his heavy teaching commitments where he probably left his greatest mark, Tarshis has continued to publish regularly. His contributions have related to international finance, the microeconomics of Keynes (most notably the aggregate supply function) and contemporary policy issues.

D.E. MOGGRIDGE

SELECTED WORKS

1938a. Real wages in the United States and Great Britain. *Canadian Journal of Economics and Political Science* 4, August, 362–76.

1938b. (With R.V. Gilbert et al.) *An Economic Program for American Democracy*. New York: Vanguard Press.

1939. Changes in real and money wages. *Economic Journal* 49, March, 150–54.

1947. *The Elements of Economics*. Boston: Houghton Mifflin.

1979. The aggregate supply function in Keynes's *General Theory*. In *Economics and Human Welfare: Essays in Honour of Tibor Scitovsky*, ed. M.J. Boskin, New York: Academic Press.

1984. *World Economy in Crisis*. Toronto: Lorimer.

BIBLIOGRAPHY

Dunlop, J.T. 1938. The movement of real and money wage rates. *Economic Journal* 48, September, 413–34.

Keynes, J.M. 1939. Relative movements of real wages and output. *Economic Journal* 49, March, 34–51.

Stein, H. 1969. *The Fiscal Revolution in America*. Chicago: University of Chicago Press.

tastes, changes in. *See* CHANGES IN TASTE.

tâtonnement and recontracting. In the current theory of general economic equilibrium, recontracting and tâtonnement (a French word meaning 'groping') are used interchangeably to denote a simplifying assumption that no actual transactions, and therefore no production and consumption activities, take place at disequilibria when prices are changed according to the law of supply and demand (Kaldor, 1934; Arrow and Hahn, 1971, pp. 264, 282). Historically speaking, however, this usage is somewhat confusing, since recontracting is originally due to Edgeworth who developed it in a direction different from that in which Walras developed his tâtonnement (Walker, 1973).

Though different interpretations are given as to whether Walras explicitly excluded disequilibrium transactions from the beginning (Patinkin, 1956, p. 533; Newman, 1965, p. 102; Jaffé, 1967, 1981), it is clear that Walras developed his theory of tâtonnement so as to exclude such transactions. To do this there are at least three methods of tâtonnement. First, we may assume that price-taking traders facing market prices cried by the *auctioneer* reveal their plans of demand and supply to the auctioneer but do not make any trade contract among themselves until the auctioneer declares that equilibrium is established. Alternatively, traders may be assumed to make trade contracts (Walras 1926, p. 242, suggested the use of tickets when production is involved) but recontract is assumed always to be possible, in the sense that contract can be cancelled without consent of the other party if market prices are changed. Finally, the effect of past contracts can be nullified by offering new demands (supplies) to offset past supplies (demands), even if it is assumed that past contracts are effective and would be carried out at the current prices when the equilibrium is established (Morishima, 1977, pp. 28–30). Since any changes in prices make the contract unfavourable to one of the parties which then wishes to cancel the trade contract, there is no difference between the three methods of tâtonnement in the behaviour of demand, supply and prices. Recontracting in this sense of tâtonnement is, however, quite different from that developed in Edgeworth's theory of recontract.

We shall start by the consideration of why this assumption of tâtonnement is necessary for the Walrasian theory of general equilibrium, which is the foundation of neoclassical economic theory. The reason lies in the structure of Walrasian economics, dichotomized between real and monetary theories. Then we analyse formal models of tâtonnement including the original one due to Walras and the modified version developed in modern theories of general equilibrium. It is followed by our assessment of the theoretical achievements and empirical relevance of Walrasian tâtonnement economics. Edgeworth's theory of recontract is reviewed in its relation to the Walrasian theory of tâtonnement. Finally, an evaluation is made on the recent studies of tâtonnement and recontracting, to show in which direction further progress should be made.

1. Walras ([1874–7] 1926) insisted that complicated phenomena can be studied only if the rule of proceedings from the simple to the complex is always observed. To understand the fundamental nature of Walrasian economics, it is convenient to make (as did Hicks, 1934) a comparison of Walrasian and Marshallian ways of applying this rule to the study of complicated economic phenomena. Both Walras and Marshall (1890) start with a very simple model of an economy and then proceed to more complex models. There is an important difference, however, between Walrasian general equilibrium analysis and Marshallian partial equilibrium analysis.

Walras first decomposes a complicated economy of the real

world into several fundamental components like consumer-traders, entrepreneurs, consumers' goods, factors of production, newly produced capital goods, and money. He then composes a simple model of a pure exchange economy by picking up a very limited number of such components, that is, individual consumer-traders and consumer's goods, disregarding the existence of all other components. Travel from this simple model to the complex proceeds by adding one by one those components so far excluded, that is, entrepreneurs and factors of production first, then newly produced capital goods, and finally money. In this journey each intermediate model, enlarged from a simpler one and to be enlarged into a more complex one, is still a closed and self-compact logical system. However, each of them is as unrealistic as the starting model, with the exception of the last, into which all the components of a real world economy have been introduced.

Marshall on the other hand studies a whole complex of a real world economy as such. Of course, he also simplifies his study at first by confining his interest to a certain limited number of aspects of the economy. But he does it not by disregarding the existence of other aspects but by assuming that other things remain equal. In this sense most of Marshall's models of an economy, though realistic, are open and not self-sufficient, since some endogenous variables (i.e. the 'other things') remain unexplained and have to be given exogenously.

The simplest model of Walrasian economics is that studied in the theory of exchange, where goods to be exchanged among individual consumer-traders are assumed simply to be endowed to them and not considered as produced at cost. There exist no production activities in this hypothetical world. The corresponding simplest model of Marshall is that of the market day, in which goods to be sold are produced goods, although the amount available for sale is, for the time being, assumed to be constant. Production does exist in this temporary model, though the level of output is assumed to be unchanged. In that Walrasian model which includes production capital goods are introduced as a kind of factor of production but investment (i.e. the production of new capital goods) simply does not exist. On the other hand, in Marshallian short-run theory, which is also a theory of production, investment is actually undertaken though the amount of currently available capital is given. In all of the Walrasian models of exchange, of production and of credit and capital formation there exists no money at all, until it is finally introduced in the theory of circulation and money. In Marshallian models on the other hand money exists from the beginning, though its purchasing power is sometimes assumed to be constant.

In other words, Marshallian theories correspond respectively to special states of the real world economy. The market day (temporary) and short-run models are just as realistic as the long-run model, where capitals are fully adjusted. Thus Marshallian models are practically useful to apply to what Hicks (1934) called particular problems of history or experience. On the other hand, Walrasian models are in general not useful for such practical purposes. They are designed to show the fundamental significance of such components of the real world economy as entrepreneurs and production, investment and the rate of interest, inventories and money, etc., by successively introducing them into simple models which are then developed into more complex ones. Walras' theoretical interest was not in the solution of particular problems but in what Hicks called the pursuit of the general principles which underlie the working of a market economy.

From our standpoint we must emphasize that all exchanges have to be non-monetary (i.e. direct exchanges of goods for goods) in all the Walrasian theories of exchange, production and capital formation and credit, since money has not yet been introduced. Relative prices (including the rate of interest) and hence consumption and production activities are determined in non-monetary real models without using money, while the role of the model of circulation and money lies only in the determination of the level of absolute prices by the use of the money (Morishima, 1977, ch. 11; Negishi, 1979, ch. 2). Thus Walrasian economics is completely dichotomized between non-monetary real theories and monetary theory, in the sense that all non-monetary real variables are determined in the former and money is neutral, that is it does not matter for the determination of such variables. 'That being the case, the equation of monetary circulation, when money is not a commodity, comes very close, in reality, to falling outside the system of equations of (general) economic equilibrium' (Walras, 1926, pp. 326–7).

2. In each of his non-monetary theories Walras tried to show the existence of a general equilibrium in its corresponding self-compact closed model. General equilibrium is a course of state in which not only each individual consumer-trader (entrepreneur) achieves the maximum obtainable satisfaction (profit) under given conditions but also demand and supply are equalized in all markets. In a large economy, how can we make such a situation possible without introducing money? What kind of process of exchange should we consider in order to establish a general equilibrium without using money? Even in the most simple case of an exchange economy, it seems in general almost impossible to satisfy all individual traders by barter exchanges, unless mutual coincidence of wants accidentally prevails everywhere. Walras ingeniously solved this difficulty by his famous tâtonnement, a preliminary process of price (and quantity) adjustment which preceeds exchange transactions and/or effective contracts.

Suppose that all the individual consumer-traders and entrepreneurs meet in a big hall. Since all of them are assumed to be competitive price takers it is convenient to assume (though Walras himself did not do so explicitly) the existence of an *auctioneer* whose only role is to determine prices. At the start the auctioneer calls all prices (including the price of a bond) at random. Individual consumers and entrepreneurs make decisions on the supply and demand of all goods, factors of production and of the bond, assuming that the prices cried by the auctioneer are fixed and that whatever amount they wish can actually be supplied and demanded at these prices. If total demand equals total supply for every good (including the factors of production and the bond) exchange takes place (or contracts are made) at these prices, and the problem is solved.

Generally, however, this will not be the case, in which event no exchange transaction should take place at all, even for a good for which total demand is equal to total supply, and every mutually agreed contract should be cancelled. The auctioneer cancels the earlier prices, which failed to establish a general equilibrium, and calls new prices by following the law of supply and demand, that is raising (lowering) the price of each good for which the demand is larger (smaller) than the supply. The same procedure is repeated until general equilibrium is established. Actual exchange transactions take place and enforceable contracts are made only when every party can actually realize its plan of demand and supply.

Prices change in the process of tâtonnement and it is generally impossible for a single trader to purchase or sell whatever amount he wishes at going prices. Nevertheless, each trader behaves on the assumption that prices are unchanged and that unlimited quantities of demand and supply can be realized at the current prices. This conjecture is justified by the very fact that no exchange transactions are made and no trade contracts are in effect during the tâtonnement, until general equilibrium is established where prices are no longer changed, and every trader can purchase and sell exactly the amount he wishes at going prices.

In a monetary economy of the real world, where of course the tâtonnement assumption cannot be made and some exchange transactions actually take place before general equilibrium is established, even a competitive trader without power to control prices has to expect price changes and to try to sell when the price is high and to buy when the price is low, though he may not always succeed in doing so. This leads to the separation of sales and purchases, a separation which is made possible only by the use of money as the medium of exchange and the store of value. In Walrasian non-monetary real models where the tâtonnement assumption is made, on the other hand, sales and purchases are synchronized when general equilibrium is established so that there is no need for money, and indeed there is no reason why the role of medium of exchange should be exclusively assigned to a single item called money. Since equilibrium prices are already fixed and unchanged almost any non-perishable good can be used if necessary as a medium of exchange.

Walras considered tâtonnement even in his final model, i.e. that of circulation and money. Since disequilibrium transactions are thus excluded and there is no uncertainty, there is no room here for money as a store of value. We have to assume therefore that people demand money only for the sake of convenience in transactions. Since all actual transactions are carried out at general equilibrium after the preliminary tâtonnement is over, however, this rationale for the demand for money is not at all convincing. The only role left for money is to determine its own price, that is the general level of prices.

3. Walras gave two solutions for general equilibrium of each of his non-monetary real models, as well as his monetary model. The first solution is the demonstration that the number of unknowns is equal to the number of independent equations, which Walras called the scientific or mathematical solution. But how can we find a solution of such equations, particularly when the number of equations is very large? The second solution of general equilibrium given by Walras (1926, pp. 162–3, 170–72) is tâtonnement itself, which is suggested by the mechanism of free competition in markets and is called the practical or empirical solution. Taking the example of the simple model of exchange these two solutions may be reformulated in modern notation as follows.

Consider an exchange economy of m goods and denote the price of and the excess demand for the jth good by p_j and E_j respectively. One condition for general equilibrium is that demand is equal to supply in all markets, that is

$$E_j(p_1, \ldots, p_m) = 0, \quad j = 1, \ldots, m. \tag{1}$$

In view of Walras' Law that

$$\sum_j p_j E_j \equiv 0, \tag{2}$$

only $(m-1)$ equations of (1) are independent, while we can assign the role of numéraire to the mth good so that $p_m = 1$, since only relative prices are relevant in a non-monetary economy. Therefore (1) is replaced by

$$E_j(p_1, \ldots, p_{m-1}) = 0, \quad j = 1, \ldots, m-1. \tag{3}$$

Equations (1) or (3) are derived from the competitive behaviour of individual consumer-traders. The ith consumer-trader is assumed to maximize his utility $U_i(x_{il}, \ldots, x_{im})$, subject to the budget constraint

$$\sum_j p_j x_{ij} = \sum_j p_j y_{ij} \tag{4}$$

where x_{ij} and y_{ij} denote respectively the gross demand for the jth good by the ith consumer-trader and the given initial holding of the jth good of the ith consumer-trader. The excess demand for the jth good is then defined as

$$E_j = \sum_i x_{ij} - \sum_i y_{ij}. \tag{5}$$

It is to be noted that excess demand is not defined in (1) and (3) explicitly as a function of the y_{ij}'s. The reason is that the y_{ij}'s are given constants and are assumed not to change through the process of exchange until the demand plans of all consumer-traders are simultaneously realized when general equilibrium is established. In other words the assumption of tâtonnement is already implicitly made in the mathematical or theoretical solution of general equilibrium.

The original form of Walrasian tâtonnement is the process of successive adjustment in each single market. Suppose the initial set of prices cried by the auctioneer $(p_1, \ldots, p_{m-1})$ does not satisfy the condition (3) of general equilibrium, and we are for example in a situation described by

$$\begin{aligned} &E_1(p_1, \ldots, p_{m-1}) > 0 \\ &E_2(p_1, \ldots, p_{m-1}) < 0 \\ &\qquad \cdots \\ &E_{m-1}(p_1, \ldots, p_{m-1}) > 0 \end{aligned} \tag{6}$$

The price of the first good p_1 is now adjusted by reference to its excess demand E, and increased in the situation (6) until an equilibrium in the first market is established, that is

$$E_1(p_1', p_2, \ldots, p_{m-1}) = 0. \tag{7}$$

Here E_1 is assumed to be decreasing with respect to p_1, an assumption which, writing the partial derivative of the excess demand function for the ith good with respect to the kth price by E_{jk}, may be symbolized by $E_{11} < 0$.

Under the new price system $(p_1', p_2, \ldots, p_{m-1})$ the remaining $m-1$ markets may or may not be in equilibrium. If the second market is out of equilibrium, again under the assumption that $E_{22} < 0$, the price of the second good is changed from p_2 to p_2' so as to satisfy

$$E_2(p_1', p_2', p_3, \ldots, p_{m-1}) = 0. \tag{8}$$

[Generally, this will upset the equilibrium in the first market (7).] Under the price system $(p_1', p_2', p_3, \ldots, p_{m-1})$, then, the price of the third good p_3 is adjusted if the third market (where $E_{33} < 0$) is out of equilibrium, upsetting the equilibrium in the second market (8) just established. In this way the last, $m-1$th market, where $E_{m-1,m-1} < 0$, is eventually cleared by changing the price system from $(p_1', \ldots, p_{m-2}', P_{m-1})$ into $(p_1', \ldots, p_{m-2}', p_{m-1}')$ so as to satisfy

$$E_{m-1}(p_{m1}', \ldots, p_{m-2}', p_{m-1}') = 0. \tag{9}$$

By this time all the markets except the last, which were once cleared successively, have generally been thrown out of their respective equilibria again. Neither the price system we have just arrived at, $(p_1', \ldots, p_{m-1}')$, nor the initial system $(p_1, \ldots, p_{m-1})$, is part of a general equilibrium. The question then is which of the systems is closer to a true general equilibrium that satisfies (3). Walras argued that the former price system is closer to equilibrium than the latter since for example $E_1(p'_1, \dots, p'_{m-1}) \neq 0$ is closer to 0 than $E_1(p_1, \dots, p_{m-1}) \neq 0$. The reason for this, according to Walras, is that the change from p_1 to p'_1 which established (7) exerted a direct influence that was invariably in the direction of zero excess demand so far as the first good is concerned. But the subsequent changes from p_2 to $p'_2, \dots, p_{m-1}$ to p'_{m-1}, which jointly moved the first excess demand away from zero exerted only indirect influences, some in the direction of equilibrium and some in the opposite direction, at least so far as the excess demand for the first good is concerned. So up to a certain point they cancelled each other out. Hence, Walras concluded, by repeating the successive adjustment of $m-1$ markets along the same lines, that is changing prices according to the law of supply and demand, we can move closer and closer to general equilibrium.

4. Walras's argument for the convergence of the tâtonnement process to general equilibrium was intended to be, if successful, the first demonstration of the existence of competitive general equilibrium (Wald, 1936). As we said above, it was merely an argument for the plausibility of such convergence of the process of tâtonnement, and cannot be considered as a rigorous demonstration of existence of equilibrium. Whether indirect influences of the prices of other goods on the excess demand of a given good cancel each other out will certainly depend on substitutability and complementarity between goods. For example, indirect influences are *not* cancelled out and the excess demand of a good *is* increased if the prices of all gross substitutes are raised and the prices of all gross complements are lowered. In addition to the Walrasian stability condition for a single market, that is $E_{jj} < 0$ for all j, therefore, some conditions on the cross-effects of prices on excess demands, that is on E_{jk}, $j \neq k$ have to be imposed so as to demonstrate convergence.

It was Allais (1943, vol. 2, pp. 486–9) who first demonstrated the convergence of Walrasian tâtonnement by assuming gross substitutability, that is, $E_{jk} > 0$ for all $j = k$. To see whether the price system moves closer and closer to the general equilibrium, which he assumes to be at least locally unique, Allais defines the distance D of a price system from the equilibrium price system as the sum of the absolute values of the value of excess demand for all goods, including the numéraire. The convergence of tâtonnement is then demonstrated by showing that this distance D is always decreased by changes in prices that are made in accordance with the law of supply and demand. His demonstration may be reformulated in our notation as follows.

The distance to the general equilibrium is defined as

$$D = \sum_j |p_j E_j| \qquad (10)$$

where the summation runs from $j = 1$ to $j = m$, and E_j is defined as a function of $p_1, \dots, p_{m-1}$ as in (3). In view of Walras' Law (2), D can be replaced either by the summation of positive excess demands

$$D_1 = \sum_j p_j \max(0, E_j) \qquad (11)$$

or by the summation of negative excess demands

$$D_2 = -\sum_j p_j \min(0, E_j) \qquad (12)$$

where $\max(0, E_j)$ denotes E_j if it is positive and 0 if E_j is negative, and $\min(0, E_j)$ denotes E_j if it is negative and 0 if E_j is positive. From (2), that is $D_1 - D_2 = 0$, it is clear that

$$D = 2D_1 = 2D_2 \qquad (13)$$

so that whether D is increasing or decreasing can be seen by checking whether D_1 or D_2 (whichever is more convenient) is increasing or decreasing.

Suppose E_1 to be positive as in (6) and that p_1 is raised following the law of supply and demand. From (12), we have

$$\partial D_2 / \partial p_1 < 0 \qquad (14)$$

since $E_{j1} > 0$ for any j such that $E_j < 0$, from gross substitutability. In other words, a change in the price of the first good from p_1 to p'_1 so as to satisfy (7) decreases the sum of negative excess demands D_2 and therefore the distance D to the general equilibrium. Suppose next that $E_2(p'_1, p_2, \dots, p_{m-1})$ is negative and p_2 is lowered to p'_2 so as to satisfy (8). From (11) this time, we have

$$\partial D_1 / \partial p_2 > 0 \qquad (15)$$

since $E_{j2} > 0$ for any j such that $E_j > 0$ from gross substitutability. In other words, a decrease in the price of the second good from p_2 to p'_2 decreases the sum of positive excess demands D_1 and therefore the distance D to the general equilibrium.

Generally, if E_j is positive and p_j is raised D is decreased, which can be seen from the fact that D_2 is decreased. Similarly, if E_j is negative and p_j is lowered again D is decreased, which can be seen from the consideration of the behaviour of D_1. Out of the general equilibrium D remains positive and there exists at least one non-numéraire good with non-zero excess demand, so that its price is changing. The distance to the general equilibrium always decreases out of equilibrium, and therefore we can move closer and closer to that equilibrium by changing prices according to the law of supply and demand, provided that gross substitutability is assumed.

Though Walras discussed the behaviour of the process of successive adjustment, he was not against the consideration of *simultaneous adjustment processes* in all markets (Uzawa, 1960; Jaffé, 1981). If we assume that adjustments take place not only simultaneously but also continuously, the tâtonnement process that each rate of change of price is governed by excess demand can be described by a set of differential equations,

$$\mathrm{d}p_j/\mathrm{d}t = a_j E_j(p_1, \dots, p_{m-1}), \qquad j = 1, \dots, m-1, \qquad (16)$$

where t denotes time and the a_j's are positive constants signifying the speed of adjustment in the jth market. The study of the behaviour of the solutions of (16), that is prices as functions of t, which was initiated by Samuelson (1941) is called the study of the *stability of competitive equilibrium* and has been extensively carried out by many mathematical economists (Arrow and Hahn, 1971, pp. 263–323; Negishi, 1972, pp. 191–206). It is well known that gross substitutability is also a sufficient condition for the *convergence of adjustment processes* like (16).

5. The idea of tâtonnement was clearly suggested to Walras from the observation of how business is done in some well organized markets in the real world, like the stock exchanges, commercial markets, grain markets, fish markets. As a matter of fact, Walras was well informed of the actual operation of the Paris Stock Exchange where disequilibrium transactions actually did not occur (Jaffé, 1981). Tâtonnement is therefore not entirely unrealistic as a model of adjustment in such special markets.

However, it is certainly very unrealistic to apply such a model of special markets to the whole economy, since preliminary adjustments are usually not made before exchange transactions and effective contracts take place, even in markets where competition, though not so well organized, functions fairly satisfactorily. Of course, Walras would have admitted this, since tâtonnement was for him not so much a description of the process of adjustment in the markets of the real world as it was the demonstration of the existence of general equilibrium, that is a limit to which tâtonnement converges. It should be so interpreted not only in the case of successive tâtonnement, which reminds us of the Gauss–Seidel method of solving a set of simultaneous equations, but also in the case of simultaneous tâtonnement (16), where time t is not real calendar time, but hypothetical process time. This is no wonder, since Walrasian non-monetary models are not intended to be faithful descriptions of the real world. They are designed rather to make clear the significance of each component of the market economy and to uncover the general principles that underlie its working.

One may feel that such an interpretation of Walrasian tâtonnement is too strict and that the behaviour of not so well organized markets can be described approximately by the tâtonnement model. Walrasian tâtonnement may be interpreted as something like the laws of motion, that work strictly speaking only in the ideal frictionless world but which can be applied approximately to the real world. The law of supply and demand can certainly be applied even in markets where there is no auctioneer, traders are dispersed, and exchange transactions take place and effective contracts are made before equilibrium of demand and supply is established.

Prices are formed differently in each exchange transaction by negotiation between relevant parties of traders. The Law of Indifference tends to prevail, however, if the transmission of information is nearly perfect, since atomistic traders know the difficulty of purchasing (selling) at prices lower (higher) than the prices offered by competitors and there are, furthermore, arbitrage activities. If demand falls short of supply, it is suicidal for atomistic sellers to offer a price higher than the average market price, while an atomistic purchaser is unable to consider a price lower than the average market price when demand exceeds supply. With disequilibrium of supply and demand, exchange transactions can take place only if demanders (suppliers) can find suppliers (demanders). If demand is deficient therefore sellers consider cutting prices or increasing marketing costs in order to attract more purchasers, since a drastic increase in sales is expected from slight falls in price or slight increases in marketing costs when information is nearly perfect. By observing such behaviour by the sellers, the purchasers also insist on price cuts. Thus price falls in the face of excess supply. Similarly, market prices rise as the result of a similar process of disequilibrium exchange transactions in the face of excess demand, in which the roles of sellers and purchasers are interchanged from the case of excess supply.

Therefore, we can extend (16) to

$$\mathrm{d}p_j/\mathrm{d}t = a_j E_j(p_1, \ldots, p_{m-1}, y_{11}, \ldots, y_{nm}),$$
$$j = 1, \ldots, m-1, \qquad (17)$$

where the E_j's are again derived from (5) but have now to be considered explicitly as functions of the y_{ij}'s, that is the stock of the jth good held by the ith consumer-trader, $i = 1, \ldots, n$, since the y_{ij}'s are no longer constants but instead are changed by disequilibrium transactions among the n consumer-traders. Here we cannot discuss in detail how the y_{ij}'s are changed as a result of transactions at disequilibria, and have to be content with the general assumption that their rates of change depend on everything, that is we have

$$\mathrm{d}y_{ij}/\mathrm{d}t = F_{ij}(p_1, \ldots, p_{m-1}, y_{11}, \ldots, y_{nm}),$$
$$i = 1, \ldots, n, \quad j = 1, \ldots, m, \qquad (18)$$

where the F_{ij}'s are unknown functions incorporating rules for exchange transactions out of equilibria. Models of an economy with (17) and (18) are called non-tâtonnement models or *non-recontracting models*.

Generally, if a non-tâtonnement or non-recontracting process (17) and (18) converges, it does so to an equilibrium that is different from that arrived at by the tâtonnement process (16), since changes in the y_{ij}'s due to disequilibrium exchange transactions have effects on (17) which do not exist in the case of (16). As Newman (1965, p. 102) correctly pointed out, however, the difference can be safely neglected, if the speed of price adjustment in every market is very high [i.e. the a_j's in (17) are very large], since then markets arrive at equilibrium prices so rapidly that the effects of disequilibrium transactions are prevented from becoming serious. Although the possibility of disequilibrium transactions is not institutionally excluded and there may well be some, most transactions are actually carried out at equilibrium so that it looks as if the assumption of tâtonnement is satisfied. In this sense, tâtonnement models can be used to describe the behaviour of non-tâtonnement or non-recontracting markets in the real world.

6. Although the tâtonnement model can be applied to markets that are not so well organized if the transmission of information is nearly perfect and the speed of price adjustment is rapid, the general equilibrium tâtonnement model (16) is still not a realistic description of the real world economy. The reason is that the role of money as the medium of exchange and a store of value is very important in the real world, while as we saw it is highly limited in a model where most exchange transactions are simultaneously carried out at equilibrium. To make our model more realistic so that sales and purchases take place at disequilibria and are separated by the use of money, therefore, we have to get rid of tâtonnement by arguing that the speed of price adjustment is not rapid in (17), so that disequilibrium transactions cannot be ignored.

If the transmission of information is perfect, the law of supply and demand can be applied even in not so well organized markets where no auctioneer exists and disequilibrium transactions take place. This is because every seller (purchaser) perceives an infinitely elastic demand (supply) curve and expects that a drastic increase in sale (purchase) is made possible by a slight reduction (increase) in price. If total demand falls short of total supply in a market then, every trader willingly reduces price or accepts a reduction in it. Similarly, if total demand exceeds total supply in a market every trader willingly raises price or accepts a rise in it.

The transmission of information may not be so perfect, however, in markets where traders are dispersed and so cannot meet in a big hall as they do in the case of Walrasian tâtonnement. Suppose that a market is segmented and transmission of information is perfect among closely related traders, but that it is not so between different segments. Individual traders are assumed to keep contact with current trade partners and not to leave the segment of the market in which they are currently located in search of more favourable trade conditions, unless either they are well informed of such conditions in other segments or trade conditions change unfavourably in the original segment. Possibly because of consideration of cost, traders are constrained by inertia and do not move unless shocked by information on other segments or by changes in the original segment.

Then even an atomistic seller (purchaser) does not perceive an infinitely elastic demand (supply) curve. A seller expects that sales cannot be increased very much by reduction of price since only those purchasers who are currently buying from him are well informed of the price reductions, and this information is not perfectly transmitted to those purchasers who belong to other segments of the market and who are not buying from him. When total demand falls short of total supply and other sellers do not raise the price, it cannot be expected that 'their' purchasers leave them in search of cheaper sellers. The same seller has to expect, however, that sales will be drastically reduced if the price is raised, since those customers who are currently buying will be well informed of this and will leave to search for cheaper sellers, which they can find easily when total demand falls short of total supply and there are many other sellers willing to sell more at the unchanged price.

Atomistic sellers perceive kinked demand curves, with a downward sloping segment for levels of sale higher than the current one, and an almost infinitely elastic segment for levels of sale lower than the current one, when the market is in excess supply. It is very likely then that price does not fall and remains sticky in the face of excess supply (Reid, 1981, pp. 65–6, 96–9; Negishi, 1979, p. 36). It may not pay to reduce price if demand cannot be increased very much. Similarly, an atomistic purchaser perceives a kinked supply curve with an upward sloping segment for levels of purchase higher than the current one, and an almost infinitely elastic segment for levels of purchase lower than the current one, when the market is in excess demand. Since the transmission of information is imperfect and the purchaser cannot attract many sellers by raising price, it may not pay to raise price even if a larger purchase is wanted at the current price. It is very likely, therefore, that price does not rise and remains sticky in the face of excess demand.

Thus prices may be sticky and may not be adjusted quickly by demand and supply in not-well-organized markets in the real world. The speed of adjustment in (17) need not be rapid enough to allow one to ignore the effects of disequilibrium transactions, so that the tâtonnement process (16) cannot then be regarded as a realistic description of adjustment in real-world markets. Walrasian tâtonnement models are, of course, not designed to describe such markets empirically. They are constructed to show how the market mechanism works beautifully under ideal conditions. No one can deny that Walrasian economics succeeded in accomplishing this purpose. The market mechanism, however, does not work so beautifully in the real world. It certainly manages to work somehow but quite often at the cost of prolonged disequilibria in markets, such as involuntary unemployment in the labour market and excess capacity in goods markets. This is why we have to supplement Walrasian economics by launching out into the study of non-Walrasian economics.

7. RECONTRACTING. Since the idea of recontracting is due originally. to Edgeworth, who developed it in a way different from Walras's tâtonnement, the implication of Edgeworth's theory of recontract has to be carefully considered in its relation to the theory of tâtonnement in Walrasian economics. These two theories are different from each other in at least two ways, namely with respect to the Law of Indifference (the uniformity of prices) and to the provisional nature of revocability of trade contracts. The first problem is discussed below, while the second will be considered in the next section.

There have been different interpretations as to whether Edgeworth's *Mathematical Psychics* (1881) excluded disequilibrium transactions or assumed the irrevocability of contracts (Walker, 1973; Creedy, 1980). Even if we assume that disequilibrium transactions are excluded, however, the theory of recontract in Edgeworth is different from the theory of tâtonnement in Walrasian economics. The Law of Indifference (i.e. the existence of uniform market prices even in disequilibria) is imposed as an axiom in the original Walrasian as well as in modern Walrasian economic theories. This axiom may be justified either through arbitrage activities or by the existence of the auctioneer, and enables individual traders to act as price takers who have only to adjust their plans of supply and demand to the given prices. Such an axiom is not imposed in Edgeworth's recontracting model.

To demonstrate his famous limit theorem (Bewley, 1973), Edgeworth starts with a simple two-good two-individual model of exchange, where a trader X offers a good x to a trader Y in exchange for a good y. If we consider the so-called Edgeworth Box diagram, any point on the contract curve, where each of two individual traders is not worse off than before exchange, can be a final settlement of trade contract which cannot be varied by recontract. To narrow down the range of possible final settlements Edgeworth introduces a second X and a second Y, each respectively identical to the first, both in tastes and initial endowments. Since identical traders have to be treated equally in any final settlement, we can still use the same box diagram. Now it can be shown that no final settlement of contract can contain points on the contract curve which give 'small' gains from trade to the X traders. Otherwise, it is 'possible for *one* of the Ys (without the consent of the other) to *recontract* with the two Xs, so that for all those three parties the recontract is more advantageous than the previously existing contract' (Edgeworth, 1881, p. 35). Similarly, it is possible to exclude as final settlements those points which give 'small' trade gains to Y traders.

In this way Edgeworth shows that the range of possible final settlements shrinks as the number of identical traders grows. If there are infinitely many traders the only remaining final settlements turn out to be precisely the points of Walrasian equilibrium, each with a uniform price line, that is the common tangent to indifference curves of X and Y passing through the point of initial endowments. In the terminology of the modern theory of cooperative games, the core of the exchange game (i.e. those allocations not blocked by any coalitions of players) consists only of the Walrasian equilibria when the numbers of the Xs and the Ys are each infinitely large. Thus Edgeworth tries to show that the recontracting process in the large economy, where traders obtain a free flow of information through the making and breaking of provisional contracts, leads to the same uniform prices that are given by the auctioneer to price-taking traders in Walrasian equilibria. Though there are no uniform market prices and individual traders are not assumed to be price-takers in Edgeworth's recontracting process, the resulting equilibrium exchanges are the same as those obtained through Walrasian tâtonnement in a large economy. In such an economy, therefore, where information is perfect, we can safely argue as if there were uniform market prices and as if traders were price-takers. In a sense, Edgeworth justified the Walrasian axiom, since axioms of theories should be assessed not by themselves but by the results derived from them. Even if the Walrasian axiom is not itself realistic, the results derived from it can be as realistic as those derived from more realistic but more complicated axioms.

In later writings Edgeworth confirmed his early position on Walras and the uniformity of prices. Walras

> describes *a* way rather than *the* way by which economic equilibrium is reached. ... Walras's laboured description of prices set up or 'cried' in the market is calculated to divert attention from a sort of higgling which may be regarded as

more fundamental than his conception, the process of *recontract* ... . The proposition that there is only one price in a perfect market may be regarded as *deducible* from the more axiomatic principle of recontract (*Mathematical Psychics*, p. 40 and context: Edgeworth, 1925, vol. 2, pp. 311–23).

We may add that even the existence of a uniform rate-of-exchange between any two commodities is perhaps not so much axiomatic as deducible from the process of competition in a perfect market (Edgeworth, 1925, vol. 2, p. 453).

8. It is possible to interpret Edgeworth's theory of bilateral exchange (Edgeworth, 1925, vol. 2, pp. 316–19) as a theory of a process where not only the rate of exchange is variable but also contracts are irrevocable. Starting from a situation with initial holdings, two goods are actually exchanged so as always to increase the utility of each of the two traders. Since exchanges are irrevocable, however, where on the contract curve this process of exchange will terminate depends on the path of exchanges as well as on the initial holdings. Hence it contrasts strongly with Walrasian tâtonnement, the equilibrium of which depends only on the initial holdings. There is no confusion, however, between this theory of Edgeworth and Edgeworth's theory of recontract interpreted in the sense of tâtonnement, since the modern extension of the former theory to the case of multiple traders is rightly called the theory of Edgeworth's *barter* process (Uzawa, 1962; Fisher, 1983, pp. 29–31).

Incidentally, Edgeworth's idea that exchanges necessarily take place only in the direction of increasing utilities can be relevant only in a barter economy. In a monetary economy an exchange of one good against another is decomposed into an exchange of the first good against money and an exchange of money against the second good. Even though the completed exchange of the two goods increases utility, its first half need not do so since in the course of the exchange process one may temporarily receive more money than one plans to keep eventually. In other words, one may impose a rule for non-monetary goods of no overfulfilment of demand and supply plans in the process of exchange, but this cannot be done for money, which has to act both as the medium of exchange and as a store of value beyond the current period.

In view of the current usage of the concept of recontracting in the sense of tâtonnement, what is confusing is the fact that Edgeworth sometimes, and particularly in his later writings, applied his recontracting model to situations where exchange transactions actually take place at disequilibria. To show that his model is of more than academic interest Edgeworth considered the case of a labour market, which each day ends in disequilibrium after exchange transactions have taken place at disequilibrium rates of exchange. From day to day, as the traders' knowledge of the state of the disequilibrium in the market changes they progressively modify their behaviour, changing the rate of exchange in such a way that the market converges to equilibrium.

Since labour service is perishable within a day and the number and dispositions of the traders are assumed to be unchanged, this process over a sequence of days is formally equivalent to the recontracting process within a day, even though in the former process contracts made on the previous days are irrevocable while in the latter disequilibrium contracts are revocable. Edgeworth insisted that in this example of a process over a sequence of days (Edgeworth, 1925, vol. 1, p. 40) traders do recontract, in the full sense of *Mathematical Psychics*. Since contracts made in earlier days are irrevocable, however, in this case to recontract implies that a new contract is made which is different from that carried out on the previous day. It does not imply the cancellation of contracts already made.

Only a formal similarity exists between these two processes of recontracting, which is due to the assumption that disequilibrium exchange transactions do not really involve a permanent redistribution of wealth. Although labour service is perishable within a day, however, the money paid against labour service certainly is not and it is likely that a redistribution of wealth does take place over a sequence of days. Even from a formal point of view, then, Edgeworth's model of the labour market is rather a pioneering instance of *non-recontracting models*.

9. No one can deny that the rigorous demonstration of the dynamic stability of tâtonnement under certain sufficient conditions has substantially improved on the original argument for the plausibility of its convergence that was made by Walras. More importantly, however, the recent studies on stability have helped us to understand the underlying economic assumptions of the Walrasian tâtonnement process itself, and made us realize its considerable differences from most price adjustment processes in actual economies. The similar studies of Edgeworth's recontracting process have been helpful in the same way.

As we have shown, Walrasian tâtonnement is a realistic approximation to some actual adjustment processes, provided that the transmission of information is perfect and the speed of adjustment is rapid, as is roughly the case in well organized markets. The problem that remains to be studied, therefore, is the nature of adjustment processes when these conditions are not satisfied, that is, when markets are not so well organized. This is the problem of non-recontracting models in non-Walrasian or disequilibrium economies.

TAKASHI NEGISHI

See also ADJUSTMENT PROCESSES; AUCTIONEER; GENERAL EQUILIBRIUM; STABILITY; WALRAS, LÉON.

BIBLIOGRAPHY

Allais, M. 1943. *Traité d'économie pure*. Paris: Imprimerie Nationale, 2nd edn, 1952.

Arrow, K.J. and Hahn, F.H. 1971. *General Competitive Analysis*. San Francisco: Holden-Day.

Bewley, T.F. 1973. Edgeworth's conjecture. *Econometrica* 41(3), May, 425–54.

Creedy, J. 1980. Some recent interpretations of *Mathematical Psychics*. *History of Political Economy* 12(2), Summer, 267–76.

Edgeworth, F.Y. 1881. *Mathematical Psychics: An Essay on the Application of Mathematics to the Moral Sciences*. London: C. Kegan Paul & Co.

Edgeworth, F.Y. 1925. *Papers Relating to Political Economy*. 3 vols, London: Macmillan.

Fisher, F.M. 1983. *Disequilibrium Foundations of Equilibrium Economics*. Econometric Society Monographs in Pure Theory, Cambridge: Cambridge University Press.

Hicks, J.R. 1934. Léon Walras. *Econometrica* 2, October, 338–48.

Jaffé, W. 1967. Walras's theory of *tâtonnement:* a critique of recent interpretations. *Journal of Political Economy* 75(1), February, 1–19.

Jaffé, W. 1981. Another look at Léon Walras's theory of *tâtonnement*. *History of Political Economy* 13(2), Summer, 313–36.

Kaldor, N. 1934. A classificatory note on the determinateness of equilibrium. *Review of Economic Studies* 1, February, 122–36.

Marshall, A. 1890. *Principles of Economics*. London: Macmillan.

Morishima, M. 1977. *Walras' Economics: A Pure Theory of Capital and Money*. Cambridge: Cambridge University Press.

Negishi, T. 1972. *General Equilibrium Theory and International Trade.* Amsterdam: North-Holland.
Negishi, T. 1979. *Microeconomic Foundations of Keynesian Macroeconomics.* Amsterdam: North-Holland.
Newman, P. 1965. *The Theory of Exchange.* Englewood Cliffs, NJ: Prentice-Hall.
Patinkin, D. 1956. *Money, Interest, and Prices: An Integration of Monetary Theory.* Evanston: Row, Peterson.
Reid, G.C. 1981. *The Kinked Demand Curve Analysis of Oligopoly: Theory of Evidence.* Edinburgh: Edinburgh University Press.
Samuelson, P.A. 1941. The stability of equilibrium: comparative statics and dynamics. *Econometrica* 9, April, 97–120.
Uzawa, H. 1960. Walras' tâtonnement in the theory of exchange. *Review of Economic Studies* 27(74), June, 182–94.
Uzawa, H. 1962. On the stability of Edgeworth's barter process. *International Economic Review* 3(2), May, 218–32.
Wald, A. 1936. Über einige Gleichungssysteme der mathematischen Ökonomie. *Zeitschrift für Nationalökonomie* 7, 637–70.
Walker, D.A. 1973. Edgeworth's theory of recontract. *Economic Journal* 83, March, 138–49.
Walras, L. 1874–7. *Éléments d'économie politique pure ou théorie de la richesse sociale.* Definitive edn, Lausanne, 1926. Trans. by W. Jaffé as *Elements of Pure Economics.* London: George Allen and Unwin; Homewood, Ill.: Richard D. Irwin, 1954.

Taussig, Frank William (1859–1940). Taussig was born on 28 December 1859 in St Louis, Missouri, and died on 11 November 1940 in Cambridge, Massachusetts. After starting college at Washington University, St Louis, he transferred to Harvard University, where he received the BA (1879), PhD (1883) and LL.B (1886). He also studied at the University of Berlin.

Taussig was one of the foremost US economists for half a century. He was on the Harvard faculty from 1885 to 1935, where he was a magisterial teacher and edited the *Quarterly Journal of Economics* from 1896 to 1936. A member of several government commissions, he was the first chairman of the US Tariff Commission, 1917–19, and an adviser to President Woodrow Wilson. He was president of the American Economic Association in 1904 and 1905. His *Principles of Economics* (1911) was the foremost US textbook for generations of economists and non-economists.

Taussig was accurately called 'the American Marshall' by Joseph Schumpeter because of his professional stature. He shared with Alfred Marshall an identification with the Ricardo–Mill tradition coupled with a willingness to integrate the ideas of marginalism; a scepticism of the mathematicization of economics; a desire to moderate conflict within the discipline; an understanding that economics was or should be more an organon of analysis, a collection of tools, than a body of doctrine; a sympathy for the working class; and a view that economics was to remain political economy, to include what Schumpeter called 'economic sociology'. He preferred J.S. Mill's *Principles of Political Economy* to any modern text, including Marshall's *Principles*, because in his view it prevented delusions as to economic questions being easy of solution. Like Marshall, too, he considered the Austrian system needlessly complex.

His principal work as an economic theorist lay in wage theory and in international trade theory and policy. In the former, he attempted to resuscitate a modified version of the wages fund theory, centring on the relative inelasticity of the short-run supply of consumer goods, which he combined with marginal productivity theory. He stressed, however the role of noncompeting groups (as part of his great realism in matters of stratification), criticized John Bates Clark's moralistic version of marginal productivity theory and argued that the frequent superior advantage in bargaining of employers meant that marginal productivity was only an upper limit, in the absence of effective competition.

In the field of international trade, in which he was the principal US figure for decades, his major concerns were the complexities of comparative advantage, the role of the specie flow mechanism and the international trade mechanism under nonspecie monetary systems, and the history and analysis of protection. His position on protectionism was complex: he affirmed free trade, accepted the infant-industry argument with considerable scepticism of its application in practice, favoured gradual lessening of tariffs and (or but) affirmed a stable tariff system rather than policies of disruptive shifts and shocks.

In other policy controversies he strenuously opposed the free coinage of silver as inflationary; criticized unemployment insurance and minimum wages as violative of traditional individual initiative; thought progressive taxation less important than the elimination of monopoly and the use of education to diffuse opportunity; and, understanding of worker reliance on unions, blamed labour–management conflict on the failure of management to exercise the responsibilities of wealth and power and to be more understanding of worker interests and ambitions.

Taussig's political economy, or economic sociology, set him off from most other leading orthodox economists. He saw society as both a structure and a struggle for power and privilege, in which an instinct of domination and an impulse of emulation were prevalent if not dominant. These ideas pervaded his *Principles*, in which he presented, for example, a functional analysis of the leisure class and, in his *Inventors and Money Makers* (1915–16) and (with C.S. Joslyn) *American Business Leaders* (1932), a further analysis of both the complex psychological bases of economic behaviour and the role of leadership in the successful operation of the market mechanism. Schumpeter wrote that Taussig was 'among those few economists who realize that the method by which a society chooses its leaders, in what, for its particular structure, is the fundamental social function ... is one of the most important things about a society, most important for its performance as well as for its fate' (Schumpeter, 1951, p. 217). In these respects, Taussig's work was compatible with institutionalism, but his establishment position apparently kept those in the latter tradition from fully appreciating his contributions. Taussig's ideas here, supplementing those of Friedrich von Wieser, had some influence on Schumpeter himself.

WARREN J. SAMUELS

See also WAGES-FUND DOCTRINE.

SELECTED WORKS

1888. *The Tariff History of the United States.* 8th edn, revised, New York: Putnam's, 1931.
1896. *Wages and Capital.* New York: D. Appleton.
1911. *Principles of Economics.* 4th edn, New York: Macmillan, 1939.
1915a. *Some Aspects of the Tariff Question.* 3rd edn, enlarged, Cambridge, Mass.: Harvard University Press, 1931.
1915b. *Inventors and Money Makers.* New York: Macmillan.
1927. *International Trade.* New York: Macmillan.
1932. (With C.S. Joslyn.) *American Business Leaders: a Study in Social Origins and Social Stratification.* New York: Macmillan.

BIBLIOGRAPHY

Opie, R. 1941. Frank William Taussig (1959–1940). *Economic Journal* 51, June–September, 347–68.
Schumpeter, J.A. 1951. *Ten Great Economists.* New York: Oxford University Press.

Tawney, Richard Henry (1880–1962). R.H. Tawney was an economic historian and socialist philosopher whose Anglican beliefs lay at the heart of his influential studies of the enduring problem of the ethics of wealth distribution. As Professor of Economic History at the London School of Economics from 1921 to 1958, he became the doyen of a school of thought which defined the subject as the exploration of the resistance of groups and individuals in the past to the imposition on them of capitalist modes of thought and behaviour.

In his first book, *The Agrarian Problem in the Sixteenth Century* (1912) – written to provide an appropriate text for his pioneering tutorial classes for the Workers' Educational Association – he examined patterns of rural development, protest and litigation surrounding the enclosure of land in Tudor England. After service in the British Army during the First World War – he was severely wounded on the first day of the Battle of the Somme – Tawney returned to his scholarship and developed the arguments which appeared in perhaps his best-known work, *Religion and the Rise of Capitalism* (1926). Here he showed how alien to the teachings of the Reformation was the assumption that religious thought had no bearing on economic behaviour. Tawney captured in classical prose the clash within religious opinion that preceded that abnegation of the social responsibility of the churches and suggested that 'religious indifferentism' was but a phase in the history of Christian thought.

In *Religion and the Rise of Capitalism* Tawney crystallized a number of ideas he had begun to consider in the pre-1914 period. In a Commonplace Book he kept from 1912 to 1914, Tawney jotted down notes on many of his religious and historical preoccupations. Among them is the simple query, 'I wonder if Puritanism produced any special attitude toward economic matters.' Over the following decade, he gathered evidence on this subject, and presented preliminary statements in the Scott Holland Memorial Lectures at King's College, London, in 1922, and in the lengthy introduction he wrote for a 1925 edition of Thomas Wilson's *Discourse on Usury* of 1569.

In the notes Tawney left concerning this facet of his historical research, there is no evidence whatsoever that he drew on the celebrated essay of Max Weber, originally published in 1905, on *The Protestant Ethic and the Spirit of Capitalism.* Indeed, a full appreciation of Tawney's Anglican concerns requires a divorce between the two partners of the so-called 'Tawney-Weber' thesis.

It is true that both men believed that (in Tawney's words) 'The fundamental question to be asked, after all, is not what kind of rules a faith enjoins, but what kind of character it values and cultivates.' They agreed as well that there was in Calvinism a corrosive force which undermined traditional doctrines of social morality in ways which would have shocked the early reformers. And they shared the view that in Protestant teaching there was an important emphasis in religious terms on the 'inner isolation of the individual' which reinforced a more general individualism of social and economic behaviour.

But what differentiates their work is the uses to which they put their interpretations of Protestantism. Weber's essay was but one part of a comprehensive study of the sociology of religion. It reflects his overriding concern with the development of what he termed the rational bureaucratic character of modern society. In both these facets of his work he charted the progressive, relentless, and irreversible demystification of the world.

Weber's essay helped foster a belief in the bleak permanence of the spirit of capitalism which Tawney laboured to refute throughout his work. *Religion and the Rise of Capitalism* was written precisely to counter the view that social indifferentism in religious thought and individualism in economic thought were unchangeable features of modern life. If Weber's purpose was to describe the demystification of the world, Tawney's was to help in the demystification of capitalism, by stripping it of some of its most powerful ideological supports, derived from one reading of the Protestant tradition.

Anglicanism is, of course, a house of many mansions, in which there is room for reactionaries and socialists alike. The view that capitalism is unchristian because it stultifies the common fellowship of men of different means and occupations has never been more than a minority view. But, at precisely the same time as he was writing *Religion and the Rise of Capitalism*, Tawney joined a number of other influential Anglicans who spoke out against capitalism as a way of life which violated the moral precepts of their faith.

This position was as evident in his essays in political philosophy as it was in his scholarship in economic history. In *The Acquisitive Society* (1921) and in *Equality* (1931), Tawney argued that capitalism was an irreligious system of individual and collective behaviour, since it was based on the institutionalization of distinctions between men based on inherited or acquired wealth. For a Christian, such divisions manifested a denial of the truth that all men are equally children of sin and equally insignificant in the eyes of the Lord. What Matthew Arnold had called the 'religion of inequality' was really the obverse of a Christian way of looking at the world.

Tawney's legacy has been particularly pervasive, because his voice had a resonance which appealed to many who did not share his religious outlook. This was in part because he wrote with the moral outrage of Marx and with the grace and eloquence of Milton. His strength lay too in the fact that his was a distinctively English voice. This did not prevent his advocacy of the comparative method in the study of economic history, best evidenced in his book *Land and Labour in China* (1932), written after an eight-month mission to China as an educational adviser to the League of Nations, and in a history of the American labour movement he wrote while adviser to Lord Halifax, British Ambassador to Washington during World War II.

But Tawney's influence lies more centrally in his writings on the moral issues posed by capitalist economic development in Britain. His call for an alternative to the cash nexus – firmly within the tradition of Owen, Ruskin and Morris – has continued to strike a chord among many people not of religious temperament who have sought indigenous answers to the problems of a society crippled by the injuries of class.

J.M. WINTER

See also FABIAN ECONOMICS; WEBER, MAX.

SELECTED WORKS

1912. *The Agrarian Problem in the Sixteenth Century.* London: Longmans.

1914: (ed., with A.E. Bland and P.A. Brown.) *English Economic History: Selected Documents.* London: Bell.

1921. *The Acquisitive Society.* London: Bell.

1924. (ed., with E. Power.) *Tudor Economic Documents.* London: Longmans.

1926. *Religion and the Rise of Capitalism.* London: Murray.

1927. (ed.) *Economic History: The Collected Papers of George Unwin.* London: Macmillan.

1931. *Equality.* London: Allen & Unwin.

1932. *Land and Labour in China.* London: Allen & Unwin.

1953. *The Attack and other Essays.* London: Allen & Unwin.

1958. *Business and Politics under James I: Lionel Cranfield as Merchant and Minister*. Cambridge: Cambridge University Press.
1964. *The Radical Tradition*. London: Allen & Unwin.
1972. *R.H. Tawney's Commonplace Book*. Ed. D.M. Joslin and J.M. Winter, Cambridge: Cambridge University Press.
1978. *History and Society. Essays by R.H. Tawney*. Ed. J.M. Winter, London: Routledge & Kegan Paul.
1979. *The American Labour Movement and Other Essays*. Ed. J.M. Winter, Brighton: Harvester Press.

BIBLIOGRAPHY
Terrill, R. 1974. *R.H. Tawney and His Times*. Cambridge, Mass.: Harvard University Press.
Winter, J.M. 1974. *Socialism and the Challenge of War*. London: Routledge & Kegan Paul.

taxation. *See* PROGRESSIVE AND REGRESSIVE TAXATION; PROPERTY TAXATION; TAXATION OF CAPITAL; TAXATION OF CORPORATE PROFITS; TAXATION OF INCOME; TAXATION OF WEALTH.

taxation of capital. Taxes on the income from capital have generated a large debate for two reasons. First, the contrast between the arguments for efficiency and equity seems to be particularly sharp here. Second, there exists a variety of views on the appropriate choice of an economic model and its parametric values that are relevant for policy. In this exposition, emphasis will be put on the dynamic aspects of a uniform tax on capital in general equilibrium. In most economies the tax on capital discriminates between different sectors (corporate capital, housing) and induces some static efficiency cost. This cost will be considered only very briefly in comparison with the dynamic efficiency cost.

1. THE IMPACT ON CAPITAL ACCUMULATION. A dynamic framework is essential in the analysis of the taxation of capital income, and it is useful to recall that there are three generic models of capital accumulation. The first is the so-called neoclassical model with an ad hoc specification of the saving function that depends on the flows of incomes and on the interest rate. Although there is little theoretical or empirical foundation for this form, a vague justification has been found in the argument that individuals may not optimize rationally over time, or that capital markets do not operate like standard intratemporal markets. However, the main value of this specification seems to be analytical expediency. In the second type of model, individuals optimize a life-time utility function with no bequest. The third model assumes that individuals care about the welfare of their next descendants as if they would be reincarnated in these descendants with the same utility function. A recursive argument implies that individuals act as if they would live forever.

Most dynamic studies on the taxation of capital income rely on one of these models, or a variation between these types. The models have different implications for the impact of the taxation of capital income on the level of capital accumulation and output, and for the method of evaluation of the tax on capital.

In the neoclassical model the tax reduces the net flow of saving (which is equal to the growth of capital on the balanced growth path at the natural rate), and has a negative impact on capital accumulation. The magnitude of the capital reduction is of course greater when the propensity to save from disposable income has a positive elasticity with respect to the rate of return, net of tax.

In the life cycle model, the capital stock behaves like the level of water in a bathtub. On the balanced growth path it is in equilibrium between the inflow of the savings of the younger generations and the outflow of the dissavings of the older generations. The impact of the tax depends on the elasticity of this equilibrium level with respect to the net rate of return to capital. The tax induces a decrease of the level of capital, if and only if the interest elasticity is positive (Diamond, 1971). A weaker condition is sufficient for a decrease of capital when there is a fixed factor of production such as land because the tax on capital induces an appreciation of land that diverts savings from capital (Chamley and Wright, 1986).

When the utility function is additively separable, the value of the interest elasticity of the aggregate stock of capital that is generated by the life-cycle process in the steady state depends mainly on two parameters. The first is the short-run elasticity of saving with respect to the interest rate, which is proportional to the intertemporal elasticity of substitution of consumption. The second is the length of an individual's horizon that determines the time span during which he can accumulate capital and consume it. When the length of an individual life tends to infinity, he has more time to save up to the point where the rate of return and the rate of time preference are equal. This implies that the elasticity of supply of the stock of capital with respect to the rate of return is larger (Summers, 1981).

In the limit case where individuals have infinite lives, this elasticity of supply is infinite. The impact of the capital income tax is negative and its magnitude depends on the elasticity of the demand for capital by firms. The long-term impact of the tax may be large, but a steady state analysis may be misleading since it neglects the transition period.

2. DYNAMIC INCIDENCE. In the short-run, an increase of the tax rate on capital falls entirely on capital income. In the neoclassical model, the dynamic impact of the tax is a lower level of capital and of the wage rate in the long run, and a higher gross rate of return. In the example of an economy where all profits are saved and all wages consumed, a well-known result is that a tax on profit with transfer to workers, lowers the level of consumption of workers in the steady state. This occurs because the tax induces a shift away from the golden rule. For more general specifications, the incidence of this is shifted at least partially to labour income (Feldstein, 1974).

The concept of factor incidence loses its meaning in an economy where the optimizing behaviour of agents is fully specified. In the life-cycle model for example, every individual goes through a worker and a capitalist phase. The proper evaluation method is the analysis of the welfare impact of the tax to which we now turn.

3. EFFICIENCY COST. A first step in the computation of the welfare cost of the tax on capital is to assume that the economy is composed of a large number of identical individuals who are price takers. In the dynamic context, these individuals become families with an infinite horizon. The welfare cost of the tax is defined either with respect to lump-sum taxation, or as the differential welfare cost with respect to alternate forms of distortionary taxation.

The method of analysis is to consider a small variation of the tax rate combined with a change of lump-sum taxation or of other tax rates to keep the total revenues invariant. An important assumption is that the tax rate is constant over time. The efficiency cost is given by the difference between the levels of welfare (or its income equivalent), as measured on the dynamic path with and without the tax changes, respectively. For convenience, the original position the economy is in a steady state. An essential aspect of the method is that individuals have perfect foresight and optimize rationally over time. Other forms of expectations (such as myopic expectations or other types), may be convenient for large models but they lead to strange results. For example, a tax on capital income could correct myopic expectations and improve welfare if the level of the capital stock is lower than in the steady state.

When the tax rate is small and there are no other taxes, the welfare cost is of the second order with respect to revenues, a result that is well known for any tax. Note that the impact on the steady state level of output is of the first order. This illustrates how comparisons between steady states that ignore transitional effects can lead to large errors.

The effect of an increase of the tax rate on capital income has two components. In the short run, the level of consumption increases. In the long run the levels of capital, output and consumption are lower than in the initial steady state. The relative weights of these two effects depend on the difference between the growth rate of the economy and the discount rate. Only in the special case where these two rates are almost equal, is the transition component relatively insignificant. The comparison between steady states is then a proper evaluation method.

Consider first the case where the labour supply is fixed, and assume that there is no other tax in the original position. Two structural parameters are important for the value of the excess burden of the tax. First, there is a positive relation between the welfare cost and the intertemporal elasticity of substitution of the utility function. This effect is related to the transition path between steady states. It vanishes when the value of the growth rate tends to that of the discount rate.

Second, the welfare cost is positively related to the elasticity of substitution between capital and labour in the production function. For plausible values of this elasticity, the relation is almost linear. The smaller the elasticity, the larger is the fraction of the tax burden shifted to labour (which is a fixed factor here). When the elasticity is equal to zero, there is no distortion.

When the labour supply is elastic, the welfare cost is larger because the tax has a negative impact on the wage rate that affects the supply of labour. The marginal efficiency cost of the capital income tax is also larger when there are other taxes in the original position.

The differential welfare cost between the taxes on capital income and labour income is not always positive. A reduction of the tax rate on capital income that is maintained over time implies a lump sum transfer to the owners of the capital in place at the time of the tax reform. Therefore, a substitution of the capital income tax by the wage tax (at rates constant overtime), is not always efficient (Auerbach, Kotlikoff and Skinner, 1984; Chamley, 1985).

When the difference between the growth rate and the discount rate is small, the magnitude of the lump-sum transfer to the old capital is negligible with respect to the welfare cost of other taxes. In this case the differential welfare cost between the taxes on the incomes of capital and labour is positive. Its value depends on the interest elasticity of the demand for capital by firms and it is independent of the parameters of the utility function.

The measurement of the efficiency cost of the tax on capital income is more difficult when the population of individuals is heterogeneous, since it may involve implicit or explicit interpersonal comparisons of income and equity tissues. Auerbach et al. (1983, 1986), use a lump-sum redistributive authority to isolate the efficiency cost in an overlapping generation model.

Finally, the stylized model of dynamic general equilibrium is potentially a useful tool for the evaluation of a capital tax that is raised on a specific sector (such as the corporate tax), when agents optimize over time. Preliminary estimates indicate that for a production technology with constant returns to scale, the cost of the intrasectoral misallocation may be greater than the intertemporal welfare cost.

4. OPTIMAL TAX RATES AND REDISTRIBUTION. The standard method for the determination of a programme of efficient tax rates on capital income is to choose somewhat arbitrarily, an origin of time, and to analyse from that point on the standard second-best problem where the tax on capital income is one of the fiscal instruments.

The distortion induced by the tax on capital income increases with the interval between the moment of the announcement and the date at which the tax is actually raised because the supply elasticity of savings with respect to the rate of return increases also with time. This implies the disturbing property that the policy of second-best is time inconsistent. Since the tax on capital income has a very low efficiency cost at the beginning of the policy horizon, an arbitrary limit may have to be imposed on the tax rate for some initial interval of time so that the policy is defined.

An interesting result is that for fairly general assumptions, the long-run efficient value of the tax rate on capital income is equal to zero when the fiscal instruments are the taxes on the incomes of capital and labour, respectively. The two main assumptions are that a steady state exists in the long run, and that some individuals have an infinite horizon with an asymptotic rate of time preference equal to the social rate of time preference. The latter assumptions is satisfied when the individual's utility function satisfies the axiom of Koopmans. It does not have to be separable between periods. The steady state is locally stable for additive utility functions and values of the tax rates that are not too large (Chamley, 1986). The same result holds when the wage tax is replaced by an ad valorem consumption tax.

On the transition to the steady state the value of the tax rate on capital income is in general different from zero. For an economy where the government expenditures fluctuate, the debt has been considered as a useful instrument for tax smoothing and the minimization of the efficiency cost of raising revenues (Barro, 1979). It is interesting to observe that when the efficiency cost of taxation is derived explicitly from price distortions, a tax on the income of capital (with a positive or negative rate), may perform the same function (Chamley 1980). Its role is to offset the intertemporal distortions that are caused by the variations of the tax rates on consumption and labour income that occur when the government budget has to be balanced in each period.

When individuals have finite lives and an operative bequest motive *à la* Barro, the standard Ramsey rules (Diamond and Mirrlees, 1981), apply for the taxation of the savings that are used in life cycle consumption. However, the taxation of intergenerational transfers is suboptimal in the second-best (i.e. when the labour tax is an alternative to the capital income tax).

The result holds under a variety of assumptions about the heterogeneity of the population (Judd, 1985), and casts some doubt on the redistributive value of capital taxation in the long run. This is in contrast to other studies that use an ad hoc specification of the processes of saving and income distribution

(Stiglitz, 1978). The result is not valid however when there are binding restrictions on negative bequests.

In a life-cycle framework the government that maximizes a social welfare function is chosen somewhat arbitrarily, as the representative of future generations. The level of the capital generated in the process of saving and dissaving for selfish life-cycle consumption, is not in general optimal when the welfare of future generations is taken into account in an intergenerational comparison.

An important issue here is whether the government can affect the level of capital directly through its saving or dissaving. If public saving is feasible, the efficient tax rates on the incomes of capital and labour on the dynamic path tend to values in the steady state that are determined by the Ramsey rules, and they depend on the price elasticities of the supply of labour and consumption at different instants (Pestieau, 1974).

When there are binding restrictions on public saving or dissaving, they can be alleviated by exploiting the differences between the timings of the taxes on labour and capital, respectively. The capital income tax is levied later in life than the labour income tax. A government that is restricted from accumulating capital, could 'entrust' the young with some capital through a labour tax, and recover it later through the capital income tax in order to place it with the next generation and so on. The opposite policy can be used when the government wants to hide the public debt from the accountants. This 'wealth carrying' function of the tax system invalidates the standard formulae for efficient taxation (Atkinson and Sandmo, 1980).

5. OTHER ISSUES. The analysis has so far omitted the adjustment cost of investment and the international mobility of capital. The adjustment costs reduce the possibilities for intra- or intertemporal distortions, and the potential welfare gains of tax reform. The international mobility of capital has the opposite effect. One possible formulation of adjustment costs is the q-theory of investment that has been applied for the corporate tax by Summers (1981).

The issues of adjustment cost and international mobility have been integrated recently in an analytical model by Bovenberg (1986), who finds that the welfare cost of the capital income tax is significantly larger in open economies compared to closed economies, only when the degree of international capital is very high.

CHRISTOPHE CHAMLEY

See also CAPITAL GAINS AND LOSSES.

BIBLIOGRAPHY

Atkinson, A.B. and Sandmo, A. 1980. Welfare implications of the taxation of savings. *Economic Journal* 90, 529–49.

Auerbach, A.J. and Kotlikoff, L.J. 1987. *Dynamic Fiscal Policy*. Cambridge: Cambridge University Press.

Auerbach, A.J., Kotlikoff, L.J. and Skinner, J. 1983. The efficiency gains from dynamic tax reform. *International Economic Review* 24, 81–100.

Barro, R.J. 1974. Are government bonds net wealth? *Journal of Political Economy* 82, 1095–117.

Barro, R.J. 1979. On the determination of the public debt. *Journal of Political Economy* 87, 940–71.

Bovenberg, L.A. 1986. Capital income taxation in growing open economies. *Journal of Public Economics*.

Chamley, C.P. 1980. Optimal intertemporal taxation and the public debt. Cowles Foundation Discussion Paper No.554.

Chamley, C.P. 1985. Efficient tax reform in a dynamic model of general equilibrium. *Quarterly Journal of Economics* 100, 335–6.

Chamley, C.P. 1986. Optimal taxation of capital income in general equilibrium with infinite lives. *Econometrica* 54, 607–22.

Chamley, C.P, and Wright, B.D. 1986. Fiscal incidence in an overlapping generation model with a fixed factor. Hoover Institution, Mimeo.

Diamond, P.A. 1965. National debt in a neoclassical growth model. *American Economic Review* 55, 1125–50.

Diamond, P.A. 1970. Incidence of an interest income tax. *Journal of Economic Theory* 2, 211–24.

Diamond P.A. and Mirrlees, J.A. 1971. Optimal taxation and public production. II: Tax rules. *American Economic Review* 61, 261–78.

Feldstein, M. 1974. Incidence of a capital income tax in a growing economy with variable savings rates. *Review of Economic Studies* 41, 505–13.

Judd, K.L. 1985. Redistributive taxation in a simple perfect foresight model. *Journal of Public Economics* 28, 59–83.

Pestieau, P. 1974. Optimal taxation and discount rate for public investment. *Journal of Public Economics* 3, 217–35.

Stiglitz, J.E. 1978. Notes on estate taxes, redistribution and the concept of balanced growth path incidence. *Journal of Political Economy* 86, S137–S150.

Summers, L. 1981. Capital taxation and capital accumulation in a life cycle growth model. *American Economic Review* 71, 533–44.

Summers, L. 1981. Taxation and corporate investment: a q-theory approach. *Brookings Papers on Economic Activity* (1), 67–127.

taxation of corporate profits. Industrial countries levy a profits tax on the earnings of corporations. The statutory rate of tax is typically close to 50 per cent; interest paid on corporate debt is deducted from the tax base; dividends earned on corporate equity are taxed at the household level under the personal income tax; and capital gains on corporate equity are taxed on a realization basis at a preferential rate of tax. Most systems of corporate taxation include a variety of special provisions: accelerated depreciation, investment tax credits, depletion allowances, and preferential tax treatment of specific industries.

As corporations undertake most industrial investments and save through retained earnings, the effects of corporation taxation on economic growth and employment are of special interest to policy makers and academic analysts. Until recently researchers calculated very high average effective tax rates on corporate capital income. Arnold Harberger (1966) calculated the average rate of tax to be 63 per cent on corporate profits and 31 per cent on non-corporate capital earnings for the United States during 1953–59. Harberger estimated the dead-weight loss resulting from the differentially high rate of corporate taxation to be about 0.5 per cent of national income. Similarly Feldstein and Summers (1979) calculated total capital taxes paid on corporate profit income to be 70 per cent in 1970.

In 1981 the United States enacted tax incentives to decrease these high effective tax rates and to stimulate investment. Similar measures, such as accelerated depreciation and capital grants, were also enacted in the United Kingdom. Following these changes, the average effective corporate tax fell quite dramatically. The tax base in the corporate sector eroded, many large corporations pay little if any tax, and the tax concessions added a number of distortions into the tax system.

The analysis of effective tax rates on marginal investment reveals significant inter-industry tax distortions. Also the effective marginal rates of tax on corporate investment are calculated to be well below both the statutory rates of tax and the average effective rates, and the effective tax rate on investment in structures approximates the statutory tax rate, while the tax on equipment is zero, or even negative.

Two theoretical contributions have challenged the conventional view that combined effects on the corporate profits tax and the personal income tax are highly distortionary and discourage corporate investment. One of these concluded that personal taxes on dividends do not increase the cost of capital financed through the retention of corporate earnings. The second theoretical insight relates to the division of corporate profits between a riskless return and a risk premium. In the context of the capital asset pricing model it has been argued that imposition of a profit tax on the risk portion of the corporate return is non-distortionary, and it is possible to raise large amounts of tax revenue without significantly affecting corporate investment. The theoretical changes and the modifications of the tax law have been so significant that recent empirical studies conclude that the marginal effective tax rate on corporate investment is only slightly higher than non-corporate investment, or even that the tax system encourages corporate investment. I shall explain how predictions about the effects of corporate taxation appear to be so sensitive to certain key analytical assumptions and to changes in research methodology.

THE HARBERGER CONTRIBUTIONS. Much of the conventional analysis of the effects of the corporate tax was developed by A.C. Harberger (1962, 1966), who characterized the corporate profits tax as a partial factor tax on corporate capital. In a world of certainty Harberger postulated that the after-tax rate of return on different investments will tend towards equality. The imposition of a differential tax on corporate investment reallocates capital to the non-corporate industries and results in a distorted equilibrium with variations across industries in the social rate of return. For a corporate investment financed by equity where all earnings are paid as dividends, the corporate profits tax will raise the before-tax corporate return by the amount of the tax relative to the non-corporate rate of return.

Harberger recognized that the preferential treatment of capital gains lowers the tax on corporate distributions if earnings are retained and fully reflected in share prices. Also in empirical work Harberger took account of the deduction of interest paid on corporate debt. But since a large share of corporate investment is financed by retained earnings, and corporations pay out roughly half of their earnings in dividends, these special tax provisions were treated as features to be incorporated into the calculation of tax rate differentials, and mere qualifications to the conclusion that corporate capital is subject to a much higher profits tax relative to non-corporate investment.

Harberger developed a two-sector model by dividing the economy into corporate and non-corporate sectors. He derived a general expression for the change in the after-tax return to capital resulting from the differential tax on capital in the corporate sector and found it to be quite complex. After estimating the relative factor intensities of the two sectors, he concluded that under a wide range of assumptions for unknown parameter values, the after-tax return to capital in the whole economy decreases by the amount of taxes collected from corporate capital. This implies that capital as a whole in the national economy bears the burden of the corporate tax. This result, derived for an economy where the amounts of capital in the two sectors are roughly equal, is a special case of a more general proposition, namely that a tax on a mobile factor in a specific industry, even a small one, will, by its reallocative effects, decrease the overall after-tax return to the mobile factor by an amount approximately equal to tax revenues. The decrease in the return to the immobile factors in the heavily taxed sectors and in the commodity prices there is offset by an increase in the return to immobile factors in the lightly taxed industries.

Harberger's conclusions on incidence were challenged by the econometric results of Krzyzaniak and Musgrave (1963), who, on the basis of time series analyses for American manufacturing, reached the startling conclusion that an increase in corporate tax liabilities of \$1.00 per unit of capital will increase before-tax profits by \$1.35. The result, a measure of short-run shifting for a fixed capital stock, implies the corporate tax is shifted by more than 100 per cent. The Krzyzaniak–Musgrave contribution was criticized by a number of writers who argued that their model was incorrectly specified. Also other empirical studies, one based on a mark-up theory of pricing, another based on a neo-classical production function approach, concluded that the degree of shifting in US manufacturing was quite low.

These results and the fact that most subsequent theoretical work on the effects of corporate tax has been carried out in a competitive framework have led to general acceptance of Harberger's conclusions on the incidence of the corporate tax. One interesting exception to this consensus is the recent theoretical contribution of Katz and Rosen (1985) who found for a model of oligopoly that an increase in the taxation of profits may raise industry after-tax profits, a result that cannot occur under either perfect competition or monopoly. The explanation of this result is that firms in an oligopolistic industry may not maximize joint profits. A tax, by shifting marginal costs, induces firms to cut output, raise prices and move to an equilibrium more in line with joint profit maximization. So the Krzyzaniak–Musgrave result of overshifting is not outside the pale of economic theory and can be rationalized using neoclassical analysis.

Harberger's second contribution is his estimates of the inefficiency resulting from the higher tax imposed on corporate capital. As a result of the corporate tax, the social (before-tax) rate of return is higher in the corporate sector. Real national income would increase if the tax distortion were eliminated and capital were reallocated to equalize rate of return across sectors. Harberger approximated the dead-weight loss of the tax differential between corporate and non-corporate investment by the expression $1/2\,\Delta KT^2$, where T is the tax differential between the two sectors and ΔK is the reallocation of capital that occurs as the results of the tax differential. Harberger developed estimates for T and used his two-sector, two-factor model to approximate ΔK. He concluded that for 1953–9, the capital stock in the corporate sector was decreased by between one sixth and one third, relative to a neutral tax system, and social welfare was decreased by about \$2 billion a year, or about seven per cent of the taxes collected on corporate earnings.

Shoven and Whalley (1972/5) and their collaborators have made the most notable contributions to recent work on general equilibrium analyses of the effects of corporate taxation. They pioneered the use of fixed point algorithms to solve general equilibrium systems, improving on the accuracy of linear approximations based on calculus. They disaggregated producing sectors, specified a large number of household income classes, and were the first to develop a fully integrated quantitative treatment of the effects of taxes on both sides of real income equations, the uses or consumption side and the sources or factor price side.

Shoven and Whalley have studied the differential efficiency properties of a large number of taxes, consumption, value-added, with and without international capital movement. They concluded that the real income of the United States would increase significantly if the corporate tax distortion were eliminated by integration of personal and corporate taxes.

One common feature of the Shoven–Whalley studies and

Harberger's contribution is the use of factor price information to estimate the allocation of capital between sectors by assuming that per-unit capital returns are equalized throughout the economy. Average effective tax rates by industry are estimated from national accounts information on capital taxes actually paid. Personal income tax paid on earnings by industries is estimated from information on dividends, retained earnings and appropriate assumptions about capital gain taxes and taxes on dividends. Depreciation rates, investment tax credits, the financial structure of different industries, dividends pay-out rates are all taken as given and enter the analysis through taxes actually paid or estimated to be paid. The key assumption of the research is that average tax rates actually paid are a good approximation of marginal tax rates.

EFFECTIVE TAX RATES. In contrast to the calculation of 'average' effective tax rates paid on existing assets, it is possible to develop a methodology to calculate 'marginal' prospective taxes on new investments. These calculations are based on the user cost of capital formula developed by Hall and Jorgenson (1967) in the investment literature. The user cost of capital or required rate of return on capital, c, gross of economic depreciation is equal to

$$\frac{c}{q} = \frac{(r^c - P - d)}{1 - u}(1 - k - uz)$$

where r^c is the cost of funds to the corporation or the return to the investor before payment of personal taxes, q is the relative price of capital goods, P is the expected inflation rate, u is the statutory tax rate, d is the true rate of economic depreciation, k is the investment tax credit rate and z is the present value of depreciation allowance per dollar of investment.

The equilibrium social rate of return on capital, s, is equal to $c/q - d$. One measure of the effective tax rate is $(s - r^c)/s$.

The user cost of capital formula shows the effects of change in various tax provisions of the tax code and inflation on effective tax rates. This approach also allows the calculation of separate rates of tax across assets, across industries, and across the corporate and non-corporate sectors.

A number of different sets of effective tax rates have been calculated, some of these inclusive of the payment of corporate tax rates and personal income taxes. Studies have assumed that firms arbitrage between real capital and corporate debt so that r^c is the after tax nominal rate $i(1 - u)$. An alternative approach is to specify different required rates of return for new shares, retained earnings, and corporate debt, and to calculate an average required rate r^c on the basis of the observed proportions for different sources of corporate finance.

Auerbach (1983) found the marginal effective tax rate in the United States to be well below average effective corporate rates since 1972. Since 1981, when accelerated depreciation was liberalized for equipment, the effective tax rate on equipment has fallen to zero, or slightly negative, while the tax rate on structures is only slightly less than the statutory rate of 46 per cent. Auerbach also found very large differences in effective tax rates across industries ranging from a maximum of 39.4 per cent to a minimum of 6.3 per cent. He calculated that tax differentials within industries and between industries within the corporate sector result in substantial efficiency losses. One of Auerbach's most interesting conclusions is that the social cost of the misallocation of capital within the corporate sector resulting from differential asset taxation increased over the same period during which the marginal tax rate on capital in the aggregate was falling.

A study on inter-country comparisons of effective tax rates edited by King and Fullerton (1984) found very low effective tax rates in the United Kingdom where a combination of immediate expensing investment and special investment grants has moved the system of personal taxation very close to a consumption base system.

In the United Kingdom a combination of depreciation rules, LIFO accounting, and the deduction of nominal interest outweighs in an inflationary environment the tax disadvantages of historical cost depreciation and the taxation of nominal capital gains. For other countries studied by King and Fullerton the overall effective taxes on corporate earnings are found to increase only slightly with the rate of inflation. But this conclusion is quite sensitive to the estimate of the marginal tax rate of the recipients of corporate interest relative to the tax rate of the corporations that profit from the deduction of higher nominal interest rate. If the tax rates were roughly equal, then tax rates would increase more significantly with inflation.

CORPORATE FINANCIAL POLICY AND TAXATION. The deductibility of interest on corporate debt favours the use of corporate debt by the corporation, while the preferential taxation of capital gains on a realization basis favours the use of retained earnings as a source of investment funds. The existence of two offsetting advantages explains why corporations have not relied exclusively on debt. Stiglitz (1973) concluded that under certainty firms should pay no dividends, retain all their earnings, and meet any additional financing needs by issuing debt. Investors in high tax brackets will find it advantageous to hold equity, while others will supply debt to the corporation. Miller (1977) postulated that a segmented equilibrium will result with some investors holding only debt and others holding only equity.

The segmentation of portfolios is at variance with reality as in the prediction that firms will pay no dividends. The introduction of uncertainty can be used to explain portfolio diversification and to justify the payment of dividends. An explanation for the payment of dividends which does not rely on uncertainty has been developed by Auerbach (1981), Bradford (1981) and King (1977). The essence of their explanation is that the potential of mature corporations to profitably reinvest all retained earnings is limited, and that the rational stockholder expects that ultimately firms will pay dividends. Corporations are characterized as permanent 'vessels' on the analogy of a savings account. The income tax on dividends is a tax on distributions stockholders expect to pay. This expectation lowers the market value of the firm below the replacement cost of its assets. (Tobin's 'q' may be less than 1.)

The market value of q for the firm is determined by investors' demand for 'new shares' issued by the firm through retained earnings. When the income tax on dividends, ϕ, is greater than c, the tax on capital gains, no dividends will be paid by the firm until q falls to the critical level $1 - \phi/1 - c$. When the market value of shares falls to this level, the investor is indifferent between the payment of an additional dollar of dividends and an additional dollar of retentions by the firm that will increase share prices by an amount equal to $q = (1 - \phi)/(1 - c)$.

One of the implications of this 'new view' of equity finance is that the rate of dividend taxation ϕ, has no effect on the cost of capital obtained by retained earnings, which can be shown to be $x = r/(1 - z)(1 - c)$, where r is the required rate of return on capital and z is the corporate tax rate. To illustrate why ϕ does not affect the return on the marginal investment and why increases in the tax on dividends are simply capitalized in the share prices, consider the case where $r = 0.05$, $c = 0$, and z is equal to 0.5. If initially $\phi = 0$, the corporation by earning 0.10 per dollar of capital can pay the stockholder his required rate of return of 0.05. If ϕ is increased to 0.50, the tax on the dividends resulting from the real investment of \$1.00 will be 0.025 after payment of the corporate and the dividend tax. But after imposition of the dividend tax, the opportunity cost of the dollar returned by the corporation is no longer equal to \$1.00 as it was when the dividend tax was zero; it has fallen to 0.50, for if it were taken out of the corporation, a dividend tax of 50 per cent would have to be paid. So the return to the investor remains unchanged at 5 per cent, i.e. $0.025/0.50 = 0.05$. The reason why the tax on dividends does not enter the cost of capital is that it reduces *both* the after-tax return on new investment financed with retentions and the value of the retentions to the stockholder.

One problem with the 'trapped equity' theory of dividends and share valuation is that it does not allow the firm to repurchase its shares or to buy other firms. If q is less than 1 firms will find it more profitable to buy firms with existing assets than to buy new capital goods. The theory also implies that any payout rate is consistent with equilibrium and does not explain the stability of the payout rate of dividends. Also, in a careful study based on British data where changes in the tax treatment of dividends have been relatively frequent, Poterba and Summers (1985) conclude that a reduction in dividend tax rates increases both dividend payout and corporate investment. So, contrary to the trapped equity theory, taxes on dividends appear to increase the cost of capital.

This evidence notwithstanding, the Auerbach–Bradford–King theory is a significant contribution as it is the only explanation of dividends under certainty, and its implications for tax policy are very important. A paper by Fullerton and Henderson (1986) which recognizes that new shares are used to finance only 5 per cent of investment and assumes that dividend taxes on financing through retained earnings do not increase the cost of capital concluded that while each class of broad investment asset (equipment, land) is taxed more lightly in the non-corporate sector, the overall rate of taxation of corporate and non-corporate capital is not very different. The importance of the welfare loss of capital tax disparities between industries is estimated to be much less than by Harberger, as the average effective tax rates used in earlier research varied much more by industry than the marginal effective tax rates used by Fullerton and Henderson. However, their results are quite sensitive to the assumption that dividend taxes do not increase the cost of funds obtained through retained earnings. If the cost of these funds which finance 61 per cent of investment are set equal to the cost of new equity, the estimated cost of capital in the corporate sector increases by 50 per cent.

CONSIDERATIONS OF UNCERTAINTY. The introduction of risk and uncertainty provides a number of alternative explanations to the payment of dividends and to the simultaneous use of equity and debt financing in corporate investment. Gordon and Malkiel (1981) criticize the predictions of certainty models and conclude that most of these are counterfactual. They argue that the possibility of stock repurchase is the mechanism by which the stockmarket will tend to value marginal real investment at its replacement cost. They also argue that firms will pursue policies so that at the margin capital gains and dividends will be equally valued. Different stockholders in a world of uncertainty hold diversified portfolios and value dividends and capital gains differently. Also under conditions of uncertainty firms will pay a stable stream of dividends to provide information about the true long-run earnings prospects of the firm.

Gordon and Malkiel emphasize the cost of formal bankruptcy and possible conflicts between bondholders and stockholders. Also the prospect of bankruptcy during periods of fiscal distress will result in efficiency costs as the firm will be constrained in investment and related business decisions. The deduction of interest under the corporate tax will promote the use of debt. But as the likelihood of bankruptcy increases with increases in the debt-equity ratio, the marginal costs of both debt and equity will rise with increased leverage and an optimal debt-equity ratio will exist.

Feldstein, Green and Sheshinski (1979) also use tax considerations and the risk of bankruptcy to establish an optimal debt-equity ratio in a model of a growing economy. For a particular tax regime, this optimal ratio along with the overall growth constraint imposed by the nation's savings rate will determine the dividend payout rate. The payment of dividends is determined as part of an optimal financial and investment plan.

These models stress uncertainty and develop predictions which are not counter factual; they explain the payment of dividends and demonstrate how the interaction between corporate and personal taxes distorts the financial behaviour of firms. These models are quite traditional in their predictions. In particular, higher taxes on dividends do increase the cost of corporate capital.

Roger Gordon (1983 with D. Fullerton; 1985) has reached the radical conclusion that the distortionary effects of the corporate tax may be quite small even when the tax collects large amounts of revenue. The essence of Gordon's arguments is that the return to corporate investment, r_c, consists of a riskless component, i and a risk premium p, i.e. $r_c = i + p$.

In the context of the capital asset pricing model, the required risk premium on a corporate investment is equal to $p = \text{cov}\{(r_c, r_m)/\text{var}(r_m)\} \cdot \bar{r}_m$ where r_m is the excess rate of return on the market portfolio and $\bar{r}_m$ is its expected value. Gordon argues that the excess return on the market portfolio is not changed by the imposition of the corporate tax as the government cannot dispose of the risk that it bears. Individuals must bear the risk through changes in other taxes or through changes in expenditures. On this assumption it follows that the covariance of the after-tax return on corporate capital is decreased by the term $(1 - t_c)$. The risk premium is not affected by the tax so the required return on the corporate capital after the imposition of the tax is equal to $r_c = [i/(1 - t_c)] + p$. If i is small relative to p the change in the marginal product of corporate capital following the imposition of the tax will be small.

Gordon's conclusion that the corporate tax is a highly efficient source of revenue as it may have small effects on investment and could raise large amounts of revenues has been challenged by Bulow and Summers (1984). They argue that while the government shares in the income risk of a corporate investment, much of the investment risk is associated with fluctuations in the price of capital goods, and the corporate tax, levied on accounting income, excludes capital gains and losses. The theoretical importance of this criticism remains to be resolved, but the empirical significance of the point has been demonstrated. Simulation work has shown that the predictions of the effects of various tax reforms are very sensitive to whether variances of corporate returns are sensitive to changes in the corporate tax.

CONCLUDING REMARKS. The traditional argument favouring the corporate tax is that it is a progressive tax and falls primarily on high income stockholders or owners of capital. Also the complete elimination of the corporate tax by a single nation may be precluded by international considerations as under existing tax treaties corporate tax revenue accrues to countries of origin. Countering these distributive arguments is a large literature on the distortionary effects of the corporate tax. With the introduction of a variety of investment incentives, the revenues of corporate tax systems have decreased and inter-asset distortions have been added while inter-sectoral distortions have decreased. Without a complete reform of accelerated depreciation, and other deductions, the overall progressivity of the tax system would not be decreased if the corporate tax were eliminated or changed to a cash flow corporate income tax. The alternative is to reform the existing system by moving to a more neutral system of depreciation and by eliminating other deductions.

The resolution of two key issues appears to be essential for the determination of the correct policy. They are: first, the extent to which income taxes on dividends increase the cost of capital raised through retained earnings, and second, the extent to which the corporate profit tax is a neutral tax on a risk premium.

PETER MIESZKOWSKI

See also TAXATION OF CAPITAL.

BIBLIOGRAPHY

Auerbach, A.T. 1979. Share valuation and corporate equity policy. *Journal of Public Economics* 11(3), June, 291–305

Auerbach, A. 1983. Corporate taxation in the US Brookings Papers on Economic Activity, Washington: Brookings Institution.

Ballard, C.L., Fullerton, D., Shoven, T.B. and Whalley, T. 1985. *A General Equilibrium Model for Tax Policy Evaluation.* Chicago: University of Chicago Press.

Bradford, D.F. 1981. The incidence and allocation effects of a tax on corporate distributions. *Journal of Public Economics* 15(1), February, 1–22.

Bulow, J.T. and Summers, L.H. 1984. The taxation of risky assets. *Journal of Political Economy* 92(1) February, 20–39.

Feldstein, M., Green T. and Sheshinski, E. 1979. Corporate financial policy and taxation in a growing economy. *Quarterly Journal of Economics* 93(3), August, 411–32.

Feldstein, M. and Summers, L. 1979. Inflation and the taxation of capital income in the corporate sector. *National Tax Journal* 32(4), December, 445–70.

Feldstein, M. 1983. *Capital Taxation.* Cambridge, Mass.: Harvard University Press.

Fullerton, D. and Gordon, R. 1983. A reexamination of the tax distortion in general equilibrium models. In *Behavioral Simulation Methods in Tax Policy Analysis*, ed. M. Feldstein, Chicago: University of Chicago Press.

Fullerton, D. and Henderson, Y.K. 1986. A disaggregate equilibrium model of the tax distortions among assets, sectors and industries. *AEI Occasional Papers,* Washington, DC; American Enterprise Institute.

Gordon, R.H. and Malkiel, B.G. 1981. Corporation finance. *How Taxes Affect Economic Behavior*, ed. H.T. Aaron and J.A. Pechman, Washington: The Brookings Institute.

Gordon, R. 1985. Taxation of corporate capital income: tax revenues versus tax distortions. *Quarterly Journal of Economics* 100(1), February, 1–27.

Hall, R. and Jorgenson, D.W. 1967. Tax policy and investment behavior. *American Economic Review* 57, June, 391–414.

Harberger, A.C. 1962. The incidence of the corporation income tax. *Journal of Political Economy* 70, June, 215–40.

Harberger, A.C. 1966. Efficiency effects of taxes on income from capital. In *Effects of Corporation Income Tax*, ed. M. Krzyzaniak, Detroit: Wayne State University Press.

Katz, M.L. and Rosen, H.S. 1985. Tax analysis in an oligopoly model. *Public Finance Quarterly* 13(1), November, 3–20.

King, M.A. 1977. *Public Policy and the Corporation.* London: Chapman & Hall.

King, M.A. and Fullerton, D. (eds) 1984. *The Taxation of Income from Capital: A Comparative Study of the US., UK., Sweden, and West Germany.* Chicago: The University of Chicago Press.

Krzyzaniak, M. and Musgrave, R.A. 1963. *The Shifting of the Corporation Tax.* Baltimore: Johns Hopkins Press.

Miller, M. 1977. Debt and taxes. *Journal of Finance* 32(2), May, 261–75.

Poterba, J.M. and Summers, L.H. 1985. The economic effects of dividend taxation. In *In Recent Advances in Corporate Finance,* ed. E.I. Altman and M.G. Subrahmayan, Homewood, Ill.: Richard D. Irwin.

Shoven, J.B. and Whalley, T. 1972. A general equilibrium calculation of the effects of differential taxation of income from capital in the US. *Journal of Public Economics* 1, 281–321.

Stiglitz, J.E. 1973. Taxation, corporate financial policy and the cost of capital. *Journal of Public Economics* 2(1), February, 1–34.

Stiglitz, J.E. 1976. The corporation tax. *Journal of Public Economics* 5(3–4), April–May, 303–11.

taxation of income. In the historical evolution of government finance, the income tax is relatively novel. It is difficult to find any evidence of a serious national income tax being used until the end of the 18th century, when William Pitt achieved the passage in Great Britain of the Act of 1799 which imposed a comprehensive income tax, complete with exemptions and abatements for dependents, on all residents of Great Britain. The tax was introduced to maintain the solvency of the British government in the face of the expense of the Napoleonic Wars. When the French had been dispatched, so too was the income tax. Seligman (1911, p. 113) quotes a contemporaneous source as stating that the repeal of the tax by Parliament 'was declared amidst the greatest cheering and the loudest exultation ever witnessed within the halls of the English Senate'. It was only decades later that income tax reappeared in Britain.

This pattern of introduction during wartime, followed by repeal and eventual, permanent reinstitution is found in the experience of other countries, as well. In the US, for example, the first income tax was introduced during the Civil War in 1862, being abandoned in 1872. It reappeared in 1894 in similar form, but was almost immediately declared unconstitutional by the Supreme Court, which found it to be a 'direct' tax not apportioned among the states according to population. The Sixteenth Amendment to the constitution was required for the permanent reimposition of the tax in 1913.

Over time, the income tax has grown in importance so that it now represents the single most important revenue source in most developed countries. In 1982 (according to OECD, 1984), for example, taxes on income and profits accounted for 45 per cent of government tax revenues in the US and Japan, 44 per cent in Canada, 38 per cent in the UK and 34 per cent in Germany. France was unusual among the leading industrialized countries in raising only 18 per cent of its revenues from these sources.

Being a direct tax on individuals, rather than an indirect tax on transactions, the income tax required a more developed government infrastructure than other revenue sources. This distinction also provides the key to understanding both why the income tax was seen as a fairer way to raise revenue and why it was so vehemently opposed. Through assessment of individuals, the income tax was better suited to the achievement of a progressive, broad-based tax structure than the agglomeration of indirect taxes and duties that preceded it. At the same time, this focus on individuals instead of transactions brought with it the perception of a challenge to individual liberty, both because of the exposure to the government of the individual's economic behaviour and the ability of government to levy arbitrarily high taxes on small groups of taxpayers (see, e.g., Blum and Kalven, 1953).

THE MEASUREMENT OF INCOME

Dating back almost to the acceptance of the income tax itself is the question of how income should be measured. What has come to be called the 'Haig–Simons' measure of income is now generally accepted as the appropriate base for an income tax (Haig, 1921; Simons, 1938). As expressed by Simons (1938, p. 50), 'Personal income may be defined as the algebraic sum of (1) the market value of rights exercised in consumption and (2) the change in the value of the store of property rights between the beginning and end of the period in question.' One may justify the Haig–Simons approach on grounds of both fairness and efficiency, the former because it treats individuals with different sources of income uniformly and the latter because it does not distort decisions of how to devote resources to the generation of income.

Yet actual income taxes vary from this definition, for reasons of both administration and politics.

Market versus non-market activities. A range of activities generates what might be considered imputed income appropriate for inclusion in the income tax base. Some, such as the imputed rent on owner-occupied housing, have been seriously evaluated in this regard. At the other extreme, few have suggested taxing the entertainment services obtained from watching television.

It is this inability to measure and tax non-market sources of income that makes the income tax inherently distortionary, for it encourages the taxpayer to substitute non-market for market activities. Such substitution may be entirely legal, as in the purchase of one's own home or the decision to take a vacation, or illegal, as in the establishment of professional cooperatives wherein members provide services to other members 'for free'.

Realizations versus accruals. The Haig–Simons measure does not distinguish between realized and unrealized increases in wealth. Yet most income tax systems include capital gains in the tax base only when they are realized, if at all. This outcome is traceable in part to the difficulty of measuring unrealized gains, although this can hardly be a problem for the vast wealth held in marketable securities. A related difficulty, often ascribed to farmers and the owners of small businesses, involves illiquid assets which would have to be sold below their going-concern values were their owners subject to taxes on associated accrued gains. Finally, property rights to capital assets may be sufficiently vague or disputed that it is difficult even to attribute ownership until gains have actually been realized. A variety of proposals to tax such accrued gains retrospectively upon realization (e.g. Vickrey, 1947) have achieved little more than academic attention.

This favourable treatment of capital gains facilitates the accumulation and transmission of wealth. It has therefore been viewed as mitigating the progressivity of the income tax system, leading some (e.g. Kaldor, 1955) to favour an individual expenditure tax on grounds of equity. At the same time, others have argued that favourable capital gains treatment serves to encourage risk-taking, which is otherwise discriminated against by the income tax system (see the discussion below).

Nominal versus real income. Income has been viewed as an appropriate measure of the individual's ability to pay, but this ability is generally viewed in real rather than money terms, an individual being no better off with twice the income at twice the price level. Price level indexation of the income tax requires two types of corrections: to the rate structure, and to the base itself. The first is required because of the progressivity of marginal tax rates, the second because capital income is measured incorrectly in the presence of inflation.

When the income tax structure has marginal tax rates that rise with nominal income, increases in the price level increase both the marginal and average tax burden on a given real income level. Correction for inflation involves indexing tax brackets to the price level, a practice adopted only in 1985 in the US and not commonly found in use elsewhere.

Capital income is generally mismeasured in an inflationary environment because changes in the real value of capital goods that are due to inflation are generally treated incorrectly by the tax system. This has led to four problems identified by the literature (see, e.g., Aaron, 1976); the understatement of costs of goods sold from inventories, the understatement of the depreciation expenses associated with the use of durable capital goods, the overstatement of income received from bonds and other nominal commitments, and the overstatement of realized capital gains. In all cases, the problem arises from a failure to apply the Haig–Simons approach to changes in the value of capital assets. There have been few attempts to ameliorate these distortions in practice.

Losses. There is no logical reason why the income tax base for an individual cannot be negative, but treating losses the same way as gains would call for a negative tax payment, that is a government refund. This outcome is not very often observed in practice. Instead, individuals with currently negative tax bases are permitted to average the current base retrospectively or prospectively with the aim of achieving a positive number. In the case of forward averaging (called carrying forward) this still amounts to the penalty of having to wait for the refund until future taxes are due.

A problem which is mathematically the same occurs under a progressive tax structure even when income is positive in every year, but fluctuating. Since marginal rates are higher in good years than bad (a milder version of what occurs when negative tax bases face a tax rate of zero), taxpayers face a higher tax in present value than if they received the same present value of income, but in a smooth stream over time. As with the treatment of losses, tax systems typically provide some imperfect form of averaging of incomes over several contiguous years to lessen this problem.

This treatment of losses and risky incomes has been viewed as discouraging the taking of risks (e.g. Domar and Musgrave, 1944), and has been one of the more valid reasons for favouring the preferential treatment normally accorded capital gains. At the same time, there is no general presumption that income taxation, in itself, discourages the taking of risks, since it not only reduces the returns to risky investments, but also the risks (Domar and Musgrave, 1944; Tobin, 1958).

DEFINING THE UNIT OF TAXATION

In addition to these problems of income measurement, there have arisen ambiguities concerning the delineation of the taxpaying unit. Questions have concerned how broadly to define to unit at a given date, and over what time interval to measure the income accruing to that unit.

Tax treatment of the family. Tax systems vary in their

treatment of related individuals. The method of treatment of family members affects the tax burden on a family because of the progressivity of the rate structure. Two individuals will generally be assessed a different tax bill if considered separately than if taxed jointly as a couple, regardless of how the rate structure is adjusted, since the total tax bill under separate taxation will depend on the distribution of taxable income between the individuals while under joint taxation it will not.

Even if families can be identified and grouped for purposes of taxation, the problem remains in deciding how to vary the tax schedule with family size. For this, one must have a measure of how to normalize income by family size to obtain a measure of the family's ability to pay. Such questions have been addressed but not often applied to the design of tax schedules.

Finally, how the family is grouped also matters if the tax-free transfer of resources through gifts and bequests is not allowed. The strict Haig–Simons approach would include gifts and bequests in the tax base of the recipient, but such transfers would never appear if occurring within the unit of taxation.

Tax treatment over time. In Simons' own description of the appropriate measurement of income, the element of time plays a crucial role, since accretions to wealth must be defined over some interval. Indeed, the difference between a tax on income and a tax on expenditures amounts to a different choice of time interval over which to measure income for purposes of taxation. If, instead of annual income, we assessed taxes on lifetime income, then individuals would pay taxes in excess of lifetime consumption only to the extent that they accumulated resources over their lifetimes.

This point has not been missed by advocates of the expenditure tax who argue that, from a lifetime perspective, individual expenditures are a better measure of ability than annual income. Under the annual income tax, individuals who consume their resources later in life face a heavier lifetime burden, paying taxes when income is initially earned and again when interest on the saved capital is received in later years. Hence the charge that the annual income tax imposes a 'double taxation' of savings (see, for example, Mill, 1848; Fisher, 1939; Kaldor, 1955).

ON THE OPTIMAL PROGRESSIVITY OF THE INCOME TAX

As soon as the income tax became ensconced as a revenue source, economists began to consider how progressive it should be. Early researchers in the utilitarian tradition focused on how rapidly the tax burden should rise with income so as to exact an equal sacrifice from each individual given the particular utility function with which people were assumed to be endowed. The answer also depended on whether one was seeking equal absolute sacrifice, equal proportional sacrifice, or equal marginal sacrifice, all measured in units of the interpersonally comparable individual utilities (Musgrave, 1959, pp. 99–105).

Perhaps the most disquieting result from this line of investigation was that the achievement of equal marginal sacrifices required the equalization of incomes across individuals, if utility functions were the same (Edgeworth, 1897). A missing element that would have altered this finding was the distortionary impact of taxes on economic behaviour. The high marginal tax rates needed to approach equality of after-tax incomes (100 per cent in the extreme case of complete equality) would undoubtedly become self-defeating, in that the after-tax incomes of all individuals would begin to fall as tax revenues ceased increasing with increases in marginal tax rates. Such an outcome would be inconsistent with any evaluation of social welfare that had Pareto efficiency as a necessary condition for an optimum.

There was thus, eventually, spawned a line of research that sought to reconcile the utilitarian aim of equal marginal sacrifice with the disincentive effects of marginal taxation. The seminal paper here is that of Mirrlees (1971), who found optimal marginal rates to be relatively low. Subsequent research has also shown that marginal tax rates should eventually approach zero at the highest incomes, a result that is not only dependent on various assumptions but also less politically controversial than one might first expect once it is recognized that it applies to marginal, not average tax rates.

Further research on the distortions of the income tax have focused on its efficiency relative to other tax bases, such as labour income and consumption expenditures. There can be no presumption that one tax would be superior to another, since each imposes distortions: the income tax affecting both the labour–leisure decision and the savings decision, the other tax systems perhaps distorting only the former choice, but doing so more severely than the income tax does. Little conclusive empirical evidence has been adduced to date on this matter, but it remains an area of active research.

ALAN J. AUERBACH

See also DIRECT TAXATION; PUBLIC FINANCE.

BIBLIOGRAPHY

Aaron, H. (ed.) 1976. *Inflation and the Income Tax*. Washington, DC: Brookings Institution.

Blum, W. and Kalven, H. 1953. *The Uneasy Case for Progressive Taxation*. Chicago: University of Chicago Press.

Domar, E. and Musgrave, R. 1944. Proportional income taxation and risk-taking. *Quarterly Journal of Economics* 58, May, 388–422.

Edgeworth, F. 1897. The pure theory of taxation. *Economic Journal* 7, December, 550–71.

Fisher, I. 1939. The double taxation of savings. *American Economic Review* 29, March, 16–33.

Haig, R. 1931. The concept of income: economic and legal aspects. In *The Federal Income Tax*, ed. R. Haig, New York: Columbia University Press.

Kaldor, N. 1955. *An Expenditure Tax*. London: Allen & Unwin.

Mill, J.S. 1848. *Principles of Political Economy*. Ed. W. Ashley, London: Longmans, 1921.

Mirrlees, J. 1971. An exploration in the theory of optimum income taxation. *Review of Economic Studies* 38(2), April, 175–208.

Musgrave, R. 1959. *The Theory of Public Finance*. New York: McGraw-Hill.

Organization for Economic Cooperation and Development. 1984. *Revenue Statistics of OECD Member Countries 1965–83*. Paris: OECD.

Seligman, E.R.A. 1911. *The Income Tax*. New York: Macmillan.

Simons, H. 1938. *Personal Income Taxation*. Chicago: University of Chicago Press.

Tobin, J. 1958. Liquidity preference as behavior towards risk. *Review of Economic Studies* 25, February, 65–86.

Vickrey, W. 1947. *Agenda for Progressive Taxation*. New York: Ronald Press.

taxation of wealth. Wealth taxation is one of the oldest methods of government revenue collection, having been used at least since the time of the Greeks. According to one source (Seligman, 1925, p. 34), Athens levied a general property tax not only on land and houses, but also on slaves, cattle, furniture, and money. Over the succeeding centuries, many types of wealth taxation have been tried, and others proposed, with perhaps no other form of taxation being the subject of such heated debate. This may strike the economist as somewhat inexplicable, since wealth taxes are in effect little more than taxes on capital income.

All assets have value because of the returns they generate, though the returns need not be in explicit form (as with business assets) but may be implicit (as with owner-occupied housing or gold). Taxing wealth on an annual basis may therefore be viewed as equivalent to taxing its return at a rate sufficient to produce the same tax revenue. However, there are a number of factors that have made wealth taxation different from capital income taxation, in practice.

First, there has been little hesitancy on the part of governments to levy specific taxes on very particular forms of wealth (e.g. land), while income taxation has more typically been broad-based. Second, taxes on income have usually been confined to income explicitly realized. This is, for example, the universal approach to capital gains taxation. Wealth taxes, such as property taxes on owner-occupied real estate, have not followed the same principle. Thus, it has been possible for taxpayers with very little liquidity but substantial wealth to be burdened with taxes well in excess of their *explicit* income. Moreover, it has generally been the case that wealth is even more unevenly distributed among the population than realized capital income.

Finally, while it is natural to expect that income taxes would not exceed 100 per cent of income, there is no comparable upper bound on wealth taxes short of the entire stock of wealth. The perception that wealth taxes threaten the rights of individual citizens through the possibility of discriminatory or unfair taking of assets is undoubtedly a factor in the controversy that has often surrounded wealth taxation.

TYPES OF WEALTH TAXATION

In discussing the history and economic effects of wealth taxation, it is useful to distinguish the primary forms of wealth taxation that have been used. There are four that may be considered important.

Property taxation. This is the oldest form of wealth taxation, dating from antiquity. It is characterized by a tax at regular intervals (e.g. yearly) on particular forms of private wealth, most commonly land, but also other forms of property. Originating in an era when land ownership was a much better measure of one's ability to pay than is currently so, property taxes have gradually been replaced and supplemented by other forms of taxation. In the US, for example, where property taxes are still relatively important, the fraction of government revenue coming from property taxation fell to less than 15 per cent by the 1950s, compared to over 50 per cent just before World War I (US Bureau of the Census 1960).

Usually based on the value of individual as sets, property taxes have typically not been progressive.

Estate taxation. Taxes on bequests and inheritances first appeared long after general property taxes. They differ from property taxes in that they are assessed only once, at death, and typically apply to most assets and liabilities bequeathed.

Estate taxes are typically quite complicated and not particularly successful either at revenue collection or wealth redistribution. Some have referred to the estate tax as a 'voluntary tax' because there are so many tax-planning devices available to reduce or eliminate the tax burden imposed on transfers of wealth.

Net worth taxation. Many countries currently supplement their revenue collections with annual taxes on personal net worth. Tax rates are typically very low, in the neighbourhood of one per cent, and may be progressive. As discussed above, this type of tax, which applies to assets net of liabilities, is very similar in effect to a tax on capital income, differing primarily in its coverage of assets which do not generate substantial current realized income.

Capital levies. In wartime, countries need vast resources over short periods of time. The preferred method of raising such funds has been the issuance of national debt, but several countries have resorted in the 20th century to the capital levy, a 'one time only' tax on existing wealth, more burdensome than annual net worth taxes but ostensibly temporary. Such levies were imposed in World War I by Germany, Czechoslovakia, Austria and Hungary, and prior to World War II by Italy and Hungary (Hicks et al., 1941). Naturally, fully unanticipated, one-time wealth taxes are non-distortionary, if not particularly fair, but the appearance of one country more than once in the above list indicates the difficulty of using capital levies unexpectedly, a problem popularly known as dynamic inconsistency.

THE ECONOMIC EFFECTS OF WEALTH TAXATION

One may start an analysis of the effects of wealth taxation by noting its similarity to the taxation of capital income, with its coincident discouragement of saving. In practice, however, different forms of wealth taxation may have different or additional effects because of their design. For example, the capital levy may be less distortionary to the extent that it is unanticipated.

The 'Single Tax'. In *Progress and Poverty*, Henry George argued for the use of a tax on the rent of unimproved land as the chief source of government revenue. Though some contemporary authors disagreed, it is fairly clear that George's tax, in hitting the return to a productive factor in extremely inelastic supply, would have imposed minimal distortions to economic behaviour. Of course, the 'Single Tax' movement that followed for many years after was invested with a fervour based on much more than the desire for Pareto efficiency.

Taxation and risk-taking. Many authors (e.g. Domar and Musgrave, 1944; Stiglitz, 1969) have noted the potentially different impact on risk-taking occurring under capital income and wealth taxes because of the failure of the latter to vary with the asset returns actually realized. That this distinction is more apparent than real under competitive conditions is now also understood. As Tobin (1958) showed, a tax on risky capital income has no effect on individual welfare and private risk-taking when the safe rate of return is zero. It may further be shown (Atkinson and Stiglitz, 1980; Gordon, 1981) that, when social risks are efficiently traded, neither does *social* risk-taking change when such a tax is levied.

These results are quite easily extended to the case when the safe rate of return is positive and the tax is on capital income *in excess* of this safe return on assets. Thus, if we view a tax on all capital income as one on the safe return to capital and one on the excess returns that compensate for risk, only the former component has economic impact. Hence, we may view a capital income tax as being equivalent to one levied on asset values multiplied by a fixed, safe rate of return, in which case it is obviously equivalent to a tax on wealth.

Note that this equivalence requires that risks be efficiently borne in the absence of taxation. Otherwise, capital income taxation may be preferred because it allows the government to pool the risks associated with different investments that individual investors have not been able to pool privately.

The Tiebout hypothesis. In the US, property taxes are used primarily to pay for local public services, and are the primary source of finance for such services. This connection means that if communities differ in their property tax burdens, one cannot ignore the implied differences in public services if it is necessary to live in a community to partake of its public services, such as education, trash removal, and police and fire protection. In the absence of such a connection, one would expect property tax differentials to be reflected in land prices. However, with governments using the taxes to pay for desired public outputs, one might expect a different result.

This notion was formalized by Tiebout (1956), who sketched a theory in which different communities levied different taxes and provided different bundles of public services, with the result being a Pareto optimal allocation, with individuals choosing their place of residence according to the bundle of local public goods and services desired. Aside from the difference between such an entrance fee and the actual property tax, there are additional theoretical problems with Tiebout's formulation (see, e.g., Bewley, 1981). Nevertheless, local wealth taxes, with competing jurisdictions, are clearly different in their impact than national wealth taxes.

Bequests and the estate tax. If annual wealth taxes discourage saving in a way similar to annual capital income taxes, one might presume the same result for estate taxes, with the large anticipated one-time burden having an important impact on lifetime saving. However, this presupposes an economic model of bequests that is by no means well accepted, i.e., that they are the manifestation of a desire to leave resources to heirs, and that they are influenced by the 'price' of an after-tax dollar in the heir's hands. At least one factor leading to bequests is the absence of efficient annuities markets, inducing the need for elderly individuals to engage in precautionary saving to provide for unanticipated health expenses or a longer than predicted lifetime. Such saving would not be influenced at all by taxes imposed after death. Hence, one might view estate taxes as being potentially less distortionary than wealth taxes on the living, but this has not been enough to overcome administrative complexity and popular opposition to strong estate taxes.

POLICY CHANGES AND IMPLICIT WEALTH TAXES

Whatever explicit taxes on wealth they impose, governments also use implicit wealth taxes whenever they change tax policies to alter the attractiveness of different assets. Perhaps the clearest example is the introduction of an investment incentive which applies only to new capital goods. Relative to a capital income tax reduction, which would favour all income-producing assets equally, such a policy would discriminate against existing assets. One may view the first policy as being equivalent to the second plus a capital levy on existing assets. A similar outcome would occur with the switch in the individual tax base from income to consumption that has been recommended by many authors over the years, with investors receiving a higher after-tax return on new investments but being saddled with unanticipated taxes on the decumulation of existing assets for consumption purposes (Auerbach et al., 1983).

Implicit wealth taxes of this sort are potentially much larger in magnitude than formal wealth taxes themselves, and might find strong resistance indeed if their explicit enactment were attempted.

ALAN J. AUERBACH

See also INHERITANCE TAXES; PROPERTY TAXATION; REDISTRIBUTION OF INCOME AND WEALTH; SINGLE TAX.

BIBLIOGRAPHY

Auerbach, A., Kotlikoff, L. and Skinner, J. 1983. The efficiency gains from dynamic tax reform. *International Economic Review* 24(1), February, 81–100.
Bewley, T. 1981. A critique of Tiebout's theory of local public expenditures. *Econometrica* 49(3), May, 713–40.
Domar, E. and Musgrave, R. 1944. Proportional income taxation and risk-taking. *Quarterly Journal of Economics* 58, May, 388–422.
George, H. 1882. *Progress and Poverty*. New York: Appleton.
Gordon, R. 1981. Taxation of corporate capital income: tax revenues versus tax distortions. National Bureau of Economic Research Working Paper No. 687, June.
Hicks, J., Hicks, U. and Rostas, L. 1941. *The Taxation of War Wealth*. Oxford: Clarendon Press.
Seligman, E. 1895. *Essays in Taxation*. 10th edn,New York: Macmillan, 1925.
Stiglitz, J. 1969. The effects of income, wealth and capital gains taxation on risk-taking. *Quarterly Journal of Economics* 83(2), May, 263–83.
Tiebout, C. 1956. A pure theory of local expenditures. *Journal of Political Economy* 64, October, 416–24.
Tobin, J. 1958. Liquidity preference as behavior towards risk. *Review of Economic Studies* 25, February, 65–86.
US Bureau of the Census 1960. *Historical Statistics of the United States*. Washington, DC: Government Printing Office.

taxes. *See* INDIRECT TAXES; INHERITANCE TAXES; LUMP-SUM TAXES; PAYROLL TAXES; PUBLIC FINANCE; SINGLE TAX; VALUE-ADDED TAX.

taxes and subsidies. The taxes and subsidies with which we shall be concerned are the *corrective* or *Pigovian* ones that could in theory be used to bring marginal private costs or benefits more closely into alignment with marginal social ones. The need for alignment arises when externalities (whether economies or diseconomies), operating at the margin, cause a divergence.

The name of Pigou is often associated with the idea, although his own statements are very cautious (1932, p. 381; 1947, pp. 99–100). That the matter is more complicated became clear from later work of Coase (1960), Buchanan and Stubblebine (1962) and others. A good summary is to be found in Turvey (1963).

Externalities may be between firms, where they are caused by technological interdependence between production functions, one firm's containing an input or an output proper to another's. They may be between consumers, one's utility function containing a variable proper to another consumer. Or they may, by an obvious extension, be between consumers and firms. Examples will be given later.

Optimizing behaviour by consumers and firms implies that marginal private costs and benefits will be equalized. If these coincide with social costs and benefits, they too will be equalized; if not, there will be a measure of market failure. Market failure means that all mutually beneficial bargains have not been struck and that it is possible to make one or more participants better off without making anyone worse off. Efficient markets (or 'Pareto efficiency') imply the exhaustion of all such opportunities.

The purpose of a corrective tax is to bridge the gap between private and social cost (if that is the side of the market we are looking at) created at the margin by an externality, and to vary with it. (As will shortly appear, this is much easier in theory than in practice.) The idea is to bring the externality to account, as it would be brought to account if internalized by a merger, not to eliminate it. It is to make an otherwise inefficient market simulate an efficient one, achieving by fiscal intervention what might (if transaction costs had not been too high) presumably have been achieved by direct negotiation between the parties.

A simple example (still on the cost side) will help to make these ideas more concrete. Assume that factory A discharges effluent into a river, increasing the purification costs of factory B, situated lower down, where it draws its water. Assume that B's costs of purification depend on the method chosen and vary with its product mix and levels of output as well as with A's output and expenditure (or lack of it) on filtration. (This example is 'simple' because at least the causation runs one way only, from A to B. If both factories drew water from a lake into which both discharged effluent, reciprocal externalities could give rise to the sort of situation commonly encountered in Game Theory.)

The complexity of designing a tax on A that would correctly measure the costs imposed on B, and vary with *them* (rather then with A's activity) as A adjusted to it (by changing the quantity and quality of water discharged) and B responded, is evident. It is also evident that, to simulate the operation of a market in which there was direct negotiation between A and B, the proceeds of the tax would have to go to B, not to the fisc. This is a simple point, often overlooked, but recognized in the older literature when reference was made to systems of taxes *and subsidies*. The latter were to go not only to those creating external economies but to those suffering external costs.

From the community's point of view the most efficient (i.e. cost-effective) configuration of water treatment systems could be along the following lines. Factory A reduces its discharge of effluent (or improves its filtration) by less than it would if taxed an amount equal to the damage caused. Instead it seeks to limit the damage by sharing the costs of operating and up-grading B's purification plant. This could be *much* more efficient, offering gains to both parties. It is an outcome that could be achieved by encouraging negotiation between the two firms, or allowing them to merge. It could not be achieved by a unilateral tax.

Internalizing an externality by merger is possible only between firms, but negotiation is possible in a wider context (between consumers, or between consumers and firms) whenever the numbers involved are not large. The problem is that the numbers often are large. Consider motorists creating congestion on a public road. Negotiation to reduce the external costs that each imposes on the others is hardly feasible. The transaction costs would be enormous. Some sort of second best solution is to be preferred. A tax on fuel, licence fees and highway rules are among the possibilities. They would at least help to reduce congestion, or limit its consequences.

Corrective taxes are best seen in this light. They are seldom a practical way of achieving Pareto efficiency. But they could be part of a second best solution to the problem of market failure. As such they are to be weighed against other second best solutions such as licences, zoning laws and outright prohibitions. In the river pollution example, if there were too many firms to make negotiation feasible, a law prohibiting the discharge of effluent, or even one prohibiting the use of river water for industrial purposes, would clearly eliminate the externality. But it would not bring about a particularly efficient state of affairs. In such circumstances the use of admittedly rough corrective taxes might be a serious alternative.

In other circumstances a combination of measures might be appropriate. A tax on tobacco is almost always designed with an eye to revenue, the demand for the commodity being inelastic, but the acceptability of the tax is probably due to widespread recognition of the external costs imposed by smokers on non-smokers. The sheer difficulty of trying to measure these costs makes a genuinely corrective tax all but impossible. So partial prohibitions in the form of non-smoking areas are common. Their creation is a much more practical approach to a common social problem than attempting to tax smokers whenever they cause inconvenience to others – or suggesting that non-smokers should pay smokers to refrain from indulging.

This brings us to a final point. In our original example, if A and B were brought to the negotiating table, the outcome of the negotiation would be very different if the laws, customs or conventions of the society gave riparian owners (a) the right to discharge effluent or (b) the right to draw clean water. The two regimes would result in two very different distributions of the potential gains. But under either regime an efficient outcome would be possible – one in which all opportunities for mutually beneficial bargains had been exhausted. Corrective taxes and subsidies are concerned with the latter, not with the distribution of the gains from trade – that is to say: with efficiency, not equity.

J. DE V. GRAAFF

See also NEUTRAL TAXATION.

BIBLIOGRAPHY

Buchanan, J.S. and Stubblebine, W.C. 1962. Externality. *Economica* 26, November, 371–84.

Coase, R.H. 1960. The problem of social cost. *Journal of Law and Economics* 3, October, 1–44.

Pigou, A.C. 1932. *The Economics of Welfare*. 4th edn, London: Macmillan.

Pigou, A.C. 1947. *A Study in Public Finance*. 3rd edn, London: Macmillan.

Turvey, R. 1963. On divergences between social cost and private cost. *Economica* 30, August, 309–13.

tax incidence. Tax incidence analysis is the study of the effects of a particular tax or a tax system on the distribution of economic welfare. The key question is who actually bears the burden of the resources transferred to the government by the tax. Actually, the total burden will generally exceed the amount of the resource transfer due to the inefficiency cost of taxes. Only with lump sum taxes will the burden be precisely equal to the revenue.

The subject of tax incidence has been discussed for many years including such classic arguments as those of Ricardo concerning the taxation of a pure rent and of Henry George regarding the possibility of a land tax. More recently, Joseph Pechman titled his 1985 book, *Who Paid the Taxes, 1966–85*. There has also been increasing awareness that there are a number of important dimensions to the question of tax incidence. There is the division of the tax burden between producers, consumers, and suppliers of factors. This particular tax incidence question is often emphasized in elementary economics classes, where the important lesson is learned that the more inelastic participant in the market bears a larger share of the burden. But there also is the classic question of the effect of taxes on the functional distribution of income (between capital and labour) and on the personal distribution of income. For many applications, there are important intergenerational incidence questions and interregional ones as well.

The most elementary lesson of the study of tax incidence is that there is not a correlation between the individual who sends the cheque to the government and the person who bears the tax burden. In the simple example of excise tax on a single good in a competitive market place, the actual incidence does not depend on whether the customer pays the tax or the seller. The only thing that matters in the partial equilibrium analysis of this situation is the relative magnitudes of the supply and the demand elasticities. To a first order approximation, the customer's share of the tax burden is given by $\eta D/(\eta D+\eta S)$ where ηD is the elasticity of demand and ηS is the elasticity of supply. A more sophisticated general equilibrium model would include income effects and cross elasticities, but the result that the person who sends in the cheque is irrelevant would continue to be valid. This is perhaps most clear in the case of the corporation income tax. The corporation sends in the money, but who bears the tax? Answering that it is the corporation is both not very insightful and probably wrong. It could be the owners of the firm, its workers, its customers, capitalists in general, or workers in general. Actually, the incidence of the corporation income tax has proven to be one of the most studied of tax incidence questions. Another example of the tax incidence being independent of the actual payer is given by the Social Security tax in the United States. While the employer and the employee pay equal amounts to the government, no economist would argue that the burden is shared in this manner. As with other taxes, the incidence of the real burden of the Social Security tax fundamentally depends on certain key elasticities; in this case, the labour demand and supply elasticities. It is often asserted that the Social Security payroll tax is fully borne by the workers. This is not true in general unless labour supply is perfectly inelastic or labour demand infinitely elastic.

The theoretically correct way to evaluate tax incidence effects is quite clear. One wants to compare the general equilibrium of the economy before the tax change with the equilibrium which occurs after the change. Ideally the general equilibrium model would be sufficiently disaggregated, would be dynamic and involve overlapping generations, and would contain all the distortions of the tax system. The economist can then examine the changes caused by the tax change, and these changes are the incidence of the tax. One could examine the changes in the welfare of each consumer, the changes in the total return to capital and labour, and the magnitude of the price changes. The difficulty with this approach has been the slowness of the development of empirical general equilibrium economics.

Perhaps the most significant development in applied tax incidence analysis was Harberger's (1962) use of the two-sector general equilibrium model to evaluate the incidence of the corporation income tax. He divides the production side of the economy into the corporate and non-corporate sectors and models the corporate income tax as a tax on the rental price of capital in the corporate sector. One of the key advantages of his general equilibrium approach over partial equilibrium methods is its ability to evaluate the impact of a partial factor tax on output markets. Harberger's model is static and often is interpreted as being a medium run model. Factors are fixed in total supply but perfectly mobile between sectors. Each sector is perfectly competitive and has a constant returns to scale production technology. There is essentially only one consumer in the model in that the government spends its money in exactly the same way as the household sector. The model is presented as a set of linear equations coming from first order optimization conditions. The linearity is strictly valid only in the limit of extremely small changes in the tax system. Harberger parameterized the model to accord roughly with the US economy of the 1950s and found that for most sets of demand and factor substitution elasticities that he examined, the corporation income tax was fully borne by the owners of capital. Since in his model the net of tax return is equated in both sectors after the tax, it is important to note that his model indicates that the owners of the non-corporate capital stock bear the burden along with those who own the corporate sector capital. Harberger's model and its applications to tax incidence are clearly presented and surveyed in McLure (1975).

Harberger's model has been criticized on a number of grounds. First, by only having two sectors, many tax interactions cannot be examined. Second, the local approximations are disturbing when what you are attempting to do is measure how large certain effects are. Third, some people questioned his assumption that the corporate tax was correctly captured as a tax on the use of capital in the corporate sector. Clearly, it is only a tax on the equity financed capital, and his model does not capture the financing decisions of the firm. Fourth, Harberger's model is a closed one. Tax incidence results are quite sensitive to the functioning of international capital markets, as demonstrated in the research of Goulder, Shoven and Whalley (1983). Despite these shortcomings, Harberger's work was seminal and established the use of general equilibrium models to evaluate tax incidence.

The general equilibrium approach has been extended in many ways. Shoven and Whalley (1972) and Shoven (1976) added additional sectors to Harberger's analysis. While they found larger efficiency losses to the corporation tax, they did not qualitatively change his functional incidence results. They found that the personal incidence pattern was 'U-shaped' in that the largest proportional burdens were suffered by the lowest and the highest income households. This result is due primarily to the fact that the lowest-income households have many elderly among them who rely primarily on capital income to finance their retirements. The highest-income households also receive a relatively high percentage of their income from capital and hence bear a significant burden of the corporation tax. Another extension was contributed by Feldstein (1974), who analysed the long-run incidence of the tax, dropping Harberger's fixed factor supply assumption. He showed that if saving is depressed by the lower after-tax return on capital, then the long-run burden of the tax may be shifted into labour due to the reduced capital–labour ratio in the economy. Bernheim (1981) presents an analytical model and Auerbach and Kotlikoff (1983) a dynamic computational general equilibrium model which describes the complete dynamic path of the economy after the introduction of a tax change. Thus, their work covers the transition path as well as the new long run steady state path of the economy.

Pechman's work is of a different nature, but is equally important. He calculates the detailed taxes paid by all households in a large microeconomic data set. He then presents numerous cross-tabulations of tax burden by income class. The results are difficult to generalize, but the results suggest that the total tax burden in the United States is much closer to proportional than a causal examination of the tax code would suggest, and that the tax system, as such, changes the distribution of income in the economy very little. The strength of his approach is its detail and the relatively high quality of the data. The weakness is the lack of economic behaviour by the agents in the economy. That is, while one can collect data on household behaviour in the presence of the current tax system, such data are, of course, unavailable in the absence of the taxes. One cannot correctly judge the impact of the tax without knowing the behavioural responses of the economy's participants. For the most part, Pechman assumes no behavioural response and calculates tax burdens accordingly. Another problem with his work, shared with many of the general equilibrium tax incidence models, is that it measures incidence at a moment in time.

Many economic theorists now feel that measuring economic welfare by examining annual income is inadequate and potentially misleading. Certainly individuals have planning horizons which exceed one year and financial markets facilitate households in smoothing consumption relative to income by borrowing and lending. The life-cycle model, with or without a bequest motive added, has many desirable attributes and implies that households maximize lifetime utility subject to a lifetime budget constraint. Clearly capital markets are not perfect in the real world, and some people may be solving their lifetime optimization problem unconstrained by this fact, while others are liquidity constrained by their current income. Nonetheless, the life-cycle model is an important one and has had a major affect on incidence analyses. The lifetime perspective suggests that it is inappropriate to examine the impact of a tax on the poor (or the rich) at a particular instant in time. Medical students with low incomes are not poor in the same sense as someone with the same income in their peak earnings years. Because of this, it has been suggested that lifetime incidence is an appropriate concept to examine.

One tax whose incidence may look different from a lifetime perspective than from a point-in-time perspective is the value added tax. This tax, which is essentially a sales tax, is regressive at any point in time because the poor tend to have a higher average propensity to consume than the rich. However, over a lifetime average propensities to consume tend to be about the same (and about unity), so the tax would look close to proportional on a lifetime incidence basis. Browning and Johnson (1979) have even suggested that it may be quite progressive because some of the poor are on public welfare programmes which are explicitly indexed for price increases and thus escape the burden entirely. Davis, St-Hilaire and Whalley (1984) attempt to calculate lifetime incidence for the entire tax system.

The fact that tax incidence differs from tax payments is most strikingly apparent when one considers tax sheltered investments. For example, the interest earned on municipal bonds is not taxed in the United States. Because of this, high tax rate individuals may choose to invest in these financial instruments. However, because of their tax preference, these securities offer a lower yield than a fully taxable bond. In fact, the yield may be only 70 per cent as great. Clearly, while the owner of this bond does not pay any taxes, he or she still bears a burden due to the tax system. In this case, the implicit tax rate is 30 per cent. This implicit but real tax incidence occurs with all tax favoured investments such as equity, real estate, and household durables. This tax incidence occurs because the tax advantage of the asset is to some extent capitalized into its price. Calculating the complete incidence of the tax system would involve this consideration, although little has been done on this empirically.

Tax incidence is an extremely important subject given the large size of the public sector in most developed countries and their habit of changing their tax systems in significant ways. There are many dimensions to tax incidence and complete analyses with endogenous economic behaviour are still the illusive goal. On the other hand, the subject has made dramatic progress in the last ten to fifteen years, and more is promised as large and realistic computable general equilibrium models become feasible.

JOHN B. SHOVEN

See also COMPUTATION OF GENERAL EQUILIBRIA; PUBLIC FINANCE.

BIBLIOGRAPHY

Auerbach, A. and Kotlikoff, L. 1983. National savings, economic welfare, and the structure of taxation. In *Behavioral Simulation Methods in Tax Policy Analysis*, ed. M. Feldstein, Chicago: University of Chicago Press.

Bernheim, B. 1981. A note on dynamic tax incidence. *Quarterly Journal of Economics*, November, 705–23.

Browning, E. and Johnson, W. 1979. *The Distribution of the Tax Burden*. Washington, DC: American Enterprise Institute.

Davies, J., St-Hilaire, F. and Whalley, J. 1984. Some calculations of lifetime tax incidence. *American Economic Review* 74(4), 633–49.

Feldstein, M. 1974. Incidence of a capital income tax in a growing economy with variable savings rates. *Review of Economic Studies* 41, 505–13.

Goulder, L., Shoven, J. and Whalley, J. 1983. Domestic tax policy and the foreign sector: the importance of alternative foreign sector formulations to results from a general equilibrium tax analysis market. In *Simulation Methods in Tax Policy Analysis*, ed. M. Feldstein, Chicago: University of Chicago Press.

Harberger, A.C. 1962. The incidence of the corporation income tax. *Journal of Political Economy* 70, 215–40.

Kotlikoff, L. and Summers, L. 1986. Tax incidence. National Bureau of Economic Research Working Paper No. 1864, March.

McLure, C., Jr. 1975. General equilibrium incidence analysis: the Harberger Model after ten years. *Journal of Public Economy* 4, 125–61.

Pechman, J.A. 1985. *Who Paid the Taxes, 1966–85*. Washington, DC: Brookings Institution.

Shoven, J.B. 1976. The incidence and efficiency effects of taxes on income from capital. *Journal of Political Economy* 84, 1261–84.

Shoven, J.B. and Whalley, J. 1972. A general equilibrium calculation of the effects of differential taxation of income from capital in the U.S. *Journal of Public Economy* 1, 281–321.

Taylor, Fred Manville (1855–1932). Taylor made his chief contribution to economic theory in his 1928 presidential address to the American Economic Association, in which he laid out the basic principles of market socialism (Taylor, 1929). He argued that rational allocation of resources could be achieved in a socialist state if three conditions are met: citizens obtain income from the state in exchange for services; income is freely spent on goods offered for sale by the state at given prices; prices are set at full costs of production. The third condition can be met through a trial-and-error method in which prices of factors of production are set at levels that clear the market. Given these costs and consumer demand, markets for finished products can be cleared by adjusting levels of output and inventories. Such a system could achieve results similar to those of a competitive private enterprise economy.

Taylor's doctorate was in philosophy from the University of Michigan (1888). He taught at Albion College 1879–92, and in the Department of Economics at Michigan from 1892 to 1929. A strong advocate of laissez-faire policies and the gold standard, Taylor was a noted expositor of economic theory, with emphasis on Marshallian partial equilibrium analysis, analytic rigour and a libertarian ideology. His *Principles* textbook (Taylor, 1911) went through nine editions from 1911 to 1925.

DANIEL R. FUSFELD

See also LANGE–LERNER MECHANISM.

SELECTED WORKS
1911. *Principles of Economics*. Ann Arbor: University of Michigan Press, 1918; New York: Ronald Press, 1921. 9th edn, 1925.
1929. The guidance of production in a socialist state. *American Economic Review* 19(1), March, 1–8. Reprinted in *On the Economic Theory of Socialism*, ed. B.E. Lipincott. New York: McGraw-Hill, 1938.

Taylor, Harriet (née Hardy, later Mrs John Stuart Mill) (1807–1858). Harriet Taylor was born in London on 8 October 1807 and died at Avignon on 3 November 1858. A Unitarian doctor's daughter, she was beautiful, mainly self-educated and of considerable intelligence. In 1826 she married a Unitarian wholesale druggist, John Taylor, and had two sons and one daughter, Helen, who became a champion of women's suffrage and higher education. Harriet, who had literary ambitions, contributed briefly and anonymously book reviews, verses and articles to the Unitarian *Monthly Repository*. In 1830 she met John Stuart Mill, also a contributor to the *Repository*. Friendship, based on mutual concern for the poor and the inferior status of women, developed into love. Their indiscreet public appearances and travels caused a scandal. In 1851, some two years after the death of John Taylor, who had reluctantly condoned the situation, they married. Mill praised Harriet in extravagant terms, which his friends, admirers and subsequent critics found false and ludicrous, particularly the inscription on her tombstone, ending WERE THERE BUT A FEW HEARTS AND INTELLECTS LIKE HERS THIS EARTH WOULD ALREADY BECOME THE HOPED-FOR HEAVEN.

It is only in recent years that her influence over his later work has received recognition. Its importance was apparent in *On Liberty*, published in 1859 after her death, and *The Subjection of Women* (1869) based on her only additional publication, 'The Enfranchisement of Women', which, with Mill's help and through his agency, appeared anonymously in the *Westminster Review* for July 1851. Her influence on his *Principles of Political Economy* was decisive. She persuaded him to include a chapter, 'On the Probable Futurity of the Labouring Classes', written partly in her own words. At her request he wrote, 'The poor have come out of leading-strings and cannot any longer be governed or treated like children ...' (Mill, 1848). In 1849 the chapter 'Of Property' was revised at her insistence. Initially she had approved the claim that in existing circumstances Socialism and Communism (they appear to have been considered synonymous) were neither realistic nor desirable since they overemphasized the importance of security. The 1848 French uprising which preceded the Republic had strengthened Harriet's left-wing bias. The argument, she now declared, was invalid and she took violent exception to a passage, to Mill most pertinent, that, 'The necessaries of life, when they have always been secure for the whole of life, are scarcely more a subject of consciousness or ... happiness than the elements' (Mill, 1848). He now confessed that further consideration would probably bring him to her side, as was almost invariably the case when a subject received their joint consideration. Against his former judgement he amended the passage to read, 'On the Communistic scheme, supposing it to be successful, there would be an end to all anxiety concerning the means of subsistence; and this would be much gained for human happiness ...' (Mill, 1849).

The third edition (1852) marked Harriet's triumph. If, Mill wrote, 'the choice were to be made between Communism with all its chances, and the present state of society with all its sufferings and injustices ... all the difficulties ... of Communism would be as dust in the balance ... .' It was, however, too soon to judge whether, at their best, 'individual agency' or left-wing doctrines 'will be the ultimate form of human society'. Mill did not exaggerate when he wrote that, but for Harriet, the left-wing argument would 'either have been absent, or the suggestions would have been made much more timidly and in a more qualified form' (Mill, *Autobiography*, edited by Helen Taylor, 1873).

JOSEPHINE KAMM

SELECTED WORKS
1851. The enfranchisement of women. *Westminster and Foreign Quarterly Review* 55.

BIBLIOGRAPHY
Mill, J.S. 1848, 1849. *Principles of Political Economy*. In *Collected Works of John Stuart Mill*, Vol. III, ed. J.M. Robson, Toronto: University of Toronto Press; London: Routledge & Kegan Paul, 1965.
Mill, J.S. 1852. *Principles of Political Economy*. 3rd edn. In *Collected Works of John Stuart Mill*, Vol. II, ed. J.M. Robson, Toronto: University of Toronto Press; London: Routledge & Kegan Paul, 1965.
Mill, J.S. 1859. *On Liberty*. 4th edn, London: Longmans & Green, 1869.
Mill, J.S. 1869. *The Subjection of Women*. London: Longmans & Green.
Mill, J.S. 1873. *Autobiography*. In *Collected Works of John Stuart Mill*, Vol. I, ed. J.M. Robson and J. Stillinger, Toronto: University of Toronto Press; London: Routledge & Kegan Paul, 1981.

Taylorism. Taylorism refers to the system of management developed by Frederick Winslow Taylor. Taylor called his system Scientific Management. Scientific management is clearly described in Taylor's two most famous works, *Shop Management* (1903) and *The Principles of Scientific Management* (1911).

Scientific management is based on the following principles:

1. Management gathers and systematizes all the workers' traditional knowledge.

2. All possible 'brainwork' is removed from the shop and centred in the planning or layout department.

3. The work should be divided into its simplest constituent elements: the tasks. Management should try to limit individual 'jobs' to a single task as far as possible.

4. Managers should specify the tasks to be done in complete detail. These tasks should be presented to the worker in written form. They should note not only what is to be done, but also how it is to be done and the exact time allowed for doing it.

5. The work should be monitored closely.

Taylor's techniques for gathering information about work was time study, the measurement of elapsed time for each component operation of a work process. Taylor also recommended that the foreman's job should be divided into more simplified task collections. Shop-floor foreman should be divided into the setting-up boss, speed boss, quantity inspector and repair boss. However, the main division was to separate work-design and manning-level decisions away from shop-floor foreman and to the planning department.

The purpose of Taylor's system was to eliminate 'soldiering', or low worker effort. This could either take the form of natural soldiering, the natural instinct and tendency for men to take it easy, or systematic soldiering, the calculated reduction of effort arising from actions and communication among groups of workers. The ultimate cause of both forms of soldiering for Taylor 'lay in the ignorance of the management as to what really constitutes a proper day's work for a workman' (1911, p. 53). Once this was determined 'scientifically', workers would be forced to comply with this standard by careful monitoring of their performance and by a differential piece-work payment system. A target rate of work would be determined by work study. If workers exceeded this target, they would receive a bonus, but bonus payments would reach a ceiling between 30 per cent and 100 per cent of the standard work rate. If workers failed to meet their targets, they would lose earnings.

There is a wide range of opinions as to the importance of Taylorism. For some, Taylorism represents the dominant theory and practice of 20th-century management (Drucker, 1954; Braverman, 1974). For others, Taylorism is viewed as having widespread ideological impact, but not much influence on practice because it was successfully resisted by workers and was too expensive for managers (Edwards, 1979). Finally, there are those who view Taylorism as an expression of important changes in management practices, but that moves towards Taylorism have not been universal. The application of Taylorism is contingent on environmental factors (Friedman, 1977; Littler, 1982).

A.L. Friedman

See also labour process; ure, andrew.

BIBLIOGRAPHY

Braverman, H. 1974. *Labor and Monopoly Capital*. New York: Monthly Review Press.

Drucker, P. 1954. *The Practice of Management*. New York: Harper & Row.

Edwards, R. 1979. *Contested Terrain*. London: Heinemann.

Friedman, A.L. 1977. *Industry and Labour*. London: Macmillan.

Littler, C.R. 1982. *The Development of the Labour Process in Capitalist Societies*. London: Heinemann.

Taylor, F.W. 1903. Shop management. In F.W. Taylor, *Scientific Management*, London: Harper & Row, 1964.

Taylor, F.W. 1911. The principles of scientific management. In F.W. Taylor, *Scientific Management*, London: Harper & Row, 1964.

teams. The economic theory of teams addresses a middle ground between the theory of individual decision under uncertainty and the theory of games. A *team* is made up of a number of decision-makers, with common interests and beliefs, but controlling different decision variables and basing their decisions on (possibly) different information. The theory of teams is concerned with (1) the allocation of decision variables (tasks) and information among the members of the team, and (2) the characterization of efficient decision rules, given the allocation of tasks and information.

For example, in the pre-computer age, airline companies had a number of ticket agents who were authorized to sell reservations on future flights with only partial information about what reservations had been booked by other agents. A team-theoretic issue would be the characterization of best rules for those agents to use under such circumstances, taking account of the joint probability distribution of demands for reservations at the different offices, the losses due to selling too many or too few reservations in total, and so forth. A second issue would be the calculation of the increase in expected profit that would be obtained by providing each agent with better information about the status of reservations at all offices, or by increased centralization of the reservation process. To calculate this increase in expected profit – the *value* of the additional information – one of course needs to know something about the best decision rules with and without the additional information. However, providing this additional information would require additional communication, transmission, processing, and storage, all of which would be costly. The value of the information puts an upper bound on the additional cost that should be incurred. The value – and cost – of the information will depend on its structure and on the structure of the team's decision problem, and not just on some simple measure of the 'quantity' of information. (For a study of the airline reservation problem, and other models of sales organization, from a team-theoretic point of view, see Beckmann, 1958 and McGuire, 1961, respectively.)

In this entry we shall sketch a formal model of team theory, the characterization of optimal team decision functions, and the evaluation of information in a team. The theory will be illustrated with a discussion of decentralized resource allocation, followed by concluding remarks on the incentive problem.

A FORMAL MODEL. We consider a *team* and M *members*. Each member m controls an *action*, say a_m. The resulting utility to the team depends on the *team action*,

$$a = (a_1, \dots, a_M),$$

and on the *state of the environment*. (Since the team members have common interests, there is a single utility for the whole team.) The state of the environment comprises all the variables about which team members may be uncertain before choosing their actions. It is determined exogenously, i.e. is not subject to the control or influence of the team members. If we denote the state of the environment by s, then we can denote the utility to the team by $u(a, s)$; the function u will be called the *payoff function* for the team.

Before choosing an action, each team member m receives an information signal, y_m. This information signal is determined by the state of the environment, say $y_m = \eta_m(s)$. (This includes the case of 'noisy' information, if the description of the state of the environment includes a description of the noise.) We shall call η_m the *information function* for member m, and the M-tuple $\eta = (\eta_1, \dots, \eta_M)$ will be called the *information structure* of the team.

Each team member m will choose his action on the basis of the information signal he receives, according to a decision function, say α_m. Thus

$$a_m = \alpha_m(y_m) = \alpha_m(\eta_m[s]). \quad (1)$$

If we use the symbol α to denote the *team decision function*, i.e., the M-tuple of individual decision functions, then the utility to the team, in *state s*, of using the information structure η and decision function α can be expressed as

$$U(s) = u[\alpha(\eta[s]), s], \quad (2)$$

To express the team's uncertainty about the state of the environment, we suppose that s is determined according to some probability distribution, ϕ, on the set S of possible states. This probability distribution may be interpreted as 'objective' or 'personal'; in the latter case it represents the beliefs of the team members (Savage, 1954). It is part of the definition of a team that its members have common beliefs, as well as common utility functions.

With the state s distributed according to the probability distribution ϕ, the utility $U(s)$ in (2) is a random variable. We shall assume that the team chooses its decision function so as to maximize the (mathematical) expectation of this utility,

$$E[U(s)] = \sum_s \phi(s)U(s) \equiv \omega(\alpha, \eta, \phi). \quad (3)$$

As a special case, suppose that the information functions of the team members are identical. In this case, the team decision problem is formally identical to a one-person decision problem in which the same person controls all of the actions. An alternative interpretation of this case is that the information is *centralized.* By contrast, if at least two team members have essentially different information functions, then we may say that the information is *decentralized.* With this definition of (informational) decentralization, we see that all organizations but the very smallest are likely to be decentralized to some extent.

The expected utility for the team depends on the team members' decision function, the team information structure, and the probability distribution of states of the environment, as well as on the 'structure' of the decision problem, i.e. the way in which the utility (2) depends on the members' action and the state of the environment. This is brought out by the notation in (3). If we want to compare the usefulness of two different information structures, we have to associate with them some corresponding decision function α and probability distribution ϕ. Since the probability distribution (sometimes called the 'prior distribution') represents either objective probabilities or the team members' common beliefs before they receive further information, it is natural to take it as a datum of the problem. On the other hand, since the decision functions can be chosen by the team, it is natural to associate with each information structure the corresponding team decision function that maximizes its expected utility (given the information structure). Thus the optimization problem for the team may be posed in two stages: (1) for a given information structure, characterize the optimal team decision function(s); (2) optimize the information structure, taking account of the costs of – or constraints on – making the information available, and with the proviso that for each information structure the team uses an optimal decision function.

More will be said below about each of these stages of the problem. However, it should be emphasized here that the choice of information structure comprises most of the organizational design choices that are not concerned with conflicts of interests or beliefs among the organization's members. The information structure is, of course, affected by the pattern of observation and communication in the team. In addition, the allocation of tasks within the team is expressed by the information structure. To see this, suppose that each member of the team were assigned an information structure; then a reassignment of decision variables to team members would be formally equivalent to reassigning information functions to decision variables.

OPTIMAL DECISION FUNCTIONS. We shall now consider the characterization of team decision functions that are optimal for a given structure of information. It will be useful to recall here the corresponding problem for a single-person decision problem (see, e.g., Marschak and Radner, 1972, ch. 2). We may use the same model and notation as in the previous section, but remembering that there is only one member of the team. The following statement provides a general characterization of the optimal decision function: *For each information signal, choose an action that maximizes the conditional expected utility given the particular signal.*

This characterization is easily derived from equations (2) and (3). In equation (3), group the terms in the sum according to the information signal associated with each state; this gives us

$$E[U(s)] = \sum_y \sum_{\eta(s)=y} \phi(s)U(s). \quad (4)$$

From (2), if $\eta(s) = y$, then the resulting utility in that state is

$$U(s) = u[\alpha(y), s]. \quad (5)$$

For each signal y, the decision-maker can choose an action $a = \alpha(y)$. Hence, combining (4) and (5) we see that, for each signal y, the decision-maker should choose $a = \alpha(y)$ to maximize

$$\sum_{\eta(s)=y} \phi(s)u(a, s). \quad (6)$$

Let $\psi(y)$ denote the probability of y, and let $\phi(s \mid y)$ denote the conditional probability of s given y. By definition,

$$\psi(y) = \sum_{y=\eta(s)} \phi(s),$$

and if $y = \eta(s)$,

$$\phi(s \mid y) = \frac{\phi(s)}{\psi(y)},$$

or

$$\phi(s) = \psi(y)\phi(s \mid y).$$

Hence (6) can be written as

$$\psi(y) \sum_{\eta(s)=y} \phi(s \mid y)u(a, s), \quad (7)$$

so that maximizing (6) is equivalent to maximizing

$$\sum_{\eta(s)=y} \phi(s \mid y)u(a, s), \quad (8)$$

which we recognize as the conditional expected utility using the action a, given the signal y. This proves the above characterization of the best decision function. (Notice that we have implicitly assumed that the signal has positive probability. There is no loss of generality in doing so; we can simply exclude from consideration all signals that have zero probability, since they do not affect the expected utility.)

The characterization of optimal single-person decision functions can be extended to the case of a team, but in a restricted way. Consider a particular team member i. If a team decision function, say $\hat{\alpha}$, is optimal, then surely i's decision function α_i is optimal given that each other member j uses $\hat{\alpha}_j$. Hence i is faced, so-to-speak, with a one person decision problem in which the other members' decision functions form part of i's 'environment'. The following is therefore a *necessary* condition for a team decision function to be optimal:

Person-by-person-Optimality Condition: For each member i, and for each signal y_i with positive probability, the corresponding action $a_i = \alpha_i(y_i)$ maximizes the team's conditional expected utility given the signal y_i and the decision functions of the other members.

Although person-by-person-optimality is necessary for optimality, it need not be sufficient. However, one can prove the following:

Theorem 1. If each member's action is a real finite-dimensional vector chosen from some open rectangle, and if for each state s the team's utility is a concave and differentiable function of the team action, then any team decision function that is person-by-person-optimal is also optimal.

(For a proof of this theorem, and an example in which a person-by-person-optimal decision function fails to be optimal, see Marschak and Radner, 1972, ch. 10, s. 3.; for a more complete treatment, see Radner, 1962.)

The person-by-person-optimality condition can be applied to yield more detailed characterizations of optimal team decision functions for special cases, e.g., in which the utility function is quadratic or piecewise-linear (see Marschak and Radner, 1972, ch. 10). A few such applications are illustrated below.

THE EVALUATION OF INFORMATION. As noted at the beginning of this discussion, many of the most interesting questions in organizational design concern the comparison of alternative information structures. One information structure is better than another to the extent that it permits better decisions; on the other hand, this improvement be obtained only at some additional cost.

We first consider the case in which the utility from the decisions is additively separable from the cost of the information structure; we shall call this the *separable case*. In this case, one is justified in defining the *gross value* of an information structure as the difference between (1) the expected utility derived from its best use and (2) the maximum utility obtainable using no information (beyond that contained in the prior probability distribution of states).

If the team has no information (the null information structure), then its decision function reduces to a single team action. The maximum expected utility that the team can obtain with the null information structure is

$$V_0(\phi) = \max_a \sum_s u(a, s). \qquad (9)$$

Hence in the separable case, the gross value of an information structure η is defined as

$$V(\eta, \phi) \equiv \max_\alpha \omega(\alpha, \eta, \phi) - V_0(\phi). \qquad (10)$$

(Cf. equation (3).)

Note that the value of an information structure depends on the prior distribution, as well as on the entire structure of the decision problem (available actions, utility function, etc.). This should make one suspect that there is no way to tell whether one information structure is more valuable than another just by examining the two information structures alone.

To examine this question more carefully, it is useful to introduce another representation of information. Consider again for the moment the single-person case; an information structure then consists of a single function from states to information signals. For any given signal, there is a set of states that give rise to that signal. This correspondence between signals and sets of states determines a partition of the set of states; each element of the partition is a set of all states that lead to a particular signal; denote this partition by (S_y). It is obvious that any two information structures that give rise to the same partition are equivalent from the point of view of the decision-maker, and in particular must have the same value. In other words, the names or labels of the signals are unimportant.

Suppose now that the set S of states of the environment, the number M of team members, and the set A of team actions are fixed. Consider the family of all team decision problems that can be formulated with the given triple (S, M, A). In other words, consider the set of all pairs (u, ϕ), where u is a utility function for the team, and ϕ is a prior distribution, compatible with (S, M, A). We shall say that one information structure *is as valuable* as another information structure if the value of the first is greater than or equal to the value of the second for all team decision problems compatible with (S, M, A). (Value is defined by equation (10).)

The following criterion provides a simple test for the relation 'as valuable as'. Of two partitions of the set S, we shall say the first is as *fine* as the second if every element of the first partition is a subset of some element of the second (the first can be obtained by 'refining' the second). Let $\eta = (\eta_1, \ldots, \eta_M)$ and $\chi = (\chi_1, \ldots, \chi_M)$ be two team information structures. We shall say that η is as fine as χ if for every team member m, η_m is as fine as χ_m. One can prove (see Marschak and Radner, 1972, Ch. 2, Sec. 6):

Theorem 2. Assume that every team member has at least three alternative actions; then the information structure η is at least as valuable as the information structure χ if and only if, for each member m, η_m is as fine as χ_m.

Theorem 2 can be extended to deal with 'noisy' information; (see, e.g., McGuire, 1972).

Since two partitions of a set need not be ranked by the relation 'as fine as', it is clear from Theorem 2 that the relation 'as valuable as' is only a partial ordering of information structures. This implies, in particular, that there is no numerical measure of 'quantity of information' that can rank all information structures in order of value, independent of the decision problem in which the information is used.

If the utility of the team decision and the cost of information are not additively separable, then an alternative definition of value of information must be used. For example, suppose that the outcome of the team decision and the cost of the information structure are both measured in dollars, and the the team is not risk-neutral, so that the team utility is some (nonlinear) function of the outcome and the cost. Then we can define the value of the information structure as the 'demand price', i.e., the smallest cost that would make the team indifferent between using the information structure and having no information beyond the prior distribution. (For further discussion of the comparison of information structures, see McGuire, 1972. For more on the value of and demand for information, see Arrow, 1972.)

DECENTRALIZATION. We have used the term informational decentralization to refer to a structure of information in which not all members have the same information function. In an economic organization the information structure is generated by processes of observation, communication, storage, and computation. For example, suppose that each team member m starts by observing a different random variable, say $\zeta_m(s)$. If there were no communication among the members before actions were taken, then each member's information would be the same as his observation – an extreme form of decentralization. On the other hand, if there were complete communication of their observations among the members, then their information functions would be identical, namely $\zeta = (\zeta_1, \ldots, \zeta_M)$. Alternatively, the latter information structure could be generated by having all members communicate their observations to a central agency, which would then compute the team action and communicate the corresponding individual action to each member. In the last two cases, we would say that the information structure is completely centralized, because all of the members' action were based on the same information.

Rarely does one encounter in a real organization the extremes of no communication or complete communication just described. Rather, one finds that numerous devices are used to bring about a partial exchange of information. The usefulness of such devices is measured by the excess of additional value (expected utility) they contribute over the costs of installing and operating them. Examples of such devices are the dissemination of reports and instructions, the formation of committees and task forces, and 'management by exception'. Formal models and a comparative analysis of some of these devices are given in (Marschak and Radner, 1972, ch. 6). In particular, this methodology is used to elucidate the value of two different forms of management by exception.

ALLOCATION OF RESOURCES IN A TEAM. For many economists, the purely competitive market represents the ideal model of economic decentralization. Indeed, in some economic literature, 'decentralization' and 'pure competition' are synonymous. The potential usefulness of market-like mechanisms to decentralize economic decision-making in a socialist economy has also been discussed by students of socialism (Lange and Taylor, 1938; Lerner, 1944; Ward, 1967).

The theory of teams provides a natural framework for the analysis of market mechanisms as a device for decentralization. For example, consider the problem of allocating resources to productive enterprises. Suppose that some resources are initially held centrally by a 'resource manager'. Before any exchange of information, the resource manager observes the supplies of centrally available resources, and each enterprise manager observes his respective local conditions of production: technology, supplies of local resources, etc. The action of the resource manager is to allocate the central resources among the enterprises. The action of an enterprise manager includes (say) the choice of techniques and the levels of inputs of local resources. The state of the environment comprises the total supplies of central resources and the local conditions.

At one extreme, the team action could be taken without any communication. In particular, the central resources would be allocated based only on the prior probability distribution of local conditions. Regarding the supplies of central resources, each enterprise manager would know only the prior probability distribution of such supplies, and the allocation rule to be used by the resource manager. We might call the resulting information structure 'routine'.

At the other extreme (complete centralization), each enterprise manager might be required to report to the resource manager all of his information about local conditions. The resource manager would then compute both the optimal decisions of the enterprises and the optimal allocation of resources. Accordingly, the resources would be allocated and the enterprise managers would the 'instructed' by the resource manager as to what actions they should take.

In a market mechanism, the resource manager would announce prices (of central resources), and the enterprise managers would respond with demands. In the literature on allocation and price-adjustment mechanisms it is usually assumed that this exchange of messages is iterated until an equilibrium of supply and demand is reached (this may require infinitely many iterations!). In a real application of such a mechanism, only a few iterations would typically be feasible, and equilibrium would not be reached. Thus one could not appeal to the theory of optimality of the equilibria of such processes. Nevertheless, the exchange of information produced by even a few iterations might be quite valuable, i.e., the information structure might be much more valuable than the 'routine' structure, and possibly close in value to that of complete centralization.

Indeed, research done to-date on models of such processes suggests that price and demand signals are strikingly efficient in conveying the information needed for good allocation decisions, even out of equilibrium (Radner, 1972; Groves and Radner, 1972; T.A. Marschak, 1959, 1972; Arrow and Radner, 1979; Groves and Hart, 1982; Groves, 1983; Hogan, 1971).

INCENTIVES IN TEAMS. The model of a team assumes that the team members have identical interests and beliefs. Thus no special incentives are required to persuade the individual members to honestly implement the given information structure or to take the decisions prescribed by the optimal team decision function. A full-fledged theory of economic organization should, of course, take account of conflicting interests and beliefs, and the resulting problems of incentives.

This article is not the place to review the growing literature on this subject, but a few comments may be useful here. In general, it is not possible to solve the 'incentive problem' costlessly. (For exceptions to this generalization, see Groves, 1973; Green and Laffont, 1979.) Thus, in an economic organization, there will be two sources of efficiency loss: (1) decentralization of information, having the effect that individual actions will be based on information that is less complete than the information jointly available to the organization as a whole; (2) conflicts of interests and beliefs among the decision-makers, leading to distortions of information and action ('game-playing'). In fact these two sources are not so easily disentangled. For example, under conditions of uncertainty and limited information, it will typically be difficult for a supervisor (or organizer) to determine whether a particular decision-maker is providing correct information or following a prescribed decision rule, since to achieve this would require the supervisor to have all of the information that is available to the subordinate. In other words, informational decentralization leads to de facto decentralization of authority. (For references to the literature on incentives and decentralization in economic organizations see Arrow, 1974; Hurwicz, 1979; Radner, 1975, 1986; and Stiglitz, 1983.)

ROY RADNER

See also EFFICIENT ALLOCATION; ORGANIZATION THEORY; SIGNALLING.

BIBLIOGRAPHY

Arrow, K.J. 1972, The value of and demand for information. Ch. 6 of McGuire and Radner (1986).

Arrow, K.J. 1974. *The Limits of Organization*. New York: Norton.

Arrow, K.J. and Radner, R. 1979. Allocation of resources in large teams. *Econometrica* 47, 361–85.

Beckmann, M.J. 1958. Decision and team problems in airline reservations. *Econometrica* 26, 134–45.

Green, J., and Laffont, J.-J. 1979. *Incentives in Public Decision-Making*. Amsterdam: North-Holland.

Groves, T. 1973. Incentives in teams. *Econometrica* 41, 617–31.

Groves, T. 1983. The usefulness of demand forecasts for team resource allocation in a stochastic environment. *Review of Economic Studies* 50, 555–71.

Groves, T. and Radner, R. 1972. Allocation of resources in a team. *Journal of Economic Theory* 3, 415–44.

Groves, T. and Hart, S. 1982. Efficiency of resource allocation by uninformed demand. *Econometrica* 50, 1453–82.

Hogan, T.M. 1971. A comparison of information structures and convergence properties of several multisector economic planning procedures. Technical Report No. 10, Center for Research in Management Science, University of California, Berkeley.

Hurwicz, L. 1979. On the interaction between information and incentives in organizations. In *Communication and Control in Society*, ed. K. Krittendorf, New York: Gordon and Breach, 123–47.

Lange, O. and Taylor, F.M. 1938. *On the Economic Theory of Socialism*. Minneapolis: University of Minnesota Press.

Lerner, A. 1944. *The Economics of Control*. New York: Macmillan.

Marschak, J., and Radner, R. 1972. *Economic Theory of Teams*. New Haven: Yale University Press.

Marschak, T.A. 1972. Computation in organizations: the comparison of price mechanisms and other adjustment processes. Ch. 12 of McGuire and Radner (1986), 237–82.
Marschak, T.A. 1959. Centralization and decentralization in economic organizations. *Econometrica* 27, 399–430.
McGuire, C.B. 1961. Some team models of a sales organization. *Management Science* 7, 101–130.
McGuire, C.B. 1972. Comparisons of information structures. Ch. 5 of McGuire and Radner (1986), 101–30.
McGuire, C.B. and Radner, R. 1986. *Decision and Organization.* 2nd edn, Minneapolis: University of Minnesota Press; originally published Amsterdam: North-Holland, 1972.
Radner, R. 1972. Allocation of a scarce resource under uncertainty: an example of a team. Ch. 11 of McGuire and Radner (1986), 217–36.
Radner, R. 1962. Team decision problems. *Annals of Mathematical Statistics* 33, 857–881.
Radner, R. 1975. Economic Planning under uncertainty. Ch. 4 of *Economic Planning, East and West,* ed. M. Bornstein, Cambridge, Mass.: Ballinger, pp. 93–118.
Radner, R. 1987. Decentralization and incentives. In *Information, Incentives, and Economic Mechanisms: Essays in Hornor of Leonid Hurwicz*, ed. T. Groves, R. Radner and S. Reiter, Minneapolis: University of Minnesota Press.
Savage, L.J. 1954. *The Foundations of Statistics.* New York: Wiley.
Stiglitz, J.E. 1983. Risk, incentives, and the pure theory of moral hazard. *The Geneva Papers on Risk and Insurance* 8, 4–33.
Ward, B. 1967. *The Socialist Economy.* New York: Random House.

technical change. The transformation of economic society from an agricultural to an industrial foundation, beginning around 1750, set in motion a process of economic change with its own inner logic of tremendous power, a logic which harnessed continual technical and organization progress to the pursuit of profit. From this has followed the sustained increase of aggregate output per person employed – the chief proximate source of increased standards of living – the progressive mechanization and automation of production methods, and the continuous development of the economic structure. Knowledge-driven economic growth is not a smooth, balanced affair with each activity advancing in step. Rather, as Schumpeter insisted, it involves disharmony and fierce competition between the new and old, a diversity of sectoral growth rates and profit rates and continual reallocation of labour and capital between activities. It is occasionally useful to study such processes as if structural change were absent, but to do so courts the danger of missing the substance and therefore the mechanisms of technical and economic change.

All productive activity involves material and energy transformation, either of form, location or time; indeed, the history of technical change is a history of invention and innovation directed to providing new inanimate energy sources, to providing means to control the application of energy, and to providing new materials on which to work. In the process, man's role as supplier of energy has been greatly diminished while his role as coordinator and controller of the production process is increasingly under threat from automation.

The economic analysis of technical progress is not a straightforward matter. The familiar tools of equilibrium economics are best suited to discussing the long-run effects of new products and methods of production; they are not well suited to analysis of the disequilibrium processes by which new technologies are generated, improved and absorbed into the economic structure. It has been traditional to divide the analysis of technical change into three branches: invention, the creation of new products and processes; innovation, the transfer of invention to commercial application; and diffusion, the spread of innovation into the economic environment. Unfortunately, this has provided a somewhat fragmented approach to the study of technical change in which interdependence and feedback between the stages has been lost, together with important elements which emphasize the continuity of technological change. A more unified approach is possible if we turn to the idea of competition as a dynamic process, in which firms seek to differentiate themselves and gain competitive advantages by introducing new products and processes. The three questions which arise from this viewpoint are: (a) by what processes is technological variety generated? (b) by what processes do different varieties acquire economic weight? and (c) by what mechanisms does the process of acquiring economic weight shape the development of technological variety?

To the first question belongs the study of firm strategy in changing its knowledge base and articulating new and improved products and processes. The role of science in modern invention, the organization of R&D activity, and the links between a firm and other knowledge-generating institutions each play a role with respect to variety and its generation. But no individual variety of product or process is significant until it acquires economic weight, and the greater the weight the greater the impacts of the new technology upon its environment. New technologies acquire weight because they are superior either from the point of view of users or from the point of view of their producers or both. This is a complex area and we as yet know relatively little of the processes by which preferences of individuals and organizations are switched to favour new technological varieties. Clearly, however, the more profitable it is to use new products and processes and the more profitable it is to supply them, the more quickly will they acquire economic weight and displace existing products and processes. The dynamics of adjustment to new opportunities depend on how different are the new technologies relative to established forms, and how the economic environment evaluates those differences relative to the standards of profit and cost. The third question contains some of the most complex questions of all, relating to the inducement mechanisms which generate and shape technological variety. Clearly there are important non-economic factors at work. However, different environments do made it profitable to develop a technology in different directions, and the experience of exploiting a technology in a given environment always gives rise to important learning phenomena which indicate an agenda for subsequent development. Technologies do not emerge into the economic sphere fully fledged but typically in immature form and evolve very much according to the bottlenecks and incentives to development which arise in their application. Progress thus tends to be localized around an obvious path of advance and to be environmentally contingent. The same technological opportunity exploited in different environments would in all probability develop in different directions. By a similar token, a technology which is mature in one environment may be developing rapidly in another. Maturity is at root an economic concept applicable to situations where the expected benefits fall short of the expected costs of advancing technology. No treatment of inducement mechanisms can fail to recognize the peculiar economics of knowledge production and dissemination: the fact that knowledge is costly and risky to produce but cheap to imitate; the public good dimension, and the difficulties of establishing property rights, for which the patent system is only an imperfect solution.

Within the development of economic thought, the study of technical change has never played a major role. Indeed, from Adam Smith onwards, and with the exception of Marx, it was progressively written out of even classical economic analysis. Thus, despite Smith's emphasis on the division of labour as a form of induced technological and organizational change, little survived in subsequent writings, apart from the maintained separation of the agricultural and manufacturing sectors as different loci of progress. Not surprisingly, no classical writer foresaw that technical progress in agricultural methods would dispel the niggardliness of nature and banish the spectre of the stationary state. By the time Robbins came to write his methodological characterization of the neoclassical scheme in 1932, not only had technical progress been handed over to the psychologists and engineers, the very nature of the questions posed by economists had changed fundamentally. Gone was the emphasis on accumulation and progress and in its place stood the analysis of the allocation of given resources under given technical conditions and, moreover, subject to a definition of competition as a state of equilibrium quite incompatible with the increasing-returns implications of the division of labour. Only Schumpeter provided a clear way forward. He insisted that technical progress be viewed as a transformation arising from *within* the capitalist system, that it was an integral part of the competitive process and that a key role was played by the entrepreneur and entrepreneurial profits in the process by which technologies acquire economic weight. Orthodox, equilibrium theory it will be noted had found no room for the entrepreneur. It has been left to the post-1945 generation of economists to reassert the importance of technological change. So far they have done so in a piecemeal, empirical fashion with little attempt to reintegrate the phenomena back into a formal framework of accumulation and structural change. Only the writings of Pasinetti (e.g. 1981) and Nelson and Winter (e.g. 1982) can be said, from quite different perspectives, to make this attempt.

SOME CONSEQUENCES OF TECHNICAL CHANGE. One of the most compelling features of production in modern industrial societies is its roundabout nature. Industrial man does not satisfy his physical and other needs by working directly upon nature, rather resources are devoted to elaborate chains of production in which raw materials (mineral or agricultural) are worked into intermediate commodities for further processing into final commodities with the aid of complex tools and machinery. Specialization and the division of labour are the natural features of such roundabout, mechanized methods as Adam Smith made clear. When discussing technical progress it is particularly important to recognize that the majority of changes occur within the structure of input–output relations which reflect the division of labour. A framework which treats this structure as a black box into which primary inputs flow and final outputs emerge, will not be a useful foundation for the study of technical progress and its effects.

To illustrate some possibilities we employ the following analytic device. Consider a self-contained component of the economic system, a sub-system, which produces a single consumption good, cloth, via three separate activities. A lathe is produced with inputs of labour and itself, a loom is produced with inputs of labour and the lathe, and final output, cloth, is produced with labour and the loom. The lathe and the loom are produced means of production, they are inputs into another productive activity. Each commodity is produced by a single product activity, subject to constant returns to scale. Imagine this sub-system to be embedded in a competitive capitalist economy, and that it is analysed in long-run equilibrium conditions in which capital invested in each activity in the sub-system supports a common rate of profits, r, and grows at the common rate, g. Given the profits rate there will be a unique pattern of relative production prices of the three commodities and a unique level of the real wage, w (ratio of money wage to the price of cloth). Similarly, given the growth rate there is a unique pattern of employment within the sub-system and a unique level of consumption per worker, c (ratio of cloth output to total employment in the sub-system). Now it is well known that higher values of r are related to lower values of w, while higher values of g are related to lower values of c. The corresponding wage-profit and consumption growth frontiers are downward sloping, satisfy the dual property that $r=g$ entails $w=c$, and have a common, finite maximum value for r and g, corresponding to zero w and zero c, respectively.

Starting from a position in which only one production process is available in each activity, consider the long-run equilibrium effects of technical change. Two basic categories of change may be considered, in each case involving changes in one or more input–output coefficients. First, *improvements* which imply no qualitative change to any output or input and only require that less of at least one existing input is used within at least one of the processes. Increased organizational efficiency which 'rearranges' the process is the typical basis of improvement. Second, *inventions* which do imply qualitative change, a physically different output (e.g. a new lathe or loom) is produced by an entirely new process. Historically, inventions are often associated with a new material basis for the productive activity; for example, the substitution of synthetic for cotton fibres in cloth-making. Such material inventions can readily be incorporated by a suitable extension of the sub-system.

Whatever the precise changes in input–output coefficients, inventions and improvements can always be classified into three groups, by comparing the properties of the new process with those of the existing process. Dominant technical changes are those which are economically superior over the entire range of profit rates consistent with the existing technology. At the *ruling* real wage and relative price structure which is supported by the 'old' method, the new process supports a higher rate of profit than the old method, and this is the basis for its superiority. Redundant technical changes are those which are economically inferior over the prevailing range of profit rates. Finally, conditional changes are those whose superiority or otherwise does depend on the prevailing relative price structure. For the invention or improvement to become an innovation it must be economically superior when evaluated at the prevailing price structure. Only dominant changes and the superior set of conditional changes satisfy this condition and can have an economic effect; that is, become innovations.

The equilibrium effects of innovations depend on the nature of the change in technology *and* the position of the corresponding process in the input–output structure. In particular, changes in machine processes have quite different consequences from changes within the cloth activity. The more important consequences may be summarized as follows.

An improvement or invention in a machine process will alter the entire relative price structure of the sub-system. At the ruling rate of profits, the price of the commodity whose method is improved is reduced relative to the price of all other produced commodities, while the price of all commodities which use the output of the improved process are reduced relative to the money wage. The further down the chain of input–output relations lies the improvement, the greater the breadth of the consequences of the technical change. Consequently, the simplest case involves an improvement to the cloth activity: cloth falls in price but the relative price of lathes and looms are unaffected. The corollary of these effects is that any technical change increases the real wage consistent with the ruling rate of profits. Corresponding to the changes in price relations are changes in the structure of employment within the sub-system. A technical improvement in a machine activity reduces the proportion of total sub-system employment absorbed by that activity, but how it redistributes employment among the other activities depends on the particular nature and location of the change in question. Any improvement in cloth, by contrast, has no effects on the equilibrium employment structure. All technical changes will increase the level of consumption per head consistent with the ruling growth rate. Naturally, the magnitudes of these effects depends on the ruling values of the growth rate and rate of profits. It is often convenient to summarize the effects of technical change in terms of the associated differences in w–r and c–g frontiers before and after the technical change. In brief all dominant changes give rise to new frontiers which lie above the ones associated with the old methods. In the case of conditional changes the old and new frontiers intersect at least once. Nothing clear-cut can be established about the effects of technical change on the aggregate degree of mechanization, whether measured by the capital–labour or the capital–output ratio. Depending on the basis of valuing the capital stock, capital intensity may increase or decrease, and the different measures may even move in opposite directions. We note that the concept of neutral technical progress has traditionally been a focus of attention in relation to the effects of progress upon the distribution of income. As an example, the traditional case of Harrod-neutral technical progress (no effect on the capital–output ratio at the ruling r and g) is achieved, trivially, with an improvement in labour productivity confined to the non-basic activity but, more generally, requires that labour productivity increase in equal proportionate amounts in each and every process. Such Harrod neutral changes leave the structure of employment and relative commodity prices unchanged. There is little doubt that neutral progress of any kind is not to be expected in practice, nor is it a particularly interesting analytic category. Indeed, at given r and g values, Hicks's neutral technical progress (no effect on the capital–labour ratio) is logically impossible in a sub-system of the kind discussed here (Steedman, 1985).

More interesting in terms of technological interdependence are the induced technical changes known as trigger effects (Simon, 1951; Fujimoto, 1983). Where technical progress occurs in a machine activity it may so alter the relative profitability of other activities in which that good is an input, that induced changes of process can be triggered within those other activities. In this way the effects of technical change in any machine activity may spread far beyond the activity in question.

This catalogue of equilibrium effects is readily generalized. The economy in aggregate can be pictured in terms of a number of sub-systems, the final outputs of which compete for their share of consumption and investment expenditure, while machine activities may be part of more than one sub-system. Technical changes associated with new final commodities, and their sub-systems can then be treated in terms of the methods outlined above. The consequences follow as before with the added complication of relative price changes in relation to patterns of final expenditure. Expanding the argument further to include many primary inputs, heterogeneous labour, say, or land, allows one to investigate the effects of progress on the distribution of primary income (the non-profit component of value added), but there are no readily generalizable results. The primary input saving bias of progress depends on both the nature of the changes in technique and their location within the economic structure.

In summary, even under the hypotheses of long-run equilibrium conditions the consequences of technical progress are complex, and are associated with changes in relative prices, real incomes and physical patterns of employment of all inputs. Unless attention is confined to progress in consumption goods, the full ramifications of technical progress can only be understood within an input–output framework. *A fortiori* one can only understand the inducements to change technology within such a framework of technological interdependence.

THE RESIDUAL DEBATE. A central focus for the literature on technical progress has been provided since the early 1950s by a debate on the measurement of total factor productivity and the implications which follow for our understanding of the growth process. Within the neoclassical tradition, the sources of economic expansion were considered to be population growth and thrift, with growth in labour productivity dependent upon the substitution of capital for labour. Despite the protests of Schumpeter that these mechanisms were of negligible significance in explaining long-term growth of capitalist economics, it was not until a series of studies demonstrated the apparent independence of output growth from accumulation that debate could be engaged. The ingenious methods of Abramovitz (1956), Solow (1957) and Kendrick (1973) showed beyond reasonable doubt that the modern growth of the US economy was in proportionate terms at least three-quarters due to increased efficiency in the use of productive inputs and not to the growth in the quantity of resource inputs *per se*. The implication was quite devastating: the explanation of economic growth appeared to lie outside the traditional concerns of economists, to constitute a residual hypothesis.

From these early studies followed a lengthy sequence of extensions and amendments creating a rich tapestry of data on the growth of the major industrialized nations, and their constituent industries. For our purposes it is the framework employed to identify the contributing sources of economic growth which is of primary interest. For the actual measurements are brittle constructs easily swayed by errors of measurement or aggregation, and particularly marked by a failure to allow for quality change in the consumption basket, the disamenities of modern growth and the valuation to be placed on enhanced leisure time. Despite the efforts to refine measures of the productive input, taking detailed account of the effects of education on labour quality (Denison, 1962) and on the accurate measurement of capital goods and their services (Jorgenson and Griliches, 1967), agreement on the size of the so-called residual element in growth remains as elusive as ever. Nonetheless, a residual clearly persists at both aggregate and industry levels of analysis.

Consider then the accepted neoclassical framework of analysis applied to a whole economy. The central organizing concept behind the early studies was the aggregate production function and the division of observed growth in output per worker into two independent and additive elements: capital–labour substitution, reflected in movements around the production function; and increased efficiency in resource use, as reflected by shifts in this function. To maintain additivity, the analysis had to be confined to marginal changes in output and input (short periods of time?) and could not be applied cumulatively to longer periods without introducing an interaction term between capital substitution and increased efficiency. Within this framework all inputs, the factor services, stand on an equal footing, and constant returns alloyed with universal perfect competition allows marginal productivity pricing to identify the contribution which each input makes to the growth of output per worker. To identify the growth of total factor productivity in a short time interval one need only subtract from the growth of output, the growth in total factor input, itself a weighted sum of the growth rates of the individual inputs. The sensitivity of such a procedure to errors of measurement will be obvious.

Some difficulties, immediately apparent from the controversy over capital and distribution, now enter the picture. From the point of view of the long-run supply of productive services, all inputs do not stand on an equal footing. In particular, the flow of capital services depends on the stocks of usable capital instruments and thus on the ability of the economic system to maintain and augment such stocks in quality and quantity. But capital instruments are produced and reproduced by productive activities which themselves are subject to increases in efficiency over time. Thus, to treat independently increases in efficiency and increases in the stock of capital goods is quite false, unless one maintains that technical progress only occurs in consumption activities. The consequences of this for the measurement of total factor productivity are severe (Rymes, 1971). To illustrate, consider an economy growing over time with a constant saving ratio, with the rate of increase in labour productivity the same in all activities, and the capital–output ratio constant. In such an economy the rate of increase in efficiency is exactly measured by the rate of increase in productivity per worker, and not by the measured increase of total factor productivity which is of a smaller magnitude. Increased efficiency makes it easier to reproduce capital goods, such that all the observed rate of increase in the capital–labour ratio (equal to the growth of output per worker) is attributable to the enhanced efficiency in the processes producing capital goods. There is no independent capital deepening to contribute to the growth of labour productivity. It is not of course surprising that when we identify labour as the only primary input then the natural measure of increased efficiency is the rate of increase of labour productivity. Capital goods are after all instruments made by labour too. All this, of course, leaves untouched a second aspect of the capital controversy; namely, the severe conditions which have to be imposed to generate an aggregate production function along which output per worker is positively associated with the quantity of capital per worker, and for which input prices may be claimed to measure the corresponding marginal products of factor services. It is perhaps for this reason that studies of residual productivity have become more prominent at the industry level with as detailed a specification as possible of the relevant physical flows of factor services. But disaggregation does not avoid the fact that the capital inputs of one activity are derived from the outputs of other activities. The growth of labour productivity in any one activity depends not only upon its own increase in efficiency but upon increased efficiency in the activities supplying it with capital goods, materials and energy. Thus we are back in the world of input–output interdependence in which the results of enhanced efficiency are imported and exported between activities in the way outlined in the previous section.

There can be no doubt as to the value of the residual productivity debate; it awakened interest in the origins and effects of technical progress and stimulated several new lines of research. However, it never did attempt to answer the question, of what is the residual composed? This remains the dominant question.

S. Metcalfe

See also INNOVATION; STRUCTURAL CHANGE.

BIBLIOGRAPHY

Abramovitz, M. 1956. Resource and output trends in the United States since 1870. *American Economic Review, Papers and Proceedings* 46, May, 5–23.

Denison, E.F. 1962. *The Sources of Economic Growth in the United States*. New York: Committee for Economic Development.

Fujimoto, T. 1983. Inventions and technical change: a curiosum. *Manchester School of Economics and Social Studies* 51(1), March, 16–20.

Harrod, R. 1948. *Towards a Dynamic Economics*. London: Macmillan.

Jorgenson, D. and Griliches, Z. 1967. The explanation of productivity change. *Review of Economic Studies* 34, July, 249–83.

Kendrick, J. 1973. *Postwar Productivity Trends in the United States, 1948–1969*. New York: National Bureau of Economic Research.

Nelson, R. and Winter, S. 1982. *An Evolutionary Theory of Economic Change*. Cambridge, Mass. and London: Belknap Press.

Pasinetti, L.L. 1981. *Structural Change and Economic Growth*. Cambridge: Cambridge University Press.

Rymes, T. 1971. *On Concepts of Capital and Technical Change*. Cambridge: Cambridge University Press.

Schumpeter, J. 1911. *The Theory of Economic Development*. Oxford: Oxford University Press, 1934.

Simon, H. 1951. Effects of technical change in a linear model. In *Activity Analysis of Production and Allocation*, ed. T.C. Koopmans, New York: John Wiley & Sons; London: Chapman & Hall.

Solow, R. 1957. Technical change and the aggregate production function. *Review of Economics and Statistics* 39, August, 312–20.

Steedman, I. 1985. On the 'impossibility' of Hicks' neutral technical progress. *Economic Journal* 95, September, 746–58.

technique, choice of. *See* CHOICE OF TECHNIQUE.

technological unemployment. *See* MACHINERY QUESTION; STRUCTURAL UNEMPLOYMENT.

temporary equilibrium.

1. THE CONCEPTUAL FRAMEWORK. The fact that trade and markets take place sequentially over time in actual economies is a trivial observation. It has nevertheless far-reaching implications. At any moment, economic units have to make decisions that call for immediate action, in the face of a future that is as yet unknown. Expectations about the unknown future play therefore an essential role in the determination of current economic variables. On the other hand, the expectations that traders hold at any time are determined by the information that they have at that date on the economy, in particular on its current and past states. Observed economic processes are thus the result of a strong and complex interaction between expectations of the traders involved and the actual realizations of economic variables.

Economists have long recognized that such an interaction should be at the heart of any satisfactory theory of economic dynamics. The temporary equilibrium approach was indeed designed quite a while ago by the Swedish school (Lindahl, 1939) and J.R. Hicks (1939, 1965), with the intent to establish a general conceptual framework that would enable economists to cope with the study of dynamical economic systems, and in particular to incorporate in their models the subtle interplay between expectations and actual realizations of economic variables that seems factually so important. Economic theorists have employed this framework in a systematic way over the last fifteen years or so, using in particular the powerful techniques of modern equilibrium and/or game theory; this effort has yielded important improvements of our understanding of monetary theory or of the choice-theoretic structure of traditional Keynesian models of unemployment, and more generally of the microeconomic foundations of macroeconomics.

Before reviewing briefly a few of these important advances, it may be worthwhile to make clear what are the basic characteristics of the temporary equilibrium approach, and to compare it with others.

To fix ideas, let us assume that time is divided into an infinite, discrete sequence of dates. We may envision first a specific institutional set-up, that was called a *futures economy* by Hicks (1946), and later generalized by Arrow and Debreu. Let us assume that markets for exchanging commodities are opened at a single date, say date 0; assume further that at that date, markets exist for contracts to deliver commodities at each and every future date $t \geqslant 0$. The specification of a 'commodity' will then involve not only the physical characteristics of the good or service to be delivered, but also the location and the circumstances ('state of nature') of the delivery. One gets then what has been called a 'complete' set of futures markets at the initial date $t=0$ (Debreu, 1959, ch. 7).

It is clear that this framework is essentially timeless. Once an equilibrium is reached at date 0 (this equilibrium may be Walrasian or the result of any other game theoretic equilibrium notion), production and trade do take place sequentially in calendar time. But the coordination of the decisions of all traders is achieved at a single date through futures markets. There is no sequence of *markets* over time, and no role for expectations, money, financial assets, or stock markets.

Let us consider next another, more dynamic, type of organization, in which markets do open in every period. In this framework, traders would exchange at every date commodities immediately available on spot markets, promises to deliver specific commodities at later dates on futures markets, as well as money, financial assets and/or stocks (of course markets must be 'incomplete' in the sense of Arrow–Debreu at every date, otherwise reopening markets would serve no purpose). To convey the following discussion most simply, let us assume away all sources of uncertainty and consider the case where the state of the economy at any date can be described by a single real number. To simplify matters further, let us assume that the state of the economy at t, say x_t, is completely determined by the forecasts $x^e_{i,t+1}$ made by all traders at date t about the future state, through the relation

$$x_t = f(x^e_{1,t+1}, \ldots, x^e_{i,t+1}, \ldots, x^e_{m,t+1}) \tag{1}$$

The temporary equilibrium map f describes the result of the market equilibrating process at date t – be it Walrasian or not – for a given set of forecasts. Of course, in the study of any particular economy, the map f will be derived from the 'fundamental' characteristics of the economy: tastes, endowments, technologies, the rules of the game, the policies followed by the Government.

The foregoing formulation does seem to take into account the observed fact that markets unfold sequentially in calendar time. It is, however, incomplete since no specification of the way in which forecasts are made at each date has been offered at this stage.

We must first discuss a concept that was introduced by Hicks himself, that of an *intertemporal equilibrium*, with self-fulfilling expectations, and that has been extensively used recently in a variety of contexts. Such an intertemporal equilibrium is defined formally, in the present framework, as an infinite sequence of states $\{x_t\}$ and of forecasts $\{x^e_{i,t+1}\}$ satisfying (1) and

$$x^e_{i,t+1} = x_{t+1} \tag{2}$$

for all dates. Although time appears explicitly in this formulation, it should be clear that this particular equilibrium concept is also intrinsically *timeless*. It is true, here again, that once an intertemporal equilibrium has been determined, production and exchange do take place sequentially in calendar time. But the inescapable truth is that all elements of the sequences of equilibrium states $\{x_t\}$ and of equilibrium forecasts $\{x^e_{i,t+1}\}$ are determined simultaneously by an outside observer. There is *no* sequential adjustment of the markets: past, present and future markets are equilibrated all at the same time. Furthermore, if one tries to give a dynamical interpretation of the foregoing equilibrium notion, in which markets do adjust sequentially, one finds that the dynamics go in the wrong direction. The formation of forecasts specified in (2) states indeed that the future equilibrium state x_{t+1} determines the current forecasts, which in turn determine the current equilibrium state x_t through (1).

The preceding discussion shows how we must proceed to describe a sequential adjustment of markets, in calendar time. We *must* add to the temporary equilibrium relationship (1) a specification of the way in which traders forecast the future at each date *as a function of their information on current and past states of the economy*. If we assume, for the simplicity of the exposition, that the only information available to traders at date t is represented by the sequence $(x_t, x_{t-1}, \ldots)$, that means that we have to add to (1), *m expectations functions* of the form

$$x^e_{i,t+1} = \psi_i(x_t, x_{t-1}, \ldots) \tag{3}$$

The equations (1) and (3) describe then in a consistent way a sequential adjustment of markets – a sequence of *temporary equilibria* – in which time goes forward, as it should. Given past history $(x_{t-1}, x_{t-2}, \ldots)$, (1) and (3) determine the current temporary equilibrium state and forecasts. Once such a temporary equilibrium is reached, production and exchange takes place at date t, and the economy can move forward to date $t+1$, where the equilibrating process is repeated.

A formulation of the sort (1) plus (3) is thus the general formulation, in fact the *only* sort of formulation that is allowed, if one wishes to describe the evolution of the economy as a *sequence* of markets that adjust one after each other.

We claim that the temporary equilibrium approach, as sketched above, is general. One should expect it accordingly to include self-fulfilling expectations as a special case. It is not difficult to verify that it is indeed so, provided that the expectations functions ψ_i satisfy a number of restrictions. Choose a particular intertemporal equilibrium. Then the associated sequence of states, say $\{\bar{x}_t\}$, is a solution of the difference equation

$$\bar{x}_t = F(\bar{x}_{t+1}) \tag{4}$$

in which $F(x) = f(x, \ldots, x)$ for all x. Consider now the economy at date t, and assume that past states have been $(\bar{x}_{t-1}, \bar{x}_{t-2}, \ldots)$. Assume that the traders know the characteristics of the economy, or at least the map F, and further that the map F is invertible (we are voluntarily vague about the domain of definitions of the functions under consideration, to simplify the present methodological discussion, but these technical details can be fixed up). The traders are then able to detect the recurrence satisfied by current and past states. If they infer that this recurrence will obtain in the future as well, their forecasting rule should satisfy, for all $i = 1, \ldots, m$

$$\psi_i(\bar{x}_t, \bar{x}_{t-}, \ldots) = F^{-1}(\bar{x}_t) \quad (5)$$

If this relation holds, $\bar{x}_t$ is indeed a temporary equilibrium state (i.e. it solves (1) and (3)) at date t, given past history $(\bar{x}_{t-1}, \bar{x}_{t-2}, \ldots)$. This will be true at all dates, and one will be able to generate any intertemporal equilibrium with self-fulfilling expectations as a sequence of temporary equilibria, provided that the traders' forecasting rules satisfy (5) at all dates, and for any sequence $(\bar{x}_t, \bar{x}_{t-1}, \ldots)$ that is part of an intertemporal equilibrium $\{\bar{x}_t\}$. The condition (5) is in fact necessary.

As we have just shown, the temporary equilibrium method includes self-fulfilling expectations as a special case. The approach is indeed much more general, since it permits to incorporate in the analysis the fact that traders usually learn the dynamics laws of their environment only gradually, and thus to study in principle how convergence toward self-fulfilling expectations may or may not obtain in the long run.

The preceding discussion was carried out in a simple one-dimensional world operating under certainty. It should be clear nevertheless that the qualitative conclusions we obtained hold as well in a more complex, multidimensional world operating under uncertainty. The general objective is, we recall, to design a conceptual framework that does justice to the fact that markets adjust sequentially in calendar time. The preceding discussion shows that, to this effect, one must specify beforehand two kinds of objects:

(1) The 'fundamental' characteristics of the economy (tastes, endowments, technologies, the institutional set up, the Government's policies, etc.). They should lead to the specification of a relation that describes, as in (1), how a temporary equilibrium is determined at any date, given past history and the current realization of exogenous variables, for a given 'state of expectations'.

(2) A description of the way in which traders form their expectations (these may be probability distributions or random variables), at any date, as a *function of the observations made in the current and past periods*. The process of expectations formation may be complex, it may involve sophisticated statistical inferences or estimations of unknown parameters, and/or it may be the result of a backward inductive procedure carried out by the traders. But the specification must generate in the end an *expectations function* for each trader, that links forecasts to current and past experience, as in (3).

The evolution of the economy is then described as a sequence of temporary equilibria, in which at each date, the current equilibrium states are determined by past history. In this framework, a number of issues arise naturally. First, one has to find the conditions under which the dynamic evolution of the economy is well defined. In other words, when does a temporary equilibrium exist? Second, does the corresponding dynamical system have long run equilibrium states, such as deterministic stationary states or cycles, and/or stationary stochastic processes, along which expectations are self-fulfilling? Under which conditions, in particular on the formation of expectations, do the sequences of temporary equilibria so generated converge to such a long run equilibrium? This is precisely the sort of questions that have attracted the attention of modern economic theorists working in temporary equilibrium theory over the last 15 years or so.

2. OVERVIEW. We turn now to a brief appraisal of this research effort, referring the interested reader to more extensive and more technical surveys that already exist in the literature, see for example Grandmont (1977, 1987).

Money and assets in competitive markets. Considering a sequence of markets opens immediately the possibility for traders to hold money and more generally, assets of various kinds for saving, borrowing, transactions purposes and/or insurance motives. The application of the modern techniques of temporary equilibrium theory to the study of monetary phenomena has led to a major reappraisal, in the seventies, of classical and neoclassical monetary theories in competitive environments. It has permitted in particular to solve an old problem that had puzzled economic theorists for some time (Hahn, 1965), namely why fiat money, which has no intrinsic value, should have a positive value in exchange in competitive markets. The answer provided by traditional neoclassical theory relied essentially upon unit-elastic price expectations and the presence of real balance or wealth effects (Patinkin, 1965). Modern temporary equilibrium methods have shown that sort of answer to be surely incomplete and presumably mistaken: intertemporal substitution effects have to play an important role, and this can be only achieved by abandoning the hypothesis of unit-elastic expectations and by introducing some degree of inelasticity of expectations with respect to current observations. The reappraisal of monetary theory by means of the temporary equilibrium method clarified greatly many confusing debates of the preceding literature: the relations between Walras's and Say's Law, the meaning and the validity of the Classical Dichotomy and the Quantity Theory of Money, the possibility of monetary authorities to manipulate the interest rates or the money supply, the existence of a 'liquidity trap' (Grandmont, 1983). The introduction of cash-in-advance constraints in temporary competitive equilibrium models of money (Grandmont and Younès, 1972, 1973) yielded important insights into the relations between its respective roles as a store of value and as a medium of exchange, and time preference, and permitted to make precise the microeconomic foundations of Milton Friedman's theory of optimum cash balances (1969). Such models of money using cash-in-advance constraints have been popular recently in macroeconomics, following the contribution of R.E. Lucas, Jr. (1980).

The introduction of assets of various kinds in competitive markets leads also to the possibility of speculation and arbitrage in capital markets. Different persons with different tastes or expectations will then be willing to trade such assets. An important question is to study the conditions ensuring the existence of a temporary equilibrium in that context. A neat answer to that problem was provided by J.R. Green (1973) and O.D. Hart (1974): there must be some agreement between the traders' expectations about future prices. That sort of result should remain at the centre of any theory of competitive financial markets.

Temporary equilibria with quantity rationing. As noted previously, a temporary equilibrium need not be Walrasian. In particular, one may consider cases where prices are set through monopolistic or oligopolistic competition at the beginning of each elementary period and remain temporarily fixed within that period. A temporary equilibrium corresponding to these prices is then achieved at each date by quantity rations that set upper or lower bounds on the traders' transactions.

It had been known for some time that traditional Keynesian macroeconomic models of unemployment involved, explicitly or implicitly, the assumption of temporarily fixed prices, as noted by Hicks himself (1965). The choice-theoretic structure of these models was rather unclear, however, which was a source of some confusion. The systematic study of temporary equilibrium models with quantity rationing undertaken in the seventies produced deep insights on this issue, and unveiled the hidden but central role played by quantity signals, as perceived by the traders in addition to the price system, to achieve an equilibrium in such models.

One major outcome of this research programme was the discovery that different types of unemployment could obtain, and even co-exist. 'Keynesian unemployment' corresponds to a situation where there is an excess supply on the labour and the goods markets. In such a situation, firms perceive constraints on their sales because demand is too low. Keynesian policies aiming at increasing aggregate demand do work in such a case. But unemployment may co-exist with an excess demand on the goods markets. In such a regime, called 'Classical unemployment' by Malinvaud (1977), the source of unemployment is rather the low profitability of productive activities. Keynesian policies do not work in that case; one has to resort to policies that restore profits, such as lowering real wages. In that respect, these results achieved a remarkable synthesis, within a unified and clear conceptual framework, between two paradigms that appeared fundamentally distinct beforehand.

The literature on this topic yielded numerous insights in particular of the connections between Keynesian models of unemployment and price-making in monopolistic or oligopolistic models of competition (see e.g. Hart (1982), on the role of inventories and productive investment in such models, on the nature of unemployment in open economies. On these and related topics, the reader will benefit greatly from consulting the books of Barro and Grossman (1976), Benassy (1982, 1986), Malinvaud (1977, 1980), Negishi (1979), Picard (1985).

Stability and learning. As we mentioned earlier, the temporary equilibrium approach includes self-fulfilling expectations as a particular case, and is in fact more general, since it can incorporate learning in the formation of the traders' expectations. An important issue is then to know when the sequences of temporary equilibria that are associated to given learning processes or expectations functions converge eventually to a long run equilibrium along which forecasting mistakes vanish. This is a difficult question, on which much work has to be done. Progress has been made up to now by looking at the stability of stationary equilibria for given learning procedures, in particular examples. One of the lessons one can draw from these studies is that stability in the temporary equilibrium dynamics with learning may be *reversed* by comparison to the apparent stability properties one gets from the dynamics with self-fulfilling expectations. For more information, see Fuchs and Laroque (1976) and Grandmont (1987, ch. 1).

J.-M. GRANDMONT

See also FIXPRICE MODELS; GENERAL EQUILIBRIUM; RATIONED EQUILIBRIA.

BIBLIOGRAPHY

Barro, R.J. and Grossman, H.I. 1976. *Money, Employment and Inflation*, Cambridge: Cambridge University Press.

Benassy, J.P. 1982. *The Economics of Market Disequilibrium*. New York: Academic Press.

Benassy, J.P. 1986. *Macroeconomics: An Introduction to the Non-Walrasian Approach*. New York: Academic Press.

Debreu, G. 1959. *Theory of Value: an axiomatic analysis of economic equilibrium*. Cowles Foundation monograph no. 17, New York: Wiley.

Friedman, M. 1969. *The Optimum Quantity of Money and Other Essays*. Chicago: Aldine.

Fuchs, G. and Laroque, G. 1976. Dynamics of temporary equilibria and expectations. *Econometrica* 44, 1157–78.

Grandmont, J.M. 1977. Temporary general equilibrium theory. *Econometrica* 45, 535–72.

Grandmont, J.M. 1983. *Money and Value: a reconsideration of classical and neoclassical monetary theories*. The Econometric Society, Monograph No. 5, Cambridge: Cambridge University Press.

Grandmont, J.M. (ed.) 1987. *Temporary Equilibrium: selected readings*. New York: Academic Press.

Grandmont, J.M. and Younès, Y. 1972. On the role of money and the existence of a monetary equilibrium. *Review of Economic Studies* 39, 355–72.

Grandmont, J.M. and Younès, Y. 1973. On the efficiency of a monetary equilibrium. *Review of Economic Studies* 40, 149–65.

Green, J.R. 1973. Temporary general equilibrium in a sequential trading model with spot and future transactions. *Econometrica* 41, 1103–23.

Hahn, F.H. 1965. On some problems of proving the existence of an equilibrium in a monetary economy. In *The Theory of Interest Rates*, ed. F.H. Hahn and F.P.R. Brechling, London: Macmillan.

Hart, O.D. 1974. On the existence of equilibrium in a securities model. *Journal of Economic Theory* 9, 293–311.

Hart, O.D. 1982. A model of imperfect competition with Keynesian features. *Quarterly Journal of Economics* 97, 109–38.

Hicks, J.R. 1939. *Value and Capital*. Oxford: Clarendon Press; 2nd edn, 1946.

Hicks, J.R. 1965. *Capital and Growth*. Oxford: Clarendon Press.

Lindahl, E. 1939. *Theory of Money and Capital*. London: Allen and Unwin.

Lucas, R.E., Jr. 1980. Equilibrium in a pure currency economy. *Economic Inquiry* 18, 203–220. Also in *Models of Monetary Economies*, ed. J.H. Kareken and N. Wallace, Minneapolis: The Federal Reserve Bank of Minneapolis, 1980.

Malinvaud, E. 1977. *The Theory of Unemployment Reconsidered*. Oxford: Basil Blackwell.

Negishi, T. 1979. *Microeconomic Foundations of Keynesian Macroeconomics*. Amsterdam: North-Holland.

Patinkin, D. 1965. *Money, Interest and Prices*. 2nd edn, New York: Harper & Row.

Picard, P. 1985. *Théorie du déséquilibre et politique économique*. Paris: Economica.

terms of trade. The two most basic questions about international trade are: What goods will each country export? and What will be the ratios at which the exports of one country exchange for those of its trading partners?

The first problem is that of 'comparative advantage'; the second that of the 'terms of trade', which is the subject of the present contribution. David Ricardo, in chapter 7 of the *Principles*, gave a definitive answer to the first question and went a long way towards the solution of the second, though it was J.S. Mill and Alfred Marshall who eventually gave the complete answer.

In the following discussion it will be convenient to assume, for simplicity, that there is only a single good exported and imported, and sometimes even that there is only a single factor of production, such as labour of a given quality. In practice, of course, we would have to use index numbers for unit values and physical volumes of exports and imports, giving rise to all the familiar problems.

CONCEPTS AND DEFINITIONS. There are a number of alternative concepts and associated statistical measures of the terms of trade. The most prominent are listed below:

(i) The *commodity* or *net barter* terms of trade. This is by far the most common meaning of the term, and is usually what is meant when the expression is used without any qualifying prefix. In principle it is the relative price of the 'exportable' in terms of the 'importable', that is the number of units of the latter obtainable for each unit of the former. It has the dimensions of 'nine waistcoat buttons for a copper disc' in the words of Lewis Carroll's 'Song of the Aged, Aged Man' in *Through the Looking Glass*, words that D.H. Robertson (1952, ch. 13) used as the motto for a delightful essay on the terms of trade. In statistical practice the commodity terms of trade are calculated as changes in the ratio of an export price index to an import price index, relative to a base year.

(ii) The *gross barter* terms of trade is a concept introduced by Taussig. It is the ratio of the *volume* of imports to the *volume* of exports. It coincides with the commodity terms of trade when trade is balanced, that is, there are no international loans or unrequited transfers. A deficit in the trade balance would cause the gross barter terms to be more favourable than the commodity or net barter terms and vice versa. This should not, of course, be interpreted as a trade deficit being necessarily preferable to balanced trade, since the additional imports now may have to be paid for by future trade surpluses.

(iii) The *income* terms of trade, sometimes also referred to as 'the purchasing power of exports'. It corresponds to the commodity terms of trade multiplied by the volume of exports. This is equal to the volume of imports under balanced trade, and exceeds or falls short of it if there is a surplus or deficit respectively in the balance of trade. In other words, it is the level of imports in real terms that can be sustained by current export earnings.

(iv) The *single factoral* terms of trade. This refers to the marginal or average productivity of a factor in the export sector, evaluated in terms of the imported good at the commodity terms of trade. The concept is meaningful for any single factor or production taken separately, though it is sometimes defined in a non-operational fashion in the literature as referring to 'units of productive power'.

(v) The *double factoral* terms of trade. This is an attempt to go behind the international exchange of commodities to the productive factors that are 'embodied' in them. Thus, if units are chosen such that a unit of labour in England produces a unit of cloth and a unit of labour in Portugal produces a unit of wine, commodity terms of trade of say five wine to one cloth would mean that a unit of English labour exchanges implicitly for five units of Portuguese labour in international trade.

The first three concepts of the terms of trade are all measurable in practice, subject to the usual index number problems. The commodity terms of trade are routinely calculated for most countries in the world by international agencies such as the UN, the World Bank and the IMF. The gross barter and income terms of trade have also been calculated for several countries.

The single factoral terms of trade, for any particular factor, can also be computed. Indeed it corresponds exactly to the concept of 'shadow prices' for primary inputs that has recently been developed in the literature on cost–benefit analysis in distorted open economies. Thus it could indicate what the value of a worker or an acre of land, engaged say in the coffee export sector, was worth in terms of imported food at the commodity terms of trade. This could serve as a valuable guide to resource allocation by comparing it with what these resources could produce in the domestic food sector.

The double factoral terms of trade, however, is either misleading if it is computed for any particular single factor in a world of more than one scarce input, or non-operational if defined amorphously as applying to units of 'productive power'. The concept is regarded by more than one economist as fundamental, and no less an authority than D.H. Robertson, in the essay referred to, called it the 'true' terms of trade. Equally eminent authorities, such as Haberler (1955) and Viner (1937), have however been more sceptical.

The concept has recently come to the fore again, after many decades of neglect, in connection with the theories of A. Emmanuel (1972) on 'unequal exchange' in trade between high-wage and low-wage countries, a form of 'exploitation' of the latter by the former. It is possible to interpret Emmanuel as saying that it is only when the double factoral terms of trade are equal to unity that there is no unequal exchange. As Emmanuel himself acknowledges, however, his argument requires equal capital intensity in the export sectors of the trading partners. We may all agree with Robert Burns that 'a man's a man for a' that' in terms of dignity and spiritual worth. It is another thing to say that skill or physical capital, both accumulated at some cost, should count for nothing, and that the only 'fair' exchange is one that takes place according to the simple labour theory of value.

Furthermore, it is clear that the commodity terms of trade can improve while the factoral terms worsen and vice versa. Thus suppose initially that one day's labour in 'North' and 'South' produces a unit of steel and coffee respectively and that the commodity terms of trade was one steel for one coffee. Suppose now that one worker in the North produces three steel, while his counterpart in the South still produces only one coffee. Let the commodity terms of trade now be two steel for one coffee. The commodity terms have doubled in favour of the South, while its factoral terms have deteriorated to two-thirds instead of unity. Which situation would the South prefer?

FUNDAMENTAL DETERMINANTS. Ricardo did not determine the terms of trade explicitly in his analysis in chapter 7 of the *Principles*. He was only able to show that the equilibrium value would be between the comparative cost ratios of the two countries, specified by the linear technologies. It was John Stuart Mill who solved the problem by his numerical example of 'reciprocal supply and demand', later refined by Marshall through the geometric device of the 'offer curves' showing the excess supplies and demands of the two goods in each country as functions of the terms of trade, the equilibrium value of which would be determined by setting world excess supply equal to zero. Marshall demonstrated the possibility of multiple equilibria and also established a criterion for stability of equilibrium that is in use to this day, in the form of the so-called Marshall–Lerner condition that the sum of the import demand elasticities has to be greater than unity.

In modern terms it is the preferences of the consumers that have to be introduced to close the model. Once these are introduced the equilibrium value(s) of the terms of trade are determined as a function of these preferences, the labour endowments and the technical coefficients of production. The subsequent development of the literature has generalized Ricardo's analysis to any number of goods, factors and countries and to variable instead of fixed technical coefficients. The determination of the terms of trade is thus technically nothing other than that of finding the equilibrium vector(s) of relative prices for general equilibrium models in which there is a world market for tradeable goods and internationally mobile factors, and national markets for non-traded, goods and internationally immobile factors.

In addition to constituting a central problem for the theory of international trade in its 'positive' aspect, the terms of trade plays if anything an even more critical role in the 'normative' dimension of evaluating the 'gains from trade'. It is crucial to keep these two facets of the terms of trade conceptually distinct, though of course they are both involved in almost every theoretical or policy problem. Another essential distinction is between the terms of trade as an *exogenously* determined parameter, as in the 'small' open economy models, and as an *endogenously* determined variable, the equilibrium value of which is altered by some change in circumstances or parameters, such as factor endowments, technology or tastes. Much confusion has been caused in the literature by failure to bear these basic distinctions in mind at all times.

In the realm of positive theory, the terms of trade generally appear in comparative statics exercises as the key dependent variable, upon which the effect of some exogenous shock is sought. As an example, consider the effect of a switch in the composition of home demand in favour of the imported good. At constant terms of trade this would create an excess demand for the imported good. Assuming Walrasian stability, this must lead to a deterioration of the home country's terms of trade for the world market to return to equilibrium.

The famous 'transfer problem' is another example of this sort of comparative statics exercise. The transfer of purchasing power, at constant terms of trade, would lead to an excess supply in the world market of the transferor's exportable, if the home propensity to consume this good is greater than that of the recipient country (the so-called 'classical presumption'). Thus the terms of trade of the tranferor would deteriorate, given Walrasian stability, imposing a 'secondary burden' on the transferor.

Finally, we may consider the effects of economic growth, in the form of exogenous changes in factor endowment or technical innovations in either sector, a literature that was stimulated by Hicks's (1953) inaugural lecture on the 'dollar shortage'. Here again the analysis consists in finding the effect of the change on excess supply or demand at constant terms of trade, and thus obtaining the direction of movement in the terms of trade necessary to clear the market, assuming stability in the Walrasian sense.

WELFARE EFFECTS. All of these exercises in positive theory of course have welfare consequences for both trading partners. In the case of the two-country transfer problem the transferor is worse off, even if the terms of trade were to move in its favour, while the recipient is better off, even if the terms of trade were to turn against it. In the case of a shift in the composition of home demand towards imports the welfare of the trading partner will rise under normal conditions (made more precise in the next paragraph) as a result of this improvement in its terms of trade. If growth in one country creates an excess demand for imports at constant terms of trade, its passive partner will also benefit from the resulting increase in the relative price of its export.

In the last two cases a country experiences an *exogenous* improvement in its terms of trade, with no alteration in its own preferences, technology or factor endowment. Must its welfare necessarily increase as a result? The answer in general is yes, unless there are domestic distortions such as monopoly or monosony in product or factor markets, exogenous wage differentials or real factor–price rigidities. A simple example of how it is possible for a country to experience a *loss* in welfare as a result of an *improvement* in its commodity terms of trade can be constructed as follows. Suppose that domestic production is completely specialized on the export good and that the real wage is fixed in terms of the imported good. At constant employment and therefore constant marginal physical productivity of labour in terms of the exported good the real wage would be lower in terms of the imported good because of the improvement in the terms of trade. This will induce a decline in employment and output until the marginal physical product of labour rises in the same proportion as the relative price of the imported good has fallen so that the original level of the real wage is restored. The terms of trade improvement, given employment and output, increases welfare, but the contraction in these variables induced by the change in the terms of trade reduces welfare. This negative effect can clearly be sufficient to outweigh the positive effect of the terms of trade gain considered in isolation, since the counteraction can be very sharp if the marginal productivity of labour schedule is assumed to be sufficiently elastic.

Haberler (1955, p. 30), in a characteristically penetrating and judicious discussion of the subject, has stated that 'other things being equal an improvement in the commodity terms of trade does imply an increase in real national income'. As our analysis of the example in the previous paragraphs shows, however, even such a cautious formulation needs to be interpreted with care. It would obviously be a mistake to compound the welfare effects of an exogenous shift in the terms of trade with the direct welfare effects of some *independent* shock. In our example, however, the terms of trade change was the sole shift in the data, the contraction of employment and output being induced by this very change in the terms of trade itself.

When the change in the terms of trade is a *consequence* of some exogenous shock, such as a change in tastes, technology or factor endowment, it is clearly erroneous to infer the total change in welfare solely from the direction of change in the terms of trade. Technological progress in the export sector that deteriorates the terms of trade can obviously leave a country better off in spite of the deterioration, even though it would of course have been still better off if the terms of trade had remained unchanged. It is this sort of consideration that has led to the introduction of concepts such as the factoral terms of trade, since these measures could show an improvement even when the commodity terms of trade deteriorate. In general, however, it is a mistake to expect any single concept of the terms of trade to be an unambiguous indicator of changes in the gains from trade when there are shifts in the fundamental determinants of tastes, technology and factor endowments.

The welfare effects of such changes can be broken into two parts: first, the effect at unchanged terms of trade, and second, the effect of the associated change in the terms of trade. The *net* effect on welfare may thus be positive or negative and need not correspond with the direction of the change in the terms of trade. Bhagwati (1958) established the possibility that the net effect on welfare of the country experiencing economic growth can be *negative*, a phenomenon that he termed 'immiserizing growth'.

Finally, we may consider the terms of trade as an objective of policy, when the country has some degree of monopoly power in international markets. The consideration of a rational policy maker, ignoring the possibility of retaliation would be to restrict trade to such an extent as to equate at the margin the benefit resulting from the improvement in the terms of trade with the loss of welfare resulting from the decline in the volume of trade. This is the famous 'optimum tariff' argument, the level of which varies inversely with the elasticity of foreign demand for imports.

SECULAR TENDENCIES. In addition to comparative statics analyses of the type considered up to now the literature also contains some more speculative hypotheses about secular tendencies in the terms of trade. In the Ricardian tradition capital accumulation and technical progress lead to a steady expansion in the supply of manufactures, while the supply of primary products is always constrained by the limited availability of 'land' and other natural resources. Ricardo's theorem for a closed economy – that growth would raise the relative price of food and therefore the rent of land until a 'stationary state' is approached – has been extended to the world economy in the form of a presumption that there would be a tendency for the terms of trade to move against manufactures and in favour of primary products. Keynes, Beveridge, Robertson and E.A.G. Robinson all took part in a long-running debate on this issue. The story that W.S. Jevons kept enormous stocks of coal in his basement is a bizarre manifestation of this phobia. W.W. Rostow (1962, chs 8 and 9) gives a very interesting review and analysis of this literature, which foreshadows the views associated more recently with the Club of Rome.

Discussions of the secular tendencies of the terms of trade since World War II, however, have been dominated by the view of Raul Prebisch (1950) and Hans Singer (1950) that the historical record shows a long-run tendency for the commodity terms of trade of the less developed countries to deteriorate. The evidence was a series showing an apparent long-run improvement in Britain's terms of trade between 1870 and 1940. Theoretical reasons given for the alleged tendency have been lower income-elasticity of demand for primary products than for manufactures, technical progress that economizes on the use of imported raw materials and monopolistic market structures in the industrial countries combined with competitive conditions in the supply of primary products. The general consensus on the statistical debate that has arisen on this issue is that there has *not* been any discernible secular trend for the commodity terms of trade of the developing countries to deteriorate (see Spraos, 1980, for a recent summary and assessment of the evidence; Lewis, 1969, presents a very interesting alternative theoretical and empirical analysis of this problem).

The Prebisch–Singer hypothesis and the more general concerns of the ongoing North–South dialogue have also spawned a number of so-called 'North–South' models, in which the interaction of an advanced industrial region with a less developed and structurally dissimilar, labour-abundant, primary producing region is studied in a dynamic context. The terms of trade play a key role in these models, since the growth rate of the South is linked to this variable through dependence on capital goods imported from the North. This and other analytical issues related to secular trends in the terms of trade are further discussed in Findlay (1981, 1984).

RONALD FINDLAY

See also COMPARATIVE ADVANTAGE; HECKSCHER–OHLIN TRADE THEORY.

BIBLIOGRAPHY

Bhagwati, J. 1958. Immiserizing growth: a geometrical note. *Review of Economic Studies* 25, June, 201–5.

Emmanuel, A. 1972. *Unequal Exchange*. New York: Monthly Review Press.

Findlay, R. 1981. The fundamental determinants of the terms of trade. In *The World Economic Order: Past and Prospects*, ed. S. Grassman and E. Lundberg, London: Macmillan.

Findlay, R. 1984. Growth and development in trade models. In *Handbook of International Economics*, ed. R.W. Jones and P.B. Kenen, Amsterdam: North-Holland, Vol. 1, ch. 4.

Haberler, G. 1955. *A Survey of International Trade Theory*. Princeton: International Finance Section.

Hicks, J.R. 1953. An inaugural lecture. *Oxford Economic Papers*, NS 5, June, 117–35.

Lewis, W.A. 1969. *Aspects of Tropical Trade 1883–1965*. Stockholm: Almqvist and Wiksell.

Prebisch, R. 1950. *The Economic Development of Latin America and its Principal Problems*. New York: United Nations.

Robertson, D.H. 1952. The terms of trade. Chapter 13 of *Utility and All That*, New York: Macmillan.

Rostow, W.W. 1962. *The Process of Economic Growth*. New York: Norton, chs 8 and 9.

Singer, H.W. 1950. The distribution of gains between investing and borrowing countries. *American Economic Review, Papers and Proceedings* 5, Supplement, May, 473–85.

Spraos, J. 1980. The statistical debate on the net barter terms of trade between primary commodities and manufactures. *Economic Journal* 90(357), March, 107–28.

Viner, J. 1937. *Studies in the Theory of International Trade*. New York: Harper Bros., ch. 9.

terms of trade and economic development. One of the most widely discussed theories concerning the terms of trade of developing countries is the Prebisch–Singer hypothesis, independently published in 1950 (Prebisch, 1950; Singer, 1950). This hypothesis proclaimed a structural tendency for the terms of trade of developing countries to deteriorate in their dealings with industrial countries. In the original form this related mainly to the terms of trade between primary commodities and manufactured goods from the industrial countries. The historical statistical basis was an analysis of British terms of trade during the period 1873–1938 which corresponded to this image of exports of manufactured goods in exchange for primary commodities.

During the first half of the 19th century the historical statistical experience regarding British terms of trade was in the opposite direction. British import prices of primary commodities such as cotton, wool, etc. increased in relation to the prices of British manufactured products (with textile manufactures prominent among exports at that time). This was in line with classical thinking according to which there would be diminishing returns in the production of primary products, due to the scarcity of land and mineral resources (Malthus, Ricardo and extended by Jevons to the cases of coal and minerals more generally). In classical thinking, up to and including John Stuart Mill, it was taken for granted that there was a tendency for the prices of primary commodities to rise in relation to manufactures, especially since the pressure of surplus population and the process of urbanization would keep wages and cost of production in manufacturing low; this was indeed in line with actual experience in the first half of the 19th century and formed the basis of Marx's theory of surplus value and was later applied by Arthur Lewis to conditions in developing countries in his emphasis on the role of unlimited supplies of labour in economic development (Lewis, 1954).

Thus when Singer in 1947/48 prepared for the United Nations his analysis of British terms of trade after 1873 (*Relative Prices of Exports and Imports of Under-developed Countries*, New York: United Nations, 1949) which subsequently formed the basis of the Prebisch–Singer hypothesis, this ran contrary to traditional thinking. Hence there was a great reluctance even to accept the empirical evidence for this period. In particular the question of transport costs and also the question of improving quality of manufactured goods were used by critical economists to contest the empirical basis of the UN study and the Prebisch–Singer hypothesis (Viner 1953; Haberler, 1961; Ellsworth, 1956 and Morgan, 1959). However, subsequent analysis has shown that correction for shipping costs and changing quality would not destroy the empirical basis for the hypothesis (Spraos, 1980 and 1983).

The extension of the Prebisch–Singer hypothesis to the post-war period has also been questioned empirically. At the time the hypothesis was formulated in 1949/50 primary commodity prices were high as a result of wartime disruption and restocking needs after the war, and rose even further subsequently in 1950/51 as a result of the Korean war. Hence while the hypothesis is empirically supported if both the 1873–1938 period and the period since 1949–50 are considered separately, some doubts have been expressed about the postwar period and about the period since 1873 considered as a whole. However the doubts about the post-war period expressed by Spraos (1983) are only partial doubts; they only applied to the net barter terms of trade (NBTT) (and even there of doubtful validity) but vanished when looked at the 'Employment Corrected Double Factorial Terms of Trade' (ECDFTT). The double factorial terms of trade take the relative productivities into account as well as relative prices. The employment correction allows for the fact that the manufactured products from the North are produced under conditions of full employment, while the South was subject to chronic unemployment. (The first part of this correction would hardly be made for current measurement.) This shift to ECDFTT seems perfectly compatible with the Prebisch–Singer hypothesis since its main concern was with the welfare impact of terms of trade upon industrial and developing countries respectively which is a matter of productivity and employment as well as prices. Moreover, more detailed analysis of the post-war period or of the whole period since 1873 seems to confirm the hypothesis empirically even as far as simple NBTT are concerned. For example, Sapsford (1985) extended Spraos' analysis into the early eighties and applied statistical analysis to the whole series since 1900 to account for the wartime break and found that the Prebisch–Singer hypothesis was strongly borne out not only for the pre-war period since 1900 and the post-war period separately, but also for the whole period in spite of the wartime upward displacement. He determined the downward trend in the NBTT over the period 1900 to 1982 as 1.2% per annum. A.P. Thirlwall (1983, pp. 52–354) and Prabirjit Sarkar in a forthcoming paper on 'The terms of trade experience of Britain since the nineteenth century' also have no doubt about the genuineness and validity of the long-term declining trend in NBTT for primary commodity exports.

The empirical basis for a continuing post-war declining trend of terms of trade of developing countries or of primary exporters, in confirmation of the Prebisch–Singer hypothesis, can of course be taken as established only if oil prices are excluded. However, this exclusion of oil prices seems fully justified. The Prebisch–Singer hypothesis clearly refers to normal international market processes while the rise in oil prices was due to the application of producer power by a producer cartel in 1973 and again in 1979 to set aside market forces. In fact the need for such producer action and the need for international commodity agreements to raise and stabilize primary commodity prices is one of the possible policy conclusions arising from the Prebisch–Singer hypothesis. It could, of course, be taken as a weakness of Prebisch–Singer that it does not allow for such reaction to market pressures; but then the OPEC case has remained fairly isolated and it is by no means certain that market pressures will not in the end have the last word.

The underlying economic argument in explaining the trend towards deteriorating terms of trade observed and projected by Prebisch–Singer can be put under four headings:

(1) Differing elasticities of demand for primary commodities and manufactured goods. Primary commodities being inputs have a lower elasticity of demand because a 10 per cent drop (rise) in the price of the primary input will only mean a fractional drop in the price of the finished product – say 2 per cent instead of 10 per cent – and hence no great effect on demand can be expected. This means that in the case of a drop in prices there is no compensation in balance-of-payments terms (or 'income terms of trade') as a result of increasing volume. In the case of food the low price elasticity of demand is due to the fact that food is a basic need – and hence much of the income set free by a fall in the price of food will be devoted to other consumption goods rather than an increase in food consumption. Today the developing countries are net importers rather than exporters of food although this was not the case when the Prebisch–Singer hypothesis was developed in 1949/50. This low elasticity of demand, especially when combined with low elasticity of supply as emphasized by the classical analysis also means that there is great instability of primary commodity prices and hence terms of trade – both upward and downward. The Prebisch–Singer analysis did not always quite clearly distinguish the disadvantages of the present system of world trade for primary exporters due to price instability from those due to a deteriorating trend. In terms of instability, the Prebisch–Singer hypothesis was much more widely accepted and for example strongly anticipated by Keynes (1938), and also in the various memoranda and proposals by Keynes at the Bretton Woods conference aiming at an International Commodity Clearing House or even a world currency based on commodities.

(2) Demand for primary commodities is bound to expand less than demand for manufactured products. This is due partly to the lower income elasticity of demand for primary products, especially agricultural products (Engel's Law), and partly to the technological superiority of the industrial countries exporting manufactures. Part of that technological superiority is devoted to economies in the use of primary commodities and also to the development of synthetic substitutes for primary commodities. The latter has been a striking feature of economic development which has markedly accelerated since it was first emphasized by Prebisch–Singer (Singer 1950). The tendency towards balance of trade deficits for developing countries arising from such divergent demand trends will enforce currency depreciations which will introduce a further circle of terms of trade deterioration (although hopefully not of income terms of trade).

(3) The technological superiority of the industrial countries means that their exports embody a more sophisticated technology the control of which is concentrated in the exporting countries and especially in the large multinational firms located in those countries. This means that the prices of manufactured exports embody a Schumpeterian rent element for innovation and also a monopolistic profit element because of the size and power of multinational firms.

(4) The structure of both commodity markets and labour markets is different in industrial and developing countries. In the industrial 'centre' countries, labour is organized in trade unions and producers in strong monopolistic firms and producers' organizations, all very powerful at various times. This means that the results of technical progress and increased productivity are largely absorbed in higher factor incomes rather than lower prices for the consumers. In the developing 'peripheral' countries, to the contrary, where labour is unorganized, the rural surplus population (Lewis, 1954) and its partial transfer into urban unemployment, open or disguised as explained in the Harris–Todaro model (Todaro, 1969) make for a situation in which results of increased productivity are likely to show in lower prices, benefiting the overseas consumer rather than the domestic producer. As long

as we deal only with domestic production, such shifts in internal terms of trade between consumers and producers may not matter too much, partly because the two bodies are largely the same people, and partly because internal terms of trade can be influenced by domestic fiscal and other policies. But in international trade, the producers and consumers are in different countries; hence a tendency for productivity improvements mainly benefiting producers in the industrial countries but not in the developing countries will clearly affect terms of trade and international income distribution. Moreover, in many developing countries some of the major 'domestic' producers benefiting from higher productivity would be foreign investors and the higher profits flowing abroad would be equivalent in results to worsening terms of trade.

It will be noted that some of the four explanations for a deteriorating trend in terms of trade of developing countries relate as much or more to the characteristics of different types of *countries* – their different level of technological capacity, different organization of labour markets, presence or absence of surplus labour, etc. – as to the characteristics of different *commodities*. This indicates a general shift in the terms of trade discussion away from primary commodities *versus* manufactures and more towards exports of developing countries – whether primary commodities or simpler manufactures – *versus* the exports products of industrial countries – largely sophisticated manufactures and capital goods as well as skill-intensive services including technological know-how itself. As already mentioned, the initial hypothesis was formulated at a time when there was relatively little export of manufactures from developing countries. Since then there has been a considerable shift towards manufactures, including intensifying the export of primary commodities embodied in more highly processed manufactures. Although the early exponents of the Prebisch–Singer approach were often criticized for recommending import substituting industrialization (ISI) as a main policy conclusion, another equally logical policy conclusion would be export substituting industrialization (ESI) to get exports away from the deteriorating primary commodities. In fact this policy advice was given by some early followers of Prebisch–Singer to countries like India, where the possibilities of ESI seemed to exist at the time. However, the fact that some of the explanation for deteriorating terms of trade now relates to the characteristics of countries rather than commodities means that even ESI, a shift away from primary commodities to manufactures in the exports of developing countries has not disposed of the problem. The type of manufactures exported by developing countries in relation to the different types of manufactures exported by the industrial countries shared some of the disadvantages pointed out by Prebisch–Singer for primary commodities in relation to manufactures.

This can be demonstrated from some recent data. Taking trend equations for the period 1954–72 we find that in constant export unit values the prices of the primary commodities of developed countries fell by an annual average of 0.73%, but those of primary commodities of developing countries fell by 1.82% p.a. (both co-efficients significant at 1% level). This difference shows the existence of both commodity and country influences reinforcing each other. Similarly it can be shown that while the terms of trade for manufactures improved, they did so less for the manufactures of developing countries than those of industrial countries. Hence the deterioration in terms of trade of developing countries during this period can be attributed to three distinct factors:

(1) the rate of deterioration in prices of their primary commodities compared with those of primary commodities exported by industrial countries;

(2) a fall in prices of the manufactures exported by developing countries relative to the manufactures exported by industrial countries; and

(3) the higher proportion of primary commodities in the exports of developing countries which means that the deterioration of primary commodities in relation to manufactures affected them more than the industrial countries.

A quantitative weighting of these three factors is difficult but a broad estimate seems to show that they are of more or less equal importance. The original Prebisch–Singer hypothesis based on characteristics of commodities emphasized only the third factor, while the more recent formulations in terms of characteristics of countries include also the first two factors. It also shows that ESI mitigates the problem but does not entirely dispose of it. The shift in emphasis from commodity factors to country factors is particularly associated with the various theories of dependency (Prebisch and the work of the UN Economic Commission for Latin America (ECLA); Furtado, 1964), of centre–periphery analysis (Seers, 1983); and particularly of unequal exchange (Emmanuel, 1972).

H.W. SINGER

See also DEVELOPMENT ECONOMICS; PERIPHERY; STRUCTURALISM.

BIBLIOGRAPHY

Ellsworth, P.T. 1956. The terms of trade between primary producing and industrial countries. *Inter-American Economic Affairs* 10, Summer, 47–65.

Emmanuel, A. 1972. *Unequal Exchange*. New York and London: Monthly Review Press.

Furtado, C. 1964. *Development and Underdevelopment*. Berkeley: University of California Press.

Haberler, G. 1961. Terms of trade and economic development. In *Economic Development for Latin America*, ed. H.S. Ellis, London: Macmillan.

Keynes, J.M. 1938. The policy of government storage of foodstuffs and raw materials. *Economic Journal* 48, September, 449–60.

Lewis, W.A. 1954. Economic development with unlimited supplies of labour. *Manchester School of Economics and Social Studies* 22, May, 139–91.

Morgan, T. 1959. The long-run terms of trade between agriculture and manufacturing. *Economic Development and Cultural Change* 8, October, 1–23.

Prebisch, R. 1950. *The Economic Development of Latin America and its Principal Problems*. New York: UN Economic Commission for Latin America.

Sapsford, D. 1985. The statistical debate on the net barter terms of trade between primary commodities and manufactures: a comment and some additional evidence. *Economic Journal* 95(379), September, 781–8.

Seers, D. 1983. *The Political Economy of Nationalism*. Oxford: Oxford University Press.

Singer, H.W. 1950. The distribution of gains between investing and borrowing countries. *American Economic Review* 40, May, 473–85.

Spraos, J. 1980. The statistical debate on the net barter terms of trade between primary commodities and manufactures. *The Economic Journal* 90(357), March, 107–28.

Spraos, J. 1983. *Inequalising Trade?* Oxford: Clarendon Press.

Spraos, J. 1985. A reply. *Economic Journal* 95(379), September, 789.

Thirlwall, A.P. 1983. *Growth and Development, with special reference to developing economies*. 3rd edn, London: Macmillan.

Todaro, M.P, 1969. A model of labour migration and urban unemployment in less developed countries. *American Economic Review* 59(1), March, 138–48.

Viner, J. 1953. *International Trade and Economic Development*. Oxford: Clarendon Press.

term structure of interest rates. The term structure of interest rates concerns the relationship among the yields of default-free securities that differ only with respect to their term to maturity. The relationship is more popularly known as the shape of the yield curve and has been the subject of intense examination by economists for over fifty years. Historically, three competing theories have attracted the widest attention. These are known as the expectations, liquidity preference, and hedging-pressure or preferred habitat theories of the term structure.

THE EXPECTATIONS THEORY. According to the expectations theory, the shape of the yield curve can be explained by investors' expectations about future interest rates. This proposition dates back at least to Irving Fisher (1896), but the main development of the theory was done by Hicks (1939) and Lutz (1940). More recent versions of the theory have been developed by Malkiel (1966) and Roll (1970; 1971).

Suppose, for example, that investors believe the prevailing level of interest rates is unsustainably high and that lower rates are more probable than higher ones in the future. Under such circumstances, long-term bonds will appear to investors as more attractive than shorter-term issues *if* both sell at equal yields. Long-term bonds will permit an investor to earn what is believed to be an unusually high rate over a longer period of time than short-term issues, whereas investors in shorter bonds subject themselves to the prospect of having to reinvest their funds later at the lower yields than are expected. Moreover, longer-term bonds are likely to appreciate in value if expectations of falling rates prove correct. Thus, if short and long securities sold at equal yields, investors would tend to bid up the prices (force down the yields) of long-term bonds while selling off short-term securities causing their prices to fall (yields to rise). Thus, a descending yield curve with short issues yielding more than larger ones can be explained by expectations of lower future rates. Similarly, an ascending yield curve with longer issues yielding more than shorter-term ones can be explained by expectations of rising rates.

Under the assumptions of the perfect-certainty variant of the expectations theory, there are no transactions costs, and all investors make identical and accurate forecasts of future interest rates. The theory then implies a formal relationship between long and short-term rates of interest. Specifically, the analysis leads to the conclusion that the long rate is an average of current and expected short rates. Consider the following simple two-period example, where only two securities exist (a one-year and a two-year bond), and investors have funds at their disposal for one or two years. Let capital *R*s stand for actual market rates (yields), while lower-case *r*s stand for expected or forward rates. Prescripts represent the time periods for which the rates are applicable, while postscripts stand for the maturity of the bonds. Thus, $t, R, 2$ indicates today's two-year rate, while $t+1, r, 1$ stands for the expected one-year rate in period $t+1$.

If investors are profit maximizers, it follows that each investor will choose that security (or combination of securities) that maximizes his return for the period during which his funds are available. Consider the alternatives open to the investor who has funds available for two years. The two-year investor will have no incentive to move from one bond to another when he can make the same investment return from buying a combination of short issues or holding one long issue to maturity. If such an investor invests one dollar in a one-year security and then reinvests the proceeds at maturity (i.e. $(1+t, R, 1)$) in a one-year issue next year, his total capital will grow to $(1+t, R, 1)(1+t+1, r, 1)$ at the end of the two-year period. Alternatively, if he invests his dollar in a two-year issue (and leaves all interest to be reinvested until the final maturity date in two years) he will have at maturity $(1+t, R, 2)^2$. In equilibrium, where the investor has no incentive to switch from security to security, the two alternatives must offer the same overall yield, i.e.,

$$(1+t, R, 2)^2 = (1+t, R, 1)(1+t+1, r, 1). \qquad (1)$$

Thus, the two-year rate can be expressed as a geometric average involving today's one-year rate and the one-year rate of interest anticipated next year.

$$(1+t, R, 2) = [(1+t, R, 1)(1+t+1, r, 1)]^{1/2}. \qquad (2)$$

If equation (2) holds, then the holding-period return for the one-year investor will also be the same whether he buys a one-year bond and holds it to maturity or buys a two-year bond and sells it after one year.

In similar fashion, the rate on longer-term issues must turn out to be an average of the current and a whole series of future short-term rates of interest. Only when this is true can the pattern of short and long rates in the market be sustained. The long-term investor must expect to earn through successive investment in short-term securities the same return over his investment period that he would earn by holding a long-term bond to maturity. In general, the equilibrium relationship is,

$$(1+t, R, N) = [(1+t, R, 1)(1+t+1, r, 1)\cdots \cdots(1+t+N-1, r, 1)]^{1/N} \quad (3)$$

The expectations theory can be extended to a world of uncertainty and it can account for every sort of yield curve. If short-term rates are expected to be lower in the future, then the long rate, which we have seen must be an average of those rates and the current short rate, will lie below the short rate. Similarly, long rates will exceed the current short rate if rates are expected to be higher in the future.

THE LIQUIDITY-PREFERENCE THEORY. The liquidity-preference theory, advanced by Hicks (1939) concurs with the importance of expectations in influencing the shape of the yield curve. Nevertheless, it argues that, in a world of uncertainty, short-term issues are more desirable to investors than longer-term issues because the former are more liquid. Short-term issues can be converted into cash at short notice without appreciable loss in principal value, even if rates change unexpectedly. Long-term issues, however, will tend to fluctuate widely in price with unanticipated changes in interest rates and hence ought to yield more than shorts by the amount of a risk premium.

If no premium were offered for holding long-term bonds, it is argued that most individuals and institutions would prefer to hold short-term issues to minimize the variability of the money value of their portfolios. On the borrowing side, however, there is assumed to be an opposite propensity. Borrowers can be expected to prefer to borrow at long term to assure themselves of a steady source of funds. This leaves an imbalance in the pattern of supply and demand for the different maturities – one which speculators might be expected to offset. Hence, the final step in the argument is the assertion that speculators are also averse to risk and must be paid a liquidity premium to induce them to hold long-term securities. Thus, even if interest rates are expected to remain unchanged, the yield curve should be upward sloping, since the yields of long-term bonds will be augmented by risk premiums necessary to induce investors to hold them. While it is conceivable that short rates could exceed long rates if investors thought that rates would fall sharply in the future, the 'normal relationship' is assumed to be an ascending yield curve.

Formally, the liquidity premium is typically expressed as an amount that is to be added to the expected future rate in arriving at the equilibrium-yield relationships described in equations (1) through (3). If we let $L, 2$ stand for the liquidity premium that should be added to next year's forecasted one-year rate, we have

$$(1+{}_tR_2)^2 = (1+{}_tR_1)(1+{}_{t+1}r_1+L_2) \qquad (4)$$

and

$$(1+{}_tR_2) = [(1+{}_tR_1)(1+{}_{t+1}r_1+L_2)]^{1/2}. \qquad (5)$$

Thus, if $L, 2$ is positive (i.e. if there is a liquidity premium), the two-year rate will be greater than the one-year rate even when no change in rates is expected. It has also been customary to assume that $L, 3$, the premium to be added to the one-year rate forecasted for two years hence (i.e. period $t+2$) is even greater than $L, 2$, so that the three-year rate will exceed the two-year rate when no change is expected in short-term rates over the next three years. In general, the liquidity-premium model may be written as

$$(1+{}_tR_N) = [(1+{}_tR_1)(1+{}_{t+1}r_1+L_2)\cdots \cdots(1+{}_{t+N-1}r_1+L_N)]^{1/N}. \qquad (6)$$

Assuming that $L, N > L, N-1 > \cdots > L, 2 > 0$, the yield curve will be positively sloped even when no changes in rates are anticipated.

THE HEDGING-PRESSURE OR PREFERRED HABITAT THEORY. Other critics of the expectations theory, including Culbertson (1957) and Modigliani and Sutch (1966), argue that liquidity considerations are far from the only additional influence on bond investors. While liquidity may be a critical consideration for a commercial banker considering an investment outlet for a temporary influx of deposits, it is not important for a life insurance company seeking to invest an influx of funds from the sale of long-term annuity contracts. Indeed, if the life insurance company wants to hedge against the risk of interest-rate fluctuations, it will prefer long, rather than short, maturities. Long-term investments will guarantee the insurance company a profit regardless of what happens to interest rates over the life of the contract.

Many pension funds and retirement savers find themselves in a wholly analogous situation. A retirement saver who has funds to invest in bonds for n periods will find an n-period pure discount (zero coupon) bond to be the safest investment. It is assumed that if investors are risk averse, they can be tempted out of their preferred habitats only with the promise of a higher yield on a bond of any other maturity. Of course, other investors such as commercial banks or corporate investors will hedge against risk by confining their purchases to short-term issues. These investors will need higher yields on longer-term issues to induce them to invest in such securities. Under this hedging-pressure theory, however, there is no reason for term premiums to be necessarily positive or to be an increasing function of maturity. Under an extreme (and somewhat implausible) form of the argument suggested by Culbertson, the short and long markets are effectively segmented; and short and long yields are determined by supply and demand in each of the segmented markets.

EMPIRICAL ANALYSIS OF THE TERM STRUCTURE. The chief obstacle to effective empirical analysis of the determinants of the term structure of interest rates has been the lack of independent evidence concerning expectations of future interest rates. Consequently, the first step in most empirical tests of the pure form of the expectations theory has been to set up some mechanism by which expectations may reasonably have been formed by market participants. Since people usually estimate the future by relying, at least in part, on historical information, this procedure has often involved the generation of forecasts of future interest rates from past values of these rates. Then investigators have sought to determine whether empirical yield curves have been consistent with these hypothetical forecasts and with the premise that investors, in fact, behave as the expectations theory claims. Thus, in essence, two theories were tested jointly: first, a theory of expectations formation and, second, a theory of the term structure. Of course, it is important to realize that any inability to confirm the expectations theory may be due to a failure to specify properly an expectations-forming mechanism rather than a failure of the theory to offer a correct explanation of the shape of the yield curve. Nevertheless, the wide body of evidence we have does suggest a general conclusion.

The expectations forming mechanisms utilized in empirical studies have been varied and inventive. They have included an error-learning mechanism (Meiselman, 1962); distributed lags on past rates (Modigliani and Sutch, 1966) or on inflation (Modigliani and Shiller, 1973; Fama, 1976); use of ex post data under an assumption that market efficiency and rationality require that ex post realizations do not differ systematically from ex ante views (Roll, 1970; 1971; Fama, 1984a and b); and survey data assumed to reflect the actual expectations of market participants (Kane and Malkiel, 1967; Malkiel and Kane, 1968; Kane, 1983). While affirming the general importance of expectations in influencing the shape of the yield curve, empirical studies have generally rejected the pure form of the expectations hypothesis. There does appear to be an upward bias to the shape of the yield curve indicating that term premiums do exist. But contrary to the liquidity-preference theory, term premiums do not increase monotonically over the whole span of forward rates. Moreover, such term premiums vary over time. In addition, there appears to be seasonal patterns in the forward rates calculated from the short end of the yield curve. While expectations are unquestionably an important determinant of the term structure, it is clear that other factors also play an important role.

TOWARD AN ECLECTIC THEORY OF THE TERM STRUCTURE. The most recent work on the term structure has recognized that many factors play a role in shaping the yield curve. It has also considered the problem of explaining the term structure as one of intertemporal general equilibrium theory. Using the methodology of modern option pricing theory, bonds of different maturities are treated symmetrically with other contingent claims. Cox et al. (1981, 1985) have built such an eclectic model that encompasses all the elements of previous theories in a way that is fully consistent with maximizing behaviour and rational expectations. Expectations of future events, risk preferences, and the characteristics of a variety of investment alternatives are all important, as are the individual preferences (habitats) of market participants about the timing of their consumption. Their approach permits the derivation of clear predictions about how changes in a wide variety of exogenous economic variables will affect the term structure. Their model is likely to spawn richer empirical work enabling us to understand better both the expectations forming mechanism and the varied influences on bond prices.

BURTON G. MALKIEL

See also INTEREST RATES.

BIBLIOGRAPHY

Cox, J., Ingersoll, J., Jr. and Ross, S. 1981. A re-examination of traditional hypotheses about the term structure of interest rates. *Journal of Finance* 36(4), September, 769–99.

Cox, J., Ingersoll, J., Jr. and Ross, S. 1985. A theory of the term structure of interest rates. *Econometrica* 53(2), March, 385–407.

Culbertson, J. 1957. The term structure of interest rates. *Quarterly Journal of Economics* 71, November, 485–517.

Fama, E. 1976. Inflation uncertainty and expected returns on treasury bills. *Journal of Political Economy* 84(3), June, 427–48.

Fama, E. 1984a. The information in the term structure. *Journal of Financial Economics* 13(4), December, 509–28.

Fama, E. 1984b. Term premiums in bond returns. *Journal of Financial Economics* 13(4), December, 529–46.

Fisher, I. 1896. Appreciation and interest. *AEA Publications* 3(11), August, 331–442.

Hicks, J. 1939. *Value and Capital.* 2nd edn, London: Oxford University Press, 1946.

Kane, E. 1983. Nested tests of alternative term-structure theories. *Review of Economics and Statistics* 65(1), February, 115–23.

Kane, E. and Malkiel, B. 1967. The term structure of interest rates: an analysis of a survey of interest-rate expectations. *Review of Economics and Statistics* 49, August, 343–55.

Lutz, F. 1940. The structure of interest rates. *Quarterly Journal of Economics* 55, November, 36–63.

Malkiel, B. 1966. *The Term Structure of Interest Rates.* Princeton: Princeton University Press.

Malkiel, B. and Kane, E. 1968. Expectations and interest rates: a cross-sectional test of the error-learning hypothesis. *Journal of Political Economy* 77(4), July–August, 453–70.

Meiselman, D. 1962. *The Term Structure of Interest Rates.* Englewood Cliffs, NJ: Prentice-Hall.

Modigliani, F. and Shiller, R. 1973. Inflation, rational expectations and the term structure of interest rates. *Economica*, NS 40(157), February, 12–43.

Modigliani, F. and Sutch, R. 1966. Innovations in interest rate policy. *American Economic Review, Papers and Proceedings* Supplement, 56, May, 178–97.

Roll, R. 1970. *The Behavior of Interest Rates.* New York: Basic Books.

Roll, R. 1971. Investment diversification and bond maturity. *Journal of Finance* 26(1), 51–66.

Thompson, Thomas Perronet (1783–1869). Appointed as the first Crown Governor of the British territory of Sierra Leone in 1808, Thompson was recalled under suspicion of financial impropriety in 1809. The real explanation for his departure, however, had more to do with the fact that the Sierra Leone Company (which had governed since 1790) found Thompson's determination to rid the colony of an apprenticeship system whose features, as he saw it, were hardly different from those of slavery, excessively disturbing. The abuses which Thompson observed had developed, it should be noted, despite the fact that the Sierra Leone Company had been set up by anti-slavery philanthropists, including William Wilberforce and the economist Henry Thornton, with the intention of returning liberated slaves from the Americas to Africa (and, it was hoped, to illustrate the profitability of an African colonial trade not based on slavery).

On his return voyage to England, Thompson was the victim of an act of piracy. His vessel was boarded by the crew of a French corvette, and while its captain entertained Thompson, the British vessel was liberated of its cargo and provisions. Once safely back in England, Thompson applied to the Prime Minister (Lord Liverpool) for another official posting, but 'in case no other situation should present itself', he considered the possibility of single-handedly introducing the study of political economy into the University of Cambridge 'in order to provide a living for myself' (letter to E.P. Sells, January 1811, cited in Johnson, 1957, p. 70). This idea was not entirely fanciful, since Thompson was a graduate of Queen's College (BA, seventh wrangler, 1802) and a fellow of that college. It transpired, however, that the first regular lectures on the subject at Cambridge were given by George Pryme in 1816, and Thompson instead re-activated his commission in the army (into which service he had switched from the navy in 1806). His command of a defeat at Muscat led to his being court martialled but acquitted (though with a reprimand for 'rashly undertaking the expedition with so small a detachment') in 1820.

In 1822 Thompson played an active role in the founding the *Westminster Review* (financed by a £4000 advance from Bentham) which aimed to provide a radical alternative to the Tory *Quarterly Review* and the Whig *Edinburgh Review*. James Mill turned down the offer of its editorship, although he did contribute to its first number (in 1824) for which Thompson himself wrote an article on the 'Instrument of Exchange'. This constituted his first published work on economics. Thompson was sole proprietor of the *Review* from 1829 until 1836 when, on his election to the reformed House of Commons for the seat of Hull (where he had been born on 15 March 1783), he transferred its ownership to William Molesworth.

In 1826 Thompson published the first of his longer tracts on economics, *An Exposition of Fallacies on Rent, Tithes, &etc.* Ostensibly an attack on the Ricardian theory of rent (indeed, Thompson re-titled its second edition *The True Theory of Rent in Opposition to Mr Ricardo and Others*), John Stuart Mill described it as 'a striking exemplification of the mistakes of an ingenious, but not thoroughly informed mind' and claimed that, in fact, Thompson's 'theory of rent differs from that of Mr Ricardo only in the expression' (1828, pp. 178–9). However, Mill's claim is open to question. Thompson argued that rent was determined by 'the limited quantity of land in comparison with the competitors for its produce' (1826, pp. 8–9) – quite how this could be said to be essentially Ricardo's theory 'in different words' is difficult to see. Not only does it fail to distinguish between extensive and intensive rent, but it ignores altogether the effect on the conditions of production of wage goods of restrictions on the importation of corn which is the key to Ricardo's argument. The only observation which needs to be made about Mill's claim is, perhaps, that it may tell us rather more about his own contribution to the decline of Ricardian economics than about Ricardo's theory of rent. That Mill could advance such a claim within five years of Ricardo's death, makes it less difficult to understand why many felt that 'little remained of Ricardo's theory' by the end of that decade.

In 1827 followed the *Catechism of the Corn Laws* which Mill pronounced 'one of the most useful works which have appeared in the present controversy' (1828, p. 186); an interesting judgement given that its opening section was based on the *Exposition.* The *Catechism* presents a list of 120 (later increased to 365) 'Proteus-like fallacies' and answers, and has been referred to as 'the arsenal whence the Anti-Corn Law League drew its best weapons' (Allibone, 1871). There then followed, during the seven years he owned the *Westminster Review* better than one hundred articles for that periodical on subjects as diverse as the reform of the House of Lords and Catholic emancipation. Most of these were republished in his multi-volume *Exercises, Political and Other* in 1842. Also to be mentioned are his opinions on currency questions (for example, 1848), where he was an opponent of 'inflationist' proposals largely on the grounds of the redistribution against workers which he saw as part of the process. In the crisis of

1847, when the Bank Act of 1844 was again the subject of hot debate, Thompson wrote: 'I hold to my opinion that there will be mischief on the Currency question. I receive more half-mad pamphlets from Birmingham' (letter to J. Bowring, April 1847, quoted in Johnson, 1957, p. 265). In 1852 he attempted to introduce into Parliament measures which would protect the value of the currency against depreciation due to new gold discoveries, but these were defeated.

There is much more that could be said of Thompson's remarkable career. He was a moral-force, class-alliance chartist (and was invited to participate in writing the draft act of parliament which was to become the People's Charter); he voted consistently with the Radicals when a member of parliament; he constructed, and published, a non-axiomatic system of geometry (Euclid without the axioms); and he invented an enharmonic organ which was exhibited at the Great Exhibition of 1851, where it received an honourable mention. He died at Blackheath on 6 September 1869.

MURRAY MILGATE AND ALASTAIR LEVY

SELECTED WORKS

1826. *An Exposition of Fallacies on Rent, Tithes, &etc.* London: Hatchard & Son. 2nd edn, re-titled *The True Theory of Rent in Opposition to Mr Ricardo and Others*, 1826.

1827. *A Catechism on the Corn Laws; with a list of fallacies and answers.* London: J. Ridgway.

1842. *Exercises, Political and Other.* 6 vols, London: E. Wilson.

1848. *A Catechism on the Currency.* London: E. Wilson.

1859. *Catechism on the Ballot; or a list of fallacies and the answers.* London: G. Brown.

BIBLIOGRAPHY

Allibone, S.A. 1859–71. *A Critical Dictionary of English Literature and British and American Authors, Living and Deceased.* 3 vols, Philadelphia: Childs & Peterson; London; N. Trübner & Co.

Johnson, L.G. 1957. *General T. Perronet Thompson: 1763–1869: His Military, Literary and Political Campaigns.* London: Allen & Unwin.

Mill, J.S. 1828. A review of the third edition of *Catechism on the Corn Laws. Westminster Review* 13, 169–87.

Thompson, William (1785–1833). Self-confessedly 'one of the idle classes', Thompson, the son of a merchant, was a substantial landowner with an estate in County Cork. He evinced an early interest in 'advanced' opinions which led to contacts with the St. Simonians in France and in 1822 his intellectual interests took him to London where he resided for a time with Bentham in Queen Square Place. Here he met some of the leading philosophical radicals and classical political economists of the day, such as Robert Torrens and James Mill. His sympathies were, however, enlisted by the expanding co-operative movement and by 1825 he was, in the words of J.S. Mill, 'the chief champion on the co-operative side' in a series of debates held in the metropolis on the subject of co-operation.

Thompson's major work of political economy, *An Inquiry into the Principles of the Distribution of Wealth* was published in 1824. In it, Thompson set out the principles which he believed should regulate economic life, namely the free direction of labour, voluntary exchanges and the use by labour of its entire product. These were the 'natural laws' which, if they prevailed, 'would produce much happiness in any community' and it was the purpose of the *Inquiry* to examine the extent to which they did prevail first, under existing economic arrangements; secondly, in a truly competitive market economy; and thirdly, under a system of mutual co-operation.

For Thompson, existing economic arrangements were governed by 'absolute violence, fraud ... the operation of unequal laws interfering with the freedom of labour ... and the perfect freedom of voluntary exchanges'. This resulted in the appropriation of labour's product by 'a class of capitalists a class of rent or land-owners, and an always imperious class of idlers'. It was these classes who, through the coercive exercise of economic and political power, 'counteract(ed) the natural laws of distribution', 'forcing labour without a satisfactory equivalent'.

Yet in the *Inquiry* Thompson seems to have accepted that force and fraud were not a necessary feature of a competitive market economy. Rather they were aberrant intrusions which obstructed its equitable functioning. Render a market economy truly free and competitive and 'the natural laws of distribution' would prevail. Thus such an economy might play a distributive role which militated strongly against substantial material inequalities. As he wrote in the *Inquiry*,

> 'tis by means of the brutal expedients of insecurity ... by the varied employments of force and terror ... that the capitalist is enabled to keep down the remuneration of labour... . The mere competition of producers, if left to the natural laws of distribution ... would be entirely of the exhilarating instead of the depressing species.'

It would act 'constantly to raise the remuneration of labour ... while ... at the same time cheapen the articles produced to society at large'. Untramelled competition would 'banish extremes of wealth and poverty' and society would enjoy 'blessings of equality comparable to those enjoyed under Mr. Owen's system of mutual co-operation by common labour'.

Yet for Thompson this was not sufficient and in the *Inquiry* he proceeds to press the case for communities of mutual co-operation where all would have an equal right to draw upon the products of co-operative labour and where the voluntary renunciation of personal rights to property would obviate any violation of the principle of security in the products of individual labour.

In the *Inquiry* communities were preferred largely because of their benign social and ethical consequences. Thus Thompson expressed anxiety over the moral tone of a society which 'retain(ed) the principle of selfishness ... as the leading motive to action' and where there was, in consequence, negligible scope for action motivated by benevolence and social concern. Such a society bred antagonism and conflict. The competitive pressures it unleashed threatened its social cohesion and harmony, while the moral corrosion it engendered was revealed in the transmutation of truth, sincerity benevolence and man himself into marketable commodities.

The publication of *Labor Rewarded* (1827) saw an even more emphatic rejection of the competitive market economy. Thus Thompson argued in this work that even in the non-slave states of America, were it existed in its purest actualized form, individual competition produced not only the moral and social evils of the kind detailed in the *Inquiry* but also general destitution and distress with labour, in many cases, securing a 'mere sufficiency of food and clothing'.

What seems to have provoked this more hostile attitude was Thompson's recognition that whatever the theoretical ideal, the reality was that 'free competition' had 'never yet practically meant anything else but a sham' for if it was to mean anything it required the existence of 'equal means of knowledge and skill, equal freedom of action, equal materials for production and accumulation, equal rights and duties' and equality of 'fortunes' when 'beginning the race of competition'. These preconditions had never been met and so the defence of competition became, in fact, a defence of inequality and exploitation.

Both in the *Inquiry* and *Labor Rewarded*, therefore, Thompson looked to the transcendence of the market through the creation of co-operative communities. By abolishing exchange these communities eliminated any possibility of exploitation and the material and moral evils which resulted from it. Their neo-autarkic nature insulated them against the vagaries of contemporary capitalism while the distribution of produce according to need freed communitarians from the fear of destitution and from the social antagonism and immorality consequent upon the individual pursuit of material gain. They were, in effect, the ideal environment for the transformation of the human base metal of the old moral order into the gold of the new moral world; a transformation which Thompson hoped to accelerate with the publication in 1830 of his *Practical Directions for the Speedy and Economical Establishment of Communities*.

The most powerful initial influence upon Thompson was Benthamite utilitarianism. This is apparent in the *Inquiry* where Thompson discussed its egalitarian implications and where he considered at length the whole problem of reconciling security with equality. However, the most profound and lasting intellectual influence was that of Owenism, though it should be stressed that Thompson helped to mould Owenite thinking as much as Owenite socialism shaped his own thought. In particular his political or, as Thompson would have preferred it, 'social economy', provided Owenites with a new range of critical tools of analysis with which to condemn the existing order and to sap the ideological defences thrown up by the popularizers of classical economics. His *Inquiry* was the *magnum opus* of co-operative political economy, far surpassing in scope and coherence anything emanating from the pen of Robert Owen.

Thompson died in 1833 and while his *Inquiry* was reprinted in 1850, its influence faded in the second half of the 19th century as co-operation assumed a commercial rather than a communitarian form.

N.W. THOMPSON

See also RICARDIAN SOCIALISTS.

SELECTED WORKS

1824. *An Inquiry into the Principles of the Distribution of Wealth most conducive to Human Happiness*. London.

1827. *Labour Rewarded. The Claims of Labor and Capital Conciliated, by One of the Idle Classes*. London.

1830. *Practical Directions for the Speedy and Economical Establishment of Communities*. London.

BIBLIOGRAPHY

Beales, H.L. 1933. *The Early English Socialists*. London: Hamish Hamilton.

Beer, M. 1953. *A History of British Socialism*. 2 vols, London: Allen & Unwin.

Cole, G.D.H. 1977. *A History of Socialist Thought*. 5 vols. Vol. 1: *Socialist Thought, The Forerunners*. London: Macmillan.

Foxwell, H.S. 1899. Introduction to the English translation of A. Menger, *The Right to the Whole Produce of Labour*. London: Macmillan.

Gray, A. 1967. *The Socialist Tradition, Moses to Lenin*. London: Longman.

Hunt, E.K. 1979. Utilitarianism and the labour theory of value. *History of Political Economy* 11, 544–71.

Hunt, E.K. 1980. The relation of the Ricardian socialists to Ricardo and Marx. *Science and Society* 44, 177–98.

Jones, G.S. 1983. Rethinking Chartism. In *Languages of Class: Studies in English working class History 1832–1982*. Cambridge: Cambridge University Press.

King, J.E. 1981. Perish Commerce! Free trade and underconsumption in early British radical economics. *Australian Economic Papers* 20, 235–57.

Lowenthal, E. 1911. *The Ricardian Socialists*. New York: Longman.

Pankhurst, R.K.P. 1954. *William Thompson, Pioneer Socialist, Feminist and Co-operator*. London: Watts.

Thompson, N.W. 1984. *The People's Science: The Popular Political Economy of Exploitation and Crisis, 1816–34*. Cambridge: Cambridge University Press.

Thornton, Henry (1760–1815). I. Henry Thornton was born in 1760, the youngest son of John Thornton, a London merchant prominent in the Russian trade. All three of John Thornton's sons were important in the business community and all three served as members of Parliament. The eldest, Samuel, followed his father in the Russian trade, was a director of the Bank of England, and its Governor between 1799 and 1801; Robert served as Governor of the East India Company for a time, but business reverses were eventually to lead to his emigration to the United States; and Henry became an extremely successful London banker. He died, probably from consumption, in 1815.

John Thornton had been an early member of the Evangelicals, as those followers of John Wesley who remained within the Church of England were called, and Henry too was among their leaders, the most famous of whom was his second cousin and close friend William Wilberforce. The movement became known as the Clapham Sect largely because their informal headquarters was Thornton's country house, located in that then outlying village. The Evangelicals were also known as 'the Party of Saints' and what we would now regard as the conventional piety and respectability of the Victorian middle classes owe much to their influence. Nevertheless their milieu was not Victorian but Georgian and Regency England, where their insistence that public policy be informed by the same high moral purpose as their private lives was profoundly radical. Their best-known accomplishment was ending Britain's participation in the slave trade in 1809, and in 1833 the abolition of slavery itself in the British Empire; but the role of their Sunday School Movement in promoting popular literacy in Britain, not to mention the influence of their British and Foreign Bible Society on 19th-century missionary activity throughout the world, is also noteworthy.

Henry Thornton was at the centre of all of these activities and many others as organizer, fund-raiser and donor. Before his marriage in 1796 he habitually devoted six-sevenths of his considerable income to charity, and perhaps a quarter thereafter. During his 33 years' service in Parliament, in addition to his work against the slave trade, he supported such progressive causes as peace with the American colonies, accommodation with France, and Catholic Emancipation. He also devoted considerable time and energy to religious writings and his great-great grandson E.M. Forster (1951) records that his posthumously published volume of *Family Prayers* was something of a Victorian bestseller which was still earning royalties for his descendants at the end of the 19th century.

Among all of this activity, Henry Thornton found time to study monetary economics. As a prominent banker and member of Parliament it was natural that he would take a practical interest in such matters, particularly given the financial turbulence associated with the French Wars of 1793–1815 and the suspension of the gold convertibility of

Bank of England notes which accompanied them. He gave evidence to the Parliamentary Committees enquiring into the circumstances of the suspension in 1797, and he was an important member of both the Commons Committee which investigated Irish Currency problems in 1804 and the famous 'Bullion Committee' of 1810. However, he was also and above all a great monetary theorist, and his outstanding treatise, *An Enquiry into the Nature and Effects of the Paper Credit of Great Britain* (1802), gives him a strong claim to be regarded as the most important contributor to monetary economics between David Hume (1752) and Knut Wicksell (1898). Only David Ricardo could seriously be regarded as his rival here.

II. The early 18th century had seen considerable progress in monetary economics, and David Hume's three essays of 1752 are rightly regarded as containing the core of classical monetary theory. They set out the quantity theory doctrine that, other things being equal, the price level varies with the quantity of money, and accompany this with an analysis of the way in which, under a commodity standard, balance of payments mechanisms operate so as to equalize price levels and distribute the precious metals among countries. Although allowing that monetary changes can have short-run effects on real output, they also develop the basic classical postulate that money is neutral in the long run, affecting only prices; and in particular they argue that the rate of interest is not a monetary phenomenon.

Banks are scarcely mentioned in Hume's analysis, and though Adam Smith (1776) paid considerable attention to them, his model was the 18th-century Scottish system. Scottish commercial banks held their reserves in claims upon London, not upon any Scottish central bank, and Scotland was a small, largely price-taking economy. Hence Smith's analysis of the interaction of bank behaviour, the price level and the balance of payments, though remarkably perceptive, was far from complete. It had little to say about the transmission mechanisms at work here and about the role of financial assets other than bank notes in the monetary system. Moreover it had nothing at all to say about central banking.

By the 1790s, the development of the English monetary system had far outstripped the growth of knowledge concerning the principles that underlay its operations, and the financial crisis which culminated in the suspension of February 1797 drew attention to this gap in most dramatic fashion. Thornton's *Paper Credit*, published in 1802 but perhaps begun as early as 1796, not only remedied this deficiency, but brought monetary theory to a level of sophistication that it was not to surpass until the end of the 19th century, as a brief sketch of its contributions will make quite evident.

III. *Paper Credit* begins with a detailed description of the contemporary English monetary system, showing how a rather wide variety of credit instruments had come to circulate as what we would now call money, alongside coin and bank notes, and it argues that the velocities of various components of this complex 'circulating medium' differ among instruments and fluctuate over time. In common with virtually every monetary economist before Irving Fisher (and many thereafter), Thornton regarded velocities of circulation as frequently unstable and he discussed in some detail how the Bank of England should behave, both to minimize the occurrence of monetary instability and to offset its consequences when it arose. Thornton was by no means the only contributor to the 'Bullionist Controversy', as the debates of the period are called, to recognize the crucial role and responsibilities of the Bank of England as a central bank, but there were many, not least among the directors of that institution, who refused to do so; and Thornton's exposition of the issues involved represents an important contribution to monetary economics.

No doubt drawing upon his own first-hand observations of the mechanisms at work during the turbulent 1790s, Thornton stressed both the crucial role and the volatility of the public's confidence in the banking system's ability to redeem its liabilities (in terms of Bank of England Notes in the case of country and private London banks, and, under convertibility, in terms of specie in the case of the Bank of England). He understood that bank customers, who were confident that they could obtain Bank of England notes or specie when they required it, would not in fact seek such accommodation, and that only those who had doubts about the convertibility of their assets would demand their redemption. Hence he argued that any initial fall in confidence could lead to a self-reinforcing drain of reserves from the system if the Bank of England responded to it by reducing lending and hence cutting down the supply of the very central bank notes that the public were demanding from country and London banks. For Thornton, the right response to such an 'internal' (i.e., within the country) drain of reserves from the Banking system was for the Bank of England to lend freely to all solvent borrowers in order to restore and maintain the public confidence in the system. In short, the by now conventional textbook analysis of the central bank's 'lender of last resort' function found its first full statement in *Paper Credit*.

But Thornton understood well enough that an internal drain was not the only possible source of pressure on reserves. An external drain associated with what we would now call an adverse balance of payments was also a possibility, and here the required remedy might be different. He was clear that, to the extent that the drain stemmed from an uncompetitively high domestic price level, it could only be remedied by monetary contraction, and hence by the central bank scaling down its loans, including those made to the rest of the banking system. In the conventional wisdom of the later 19th century concerning sound central bank practice, an external drain was always appropriately to be met by such measures, but Thornton (unlike Ricardo, who is the true father of that conventional wisdom) was more subtle than this in his analysis.

For him, money wages were sticky and any sudden monetary contraction carried with it the danger of disrupting markets and causing real output and employment to fall, a danger to be avoided if at all possible. Hence when developing the implications for Bank of England policy of his pioneering analysis of what was later to be called 'the transfer problem', he advocated that temporary drains of specie abroad, associated with bad harvests or once and for all subsidy payments to allies, be accompanied by as little domestic monetary contraction as seemed to that institution to be prudent. Under arrangements prevailing after 1797, he was even willing to entertain temporary departures of sterling from par with specie in the face of temporary external drains rather than risk the domestic disruption that might accompany monetary contraction. Thornton was thus in *Paper Credit* far from being an advocate of an automatic gold standard, and his views have something in common with those of such later advocates of managed paper currency as Thomas Attwood – not to mention John Maynard Keynes, as certain commentators, notably Hicks (1967) and Beaugrand (1981) have pointed out.

IV. McCulloch (1845), who confused Henry with his brother Samuel, regarded *Paper Credit* as being too partial to the

Bank of England in its arguments, but though it may certainly be regarded as a defence of that institution's behaviour during the early years of the restriction, it is nevertheless a critical defence. Even so, by 1810, Henry Thornton was a prominent member of the Bullion Committee, and had become one of the Bank's sternest critics, advocating, both as a signatory to the Committee's Report (Cannan, 1919) and in two Commons speeches on the Report, that the obligation to redeem its notes in specie be reimposed upon it as soon as possible, a measure which was designed to narrow considerably the scope for discretion left to the Bank when confronted with an external drain.

Thornton's policy stance had changed between 1802 and 1810, but there is no evidence that his underlying analytic views were any different. First and foremost, and despite certain affinities, mentioned above, between his work and that of subsequent advocates of managed paper standards, Henry Thornton was always, as Hicks (1967) has put it, a 'hard money' man as far as long-run policy questions were concerned. He regarded the maintenance of the specie value of Bank of England liabilities as the proper overriding end of monetary policy. After 1797 he expected the Bank of England, subject to certain caveats about bad harvests and once and for all transfers, to manage its discounts so as to stabilize the exchange rate and the price of specie. In 1802 he believed that the Bank could be trusted to do so without the check of convertibility, but by 1810 he had changed his mind.

Though the actual conduct of monetary policy, particularly after 1811, shows that, luckily for Britain, they did not always practise what they preached, the directors of the Bank declared themselves firmly committed to the so-called 'Real Bills doctrine' in their evidence to the Bullion Committee, as they did in many other statements. This doctrine distinguishes between 'real bills', drawn to finance goods in the process of production and distribution, and 'fictitious bills' those which simply represent a debt with no corresponding real asset to back them. It then argues that a banking system in general, and a Central Bank in particular, which confines its activities to the discount of the former, cannot affect the price level. The quantity of money generated by following such practices will, so it is claimed, vary with the volume of output and adjust itself automatically and passively to the 'needs of trade'.

Thornton had considered and comprehensively refuted this bundle of fallacies in *Paper Credit*. He had shown that, because there is no necessary relationship between the period for which commercial bills are discounted and the period of time that elapses between the beginning of the production of a particular unit of output and its final consumption, the distinction between 'real' and 'fictitious' bills was specious. Distinguishing between credit *per se*, and the role of credit instruments as components of the circulating medium, he had also shown how money, even if created against the security of good quality commercial bills, could influence the price level. Finally, and crucially, he had shown that the demand of manufacturers and merchants for bank credit would vary with the relationship between the banking system's lending rate and the expected rate of profit in such a way that, if the latter were high relative to the former, potentially unlimited monetary expansion and inflation could be generated by a banking system whose central authority took the Real Bills doctrine as its sole operating guide.

These arguments of Thornton's play a central role in the 1810 *Report* of the Bullion Committee and reflect his influence on that document. The explicit rejection of them by the Directors of the Bank of England, not to mention widespread concern about inflation during 1809–10, was a crucial factor in persuading the Committee in general, and Thornton in particular as one of its key members, to recommend that the constraint of specie convertibility be reimposed upon the Bank as soon as possible, a recommendation which was, of course, rejected by Parliament in 1811 along with the rest of the *Bullion Report*.

V. The reader familiar with the later literature of monetary economics will recognize the essentially Wicksellian (e.g. 1898) flavour of Thornton's discussion of the relationship between bank lending policies and inflation. In a parliamentary speech of 1811 on the Bullion Report he elaborated on his earlier analysis by allowing for the influence of inflation expectations on the perceived real interest burden implied by any given nominal bank lending rate. This insight, which plays only an occasional and peripheral role in Wicksell's work, was of course central to the contributions of another great monetary theorist, Irving Fisher (1896). Moreover in his analysis of these matters, Thornton developed a version of what was later to be called the 'forced saving' doctrine which played an important role in early 20th-century business cycle theory. In the light of all this, it would be easy to jump to the conclusion that Thornton's work was well known to his successors. However it was not.

Failing health and a relatively early death removed Henry Thornton from the centre of monetary controversy just as David Ricardo came to the height of his powers and influence. It was Ricardo and not Thornton who was destined to become the recognized authority to whom 19th-century monetary economists working within the classical tradition looked for guidance in matters of monetary theory. As Hutchison (1968) points out, J.S. Mill (1848) was the last important 19th-century author to recognize Thornton's contributions. Thereafter, his name faded from view, and was not even known to Wicksell; it is largely due to the efforts of Jacob Viner (1924 and 1937) and particularly Friedrich von Hayek (1939) that his true stature has come to be appreciated in the 20th century. Nevertheless, his ideas were well known to his contemporaries, not least to Ricardo, and as transmitted by them, not always without a certain loss of subtlety, they permeate 19th-century classical monetary theory. Thus if Henry Thornton's name was often forgotten by economists, his contributions to the subject were certainly not. For most men, this would be small consolation indeed, but one suspects that so benevolent and self-effacing a man as Henry Thornton might have been content with such an outcome.

DAVID LAIDLER

See also HUME, DAVID; QUANTITY THEORY OF MONEY.

SELECTED WORKS

1802. *An Enquiry into the Nature and Effects of the Paper Credit of Great Britain.* Together with his evidence given before the Committees of Secrecy of the two Houses of Parliament in the Bank of England, March and April 1797, some manuscript notes, and his speeches on the Bullion Report, May 1811. Edited with an introduction by F.A. von Hayek, London: George Allen & Unwin, 1939. Reprinted, London: Frank Cass & Co.; New York: Augustus Kelley, 1962.

BIBLIOGRAPHY

Beaugrand, P. 1981. *Henry Thornton: un precurseur de J.M. Keynes.* Paris: Presses Universitaires de France.

Cannan, E. (ed.) 1919. *The Paper Pound of 1797–1821: The Bullion Report.* London: P.S. King & Son. 2nd (1921) edn, reprinted New York: Augustus M. Kelley, 1969.

Fisher, I. 1896. Appreciation and interest. *AEA Publications* 3(11), August, 331–442.
Forster, E.M. 1951. Henry Thornton. In E.M. Forster, *Two Cheers for Democracy*, London: Abinger. Reprinted, London: Edward Arnold, 1972.
Hayek, F.A. von. 1939. Introduction to Thornton (1802).
Hicks, J.R. 1967. Thornton's *Paper Credit*. In *Critical Essays in Monetary Theory*, London: Oxford University Press.
Hume, D. 1752. Of money; Of the balance Of trade; Of interest. In D. Hume, *Essays, Moral, Political and Literary*, London. Reprinted London: Oxford University Press, 1962.
Hutchison, T.W. 1968. Thornton, Henry. In *International Encyclopaedia of the Social Sciences*, New York: Macmillan and Free Press, Vol. 16.
McCulloch, J.R. 1845. *The Literature of Political Economy*. London.
Mill, J.S. 1848. *Principles of Political Economy with Some of Their Applications to Social Philosophy*. London: Parker.
Smith, A. 1776. *An Inquiry into the Nature and Causes of the Wealth of Nations*. Ed. R.H. Campbell, A.S. Skinner and W.B. Todd, Oxford: Clarendon Press, 2 vols, 1976.
Viner, J. 1924. *Canada's Balance of International Indebtedness 1900–1913*. Cambridge, Mass.: Harvard University Press.
Viner, J. 1937. *Studies in the Theory of International Trade*. New York: Harper Bros.
Wicksell, K. 1898. *Interest and Prices*. Trans. R.F. Kahn, London: Macmillan for the Royal Economic Society, 1936.

Thornton, William Thomas (1813–1880). Thornton was born in Buckinghamshire and lived three years in Malta and five years in Constantinople. In 1836 he obtained a clerkship in the East India House and later (1858) became secretary for public works to the India Office. His expertise had a wide range, from literary works to political economy. Thornton's economic works were praised by his friend J.S. Mill, who referred to his work on population in the *Principles* and used Thornton's arguments for his recantation of the strict wages-fund theory (Mill, 1869). Thornton's fortunes with Marshall were less stable. Marshall was doubtful about the critique of the law of supply and demand as the determinant of wages but appreciated Thornton's style and his work on trade unions (Marshall, 1975, pp. 117–20, 263; 1960, p. 365).

In 1846 Thornton published a book on population based on the wages-fund theory, and then in 1869 he published *On Labour* presenting his critique. The latter book appeared after Longe's contribution on the same topics, and followed Longe's reasoning. Longe's originality was recognized by the Political Economy Society (Hollander, 1903, p. 5), and the possibility of Thornton's plagiarism was discussed by various authors (Hollander, 1903; Schumpeter, 1954, pp. 669–70).

Thornton's critique of the wages fund aimed mainly to show, with many detailed examples, that supply-and-demand adjustments of prices to quantities and vice versa did not occur in the real world. First of all Thornton considered prices as usually 'reserved', hence not flexible in relation to changes in quantities. Even in the case of unreserved prices, quantities would not adjust symmetrically to relative changes in supply and demand. Thornton in fact considered prices and quantities as separately determined. He thought that although it is usually true that prices rise when demand exceeds supply, it is not true that demand decreases if prices increase (Thornton, 1870, pp. 58–64). Moreover, prices can remain stable if demand and supply change (p. 67), and, even more devastating for supply-and-demand theories, demand and supply are not brought into equilibrium, as general case, by changes in prices (pp. 73–5).

Thornton does acknowledge the role of competition among buyers and sellers as a determinant of prices, but he does not assume any systematic behaviour which could justify the idea of general laws of prices.

When Thornton moves from his critique of supply-and-demand prices to its application to the determination of wages, his alliance with Longe against the dogmatism of theories assuming a mechanical determinacy of wages emerges clearly (Thornton, 1970, pp. 82–5; McNulty, 1980, p. 80). Thornton sees insecurity as the basis for the specificity of labour as a commodity. Although labour is sold at unreserved price, there is still no mechanism which can be assumed to adjust quantities to prices. For this reason and because the demand for labour cannot be considered a definite fund – as it depends on capitalists' consumption and expectations – wages cannot be considered as determinate within the supply-and-demand allocation of labour (ibid, pp. 85–105).

On the question of labour relations Thornton was a great supporter of Cooperation. Cooperation was considered a possible alternative to class war and strikes, and the basis for an alliance between labour and capital. Cooperation was debated in the Unions at the time (Webb [1894] 1920, p. 225) and it reconciled Thornton with his friend J.S. Mill with regard to policies if not to theories.

A. PICCHIO

See also MILL, JOHN STUART; WAGE-FUND DOCTRINE.

SELECTED WORKS

1846. *Overpopulation and its remedy; or, an enquiry into the extent and causes of the distress prevailing among the labouring classes of the British Islands*. London: Longman, Brown, Green, & Longmans.
1848. *A Plea for Peasant Proprietors*. London: J. Murray.
1854. *Zohrab; or a midsummer day's dream; and other poems*. London.
1867a. What determines the price of labour or rate of wages? *Fortnightly Review*, May.
1867b. Stray chapters from a forthcoming work on labour. *Fortnightly Review*, October–December.
1869. *On Labour, its wrongful claims and wrightful dues; its actual present and possible future*. London: Macmillan.
1873. Old fashioned ethics and common-sense metaphysics with some of their applications. London: Macmillan.
1875. *Indian Public Works, and cognate Indian topics*. London: Macmillan.
1878. *Horatius Flaccus, Word for Word from Horace. The Odes literally versified by William Thomas Thornton*. London.

BIBLIOGRAPHY

Hollander, J.H. 1903. Introduction to F.D. Longe, *The Wages Fund Theory*. Baltimore: Johns Hopkins Press.
McNulty, P.J. 1980. *The Origins and Development of Labor Economics*. Cambridge, Mass.: Harvard University Press.
Marshall, A. 1975. *The Early Economic Writings of Alfred Marshall, 1867–1890*. Vols I and II, ed. J.K. Whitaker, London: Macmillan.
Schumpeter, J.A. 1954. *History of Economic Analysis*. New York: Oxford University Press.
Webb, S. and B. 1894. *The History of Trade Unionism*. London: Longman & Co. Revised edn, 1920.

Thünen, Johann Heinrich von (1783–1850). Thünen was born in Canarienhausen (Oldenburg) on 24 June 1783. He died on his estate Tellow (Mecklenburg), near Rostock, on 22 September 1850. His paternal ancestors were farmers; despite the 'von', they did not belong to the aristocracy.

After his father's early death, Thünen's mother married a timber merchant. The boy grew up in a small town on the northern seaboard, where he obtained a good, but short, high-school education. As an apprentice he got to know hard manual labour on a farm. There followed academic studies on all aspects of agronomy, including natural sciences, mathematics and economics, at the agricultural colleges of Gross-Flottbeck and Celle (where he heard Thaer) and at the University of Göttingen (where he read Adam Smith). Nevertheless, Thünen remained essentially a scientifically gifted autodidact. During this period (around 1803), he seems to have conceived the idea of his 'isolated state'.

Newly married to the daughter of a respected landowner, Thünen first operated a rented estate. In 1809, with the inheritance from his father, he bought from his brother-in-law the rather run-down estate of Tellow with about 1200 acres of land. Though his heart was in his intellectual pursuits rather than in practical farming, he succeeded in gradually paying off his initial debt and in raising the value of his property, leaving to his four children a prosperous estate with ample liquid funds.

Like Quesnay, who came from a similar background, Thünen made the farm his economic paradigm. With the Physiocrats and Thaer, he belongs to those representatives of the Enlightenment who regarded improvements in agriculture as the key to economic progress. For his estate he kept meticulous accounts, which he used to compute optimal solutions to management problems. He was a model employer with philanthropic, if somewhat paternalistic, ideas on social policy, who established a profit-sharing plan for his employees.

Of Thünen's *magnum opus*, 'The Isolated State with Respect to Agriculture and Political Economy', the first part, including the analysis of rent, location and resource allocation, appeared in 1826 after more than 20 years of work. The second part, containing the marginal productivity theory of distribution, only appeared in 1850. Additional papers, including important contributions on forestry, were published in 1863 by Thünen's biographer, H. Schumacher. All of this material is united in the third edition of 1875, but Waentig's later edition and also the English translations are limited to part I and the first (and more important) half of part II. Additional material was published by Braeuer in his volume of selected works, which also includes a bibliography of Thünen's writings. The literary remains, including unpublished manuscripts, are preserved in the Thünen-Archiv at the University of Rostock.

It has been said that Thünen was a prophet with little honour in any country, and even less in his own. This is inaccurate. It is true that he was at first disappointed about the reception of his book. Nevertheless, by 1827 he was an internationally known authority on agriculture, and the first edition was sold out within seven years. Tellow became a mecca for agronomists, attracting visitors from all over Europe. In 1830, Thünen was made a *doctor philosophiae honoris causa* by the University of Rostock. Politically a progressive liberal, he was elected to the National Assembly in Frankfurt in 1848, but could not attend because of his declining health. In the same year, the town of Teterow, with flags flying and bands playing, made him an honorary burgher. Like Quesnay, he died revered as a sage.

Thünen's scientific achievements are at different levels. In agronomy he made important contributions to the 'statics' of the soil, which are concerned with the steady state where fertility, by suitable crop rotation and fertilization, is maintained at an optimal level. In economics his most fundamental contribution is the method of deriving economic propositions from explicit optimizing models. By 1824 (as

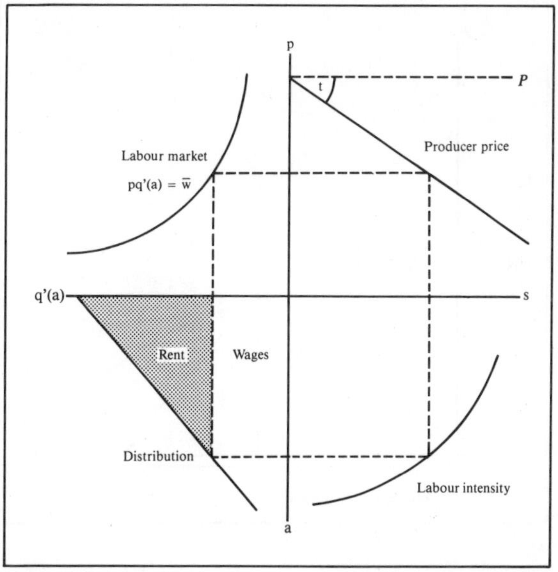

Figure 1

Braeuer reports) this had led him to the differential calculus, which he may thus have been the first to apply to economic problems. At a time when German economists liked to criticize Adam Smith for his 'rationalism', Thünen criticized him for his lack of an explicit theory, which he undertook to provide. In mathematical elegance his contribution falls far short of Cournot's, but it exceeds the latter in breadth and depth. It makes Thünen one of the patron saints of modern economics.

A more specific contribution is Thünen's theory of rent, location and resource allocation. In terms of modern economics, its elements can be summarized as follows. Suppose rye is sold in a central city at a given market price P. Production takes place on an unlimited plain of uniform fertility. Transportation to the market over s miles costs ts per bushel. The producer price, p, therefore, declines with increasing distance according to $p = P - ts$, as illustrated in the NE quadrant of Figure 1. Output per acre depends on labour per acre according to $q = q(a)$. At each producer price, the manager selects his method of production in such a way that the marginal product of labour, $q'(a)$, evaluated at the producer price, equals the given (and uniform) wage rate, as described in the NW quadrant. The curve in the SW quadrant expresses the decline in the marginal product of labour as increasingly more labour-intensive methods are applied. The area 'below' the marginal product curve is total product. While the rectangle $q'(a)a$ goes to wages, the shaded residual represents land rent. The curve in the SE quadrant, finally, shows labour intensity as a diminishing function of distance.

The solid curve in Figure 2 graphs land rent from rye production as a diminishing function of distance. Similar rent–distance curves can be constructed for other products like vegetables or lumber. They are represented by, respectively, the dotted and the broken curve. At each distance the farmer will plant the product promising the highest rent. This results in Thünen's famous rings. For a given product there may also be rings of different technologies.

In analysing the comparative statics of the 'isolated state', Thünen shows that lower transportation costs and more

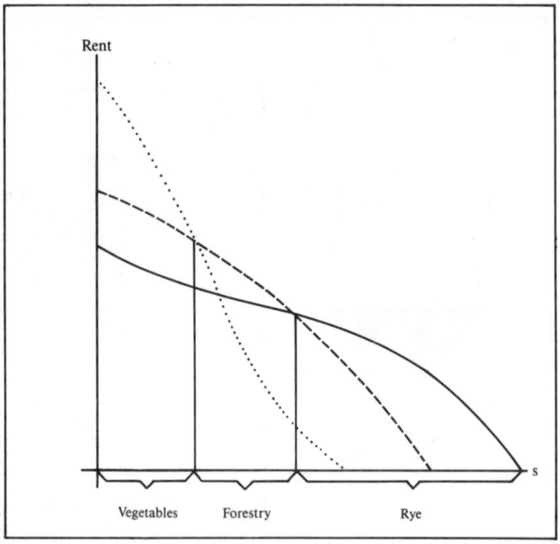

Figure 2

rapidly diminishing returns tend to increase the distance from the city at which a good is produced or a technology is used. It is important to note that Thünen provides not only a theory of location, but also of factor intensities. That the relative efficiency of different technologies depends on market conditions is one of the main propositions he wanted to demonstrate.

The basic model is extended by Thünen in numerous directions. If the required quantities are given, the model determines their market prices. Since the rural workers do not generally pay the given city prices, their money wages will not actually be uniform. Freight costs may not be proportionate to distance. Substitutes and joint products are discussed. To the flows of agricultural products to the market centre, Thünen adds the reverse flows of consumer goods and means of production (like manure) and he pays attention to the unequal quality of the soil. The problem of the spatial distribution of several cities is raised, though not solved. It is finally shown that agricultural protection, by reducing the efficiency of land use, makes both parties worse off and that land taxes do not distort allocation. Despite its richness, Thünen's analysis remains partial in the sense that it does not determine a general spatial equilibrium. His notions about the price mechanism are crude. The long-winded discourse is replete with empirical calculations, relating Thünen's analysis to his account books down to the most minute details.

By applying his optimizing approach to factor inputs, Thünen became one of the originators of the marginal productivity theory of distribution. Using the Ricardian subterfuge of a rentless margin of cultivation, he explains his basic idea in the following words:

> Output p is the joint product of labour and capital. How should the share of each factor in the joint product be measured? We measured the effectiveness of capital by the increment in the output per worker due to an increase in the capital he works with. In this context, labour is constant, but capital is a variable magnitude. Suppose now that this procedure is continued, but in the reverse sense of considering capital as constant and labour as growing. In this case, in a large-scale operation, the effectiveness of labour (the contribution of the worker to output) is recognized from the increment in total output due to the augmentation of workers by one (II, §19).

As in Turgot, the output increments, from both capital and labour, are postulated to decline with an increasing factor input. The profit-maximizing entrepreneur will determine each factor input in such a way that the sales proceeds from the last unit are equal to the given factor price. This implies that at the point of minimum cost the ratio of factor prices is equal to the ratio of what today would be called their marginal products. The word 'marginal' does not occur, but the expressions 'margin' or 'limit' are constantly used.

From the laws that govern actual distribution, Thünen, deeply concerned with the 'social problem', proceeded to the laws that ought to govern it. This led him to the most controversial of his achievements, his famous 'natural wage' formula. In Thünen's economy, per capita output, p (measured in rye), depends on capital per worker, q (measured in terms of the tools a worker can make in a year). Output is divided between the wage, w, and the rental on capital, r, according to $p(q)=w+rq$. In sharp contrast to later notions, savings are supposed to come out of wages while property income is consumed. Specifically, savings are the excess of wages over some subsistence minimum, a. The economy is growing by the construction of new farms at the rent-less margin of cultivation.

With interest rate $(p-w)/wq$, the return on savings is

$$R=\frac{p-w}{wq}(w-a).$$

Thunen's 'natural wage' maximizes R on the assumption of fixed q (and thus p). By equating $\mathrm{d}R/\mathrm{d}w$ to zero, the natural wage is easily determined as the geometric mean of p and a, $w=\sqrt{pa}$.

Thünen's cumbersome exposition has given rise to many misunderstandings. Some (including Marshall) argued that the correct interest rate would have been $(p-w)/q$. In this case, the natural wage turns out to be the arithmetic mean $w=\frac{1}{2}(p+a)$ (as already suggested by Knapp). This criticism would be valid for a one-sector economy in which q is simply a stock of rye. Actually Thünen (as noted by Samuelson) considers a (rudimentary) two-sector economy in which capital goods are produced by labour only (at constant cost). Thünen is right, therefore, in valuing q at the wage rate w.

Another objection (raised, among others, by Wicksell and strongly reiterated by Samuelson) concerns the postulated constancy of q. After all, an increase in w presumably leads to an increase in q (and thus in p). Thünen anticipated this objection, for he supplemented his mathematical derivation, both verbally and by numerical examples, with a cogent explanation of how the overall maximum of R is to be found by searching over different q (and thus p). In fact, if output and marginal productivity wages are allowed to adjust to changes in q, the necessary condition for a maximum, as Dorfman (1986) showed, is again Thünen's square-root formula.

Many have thought Thünen's natural wage to be inconsistent with his own marginal productivity theory. If wages correspond to the marginal product of labour, how can they at the same time be expected to conform to some particular social ideal? This objection, however, loses its force once it is realized that Thünen (as observed by Dickinson) determined the capital/labour ratio at which the marginal productivity wage happens to be equal to his natural wage.

The fundamental objection to the natural wage formula is that it makes no sense for workers to be interested in the returns on their savings only. What Thünen seems to have been groping for, more than a century before Phelps et al., was a 'Golden Rule' of capital accumulation leading to some sort of optimal growth path. (In a one-sector model, the arithmetic variant of the natural wage has indeed such properties; they are analysed in Samuelson, 1986.) He never got it right; in such an optimization problem, the savings parameter, a, can hardly be treated as given. Thünen regarded his formula as important enough to have it engraved on his tombstone in the churchyard of Belitz. It commemorates a brilliant failure.

Part III of the 'Isolated State' is concerned with the efficiency of forest management, thereby extending the incomplete treatment in Part I. The detailed analysis of the optimal spacing of trees is of interest mainly to forest engineers. In analysing the optimal rotation period, however, Thünen makes another important contribution to economic theory. He had already pointed out in Part I that the value of a forest should not be measured by the sales value of the timber if the trees are cut today, but rather by the present value of the timber if the trees are cut and sold at the end of the optimal rotation period. In an efficient operation, the latter exceeds the former; if not, the trees should be cut at once. Efficient forest management is thus interpreted as a problem of capital and interest, providing economic theory with one of its most fruitful paradigms.

Thünen's optimality criterion, in contrast to Wicksell and Fisher, is not the equality of the marginal product of capital and the rate of interest, which, by disregarding the value of land, results in cutting trees too late. As Manz (1986) has shown, Thünen was probably the first to use the correct criterion of maximal land rent, which shortly afterwards was so brilliantly developed by Faustmann. The formula derived in Part III is flawed by incorrect discounting, and the exposition is clumsy. Nevertheless, with respect to substantive content, the capital theory implied in Thünen's forest model is superior to Böhm-Bawerk's and it was not surpassed in economic science before Wicksell.

JÜRG NIEHANS

See also LOCATION OF ECONOMIC ACTIVITY; MARGINAL PRODUCTIVITY THEORY; MONOCENTRIC MODELS IN URBAN ECONOMICS.

SELECTED WORKS

1826–63. *Der isolierte Staat in Beziehung auf Landwirtschaft und Nationalökonomie*. Pt I: *Untersuchungen über den Einfluss, den die Getreidepreise, der Reichtum des Bodens und die Abgaben auf den Ackerbau ausüben*. Hamburg: Perthes, 1826. 2nd edn, Rostock: Leopold, 1842. Pt II: *Der naturgemässe Arbeitslohn und dessen Verhältniss zum Zinsfuss und zur Landrente*. Rostock: Leopold; 1st section 1850; 2nd section 1863. Pt III: *Grundsätze zur Bestimmung der Bodenrente, der vorteilhaftesten Umtriebszeit und des Werts der Holzbestände von verschiedenem Alter für Kieferwaldungen*, Rostock: Leopold, 1863.

1951. *Ausgewählte Texte*. Ed. Walter Braeuer, Die grossen Sozialökonomen, Vol. VII. Meisenheim: Hain, 1951. English translations: Pt I: *Von Thünen's Isolated State*. Ed. Peter Hall, trans. Carla M. Wartenberg, Oxford: Pergamon Press, 1966. Pt II, section 1, in Bernard W. Dempsey, *The Frontier Wage*, Chicago: Loyola University Press, 1960.

BIBLIOGRAPHY

Braeuer, W. 1950. Der Mathematiker-Oekonom. Zur Erinnerung an Johann Heinrich von Thünen. *Kyklos* 4(2/3), 150–71.

Buhr, W. 1983. Mikroökonomische Modelle der von Thünenschen Standorttheorie. *Zeitschrift für Wirtschafts- und Sozialwissenschaften* 103(3), 587–627.

Bulow, F. 1958. Johann Heinrich von Thünen als forstwirtschaftlicher Denker. Zur Erinnerung an den 175. Geburtstag Johann Heinrich von Thünens am 24. Juni 1783. *Weltwirtschaftliches Archiv* 80(2), 183–233.

Dickinson, H.D. 1969. Von Thünen's economics. *Economic Journal* 79(316), December, 894–902.

Dorfman, R. 1986. Comment: P.A. Samuelson, 'Thünen at two hundred'. *Journal of Economic Literature* 24.

Ehrenberg, R. 1905a. Johann Heinrich von Thünen. *Thünen-Archiv. Organ für exakte Wirtschaftsforschung*, Vol. 1.

Ehrenberg, R. 1905b. Thünen's erste wirtschaftswissenschaftliche Studien. *Thünen-Archiv. Organ für exakte Wirtschaftsforschung*, Vol. 1.

Ehrenberg, R. 1905c. Thünen und Thaer. *Thünen-Archiv. Organ für exakte Wirtschaftsforschung*, Vol. 1.

Ehrenberg, R. 1909. Entstehung und Wesen der wissenschaftlichen Methode Johann Heinrich von Thünen's. *Thünen-Archiv. Organ für exakte Wirtschaftsforschung*, Vol. 2.

Franz, G. (ed.) 1958. Johann Heinrich von Thünen. *Zeitschrift für Agrargeschichte und Agrarsoziologie* (Special issue) 6, Frankfurt: DLG.

Knapp, G.F. 1865. *Zur Prüfung der Untersuchungen Thünen's über Lohn und Zinsfuss im isolierten Staate*. Braunschweig: Vieweg.

Krzymowski, R. 1928. Graphical presentation of Thünen's theory of intensity. *Journal of Farm Economics* 10, October, 461–82.

Leigh, A.H. 1946. Von Thünen's theory of distribution and the advent of marginal analysis. *Journal of Political Economy* 54, December, 481–502.

Manz, P. 1986. Forestry economics in the steady-state. The contribution of J.H. von Thünen. *History of Political Economy* 18(2), Summer, 281–90.

Moore, H.L. 1895. Von Thünen's theory of natural wages. *Quarterly Journal of Economics* 9, April, 291–304; July, 388–408.

Salin, E. 1926. Der isolierte Staat 1826–1926. *Zeitschrift für die gesamte Staatswissenschaft* 81(3), 410–31.

Samuelson, P.A. 1983. Thünen at two hundred. *Journal of Economic Literature* 21(4), December, 1468–88.

Samuelson, P.A. 1986. Yes to Robert Dorfman's vindication of Thünen's natural-wage derivation. *Journal of Economic Literature* 24.

Schneider, E. 1959. Johann Heinrich von Thünen und die Wirtschaftstheorie der Gegenwart. *Schriften des Vereins für Sozialpolitik* 14, 14–28.

Schumacher, H. 1868. *Johann Heinrich von Thünen. Ein Forscherleben*. Rostock: Leopold.

Seedorf, W. and Seraphim, H.-J. (eds) 1933. *Johann Heinrich von Thünen zum 150. Geburtstag. Versuch der Würdigung einer Forscherpersönlichkeit*. Rostock: Hinstorffs.

Woermann, E. 1959. Johann Heinrich von Thünen und die landwirtschaftliche Betriebslehre der Gegenwart. *Schriften des Vereins fuř Sozialpolitik*, 14, 28–45.

Tiebout, Charles Mills (1924–1968). Tiebout was born in Norwalk, Connecticut, took his BA from Wesleyan University in 1950, and his PhD from the University of Michigan in 1957. After holding appointments at Northwestern (1954–8) and the University of California at Los Angeles (1958–62), he became professor of economics and business administration at the University of Washington at Seattle in 1962. He died on 16 January 1968. By far his most important work was his 'Pure theory of local public expenditure' which appeared in the October number of the *Journal of Political Economy* for 1956, from which is derived the so-called Tiebout Hypothesis which is the subject of a separate entry in this Dictionary. However, his work on problems in regional and urban economics was more extensive than this one theoretical article on the local provision of public goods might suggest.

For example, in the volume of the *Journal of Political Economy* that carried his essay on public goods, there also appeared a paper which examined the effects of export growth on the pattern of regional economic development. This analysis represents an attempt to apply a Keynesian model of income determination to regional development. Tiebout argued that exports are only one of a number of sources that act to determine the growth of regional income, and through what appears to be the first application of the foreign-trade multiplier to regional analysis he attempts to reach conclusions as to the relative significance of regional exports vis-à-vis regional demand as a source of income generation. Principal among these, is that export-led regional growth is likely to be most effective when the regional base is small.

This paper was followed by work on the construction and use of regional and inter-regional input-output models (1957), which itself produced empirical investigations into the regional distribution of economic activity in the American states of California (1963) and of Washington (1969). The results of these studies were still appearing after Tiebout's early death – especially to be noted in this regard is his inter-regional input-output model of the linkages between the economies of Washington and California (1970). Add to this his work on the regional impact of the Federal government's dispensation of its defence and space budgets (1964), and it becomes fairly clear that to record Tiebout's name solely in regard to his contribution to the pure theory of public goods would be to present a rather one-sided picture of his scientific interests.

MURRAY MILGATE

SELECTED WORKS

1956a. A pure theory of local public expenditures. *Journal of Political Economy* 64, 416–24.

1956b. Exports and regional economic growth. *Journal of Political Economy* 64, 160–64.

1957. Regional and inter-regional input-output models: an appraisal. *Southern Economic Journal* 24, 140–47.

1960a. Community income multipliers: a population growth model. *Journal of Regional Science* 2, 75–84.

1960b. Economies of scale and metropolitan governments. *Review of Economics and Statistics* 42, 442–4.

1963. (With W.L. Hansen.) An intersectoral flows analysis of the Californian economy. *Review of Economics and Statistics* 45, 409–18.

1964. (With R.S. Peterson.) Measuring the impact of regional defence-space expenditures. *Review of Economics and Statistics* 46, 421–8.

1969. An empirical regional input-output model: the state of Washington. *Review of Economics and Statistics* 51, 334–40.

1970. Inter-regional input-output: an empirical California-Washington model. *Journal of Regional Science* 10, 133–52.

Tiebout hypothesis. The essence of the Tiebout hypothesis is that there exists a mechanism for preference revelation regarding publicly provided goods so long as consumer-voters can choose among 'jurisdictions'. The obvious application – the one both Tiebout and his followers had in mind – is that of a large number of autonomous suburban jurisdictions providing those goods which are generally in the domain of local governments, such as primary and secondary education, police and fire protection, sewer and water provision.

Tiebout's basic insight is laid out in his famous 1956 paper. It is worth noting that he offered his model as an antidote to Samuelson's rather gloomy results on the economy's inability to 'find' solutions to the efficient provision of public goods. In Samuelson's (1954) public-goods world (previously laid out by Bowen, 1943)) consumers do not find it in their interest to reveal their preferences for public goods, since preference revelation merely results in a larger payment and essentially no increase in actual provision. As a consequence, voting schemes generally produce a below-optimum level of public goods. But Tiebout has endowed his consumers with another preference-revelation mechanism – mobility. By moving to a jurisdiction with his preferred level of local public services, the consumer simultaneously reveals his preferences and ends up on his demand curve. So long as there is a sufficient variety of jurisdictions, all consumers can get on (or at least close to) their demand curves.

Tiebout's insight is disarmingly simple – if there are different jurisdictions in a metropolitan area which offer, say, different levels of education, then the high demanders will go to the jurisdiction which supplies better schools. But despite this simplicity, he displayed considerable care in his characterization of many aspects of the problem. In defining local public goods, he substitutes non-excludability for Samuelson's famous non-rivalry. He also discussed the behaviour of bureaucrats. And he recognized that his results would break down if there were interjurisdictional spillovers. In other words, his insight was much deeper than 'voting with your feet'.

The Tiebout model lay fallow for over a decade after its publication. Interest was finally sparked by the publication of Oates's (1969) study of the effects of local taxes and school expenditures raised property values by a comparable magnitude. The conclusion was obvious – consumers think about schools and taxes when making their location decisions. Tiebout's statement regarding consumer behaviour appeared vindicated. (As we will see, capitalization plays a far greater role in modern versions of the Tiebout hypothesis than providing empirical support for Tiebout's behavioural claims.)

After publication of Oates's paper, economists began to study the theoretical underpinnings of the Tiebout model with more care. An important weakness in Tiebout's original treatment is that of the pricing mechanism associated with the local public goods. He simply speaks loosely about jurisdictions with high expenditure and high taxes. But without further specification, there is a serious free-rider problem. Consider the case of a jurisdiction with a high property tax rate to finance high-quality schools. Low-income people (who would not buy much housing anyway) could move in, buy the housing they demand, and acquire their high-quality schools at less than cost. This problem was first addressed by Ellickson (1971), who noted that free riding is not a serious problem so long as housing and local public services are sufficiently strong complements. In such a world stratification by public service demand is voluntary. But the conditions for voluntary stratification are very restrictive, and there is no reason to believe that they hold in general.

Then, in a simple but extreme model, Hamilton (1975) noted that free riding could be eliminated by careful use of zoning and building controls. A property tax, coupled with the right dose of zoning, becomes a lump-sum tax, or better yet, a price, with all its attendant efficiency properties. Citizens of a rich jurisdiction could safely tax themselves sufficiently to finance their demanded level of public services, secure in the knowledge that the zoning code would protect them from free riders.

There are two obvious problems even with the less restrictive (1976) version of this model. First, local public goods are assumed to be produced under constant returns to jurisdiction size – as contrasted with Tiebout's U-shaped average cost curve. And second – related to but stronger than the first – there are no impediments to jurisdiction formation. Given these assumptions the world is populated by perfectly stratified (according to public-service demand) jurisdictions in which taxes are equal to average cost. Since the metropolitan area offers a wide range of such jurisdictions, each of which provides services at average (equals marginal) cost, the consumer faces the same budget constraint that he would if local public services were marketed through department stores. The perfect-competition paradigm carries over completely. Note also that the tax instrument is of critical importance if the efficiency or even existence of a Tiebout equilibrium is to be achieved. Westhoff (1977) has analysed the Tiebout world in which the public sector is financed by an income tax (with no zoning or analogous restrictions on entry) and found that equilibria exist only under fairly extreme assumptions.

At this point it is worthwhile to reconsider the capitalization results obtained in Oates (1967), which found (among other things) property value premia in jurisdictions with high school expenditure. Upon reflection, it is clear that this capitalization effect is part of the price people pay for the privilege of consuming high-quality schools. Taxes cover the cost of providing these schools; the presence of capitalization effects implies that the demand price (for the marginal consumer) exceeds production cost. This in turn can be interpreted as evidence of excess demand for high-quality schools. In the flexible-communities model discussed above, this should give rise to high-expenditure community formation, which in turn should eliminate the capitalization effect. Under this interpretation the Oates capitalization effect is the Tiebout analogue to short-run profit in the competitive model.

When community formation is free, when public services are produced according to constant costs, and when stratification (either voluntary or by fiat) is perfect, the Tiebout model is a simple and elegant extension of the competitive model.

There are two major remaining complications of the Tiebout model, each representing a step toward realism and each casting at least some measure of doubt upon the efficiency and even the existence of Tiebout equilibrium. The first complication is the existence of incomplete stratification, possibly due to institutional restrictions on jurisdiction formation or increasing returns in the provision of public services, or to limitations on the ability of jurisdictions to prevent free riders. The second complication concerns the nature of the technology in a fundamental way. There is mounting evidence that the cost of providing many local public services is heavily influenced by characteristics of the jurisdiction's residents, indicating that these characteristics enter into the production function for the services. There has been a great deal of research on the first of these complications, but virtually none on the second. I discuss them in turn below.

If stratification by demand is perfect, and if everybody faces an average-cost (equals marginal cost) price, then local governments have virtually no role to play. Every electoral issue receives unanimous consent (or unanimous rejection). Jurisdiction size is a matter of indifference to current residents (as well as to the local officials). But once we remove the constant-cost and perfect-stratification assumptions we cannot ignore the role of the voting process. And we cannot be sure that migration behaviour of consumers is efficiency-enhancing. Suppose for example that jurisdictions have not achieved sufficient size to exhaust scale economies. A consumer migrating from jurisdiction A to jurisdiction B raises cost in A and reduces cost in B. With non-constant returns the welfare effects of migration are not strictly internal to the migrant. This of course removes the presumption of efficiency from any Tiebout equilibrium. But the presumption of existence is also weakened; depending upon the instruments available to local governments, they might wage war for migrants, manipulating their public-service offerings in efforts to slide down their average cost curves. An interesting set of 'failure' examples is contained in Bewley (1981). In the most interesting of his failure examples, there are fewer jurisdictions than there are desired consumption bundles – either by assumption or through invocation of increasing returns.

The objections raised by Bewley and others suggest the importance of looking at community formation, and at the diversity among communities which would be required to adequately approximate the range of choice envisioned in the Tiebout model. Do the various jurisdictions in our cities generally offer enough choice to satisfy the requirements of the Tiebout model? The first impediment to such diversity would seem to be increasing returns. And to address this we need to examine the range of goods offered by local governments. On such examination, it seems clear that the empirical case for or against Tiebout must be built on public education. Education absorbs almost half of aggregate local spending in the United States, and no other item accounts for more than about 10 per cent. In addition, much of the typical non-education budget is devoted to such things as sewer, water and street maintenance. Although a few decades ago people may well have shunned certain cities because of the state of their sewers, it seems highly unlikely that jurisdiction choice is based on 'shopping' for one's demanded level of sewer service today.

As regards education, the best available evidence suggests that any increasing returns to community size are dissipated at a population of about 10,000. This evidence comes from work by Bergstrom and Goodman (1973) and Borcherding and Deacon (1972), and results from an examination of the relationship between expenditure and community size. Both sets of results find per capita expenditure invariant with community size above about 10,000. The 'simplest' interpretation of this finding is that unit cost does not vary with population. But an alternative explanation is that demand is unit elastic with respect to price, in which case one cannot tell anything about scale economies by regressing expenditure on scale.

Despite doubts about the interpretation of the empirical results on scale economies in education, there is no evidence which clearly points to scale economies beyond some modest scale. In fact, the reason for doubting scale economies extends beyond evidence from the expenditure–scale regressions described above. In the presence of scale economies, large jurisdictions should have a cost advantage over small ones, which should be reflected in property values. The failure of capitalization studies to find such an effect lends support to the presumption of constant returns.

All of this means that we have no particular reason to believe that scale economies are an impediment to wide community choice. Of course it is still possible that jurisdiction variety fails to arise for some other reason. Henderson (1985), however, has examined the data on jurisdiction formation and has discovered, somewhat surprisingly, that jurisdiction formation in most urban areas approximates population growth.

In conclusion, the concerns over community variety and formation raised by Bewley and others need to be taken seriously. But the evidence for scale economies, and for insufficient community variety, is not fully convincing.

The next issue to be addressed concerns the nature of the production function for education. Suppose we accept the view expressed above that education is the only good for which Tiebout-sorting and provision are relevant. Further, we will accept the notion that education is produced under constant returns to community size. One fundamental question, which has not been addressed by any of the Tiebout modellers, remains to be addressed.

Suppose the technology for producing education contains child and parent characteristics as one of its arguments. Both the casual and published evidence for this is overwhelming. Casual support can be found by noting that per-pupil expenditure on education is frequently higher in central cities than in their suburbs; yet nobody thinks education quality is higher in central cities. The statistical evidence is at least as compelling. Whenever one regresses a measure of education output – say, test sources or annual improvements in test scores, characteristics of parents and peers have strong explanatory power. (Indeed, the embarrassing aspect of these studies is that measures of purchased inputs, such as class size and teacher characteristics, frequently have no explanatory power at all.) (See Hanushek (1986) for a thorough review of the economics of schooling.) Then we cannot model the Tiebout world as a choice set of communities offering education at a certain price, waiting like grocers for households to purchase their wares. For the quality of education depends upon the characteristics of the households who arrive.

It is highly likely in such a world that voluntary Tiebout sorting is unstable, as those households with 'bad' production inputs chase those with 'good' inputs. The problem is that sorting according to quantity demanded is not the end of the story; stability may well require that we separate high demanders who are cheap to educate from high demanders who are expensive to educate.

A second problem arises when we consider efficiency. Much like the world with increasing returns, we now have two efficiency objectives to worry about. First, we continue to have the traditional Tiebout objective of satisfying a variety of demands with a variety of offerings. But we now have a second objective, namely minimizing cost. Depending on the nature of the technology, there may be large cost savings associated with (say) placing a few high-motivation children in each classroom. The performance gains (cost savings) achieved by the other students might more than compensate the increased cost of educating these children in a non-enriched environment. In such a world there are externalities associated with ability-mixing. As there seems to be no obvious mechanism for internalizing these externalities, we have no reason to anticipate that Tiebout sorting will lead to an efficient outcome, even under the most favourable assumptions on every aspect of the problem except the technology.

BRUCE W. HAMILTON

See also LOCAL PUBLIC FINANCE; PROPERTY TAXATION; PUBLIC FINANCE; REGIONAL ECONOMICS; URBAN ECONOMICS.

BIBLIOGRAPHY

Bergstrom, T. and Goodman, R. 1973. Private demand for public goods. *American Economic Review* 63, June, 280–96.

Bewley, T.F. 1981. A critique of Tiebout's theory of local public expenditures. *Econometrica* 49, May, 713–40.

Borcherding, T. and Deacon, R. 1972. The demand for the services of non-Federal Governments. *American Economic Review*, 62, December, 891–901.

Bowen, H.R. 1943. The interpretation of voting in the allocation of economic resources. *Quarterly Journal of Economics* 58, November, 27–48.

Ellickson, B. 1971. Jurisdictional fragmentation and residential choice. *American Economic Review* 61, December, 334–9.

Hamilton, B.W. 1975. Zoning and property taxation in a system of local governments. *Urban Studies* 12(2), June, 205–11.

Hamilton, B.W. 1976. Capitalization of intrajurisdictional differences in local tax prices. *American Economic Review* 66(5), December, 743–53.

Hanushek, E.A. 1986. The economics of schooling. *Journal of Economic Literature* 24, September, 1141–77.

Henderson, J.V. 1985. The Tiebout Model: bring back the entrepreneurs. *Journal of Political Economy* 93, April, 248–57.

Oates, W.E. 1969. The effects of property taxes and local public spending on property values: an empirical study of tax capitalization and the Tiebout hypothesis. *Journal of Political Economy* 77(8), November–December, 957–71.

Samuelson, P.A. 1954. The pure theory of public expenditure. *Review of Economics and Statistics* 36, November, 387–9.

Tiebout, C. 1956. A pure theory of local expenditures. *Journal of Political Economy* 64, October, 416–24.

Westnoff, F. 1977. Existence of equilibria in economies with a local public good. *Journal of Economic Theory* 14, 84–112.

tight money. This term, like many others in financial economics, has no single and precise meaning because over the years debate has come inevitably to reflect the complexity of financial realities. But some pointers towards definition may usefully be made. First, the reference is to tightness of the supply of money relative to the demand for it. Recognition of this point, elementary yet easily overlooked in the heat of practical controversy, immediately indicates the problem that tightness/ease is typically difficult to identify – much less to measure – with any confidence. For example, while interest-rate levels are frequently regarded as appropriate indicators, low and/or falling rates can indicate monetary ease if they reflect supply expanding more rapidly than demand, but could reflect tightness if demand has contracted – say because of collapsing sales and profits – so that equilibrium interest rate levels would be lower still.

Second, we must ask *what* is in tight supply. In some earlier phases of discussion, notably in the late 19th and early 20th centuries, attention was focused on the inelasticity of the supply of currency under gold-standard régimes, in the face of rising demand to finance transactions as boom conditions developed, and of the need to bolster confidence as those conditions gave way to liquidity difficulties around the peak of the cycle. Thus (over-)tight money was seen as evidence of failure to solve one aspect of the problem of sound money.

The abandonment of the gold standard, and the development of smoothing techniques by central banks, caused this particular difficulty to fade. In later phases, attention has shifted towards inelasticity of the supply of bank credit, whether in the sense of the flow of bank lending or in that of the stock of bank deposits, and whether occurring as a result of the autonomous operation of the market or of policy measures taken by the monetary authorities. Though definition is often not made explicit, most discussion probably has made implicit reference to policy-induced restriction of the flow of bank lending, from the supply side. Such restriction would normally be accompanied by a tendency for short-term interest rates to rise relative to what would otherwise have occurred, but probably also by expansion of Keynes's 'fringe of unsatisfied borrowers' in imperfect credit markets. Dear money, that is to say, may be caused by tightness of money, but tightness is not necessarily fully reflected in price.

This last point draws our attention to the undoubted fact that the impact of tight money is by no means likely to be evenly distributed over the population of transactors in an economy. Awareness of this fact has doubtless been one reason prompting the question (G.L. Bach, in Carson, 1963),

'How discriminatory is tight money?' Before outlining Bach's own answer to this question, it is necessary to emphasize that his discussion relates to the earlier of two phases into which the post-1945 history of this issue naturally divides. In that earlier phase, covering roughly the years to 1970, 'tightness' of money was both an occasional and (by later standards) a distinctly modest phenomenon. Since 1970, in the era of anti-inflationary monetary targets, tightness has tended to be both more continuous and more severe.

Bach's evidence in fact related primarily to the years 1955–7, and to the USA. He found little evidence to support one common hypothesis, that tight money caused discrimination against small business borrowers in favour of larger ones – a conclusion reinforced by indications that, in the conditions of this earlier phase at least, small businesses could respond to restrictions on the supply of bank credit by taking relatively more net trade credit. On the other hand, the investigation provided additional support for another form of discrimination that is so widely recognized, especially for the earlier phase, as to be hardly open to dispute: because interest rates in the mortgage market were, for institutional reasons, 'sticky' relative to market rates, the overall availability of mortgage finance was undoubtedly somewhat reduced in periods of relative monetary tightness.

One other kind of discriminatory effect of tight money and higher-than-otherwise interest rates has been widely discussed. This is the effect on income distribution. Banks, for example, have been supposed to gain from tight money, on account of the so-called endowment element arising from their zero-interest deposits on current account, so that generally rising interest rates tended to increase the differential between average income on assets and average cost of liabilities. This argument was doubtless valid, though its effects were offset in periods of monetary ease. Its importance has in any case declined with the spread (from the early 1980s) of mechanisms for paying interest on current accounts.

More generally, tight money has been argued to have differential implications for creditors and debtors. Their nature, however, is ambiguous. On the creditor side, for example, new lenders benefit from higher interest rates, but existing lenders may suffer from decline in the market value of fixed-interest assets. These changes are mirrored on the debtor side, but individuals are frequently both debtors and creditors, and groups of transactors (e.g. the company sector) will certainly include both. So, while it must be recognized that tight money (like the inflationary situation it is usually designed to counter) will cause some to gain and others to lose, no cogent generalization is possible.

In any case, the major controversy over tight money concerns not its differential, but its general, impact. Any discriminatory effects are more or less incidental to its normal purpose (when it results from policy decisions) of reducing the level of aggregate demand and associated inflationary pressures in the economy. In examining this matter, it is again desirable to distinguish between the earlier and the later phases of the post-1945 era.

Before 1970, Gurley and Shaw (1960) had provided rigorous exposition of a theoretical standpoint, applied in the 1959 Radcliffe Report to then-contemporary UK institutions and conventions, which postulated that the effects of limited tightness of money could be circumvented by economic agents with relative ease. The main focus of the argument was on the operation of financial intermediaries other than banks, many of which (notably, but far from exclusively, UK building societies and US savings and loan associations) issued liabilities that were relatively close substitutes for bank deposits – certainly as stores of value, and to some extent also as exchange media. These non-bank financial intermediaries could attract additional deposits by relatively small interest-rate increases (the bank-deposit preference schedule was interest-elastic owing to the existence of close substitutes), and use the funds to finance loans to agents affected by a squeeze on bank credit. So, the effects of tight money would be neutralized by rerouting of fund flows, reflected in rising velocity of circulation, and in interest-rate increases that tended to be insignificant given a relatively interest-inelastic marginal efficiency of capital schedule.

The force of such arguments clearly depended, *inter alia*, on the maintenance of confidence by (real) investors, and that confidence in turn rested in part on the absence of threats to the stability of the financial system. Periods of more severe monetary tightness since about 1970 have been characterized by such threats (cf. the 1974 secondary banking crisis in the UK and elsewhere), in a manner giving practical force to theoretical ideas associated – in the modern period – primarily with the writings of Hyman Minsky, progenitor of the so-called 'financial instability thesis'. One central strand of these ideas relates to the pattern of company finance during the cycle upswing. It sees non-financial companies as prone, in this phase, to euphoric expectations which result in financing patterns (relatively more external finance compared with internal, bond finance compared with equity, short-term borrowing compared with long) causing deterioration of the financial strength of balance-sheet positions. Because rather similar influences affect the condition of financial intermediaries, bank and non-bank, the liquidity problems typical of the cycle peak can easily cause a finance shortfall resulting in inability to meet by due date cash-payment commitments that prove to have been based on over-optimistic expectations. In such 'fragile' circumstances, tight money can cause insolvency and bankruptcy, tending to spread because of interdependence between transactors (A's ability to fulfil commitments to B is undermined if C fails to fulfil commitments to A ...). Therefore central banks will have powerful incentive to acquiesce in easy money conditions – which, if crisis is indeed thereby forestalled, may be followed by a new inflationary boom in a sequence that monetarist models inevitably misinterpret.

The argument just outlined explains why central banks tend, at least in the late upswing and peak phases of the cycle, to give priority to what the present writer has labelled *support* objectives as opposed to those *control* objectives whose potential has been inappropriately over-emphasized by monetarist/neoclassical theorizing. In turn, the necessary concern with support objectives explains why, even in the later postwar phase of supposedly continuous tight contra-inflationary money supply targets, the effective degree of tightness (in any case impossible to measure with any precision) has probably tended to be less than it might appear on a superficial view. The Bank of England in the first half of the 1980s, for example, has responded to high private sector demand for bank loans by 'overfunding' (selling more government debt than needed to finance current spending requirements); thus negative bank lending to the public sector, in the face of high levels of lending to the private sector, facilitates the achievement of money supply targets. But to offset the resultant squeeze on bank reserve ratios, the Bank has been ready to buy commercial bills of exchange from the banks, adding to its so-called 'bill mountain', but permitting private sector borrowing to continue with little effective check.

Emphasis on this kind of sophisticated combination of tightening/loosening measures, however, should not be exaggerated to the point of arguing that tightness of money has never been sufficient to frustrate private sector spending plans. There have been periods (during what we have called the later, post-1970 phase) in which, partly to persuade markets to absorb enough government debt to enable money-supply targets to be met, apparent real interest rates have been at levels extremely high by reference both to long-term historical experience and to current profit levels. This may well have been due as much to market reaction against earlier experience of negative real interest rates as to the direct effects of current monetary policy, so that it is debatable how far the phenomenon should be regarded as the outcome of tight money; it might more appropriately be regarded as the price of earlier weakness in such areas as fiscal and incomes policies. Be that as it may, there is little doubt that in such periods private-sector agents have suffered considerable damage (see, e.g. Miller and Lonie, 1978). High real interest rates reduce the profitability of the operations of existing borrowers. *Falling* inflation rates adversely affect cash-flow projections for operations proposed to be financed by new loans. There is a general tendency to decline of credit-worthiness, which explains how valid cries of pain from borrowers and valid claims by banks to be meeting all credit-worthy demands can co-exist, and probably also is part of the explanation of generally rising levels of company liquidations and bankruptcies. The fruits of inflation are bitter, but on the view taken here monetarist doctrine is inadequate to explicate either inflation's cause or its cure.

A.B. Cramp

See also DEAR MONEY.

BIBLIOGRAPHY

Carson, D. ed. 1963. *Banking and Monetary Studies*. Homewood: Richard D. Irwin.

Gurley, J.G. and Shaw, E.S. 1960. *Money in a Theory of Finance*. Washington, DC: Brookings Institution.

Miller, E. and Lonie, A. 1978. *Micro-economic Effects of Monetary Policy*. London: Martin Robertson.

time preference. Time preference is the insight that people prefer 'present goods' (goods available for use at present) to 'future goods' (present expectations of goods becoming available at some date in the future), and that the social rate of time preference, the result of the interactions of individual time preference schedules, will determine and be equal to the pure rate of interest in a society. The economy is pervaded by a time market for present as against future goods, not only in the market for loans (in which creditors trade present money for the right to receive money in the future), but also as a 'natural rate' in all processes of production. For capitalists pay out present money to buy or rent land, capital goods, and raw materials, and to hire labour (as well as buying labour outright in a system of slavery), thereby purchasing expectations of future revenue from the eventual sales of product. Long-run profit rates and rates of return on capital are therefore forms of interest rate. As businessmen seek to gain profits and avoid losses, the economy will tend toward a general equilibrium, in which all interest rates and rates of return will be equal, and hence there will be no pure entrepreneurial profits or losses.

In centuries of wrestling with the vexed question of the justification of interest, the Catholic scholastic philosophers arrived at highly sophisticated explanations and justifications of return on capital, including risk and the opportunity cost of profit foregone. But they had extreme difficulty with the interest on a riskless loan, and hence denounced all such interest as sinful and usurious.

Some of the later scholastics, however, in their more favourable view of usury, began to approach a time preference explanation of interest. During a comprehensive demolition of the standard arguments for the prohibition of usury in his *Treatise on Contracts* (1499), Conrad Summenhart (1465–1511), theologian at the University of Tübingen, used time preference to justify the purchase of a discounted debt, even if the debt be newly created. When someone pays \$100 for the right to obtain \$110 at a future date, the buyer (lender) doesn't profit usuriously from the loan because both he and the seller (borrower) value the future \$110 as being worth \$100 at the present time (Noonan, 1957).

A half-century later, the distinguished Dominican canon lawyer and monetary theorist at the University of Salamanca, Martin de Azpilcueta Navarrus (1493–1586) clearly set forth the concept of time preference, but failed to apply it to a defence of usury. In his *Commentary on Usury* (1556), Azpilcueta pointed out that a present good, such as money, will naturally be worth more on the market than future goods, that is, claims to money in the future. As Azpilcueta put it:

> a claim on something is worth less than the thing itself, and . . . it is plain that that which is not usable for a year is less valuable than something of the same quality which is usable at once (Gordon, 1975, p. 215).

At about the same time, the Italian humanist and politician Gian Francesco Lottini da Volterra, in his handbook of advice to princes, *Avvedimenti civili* (1574), discovered time preference. Unfortunately, Lottini also inaugurated the tradition of moralistically deploring time preference as an over-estimation of a present that can be grasped immediately by the senses (Kauder, 1965, pp. 19–22).

Two centuries later, the Neapolitan abbé, Ferdinando Galiani (1728–87) revived the rudiments of time-preference in his *Della Moneta* (1751) (Monroe, 1924). Galiani pointed out that just as the exchange rate of two currencies equates the value of a present and a spatially distant money, so the rate of interest equates present with future, or temporally distant, money. What is being equated is not physical properties, but subjective values in the minds of individuals.

These scattered hints scarcely prepare one for the remarkable development of a full-scale time preference theory of interest by the French statesman, Anne Robert Jacques Turgot (1727–81), who, in a relatively few hastily written contributions, anticipated almost completely the later Austrian theory of capital and interest (Turgot, 1977). In the course of a paper defending usury, Turgot asked: why are borrowers willing to pay an interest premium for the use of money? The focus should not be on the amount of metal repaid but on the usefulness of the money to the lender and borrower. In particular, Turgot compares the 'difference in usefulness which exists at the date of borrowing between a sum currently owned and an equal sum which is to be received at a distant date', and notes the well-known motto, 'a bird in the hand is better than two in the bush'. Since the sum of money owned now 'is preferable to the assurance of receiving a similar sum in one or severai years' time', returning the same principal means that the lender 'gives the money and receives only an assurance'. Therefore, interest compensates for this difference in value by a sum proportionate to the length of the delay. Turgot added that what must be compared in a loan transaction is not the value of money lent with the value repaid, but rather the 'value of the *promise* of a sum of money compared to the value of money available now' (Turgot, 1977, pp. 158–9).

In addition, Turgot was apparently the first to arrive at the concept of *capitalization*, a corollary to time preference, which holds that the present capital value of any durable good will tend to equal the sum of its expected annual rents, or returns, discounted by the market rate of time preference, or rate of interest.

Turgot also pioneered in analysing the relation between the quantity of money and interest rates. If an increased supply of money goes to low time preference people, then the increased proportion of savings to consumption lowers time preference and hence interest rates fall while prices rise. But if an increased quantity goes into the hands of high time preference people, the opposite would happen and interest rates would rise along with prices. Generally, over recent centuries, he noted, the spirit of thrift has been growing in Europe and hence time preference rates and interest rates have tended to fall.

One of the notable injustices in the historiography of economic thought was Böhm-Bawerk's brusque dismissal in 1884 of Turgot's anticipation of his own time-preference theory of interest as merely a 'land fructification theory' (Böhm-Bawerk, I, 1959). Partly this dismissal stemmed from Böhm's methodology of clearing the ground for his own positive theory of interest by demolishing, and hence sometimes doing injustice to, his own forerunners (Wicksell, 1911, p. 177). The unfairness is particularly glaring in the case of Turgot, because we now know that in 1876, only eight years before the publication of his history of theories of interest, Böhm-Bawerk wrote a glowing tribute to Turgot's theory of interest in an as yet unpublished paper in Karl Knies's seminar at the University of Heidelberg (Turgot, 1977, pp. xxix–xxx).

In the course of his demolition of the Ricardo–James Mill labour theory of value on behalf of a subjective utility theory, Samuel Bailey (1825) clearly set forth the concept of time preference. Rebutting Mill's statement that time, as a 'mere abstract word', could not add to value, Bailey declared that 'we generally prefer a present pleasure or enjoyment to a distant one', and therefore prefer present goods to waiting for goods to arrive in the future. Bailey, however, did not go on to apply his insight to interest.

In the mid–1830s, the Irish economist Samuel Mountifort Longfield worked out the later Austrian theory of capital as performing the service for workers of supplying money at present instead of waiting for the future when the product will be sold. In turn the capitalist receives from the workers a time discount from their productivity. As Longfield put it, the capitalist

> pays the wages immediately, and in return receives the value of [the worker's] labour,... [which] is greater than the wages of that labour. The difference is the profit made by the capitalist for his advances ... as it were, the discount which the labourer pays for prompt payment (Longfield, 1834).

The 'pre-Austrian' time analysis of capital and interest was most fully worked out, in the same year 1834, by the Scottish and Canadian eccentric John Rae (1786–1872). In the course of attempting an anti-Smithian defence of the protective tariff, Rae, in his *Some New Principles on the Subject of Political Economy* (1834), developed the Böhm-Bawerkian time analysis of capital, pointing out that investment lengthens the time involved in the processes of production. Rae noted that the capitalist must weigh the greater productivity of longer production processes against waiting for them to come to fruition. Capitalists will sacrifice present money for a greater return in the future, the difference – the interest return – reflecting the social rate of time preference. Rae saw that people's time preference rates reflect their cultural and psychological wilingness to take a shorter or longer view of the future. His moral preferences were clearly with the low time preference thrifty as against the high time preference people who suffer from a 'defect of the imagination'. Rae's analysis had little impact on economics until resurrected at the turn of the 20th century, whereupon it was generously hailed in the later editions of Böhm-Bawerk's history of interest theories (Böhm-Bawerk, I, 1959).

Time preference, as a concept and as a foundation for the explanation of interest, has been an outstanding feature of the Austrian School of economics. Its founder, Carl Menger (1840–1921), enunciated the concept of time preference in 1871, pointing out that satisfying the immediate needs of life and health are necessarily prerequisites for satisfying more remote future needs. In addition, Menger declared, 'all experience teaches that we humans consider a present pleasure, or one expected in the near future, more important than one of the same intensity which is not expected to occur until some more distant time' (Wicksell, 1924, p. 195; Menger, 1871, pp. 153–54). But Menger never extended time preference from his value theory to a theory of interest; and when his follower Böhm-Bawerk did so, he peevishly deleted this discussion from the second edition of his *Principles of Economics* (Wicksell, 1924, pp. 195–6).

Böhm-Bawerk's *Capital and Interest* (1884) is the *locus classicus* of the time preference theory of interest. In his first, historical volume, he demolished all other theories, in particular the productivity theory of interest; but five years later, in his *Positive Theory of Capital* (1889), Böhm brought back the productivity theory in an attempt to combine it with a time preference explanation of interest (Böhm-Bawerk, I, II, 1959). In his 'three grounds' for the explanation of interest, time preference constituted two, and the greater productivity of longer processes of production the third, Böhm ironically placing greatest importance upon the third ground. Influenced strongly by Böhm-Bawerk, Irving Fisher increasingly took the same path of stressing the marginal productivity of capital as the main determinant of interest (Fisher, 1907, 1930).

With the work of Böhm-Bawerk and Fisher, the modern theory of interest was set squarely on the path of placing time preference in a subordinate role in the explanation of interest: determining only the rate of consumer loans, and the supply of consumer savings, while the alleged productivity of capital determines the more important demand for loans and for savings. Hence, modern interest theory fails to integrate interest on consumer loans and producer's returns into a coherent explanation.

In contrast, Frank A. Fetter, building on Böhm-Bawerk, completely discarded productivity as an explanation of interest and constructed an integrated theory of value and distribution in which interest is determined solely by time preference, while marginal productivity determines the 'rental prices' of the factors of production (Fetter, 1915, 1977). In his outstanding critique of Böhm-Bawerk, Fetter pointed out a fundamental error of the third ground in trying to explain the return on capital as 'present goods' earning a return for their productivity in the future; instead, capital goods are *future* goods, since they are only valuable in the expectation of being used to produce goods that will be sold to the consumer at a future date (Fetter, 1902). One way of seeing the fallacy of a productivity explanation of interest is to look at the typical practice of any current microeconomics text: after explaining marginal productivity as determining the demand curve for factors with wage rates on the y-axis, the textbook airily shifts to interest rates on the y-axis to illustrate the marginal productivity determination of interest. But the analog on the y-axis should not be interest, which is a ratio and not a price, but rather the *rental price* (price per unit time) of a capital good. Thus, interest remains totally unexplained. In short, as Fetter pointed out, marginal productivity determines rental prices, and time preference determines the rate of interest, while the capital value of a factor of production is the expected sum of future rents from a durable factor discounted by the rate of time preference or interest.

The leading economist adopting Fetter's pure time preference view of interest was Ludwig von Mises, in his *Human Action* (Mises, 1949). Mises amended the theory in two important ways. First, he rid the concept of its moralistic tone which had been continued by Böhm-Bawerk, implicitly criticizing people for 'under'-estimating the future. Mises made clear that a positive time preference rate is an essential attribute of human nature. Secondly, and as a corollary, whereas Fetter believed that people could have either positive or negative rates of time preference, Mises demonstrated that a positive rate is deducible from the fact of human action, since by the very nature of a goal or an end people wish to achieve that goal as soon as possible.

MURRAY N. ROTHBARD

See also BÖHM-BAWERK, EUGEN VON; FISHER, IRVING; IMPATIENCE.

BIBLIOGRAPHY

Bailey, S. 1825. *A Critical Dissertation on the Nature, Measure, and Causes of Value*. New York: Augustus M. Kelley, 1967.

Böhm-Bawerk, E. von. 1884–9. *Capital and Interest*, Vols I and II. 4th edn, South Holland, Ill.: Libertarian Press, 1959.

Fetter, F.A. 1902. The 'Roundabout process' in the interest theory. *Quarterly Journal of Economics* 17, November, 163–80. Reprinted in F.A. Fetter, *Capital, Interest and Rent: Essays in the Theory of Distribution*, ed. M. Rothbard, Kansas City: Sheed Andrews and McMeel, 1977.

Fetter, F.A. 1915. *Economic Principles*, Vol I. New York: The Century Co.

Fetter, F.A. 1977. *Capital, Interest, and Rent: Essays in the Theory of Distribution*. Ed. M. Rothbard, Kansas City: Sheed Andrews and McMeel.

Fisher, I. 1907. *The Rate of Interest*. New York: Macmillan.

Fisher, I. 1930. *The Theory of Interest*. New York: Kelley & Millman, 1954.

Gordon, B. 1975. *Economic Analysis Before Adam Smith; Hesiod to Lessius*. New York: Barnes & Noble.

Kauder, E. 1965. *A History of Marginal Utility Theory*. Princeton: Princeton University Press.

Longfield, S.M. 1971. *The Economic Writings of Mountifort Longfield*. Ed. R.D.C. Black, Clifton, NJ: Augustus M. Kelley.

Menger, C. 1871. *Principles of Economics*. Ed. J. Dingwall and B. Hoselitz, Glencoe, Ill.: Free Press, 1950.

Mises, L. von. 1949. *Human Action: a treatise on economics*. 3rd revised edn, Chicago: Regnery, 1966.

Monroe, A. (ed.) 1924. *Early Economic Thought*. Cambridge, Mass.: Harvard University Press.

Noonan, J.T., Jr. 1957. *The Scholastic Analysis of Usury*. Cambridge, Mass.: Harvard University Press.

Rae, J. 1834. *Some New Principles on the Subject of Political Economy*. In *John Rae: Political Economist*, ed. R.W. James, Toronto: University of Toronto Press, 1965.

Turgot, A.R.J. 1977. *The Economics of A.R.J. Turgot*. Ed. P.D. Groenewegen, The Hague: Martinus Nijhoff.

Wicksell, K. 1911. Böhm-Bawerk's theory of interest. In K. Wicksell, *Selected Papers on Economic Theory*, ed. E. Lindahl, Cambridge, Mass.: Harvard University Press, 1958.

Wicksell, K. 1924. The new edition of Menger's *Grundsatze*. In K. Wicksell, *Selected Papers on Economic Theory*, ed. E. Lindahl, Cambridge, Mass.: Harvard University Press, 1958.

time series analysis. Any series of observations ordered along a single dimension, such as time, may be thought of as a time series. The emphasis in time series analysis is the study of dependence among the observations at different points in time. What distinguishes time series analysis from general multivariate analysis is precisely the temporal order imposed on the observations. Many economic variables, such as prices, sales, stocks, GNP and its components, are observed over time; in addition to being interested in the interrelationships among these variables, we are also concerned with relationships among the current and past values of one or more of them, that is, relationships over time.

The study of time series of, for example, astronomical observations predates recorded history. Early writers on economic subjects occasionally made explicit reference to astronomy as the source of their ideas. For example, in 1838 Cournot said, 'As in astronomy, it is necessary to recognize the *secular* variations which are independent of the periodic variations' (Cournot, 1838, translation 1927). Jevons (1884) remarks that his study of short-term fluctuations uses the methods of astronomy and meteorology. During the 19th century interest in, and analysis of, social and economic time series evolved independently of parallel developments in astronomy and meteorology. (See Nerlove et al., 1979, pp. 1–21, for an historical survey.)

One of the earliest methods of analysing time series thought to exhibit some form of periodicity is harmonic analysis. In this type of analysis, the time series, or some simple transformation of it, is assumed to be the result of superposition of sine and cosine waves of different frequencies. However, since summing a finite number of such strictly periodic functions always results in a perfectly periodic series, which is seldom observed in practice, it is usual to add a stochastic component, sometimes called 'noise'. Thus one is led to search for 'hidden periodicities', that is the unknown frequencies and amplitudes of sinusoidal fluctuations hidden amidst noise. The method for doing so is *periodogram analysis*, suggested by Stokes (1879) and used by Schuster (1898) to analyse sunspot data and later by others, principally William Beveridge (1921, 1922), to analyse economic time series.

Spectral analysis is a modernized version of periodogram analysis modified to take account of the stochastic nature of the entire time series, not just the noise component. If it is assumed that economic time series are fully stochastic, it follows that the older technique is inappropriate to their analysis and that considerable difficulties in the interpretation of the periodograms of economic series may be encountered.

At the time when harmonic analysis proved to be inadequate for the analysis of economic and social time series, another way of characterizing such series was suggested, more or less simultaneously, by the Russian statistician and economist, Eugen Slutsky (1927), and the British statistician, G.U. Yule (1921, 1926, 1927). Slutsky and Yule showed that if we begin with a series of purely random numbers and then take sums or differences, weighted or unweighted, of such numbers, the new series so produced has many of the apparent cyclic properties that were thought at the time to characterize economic and other time series. Such sums or differences of purely random numbers and sums or differences of the resulting series are the basis for the autoregressive moving-average (ARMA) processes which are the basis for modelling many kinds of time series. There is, however, nothing incompatible with looking at time series as generated by processes of this sort and the way spectral analysis looks at them. The remainder of this entry explores the complementarities of these two approaches to the analysis of economic time series.

1. BASIC THEORY

1.1 Stationarity and ergodicity of time series processes. Consider a random variable x_t, where $t \in T$, the set of integers; the infinite vector $\{x_t, t \in T\}$ is called a discrete time series. Let $T_k = \{t_1, \ldots, t_k\}$ be a subset of k elements of T; the distribution of the finite dimensional vector $\{x_t, t \in T_k\}$ is a well-defined multivariate distribution function, $F_{T_k}(\cdot)$. The time series $\{x_t, t \in T\}$ is said to be *strictly stationary* if, for any finite subset T_k of T and any integer τ, the distribution function of $\{x_t, t \in T_k + \tau\}$ is the same as the distribution function of $\{x_t, t \in T_k\}$ that is, for an arbitrary finite subset of the index set. The distribution function of the finite vector of observations on x_t is invariant with respect to the origin from which time is measured. All the unconditional moments of the distribution function, if they exist, are independent of the index t; in particular,

$$Ex_t = \mu$$
$$\gamma(\tau) = E[x_t - \mu][x_{t+\tau} - \mu], \tag{1}$$

where $\gamma(\tau)$ is the autocovariance function and depends only on the difference in indices, τ. Time-series processes for which (1) holds, but which are not necessarily strictly stationary according to the definition above, are said to be *weakly stationary, covariance stationary*, or *stationary to the second order*.

Time-series processes for which $F_{T_k}(\cdot)$ is multivariate normal for any subset T_k of T are called *Gaussian processes*. For Gaussian processes covariance or weak stationarity implies strong stationarity.

In practice, we usually observe only a finite subset of one realization of a time series (from a set of many potential realizations corresponding to drawings from $F_{T_k}(\cdot)$). The question is whether a valid inference can be made about the movements of $F_{T_k}(\cdot)$ from one such observation, for example, from the time averages of sums or sums of products of the observed values. If the process is what is known as *ergodic*, time averages of functions of the observations on the time series at $k = N$ time points converge in mean square to the corresponding expectations. (See Priestley, 1981, pp. 340–43; Doob, 1953, p. 465.) While ergodicity is a deep mathematical property of the distribution function characterizing the time series in question, its meaning for a stationary time series is essentially independence of observations far enough apart in time. Thus, for example, the series generated by $x_t = r\, e^{i(\lambda t + \phi)}$, where $r \sim N(\mu, 1)$, λ fixed, and ϕ uniformly distributed on the interval $[-\pi, \pi]$ is stationary but not ergodic.

1.2 The Wold decomposition and general linear processes. Let $\{\epsilon_t\}$ be a time series generated by a process of independent, identically distributed random variables with zero mean and variance σ^2. (Such a series is often called 'white noise'.) The infinite, one-sided moving average (MA)

$$x_t = \sum_{j=0}^{\infty} b_j \epsilon_{t-j}, \quad \sum_{j=0}^{\infty} b_j^2 < \infty, \quad b_0 = 1, \tag{2}$$

is also a well-defined stationary process with mean 0 and variance $\sigma^2 \Sigma_0^\infty b_j^2$. Processes of this form and, more generally, processes based on an infinite two-sided MA of the same form are called *linear processes*, are always ergodic, and play a key role in time series analysis (Hannan, 1970).

The importance of the process (2) is underscored by the Wold Decomposition Theorem (1938) which states that any weakly stationary process may be decomposed into two mutually uncorrelated component processes, one an infinite one-sided MA of the form (2) and the other a so-called linearly deterministic process, future values of which can be predicted exactly by some linear function of past observations. The linearly deterministic component is non-ergodic.

2. LINEAR PROCESSES IN TIME AND FREQUENCY DOMAINS

2.1 Autocovariance and autocovariance generating functions. The autocovariance function of a stationary process, defined in (1) above, or its matrix generalization for vector processes, provides the basic representation of time dependence for weakly stationary processes. For the stationary process defined in (2), it is

$$\gamma(\tau) = \sigma^2 \sum_{j=0}^{\infty} b_j b_{j+\tau}. \tag{3}$$

The autocovariance generating transform is defined as

$$g(z) = \sum_{-\infty}^{\infty} \gamma(\tau) z^\tau \tag{4}$$

in whatever region of the complex plane the series on the right-hand side converges. If the series $\{x_t\}$ is covariance stationary, convergence will occur in an annulus about the unit circle. The autocovariance generating transform for the one-sided MA defined in (2) is

$$g(z) = \sigma^2 B(z) B(z^{-1}) \tag{5}$$

where

$$B(z) = \sum_{k=0}^{\infty} b_k z^k.$$

If $B(z)$ has no zeros on the unit circle, the process defined in (2) is invertible and also has an infinite autoregressive (AR) representation as

$$A(L) x_t = \epsilon_t, \tag{6}$$

where L is the lag operator such that $L^j x_t = x_{t-j}$ and $A(L) = a_0 + a_1 L + a_2 L^2 + \cdots$.

Processes having an autocovariance generating transform which is a rational function of z are the so-called autoregressive moving average (ARMA) processes. If the ARMA process is both stationary and invertible, $g(z)$ may be written.

$$G(z) = \frac{P(z)P(z^{-1})}{Q(z)Q(z^{-1})} = \sigma^2 \frac{\prod_{k=1}^{m} (1 - \beta_k z)(1 - \beta_k z^{-1})}{\prod_{j=1}^{n} (1 - \alpha_j z)(1 - \alpha_j z^{-1})} \tag{7}$$

where $|\beta_k|, |\alpha_j| < 1$, all j, k. Then

$$Q(L) x_t = P(L) \epsilon_t, \tag{8}$$

where

$$Q(L) = \prod_{j=1}^{n} (1 - \alpha_j L) \quad \text{and} \quad P(L) = \prod_{k=1}^{m} (1 - \beta_k L),$$

is the corresponding ARMA model.

2.2 Spectral density functions. The spectral density function of a linearly non-deterministic stationary process with autocovariance generating transform (5) is proportional to the value of this function on the unit circle by a factor $1/2\pi$:

$$f(\lambda) = (1/2\pi)g(e^{i\lambda}) = (\sigma^2/2\pi)B(e^{i\lambda})B(e^{-i\lambda})$$
$$= (1/2\pi)\sum_{-\infty}^{\infty}\gamma(\tau)e^{-i\lambda\tau}, \qquad -\pi \leqslant \lambda < \pi. \tag{9}$$

That is, the spectral density function is the Fourier transform of the autocovariance function.

Characterization of time series by their autocovariance functions is time-domain analysis; characterization by means of their spectral density functions is frequency domain analysis. Either represents a valid way to view the temporal interdependencies of a time series.

The spectral density function for a linearly non-deterministic, stationary, real-valued time series is a real-valued, non-negative function, symmetric about the origin, defined in the interval $[-\pi, \pi)$:

$$f(\lambda) = (1/2\pi)\left[\gamma(0) + 2\sum_{\tau=1}^{\infty}\gamma(\tau)\cos\lambda\tau\right]. \tag{10}$$

Moreover,

$$E(x_t - \mu)^2 = \int_{-\pi}^{\pi} f(\lambda)\,d\lambda, \tag{11}$$

so that the spectral density function is a frequency-band decomposition of the variance of $\{x_t\}$.

When the process generating $\{x_t\}$ is merely stationary, that is, when $\{x_t\}$ may have a linearly deterministic component, the result corresponding to (10) is

$$\gamma(\tau) = \int_{-\pi}^{\pi} e^{i\lambda\tau}\,dF(\lambda), \tag{12}$$

where $F(\lambda)$ is a distribution function (Doob, 1953, p. 488).

The autocovariance function, its generating transform and the spectral distribution function all have natural generalizations to the multivariate case, that is, where $\{x_t\}$ can be thought of as a vector of time-series processes.

The estimation and analysis of spectral density and distribution functions play an important role in all forms of time-series analysis. More detailed treatments are Doob (1953), Fishman (1969), Koopmans (1974), Fuller (1976), Nerlove et al. (1979, ch. 3), and Priestley (1981).

2.3 Unobserved components (UC) models. In the statistical literature dealing with the analysis of economic time series it is common practice to classify the types of movements that characterize a time series as trend, cyclical, seasonal, and irregular. The idea that a time series may best be viewed as being composed of several unobserved components is by no means universal, but it plays a fundamental role in many applications, for example, the choice of methods for seasonal adjustment. Nerlove et al. (1979, ch. 1) review the history of the idea of unobserved components in economics from its origin early in the 19th century.

In the 1960s, Nerlove (1964, 1965, 1967) and Granger (1966) suggested that the typical spectral shape of many economic time series could be accounted for by the superposition of two or more independent components with specified properties. There are basically two approaches to the formulation of UC models: First, Theil and Wage (1964) and Nerlove and Wage (1964), Nerlove (1967) and Grether and Nerlove (1970) choose the form of components in such a way as to replicate the typical spectral shape of the series which represents their superposition. For example, let T_t represent the trend component, C_t the cyclical, S_t the seasonal, and I_t the irregular; the observed (say, monthly) series is

$$y_t = T_t + C_t + S_t + I_t,$$

where

$$T_t = a_0 + a_1 t + a_2 t^2 + \cdots + a_p t^p,$$

$$C_t = \frac{1 + \beta_1 L + \beta_2 L^2}{(1 - \alpha_1 L)(1 - \alpha_2 L)}\epsilon_{1t},$$

$$S_t = \frac{1 + \beta_3 L + \beta_4 L^2}{1 - \gamma L^{12}}\epsilon_{2t},$$

$$I_t = \epsilon_{3t},$$

and $\epsilon_{1t}, \epsilon_{2t}$, and ϵ_{3t} are i.i.d. normal variables with variances σ_{11}, σ_{22}, and σ_{33}, respectively. This approach has been carried forward by Harvey (1984), Harvey and Peters (1984) and Harvey and Todd (1984).

Second, an alternative is to find a well-fitting ARMA model (possibly fit after differences of the original series have been taken to remove trend and, given sufficient a priori restrictions on spectral properties of the components to identify them, to derive the components from the empirical model. See Box, Hillmer and Tiao (1978), Pierce (1978, 1979), Burman (1980), Hillmer and Tiao (1982), Hillmer, Bell and Tiao (1983), Bell and Hillmer (1984), Burridge and Wallis (1984), and Maravall (1981, 1984). The basis of this procedure is the fact that every stationary UC model, or the stationary part of every UC model, has an equivalent ARMA form, the so-called canonical form of the UC model (see Nerlove and Wage, 1964; Nerlove et al., 1979, ch. 4).

3. SPECIFICATION, ESTIMATION, INFERENCE AND PREDICTION

3.1 Autocovariance and spectral density functions. Suppose we have a finite number of observations of a realization of the process generating the time series $\{x_t, t \in T\}$, say, $x_1, \ldots, x_T$. The natural way to estimate μ is by

$$\bar{x} = (1/T)\sum_{t=1}^{T} x_t. \tag{14}$$

Suppose we have done so and the sample observations in fact represent deviations from the sample mean $\bar{x}$. (This new process now has zero mean.) There are basically two ways to estimate $\gamma(\tau)$ defined in (1): the first is a biased estimate

$$c(\tau) = (1/T)\sum_{t=1}^{T-|\tau|} x_t x_{t+|\tau|},$$
$$\tau = 0, \pm 1, \ldots, \pm M, M \leqslant (T-1). \tag{15}$$

The second is an unbiased estimate

$$\tilde{c}(\tau) = [1/(T - |\tau|)]\sum_{1}^{T-|\tau|} x_t x_{t+|\tau|},$$
$$\tau = 0, \pm 1, \ldots, \pm M, M \leqslant T - 1. \tag{16}$$

Although $c(\tau)$ is biased in finite samples, it is asymptotically unbiased. The difference between $c(\tau)$ and $\tilde{c}(\tau)$ that is important for estimation is that $c(\tau)$ is a positive definite function of τ whereas $\tilde{c}(\tau)$ is not (Parzen, 1961, p. 981). The variance and covariances of the estimated autocovariances are derived, *inter alia*, by Hannan (1960), and Anderson (1971).

As $T \to \infty$, both tend to zero, as the estimates are asymptotically uncorrelated and consistent. However, the variance relative to the mean does not approach zero as τ increases at the same rate as T:

$$E[c(\tau) - Ec(\tau)]^2/Ec(\tau) \to \infty \quad \text{as} \quad \tau/T \to 1. \tag{17}$$

This property accounts for the failure of the estimated autocorrelation function

$$r(\tau) = c(\tau)/c(0) \tag{18}$$

to damp down as $\tau \to \infty$ as it should for a stationary, linearly non-deterministic process (Hannan, 1960, p. 43).

The 'natural' estimator to employ for the spectral density function is that obtained by replacing $\gamma(\tau)$ in (10) by $c(\tau)$ or $\tilde{c}(\tau)$. The estimator so obtained is proportional, at each frequency, to a sample quantity called the periodogram:

$$I_T(\lambda) = (2/T)\left|\sum_1^T e^{i\lambda t} x_t\right|^2 \tag{19}$$

usually evaluated at the equispaced frequencies

$$\lambda = 2k\pi/T, \qquad k = 0, 1, \ldots, [T/2] \tag{20}$$

in the interval $[0, \pi]$. Although, for a stationary, nonlinearly deterministic process, the periodogram ordinates are proportionately asymptotically unbiased estimates of the spectral densities at the corresponding frequencies, they are not consistent estimates; moreover, the correlation between adjacent periodogram ordinates tends to zero with increasing sample size. The result is that the periodogram presents a jagged appearance which is increasingly difficult to interpret as more data become available.

In order to obtain consistent estimates of the spectral density function at specific frequencies, it is common practice to weight the periodogram ordinates over the frequency range or to form weighted averages of the autocovariances at different lags. There is a substantial literature on the subject. The weights are called a 'spectral window'. Essentially the idea is to reduce the variance of the estimate of an average spectral density around a particular frequency by averaging periodogram ordinates which are asymptotically unbiased and independently distributed estimates of the corresponding ordinates of the spectral density function. Related weights can also be applied to the estimated autocovariances which are substituted in (10); this weighting system is called a 'lag window'. Naturally the sampling properties of the spectral estimates depend on the nature of the 'window' used to obtain consistency. The literature on this topic is summarized in Priestley (1981, pp. 432–94).

3.2 ARMA models. The autocovariance function and the spectral density function for a time series represent relatively non-parametric ways of describing the data. An alternative approach is to specify and estimate an ARMA model after transforming the data to render the series stationary. This means choosing the orders of the polynomials P and Q in (7) and (8) and perhaps also specifying that one or more coefficients may be zero or placing other restrictions on P and Q. The problem then becomes that of estimating the parameters of the model.

Despite the poor statistical properties of the estimated autocovariance function and a related function called the partial autocorrelation function, these are usually used to specify the orders of the polynomials P and Q. More recently Akaike (1970, 1974) has introduced a new expression called Akaike's information criterion (AIC). This is a very general criterion, which is based on information theoretic conceptions and can be used for statistical model identification in a wide range of circumstances. When a model involving k independently estimated parameters is fit, the AIC is defined as

$$\text{AIC}(k) = -2 \log[\text{maximized likelihood}] + 2k. \tag{21}$$

The appropriate value of k is that at which AIC attains its minimum value.

Once the orders of the AR and MA components have been determined a variety of maximum-likelihood or approximate maximum likelihood methods are available to estimate the parameters. Newbold (1974) shows that if x_t is characterized by (8) with $\epsilon_t \overset{iid}{\sim} N(0, \sigma^2)$ then the exact likelihood function for the parameters of $P(\cdot)$ and $Q(\cdot)$ is such that the maximum-likelihood estimates of the parameters and the least-squares (LS) estimates (in general highly nonlinear) are asymptotically identical. Only in the case of a pure AR model are the LS estimates (conditional on the initial observations) linear. Various approximations have been discussed (Box and Jenkins, 1970; Granger and Newbold, 1977; Nerlove et al., 1979, pp. 121–25).

Exact maximum-likelihood estimation of ARMA models has been discussed by, *inter alia*, Newbold (1974), Anderson (1977), Ansley (1979), and Harvey (1981). Following Schweppe (1965), Harvey suggests the use of the Kalman filter (1960) to obtain the value of the exact-likelihood function numerically, which may be maximized by numerical methods. The Kalman filter approach is easily adapted to the estimation of UC models in the time domain.

An alternative to exact or approximate maximum-likelihood estimation in the time domain was suggested by Hannan (1969). Estimates may be obtained by maximizing an approximate likelihood function based on the asymptotic distribution of the periodogram ordinates defined in (19). These are asymptotically independently distributed (Brillinger, 1975, p. 95), and the random variables $2I_t(\lambda)/f(\lambda)$ have an asymptotic χ^2 distribution with two degrees of freedom (Koopmans, 1974, pp. 260–65). This means that the asymptotic distribution of the observations, $\{x_1, \ldots, x_T\}$ is proportional to

$$\prod_{j=0}^{[T/2]} [1/f(\lambda_j)] \exp[-I(\lambda_j)/f(\lambda_j)]$$

where $\lambda_j = 2j\pi/T$, $j = 0, \ldots, [T/2]$, are the equi-spaced frequencies in the interval $[0, \pi]$ at which the periodogram is evaluated. (See also Nerlove et al., 1979, pp. 132–6). Since the true spectral density $f(\lambda)$ depends on the parameters characterizing the process, this asymptotic distribution may be interpreted as a likelihood function. Frequency domain methods, as these are called, may easily be applied in the case of UC models.

Whether approximate or exact maximum-likelihood estimation methods are employed, inference may be based on the usual criteria related to the likelihood function. Unfortunately, serious difficulties may be encountered in applying the asymptotic theory, since the small sample distributions of the MLE's are known to be extremely different from the limiting distributions in important cases. (See Sargan and Bhargava, 1983; Anderson and Takemura, 1984.)

3.3 Prediction and extraction. The problem of prediction is essentially the estimation of an unknown future value of the time series itself; the problem of extraction, best viewed in the context of UC models described in section 2.3 above, is to estimate the value of one of the unobserved components at a particular point in time, not necessarily in the future. Problems of trend extraction and seasonal adjustment may be viewed in this way (Grether and Nerlove, 1970). How the prediction (or extraction) problem is approached depends on whether we are assumed to have an infinite past history and, if not, whether the parameters of the process generating the time series are assumed to be known or not. In practice, of course, an infinite past history is never available, but a very long history is nearly equivalent if the process is stationary or can be transformed to stationarity. It is usual, as well, to restrict attention to linear predictors, which involves no loss of generality if the processes considered are Gaussian and little loss if merely linear. To devise a theory of optimal prediction or extraction requires some criterion by which to measure the accuracy of a particular candidate. The most common is the minimum mean-square error (MMSE) criterion which is also the conditional expectation of the unknown quantity.

The theory of optimal prediction and extraction due to Kolmogorov (1941) and Wiener (1949) and elaborated by Whittle (1963) for discrete processes assumes a possibly infinite past history and known parameters. Consider the linear process defined by (2). Since the ϵ_t are i.i.d. zero mean with variance σ^2, it is apparent that the conditional expectation of x_{t+v} given the infinite past to t is

$$\hat{x}_{t+v} = b_v \epsilon_t + b_{v+1}\epsilon_{t-1} + \cdots. \tag{22}$$

Of course, even if the parameters b_j, $j = 0, 1, \ldots$, are assumed to be known, the series $\{\epsilon_t\}$ is not directly observable. The ϵ_t's are sometimes called the *innovations* of the process, since it is easy to show that $\epsilon_{t+1} = x_{t+1} - \hat{x}_{t+1}$ are the one-step ahead prediction errors. If the process is invertible, it has the autoregressive representation (6) and so can be expressed solely in terms of the, generally infinite, autoregression

$$\hat{x}_{t+v} = D(L)x_t, \tag{23}$$

where the generating transform of the coefficients of D is

$$D(z) = \frac{1}{B(z)}\left[\frac{B(z)}{z^v}\right]_+. \tag{24}$$

The operator $[\cdot]_+$ eliminates terms having negative powers of z. (The Wiener–Kolmogorov theory is more general than this, since $\{x_t\}$ is allowed to be any non-deterministic, stationary process.)

The problem of extraction may best be viewed in the context of multiple time series; in general we wish to 'predict' one time series $\{y_t\}$ from another related series $\{x_t\}$. It is not necessary that the series $\{y_t\}$ actually be observed as long as its relationship to an observed series $\{x_t\}$ can be described. (See Nerlove et al., 1979, ch. 5.)

The Kalman filter approach (1960) to prediction and extraction is both more special and more general than the Wiener–Kolmogorov theory: attention is restricted to finite parameters, linear processes (effectively ARMA models if the processes considered are stationary), but these processes need not be stationary. The parameters may vary with time, and we do not require an infinite past. This approach represents a powerful tool of practical time-series analysis and may be easily extended to multiple time series. A full discussion, however, requires a discussion of 'state-space representation' of time series processes and is beyond the scope of this entry. (See Anderson and Moore, 1979.)

4. MULTIPLE TIME SERIES ANALYSIS

A general treatment of multiple time-series analysis is contained in Hannan (1970). The two-variable case will serve to illustrate the matter in general. Two stationary time series $\{x_t\}$ and $\{y_t\}$ are said to be jointly stationary if their joint distribution function does not depend on the origin from which time is measured. Joint stationarity implies, but is not in general implied by, weak or covariance joint stationarity; that is, $\mathrm{cov}(x_t, y_s)$ is a function of $s - t$ only. In this case the cross-covariance function is

$$\gamma_{yx}(\tau) = E[y_t - \mu_y][x_{t-\tau} - \mu_x], \tag{25}$$

where $\mu_x = Ex_t$ and $\mu_y = Ey_t$. Note that $\gamma_{yx}(\tau)$ and $\gamma_{xy}(\tau)$ are, in general, different. The cross-covariance generating function is defined as

$$g_{yx}(z) = \sum_{-\infty}^{\infty} \gamma_{yx}(\tau) z^\tau \tag{26}$$

in that region of the complex plane in which the right-hand side of (26) converges. For two jointly stationary series this occurs in an annulus containing the unit circle. In this case, the cross-spectral density function is defined as

$$f_{yx}(\lambda) = (1/2\pi) g_{yx}(e^{i\lambda}). \tag{27}$$

Since $\gamma_{yx}(\tau)$ and $\gamma_{xy}(\tau)$ are not equal, the cross-spectral density function is complex valued. The real part is called the co-spectral density and the complex part, the quadrature spectral density, and written

$$f_{yx}(\lambda) = c_{yx}(\lambda) + iq_{yx}(\lambda). \tag{28}$$

In polar form, the cross-spectral density may be written

$$f_{yx}(\lambda) = \alpha_{yx}(\lambda)\exp[i\phi_{yx}(\lambda)], \tag{29}$$

where $\alpha_{yx}(\lambda) = [c^2_{yx}(\lambda) + q^2_{yx}(\lambda)]^{1/2}$ is called the amplitude or gain, and where $\phi_{yx}(\lambda) = \arctan\{-q_{yx}(\lambda)/c_{yx}(\lambda)\}$ is called the phase. Another useful magnitude is the coherence between the two series, defined as

$$\rho_{yx}(\lambda) = \frac{|f_{yx}(\lambda)|^2}{f_{xx}(\lambda) f_{yy}(\lambda)}, \tag{30}$$

which measures the squared correlation between y and x at a frequency λ. Clearly, $\rho_{yx}(\lambda) = \rho_{xy}(\lambda)$. Estimation of cross-spectral density functions and related quantities are discussed in Priestley (1981, pp. 692–712).

The formulation of ARMA and UC models discussed earlier may easily be extended to the multivariate case by interpreting the polynomials in the lag operator as matrix polynomials and the scalar random variables as vectors. Although these models bear a superficial resemblance to the corresponding univariate ones, their structure is, in fact, much more complicated and gives rise to difficult identification problems. In the univariate case, we can formulate simple conditions under which a given covariance function identifies a unique ARMA or UC model, but in the multivariate case these conditions are no longer sufficient. Hannan (1970, 1971) gives a complete treatment. More recently state-space methods have been employed to study the structure of multivariate ARMA models (Hannan, 1976 and, especially, 1979).

5. APPLICATIONS

Time series analytic methods have many applications in economics; here we consider four: (1) Forecasting, (2) Description of seasonality and seasonal adjustment, (3) Analysis of the cyclic properties of economic time series, and (4) Dynamic econometric modelling.

5.1 Forecasting. Time-series models, together with associated methods of trend removal, such as differencing, are widely used in forecasting economic time series. In addition there is a close relationship between the forecasts generated in this way and the forecasts based on the so-called final form of an econometric model.

One of the simplest forecasting procedures is exponential smoothing based on the relationship

$$\hat{y}_{t+1,t} = (1-\theta)y_t + \theta\hat{y}_{t,t-1}, \qquad (31)$$

where y_t is the observed series, $\hat{y}_{j,k}$ is the forecast of the series at time j made on the basis of information available up to time k. Muth (1960) showed that (31) gives an optimal (MMSE) forecast if the model generating the time series is $y_t - y_{t-1} = \epsilon_t - \theta\epsilon_{t-1}$. Time series which are stationary *after* differencing are said to be generated by autoregressive integrated moving-average (ARIMA) processes. Holt (1957) and Winters (1960) generalize the exponential smoothing approach to models containing more complex trend and seasonal components. Further generalization and proofs of optimality are contained in Theil and Wage (1964) and Nerlove and Wage (1964).

Box–Jenkins procedures (Box and Jenkins, 1970) are based on general ARIMA models of time series processes. The developments discussed in the preceding paragraph led to the more general development of UC models, which give rise to restricted ARIMA model forms (Nerlove et al., 1979).

State-space representations of these models permit the application of the Kalman filter to both estimation and forecasting. Harvey (1984) presents a unified synthesis of the various methods.

5.2 Description of seasonality and seasonal adjustment. Many economic time series exhibit fluctuations which are more or less periodic within a year or a fraction thereof. The proper treatment of seasonality, whether stochastic or deterministic, is the subject of a large literature, summarized rather selectively in Nerlove et al. (1979, ch. 1).

Spectral analysis has been used to detect the presence of seasonality (Nerlove, 1964). Deterministic seasonality, just as deterministic trend, offers no great conceptual problems but many practical ones. Stochastic seasonality is best viewed in terms of UC models (Grether and Nerlove, 1970). Appropriate UC models may be determined directly or by fitting an ARIMA model and deriving a related UC model by imposing sufficient a priori restrictions (Hillmer and Tiao, 1982; Bell and Hillmer, 1984).

5.3 Analysis of the cyclic properties of economic time series. Suppose that the time series $\{x_t\}$ is a linearly non-deterministic stationary series and that the series $\{y_t\}$ is formed from $\{x_t\}$ by the linear operator

$$y_t = \sum_{j=m}^{n} w_j x_{t-j}, \quad \sum_{m}^{n} w_j^2 < \infty. \qquad (32)$$

Such an operator is called a time-invariant linear filter. Analysis of the properties of such filters plays an important role in time series analysis since many methods of trend estimation or removal and seasonal adjustment may be represented or approximated by such filters. More interestingly, systems of simultaneous econometric equations can also be viewed in this manner and their dynamic stochastic properties studied by analysing the properties of approximating filters. An interesting example which combines both elements is given by Adelman (1965) who showed that the 20-year long swings in various economic series found by Kuznets (1961) may well have been the result of the trend filtering operations used in preliminary processing of the data. For a fuller treatment see Nerlove et al. (1979, pp. 53–7).

5.4 Dynamic econometric modelling. There is a close connection between multivariate time-series models and the structural, reduced and final forms of econometric models: the standard simultaneous-equations econometric model (SEM) is a specific and restricted case.

Suppose that a vector of observed variables y_t may be subdivided into two classes of variables, 'exogenous', $\{x_t\}$, and endogenous, $\{z_t\}$. A dynamic, multivariate simultaneous linear system may be written

$$\begin{bmatrix} \Psi_{11}(L) & \Psi_{12}(L) \\ 0 & \Psi_{22}(L) \end{bmatrix} \begin{pmatrix} z_t \\ x_t \end{pmatrix} = \begin{bmatrix} \Theta_{11}(L) & 0 \\ 0 & \Theta_{22}(L) \end{bmatrix} \begin{pmatrix} \epsilon_{1t} \\ \epsilon_{2t} \end{pmatrix} \qquad (33)$$

where $\Psi_{ij}(\cdot)$ and $\Theta_{ij}(\cdot)$, $i, j = 1, 2$, are matrix polynomials in the lag operator L. Such systems are known as ARMAX models and conditions for their identification are given by Hatanaka (1975). The reduced form of the system is obtained by solving for $\{y_t\}$ in terms of $\{x_t\}$. The final form is then obtained by eliminating the lagged z's; see Zellner and Palm (1974) and Wallis (1977).

MARC NERLOVE AND FRANCIS X. DIEBOLD

See also ARIMA MODELS; AUTOCORRELATION; FORECASTING; MAXIMUM LIKELIHOOD; MULTIVARIATE TIME SERIES MODELS; PREDICTION; SPECTRAL ANALYSIS; STATIONARY TIME SERIES.

BIBLIOGRAPHY

Adelman, I. 1965. Long cycles – fact or artifact? *American Economic Review* 60, 443–63.

Akaike, H. 1970. Statistical predictor identification. *Annals of the Institute of Statistical Mathematics* 22, 203–17.

Akaike, H. 1974. A new look at the statistical model identification. *IEEE Transactions on Automatic Control* 19, 716–23.

Anderson, B.D.O. and Moore, J.D. 1979. *Optimal Filtering*. Englewood Cliffs: Prentice-Hall.

Anderson, T.W. 1971. *The Statistical Analysis of Time Series*. New York: John Wiley.

Anderson, T.W. 1977. Estimation for autoregressive moving average models in the time and frequency domains. *Annals of Statistics* 5, 842–65.

Anderson, T.W. and Takemura, A. 1984. Why do noninvertible moving averages occur? Technical Report No. 13, Department of Statistics, Stanford University.

Ansley, C.F. 1979. An algorithm for the exact likelihood of a mixed autoregressive-moving average process. *Biometrika* 66, 59–65.

Bell, W. and Hillmer, S. 1984. Issues involved with seasonal analysis of economic time series. *Journal of Business and Economic Statistics* 2, 291–349.

Beveridge, W.H. 1921. Weather and harvest cycles. *Economic Journal* 31, 429–52.

Beveridge, W.H. 1922. Wheat prices and rainfall in western Europe. *Journal of the Royal Statistical Society* 85, 412–59.

Box, G.E.P., Hillmer, S.C. and Tiao, G.C. 1978. Analysis and modeling of seasonal time series. In *Seasonal Analysis of Economic Time Series*. ed. A. Zellner, Washington, DC: US Department of Commerce, Bureau of the Census, 309–44.

Box, G.E.P. and Jenkins, G.M. 1970. *Time Series Analysis: Forecasting and Control*. San Francisco: Holden-Day.

Brillinger, D.C. 1975. *Time Series: Data Analysis and Theory*. New York: Holt.

Burman, J.P. 1980. Seasonal adjustment by signal extraction. *Journal of the Royal Statistical Society*, Series A, 143, 321–37.

Burridge, P. and Wallis, K.F. 1984. Calculating the variance of seasonally adjusted series. Working Paper, University of Warwick.

Cournot, A.A. 1838. *Researches Into the Mathematical Principles of the Theory of Wealth*. Trans. N.T. Bacon, New York: Macmillan, 1927.

Doob, J.L. 1953. *Stochastic Processes*. New York: John Wiley.

Fishman, G.S. 1969. *Spectral Methods in Econometrics*. Cambridge: Harvard University Press.

Fuller, W.A. 1976. *Introduction to Statistical Time Series.* New York: John Wiley.
Granger, C.W.J. 1966. The typical spectral shape of an economic variable. *Econometrica* 34, 150–61.
Granger, C.W.J. and Newbold, P. 1977. *Forecasting Economic Time Series.* New York: Academic Press.
Grether, D.M. and Nerlove, M. 1970. Some properties of 'optimal' seasonal adjustment. *Econometrica* 38, 682–703.
Hannan, E.J. 1960. *Time Series Analysis.* London: Methuen.
Hannan, E.J. 1969. The estimation of mixed moving average autoregressive systems. *Biometrika* 56, 223–5.
Hannan, E.J. 1970. *Multiple Time Series.* New York: John Wiley.
Hannan, E.J. 1971. The identification problem for multiple equation systems with moving average errors. *Econometrica* 39, 751–65.
Hannan, E.J. 1976. The identification and parameterization of ARMAX and state space forms. *Econometrica* 44, 713–23.
Hannan, E.J. 1979. The statistical theory of linear systems. In *Developments in Statistics*, ed. P.R. Krishnaiah, New York: Academic Press, 83–121.
Harvey, A.C. 1981. *The Econometric Analysis of Time Series.* Oxford: Allan.
Harvey, A.C. 1981. *Time Series Models.* Oxford: Allan.
Harvey, A.C. 1984. A unified view of statistical forecasting procedures. *Journal of Forecasting* 3, 245–75.
Harvey, A.C. and Peters, S. 1984. Estimation procedures for structural TSM's. Working Paper, London School of Economics.
Harvey, A.C. and Todd, P.H.J. 1984. Forecasting economic time series with structural and Box–Jenkins models: a case study (with discussion). *Journal of Business and Economic Statistics* 1, 299–315.
Hatanaka, M. 1975. On the global identification of the dynamic simultaneous equations model with stationary disturbances. *International Economic Review* 16, 545–54.
Hillmer, S.C. and Tiao, G.C. 1982. An ARIMA-model-based approach to seasonal adjustment. *Journal of the American Statistical Association* 77, 63–70.
Hillmer, S.C., Bell, W.R. and Tiao, G.C. 1983. Modeling considerations in the seasonal analysis of economic time series. In *Applied Time Series Analysis of Economic Data,* ed. A. Zellner. Washington, DC: Dept. of Commerce, Bureau of the Census, 74–100.
Holt, C.C. 1957. Forecasting seasonals and trends by exponentially weighted moving averages. ONR Research Memorandum No. 52, Carnegie Institute of Technology.
Jevons, W.S. 1884. *Investigations in Currency and Finance.* London: Macmillan.
Kalman, R.E. 1960. A new approach to linear filtering and prediction problems. *Transactions of the American Society of Mechanical Engineers. Journal of Basic Engineering*, Series D 82, 35–45.
Kolmogorov, A. 1941. Interpolation und Extrapolation von Stationären Zufäligen Folgen. *Bulletin of the Academy Science (Nauk), USSR, Mathematical Series* 5, 3–14.
Koopmans, L.H. 1974. *The Spectral Analysis of Time Series.* New York: Academic Press.
Kuznets, S. 1961. *Capital and the American Economy: Its Formation and Financing.* New York: NBER.
Maravall, A. 1981. *Desestacionalizacion y Politica Monetaria.* Economic Studies 19, Bank of Spain, Madrid.
Maravall, A. 1984. Model-based treatment of a manic depressive series. Working Paper, Bank of Spain, Madrid.
Muth, J.F. 1960. Optimal properties of exponentially weighted forecasts. *Journal of the American Statistical Association* 55, 299–305.
Nerlove, M. 1964. Spectral analysis of seasonal adjustment procedures. *Econometrica* 32, 241–86.
Nerlove, M. 1965. A comparison of a modified Hannan and the BLS seasonal adjustment filters. *Journal of the American Statistical Association* 60, 442–91.
Nerlove, M. 1967. Distributed lags and unobserved components in economic time series. In *Ten Economic Essays in the Tradition of Irving Fisher*, ed. W. Fellner, et al., 126–69, New York: John Wiley.
Nerlove, M., Grether, D.M. and Carvalho, J.L. 1979. *Analysis of Economic Time Series.* New York: Academic Press.
Nerlove, M. and Wage, S. 1964. On the optimality of adaptive forecasting. *Management Science* 10, 207–24.
Newbold, P. 1974. The exact likelihood function for a mixed autoregressive-moving average process. *Biometrika* 61(3), 423–6.
Parzen, E. 1961. An approach to time series analysis. *Annals of Mathematical Statistics* 32, 951–89.
Pierce, D.A. 1978. Seasonal adjustment when both deterministic and stochastic seasonality are present. In *Seasonal Analysis of Economic Time Series,* ed. A. Zellner, Washington, DC: Department of Commerce, Bureau of the Census, 242–80.
Pierce, D.A. 1979. Signal extraction error in nonstationary time series. *Annals of Statistics* 7, 1303–20.
Priestley, M.B. 1981. *Spectral Analysis and Time Series.* New York: Academic Press.
Sargan, J.D. and Bhargava, A. 1983. Maximum likelihood estimation of regression models with moving average errors when the root lies on the unit circle. *Econometrica* 51(3), May, 799–820.
Schuster, A. 1898. On the investigation of hidden periodicities with application to the supposed 26-day period of meteorological phenomena. *Terrestrial Magnetism and Atmospheric Electricity* [now *Journal of Geophysical Research*], 3, 13–41.
Schweppe, F.C. 1965. Evaluation of likelihood functions for Gaussian signals. *IEEE Transactions on Information Theory* 11, 61–70.
Slutsky, E. 1927. The summation of random causes as the source of cyclic processes. *Econometrica* 5, April 1937, 105–46.
Stokes, G.C. 1879. Note on searching for hidden periodicities. *Proceedings of the Royal Society* 29, 122–5.
Theil, H. and Wage, S. 1964. Some observations on adaptive forecasting. *Management Science* 10, 198–206.
Wallis, K.F. 1977. Multiple time series analysis and the final form of econometric models. *Econometrica* 45(6), September, 1481–97.
Whittle, P. 1963. *Prediction and Regulation by Linear Least-squares Methods.* London: English Universities Press.
Wiener, N. 1949. *The Extrapolation, Interpolation and Smoothing of Stationary Time Series with Engineering Applications.* New York: John Wiley.
Winters, P.R. 1960. Forecasting sales by exponentially weighted moving averages. *Management Science* 6, 324–42.
Wold, H.O. 1938. *A Study in the Analysis of Stationary Time Series.* Stockholm: Almqvist and Wiksell.
Yule, G.U. 1921. On the time-correlation problem, with special reference to the variate-difference correlation method. *Journal of the Royal Statistical Society* 84, July, 497–526.
Yule, G.U. 1926. Why do we sometimes get nonsense correlations between time series? A study in sampling and the nature of time series. *Journal of the Royal Statistical Society* 89, 1–64.
Yule, G.U. 1927. On a method of investigating periodicities in disturbed series with special reference to Wolfer's sunspot numbers. *Philosophical Transactions of the Royal Society of London* Series A, 226, 267–98.
Zellner, A., and Palm, F. 1974. Time series analysis and simultaneous equation econometric models. *Journal of Econometrics* 2, 17–54.

Tinbergen, Jan (born 1903). Tinbergen was born in The Hague, Netherlands, in 1903. He studied mathematical physics at Leiden, received his doctorate in 1929 and then joined the Central Bureau of Statistics at The Hague. For a period in the Thirties (1936–8) he worked at the League of Nations in Geneva under Alexander Loveday. After World War II he became Director of the Central Planning Bureau at The Hague and served in the capacity from 1945 to 1951. Tinbergen was appointed an extraordinary Professor of Economics at the Netherlands School of Economics in 1933. On his retirement from the Directorship of the Central Planning Bureau in 1955 this was made into a full Professorship with a focus on development problems of less developed countries, which he held till 1973. Together with Ragnar Frisch, Tinbergen was awarded the first Nobel Memorial Prize in Economics in 1969. He was also elected the first Chairman of the UN Committee on Development Planning.

Tinbergen's work in economics is best viewed as a product of his scientific curiosity and deep interest in social problems. Tinbergen studied physics under P. Ehrenfest, himself a student of L. Boltzmann and author, with his wife, T. Ehrenfest, of one of the most important contributions ever made to statistical mechanics. Ehrenfest was influential in directing Tinbergen's attention to mathematical formulations of economic problems and Tinbergen's dissertation (1929) dealt with minimum problems in physics and economics.

Tinbergen's first two major papers dealt with what are described these days as 'cobweb theorems' (1930a) and shipbuilding cycles (1930b). While developing the latter, Tinbergen introduced for the first time in economics a mixed difference – differential equation which played a role in Frisch's well-known paper on cycles in the volume of essays in honour of G. Cassel (Frisch, 1933), and more importantly in Kalecki's macrodynamic model which was first published in *Econometrica* (1935). By any standard, Tinbergen's early work in economic dynamics was highly innovative in a theoretical sense. But his interest went beyond purely theoretical issues and he began his work on economy-wide models to understand better the dynamic functioning of an economy. Here again, he was interested in a threefold problem: theory construction, testing, and subsequent application to the solution of specific policy problems.

The earliest formulation of this threefold approach is furnished by his paper written for the Dutch Economic Association, 'An economic policy for 1936'. This paper, subsequently translated into English (1959), is notable among other things for including a clear enunciation of what was subsequently called the 'Phillips curve'. Tinbergen found little statistical evidence for the 'acceleration principle' and relied instead on the 'profits principle', also used by Kalecki.

Tinbergen was invited by the League of Nations to extend his work on quantitative analysis of the Dutch economy as part of its two-part project on business cycles, of which the first part was carried out by G. Haberler. While Haberler's work, 'Prosperity and Depression', consisted of a verbal discussion of various business cycle theories, Tinbergens's attempt was directed towards quantification of different theories of the cycle as testable hypotheses. His work for the League of Nations was published in two volumes (1939). The first volume presented his exposition of the appropriate statistical method in relation to explanation of investment fluctuations. The second volume dealt with a statistical analysis of business cycles in the United States between 1919 and 1932. The first volume was reviewed by J.M. Keynes, who raised numerous issues of a critical nature, including important ones on 'specification biases' and 'simultaneous equation biases' which were discussed more extensively only much later. While Tinbergen's statistical technique was simple, consisting of multiple regression analysis supplemented by Frisch's work on 'confluence analysis', he succeeded in demonstrating in volume II of his work, which Keynes did not review, the existence of damped periodic movements without having to invoke special factors for explaining turning points in the context of business cycle discussions. Tinbergen's approach towards modelling, economy-wide interrelationships in quantitative forms, became highly influential with the passage of years. While numerous important contributions have been made in this area, the work of Lawrence Klein deserves special mention. In retrospect, the Keynes – Tinbergen debate is best viewed as an important milestone in the development of econometrics, as Tinbergen's pioneering work, despite its great innovative quality, was naturally not free from limitations, either as a 'Technique of discovery, or as a technique of Criticism' to borrow Keynes's expression.

Most of Tinbergen's applied work was based on the use of linear difference equations, which he especially favoured over the use of differential equations. This was because Tinbergen believed that discrete time models were more appropriate for economic analysis where data was collected on the basis of discrete intervals. This was also consonant with the notions of 'sequence models' which were being contemporaneously developed by E. Lundberg and others. Tinbergen accepted Frisch's formulation that wave-like movements were produced in economic quantities because of a combination of a damped inner structure and the existence of exogenous shocks. Frisch was indebted in this respect to the earlier suggestion of Wicksell and to the statistical work of Yule and Slutsky. In a little known paper, Tinbergen tried to explore whether alternative models were theoretically possible, and in so doing produced the first *formal* analysis of a non-linear dynamical system (1944) in simple economic terms. Subsequent work by Hicks and, more especially, by Goodwin, took this line of reasoning much further.

Tinbergen's interest in growth problems dates back from the 1940s, when he presented his mathematical theory of trend movements (1942), a paper which hardly attracted any attention until the late 1950s (1959). While it has generally been relegated to the status of a precursor to the contribution by Solow towards a neoclassical model of growth, this paper deserves special attention as Tinbergen gave a very prominent place to technical progress, besides using a mass of statistical literature.

Since the end of World War II, Tinbergen has largely worked on three problems: theory of policy models, problems of developing economies, and theory of personal distribution of incomes. His work on policy models was directly related to his prewar work, notably to his paper on 'An economic policy for 1936'. The other two areas were new to him.

As part of his postwar job as Director of the Central Planning Bureau, Tinbergen decided to systematize the bases on which policy could be formulated in regard to issues that chiefly interested the government, that is, full employment, price stability, and equilibrium in the balance of payments. He demonstrated that, in general, these three objectives could not be achieved without the use of three specific instruments. Contemporaneously with Frisch and Bent Hansen, he developed the logic of a simple type of decision model that has been greatly influential. While the result on the equality of instruments and targets is widely known (a result which is valid only in the case of linear systems without boundary conditions), the important contribution was in identifying the basic structure of a policy problem which was generally the inverse of what he called the 'analytical problem'. H. Theil and H.A. Simon extended the policy model by introducing stochastic elements.

Since 1954, Tinbergen has devoted most of his time to the problem of economic development of the less developed countries. He has been an adviser to many national governments, to his own country on development aid, and to various international organizations. He has advocated a reformist policy for the developing countries and developed countries alike. While Tinbergen's efforts in this work are very highly esteemed by all those who see the need to reshape the international order, analytically speaking Tinbergen's contributions during this period consist of the following: (a) his work on semi-input–output analysis, which makes an imaginative use of the distinction between tradeables and non-tradeables for purposes of project appraisal. This idea has been developed by B. Hansen and others; (b) a theory of an optimum international division of labour, based on an extension of the Heckscher–Ohlin model; and (c) his proposal of a commodity reserve currency, developed along with N. Kaldor and A.G. Hart.

Tinbergen's work throughout has been characterized by adherence to the principle of successive approximation, importance of measurement, and policy relevance. As an economist, Tinbergen has been an auto-didact and belongs to no particular school. His great quest has been always to use economics to determine the contours of a more humane society. His research amply reflects this feature, along with his scientific imagination and sense of empirical relevance.

SUKHAMOY CHAKRAVARTY

See also ECONOMETRICS.

SELECTED WORKS

1929. *Minimumproblemen in de natuurkunde en de ekonomie.* Amsterdam: J.H. Paris.

1930a. Bestimmung und Deutung von Angebotskurven. Ein Beispiel. *Zeitschrift für Nationalokonomie* 1(5), April, 669–79.

1930b. Ein Schiffbauzyklus? *Weltwirtschaftliches Archiv*. In *Selected Papers,* 1959.

1936. An economic policy for 1936. Paper read before the Dutch Economic Association. In *Selected Papers,* 1959.

1939. *Statistical Testing of Business Cycles Theories.* Vols I and II, Geneva: League of Nations.

1942. Zur Theorie der langnistigen Wirtschaftsentwicklung. *Weltwirtschaftliches Archiv.* Translated as 'On the theory of trend movements' in *Selected Papers,* 1959.

1944. Ligevaegtstyper og Konjunkturbevaegelse. *Nordisk Tidsskrift for Tekniskökonomie.* Trans. as 'Types of equilibrium and business cycle movements' in *Selected Papers,* 1959.

1945. *International Economic Cooperation.* Amsterdam: Elsevier.

1951. *Business Cycles in the United Kingdom, 1870–1914.* Amsterdam: North-Holland.

1952. *On the Theory of Economic Policy.* Amsterdam: North-Holland.

1956a. *Economic Policy: Principles and Design.* Amsterdam: North-Holland.

1956b. *The Design of Development.* Baltimore: Johns Hopkins Press.

1959. *Selected Papers.* Ed. L.H. Klaassen et al., Amsterdam: North-Holland.

1968. *Development Planning.* London: Weidenfeld & Nicolson.

1975. *Income Distribution.* Amsterdam: Elsevier.

BIBLIOGRAPHY

Bos, H.C. 1979. Jan Tinbergen. In *International Encyclopaedia of the Social Sciences,* Vol. 18, Biographical Supplement, New York: Free Press.

Hansen, B. 1969. Jan Tinbergen. *Swedish Journal of Economics* 71, 325–36.

Frisch, R. 1933. Propagation and impulse problems in dynamic economics. In *Economic Essays in Honour of Gustav Cassel,* London: Allen & Unwin.

Kalecki, M. 1935. A macrodynamic theory of business cycles. *Econometrica* 3, July, 327–44.

Keynes, J.M. 1939. *Collected Works,* Vol. 14. London: Macmillan, 1973, 285–320.

Klaassen, L.H., Koyck, L.M. and Witteveen, H.J. (eds) 1959. *Selected Papers by Jan Tinbergen.* Amsterdam: North-Holland.

Pronk, J.P. 1970. Bibliography 1959–1969 of Prof. Dr. J. Tinbergen. *De Economist* 118(2), March–April, 155–72.

Tintner, Gerhard (1907–1983). Gerhard Tintner was born in Nuremberg, Germany, of Austrian parents, and educated in Vienna, completing his doctorate in economics, statistics and law at the University of Vienna in 1929. Tintner was much ahead of his time in important respects. First, he made early and significant contributions toward the development of a theory of behaviour under uncertainty (cf. Tintner 1941a and b, 1942a, b and c). Second, he consistently stressed the need for a broad view of probability in the behavioural sciences and economics (Tintner 1960, 1968a). His seminal article 'Foundations of probability and statistical inference' (1949) started from Carnap's view of probability as *degree of confirmation* and raised issues some of which are now being debated in current reformulations of econometric methodology (Harper and Hooker (eds), 1976; Koch and Spizzichino (eds), 1982). Third, he firmly believed that the tools of modern disciplines such as cybernetics and system theory should be adapted and used to gain insight into individual and social behavior, which is the basis of all applied economic models (cf. Tintner and Sengupta, 1972).

Tintner's first book (1935) was written as part of the programme of the Austrian Institute for Trade Cycle Research. In it Tintner applied Anderson's (1927) variate difference method to some 300 series of commodity prices from 1845 to 1914. Under certain assumptions, this method eliminated (most of) the random component from each series, leaving the systematic component for further study; Tintner (1940) presented a more complete statement of the method.

By 1935, Tintner had become enthusiastic about the work of the American mathematicians G.C. Evans (1922, 1924, 1930) and C.F. Roos (1925, 1934), who were applying calculus of variations to theoretical problems in economic dynamics. It appears that Tintner hoped to make a major breakthrough by extending the Evans–Roos approach. From 1936 to 1942 he published a series of brilliant articles (1936, 1937, 1938a and 1938b, 1939, 1941a and 1941b, 1942a, 1942b and 1942c) on such topics as maximization of utility over time, the theoretical derivation of dynamic demand curves, and the pure theory of production under technological risk and uncertainty; his last article of this type was 'A note on welfare economics' (1946a). Apparently these articles attracted little attention under the disturbed conditions of the time and were not consulted by the young economists who applied similar methods in the 1950s and 1960s to the theory of economic growth and uncertainty. Tintner's work on dynamic economic theory deserves a thorough reappraisal.

The early literature on linear programming dealt exclusively with the deterministic case. Tintner (1955) and Charnes and Cooper (1959) were the first to develop theories and methods for dealing with the various stochastic cases in which inputs, outputs, technical coefficients and/or constraints are subject to random disturbances. Tintner's development of an active approach to stochastic programming (as opposed to a passive approach) pointed the way to current research on self-tuning control combining both estimation and regulation (Sengupta, 1985). Tintner's students and others also made important contributions to stochastic programming; by the late 1970s its literature included several hundred articles and a number of books – see, for example, Kolbin (1977), Tintner and Sengupta (1972), van Moeseke (1965), and Sengupta (1972, 1982).

A selected bibliography of Tintner's publications through 1967 is included in Fox et al. (1969). Tintner spent the bulk of his career at Iowa State University (1937–62) and the University of Southern California (1963–73). From 1973 until shortly before his death (in Vienna, 13 November 1983) he was professor of econometrics at the Technische Universität in Vienna and Honorary Professor at the University of Vienna. His textbooks (Tintner 1952, 1953) had considerable influence on the teaching of econometrics and he also published important articles on multivariate analysis, time series analysis and homogeneous systems in mathematical economics.

KARL A. FOX

SELECTED WORKS

1935. *Prices in the Trade Cycle*. Vienna: Julius Springer.
1936. A note on distribution of income over time. *Econometrica* 4, January, 60–66.
1937. Monopoly over time. *Econometrica* 5, April, 160–70.
1938a. The maximization of utility over time. *Econometrica* 6, 154–8.
1938b. The theoretical derivation of dynamic demand curves. *Econometrica* 6, October, 375–80.
1939. Elasticities of expenditure in the dynamic theory of demand. *Econometrica* 7, July, 266–70.
1940. *The Variate Difference Method*. Cowles Commission Monograph No. 5, Bloomington, Indiana: Principia Press.
1941a. The theory of choice under subjective risk and uncertainty. *Econometrica* 9, July–October, 298–304.
1941b. The pure theory of production under technological risk and uncertainty. *Econometrica* 9, July–October, 305–12.
1942a. A contribution to the non-static theory of choice. *Quarterly Journal of Economics* 56, February, 274–306.
1942b. A contribution to the non-static theory of production. In *Studies in Mathematical Economics and Econometrics: in memory of Henry Schultz*, ed. O. Lange et al., Chicago: University of Chicago Press.
1942c. The theory of production under nonstatic conditions. *Journal of Political Economy* 50, October, 645–67.
1946. A note on welfare economics. *Econometrica* 14, January, 69–78.
1949. Foundations of probability and statistical inference. *Journal of the Royal Statistical Society*, Series A (General) 112, Part III, 251–79.
1952. *Econometrics*. New York: Wiley; London: Chapman & Hall.
1953. *Mathematics and Statistics for Economists*. New York: Rinehart.
1955. Stochastic linear programming with applications to agricultural economics. In *Symposium on Linear Programming*, Vol. 1, Washington, DC: National Bureau of Standards.
1960. *Handbuch der Ökonometrie*. Berlin: Springer-Verlag.
1968. *Methodology of Mathematical Economics and Econometrics*. Chicago: University of Chicago Press. Also issued as Vol. II, No. 6, of the *International Encyclopedia of Unified Science*, Chicago: University of Chicago Press.
1972. (With J.K. Sengupta.) *Stochastic Economics: stochastic processes, control, and programming*. New York: Academic Press.

BIBLIOGRAPHY

Anderson, O. 1927. On the logic of the decomposition of statistical series into separate components. *Journal of the Royal Statistical Society* 90, Part III, 548–69.
Charnes, A. and Cooper, W.W. 1959. Chance-constrained programming. *Management Science* 6(1), October, 73–9.
Evans, G.C. 1922. A simple theory of competition. *American Mathematical Monthly* 29, November–December, 371–80.
Evans, G.C. 1924. The dynamics of monopoly. *American Mathematical Monthly* 31, February, 77–83.
Evans, G.C. 1930. *Mathematical Introduction to Economics*. New York: McGraw-Hill.
Fox, K.A., Sengupta, J.K. and Narasimham, G.V.L. (eds) 1969. *Economic Models, Estimation and Risk Programming: Essays in Honor of Gerhard Tintner*. Berlin and New York: Springer-Verlag.
Harper, W.L. and Hooker, C.A. (eds) 1976. *Foundations of Probability Theory, Statistical Inference and Statistical Theories of Science*, Vol. II. Dordrecht: D. Reidel.
Koch, G. and Spizzichino, F. (eds) 1982. *Exchangeability in Probability and Statistics*. Amsterdam: North-Holland.
Kolbin, V.V. 1977. *Stochastic Programming*. Dordrecht: D. Reidel.
Moeseke, P. van. 1965. Stochastic linear programming. *Yale University Economic Essays* 5(1), Spring, 197–253.
Roos, C.F. 1925. A mathematical theory of competition. *American Journal of Mathematics* 47, 163–75.
Roos, C.F. 1934. *Dynamic Economics*. Cowles Commission Monograph No. 1, Bloomington, Indiana: Principia Press.
Sengupta, J.K. 1972. *Stochastic Programming: methods and applications*. Amsterdam: North-Holland.
Sengupta, J.K. 1982. *Decision Models in Stochastic Programming*. Amsterdam: North-Holland.
Sengupta, J.K. 1985. *Information and Efficiency in Economic Decision*. Dordrecht: Martinus Nijhoff.

Titmuss, Richard Morris (1907–1973). Best known as a standard-bearer for the postwar welfare state in Britain, Richard Titmuss was a constant critic of what he saw as the narrow and inhumane doctrines of conventional economics and economists. He reserved particular disdain for those who would have it that the social relationships between individuals which sprang up as a consequence of market exchange were 'natural', desirable, and the very pre-requisites of freedom: 'as freedoms are lost in the marketplace ... truth is an accompanying victim' (1971, p. 240). Inasmuch as Titmuss envisaged individuals as constituent parts of a larger moral community, he carried forward into the postwar world a familiar strand of British social thought which had its origins in the 19th century. But in doing so he changed it in many quite fundamental ways. Marx had omitted any attempt to formulate a morality for a new society (Titmuss, 1971, p. 195), so there was little to be mined from that source. And if only because the postwar world offered new options, Titmuss's vision of the role of social policy in shaping a better community was of neither a reformist, a democratic socialist, nor an old Tory kind. Towards the end of his life, in his well-known book *The Gift Relationship* (1971), he attempted to marry it with a kind of Durkheimian conception of social policy as an instrument of social solidarity and moral regulation.

Titmuss left school at the age of fifteen, and during World War II found his way into the history section of the Cabinet Office. In 1949 he worked with the Medical Research Council. In 1950 he moved to the London School of Economics as professor of social administration.

Two examples may serve to highlight Titmuss's attacks on economics. The first is his *Income Distribution and Social Change* (1962) in which he takes issue with those economists who he believed were arguing at the time that postwar Britain, as well as enjoying full employment, had experienced as marked 'narrowing of inequality'. The criticism consists of a familiar theme: that 'economic' categories used in statistical 'studies of inequality' focused almost exclusively upon the distribution of pecuniary income, thereby ignoring, argued Titmuss, not only other economic factors (like 'wealth') which bear importantly on the question of inequality, but also the extent to which there could be said to be increased equality of access to social services, health care, housing and the like. There is little doubt that he was basically right on this score – the usual indicators of income are quite narrowly defined. The problem is that it is difficult to move from this observation to the claim that the real dimensions of inequality had been forgotten by economists writing explicitly and exclusively about the inequality in the distribution of income (presumably not a useless task). What Titmuss wanted was *more* analysis, what the economists gave him was only a *part* of the story – but the claim that they falsely told their part, however, seems an exaggeration.

The second example is *The Gift Relationship*. Here, however, the charge is more substantial. Titmuss seems to argue that orthodox economic analysis places undue emphasis upon a social psychology of self-interested action, thus denying the human capacity for other-oriented action. It focuses on taking rather than giving. In a sense, Titmuss's view of the social psychology of individuals requires what writers like Durkheim might have called an 'elementary form' of religious life. Of course, the 'religion' is secular, but the function it performs is akin to that performed by 'religion' in traditional societies. That Titmuss thought this re-orientation possible, is evidenced by his strong preference for the voluntary blood donor system of Britain over the market-based system of the USA.

MURRAY MILGATE

SELECTED WORKS

1938. (With F. Le Gros Clark.) *Poverty and Population*. London: Macmillan.

1943. *Birth, Poverty and Wealth*; a study of infant mortality. London: Hamish Hamilton Medical Books.

1950. *Problems of Social Policy*. London: HMSO.

1956a. (With B. Abel-Smith.) *The Cost of the National Health Service*. Cambridge: Cambridge University Press.

1956b. *The Social Division of Welfare*. Liverpool: Liverpool University Press

1958. *Essays on the Welfare State*. London: George Allen & Unwin.

1962. *Income Distribution and Social Change: A Critical Study in British Statistics*. London: George Allen & Unwin.

1968. *Commitment to Welfare*. London: George Allen & Unwin.

1971. *The Gift Relationship: From Human Blood to Social Policy*. London: George Allen & Unwin.

tobits. *See* LOGITS, TOBITS AND PROBITS.

Tocqueville, Alexis Charles Henri Clérel de (1805–1859). Alexis de Tocqueville was born at Verneuil, in Normandy, France, on 29 July 1805. In 1831 he journeyed to the United States with his friend Gustave de Beaumont to study the American penal system. He then wrote *Democracy in America*, the first volume of which appeared in 1835, the second in 1840. Tocqueville was a member of the French chamber of deputies and served briefly as Minister of Foreign Affairs in the republic established after the Revolution of 1848. The events of this period are recounted in his *Recollections* (1893). Tocqueville was among those arrested during the coup d'état of Louis Napoleon on 2 December 1851, and he subsequently retired from public life. Tocqueville devoted his last years to a major study of the French Revolution, although he completed only the first volume before his death. This appeared as *The Old Régime and the French Revolution* in 1856. He died at Cannes on 16 April 1859.

Tocqueville was interested in the political, cultural, and, to a lesser extent, economic consequences of 'democracy', by which he meant not representative government or political arrangements of any sort, but 'equality of conditions'. (John Stuart Mill would argue that Tocqueville had confounded the effects of 'democracy' with the tendencies of modern commercial society.) By equality of conditions, Tocqueville meant neither the absence of classes nor mere equality of opportunity, but something like rough social equality, including, especially, the absence of the legally prescribed hierarchy of social groups characteristic of 'aristocratic' societies.

Tocqueville's major intellectual, not to say political, preoccupation was discovering how 'liberty' might be preserved under democratic conditions. By 'liberty' Tocqueville meant above all the local control and administration of a community's common affairs by a politically engaged and civic-minded populace. He was thus a strong critic of both the administrative centralization of the state and the narrow, self-interested 'individualism' of bourgeois society. This explains Tocqueville's appeal to those on both the right and left of the political spectrum.

Tocqueville's search for the institutional and ideological supports of liberty under democratic conditions was the ulterior purpose of his journey to the United States, a country which had managed to combine democracy and liberty. In *Democracy in America*, Tocqueville analysed a number of factors which he believed helped to maintain political liberty in the United States, including administrative decentralization, the profusion of voluntary associations, and what he termed 'self-interest properly understood', that is, a disposition to devote part of one's time and wealth for the good of the community. *The Old Régime and the French Revolution*, by contrast, explored the failure of France's revolutionary transition to democracy to produce a stable liberal regime; this Tocqueville attributed principally to the immense administrative centralization of the pre-revolutionary period and the consequent degradation of French political culture.

Tocqueville's reflections on economic matters are few. In fact, he once 'confessed' to Naussau Senior that he 'was insufficiently informed on this important portion of human science'. In *The Old Régime*, however, Tocqueville did not hesitate to criticize the Physiocrats, whom he believed perhaps best represented the abstract and utopian type of intellectual nourished by the illiberal environment of pre-revolutionary France. Tocqueville thought that the Physiocrats lacked any concern for political, as opposed to economic, liberty, offering only the 'intellectual panacea' of universal education.

> They were for abolishing all hierarchies, all class distinctions, all differences or rank, and the nation was to be composed of individuals almost exactly alike and unconditionally equal. In this undiscriminated mass was to reside, theoretically, the sovereign power; yet it was to be carefully deprived of any means of controlling or even supervising the activities of its own government.

Tocqueville's reflections on economic matters in *Democracy in America* comprise only a few pages of that voluminous work. Tocqueville argued that rents tend to rise and the terms of leases to shorten in democracies owing to the dissolution of the close, customary relationship between landlord and tenant and its replacement by the impersonal contract. He also thought that democratic conditions made it easier for workmen to combine and pressure their employers for higher wages; he thus argued that 'a slow, progressive rise in wages is one of the general laws characteristic of democratic societies'. At the same time, Tocqueville feared that the very richest industrialists could wait out strikes and force permanently lower wages on their workers. In fact, Tocqueville believed that a dangerous business or industrial 'aristocracy' might arise within the womb of democratic society. However, this potential aristocracy was not to be greatly feared, Tocqueville thought, since industrialists seldom look beyond their own interests and share no common traditions or corporate spirit; still, Tocqueville warned, 'if ever again permanent inequality of conditions and aristocracy make their way into the world, it will have been by that door that they entered'.

J. GOODWIN

SELECTED WORKS

1835. *Democracy in America*, Vol. 1. Ed. J.P. Mayer, trans. G. Lawrence, New York: Doubleday, 1969.

1840. *Democracy in America*, Vol. 2. Ed. J.P. Mayer, trans. G. Lawrence, New York: Doubleday, 1969.

1856. *The Old Régime and the French Revolution*. Trans. S. Gilbert from the 4th French edn of 1858, New York: Doubleday, 1955.

1872. *Correspondence and Conversations of Alexis de Tocqueville with Naussau William Senior, 1834–1859*. 2nd, edn. ed. M.C.M. Simpson. Reprinted, New York: A.M. Kelley, 1968.
1893. *Recollections*. Ed. J.P. Mayer and A.P. Kerr, trans. G. Lawrence, New York: Doubleday, 1970.

Tooke, Thomas (1774–1858). Thomas Tooke, the leading member of the Banking School, was born at St Petersburg in 1774, the eldest son of William Tooke, historian of Russia and man of letters, at that time chaplain to the English church at St Petersburg. Not a professional scientist but an active man of business of comfortable social standing, Thomas was successively a partner in the London firms of Stephen Thornton & Co. and Astell, Tooke & Thornton, Russian merchants, and was governor of the Royal Exchange Corporation and chairman of the St. Katharine's Dock Company. In 1802 he married Priscilla Combe, by whom he had three sons.

As an early supporter of the free trade movement, he drew up the Merchants' Petition of the City of London, which contained the statement of the principles of free trade and was presented to the House of Commons in May 1820. He gave evidence on monetary questions before several parliamentary committees, from the Resumption Committees of 1819 to the Committees on Bank Acts in the 1850s. Tooke was elected Fellow of the Royal Society in March 1821; shortly afterwards, with Ricardo, Malthus, James Mill and others, he founded the Political Economy Club and took a prominent part in its discussions until very late in his life. He died in London on 26 February 1858. A few days later, in a letter to Engels, Marx wrote: 'Friend Thomas Tooke has died, and with him the last English economist of any value' (Letter of 5 March 1858, in Marx and Engels, 1983, p. 284).

Tooke's writings may be divided into two groups, two phases of his work which it is useful to distinguish for a better appraisal of his contribution. The first phase consists essentially in a systematic attempt to collect and analyse as much historical material and statistical information as possible, connected with price changes in England from 1793 onwards: a thorough observation of facts, aimed at understanding the determinants of fluctuations in the domestic price level. This phase is represented by his writings from 1823 to 1838 – from Tooke's first pamphlet *Thoughts and Details on the High and Low Prices of the Thirty Years from 1793 to 1822* to the first two volumes of his *History of Prices*, that is to say, with his *Considerations on the State of the Currency* (1826) *and* the two *Letters* to Lord Grenville (1829) in between. In the second group of writings, Tooke finally brings into focus and elaborates a few significant general principles which he gradually became certain could be derived from his observation of facts; moreover, he fully perceives the conflict between those principles and the prevailing notions, and copes with the arguments of his critics. This second phase of Tooke's work covers the writings from Vol. III of the *History* (1840) to Volumes V–VI (1857, a year before Tooke's death) and comprises his *Inquiry into the Currency Principle* (1844) – the most representative and outstanding piece, together with Vol. IV of the *History* (1848), of Tooke's voluminous work.

The main result emerging from Tooke's observation of facts in the first group of writings can be summarized as follows: the great fluctuations of prices that occurred in the 45 years following 1792 must be attributed to circumstances affecting the conditions of supply of commodities, rather than to the alterations in the system of the currency – the latter being represented by the suspension of convertiblity from 1793 and its resumption after 1819 (by the Resumption Act of 1819). The prevailing view was that the value of the currency had been depreciated by the suspension, and enhanced by the contraction in the amount of circulating medium that the resumption of convertibility was alleged to have brought about. According to Tooke, 'the most extensive induction of facts' made it apparent that the phenomena of high prices from 1792 to 1819 and of the comparatively low prices after 1819, did not originate in the variations in the quantity of money (independently of whether the latter proceeded from the alterations in the system of the currency or from any other cause). The great fluctuations of prices originated instead from alterations in the cost of production and from other 'accidents' affecting supply: the character of the seasons (more unfavourable on the average from 1793 to 1818 than from 1818 to 1837); marked variations in the cost of imported commodities, as well as in the existence and removal of various obstacles (revolutions, wars) from the several sources of foreign supply; significant improvements in machinery and sciences generally, all tending to reduce the cost of production of numerous commodities (or to provide cheaper substitutes). In Volume II of the *History*, the rate of interest is listed for the first time amongst the causes of the high and of the low prices in the period under consideration – 'a higher rate of interest constituting an increased cost of production' and 'a reduction of the general rate of interest' leading 'to reproduction at a diminished cost' (1838, pp. 847 and 849). As we shall see, this is in our view the crucial point upon which hinge those aspects of Tooke's contribution that are most relevant for the modern scholar of capitalism.

The connection between money and prices occupies the centre of the stage in the second group of Tooke's writings: 'the prepossession or prejudice', as he puts it, that the quantity of money must have a direct influence on the prices of commodities. By 'money' must be understood, Tooke insists in pointing out to the supporters of the Currency Theory, not only coin and paper money (bank notes), but also cheques, bills of exchange, settlements and whatever form of paper credit which may come to be a component part of the circulating medium, performing the functions of money in daily transactions. By 1844 he was fully convinced

> that the prices of commodities do not depend upon the quantity of money indicated by the amount of bank notes, nor upon the amount of the whole of the circulating medium; but that, on the contrary, the amount of the circulating medium is the consequence of prices (1844, p. 123).

Tooke's evidence for this conclusion was ultimately the fact that the banks, including the Bank of England, did not appear to have the power to add to the quantity of money in circulation – unless other independent circumstances, such as an extension of trade and a rise in prices, were 'coincidently' in progress (1844, p. 66); nor did the banks appear to have the power to diminish the total amount of the circulation. Banks may withold loans and discounts, and may refuse any longer to issue their own notes, but those loans, discounts and notes will be replaced in due course, Tooke argues, 'by other expedients calculated to answer the same purpose' (ibid., p. 122). Only compulsory paper money issued directly by a government in payment for goods and services (like the French *assignats*) constitutes a fresh source of demand, so that alterations in its quantity act directly as an originating cause on prices (see 1844, pp. 68–78; 1848, pp. 183–97).

The power of the banks to expand and contract the quantity

of the circulating medium at pleasure, was taken for granted by the Currency School and by most writers. It was a challenging task, for Tooke and the Banking School, to convince those writers of the lack of such a power, and, in consequence, of the fact that such alterations in the quantity of money as do actually occur are the *effect* of increased transactions and prices, and not the *cause* of them. Tooke has the great merit of having succeeded in bringing into focus the heart of the matter: the question of the effects of changes in the rate of interest on the inducement to purchase commodities. 'Abundance of money' – i.e. a high disposition on the part of the banks to make advances in the way of loan or discount – results in the first place in a high price of securities and a low rate of interest; thus the power of the banks to add to the amount of the circulating medium, and hence to act as an originating cause on trade and prices, will ultimately depend on whether a low rate of interest supplies the *stimulus* to purchase commodities. Tooke points out that actual experience does not validate the notion that the facility of borrowing at a low rate of interest, not only confers the power of purchasing commodities, but also affords the motive and inducement to do it. 'The error', he says, 'is in supposing the *disposition* or *will* to be co-extensive with the power' (1844, p. 79). No relation of cause and effect between variations in the rate of interest and variations in the demand for commodities can be inferred from trustworthy evidence (cf. 1857, Vol. V, p. 345).

The questions of the connection between money and prices and between the rate of interest and the price level are thus clearly seen as two sides of the same coin. Arguing against the dominant opinion that a low rate of interest raises prices and that a high rate depresses them, Tooke actually maintained that a persistent reduction in the rate of interest constitutes a reduction in the cost of production, which could not fail, by the competition of the producers, to bring about a fall of prices (cf. 1844, p. 81). He went so far as to state that it is difficult to find evidence of facts more in contrast with the influence ascribed to a low rate of interest in raising prices and viceversa: 'The theory is not only not true, but the reverse of the truth' (ibid., p. 84).

It is important to notice that Tooke's conception of the relation between the rate of interest and the price level, and the connected notion of 'endogenous money' (as we would now call his view of the relation between money and prices), are in no way contingent upon the particular currency system of his day, with the relevant part played in it by precious metals. Rather, it is the denial of any power on the part of the banks to regulate at will the amount of the circulating medium, together with the emphasis on the circumstances affecting supply, that provide Tooke with the basis for his criticism of the idea that every influx or efflux of the precious metals must cause a rise and fall of prices, independently of circumstances connected with the cost of production of commodities. On that same basis he opposes the prevailing view that the discovery of a gold mine within the premises of the Bank of England – Ricardo's famous assumption in his first pamphlet (1811) – would necessarily raise the prices of commodities. And he argues that for an increased production of gold to be associated with a permanent rise in the prices of commodities, measured in gold, the increased production must be the consequence either of the discovery of more fertile mines, or of improved methods of working the existing ones (1848, pp. 199 et seq.; 1857, Vol. VI, pp. 413–4).

Monetary policy questions, naturally, permeate all of Tooke's writings. The chief place amongst them is occupied by the Bank Charter Act of 1844 and the controversies that both preceded and followed its implementation – controversies centred upon the idea of a separation of the business of the note-issue from the banking business of the Bank of England. This idea, opposed by Tooke, was given statutory effect by the Act, and brought about in due time many of the shortcomings that had been foreseen by Tooke (for an extensive critical account of Tooke's views on banking policy, see Gregory, 1928; 1929, Vol. I).

On several policy issues that are still relevant today, the modern orthodox scholar of monetary questions and central banking policy is likely to find himself more in agreement with Tooke's views than with those of the supporters of the Currency School. This hardly applies, however, to those views of Tooke's which are more strictly connected with his conception of the relation between money and prices, and of the influence of the rate of interest on the price level. As an important example of one such view, one may refer to Tooke's contention that, as the Bank of England and the banks collectively cannot arbitrarily change the amount of the circulating medium, nor operate through that medium on the prices of commodities, the only 'infallible means' they have to influence foreign exchanges – 'so as to arrest a drain, or to resist an excessive influx' – is by a forcible operation on securities: a great advance in the rate of interest on the one hand, or a great reduction of it in the other. Now, the articulated line of argument laid down by Tooke in discussing the power of the central bank to influence foreign exchanges (cf. 1844, pp. 123–4), appears on the whole no less alien from today's quantity of money approach to problems of general prices than it was at Tooke's day.

Besides Marx (cf. above, and also 1857–8; 1859), Tooke's most outstanding contemporaries who praised his work and ideas were Malthus (1823) and J.S. Mill (1844; 1852, ch. XXIV, pp. 203–4). (Malthus's appreciation, however, must not be overrated: he tends to understand Tooke's early contribution merely as a confirmation of his own views on value against those of Ricardo – namely, 'that everything must be attributed to supply and demand', rather than simply to 'labour and the costs of production'; 1823, p. 218). The most strenuous opponent of Tooke's ideas and policy recommendations was Robert Torrens (1840, 1844, 1848). This author's criticisms grew increasingly severe as Tooke's work advanced with the development of more general principles from the empirical analyses. By 1844, Tooke's thesis that the prices of commodities do not depend upon the quantity of money is referred to and criticized as 'the most astonishing of the many astonishing fallacies' (Torrens, 1844, p. 43). Torrens's criticisms are extensively dealt with by Tooke in Vol. IV of the *History of Prices* (1848), and by Fullarton (1844) and Wilson (1847).

If Torrens was the most outstanding critic of Tooke amongst classical economists, Knut Wicksell, the father of 20th-century monetary theory, has been his most outstanding critic since the inception of marginalism. Wicksell's conceptions ultimately constitute the main reference-point of this century's (not so large) literature in which Tooke's work and ideas are somehow taken into consideration, starting from Gregory's *Introduction* to the *History of Prices* (1828). In fact, we can look today at Tooke and Wicksell as the chief exponents of two alternative ways of reasoning about the connection between money and prices. Wicksell's criticisms of Tooke's view are somewhat vitiated by their being mostly based upon the interest elasticity of the demand for loan capital, as postulated by the marginalist theory (see 1898, ch. 7; 1906, pp. 175–208). There is, however, one important criticism which does not reflect Wicksell's tendency to superimpose upon Tooke's view his own theory. He criticizes Tooke's reasoning about the effect of the rate of interest on the cost of production and commodities prices, as entailing that every persistent move in either direction would cause a progressive divergence of both interest and prices from their initial levels: a persistent reduction in the rate of interest

> would lead to a reduction ... in the demand for loans by business people, money would flow into the banks and would cause a further reduction of interest rates, and so on, until the rate fell to nil – In other words, the money rate of interest would be in a state of unstable equilibrium (Wicksell, 1906, p. 187).

This conclusion actually follows, not from Tooke's view of the influence of the rate of interest on prices, but from his conception of the rate of interest as a magnitude 'entirely governed by the supply of and demand for monied capital', on which the central bank can exercise only a *temporary* influence (1826, sect. I; 1857, pp. 556–7; see also Newmarch, 1857, pp. 66–72).

Not to have acknowledged that the monetary authorities do have the power of determining the rate of interest – albeit a power exercised under a wide range of constraints – constitutes, in our opinion, the main shortcoming of Thomas Tooke and the Banking School.

MASSIMO PIVETTI

SELECTED WORKS

1823. *Thoughts and Details on the High and Low Prices of the Last Thirty Years.* London: John Murray.
1826. *Considerations on the State of the Currency.* London: John Murray.
1829a. *A Letter to Lord Grenville, on the effects ascribed to the resumption of cash payments on the value of the currency.* London: John Murray.
1829b. *A Second Letter to Lord Grenville, on the currency in connexion with the corn trade and on the corn laws, to which is added a postscript on the present commercial stagnation.* London: John Murray.
1838. *A History of Prices and of the State of the Circulation from 1793 to 1837.* 2 vols, London: Longman, Orme, Brown, Green & Longmans.
1840. *A History of Prices and of the State of the Circulation in 1838 and 1839, with remarks on the corn laws and some of the alterations in our banking system.* London: Longman, Orme, Brown, Green & Longmans.
1844. *An Inquiry into the Currency Principle; the connection of the currency with prices and the expediency of a separation of issue from banking.* 2nd edn, Series of Reprints of Scarce Works on Political Economy No. 15. London: London School of Economics and Political Sciences, 1959.
1848. *A History of Prices and of the State of the Currency from 1839 to 1847 inclusive: with a general review of the currency question and remarks on the operation of the Act 7 & 8 Vict. 32.* London: Longman, Brown, Green & Longmans.
1856. *On the Bank Charter Act of 1844, its Principles and Operations; with suggestions for an improved administration of the Bank of England.* London: Longman, Brown, Green & Longmans.
1857. (With W. Newmarch.) *A History of Prices and of the State of the Circulation During the Nine Years 1848–1856* (in Two Volumes; forming the fifth and sixth volumes of the history of prices from 1792 to the present time). London: Longman, Brown, Green, Longmans & Roberts.

BIBLIOGRAPHY

Fullarton, J. 1844. *On the Regulation of Currencies; being an examination of the principles on which it is proposed to restrict, within certain fixed limits, the future issues on credit of the Bank of England, and of the other banking establishments throughout the country.* London: John Murray.
Gregory, T.E. 1928. *An Introduction to Tooke and Newmarch's A History of Prices and of the State of the Circulation from 1792 to 1856.* Series of Reprints of Scarce Works on Political Economy No. 16. London: London School of Economics and Political Sciences, 1962.
Gregory, T.E. 1929. *British Banking Statutes and Reports, 1832–1928.* 2 vols, London: Oxford University Press.
Johnson, A. 1856. *Currency Principles versus Banking Principles; being strictures on Mr Tooke's pamphlet on the Bank Charter Act of 1844.* London: Richardson Brothers.
Malthus, T.R. 1823. Review of Tooke's 'Thoughts and Details on the High and Low Prices of the Last Thirty Years'. *Quarterly Review* 29, April, 214–39.
Marx, K. [1857–8]. *Grundrisse* (Rough Draft): *Foundations of the Critique of Political Economy.* Harmondsworth: Penguin, 1973.
Marx, K. 1859. *A Contribution to the Critique of Political Economy.* Moscow: Progress Publishers, 1978.
Marx, K. and Engels, F. 1983. *Collected Works.* London: Lawrence & Wishart, Vol. XL.
Mill, J.S. 1844. Review of Tooke's 'An Inquiry into the Currency Principle'. *Westminster Review*, March–June.
Mill, J.S. 1852. *Principles of Political Economy, with Some of Their Applications to Social Philosophy.* 3rd edn. London: John W. Parker and Son.
Newmarch, W. 1857. Evidence before the Select Committee of the House of Commons on Bank Acts, 5th June. In Gregory (1929), Vol. II.
Ricardo, D. 1811. *The High Price of Bullion, a Proof of the Depreciation of Bank Notes.* 4th edn. In *The Works and Correspondence of David Ricardo*, ed. P. Sraffa, Vol. 3. Cambridge: Cambridge University Press, 1966.
Ricardo, D. 1811. *Reply to Mr Bosanquet's Practical Observations on the Report of the Bullion Committee.* In *The Works and Correspondence of David Ricardo*, ed. by P. Sraffa, Vol. 3. Cambridge: Cambridge University Press, 1966.
Torrens, R. 1840. *A Letter to Thomas Tooke, esq. in reply to his objections against the separation of the business of the Bank into a department of issue, and a department of deposit and discount: with a plan of bank reform.* London: Longman, Orme, Brown, Green & Longmans.
Torrens, R. 1844. *An Inquiry into the Practical Working of the Proposed Arrangements for the Renewal of the Charter of the Bank of England, and the Regulation of the Currency: with a refutation of the fallacies advanced by Mr Tooke.* London: Smith, Elder & Co.
Torrens, R. 1848. *The Principles and Practical Operation of Sir Robert Peel's Bill of 1844 Explained and Defended against the Objections of Tooke, Fullarton, and Wilson.* London: Longman, Brown, Green & Longmans.
Wicksell, K. 1898. *Interest and Prices.* London: Macmillan, 1936.
Wicksell, K. 1906. *Lectures on Political Economy.* Vol. II: *Money.* London: Routledge & Kegan Paul, 1962.
Wilson, J. 1847. *Capital, Currency, and Banking; being a collection of a series of articles published in the 'Economist' in 1845, on the principles of the Bank Act of 1844, and in 1847, on the recent monetarial and commercial crisis; concluding with a plan for a secure and economical currency.* London: The Economist.

Torrens, Robert (1780–1864). Torrens, if not in the top rank of the classical economists, or in the class for example of Ricardo, Senior or John Stuart Mill, certainly was of the second rank and was the equal of, or even above, James Mill or McCulloch in terms of originality, theoretical reasoning and the range of economic topics that he considered. His work was almost completely neglected in the years after his death in 1864 and his re-emergence to his rightful place as an important member of the Classical School was initially due to Seligman in his famous article 'On Some Neglected British Economists' (1913) and later to the definitive study by Lionel Robbins (1955). In recent years Torrens has also come to the fore again because of the debates surrounding the Sraffa interpretation of Ricardo.

Robert Torrens was a most prolific writer and produced a vast quantity of books and pamphlets on all sorts of economic matters for over fifty years. His first publication appeared in 1808 (*The Economists Refuted*) and his last in 1858 (*Lord Overstone on Metal and Paper Currency*). He managed all of this against the background of an extremely busy life that included several different careers. He was a professional soldier – a Colonel in the Marines – and was decorated for gallantry at the battle of Anholt. Subsequently he became the proprietor of the Globe Newspaper, a member of Parliament, the planning genius behind the colonization and development of New South Wales, a founder member of the Political Economy Club and many other things besides. He even found time to write two never-read novels, the *Hermit of Killarney* and *Coelibia in Search of Husband*, both of which contain hefty chunks of economic discourse.

His specific contributions to economics may be dealt with under the general headings of microeconomics; theory of money and banking, commercial policy and colonization.

Torrens's main contributions to microeconomics concerned the Ricardian system. He objected to the search for an absolute, invariant measure of value and also tried to replace the labour quantity theory of value with a capital theory of value – where relative commodity values are determined by relative capital inputs. He did not however fully realize that his definition of capital combining wages and materials was different from Ricardo's which was really only wages.

On the other hand, and somewhat inconsistently it is now clear (see Laner, 1982; de Vivo, 1985) that Torrens fully understood the corn-ratio theory of profits, that Sraffa ascribed to Ricardo, and that he (Torrens) derived this from Ricardo. He also saw, following Ricardo that given the agricultural rate of profit, the price of manufactured goods relative to corn, was given. All of this is clearly spelt out in the second edition of *An Essay on the External Corn Trade* (1820) and must therefore lead one to doubt Hollander's argument (1979) that Ricardo did not mean the corn-ratio theory of profit and the key role of the agriculture sector in his analysis to be taken too seriously.

In the first edition (1815) of the *Essay* Torrens has a clear statement of the principle of comparative advantage well before its more popularly ascribed origins in Ricardo's *Principles* (1819). He makes a clear distinction between absolute and comparative advantage and indeed he actually hints at this distinction in his earlier *Economist Refuted* (1808).

In the field of money and banking Torrens is best known for his championing of the Currency School in their debate with the Banking School. Essentially the currency principle was that a mixed currency, that is, a currency consisting of notes and coins, should be regulated so that movements in it were the same as under a purely metallic currency. Unlike the bullionists, however, the Currency School did not believe that convertibility alone would achieve the conformability of a mixed currency to a metallic one. To this end, Torrens may claim to have been the originator of the plan, activated in the Bank Charter Act of 1844, to separate the issue and banking department of the Bank of England. This he did in his *Letter to Lord Melbourne* (1837) and he later vigourously defined the legislation in his *Principles and Practical Operation of Sir Robert Peel's Bill of 1844* (1848).

Students of Torrens find an inconsistency with this aspect of his monetary thinking and his earlier exposing of the anti-bullionist position; in particular his *Essay on Money and Paper Currency* (1812) is a strong plea for a paper currency without convertibility and relying on the real bills doctrine to prevent excess issue. The reasons for abandoning this extreme anti-bullionist position and his switch to the Ricardian live are explained in his *On the Means of Establishing a Cheap, Secure and Uniform Currency* (1828).

Torrens's main contribution to the theory of commercial policy was to suggest a modification of the general classical case for free trade. He pointed out, and was amongst the first to do so, that a country might alter its terms of trade in its favour by use of an import tariff. In a series of letters to Lord John Russell (published in 1844 as *The Budget*) he argued the case for what he termed 'reciprocity'. that is, if some countries had tariffs unilateral free trade was a mistaken policy and in these cases reciprocal tariffs should be adopted. Against the change that he was abandoning the central classical (Ricardian) belief in free trade, Torrens replied that he was just applying the logic of the Ricardian analysis.

Finally, Torrens had a significant influence on the theory and practice of colonization. Along with most of the later classical economists he rejected the Smithian view that colonies were of no economic benefit to the colonial power. Much of the later classical case for Colonies was based on the view that colonies would provide profitable investment outlets to offset a declining rate of profit at home. Torrens used this argument in some of his later writings but his main argument was that colonies were an ideal solution to the Malthusian overpopulation problem. In this view he was undoubtedly influenced by his interpretation of the causes of Irish poverty – a country incidently where Torrens was born and in general its problems had a profound effect on his thinking.

In terms of colonization policy Torrens, like Wakefield, was opposed to the movement of labour on to free land on the grounds that this would lead to a dispersed population and land holdings of sub-optimal size. He advocated systematic colonization with the price of land set sufficiently high that large units of capital would have to be amassed before the immigrant labourers became independent farmers.

B.A. Corry

SELECTED WORKS

1820. *An Essay on the External Corn Trade*. London: Longman, Rees, Orme, Brown & Green.

1821. *An Essay on the Production of Wealth*. London: Longman, Hurst, Rees, Orme, & Brown.

1835. *Colonization of South Australia*. London: Longman, Rees, Orme, Brown, & Green.

1838. *A Letter to the Right Honourable Lord Viscount Melbourne*. London: Longman, Rees, Orme, Brown & Green.

1840. *The Budget*. London: Smith, Elder & Co.

1847. *On the Operation of the Bank Charter Act of 1844*. London: Smith & Elder.

BIBLIOGRAPHY

De Vivo, G. 1985. Robert Torrens and Ricardo's 'corn-ratio' theory of profits. *Cambridge Journal of Economics* 9(1), March, 89–92.

Langer, G.F. 1982. Further evidence for Sraffa's interpretation of Ricardo. *Cambridge Journal of Economics* 6(4), December, 397–400.

Robbins, L.C. 1958. *Robert Torrens and the Evolution of Classical Economics*. London: Macmillan & Co. (This book includes brief summaries of all of Torrens's writings.)

total factor productivity. In the post-World War II period 'growth accounting' became a popular field in macroeconomics. This branch of applied economics sought to measure the contribution to the overall growth of the economy of the 'immediate' sources of growth, that is, the inputs into some kind of implicit production function for the whole economy. The core of this analysis was the determination of the contribution of labour and capital to the growth of output, with that part of growth still unaccounted for being alternatively referred to as technical progress, our ignorance, increased efficiency or total factor productivity (Domar, 1961, 1962).

The starting point of the accounting procedure was to specify the mathematical form by which the two inputs were to be combined in order to obtain a measure of total factor input, together with some rules for weighting their contribution (Fabricant, 1954; Kendrick, 1961; Denison, 1974, 1979). For example write (1)

$$A = Q/(K^{\omega_1} L^{\omega_2})$$

where Q, K and L are total output, the capital stock and the labour force respectively, w_1 and w_2 are weights and A is the geometric index of the total factor productivity. For convenience the expression is then transformed into growth rates giving (2) $A' = Q' - w_1 K' - w_2 L'$ where A', Q', K' and L' represent rates of growth of the variables.

The numerical values chosen for the weights were usually the share of output or income accruing to capital and labour in the particular country or P/Q and W/Q, where P and W are total profits and wages, respectively. Since total profits and wages exhaust total output, that is, $P/Q + W/Q = 1$, the assumption of constant returns to scale was made an important part of the exercise.

The justifications of the weighting schemes in growth accounting have never been convincing nor have they been well defended. For example, in short-run and long-run equilibrium under competitive conditions, factor shares do measure the contributions of each input, but the real world hardly conforms to the model of perfect competition whether in or out of equilibrium. What kind of bias this weighting procedure might introduce has never been made clear.

SOME IMPLICATIONS. The weighting of capital's and labour's contributions by the share of income accruing to each factor had two important and unmistakable results. First, it reduced the share of capital's contribution to the growth of output to near insignificance. Thus, using equation (2) the contribution of capital to growth can be written $(P/Q)\cdot Q'$ or, expressed as a ratio of the total growth of output, $[(P/Q)\cdot Q']/Q'$. If it is then recognized that over a period of 10 to 20 years the rates of growth of capital and output in an economy are approximately equal, that is, $K' \simeq Q'$, the percentage contribution of the growth of the capital stock to output growth is simply P/Q, the share of profits in output.

The unimportance of capital is brought out quite clearly in a growth accounting study of the 1950s and 1960s, a period of rapid recovery and extraordinary growth in most of the capitalist economies, in which the contributions of capital formation by business and households were calculated separately (Denison, 1967). In a sample of eight Northwest European countries treated as a single country, profits earned on non-residential plant and equipment as a share of output produced was about 14 per cent. The same ratio for the United States was 11 per cent. This means that following this accounting method only something like 10 to 15 per cent of growth can be accounted for by capital formation in non-residential plant and equipment.

If during this period the rate of growth of capital had been zero, the rate of growth of output would have fallen from 4.7 to 4.1 per cent in Northwestern Europe and from 3.4 to 3.0 per cent in the United States. Clearly according to the growth accounting methods, investment by business is a minor source of economic growth. Given the fact that this was a period of recovery and rapid development of new industries requiring new production technologies, serious questions have been raised about the reliability of the growth accounting procedure.

A SECOND IMPLICATION. Growth accounting procedures lead to another important result: an inability to explain very much of the actual growth performance on the basis of what has usually been considered by economists to be the two key sources of growth, the growth of capital and labour. Study after study utilizing the growth accounting framework found that after the contributions of the two inputs had been taken into account A'/Q' remained unusually large, for instance, of the order of magnitude of one-half. Whether this residual is referred to as efficiency, technical progress or total factor productivity, critics have been quick to point out that, at best, something is clearly missing in the analysis.

The response to the inability to explain much of growth by considering only the two factor inputs has been to devise new measures of the inputs and to introduce additional inputs to account for the unexplained part of growth. Obviously in principle it is possible to account eventually for all the residual part of growth in this way, although critics have also argued that the whole approach may be seriously flawed. The procedure lends itself to a charge of arbitrariness since no test is offered to justify the inclusion of the new measurements and new variables (other than their 'reasonableness').

Additional inputs suggested include economies of scale, R&D outlays, technical progress based on innovations and the reallocation of labour. The introduction of scale economies as an explanatory factor implies that any weighting procedure which initially assumes constant returns to scale is incorrect. It also suggests that there may be interaction effects between the rates of growth of the factor inputs and total factor productivity, A'. Furthermore, since it is difficult to reallocate labour and to implement innovations in general and R&D results in particular without providing new capital, a similar interaction between capital formation and that part of total factor productivity attributed to reallocation of labour, technical progress and R&D outlays is suggested. Taking account of these interactions would certainly increase the contribution of capital and total factor inputs to growth.

More generally, this recognition of interaction effects calls into question any growth accounting procedure that assumes that the rate of growth of factor inputs, especially capital, can be separated from that part of growth attributed to the various inputs used to reduce the size of A' (Nelson, 1964, 1981). This point is given added force when it is recalled that the growth process throughout the modern history of capitalism has been one of unbalanced growth in which some sectors decline in importance at the same time as others rise (Schumpeter, 1912; Svennilson, 1954). It has been the rapid-growth industries that have experienced relatively high rates of growth of total factor productivity and technical progress. Given the pronounced non-malleability and immobility of capital this technical progress and growing efficiency could not have occurred without capital formation.

ACCOUNTING FOR STAGNATION. What has just been said is relevant in evaluating the growth accounting explanations of the stagnation in capitalist economies that began in the early 1970s and continues today. Rates of growth of output have slowed noticeably as have rates of growth of the capital stock.

Using the traditional growth-accounting technique the role of reduced capital formation in the current stagnation has been found to be slight (Bosworth, 1982). These results should be neither surprising nor acceptable as an explanation of the current stagnation. Rather these findings should be an additional reason for questioning the growth-accounting framework.

JOHN CORNWALL

See also GROWTH ACCOUNTING; PRODUCTIVITY: MEASUREMENT PROBLEMS; VINTAGES.

BIBLIOGRAPHY

Bosworth, B. 1982. Capital formation and economic policy. *Brookings Papers on Economic Activity* 2, 273–317.
Denison, E. 1967. *Why Growth Rates Differ: Postwar Experience in Nine Western Countries.* Washington, DC: Brookings.
Denison, E. 1974. *Accounting for United States Economic Growth, 1929–1969.* Washington, DC: Brookings.
Denison, E. 1979. *Accounting for Slower Economic Growth: The United States in the 1970s.* Washington, DC: Brookings.
Domar, E. 1961. On the measurement of technological change. *Economic Journal* 71, December, 709–29.
Domar, E. 1962. On total productivity and all that. *Journal of Political Economy* 70, December, 597–608.
Fabricant, S. 1954. *Economic Progress and Economic Change.* National Bureau of Economic Research, 34th Annual New York: National Bureau of Economic Research .
Kendrick, J. 1961. *Productivity Trends in the United States.* Princeton: Princeton University Press.
Nelson, R. 1964. Aggregate production functions and medium-range growth projections. *American Economic Review* 54(5), September, 575–606.
Nelson, R. 1981. Research on productivity growth and productivity differences: dead ends and new departures. *Journal of Economic Literature* 19(3), September, 1029–64.
Schumpeter, J.A. 1912. *The Theory of Economic Development. An inquiry into profits, capital, credit, interest, and the business cycle.* Trans. R. Opie, Cambridge, Mass.: Harvard University Press, 1934. Reissued, New York: Oxford University Press, 1961.
Svennilson, I. 1954. *Growth and Stagnation in the European Economy.* Geneva: EEC.

town planning. *See* URBAN ECONOMICS.

Townshend, Hugh (1890–1974). Townshend is an anomaly amongst economists, for he owes his reputation almost entirely to one brilliant article. He took a First in Mathematics at Cambridge in 1912 and stayed on to prepare for the Civil Service examinations under Keynes's supervision. He served with the Post Office, where his duties included economic forecasting.

His correspondence with Keynes over the just-published *General Theory* (Keynes, 1979) reveals both the extent of Townshend's intellectual grasp of that complex and difficult book and something, whether derived from his studies with Keynes or innate in his temperament, which allowed him to accept aspects of *The General Theory* which others resisted. These qualities bore fruit in the famous 12-page article, published as a Note in the *Economic Journal* (1937a). This note takes issue with Hicks's attempt, in his review of the *General Theory* (1936), to transform the theory of liquidity preference into a mirror image of loanable funds theory by Walras' Law. Townshend saw that this was an attempt to retain the link between prices and the flow concepts of cost and demand. In contrast, he argued, it was in the nature of Keynes's liquidity preference theory that expectations of the future could change the value of assets overnight and be reflected in market prices of those assets even in the absence of actual trading. Thus current prices could be determined by subjective as well as objective factors and future prices were indeterminate.

Townshend's achievement was to 'follow liquidity preference theory where it led: to the destruction of determinate price' (Shackle, 1967). Keynes had left this implicit.

Townshend's restatement required the courage to go against established modes of thought: whether by temperament or because they are imbued with outdated conceptions of science, most economists are determinists. Townshend's stock can only rise as the methodological change that has occurred in science becomes known across the divide between science and the arts.

Townshend also wrote four book reviews for the *Economic Journal* (1937b, 1938, 1939, 1940) which show a breadth of conception and keenness of intellect from which one wishes Economics had benefited more.

VICTORIA CHICK

SELECTED WORKS

1937a. Liquidity-premium and the theory of value. *Economic Journal* 47, March, 157–69.
1937b. Review of R.G. Hawtrey, *Capital and Employment. Economic Journal* 47, June, 321–6.
1938. Review of G.L.S. Shackle, *Expectations, Investment and Income. Economic Journal* 48, September, 520–23.
1939. Review of H. Munro, *Principles of Monetary-Industrial Stability. Economic Journal* 49, March, 102–5.
1940. Review of F. Hayek, *Profits, Interests and Investment. Economic Journal* 50, March, 99–103.

BIBLIOGRAPHY

Hicks, J.R. 1936. Mr. Keynes's theory of employment (review article). *Economic Journal* 46, June, 238–53.
Keynes, J.M. 1936. *The General Theory of Employment, Interest and Money.* London: Macmillan.
Keynes, J.M. 1973, 1979. *Collected Writings of J.M. Keynes,* vols. XIV, XXIX. ed. D.E. Moggridge. London: Macmillan.
Shackle, G.L.S. 1967. *The Years of High Theory: Invention and Tradition in Economic Thought, 1926–1939.* Cambridge: Cambridge University Press.

Toynbee, Arnold (1852–1883). Arnold Toynbee, best known for his lectures on the industrial revolution (published posthumously in May 1884), was during the late 1870s and early 1880s a major influence on the shape and direction of the interest at Oxford in socio-economic questions and their history.

Born in London on 23 August 1852, Arnold Toynbee was the fourth child and second son of Dr Joseph Toynbee, FRS, a philanthropist and a successful aural surgeon. Initial plans for his education at Rugby were first delayed by an accident at the age of 13 or 14 which resulted in severe concussion and, in the long run, in recurring migrains, impeding prolonged mental exertion. These plans were finally shelved for financial reasons following Joseph Toynbee's death in a laboratory accident. After two unprofitable years in a military preparatory school, and some classes at King's College, London, Toynbee's education was reduced to long periods of solitary reading.

He developed an independent if unsystematic bent, coupled with overconfidence in his capability to master on his own any subject which might catch his attention.

Having come into a modest inheritance from his father's estate at the age of 21, Toynbee entered Pembroke College,

Oxford, in January 1873 with the intention of reading for Greats. He shortly afterwards migrated to Balliol, which he found socially and intellectually more attractive. For health reasons he eventually settled for a Pass degree, obtained in 1878. However, he had impressed the college sufficiently to be offered a tutorship in charge of the candidates for the Indian Civil Service. In 1881 he was appointed Senior Bursar, and at the time of his death was about to be elected Fellow. Toynbee had meanwhile become involved in a number of public causes, all of which may be seen as related to efforts to revive Liberalism as a radical-reformist movement. These included church reform aimed at the democratization of Church of England government on the parish level, adult education through the cooperative movement, rural reform, Irish land reform, and municipal politics. In 1883 he stood, unsuccessfully, as a Liberal candidate for one of the North Ward seats on the Oxford City Council (represented by T.H. Green until his death in 1882) and Toynbee may well have contemplated the possibility of a political career. His academic interests reflect his search for a scientifically reasoned programme for comprehensive reform, while his inquiries were greatly influenced by a fear of the consequences of rising working-class radicalism.

The industrial revolution lectures, delivered in 1881–2, offered a liberal interpretation of industrialization and its political, social and economic consequences as an alternative to both socialist and laissez-faire views of industrial society. Despite their ideological bias and fragmentary form they constituted an important departure in English economic history. They demonstrated the usefulness of an historical approach to the study of industrial society, thereby suggesting an alternative to economic theory, which at the time was increasingly regarded as either morally or ideologically unacceptable or as inapplicable to current conditions. Hence Toynbee directly contributed to the Oxford inclination towards an empirical and historical approach to the study of socio-economic questions. In addition, Toynbee outlined the possibility of an historical and, thereby, a relativist consideration of economic theories, seen as reflecting historical circumstances in which they were formed and, while of a limited general application, of considerable interest to the historian. Finally, and perhaps most importantly, the industrial revolution lectures suggested an autonomous approach to the study of economic history, based on its own type of primary sources, in which economic circumstances were not placed in causal subservience to political developments (as in the work of W. Cunningham). Toynbee's approach was ideologically and philosophically acceptable to the next generation of economic historians. It was not materialistic yet it tended to regard economic change in terms of general impersonal trends rather than attributing it to the conscious action of narrow interest groups (as in the work of J.E.T. Rogers).

Following an attempt to convince a hostile London audience of the futility of land nationalization and the desirability and attainability of liberal alternatives, Toynbee suffered a nervous breakdown. While convalescing he contracted meningitis and died at the age of 30, widely hailed as a martyr to the cause of social harmony and to the type of reformism which became known as New Liberalism. His reputation and martyrdom contributed to the popularity of the university settlements, beginning with Toynbee Hall, and a general interest at Oxford and Cambridge in social and economic reform. His importance as an economic historian, however, emerged only with the development of the study some years after his death.

A. Kadish

See also INDUSTRIAL REVOLUTION.

SELECTED WORKS

A partial collection of Toynbee's work including a reconstruction of his industrial revolution course based on his and on some of his student's notes was edited by his friend Alfred Milner and published posthumously as *Lectures on the Industrial Revolution in England. Popular addresses, notes and other fragments*, London: Rivingtons, 1884.

'Progress and Poverty' a criticism of Mr H. George: being two lectures delivered in ... London (London: Kegan Paul, 1883) was published in pamphlet form and appended to the 2nd edition (1887) of *Lectures on the Industrial Revolution in England.*

BIBLIOGRAPHY

Kadish, A. 1986. *Apostle Arnold. The Life and Death of Arnold Toynbee (1852–1883)*. Durham, North Carolina: Duke University Press.

Montague, F.C. 1889. *Arnold Toynbee*. Baltimore: Johns Hopkins University Studies in Historical and Political Science.

Tozer, John Edward (1806–1877). Tozer was born at Woolwich in 1806 and died in London in 1877. He was privately educated and at the age of twenty-six was admitted as a 'Pensioner' of Caius College, Cambridge. He immediately showed his ability in mathematics by carrying off the first prize in 1833 and 1834. In the four years after his graduation in 1836, Tozer wrote two essays on mathematical economics, the first on 'Machinery' (1838), and the second on 'Landlords' (1840). However, soon after the publication of these two papers he abandoned economics and went into law, in which he achieved distinction. Later he went into university administration.

Tozer's two papers on economics represent a systematic application of mathematical reasoning to political economy. In that period Whewell, at Trinity College, Cambridge, was trying to introduce mathematical analysis into economics and Tozer adopted his method. Like Whewell, Tozer believed that mathematics, because it turned economics into a 'science' characterized by a series of propositions leading to 'axiomatic truths', was not only appropriate but necessary to the subject (Tozer, 1838, pp. 1–2).

Of the two essays on economics, that on 'Machinery' is by far the more interesting. In this paper, Tozer wants to provide a mathematical basis for the idea that the employment of machinery always increases the wealth of community. His final conclusion is that the capitalist is 'not only ... unable to secure his own advantage at the expense of any other class, he cannot even prevent a general participation in the benefit' (Tozer, 1838, p. 10).

However, the most original feature of this paper is Tozer's mathematical treatment of the problem of machinery. In particular the calculation of the annuity and the algebraic formulation of the construction period of machinery can undoubtedly be regarded as a sophisticated contribution to the fixed-capital debate of that time.

G. Campanelli

See also MACHINERY QUESTION.

SELECTED WORKS

1838. *Mathematical Investigation of the Effect of Machinery on the Wealth of a Community in which it is Employed and on the Fund for the Payment of Wages*. Cambridge: Cambridge Philosophical Society, Transaction 6.

1840. *On the Effect of the non-Residence of Landlords on the Wealth of a Community*. Cambridge: Cambridge Philosophical Society, Transaction 7.

trade. *See* FOREIGN TRADE; INTERNATIONAL TRADE.

trade, gains from. *See* GAINS FROM TRADE.

tradeable and non-tradeable commodities. The distinction between internationally tradeable and non-tradeable commodities lies at the heart of the reason for the development of the theory of international trade as an area of economics distinct from the general theory of value. If the latter approach were adopted, nations would simply be a collection of production and consumption units, each with its own monetary and political system. The international trade literature has, however, imposed the assumption that certain classes of commodities are non-tradeable. Accordingly, there exist purely domestic markets as well as international markets, and this is the most important distinguishing feature of the international trade literature.

The early classical economists made a clear distinction between products, which were assumed to be internationally tradeable, and factors of production such as land, labour and capital, which were assumed to be non-tradeable internationally but perfectly mobile within each nation. This distinction, which is central to the writings of such eminent classical theorists as Ricardo, Torrens, Mill and Bastable, was carried on by early 20th-century writers such as Taussig (1927), Yntema (1932), Ohlin (1933), Haberler (1936), and Mosak (1944). The modern literature, initiated perhaps by Samuelson (1953), has continued with the same model.

The traditional international trade model, therefore, contains non-tradeable commodities. However, they are in the form of non-producible factors of production rather than products and this provides important structure to the traditional model. Moreover, and perhaps more importantly, further structure is imposed by assuming that the non-tradeable factors are in fixed supply. As a result, consumer preferences do not play a role in the market for non-tradeable commodities. It therefore follows that the traditional model of trade encompasses non-tradeable commodities in a very special way.

A more general, and more useful way to deal with non-tradeables is to define a set of commodities that are non-tradeable, and allow this set to include *products* as well as factors. While the existence and importance of non-tradeable commodities in the form of products has been recognized as early as, for example, Ohlin (1933, ch. 8), Haberler (1936, pp. 34–5) and Taussig (1927, ch. 5), it has not been until relatively recent times that non-tradeable products have been explicitly incorporated into international trade models. For surveys of the recent literature see, for example, McDougall (1970) and Woodland (1982, ch. 8).

There is the fundamental question of why certain commodities are not traded internationally. Some may be non-traded because of their intrinsic nature; they are simply not transportable. Others may be transportable and hence tradeable but are not actually traded because it is unprofitable to do so due to the costs of transportation or other expenses such as tariffs. Finally, products may be tradeable, but trade in them may be illegal – an extreme form of trade quota.

While it has long been recognized that there is a difference between a commodity being tradeable and its actually being traded, and that the difference arises as a result of the profitability of trade, few models actually deal with non-traded commodities in this way. (Hadley and Kemp (1966) and Woodland (1968) explicitly model transport costs and thus endogenize the division into traded and non-traded commodities.) Rather, it is typically assumed that transport costs are zero for some commodities (tradeable) and infinite, or, at least, sufficiently large for others (non-tradeable) so as to preclude their trade.

The existence of non-tradeable commodities as well as tradeable commodities implies that some markets are domestic while others are international. However, this does not mean that the domestic markets operate in isolation from international markets. On the contrary, the prices of domestic (non-tradeable) commodities will be influenced by activities in the international markets. Though of less apparent interest, the reverse is also true: the prices of internationally traded commodities are influenced by activities in domestic markets. The various national markets for non-tradeable commodities are, of course, connected only indirectly via the international markets for tradeable commodities.

Let $p=(p_t, p_n)$ denote the partition of the price vector for a nation into tradeable and non-tradeable commodities, and let $X(p)=(X_t(p), X_n(p))$ denote the vector of excess supply functions correspondingly partitioned. If the foreign nation's functions and variables are distinguished by an * the equilibrium conditions for internationally tradeable commodities and the non-tradeable commodities of the home and foreign nations may be written as:

$$X_t(p_t, p_n) + X_t^*(p_t, p_n^*) = 0 \tag{1}$$

$$X_n(p_t, p_n) = 0 \tag{2}$$

$$X_n^*(p_t, p_n^*) = 0. \tag{3}$$

Under reasonable regularity conditions the market equilibrium conditions for the domestic commodities in the home nation, (2), may be solved for p_n as a function of p_t, as $p_n = P_n(p_t)$. Similarly, (3) may be solved as $p_n^* = P_n^*(p_t)$. Thus, the equilibrium conditions for domestic commodities provide the connection between the prices of tradeable commodities and the prices of domestic or non-tradeable commodities. An elegantly simple analysis of the connection between the markets for tradeable and non-tradeable commodities is provided by Jones (1974).

A significant amount of the international trade literature has been devoted to the relationship between prices of tradeable and non-tradeable commodities. Within the context of factors being the only non-tradeable commodities, there are several famous propositions that emerge. The Stolper–Samuelson (1941) theorem indicates, within a two-product, two-factor model, that if the relative price of one product increases then one factor price will increase proportionately more and the other factor price will fall. The factor whose price increases, and whose real income therefore increases, is the one used relatively intensively by the product whose price increases. Second, the factor–price equalization theorem provides conditions under which the factor–price vectors, here p_n and p_n^*, are the same in the two nations despite differences in factor supplies. The required conditions are that each nation should have the same production technology and that their endowment vectors be sufficiently close so that each nation is diversified and produces the same set of traded goods (Samuelson, 1953; McKenzie, 1955; Dixit and Norman, 1980).

The reason why non-tradeable commodities complicate the analysis of many problems in international trade theory is that whenever there is a disturbance to equilibrium, there will be an effect on the markets for non-tradeables. The price of non-tradeables will have to adjust to restore equilibrium. This adjustment of prices will, in general, affect the variable of interest and may yield different qualitative results than obtained from a model without non-tradeable commodities (factors, or products). Much of the literature is concerned with the question of how the introduction of non-tradeable products affects results obtained from models with only tradeable products. However, some recent literature has gone the other way, enquiring whether trade in one or more factors alters results obtained assuming all factors are non-tradeable.

As an example of the role that non-tradeable products can play, take the case of an increase in the international price for a nation's import good. If there are just two traded products, a single consumer, and all non-tradeable commodities are factors in fixed supply, then it is well known that the quantity of imports will fall. The introduction of a third product that is consumed but not traded can upset this result. The rise in the price of the imported product causes imports to change directly, and indirectly via the consequent change in the price of the non-tradeable product. The total effect consists of a substitution effect and an income effect. The substitution effect is to reduce imports. The direct effect of the reduced real income is to reduce imports, while the indirect effect causes the quantity demanded and hence the price of the non-tradeable product to fall (ruling out inferiority). This fall in price causes a reduction in the outputs of both the imported and non-tradeable goods if they are net complements. If this indirect reduction is sufficiently strong to outweigh the direct positive effect of the increase in the price of the imported product, the quantity of imports will rise. Thus arises the paradoxical case where an increase in the price of the imported product causes the level of imports to rise. This case occurs because of the net complementarity between the imported and non-tradeable products and manifests itself through the income effect on consumption.

It is noteworthy that many of the difficulties that occur when non-tradeable products are included in a model arise in the consumption sector. In the example of the previous paragraph, if there is a fixed demand for the non-tradeable product the indirect income effect vanishes and so the quantity of imports falls in response to a rise in their price. Alternatively, one can ensure this result by assuming that the non-tradeable and imported products are net substitutes.

For some problems the existence of non-tradeable commodities does not have any substantial influence upon the solution. The prices of non-tradeable products can be eliminated from the equilibrium conditions by first solving for their prices in terms of the prices for tradeables, and then substituting into the excess supply functions for tradeables. This yields

$$\tilde{X}(p_t) = X_t(p_t, P_n(p_t)). \tag{4}$$

These resulting 'reduced form' excess supply functions can then be used directly to analyse various problems. As an example, the usual stability conditions for international equilibrium can be applied to the reduced form excess supply functions assuming that domestic markets clear instantly. The problem of the effect of a transfer of income upon the terms of trade can be similarly handled. For details on the reduced form approach to non-tradeables see Dixit and Norman (1980, pp. 89–92) and Woodland (1982, pp. 172–3, 218–22). Those that prefer to deal with the structural form include Komiya (1967), McDougall (1970) and Jones (1974).

For other problems, the existence of non-tradeable commodities has to be explicitly taken into account. Some specific instances are as follows:

(a) In the case of shadow pricing of commodities for the purpose of evaluating the welfare effects of a public project in the presence of tariffs, the existence of non-tradeable commodities provides special complications. While tradeable commodities should be evaluated using world prices, the appropriate shadow prices for non-tradeable commodities depends in a complex way upon technology and taste conditions. See, for example, Warr (1982) for details.

(b) Several analyses of technological advances in the production of a traded product upon the output levels of other traded goods, and upon the real exchange rate, have focused attention upon the role played by non-tradeable commodities. In general, the effect of the 'boom' upon the other tradeable's production is ambiguous, stemming partly from the adjustments in the market for non-tradeables. For details, see Corden and Neary (1982) and references therein.

(c) The effect of the introduction of non-tradeable products upon the Stolper–Samuelson, Rybczynski and factor–price equalization theorems has been thoroughly analysed by Ethier (1972). In the case of the Stolper–Samuelson theorem, a change in the relative price of tradeable products induces a change in the price of the non-tradeable product. This has a further effect upon factor prices. The question of whether a particular factor gains in real income depends upon the directions of these price changes, and can only be answered from knowledge of the technology and preferences.

(d) The 'purchasing power parity' theory of exchange rates states that the relative value of currencies equals the relative purchasing power of each currency in its domestic markets. Clearly, the existence of non-tradeable commodities with different prices across countries will cause the purchasing power of each currency to be different independently of the value of the exchange rate.

(e) The analysis of the effects of devaluation is also affected by the existence of non-tradeable products. An example of such an analysis is Dornbusch (1973), who concludes that his basic results hold up when a non-tradeable product is introduced into the model.

(f) The welfare implications of tariff reform depend upon the existence of non-tradeable products. Hatta (1977) has shown that the policy of reduction of the highest rate of import duty to the next highest is welfare improving if non-tradeable and tradeable products are net substitutes. If they are sufficiently complementary, the policy may reduce welfare.

It is somewhat surprising that non-tradeable products (as opposed to factors) have only recently been given explicit attention in the literature, given that most economic activity is in the markets for domestic products. Perhaps future studies will introduce non-tradeable products automatically, except where a reduced form analysis is applicable, and give more attention to the endogeneity of the division of commodities into traded and non-traded groupings.

A.D. WOODLAND

See also INTERNATIONAL TRADE; PROJECT EVALUATION.

BIBLIOGRAPHY

Corden, W.M. and Neary, J.P. 1982. Booming sector and de-industrialization in a small open economy. *Economic Journal* 92, December, 825–48.

Dixit, A.K. and Norman, V. 1980. *Theory of International Trade.* Cambridge: Cambridge University Press.

Dornbusch, R. 1973. Devaluation, money, and nontraded goods. *American Economic Review* 63, December, 871–80.

Ethier, W. 1972. Non-traded goods and the Heckscher-Ohlin model. *International Economic Review* 13(1), February, 132–47.

Haberler, G. 1933. *The Theory of International Trade with its Applications to Commercial Policy*. Trans. from the German, London: William Hodge, 1936.

Hadley, G. and Kemp, M.C. 1966. Equilibrium and efficiency in international trade. *Metroeconomica* 18(2), May–August, 125–41.

Hatta, T. 1977. A recommendation for a better tariff structure. *Econometrica* 45(8), November, 1859–69.

Jones, R.W. 1974. Trade with non-traded goods: the anatomy of interconnected markets. *Economica* 41, May, 121–38.

Komiya, R. 1967. Non-traded goods and the pure theory of international trade. *International Economic Review* 8(2), June, 132–52.

McDougall, I.A. 1970. Non-traded commodities and the pure theory of international trade. In *Studies in International Economics*, ed. I.A. McDougall and R.H. Snape, Amsterdam: North-Holland.

McKenzie, L.W. 1955. Equality of factor prices in world trade. *Econometrica* 23(3), July, 239–57.

Mosak, J.L. 1944. *General Equilibrium Theory in International Trade*. Bloomington: Principia Press.

Ohlin, B. 1933. *Interregional and International Trade*. Cambridge, Mass.: Harvard University Press. Reprinted 1952.

Samuelson, P.A. 1953. Prices of factors and goods in general equilibrium. *Review of Economic Studies* 21(1), 1–20.

Stolper, W. and Samuelson, P.A. 1941. Protection and real wages. *Review of Economic Studies* 9, November, 58–73.

Taussig, F.W. 1927. *International Trade*. New York: Macmillan. Reprinted New York: Kelley, 1966.

Warr, P.G. 1982. Shadow pricing rules for non-traded commodities. *Oxford Economic Papers* 34, 305–25.

Woodland, A.D. 1968. Transportation in international trade. *Metroeconomica* 20(2), May–August, 130–5.

Woodland, A.D. 1982. *International Trade and Resource Allocation*. Amsterdam: North-Holland.

Yntema, T.O. 1932. *A Mathematical Reformulation of the General Theory of International Trade*. Chicago: University of Chicago Press.

trade cycle. The dynamics of capitalist economies are characterized by two facts: sustained growth of production and employment and wide oscillations of these magnitudes and the level of prices as well. This oscillatory behaviour of economic activity as a whole is indeed the subject of trade cycle theory. The use of the word 'cycle', besides pointing to alternation of ups and downs, also suggests the idea that oscillations are somewhat regular.

Concerning the occurrence and regularity of the cycle there exist two entirely different positions. According to one line of thought, it is possible to explain it exogenously. The economic system by itself would not display any tendency to fluctuate regularly but for the influence of external cyclical impulses such as the alternation of seasons. A more sophisticated version of this principle recognizes that external impulses do not even have to be cyclical in order to induce regular fluctuations of the system. This approach, which is very old and recurrent among economists, reflects an essentially pessimistic view about their ability to explain a prominent feature of modern economies.

The opposite opinion holds that the generation and the persistence of cycles are totally or mainly endogenous to the economic system. This is an idea rather difficult to argue cogently. One can fairly easily represent a dynamic system characterized by a succession of expansions and contractions. It is a much harder task to define rigorously a system whose oscillations persist indefinitely, independent of external impulses, with amplitude and frequency determined solely by the structural parameters. Only recently has the economics profession acquired the necessary mathematical tools to solve this problem satisfactorily.

A possible third alternative – which possesses some elements of the other two – is to postulate that oscillations are normally damped and would therefore eventually die out, were they not continually revived by erratic shocks that resupply the system with the energy needed to sustain the cyclical motion. We shall return to this idea later since its discussion merges into that of some recent developments in economic dynamics.

The very existence of specific (and measurable) cycles of different lengths has been the object of heated discussions among economists. Joseph Schumpeter, the author of a monumental historical investigation on business cycles (1939), detected three main types of cycles. The shortest ones, named after the economist Joseph Kitchin, would last approximately three years. The intermediate ones (the Juglar cycles) would comprise three Kitchins and last approximately ten years. Finally, the 'long waves' (Kondratieff) would reflect major technological innovations and extend over 50–60 years.

Subsequent empirical research failed to find conclusive evidence of the actual existence of such regularities in the ups and downs of capitalist economies. And yet the recession of the 1970s has prompted a renewed interest in Schumpeter's work and one hears economists speak once again of the Kondratieff cycle.

Two considerations are here in point. First of all, the (courageous) formulations of hypotheses concerning the exact shape and duration of cycles and the subsequent discussions thereof provided fresh evidence as well as new and better tools of analysis, which greatly improved our knowledge of the subject, even when those hypotheses were eventually discarded. Secondly, in the last fifty years, economic agents' improved understanding of fluctuations, and the vastly increased public intervention to counteract their most negative consequences, have certainly modified both the economic mechanisms that produce those fluctuations and people's expectations about them. On this point too we shall have to return.

The discussion of long waves naturally leads one to consider trend in relation to cycle. Indeed the rising phase of a very long cycle may not be distinguishable over a certain period of time from sustained growth. The presence of a trend itself raises a number of problems. First of all, we would like to understand the economic forces that determine it. In most analyses of growth and cycle one assumes that trend is determined mainly by such long-run factors as population growth and technical progress. The latter, however, are usually represented by given functions of time, which is tantamount to admitting that we do not know much about them.

On the other hand, the causal relation may well run in the opposite direction: that is to say, in an economy characterized by sustained expansion, both population growth and productivity might be stimulated by general prosperity, the latter being determined by other factors. In most economic systems there obviously exist 'hereditary factors' owing to which the 'long run' is resolved into a chain of 'short run' events. For instance, technical progress – at least that of the 'learning by doing' type – depends on the cumulative levels of production (or investment) over a more or less distant past. Moreover, both productivity and desired consumption display important 'ratchet effects', that is, they move more easily upwards than downwards. All these considerations suggest a dependence of trend on the cyclical path actually followed by the economy. However, a rigorous analysis of the process through which this influence is exerted is still lacking.

There also exists an inverse causal relation running from trend to cycle; that is, the characteristics of a cycle, in particular its amplitude and duration, are markedly different according whether the economy is in a phase of stagnation or prosperity.

Unfortunately, the question of the relation between cycle and trend remains to these days one of the many obscure points of economic theory. Most models tend to overcome this difficulty by assuming that short run (cycle) and long run (trend) may be dealt with separately and then re-combined in a 'cyclical growth model'. This procedure, however, requires rather formidable (and usually hidden) hypotheses; in particular, the relevant dynamic equations of the model must be linear, so that one may apply the principle of superposition of solutions of a dynamic model. The different authors' explanations of the trade cycle are better investigated in the wider context of their economic theories as a whole and nothing close to a comprehensive survey may be attempted here. We shall only try to put the contemporary discussions into a historical prospective, without which it would be difficult to understand what the various theories state and why.

Broadly speaking, we can identify three main phases in the development of cycle theory.

The first phase – the classical one – comprises the works of economists who wrote in the 18th century and in the first half of the 19th century. These writers did not provide a true scientific explanation of the cycle, but addressed certain basic questions whose understanding would prove essential to subsequent developments. In particular, classical economists debated the question of the stability of economic systems with a view to establishing whether capitalist economies possess an inherent tendency to equilibrium, that is, whether they are able to generate and maintain prices and quantities consistent with one another as well as with the structural parameters of the system. This problem, formulated by Adam Smith in terms of the 'invisible hand', was discussed in the first half of the 19th century mainly in relation to the possibility (or probability) of general crises of overproduction. In this context, Say (1803), Ricardo (1817) and James Mill (1821) shared the opinion that production always creates its own demand and no general overproduction is therefore possible. Lauderdale (1804), Sismondi (1819) and especially Malthus (1820) dissented and pointed out that accumulation (saving) is not simply a redistribution of expenditure between consumption and investment goods. If incentive to invest is lacking or too weak, saving may well result in a general lack of expenditure and a consequent decline of production and employment.

The idea that capitalist economies have an intrinsic tendency to disequilibrium was also argued, in a very different context and with different overtones, by Karl Marx. Marx never produced a rigorous explanation of the cycle but his ideas provided inspiration to contemporary writers, in particular Kalecki and Goodwin. Marx, too, opposed the so-called Say's Law and pointed out that in a market economy, where purchases and sales are disjoint operations connected by the intermediation of money, discrepancies between demand and supply are always possible, not only in each individual sector but also in the economy as a whole. In volume I of *Das Kapital* (1867), Marx came close to formulating a self-consistent model of the cycle. Accumulation of capital, Marx argues, by reducing the rate of unemployment (the 'reserve industrial army'), pushes up wages (down profits), thus discouraging further investment. The ensuing recession brings about higher unemployment, leading to lower wages (higher profits) and therefore re-establishing the profitability of accumulation. This cyclical mechanism would be reformulated rigorously one century later by Richard Goodwin (1967) and others, to provide a 'classical theory of the cycle' based on the interaction of capital accumulation and distribution of income.

A second phase in the theory of the cycle, which we can locate between 1850 and 1930, may be termed 'modern' and among its forerunners we shall mention Juglar (1862), Jevons (1884) and Tugan-Baranowsky (1901). In this phase the cycle as such became an object of specific investigation. Economists then attempted to define hypotheses and construct theories to explain the 'true and fundamental' causes of economic fluctuations.

Broadly speaking, we can distinguish three main 'explanations' of the cycle, namely: (i) a monetary theory; (ii) an overinvestment theory, in its turn subdivided into a monetary and a real variation; (iii) an underconsumption theory. We shall briefly present the main ideas of the leading exponents of each group of theories. Separate consideration will be given to Keynes's contribution, which marks a watershed between modern and contemporary cycle theories.

The monetary theory of the trade cycle has been most forcefully argued by Ralph Hawtrey (1919). According to this author, the rising phase of the cycle is caused by credit expansion, realized mainly through a reduction of the rate of interest. This induces inventory accumulation by dealers, whose increased demand in turn stimulates producers' expenditure. The rise in demand for investment and consumption goods brings about a undesired *reduction* of the inventory–sales ratio to which dealers respond with further accumulation. A self-sustaining expansionary process ensues – possibly reinforced by secondary speculative waves – and will continue as long as monetary expansion goes on.

However, Hawtrey argues, insofar as the monetary system is constrained by a link between global liquidity and a real asset whose quantity is limited, monetary expansion must come to an end. Monetary flows, moreover, tend to generate fluctuations of real variables, owing to the lagged response of the demand for money to changes in income. Thus, in the ascending phase of the cycle, demand for money does not grow *pari passu* with expenditure and consumers' income. Consequently the banking system experiences net monetary inflows, which permit it to pursue an expansionary policy. However, as soon as demand for money catches up with income, banks' liquidity deteriorates, forcing them sooner or later to increase the rate of interest and squeeze credit. This initiates a downwards cumulative process. In a recession the lagged response of the demand for money will again act as a brake, slowing down the decline of the real output and employment. Eventually excess liquidity will reappear, the rate of interest will be reduced and the cycle will start anew.

The overinvestment theory of the cycle in its monetary version is perhaps best represented by Hayek's so-called 'concertina effect', as described in his book *Prices and Production* (1931).

Two ideas here play a crucial role. The first one is a typically neo-Austrian proposition stating that capital intensity (assumed to be unambiguously measurable) is an inverse function of the rate of interest. The second idea is based on the distinction between voluntary and forced saving. An increase in voluntary saving is accompanied by a reduction in the rate of interest and by an increase in capital intensity. While these adjustments take place, the system remains in equilibrium and no fluctuations arise. On the contrary, when saving is forced by an excessive credit expansion, investment is no longer constrained by *ex-ante* saving. Owing to the unduly low rate of interest, the production process becomes too 'indirect', that is, there will be an excessive development of those stages of production which are more removed from the final, consumption stage.

In sum, according to Hayek's theory, the structure of demand and in particular the distribution between investment and consumption goods is determined by the propensity to save, whereas the structure of production is a function of the rate of interest. In equilibrium the rate of interest is fixed so as to make those two structures consistent. Excess credit causes an overproduction of capital goods, which must eventually manifest itself through increased profitability in the consumption good sector and corresponding losses in the investment sector. The latter will therefore experience a crisis that will turn the boom into a recession.

It is interesting to observe that in both Hawtrey's and Hayek's theories the culprit for the recession is the banking system, which keeps the rate of interest too low during expansion. However, for Hayek this leads to an undue 'lengthening' of the production process, bound to be reversed when the supply of money ceases to grow at an excessive rate. For Hawtrey, a low rate of interest provokes an excessive rise in global demand *vis-à-vis* the available stock of money.

A real version of the overinvestment theory of the cycle was put forward by Wicksell (1907) and Schumpeter, whose ideas on this subject are best summarized in the already quoted treatise (1939). These authors shared the view that growth and cycle are intrinsically related, and the main theoretical problem in this context is to explain why economic expansion does not take place smoothly, 'as trees grow', but why it occurs in leaps and bounds. Wicksell and Schumpeter also agreed that the oscillatory behaviour of capitalist economies is related to the process of innovation through which the employment of limited quantities of primary factors (labour and land) results in increasingly greater amounts of consumption and investment goods. Essentially the trade cycle depends on the fact that innovations, that is, the introduction of new techniques, new products and new markets, are not distributed uniformly in time, but take place in a discontinuous manner, in groups or 'swarms'.

Schumpeter especially emphasized the role of entrepreneurial activity in the generation of business cycles. Since innovation implies a break of routine, it cannot occur smoothly but requires a minimum critical amount of energy to overcome inertia. Such energy is provided by exceptional individuals who possess the courage, strength and imagination necessary to 'do things differently'. Once these few pioneers have opened the way, many others will follow to share in the extra-profits made available by innovation. This is a self-defeating process, though. Insofar as the new methods or products have been absorbed by the market, prices and profits will fall, terminating the boom and reversing the direction of the cycle. Secondary waves may amplify the oscillations, bringing about overoptimistic booms followed by severe slumps.

For Schumpeter and Wicksell alike, however, not everything about recession is bad, provided the worst consequences of deep depressions can be avoided. Recession is indeed a phase of adjustment during which innovations are 'digested' and leads the economy to an intrinsically superior stage. Recession, so to speak, realizes what the boom had promised: a permanently increased flow of commodities, reduced costs, entrepreneurial profits transformed into higher incomes of the other social classes. Schumpeter insisted upon the Darwinian function of (normal) recessions, during which 'lame ducks' are eliminated and only the stronger and more efficient survive. Similar arguments would be employed in the 1980s on both sides of the Atlantic Ocean to justify severe anti-inflationary policies.

The best-known exponent of underconsumption theories of the cycle was undoubtedly Hobson (1922). His theory of investment did not differ much from that of Wicksell and Schumpeter and he shared their view that investment opportunities are basically determined by the needs of development, which are in turn governed by technical changes and population growth.

According to Hobson, though, depressions are caused by insufficient expenditure, which in capitalist economies arises from a skew distribution of income. Increases in income are accompanied by more than proportional increases in saving, leading to overinvestment first and overproduction later. Hobson did not believe in the efficacy of the traditional remedies to overproduction, namely a reduction in the rate of interest and in the level of prices. As concerns the former, he was of the opinion that saving responded little, if at all, to changes in the interest rate. On the other hand, changes in prices are too sluggish to counteract undesired changes in real variables. Instead actual economies eliminate excess saving in the most inefficient and painful way, that is, through depression and unemployment.

Hobson's arguments are clear anticipation of certain Keynesian ideas which would become very popular a few decades later.

It may be noticed that both the overinvestment and the underconsumption theories locate the origin of the crises in a 'vertical' imbalance between the investment and consumption sectors, an idea which had already been discussed by Marx, Rosa Luxemburg and Tugan-Baranowsky. Those theories differ from one another concerning which of the two sectors is overexpanded, the investment sector according to the former, the consumption sector to the latter. Both of them, moreover, could be comprised under the more general label of overcapitalization theories, but the one (underconsumption) argues that there are too many capital goods (and consequently too many consumption goods) *vis-à-vis* global demand, the other (overinvestment) maintains that there is excess accumulation *vis-à-vis* saving. It follows that policy recommendations suggested by the supporters of these theories conflict: a reduction of consumption according to overinvestment; a redistribution of income leading to greater consumption according to underconsumption theory.

Keynes's own theory of the cycle – as distinguished from Keynesian theories – constitutes a *trait d'union* between the modern and the contemporary phase. Even if all the elements necessary to build a true model of the cycle exist in Keynes's work, this task was left to his followers. We shall describe here the essence of Keynes's argument as it appears in the *General Theory* (1936).

At an abstract level, Keynes was fully aware that cyclical motion must result from alternations in the relative strength of expansive and contractive forces, to wit that the cycle must be non-linear. The changes in the balance between expansive and contractive forces may take place smoothly or abruptly, the latter case being more frequently in a boom, the former in a slump. These ideas would be further developed by younger economists inspired by Keynes, in particular by Kaldor and Goodwin.

For Keynes the trade cycle is a complex mechanism but its most important manifestations are the fluctuations of the marginal efficiency of capital, which is determined by psychological as well as economic considerations, and primarily depends on abundance or scarcity of capital goods, their cost and expectations about their future returns. Most often a recession is precipitated by a turnaround of expectations, which, to Keynes, is a much more decisive factor than the increase in the rate of interest sometimes associated with it.

In the last part of the boom, entrepreneurs' optimism offsets all the other unfavourable circumstances: excess capital goods, increasing costs and a high rate of interest. Estimates of future returns to assets are distorted and exaggerated by ignorance, speculation, and vested interests of financial intermediaries and asset-owners. When finally the overoptimistic forecasts are falsified by facts, there follow excessive and even catastrophic readjustments. The increase in liquidity preference that usually accompanies the decrease in the marginal efficiency of capital aggravates the situation and nullifies the effects of expansive monetary measures.

At this point, Keynes contrasts his own theory with that based on overinvestment and observes that the latter is an ambiguous term. If overinvestment means that capital goods in general are so abundant that no investment project can be found whose expected return could justify the cost, then, according to Keynes, this is a rare occurrence even at the peak of a boom. Instead – Keynes continues – investment is excessive either in the sense that actual returns are lower than those on the expectations of which the decision to invest has been taken, or in the sense that severe unemployment makes investment superfluous. It follows that in a recession the right remedy is to reduce, not to increase, the rate of interest.

On the other hand, Keynes thought that the essential propositions of the underconsumption theory were substantially correct. Under capitalist rules of the game, the volume of investment is not controlled, let alone planned, and depends on the vagaries of the marginal efficiency of capital, with a rate of interest systematically kept above a conventional minimum. In this situation, in order to maintain high rates of employment it may well be necessary to stimulate consumption. Keynes's only criticism of the underconsumption theory is its neglect of the possibility of stimulating investment directly. But this – according to Keynes – is a matter of expediency rather than theory.

The modern phase of the cycle theory was characterized by a rich theoretical investigation which led to a deeper understanding of the dynamics of capitalist economies. It did not result, however, in the production of true models, that is, sets of rigorously formulated propositions containing the (necessary and) sufficient conditions to represent in idealized form the cyclical behaviour of the economy. The 'contemporary' phase of cycle theory – from the 1930s onwards – does not consist so much in the search for new explanations of the 'enigma of the cycle' (Wicksell, 1907) as in the attempt to analyse in a rigorous manner concepts and ideas put forward by earlier writers in an intuitive form.

The foundations of the mathematical theory of the trade cycle were laid down mostly in the 1930s, and the early works in this field (Frisch, 1933; Tinbergen, 1959: Kalecki 1935, 1943; and Samuelson, 1939) were characterized by a distinctly Keynesian flavour. Keynes's own writings – and of course even more so the world crisis – had convinced a growing number of economists that the free functioning of the market was more likely to lead to an oscillatory behaviour of income, employment and prices, than to full employment equilibrium.

Multiplier-accelerator theory, in different versions and with different refinements, rapidly became predominant in the decades immediately before and after World War II.

In the 1960s, however, the economics profession's attention turned away from the problem of the cycle. Several reasons contributed to this change, but four of them seem to stand out as crucial.

First of all, economic events after World War II seemed to suggest that business cycles had become obsolete. After a phase of settlement following the turmoil of the war, the world economy (or at least that of the major industrialized countries) seemed to have entered an epoch of sustained growth without (or with only minor) fluctuations. Economists, and especially the younger ones, were quick to respond to the current social and political mood.

Secondly, the prevailing models of the cycle, those of Keynesian inspiration, suffered from a major drawback. The solution of such models consists of fluctuations, perfectly regular in the sense that a certain periodic orbit, once established, repeats itself over and over again.

In such a situation, economic agents would sooner or later notice the periodic character of the dynamics of the system and learn to calculate the amplitude and frequency of the cycles. This in turn would lead to a revision of their expectations. The behavioural hypotheses of the model – on which the cyclical motion of the system depends – would no longer be tenable and the model itself would have to be reformulated. Incidentally, this criticism of the deterministic models of the cycle is perhaps the most important element of truth in the theory of rational expectations.

Thirdly, historical data on the main economic variables do not confirm the periodic regularity predicted by the model.

Finally, and partly in response to the theoretical difficulties mentioned above, there has recently been a revival of what we would call the 'static prejudice' in economics, whose most explicit expression is perhaps 'equilibrium business cycle theory'. In a nutshell, this theory describes the working of the economy by means of a model whose deterministic part is characterized by a unique, stable equilibrium. A stochastic part is added to it which depends on imperfect information of economic agents, whose decisions are therefore mistaken. With rational expectations these errors are 'white noise', i.e. they are normally distributed above and below the optimal (equilibrium) values. The resulting fluctuations of the system are non-periodic but bounded and their amplitude and frequency can be estimated statistically. This approach is reminiscent of certain early ideas first developed in the 1920s and 1930s by Slutsky (1927), Hotelling (1927), Yule (1927), Frisch (1933) and later by Kalecki (1954), to explain the persistence of the cycle. However – as Hicks commented long ago (1950) – when the random factors 'explain' a substantial part of the deviations of a system from its equilibrium position, the proposed theory amounts to a confession of ignorance.

Mentioning a 'static prejudice' in economics raises a few methodological questions, discussion of which is perhaps the best way to introduce the recent developments in the theory of the cycle (and, more generally in economic dynamics) and to conclude this essay.

In spite of the great practical importance of the problems discussed and the high intellectual quality of the results obtained, cycle theory has generally been regarded as an interesting but as a whole marginal branch of economics, whose exponents as such rarely managed to hold centre stage in professional debates.

The great theoretical systems developed in the 18th and 19th centuries, for example, those of Ricardo and of Walras, were more suited to the explanation of interdependence of economic variables, rather than their evolution in time. This problem is better formulated by means of a system of algebraic equations, whose solution (not necessarily unique) is a set of values of the variables – typically prices of commodities and quantities produced – which is consistent with the postulated relationships and the exogenously fixed parameters. The equations themselves define certain equilibrium conditions, for example, equality of demand and supply, or uniformity of the rate of profits. Uniqueness and stability of equilibrium are deemed to be desirable properties of the model, in a descriptive as well as in normative sense. Indeed only stable systems are observable. Multiple equilibria, on the other hand, are not satisfactory for two reasons. First of all, in the general case they are alternatively stable and unstable; secondly, the multiplicity of equilibria introduces a certain amount of relativism as far as their optimality properties are concerned.

Discussion of stability must bring (and historically has brought) dynamic considerations into the picture. Early writers provided intuitive, but not very cogent stories arguing that the system 'tended to' or 'gravitated towards the natural or equilibrium values and prices'. Walras took a step forward, providing a principle (Walras' Law) which shows that, under the postulated maximizing behaviour, disequilibria of notional demands and supplies cannot be entirely haphazardous, but most take place according to certain rules (i.e. the value of total excess demand must be equal to zero). This led to rather optimistic considerations as far as stability of competitive equilibrium was concerned, but was a far cry from a rigorous statement of the problem.

A deeper understanding of the intricacies of non-equilibrium behaviour of dynamical systems and more powerful mathematical techniques were required. Fundamental progress along this line was made in the interwar period (Hicks, 1939) and more so during and after World War II, when certain necessary mathematical results became available to economists. (The list of important contributions is too long to be quoted exhaustively here: we shall only mention Samuelson, 1941, 1942; Metzler, 1945; Morishima, 1952; Arrow and Hurwicz, 1958.)

The conclusions were rather dismaying though, since a rigorous analysis showed that sufficient stability conditions entailed the most heroic assumptions on the specifications of the system.

Economists' overwhelming preoccupation with equilibrium explains their neglect of cycle theory. Indeed cycle theory must by definition concern itself with off-equilibrium states of the system. Empirical observation suggests that the economy is not normally in equilibrium, but fluctuates without ever coming to rest or, if we except relatively rare historical occurrences, without 'exploding'. Is this restlessness only the result of random external shocks, or is it a structural characteristic of the system, owing to the operation of endogenous mechanisms? In dealing with this problem the cycle theorist is naturally led to posing typically dynamic questions such as 'what are economic agents' reactions to non-equilibrium, and therefore unsatisfactory situations?'; or, more generally, 'what laws of motion govern the system, starting from a given, generally off-equilibrium state?'

An exact formulation of this problem required an even more sophisticated analytical apparatus than was the case with static theory. Its natural mathematical set-up is a system of differential (or difference) equations, whose solution is a set of *functions* of time which, given the initial conditions, describes, so to speak, the history of the variables under consideration. The fact that the relevant part of theory of differential equations became available to economists at a rather late date is perhaps a further explanation of their preference for static rather than dynamic problems.

In discussing the problem of fluctuations, economists must soon run up against the question of linearity. Most systems, as described by economists' models, are linear; that is, the coefficients that appear in those models do not depend on the variables or their derivatives with respect to time. The crucial importance of this assumption can be appreciated by considering how it affects the analysis of stability. From the point of view of linear analysis, equilibrium is either stable or unstable. A disturbance is therefore followed by a return to rest in the former case, or by an indefinite increase in the magnitude of the deviation in the latter. But this is a very rough description of the behaviour of an economic system. Linear analysis, by its very nature, completely disregards the effect of the size of disturbances. Indeed an economy may be stable with respect to small deviations from equilibrium, but not so when those deviations are large. On the other hand, an economy may be locally unstable, in the sense than it does not show any tendency to return to its equilibrium position when subjected to small shocks, but it may possess self-correcting mechanisms which only operate far from equilibrium. In either case, the conclusions reached by means of a linearization around the equilibrium point would be misleading.

The linear approximation is unsatisfactory not only because it provides a simplified and therefore distorted picture of reality. A much more fundamental shortcoming is that there exist certain phenomena (economic or otherwise) which cannot be idealized at all by means of linear models. In particular, it is well known that a system of linear differential (or difference) equations, if structurally stable, cannot describe sustained oscillations, that is, oscillations that do not expire or explode.

The discovery that certain basic questions of economic dynamics, in particular persistent cycles, could not be tackled effectively by means of linear models led an increasing number of economists to make use of non-linear methods of analysis. In so doing, they experienced what Poincaré – to whom modern dynamic analysis owes more than to anybody else – had described several decades earlier. The study of the cycle had proved precious to the analyst, all the more so since it constituted a first necessary step into the mysterious and hitherto inaccessible realm of non-equilibrium dynamics.

At that point the phrase 'cycle theory' became an elliptical expression designating not a particular problem, but economic dynamics as a whole or, more appropriately, a method for investigating dynamic processes in economics. But from the analysis of fluctuations economists have obtained much more than a number of new methods and mathematical tools. The most aware of them have undergone a true cultural revolution that Frisch already in the early Thirties (1933) thought would be as important to economics as the transition from classical to quantum mechanics had been to physics.

Equilibrium states, stable and unstable and even limit cycles have now been revealed as rather special configurations in a much more complex and morphologically rich theoretical universe. As soon as the linearity assumption has been dropped, even a simple model may exhibit a very complicated behaviour.

The objection may be raised that this is very nice, but what does it have to do with real systems, in our case real economies? On the contrary, recent developments in dynamic theory have finally provided economists with tools of analysis such that theoretical results are, at least qualitatively, comparable with empirical observations. Take, for example, so-called chaotic behaviour. This characterizes a large class of dynamic models, economic or otherwise and, in common parlance, describes irregular fluctuations of a type that has so far been exclusively associated with random (and therefore essentially unexplained) disturbances. After all, what could be more realistic than irregular, but bounded fluctuations of income, employment and prices, and what more unrealistic than a stable unique equilibrium point?

Clearly cycle theory and, more generally, economic dynamics is in a state of transition. To produce theoretically meaningful and socially relevant models of real systems, economists must fulfil two main requirements:

(i) to define mechanisms of adjustment that realistically describe economic agents' behaviour in disequilibrium;

(ii) to employ techniques of analysis suitable to study the dynamic systems resulting from the operation of those mechanisms.

Recent developments have contributed substantially to solve some of the problems in (i). Instead, off-equilibrium behaviour of economic agents remains to this day a rather fuzzy area of economic investigation.

A. Medio

See also AGGREGATE DEMAND AND SUPPLY ANALYSIS; BUSINESS CYCLES; PREDATOR-PREY MODELS.

BIBLIOGRAPHY

Arrow, K.J. and Hurwicz, L. 1958. On the stability of the competitive equilibrium. *Econometrica* 26, October, 522–52.

Frisch, R. 1933. Propagation problems and impulse problems in dynamic economics. In *Economic Essays in Honour of Gustav Cassel*, London: G. Allen & Unwin.

Goodwin, R.M. 1950. A non-linear theory of the cycle. *Review of Economics and Statistics* 32, November, 316–20.

Goodwin, R.M. 1951. The non-linear accelerator and the persistence of business cycles. *Econometrica* 19, January, 1–17.

Goodwin, R.M. 1953. Econometrics in business cycle analysis. In *Readings in Business Cycles and National Income*, ed. R.V. Clemence and A.H. Hansen, New York: Norton.

Goodwin, R.M. 1955. A model of cyclical growth. In *The Business Cycle in the Post-War World*, ed. E. Lundberg, London: Macmillan.

Goodwin, R.M. 1967. A growth cycle. In *Socialism, Capitalism and Economic Growth*, ed. C.H. Feinstein, Cambridge: Cambridge University Press.

Hawtrey, R.G. 1919. *Currency and Credit*. London: Longmans.

Hayek, F. 1931. *Prices and Production*. London: G. Routledge & Sons.

Hicks, J.R. 1939. *Value and Capital*. Oxford: Clarendon Press.

Hicks, J.R. 1950. *A Contribution to the Theory of the Trade Cycle*. Oxford: Clarendon Press.

Hobson, J.A. 1922. *The Economics of Unemployment*. London: G. Allen & Unwin.

Hotelling, H. 1927. Differential equations subject to error, and population estimates. *Journal of the American Statistical Association* 22, 283–314.

Jevons, W.S. 1884. *Investigations in Currency and Finance*. London: Macmillan.

Juglar, C. 1862. *Des crises commerciales, et leur retour périodique en France, en Angleterre, et aux Etats-Unis*. Paris: Guillaumin.

Kaldor, N. 1940. A model of the trade cycle. *Economic Journal* 50, March, 78–92.

Kalecki, M. 1935. A macrodynamic theory of business cycles. *Econometrica* 3, July, 327–44.

Kalecki, M. 1943. *Studies in Economic Dynamics*. London: G. Allen & Unwin.

Kalecki, M. 1954. *Theory of Economic Dynamics*. London: G. Allen & Unwin.

Kalecki, M. 1968. Trend and business cycle reconsidered. *Economic Journal* 78, June, 263–76; corrigendum, September, 729.

Kalecki, M. 1971. *Selected Essays on the Dynamics of the Capitalist Economy 1933–1970*. Cambridge: Cambridge University Press.

Lauderdale, J.M. 1804. *An Inquiry into the Nature and Origin of Public Wealth and into the Means and Causes of its Increase*. Edinburgh: A. Constable & Co.; London: Hurst, Robinson & Co.

Lucas, R. 1981. *Studies in Business Cycle Theory*. Oxford: Basil Blackwell.

Metzler, L.A. 1945. The stability of multiple markets: the Hicks conditions. *Econometrica* 13, October, 277–92.

Mill, J. 1821. *Elements of Political Economy*. London: Baldwin, Cradock & Joy.

Morishima, M. 1952. On the laws of change of price-system in an economy which contains complementary commodities. *Osaka Economic Papers* 1, May, 101–13.

Samuelson, P.A. 1939. Interactions between the multiplier analysis and the principle of acceleration. *Review of Economics and Statistics* 21, May, 75–8.

Samuelson, P.A. 1941–1942. The stability of equilibrium. Pt. I: comparative statics and dynamics; Pt. II: linear and non-linear systems. *Econometrica* 9, April 1941, 97–120; 10, January 1942, 1–25.

Say, J.B. 1803. *Traité d'économie politique*. Paris: Déterville.

Schumpeter, J.A. 1939. *Business Cycles: A Theoretical, Historical and Statistical Analysis of the Capitalist Process*. New York and London: McGraw-Hill.

Sismondi, J.C.L. 1819. *Nouveaux principes d'économie politique*. Paris: Delaunay.

Slutzky, E. 1937. The summation of random causes as the source of cyclical processes. *Econometrica* 5, April, 105–46.

Tinbergen, J. 1959. *Selected Papers*. Ed. L.H. Klaassen, Amsterdam: North-Holland.

Tugan-Baranowsky, M. 1901. *Studien zur Theorie und Geschichte der Handelskrisen in England*. Jena.

Wicksell, K. 1907. Krisernas gåta. *Statskonomisk Tidsskrift*, 255–84. Trans. by C.G. Uhr as 'The enigma of business cycles', *International Economic Papers* No. 3, 1953, 58–74.

Yule, G.U. 1927. On a method of investigating periodicities in disturbed series. *Philosophical Transactions of the Royal Society of London*, Series A 226, April, 267–98.

trade subsidies. That it may be in the interest of a prince or nation to subsidize foreign trade is an ancient doctrine. However, the manner in which subsidization has been justified and the means by which it has been effected have changed radically over the years. In the 17th and 18th centuries, the subsidization of exports was a corollary of the general Mercantilist doctrines of the time (Viner, 1937); and the British Navigation Acts were defended, even by Adam Smith (1776), as ensuring that England would be adequately provided with ships and sailors in time of war. In the 19th century, Alexander Hamilton and the economists List, J.S. Mill and Bastable argued that industries which in the face of foreign competition are unprofitable but which are capable of learning might qualify for temporary support (see Kemp, 1974, for a modern statement of this 'infant industry' doctrine). And some 20th-century economists have advocated export subsidies as a means of alleviating unemployment.

Subsidization may be direct or indirect. Direct subsidies to trade are simply negative taxes and have repercussions which are, in all details, the opposite of those associated with taxes. An indirect subsidy, on the other hand, may take the form of a 'tax holiday', easy credit, cheap power or free infrastructure. The amount of the subsidy may bear a simple relationship of constant proportionality to the volume of trade (a *specific* subsidy) or to the value of trade (an *ad valorem* subsidy). Or it may be determined by a more complicated formula, as with the variable levy on the agricultural imports of the European Economic Community, the purpose of which is to stabilize internal producers' prices; for a comparison of the welfare implications of the variable levy and alternative stabilization devices, see Young and Kemp (1982).

Formal economic analysis has focused on direct trade subsidies which, as we have noticed, are simply negative taxes. Much of that analysis has dealt with highly simplified worlds with just two primary factors and two traded goods. The following propositions have emerged.

(a) To each *ad valorem* rate of export subsidy there corresponds an *ad valorem* rate of import subsidy with the same impact on world and domestic price ratios (Lerner's (1936) Symmetry Theorem).

(b) A subsidy to imports or exports will normally turn the terms of international trade against the policy-making country; but exceptions are possible, as noted by Marshall (1926), Lerner (1936) and Kemp (1966).

(c) A subsidy to imports or exports will normally turn the domestic price ratio against the subsidized good and therefore will normally turn the distribution of income against whichever factor is used relatively intensively in the subsidized industry; but Lerner (1936) has noted that exceptions are possible.

However, in recent years attention has moved to a more policy-relevant range of questions. Working with models which accommodate any number of traded and non-traded goods, economists have considered the implications for national welfare of prescribed patterns of change in taxes and subsidies on trade. Of particular interest is the discovery that, under certain conditions, a small country will benefit from a uniform proportionate reduction in all specific taxes and subsidies and from a reduction in that tax or subsidy which has the largest absolute value to the level of the next largest tax or subsidy (see Lloyd, 1974; Hatta, 1977; Fukushima, 1979, 1981).

Economists have been much occupied with the implications of trade subsidies for national welfare. However, it should not be inferred from their choice of research topic that prevailing trade subsidies are, on the whole, designed by legislatures to promote the national interest. Most subsidies are monuments to past and present sectional interests.

MURRAY C. KEMP

See also EFFECTIVE PROTECTION.

BIBLIOGRAPHY

Fukushima, T. 1979. Tariff structure, nontraded goods and the theory of piecemeal policy recommendations. *International Economic Review* 20(2), June, 427–35.

Fukushima, T. 1981. A dynamic quantity adjustment process in a small open economy, and welfare effects of tariff changes. *Journal of International Economics* 11(4), November, 513–29.

Hatta, T. 1977. A recommendation for a better tariff structure. *Econometrica* 45(8), November, 1859–69.

Kemp, M.C. 1966. Note on a Marshallian conjecture. *Quarterly Journal of Economics* 80, August, 481–4.

Kemp, M.C. 1974. Learning by doing: formal tests for intervention in an open economy. *Keio Economic Studies*, October, 1–7.

Lerner, A.P. 1936. The symmetry between import and export taxes. *Economica* 3, August, 306–13.

Lloyd, P.J. 1974. A more general theory of price distortions in open economies. *Journal of International Economics* 4(4), November, 365–86.

Marshall, A. 1926. Memorandum on fiscal policy. In *Official Papers by Alfred Marshall*, ed. J.M. Keynes, London: Macmillan, 1926.

Smith, A. 1776. *An Inquiry into the Nature and Causes of the Wealth of Nations*. Ed. E. Cannan. Reprinted, New York: Modern Library, 1937.

Viner, J. 1937. *Studies in the Theory of International Trade*. London: George Allen & Unwin.

Young, L. and Kemp, M.C. 1982. On the optimal stabilization of internal producers' prices in international trade. *International Economic Review* 23(1), February, 123–41.

trade unions. When they formulated their classic definition of a trade union, Sidney and Beatrice Webb had in view the long struggle of groups of English workers to maintain associations that could stand up to employers and gain acceptance by the community. 'A trade union,' they said, 'is a continuous association of wage earners for the purpose of maintaining or improving the conditions of their working lives' (1894, p. 1). An economist starting from the assumption of the ultimate rationality of decisions is likely to see the trade union as a cartel or monopoly intended to maximize the benefits of its members. An intermediate view recognizes that men and women join trade unions for reasons that arise out of imperfections of the labour market. Because of the slow response of employment to lower labour cost, the job seekers in any one district will be confronted at a given time with a limited number of jobs: if then they exceed that number, even by one, and compete with each other by underbidding, the wage can be brought down to a limit set by bare subsistence or the level of support in unemployment.

But even suppose that the numbers of vacancies and applicants match exactly: then if the employer and an individual applicant cannot reach agreement on the rate for the job, so that for the time being the employer lacks a workman and the applicant has no job or pay, which is in the greater trouble? As Adam Smith said, 'In the long run the workman may be as necessary to his master as his master is to him; but the necessity is not so immediate.' The applicants here are evidently unable to move away readily to other employers: those with whom they are dealing are monopsonists or oligopsonists. Against this, they try to maintain a monopoly. They agree to hold out for a minimum in common. They want to keep up the price of their work by limiting the supply. They also want to safeguard their jobs against a drop in demand – they aim to establish a property in jobs. To these ends they defend lines of demarcation, within which they have the sole right to work, or they allow only approved entrants, in limited numbers, to acquire certain skills, or to be recruited for certain purposes. The defensive object of preventing their rates being undercut or their labour being displaced by outsiders merges here into the calculated purpose of pushing up their earnings by restricting supply.

In modern Western economies, trade union membership has also been maintained or extended, especially among white collar workers; by the need to renegotiate the pay of all employees to compensate for changes in the cost of living; the addition of an improvement factor in real terms has also been regarded as defensive from the point of view of any one group, which would otherwise fall behind the others. Beyond these issues of the rate of pay and job security are those that arise at the place of work. People join trade unions to secure protection against discrimination and arbitrary treatment by management, and the negotiation and observance of a code governing discipline, grievance procedure, promotion, redundancy, the pace of work, and the like.

FACTORS AFFECTING MEMBERSHIP. These forces making for trade union membership have arisen and taken effect only in certain conditions. Where trade unions emerged, their form and function differed widely in different societies. In the Western democracies, the proportion of employees unionized has varied widely over time and between countries (Bain and Price, 1960); sometimes it has fallen even against the trend of economic growth, notably in the USA since the 1960s. In full employment, and in places where the individual had access to a number of alternative employers, or to natural resources like the American open frontier, he would feel able to fend for himself. The absence of observed falls in wage rates down the centuries (Phelps Brown and Hopkins, 1981) implies that custom and tacit understandings can maintain rates in the absence of overt trade unionism. Individuals whose qualifications, temperaments, and entries into employment interest them in personal advancement are not likely to become trade unionists; but these factors deterring clerical, administrative and managerial employees from membership have been offset by the growth of offices in size and impersonality, and the need of staff to negotiate frequent salary rises to offset inflation. The ability of manual workers to form their own trade unions has depended upon leaders coming forward from their ranks who were literate, upright, and skilful in administration; the workers themselves must be able to keep up a subscription, and have the discipline to sustain a stoppage. Where those conditions are lacking, as in much of the Third World, trade unions tend to be organized by outsiders, often a political party.

In all countries, the ability of trade unions to maintain themselves and function depends on the provisions of the law and their application in the courts: landmarks here were the immunity from civil liability conferred on British trade unions in 1906, and the promotion of trade unionism and collective bargaining by American legislation in the 1930s. Linked with this is the attitude of the employers: whereas those in France, Germany and the United States generally felt themselves justified, down to 1914 and sometimes later, in resisting trade unionism, many British employers had come to accept it as a means of stabilizing industrial relations. In the Soviet-type economies, discontent with the conditions of employment leading to combined action can result only in a political revolt: trade unions exist by name, but only to administer social benefits and maintain the control of the party within the establishment.

Trade unions thus have to be viewed in their local variety and historical setting. 'Where we expected to find an economic thread for a treatise,' the Webbs wrote in the Preface to their *History of Trade Unionism* (1894), 'we found a spider's web; and from that moment we recognized that what we had first to write was not a treatise, but a history.'

TRADE UNIONS AS MONOPOLIES. None the less, there are economic threads to be followed through. One is the effect of the trade union on the relative pay of its members. Here the theory of the monopoly power of the trade union directs attention to the elasticity of substitution between the members' labour and other factors of production, and to the elasticity of demand for the product. Substantially, much depends on the possibility of the labour being replaced by equipment, and of the trade union gaining control of this if it were introduced. It is in the firms and industries themselves most strongly placed in the market, and able to retain ample margins, that trade unions are likely to maintain levels of pay above those obtaining elsewhere for similar grades of labour. The employers concerned are thus paying what seems more than the supply price of labour to them, and the differences found in surveys in the rates paid even in adjacent firms suggest that this is so; the trade unions may be said to share in the monopoly power of the employers. They may also acquire monopoly power directly by restricting supply and by forcing demand.

Craft unions have restricted supply by limiting the numbers of apprentices; when a trade is being organized for the first time, attacks on non-members who are continuing to work for less than the union rate serve either to exclude or recruit them; and this shades into the general purpose of the rule that no one shall undertake work of a certain kind unless he or she holds a union card, which serves more for recruitment than for exclusion. The pre-entry closed shop provides the most complete control. A trade union that organizes all the existing workers in an industry has to reckon with the possibility of the market being invaded by the products of non-members newly employed elsewhere – except in those cases where of its nature the produce must be supplied in the place where it is consumed.

Trade unions force demand by rules preventing work being taken away from their members, such as compositors' work being done by advertisers, or builders' work by the makers of pre-fabricated components; by stopping other workers doing jobs in the territory to which they claim exclusive rights; and by resisting the application of labour-saving equipment to their own work. Many restrictive prices are intended to maintain or increase the input of labour per unit of output.

The monopoly power of a group of workers who form an essential link in a chain of production but account for a small part of the whole cost, appears great. Adam Smith instanced the half dozen woolcombers who were needed to keep a thousand spinners and weavers at work. Marshall asked why the bricklayers of his day did not get 'an enormous rise' by pushing their own rate up. This power is in fact limited by the employer's powers of resistance. He may redesign process or product, so as to by-pass the labour in question; he may put the work out to subcontract, or import components; at the limit, he may move the whole operation to a location where the trade union is not in control. His resistance to a claim by the union will also be stiffened by his knowledge that other groups in his employ will have regard to relativities, and will base their own claims on concessions he makes to the union.

COLLECTIVE BARGAINING. The most widely available use of monopoly power is the pushing up of the rate of pay by bargaining, which leaves it to employers to restrict the supply by the limitation of the number they engage at the higher rate. If we consider in the first place a negotiation whose effects are largely confined to the immediate parties, bargaining power proper may be defined as the power to inflict loss by withholding consent. It is understandable that if two parties cannot agree upon the terms of an agreement to work together, they should suspend operations meanwhile. But this suspension is not a merely negative act, for it puts each party into difficulties. Workers are left without pay. Craft unions have often had funds from which to issue strike pay; other unions, needing to keep subscriptions low, pay none, but have sometimes been able to maintain long strikes none the less with the aid of contributions from other unionists and the public. There has been a risk of the vacant places being filled by disloyal members of the union, or by imported blacklegs who will be kept on when the dispute is settled. These difficulties increase the longer the stoppage goes on. But so do those of the employer. There is the immediate loss of profitable operation, and in some industries this cannot in the nature of things be made good by increased output when work is resumed. There is the likelihood that customers will resort to other suppliers meanwhile, and the possibility that some of them will never return. Firms that have been unprofitable, though on that account they cannot easily afford a rise, may not however be able to hold out against settling for one, because of their attenuated cash flow. The actual experience of increasing difficulty makes the parties willing to modify the terms for which they stood out when the stoppage began: there is convergence, and they reach agreement. Such at least is a natural interpretation of the observation that most stoppages have ended in a compromise. Reflecting on this, J.R. Hicks inferred (1932, chapter 7) that if the parties estimated each other's powers of resistance accurately beforehand, there would be no stoppage, but agreement would be reached at once on the terms reached only at the end of a stoppage that occurs when the parties do not know those powers, or misconceive them, and find out the facts by painful experience.

That most agreements are reached without a stoppage does not mean that bargaining power is not exerted. But more enters into the reaching of an agreement than bargaining power. The matter to be negotiated is the terms and conditions on which a joint activity is to be carried on by the parties in future, and this is not, like the price of a horse, to be haggled over between two people who may never deal with each other again: the relation between parties who continue to be indispensable to one another is more nearly matrimonial. The parties are therefore open to influence by the thought of what is fair and reasonable in the terms on which they can work together. Trade unionists may be moved by the aim, not of receiving the greatest possible gain, but of obtaining what is justly due to them, or of righting a wrong. Where justice is at stake they will fight without weighing the cost against the gain.

Another consideration in their conduct of a negotiation is their determination to avoid subservience. They refuse to accept the force of the remark that the improvements in terms achieved by a strike will not make good the wages lost in the strike until after many years: for that is an argument to show that the employer's superior resources should always oblige the workers to accept his terms. Bargaining may turn again into warfare, in which trade unionists whose blood is up will make sacrifices according to no maximizing calculus, and will attack blacklegs with patriots' hatred for a traitor.

So far, the bargaining power of the trade union has been considered as if it were exerted by one of two parties facing each other in isolation; but the power of many unions is enhanced by the impact of their strikes on third parties and on the community. The third parties who are most likely to be disturbed by the stoppage of the employer's activity, and interested in his reaching an early settlement, are the firms who supply him with substantial parts of their own output, and those who depend on him for supplies that they cannot readily replace from stock or from other sources. A trade union that can withhold the supply of an essential product or service from a whole region can force the intervention of the government.

In 1893 the power of the English Miners' Federation to cut off much of the country's heat, light and inland transport brought about what was unthinkable a short time before – the intervention of Government to effect a settlement. When the French railwaymen went on strike the Government broke the strike by mobilizing them for military service. A strike of the British miners that threatened to bring the whole country to a halt in 1912 was settled by an Act of Parliament that gave the miners much of what they had claimed. Where the Government has to settle a national emergency dispute, it cannot force the trade unionists to resume work on terms that they reject as unfair and unreasonable, but it can apply a substantial coercive force to the employers.

Control of essential supplies and services offered certain trade unions great power in this way, and the Triple Alliance of miners, transport workers and railwaymen was formed in Great Britain to exploit it; but the Government for its part built up a detailed organization, held in reserve against an emergency, for the maintenance of supplies. In the USA, the Taft–Hartley Act of 1947 provided that in a strike that creates a national emergency the President might take the business concerned into public possession for eighty days, during which the employees must return to work while a fact-finding board reported on the circumstances of the dispute. With the extension of trade unionism in the public sector and in services in Great Britain, the object of strikes has shifted from inflicting loss on the employer to demonstrating discontent by disrupting the activities of the community, and inflicting hardship on the parents of schoolchildren or on invalids or commuters.

TRADE UNIONS AND THE LAW. The bargaining power of trade unions depends upon legal privilege. Employers may refuse to recognize a trade union unless the law obliges them to do so. In a strike, labour is commonly withdrawn in breach of the individual worker's contract of employment; losses are usually inflicted on third parties. In the USA, employers were able to inhibit many forms of trade union action by obtaining injunctions against them from the courts, until the Norris-La Guardia Act of 1932. If those who suffer damages are able to bring civil actions to recover them, most strikes will be impossible: British trade unions have operated under the shelter of immunities that were given outright statutory form by the Trade Disputes Act 1906. Many strikes, again, will not be effective unless pickets are posted to turn back men and women who want to go on working, or stop supplies moving: the effectiveness of legal provisions designed to regulate picketing depends on the possibility and practice of enforcement. Not only the activities but the very existence of a trade union, as a combination in restraint of trade, are anomalous in a country whose common law protects the freedom of the individual to use his labour and property. In these countries the law has found a place for the trade union by way of large exception, rather than by the conferment of delimited rights.

The close bearing of the law on trade union activities has led the trade unions to bring pressure to bear on the legislature. The entering of representations on particular measures was the original purpose of the British Trades Union Congress, and the policy of the American Federation of Labour under Gompers. In later years the British trade unions have become the principal financial support of the Labour Party, and the American leadership has become associated with the Democratic Party. A main reason for association between European trade unions and a political party is the sharing of social principles and ideals, and in France and Italy different groups of trade unions are linked with different parties.

THE BARGAINING AREA. Bargaining power cannot be considered apart from the bargaining area within which it is exerted. What that area shall be in a given case is the outcome of historical factors. Sometimes the initiative in shaping the present area has been taken by employers, sometimes by trade unionists. American employers, perhaps because they were highly individualistic and competitive, have generally been loath to associate, even for the legitimate purpose of collective bargaining, and the plant contract has predominated. The British tradition has been that of the craft union that has tried to make one rate obtain for all engagements, and maintain it through times of slack trade; here the wider the front that could he held, the better, and trade union policy drew together the major employers of each district. Through World War I this extended to industry-wide bargaining. 'Putting a floor under competition' throughout an industry in that way was a step towards turning it into a cartel. It might seem to offer the trade unions concerned the opportunity to push up their pay as far as the elasticity of demand for the products of the industry would let them. The difference between wages in the 'sheltered' and 'unsheltered' industries in the interwar years suggests that some effect of that kind did come about, if only in resisting downward pressure. More positive effects are less likely because employers' resistance will be based on their expectation of price rises stimulating competition from fresh sources at home as well as abroad.

Ideally, trade unions use establishment bargaining (the plant contract) to combine central control of 'the rate for the job' in all establishments, with whatever extra benefits can be extracted from the profitability of particular firms; but in hard times the local or union branch may prefer job security to maintenance of rates, and make concessions. Whereas industry-wide agreements are limited to simple provisions capable of general application, the American plant contract is generally voluminous, and provides rules for all manner of working practices and procedures in the plant. The trade union can therefore undertake to submit any dispute arising during the currency of the contract to arbitration, as the arbitrator can interpret and apply the relevant rule to the facts of the case.

TRADE UNIONISM AT THE PLACE OF WORK. Whether or not the trade unionists working in an establishment negotiate their own agreement with management, they are concerned with issues arising within its walls. Such issues include the allocation and pace of work; discipline; promotion; redundancies; and the processing of grievances. Under the law of the USA, the sole negotiating rights for all the manual workers of an establishment can be vested in one union; the officers of its local branch will then represent them on all these issues. In a British establishment the workers may belong to a number of unions, but the shop stewards elected by the members of the different unions come together in a council, which provides unified representation in meetings with management; its convenor may be wholly occupied with administrative business. Where the roots of trade unionism run back to handicrafts, the workshop is the arena in which the issues arise which bind the member to the union and over which sterner battles have been fought, as new machines and methods have come in, than have been caused by disputes about pay.

It has long been the aim of some trade unions in Europe, but not in the USA, to transcend the adversary system which opposed their members to management at the place of work. Many have sought to do this by a political revolution that would abolish capitalism, but equally in the social democracies, part of the case for nationalization has been that it would substitute public appointment for the irresponsibility of the private employer. Some trade unions have been more concerned with the substance of face-to-face relations, and the possibilities of workers' control and self-management. Interest has therefore attached to the statutory provision in the laws of some European countries, especially Germany, for works councils and the appointment of directors to represent the workers on supervisory boards. The general verdict on the German provisions is that the works councils – where the franchise extends to all employees, but the representatives are in practice the trade unionists – are greatly valued by the trade unions as a means of consultation and joint consideration of management issues; but the appointment of 'worker directors', though a mark of status whose removal would be resented, is not found to confer benefits that are actively felt.

THE IMPACT OF THE TRADE UNION ON PAY. Some estimate of the effects that trade unions have taken can be made by comparing the behaviour of pay in periods of trade union activity and at other times. In a number of Western countries there was a rapid extension of membership, for example, in the years following 1890; in Great Britain membership doubled during World War I; in many Western countries again, but not in the USA, membership rose in the years of full employment after World War II. When such indications as these of trade union strength and activity are set against the economic record, certain inferences suggest themselves about the extent to which trade unions may have changed the course of events, at large and in detail.

It appears that their effect on the general level of money wage rates has been in part to reinforce the ratchet effect which stops those rates dropping back and which has long been present even in the absence of combination: the much smaller reductions of wages in the organized trades in the USA in the great depression of 1929–34 is particularly striking. Generally it was observed that when the falling phase of the eight-year cycle brought wage cuts, the trade union deferred them or even staved them off altogether. Correspondingly, in the rising phase trade unionists were able to get a rise earlier than unorganized workers in their place would have done. But it has not appeared that even widespread and solid trade unionism has been able to push up the general level of money wage rates in a hard market environment, that is, when employers generally have not been able to pass higher costs on in higher prices. The case has been different when the expectation of the employers, reinforced by the commitments of government, allow the negotiation of wage rises needed to keep the workers concerned in line with others, even though product prices must be raised in consequence: in these conditions associated with full employment the trade unions decide the course of the price level jointly with that of money wage rates.

The effect of trade unions on the level of real wages depends on their effect in the first place on productivity, or output per head, and then on their effect on distribution, or the share of output that accrues to the worker. That the 'restrictive practices' enforced by those unions whose control of employment is close enough serve to reduce productivity is evident from their nature, and from the willingness of managers to pay for their removal; but there are understandings about stints and working practices among unorganized workers too, and management must accept some understanding about these issues in any negotiated agreement with its workforce – the question is where the line shall be drawn. If changes in the strength of trade unionism have affected changes in productivity over time, it has been as only one among other and stronger influences: though the activity and spirit of the New Unionism in Great Britain were held responsible for the check to productivity that became conspicuous there at the beginning of the 20th century, the extension of trade union membership, and of trade union activity at the place of work in the 1950s and 1960s occurred at a time when the rise of productivity was exceptionally fast and sustained.

The effect of trade unions on distribution is illuminated by the evidence from a number of countries of trends that have kept real wages proportionate to productivity, that is, to real output per head (Phelps Brown and Browne, 1968). Whatever the course of money wages, and whatever trade unions may have done at certain times to make them rise faster, the prices of products must have been adjusted so as to maintain a given ratio of wage to product; and in periods such as 1874–89 and 1923–37 in Great Britain, when money wages did not rise at all from end to end but productivity rose, the real wage was raised by a fall in prices. A further implication is that the proportionate division of the product between pay and profits has been constant. But this division, and the stability in the ratio of the real wage to productivity, has been subject to occasional displacement, in which that ratio has been raised.

In depression and deflation, the power of the trade union to resist cuts compresses profit margins, and it appears that when the upheaval is sufficiently thoroughgoing, as after World War I, norms and expectations are permanently shifted, and the previous share of profits may never be restored.

Evidently the rise in the standard of living which has transformed the condition of the working population of the western world since 1850 seems to owe nothing directly to trade union pressure for higher wages. Trade unions appear to have taken more effect on distribution as anvil than as hammer. But these inferences from the behaviour of the general level of wages are compatible with substantial influence of the trade unions on the structure of pay. Particular groups may have gained by unionization. One effect of unionization is that it reduces the dispersion of rates for labour of the same type of grade, which otherwise is commonly wide, even in the same locality. Inquiries have also agreed in finding that unionization lifts the organized relatively to the unorganized. Collectively, this shows itself in the rise obtained when a group first bargains; but this is only an impact effect. There has been a cyclical pattern of variation between the wages of organized and unorganized workers, but not progressive divergence. Whether trade unions have changed the differential for skill depends on whether the skilled grades are organized and negotiate separately, or, if they belong to a general union, on their political influence within it. In Sweden in the 1950s and 1960s the pay structure was compressed by agreements made at the national level in pursuance of the egalitarian philosophy of the Landsorganisationen, the national trade union organization; but differentials were restored by wage drift on the shop floor. Statistical studies have shown that individuals who belong to trade unions earn substantially more than non-members when allowance is made for the factors making up personal earning capacity: the difficulty is to be sure that all such factors have been taken into account.

COST PUSH, STAGFLATION AND INCOMES POLICIES. The ability of trade unions to push up the general level of pay when employers are not constrained from raising prices became an engine of cost inflation in the 1960s, when trade unionists sloughed off the cautious expectations formed in harder times, and began raising their claims. Various forms of incomes policy were devised to persuade or require the trade unions to accept rises in money wages that did not outrun the prospective rise in productivity. But for the individual trade unionist, a rise in the money wage was equally a rise in the real wage at the time it was given; and experience showed that the tolerance of trade unionists for policies that required them to accept less than full compensation for rises in the cost of living, was limited. When in the 1970s recession brought back constraints on employers, the trade unionists' expectations and claims persisted, and the combination of unemployment and cost inflation was known as stagflation. It was widely recognized that in these circumstances an expansion of demand would be effective in reducing unemployment only if it was not used by trade unionists in jobs to push their pay up, and that it would therefore have to be accompanied by some form of agreement on restraint between the government and the trade unions.

HENRY PHELPS BROWN

See also ARBITRATION; COLLECTIVE BARGAINING; INDUSTRIAL RELATIONS; STRIKES.

BIBLIOGRAPHY

Bain, G.S. and Price, R. 1960. *Profiles of Union Growth*. Oxford: Blackwell.

Hicks, J.R. 1932. *The Theory of Wages*. 2nd edn, London: Macmillan, 1963.

Phelps Brown, E.H. and Hopkins, S.V. 1955. Seven centuries of building wages. *Economica* 22, August, 87. Reprinted in E.H. Phelps Brown and S.V. Hopkins, *A Perspective of Wages and Prices*, London and New York: Methuen, 1981.

Phelps Brown, E.H. and Browne, M.H. 1968. *A Century of Pay: the course of pay and production in France, Germany, Sweden, the United Kingdom, and the United States of America, 1860–1960*. London: Macmillan.

Smith, A. 1776. *An Inquiry into the Nature and Causes of the Wealth of Nations*. Ed. E. Cannan. Reprinted, London: Methuen, 1961.

Webb, S. and B. 1894. *The History of Trade Unionism*. 2nd edn, London: Longmans, 1920.

transaction costs. Transaction costs arise from the transfer of ownership or, more generally, of property rights. They are a concomitant of decentralized ownership rights, private property and exchange. In a collectivist economy with completely centralized decision-making they would be absent; administrative costs would take their place.

In modern economies a substantial, and probably increasing, proportion of resources is allocated to transaction costs. Nevertheless, up to World War II economic theory had virtually nothing to say about them. Over the last few decades a large and diverse literature has developed, but the analytic complexities are such that success still is only partial; important problems remain unsolved.

TRANSACTION TECHNOLOGY. Transaction costs, like production costs, are a catch-all term for a heterogeneous assortment of inputs. The parties to a contract have to find each other, they have to communicate and to exchange information. The goods must be described, inspected, weighed and measured. Contracts are drawn up, lawyers may be consulted, title is transferred and records have to be kept. In some cases, compliance needs to be enforced through legal action and breach of contract may lead to litigation.

Transaction costs face the individual trader in two forms, namely (1) as inputs of his own resources, including time and (2) as margins between the buying and the selling price he finds for the same commodity in the market.

The transaction technology specifies what resource inputs are required to achieve a given transfer. It may be formalized in a 'transaction function' analogous to a production function. In principle, each such function relates to a specific pair (or, more generally, group) of economic agents. In this respect transaction costs are analytically analogous to transportation costs, which relate to a pair of locations. In one way or another, transaction costs are incurred in an effort to reduce uncertainty. For many purposes it may nevertheless be an efficient research strategy to proceed *as if* transaction costs occurred even under full certainty. Transaction costs then become, as Stigler (1967) put it, 'the costs of transportation from ignorance to omniscience'.

While transaction costs are analogous to transportation costs in some respects, they are quite different in others. This is because they relate not to individual commodity flows, but to pairs (or, more generally, to groups) of such flows. There must be a *quid pro quo* in every single transaction. This requirement imposes constraints for which there is no spatial counterpart. While in a Walrasian equilibrium each trader has to observe only his budget constraint, in a transaction cost equilibrium he

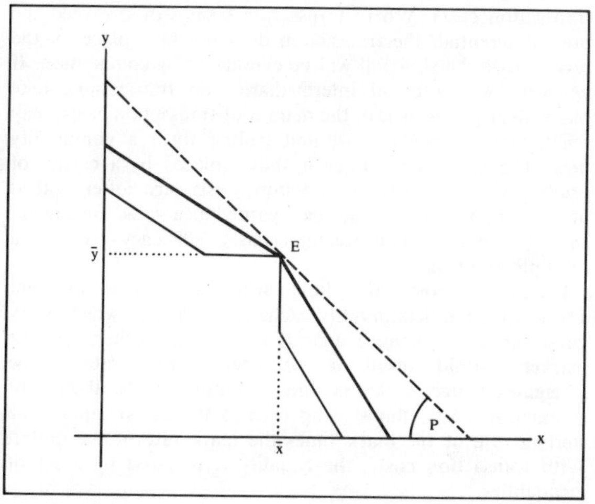

Figure 1

has to balance his account with every other trader. This gives rise to an additional set of shadow prices, reflecting the burden of the bilateral balance requirement (Niehans, 1969).

Transaction functions may exhibit diminishing, constant, or increasing returns. Scale economies are often pronounced; in many cases, transaction costs are virtually independent of the quantity transferred. The scale effects may relate to the size of the individual transaction, to the size of the participating firm or to the size of the market as a whole.

Only for simple exchange will a transaction function, built in analogy to a production function, provide an adequate description of transaction technology. Many contracts, particularly the more important ones, are far more complicated, often assuming a bewildering (and expensive) complexity. As a consequence, transaction costs become difficult, and perhaps impossible, to quantify. The analysis of more complex contracts, institutions and economic arrangements has thus been forced to rely more on qualitative than on quantitative methods.

THE VOLUME OF TRANSACTIONS. Transaction costs, by and large, reduce the volume of transactions. In general equilibrium without transaction costs, the network of exchanges is indeterminate; there is no constraint on the gross trading volume. With increasingly costly transactions, individuals have an ever stronger incentive to economize transactions.

This can be clearly seen in a single market in which x is exchanged against y. In the budget constraint confronting an individual trader, proportional transaction costs produce a kink. If they amount to θ units of y for every unit of x bought or sold, the constraint will look like the heavy line in Figure 1, where $\bar{x}$ and $\bar{y}$ mark the initial endowment. Depending on the shape of the indifference curves, the individual may wish to buy x (selling y), to buy y (selling x), or not to trade at all. A shift in the market price will let the budget constraint swivel around E. The important point is that, because of the kink, there is a *range* of prices for which trade remains zero.

The reciprocal demand curves for two representative traders will, with transaction costs, have a kink at the origin (Figure 2). This may have the consequence that trade remains at zero (as illustrated) despite considerable changes in tastes and/or endowments. If transaction costs also have a fixed component, the budget constraint assumes the shape of the thin line in Figure 1, and the reciprocal demand curves have an empty space around the origin (not illustrated). The larger transaction costs, both variable and fixed, the more likely it is that equilibrium is at the no-trade point. In a multimarket framework, therefore, transaction costs can explain why certain potential markets, either for present or future goods, do not exist (Niehans, 1971). There have been numerous studies applying these general considerations to particular markets.

One way of economizing on costly market transactions is the establishment of firms. Coase (1937) regarded the cost of using the price mechanism as the main reason for the existence of firms. For Williamson (1979, 1981) transaction costs are not only the key to an institutional theory of the firm but also to a new type of institutional economics.

THE BUNCHING OF TRANSACTIONS. Fixed transaction costs tend to result in a bunching of transactions. This effect has played a major role in explaining the demand for money. Cash balances are held because for short holding periods the costs of buying and selling an earning asset are too high compared to its yield (Hicks, 1935). Using an elementary inventory model with a sawtooth pattern of total assets, Baumol (1952) and Tobin (1956) derived algebraic demand functions for the demand for money. With fixed transaction costs, the demand for money would rise only with the square root of total assets, but this property does not hold in more general models. There is a vast literature applying the Baumol/Tobin approach to problems of monetary economics. In the history of economic thought few quantitative models of comparable simplicity have inspired more widespread uses.

EFFICIENCY. Compared to an imaginary state with costless transactions, transaction costs inevitably reduce welfare. In the individual optimization model of above, the set of consumption possibilities shrinks. The welfare loss is reflected partly in the resources allocated to transactions and partly in the suppression of exchanges that would otherwise have been mutually beneficial.

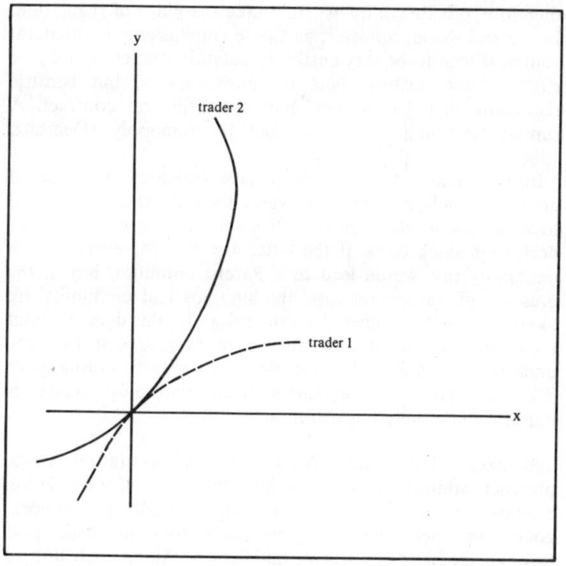

Figure 2

The more interesting question is whether transaction costs make an economy inefficient. A number of contributions to it are surveyed by Ulph and Ulph (1975). The mere fact that the Walrasian auctioneer uses up resources, reflected in a spread between selling and buying prices, does not in itself create efficiency problems. However, increasing returns in transaction technology, particularly in the form of fixed transaction costs, may lead to distortions. It is well known that in the presence of scale economies competition may not lead to an efficient allocation of resources.

Hahn (1971) took the view that transaction costs generally result in an inefficient equilibrium because the multiplicity of budget constraints reduce consumption possibilities. Kurz (1974a, 1974b) made it clear, however, that the alleged inefficiency may just be due to an inappropriate efficiency concept. The real question is whether, with given initial allocation and given transaction technology, the resulting equilibrium could be improved upon by a Pareto-superior reallocation, even though this would again cost resources. In the absence of scale economies, the discussion has produced no reason why, in this sense, transaction costs should generally cause inefficiency.

Efficiency problems also arise in a more general context. Simple exchange is a bilateral transaction. More complicated transactions may range from triangular exchange to multilateral contracts with a large number of parties. With increasing complexity, transaction costs tend to increase very rapidly. Even triangular contracts, therefore, are relatively rare and for more complex transactions the costs may rapidly become prohibitive. This is the basic reason for the emergence of market economies consisting of a network of bilateral exchanges. Politics may be interpreted as the arena in which multilateral transactions are typically made.

In a sense, any deviations from Pareto-optimality can be attributed to transaction costs, because in their absence all opportunities for Pareto-superior contracts would be realized. This is the so-called 'Coase theorem' (Coase, 1960). If, for example, the externalities of water pollution give rise to a social loss, one can imagine a multilateral abatement contract providing for payments from the sufferers to the polluters which is beneficial to all. In a world without transaction costs, therefore, private contracts could take the place of regulation. In the real world, however, as Coase emphasized, multilateral contracts tend to be very costly. Regulation, therefore, may be efficient, not because there is an externality, but because regulation may be cheaper than a multilateral contract. A similar reasoning can be applied to monopoly (Demsetz, 1968).

Buchanan and Tullock (1962) have extended this type of analysis to political decisions, where the individual is assumed to weigh his benefit from collective action against his share of decision-making costs. If the latter are zero for everybody, a unanimity rule would lead to a Pareto optimum, but in the presence of transaction costs the high costs of unanimity are likely to result in other decision rules. In the debate about these propositions it has often been pointed out that the underlying definition of transaction costs may be tautological: Whatever produces deviations from Pareto-optimality is implicitly interpreted as a transaction cost.

ARBITRAGE. Transaction costs, like transportation costs, obstruct arbitrage, thus impeding the Law of One Price. Suppose, in an efficient and competitive exchange network, goods, on their way from producers to consumers, pass through the hands of several middlemen. Along each link of the network the increase in price will just pay for the marginal transaction costs. Where transaction costs would exceed the price differential, the transaction does not take place; in the reverse case the shortfall will be eliminated by competition. If between two potential intermediaries no transactions take place, their prices, within the margin of transaction costs, may fluctuate independently without calling forth a commodity flow. The one market price is thus replaced by a cluster of prices. Markets with transaction costs are often called 'imperfect'. This should not be regarded as a value judgement. In the presence of transaction costs, efficiency requires a multiplicity of prices.

Transaction costs also limit arbitrage between different assets. In a multicommodity exchange system in which every good can be exchanged against each of the others, perfect markets would result in consistent 'cross rates'. The foreign-exchange market is a good example: in the absence of transaction costs, the sterling rate of the dollar equals the sterling rate of the mark times the mark rate of the dollar. With transaction costs, the equality is replaced by a set of inequalities.

The influence of transaction costs on asset arbitrage was studied for many particular markets, including those for Eurocurrencies (Frenkel and Levich, 1975), bonds of different types (Litzenberger and Rolfo, 1984) and maturities (Malkiel 1966), stocks (Demsetz, 1968, is the forerunner of many studies), take-overs (Smiley, 1976), stock options (Phillips and Smith, 1980) and commodities (Protopapadakis and Stoll, 1983).

INTERMEDIATION. Imagine an economy in which all exchange consists of bilateral barter. In the absence of transaction costs it would make no difference who trades with whom; on their way from producers to consumers, commodities could pass through any number of hands. The presence of transaction costs makes the exchange network determinate. In such a network, certain traders, in view of their lower transaction costs, probably emerge as middlemen, brokers or intermediaries (Niehans, 1969). A pure intermediary makes his contribution to the social product, abstracting from any associated contribution to production, by helping other traders to economize on transaction costs. Transaction costs, therefore, are the key to an understanding of intermediation and of the structure of markets.

This is especially important in asset markets. For many consumer goods, particularly perishable ones, transaction costs are too high for them to pass through many hands. However, for assets like deposits, securities, foreign exchange, commodity contracts, gold options, insurance contracts, and mortgages, transaction costs are low enough to permit complicated intermediary networks. Benston and Smith (1976) thus argued convincingly that transaction costs are the *raison d'être* of financial intermediaries.

The Eurodollar market offers an instructive example. In the interwar period it became customary to regard banks primarily as producers of money and possibly other liquid assets. From this point of view, the emergence and the functioning of the Eurodollar market appeared as a 'puzzle'. The puzzle was easily solved once it was realized that the market for dollar funds (and other currencies) tended to move wherever transaction costs were lowest (Niehans and Hewson, 1976). The more transaction costs decline under the pressure of financial innovation, the more highly developed will be the division of labour in financial services, the more elaborate the structure of the financial system and the higher the flow of daily transactions compared to the stocks of traded assets. It is tempting, therefore, to interpret the rapid changes in financial markets in recent years largely as a consequence of changing transaction costs.

MEDIA OF EXCHANGE. Transaction costs are also responsible for the use and choice of media of exchange. The lower transaction costs on a given commodity, the more likely that this commodity will serve as money. Thanks to low transaction and holding costs, money helps to save resources that would otherwise have been used up in transactions. More important, it extends the scope of mutually beneficial exchange. In a world with transaction (and holding) costs, money thus has (indirect) utility even though, being a mere token money, it may have no direct utility.

Though this insight is old, its analytical implementation has made progress only in the last two decades. A simple expedient is to express transaction costs as a declining function of cash balances and then treat them like other costs (Saving, 1971, 1972), but this begs the question how exactly such a function is determined.

The services of money for the individual consumer in the presence of transaction costs were analysed by Bernholz (1965, 1967) and, more fully, by Karni (1973). A rigorous analysis would have to be based on a general-equilibrium model of bilateral barter with transaction costs, which is not yet available. Since cash balances are an inventory, this needs to be a multiperiod model in which endowments, tastes and perhaps technology are subject to fluctuations. In order to model such fluctuations in an equilibrium framework, one might visualize those changes in the form of infinite stationary motion in which successive 'days' or 'seasons' are different, but successive 'years' are the same.

Such an economy will generally exhibit a complex pattern of markets in which a given commodity is traded against many (though not all) other commodities. If, from this arbitrary starting point, transaction costs are gradually lowered for one particular good, this good appears as the *quid pro quo* in an increasing number of transactions, while other barter exchanges disappear. There may also be cases with several moneys, each with its comparative advantages (Niehans, 1969). If transaction costs on the medium of exchange (and also its holding costs) are low enough, it will be used as a general medium of exchange. If, in the limit, money can be transferred, produced and held without cost, one arrives at the special case of a Walrasian economy with an integrated budget constraint and neutral money (Niehans, 1971, 1975, 1978), but, in contrast to Walras, with a determinate exchange network.

The rigorous mathematical analysis of the existence, uniqueness and efficiency of monetary equilibria with transaction costs made some progress during the 1970s (see Honkapohja, 1977, 1978a, 1978b and the literature given there). Since then, progress has been slow. The difficult process of adapting the traditional concepts of general-equilibrium analysis to the requirements of an intertemporal transaction-cost economy is still incomplete. This is one area where rigour so far has been at the expense of substance.

JÜRG NIEHANS

See also ECONOMIC ORGANIZATION AND TRANSACTION COSTS; MONEY AND GENERAL EQUILIBRIUM THEORY.

BIBLIOGRAPHY

Baumol, W.J. 1952. The transactions demand for cash: an inventory theoretic approach. *Quarterly Journal of Economics* 66(4), 545–56.

Benston, G.J. and Smith, C.W. 1976. A transactions cost approach to the theory of financial intermediation. *Journal of Finance* 31(2), 215–31.

Bernholz, P. 1965. Aufbewahrungs- und Transportkosten als Bestimmungsgründe der Geldnachfrage. *Schweizerische Zeitschrift für Volkswirtschaft und Statistik* 101(1), 1–15.

Bernholz, P. 1967. Erwerbskosten, Laufzeit und Charakter zinstragender Forderungen als Bestimmungsgründe der Geldnachfrage der Haushalte. *Zeitschrift für die gesamte Staatswissenschaft* 123(1), 9–24.

Buchanan, J.M. and Tullock, G. 1962. *The Calculus of Consent; Logical Foundations of Constitutional Democracy*. Ann Arbor: University of Michigan Press.

Coase, R.H. 1937. The nature of the firm. *Economica* 4(16), 386–405.

Coase, R.H. 1960. The problem of social cost. *Journal of Law and Economics* 3, 1–44.

Demsetz, H. 1968. The cost of transacting. *Quarterly Journal of Economics* 82(1), 33–53.

Frenkel, J.A. and Levich, R.M. 1975. Covered interest arbitrage: unexploited profits? *Journal of Political Economy* 83(2), 325–38.

Hahn, F.H. 1971. Equilibrium with transaction costs. *Econometrica* 39(3), 417–39.

Hicks, J.R. 1935. A suggestion for simplifying the theory of money. *Economica* 2(1), 1–19.

Honkapohja, S. 1977. Money and the core in a sequence economy with transaction costs. *European Economic Review* 10(2), 241–51.

Honkapohja, S. 1978a. A reexamination of the store of value in a sequence economy with transaction costs. *Journal of Economic Theory* 18(2), 278–93.

Honkapohja, S. 1978b. On the efficiency of a competitive monetary equilibrium with transaction costs. *Review of Economic Studies* 45(3), 405–15.

Karni, E. 1973. Transactions costs and the demand for media of exchange. *Western Economic Journal* 11(1), 71–80.

Kurz, M. 1974a. Equilibrium in a finite sequence of markets with transactions cost. *Econometrica* 42(1), 1–20.

Kurz, M. 1974b. Arrow-Debreu equilibrium of an exchange economy with transaction cost. *International Economic Review* 15(3), 699–717.

Litzenberger, R.H. and Rolfo, J. 1984. Arbitrage pricing, transaction costs and taxation of capital gains: a study of government bonds with the same maturity date. *Journal of Financial Economics* 13, 337–51.

Malkiel, B.G. 1966. *The Term Structure of Interest Rates: Expectations and Behavior Patterns*. Princeton: Princeton University Press.

Niehans, J. 1969. Money in a static theory of optimal payment arrangements. *Journal of Money, Credit and Banking* 1(4), 706–26.

Niehans, J. 1971. Money and barter in general equilibrium with transactions costs. *American Economic Review* 61(5), 773–83.

Niehans, J. 1975. Interest and credit in general equilibrium with transactions costs. *American Economic Review* 65(4), 548–66.

Niehans, J. 1978. *The Theory of Money*. Baltimore: Johns Hopkins University Press.

Niehans, J. and Hewson, J. 1976. The eurodollar market and monetary theory. *Journal of Money, Credit and Banking* 7(1), 1–27.

Phillips, S.M. and Smith, C.W. 1980. Trading costs for listed options: the implications for market efficiency. *Journal of Financial Economics* 8, 179–201.

Protopapadakis, A. and Stoll, H.R. 1983. Spot and futures prices and the Law of One Price. *Journal of Finance* 38(5), 1431–55.

Saving, T.R. 1971. Transactions costs and the demand for money. *American Economic Review* 61(3), 407–20.

Saving, T.R. 1972. Transactions costs and the firm's demand for money. *Journal of Money, Credit and Banking* 4(2), 245–59.

Smiley, R. 1976. Tender offers, transactions costs and the theory of the firm. *Review of Economics and Statistics* 58(1), 22–32.

Stigler, G.J. 1967. Imperfections in the capital market. *Journal of Political Economy* 75(3), 287–92.

Tobin, J. 1956. The interest-elasticity of transactions demand for cash. *Review of Economics and Statistics* 38(3), 241–7.

Ulph, A.M. and Ulph, D.T. 1975. Transaction costs in general equilibrium theory: a survey. *Economica* 42(168), 355–72.

Williamson, O.E. 1979. Transaction-cost economics: the governance of contractual relations. *Journal of Law and Economics* 22(2), 233–61.

Williamson, O.E. 1981. The modern corporation: origins, evolution, attributes. *Journal of Economic Literature* 19(4), 1537–68.

transfer of technology. Economists have long recognized that the transfer of technology is at the heart of the process of economic growth, and that the progress of both developed and developing countries depends on the extent and efficiency of such transfer. But until recently, there has been surprisingly little systematic analysis of the transfer of technology. During the 1960s and 1970s, the process of international technology transfer was modelled largely in terms of the concept of the product life cycle (see Vernon, 1966), according to which there is a fairly definite sequence in the relationship between technology and trade, whereby the United States tends to pioneer in the development of new products, enjoying for a time a virtual monopoly. After an innovation occurs, the innovator services foreign markets through exports, according to this model. As the technology matures and foreign markets develop, companies begin building plants overseas, and US exports may be displaced by production of foreign subsidiaries. The concept of the product life cycle has had a great influence because it has been able to explain the train of events in many industries.

However, recent evidence indicates that the situation has changed, and that the product life cycle is less valid than in the past (see Mansfield et al., 1982). At present, the principal channel through which new technologies are exploited abroad during the first five years after their commercialization seem to be foreign subsidiaries, not exports. Thus, the 'export stage' of the product cycle has often been truncated and sometimes eliminated. Particularly for new products, firms frequently begin overseas production within one year of first US introduction. In some industries such as pharmaceuticals, new products commonly are introduced by US-based firms more quickly in foreign markets than in the US (due in part to regulatory considerations). For new processes, on the other hand, the 'export stage' continues to be important.

This change in the process of international technology transfer and trade reflects the fact that many US-based (and foreign-based) firms have come to take a worldwide view of their operations. Many of them have in place extensive overseas manufacturing facilities, as well as substantial R and D activities located abroad. Given the existing worldwide network of facilities and people, firms are trying to optimize the operation of their overall operations. This may mean that some of the technology developed in the US may find its *initial* application in a Belgian subsidiary, or that an innovation developed in its Belgian subsidiary may find its *initial* application in the firm's Mexican subsidiary, and so on.

Another reason why the product life cycle is less valid than in the past is that technology is becoming increasingly internationalized. In the pharmaceutical industry, frequently it is no longer true that a new drug is discovered, tested, and commercialized, all within a single country. Instead, the discovery phase frequently involves collaboration among laboratories and researchers located in several different countries, even when they are within the same firm. And clinical testing generally becomes a multi-country project. Even in the later phases of drug development, such as dosage formulation, work often is done in more than one country. In contrast, the product life cycle seems to assume that innovations are carried out in a single country, generally the US, and that the technology stays exclusively within that country for a considerable period after the innovation's initial commercial introduction.

To analyse the international transfer of technology, econometricians have expanded the production function approach to the study of the effects of research and development (R&D) on productivity. For example, Mansfield (1984) has investigated the effect of American multinational firms' overseas R&D expenditure on their rate of increase of total factor productivity. In a particular firm, the production function is assumed to be:

$$Q = A\, e^{\lambda t} R_d^{\beta_1} R_o^{\beta_2} L^{v} K^{1-v}, \tag{1}$$

where Q is the firm's value added, R_d is the firm's stock of domestic R and D capital, R_o is its stock of overseas R and D capital, L is its labour input, and K is its stock of physical capital. Thus, the annual rate of change of total factor productivity is

$$\rho = \lambda + \theta_1 \frac{\mathrm{d}R_d/\mathrm{d}t}{Q} + \theta_2 \frac{\mathrm{d}R_o/\mathrm{d}t}{Q}, \tag{2}$$

where $\theta_1 = \delta Q/\delta R_d$, and $\theta_2 = \delta Q/\delta R_o$. And based on the usual assumptions,

$$\rho = \lambda + a_1 \frac{X_d}{Q} + a_2 \frac{X_o}{Q}, \tag{3}$$

where X_d is the firm's domestic R&D expenditures, and X_0 is its overseas R&D expenditures in the relevant year. Estimates of a_1 and a_2 were obtained for a sample of chemical and petroleum firms for 1960–76. The estimate of a_2 is positive, statistically significant, and relatively large, indicating the importance of this form of international technology transfer.

How quickly a nation begins producing a new product seems to depend in part on how much it spends on R&D in the relevant industrial field. Both for entire nations and individual firms, R&D provides a window opening on various parts of the environment, and it enables the nation or firm to evaluate external developments and react more quickly to them. In some economic models, R&D is viewed as an invention-producing or innovation-producing activity. While correct as far as it goes, this view misses much of the point of R&D, which also is aimed at a quick response to rivals and at clever modification, adaptation, and improvement of their results.

Technology frequently is neither easy nor cheap to transfer. On the average, technology transfer costs seem to average about 20 per cent of the total cost of establishing an overseas plant. Thus, although many economists regard existing technology as something that can be made available to all at zero social cost, this simply is untrue. Furthermore, transfer costs vary considerably, especially according to the number of previous applications of the innovation and how well the innovation is understood by the parties involved. It is equally inappropriate, therefore, to make sweeping generalizations about the size of the costs involved. For instance, technology transfer in chemical and petroleum refining displays relatively low transfer costs, presumably because it is possible to embody sophisticated process technology in capital equipment, which in turn facilitates the transfer process.

In some instances, technology is transferred from one organization to another with the help, or at least the consent, of the owner of the technology. In other instances, much or all of the technology is revealed by the innovation itself. In some fields, reverse engineering – which, crudely speaking, involves analysing and tearing a product apart to see what it consists of and how it is made – is a well developed art. Even if a new product is not subject to reverse engineering, it may be possible to 'invent around' the patents on which it is based, if it is patented. Because much of the relevant technology frequently is transferred (more or less involuntarily) to potential imitators, the costs of imitating an innovation frequently are substantially lower than the cost of the innovation itself.

Imitation costs are a very important, if neglected, topic. If imitation costs are substantially below the cost to the innovator of developing the innovation, there may be little or no incentive for the innovator to carry out the innovation. Imitation costs also affect concentration, since an industry's concentration level will tend to be relatively low if its members' products and processes can be imitated cheaply. Based on the available evidence, it appears that the average ratio of imitation cost to innovation cost is about 0.65, and the average ratio of imitation time to innovation time is about 0.70. The ratio of imitation cost to innovation cost tends to be inversely related to the proportion of the product's innovation cost that goes for research (as opposed to development, physical capital, and startup). Also, patents have an effect on imitation costs, although this effect (outside the pharmaceutical industry) seems generally to be modest. In the sample provided in Mansfield, Schwartz and Wagner (1981), the median increase in imitation cost due to patent protection was about 10 per cent.

EDWIN MANSFIELD

See also DIFFUSION OF TECHNOLOGY; PRODUCT CYCLE.

BIBLIOGRAPHY

Mansfield, E. 1984. R&D and innovation: some empirical findings. In *R and D, Patents, and Productivity*, ed. Z. Griliches, Chicago: University of Chicago.

Mansfield, E., Schwartz, M. and Wagner, S. 1981. Imitation costs and patents: an empirical study. *Economic Journal* 91, December, 907–18.

Mansfield, E. et al. 1982. *Technology Transfer, Productivity, and Economic Policy*. New York: W.W. Norton.

Vernon, R. 1966. International investment and international trade in the product cycle. *Quarterly Journal of Economics* 80, May, 190–207.

transfer payments. A transfer transaction is unlike an exchange transaction. The latter, which is the main concern of market economists, involves two trading partners both of whom give up something of value in search of mutual gain. The former involves a donor and a recipient, with the donor giving up something of value without receiving anything in return. Transfers can be made between one person and another or from one organization such as a government to another. The transaction can be explicit as in the case of a stated gift to a certain person or quite diffuse as in the case of a subsidy to anyone who produces or consumes a specific consumer good. Transfers, which may take the form of income or wealth, can be voluntary or involuntary and may be motivated either by altruism of the donor of malevolence of the recipient.

The study of transfer payments can take one in many directions. However, the most common direction is that given by national income accountants in reference to transfer payments to persons. In the United States this term is restricted mainly to payments from government and business to the personal or household sector (United States, 1981, p. xi). Government payments recorded under this heading include cash benefits paid out under social insurance and public assistance programmes as well as programmes for government employees, veterans and students. Also included are certain cash payments to nonprofit organizations which are considered part of the household sector. In addition to those cash payments, some in-kind benefits, notably health care under social insurance and food stamps, are included. The total of government transfer payments to persons equalled about 10 per cent of GNP in the 1980s.

A much smaller amount is recorded as business transfers to persons, which include corporate gifts to non-profit organizations, consumer bad debts, liability claims for personal injuries, thefts and forgeries, and cash prizes. The national income accounts also show a similarly small flow of transfer payments to foreigners from the domestic household sector and the government sector.

United States national income accounting practice emphasizes monetary benefits, it uses a one-year accounting period to help distinguish a transfer from an exchange, and it excludes transfers which do not cross sectors but occur within the polyglot household sector. This accounting practice is criticized both for items it leaves out and for some of those it includes. Questions raised include the following. Should social insurance benefits paid for by the recipient in a prior year be classified as deferred wages rather than as transfers? Why are health care under social insurance and food stamps included, while many other non-monetary benefits – for example, education – are not? Why are benefits paid out by private pension funds and group health insurance plans not counted as transfer payments to persons? Should corporations' payments of interest and dividends be classified as business transfer to persons on the grounds that unlike the return to physical capital owned by the corporation, the payment by the corporation to the owner of financial assets may not relate to current changes in real capital and land supplied to the productive process? (This classification is followed in the United Nations' System of National Accounts, United Nations, 1968.) Should capital gains and losses be recognized as transfers? (Eisner, 1984).

These questions are all difficult ones for national income accountants, who see their role primarily as one of measuring output produced in a year. For this purpose the activities of business and government are of major importance and the flow of income to and within the household sector is of lesser significance. To the extent that it is desirable to show more of the income received by persons, modifications of the personal or household sector and a broader definition of transfer are needed. Such changes include (1) dividing this sector into separate sub-sectors for consumer units, nonprofit institutions, and private pension and group insurance organizations, and (2) identifying more in-kind government benefits as transfer to persons (Ruggles and Ruggles, 1982).

While national income accountants have been slow to move on this question, other scholars have take steps to widen the inquiry. One group of economists has undertaken to show how all taxes and all government spending, including that for public goods, affect the distribution of income. Public goods are, of course, particularly difficult to allocate among specific families. This kind of study relies upon tax records, records of expenditures under public programmes, and household surveys of family income and expenditures classified by size and composition of families (Gillespie, 1965; Reynolds and Smolensky, 1977). In general, such studies find that while tax systems are only slightly redistributive from rich to poor, government expenditures are more clearly so.

Still another group of economists, this one led by Boulding (1973), see the phenomenon of transfer as much more fundamental than is suggested by any list of formal public and private redistributive programmes. They envision every economy as comprising two co-existing systems, a market system and a transfer or 'grants' system. The latter enters into almost all producer as well as consumer decisions. Grants arise not only from government expenditures but also, implicitly, from such regulatory actions as restrictions on trade, occupational licensing, and the setting of wage rates and work rules by collective bargaining.

A third group can be identified as staking out a middle ground for the study of transfers. This middle ground is based on a concept of a redistributive budget or a social budget. It starts with a list of explicit, as distinct from Boulding's implicit, transfers, and it excludes transfers of public goods. The private goods that go to specified consumer units include cash benefits and such in-kind benefits as education and health care. A number of nations, including the United States and the Federal Republic of Germany, have made use of social budgets, and the OECD recently developed a standard reporting pattern for use in comparing the social spending of its member nations (OECD, 1985). Social spending grew faster than total government spending in all OECD nations from 1960 to about 1975. The ratio of social spending to GNP averaged 25.6 per cent in those nations in 1981, with a low of 13.4 per cent in Greece and a high of 37.6 per cent in Belgium. The United States and the United Kingdom were each a few percentage points below the average.

Lampman (1984) has proposed a two-way expansion of the social budget to make it more useful for comparison across nations and over time. First, he adds the role played by private alternatives to government delivery of social benefits. In so doing he implements the subsectoring of the household sector referred to above in the discussion of national income accounting. He conceives of transfers as flowing from families to families as direct gifts from one family to another and also via intermediary organizations including government, private philanthropies such as churches and private schools, and private pension funds and group health insurance plans. Secondly, he adds information to show the other side of the budget, detailing which families pay for the total of current benefits received.

Using this scheme of an expanded social budget, Lampman finds that the ratio of social spending to GNP in the United States in 1978 was 27.6 per cent inclusive of 19.6 per cent via government intermediaries. The private role of 8 per cent was made up of 4 per cent interfamily direct giving, 3.6 per cent private group insurance, and 0.6 per cent philanthropic giving. Over half of all social benefits as defined take the form of cash, and most of the in-kind benefits are education and health care services. The largest share of cash benefits goes to the retired aged and about a third of all benefits go to the pre-transfer poor.

It is important to relate the definition of transfers from and to persons to the widespread recognition that they may influence patterns of consumption, saving, investment in human capital, family composition, and work effort. Improved quantitative information may help to resolve questions of why social spending has increased. Is it due to market failure to deal with externalities and high costs of information and transactions, or is it due to government failure to identify the optimal quantities of transfer?. Further, such information may assist in the illumination of the social benefits and social costs that flow from recent expansion of social spending (Wilson and Wilson, 1982).

ROBERT J. LAMPMAN

See also NEGATIVE INCOME TAX; POOR LAW; SOCIAL SECURITY.

BIBLIOGRAPHY

Boulding, K.E. 1973. *The Economy of Love and Fear: A Preface to Grants Economics*. Belmont: Wadsworth.

Eisner, R. 1984. Transfers in a total income system of accounts. In *Economic Transfers in the United States*, ed. M. Moon, Studies in Income and Wealth, Vol. 49, Chicago and London: University of Chicago Press, 9–35.

Gillespie, W.I. 1965. The effects of public expenditures on the distribution of income. In *Essays in Fiscal Federalism*, ed. R.A. Musgrave, Washington, DC: Brookings Institution.

Lampman, R.J. 1984. *Social Welfare Spending: Accounting for Changes from 1950 to 1978*. Orlando: Academic Press.

OECD. 1985. *Social expenditure: 1960–1990*. OECD: Paris.

Reynolds, M. and Smolensky, E. 1977. *Public Expenditures, Taxes, and the Distribution of Income: The U.S. 1950, 1961, 1970*. New York: Academic Press.

Ruggles, R. and Ruggles, N.D. 1982. Integrated economic accounts for the United States, 1947–1980. US Department of Commerce, *Survey of Current Business* 62, May, 1–53.

United Nations, Department of Economic and Social Affairs. 1968. System of national accounts. In *Studies in Methods*, Series F, No. 2, rev.3, New York.

US Department of Commerce. 1981. *The National Income and Product Accounts of the United States 1929–76. Statistical Tables*. Washington, DC: Government Printing Office.

Wilson, T. and Wilson, D.J. 1982. *The Political Economy of the Welfare State*. London: Allen & Unwin.

transfer pricing. A 'transfer price' is the price attached by a business enterprise to transactions between different divisions or affiliates under its ownership. Every large firm sets such internal accounting prices to monitor the performance of its various operating divisions. Where the divisions are given some managerial autonomy, transfer prices are also central to each unit's decision-making process: they enable each internal 'market' to clear efficiently. Transfer prices exist whether a firm is confined to a single location or country, or is spread over several different countries. They are needed to value internal transfers not only of goods but also of technology, management, finance or other services.

Transfer prices in this internal-accounting sense have no economic welfare or policy implications. As such, they have attracted little economic interest (but see the classic article by Hirshleifer, 1956, and a recent paper by Diewert in Rugman and Eden, 1985). Most attention has been focused on internal prices that are set by transnational companies on intra-firm transactions across national boundaries. Transfer prices of this sort do affect national welfare and government revenues. By altering relative transfer prices between different kinds of transactions, a transnational company can show its earnings in different forms in a particular country (e.g. less as dividends and more as royalties or interest) to minimize its tax liabilities there. By altering transfer prices for a given form of intra-firm trade, a transnational company can transfer pre-tax profits from one country to another to maximize its global post-tax profits.

There is no necessary correspondence between transfer prices set by transnational companies for internal management control and those used for taxation and external auditing. The two can deviate widely if external circumstances make this profitable and feasible. There are few internal constraints to a firm using different sets of prices for different purposes. Indeed, there is widespread evidence that similar price manipulations are undertaken by unrelated firms colluding to evade official restrictions or to lower tax burdens – a much more difficult arrangement than the adjusting of internal prices by one firm.

The financial press and tax journals regularly carry reports of transfer pricing manipulations, tax havens, and related disputes between transnational companies and fiscal authorities. A large body of complex writing and interpretation has grown up around the most influential of the tax provisions dealing with transfer pricing, Section 482 of the US Internal Revenue Code (Verlage, 1975), which proposes several ways of dealing with what is clearly a widespread problem. The international business literature also offers advice on the use of transfer prices to maximize net profits (Robbins and Stobaugh, 1973, is a good example). Yet interestingly, in recent years, as public concern has grown about transfer pricing (especially in developing countries) this literature has attempted to play down this aspect of corporate strategy. This does not indicate that the scope or impact of transfer pricing has decreased, only that its practice is more discreet and more closely monitored by national governments.

The fact that transfer pricing raises legitimate national concerns has aroused a reaction in some recent economic analyses of transnational companies (a brief exposition is given in the introduction to Rugman and Eden, 1985). Some exponents of the theory that transnational companies are the most efficient form of internalization of imperfect markets (for knowledge and skills) argue that the transfer prices set by transnational companies will also be the most efficient possible. Thus any attempt at regulation may create inefficiency and resource misallocation. Actual transfer prices will, by this reasoning, differ from efficient ones only if there are 'distortions' that create incentives for profit shifting across countries. The optimal policy would then be to remove all 'distortions' and leave transnational companies free to set efficient transfer prices.

This argument begs several questions. It is not clear that transnational companies in fact choose 'efficient' transfer (marginal-cost) prices even for internal management purposes. The marginal-cost rule recommended in theory has several practical problems (Verlage, 1975). The possibility for double (or multiple) bookkeeping breaks any link between managerial shadow prices and declared prices. Thus, regulation of the latter need not affect real operations by transnational companies unless, as Horst (1971) assumes in a widely quoted but highly simplified model of transnational company activity, there are limits to declared prices set by governments. The postulate that all government policies that deviate from a competitive market are 'distortions' is open to severe criticism on many counts. Nevertheless, there remains a valid point about the best policy towards transfer pricing, to which reference is made later.

The scope for transfer pricing is extensive. Intra-firm trade by transnational companies represents a significant proportion of trade by major industrial countries (Plasschaert, 1979; Helleiner, 1982). Between a third and a half of total manufactured exports, and a slightly smaller proportion of imports, are between 'related' parties. In addition, substantial sums are exchanged within transnational companies for royalties, fees, interest and the like. Even modest changes in the prices set on such transactions can have large effects on profits declared in particular countries.

The incentives to declare greater or lesser earnings in particular countries depend on several factors. Different tax and tariff rates are the most obvious, and probably the most important for developed countries. Restrictions on dividend remission, controls on royalities and fees, threat of price controls, forced equity participation by nationals, exchange rate instability and trade union militancy are others, with greater significance in developing countries.

The possible dangers of transfer pricing to developing countries were first highlighted by evidence from Colombia by Lall (1973) and Vaitsos (1974). Subsequent evidence suggested that the practice was widespread (see papers by Benvignati, Chudson, Natke and Lecraw in Rugman and Eden, 1985), though the nature of the problem made it very difficult to establish correctly the extent of transfer pricing manipulations. The evidence also suggested that its incidence was highly uneven: certain products traded by relatively few large transnational companies among relatively few countries comprised the main 'area of concern' (Lall, 1979). Many standardized products were not prone to intra-firm trade. If they were, their prices were easy to check with reference to open markets. The real problems arose for products that were highly specific to individual firms, for which no easy reference prices existed and for which the complex structure of innovation and production made the calculation of a correct reference price extremely difficult. Similar problems existed for intra-firm transactions in technology and services (Kopits, 1976).

Some early attempts to analyse and regulate transfer prices used as reference prices the quotations of imitating suppliers. This was particularly true of the pharmaceutical industry, where innovations were easy to copy and where new products were priced several times above marginal cost. It was realized over time that this was unfair to the innovating transnational companies. Most governments in the industrialized countries gave up attempts to calculate arm's-length prices for highly specific commodities and resorted instead to checking that similar prices were declared in different destinations, and to simple bargaining with the transnational companies over the 'correct' share of their revenues.

The inherent problems of detecting transfer-pricing abuse in the case of specific commodities and services make it easier for transnational companies to use the tool discreetly. This also makes it cumbersome and expensive for authorities to monitor such prices with any pretence at precision or fairness. There are other costs in mounting a major war on transfer-pricing abuse. A complex regulatory apparatus may scare off new investments. Effective high tax rates may induce existing investors to reduce their activity in that location or pull up stakes completely. In a neoclassical world, where policy 'distortions' reduce economic welfare, transfer pricing actually counteracts welfare losses by enabling transnational companies to get around government interventions (see Aliber in Rugman and Eden, 1985). In the real world, tough bargaining and regulation by host governments can indeed kill the goose that lays the golden eggs (as almost happened in the 1970s in the Andean Pact countries).

Does this mean that governments should not attempt to check transfer prices at all? For products which have competitive arm's-length prices, the possibilities of abuse are limited and the limits should be enforced by the authorities. For others, some monitoring and cross-border exchange of tax/price information are desirable. This is precisely what revenue authorities in Europe and North America are doing. An alternative solution, unitary taxation (taxing transnational companies on global profits allocated to a particular jurisdiction on the basis of its share of their total sales or employment), has the attraction of simplicity. As recent experience in the US shows, this is politically difficult to implement, and has various fiscal problems (see Chudson in Rugman and Eden, 1985). Moreover, the limits to taxability of transnational companies in particular host countries have been noted. Given all this, a harmonization of tax regimes and the creation of relatively favourable business environments for transnational companies seem to offer the best way of attracting transnational companies and retaining a legitimate share of revenues. This may need to be supported by some form of international arbitration of tax disputes for difficult cases, along lines suggested by Shoup (in Rugman and Eden, 1985). Clearly the problem will remain, and there can be no ideal solution.

SANJAYA LALL

See also MULTINATIONAL CORPORATIONS.

BIBLIOGRAPHY

Helleiner, G.K. 1982. *Intra-Firm Trade and Developing Countries.* London: Macmillan.

Hirshleifer, J. 1956. On the economics of transfer pricing. *Journal of Business* 29, July, 172–84.

Horst, T. 1971. The theory of the multinational firm: optimal behaviour under different tariff and tax rates. *Journal of Political Economy* 79(5), September–October, 1059–72.

Kopits, G.K. 1976. Intrafirm royalties crossing frontiers and transfer-pricing behaviour. *Economic Journal* 86(344), December, 791–805.

Lall, S. 1973. Transfer-pricing by multinational manufacturing firms. *Oxford Bulletin of Economics and Statistics* 35(3), August, 173–95.

Lall, S. 1979. Transfer pricing and development countries: some problems of investigation. *World Development* 7(1) January, 59–71.

Plasschaert, S. 1979. *Transfer Pricing and Multinational Corporations.* Farnborough: Saxon House.

Robbins, S. and Stobaugh, R. 1973. *Money in the Multinational Enterprise.* New York: Basic Books.

Rugman, A.M. and Eden, L. 1985. *Multinationals and Transfer Pricing.* London: Croom Helm.

Vaitsos, C.V. 1974. *Intercountry Income Distribution and Transnational Corporations.* Oxford: Clarendon Press.

Verlage, H.C. 1975. *Transfer Pricing for Multinational Enterprises.* Rotterdam: Rotterdam University Press.

transfer problem. Development of the theoretical literature on the transfer problem mirrors the historical context within which the issue first arose. In 1919, as part of the Treaty of Versailles, Germany was required to make reparations payments to the European powers to which it surrendered. An international commission was established and vested with responsibility for determining the magnitude of German reparations. Its proceedings were marked by continuous dispute over Germany's willingness and capacity to pay: the initial figure arrived at was repeatedly revised downward, reflecting new realities and changing perceptions of economic and political conditions in Europe, until German reparations were all but eliminated following the Hoover Moratorium of 1931 (for further discussion of historical developments see Eichengreen, 1986).

Initially, much discussion of Germany's capacity to pay proceeded on the basis of constant international prices and assumed that governments could automatically engineer the required changes in spending on traded goods at home and abroad. But Keynes (1929), in an article which introduced the phrase 'transfer problem' into the professional literature, argued that a country required to make a fixed transfer of purchasing power to another would suffer a secondary burden in the form of a further decline in its purchasing power due to an induced deterioration in its international terms of trade. This secondary burden might be so large as to reduce the value of traded-goods production in the transfer-making country to an amount less than the required transfer. Ohlin (1929) argued in response that a secondary benefit – or terms of trade improvement – was as likely to occur. The subsequent theoretical literature can be interpreted as attempting to resolve this dispute over which way the international terms of trade will move in the wake of a transfer, and of exploring the conditions under which various special cases – such as the terms of trade deteriorating sufficiently that the transfer of a given amount of purchasing power becomes impossible to effect, or the terms of trade improving sufficiently that the recipient is actually made worse off by receipt of its transfer – may or may not arise (Leontief, 1936).

The fundamental insight of the early literature on the transfer problem can be stated simply, following Pigou (1932), using a two-country, two-commodity model of international trade. To highlight the central point, assume initially that production of both goods is exogenously given and that all income is devoted to consumption. If the markets for both commodities clear, then by Walras' Law we need only consider one, for example the good exported by the home country, where that good is denoted x. The total supply of x must equal the sum of domestic and foreign demands:

$$S + S^* = D(y, p) + D^*(y^*, p) \tag{1}$$

where S and S^* designate domestic and foreign supplies, taken as exogenous for the moment (with asterisks denoting foreign values throughout), and D and D^* domestic and foreign demands (each of which depends on real income and relative prices). Now assume that an amount T of purchasing power is transferred from the home to the foreign country. Domestic demand for x falls by $D_y T$ where D_y is the home country's marginal propensity to consume x out of income, while foreign demand for this good rises by $D^*_{y^*} T$, where $D^*_{y^*}$ is the foreign country's marginal propensity to consume x, also its marginal propensity to import. Equilibrium in the market for x at the initial prices requires that an export surplus in the amount T results from income effects alone – in other words, that $(D_y + D^*_{y^*})T = T$, or $D_y + D^*_{y^*} = 1$. If $D_y + D^*_{y^*} < 1$, the combined marginal propensities to spend on x out of income are too small to generate a sufficient surplus at initial relative prices. This is the 'orthodox' case in which the transfer-making country's terms of trade deteriorate, creating a secondary burden (Samuelson, 1952, 1971). If $D_y + D^*_{y^*} > 1$, then to the contrary the transfer-making country's terms of trade improve.

The subsequent literature consists almost entirely of variations upon this theme. Once adjustments in production are introduced, the terms of trade will deteriorate when the bias in tastes in each country toward consumption of the exportable good is greater than the bias in production due to international differences in factor endowments or technologies, where the meaning of 'bias' is made precise by Jones (1975). Transport costs, by increasing the correlation within countries of patterns of production and consumption, reinforce the orthodox presumption of a secondary burden (Samuelson, 1952). Once the assumption of the equality of income and expenditure is relaxed, then in the context of a simple Keynesian model whether the demand for x rises or falls will depend not only on any international differences in consumers' tastes but in addition on their marginal propensities to save. If for example purchasing power is transferred from a country with a low savings propensity to one with a high one, demand will decline further than when consumption is constrained to equal income, and the transfer-making country will in consequence be more likely to experience a secondary burden (Metzler, 1942; Meade, 1951; Johnson, 1953; Jones, 1976). Once nontraded goods are introduced, a number of new possibilities arises, since there exists another commodity whose relative price may have very different effects on the supply and demand for x (Samuelson, 1954). Introducing a third country has many of the same effects as introducing a third commodity: by adding an additional set of supply and demand elasticities and the possibility of complementarity in production and consumption, it makes possible a number of cases – such as a transfer which immiserizes the recipient country – whose existence is inconsistent with market stability in two-country models (on the stability question, see Samuelson, 1947; Johnson, 1956; for extensions of the analysis to more than two countries, see Bhagwati, Brecher and Hatta, 1983, and Majumdar and Mitra, 1985.

Most of this recent work has been stimulated by the theoretical conundra raised by the transfer problem. Some research, however, has been motivated by other empirical contexts in which international transfers arise. For example, Balogh and Graham (1979) and Lipton and Sachs (1983) have considered the oil price increases of the 1970s as an international transfer under the assumption that the demand for oil is relatively inelastic. Others have viewed as a transfer the real interest shocks experienced by developing countries faced with the burden of an external debt, and modelled the effects of default by sovereign debtors as a transfer away from creditor countries. Many of these studies reflect the influence of recent work on intertemporal aspects of macroeconomic adjustment, emphasizing for example likely differences in the response to temporary and permanent transfers, and different relative price movements in the short and long runs.

BARRY EICHENGREEN

See also KEYNES, JOHN MAYNARD; OHLIN, BERTIL GOTTHARD; REPARATIONS.

BIBLIOGRAPHY

Balogh, T. and Graham, A. 1979. The transfer problem revisited: analogies between the reparations payments of the 1920s and the problems of the OPEC surpluses. *Oxford Bulletin of Economics and Statistics* 41(3), August, 183–91.

Bhagwati, J.N., Brecher, R.A. and Hatta, T. 1983. The generalized theory of transfers and welfare. *American Economic Review* 73, 606–18.

Eichengreen, B. 1986. Macroeconomics and history. In *The Future of Economic History*, ed. A. Field, Boston: Martinus Nijhoff.

Johnson, H.G. 1953. The reparations problem: a correction. *Economic Journal* 63, 724–5.

Johnson, H.G. 1956. The transfer problem and exchange stability. *Journal of Political Economy* 64, 212–25.

Jones, R. 1975. Presumption and the transfer problem. *Journal of International Economics* 5, 263–74.

Jones, R. 1976. Terms of trade and transfers: the relevance of the literature. In *The International Monetary System and the Developing Countries*, ed. D.M. Leipziger, Washington, DC: AID.

Keynes, J.M. 1929. The German transfer problem. *Economic Journal* 39, 1–17.

Leontief, W. 1936. Note on the pure theory of capital transfer. In *Explorations in Economics: Notes and Essays in Honor of F.W. Taussig*, New York: McGraw-Hill.

Lipton, D. and Sachs, J. 1983. Accumulation and growth in a two-country model: a simulation approach. *Journal of International Economics* 15, 135–60.

Majumdar, M. and Mitra, T. 1985. A result on the transfer problem in international trade theory. *Journal of International Economics* 19, 161–70.

Meade, J. 1951. *The Balance of Payments*. London: Royal Institute of International Affairs.

Metzler, L.A. 1942. The transfer problem reconsidered. *Journal of Political Economy* 50, 397–414.

Ohlin, B. 1929. The reparation problem: a discussion. *Economic Journal* 39, 172–83.

Pigou, A.C. 1932. The effects of reparations on the ratio of international exchange. *Economic Journal* 42, 532–43.

Samuelson, P. 1947. *Foundations of Economic Analysis*. Cambridge, Mass.: Harvard University Press.

Samuelson, P. 1952. The transfer problem and transport costs: the terms of trade when impediments are absent. *Economic Journal* 62, 278–304.

Samuelson, P. 1954. The transfer problem and transport costs II. *Economic Journal* 64, 264–89.

Samuelson, P. 1971. On the trail of conventional beliefs about the transfer problem. In *Trade, Balance of Payments and Growth*, ed. J. Bhagwati et al., Amsterdam: North-Holland.

transformation of statistical variables. Transformations of many kinds are used in statistical method and theory including simple changes of unit of measurement to facilitate computation or understanding, and the linear transformations underlying the application and theory of multiple regression and the techniques of classical multivariate analysis. Nevertheless the word transformation in a statistical context normally brings to mind a non-linear transformation (to logs, square roots, etc.) of basic observations done with the objective of simplifying analysis and interpretation. The present entry focuses on that aspect.

Mostly we discuss problems in which variation in a univariate response variable, y, is to be explained in terms of explanatory variables $x_1, \dots, x_p$; the terminology here is self-explanatory and avoids overuse of the words dependent and independent! We consider transformations of y and/or some or all of the explanatory variables. Note that where a number of variables are of very similar kinds, it may be sensible to insist on transforming them in the same way.

A brief historical note is desirable. Until the wide availability of computers, the majority of relatively complicated statistical analyses used the method of least squares or fairly direct elaborations thereof. Particular requirements of these methods are linear representations of the expected response, constancy of variance and normality of distribution of errors. When the data manifestly do not obey one or more of these conditions, transformation of variables provides a flexible and powerful technique for recovering a situation to which well-understood methods of analysis are reasonably applicable and thus greatly extends the range of applicability of those methods. With powerful and sometimes even flexible computing facilities now commonplace, such transformations, while remaining important, are less so than they used to be, because it is now feasible to develop special models for each specific application and to implement an appropriate analysis from first principles.

PURPOSE OF TRANSFORMATIONS. The key assumptions of the 'classical' methods mentioned above are (a) simplicity of structure, additivity, linearity, absence of interaction; (b) constancy of variance; (c) normality of error distribution. Independence of errors is another very important assumption, needing especially careful consideration in the case of time series data, but is not particularly relevant in the present discussion.

While the relative importance of (a)–(c) depends on the context, they are listed in broadly decreasing order of importance. Linear relations are easy to specify and understand; absence of interaction, for example that important relations retain their form for different groups of data, is important not only for understanding but also as a basis for extrapolation to new groups of data.

Constancy of variance has a triple role. If the pattern of variance is of intrinsic interest, constancy of variance is a reference level for interpretation. If the effect of explanatory variables on whole distributions is of interest, constancy of variance suggests that only changes in location need be studied. Finally constancy of variance is required for various technical statistical reasons. Appreciable changes in variance vitiate standard errors and tests of significance and will lead to a general loss of efficiency; the method of weighted least squares can be used when the nature of the changes in variance is at least roughly known.

The assumption of normality of error distributions is particularly important if the ultimate objective is prediction in the tails of a distribution. Otherwise appreciable non-normality is sometimes an indication that a quite different distributional formulation is called for, sometimes a warning about the occurrence of aberrant values in the data and more broadly is a sign of potential loss of efficiency and possible failure of tests of significance.

The possibility of approximately satisfying all three requirements simultaneously is often an expression of rational optimism, to be assumed although not taken for granted.

An important aspect of any statistical analysis is the presentation of conclusions in a simple form and this may demand reinterpretation of conclusions on to the original scale of measurement.

CONSTRUCTION OF TRANSFORMATIONS. We now discuss in outline a number of techniques for choosing a suitable transformation.

The two most important techniques are probably previous experience of similar data, and the application of diagnostic checks to the analysis of untransformed data. In the latter case it may be clear that 'pulling in' either of the upper tail or of the lower tail of the data would be helpful.

To stabilize variance, a widely used technique is to establish either empirically or theoretically a relation between variance and mean. If for observations of true mean μ the variance is $v(\mu)$, then it is easy to show by local linearization that the transformation

$$y \rightarrow \int_0^y \mathrm{d}x/\sqrt{v(x)}$$

will induce observations of approximately unit variance. A common possibility is to find $v(\mu)$ approximately of the form $a\mu^b$, often established by plotting log sample variance against log sample mean, when a line of slope b should result. This leads to a power transformation except for $b = 2$, when a log transformation is indicated. The z transformation of correlation coefficients, r,

$$r \rightarrow \tfrac{1}{2}\log\{(1+r)/(1-r)\}$$

Is historically the first example of this argument, the relation between mean and variance being obtained theoretically.

Some simple equations expressing non-linear relations have simple linearizing transformations, of which the most common and important is the relation

$$y = \alpha x_1^{\beta_1} x_2^{\beta_2},$$

which is linearized by taking logs of all variables. A more empirical approach, not in fact much used in practice, is to search within some family of possible transformations for one which minimizes a measure of non-linearity or interaction.

A much more formal approach to the choice of a transformation is to start with some parametric family of transformations $y \rightarrow y^{(\lambda)}$ of which the most important is normally the family of power transformations, including as a limiting case the log transformation. The unknown parameter λ indexes the transformation that is appropriate. If now it is assumed that for some unknown λ the transformed values satisfy all the standard assumptions of some special convenient model, such as the normal theory general linear model, formal methods of estimation, in particular the method of maximum likelihood, can be applied to estimate λ, to see whether there is evidence that a transformation really does improve fit, to compare the values of λ in several unrelated sets of data, and so on. The calculations are relatively simple and straightforward. The usual procedure is to choose as a scale for analysis that corresponding to a simple value of λ reasonably consistent with the data.

Transformations to normality are always possible for a single continuous distribution, because any continuous distribution can be transformed into any other. Normalizing transformations are quite widely used in theoretical arguments; their direct use in the analysis of empirical data is on the whole rather less common, essentially for the reasons outlined above.

SOME FURTHER DEVELOPMENTS. The topics outlined above have an extensive literature. Some recent points of discussion and open issues are as follows:

(i) There are no good techniques for the transformation of multivariate distributions other than component by component.

(ii) Transformation selection by methods that are robust to outliers have been discussed, although in many practical situations it is the extreme observations that carry the most information about the appropriateness of transformations and whose accommodation is particularly important.

(iii) Following the choice of a transformation estimation and interpretation of effects is usually carried out on the transformed scale as if this had been given a priori. The appropriateness and justification of this has been the subject of lively discussion.

(iv) It is possible to transform to simple models other than the standard normal ones, for example to the exponential based models so useful in the analysis of duration data.

(v) The main procedures discussed above involve an interpretation essentially in terms of the expected response on the transformed scale. An alternative approach postulates that the expected value of the response on the original scale is a suitable non-linear function of a linear combination of explanatory variables. To distinguish empirically between these formulations is likely to require a large amount of high quality data.

(vi) Methods can be developed for estimating transforming functions totally non-parametrically. Such an approach uses a great deal of computer time.

D.R. COX

See also NON-LINEAR METHODS IN ECONOMETRICS; REGRESSION AND CORRELATION ANALYSIS.

BIBLIOGRAPHY

Bartlett (1943) gives an excellent account of the early work; Box and Cox (1964) discuss the estimation of transformations via the likelihood and Bayesian methods. Butter and Verbon (1982) describe economic applications in some depth. Bickel and Doksum (1981) and Box and Cox (1982) give opposing views of estimation following a transformation.

Bartlett, M.S. 1947. The use of transformations. *Biometrics* 3, 39–52.

Bickel, P.J. and Doksum, K.A. 1981. An analysis of transformations revisited. *Journal of the American Statistical Association* 76, 296–311.

Box, G.E.P. and Cox, D.R. 1964. An analysis of transformations. *Journal of the Royal Statistical Society*, Series B 26, 211–43.

Box, G.E.P. and Cox, D.R. 1982. An analysis of transformations revisited, rebutted. *Journal of the American Statistical Association* 77, 209–10.

den Butter, F.A.G. and Verbon, H.A.A. 1982. The specification problem in regression analysis. *International Statistical Review* 50, 267–83.

transformation of variables in econometrics. Economic theory usually fails to describe the functional relationship between variables (the CES production function being an exception). In econometrics, implications of simplistic choice of functional form include the danger of misspecification and its attendant biases in assessing magnitudes of effects and statistical significance of results. It is safe to say that when functional form is specified in a restrictive manner a priori before estimation, most empirical results that have been debated in the professional literature would have had a modified, even opposite, conclusion if the functional relationship had not been restrictive (see Zarembka, 1968, p. 509, for an illustration; also, Spitzer, 1976).

Most econometric research is not based on a large enough sample size for elaborate functional relationships to be meaningful. Therefore, a functional relationship which preserves additivity of effect (as in the linear model), but is more general than the usual choice between linear and linear-in-logarithmic models, ought to be sufficiently general. A transformation of variables in the form

$$y^{(\lambda)} = \begin{cases} (y^{\lambda} - 1)/\lambda, & \lambda \neq 0 \\ \ln y, & \lambda = 0 \end{cases}$$

offers a solution, where we note that lim $\lambda \to 0$ in the upper expression is in fact ln y, the lower expression.

Such transformations can be applied both to the dependent and independent variables with additivity of effect preserved on the transformed variable(s). The linear and linear-in-logarithmic models are both special cases ($\lambda = 1$ and $\lambda = 0$ for all variables, respectively). The transformation on the dependent variable may be different from those for the independent variables and different transformations may be applied to different independent variables, with corresponding increases in the parameter space (an obvious extension not elaborated upon here). It is important to note that a constant term must be included as an independent variable in order to preserve invariance of estimates of a transformation on a variable to changes in units of measurement for that variable (Schlesselman, 1971); otherwise the form y^{λ} or y^{λ}/λ would have to be used.

Usual econometric practice with a linear model, in this case in transformed variables, is to add an error term with a normal distribution of zero mean and constant variance (actually, here, only approximately normal since negative values on a transformed dependent variable would generally be truncated). Using maximum likelihood estimation, Box and Cox (1964) follow this approach. However, Amemiya and Powell (1981) have questioned such a procedure on grounds that the error distribution must be truncated and they show with the example of a gamma distribution on the dependent variable before transformation that the Box and Cox procedure is inconsistent and typically leads to quite different results than their statistically proper procedure. Nevertheless, Draper and Cox (1969) have shown that, as long as the error term is reasonably symmetric, the Box and Cox procedure is robust. (The apparent discrepancy between Draper and Cox and Amemiya and Powell is presumably that the latters' assumed gamma distribution on the untransformed dependent variable need not imply a 'reasonably' symmetric distribution of the transformed variable. The issue deserves further research.)

Following usual practice in its assumed normality (albeit here truncated) of the error term, along with independent and identically distributed terms, the iterated ordinary least squares is conceptually the simplest procedure for estimation. If σ^2 is the constant variance of the error distribution and N is the number of observations, then the maximized log-likelihood L for given λ is, except for a constant,

$$-\tfrac{1}{2}N \ln \hat{\sigma}^2(\lambda) + (\lambda - 1) \sum_{i=1}^{N} \ln y_i,$$

or, with the specific sample of y scaled by its geometric mean so that the latter term is zero,

$$L_{\max}(\lambda) = -\tfrac{1}{2}N \ln \hat{\sigma}^2(\lambda).$$

To maximize over the the whole parameter space, simply take alternative values of λ; the one that minimizes $\hat{\sigma}^2(\lambda)$ maximizes the log likelihood (a procedure almost any simple least squares programme can handle). Estimates of parameters for independent variables are also thus provided, while (as emphasized by Spitzer, 1982a, p. 311) their standard errors should be obtained from the information matrix. An approximate $100(1-\alpha)$ per cent confidence region for λ can be obtained from

$$L_{\max}(\hat{\lambda}) - L_{\max}(\lambda) < \tfrac{1}{2}\chi_1^2(\alpha).$$

For example, for a 95 per cent confidence interval ($\alpha = 0.05$), the region can be obtained from $L_{\max}(\hat{\lambda}) - L_{\max}(\lambda) < 1.92$. (Beauchamp and Kane (1984), give a survey of other estimation procedures, including Spitzer's (1982b) modified Newton algorithm preferred by him for its greater computational efficiency.)

The above has assumed that the error distribution is homoskedastic across observations on the dependent variable as transformed by the true λ. While such an assumption is relaxingly convenient, there is no obvious justification for it. Zarembka (1974, pp. 87–95) has analysed the circumstance in which heteroskedasticity of the error term obtains and shows that an incorrect assumption of homoskedasticity implies that the resulting maximum-likelihood procedure is biased asymptotically away from the true λ toward that transformation which more nearly stabilizes the error variance. Other parameters will also fail to be consistently estimated. For example, if the variance of the untransformed dependent variable y_i is constant, the bias is toward $\lambda = 1$; if the coefficient of variation of y_i is constant, the bias is toward $\lambda = 0$.

To estimate consistently the model under heteroskedasticity, some assumption concerning its pattern seems required. Zarembka (1974, pp. 93–5) considers the case where the variance of y_i is related to the power of the expectation of the transformed y_i. Lahiri and Egy (1981) consider the case where the variance of the transformed y_i is related to a power of any exogenous variable while Gaudry and Dagenais (1979) relate that variance to a function of several exogenous variables. Seaks and Layson (1983) consider the case where the variance of the transformed dependent variable is related to the square of one of the independent variables, while they also include autocorrelation in the error terms as an additional possibility (a problem first tackled for such transformation-of-variables models by Savin and White, 1978; see also Gaudry and Dagenais, 1979). Most show through examples the actual importance of confronting the possibility of heteroskedasticity. In the absence of specifying a structure for heteroskedasticity, Tse (1984) suggests a Lagrange multiplier test for its possible presence.

Almost all empirical uses of transformation of variables still use the conventional assumptions of normally and independently distributed error terms of constant variance (with exceptions such as Blaylock and Smallwood, 1982). In econometrics, examples of the wide range of applications of transformations of variables have included the elasticity of factor substitution in neoclassical production economics (and its possible variability), economies of scale in banking, the rate of technical progress represented in the 'Indianapolis 500', willingness to pay for automobile efficiency, economic depreciation of used buildings, capital asset pricing models, elasticities of demand for consumption (and specifically, meat, food, radios, and air quality), elasticities of the demand for money (and a possible 'liquidity trap') and for imports, demand for leisure and non-pecuniary job characteristics, relation of earnings to schooling and cognitive abilities, wage and rent gradients and the price elasticity of demand for urban housing, and elasticities of interstate migration.

PAUL ZAREMBKA

See also NON-LINEAR METHODS IN ECONOMETRICS; REGRESSION AND CORRELATION ANALYSIS.

BIBLIOGRAPHY

Amemiya, T. and Powell, J.L. 1981. A comparison of the Box–Cox maximum likelihood estimator and the non-linear two-stage least squares estimator. *Journal of Econometrics* 17, 351–81.

Beauchamp, J.J. and Kane, V.E. 1984. Application of the power-shift transformation. *Journal of Statistical Computation and Simulation* 19, 35–58.

Blaylock, J.R. and Smallwood, D.M. 1982. Analysis of income and food expenditure distributions: a flexible approach. *Review of Economics and Statistics* 64, 104–9.

Box, G.E.P. and Cox, D.R. 1964. An analysis of transformations. *Journal of the Royal Statistical Society*, Series B 26, 211–43.

Draper, N.R. and Cox, D.R. 1969. On distributions and their transformation to normality. *Journal of the Royal Statistical Society*, Series B 31, 472–6.

Gaudry, M.J.I. and Dagenais, M.G. 1979. Heteroskedasticity and the use of Box-Cox transformations. *Economics Letters* 2, 225–9.

Lahiri, K. and Egy, D. 1981. Joint estimation and testing for functional form and heteroskedasticity. *Journal of Econometrics* 15, 299–307.

Savin, N.E. and White, K.J. 1978. Estimation and testing for functional form and autocorrelation. *Journal of Econometrics* 8, 1–12.

Schlesselman, J. 1971. Power families: a note on the Box and Cox transformation. *Journal of the Royal Statistical Society*, Series B 33, 307–11.

Seaks, T.G. and Layson, S.K. 1983. Box–Cox estimation with standard econometric problems. *Review of Economics and Statistics* 65, 160–64.

Spitzer, J.J. 1976. The demand for money, the liquidity trap, and functional forms. *International Economic Review* 17, 220–27.

Spitzer, J.J. 1982a. A primer on Box–Cox estimation. *Review of Economics and Statistics* 64, 307–13.

Spitzer, J.J. 1982b. A fast and efficient algorithm for the estimation of parameters in models with the Box–Cox transformation. *Journal of the American Statistical Association* 77, 760–66.

Tse, Y.K. 1984. Testing for linear and log-linear regressions with heteroskedasticity. *Economics Letters* 16, 63–9.

Zarembka, P. 1968. Functional form in the demand for money. *Journal of the American Statistical Association* 63, 502–11.

Zarembka, P. 1974. Transformation of variables in econometrics. In *Frontiers in Econometrics*, ed. P. Zarembka, New York: Academic Press.

transformation problem The 'transformation problem' is at the heart of the Marxian labour theory of value. The topic has always been the subject of sharp controversy. The controversy reflects not only the general ideological conflicts that surround all Marxist ideas, but also the disagreement among Marxists themselves about the nature of the labour theory of value. After defining the problem in Marx's terms, we first present Marx's solution and the claims which he makes regarding its properties. This discussion is then followed by a brief critical review of the various solutions which have been proposed since Marx.

THE 'TRANSFORMATION PROBLEM'. To Marx, the value of a commodity consisted of the labour embodied in the means of production that were used up in the production of the commodity (dead labour) and the labour expended in the current production period (living labour).

$$W = L_d + L_l \tag{1}$$

where W is value, L_d is dead labour, and L_l is living labour. Living labour can be separated into necessary labour L_n and surplus labour, L_s. Necessary labour is that proportion of living labour that creates the value equivalent of the worker's wages and surplus labour is the remaining living labour time during which the value equivalent of surplus value is created. Thus, the following equation holds:

$$W = L_d + L_n + L_s \tag{2}$$

In actual pricing processes, Marx believed that capitalists summed up the costs of production and then added a percentage markup, which was determined by the average rate of profit. Thus the formula for equilibrium prices is:

Price of Prod = cost of commodities + cost of labour + Profit markup or, using p for the prices of production, c for constant capital, v for variable capital, and r for the rate of profit, we have:

$$P = c + v + r(c + v)$$

where $r + s/c + v$ and $r(c+v) = s/c + v(c+v) = s$.

The general correspondence between the various types of labour and the cost-components of price is obvious:

$$\begin{array}{ccccccc} W & = & L_d & + & L_n & + & L_s \\ \updownarrow & & \updownarrow & & \updownarrow & & \updownarrow \\ P & = & c & + & v & + & r(c+v). \end{array}$$

Price corresponds to value, constant capital corresponds to dead labour; variable capital corresponds to necessary labour; and profit corresponds to surplus value.

The most important reason why this correspondence is not proportional or one-to-one, however, is that the production of different commodities involves unequal organic compositions of capital (defined as either c/v or L_d/L_l). The exchange of commodities at values is thus incompatible with equal rates of profit. Given two industries which exchange at values, their rates of profit can only be equal if their organic compositions are equal:

$$r_1 = \frac{s_1/v_1}{c_1/v_1 + 1} = \frac{s_2/v_2}{c_2/v_2 + 1}.$$

Since the rates of surplus will be equalized through competition between workers, it follows that equal rates of profit imply equal organic compositions $(c_1/v_1) = (c_2/v_2)$. Marx argued that this would not be the case in general and that (c/v) varied significantly from sector to sector.

MARX'S SOLUTION. Marx's solution to the problem was to transform values into prices of production which correspond to equalized rates of profit. In chapter 9 of Volume III of

Capital he presents a table with five sectors and transforms values to prices of production by the following procedure. First he calculates the average rate of profit as:

$$\frac{\sum S_i}{\sum (c_i + v_i)}$$

Once given the average rate of profit, r, he recalculates all of the prices according to the formula:

$$(1+r)(c_i+v_i)$$

Marx was anxious to show that the essence of the labour theory of value and the theory of surplus value can be preserved when the transition is made from values to prices. Prices, he argued, are merely transformed values and profit is redistributed surplus value. In order to show the consistency of this view he made the following two claims concerning the aggregates in his transformation solution: 1. The sum of values = the sum of prices; 2. The sum of surplus value = the sum of profit.

> The sum of the profits for all the different spheres of production must accordingly be equal to the sum of surplus values, and the sum of prices of production for the total social product must be equal to the sum of its values (Marx [1867], 1981, p. 273).

The equality of these aggregates was used by Marx to argue that only a redistribution has occurred and nothing has actually been created or destroyed in the transformation from values to prices.

THE REPRODUCTION SCHEME ARGUMENT: BORTKIEWICZ, SWEEZY, SETON. Following the publication of Marx's solution to the transformation problem, a number of critics pointed out that Marx had not completely solved the transformation problem. In his solution, Marx had transformed the output prices while the input prices remained in values. This was an inadequate solution, it was argued, since capitalists buy inputs at prices and not values. In addition, the output price of one commodity is the input price of another. In his famous 1907 article, Bortkiewicz attempted to solve the transformation problem by simultaneously transforming both inputs and outputs (Bortkiewicz, 1907). But in his result he found that he could obtain only one of the two claims made by Marx. Either total prices were equal to total values or total surplus value was equivalent to total profit, but not both. He considered this as an important criticism of the labour theory of value.

In 1942, Sweezy built on the Bortkiewicz result using a three sector reproduction scheme. Although Bortkiewicz used this apparatus as a matter of convenience, Sweezy argued that the transformation procedure should 'not result in a disruption of the conditions of simple reproduction' (Sweezy, 1942, p. 114). Sweezy went beyond Bortkiewicz, and claimed that his solution would satisfy both of Marx's claims. He obtained such a result by assuming that the output of the luxury sector is equal to unity, and assuming that this sector also has the average organic composition. He argued that these two assumptions are reasonable since the output of the luxury sector can be considered the money commodity, and to avoid price/value deviations in the money commodity, its organic composition must be set equal to the average of the first two sectors. Seton later provided a proof of Sweezy's example.

Unfortunately, Sweezy's success is a result of his assumptions. First, since surplus value is equal to the output of the luxury sector, setting this output equal to one in both prices and values ensures that total surplus value will equal total profit. The assumption of a socially average organic composition in the third sector obtains the second condition. If the sum of the organic compositions of department I and department II is equal to that of department III, and department III's output is set equal in prices and values, then the sum of prices and values in departments I and II must also be equal. Not only are Sweezy's results true by definition, but these two assumptions are unnecessarily restrictive for a convincing solution to the transformation problem.

NORMALIZATION BY SRAFFA'S STANDARD COMMODITY: MEDIO. In general, it can be said that, lacking an invariant measure of value, it has proven impossible to obtain a transformation solution in which the equalities between values and prices as well as profit and surplus value can be simultaneously maintained without the aid of extremely restrictive assumptions. When Sraffa's standard commodity became widely known there was initially some hope that it might provide such an invariant measure. This hope was quickly abandoned, however, when it was realized how restrictive the nature of the invariance of Sraffa's standard commodity is.

Marx, however, suggested a third method for linking prices to labour values. It is within the context of this third method that Alfredo Medio (1972) demonstrated that Sraffa's standard commodity could provide an important analytical tool for the Marxist labour theory of value. Marx realized that if a commodity could be found that was produced with the socially average organic composition of capital, then the rate of profit which could be obtained in the production and sale of that commodity would be identical whether all commodities were sold at their labour values or at their transformed money prices. Therefore, the rate of profit on that commodity would be determined entirely by labour values. Moreover, since competition tended to equalize all profit rates, it could be shown that the socially average rate of profit (by virtue of which all price calculations could be made with a cost-of-production theory of prices) would correspond to the rate of profit on the average commodity – a rate determined entirely by labour value calculations. If a numeraire that equates aggregate profit and aggregate surplus value (or equates the aggregate of values and prices) cannot be found, then an average industry whose rate of profit is determined by labour values suffices to connect the labour value analysis and the price analysis.

Medio demonstrated that in the industry producing Sraffa's standard commodity, the Marxian formula for the rate of profit, $r = (s/v)/(c/v + 1)$, always holds true. In Medio's demonstration the profit rate (r) is the money rate of profit by which capitalists mark up their money costs to arrive at prices. The rate of exploitation, or rate of surplus value (s/v), is defined in labour value terms. It is the rate at which surplus value is created in the sphere of production, and hence it is equal in all industries. The organic composition of capital (c/v), however, has a special meaning in Medio's formulation. It is determined by labour values alone, and is a weighted average of all of the production processes that make up the industry that produces the standard commodity.

Medio's solution has been criticized by the observation that a standard commodity does not actually exist, and that a hypothetical form of measurement is a weaker claim than that sought by Marx.

THE ITERATIVE METHOD AND BALANCED GROWTH: SHAIKH. Anwar Shaikh's popular solution to the transformation problem has been published in two important papers with a seven year gap (Shaikh, 1977; 1984). In his 1977 paper on the transformation problem, Shaikh is concerned with establishing a link between Marx's method and what he considers the 'correct' prices obtained by Bortkiewicz. Instead of developing a new mathematical apparatus, all one had to do, according to Shaikh, is to iterate Marx's procedure. If one takes Marx's prices of production and uses them as inputs, and then uses Marx's procedure again to obtain new prices of production, and so on, one converges on the set of Bortkiewicz prices. Shaikh's actual procedure, however, makes a number of assumptions which are found in Bortkiewicz but may not be in Marx. He sets the sum of prices equal to the sum of values in each step, and adjusts the money wage at every step so that the workers consume a certain bundle of commodities at the previous period's prices. Shaikh's procedure does obtain the set of prices consistent with the Bortkiewicz method, but also like Bortkiewicz, he obtains only one of Marx's aggregates. In Shaikh's solution total surplus value is not equal to total profit. Why not? This is the issue discussed in his 1984 paper.

In his 1984 paper, Shaikh argues that the transformation solution should not adopt ad hoc assumptions to obtain both of Marx's aggregates. Instead, he reasons, we should actually expect total surplus value and total profit to differ. This difference is due to the price-value deviations and the size of the luxury sector. When price-value deviations exist in the luxury sector, surplus value can be gained or lost through the circuits of revenue. His proof of this argument utilizes the assumption of balanced growth. In a situation of balanced growth he shows that the difference between surplus value and profit can be shown to be proportional to the price-value deviation in the sector producing luxury products. Such a result is very close to the well known property of von Neumann systems that when an economy is at maximum balanced growth and one of Marx's claims is assumed, then the other will automatically follow. Unfortunately, Shaikh's result cannot hold in a real economy where balanced growth is not satisfied.

THE 'NEW SOLUTION': DUMÉNIL, LIPIETZ AND FOLEY. What is being called the 'new solution' to the transformation problem by a small but growing group of Marxist economists was first introduced to English-speaking readers by Lipietz (1982). but the original solution was formulated by Duménil (1980) and later 'discovered' independently by Duncan Foley (1982). The new solution entails two important assumptions which are traced back to Marx. The first is that (the sum of prices equals the sum of values) should be modified to read: the sum of the prices of the net product (defined as the value added) should be the sum of the values of the net product. The second assumption is that distribution must be defined ex post, as either the value of the money wage which workers receive (Foley, 1982), or the bundle of consumption goods which the workers buy valued at prices (Duménil, 1980). Once these two assumptions are made any set of values can be transformed into any set of prices with the property that both of Marx's aggregates hold.

Duménil and Foley make two arguments for the adoption of their unique normalization procedure on the net product. First, they claim that such a normalization avoids double counting (Duménil, 1983–4, p. 442). In addition, they both argue that such a normalization conforms to Marx's view of what value is. Value 'is the linking of the total labour expended in a given period with the production associated with it, that is, the net product' (Duménil, 1983–4, p. 442). In addition, they argue that wages must be evaluated on the basis of prices and not as the value of a wage bundle. This view of distribution avoids the problem that when prices deviate from values, the rate of exploitation in price terms depends on the particular set of goods which workers buy and is not settled in the production process. They further argue that, in the previous formulations, if any part of the wage is saved the rate of surplus value becomes incalculable. Foley goes further than Duménil and argues that the wage should not be considered as a bundle at all. Wages are a sum of money, he claims, which can be used to buy any goods at the existing set of prices. In addition, unlike a wage bundle, the money wage conceals the exploitative nature of capitalist relations (Foley, 1982, p. 43).

One argument which has been posed against this view is that in the set of 'new solution' prices of production the sum of the values of constant capital does not equal the total sum of its prices. A convincing argument justifying this result must be established. In addition, the distribution assumption requires ex post knowledge. The actual set of prices must be known before the rate of wages can be established. One cannot move step by step from values into prices. The two realms must be considered separately while the new solution only provides a mapping procedure from one to the other.

SUMMARY AND IMPLICATIONS. The transformation problem arose from the attempt to show that the labour theory of value is consistent with the money prices of exchange. Marx's two claims that total prices should be equal to total values and total surplus value should be equal to total profit have traditionally been considered a prerequisite to the argument that prices are merely transformed values and profit is redistributed surplus value. We have shown that this result can be obtained by using numerous different assumptions. Some of these procedures hold total prices and values constant but require special assumptions to obtain an equality between surplus value and profit, others do the reverse. Many of these assumptions are clearly unjustifiable while others are rather more realistic. The 'new solution' of Duménil and Foley obtains both aggregates but finds a discrepancy between constant capital in price and value terms, while Medio's solution holds that equality of the rate of profit in value and money terms is more important than either of the two more traditional equalities.

It is clear from the literature on the 'transformation problem' that its resolution will not be merely a mathematical exercise. The ground of this continuing debate in the future will, instead, concern the social and economic implications of the competing assumptions which are adopted and their compatibility with the tenets of the labour theory of value. This, however, will be a complex debate since Marxists themselves have strong disagreements about the specific nature of the labour theory of value as well as its role or function within the Marxist theoretical system.

E.K. HUNT AND MARK GLICK

See also BORTKIEWICZ, LADISLAUS VON; SWEEZY, PAUL MALOR; VALUE AND PRICE.

BIBLIOGRAPHY

Bortkiewicz, L. 1907. Value and price in the Marxian system. Trans. in *International Economic Papers* No. 2, 1952, 5–61.

Duménil, G. 1980. *De la valeur aux prix de production*. Paris: Economica.

Duménil, G. 1983–4. Beyond the transformation riddle: a labor theory of value. *Science and Society* 47(4), Winter, 427–50.

Foley, D. 1982. The value of money, the value of labor power and the Marxian transformation problem. *Review of Radical Political Economics* 14(2), Summer, 37–47.

Lipietz, A. 1982. The so-called 'transformation problem' revisited. *Journal of Economic Theory* 26(1), 59–88.
Marx, K. 1867.*Capital*, Vol. I. Harmondsworth: Penguin, 1981.
Medio, A. 1972. Profits and surplus value: appearance and reality in capitalist production. In *A Critique of Economic Theory*, ed. E.K. Hunt and J. Schwartz, New York: Penguin.
Seton, F. 1957. The 'transformation problem'. *Review of Economic Studies* 24, June, 149–60.
Shaikh, A. 1977. Marx's theory of value and the 'transformation problem'. In *The Subtle Anatomy of Capitalism*, ed. J. Schwartz, Santa Monica: Goodyear.
Shaikh, A. 1984. The transformation from Marx to Sraffa. In *Ricardo, Marx, Sraffa*, ed. E. Mandel, London: Verso.
Sweezy, P. 1942. *The Theory of Capitalist Development*. New York: Monthly Review Press, ch. 7.

transformations and invariance. Theories of measurement have applications throughout economics. Some applications are familiar because they are firmly established in the literature (think of utility theory and price indexes). But some are yet to be incorporated into the wider literature and many potential applications remain to be made. This entry does not survey the applications or the theories (see Pfanzagl, 1968, and Krantz et al., 1971 on theories of measurement), but (1) attempts to explain a certain kind of invariance principle and (2) shows how the principle can be applied to economic analysis.

The invariance principle can be expressed somewhat loosely like this: a relation S between the numbers that represent measures of things is interesting (in the sense that it possibly represents a relation between the things themselves) only so far as it is invariant under all permissible changes in the scales of measurement of the things. If a relation S meets this condition, we may reasonably hope that it expresses in the language of numbers a statement that is true of the world; if not, we have no such hope, for the failure of S to hold under all permissible selections of scales shows that it is a property of our analysis of the world, not of the world itself, because the selection of measurement scales is intrinsically arbitrary.

This principle is rarely discussed in economics but it lies behind a number of familiar propositions. Modern economists know that diminishing marginal utility is not an interesting property of an ordinal utility function because it is not invariant under increasing transformations of the utility function. And they compare elasticities, not slopes, of demand functions because order relations among the elasticities, but not among the slopes, are invariant under changes in the measurement scales for prices and commodities. This invariance does not prove that corresponding order relations exist among the demand functions of the real world, but it allows us to hope so.

By demand functions of the real world, I mean functional relations between commodities and prices, not between their measurements. I do not take the extreme operationalist view that all empirical laws are simply relations between measurements. This view seems untenable if for no other reason than the many relations that surely predated the development of the number systems: preference relations, production functions, hierarchical relations, and so on through a long list. Popper (1963) gives additional objections to operationalism.

Extreme operationalism is one of several conceptual schemes, or schema, for thinking about the relations among measurement, empirical laws, and numerical laws. It is the schema that recognizes no distinction between empirical laws (true statements about the world) and numerical laws (true statements about the numbers that measure the world's things). Three alternative schema are explained in the next section.

Usage. Throughout the entry, R denotes the set of real numbers (reals), R_+ the non-negative reals, and R_{++} the positive reals. A function $f\colon A \rightarrow B$ has a domain in A and a range in B. If the domain is A, the function is *on A* (otherwise *from A*). If the range is B, the function is *onto B* (otherwise *into B*). 'From' and 'into' are understood; 'on' and 'onto' must be stated.

1. THINGS AND THEIR MEASURES

The basic objects of economic behaviour belong to a different category of thought than the numbers that represent them, and relations among these objects belong to a different category than relations among numbers. The goal of economic analysis is to understand the basic objects and the economically interesting relations among them, but this goal is pursued by analysing relations among numbers. Economics is *about* two categories – basic objects and their relations – but it is *performed on* two other categories – numbers and their relations. These two pairs of distinct categories are linked by a fifth category, consisting of the scales of measurement of the basic objects. The linkage is not one-to-one, however, for the scales are not unique.

The distinctions among these categories are central to the part of measurement theory that deals with meaningfulness (a subject discussed by the authors cited above and by many others including Ramsay (1976) and Falmagne and Narens (1983)). The distinctions may be illustrated by an example in which the basic objects are three types of commodities and the relation of interest among them is production. The classic works in production theory verbally describe a two-input–one-output production function as a specified kind of relation between two input commodities and one output commodity, but they formally define it as a real-valued function of two real variables that obeys certain axioms (see Shephard, 1970, for example). This equivocation may be explained by a schema. All three of the schema to be mentioned have two elements in common: first, the sets C_k consisting of all commodities of type k ($k = 1, 2, 3$), and second, a function $\pi\colon C_1 \times C_2 \rightarrow C_3$ showing which commodity of type 3 is producible by a bundle of the other two.

The most completely specified (that is, least general) schema is that of Dimensional Analysis. In this schema, commodities are regarded as physical quantities in the sense of Whitney (1968) or the more general sense of Krantz et al. (1971), thus paving the way for an application of Luce's (1978) theorem on meaningfulness to π. Then π is a dimensionally invariant relation and may be analysed with the tools of Dimensional Analysis (Bridgman, 1922; Kurth, 1965; de Jong, 1967; Krantz et al., 1971). These tools, familiar to all physicists and engineers, are virtually unknown among modern economists. Jevons's prelude to a rigorous theory of economic dimensions in the second edition of *The Theory of Political Economy* (1879, 1965) was advanced a little by Wicksteed in Palgrave's *Dictionary of Political Economy* and then allowed to die. De Jong's attempted revival (1967) was ignored. Economists just lost interest. Whether this says something about economists or about economics is far from clear. What is clear is that until commodities are rigorously examined in terms of the axioms of physical quantities, the Dimensional Analytic schema will remain problematic for economics.

A more general schema, which subsumes Dimensional analysis, is that of Conjoint Measurement (Luce and Tukey, 1964; Krantz et al., 1971; Luce and Cohen, 1983), which characterizes π and the C_k as a unified object of thought (C_1, C_2, C_3, π) and obtains numerical representations of the C_k and π simultaneously. Although this powerful and rapidly developing theory seems naturally suited to economics, its potential applications remain largely unexplored outside the area of decisions under risk.

Although we do not employ an explicit measurement schema in formal economic analysis, our customary procedures embody one implicitly. When we speak of a (two-input, one-output) production function as a real-valued function of two real variables, we have implicitly introduced scales of measurement for the commodities and represented the production function π by what Falmagne and Narens (1983) call a 'numerical code'. Let us make this schema more explicit under the strong assumption that all the measurement scales are ratio scales (unique up to a positive multiplier).

A measurement scale for the type-k commodity is a homomorphism between C_k and R_+, that is, it preserves the algebraic structure of C_k. In assuming ratio scales, we are attributing so much structure to C_k that its homomorphisms are severely limited. The validity of such an attribution is a promising subject for research; here we take it for granted.

When spelled out in sufficient detail to yield an application to production theory, our schema consists of six elements. (1) the sets C_k of commodities of type k. (2) The assumed production function π: $C_1 \times C_2 \rightarrow C_3$. (3) A clear distinction between commodities and numbers. (4) The assumption that, nevertheless, commodities share sufficiently many properties of the real numbers that their homomorphisms, or scales, are determined up to a positive multiplication. The set of scales for type-k commodities is H_k, with members $h_k, h'_k, \ldots$; the cartesian product $H_1 \times H_2 \times H_3$ is written as H. We need not decide at this point whether all members of H are available in a system of coherent units. (5) The representation of π by a *general numerical code* F: $R_+ \times R_+ \times H \rightarrow R_+$ defined under the conditions

$$x_k = h_k(c_k), \qquad k = 1, 2, 3 \tag{1}$$

$$c_3 = \pi(c_1, c_2) \tag{2}$$

by

$$x_3 = F(x_1, x_2; h_1, h_2, h_3). \tag{3}$$

This representation is general because it holds for all h_k that yield coherent units (i.e. all 'admissible' h_k). It does not appear in practice, where we employ the sixth element. (6) The selection of an arbitrary admissible member h from H and the representation of F (and hence π) by a *special numerical code* f_h: $R_+ \times R_+ \rightarrow R_+$ defined by

$$f_h(x_1, x_2) = F(x_1, x_2; h_1, h_2, h_3), \tag{4}$$

which holds only for the scales h_1, h_2, h_3.

The sixth element of our schema actually consists of a set of special numerical codes like (4), one for each admissible triple of scales. Since every such triple can be expressed in terms of the fixed triple (h_1, h_2, h_3) by (r_1h_1, r_2h_2, r_3h_3) for some positive numbers r_1, r_2, r_3, and every measure x_k in the fixed scale h_k becomes r_kx_k in the scale r_kh_k, we can write any special numerical code in the generic form

$$f_{rh}(r_1x_1, r_2x_2) = F(r_1x_1, r_2x_2; r_1h_1, r_2h_2, r_3h_3). \tag{5}$$

In practice, of course, the subscripts h and rh are omitted from the functional symbol f.

This schema is one way of making explicit the assumptions and conventions that precede – and link to the world – a typical economic analysis of production, which focuses on a special numerical expression of π.

The preceding references to commodities, ratio scales, and production are only intended to fix ideas. When generalized in the obvious manner, the schema covers all the relations between basic objects that can be represented by functions whose domains and ranges are vectors of real numbers. It leads directly to the following question and sometimes to its answer: What can we learn about f_h and f_{rh}, and thus indirectly about π, from the fact that both f_h and f_{rh} represent π? To answer this question we must know the type of scale in each H_k and something about the relations (if any) among the H_k. In many cases, such knowledge is sufficient for the discovery of interesting properties of π or of unexpected implications of our formal theory of π. In other words, we can learn something about the relations among things – or at least about our theories of such relations – by considering how the things are measured. This remarkable fact ought to be known more widely. We demonstrate its utility by means of the special case of our schema as outlined above.

2. AN INVARIANCE CONDITION

For notational simplicity we may omit the subscript h from the functions f_h and f_{rh} defined in equations (4) and (5) (we are keeping h fixed), denoting them by f and f_r. Since these functions represent the same production function π, we have

$$f(x_1, x_2) = h_3(c_3) = h_3[\pi(c_1, c_2)] \tag{6}$$

$$f_r(r_1x_1, r_2x_2) = r_3h_3(c_3) = r_3h_3[\pi(c_1, c_2)]. \tag{7}$$

If $f(x_1, x_2) > 0$, eqs (6) and (7) imply

$$\frac{f_r(r_1x_1, r_2x_2)}{f(x_1, x_2)} = r_3. \tag{8}$$

Clearly, for all $(x_1, x_2), (y_1, y_2), \ldots, (z_1, z_2)$ representing input bundles associated with positive ouputs, we have

$$\frac{f_r(r_1x_1, r_2x_2)}{f(x_1, x_2)} = \frac{f_r(r_1y_1, r_2y_2)}{f(y_1, y_2)} = \cdots = \frac{f_r(r_1z_1, r_2z_2)}{f(z_1, z_2)}, \tag{9}$$

showing that the ratio r_3 depends only on r_1 and r_2. Denoting this dependence by $\phi(r_1, r_2)$, we obtain the equation

$$f_r(r_1x_1, r_2x_2) = \phi(r_1, r_2) f(x_1, x_2). \tag{10}$$

Equation (10) is an invariance condition. It states that the special numerical codes f and f_r of π are related by a positive multiplier that depends only on the multipliers r_1 and r_2. Therefore, properties expressed in terms of the 'internal structure' of f are invariant under changes of the scales for commodities 1 and 2. (See Leontief, 1947, for a discussion of 'internal structure'; it is a part of the theory of functional equations, for which Aczel, 1966, is a valuable reference.) Equation (10) embodies the invariance principle stated at the beginning of this entry.

Equation (10) is a functional equation in the three functions f_r, ϕ, and f. Given that any two of these functions have positive values at (1,1), equation (10) implies three additional functional equations, one for each function, and all three equations have the same form. The key steps in obtaining these equations use the relations (similar to relation (9)),

$$\frac{f_{sr}(s_1r_1x_1, s_2r_2x_2)}{f(x_1, x_2)} = \cdots = \frac{f_{sr}(s_1r_1z_1, s_2r_2z_2)}{f(z_1, z_2)} \equiv \psi(s_1r_1, s_2r_2)$$

and

$$\frac{f_{sr}(s_1r_1x_1, s_2r_2x_2)}{f_r(r_1x_1, r_2x_2)} = \cdots = \frac{f_{sr}(s_1r_1z_1, s_2r_2z_2)}{f_r(r_1z_1, r_2z_2)} \equiv \epsilon(s_1, s_2).$$

These relations follow because the transformations $x_k \rightarrow s_kr_kx_k$

can be decomposed into $x_k \to r_k x_k \to s_k r_k x_k$. Using the definitions of ϕ, ψ, and ϵ, it can be shown under relatively mild conditions that f satisfies the functional equation

$$f(t_1 x_1, t_2 x_2) = \frac{f(t_1, t_2) f(x_1, x_2)}{f(1, 1)}. \qquad (11)$$

Equation (11) is a stronger invariance condition. It may be interpreted two ways. On the first, t_1 and t_2 represent scale transformations for a fixed input bundle

$$(c_1, c_2) = [h_1^{-1}(x_1), h_2^{-1}(x_2)],$$

and we see that these transformations affect f only by multiplying all its values by a positive constant $f(t_1, t_2)/f(1, 1)$. On this interpretation, (11) holds for all $(x_1, x_2) \in h_1(C_1) \times h_2(C_2)$ such that $f(x_1, x_2) > 0$ but only for all *admissible* t_1, t_2. On the second interpretation, t_1 and t_2 represent variations in input bundles as measured on a fixed scale, so that $(t_1 x_1, t_2 x_2) = [h_1(t_1 c_1), h_2(t_2 c_2)]$. On this interpretation, (11) holds for the same bundles (x_1, x_2) as before and for all $(t_1 x_1, t_2 x_2)$ such that $(t_1 c_1, t_2 c_2)$ is defined and productive.

We may thus draw a general conclusion: whenever a relation among basic objects can be represented by a functional relation among the measures of the objects, the function will obey an invariance condition. If all the measures are on ratio scales, the invariance condition takes the form of (10) or (11), but in general each combination of types of scales induces its own form of invariance condition. Thus an appropriate invariance condition is a logical consequence of more fundamental hypotheses, and the invariance principle is positive, not normative, when a basic empirical relation exists.

There are, of course, many cases in which the problem is not to represent a specified empirical relation but to define a theoretical relation among basic objects by first defining a relation among their measurements and then attributing a corresponding relation to the objects themselves. Such a relation need have no empirical counterpart.

A price index P_t, for instance, defined in terms of the measures $P_{1t}, \ldots, P_{2t}$ of n individual prices at time t, is supposed to permit us to compare 'the average price level' (APL) at times 1 and 2 by comparing the values of P_1 and P_2. We say that APL_1 is higher than APL_2 if and only if $P_1 > P_2$, or, more generally, that $APL_1, \ldots, APL_k$ are in relation S_A if and only if $P_1, \ldots, P_k$ are in relation S_P. The relation S_A is not a preexisting relation *represented* by S_P but is *defined* by it.

For another example, let A be a set of social states in the sense of Arrow (1951) and $u_i\colon A \to R$ be the ith person's utility function $(i = 1, \ldots, n)$. A social welfare function $w\colon A \to R$ is defined by $w(a) = f[u_1(a), \ldots, u_n(a)]$, where $f\colon R^n \to R$ is some function that obeys specified conditions. We say that state b is 'socially better' than state c if and only if $f[u_1(b), \ldots, u_n(b)] > f[u_1(c), \ldots, u_n(c)]$. This comparison between social states does not exist independently of the comparison between the values of f.

In such cases the invariance principle is normative and an appropriate invariance condition (Osborne, 1976a) must be imposed. This condition is usually only one of a set of conditions that the relation among measures must meet. In some cases the full set of conditions cannot be met by any such relation. Examples occur in the theories of price indexes (Fisher, 1911) and social welfare functions (Osborne, 1976b).

3. AN APPLICATION

The implications of (11) depend on the qualitative structure of the part of $C_1 \times C_2$ that can be physically realized and that yields positive output of commodity 3. There are a number of interesting special cases, of which we can consider only one.

Suppose that for all $t > 0$ such that f is defined,

$$f(x_1, x_2) > 0 \text{ implies } f(tx_1, tx_2) > 0. \qquad (12)$$

(The restriction on t follows from the necessity that tc_k be in C_K when $c_k \in C_k$.) Then f is homothetic: for if (x_1, x_2) and (y_1, y_2) are on the same isoquant, so that $f(x_1, x_2) = f(y_1, y_2)$, then by (11) with $t_1 = t_2 = t$, $f(tx_1, tx_2) = f(ty_1, ty_2)$; so (tx_1, tx_2) and (ty_1, ty_2) are on the same isoquant.

Homotheticity follows from the invariance condition and the assumption stated in (12). This assumption can be recast into a weaker form that is common in theoretical work (let (x_1, x_2) and (y_1, y_2) lie on the lowest positive isoquant and confine t to values greater than 1). The invariance condition follows, under mild conditions, from our schema. Essentially, then, empirical evidence against homotheticity would indicate defects in the schema. One obvious potential defect is the assumption of ratio scales, which, after all, still awaits a searching examination. The alternatives to ratio scales that have received much attention in measurement theory are ordinal, interval, and log-interval scales. Ordinal and interval scales are familiar in economics from utility and expected-utility theories. Log-interval scales h are unique up to transformations $h \to rh^s$, $r, s > 0$. The literature of economics would look very different if any of these alternatives were thought appropriate for commodities. Suppose the measure of commodity 1 were unique up to the transformation $x_1 \to r_1 x_1^{s_1}$, for instance. Then the price elasticity of demand, e, would be unique up to the transformation $e_1 \to s_1 e_1$, and the demand for commodity 1 would be more or less elastic than that for commodity 2 depending on our arbitrary choice of scales for measuring the commodities. This does not, of course, justify the assumption of ratio scales, but it indicates how radical the effects of abandoning the assumption would be.

Another potential defect in the schema is the assumption that a production function exists – or, in other words, that a production process can be modelled by a real-valued function of real variables. Georgescu-Roegen has energetically disputed this assumption on a number of occasions (e.g. 1970). But to follow up his line of thought would take us out of the realm of invariance into that of production.

DALE K. OSBORNE

See also HOMOGENEOUS AND HOMOTHETIC FUNCTIONS; MEANINGFULNESS AND INVARIANCE.

BIBLIOGRAPHY

Aczel, J. 1966. *Lectures on Functional Equations and Their Applications.* New York: Academic Press.

Arrow, K.J. 1951. *Social Choice and Individual Values.* New York: John Wiley and Sons.

Bridgman, P.W. 1922. *Dimensional Analysis.* New Haven: Yale University Press.

de Jong, F.J. 1967. *Dimensional Analysis for Economists.* Amsterdam: North-Holland Publishing Co.

Falmagne, J.C. and Narens, L. 1983. Scales and meaningfulness of quantitative laws. *Synthese* 55, 287–325.

Fisher, I. 1911. *The Purchasing Power of Money.* New York: The MacMillan Co.

Georgescu-Roegen, N. 1970. The economics of production. *American Economic Review* 60, 1–9.

Jevons, W.S. 1965. *The Theory of Political Economy*. 5th ed. New York: Augustus M. Kelley.
Krantz, D.H., Luce, R.D., Suppes, P. and Tversky, A. 1971. *Foundations of Measurement* I. New York: Academic Press.
Kurth, R. 1965. A note on dimensional analysis. *American Mathematical Monthly* 72, 965–9.
Leontief, W. 1947. Introduction to the internal structure of functional relationships. *Econometrica* 361–73.
Luce, R.D. 1978. Dimensionally invariant numerical laws correspond to meaningful qualitative relations. *Philosophy of Science* 45, 1–16.
Luce, R.D. and Cohen, M. 1983. Factorizable automorphisms in solvable conjoint structures, I. *Journal of Pure and Applied Algebra* 27, 225–61.
Luce, R.D. and Tukey, J.W. 1964. Simultaneous conjoint measurement: A new type of fundamental measurement. *Journal of Mathematical Psychology* 1, 1–27.
Osborne, D.K. 1976a. Unified theory of derived measurement. *Synthese* 33, 455–81.
Osborne, D.K. 1976b. Irrelevant alternatives and social welfare. *Econometrica* 44, 1001–15.
Pfanzagl, J. 1968. *Theory of Measurement*. New York: John Wiley & Sons.
Popper, K. 1963. *Conjectures and Refutations*. London: Routledge & Kegan Paul.
Ramsay, J.O. 1976. Algebraic representation in the physical and behavioral sciences. *Synthese* 33, 419–53.
Shephard, R.W. 1970. *Theory of Cost and Production Functions*. Princeton: Princeton University Press.
Whitney, H. 1968. The mathematics of physical quantities. *American Mathematical Monthly* 75, 115–38, 227–56.

transformations in economics. *See* TRANSFORMATIONS AND INVARIANCE.

transitivity. Transitivity is formally just a property that a binary relation might possess, and thus one could discuss the concept in any context in economics in which an ordering relation is used. Here, however, the discussion of transitivity will be limited to its role in describing an individual agent's choice behaviour. In this context transitivity means roughly that if an agent choses *A* over *B*, and *B* over *C*, that agent ought to choose *A* over *C*, or at least be indifferent. On the surface this seems reasonable, even 'rational', but this ignores how complicated an agent's decision making process can be. For an excellent discussion of this issue see May (1954). Given a model of agent behaviour, transitivity can be imposed as a direct assumption, or can be an implication of the model for choice behaviour. The standard model of agent behaviour in economics is that the agent orders prospects by means of a utility function, which in effect assumes transitivity. With appropriate continuity and convexity restrictions on utility functions, the model allows one to demonstrate that: (1) Individual demand functions are well defined, continuous, and satisfy the comparative static restriction, the Strong Axiom of Revealed Preference (SARP). (In the smooth case, this corresponds to the negative semidefiniteness and symmetry of the Slutsky matrix.) (2) Given a finite collection of such agents with initial endowments of goods, a competitive equilibrium exists. What will be discussed in the remaining part of this entry is to what extent one can obtain results analogous to (1) and (2) above while using a model of agent behaviour which does not assume or imply transitive behaviour. To keep the discussion as simple as possible, we will only consider the situation in which the agent's set of feasible commodity vectors is the non-negative orthant of n-dimensional Euclidean space, and the agent's problem is to choose a commodity vector x when faced with positive prices and income. A vector p in the positive orthant of Euclidean n-space will denote the vector of price-income ratios, or a 'price' system.

Two models of agent behaviour which have a long history in economics will now be described. The first, which will be called the 'local' theory, takes as its primitive the assumption that if an agent is currently consuming at a vector x, he is able to determine if an infinitesimal change in x, say x to $x + \mathrm{d}x$, is a change for better or worse. This idea is represented by a function $x \rightarrow g(x)$, mapping each vector x into a n-vector $g(x)$ such that a small movement from x in the direction of y is an improvement if $g(x)(y-x)>0$, and not an improvement otherwise. Given a price system p, an affordable x is an equilibrium point for the agent if $g(x)(y-x)\leqslant 0$ for all affordable y. That is, no small movement from x in the direction of an affordable y is an improvement. A basic question is whether for every p, an equilibrium x exists. This approach goes back at least to Pareto, and most economists, including Pareto, concerned themselves with the 'integrability' problem; when is there a quasi-concave utility function such that $g(x)$ is a positive scalar multiple of the vector of marginal utilities, for each x? Note that if an agent has a differentiable quasi-concave utility function u, and one defines g by $g(x)=\lambda(x)Du(x)$ for any $\lambda(x)>0$, then $g(x)(y-x)>0$ is equivalent to $Du(x)(y-x)>0$, and this implies $u(x+t(y-x))>u(x)$ for t positive and sufficiently small. Thus if g is 'integrable', the agent acts as if he maximizes a utility function, and thus results (1) or (2) above will be satisfied. Some economists, however, believed that the local theory could be used to describe agent behaviour without assuming the integrability conditions. Most notable is the work of Allen (1932), Georgescu-Roegen (1936; 1954) and Katzner (1971). Without the integrability conditions and the implied utility function (and thus implied transitivity) the existence of an equilibrium x given any p is nontrivial. This problem was solved by Georgescu-Roegen (1954), who showed that if g is continuous and g satisfied the 'Principal of Persistent Nonpreference' (PPN), that is, $g(x)(y-x)<0$ implies $g(y)(x-y)>0$, then an equilibrium point will exist in any budget set. It should be noted that the integrability problem mentioned above requires PPN (for quasi-concave utility), as well as the Frobenius conditions for mathematical integrability. It is easy to show that Georgescu-Roegen's assumptions imply that the resulting demand correspondence will be upper-hemicontinuous.

The second basic approach to modeling agent behaviour will be called the 'global' theory. In this approach, the primitive of the theory is a binary relation R on the commodity space with xRy having the interpretation 'x is at least as good as y'. Define the strict preference relation P by xPy is equivalent to not yRx. (P could also be taken as the primitive.) Given a price system p, an affordable x in an equilibrium point if yPx implies $py>1$, i.e., any vector y preferred to x is not affordable. A basic question is whether such an equilibrium point will exist. This approach dates back to Frisch (1926), and the usual approach was to specify conditions on R which imply R has a representation by a continuous utility function, i.e., $u(x)\geqslant u(y)$ equivalent to xRy. This problem was solved by Debreu (1954), who showed that R must be reflexive, complete, transitive, and continuous. With the addition of appropriate convexity conditions, this approach yields the results (1) and (2) above. However, in a remarkable paper, Sonnenschein (1971) showed that one could remove transitivity from the list of standard assumptions and still have a well defined demand correspondence which is upper-hemicontinuous. Specifically, he demonstrated that if R is continuous, reflexive, and $P(x) = \{y : yPx\}$ is convex for all x, then an equilibrium point will exist in any budget set, and the resulting demand correspondence is upper-hemicontinuous. (He also assumed R is complete, but that assumption was used only to show that an equilibrium point is comparable to every affordable y.) Note that if g represents local theory, and g is continuous, then the R defined by xRy is equivalent to $g(x)(y-x) \leqslant 0$, satisfies Sonnenschein's conditions, and an equilibrium x for R is an equilibrium point for g, in any budget. Thus Sonnenschein demonstrated that Georgescu-Roegen's condition PPN is not necessary for the existence of equilibrium points in a budget set.

In order to resolve question (1) above, a theory must predict a unique equilibrium point in each budget set, in order to get a well defined demand function. In the local theory, if one assumes $g(x) \neq 0$ for all x and strengthens PPN to SPPN: $g(x)(y-x) \leqslant 0, x \neq y$ implies $g(y)(x-y) > 0$, then the equilibrium point x will be unique in any budget, and the resulting demand function will be continuous and satisfy the Weak Axiom of Revealed Preference (WARP). Thus the local theory, without assuming mathematical integrability (implied transitivity), yields a theory of individual demand functions satisfying WARP. On the other hand, given a continuous demand function h satisfying WARP, if h has a continuous inverse, then $g = h^{-1}$ yields a local theory with g satisfying SPNN and generating h. Now consider the global theory. If R is represented by a continuous, strictly quasi-concave nonsatiated utility function, then R will be reflexive, complete, transitive, strongly convex, and nonsatiated. If one simply removes the assumption of transitivity from this list, then Sonnenschein's result implies that an equilibrium point will exist, and the remaining assumptions imply that this point will be unique, and that the resulting demand function will be continuous and satisfy WARP (see Shafer, 1974). Furthermore, Kim and Richter (1986) showed, that with a slight variation in the assumptions on R, any continuous demand function h satisfying a modified version of WARP can be generated by such an R. Thus, from the point of view of having single valued demand functions, the absence of transitivity, either assumed as in the global theory or implied as in the local theory, is essentially equivalent to Samuelson's theory of observed demand satisfying WARP. Since WARP includes the 'law of demand', i.e., normal goods have downward sloping demand, in my view little is lost by not assuming transitivity.

Now question (2) above, the problem of existence of competitive equilibrium will be discussed. Again, Sonnenschein observed that if one took the standard assumptions on R normally used in proofs of existence of a competitive equilibrium, and removed the transitivity assumption, then demand correspondences would be well defined and convex valued, and the standard proof techniques would still work, so equilibrium would exist. Thus transitivity is irrelevant to demonstrating the internal consistency of the competitive model. Note, however, that the assumptions needed by Sonnenschein to demonstrate that individual demand correspondences are well defined and upper-hemicontinuous, namely continuity and convex preferred sets, are too weak to ensure convex valued demand correspondences. Nevertheless, Mas-Colell (1974) demonstrated that with only these assumptions on preferences, competitive equilibria will exist. Thus the only properties of individual preferences which are important to the existence of competitive equilibrium are continuity and convexity.

WAYNE SHAFER

See also ACYCLICITY; INTEGRABILITY OF DEMAND; ORDERINGS.

BIBLIOGRAPHY

Allen, R.G.D. 1932. The foundations of a mathematical theory of exchange. *Economica* 12, 197–226.

Debreu, G. 1954. Representation of a preference ordering by a numerical function. In *Decision Processes*, ed. R.M. Thrall, C.H. Combs and R.L. Davis, New York: Wiley, 159–65.

Frisch, R. 1926. Sur un problème d'économie pure. *Norsk matematisk forenings skrifter* 16, 1–40.

Georgescu-Roegen, N. 1936. The pure theory of consumer's behavior. *Quarterly Journal of Economics* 50, August, 545–93.

Georgescu-Roegen, N. 1954. Choice and revealed preference. *Southern Economic Journal* 21, October, 119–30.

Katzner, D. 1971. Demand and exchange analysis in the absence of integrability conditions. In *Preferences, Utility, and Demand*, ed. J. Chipman et al., New York: Harcourt, Brace, Jovanovich, 254–70.

Kim, T. and Richter, M. 1986. Nontransitive-nontotal consumer theory. *Journal of Economic Theory* 38, April, 324–63.

Mas-Colell, A. 1974. An equilibrium existence theorem without complete or transitive preferences. *Journal of Mathematical Economics* 1, 237–46.

May, K. 1954. Intransitivity, utility, and aggregation in preference patterns. *Econometrica* 22, January, 1–13.

Shafer, W. 1974. The nontransitive consumer. *Econometrica* 42, 913–19.

Sonnenschein, H. 1971. Demand theory without transitive preferences, with applications to the theory of competitive equilibrium. In *Preferences, Utility and Demand*, ed. J. Chipman et al., New York: Harcourt, Brace, Jovanovich, 215–23.

transport. The obvious definition of 'transportation' is the movement of goods or people over space. But conventionally we do not include short trips inside the household or office or warehouse or factory as part of transport; such activities of movement are reckoned to be part of the household chore or industrial process. Only movements outside the home or factory are normally reckoned to require the services of the transport sector, as normally defined. In many definitions of 'transport', particularly in Western industrialized countries, non-motorized forms of carriage are excluded. Walking trips or manually hauled freight, bicycle journeys and even animal-powered journeys are usually excluded – except in those cases where walking may play a ubiquitous role, or in cities such as Amsterdam and Cambridge, where bicycles are a common form of transit. In third world countries, however, such manual or animal-powered operations still play a significant, perhaps a major role in the sector. Even in the mid-1980s it is very likely that, considering only passenger trips of over one kilometre in length, the vast majority in the third world are walked (World Bank, 1985).

In measuring the size of the transport sector, these issues of definition must constantly be borne in mind. If we confine the transport sector to mechanical carriage, then it is likely that in most Western industrialized countries, transport accounts for about 10 to 12 per cent of the gross domestic product (GDP). As well as excluding walking and cycling, this percentage does not take into account the value of time that people and goods spend in transit. If some allowance is made for this time (at values discussed below), then the percentage would rise to over 15 per cent, and perhaps as much as 20 per cent, of GDP. In primitive societies in the third world, such as the Sahel countries of Africa, the percentage is likely to be much higher, whereas in the constrained city states of Singapore and Hong Kong it is rather lower.

Throughout the world the dominant form of transport is by road. In the Western industrialized countries, some 75 to 85 per cent of transport sector resources are attributed to truck, bus or car. The remaining 15 to 25 per cent are distributed over rail, water and air, depending on geographical, historical and political conditions. In the third world this dominance of road transport, with one or two important exceptions such as India, tends to be even more pronounced. Transport by truck, bus and car is growing at rates higher than the growth of GNP in much of the third world.

INSTITUTIONS AND ORGANIZATIONS. The institutional structure of transport tends to be broadly similar in all countries. The road transport industry is typically organised in small, even very small, owner-driver units operating in a competitive, if often regulated, environment. Railways, *per contra*, are generally large monopolies almost always owned and, in principle at least, regulated by the state. State-owned airline monopolies are still the normal form of organization, the outstanding exceptions being the United States. But there is some evidence of a trend towards competition and private ownership in air transport. Ocean transport, especially the bulk-cargo business, is mainly in the hands of competitive private owners. Many countries have state-owned shipping lines, but although they often have reserved cargoes, they generally try to compete for free cargo.

The institutional and organizational structure of transport has affected the study of transport economics – and perhaps even the results of such studies have influenced government policies and so affected institutional forms. Transport economics has hardly been one of the central concerns of the discipline of economics. Yet over the years it has provided a fruitful field for the development of ideas which turn out to have a wide field of application.

MONOPOLY POWER AND REGULATIONS. In the 19th century, apart from the interest in transport costs as some sort of natural barrier to trade, the interests of economists centred mainly on the problems of controlling what were widely thought to be natural monopolies. Regulation of tariffs and fares pre-dated the railways, but the rapid expansion of steam locomotion raised the issue of control and regulation to the centre of political dispute.

From the middle of the 19th century, laws were passed prohibiting 'undue' (UK) or 'unfair' (USA) preference in the fixing of rail freight rates and fares. Behind this legislation lay the widespread fear that the railways would use their monopolistic bargaining powers to discriminate against the small shipper and *a fortiori* against the individual passenger. From the last quarter of the 19th century the hazy ideas on which this legislation was based were redefined by Marshall, Taussig, Edgeworth, Pigou and Ramsey. The theory of a discriminating monopoly provided a rationalization for 'charging what the traffic will bear', as well as providing the basis of modern theories of optimum taxation and utility pricing.

Besides requiring what were thought to be fair prices, the law had something to say about the provision of services. The general idea was to prevent the railways using withdrawal, or the threat of withdrawal, as a way of avoiding their common carrier obligation to provide adequate service. The implication was that the railways should maintain services even if that implied that loss-making services had to be cross-subsidized from profitable ones. Throughout the 20th century the closure of a rail line or even the withdrawal of a service has entailed major political or legal action.

The railways were never the absolute monopolists of popular fable. Their power was much restricted by other rail companies, water transport and highway competition. Initially, unregulated trucks and buses grew rapidly after World War I and were said to be 'creaming' off the railways' profitable traffic of commodities with a high value relative to bulk. Thus the railways argued that they were left with the low-value, bulky traffic such as coal and minerals, which could not bear a high freight rate. The railways and established large truckers complained that the trucking industry, and particularly new entrants, were indulging in 'wasteful competition' with cut-throat tariffs. These complaints, in addition to excessive, repeated bankruptcies in the 1930s, led in Britain to the substantial control of entry and fares, and in the USA and Germany to trucking and bus tariffs.

In the 1930s, 1940s and much of the 1950s, transport economists were concerned largely with the examination of the consequences, and a judgement of the efficacy, of the restrictive rail legislation of the previous century and new regulatory mechanism imposed on trucks and buses. Gilbert Walker (UK), James Nelson (USA) and Walter Eucken (Germany) showed that the conventional wisdom was quite discredited by the evidence (Walker, 1948). The common understanding that the railways made profits from their high-value traffic and lost money on their bulk traffic was quite wrong – the opposite of the truth. (In Gilbert Walker's aphorism, the railways' traffic cream was at the bottom, not the top, of the bottle.) Second, it was shown that the preregulation bankruptcy rates of truckers were unusually low, not high, and that regulation was primarily an obstacle to efficiency and innovation. Third, the scholars demonstrated that regulation entailed absurd wastes of resources in empty back-hauls, idle capacity and, in the United States, circuitous routings (*see* REGULATION AND DEREGULATION). They showed the unmistakable signs of what came later to be called the captive regulatory agency. (It was perhaps the sign of the times that they did not extend their analysis to the wastes that restrictive trades union behaviour so encouraged.) The rapid accumulation of evidence of the waste, inefficiency and inequity of regulation was the main factor behind the deregulation movement which gathered momentum in the 1950s and 1960s, culminating in the extensive deregulations of the 1970s and 1980s (Keeler, 1983).

Although (in 1985) it is rather too soon to give a definitive view of the effects of deregulation, the interim result appear to be entirely consistent with the implications suggested by transport economists such as Walker and Nelson. No evidence of 'wasteful competition', whatever that omnibus term may mean, can be readily detected in the deregulated trucking industry (e.g. in the UK or Australia). And freedom has meant a large increase in efficiency with lower fares, as in the United States airline industry. Significantly, there has been little evidence of any movement to re-regulate those industries which have been freed (Friedlander, 1981).

The precise process of deregulation has varied considerably, depending on political and social conditions and whether or not the industry has substantial elements of public ownership. Most of the railroads of the world had been taken into public ownership by the 1950s, the most notable exception being those in the United States. Regulations requiring the privately owned rail companies to maintain unprofitable services, limitations on their pricing policies, and notorious featherbedding and restrictive practices had all served to render them financially nonviable and dependent on subsidies from the state. The flight of private capital from such an unpromising industry was countered by nationalization. With persistent regulation, however, changing the ownership did not have any substantial beneficial effect on what had come to be called the railway problem, except to make the railways more subject to political pressure and union militancy. The financial deficits waxed rather than waned – to become a major worry to finance ministers all over the world. The fear that such deficits would grow even faster if road transport were free to compete with rail has been one of the main constraints on deregulation of trucking and buses in continental Europe and Japan, thus providing an example of the chain reaction that is typical of regulation. It is unlikely that there will be any substantial privatization and deregulation of railways in the foreseeable future. On the other hand, because of the example of the United States, there does seem both scope and hope for substantial deregulation and privatization of the airline industry in Europe, together with some further freeing of trucks and buses.

SUPPLY AND COST. From the 1950s onwards the content of transport economics changed considerably. Although work continued on the issues of law and regulation, the new transport economists were more interested in the analysis and, above all, the measurement of economic phenomena in transport. Analysis primarily took the form of seeking to refine and develop basic spatial models of economic activity and the specification of the salient characteristics of transport supply and demand.

From the *supply* side, one of the main aims has been to determine the structure of the production function and its dual, the cost function. In particular, the implementation of regulations often, implicitly at least, required evidence on costs. But the theoretical as distinct from the political rationalization for subsidies to rail, ports, airports and so on, required demonstration of substantial economies of scale. The earliest studies of rail costs focused on whether total costs varied less than proportionately to the variation of traffic. Lumpiness in the production of transport services and discontinuous jumps in the cost function had been recognized in the 19th century (Lardner, 1850). The track is fixed and so its costs vary little with respect to traffic, until an additional track is needed. By plotting railway costs against ton-miles, the first studies suggested that there were considerable economies of scale in the average railway operation.

Perhaps the most important development in cost function analysis from the late 1950s onwards was the integration of the engineering and economic approaches (Wohl and Hendrickson, 1984). Both models and data were taken over from engineering and interpreted in economic terms, often thereby improving the engineers' interpretation and forecasts. The engineering–economics applications were particularly fruitful in pipelines, airlines and shipping, but above all in the analysis of road traffic. For example, economic interpretation of the traffic engineers' gravity model provided new insights, both economic and engineering. Old data could be usefully reworded and reinterpreted. Perhaps the most important particular benefit was in the analysis of the social costs of congestion and the development of better systems of user costs for highways and urban streets. The various statistical models of the theory of queues and basic principles from the theory of fluid dynamics have proved useful bases for modelling traffic flow, with results that have been interpreted in terms of social costs of congestion.

The specification of the transportation process in terms of its engineering elements, the attribution of unit costs to inputs and the development of a *synthetic cost function* have been particularly useful for modelling the multiproduct nature of transport services. The carriage of a consignment or passenger from point A to point B in a particular time interval is a service distinct from, and with finite substitutability for, another service from C to D in another time interval. Yet clearly *some* aggregation is required over space and time. Transportation firms themselves tend to think and to price their services in terms of aggregates, but in the econometric analysis such aggregation still tends to be rather *ad hoc*.

The basic theoretical requirement of aggregation – additive separability – does not readily apply to most transportation processes. Moreover, the variability of marginal costs due to the variations in load factor, or empty capacity, makes it particularly hazardous to aggregate outputs. (The marginal costs of freight when capacity is full may be more than three times the marginal costs where there is empty space to be filled on a back-haul.)

The levels of costs that have emerged from the econometric–engineering studies have been most useful for comparative purposes. For example, one important application is whether a rail, subway or bus system should be developed to deal with the increased demand for urban passenger transport. As shown in World Bank (1985), such comparative studies have shown that subway rail systems costs two or three times that of alternative bus systems.

The most important application of the cost model is the issue of the existence and extent of economies of scale. As the 19th-century studies suggested, railways experience substantial economies of scale; more recent studies have shown their cost elasticities ranging from 0.35 to 0.80. By using their fixed assets (particularly the track) more intensively, unit costs can be much reduced. In road transport, *per contra*, scale economies are quickly exhausted, and the trucking and bus firms soon reach their minimum-cost outputs. (Such results are consistent with the ubiquity of the small firm for both bus and trucking operations in an unregulated environment.) Similarly for airlines, the evidence suggests that, for the prevailing size of airline in the United States, there are no signs of scale economies.

Refinements of the production function, and in particular the cost function, have included the elaboration of the specification of qualitative characteristics of the output of services (so-called hedonic measurements) and the influence of the stochastic nature of demand on costs. It was always clear that quality of service played a dominant role in the valuation of transport services. Speed of delivery (freight) and time of trip (passenger) as well as comfort and safety were the necessary *ceteris paribus* of competitive studies of cost functions. But shipper and passenger valuations of such quality-of-service variables must be incorporated in cost models if the results are to have useful validity.

The value which is to be attributed to time is also a parameter of some, often critical, importance. Although time is often important even in freight transport, it is clearly of crucial importance in passenger transit. Many comparisons of cost also involve differences in the time of trip, so that some evaluation of time savings is necessary in order to draw implications. The market value of time can be observed as people trade off time against money in decisions such as the use of a toll road rather than a free highway, or in taking an air trip rather than a surface trip. From studies of these situations, the dispersions of the implicit values of time have been considerable, yet some signs of regularity have been observed (Winston, 1985). Thus: (a) if the person is travelling on his firm's time, the savings of time can be valued at the wage costs per hour of the person involved; (b) if he is travelling during his leisure time and in a vehicle, then he values time saved at roughly one-third to one-quarter of his earnings during his working time; and (c) if he is waiting at the bus stop or rail platform, then he values such waiting time about as much as his wage rater per hour (World Bank, 1985). These are the trade-offs observed in the market for time of trip, and in a competitive system these trade-offs will be reflected in the decisions of competitive firms in their production functions.

Safety is yet another characteristic of transport services, again particularly passenger services, which is implicit but important. Indeed, traffic accidents are a major source of mortality in developing countries (World Bank, 1985). The valuation of injury or loss of life is fraught with daunting philosophical difficulties. But fortunately we do not need to ask, let alone answer, the questions concerned with the 'value of a life'. In practice the person travelling makes an implicit decision about the change in the probability of losing his life (or being injured, etc.) and the cost involved. No one 'buys' a life, either his own or that of any other person, on the market (except for certain villains); but people do implicitly value *changes in the probability of being killed or injured.* This trade-off between safety and money and time is practised when a man jay-walks or when he skips a servicing of the brakes and steering of his motor car. Little research, however, has been pursued to discover these implicit valuations. Most of the valuations of life and limit which are employed in practical applications, such as highway construction and road-use regulations, have been calculated from the money costs of damage, loss of useful output while incapacitated, the costs of medical services, and some notional sum for pain and discomfort.

Finally, there is the problem of allowing for other externalities or 'the social and environmental effects' of transport activities. Air pollution, noxious noise and the disfigurement of the landscape with perhaps the loss of part of the 'national heritage' are the most important items considered in such calculations. The best measure of the cost is the loss of rent of facilities, such as houses, shops, land, and so on, which are affected. This loss of rent needs to be inserted in a dynamic model of the adjustment process; then one can find the capitalized net present value of the disamenity created by the new transport facility. The most sophisticated applications of this environmental model have been for aircraft noise shadows associated with new runways at airports (Walters, 1978). The valuation of loss of amenity is generally carried out by some version of the Clawson method.

THE DEMAND FOR TRANSPORT. The reaction of people and firms to a reduction or increase of fares, transport costs or freight rates has always been a central issue of economic development. A general knowledge of what were later to be called demand elasticities has been incorporated in tariffs and fares since classical times. The principle of charging 'what the traffic will bear' and fixing freight rates proportional to the value per kilogram of the commodity was a primitive but effective way of discriminating according to the inverse of the elasticity of demand.

The systematic study of transport demand by professional economists and statisticians began after World War II. The first studies were generally statistical analyses of aggregate data, where the emphasis was primarily on modal choice. The distribution of aggregate freight traffic modes was analysed by regression analysis. It was, however, difficult to interpret the results in the usual form of elasticities of demand or substitution, since the functional forms and theoretical specification had no obvious basis in economic theory of either the firm or of the consumer. Moreover, the levels of aggregation tended to be too large to be of use in deriving useful estimates of parameters. The thrust of much research in the 1970s and 1980s changed to disaggregated data and models. The functional forms were derived from the traditional theory of the consumer (for passenger travel) and from the cost-minimizing motive of the theory of the firm (for freight transportation).

For passenger transport, perhaps the most important econometric development was that of the logit and probit models (Winston, 1985). This models the discrete choice of transportation mode in terms of maximizing utility, attributing to each individual a random element of utility which describes his peculiarities and unobservable tastes for travel. Thus, for any given measured characteristics of the population and for given conditions of transportation, one will observe a certain fraction using a particular model. This probability of using that mode is then described as a functional form of the characteristics of the modes and, of course, other social and economic characteristics of the traveller.

Essentially these models give decision rules for discrete choices. In another sense they provide a statistical description of our ignorance, by specifying a probability density distribution to delineate what we do *not* know about the choice of mode. One objective is to try to reduce this degree of ignorance by defining groupings, such as commuters and shoppers, which have distinctly different patterns of behaviour. A second objective is the joint modelling both of the decision on which mode to use and the choice of another continuous variable, such as frequency of trip or (in the case of freight transport) the size of the consignment or shipment. The continuous choice decision is then contingent upon the discrete decision on mode. This opens up a rich seam of possible models.

Notwithstanding the statistical complexities of these models, there are some basic economic constraints on transport demand. First it is a *derived* demand and so must conform to the Marshallian laws. If there is no conceivable substitution of different modes or markets, then the market elasticity of demand for transport is measured by the multiple of the final market elasticity of demand for the commodity and the fraction of the final price accounted for by transport costs. On such assumptions elasticities of demand are low, even very low. The transport of such items as lumber, minerals and even coal – especially by ocean – approximates such conditions. Studies have confirmed that the freight–tariff elasticities are indeed very low – less than 0.1 (in absolute terms). Yet very few transport operations conform closely to these assumptions. Even in the case of minerals, coal or timber, there is often an alternative source which topples the demand curve from its near vertical slope. Since alternative sources probably become available in discrete jumps, it may well be that the elasticity is very low within a small range, but as the alternative becomes profitable, the elasticity rises substantially. Thus one finds that historically, as transport costs have declines in real terms, the near monopoly of local sources has been eroded as more distant sources become profitable to tap. For freight operations where other *modes* are competitive, the market elasticity of demand for any given mode tends to be very high (absolutely) because of the ease of substitution, for example of truck for rail, or air for truck.

Even in freight transport it seems that transit time is of considerable importance in defining the quality of the service. Speeding the transit and, perhaps even more important, improving its reliability, are attributes which command high premiums for many goods. The shipper saves on inventory costs and maintains a tighter control of the production and distribution process. The numerical values of freight elasticities of demand with respect to time of transit tend to be of the order of 0.4 to 0.7 for all commodities except for bulk-hauled minerals. The more speedy transit by truck has explained much of the switch of traffic from slow rail to fast truck in the past half century.

The time-of-trip and, *a fortiori*, the waiting time are even more important in explaining the modal choice of passengers, particularly in city transportation. The time-of-trip elasticity tends to be larger (absolutely) than the fare elasticity. But for most studies of passenger travel the market elasticities tend to be less than one (in absolute terms) for a particular model. The main exceptions are for leisure travel by rail, bus and air, where the elasticities tend to be around two. This is consistent with the profitability of the policy of some railways in promoting cheap 'excursion fares' as a way of segmenting the market. Of course, individual airlines or buses, in a competitive environment, will always find that the elasticities with respect to both price and time will be considerably larger than the corresponding market elasticities. So an individual operator will have the greater incentive to keep his fares low and beat the competition. The relatively low elasticity of demand for the mode, compared with the high elasticities for competitive firms within a particular mode (excepting perhaps the railroads), illustrates the value of ensuring a competitive discipline on both pricing and quality of service characteristics.

The high value that people place on time and convenience has many other implications for the structure of transportation services. For example, it may be much better to have more frequent (if more costly) services than those which are produced by choosing vehicles and equipment that minimize the costs to the operator. The competitive operators might well find that the savings in pecuniary cost by adopting the large vehicle with substantial economies of scale are more than offset by the reduction in demand for their services caused by the lower frequency of service – and so longer waiting times. The higher the levels of income of the passengers, the greater the value that they will place on high frequencies and greater convenience.

INVESTMENT. The main use of the studies of production and cost functions, on the one hand, and the demand functions, on the other, is to develop a critique of pricing policy and to provide a basis for investment appraisal. The basic criterion is to find the net present value (NPV) of future revenues and outgoings by discounting with a rate of interest that measures the marginal productivity of capital in alternative uses. The rule is that the investment is worthwhile if the NPV exceeds zero. There are many alternative criteria which have been suggested to supplement or supplant the NPV principle, such as the benefit–cost ratio, the first-year rate of return and the implicit rate of return. Although the latter is useful as an evocative and easily understood 'rate of profit', none should be allowed to supplant the NPV method, since all may involve substantial error in application.

The benefits and costs to be entered into the calculation normally assume that the price of the service is, under competitive market conditions, an appropriate indication of the value that the consumer places on the marginal unit that he buys, and that the supply price is competitively determined and reflects marginal costs. These general conditions seem to be widely satisfied in the road sector, and in rather more qualified ways in rail, airlines and ocean or inland waterway transport.

Many of the complications of investment appraisal arise, as in the cost studies, from the multiproduct nature of the services. An improvement of a particular road may displace traffic or generate new vehicle flows on many another facility, and it is often very important to take into account such secondary effects, such as the benefits which consumers may lose (or gain) through the additional congestion (or decongestion) of existing highways. The procedure recommended by theory is to measure the areas under the demand curves for individual roads, while holding the cost conditions on all other roads fixed. This tedious process can be circumvented if one is willing to assume, first, that all demand curves are compensated, and second, that we may approximate the demand curve for the services of the road by a linear form over the relevant range of traffic. Then the gain to road users is

$$-0.5\sum_i (q_{1i}-q_{0i})(p_{1i}-p_{0i})$$

where q_{0i} is the number of i-type trips without the project, q_{1i} is the number of i-type trips with the project and p_{0i} and p_{1i} are the associated prices of trips.

This procedure is much simpler than the traditional Marshallian method of moving one price at a time, and it works well in practical situations. Yet it is important to recall that it depends crucially on the efficacy of the modelling system for road traffic and on the various valuations of cost, particularly the cost of time.

It is relatively easy to estimate the benefits of the increase in efficiency of the use of assets, such as vehicles or runways or terminal capacity. One can estimate the expenditure so avoided by making verifiable assumptions about the rates of utilization. In practice most investment appraisals involving passengers turn critically on the modelling of time savings and the valuation of such savings. Occasionally problems of valuation are of dominant importance in investments in freight transport (such as the widening of the Suez Canal) when there is expected to be a large and persistent overhang of excess capacity for some years; but such cases are the exception rather than the rule.

By the late 1960s most OECD governments had developed systematic procedures for the appraisal of government investments in transport. Such an approach enabled governments more readily to identify white elephants and to sequence their programme in a more efficient way. However, it is not at all clear that the improved appraisals had any substantial effect on programmes, at least until the austerities of the mid-1970s. For example, the interstate highway system in the United States saw considerable overinvestment in roads that carried little traffic. The political pressures for particular investments were often of much more importance in the decision-making process than any rational calculations of costs and benefits (Walters, 1978). The list of undesirable and loss-making projects is depressingly long and formidable for most countries. Apart from such prominent cases as Concorde, one must include perhaps most railway and subway investment, many airports, and some ports on such a list.

THE POLITICAL ECONOMY OF TRANSPORT – INEQUITY AND INEFFICIENCY. Most transport activities normally involve considerable state intervention, not merely state participation but often actual ownership of transport concerns. Hence the problem of understanding transportation industries, the consequences of exogenous change and the effects of policies need to be studied in terms of the political process and the power of interest coalitions. Many democratic legislatures have arrogated to themselves the power to control closely the services, rates and fares, investment and manning programmes of state-owned or regulated industries. This power is most obviously demonstrated in the inability to reduce unprofitable rail, bus or airline services. Coalitions of legislature members will form to block withdrawal of service or closure of the line, even though the benefits derived by the constituents comprise only a small fraction of the total cost involved in providing the service. Although it would be more efficient to 'buy off' the users of the service, a sense of misplaced propriety combined with legal constraint has inhibited the development of such side-payments.

Because of the concentration of ownership – usually in the state itself – railways and ports tend to be fertile ground for the formation of powerful trades unions. By exercising control over the arteries of commerce, the unions can exact much danegeld. Perhaps more important is that their power is deployed in legislatures and executive branches of government. Such power can be quite awesome – as for example that which the railway trade union exercised in Argentina in the 1950s and 1960s.

Although the problem of exercising control and financial discipline over state-supported or state-owned industries has been seen to be of crucial importance – at least since the end of World War II – little progress appears to have been made. The (Herbert) Morrison formula, used in the UK, was to allow the nationalized railways to operate without political interference in day-to-day decision-making, the legislature and executive having control only over broad policy issues. And the public corporation was to be required to cover its costs, 'taking one year with another'. The failure of the Morrison approach was complete. Not only was there continuous political interference and substantial and persistent large losses, political control over the strategy was, until the 1980s, largely dominated by the trades unions. Conditions in other OECD countries, although varying in detail, are quite similar. Even in the Third World countries, such as India, the power of the rail unions (together with the bureaucrats of Indian Railways) has been sufficient to keep competitive road operators under very large handicaps, and to maintain rail operations when they should long have been superseded by road.

The solutions to the overweening power of nationalized transport organizations and their trades unions, and the politicization of transport decisions, have not come easily. Perhaps the best approach is the privatization of such large bureaucratic organizations. The United States with its dispersion of ownership of railroads seems to have avoided many of the problems that affect other OECD countries with their nationalized concerns. (In the United States the exception has been Amtrak, the subsidized passenger service.) But, once nationalized, it is not easy to disentangle the integrated system and dispose of its parts. This approach has proved much more successful in the case of the ports (perhaps in the latter half of the 1980s, airports as well) airlines and even buses (World Bank, 1985). Various other approaches have been proposed, such as a constitutional limitation on the legislature's directives combined with suitable incentive payments for staff and management; but such solutions have yet to be tried. The inefficiencies of state-owned and regulated systems remain the major problem.

PRODUCTIVITY, TECHNOLOGY AND THE DEVELOPMENT OF TRANSPORT. Over the historical record the measures of the productivity of many transport industries have shown a creditable performance, relative to most other industries. The only marked exceptions are the railways and urban buses. For highway transport, airlines and certain shipping services, the gains in productivity have exceeded those in most manufacturing industries. In large part such gains have been due to the improvement of equipment used by the transport industries. The increase in the efficiency of aircraft, ships and road vehicles have been both sustained and, in some cases, dramatic. In the decades from 1950 and 1980 one of the main gains in efficiency was due to the increased capacity of equipment – the jumbo tankers and aircraft. The variety and quality of service, however, have also expanded considerably.

One of the most important innovations was a product of the transport industries as such, namely, containerization and its forerunner, palletization. This simplified the handling problems for freight (particularly for non-bulk, non-mineral consignments), greatly reduced inputs of unskilled labour, speeded up transit and reduced pilferage and damage. Containerization, having transformed ports, shipping and much trucking, has still (in 1985) much more potential penetration ahead, with profound effects on distribution systems.

The silicon chip must affect the future of transport. The use of the developing information technology is still very much in its infancy in the transport sector. The potential is great. For example, a computerized road-pricing system for urban areas is now feasible, and prototypes are being tested (World Bank, 1985), while plausible control and guidance systems have gone beyond the drawing-board stage. But the range of profitable application cannot be foreseen.

Most of the gain in future productivity and reductions of cost may come from institutional change. It has been shown that privatization of public sector transport operations often has a dramatic effect in reducing costs and improving the quality of the service (World Bank, 1985). Private provision of urban bus services usually costs about 50 and 60 per cent of the costs of public provision, and the private airlines in the United States provide services which are only about 40 per cent of the (adjusted) costs of the state-owned airlines in Europe. In addition, the record of the private sector in promoting and paying for innovations is far better than that of the public sector firms. However, whether such innovations will persist in the face of the opposition of vested interests is a question which must remain unanswered.

A.A. WALTERS

See also CONGESTION; DERIVED DEMAND; INDUSTRIAL ORGANIZATION; REGULATION AND DEREGULATION.

BIBLIOGRAPHY

Caves, D., Christensen, L. and Swanson, J. 1981. Productivity, growth, scale economies and capacity utilization in US railroads, 1955–1974, *American Economic Review* 71(5), December, 994–1002.

Friedlander, A.F. 1981. *Freight Transport Regulation*. Cambridge, Mass.: MIT Press.

Hotelling, H. 1938. The general welfare in relation to problems of taxation and of railway and utility rates. *Econometrica* 6, July, 242–69.

Keeler, T.E. 1983. *Railroads, Freight and Public Policy*. Washington, DC: Brookings Institution.

Lardner, D. 1850. *Railway Economy: A Treatise on the New Art of Transport*. New York: Harper & Bros. Reprinted, New York: A.M. Kelley, 1968.

Meyer, J., Peck, M.J., Stenason, J. and Zwick, C. 1959. *The Economics of Competition in the Transportation Industries*. Cambridge, Mass.: Harvard University Press.

Walker, G. 1948. *Road and Rail*. London: Allen & Unwin.

Walters, A.A. 1968. *The Economics of Road User Charges*. Baltimore: Johns Hopkins Press.

Walters, A.A. 1978. Airports – an economic survey. *Journal of Transport Economics and Policy* 12, May, 125–60.
Winston, C. 1985. Conceptual developments in the economics of transportation: an interpretive survey. *Journal of Economic Literature* 23, March, 57–94.
Wohl, M. and Hendrickson, C. 1984. *Transportation Investment and Pricing Principles: An Introduction for Engineers, Planners and Economists*. New York: John Wiley & Sons.
World Bank. 1985. *Urban Transport Sector Policy Paper*. Washington, DC.

Triffin, Robert (born 1911). Triffin was born in 1911 in the pleasant Belgian village of Flobecq. After a brilliant school career, a scholarship enabled him to study law and economics at the university of Louvain. Another scholarship sent him to Harvard, where he got a thorough grounding in theory with Schumpeter and Leontief. His 1938 dissertation, 'Monopolistic Competition and General Equilibrium Theory', earned a Wells Prize and was published in 1940.

After a brief return to Belgium, he was appointed instructor at Harvard, and was soon cut off from Europe by the outbreak of the war. In 1942 he joined the Federal Reserve Board to organize a research section on Latin America. This launched him on his parallel career of advising Central Banks on reform of monetary and exchange arrangements. He rapidly developed what was to remain a main characteristic of his work in this area: a flair for practical suggestions and an imagination that provided alternatives in case of political objections to the first proposals. His success in a number of Latin American countries led to his appointment in 1946 as head of the exchange control division in the newly-created International Monetary Fund. Moving to Europe as IMF chief representative, he developed a proposal for the European Clearing Union. Having later transferred to the State Department, he succeeded in negotiating his proposal through OEEC, and became the recognized father of the European Payment Union of 1950.

Triffin left the State Department after a policy disagreement, and went to Yale where he stayed from 1951 to 1977. There he published his two classic works: *Europe and the Money Muddle* in 1957; *Gold and the Dollar Crisis* in 1959 and 1960. The first book reviews the European Monetary experience, using an integrated analysis of the money supply and the balance of payments. It proclaims the end of the 'dollar shortage' and explains the dilemma of the gold-exchange standard in the absence of an adequate supply of gold: either the key-currency country maintains equilibrium in its balance of payments, and other countries will experience a shortage of the reserves needed to support an expansion of trade and transactions, with an attendant brake on growth; or the desirable growth of world reserves will be preserved only through persistent increases in the liabilities of the key-currency country, raising increasing doubts about its ability to redeem such liabilities, especially when they begin to exceed the country's dwindling gold reserves. The second book, shorter and less analytic, goes further: it contains a bold prophecy of a dollar glut, bound in time to bring down the gold exchange standard. The fate experienced by sterling in the interwar years was bound to catch up with the dollar as well.

The second part of the book contained the famous 'Triffin Plan' to obviate these dangers: on the one hand, the controlled creation of an international reserve instrument by the IMF; on the other hand, regional monetary arrangements, with emphasis on European integration.

The announced dollar glut did indeed develop over the following years with the predicted consequences; the gold parity rate was first abandoned, then the dollar became inconvertible. The first policy prescription was timidly followed with the creation of Special Drawing Rights, but without the essential element of conversion of dollar balances. Indeed the excessive accumulation of such balances has since been denounced by Triffin as the main factor in the inflationary development of the Seventies, and as an unwarranted capital inflow into the USA, which on the contrary should be a leading exporter of capital.

The other prescription was more successful, and Triffin moved back to Europe (and the University of Louvain) in order to participate more fully in the emergence and development of the European Monetary System.

He has been throughout a most active participant in the debate on money and exchanges. In a continuous stream of studies, papers and memoranda, he has pressed forward for advances on the two fronts of international monetary reform and European integration.

His reputation as an analyst and skilled deviser of techniques has led to his being called in as a consultant all over the world, on domestic as well as regional monetary issues.

Triffin has remained a much concerned 'citizen of the world' and has applied his policy-oriented brand of 'economics of persuasion' not only to his particular area of expertise, but also to the issues of development and disarmament.

ALBERT KERVYN

SELECTED WORKS

As a policy-oriented persuader, Triffin has been a prolific writer. In his attempt to reach a wide public for his ideas, he gives the impression of never having refused a contribution. As a result a complete bibliography would include well over 300 items – many in less accessible publications. The following list is therefore highly selective.

1940. *Monopolistic Competition and General Equilibrium Theory*. Cambridge, Mass.: Harvard University Press.
1957. *Europe and the Money Muddle*. New Haven: Yale University Press.
1960a. *Statistics of Sources and Uses of Finance, 1948–58*. Paris: OEEC.
1960b. *Gold and the Dollar Crisis*. New Haven: Yale University Press.
1964. *The Evolution of the International Monetary System*. Princeton Studies in International Finance No. 12, Princeton: Princeton University Press.
1966. *The World Money Maze*. New Haven: Yale University Press.
1969. The thrust of history in international monetary reform. *Foreign Affairs* 47(3), April, 477–92.
1971. The use of SDR finance for collectively agreed purposes. *Banca Nazionale del Lavoro Quarterly Review* 96, March, 3–12.
1973. The role of developing European monetary union. In *Europe and the Evolution of the International Monetary System*, ed. A.K. Swoboda, Leiden: Sijthoff.
1975. The Community and the disruption of the world monetary system. *Banca Nazionale del Lavoro Quarterly Review* 112, March, 3–35.
1976. Size, sources and beneficiaries of international reserve creation, 1970–74. In *Economic Progress, Private Values and Public Policy*, ed. B. Balassa and R. Nelson, New Haven: Yale University Press.
1978a. 'Europe and the money muddle' revisited. *Banca Nazionale del Lavoro Quarterly Review* 124, March, 49–65.
1978b. *Gold and the Dollar Crisis: Yesterday and Today*. Princeton Essays in International Finance No. 132, Princeton: Princeton University Press.
1978c. The international role and fate of the dollar. *Foreign Affairs* 57(2), 269–86.
1981a. Le système monétaire Européen dans le cadre du système monétaire mondial. *Banque* 55(406), May, 535–40.
1981b. An economist's career: What? Why? How? *Banca Nazionale del Lavoro Quarterly Review* 139, September, 239–59.

1981c. The first two years of FECOM transactions. *EEC Economic Papers* No. 2, July.
1984a. How to end the world 'infession'. In *Europe's Money*, ed. R.S. Masera and R. Triffin, Oxford: Clarendon Press.
1984b. Une tardive autopsie du Plan Keynes de 1943. *Revue d'économie politique.*
1986. Correcting the world monetary scandal. *Challenge*, January.

Trosne, Guillaume François le. *See* LE TROSNE, GUILLAUME FRANÇOIS.

Trotsky, Lev Davidovitch (1879–1940). Born in 1879, the son of Jewish farmers living near the Black Sea, Trotsky became an important political figure by the time of the Second Congress of the Russian Social Democratic Party in 1903. Disagreeing with Lenin's centralizing view of party organization, Trotsky either favoured the Mensheviks or attempted to mediate between them and the Bolsheviks until making his peace with Lenin in 1917. In the 1905 Revolution he served as chairman of the St Petersburg Soviet, drawing upon that experience to develop the theory of 'permanent revolution' in his book *Results and Prospects*. In the 1917 Revolution Trotsky ranked second only to Lenin among Bolshevik party leaders. He orchestrated the seizure of power and subsequently organized and led the Red Army in the civil war. During the early 1920s Trotsky's political influence waned, and by the middle of the decade he became the political leader and intellectual mentor of the Left Opposition to Stalin. Defeated by Stalin in the intra-party struggle, in 1929 Trotsky was deported from the Soviet Union. In exile he edited *Biulleten' Oppozitsii* (Bulletin of the Opposition) and published numerous other writings critical of Stalinist policy, the most important being *The Revolution Betrayed.* Unable to answer Trotsky's criticisms on intellectual grounds, in August 1940 Stalin replied in the only way he knew: he had Trotsky assassinated in Mexico, his last place of exile.

In *Results and Prospects* (first published in 1906), Trotsky predicted that Russian backwardness would guarantee the revolution in permanence. Surrounded by stronger enemies, the Russian state had prevented the nobility from becoming politically independent. The nobility were mere tax collectors, extracting revenue from the peasants in order to promote development; and the bourgeoisie, likewise, were weaker than their Western counterparts, for much of the economy was built with foreign loans, serviced by grain exports. The proletariat, in contrast, enjoyed disproportionate strength. Few in number, Russian workers were concentrated in large factories organized around foreign technology. Trotsky predicted that the proletariat would overthrow the autocracy, by-passing the bourgeois revolution, but would then confront a counter-revolutionary alliance when it implemented its programme. The counter-revolution would be supported by Germany, Austria and France, who would be anxious to prevent the revolution's spread and to safeguard their investments. When these countries mobilized, however, they would drive their own workers to revolt, thereby making the revolution permanent both domestically and internationally.

Aware of Russia's historical dependence on the world economy, Trotsky characteristically viewed economic issues in an international context. Modern industry, he believed, had become so capital intensive that production could only be profitable through specialization in service of the world market. It was in the nature of socialism to emancipate the productive forces from the fetters of the nation state. A victory of the proletariat in the leading countries would mean 'a radical restructuring of the very economic foundation in correspondence with a more productive international division of labour, which is alone capable of creating a genuine foundation for a socialist order' (Trotsky Archives, No. T-3148).

When the international revolution did not come to Soviet Russia's aid as Trotsky had expected, he continued to insist that industrialization must draw upon the resources of the world market. Opposing Stalin's notion of an isolated socialist state (Socialism in One Country), he argued that 'a properly regulated growth of export and import with the capitalist countries prepares the elements of the future commodity and product exchange [which will prevail] when the European proletariat assumes power and controls production' (*Trotsky Archives* No. T-3034). Soviet Russia's relation to the West would involve a dialectic of cooperation and struggle in which the Soviet state would regulate its 'dependence' on capitalism through its monopoly of foreign trade. The alternative, the Stalinist vision of autarky, would mean reliance 'on the curbed and domesticated productive forces, that is ... on the technology of backwardness' (Trotsky, 1947, p. 53).

Uppermost in Trotsky's mind throughout the 1920s was the need not only to preserve access to foreign technology, but also to reduce domestic prices in order to maintain the trade monopoly. In 1923 he warned the party that 'Contraband is inevitable if the difference between external and internal prices goes beyond a certain limit ... contraband, comrades ... undermines and washes away the monopoly' (*Dvenadstatyi s'ezd RKP* (b), 1923, p. 372; 12th Congress of the Russian Communist Party (Bolsheviks)). Without this protection for new Soviet industries, planned growth would be impossible.

For the promotion of new industrial construction, Trotsky proposed to supplement domestic tax revenues by taking advantage of Europe's need for foreign markets and by pursuing all manner of credits:

> What does foreign credit do for our economic development? Capitalism makes advances to us against our savings which do not yet exist ... As a result, the foundations of our development are extended ... The dialectics of historical development have resulted in capitalism becoming for a time the creditor of socialism. Well, has not capitalism been nourished at the breasts of feudalism? History has honoured the debt (*Pravda*, 20 September 1925).

In addition to making use of foreign credits, Trotsky hoped to resume the tsarist pattern of exporting grain in exchange for finished goods. In 1925 he predicted that the Soviet economy would be unable to satisfy more than a fraction of its need for new equipment:

> We must not ... forget for a moment the great mutual dependence which existed between the economies of tsarist Russia and world capital. We must just bring to mind the fact that nearly two-thirds of the technical equipment in our works and factories used to be imported from abroad. This dependence has hardly decreased in our own time, which means that it will scarcely be economically profitable for us in the next few years to produce at home the machinery we require, at any rate, more than two-fifths of the quantity, or at best more than half of it (*Pravda*, 20 September 1925).

Trotsky hoped to reconcile a high level of foreign trade with socialist protectionism through strict determination of priorities. Soviet industries should economize on scarce capital, specialize in those products in greatest demand, standardize output and reduce costs, while leaving the remaining needs to be met by low-cost imports. A system of comparative coefficients should be devised by the planners, comparing the cost and quality of Soviet products with foreign competition. A poor coefficient would then signal the advisability of imports in the short run and of re-equipment in the long run, as new resources became available. 'A comparative coefficient is the same for us as a pressure gauge for a mechanic on a locomotive. The pressure of foreign production is for us the basic factor of our economic existence. If our relation to this production is [unsatisfactory], then foreign production will sooner or later pierce the trade monopoly' (*Ekonomicheskaia Zhizn'* 18 August 1925).

In spite of his balanced approach to industrialization, official Soviet historiography insists that Trotsky was a 'super-industrializer', determined to plunder the peasantry. In reality he attempted more systematically than any of his contemporaries to avert the crisis of forced industrialization by balancing the needs of the peasantry against those of industry through a policy of 'commodity intervention'. To the extent that export-oriented growth clearly depended upon the peasants bringing grain to market, Trotsky was quite aware that the most urgent consumer needs would also have to be satisfied through imports. The world market was to function as a 'reserve' for both light and heavy industry. The 'goods famine', or the chronic shortage of consumer goods, was 'obvious and incontestable proof that the distribution of national economic resources between state industry and the rest of the economy has ... acquired the necessary proportionality' (*Trotsky Archives*, No. T-2983). The real enemies of the peasantry, in Trotsky's view, were the authors of Socialism in One Country – Stalin, who saw only the needs of the machine-building industries, and Bukharin, who urged the peasant to 'enrich' himself without seriously considering the need to provide consumer goods upon which these savings might be spent.

It was Trotsky's concern for the legitimate needs of workers and peasants alike which led him in the 1930s to reconsider the role of market forces, for a time at least, in socialist planning. As early as 1925 he had warned that it was 'impossible to push industrialization forward with the aid of unreal credits' (Trotsky, 1955, p. 186). During the first five-year plan he called for restraints upon the inflationary financing of heavy industry and 'strict financial discipline', even at the expense of closing down enterprises. A stable currency, in turn, would provide an instrument whereby the masses themselves could democratically control production decisions from below. 'The innumerable living participants in the economy,' Trotsky wrote in 1932,

> state and private, collective and individual, must announce their needs and their respective intensities not only through the statistical calculations of the planning commissions, but also by the direct pressure of supply and demand. The plan ... [must be] verified, and in an important measure must be achieved through the market (*Biulleten' Oppozitsii* XXXI, 1932, p. 8).

A planned market, free trade unions, and restoration of soviet democracy: these were the three elements without which any talk of socialism was a mockery.

> If there existed the universal mind described in the scientific fantasy of Laplace – a mind which might simultaneously register all the processes of nature and society, measure the dynamic of their movement and forecast the results of their interactions – then, of course, such a mind could *a priori* draw up a faultless and exhaustive economic plan, beginning with the number of hectares of wheat and ending with buttons on a waistcoat. True, it often appears to the bureaucracy that it possesses just such a mind: and that is why it so easily emancipates itself from control by the market and by soviet democracy. The reality is that the bureaucracy is cruelly mistaken in its appraisal of its own spiritual resources (*Biulleten' Oppozitsii* XXXI, 1932, p. 8).

In *The Revolution Betrayed*, his most thorough critique of Stalinist 'planomania', Trotsky concluded that the real basis of bureaucratic power had nothing to do with Stalin's pompous claims of industrial triumphs; the horrible truth was that the whole bureaucratic edifice had come to rest upon nothing more profound or despicable than an ability to manufacture poverty. Queues were the foundation of Soviet power and the innermost secret of the police state:

> The basis of bureaucratic rule is the poverty of society in objects of consumption. When there are enough goods in a store, the purchasers can come whenever they want to. When there are few goods, the purchasers are compelled to stand in line. When the lines are very long, it is necessary to appoint a policeman to keep order. Such is the starting point of the Soviet bureaucracy. It 'knows' who is to get something and who has to wait (Trotsky, 1945, p. 112).

Historians will continue to debate whether Trotsky's policies might have avoided forced collectivization and the excesses of Stalin's five-year plans. On one point, however, there can be no dispute: Trotsky was perfectly correct to conclude that Stalin's pursuit of autarky had more in common with the ideals of Hitler than with those of Marx. The Russian revolution, confined to a single backward country, did not lead to the emancipation of the proletariat. Trotsky attempted to reinterpret and apply Marxism to the unexpected conditions of an isolated revolutionary experiment. He did not win the battle against Stalin. He did, however, help to explain and attempt to avert one of the great tragedies of the 20th century.

RICHARD B. DAY

SELECTED WORKS

The Permanent Revolution and Results and Prospects. Trans. John G. Wright and Brian Pearce, London: New Park Publications, 1962.

Terrorism and Communism. Ann Arbor: University of Michigan Press, 1963.

The New Course. Ann Arbor: University of Michigan Press, 1965.

Towards Socialism or Capitalism? London: Methuen & Co., 1926.

The Platform of the Left Opposition. (1927). London: New Park Publications, 1963.

My Life. New York: Grosset & Dunlap, 1960.

The History of the Russian Revolution. Trans. Max Eastman, London: Victor Gollancz, 1965.

The Revolution Betrayed. New York: Pioneer Publishers, 1945.

Stalin; An Appraisal of the Man and His Influence. London, Hollis & Carter, 1947.

Biulleten' Oppozitsii (Bulletin of the Opposition). New York: Monad, 1973.

BIBLIOGRAPHY

Day, R.B. 1973. *Leon Trotsky and the Politics of Economic Isolation*. London: Cambridge University Press.

Deutscher, I. 1954. *The Prophet Armed. Trotsky: 1879–1921*. London: Oxford University Press.

Deutscher, I. 1959. *The Prophet Unarmed. Trotsky: 1921–1929.* London: Oxford University Press.
Deutscher, I. 1963. *The Prophet Outcast. Trotsky: 1929–1940.* London: Oxford University Press.
Howe, I. 1978. *Leon Trotsky.* New York: Viking, 1978.

trusts. *See* ANTI-TRUST POLICY.

Tsuru, Shigeto (born 1912). Tsuru was born on 6 March 1912 in Oita and brought up in Nagoya. Political disapproval of his involvement in a socialist study group led to his leaving Japan for the United States in 1931.

After receiving a PhD at Harvard in 1940, he taught there briefly as a lecturer. During that period, he married Masako Wada, the niece of Marquis Koichi Kido. They left the United States for Japan in 1942 on board a ship exchanging citizens during wartime.

During the reconstruction of Japan after World War II, he served first in the Ministry of Foreign Affairs and later as the vice minister of the Economic Stabilization Board, where he took part in the preparation of the first issue of the Board's Economic White Paper.

In 1948, he was appointed Professor of Economics at Hitotsubashi University, where he later served for nine years as the director of the Institute of Economic Research and for three years as president of the university from 1972 until retirement. Since retiring, he has served as an adviser to the Asahi newspaper. He then assumed a professorship at Meijigakuin University.

Tsuru's analytical works in economics are based on his wide background in the area of both Marxian and modern economics. His principal studies have been incorporated in the *Collected Works of Shigeto Tsuru* (1976). These constitute thirteen volumes, and the last one, in English, is entitled *Towards a New Political Economy*.

The main areas of the author's interests which have developed from his Harvard days encompass Marxian methodology, business cycle theories and their application to Japan's economic development. A continuing emphasis in the studies is on aspects of the development of capitalism in Japan. His book *Has Capitalism Changed?* (1961) reflects this particular interest.

Tsuru is one of the first economists in Japan to have drawn the attention of the general public to environmental problems by applying his unusual skills in putting academic concepts into the language of ordinary people.

TSUNEO NAKAUCHI

SELECTED WORKS
1961. *Has Capitalism Changed?* Tokyo: Iwanami Shoten Publishers.
1976. *Collected Works of Shigeto Tsuru.* 13 vols, Tokyo: Kodansha. Vol. 13, *Towards a New Political Economy*, is in English.

Tucker, George (1775–1861). American economist and statistician, he was born in Bermuda, the offspring of a family prominent there and in Virginia. When he joined the faculty of the University of Virginia in 1825, he had already made a name for himself as a lawyer, man of letters and member of Congress.

Among Tucker's economic writings, *The Laws of Wages, Profits and Rent, Investigated* (1837) stands out as a theoretical contribution. Instead of Ricardo's labour theory of value he proposes a supply and demand theory. Ricardo had related rent to the original and indestructible powers of the soil, while according to Tucker rent arises because land yields a surplus. Ricardo had taught that profits tend to decline with rising money wages. To Tucker, the decline of profits reflected the movement from high-yielding investment projects to low-yielding ones. Wages, according to Ricardo, would remain at subsistence level. Tucker did not deny this, but called attention to the diminished quality of subsistence, which, as population grows, shifts to nutrients that require less land; for example, from meat to cereals to potatoes.

Tucker's pioneering work in statistics and demography, *Progress of the United States in Population and Wealth in Fifty Years as Exhibited by the Decennial Census* (1843), includes an early estimate of the national income – $62 per capita – and the prediction of the 'euthanasia' of slavery once the institution would no longer pay for itself.

Tucker's contributions demonstrate the high achievements of the Southern contingent among *antebellum* economic writers in the United States. His views about slavery, free trade and manufacture diverged from the pattern characteristic of the South and attest to the independence of his mind.

HENRY W. SPIEGEL

SELECTED WORKS
1837. *The Laws of Wages, Profits and Rent, Investigated.* Philadelphia: E.L. Carey & A. Hart.
1843. *Progress of the United States in Population and Wealth in Fifty Years as Exhibited by the Decennial Census.* New York: Press of Hunt's merchant's magazine; Boston: Little & Brown.

BIBLIOGRAPHY
Dorfman, J. 1946. *The Economic Mind in American Civilization 1776–1865.* Vol. II, New York: Viking.
Dorfman, J. 1964. George Tucker and economic growth. In G. Tucker, *The Theory of Money and Banks Investigated*, first published 1839, reprinted Clifton, NJ: Kelley.
Snavely, T.R. 1964. *George Tucker as Political Economist.* Charlottesville: University Press of Virginia.

Tucker, Josiah (1713–1799). Born in Laugharne, Carmarthenshire, Tucker was Dean of Gloucester from 1758 until his death, and was also a rector in Bristol for over 50 years. Although his career as an ecclesiastic was a long and honourable one, he was best known in his own day for his active part in many contemporary controversies. Whether the subject was the naturalization of foreign Protestants and Jews, the undesirable effect of low-priced liquors, or the cruel custom of cock-throwing on Shrove Tuesday, his pen was always ready. He was responsible for the earliest study of the Methodist movement and the first substantial critique of Locke's political philosophy. The themes which recurred most often were his opposition to monopolies and his hatred of war. His interest in political affairs was not confined to the press: he participated in several Bristol elections as the local Whig agent.

Tucker's period of greatest notoriety came during the American Revolution. In a steady stream of publications he rejected both the conciliation policy of Burke and that of war. Although he had no sympathy for the ideas espoused by the more radical Americans and their supporters in Britain, he saw no economic reason for attempting to retain the colonies by force, since he was convinced that they would willingly trade with her as long as it was in their interest to do so.

In his *Essay on Trade* (1749) Tucker recognized the need for a scientific study of what is now called economics but only the first part of what was to be his 'great work' on the subject was ever printed, and then only for circulation among friends. However, his other works, which contained the bulk of his ideas, were known to Quesnay and Turgot (who translated one of them) well before the Physiocrats' first writings appeared, and several of his books were to be found in Adam Smith's library. These ideas included: self-love as a socially useful drive, labour as the true source of wealth, and the importance of machinery as a means of increasing that wealth. His aim was to encourage high productivity which would lead, in turn, to lower prices, increased demand, and more jobs. Anything which obstructed the free circulation of labour and capital, especially regulations supporting vested interests, should be eliminated. On the other hand, Tucker did not expect that self-interest and the public good would always coincide; some legislation was necessary to encourage that happy outcome by making what was socially desirable also profitable.

Tucker's most significant contribution may have been his argument against the notion put forward by David Hume that rich countries were likely over time to lose their wealth to poorer ones. Tucker eventually convinced Hume that the factors which made a nation rich in the first place tended to give it a practically insurmountable advantage over its less wealthy neighbours. Since Britain enjoyed such an advantage, once Tucker's reasoning was accepted, as it was by Pitt in the 1780s, opposition to free trade could be disarmed and the way cleared for its triumph in the 19th century.

G. Shelton

SELECTED WORKS

1749. *A Brief Essay on the Advantages and Disadvantages which Respectively Attend France and Great Britain with Regard to Trade [The Essay on Trade].*

1751–2. *Reflections on the Expediency of a Law for the Naturalisation of Foreign Protestants.* Part I (1751), Part II (1752).

1753. *Letters to a Friend Concerning Naturalisation.*

1755. *The Elements of Commerce and Theory of Taxes.*

1757. *Instructions for Travellers.*

1774. *Four Tracts Together With Two Sermons on Political and Commercial Subjects.* Gloucester and London: Raikes & Rivington.

1775. *A Letter to Edmund Burke.*

1781. *A Treatise Concerning Civil Government.*

BIBLIOGRAPHY

Clark, W.E. 1903. *Josiah Tucker, Economist.* New York: Columbia University Press.

Schuyler, R.L. (ed.) 1931. *Josiah Tucker, a Selection from his Economic and Political Writings.* New York: Columbia University Press.

Semmel, B. 1965. The Hume-Tucker debate and Pitt's trade proposals. *Economic Journal* 75, December, 759–90.

Shelton, G. 1981. *Dean Tucker and Eighteenth-Century Economic and Political Thought.* London: Macmillan.

Tugan-Baranovsky, Mikhail Ivanovich (1865–1919). Of mixed Ukrainian-Tartar origin, Tugan-Baranovsky was born in the Kharkov province, and graduated from Kharkov university in 1888. His *Magister* dissertation for Moscow University was on industrial cycles in Great Britain, and he spent six months of his research time in London in 1892. There could scarcely have been a more masterly master's thesis. It was published in 1894. While criticizing crude underconsumptionist theories, and pointing out that 'the process of production creates its own market', especially for producers' goods, he went on to stress that the simple model derived from J-B Say assumes that 'the entrepreneur, before beginning production, has a wholly correct and accurate knowledge of the requirements of the market and of the output of every branch of industry'. He cited Moffat's phrase 'the continuous struggle between the requirements of unknown demand and the fluctuations of unknown supply'. He contrasted the 'propensity to save' with the output of capital goods of various types, and with the opportunities to invest, which can and do get out of line with one another. He collected much empirical data. In the words of Alvin Hansen, 'he began a new way of thinking about the problem' of business cycles (Hansen, 1951, p. 281).

His doctoral dissertation was another masterpiece, full of original research, *The Russian factory, past and present (Russkaya fabrika v proshlom i nastoyashchem)*, which has recently appeared in English translation. This was a major contribution to economic history. In vivid and well-written pages, Tugan-Baranovsky shows the great importance of the state and of serfdom, and the subsequent growth of market-orientated industries based on free labour (though some workers were serfs on quit-rent, a few of whom became serf millionaires). He also made stimulating observations concerning 'natural' and 'artificial' industrialization, relevant to today's concerns with economic development.

His major contribution to economic theory was *Osnovy politicheskoi ekonomii*, which went through many editions, and represented an attempt at a synthesis between marxist political economy (the labour theory of value) and subjective value theory. He considered that the marginalist ignored 'the objective conditions of production', while marxists failed to recognize that not only objective factors but also subjective valuations were an integral part of a theory of value. He argued that Marx confused value (*Wert*) with cost (*Kosten*). He basically supported Marx's theory of exploitation, but defined 'surplus value' as equal to the value of the *products* acquired (consumed) by the capitalists, which earned him criticism from Kondratiev and Struve. He retained from his early marxism the belief that economists should regard Man as not just another factor of production. If horses could write economics, there would be a horse theory of value.

Tugan-Baranovsky to the end of his life retained a particular interest in agriculture and in (voluntary) cooperation. One of his last articles drew attention, prophetically, to the effect of the egalitarian land redistribution of 1917–18 on the marketing of foodstuffs.

His academic career was mainly in the University of St Petersburg, though he was dismissed in 1899 for 'political unreliability' and only reinstated in 1905, as a *privatdozent*. His election to the chair of political economy in 1913 was vetoed by the Minister of Education. Re-elected in 1917, he did not take up his appointment, but returned to his native Ukraine. He became Academician, dean of the Faculty of Law of Kiev, chairman of the Ukrainian cooperatives, president of the Ukrainian economic association, and for a short period Minister of Finance, amid turmoil and civil war. He died in 1919, on his way to Odessa to board a ship for France. He must be seen as the most original of the Russian economists of his generation. Alas, in the Soviet Union he is known chiefly as a 'legal-marxist' opponent of Lenin, and few have the opportunity to study his works, though *The Russian Factory* was reprinted.

Alec Nove

SELECTED WORKS

1894. *Promyshlennye krizisy v sovremennoi Anglii* (Industrial crises in contemporary Britain). St Petersburg. 2nd Russian edn. trans. into French by Joseph Schapiro as *Les crises industrielles en Angleterre*, Paris: M. Giard & E. Briere, 1913.

1898. *Russkaia fabrika v proshlom i nastoiashchem.* (The Russian factory, past and present.) St Petersburg. 3rd Russian edn. trans. by Arthur Levin and Claora S. Levin, under the supervision of Gregory Grossman, as *The Russian Factory*, Homewood: R.D. Irwin, for the American Economic Association, 1970.

1905. *Teoreticheskie osnovy marksizma.* (The theoretical foundations of Marxism.) St Petersburg. Trans. into German as *Theoretische Grundlagen der Marxismus*, Leipzig: Duncker & Humblot, 1905.

1906. *Souremennyi sotsializm v svoem istoricheskom razuitii.* Trans. by M.I. Redmount as *Modern Socialism in its Historical Development*, London: S. Sonnenschein & Co., 1910. Reprinted New York: Russell & Russell, 1966.

1914a. *Ekonomicheskaia priroda kooperativov i ikh klassifikatsiia* (The economic nature of cooperatives and their classification). Moscow.

1914b. *Ocherki iz noveishei istorii politicheskoi ekonomii i sotsializma* (Outlines of the recent history of political economy and of socialism). St. Petersburg.

1917. *Osnovy politicheskoi ekonomii* (Foundations of political economy). Petrograd.

1918. *Sotsializm kak polozhitelnoe uchenie* (Socialism as a positive subject). Petrograd.

Tugwell, Rexford Guy (1891–1979). Rexford Guy Tugwell was born in 1891. As an undergraduate at the Wharton School, he was jarred by textbooks reciting classical economic theories but ignoring real life; he wrote:

> I am sick of a nation's stenches,
> I am sick of propertied czars,
> I will roll up my sleeves,
> – make America over!

This did not bespeak revolutionary inclinations; it merely noted the unacceptable and his resolve to do something about it.

As head of the Economics Department in Columbia College, the undergraduate school in Columbia University, Tugwell stood against the graduate economics faculty; he insisted that more of the best economists should be assigned to teach undergraduates who later would vote upon or directly make public policies, rather than being used excessively in the graduate faculty to shape economics professors. And to counteract classical texts, he wrote for classroom use an institutional study, *American Economic Life and the Means of Its Improvement*. And, *The Industrial Discipline and the Governmental Arts*, showing preference for national economic planning.

During F.D.R.'s last two years as Governor of New York, Tugwell joined in advising how a President should fight the Great Depression. His revealing book, *The Brains Trust*, depicted F.D.R.'s innate conservatism but also made clear that his advisers prompted him toward boldness and experimentation.

Tugwell next served as Assistant and then Undersecretary in the Department of Agriculture. In these posts, his fight for improved pure food and drug laws stirred up violent opposition, and his outspoken liberalism made him a whipping boy for the Administration. More proximately, his siding with Jerome Frank, General Counsel of the Agricultural Adjustment Administration, and others on behalf of small rather than the large farmers championed on Capitol Hill led to his being transferred to head the Resettlement Administration, initiating towns like Greenbelt, Maryland.

However, his most vital role in Washington was as leader of an informal but influential group favouring centralized national planning, rather effective during the 'first New Deal'. A second informal group, led intellectually by Louis D. Brandeis (and fortified by his Supreme Court votes) and Felix Frankfurter, turned action considerably toward the 'second New Deal', marked by a slowdown of strong policies, and with much inveighing against 'the curse of bigness' and 'economic royalists'.

Rex's ideas were in no way totalitarian; they urged peacetime application, with appropriate modifications, of the type of comprehensiveness economic planning later used during World War II, with large interpenetration between Government and business. Sensing increasing frustration and official rejection, Tugwell left the Government to become Vice-President of American Molasses Company and the Chairman of the New York City Planning Commission. Roosevelt then appointed him the first Governor of Puerto Rico, with good accomplishments as reported in *The Stricken Land.*

Thereafter, Tugwell taught planning at the University of Chicago, and finally spent many years at the Hutchins Center for the Study for Democratic Institutions in Santa Barbara. His views never altered, that New Deal 'patchwork' would never work and that centralized national planning was imperative. Coming to feel that current trends in economics were hopeless and incorrigible, he turned to institutional proposals for rearranging the structure of government. Hence, his monumental work, *The Emerging Constitution.* He knew that none of his recommendations would be adopted, but felt that stating them would be of value. His many books about the Presidency included *The Democratic Roosevelt*, beautifully written like all his work, and an objective and critical evaluation of one whom he admired endlessly. It is probably the most revealing book about F.D.R.

At memorial services in 1979, I spoke of a man who, among all whom I got to know during a half century of public service, was truly one of 'the best and the brightest'.

LEON H. KEYSERLING

SELECTED WORKS

Tugwell's publications are far too numerous to be listed here, but those listed are representative of his work and interests.

1922. *The Economic Basis of Public Interest.* Menasha, Wisconsin: George Banta Publishing Company.

1924. *The Trend of Economics* (editor and contributor). New York: Knopf.

1925. (With Thomas Monroe and Roy E. Stryker.) *American Economic Life and the Means of its Improvement.* New York: Harcourt, Brace.

1927. *Industry's Coming of Age.* New York: Harcourt, Brace.

1932. *Mr. Hoover's Economic Policy.* New York: John Day.

1933. *The Industrial Discipline and the Governmental Arts.* New York: Columbia University Press.

1934. (With Howard C. Hill.) *Our Economic Society and its Problems* New York: Harcourt, Brace.

1934–5. *Redirecting Education* (ed. with Leon H. Keyserling, and contributor). New York: Columbia University Press. Vol. 1, 1934; Vol. 2, 1935.

1947. *The Stricken Land: The Story of Puerto Rico.* Garden City, New York: Doubleday.

1957. *The Democratic Roosevelt.* Garden City, New York: Doubleday.

1967. *The Light of Other Days.* Garden City, New York: Doubleday.

1967. *F.D.R.: Architect of an Era.* New York: Macmillan.

1968. *The Brains Trust.* New York: Viking.

1974. *The Emerging Constitution.* New York: Harper's Magazine Press.

1982. (Posthumous.) *To the Lesser Heights of Morningside.* Philadelphia: University of Pennsylvania Press (Introduction by Leon H. Keyserling).

tulipmania. The term refers to situations in which some prices behave in a way that appears not to be fully explainable by economic 'fundamentals'. Keynes (1936, ch. 12) has a discussion of this type of phenomenon. Modern theory pays a great deal of attention to equilibria that may resemble tulipmanias, but which are consistent with standard demand-supply analysis under the assumption of Perfect Foresight or Rational Expectations.

An example will serve to convey the flavour of the main issues. Let q_t be the price of land at time t, and let $R>0$ be the net rent (in terms of output) of one unit of land per unit of time (momentarily, R is assumed constant over time); moreover, let $r>0$ be the competitive real rate of interest (assumed, momentarily, constant over time). In the absence of uncertainty, the equilibrium rate of return on land must equal the rate of interest; more specifically, in equilibrium

$$(R+q_{t+1})/q_t=1+r \qquad (1)$$

Let $t=0$ be the 'present'; if q_0 is given, then (1) determines the unique equilibrium path of q for all $t>0$. On the other hand, if q_0 has to be determined by equilibrium conditions, equation (1) is clearly insufficient. If equilibrium does not impose any further constraints on the path of q, then there exists a *continuum* of equilibrium paths of q – one path for each possible initial price of land, q_0.

Equation (1) can be expressed as

$$q_{t+1}=(1+r)q_t-R \qquad (2)$$

Equation (2) exhibits a unique steady-state q equal to R/r; if $q_0>R/r$, for example, the price of land will increase without limit. Since the rental on land and the rate of interest are constant, this type of path appears not to be related to economic 'fundamentals'. However, if (2) is the only equilibrium condition for the price of land, these apparent tulipmanias would be consistent with standard general equilibrium analysis. Notice that along an unstable path the price of land rises (falls) essentially because it is expected to rise (fall). There is, however, nothing in the logic that contradicts standard economic theory.

Obviously, the crux of the matter is whether there are constraints other than the above (equations (1) and (2)). In an overlapping-generations model, for example, the boundless increase in the price of land may not be consistent with equilibrium, because the time might come when future generations simply could not afford to buy the land. On the other hand, paths that originate at $q_0<R/r$ will eventually exhibit negative prices – a situation that may be ruled out in equilibrium if one assumes nonsatiation. Wallace (1980), however, has shown examples of the above-type of equilibrium indeterminacy in the context of monetary models with overlapping generations. He showed that there may exist a continuum of paths, each of which exhibits hyperinflation even when money supply remains constant.

In a richer model both R and r will become functions of the price of land, q. Calvo (1978) shows that in an otherwise standard overlapping-generations model, the equilibrium price of land (or capital) may be governed by a stable difference equation – not an unstable one like equation (2) – which immediately implies the existence of a continuum of equilibria around the steady state. It should be noted, however, that these equilibria are stable – they all converge to the steady state. The fact remains, nevertheless, that nothing would impede this economy from jumping from one stable equilibrium solution to another in the continuum without any change in technology or tastes. Azariadis (1981) has further shown that if there is a continuum of Perfect Foresight equilibria which converge to the steady state, then one can also find stochastic equilibrium solutions, each of which contingent on the development of one or more random variables. These random variables may have nothing to do with the structure of the economy (he called his equilibrium behaviour 'extraneous uncertainty'). Finally, Grandmont (1985) gives conditions under which some of these multiple solutions exhibit a cyclical pattern.

There seems to be some controversy about what to conclude from the existence of a continuum of equilibrium paths. Calvo (1978) asserts that a continuum of equilibria is inconsistent with the Rationality of Expectations Hypothesis. McCallum (1983) argues that multiplicity of equilibria is not necessarily a problem. He proposes a method of obtaining uniqueness by restricting one's attention to certain types of solutions. Yet, there are authors (e.g. Grandmont, 1985) that appear to believe in the power of indeterminate-equilibrium models for descriptive purposes.

GUILLERMO A. CALVO

See also BUBBLES; 'HAHN PROBLEM'.

BIBLIOGRAPHY

Azariadis, C. 1981. Self-fulfilling prophecies. *Journal of Economic Theory* 25, December, 380–96.

Calvo, G.A. 1978. On the indeterminacy of interest rates and wages with perfect foresight. *Journal of Economic Theory* 19, December, 321–37.

Grandmont, J.-M. 1985. On endogenous competitive business cycles, *Econometrica* 53, September, 995–1045.

Keynes, J.M. 1936. *The General Theory of Employment, Interest and Money*. London: Macmillan.

McCallum, B.T. 1983. On non-uniqueness in rational expectations models: an attempt at perspective. *Journal of Monetary Economics* 11, March, 139–67.

Wallace, N. 1980. The overlapping generations model of fiat money. In *Models of Monetary Economies*, ed. John H. Kareken and Neil Wallace, Federal Reserve Bank of Minneapolis.

Turgot, Anne Robert Jacques, Baron de L'Aulne (1727–1781). Economist, philosopher and administrator, Turgot was born in Paris, in 1727, the third son of a well-established Norman family with a long tradition of public service in the magistrature. Destined originally for a career in the church, his education was extensive. Because of shyness, his education commenced at home with a private tutor; continued at the Collèges Duplessis and Bourgogne where, among other things, he studied the philosophical systems of Newton and Locke. In October 1746 he entered the Seminary of Saint-Sulpice in preparation for the priesthood. From June 1749 to early 1751 he was resident student at the Maison de Sorbonne, an annex of the Theological Faculty of the University of Paris. His already considerable academic distinction lead to his election to the office of prior in 1750. This honorary position inspired two of his earliest works, of which the second, *Philosophical Review of the Successive Advances of the Human Mind* (Turgot, 1750a) contained a demonstration of the importance of economic surplus for the development of civilization as part of his four stages theory of human progress:

> Tillage ... is able to feed more men than are employed in it ... Hence towns, trade, the useful arts and accomplishments, the division of occupations, the differences in education, and the increased inequality in the conditions of life. Hence leisure ... (and) the cultivation of the arts (Turgot, 1750a, p. 43).

His father's death in early 1751 possibly saved Turgot from having to take his final vows, since his inheritance provided sufficient income to commence the administrative career he desired. He gained appointment to some judicial positions, including that of Master of Requests in early 1753, the stepping stone to a career as provincial intendant. During the 1750s, Turgot's prolonged residence in Paris allowed immense intellectual activity but left time for extensive travels through France when accompanying Gournay on his official tours of inspection of French industry. His contributions to the *Encyclopédie* (Turgot, 1756, 1757a, 1757b), ranging from articles on Etymology, Existence and Expansibility to Fairs and Foundations, spread his fame as a philosopher and gained him the friendship of Voltaire, whom he visited in 1760 during his only journey abroad.

Although Turgot's interest in economics had commenced as early as 1749 when he wrote a critique of Law's system of paper currency and such interest was maintained in the Sorbonne orations and other early writings, it was considerably stimulated by Gournay's friendship. Gournay's death inspired Turgot's famous eulogy (Turgot, 1759) and earlier he had encouraged Turgot's translation of Tucker (Turgot, 1755), Turgot's comments on Gournay's notes to the translations of Child (Turgot, 1753–4), and most probably, aspects of the content of Turgot's two economic articles for the *Encyclopédie* (1757a and 1757b). Gournay's friendship was particularly important because it brought Turgot's economics under more substantial English influence as compared with Physiocracy (Goroenewegen, 1977, p. xiv). Turgot's first meeting with Quesnay cannot be precisely dated. It may not have occurred till 1756 or 1757 when their mutual association with the *Encyclopédie* may have brought them together. Turgot (1759), p. 26) cites Quesnay's contributions with considerable approval, indicating that his generally good relations with the Physiocrats must by then have been well established. His presence at Quesnay's meeting in the Entresol at Versailles as a 'handsome young Master of Requests' was in any case recorded by Mme de Hausset (n.d., pp. 117–119). A life-long friendship with Du Pont de Nemours, which began in 1763 must have strengthened good relations with the Physiocrats even further. Another enduring friendship was made with the philosopher and mathematician, Condorcet. Both friends produced memoirs of Turgot's life after his death (Du Pont, 1782; Condorcet, 1786).

In 1761 Turgot was appointed Intendant of Limoges, a large district containing most of the provinces of Limousin and Angoumois, and this position he filled with distinction for thirteen years. The task of the 18th-century intendant, a post compared by Morley (1886, p. 112) to that of Chief Commissioner in a large district of the former British Empire in India, were many:

> He had to collect direct taxation, rectify justice, promote the arts of agriculture, encourage industry and commerce ... Everything came within the scope – sanitation and public order, morality and poor relief, the recruiting and billeting of soldiers, military equipment, rations and transport, religious processions and the pairs of churches, colleges and libraries, parochial and municipal finance (Dakin, 1939, pp. 27–8, the standard source for details of Turgot's administrative career as intendant).

Despite this cumbersome and heavy administrative load, Turgot managed to introduce some reforms. These included changes to the assessment and collection of the taille, transmutation of the *corvée* and the *milice* into money payments, and establishing public workshops to alleviate hardships suffered by the population of his province during the long and severe famine of 1769 to 1772. Many of his better known economic writings date from this period: first of all, his *Reflections on the Production and Distribution of Wealth* (Turgot, 1766a but not published till 1769–70 in serial form in the *Ephémérides*), a draft for a paper on value and money (Turgot, 1769), observations on two winning entries in a prize competition he had organized on the subject of taxation (Turgot, 1767a and 1767b), and a series of memoranda connected with the ministration of his province in which he pleaded with the central authorities for reforms on the basis of carefully elucidated theoretical principles. The more important of these deal with taxation in general (Turgot, 1763), mines and quarries (Turgot, 1767a), the grain trade (Turgot, 1770a), the rate of interest (Turgot, 1770b) and the trade mark on iron products (Turgot, 1773). His administrative work permitted regular but infrequent visits to Paris to see friends and attend the salons of Mme de Graffigny, Mme de Geoffrin and later, Mlle de Lespinasse. Apart from the French intelligentsia, he there became acquainted with foreign notables like Hume, Adam Smith, Franklin and Gibbon. The exile imposed by his administrative position also inspired a substantial correspondence with Du Pont de Nemours, Condorcet, and his personal secretary, Caillard, making up a large part of the five volume edition of his works as edited by Schelle (1913–23). Schumpeter (1954, p. 248) notes a further significant aspect about Turgot's administrative career: 'nearly all his creative work must have been done between 18 and 34 because during the 13 years at Limoges, Turgot can have had but scanty leisure, during his nearly 2 years of ministerial office, practically none.'

Louis XVI's succession to the throne in 1774 marks the next stage in Turgot's career; his membership of the Royal Council, first as Minister of the Navy (from 20 July 1774), then as Minister of Finance (from 24 August 1774 to 12 May 1776, the date of his dismissal). While lamenting the fact that so much more could have been done, Du Pont de Nemours (1782) summarized Turgot's career as minister in terms of the reforms accomplished. These included restoration of the domestic free trade in grain, abolition of many small, local duties and other constraints on trade, and the January 1776 measures, of which partial suppression of the guilds and replacing the *corvée* with a more general land tax were the more controversial measures. These last, now generally known as the six Edicts, ultimately caused his downfall even though he did secure royal support for their forcible registration at a famous *Lit de Justice*. As an 'experience in economic politics, an exception to the general rule that French ministers of finance are financiers rather than economists', Faure (1961) gives a detailed account of Turgot's ministerial experience and the opposition it encountered almost from the start during the grain riots of early 1775 and the intrigues surrounding the campaign to prevent registration of his 1776 Edicts. The reforms Turgot had accomplished were reversed within six months from his downfall, and 'leisure and complete freedom as the principal net product from my two years in the ministry' was how he himself sarcastically summed up his achievements in a letter to Caillard (Schelle, 1913–23, V, p. 488). The period of retirement in the five years which remained of his life were not years of inactivity.

> The sciences which he had formerly cultivated, easily filled up his time; he studied mathematics, he sought to bring the thermometer to greater precision, he searched with l'Abbé Rochon, after various expeditious convenient, and cheap methods of multiplying copies of writing to supply the

place of printing,... he preserved all his passion for literature and poetry ... (Condorcet, 1786, pp. 255–62).

In 1778 he was elected President of the Académie des Inscriptions et des Belles Lettres. He died in Paris in March 1781 from gout, a family illness that had steadily wrecked his health, worsening particularly during the last decade of life.

Although Turgot is now largely remembered as a very important 18th-century French economist and a pre-revolutionary reformist finance minister, such an assessment fails to reflect his youthful ambitions and work. Meek (1973, pp. 1–2) indicates that

> Turgot set out from the beginning with the conscious intention of becoming a polymath rather than a specialist ... . A list of works to be written ... begins with 'The Barcimedes', a tragedy, and ends with 'On Luxury, Political Reflections', and in between these are forty-eight others, including works on universal history, the origin of languages, love and marriage, political geography, natural theology, morality and economics, as well as numerous translations from foreign languages, literary works, and treatises on scientific subjects ... What is (especially) remarkable is ... that Turgot managed, during his short life of only fifty-four years, to make some contribution to so many of them, or at least to retain an active and intelligent interest in them.

Turgot was therefore considerably more than an economist, and some of the qualities Meek listed needed to be highlighted to underscore that fact. In the first place, he was a superb linguist, 'reading seven languages – Greek, Latin, Hebrew, Spanish, German, Italian, and English, the last three of which he spoke fluently' (Dakin, 1939, pp. 10–11) and from some of which he published poetry translations (Turgot, 1760, 1762, 1778). This linguistic skill is reflected in his magnificent library, the catalogue of which (Tsuda, 1974) demonstrates his ability to profit from the economic writings of other countries. Secondly, his wider interests influence the interpretation to be given to his economics. Turgot's contributions cannot be simply assessed in terms of his importance in fashioning certain parts of the marginalists' toolbox, as done, for example, by Schumpeter (1954). He is far more correctly depicted as 'an author of transition between the Physiocrats at the end of the eighteenth century and the English classical economists at the start of the nineteenth' (Bordes, 1981, p. xvi), that is, the true contemporary of those like Smith, Steuart, Condillac, Verri and Beccaria producing economic treatises building on Physiocracy in that quarter century ending in 1776 during which political economy emerged as the science of the reproduction, circulation and distribution of wealth (see Groenewegen, 1983a). Although, apart from the skeleton form of his *Reflections* (Turgot, 1766a), Turgot never completed such a treatise, this skeleton combined with his youthful views on social progress allows his economics to be depicted as something essential to the understanding of historical stages (see Finzi, 1981). The reduced emphasis on the economics developed by him as a by-product of his administrative career this implies prevents his depiction as a 19th-century liberal (see Morley, 1886; Bourrinet, 1965) or as a general precursor of equilibrium theory (Nogaro, 1944, pp. 26–7; Bordes, 1981, pp. xxvi–xxviii).

Schelle (1913–23, I, pp. 29–30, 79) draws attention to the fact that the young Turgot was interested above all in sociology, shown by his attempts at analysing causes of progress and decay in taste, science and the arts, and that this analytical interest was enhanced by studying the formation of languages, because etymology provides valuable clues not only to the progression of ideas but to the needs from which ideas originate. Turgot's early work on language formation and social progress appears to have suggested the importance of economic factors in explaining this process, and that the means by which peoples gain their subsistence, determining as it does their access to economic surplus, is particularly important to explain the manner in which societies, morals, laws, the arts and the sciences gradually develop. Turgot (1750b, p. 172) explicitly relates certain characteristics in the formation of languages to stages of hunters, shepherds and husbandmen with their different requirements for communication. The notion of progress between these stages is implied in his critique (Turgot, 1751a, pp. 242–3) of the alleged virtues of equality in the savage state where he shows that by preventing the division of labour and the accumulation of capital on which abundance and secure subsistence depend, such equalities also prevent progress in the sciences and arts. The subsequent fragment *On Universal History* (Turgot, 1751b) combines these elements into 'a quite advanced statement of the four stages theory – or at any rate a three stages theory, with a distinct hint of the fourth stage' (Meek, 1977, p. 22).

Although Turgot's *On Universal History* was not completed, its basic notions stayed with him for the rest of his life and in a number of aspects received further development. The systematic attempt to explain general progress by stages from hunters, shepherds, farmers to a commercial society to a large extent provides the basis on which Turgot constructed his analysis of the production and distribution of wealth in the *Reflections*, as is explicitly recognized in his discussion of cattle as a form of moveable wealth (Turgot, 1766a, pp. 66–7). Moreover, the whole of the *Reflections* is imbued with Turgot's sociological concerns with nature of progress and historical development, thereby reinforcing the need to interpret its contents in terms of stadial development. Such a view is also appropriate for its alleged original purpose as providing explanations to accompany an extensive questionnaire on the Chinese economy and society which he had prepared for two young Chinese students in 1766 (see Groenewegen, 1977, pp. xvii–xix). This aspect of the *Reflections* may be demonstrated from a summary of its contents, a process facilitated by the parts into which Du Pont divided it for publication in *Ephémérides*.

Under this subdivision (Turgot, 1766a, pp. 43–56); the first part of the *Reflections* analyses the basic features of the production and distribution of wealth within an agricultural society. Although capital advances are used in such a society, the distributional aspect of such use is ignored at this stage except for its final sections dealing with what for Turgot were contemporary manifestations of agricultural production (1766a, pp. 56–6). Turgot argues at the outset that such an agricultural society presumes a division of labour, a natural consequence of its inequality of property ownership. Hence it presumes a specific set of class relations, that is, division of society between a proprietors' class owning land and living from its surplus produce without a need to work, and working classes without property earning their living from their labour. Within this working class, the division of labour divides those cultivating the soil to produce food and raw material or products of prime necessity from artisans who transform those primary materials into forms more suitable for people's use. Because artisans depend on those working in agriculture for their livelihood, Turgot calls them a stipendiary class. Because they only transform existing wealth without generating a surplus, Turgot calls them a sterile class to contrast their work with that in agriculture which produces such a surplus and thereby generates new wealth. In this way Turgot demonstrates the appropriateness of Physiocratic class analysis for understanding agricultural society.

At the end of this discussion Turgot suggests that the relationship between proprietors and the working classes in agriculture is itself subject to change with respect to the manner in which proprietors draw the surplus from the land through the organization of production. The method springing first to mind, landlords hiring wage labour for themselves, Turgot views as an unlikely candidate to be first from the perspective of actual historical development. Slavery appears to have been first in this regard. Though Turgot saw slavery persisting in colonial societies, elsewhere economic circumstances, combined with humanity and landlord's convenience gradually transformed slavery first into bondage of the soil and then vassalage, where former serfs become tenants and surplus product rent and other stipulated dues. One such tenancy, the dominant form in Turgot's France, was share cropping or *métayage* in which the landlord made the advances in return for a fixed part of the produce; another, more advanced form existed where a capitalist farmer, or entrepreneur (Turgot, 1766b, pp. 28–9) rented the land from the proprietor for a specified rent and period of time, himself providing the necessary advances for cultivation. Capitalist farming or *la grande culture* had begun to emerge in France during Turgot's time, and the farmer/entrepreneur class it created 'has a quite distinct status from that of the ploughman/sharecropper. He does not earn his living by the sweat of his brow like labourers but by employing his capital in a lucrative manner like the shipowners of Nantes and Bordeaux employ theirs in maritime trade' (Turgot, 1766b, p. 29). As nations become more wealthy, and capital accumulates, a new proprietors' class is created who live without working from the revenue of money or capital. The section which opens the second part of the *Reflections* draws attention to this feature by dealing with 'capitals in general and the revenue of money'.

Explanations of the origin and use of capital, and its impact on 'the system of distribution of wealth which I have just outlined' (Turgot, 1766a, p. 56) requires an elementary acquaintance with the theory of money, commerce, exchange and value and hence some retracing of steps. After this disgression, which contains little that is new, Turgot presents a fascinating analysis on both the uses of capital and its origins through accumulation and thrift. Turgot discusses accumulation and thrift both historically and analytically. Historically, accumulation is associated with slavery and surplus product from land: analytically, prudence and a desire for self-improvement are seen as major motives for thrift. Turgot argues that the savings process is greatly facilitated by the introduction of money but that this raises new complications such as a need to distinguish saving, hoarding and investment. Turgot's saving–investment analysis denied the possibility that money savings were able to induce substantial leakages from the circular flow because hoarding was seen as irrational and money had only a limited role as a store of value. Turgot argued that savings were immediately transformed into investment (see Groenewegen, 1971).

Turgot's analysis of the productive use of capital and its social implications is presented in the second and third parts of the *Reflections*. These reveal the degree to which his economics had departed from Physiocracy and anticipated views subsequently developed by Adam Smith. First of all, Turgot's exposition extends the use of capital to all sectors of industry thereby not confining it to agriculture as Quesnay had done. Secondly, Turgot, like Smith, links an increasing need for capital in production with extensions of the division of labour and a consequent lengthening of the time period of production. Thirdly, Turgot associates the provision of capital to industry with a new class of society, the capitalist/entrepreneur as owners of moveable wealth, who invest these resources to reap a return. Hence the working classes of agriculture, manufacturing and trade 'may be divided into two orders of men, that of the Entrepreneurs of Capitalists, who make all the advances, and that of the mere wage earning workmen' (Turgot, 1766a, pp. 72–3). Of special significance for analysing distribution, this new class appropriates the resources by which it can live without labour through the creation of interest and profit as a new income type. Profit in this context, is clearly associated by Turgot with a return on productive investment, comprising an interest component, a premium for risk and remuneration for the time and trouble of the entrepreneur in supervising the investment. Part of the *Reflections* therefore suggests that the quantitative changes of gradual capital accumulation (perhaps first experienced within agriculture) by a qualitative leap create a new stage of society, the commercial or capitalist stage (see Meek, 1973, pp. 21–6).

However, this view is partially contradicted in some of the *Reflections*' later sections. These reveal the new class as mere lenders of money and show Turgot equivocating on whether interest and profit have the same disposable status as the net product of land. Such aspects of Turgot's work show that for him 'commercial society' perhaps remained 'incorporated into the agricultural state [never becoming] a separate stage, characterised and led by an internal logic of its own' (Finzi, 1982, p. 116), and reinforce the position that Turgot's analytical schema is a transition from the Physiocrats to subsequent classical political economy retaining that ambiguous relationship between capital and land, rent and interest, not really resolved analytically until Ricardo's distribution analysis (see Cartelier, 1981).

Despite this ambivalence in depicting the final stage of social progress, these sections of the *Reflections* also contain some of Turgot's most analytically significant contributions to economics. Having shown that 'capitals are the indispensable foundation of all lucrative enterprises' and that the continual reproduction of these capitals 'with a steady profit' constitutes 'the true idea of the circulation of money' the disturbance of which may cause economic decline (1766a, pp. 75–6), Turgot analyses the mutual interrelationship of the returns on various types of investment and the rate of interest. Interest itself is shown by Turgot to be determined by the demand for and supply of loanable funds, the demand arising from both consumption and investment needs. These investment needs, or employments of capital as Turgot calls them, are described as five: purchasing a landed estate, which yields least; lending a capital at interest the return of which is greater; and investing in agricultural, manufacturing or commercial enterprises, the return of which is greatest. Irrespective of these inequalities in yield to the various employments of capital, Turgot argues that competition combined with capital mobility causes a tendency to equilibrium between them.

> As soon as the profits resulting from an employment of money, whatever it may be, increase or diminish, capitals turn in that direction or withdraw from other employments, or withdraw and turn towards other employments, and this necessarily alters in each of these employments, the relation between the capital and the annual product (1766a, p. 87).

This investment analysis must be seen as a substantial advance on the earlier literature, and hence as a major contribution to economics.

Turgot's other economic writings can be seem as supplementing the analytical framework of the *Reflections*. This can be particularly illustrated from his theory of value, the outlines of which had been developed by the early 1750s (Schelle, 1913–23, I, p. 385). Its foundation rested on a relationship between current (market) price and fundamental value dependent on competition and resources mobility. Subsequently (Turgot, 1767b, p. 120,n.) this proposition is elaborated to demonstrate that the market price of a commodity 'ruled as it is by supply and demand' and liable to 'very sudden fluctuations' though 'not in any essential proportion to the fundamental value,... has a tendency to approach it continually, and can never move far away from it permanently'. Turgot therefore developed the classical position which saw 'natural prices' as the centres of gravitation for market prices. Elaborations on the elementary theory of wages of the *Reflections* (1766a, pp. 45–6) are made within this value framework. Turgot did this in a letter to Hume where on the argument that taxes increase 'the fundamental price of labour' or 'the cost of his subsistence', a tax on wages must be rapidly absorbed in market wage rates (Schelle, 1913–23, II, pp. 662–3). The *Reflections* was confined to brief explanations of the current or market price; the unfinished 'Value and Money', with its unsuccessful attempts at determining value in various exchange situations, appears as an elaboration of the underlying competitive theory rather than as a new departure towards a more subjective value theory. Turgot's famous analysis of the 'law of variable proportions' (Schumpeter, 1954, pp. 260–61) may also be noted here. This arose in criticism of a common Physiocratic assumption that product was invariably proportional to advances. Turgot (1767b, pp. 111–12) argued instead that as 'advances are gradually increased up to the point where they yield nothing, each increase would be less and less productive', thereby clearly recognizing the possibility of diminishing returns.

On the basis of these contributions, Schumpeter (1954, pp. 260–1, 307, 332) argued the Turgot was a writer in advance of his time by anticipating much of what became important after the 'marginal revolution'. Turgot's analysis of the market mechanism are reminiscent of Böhm-Bawerk and Menger; his 'interest and capital theory ... clearly foreshadowed much of the best thought in the last decades of the nineteenth century'. However, it seems more reasonable to conclude 'that the resemblance between Turgot's economics and that of post-1870 writers is superficial' and that both in temperament and thrust his economics is part of the classical tradition (Groenewegen, 1982). His development of the Physiocratic notion of reproduction (Turgot, 1763, 1766a, pp. 75–6) and his emphasis on the principle of competition as regulator of the rate of interest, wages and values in general, are firmly within that 'classical tradition rehabilitated by Sraffa' (Ravix and Romani, 1984, p. 145).

Turgot's strong laissez faire position, which turned him into the patron saint of the French liberal economics tradition of the middle of the 19th century, was most systematically expounded in his eulogy of Gournay (1759). This rested on the principle that unrestrained self-interest yields the best results in economic activity, a principle he applied wherever he could during his administrative career. It justified his pleas (1770b) and subsequent imposition of domestic free trade in grain, his criticism of the prevalent regulation of lending at interest (1770a), and the suppression of the guilds in one of his famous 1776 Edicts. More important is his discussion of taxation principles. Turgot's major paper on the subject (Turgot, 1763), after setting out some general principles, defends the concept of the single tax on net product on the basis of Physiocratic theory. However, he identifies difficulties in its implementation. These need detailed examination if the benefits of the policy are to be achieved. More generally, it can be said of his policy implementation that though based on broad principles, these were in practice always modified to cater for actual circumstances.

Turgot's work and its importance in the history of economics have occasionally been vigorously debated, most notably in the controversies over the degree of influence he exerted on Adam Smith and Böhm-Bawerk's interpretation of his capital and interest theory. An assessment of the evidence (Groenewegen, 1969) suggests that Turgot influenced Smith on only a few fairly specific points and that the broad similarities (and differences) in their economic systems are largely explained by their common heritage of British and French predecessors. The quarrel over Böhm-Bawerk's interpretation of Turgot's interest theory (involving Cassel, Wicksell and Marshall) is more instructive for the light it sheds on the participants than for discovering Turgot's views on the subject. For example, it can be suggested that Böhm-Bawerk's position may have been influenced by his considerable youthful debts to Turgot's theory while Marshall's involvement may be explained by antipathy to the Austrian economists and some striking similarities between his and Turgot's interest theory (see Groenewegen, 1983b). This debate highlights his analytical contributions to interest and capital theory.

The doctrine of social progress, which played such an important part in establishing Turgot's vision, was also applied by him to his history of ideas. In his fragment *On Universal History* (1751b, pp. 95–6) a cumulative notion of intellectual progress is presented, in which ideas are seen to develop necessarily from the systems of predecessors; each scientist, as it were, standing on the shoulders of those who came before. Two decades later, Turgot applied this doctrine to the history of economics when defending Melon, the financial economist, against Du Pont's charge that Melon's work was historically unimportant because it was wrong. 'Someone entering the world after Montesquieu, Hume, Cantillon, Quesnay, M. de Gournay, etc. is less struck by the merit arising from Melon's priority because he does not appreciate it; for him it is no more than a date, and when he reads him, he knew already more than his book' (Turgot to Caillard, 1 January 1771, Schelle, 1913–23, III, p. 500). This line of thought can be applied to Turgot himself. He built on the work of Montesquieu, Hume, Cantillon, Quesnay and Gournay, thereby becoming a major participant in contructing 18th-century classical political economy with noteworthy contributions of his own particularly to the theory of value, capital and interest, production and distribution.

Turgot's works were collected on three occasions: by his friend Du Pont (1808–11), by Daire and Dussard (Turgot, 1844), and by Schelle (1913–23) together with a biography and associated material. Few of his writings were published in his lifetime, but from 1788 to 1792 some of his major economic writings were republished by his friends Condorcet and Du Pont. Comparison of these texts, manuscript versions and the text of the collected works, suggest differences attributable to Du Pont, who edited the text for ideological and occasionally political reasons (see Groenewegen, 1977, pp. xxxiv–xxxvi). Schelle first drew attention to, and then removed, many of these corrections, but was not completely successful in this. For this reason, and because of its omissions, particularly of subsequently discovered items from Turgot's voluminous correspondence, Schelle's edition can no longer be described as definitive. Preparing such an edition of Turgot's works awaits both the generous financing required for the task and the services of a devoted editor.

PETER GROENEWEGEN

See also PHYSIOCRATS; SMITH, ADAM.

SELECTED WORKS

1749. *Letter to M. l'abbé de Cicé on the replacing of Money by Paper*, also known as the *'Letter on paper money'*. Trans. in Groenewegen (1977), 1–8.

1750a. *Philosophical Review of the Successive Advances of the Human Mind*. Trans. in Meek (1973), 44–59.

1750b. Remarques critiques sur les Réflexions Philosophiques de Maupertuis *Sur l'Origine des langues et la signification des mots*. In Schelle (1913–23), Vol. I, 15–79.

1751a. Lettre à Madame de Graffigny sur les *Lettres d'une Péruvienne*. In Schelle (1913–23), Vol. I, 241–55.

1751b. *On Universal History*. Trans. in Meek (1973), 61–118.

1753–4. *Remarks on the Notes to the Translation of Josiah Child [by Gournay]*. Trans. in Groenewegen (1977), 9–13.

1755. *Reflections on the Expediency of a Law for the Naturalisation of Foreign Protestants*, by Josiah Tucker, translated into French with notes by Turgot. London and Paris.

1756. *Etymologie, Existence, Expansibilité*. In *Encyclopédie ou Dictionnaire Raisonné des Sciences, des Arts, et Des Métiers*. Vol. 6, Paris.

1757a. *Fairs and Markets*. Trans. in Groenewegen (1977).

1757b. *Foundations*. Trans. as Article I in the Appendix to Condorcet, *Life of M. Turgot*, London, 1787.

1759. *In Praise of Gournay*. Trans. in Groenewegen (1977).

1760. *Salomon Gessner, la Mort d'Abel, Poème*. Traduit par M. Huber [et Turgot], Paris.

1762. *Salomon Gessner, Idylles et Poèmes Champêtres*. Traduit par M. Huber [et Turgot], Lyon.

1763. *Plan for a Paper on Taxation in General*. Trans. in Groenewegen (1977).

1766a. *Reflections on the Production and Distribution of Wealth*. Trans. in Groenewegen (1977).

1766b. *On the Characteristics of La Grande and La Petite Culture*. In *Quesnay, Farmers 1756 and Turgot, Sur la Grande et la petite Culture*, ed. P. Groenewegen, Reprints of Economic Classics, Series 2, No.2. Sydney: University of Sydney, 1983.

1767a. Extract d'un mémoire de M.C. qui contient les Principes de l'administration politique, sur la propriété des carrieres et des mines, et sur les règles de leur exploitation. In *Ephémérides du Citoyen*, Vol. VII, Paris, 33–118.

1767b. *Observations on a Paper by Saint-Péravy*. Trans. in Groenewegen (1977).

1767c. *Observations on a Paper by Graslin*. Trans. in Groenewegen (1977).

1769. Value and money. Trans. in Groenewegen (1977).

1770a. *Letters on the Grain Trade*. Extracts trans. in Groenewegen (1977).

1770b. *Paper on Lending at Interest*. Extracts trans. in Groenewegen (1977).

1773. *Letter to l'abbé Ternay on the 'Marque des Fers'*. Trans. in Groenewegen (1977).

1778. *Virgile, Didon, Poème en vers métrique hexamètres, divisés en trois chants, traduit du 4e livre de l'Enéide*. n.p.

1808–11. *Oeuvres de Turgot précédées et accompagnées de mémoires et de notes sur son vie, son administration et ses ouvrages*. Ed. P.S. du Pont de Nemours, Paris.

1844. *Oeuvres de Turgot, nouvelle édition*. Ed. Eugéne Daire and Hyppolite Dussard, Paris.

BIBLIOGRAPHY

Bordes, C. 1981. Présentation. In *Turgot, économiste et administrateur*, ed. C. Bordes and S. Morange, Paris: Presses Universitaires de France.

Bourrinet, J. 1965. Turgot, théoricien de l'individualisme libéral. *Revue d'histoire économique et sociale* 43(4), 465–89.

Cartelier, J. 1981. La contradiction terre/capital-argent chez Turgot. In *Turgot, économiste et administrateur*, ed. C. Bordes and J. Morange, Paris: Presses Universitaires de France.

Condorcet, J.A.N. Caritat de. 1786. *The Life of M. Turgot, Controller-General of the Finances of France in the Years 1774, 1775 and 1776*. Translated from the French with an Appendix, London, 1787.

Dakin, D. 1939. *Turgot and the Ancien Régime in France*. London: Methuen.

Du Pont, P.S. 1782. *Mémoires sur la vie et les ouvrages de M. Turgot*. Philadelphia and Paris.

Faure, E. 1961. *La disgrâce de Turgot, 12 Mai 1776*. Paris: Gallimard.

Finzi, R. 1981. Turgot: l'histoire et l'économie: 'Nécessité' de l'économie politique? 'Historicité' des lois économiques? In *Turgot, économiste et administrateur*, ed. C. Bordes and J. Morange, Paris: Presses Universitaires de France.

Finzi, R. 1982. The theory of historical stages in Turgot and Quesnay. *Kenzei, Kenkyu* 33(2), April, 109–18.

Groenewegen, P.D. 1969. Turgot and Adam Smith. *Scottish Journal of Political Economy* 16(3), November, 271–87.

Groenewegen, P.D. 1971. A re-interpretation of Turgot's theory of capital and interest. *Economic Journal* 81(2), June, 327–40.

Groenewegen, P.D. 1977. *The Economics of A.R.J. Turgot*. The Hague: Martinus Nijhoff.

Groenewegen, P.D. 1982. Turgot: forerunner of neo-classical economics? *Kenzei, Kenkyu* 33(2), April, 119–33.

Groenewegen, P.D. 1983a. Turgot, Beccaria and Smith. In *Italian Economics, Past and Present*, ed. P. Groenewegen and J. Halevi, Sydney: Frederick May Foundation.

Groenewegen, P.D. 1983b. Turgot's place in the history of economic thought: a bi-centenary estimate. *History of Political Economy* 15(4), 585–616.

Hausset, Mme de. (n.d.) *Secret Memoirs of the Court of Louis XV and XVI, taken from the Memoir of Madame of Hausset, Lady's maid to Madame de Pompadour and from the Journal of the Princess Lamballe*. London: Grolier Society.

Meek, R.L. (ed.) 1973. *Turgot on Progress, Sociology and Economics*. Cambridge: Cambridge University Press.

Meek, R.L. 1977. Smith, Turgot and the four stages theory. In R.L. Meek, *Smith, Marx and After*, London: Chapman & Hall, 18–32.

Morley, J. 1886. Turgot. In *Critical Miscellanies*. Vol. 2, London: Macmillan.

Nogaro, B. 1944. *Le développement de la pensée économique*. Paris: Pichon and Durand-Auzias.

Ravix, J.T. and Romano, P.M. 1984. Argent, 'Capital' et reproduction chex Turgot. In R. Arena et al., *Production, circulation et monnaie*, Paris: Presses Universitaires de France.

Schelle, G. 1913–23. *Oeuvres de Turgot et documents le concernant*. Paris: Félix Alcan.

Schumpeter, J.A. 1954. *History of Economic Analysis*. New York: Oxford University Press; London: Allen & Unwin.

Tsuda, T. 1974. *Catalogue des livres de la bibliothèque de Turgot*. Tokyo: Hitotsubashi University.

turnpike theory. The classical economists discussed the eventual convergence of the economy to a stationary state as a consequence of the growth of population and the accumulation of capital, in the absence of continual technical progress or continual expansion of natural resources (Mill, 1848, Book IV, ch. V). In their theories they proposed a natural level of real wages equal to subsistence wages and a natural rate of profit just sufficient to prevent decumulation of capital. With a given amount of land and given methods of production, wages and profits would tend to these levels. Both the classical and the neoclassical economists also described a progressive state of the economy where capital accumulates faster than population grows and where technical improvements occur. Cassel (1918, ch. 1, section 6) explicitly considers a 'uniformly progressing state' in which resources and population grow at the same constant rate. However, there is no suggestion that competitive equilibrium converges to such a state.

Ramsey (1928) introduced another type of convergence result in which population, natural resources, and technology are constant but capital is accumulated in an optimal way, that is, in a way to maximize in some sense the sum of utility from consumption over the future. In an aggregative model with one good he describes an optimal path for the capital stock that converges over time to the stock providing the maximum sustainable utility.

A second development in capital theory occurred a few years later and provided the second component of the eventual asymptotic theory for optimal paths. A disaggregated model of capital accumulation was described by von Neumann (1937). In this model there were many alternative production processes with many capital goods as inputs and as outputs. However, labour inputs and consumption did not appear explicitly. In effect, labour was treated as an intermediate product produced by given consumption processes, which were integrated into the processes presented in the model. These processes had stocks of goods as their only inputs and outputs, so all flows of services and intermediate products were suppressed through integration with other processes. Also there were no scarce non-producible goods (natural resources). In this model with a finite number of goods and processes von Neumann proved that there exists a kind of competitive equilibrium in which the maximal rate of uniform expansion of capital stocks is achieved. He proved that this equilibrium is supported by prices in the sense that activities in use earn zero profits and other activities earn zero or negative profits. Also the interest rate implicit in the price system is equal to the maximum rate of expansion.

A TURNPIKE IN THE VON NEUMANN MODEL. The von Neumann model may be defined by an input matrix $A = [a_{ij}]$ and an output matrix $B = [b_{ij}]$. The term $a_{ij} \geqslant 0$ represents the input of the ith good needed at a unit level of the jth activity, and $b_{ij} \geqslant 0$ represents the output of the ith good achieved at a unit level of the jth activity. There are n goods and m activities so A and B are $n \times m$. Inputs occur at the start of a production period, which is uniform for all activities, and outputs appear at the end of the period. Goods at different levels of depreciation are treated as different goods but the number of goods may be as large as needed to achieve an adequate approximation to reality.

An equilibrium of the von Neumann model is defined by a price vector $p \geqslant 0$, a vector of activity levels $x \geqslant 0$, and a rate of expansion $\alpha > 0$ which satisfy the relations (1) $Bx \geqslant \alpha Ax$, (2) $pB \leqslant \alpha pA$, and (3) $pBx > 0$. Relation (1) provides that output is adequate to supply next period's input requirements. Relation (2) implies that no activity is profitable. Relation (3) implies that some good that is produced has a positive price. Since the relations are homogeneous in x and p, x and p may be chosen to satisfy $\Sigma_1^m x_j = 1$ and $\Sigma_1^n p_i = 1$. If (1) is multiplied on the left by p and (2) on the right by x, we find that $pBx = \alpha pAx > 0$. Therefore, some activities are used and they earn zero profits.

Assume the conditions (1) $a_{ij} > 0$ for some i and any j, (2) $b_{ij} > 0$ for some j for any i and (3) if α' is the maximum value of α such that $Bx \geqslant \alpha Ax$ holds for some $x \geqslant 0$, $\neq 0$, then $Bx > 0$ (irreducibility). With these conditions (essentially) von Neumann proved that the model has a unique equilibrium, after normalizing x and p, and that the equilibrium value of α is the maximal rate of proportional expansion.

The turnpike name was applied to an asymptotic result for the von Neumann model by Dorfman, Samuelson and Solow (Dosso) (1958). They consider paths of accumulation starting from given initial stocks which maximize the size of terminal stocks at the end of the period of accumulation where the proportions of goods in the terminal stocks is specified in advance. They show that for sufficiently long paths which are maximal in this sense the configuration of stocks will be within an arbitrary neighbourhood of the von Neumann equilibrium for all but an arbitrary fraction of the time. This theorem gives the von Neumann equilibrium, which is called 'the turnpike', a general significance for efficient accumulation. An efficient path may be supported by prices just as the equilibrium path is. The turnpike theorem was conjectured by Samuelson (1966) in an unpublished Rand research memorandum as early as 1949. The Dosso theorem is a local result which was proved (not quite completely) for a two sector model. It was extended in a rigorous way to an n sector model by McKenzie (1963).

A global turnpike theorem was proved for a von Neumann model with many capital goods by Radner (1961), who also introduced the 'value loss' method of proof. This method of proof has been very productive of other turnpike results in subsequent years. Radner's model also allows an infinity of processes and joint production. The equilibrium theorem was extended to this context by Gale (1956). We will consider Radner's theorem in the model with a finite list of processes. Make a further assumption, (4) if (x, p, α) is a von Neumann equilibrium and $x^1 \neq 0$ is any other vector of activity levels, $p(B - \alpha A)x^1 < 0$. With this assumption Radner proved a 'value loss' lemma which may be stated in this way, for any $\epsilon > 0$ there is $\delta < 1$ such that $pBx^1 \leqslant \delta(\alpha pAx^1)$, if x^1 is any vector of activity levels, and $|x^1/|x^1| - x/|x\|| > \epsilon$. With this lemma it is easy to prove a turnpike theorem.

Let a sequence of capital stock vectors, $(y_0, y_1, \ldots, y_T)$ be a path if there is a corresponding sequence of activity vectors $(x_1, x_2, \ldots, x_T)$ such that $y_t = Ax_{t+1}$ for $t = 0, \ldots, T-1$, and $y_t \leqslant Bx_t$ for $t = 1, \ldots, T$. Assume that the vector y_0 of initial stocks satisfies $y_0 > 0$. Then by disposal $y < y_0$ may be chosen so that $y = Ax$ and (x, p, α) is a von Neumann equilibrium. Then $(y, \alpha y, \ldots, \alpha^T y)$ is a feasible path (the comparison path). Suppose $(y_0, y_1, \ldots, y_T)$ is a maximal path. Then the value loss lemma implies that for any $\epsilon > 0$ there is $\delta < 1$ such that $\delta \alpha p y_t \geqslant p y_{t+1}$ when $|x_t/|x_t| - x/|x\|| > \epsilon$. But the equilibrium conditions imply $\alpha p y_t \geqslant p y_{t+1}$. Thus if $x_t/|x_t|$ is outside the ϵ-neighbourhood of $x/|x|$ for τ periods then for $T > \tau$ it will be true that

$$\delta^\tau \alpha^T p y_0 \geqslant p y_T. \tag{1}$$

Let the desired configuration of terminal stocks be given by the vector $\bar{y}$. Define a utility function on terminal stocks by $\rho(z) = \min z(i)/\bar{y}(i)$ over $i = 1, \ldots, n$. Then $(y_0, \ldots, y_T)$ maximal implies

$$\rho(y_T) \geqslant \rho(\alpha^T y) = \alpha^T \rho(y). \tag{2}$$

Since $y > 0$, $\rho(y) > 0$. Now choose the length of the equilibrium price vector p so that $p(i) \geqslant 1/\bar{y}(i)$ for some i with $p(i) > 0$. This implies that

$$pz \geqslant z(i)/\bar{y}(i) \geqslant \rho(z). \tag{3}$$

Combining (1), (2), and (3), gives the sequence of inequalities

$$\alpha^T \rho(y) \leqslant \rho(y_T) \leqslant p y_T \leqslant \delta^\tau \alpha^T p y_0 \tag{4}$$

The first and last terms of (4) imply that δ^τ cannot exceed $\rho(y)/py_0$, which is a well defined positive number. Thus (4) implies that an integer $\bar{\tau}$ exists such that $x_t/|x_t|$ cannot lie outside the ϵ-neighbourhood of $x/|x|$ for more than $\bar{\tau}$ periods regardless of the length T of the accumulation path. Since y and y_t are linear transforms of x and x_{t+1}, an analogous statement holds for y and y_t. This is a stronger form of the conclusion of the original Dosso theorem.

A TURNPIKE IN THE RAMSEY MODEL. Ramsey's aggregative model of capital accumulation was extended to a model with a growing population by Koopmans (1965). Koopmans defines optimality as the maximization of a sum of per capita utilities. When utility is not discounted, he proves that the optimal path converges monotonically to the stock that provides maximum sustainable per capita utility. However, he is also able to treat the case of discounted utility, a case which was not analysed in a satisfactory way by Ramsey. The optimal path of stocks in the discounted case is shown to converge monotonically to the stock for which the marginal product of capital is equal to the sum of the rate of population growth and the rate of discount on utility. The generalization of this result to the many goods case proved very difficult and was only achieved much later by Scheinkman (1976) and Cass and Shell (1976). Also Cass (1966) proved a turnpike theorem for this discounted model with a per capita objective in the sense of Dosso where the accumulation period is finite and a terminal stock is specified. This was proved in an aggregative model.

The spirit of the original turnpike theorem is not well preserved in the aggregative model since the emphasis in the original theorem lies on the relative composition of the capital stock. Samuelson and Solow (1956) generalized the original Ramsey analysis to many goods in a model based on a strictly concave social production function. However, the first rigorous proof of a turnpike result in a Ramsey setting with growing population and more than one capital good was given by Atsumi (1965) in a neoclassical model with two goods, the Dosso model with a Ramsey style objective stated in terms of utility sums. On analogy with the theorem of von Neumann, Atsumi established the existence of a unique maximal balanced growth path along which capital stocks expand at the rate of population growth. The path is maximal in the sense that per capita consumption is maximized over the set of balanced growth paths expanding at the rate of population growth. However, the path is also the only such balanced growth path that is efficient. It is price supported like the von Neumann path, except that consumption goods are now teated as net output rather than as intermediate product. The rate of interest is equal to the growth rate as in von Neumann's case. If the growth rate of population is zero the balanced growth path represents capital saturation, or Ramsey's bliss.

In order to prove the turnpike theorem Atsumi proved a value loss lemma analogous to Radner's lemma for the von Neumann model. He also gave a new definition of an optimal path, that a path is optimal if its utility sums over sufficiently longer initial periods exceed the utility sums of any given alternative path over the same periods. This criterion, in variant forms, is called the overtaking criterion. It was proposed in the same journal issue in a slightly different form, allowing 'eventually equalling' as well as 'exceeding', by Weiszäcker (1965), who used it to discuss the existence of optimal paths. Atsumi proves that infinite optimal paths converge to the maximal balanced growth path. He also proves a theorem for finite optimal paths with assigned terminal stocks analogous to the Dosso theorem.

Turnpike theorems for the general multisector model with a Ramsey objective and a von Neumann technology were first proved by Gale (1967) and McKenzie (1968). Their order of proof does not differ from that of Atsumi, which is, in turn, parallel to the proof used by Radner in the model with maximal growth as an objective. It is simplest to stay close to to the von Neumann model. Let Y represent a reduced model for the activity of one period where $(u, y, -x)$ is a typical element of Y. In the typical element, u is a real number giving a per capita utility level for the period, $y \geqslant 0$ is a vector of terminal stocks, and $x \geqslant 0$ is a vector of initial stocks. There are n goods. Since Y is independent of time and of past activities, this model does not allow depletable natural resources or technical progress. Assume

I. Y is a closed convex subset of $2n+1$ dimensional Euclidean space. Also $(u, y, -x) \in Y$ implies that $(u', y', -x') \in Y$ when $u' \leqslant u$, $0 \leqslant y' < y$, and $x' \geqslant x$, that is, there is free disposal.

II. There is $\bar{x}$ such that $(u, y, -\bar{x}) \in Y$ and $y > \bar{x}$, that is, $\bar{x}$ is expansible.

III. (a) For any ξ, there is η such that $|x| \leqslant \xi$ and $(u, y, -x) \in Y$ implies $u < \eta$ and $|y| < \eta$. (The output from bounded input is bounded.) (b) There is ζ, and $\gamma < 1$, such that $(u, y, -x) \in Y$ and $|x| \geqslant \zeta$ implies $|y| < \gamma |x|$. (All paths are bounded.)

IV. If $(u^*, k^*, -k^*) \in Y$ and $u^* \geqslant u$ for any $(u, x, -x) \in Y$, then k^* is expansible.

A path in this model is a sequence $(u_t, k_t, -k_{t-1})$, $t = 1, \ldots, T$, with T finite or infinite and $(u_t, k_t, -k_{t-1}) \in Y$ for each t. The existence of k^* which defines a path of maximal utility at balanced growth is guaranteed by assumptions I, II, and III. It may be proved that a price vector $p^* \geqslant 0$ exists which satisfies the support property.

$$u + p^*(y - x) \leqslant u^* + p^*(k^* - k^*) = u^*, \quad \text{for any } (u, y, -x) \in Y. \quad (5)$$

Define the von Neumann facet F of the technology set Y as all $(u, y, -x) \in Y$ such that $u + p^*(y - x) = u^*$. This means there will be no value loss when the path of accumulation lies on F. However, when the path is off F, a value loss lemma due to Atsumi (1965) applies and for any $\epsilon > 0$ there is $\delta > 0$ such that if $(u, y, -x)$ lies outside the ϵ-neighbourhood of F it follows that

$$u + p^*(y - x) \leqslant u^* - \delta. \quad (6)$$

As before a comparison path is found, but no longer simply by disposal to an equilibrium. A lemma due to Gale (1967) implies that a path exists from any expansible stock to any other expansible stock. Thus k_0 expansible and k^* expansible (Assumption IV) implies that a path exists from k_0 to $k_s = k^*$ for some integer s. Then $k_t = k^*$ may be maintained indefinitely for $t > s$.

With this preparation the proof of the turnpike theorem as given by McKenzie (1968) is straightforward. Let u_1 be the utility sum along the approach to k^* from k_0 along the comparison path and let $(u_t, k_t, -k_{t-1})$, $t = 1, 2, \ldots$, be an optimal path by the overtaking criterion. Suppose the optimal path lies outside the ϵ-neighbourhood of F for τ periods. Let $\bar{t}$ be the period in which the optimal path overtakes the comparison path and let $T > \bar{t}$ be chosen arbitrarily. Consider the inequalities

$$(T - s)u^* + u_1 \leqslant \sum_1^T u_t \leqslant Tu^* - \sum_1^T p^*(k_t - k_{t-1}) - \tau\delta$$
$$= Tu^* - p^*(k_T - k_0) - \tau\delta. \quad (7)$$

The first inequality is justified by $T > \bar{t}$ and optimality. The second inequality follows from (5) and (6). However, (7) implies that $\tau \leqslant (su^* - u_1)/p^*(k_T - k_0)$, which is a constant. Since ϵ is arbitrary, it is clear that an optimal path converges to F. Indeed, as one might suspect from (7), paths that are any good converge to F, since paths that do not converge become indefinitely worse than the comparison path. Also there is no difficulty in proving the analogue of the Dosso type of theorem for finite paths when terminal stocks are specified.

In order to prove that optimal paths converge to a maximal balanced path or, in per capita terms, a maximal stationary path, the assumptions must be strengthened. The most general assumption is that the von Neumann facet F is stable, in the sense that all paths that remain on the facet forever converge uniformly to a maximal stationary path. The assumption in this general form was proposed by Inada (1964) for the von Neumann model. Then it may be proved that a path which converges to a stable facet must also converge to the stable point on the facet (see McKenzie, 1968). The simplest case arises when $F = \{(u^*, k^*, -k^*)\}$. This is analogous to the case analysed by Radner for the von Neumann model. It is implied if it is assumed that the technology set Y is strictly convex. However, it should be noted that strict convexity of Y is not consistent wtih neoclassical models of production when goods are produced by independent industries, even though consumer utilities are strictly concave functions of consumption. Indeed, as Bewley (1982) has pointed out, it is not consistent with the use of machines in production since an input of m machines leads to an output of m older machines at the end of the period. The behaviour of paths on F may be studied by means of difference equations which are defined in terms of points $(u^j, y^j, -x^j) \in F$ that span F. In the analogous problem for the von Neumann case this was done explicitly for the generalized Leontief model by McKenzie (1963). However, the time that can be spent outside an ϵ-neighbourhood of the turnpike by an optimal path is no longer a given number of periods but a given fraction of the total time of accumulation. Even though the facet is not stable, it was proved by Brock (1970) that if the maximal stationary path is unique the average capital stock of an optimal path over time converges to the capital stock of the maximal stationary path.

RAMSEY MODELS WITH DISCOUNTING. Turnpike theorems for Ramsey models with von Neumann technologies and positive discounting of utility are much harder to prove. The difficulty is that discounting utility implies discounting value losses, so value loss is bounded and need not exceed the loss from going over to a comparison path. The first theorems were due to Scheinkman (1976) and Cass and Shell (1976). These were global results proved for models defined by differentiable functions. Also the theorems are proved for discount factors sufficiently close to 1. Scheinkman showed for discount factors close to 1 and with Y strictly convex that the optimal path would visit a small neighbourhood of the maximal stationary path at least once. Then he showed that if this neighbourhood were small enough the path would not leave it but would in fact converge to the maximal stationary path.

The reduced model that is frequently used for the multisector Ramsey case with discounting expresses per capita utility over a period by a function $u(x, y)$ where x is the vector of initial stocks per capita and y is the vector of terminal stocks per capita. The function expresses the maximum utility achievable during the period given these end conditions. It is assumed that utility in one period is independent of events that occur in other periods except as they influence the initial or terminal stocks of that period. The technology set Y described for the model without discounting corresponds to the epigraph of the function u. The function u is defined on a convex set D contained in the positive orthant of a Euclidean space of dimension $2n$, the Cartesian product of the space of initial stocks and the space of terminal stocks. Let the discount factor be $\rho < 1$. The assumptions are

I′. The utility function $u(x, y)$ is concave and upper semi-continuous. If $(x, y) \in D$, then $(z, w) \in D$ for all $z \geqslant x$ and all w such that $0 \leqslant w \leqslant y$. Also $u(z, w) \geqslant u(x, y)$ holds (free disposal).

II′. There is $\bar{x}$ such that $(\bar{x}, y) \in D$ and $\rho y > \bar{x}$, that is $\bar{x}$ is ρ-expansible.

III′. (a) For any ξ, there is η such that $|x| \leqslant \xi$ and $(x, y) \in D$ implies $|y| < \eta$. (b) There is ζ and $\gamma < 1$, such that $(x, y) \in D$ and $|x| \geqslant \xi$ implies $|y| < \gamma |x|$.

These assumptions are closely parallel to the assumptions of the undiscounted Ramsey model except that the expansibility assumption is strengthened. It is easily seen that any neoclassical model with utility defined on consumption and labour services and a production function that converts inputs of labour services, initial stocks of capital, and natural resource flows into outputs of capital goods and consumption goods corresponds uniquely to a reduced model. The utility function of the reduced model is derived by maximizing the utility of consumption and labour services given the initial and terminal stocks of capital goods. Upper semi-continuity of utility carries over from the neoclassical model to the reduced model.

A path is a sequence $\{k_t\}$, $t = 1, 2, \ldots$, such that $(k_{t-1}, k_t) \in D$ for all t. A path $\{k_t\}$ is optimal if $\Sigma_1^\infty \rho^t u(k_{t-1}, k_t) \geqslant \Sigma_1^\infty \rho^t u(k'_{t-1}, k'_t)$ holds for every path $\{k'_t\}$. On Assumptions I′, II′, and III′ it may be proved that a stationary path with $k_t = k$, all t, exists which is price supported in the sense that there exists a vector $q \geqslant 0$ such that

$$u(z, w) + qw - \rho^{-1}qz \leqslant u(k, k) + qk - \rho^{-1}qk \quad \text{for all } (z, w) \in D. \qquad (8)$$

We may use the relation (8) to prove that $k_t = k$ defines an optimal path from k. Let k'_t be any path from k with $k'_0 = k$. Then summing the relations (8) over the path gives for any $T \geqslant 1$,

$$\sum_1^T [\rho^t u(k'_{t-1}, k'_t) - u(k, k)] = \rho^T q(k - k'_T) - \sum_1^T \delta_t. \qquad (9)$$

where $\delta_t \geqslant 0$. Since k'_T is non-negative and bounded, and $\rho^T \to 0$ as $T \to \infty$, in the limit the right-hand side of (9) is less than or equal to 0 which establishes the optimality of $\{k_t\}$.

In the discounted model it is also useful to have prices to support any optimal path. Let $V(x) = \sup \Sigma_1^\infty \rho^t u(k_{t-1}, k_t)$ over all paths $\{k_t\}$, $t = 0, 1, \ldots$, with $k_0 = x$. Put $V(x) = -\infty$ if no path from x exists. Define a sufficient stock as a stock from which there exists a path that reaches an expansible stock in finite time. It has been proved by McKenzie (1974), extending a result of Weitzman (1973), that a price sequence $\{q_t\}$ exists for any optimal path $\{k_t\}$ that starts from a sufficient stock k_0. This price sequence satisfies

$$u(k_t, k_{t+1}) + q_{t+1}k_{t+1} - \rho^{-1}q_t k_t \geqslant u(x, y) + q_{t+1}y - \rho^{-1}q_t x, \quad \text{for all } (x, y) \in D, \qquad (10)$$

and

$$V(k_{t+1}) - q_{t+1}k_{t+1} \geqslant V(y) - q_{t+1}y, \quad \text{for all } y \text{ such that } V(y) > -\infty, \quad \text{for } t > \tau, \qquad (11)$$

where τ is independent of ρ.

Using the prices q_t as well as the prices $q(\rho)$ that support a stationary optimal path $k(\rho)$ allows the definition of a symmetric value loss function $L(t) = [q_t(\rho) - q(\rho)(k_t(\rho) - k(\rho)]$ which can play a crucial role in proving turnpike theorems for this model. It should be kept in mind that $L(t)$ depends on ρ and on the particular $k(\rho)$ as well.

If one writes (10) with $(x, y) = [k(\rho), k(\rho)]$ and then writes (10) again with the roles of k_t and $k(\rho)$ reversed, with the support prices of $k(\rho)$, that is, $[q(\rho), q(\rho)]$ in place of (q_t, q_{t+1}), subtracting the second version of (10) from the first gives the result

$$L(t+1) - \rho^{-1}L(t) \geqslant 0. \tag{12}$$

Doing the same operation with (11) gives

$$L(t) \leqslant 0. \tag{13}$$

Then using $L(t)$ in a similar manner to the asymmetric value loss for the undiscounted model a turpike result may be proved for paths which start from a sufficient stock.

Define a von Neumann facet $F[k(\rho)]$ for this model as the set of all $(x, y) \in D$ such that $u(x, y) + q(\rho)y - \rho^{-1}q(\rho)x = u[k(\rho), k(\rho)] + (1 - \rho^{-1})q(\rho)k(\rho)$. This is the projection of a flat in the graph of the function $u(x, y)$ on the commodity space. There is a von Neumann facet for every non-trivial stationary optimal path, that is, for every stationary optimal path $k(\rho)$ which satisfies the condition that $u[k(\rho), k(\rho)]$ is maximal over the set of (x, y) such that $\rho y - x \geqslant (\rho - 1)k$. If $\rho = 1$, this set is the same as that over which $u(k, k)$ is maximal. Say that a point $(x, y) \in D$ is supported by the prices (p, q) if $u(x, y) + qy - \rho^{-1}px \geqslant u(z, w) + qw - \rho^{-1}pz$ for any $(z, w) \in D$.

Two additional assumptions are made. Let $\bar{\rho}$ be a value of ρ for which D satisfies assumption II′. Assume

IV′. If (p, q) are support prices for some point of the von Neumann facet $F[k(\rho)]$ where $\bar{\rho} \leqslant \rho \leqslant 1$, then $(p, q) = [q(\rho), q(\rho)]$.

In other words, the von Neumann facet has a unique support. Assumption IV′ implies that $L(t)$ is zero on $F[k(\rho)]$ and that $L(t)$ is close to zero in a small neighbourhood of $F[k(\rho)]$. This assumption is needed since $k_t(\rho)$ need not be near $k(\rho)$ even though $[k_t(\rho), k_{t+1}(\rho)]$ is near $F[k(\rho)]$.

The second assumption is needed to obtain a uniform value loss condition which is analogous to (6) in the undiscounted model for all $F(k(\rho))$, $\bar{\rho} \leqslant \rho < 1$. Let $\delta(k(\rho), (x, y))$ be the deficiency of the right-hand side of (10) when $k_t = k_{t+1} = k(\rho)$ and $q_t = q_{t+1} = q(\rho)$. Assume

V′. For any $\epsilon > 0$ there is $\delta > 0$ such that $|x| < \xi$ and (x, y) outside the ϵ-neighbourhood of $F[k(\rho)]$ implies that $\delta[k(\rho), (x, y)] > \delta$ for any ρ with $\bar{\rho} \leqslant \rho < 1$ and any choice of $k(\rho)$.

Rewrite (12) in the form

$$L(t+1) - L(t) \geqslant (\rho^{-1} - 1)L(t) + \delta. \tag{14}$$

As a consequence of V' the value loss δ may be chosen uniformly over ρ and $k(\rho)$. Then ρ may be chosen so that $(\rho^{-1} - 1)L(0) \geqslant -\delta/2$, uniformly. Moreover, this condition continues to hold for $t \geqslant 0$ which implies that $L(t)$ grows by an indefinite amount unless the path enters the ϵ-neighbourhood of $F(k(\rho))$. This it must do or violate (13). Then using Assumption IV′ the existence may be established of an ϵ'-neighbourhood to which the path is subsequently confined. Also the ϵ'-neighbourhood can be made arbitrarily small by the choice of ϵ. For the details of this argument see McKenzie (1983). It is not implied that the $k(\rho)$ are unique or that cyclic paths, or even chaotic paths, are absent. However, these paths must eventually lie in the ϵ'-neighbourhood. The larger is the neighbourhood chosen, the smaller the discount factor that may be allowed. It is implied that all $k(\rho)$ for a given ρ lie in the ϵ'-neighbourhood of any one of the $F(k(\rho))$. An example using the discounted utility function $\rho^t u(x, y) = \rho^t x^{\beta}(1 - y)^{1-\beta}$, $0 < \rho \leqslant 1$, $0 < \beta < 1$, is described in McKenzie (1983).

As in the undiscounted model it is possible to go beyond facet stability on further assumptions. Most simply if strict concavity of $u(x, y)$ is assumed the von Neumann facets are trivial since $F[k(\rho)] = \{k(\rho)\}$. Then a neighbourhood theorem is implied for the nontrivial optimal stationary paths, each of which must lie within ϵ of any other. Indeed, it may be shown for differentiable $u(x, y)$ that the optimal stationary path is unique for ρ near enough to 1 (Brock, 1973). Indeed, Boldrin and Montrucchio (1986b) have a simple condition on ρ in terms of the concavity of u which implies uniqueness. Even without strict concavity convergence to a neighbourhood of $k(\rho)$ may be proved if it is assumed that $k(1) = k^*$ is unique (in any case the set of maximal stationary paths is convex) and that the von Neumann facet $F(k^*) = F$ is stable in the sense that all paths in F converge uniformly to (k^*, k^*).

Suppose $u(x,y)$ is strictly concave and twice continuously differentiable. Also assume that the Hessian matrix of u is negative definite at (k^*,k^*). Then ρ may be chosen close enough to 1 so that the matrix

$$Q(\rho) = \begin{bmatrix} \rho u_{xx} & \rho u_{xy} \\ u_{yx} & u_{yy} \end{bmatrix}$$

evaluated at $(k(\rho), k(\rho))$ is negative definite. Here $u_{xy} = \partial^2 u(x, y)/\partial x \partial y$, and analogously for the other blocks for $Q(\rho)$. If k_0 is sufficient, the neighbourhood turnpike theorem implies that the path is eventually confined to a neighbourhood where $Q(\rho)$ is negative definite when ρ is chosen sufficiently near 1. If this neighbourhood is small enough it may be shown that $L(t+1) - L(t)$ is positive and $L(t) \leqslant 0$ will be violated unless $k(t)$ converges to k^*(McKenzie, 1985). The condition $Q(\rho)$ negative definite assumed over the interior of D was proposed by Brock and Scheinkman (1978) and used to prove a global turnpike theorem.

An asymptotic result is also available when the von Neumann facets have positive dimension. The conditions needed are $Q(\rho)$ negative definite at (k^*, k^*) in directions leading immediately off the facet F, the absence of cyclic paths on F, and the condition that the stable manifold at (k^*, k^*) have a tangent plane whose projection on the input space covers a neighbourhood of k^*. The implications of these conditions for the neoclassical model without joint production have been studied by Takahashi (1985).

The turnpike theorems for the multisector Ramsey model thus far described depend on discount factors near 1. There are some theorems, however, which are free of this condition. Suppose $u(x, y)$ is twice continuously differentiable in the interior of D and strictly concave. Under Assumptions I′–V′ a necessary and sufficient condition for the optimality of a path $\{k_t\}$ which is bounded away from the boundary of D is

$$u_2(k_{t-1}, k_t) + \rho u_1(k_t, k_{t+1}) = 0, \tag{15}$$

for $t = 1, 2, \ldots,$ Araujo and Scheinkman (1977) consider the Jacobian of the infinite sequence of equations given by (15). They define a notion of dominant diagonal blocks for the Jacobian and show that this, together with local asymptotic stability, implies that k_t converges to $k(\rho)$. However, the assumption of local stability has been shown to be unnecessary (McKenzie, 1977). The dominant diagonal block condition is independent of ρ.

An interesting special case arises where $u_{12}[k(\rho), k(\rho)]$ is nonsingular and symmetric and the linearization of (15) at $k_{t-1} = k_t = k_{t+1} = k(\rho)$ does not have roots of unit modulus. Then the dominant diagnoal block condition for the optimal stationary path $k_t = k(\rho)$ is necessary and sufficient for local stability (Dasgupta and McKenzie, 1985). However, the dominant diagonal block condition is sufficient for global stability, so in this case it is necessary and sufficient for global stability.

Another approach ot turnpike theory which is independent of ρ has been found by Boldrin and Montrucchio (1986a). Assume that $u(x, y)$ is concave and strictly concave in y. Define the binary relation P by yPx if and only if $u(x, x) + \rho V(x) < u(x, y) + \rho V(y)$, where V is the value function. Let the projection of D on the space of initial stocks be a compact set X. P is said to be acyclic if there is no sequence $(x_1, \ldots, x_n)$ such that $x_{i+1} P x_i$ for $i = 1, \ldots, n$, when x_{n+1} is set equal to x_1. Define the policy function $f(x)$ equal to the maximizer of $u(x, y) + \rho V(y)$ over y. Then $f(x)Px$ holds whenever $f(x) \neq x$. Any optimal path is generated by repeated applications of f. Suppose the optimal stationary path $k_t = k(\rho)$ is unique. Then if P is acyclic, all optimal paths converge to $k(\rho)$. But it may be seen that P is acyclic if and only if $\Sigma_1^n u(x_t, x_t) \geqslant \Sigma_1^n u(x_t, x_{t+1})$, for every path $(x_1, \ldots, x_n)$ and $x_{n+1} = x_1$. This condition holds, for example, if $u(x, y) = \phi(x) + \psi(y - x)$, which has been referred to as the separable case. This case occurs in some models of investment by the firm in which u is a profit function (see Treadway, 1971).

TURNPIKE THEOREMS FOR COMPETITIVE EQUILIBRIA. In recent years the circle has been completed and turnpike theorems have led to asymptotic results for the theory of competitive equilibrium. These results bear some analogy to the convergence to a stationary state described by the classical economists. However, the modern results are based on capital accumulation in the absence of a population dynamics. There is also an analogy to the Dosso theorems on efficient capital accumulation in the von Neumann model, but now it is utility maximization rather than efficient capital accumulation that defines the path.

The equilibrium model with many households was described briefly by Ramsey but the first serious analysis of the model was given by Becker (1980), who verified Ramsey's conjecture that the long-run equilibrium would place all capital in the hands of the most thrifty households. Subsequently Bewley (1982) applied the turnpike results of optimal growth theory to prove that the competitive equilibrium path with infinitely lived households, who hold identical discounts on future utility from consumption, will converge to a stationary equilibrium. He made use of the duality of competitive equilibrium and a social optimum which was described by Negishi (1960).

Bewley presents an equilibrium model in which production over the infinite horizon is decentralized to a finite number of firms that possess in each period strictly concave production functions which are twice continuously differentiable. Similarly the consumers, who are finite in number, have strictly monotone, strictly concave, and twice continuously differentiable utility functions in each period. Zero production is possible and primary inputs are necessary for production. Each firm maximizes its profit over the future at present prices. Each consumer maximizes his discounted utility sums from consumption over the future subject to a budget constraint derived from the value of his endowment of primary goods (assumed the same in each period) and his share of firms' profits, all calculated at present prices. To guarantee income each consumer is assumed to have a positive endowment of some primary good which is also a consumption good. It is feasible to produce a positive amount of all goods in all periods. Finally it is assumed that in any stationary equilibrium (with transfer payments) every firm has positive initial stocks of all produced goods. Transfer payments must be allowed in the stationary equilibrium since the consumer's budget is balanced only over the infinite horizon, so that asymptotically he may be (in effect) a debtor or a creditor and (in effect) pay or receive interest.

An equalibrium is a feasible allocation $\{x_h(t), y_f(t)\}$, $t = 1, 2, \ldots$, where h indexes consumers and f indexes firms, together with a price vector $p(t)$ such that $\Sigma_0^\infty p(t) < \infty$, and where each consumer maximizes utility and each firm maximizes profit. In a stationary equilibrium the budget constraint for consumers is written $px(t) \leqslant px_h(t)$ to take account of the transfer payments which may occur. It is proved that if all consumers have the same discount factor and this discount factor is sufficiently close to 1, then the allocation of the competitive equilibrium converges exponentially to the allocation of a stationary equilibrium with transfers $(\bar{x}_h(t), \bar{y}_f(t), \bar{p}(t))$.

The proof that the equilibrium converges to a stationary state is given by identifying the competitive equilibrium with the maximization of a weighted sum of consumers' utilities which is given by $V(K) = \sup \Sigma_{t=0}^{\infty} \rho^t \Sigma_h \Lambda_h^{-1} U_h(x_h(t))$. The weights Λ_h^{-1} are the inverses of the marginal utilities of expenditure, and ρ is the discount factor on future utility, K is the vector of initial stocks of capital (produced goods), V is a maximum of the weighted utility sum over all consumption streams consistent with the initial stocks K, the endowments, and the production functions of the firms. Bewley shows that $V(K(t))$ may be used as a Lyapounov function to establish that $K(t)$ converges to $\bar{K}$ which is the vector of stocks of a stationary optimal path for the optimal growth problem and of a stationary competitive equilibrium with transfers that corresponds to it. The proof depends on the consumers' utility functions being concave, not just quasi-concave. Bewley's theorem differs from the other asymptotic theorems we have considered in that the stationary state depends on the initial stocks since they affect the weights Λ_h^{-1}, that is, the relative wealth of consumers.

Other theorems analogous to Bewley's have been proved by Yano (1984a, 1985). Yano describes a model with a production sector given by a cone with a cross-section which is strictly convex in the neighbourhood of the path achieving maximum sustainable utility. This is analogous to the model used by Radner for the Dosso problem. As a consequence the production sector does not have a multiplicity of firms with distinct technologies since this would lead to flats in the production cone. However, his consumers are allowed to have different tastes and endowments. He dispenses with differentiability and proves a neighbourhood turnpike theorem similar to McKenzie's but applying to a competitive equilibrium path. The turnpike depends on consumer endowments and initial stocks as in Bewley's analysis.

Yano also shows (1984b) that the turnpikes in the discounted model can be brought within an ϵ-neighbourhood of a stationary competitive equilibrium without discounting for arbitrary $\epsilon > 0$ for an appropriate choice of ρ and a given initial distribution of capital. In this sense the equilibrium turnpike has an invariance to initial stocks typical of the turnpikes of optimal growth theory. The explanation is that as ρ converges to 1, the importance of initial stocks compared with future endowments becomes negligible in determining the wealth of the consumer. The stationary competitive equilibrium without discounting is based upon the capital stocks that achieve capital saturation, as at Ramsey's bliss point. Thus there is no interest income and by homogeneity of production there is no profit. In other words, consumer wealth is independent of ownership shares in profits (which are zero) or in capital stocks (which have zero rental income). However, the distribution of endowments remains important, both of personal skills and of natural resources.

Some progress has been made toward handling the case of consumers whose discounts on future utility differ without leading to an asymptotic state in which all capital is in the hands of a few patient consumers. To avoid this outcome it is assumed that the discount on future utility depends on the level of utility achieved, either by the consumption of the current period or by the entire future consumption stream. Lucas and Stokey (1984) consider a model with one consumption good and many capital goods. They use a device of Koopmans (1960) to write the utility of a consumption stream ${}_1C = (C_1, C_2, \ldots)$ in terms of the first period consumption and the utility of the stream ${}_2C = (C_2, C_3, \ldots)$, that is, $U({}_1C) = W(C_1, U({}_2C))$. In the case of additively separable utility the formula appears as $U({}_1C) = U(C_1) + \rho U({}_2C)$, where $\rho \leqslant 1$ is the discount factor. This suggests that the subjective discount factor implied by W be defined by W_2, the derivative of W with respect to its second argument. Consider constant paths ${}_1C = (C, C, \ldots)$. Lucas and Stokey assume, unlike Fisher (1930), that along constant paths the discount factor W_2 is a decreasing function of C. They prove in their model that the stationary state of the perfect foresight economy is unique on this assumption. They also prove a turnpike theorem for the competitive equilibrium of a two consumer model without production.

More recently Epstein (1987), using a continuous time version of the Lucas and Stokey model has succeeded in proving a turnpike theorem for a model with many consumers whose utility functions and implied discount factors may differ. He defines the implicit rate of time preference as equal to minus the proportional rate of change of marginal utility along a locally constant path. The corresponding periodwise discount factor would be approximately $\rho = 1 - r$. Then r is a function of current consumption and the utility of future consumption. However, he assumes r to be independent of current consumption but increasing in the utility of future consumption. He is able to prove with this assumption that all Pareto optimal paths of accumulation converge to a unique stationary path. Thus by the first welfare theorem all competitive equilibria converge to a unique stationary equilibrium. However, these results depend on implicit rates of time preference sufficiently close to 0, or else own rates of return in production sufficiently close to 0. Unlike the stationary equilibria of Bewley and Yano, this equilibrium is independent of initial stocks and their distribution of ownership. All that matters finally for the wealth of consumers are their endowments, repeated each period, and their rates of time preference. Such a result is compatible with classical ideas. The methods used by Epstein in his proof are derived from the work of Brock and Scheinkman (1976) in a differentiable multi-sector Ramsey model.

It should be pointed out that the assumptions made by these writers on the function W or U imply a weak form of separability between present and future consumption. Loosely speaking the ranking of future consumption bundles is not affected by current consumption, nor *a fortiori* by past consumption. Thus intuitively what is done by their formulation is to make the rate of time preference, or the implicit discount factor, depend on present consumption and the utility of the future consumption stream.

FURTHER GENERALIZATIONS. Turnpike theorems have also been generalized to allow habit formation so that current preferences are affected by past consumption (for example, Samuelson, 1971; Heal and Ryder, 1973). It has been shown by Epstein (1986) that the turnpike theorems hold in these circumstances if and only if a form of asymptotic independence holds or that the effect of earlier consumption on current preferences fades out over time.

The theorems on the correspondence of turnpike theorems for optimal paths and for equilibrium paths have been extended in two ways. Coles (1985) proved asymptotic convergence to the von Neumann facet in a model like that of Yano where separable additive utility is assumed and the discount factors of consumers may differ. This extension allows the use of capital equipment in production without introducing interdependence between industries.

On the other hand, the Bewley theorems were extended by Marimon (1984) to a stochastic model. The preferences and technology, as well as the discount factors and endowments, are made to depend on a stationary and transitive stochastic process. The equilibrium is that of a complete Arrow–Debreu market in which consumers own given shares of the firms and all trading occurs at the initial date. Marimon proves that the equilibrium allocation converges almost surely to the allocation of a stationary equilibrium with transfer payments. This result holds when the discount factors are sufficiently close to 1, almost surely. From the viewpoint of optimal growth his results generalize those of Brock and Mirman (1972) for the one sector model, those of Evstigneev (1974) for the undiscounted multisector model, and those of Brock and Majumdar (1978) for the discounted multisector model.

Conditions have been found to guarantee the presence of cycles in models of economic growth and by the same token in models of competitive equilibrium. These results are relevant to the study of endogenous cycles in competitive economies, a study which has been pursued in overlapping generations models by Grandmont (1985). In the context of optimal growth models Benhabib and Nishimura (1985) have given sufficient conditions for robust periodic optimal paths in Ramsey models with additively separable utility and neoclassical technology. The utility function is strictly concave and there is one capital good. If $u(x,y)$ is the reduced form utility function the basic condition for oscillations on interior optimal paths in the discrete time model is that $u_{12}(x,y) < 0$ hold throughout the interior of D, the domain of definition of u. This says that larger initial stocks (an increase in wealth) cause the marginal utility of terminal stocks to be smaller (saving is discouraged). However, added conditions are needed to ensure sustained oscillations which are robust to small perturbations of the model. In particular, it is assumed there is a ρ such that $u_{22} + \rho u_{11} > (1 + \rho)u_{12}$ where the derivatives are evaluated at a nontrivial stationary optimal path.

This line of research has been further advanced by Boldrin and Montrucchio (1985). Consider a multisector Ramsey model defined by a reduced utility function $u(x, y)$. Assume that $u(x, y)$ is defined over a compact set $D \subset XxX \subset R^n_+ \times R^n_+$, where X is the projection of D on the first factor. Let $u(x, y)$ be continuous and concave, strictly concave in y, strictly increasing in x and strictly decreasing in y. Define the optimal policy function $f(x) = y$ where y is the unique vector of terminal stocks for the first period of an optimal path, when x is the vector of initial stocks. Let θ map X into X and assume that it may be extended to be twice continuously differentiable on X. Then there exists $\rho^* > 0$ such that, given any ρ with $0 < \rho \leqslant \rho^*$, θ is the policy function for some Ramsey problem satisfying the usual assumptions. Since the policy function can be chosen freely, it follows that no complex behaviour of optimal paths can be excluded, in particular chaotic paths are possible. Boldrin and Montrucchio also provide a way of calculating a possible value for ρ^* in terms of the diameter of X and bounds on the derivatives of θ.

Another direction of generalization is to models with non-convex technologies. The principal turnpike results that have been proved with non-convexity are concerned with one good Ramsey models of optimal growth in which the production function has an initial phase of increasing returns followed by a terminal phase of decreasing returns (for example, Skiba, 1978; Majumdar and Mitra, 1982; Dechert and Nishimura, 1983). Optimal paths in differentiable models with discrete time and discounted utility converge to steady states, that is, stationary paths, among which the origin is included. Nontrivial steady states are solutions of $f'(x) = \rho^{-1}$, where $f(x)$ is a differentiable production function. There cannot be more than two nontrivial steady states, k_* in the concave region and k^* in the convex region, and there may be none. Every optimal path converges to a steady state. If the discount factor ρ is near 1, optimal paths converge to k^*. If ρ is small enough, they converge to 0. For intermediate values of ρ the turnpike depends on the initial capital stock. There is a critical value k_c such that $k_0 < k_c$ implies that optimal paths converge to the origin and $k_0 > k_c$ implies that optimal paths converge to k^*. *If* $k_c = k_*$, then $k_t = k_*$, $t = 0, 1, \ldots$, is the unique optimal path from $k_0 = k_c$.

The theorems that have been reviewed are all concerned with the convergence of optimal paths to stationary optimal paths. However, the method of the proofs is to show that optimal paths converge to one another. Thus it is not really necessary that the reduced utility function be constant over time. Loosely speaking, constancy may be replaced by variation within bounds. The variation of the reduced utility function may reflect a varying production function and a varying utility function over consumption bundles. Examples of this approach are found in Keeler (1972), McKenzie (1974; 1976; 1977) Mitra (1979) and Brock and Magill (1979).

The account of turnpike theorems has concentrated on the discrete time model, which is descended from the early von Neumann growth model and the Dosso model. There is a considerable literature on the continuous time model which is related to the literature on investment in the firm and to the engineering literature on optimal control. With a continuous time model some results become available from the theory of differential equations which permit further theorems to be proved on the asymptotic behaviour of optimal paths. Many of these results are found in Brock and Scheinkman (1977). Particularly complete results for the local problem were found by Magill (1977). Also the asymptotic results of optimal growth theory have been applied in areas which have not been reviewed, for example, in the theory of finance (see Brock, 1982).

LIONEL W. MCKENZIE

See also MULTISECTOR GROWTH MODELS; VON NEUMANN RAY.

BIBLIOGRAPHY

Araujo, A.P. de and Scheinkman, J.A. 1977. Smoothness, comparative dynamics, and the turnpike property. *Econometrica* 45, 601–620.

Atsumi, H. 1965. Neoclassical growth and the efficient program of capital accumulation. *Review of Economic Studies* 32, 127–36.

Becker, R.A. 1980. On the long-run steady state in a simple dynamic model of equilibrium with heterogeneous households. *Quarterly Journal of Economics* 94, 375–82.

Benhabib, J. and Nishimura, K. 1985. Competitive equilibrium cycles. *Journal of Economic Theory* 35, 284–306.

Bewley, T.F. 1982. An integration of equilibrium theory and turnpike theory. *Journal of Mathematical Economics* 10, 233–68.

Boldrin, M. and Montrucchio, L. 1986. On the indeterminacy of capital accumulation paths. *Journal of Economic Theory* 40, 26–39.

Boldrin, M. and Montrucchio, L. 1986a. Acyclicity and stability for intertemporal optimization models. Working Paper, University of Rochester. March.

Boldrin, M. and Montrucchio, L. 1986b. Private communication.

Brock, W.A. 1970. On existence of weakly maximal programmes in a multi-sector economy. *Review of Economic Studies* 37, 275–80.

Brock, W.A. 1973. Some results on the uniqueness of steady states in multisector models of optimum growth when future utilities are discounted. *International Economic Review* 14, 535–59.

Brock, W.A. 1982. Asset prices in a production economy. In *The Economics of Information and Uncertainty*, ed. J.J. McCall, Chicago: University of Chicago Press.

Brock, W.A. and Magill, M. 1979. Dynamics under uncertainty. *Econometrica* 47, 843–68.

Brock, W.A. and Majumdar, M. 1978. Global asymptotic stability results for multisector models of optimal growth with uncertainty when future utilities are discounted. *Journal of Economic Theory* 18, 225–43.

Brock, W.A. and Mirman, L. 1972. Optimal economic growth and uncertainty: the discounted case. *Journal of Economic Theory* 4, 479–513.

Brock, W.A. and Scheinkman, J. 1976. The global asymptotic stability of optimal control systems with applications to the theory of economic growth. *Journal of Economic Theory* 12, 164–90.

Brock, W.A. and Scheinkman, J. 1977. The global asymptotic stability of optimal control with applications to dynamic economic theory. In *Applications of Control Theory to Economic Analysis*, ed. J.D. Pitchford and Jose A. Scheinkman. Amsterdam: North-Holland.

Brock, W.A. and Scheinkman, J. 1978. On the long-run behavior of a competitive firm. In *Equilibrium and Disequilibrium in Economic Theory*, ed. G. Schwödiauer. Dordrecht, Holland: D. Reidel.

Cass, D. 1966. Optimum growth in an aggregative model of capital accumulation: a turnpike theorem. *Econometrica* 34, 833-50.

Cass, D. and Shell, K. 1976. The structure and stability of competitive dynamical systems. *Journal of Economic Theory* 12, 31–70.

Cassel, G. 1918. *Theoretische Sozialökonomie*. Trans. from the 5th German edn. as *Theory of Social Economy*, New York: Harcourt, Brace, 1932.

Coles, J.L. 1985. Equilibrium turnpike theory with constant returns to scale and possibly heterogeneous discount factors: *International Economic Review* 26, 671–80.

Dasgupta, S. and McKenzie, L.W. 1985. A note on comparative statics and dynamics of stationary states. *Economic Letters* 18, 333–8.

Dechert, W.D. and Nishimura, K. 1983. A complete characterization of optimal growth paths in an aggregated model with a non-concave production function. *Journal of Economic Theory* 31, 332–54.

Dorfman, R., Samuelson, P. and Solow, R. 1958. *Linear Programming and Economic Analysis*. New York: McGraw-Hill.

Epstein, L.G. 1986. Implicitly additive utility and the robustness of turnpike theorems. *Journal of Mathematical Economics* 15, 111–28.

Epstein. L.G. 1987. The global stability of efficient intertemporal allocations. *Econometrica* 55, 329–56.

Evstigneev, I.V. 1974. Optimal stochastic programs and their stimulating prices. In *Mathematical Models in Economics*, ed. J. Łoś and M. Łoś, Amsterdam: North-Holland.

Fisher, I. 1930. *The Theory of Interest*. New York: Macmillan.

Gale, D. 1956. The closed linear model of production. In *Linear Inequalities and Related Systems*, ed. H.W. Kuhn and A.W. Tucker. Princeton: Princeton University Press.

Gale, D. 1967. On optimal development in a multi-sector economy. *Review of Economic Studies* 34, 1–18.

Grandmont, J.M. 1985. On endogenous business cycles. *Econometrica* 53, 995–1046.

Heal, G. and Ryder, H. 1973. An optimum growth model with intertemporally dependent preferences. *Review of Economic Studies* 40, 1–33.

Inada, K. 1964. Some structural characteristics of turnpike theorems. *Review of Economic Studies* 31, 43–58.

Keeler, E.B. 1972. A twisted turnpike, *International Economic Review*, 13, 160–66.
Koopmans, T.C. 1960. Stationary ordinal utility and time perspective. *Econometrica* 28, 287–309.
Koopmans, T.C. 1965. The concept of optimal economic growth. In *The Econometric Approach to Development Planning*, Pontificae Academiae Scientiarum Scripta Varia No. 28, Amsterdam: North-Holland.
Lucas, R. and Stokey, N. 1984. Optimal growth with many consumers. *Journal of Economic Theory* 32, 139–71.
Magill, M.J.P. 1977. Some new results on the local stability of the process of capital accumulation. *Journal of Economic Theory* 15, 174–210.
Majumdar, M. and Mitra, T. 1982. Intertemporal allocation with a non convex technology: the aggregative framework. *Journal of Economic Theory* 27, 101–136.
Marimon, R. 1984. General equilibrium and growth under uncertainty: the turnpike property. Discussion Paper No. 624. Northwestern University, August, 1984.
McKenzie, L.W. 1963. Turnpike theorems for a generalized Leontief model. *Econometrica* 31, 165–80.
McKenzie, L.W. 1968. Accumulation programs of maximum utility and the von Neumann facet. In *Value, Capital, and Growth*, ed. J.N. Wolfe, Edinburgh University Press.
McKenzie, L.W. 1974. Turnpike theorems with technology and welfare function variable. In *Mathematical Models in Economics*, ed. J. Łoś and M.W. Łoś, New York: American Elsevier.
McKenzie, L.W. 1976. Turnpike theory. *Econometrica* 44, 841–65.
McKenzie, L.W. 1977. A new route to the turnpike. In *Mathematical Economics and Game Theory*, ed. R. Henn and O. Moeschlin. New York: Springer-Verlag.
McKenzie, L.W. 1983. Turnpike theory, discounted utility, and the von Neumann facet. *Journal of Economic Theory* 30, 330–52.
Mill, J.S. 1848. *Principles of Political Economy*. Parker, London. New edn, London: Longmans, Green, 1909.
Mitra, T. 1979. On optimal growth with variable discount rates: existence and stability results. *International Economic Review* 20, 133–46.
Negishi, T. 1960. Welfare economics and existence of an equilibrium for a competitive economy. *Metroeconomica* 12, 92–7.
Radner, R. 1961. Paths of economic growth that are optimal with regard only to final states. *Review of Economic Studies* 28, 98–104.
Ramsey, F. 1928. A mathematical theory of savings. *Economic Journal* 38, 543–59.
Samuelson, P.A. 1966. Market mechanisms and maximization. In *The Collected Scientific Papers of Paul Samuelson*, Vol. 1, ed. J. Stiglitz, Cambridge, Mass., M.I.T. Press, 425–92.
Samuelson, P.A. 1971. Turnpike theorems even though tastes are intertemporally interdependent. *Western Economic Journal* 9, 21–6.
Samuelson, P.A. and Solow, R.W. 1956. A complete capital model involving heterogeneous capital goods. *Quarterly Journal of Economics* 70, 537–62.
Scheinkman, J. 1976. On optimal steady states of n-sector growth models when utility is discounted. *Journal of Economic Theory* 12, 11–20.
Skiba, A.K. 1978. Optimal growth with a convex-concave production function. *Econometrica* 46, 527–40.
Takahashi, H. 1985. Characterizations of optimal programs in infinite horizon economies. PhD thesis, University of Rochester.
Treadway, A.B. 1971. The rational multivariate flexible accelerator. *Econometrica* 39, 845–55.
von Neumann, J. 1937. Über ein Okonomisches Gleichungssystem und eine Verallgemeinerung des Brouwerschen Fixpunktsätzes. *Ergebnisse Eines Mathematischen Kolloquiums*, 8, 73–83. Translated in *Review of Economic Studies* 13, (1945), 1–9.
von Weiszäcker, C.C. 1965. Existence of optimal programs of accumulation for an infinite time horizon. *Review of Economic Studies* 32, 85–104.
Weitzman, W.L. 1973. Duality theory for infinite horizon convex models. *Management Science* 19, 783–9.
Yano, M. 1984a. Competitive equilibria on turnpikes in a McKenzie economy, I: a neighborhood turnpike theorem. *International Economic Review*, 25, 695–718.
Yano, M. 1984b. The turnpike of dynamic general equilibrium paths and its insensitivity to initial conditions. *Journal of Mathematical Economics* 13, 235–54.
Yano, M. 1985. Competitive equilibria on turnpikes in a McKenzie economy, II: an asymptotic turnpike theorem. *International Economic Review* 26, 661–70.

Twiss, Travers (1809–1897). In economics, Twiss's reputation rests primarily upon two contributions: one on the machinery question and the other a 'View of the Progress of Political Economy in Europe since the Sixteenth Century' (1847) of some three-hundred pages. Both of these works originated in lectures during his tenure as Drummond Professor of Political Economy at Oxford (1942–7). The latter numbers with McCulloch's much shorter *Historical Sketch of the Rise and Progress of the Science of Political Economy* (1926) as being among the first significant histories of the discipline published in English. The only works of comparable significance in the area which pre-date it appeared in French: Blanqui's *Historie de l'économie politique en Europe* (1837–8) and Jean Paul Alban de Villeneuve-Bargemon's *Historie de l'économie politique* (1836-8 and 1841). Twiss acknowledges his debt to the abovementioned authors, but has been criticised (for example, by Cossa) for a tendency to rely too heavily upon second-hand sources in the construction of his argument.

The published versions of his lectures at Oxford are all that Twiss left to the literature of economics.

Twiss was born in London on 19 March 1809 and died there on 14 January 1897, and was educated at University College, Oxford, taking his BA (in mathematics and classics) in 1830. From 1830 until 1863 he was a fellow of that college. In 1835 he commenced the study of law in Lincoln's Inn and was admitted to the Bar in 1840. Following his term as Drummond Professor (in which he succeeded Merivale) he turned more and more to the study of international law, and in 1852 he was elected to the chair in that field at King's College, London. In 1855 he moved to Oxford as Regius Professor of Civil Law, where he remained until 1870. In 1867 he became the Queen's advocate-general, and was knighted in 1868.

At this point occurred 'the catastrophe which put an end to his official career', as the original edition of this *Dictionary* put it. It seems that in 1872, Twiss instituted an action for malicious libel with intent to extort against a solicitor who had put about statements impugning the moral propriety of Twiss's wife. As the case proceeded, Lady Twiss was called to testify. However, an arduous cross-examination proved to be too much for her, and she departed London before its conclusion, thus causing Twiss's case to collapse and precipitating his resignation from all offices. Of course, it is not surprising (given the climate of the times) that Lady Twiss's breakdown should have been interpreted as telling evidence against her – but from what we now know of these extraordinary Victorian public rituals over sexual behaviour and preference, and of the pressures placed on the principal actors in such notorious trials, a rather different verdict might just as plausibly be drawn from the episode. From the point of view of individual and social psychology, however, even more interesting is the question of just why these kinds of cases were voluntarily brought before the courts in the first place.

MURRAY MILGATE

SELECTED WORKS

1845. *On Certain Tests of a Thriving Population*. London.
1847. *View of the Progress of Political Economy in Europe Since the*

Sixteenth Century. London: Longmans, Brown, Green, and Longmans.
1861. *Law of Nations considered as Independent Political Communities*. Oxford: Oxford University Press.

two-sector models. Problems of interest in economic theory, both from the theoretical and policy points of view, occur only when there exist a multitude of goods and services, each of which is either produced by different technologies or utilized for different purposes in consumption. However, it is often the case that an economic system with a multitude of goods and services is too complicated to analyse effectively and to derive conclusions of any practical use. Two-sector models enable us to bring forth essential elements of the economic mechanisms in a more complicated real world while still making it possible to analyse graphically the basic structure of equilibrium and to understand the policy implications within the framework of the two-sector analysis. The two-sector analysis plays a particularly important role in trade theory and in growth theory.

A typical two-sector model concerns itself with an economy in which there exist two productive sectors, to be referred to as sector 1 and sector 2, respectively. In the context of growth theory, one sector produces consumption goods and the other investment goods. Both goods are assumed to be composed of homogeneous quantities and to be produced by two factors of production, capital and labour. Both capital and labour are also assumed to be composed of homogeneous quantities.

In each sector, production is assumed to be subject to constant returns to scale and diminishing marginal rates of substitution between capital and labour. Joint products are excluded and external (dis-)economies do not exist. The output in each sector is determined by the quantities of capital and labour allocated to that sector. In sector j, let Y_j be the quantity of good j produced by the input of capital and labour by the quantities K_j and L_j, respectively, then we may write

$$Y_j = F_j(K_j, L_j), \qquad j = 1, 2. \tag{1}$$

For each j, the production function $F_j(K_j, L_j)$ is linear homogeneous and continuously differentiable, so that the marginal rate of substitution between capital and labour is well defined.

Let K and L be the quantities of capital and labour which exist in the economy at a particular moment of time. If both capital and labour are assumed to be freely transferred from one sector to another and both are fully employed, then we have

$$K_1 + K_2 = K, \quad L_1 + L_2 = L. \tag{2}$$

In a typical two-sector model, it is often assumed that the allocation of two factors of production is perfectly competitive, so that in each sector the wage w is equal to the marginal product of labour and the rentals r of capital goods to the marginal product of capital:

$$w = p_j \frac{\partial F_j}{\partial L_j}, \qquad r = p_j \frac{\partial F_j}{\partial K_j}, \tag{3}$$

where p_j is the price of good j.

In what follows, good 1 is taken as the numéraire, so that $p_1 = 1$ and $p_2 = p$.

Since production is assumed to be subject to constant returns to scale, the model is reduced to one involving per capita quantities only. Let us introduce the following notation:

$k = K/L$: the capital–labour ratio in the economy as a whole,
$k_j = K_j/L_j$: the capital–labour ratio in sector j,
$y_j = Y_j/L$: output of good j per capita,
$v_j = L_j/L$: the proportion of labour allocation in sector j,
$\omega = w/r$: the wage–rental ratio.

The relations (1)–(3) are then reduced to the following:

$$y_j = f_j(k_j)v_j, \tag{4}$$

where $f_j(k_j) = F_j(k_j, 1)$,

$$v_1 = \frac{k - k_2}{k_1 - k_2}, \qquad v_2 = \frac{k_1 - k}{k_1 - k_2}, \tag{5}$$

$$\omega = \frac{f_j(k_j)}{f_j'(k_j)} - k_j, \tag{6}$$

$$p = \frac{f_1'(k_1)}{f_2'(k_2)}, \tag{7}$$

$$y_1 = f_1(k_1)\frac{k - k_2}{k_1 - k_2}, \qquad y_2 = f_2(k_2)\frac{k_1 - k}{k_1 - k_2}. \tag{8}$$

The relation (6) means that the wage–rentals ratio ω is equal to the marginal rate of substitution between capital and labour. The capital–labour ratio k_j which satisfies (6) is uniquely determined for given wage–rentals ratio ω; it may be written $k_j = k_j(\omega)$, which is referred to as the optimum capital–labour ratio corresponding to the wage–rentals ratio ω. It is easily seen that the optimum capital–labour ratio $k_j(\omega)$ is an increasing function of the wage–rentals ratio ω. In fact, by differentiating (6) with respect to ω, we get

$$\frac{dk_j}{d\omega} = -\frac{[f_j'(k_j)]^2}{f_j(k_j)f_j''(k_j)} > 0, \tag{9}$$

because of the diminishing marginal rate of substitution condition: $f_j'(k_j) > 0$ and $f_j''(k_j) < 0$.

The relationships between the price ratio p and the wage–rentals ratio ω may be obtained by differentiating (7) logarithmically, and noting (9):

$$\frac{1}{p}\frac{dp}{d\omega} = \frac{1}{\omega + k_2(\omega)} - \frac{1}{\omega + k_1(\omega)}. \tag{10}$$

Hence, we have the following proposition:

The relative price p of good 2 is an increasing or decreasing function of wage–rental ratio ω according to whether good 1 is more or less capital-intensive than good 2.

In particular, if good 1 is always more capital-intensive than good 2, then the relative price p of good 2 (with respect to the price of good 1) is an increasing function of the wage–rentals ratio ω. The latter is indeed nothing but the essence of the factor–price–equalization theorem. In this case, we can see from (8) that, as the endowment ratio k is increased, the output of good 1 is increased and that of good 2 is decreased, provided that the wage–rentals ratio ω or relative price p remains constant.

The wage–rentals ratio ω or price ratio p is determined once the demand conditions are specified.

The allocation of capital and labour between two sectors in the perfectly competitive situation, as described above, may be viewed from another point of view. It is easily seen that the allocation of capital and labour which satisfies (1)–(3) is nothing but the solution of the following optimum problem:

Find the allocation (K_1, K_2, L_1, L_2) which maximizes the national product

$$Y = p_1 Y_1 + p_2 Y_2$$

subject to the constraints (1) and

$$K_1 + K_2 \leqslant K, \quad L_1 + L_2 \leqslant L. \qquad (2')$$

In fact, wage w and rentals r are the Lagrange multipliers associated with the constraints (2′).

The set of all combinations (Y_1, Y_2) of two goods satisfying (1) and (2′) then is a convex set, to be referred to as the production possibility set. It is the set of all possible combinations of the quantities of two goods which can be produced from the given endowments of capital and labour, K and L. The competitive allocations of capital and labour then result in those combinations of two goods for which the national product, evaluated at prices p_1 and p_2, is maximized.

These observations lead us to the following conclusion. Namely, if the demand conditions are those obtained by an optimization of a certain community preference ordering, then the equilibrium prices and outputs are uniquely determined.

The analysis may be carried out in terms of a geometric presentation. For the given techniques of production and the given factors of production, the set of all possible combinations of two goods produced in the two-sector economy is represented by the production possibility set, as shown by the shaded area in Figure 1. In Figure 1, the quantities of good 1 and good 2 are measured along the abscissa and ordinate, respectively, and the boundary curve of the production possibility set is the transformation curve F_1F_2, showing the maximum quantity of one good that can be produced, given a specific quantity of the other to be produced. The transformation curve is concave toward the origin and the tangent at each point on the transformation curve has a slope equal to the relative price of two goods, as shown in Figure 1. It is possible to prove these properties by using the contract box, as in Figure 2. In Figure 2, the endowments of capital and labour are measured along the sides of the box, and the allocations of capital and labour between two sectors are entered in the box from opposite corners. An efficient allocation of factors of production is realized only at a point at which two isoquants are tangent to each other. The efficient locus in the contract box corresponds to the transformation curve in Figure 1. The configuration

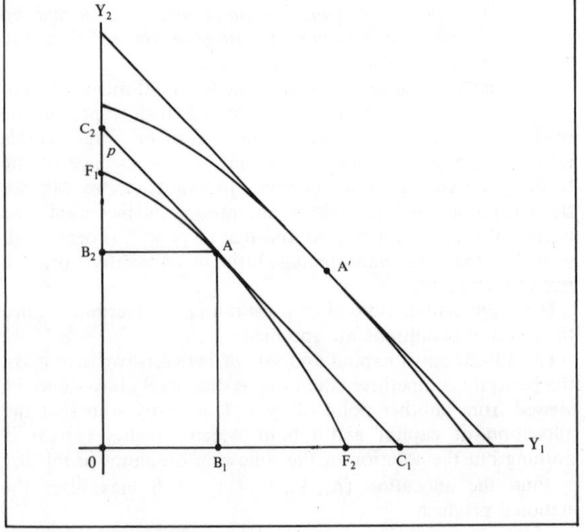

Figure 1 The transformation curve

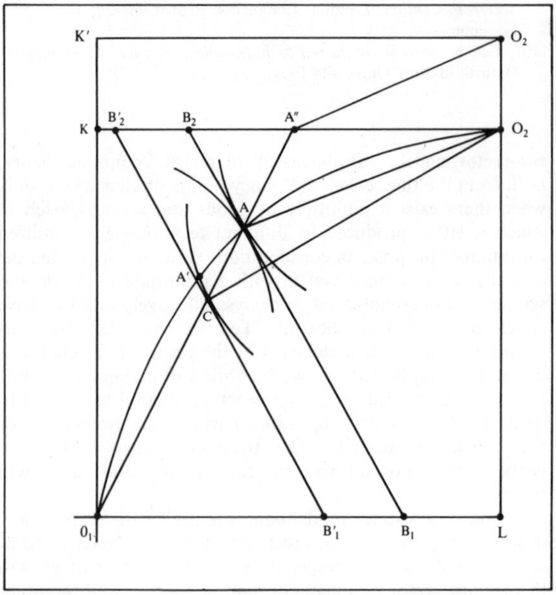

Figure 2 The contract box

described in Figure 2 represents the case where good 1 is more capital-intensive than good 2. Let the point A in Figure 1 correspond to the point A in the contract box in Figure 2. Suppose the quantity of good 1 to be produced is reduced by ΔY_1 and the production of good 2 is increased by ΔY_2, resulting in a shift from A to A' along the efficiency locus. At point A, the isoquants in two sectors have a common tangent; let B_1 and B_2 be the points on the labour-side at which the tangent line at A intersects. The two distances, O_1B_1 and O_2B_2, measure the values of the two goods produced, p_1Y_1/w and p_2Y_2/w, respectively. Let C be the point at which O_1A intersects with the isoquant passing through A', and let B_1' and B_2' be the points on the labour-side at which the tangent line at C intersects. Then $B_1'B_1 = p_1\Delta Y_1/w$ and $B_2'B_2 \simeq p_2\Delta Y_2/w$, where the symbol $\simeq$ indicates that both sides are approximately equal, converging to the equality as ΔY_1 approaches to 0. Hence, $\Delta Y_1/\Delta Y_2 \simeq p_2/p_1$.

As the output of good 1 is reduced, the point A moves toward O_1 along the efficiency locus. Then the optimum capital–labour ratio, which is represented by LAO_1B_1, is increased, and the tangent line at A' is steeper than that at A, indicating an increase in the price ratio p_2/p_1. The transformation curve thus is shown to be concave toward the origin and the tangent at each point on it is equal to the price ratio.

The relationships between the price ratio and the wage-rentals ratio may also be discussed in terms of a two-dimensional diagram, as in Figure 3. Suppose good 1 is more capital-intensive than good 2. For the given wage-rentals ratio ω, the unit by which good 2 is measured is so adjusted that $p_2/p_1 = 1$ and the unit-isoquants for both goods share the same cost line CC, as shown in Figure 3. The distance OC along the abscissa measure $p_1/w = p_2/w$. Suppose the wage–rentals ratio is increased from ω to ω'. Then at the new wage–rentals ratio ω', the configuration of the cost lines in two sectors must be of the form described in Figure 3. Namely, $OB_1 < OB_2$; hence, $p_1'/w' < p_2'/w'$, implying $p_2'/p_1' < 1 = p_2/p_1$. Thus we have proved that, as the wage–rentals ratio is increased, the price of a good

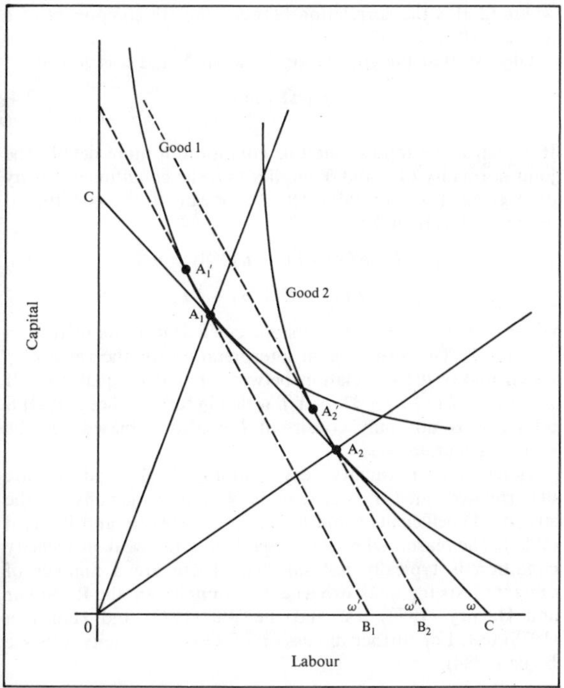

Figure 3 The relationships between price ratio p and wage – rentals ratio ω

which is more labour-intensive has been increased relative to that of a less labour-intensive good.

The effect of an increase in the endowment of either capital or labour may also be analysed in terms of the contract box. Suppose the endowment of capital is increased from K to K' so that the new contract box is indicated by $O_1LO_2'K'$ in Figure 2. If the relative price $p = p_2/p_1$ remains unchanged, then the factor price ratio $\omega = w/r$ also remains unchanged. Let A'' be the point at which the extension of O_1A intersects with the line originating from O_2' which is parallel to O_2A. Then at the new configuration, the output of good 1 is increased by AA'', while the output of good 2 is decreased from O_2A to $O_2'A'$. Thus we have shown the proposition, known as the Rybczynski theorem: An increase in the endowment of capital increases the output of a good which is more capital-intensive than the other, while decreases the output of another good which is less capital-intensive, provided the price ratio of the two goods remains constant. The resulting shift in the transformation curve is described in Figure 3, where the efficient point A moves to A' in the new environment.

H. UZAWA

See also FACTOR–PRICE FRONTIER.

two-stage least squares and the k-class estimator. Two-stage least squares (TSLS) is a method of estimating the parameters of a single structural equation in a system of linear simultaneous equations. The TSLS estimator was proposed by Theil (1953a, 1961) and independently by Basmann (1957). The early work on simultaneous equation estimation was carried out by a group of econometricians at the Cowles Commission. This work was based on the method of maximum likelihood. Anderson and Rubin (1949) proposed the limited information maximum likelihood (LIML) estimator for the parameters of a single structural equation.

Although introduced later, TSLS was by far the most widely used method in the 1960s and the early 1970s. The explanation involves both the state of computer technology and the state of statistical knowledge among applied econometricians. By the end of the 1950s computer programs for ordinary least squares were available. These programs were simpler to use and much less costly to run than the programs for calculating LIML estimates. Among the applied econometricians relatively few had the statistical training to master Cowles Commission Monograph 14 (1953), which is the classic exposition of maximum likelihood methods of simultaneous equations estimation. Owing to advances in computer technology and, perhaps, also better statistical training, the popularity of TSLS started to wane by the end of the 1970s. In particular, the cost of calculating LIML estimates was no longer an important constraint.

There are many structural estimators in addition to TSLS and LIML. The problem is to decide which estimator to use. The presumption is that choice depends on the statistical properties of the estimators and how the estimators compare. The statistical properties have been intensively investigated in the case of a model of a single structural equation with normal errors and no lagged dependent variables. In this case some useful results have been recently established on the comparison of estimators. In order to discuss these results certain statistical concepts have to be introduced. I shall try to present these concepts informally, but with enough rigour so as not to be misleading. More research is required to establish the statistical properties of estimators for models with non-normal error specifications and for models with dynamics.

The model with normal errors and no lagged dependent variables is presented in section 1. Section 2 defines the concept of a consistent estimator and discusses the properties of the least squares method. Section 3 shows that there is an abundance of consistent estimators and section 4 defines the property of asymptotic efficiency. Some interpretations of the TSLS method are given in section 5 and the k-class family of estimators is defined in section 6. The results on the comparison of estimators are reported in section 7 and the concluding comments are in section 8.

1. THE MODEL. Consider the structural equation

$$y = Y\gamma + X_1\beta + u = Z\delta + u \tag{1.1}$$

where y is a $T\times 1$ vector and Y is a $T\times(L-1)$ matrix of observations on the included endogenous variables and X_1 is a $T\times K_1$ matrix of observations on the included exogenous variables. It is assumed that the system can be solved for y and Y in terms of the exogenous variables and the errors. The solution is called the reduced form of the system. The reduced form can be written as

$$\begin{aligned}[y, Y] &= [X_1, X_2]\begin{bmatrix}\pi_1 & \Pi_1\\ \pi_2 & \Pi_2\end{bmatrix} + [v, V]\\ &= X[\pi, \Pi] + [v, V] \qquad (1.2)\end{aligned}$$

where X_2 is a $T\times K_2$ matrix of observations on the exogenous variables excluded from (1.1) but appearing elsewhere in the system. It is assumed that $X = [X_1, X_2]$ is a matrix of constants and has full column rank. The rows of $[v, v]$ are assumed to be independent normal vectors with mean zero and positive definite covariance matrix

$$\Omega = \begin{bmatrix} \omega_{11} & \omega_{12}^{\mathrm{T}} \\ \omega_{12} & \Omega_{22} \end{bmatrix}. \tag{1.3}$$

In other words, the rows of $[y, Y]$ are independently normally distributed with conditional means given by the rows of $X[\pi, \Pi]$ and with the same conditional covariance matrix which is given by Ω.

In Tintner's (1952, pp. 176–9) two equation model of the American meat market the endogenous variables are meat consumption and meat price and the exogenous variables are disposable income, the unit cost of meat processing and the cost of agricultural production. The demand equation omits the cost variables.

The relation between the structural parameters and the reduced form parameters is found by post-multiplying the reduced form (1.2) by the vector $[1, -\gamma^{\mathrm{T}}]^{\mathrm{T}}$. This gives relations

$$\pi_1 - \Pi_1\gamma = \beta, \tag{1.4}$$

$$\pi_2 - \Pi_2\gamma = 0 \tag{1.5}$$

and

$$u = v - V\gamma. \tag{1.6}$$

The coefficients of the structural equation (1.1) are identified if they can be uniquely determined from knowledge of $[\pi, \Pi]$. If rank $\Pi_2 = \text{rank}[\pi_2, \Pi_2] = L - 1$, then (1.5) can be solved for a unique value of γ. Given a value of γ, (1.4) uniquely determines β. Hence, the rank condition for identification is that rank $\Pi_2 = \text{rank}[\pi_2, \Pi_2]$. It is assumed that the rank condition for identification is satisfied and hence that the so-called order condition, $K_2 \geqslant L - 1$, is also satisfied. From (1.6) it follows that the components of u are independently normally distributed with mean zero and variance $\sigma^2 = \omega_{11} - 2\omega_{12}\gamma + \gamma^{\mathrm{T}}W_{22}\gamma$. For an exposition of simultaneous equation models see Hausman (1983).

2. ORDINARY LEAST SQUARES. The problem is to find an estimator of the parameters γ and β which has good statistical properties. An obvious question is whether ordinary least squares (OLS) is a good estimator. The answer depends on whether a certain correlation is zero.

An estimation method defines a random variable for each sample size and hence a sequence of random variables indexed by the sample size. A sequence of random variables $\{X_n\}$ is said to converge to a constant c in probability if

$$\lim_{n\to\infty} P(|X_n - c| > \epsilon) = 0, \qquad \text{for any } \epsilon > 0.$$

We write $\operatorname{p\,lim} X_n = c$. A sequence of $n \times m$ random matrices is said to converge in probability if each element converges. Let θ_{T} be an estimator of the parameter θ which converges to θ_0 in probability where θ_0 denotes the true parameter value. The estimator θ_{T} is said to be a consistent estimator for θ.

The OLS estimator of δ is

$$d = [Z^{\mathrm{T}}Z]^{-1}Z^{\mathrm{T}}y = \delta + [Z^{\mathrm{T}}Z]^{-1}Z^{\mathrm{T}}u. \tag{2.1}$$

If this estimator converges in probability to a constant, then that constant is given by

$$\operatorname{p\,lim} d = \delta + [\operatorname{p\,lim} Z^{\mathrm{T}}Z/T]^{-1} \operatorname{p\,lim} Z^{\mathrm{T}}u/T. \tag{2.2}$$

It is conventional to impose assumptions on X such that as the sample size increases the term in square brackets converges in probability to a matrix of constants and the correlation between X and $[v, V]$ and hence between X and u converges in probability to zero. The OLS estimator is a consistent if

$$\begin{aligned} \operatorname{p\,lim} Y^{\mathrm{T}}u/T &= \operatorname{p\,lim}[X\Pi + V]^{\mathrm{T}}u/T \\ &= \operatorname{p\,lim} V^{\mathrm{T}}u/T = w_{12} - \Omega_{22}\gamma = 0 \end{aligned} \tag{2.3}$$

where (2.3) is the correlation between the tth component of u and the tth row of V.

Observe that the correlation between Y and u is zero if

$$\gamma = \Omega_{22}^{-1}\omega_{12}. \tag{2.4}$$

It is instructive to examine this condition in more detail. The joint normality of y and Y implies that the conditional density of y given Y is normal where the mean of the conditional density is linear in Y:

$$\begin{aligned} E(y \mid Y) &= E(y) + [Y - E(Y)]\Omega_{22}^{-1}\omega_{12} \\ &= [E(y) - E(Y)\alpha] + Y\alpha \end{aligned} \tag{2.5}$$

where $\alpha = \Omega_{22}^{-1}\omega_{12}$ is the true slope coefficient in the regression of y on Y. This provides an interpretation for the value of γ which makes the correlation between Y and u equal zero. If $\alpha = \gamma$, then $E(y \mid Y) = Y\gamma + X_1\beta$ which in turn implies that OLS estimator is not only consistent but also unbiased for the structural parameters.

Under the normality assumption, if Y and u are uncorrelated, then Y is said to be weakly exogenous for the structural coefficients γ and β. See Engle, Hendry and Richard (1983). The reason OLS is not used is that the weak exogeneity condition is typically not satisfied. There are a number of different tests for weak exogeneity. Examples are the Revankar and Hartley (1973) test and the Wu (1973) and Hausman (1978) test. For further discussion of weak exogeneity tests see Engle (1984).

3. A PLETHORA OF CONSISTENT ESTIMATORS. When the weak exogeneity condition fails the OLS estimator is not consistent. In fact, there is an abundant supply of consistent estimators. The standard textbook treatment of structural estimation usually begins with the indirect least squares (ILS) method. The starting point for this method is the sample analogue of (1.5):

$$p_2 = P_2 g \tag{3.1}$$

where $[p_2, P_2]$ is the OLS estimate of the $K_2 \times L$ reduced form coefficient matrix $[\pi_2, \Pi_2]$. The OLS estimator is

$$[p_2, P_2] = [X_2^{\mathrm{T}}M_1X_2]^{-1}X_2^{\mathrm{T}}M_1[y, Y] \tag{3.2}$$

where $M_1 = I - X_1^{\mathrm{T}}[X_1^{\mathrm{T}}X_1]^{-1}X_1$ and $X_2^{\mathrm{T}}M_1X_2$ is the sum of squared residuals from the OLS regression of X_2 on X_1. Since the reduced form equations satisfy the assumptions of the classical normal linear regression model, the OLS estimator (3.2) is minimum variance unbiased and consistent.

The structural equation (1.1) is defined to be just-identified if $K_2 = L - 1$ and over-identified if $K_2 \geqslant L - 1$. Since it is assumed that the structural equation (1.1) is identified, the rank of Π_2 and of P_2 is $L - 1$. If $K_2 = L - 1$, the rank of $[p_2, P_2]$ is $L - 1$ so that p_2 is in the column space of P_2. Hence, when the equation is just-identified the estimator defined by (3.1) is given by

$$\hat{\gamma} = P_2^{-1}p_2 \tag{3.3}$$

since P_2 is square. This is the ILS estimator and it is easy to show that it is consistent since $[p_2, P_2]$ is consistent for $[\pi_2, \Pi_2]$. Once the estimate of γ is uniquely determined, the sample analogue of (1.4) is used to determine the estimate of β. The ILS method is available only in the just-identified case. This is because when $K_2 > L - 1$ the rank of $[p_2, P_2]$ is L with probability one so that (3.1) has no solution.

In the over-identified case there are several possibilities of obtaining a consistent estimator. One is to throw enough rows of $[p_2, P_2]$ to bring its rank down to $L - 1$. As Goldberger

(1964, p. 328) remarks, consistent estimates are still obtained, but this procedure is not recommended since it is arbitrary and since discarding information results in a loss of efficiency. A consistent estimator of γ can obtained by regressing p_2 on P_2. This gives the estimator

$$\gamma^* = [P_2^{\mathrm{T}}P_2]^{-1}P_2^{\mathrm{T}}p_2. \tag{3.5}$$

This estimator does not have any of the disadvantages noted above by Goldberger. When the question is just-identified it reduces to the ILS estimator.

If the rank of $[p_2, P_2]$ were always $L-1$ and if the aim were to obtain an estimator with good large sample properties, then the analysis of structural estimation need go no further. This is because ILS is not only consistent, but asymptotically efficient.

4. A MATTER OF EFFICIENCY. A widely used criterion for choosing among consistent estimators is asymptotic efficiency. Asymptotic efficiency is defined for estimators which have limiting normal distributions. A sequence of random variables $\{X_n\}$ is said to converge to a variable X in distribution if the distribution function F_n of X_n converges to the distribution function F of X at every continuity point of F. The distribution function F is called the limit distribution of $\{X_n\}$. For consistent estimators the limit distribution is simply a point. Under appropriate general conditions TSLS and LIML are consistent and when normalized by multiplying by the square root of the sample size both estimators converge in distribution to the same limiting (asymptotic) normal distribution, where the covariance matrix of the limiting normal distribution is the inverse of the standardized Fisher information matrix. This convariance matrix is also referred to as the Cramer–Rao lower bound.

In the class of consistent and asymptotically normal (CAN) estimators of the parameter θ the mean of the limiting normal distribution is equal to the true parameter value, say θ_0, for all estimators in the class. On the other hand, the covariance matrix of the limiting normal distribution, which is called the asymptotic variance, may be different for different CAN estimators. Hence it is natural to define the best CAN estimator as the one with the smallest asymptotic variance. At one time statisticians belived that the minimum asymptotic variance was given by the Cramer–Rao lower bound. This was proved wrong, but despite this, there are good reasons for continuing the practice of defining a CAN estimator to be asymptotically efficient if it achieves the Cramer–Rao lower bound. An asymptotically efficient estimator is said to be best asymptotically normal or BAN for short. For a discussion of asymptotic efficiency see Amemiya (1985, Ch. 4).

From the point of view of large sample properties the reason TSLS merits attention is that it is a BAN estimator. In the just-identified case ILS is identically equal to the TSLS and the LIML estimators and hence is a BAN estimator. As will become apparent, in the over-identified case there are many BAN estimators in addition to TSLS and LIML.

5. TWO STAGE LEAST SQUARES. The TSLS estimator is defined by

$$\hat{\delta} = [Z^{\mathrm{T}}X(X^{\mathrm{T}}X)^{-1}X^{T}Z]^{-1}Z^{\mathrm{T}}X(X^{\mathrm{T}}X)^{-1}X^{\mathrm{T}}y. \tag{5.1}$$

Theil (1971, ch. 9.5) gives two interpretations for this formula. In the first the structural equation (1.1) is multiplied by $(X^{\mathrm{T}}X)^{-1}X^{\mathrm{T}}$:

$$\begin{aligned}(X^{\mathrm{T}}X)^{-1}X^{\mathrm{T}}y &= (X^{\mathrm{T}}X)^{-1}X^{\mathrm{T}}Y\gamma + (X^{\mathrm{T}}X)^{-1}X^{\mathrm{T}}X_1\beta \\ &\quad + (X^{\mathrm{T}}X)^{-1}X^{\mathrm{T}}u \\ p &= P\gamma + (X^{\mathrm{T}}X)^{-1}X^{\mathrm{T}}X_1\beta + (X^{\mathrm{T}}X)^{-1}X^{\mathrm{T}}u. \end{aligned} \tag{5.2}$$

The error term $(X^{\mathrm{T}}X)^{-1}X^{\mathrm{T}}u$ is normally distributed with mean zero and covariance matrix $\sigma^2(X^{\mathrm{T}}X)^{-1}$ and the correlation between P and $(X^{\mathrm{T}}X)^{-1}X^{\mathrm{T}}u$ converges in probability to zero:

$$\begin{aligned} &\operatorname{p\,lim}[(P-\Pi)^{\mathrm{T}}(X^{\mathrm{T}}X/T)^{-1}(X^{\mathrm{T}}u/T)] \\ &= \operatorname{p\,lim}[(V^{\mathrm{T}}X/T)(X^{\mathrm{T}}X/T)^{-1}(X^{\mathrm{T}}X/T)^{-1}(X^{\mathrm{T}}u/T)] \\ &= 0 \end{aligned} \tag{5.3}$$

when assumptions are imposed on X such that $X^{\mathrm{T}}X/T$ converges to a non-singular matrix of constants and $X^{\mathrm{T}}V/T$ and $X^{\mathrm{T}}u/T$ both converge in probability to zero. Since in large samples (5.2) approximately satisfies the assumptions of the generalized normal linear regression model, it is tempting to apply generalized least squares (GLS) to (5.2) to estimate δ. The GLS estimator is obtained by multiplying (5.2) by $(X^{\mathrm{T}}X)^{1/2}$ and applying OLS. This yields the TSLS estimator. The TSLS estimator does not have the finite sample properties of the GLS estimator in the generalized normal linear regression model since (5.2) does not fully satisfy the assumptions of that model. Proofs of the large sample properties of TSLS are given in Theil (1971, ch. 10) and Amemiya (1985, ch. 7).

The second interpretation is the source of the name TSLS. Write the structural equation (1.1) as

$$y = [X\Pi, X_1]\begin{bmatrix}\gamma \\ \beta\end{bmatrix} + u + (Y - X\Pi)\gamma. \tag{5.4}$$

Since the matrix $[X\Pi, X_1]$ is not stochastic, it is not correlated with the compound error term $u+(Y-X\Pi)\pi$. It is easy to show that rows of this error term are independently normally distributed with zero mean and constant variance. Hence, the obvious estimation procedure is to apply OLS to (5.4). The difficulty is that Π is unknown. The solution to this difficulty is a two stage procedure. In the first stage, the portion of the reduced form equation (1.2) which is for Y is estimated by OLS in order to obtain an estimate of Π. The OLS estimator of Π is $P=[X^{\mathrm{T}}X]^{-1}X^{\mathrm{T}}Y$. In the second stage XP is substituted for $X\Pi$ in (5.4), or, equivalently, for Y in the structural equation (1.1), and the resulting equation is estimated by OLS. The estimates of γ and β are the TSLS estimates.

The next two interpretations of TSLS use the sample analogue of (1.4) as a starting point. The TSLS estimator of γ is defined by

$$\hat{\gamma} = [P_2^{\mathrm{T}}X_2M_1X_2P_2]^{-1}P_2^{\mathrm{T}}X_2^{\mathrm{T}}M_1X_2p_2, \tag{5.5}$$

from which it is easy to verify that TSLS reduces to the ILS in the just-identified case. Anderson and Sawa (1973) provide a motivation for this formula. Premultiplying the structural equation (1.1) by $[X_2^{\mathrm{T}}M_1X_2]^{-1}X_2^{\mathrm{T}}M_1$ gives

$$p_2 = P_2\gamma + w \tag{5.6}$$

where w is normally distributed with zero mean and covariance $\omega^2[X_2^{\mathrm{T}}M_1X_2]^{-1}$ where ω^2 is Ω pre- and postmultiplied by $[1, -\gamma^{\mathrm{T}}]^{\mathrm{T}}$. Since the correlation between P_2 and w converges in probability to zero, in large samples (5.6) approximately satisfies the assumptions of the generalized linear regression model. Applying generalized least squares (GLS) to (5.6) gives (5.5). Another interpretation of (5.5) is that it is the estimator which minimizes

$$[1, -g^{\mathrm{T}}]W_1\begin{bmatrix}1 \\ -g\end{bmatrix} = (p_2 - P_2g)^{\mathrm{T}}X_2^{\mathrm{T}}M_1X_2(p_2 - P_2g) \tag{5.7}$$

where $W_1 = [y, Y]^{\mathrm{T}}M_1[y, Y]$ is the matrix of the sum of squared residuals from the OLS regression of $[y, Y]$ on X_1. The expression (5.7) is the GLS criterion function for (5.6) since the GLS estimator minimizes (5.7), that is, the TSLS estimator (5.5) minimizes (5.7).

6. THE k-CLASS FAMILY. The k-class family of estimators of δ is defined by

$$\hat{\delta}_k = [Z^{\mathrm{T}}(I - kM)Z]^{-1}Z^{\mathrm{T}}(I - kM)y \qquad (6.1)$$

where $M = I - X(X^{\mathrm{T}}X)^{-1}X$. This family was introduced by Theil (1953b, 1961). It includes the OLS estimator ($k = 0$) and the TSLS estimator ($k = 1$).

A remarkable fact is that the k-class family also includes LIML. The LIML estimator is obtained by setting $k = \lambda_0$, where λ_0 is the smallest root of

$$|W_1 - \lambda W| = 0. \qquad (6.2)$$

In the determinantal equation W_1, which is defined in section 5, is the sum of squared residuals from the OLS regression of $[y, Y]$ on X_1 and $W = [y. Y]^{\mathrm{T}}M[y. Y]$ which is the sum of squared residuals from a regression of $[y, Y]$ on X. The LIML estimator of γ minimizes the variance ratio

$$\frac{[1, -g^{\mathrm{T}}]W_1\begin{bmatrix}1\\-g\end{bmatrix}}{[1, -g^{\mathrm{T}}]W\begin{bmatrix}1\\-g\end{bmatrix}}. \qquad (6.3)$$

Another interpretation of LIML is that it maximizes the likelihood function of $[y, Y]$ subject to the restriction $\pi_2 - \Pi_2\gamma = 0$.

The k-class estimator $\hat{\delta}_k$ is consistent if $\mathrm{p\,lim}(k - 1) = 0$ and has the same limiting distribution as TSLS if $\mathrm{p\,lim}\, T^{1/2}(k - 1) = 0$. These conditions are clearly not satisfied when $k = 0$ and hence by OLS. The proof that these conditions are satisfied for LIML is based on a result in Anderson and Rubin (1950).

7. EXACT DISTRIBUTIONS AND SECOND ORDER APPROXIMATIONS. The limiting distribution of an estimator is an approximation to the finite sample distribution where the accuracy of the approximation gets better as the sample size increases. The exact finite sample distributions of TSLS and LIML are different. This illustrates the fact that not all the BAN estimators have the same finite sample distribution. The question is whether the differences in the finite sample distributions are important when choosing a BAN estimator. The answer depends on the sample size used in estimation of simultaneous equation models.

The accuracy of the limiting normal approximation to the distributions of the TSLS and LIML estimators has been investigated for the case of two endogenous variables. In these studies the two estimators are normalized such that the limiting distribution is standard normal. From a study of the tables and graphs of the distributions Anderson (1982) concludes:

> For many cases that occur in practice (perhaps most), the standard normal theory is inadequate for the TSLS estimator. Even though the moments of the LIML estimator are not finite, the standard normal distribution is a fairly good approximation to the actual distribution.

This finding implies that in many cases of practical interest the differences between the finite sample distributions of TSLS and LIML are important when deciding which estimator to use.

There are several ways to compare BAN estimators on the basis of finite sample properties. One is to use the exact distributions of the estimators. The exact finite sample distributions of TSLS and LIML have been examined using analytical and Monte Carlo techniques. For a survey of the results see Phillips (1983). The exact distributions are usually very complicated and as a result it is difficult to draw meaningful general conclusions. It is also difficult to draw general conclusions from the Monte Carlo studies.

Another approach is to use an approximation which is closer to the exact distribution. Let θ_{T} be a BAN estimator of the parameter θ. The procedure is to approximate the distribution of $T^{1/2}(\theta_{\mathrm{T}} - \theta)$ by the first three terms in an asymptotic expansion of the distribution in powers of $T^{-1/2}$: the expansion of the distribution is to terms of order $0(T^{-1})$ where the first term in the expansion is the limiting normal distribution of the BAN estimator. This expansion is described as second-order by some statisticians and third-order by others. We will use the former description and call the distribution based on this expansion the second-order approximate distribution. The first moment of this distribution is the (second-order) approximate bias of the estimator and the mean squared error is the (second-order) approximate mean squared error. For an excellent treatment of second-order asymptotic theory see Rothenberg (1984).

Anderson, Kunitomo and Morimune (1986) compared various single equation estimators on the basis of second-order approximate distributions. One criterion used for comparing alternative estimators was the approximate mean squared error. Another was the probability of concentration of the second-order approximate distribution about the true parameter value. They show that approximate mean squared errors of the fixed k-class estimators are greater than or equal to that of a modified LIML estimator. Similar results are obtained using the probability of concentration. As a consequence, they do not recommend using the fixed k-class estimators including the TSLS estimator.

A BAN estimator can be approximately corrected for bias by subtracting the approximate bias. Since the approximate bias will generally depend on the unknown parameter, this parameter is replaced by its BAN estimator to give an (second-order) approximate unbiased estimator. Under certain regularity conditions on the large sample expansions Takeuchi and Morimune (1985) prove that the approximate unbiased LIML estimator is second-order efficient: in the class of all approximate unbiased BAN estimators the approximate mean squared error of the approximate unbiased LIML estimator is at least as small as that of any other estimator. In this context the approximate mean squared error is equal to the second-order approximate variance. Anderson and his associates (1985) prove that the property of second-order efficiency is shared by other estimators including a Bayes estimator proposed by Dreze (1976) and a modification of LIML proposed by Fuller (1977). The approximate unbiased TSLS estimator is not second-order efficient.

The distribution of an estimator can also be approximated by expanding the distribution in powers of the structural error variance σ and letting σ go to zero. Anderson and his associates also compare the estimators using the small disturbance expansion. This does not alter the recommendations even though the uniform domination by one estimator over others is not necessarily obtainable using small disturbance expansions.

8. CONCLUSION. There is a caveat which must be kept in mind when considering the results reported by Anderson (1982) and Anderson et al. (1986). These results are for the model specified in section 1. This model may not be plausible in many empirical applications owing to the presence of non-stationary and possibly non-normal errors. In particular, the covariance matrix of the errors may be time varying. Most of the models which have been estimated incorporate dynamics. The dynamic specification and the values of the

roots of the associated characteristic equation may have an important influence on the finite sample distributions. The next step is to examine the finite sample distributions in models with more general error processes and in models with dynamics. Taking this next step seems to be a difficult one and so the final verdict on TSLS has still to be reached.

N.E. SAVIN

See also INSTRUMENTAL VARIABLES.

BIBLIOGRAPHY

Amemiya, T. 1985. *Advanced Econometrics*. Cambridge, Mass.: Harvard University Press.

Anderson, T.W. 1982. Some recent developments on the distribution of single-equation estimators. In *Advances in Econometrics*, ed. W. Hildenbrand, Cambridge: Cambridge University Press.

Anderson, T.W. and Rubin, H. 1949. Estimator of the parameters of a single equation in a complete system of stochastic equations. *Annals of Mathematical Statistics* 20, 46–63.

Anderson, T.W. and Rubin, H. 1950. The asymptotic properties of estimates of the parameters of a single equation in a complete system of stochastic equations. *Annals of Mathematical Statistics* 21, 570–82.

Anderson, T.W. and Sawa, T. 1973. Distributions of estimates of coefficients of a single equation in a simultaneous system and their asymptotic expansions. *Econometrica* 41, 683–714.

Anderson, T.W., Kunitomo, N. and Morimune, K. 1986. Comparing single equation estimators in a simultaneous equation system. *Econometric Theory* 2, 1–32.

Basmann, R.L. 1957. A generalized classical method of linear estimation of coefficients in a structural equation. *Econometrica* 25, 77–83.

Drèze, J.H. 1976. Bayesian limited information analysis of the simultaneous equations model. *Econometrica* 44, 1045–75.

Engle, R.F. 1984. Wald likelihood ratio and Lagrange multiplier tests. In *Handbook of Econometrics*, ed. Z. Griliches and M.D. Intriligator, Amsterdam: North-Holland.

Engle, R.F., Hendry, D.F. and Richard, J.-F. 1983. Exogeneity, *Econometrica* 51(2), 227–304.

Fuller, W.A. 1977. Some properties of a modification of the limited information estimator. *Econometrica* 45, 939–53.

Goldberger, A.S. 1964. *Econometric Theory*. New York: John Wiley.

Hausman, J. 1978. Specification tests in econometrics. *Econometrica* 46, 1251–71.

Hausman, J. 1983. Specification and estimation of simultaneous equation models. In *Handbook of Econometrics*, ed. Z. Griliches and M.D. Intriligator, Amsterdam: North-Holland.

Koopmans, T.C. and Hood, W.C. 1953. The estimation of simultaneous linear economic relationships. In *Studies in Econometric Method*, ed. W.C. Hood and T.C. Koopmans, New York: John Wiley.

Phillips, P.C.B. 1983. Exact small sample theory in the simultaneous equation model. In *Handbook of Econometrics*, ed. Z. Griliches and M.D. Intriligator, Amsterdam: North-Holland.

Revankar, H.S. and Hartley, M.J. 1973. An independence test and conditional unbiased predictions in the context of simultaneous equation systems. *International Economic Review* 14, 625–31.

Rothenberg, T.J. 1984. Approximating the distributions of econometric estimators and test statistics. In *Handbook of Econometrics*, ed. Z. Griliches and M.D. Intriligator, Amsterdam: North-Holland.

Takeuchi, K. and Morimune, K. 1985. Third-order efficiency of the extended maximum likelihood estimator in a simultaneous equation system. *Econometrica* 53, 177–200.

Theil, H. 1953a. Repeated least-squares applied to complete equation systems. The Hague: Central Planning Bureau (mimeographed).

Theil, H. 1953b. Estimation and simultaneous correlation in complete equation systems. The Hague: Central Planning Bureau (mimeographed).

Theil, H. 1961. *Economic Forecasts and Policy*. 2nd edn, Amsterdam: North-Holland.

Theil, H. 1971. *Principles of Econometrics*. New York: John Wiley.

Tintner, G. 1952. *Econometrics*. New York: John Wiley.

Wu, De-Min. 1973. Alternative tests of independence between stochastic regressors and disturbances. *Econometrica* 41, 733–50.

U

unbiased technical change *See* BIASED AND UNBIASED TECHNICAL CHANGE.

uncertainty. Nothing is more certain than the prevalence of uncertainty about the consequences of any economic decision. It is therefore entirely appropriate that uncertainty has been the subject of a large literature that grew out of important work in the early 1950s, and is still flourishing, as testified by the number of recent surveys and books such as Balch, McFadden and Wu (1974), Diamond and Rothschild (1978), Hirshleifer and Riley (1979), Lippman and McCall (1981), Fishburn (1982), Schoemaker (1982), Sinn (1983). No attempt will be made here to provide a comprehensive new survey. Rather, the devices of state contingent consequence functions and state preferences will be explained, and various types of uncertainty categorized. Following the pioneering work of Ramsey (1926, 1950), Savage (1954), and Anscombe and Aumann (1963) in particular, I shall discuss decision theory and when uncertainty can be described by subjective probabilities, based on an analysis of decision trees in the spirit of Raiffa (1968). While uncertainty *per se* can be largely treated through devices such as Debreu (1959) state contingent commodity contracts, the problems posed by asymmetric information and the lack of common knowledge are much more fundamental and intractable.

STATES OF THE WORLD AND CONTINGENT CONSEQUENCES. Economics is the scientific study of decisions affecting the allocation of scarce resources between competing ends. *Uncertainty* arises whenever a decision can lead to more than one possible consequence. Following Savage (1954, ch. 2) the term *state of the world* is commonly used to describe whatever determines the uncertain consequence of a decision. Formally, states of the world s in the set S, decisions d in the set D, and consequences c in the set C must be defined in a way which ensures that the consequences $c(d, s)$ of any decision d in any state of the world s is uniquely determined. Thus, states of the world must be defined so finely that no decision can possibly have more than one consequence in a given state of the world. Given the set S of possible states of the world, any decision d gives rise to a *contingent consequence function* (CCF) γ_d mapping S into the set of consequences C, given by:

$$\gamma_d(s) = c(d, s) \qquad (\text{all } s \in S) \tag{1}$$

Savage (1954) even defines an 'act' (or decision) as such a contingent consequence function, but this may be confusing because decisions which seem very different a priori may lead to identical CCFs. Jeffrey (1974) especially seriously questions whether decisions can ever have their consequences described so precisely in practice, and Jeffrey (1965) and Bolker (1967) have constructed a decision theory without using CCFs. But one might argue that their objections can be met by employing a much richer space of consequences.

CATEGORIES OF ECONOMIC UNCERTAINTY. In economics several different kinds of uncertainty arise, according to what aspect of the 'state of the world' is being considered. The first kind is *exogenous uncertainty*, concerning variables like consumers' tastes and firms' technologies which the economist usually treats as exogenous. An obvious example is the weather which affects both consumers' tastes and farmers' production possibilities in predictable ways. Other examples are medical uncertainties affecting a person's contracting a disease and recovery from it, as well as various kinds of accident. Often insurance against adverse exogenous uncertainty is available.

No economic system can reduce exogenous uncertainty, although insurance may help to mitigate its impact upon individuals. Other kinds of uncertainty, however, concern the operation of the economic system itself. In market economies, a buyer may be uncertain whether he will meet a suitable seller, and vice versa. Both may be uncertain about the terms at which trade will take place, as in the extensive literatures on search theory and bargaining. Such uncertainty can be reduced, to some extent, by individuals who take the trouble to search extensively. It can also be created by sellers who change their prices frequently and unpredictably, as currently exemplified by de-regulated airlines in the USA. Such uncertainty is *endogenous*; it results from the decisions of economic agents, which it is the task of the economist to explain and/or predict. Notice too that endogenous and exogenous uncertainty can interact, as when a dam bursts because of a combination of cost-cutting carelessness by the constructor – which is endogenous – and an exceptionally severe rainstorm – which is exogenous. The unhealthy effects of cigarette smoking also result from a combination of endogenous decisions affecting smoking and exogenous factors determining a smoker's susceptibility to disease.

An important kind of uncertainty in modern economies concerns economic policy and its impact on the tax system, interest rates, the provision of public goods, etc. This is *policy uncertainty* which, to the economist at least, is really a form of exogenous uncertainty, since it is the task of political science to explain policy.

Finally, a recent development is work on *extrinsic uncertainty*, due to Cass and Shell (1983). By 'extrinsic' uncertainty, they mean that there is no uncertainty about the usual exogenous variables such as tastes and technology, which would constitute 'intrinsic' uncertainty of a kind one naturally expects to affect the allocation of resources in an economy. They give 'sunspots' as an example of extrinsic uncertainty. They show that, in market economies where there are some agents who cannot insure themselves against extrinsic uncertainty before they are born, there may exist 'sunspot' equilibria in which the allocation depends upon the outcome of extrinsic uncertainty. This may be so even though there is a unique equilibrium in which extrinsic uncertainty does not matter. Thus the 'sunspot' equilibrium is not just some randomization of 'non-sunspot' equilibria, and the competitive market system is quite capable of producing uncertainty which is completely unrelated to any intrinsic uncertainty. It should be added that recent work on equilibrium with incomplete financial markets shows that there is likely to be a continuum of multiple equilibria, which suggests an even more prevalent form of extrinsic uncertainty regarding equilibrium prices and the resulting allocation of resources.

FROM STATE PREFERENCES TO RANDOM CONSEQUENCES. Earlier, contingent consequence functions (CCFs) were defined to describe uncertainty about the consequences of a decision. Particular examples of CCFs are the contingent commodity contracts of Debreu (1959, ch. 7). Arrow's (1953) ingenious device of contingent securities is closely related, provided that agents always foresee correctly at what prices they will be able to trade later on. For the 'Arrow–Debreu' theory of complete markets, it suffices to postulate that consumers have 'regular' preferences – obeying the standard properties – over the space of contingent commodity bundles, with goods distinguished by the state of the world in which they are available, as well as by physical properties including location and date. Indeed, a great deal of standard economic analysis applies in this case, as was realized by Hirshleifer (1966). His 'state-preference' approach to economic decisions under uncertainty relies precisely upon preferences over contingent commodity bundles.

The state preference approach makes no explicit reference to probabilities of states of the world, although implicitly a consumer's marginal willingness to pay for consumption in a specific state s will be higher, the more likely the occurrence of state s is believed to be. This observation suggests that it may be useful to consider how state preferences depend upon probabilities in those cases where probabilities are known. Of course, this is the subject of expected utility theory, discussed below, whose origins can be traced back at least to D. Bernoulli's (1738) attempt to resolve the 'St Petersburg paradox'. If probabilities are indeed known, then two CCFs which yield the same probability distribution of consequences may be regarded as equivalent. For example, suppose there are three states s_1, s_2, s_3 each with probability 1/3. Let c_1, c_2 be any pair of consequences. Then the three CCF's γ_1, γ_2, and γ_3 given by:

$$\begin{aligned} &\gamma_1(s_1) = c_1, \quad \gamma_1(s_2) = c_1, \quad \gamma_1(s_3) = c_2 \\ &\gamma_2(s_1) = c_2, \quad \gamma_2(s_2) = c_1, \quad \gamma_2(s_3) = c_1 \\ &\gamma_3(s_1) = c_1, \quad \gamma_3(s_2) = c_2, \quad \gamma_3(s_3) = c_1 \end{aligned} \tag{2}$$

all yield the same probability distribution of consequences, in which c_1 occurs with probability 2/3 and c_2 occurs with probability 1/3.

So, if every state of the world s happens to have an associated probability π_s, then uncertain consequences are equivalent to random consequences. For, given any CCF $\gamma: S \to C$, there is an associated probability distribution $\mu(\gamma, \pi)$ on C defined by:

$$\mu(\gamma, \pi)(B) = \sum_{s \in S(\gamma, B)} \pi_s \tag{3}$$

for every set of consequences B, a subset of C, where:

$$S(\gamma, B) = \{s \in S \mid \gamma(s) \in B\}. \tag{4}$$

(There are some technical problems of measurability here, which I shall avoid by assuming that the set S of possible states of the world is finite.)

Thus, corresponding to a preference ordering $\succsim$ on the space $M(C)$ of probability distributions over C, and to the probability distribution π on S the set of states of the world, there exists a unique corresponding preference ordering $\succsim(\pi)$ on the set S^C of CCF's $\gamma: S \to C$, with:

$$\gamma_1 \succsim (\pi) \gamma_2 \Leftrightarrow \mu(\gamma_1, \pi) \succsim \mu(\gamma_2, \pi) \tag{5}$$

for all pairs $\gamma_1, \gamma_2: S \to C$. Preferences over probability distributions in $M(C)$ then induce preferences over CCF's because each CCF γ gives rise to a unique probability distribution μ_γ in $M(C)$.

In principle, one could go on to ask whether, even if probabilities π_s are not known, there may be a (unique) probability distribution $\bar{\pi}$ on S such that $\succsim(\bar{\pi})$ is the preference ordering for CCF's.

If this is true for a unique probability distribution $\bar{\pi}$ on S, then one can say that $\bar{\pi}$ is the *subjective probability distribution*. The existence of subjective probabilities for general preferences $\succsim$ over $M(C)$ may appear to be a problem of some theoretical interest, in the spirit of Machina's (1982) recent work. Yet, understandably, the literature has concentrated upon a particularly appealing special case, in which the preference ordering $\succsim$ has an expected utility representation, relying upon the independence axiom which I shall discuss next. This leads to the theory of the simultaneous determination of subjective probabilities and utility which Savage (1954) and Anscombe and Aumann (1963) based on the fundamental ideas of Ramsey (1926, 1950) who was in turn apparently stimulated by Keynes (1921).

THE INDEPENDENCE AXIOM AND EXPECTED UTILITY. The independence axiom can be motivated as follows, using an idea due to Raiffa (1968, pp. 82–83). Suppose there is a decision tree with a chance node n_0, which is succeeded either by node n_1 with probability λ (where $0 < \lambda \leqslant 1$) or by node n_2 with probability $1 - \lambda$. Suppose too that at n_1 the decision maker chooses between two acts a_1 and a_2, and that act a_j results in the random consequence $\mu_j \in M(C)$ $(j = 1, 2)$. At n_2, on the other hand, there is no decision to make and the random consequence is μ_0. Then the decision maker chooses a_1 over a_2 at node n_1 if and only if he prefers μ_1 to μ_2. On the other hand, at node n_0, the decision maker will plan to choose a_1 over a_2 if and only if the random consequence $\lambda\mu_1 + (1 - \lambda)\mu_0$ is preferred to the alternative random consequence $\lambda\mu_2 + (1 - \lambda)\mu_0$. For, when μ_0 is still a possible random consequence because the decision maker does not know whether n_1 or n_2 will occur, the random consequence of planning to choose a_j if n_1 does occur is indeed $\lambda\mu_j + (1 - \lambda)\mu_0$ $(j = 1, 2)$. Thus, requiring plans to be consistent with actual later choices implies that:

$$\lambda\mu_1 + (1 - \lambda)\mu_0 \succsim \lambda\mu_2 + (1 - \lambda)\mu_0 \Leftrightarrow \mu_1 \succsim \mu_2 \tag{6}$$

for all random consequences μ_0, μ_1 and μ_2 and for all λ satisfying $0 < \lambda \leqslant 1$. This is the *independence axiom*, originally formulated by Samuelson (1952).

The *expected utility hypothesis* requires the existence of a "von Neumann-Morgenstern utility function" (NMUF) v, defined on C the space of consequences, with the property that for all pairs μ', μ'' of random consequences in $M(C)$:

$$\mu' \succsim \mu'' \Leftrightarrow E_{\mu'} v \geqslant E_{\mu''} v \tag{7}$$

where $E_\mu v$ is defined, for every μ in $M(C)$, as the expected utility expression:

$$E_\mu v = \sum_{c \in C} \mu(\{c\}) v(c) \tag{8}$$

The NMUF v can be replaced by any other NMUF $\tilde{v}$ which is cardinally equivalent, in the sense that:

$$\tilde{v}(c) \equiv \alpha v(c) + \beta \tag{9}$$

for some positive multiplicative constant α and an arbitrary additive constant β.

It is easy to check that the expected utility hypothesis implies the independence axiom. The converse is not true; without an extra assumption such as preferences being continuous in probabilities, the independence axiom does not imply the expected utility hypothesis – one can still have multidimensional or lexicographic utilities (see Hausner (1954), Thrall (1954) and Skala (1975)). But such a continuity condition or "Archimedean axiom" is sufficient (see Herstein and Milnor, 1953) and is anyway mostly just a technical requirement.

THE SURE-THING PRINCIPLE. Now we can return to the question posed earlier concerning the existence of subjective probabilities, but making use of the expected utility framework. Given that the preference ordering $\succsim$ is represented by the expected utility expression $E_\mu v$, do there exist unique subjective probabilities $\pi_s (s \in S)$ for which the preference ordering $\succsim(\pi)$ on C^S, the space of CCF's, is represented by the subjectively expected utility expression:

$$\sum_{s \in S} \pi_s v(\lambda(s)) \tag{10}$$

Just as the independence axiom is necessary for (7) to hold, a corresponding 'sure-thing principle' is required if (10) is indeed to represent the ordering $\succsim(\pi)$. This sure-thing principle has a similar motivation, moreover. Indeed, suppose that there is a decision tree in which 'nature' determines at node n_0 which of two disjoint events, either E or F, occurs. If E occurs at n_0, then the next node of the tree is n_1 at which the decision maker chooses between the two acts a_1 and a_2; if a_j is chosen, the consequences are described by $\gamma_j(s)$ $(s \in E; j = 1, 2)$. On the other hand, if F occurs at n_0, there is no decision to make, and the consequences are described by $\gamma(s)$ $(s \in F)$. Now the decision maker chooses a_1 over a_2 at n_1 if and only if the CCF γ_1: $E \to C$ is preferred to the alternative CCF γ_2: $E \to C$. On the other hand, suppose that the two CCF's $\bar{\gamma}_j$: $S \to C$ $(j = 1, 2)$ are defined by:

$$\bar{\gamma}_j(s) = \begin{cases} \gamma_j(s) & (s \in E) \\ \gamma(s) & (s \in F). \end{cases} \tag{11}$$

Then the decision maker at node n_0 will plan to choose a_1 over a_2 if and only if he prefers the CCF $\bar{\gamma}_1$ to $\bar{\gamma}_2$, because the CCF $\bar{\gamma}_j$ is what results from a combination of the uncertainty at node n_0 about the event E or F with the consequences of choosing act a_j at node n_1. For consistency of plans with actual choices later on, it must be true that:

$$\bar{\gamma}_1 \succsim_S^* \bar{\gamma}_2 \Leftrightarrow \gamma_1^E \succsim_E^* \gamma_2^E \tag{12}$$

where $\succsim_S^*$ denotes the preference ordering over C^S, the space of CCF's γ: $S \to C$, and $\succsim_E^*$ is the preference ordering over C^E, the space of restricted CCF's γ^E: $E \to C$ conditional upon event E having occurred. The equivalence (12) is the *sure-thing principle*, so called because the same CCF $\gamma(s) (s \in F)$ is a 'sure-thing', regardless of whether a_1 or a_2 is chosen at n_1. Really, both the sure-thing principle and the independence axiom are like weak dominance relations which feature prominently in both decision theory and game theory (cf. Arrow, 1971, p. 50).

Another appealing restriction on preferences arises when a restricted CCF γ^E: $E \to C$ yields the same consequence c in every state s of E. Then γ^E is effectively identical to the sure consequence c. So the *sure consequence principle* (which is closely related to the sure thing principle as defined above; indeed, that corresponds to Savage's (1954) P2, while the new principle corresponds to P3, and both seem regarded by Savage as part of his "sure thing principle") requires the existence of a *sure consequence preference ordering* $\succsim_C$ on the set of consequences C such that:

$$\text{If} \quad \gamma_1(s) = c_1, \quad \gamma_2(s) = c_2 \quad (\text{all } s \in E),$$

then

$$\gamma_1^E \succsim_E^* \gamma_2^E \Leftrightarrow c_1 \succsim_C c_2 \tag{13}$$

for every event E and pair of consequences c_1, c_2.

HORSE LOTTERIES AND SUBJECTIVE PROBABILITIES. Savage (1954) and Arrow (1965, 1971) proceed to derive subjective probabilities from a number of additional postulates, in particular one called "ordering of events" whose motivation is not nearly so appealing to this author as the independence axiom or the sure-thing principle. In addition, Savage and Arrow both assume that events can be partitioned arbitrarily finely so that, in the end, to every possible number p between zero and one, there exist events with subjective probabilities arbitrarily close to p. An alternative and simpler derivation of subjective probabilities was first suggested by Anscombe and Aumann (1963) through the device of "horse lotteries", which combine uncertain states of the world determined by nature with "extraneous uncertainty" determined through artificial lotteries with known probabilities.

Formally, a *horse lottery* is a probability distribution μ on C^S, the space of CCF's. The uncertain consequence of a horse lottery therefore depends both on the realization of a random process with known probabilities μ and on the state of the world s. The probability distribution μ is therefore really the joint multivariate distribution of the random consequences $\gamma(s)$ $(s \in S)$.

The independence axiom is equally appealing for horse lotteries. Together with continuity in probabilities, it implies the existence of an NMUF U^E for every $E \subset S$, defined on C^E the space of CCF's, whose expected value represents preferences on $M(C^E)$. The sure-thing principle is justified for *independent* random CCF's in the sense that for any $\mu_1^E, \mu_2^E \in M(C^E)$ and $\mu^F \in M(C^F)$, where E and F are disjoint:

$$\mu_1^E \times \mu^F \succsim_S^* \mu_2^E \times \mu^F \Leftrightarrow \mu_1^E \succsim_E^* \mu_2^E \tag{14}$$

where for $j = 1, 2$, $\mu_j^E \times \mu^F$ is the random CCF $v_j \in M(C^S)$ for which:

$$v_j(\{\gamma^E, \gamma^F\}) = \mu_j^E(\{\gamma^E\}) \times \mu^F(\{\gamma^F\}) \tag{15}$$

for all $\gamma^E \in C^E, \gamma^F \in C^F$.

Horse lotteries also suggest a *random* sure consequence principle, as follows. Suppose that $\mu_1, \mu_2 \in M(C^E)$ each have the property that consequences in different states of the world are perfectly correlated, so that for $j = 1, 2$ one has $\mu_j(\{\gamma^E\}) = 0$ unless there is a constant consequence c for which $\gamma^E(s) = c$ (all $s \in E$). Then μ_j is equivalent to a random "sure consequence" distribution λ_j on C with the property that:

$$\lambda_j(\{c\}) = \mu_j(\{\gamma^E | \gamma^E(s) = c \text{ (all } s \in E)\} \tag{16}$$

The natural counterpart of (13) then requires the existence of an NMUF v on C, independent of E, whose expected value represents the preference ordering for all pairs of random sure consequences – this is the *random sure consequence principle.*

Invoking the axioms so far – the independence axiom, the sure-thing principle for independent random CCF's, the random sure consequence principle, and continuity in probabilities – does not quite suffice to guarantee the existence of subjective probabilities. If there are only two possible consequences in the set C, preferences which amount to preferring known probabilities, as against "unreliable probabilities," are still possible, as in "Ellsberg's paradox" (1961) – see also Drèze (1974) and Gärdenfors and Sahlin (1982). When, however, C contains at least three consequences, of which no two are indifferent according to the ordering $\succsim_C$, then there do exist an NMUF v on C and positive constants $\alpha_s (s \in S)$ such that, for every $E \subset S$ and all CCF's $\gamma_1^E, \gamma_2^E: E \to C$:

$$\gamma_1^E \succsim_E^* \gamma_2^E \Leftrightarrow \sum_{s \in E} \alpha_s v[\gamma_1(s)] \geqslant \sum_{s \in E} \alpha_s v[\gamma_2(s)]. \quad (17)$$

Thus the utility function

$$U^E(\gamma^E) = \sum_{s \in E} \alpha_s v(\gamma(s))$$

represents $\succsim_E^*$ over C^E, the space of CCF's $\gamma^E: E \to C$, and its expected value represents preferences over $M(C^E)$, the set of random CCF's. Normalizing by taking:

$$\pi(s \mid E) := \alpha_s \Big/ \sum_{s' \in E} \alpha_{s'}, \qquad (s \in E) \quad (18)$$

implies that the NMUF U^E on C^E takes the subjectively expected utility form:

$$U^E(\gamma^E) = \sum_{s \in E} \pi(s \mid E) v[\gamma(s)] \quad (19)$$

(ignoring an irrelevant positive multiplicative constant). Notice that one of the assumptions of Anscombe and Aumann (1963), Harsanyi (1978) and Myerson (1979) is logically entailed by the assumptions given here; specifically, the assumption that preferences on $M(C^E)$ depend only on the marginal probabilities $\mu(s) \in M(C)$ for every state $s \in E$. This is immediate from the fact that the expected value of (19) can be written in the form:

$$E_\mu U^E(\gamma^E) = \sum_{s \in E} \pi(s \mid E) E_{\mu(s)} v[\gamma(s)] \quad (20)$$

where $\mu(s)$ is the marginal distribution of consequences in state s induced by the joint distribution μ of CCG's.

It is noteworthy that each α_s must be *positive* so there can be no zero probabilities in this formulation. Zero probabilities give rise to inconsistencies in some decision trees if an event with zero probability does occur, because acts which were originally indifferent will cease to be indifferent, in general. Events which cannot occur must be omitted from the decision tree. Of course, the finiteness of the set S is crucial here.

Also noteworthy is the fact that consistency implies Bayes' rule (Weller, 1978) because for any pair of events E' and E'':

$$\pi(E' \mid E'') = \sum_{s \in E'} \pi(s \mid E'') = \sum_{s \in E' \cap E''} \alpha_s \Big/ \sum_{s' \in E''} \alpha_{s'}$$

from which it follows that:

$$\pi(F \mid E \cap G) = \pi(E \mid F \cap G)\pi(F \mid G)/\pi(E \mid G). \quad (21)$$

This is indeed Bayes' rule for the posterior probability of F given E and G, in terms of the prior probability of F given G and the likelihood of E given F and G. In particular, (21) is equivalent to:

$$\frac{\pi(F_1 \mid E \cap G)}{\pi(F_2 \mid E \cap G)} = \frac{\pi(E \mid F_1 \cap G)\pi(F_1 \mid G)}{\pi(E \mid F_2 \cap G)\pi(F_2 \mid G)} \quad (22)$$

which has posterior probabilities proportional to the product of prior probabilities with likelihoods.

CONTINGENT FEASIBILITY OF CONSEQUENCES. The above discussion treated the space of consequences C as the same in every state of the world. Yet as Jones-Lee (1979) and others have rightly emphasized, when uncertainty concerns events such as death or injury, not all consequences are feasible in every state. So let C_s denote the set of consequences which are possible in state s, for every $s \in S$, and let C denote $\cup_{s \in S} C_s$. For every $E \subset S$, let C^E denote the product space $\Pi_{s \in E} C_s$.

In this more general framework, the sure-thing principle (12) retains its appeal, as does the sure-consequence principle (13) provided that CCF's $\gamma^E: E \to C$ are restricted to satisfy the obvious requirement:

$$\gamma^E(s) \in C_s \qquad (\text{all } s \in E) \quad (23)$$

Equation (17) no longer follows from the independence axiom, the sure-thing principle, the sure consequence principle, and continuity of probability, even if C does contain at least three members. To rule out Ellsberg-like paradoxes, it suffices to assume that there are two states s', s'' and three consequences c_1, c_2, c_3 – no two of which are indifferent according to the sure consequence ordering $\succsim_C$ – such that c_1, c_2, c_3 all belong to $C_{s'} \cap C_{s''}$. Even then, however, all that can be shown is the existence of state dependent NMUF's $w(s, \cdot)$, defined on C_s for every $s \in S$, such that the NMUF whose expected value represents preferences on $M(C^E)$ takes the additive form:

$$U^E(\gamma^E) = \sum_{s \in E} w[s, \gamma(s)]. \quad (24)$$

Following Wilson (1968) and Myerson (1979), the function w is called an *evaluation function*.

One problem which remains in showing that (24) can be expressed in the form (19) for well defined subjective probabilities $\pi(s \mid E)$ is that the probabilities may not be uniquely defined; obviously this happens whenever S can be partitioned into two events S' and S'' such that $\cup_{s \in S'} C_s$ and $\cup_{s \in S''} C_s$ are disjoint. To overcome this difficulty, Karni, Schmeidler and Vind (1983) assume that there is some set of all positive probabilities $\bar{\pi}_s (s \in S)$ such that the decision-maker could conceivably be convinced that these were the true probabilities, and would then maximize the expected value accordingly. Here, the expected value is the following sum (where the first sum is as c^E varies over the whole of C^E):

$$\sum \mu(c^E) \sum_{s \in E} \bar{\pi}_s v(c_s) \quad (25)$$

for every $\mu \in M(C^E)$ and $E \subset S$, where v is a well defined NMUF on C, the whole set of possible consequences. Now, when state s is known to have occurred, (24) implies maximizing the expected value of $w(s, c)$ while (25) implies maximizing the expected value of $v(c)$. So these must be cardinally equivalent NMUF's, which implies that there exist positive multiplicative constants α_s and arbitrary additive constants β_s such that:

$$w(s, c) = \alpha_s v(c) + \beta_s \qquad (\text{all } s \in S,\ c \in C_s) \quad (26)$$

Ignoring the irrelevant additive constants and normalizing using (18), gives the subjectively expected form (19) of (24). The positive conditional probabilities $\pi(s \mid E)$ emerge as before as marginal rates of substitution, in effect, between measures of von Neumann–Morgenstern utility in state s and in event E, whenever $s \in E \subset S$.

The crucial new assumption here, of course, was the possibility of having objective probabilities $\bar{\pi}_s (s \in S)$. Yet this is obviously a necessary condition for the existence of subjective probabilities, because having subjective probabilities become objectively known should not affect behaviour. It is interesting that the same condition is also sufficient; indeed, only *one* set of possible objective probabilities are needed, whereas when probabilities are unknown one could well argue that whole ranges of objective probabilities should be viewed as possibilities.

Maximization of subjectively expected utility has been called *Bayesian rationality* by Harsanyi (1975, 1978) and others. The last few sections have presented the following six sufficient conditions for Bayesian rationality – (i) existence of a preference ordering, (ii) the independence axiom, (iii) continuity with respect to objective probabilities, (iv) the sure-thing principle, (v) the sure consequence principle, and (vi) rationality (in the sense of the previous five conditions) for some possible set of probabilities attached to states of the world.

BAYESIAN RATIONAL SOCIAL CHOICE WITH COMMON PROBABILITIES. So far I have considered rationality just for individual choice under uncertainty. But the same standards of rationality apply to policy objectives as well, which are the subject of Arrow's (1951, 1963) social choice theory. When there is uncertainty, however, Harsanyi's (1955) approach seems more suitable. There must exist subjective probabilities $\pi_s (s \in S)$ for society and a 'von Neumann–Bergson social welfare function' (NMBSWF) W such that the social objective is to maximize the expected value of:

$$W^E(c^E) = \sum_{s \in E} \pi(s \mid E) w(c_s). \tag{27}$$

Suppose that society consists of individuals in the finite membership set M. To ensure the existence of subjective probabilities, suppose that it is possible for all individuals to know that $\bar{\pi}_s (s \in E)$ are the true probabilities. In this case, society's NMBSWF is:

$$\bar{W}^E(c^E) = \sum_{s \in E} \bar{\pi}_s w(c_s) \tag{28}$$

while each individual i has an NMUF of the form:

$$\bar{U}_i^E(c^E) = \sum_{s \in E} \bar{\pi}_s v_i(c_s). \tag{29}$$

As shown by Harsanyi (1955) and (under less restrictive conditions) by Border (1985), the usual Pareto condition of social choice theory then implies the existence of positive welfare weights ω_i $(i \in M)$ for which:

$$w(c_s) = \sum_{i \in M} \omega_i v_i(c_s). \tag{30}$$

Returning to (27), this now becomes:

$$W^E(c^E) = \sum_{s \in E} \pi(s \mid E) \sum_{i \in M} \omega_i v_i(c_s). \tag{31}$$

When each individual i has his own subjective probabilities $\pi_i(s \mid E)$, i's objective is

$$U_i^E(c^E) = \sum_{s \in E} \pi_i(s \mid E) v_i(c_s) \tag{32}$$

and the usual Pareto condition is then generally violated unless

$$\pi_j(s \mid E) = \pi(s \mid E) \qquad (\text{all } i \in M). \tag{33}$$

whenever $s \in E \subset S$. Thus Paretian social choice experiences difficulties except when individuals have identical subjective probabilities, as was first realized by Diamond (1967). In particular, there is a contradiction between the ex-ante and ex-post approaches to welfare economics under uncertainty. For the ex-ante approach suggests combining individuals' ex-ante expected utilities into an ex-ante social welfare function, such as the expected value of:

$$\sum_{i \in M} \omega_i \sum_{s \in E} \pi_i(s \mid E) v_i(c_s). \tag{34}$$

Whereas the ex-post approach suggests taking the socially expected value of ex-post social welfare:

$$\sum_{s \in E} \pi(s \mid E) \sum_{i \in M} \omega_i v_i(c_s) \tag{35}$$

which generally differs from (34) unless (33) is satisfied. Apart from Diamond (1967), the contrast between ex-ante and ex-post has been discussed by Starr (1973) and many others, including Hammond (1983).

These difficulties for Paretian social choice and welfare economics have proved intractable. One feels that the ex-ante approach embodied in (34) pays too much heed to probabilities $\pi_i(s \mid E)$ that may be based on poor information. Yet the ex-post approach smacks of paternalism if the probabilities $\pi(s \mid E)$ are imposed, as it seems that they must be. A possible resolution may be to construct individual types t_i $(i \in M)$ broadly enough, as in Mertens and Zamir's (1985) recent elaboration of Harsanyi's (1967, 1968) games of incomplete information, so that there is a common joint conditional prior probability distribution $\pi^*(s, t^M \mid E)$ on combinations of social states s and profiles $t^M = (t_i)_{i \in M}$ of individuals' types, for every $E \subset S$. Then, provided that $\bar{t}^M$ is known, the natural NMBSWF to use is:

$$\sum_{s \in E} \pi^*(s \mid \bar{t}^M, E) \sum_{i \in M} \omega_i v_i(c_s) \tag{36}$$

with probabilities conditional upon $\bar{t}^M$ and E. This is so even though each individual i, knowing only t_i, desires to maximize the expected value of the sum over all possible t^M of:

$$\sum_{s \in E} \pi^*(s, t^M \mid t_i, E) v_i(c_s) \tag{37}$$

with probabilities conditional upon t_i and E, and even though the Pareto condition is then violated in general unless it happens that:

$$\pi^*(s \mid \bar{t}^M, E) = \pi^*(s, t^M \mid t_i, E) \qquad (\text{all } s \in E,\ i \in M) \tag{38}$$

which generally implies that $\pi^*(s \mid t^M, E)$ is independent of t^M—i.e., individuals have common subjective probabilities. If t^M is not known, the natural NMBSWF is the sum over all possible t^M of:

$$\sum_{s \in E} \pi^*(s, t^M \mid E) \sum_{i \in M} \omega_i v_i(c_s). \tag{39}$$

This is only a *possible* resolution, however, whose full implications remain unexplored as this is written. Reconciling conflicting subjective probabilities raised conceptual issues far beyond anything else yet discussed in this essay.

DIFFERENCES IN INDIVIDUALS' INFORMATION. In the discussion of single person decision theory, uncertainty was handled in principle by the device of contingent consequence functions. Thereafter conditions were given for a person's decisions to be Bayesian rational – i.e., correspond to maximizing the expected value of an NMUF, attaching subjective probabilities to each state of the world. Provided that all individuals also share the same information and the same subjective probabilities throughout, it is also straightforward in principle to use contingent consequence functions (or Debreu's contingent commodity contracts in economies) in order to adapt any piece of standard static economic analysis to allow for uncertainty. It is true that expected utility maximization introduces a special additive structure to preferences which permit special results to be derived, as in the theory of risk-aversion. But really this is incidental rather than fundamental.

As the discussion of the previous section begins to illustrate, fundamental new issues arise once one recognizes that individuals do not all share the same information and probability beliefs. There, the contrast between ex-ante and ex-post and the dilemma posed for Paretian social choice and welfare economics were noted. Far more important, however, is the realization that the environment in which an individual makes decisions is not just determined by an uncertain 'state of the world' which is chosen passively by 'nature' who, one presumes, has no objectives of her own. In addition, in a game of imperfect or incomplete information, there is uncertainty about the strategic choices by other 'players' who may well have very definite objectives (even if there is uncertainty about these objectives, as indeed there is in games of incomplete information). Such uncertainty is much better able to justify Knight's (1921) claim that 'risk' offers no profit opportunities whereas 'uncertainty' does – after all, complete Arrow–Debreu markets for contingent commodities may well remove profit opportunities that arise from uncertain states of the world, but not those that result because some traders are better informed than others about profit opportunities.

So, uncertainty *per se* really introduces little that is fundamentally new into economics. It is when individuals have different information as well that the position changes dramatically.

PETER J. HAMMOND

See also DECISION THEORY; EXPECTATIONS; EXPECTED UTILITY AND MATHEMATICAL EXPECTATION; EXPECTED UTILITY HYPOTHESIS; RISK.

BIBLIOGRAPHY

Anscombe, F.J. and Aumann, R.J. 1963. A definition of subjective probability. *Annals of Mathematical Statistics* 34, 199–205.

Arrow, K.J. 1951. *Social Choice and Individual Values*. New York: John Wiley; 2nd edn, New Haven: Yale University Press, 1963.

Arrow, K.J. 1953, 1963. The rôle of securities in the optimal allocation of risk-bearing. *Review of Economic Studies* 31, 91–6; first published as 'Le rôle des valeurs boursières pour la répartition la meilleure des risques', *Économetrie* (Colloques Internationaux du Centre National de la Recherche Scientifique) 11, 41–7; reprinted as ch. 4 of Arrow (1971) and as ch. 3 of Arrow (1983).

Arrow, K.J. 1965. *Aspects of the Theory of Risk-Bearing*. Helsinki: Yrjö Jahnsson Foundation.

Arrow, K.J. 1971. *Essays in the Theory of Risk-Bearing*. Amsterdam: North-Holland and Chicago: Markham.

Arrow, K.J. 1983. *Collected Papers of Kenneth J. Arrow, 2: General Equilibrium*. Cambridge, Mass.: The Belknap Press of Harvard University Press.

Balch, M., McFadden, D. and Wu, S. (eds) 1974. *Essays on Economic Behavior under Uncertainty*. Amsterdam: North-Holland.

Bernoulli, D. 1738. Specimen theoriae novae de mensura sortis. *Commentarii academiae scientiarum imperialis Petropolitanae* 5, 175–92. Translated by L. Sommer (1954) as 'Exposition of a new theory on the measurement of risk', *Econometrica* 22, 23–36.

Bolker, E.D. 1967. A simultaneous axiomatization of utility and subjective probability. *Philosophy of Science* 34, 333–40.

Border, K.C. 1985. More on Harsanyi's utilitarian cardinal welfare theorem. *Social Choice and Welfare* 1, 279–81.

Cass, D. and Shell, K. 1983. Do sunspots matter? *Journal of Political Economy* 91, 193–227.

Debreu, G. 1959. *Theory of Value: An Axiomatic Analysis of General Equilibrium*. New York: John Wiley.

Diamond, P.A. 1967. The role of a stock market in a general equilibrium model with technological uncertainty. *American Economic Review* 57, 759–76.

Diamond, P.A. and Rothschild, M. (eds) 1978. *Uncertainty in Economics: Reading and Exercises*. New York: Academic Press.

Drèze, J.H. 1974. Axiomatic theories of choice, cardinal utility and subjective probability: A review. In *Allocation under Uncertainty* ed. J.H. Drèze, London: Macmillan, 3–23.

Ellsberg, D. 1961. Risk, ambiguity and the Savage axioms. *Quarterly Journal of Economics* 75, 643–69.

Fishburn, P.C. 1982. *The Foundations of Expected Utility*. Dordrecht: Reidel.

Gärdenfors, P. and Sahlin, N.-E. 1982. Unreliable probabilities, risk taking, and decision making. *Synthèse* 53, 361–86.

Hammond, P.J. 1983. Ex-post optimality as a dynamically consistent objective for collective choice under uncertainty. In *Social Choice and Welfare*, ed. P.K. Pattanaik and M. Salles, Amsterdam: North-Holland, 175–205.

Harsanyi, J.C. 1955. Cardinal welfare, individualistic ethics, and interpersonal comparisons of utility. *Journal of Political Economy* 63, 309–21.

Harsanyi, J.C. 1967, 1968. Games with incomplete information played by 'Bayesian' players, I–III. *Management Science; Theory* 14, 159–82, 320–34 and 486–502.

Harsanyi, J.C. 1975. Nonlinear social welfare functions: do welfare economists have a special exemption from Bayesian rationality? *Theory and Decision* 6, 311–32.

Harsanyi, J.C. 1978. Bayesian decision theory and utilitarian ethics. *American Economic Review, Papers and Proceedings* 68, 223–8.

Hausner, M. 1954. Multidimensional utilities. In R.M. Thrall et al. (eds) (1954), 167–90.

Herstein, I.N. and Milnor, J. 1953. An axiomatic approach to measurable utility. *Econometrica* 21, 291–7.

Hirshleifer, 1966. Investment decision under uncertainty: applications of the state-preference approach. *Quarterly Journal of Economics* 80, 252–77.

Hirshleifer, J. and Riley, J.G. 1979. The analysis of uncertainty and information: an expository survey. *Journal of Economic Literature* 17, 1375–421.

Jeffrey, R.C. 1965. *The Logic of Decision*. New York: McGraw-Hill.

Jeffrey, R.C. 1974. Frameworks for preference. In Balch, McFadden and Wu (1974), 74–9.

Jones-Lee, M.W. 1979. The expected conditional utility theorem for the case of personal probabilities and state conditional utility functions: a proof and some notes. *Economic Journal* 89, 834–49.

Karni, E., Schmeidler, D. and Vind, K. 1983. On state dependent preferences and subjective probabilities. *Econometrica* 51, 1021–31.

Keynes, J.M. 1921. *A Treatise on Probability*. London: Macmillan.

Knight, F.H. 1921, 1971. *Risk, Uncertainty and Profit*. Chicago: University of Chicago Press.

Kyburg, H.E., Jr. and Smokler, H.E. (eds) 1964. *Studies in Subjective Probability*. New York: John Wiley.

Lippman, S.A. and McCall, J.J. 1981. The economics of uncertainty: selected topics and probabilistic methods. In *Handbook of Mathematical Economics*, Vol. 1, ed. K.J. Arrow and M.D. Intriligator, Amsterdam: North-Holland, 211–84.

Machina, M. 1982. 'Expected utility' analysis without the independence axiom. *Econometrica* 50, 277–323.

Mertens, J.-F. and Zamir, S. 1985. Formalization of Harsanyi's notions of 'type' and 'consistency' in games with incomplete information. *International Journal of Game Theory* 14, 1–29.

Myerson, R.B. 1979. An axiomatic derivation of subjective probability, utility and evaluation functions. *Theory and Decision* 11, 339–52.

Raiffa, H. 1968. *Decision Analysis: Introductory Lectures on Choices under Uncertainty*. Reading, Mass.: Addison-Wesley.

Ramsey, F.P. 1926. Truth and probability. In F.P. Ramsey, *The Foundations of Mathematics and Other Logical Essays*, ed. R.B. Braithwaite, New York: Humanities Press, 1950, and in Kyburg and Smokler (1964).

Samuelson, P.A. 1952. Probability, utility and the independence axiom. *Econometrica* 20, 670–8.

Savage, L.J. 1954. *The Foundations of Statistics*. New York: John Wiley, and Dover. 2nd revised edn, 1972.

Schoemaker, P.J.H. 1982. The expected utility model: its variants, purposes, evidence and limitations. *Journal of Economic Literature* 20, 529–63.

Sinn, H.-W. 1983. *Economic Decisions Under Uncertainty*. Amsterdam: North-Holland.

Skala, H.J. 1975. *Non-Archimedean Utility Theory*. Dordrecht: D. Reidel.

Starr, R. 1973. Optimal production and allocation under uncertainty. *Quarterly Journal of Economics* 87, 668–90.

Thrall, R.M. 1954. Applications of multidimensional utility theory. In R.M. Thrall et al. (eds), 181–6.

Thrall, R.M., Coombs, C.H. and Davis, R.L. (eds) 1954. *Decision Processes*. New York: John Wiley.

Weller, P.A. 1978. Consistent intertemporal decision making under uncertainty. *Review of Economic Studies* 45, 263–6.

Wilson, R.B. 1968. The theory of syndicates. *Econometrica* 36, 119–32.

uncertainty and general equilibrium. One of the notable intellectual achievements of economic theory during the past years has been the rigorous elaboration of the Walras–Pareto theory of value; that is, the theory of the existence and optimality of competitive equilibrium. Although many economists and mathematicians contributed to this development, the resulting edifice owes so much to the pioneering and influential work of Arrow and Debreu that in this paper I shall refer to it as the 'Arrow–Debreu theory'. (For comprehensive treatments, together with references to previous work, see Debreu, 1959, and Arrow and Hahn, 1971.)

The Arrow–Debreu theory was not originally put forward for the case of uncertainty, but an ingenious device introduced by Arrow (1953), and further elaborated by Debreu (1953), enabled the theory to be reinterpreted to cover the case of uncertainty about the availability of resources and about consumption and production possibilities. (See Debreu, 1959, ch. 7, for a unified treatment of time and uncertainty.)

Subsequent research has extended the Arrow–Debreu theory to take account of (1) differences in information available to different economic agents, and the 'production' of information, (2) the incompleteness of markets, and (3) the sequential nature of markets. The consideration of these complications has stimulated the developments of new concepts of equilibrium, which will be discussed in this article under the headings: (1) temporary equilibrium, (2) equilibrium of plans, prices, and price expectations, and (3) rational expectations equilibrium. The consideration of these features of real-world markets has also made possible a general-equilibrium analysis of money and securities markets, institutions about which the original Arrow–Debreu theory could provide only limited insights.

REVIEW OF THE ARROW–DEBREU MODEL OF A COMPLETE MARKET FOR PRESENT AND FUTURE CONTINGENT DELIVERY. In this section I review the approach of Arrow (1953) and Debreu (1959) to incorporating uncertainty about the environment into a Walrasian model of competitive equilibrium. The basic idea is that commodities are to be distinguished, not only by their physical characteristics and by the location and dates of their availability and/or use, but also by the environmental event in which they are made available and/or used. For example, ice cream made available (at a particular location on a particular date) if the weather is hot may be considered to be a different commodity from the same kind of ice cream made available (at the same location and date) if the weather is cold. We are thus led to consider a list of 'commodities' that is greatly expanded by comparison with the corresponding case of certainty about the environment. The standard arguments of the theory of competitive equilibrium, applied to an economy with this expanded list of commodities, then require that we envisage a 'price' for each commodity in the list, or, more precisely, a set of price ratios specifying the rate of exchange between each pair of commodities.

Just what institutions could, or do, effect such exchanges is a matter of interpretation that is, strictly speaking, outside the model. I shall present one straightforward interpretation, and then comment briefly on an alternative interpretation.

First, however, it will be useful to give a more precise account of concepts of environment and event that I shall be employing. The description of the 'physical world' is decomposed into three sets of variables: (1) decision variables, which are controlled (chosen) by economic agents; (2) environmental variables, which are not controlled by any economic agent; and (3) all other variables, which are completely determined (possibly jointly) by decisions and environmental variables. A state of the environment is a complete specification (history) of the environmental variables from the beginning to the end of the economic system in question. An event is set of states; for example, the event 'the weather is hot in New York on July 1, 1970' is the set of all possible histories of the environment in which the temperature in New York during the day of July 1, 1970, reaches a high of at least (say) 75°F. Granted that we cannot know the future with certainty, at any given date, there will be a family of elementary observable (knowable) events, which can be represented by a partition of the set of all possible states (histories) into a family of mutually exclusive subsets. It is natural to assume that the partitions corresponding to successive dates are successively finer, which represents the accumulation of information about the environment.

We shall imagine that a 'market' is organized before the beginning of the physical history of the economic system. An elementary contract in this market will consist of the purchase (or sale) of some specified number of units of a specified commodity to be delivered at a specified location and date, if and only if a specified elementary event occurs. Payment for this purchase is to be made now (at the beginning), in 'units of account', at a specified price quoted for that commodity-location-date-event combination. Delivery of the commodity in more than one elementary event is obtained by combining a suitable set of elementary contracts. For example, if delivery of one quart of ice cream (at a specified location and date) in hot weather costs \$1.50 (now) and delivery of one-quart in non-hot weather costs \$1.10, then sure delivery of one quart (i.e., whatever the weather) costs \$1.50 + \$1.10 = \$2.60.

There are two groups of economic agents in the economy: producers and consumers. A producer chooses a production plan, which determines his input and/or output of each commodity at each date in each elementary event. (I shall henceforth suppress explicit reference to location, it being understood that the location is specified in the term commodity.) For a given set of prices, the present value of a production plan is the sum of the values of the inputs minus the sum of the values of the outputs. Each producer is characterized by a set of production plans that are (physically) feasible for him: his production possibility set.

A consumer chooses a consumption plan, which specifies his consumption of each commodity at each date in each elementary event. Each consumer is characterized by: (1) a set of consumption plans that are (physically, psychologically, etc.) feasible for him, his consumption possibility set; (2) preferences among the alternative plans that are feasible for him; (3) his endowment of physical resources, i.e., a specification of the quantity of each commodity, e.g., labour, at each date in each event, with which he is exogenously endowed; and (4) his shares in each producer, that is, the fraction of the present value of each producer's production plan that will be credited to the consumer's account. (For any one producer, the sum of the consumers' shares is unity.) For given prices and given production plans of all the producers, the present net worth of a consumer is the total value of his resources plus the total value of his shares of the present values of producers' production plans.

An equilibrium of the economy is a set of prices, a set of production plans (one for each producer), and a set of consumption plans (one for each consumer), such that (a) each producer's plan has maximum present value in his production possibility set; (b) each consumer's plan maximizes his preferences within his consumption possibility set, subject to the additional (budget) constraint that the present cost of his consumption plan not exceed his present net worth; (c) for each commodity at each date in each elementary event, the total demand equals the total supply; i.e., the total planned consumption equals the sum of the total resource endowments and the total planned net output (where inputs are counted as negative outputs).

Notice that (1) producers and consumers are 'price takers'; (2) for given prices there is no uncertainty about the present value of a production plan or of given resource endowments, nor about the present cost of a consumption plan; (3) therefore, for given prices and given producers' plans, there is no uncertainty about a given consumer's present net worth; (4) since a consumption plan may specify that, for a given commodity at a given date, the quantity consumed is to vary according to the event that actually occurs, a consumer's preferences among plans will reflect not only his 'tastes' but also his subjective beliefs about the likelihoods of different events and his attitude towards risk (Savage, 1954).

It follows that beliefs and attitudes towards risk play no role in the assumed behaviour of producers. On the other hand, beliefs and attitudes towards risk do play a role in the assumed behaviour of consumers, although for given prices and production plans each consumer knows his (single) budget constraint with certainty.

I shall call the model just described an 'Arrow–Debreu' economy. One can demonstrate, under 'standard conditions': (1) the existence of an equilibrium, (2) the Pareto optimality of an equilibrium, and (3) that, roughly speaking, every Pareto optimal choice of production and consumption plans is an equilibrium relative to some price system for some distribution of resource endowments and shares (Debreu, 1959).

In the above interpretation of the Arrow–Debreu economy, all accounts are settled before the history of the economy begins, and there is no incentive to revise plans, reopen the market or trade in shares. There is an alternative interpretation, which will be of interest in connection with the rest of this entry but which corresponds to exactly the same formal model. In this second interpretation, there is a single commodity at each date – let us call it 'gold' – that is taken as a numeraire at the date. A 'price system' has two parts: (1) for each date and each elementary event at that date, there is a price, to be paid in gold at the beginning date, for one unit of gold to be delivered at the specified date and event; (2) for each commodity, date, and event at that date, there is a price, to be paid in gold at that date and event, for one unit of the commodity to be delivered at that same date and event. The first part of the price system can be interpreted as 'insurance premiums' and the second part as 'spot prices' at the given date and event. The insurance interpretation is to be made with some reservation, however, since there is no real object being insured and no limit to the amount of insurance that an individual may take out against the occurrence of a given event. For this reason, the first part of the price system might be better interpreted as reflecting a combination of betting odds and interest rates.

Although the second part of the price system might be interpreted as spot prices it would be a mistake to think of the determination of the equilibrium values of these prices as being deferred in real time to the dates to which they refer. The definition of equilibrium requires that the agents have access to the complete system of prices when choosing their plans. In effect, this requires that at the beginning of time all agents have available a (common) forecast of the equilibrium spot prices that will prevail at every future date and event.

EXTENSION OF THE ARROW–DEBREU MODEL TO THE CASE IN WHICH DIFFERENT AGENTS HAVE DIFFERENT INFORMATION. In an Arrow–Debreu economy, at any one date each agent will have incomplete information about the state of the environment, but all the agents will have the same information. This last assumption is not tenable if we are to take good account of the effects of uncertainty in an economy. I shall now sketch how, by a simple reinterpretation of the concepts of production possibility set and consumption possibility set, we can extend the theory of the Arrow–Debreu economy to allow for differences in information among the economic agents.

For each date, the information that will be available to a given agent at that date may be characterized by a partition of the set of states of the environment. To be consistent with our previous terminology, we should assume that each such information partition must be at least as coarse as the partition that describes the elementary events at that date; i.e. each set in the information partition must contain a set in the elementary event partition for the same date.

For example, each set in the event partition at a given date might specify the high temperature at that date, whereas each set in a given agent's information partition might specify only whether this temperature was higher than 75°F. or not. Or the event partition at a given date might specify the temperature at each date during the past month, whereas the information partition might specify only the mean temperature over the past month.

An agent's information restricts his set of feasible plans in the following manner. Suppose that at a given date the agent knows only that the state of the environment lies in a specified set A (one of the sets in his information partition at that date), and suppose (as would be typical) that the set A contains several of the elementary events that are in principle observable at that date. Then any action that the agent takes at that date must necessarily be the same for all elementary events in the set A. In particular, if the agent is a consumer, then his consumption of any specified commodity at that date must be the same in all elementary events contained in the information set A; if the agent is a producer, then his input or output of any specified commodity must be the same for all events in A. (I am assuming that consumers know what they consume and producers what they produce at any given date.)

Let us call the sequence of information partitions for a given agent his information structure and let us say that this structure is fixed if it is given independent of the actions of himself or any other agent. Furthermore, in the case of a fixed information structure, let us say that a given plan (consumption or production) is compatible with that structure if it satisfies the conditions described in the previous paragraph, at each date.

Suppose that the consumption and production possibility sets of the Arrow–Debreu economy are interpreted as characterizing, for each agent, those plans that would be feasible if he had 'full information' (i.e. if his information partition at each date coincided with the elementary event partition at that date). The set of feasible plans for any agent with a fixed information structure can then be obtained by restricting him to those plans in the full information possibility set that are also compatible with his given information structure.

From this point on, all of the machinery of the Arrow–Debreu economy (with some minor technical modifications) can be brought to bear on the present model. In particular, we get a theory of existence and optimality of competitive equilibrium relative to fixed structures of information for the economic agents. I shall call this the 'extended Arrow–Debreu economy'. (For a fuller treatment, see Radner, 1968, 1982.)

CHOICE OF INFORMATION. There is no difficulty in principle in incorporating the choice of information structure into the model of the extended Arrow–Debreu economy. I doubt, however, that it is reasonable to assume that the technological conditions for the acquisition and use of information generally satisfy the hypotheses of the standard theorems on the existence and optimality of competitive equilibrium.

The acquisition and use of information about the environment typically require the expenditure of goods and services; i.e., of commodities.

If one production plan requires more information for its implementation than another (i.e., requires a finer information partition at one or more dates), then the list of (commodity) inputs should reflect the increased inputs for information. In this manner a set of feasible production plans can reflect the possibility of choice among alternative information structures.

Unfortunately, the acquisition of information often involves a 'set-up cost'; i.e., the resources needed to obtain the information may be independent of the scale of the production process in which the information is used. This set-up cost will introduce a nonconvexity in the production possibility set, and thus one of the standard conditions in the theory of the Arrow–Debreu economy will not be satisfied (Radner, 1968).

Even without set-up costs, *there is a general tendency for the value of information to exhibit 'increasing returns', at least at low levels*, provided that the structure of information varies smoothly with its cost. This striking phenomenon leads to discontinuities in the demand for information. (For a precise statement, see Radner and Stiglitz, 1984.)

There is another interesting class of cases in which an agent's information structure is not fixed, namely, cases in which the agent's information at one date may depend upon production or consumption decisions taken at previous dates, but all actions can be scaled down to any desired size. Unfortunately space limitations prevent me from discussing this class in the present article.

CRITIQUE OF THE EXTENDED ARROW–DEBREU ECONOMY. If the Arrow–Debreu model is given a literal interpretation, then it clearly requires that the economic agents possess capabilities of imagination and calculation that exceed reality by many orders of magnitude. Related to this is the observation that the theory requires in principle a complete system of insurance and futures markets, which appears to be too complex, detailed, and refined to have practical significance. A further obstacle to the achievement of a complete insurance market is the phenomenon of 'moral hazard' (Arrow, 1965).

A second line of criticism is that the theory does not take account of at least three important institutional features of modern capitalist economies: money, the stock market, and active markets at every date.

These two lines of criticism have an important connection, which suggests how the Arrow–Debreu theory might be improved. If, as in the Arrow–Debreu model, each production plan has a sure unambiguous present value at the beginning of time, then consumers have no interest in trading in shares, and there is no point in a stock market. If all accounts can be settled at the beginning of time, then there is no need for money during the subsequent life of the economy; in any case, the standard motives for holding money are not applicable.

On the other hand, once we recognize explicitly that there is a sequence of markets, one for each date, and no one of them complete (in the Arrow–Debreu sense), then certain phenomena and institutions not accounted for in the Arrow–Debreu model become reasonable. First, there is uncertainty about the prices that will hold in future markets, as well as uncertainty about the environment.

Second, producers do not have a clear-cut natural way of comparing net revenues at different dates and states. Stockholders have an incentive to establish a stock exchange, since it enables them to change the way their future revenues depend on the states of the environment. As an alternative to selling his shares in a particular enterprise, a stockholder may try to influence the management of the enterprise in order to make the production plan conform better to his own subjective probabilities and attitude towards risk.

Third, consumers will typically not be able to discount all of their 'wealth' at the beginning of time, because (a) their shares of producers' future (uncertain) net revenues cannot be so discounted and (b) they cannot discount all of their future resource endowments. Consumers will be subject to a sequence of budget constraints, one for each date (rather than to a single budget constraint relating present cost of his consumption plan to present net worth, as in the Arrow–Debreu economy).

Fourth, economic agents may have an incentive to speculate on the prices in future markets, by storing goods, hedging, etc. Instead of storing goods, an agent may be interested in saving part of one date's income, in units of account, for use on a subsequent date, if there is an institution that makes this possible. There will thus be a demand for 'money' in the form of demand deposits.

Fifth, agents will be interested in forecasting the prices in markets at future dates. These prices will be functions of both the state of the environment and the decisions of (in principle, all) economic agents up to the date in question.

Sixth, if traders have different information at a particular date, then the equilibrium prices at that date will reflect the pooled information of the traders, albeit in a possibly complicated way. Hence traders who have a good model of the market process will be able to infer something about other traders' information from the market prices.

EXPECTATIONS AND EQUILIBRIUM IN A SEQUENCE OF MARKETS. Consider now a sequence of market at successive dates. Suppose that no market at any one date is complete in the Arrow–Debreu sense; i.e., at every date and for every commodity there will be some future dates and some events at those future dates for which it will not be possible to make current contracts for future delivery contingent on those events. In such a model, several types of 'equilibrium' concept suggest themselves, according to the hypotheses we make about the way traders form their expectations.

Let us place ourselves at a particular date-event pair; the excess supply correspondence at that date-event pair reflects the traders' information about past prices and about the history of the environment up through that date. If a given trader's excess supply correspondence is generated by preference satisfaction, then the relevant preferences will be conditional upon the information available. If, furthermore, the trader's preferences can be scaled in terms of utility and subjective probability, and conform to the Expected Utility Hypothesis, then the relevant probabilities are the conditional probabilities given the available information. These conditional probabilities express the trader's expectations regarding the future. Although a general theoretical treatment of our problem does not necessarily require us to assume that traders' preferences conform to the Expected Utility Hypothesis, it will be helpful in the following heuristic discussion to keep in mind this particular interpretation of expectations.

A trader's expectations concern both future environmental

events and future prices. Regarding expectations about future environmental events, there is no conceptual problem. According to the Expected Utility Hypothesis, each trader is characterized by a subjective probability measure on the set of complete histories of the environment. Since, by definition, the evolution of the environment is exogenous, a trader's conditional subjective probability of a future event, given the information to date, is well defined.

It is not so obvious how to proceed with regard to traders' expectations about future prices. I shall contrast two possible approaches. In the first, which I shall call the *perfect foresight* approach, let us assume that the behaviour of traders is such as to determine, for each complete history of the environment, a unique corresponding sequence of price system, say $\phi_t^*(e_t)$, where e_t is the particular event at date t. If the 'laws' governing the economic system are known to all, then every trader can calculate the sequence of functions ϕ_t^*. In this case, at any date-event pair a trader's expectations regarding future prices are well defined in terms of the functions ϕ_t^* and his conditional subjective probability measures on histories of the environment, given his current information. Traders need not agree on the probabilities of future environmental events, and therefore they need not agree on the probability distribution of future prices, *but they must agree on which future prices are associated with which events.* I shall call this last type of agreement the condition of *common price expectation functions.*

Thus, the perfect foresight approach implies that, in equilibrium, traders have common price expectation functions. These price expectation functions indicate, for each date-event pair, what the equilibrium price system would be in the corresponding market at that date-event pair. Pursuing this line of thought, it follows that, in equilibrium, the traders would have strategies (plans) such that, if these strategies were carried out, the markets would be cleared at each date-event pair. Call such plans *consistent.* A set of common price expectations and corresponding consistent plans is called an *equilibrium of plans, prices, and price expectations.*

This model of equilibrium can be extended to cover the case in which different traders have different information, just as the Arrow–Debreu model was so extended. In particular, one could express in this way the hypothesis that a trader cannot observe the individual preferences and resource endowments of other traders. Indeed, one can also introduce into the description of the state of the environment variables that, for each trader, represent his alternative hypotheses about the 'true laws' of the economic system. In this way the condition of common price expectation functions can lose much of its apparent restrictiveness.

The situation in which traders enter the market with different non-price information presents an opportunity for agents to learn about the environment from prices, since current market prices reflect, in a possibly complicated manner, the non-price information signals received by the various agents. To take an extreme example, the 'inside information' of a trader in a securities market may lead him to bid up the price to a level higher than it otherwise would have been. In this case, an astute market observer might be able to infer that an insider has obtained some favourable information, just by careful observation of the price movement. More generally, *an economic agent who has a good understanding of the market is in a position to use market prices to make inferences about the (non-price) information received by other agents.*

These inferences are derived, explicitly or implicitly, from an individual's 'model' of the relationship between the non-price information received by market participants and the market prices. On the other hand, the true relationship is determined by the individual agents' behaviour, and hence by their individual models. Furthermore, economic agents have the opportunity to revise their individual models in the light of observations and published data. Hence, there is a feedback from the true relationship to the individual models. An equilibrium of this system, in which the individual models are identical with the true model, is called *rational expectations equilibrium.*

This concept of equilibrium is more subtle, of course, than the ordinary concept of the equilibrium of supply and demand. In a rational expectations equilibrium, not only are prices determined so as to equate supply and demand, but individual economic agents correctly perceive the true relationship between the non-price information received by the market participants and the resulting equilibrium market prices. This contrasts with the ordinary concept of equilibrium in which the agents respond to prices but do not attempt to infer other agents' non-price information from the actual market prices.

Research on rational expectations equilibrium is quite recent, and the subject has not been fully explored. Nevertheless, several important insights have already been obtained; these insights will be sketched below.

Although it is capable of describing a richer set of institutions and behaviour than is the Arrow–Debreu model, the perfect foresight approach is contrary to the spirit of much of competitive market theory in that it postulates that individual traders must be able to forecast, in some sense, the equilibrium prices that will prevail in the future under all alternative states of the environment. Even if one grants the extenuating circumstances mentioned in previous paragraphs, this approach still seems to require of the traders a capacity for imagination and computation far beyond what is realistic. An equilibrium of plans and price expectations might be appropriate as a conceptualization of the ideal goal of indicative planning, or of a long-run steady state toward which the economy might tend in a stationary environment.

These last considerations lead us in a different direction, which I shall call the *bounded rationality* approach. This approach is much less well defined, but expresses itself in terms of various retreats from the hypothesis of 'fully rational' behaviour by traders, e.g., by assuming that the trader's planning horizons are severely limited, or that their expectation formation follows some simple rules-of-thumb. An example of the bounded-rationality approach is the theory of *temporary equilibrium.*

In the evolution of a sequence of momentary equilibria, each agent's expectations will be successively revised in the light of new information about the environment and about current prices. Therefore, the evolution of the economy will depend upon the rules or processes of expectation formation and revision used by the agents. In particular, there might be interesting conditions under which such a sequence of momentary equilibria would converge, in some sense, to a (stochastic) steady state. This steady state, for example stationary probability distribution of prices, would constitute a fourth concept of equilibrium.

Of the four concepts of equilibrium, the first two are perhaps the closest in spirit to the Arrow–Debreu theory. How far do the conclusions of the Arrow–Debreu theory (existence and optimality of equilibrium) extend to this new situation? We turn now to this question.

EQUILIBRIUM OF PLANS, PRICES AND PRICE EXPECTATIONS. Consider now the model of perfect-foresight equilibrium sketched above, in which the agents have common information at every date-event pair (for a precise description of the model, see Radner, 1972). Three features of the situation are different from the Arrow–Debreu model: (1) there is a sequence of markets (or rather a 'tree' of markets), one for each date-event pair, no one of which is complete; (2) for each agent, there is a separate budget constraint corresponding to each date-event pair; (3) even if there is a natural bound on consumption and production, there is no single natural bound on the *positions* that traders can take in the markets for securities, if short sales are permitted; (4) there is no obvious objective for each firm to pursue, since each firm's profit is defined only for each date-event pair.

To deal with points (3) and (4), make the following assumptions. Regarding (3), although there is no *single* natural bound on traders' positions, *some* bound is natural; for example, a commitment to deliver a quantity of a commodity vastly greater than the total supply would not be credible to moderately well-informed traders. Regarding (4), assume that the manager of each firm has preferences on the sequence of net revenues that can be represented by a continuous, strictly concave utility function. In other respects, we make the 'standard' assumptions of the Arrow–Debreu model.

I first discuss the question of existence of equilibrium, but before paraphrasing the existence theorem I must define what I shall call a *pseudo-equilibrium*.

The definition of pseudo-equilibrium is obtained from the definition of equilibrium by replacing the requirement of consistency of plans by the condition that at each date and each event the difference between total saving and total investment (by consumers) is smaller at the pseudo-equilibrium prices than at any other prices.

One can prove (Radner, 1972) that under assumptions about technology and consumer preferences similar to those used in the Arrow–Debreu theory, and with the additional assumptions sketched above: (1) there exists a pseudo-equilibrium; (2) if in a pseudo-equilibrium the current and future prices on the stock market are all strictly positive, then the pseudo-equilibrium is an equilibrium; (3) in the case of a pure exchange economy, there exists an equilibrium.

The crucial difference between this theorem and the corresponding one in the Arrow–Debreu theory seems to be due to the form taken by Walras's Law, which in this model can be paraphrased by saying that saving must be at least equal to investment at each date in each event. This form derives from the replacement of a single budget constraint (in terms of present value) by a sequence of budget constraints, one for each date-event pair.

Hart (1975) has shown that without a bound on traders' positions an equilibrium need not exist, even in pure-exchange economies. Geanakoplos and Polemarchakis (1986) have shown that, in a pure-exchange economy, if all securities (for future delivery) are denominated in the same real commodity (possibly composite), then equilibrium exists. Duffie and Shafer (1985, 1986, 1987) have demonstrated the *generic* existence of equilibrium with a general structure of incomplete asset markets. (Roughly speaking, equilibrium is said to exist *generically* in a given model if, for any vector of parameters for which an equilibrium does not exist, there are arbitrarily small perturbations of the parameters for which an equilibrium does exist.)

In the above model with production the 'shareholders' have *un*limited liability, and therefore have a status more like that of partners than of shareholders, as these terms are usually understood. One way to formulate limited liability for shareholders is to impose the constraint on producers that their net revenues be non-negative at each date-event pair. However, in this case producers' correspondences may not be upper semicontinuous. This is analogous to the problem that arises when, for a given price system, the consumer's budget constraints force him to be on the boundary of his consumption set. In the case of the consumer, this situation is avoided by some assumption; see Debreu (1959, notes to ch. 5, pp. 88–9) and Debreu (1962). However, for the case of the producer, it is not considered unusual in the standard theory of the firm that, especially in equilibrium, the maximum profit achievable at the given price system could be zero (e.g., in the case of constant returns to scale).

What are conditions on the producers and consumers that would directly guarantee the existence of an equilibrium, not just a pseudo-equilibrium? In other words, under what conditions would the share markets be cleared at every date-event pair? Notice that if there is an excess supply of shares of a given producer j at a date-event pair (t, e), then at date $(t+1)$ only part of the producer's revenue will be 'distributed'. One would expect this situation to arise only if his revenue is to be negative in at least one event at date $t+1$; thus at such a date-event pair the producer would have a deficit covered neither by 'loans' (i.e. not offset by forward contracts) nor by shareholders' contributions. In other words, the producer would be 'bankrupt' at that point.

One approach might be to eliminate from a pseudo-equilibrium all producers for whom the excess supply of shares is not zero at some date-event pair, and then search for an equilibrium with the smaller set of producers, etc. successively reducing the set of producers until an equilibrium is found. This procedure has the trivial consequence that an equilibrium always exists, since it exists for the case of pure exchange (the set of producers is empty)! This may not be the most satisfactory resolution of the problem, but it does point up the desirability of having some formulation of the possibility of 'exit' for producers who are not doing well.

Generic existence of equilibrium with production (and stock markets) has been demonstrated under sufficiently strong 'regularity' conditions (e.g. smoothness of preferences and production sets, etc.). (See Duffie and Shafer, 1986; Burke (1986); and the references cited below.)

Although the above model with production does not allow for 'exit' of producers (except with the modification described in the preceding paragraph), it does allow for 'entrance' in the following limited sense. A producer may have zero production up to some date, but plans to produce thereafter; this is not inconsistent with a positive demand for shares at preceding dates.

The creation of new 'equity' in an enterprise is also allowed for in a limited sense. A producer may plan for a large investment at a given date-event pair, with a negative revenue. If the total supply of shares at the preceding date-event pair is nevertheless taken up by the market, this investment may be said to have been 'financed' by shareholders.

The above assumptions describe a model of producer behaviour that is not influenced by the shareholders or (directly) by the prices of shares. A common alternative hypothesis is that a producer tries to maximize the current market value of this enterprise. There seem to me to be at least two difficulties with this hypothesis. First, there are different market values at different date-event pairs, so it is not clear how these can be maximized simultaneously. Second, the market value of an enterprise at any date-event pair is a price, which is supposed to be determined, along with other prices, by an equilibrium of supply and demand. The 'market-value-maximizing' hypothesis would seem to require the producer to predict, in some sense, the effect of a change in his plan on a price *equilibrium*: in this case, the producers would no longer be price-takers, and one would need some sort of theory of general equilibrium for monopolistic competition.

There is one circumstance in which the value of the firm can be defined unambiguously, given the system of present prices and common expectations about future prices. Call a price system *arbitrage-free* if it is not possible to make a sure, positive cash flow from trading, without a positive investment. An equilibrium price system is, *a fortiori*, arbitrage-free. One can show (see Radner, 1967; Harrison and Kreps, 1979; Duffie and Shafer, 1986) that an arbitrage-free price system implicitly determines a system of 'insurance premiums' for a corresponding family of events. This means that, by suitable trading one can insure oneself against the occurrence of any of these events. If these events include all of the uncertain events that may affect the (uncertain) revenues of the firm, then they can be used in a natural way to define a present value of the firm at any date-event pair, for any production plan of the firm, and no probability judgements are needed to calculate the value. On the other hand, if the family of 'insurable events' is not rich enough, then the value is a random variable, and stockholders may not agree on its probability distribution.

OPTIMALITY. Recall that in the extended Arrow–Debreu model, under 'standard' conditions, equilibria are Pareto-optimal, and (roughly speaking) vice-versa. The same results do not hold for the case of incomplete markets. Of course, if markets are incomplete, one could at best expect equilibria to be optimal relative to some constrained set of resource reallocations. With a fairly natural definition of 'constrained optimality', Geanakoplos and Polemarchakis (1986) have shown that, generically, equilibria of pure exchange are not optimal. Indeed, Hart (1975) gave an example of a model of incomplete markets in which there is a multiplicity of equilibria, which can be ranked by the Pareto criterion.

RATIONAL EXPECTATIONS EQUILIBRIUM. In a market for commodities whose future utility is uncertain, the equilibrium prices will reflect the information and beliefs that the traders bring to the market, as well as their tastes and endowments. If the traders have different nonprice information, this situation presents an opportunity for each trader to make inferences from the market prices about other traders' information. An example of this phenomenon is recognized by the everyday expression, 'judging quality by price'. The term *rational expectations equilibrium* is applied to a model of market equilibrium that takes account of this potential informational feedback from market prices.

We may make the convention that the future utility of the commodities to each trader depends on the *state of the environment*. With this convention, we can model the inferences that a trader makes from the market prices and his own nonprice information signal by a family of conditional probability distributions of the environment given the market prices and his own nonprice information. We shall call such a family of conditional distributions the trader's *market model*. Given such a market model, the market prices will influence a trader's demand in two ways: first, through his budget constraint, and second, through his conditional expected utility function. It is this second feature, of course, that distinguishes theories of rational expectations equilibrium from earlier models of market equilibrium.

Given the traders' market models, the equilibrium prices will be determined by the equality of supply and demand in the usual way, and thus will be a deterministic function of the joint nonprice information that the traders bring to the market. In order for the market models of the traders to be 'rational', they must be consistent with that function. To make this idea precise, it will be useful to have some formal notation. Let p denote the vector of market prices, e denote the (utility-relevant) state of the environment, and s_i denote traders i's nonprice information signal ($i = 1, \ldots, I$). The joint nonprice information of all traders together will be denoted by $s = (s_1, \ldots, s_I)$. We shall call s the 'joint signal'. (The term 'state of information' is also commonly applied to this array.) Trader i's market model, say m_i, is a family of conditional probability distributions of e, given s_i and p. Given the traders' market models, the equilibrium price vector will be some (measurable) function of the joint nonprice information, say $p = \phi(s)$.

To model the required rationality of the traders' models, suppose that, for each i, trader i has (subjective) prior beliefs about the environment and the information signals that are expressed by a joint probability distribution, say Q_i, of e and s. These prior beliefs need not, of course, be the same for all traders. Given the price function ϕ, a *rational* market model for trader i would be the family of conditional probability distributions of e, given s_i and p, that are derived from the distribution Q_i and the price function ϕ; thus (supposing e and s to be discrete variables),

$$m_i(e'|s_i', p') = \text{Prob}_{Q_i}(e = e'|s_i' \text{ and } \phi(s) = p'). \quad (1)$$

A given price function ϕ, together with the rationality condition (1), would determine the total market excess supply for each price vector p and each joint information signal s, say $Z(p, s, \phi)$. Note that the excess supply for any p and s *depends also on the price function* ϕ, since (in principle) the entire price function is used to calculate the conditional distribution in (1). I can now define a *rational expectations equlibrium* (REE) to be a price function ϕ^* such that, for (almost) every s, excess supply is zero at the price vector $\phi^*(s)$, i.e.,

$$Z(\phi^*(s), s, \phi^*) = 0, \quad \text{for a.e. } s. \quad (2)$$

The formal study of rational expectations equilibrium was introduced in Radner (1967); it was taken up independently by Lucas (1972) and Green (1973), and further investigated by Grossman, Jordan, and others. We shall make no attempt here to provide complete bibliographic notes on the subject; for this the reader is referred to Radner (1982, Sec. 7.1, 7.4). The particular definition given above can be criticized on several grounds, and we shall return to this point below.

I should emphasize that I am concerned here with the aspect of 'rational expectations' in which traders make inferences from market prices about other traders' information, a phenomenon that is only of interest when traders do not all have the same nonprice information. The term 'rational expectations equilibrium' has also been used to describe a situation in which traders correctly forecast (in some sense or other) the probability distribution of future prices. (See Radner (1982) for references to the work of Muth and others on this topic.)

The concept of REE has been used to make a number of interesting predictions about the behaviour of markets (see, for example, Futia (1979, 1981) and the references cited there). A sound foundation for such applications requires the investigation of conditions that would ensure the existence and stability of REE, and this investigation has revealed a set of problems that are more difficult and more subtle than those encountered in ordinary equilibrium analysis.

If markets are incomplete, the existence of REE is not assured by the 'classical' conditions of ordinary general equilibrium analysis. Even under such conditions, if traders condition their expected utilities on market prices, then their demands can be discontinuous in the price function. Specific examples of the nonexistence of REE due to such discontinuities were given by Kreps (1977), Green (1977), and others.

These examples naturally led theorists to question whether the absence of REE is pervasive or is confined to a 'negligible' set of such examples. Indeed, this question was already anticipated by Green, whose example is robust to perturbations of the density function describing the environment, but not to perturbations of traders' characteristics. The work of Radner, Allen, and Jordan (see Jordan and Radner, 1982, for references) provided – in a certain context – an essentially complete answer, which can be loosely summarized in the statement that *REE exists generically except when the dimension of the space of private information is equal to the dimension of the price space.* (Recall that REE exists *generically* in a given model if, for any vector of parameters values for which REE does not exist, there are arbitrarily small perturbations of the parameters for which REE does exist.) Furthermore, if the dimension of the space of private information is strictly *less* than the dimension of the price space, then generically there is a REE that is *fully revealing*, i.e., in which the price reveals to each trader all the nonprice information used by *all* traders (Radner, 1979; Allen, 1981).

EQUILIBRIUM AND LEARNING WITH IMPERFECT PRICE MODELS. The nonexistence of rational expectations equilibrium illustrated in section 2 can be traced to discontinuities in the demand function with respect to the price function. In a sense, these discontinuities arise because the theory postulates that, in equilibrium, *the traders know the price function perfectly, and the price function is perfectly accurate.* To see this, consider the example of section 2, in which there are two traders, one who is initially fully informed about the environment and one who is initially uninformed. Suppose that there are two possible information signals, s', and s'', let ϕ_n be a sequence of price functions, and define

$$p'_n = \phi_n(s'), p''_n = \phi_n(s'').$$

Suppose that, for every n, $p'_n \neq p''_n$, but that the two sequences, (p'_n) and (p''_n), both converge to a common value, say p_0. Finally, define the price function ϕ_0 by $\phi_0(s') = \phi_0(s'') = p_0$. Thus each price function in the sequence is revealing, but the limit price function is not. Therefore, for each $n > 0$ the second trader's demands at the two prices will be different, and these differences will not tend to zero as n increases because although the differences between p'_n and p''_n are tending to zero the two prices reveal the respective signals, s' and s'', as long as the prices are different. On the other hand, in the limit trader 2 cannot infer the information signal from the price, since the limit price function is not revealing. Hence, in the limit, trader 2's expected utility will not be conditioned on the signal s, and so his demand will (typically) have a discontinuity at the limit price function. This follows from the (implicit) assumption that, *no matter how close* $\phi(s')$ and $\phi(s'')$ are, if they are different then trader 2 can infer the signal s from the price.

Let us now modify the description of the market, by replacing the assumption that each trader knows a (perfectly accurate) forecast function with the assumption that each trader has an 'econometric' model of how equilibrium prices are determined. Let E denote the set of environments e, let S denote the set of pooled information signals s, and let Δ denote the set of all nonnegative price vectors, normalized so that the sum of all prices is unity. Trader i's econometric model of price determination, which we shall call his *price model*, is characterized by a family, $\psi_i(p|s)$, of strictly positive conditional probability density functions on the set Δ of possible price vectors. (This includes, as a special case, the typical econometric model in which a 'disturbance' with a probability density function is added to a deterministic relationship.) The joint probability distribution, for trader i, of the variables e, s, and p is determined by his probability distribution Q_i on $E \times S$ together with his price model, ψ_i.

One can show that, for each trader i, maximizing conditional expected utility given s_i and p is equivalent to maximizing

$$E_{Q_i}[u_i(x_i, e)\psi_i(p|s)|s_i], \tag{3}$$

where $E_{Q_i}[\cdot|s_i]$ denotes conditional expectation with respect to the probability measure Q_i, given s_i. Given s, an equilibrium is characterized by a price vector p^* and an I-tuple (x_i^*) of demand vectors such that, for each i, x_i^* maximizes (3) subject to $x_i \geqslant 0$ and a budget constraint, and such that excess demand is zero.

One can show that, with suitable assumptions, *an equilibrium exists for almost every s.* The assumptions are in two sets.

Those in the first set concern the trader's models of price determination. They express the two ideas that (1) each trader's price model is appropriately continuous in the price vector p, and (2) no trader's price model could predict the equilibrium price perfectly from the joint signal s. Formally, we assume that, for every trader i:

$\psi(\cdot|s)$ is continuous on Δ, and strictly positive on its interior, for almost every s; (4a)

$\psi_i(p|\cdot)$ is majorized in absolute value by an integrable function on S, *uniformly in p*. (4b)

The assumptions in the second set are standard in the theory of exchange equilibrium and in expected utility theory; they are omitted here (see Jordan and Radner, 1982, section 4).

With only these assumptions, the resulting equilibrium has no obvious 'self-fulfilling' or 'rational' expectations property. A minimal requirement along these lines is that an equilibrium price p^* not be 'inconsistent' with any trader's model of price determination. One way to express this formally is to require that p^* be in the support of $\psi_i(\cdot|s)$, considered as a probablity density on Δ. But this follows from the assumption that $\psi_i(p|s)$ is strictly positive on the interior of Δ. This expresses the idea that, given any exogenous signal s_i, trader i's model ψ_i *does not exclude as impossible any open set of equilibrium price vectors.*

A more stringent 'rational expectations' requirement would concern the opportunities that traders might have for learning from experience. For example, suppose that there is a market at each of a succession of dates t, and that the successive exogenous vectors (e_t, s_t) are independent and identically distributed. Suppose further that at the beginning of date t trader i knows the *past* history of environments, prices, and his own nonprice information. On the basis of this history he updates his initial market model to form a current market model. These current market models, together with the nonprice information signals at date t, then determine an equilibrium price at date t, say p_t^*, as above. The updating of models constitutes the *learning* process of the traders. For a given learning process, one might ask whether the process converges in any useful sense, and if so, whether the models are asymptotically consistent with the (endogeneously determined) actual relationship between signals and equilibrium prices, i.e. whether they converge to a REE. In this case one would say that the REE is *stable* (relative to the learning process).

Thus far, answers to this question are only fragmentary. Bray (1982) has studied a simple linear asset-market model in which, at each date, each trader i updates his model by calculating an ordinary least-squares estimates of the regression of e on p and s_i, using all the past values (e_i, p_t^*, s_{it}). For this example, Bray proves stability.

On the other hand, Blume and Easley (1982) present a somewhat less optimistic view of the possibility of learning rational expectations. They define a class of learning procedures by which traders use successive observations to form their subjective models, where the term model for trader i means a conditional distribution of s, given s_i and p. They show that rational expectations equilibria are at least 'locally stable' under learning, but that learning processes may also get stuck at a profile of subjective models that is not an REE. The learning procedures defined by Blume and Easley are applied to a fairly general class of stochastic exchange environments that do not process the special linear structure of the above example. However, to accommodate this additional generality, Blume and Easley constrain traders to choose their subjective models from a fixed finite set of models and convex combinations thereof. Hence for some profiles of subjective models, market clearing may result in a 'true' model that lies outside the admissible set. It is then intuitively plausible that a natural learning procedure could get stuck at a profile of subjective models that differs from the resulting true model but is in some sense the best admissible approximation to the true model, even if the admissible set contains an REE model. This phenomenon is illustrated in section 5 of their paper.

ROY RADNER

See also ARROW–DEBREV MODEL; GENERAL EQUILIBRIUM; PERFECT FORESIGHT; RATIONAL EXPECTATIONS; TEMPORARY EQUILIBRIUM.

BIBLIOGRAPHY

Most of the literature on incomplete markets and on rational expectations equilibrium is quite recent, and many interesting papers are still unpublished at the time this is being written. Further results and references can be found in (Radner, 1982), Jordan and Radner (1982), Youné's (1985), Allen (1986), Geanakoplos and Polemarchakis (1986), and Duffie and Shafer (1986).

Allen, B. 1981. Generic existence of completely revealing equilibria for economies with uncertainty when prices convey information. *Econometrica* 49, 1173–99.

Allen, B. 1986. General equilibrium with rational expectations. Ch. 1 of *Contributions to Mathematical Economics: Essays in Honor of Gerard Debreu*, ed. A. Mas-Colell and W. Hildenbrand, Amsterdam: North-Holland, 1–23.

Arrow, K.J. 1953. Le rôle de valeurs boursières pour la repártition la meilleure des risques. *Econométrie*, 41–48. Trans. as 'The role of securities in the optimal allocation of risk-bearing', *Review of Economic Studies* 31, (1964), 91–6.

Arrow, K.J. 1965. *Aspects of the Theory of Risk-Bearing*. Helsinki: Yrjo Johansson Foundation.

Arrow, K.J., and Hahn, F.H. 1971. *General Competitive Analysis*. San Francisco: Holden-Day.

Blume, L.E. and Easley, D. 1982. Learning to be rational. *Journal of Economic Theory* 26, 340–51.

Bray, M. 1982. Learning, estimation, and the stability of rational expectations *Journal of Economic Theory* 26, 318–39.

Burke, J. 1986. Existence of equilibrium for incomplete market economies with production and stock trading. Texas A&M University (unpublished).

Debreu, G. 1953. Une économie de l'incertain. Electricité de France, Paris, mimeo.

Debreu, G. 1959. *Theory of Value*. New York: Wiley.

Debreu, G. 1962. New concepts and techniques for equilibrium analysis. *Intermaterial Economic Review* 3, 257–73.

Duffie, D. and Shafer, W. 1985. Equilibrium in incomplete markets I: a basic model of generic existence. *Journal of Mathematical Economics* 14, 285–300.

Duffie, D. and Shafer, W. 1986. Equilibrium and the role of the firm in incomplete markets. Research Paper No. 915, Graduate School of Business, Stanford University, November.

Duffie, D. and Shafer, W. 1987. Equilibrium in incomplete markets II: Generic existence in stochastic economies. *Journal of Mathematical Economics* 15, 199–216.

Futia, C.A. 1979. Stochastic business cycles. AT&T Bell Laboratories, Murray Hill, N.J. (unpublished).

Futia, C.A. 1981. Rational expectations in stationary linear models. *Econometrica* 49, 171–92.

Geanakoplos, J. and Polemarchakis, H. 1986. Existence, regularity, and constrained suboptimality of competitive allocations when the asset market is incomplete. In *Uncertainty, Information, and Communication: Essays in Honor of Kenneth Arrow*, ed. W.P. Heller, R.M. Starr, and D.A. Starrett, Vol. III, 65–95.

Green, J. 1973. Information, inefficiency, and equilibrium. Discussion Paper 284, Harvard Institute of Economic Research, Cambridge.

Green, J. 1977. The nonexistence of informational equilibria. *Review of Economic Studies* 44, 451–63.

Harrison, J.M. and Kreps, D.M. 1979. Martingales and arbitrage in multiperiod securities markets. *Journal of Economic Theory 20*, 381–408.

Hart, O. 1975. On the optimality of equilibrium when the market structure is incomplete. *Journal of Economic Theory* 11, 418–43.

Jordan, J.S. and Radner, R. 1982. Rational expectations in microeconomic models: an overview. *Journal of Economic Theory* 26, 201, 201–23.

Kreps, D.M. 1977. A note on 'fulfilled expectations' equilibria. *Journal of Economic Theory* 14, 32–43.

Lucas, R.E. 1972. Expectations and the neutrality of money. *Journal of Economic Theory* 4, 103–24.

Radner, R. 1967. Equilibre des marchés à terme et au comptant en cas d'incertitude. *Cahiers d'Econométrie CNRS*, Paris, 4, 35–52.

Radner, R. 1968. Competitive equilibrium under uncertainty. *Econometrica* 36, 31–58.

Radner, R. 1972. Existence of equilibrium of plans, prices, and price expectations in a sequence of markets. *Econometrica* 40, 289–304.

Radner, R. 1979. Rational expectations equilibrium: generic existence and the information revealed by prices. *Econometrica* 47, 655–667.

Radner, R. 1982. Equilibrium under uncertainty. Ch. 20 in *Handbook of Mathematical Economics*, ed. K.J. Arrow and M.D. Intriligator, Vol. II, Amsterdam: North-Holland, 923–1006.

Radner, R. and Stiglitz, J.E. 1984. A nonconcavity in the value of information. In *Bayesian Models in Economic Theory*, ed. M. Boyer and R.E. Kihlstrom, Amsterdam: North-Holland, 33–52.

Savage, L. J. 1954. *The Foundations of Statistics*. New York: Wiley.

Younès, Y. 1985. Competitive equilibrium and incomplete market structures. Economics Department, University of Pennsylvania, revised October 1986 (unpublished).

underconsumption. 'Underconsumption' is the label given to theories which attribute the failure of the total output of an economy to continue to be sold at its cost of production (including normal profit) to too low a ratio of consumption to output. According to underconsumption theories, such deficient consumption leads either to goods being able to be sold only at below-normal rates of profit, or to goods not being able to be sold at all. These effects are seen as leading in turn to cutbacks in production and increases in unemployment. Underconsumption theories are thus amongst those which seek to explain cyclical or secular declines in the rate of economic growth.

Where underconsumption exists in the sense that the ratio of consumption to output is below the optimum level, it follows that the ratio of 'unconsumed' output to total output must be too high. For the period in which underconsumption breaks out, underconsumptionists in general both identify this 'unconsumed' output with saving, and equate saving with investment. Thus Haberler, to whose 1937 analysis of underconsumption and related theories the reader should turn for the best extended treatment of the subject, wrote that in 'its best-reasoned form ..., the under-consumption theory uses "under-consumption" to mean "over-saving" ', and that in 'the under-consumption or over-saving theory ... savings are, as a rule, invested ...' (Haberler, 1937, pp. 115 and 117).

While the theories advanced by underconsumptionists overlap with some other macroeconomic theories in certain ways, their basic characteristics make them distinct in other respects. Underconsumption theories share with Keynesian theories, for example, the characteristic that they are 'demand-side' (as opposed to 'supply-side') theories. However, there is a fundamental difference between the two, in that Keynesian theories attribute the failure of total output to reach the full employment level to a deficiency of *aggregate* demand. The two types of theory consequently have different implications. As Robbins succinctly put it, with reference to the underconsumptionist J.A. Hobson, for 'Mr Keynes, one way out of the slump would be a revival of investment; for Mr Hobson, this would simply make matters worse' (Robbins, 1932, p. 420). A further difference between the two lies in the fact that, by contrast with Keynesian theories, hoarding plays no part in underconsumption theories. Underconsumptionists in general confine their analyses to the real sector of the economy, and where monetary factors are discussed at all they are treated as secondary.

There are also some connections between underconsumption theories and the accelerator theory of investment. As Haberler pointed out, the acceleration principle can be used 'in support of a special type of the under-consumption theory of the business cycle' (Haberler, 1937, p. 30). More importantly, a variant of the principle can be seen as underlying all underconsumption theories. When first expounded by J.M. Clark, the acceleration principle was used to explain the level of activity in the investment goods sector of an economy by changes in the demand for finished goods. In essence, underconsumptionists base their theories on the idea that changes in the demand for consumption goods determine the future level of activity in the investment goods sector. By this means they draw the conclusion that the level of activity in the economy as a whole is wholly determined by consumption demand.

In a review of Harrod's *Towards a Dynamic Economics*, Joan Robinson suggested that 'Mr Harrod's analysis provides the missing link between Keynes and Hobson' (Robinson, 1949, p. 80). The resemblance of underconsumption theories to growth models of the Harrod–Domar type is in fact greater than their resemblance to Keynesian theories. As Domar pointed out in the *American Economic Review* article expounding his growth model, he shared with Hobson a concern with the capacity-creating effect of investment, a question which Keynes hardly touched on in the *General Theory*. The essential features of underconsumption theories can in fact be captured by a growth model of the Harrod–Domar type, in which however the driving force is provided not by the rate of growth of investment but by the rate of growth of consumption. Such a model is particularly appropriate in the case of those theories which treat underconsumption as a secular rather than a cyclical phenomenon.

There are connections too between underconsumption theories and explanations of 'economic crises' in terms of 'disproportionate production', to use Marx's terminology. By 'disproportionate production' Marx meant an allocation of labour time between sectors or industries other than that required to satisfy social need as reflected in demand. Now underconsumption involves an allocation of too few resources to the consumption goods sector and too many resources to the investment goods sector. But as Haberler pointed out, such 'vertical disproportion' should be distinguished from 'horizontal disproportion'. And unlike cases of horizontal disproportion (if optimal stock levels are ignored), vertical disproportion, involving industries not equidistant from consumption goods industries, cannot be rectified immediately by a return to 'proportionate' production. For the excessive production of investment goods consequent upon underconsumption leaves a legacy in the form of excessive productive capacity. Underconsumption theories thus should be distinguished from the more general category of 'disproportionality' theories; the disproportionality element they incorporate is specific and has distinctive consequences.

Over-investment theories provide a different example of vertical disproportion. As they are defined by Haberler, over-investment theories offer an explanation of the excessive aggregate demand characteristic of an economy during the upswing of a trade cycle. Therefore they also belong to a different category from underconsumption theories, even though the deficiency of consumption characteristic of the latter is accompanied by excessive investment.

Despite their basic similarities, underconsumption theories differ as to the cause of, and hence remedies for, underconsumption. A view to be found in the writings of some underconsumptionists, especially the less well known ones, is that underconsumption is due to total purchasing power falling short of the value of output. Since all the value of output accrues to the owner of one factor of production or another, this proposition as it stands cannot be sustained. This view as to the cause of underconsumption should not be confused, however, with a superficially similar view relating to its effects, which is at least implicit in all underconsumptionist thinking. This is the idea that income is generated not by production but by purchases of what is produced. In underconsumptionist writings, by contrast for example with Keynesian writings, income may fall short of the value of output.

How this may be so is perhaps best seen in terms of period analysis. An outbreak of underconsumption will lead in the first period to excessive saving accompanied by excessive investment. In the second period the resulting additional capacity will be used, and unless there is an increase in consumption the level of output will exceed the demand for it; hence in this period the income generated by purchases will fall short of the value of output, while at the same time saving, if it is defined as that part of income (as opposed to output) not consumed, will just match investment demand. The deficient demand in the second period will lead in the third period to actual output falling short of potential output, that is to excess capacity, with saving however continuing to equal investment.

One underconsumptionist who clearly did not attribute underconsumption to lack of purchasing power is Malthus. In his correspondence with Ricardo, Malthus instead took the position that 'a nation must certainly have the power of purchasing all that it produces, but I can easily conceive it not to have the will' (Sraffa, 1952, p. 132). Like some other underconsumptionists, notably Sismondi and Hobson, Malthus believed that one cause of underconsumption is to be found in the limited capacity of human beings to expand their wants, at least in the short run. It was Malthus's view that men have a tendency towards indolence once their needs for necessaries are satisfied. If in the face of such limited growth in human wants capital accumulation continues apace, the resulting increase in productive capacity will fail to be matched by an equal increase in consumer demand. The remedy for this state of affairs, suggested Malthus, is an increase in commerce, both domestic and foreign, so as to stimulate tastes by exposing the population to new products.

Most commonly, however, underconsumptionists find the

cause of underconsumption in a maldistribution of income. The underlying argument is simple. If different economic classes have different propensities to consume, the distribution of an excessive share of income to classes with a relatively low propensity to consume will result in underconsumption. Underconsumptionists agree that a remedy cannot be found by a redistribution of income towards the capitalist class, which they see as having a relatively high propensity to save. They differ, however, on the question of the class to which income should in cases of underconsumption be redistributed. The earliest underconsumptionists ruled out a redistribution of income towards workers, perhaps partly because it was incompatible with their adherence to the wages fund doctrine, according to which total wages are fixed by the capital set aside in advance to pay them. They advocated rather a redistribution of income towards landlords. The first underconsumptionist to advocate a redistribution of income towards workers was Sismondi, whose example was followed by most later underconsumptionists.

Underconsumption theories were first put forward in the 19th century. While some 17th- and 18th-century writers, most notably Mandeville and the Physiocrats, advocated an increase in expenditure on consumption goods, none of them linked this with a corresponding reduction in investment. Therefore although they may be seen as predecessors of Keynes, they should not be classified as underconsumptionists. The first to advance an underconsumption theory in the sense outlined above was Lauderdale, in *An Inquiry into the Nature and Origin of Public Wealth* (1804). Perhaps the best known of the subsequent underconsumptionists are Malthus, Sismondi, Rodbertus, Hobson and Rosa Luxemburg. For a fuller (and sometimes different) account of the theories of these and other underconsumptionists than is possible here, the reader should turn to Bleaney (1976) or Nemmers (1956). Further, additional light has been shed on the overall nature of underconsumptionist theories by the several attempts that have been made to express the theory put forward by Malthus in the form of a model, notably by Eagly (1974), Eltis (1980) and Costabile and Rowthorn (1985).

While some underconsumption theories were largely prompted by current or expected economic events, in other cases the inspiration was mainly intellectual. Both factors seem to have been important in the case of Lauderdale, the earliest underconsumptionist. Lauderdale was in part reacting against the praise of parsimony by Adam Smith, but he was also alarmed at the prospect of the British government using its revenue after the end of the Napoleonic wars for the purpose of capital accumulation in place of wartime consumption. More generally, as a precaution against underconsumption, Lauderdale advocated a lessening of the current inequality of wealth, as Malthus was also to do. By contrast Spence, in *Britain Independent of Commerce* (1807), developed an underconsumption theory on the basis of physiocratic ideas. His solution for underconsumption was encouragement of consumption by landlords, so as to restore the income of the manufacturing class to its former level.

His correspondence with Ricardo shows that Malthus had developed underconsumptionist views by 1814. This fact is doubly significant. It proves both that Malthus's underconsumptionism preceded the depressed economic conditions which followed the ending of the Napoleonic wars in 1815, rather than being a response to them, and that Marx's charge that Malthus plagiarized Sismondi is unfounded. The underconsumptionist elements in Malthus's thinking are to be found not only in his correspondence with Ricardo, but also in his *Principles of Political Economy Considered with a View to their Practical Application* (1820). The latter had an influence on the underconsumption theory put forward in Chalmers' *Political Economy* (1832). It may also have provided a stimulus for the underconsumption theory advanced in a pamphlet entitled *Considerations on the Accumulation of Capital* (1822). Published anonymously, this pamphlet was written by Cazenove, the friend of Malthus who was later to edit (also anonymously) the second edition of Malthus's *Principles*.

Like Lauderdale, Sismondi reacted against Adam Smith's views on parsimony, and like Malthus he had become an underconsumptionist by the end of the Napoleonic wars, as is evidenced by the material contained in the article entitled 'Political Economy' which Sismondi wrote in 1815 for Brewster's *Edinburgh Encyclopaedia.* A complete account of Sismondi's underconsumption theory is only to be found, however, in his *Nouveaux principes d'économie politique* (1819). Here Sismondi argued that where producers supply a large anonymous market, competition for profits leads each of them on the one hand to overestimate the demand for the commodity he produces and overaccumulate capital accordingly, and on the other hand so to depress wages that they grow at a slower rate than profits. Sismondi's remedies for underconsumption include organization of industry on a local basis, and a redistribution of income towards wages.

For a discussion of possible sources of the underconsumptionist elements in the writings of Robert Owen and the Ricardian Socialists the reader is referred to King (1981). A more comprehensive underconsumption theory than in those writings is to be found in Rodbertus's 'second letter' to von Kirchmann, published in 1850–51. Rodbertus was reacting against the ideas of Jean Baptiste Say and his followers. His own view was that in a *laissez faire* economy underconsumption must inevitably emerge and worsen, because 'natural' laws will ensure that an ever increasing productivity of labour will be accompanied by an ever decreasing share of income going to wages. His remedy was 'rational' intervention in the economy to counteract these 'natural' laws.

The emphasis in Marx's economic theory on the necessity in a capitalist economy for value not only to be generated in production but also realized by sale makes that theory well adapted to use in the development of an underconsumption theory. Marx himself gave substantial praise to Sismondi for his exposition of such a theory, and there are several passages in Marx's own writings which put forward an underconsumptionist view. On the other hand, there is a well-known passage in Volume II of *Capital* which condemns underconsumption theories in no uncertain terms, and in any case there are other elements in his economic theory which are so much more important to Marx that he is not usually classified as an underconsumptionist. Many, though by no means all of his followers have in fact condemned underconsumption theories. Examples of such condemnation are to be found in some of Lenin's writings, notably his pamphlet entitled *A Characterisation of Economic Romanticism (Sismondi and our Native Sismondists)*, written in 1897. This pamphlet was particularly directed at the underconsumptionist views of the Russian 'Populists', or 'Narodniks', who had argued that capitalism could not survive in Russia without the consumer markets provided by its then-dwindling peasant economy. It was Lenin's view that for the development of capitalism expansion of the market for investment goods is more important than expansion of the market for consumption goods.

Amongst Marx's earlier followers, those who most strongly supported the underconsumptionist element in Marx's thinking were Kautsky and Rosa Luxemburg. Rosa Luxemburg's main arguments were set out in *The Accumulation of Capital* (1913). Contrasting the ever-growing generation of value in a capitalist economy with the inability of workers and unwillingness of capitalists to realize that value by increasing their consumption, she crossed swords with Tugan Baranovski, who had argued that capitalists 'see to it that ever more machines are built for the sake of building – with their help – ever more machines' (Luxemburg, 1913, p. 335). Rosa Luxemburg took the same view as that advanced by J.B. Clark, in his introduction to the English translation of Rodbertus's 'second letter' to von Kirchmann, namely that 'this case presents no glut: but it is an unreal case' (Rodbertus, 1898, p. 15). She concluded that because it was inevitably faced by increasing underconsumption, a capitalist economy could only survive as long as it was able to dispose of its surplus to non-capitalist consumers, either at home or abroad, the latter accounting in her view for policies of imperialism. Apart from Rosa Luxemburg, others who have both drawn on Marx's ideas and made use of underconsumption theory include Sweezy in *The Theory of Capitalist Development* (1942), Baran and Sweezy in *Monopoly Capital* (1966) and Emmanuel in *Unequal Exchange* (1969).

A causal connection between underconsumption and policies of imperialism was also argued to exist by the non-Marxist writer J.A. Hobson, in *Imperialism: a Study* (1902). Jointly with A.F. Mummery, Hobson had reacted to the depression in trade in the 1880s by putting forward an underconsumption theory in *The Physiology of Industry* (1889), which was the first underconsumptionist work actually to use the term 'underconsumption'. In this book Mummery and Hobson argued that the sole source of demand for investment goods is demand for consumption goods. From this they drew the conclusion, as Malthus had done, that there exists an optimum ratio between saving (investment) and spending (consumption). Like Sismondi, they stressed the role of competition in causing supply to exceed demand. They went beyond the earlier underconsumptionists, however, in specifically arguing that neither a fall in the rate of interest nor a fall in the price level could remedy a state of depression brought about by underconsumption. Hobson's subsequent restatement of this theory, with various amplifications, made him the most influential 20th-century exponent of underconsumption theories.

In *The Physiology of Industry* Mummery and Hobson drew the policy conclusion that 'where Under-consumption exists, Savings should be taxed' (Mummery and Hobson, 1889, p. 205). In his later works, however, from *The Problem of the Unemployed* (1896) on, Hobson laid most stress on a redistribution of income from what he called 'unearned income' (income unrelated to effort) to wages as the main remedy for underconsumption. The most comprehensive expositions of Hobson's underconsumption theory are to be found in *The Industrial System* (1909), which is characterized by a more extensive treatment of underconsumption in a growing economy, *The Economics of Unemployment* (1922), and *Rationalisation and Unemployment* (1930).

Other 20th-century exponents of underconsumption theories include Foster and Catchings, in a number of jointly written books. The theories of Major Douglas, however, with their lack of reference to over-investment and their emphasis on the role of money and credit, do not fit well into the underconsumptionist category.

Underconsumption theories have never been acceptable to orthodox economists, perhaps partly because underconsumptionists in general have lacked rigour in the exposition of their ideas, and partly because underconsumption theories have been seen as a threat to the saving necessary for economic growth in particular, and to capitalism in general. They have also attracted less attention since 1936 then before, because Keynes's *General Theory* satisfied the needs of many of those whose intuitions led them to seek a 'demand-side' explanation of economic depression. However, underconsumption theories can be argued still to provide a useful supplement to Keynesian theories, as a reminder that there is a limit to the extent to which employment can be increased by increases in investment alone. There is perhaps some recognition of this in the distinction which is now commonly made as to whether the current need is for an 'investment-led' or a 'consumption-led' recovery.

MICHAEL SCHNEIDER

See also HOBSON, JOHN ATKINSON; KEYNES, JOHN MAYNARD.

BIBLIOGRAPHY

Baran, P.A. and Sweezy, P.M. 1966. *Monopoly Capital*. New York: Monthly Review Press.

Bleaney, M. 1976. *Underconsumption Theories: a history and critical analysis*. London: Lawrence & Wishart.

Cazenove, J. 1822. *Considerations on the Accumulation of Capital and its Effects on Profits and on Exchangeable Value*. London: J.M. Richardson. Published anonymously.

Chalmers, T. 1832. *On Political Economy, in Connexion with the Moral State and Moral Prospects of Society*. Glasgow: William Collins.

Costabile, L. and Rowthorn, R.E. 1985. Malthus's theory of wages and growth. *Economic Journal* 95, June, 418–37.

Domar, E.D. 1947. Expansion and employment. *American Economic Review* 37, March, 34–55.

Eagly, R.V. 1974. *The Structure of Classical Economic Theory*. Oxford: Oxford University Press.

Eltis, W.A. 1980. Malthus's theory of effective demand and growth. *Oxford Economic Papers* 32, March, 19–56.

Emmanuel, A. 1969. *Unequal Exchange: A Study of the Imperialism of Trade*. New York: Monthly Review Press, 1972.

Haberler, G. 1937. *Prosperity and Depression*. Geneva: League of Nations.

Hobson, J.A. 1896. *The Problem of the Unemployed*. London: Methuen.

Hobson, J.A. 1902. *Imperialism: A Study*. London: Nisbet.

Hobson, J.A. 1909. *The Industrial System*. New York: Longmans.

Hobson, J.A. 1922. *The Economics of Unemployment*. London: Allen & Unwin.

Hobson, J.A. 1930. *Rationalisation and Unemployment*. London: Allen & Unwin.

Keynes, J.M. 1936. *The General Theory of Employment, Interest and Money*. London: Macmillan.

King, J.E. 1981. Perish commerce! Free trade and underconsumption in early British radical economics. *Australian Economic Papers* 20(37), December, 235–57.

Lenin, V.I. 1897. A characterisation of economic romanticism (Sismondi and our native Sismondists). In V.I. Lenin, *Collected Works*, Vol. II, Moscow: Foreign Languages Publishing House, 1962.

Luxemburg, R. 1913. *The Accumulation of Capital*. Trans. A. Schwarzschild, with an introduction by Joan Robinson, London: Routledge & Kegan Paul, 1951.

Malthus, T.R. 1820. *Principles of Political Economy Considered with a View to their Practical Application*. London: Murray.

Malthus, T.R. 1836. *Principles of Political Economy Considered with a View to their Practical Application*. 2nd edition, London: William Pickering.

Marx, K. 1885. *Capital*. Vol. II, Moscow: Foreign Languages Publishing House, 1957.

Mummery, A.F. and Hobson, J.A. 1889. *The Physiology of Industry*. London: Murray.

Nemmers, E.E. 1956. *Hobson and Underconsumption*. Amsterdam: North-Holland.
Robbins, L. 1932. Consumption and the trade cycle. *Economica* 12, November, 413–30.
Robinson, J. 1949. Mr Harrod's dynamics. *Economic Journal* 59, March, 68–85.
Rodbèrtus, K. 1898. *Overproduction and Crises*. London: Swan Sonnenschein.
Sismondi, J.C.L. 1815. *Political Economy*. New York: Kelley, 1966.
Sismondi, J.C.L. 1819. *Nouveaux principes d'économie politique*. Paris: Delaunay.
Spence, W. 1807. Britain independent of commerce. In *Tracts on Political Economy*, London: Longman, Hurst, Orme & Brown, 1822.
Sraffa, P. (ed.) 1952. *Works and Correspondence of David Ricardo*. Vol. VI, Cambridge: Cambridge University Press.
Sweezy, P.M. 1942. *The Theory of Capitalist Development*. New York: Monthly Review Press.

undertaker. *See* ENTREPRENEUR.

unemployment. Unemployment can be divided into different types according to the reasons for its occurrence. Some types are relatively uncontroversial from a theoretical point of view. For example, there is frictional unemployment which arises when a person is temporarily unemployed between jobs. Similarly, there is structural unemployment when people find their skills are not employable because they have become technologically redundant or there is no demand for them in the particular part of the country where they live. These sorts of unemployment will be discussed later. By comparison, there is an enduring controversy associated with the attempts to unravel what, if any, are the differences between Classical and Keynesian unemployment. It is this controversy and the policy debate that flows from it which occupies most of the immediate discussion.

The macroeconomists' use of the term Classical, and the designation New Classical for contemporary theorists in this tradition, is somewhat idiosyncratic. This is not the economics of Smith, Ricardo and Marx. Indeed, Neoclassical would be a much more appropriate label. The intuition behind their analysis of unemployment comes from the standard apparatus of supply and demand curves: and the conclusion is drawn that if the labour market does not equilibrate, it must be because the price, in this case the real wage, is set at an inappropriate level.

The demand for labour emanates from the profit maximizing decisions of firms. Under competitive conditions, this leads firms to equate the real wage with the marginal physical product of labour. Hence the demand for labour schedule is a direct reflection of the marginal physical product of labour function. With a well-behaved aggregate production function, the marginal physical product of labour will be a decreasing function of the level of employment, and so the demand for labour varies inversely with the real wage. Consequently, if the supply of labour exceeds the demand and there is a problem of unemployment, then the solution lies with a fall in the real wage as this will prime the quantity of labour demanded and close the unemployment gap.

There are two conceptually separate reasons why the real wage may fail to adjust to the competitive equilibrium value as far as the New Classical Macroeconomics is concerned. Firstly, the institutions of the economy may not correspond to those of a competitive economy: information may be costly, there may be traces of monopoly, etc. Within this institutional context, markets are assumed to clear and the associated level of unemployment is termed the 'natural' rate of unemployment.

> The 'natural rate of unemployment' ... is the level that would be ground out by the Walrasian system of general equilibrium equations, provided there is imbedded in them the actual structural characteristics of the labor and commodity markets, including market imperfections, stochastic variability in demands and supplies, costs of gathering information ... and so on (Friedman, 1968, p. 8).

Consequently, one way that unemployment might be tackled is through policies which attempt to lower the 'natural' rate by removing market imperfections. The policy discussion here does not differ significantly from the Classical analysis of what to do about unemployment. These policies will be considered later in more detail when the topics of frictional and structural unemployment are taken up.

By comparison, the second source of an inappropriate real wage is more distinctively New Classical Macroeconomic. The real wage may deviate from its equilibrium value because workers hold incorrect expectations with respect to the rate of inflation. The point here is that workers bargain over the money wage and hence they will settle for a real wage which unintentionally deviates from the equilibrium value whenever inflation is not accurately anticipated. Unanticipated inflation of this sort forces a wedge between unemployment and its 'natural' level. The policy implications of this analysis revolve around the conduct of demand management policies, and can best be appreciated once Keynes's analysis and policy prescriptions have been introduced.

In the *General Theory*, Keynes disputed the Classical analysis of unemployment and the associated policy prescriptions. He distinguished another category of 'involuntary' unemployment that had something to do with inadequate demand in final commodity markets and which could be remedied with the management of demand by fiscal and possibly monetary policy.

Keynes's *General Theory* is a masterful book, but it is sufficiently ambiguous at crucial points to admit several interpretations of this claim. The dominant view, at least until the late 1960s, is sometimes referred to as the neoclassical-synthetic interpretation and focuses on the role of nominal wage inflexibility in the *General Theory*. As the title might suggest, according to this interpretation, once the *General Theory* is stripped of its rhetoric, it turns out that unemployment results from an inflexible money wage which prevents the real wage from adjusting downwards to prime the demand for labour. In other words, hidden amongst the claims to be providing a General Theory of which Classical theory is a special case, is a piece of theoretical analysis that looks suspiciously like the Classical and New Classical Macroeconomic diagnosis of unemployment as a problem flowing from an inappropriate real wage.

To appreciate this conjecture, consider what would happen in Keynes's model if money wages were allowed to fall in response to unemployment. Initially, with unchanged final commodity prices, this would lead to a fall in the real wage which would increase employment and the output supplied. But, given the initial level of aggregate demand, this increase in aggregate supply will put downward pressure on final commodity prices. As prices fall aggregate demand starts to increase and aggregate supply begins to shrink back because the real wage is creeping up again. Eventually, the economy equilibrates at a lower real wage with higher output and aggregate demand. It is the initial excessive fall in the real wage that creates the excess supply which is necessary if final prices are to fall and prime the increase in aggregate demand to sustain a higher equilibrium level of output. The only circumstances in which this adjustment process would lead the economy back to the same level of employment is if aggregate demand is insensitive to changes in the general level of prices. Here, the increase in aggregate supply which put pressure on final commodity prices would only be removed when final commodity prices have fallen in line with the drop of the money wage to restore the original real wage. Since aggregate demand does not increase as prices fall, the only way the market can re-equilibrate here is through supply reverting to its original value and this will happen once prices have fallen sufficiently to recreate the original real wage.

There was some dispute over the possibility of aggregate demand being insensitive to changes in the general level of prices. But, even within Keynes's model of aggregate demand it is difficult to hold the idea of insensitivity, especially once the real balance effect is acknowledged. From this vantage point, though, granted there is not much new theory in Keynes, it is still possible to see merit in Keynes's policy prescription. An increase in aggregate demand may well be an altogether simpler and quicker way of producing the necessary reduction in the real wage by increasing the general level of prices with a constant money wage, rather than waiting on falls in the money wage to do the trick.

However, even this restricted claim for Keynes is disputed by the New Classical Macroeconomics. After the experience of rapid wage and price changes in the 1970s, it is not very plausible to assume the kind of money illusion which is implicit in the neoclassical-synthetic story of constant money wages. Instead, the New Classical Macroeconomics argues that money wages will be set, given a particular expectation of the rate of inflation, to achieve an equilibrium real wage. Consequently, as noted above, the real wage will only deviate from its equilibrium value when there is unanticipated inflation. The twist to the policy argument comes when a particular version of Rational Expectations is introduced to help analyse the circumstances in which there is unanticipated inflation.

The rational agents of New Classical Macroeconomics use available information to generate expectations which do not suffer from systematic errors. Agents in this world will realise it is demand management policies that influence the rate of inflation; and so it is only unanticipated changes in policy which will create unanticipated inflation. But, any systematic policy rule of the sort advocated by Keynes (i.e. expand/contract demand when unemployment is above/below the target unemployment level) cannot remain unanticipated for long. Rational agents will learn the rule through experience and once learnt the effects of the policy become anticipated. When the policy is anticipated in this fashion it no longer affects output and employment because it does not cause unanticipated inflation. This is the famous policy impotence proposition of Sargent and Wallace (1975). The only kind of policy that would affect unemployment in these circumstances is a completely random one, because only a truly random policy cannot be anticipated. However, it is not at all clear what advantages a government could see in pursuing a random demand policy of this sort since it would only generate random perturbations in unemployment about the 'natural' rate. Ironically, the New Classical Macroeconomics might say, it was the inflation produced by Keynesian inspired expansionary demand policies that undermined the money illusion upon which the efficacy of those policies depended.

The neoclassical-synthetic interpretation of Keynes was always controversial with those like Joan Robinson who had been influential in the development of the *General Theory*. She dubbed it 'bastard Keynesianism'. However, it was not until the late 1960s that an alternative reading of Keynes, sharing many of the insights of Joan Robinson and others from that critical tradition, gained a wide currency. It is perhaps conceding a little too much to the sociology of knowledge to suggest that the success of this reappraisal of Keynes owed much to the fact that it was firmly located in the tradition of neoclassical general equilibrium theory. Nevertheless, whatever its origins and relation to earlier ideas, the reappraisal of Keynes establishes a firm theoretical base for answering the New Classical Macroeconomic argument and restoring a role for Keynesian-type demand management policies.

There are two substantive parts to the reappraisal. Firstly, that Keynes was arguing it is extremely likely an economy will go to work with a non-Walrasian equilibrium price vector. The reasons for this are much more general than the ad hoc suggestion that the money wage is inflexible. They revolve around the congenital problem of all economies located in historical time, the existence of uncertainty. Uncertainty is a keyword in the Robinson approach. But, in neoclassical hands the concept of uncertainty is usually cashed in with the idea that the informational base of the economy is imperfect: there is inadequate information, misinformation, impacted information, asymmetric information, etc. Informational disorders of this sort can then be used to explain the existence of wage stickiness; in the sense not of a constant money wage but of a failure of wages to move to clear the market. It is poor information which prevents agents in the labour market from pursuing the mutually beneficial exchanges which could be realized through setting an equilibrium wage. However, once the point about information problems is recognized, it tends to shift the focus of attention away from the labour market to financial markets because it is intertemporal decisions which are liable to suffer particularly from these informational difficulties. Put it this way: uncertainty is bound to attach with force to those decisions like investment which depend on expectations with respect to a distant future; and this can greatly complicate the business of coordinating savings and investment in financial markets.

Leijonhfvud (1968) and Minsky (1975) provide two accounts in this tradition of how it is the complex intervention of uncertainty which prevents the interest rate from adjusting to equilibrate savings and investment. The failure of financial markets in this regard throws the burden of adjustment on to goods markets, where uncertainty again in the form of initial price stickiness will produce quantity adjustments. This takes the story on to the second part of the reappraisal. Before taking up that part explicitly, it is perhaps worth noting that, aside from the specific role of uncertainty in this account, there is a general point here which any general equilibrium theorist should appreciate. Namely, that in the context of a general equilibrium system it makes no sense to locate the source of market failure in the market in which it happens to occur. In a general equilibrium system, everything depends on everything else that is happening in the economy, and consequently it need not be the agents in the labour market who are responsible for the failure to generate the Walrasian equilibrium price vector. To paraphrase a famous comment by Lerner, the fault may well lie in the market for peanuts.

The second part of the reappraisal suggests Keynes was introducing a new set of dynamics for an economy which trades with such a vector of false prices. A variety of non-Walrasian equilibrium states, where markets do not clear in the accepted sense, can arise from this process of false trading. In general, the insights of Walrasian equilibrium analysis do not carry over to these other states: and in particular a fall in the real wage may not, but an increase in aggregate demand could, prime employment. The analysis of trading at false prices here turns on a distinction between 'notional' and 'effective' demands and supplies.

Patinkin (1956) is now credited with first making this distinction explicit in the labour market. The 'notional' demand for labour is the old demand for labour which is to be found in the classical model where competitive firms equate the real wage with the marginal physical product of labour. However, this is only the effective demand for labour if firms are able to sell all the output which would be produced at each level of employment. When firms are constrained in final commodity markets by a particular level of demand, then even though the real wage may fall the effective demand for labour need not increase because although it would be notionally profitable to hire more workers and sell more output at the lower wage, the constraint of final demand undercuts this calculation: no more goods can be sold in the market and so it makes no sense to hire additional labour.

Clower (1965) plots the reverse influence of how the constraint workers encounter in the labour market produces a wedge between the notional and effective demands for final commodities. Thereby providing an alternative explanation of why a quantity variable appears in the Keynesian consumption function. Barro and Grossman (1971) put the two together, assume that trades take place on the short side of the market, and derive Keynes's multiplier adjustment process. So when economies trade with a vector of false prices and adjustment occurs with quantities on the short side of the market, the famous deviation amplifying Keynesian dynamics can be derived.

Once the two parts of the reappraisal are put together, it is easy to see how the reappraisal lends support to Keynes's claim to have offered a more general theory, of which Classical economics was a special case. Uncertainty means you typically operate with a vector of false prices, false trading ensues with its deviation-amplifying dynamics until a non-Walrasian equilibrium state is reached, and where this state is characterized by unemployment it may be remedied through expansionary aggregate demand policies. Only in the special case where informational difficulties are not important would the economy operate with the Walrasian equilibrium price vector, with the resulting trades producing a Walrasian equilibrium, thus obviating the need for Keynesian activist demand policies.

The position of the New Classical Macroeconomics and its dispute with Keynesian type policy recommendations also becomes clearer with the benefit of the reappraisal. In effect, the New Classical Macroeconomics has defined away the informational problems which are central to Keynes with the twin assumptions of market clearing prices and rational expectations. Indeed, once information difficulties are introduced in New Classical models in the form of gradual price adjustment, then rational expectations can still be maintained and there is a role for Keynesian-like policies (see Buiter, 1980). Equally, if the information difficulties only apply to the formation of rational expectations, say because of non-convergence in the learning process, then even with market clearing prices there remains a place for demand management.

At this stage it may be tempting to declare the rout of Classical and New Classical Macroeconomic analysis of unemployment. After all, it seems impossible to doubt there are significant information problems in the real world. We do not have crystal balls, and learning to remove systematic errors in expectations is no simple matter when our ignorance affects the data set from which we are trying to discover the true relationships between variables. The point being that expectations influence behaviour and so misinformed expectations produce economic outcomes that deviate from those which would be observed in a rational expectations equilibrium and so there is no guarantee that those outcomes will provide any clue to the rational expectations equilibrium relationship between variables. Furthermore, the New Classical Macroeconomics' random errors explanation of unemployment movements appears to come up against a brute empirical fact, the business cycle: unemployment movements are far from random, they exhibit a strong pattern of serial correlation.

Some caution is in order, however, before the declaration of a Keynesian celebration. Firstly, several ingenious explanations of the business cycle have been mounted within the New Classical Macroeconomic framework. Some revolve around cyclical changes in the 'natural' rate itself, occasioned by intertemporal substitutions of labour for leisure or deviations from the trend growth in the capital stock which take place in response to random variations in demand. Others rationalize persistence when there are random oscillations of demand by introducing inventories which spread the adjustment to a disturbance over several time periods (see Lucas, 1981).

Secondly, there are two non-Walrasian equilibrium states in Barro and Grossmans's (1971) model that are characterized by unemployment. One exhibits all the Keynesian properties, the demand for labour is invariant to the real wage and employment can only be increased if aggregate demand rises in final commodity markets. The other has all the classical properties, increasing aggregate demand per se will not help unemployment, what is required is a fall in the real wage. Which non-Walrasian state the economy finds itself in depends on the precise vector of false prices with which the economy has gone to work. So, just because an economy suffers from unemployment, it cannot be presumed that it is Keynesian in origin and will respond to expansionary demand policies. In addition, even if the Keynesian non-Walrasian regime obtains rather than the classical one, the effective demand for labour could still depend in more general models on the real wage. Changes in the real wage could have effects on the level of aggregate demand, via for example redistribution effects; or the fall in the real wage could arise from a depreciation in the exchange rate which alters international demand for domestic goods, thus influencing the effective demand for labour. The direction of influence is, of course, ambiguous and it remains the case that the full Walrasian equilibrium could not be achieved by changes in the real wage alone.

In other words, even if information difficulties are acknowledged and trades occur at false prices, it does not follow that all unemployment deviations from the 'natural' rate can be remedied through Keynesian demand manipulations. Real wage adjustments may be required. In this way, the insights of Classical and New Classical Macroeconomics carry over to a world where there is uncertainty. What has become clear, however, is that Classical and New Classical Macroeconomics do not hold the monopoly on what happens in a world where there is uncertainty: Keynes's theoretical credentials have been restored.

In fact, it could be argued that the recent discussion of Keynes and the New Classical Macroeconomics, rather than proving decisive on one side of the dispute or the other, has revealed a deep underlying consensus on the theory of unemployment. The rational expectations component of the New Classical Macroeconomics, particularly its critique of arbitrary expectation assumptions, is pushing economic analysis in exactly the same direction as the reappraisal. Even, if it comes at the issue from a slightly different direction, the issue is very definitely information and its processing. In short, there is perhaps a surprising level of agreement that the informational base of an economy is crucial in determining its functioning and the appropriate role for policy. From this position, the disagreement only surfaces over the diagnosis of the degree of imperfection in the informational bases of economies in the real world.

Before concluding the discussion on this aspect of unemployment, it is worth developing briefly the Kaleckian tradition which explicitly draws on Robinson's emphasis on uncertainty arising from economies operating in historical time. Typically, uncertainty and history license a different set of microfoundations in this tradition. This is not the place to elaborate these foundations. But, what is interesting is that they yield surprisingly similar implications for the analysis of unemployment (see Rowthorn, 1980). Unemployment is still influenced by aggregate demand, but it now also regulates class conflict. Both the real wage and profit expectations of workers and firms are affected by the level of unemployment. A 'natural' rate of unemployment now emerges in the same sense that it is the level of unemployment where inflation is anticipated. The only difference, albeit one with important normative implications, is that this rate no longer corresponds to the adjusted Walrasian market clearing value. It is for this reason that the less normatively charged term, NAIRU (the non accelerating inflation rate of unemployment) is often preferred to the title 'natural' to describe this level of unemployment. Indeed, it would be pure serendipity if this level coincided with what would otherwise be called the full employment level of unemployment in the Walrasian world. Instead, it is the level of unemployment where the otherwise conflicting real wage and profit expectations of workers and firms are reconciled. At other levels of unemployment these aspirations are inconsistent and a reconciliation is achieved through unanticipated inflation which frustrates one set of the claims on output. Again, though, how long unemployment can persist at such a non-'natural' level will depend on the degree of price stickiness and the expectation generating mechanisms.

To summarize, there is widespread agreement in macroeconomics that when there are informational inadequacies leading to sticky prices and difficulties forming expectations, unemployment can deviate from its 'natural' level. In such circumstances, there may be a part for Keynesian demand management policies to play in influencing unemployment. Where there is disagreement is over the normative properties of the 'natural' rate and over the likelihood of these information disorders being important in the economies of the real world.

Of course, unemployment can also be influenced by policies directed at the 'natural' rate itself. These are sometimes referred to as supply side policies to distinguish them from the demand manipulations designed to alter unemployment through changing its relation to the 'natural' rate.

Two sorts of unemployment which pop up in both the orthodox market clearing and Kaleckian accounts of the 'natural' rate are frictional and structural unemployment. Search theoretic explanations of frictional unemployment typically isolate the level of unemployment benefits as important in determining the length of search since this affects the calculation of costs versus expected benefits of search. Similarly, any measure which improves the flow of information about job vacancies in the labour market is likely to lower frictional unemployment. In addition, the age and sex composition of the labour force is probably important. It is a feature of the gender stratification of most economies that women enter and re-enter the labour force more frequently than men and because each re-entry is often accompanied by a period of frictional unemployment, an increase in the share of women in the labour force tends to increase the economy-wide proportion of frictional unemployment. Likewise young people tend to chop and change jobs more often than older people and so an increase in their share raises the overall level of frictional unemployment. It is not obvious how policy can alter the age-sex composition itself, but it could be directed at this aspect of gender stratification.

The geographic dimension of structural unemployment could be ameliorated with encouragements to mobility. The skill aspect depends on whether the evolution of the skills of the labour force keep pace with the changing requirements associated with technological advance. There is a rather obvious role for policy here in the provision of educational, training and re-training facilities.

The extent of monopoly in product and factor markets will also influence the 'natural' rate. From the market clearing perspective trades unions are the obvious market imperfection which produces an equilibrium real wage above the competitive value with a corresponding lower level of employment. By contrast, it is monopoly in product markets which attracts the Kaleckian attention. The degree of monopoly influences the profit expectations of firms positively and consequently produces a direct relationship with the 'natural' rate. The difference here is really only a matter of emphasis: which type of monopoly excites immediate interest. Where the Kaleckians depart decisively in their analysis of the 'natural' rate is on what determines the wage expectations of workers.

For Kaleckians, the wage expectations of workers depend on the historical and social circumstances of the time. This may seem a bit woolly, but it has its uses. For example, it enables a careful politico-historical explanation of the surge in wage militancy which is thought to have occurred in many European countries in the late 1960s. More generally, it locates the distribution of income, which is central to their view of the 'natural' rate, strongly in the political arena and this makes the 'natural' rate susceptible to a range of policies from social contracts, national economic assessments, to incomes policies to industrial policies: in fact, anything that might directly or indirectly bear on questions of distribution.

One of the more intriguing possibilities, which gives a twist to the earlier policy debate, is that the government's demand policies may themselves influence the 'natural' rate. Friedman (1977) acknowledges such a possibility. He argues that the variability of inflation is directly related to the level of inflation. So, more noise enters into price signals at higher rates of inflation, with the result that the 'natural' rate rises with the rate of inflation. This provides the ammunition to extend the argument against Keynesian demand activism into one where steady demand growth is targeted for low rates of inflation.

Tobin (1980) envisages a different connection:

> It is hard to resist or refute the suspicion that the operational NAIRU gravitates towards the average rate of unemployment actually experienced. Among the mechanisms which produce that result are improvements in unemployment compensation and other benefits enacted in response to higher unemployment, loss of on-the-job training and employability by the unemployed, defections to the informal and illegal economy, and a slowdown in

capital formation as business firms lower their estimates of needed capacity (p. 60).

If such hysteresis effects are accepted, then an expansionary demand policy which lowers unemployment 'temporarily' below the 'natural' rate will have a permanent influence because it contributes to reducing the 'natural' rate itself. In the most recent world recession, there is no evidence of unemployment compensation changing in this way. There is some evidence that the loss of on-the-job training has contributed to a rise in the numbers structurally unemployed: this effect can be most easily seen in the growth of long term unemployment. And, overall, it is clear in a number of countries that the 'natural' rate has risen during the course of the world recession of the early 1980s. Consequently, there is some basis for accepting this idea of cumulative causation applied to the 'natural' rate itself; and this provides a contrary presumption to that of Friedman in favour of expansionary demand policies.

One way of appreciating this policy implication and summarizing the whole discussion, is through the language of Phillips curves. The original Phillips curve suggested there was a trade-off between inflation and unemployment which could be exploited by governments with their manipulation of aggregate demand. Friedman (1968) interpreted this curve as a short run reflection of the aggregate supply function arising only when inflation was unanticipated: in the long run when inflation is anticipated there is no trade-off, the Phillips curve is vertical and unemployment does not deviate from its 'natural' rate. The New Classical Macroeconomics collapsed the long run here into the short run with the addition of their version of rational expectations. There is no scope for systematic Keynesian demand manipulations to influence unemployment in the short or long run: any systematic manipulation will become anticipated and once anticipated it ceases to have an effect on output and employment.

The reappraisal of Keynes has made clear that the conditions where this conclusion holds are rather special. If an economy suffers from informational problems producing either sticky prices or difficulties with the formation of rational expectations, then the operative Phillips curve is one of the so-called short run versions and there is a role for demand management. Acknowledging hysteresis effects tends to reinforce this conclusion by providing grounds for the belief that the 'long' run of the inflation anticipated Phillips curve is not vertical: rather it too exhibits a trade-off between the 'natural' rate and the fully anticipated rate of inflation. Friedman's (1977) contrary argument that the 'natural' rate rises with the rate of inflation, of course, points policy in the opposite direction.

To conclude, the theoretical and policy debate over unemployment turns on two sets of issues. The first concerns the pervasiveness and influence of uncertainty (or informational problems) as this affects the potential for demand policies to manage the relation between unemployment and the 'natural' rate. Secondly, there are disputes over the determinants of the 'natural' rate and this generates a controversy over the appropriate supply side policies. The two issues are connected. The hysteresis argument links demand policies to the determination of the 'natural' rate. But, more generally, it is the perception of uncertainty as endemic that contributes to the alternative Kaleckian micro foundations which are at the root of the dispute over supply side policies for the 'natural' rate. In short, all macroeconomists might agree with Angelica in Congreve's *Love For Love*, 'Uncertainty and expectation are the joys of life': or at least, they are the joys of macroeconomic theorizing on employment.

SHAUN HARGREAVES-HEAP

See also INVOLUNTARY UNEMPLOYMENT; NATURAL RATE OF UNEMPLOYMENT.

BIBLIOGRAPHY

Barro, R.J. and Grossman, H.I. 1971. A general disequilibrium model of income and unemployment. *American Economic Review* 61, 82–93.

Buiter, W.H. 1980. The macroeconomics of Dr Pangloss. *Economic Journal* 90, 34–50.

Clower, R.W. 1965. The Keynesian counter-revolution: a theoretical appraisal. In *The Theory of Interest Rates*, ed. F.H. Hahn and F. Brechling, London: Macmillan.

Friedman, M. 1968. The role of monetary policy. *American Economic Review* 58, 1–17.

Friedman, M. 1977. Inflation and unemployment. *Journal of Political Economy* 85, 451–72.

Keynes, J.M. 1936. *The General Theory of Employment, Interest and Money*. London: Macmillan.

Leijonhufvud, A. 1968. *On Keynesian Economics and the Economics of Keynes*. New York: Oxford University Press.

Lucas, R.E. 1980. *Studies in Business Cycle Theory*. Oxford: Blackwell.

Minsky, H. 1975. *John Maynard Keynes*. London: Macmillan.

Patinkin, D. 1956. *Money, Interest and Prices*. New York: Harper & Row.

Rowthorn, R. 1980. *Capitalism, Conflict and Inflation*. London: Lawrence & Wishart.

Sargent, T.J. and Wallace, N. 1975. Rational expectations, the optimal monetary instrument, and the optimal money supply rule. *Journal of Political Economy* 83, 241–54.

Tobin, J. 1980. Stabilization policy ten years after. *Brookings Papers on Economic Activity* No. 1, 19–71.

unemployment benefit. *See* SOCIAL SECURITY.

unequal exchange. Marxists have long attempted to explain the uneven development of 'productive forces' (labour productivity) and the resulting income differences in the world capitalist economy primarily by means of the 'surplus drain' hypothesis (see Emmanuel, 1972; Andersson, 1976). Adopting Prebisch's division of the world capitalist economy into the 'centre' and 'periphery', Marxists have argued that surplus transfer has restrained the economic development of the periphery and exacerbated its income gap vis-à-vis the centre.

Before Emmanuel's work, the surplus transfer argument consisted of a loose intertwining of Prebisch's thesis over the secular deterioration of the terms of trade in the periphery, Marx's writings on 'the colonial question', and Lenin's theory of imperialism. Although presented inelegantly in terms of Marx's tableaux, Emmanuel introduced a coherent surplus drain theory utilizing Marx's transformation of values into production prices.

Emmanuel (1972) formulated his theory of surplus transfer through unequal exchange by comparing values with Marxian prices of production (see Okishio, 1963, pp. 296–8). Subsequently, Braun (1973) introduced unequal exchange utilizing Sraffa's framework (see Evans's, 1984, critical survey), Bacha (1978) introduced a neoclassical counterpart, and Shaikh (1979) suggested an alternative preserving Marx's theory of value.

Departing from recent reformulations, it is helpful to explain Emmanuel's unequal exchange theory within its original Marxist framework. The value (t) of a product is the sum of constant capital (c), variable capital (v), and surplus value (s), whereas its corresponding Marxian production price (p) includes the average profit rate (r):

$$t = c + v + s \quad (1)$$

$$p = (1 + r)(c + v) \quad (2)$$

In a world capitalist system consisting of the centre (A) and periphery (B) as trading partners, unequal exchange is defined as the difference (g) between Marxian production prices and values (see Marelli, 1980, p. 517). In fact, unequal exchange compares two terms of trade under different assumptions about the wage rate in each country:

$$g_i = p_i - t_i \quad i = \text{A,B} \tag{3}$$

A positive g denotes a *surplus gain* for exporters, while a negative g denotes a *surplus loss*.

Emmanuel's theory rests on the assumptions of a single world-wide profit rate resulting from international capital mobility, and the existence of a wage gap resulting from the immobility of labour from the periphery to the centre. The wage rate is an independent variable. Based on these assumptions, Emmanuel showed that unequal exchange depends on a country's rate of surplus value and on its organic composition of capital in relation to world average. Subtracting (1) from (2), we obtain:

$$g_i = r(c_i + v_i) - s_i \tag{4}$$

now consider these definitions:

(a) $s_i = e_i v_i$ rate of surplus value,
(b) $r = e/(1+k)$ average profit rate,
(c) $c_i = k_i v_i$ organic composition of capital.

After substituting the definitions for the rate of surplus value, the average profit rate, and the organic composition of capital into equation (4), we obtain a formula to measure unequal exchange:

$$g_i = v_i\left\{e\frac{1+k_i}{1+k} - e_i\right\}. \tag{5}$$

Unequal exchange will disappear when the profit rate of the centre or the periphery approaches the world average profit rate, i.e. $r_i = r$. This is satisfied when these conditions hold:

$$\text{(i) } e_i = e \quad \text{and} \quad \text{(ii) } k_i = k.$$

Emmanuel's distinction between the *broad* and *strict* definitions of unequal exchange can be easily understood by referring to equation (5). Even when the wage rates and thus the rates of surplus are equalized between the centre and the periphery, unequal exchange in the 'broad sense' occurs resulting from differences in the organic composition of capital. This type of unequal exchange can also exist *within* a country because of the differences in the organic composition of capital among sectors.

If condition (i) is satisfied and the rates of surplus value in the centre and periphery are equalized, the unequal exchange equation (5) becomes:

$$g_i = v_i e\left\{\frac{1+k_i}{1+k} - 1\right\}. \tag{5'}$$

As a result, there will be a surplus gain through trade when the individual organic composition of capital exceeds the world average. Likewise, if condition (ii) is satisfied and the organic compositions of capital are equal in both the centre and the periphery, the unequal exchange equation (5) becomes:

$$g_i = v_i(e - e_i). \tag{5''}$$

In this case, corresponding to Emmanuel's unequal exchange in the 'strict sense', there will be a surplus gain through trade when the world average rate of surplus value exceeds the individual rate.

The periphery tends to transfer surplus through trade because its rate of surplus value is higher than the world average, resulting from an international wage gap favouring workers in the centre. Therefore, even if the organic compositions of capital are equalized, unequal exchange results from the existence of a wage gap between the centre and the periphery, expressed as the rate of surplus value being lower in the centre than in the periphery (the rate of surplus value can be expressed as one over the value of labour power or 'wage share' minus one, $e = (1/w) - 1$). According to Emmanuel, unequal exchange in the 'strict sense' characterizes the trade relations between the centre and periphery.

Emmanuel's (1972, p. 61) basic conclusions is that 'the inequality of wages as such, all other things being equal, is alone the cause of the inequality of exchange'. As a corollary, Emmanuel (1972, p. 131) argued that 'by transferring, through non-equivalent [exchange], a large part of its surplus to the rich countries, [the periphery] deprives itself of the means of accumulation and growth'. Thus, an important implication of Emmanuel's theory is that a widening wage gap leads to a deterioration of the periphery's terms of trade, and a subsequent reduction in its rate of economic growth.

Emmanuel's work generated an interesting international debate. One contentious issue is the relationship of Emmanuel's theory to Marx's theory of value, leading to reformulations of Emmanuel's theory within the context of the Marx–Sraffa debate (Gibson, 1980; Mainwaring, 1980; Dandekar, 1980; Evans, 1984; Sau, 1984). Another view holds that Emmanuel's theory does not sufficiently explain uneven development because it omits the 'blocking of the productive forces' by entrenched and reactionary social classes in the periphery (Bettelheim, in the Appendix to Emmanuel, 1972). Bettelheim also argues that the rate of surplus value is higher in the centre resulting from its higher labour productivity, thus giving rise to unequal exchange reversal.

At the same time, Amin (1977) has emphasized non-specialized trade between the centre and the periphery, claiming the 'end of a debate', while the debate survived a virulent 'exchange of errors' among Marxists in India (see Dandekar, 1980; Sau, 1984). De Janvry and Kramer (1979) criticize unequal exchange as a theory of underdevelopment because capital mobility tends to eliminate wage differences by exhausting the 'reserve army' in the periphery, an argument which is challenged by Gibson (1980). Andersson (1976) surveys some pre-Emmanuel views, adding a formalization similar to Braun (1973), while Liossatos (1979) and Marelli (1980) have recast Emmanuel's theory in a modern, Morishima-like Marxian framework.

Although Emmanuel's primary objective involves 'model building', it is important to recognize that his references to standard trade theory are dated, largely confined to the literature of the 1950s, perhaps indicating that his work suffered from a long gestation period. Therefore, one should be cautious about treating Emmanuel's work as a critique of standard trade theory. Outside of Ricardian and Marxian circles, the reception of Emmanuel's work has been tepid if not neglectful.

Looking ahead, Harris (1975) suggests that a convincing theory of economic development should include a theory of value and distribution and a theory of accumulation on a world scale. Emmanuel's theory of unequal exchange, especially in subsequently more rigorous formulations (Andersson, 1976; Liossatos, 1979; Marelli, 1980; Gibson, 1980; Evans, 1984; Sau, 1984) has an assured place in this curriculum. In this way, Emmanuel's theory of unequal exchange is definitely linked to the original theory of Prebisch, Singer, Lewis and Baran, on trade and development.

EDNALDO ARAQUEM DA SILVA

See also PERIPHERY.

BIBLIOGRAPHY

Amin, S. 1977. *Imperialism and Unequal Development*. New York: Monthly Review Press.

Andersson, J. 1976. *Studies in the Theory of Unequal Exchange Between Nations*. Abo: Abo Akademi.

Bacha, E. 1978. An interpretation of unequal exchange from Prebisch–Singer to Emmanuel. *Journal of Development Economics* 5(4), December, 319–30.

Braun, O. 1973. *International Trade and Imperialism*. Atlantic Highlands, NJ: Humanities Press, 1984.

Dandekar, V. 1980. Unequal exchange of errors. *Economic and Political Weekly* 15(13), March, 645–48. Continued in 16(6), February 1981, 205–12.

De Janvry, A. and Kramer, F. 1979. The limits of unequal exchange. *Review of Radical Political Economics* 11(4), Winter, 3–15.

Emmanuel, A. 1972. *Unequal Exchange: A Study of the Imperialism of Trade* (with additional comments by Charles Bettelheim). New York: Monthly Review Press.

Evans, D. 1984. A critical assessment of some neo-Marxian trade theories. *Journal of Development Studies* 20(2), January, 202–26.

Gibson, B. 1980. Unequal exchange: theoretical issues and empirical findings. *Review of Radical Political Economics* 12(3), Fall, 15–35.

Harris, D. 1975. The theory of economic growth: a critique and reformulation. *American Economic Review* 65(2), May, 329–37.

Liossatos, P. 1979. Unequal exchange and regional disparities. *Papers of the Regional Science Association* 45, November, 87–103.

Mainwaring, L. 1980. International trade and the transfer of labour values. *Journal of Development Studies* 17(1), October, 22–31.

Marelli, E. 1980. An intersectoral analysis of regional disparities in terms of transfers of surplus value. *Revista internazionale di scienze economiche e commerciali* 27(6), June, 507–26.

Okishio, N. 1963. A mathematical note on Marxian theorems. *Weltwirtschaftliches Archiv* 91(2), 287–98.

Sau, R. 1984. *Underdeveloped Capitalism and the General Law of Value*. Atlantic Highlands, NJ: Humanities Press.

Shaikh, A. 1979. Foreign trade and the law of value: Part I. *Science and Society* 43(3), Fall, 281–302. Part II was published in 44(1), Spring.

uneven development. In considering the general character of the process of capitalist development as it has appeared historically across many different countries over a long period of time, one of its most striking characteristics is the phenomenon of uneven development. By this is meant specifically that the process is marked by persistent differences in levels and rates of economic development between different sectors of the economy.

This differentiation appears at many levels and in terms of a multiplicity of quantitative and qualitative indices. Relevant measures which sharply identify the pattern of differentiation would include, for instance, the level of labour productivity in different sectors, the level of wages, occupational and skill composition of the labour force, the degree of mechanization of production techniques, the level of profitability as measured by sectoral rates of profit, the size structure of firms, and rates of growth at the sectoral level. This phenomenon appears regardless of the level of aggregation or disaggregation of the economy, except for the extreme case of complete aggregation – in which case, of course, one cannot say anything about the structural properties of the economy. For example, it appears at the level of comparing the broad aggregates of manufacturing industry and agriculture. It appears also at the level of individual industries within the manufacturing sector. It appears on a regional level as well as on a global scale within the international economy. In this latter context, one form that it takes is the continued differentiation between underdeveloped and advanced economies, usually identified as the problem of underdevelopment.

These disparities appear from observing the economy as a whole at any given moment and over long periods of time. And while the relative position of particular sectors may change from one period to another, nevertheless, there is always a definite pattern of such differentiation. We might say, therefore, and certainly it is an implication of these observations, that these disparities are continually reproduced by the process of development. Uneven development, in this sense, is an intrinsic or inherent property of the economic process. Far from being merely transitory, it seems to be a pervasive and permanent condition.

Now, it is an equally striking fact that, when we examine the theoretical literature on economic growth, we find the completely opposite picture. In particular, the dominant conception of the growth process that has motivated the post-World-War II literature is one that is constructed in terms of uniform rates of expansion in output, productivity and employment in all sectors of the economy. It is largely a literature of steady-state growth. Furthermore, much of existing economic theory predicts that, given enough time, many of the features of differentiation which we observe empirically would tend to wash out as a result of the operation of competitive market forces. Such differentiation should therefore be viewed only as a transitory feature of the economic process. But, in fact, we observe the opposite.

Thus, on the one side, we find a historical picture of uneven development as a persistent phenomenon. On the other side, we find a theory which essentially negates and denies this fact. It is as if the theory existed on one side and the historical reality on the other, and never the twain shall meet. However, it is possible to go some of the way towards bridging this gap. Accordingly, I consider here a strategy for analysis of uneven development that breaks through the narrow limits of the existing steady-state theory and advances towards a historically and empirically relevant theory. A detailed review and critique of the analytic foundations of steady-state theory is presented in Harris (1978; 1985).

THE ANALYSIS OF UNEVEN DEVELOPMENT. In order to go beyond the analysis of steady-state growth, it is necessary to start by recognizing the intrinsic character of the individual firm as an expansionary unit of capital. Various efforts have been made to develop a theory of the firm on this basis. (See, for instance, Penrose, 1959; Baumol, 1959; and Marris, 1967.) In this conception, growth is the strategic objective on the part of the firm. This urge to expand is not a matter of choice. Rather, it is a necessity enforced upon the firm by its market position and by its existence within a world of firms where each must grow in order to survive. It is reinforced also by sociological factors, such as the social status and power associated with being the owner, director, or manager of an expanding enterprise. It is this character of the firm which constitutes the driving force behind the process of expansion of the economy.

This is a crucial starting point because it establishes the idea of growth as the outcome of a process which is driven by active agents and not by exogenous factors. In particular, in the context of the capitalist economy, growth is the outcome of the self-directed and self-organizing activity of firms, each seeking to expand and to improve its competitive position in relation to the rest. Once this principle is recognized it becomes possible to move towards an understanding of the problem of uneven development.

The imperative of growth impels the firm constantly to seek out new investment opportunities wherever they are to be found. Such investment may occur in existing product lines, in new products and processes, or in the takeover of existing firms. The emergence of growth centres or leading sectors is a reflection of this underlying process. It is a consequence of the effort on the part of many firms to create or to rush into those spheres in which a margin of profitability exists that allows them to capture new growth opportunities. Such new spheres are always being opened up as a consequence of the ongoing innovative activity of firms and the competitive interactions among them. It is this constant flux, consisting of the emergence of new growth centres, their rapid expansion relative to existing sectors, and the relative decline of other sectors, which shows up in the economy as a whole as uneven development.

The form that this process takes, as it appears at the level of particular industries and product lines, has been well documented through empirical research. These studies show that the growth of many new industries and products follows a life-cycle pattern which may be represented by an S-shaped curve as in Figure 1. There are correspondingly three phases of expansion. In the initial phase, total output of the new industry is a minute share of the overall aggregate output in the economy and the rate of growth of output is low. This is followed by a phase of rapid growth in which this sector's output expands rapidly relative to overall output and its share of aggregate output grows. Then there is a third phase in which the sector reaches a threshold beyond which the growth rate tends to level off and perhaps to decline.

Of course, the process does not come to an end at that point. We must understand this sequence, schematically described here, as but a small segment of the time sequence characterizing the historical evolution of the economy. Given that firms are growing, making profits, and seeking to continue to grow, it would be necessary for them, having entered into phase III, to launch out into new sectors. They will therefore actively seek to find new products that will initiate a corresponding new sequence.

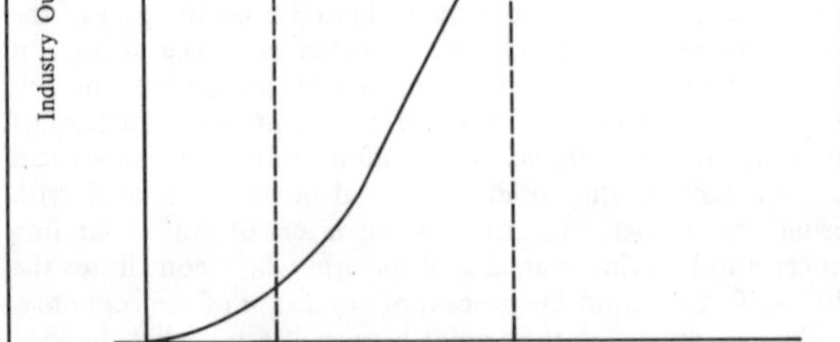

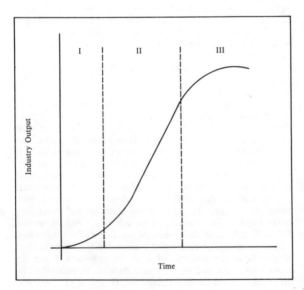

Figure 1 Life-cycle of an industry

It follows that we can map out the dynamic evolution of the economy in terms of *a sequential process*, where the overall growth is accountable for on the basis of (1) the individual growth of particular new sectors, (2) the growth of pre-existing sectors, each of which is growing at a different rate depending on the particular phase reached in its life-cycle, and (3) the constant accretion of new sectors into the economy owing to the introduction of new products. In this context also, the relative position of any region or country on a relevant index of development could be seen as a matter of the particular products or industries it has managed to capture as a result of the previous pattern of accumulation and the ongoing activity of firms operating within it and the particular timing of their entry into the life-cycle of new products.

We can go further in understanding the anatomy of this process if we take account of the technological innovation process tied up with it. In this connection it is helpful to draw upon Kuznets's suggestive characterization of general features of the innovation process for 'major' innovations. Specifically, Kuznets (1979) identifies a sequence of four distinct phases as constituting the life-cycle of an innovation. It begins with a *pre-conception* phase in which necessary scientific and technological preconditions are laid. This is followed by a phase of *initial application* involving the first successful commercial application of the innovation. Then comes the *diffusion* phase marked by spread in adoption and use of the innovation throughout the economy along with continued improvements in quality and cost. Finally, there is a phase of *slowdown* and *obsolescence* in which further potential of the innovation is more or less exhausted and even some contraction may occur. This taxonomy is useful and suggestive in pointing to a certain internal logic of the innovation process related to 'the purely technological problems in breaking through to an effective invention and resolving the difficulties in development, prototype production, etc,... [and] ... the complementary and other organizational and social adjustments that would assure adequate diffusion and economic success' (pp. 64–5). It suggests, furthermore, that different firms, regions, and countries may be differently situated in terms of their capacity to undertake or enter the innovation process and hence to realize the growth advantages/disadvantages associated with different phases of that process. The case for such differentiation has been cogently argued, for instance, by Hirsch (1967).

The anatomy of this process can be further understood by taking account of its connection with the changing firm-structure of the industry. In particular, it has been observed that, for many industries, there is a proliferation of small firms in phase I of the industry's life cycle. But as the diffusion of the product occurs and growth speeds up, there is a 'shaking out' process by which many of the smaller firms disappear and the available market is concentrated in the remaining firms. When the industry reaches 'maturity', in phase III, there is a high degree of concentration.

This association between industry life cycle and firm-structure of the industry suggests that the dynamic of expansion through innovation is simultaneously a process of the concentration of capital. Further investigation of this link may provide a key to understanding the internal mechanisms and forces which feed the expansion process and account for its character as a process of uneven development. Without going into these in depth, it may be suggested here that there are a number of factors at work.

One is the phenomenon of economies of scale in production and marketing. Such economies give to the larger firms a decisive advantage in exploiting an innovation. Small firms may well have special advantages in the research and development phase of innovation and, in many cases, are observed to lead the process in that phase. But they often lose out to the larger firms at the stage of standardization, mass production and mass marketing of the product. The larger firms, on their part, may gain from foregoing the risks associated with the first phase and choosing to enter at a later stage through adoption of a proven innovation or takeover of a successful firm.

Another factor is the power of finance. The capacity to command finance is a powerful lever in the expansion process, deriving its significance from the substantial financial outlays involved in product development, production, and marketing, that have to be made well in advance of sales. This capacity depends both on the generation of internal funds and on access to external funds. Large firms have an advantage here because of their larger profits, to begin with, and because of their superior ability to borrow.

Because of these complementary relationships one might say that it is the large firms which drive the process, at least within certain phases of it. It is still a process which is driven by the expansion of firms, but it turns out that some firms are more equal than others in this process.

What role is to be assigned to demand as a factor in this process? At the level of individual consumer products or industries, a common conception is that demand acts as an autonomous factor with a definite influence on the life-cycle pattern of evolution of the product. That influence is exerted in the early phase of introduction of a new product because of an element of resistance due to 'habit' formed in a customary pattern of consumption. It is exerted also in the maturity phase because of the operation of 'saturation effects' in consumption. But there are reasons to doubt the strength and effectiveness of such factors, as well as their supposed autonomy.

First of all, in an economy undergoing regular and rapid change, it is not evident what role there is for habit except for the habit of change itself. The experience of and adaptation to change may create a high degree of receptivity to change. What then becomes decisive in the evolution of demand for consumer goods is the growth of income, and the changing relative prices and quality of products.

Second, insofar as these latter factors are crucial to the formation of demand, it may be argued that there is a certain self-fulfilling aspect of the expansionary process at the level of industry demand. In particular, investment generates the demand that provides the market for the new products which the investment itself creates. This occurs in two ways. First, investment generates income both directly in the sector undergoing rapid expansion and indirectly, via backward and forward linkages, through the stimulation of demand and investment in other sectors. In this respect, structural interdependence in the economy at the level of both production and expenditure patterns, allows for the possibility of a certain mutual provisioning of markets when expansion takes place on a broad front. Second, as a new product unfolds through the stages of the innovation process, it undergoes both improvements in quality and a decline in price relative to other products. This development provides a substantive basis for making inroads into the market for existing closely related products and hence promotes demand through a shift from 'old' to 'new' products. It is perhaps this *shift effect* which is mistakenly identified as a *saturation effect* by adopting a one-sided and static view of a dynamic and interdependent process.

Of course, though investment generates demand in these various ways, there is no guarantee that in the aggregate there is always sufficient demand for all products. It is here that the argument comes full circle, so to speak, back to the problem of overall effective demand that motivated the early post-war growth theory initiated by Harrod (1948) and Domar (1957). This problem was a central focus of the analysis of steady-state growth. It appears now that it cannot be escaped in making the transition to the analysis of uneven development.

In general, it must be recognized here that all of the preceding argument concerns the pattern of sectoral growth viewed at the level of individual industries, products, and firms. There is nothing in that argument to indicate how the pattern of sectoral growth translates into aggregate expansion at the level of the economy as a whole, or how the various sectoral patterns fit together to form a complete whole. This is a substantive problem requiring further analytical treatment on its own terms. Its significance derives from the recognition that the economy as a whole is not just the sum of its parts. Hence, the motion of the economy cannot simply be deduced from the movement of its parts.

Another aspect of the problem is associated with the manifold and complex ways in which growth in one sector mutually conditions and is conditioned by growth in all other sectors. Such mutual interaction is a necessary consequence of economic interdependence. The existence of such interaction implies that there is a certain cumulative effect intrinsic in the growth process. Understanding the exact mechanisms through which this effect operates is one of the central analytical problems for the analysis of uneven development.

DONALD J. HARRIS

See also TERMS OF TRADE AND ECONOMIC DEVELOPMENT.

BIBLIOGRAPHY

Baumol, W.J. 1959. *Business Behaviour, Value and Growth*. New York: Harcourt, Brace and World.

Domar, E.D. 1957. *Essays in the Theory of Economic Growth*. New York: Oxford University Press.

Harris, D.J. 1978. *Capital Accumulation and Income Distribution*. Stanford: Stanford University Press.

Harris, D.J. 1985. The theory of economic growth: from steady states to uneven development. In *Contemporary Issues in Macroeconomics and Distribution*, ed. G. Feiwel, London: Macmillan.

Harrod, R.F. 1948. *Towards a Dynamic Economics*. London: Macmillan.

Hirsch, S. 1967. *Location of Industry and International Competitiveness*. Oxford: Clarendon Press.

Kuznets, S. 1979. Technological innovations and economic growth. In *Growth, Population, and Income Distribution, Selected Essays*. New York: Norton.

Marris, R. 1967. *The Economic Theory of 'Managerial' Capitalism*. London: Macmillan.

Penrose, E.T. 1959. *The Theory of the Growth of the Firm*. Oxford: Blackwell.

unintended consequences. *See* INVISIBLE HAND; SELF-INTEREST.

uniqueness of equilibrium. In general equilibrium theory, equilibrium prices may be interpreted as those prices which coordinate the buying and selling plans of all the various agents in the economy; equivalently, they may be interpreted as the values of the commodities. Such values will only be well defined if there is only one system of coordinating prices, that is, if the equilibrium is unique. If this does not obtain then at least the set of equilibrium price systems should not be too large, that is, there should be only a finite number of equilibria.

The question of uniqueness was first posed by Walras (1874–7), but received its first systematic treatment by Wald (1936). In the present discussion we commence with a formal definition of uniqueness. We then note that there may be multiple, and even infinitely many, equilibria, but show that the latter possibility is unlikely. In the light of this we examine various conditions which are sufficient to ensure that equilibrium is unique. Finally, we note some problems which may arise in the presence of multiple equilibria.

We may represent an economy with n commodities by the excess demand function $f\colon S \to R^n$, where $S = R^n_+ - 0$. The interpretation of this is that $f(p)$ is the vector of aggregate excess demands (positive) or excess supplies (negative) expressed at the price system p. Under some reasonable assumptions on the underlying parameters of the economy, that is the individual preferences and endowments, this excess demand function has the following properties:

Homogeneity: $f(tp) = f(p)$ for all positive t.

Walras' Law: $p \cdot f(p) = 0$ for all p.

Desirability: $f_i(p)$ is infinite if $p_i = 0$.

Differentiability: f is continuously differentiable.

The price system p is an equilibrium price system if $f(p) = 0$. Because of desirability it is clear that if p is an equilibrium then p is strictly positive. We shall denote by E the set of equilibrium prices. Now if p is in E then so is tp for any positive t (because of Homogeneity), so we take the equilibrium p to be unique if q is in E implies that $q = tp$ for some positive t. Equivalent formulations specify that the equilibrium p is unique if it is the only equilibrium in the unit simplex in R^n, or if it is the only equilibrium with, say, $p_n = 1$. Of course, the question of uniqueness of equilibrium only arises if there is at least one equilibrium: however, under the above four conditions on the excess demand function this existence is assured (Debreu, 1959).

The first point to note is that equilibrium may well not be unique: indeed, there may be infinitely many equilibria. This follows from the fact that the above four conditions are, at the most, the only restrictions which economic theory places on the excess demand function (Debreu, 1970). It is therefore straightforward to construct examples of economies with many equilibria, and even of economies in which all positive prices are equilibrium prices.

In the light of this point we first consider the likelihood of encountering an infinite number of equilibria. Let $F(p)$ be the Jacobian of excess supply, that is of $-f$, at p with the last row and last column deleted. We lose no information in working with F rather than with the full Jacobian: simply because we can set $p_n = 1$ without loss of generality (Homogeneity) and because if $f_i(p) = 0$ for all i other than n then $f_n(p) = 0$ (Walras' Law). The economy is said to be regular if $F(p)$ is of full rank at all p in E. The importance of this is that almost all economies are regular, in that the set of economies which are not regular, or critical economies, is a closed null subset of the set of all economies, as may be shown using Sard's theorem (Debreu, 1970).

With this in mind we may now observe that the number of equilibria in a regular economy is finite. This may be shown, using the Poincaré–Hopf index theorem, by defining the index $i(p) = 1$ if the determinant $\det F(p) > 0$ and $i(p) = -1$ if $\det F(p) < 0$ and noting that the sum of $i(p)$ over all p in E is 1 (Dierker, 1972). This result has two immediate corollaries: the first is that the number of equilibria in a regular economy is odd; the second is that if $\det F(p)$ is positive for all p in E then equilibrium is unique. Taking the above two results together we note that in almost all economies the number of equilibria is finite.

The economic interpretation of $\det F(p)$ being positive in the two-dimensional case is that excess demand is 'downward-sloping' (or excess supply 'upward-sloping'). It is intuitively clear that this ensures uniqueness. In the general case, however, the economic interpretation of this property is not so clear; we therefore examine some more interpretable properties which ensure uniqueness.

An economy with excess demand function f has the revealed preference property if $p \cdot f(q) > 0$ wherever p is in E and q is not in E. It is well known that if g is an individual's excess demand function then $q \cdot g(p) \leqslant 0$ (that is $g(p)$ is available to the individual at price q) implies that $p \cdot g(q) > 0$ (that is $g(q)$ is not available at price p). If all individuals are identical this property will hold in aggregate, where, if p is in E, $q \cdot f(p) = 0$ immediately, so that $p \cdot f(q) > 0$ if q is not in E. Thus if all agents are identical the economy has the revealed preference property. In fact the essential reason why the property holds if all agents are identical is that there is then no trade at equilibrium. It can readily be seen that the property holds if there is no trade at equilibrium for whatever reason. This becomes relevant if we consider today's endowments as being the result of yesterday's trading, with no intervening consumption or production.

Now assume that f has the revealed preference property and let p and q be in E but suppose that r, a proper linear combination of p and q, is not in E. Then $p \cdot f(r) > 0$ and $q \cdot f(r) > 0$ so that $r \cdot f(r) > 0$, which contradicts Walras' Law. This shows that E is convex. Since in almost all economies E is finite, and the only finite convex set is a singleton, it follows that in almost all economies with the revealed preference property equilibrium is unique.

An economy with excess demand function f has the gross substitute property if $p_i > q_i$ and $p_j = q_j$ for each $j \neq i$ imply that $f_j(p) > f_j(q)$ for each $j \neq i$. If this property obtains then Walras' Law implies that excess demand must be 'downward-sloping'. The interpretation of this is that all commodities are substitutes for each other (in the gross sense, that is including income effects as well as substitution effects). In fact, the gross substitutes property implies the revealed preference property; instead of showing this implication we will demonstrate directly that the gross substitutes property ensures uniqueness.

Let p be in E and for any $q \neq p$ define $m = \max_i q_i/p_i = q_k/p_k$ say, and let $r = mp$. Then $r_i \geqq q_i$ for each i with equality for $i = k$ and inequality for some $i \neq k$, so by repeated use of the gross substitutes property we have $f_k(r) > f_k(q)$. But by Homogeneity $f(r) = f(p) = 0$, so that $f_k(q) < 0$ and q is not in E. Thus equilibrium is unique.

If $p_i > q_i$ and $p_j = q_j$ for each $j \neq i$ imply that $f_j(p) \geqq f_j(q)$ for each $j \neq i$ then the economy has the weak gross substitutes property. Arguments analogous to that above show that in this case E is convex, so that in almost all economies equilibrium is unique. Alternatively, if the economy is, in addition, connected in some specific sense, then equilibrium is definitely unique.

Finally, we should note that these properties of revealed preference and gross substitutes do not depend on differentiability. If we accept differentiability there are other properties which ensure uniqueness. One such is diagonal dominance, which is that F has a positive diagonal and that there are some units in which commodities can be measured such that each of their excess demands are more sensitive to a change in their own price than they are to a change in all other non-numeraire prices combined.

It is clear from the above discussion that uniqueness is a strong property. If it does not obtain equilibrium prices will still coordinate individual agents' plans, but they will not, of course, define values uniquely.

One more specific problem which arises under multiple equilibria concerns stability. Assume that we have a process for changing prices such that no change is made in equilibrium and define an equilibrium price p to be stable under this process if prices converge to p whatever their initial values. Then if there are two equilibria, say p and q, neither can be stable: the path starting at p will remain at p so that q is not stable, and conversely. This problem may be avoided by considering only system stability, that is by defining the set E of equilibrium prices to be stable if all paths converge to E. It may also be avoided by considering only local stability, that is by defining p to be stable if prices converge to p given initial values sufficiently close to p. It is clear that even local stability requires equilibria to be separated, and thus finite. As we have seen, this applies in a regular economy; in this case the index theorem then implies that if there are $2k+1$ equilibria (we know the number to be odd) then $k+1$ will typically be locally stable and k unstable.

A further specific problem which arises under multiple equilibria concerns comparative statics. Assume that we want to compare the set of equilibria E of the economy with the set of equilibria E' of some new economy obtained from the original economy by some specified parameter change. If there are multiple equilibria we may be able to say very little: for example if p is in E and both p' and q' are in E' and $p'<p<q'$ all comparative statics results are ambiguous. However, in regular economies, where not only are equilibria separated but also the elements of E and of E' correspond to one another in a natural one-to-one way, this problem may be avoided by considering only local comparative statics, interpreted analogously to local stability.

MICHAEL ALLINGHAM

See also GENERAL EQUILIBRIUM; REGULAR ECONOMIES

BIBLIOGRAPHY

Debreu, G. 1959. *Theory of Value*. New York: Wiley.

Debreu, G. 1970. Economies with a finite set of equilibria. *Econometrica* 38(3), May, 387–92.

Dierker, E. 1972. Two remarks on the number of equilibria of an economy. *Econometrica* 40(5), September, 867–81.

Wald, A. 1936. Über einige Gleichungssysteme der mathematischen Ökonomie. *Zeitschrift für Nationalökonomie* 7; trans. as: On some systems of equations of mathematical economics, *Econometrica* 19, October 1951, 368–403.

Walras, L. 1874–7. *Eléments d'économie politique pure*. Definitive edn, Lausanne: Corbaz, 1926. Translated by W. Jaffé as *Elements of Pure Economics*, London: George Allen & Unwin, 1954.

universalist economics. *See* SPANN, OTHMAR.

Uno, Kozo (1897–1977). A prominent Japanese Marxian economist known especially for his rigorous and systematic reformulation of Marx's *Capital*. Born in Kurashiki in western Japan in a year of intense social unrest, Uno early took an interest in anarcho-syndicalism and Marxism. Not being of an activist temperament, however, he strictly disciplined himself to remain, throughout his life, within the bounds of independent academic work. For this deliberate separation of theory (science) from practice (ideology) he was frequently criticized. After studying in Tokyo and Berlin in the early 1920s, Uno taught at Tohoku University (1924–38), the University of Tokyo (1947–58) and Hosei University (1958–68). During most of the war years he kept away from academic institutions. He authored many controversial books, especially after the war. His 11-volume *Collected Works* were published by Iwanami-Shoten in 1973–4.

The problem with Marx's *Capital*, according to Uno, is that it mixes the theory and history of capitalism in a haphazard fashion (described as 'chemical' by Schumpeter) without cogently establishing their interrelation. Uno's methodological innovation lies in propounding a stages-theory of capitalist development (referring to the stages of mercantilism, liberalism, and imperialism) and using it as a mediation between the two.

Capitalism is a global market-economy in which all socially needed commodities tend to be produced as value (i.e. indifferently to their use-values) by capital. This tendency is never consummated since many use-values in fact fail to conform to this requirement. Only in theory, which synthesizes 'pure' capitalism, can one legitimately envision a complete triumph of value over use-values. The inevitable gap between history, in which use-values appear in their raw forms, and pure theory in which they are already idealized as merely distinct objects for use, must be bridged by stages-theory, which structures itself around use-values of given types (as 'wool', 'cotton', and 'steel' respectively typify the use-values of the three stages).

Uno's emphasis on 'pure' capitalism as the theoretical object has invited many uniformed criticisms. His synthesis of a purely capitalist society as a self-contained logical system follows the genuine tradition of the Hegelian dialectic, and is quite different from axiomatically contrived neoclassical 'pure' theory. Unlike the latter which takes the capitalist market for granted, Uno's theory logically generates it by step-by-step syntheses of the ever-present contradiction between value and use-values. The pure theory of capitalism is thus divided into the three doctrines of circulation, production, and distribution according to the way in which this contradiction is settled. By specifically articulating the abiding dialectic of value and use-values, already present in *Capital*, Uno has given Marxian economic theory its most systematic formulation, a formulation which militates against the two commonest Marxist errors known as voluntarism and economism.

Uno's approach is not dissimilar to Karl Polanyi's in appreciating the tension between the substantive (use-value) and the formal (value) aspect of the capitalist economy. Unlike Polanyi, however, Uno ascribes more than relative importance to capitalism, in the full comprehension of which he sees the key to the clarification of both pre-capitalist and post-capitalist societies. Thus Uno's approach reaffirms and exemplifies the teaching of Hegel (and Marx) that one should 'learn the general through the particular', and not the other way round.

T. SEKINE

BIBLIOGRAPHY

Albritton, R. 1984. The dialectic of capital: a Japanese contribution. *Capital and Class* 22, 157–76.

Albritton, R. 1985. *A Japanese Reconstruction of Marxist Theory*. London: Macmillan,

Itoh, M. 1980. *Value and Crisis, Essays in Marxian Economics in Japan*. New York: Monthly Review Press.

Sekine, T.T. 1975. Uno-Riron: a Japanese contribution to Marxian political economy. *Journal of Economic Literature* 13, 847–77.

Sekine, T.T. 1984. *The Dialectic of Capital, a Study of the Inner Logic of Capitalism*. Tokyo: Toshindo Press.

Uno, K. 1980. *Principles of Political Economy, Theory of a Purely Capitalist Society*. Translated from the Japanese by T.T. Sekine, Brighton: Harvester Press.

unproductive consumption. *See* PRODUCTIVE AND UNPRODUCTIVE CONSUMPTION.

unproductive labour. *See* PRODUCTIVE AND UNPRODUCTIVE LABOUR.

urban economics. Large cities and urban areas exist because it is advantageous to pursue production and consumption activities in a spatially concentrated fashion. Cities are characterized by high population densities, congested intra-city movement, expensive land and the substitution of capital for land. Since persons and firms interact in high density concentrations, the essence of urban economics is the analysis of externalities, neighbourhood effects and related forms of market failure. Traffic congestion, agglomeration economies, pollution, racial segregation, and the provision of public goods all involve externalities and jointness in consumption or production.

Urban economics addresses two central positive issues. First, it explains the internal form, or the density gradient, of a city vis-à-vis a centralized place of employment, the central business district (CBD); and second, it analyses the determinants of relative city size.

The density gradient is a measure of the rate at which population or employment density declines in space as a function of commuting distance from the CBD. The declines in these densities are non-linear, approximately exponential; absolute densities, and land rents, decline very rapidly as distance from the CBD increases. Historically, urban density gradients have become flatter, cities have become much less dense, more decentralized, more suburbanized. This rapid development of suburban areas has eroded the fiscal bases of central cities, and in the United States, large portions of older central cities have become racially segregated low-income ghettoes. A basic concern of social policy is with the effects of this spatial concentration on the poor themselves, and on the general community.

The analysis of urban hierarchies, or the system of cities, abstracts from the internal structure of cities and studies the determinants of the size of different cities. Recent studies have emphasized the relationship between city size and productivity. Economies of scale in production are either localization economies, which are external to the firm but internal to the industry, or urbanization or agglomeration economies, which depend on the size of the metropolitan area. These economies of scale interact with various diseconomies to produce varying levels of utility, or real income, at different levels of population. An important policy issue is whether decentralized migration and firms' location decisions result in an efficient system of cities. Some countries, such as the United Kingdom and France, have evidently decided that they do not. In response to externalities such as pollution and congestion, they have restricted the growth of their largest cities and have built new towns as part of their policies to decentralize urban development.

Urban economics analyses the spatial distribution of the population and the policies designed to change the distribution of the population within cities, between cities, and between urban and rural areas. The basic objective of this branch of economics is to study market failures, and to help design public policies to improve upon the shortcomings of non-coordinated allocative decisions in urban areas.

HISTORICAL REVIEW. As structures are durable and can be maintained indefinitely, the structure of a city at a particular point in time will strongly reflect its historical development. Variations in average residential densities across American cities are highly correlated with the size of the city and average age of the housing stock. Although the typical densities of new suburban development in older metropolitan areas (Boston) and new metropolitan areas (Houston) may be similar, the overall structure of these two cities is quite different because of cumulative urban development. A historical perspective is therefore very important for understanding variations in urban structure within metropolitan areas and across cities.

In the 19th century intra-city movements of persons and goods were very expensive, and cities were relatively small and very compact. Virtually all employment was located within one to three miles of the central business districts with workers' residences often located close to their places of employment. Within cities, freight was transported by horse and wagon, and communication between firms was either through messages or face-to-face meetings. The horse-drawn carriage and rail-guided horse and wagon were expensive means of transportation relative to earnings and were used primarily by higher income groups.

In the late 19th century the development of electric traction permitted the running of clean subways and trolley cars. This technological change led to an increase in city size and the decentralization of urban areas. A more dramatic, far-reaching transportation innovation was the development of the automobile and the truck. The effects of this innovation continue to the present day as automobile ownership becomes more ubiquitous throughout the world. In the United States over 90 per cent of adults drive cars and the vast majority of households, including the poorest quintile group, own automobiles.

The truck was first used in intra-city movements of freight and then increasingly for inter-city transportation, after the more recent development of interstate highways and outer-circumferential routes. Improvements in the long-distance truck and intra-city automobile transportation permitted firms to draw workers from a wider area, and to locate in less expensive, less dense suburban locations in more efficient one-storey continuous process operations. Industries and residences have decentralized in cities throughout the world.

EXPLANATIONS OF INTRA-METROPOLITAN DECENTRALIZATION. In the United States, and in some other industrial countries, the decentralization of activity within urban areas has been accompanied by an increased concentration of low income groups in central cities. In 1983 the median income of families resident in American central cities was 70 per cent of the median income of suburban communities. A large portion of the growing income disparity between the central city and suburbs is explained by the increased concentration of poor black families in central cities. The median income of suburban black households is 45 per cent higher than that of black families residing in central cities.

Two somewhat conflicting explanations have been offered for suburbanization of metropolitan areas. One, based on the monocentric model of urban areas, stresses technological change, decreasing transportation costs, the increased use of the automobile, rising real incomes, and population growth. The alternative explanation stresses lower suburban tax rates and a variety of central city social factors: high crime rates, congestion, smog, poor schools and neighbourhood blight. According to this explanation middle income families move to the suburbs to escape these problems.

To formulate appropriate public policies it is important to identify the relative contributions of different factors causing intra-metropolitan decentralization. If suburbanization is largely explained by technological changes that permitted the transformation of a compact, highly dense city to a more sprawling city form, and if the success of the suburbs is explained by the revealed preference of more affluent households for new housing and land-intensive residential patterns, the case of public intervention in rebuilding the central cities is weak. Intervention and fiscal aid to central cities need to be justified primarily on distributive grounds, to improve the level of public services and the general quality of life for poorer residents of the central city.

If, on the other hand, fiscal distortions, crime and the quality of education are important causes of decentralization, the case is much stronger for a broad set of policies to stem the potentially unstable cumulative decline of central cities. Fiscal distortions decrease the overall level of national income by dissipating production and consumption economies. The case for public intervention will rest on considerations of allocative efficiency, as well as redistributive objectives.

The monocentric model of urban areas assumes that employment is concentrated at the CBD and that households make residential location decisions by trading off commuting costs and higher housing costs close to the CBD. If households are identical in terms of income and preferences, an equilibrium set of housing prices must yield the same level of real income at all residential locations. Housing services are produced with inputs of land and capital and it is possible to substitute capital for land by building multi-storey residential structures. The substitution of capital for land explains the rapid decline of both density and land values close to the CBS, and the less rapid declines at more distant locations.

A key concept in this analysis of urban form is the bid rent function, or the rent offer curve. Firms and households bid for land at different locations. The equilibrium structure of land rents requires that firms have no incentive to move; they earn zero profits at all locations or in the case of households achieve an equal level of utility (real income). Although there is no well-developed theory on intra-urban employment location, some firms, even if they ship all of their output for sale at the CBD, will have an incentive to move to the suburbs to take advantage of lower land prices and lower wages. As employment decentralizes, a negative wage gradient will evolve as suburban residents will accept lower wages in suburban employment to offset commuting costs to the CBD.

It is important to note that the monocentric model as developed by Mills (1972) and Muth (1969) is an equilibrium model. The capital (housing) stock is assumed to be malleable so that in effect the city is 'rebuilt' in each period. Under certain simplifying assumptions, the monocentric model yields a negative exponential density function of the form

$$D(u) = D_0 e^{-\gamma u}$$

where $D(u)$ is the residential density, u miles from the CBD, and D_0 is the density next to the CBD. The model predicts that as the population of the metropolitan area increases D_0 will increase, but there is no prediction on the relationship between city size and the density gradient γ. However, it can be argued that larger cities will be more decentralized, and γ will be smaller in absolute size as large metropolitan areas will support more subcentres for shopping and employment.

The effects of rising real income on urban structure are ambiguous. Rising real incomes will increase the demand for housing and land and will lead to suburbanization. However, as rising real incomes increase the time costs of commuting, it is uncertain whether increases in real income, other things equal, will result in a more decentralized urban structure. The empirical evidence indicates that the income elasticity of the demand for housing is only slightly larger than the income elasticity of commuting costs. Also there is no empirical evidence that the rent offer curves get flatter as the incomes of households increase. Consequently the location of high income groups in suburbs *cannot* be explained by a high income elasticity of demand for housing relative to increases in commuting expenses. In fact, there is some evidence that, other things equal, high income groups will outbid lower income groups for high quality suburban sites with better access to central city employment.

The long-run equilibrium portrayed in static models of urban spatial structure may, in fact, never be achieved. Anas (1978) and Harrison and Kain (1974) have developed models based on the assumption that residential capital is very durable and non-malleable. According to this model, the city does not develop by being 'rebuilt' in every period; rather, urban form depends on a set of incremental investment decisions. City development takes place in rings moving outwards from the city centre. Each ring represents a historical period of growth. The development process is assumed to be myopic, so housing of a particular vintage incorporates the income and transportation conditions that prevail at the time of construction.

One implication of this formulation is that urban development is a cumulative process and that two cities of the same size and income levels may have very different density structures depending on their historical pattern of development. The cities that had substantial population in 1900 will be of a different form than the new cities developed after the widespread introduction of the automobile.

The most striking implication of the assumption of durable, non-convertible capital is that rising incomes or declining transportation costs will lead to the obsolescence of central city housing and to abandonment. As development proceeds outwards from the city centre, the oldest housing will be small, reflecting lower real income in the past. With increases in real income, rental income on the older housing will fall, and if income growth is large enough the oldest housing will ultimately become economically obsolete.

However, as Wheaton (1982) noted, this conclusion forgets that older sites can be redeveloped. Wheaton showed that reconstruction will occur at the most central locations and that the densities of the redeveloped sites will be greater than that of replaced use. According to this formulation, the central city is developed first, and for a long period new construction occurs at the fringe, but as the city continues to grow, central redevelopment will displace at least some new construction in the suburbs. Even in the absence of different income groups then, the urban development process will go through stages in which a central city first declines and is then reconstructed.

Wheaton has also shown, in a perfect foresight model, that for a growing city it will be efficient to withhold some land from premature development. For example, some land close to the CBD that will be especially valuable in the future as high density business development will not be developed currently as lower density residential property. This result illustrates the social value of land speculation, and partially counters criticism of urban sprawl. Land markets do not work perfectly, but city planning designed to curb urban sprawl and proposals to impose differentially high taxes on vacant land may be myopic and inefficient. Similarly, abandonment of certain housing units, or even whole neighbourhoods, is not necessarily evidence of market failure even when redevelopment occurs after a long lag. The current value of the cleared land may simply be less than demolition and clearing costs.

A vintage model of a durable housing stock assuming myopic foresight has been developed by Cooke and Hamilton (1984) to explain the tendency for high income groups to reside in suburban areas. These authors assume a demand function for housing based on income and price and a particular distribution of income. According to this model, in the decade beginning in 1900 a housing stock was built to house the population, and the characteristics of the houses built during that decade reflected income and price conditions at that time. A variety of housing types accommodated persons of different incomes. In the next decade, 1910, a new distribution of income determined an updated housing demand distribution. This new demand distribution that set the rents on the first period's stock of housing. Units in excess supply filtered down the income distribution to low income groups.

New units were built on the periphery of the city as income grew over time, leaving smaller houses in high density neighbourhoods in the central city. These older, less desirable units tended over time to be occupied by low-income groups, while more affluent households lived in larger, newer housing in the suburbs. This version of the filtering model of housing predicts a growing income disparity between the central city and the suburbs solely in terms of the age and characteristics of the housing stocks. According to this analysis, the fiscal and social problems of central cities caused by high concentrations of low-income population in these areas may be largely a reflection of the way housing markets operate.

Some writers have stressed changes in transportation modes as the basis of central city revival or redevelopment. Historically, when everyone walked to work the centre of the city was an area of high prestige. However, upon the successive development of the omnibus, the commuter tram, the streetcar, and finally the automobile, all expensive modes of transportation relative to earnings at their time of introduction, the suburbs became the prestigious areas. Only recently, when the cost of car ownership relative to income has fallen and the ownership of cars for households in the lowest income quintile in the United States has increased to over 60 per cent, are lower income groups able to commute to suburban properties. The more equal access to the most effective means of transportation suggests that more affluent households will move back to the central city and low and moderate income groups will move increasingly to the suburbs.

Most empirical investigations of the factors behind decentralization have utilized cross-section data for American cities. Muth (1969) estimated density gradients for 46 American cities in 1950 and found car registrations, the intra-metropolitan distribution of employment and the proportion of the central city population which was black to be the most consistent variables in explaining variation in density gradients across cities. Muth also concluded that the physical characteristics of the central city, such as the age and condition of the housing stock, do not have a significant effect on decentralization. A careful study by Mills and Price (1984) explaining a cross section of density gradients for 1970 also concluded that a set of measures of central city social problems – race, crime, and taxes – adds almost nothing to the explanation of suburbanization.

Several other studies, using other measures of decentralizations and different time periods, concluded that the net fiscal surplus received by middle-class families in central-city versus suburban locations does affect their residential location. Also, there is evidence for the 1970s that school desegregation led to a sharp drop in white enrolments in central city schools. A significant majority of affluent households that continue to reside in the central city do not have school-aged children. Evidence of racial prejudice also appears from empirical work on white–black housing cost differentials. Studies based on 1970s data show lower housing prices and rents in black neighbourhoods. These differentials, approaching 20 per cent, confirm models of prejudice that predict whites are willing to pay a premium to maintain a distance from racial integration.

The most persuasive evidence that recent government transportation and housing policies, racial tensions and other central city problems are *not* the primary explanations of suburbanization is historical evidence on declining density gradients throughout the world. Mills and Tan (1980) have assembled evidence on the flattening of density functions, a measure of decentralization for a large number of developed countries. Some of the evidence goes back into the early 19th century. The evidence for European and American cities shows that decentralization is *not* a post-World War II phenomenon and there is relatively little variability from one decade to the next at the rate at which decentralization has occurred.

The demonstration that density gradients have been decreasing throughout the world for a hundred years is an important achievement. This result shows that suburbanization has occurred in countries without the social problems characteristic of American cities. Decentralization must be rooted in technological changes, the interaction between employment and residential decentralization and the growth of real income. Cities have simply changed form, and there is little reason for public policy to try to change the less dense, more decentralized urban structure.

Yet our understanding of urban decentralization, past and future, remains imperfect. First, relative transportation costs have not been directly introduced into the econometric investigations of density gradients. Second, there are difficulties with dismissing the role of social and racial factors in explaining suburbanization. A summary statistic, the density gradient, may be too aggregative a measure to capture the effects of fiscal and related neighbourhood effects. Moreover, the idea that rich households have a high income elasticity of demand for the newest, most desirable housing that is located in the suburbs is a very short step away from the idea that the same households have the same high income elasticity of demand for the best schools and the safest, low density neighbourhoods, which are also located in the suburbs. Nevertheless, existing empirical research provides very partial support for the importance of social factors as determinants of intra-metropolitan decentralization.

THE SIZE DISTRIBUTION OF URBAN AREAS AND OPTIMAL CITY SIZE. The distribution of city sizes is skewed to the right as there are many small cities and few very large ones. Early explanations of the size distribution of cities emphasized specialization of economic function and the role of cities as central market places. The foundation of this theory is the number of rural residents that can be served by cities of the smallest size. The rural residents buy a variety of goods and retail and personal services produced by these cities. One step higher in the city hierarchy are towns that provide more specialized functions to their own populations, and to urban areas of the next smallest size. City size increases as cities become more specialized, and the more specialized the functions, the smaller the number of cities. Beckmann (1958) has shown that the simple model, grounded in the idea that urban areas are service areas for the farm population, can be used to generate the rank-size rule where the second largest urban area has half the population of the largest city and the third largest has one-third the population of the largest and so on.

In contrast to traditional considerations of specialization and exchange, recent work on city size has emphasized amenity characteristics, such as climate, and the interaction between economies and diseconomies of scale. This analysis seeks to explain the level of per capita real income, or utility, as a function of a city's total population. In the simplest versions of these models there are two production activities and two consumption goods, a manufactured good and housing services. The production of the export good is subject to increasing returns to scale while the production of housing services, which requires land space and involves commuting, is subject to decreasing returns. At low population levels it is postulated that the economies of scale outweigh the diseconomies and that real income increases with increases in population. As the city grows it becomes more spread out, more congested, and at larger population levels diseconomies of scale outweigh at the margin additional economies, and utility per capita reaches a maximum and declines with further increases in population. The relationship between individual utility and population size is bell-shaped.

The economies of scale can be consumption economies as well as production economies. One example of a consumption economy is a non-rival public good whose price or cost per person is inversely proportional to the size of the population. Also the variety and quality of various private consumption goods increases with population size. Increases in city size are associated with a variety of subtle advantages as well as a number of more obvious disadvantages.

Interaction between economies and diseconomies of scale and the implied differences in relative prices and differences in consumption bundles across cities explain differences in money wages across cities, and the co-existence of the same industries in cities of varying size. The higher money wages paid to workers in larger cities are made possible by higher labour productivity in these cities. Different industries will be subject to varying economies of scale, and city size will vary according to the industries in which they are specialized. The existence of consumption economies also decreases the likelihood that maximum per capita utility is determined at a unique population level.

As a particular city grows, congestion and related diseconomies may outweigh production economies and per capita at medium population levels and utility will decrease. However if growth continues the larger population generates a number of consumption economies (lower per-capita costs for public services, more varied recreation), per-capita utility will again rise with population. Similarly, the growth and development of a particular city may occur very rapidly over a short period of time as increases in population improve the quality of life in the city. This improvement leads to further in migration of population, and growth continues until it is slowed by diseconomies of scale.

For some policy purposes it is important to determine whether production economies are economies of localization, which are internal to each industry in a particular city, or are economies of urbanization, or agglomeration economies, which are external to individual industries. These reflect the advantages of operation in cities with larger labour forces, diverse suppliers and customers. Empirical research indicates that external economies of scale are primarily those of localization, not urbanization, and they peter out as city size increases. Thus finding suggests that cities should be specialized and that smaller cities will be specialized, and it enhances the case for coordinating firm location decisions. For example, if a city becomes too large it will be difficult to develop secondary production centres as dispersal will require coordination by industry.

Localization economies also explain why industrial activity in less developed countries is typically concentrated in a primary city. In these countries business, financial services and quality public services are initially very scarce. As industrialization begins it is quite natural for new manufacturing firms to establish themselves in the largest city, and the advantages of newly developed localization economies acts as a magnet for new firms. Coordination at the early stages of industrialization might be needed to avoid the disadvantages of future industrial concentration.

The United Kingdom and France have actively pursued policies to disperse employment and population away from their principal economic regions, London and Paris. These policies were designed to counteract the concentration of manufacturing investments in the capital regions. Although economic activity continues to shift to southeast England, the population of greater London has declined, and manufacturing in England and France has been dispersed. The benefits of population dispersal have not been quantified, but these policies are relatively non-controversial and remain in effect.

In contrast, the United States has not attempted to limit the size of its largest cities, and there is little support for a national policy on population distribution. This is explained by the greater degree of political decentralization in the United States and by the very rapid decrease in primacy. Between 1940 and 1980 the population of the New York metropolitan area as a percentage of total US population fell from 18.6 per cent to 10.2 per cent. A number of the largest metropolitan areas grew very slowly or declined during the 1970s. Much of the growth of the US population occurred in the South and Southwest, regions with smaller cities and less urbanization. Market forces appear to be controlling the growth of the largest cities and promoting a more diversified national urban structure.

Regional income differentials have narrowed in the United States and, after adjusting for cost-of-living differences, differences in real incomes across broad regions have virtually disappeared. Migration into the high-income West coast region has decreased incomes there while migration of unskilled farm population from the South to the industrial North and of capital and skilled white collar labour into the South have eliminated North–South income differentials.

These equalizing trends may be unique to the United States. Some anti-neoclassical writers have described European regional development as highly unstable and leading to an extremely skewed urban structure because of a highly unstable process of cumulative causation. Whatever the case may be for European development, this process clearly does not apply to the US. In fact, post-war regional trends and urban development in the US are basically consistent with neoclassical considerations of comparative or differential costs, along with internal migration towards warmer, more rapidly growing areas.

A fundamental reason for questioning the advisability of restricting the size of the largest cities is Tolley's (1974) result that large cities may be too small relative to their optimal size when their internal organization is inefficient because of the existence of pollution and congestion externalities.

Tolley argues that pollution and congestion decrease amenity values in a city, decrease the supply of residents and increase nominal wages. In the absence of taxes on pollution and congestion the real income or utility of a city is below its optimal level for any given population level. This result implies that the primary policies of dealing with inefficiencies in large cities should attack the problems at their source, and regulate or price externalities. Pollution and congestion are related to population size, but the technological links may be quite weak and indirect. The efficient, direct solution to the externality problems is to modify polluting production processes and to change commuting patterns, and/or the structure of the transportation network.

This argument, with its conclusion that inefficiently organized cities may be too small, does not rule out the need for a coordinating national population policy to achieve a first best outcome. In general, decentralized policies initiated by local governments to deal with pollution and congestion, though necessary for efficiency, are not sufficient to achieve full efficiency in the distribution of a nation's population.

The general condition for the efficient allocation of population between cities or regions, *given that the internal organization of each city is efficient*, is the difference between social marginal product and the social marginal cost of maintaining a person at a given level of utility equalized across cities. To illustrate, for large cities L, and small cities S,

$$SMP_L - SMC_L = SMP_S - SMC_S.$$

If large cities are overpopulated relative to small cities then

$$SMP_L - SMC_L < SMP_S - SMC_S.$$

One model with non-rival public goods illustrates that free migration between cities will not be inefficient when utility is equalized across cities and each city is efficiently organized. There are two cities each with a finite amount of land space. One city has more land, supports a larger population, and has a lower tax price per capita for public goods. Some writers conjecture that the advantage would result in an excessively large population in the larger city. It has been shown that a non-coordinated or decentralized equilibrium will be inefficient unless per capita taxes are equalized across cities, and this will occur only in very special circumstances. Also empirical evidence supports the expectation that the large city will be overpopulated relative to the social optimum.

A very similar result obtains when Pigovian taxes are imposed by local governments to control pollution. The outcome is suboptimal relative to a first best national policy which adopts different tax rates in cities of varying size but which requires equal transfers per capita. When capital and labour are the production inputs and pollution is harmful to labour but not to capital, the optimal solution requires the conservation of labour and a high wage rate. A decentralized equilibrium undermines the optimal solution when larger per capita taxes are collected in the larger, more heavily polluted communities, and are transferred to local labour. The condition of equal per capita transfers requires a nationally administered pollution policy.

Variability in the quality of urban sites also results in coordination problems in a developing country undergoing urbanization. The first cities will be developed on superior sites, often on the coast. Interior sites will not be developed until the coastal cities are large, polluted and congested. Interior development will begin when real income in the two regions is equal. Because of economies of scale, real incomes in the interior cities and in coastal cities will increase as the population migrates from the congested coast to the emerging interior cities.

The improvement in welfare throughout the nation establishes that the development of interior sites occurred too late, i.e., the urban population of the nation became large enough and real income low enough so pioneers began tricking into the interior. One policy superior to laissez-faire development to coordinate migration into the interior to guaranteeing residents a certain level of real income. This policy, if timed correctly, will not require fiscal transfers between cities. The first best policy will require a still earlier development of the interior and will require fiscal transfer between cities (regions).

The need for coordination in the development of cities arises from economies of scale and variations in the quality of urban sites, which result in a lumpiness problem. J.V. Henderson (1985) has argued that if there exist a large number of cities and cities can be replicated, the lumpiness problem becomes less significant. In the extreme case where the number of cities becomes very large and individual cities approximate their efficient size, a constant returns-to-scale world is approached. This result suggests that the importance of intervention in the shaping of the system of cities will vary from country to country. The spontaneous development of new, efficient cities in a relatively short period is much more likely in a large country with a varied urban structure than in countries with small populations, such as Australia, Argentina and Canada, or in countries with large populations but with an underdeveloped urban system consisting of a small number of large cities.

CONGESTION AND OTHER FORMS OF MARKET FAILURE IN URBAN AREAS. The principal urban externality is congestion, which is related to peak-hour work-trips made to the CBD. Commuters take account of the average level of congestion in deciding whether and when to travel, but do not account for the additional congestion costs they impose on other commuters. The divergence between marginal and average congestion cost is large, and calls for congestion tolls that would vary according to time of day. The tolls would finance highway construction, and it can be shown that when the long-run marginal cost of highway capacity is constant, the optimum congestion toll will just finance a road system that has been carried out to the optimum level.

There are administrative problems in setting tolls and, more significantly, there is no political support for them. Consequently, there is too much commuting to the CBD by automobile, the rent gradient is flatter than it would be with congestion tolls and residential location is more decentralized. The absence of congestion tolls distorts land values, and market prices of land close to the CBD are below their social value. The use of distorted land values by highway planners to determine highway capacity will lead to an excessive allocation of land to roads. Without congestion tolls, attempts to alleviate congestion in certain bottleneck situations by increasing capacity will have little social value as additional traffic simply fills the increased capacity of the bottleneck. Also because of the increased reliance on the automobile, congestion, especially in the largest cities such as New York, has gotten worse over time.

These conclusions notwithstanding, the principal solution to urban congestion is the expansion of the highway system. In the United States 90 per cent of work trips and 95 per cent of all trips in urban areas are made by private automobile. Due to the decentralization of employment within metropolitan areas, only 15 per cent of work trips are towards the CBD. Public transit is relatively inconvenient for reverse-direction and circumferential commutes.

During the 1970s the US Congress established new grant programmes to subsidize operating expenses of local transit systems and provide 80 per cent of the construction costs of new subway systems. Passenger contributions fell to 38 per cent of operating expenses, and new rail systems were built in Washington, San Francisco and several southern cities with relatively low population densities. While the real value of transit taxes decreased, the subsidy programmes failed to increase transit travel significantly on existing systems. The ridership on new rail systems was overprojected by a factor of two, these expensive systems ran large operating losses and the cost per auto trip avoided was very high.

As expressways near the centre of CBDs are very expensive, peak-hour users are also heavily subsidized, although as a group urban highway users provide more in highway tax revenues than is spent on highway expenditures. Further subsidies to local transit to offset the subsidy to peak-hour highway users will increase travel in general, thus misallocating resources. A more appropriate step might be to decrease federal subsidies to all forms of local transportation.

Even in the absence of congestion tolls, evidence has accumulated that highways are underbuilt in metropolitan areas. Some urban travel-demand models have found very high values of travel time and very high willingness to pay for the benefits of the private automobile. Benefit–cost analyses have concluded that additional lanes of highway could pay for themselves in one year alone. And a study on the benefits of giving buses preferential treatment in an *expanded* system of urban roads concluded that an expanded all-auto system would also yield substantial benefits.

In very large cities such as New York a significant expansion of the highway system is not feasible because of high construction costs and social disruption. For very dense cities, congestion tolls seem to be essential instruments of policy as congestion is most pronounced and extension of highway capacity most difficult. Given the diversity of city type and differences in density across cities, there is a strong case for decentralized urban transportation policies and solutions tailored to the needs of specific cities. Congestion tolls represent an important financial instrument in effecting decentralization.

Unpriced accessibility poses problems similar to unpriced congestion. Koopmans and Beckmann (1957), in a classic paper, argued that if there are *n* indivisible plants to be assigned to *n* sites, and if plants sell intermediate products to one another, no price system will sustain any assignment of plants to sites. Subsequent research reveals that this theorem is incorrect and there are cases where land markets will clear. The explanation of the problem is that firms differ in their preferences for sites first *qua* sites, and second because of transportation costs resulting from interplant trade. The market breaks down because it fails to price accessibility to other plants, *and* the locational preferences of firms for sites *qua* sites is not strong enough to establish locational stability by overcoming these externalities.

Firms and households also may not account for negative externalities in making locational decisions; the glue factory may choose to locate in a high-quality residential neighbourhood. Empirical studies on the effects of non-conforming land uses on residential property value have generally found that they are very small or affect only a small number of adjacent properties, a finding which undermines the traditional basis for land use regulations (zoning). Evidence has also accumulated that, rather than improving the efficiency of land markets, regulations have distorted development and are used to exclude low-income groups from many suburban communities. By restricting the amount of land for apartments, they increase the cost of moderate income housing.

Reliance on the residential property tax for local finance results in exclusionary zoning, but the incentives to exclude and to limit new development go well beyond fiscal considerations. For instance, the residents of a partially developing community have a high incentive to restrict development since they rarely own the undeveloped land in the community and have no interest in the value of this land. Furthermore, they may also have a preference for low density development, open space and ecological protection. Finally, they do not have to compensate the owners of the undeveloped land and by restricting development they increase the value of their properties. One empirical study has concluded that in a metropolitan area with highly concentrated zoning authorities, development controls have increased housing prices by 50 per cent.

Another example of public intervention in the United States was the urban renewal programmes introduced in the 1950s and 1960s. The local agencies, heavily subsidized by the federal government, bought buildings in blighted neighbourhoods, cleared the land and auctioned the land to private developers. The market value of cleared land was well below the original cost plus demolition.

The justification for public intervention in redevelopment is the existence of neighbourhood effects and interdependencies between property owners. Efficient redevelopment is more likely to be undertaken if coordinated. Fragmented ownership of properties complicated the assembly of a number of neighbourhood properties because of the possibility of price gauging by a small number of holdouts.

The criticism of past urban renewal programmes is that they were operated without any relevant criteria for expenditures as they were heavily subsidized. Yet local authorities should use eminent domain to assemble properties when benefits of coordinated redevelopment exceed costs.

POVERTY AND RACE. A significant social problem in many industrial countries is unemployment and poverty among the youth who are concentrated in the central cities. In the United States the poor are disproportionately black, and residential patterns in American cities are highly segregated by race. Only a small portion of the observed patterns of segregation can be explained by income and family structure. Social concern over urban decentralization is closely related to the fiscal problems of central cities and to racial equality. Suburbanization in housing and employment diminishes the employment, housing and educational prospects for minorities who are concentrated in central cities.

The income gap between individual black workers and whites has narrowed significantly, but many black families have not shared in these gains because an increasing number of black families are headed by women. The incidence of poverty in many central city neighbourhoods has increased over time and there is evidence of the bifurcation of black America as more successful blacks move out of ghetto areas. There is little understanding of the causes of the increased instability of black families, though the compensatory welfare programme has had little effect on changes in black family structure.

Existing patterns of racial segregation are explained by the prejudice of whites. There are many empirical studies on the effects of prejudice and discrimination on black/white housing price differentials. The studies with data for the 1960s, when substantial number of blacks migrated to northern areas, showed that blacks paid 10–15 per cent more for housing of the same quality. During the 1970s black urbanization slowed and the weight of the empirical evidence shifted as 1970s data showed that housing prices in black neighbourhoods were 20 per cent lower than comparable housing in white areas. This research supports the view that whites are prejudiced and will not rent or buy in largely black residential areas. Thus, even if open housing laws were rigorously enforced, residential segregation would remain as blacks would find it cheaper to live in black areas.

One argument for opening up the suburbs to blacks at all income levels is the importance of neighbourhood effects on the quality of life and on individual behaviour. A small minority of individuals victimize all of the residents of lower income black areas. A specific benefit of greater racial and class integration resulting from suburbanization might be higher educational attainment by low achievers. The results of empirical studies on the importance of peer-group effects on educational achievement are mixed. One study found that students of all levels of achievement gain by being in classes with higher levels of average achievement. Other studies found peer-group effects to be small, or insignificant.

As employment has decentralized to the suburbs, residential segregation may diminish the employment and income prospects of minorities. Some empirical evidence for the 1960s was developed which linked the employment rate of blacks in an area to residential location and to distance of the location from major black ghettoes. The results were used to argue that the dispersal of black settlement would increase the employment of blacks.

More recently, there are reports of severe labour shortages of unskilled workers in affluent suburban areas at a time when the unemployment rate of black youth has increased absolutely, and relative to the unemployment of white youth. This seems to confirm the importance of the link between housing segregation and deteriorating employment prospects for non-whites. But systematic research on this topic, though limited in quantity, has not established the importance of residential location as a determinant of earnings. One study, after controlling for education, occupation, experience and other factors, found the income difference of black residents in the suburbs and in the central city to be no larger than five per cent. This is a small effect relative to the estimate of the racial discrimination effect of 15 per cent and relative to the 20 per cent difference in black–white earnings that is attributed to differences in education and related human capital endowments.

A special survey of the employment problems of inner-city youth confirms the weak evidence for the spatial mismatch hypothesis. In Chicago, where some residential areas are close to clusters of factories and jobs and other residential areas are not, it was found that proximity to jobs does not help non-white youth. Even when the jobs were nearby, white youths got them.

The general subsidization of public transit is a cost-ineffective method of increasing the mobility of the poor as this group accounts for only 25 per cent of transit trips and low-income ridership is concentrated on short trips in the central city. Also the diversity of origins and destinations of the poor who commute to the suburbs makes *existing* public transit an ineffective transportation system for their needs. However, if transportation access is the primary cause of the employment problems of central-city minority residents, the solution would be straight-forward and relatively inexpensive. Special programmes could be introduced where public transit could be restructured by providing more individualistic door-to-door service with smaller vehicles. Furthermore, if labour shortages in the suburbs exist and there is unemployment in the central city, firms should have the incentive to transport workers to suburban job sites.

CONCLUDING REMARKS. Urban economics has developed rapidly, and a large theoretical and empirical literature now exists. The work on urban structure is perhaps most advanced as this knowledge is based on both theory and quantitative research. There have been substantial advances in research sub-areas such as transportation, housing markets, and urban public finance. The work on optimal city size and system of cities has advanced theoretically, but considerably more empirical research is needed on the contributions of various economies and diseconomies of scale to economic welfare.

Despite the vast literature on the subject, little is known about the most effective solutions to urban poverty and related social pathologies such as crime and the unstable structure of low-income families. One important conclusion, though based on a very small number of empirical studies, is that the spatial isolation of the poor is not a primary determinant of their employment and income.

Perhaps the most significant contribution of urban economics is that it has demonstrated, despite outward evidence of sprawl, blight and racial segregation, that decentralized market forces do a reasonably good job in allocating resources. Sound rationalizations can be provided for sprawl and land speculation, and for abandonment of housing in the growing, changing cities. Governmental intervention in the allocative process should be used sparingly, given the history of past mistakes and the inefficiencies of existing land-use regulations. The theoretical basis for various forms of public intervention exists but poverty is the primary cause of the most acute urban problems, not the lack of governmental planning of urban structure.

PETER MIESZKOWSKI

See also CONGESTION; LOCAL PUBLIC FINANCE; MONOCENTRIC MODELS IN URBAN ECONOMICS; REGIONAL ECONOMICS; TIEBOUT HYPOTHESIS.

BIBLIOGRAPHY

Anas, A. 1978. Dynamics of urban residential growth. *Journal of Economics* 5(1), January, 66–87.

Beckmann, M.J. 1958. City hierarchies and the distribution of city size. *Economic Development and Cultural Change* 6, April, 243–8.

Cooke, T.W. and Hamilton, B.W. 1984. Evolution of urban housing stocks: a model applied to Baltimore and Houston. *Journal of Urban Economics* 16(3), November, 317–38.

Harrison, D. and Kain, J.F. 1974. Cumulative urban growth and urban density functions. *Journal of Urban Economics* 4(1), *January*, 113–17.

Henderson, J.V. 1985. *Economic Theory and Cities*. 2nd edn, New York: Academic Press.

Koopmans, T.C. and Beckmann, M. 1957. Assignment problems and the location of economic activities. *Econometrica* 25, January, 53–76.

Mills, E.S. 1972. *Studies in the Structure of the Urban Economy*. Baltimore: Johns Hopkins Press.

Mills, E.S. and Tan, J.D. 1980. A comparison of urban population density functions in developed and developing countries. *Urban Studies* 17(3), October, 313–21.

Mills, E.S. and Price, R. 1984. Metropolitan suburbanization and central city problems. *Journal of Urban Economics* 15(1), January, 1–17.

Muth, R.F. 1969. *Cities and Housing*. Chicago: University of Chicago Press.

Tolley, G.S. 1974. The welfare economics of city bigness. *Journal of Urban Economics* 1(3), July, 324–45.

Wheaton, W.C. 1982. Urban spatial development with durable but replaceable capital. *Journal of Urban Economics* 12(1), July, 53–67.

urban housing. The specifics of history and geography indicate a vast array of urban housing types and patterns within equally divergent sets of urban circumstance. The problem is to bring all this particularity and variety into a frame of reference that will help us understand the social, economic, cultural and political significance of urban housing.

Housing means more than just shelter from the elements. It defines a space of social reproduction that necessarily reflects gender, familial, and other types of social relations. It can also function as a place of manufacture and commerce, of leisure, education and religious observance, of ordered social intercourse. Whether or how it performs such functions depends on the nature of the social order – its dominant mode of production, consumption and reproduction, its hegemonic class, gender and ethnic relations, its cultural requirements and form of urbanization.

The separation of working and living in the capitalist city, for example, arises out of a mode of production founded on wage labour. In the medieval city working and living were often kept under the same roof. In many pre-capitalist muslim cities, on the other hand, concern over privacy and the seclusion of women pushed the activities of artisans and traders out of the house and into the streets and markets. Thus did gender relations in one place forge a pattern of uses made necessary by class relations in another.

The ability of the house to accommodate diverse functions has also varied considerably. Apart from technological and organizational limitations on housing construction and design (interior plumbing being perhaps the most important), competition for urban space and housing costs sometimes make it impossible to meet basic needs within the house. Working class immigrants to 19th-century Paris, for example, found such limited accommodation that most were forced to eat on the streets or in the cafés and cabarets. Recent muslim immigrants into Ibadan likewise find it hard to procure housing suited to the perpetuation of kinship relations. In both cases, problems of urban housing provision forced sometimes disruptive social adaptations. Eating out in the modern American city has, however, a quite different social signification (particularly for the upper classes), reflecting in part the attractions of urban alternatives and the limitations of time (rather than space) in a society where the role of women has undergone a significant transformation.

Considerations of law, social structure and culture therefore intersect with those of economy and technology to dictate the status of housing provision and use. Courtyards and compounds – the former being the oldest of all known urban housing types – suit a kinship system and can be easily adapted, as they have in the muslim world, to societies where polygamy and the seclusion of women are important. Within compounds, housing units are built or allowed to collapse as households form or dissolve within the kinship frame. Increasing density and the shift from collective to private property ownership put pressures on such flexible use of space, though the populations in the muslim quarters of even the highest-density African and Asiatic cities go to extraordinary lengths to preserve such possibilities by elaborate use of rooftops and interior adjustments of housing design. While kinship does not necessarily die out with modern high-rise apartment block living, it does become harder to sustain. This accounts for the social preference in many third-world cities for squatter settlements that subvert private property rights and permit the replication of more traditional social structures within more flexible spaces than those provided by public or commercial housing systems (often based on nuclear family concepts).

Housing construction entails more than a simple technological capacity to defy the laws of gravity and vault a roof over covered space. Though building technologies have changed over the ages housing styles have remained remarkably persistent. Geographical variation is much more emphatic because housing has to respond to different environmental conditions (climate, drainage, disease, etc.) using local construction materials and labour skills. The house also embodies local cultural preferences for light, ventilation and privacy, while responding to the needs of security, mobility, economy, and social structure. The range of primitive housing types extends from the eskimo igloo through the Berber tent to the cave dwelling, the wattle hut, the log cabin, and the adobe house. Out of these primitive house types a wide variety of vernacular pre-industrial architectures were evolved (see Rapoport, 1969), many of which could be adapted to urban circumstances.

But urbanization always imposes social, economic and political as well as physical constraints. Modifications to rural vernacular led urban housing to evolve in quite distinctive ways. Furthermore, the pursuit of permanence and physical symbols of authority led to a much greater emphasis upon monumental forms of building in urban settings. These required new techniques and styles, elements of which could be incorporated into house building activity, in the first instance for the ruling class but later on for less privileged strata. Urbanization therefore entailed a complex interaction between these monumental styles and urban vernacular (Kostof, 1985). Traditional vernacular forms do not necessarily disappear however. They can be reimported by rural migrants (in the contemporary shanty towns), or resurrected by architects as better physical or commercial adaptations (as with the use of Japanese or Islamic open style housing in California).

Urban housing cannot be understood independently of the kind of urbanization in which it is embedded. Urbanization depends upon the production, appropriation and geographical concentration of economic surpluses under the aegis of some ruling class. Different modes of production and appropriation associate with different class structures and produce different types of urbanization. The theocratic cities of the ancient world, meso-America and pre-colonial Africa had much in common with each other in spite of wide separations in time and space, than they did with the bureaucratic cities of the Orient and Asia, the classical urbanization of Greece and Rome, the feudal cities of medieval Europe, the industrial and so-called 'post industrial' cities of advanced capitalism, and the contemporary cities of the neo-colonial or socialist bloc worlds. The quantities, qualities, and functions of urban housing reflect and help create such differences.

The organization of space and of dwelling units in a theocratic city that depended on the direct appropriation of agricultural surpluses expressed the symbolic and hierarchical requirements of the theocratic order. Where people lived and the nature and style of their building symbolized social position directly. As theocratic cities evolved into bureaucratic centres of organized political and military power, leavened by some degree of market exchange and artisanal production, so the organization of space and housing provision had to be opened up to more divergent functions and influences. It was, however, still subject to state regulation because location, style and function continued to signify positions of relative power and prestige within the social order. Political and social conflict over housing has often been, therefore, a signal of deeper stresses in society. Transitions from one mode of production and class domination to another have always coincided with rapid shifts in the forms and functions of urban housing. This general theme can perhaps best be illustrated by the evolution of urban housing in the passage from Western feudalism to capitalism and beyond.

Urbanization under feudalism was supported primarily out of the direct extraction of economic surpluses from the land (tithes, money rents, taxes) or their accumulation out of often tightly controlled trade. Towns were religious, political and military centres with ancillary market activities and artisanal production. Buildings, even those alienable under laws of private property, were not generally produced as commodities but as use values. Even though regulated guild labour (the predominant form of organization of construction) was frequently pushed to adapt vernacular or imported building styles for purposes of conspicuous display, the tight ordering of the social structure made the unrestrained flouting of individual wealth through building dangerous. Even as late as the 17th century, Louis XIV of France would brook no rivals in house building and the aristocracy applied the same pressure to a nascent bourgeoisie. Only in the Italian city states did a more powerful and autonomous merchant class permit a broader basis to conspicuous housing consumption (with effects visible to this day).

Merchants, shopkeepers, artisans and administrative officials built soberly under the jealous eye of church and state, but did so on a sufficient scale to house themselves, their families, servants, apprentices and employees. Only wage labourers (of which there were always fluctuating numbers) and the urban poor were forced to find independent means of shelter. Shanty towns, though frequent, were ephemeral and frowned on by authority, forcing the conversion of older structures into overcrowded lodging houses for rent. This commodification of housing had important consequences. Not only did it force the urban poor to become wage labourers in order to pay their rooming costs, but it also stimulated the production of housing as a speculative commodity wherever the wage labourers increased in numbers. Sold to landlords anxious to turn a profit out of the labourers' paltry wages, the new housing was cheaply built (often by casual rather than craft labour), thus forming the instant slums of many medieval towns. Ironically, the only other strata served by such speculative building were the aristocrats and high state functionaries needing to rent temporary accommodations close to the centres of political power.

The commodification of housing within the medieval frame had all kinds of social and physical consequences. Not only did it open up location and house building to the power of money and markets, but it also hinted at radical changes in social relations that came to fruition only with the rise of industrial capitalism. Entrepreneurial activity in building and the widespread use of wage labour in construction was an important and often underestimated step in the transition from feudalism to capitalism.

Speculative house building was of two types. 'It is', noted Marx, 'the ground rent, and not the house, which forms the actual object of building speculation in rapidly growing cities.' The traditional power of landowners remained unchallenged while the builders remained under-capitalized and weak, usually beholden to the superior financial power of the landed capitalists. This style of speculation produced the large estates of upper class housing in older urban centres as well as in the new spas and resorts. The Georgian terraces in England provide excellent examples (Chalkin, 1974). This system would later be adapted in England to the production of densely packed back-to-back housing for workers in industrial cities.

Speculative builders were of a different breed. Viewing land as just one of many inputs to their production process, they sought to produce housing for profit. Originating as craft workers who organized other craft workers and casual labour into an entrepreneurial production system, they were initially short on capital and credit, remained small-scale and locked into vernacular designs using traditional construction methods. Though entrepreneurial, they found it difficult to liberate themselves from the overwhelming power of landowners. And even when they could, the tyranny of lot size and land scarcity, coupled with lack of effective demand, constrained what they could build (awkward lot size played a key role, for example, in shaping the extraordinary design of New York's tenement housing). Only when finance capital (armed with new institutions and powers) came to control both land development and building jointly, did the industrialization of urban housing production become possible.

The rise of industrial capitalism changed the face of urbanization. The industrial city's business was the production of surpluses through the exploitation of wage labour in production organized within the urban frame. The radical reorganization of labour processes under industrial capitalism undermined craft distinctions and reorganized an ever-growing working class into a hierarchy of skills and authority positions to which there corresponded a hierarchy of wage rates. The housing needs of this vast and growing mass of heterogeneous wage labourers had to be met by commodity production. But how? Industrial capitalism had to find an answer to that question or simply collapse under the weight of its own inability to assure the reproduction of labour power as its most valuable commodity.

The conversion of pre-existing structures to lodging houses, tenements and rooming units, and the opening up of damp cellars and attics ill-protected from the elements formed one set of solutions. To this were added the efforts of speculative builders creating blocks of housing here (the back-to-backs of Britain, the *cités ouvrières* of France, the terrace housing of the United States) or jerry-built structures on odd land lots there. Only occasionally did employers seek to provide worker housing on their own account (Bourneville and Port Sunlight in England; Lowell and Pullman in the United States). Short of capital and low on income, most workers were forced to rent, and although the quality of housing varied, the net effect was to produce the dramatic overcrowding and all the signs of physical and social breakdown that made the industrial city such an appalling place. The more privileged strata of wage workers and the middle and upper classes for their part increasingly used their money power to escape contact with what they saw as dens of disease, vice and misery (to say nothing of the threats of the urban rabble). As early as 1844, Engels showed how suburbanization (later aided and abetted by revolutions in urban mass transportation) and residential differentiation reflected class-bound stratifications in money power. The housing spaces of the capitalist city came to be seen as 'natural' outcomes of competition and the commodification of housing provision and use in spatially segregated markets.

Bourgeois concerns over health, social unrest (the 'housing question' played an important role in sparking such events as the Paris Commune as well as movements towards municipal socialism) and the qualities of labour power, coincided with strengthening working-class movements to produce substantial housing reform movement throughout the capitalist world in the latter half of the 19th century. If commodity provision and delivery (through landlordism) could not meet the needs and aspirations of the mass of urban workers, then other solutions to the housing question had to be found.

The first solution was to treat housing as an inalienable use value. Social housing produced through state action became a conspicuous feature of urban housing in all advanced capitalist countries in the 20th century, with the exception of the United States. The quantity, quality and location of this housing depends upon state policies (a question of political power and class interests), fiscal restraints (the tax base and borrowing costs), and the ability to organize production (land procurement, industrialization of building technologies, economies of scale, etc.). Organized state planning of housing provision was problematic, at least in part because it smacked heavily of some transition from capitalism to socialism. The second solution, therefore, was to reorganize housing provision around the principle of home ownership ('the last defence against bolshevism', as the head of the British Building Society movement put it in the 1920s). This solution depended upon rising worker incomes and job security coupled with new financial instruments that organized flows of savings and mortgage credit to the more privileged segments of the working class. State support was essential to the creation of such conditions, both in legalizing limited trade union power and supporting homeownership mortgage markets. Once the mass market had been clearly established (particularly after World War II), speculative building could gear up to mass produce privatized housing (the suburban building estates, the Levittowns, etc.). Revolutions in building technology together with the declining power of landowners relative to finance capital and the state, transformed housing provision. And finally, with increasing interest in tools for government intervention after the depression of the 1930s, housing became a target of fiscal and monetary policy. In the United States, for example, government policies accelerated suburbanization and access to individualized homeownership after 1945 so as to contain business cycles and sustain the post-war boom. The consequent deterioration of inner-city housing was an unfortunate side effect that played an important role in massive urban unrest. Housing continues to be a central issue in many urban social movements as well as in local and national politics.

Disparities in money power, modified by legal conditions of tenure and state intervention, typically generate marked residential differentiation in housing types and qualities. While the focus on the nuclear family is very strong, housing is still used to signal status, prestige and class power as well as life-style preferences, cultural affinity, gender relations and religious or ethnic identity. The 'housing question' remains a serious social and political issue in advanced capitalist cities and periodically becomes the focus of intense political struggles that sometimes touch at the very root of the capitalist form of urbanization. That this is so testifies to the cogency of Engels' remark that the 'manner in which the need for shelter is satisfied furnishes a measure for the manner in which all other necessities are supplied'.

D. Harvey

See also HOUSING MARKETS; PROPERTY TAXATION.

BIBLIOGRAPHY

Abrams, C. 1964. *Man's Struggle for Shelter in an Urbanizing World.* Cambridge, Mass.: MIT Press.

Ball, M. 1981. The development of capitalism in housing provision. *International Journal of Urban and Regional Research* 5, 145–77.

Burnett, J. 1978. *A Social History of Housing, 1815–1970.* Newton Abbott: David and Charles.

Chalkin, C. 1974. *The Provincial Towns of Georgian England: a Study of the Building Process.* London: Edward Arnold.

Dwyer, D. 1975. *People and Housing in Third World Cities.* London: Longmans.

Engels, F. 1844. *The Condition of the Working Class in England.* London: Parker, 1974.

Harvey, D. 1985. *The Urbanization of Capital.* Oxford: Blackwell.

Houdeville, L. 1969. *Pour une civilisation de l'habitat.* Paris: Editions Ouvrières.

Kostof, S. 1985. *A History of Architecture: Settings and Rituals.* Oxford: Oxford University Press.

Rapoport, A. 1969. *House Form and Culture.* Englewood Cliffs, NJ: Prentice-Hall.

Schwerdtfeger, F.W. 1982. *Traditional Housing in African Cities.* New York: Wiley.

Vance, J. 1966–7. Housing the worker. *Economic Geography* 42, 294–325; 43, 94–127.

Ure, Andrew (1778–1857). Andrew Ure, MD, was professor of chemistry and natural science at Anderson's College, Glasgow from 1804 to 1830. In 1830, he introduced the word 'thermostat' into the English language in conjunction with a patent that he secured (Standfort, 1982, p. 659). At about the same time, he moved to London to serve as a consultant in analytical chemistry to the Board of Customs. From 1832 to 1834, his major research assignment was to ascertain the wastage rate of raw material in sugar refining in order to determine the rebates on raw sugar import duties that British refiners could legitimately claim. Ure (1843, p. iv) complained that his research saved the exchequer £300,000 but yielded him only £800 in remuneration and cost him his health.

To recuperate, he 'spent several months in wandering through the factory districts of Lancashire, Cheshire, Derbyshire, &c., with the happiest results to his health; having everywhere experienced the utmost kindness and liberality from the mill-proprietors' (Ure, 1835, p. viii). Two important books were the result. *The Philosophy of Manufactures* (1835) and *The Cotton Manufactures of Great Britain* (1836) are detailed technical treatises on the industry at the heart of Britain's industrial revolution, interlaced with commentary on the salutary moral, intellectual, and physical effects of factory life on the workers.

Ironically, it was Karl Marx who established Ure's place in the history of economics. Ure's blatantly pro-capitalist stance, combined with his obvious technical expertise, made him the perfect 'horse's mouth' in Marx's attempt to show how capitalists used technology to throw adult males out of work and turn women and children into mere appendages of the machine. Marx (1867 [1977], pp. 560, 563–4) invoked the authority of Ure, who, in the conflict-ridden 1830s, argued that the diffusion of more automated technology would 'put an end ... to the folly of trades' unions', proving that 'when capital enlists science into her service, the refractory hand of labour will be taught docility' (Ure, 1835, pp. 23, 368).

Writing some three decades later, however, Marx failed to distinguish pro-capitalist ideology from ongoing reality. Contrary to Ure and Marx, adult male workers had not been definitively humbled, even in the presence of mechanization. Rather, certain groups of workers had maintained substantial control of work organization and had built up considerable union power (Lazonick, 1979). In effect, Marx's uncritical use of Ure provided the 'evidence' needed to confirm that, in their confrontation with capitalists armed with technology, workers had 'nothing to lose but their chains'. Theory and history were parting company in Marx's theory of capitalist development (Lazonick, 1986).

William Lazonick

See also TAYLORISM.

SELECTED WORKS

1835. *The Philosophy of Manufacture*. London: Knight.

1836. *The Cotton Manufacture of Great Britain*. London: Knight.

1843. *The Revenue in Jeopardy from Spurious Chemistry*. London: Ridgway.

BIBLIOGRAPHY

Lazonick, W. 1979. Industrial relations and technical change: the case of the self-acting mule. *Cambridge Journal of Economics* 3, September, 231–62.

Lazonick, W. 1986. Theory and history in marxian economics. In *The Future of Economic History*, ed. A.J. Field, The Hague: Kluwer-Nijhoff.

Marx, K. 1867. *Capital*, Volume I. New York: Vintage, 1977.

Standfort, J.T. 1982. Thermostat. In *Encyclopedia Americana* Vol. 26, New York: Grolier.

user cost. John Maynard Keynes developed the concept of user cost as a significant component of the supply price of any business enterprise. By introducing user cost as an expectational variable, Keynes hoped to bring the existing unrealistic economic theory back 'to reality' (Keynes, 1936, p. 146). Keynes believed that the concept of user cost had 'an importance ... for the theory of value which has been overlooked' (ibid., p. 66).

Keynes's *General Theory* was based on Marshall's micro (value) theory foundations enlarged by Keynes's chapter 5 argument that entrepreneurial expectations determine output and employment. Accordingly, for theoretical completeness, Keynes had to augment Marshall's analysis of value theory with the concept of user costs, to show how profit-seeking entrepreneurs, in an uncertain world, would have 'no choice but to be guided by these expectations' (Keynes, 1936, p. 46) in deciding today's employment hiring and production flow schedules.

While borrowing the name 'user cost' from Alfred Marshall (1890), Keynes's user cost notion involved components of cost different from those in Marshall's concept. Marshall believed that user cost was simply the additional 'wear and tear of plant' caused by current use of equipment compared to leaving it unused. Keynes, on the other hand, defined user cost as 'the reduction in value of the equipment due to using it as compared to not using it, *after allowing for the cost of the maintenance and improvements*' (1936), (p. 70; italics added). For Keynes, therefore, user cost was based on the idea of entrepreneur's intertemporal (profit) opportunity costs; that is, the sacrifice of expected future profits due to using equipment today rather than in the future.

Calendar time is a device which prevents everything from happening at once. Production takes time and hence profit-maximizing enterprises must make current production decisions based on expectations of future outcomes. The firm uses long-lived durable equipment in its production process; the present value of this equipment depends on expectations of the costs of future production flows *and* future sales from this equipment. The flow of production undertaken in time period t_1 will affect both the future ability of the firm to produce *and* the future market conditions it will face, and hence its ability to make profits in time period t_2 (as well as in periods further in the future).

Normally, use of any equipment in t_1 will impair its ability to render service in future periods, thereby raising future costs of production and/or affecting future investment decisions in new plant and equipment. More importantly, any rate of production and sales in the present period can often be expected to affect market demands (and hence profit opportunities) in the future. Current profit-maximizing production decisions, in an intertemporal setting, will therefore not only involve estimates of current market conditions and current prime labour and materials costs, but they must also involve potential expected changes in future costs and market demands and hence future profit opportunities vis-à-vis leaving the plant and equipment idle.

For Keynes, user cost involved these expected changes in future profit opportunities arising from the current use of equipment in the production process. In a world where the economic horizon extends beyond a single future period, the user cost attributable to any current period production flow will be equal to the discounted (present) value of the expected greatest potential profit change due to using equipment compared to leaving it idle.

The additional 'wear and tear of plant' caused by current use equipment compared to leaving it unused was first identified, by Marshall, as *the* user cost which was associated with the prime or short-run marginal costs of production. Pigou (1933, p. 42), however, expressedly assumed that the differences in wear and tear suffered by equipment by being used in the production process as compared to being left idle could be ignored as being of 'secondary importance', so that one could assume that disinvestment in equipment through use, as opposed to time depreciation, was zero. Most economists writing in the 1920s and 1930s either followed Pigou's lead in assuming the cost of use depreciation to be negligible, or else argued that the costs of additional wear and tear would be equal to the additional maintenance costs necessary to restore the equipment to its original pre-use condition. In the latter case, marginal maintenance costs encompassed Marshall's user cost concept.

Keynes, on the other hand, believed that user cost or 'the marginal disinvestment in the firm's own equipment involved in producing marginal output' (Keynes, 1936, p. 67) could differ substantially from marginal maintenance costs. Hence user cost could affect employment and production decisions more than what would be expected merely from correctly accounting for the components of maintenance expenditures into (1) those overhead expenditures for maintenance which had to be made only if the machine was idle and (2) those maintenance costs incurred only if the machine was used. Even if the potential maintenance costs incurred only if equipment is idle might offset the marginal maintenance cost of using equipment (where the latter was included in variable costs), Keynes (ibid., p. 67) insisted that it was 'illegitimate' to assume marginal user cost was zero and hence would not affect entrepreneurial production and employment decisions.

To drive home his point that marginal user costs differed from marginal maintenance costs, Keynes used what he believed was an obvious example – namely, the mining of mineral raw materials. The example used had been worked out in detail in his earlier *Treatise on Money* (1930, vol. 2, ch. 29), where Keynes demonstrated that, in a recession, the production of material goods today depended on the entrepreneurial expectations of when the market's surplus stock of materials will disappear. In the case of the production of raw materials, as Keynes put it, 'if a ton of copper is used today, it cannot be used tomorrow and the value which the copper would have for the purposes of tomorrow must clearly be reckoned as part of the [today's] marginal costs' (Keynes, 1936, p. 73).

The user costs associated with the mining or production of any mineral is, Keynes (ibid., p. 73) noted, but 'an extreme case' of user costs associated with any current production flows using existing durables.

Keynes's concept of user costs highlighted the fact that when the same equipment can be used either in today's or tomorrow's production flows, then *prime production costs as well as market demand conditions are (or at least may be expected to be) time interdependent.* Hence expectations regarding this intertemporal interdependence will affect today's employment and production decisions.

Furthermore, when future economic outcomes are due to a nonergodic stochastic process so that the future is uncertain (i.e. future events are not statistically predictable based on the historical evidence), then expected changes in future profit opportunities on the basis of expected future costs and/or future demand conditions (the user costs of utilizing equipment today) can only be guessed at. Hence, forward-looking profit-maximizing employment decisions in a nonergodic, calendar time setting, must necessarily be subjective and uncertain – and the uncertainty (nonstatistical predictability) of future economic events is one of the essential characteristics that made Keynes's monetary system operate differently from a 'real exchange' system where money was a veil. Thus, for Keynes, the user cost construction was an essential aspect for bringing economic theory 'back to reality' (Keynes, 1936, p. 146) where the non-neutrality of money in an uncertain environment dominated economic decision-making processes.

If different firms foresee different future situations, even if they currently possess identical equipment, there will not be any simple, uniform profit-maximizing production decision amongst the competing firms. In such a world of nonergodic uncertainty, therefore, where different agents can, with the same historical information, perceive different futures, there can be no such thing as a unique path of optimal resource allocation over future time.

Keynes's user cost analysis, as developed in *The General Theory*, was one way Keynes attempted to introduce the reality of 'the bundle of vague and more various possibilities' (Keynes, 1936, p. 24) which are the basis of entrepreneurial expectations in a statistically nonpredictable, nonergodic world; where these expectations are the determinant on today's production decisions. Keynes (1936, p. 146) argued that the assumptions of orthodox economic theory regarding the predictability of the future (what today's neoclassical economists call rational expectations, i.e. the absence of systematic errors in entrepreneurial expectations) introduced 'a large element of unreality'. By introducing the concepts of user cost and the marginal efficiency of capital (both based on expectations in an uncertain, non-ergodic world), Keynes hoped to bring microeconomic theory 'back to reality, whilst reducing to a minimum the necessary degree of adaption' (1936, p. 146).

Since Keynes's 1936 analysis, user costs have been mainly developed and applied to the question of the intertemporal production flows from depletable resources by many economists (e.g. Adelman, 1972; Bain, 1937; Davidson, 1963; Davidson, et al., 1974; Neal, 1942; Scott, 1953; Weintraub, 1949). In general however, economists have not significantly developed the concept of user costs as an intertemporal opportunity cost in the traditional analysis of non-mineral production processes using durable equipment – despite Keynes's suggestion. Nor have many economists used the concept for the analysis of intertemporally related demand conditions.

Weintraub is the only economist who has developed the user cost concept of across-time profit opportunities with intertemporally related demands of monopolistically competitive firms (especially in a world where consumers buy often on the basis of habit, follow fashion trends or purchase replacements for their existing stock of durables). For example, production and sales this period at 'special' prices can affect future profit opportunities by altering future demands relative to future production costs. Thus, although not often recognized as such, negative user cost considerations are involved in 'introductory offer' situations where future demands are complementary to current sales (Weintraub, 1949, p. 381).

PAUL DAVIDSON

See also AGGREGATE SUPPLY FUNCTION.

BIBLIOGRAPHY

Adelman, M.A. 1972. *The World Petroleum Market*. Washington, DC: Resources for the Future.

Bain, J.S. 1937. Depression pricing and the depreciation function. *Quarterly Journal of Economics* 51, August, 705–15.

Davidson, P. 1963. Public problems of the domestic crude oil industry. *American Economic Review* 53, March, 85–108.

Davidson, P. et al. 1974. Oil: its time allocation and project independence. *Brookings Papers on Economic Activity* No. 2, Summer, 411–48.

Keynes, J.M. 1930. *A Treatise on Money*. Vol. 2, London: Macmillan.

Keynes, J.M. 1936. *The General Theory of Employment, Interest and Money*. New York: Harcourt, Brace.

Marshall, A. 1890. *Principles of Economics*. London: Macmillan

Neal, A.C. 1942. *Industrial Concentration and Price Inflexibility*. Washington, DC: American Council on Public Affairs.

Pigou, A.C. 1933. *The Theory of Unemployment*. London: Macmillan.

Scott, A.D. 1953. Notes on user cost. *Economic Journal* 63, June, 368–84.

Weintraub, S. 1949. *Price Theory*. New York: Pitman.

user fees. The genealogy of the term 'user fees' (or, synonymously, 'user charges') is neither long nor coherent. Neither Marshall nor Pigou appears to have used the term. The term was in common usage in the USA during the early post-World War II years; see e.g. Stockfisch (1960). Throughout its short history, the term seems to have been employed much more frequently in the United States than elsewhere. Since about 1970, the term has appeared in the indexes of most US public finance textbooks.

No writer has provided a careful definition of the term or distinguished it from similar terms. Rosen (1985) defines a user fee as a price charged for a commodity or service produced by a government. Some writers appear to restrict the term to charges for services produced by governments. To add confusion, many writers apply the term 'user fee' to charges levied by a government for the discharge of wastes to the air and water environment. In this usage, the term is synonymous with 'effluent fee'. Although most economists believe that governments should protect the environment by fees or regulations, since the environment has the characteristics of a public good, the environment is not in any reasonable sense a commodity or service produced by a government.

How is a user fee distinguished from two related concepts, a benefit tax and a price? There is a legal and constitutional difference between fees and taxes levied by governments, but the issue here is the economic content of the terms.

A benefit tax is any tax levied proportionately to benefits received by the taxpayer from a commodity or service provided by a government. The appropriate distinction is that a fee is paid only if the consumer decides freely to consume the commodity or service, whereas the taxpayer may be forced to pay a benefit tax even though he or she is not free to decide whether to consume the commodity or service. If the term 'benefit tax' is restricted to taxes whose amounts are no greater than the value to the taxpayer of the commodity or service consumed, the important distinction disappears. No rational consumer would refuse to pay a tax which is less than the benefit which the consumer receives from commodities or services financed by the tax. Thus, the distinction between voluntary and involuntary payment becomes unimportant. In practice, governments levy many taxes in the name of benefits even though they are larger than the benefits derived from the commodity or service provided. Most ostensibly benefit taxes are only approximations to fees for the commodity or service consumed. A gasoline tax is an approximation to a fee for road consumption or congestion and pollution externalities. The Tiebout theory (1956) implies that all local government taxes can be viewed as benefit taxes.

There seems to be no important distinction between a user fee and a price except that the term 'user fee' is used when government is the supplier. Public finance economists frequently use the term 'user fee' when reference is to a service, such as electricity, provided by government, even though the service is sometimes provided by private suppliers and the charge is then referred to as a price.

Why make the distinction between a user fee and a price? There seems to be no justification except to identify the supplier. Yet that typically is, and always could be, clear from the context. It appears to be unjustified to coin a different, and indeed clumsy, term merely to identify the supplier. One suspects that some intellectual product differentiation is behind the distinction.

EDWIN S. MILLS

See also ENVIRONMENTAL ECONOMICS; EXTERNALITIES; WATER RESOURCES.

BIBLIOGRAPHY

Rosen, H. 1985. *Public Finance*. Homewood, Ill.: Richard D. Irwin.

Stockfisch, J.A. 1960. Fees and service charges as a source of city revenue: a case study of Los Angeles. *National Tax Journal* 13(2), June, 97–121

Tiebout, C. 1956. A pure theory of local expenditures. *Journal of Political Economy* 64, 416–24.

Usher, Abbot Payson (1884–1965). Usher occupied the chair of European economic history at Harvard University from 1936 to 1949 and was surely the most productive and original scholar to occupy this post. For economists of later decades, his most significant book was *A History of Mechanical Inventions* (1st edn, 1929; 2nd edn, 1954). In it he identified invention as a four-stage process in which the individual inventor, being seized of a problem in the presence of the intellectual and physical elements for a solution, achieves the primary insight (called by Usher the 'saltatory act' and by his students the 'ah-ha!' or 'Eureka' moment) and completes the invention through a stage of 'critical revision'. Usher's work here became noticed by economists when it was taken up by J.A. Schumpeter to form the historical basis of his descriptive and theoretical work on Business Cycles (1939) and also through its relation to the Kondratieff 'long waves' based on the clustering of a few major inventions at discrete points in and around the 19th century (1770–80, 1840–60, 1890–1910). At a time when economists treated technological change as an element as exogenous to economics as physical geography, Usher alone thought it worth examining as a complex socio-economic 'thread' in history. In this he was the forerunner of such modern students as Schmookler, Mansfield, Ruttan, Nelson and Rosenberg, though his book largely emphasized the technical (supply side) aspects of the process.

The identification of Usher with the study of technological change is unfortunate, since his many monographs and articles, his two textbooks, and his classroom teaching reveal a comprehensive grasp of the experience of the West in economic life and organization in all its major aspects. It is perhaps fair to say that his mind was fascinated with those points where societies face Nature. Population growth, geographical resource patterns, transport, industrial location, technology, physical costs and physical constraints on social action and organization were the themes around which his view of economic history was organized. His insights were those of the engineer, not those of the sociologist.

This bias in Usher's work undoubtedly derived from a deep-seated liberal ideology which regulated both his topics and his methods of research. He looked on economic history not simply as an interesting outlet for scientific curiosity but as an instrument to help societies achieve a rational control over their environment. But, himself the most modest and unpolitical of men, he evidently saw little use to studies where the social control to which they could lead impinged on the individual's personal and private life and values. And methodologically Usher was a committed empiricist. He evinced, and often reiterated, a deep distrust of what he called the idealistic formulations of Marx, Weber, and Parsons. Yet his admiration of the British school typified by Clapham was moderated by an uneasiness over its commitment to a purely literary or descriptive methodology. He was most at home in the study of specific limited topics in which a quantifiable trend could be observed over a long period and where measurement and economic theory of a Marshallian variety could be employed. His concrete applications of the German theories and models of industrial location were particularly powerful, and inspired the later work of E. Hoover, W. Isard and others. He must be accounted, along with S. Kuznets and A. Gerschenkron as a patriarch of the so-called 'new' economic history in the United States, and of those three, Usher's grasp of the relation between theory, measurement and the phenomena of historical change must be accounted to have been the most philosophical and careful, and the best exemplified in concrete historical studies.

WILLIAM N. PARKER

SELECTED WORKS

A bibliography of Usher's writings is contained in Lambie (ed.), (1956). This volume also contains an essay on Usher's thought and writings. See also the article by John Dales in the *International Encyclopedia of the Social Sciences*, Vol. 16 (1968), pp. 271–4, and the generous memorial tribute by A. Gerschenkron, retained in the files of the Harvard Department of Economics.

Among Usher's books and articles, *A History of Mechanical Inventions* (1929; 1954), and his two advanced level texts, *An Introduction to the Industrial History of England* (1920) and (with W. Bowden and M. Karpovich), *An Economic History of Europe since 1750* (1937) were the most durable and highly valued by students. His major contributions to early modern European economic history are *The History of the Grain Trade in France, 1400–1710* (1913) and *The Early History of Deposit Banking in Mediterranean Europe* (1943). Usher's attitudes toward economic history and methodology are best stated in three articles, (1932, 1949 and 1951) and in chapter 4 of *A History of Mechanical Inventions.* His attitude toward economics and economic policy is well stated in his 1934 address to the American Economic Association.

1913. *The History of the Grain Trade in France, 1400–1710.* Cambridge, Mass.: Harvard University Press.

1920. *An Introduction to the Industrial History of England.* Boston: Houghton Mifflin.
1929. *A History of Mechanical Inventions.* 2nd edn, Cambridge, Mass.: Harvard University Press, 1954.
1932. The application of the quantitative method to economic history. *Journal of Political Economy* 40, 186ff.
1934. A liberal theory of constructive statecraft (Address to the American Economic Association). *American Economic Review, Papers and Proceedings* 24, 1–10.
1937. (With W. Bowden and M. Karpovich.) *An Economic History of Europe since 1750.* New York: American Book Company.
1943. *The Early History of Deposit Banking in Mediterranean Europe.* Cambridge, Mass.: Harvard University Press.
1949. The significance of modern empiricism for history and economics. *Journal of Economic History* 9, 137–55.
1951. Sir John Howard Clapham and the empirical reaction in economic history. *Journal of Economic History* 11, 148–53.

BIBLIOGRAPHY

Dales, J. 1968. Usher, Abbot Payson. In *International Encyclopedia of the Social Sciences*, New York: Macmillan, Vol. 16, 196.
Gerschenkron, A. 1965. Abbot Payson Usher: a memorial tribute. Files of the Department of Economics, Harvard University.
Lambie, J. (ed.) 1956. *Architects and Craftsmen in History. Festschrift für Abbot Payson Usher.* Veröffentlichungen der List Gesellschaft, Vol. 2, Tübingen: J.C.B. Mohr (Paul Siebeck).

usury. Usury, in the scholastic economic thought of the Middle Ages, referred to a lender's intention to obtain more in return than the principal amount of the loan. As a general rule this meant that any interest-taking was usurious and forbidden, whereas in modern parlance only exorbitant interest is considered usurious. Usury was outlawed by lay and clerical authorities, who addressed the prohibition at first only to the clergy but expanded it later to lay persons as well and repeated it frequently and in strong terms.

In the age of faith during which scholastic economic thought flourished, the authorities that outlawed interest would justify their view by reference to the Bible, several passages of which are critical of interest-taking. Another consideration, later fortified by the thought of Aristotle, was the view that money was barren – which, of course, it is if kept in a strongbox or under a mattress. Still another consideration looked at interest as a payment for the passage of time, something considered not to be the private property of the creditor. References were also made to the Roman-law distinction between fungible and non-fungible goods, the former being moveable goods that are measured by number or weight and consumed by use, such as food or fuel. Fungibles are repaid by being returned in their species rather than individually. In varying formulations and for various reasons, the scholastic authorities forbade interest on the loan of fungibles or certain fungibles. Some stressed that the borrower bears the risk of the loss of the good and is obliged to return its equivalent even if the original amount that was borrowed has been stolen or lost. Others emphasized that in the case of fungibles use and consumption coalesce and that a separate charge for use in addition to the claim for return would require payment twice for the same thing. Attention was drawn to the evil effects of usury on the community and it was held that usury violated the commands of charity, justice and natural law.

The enforcement of the canonical prohibition of usury largely relied on the conscience of the faithful, who would make restitution or abstain from interest-taking rather than die in sin and be refused a Christian burial. The frequent reiteration of the usury prohibition points to the fact that many could not resist temptation. There was even a wolf in sheep's clothing who urged Saint Bernardin of Siena on to preach more insistently against usury. Little did the Saint know that the person in question was the town's most notorious usurer, who was eager to discourage his competitors.

Under the primitive economic conditions that prevailed during the early Middle Ages the typical loan may have been a consumption loan, where the potential for the exploitation of the lender is stronger than it is in the case of production loans. During the later Middle Ages, when flourishing cities were replete with commercial activities, ways were found to secure the lender of funds a return over and above the principal. As time went on, these devices to avoid the effects of the usury prohibition became so numerous and potent as to leave the prohibition an empty shell.

To begin with, it had for long been allowed to employ interest as a means of economic warfare by charging it to political enemies such as the Saracens during the Crusades. Second, and of greater practical significance, it became an established rule that the loan contract might include a provision arranging for a conventional penalty to be paid by the borrower if he failed to return the principal at the appointed time, that is, in the case of default. Third, default itself came to constitute in time a justification for charging interest. By means of these provisions the parties to the loan contract, by arranging for very short loans and simulating default, could make interest look respectable. Fourth, it became recognized that if the creditor would suffer damage on account of the loan, having perhaps himself to borrow from others at usurious terms, he could claim compensation for the damage. Fifth, more haltingly, it was also allowed that the lender be compensated for the gain that escaped him because he granted the loan. Thus a lender who used capital in his business could claim compensation under this title, which would legitimize a wide range of financial transactions. Sixth, although many loans were secured by pledges, an element of risk-taking was inherent in virtually all of them. In view of this consideration, interest was allowed as a risk-premium. Seventh, since the legal form in which the financial transaction was clothed was of crucial importance, the owner and prospective user of loan funds, instead of arranging for a loan, might form a partnership, with profit and loss divided among them in various ways. Eighth, persons reluctant to assume the burden of entrepreneurship could obtain a return on their money by investing it in annuities. They would turn over their funds to a private or public agency that promised to deliver them the annual return from a productive asset. Ninth, a banker might accept deposits without expressedly promising interest but rewarding the depositors with payments ostensibly in the nature of gifts. This was indeed a characteristic feature of early deposit-banking. Tenth, the parties might engage in a credit transaction involving a bill of exchange. As the name of this credit instrument implies, it used originally to be drawn on a foreign locality, with the opportunity of employing a foreign-exchange rate that would favour the creditor and yield him a return in excess of the principal. Such was indeed the origin of the bill of exchange, later as often used in domestic transactions as in foreign ones. In England, the first legal case dealing with an inland bill of exchange occurred in 1663.

The Christian society of the time persecuted and discriminated against the Jews in many ways. With their opportunities for making a living severely restricted, and with the canonical injunction not addressed to them, many were driven into money-lending at interest. Some were busy in lowly pawnshops, others served as bankers to princes and popes.

With the coming of the age of individualism and *laisser faire* the usury doctrine fell into disuse. When in the 1820s and 1830s inquiries were made with the ecclesiastical authorities in Rome as to what should be done in cases where the faithful had charged interest as allowed by the law of the land, the response invariably was that they were not to be troubled. An Irish priest, Fr. Jeremiah O'Callaghan, who insisted on the application of the original usury rule in all its strictness, was suspended from office by his bishop. In the twentieth century, the Code of Canon Law of 1917 allowed a creditor to accept the legal rate of interest and under certain circumstances even more. The Code of Canon Law of 1983 goes still farther by imposing a *duty* to pay interest when due on an administrator of ecclesiastical goods who has incurred a debt.

Secular legislation became permissive during the sixteenth century. For example, in England after the break with Rome interest up to 10 per cent was allowed by law in 1546. After some wavering this rule was confirmed in 1571. The legal maximum was gradually reduced, but in 1854 the usury laws were abolished altogether.

The economists' reaction to the usury rule mirrored the temper of their time. Turgot, in his *Memorial on Money Loans* of 1769, poked fun at the casuistry of the scholastics and insisted that Christ in no way had intended to condemn all lending at interest. A few years later, in 1787, Bentham published his *Defence of Usury*, in which he took Adam Smith to task for endorsing legislation that put a ceiling on interest rates and in which he made a strong plea for absolute liberty in setting up the terms of loans. It is not known whether Bentham converted Smith, who, however, did not appear to be offended and sent Bentham a gift shortly before Smith's death in 1790. In our own time, the usury doctrine was defended by Keynes, who himself favoured low rates of interest. In the *General Theory*, Keynes praised the scholastics for having attempted to keep the schedule of the marginal efficiency of capital high, while keeping down the rate of interest (p. 352). However much these opinions vary, it is likely that the usury rule had the important effect of channeling funds into equity investments rather than loans. Thereby the usury rule helped to nourish a spirit of enterprise that eased the march into capitalism, the same capitalism which, in turn, brought about the usury's rule downfall.

HENRY W. SPIEGEL

See also AQUINAS, ST TOMAS; JUST PRICE; SCHOLASTIC ECONOMIC THOUGHT.

BIBLIOGRAPHY

Consult Spiegel (1983, pp. 63–9, 696–70, with ample bibliography); Noonan (1957), the work of a legal historian; Nelson (1969), a sociological study inspired by the ideas of Max Weber; Baldwin (1970, Part IV), an historical study of the views of 12th-century churchmen, and the other works cited below. Langholm (1984) offers a new interpretation of the scholastic theory of usury on the basis of recently discovered medieval treatises.

Baldwin, J.W. 1970. *Masters, Princes and Merchants*. 2 vols, Princeton: Princeton University Press, Part IV.

Langholm, O. 1984. *The Aristotelian Analysis of Usury*. Bergen: Universitetsforlaget; distributed in the USA by Columbia University Press, New York.

Nelson, B.N. 1969. *The Idea of Usury*. 2nd edn, enlarged, Chicago: University of Chicago Press.

Noonan, J.T. Jr. 1957. *The Scholastic Analysis of Usury*. Cambridge, Mass.: Harvard University Press.

Poliakov, L. 1965. *Jewish Bankers and the Holy See from the Thirteenth to the Seventeenth Century*. Trans. by M. Kochan, London: Routledge & Kegan Paul, 1977.

Spiegel, H.W. 1983. *The Growth of Economic Thought*. Revised and expanded edn, Durham, North Carolina: Duke University Press.

Viner, J. 1978. Four articles on religious thought and economic society. *History of Political Economy* 10(1), Spring, 9–45; 46–113; 114–50; 151–89. Also available as *Religious Thought and Economic Society: Four chapters of an unfinished work by Jacob Viner*, ed. J. Melitz and D. Winch, Durham, North Carolina: Duke University Press, 1978.

utilitarianism.

Intense, long, certain, speedy, fruitful, pure –

Such marks in *pleasures* and in *pains* endure.
Such pleasures seek if *private* be thy end;
If it be *public*, wide let them *extend*.
Such *pains* avoid, whichever be thy view;
If pains *must* come, let them *extend* to few.

Jeremy Bentham added these 'memoriter verses' to a revised edition of *An Introduction to the Principles of Morals and Legislation* to fix in the reader's mind those points 'on which the whole fabric of morals and legislation may be seen to rest' (Bentham, 1789, p. 38). And indeed, although his formulation equates utility with pleasure in a way that many contemporary utilitarians would reject, Bentham does implicitly identify the central propositions that continue to inform philosophical utilitarianism today: i.e. (1) individual well-being ought to be the end of moral action; (2) each individual is to 'count for one and no more than one'; and (3) the object of social action should be to maximize general utility (or, in Bentham's phrase, to promote the greatest happiness of the greatest number).

This moral position was not, of course, original to Bentham. It was held in some form by a wide array of 18th-century writers – the English theologians Brown, Tucker and Paley, as well as the French *philosophes* Helvetius and Holbach. The distinctive doctrine associated with Bentham and James Mill, however, was first labelled *utilitarianism*. Originally coined by Bentham, and subsequently rediscovered by John Stuart Mill in a novel by Galt, the term entered the general lexicon in the 1820s. It connoted a systematic ideology composed of sensationalist psychology, ethical hedonism, classical economics, and democratic politics. Early utilitarianism – also known as Philosophical Radicalism – inspired an influential movement of reform in English law and politics during the early 19th century. But more important, the philosophy of utility as articulated by Bentham and revised by his successors has retained a central place in the theoretical debates that have dominated economics, sociology, and moral and political philosophy into the 20th century.

BENTHAM'S THEORY OF UTILITY. Bentham's theoretical innovations were not striking; like earlier utilitarians he stated both that men are in fact pleasure-seeking creatures and that the promotion of general pleasure or happiness should be the criterion of moral goodness. But Bentham's utilitarianism aspired to be both scientific and systematic. It derived these scientific pretensions from three tendencies that were particularly pronounced in his thought. First, he held a reductionist version of the empiricist theory of mind in which ideas – born of sensations – were formed by mental associations prompted by the urges of pleasure and pain. Bentham assumed that there was a correct association of ideas that would yield a correspondingly rationalized language. He believed that this rationalization of language was a necessary prerequisite to the proper calculation of self-interest, and always held to the Enlightenment hope that moral language could be made scientific by purging it of irrationalities and illusions. Second, Bentham stated unequivocally that pleasure is homogeneous and thus quantifiable. He used mathematical 'metaphors' – the felicific calculus, axioms of mental pathology, the table of the springs of action – images that suggested concreteness and precision. Finally, he gave detailed and systematic attention to 'sanctions', i.e. painful disincentives to action. Unlike the theological utilitarians, he neglected the godly sanction and concentrated on those earthly penalties of public opinion and legal punishment that could be placed under the influence or control of the legislator.

Bentham's importance lay not in these refinements of utilitarianism, except insofar as they apparently strengthened its claim to certainty, but rather in his lucid and single-minded application of the doctrine to criticize the 'fallacies' of English public discourse. In this crusade he attacked both the authority of custom and the 'anarchical' philosophy of natural rights. Bentham's rhetorical assault on the French Declarations of Rights was occasioned by his recoil from the Terror, but his arguments against the language of rights remained consistent throughout his life. He makes two powerful claims: (1) rights are not anterior to political society but are created by law; hence an inalienable or non-legal right is a self-contradictory notion; and (2) a philosophy of natural rights offers no way to adjudicate the competing claims of such rights to priority; a non-legal moral right is a 'criterionless notion' (Hart, 1982, p. 82). This distinction between law and morals is further developed by Austin and is fundamental to the legal positivist tradition, as well as to contemporary criticisms of rights-based moral theories.

If natural rights offered no clear theory to guide moral or social choice, utility, according to Bentham, did offer such guidance. The main body of his work lay in substituting utility for alleged logical fictions as a rationale for legislation. In his extensive writings on penal law, for example, he attempted to provide a 'calculus of harm' to facilitate the legislator's task of imposing the minimum sanction that would deter certain undesirable actions. Because Bentham's reformist ambitions encompassed civil and constitutional law, his work also touched directly on contentious public issues, such as abolition of the corn laws and reform of the suffrage. Bentham was a Smithian in economics and became a radical democrat in politics, but the logic of the original connections between utilitarianism and economic and political reform become clearer by considering the contributions of James Mill.

JAMES MILL AND PHILOSOPHICAL RADICALISM. According to J.S. Mill, 'it was my father's opinions which gave the distinguishing character to the Benthamic or utilitarian propagandism of the time' (Mill, 1873, p. 72). This propagandism was energetically carried out by a small group of self-styled Philosophical Radicals, including Francis Place, Joseph Hume, George Grote, Arthur Roebuck, Charles Buller, Sir William Molesworth, and – most important – John Stuart Mill. In a series of articles in the *Westminster Review* (beginning in 1824), they launched a political movement to begin the radical revitalization of English public life.

Bentham's work on sanctions (and some of his theoretical statements) suggest that individual interests would have to be associated 'artificially' through the manipulation of legal penalties. At the same time his faith in the general harmony between individual interests and the public interest implies that interests are harmonized 'spontaneously' (see Halevy, 1903). Among Bentham's political disciples, and largely through the influence of James Mill, this tension was resolved decisively in favour of the latter conception. Underlying the Philosophical Radicals' programme lay a dogmatic belief that the sum of enlightened self-interests would yield the general interest, in both economics and politics. It was the scientific reformer's job to attack the systematic distortions of self-interest that were charged to the account of 'King and Company', i.e. to the crown, the aristocracy, and the church.

In economics, the Philosophical Radicals endorsed the 'system of natural liberty' and the classical economic programme of competition, minimal state interference, free trade, and the abolition of monopolies. Given the rule of law necessary to produce a sense of individual security, men would be spurred to productive labour and to a rational pursuit of their interests by the operation of the natural sanctions of hunger and desire for satisfaction. Self-interested exchanges would then lead to the establishment of ever-wider markets and eventually to the production of the greatest possible satisfaction of wants. The principle of 'utility' was thus linked to an economic programme; however, the central problem of theoretical economics, i.e. the notion of 'value', was not conceptualized directly in utilitarian terms.

One could argue that there is an inherently democratic and critical dimension to the politics of utilitarianism because of the assumption that every man is the best judge of his interest, and because of the perception that individual freedom is necessary to recognize and formulate 'rational' interests. But the democratic logic of the original utilitarian radicals, put forward most forcefully in James Mill's *Essay on Government* (1820) was tailored closely to the historical problem of reforming the British aristocratic polity. James Mill argued that government is by definition rule by some group that is less than the whole 'people'. The circumstances of power, however, tempt these rulers to aggrandize themselves in a fashion neither in their own nor the people's long-term interests. They develop corporate, or in Bentham's terms, 'sinister' interests. This aristocratic corruption can be checked only through democratic representative institutions. Philosophical Radicals insisted on breaking the hold of Britain's aristocratic elite through education of the electorate, extension of the suffrage, frequent Parliaments, and the secret ballot. This sort of radicalism was distinguished from that of other democrats by its appeal to a science of politics rather than to the rights – natural or prescriptive – of Englishmen, and from that of liberal Whigs by its ahistorical and doctrinaire view of that 'science'. In the wake of the highly charged but inconclusive debates of the French revolutionary period, the appeal of a rational arbiter in politics was very attractive, especially to Britain's small emerging 'intelligentsia'. The Radicals' endorsement of the neutral standard of utility had strong affinities with the views of certain continental radicals who attempted to exorcize the terrors of the French Revolution by repudiating its language while retaining the substance of moderate republicanism (Welch, 1984). In both cases, however, the reformers overestimated the attractions of their programme for the middle classes, and underestimated the possibility of the growth of a distinctively working-class consciousness. In England, the Philosophical Radicals never achieved their goal of creating a fundamental political realignment, although they clearly had an ideological impact much greater than their immediate political one.

J.S. MILL. The most famous proselytizer of Philosophical Radicalism, and its most notable apostate, was John Stuart Mill. Although Henry Sidgwick has often been called the last 'classical' utilitarian, the name can better be applied to Mill in the sense that he was the last thinker to attempt to integrate a utilitarian moral and social theory with a full-blown psychology and a theory of politics. In politics Mill came to question the iron-clad logic of his father's *Essay*, to distrust the tendency to uniformity that he perceived in democracy, and to seek a theory of counterpoise and leadership. In economics he was both the last important thinker in the classical tradition and a sharp critic of existing capitalism. But his intent in all of his writings was, as he said, to modify the structure of his beliefs without totally abandoning the foundations.

An important discussion of the moral foundations of those beliefs can be found in *Utilitarianism* (1861). The argument here rests, inauspiciously enough, on the 'naturalistic fallacy' that underlay the work of Bentham and so many other 18th-century moralists; Mill's case for the moral worth of happiness rests on the 'fact' that people desire it:

> ... the sole evidence it is possible to produce that anything is desirable, is that people do actually desire it ... No reason can be given why the general happiness is desirable except that each person, so far as he believes it to be attainable, desires his own happiness (p. 44).

By 'desirable' Mill clearly seems to mean 'ought to be desired' rather than the less problematical 'can be desired'. Mill, then, was not unduly troubled by Bentham's psychological hedonism, which he largely shared, or by the derivation of ethical hedonism from this descriptive theory. Rather what bothered Mill was the suggestion that this psychological theory implied (1) a narrow materialistic view of pleasure, and (2) *egoistic* hedonism (i.e. the notion that every person ought to maximize his own pleasure). Egoistic hedonism, Mill correctly intuited, is not an ethical theory at all. To meet the first problem Mill proposed his notorious defence of qualitative differences in pleasure, a defence that only contributed to the common view that *Utilitarianism* is a casebook of logical blunders. For if there are higher and lower pleasures, it has often been pointed out, another standard than pleasure is clearly implied as the criterion of judgement between them. This tension between 'utility' and some notion of 'moral perfection' runs unresolved through most of Mill's mature works, and reappears in his defences of liberty and of democracy. To meet the second objection, Mill is careful to state, more clearly than his predecessors, that utilitarianism is a system of *ethical* hedonism, i.e. that the criterion applied to individual moral action is general happiness not individual interest. The difficult question, of course, is how to account for the motivation to moral action, given the psychological assumption that people act only to increase their own satisfactions. Mill moves away from Bentham's tendency to see the problem as one of 'conditioning' the agent to recognize the general interest as his self-interest, and offers a more sophisticated theory (reminiscent of Hume) of sympathy or disinterested altruism and its empirical connections with a sense of justice.

The power of Philosophical Radicalism as it entered the ideological arena (in a time when seismic political and industrial change had unsettled forms of social intercourse) was that it fused psychology, economics, and moral and political theory into a compelling 'fit', just how compelling a study of J.S. Mill's intellectual development would confirm. But this synthesis soon began to unravel in the hands of both friends and critics.

UTILITARIANISM: RECONSTRUCTIONS AND INFLUENCE

If utilitarianism were only the doctrine of an unsuccessful 19th-century sect of reformers, it would hardly be of much contemporary interest. But as the exemplar of a 'type' of analysis, a type often held to be radically defective, it has served and continues to serve as a point of departure in discussions of economic, social and moral theory.

Utilitarianism and economics. Utilitarianism has overtly triumphed in only one area of what were once termed the moral sciences, namely, economics. Indeed, the idea of welfare economics, i.e. of determining a 'welfare function', is irreducibly utilitarian in the sense that it seeks to measure individual want-satisfaction and to construct indices of utility. The principle of decreasing marginal utility, which was to give a decisive turn to the evolution of modern economics when applied to the determination of value, was clearly stated by Bentham for the case of money (*Principles of the Civil Code*, 1802). Paradoxically, however, the roots of the marginalist revolution cannot be traced to the formulations of the original utilitarians in any straightforward way. The technical innovations of Gossen, Jevons, Menger and Walras seem to have come at least in part from a greater sensitivity to the market position of consumers. Since then, the increasingly sophisticated mathematical structure of utility theory has generated many of the innovations that have dominated debates within the field.

The early marginalists, however, continued to think of utility in terms of the pleasurable sensations associated with consuming a good. They generally defended the cardinal measurability of utility; some even dreamed of a 'hedomiter' to measure it. The important theoretical break with the classical tradition was to abandon this notion of pleasure as a quality inherent in a good that could be measured in favour of a theory of choice based on the possibility of ranked individual preferences. However, although the problem underlying welfare economics is today construed differently – not as measurement of pleasure but as ranking of preferences – the analysis is still fundamentally akin to Bentham's calculus. Indeed, insofar as economists have addressed the larger issue of intellectual debts and affinities, they have acknowledged the formative influence of the classic utilitarians (see Harsanyi, 1977). The issue that philosophically-inclined economists must address is that of the reach of this sort of analysis. Deep divisions remain about what sorts of issues a utilitarian theory of social choice can illuminate, and about whether the attempted solutions are morally compelling. The former issue has been posed most trenchantly by sociologists; the latter by moral philosophers.

Utilitarianism and sociology. If the hypothesis of the rational economic maximizer has been retained in economics because of its heuristic strength in addressing a range of econometric questions, it was abandoned by the earliest of 'sociologists' because of its perceived heuristic weakness. From the beginning of the 19th century, social theorists have criticized methodological 'individualism' as incapable of generating insights into social life because such a view does not attribute constitutive power to social forces, but rather takes individual desires, purposes, and aspirations as the starting point of social analysis.

Sociology was born of the perceived problematic status of order in societies that had, at least in theory, repudiated the ties of 'tradition'. From St. Simon and Comte through Durkheim to Talcott Parsons, sociologists have singled out utilitarianism as singularly incapable of illuminating this problem. For these theorists, utilitarianism represents the notion of society conceived as a set of competing egoisms; this notion is thought to be peculiarly congenial to the English-speaking world and is often loosely and simplistically equated with liberalism. On this view, the utilitarian pedigree includes Hobbes, Locke and Smith, and its progeny the evolutionary utilitarianism of Spencer and McDougall. Durkheim's attack on Herbert Spencer (in *The Division of Labor*, 1893) can be taken as paradigmatic of the sociological critique.

Spencer was greatly attracted by organic analogies, but he applied them to social analysis in a way that radically maintained the notion that consciousness exists only in the individual 'parts' of society. He developed a strict utilitarian theory of ethics, which described the moral ideal as the individual pursuit of long-term pleasures (a calculation that involved cooperation with others through self-interested exchanges). The relative predominance of this sort of calculus over one in which individuals sought immediate gratification distinguished advanced from primitive societies. Durkheim argues that Spencer, and by extension individualist social theory, is not only inadequate but incoherent conceptually in its reliance on the notion of exchange to comprehend the patterning of social life. Formalized exchange makes sense only against the background of a culture that has internalized a particular set of social norms. Talcott Parsons takes up the theme insistently in *The Structure of Social Action* (1937). He argues that any theory which postulates the 'randomness of ends' cannot account for the ultimate reconciliation of those ends in society except by unacknowledged assumptions, sleight of hand, or a providential *deus ex machina*. Thus, on Parsons' view, an analogous function is served by the Leviathan (for Hobbes); God and natural law (for Locke), the invisible hand (for Smith); and the necessities of evolution (for Spencer). Bentham's utilitarian policy oscillates uneasily between Leviathan and the prior assumption of a natural harmony.

According to many sociologists, then, utilitarianism as the quintessential 'individualist' social theory is fundamentally wrongheaded because individuals are defined, shaped, and constrained within social structures. Nevertheless, a reconstructed and simplified 'utilitarianism' remains the indispensable foil from which they delineate and justify the contributions of their own discipline.

Utilitarianism and philosophy. The debate engaged between utilitarians and sociologists is between an intentionalist versus a structuralist theory of action, between a theory that heuristically treats individual preferences as random and one that emphasizes the determining constraints on those preferences. The moral philosopher engaged with utilitarianism – either as advocate or critic – has a rather different perspective and set of questions, although the philosophic criticism, especially those of 'communitarian' critics, sometimes overlap with those of sociologists. In general, however, the debates within moral philosophy take place within the camp of liberal 'individualism', in the sense that they have focused on the problems of individual moral agency. Philosophers do not ask how we can understand social order, but rather how we can judge the rightness or wrongness of individual action. The utilitarian answer (i.e. by the goodness or badness of the action's consequences) can be taken as the starting point for constructing both an analysis of moral judgements and a system of normative ethics. The utilitarian tradition of the philosophers, however, differs from that of the sociologists; it harks back to Hume and Shaftesbury rather than to Hobbes, and forward to Sidgwick, Edgeworth and Moore, rather than to Spencer. In an attempt to give a general account of moral thinking, modern philosophers have drawn on this tradition to refine ever more subtle versions of utilitarianism.

Much of this literature focuses on the arena of personal ethics. However, the public dimension – so obvious among the Philosophical Radicals who employed utility principally as an argument for or against public rules, institutions and policies – has always been implicit. Contemporary discussion of the issue occurs largely within an overlapping group of practically minded philosophers and philosophically minded welfare economists. A utilitarian theory of social justice has been explicitly argued for in the works of such thinkers as R.M. Hare, J.J.C. Smart, P. Singer and J. Harsanyi. They endorse utility, as did the classical thinkers, as the only reasonable criterion of justice in a secular society.

Philosophical utilitarianism. There are three separate but related issues that have been crucial in the evolution of utilitarian moral theories. The first, that of justifying the imperatives of utility, has produced a measure of agreement among contemporary utilitarians and at least some of their critics. The second and third, how to decide what is a good consequence, and how to determine the right way to assess these consequences, have spawned a host of subtle distinctions that continue to preoccupy and provoke theoretical argument.

The problem of justification in utilitarianism is best approached through the work of Henry Sidgwick (*The Methods of Ethics*, 1874). Unlike Bentham or J.S. Mill, Sidgwick did not base his utilitarianism on the psychological theory that individuals always act to obtain their own good. He does argue that desirable or pleasant states of consciousness are the only intrinsic good, and that an act is objectively right only if it produces more good than any other alternative act open to the agent, but he presents these principles as moral imperatives, implicit in common sense morality, not descriptions of actual behaviour. They come to us through a sort of moral intuition that is self-evident and not susceptible of further analysis. Sidgwick narrowed the focus of utilitarianism to a theory of moral choice, theoretically separable from any particular metaphysical doctrine, psychological theory, or political and institutional programme. He distanced himself not only from the sensationalist psychology of the earlier radicals, but also from their democratic reformism. This narrowed field is still characteristic of much, though not all, contemporary utilitarian theory. However, the arguments advanced for why we should accept utilitarian moral precepts have changed. Although he clarified the problem of justification by recognizing the illegitimacy of the slide from 'is' to 'ought', Sidgwick's own theory of moral intuitions proved extremely vulnerable.

The 20th-century analytic movement in philosophy has tended to discredit the notion of a proof of normative ethics altogether, and to disregard 'intuition' as vague and arbitrary. Nevertheless, the analytic philosopher's preoccupation with the meaning of moral language and the types of moral reasoning that are valid has led to a widespread belief that, even in the absence of epistemological certainty, good moral arguments can be distinguished from bad ones, fallacious statements from true ones. It is on this basis (greater plausibility or reasonableness) that arguments for utility are generally defended. Given some ultimate attitude that is acknowledged to be shared (usually generalized benevolence) the utilitarian hopes to convince others that his system of ethics is more plausible, that is, less prone to conceptual confusions and more coherent, than either unreflective moral sentiments, or some alternative general account of these sentiments. Insofar as some moral critics share the desire to apply to moral argument the established canons of rationality, there is common ground for discussion of the utilitarian viewpoint. John Rawls's *Theory of Justice* (1971) is developed largely through an antagonistic dialogue with utilitarianism on just this common ground.

A second issue that has been important in debates within the utilitarian moral tradition is the problem of how consequences are to be defined. A 'consequentialist' moral theory is one in which the results of action, not the motives to action, are the objects of rational assessment. Bentham, for example, stated that 'there is no such thing as any sort of motive that is in itself a bad one' (1789, p. 100). The classic discussion of this issue took place within the rubric of hedonism; pleasure – in narrow or more expansive senses – was the desired end of moral action. G.E. Moore (*Principia Ethica*, 1903), building on the dissatisfactions already expressed by J.S. Mill, offered a theory of 'ideal' utilitarianism that was consequentialist, but not hedonistic. Moore argued that pleasure was but one of many desirable goods, among which he included truth and beauty. Another answer to this question arises from the attempt to accommodate the common sense moral judgement that it is better to relieve suffering than to promote pleasure. Hence the so-called 'negative' utilitarianism attributed to Karl Popper, which argues that moral experience is uniquely concerned with the prevention of harm to others.

Among many contemporary thinkers the problem of defining the good is thought to be obviated by considering the good in terms of maximizing 'preferences'. The power of legitimation falls, in this view, on the process of choice, not on what is chosen; it is 'topic neutral'. Despite the intuitive appeal and apparent methodological advantages of this reformulation, the constraints imposed by the process of 'sum-ranking' and by the theory of rationality, as well as by common empirical assumptions about what people *do* in fact choose, lead choice-based utilitarianism inexorably back to the notion of maximizing 'well-being' or 'interest'.

The most important distinction developed within modern utilitarianism is that between 'act' and 'rule' utilitarianism, or 'unrestricted' and 'restricted' utilitarianism. This distinction has to do with the proper procedure for determining consequences. The modern statement of the problem dates back to R.F. Harrod (1936), but the intuitive sense of the distinction is quite old and is certainly present in the classical thinkers, who are usually classed as act utilitarians.

An act utilitarian assesses the rightness of an action directly by its consequences, i.e. he judges that action A is to be chosen because the total happiness expected to be produced by A exceeds that of any alternative action open to the agent. This position has been criticized in a number of ways (for instance, it is said to hold the agent to an impossibly exigent standard of behaviour), but the most serious objections have centred on the possibility that the course of action that would be chosen on act utilitarian principles would clash violently with common sense moral judgements. Two examples, separated by two centuries, bring out the nature of this objection.

The utilitarian William Godwin (1793) argued that, if given a choice between saving one's mother from a burning building or saving a great man whose works were more likely to benefit mankind, one ought to save the great man and leave one's mother to the fire. A modern critic of utilitarianism, H.J. McCloskey (1963), offers one version of a familiar example involving not personal but public ethics. A small-town sheriff would be able to prevent serious public disturbances (in which hundreds would surely die) if he were to execute an innocent person as a scapegoat. (One could present the case, McCloskey argues, in such a way that the sheriff is certain both that his act will not be found out and that the riots will occur.) A strict utilitarian would have to recognize that, on his principles, the correct moral choice would be to kill an innocent person. Or at least he would have to recognize that such a judgement was theoretically possible. Utilitarianism, then, seems to commit one to the possibility of acting in ways abhorrent to the common sense of domestic obligation and justice. To avoid these implications, many have proposed differing versions of rule utilitarianism.

A rule utilitarian assesses the rightness of an action by asking whether it would have good consequences if it became part of general practice. Thus general rules, like 'promises must be kept', are given moral status indirectly through their role in fostering long-term utility. All utilitarians have recognized the indirect utility of rules like promise-keeping, if only as short-cuts ('rules of thumb') to the process of calculating consequences. Bentham and Mill, for example, distinguished between first-order harm and the second-order evil that comes from the example of law-breaking. However, attempts to defend a distinctive rule utilitarian position have proved problematical. Either rule utilitarianism collapses into act utilitarianism in disputed cases (e.g. when general rules conflict), or it departs from the particular utilitarian viewpoint by asserting that some rules are so necessary as to become good in themselves. Many have attempted to gain a foothold on the slippery slope between these two possibilities and the issue has generated a substantial literature.

CRITICISMS. One line of criticism of moral utilitarianism has always been 'technical', i.e. it has referred to the impossibility of inter-personal comparisons of utility. In 1879 a now-forgotten professor of jurisprudence argued:

> There is an illusive semblance of simplicity in the Utilitarian formula ... it assumes an unreal concord about the constituents of happiness and an unreal homogeneity of human minds in point of sensibility to different pains and pleasures ... Nor is it possible to weigh bodily and mental pleasures and pains one against the other; no single man can pronounce with certainty about their relative intensity even for himself, far less for all his fellows (T.E. Cliffe Leslie, 1879, 45–6).

The idea that utility is cardinally measurable was basic to Bentham's enterprise, and has always been criticized on the grounds that pleasures are incommensurable. Far from resolving these problems, the economic theory of social choice has merely transposed them into different terms. Many versions of the theory depend heavily on a system of cardinalization derived from the work of von Neumann and Morgenstern on decisions taken under uncertainty. Yet these arguments have always encountered great scepticism (Georgescu-Roegen, 1954). At issue is the notion of the substitutability of satisfactions. Many would argue that altruistic preferences, or preferences that are 'public' cannot be translated into preference schedules. And a persistent problem is the inability to deal in a satisfactory way with equity in distribution.

A related but more fundamental line of criticism asserts that utilitarians radically misconstrue the moral experience. If sociologists are concerned with the alleged poverty of social insight that a theory of utility-maximizing individuals offers, moral philosophers have been haunted by the unnecessary impoverishment of those individuals, and by the narrowing and distorting of individual moral judgement. When Themistocles proposed to burn the ships of Athens' allies in order to secure Athenian supremacy, Aristides is supposed to have answered, 'The project would be expedient but it is unjust.' The fundamental insight that expedience and justice are at some level qualitatively distinct forms the essence of this critical perspective. 19th-century critics focused on the inability of utilitarians to comprehend duties to God and country, and hence emphasized the virtues of 'excellence', 'reverence', 'nobility' and 'honour'. 20th-century critics focus on the lack of understanding of the moral person and of duties to oneself (hence their emphasis on 'integrity', 'commitment', and 'self-respect'). Implicit in both these views is the judgement that the psychological assumptions that utilitarianism must make are so narrow and implausible as to render the theory either inadequate, or positively pernicious.

Finally, there is the problem of the cultural and institutional correlates that might accompany the adoption of utilitarianism as the criterion of social justice. Utilitarianism as a practical movement was wedded to a particular theory of politics. Yet this connection between utilitarianism and liberal democracy was largely historical and fortuitous rather than logical. The institutional implications of preference utilitarianism have not been extensively discussed, but they have aroused numerous fears and doubts among its critics. One approach to the problem is to consider again the ambiguity present in Bentham's use of the concept of interests. On the one hand, he takes interests 'as they are'. On the other, he distinguishes between existing interests, and interests that are 'well-understood'. Both conceptions have led to misgivings about the institutional implications of utilitarianism.

The idea of giving people what they happen to desire, or what they 'prefer', has much to recommend it; it seems both benevolent and non-intrusive. Yet, as social theorists have long pointed out, what grounds do we have for accepting the 'givenness of wants'? Within debates over social choice this issue has reemerged in the form of the question 'why should individual want satisfaction be the criterion of justice and social choice when individual wants themselves may be shaped by a process that preempts the choice?' (Elster, 1982, p. 219). The use of existing preferences – especially given the severe restrictions on the types of preferences that can usefully be considered – may be a way of predetermining certain outcomes, of reinforcing what people regard as likely or possible in their present situation. Or so argue many critics who have seen in utilitarianism a complacent one-dimensional defense of the status quo.

Yet the concept of 'well-understood interests' (or the analogous 'true preferences') raises the question of the conditions under which these interests and preferences are revealed to be rational or true. One image that has reappeared – especially in the literature on private ethics – is the notion of the rational utilitarian floating in a sea of traditional moralists. Because the notion of a social utility function seems to imply the need for a central directing agency – an assumption itself often challenged from a pluralist perspective – the elitism implicit in the preceding image has often suggested the idea of a manipulating elite, or at best of a benevolent despotism.

CONCLUSION. Utilitarianism began and continues to be developed on the premise that intuitions of the divine, of tradition, or of natural law and rights have been discredited beyond rehabilitation as criterions of moral choice in a secular world shorn of metaphysics. Yet this view has always been challenged, and is today sharply contested by a resurgence of 'discredited' views. Insights into the underlying structure of social life are again sought in 'contract', 'rights' or 'community' by thinkers (one might mention such different theorists as Rawls, Nozick, McIntyre and Walzer) who argue that other traditions of thought correspond better to the articulation of the dilemmas of moral and public life. These same theorists, however, share a preoccupation with disposing of the claims of utilitarianism as a necessary prelude to developing their own positions. Indeed, utilitarianism apparently has a special status in the evolution of modern social inquiry, not just because well-being is the modern obsession, or because the model of the 'science' of economics is seductive in an age of science, but because utilitarians claim to offer a criterion of neutrality among competing conceptions of the good life in a pluralistic and antagonistic world. Thus, to many, some version of the theory of utility has a compelling claim on our intellectual attention. If it is ultimately rejected, the imagery is nevertheless that of a 'journey away from' or 'beyond' utilitarianism (see Sen and Williams, 1982). Utilitarianism has achieved a paradoxical status; it dominates the landscape of contemporary thought in the social sciences not of its own commanding presence, but because it has been necessary to create and recreate it in order to map out the relevant terrain. Its critics claim to look forward to the day when 'we hear no more of it' (Williams, 1973, p. 150), yet it continues to figure as the alter-ego of much modern moral and social inquiry.

C. WELCH

See also BENTHAM, JEREMY; CHADWICK, EDWIN; EDGEWORTH, FRANCIS YSIDRO; HEDONISM; MILL; JOHN STUART; PLEASURE AND PAIN; SIDGWICK, HENRY.

BIBLIOGRAPHY

Bentham, J. 1789. *An Introduction to the Principles of Morals and Legislation*. Ed. J.H. Burns and H.L.A. Hart, London: Athlone Press, 1970.

Bentham, J. 1802. *Principles of the Civil Code*, Vol. 1. In *The Complete Works of Jeremy Bentham*, 11 vols, ed. J. Bowring, New York: Russel & Russel, 1962.

Cliffe Leslie, T.E. 1879. *Essays in Political and Moral Philosophy*. London: Longmans, Green.

Durkheim, E. 1893. *The Division of Labour in Society*. New York: Free Press, 1964.

Elster, J. 1982. Sour grapes – utilitarianism and the genesis of wants. In Sen and Williams (1982).

Georgescu-Roegen, N. 1954. Choice, expectations, and measurability. *Quarterly Journal of Economics* 68, 503–34. Reprinted in N. Georgescu-Roegen, *Analytical Economics: Issues and Problems*, Cambridge, Mass.: Harvard University Press, 1966.

Halévy, E. 1903. *The Growth of Philosophical Radicalism*. Trans. M. Morris, Boston: Beacon, 1960.

Hamburger, J. 1965. *Intellectuals in Politics: John Stuart Mill and the Philosophical Radicals*. New Haven: Yale University Press.

Harrod, R.F. 1936. Utilitarianism revised. *Mind* 45, 137–56.

Harsanyi, J.C. 1977. Morality and the theory of rational behaviour. *Social Research*, Winter. Reprinted in Sen and Williams (1982).

Hart, H.L.A. 1982. *Essays on Bentham: Studies in Jurisprudence and Political Theory*. Oxford: Clarendon Press.

Lyons, D. 1965. *Forms and Limits of Utilitarianism*. Oxford: Clarendon Press.

McCloskey, H.J. 1963. A note on utilitarian punishment. *Mind* 72, 599.

Mill, J.S. 1861. *Utilitarianism*. New York: Bobbs-Merrill, 1957.

Mill, J.S. 1873. *Autobiography*. New York: Columbia University Press, 1944.

Moore, G.E. 1903. *Principia Ethica*. Cambridge: Cambridge University Press.

Parsons, T. 1937. *The Structure of Social Action: A Study in Social Theory with Special Reference to a Group of Recent European Writers*. Glencoe, Ill.: Free Press.

Plamenatz J. 1970. *The English Utilitarians*. Oxford: Blackwell.

Rawls, J. 1971. *A Theory of Justice*. Cambridge, Mass.: Harvard University Press.

Ryan, A. 1974. *J.S. Mill*. London: Routledge.

Sen, A.K. 1970. *Collective Choice and Social Welfare*. San Francisco: Holden-Day.

Sen, A.K. and Williams, B. 1982 (eds). *Utilitarianism and Beyond.* Cambridge: Cambridge University Press.
Sidgwick, H. 1874. *The Methods of Ethics.* 7th edn, London: Macmillan, 1907.
Smart, J.J.C. and Williams, B. 1973. *Utilitarianism: For and Against.* Cambridge: Cambridge University Press.
Stephen, L. 1900. *The English Utilitarians.* 3 vols, New York: Peter Smith, 1950.
Welch, C. 1984. *Liberty and Utility: the French Ideologues and the Transformation of Liberalism.* New York: Columbia University Press.

utility. Utility is a term which has a long history in connection with the attempts of philosophers and political economists to explain the phenomenon of value. It has most frequently been given the connotation of 'desiredness', or the capacity of a good or service to satisfy a want, of whatever kind. Its use with that meaning can be traced back at least to Gershom Carmichael's 1724 edition of Pufendorf's *De Officio Hominis et Civis Iuxta Legem Naturalem*, and arguably came down to him through the medieval schoolmen from Aristotle's *Politics*.

Utility in the sense of desiredness is a purely subjective concept, clearly distinct from usefulness or fitness for a purpose – the more normal every day sense of the word and the first meaning given for it by the *Oxford English Dictionary*.

While most political economists of the 18th and 19th centuries used the term in this subjective sense, the distinction was not always kept clear, most notably in the writings of Adam Smith. In a famous passage in the *Wealth of Nations* Smith wrote:

> The word VALUE, it is to be observed, has two different meanings, and sometimes expresses the utility of some particular object, and sometimes the power of purchasing other goods which the possession of that object conveys. The one may be called 'value in use'; the other, 'value in exchange'. The things which have the greatest value in use have frequently little or no value in exchange; and, on the contrary, those which have the greatest value in exchange have frequently little or no value in use. Nothing is more useful than water; but it will purchase scarce any thing; scarce any thing can be had in exchange for it. A diamond, on the contrary, has scarce any value in use; but a very great quantity of other goods may frequently be had in exchange for it (1776, Book I, ch. IV).

Smith has sometimes been accused, because of the wording of this passage, of falling into the error of claiming that things which have *no* value in use can have value in exchange, which is tantamount to saying that utility is not a necessary condition for a good to have value. It would appear, however, that Smith was not here using the theme 'value in use', or utility, in the subjective sense of desiredness but in the normal objective sense of usefulness (cf. Bowley, 1973, p. 137; O'Brien, 1975, pp. 80 and 97). Most other classical economists and even Smith himself in his *Lectures on Jurisprudence*, used the term in its subjective sense, but the passage in the *Wealth of Nations* gave rise to considerable confusion and misinterpretation. Nor was this the only source of confusion in the early writing on the subject: even those who used the term utility in its subjective sense were not always clear as to whether it should be considered a feeling in the mind of the user or a property of the good or service used. Thomas De Quincey, for example, referred to the 'intrinsic utility' of commodities (*Logic of Political Economy*, 1844, p. 14).

Most classical economists, however, were not greatly concerned with the subtleties of meaning which the term utility might contain. Generally they used it in the broad sense of desiredness, and Ricardo employed it in a typically classical way when he wrote

> Utility then is not the measure of exchangeable value, although it is absolutely essential to it. If a commodity were in no way useful – in other words, if it could in no way contribute to our gratification – it would be destitute of exchangeable value, however scarce it might be, or whatever quantity of labour might be necessary to procure it (*Principles of Political Economy and Taxation*, 1817, ch. I, sect. I).

'Useful' here is interpreted as 'contributing to gratification' but the very word carries an echo of Smith's confusion.

For Ricardo and others in the mainstream classical tradition down to J.S. Mill and Cairnes utility became a necessary but not a sufficient condition for a good to possess value. In this context, the utility referred to was generally the total utility of the good to the purchaser, or the utility of a specific quantity which is all that is available in the circumstances of the example – for example, the utility of a single item of food to a starving person.

As a result of this approach it followed, in the words of J.S. Mill, that 'the utility of a thing in the estimation of the purchaser is the extreme limit of its exchange value: higher the value cannot ascend; peculiar circumstances are required to raise it so high' (*Principles of Political Economy*, 1848, Book III, ch. II, §.1). Classical economists like Mill accepted the view put forward by J.B. Say that 'labour is not creative of objects, but of utilities' but could see the weakness in Say's contention that price measured utility. Clearly in the case of competitively produced commodities it did not and it was cost of production and not utility (in the total sense) which determined value.

Since the classical economists were mainly interested in 'natural' rather than 'market' price, that is, in long-run normal values which were mainly determined by supply and cost, the fact that they had no theory to explain fully the relationships between utility, demand and market price was not a matter of concern to most of them. Nevertheless in the period from about 1830 to 1870 a number of attempts were made to work out these relationships more fully or to clarify aspects of them. Some of these attempts took place in Britain, within the framework of the classical system, but not surprisingly some of the best work was done at this time in France, where the tradition of demand analysis was stronger.

The full explanation of the relation between utility and demand requires the distinction between total utility and increments of utility, and the recognition of the principle that consumption of successive increments of a commodity yields not equal but diminishing increments of satisfaction or utility to the consumer. A number of writers in the mid-19th century showed an understanding of this point, but only a few stated it explicitly and correctly. Among those in Britain who did so were William Foster Lloyd (*A Lecture on the Notion of Value, delivered before the University of Oxford in Michaelmas Term*, 1833) and Nassau Senior (*Outline of the Science of Political Economy*, 1836), but neither proceeded to develop their insights into a complete theory of the relationship between utility, demand and market values.

The French engineer A.J. Dupuit was the first to present an analysis which clearly explained the concept of marginal utility and related it to a demand curve, in his paper 'On the Measurement of the Utility of Public Works' (*Annales des*

Ponts et Chaussées, Vol. VIII, 1844; English translation in *International Economic Papers*, No. 2, 1952, pp. 83–110). Dupuit also extended his analysis to show that the total area under the demand curve represents the total utility derived from the commodity; deducting from this the total receipts of the producer he arrived at the 'utility remaining to consumers' or what was later to be termed 'consumers' surplus'.

The significance of Dupuit's contribution is now well recognised, but at the time of its appearance it had little impact. The same is even more true of the work of Hermann Heinrich Gossen, one of the few German contributors to utility theory in this period. His book *Entwicklung der Gesetze des Menschlichen Verkehrs*, published in 1854, contained not only a statement of the 'law of satiable wants', or diminishing marginal utility, but also of the proposition that to maximize satisfaction from any good capable of satisfying various wants it must be allocated between those uses so as to equalize its marginal utilities in all of them.

Gossen's analysis of the principles of utility maximization was thus more complete than any which had preceded it. Yet his one book, which foreshadowed many features of general equilibrium as well as utility theory, received virtually no attention until 1878, twenty years after the author's death, when Robert Adamson, W.S. Jevons's successor as Professor of Philosophy and Political Economy at Manchester, obtained a copy of it and drew it to the attention of Jevons himself.

By that time the whole character of utility analysis and its place in economic theory had begun to change significantly. This change is usually dated from the very nearly simultaneous publication of Jevons's *Theory of Political Economy* in England and Menger's *Grundsätze der Volkswirtschaftslehre* in Austria, both in 1871, and Walras's *Eléments d'économie politique pure* in Switzerland in 1874. All these works contained a treatment of the theory of value in which the analysis of diminishing marginal utility (under a variety of other names) played a considerable part, but each of the three authors seems to have arrived independently at the main ideas of his theory without indebtedness to the others or to the predecessors already mentioned above.

This remarkable example of multiple discovery in the history of ideas has come to be known as 'the Marginal Revolution'. Discussion of its causes and character lies outside the scope of this article, but it is generally accepted that, as Sir John Hicks has said, 'the essential novelty in the work of these economists was that instead of basing their economics on production and distribution, they based it on exchange' (Hicks, 1976, p. 212).

A major element in this 'shift in attention' undoubtedly was a change from the classical concept of value in use, or total utility, as a necessary but not sufficient condition to explain the normal values of freely reproducible commodities, to the concept of what Jevons called 'the degree of utility' and of adjustments in it, through exchange of quantities of goods held or consumed, in order to maximize satisfaction. Marginal analysis can, however, be applied to questions of production and distribution as well as consumption, and hence the 'Marginal Revolution' involved more than a new stage in the development of utility theory.

Although all three pioneers of the Marginal Revolution did contribute to that development they also contributed in other ways to the theory of pricing and exchange. Perhaps only for Jevons was the theory of utility genuinely central to the structure of his economic work. On the opening page of his *Theory of Political Economy* he emphatically asserted that '*value depends entirely upon utility*' and he went on to say that 'Political Economy must be founded upon a full and accurate investigation of the conditions of utility' (1871, p. 46). Jevons indeed appears to have shared with his classical predecessors the view that a theory of value must go beyond the phenomena of demand and supply to some more fundamental explanation which for him was to be found in utility rather than in labour. 'Labour is found often to determine value, but only in an indirect manner, by varying the degree of utility of the commodity through an increase or limitation of supply' (Jevons, 1871, p. 2).

Apart from differences of terminology, Walras's treatment of utility in relation to the problem of exchange had substantial similarities with that of Jevons; but Walras saw the problem in a different context.

> His whole attention was focused on market pheomena and not on consumption ... while the driving force in the theory of exchange is, as Walras saw it, the endeavour of all traders to maximise their several satisfactions, it is marketplace satisfactions rather than dining-room satisfactions which Walras had in mind (Jaffé, 1973, pp. 118–19).

For Menger, as for Walras, the concepts of utility theory formed only a part of a much large analytical structure (concerned in his case not so much with equilibrium as with development), but unlike both Walras and Jevons he refused to state his theories in mathematical terms.

Menger developed a theory of economizing behaviour showing how the individual would seek to satisfy his subjectively felt needs in the most efficient manner. In the process he elaborated the essential propositions of a theory of maximizing behaviour for the consumer, but he expressed them in terms of the satisfaction of needs by the consumption of successive units of goods. In his discussion of this process Menger used the same phrases – use-value and exchange-value – which Smith had used almost a century earlier, and with similar connotations. Use-value he defined as 'the importance that goods acquire for us because they *directly* assure us the satisfaction of needs that would not be provided for if we did not have the goods at our command. Exchange value is the importance that goods acquire for us because their possession assures the same result *indirectly*' (Menger [1871], 1950, p. 228). Menger did use the term 'utility', but not as a synonym for use-value; he viewed it as an abstract relation between a species of goods and a human need, akin to the general term 'usefulness'. As such it constituted a prerequisite for a good to have economic character, but had no quantitative relationship to value.

The three pioneers of the Marginal Revolution thus saw the problem of the relationship of utility to exchange value in different contexts and expressed their solutions to it in different ways. Inevitably also their first solutions were incomplete in various respects. For example the precise relationships between the individual's utility function and demand function, the market demand function and the market price were not clearly specified in some of the earlier formulations; it remained for later contributors such as Marshall, Wicksteed and Edgeworth to deal with these points.

Nevertheless, despite their differences of terminology and approach, the writings of the pioneers did contain a common core which gradually gained wider acceptance, and by 1890, with the appearance of Marshall's *Principles of Economics* it seemed that the new analysis of market values had been effectively integrated with an analysis of supply and cost which served to explain long-run 'normal' values. It did provide some things which the classical system had not contained, among them a consistent theory of consumer behaviour, expressed in terms of utility.

So in 1899 it was possible for Edgeworth to write that:

> the relation of utility to value, which exercised the older economists, is thus simply explained by the mathematical school. The value in use of a certain quantity of commodity corresponds to its total utility; the value in exchange to its marginal utility (multiplied by the quantity). The former is greater than the latter, since the utility of the final increment of commodity is less than that of every other increment (Edgeworth, 1899, p. 602).

At this stage utility analysis appeared to have evolved to something approaching finality, and in 1925 Jacob Viner could still say:

> In its developed form it is to be found sympathetically treated and playing a prominent role in the exposition of value theory in most of the current authoritative treatises on economic theory by American, English, Austrian, and Italian writers.

Yet Viner immediately went on to add:

> In the scientific periodicals, however, in contrast with the standard treatises, sympathetic expositions of the utility theory of value have become somewhat rare. In their stead are found an unintermittent series of slashing criticisms of the utility economics (Viner [1925], 1958, p. 179).

The principal criticisms which Viner noted were the apparent involvement of utility theory with hedonistic psychology and the problems of measuring welfare in terms of utility. In later years questions of the measurement and summation of utility came to trouble economists more and more.

The two basic problems involved here are whether utility can be measured cardinally or simply ordinally, and whether interpersonal comparisons of utility are possible. The pioneers of the Marginal Revolution were not unaware of these problems; Jevons nowhere attempted to define a unit of utility, and indeed said that 'a unit of pleasure or pain is difficult even to conceive', but he went on to say that 'it is from the quantitative effects of the feelings that we must estimate their comparative amounts' (Jevons, 1871, p. 14). However they may be estimated, Jevons did not hesitate to refer to 'quantity of utility', and his whole analysis proceeds by treating utility as if it could be measured. The question was not examined in detail by Walras or Menger, but both their analyses treat utility as cardinally measurable.

On the question of interpersonal comparisons of utility, Menger and Walras seemed to find no difficulty, and Walras was prepared to speak of a 'maximum of utility' for society (Walras [1874], 1954, p. 256). Jevons on the other hand declared that 'every mind is ... inscrutable to every other mind, and no common denominator of feeling seems possible' (Jevons, 1871, p. 211) – but this did not always prevent him from comparing and aggregating utilities.

In the early editions of his *Principles of Economics* Marshall fully accepted the idea of utility as cardinally measurable and allowed the possibility if not of interpersonal certainly of inter-group comparisons of utility (1890, pp. 151 and 152). In later years he became more reticent and defensive on these points, and he was always more concerned than Jevons with the effects of feelings rather than the feelings themselves; yet cardinal utility always remained the basis of Marshall's demand theory.

Now, as Sir John Hicks said:

> if one starts from a theory of demand like that of Marshall and his contemporaries, it is exceedingly natural to look for a welfare application. If the general aim of the economic system is the satisfaction of consumer wants, and if the satisfaction of individual wants is to be conceived of as a maximising of utility, cannot the aim of the system be itself conceived of as a maximising of utility – universal utility, as Edgeworth called it? If this could be done and some measure of universal utility could be found, the economist's function could be widened out, from the understanding of cause and effect to the judgement of the effects – whether, from the point of view of want-satisfaction, they are to be judged as successful or unsuccessful, good or bad (Hicks, 1956, p. 6).

This was, in effect, the task which was undertaken by Marshall's successor, A.C. Pigou, in his *Economics of Welfare* (1920; earlier version published under the title *Wealth and Welfare*, 1912). Pigou made no attempt to establish a measure of universal utility; instead he took what Marshall had called 'the national dividend', aggregate real income, as the 'objective counterpart' of economic welfare. Pigou argued that economic welfare would be greater when aggregate real income increased, when fluctuations in its amount were reduced, and when it was more equally distributed among persons. It was in the context of this last point that interpersonal utility comparisons were most evident; Pigou argued that

> the old 'law of diminishing utility' thus leads securely to the proposition: Any cause which increases the absolute share of real income in the hands of the poor, provided that it does not lead to a contraction in the size of the national dividend ... will in general, increase economic welfare' (1920, p. 89).

In the 1930s most economists became increasingly uncomfortable with the idea of measurement and interpersonal or intergroup comparisons of utility. In 1934, in a famous article entitled 'A Reconsideration of the Theory of Value', Hicks and Allen used the technique of indifference curves originated by Edgeworth and developed by Walras's successor at Lausanne, Vilfredo Pareto, in presenting a theory of consumer behaviour involving only ordinal comparisons of satisfaction. A few years later a further step towards eliminating what were now considered dubious psychological assumptions from that theory was taken by treating consumer behaviour solely on the basis of revealed preference.

Accompanying these changes there was a movement away from the type of welfare economics developed on the basis of utility theory by Marshall and Pigou towards that based on Pareto's concept of an economic optimum as a position from which it is impossible to improve anyone's welfare without damaging that of another.

Indifference analysis and revealed preference theory are now standard features of microeconomic theory; but the utility concept has not disappeared; the most widely used introductory economics texts still tend to begin their treatments of household behaviour with an account of utility theory.

R.D. COLLISON BLACK

See also ECONOMIC THEORY AND THE HYPOTHESIS OF RATIONALITY; OPHEMILITY; PREFERENCES; GOSSEN, HERMANN HEINRICH

BIBLIOGRAPHY

Bowley, M. 1973. Utility, the paradox of value and 'all that' and classical economics. In M. Bowley, *Studies in the History of Economic Theory before 1870*, London: Macmillan.

Dupuit, A.J. 1844. On the measurement of the utility of public works. *Annales des Ponts et Chaussées*, 2nd Series, Vol. VIII. Translated in *International Economic Papers* No. 2, 1952, London: Macmillan, 83–110.

Edgeworth, F.Y. 1899. Utility. In *Dictionary of Political Economy*, Vol. III, ed. R.H.I. Palgrave, London: Macmillan, 602.
Gossen, H.H. 1854. *Entwicklung der Gesetze des menschlichen Verkehrs und der daraus Fliessenden Regeln für menschliches Handeln*. Brunswick: Viewig. Translated as *The Laws of Human Relations and the Rules of Human Action Derived Therefrom*, Cambridge, Mass.: MIT Press, 1983.
Hicks, J.R. 1956. *A Revision of Demand Theory*. Oxford: Clarendon Press.
Hicks, J.R. 1976. 'Revolutions' in economics. In *Method and Appraisal in Economics*, ed. S.J. Latsis, Cambridge: Cambridge University Press.
Hicks, J.R. and Allen, R.G.D. 1934. A reconsideration of the theory of value. *Economica*, NS 1, 52–76; 196–219.
Howey, R.S. 1960. *The Rise of the Marginal Utility School, 1870–1889*. Lawrence, Kansas: University of Kansas Press.
Jaffé, W. 1973. Léon Walras's role in the 'marginal revolution' of the 1870s. In *The Marginal Revolution in Economics*, ed. R.D. Collison Black, A.W. Coats and C.D. Goodwin, Durham, North Carolina: Duke University Press.
Jevons, W.S. 1871. *The Theory of Political Economy*. London: Macmillan.
Kauder, E. 1965. *A History of Marginal Utility Theory*. Princeton: Princeton University Press.
Lloyd, W.F. 1833. A lecture on the notion of value, delivered before the University of Oxford in Michaelmas Term 1833. Reprinted in *Economic History*, supplement to the *Economic Journal*, No. 2, (1927), 168–83.
Marshall, A. 1890. *Principles of Economics*. 9th (Variorum) edn, ed. C.W. Guillebaud, London: Macmillan, 1961.
Menger, C. 1871. *Grundsätze der Volkswirtschaftslehre*. Trans. by J. Dingwall and B.F. Hoselitz as *Principles of Economics*, Glencoe, Ill.: Free Press, 1951.
Mill, J.S. 1848. *Principles of Political Economy*. Ed. W. J. Ashley, London: Longmans, 1909.
O'Brien, D.P. 1975. *The Classical Economists*. Oxford: Clarendon Press.
Pigou, A.C. 1912. *Wealth and Welfare*. Expanded and republished as *The Economics of Welfare*, London: Macmillan, 1920.
Ricardo, D. 1817. *The Principles of Political Economy and Taxation*. Vol. I of *The Works and Correspondence of David Ricardo*, ed. P. Sraffa, Cambridge: Cambridge University Press, 1951.
Senior, N.W. 1836. *An Outline of the Science of Political Economy*. London: W. Clowes. Reprinted, London: Allen & Unwin, 1938.
Smith, A. 1776. *An Inquiry into the Nature and Causes of the Wealth of Nations*. Ed. R.H. Campbell and A.S. Skinner, Oxford: Clarendon Press, 1976.
Stigler, G.J. 1950. The development of utility theory. Pts. I and II. *Journal of Political Economy* 58, 307–27; 373–96. Reprinted in G.J. Stigler, *Essays in the History of Economics*, Chicago: University of Chicago Press, 1965.
Viner, J. 1925. The utility concept in value theory and its critics. *Journal of Political Economy* 33, 369–87. Reprinted in J. Viner, *The Long View and the Short*, Glencoe, Ill.: Free Press, 1958.
Walras, L. 1874. *Eléments d'économie politique pure*. Lausanne: Corbaz et Cie. Trans. by W. Jaffé as *Elements of Pure Economics*, London: Allen & Unwin, 1954.

utility, degree of. *See* DEGREE OF UTILITY.

utility, interpersonal comparisons of. *See* INTERPERSONAL COMPARISONS OF UTILITY.

utility maximization. *See* COST MINIMIZATION AND UTILITY MAXIMIZATION.

utility theory and decision theory. The conjunction of utility theory and decision theory involves formulations of decision making in which the criteria for choice among competing alternatives are based on numerical representations of the decision agent's preferences and values. Utility theory as such refers to these representations and to assumptions about preferences that correspond to various numerical representations. Although it is a child of decision theory, utility theory has emerged as a subject in its own right as seen, for example, in the contemporary review by Fishburn (*see* REPRESENTATION OF PREFERENCES). Readers interested in more detail on representations of preferences should consult that entry.

Our discussion of utility theory and decision theory will follow the useful three-part classification popularized by Luce and Raiffa (1957), namely decision making under certainty, risk, and uncertainty. I give slightly different descriptions than theirs.

Certainty refers to formulations that exclude explicit consideration of chance or uncertainty, including situations in which the outcome of each decision is known beforehand. Most of consumer demand theory falls within this category.

Risk refers to formulations that involve chance in the form of known probabilities or odds, but excludes unquantified uncertainty. Games of chance and insurance decisions with known probabilities for possible outcomes fall within the risk category. Note that 'risk' as used here is only tangentially associated with the common notion that equates risk with the possibility of something bad happening.

Uncertainty refers to formulations in which decision outcomes depend explicitly on events that are not controlled by the decision agent and whose resolutions are known to the agent only after the decision is made. Probabilities of the events are regarded either as meaningless, unknowable, or assessable only with reference to personal judgement. Situations addressed by the theory of noncooperative games and statistical decision theory typically fall under this heading.

A brief history of the subject will provide perspective for our ensuing discussion of the three categories.

HISTORICAL REMARKS. The first important paper on the subject was written by Daniel Bernoulli (1738) who, in conjunction with Gabriel Cramer, sought to explain why prudent agents often choose among risky options in a manner contrary to expected profit maximization. One example is the choice of a sure $10,000 profit over a risky venture that loses $5000 or gains $30,000, each with probability 1/2. Bernoulli argued that many such choices could be explained by maximization of the expected utility ('moral worth') of risky options, wherein the utility of wealth increases at a decreasing rate. He thus introduced the idea of decreasing marginal utility of wealth as well as the maximization of expected utility.

Although Bernoulli's ideas were endorsed by Laplace and others, they had little effect on the economics of decision making under risk until quite recently. On the other hand, his notion of decreasing marginal utility became central in consumer economics during the latter part of the 19th century (Stigler, 1950), especially in the works of Gossen, Jevons, Menger, Walras and Marshall.

During this early period, utility was often viewed as a measurable psychological magnitude. This notion of intensive measurable utility, which was sometimes represented by the additive form $u_1(x_1)+u_2(x_2)+\cdots+u_n(x_n)$ for commodity bundles $(x_1, x_2, \ldots, x_n)$, was subsequently replaced in the ordinalist revolution of Edgeworth, Fisher, Pareto, and Slutsky by the view that utility represents nothing more than the agent's preference ordering over consumption bundles. A revival of intensive measurable utility occurred after 1920 when Frisch, Lange and Alt axiomatized the notion of comparable preference differences, but it did not regain the prominence it once held.

Bernoulli's long-dormant principle of the maximization of expected utility reappeared with force in the expected utility theory of von Neumann and Morgenstern (1944, 1947). Unlike Bernoulli and Cramer, who favoured an intensive measurable view of utility, von Neumann and Morgenstern showed how the expected-utility form can arise solely from simple preference comparisons between risky options. They thus accomplished for decision making under risk what the ordinalists accomplished for demand theory a generation earlier.

Although little noted at the time, Ramsey (1931), in an essay written in 1926 and published posthumously, attempted something more ambitious than the utility theory for risky decisions of von Neumann and Morgenstern. Ramsey's aim was to show how assumptions about preferences between uncertain decisions imply not only a utility function for outcomes but also a subjective or personal probability distribution over uncertain events such that one uncertain decision is preferred to another precisely when the former has greater subjective (probability) expected utility. Ramsey's outline of a theory of decision making under uncertainty greatly influenced the first complete theory of subjective expected utility, due to Savage (1954). Savage also drew heavily on Bruno de Finetti's seminal ideas on subjective probability, which are similar in ways to views espoused much earlier by Bayes and Laplace.

During the historical period, several unsuccessful proposals were made to replace 'utility' by a term better suited to the concepts it represents. Despite these failures, the terms *ordinal utility* and *cardinal utility*, introduced by Hicks and Allen (1934) to distinguish between the ordinalist viewpoint and the older measurability view of utility as a 'cardinal magnitude', caught on. Present usage adheres to the following measurement theoretic definitions.

Let $\succ$ denote the relation *is preferred to* on a set X of decision alternatives, outcomes, commodity bundles, or whatever. Suppose preferences are ordered and can be represented by a real valued function u on X as

$$x \succ y \Leftrightarrow u(x) > u(y), \qquad (1)$$

for all x and y in X. We then say that u is an *ordinal utility function* if it satisfies (1) but is subject to no further restrictions. Then any other real function v that preserves the order of $\succ$, or satisfies (1) in place of u, is also an ordinal utility function, and all such functions for the given $\succ$ are equivalent in the ordinal context. A different preference ordering on X will have a different equivalence class of order-preserving functions. If u is also required to be continuous, we may speak of continuous ordinal utility.

If u satisfies (1) and is restricted by subsidiary conditions in such a way that v also satisfies (1) *and* the subsidiary conditions if and only if there are numbers $a>0$ and b such that

$$v(x) = au(x) + b, \qquad \text{for all } x \text{ in } X, \qquad (2)$$

then u is a *cardinal utility function* and is said to be unique up to a positive $(a>0)$ linear transformation. Subsidiary conditions that force (2) under appropriate structure for X include additivity $u(x_1, \ldots, x_n) = u_1(x_1) + \cdots + u_n(x_n)$ with $n \geqslant 2$, the linearity property $u[\lambda p + (1-\lambda)q] = \lambda u(p) + (1-\lambda)u(q)$ of expected utility, and the ordered preference-difference representation $(x, y) \succ^* (z, w) \Leftrightarrow u(x) - u(y) > u(z) - u(w)$. Only the last of these, where $(x, y) \succ^* (z, w)$ says that the intensity of preference for x over y exceeds the intensity of preference for z over w, involves a view of preference that goes beyond the basic relation $\succ$.

DECISIONS UNDER CERTAINTY. Representation (1) is the preeminent utility representation for decision making under certainty. It presumes that the preference relation $\succ$ is

asymmetric: if $x \succ y$ then not $(y \succ x)$,

negatively transitive: if $x \succ z$ then $x \succ y$ or $y \succ z$,

and, when X is uncountably infinite, that there is a countable subset C_0 in X such that, whenever $x \succ y$, there is a z in C_0 such that $x \succsim z \succsim y$, where $x \succsim z$ means not $(z \succ x)$. An asymmetric and negatively transitive relation is often referred to as a *weak order*, and in this case both $\succ$ and its induced indifference relation $\sim$, defined by

$$x \sim y \text{ if neither } x \succ y \text{ nor } y \succ x,$$

are *transitive*, that is $(x \succ y, y \succ z) \Rightarrow x \succ z$ and $(x \sim y, y \sim z) \Rightarrow x \sim z$. If X is a connected and separable topological space, the countable C_0 condition can be replaced by the assumption that the preferred-to-x set $\{y: y \succ x\}$ and the less-preferred-than-x set $\{y: x \succ y\}$ are open sets in X's topology for every x in X. When this holds, u can be taken to be continuous. If the countable C_0 condition fails when $\succ$ is a weak order, (1) cannot hold and instead we could represent $\succ$ by vector-valued utilities ordered lexicographically. For details and further references, see Fishburn (1970, 1974).

Economics is often concerned with situations in which any one of a number of subsets of X might arise as the feasible set from which a choice is required. For example, if X is a commodity space $\{(x_1, \ldots, x_n): x_i \geqslant 0 \text{ for } i = 1, \ldots, n\}$, then the feasible set at price vector $p = (p_1, \ldots, p_n) > (0, \ldots, 0)$ and disposable income $m \geqslant 0$ is the *opportunity set* $\{(x_1, \ldots, x_n): p_1x_1 + \cdots + p_nx_n \leqslant m\}$ of commodity bundles that can be purchased at p and m. The allure of (1) in such situations is that the same u can be used for choice by maximization of utility for each non-empty feasible set Y so long as the set

$$\max_u Y = \{x \text{ in } Y: u(x) \geqslant u(y) \text{ for all } y \text{ in } Y\}$$

is not empty. The existence of non-empty $\max_u Y$ is assured if Y is finite or if it is a compact subset of a connected and separable topological space on which u is upper semi-continuous.

When (1) holds, the set

$$\max \succ Y = \{x \text{ in } Y: y \succ x \text{ for no } y \text{ in } Y\}$$

of maximally-preferred elements in Y is identical to $\max_u Y$. On the other hand, $\max \succ Y$ can be non-empty when no utility function satisfies (1). For example, if X is finite, then $\max \succ Y$ is non-empty for every non-empty subset Y of X if, and only if, X contains no preference cycle, that is no $x_1, \ldots, x_m$ such that $x_1 \succ x_2 \succ \cdots \succ x_m \succ x_1$. In this case it is always possible to define u on X so that, for all x and y in X,

$$x \succ y \Rightarrow u(x) > u(y). \qquad (3)$$

Then choices can still be made by maximization of utility since $\max_u Y$ will be a non-empty subset of $\max \succ Y$. However, if $\succ$ has cycles, then the principle of choice by maximization breaks down.

The situation for infinite X and suitably constrained feasible sets is somewhat different. Sonnenschein (1971) shows for the commodity space setting that $\succ$ can have cycles while every opportunity set Y has a non-empty $\max \succ Y$. His key assumptions are a semicontinuity condition on $\succsim$ and the assumption that every preferred-to-x set is convex. Thus, choice by maximal preference may obtain when $\succ$ can be characterized by neither (1) nor (3).

Max$\succ Y$ for opportunity sets Y in commodity space is the agent's *demand correspondence* (which depends on p and m) or, if each max$\succ Y$ is a singleton, his *demand function*. The revealed preference approach of Samuelson and others represents an attempt to base the theory of consumer demand directly on demand functions without invoking preference as an undefined primitive. If $f(p,m)$ denotes the consumer's unique choice at (p,m) from the opportunity set there, we say that commodity bundle x is *revealed to be preferred to* commodity bundle y if $y \neq x$ and there is a (p,m) at which $x = f(p,m)$ and $p_1 y_1 + \cdots + p_n y_n \leqslant m$. Conditions can then be stated (Uzawa, 1960; Houthakker, 1961; Hurwicz and Richter, 1971) for the revealed preference relation such that there exists a utility function u on X for which $\max_u Y = \{f(p,m)\}$ when Y is the opportunity set at (p,m), for every such Y.

The revealed preference approach in demand theory has stimulated a more general theory of choice functions. A *choice function* C is a mapping from a family of non-empty feasible subsets of X into subsets of X such that, for each feasible Y, $C(Y)$ is a non-empty subset of Y. The *choice set* $C(Y)$ describes the 'best' things in Y. Research in this area has identified conditions on C that allow it to be represented in interesting ways. Examples appear in Fishburn (1973, chapter 15) and Sen (1977). One is the condition

$$\text{if } Y \subseteq Z \text{ and } Y \cap C(Z) \text{ is non-empty,}$$

$$\text{then } C(Y) = Y \cap C(Z).$$

When every two-element and three-element subset of X is feasible, this implies that the revealed preference relation $\succ_r$, defined by $x \succ_r y$ if $x \neq y$ and $C(\{x,y\}) = \{x\}$, is a weak order. The weaker condition

$$\text{if } Y \subseteq z \text{ then } Y \cap C(Z) \subseteq C(Y)$$

implies that $\succ_r$ has no cycles when every non-empty finite subset of X is feasible.

DECISIONS UNDER RISK. Let P be a convex set of probability measures on an algebra $\mathscr{A}$ of subsets of an outcome set X. Thus, for every p in $\mathscr{P}$, $p(A) \geqslant 0$ for all $\mathscr{A}$ in $\mathscr{A}$, $p(X) = 1$, and $p(A \cup B) = p(A) + p(B)$ whenever A and B are disjoint sets in $\mathscr{A}$. *Convexity* means that $\lambda p + (1-\lambda)q$ is in $\mathscr{P}$ whenever p and q are in $\mathscr{P}$ and $0 \leqslant \lambda \leqslant 1$. We assume that each $\{x\}$ is in $\mathscr{A}$ and each measure that has $p(\{x\}) = 1$ for some x in X is in $\mathscr{P}$.

The basic expected utility representation is, for all p and q in $\mathscr{P}$,

$$p \succ q \Leftrightarrow \int_X u(x)\,\mathrm{d}p(x) > \int_X u(x)\,\mathrm{d}q(x), \tag{4}$$

where u is a real valued function on X. When u satisfies (4), it is unique up to a positive linear transformation. The expected utility representation follows from the preference axioms of von Neumann and Morgenstern (1947) when each p in $\mathscr{P}$ has $p(A) = 1$ for a finite A in $\mathscr{A}$. Other cases are axiomatized in Fishburn (1970, 1982a). The most important axiom besides weak order is the *independence condition* which says that, for all p, q and r in P and all $0 < \lambda < 1$,

$$p \succ q \Rightarrow \lambda p + (1-\lambda)r \succ \lambda q + (1-\lambda)r. \tag{5}$$

If \$5000 with certainty is preferred to a 50-50 gamble for \$12,000 or \$0, then (5) says that a 50-50 gamble for \$5000 or −\$20,000 will be preferred to a gamble that returns \$12,000 or \$0 or −\$20,000 with probabilities 1/4, 1/4 and 1/2 respectively: $r(-\$20{,}000) = 1$ and $\lambda = 1/2$.

The principle of choice for expected utility says to choose an expected-utility maximizing decision or measure in the feasible subset $\mathscr{Q}$ of $\mathscr{P}$ when wuch a measure exists. Since convex combinations of measures in $\mathscr{Q}$ can be formed at little or no cost with the use of random devices, feasible sets are often assumed to be convex. Although this will not create a maximizing combination when none existed prior to convexification under the usual expected utility model, it can create maximally-preferred measures in more general theories that allow cyclic preferences. Convex feasible sets are also important in the minimax theory of noncooperative games (Nash, 1951) and economic equilibrium without ordered preferences (Mas-Colell, 1974; Shafer and Sonnenschein, 1975).

Expected utility for the special case of monetary outcomes has sired extensive literatures on risk attitudes (Pratt, 1964; Arrow, 1974) and stochastic dominance (Whitmore and Findlay, 1978; Bawa, 1982). Risk attitudes involve curvature properties of an increasing utility function ($u'' < 0$ for risk aversion) and their economic consequences for expected-utility maximizing agents. Stochastic dominance relates shape features of u to distribution function comparisons. For example, $\int u\,\mathrm{d}p \geqslant \int u\,\mathrm{d}q$ for all increasing u if and only if $p(\{x : x \geqslant c\}) \geqslant q(\{x : x \geqslant c\})$ for every real c.

Alternatives to expected utility maximization with monetary outcomes base criteria for choice on distribution function parameters such as the mean, variance, below-target semivariance, and loss probability (Markowitz, 1959; Libby and Fishburn, 1977). The best known of these are mean (more is better)/variance (more is worse) models developed by Markowitz (1959), Tobin (1965) and others. Whether congruent with expected utility or not (Chipman, 1973), such models assume that preferences between distributions depend only on the parameters used.

Recent research in utility/decision theory of risky decisions has been motivated by empirical results (Allais and Hagen, 1979; Kahneman and Tversky, 1979; Slovic and Lichtenstein, 1983) which reveal systematic and persistent violations of the expected utility axioms, including (5) and transitivity. Alternative utility models that weaken (5) but retain weak order have been proposed by Kahneman and Tversky (1979), Machina (1982), and others. A representation which presumes neither (5) nor transitivity is axiomatized by Fishburn (1982b).

DECISIONS UNDER UNCERTAINTY. We adopt Savage's (1954) formulation in which each potential decision is characterized by a function f, called an *act*, from a set S of *states* into a set X of *consequences*. The consequence that occurs if f is taken and state s obtains is $f(s)$. Exactly one state will obtain, the agent does not know which it is, and the act chosen will not affect its realization. Examples of states are possible temperatures in central London at 12 noon next 14 July and possible closing prices of a company's stock next Thursday.

Suppose S and the set F of available acts are finite, and that there is a utility function u on X that satisfies (1) and perhaps other conditions. Choice criteria that avoid the question of subjective probabilities on $\mathscr{S}$ (Luce and Raiffa, 1957, chapter 13) include

maximim utility: choose f to maximize $\min_S u[f(s)]$;

minimax loss: choose f to minimize

$$\max_S \left\{ \max_F u[f(s)] - u[f(s)] \right\};$$

Hurwicz α: given $0 \le \alpha \le 1$, choose f to maximize

$$\alpha \max_S u[f(s)] + (1-\alpha) \min_S u[f(s)].$$

Maximin, which maximizes the worst that can happen, is very conservative. Minimax loss (or regret), which is less conservative than maximin, minimizes the maximum difference between the best that could happen and what actually happens. Hurwicz α ranges from maximin ($\alpha=0$) to 'maximax' ($\alpha=1$).

Another criterion maximizes the average value of $u[f(s)]$ over s. This is tantamount to the subjective expected utility model with equal probability for each state.

Subjective probability as developed by Ramsey, de Finetti and Savage quantifies partial beliefs by the extent to which we are prepared to act on them. If you would rather bet £100 on horse A than on horse B then, *for you*, A has the higher probability of winning. If your beliefs adhere to appropriate axioms for a comparative probability relation $\succ^*$ on the algebra $\mathscr{S}$ of subsets of S (Fishburn, 1986) then there is a probability measure ρ on $\mathscr{S}$ such that, for all A and B in $\mathscr{S}$, $A\succ^* B \Leftrightarrow \rho(A) > \rho(B)$.

Savage's axioms for $\succ$ on F (Savage, 1954; Fishburn, 1970, chapter 14) imply the existence of a bounded utility function u on X and a probability measure ρ on $\mathscr{S}$ such that, for all f and g in F,

$$f \succ g \Leftrightarrow \int_S u[f(s)]\,\mathrm{d}\rho(s) > \int_S u[g(s)]\,\mathrm{d}\rho(s), \quad (6)$$

with u unique up to a positive linear transformation and ρ unique. His axioms include weak order, independence axioms that in part yield the preceding representation of $\succ^*$, and a continuity condition. Many other people (Fishburn, 1981) have developed alternative axiomatizations of (6) and closely-related representations.

Recent alternatives to Savage's subjective expected utility theory have been motivated by the empirical results cited in the preceding section and by Ellsberg's (1961) challenges to the traditional subjective probability model. Suppose an urn contains 30 red balls and 60 others that are black and yellow in an unknown proportion. One ball is to be drawn at random. Many people are observed to prefer a bet on *red* rather than *black*, and a bet on *black or yellow* rather than *red or yellow*. By the traditional model, the first preference gives $\rho(\text{red}) > \rho(\text{black})$ and the second gives $\rho(\text{black}) > \rho(\text{red})$.

Schmeidler (1984) axiomatizes a utility model that replaces the additive probability measure ρ in (6) by a monotone $[A \subset B \Rightarrow \rho(A) \leqslant \rho(B)]$ but not necessarily additive measure and argues that his model can accommodate Ellsberg's phenomena. A different model (Loomes and Sugden, 1982) uses additive ρ but accommodates other violations of independence and cyclic preferences.

Maximization of subjective expected utility is the core principle of Bayesian decision theory (Savage, 1954; Raiffa and Schlaifer, 1961; Winkler, 1972). This name, used in distinction to classical methods of statistical analysis pioneered by R.A. Fisher, Jerzy Neyman, Egon Pearson, and Abraham Wald, recognizes the unabashed use of subjective probability and the revision of probabilities in light of new evidence by the basic formula of conditional probability known as Bayes's Theorem.

A typical problem is statistical decision theory is to decide which of several possible experiments, if any, to perform for the purpose of gathering additional information that will be used in a subsequent decision. In the Bayesian approach, the primary states that occasion the need for further information can be enriched to incorporate potential experimental outcomes in such a way that (6) refers to the entire decision process. The problem can then be decomposed, as is usually done in practice, to compute optimal subsequent decisions based on particular experiments and their possible outcomes. Decision functions for each experiment that map outcomes into best subsequent acts can then be compared to determine a best experiment. Various methods of analysis in the Bayesian mode are described and illustrated in Raiffa and Schlaifer (1961).

PETER C. FISHBURN

See also DECISION THEORY; EXPECTED UTILITY AND MATHEMATICAL EXPECTATION; EXPECTED UTILITY HYPOTHESIS.

BIBLIOGRAPHY

Allais, M. and Hagen O. (eds) 1979. *Expected Utility Hypotheses and the Allais Paradox*. Dordrecht: Reidel.

Arrow, K.J. 1974. *Essays in the Theory of Risk Bearing*. Amsterdam: North-Holland.

Bawa, V.S. 1982. Stochastic dominance: a research bibliography. *Management Science*. 28, 698–712.

Bernoulli, D. 1738. Specimen theoriae novae de mensura sortis. *Commentarii Academiae Scientarium Imperalis Petropolitanae*. 5, 175–92. Trans L. Sommer, *Econometrica* 22, (1954), 23–36.

Chipman, J.S. 1973. The ordering of portfolios in terms of mean and variance. *Review of Economic Studies* 40, 167–90.

Ellsberg, D. 1961. Risk, ambiguity, and the Savage axioms. *Quarterly Journal of Economics* 75, 643–69.

Fishburn, P.C. 1970. *Utility Theory for Decision Making*. New York: Wiley.

Fishburn, P.C. 1973. *The Theory of Social Choice*. Princeton: Princeton University Press.

Fishburn, P.C. 1974. Lexicographic orders, utilities, and decision rules: a survey. *Management Science* 20, 1442–71.

Fishburn, P.C. 1981. Subjective expected utility: a review of normative theories. *Theory and Decision* 13, 139–99.

Fishburn, P.C. 1982. *The Foundations of Expected Utility*. Dordrecht: Reidel.

Fishburn, P.C. 1982. Nontransitive measurable utility. *Journal of Mathematical Psychology* 26, 31–67.

Fishburn, P.C. 1986. The axioms of subjective probability. *Statistical Science* 1, 335–45.

Hicks, J.R. and Allen, R.G.D. 1934. A reconsideration of the theory of value, I, II. *Economica* 1, 52–75, 196–219.

Houthakker, H.S. 1961. The present state of consumption theory. *Econometrica* 29, 704–40.

Hurwicz, L. and Richter, M.K. 1971. Revealed preference without demand continuity assumptions. In *Preferences, Utility, and Demand*, ed. J.S. Chipman, L. Hurwicz, M.K. Richter and H.F. Sonnenschein, New York: Harcourt Brace Jovanovich.

Kahneman, D. and Tversky, A. 1979. Prospect theory: an analysis of decision under risk. *Econometrica* 47, 263–91.

Libby, R. and Fishburn, P.C. 1977. Behavioural models of risk taking in business decisions: a survey and evaluation. *Journal of Accounting Research* 15, 272–92.

Loomes, G. and Sugden, R. 1982. Regret theory: an alternative theory of rational choice under uncertainty. *Economic Journal* 92, 805–24.

Luce, R.D. and Raiffa, H. 1957. *Games and Decisions*. New York: Wiley.

Machina, M.J. 1982. 'Expected utility' analysis without the independence axiom. *Econometrica* 50, 277–323.

Markowitz, H. 1959. *Portfolio Selection*. New York: Wiley.

Mas-Colell, A. 1974. An equilibrium existence theorem without complete or transitive preferences. *Journal of Mathematical Economics* 1, 237–46.

Nash, J. 1951. Non-cooperative games. *Annals of Mathematics* 54, 286–95.

Pratt, J.W. 1964. Risk aversion in the small and in the large. *Econometrica* 32, 122–36.

Raiffa, H. and Schlaifer, R. 1961. *Applied Statistical Decision Theory*. Boston: Division of Research, Graduate School of Business, Harvard University.

Ramsey, F.P. 1931. Truth and probability. In *The Foundations of Mathematics and other Logical Essays*, ed. R.B. Braithwaite, New York: Harcourt, Brace. reprinted in *Studies in Subjective Probability*, ed. H.E. Kyburg and H.E. Smokler, New York: Wiley, 1964, 61–92.

Savage, L.J. 1954. *The Foundations of Statistics*. New York: Wiley. 2nd rev. edn, Dover Publications, 1972.

Schmeidler, D. 1984. Subjective probability and expected utility without additivity. Reprint no.84, Institute for Mathematics and its Application, University of Minnesota.

Sen, A. 1977. Social choice theory: a re-examination. *Econometrica* 45, 53–89.

Shafer, W. and Sonnenschein, H. 1975. Equilibrium in abstract economies without ordered preferences. *Journal of Mathematical Economics* 2, 345–8.

Slovic, P. and Lichtenstein, S. 1983. Preference reversals: a broader perspective. *American Economic Review* 73, 596–605.

Sonnenschein, H.F. 1971. Demand theory without transitive preferences, with applications to the theory of competitive equilibrium. In *Preferences, Utility, and Demand*, ed. J.S. Chipman, L. Hurwicz, M.K. Richter and H.F. Sonnenschein. New York: Harcourt Brace Jovanovich, 215–23.

Stigler, G.J. 1950. The development of utility theory: I, II. *Journal of Political Economy* 58, 307–27, 373–96.

Tobin, J. 1965. The theory of portfolio selection. In *The Theory of Interest Rates*, ed. F.H. Hahn and F.P.R. Brechling, New York: Macmillan, 3–51.

Uzawa, H. 1960. Preference and rational choice in the theory of consumption. In *Mathematical Methods in the Social Sciences, 1959*, ed. K. J. Arrow, S. Karlin and P. Suppes, Stanford, California: Stanford University Press, 129–48.

von Neumann, J. and Morgenstern, O. 1944. *Theory of Games and Economic Behavior*. Princeton, NJ: Princeton University Press. 2nd edn, 1947; 3rd edn, 1953.

Whitmore, G.A. and Findlay, M.C. (eds) 1978. *Stochastic Dominance*. Lexington, Mass.: Heath.

Winkler, R.L. 1972. *An Introduction to Bayesian Inference and Decision*. New York: Holt, Rinehart and Winston.

utopias. The word 'utopia' is derived from a Greek term meaning 'no place'. A utopia is a fictional account of a perfect or ideal society which in its economic aspect is usually stationary and often includes community of goods. Many proposals for social reform have included elements inspired by utopias, and most utopias at least tacitly plead for social change. There is no single utopian tradition and thus no unilinear relationship between 'utopia' and the history of economic thought. Insofar as the provision of a subsistence for mankind has been the aim of all forms of normative economic thought, however, the mode of thinking about perfect or harmonious societies termed 'utopian' has usually presented itself as the most comprehensive answer to the riddles offered by economic writers. Particularly in the modern period this has involved the use of science and technology to solve economic problems. In turn, the most ambitious plans to settle all economic difficulties have themselves often verged upon the utopian (in the sense of being particularly fanciful or unachievable). A clarification of this relationship requires distinguishing utopian thought from at least four related modes of speculation. In millenarianism, all social problems are disposed of through divine intervention, often in the form of the Second Coming of Christ, at which time a perfect society is founded. In the medieval English poetic vision described in the 'Land of Cockaygne' and similar works, all forms of scarcity are dissolved in a fantasy of satiety, where desires remain fixed while their means of satisfaction increase without labour and are consumed without effort. In arcadias, a greater stress is given to the satisfaction of 'natural' desires alone and to the equal importance of a spiritual and aesthetic existence. In what has been termed the 'perfect moral community' the necessity for a prior change in human nature and especially in human wants is also assumed and more attention is given to spiritual regeneration as the basis of social harmony.

In all forms of ideal societies the problem of wants or needs is central. The utopian tradition has tended to accept the central tension between limited resources and insatiable appetites, neither ignoring the problem nor assuming any essential change in human nature (Fuz (1952) has termed 'utopias of escape' those which begin with the assumption of plenty, 'utopias of realization' those which presume scarcity as a starting-point). Most utopias attempt instead to control the key forms of social malaise (crime, poverty, vice, war, etc.) which result from human frailty, giving greater stress to the best organization of social institutions rather than idealizing either nature (as in the Land of Cockaygne) or man (as does the perfect moral commonwealth), and relying upon designs fostered by human ingenuity rather than those derived from divine foresight. In economic as well as other aspects, utopias seek the perfection of a completely ordered and detailed social model rather than an interim solution to or partial reform of present disorders. In the imaginative grasp of possibility and presumptive omniscience of exactitude lies the charm and utility as well as the overperfectionist dangers of utopian schemes. Seeking at once to preserve the best of the past and to design an ideal future, utopias have themselves often served as models for judging the adequacy of the present as well as – particularly in the areas of science and technology – its logical development.

As a general rule the economic aspect of the utopian tradition can be understood as moving from a central concern with the maintenance of limited wants and (very often) a community of goods to solve problems of production and distribution, to a greater reliance upon the productive powers provided by science, technology and new forms of economic organization, with less strenuous demands being made for a denial of 'artificial' needs. In this sense the history of utopias mirrors both economic history and the history of economic thought insofar as the latter has legitimized that potential for satisfying greater needs for which scientific and technological development have provided the chief basis. As mainstream liberal political economy came to relinquish the ideal of economic regulation in the 18th century, relying instead upon the development of the market to overcome scarcity, utopianism also shifted its emphasis away from the creation of virtue and towards that of organized superfluity and affluence, often in combination with centralized economic planning and organization. Technology has been presumed to have brought a diminution in the amount of socially necessary labour without the necessity for a concomitant reduction in wants. The inevitability of an extreme division of labour has also been supplanted by the vision of alternating forms of more interesting and creative employment in many modern utopias. Contemporary utopianism both builds upon the promises of technology, and remains critical of forms of social organization which fail to develop this potential or to curb its harmful excesses. No longer content to offer a transcendent image of possibility, modern utopianism is moreover committed to the problem of actualizing planned and ideal societies.

Though the utopian genre is usually dated from the publication of Thomas More's *Utopia* (1516), the proposal of a community of goods as a major element in the solution to economic disorder is much older. An important antecedent was Plato's *Republic* (*c*360 BC), in which the ruling Guardians alone shared their goods in common as a means of ensuring the least conflict between private and public interest. At the end of the 2nd century AD Plutarch wrote his life of the mythical Spartan legislator Lycurgus, who ended avarice, luxury and inequality by an equal division of lands, the replacement of gold and silver by iron coinage, and various sumptuary laws. Though Aristotle was an early and influential critic of Plato's communism, the idea that a community of goods was the ideal state of property survived in various forms in the early Christian era. The very ancient image of a mythical Golden Age of flowing milk and honey which appeared in Hesiod (*c*750 BC), Ovid, and the Stoic-influenced account of the Isles of the Blessed here found a counterpart in the imagery of Paradise and the Garden of Eden, and it was universally assumed that the institution of private property could only have resulted from the Fall and the expulsion of Adam and Eve from Paradise. Some community of goods existed among the Jewish sect of the Essenes, in the early Christian Church as well as later monastic movements, and there was later considerable debate as to whether the Apostles had intended this to hold amongst themselves or for all mankind. But early on the Church offered a robust defence of the naturalness of private property on the grounds that it produced greater peace, order and economic efficiency. Charity, however, and especially the support of the poor in times of necessity, was regarded as the duty accompanying the private ownership of goods on an earth intended by God to be sufficient for the sustenance of all.

This was the tradition which Thomas More, with one eye on Plato and another, perhaps, on the potential of the New World, was to overthrow. In More the possibility of secular, social improvement was revived and now recrafted in a new image of fantasy. Both at this time and later, rapid economic change in Britain was a key reason for the Anglo-centric character of much of the utopian tradition. No doubt angered by the effects of land enclosures on the poor, More gave to the Utopians not only equality but also plenty, six hours' daily work (and more dignity to their activity than had done the ancient utopias), and a rotation of homes every ten years and of town and country inhabitants more frequently. Public markets made all goods freely available, while public hospitals cared for the sick. National plenty and scarcity were to be balanced by compensatory distribution, while the surplus was in part given away to the poor of other countries and in part sold at moderate rates. Iron was to be esteemed higher than silver or good, while jewels and pearls were treated as mere baubles fit only for children. Needs were clearly fixed and limited to the level of comforts. With the conquest of the fear of want, greed was largely eliminated, while pomp and excess derived from pride alone were prohibited by law.

The mid-16th century saw a variety of radical Protestant attempts and plans to emulate the purported communism of the early Church (e.g. in the Hutterite Anabaptism of Peter Rideman), and a considerable augmentation to anti-luxury sentiments within a few of the Protestant sects. A preference for agriculture and hostility to luxury typifies most Renaissance utopias, for instance Johann Günzberg's *Wolfaria* (1621), Andreae's *Christianopolis* (1619) (in which a guild model was of some importance), Campanella's *City of the Sun* (1623) (in which slave labour was first abolished in a utopia), and Robert Burton's *Anatomy of Melancholy* (1621) which included a powerful attack upon avarice as well as a national plan for land utilization, the management of economic resources by a bureaucracy, communal granaries, and the public employment of doctors and lawyers. Francis Bacon's *New Atlantis* (1627) was less concerned with the details of economic organization than with the justification of the rule of scientists, and established a paradigmatic attitude towards technology often repeated in later utopias. Bacon also paid some heed to the dangers posed by novelties generally to social order, while Samuel Gott's *Nova Solyma* (1648) was more severe in its condemnation of luxury and intolerance of waste. Of the utopias of the English civil war period, two are particularly worthy of note. Gerrard Winstanley's *The Law of Freedom in a Platform* (1652) developed the Diggers' efforts to reclaim common land for the poor into a scheme for the communal ownership of all land which included universal agricultural labour to age 40. Public storehouses were to make all necessary goods freely available as needed, while domestic buying and selling and working for hire were prohibited. Gold and silver were to be used for external trade alone. Better known was James Harrington's *Oceana* (1656), which popularized the proposal for agrarian laws in order to prevent the predominance of the aristocracy and urged a limit upon dowries and inheritance for similar reasons.

The late 17th century occasioned a profusion of welfare or full employment utopias in Britain (only in the following century would France see as rich a development of a genre). At this time schemes for practical, immediate social reform and utopias proper were often not far removed. It is in this period, too, that we begin to find a shift away from a concern with a limited demand and the satisfaction of only natural wants towards a conception of maximized production with the full employment of people and resources and a minimization of waste (goals to some extent shared by mainstream Mercantilism). Such aims are evident in, for example, *A Description of the Famous Kingdom of Macaria* (1641), where most legislation is concerned with regulating the production of wealth, Peter Chamberlen's *The Poore Man's Advocate* (1649), which included a detailed scheme for the joint-stock employment of the poor to be supervised by public officials, Peter Plockhoy's *A Way Propounded to Make the Poor in These and Other Nations Happy* (1659), which proposed the resettlement into communities of an elite of artisans, husbandmen and traders, and John Bellers' *Proposals for Raising a Colledge of Industry* (1695), in which the wealthy would help to found communities where the poor were to support them while also providing a decent subsistence for themselves. In such plans, solutions to economic distress tended to focus increasingly upon isolated communities rather than the nation-state, and upon segments of the population rather than, for example, all the poor. It has been suggested (by J.C. Davis, 1981) that this implied a waning confidence in the ability of the state to tackle the problem of poverty, and certainly it seems evident that the Act of Settlement of 1662 transferred this burden to individual parishes and away from central government.

The period between 1700 and 1900 marks not only the great age of utopian speculation, but also the period in which economic practice and utopian precept become increasingly intertwined. In addition, it was here that a community of goods ceased to be the *sine qua non* of utopian ideas of property, and that the liberal view of the benefits of private property ownership itself was expressed in utopian form. This entailed a combination of utopian thought and the theory of progress, though in the genre as a whole the two are usually understood as contradictory. In both modern socialism and classical political economy, then, needs are perceived as virtually unlimited, and social harmony is contingent largely upon their fulfillment. The homage to *homo oeconomicus* is usually understood to have begun in Daniel Defoe's *Robinson Crusoe* (1719), and was at its most exalted in Richard Cobden and John Bright's mid-19th-century claims about the universal peace which would be incumbent upon the global extension of free trade. One of its first serious challenges was in John Stuart Mill's acceptance after 1850 of the desirability of a steady-state economy in which further economic development was avoided. Many 18th-century utopias were devoted to the notion of progress (e.g. Mercier's *L'An 2440* (1770) and Condorcet's *L'Esquisse d'un Tableau historique des progrès de l'ésprit humain* (1794)). In others the critique of commercial society took various forms, such as Swift's gentle satire in *Gulliver's Travels* (1726), where the Houyhnhnms showed great disdain for shining stones and distributed their produce according to need, or Rousseau's more biting castigation of civilization in his *Discours sur l'origine de l'inégalité* (1755). Similar criticisms were developed into the foundations of modern communism in the writings of Raynal, Mercier, Mably, Morelly, Babeuf and in Britain, Spence and Godwin. In many of these the Spartan model was of some importance, and luxury seen as a principal source of working class oppression as well as general moral corruption.

Though the entire utopian edifice was severely shaken by the pessimistic prognosis of Malthus' *Essay on Population* (1798), the first half of the 19th century witnessed the widespread foundation of small 'utopian socialist' ideal communities which aimed to bring utopian goals into practice, and which could be essentially communistical (Robert Owen, Etienne Cabet) or semi-capitalist (Charles Fourier). Other plans concentrated upon the nation-state and the beneficial development of large-scale industry (Saint-Simon), a pattern which was to become increasingly dominant as the potential role of machinery in creating a new cornucopia became evident. (Some disenchantment with this view occurred later, however, for example in William Morris's *News from Nowhere* (1890), with its preference for rustic and artisanal virtues.) Considerably more attention came to be paid in the early 19th century (by Owen and Fourier, e.g.) to the disadvantages of too narrow a division of labour and the benefits of task rotation. At mid-century began the most compelling radical vision of the age in the works of Marx and Engels, whose plans qualify as utopian in the degree to which they inherited overly optimistic assumptions about human nature, technology and social organization in a future society in which private property and alienation were to be superseded. The last twenty years of the century found at least in Britain and America a virtually continuous outpouring of planned economy utopias, of which the best known are Edward Bellamy's *Looking Backward* (1887), which included provisions for the abolition of money, equal wages and credit for all, and an industrial army, W.D. Howells's *A Traveller from Altruria* (1894), and H.G. Wells's *A Modern Utopia* (1905), which made some effort to incorporate a conception of progress into the ideal image of the future, and included a mixed rather than wholly publicly owned economy.

In the 20th century utopianism has faltered in face of some of the consequences of modernity, and speculation has often taken the form of the negative utopia or dystopia. In the most famous of these, George Orwell's *Nineteen Eighty-Four* (1949), both capitalist aggression and inequality and communist despotism were criticized, with a central thesis of the work being the prevention of the majority enjoying the benefits of mass production via the deliberate destruction of commodities in war. More satirical of the hedonist utopia is Aldous Huxley's *Brave New World* (1932), though Huxley's later *Island* (1962) is a positive utopia which criticises the spiritual impoverishment of an overly-materialistic civilization. Late 20th century popular utopianism has included some works of science fiction, the libertarian speculation of Murray Rothbard and Robert Nozick (*Anarchy, State, and Utopia*, 1974), and the steady-state environmentalism of Ernest Callenbach's *Ecotopia* (1975). With the progressive extension of both machinery and the welfare state, utopias developing such themes optimistically have declined. To those sated with goods some of the attractions of the consumerist paradise have faded. Technological determinism has often seemingly rendered forms of economic organization unimportant. Two world wars and the spectre of nuclear catastrophe have dented confidence in human perfectibility, while half a century's experimentation with centrally planned communism has lent little credence to the view that this provides the surest path to moral and economic improvement. Nor is 'growth' any longer an uncritically accepted ideal even amongst those who have not yet experienced its effects. Nonetheless the utility of utopias to economic thought is undiminished, for they offer both illumination into important aspects of the history of economic ideas (especially in the areas of welfare and planning), as well as an imaginative leap into possible futures into which more positivist and empirically based thinking fears to wander. If 'progress' can be realized without 'growth', it will likely first persuasively appear in utopian form.

GREGORY CLAEYS

See also ANARCHISM; FULL COMMUNISM; INDIVIDUALISM; SOCIALISM.

BIBLIOGRAPHY

Adams, R.P. 1949. The social responsibilities of science in *Utopia, New Atlantis* and after. *Journal of the History of Ideas* 10, 374–98.

Armytage, W.H.G. 1984. Utopias: the technological and educational dimension. In *Utopias*, ed. P. Alexander and R. Gill, London: Duckworth.

Boguslaw, R. 1965. *The New Utopians: A Study of System Design and Social Change*. Englewood Cliffs, NJ: Prentice-Hall.

Bowman, S. 1973. Utopian views of man and the machine. *Studies in the Literary Imagination* 6, 105–20.

Claeys, G. 1986. Industrialism and hedonism in Orwell's literary and political development. *Albion* 18.

Claeys, G. 1987. *Machinery, Money and the Millennium. From Moral Economy to Socialism*. Oxford: Polity Press.

Dautry, J. 1961. Le pessimisme économique de Babeuf et l'histoire des Utopies. *Annales Historiques de la Révolution Francaise* 33, 215–33.

Davis, J.C. 1981. *Utopia and the Ideal Society. A Study of English Utopian Writing 1516–1700*. Cambridge: Cambridge University Press.

Eurich, N. 1967. *Science in Utopia*. Cambridge, Mass.: Harvard University Press.

Farr, J. 1983. Technology in the Digger Utopia. In *Dissent and Affirmation: Essays in Honor of Mulford Sibley*, ed. A.L. Kalleberg, J.D. Moon and D. Sabia, Bowling Green: Bowling Green University Popular Press.

Flory, C.R. 1967. *Economic Criticism in American Fiction, 1792 to 1900*. New York: Russell & Russell.

Fogg, W.L. 1975. Technology and dystopia. In *Utopia/Dystopia?*, ed. P.E. Richter, Cambridge, Mass.: Schenkman.

Fuz, J.K. 1952. *Welfare Economics in English Utopias from Francis Bacon to Adam Smith*. The Hague: Martinus Nijhoff.

Gelbart, N. 1978. Science in French Enlightenment Utopias. *Proceedings of the Western Society for French History* 6, 120–28.

Goodwin, B. 1984. Economic and social innovation in Utopia. In *Utopias*, ed. P. Alexander and R. Gill, London: Duckworth.

Gusfield, J. 1971. Economic development as a modern utopia. In *Aware of Utopia*, ed. D.W. Plath, Urbana: University of Illinois Press.

Hall, A.R. 1972. Science, technology and utopia in the seventeenth century. In *Science and Society 1600–1900*, ed. P. Mathias, Cambridge: Cambridge University Press.

Hont, I. and Ignatieff, M. 1983. Needs and justice in the *Wealth of Nations:* an introductory essay. In *Wealth and Virtue: the Shaping of Political Economy in the Scottish Enlightenment*, ed. I. Hont and M. Ignatieff, Cambridge: Cambridge University Press.

Hudson, W. 1946. Economic and social thought of Gerrard Winstanley: was he a seventeenth-century marxist? *Journal of Modern History* 18, 1–21.
Hymer, S. 1971. Robinson Crusoe and the secret of primitive accumulation. *Monthly Review* 23, 11–36.
King, J.E. 1983. Utopian or scientific? A reconsideration of the Ricardian Socialists. *History of Political Economy* 15, 345–73.
Klassen, P.J. 1964. *The Economics of Anabaptism 1525–60*. The Hague: Mouton.
Krieger, R. 1980. The economics of Utopia. In *Utopias: the American Experience*, ed. G.B. Moment and O.F. Kraushaar, London: Scarecrow Press.
Landa, L. 1943. Swift's economic views and Mercantilism. *English Literary History* 10, 310–35.
Leiss, W. 1970. Utopia and technology: reflections on the conquest of nature. *International Social Science Journal* 22, 576–88.
Levitas, R. 1984. Need, nature and nowhere. In *Utopias*, ed. P. Alexander and R. Gill, London: Duckworth.
MacDonald, W. 1946. Communism in Eden? *New Scholasticism* 20, 101–25.
MacKenzie, D. 1984. Marx and the machine. *Technology and Culture* 25, 473–502.
Manuel, F.E. and Manuel, F.P. 1979. *Utopian Thought in the Western World.* Oxford: Basil Blackwell.
Mumford, L. 1967. Utopia, the city and the machine. In *Utopias and Utopian Thought*, ed. F.E. Manuel, Boston: Beacon Press.
Novak, M. 1976. *Economics and the Fiction of Daniel Defoe*. New York: Russell & Russell.
Perrot, J.-C. 1982. Despotische Verkunft und ökonomische Utopie. In *Utopieforschung. Interdisziplinäre Studien zur neuzeitlichen Utopie*, ed. W. Vosskamp, Stuttgart: J.B. Metzlersche Verlagsbuchhandlung.
Pocock, J.G.A. 1980. The mobility of property and the rise of eighteenth-century sociology. In *Theories of Property, Aristotle to the Present*, ed. A. Parel and T. Flanagan, Waterloo: Wilfred Laurier University Press.
Sargent, L.T. 1981. Capitalist eutopias in America. In *America as Utopia*, ed. K.M. Roemer, New York: Burt Franklin.
Schlaeger, J. 1982. Die Robinsonade als frühbürgerliche 'Eutopia'. In *Utopieforschung. Interdisziplinäre Studien zur neuzeitlichen Utopie*, ed. W. Vosskamp, Stuttgart: J.B. Metzlersche Verlagsbuchhandlung.
Schoeck, R.J. 1956. More, Plutarch, and King Agis: Spartan history and the meaning of *Utopia. Philological Quarterly* 35, 366–75.
Segal, H. 1985. *Technological Utopianism in American Culture.* Chicago: Chicago University Press.
Sibley, M.Q. 1973. Utopian thought and technology. *American Journal of Political Science* 17, 255–81.
Soper, K. 1981. *On Human Needs: Open and Closed Theories in Marxist Perspectives*. London: Harvester Press.
Springborg, P. 1981. *The Problem of Human Needs and the Critique of Civilisation*. London: George Allen & Unwin.
Steintrager, J. 1969. Plato and More's *Utopia. Social Research* 36, 357–72.
Taylor, W.F. 1942. *The Economic Novel in America*. Chapel Hill: University of North Carolina Press.
Thompson, N.W. 1985. *The People's Science. The Popular Political Economy of Exploitation and Crisis, 1816–34*. Cambridge: Cambridge University Press.
Welles, C.B. 1948. The economic background of Plato's communism. *Journal of Economic History* 8, 101–14.

V

Valeriani, Luigi Molinari (1758–1828). Born at Imola, near Bologna, Valeriani was a learned man, and well acquainted with the classical languages; he studied poetry, physics, law, and economics. He was appointed in 1797 a member of the legislative body in Milan, and in 1801 professor of public economy at the university of Bologna where Pellegrino Rossi was his pupil.

In his day Valeriani was widely known; he wrote many works, some of which were never published. Though diffuse and obscure in style, his writings deserve attention for the learning they display and a certain originality of conception. Trained both as a lawyer and an economist, his writings bear especially on the relation between economics and law. He devoted himself with assiduity to the theory of value, and wrote a book on the subject. He maintains that the law of value depends rigidly on supply and demand, supporting this theory with a geometrical illustration from the relative quantities of both; he combats the theory of cost of production and engaged in a controversy on this question with Melchiorre Gioja. In illustrating the theory of value he employs mathematical formulae. These are, however, not employed as a means of investigating the phenomena of prices, but are only symbols employed to express in mathematical language economic laws already known – as Montanari justly said.

[UGO RABBENO]

Reprinted from *Palgrave's Dictionary of Political Economy*.

SELECTED WORKS

1806. *Del prezzo cose tutte mercantili.*
1807. *Trattato sulle misure.*
1823. *Trattato dei cambi.*
1827. *Saggio di erotemi di quella parte del gius delle genti e pubblico che dicesi pubblica economia.*

BIBLIOGRAPHY

Cavazzoni-Pederzini, A. 1859. *Intorno alla vita, opere e dottrine di L. Molinari Valeriani.*
Cossa, L. 1891–1901. Saggi bibliografica di economia politica. *Giornale degli economisti.*
Cossa, L. 1893. *Introduction to the Study of Political Economy.* Trans. L. Dyer, London: Macmillan.
Lampertico, F. 1904. Della vita e degli scritti di Luigi Valeriani Molinari, economista. *Atti della Reale Academia dei Lincei* 11(1), Rome.
Montanari, G. 1892. *La matematica applicata all' economia politica da Cesare Beccaria, Guglielmo Silio, Luigi Molinari Valeriani.* Ed. A. Scialoja.
Montanari, G. 1804. Della moneta trattato mercantile. *Economia politica* 44, Milan.
Montanari, G. 1876. *Notizie e lettere inedite de G. Montanari.* Modena: G. Campori.
Rossi, P.L.E. 1863–7. *Oeuvres complètes.* Paris.

valued-added tax. A Value-Added Tax (VAT) is a tax upon a business firm's contribution to the market value of the good or service it produces. A consequence of such taxation is that the total tax upon any *final* good or service is levied in stages. Viewed in this light, the VAT is more a method of collecting a tax as opposed to a unique form of tax. Depending upon the treatment accorded depreciation, the VAT has been held to be equivalent to a proportional tax upon income (IVA), consumption (CVA), or *final* output (GVA). Moreover, in its consumption tax mode (CVA), if it had been in existence sufficiently long, it approximates a proportional tax upon wages (WVA). These equivalences apply to a VAT levied in its purest form. Considerations of administration and politics make departure from the pure cases most likely. To the extent they do, the VAT will take on a character of its own. This is particularly significant for cases in which the tax is adopted by regional governments within a confederation.

Interest in the VAT surfaced initially during the 1920s as a variant of sales taxation. Because the tax only applied to value-added rather than total receipts, the cascade features of many forms of sales taxes could be avoided. This is, multiple taxation of the same input at the intermediate and final points of sale is eliminated. The taxation of value-added has also been defended on the grounds that it promotes a closer approximation to the benefit principle than its major alternative – corporate profits taxation. Firms absorb governmental services whether or not they earn profits. Not only is greater equity thereby achieved, but efficiency may be promoted as well. For unless government services are pure public goods, efficient resource allocation requires that firms be charged for their use. Most recently, value-added taxation has been advocated on the grounds that it is more conducive to economic growth and balance-of-payments stability than the corporate profits tax.

EQUIVALENCES. The various forms of VAT differ solely in the way in which depreciation is treated. Under a GVA no allowance is given for depreciation. Under an IVA economic depreciation is deductible from the tax base. Finally, under a CVA firms are allowed immediate expensing of investment outlays – i.e. instantaneous depreciation. The equivalence between the IVA and the proportional income tax follows at once from the firm's income statement.

$$\text{PROFITS} = \text{SALES} - \text{COST OF MATERIALS} - \text{DEPRECIATION}$$
$$- \text{WAGES} - \text{INTEREST} - \text{RENTS}$$

By simply rearranging the terms of this definition, we find that

$$\text{TAX BASE} = \text{SALES} - \text{COST OF MATERIALS} - \text{DEPRECIATION}$$
$$= \text{WAGES} + \text{RENTS} + \text{INTEREST} + \text{PROFITS}$$

Thus, the tax base of the firm is equal to its factor payments. Since the effects of a tax are the same whether the legal liability for the tax is imposed upon the buyer or seller in a transaction, it follows that the IVA levied upon the firm is equivalent to a proportional income tax levied upon factor income recipients.

The equivalence of a GVA to a sales tax upon final output is also easily established. Once again we can use the firm's income statement to derive the equivalence.

TAX BASE = SALES − COST OF MATERIALS

= WAGES + RENTS + INTEREST + PROFITS

+ DEPRECIATION

The latter expression, when summed over all firms in the economy, equals GNP, which, in turn, equals total final sales in the economy.

Finally, that a CVA is equivalent to a proportional tax upon consumption can be established by the definition of the firm's tax base.

TAX BASE = SALES − COST OF MATERIALS − CAPITAL OUTLAYS

This, when summed over all firms, yields GNP − AGGREGATE INVESTMENT, which is equal to aggregate consumption. In effect, the CVA amounts to a retail sales tax collected at the different stages of the production process.

That a CVA, if in effect long enough, approximates a tax upon wages, can be seen by observing that immediate expensing of capital outlays effectively offsets any future tax burden on the income from the new capital. Hence, if all capital in place had been so expensed, the tax burden must fall entirely upon labour income. A CVA is thus equal to a tax upon current wages and a capital levy upon the capital that was in place at the time of enactment. Over time, the importance of the capital levy aspect of the CVA will diminish, so that after some point in time the tax will have an incidence identical to a wage tax.

ECONOMIC EFFECTS. Given these equivalences, the economic effects of VAT will be the same as that of its equal partner. Since the economics of income and consumption taxes has received extensive treatment elsewhere, there is little reason for repeating it here. Suffice it to say that the CVA will promote capital accumulation the most, followed by the IVA, and then the GVA. This follows directly the generosity extended capital consumption allowances under the different schemes. The presumption also is that the variants will share the same ranking with respect to income inequality, reflecting the fact that capital income is more concentrated than labour income.

BORDER ADJUSTMENTS. Much has been made in the literature of the fact that, in open economies a VAT could be levied upon production *or* consumption. The tax will fall upon production if no border adjustments are made with respect to the tax. Similarly, if imports are subjected to the VAT, while exported goods are exempt in full, the tax is alleged to fall upon consumption – i.e., all goods used up within the economy are subject to the same rate of tax, while goods shipped outside the economy are unaffected. These different treatments are usually referred to as the origin and destination principles, respectively. The destination principle is usually favoured because it is neutral towards international trade. The relative prices of imported and domestic goods are unaffected as are the relative prices of exported goods and those prevailing in world markets. Despite the prevailing wisdom, the distinction between the two principles of border adjustment may be vacuous – at least in the long run. This is most easily seen within the context of a flexible exchange rate system. The origin principle amounts to a *de facto* devaluation of a nation's currency. As such, it can be counteracted by a formal appreciation of the exchange rate. The latter will follow naturally if the monetary authorities do not allow the VAT to be reflected in higher goods prices. This will require that factor prices fall so as to absorb the tax. Such a set of price adjustments will lead to exactly the same impact on the terms of trade as would be realized under the destination principle. The fall in factor prices negates the cost effect of VAT upon exports and keeps domestic goods' prices in line with those of imports. Note that, under the destination principle, if the monetary authorities refused to permit the VAT to be passed along in higher prices, exports would be stimulated and imports restricted. Thus, the alleged neutrality of the destination principle rests upon the monetary authorities willingness to ratify price increases. Even if they do, however, the outcome may not be materially different under the origin principle. For here the stimulus to imports and retardation of exports that would result initially would cause the exchange rate to depreciate – offsetting the effect of the tax. Thus the superiority of the destination principle rests with the presumption that the monetary authorities would permit prices to rise and that the necessary depreciation of the exchange rate associated with the origin principle would take some time to materialize.

ADMINISTRATION ISSUES. There are three alternative ways of collecting the tax: (1) the addition method; (2) the subtraction method; (3) the credit method. Under the first method factor payments (plus a suitable allowance for depreciation) are added to arrive at the tax base. This approach makes most sense if the origin principle is sought. The subtraction method requires that firms subtract their purchases from sales to determine their tax base. The credit method is much the same as the subtraction method with an added degree of incentive for taxpayer compliance. Here the firm is taxed fully on its receipts and is allowed a credit for any value-added taxes shown on invoices from suppliers. Hence the firm has a monetary incentive to see that its suppliers document their tax liability. The credit approach makes most sense when the destination principle is used. Here, credits to exporters are easily arranged, and taxation of imports follows directly.

OTHER ISSUES. The value-added tax has also substantial possibilities for sub-national units. While such governments often employ a close cousin to the VAT – the retail sales tax – there may be advantages of using VAT alongside or as a substitute for a retail sales tax. For one thing, since it is collected in stages, the VAT is not as vulnerable to evasion as a single stage levy. Second, it is easier to target preferential rates under the VAT than under the retail sales tax. For example, if it is decided to give relief to producers of certain intermediate goods – for example, farmers – this can be done without having to exempt food expenditures entirely. The issue of border adjustments is much more substantive for the application of VAT at the sub-national level. For here the exchange rate is fixed, the money supply is endogenous, and, most importantly, factors of production are mobile. The latter means that if the origin principle is used and the VAT is not a perfect benefit tax, the region will suffer an increase in imported goods, a decrease in exports, and a reduction in population and capital stock. Thus, sub-national governments should probably opt for the destination principle. Oddly, the only state in the USA which has adopted a VAT, Michigan, uses a variant of the origin approach.

Finally, there has been some question as to whether the value-added tax fosters the growth of government. A VAT can be a prodigious revenue producer because it can be levied on a very broad base and need not be subject to the exemptions, deductions, and exclusions associated with the income tax. Moreover since the point of collection is the firm, it remains relatively invisible to the average taxpayer. This is in sharp contrast to the personal income tax and the payroll tax, two principle sources of direct tax revenue. The VAT is also less visible than the two principal forms of indirect taxation widely in use – the sales tax and the property tax. Only the corporate income tax compares in obscurity to the average citizen. But here, the tax is highly visible to the business community which it affects, and this group has been very vigorous in opposing increases in tax burdens. Indeed, their success is such that many observers believe that the corporate income tax in the USA has been effectively repealed via liberalized depreciation rules and tax credits for investment. While the VAT is the legal liability of business, its incidence is upon consumers and factor earners. Hence, business firms may not be as vigilant in opposing increases in VAT once the system is in place. The preceding remarks explain the rather paradoxical result that conservatives, who usually support reduced taxation for business and investment, oppose the adoption of VAT. The opposition stems from a conviction that the VAT will give rise to a larger public sector than would otherwise be the case. To support this claim they point to those countries in Europe which have adopted a VAT. Almost without exception, these countries lie well above the median for the share of GNP represented by government. Thus, the spread of value-added taxation may hinge upon its political as opposed to economic characteristics.

William H. Oakland

See also CONSUMPTION TAXATION; NEUTRAL TAXATION; OPTIMAL TAXATION.

value analysis. *See* MARXIAN VALUE ANALYSIS.

value and price. The problem of the relationship between value and price – the so called Transformation Problem – is a central issue in Marxian economics. In one sense it can be posed as a technical or mathematical problem of deriving a set of prices from a given set of value equations. But if it were only a technical problem then it should have a definite answer – either a solution exists or it does not. It is surprising therefore that this problem has continued to attract succeeding generations of economists since the date of publication of Volume 3 of *Capital* in 1894 (Marx, 1894).

The debate shows no signs of abating and seems a rare example of a problem which continues to invite new solutions or versions in new mathematical language of the old solution. There can rarely have been a question in economic theory which has been solved so many times in so many different mathematical languages but yet not resolved finally. This continuing fascination of the Transformation Problem leads one to suspect that there is more than a technical issue at stake.

The *locus classicus* of the debate is chapter IX of *Capital* Vol. 3 (3/IX), which was published posthumously by Engels from notes left by Marx. There is evidence however that the material contained in this volume was written some time in the 1860s before the publication of *Capital* Vol. 1 (Marx, 1867). This is of more than biographical interest in the debate. In Vol. 1, Marx developed his theory on the explicit assumption that values and prices were proportional to each other. This was done in awareness of two qualifying conditions; *first* that this was a special case and generally value and prices were related systematically but not proportionally, but *second* that values and value relations were unobservable, latent or structural whereas prices were observable, actual and phenomenal. The hidden nature of value relations – commodity fetishism – is crucial to Marx's argument and hence it would have been totally uncharacteristic of Marx's approach not to have foreseen that values and prices diverge from each other.

This divergence of prices from values emerged as a central result of 3/IX and was seized upon by Böhm-Bawerk in his *Karl Marx and the Close of His System* (1896; Sweezy, 1949) as a basic deficiency and disproof of Marx's theory of profits. He took it to be a complication that may have arisen in Marx's work after he had written the first volume and an impression was conveyed that the price value divergence, being contrary to the proportionality assumed in Vol. 1, invalidated the conclusions in that volume.

If Böhm-Bawerk was able to gain and convey this impression it was because Marx's attempt at solving the Transformation Problem *looks* unfinished. Having derived a numerical solution for prices from a set of value equations, as we will see below, Marx confronts the divergence as a puzzle and then spends some pages tacking around the problem but in no way presenting it as a systematic outcome. Thus it could be thought from reading 3/IX that the Transformation Problem was left unsolved.

THE PROBLEM. Marx's theory of profit was that profits were the money form of surplus value produced by labour during the production process. The conversion of surplus value into profits was accomplished not at the level of the firm but of the whole economy. This conversion had to be effected in the context of a contractual purchase of labour by employers (i.e. no extraeconomic coercion) and secondly, the rate of profit had to be equal in all activities. The first consideration meant that the wage rate – the exchange value of the commodity sold by the labourer and bought by the employer – was determined on the same principles as any other commodity. Thus the existence of surplus value had to be reconciled with an economic determination of the exchange value of the commodity labour power.

To drive a wedge between the product of labour and its price, Marx used the accepted distinction between use value and exchange value of a commodity. The commodity in question, labour power, is the labourer's potential for production. The use-value of labour power to the purchaser of the commodity – the capitalist employer – was measured in terms of the total labour time contracted to be spent by the labourer in production – the length of the working day in hours. The exchange value of labour power, like that of any other commodity, was the amount of labour time required for its reproduction, measured by the labour time equivalent of the basket of wage goods purchasable by the given wage. Having thus obtained two commensurable measures of the use value and the exchange value of labour power, the wedge between them was identified as surplus value, produced by the labourer but retained by the purchaser of labour power, the capitalist employer.

Now the total value of a commodity comprised the value contained in the materials used up in the production process – raw materials and energy used as well as the wear and tear of the fixed means of production – which Marx labelled *constant capital* (c) and the total value contributed by labourers. The latter consists of the exchange value of the wage, i.e. of paid labour, labelled variable capital (v) by Marx, and surplus labour (value) (s) which was the remainder. Given this framework the proportion of surplus value to value paid for (constant capital plus variable capital) is defined as the (value) rate of profit. This quantity can be expressed as a product of the rate of surplus value (s/v) and the organic composition of capital ($c/c+v$). Thus, the (value) rate of profit ρ in the ith economic activity

$$p_i = \frac{s_i}{v_i}\left[1 - \frac{c_i}{(c_i + v_i)}\right] = r_i(1 - g_i) \qquad (1)$$

where r_i is the rate of surplus value and g_i is the organic composition of capital. But if this were the basis of actual profits, activities with higher proportion of living labour would earn a higher rate of profit (given identical rates of exploitation) relative to one with the lesser labour intensive activity. But since we have to provide for equal rates of profit in all activities, a further step has to be taken to reconcile the theory of unequal value rates of profit with equal actual (or price) rates of profit.

Marx envisaged a pooling of surplus value from all activities at the level of economy and then its redistribution in a transformed form as profits equiproportional to the amount of capital (fixed and variable) invested in each activity. This was done by the price of a product departing from its unit value. The ratio would be above one for activities with organic composition of capital above average and below one for those below average. This condition will reconcile the unequal value rates of profit, given equal rates of surplus value with equal (price) rates of profit. Indeed for Marx this gives a usable rule to predict transfer of surplus value from one sector to another as he did use in his chapter on Absolute Rent (3/XLV).

The problem is however that the numerical example used in 3/IX contained a conceptual error (though this is disputed as we shall see below) which gave the calculations a tentative, half-finished, unsolved appearance. This can be best explained by setting out Marx's numerical example but in a more general notation. He took five activities labelled $i = 1, \ldots, 5$, each using as inputs constant capital c_i and variable capital v_i with the g_i being different in each activity from the other. The output of the activities were not specifically identified nor was it clear whether they were of the constant capital or the variable capital category. To keep the inputs and outputs separate therefore let input prices be labelled p_c, p_v and output prices p_i.

The value of output can be expressed as

$$\begin{aligned} y_i &= c_i + v_i + s_i = \{[1 + r(1 - g_i)]/(1 - g_i)\}v_i \\ &= [(1 + \rho_i)/(1 - g_i)]v_i \qquad (2) \end{aligned}$$

In equation (2), we have used equation (1) and assumed as Marx did that the rate of exploitation is identical in all activities. (All the variables total value y_i as well as c_i, v_i could be interpreted as being per unit of physical output if thought convenient.) Corresponding to (2), the price (total revenue) of output was written by Marx as

$$p_i = (1 + \pi)(c_i + v_i) = ((1 + \pi)/(1 - g_i))v_i \qquad (3)$$

Again but especially in this case, variables could be thought of in terms of per unit of output.

To determine π, the actual (price) rate of profit, Marx imposed the condition that the sum of surplus values in all activities was equal to the total of profits over all activities i.e.

$$\sum_i s_i = r \sum_i v_i = \pi \sum_i (c_i + v_i). \qquad (4a)$$

Since however his five units were taken to be of the same size in terms of total value, he also trivially obtained an alternative normalization condition that the total value produced equalled total revenue, i.e.

$$\sum y_i = \sum p_i \qquad (4b)$$

Using the normalization conditions notice that (2) and (3) together yield

$$p_i/y_i = (1 + \pi)/(1 + \rho_i) = (1 + r(1 - g))/(1 + r(1 - g_i)). \qquad (5)$$

Thus strict proportionality of prices and values can only hold if either the rate of exploitation is zero i.e. no exploitation or for the case of identical organic compositions of capital $g_i = g$. Given (4b) it was not difficult to see that the price value differences cancel out in the aggregate. While Marx found some positive and some negative deviations of p_i from y_i, he had no precise explanation to offer at this stage. It is obvious however as he saw that (5) implies

$$p_i/y_i \gtrless 1 \quad \text{as} \quad g_i \gtrless \bar{g} \quad \text{where} \quad \bar{g} = \sum \bar{c}_i \Big/ \sum (c_i + v_i).$$

The problem with Marx's calculation is not that prices diverge from values; that they must, but that the specification of (3) is mistaken if (5) holds. The correct way to write the price equation is to weight the inputs by their respective prices, i.e.

$$p_i = (1 + \pi)(p_c c_i + p_v v_i). \qquad (3a)$$

At one level, we can see that Marx made a mistake in considering the cost of inputs in value terms rather than in price terms. It has been argued however (Shaikh, 1977; Morishima and Catephores, 1975) that (2)–(5) can be thought of as the first stage of an ergodic process. By substituting the values obtained by (5) into (3) to modify the input prices, the calculations will converge so that the prices in (5) and (3) would be consistent with each other.

But this can only be done if the physical specification of c_i and v_i is matched to one or more of the commodities produced. If this is not done then we have two more prices than we can solve for. It was Bortkiewicz's merit to have reformulated Marx's problem using Marx's Reproduction Schemes outlined in *Capital* Vol. 2 to allow for matching specification of physical outputs and inputs with constant and variable capital. This allowed him to reduce the size of the problem (the number of unknowns) and allow for aggregate availability constraints on inputs and outputs. He took a model with three commodities (industries or departments) with Department 1 'capital' good (constant capital), Department 2 'wage' good (variable capital) and Department 3 capitalists' consumption (luxury) good. Thus, two of his three commodities were inputs as well as outputs in the production process i.e. they are basic in the sense of Sraffa but the third one is an output to be consumed but not an input.

Let the three departments (commodities) be denoted as $j = 1, 2, 3$. The value equations are the same as in Marx but Bortkiewicz's treatment allows a clearer input–output demarcation. Thus, the value equations can be written

$$y_j = y_{1j} + (1 + r)y_{2j} \qquad (6)$$

where y_{ij} is the input of good i in the output of good j etc. The price equations are

$$p_j = (1 + \pi)\sum_i p_i y_{ij}. \qquad (7)$$

Bortkiewicz preserved (4a) as the normalization condition. But in addition he took care to ensure that the conditions of simple reproduction were satisfied. Thus, he imposed for the two inputs

$$y_i = \sum_i y_{ij}, \quad i = 1, 2. \qquad (8)$$

But having implicitly chosen his magnitudes to satisfy (4b) as well, he imposed a condition

$$\sum_j s_j = y_3. \qquad (9)$$

While (8) are conditions on total availability of inputs to sustain the required level of output, equation (9) is a 'consumption function' for the recipients of surplus value. As there is no accumulation by assumption, we require that all surplus value is spent on the 'luxury good' produced by Department 3.

Thus Bortkiewicz correctly formulated the problem and even put it in the appropriate general equilibrium framework lacking in Marx's formulation in 3/IX. The solution is straightforward and need not be given here (see Sweezy, 1942, 1949; Desai, 1979). This should have settled any debate about the problem. It emerges that prices are systematic functions of values but are not proportional to them. But the solution was published in German in 1907 and did not become generally known until Sweezy described it in his *Theory of Capitalist Development*, nor did it become available until Sweezy's translation of it in 1949. Within this forty-year interval, economists' knowledge of the linear model had advanced as a result of the works of Leontieff and von Neumann. It was obvious therefore that the problem could be reformulated in these terms. Winternitz proposed such a formulation in 1949 and full general solution in terms of n goods was given by Morishima and Seton (1961). Roemer (1980) has shown that the linearity assumption can be dropped and a solution in the 'Arrow–Debreu language' can be obtained.

Two areas of controversy arose during the 1970s. First was whether it was necessary to go through the transformation problem at all to solve for prices from physical input-output data. This was raised by Samuelson (1971). Second is a more serious question about the conditions required for solution when there is joint production in the von Neumann–Sraffa sense.

Samuelson's point can be simply made. In order to arrive at value equations such as (2) or (6), we have to translate the data which are in terms of physical output flows and labour inputs into the direct and indirect labour content of inputs. After such a translation, we proceed with the transformation. But as we know from input–output analysis, from the physical input data, one can directly solve for prices from the dual of the Leontieff matrix. If one thought of the purpose of the exercise to provide merely a set of prices consistent with a set of values, he is entirely right. What the criticism misses, however, is that if we were to follow Marx's purpose in providing a theory of profits, the separation of labour input into paid and unpaid components (which assumes a political economic background) and the use of the concept of the rate of exploitation are required. If one is to reject Marx's theory of profits, it can be done quite independently of the Transformation Problem, as Wicksteed was able to do even before the publication of *Capital* Vol. 3 since he rejected the labour theory of value, classical or Marxian, as such (Wicksteed, 1884; see Desai, 1979, for details).

The second line of criticism is much more serious. This is because it claims that positive surplus value is neither necessary nor sufficient for positive profits i.e. it denies the existence of any mapping from values to prices that can satisfy certain general conditions. The problem is with Marx's treatment of fixed capital. In his formulation of the value equations, Marx takes a flow measure of non-labour inputs. This suffices if all capital equipment has only one period life since then the stock and flow measures are equivalent. But if the capital equipment lives beyond the production period some account has to be taken of this in writing the value and prices equations. Bortkiewicz was also able to formulate this problem with different rates of turnover of capital i.e. different lengths of life in another, even lesser known, paper of his (Bortkiewicz, 1906–7). But he took the rates of turnover to be fixed and known in advance. This is less general than one wishes (see Desai (1979) for a description). Marx can be said to have used implicitly a neoclassical accounting whereby the rental on capital correctly measures its productive contribution. But as Morishima (1973) points out a von Neumann accounting scheme in a 'joint production' model is more appropriate.

It was Steedman (1977) who first constructed a numerical example in which there is negative surplus value but positive profit. This is an example of the generic case of non-convexities which are known to arise in activity analysis (Koopmans, 1951). Steedman made it however an argument for abandoning Marxian value theory in favour of a Ricardo–Sraffa formulation. This suggestion has parallels with Samuelson's suggestion since the detour via labour values can be shown to be misleading in some cases. It has also been pointed out that the non-convexity problem can arise in the Ricardo–Sraffa scheme just as much as in the Marx scheme. Morishima (1973, 1975) has taken the view that all that is necessary is to reformulate the value price problem under joint production with appropriate inequality constraints so that non-negativity of (surplus) values and prices are assured. This would seem the more rigorous formulation. The question does remain however of the behavioural foundations of the mechanism that will ensure that in a capitalist economy, only activities with positive surplus values are chosen.

The transformation problem thus continues to fascinate economists even as they debate its relevance. It formed the basis in Bortkiewicz's case for an early formulation of a general equilibrium problem in linear terms. It has been argued that it is more appropriate for planning calculations in a socialist economy than in a capitalist economy whose workings it was supposed to illuminate (Samuelson and Weiszacker, 1971; Morishima, 1973). To Marxists as to their opponents, more important issues such as the moral justification for capitalism seem to be at stake in the solution or non-solution of this seemingly arid technical problem. This is one reason why it will no doubt go on attracting new solutions and new attacks.

MEGHNAD DESAI

See also BORTKIEWICZ, LADISLAUS VON; SWEEZY, PAUL MALOR.

BIBLIOGRAPHY

Böhm-Bawerk, E.R. von. 1896. Zum Abschluss des Marxschen System. In *Staatswissenschaftliche Arbeiten: festgaben für Karl Knies*, ed. O.V. Boenig, Berlin. Trans. as 'Karl Marx and the close of his system' in Sweezy (1949).

Bortkiewicz, L. von. 1906–7. Wertrechnung und Preisrechnung im Marxschen System. *Archiv fur Sozialwissenschaft und Sozialpolitik*, July 1906, July and September 1907. Trans. as: Value and price in the Marxian system. In *International Economic Papers* No. 2, ed. Alan T. Peacock et al., London and New York: Macmillan, 1952.

Bortkiewicz, L. von. 1907. Zur Berichtigung der grundlegenden theoretischen konstruktion von Marx im dritten Band des 'Kapital'. *Jahrbucher für Nationalökonomie und Statistik*, July. Trans. as: 'On the Correction of Marx's Fundamental Theoretical Construction in the Third Volume of *Capital*' as Appendix in Sweezy (1949).

Desai, M. 1979. *Marxian Economics*. Oxford: Basil Blackwell.

Koopmans, T.C. 1951. *Activity Analysis of Production and Allocation.* Cowles Commission Monograph No. 13, New York: John Wiley.
Marx, K. 1894. *Das Kapital*, Volume III. Ed. F. Engels, Hamburg: Otto Meissner.
Morishima, M. 1973. *Marx's Economics: A Dual Theory of Value and Growth*. Cambridge: Cambridge University Press.
Morishima, M. and Catephores, G. 1975. The transformation problem: a Markov process. In *Value Exploitation and Growth – Marx in the Light of Modern Economic Theory*, ed. M. Morishima, New York: McGraw–Hill.
Morishima, M. and Seton, F. 1961. Aggregation in Leontief matrices and the labour theory of value. *Econometrica* 29, 203–20.
Roemer, J. 1980. A general equilibrium approach to marxian economics. *Econometrica* 48, March, 505–30.
Samuelson, P.A. 1971. Understanding the marxian notion of exploitation: a summary of the so-called transformation problem between marxian values and competitive prices. *Journal of Economic Literature* 9(2), June, 399–431.
Samuelson, P.A. 1972. *The Collected Scientific Papers of Paul A. Samuelson*, Vol. 3. Ed. Robert C. Merton, Cambridge, Mass.: MIT Press.
Samuelson, P.A. and Weiszacker, C. 1971. A new labour theory of value for rational planning through the use of the bourgeois profit rate. *Proceedings of the National Academy of Sciences*, June. Also in Samuelson (1972).
Schwartz, J. 1977. *The Subtle Anatomy of Capitalism*. Santa Monica, California.
Shaikh, A. 1977. Marx's theory of value and the transformation problem. In Schwartz (1977).
Steedman, I. 1977. *Marx after Sraffa*. London: New Left Books.
Sweezy, P.M. 1942. *The Theory of Capitalist Development*. New York: Monthly Review Press.
Sweezy, P.M. (ed.) 1949. *Karl Marx and the Close of His System* by E. von Böhm-Bawerk and Böhm-Bawerk's criticism of Marx by Hilferding. New York: Augustus Kelly.
Wicksteed, P.H. 1884. Das Kapital: a criticism. First published in *Today*, October 1884, reprinted in P.H. Wicksteed, *The Commonsense of Political Economy* Vol. II, 1933.
Winternitz, J. 1948. Values and prices: A solution of the so-called transformation problem. *Economic Journal* 58, 276–80.

value judgements.

THE CLAIM OF OBJECTIVE VALIDITY. One may define value judgements as judgements of approval or disapproval claiming objective validity. Many of our judgements of approval and disapproval do not involve such claims. When I say that I like a particular dish, I do not mean to imply that other people ought to like it too or that those disliking it are making a mistake. All I am doing is expressing my personal preference and my personal taste. (But an expert chef or an expert food critic may very well claim that his judgements about food have some degree of objective validity – in the sense that other gastronomic experts would tend to agree with his judgements. Of course, it is an empirical question whether his claim would be justified and, more generally, how much agreement there is in fact among expert judges of food.) Yet when I say that Hitler's murder of many millions of innocent people was a moral outrage, I do mean to do more than express my personal moral attitudes and do mean to imply that anybody who tried to defend Hitler's actions would be morally wrong.

In claiming objective validity, value judgements resemble factual judgements (both those dealing with empirical facts and those dealing with logical-mathematical facts). But they resemble judgements of personal preference in expressing human attitudes (those of approval or disapproval) rather than expressing beliefs about matters of fact, as factual judgements do. But this immediately poses a difficult philosophical problem: We can understand what it means for factual judgements to be objectively valid, i.e., to be true, or to be objectively invalid, i.e., to be false. They will be true if they describe the relevant facts as these facts actually are, and will be false if they fail to do so. But in what sense can judgements expressing human attitudes be objectively valid or invalid?

It seems to me that this can happen in at least two different ways. Such judgements can be objectively invalid either because they are contrary to the facts or because they are based on the wrong value perspective. Value judgements can be contrary to the facts in the following sense: When we form our attitudes, we do so on the basis of some specific factual assumptions so that our attitudes and our judgements expressing these attitudes will be contrary to the facts if they are based on false factual assumptions. Mistaken factual assumptions may vitiate both our value judgements about instrumental values and those about intrinsic values. Thus, if I approve of using A as a means to achieve some end B, I will do this on the assumption that A is causally effective in achieving B. Hence, my approval will be mistaken if this assumption is incorrect. Likewise, if I approve of A as an intrinsically desirable goal, I will do this on the assumption that A has some qualities I find intrinsically attractive. My approval will be mistaken if in fact A does not possess these qualities.

Another way of value judgement may be objectively invalid is by being based on a value perspective different from the one it claims to have. For example, I may claim that my support for some government policy is based on its being in the public interest, even though actually it is based on its being in my own personal interest. Or, I may praise a very undistinguished novel as a great work of art merely because it supports my own political point of view. When a person claims to base his value judgement on one value perspective though actually he bases it on another, he may be simply lying, being fully aware of not telling the truth. Another possibility is that he is unaware, or only half aware, of using a value perspective different from the one he claims to use. (Likewise, when a person is making a value judgement based on false factual assumptions, he may or may not be fully aware of the falsity of these assumptions.)

DISAGREEMENTS IN VALUE JUDGEMENTS. As we all know, disagreements in value judgements are extremely common and in many cases are very hard, or even impossible, to resolve. It seems to me that in most cases careful analysis would show that these disagreements about values are based on disagreements about the facts. Yet, they may be very hard to resolve because these factual disagreements may be about very subtle facts about which reliable information is very hard, or even impossible, to obtain. For instance, our value judgements about a person's behaviour will often crucially depend on what we think his motives are. Some observers may attribute very noble motives to him, while others may do the opposite. Yet, the available evidence might be consistent with either assumption. Other value judgements we make may hinge on our predictions about future facts. Thus, different economists may advocate very different economic policies because they have very different expectations on the likely effects of specific policies – even if their ultimate policy objectives are much the same. Yet, at the present stage of our knowledge about the economic system, we may be unable to tell with any degree of confidence which predictions are right and which are wrong.

Of course, we could avoid most of these disagreements if we refrained from making value judgements until we could ascertain with some assurance that the factual assumptions underlying the value judgements we want to make are correct.

But this would require more intellectual self-discipline than most of us can muster. We have to act one way or another; and it is psychologically much easier for us to act if we can manage to entertain value judgements justifying our actions – even if the factual assumptions underlying these value judgements go far beyond, or are even clearly inconsistent with, the available evidence.

Let me add that most disagreements in value judgements are not disagreements about what the basic values of human life actually are. Rather, most disagreements are about the relative weights and the relative priorities to be assigned to different basic values. Some individuals and some societies will learn from their experience – possibly based on a very idiosyncratic personal or national history – that things tend to work out best if value A is given far greater weight than value B is. Other individuals and other societies will reach very much the opposite conclusion on the basis of their experience. Once a given ranking of these two values has been adopted, it may be retained for a long time even when conditions change and make this ranking utterly inappropriate. For instance, an individual or a society that suffered a good deal from lack of individual freedom may be so preoccupied with political liberty as to neglect the need for social discipline – even under conditions that would make the need for social discipline paramount.

Besides disagreements about the facts, another source of value conflicts are philosophical disagreements about the correct value perspectives to be used in making various classes of value judgements. For instance, even if two people agree about all the relevant facts, they may still make conflicting moral value judgements if they disagree about the nature of morality and, therefore, disagree about the nature of the moral perspective to be used in making moral value judgements. (For instance, one individual may favour a utilitarian interpretation of morality (see, e.g., Harsanyi, 1977), while the other may favour an entitlement interpretation (see Nozick, 1974).) In the same way, disagreements about the nature of the aesthetic perspective to be used in making aesthetic value judgements may lead to disagreements about the artistic quality of various works of art.

VALUE JUDGEMENTS IN ECONOMICS. There was a time when many economists wanted to ensure the objectivity of economic analysis by excluding value judgements, and even the study of value judgements, from economics. (A very influential advocate of this position has been Robbins, 1932.) Luckily, they have not succeeded; and we now know that economics would have been that much poorer if they had.

After some important preliminary work in the Thirties and the Forties, mainly in welfare economics, a new era in the study of economically relevant value judgements, has started with Arrow's *Social Choice and Individual Values* (1951). This book has shown how to express alternative value judgements in the form of precisely stated formal axioms, how to investigate their logical implications in a rigorous manner, and how to examine their mutual consistency or inconsistency. Arrow's book and the research inspired by it have greatly enriched economic theory not only in welfare economics but also in several other fields, including the theory of competitive equilibrium. It has given rise to a new subdiscipline called *public choice theory*, which is a rigorous study of voting and of alternative voting systems and which has made important contributions to the study of alternative political systems and of alternative moral codes and, more indirectly, to the study of alternative economic systems as mechanisms of social choice.

Of course, value judgements often play an important role in economics even when they are not the main subjects of investigation. They influence the policy recommendations made by economists and their judgements about the merits of alternative systems of economic organization. But this need not impair the social utility of the work done by economists as long as it is work of high intellectual quality and as long as the economists concerned *know* what they are doing, *know* the qualifications their conclusions are subject to, and *tell* their readers what these qualifications are. In particular, intellectual honesty requires economists to *state* their political and moral value judgements and to make clear how their conclusions differ from those that economists of different points of view would tend to reach on the problems under discussion. What is no less important, they should make clear how *uncertain* many of their empirical claims and their predictions actually are. This is particularly important in publications addressed mainly to people outside the economist profession.

JOHN C. HARSANYI

See also ENTITLEMENTS; INTERPERSONAL UTILITY COMPARISONS; PHILOSOPHY AND ECONOMICS; POSITIVISM.

BIBLIOGRAPHY

Arrow, K.J. 1951. *Social Choice and Individual Values*. New York: Wiley.

Harsanyi, J.C. 1977. Morality and the theory of rational behavior. *Social Research* 44, 623–56.

Nozick, R. 1974. *Anarchy, State and Utopia*. Oxford: Blackwell.

Robbins, L. 1932. *An Essay on the Nature and Significance of Economic Science*. London: Macmillan.

value of life. It is not identified lives but statistical lives – the reduction of some mortal hazard to some part of the population – whose value is our topic. But the prolongation of individual lives is getting increased attention, and it deserves some of ours before we get on with the main business.

'Our society values life', a California judge commented when he ordered force-feeding for a quadriplegic woman who wished to die and had asked the hospital's help in starving to death. Medical technology now provides, and medical institutions often require, procedures that prolong lives expensively and indefinitely even when the life is of dubious quality to the patient. These are procedures that the deciding institutions either cannot deny or will not permit to be withdrawn, and they are independent of any assessment of value of the life extension procured. In some cases rejoicing is unanimous when death mercifully terminates an effort to prolong life.

Even assessing the value of statistical lifesaving – reducing some small carcinogenic hazard – is not universally considered properly subject to a comparison of costs and benefits. In the US government there has been controversy whether the cost per life saved should be a consideration in occupational-safety decisions: even the courts have had difficulty construing the legislation to permit taking costs into account. Nor is it generally accepted that hazardous activities should always be relocated to less densely populated areas where fewer would be at risk. Marginal outlays per expected life saved vary among agencies by two orders of magnitude.

In economics, valuing life means the prevention of death, not the creation of people who might never have existed. The economics of overpopulation can draw an economist's attention, but nobody measures the welfare gain to sterile parents of a steady supply of births for adoption. Economies of scale to population size in a sparsely populated area are easy to handle; but the value of simply having more 'lives' – more people born to enjoy life – is rarely discussed in our profession. It is only philosophers (Parfit, 1984, pp. 351–454, 487–90), and few of them, who write about 'whether causing someone to exist can benefit this person'. Our topic is therefore asymmetrical. I confine this essay to the value of preventing deaths because that is what the subject has been, but we can hope that the next Palgrave may have a more symmetrical topic to pursue.

WORTH TO WHOM?

The first principle that ought to bear on what it is worth to save a statistical life – to reduce a mortal risk to some part of the population – is that there ought to be some person or collection of persons to whom it is worth something. To whom is it worth something to reduce the risk of death to some identified part of the population? We can begin with the people at risk. They may not be good at calculating risks and handling probabilities and expected values; they may give exaggerated emphasis to risks that are mysterious or sensational; but if they are susceptible, they care; and unless their attitude is wholly superstitious they are likely to recognize that reducing statistical risks to their own and their families' lives is worth paying for. What is at stake is not only life itself but grief and the permanent loss of parents, children and spouses.

Many of the people targeted for risk reduction will be financially responsible for others. The family has an economic interest in the parent's continued living. The importance of the parent's livelihood, in contrast to his living, will depend on the private and public insurance and other arrangements to care for his dependents.

Social and private insurance, charities, and all the claims that the deceased's family will exercise introduce another set of interests – all the people and institutions that are sources or recipients of transfers on account of the death. The fact that in one respect the transfers cancel out – the dependents of the deceased showing receipts equivalent to the public and private payments to them – does not make them uninteresting. The transfers change and broaden the answer to the question, to whom is it worth something that these deaths be prevented.

Transfers can go in either direction. Some of the current discussions of health policy neglect this important fact. It is often alleged that people who smoke impose costs on the health-care system and should be penalized through higher cigarette taxes or health insurance premiums. But the typical lung cancer victim enriches the society he leaves behind. The median age for lung cancer is 65 and most victims are dead within a year; the median male retirement age in the United States is about 63; a 65-year-old male victim loses an expected fifteen years of life. Discounting at 5 per cent, if he is without dependents he relinquishes upwards of $50,000 in social security benefits, and if he was at the median income level during his pre-retirement years he may relinquish a like amount in private pensions. His terminal illness inflicts a small fraction of that on the health insurers (and he will not be around to be hospitalized again later in life).

Lung cancer reminds us that our financial stakes in the continued living of those among us who are at risk can be positive or negative. Aggregating the financial interests, positive and negative, that different people may have in the demise or longevity of some segment of the population is simpler than distinguishing local and national tax payer interests, occupational interests in shared retirement funds, or policyholder interests in the claims exercised on a life insurance company. For policy purposes the question of who has interest in reducing (or not reducing) some mortal risk may be as important as how big the algebraic sum of those interests is.

So far we have identified two sources of 'value' for enhanced survival, the 'consumer interest' of a family in its own survival and the externalities that take mainly the form of transfers to or from the consuming unit. Whether it makes sense to add up the transfers into a net figure and add that figure to the consumer's own value will depend on the purpose for which some calculation of worth is desired. If the purpose, for example, is to see whether there are enough votes to support a programme that may save lives there may be jurisdictional constraints on the components that go into one's estimate of worth.

There are other interests. One that has received attention is the Gross National Product that is lost when a person dies (Rice, 1967; Hartunian, Smart and Thompson, 1981, pp. 41–56). The 'value' of the lives lost in motorcycle accidents that could have been saved with helmets has been approximated by the discounted lifetime earnings of the kinds of people who die in motorcycle accidents – mostly young men without dependents. But it is difficult to identify anyone to whom this loss accrues. The motorcyclist dies and this piece of the GNP disappears, but so does the person who was going to consume most of it. The economy does not miss him. He could as well have moved to another country. We can of course consider the taxes he paid and the exhaustible public benefits that he consumed, but we did that already in considering those transfers. It is not worth anything to the economy to spare his life. (The point can be reduced to absurdity by observing that a modest extension of this methodology discovers that abortions in the United States are 'costing the economy' a quarter of a trillion dollars every year.)

CONCERN FOR OTHERS' LIVES

To this point I have looked at selfish interests. What about our compassionate interest in the longevity of fellow citizens, or our charitable interests in the lives of those who are especially at risk because their poverty exposes them to hazards? What is the government's obligation for the safety of its citizens and how should it assess the worth of a programme, regulatory or budgetary, that may save some expected number of lives?

The question especially arises because many of the activities that promise to reduce mortality are public goods. We can find motorcycle helmets, smoke detectors and seatbelts in the market, but if we want more effective treatment for coronary heart disease we have to expect publicly financed medical research to carry the burden. (The research, of course, does not have to be financed by our own government to benefit us, as rescue and regulation would.)

How should the government, then, evaluate the lifesaving consequences of an activity that requires budgetary outlays or imposes regulatory costs on its citizens? Take the question on two assumptions, first that all families share equally in the potential benefits and, second, that programmes discriminate in their benefits by age, wealth, occupation, health status, or geographical location. 'Sharing equally' could mean either of two things: equal reductions in some risk of dying, or equal extensions of life expectancy, the difference depending mainly on age. If we take families as the sharing units, age differences will average out somewhat (and we can avoid the questions whether or not to count a foetus as a child). For simplicity assume that if citizens share equally in the expected reduction of mortality they also share equally in the associated transfers. This assumption is certainly false and is introduced only to reduce the scope of this essay.

In a first approximation I see no reason why a legislator or administrator should not approach mortal-risk-reducing activities in the same way he approaches activities that raise productivity, save time, reduce annoyance, provide entertainment, or reduce the discomforts of nonfatal illness (Schelling, 1968; Mishan, 1971; Zeckhauser, 1975). Specifically, one considers how the beneficiaries value the reduced mortality compared with what they could have procured with lower taxes or prices. It is always the case that some citizens value these things differently from others even when they benefit equality; that is in no way peculiar to risk reduction.

A way in which mortal-risk reduction differs from other benefits is in the lesser likelihood that the beneficiaries of reductions in small risks can articulate what it is worth to them or even discuss it reasonably when the issue arises. Traffic lights that reduce congestion are more susceptible to public hearings to establish their money values than lights primarily intended to save children's lives. On the other hand there is an economy of information to be enjoyed in connection with lifesaving if the principle can be adopted that, where all the citizens share equally in the reduced mortality, all benefits will be measured proportionately to the lives saved. (Or, if people so choose, life-years saved; see below.) If lifesaving is valued identically for traffic lights, cancer research, and police protection, one good determination of the 'value of lives saved' can be used repeatedly within any jurisdiction in which the character of the population has not changed much since that determination was made. This kind of determination has rarely if ever been done in any jurisdiction, but the same can probably be said of the value of noise reduction. The problem is not in the theory.

The hard issues arise when the benefits are not shared equally, and especially when the beneficiaries of a risk-reducing activity will be poor, or the innocent victims of the location of some hazardous activity. The debate in this case is familiar. Economists usually argue that if the beneficiaries are going to pay for the activity it is their valuations that should govern the decision. And even if it is difficult to penetrate their valuations it can be concluded that the poor will value risk reduction, compared to the other things that money will buy, less than the well-to-do.

It is only one step to the corollary that when the poor are to be provided greater safety at the expense of the well-to-do it should still be their privilege to request cash instead that they can spend as they please on other things they value more than the reduction in some life-threatening hazard. Institutionally, however, it is usually not the case that funds available for reducing mortal hazards can be transferred to procurement of whatever the beneficiaries want even more.

There is an argument here that economics cannot resolve. In the days when the *Titanic* hit an iceberg there were lifeboats for first class and tourist, steerage was expected to go down with the ship. The economic efficiency of that arrangement does not necessarily make it appealing; and even letting the poor travel cheaply on densely packed separate ships with no first class and no lifeboats can be objected to on grounds that are not easily dismissed by mere reference to economic efficiency.

SOME TECHNICAL ISSUES

Life vs. risk. Despite emphasis that our topic is *risk reduction*, there is temptation to talk about the value of a *life* saved. If an individual will pay annually (or forego in wages) $100 to reduce some mortal risk to himself from 1:10,000 annually to 1:20,000 – a reduction of 1:10,000 – it is convenient to say that he 'values his own life' at $2 million. That sounds as if, confronted with certain death, he would come up with $2 million to stay alive. But that is not what we meant, and it does not follow from the small-risk calculation. (In particular, there would be income effects if the risk-eliminating payment rose from $100 to $100,000.) What we mean is that 20,000 identical individuals identically at risk would collectively pay $2 million for each yet unidentified averted death among themselves. A terminological proposal is suggested by the unit of measure in part-time hiring, the FTE, 'full-time equivalent'; we can say that our subject values reducing the risk to his own life at $2 million per FLE, 'full life equivalent'.

Years of life saved. 'Saving a life' by reducing some mortal risk means only prolonging it; death eventually ensues. An alternative to the worth per life 'saved' would be the worth per 'year of life' saved. And not all years are worth the same. Some index of 'quality-adjusted life-years' has been proposed. These approaches are alternatives: we can impute more value to young lives than old, or measure benefits in life-years to the same effect.

Insurance. The availability of life insurance should have a powerful influence on the value of risk reduction to the person who provides for a family. Just as one might make heroic and uneconomic investments in fire safety to protect a home or farm that represented all of one's assets if insurance were unavailable, extreme precautions against the risk of death might appear necessary for the young parents of triplets if life insurance could not be procured. Thus any of the institutions that insure the welfare of dependent survivors can help to avoid inefficient investments in longevity. Similarly, older people without dependents might make collectively inefficient investments in longevity out of wealth that they would lose if they died; life annuities are a contractual solution.

Risk and anxiety. The elimination of certain mortal risks, besides saving lives, can reduce anxiety. Fear can afflict those who survive as much as those who die, so it is not double counting to include reduced anxiety among the benefits. But anxiety or concern, according to some studies, is not proportionate to the risk (Starr and Whipple, 1980). Some of it appears due to the stimuli that remind people of the danger, for example stories of violence on the streets at night. Two policy questions result. One is whether governments might wisely and properly give disproportionate emphasis – pay more per life actually saved – where the risks generate extraordinary anxiety, on grounds that the anxiety is commensurate in its impact on welfare with the actual incidence of death. (This would be like weighing nonfatal illness along with the fatal.) The second is whether a responsive government should deploy its resources toward those risks that citizens express most concern about, even when the government has evidence that those concerns are based more on imagination than on fact.

There are two possibilities here. One is that citizens grossly exaggerate some risk – a food additive, radioactivity, night-time violence – and the government knows that the public is simply wrong. The other is that citizens have preferences that are not confined to the arithmetic of life expectancy and consider certain horrors – perhaps those that their minds insist on dwelling on – more worth eliminating than others.

Discounting. Many policies entail current investment in future safety or reduced future mortality. (The two are not the same:

exposure to asbestos or radiation increases the likelihood of cancer some decades later.) The question of discounting arises: is a death averted twenty years hence, or a hundred, worth less than a death averted today? Again: 'worth' to whom? People today who would bear the cost of averting that death a century hence can be expected to be less interested than they would be in averting a death that could be their own or their families', i.e. a death today, just as people who might bear the cost of saving lives in some remote part of the world, not being potential beneficiaries, would have to think of it as charity, not personal safety, and might be less interested.

But many programmes for health and safety are charitably motivated, that is, the expenses are incurred by people who do not expect to benefit. Should they discount future lives saved? There are economic arguments for discounting not the 'lives' but the money value imputed to a future life saved by some expenditure today. (1) Money spent today to save lives in the future could be invested instead to yield a larger lifesaving budget when the time comes, saving more lives. (2) Technological progress may make lifesaving cheaper in the future; wait and take advantage of the lower prices. (3) There is uncertainty about what hazards may disappear in the interim or cease to be lethal, and some of today's outlay will have procured no benefit. (4) And people may be richer in the future and better able to spend their own money to save their own lives. If one does not discount lives saved, the first two arguments together imply a higher marginal productivity in future lifesaving, and that all lifesaving resources should be channelled toward future lives until the marginal costs of future lifesaving have risen to that of current lifesaving. That that is not done is probably evidence that people do discount future lives whether or not they realize that they do.

Implicit valuations. It is sometimes argued that we should look at the implicit valuations expressed in social policy to 'discover' what 'our society' considers lives to be worth. In the United States there are tens of thousands of coronary bypass operations per year at a cost of $25,000 each. Most are undertaken in the hope of prolonging life. Since this surgical technique has been around for only a decade the data on its contribution to life extension are indecisive but suggest that the contribution is at most a year. (Some studies dispute any positive contribution.) Americans apparently acquiesce in the procurement of extended life at $25,000 or more per year. At that rate an averted lung cancer in a 65-year-old is worth (discounted at 5 per cent) upwards of $250,000, a youthful motorcycle fatality upwards of $500,000. These may not be bad numbers; but they do not reflect any explicit determination that the cost of bypass surgery is a reasonable price to pay for the life extension that on average it produces.

Market evidence. Some investigators have examined the relation of wage differentials among occupations or industries to the risk differentials, as measured by accidental deaths and work-related fatal illnesses (Viscusi, 1983). Econometric analysis leads to estimates of implicit own-life FLEs – the income workers forego to work in safer occupations. In 1980 prices, implicit FLEs are obtained over the range from roughly one to five million dollars, with workers in the extremely risky occupations 'revealing' implicit FLEs under one million. The different estimates are partly due to different data and methodologies but probably reflect also individual differences in willingness to trade money against risk of death, and some consequent sorting into the more and the less risky occupations.

THOMAS C. SCHELLING

See also ADVERSE SELECTION; HEALTH, ECONOMICS OF; LIFE INSURANCE; PUBLIC HEALTH.

BIBLIOGRAPHY

Hartunian, N. S., Smart, C.N. and Thompson, M.S. 1981. *The Incidence and Economic Costs of Major Health Impairments.* Lexington: Lexington Books.

Mishan, E.J. 1971. Evaluation of life and limb: a theoretical approach. *Journal of Political Economy* 79, 687–705.

Parfit, D. 1984. *Reasons and Persons.* Oxford: Clarendon Press.

Rice, D. 1967. Estimating the costs of illness. *American Journal of Public Health* 57, 424–40.

Schelling, T.C. 1968. The life you save may be your own. In *Problems in Public Expenditure Analysis*, ed. S.B. Chase, Jr., Washington, DC.: The Brookings Institution.

Starr, C. and Whipple, C. 1980. Risks of risk decisions. *Science* 208, 1114–19.

Viscusi, W.K. 1983. *Risk By Choice.* Cambridge, Mass.: Harvard University Press.

Zeckhauser, R.J. 1975. Procedures for valuing lives. *Public Policy* 23, 419–64.

value of time. Time is a scarce resource or, to use a popular adage – 'time is money'. The value of time depends on its usage and the complementary resources used with it. Firms pay for their workers' time according to the workers' value or marginal product. Households naturally place a value on their time when they sell it in the market, but they also assign a value to the time they use in the home sector. This value determines (and is sometimes determined by) the optimum combination of activities a person engages in, and the optimum combination of goods and time used in each activity. It affects the supply of labour and the demand for goods.

The recognition of the importance of time for many economic decisions related and unrelated to the labour market (e.g., schooling; transportation) is not new. The generalization of the model is associated with Becker's (1965) theory of home production. Becker (following Mincer, 1963) reformulates traditional consumption theory by shifting the focus of analysis from goods to activities ('commodities', in his terms). By this approach the source of the household's welfare is its activities, which in turn, are a combination of goods and time. Welfare is maximized subject to home technology, the budget constraint, and the time constraint. Formally, the welfare function depends on the activity levels (Z_i)

$$U = U(Z_1, \ldots, Z_n)$$

where each activity is 'produced' through a combination of goods (X_i) and time (T_i)

$$Z_i = d_i(X_i, T_i).$$

The consumer's welfare is maximized subject to the budget constraint

$$\Sigma P_i X_i = W(Z_n) + V$$

and the time constraint

$$\Sigma T_i = T,$$

where P_i denote prices, $W(Z_n)$ is labour income (Z_n denoting the activity work in the market), V is non-labour income, and T is the total time available.

The maximization of welfare subject to the home production technology and the time and budget constraints yields the optimum allocation of activities:

$$\partial U / \partial Z_i = \lambda \hat{\Pi}_i,$$

and the optimum combination of inputs in the production of each activity

$$(\partial Z_i/\partial T_i)/(\partial Z_i/\partial X_i) = \hat{W}/P_i,$$

where λ denotes the marginal value of income, $\hat{\Pi}_i$ is the shadow price of activity i, and $\hat{W}$ is the shadow price of time. The shadow price of the activity equals its marginal cost of production

$$\hat{\Pi}_i = P_i(\partial X_i/\partial Z_i) + \hat{W}(\partial T_i/\partial Z_i).$$

Thus an increase in the shadow price of time leads to substitution of time in favour of goods and a substitution from time-intensive to goods-intensive activities.

When there are no external constraints on hours of market work the value people place on their time depends on their marginal wage rate

$$\hat{W} = w + (u_n/\lambda),$$

where w is the marginal wage rate (the change in earnings as a result of a change in market work net of taxes and any expenditures associated with work) and u_n denotes the marginal utility of labour. However, even when one is not free to change one's working hours the shadow price of time increases with wages and with income because of the increase in time scarcity.

The importance of the value of time to allocative decisions has been shown in a wide range of contexts: fertility (Becker, 1960; Willis, 1973; Schultz, 1975), health (Grossman, 1972) and most notably, labour supply and transportation. Thus, women with higher wages have higher opportunity costs of raising children and therefore tend to reduce fertility, substituting 'quality' for 'quantity'. Travellers who place a high value on their time prefer faster but more expensive modes of transport to slower and cheaper modes. Married women with young children or with high earning husbands place higher value on their time and are, therefore, more reluctant to participate in the labour force.

Theory predicts that the shadow price of time changes with the person's wage rate. It does not imply that the two are equal; they differ if the marginal net wage differs from the average wage, when labour involves direct utility (or disutility), or when it is assumed that the utility generated by an activity depends on the time inputs involved (Bruzelius, 1979).

The value of time saving is a major component of the benefits of the investment in many transportation projects (Beesley, 1965; Tipping, 1968). To evaluate the shadow price of time transportation economists studied the trade-off between time and money implicit in the choice of modes of transport, choice of route, location decision, and demand for travel. Studying commuter choices it is found that the value placed by commuters on their time is only 1/5 to 1/2 of their wage rate. The value of walking and waiting time is found to be 2.5–3.0 times greater than the value of in-vehicle time. Differences in convenience, comfort, effort, etc. are reflected in estimates of time value in bus travel that are higher than travel by car, and values that tend to increase with the length of the trip. Finally, differences between the gross and the net wage and constrained working hours result in estimates that are higher for business travel than for personal travel. (For a recent discussion of the estimating methods and results see Bruzelius, 1979.)

A second source for the study of the value of time at home is labour-force-participation behaviour. A person is supposed to participate in the labour force if the wage he is offered exceeds the value of his marginal productivity at home – that is, his value of home time. Studying the labour force participation patterns of US married women Gronau (1973) found that the value of time of these women increases with their schooling (most noticeably with college attendance). It is little affected by the husband's schooling and income and by age, and increase sharply when the family has children. Having a child under 3 years of age increases the value of its mother's time at home by over 25 per cent (in particular if she has a college education), but this effect diminishes as the child grows older.

R. GRONAU

See also FAMILY; GENDER; HOUSEHOLD PRODUCTION; LEISURE; LABOUR SUPPLY OF WOMEN

BIBLIOGRAPHY

Becker, G.S. 1960. An economic analysis of fertility. In *Demographic and Economic Change in Developed Countries*, University-National Bureau Conference Series, No. 11, Princeton: Princeton University Press.

Becker, G.S. 1965. A theory of the allocation of time. *Economic Journal* 75, September, 493–517.

Beesley, M.E. 1965. The value of time spent in travelling; some new evidence. *Economica* 45, May, 174–85.

Bruzelius, N. 1979. *The Value of Travel Time*. London: Croom Helm.

Gronau, R. 1973. The effect of children on the housewife's value of time. *Journal of Political Economy* 81(2), March–April, Supplement, 168–99.

Grossman, M. 1972. On the concept of health capital and the demand for health. *Journal of Political Economy* 80(2), March–April, 223–55.

Mincer, J. 1963. Market prices, opportunity costs, and income effects. In *Measurement in Economics: Studies in Mathematical Economics and Econometrics in Memory of Yehuda Grunfeld*, ed. C. Christ et al., Stanford: Stanford University Press.

Schultz, T.W. (ed.) 1975. *Economics of the Family: marriage, children, and human capital*. London and Chicago: Chicago University Press for the National Bureau of Economic Research.

Tipping, D.G. 1968. Time savings in transport studies. *Economic Journal* 78, December, 843–54.

Willis, R.J. 1973. A new approach to the economic theory of fertility behavior. *Journal of Political Economy* 81(2), March–April, Supplement, 14–64.

Vanderlint, Jacob (*d.* 1740). A timber merchant at Blackfriars, London, about whose life little is known except that in 1734 he published *Money Answers All Things, or an Essay to make Money Plentiful among all Ranks of People and increase our Foreign and Domestick Trade*. This work appears to have received little attention during the 18th century until Dugald Stewart referred to it as anticipating the Physiocrats on the single tax of land rent and on free trade. Stewart compared him also with David Hume 'in point of good sense and liberality' (Stewart, 1794, pp. 342, 343, 346). McCulloch used Stewart's opinions on several occasions (e.g. 1845, p. 162) and may have provided the basis for Marx's charge (1878, p. 327, cf. 1867, p. 124, n.1) that 'Hume follows step by step, and often even in his personal idiosyncrasies' Vanderlint's work.

The essay itself presents a complex argument supporting a proposal for alleviating the distress from a diagnosed trade depression (pp. 134–48). This was designed to ensure prosperity for all including the labouring poor to whose plight Vanderlint was most sympathetic (pp. 72–7, 83, 88, 100). As Vanderlint explains in the opening remarks of his preface, reducing labour costs is the best way to stimulate domestic and foreign trade; the problem is how to achieve this end without the reduction in domestic demand following a cut in money wages. Vanderlint's solution rests on his proposal to extend agriculture by making more labour and land available for cultivation (pp. 117–19, 163–8). Assuming constant returns (pp. 81–2) this policy leads to increased agricultural produce, the starting point for his causal analysis. As Vickers (1960, p. 180) demonstrates, Vanderlint argues that increased agricultural produce lowers the price of wage goods, hence the money wage level, hence cost of production, hence favourably affects the balance of trade by increasing export competitiveness, increasing money supply, which increases demand for output in general and brings about full employment and prosperity. Vanderlint combines real and monetary factors in this analysis as Hume was to do two decades later. Aware of the specie mechanism (see Viner, 1937, pp. 83–4), Vanderlint suggests ways of neutralizing monetary effects on the prices of provisions. He also provides interesting reflections on war and peace, marriage, luxury, and more equal distribution of income and taxation. His analysis is enriched by empirical material drawn from contemporary political arithmetick sources.

PETER GROENEWEGEN

BIBLIOGRAPHY

McCulloch, J.R. 1845. *The Literature of Political Economy*. London: LSE reprint, 1938.

Marx, K.H. 1867. *Capital*. Moscow: Foreign Languages Publishing House, 1959.

Marx, K.H. 1878. From the critical history. In F. Engels, *Anti-Dühring*, Moscow: Foreign Languages Publishing House, 1954.

Stewart, D. 1794. *Account of the Life and Writings of Adam Smith, L.L.D.* In *Adam Smith, Essays on Philosophical Subjects*, ed. W.P.D. Wightman, J.C. Bryce and I.S. Ross, Oxford: Clarendon Press, 1980.

Vanderlint, J. 1734. *Money Answers All Things or, An Essay to Make Money sufficiently plentiful*. New York: Johnson Reprint Corporation, n.d.

Vickers, D. 1960. *Studies in the Theory of Money 1690–1776*. London: Peter Owen.

Viner, J. 1937. *Studies in the Theory of International Trade*. New York: Harper & Brothers.

Vansittart, Nicholas, Lord Bexley (1766–1851). Son of Henry Vansittart, sometime governor of Bengal, Vansittart took his MA degree at Oxford in 1791, and was called to the bar at Lincoln's Inn, where he became a bencher in 1812. He was MP for Hastings in 1796, and in 1801 was sent as minister plenipotentiary with Parker and Nelson to Copenhagen to endeavour to detach Denmark from the Northern Alliance. In April 1801 he was appointed joint-secretary to the treasury by Addington.

Between 1802 and 1812 he sat for Old Sarum, and afterwards for Harwich. In 1804 he was a lord of the treasury in Ireland and in the following year secretary to the lord lieutenant. He was reappointed joint secretary to the treasury, 1806–7, under Grenville's administration; and in 1812 became a cabinet minister, succeeding Perceval as chancellor of the exchequer. He held this office during Lord Liverpool's administration until January 1823, when he retired, and was raised to the peerage. He remained in the cabinet as chancellor of the duchy of Lancaster until 1828. He died 8 February 1851, in his 85th year.

Vansittart was a poor debater, with feeble voice and indistinct utterance, but he at one time had a certain financial reputation, and his gentle manners and benevolent character secured the attention which his natural abilities were unable to command. The eleven years during which he was chancellor of the exchequer were from a financial point of view perhaps the most critical England ever saw, but Vansittart never showed dexterity either in imposing or in remitting taxation. He introduced no measure of first importance. He was not responsible for the repeal of the income tax in 1816, the surrendering of the war malt tax, nor the return to cash payments. His resolutions on the report of the Bullion Committee have not added to his fame, and a praiseworthy scheme for converting the navy five per cents to four per cents in 1822 was coupled with an objectionable proposal to farm the pensions known as the 'dead weight annuity'. He introduced alterations into the sinking fund far from successful. He was simply an honest and industrious clerk, finally dismissed from his office with little ceremony.

[H.R. TEDDER]

Reprinted from *Palgrave's Dictionary of Political Economy*.

SELECTED WORKS

1793. *Reflections on the Propriety of an immediate Conclusion of the Peace*. London.

1794. *A Reply to the addressed to Mr. Pitt by Jasper Wilson*. London.

1796a. *Letter to Mr. Pitt on the conduct of the Bank directors*. London.

1796b. *An Inquiry into the state of the Finances of Great Britain, in answer to Mr. Morgan's Facts*. London.

1811. *Substance of two Speeches on the Bullion Question*. London.

1813. Outline of a plan of finance proposed to be submitted to parliament. *Pamphleteer* 1, 255.

1815a. The Budget of 1815. *Pamphleteer* 6, 27.

1815b. Speech ... February 20 1815 in the Committee of Ways and Means. *Pamphleteer* 6, 1.

1818. Speech 16 March 1818 on a Grant of £1M for (Churches). *Pamphleteer* 12, 3.

1819. Speech of the Chancellor of the Exchequer on the budget of 1819. *Pamphleteer* 15, 1.

BIBLIOGRAPHY

Attwood, T. 1817. *Letter to N. Vansittart on the Creation of Money and ... upon the National Prosperity*. Birmingham.

Colchester, Lord. 1861. *Diary and Correspondence of Charles, Lord Colchester by his son*. 3 vols, London.

Dunn, W. 1820. The Vansittart plan of finance. *Pamphleteer* 16, 263.

Walpole, S. 1878–86. *History of England*. 5 vols, London.

Varga, Evgeny (Jenö) (1879–1964). Soviet economist, political activist and analyst, Varga was born in Nagytétény, Hungary, on 6 November 1879, and died in Moscow on 7 November 1964. He was a college teacher, economic journalist, Professor of Political Economy (1918) and People's Commissar of the Hungarian Soviet Republic in 1919. He was forced to leave Hungary in the first days of August 1919 for Austria (where he was detained for several months). While in exile, he worked for the Secretariat of the Communist International in Moscow and the Soviet Trade Mission in Berlin. From 1927 to 1947 he held the position of Director of the Institute of World Economy and World Politics, and from 1929 to 1964 he was a Full Member of the USSR Academy of Sciences.

In feudal-capitalist Hungary of the declining Habsburg Monarchy and two subsequent short-lived revolutions, Varga systematically covered all vital economic policy issues, including industrialization (1912), land reform, and inflation (1918). His experience as Commissar he summed up in 'The economic policy problems facing the proletarian dictatorship' (1920).

In the following period of capitalism, imperialism, colonialism, fascism and war, he found confirmation for many basic tenets of Marxism: in *The Great Crisis and its Political Consequences. Economics and Politics, 1928–1924* (1935) he empirically demonstrated the validity of the theories of exploitation, imperialism, class warfare and crises, and correctly foresaw the inescapable drift towards war and revolution.

After decades of exceptionally intensive research and varied experience (which permitted him to become one of the chief architects of Hungary's spectacularly successful Forint stabilization), he published 'Changes in the Capitalist Economy following the Second World War' (1946). Now he attributed lasting importance to reinforced state control, rising consumption shares, decolonization and the increased role of international credit in the capitalist economy and, accordingly, doubted the fatality of world crises and world wars.

These conclusions were officially rejected in the Soviet Union and he was demoted from his leading Institute position (1947). But after some interruption he resumed scientific work and restated and extended his theses (1953, 1964). His Selected Works were posthumously published in three volumes (1974).

RUDOLF NÖTEL

SELECTED WORKS

1912. Az ipartelepülés és Magyarország iparosodásának problémája (The location of industry and the problem of Hungary's industrialization). *Közgazdasági Szemle*, May, 303–13; June, 393–411.

1918. *A pénz: uralma a békében, bukása a háboruban* (On money: its peace-time power and war-time collapse). Budapest: Népszava.

1920. *Die wirtschaftspolitishen Probleme der proletarischen Diktatur* (The economic policy problems facing the proletarian dictatorship). 2nd edn, Vienna: Verlag der Arbeiterbuchhandlung.

1935. *The Great Crisis and its Political Consequences. Economics and Politics, 1928–1934.* London: Modern Books.

1946. *Izmeneniia v ekonomike kapitalizma v itoge vtoroi mirovoi voiny* (Changes in the capitalist economy as a result of the Second World War). Moscow: Gospolitizdat.

1953. *Osnovnye voprosy ekonomiki i politiki imperializma – posle vtoroi mirovoi voiny* (Basic problems of imperialist economics and politics – after the Second World War). Moscow: Gospolitizdat.

1964. *Politico-economic Problems of Capitalism.* First published in Russian. Moscow: Progress Publishers, 1968.

1974. *Kapitalizm posle vtoroi mirovoi voiny. Izbrannye proizvedeniia* (Capitalism after the Second World War). In Selected Works, Moscow: Nauka; includes a bibliography listing 749 titles.

BIBLIOGRAPHY

Sociological Institute of the CC of the HSWP. 1979. *Varga Jenö müveinek bibliográfiája.* A bibliography listing 1158 titles and editorial contribution to 30 volumes. Budapest: MSZMP KB Társadalomtudományi Intézete.

variable capital. *See* CONSTANT AND VARIABLE CAPITAL.

Veblen, Thorstein (1857–1929). Thorstein Veblen has become known to the general public primarily as a sardonic social critic, his classic of this genre being *The Theory of the Leisure Class*. Professionally, however, he was an economist, the first editor of *The Journal of Political Economy*, and wrote extensively on methodological issues in economics. 'Institutionalist' economics – an important school for several decades – counted Veblen among its inspirations, along with John R. Commons, and featured such latter-day followers of Veblen as Wesley Clair Mitchell and John Maurice Clark.

Thorstein Veblen was born in 1857 in a Norwegian immigrant farming community in Wisconsin. He grew up speaking Norwegian, and only in his teens began speaking English. At Carleton college, Veblen studied under John Bates Clark, a leading theorist in the then-new school of neoclassical economics, a kind of economics at which Veblen was later to aim his most scathing attacks. Clark was only the first of the intellectual giants of the day under whom Veblen studied – and whose ideas Veblen later repudiated. As a graduate student at Johns Hopkins University, Veblen studied under the celebrated philosopher Charles Sanders Peirce, founder of the 'pragmatist' school, made more widely known by William James and John Dewey. At Yale University, from which Veblen eventually received his PhD in philosophy, he studied economics under William Graham Sumner, better known as the leading American 'Social Darwinist'.

Veblen's education made him marginal to the world in which he had grown up, where his father was the only one to send his children to college. He was also marginal to the academic institutions in which he struggled financially to get an education, and where his rough-hewn manners, unkempt appearance and Bohemian way of life set him apart from other students. His scepticism about religion and his personal eccentricities left him unwanted as a faculty member at many American colleges and universities, during an era when such institutions were often church-affiliated and when such affiliation was by no means nominal.

For seven long years, from 1884 to 1891, Veblen was unemployed, living off his family and then off his wife's family. Finally in 1891, at the age of 34, Veblen took a fellowship in economics at Cornell University. The following year, the newly opened University of Chicago hired his mentor, J. Laurence Laughlin, who took Veblen along as a teaching fellow. After four years he was promoted to instructor, and was made managing editor of the *Journal of Political Economy.*

Although Veblen's academic career began late in life, the lost years were not entirely lost, for they were years of wide reading and creative thought. In the 1890s he published numerous articles in both sociological and economic learned journals. In 1899, at the age of 42, came his first and most famous book, *The Theory of the Leisure Class.*

Veblen's writings, whether learned or popular, economic or sociological, were pervaded by notions of evolution – not biological evolution as in Darwin, but social evolution and, in particular, the evolution of ways of thinking. Whether he wrote in *The American Journal of Sociology* about 'The Beginnings of Ownership' and 'The Barbarian Status of Women', or in *The Quarterly Journal of Economics* about 'The Preconceptions of Economic Science' and 'Why is Economics Not an Evolutionary Science?', Veblen's thought was full of Darwinian notions of evolving adaptations to changing environments. But whereas the Social Darwinists emphasized the socially beneficial outcomes of these processes, Veblen emphasized the anachronistic survivals of earlier times that lingered on counterproductively because thinking lagged far behind changing realities. Economics was characterized as 'helplessly behind the times' precisely because its approach was not evolutionary.

The theories of conventional neoclassical economics were criticized, not as being incorrect in themselves but because they 'confine the attention' to narrow, incidental phenomena and 'exclude from theoretical inquiry' the broader cultural context in which economic activity evolves. The economic models in which adjustments take place 'without lag, leak, or friction' were seen as wholly unrealistic by Veblen. Yet this was not the naive complaint, sometimes voiced by later institutionalist economists, that the theoretical models did not photographically reproduce all the obtrusive features of the real world. Veblen recognized that, for a theory to be 'serviceable', it did not have to be 'true to life'. But he argued that the particular assumptions of neoclassical economics left out precisely what he considered most important to investigate – how and why economies continually evolve structurally rather than simply grow quantitatively. Neoclassical economics, according to Veblen, could not 'deal with phenomena of growth except so far as growth is taken in the quantitative sense of a variation in magnitude, bulk, mass, number, frequency'.

The kind of inquiry which Veblen wished economics to become was unlike any which had existed before him and unlike any which has come after him. It would have sought the wider social and cultural causes and consequences of evolutionary changes in economic patterns, such as the change from a hunting and fishing society to farming and from handicrafts to industrial production. Clearly, neither classical nor neoclassical economics attempted anything of the sort. Veblen criticized them for asking the wrong questions rather than giving the wrong answers to the questions they chose to ask. In the process, he generated much sarcasm and many aphorisms used later by others for still more sweeping – and more naive – attacks on economics.

Veblen's own attempts at understanding the evolution of economic patterns in a wider social context blurred the line between economics and sociology or history, and indeed blurred the line between empirical investigation and self-indulgent speculation. When he wrote of 'The Economic Theory of Woman's Dress' or *The Instinct of Workmanship*, he was clearly in a twilight zone. Indeed, no hard and fast line can be drawn between his economic and non-economic writings.

Institutionalist economics, as practised by Veblen, was quite different from some of its later variants, in part because of Veblen's definition of institutions. For Veblen, institutions were not organizations, but rather 'settled habits of thought, common to the generality of men'. They were the 'usage, customs, canons of conduct, principles of right and propriety' reigning at a given time and place. Sometimes these principles were incorporated into organization entities but mere *descriptions* of those organizations (in the manner of later institutionalist economists) were not an *analysis* of the evolution of the underlying social and cultural visions that gave them meaning. Veblen wished to analyse rather than describe. He did not wish to emulate the Historical School of economists, arguing that 'the historical school can scarcely be said to cultivate a science at all, their aim being not theoretical work'. Veblen's aim was theoretical work, however much later institutionalists engaged in exhaustive descriptions with *ad hoc* conclusions.

While Veblen was a theorist, in the sense of producing many theories, he was neither a systematic analyst nor a systematic tester of theories against empirical evidence. Pre-emptive assertions, with selective illustrations and dismissive references to opposing views, were Veblen's usual style.

Empirical facts were not lacking in Veblen, but empirical evidence was. A large amount of descriptive information can be found in Veblen's writings, but seldom related in any systematic way to specific hypotheses derived from a general theory. This became part of his legacy to institutionalist economics. One of Veblen's early articles on wheat prices was a model of the bland statistical–descriptive style that became the hallmark of the early National Bureau of Economic Research, founded by Veblen's student Wesley C. Mitchell.

Through Mitchell, J.M. Clark, and other student-disciples, Veblen made an impact on economics beyond his own career or lifetime. His writings supplied an arsenal of arguments and aphorisms for social critics inside and outside economics. But, for the longer run, the technical development of economics left institutional economics far behind, and even the National Bureau eventually became part of the newer theoretical and econometric trends. It is difficult to see how economics as it exists today is any different from what it would have been had there been no Thorstein Veblen. Still, he had his time in the sun.

THOMAS SOWELL

See also INSTITUTIONAL ECONOMICS.

SELECTED WORKS

1899. *The Theory of the Leisure Class*. New York: Macmillan.

1904. *The Theory of Business Enterprise*. New York: Charles Scribner's Sons.

1919. *The Place of Science in Modern Civilization*. New York: Huebsch. Reprinted, New York: Viking Press, 1946.

BIBLIOGRAPHY

Dorfman, J. 1934. *Thorstein Veblen and His America*. New York: Viking Press.

Riesman, D. 1953. *Thorstein Veblen: a Critical Interpretation*. New York: Seabury Press.

Sowell, T. 1967. The 'evolutionary' economics of Thorstein Veblen. *Oxford Economic Papers* 19, July, 177–98.

Sowell, T. 1969. Veblen's *Higher Learning* after fifty years. *Journal of Economic Issues*, December 66–78.

Vecchio, Gustavo del (1883–1972). Del Vecchio was born at Lugo in Romagna on 22 June 1883, and died in Rome on 6 September 1972. He initially attended the university in Rome, where he followed the history of philosophy course under Antonio Labriola. He continued his studies in Bologna, where he was greatly influenced by the teaching of Tullio Martello, follower of Francesco Ferrara's work. His post-graduate studies, which were completed in Berlin, gave Del Vecchio's entire work a wide cultural outlook, influenced by historical, philosophical and sociological factors, as well as purely economic considerations. He became Professor of Political Economy at the Universities of Trieste and Bologna, and Professor of Public Finance at the University of Rome. He lectured at the Bocconi University of Milan, where he was Chancellor from 1934 to 1938. During this last year he was forced to give up his teaching because of the anti-semitic measures adopted by the Fascist government. He went into exile in Switzerland in the latter years of World War II, and on his return to Italy started teaching once again. He was Minister of the Treasury from 1947 to 1950, but these public duties represented only a brief intermission in his life as a dedicated academic.

Del Vecchio's scientific work shows that he constantly tried to unify the tradition of Italian economic thought, whose main personality was Francesco Ferrara, with the theories of equilibrium, whether of the approach suggested by Marshall, or by Walras and Pareto. He was, moreover, profoundly influenced by the work of Maffeo Pantaleoni in the task of constructing an economic dynamics, to be understood not merely as a modification of static analysis, but as a building of a new economic framework. On the one hand, in a series of books which lasted from 1922 to 1950, Del Vecchio realized a unified exposition of political economy, public finance and economic policy, which he believed to be 'successive stages in the passage from a major to a minor level of abstraction in a unique theoretical framework'. On the other hand, on the academic plane, he carried out pioneering analyses which have received wide recognition in the literature (by Schumpeter, Ohlin, Knight and Stigler, among others). In particular, his research into the application of the marginal principle to money can be traced back to 1909; this research was started with the previously scarcely recognized Walrasian analysis of money, but criticizing some aspects of it and carrying out original developments. Among his important early works are his analyses of the process of the formation of savings which (in 1915) he linked not to the interest rate (the generally held view) but to the quality of income, that is, to its sources. He also carried out important research into the process of accumulation which he felt could not be explained purely in terms of economic factors; he believed that in order to obtain a realistic understanding of the whole accumulation process, it was necessary that non-economic factors should also be taken into account. His contributions to the pure theory of international trade, to the concept of risk as an uncertainty related to the passing of time, and to the empirical investigation into consumer behaviour by means of the investigations of relations between income and consumption have all been recognized. From all his contributions emerges the need to analyse the economy from a broader perspective, avoiding the aridity of abstraction and formalism.

F. CAFFÈ

SELECTED WORKS

1909. I principi della teoria economica della moneta. *Giornale degli Economisti.*
1912. Relazioni tra entrata e consumo. *Giornale degli Economisti.*
1915. *Lineamenti generali della teoria dell'interesse.* Rome: Atheneum.
1928. Teoria economica dell'assicurazione. *Annali di Economia dell'Universita Bocconi,* Milan.
1936. *Progressi della teoria economica.* Padua: Cedam.
1930. *Grundlinien der Geldtheorie.* Tübingen: J.C.B. Mohr (Paul Siebeck).
1932. *Ricerce sopra le teoria generale della moneta.* Milan: Università Bocconi.
1956. *Vecchie e nuovo teorie economiche.* Turin: Utet.
1961. *Economia generale.* Turin: Utet.
1983. *Anthology of the Writings of Gustavo del Vecchio on the Centenary of His Birth.* Milan: F. Angeli.

veil of money. *See* NEUTRALITY OF MONEY.

velocity of circulation. The *velocity of circulation* of money is V in the *identity of exchange*

$$MV \equiv PT \tag{1}$$

which is due to Irving Fisher (1911). On the left-hand side, M is the stock of money capable of ready payment, i.e. currency and demand deposits, or, in modern parlance, M_1; on the right, P is the price level and T stands for the volume of trade. PT is usually identified with total transactions at current value, which must be identically equal to total payments. All these variables are aggregates. The identity defines V as PT/M, that is the ratio of a flow of payments to the stock of money that performs them; its dimension is time^{-1}.

Apart from defining V, the identity (1) also serves for rudimentary quantity theories of money. If V is assumed constant, we have a theory of money demand, with PT determining M. Again, with both V and T constant, changes in M imply changes in P; this is still a popular explanation of inflation, with 'too much money chasing too little goods'. The above quantity theory of money demand has however long been replaced by a more sophisticated argument, whereby money demand is determined along with demand for other assets by yield and liquidity differentials and by net wealth or income Y. This has led, by analogy, to the unfortunate term *income velocity* for the ratio Y/M. It should not be thought that Y here acts as a proxy for PT of the earlier theory: the underlying argument is quite different, and if Y is a proxy at all it represents net wealth. The term velocity is inappropriate in this context. We shall here reserve it for the *transactions velocity* V as defined above, and for its constituent parts.

This V has no place in modern economic analysis; it attracted some interest in the decades before 1940. When we divide M into currency M_c and demand deposits M_d, and acknowledge that there are several different types of transaction, (1) becomes

$$M_cV_c + M_dV_d = \sum_j P_jT_j. \tag{2}$$

Among the variables in this expression, M_d and V_d are in principle observable at short notice, and in the absence of production indices and of national income estimates M_dV_d (or M_dV_d/P) is a useful indicator of economic activity. It was used as such by authors like Angell (1936), Edie and Weaver (1930), Keynes (1930) and Snyder (1934). As for the data, M_d is demand deposit balances, available from banking returns, and V_d is the ratio of debits to balances, which can also be obtained from banks. The US Federal Reserve Board has long published monthly statistics of this *debits ratio* or *deposit turnover rate*, and still does so; there have been some drastic changes in definition and coverage over the years. The Bank of England provided a similar series from 1930 to 1938. Comparable statistics are available for several other countries.

The main trouble with this approach is that there is more than one type of transaction, and that (bank) payments are not limited to transactions in connection with current production. Some debits even have no economic meaning at all, as when a depositor has several accounts, and shifts funds between them, or when currency is withdrawn. Moreover bank debits can also reflect the sale of capital assets, income transfers, and money market dealings. The latter are by far the largest single category of turnover. These elements hinder the interpretation of V_d, and various attempts have been made to identify and remove them. We refer to Keynes' distinction between *industrial* and *financial* circulation, and to the Federal Reserve's practice of separately recording turnover in major financial centres. Failing a detailed classification of debits by the banks, however, all corrections are limited to approximate adjustments.

The observed value of V_d thus varies considerably with the definition of the relevant payments. For the US we quote the overall annual V_d, inclusive of financial transactions and the money market. This gross V_d rose from just under 30 in 1919 to about 35 in 1929, and then declined until 1945 when it was under 15. After the war it started on a long rise. It was about 50 by 1965, and from then onwards it soared to over 400 in 1984 (Garvy and Blyn, 1970; Federal Reserve Bulletin). In Britain, *net* velocity, exclusive of the money market, was roughly stable at values between 15 and 20 from 1920 to 1940; later it rose from 20 in 1968 to 40 in 1977 (Cramer, 1981). In the Netherlands, similarly defined net debits series show a V_d of between about 40 in 1965 and 45 in 1982 (Boeschoten and Fase, 1984).

It is hard to find a single common interpretation of these movements. The development in the US until the 1960s suggests strong business cycle effects, but the enormous later increase of gross V_d must in large part be due to new techniques like overnight lending and repurchase agreements.

These generate a huge amount of debits on the basis of quite small average balances. New banking techniques that go hand in hand with improved cash management explain increases in V_d outside the money market, too. The process is induced by the pressure of rising interest rates. Increased speed and precision of bank transfers permit a reduction of working balances at a given turnover level, and the reduction of demand moreover calls forth additional debits, as when idle funds are shifted to time deposits. Debits may thus increase *because* balances are reduced, and the rise of V_d is accentuated.

As regards currency payments, the currency stock M_c is well documented, but the estimation of velocity V_c or payments M_cV_c presents intractable problems. There are two solutions, but both use major assumptions that defy verification.

The first method is based on the redemption rates of worn-out banknotes of different denominations. Under stationary conditions these rates are the reciprocal of average lifetime, and this turns out to be positively related to face value. While this may well be due to more careful handling of the larger notes, it is usually inferred from this that larger denominations circulate less rapidly and are hoarded more often, and for longer periods, than small notes. Laurent (1970) uses these specific redemption rates to estimate currency payments. He assumes that a banknote is redeemed if and only if it has completed G transfers. Assigning G transfers to notes that are redeemed, and $\frac{1}{2}G$ to notes still in circulation, he builds up cumulative estimates of the transfers performed by each US denomination from 1861 onwards. This yields annual transfers by denomination, and hence total currency payments per year, ignoring coins. All estimates are of course a multiple of the unknown G, which is regarded as a physical constant like the number of times a note can be handled. Laurent assumes implicitly that it equals the number of payments a note can perform in its lifetime. He constructs currency payments series for various G, adds bank debits, and examines the correlation of this sum with GNP over the period 1875 to 1967. The maximum correlation occurs at $G=129$, and this value is adopted. Since currency in circulation, bank debits, and GNP all share the same real growth and price movements, the constructed payment series will be closely correlated with GNP for *any* G, and the maximum correlation is not a good criterion for determining this constant. It is moreover uncertain that G *is* constant. Laurent's estimates of currency payments imply that V_c is about 30 from 1875 to 1890; it then rises to a peak of 120 in 1928, and thereafter declines steeply to 32 in 1945, remaining at that level since. We shall argue that this level is too high.

The second method of estimating currency payments is due to Fisher (1909). He observes that most people obtain the currency they spend from banks, and that most recipients return their takings to banks. The currency circulation thus consists of *loops* of payments connecting withdrawals with deposits, and currency payments can be established by multiplying aggregate withdrawals (or deposits) by the average number of intervening payments, or the *loop length*. Withdrawals and deposits are of course recorded at the banks, and should be readily available statistics (although in fact they are not); as for the loop length, there is no way of measuring it, and it must be inferred from common sense considerations. In consumer spending the loop consists of a single payment, as households draw cash from the banks and spend it at retail shops that deposit all their takings. This is of course a minimum: some agents do not deposit their currency receipts, but spend them; some agencies, like post offices or stores that cash customers' cheques, act in a double capacity, paying out currency they have received and thus doubling the number of payments it performs before returning to the banks. Such considerations together suggest an average loop length of about two for present-day industrialized countries.

In recent years, V_c has been estimated for two countries for which series or estimates of cash withdrawals could be established. Fisher's method gives a constant V_c of about 18.5 for Britain over the period 1960–78 (Cramer, 1981). For the Netherlands, a combination of Laurent's and Fisher's methods gives a constant value of about 15.3 for the years 1965–82 (Boeschoten and Fase, 1984). These results suggest that currency velocity is a constant, as if it were set by physical limitations to the speed of currency circulation, and that it lies between 15 and 20.

This estimate often arouses strong feelings, as casual observation suggests that currency performs far more than 15 or 20 payments a year. A higher value of V_c does however mean higher currency payments M_cV_c, and it is not at all clear where these take place. Even with a velocity of 15 this is a problem, for at this value currency payments in most countries far exceed consumer spending, let alone retail sales. Yet consumer spending is commonly believed to be the major repository of cash. A fair proportion must by our estimate take place elsewhere, and it appears that crime or the informal economy cannot account for this vast amount. Over and again the currency stock is much larger than common sense would suggest. Where are these payments made? Where is all the currency used or hoarded? The plain answer is that no one knows, and that very few people care. Attempts to find the answer by a sample survey have failed (Cramer and Reekers, 1976).

The above results suggest that even for current transactions (excluding the money market) bank velocity is larger than currency velocity, so that the steady and continuing shift from currency to demand deposits must mean a gradual increase in the overall velocity V.

J.S. CRAMER

See also DEMAND FOR MONEY: EMPIRICAL STUDIES.

BIBLIOGRAPHY

Angell, J.W. 1936. *The Behaviour of Money*. New York: McGraw-Hill.

Boeschoten, W.J. and Fase, M.M.G. 1984. *The Volume of Payments and the Informal Economy in the Netherlands 1965–1982*. Monetary Monographs no. 1, Amsterdam: de Nederlandsche Bank, and Dordrecht: Nijhoff.

Cramer, J.S. 1981. The volume of transactions and of payments in the United Kingdom, 1968–1977. *Oxford Economic Papers* 33(2), July, 234–55.

Cramer, J.S. and Reekers, G.M. 1976. Money demand by sector. *Journal of Monetary Economics* 2(1), January, 99–112.

Edie, L.D. and Weaver, D. 1930. Velocity of bank deposits in England. *Journal of Political Economy* 38, August, 373–403.

Fisher, I. 1909. A practical method for estimating the velocity of circulation of money. *Journal of the Royal Statistical Society* 72, September, 604–11.

Fisher, I. 1911. *The Purchasing Power of Money*, 2nd edn, 1922. Reprinted New York: Kelley, 1963.

Garvy, G. and Blyn, M.R. 1970. *The Velocity of Money*. New York: Federal Reserve Bank, available from Microfilm International, Ann Arbor and London.

Keynes, J.M. 1930. *A Treatise on Money*. London: Macmillan.

Laurent, R.D. 1970. Currency transfers by denomination. PhD Dissertation, University of Chicago.

Snyder, C. 1934. On the statistical relation of trade, credit, and prices. *Revue de l'Institut International de Statistique* 2, October, 278–91.

vent for surplus. Conventionally, international trade theory focuses attention on the pattern of comparative costs existing at a point of time on the basis of the given resources and technology of the trading countries. Adam Smith, writing before the theory of comparative costs became formalized as a cross-section type of analysis, was concerned with the process of interaction between trade and development over a period of time. Thus his writings provide a more promising starting point for the study of the historical process of export expansion and economic development in the underdeveloped countries (Williams, 1929; Myint, 1958 and 1977).

Actually, there were two strands in Adam Smith's analysis: the first, which may be called the 'productivity' theory, emphasized the role in international trade in widening the extent of the market and the scope for division of labour and specialization, thereby raising the productivity of labour by encouraging technical progress and enabling the trading country to enjoy increasing returns by overcoming technical indivisibilities imposed by the narrowness of the home market; the second, which may be called the 'vent for surplus' theory, emphasized the role of international trade in providing a wider market outlet or the 'vent' for the surplus productive capacity which would have remained underutilized in the absence of international trade.

When applied to the historical experience of the expansion of primary exports from the underdeveloped countries, Smith's 'productivity' theory of trade suggested too optimistic a picture of the rise in labour productivity through specialization and the possibility of reaping increasing returns through export expansion. It is true that the introduction of foreign investment and technology raised labour productivity in the mining and plantation exports. But this was usually of a one-off character and the subsequent expansion of output relied heavily on an abundant supply of unskilled labour at low wages. When the local labour supply was exhausted, the typical reaction was to recruit immigrant foreign labour from countries such as India and China with their vast reservoir of cheap labour, rather than to economize local labour and raise its productivity. This fell short of Adam Smith's optimistic vision of division of labour, with specialization continually raising labour's productivity. Smith's 'productivity' theory also did not accord with the typical process of expansion of peasant exports. Here, apart from the improvements in transport and communications and law and order, there was no significant improvement in agricultural techniques and the productivity of resources. Peasant exports simply expanded by bringing more land under cultivation and drawing upon the underemployed labour from the subsistence economy (Myint, 1954).

This left unanswered the question of why the primary exports from the underdeveloped countries expanded so rapidly and in a sustained manner when these countries were opened up to multinational trade in the latter half of the 19th century or the early 20th century. Smith's vent for surplus theory serves to fill this gap. The typical process of expansion of primary exports may be looked upon as a long 'transition process' during which the expected tendency to diminishing returns was held in check by drawing upon the underutilized or the surplus natural resources and labour into export production; that is to say, exports expanded approximately under conditions of constant returns during the vent for surplus phase in many peasant export economies of South-East Asia and Africa seems to have continued rather longer than expected, lasting well into the recent postwar decades.

The significance of the vent for surplus theory for the study of the underdeveloped countries may be elaborated as follows. Under normal conditions (i.e. in the absence of short-run economic fluctuations), there is generally a gap in any country between the actual level of production attained and the theoretically attainable level of production with the 'given' resources and technology idealized in international trade theory as the production possibility frontier. This gap between the actual and the attainable level of output may be expected to be wider for the underdeveloped countries than for the developed countries, even if both were pursuing similar economic policies. An important reason for this may be traced to the fact that the domestic economic organization of the poorer countries is less well developed. Specifically, it is characterized by a poor internal system of transport and communications, by an incomplete development of the markets, particularly for the factors of production, and by an inadequate development of the administrative and fiscal machinery of the government. According to the vent for surplus theory, a substantial reserve of 'surplus' resources is likely to exist in a traditional economy not yet fully opened up to external economic relations, reflecting the underdeveloped nature of the domestic economic framework. In such a setting, international trade would provide a major force for economic development. It would bring about not only 'direct gains' from trade in the form of cheaper imports raising the economic welfare of the country, but also important 'indirect gains' transforming the organization of the domestic economy: through the extension and development of the exchange economy in the traditional agricultural sector, through the improvements in transport and communications and through a better provision of public services financed by increasing government revenue from the expanding exports (Myint, 1958).

Further, the vent for surplus theory suggests that the 'direct gains' from trade would also be much larger than those envisaged in the conventional theory of multinational trade. In the conventional trade theory, the resources are assumed to be fully employed before a country enters into international trade and export production can be expanded only at the cost of contracting output for the domestic market. The gains from trade are therefore confined to the gains in allocative efficiency obtained by reallocating the given and fully employed resources according to the comparative advantage offered by international trade. In contrast, according to the vent for surplus theory, there is a considerable scope for expanding the exports of an underdeveloped country *without* contracting output for domestic consumption-by drawing upon the surplus land and labour. Thus the gains from trade would be larger because imports can be obtained with little or no resource cost. This hypothesis is supported by the experiences of the peasant export economies in South-East Asia and Africa. In Burma and Thailand, where rice happened to be both the main food crop and the export crop, rice exports expanded very rapidly for many decades without any contraction in the domestic food supply. If anything, it is possible to argue that the domestic food supplies of these countries were made more secure through the development of a large exportable surplus of rice brought about by the extension of cultivation to unused land. Similarly, African peasant economies such as Ghana, Nigeria or Uganda were able to expand their peasant exports in the prewar decades without any appreciable reduction in their domestic food production. Indeed, in the initial phase of export expansion export crops such as cocoa or cotton were usually interplanted with the food crops, such as yam, on the newly cleared pieces of land so that export production and domestic food production tended to increase together (Myint, 1963, chs 3 and 4).

The vent for surplus phase of peasant export expansion has continued somewhat longer than one would have expected at first sight. This is so because the existence of the 'unused' land is not given once for all in a physical sense by the geographical area but depends importantly on the improvements in transport and communications and the growth of the market system (the 'unused' labour being replenished by population growth). Thus, it is noteworthy that Thailand, which has been expanding her rice exports on a vent for surplus basis since the early 1900s, still managed to go through a rapid phase of expansion of new peasant exports, such as maize and tapioca in the 1960s and 1970s-mainly through an improvement in internal transport (Myint, 1972, chs 1 and 4). Similarly, in the 1950s and the 1960s, many African countries experienced a rapid expansion of new peasant exports, notably the tropical beverages, by bringing more land under cultivation. In particular, Ivory Coast continued with its rapid expansion of exports during the 1960s and 1970s. It is true that in recent times the expansion of peasant exports from many South-East Asian and African countries has slackened. In some countries, such as the Philippines, this is due to a genuine exhaustion of the supply of exploited land, which seems to have occurred by the end of the 1950s (Hayami and Ruttan, 1985, ch. 10). In other countries, particularly those in Africa, the slackening in peasant export production may be attributed not to the end of the vent for surplus phase, but to the very unfavourable prices fixed for the peasant producers by the State Agricultural Marketing Boards (World Bank, 1981, ch. 5) and, in some countries, to political instability. Sooner or later, of course, the vent for surplus phase of agricultural expansion will come to an end with the growing population pressure on limited land. But as suggested by the more recent phases of peasant export expansion in countries such as Thailand and the Ivory Coast, the possibility for the vent for surplus mechanism may not as yet be completely exhausted-given the policies of providing adequate incentives to the peasant farmers and political stability.

The vent for surplus theory may be extended on a somewhat different basis to the agricultural surpluses of the advanced countries such as the United States and the EEC countries. The reason for this type of surplus productive capacity is of course not the underdevelopment of the domestic economic organization, but the various farm support programmes induced by powerful political pressure (Hayami and Ruttan, 1985, ch. 8). Despite this, however, it is instructive to study the international trade and aid policies of the advanced countries in terms of the vent for surplus theory and the desire to find an international outlet from the existing surplus productive capacity, rather than in terms of adapting their productive capacity to the world market demand.

H. MYINT

See also CLASSICAL ECONOMICS.

BIBLIOGRAPHY

Caves, R.E. 1965. 'Vent for surplus' models of trade and growth. In *Trade, Growth and the Balance of Payments*, ed. R.E. Baldwin et al., Chicago: Rand McNally; Amsterdam: North-Holland.

Hayami, Y. and Ruttan, V.W. 1985. *Agricultural Development: an International Perspective*. Baltimore: Johns Hopkins Press.

Myint, H. 1954. An interpretation of economic backwardness. *Oxford Economic Papers* 6, June, 132–62.

Myint, H. 1958. The 'classical theory' of international trade and the underdeveloped countries. *Economic Journal* 68, June, 317–37.

Myint, H. 1963. *The Economics of the Developing Countries*. London: Hutchinson.

Myint, H. 1972. *Southeast Asia's Economy: Development Policies in the 1970s*. Harmondsworth: Penguin Books.

Myint, H. 1977. Adam Smith's theory of international trade in the perspective of economic development. *Economica* 44, August, 231–48.

Smith, A. 1776. *An Inquiry into the Nature and Causes of the Wealth of Nations*. Ed. E. Cannan, London: Methuen, 1950.

Williams, J.H. 1929. The theory of international trade reconsidered. *Economic Journal* 39, June, 195–209.

World Bank. 1981. *Accelerated Development in Sub-Saharan Africa: agenda for action*. Washington, DC: World Bank.

Verdoorn's Law. One of the most notable features of the postwar economic performance of the advanced countries has been the substantial and persistent differences between the various economies in their rates of growth of productivity and output. Yet these disparities are merely one aspect of the more general picture of economic development. Since the beginning of the Industrial Revolution, at which time there appears to have been little variation between areas in terms of per capita income, some countries have achieved a sustained growth in productivity whilst others have shown little or no improvement. The reasons for this, of course, remain a source of controversy.

Verdoorn's Law is an empirical generalization that provides the basis for one such explanation. Although originally discussed in terms of the differences in productivity growth of the advanced countries, the law is now recognized as having a wider significance for the more general process of economic growth and development.

In its simplest form, the law states that there is a close relationship between the long run growth of manufacturing productivity and that of output. (The law has also been found to hold for public utilities and the construction industries but not for any other sector of the economy.) The importance of the law is that it suggests that a substantial part of productivity growth is endogenous to the growth process, being determined by the rate of expansion of output through the effect of economies of scale.

The development of this approach to the theory of economic growth owes much to the writings of Lord Kaldor (see, in particular, Kaldor, 1978a and 1978b, and the symposium on Kaldor's growth laws published in the 1983 edition of the *Journal of Post Keynesian Economics*). Indeed, interest in the law primarily dates from Kaldor's (1966) inaugural lecture which examined why the United Kingdom had grown so much more slowly over the postwar period than most other industrial countries. (It was P.J. Verdoorn, however, who had first discussed the relationship between productivity and output growth in an article published in 1949. The paper was written in Italian which may explain why it had largely escaped notice, with the notable exception of Colin Clark (1957), until Kaldor drew attention to it. Kaldor was also the first to discuss the broader implications of the law for economic growth.)

In the inaugural lecture, Kaldor observed that there was a close relationship for the advanced countries between the growth of manufacturing output per worker (p) and that of output (q). When the Verdoorn Law was estimated in the form $p=a+bq$ using cross-country data for twelve advanced countries over the early postwar period, it was found that the estimate of b, the 'Verdoorn coefficient', took a value of about one half. (Other studies have discovered similar results using cross-industry, time-series and regional data for both the advanced and the less developed countries.) Since the exponential growth of productivity is definitionally equal to the difference between output and employment growth (e), the law is sometimes expressed as $e = -a + (1-b)q$. But the implications are the same. An increase in the growth of output will cause an increase in the growth of employment of about half a percentage point and an increase in productivity growth of a similar magnitude. Kaldor argued that this implies that manufacturing is subject to substantial increasing returns to scale.

The emphasis on the role of economies of scale as an important factor in determining the rate of economic progress has a long history. It is the basis of Adam Smith's (1776) principle enunciated in the opening sentence of Book I of *The Wealth of Nations* that '[the] greatest improvement in the productive powers of labour, and the greater part of the skill, dexterity, and judgement with which it is anywhere directed, or applied, seem to have been the effect of the division of labour'. The latter in turn is limited by the extent of the market. This is nothing more than the phenomenon of economies of scale, in the broad sense of the term. The theme was subsequently elaborated in Allyn Young's (1928) classic paper. In particular, Young argued that an important implication is that the capital–labour ratio is not to be understood as a response to relative factor prices but is primarily determined by the scale of production. He further stressed that economies of scale are primarily a macroeconomic phenomenon, the result of increased inter-industry specialization. (But it should be emphasized that the law has been found to apply to individual manufacturing industries.)

Another major tenet of the argument is that the law reflects both static and dynamic economies of scale. The former is a function of the volume of output and the gains in productivity from this source are reversible – if output contracts so the benefits of scale will be lost. Dynamic returns to scale, on the other hand, reflect such factors as 'learning by doing' and are usually ascribed to the rate of growth of output. These gains in productivity represent the acquisition of knowledge concerning more efficient methods of production and as such are irreversible. Substantial gains in productivity have been found to arise from this source even in the absence of any gross investment. A more rapid expansion of production will also lead to (as well as be the result of) a greater rate of innovation and a climate more favourable to risk taking. Investment will also be more efficiently used if it is introduced as part of a planned modernization scheme under conditions of rapidly expanding output rather than added, in an ad hoc manner, to existing capacity in stagnating industries. (Lamfalussy, 1963, has termed these 'enterprise' and 'defensive' investment, respectively.)

For the law to provide evidence of the degree of returns to scale, it must be interpreted as reflecting a production relationship such as a form of the technical progress function. This being the case, the law is now usually specified as including the growth of the capital stock. This allows a separation to be made between the growth of productivity due to the greater use of machinery and that resulting from increasing returns to scale, per se. The inclusion of the growth of capital has not led to any major revision of the interpretation of the law.

The technical progress function was developed by Kaldor in an attempt to avoid the misleading dichotomy of growth into shifts of the production function and movements along the function. It is therefore all the more ironic that Verdoorn (1949, 1980) himself regards the law as being derived from the neoclassical Cobb–Douglas production function, although with the latter expressed in terms of growth rates. (The *linear* technical progress function may also be integrated to yield a conventional production function, although this is not necessarily true of the non-linear specifications.) Nevertheless, a paradox arises in that the estimation of the law using the *levels* of the various variables (the 'static Verdoorn Law') suggests either constant or small increasing returns to scale, whereas large estimates are obtained by estimating the 'dynamic law' using the same data sets. One explanation is that while the Verdoorn Law may be derived by differentiating a Cobb–Douglas production function with respect to time, it does not follow that the latter is the correct underlying structure. Integrating the law will lead to innumerable structures, depending upon the constant of integration.

The implications of Verdoorn's Law are far-reaching. It suggests that there is an inherent tendency for growth to proceed in a self-reinforcing manner and provides an economic rationale for Myrdal's (1957) notion of 'cumulative causation'. An increase in output causes a faster growth of productivity for the reasons already noted. Provided all the gains are not absorbed by increased real wages, countries (or firms) will experience an increasing cost advantage over their competitors. Improvements in the non-price aspects of competition, such as quality, are also positively related to productivity growth. Of course, growth is not observed to be explosive and formalizations of the cumulative causation model show how the growth of various countries may converge to (differing) equilibrium rates.

(However, it has been suggested that the Verdoorn Law may simply result from this reverse causation from productivity to output growth. Large differences in *exogenous* productivity growth could lead to variations in output growth through the price mechanism – the 'Salter effect'. This could generate a Verdoorn-type relationship even though constant returns to scale prevail. However, the evidence suggests that this is unlikely to be significant for total manufacturing or for an individual industry, although it may be an important factor in cross-industry studies.)

Since the Verdoorn Law shows that differences in productivity growth are caused by variations in the growth of output, the problem is to explain why disparities in the latter arise. In the inaugural lecture, Kaldor argued that the United Kingdom's economic problems stemmed from the limited supply of labour available to the manufacturing sector and it was this that prevented a faster rate of growth. If this is the case, the Verdoorn Law may be mis-specified since employment and not output growth should be the regressor (Rowthorn, 1975). When this specification (sometimes confusingly known as Kaldor's Law) is estimated, most studies find that constant returns to scale prevail. However, Kaldor later retracted his earlier position. The long run growth of the advanced countries (and, equally, the less developed countries) is not determined by the exogenously given growth of factor inputs but rather by the growth of 'effective demand'. Under these circumstances, the original specification of the law is to be preferred, although the very nature of the cumulative causation mechanism suggests that both output and employment growth may be jointly determined.

The importance of the rate of growth of demand as the driving force behind the pace of economic growth extends beyond the issues concerning the correct specification of the law. Long-run growth is best understood in a Keynesian (or, more appropriately, 'Kaldorian') framework. The rate of capital accumulation cannot be seen as an independent determinant of development since it is as much a result as a cause of the growth of output. The evidence further suggests that labour supplies were not a serious factor in limiting the growth of the advanced countries even during their most rapid expansionary phase which lasted from the end of World War II until 1973 (Cornwall, 1977). There was either disguised unemployment in the primary and tertiary sectors or sufficient immigration to satisfy the demand for labour emanating from the manufacturing sector. The question naturally arises as to what is it that determines the growth of exogenous demand. In the early stages of development it is the growth of the agricultural surplus and the rate of land-saving innovations. With industrialization and the decline of the importance of agriculture, the key determinant becomes the growth of exports. This provides a source of the growth of autonomous demand both directly through the Harrod foreign trade multiplier and indirectly by relaxing the balance of payments constraint. Growth can thus be regarded as being 'export-led'.

An important result of this approach is that, given the cumulative nature of economic growth, there is no inherent tendency for free trade to be to the benefit of all countries. Trade liberalization may well lead to a further deterioration in the growth of those countries which are already lagging as they find they become increasingly less competitive internationally. This is, of course, the converse of the inference that is sometimes drawn from the neoclassical theory of trade.

J.S.L. McCombie

See also CUMULATIVE CAUSATION; INCREASING RETURNS.

BIBLIOGRAPHY

Clark, C. 1957. *The Conditions of Economic Progress*. 3rd edn, London: Macmillan.

Cornwall, J. 1977. *Modern Capitalism: Its Growth and Transformation*. London: Martin Robertson.

Kaldor, N. 1966. *Causes of the Slow Rate of Economic Growth of the United Kingdom: An Inaugural Lecture*. Cambridge: Cambridge University Press.

Kaldor, N. 1978a. *Further Essays on Economic Theory*. London: Duckworth.

Kaldor, N. 1978b. *Further Essays on Applied Economics*. London: Duckworth.

Lamfalussy, A. 1963. *The United Kingdom and the Six. An Essay on Economic Growth in Western Europe*. London: Macmillan.

Myrdal, G. 1957. *Economic Theory and Underdeveloped Regions*. London: Duckworth.

Rowthorn, R.E. 1975. What remains of Kaldor's Law? *Economic Journal* 85, March, 10–19.

Salter, W.E.G. 1960. *Productivity and Technical Change*. Cambridge: Cambridge University Press.

Smith, A. 1776. *An Inquiry into the Nature and Causes of the Wealth of Nations*. Ed. E. Cannan, London: Methuen, 1961.

Thirlwall, A.P. (ed.) 1983. Symposium: Kaldor's growth laws. *Journal of Post Keynesian Economics* 5(3), Spring.

Verdoorn, P.J. 1949. Fattori che regolano lo sviluppo della produttività del lavoro. *L'Industria* 1, 45–53.

Verdoorn, P.J. 1980. Verdoorn's Law in retrospect: a comment. *Economic Journal* 90, June, 382–5.

Young, A.A. 1928. Increasing returns and economic progress. *Economic Journal* 38, December, 527–42.

Vernon, Raymond (born 1913). Vernon has been a most prolific writer on international economic relations in the post World War II era. His writings reflect a multi-faceted career which includes nearly two decades in government service, a short stint with private business, three years as director of the New York Metropolitan Region Study and, since 1959, a fruitful association with Harvard University, first at the Business School, where he was the leading figure in the teaching and research of international business, and later at the John F. Kennedy School of Government, where he was incumbent of the Clarence Dillon Chair of International Affairs until his retirement.

The policy orientation of his writing and the acute awareness it reflects of the interests and point of view of foreign governments, their institutional make up and constraints, surely owe much to his years of service with the State Department. His abiding interest in the restructuring of international trade, investment and payments systems, economic development, especially of Latin America, and economic relations between East and West must be similarly attributed to his State Department experience.

One of Vernon's early analytical contributions concerns the economics of location. In the New York Metropolitan Region Study he adapted the notion of 'external economies' to the specific environment of urban agglomeration. The term was used by him to characterize the cost advantage enjoyed by firms located in urban centres because of their closeness to sources of information and to a large variety of specialized services. The availability of these services and their low costs determine the characteristics of industries, such as electronics, fashion goods, printing and publishing, which tend to flourish in agglomerates despite the high costs of more conventional production factors such as labour, space and transportation.

Information and specialized services also figure prominently in Vernon's extensive writings on the multinational corporation. In this case, Vernon has shown how information and specialized services are internalized and transformed into proprietary knowledge, which is used by the firm to obtain a monopolistic position in the domestic and international markets. This position is extended from the early to the mature phase of the 'product cycle' by transferring production to subsidiaries located in countries where conventional production factors are least costly, while retaining the location of the head office in the most developed markets where the new product and process specifications originate.

Alone and in collaboration with colleagues and doctoral students at the Harvard Business School, Vernon published numerous books and articles about the multinationals. He studied their dominant role in world production and trade of technology-based industries on the one hand the resource-based ones on the other, using the 'product cycle' as well as the more traditional industrial organization models to explain their distinct competitive structure, their insoluble conflicts with both their host and home governments, conflicts which evolve through a predictable cycle of power relations which Vernon aptly termed the 'obsolescing contract'.

His books *Sovereignty at Bay* (1971) and *Storm over the Multinationals* (1977), which summarize his work on the multinational corporation, will be regarded as major contributions to our knowledge of the multinational corporations for many years to come.

Business–government relations had been dealt with by Vernon early in his career as a civil servant. He returned to the theme in his work on the multinationals. The subject figures even more prominently in his more recent work conducted at the Kennedy School of Government, which focuses on state-owned enterprises and on government relations with private sector firms against the background of the energy crisis of the mid-seventies and its aftermath.

In *Two Hungry Giants*, which compares US and Japanese responses to the threat of resource shortage, Vernon attributes Japan's superior performance to the skilful way in which the Japanese government managed to harness private sector corporations to the 'national interest'.

Marxist doctrine claims that the state is being used by capitalists to advance their class interests. Vernon's analysis offers a less dogmatic view of the role of the state: to enhance their goals, even governments of 'market economies' increasingly use both state and privately owned enterprises as instruments of national policy.

S. Hirsch

SELECTED WORKS

1971. *Sovereignty at Bay: The Multinational Spread of U.S. Enterprises*. New York: Basic Books.

1977. *Storm over the Multinationals: The Real Issues*. Cambridge, Mass.: Harvard University Press.

1983. *Two Hungry Giants: The United States and Japan in the Quest for Oil and Ores*. Cambridge, Mass.: Harvard University Press.

Verri, Pietro (1728–1797). Italian economist, administrator and philosopher, Verri was born in Milan in 1728, educated in Rome and Parma, served with Austria in the Seven Years War and at this time was introduced to the study of economics by General Henry Lloyd (Venturi, 1978, 1979). His economic writings of the 1760s, such as *Elementi di Commercio* (1760) and the dialogues on monetary disorders in the State of Milan (1762) led to his appointment to a number of positions in the Austrian civil service in Milan. His administrative achievements include the abolition of tax farming (1770) and lowering and simplifying the tariff (1786). From 1764 to 1766 he edited with his brother Alessandro the periodical *Il Caffè* which attracted contributions on economics from Beccaria and Frisi as well as himself (Verri, 1764). His most important economic publication, *Reflections on Political Economy* appeared in 1771, went through numerous editions and was translated into French, German and Dutch and more recently, into English. Other economic works on monetary and trade questions, including his 1769 pamphlet advocating freedom of the domestic corn trade contribute to his reputation as a most important 18th-century Italian economist (McCulloch, 1845, pp. 26–7). More recently he has been noted for inspiring early developments in mathematical economics (Theocharis, 1961, pp. 27–34). He died in 1797.

Verri's *Reflections* is a complete treatise on political economy, reminiscent of Turgot's work (1766) with its tight, logical framework and division into fairly short sections. Although these cover a wide range of subjects, they are interconnected by the basic theme of the work, the increase in annual reproduction of the nation through trade of surplus product which Verri related to the balance of production and consumption. This ratio or balance is the key concept in Verri's economic analysis, since it not only influences economic growth but also value (it approximates the ratio of sellers to buyers at home and abroad), the rate of interest (it represents thriftiness conditions) and, via its influence on the balance of trade it also determines national money supply. An excess of production over consumption lowers the price level and the rate of interest, expands the money supply, animates industry and facilitates the collection of taxes. Some features of this analysis may be specifically noted. Verri does not appear to have been aware of the importance of capital, as is demonstrated in his general discussion of production (sections 26–8) and his treatment of the interest rate as a monetary phenomenon (sections 14–15). Secondly, his emphasis on supply and demand (used to determine all prices including the rate of interest) combined with references to utility and scarcity in the context of value (section 4) explains why this part of his work has been linked with marginalist economics. The last eleven sections discuss taxation and public finance, including a presentation of five canons of taxation (section 30), a tax incidence analysis arguing against the Physiocratic view that all taxes fall on the landlord (sections 32–3) and a plea for indirect consumption taxation as a fair and administratively easy way to raise revenue. Anti-physiocratic elements in his economics are not confined to tax issues, but apply to his discussion of special classes (section 24), the importance of agriculture (section 28) and are apparent in his view that free trade should be largely confined to domestic activity (section 40). Verri's *Reflections* were highly regarded when they appeared, and could be found, for example, in Smith's library. His work, though now largely ignored, may therefore have exerted greater influence than is generally believed.

Peter Groenewegen

SELECTED WORKS

1760. *Degli elementi di commercio*. In *Scrittori classici italiani di economia politica*, parte moderna, ed. P. Custodi, Milan, 1804, Vol. XVII, 328–35.

1762. *Dialogo sui disordine delle monete nello stato di Milano nel 1762*. In *Scrittori classici italiani di economia politica*, parte moderna, ed. P. Custodi, Milan, 1804, Vol. XVI, 277–94.

1764. Considerazioni sul lusso. In *Scrittori classici italiani di economia politica*, parte moderna, ed. P. Custodi, Milan, 1804, Vol. XVII, 336–48.

1771. *Reflections on Political Economy*. Trans. B. McGilvray and ed. P. Groenewegen, Reprints of Economic Classics, Series 2, No. 4, Sydney: University of Sydney, 1986.

BIBLIOGRAPHY

McCulloch, J.R. 1845. *The Literature of Political Economy*. London: LSE reprint, 1938.

Theocharis, R.D. 1961. *Early Developments in Mathematical Economics*. London: Macmillan.

Venturi, F. 1978. Le 'Meditazioni sulla economia politica' di Pietro Verri: edizioni, echi e discussioni. *Rivista storica Italiana* No. 3.

Venturi, F. 1979. Le avventure del generale Henry Lloyd. *Rivista storica Italiana* No. 2, 3.

vertical integration. An important task of economic theory, and certainly the central question with which the economics of organization is concerned, is to explain the allocation of economic activity across firm, market and hybrid modes. As discussed below, the study of vertical integration is not merely germane to but is a core feature of this inquiry. Interestingly, moreover, the patterns and regularities discovered in the study of vertical integration repeat themselves, with variation, across a wide class of other issues – including vertical market restrictions, labour market organization, regulation, corporate governance, and even family organization.

The study of vertical integration has mainly fallen to specialists in Industrial Organization. This has developed in three parts, the first of which operated within (indeed, was instrumental to the development of) the firm-as-production-function framework. Inasmuch as the 'natural' boundaries of the two trading entities were taken as given, attention was wholly concentrated on the *ex ante* bargain that determined the price and quantity at which product was traded between successive (bilateral) stages of production.

This narrow formulation of the issues contributed to public policy scepticism over vertical integration in the Industrial Organization arena. Since, moreover, vertical integration and the use of vertical market restrictions are closely linked – where vertical restraints include such practices as tie-ins, block booking, customer and territorial restrictions, exclusive dealing and the like – public policy scepticism toward vertical integration was deepened and took the form of hostility when contractual restrictions were brought under review. The 'inhospitality tradition' within antitrust thus held that vertical market restrictions were presumptively unlawful. A different assessment of vertical integration and vertical restraints awaited an alternative conception of the firm.

The modern theory of vertical integration maintains that firm and market are alternative modes of organization and that the boundary of the firm is problematic, hence needs to be derived. Although this transaction cost economics conception of the firm-as-governance-structure was first advanced fifty years ago (Coase, 1937), it lacked operationality and languished for most of the next thirty-five years (Coase, 1972). The past fifteen years, by contrast, have witnessed renewed attention to and operational headway on transaction cost matters. Public policies toward vertical integration and vertical market restrictions have been significantly reshaped in the process.

A third literature dealing with vertical integration has also appeared during the past fifteen years in which issues of uncertainty, often in conjunction with efficient risk bearing, are featured. The public policy ramifications of this literature are less fully developed. Out of respect for space considerations, interested readers are referred to Blair and Kaserman (1983, ch. 5).

1. WHAT ARE THE QUESTIONS?

Any theory of economic organization that purports to deal with vertical integration must address itself to the following central issues:

(i) Of the endless number of activities into which a firm potentially could integrate, what are the distinguishing features of those activities that are integrated and those that are not? A *discriminating* theory of vertical integration is thus the objective.

(ii) Although a technological view of the firm commonly distinguishes between activities that belong to a 'core technology' and those that are located in the 'periphery' – where the integration of the former is taken for granted while the latter is problematic – is it the case that core and periphery differ in kind, or does a common theory of integration apply to both?

(iii) Unless integration involves costs as well as benefits, vertical integration will know no limits. Of necessity, therefore, the following question must be asked and answered: Why can't a large firm do everything that a collection of small firms can do and more?

(iv) When does vertical integration pose public policy concerns and why?

2. THE APPLIED PRICE THEORY TRADITION

The immediate post-war literature in Industrial Organization was mainly informed by what Coase (1972) referred to as the 'applied price theory' approach in which the firm-as-production-function was featured. Technology was thus assigned a key role. Also, although there were very real differences among them, all variants of the applied price theory approach were unified in one striking respect: they all employed a monopoly presumption. This led to Coase's wry remark that 'if an economist finds something – a business practice of one sort or another – that he does not understand, he looks for a monopoly explanation' (1972, p. 67).

2.1 Bilateral monopoly. The oldest explanation for vertical integration, and the only one that is included in most microeconomics textbooks, is bilateral monopoly. Machlup and Tabor trace the evolution of this through 1960. As they observe, this literature includes some of the greatest names in economics – from Cournot through Edgeworth, Pareto, Zeuthen, and Stackelberg. This scholarship reached the conclusion that while optimal output between the parties might be realized, the division of profits between bilateral monopolists was indeterminate (Machlup and Tabor, 1960, p. 112). Subsequent work in this tradition emphasized efficient factor proportions (McKenzie, 1951). A combined efficient factor proportions–monopoly power framework for assessing vertical integration has since been developed by Vernon and Graham (1971), Schmalensee (1973), Warren-Boulton (1974) and Westfield (1981).

Albeit instructive, this literature is beset by a number of loose ends or anomalies. These include:

(1) Since, in a static framework, the parties can reach the same disposition of the bilateral monopoly gains by selling a specified quantity of product at an agreed upon produce price as they can by selling specified assets at an agreed upon asset price, why should they prefer the latter?

(2) Integrated firms, using the production function apparatus, can never do worse than and will normally do better than nonintegrated rivals. Why, therefore, do firms not integrate everything?

(3) Unified ownership and autonomous contracting are merely two poles of a distribution of alternative models of organization. What explains intermediate or hybrid modes of contracting?

(4) More generally, if the real problems of trading are of an intertemporal kind in which successive adaptations to uncertainty are needed, do the problems of economic organization have to be recast in a larger or even different framework?

2.2 Price discrimination. The main explanation for vertical integration, vertical market restrictions, and nonstandard contracting more generally advanced by the 'Chicago School' was price discrimination. As Burstein (1960) makes clear, much of this work was inspired by Aaron Director. But Stigler also made important contributions to this tradition.

Actually, Stigler's main treatment of vertical integration is rather eclectic. It combines a life cycle theory with a price theoretic treatment of the issues (1951). In price theoretic terms, vertical integration was viewed as a device by which sales taxes on intermediate product could be avoided and quotas and price controls could be circumvented (1951, pp. 136–7). Also, backward vertical integration may vitiate monopoly margins, while forward integration can facilitate price discrimination among buyers: 'Monopoly is a devious thing ... A firm cannot practice price discrimination in the stages in which it does not operate' (Stigler, 1951, p. 138). This last argument has subsequently been developed by Perry, both in general and with respect to the aluminum industry (1978, 1980). Price discrimination is also invoked to explain such nonstandard practices as tie-ins (Burstein, 1960) and block booking (Stigler, 1963).

Operating out of this monopoly presumption, Stigler advised that vertical integration 'loses its innocence if there is an appreciable degree of monopoly control at even one stage of the production process'. Specifically, a 20 per cent firm should be prohibited from acquiring more than a 5 or 10 per cent share in any industry from which it buys or to which it sells (Stigler, 1955, p. 224).

2.3 Barriers to entry. If the efficient boundaries of the firm are defined by technology, which is a widely held belief, then surely any effort to expand or otherwise alter those boundaries is suspect, which is also a widely held belief. Thus Bain observed with respect to the first that 'the cases of clear economies of integration generally involve a physical or technical integration of the processes in a single plant'. Thermal economies from the integration of iron-and-steel-making is offered as an example (Bain, 1968, p. 381). By contrast, the evident or proximate cause for vertical integration that does not have such a 'physical or technical aspect' is monopoly. The rationale for forward integration out of manufacturing into distribution 'is evidently the increase of the market power of the firms involved rather than a reduction in cost' (Bain, 1968, p. 381).

This entry barrier rationale for vertical integration is noteworthy in three respects: (1) it implicitly assumes that the only feasible way to organize tasks that bear a check-by-jowl relation to each other – by reason of proximity economies (of thermal, transportation, inventory, or related kinds) – is under unified ownership; (2) it disregards economies that have non-technological origins; and (3) the monopoly presumption is wilfully and expressly invoked to explain integration between stages which lack a tight technological linkage. All three features can be disputed. Thus thermal and related economies merely warrant that successive stages be located in a cheek-by-bowl relation to each other. Unless unified ownership of such stages is the only feasible way to organize such an interface – which plainly it is not, since the two stages could be linked by long term contract – then vertical integration is not uniquely implied. The first assumption is thus incorrect.

The disregard for economies that have non-technological origins is not because these were thought to be important. The reason, instead, is that they were not thought of at all. The production function framework simply ignored the possibility that comparative transaction cost economies might sometimes accrue to vertical integration. Since economic organization was presumed to be purposeful, the burden of explaining nonstandard forms was assigned to monopoly wherever tight technological linkages were missing.

2.4 Strategic purposes. Related to but really different from the barrier to entry arguments is the argument that vertical integration can impose added costs on rivals. This point was made, if not developed, by Alfred Marshall, who observed that if, in a small country, spinning and weaving were joined, 'the monopoly so established will be much harder to shake than would either half of it separately' (1920, p. 495). Bain likewise held that vertical integration may be undertaken strategically as a means by which to 'disadvantage, weaken, eliminate, or exclude non-integrated competitors' (1968, pp. 360–62). And Stigler observed that integration 'becomes a possible weapon for the exclusion of new rivals by increasing the capital requirements for entry into the combined integrated production processes' (1955, p. 224). More generally, if the requisite preconditions are satisfied, vertical integration may qualify as a member of the family of activities that Salop and Scheffman examine in the context of strategies designed to 'raise rival's costs' (1983).

It is noteworthy, however, that the strategic use of vertical integration does not derive from a simple price theoretic treatment of the issues. Implicitly, those who invoke these arguments are relying on unspoken transaction cost features. Thus, qualified suppliers into one but not both stages of an industry will not be deterred by pre-existing integration *unless* such integration is the source of *contractual breakdowns* among non-integrated (independent) traders. And potential entrants who are qualified at both stages will have no added problems in the capital market unless it is costly to display their true attributes – which is sometimes the case but also has transaction cost origins.

The applied price theory conception of firm and market structure was and remains central to the economics of organization. It nevertheless answers the set of questions set out in Section 1, above, in a disconcerting way. It thus (1) is able to supply an affirmative rationale for only a small number of transactions; (2) regards the technological core and peripheral activities as different in kind; (3) ignores the question of why a large firm is unable to do every thing that a collection of small firms can do and more; and (4) notwithstanding these concerns, it confidently advises public policy to adopt very stringent limits on vertical mergers and forbids vertical contractual restraints.

3. TRANSACTION COSTS

Two sweeping critiques of the firm-as-production-function approach to economic organization appeared in 1972, the one by Coase and the other by Richardson. Both argued that the study of economic organization was inadequately served by the applied price theory tradition and that a much wider range of organizational structures than were admitted by the usual firm or market dichotomy needed to be acknowledged.

The aforementioned implausibility of the technology/monopoly story was one of the problems. There were too many loose ends; there were too many forced fits. Also, the technology/monopoly story made little or no provision for hybrid modes. Since these were plainly an important part of the organizational landscape, to what were they responsive?

Here as elsewhere, it takes a theory to contest a theory. Although Coase had advanced an alternative hypothesis in his classic 1937 article 'On the Nature of the Firm' – namely, that transaction cost differences are responsible for the decision to organized transactions in firms rather than markets (or the reverse) – this argument had made little headway against the neoclassical firm-as-production-function construction over the next thirty-five years. There having been no effort to operationalize the transaction cost insight, the alternative hypothesis had gone nowhere during this interval: 'We know very little about the cost of conducting transactions on the market or what they depend on; we know next to nothing about the effects on costs of different groupings of activities within firms' (Coase, 1972, p. 64).

Actually, this somewhat overstates the case. Although transaction cost arguments had made little headway in assessing vertical integration, there was a growing awareness that transaction costs played a central role in understanding market failure. Arrow's early puzzlement over the problems that attend markets for information (1962) led to the conclusion that a more general formulation of the condition of market failure was needed: 'market failure is not absolute; it is better to consider a broader category, that of transaction costs, which in general impede and in particular cases completely block the formation of markets' (Arrow, 1969, p. 48).

The use of internal organization rather than markets can be interpreted in these terms. But inasmuch as internal organization experiences transaction costs of its own, the question is what factors are responsible for shifting the balance of costs one way rather than another.

Posing the issue this way discloses that transaction cost assessments are fundamentally comparative in nature. Such comparisons are facilitated by (1) making the transaction the basic unit of analysis, which is what Commons (1934) had recommended, and (2) adopting a contracting orientation. If, in fact, many transactions can be organized within many different organizational alternatives, which becomes evident upon supplanting a technological by a contracting approach to economic organization, what factors are responsible for *differential* transaction cost strains when each mode of governance is provisionally assigned the task of organization?

A three-part argument is needed. The first part was the realization that contractual difficulties could only be assessed in relation to the behavioural attributes of human actors. What Knight had felicitously referred to as 'human nature as we know it' (1921, p. 270) thus had to be plumbed. Rather than regard behavioural assumptions casually or as a matter of convenience, therefore, such assumptions were expressly addressed up-front. Second, transactions themselves needed to be decomposed. What are the critical dimensions with respect to which transactions differ? Third, what are the costs and competencies of alternative modes of organization for managing transactions? The object is to develop a discriminating approach to economic organization whereby transactions are assigned to governance structures in a transaction cost economizing way.

3.1 Behavioural assumptions. The behavioural assumptions of transaction cost economics differ from those of neoclassical economics in both rationality and self-interest seeking respects. The hyperrationality assumption of orthodoxy is supplanted by the weaker assumption of bounded rationality – where bounded rationality has reference to behaviour that is '*intendedly* rational, but only *limitedly* so' (Simon [1947], 1961, p. xxiv). The simple self-interest seeking assumption of orthodoxy is supplanted by the stronger assumption of opportunism – where the latter has reference to self-interest seeking with guile (Williamson, 1975, pp. 26–30). Solemn promises to behave 'responsibly' are not, without more, self-executing in a world in which economic agents are given to opportunism.

3.2 Dimensions. Among the more critical dimensions with respect to which transactions differ are these: the frequency with which they recur; the uncertainty to which they are subject; and asset specificity. This last turns out to be especially important.

It is now generally accepted that recurrent contracting prospectively poses problems

> if either (1) efficient supply requires investment in special-purpose, long-life equipment, or (2) the winner of original contract acquires a cost advantage, say by reason of 'first mover' advantages (such as unique location or learning, including the acquisition of undisclosed or proprietary technical and managerial procedures and task-specific labour skills) (Williamson, 1971, p. 116).

More generally, the problem is one of *ex post* small numbers bargaining brought on by a condition asset specificity, of which five kinds have been identified: site specificity, physical asset specificity, human asset specificity, dedicated assets (Williamson, 1983; 1985), and brand name capital (Klein and Leffler, 1981). Expressed in Marshallian terms, the contracting problems posed by asset specificity are due to 'potentially appropriable quasi-rents' (Klein, Crawford and Alchian, 1978).

Identity of the contracting parties becomes crucial when asset specificity intrudes. This contradicts the neoclassical assumption that transactions take place within markets where 'faceless buyers and sellers ... meet ... for an instant to exchange standardized goods at equilibrium prices' (Ben-Porath, 1980, p. 3). Facelessness is violated wherever the supply of goods or services is supported by investments in durable, transaction specific assets. By definition, these investments have been specialized – either from the outset or during contract execution – to the needs of the trading parties. Since these assets cannot be redeployed to alternative uses or by alternative users without the sacrifice of productive value, the parties to such transactions are effectively operating in an *ex post* bilateral contracting relation.

Thus even though there may have been large numbers of qualified bidders at the outset, if the winner of the original bid thereafter enjoys a sunk cost advantage, parity bidding at contract renewal intervals cannot be presumed. Instead, such transactions undergo a 'fundamental transformation'. What had been an *ex ante* large numbers bidding condition thus becomes a small numbers supply condition thereafter. This transformation is the main factor that is responsible for the decision to remove transactions from markets and organize them internally.

Not only does the transaction cost approach to vertical integration discriminate among transactions mainly in terms of asset specificity differences, but it furthermore acknowledges that classical market contracting and centralized hierarchy are but two poles on the distribution of feasible organization forms. Albeit preliminarily, the leading empirical studies (Monteverde and Teece, 1982; Stuckey, 1983; Anderson and Schmittlein, 1984; Palay, 1984, 1985; Joskow, 1985; Spiller, 1985) broadly support the predictions of transaction cost theory.

3.3 Responses to the questions. Transaction cost economics is thus responsive to the first of the four key questions posed in section 1: it advances a discriminating theory of vertical integration based largely on differences in asset specificity (the predictions of which appear to be supported by the facts). It is furthermore responsive to each of the three remaining questions posed.

Thus consider question (ii): Do core and periphery differ in degree or in kind? Applied price theory appeals to technology to explain the core and invokes monopoly to explain the periphery. The two therefore differ in kind. Transaction cost economics holds otherwise. It maintains that both core and periphery are explained by asset specificity. (Although all forms of asset specificity are observed in the core, site specificity is what most distinguishes core from peripheral activities. A common theory of asset specificity otherwise applies to core and periphery alike – which is to say that they differ in degree rather than in kind.)

Whereas the limits to firm size anomaly was not one for which applied price theory had an answer, it helped pose the issue nonetheless. Thus Knight observed that 'diminishing returns to management is a subject often referred to in economic literature,... in regard to which there is dearth of scientific discussion' (1921, p. 286, no.1). He subsequently urged, moreover, that 'The relation between efficiency and size is one of the most serious of theory ... . [Since] the possibility of monopoly gain offers a powerful incentive to continuous and unlimited expansion of the firm, [this] force must be offset by some equally powerful one making for decreased efficiency ... with growth in size, if even boundary competition is to exist' (Knight, 1965, p. xxiii). The issue was subsequently restated by Coase as follows: 'Why, if by organizing one can eliminate certain costs and in fact reduce the cost of production, are there any market transactions at all? Why is not all production carried on by one big firm?' (1937, p. 340). More generally, the issue is that put in question (iii), above: Why can't a large firm do everything that a collection of small firms can do and more?

Although there has been a widespread readiness to 'assume, as we must' that such limits exist (Young, 1928, p. 539), plainly this is not a satisfactory response to the query. The persistent failure to craft a better response is largely explained by the fact that the sources of 'bureaucratic failure' are so poorly understood. A second problem is that assessing bureaucratic failure is unavoidably a comparative institutional issue. Third, and related to both, assessing bureaucratic failure is an interdisciplinary issue. Economists, however, rarely possess the requisite knowledge of internal organization to perform these comparative assessments, while sociologists, who have deep knowledge of internal organization and its pathology, are rarely interested in the comparative analysis of differential efficiency.

Modest progress in assessing the limits of internal organization has nevertheless appeared. The differential efficacy of incentives in firm and market contexts plays the central role in a property rights approach (Grossman and Hart, 1986), while the transaction cost approach invokes a combination of incentive and bureaucratic disabilities (Williamson, 1985, ch. 6).

Consider finally the public policy issue posed in 1.1 (iv): When does vertical integration present troublesome antitrust concerns? These issues are addressed in the entry on ANTITRUST POLICY. Suffice it to observe here that the 'monopoly presumption' of the applied price theory era has been supplanted by a more favourable regard for organizational variety in all of its forms.

OLIVER E. WILLIAMSON

See also ANTITRUST POLICY; ECONOMIC ORGANIZATION AND TRANSACTIONS COSTS; INCREASING RETURNS.

BIBLIOGRAPHY

Anderson, E. and Schmittlein, D. 1984. Integration of the sales force: an empirical examination. *Rand Journal of Economics* 15, Autumn, 385–95.

Arrow, K.J. 1962. Economic welfare and the allocation of resources of invention. In National Bureau of Economic Research, *The Rate and Direction of Inventive Activity: Economic and Social Factors*, Princeton: Princeton University Press, 609–25.

Arrow, K.J. 1969. The organization of economic activity: issues pertinent to the choice of market versus nonmarket allocation. In *The Analysis and Evaluation of Public Expenditure: The PPB System*, Vol. 1, U.S. Joint Economic Committee, 91st Congress, 1st Session; Washington, DC: Government Printing Office, 59–73.

Bain, J. 1956. *Barriers to New Competition*. Cambridge, Mass.: Harvard University Press.

Bain, J. 1959. *Industrial Organization*. New York: John Wiley & Sons.

Bain, J. 1968. *Industrial Organization*. 2nd edn, New York: John Wiley & Sons.

Ben-Porath, Y. 1980. The F-connection: families, friends, and firms and the organization of exchange. *Population and Development Review* 6, March, 1–30.

Blair, R. and Kaserman, D. 1983. *Law and Economics of Vertical Integration and Control*. New York: Academic Press.

Burstein, M. 1960. A theory of full-line forcing. *Northwestern University Law Review* 55, March–April, 62–95.

Coase, R.H. 1937. The nature of the firm. *Economica* 4, 386–405. Reprinted in *Readings in Price Theory*. ed. G.J. Stigler and K.E. Boulding, Homewood, Ill.: Richard D. Irwin, 1952.

Coase, R.H. 1972. Industrial organization: a proposal for research. In *Policy Issues and Research Opportunities in Industrial Organization*, ed. V.R. Fuchs, New York: National Bureau of Economic Research, 59–73.

Commons, J.R. 1934. *Institutional Economics*. New York; Macmillan.

Grossman, S.J. and Hart, O.D. 1986. The costs and benefits of ownership: a theory of vertical integration. *Journal of Political Economy* 94, July, 691–719.

Joskow, P.L. 1985. Vertical integration and long-term contracts. *Journal of Law, Economics and Organization* 1, Spring, 33–80.

Klein, B., Crawford, R.A. and Alchian, A.A. 1978. Vertical integration, appropriable rents, and the competitive contracting process. *Journal of Law and Economics* 21, October, 297–326.

Klein, B. and Leffler, K.B. 1981. The role of market forces in assuring contractual performance. *Journal of Political Economy* 89, August, 615–41.

Knight, F.H. 1921. *Risk, Uncertainty and Profit*. New York: Harper & Row, 1965.

McKenzie, L. 1951. Ideal output and the interdependence of firms. *Economic Journal* 61, December, 785–803.

Machlup, F. and Tabor, M. 1960. Bilateral monopoly, successive monopoly, and vertical integration. *Economica*, May, 101–19.

Marshall, A. 1920. *Principles of Economics*. 8th edn, London and New York: Macmillan, 1948.

Mason, E. 1957. *Economic Concentration and the Monopoly Problem*. Cambridge, Mass.: Harvard University Press.

Masten, S. 1984. The organization of production: evidence from the aerospace industry. *Journal of Law and Economics* 27, October, 403–18.

Modigliani, F. 1958. New developments on the oligopoly front. *Journal of Political Economy* 66, June, 215–32.

Monteverde, K. and Teece, D. 1982. Supplier switching costs and vertical integration in the automobile industry. *Bell Journal of Economics* 13, Spring, 206–13.

Palay, T. 1984. Comparative institutional economics: the governance of rail freight contracting. *Journal of Legal Studies* 13, June, 265–88.

Palay, T. 1985. The avoidance of regulatory constraints: the use of informal contracts. *Journal of Law, Economics and Organization* 1, Spring, 155–75.

Perry, M. 1978. Price discrimination and vertical integration. *Bell Journal of Economics* 9, Spring, 209–17.

Perry, M. 1980. Forward integration by Alcoa. *Journal of Industrial Economics* 29, September, 37–53.

Richardson, G.B. 1972. The organization of industry. *Economic Journal* 82, September, 883–96.

Robinson, J. 1933. *The Economics of Imperfect Competition*. London: Macmillan.

Salop, S. and Scheffman, D. 1983. Raising rivals' costs. *American Economic Review* 73, May, 267–71.

Schmalensee, R. 1973. A note on the theory of vertical integration. *Journal of Political Economy* 81, March–April, 442–9.

Simon, H.A. 1947. *Administrative Behavior*. 2nd edn, New York: Macmillan, 1961.

Spiller, P. 1985. On vertical mergers. *Journal of Law, Economics and Organization* 1, Fall, 285–312.

Stigler, G.J. 1951. The division of labor is limited by the extent of the market. *Journal of Political Economy* 59, June, 185–93.

Stigler, G. 1955. Mergers and preventive antitrust policy. *University of Pennsylvania Law Review* 104, November, 176–84.

Stigler, G. 1963. United States *v* Loew's Inc.: a note on block booking. *Supreme Court Review*, 152–64.

Stigler, G. 1968. *The Organization of Industry*. Homewood, Ill.: Richard D. Irwin.

Stuckey, J. 1983. *Vertical Integration and Joint Ventures in the Aluminum Industry*. Cambridge, Mass.: Harvard University Press.

Sylos-Labini, P. 1956. *Oligopoly and Technical Progress*. Trans. E. Henderson, Cambridge, Mass.: Harvard University Press, 1962.

Vernon, J.M. and Graham, D.A. 1971. Profitability of monopolization by vertical integration. *Journal of Political Economy* 79, July–August, 924–5.

Warren-Boulton, F.R. 1974. Vertical control with variable proportions. *Journal of Political Economy* 75, April, 123–38.

Westfield, F. 1981. Vertical integration: does product price fall? *American Economic Review* 71, June, 334–46.

Williamson, O.E. 1971. The vertical integration of production: market failure considerations. *American Economic Review* 61, May, 112–23.

Williamson, O.E. 1975. *Markets and Hierarchies: Analysis and Antitrust Implications*. New York: Free Press.
Williamson, O.E. 1983. Credible commitments: using hostages to support exchange. *American Economic Review* 73, September, 519–40.
Williamson, O.E. 1985. *The Economic Institutions of Capitalism*. New York: Free Press.
Young, A. 1928. Increasing returns and economic progress. *Economic Journal* 38, December, 527–42.

Vickrey, William Spencer (born 1914). Vickrey was born in Canada in 1914. He was educated at Yale and Columbia, joining the faculty of the latter institution after World War II and maintaining that association for the remainder of his professional career. Possessing a fertile and original mind, Vickrey became as famous for the number of pioneering ideas that were embedded quietly in his works and went unnoticed until later as for his more immediately recognized work on taxation, transportation, and public utility pricing.

Vickrey began his professional career as a researcher for a tax study, and he devoted most of his attention before and during World War II to problems in public finance (especially taxation), in which he became a leading authority, his 1947 *Agenda for Progressive Taxation* becoming a classic in the field. In 1949/50 he joined Carl Shoup's Tax Mission to Japan and (with Shoup) laid the foundations for the postwar tax structure of Japan. In later years he took part in several other international tax advisory missions.

He was an applied theorist who was impatient with a display of technique for its own sake, but always careful to ensure that there was a firm theoretical underpinning to his policy-oriented analysis. If the state of art was insufficient in this respect, Vickrey would first fill the theory gap, then attack the policy problem fully armed. His contributions to theory were made out of a need to solve a problem for policy purposes.

In his 1960 *Quarterly Journal of Economics* paper, Vickrey raised the problem of truthful revelation of preferences and of the strategic advantage of concealing them. In his 1961 *Journal of Finance* paper, he considered market mechanisms (rules for auctions and sealed bidding contests) in relation to the incentives provided for truthful revelation. At the time there was little interest within the profession in the problems of incentive compatibility, but these papers were recognized two decades later as pioneering contributions to the field.

Vickrey had a strong interest in the optimal pricing of public utilities and transport, and made many contributions in this field. He had a strong and continuing interest in urban transportation in particular, and was involved with many studies of fare structures for urban rapid transit systems in the United States and elsewhere. He laid much emphasis on congestion and peak load effects and was a strong proponent of pricing relative to congestion at the time of use, even suggesting engineering solutions to the problems of monitoring tolls for urban automobile use.

K.J. LANCASTER

See also AUCTIONS; BIDDING; INCENTIVE COMPATIBILITY.

SELECTED WORKS

1949. *Agenda for Progressive Taxation*. Ronald Press. Reprinted, New York: Augustus M. Kelley, 1971.
1960. Utility, strategy, and social decision rules. *Quarterly Journal of Economics* 74, 507–35.
1961. Counterspeculation, auctions, and competitive sealed tenders. *Journal of Finance* 16, 8–37.
1963. Pricing in urban and suburban transport. *American Economic Review*. 53, 452–65.
1969. Congestion theory and transport investment. *American Economic Review* 59, 251–60.

Viner, Jacob (1892–1970). Jacob Viner, the economic theorist and historian of economic thought, was born and raised in Montreal, the son of immigrant parents from eastern Europe. As an undergraduate he attended McGill University, where he was taught economics by Stephen Leacock, the famous humourist. Leacock used texts by Mill and Walker, Milk and Water, as the students referred to them, showing 'good judgment' according to an account that Viner gave later in life. For graduate work he went to Harvard, where he earned a PhD in 1922. He was a student and eventually became a close friend of Frank W. Taussig, the well-known authority on economic theory and international economics. At that time and during the earlier part of Viner's career he and Taussig were rare specimens in what was, except for a very few others, essentially a 'wasp' establishment. But in other respects their background was quite different. Viner was a self-made man who had emancipated himself from the immigrant quarter of Montreal, while Taussig was born into a patrician family with wealth and native culture.

Taussig's specialities were the fields to which Viner himself was drawn and in which he earned great distinction, in addition to his perhaps even more distinguished work in the history of economics, where his accomplishments were almost without rival.

During the two world wars, during the Great Depression, and on and off at other times, Viner did consulting and other work in Washington, but he was foremost an academic, who taught at the University of Chicago in 1916–17 and from 1919 to 1946, when he went to Princeton and taught there until his retirement in 1960. Viner advanced rapidly at Chicago, where the department then was headed by J.M. Clark, and he became a full professor at age 32. A few decades earlier, in the same department, Veblen had risen to the rank of assistant professor only at age 43. But Veblen had defied convention both in his writings and personal life.

Viner's tenure at Chicago coincided in part with his editorship of the *Journal of Political Economy* for a period of eighteen years. Most of the time the post was held jointly with Frank H. Knight, who, after having earlier spent two years at Chicago, returned to it in 1927. Both men imprinted on the journal the mark of their own great gifts.

Viner's contributions to economic theory and the history of economic thought are embodied in periodical articles that were reprinted in book form in 1958 under the title *The Long View and the Short*. His contributions to general theory consist principally of two remarkable articles, one published in 1921 and the other ten years later. Of the two, the second on 'Cost curves and supply curves' (Viner, 1958, pp. 50–78) made an immediate and powerful impact on the profession. Written, as it was, by a then well-established scholar, it contained virtually the whole of the modern exposition, graphic and otherwise, of the theory of cost, including the envelope curve, about which Viner had a legendary dispute with his mathematically more proficient Chinese draftsman. It also contained, perhaps for the first time in print, the words 'marginal revenue'. All this matter eventually entered into the elementary textbooks. Viner's accomplishment paralleled that of Knight, whose graphic portrayal of the theory of production in *Risk, Uncertainty and Profit* (1921) likewise entered into the mainstream of economic theory and became the basis for the textbook treatment of the matter. Among the two great scholars there was forged a substantial portion of partial equilibrium analysis as it evolved during the first half of the 20th century.

Viner's earlier article, published in 1921 and covering barely five pages in the reprint of 1958, was in some respects an even more dazzling achievement than the later and much better-known one. Five years ahead of Sraffa, six years ahead of the publication of Joan Robinson's and Chamberlin's books on the subject, Viner developed here, in a short paragraph, the outlines of the theory of monopolistic competition. He writes of inflexible prices, 'differentiation' of products, advertising, non-price competition and other characteristics of markets that are neither fully competitive nor completely monopolistic. In such markets producers may succeed in creating a special demand for their products. They can then to some extent determine prices independently of the prices charged by their competitors and still maintain their sales (Viner, 1958, pp. 5–6). In the same context Viner also developed, in a few sentences, the theory of what became later known as the kinky demand curve, 18 years ahead of Sweezy's article on the subject.

These were indeed path-breaking contributions, but their existence was virtually ignored until Viner's article was reprinted in 1958. The place of the original contribution – L.C. Marshall (ed.), *Business Administration*, University of Chicago Press, 1921 – was not exactly obscure but elusive nevertheless from the standpoint of a reader looking for innovations in economic theory. Chamberlin did not mention Viner in the bibliographies that he appended to successive editions of his book and which eventually listed around 1500 items. As regards the kinky demand curve, there is no reference to Viner in Sweezy's article in the *Journal of Political Economy* for 1939, of which Viner then was the co-editor, nor in Stigler's critique published in the same journal in 1947. All this is an unresolved puzzle. No one knows why Viner never developed more fully the ideas sketched in his brief article of 1921 and why he, who in other contexts did not shy away from announcing his priority, remained silent about this one. The ideas surely were his own and not derived from an oral tradition at Harvard, whose only potential fount, Allyn Young, came to Harvard only in 1920, when Viner was already teaching at Chicago. He could not very well have anticipated unfriendly criticism, because the Chicago of the 1920s, where J.M. Clark had a senior position, was not the Chicago of the later so-called Chicago School, all of whose leaders, beginning in the mid-1940s, voiced disapproval of the theory of monopolistic competition.

Viner not only had an analytical mind that was stocked with original ideas, but combined with this a stupendous book learning that within the scope of the humanities and social sciences, and especially their history, was virtually universal and gave special depth to his studies in the history of economics. He was perhaps not as scintillating a writer as Schumpeter, nor did he turn out, as did Schumpeter, a comprehensive treatise on the subject, but his work, scattered in periodical articles, contains far more reliable and judicious interpretations of such matters as utilitarianism, classical, and Marshallian economics. The most important of Viner's articles on the history of economics were reprinted in Part II of the collection published in 1958. Their coverage extends all the way from the mercantilists to Marshall and Schumpeter. The essay on mercantilist thought shows the mercantilists in pursuit both of power and wealth as ultimate ends of national policy. Another on Adam Smith demonstrates, among other matters, that Smith was not a doctrinaire advocate of laissez faire, a quality that he shares with Viner. Smith was a favoured subject of Viner's studies, and in 1965 he contributed an introduction of 145 pages to a new edition of Rae's *Life of Adam Smith*, the standard biography. An essay about the utility concept in value theory defends the concept against its critics. Writing about Bentham and J.S. Mill, Viner clarifies the meaning of the former's hedonic calculus and by restricting it to comparisons between pain and pleasure contributes to the rehabilitation of this concept, for which, he believes, an idea of Benjamin Franklin's may have been the inspiration. Mill and Marshall are both viewed in their Victorian setting. The former's *Principles*, a combination of 'hard-headed rules and utopian aspirations', was 'exactly the doctrine that Victorians of goodwill yearned for' (p. 330). Marshall fitted into the Victorian age that was complacent about the present and optimistic with respect to future progress.

Except for the collection of his articles published in 1958 and two posthumous publications, all of Viner's books are about international economics, with a collection of his articles in this field, titled *International Economics*, published in 1951. His work in international economics covers virtually all its phases – theory, history of thought, and policy – with occasional use of empirical material. His earliest book, *Dumping* (1923), contained the first comprehensive and systematic study of this subject. It was followed a year later by Viner's doctoral dissertation on *Canada's Balance of International Indebtedness, 1900–1913*, which was written on the suggestion of Taussig, who directed a number of related empirical studies designed to demonstrate the operation of the balance-of-payments adjustment process. In 1937 there was published Viner's masterwork, *Studies in the Theory of International Trade*, which blends in an inimitable manner theoretical analysis and erudite doctrinal history. Its aim was to trace the evolution of the modern theory of international trade. It starts out with the mercantilists and continues with the bullionist controversies, the currency school–banking school controversy, the international mechanism of adjustment, and the doctrine of the gains from trade. In Viner's view, the comparative-cost doctrine is dependent on a real-cost theory of value rather than on opportunity cost. While this view was not in tune with the time, there are many forward-looking sections in the book, including references to a lecture given by Viner in 1931 in which later models of Lerner, Leontief and Hicks were anticipated.

In 1950 Viner published *The Customs Union Issue*, which contained the distinction between trade creation and trade diversion, the starting point of later discussions of the matter. Viner's articles on *International Economics*, collected in 1951, start with one on the most-favoured-nation clause and end with an essay on the economic foundations of international organizations. Many of the articles are indispensable for the study of the policy issues of the time. In 1952 Viner made his contribution to the emerging field of economic development in a book on *International Trade and Economic Development*. In this work he took a far less favourable view of a number of public policies designed to accelerate economic development than was commonly held at that time. He refused to identify agriculture with poverty, stressed that industrialization was more often a consequence than a cause of prosperity, and placed the main burden of promoting development on the underdeveloped country itself.

Viner had for long been interested in theological ideas, especially of the more remote past, and after his retirement he started out on a project designed to explore the relationship between religious and economic thought. This great project proved open-ended. After Viner's death only two fragments were published, one on *The Role of Providence in the Social Order* (1972), and the other on *Religious Thought and Economic Society* (1978). The first of these works is an original accomplishment that traces the derivation of a number of economic ideas from theological precedents, for example, the theory of international trade that is grounded in differences in factor endowments, Smith's invisible hand, and the providential origin of social inequality that was claimed in the past. The second work is written along more conventional lines and reviews the economic doctrines of the Fathers of the Church, of the Scholastics, secularizing tendencies in later Catholic social thought, and Protestantism and the rise of capitalism. This last chapter contains a critical analysis of the Weber–Tawney thesis of the Calvinist origin of capitalism.

To place Viner's work into its proper historical setting, a word is in order about his relation to the Chicago School. A common conception takes his membership or leadership in this school for granted, but this view is mistaken. Viner himself said that much in a remarkable letter to Patinkin written shortly before his death (Patinkin, 1981, p. 266; the letter is also reproduced by Reder, 1982, p. 7). It must be remembered that at the time when Viner taught at Chicago, the designation 'Chicago School' was not yet a commonly used term. To be sure, Viner's views about laissez faire, Keynesian economics and government intervention had something in common with the views held by representatives of the Chicago School, but on the whole he was a more pragmatic thinker and more aware of the need for qualification and consideration of circumstances of time and place. Moreover, Viner, from whom stems the definition, economics is what economists do, would not have felt comfortable within the confines of a school, especially of one that at times has come close to defining economics as the study of competitive markets. The early leaders of what later became known as the Chicago School were Henry Simons and Knight, not Viner. Like no one else, Knight had a charismatic appeal that yielded conversions to libertarianism in his classroom – James Buchanan has testified to this – and that made him the more likely founder of a school. It is significant also that Viner, and, for that matter, Knight too, urged deficit spending during the Great Depression. Viner called the plea for an annual balanced budget a mouldy fallacy (Viner, 1933, p. 129). He was critical of Hayek's libertarianism (Viner, 1961). He denied that competition was both a norm and normal, pointing out instead that

> monopoly is so prevalent in the markets of the western world today that discussions of the merits of the free competitive market as if that were what we are living with or were at all likely to have the good fortune to live with in the future seem to me academic in the only pejorative sense of that adjective.

He also insisted that 'no modern people will have zeal for the free market unless it operates in a setting of 'distributive justice' with which they are tolerably content' (Viner, 1960, pp. 66, 68). (The article in which Viner developed these ideas was ostensibly an exposition of the *rhetoric* of laissez faire, an early exercise in an approach that D.N. McCloskey was to apply on a wider scale more than a quarter century later.) Against Friedman Viner supported discretionary monetary management rather than conduct in conformity with a 'rule' (Viner, 1962). And, last but not least, it was Viner who created the substance of the theory of monopolistic competition, which in a peculiar dialectic was later to become the target of the Chicago School.

HENRY W. SPIEGEL

See also CHICAGO SCHOOL.

SELECTED WORKS

1923. *Dumping: A Problem in International Trade*. Chicago: University of Chicago Press.

1924. *Canada's Balance of International Indebtedness, 1900–1913: An Inductive Study in the Theory of International Trade*. Cambridge, Mass.: Harvard University Press.

1930. *Lectures in Price and Distribution Theory*. Economics 301, University of Chicago, Summer Quarter, 1930; ed. M.D. Ketchum, 1931, Mimeo.

1933. Inflation as a remedy for depression. In *Proceedings of the Institute of Public Affairs*, Seventh Annual Session, Athens, Georgia: University of Georgia.

1937. *Studies in the Theory of International Trade*. New York: Harper.

1950. *The Customs Union Issue*. New York: Carnegie Endowment for International Peace; London: Stevens.

1951. *International Economics: Studies*. Glencoe, Ill.: Free Press.

1952. *International Trade and Economic Development: Lectures Delivered at the National University of Brazil*. Glencoe, Ill.: Free Press; Oxford: Clarendon Press.

1958. *The Long View and the Short: Studies in Economic Theory and Policy*. Glencoe, Ill.: Free Press. (With bibliography.)

1960. The intellectual history of laissez faire. *Journal of Law and Economics* 3, October, 45–69.

1961. Hayek on freedom and coercion. *Southern Economic Journal* 2(3), January, 230–36.

1962. The necessary and the desirable range of discretion to be allowed to a monetary authority. In *In Search of a Monetary Constitution*, ed. L.B. Yeager, Cambridge, Mass.: Harvard University Press.

1963. Review article on C.B. Macpherson's *Political Theory of Possessive Individualism: Hobbes to Locke*. *Canadian Journal of Economics and Political Science* 29(4), November, 548 ff.

1965. Guide to John Rae's 'Life of Adam Smith'. Introduction to J. Rae, *Life of Adam Smith*, New York: Kelley.

1972. *The Role of Providence in the Social Order: An Essay in Intellectual History*. Philadelphia: American Philosophical Society.

1978. *Religious Thought and Economic Society: Four Chapters of an Unfinished Work*. Ed. J. Melitz and D. Winch, Durham, North Carolina: Duke University Press. Also published in *History of Political Economy* 10(1), Spring 1978, 9–189.

BIBLIOGRAPHY

Baumol, W.J. and Seiler, E.V. 1979. Jacob Viner. *International Encyclopedia of the Social Sciences*, Vol. 18, Biographical Supplement, New York: Free Press.

Davis, J.R. 1971. *The New Economics and the Old Economists*. Ames: Iowa State University Press.

Machlup, F. 1972. What was left on Viner's desk. *Journal of Political Economy* 80(2), March-April, 353–64.

Machlup, F., Samuelson, P.A. and Baumol, W.J. 1972. In Memoriam, Jacob Viner (1892–1970). *Journal of Political Economy* 80(1), January-February, 1–15.

Patinkin, D. 1981. *Essays on and in the Chicago Tradition*. Durham, North Carolina: Duke University Press.

Reder, M.W. 1982. Chicago economics: permanence and change. *Journal of Economic Literature* 20(1), March, 1–38.

Robbins, L. 1970. *Jacob Viner: A Tribute*. Princeton: Princeton University Press.

Samuels, W.J. (ed.) 1976. *The Chicago School of Political Economy*. Published jointly by the Association for Evolutionary Economics and Division of Research, Graduate School of Business Administration, Michigan State University, East Lansing.

Winch, D. 1981. Jacob Viner. *American Scholar* 50(4), Autumn, 519–25.

vintages. Investment represents the acquisition of capital goods at a given point of time. The quantity of investment is measured in the same way as the durable goods themselves.

For example, investment in equipment is the number of machines of a given specification and investment in structures is the number of buildings of a particular description. The price of acquisition of a durable good is the unit cost of acquiring a piece of equipment or a structure.

By contrast with investment, capital services are measured in terms of the use of a durable good for a stipulated period of time. For example, a building can be leased for a period of years, an automobile can be rented for a number of days or weeks, and computer time can be purchased in seconds or minutes. The price of the services of a durable good is the unit cost of using the good for a specified period.

AGGREGATION OVER VINTAGES. We can refer to durable goods acquired at different points of time as different *vintages* of capital. The flow of capital services is a quantity index of capital inputs from durable goods of different vintages. Under perfect substitutability among the services of durable goods of different vintages, the flow of capital services is a weighted sum of past investments. The weights correspond to the relative efficiencies of the different vintages of capital.

The durable goods model of production is characterized by price-quantity duality. The rental price of capital input is a price index corresponding to the quantity index given by the flow of capital services. The rental prices for all vintages of capital are proportional to the price index for capital input. The constants of proportionality are given by the relative efficiencies of the different vintages of capital.

We develop notation appropriate for the intertemporal theory of production by attaching time subscripts to the variables that occur in the theory. We can denote the quantity of output at time t by y_t and the quantities of J inputs at time t by $x_{jt}(j = 1, 2, \ldots, J)$. Similarly, we can denote the price of output at time t by q_t and the prices of the J inputs at time t by $p_{jt}(j = 1, 2, \ldots, J)$.

In order to characterize capital as a factor of production, we require the following additional notation:

A_t – quantity of capital goods acquired at time t.
$K_{t,\tau}$ – quantity of capital services from capital goods of age τ at time t.
$p_{A,t}$ – price of acquisition of new capital goods at time t.
$p_{K,t,\tau}$ – rental price of capital services from capital goods of age τ at time t.

To present the durable goods model of production we first assume that the production function, say F, is homothetically separable in the services of different vintages of capital:

$$y_t = F[G(K_{t,0}, K_{t,1} \ldots K_{t,\tau} \ldots), x_{2t} \ldots x_{Jt}]. \qquad (1)$$

Where K_t is the flow of capital services, we can represent this quantity index of capital input as follows:

$$K_t = G,$$

where the function G is homogeneous of degree one in the services from capital goods of different ages.

If we assume that the quantity index of capital input K_t is characterized by perfect substitutability among the services of different vintages of capital, we can write this index as the sum of these services:

$$K_t = \sum_{\tau=0}^{\infty} K_{t,\tau}.$$

Under the additional assumption that the services provided by a durable good are proportional to initial investment in this good, we can express the quantity index of capital input in the form:

$$K_t = \sum_{\tau=0}^{\infty} d_\tau A_{t-\tau}. \qquad (2)$$

The flow of capital services is a weighted sum of past investments with weights given by the relative efficiencies $\{d_\tau\}$ of capital goods at different ages.

Under constant returns to scale we can express the price of output as a function, say Q, of the prices of all inputs. The price function Q is homothetically separable in the rental prices of different vintages of capital:

$$q_t = Q[P(p_{K,t,0}, p_{K,t,1} \ldots p_{K,t,\tau} \ldots), p_{2t} \ldots p_{Jt}]. \qquad (3)$$

Where $p_{K,t}$ is a price index of capital services, we can represent this index as follows:

$$p_{K,t} = P,$$

where the function P is homogeneous of degree one in the rental prices of capital goods of different ages.

Under perfect substitutability among the services of different vintages of capital, we can write the price index of capital input P as the price of the services of a new capital good:

$$p_{K,t} = p_{K,t,0}.$$

Under the additional assumption that the services provided by a durable good are proportional to the initial investment, we can express the rental prices of capital goods of different ages in the form:

$$p_{K,t,\tau} = d_\tau p_{K,t}, \qquad (\tau = 0, 1, \ldots). \qquad (4)$$

The rental prices are proportional to the rental price of capital input with constants of proportionality given by the relative efficiencies $\{d_\tau\}$ of capital goods of different ages.

Given the quantity of capital input K_t, representing the flow of capital services, and the price of capital inputs $p_{K,t}$, representing the rental price, capital input plays the same role in production as any other input. We next derive the prices and quantities of capital inputs from the prices and quantities for acquisition of durable goods $p_{A,t}$ and A_t.

VINTAGE ACCOUNTING. We being our description of the measurement of capital input with the quantities estimated by the perpetual inventory method. Taking the first difference of the expression for capital stock in terms of past investments (2), we obtain:

$$K_t - K_{t-1} = A_t + \sum_{\tau=1}^{\infty} (d_\tau - d_{\tau-1}) A_{t-\tau},$$

$$= A_t - R_t,$$

where R_t is the level of replacement requirements in period t. The change in capital stock from period to period is equal to the acquisition of investment goods less replacement requirements.

We turn next to a description of the price data required for the measurement of the price of capital input. There is a one-to-one correspondence between the vintage quantities that appear in the perpetual inventory method and the prices that appear in our vintage price accounts. To bring out this correspondence we use a system of present or discounted prices. Taking the present as time zero, the discounted price of a commodity, say q_t, multiplied by a discount factor:

$$q_t = \prod_{s=1}^{t} \frac{1}{1+r_s} p_t.$$

The notational convenience of present or discounted prices results from dispensing with explicit discount factors in expressing prices for different time periods.

In the correspondence between the perpetual inventory method and its dual or price counterpart the price of acquisition of a capital good is analogous to capital stock. The price of acquisition, say $q_{A,t}$ is the sum of future rental prices of capital services, say $q_{K,t}$, weighted by the relative efficiencies of capital goods in all future periods:

$$q_{A,t} = \sum_{\tau=0}^{\infty} d_\tau q_{K,t+\tau+1} \tag{5}$$

This expression may be compared with the corresponding expression (2) giving capital stock as a weighted sum of past investments.

Taking the first difference of the expression for the acquisition price of capital goods in terms of future rentals (5), we obtain:

$$\begin{aligned} a_{A,t} - q_{A,t-1} &= -q_{K,t} - \sum_{\tau=1}^{\infty} (d_\tau - d_{\tau-1}) q_{K,t+\tau}, \\ &= -q_{K,t} + q_{D,t}, \end{aligned}$$

where $q_{D,t}$ is depreciation on a capital good in period t. The period-to-period change in the price of acquisition of a capital good is equal to depreciation less the rental price of capital. Postponing the purchase of a capital good makes it necessary to forego one period's rental and makes it possible to avoid one period's depreciation. In the correspondence between the perpetual inventory method and its price counterpart, investment corresponds to the rental price of capital and replacement corresponds to depreciation.

We can rewrite the expression for the first difference of the acquisition price of capital goods in terms of undiscounted prices and the period-to-period discount rate:

$$p_{K,t} = p_{A,t-1} r_t + p_{D,t} - (p_{A,t} - p_{A,t-1}), \tag{6}$$

where $p_{A,t}$ is the undiscounted price of acquisition of capital goods, $p_{K,t}$ the price of capital services, $p_{D,t}$ depreciation, and r_t the rate of return, all in period t. The price of capital services $p_{K,t}$ is the sum of return per unit of capital $p_{A,t-1} r_t$, depreciation $p_{D,t}$, and the negative of revaluation, $p_{A,t} - p_{A,t-1}$. To apply this formula we require a series of undiscounted acquisition prices for capital goods $p_{A,t}$, rates of return r_t, depreciation on new capital goods, $p_{D,t}$, and revaluation of existing capital goods $p_{A,t} - p_{A,t-1}$.

To calculate the rate of return in each period we set the formula for the rental price $p_{K,t}$ times the quantity of capital K_{t-1} equal to property compensation. All of the variables entering this equation – current and past acquisition prices for capital goods, depreciation, revaluation, capital stock, and property compensation – except for the rate of return, are directly observable. Replacing these variables by the corresponding data we solve this equation for the rate of return. To obtain the capital service price itself we substitute the rate of return into the original formula along with the other data. This completes the calculation of the service price.

In the perpetual inventory method data on the quantity of investment goods of every vintage are used to estimate capital formation, replacement requirements, and capital stock. In the price counterpart of the perpetual inventory method data on the acquisition prices of investment goods of every vintage is required. In the full price-quantity duality that characterizes the vintage accounts, capital stock corresponds to the acquisition price of durable goods and investment corresponds to the rental price of capital services.

CONCLUSION. The distinguishing feature of capital as a factor of production is that durable goods contribute capital services to production at different points of time. The services provided by a given durable good are proportional to the initial investment. In addition, the services provided by different durable goods at the same point of time are perfect substitutes. The weights correspond to the relative efficiencies of the different vintages of capital. The durable goods model of production was originated by Walras (1954) and is discussed in greater detail by Jorgenson (1973) and Diewert (1980).

The durable goods model is characterized by price-quantity duality. The rental price of capital input is a price index corresponding to the quantity index given by the flow of capital services. The rental prices for all vintages of capital are proportional to the price index for capital input. The constants of proportionality are given by the relative efficiencies of the different vintages of capital. The dual to the durable good model of production was introduced by Hotelling (1925) and Haavelmo (1960). The dual to this model has been further developed by Arrow (1964) and Hall (1968).

The acquisition prices for capital goods of each vintage at each point of time together with investments of all vintages at each point of time constitute the basic data on quantities and prices. These data can be employed in generating the complete vintage accounting system originated by Christensen and Jorgenson (1973) and described by Jorgenson (1980). Price and quantity data that we have described for a single durable good are required for each durable good in the system. These data are used to derive price and quantity indexes for capital input in the theory of production presented in the entry on PRODUCTION FUNCTIONS.

DALE W. JORGENSON

See also PRODUCTION FUNCTIONS; TECHNICAL CHANGE.

BIBLIOGRAPHY

Arrow, K.J. 1964. Optimal capital policy, the cost of capital, and myopic decision rules. *Annals of the Institute of Statistical Mathematics* 16, pp. 16–30.

Christensen, L.R. and Jorgenson, D.W. 1973. Measuring economic performance in the private sector. In *The Measurement of Economic and Social Performance*, ed. M. Mess, New York: Columbia University Press for the National Bureau of Economic Research.

Diewert, W.E. 1980. Aggregation problems in the measurement of capital. In *The Measurement of Capital*, ed. D. Usher. Chicago: University of Chicago Press.

Haavelmo, T. 1960. *A Study in the Theory of Investment*. Chicago: University of Chicago Press.

Hall, R.E. 1968. Technical change and capital from the point of view of the dual. *Review of Economic Studies* 35(1), January, 35–46.

Hotelling, H.S. 1925. A general mathematical theory of depreciation. *Journal of the American Statistical Association* 20, September, 340–53.

Jorgenson, D.W. 1973. The economic theory of replacement and depreciation. In *Econometrics and Economic Theory*, ed. W. Sellekaerts. New York: Macmillan, 189–221.

Jorgenson, D.W. 1980. Accounting for capital. In *Capital, Efficiency, and Growth*, ed. G. von Furstenberg. Cambridge: Ballinger, 251–319.

Walras, L. 1874. *Elements of Pure Economics*. Trans. W. Jaffé, Homewood: Irwin, 1954.

Viti de Marco, Antonio de (1858–1943). Italian economist and politician; born in Lecce on 30 September 1858; died in Rome on 1 December 1943. He graduated in law at the University of Rome in 1881 and embarked on an academic career, first teaching political economy and then public finance at Camerino, Macerata and Pavia. In 1887–8 he took up the post of teaching public finance in the Faculty of Law in Rome, where he remained until 1931. From 1901 until 1921, with only a brief intermission, he was a member of the Italian Parliament. He attempted unsuccessfully to found a liberal democratic group whose main aim was to fight the protectionism and exploitation of Southern Italy. The volume entitled *Un trentennio di lotte politiche (1894–1922)* is a testimony to his political ideas. In keeping with his political beliefs, he avoided taking the oath of allegiance to the fascist regime by giving up his university post in 1931. De Viti de Marco's cultural interests led him, together with some other economists, to complete the purchase in 1890 of the *Giornale degli Economisti*, of which he was co-editor until 1919 with Maffeo Pantaleoni, Ugo Mazzola and, later on, with Vilfredo Pareto. It was in this way that the *Giornale degli Economisti* became the most authoritative voice of liberal Italian thinking.

De Viti de Marco was not a prolific writer – he spent much time patiently revising his own works – but he exerted a fundamental influence on the typically Italian tradition of creating a 'pure' theory of public finance. He dedicated his first essay (*Il carattere teorico dell'economia finanziaria*) in 1888 to this particular area of economic research. At the same time he studied monetary and credit problems, on which in 1898 he published the volume entitled *La funzione della Banca*, which he revised several times before the definitive edition was published in 1934. De Viti de Marco's name, however, is primarily connected with his *Principi di Economia Finanziaria*, which was the subject of various drafts and revisions in 1923, 1928, 1934 and 1939. The definitive edition of this work contains a masterly preface by Luigi Einaudi which fully upholds 'for spontaneous universal recognition' the position of supremacy held by De Viti de Marco over other researchers in the field of public finance . In addition, when the book was translated into English, it was generally judged to be 'the best book ever written on public finance'. De Viti de Marco's *Principi* has been translated into all major foreign languages, and it embodies the most complete attempt to construct an 'economic' theory of the entire financial system, whose final aim is the systematic application of the theory of marginal utility to financial problems.

The origins of De Viti de Marco's beliefs can be traced to the work of Francesco Ferrara, in as much as the latter believed public spending to be an integral part of the study of public finance, and recognized the productive aspect of the public services. The significance of the study of financial problems had already been foreseen in the writings of Maffeo Pantaleoni and Ugo Mazzola. But it was De Viti de Marco who, after forty years of methodical work, advanced the economic concept of public finance based on two abstract types of political constitution of the State: a monopolist state in which a privileged oligarchy acts in its own interests in the decisions concerning the levying of taxes and the distribution of public expenditures; and a cooperative state where the interests of tax-payers and those who are entitled to benefit from the services of the state coincide. This latter type of state was referred to most extensively by De Viti de Marco in his work in order to examine the whole fiscal problem, because in the cooperative state choices and the decisions are reduced to economic calculus on an individualistic level and the resulting finance is devoid of any coercive character. The precise reasoning of this premise and its rigorous development explain why De Viti's work was internationally acclaimed. It also explains the criticisms of those who followed a sociological approach and did not consider economic calculus at an individual level to be a valid basis for collective decisions. But De Viti's undisputed merit lies in his having created a scientific model which has remained a point of reference and a focus of discussion for alternative ideas about the nature, the causes and the effects of fiscal phenomena.

F. Caffè

SELECTED WORKS

1885. *Moneta e prezzi*. Città de Castello: S. Lapi.

1888. *Il carattere teorico dell'economia finanziaria*. Rome: Pasqualucci.

1898a. *Saggi di economia e di finanza*. Edited from the *Giornale degli Economisti*, Rome.

1898b. *La funzione della Banca*. Rome: Accademia dei Lincei.

1930. *Un trentennio di lotte politiche*. Rome: Collezione Meridionale Editrice.

1932. *Grundlehren der Finanzwirtschaft*. Tübingen: J.C.B. Mohr.

1934a. *La funzione della Banca*. Revised and definitive edn, Turin: Einaudi.

1934b. *Principi di economia finanziaria*. Turin: Einaudi.

1934c. *Principios fondamentales de economia financier*. Madrid: Editorial Revista de Derecho Privado.

1936. *First Principles of Public Finance*. Trans. E.P. Marget, New York: Harcourt, Brace & Co.

BIBLIOGRAPHY

Buchanan, J.M. 1960. 'La scienza delle finanze': the Italian tradition in fiscal theory and political economy. In J. Buchanan, *Selected Essays*, Chapel Hill: University of North Carolina Press.

Cardini, A. 1985. *Antonio De Viti de Marco*. Bari: Laterza.

Ricci, U. 1946. Antonio De Viti de Marco. *Studi Economici*, March.

Volterra, Vito (1860–1940). A mathematician by vocation, Volterra graduated at the Scuola Normale in Pisa in 1882 and obtained the Chair of Rational Mechanics at the University of Pisa in 1883. Subsequently he held chairs at the Universities of Turin and Rome. He became a Senator in 1905, was President of the Consiglio Nazionale delle Ricerche, of the Academia dei Lincei, Fellow of the Royal Society, etc. In 1931 he refused to take the required oath of loyalty to the Fascist government and was deprived of his Rome chair and forced to resign from all Italian scientific academies.

Volterra is renowned for his contributions to pure and applied mathematics. He is recognized as the founder of the general theory of functionals (1887, 1927a, 1929). In biological mathematics (independently of Lotka, who had examined the two-species case earlier) he introduced the prey-predator equations generalized to n species (1926, 1927b, 1931).

In 1906, Volterra reviewed Pareto's *Manuale*. Pareto, in treating the problem of integrating the differential equation of the indifference curve to obtain the 'ophelimity' (the utility function) had stressed the case in which the 'elementary ophelimity' (the marginal utility) of each good was a function solely of the quantity of that good, giving the impression that this was the case in which the integration could be performed with certainty. Volterra reminded Pareto that in the two-variable case there always exists an integrating factor so that it is always possible to perform the integration; he also pointed out that – as there exists an infinite number of integrating factors – the utility function is, in general, indeterminate. The real integrability problem arises when one has to deal with more than two commodities, and Volterra invited Pareto to go more fully into this problem. This was the beginning of the integrability problem in the theory of consumer demand.

Although (1906) was Volterra's only contribution to economic theory, his work is of interest to economists for at least other two reasons. One is his functional analysis, now so important in problems involving infinite horizons, numbers of goods, etc. This, however, is like any other important mathematical tool whose availability enabled and continues to enable mathematical economists to solve their problems (for example, fixed point theorems or Liapunov's second method). The other and more important reason is his study of predator–prey equations, which directly inspired an economic model, Goodwin's growth cycle (1965): 'Finally, at some happy moment, I remembered Vito Volterra's formulation of the struggle for existence, and suddenly all became clear to me' (Goodwin's foreword to Vercelli (ed.), 1982, p. 72). This is a two-class model which can be reduced to a system of two differential equations of the Lotka–Volterra type (the variables are the workers' share of the product and the employment ratio). The result is a growth cycle; i.e. the economy grows, but with cycles in growth rates. Goodwin's was the first successful attempt at integrating (not merely superimposing) growth and cycles, and his seminal paper has given rise to many important developments which use predator–prey equations as the basic tool (see, e.g., Izzo, 1971; Desai, 1973; Vercelli (ed.), 1982; Goodwin, Krüger and Vercelli (eds), 1984).

GIANCARLO GANDOLFO

See also FUNCTIONAL ANALYSIS; INTEGRABILITY OF DEMAND; PREDATOR-PREY MODELS.

SELECTED WORKS

A full bibliography is included in Whittaker's biography of Vito Volterra (originally published in 'Obituary Notices of the Royal Society' 1941) as reproduced and completed in the 1959 reprint of (1929). This biography also contains a detailed evaluation of Volterra's scientific work. Volterra's scientific papers have been collected in five volumes by the Accademia Nazionale dei Lincei as V. Volterra, *Opere matematiche: memorie e note*, Rome: Cremonese for the Accademia nazionale dei Lincei, 1954–62; the fifth volume includes the complete bibliography of Volterra's works.

1887. Sopra le funzioni che dipendono da altre funzioni. *Rendiconti della R. Accademia dei Lincei*, series IV, 3(2). Reprinted in *Opere*, Vol. I.

1906. L'economia matematica ed il nuovo manuale del Prof. Pareto. *Giornale degli economisti* 32, April, 296–301. Reprinted in *Opere*, Vol. III.

1926. Variazioni e fluttuazioni del numero di individui in specie animali conviventi. *Memorie della R. Academia dei Lincei*, series VI, 2, 31–113.

1927a. *Teoria de los funcionales y de las ecuaciones integrales e integro-diferenciales*. Conferencias explicadas en la Facultad de Ciencias de la Universidad, 1925, redactadas por L. Fantappié. Madrid: Imprenta Clasica Española.

1927b. Variazioni e fluttuazioni in specie animali conviventi. *Rendiconti del R. Comitato talassografico italiano*, Memoria CXXXI. Reprinted in *Opere*, Vol. V.

1929. *Theory of functionals and of integral and integro-differential equations*. London: Blackie & Son (revised English translation of 1927a). Reprinted (with a Preface by G.C. Evans and the Biography by E. Whittaker), New York: Dover, 1959.

1931. *Leçons sur la théorie mathématique de la lutte pour la vie*. Paris: Gauthier-Villars.

BIBLIOGRAPHY

Desai, M. 1973. Growth cycles and inflation in a model of the class struggle. *Journal of Economic Theory* 6(6), December, 527–45.

Gandolfo, G. 1971. *Mathematical Methods and Models in Economic Dynamics*. Amsterdam: North-Holland, 409–16 and 436–42.

Goodwin, R.M. 1965. A growth cycle. Paper presented at the First World Congress of the Econometric Society, Rome. Published in *Socialism, Capitalism and Economic Growth: Essays presented to Maurice Dobb*, ed. C.H. Feinstein, Cambridge: Cambridge University Press, 1967. Reprinted in *Essays in Economic Dynamics*, ed. R.M. Goodwin, London: Macmillan, 1982.

Goodwin, R.M., Krüger, M. and Vercelli, A. (eds) 1984. *Nonlinear Models of Fluctuating Growth*. Berlin: Springer-Verlag.

Izzo, L. 1971. La moneta in un modello di sviluppo ciclico. In L. Izzo, *Saggi di analisi e teoria monetaria* II, Milano: F. Angeli.

Vercelli, A. (ed.) 1982. Non-linear theory of fluctuating growth. *Economic Notes*, September–December, 69–190.

von Böhm-Bawerk, Eugen. *See* BÖHM-BAWERK, EUGEN VON.

von Hayek, Friedrich. *See* HAYEK, FRIEDRICH ANTON.

von Mises, Ludwig. *See* MISES, LUDWIG EDLER VON.

von Neumann, John (1903–1957).

HIS LIFE. Jansci (John) von Neumann was born to Max and Margaret Neumann on 28 December 1903 in Budapest, Hungary. He showed an early talent for mental calculation, reading and languages. In 1914, at the age of ten, he entered the Lutheran Gymnasium for boys. Although his great intellectual (especially mathematical) abilities were recognized early, he never skipped a grade and instead stayed with his peers. An early teacher, Laslo Ratz, recommended that he be given advanced mathematics tutoring, and a young mathematician Michael Fekete was employed for this purpose. One of the results of these lessons was von Neumann's first mathematical publication (joint with Fekete) when he was 18.

Besides his native Hungarian, Jansci (or Johnny, as he was universally known in his later life) spoke German with his parents and a nurse and learned Latin and Greek as well as French and English in school. In 1921 he enrolled in mathematics at the University of Budapest but promptly left for Berlin, where he studied with Erhard Schmidt. Each semester he returned to Budapest to take examinations without ever having attended classes. While in Berlin he frequently took a three-hour train trip to Göttingen, where he spent considerable time talking to David Hilbert, who was then the most outstanding mathematician of Germany. One of Hilbert's main goals at that time was the axiomatization of all of mathematics so that it could be mechanized and solved in a routine manner. This interested Johnny and led to his famous 1928 paper on the axiomatization of set theory. The goal of Hilbert was later shown to be impossible by Kurt Gödel's work, based on an axiom system similar to von Neumann's, which resulted in a theorem, published in 1930, to the effect that every axiomatic system sufficiently rich to contain the positive integers must necessarily contain undecidable propositions.

After leaving Berlin in 1923 at the age of 20, von Neumann studied at the Eidgenossische Technische Hochschüle in Zurich, Switzerland, while continuing to maintain his enrolment at the University of Budapest. In Zurich he came into contact with the famous German mathematician, Hermann Weyl, and also the equally famous Hungarian mathematician, George Polya. He obtained a degree in Chemical Engineering from the Hochschüle in Zurich in 1925, and completed his doctorate in mathematics from the University of Budapest in 1926. In 1927 he became a privatdozent at the University of Berlin and in 1929 transferred to the same position at the University of Hamburg. His first trip to America was in 1930 to visit as a lecturer at Princeton University, which turned into a visiting professorship, and in 1931 a professorship. In 1933 he was invited to join the Institute for Advanced Study in Princeton as a professor, the youngest permanent member of that institution, at which Albert Einstein was also a permanent professor. Von Neumann held this position until he took a leave of absence in 1954 to become a member of the Atomic Energy Commission.

Von Neumann was married in 1930 to Marietta Kovesi, and his daughter Marina (now a vice-president of General Motors) was born in 1935. The marriage ended in a divorce in 1937. Johnny's second marriage in 1938 was to Klara Dan, whom he met on a trip to Hungary. They maintained a very hospitable home in Princeton and entertained, on an almost weekly basis, numerous local and visiting scientists. Klara later became one of the first programmers of mathematical problems for electronic computers, during the time that von Neumann was its principal designer.

In 1938 Oskar Morgenstern came to Princeton University. His previous work had included books and papers on economic forecasting and competition. He had heard of von Neumann's 1928 paper on the theory of games and was eager to talk to him about connections between game theory and economics. In 1940 they started work on a joint paper which grew into their monumental book, *Theory of Games and Economic Behavior* published in 1944. Their collaboration is described in Morgenstern (1976).

Von Neumann became heavily involved in defence-related consulting activities for the United States and Britain during the World War II. In 1944 he became a consultant to the group developing the first electronic computer, the ENIAC, at the University of Pennsylvania. Here he was associated with John Eckert, John Mauchly, Arthur Burks and Herman Goldstine. These five were instrumental in making the logical design decisions for the computer, for example, that it be a binary machine, that it have only a limited set of instructions that are performed by the hardware, and most important of all, that it run an internally stored programme. It was acknowledged by the others in the group that the most important design ideas came from von Neumann. The best account of these years is Goldstine (1972). After the war von Neumann and Goldstine worked at the Institute of Advanced study where they developed (with others) the JONIAC computer, a successor to the ENIAC, which used principles some of which are still being used in current computer designs.

In 1943 von Neumann became a consultant to the Manhattan Project which was developing the atomic bomb in Los Alamos, New Mexico. This work is still classified but it is known that Johnny performed superbly as a mathematician, an applied physicist, and an expert in computations. His work continued after the war on the hydrogen bomb, with Edward Teller and others. Because of this work he received a presidential appointment to the Atomic Energy Commission in 1955. He took leave from the Institute for Advanced Study and moved to Washington. In the summer of 1955 he fell and hurt his left shoulder. Examination of that injury led to a diagnosis of bone cancer which was already very advanced. He continued to work very hard at his AEC job, and prepared the Silliman lectures (von Neumann, 1958), but was unable to deliver them. He died on 8 February 1957 at the age of 53 in the Walter Reed Hospital, Washington, DC.

THE THEORY OF GAMES. Without question one of von Neumann's most original contributions was the theory of games, with which it is possible to formulate and solve complex situations involving psychological, economic, strategic and mathematical questions. Before his great paper on this subject in 1928 there had been only a handful of predecessors: a paper by Zermelo in 1912 on the solution in pure strategies of chess; and three short notes by the famous French mathematician E. Borel. Borel had formulated some simple symmetric two-person games in these notes, but was not able to provide a method of solution for the general case, and in fact conjectured that there was no solution concept applicable to the general case. For a commentary on the priorities involved in these two men's work see the notes by Maurice Frechet, translations (by L.J. Savage) of the three Borel papers, and a commentary by von Neumann, all of which appeared with von Neumann (1953).

The three main results of von Neumann's 1928 paper were: the formulation of a restricted version of the extensive form of a game in which each player either knows nothing or everything about previous moves of other players; the proof of the minimax theorem for two-person zero-sum games; and the definition of the characteristic function for and the solution of three-person zero-sum games in normal form. Von Neumann also carried out an extensive study of simplified versions of poker during this time, but they were not published until later.

The *extensive* form of a game is the definition of a game by stating its rules, that is, listing all of the possible legal moves that a player can make for each possible situation he can find himself during a play of the game. A *pure strategy* in a game is a much more complicated idea; it is a listing of a complete set of decisions for each possible situation the player can find himself. A complete enumeration of all possible strategies shows that the number of such strategies is equal to the product of the number of legal moves for each situation, which implies that there is an astronomical number of possible strategies for any non-trivial game such as chess. Most of these are bad, and would never be used by a skilful player, but they must be considered to find its solution. The *normalized* form of a game is obtained by replacing the definition of a game as a statement of its rules, as is done in its extensive form, by a listing of all of the possible pure strategies for each player. To complete the normalized form of the game, imagine that each player has made a choice of one of his pure strategies. When pitted against another a unique (expected) outcome of the game will result. For the moment we will imagine that the outcome of the game is monetary, and therefore each player gets a 'payoff' at the end of the game which is actually money. (Later we will replace money by 'utility'.) If the sum of the payments to all players is zero the game is said to be *zero-sum*; otherwise it is a *non-zero-sum* game.

The normalized form of a game is also called a *matrix game*, and any real mxn matrix can be considered a two-person zero-sum game. The row player has m pure strategies, $i = 1, \ldots, m$, and the column player has n pure strategies, $j = 1, \ldots, n$. If the row player chooses i and the column player chooses j then the payoff $a(i,j)$ is exchanged between them, where $a(i,j) > 0$ means that the row player receives $a(i,j)$ from the column player, while a negative payoff means that the column player receives the absolute value of that amount from the row player.

The importance of the careful analysis of the extensive and normalized forms of a game is that it separates out the concept of strategy and psychology in any discussion of a game. As an example, in poker bidding high when having a weak hand is commonly called 'bluffing', and considered an aggressive form of play. As a result of this formulation, and the solution of simplified versions of the game von Neumann showed that in order to play poker 'optimally' it is necessary to bluff part of the time, i.e., it is a required part of the strategy of any good poker player. A similar analysis for simplified bridge shows that a required part of an optimal bridge strategy is to signal, via the way one discards low cards in a suit, whether the player holds higher cards in that suit.

The analysis of special kinds of games shows that some of them can be solved by using pure strategies. This class includes the games of 'perfect information' such as the board games of chess and checkers. However, even such a simple game as matching pennies shows that an additional strategic concept is needed, namely, that of a 'mixed strategy'. This concept appeared first in the context of symmetric two-person games in Borel's 1921 paper. Briefly, a mixed strategy for either player is a finite probability function on his set of pure strategies. For matching pennies the common strategy of flipping the penny to choose whether to play heads or tails is a mixed strategy that chooses both alternatives with equal probability (1/2), and is, in fact, an optimal strategy for that game.

We now discuss the way that von Neumann made precise the definition of a solution to a matrix game. Let A be an arbitrary *mxn* matrix with real number entries. Let x be an m-component row vector, and let f be an m-component column vector all of whose components are ones. Then x is a *mixed strategy* vector for the row player in the matrix game A if it satisfies: $xf = 1$ and $x \geqslant 0$. Similarly, let y be an n-component column vector, and let e be an n-component row vector of all whose components are ones. Then y is a *mixed strategy* vector for the column player in the matrix game A if it satisfies: $ey = 1$ and $y \geqslant 0$. Mixed strategy vectors are also called *probability* vectors because they have non-negative components that sum to one, and hence could be used to make a random choice of a pure strategy by spinning a pointer, choosing a random number, etc. To complete the definition of the solution to a game, we need a real number v, called the *value of the game*. The solution to the matrix game A is now a triple, a mixed strategy x for the row player, a mixed strategy y for the column player, and a value v for the game: these quantities must solve the following pair of (vector) inequalities:

$$xA \geqslant ve \quad \text{and} \quad Ay \leqslant vf.$$

Because these are linear inequalities, one might suspect (and would be correct) that the optimal x, y and v can be found by using a linear programming code and a computer.

However, in the 1920s it was not clear that such a solution existed. In fact, Borel conjectured that it did not. The most decisive result of von Neumann's 1928 paper was to establish, using an argument involving a fixed point theorem, his famous *minimax theorem* to the effect that for an arbitrary real matrix A there exists a real number v and probability vectors x and y such that

$$\underset{x}{Maximum}\ \underset{y}{Minimum}\ xAy = \underset{y}{Minimum}\ \underset{x}{Maximum}\ xAy$$

This theorem became the keystone not only for the theory of two-person matrix games, but also for n-persons games via the characteristic function (to be discussed later).

We now discuss the major differences between von Neumann and Morgenstern (1944) and von Neumann's 1928 paper. The information available to each player was assumed, in the 1928 paper, to be the following: when required to move, each player knows either everything about the previous moves of his opponents (as in chess), or nothing (as in matching pennies). By using information trees, and partitioning the nodes of such trees into information sets, in 1944 this concept was extended to games in which players have only partial information about previous moves when they are required to make a move. This was a difficult but major extension, which has not been substantially improved upon since its exposition in the 1944 treatise.

A second major change in the basic theory of games was in the treatment of payoff functions. In the 1928 paper payoffs were treated as if they were monetary, and it was implicitly assumed that money was regarded as equally important by each of the players. In order to take into account the well-known objections, such as those of Daniel Bernoulli, to the assumption that a dollar is equally important to a poor man as a rich man, a monetary outcome to a player was replaced by the *utility* of the outcome. Although Bernoulli had suggested that the utility of x dollars should be the natural logarithm of x, so that the addition of a dollar to a rich man's fortune would be valued less than the addition of a dollar to a poor man's fortune, this specific utility concept was never universally accepted by economists. So utility remained a fuzzy, intuitive concept. Von Neumann and Morgenstern made the absolutely decisive step of axiomatizing utility theory, making it unambiguous and they can properly be said to have started the modern theory of utility, not only for game theory, but for all of economics and the social sciences.

Almost two-thirds of the 1944 treatise consists of the theory of n-person constant-sum games, of which only a small part, the three person zero-sum case, appears in the 1928 paper. When $n > 2$, there are opportunities for cooperation and collusion as well as competition among the players, so that there arises the problem of finding a way to evaluate numerically the position of each player in the game. In 1928 von Neumann handled this problem for the zero-sum case by introducing the idea of the *characteristic* function of a game defined as follows: For each *coalition*, that is, subset S of players, let $v(S)$ be the minimax value that S is assured in a zero-sum two-person game played between S and its complementary set of players.

To describe the possible division of the total gain available among the players the concept of an imputation, which is a vector $(x(1), \ldots, x(n))$ where $x(i)$ represents the amount the player i obtains, was introduced. For a coalition C in a constant-sum game $v(C)$ is the minimum amount that the coalition C should be willing to accept in any imputation, since by playing alone against all the other players, C can achieve that amount for itself. Except for this restriction there is no other constraint on the possible imputations that can become part of a solution. An imputation vector x is said to *dominate* imputation vector y if there exists a coalition C such that (1) $x(i) \geqslant y(i)$ for all i in C, and (2) the sum of $x(i)$ for i in C does not exceed $v(C)$. The idea is that that the coalition C can 'enforce' the imputation x by simply threatening to 'go it alone', since it can do no worse by itself.

One might think, or hope, that a single imputation could be taken as the definition of a solution to an n-person constant-sum game. However, a more complicated concept is needed. By a von Neumann–Morgenstern solution to an n-person game is meant a set S of imputations such that (1) if x and y are two imputations in S then neither dominates the other; and (2) if z is an imputation not in S, then there exists an imputation x in S that dominates z. Von Neumann and Morgenstern were unable (for good reasons, see below) to prove that every n-person game had a solution, even though they were able to solve every specific game they considered, frequently finding a huge number of solutions.

At the very end of the 1944 book there appears a chapter of about 80 pages on general non-zero-sum games. These were formally reduced to the zero-sum case by the technique of introducing a fictitious player, who was entirely neutral in terms of the game's strategic play, but who either consumed any excess, or supplied any deficiency so that the resulting $n+1$ person game was zero-sum. This artifice helped but did not suffice for a completely adequate treatment of the non-zero-sum case. This is unfortunate because such games are the most likely to be found useful in practice.

About 25 years after the treatise appeared, William Lucas (1969) provided as a counter-example, a general sum game that did not have a von Neumann–Morgenstern solution. Other solution concepts have been considered since, such as the Shapley value, and the core of a game.

One of the most interesting non zero-sum games considered in that chapter was the so-called *market game*. The first example of a market game (though it was not called that) was the famous horse auction of Böhm-Bawerk, published in 1881. The horses had identical characteristics, each of 10 buyers had a maximum price he was willing to bid, and each of 8 sellers had a minimum price he was willing to accept. Böhm-Bawerk's solution was to find the 'marginal pairs' of prices, which turned out to be included in the von Neumann–Morgenstern solution to this kind of game. Later work on this problem was done by Shapley and Shubik (1972) and Thompson (1980, 1981).

THE EXPANDING ECONOMY MODEL. Another of von Neumann's original contribution to economics was von Neumann (1937), which contained an expanding economy model unlike any other economic model that preceded it. When von Neumann gave a seminar to the Princeton economics department in 1932 on the model, which was stated in terms of linear inequalities not equations, and whose existence proof depended upon a fixed point theorem more sophisticated than any published in the mathematics literature of the time, it is little wonder that he made no impression on that group. He repeated his talk on the subject at Karl Menger's mathematical seminar in Vienna in 1936, and published his paper in German in 1937 in the seminar proceedings. The paper became more widely known after it was translated into English and published in *The Review of Economic Studies* in 1945 together with a commentary by Champernowne.

Von Neumann's model consists of a closed production economy in which there are m processes and n goods. In order to describe it we use the vectors e and f previously defined together with the following notation:

x is the $m\times 1$ intensity vector with $xf=1$ and $x\geqslant 0$.

y is the $1\times n$ price vector with $ey=1$ and $y\geqslant 0$.

$\alpha=1+a/100$ is the expansion factor, where a is the expansion rate.

$\beta=1+b/100$ is the interest factor, where b is the interest rate.

The model satisfies the following axioms:

Axiom 1.	$xB\geqslant\alpha xA$ or $x(B-\alpha A)\geqslant 0$.
Axiom 2.	$By\leqslant\beta Ay$ or $(B-\beta A)y\leqslant 0$.
Axiom 3.	$x(B-\alpha A)y=0$.
Axiom 4.	$x(B-\beta A)y=0$.
Axiom 5.	$xBy>0$.

Axiom 1 makes the model closed, i.e., the inputs for a given period are the outputs of the previous. Axiom 2 makes the interest rate be such that the economy is *profitless*. Axiom 3 requires that overproduced goods be *free*. Axiom 4 forces inefficient processes not to be used. And Axiom 5 requires the total value of all goods produced to be positive.

In order to demonstrate that for any pair of nonnegative matrices A and B, solutions consisting of vectors x and y and numbers α and β exist, an additional assumption was needed:

$$\text{Assumption V. } A+B>0.$$

This assumption means that every process requires as an input or produces as an output some amount, no matter how small, of every good. With this assumption, and the assumption that natural resources needed for expansion were available in unlimited quantities, von Neumann showed that necessarily $\alpha=\beta$, that is, that the expansion and interest factors were equal. In his paper, von Neumann proved a sophisticated fixed point theorem and used it to prove the existence theorem for the EEM.

D.G. Champernowne (1945) provided the first acknowledgement that the economics profession had seen the article, and also provided its first criticisms. We mention three:

(1) Assumption V which requires that every process must have positive inputs or outputs of every other good was economically unrealistic.

(2) The fact that the model has no consumption, so that labour could receive only subsistence amounts of good as necessary inputs for production processes also seem unrealistic.

(3) The consequence of Axiom 3 that overproduced good should be free is too unrealistic.

Criticisms 1 and 2 were removed by Kemeny, Morgenstern, and Thompson (1956), who replace Assumption V by:

Assumption KMT-1. Every row of A has at least one positive entry.

Assumption KMT-2. Every column of B has at least one positive entry. The interpretation of KMT-1 is that every process must use at least one good as an input. And the interpretation of KMT-2 is that every good must be produced by some process. With these assumptions they were able to show that there were a finite number of possible expansion factors for which intensity and price vectors existed satisfying the axioms. They also showed how consumption could be added into the model, which responded to criticism 2.

An alternative way of handling these criticisms appears in Gale (1956).

In Morgenstern and Thompson (1969, 1976), the third criticism above was answered by generalizing the model to become an 'open economy'. In such an economy the price of an overproduced good cannot fall below its export price, and it cannot rise above its import price. Generalizations of the open model have been made by Los (1974) and Moeschlin (1974).

VON NEUMANN'S INFLUENCE ON ECONOMICS. Although von Neumann has only three publications that can directly be called contributions to economics, namely, his 1928 paper on the theory of games, his 1937 paper (translated in 1945) on the expanding economy model and his 1944 treatise (with Morgenstern) on the theory of games, he had enormous influence on the subject. The small *number* of contributions is deceptive because each one consists of several different topics, each being important. We discuss these separately.

The expanding economy model, von Neumann (1937) consisted of two parts: the first input–output equilibrium model that permits expansion; and second the fixed point theorem. The linear input–output model is a precursor of the Leontief model, of linear programming as developed by Kantorovich and Dantzig, and of Koopman's activity analysis. This paper, together with A. Wald (1935) raised the level of mathematical sophistication used in economics enormously. Many current younger economists are high-powered applied mathematicians, in part, because of the stimulus of von Neumann's work.

The theory of games, von Neumann (1928) and von Neumann and Morgenstern (1944), was an enormous contribution consisting of several different parts: (1) the axiomatic theory of utility; (2) the careful treatment of the extensive form of games; (3) the minimax theorem; (4) the concept of a solution to a constant-sum n-person game; (5) the foundations of non-zero-sum games; (6) market games. Each of these topics could have been broken into a series of papers, had von Neumann taken the time to do so. And he could have forged a brilliant career in economics by publishing them. However, he found that making an exposition of the results that he had worked out in notes or in his head was less interesting to him than investigating still other new ideas.

Von Neumann's indirect contributions, such as the theory of duality in linear programming, computational methods for matrix games and linear programming, combinatorial solution methods for the assignment problem, the logical design of electronic computers, contributions to statistical theory, etc. are equally important to the future of economics. Each of his contributions, direct or indirect, was monumental and decisive. We should be grateful that he was able to do so much in his short life. His influence will persist for decades and even centuries in economics.

GERALD L. THOMPSON

SELECTED WORKS

1928. Zur Theorie der Gesellschaftsspiele. *Mathematische Annalen* 100, 295–320.

1937. Über ein ökonomisches Gleichungssystem und eine Verallgemeinerung des Brouwerschen Fixpunktsatzes. *Ergebnisse eines mathematische Kolloquiums* 8, ed. Karl Menger. Trans. as 'A model of general equilibrium', *Review of Economic Studies* 13, (1945–6), 1–9.

1944. (With O. Morgenstern.) *Theory of Games and Economic Behavior*. Princeton: Princeton University Press. 2nd edn, 1947; 3rd edn, 1953.

1947. Discussion of a maximum problem. Unpublished working paper, Princeton, November, 9 pp.

1948. A numerical method for determining the value and the best strategies of a zero-sum two-person game with large numbers of strategies. Mimeographed, May, 23 pp.

1953a. Communications on the Borel notes. *Econometrica* 21, 124–5.

1953b. (With G.W. Brown.) Solutions of games by differential equations. In *Contributions to the Theory of Games,* Vol. 1, ed. H.W. Kuhn and A.W. Tucker, Annals of Mathematics Studies No. 28, Princeton: Princeton University Press.

1953c. (With D.B. Gillies and J.P. Mayberry.) Two variants of poker. In *Contributions to the Theory of Games,* Vol. 1, ed. H.W. Kuhn and A.W. Tucker, Annals of Mathematics Studies No. 28, Princeton: Princeton University Press.

1954. A numerical method to determine optimum strategy. *Naval Research Logistics Quarterly* 1, 109–15.

1958. *The Computer and the Brain*. New Haven: Yale University Press.

1963. *Collected Works, Vols* I–VI. New York: Macmillan.

BIBLIOGRAPHY

Champernowne, D.G. 1945–6. A note on J. von Neumann's article. *Review of Economic Studies* 13, 10–18.

Debreu, G. 1959. *Theory of Value: an axiomatic analysis of economic equilibrium.* Cowles Foundation Monograph No. 17, New York: Wiley.

Gale, D. 1956. The closed linear model of production. In *Linear Inequalities and Related Systems,* ed. H.W. Kuhn and A.W. Tucker, Princeton: Princeton University Press. A counter-example showing that optimal prices need not exist in Gale's original model was published by J. Hulsman and V. Steinmitz in *Econometrica* 40, (1972), 387–90. Proof of the existence of optimal prices in a modified Gale model was given by A. Soyster in *Econometrica* 42, (1974), 199–205.

Goldstine, H.H. 1972. *The Computer from Pascal to von Neumann.* Cambridge, Mass.: MIT Press.

Heims, S.J. 1980. *John von Neumann and Norbet Wiener*. Cambridge, Mass.: MIT Press.

Kemeny, J.G., Morgenstern, O. and Thompson, G.L. 1956. A generalization of von Neumann's model of an expanding economy. *Econometrica* 24, 115–35.

Los, J. 1974. The existence of equilibrium in an open expanding economy model (generalization of the Morgenstern–Thompson Model). In *Mathematical Models in Economics*, ed. J. and M.W. Los, Amsterdam and New York: North-Holland Publishing Co.

Lucas, W. 1969. The proof that a game may not have a solution. *Transactions of the American Mathematics Society* 137. 219–29.

Luce, R.D. and Raiffa, H. 1957. *Games and Decisions: Introduction and Critical Survey*. New York: John Wiley & Sons.

Moeschlin, O. 1974. A generalization of the open expanding economy model. *Econometrica* 45, 1767–76.

Morgenstern, O. 1958. Obituary, John von Neumann, 1903–57. *Economic Journal* 68, 170–74.

Morgenstern, O. 1976. The collaboration between Oskar Morgenstern and John von Neumann on the theory of games. *Journal of Economic Literature* 14, 805–16.

Morgenstern, O. and Thompson, G.L. 1969. An open expanding economy model. *Naval Research Logistics Quarterly* 16, 443–57.

Morgenstern, O. and Thompson, G.L. 1976. *Mathematical Theory of Expanding and Contracting Economies*. Boston: Heath–Lexington.

Oxtoby, J.C., Pettis, B.J. and Price, G.B. (eds) 1958. John von Neumann 1903–1957. *Bulletin of the American Mathematical Society* 64(3), Part 2.

Shapley, L.S. 1953. A value for n-person games. In *Contributions to the Theory of Games* II, ed. H.W. Kuhn and A.W. Tucker, Princeton: Princeton University Press.

Shapley, L.S. and Shubik, M. 1972. The assignment game. I: the core. *International Journal of Game Theory* 1, 111–30.

Shubik, M. 1982. *Game Theory in the Social Sciences: Concepts and Solutions*. Cambridge, Mass.: MIT Press.

Shubik, M. 1985. *A Game Theoretic Approach to Political Economy*. Cambridge, Mass.: MIT Press.

Thompson, G.L. 1956. On the solution of a game-theoretic problem. In *Linear Inequalities and Related Systems,* ed. H.W. Kuhn and A.W. Tucker, Princeton: Princeton University Press.

Thompson, G.L. 1980. Computing the core of a market game. In *Extremal Methods and Systems Analysis,* ed. A.V. Fiacco and K.O. Kortanek, Berlin: Springer-Verlag.

Thompson, G.J. 1981. Auctions and market games. In *Essays in Game Theory and Mathematical Economics in Honor of Oskar Morgenstern*, ed. R.J. Aumann et al., Mannheim: Bibliographisches Institut Mannheim.

Wald, A. 1935. Über die eindeutige positive Losbarkeit der neuen Produktionsgleichungen. *Ergebnisse eines Mathematischen Kolloquiums*, ed. K. Menger 6, 12–20.

von Neumann–Morgenstern utility function. *See* EXPECTED UTILITY HYPOTHESIS.

von Neumann ray. The von Neumann ray determines the proportions of maximal balanced growth in a von Neumann technology. The economic growth trajectory, which realizes the maximum possible growth rate, that the economy could withstand for infinite time is located on this ray. Let us give a more formal discription of the problem being discussed. The trajectory $x(0), \ldots, x(t), \ldots$ generated by this technology is called stationary if the proportions between goods in the state $x(t)$ are independent of time t. A stationary trajectory can be written in the form $x(t) = \gamma^t x$ where $x = x(0)$ is the initial state. This trajectory is generated by a technologically feasible activity (x, y) under which $\gamma x \leqslant y_1$. Usually a stationary trajectory is called the trajectory of balanced growth (although actual growth will take place only for $\gamma > 1$). The maximum number γ which enables a balanced growth is called the von Neumann (or technological) rate of growth for the technology Z. Thus the technological rate α is the solution of the following optimization problem find $\alpha = \max \gamma$ subject to

$$(x, y) \in Z, \qquad y \geqslant \gamma x.$$

If $y \geqslant \alpha x$, the process (x, y) is called the von Neumann activity (process), the corresponding vector x – the von Neumann vector and the ray passing through x – the von Neumann ray.

J. von Neumann in his pioneering paper (1937) established that a stationary price trajectory corresponds to the growth rate α, i.e., there exists a sequence $p(0), p(1), \ldots, p(t), \ldots$ of price vectors such that $p(t) = \alpha^{-t}p$ and $pw \leqslant \alpha pv$ for all $(v, w) \in Z$ (this means exactly that $p(t)$ is a price trajectory). The vector p appearing in the definition of this trajectory is called the von Neumann price vector.

Thus for every von Neumann technology Z we can find the number α which is the solution of the problem (*), and a technologically feasible activity (x, y) and a price vector p satisfying the relations

$$(x, y) \in Z, \quad \alpha x \leqslant y, \quad pw \leqslant \alpha pv, \quad ((v, w) \in Z) \qquad (**)$$

It can occur in degenerate cases that $p = 0$, i.e. all goods serving as inputs in a von Neumann process have zero prices. We shall exclude this (senseless from the economic point of view) situation and call $(\alpha, (x, y), p)$ a von Neumann equilibrium if it satisfies (**) (where α is the solution of the problem (*) and $px > 0$. The equilibrium has the following economic interpretation. If in the initial time period $t = 0$ the system is in the state $x(0) = X$ then it can develop with the maximum possible rate of growth α (the same for all goods) maintaining the initial proportions between goods. This development is implemented by the activity (x, y). It is possible to choose time-constant prices in such a manner that the interest factor pw/pv (equal to 1 + the rate of return) for any technologically admissible activity (v, w) does not exceed α. For the activity (x, y) this interest factor is maximal and equals α.

Using the notion of characteristic prices we can say that the stationary equilibrium trajectory of the economic system moving along the von Neumann ray with the rate α admits as a characteristic a stationary price trajectory with the same price decline rate α.

Now we consider a von Neumann technology in the narrow sense Z. Recall that it is defined by an input matrix A and an output matrix B. For this technology the conditions (**) reduce to the following inequality system $\alpha Au \leqslant Bu$, $pb \leqslant \alpha pA$ where u is an m-vector of intensities.

Let the vectors u, p satisfy this system with

$$\alpha = \max\{\gamma : \gamma Au \leqslant Bu, u \geqslant 0\}$$

Then p is the vector of von Neumann prices, u is the so-called vector of von Neumann intensities; it determines the equilibrium vector $x = Au$.

In terms of equilibrium it is posible to characterize goods for which growth at a rate exceeding the von Neumann growth rate α is technologically possible. Let (x, y) be an activity such that the output of good i is greater than its input multipled by α. Then it can be easily seen that the equilibrium price of the good i is equal to zero; in other words, this good is free. In short, this property of the equilibrium can be stated as follows: if the growth rate for some good exceeds the technological growth rate, then this good is free.

Now we point out another property of equilibrium for a von Neumann technology, in the narrow sense defined by an input matrix A and an output matrix B. The pair (a, b), where a is the ith column of A, b is the ith column of B, defines the ith basic activity of this technology. To every basic activity we can associate its interest factor pb/pa. We can choose among the basic activities the most profitable ones, i.e. those for which the interest factor is maximal (equal to pb/pa). An important property of an equilibrium activity (x, y) is that it can be obtained by a joint use (with some intensities) only of the most profitable activities. If **u** is a von Neumann intensity vector then its components corresponding to the activities with non-maximal profitability are equal to zero.

We characterized the growth rate from a purely technological point of view. If the technology Z is 'indecomposable', i.e. for the production of some goods all goods are (directly or indirectly) used, then this growth rate admits an economic description. To demonstrate this consider stationary price trajectories, i.e. sequences of the form.

$$q, \beta^{-1}q, \ldots, \beta^{-t}q, \ldots \qquad (***)$$

where q is the price vector such that $qw \leqslant \beta qv$ for all technologically admissible activities (v, w). If q is given then the minimal number β for which the sequence (***) is a price trajectory coincides with $\beta(q) = \max\}(q(w)/q(v) : (v, w) \in Z\}$ which is the maximal (at prices q) growth rate. The quantity $\beta(q) - 1$ is the maximal rate of return at prices q,

The economic growth rate for the technology Z is the minimal number β for which a stationary price trajectory exists. If this trajectory is generated by a price vector p, i.e. has the form

$$p(0), \ldots, p(t), p(t + 1), \ldots$$

with $p(t) = \beta^{-1}p$ then the vector p is such that the maximal rate of return $\beta(p) - 1$ defined by p does not exceed the rate of return $\beta(q) - 1$ for any price vector q.

It turns out that if the technology Z is indecomposable in the aforementioned sense then the economic growth rate β coincides with the technological growth rate α, the prices p with the minimal rate of return $\beta(p) - 1$ being von Neumann prices. To clarify the situation, introduce the following definition. The number α for which there exist an activity (x, y) and a vector p satisfying (**) and the inequality $px > 0$ is called a growth rate. It turns out that for the indecomposable nondegenerate case the technology admits only one growth rate which is simultaneously the technological and the economic one. Thus if some number α, for some $(x, y)) \in Z$ and p the inequalities (**) and $px > 0$ are satisfied, then α simultaneously solves the problems of maximizing the rate of reproduction and of minimizing the rate of return $\beta(p) - 1$.

In the decomposable case the situation is much more tangled: several growth rates can exist. Nevertheless their number does not exceed the number of goods.

Further we shall consider only indecomposable technologies. Let $x = x(0)$ be a vector with non-negative components representing the endowments at the moment $t = 0$. Choosing in one way or another the activities we can form various trajectories of length T beginning in $x(0)$. Among those of special interest are trajectories which are optimal in terms of some price vector q. If the point $x(0)$ belongs to the von Neumann ray and q coincides with the von Neumann price vector then optimal behaviour consists in moving with the maximum technologically possible rate α along the von Neumann ray. It turns out that for a sufficiently wide class of initial states $x(0)$ and vectors q the optimal trajectories must grow with a rate which differ little from α.

Let us discuss this in more detail. Let p be the von Neumann price vector. If the trajectory $x(0), \ldots, x(T)$ of length T is such that for a sufficiently large number of moments t the inequality $px(t + 1)/px(t) \leqslant \gamma$ with $\gamma < \alpha$ holds then the mentioned trajectory cannot be optimal. This assertion can be elaborated in many ways. It has a very elegant and transparent geometrical interpretation.

Consider a von Neumann technology Z and choose among its activities the most profitable ones (i.e. those with the maximal rate of return according to von Neumann prices p).

These activities form a facet of the convex cone Z which is called a von Neumann facet. The further it is from the von Neumann facet the less profitable is any activity. Thus, an overwhelming majority of the activities taking part in the construction of the optimal trajectory lie near the von Neumann facet. Such assertions are usually caled turnpike theorems in the weak form. More precisely, the number of activities lying 'far' from the facet does not exceed some number independent of the length of the trajectory. Under some additional assumptions the activities essentially different from the facet can occur only at the beginning and the end of the trajectory (turnpike theorem in the strong form). Finally, some additional assumptions guarantee that the activities forming the trajectory simply belong to the facet (turnpike theorem in the strongest form).

Suppose that Z is a von Neumann technology in the narrow sense. Then the von Neumann facet has as its extreme rays the most profitable basic activities. We recall that every activity (v, w) from Z is formed as a combination of basic activities with some intensities. The closeness of (v, w) to the facet means that in its formation the most profitable activities are used with substantially greater intensities than the other activities. This activity belongs to the facet if only the most profitable activities are actually used.

We mention now the case when there is only one most profitable activity (x, y) (this case is typical for the technologies described by production functions). The von Neumann facet in this case coincides with the ray passing through the $2n$-dimensional vector (x, y). Instead of deviation of the activities from this ray we can speak about the deviation of the trajectory itself (more precisely, of its state $x(t)$) from the von Neumann ray which in this case is spanned by the vector x. The fact that a point has a small deviation from the von Neumann ray means simply that the proportions between its coordinates differ insignificantly from the proportions on the ray. This permits us to interpret the turnpike theorems from another point of view, for example, the theorem in the strong form means that the proportions between products for the states of the optimal trajectory can differ substantially from those on the ray only at the beginning and the end of the trajectory. (The first is caused by the difference of the initial state $x(0)$ from the von Neumann vector x, the second by the difference of the optimality criterion from the vector of von Neumann prices.)

A. Rubinov

BIBLIOGRAPHY

Kemeny, J., Morgenstern, O. and Thompson, G. 1956. A generalization of the von Neumann model of an expanding economy. *Econometrica* 24, 115–35.

Makarov, V.L. and Rubinov, A.M. 1977. *Mathematical Theory of Economic Dynamics and Equilibria.* New York: Springer-Verlag.

Nikaido, H. 1964. Persistence of continual growth near the von Neumann ray: a strong version of the Radner turnpike theorem. *Econometrica* 32, 1–2, 151–63.

Radner, R. 1961. Paths of economic growth that are optimal with regard only to final states; a turnpike theorem. *Review of Economic Studies* 28, 98–104.

von Neumann, J. 1945–6.A model of general economic equilibrium. *Review of Economic Studies.* 13, 1–9.

von Neumann technology. The von Neumann technology is a convenient tool for the description and analysis of a wide variety of economic systems. It can be considered a special form of describing the production possibility set (i.e. the production process of the economic system, a form mostly designed for mathematical research of development dynamics).

The production process of this technology is determined by definition of input and output of goods corresponding to contiguous time intervals. An arbitrary production process can be described in this framework by introducing additional intermediate goods. We give a more formal description of the considered situation. Consider an economy with n goods, where we understand the term 'goods' in a very broad sense. Depending on the economic situation we can number among the goods not only goods in the usual sense of the world but also various types of capital, labour, natural resources as well as some conditional goods (e.g. the effect of consumption of some other goods).

A technology is a set Z consisting of technologically feasible processes (activities) Z. Every activity transforms a given set of goods (input vector) into another set (outout vector). Thus formally the activity is represented by a pair of vectors $Z = (x, y)$, where x is the input vector and y the output vector, both of them being n-dimensional vectors with non-negative components.

Considering the technology we assume that all technologically admissible activities have the same duration (a unit time interval). This hypothesis is based on the assumption that a long-run process can be decomposed into several processes of unit length. As a result of this decomposition intermediate goods (e.g. capital vintages or unfinished products) can be introduced.

Now we point out the essential features of the von Neumann technology Z.

(1) Any activity can be used at any intensity: i.e. $(x, y) \in Z$, $\lambda \geqslant 0$ implies $\lambda(x, y) \in Z$. This property reflects the possibility of an unlimited use of resources.

(2) Any two activities can be used jointly: $(x, y) \in Z$, $(u, v) \in Z$ implies $(x + u, y + u) \in Z$.

Geometrically (1) and (2) mean that the von Neumann technology can be described by a convex cone.

(3) All goods can be produced. This means (together with (2)) that there exists an activity (x, y) such that all coordinates of the vector y are positive.

(4) Non-zero output is impossible without input.

The von Neumann technology Z in the narrow sense (in another terminology: the von Neumann model, the model of an expanding economy) is defined through specification of m activities which are termed basic; it is the set of all input–output vectors which can be obtained by the joint use of the basic activities with arbitrary intensities. Geometrically, Z is a polyhedral cone with activities as its extreme rays. Algebraically, it is convenient to define Z by a pair of $m \times n$-matrices: the input matrix A and the output matrix B. If (a, b) is the ith basic activity, the vector a is the ith column of the matrix A, b is the ith column of the matrix B. Then

$$Z = \{(x, y): x = Au, yBu, u \geqslant 0\}$$

where u is an m-vector of intensities. The condition (3) (resp. 4) is equivalent to the absence of zero columns in the matrix A (resp. to the absence of zero rows in the matrix B). These properties were formulated by Kemeny, Morgenstern and Thompson in 1956. von Neumann in his fundamental paper (1937; English translation: 1946) assumed a stronger condition: in every activity every good is either consumed or produced.

The von Neumann technology in a broad sense (in another terminology: the Neumann–Gale model) is merely a closed (in the topological sense) set for which the conditions (1)–(4) are fulfilled. It was introduced by Gale in 1956. Such technologies arise, for example, in connection with the use of production functions.

The von Neumann technology is a formal mathematical object that can be used for modelling various economic situations. One such situation was considered by J. von Neumann. He studied a closed economic system (i.e. having no connections with the outer world). The production possibilities of the system are given by the input and output matrices. There is no outflow of consumption, the process of production includes the reproduction of labour force, the workers save nothing, all capitalists' returns are invested. In other works, von Neumann abstracts from consumption and savings and concentrates solely on the process of production. A detailed analysis of the underlying economic assumptions is given in (Champernowne, 1946).

Some deep generalizations of the von Neumann technology describing an open economy and explicitly taking into account consumption, labour and wages were studied by Morgenstern and Thompson and by J. Los and his pupils.

Various modifications of this model in the framework of a von Neumann technology (possibly, in a broad sense) can be given. As an example we describe a simple macroeconomic model of a firm. Let $F(K, L)$, the production function describing the performance of the firm where K is the capital and L the labour force. It is supposed that any part of the output $F(K, L)$ obtained with the capital K and the labour force L can be turned into investment I, the remaining part being used for purchasing the labour force l. The wage rate ω and the capital deterioration rate μ are given. The set of states (k, l) the firm can reach (in a unit time interval) from the state (K, L) is described by a system of inequalities

$$0 \leqslant k \leqslant (1-\mu)k + I, \quad I + \omega l \leqslant F(k, l), \quad l \geqslant 0, I > 0. \quad (*)$$

If the function F satisfies the traditional assumptions of concavity and homogeneity of degree 1 then the set of activities $((K, L), (k, l)$ satisfying (*)) is a von Neumann technology (in a broad sense).

The von Neumann technology is often used for representing the production part in various models of economic dynamics. Models with utility functions explicitly taking into account consumption, as well as dynamic Leontief models can be stated and analysed in this framework as well. We note furthermore than many other problems not connected with economic dynamics can be embedded into a von Neumann technology scheme, in particular, 'bottleneck problems'.

Thus with the help of the von Neumann technology we can study a demographic model of population movement, based on the following hypothesis: the number of marriages between men and women under certain ages is proportional to the minimum of the numbers of unmarried men and women under these ages. Men and women under certain ages, and also their newly created families which are distinguished according to the terms of their existence, play the role of 'products' here.

The technological activities describe a shift of 'products' from one age group to another, and the processes of family increase and decrease.

As a rule the von Neumann technology is analysed from two viewpoints. First, equilibrium states of the economic system can be determined in these terms. J. von Neumann introduced it specially for this purpose. Second, this technology is a convenient tool for analysing development trajectories of the economic system. Both directions are closely interconnected. The concept of von Neumann equilibrium (geometrically: the von Neumann ray) is extremely important in these problems. Here we focus our attention on the trajectory concept.

In many situations modelled with the von Neumann technology it is reasonable to guess that the development of the underlying economic system is such that the input vector at the beginning of some time period does not exceed the output vector at the end of the preceding period. First of all, it is true for the original von Neumann construction; the same holds true for the model of the firm described in (*). Thus we can give the following formal definition. The sequence $x(0), \dots, x(T)$ is called a trajectory of length T generated by a von Neumann technology Z if the relations

$$(x(t), y(t+1)) \in Z, x(t+1) \leqslant y(t+1), \quad t = 0, 1, \dots, T-1$$

hold for some vectors $y(t)$. The trajectories which are optimal in the sense that, the output value $p(T)\, x(T)$ at moment T is greater than or equal to the output value for any other trajectory beginning at $x(0)$ are of special interest here ($p(T) \geqslant 0$ is the given price vector at the moment T, px is the scalar product of the vectors p and x).

Sometimes efficient trajectories $x(0), \dots, x(T)$ are considered. Efficiency means that from the point $x(0)$ it is impossible to reach in T steps the point $\lambda x(t)$ with $\lambda \geqslant 1$; in other words trajectories of the form $x(0), \dots, \lambda x(T)$ do not exist. Under some natural assumptions on the technology the trajectory is efficient if and only if there exists a price vector $p(T)$ for which the trajectory is optimal. One can consider infinite trajectories $x(0), \dots, x(t),\ x(t+1), \dots$ as well. An infinite trajectory is called efficient if each of its segments $x(0), \dots, x(t)$ is efficient for any $t > 0$. The interest is infinite efficient trajectories is not motivated solely by the desire to understand the system's behaviour in the far future. Much more concretely, the fact that $x(1)$ must belong to the infinite efficient trajectory beginning at $x(0)$ is often a very restrictive assumption, which allows us to determine uniquely the output $x(1)$ among all feasible outputs generated by the input $x(0)$.

The von Neumann technology Z generates not only the trajectories of goods describing the material flows in the economy but the price trajectories describing the financial flows. It is supposed that the price vector $q \geqslant 0$ at the moment $t+1$ (given the price vector p at the moment t) is chosen in such a manner that the value of any output y (at moment $t+1$) does not exceed the value of the input x at moment t). Thus we have the following definition: the sequence $p(0), \dots, p(t), \dots$ is a price trajectory if $p(t+1)\ y \leqslant p(t)x$ for all $(x, y) \in Z$, $t = 0, 1 \dots$. If $x(0), \dots, x(t), \dots$ is a goods trajectory, and $p(0), \dots, p(t), \dots$ is a price trajectory, then the inequalities

$$p(0)x(0) \geqslant p(1)x(1) \geqslant \dots p(t)x(t) \dots$$

are valid.

Let us consider now the case of a von Neumann technology (in the narrow sense) given by an input matrix A and an output matrix B. The (goods) trajectory $x(0), \dots, x(t)$ generated by the technology Z is determined by the sequence of intensity vectors $u(t)$ such that $Bu(t) \geqslant Au(t+1)$. This sequence is called the intensity trajectory. In this case the price trajectory is a sequence $p(t)$ such that $p(t+1)B \leqslant p(t)A$.

The efficient trajectory $x(0), \dots, x(t), \dots$ generated by some von Neumann technology Z can be characterized by a system of 'shadow prices' $p(0), \dots, p(t), \dots$. The corresponding result (often called the characteristic theorem) is in a sense analogous to the duality theorem of linear programming and can be interpreted in a similar manner. Under some natural additional assumptions it is: the trajectory $x(0), \dots, x(t), \dots$ is efficient if and only if there exists a price trajectory $p(0), \dots, p(t), \dots$ such that $p(t) \neq 0$ for all t and

$$p(0)x(0) = p(1)x(1) = \cdots = p(t)x(t) = \cdots$$

All this can be fully carried over to the case when at every moment t a new technology $Z(t)$ is used. The discussion of trajectory properties and, in particular, the characteristics theorem is contained in Makarov and Rubinov (1977).

V. Makarov and A. Rubinov

See also GENERAL EQUILIBRIUM; LINEAR MODELS; VON NEUMANN RAY.

BIBLIOGRAPHY

Champernowne, D.G. 1945–6. A note on J. von Neumann's article on 'A model of general economic equilibrium'. *Review of Economic Studies* 13, 10–18.

Gale, D. 1956. The closed linear model of production. In *Linear Inequalities and Related Systems*, ed. H.W. Kuhn and A.W. Tucker, Annals of Mathematics Studies No. 38. Princeton: Princeton University Press.

Kemeny, J., Morgenstern, O. and Thompson, G. 1956. A generalization of the von Neumann model of an expanding economy. *Econometrica* 24, 115–35.

Los, J. 1978. Mathematical theory of von Neumann economic models. Report on recent results. *Colloquia Mathematica* 40(2), 327–46.

Makarov, V.L. and Rubinov, A.M. 1977. *Mathematical Theory of Economic Dynamics and Equilibria*. New York: Springer-Verlag.

Morgenstern, O. and Thompson, G. 1976. *Mathematical Theory of Expanding and Contracting Economies*. Lexington, Mass: D.C. Heath

von Neumann, J. 1945–6. A model of general economic equilibrium. *Review of Economic Studies* 13, 1–9.

von Thünen, J. H. *See* THÜNEN, JOHAN HEINRICH VON.

voting. Virtually all economic doctrines prescribe that certain activities – for example, the provision of public goods – be undertaken by government. Accordingly, such doctrines implicitly prescribe that certain allocative decisions – for example, determining the level of supply of public goods – be made by political rather than market processes. Thus voting (and government decision making generally), though logically a part of political science, is of clear relevance to economic theory.

Historically, economists have contributed at least as much as political scientists to the pure theory of voting. The theory of voting has its origins in the work of such enlightenment philosophers and mathematicians as Borda, Condorcet and Laplace. Little further progress was made until some forty years ago when the economist Duncan Black wrote a series of articles (most notably Black, 1948) on the logic of committees and elections, which were subsequently consolidated into a book (Black, 1958). Since Black revived the subject, a number of economists and political scientists have made important contributions. Indeed, the theory of voting has to some extent been subsumed by the more recent and abstract theory of social choice, which was virtually invented by the economist Kenneth Arrow (1951).

Here we review the generic voting problem of selecting, on the basis of the declared preferences of several individuals, one alternative out of a set of alternatives. The voting body may be a small committee, a legislature, or a mass electorate. The alternatives may be proposed budgets, programmes, policies, or candidates for some single office – the common problem is that several alternatives are available from which exactly one must be chosen. (We exclude, therefore, the somewhat different problem of voting for representative bodies, to which several candidates may be elected simultaneously.)

The simplest voting problem is that in which there are just two alternatives, one of which is to be chosen. In this case, voting by simple majority rule strikes most people as fair and reasonable. Each voter votes for one or other alternative (or abstains), and whichever alternative receives more votes is selected. May (1952) formalized our intuition concerning majority rule: he identified four conditions that we probably want a voting rule to meet in a two-alternative contest, and he demonstrated that majority rule, and only majority rule, meets these conditions. May's conditions are: *decisiveness* – however people vote, there is always a clear outcome (even if that is 'social indifference', i.e., a tie); *anonymity* (of voters) – we do not need to know who cast which votes to determine the outcome; *neutrality* (between alternatives) – if everyone voted in the opposite fashion (or continued to abstain), the other alternative would win (or, if the outcome were initially a tie, it would remain a tie); and *positive responsiveness* – if alternative A at least ties B and someone then changes his vote to make it more favourable to A (i.e., by voting for A instead of abstaining or voting for B, or by abstaining instead of voting for B), A then wins. May demonstrated that majority rule meets these four conditions and is the only decision rule that does so. (Decision rules distinct from majority rule can meet any three of them.)

In sum, voting based on majority rule to choose between two alternatives is essentially straightforward, though objections can still be raised against it. One common objection is that, on any particular decision, the winning majority may be, in some sense, 'wrong' or misinformed. Another objection, stated in terms of political theory, is that an 'apathetic' majority (with only weak preferences for alternative A) may override an 'intense' minority (with strong preferences for alternative B); in economic terms, there is no assurance – supposing that some interpersonal accounting of costs and benefits is possible – that selection of A provides to the group as a whole greater benefits net of costs than selection of B. Finally, it may be remarked that, in some circumstances, one or more of May's conditions – and thus also majority rule itself – may not seem so fair and reasonable; an example may be provided if alternative A represents a fundamental change in constitutional arrangements and B represents maintenance of the constitutional status quo, in which case it may well seem appropriate to treat the alternatives in a non-neutral fashion (by, for example, requiring greater than majority support for the selection of A).

But more vexing problems arise when the domain of choice is expanded to three or more alternatives. Many different apparently fair and reasonable voting procedures are possible (and in actual use), all of which reduce to simple majority rule in the event there are just two alternatives, but which operate differently in the event there are three or more alternatives. It is not clear which, if any, of these procedures is the 'natural' or appropriate extension of simple majority rule. On closer inspection, they all have serious flaws – that is, they turn out not to be so fair and reasonable; indeed such flaws appear to be unavoidable in the general case.

With three or more alternatives, a procedure may require voters to declare their preferences either 'nominally' or 'ordinally' – a distinction that collapses when just two alternatives are being voted on. Under a *nominal* procedure, each voter divides the alternatives into two sets – those he votes for and (implicitly) those he votes against. Under an *ordinal* procedure, each voter ranks orders the alternatives according to his preferences. (There are other ballot forms, but they are rarely used in practice.)

For descriptive purposes, we may assign commonly used voting procedures that select one alternative out of many to three broad types (for a more extended recent discussion see Dummett, 1984), which we may label *aggregation* procedures, *elimination* procedures, and *sequential binary* procedures. To simplify the following discussion, we sidestep the question of how procedures may break ties and we suppose voters are never indifferent between alternatives.

An aggregation procedure takes declared preferences and

aggregates them in a single step to determine the selected alternative; thus only one vote is taken. The simplest voting procedure is *plurality* (or 'first-past-the-post') voting: on a nominal ballot, each voter votes for no more than one alternative; the aggregation rule selects the alternative with the most votes. A recently proposed variant is *approval* voting (Brams and Fishburn, 1982): on a nominal ballot, each voter votes for any number of alternatives; the aggregation rule is the same as plurality. The most common aggregation procedure using an ordinal ballot is *preferential* (or *Borda count*) procedure. The aggregation rule is this: if there are *m* alternatives altogether, an alternative is awarded *m* points for each ballot on which it is ranked first, *m–1* points for each on which it is ranked second, and so forth; the alternative with the most points is selected.

An elimination procedure initially aggregates declared preferences in some fashion, on the basis of which weaker alternatives are eliminated. A new vote is then taken on the remaining alternatives. (If an ordinal ballot was used at the outset, the original ballots can be reaggregated with the eliminated alternatives deleted from each ranking.) Elimination and revoting (or reaggregation) continue until every alternative but one has been eliminated. *Plurality plus runoff* voting initially aggregates in the manner of plurality voting, eliminates all alternatives except those receiving the most and second most votes, and holds a simple majority vote runoff between these two. The *alternative vote* procedure also aggregates in the manner of plurality voting, but only the alternative with the fewest number of votes is eliminated at each stage; thus *m-1* votes are required altogether. The *exhaustive* (or *Coombs*) procedure uses an ordinal ballot and eliminates from among the remaining alternatives the one with the most last-place, rather than the fewest first-place, preferences. Still other elimination procedures aggregate in the manner of preferential voting.

A sequential binary procedure is a voting procedure of the parliamentary type, in which a sequence of binary choices (e.g., yes or no) is put to the voters. A very simple sequential binary procedure – which approximately (but not exactly) mimics Anglo-American parliamentary voting – is what Black called *ordinary committee* procedure and is now generally referred to as *standard amendment* procedure: two alternatives are paired for a simple majority vote, the winner is paired with a third alternative for a second vote, and so forth until every alternative has entered the voting. The alternative that wins the final vote is selected. Another sequential procedure is variously referred to as *sequential elimination* or *successive* procedure: each alternative in turn is voted up or down on a simple majority vote; the first alternative to receive majority support is selected; if every alternative but one has been rejected, the one remaining alternative is selected by default. Under any sequential procedure, the alternatives must be placed in some kind of voting order; this raises the possibility that such procedures may violate the spirit of May's neutrality condition, in that whether an alternative is selected may depend on when it enters the voting.

The reader may easily check that each procedure described above reduces to simple majority rule in the event that there are just two alternatives. Moreover, at first blush, they all appear to be fair and reasonable – in any case, certainly not perverse. Thus each procedure appears to be a natural extension of simple majority rule when the domain of choice is expanded beyond two alternatives. However, the reader may also check that, for given declarations of preferences by voters, each procedure may imply a different selected alternative. By way of partial illustration, consider the following declaration of preferences over four alternatives (the number above each ordering indicates the number of voters declaring such preferences):

Example 1	*4*	*4*	*2*	*9*
first preference	A	B	B	C
second preference	B	A	D	D
third preference	D	D	A	A
fourth preference	C	C	C	B

Under plurality voting, C is selected (with 9 votes, as opposed to 6 for B, 4 for A, and none for D). Under approval voting, if we suppose that each voter votes for his top two alternatives, D wins (with 11 votes, as opposed to 10 for B, 9 for C, and 8 for A). Under plurality plus runoff voting, B is selected (the runoff is between B and C and the four voters whose first preference A has been eliminated prefer B to C). The alternative vote, in this case, works in just the same way as plurality plus runoff. Exhaustive voting selects D (C, with 10 last-place preferences, is eliminated first, then B with the 9 last-place preferences, and then A). Preferential voting selects A (with 50 points, as opposed to D with 49 points, C with 46 points, and B with 45 points). With respect to sequential binary procedures, voting under both amendment and successive procedures voting can select any alternative other than C (which loses every possible pairwise vote), depending on the voting order (specifically, the alternative other than C that enters the voting last is selected).

In choosing among competing voting procedures, an appealing approach is to do what May did for simple majority rule – that is, identify a set of attractive criteria and then determine which procedure uniquely meets them. (See, for example, Young, 1974.) The problem here is that different procedures meet different sets of criteria, and no procedure meets all criteria that we might regard as necessary for a fair and reasonable system to meet. (In effect, voting theory runs up against Arrow's 'general impossibility theorem' in social choice theory; cf. Arrow, 1951.)

A particularly severe flaw that affects all these voting procedures is that they are subject to *agenda manipulation* – that is, individuals who can add alternatives to, or delete alternatives from, the agenda of choice can influence the outcome *even if the alternatives that may be added or deleted cannot themselves win*. (It is this property of plurality voting that makes the presence or absence of 'third-party' candidates, who cannot themselves win, so significant in British parliamentary elections or US Presidential elections.) Consider Example 1 again. If all four alternatives are on the agenda, C is selected under plurality voting, but if A is removed from the agenda (and thus deleted from each preference ordering), B is selected. (This is why B wins under plurality plus runoff voting. More generally, it is only because the elimination of alternatives can alter the relative strength of surviving alternatives under aggregation procedures that there is any reason to devise elimination versions of these procedures.) Similar illustrations could be provided for other procedures. Thus voting under such procedures violates the Weak Axiom of Revealed Preference – which economists usually take to be an aspect of rational choice – and indeed weaker consistency criteria as well.

Let us now consider one apparently attractive approach to extending simple majority rule to the multi-alternative case that none of the procedures described above exactly implements (for good reason, it turns out). Let us consider the *majority preference relation* – that is, simple majority rule between all pairs of alternatives. Consider the following declaration of preferences by five voters (we will discuss the 'social ordering' momentarily):

Example 2	*2*	*1*	*2*	*Social ordering*
first preference	A	B	C	B
second preference	B	A	B	A
third preference	C	C	A	C

We may note that B, though it has the fewest first preferences and would lose under many procedures, has a particular strength and perhaps a strong claim to be the alternative that should be selected. This is due to the fact that B can defeat each other alternative in a pairwise vote (or 'straight fight') under simple majority rule. An alternative that can do this is called the *Condorcet winner*, and the criterion for voting procedures which requires that the Condorcet winner be the selected alternative is called the *Condorcet criterion.* Every procedure described above, other than the standard amendment procedure, violates this criterion – that is, we can find some declaration of preferences such that the procedure selects an alternative other than the Condorcet winner.

The approach of looking at pairwise contests based on majority rule apparently has this further attraction: for the example above, we can identify not only the Condorcet winner but a 'social ordering' based on majority rule, as shown above – that is, A is majority preferred to both B and C, and B is majority preferred to C. Given such a 'social ordering', if it turned out that A was in fact not a feasible alternative, the group could simply move to B as its second 'social preference'. The majority preference relation, moreover, is quite immune to agenda manipulation, as majority preference between two alternatives depends only on individual preferences between the same two alternatives and is unaffected by the presence or absence of other alternatives or by changes in individual preferences among alternatives other than the two in question.

The majority preference relation has further descriptive significance. Most electoral and legislative voting rules are *majoritarian* in nature – that is, they empower any majority of voters acting in concert to select whatever alternative that majority agrees upon. Thus to say A is majority preferred to B is equivalent to saying, in the language of cooperative game theory, that A *dominates* B, i.e., that there is a coalition of individuals who all prefer A to B and who collectively have the power to bring about A. The Condorcet winner is, therefore, the *undominated* or *core* alternative. Thus, if voters treat voting as a game of strategy in which coalitions can form freely, the outcome will be determined by the majority preference relation, independent of the particular (majoritarian) voting procedure nominally in use.

It may appear, therefore, that we have satisfactorily solved the problem of generalizing majority rule to the multi-alternative case, but unfortunately we have not. The reason is that majority preference (like game-theoretic domination) does not in general generate a 'social ordering'. This is illustrated by Example 1, in which it may be checked that, in pairwise votes, A defeats B, B defeats D, and D defeats A. (It was for this reason that the selected alternative under amendment procedure depended on the order of voting.) This phenomenon is variously called the 'paradox of voting', the 'Condorcet effect', the 'Arrow problem' and the phenomenon of 'cyclical majorities'. It is most simply illustrated by the following three voter, three alternative example.

Example 3	*1*	*1*	*1*
first preference	A	B	C
second preference	B	C	A
third preference	C	A	B

This phenomenon evidently was first discovered by Condorcet, and it was then alternately forgotten and rediscovered until the work of Black and Arrow appeared in the late 1940s. It results from some declarations of preferences (e.g., Example 3) but not others (e.g., Example 2). The question naturally occurs of whether we can specify general conditions on preference declarations under which the paradox of voting does, and does not, occur.

The most obvious condition that excludes the paradox is *majority consensus,* i.e., a majority of voters declare the same preferences; but we may note that this does not explain the absence of paradox in Example 2. What is true in Example 2 is that the declared preferences are – to use the term introduced by Black (1948) – *single-peaked.* (See Sen, 1966, for generalization of this concept.) What this means is that the declared preferences are consistent with the supposition that the alternatives are perceived by all voters as arrayed along a single dimension of evaluation. For example, three alternatives might be arrayed along an ideological dimension such that one is the (relatively) 'leftist' alternative, another is the (relatively) 'rightist' alternative, and the third is the 'centrist' alternative that represents a compromise between the other two. If all voters structure their preferences accordingly, it follows that there is some alternative – namely, the centrist one – that no voter ranks last. Then in turn it follows that either an absolute majority of voters prefers one or other extreme alternative or the centrist alternative defeats each extreme alternative in a pairwise majority vote (since the voters who most prefer one extreme alternative prefer the centrist alternative to the other extreme); in any event there is a Condorcet winner. It may be checked that the declared preferences in Example 2 meet the single-peakedness condition (with B the alternative that no one ranks last), while the preferences in Example 3 do not.

The notion of single-peaked preferences extends readily to a continuum of alternatives. Each voter has an *ideal point* of highest preference or maximum utility somewhere along the continuum and his utility declines as distance from his ideal point increases in either direction.

Whether alternatives are discrete points along a dimension or a continuum of points, if preferences are single-peaked voter ideal points can be rank ordered from left to right (or whatever is the nature of the evaluative dimension). It then follows that the alternative M corresponding to the median of voter ideal points is the Condorcet winner. This is the *median voter theorem* due originally to Black (1948, 1958). Consider any point A to the left of M. M is preferred to A by the median voter and all voters whose ideal points lie to the right of M and, by definition of a median point, this is a majority of the voters. Obviously the same argument can be made for any point B to the right of M. Thus M defeats every other point and is the Condorcet winner.

The notion of single-peaked preferences can be generalized to a multidimensional space of alternatives, where each point in the space represents a different combination of policies, programmes, appropriations, points on distinct evaluative dimensions, or whatever. Generalized to this setting, the notion requires that all voter preferences with respect to sets of alternatives lying on any straight line through the space be single-peaked. This is equivalent to the standard economic assumption that individual preferences on a space (of, for example, commodity bundles) be convex. But, in the multidimensional case, there almost never is a point that is the median ideal point in all directions, so there is almost never a Condorcet winner, and cyclical majorities almost always exist (Plott, 1967). Moreover, it turns out that, in the almost certain event that there is no Condorcet winner, a massive majority cycle encompasses all points in the space (McKelvey, 1979). Despite all this, recent work indicates that, even in the multidimensional case, common voting processes, in particular those of a competitive nature, lead to selection of more or less centrist alternatives.

Throughout the discussion thus far, we have consistently sidestepped one further complexity in voting. Voting procedures operate on the *declared preferences* on voters. The question arises of whether it always is expedient for voters to declare (or reveal) their 'honest' or 'sincere' preferences. In fact, it is well known to both students and practitioners of politics that, under common voting procedures, voters who cast 'honest' votes may regret doing so. For example, suppose the preferences displayed in Example 1 are actually the honest preferences of all voters. Under plurality voting, alternative C is selected, if preferences are honestly revealed. But it would be to the advantage of the four voters whose preference ordering appears in the first column to declare their preferences otherwise, specifically by ranking B first, for then B – which they all prefer to C – would be selected. For another example, suppose the preferences displayed in Example 3 are actually honest preferences. Under standard amendment procedure with the alternatives voted on in alphabetical order, A defeats B in the initial vote and C, which defeats A in the second vote, is ultimately selected. However, if the voter whose preference ordering appears in the first column were to vote insincerely for B instead of A at the first vote, B would be ultimately selected and that voter prefers B to C. In general, if voting is treated as a game of strategy, voting in a manner that reveals true preferences may not be the best strategy.

Several questions then naturally occur. First, if voting is treated as a game of strategy, is it possible to identify 'best' strategies for all voters? If so, and if all voters use their best strategies, is the selected alternative different from what would be selected if all voters used honest strategies? (Note that, in the two examples above, we did not consider possible counter-strategies of the remaining voters.) If the outcomes are different, how do the 'strategic' and 'honest' outcomes compare? Finally, it is possible to design a voting procedure such that best and honest strategies always coincide for all voters – that is, can we devise a 'strategy proof' voting procedure?

The first question was first systematically treated by Farquharson (1969), who introduced the concept of *sophisticated* voting, i.e., voting that is strategically optimal, which is in general different from *sincere* voting, i.e., voting that honestly reveals preferences. Farquharson stated a theorem that says this: if no voters are indifferent between alternatives, sophisticated voting under any sequential binary procedure is determinate, i.e., the game of strategy has a definite solution. However, Farquharson's method for solving such voting games, based on successive elimination of dominated strategies, is cumbersome to employ in even the simplest situation and, for all practical purposes, impossible to employ if there are more than a few voters or alternatives. Fortunately, an alternative definition of sophisticated voting under sequential binary procedures, and an alternative and much easier method of solution, exist. This is the *multi-stage* or *tree* method, which has been definitively characterized by McKelvey and Niemi (1978).

Using this method, sophisticated voting outcomes under binary procedures may easily be identified and compared with sincere outcomes. First, sincere and sophisticated outcomes often diverge – that is, strategic behaviour on the part of all voters does not necessarily 'cancel out'. Second, and perhaps contrary to 'common sense' expectations, sophisticated voting outcomes are, by several criteria, superior to sincere outcomes. (For example, sophisticated voting, but not sincere, always complies with the Condorcet criterion.) Third, if voting is sincere, alternatives are favoured by being placed later in the voting order; if voting is sophisticated, the reverse is true. Finally, these differential effects are magnified to the extent that majority preference is cyclical.

With respect to the final question, voting theorists conjectured for many years that a strategy proof voting procedure could not exist, but two fundamental problems stood in the way of decisively demonstrating this. First, it is not at all clear how to define the class of objects that we might call 'voting procedures'. Thus, no matter how many procedures we can demonstrate to be vulnerable to strategy, there seems always to be the logical possibility that something else exists that we might be willing to call a 'voting procedure' and that is strategy proof. Second, especially with more exotic procedures (e.g., approval voting), it is not always clear what constitutes 'sincere' or 'honest' voting.

Gibbard (1973) neatly sidestepped both of these problems and proved the conjecture. He did this by solving a much more general problem in game theory. First, he said, however we define the set of all voting procedures, it is certainly a subset of all 'game forms', where a *game form* is a game (in the sense of game theory) minus the preferences of players over outcomes. A game form is *dictatorial* if there is some player who, for every outcome of the game, has a strategy that is *decisive* for that outcome, i.e., its selection guarantees that outcome, regardless of the strategy selections of the other players. In a game, a strategy is *dominant* for a player if he would never regret selecting it, regardless of the strategies selected by other players. A game form is *straightforward* if it gives every player, for all possible preferences over outcomes, a dominant strategy. Gibbard then proved (using Arrow's theorem) that every straightforward game form with three or more outcomes is dictatorial.

Now suppose that a voting procedure is strategy proof. Then no voter, regardless of his preferences, can ever have reason to regret voting sincerely, regardless of how other voters vote. But this means that every voter, regardless of his preferences, must always have a dominant strategy (which, moreover, must be a sincere strategy). But, even apart from the requirement that the dominant strategies be sincere, this requires that the voting procedure be a straightforward game form. Thus, once we move beyond choice between just two alternatives, and at the same time make selection depend on the declared preferences of more than one individual, we cannot avoid the possibility that individuals may have an incentive to declare other than their true preferences.

NICHOLAS R. MILLER

See also BLACK, DUNCAN; BORDA, JEAN-CHARLES DE; CARROLL, LEWIS; CONDORCET, MARQUIS DE; PUBLIC CHOICE; SOCIAL CHOICE.

BIBLIOGRAPHY

Arrow, K.J. 1951. *Social Choice and Individual Values.* Cowles Foundation Monograph No. 17, New York: Wiley.

Brams, S. and Fishburn, P. 1983. *Approval Voting.* Boston: Birkhauser.

Black, D. 1948. On the rationale of group decision-making. *Journal of Political Economy* 56(1), February, 23–34.

Black, D. 1958. *The Theory of Committees and Elections.* Cambridge: Cambridge University Press.

Dummett, M. 1984. *Voting Procedures.* Oxford: Clarendon Press.

Farquharson, R. 1969. *Theory of Voting.* New Haven: Yale University Press.

Gibbard, A. 1973. Manipulation of voting schemes: a general result. *Econometrica* 41(4), July, 587–601.
May, K. 1952. A set of independent necessary and sufficient conditions for simple majority rule. *Econometrica* 20(4), October, 680–84.
McKelvey, R. 1979. General conditions for global intransitivities in formal voting models. *Econometrica* 47(5), September, 1085–112.
McKelvey, R. and Niemi, R. 1978. A multistage game representation of sophisticated voting for binary procedures. *Journal of Economic Theory* 18(1), June, 1–22.
Plott, C. 1967. A notion of equilibrium and its possibility under majority rule. *American Economic Review* 57(4), September, 787–806.
Sen, A.K. 1966. A possibility theorem on majority decisions. *Econometrica* 34(2), April, 491–9.
Young, H.P. 1974. An axiomatization of Borda's rule. *Journal of Economic Theory* 9(1), September, 43–52.

Voznesensky, Nikolai Alekseevich (1903–1950). Voznesensky (born the son of a timber dealer in Teploe, Russia, on 18 November 1903; executed on 30 September 1950) joined the Bolshevik Party in 1919 and studied political economy at the Institute of Red Professors, Moscow, where he stayed on as lecturer. His publications – fewer than 30, his culminating manuscript being destroyed by the police – have been analysed by Harrison (1985) and Sutela (1984). In a concept later to be termed 'unbalanced growth' by A. O. Hirschman, he saw that the national plan 'must localize bottlenecks, not for adapting them, but for doing away with them'. Ranging himself against those who argued that comprehensive planning invalidated money calculations, he had by 1935 embraced the position – which was to figure in Stalin's indictment of him in 1949 – that money would have a distributive function even when all means of production had been nationalized. His association with the Leningrad circle which eventually led to his execution also began in 1935, for A.A. Zhdanov, having replaced the assassinated S.M. Kirov as Leningrad Party Secretary, invited Voznesensky to lead that city's plan organization under an Executive Committee headed by A.N. Kosygin.

Voznesensky was promoted to the chairmanship of the USSR State Planning Committee in January 1938 and brought order into the chaos resulting from the 1937 Great Purge (Voznesensky, 1938, 1940; Harrison, 1985), but so inadequate were his plans for a war economy both before and after the German attack of June 1941 that Zhdanov's rivals, G.M. Malenkov and L.P. Beria (Ra'anan, 1983) ran the newly created State Defence Committee, from which Voznesensky was excluded until February 1942. He regained chairmanship of the Planning Committee in December 1942, and achieved in 1943 a peak of armaments production and economic expansion in the unoccupied territory. He allowed market forces to operate in the household sector, alongside rations at controlled prices, absorbing some of the inflation in purchasing power through highly taxed off-ration prices in state shops, and intended to liquidate the inflationary overhang generated by free sales by farmers in a monetary reform as soon as the war ended (though famine caused postponement and retail price restructuring until December 1947).

At the height of Voznesensky's economic leadership (he was elected Academician in 1943) an unsigned editorial, 1943, condemned the 'voluntarism' which disregarded the 'objectively-determined process of development' and confirmed, as had been adumbrated in 1941 (Kaser, 1965), that a law of value operated under socialism. His postwar Reconstruction Plan evoked 'economic levers in the organization of production and distribution, such as price, money, credit, profit and incentives' (*Selected Works*, 1979, p. 465): he brought in Kosygin as Minister of Finance to oversee the cut in subsidies required by his reform of wholesale prices; the measures which took effect on 1 January 1949 would have been a major contribution to rational economic management (Kaser, 1950).

Political realignments led to Voznesensky's dismissal within weeks of his reform and his eventual execution without trial; the life of the dismissed Kosygin, in Khrushchev's later words, 'hung by a thread'. Stalin reversed the reform of both retail and wholesale prices and soon (Stalin, 1952) limited the role of 'commodity relations' to the interface of the socialist sector with non-state entities (such as collective farmers and foreigners), vilifying Voznesensky's analysis of the war economy (Voznesensky, 1948) for the very 'voluntarism' that the author rejected. The death or disgrace of those in the Leningrad circle was a triumph, albeit short-lived, for Beria and Malenkov in a political power struggle, but the open disputations were on economic issues: on one, to stop dismantling capital in the Soviet Zone of Germany in favour of current deliveries, Voznesensky had been right; in the others – where E.S. Varga argued that east Europe should be allowed to be 'state capitalist' with market relations with the West and that Keynesian policies had halted the 'general crisis of capitalism' – he had been wrong.

M.C. Kaser

SELECTED WORKS
1938. K itogam sotsialisticheskogo vosproizvodstva vo vtoroi piatiletke (On the results of socialist reproduction in the second Five-year Plan). *Bol'shevik* No. 2. In *Selected Works*, 346–62.
1940. Tri stalinskie piatiletki stroitel'stva sotsializma (Three Stalinist Five-year Plans for building socialism). *Bol'shevik* No. 1. Not reproduced in *Selected Works*.
1948. *The War Economy of the USSR in the Period of the Patriotic War*. Washington, DC: Public Affairs Press and the American Association of Learned Societies. Translation of *Voennaia ekonomika SSSR v period Otechestvennoi voiny*, Moscow: Gospolitizdat. In *Selected Works*, 484–604.
1979. *Izbrannye proizvedeniia 1931–1947* (Selected Works 1931–1947). Moscow: Izdatel'stvo politicheskoy literatury.

BIBLIOGRAPHY
Harrison, M. 1985. *Soviet Planning in Peace and War, 1938–1945*. Cambridge: Cambridge University Press.
Kaser, M.C. 1950. Soviet planning and the price mechanism. *Economic Journal* 60, March, 81–91.
Kaser, M.C. 1965. Le débat sur la loi de la valeur en URSS. Etude rétrospective 1941–1953. *Annuaire de l'URSS 1965*, Paris: CNRS.
Ra'anan, G.D. 1983. *International Policy Formation in the USSR: Factional 'Debates' during the Zhdanovshchina*. Hamden, Conn.: Archon.
Pod znamenem marxizma (Under the banner of Marxism). 1943. No. 7–8. Editorial.
Stalin, J.V. 1952. *Economic Problems of Socialism in the USSR*. Moscow: Foreign Languages Publishing House. (Translation of *Ekonomicheskie problemy sotsializma v SSSR*, Moscow.)
Sutela, P. 1984. *Socialism, Planning and Optimality. A Study in Soviet Economic Thought*. Commentationes Scientiarum Socialium No. 25, Helsinki: Societas Scientiarum Fennica.
Varga, E.S. 1946. *Izmeneniia v ekonomike kapitalizma v itoge vtoroi mirovoi voiny* (Changes in the economy of capitalism as a result of the Second World War). Moscow: Gospolitizdat.

vulgar economy. Karl Marx used the epithet 'vulgar economy' to describe certain analytical positions which, beginning in classical political economy in the works of Malthus, Say, some of the post-Ricardians including John

Stuart Mill, developed eventually into an 'analytical system' (as in Say) and took an 'academic form' (as in the writings of Roscher, among others) (see *Theories of Surplus Value*, Vol. III, pp. 500–502). The epithet was not simply a derogatory label but had thus a specific analytical content and significance. Marx contrasted sharply the 'vulgar' from the classical political economy, the latter comprising of 'all the economists who since the time of W. Petty have investigated the real internal framework of bourgeois relations of production' (*Capital*, Vol. I, pp. 174–5). Vulgar economy, while drawing upon the materials provided by scientific political economy – and therefore lacking in originality – ruminated instead over the 'appearances'. Marx saw, in the capitalist production, 'more than in any other', a 'reality', 'the inner physiology of the system' – which was captured in scientific political economy, in their analysis locating the generation of surplus in production, in their theory explaining the manner in which surplus is appropriated by the owners of the means of production and distributed as the tripartite revenues of rents, profits and wages, and which brought to light the inevitable and endemic conflicts of class interests and thence the contradictions incipient in the processes of generation, distribution and accumulation of surplus. Marx was himself to build his theory on the rudiments provided by political economy. However, this 'reality' hides behind 'appearances' which assume forms and emerge as esoteric concepts and categories of analysis pertaining to the sphere of exchange where 'Freedom, Equality, Property and Bentham' reign supreme; exchange appears as between 'equivalents', governed entirely by competition on the market. Also, the true social relations take fetishistic forms in 'false consciousness', forming the subjectivist perceptions of the participant agents of production. Marx attacked vulgar political economy for remaining at the level of these 'appearances'; since these often reflected perceptions of the bourgeois agents of production, vulgar economy tends to defend, rationalize and therefore to serve the interests of the bourgeois class. While Marx thus recognized, in vulgar political economy, an explicit or implicit ideological function, providing apologetics for the bourgeoisie, his critique was not confined only to the ideological; he painstakingly traced its analytical roots and development and criticized the logical inconsistencies and ambivalences of their theoretical positions.

For Marx, the significant achievement of scientific political economy was in tracing the source of surplus in production and identifying the role of labour as a cause of value and the source of surplus value. It grasped the 'internal interconnections' of capitalist production through recognizing the different roles that the 'agents' – land, capital and labour – played in the process of production and in generating value and the different principles by which their revenues were governed. It identified the constraint binding upon the wage–profit relation. In contrast, vulgar political economy adopted the 'trinity formula' concerning the form and sources of these revenues. Treated as having a symmetric coordinate status, land was seen as the source of rent and capital, of profits just as labour is of wages, it being held that the agents are all paid according to their productivity. Thus land as well as capital is as much a source of value and of surplus as labour. Thus 'we have complete mystification of the capitalist mode of production, the conversion of social relations into relations among things'; to Marx, the entitlement to surplus in the form of rents and profits, originating from the property relations, is here confounded with the creation of surplus by the material means themselves. Further, through giving a symmetric role and status to the trinity, by envisaging their revenues as determined by the same process of competition, and independently of each other, a harmonious view of classes was constructed. This view, explaining distributive revenues in 'doctrinaire language' helped their theory to conform to the bourgeois perceptions: wages appeared as the competitive return to labour and, analogously, as Senior proposed, profits as the recompense for abstinence. The rise in distributive revenues of any one class, reflecting its enhanced productive contribution could not interfere with others' revenues which were determined alike but independently.

Marx sees the roots of the later vulgar economy in certain 'vulgar representations' or 'elements' in classical political economy. While generously praising the masterly vision of Adam Smith for fathoming 'the inner connection' and, for the first time, describing and providing 'a nomenclature and corresponding mental concepts' for 'the external, apparent forms of its life', Marx criticizes, at length, an important 'vulgar' element in Smith: when Smith constructs the natural price of a commodity from adding up wages, rents and profits, determined independently of each other and separately, they become *sources of value* instead of having 'a source *in* value'. After having revealed the intrinsic connection among wages and profits, Smith leaps into 'the connection as it appears in competition'. Marx attaches a great historical significance to Ricardo, 'for science' in that he brought back 'the inner connection – the contradiction between the apparent and the actual movement of the system and brought into the open the objective basis for the inescapable antagonism of class interests'.

This apart, Marx also discusses a number of other shortcomings of classical political economy that provided scope for vulgarization, such as their inadequate recognition of the historical and transient character of the capitalist mode, of the full implications of labour-power becoming a 'commodity' and of capital as a 'social relation' apart from its 'material form'; of the processes of transforming surplus value into profits and of the intervention of money into barter and the evolution of its functions over the advancing stages of capitalist accumulation. All these inadequacies were exploited by vulgar political economy in building up a sanguine and harmonious view of the functioning and growth of the capitalist system, whereas Marx found the system ridden with internal contradictions and recurrent crises.

Marx traced the growth of vulgar political economy and its ascendancy over scientific political economy in terms of the concrete conditions of the historical stages of class struggle. He saw the period between 1820 and 1830 as the last decade of scientific activity when Ricardo's theory was popularized and extended and when 'unprejudiced polemics' was possible. By 1830, the bourgoisie had conquered political power in France and England, their ascendancy over the landed interests was firmly established while the class struggle of labour was assuming threatening proportions. 'It sounded the knell of scientific bourgeois economics. It was thenceforth no longer a question whether this or that theorem was true but whether it was useful to capital or harmful, expedient or inexpedient' (Preface to the second edition, *Capital*, Vol. I).

Vulgar political economy itself passed through analytical stages in the period. Marx notices: 'Only when political economy has reached a certain stage of development and has assumed well-established forms – that is, after Adam Smith – does ... the vulgar element become a special kind of political economy.' Thus, Say separates the vulgar notions in Smith's work (such as the supply and demand determination of value) and puts them forward as a distinct system. Borrowing from the advancing political economy, vulgar economy also thrives:

after Ricardo, particularly, the decline of his theory sets in; the erosion and obfuscation occurring in the hands of his own followers. The hostility to Ricardian theory was sharpened by the use made of labour theory by the utopian writers who, on the basis of their naive interpretation, advocated a radical change in social order. Vulgar political economy becomes increasingly apologetic, as in Bastiat, with the capital-labour confrontation emerging sharply in society, until it assumes a further 'academic form' where apologetics was concealed in an 'insipid erudition' (Marx refers to Roscher as a 'master of this form'!) (1861–3, Vol. III, pp. 500–502.)

What emerges from Marx's detailed critique, particularly in the *Theories of Surplus Value*, is that his attack was not only ideological but also analytical. While a fully-fledged alternative system to replace classical political economy had not yet emerged in Marx's time, the latter had been eroded and conditions become ripe for its subversion.

KRISHNA BHARADWAJ

See also MARX, KARL HEINRICH.

BIBLIOGRAPHY

Marx, K. 1861–3. *Theories of Surplus Value*, Vols. I–III. London: Lawrence & Wishart, 1972.

Marx, K. 1890. *Capital*, Vol. I. 4th edn, London: Pelican Marx Library, 1976.

Marx, K. 1894. *Capital*, Vol. III. Moscow: Progress Publishers, 1974.

W

wage flexibility. The importance of wage flexibility arises from the fact that, in a wide range of economic models, there is an inverse relationship between wages and employment. Unemployment is thus associated with wages in excess of the full employment level, and the persistence of unemployment then depends on how quickly wages adjust in the face of unemployment. It is often argued that if wages were very flexible, unemployment would be eliminated quickly and automatically by wage cuts, and that consequently any persistence of unemployment must be ascribed to wage inflexibility.

While wage inflexibility plays a crucial role in explaining unemployment in both Classical and Keynesian models, the mechanism through which it does so is quite different in the two cases. Following Barro and Grossman (1971) and Malinvaud (1977) it is useful to distinguish 'Classical' from 'Keynesian' unemployment. Classical unemployment occurs where the real wage exceeds the marginal product of labour at full employment, so that it is not profitable for firms to employ the whole labour force. It can only be reduced by cuts in real wages which make it profitable for firms to take on more workers at the margin.

Keynesian unemployment is caused by a deficiency of aggregate demand, but in most standard presentations of the Keynesian model aggregate demand is determined, to a greater or lesser extent, in nominal terms so that a cut in money wages, and hence in prices, tends to raise real aggregate demand. Thus it is the inflexibility, or downward rigidity, of money wages which is the crucial assumption in explaining the persistence of unemployment in standard presentations of the Keynesian system. (For a very full documentation of this point see Leijonhufvud, 1968.)

Wage bargaining is generally conducted in money terms, and wage flexibility is thus generally interpreted in terms of the responsiveness of money wage settlements to changes in economic conditions. But the effectiveness of money wage flexibility in reducing unemployment depends on the interaction of wage-setting and price-setting behaviour. As Keynes stressed in the *General Theory* (1936, chs 2 and 19), if a change in money wages leads to an equi-proportionate change in prices, as the standard economic theory of competitive markets might lead one to expect, it will leave the real wage unchanged. Thus, in the Keynesian system, the wage bargain has no direct effect on the real wage. At the other extreme, in their general disequilibrium model, Barro and Grossman (1971) take the price level as fixed. In their model a fall in money wages will reduce real wages but, because there is no fall in prices, there is no stimulus to aggregate demand, and hence a fall in money wages will not help remove Keynesian unemployment.

Price-setting behaviour is important for a second reason. While wage bargains are generally conducted in money terms, it is now generally accepted that what is at issue is the real wage. There is much empirical support for the theoretical proposition that workers do not suffer from 'money illusion' (especially in countries which have had some experience of inflation), and the money wage claim is best regarded in terms of some desired real wage to be attained in the wage bargain.

The desired outcome of the wage bargain may thus be written

$$w^* = p + q - \alpha_1(u - \bar{u}), \qquad \alpha_1 > 0 \qquad (1)$$

where all variables are measured in logarithms, w^* is the desired money wage, p the price level, q labour productivity, u the unemployment rate and $\bar{u}$ a measure of 'equilibrium' unemployment in a sense to be defined below.

Equation (1) is sufficiently general to be consistent with a number of models of wage determination. Under perfect competition, it describes the equilibrium wage, given the size of the labour force, in which case $\bar{u}$ represents frictional and voluntary unemployment, determined by search behaviour, work-leisure preferences and the like. In models in which wages are not necessarily set to clear the market, the impact of trade union bargaining power or other non-competitive influences which shift the wage equation can be captured in $\bar{u}$.

In general, wages do not adjust instantaneously to the desired level, in part because perceptions, or expectations, of the relevant variables may be slow to adjust (Friedman, 1968) and in part because of rigidities in the adjustment process itself, associated for example with the existence of wage contracts (Fischer, 1977; Taylor, 1980). In a simplified representation, actual wages might be determined according to

$$w = \beta_1 w^* + (1 - \beta_1)w_{-1}, \qquad 0 < \beta_1 < 1 \qquad (1')$$

where w is the actual, and w_{-1} the one period lagged, money wage.

The price equation may be written

$$p^* = w - q - \alpha_2(u - \bar{u}), \qquad \alpha_2 > 0 \qquad (2)$$

where p^* is the firm's desired price, $(w - q)$ is a measure of unit cost and α_2 measures the impact of the level of economic activity on the price mark-up. (The constant term in the equation is suppressed, but changes in, e.g., material prices can be represented by a change in q.) Equation (2) is consistent with price-setting behaviour by firms operating in competitive or non-competitive markets (with a given degree of monopoly power).

Product prices may not adjust instantaneously due to slow adjustment of perceptions (or expectations), transactions costs

$$p = \beta_2 p^* + (1 - \beta_2)p_{-1}, \qquad 0 < \beta_2 < 1. \qquad (2')$$

These equations define the adjustment behaviour of wages and prices

$$\Delta w = \frac{\beta_1}{1-\beta_1}[p + q - w - \alpha_1(u - \bar{u})] \tag{3}$$

$$\Delta p = \frac{\beta_2}{1-\beta_2}[w - q - p - \alpha_2(u - \bar{u})]. \tag{3'}$$

For equilibrium ($\Delta w = \Delta p = 0$) we evidently require

$$\left.\begin{aligned} w &= p + q \\ u &= \bar{u} \end{aligned}\right\} \tag{4}$$

with unemployment at the equilibrium rate and real wages equal to labour productivity.

To examine the response of the system to a change in aggregate demand, we assume for simplicity that nominal aggregate demand (m) is determined exogenously and that unemployment responds to real aggregate demand according to

$$u = \bar{u} - \frac{1}{\gamma}(m - p), \qquad \gamma > 0 \tag{5}$$

Substituting (5) into (3) and (3′) allows the wage-price system to be converted to a representation of the economy in terms of money wages and unemployment.

$$\Delta w = \frac{\beta_1}{1-\beta_1}[m + q - w + (\gamma - \alpha_1)(u - \bar{u})] \tag{6}$$

$$\Delta u = \frac{\beta_2}{\gamma(1-\beta_2)}[w - q - m - (\gamma + \alpha_2)(u - \bar{u})] + \Delta\bar{u} - \frac{1}{\gamma}\Delta m \tag{6'}$$

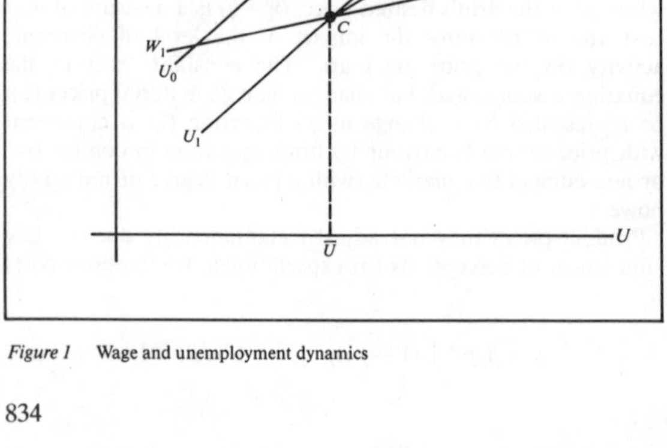

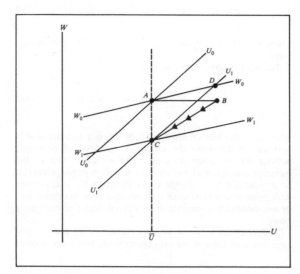

Figure 1 Wage and unemployment dynamics

new equilibrium loci $w_1 w_1$ and $u_1 u_1$ relating to the reduced level of nominal demand, m_1.

The equilibrium of this system is given by equation (4), as before, together with $m = p$. Its dynamic behaviour is depicted in Figure 1. The equilibrium loci $\Delta w = 0$ and $\Delta u = 0$ are depicted, at some given level of demand m_0, by the lines $w_0 w_0$ and $u_0 u_0$ respectively with the equilibrium of the system at point A. (The ww locus is drawn upward sloping since empirically one would expect γ to be greater than α_1.) If demand is now reduced to some lower level (m_1) initially, with given wages and prices, unemployment will rise and the system will move to point B. The higher unemployment will cause wages and prices to fall and the economy will move along the path BC, the final equilibrium position C being defined by the intersection of the

The crucial issue is the speed at which the economy progresses along the path BC. This speed is jointly determined by the parameters of equations (6) and (6′) and hence on the flexibility of prices (β_2) as much as of wages (β_1). The algebraic solution to equations (6) and (6′) is standard, and while there is no simple analytical expression for the speed of adjustment it can be confirmed that adjustment is quicker the larger the values of the demand effects on wages and prices (α_1 and α_2) and the greater the flexibility of wage and price adjustment (β_1 and β_2).

The response of the economy to a real shock, such as a change in productivity, the terms of trade or the burden of taxation, can be represented by a change in the variable q. It is clear from equations (6) and (6′) that the response of money wages and unemployment to a change in q, if it enters the two equations symmetrically, will be the same as the response to a demand shock, m. There has, however, been much discussion in the literature (e.g., Bruno and Sachs, 1985; Grubb, Jackman and Layard, 1983) of the idea that real shocks affect firms' pricing decisions but do not alter desired real wages in the wage bargain. Thus, for example, an adverse productivity or terms-of-trade shock might shift the equilibrium unemployment locus from $u_0 u_0$ to $u_1 u_1$ in Figure 1, while leaving the equilibrium wage locus unchanged at $w_0 w_0$. The economy would then move to a new equilibrium at point D, with the unemployment rate given by

$$u = \bar{u} - \frac{\Delta q}{\alpha_1 + \alpha_2} \tag{7}$$

where Δq is the change in productivity. It will be noted from the figure that a fall in productivity may in these circumstances raise money wages. The reason is that a fall in q raises costs and hence prices, and increased prices will tend to raise money wages. Money wages will rise as long as the price effect outweighs the wage-depressing effect of higher unemployment.

The 1970s were characterized by particularly severe adverse supply shocks, in particular the oil price increases of 1973 and 1979 and slowdown of productivity growth throughout the industrialized world. The above analysis suggests that the capacity of an economy to adjust to such shocks will depend above all on the extent to which wage claims are moderated. Empirically there appears much support for the view that the more 'corporatist' the structure of wage bargaining in the economy (i.e., the more centralized the wage bargain) the more quickly are such supply shocks reflected in wage settlements (Bruno and Sachs, 1985, ch. 11). Austria and Sweden are cited as examples of countries where the wage bargain is struck at the national level, involving centralized unions covering the bulk of the labour force, employers' associations and government. Corporatism is seen as helpful to the rapid assimilation of productivity changes and the like into the wage bargain both because it focuses attention on macroeconomic performance and because it avoids inter-union rivalry. In a decentralized system, individual wage bargainers may know about their individual sector but not about general macroeconomic developments, and may therefore be slow to adjust to macroeconomic shocks. Each group is reluctant to change its own wage if it is uncertain whether others will follow, because of concern over relative wages (Taylor, 1980). Wage flexibility thus suffers from the 'paradox of isolation': each group might like to adjust its wage if it could be sure that similar adjustments would be made throughout the economy, but in a decentralized system there is no coordinating mechanism.

Finally, it may be noted that a rigidity of nominal wage rates, although it raises the unemployment costs of demand deflation, reduces the short-run costs of supply shocks. In Figure 1, the progress of the economy from point A to point D is made slower if money wages are slower to adjust, and hence unemployment takes longer to emerge. A supply shock will raise prices and, if money wages are inflexible, the increase in prices will reduce real wages and thereby maintain employment. In this sense, real wage flexibility may be seen as the opposite of nominal wage flexibility (Sachs, 1979). A number of authors (Bruno and Sachs, 1985) have attributed the relatively strong performance of the United States economy since 1973 to a combination of a very high degree of nominal wage inflexibility (resulting in part from long-term wage contracts) and, over much of the period, demand expansionary policies. By contrast, in economies with more flexible money wages, meeting supply contraction by demand expansion would simply add faster inflation to higher unemployment.

RICHARD JACKMAN

See also TRADE CYCLE; WAGES, REAL AND MONEY.

BIBLIOGRAPHY

Barro, R.J. and Grossman, H.I. 1971. A general disequilibrium model of income and employment. *American Economic Review* 61(1), March, 82–93.

Bruno, M. and Sachs, J. 1985. *Economics of Worldwide Stagflation*. Oxford: Basil Blackwell.

Fischer, S. 1977. Long-term contracts, rational expectations and the optimal money supply rule. *Journal of Political Economy* 85(1), February, 191–205.

Friedman, M. 1968. The role of monetary policy. *American Economic Review* 58, March, 1–17.

Grubb, D., Jackman, R.A. and Layard, R. 1983. Wage rigidity and unemployment in OECD countries. *European Economic Review* 21(1–2), March–April, 11–39.

Keynes, J.M. 1936. *The General Theory of Employment, Interest and Money*. London: Macmillan

Leijonhufvud, A. 1968. *On Keynesian Economics and the Economics of Keynes*. New York: Oxford University Press.

Malinvaud, E. 1977. *The Theory of Unemployment Reconsidered*. Oxford: Basil Blackwell.

Okun, A. 1975. Inflation: its mechanics and welfare costs. *Brookings Papers on Economic Activity* No. 2, 351–401.

Sachs, J. 1979. Wages, profits and macroeconomic adjustment: a comparative study. *Brookings Papers on Economic Activity* No. 2, 269–193.

Taylor, J.B. 1980. Aggregate dynamics and staggered contracts. *Journal of Political Economy* 88(1), February, 1–23.

wage fund doctrine. A central part of classical analysis and closely related to the advances theory of capital, this doctrine lost support in the 1870s because of its association with unacceptable ideas on wages and trade unions. This loss was reinforced by J.S. Mill's authoritative 'recantation'. However, the doctrine was reaffirmed by Jevons and Böhm-Bawerk and survived at a high level of abstraction in neoclassical capital and production theory. This essay starts with the classical statement of J.S. Mill (1848), notices the recantation in 1869, and then looks both backwards to the 18th-century origins of the theory, and forwards to its post-classical developments.

Capital, says Mill, is a stock, previously accumulated, of the products of former labour. Because production takes time between the employment of labour and natural agents and the availability of their product, capital provides the shelter, protection, tools and materials which the work requires, and feeds and otherwise maintains the labourers during the process.

> Wages, then, depend mainly upon the demand and supply of labour; or as it is often expressed, on the proportion between population and capital. By population is here meant the number only of the labouring class, or rather of those who work for hire; and by capital only circulating capital, and not even the whole of that, but the part which is expended in the direct purchase of labour. To this, however, must be added all funds which, without forming a part of capital, are paid in exchange of labour, such as the wages of soldiers, domestic servants, and all other unproductive labourers. There is unfortunately no mode of expressing by one familiar term, the aggregate of what has been called the wages-fund of a country: and as the wages of productive labour form nearly the whole of that fund, it is usual to overlook the smaller and less important part, and to say that wages depend on population and capital. It will be convenient to employ this expression, remembering, however, to consider it as elliptical, and not as a literal statement of the entire truth.
>
> With these limitations of the terms, wages not only depend upon the relative amount of capital and population, but cannot, under the rule of competition, be affected by anything else. Wages (meaning, of course, the general rate) cannot rise, but by an increase of the aggregate funds employed in hiring labourers, or a diminution in the number of the competitors for hire; nor fall, except either by a diminution of the funds devoted paying labour, or by an increase in the number of labourers to be paid (Mill [1848], 1965, pp. 337–8).

This statement of the doctrine, agreeing in essentials with the views of Mill's contemporaries, for example, McCulloch and Senior, is followed by the conclusion that high wages require restraints on population growth.

In the recantation contained in his 1869 *Fortnightly Review* article on his friend Thornton's book, *On Labour*, Mill repeats the doctrine (Mill [1869], 1967, pp. 643–4) only to reject it immediately as a 'true representation of the matter of fact'. His grounds are simply that at any time the limit to the fund available to pay wages is not in practice fixed, because it includes 'the aggregate means of the employing classes'. The limit to the rise in wages is set by how much would drive the employer out of business. In the first six editions of his *Principles* Mill had said that if combinations of workmen 'aimed at obtaining actually higher wages than the rate fixed by supply and demand – the rate which distributes the whole circulating capital of the country among the entire working population – this could only be accomplished by keeping a part of their number permanently out of employment'. In the seventh edition (1871) the first part of this was replaced by '[workmen] would also have a limited power of obtaining, by combination, an increase of general wages at the expense of profits. But the limits of this power are narrow; and were they to attempt to strain it beyond those limits, this could only be accomplished [etc.]' (Mill [1871], 1965, p. 930). The explanation and political significance of Mill's disavowal are still the subject of academic debate; see, for example, Hollander (1985).

The idea of capital as a wages fund arises from the idea of capital as an advance to sustain labour during the period output takes to fructify, or be produced. The theory emerges naturally in commercially agricultural and mercantile economies, and became a foundation stone of the developing economics of the late 18th century in Western Europe. The idea was expressed by Cantillon, Quesnay and Hume, and developed more fully by Turgot and Smith.

In prefacing his discussion of capital, or stock, Smith (1776) observes that the division of labour presupposes a previous accumulation of stock of provisions, materials and tools. He asserted that as the division of labour increases, in order to maintain constant employment, not only an unchanged stock of provisions but also a growing stock of materials and tools is necessary (Smith [1776], 1976, pp. 276–7). Smith's emphasis on the prior accumulation of this growing stock of materials and tools as a precondition of growth of employment, together with his attention to the dependence of wages on the relative rates of growth of capital stock and employment, is the foundation of all later discussion, especially of the British school.

Furthermore, Smith recognized that although the growth of capital could outstrip the growth of population, thus allowing wages to rise for lengthy periods, population growth being responsive to wages above a subsistence level could in the long run reduce wages to that level. This even-handed recognition of various possibilities also influenced later discussion. However, Malthus's contribution, popularly interpreted as a prediction of an inevitable approach of wages to near starvation levels, coupled with the acceptance of a fixed wage fund, provided the basis in the early 19th century of pro-employer journalism and other advocacy which was both dismal and anti-trade union. The 'iron law' of Lassalle and later socialists stemmed more from popular Malthusianism than from the wage fund, and the majority of British economists, however dismal they may have appeared, cannot be accused of Malthusian predictions and pro-employer advocacy.

Wage fund doctrine, in which the wage rate is determined by supply and demand for labour, the demand for labour depending on the size of the wage fund, may be and has been interpreted variously, both in the early 19th century and today. How wide the net of the doctrine is cast, and whether it is co-extensive with the advances theory of capital, are largely matters of intent. Ricardo, for instance, defines the natural price of labour as the price necessary to enable workers 'to subsist and to perpetuate their race, without either increase or diminution' (Ricardo [1817], 1951, p. 93). Following Smith, he envisages differences between the market price and the natural price to cause changes in the labour force (through population change) which eventually equate market and natural prices at zero labour force change. Thus, if the attention is focused on natural price Ricardo (like Marx) may be said to hold a theory in which the wage rate is exogenous at a given subsistence level. However, if attention is focused on market price, Ricardo adheres to a distinctly Smithian wage fund doctrine, with increases in capital giving rise to increased demand for labour, and consequential changes in market price and in labour supply performing equilibrating functions which may be so slow that, as Ricardo says, they may be overtaken by fresh increases in capital. Failure to recognize both views in Ricardo has led some modern commentators to contrast Ricardo, holding the former view, with the anti-Ricardians, holding the latter view.

Regarding the statement that the ratio of wage fund to labour force determines the wage rate as largely self-evident, the discussion of most early 19th-century economists centred on the equilibrating effect of changes in market rate on labour supply, and the relation of wage fund to stock of capital. Malthus (1820) and McCulloch (1825), for instance, state quite clearly that because the labour supply cannot quickly adjust to changes in the market rates (McCulloch refers to a delay of eighteen to twenty years), the natural rate will move to some extent with the market rate, good times allowing workers to raise their standards, bad times forcing them to lower them. There was general agreement with Ricardo that the equilibrating mechanism would work only slowly or weakly, although there were differences, Malthus, for instance, preferring to replace Ricardo's definition of natural price (because it presupposes a stationary state) by a definition which requires 'an average supply of labourers'.

The discussion of fixity of the wage fund brought forth a variety of ideas. Malthus argued that a change in the wage fund does not necessarily imply a change in the demand for labour, giving several reasons: for example, a fall in the price of raw produce, if sudden, may because of general distress reduce the demand for labour; while an increase in circulating capital for the production of luxuries may not increase the demand for labour (Ricardo agreed with him). However, Malthus believed that increased use of fixed capital was associated with increased use of circulating capital and increased demand for labour, provided the market for the produce increased in proportion. This relatively subtle analysis of the relation of capital and labour in production was quite common. Senior (1836), for instance, who like McCulloch supported assisted emigration and deprecated wage subsidies on liberal Malthusian grounds, distinguishes the wage fund from capital, interpreting the former as a stock of means of production to supply workers with their future needs. The size of the fund depends on the productiveness of labour (which in turn depends on the use of capital), and on the extent to which labour is diverted from the production of wage goods, for example, by high levels of rent, taxation and profit. The determinants of profit lead Senior to a discussion of the length of the period of advances which foreshadows Jevons and Böhm-Bawerk.

Obviously, despite inconsistencies and the problems of interpretation, classical wage fund doctrine could be rich and sophisticated, although historians of the doctrine (Taussig, 1896; Blaug, 1958) have argued that views about the fund were both varied and vague. Nevertheless, mid-century critics like Longe and Thornton certainly fastened their attack on the fixity of the wage fund, and J.S. Mill was sufficiently embarrassed by the attack to accept the criticism. Part of the problem was the undeveloped analysis of substitution between fixed capital, raw materials and labour (the first two being usually simply subtracted from total capital leaving a wage fund as a residual). Cairnes, who was unhappy with the recantation, attempted a reconciliation (1874) by contrasting the ratio (presumably given for each industry) of capital to labour with the ratio of capital to wage fund. A change in the supply of labour, causing the wage rate to alter, would alter the distribution of labour between industries and change the size of the wage fund.

In the subsequent evolution of capital and production theory, the advances theory was further developed by Jevons and Böhm-Bawerk. Jevons (1871), while rejecting the wage fund doctrine as a truism, defined capital as a subsistence fund with a time dimension, and the Austrian, Böhm-Bawerk (1889), contributed the seminal idea of a variable period of production (during which advances are made) whose optimal length is chosen by the capitalist. In this, Böhm-Bawerk may have been anticipated by Ricardo. Wicksell (1893) interpreted Böhm-Bawerk and Jevons in a general equilibrium framework, explaining capital as in essence a fund of the produced means of production, but including exhaustible resources and excluding permanent improvements (i.e. broadly containing Smith's provisions, materials and tools), whose value in a stationary state is approximated by the annual wage bill and payments for primary resources, plus the interest accumulated over the period of production.

Thus at a high level of abstraction the classical dictum that the wage rate is determined by the ratio of wage fund to labour force was replaced by a typical neoclassical equilibrium relationship: the value of capital per unit of labour equals (approximately for low rates of interest) the wage rate multiplied by the period of production. Later writers on capital (e.g. Hayek, 1941) avoided the concept of period of production, for the same reason that the most recent theorists have found it difficult to use the concept of capital itself (Pasinetti, 1977). However, despite these modern theoretical developments which have diluted simple ideas, it is possible that in much of the modern underdeveloped world the simple 18th-century idea of the wage fund, like the equally simple ideas of the quantity theory of money and the labour theory of value, may retain practical relevance.

C.A. Blyth

See also CLASSICAL ECONOMICS; LONGE, FRANCIS DAVID; MILL, JOHN STUART, AS ECONOMIC THEORIST.

BIBLIOGRAPHY

Blaug, M. 1958. *Ricardian Economics*. New Haven: Yale University Press.

Böhm-Bawerk, E. von. 1889. *Positive Theory of Capital*. South Holland, Ill.: Libertarian Press, 1959.

Cairnes, J.E. 1874. *Some Leading Principles of Political Economy and their Applications*. London: Macmillan.

Hayek, F.A. 1941. *The Pure Theory of Capital*. London: Routledge.

Hollander, S. 1985. *The Economics of John Stuart Mill*. Oxford: Blackwell.

Jevons, W.S. 1871. *The Theory of Political Economy*. 3rd edn, London: Macmillan, 1888.

McCulloch, J.R. 1825. *The Principles of Political Economy*. London: Murray, 1870.

Malthus, T.R. 1820. *Principles of Political Economy*. New York: Augustus M. Kelley, 1968.

Mill, J.S. 1848. *Principles of Political Economy*. In *The Collected Works of John Stuart Mill*, Vols II and III (variorum edition), Toronto: University of Toronto Press, 1965.

Mill, J.S. 1869. Thornton on Labour and its Claims. In *The Collected Works of John Stuart Mill*, Vol. V, Toronto: University of Toronto Press, 1967.

Pasinetti, L.L. 1977. *Lectures on the Theory of Production*. New York: Columbia University Press.

Ricardo, D. 1817. *On the Principles of Political Economy and Taxation*. In *The Works and Correspondence of David Ricardo*, Vol. I, ed. P. Sraffa, Cambridge: Cambridge University Press, 1951.

Senior, N. 1836. *An Outline of the Science of Political Economy*. London: Allen & Unwin, 1938.

Smith, A. 1776. *An Inquiry into the Nature and Causes of the Wealth of Nations*. Vol. I, Oxford: Clarendon Press, 1976.

Taussig, F.W. 1896. *Wages and Capital*. London: London School of Economics and Political Science, 1935.

Wicksell, K. 1893. *Value, Capital and Rent*. London: Allen & Unwin, 1954.

wage goods. The concept of 'wage goods' had socio-political as well as economic significance in the early history of distribution theory. The 'necessaries' that comprised the subsistence of workers set them apart, as a class, from landowners and capitalists who consumed luxuries and conveniences.

Important pre-Smithian arguments were predicated on the wage goods concept. Mercantilist writers, while chiefly concerned with augmenting national gold stocks, attributed the superiority of advanced countries to the new technologies which they were able to support with their large stocks of wage goods. These goods originated as surpluses produced by farm workers and were advanced to 'free hands' by merchant capitalists. Most writers urged that the quantity of wage goods paid be limited to subsistence needs on the premise that 'idleness will not be totally rooted out, until people are forced in one way or another to give up both superfluity and days of recreation' (Steuart, *Inquiry II*, p. 691).

Beginning with Adam Smith, classical writers incorporated the wage goods concept into more sophisticated theoretical analyses. For example, Book I of *The Wealth of Nations*, makes it clear that 'capitalistic' production, which is roundabout and time consuming but more productive than direct methods, is possible only because capital in the form of materials and wage goods is available to be advanced to labour. As Smith observed (Introduction: Book II):

> A weaver cannot apply himself entirely to his peculiar business, unless there is beforehand stored up somewhere, either in his own possession or in that of some other person, a stock sufficient to maintain him and to supply him with the materials and tools of his work, till he has not only completed, but sold his web. This accumulation must, evidently, be previous to his applying his industry for so long a time to such a peculiar business.

Smith interprets wage goods more broadly than earlier writers did by including in the concept not only worker 'necessaries' but also 'conveniences of life'. His rudimentary 'wage fund' theory interpreted the stock of wage goods as constituting a demand for labour. Coupled with the simplistic assumption that labour supply is equal to the country's total population, it led to the thesis that the general real wage level in the economy reflects the ratio between the stock of wage goods and the population. As the real counterpart of money wages, the wage goods concept also became the basis for Smith's theory of the relationship between corn prices and money wages. Because corn was the chief article of labour's subsistence, Smith thought the worker's money wage to be more dependent on the average price of corn than it is on the price of meat or rude produce generally (1776, p. 187). The chapter entitled 'Of Wages' explains both the money (or nominal) price of labour and its price in corn, and argues that corn prices are the regulator of all other commodity prices (1776, pp. 476–7).

The notion that *parsimony* or *abstinence* from consumption is a prerequisite for the production of wage goods (or their monetary equivalent, *the wage fund*) is particularly relevant because it sanctions capitalist profits as a separate class income. Profit came to be viewed as an *earned* and, therefore, proper income share quite early in the history of economics, precisely because the dependence of workers on masters who advance them both maintenance and the materials of their work was recognized.

David Ricardo made the concept of 'wage goods' central to the problem of explaining the distributive (or income) shares, on the premise that these enter into the production of *all* products while non-wage (luxury) goods do not. Ricardo's 'fundamental theorem of distribution' which turns on a rigid distinction between wage goods and luxury goods, implies that the general rate of profits and thus of all income shares, depends chiefly on conditions of production in the wage goods (i.e. 'corn') sector and the real wage.

On occasion, both Ricardo and Thomas Malthus distinguished between 'absolute necessaries' and wage goods (Ricardo letter dated 29 November 1820, *Works* Vol. VIII, p. 311) in examining the components of capital and the ability of income receivers to pay taxes and/or support savings. It is in this context that he noted that more is generally allotted to the labourer under the name of wages than is sufficient for maintaining him and his family (*Works*, I, pp. 421–2).

Modern writers have generally dismissed the classical distinction between wage goods and non-wage goods on the ground that all commodities are consumed by workers and non-workers. Nevertheless, the wage goods concept was revived by A.C. Pigou in *Industrial Fluctuations* (1927, pp. 115–16) and *Theory of Unemployment* (1933, Part 1, chs 4 and 5). His 1933 work introduces the notion of the representative wage earner who buys both necessaries and luxuries. The proportions of purchase may vary if tastes change or relative prices become altered by changes in productive technique or the demands of non-wage earners for goods (pp. 12–18). Analogously, alterations in money wages, other things remaining constant, may alter the proportions in which the representative wage earner makes his purchases. These facts make it difficult to determine precisely what a wage good unit is in given circumstances (pp. 18–20).

J.M. Keynes also made important use of the wage goods concept in his *General Theory of Employment Interest and Money* (1936). His concern was that inflationary bank policy, in raising the average price of wage goods and thereby reducing the *real* wage rate, would be unable to assure that all labour markets would clear. Keynes's argument was that bank policy can satisfy 'the first postulate of classical theory' by increasing the demand for labour, but it cannot fulfill the second postulate which requires that the labour supply decrease sufficiently to clear the market because the real wage rate (i.e. the price of wage goods) may not measure the disutility of labour (Keynes 1936, chs 2 and 19, Appendix A; Rima, 1984). Failure of the market to satisfy the second postulate underlies Keynes's notion of involuntary unemployment.

INGRID H. RIMA

BIBLIOGRAPHY

Keynes, J.M. 1936. *The General Theory of Employment, Interest and Money*. Reprinted in *The Collected Writings of John Maynard Keynes*, Vol. VII, London: Macmillan, 1973.

Pigou, A.C. 1927. *Industrial Fluctuations*. London: Macmillan.

Pigou, A.C. 1933. *The Theory of Unemployment*. London: Macmillan.

Rima, I. 1984. Involuntary unemployment and the respecified labor supply curve. *Journal of Post-Keynesian Economics* 6(4), Summer, 540–50.

Steuart, Sir J. 1767. *An Inquiry Into the Principles of Political Economy*. Ed. A.S. Skinner, Chicago: University of Chicago Press, 1966.

Smith, A. 1776. *An Inquiry Into the Nature and Causes of the Wealth of Nations*. New York: Modern Library, 1937.

Sraffa, P. (ed.) 1951–2. *Works and Correspondence of David Ricardo*. Vols I and VIII, Cambridge: Cambridge University Press.

wage indexation. Wage indexation is a mechanism designed to adjust wages to information that cannot be foreseen when the wage contract is negotiated. A wage contract with indexation clauses will specify the wage base (i.e. the money wage applicable in the absence of new information), the indexation formula that will be used to update wages, and how often updating will occur. Most traditional discussion has focused on wage indexation to the price level as a mechanism to stabilize real wages in the presence of inflation. More recently, however, attention has shifted to indexation to a wider set of indicators. These indicators include both richer price information (such as the value added price deflator and the terms of trade) as well as rules designed to index wages to indicators measuring the level of nominal activity (such as nominal GNP). Concurrently, growing attention has been given to the potential role of wage indexation in affecting the will and ability to reduce inflation.

The economic evaluation of the role and desirability of wage indexation is inherently tied to the assessment of the functioning of the labour market and the role of wage contracts. If labour markets are cleared continuously, as in an auction market (i.e. if wages are adjusted continuously to equate the demand and the supply of labour), wage contracts serve no purpose and indexation clauses are either redundant or diminish welfare. On the other hand, the potential role of various wage indexation schemes grows the further we move away from an auction labour market. Consequently, an analysis regarding the role of wage indexation invites a specification of the nature of the deviations from an auction labour market and of the disequilibrium mechanism applied in that market. Indeed, challengers of the usefulness and relevance of wage indexation have remarked on the lack of rigorous understanding of the postulated deviations from auction market behaviour (see Barro, 1977). At the same time, a growing body of research has proceeded on the assumption that the existence of nominal contracts with limited degrees of indexation provides enough evidence to reject an auction labour-market clearing hypothesis (see Fischer, 1977b). This assumption has justified studies of the economics of wage indexation in models that lack a rigorous general equilibrium framework, but still provide insights into complicated economic environments. We start with a review of analytical studies on wage indexation, continue with overview of experience with wage indexation in various countries, and close with some interpretative remarks.

ANALYTICAL ASPECTS OF WAGE INDEXATION. The usefulness of indexing wages to the price level has been the subject of considerable research, and perceptive comments on the topic can be found in publications going back to Keynes's *General Theory of Employment, Interest and Money* (1936). A renewed interest in the question was generated by Gray (1976, 1978) and Fischer (1977a), who integrated the rational expectation hypothesis with nominal contracts. They considered an economy where nominal contracts preset the contract wage before the realization of stochastic shocks. The rational expectation hypothesis is invoked to determine the contract wage, which is set at a level that is expected to clear the labour market. The contract agreement also specifies the degree of wage indexation to unanticipated inflation. A complete indexation implies real wage rigidity, whereas the absence of indexation entails nominal wage rigidity in which changes in the price level directly affect the real wage. The contract specifies also the determination of employment rule, which is assumed to be demand determined. Consequently, in general employment will deviate from the flexible equilibrium level (i.e. from the employment level that will prevail in an economy where the wage is set as to clear the labour market continuously). The optimal degree of indexation is designed so as to minimize the expected squared output deviations from its market clearing level. This can be shown to be equivalent to minimizing the deadweight loss in the labour market for risk neutral agents (see Aizenman and Frenkel, 1985). The optimal degree of wage indexation is a compromise between two opposing forces: the wish to neutralize the potential output consequences of monetary (nominal) shocks by keeping real wages stable, and the wish to reduce real wages in the presence of adverse real shocks. The first goal is accomplished by complete wage indexation to prices, and the second by partial indexation. Optimal indexation balances between these two forces, implying that greater importance of monetary relative to real shocks will be associated with higher indexation. Such an indexation scheme implies that the real sector is not insulated from monetary variability (see Gray, 1976 and Fischer, 1977a). As a result, optimal indexation will tend to stabilize output around its full equilibrium level while it will tend to increase the volatility of prices.

Subsequent research had raised several important questions, for instance why wages are contingent only on prices and not on other relevant information. As Barro (1977) and Karni (1983) have pointed out, optimal contingencies will allow wages to adjust to all relevant information, thereby clearing the labour market continuously and eliminating the output effects of monetary policy. The fact that we find no contracts with rich sets of contingencies suggests, however, that it will be very costly to collect and process all the information needed to write and enforce full contingency contracts (see Fischer, 1977b and Blanchard, 1979). Another related question is the underlying justification of the disequilibrium hypothesis. As demonstrated by Cukierman (1980) the indexation derived by Gray is affected by the disequilibrium hypothesis. It can be shown, however, that this issue becomes inconsequential once we approach a full contingency contract because such a contract will clear the market independently of the disequilibrium hypothesis (see Aizenman and Frenkel, 1985).

Further developments regarding wage indexation have extended the analysis to open economies. Flood and Marion (1982) showed that optimal indexation is determined by the exchange rate regime, whereas Aizenman and Frenkel (1985) demonstrated that optimal indexation is only one among many potential policies, and that there is a close linkage between wage indexation, monetary policy, and exchange rate policies.

A relevant consideration in these discussions is the set of indicators to which the wage is indexed. Most of the above studies derived optimal indexation rules in terms of the underlying structural parameters (like the elasticities of demand in the money and labour market). While these results are informative, their usefulness is limited by the degree of availability of information regarding the underlying structure. In an environment with limited and costly information indexation rules that use easily available data, without relying on the structural parameters, should have natural advantage. Such rules were studied by Marston and Turnovsky (1985) who investigated the usefulness of wage indexation to the GNP price deflator and to the GNP in the context of energy shocks. Aizenman and Frenkel (1986) pursued related research, showing that if the elasticity of demand for labour exceeds the elasticity of supply, then indexing nominal wages to nominal GNP is preferable to indexing to the value added price index, and this, in turn, is preferable to indexation to the CPI (this ranking is reversed when the elasticity of the supply of labour exceeds the elasticity of demand). Similar results are applicable for ranking the usefulness of targeting monetary policy to the above indicators. Taking another research direction, Fethke and Policano (1984) addressed the usefulness of coordinating the timing of wage negotiations in a multisectoral economy. They concluded that when disturbances are driven primarily by relative shocks (i.e. shocks that hit the two sectors differentially) staggered negotiation is optimal.

Once we place wage indexation in its proper perspective as a macroeconomic policy instrument, a natural question arises regarding the linkages between wage indexation and other policies such as taxes and assets indexation (see Friedman, 1974), the risk-sharing effects of indexation (see Azariadis, 1978) and wage renegotiation (see Gray, 1978 and Aizenman, 1984). Further analysis and references regarding these important topics can be found in a useful conference volume (Dornbusch and Simonsen, 1983).

EXPERIENCE WITH WAGE INDEXATION. The experience with indexation of the last decades has been mostly with various degrees of wage indexation to the CPI. The precise indexation policy differs across countries considerably, depending on the centralization of the wage negotiation process and the degree to which wage indexation is viewed as income policy instead of as an instrument to enhance the efficiency of the labour market. For example, in the United States wage indexation is allowed, but there are no guidelines and the details of the indexation schemes are left for the contract negotiation. In Europe, Latin America, and Israel labour negotiation tends to be more centralized, and the indexation provisions tend to be dictated by a centralized policy maker. Some countries (for instance, Italy and Brazil) have applied wage indexation as an implicit income policy. This was done by imposing a rigid base wage and a high degree of wage indexation (and in some cases with a cap at high income levels). Such a policy is a poor substitute for direct income policy because it generates distortions in the labour market. These distortive effects increase in periods associated with real shocks, such as changes in input prices and in aggregate demand. Other countries have attempted to design partial indexation as a device to allow real wage flexibility in the presence of terms of trade shocks (see Brenner and Patinkin, 1977).

While experience with indexation differs across countries, several observations appear to be common to them all. *First*, the degree of indexation to the price level and the frequency of wage adjustment tend to go up with the level and volatility of inflation (see Ehrenberg et al., 1983 and Kleiman, 1977). *Second*, a higher indexation rate tends to reduce linkages between excess demand forces in the labour market and wages (see Sachs, 1983). *Third*, limited indexation seems not to be a controversial issue for countries with stable and relatively low inflation rates. For countries with high and volatile inflation the desirability of wage indexation is an important policy issue when attention shifts to curbing that inflation. In various countries in the last decades we have observed the adoption of indexation at low and moderate inflation rates. Once inflation has risen to intolerable levels, however, the policy maker has tended to couple abrupt disinflationary policies with disindexation policies (for example in Iceland in 1983 and in

Israel in 1985). This tendency is related to the fact that a typical indexation scheme adjusts wages to lagged inflation, implying that it builds in inertia, thereby a policy of disinflation will tend to raise real wages during the transition, generating unemployment (see Simonsen, 1983 and Fischer, 1984).

CONCLUDING REMARKS. The role of nominal contracts and the potential role of wage indexation and macro policies are major research topics in macro-economics. In recent years we have witnessed considerable development in this area, achieved by integrating the rational expectation hypothesis into models where transaction costs prevent continuous auction market clearing. The present state of theoretical research is, however, far from satisfactory. On the one hand, the theoretical papers reviewed above do not offer a framework that will satisfy 'purists', although they allow assessment of important policy issues in the presence of realistic contracts. On the other hand, 'purists' have not so far been able to explain the existence of nominal contracts of the type observed in various segments of the labour market. Interesting research directions that may provide further clues are frameworks that will recognize and model economic environments where decisions are costly. These costs stem from the observation that data gathering and screening are not free, and that resources are lost in the negotiation process. Such a framework will put a premium on simpler decision rules requiring less frequent negotiation, and nominal wage contracts may be one important example of such rules. The research into nominal contracts reviewed above is, we may hope, a step in that challenging direction.

The experience with wage indexation to prices suggests that greater attention should be given to the design of tractable indexation rules that will generate real wage flexibility in the presence of real shocks while retaining the purchasing power of wages in the presence of nominal disturbances. Such rules should be based upon widely available information. A candidate that deserves further exploration is wage indexation to nominal GNP. Simple-minded rules for indexation to the CPI have several potential disadvantages. They prevent real wage and employment adjustment in the presence of real shocks, thereby causing suboptimal employment. In the presence of nominal shocks and inflation, indexation to prices can generate dynamic inconsistencies – in the short- and intermediate-run it mitigates the losses associated with unanticipated inflation, but it thereby reduces the will to follow policies that are prudent with regard to inflation, causing higher inflation in the long run. Once the policy maker attempts to disinflate, the indexation scheme may exacerbate the welfare costs associated with the transition to lower inflation. Thus, a policy device that is viewed as useful in the short run can be harmful in the long run.

Consequently, indexation rules are not a substitute for prudent macro-policies. Rules that index wages to nominal income or to the GDP deflator can serve a useful role as part of macro-policies that recognize the need to undergo real adjustment in the presence of real shocks. At the same time, they are deceptive and harmful if they are used as income policy tools in an attempt to maintain the purchasing power of wages in economies exposed to productivity and terms-of-trade shocks.

JOSHUA AIZENMAN

BIBLIOGRAPHY

Aizenman, J. 1984. Optimal wage re-negotiation. *Journal of Monetary Economics* 13(2), March, 251–62.

Aizenman, J. and Frenkel, J.A. 1985. Optimal wage indexation, foreign exchange intervention, and monetary policy. *American Economic Review* 75(3), June, 402–23.

Aizenman, J. and Frenkel, J.A. 1986. Supply shocks, wage indexation, and monetary accommodation. *Journal of Money, Credit and Banking* 18, August.

Azariadis, C. 1978. Escalation clauses and the allocation of cyclical risks. *Journal of Economic Theory* 18(1), June, 119–55.

Barro, R.J. 1977. Long-term contracting, sticky prices, and monetary policy. *Journal of Monetary Economics* 3(3), July, 305–16.

Blanchard, O.J. 1979. Wage indexation rules and the behavior of the economy. *Journal of Political Economy* 87(4), August, 798–815.

Brenner, R. and Patinkin, D. 1977. Indexation in Israel. In *Inflation Theory and Anti-Inflation Policy*, ed. E. Lunberg, London: Macmillan.

Cuklerman, A. 1980. The effects of wage indexation and macroeconomic fluctuations. *Journal of Monetary Economics* 6(2), April, 147–70.

Dornbusch, R. and Simonsen, M.H. (eds) 1983. *Inflation, Debt. and Indexation.* Cambridge, Mass.: MIT Press.

Ehrenberg, R., Danziger, L. and San, G. 1983. Cost of living adjustment clauses in union contracts: a summary of results. *Journal of Labor Economics* 1(3), 215–45.

Fethke, G. and Policano, A. 1984. Wage contingencies, the pattern of negotiation and aggregate implications of alternative contract structure. *Journal of Monetary Economics* 14(2), September, 151–70.

Fischer, S. 1977a. Wage indexation and macro-economic stability. In *Stabilization of Domestic and International Economy*, ed. K. Brunner and A.H. Meltzer, *Journal of Monetary Economics*, Supplementary, 5, 107–47.

Fischer, S. 1977b. Long term contracting, sticky prices, and monetary policy: a comment. *Journal of Monetary Economics* 3(3), July, 317–23.

Fischer, S. 1984. Real balances, the exchange rate and indexation: real variables in disinflation. NBER Working Paper No. 1497, November.

Flood, R.P. and Marion, N.P. 1982. The transmission of disturbances under alternative exchange-rate regimes with optimal indexing. *Quarterly Journal of Economics* 97(1), February, 43–66.

Friedman, M. 1974. *Monetary Correction.* Washington, DC: American Enterprise Institute.

Gray, J.A. 1976. Wage indexation: a macro-economic approach. *Journal of Monetary Economics* 2, April, 221–35.

Gray, J.A. 1978. On indexation and contract length. *Journal of Political Economy* 86(1), February, 1–18.

Karni, E. 1983. On optimal wage indexation. *Journal of Political Economy* 91(2), April, 282–92.

Keynes, J.M. 1936. *The General Theory of Employment, Interest and Money.* London: Macmillan.

Kleiman, E. 1977. Monetary correction and indexation: the Brazilian and Israeli experience. *Explorations in Economic Research* 4(1), Winter, 141–76.

Marston, R.C. and Turnovsky, J.S. 1985. Imported material prices, wage policy, and macroeconomic stabilization. *Canadian Journal of Economics* 18(2), May, 273–84.

Sachs, J. 1983. Real wages and unemployment in the OECD countries. *Brookings Papers on Economic Activity* No. 1, 255–304.

Simonsen, M.H. 1983. Current theory and the Brazilian experience. In *Inflation, Debt, and Indexation*, ed. R. Dornbusch and M.H. Simonsen, Cambridge, Mass.: MIT Press.

wage labour. *See* CAPITAL AS A SOCIAL RELATION.

wages, iron law of. *See* IRON LAW OF WAGES.

wages, real and money. Our knowledge of the movements of real wages from the 12th century onwards in southern England, and later in western Europe, shows them as dominated by the varying pressure of population. A great rise of the English population in the 12th and 13th centuries brought output per head down to a level so low that a bad harvest brought famine. But the Black Death may well have reduced the population by a third, and its periodic recurrence kept numbers down. It was followed by a remarkable rise in the real wage: as indicated by the purchasing power of the wage-rate of the building craftsman or labourer, the real wage rose early in the 15th century to a high level that it sustained for a hundred years. This plateau was as high as any level to be reached, according to the same limited measure, until the second half of the 19th century. But in the 16th century the renewed pressure of population brought food output per head and real wages down again, so that after 1600 the index was running at about half its level of a century before, and in the wage-earner's world famine was recurrent again. A slow but persistent trend of recovery set in after the Civil War. At the mid-18th century a rise of standards of living conspicuous to contemporaries coincided with the onset of a new growth of population, but also an agrarian revolution, which mitigated the fall in real wages that was caused by the Napoleonic Wars.

It was at this time that economists developed a systematic account of the determination of real and monetary wages. Their analysis of supply and demand by way of the subsistence level and the amount of capital or the wages fund, though purporting to be abstract and rigorous, was effectively transcribed from current circumstances. Real wages were seen to be pressed down perpetually towards the level of subsistence by the gravitational force of population pressure. If they were above that level, the propensity of mankind to marry early and beget numerous children would before long increase the number seeking maintenance from 'the funds destined for the employment of labour', that is, the wages fund. If the real wage fell below the subsistence level, marriages would be put off, and hunger and disease would take their toll of existing families, until the wages fund, spread over a diminished labour force, provided a real wage at the subsistence level again. The political economists saw that most payments of wages gave the worker the means of immediate consumption well before the product of his own week's work became available; the wages fund was there in effect to make loans. They went on hastily to assume that the fund could be increased only by the savings of the propertied classes; and inferred that this was the only way in which real wages in the aggregate could be raised. Trade unions could raise the real wages of one group only at the expense of the rest. It was when John Stuart Mill (1869) opened his eyes to the situation of the employer, who could at need divert part of his cash flow to swell his pay packets, that he abandoned the notion of a distinct and predetermined wages fund.

That the political economists were so hasty in taking up that notion may be explained by their preoccupation with population pressure as much the more variable and disturbing term in the equation. But from the mid-19th century onwards it began to appear that advances in productivity more than offset that pressure: despite the continuing rise in numbers, real wages rose. It was in this setting that economists began to derive the real wage from the marginal product. This application of the marginal analysis of demand to a factor of production was made notably by J.B. Clark (1899) and Alfred Marshall (1890). The principle that the real wage tends to equal the marginal physical product has a firm theoretical basis, in that costs will be minimized when the marginal value products of all factors are proportioned to their prices, and profits will be maximized when these two variables are equal. The marginal productivity theory of wages therefore rests upon belief in the pervasiveness and effectiveness of the drives towards costs minimization and profit maximization in the real world. It has been objected that the theory credits the employer with accurate knowledge, and with an ability to vary the intake of factors, that empirical studies show he lacks: actual employers do not approach wages and employment as the textbooks suppose. But our view should not be bounded by the fixity of circumstances in the short run. Adjustments take place by degrees, or by reconstruction, so that in the course of time the structure of production partakes of the flexibility with which the theory of marginal productivity endows it. As these changes come about, those employers who fail, explicitly or implicitly, to apply the marginal calculus are exposed to the risk of supersession by more efficient competitors. Where any one employer combines labour with other factors in fixed proportions, the variation of proportions may be effected by the choice of buyers between different outputs. The elements, therefore, that the theory of marginal productivity sees as determining the real wage can be accepted as shaping the path that real wages tend to follow through time; though the actual adjustments made within any one firm or the market may be less for years together than the theory calls for.

There is this further reason for accepting the marginal productivity theory, that it provides a hypothesis on which we can account for the movement of real wages and associated variables in a number of Western countries since 1860 (Phelps Brown and Browne, 1968; Samuelson, 1980, fig. 27–3). Real wages rose, or failed to rise, in proportion to the movements of productivity, that is, of output per head in the whole occupied population. The rate of profit varied cyclically within a band that lay about 10 per cent and itself showed no trend. The capital/output ratio lay within a band whose midpoint was about 2.5. It was implicit in the last two observations that the division of the net product between labour as a whole and capital showed no trend, though it varied cyclically; but it was subject to a displacement through the two world wars. These regularities challenge explanation. It has been shown that they would arise if enterprise and investment were at work pervasively within an aggregate production function that is linear and homogeneous of the first degree, such as the Cobb-Douglas function, on two assumptions-that factors are remunerated according to their marginal products, and that the yield of the function with given inputs is progressively increased over time by a technical progress factor (Solow, 1957). With such a function, the marginal product of labour will be a constant proportion of its average product, that is, of productivity, as the inputs of labour and capital vary. The division of the product between labour and capital will also be constant. But to account for the stability of the rate of profit and of the capital/output ratio we have to introduce the technical progress factor, and the observation that this has operated, as a fact of history, so as to produce the degree of stability observed.

The mind may boggle at the degree of simplification required by an aggregate production function. There is attraction, therefore, in proceeding more realistically, and simply fixing upon the endeavour of employers generally to secure a normal profit, under the pressures of bargaining with their workers and competition among themselves. This endeavour acts to stabilize the rate of return on capital. If we add, again as a fact of history, stability of the capital/output ratio thanks to technical progress, we account for stability of the proportionate shares of capital and labour. But unless we introduce some internal equilibrating process, such as the marginal productivity principle, we cannot account for stability in the relation between the real wage and productivity: and of all the stable relations observed, this is the most unmistakeable.

Three factors must be added to that basic relation. One concerns the varying terms on which the industrial worker can obtain foodstuffs and raw materials. There have been long cycles in the terms of trade between factory and farm, or plantation; when agricultural depression has coincided with industrial, cheap food has kept real wages up at a time of low money wages. The second factor is the ability of trade unions to raise real wages by shifting the distribution of the product. The share of profits was generally smaller after both world wars-after the first, through the resistance of money wages to the deflationary pressure of 1920–22; after the second, through the cost push exerted by the trade unions. This latter European trend was contrasted with the lower trend of real wages in the United States, which was linked with the greater expansion of employment there. Thirdly, in recent years the increase of forms of social benefit, accruing to the household of the wage-earner in his or her capacity as a citizen, has given rise to the concept of 'the social wage'. This together with the increased incidence of direct taxation on wage-earners is taken into account in reckoning changes in their standard of living, which may diverge from those in real earnings from employment.

The course of money wages, as that can be traced mainly in the rates of building workers in Southern England from the 13th century onwards (Phelps Brown and Hopkins, 1981), has two striking features-the absence of falls, and the presence of long periods of constancy in the prevailing rate. Both may be ascribed to the power of custom; but there was probably also latent if not overt trade unionism, ready to come into action to resist any attempt to cut rates. The constancy of the wage-rate is the more noteworthy when the cost of foodstuffs fluctuated widely with the harvest from one year to another: it was common for the food prices of the dearest year within any decade to be near double those of the cheapest. Since the ratchet effect stopped the wage-rate from falling back, rises cumulated. By the end of the Napoleonic Wars there had been three major lifts. The first came as a result of the Black Death: the labour force was now reduced, probably by a third, over against undiminished resources in land and the same stock of money. After a hundred years of extraordinarily level trend in prices and money wages came the second lift, in the great Tudor inflation. Through the debasement of the currency and the cheapening of silver this doubled the wage rate between 1532 and 1580; but it has been noted above that through the same century food prices rose so much more than the monetary factory alone would have raised them, as to transmit to real wages the severe reduction demanded by population pressure. The third major lift came, again from the monetary side and in the presence of rising population, through the Napoleonic Wars.

With the extension of industry, and the appearance of data for more countries, in the course of the 19th century, a new pattern appears, that of the eight-year trade cycle. The movement of British money wages in this cycle was summarized by Phillips (1958) in a curve which was taken by many economists to show that the general level rose and fell in accordance with the balance of aggregate supply and demand in the labour market, as that was shown by the rate of unemployment. This provided an equation for the endogeneous determination of what it seemed could otherwise be taken only as imposed from without, by historical forces. But a given rate of unemployment had been associated with quite different wage changes, according as it occurred in the rising or falling phases of the cycle; and in recent years regions with different rates of unemployment had obtained much the same wage rise. It seemed likely therefore that unemployment served not as a measure of the balance of supply and demand, but as an indicator of the phase and intensity of the cycle, and the associated expectations. With these changes of phase, on the employers' side, would go changes in the strength of their resistance to their workers' claims, as the profitability of their operations and their markets' toleration of price rises varied. The view workers took of the reasonableness of changes in money wages during the cycle was influenced by their impression of their employers' current capacity to pay, and by changes in the cost of living.

This cyclical process resulted typically in a rise of five per cent or more in money wages in the rising phase and boom, with the loss of two or three per cent in the ensuing recession, so that, if this were all, money wages would have risen cumulatively over time. But it was not all. Prices in the market for the products of the labour concerned, or for the raw materials it used and the foodstuffs it consumed, were subject to long waves. In phases of downward pressure on prices, the ceiling over the upward thrust of wage-earners was itself being lowered, and the upward trend of money wages might be brought down, or disappear altogether, as it did in Great Britain during the great Victorian depression of the 1870s and 1880s. In phases of rising prices in world markets, money wages too could rise more. Examination of the trends of money wages over longer periods thus displays the ultimate ascendancy of the forces determining the product price level.

At the same time, a normative process has regulated the relation between money wages and prices, so as to keep real wages on a trend parallel to that of productivity. In times of hard market environment, when product prices have had the upper hand, it is money wages that have had to perform the adjustment. There have been periods of some length, in the Victorian depression and the interwar years, when they did not rise at all from end to end, but this was compatible with a substantial rise in real wages. In the years after World War II in which the market environment offered less resistance to the raising of prices, it was possible for cost push to take the initiative, and achieve progressive wage rises, to which prices had to be adjusted. Money wages can rise relatively to product prices according to the rise in productivity and the possibility of reducing profit margins.

The interwar years can be set within the above scheme of forces, but after 1945 the eight-year cycle did not appear again. Instead, an investment boom set in, of unprecedented duration. It was accompanied throughout most of the Western economies by a progressive rise in productivity, and by an experience of sustained demand in product and labour markets that fostered the expectation of its continuance. Employers had little reason to offer costly resistance to claims for rises in money wages when, so far as these were not offset by higher productivity, they could probably be covered as part of a general movement towards higher prices, without loss of business. Analysts used to tracing inflation to excess of monetary demand were eventually driven to recognize that here was an inflation taking its rise in cost push. The remedy was found in incomes policy. In a number of Western countries the endeavour was made to keep the rise of the general level of money wages down to that of productivity by exhortation, by agreement between central organizations of trade unions and of employers, or by restraints and controls imposed by government; these latter might be supported by price controls. But attempted controls all suffered from the lack of an effective sanction agains the strike in a democratic society; and though real wages might be maintained in the end if all wage-earners gave up their claims to higher money wages, the members of any one group could see that if they gave up their own claim they were losing here and now the opportunity of raising their own real wages. The experience of money and real wages rising year by year for more than twenty years imparted an increasing momentum to expectations; about 1969 in a number of European countries the rate of cost push began to rise. But this was just at the time when the great boom began to run out, and unemployment to mount. This brought no immediate or commensurate check to the rise of money wages. Governments wishing to relieve the unemployment of the 1970s were then inhibited from raising effective demand by the fear that the additional purchasing power would simply be absorbed by higher money wages for those already employed. The contrast was drawn between the buoyancy of money wages that resulted at this time from the expectations and cohesion of the European wage-earners, and the smaller rise in the more dispersed and individualist labour market of the United States. The autonomy of the level of money wages, as a determinant of the price level, presented itself as a major problem of economic helmsmanship.

HENRY PHELPS BROWN

BIBLIOGRAPHY

Clark, J.B. 1899. *The Distribution of Wealth*. New York and London: Macmillan.

Marshall, A. 1890. *Principles of Economics*. 1st edn, London: Macmillan.

Mill, J.S. 1869. Thornton on labour and its claims. In *Essays on Economics & Society*, Vol. II, ed. J.M. Robson, Toronto: University of Toronto Press; London: Routledge & Kegan Paul, 1967.

Phelps Brown, E.H. and Browne, M.H. 1968. *A Century of Pay: the course of pay and production in France, Germany, Sweden, the United Kingdom, and the United States of America, 1860–1960*. London: Macmillan.

Phelps Brown, E.H. and Hopkins, S.V. 1981. *A Perspective of Wages and Prices*. London and New York: Methuen.

Phillips, A.W. 1958. The relation between unemployment and the rate of change of money wage rates in the United Kingdom, 1861–1957. *Economica* 25(100), November, 283–99.

Samuelson, P.A. 1980. *Economics*. 11th edn, Tokyo and London: McGraw-Hill, Koga Kusha.

Solow, R.M. 1957. Technical change and the aggregate production function. *Review of Economics and Statistics* 39, August, 312–20.

wages in classical economics. Recent discussions stimulated by Piero Sraffa's editorial introduction and Commentaries on Ricardo (*Works*, Vols I–XI) and his slim but significant volume, *Production of Commodities by Means of Commodities* (1960) have brought to light the distinctive characteristics of the approach and structure of classical theory of value and distribution as contrasted with those of the marginalist theory which has dominated since the 1870s. The role of wages in classical theory needs to be perceived within the structure of its value and distribution theory, which analysed the central questions as to how surplus is generated, appropriated and distributed in a circular process of reproduction and further investigated into how these shaped and were, in turn, shaped by the process of accumulation. A central notion to the theory is that of surplus or 'social net product', defined as gross output of the economy produced during the chosen period minus 'productive consumption'; the latter, being the material means of production and the requisites for the sustenance of labour engaged in production. Through the various stages of theoretical advancement, from Petty and Boisguillebert to Smith, Ricardo and Marx, the various categories and constituents of net product, and of the means of production, the classes of surplus appropriators and sharers, the forms of exchange and rules of surplus distribution, altered, reflecting historical developments and the relevant analytical perceptions.

Wages were treated as a part of the productive consumption, an essential material necessity of production, whatever may be the historical form of labour (and correspondingly, the *form* of its revenue). The sustenance of the labour had to be provisioned as a prior condition: the Physiocrats were the first to theorize about wages as being 'advances' of subsistence. The necessity for wages to be advanced was particularly evident in agriculture, the central focus of their inquiry. The idea of a 'uniform', 'given wage' materialized along with labour becoming progressively a 'commodity' and with the establishment of capitalist relations. The non-wage incomes were considered as residual incomes, as paid out of surplus emerging at the end of the productive cycle; hence not a 'material necessity' as was the sustenance of labour; wages were thus seen as physical costs of reproducing labour, in contrast to, as material incentives to induce efforts or disutility of effort as in later theory.

Adam Smith conceptualized features of capitalist production (reflected in the 'net product' no more confined solely to agriculture as in the Physiocrats, and in the emergence of the free wage labourer and of the 'capitalist'), of distribution (the tripartite division of social classes and the respective revenues – wages, profits and rents – with their diverse origins and nature), and of exchange (reflected in the relevant categories of 'natural price' and 'market price'); and, formalized the regime of competition (the tendency towards uniform rate of profit and wages). Ricardo, while accepting the general framework of analysis, criticized certain inconsistencies and ambiguities of Smith's, particularly in relation to the theory of distribution (profit); namely, Smith's suggestion that the rate of profit was determined by competition of capitals and that the natural rates of wages, profits and rents were determined independently of each other and were thus the independently determined 'causes' of 'natural price'. Ricardo focused on the question of distribution, purporting to demonstrate that 'profits depend upon wages'. It is in the determination of the rate of profit, defined as the social net product (or surplus, as above, after 'getting rid of rent'), divided by the value of capital ('productive consumption'), that Ricardo faced the need to have a consistent theory of value to measure the heterogeneous aggregates involved in this determination (see Sraffa's introduction to *The Collected Works of David Ricardo*, Vol. I, 1951). Ricardo formulated and used the labour theory of value for the purpose.

As brought out by Sraffa (1951), it is in Ricardo's *Essay on Profits* (1815) and his generalization of the corn rate of profit of the *Essay* into the general rate of profit in *Principles*, using the labour theory of value, that the underlying structure of the classical theory of value and distribution becomes transparently evident. In Marx, the same basic structure continues and his scheme of prices of production is presented in a many-commodities framework in Sraffa's *Production of Commodities* (1960). We find therein, given social output levels and composition, given methods of production and given the wage, under the competitive assumption of uniformity of profit and wage, the rate of profit and prices of products are simultaneously determined.

This structure implies that the determination of prices and distribution would need to be carried out, taking the output levels and methods of production and wage as provisional data; this is not to rule out the interaction among accumulation (changes in output), changes in technology and changes in wages – indeed, the classical writings, as we see below, were deeply concerned about these interactions. The analysis is carried out in separate stages so that, for the derivation of distributive shares, at any stage, these are taken as provisional data.

The determination of wages itself is explained in classical theory in terms of a variety of historical and socio-economic factors. The role of wages, as 'given' in the value-scheme, needs to be contrasted with the neoclassical theory wherein the prices of 'factors of production' along with prices of commodities are determined simultaneously with quantities of outputs, employing the same mechanism of demand and supply relations for factors and commodities; for which purpose, factor endowments, technological possibilities and consumer preferences are taken as data. Given these, the relevant supply and demand functions are generated on the basis of the universal application of the price-guided 'substitution' principle.

In the very early theories, the idea that subsistence wage was a physiological minimum appeared as an axiom derived from the prevalent conditions under which the ordinary, unskilled labour was performed. However, even with the Physiocrats, the idea of a 'given' wage (rather than a *fixed* minimum subsistence) was emerging prominently. While a tendency for wages to be restored to a certain norm was recognized, the norm itself was determined by customs, conventions, 'political necessity' (as in Steuart) and variations in it were discussed in the context of the effect of accumulation, migration or changes in population or, vice versa.

Adam Smith, with his distinction between 'natural' and 'market' price of labour was to synthesize preceding discussions on wages into a much more interesting theory. We find in Smith, a graphic expression of the inequitous bargaining position of 'masters' and workmen and the ensuing social struggle. Wage is also influenced by the pace of accumulation so that the 'norms' (or 'natural price') of labour would be low, medium or high depending upon the stage of development of the country and while Smith acknowledged a tendency for wages to gravitate to the natural level, (so that, he argued, that money wages would move sympathetically with prices of provisions), the norm itself was variable, depending upon whether the economy was declining, stationary or progressive. Smith opposed, in fact, the Mercantilist belief (and policy prescription) that low wages were necessarily advantageous as they stimulated hard work and afforded a commercial advantage through cheapness of the products; Smith argued, on the contrary, that 'a plentiful subsistence' stimulates productivity ('where wages are high, accordingly, we shall always find the workmen more active, diligent and expeditious, than when they are low' p. 81); Smith highlighted the importance of stimulating productivity of labour as it was the surplus produce over and above the necessary wage that would be the fund for accumulation. It was the annual produce of productive labour which constituted the wealth of a nation and not the accumulation of species (Smith's emphasis on division of labour as stimulating productivity of labour arises from such a perspective). What is characteristic of the view, and distinctly different the marginalist theory, is that there is no necessary functional relation between labour productivity and the wage. He did not however define any quantitative limit on 'plentiful subsistence' and did not draw the implications of the inverse wage-profit relation which Ricardo focused upon, under, however, 'given methods of production'.

Smith discussed, following Cantillon, wage differentiation among different categories of workers arising due to different degrees of 'hardship and ingenuity'. These differences cannot be accurately measured but Smith referred to 'the higgling and bargaining' on the market from which arises a 'scale', which, once formed, shows little variation. The subsistence of an unskilled labour was taken as the basic-level norm, with wages of other categories maintaining a proportion to it. The levels of wage were not explained by 'productivity' of the worker (if they were, a circularity in reasoning would be involved) but were the cost of reproduction of labour of the particular kind at the *norm* of maintenance which was generated by custom, convention, cost of training and of rearing the requisite skills and, in general, by 'the higgling and bargaining of the market'. That wages were basically looked upon from the point of view of the needs of reproduction of labour is evident when, for example, Smith argues that the minimum wage or the natural price of labour is lower for the free workman than for the slave. The slave is 'dearer' than the free labourer because the latter looks after his 'wear and tear' whereas the 'fund for replacing "wear and tear" is wastefully and disorderly administered by a "negligent master or careless overseer" ' (p. 81). It is also evident in the provision for cost of training in the wage of a skilled labourer.

In Ricardo, the distinction between 'natural wage' and 'market wage' is analysed more systematically: while the natural price of labour is considered to be 'that price which is necessary to enable the labourers, one with another, to subsist and perpetuate their race, without increase or diminution', it is not necessarily the physiologically fixed minimum level of wages. It can vary from region to region and time to time and incorporates a large element of 'custom and habit', which may render 'comforts' necessaries. There remains active, however, a tendency whereby fluctuations in wages (i.e. in 'market price of labour') gravitate to restore the natural wage. The forces that generate these deviations were analysed by Ricardo in terms of 'supply' and 'demand' for labour; when the market price of labour exceeds the natural price, a stimulus is provided for an increase in population; consequently, increasing the supply of labour. The reverse is the case when the market price of labour falls short of the 'natural price'. Thus, given the demand for labour at any time, the adjustment occurred through the changes in the supply of labour – which adaptations, however, could be slow and may lead sometimes to a higher market price for a long period. The demand for labour would itself be dependent on the pace of accumulation and increase in capital. Ricardo distinguished between the two effects of accumulation: the 'increase' of capital (defined as 'food, clothing, tools, raw materials, machinery, necessaries of labour etc.') could affect the natural wage, if, along with the increase in the quantity of capital, its 'value' also increased. By the latter, Ricardo referred to the increasing difficulty of production (requiring higher labour) of the means of production, particularly food and necessaries of labour. Such a difficulty was envisaged by Ricardo especially in the production of food; in which case, the natural wage would increase along with the prices of provisions (unless the non-food necessaries of labour fell in value to compensate for the rise in food). If such is not the case, the natural price of labour would be unaffected. However, in either situation, Ricardo argued that there would be a tendency for the 'market price of labour' to rise, following the accentuation of demand for labour and this would set up the tendency for supply of labour to so adjust as to restore the wages to their natural level. How rapidly or closely this could happen therefore depended upon the effects of accumulation on the natural wage and the extent of stimulus given to demand for labour.

Certain clarifications need to be made regarding the peculiarities of Ricardo's analysis of the 'supply and demand factors'. First, while the 'supply' and 'demand' come into play to determine the variations of 'market price of labour', these are fluctuations around a 'natural wage' (and, anchored to it) which is determined exogeneously. For example, nowhere does Ricardo argue that the wage would be pushed permanently below the natural wage *in order to* achieve *full* absorption of labour. (The logical inference in the case of the marginalist supply and demand determined equilibrium would be that, at the 'equilibrium' wage, there should be full utilization of labour.) Smith, too, emphasized the conventional limits to depressing wages below a certain minimum, adopted by 'common humanity'. (In *Theory of Moral Sentiments*, he was to elucidate the rise of conventions and morality which renders a certain social order viable.) The second peculiarity is that Ricardo's population dynamics works in order to adjust the supply of labour to a demand that is generated by the process of accumulation which is independently determined. This is to be contrasted with the supply and demand mechanism that works in the 'factor-markets' in the neoclassical theory. In Ricardo's theory, it is the aggregate supply of labour that is altering. In the marginalist theory, the 'factor endowments' are given so that it is the relative demands and supplies of the different factors of production which are generated because of the price-guided substitution that occurs in the commodity and factor markets. The interplay of supply and demand forces in the labour market can no more be separated from other, factor and output, markets as the determination of wages in the labour market can happen only simultaneously with the determination of all other prices and all other quantities. In Ricardo, the demand for labour generated by accumulation (and, the variations in outputs that this process involves) is taken as independently given and the supply of labour adjusts only if market wages deviate from the 'natural'. Further, Ricardo does not posit any positive functional relationship between the growth of stock of capital and the rate of profit – as is presumed by 'modern' interpretations. While a certain minimum rate of profit was expected for investment to be positive, no monotonic positive relation such as above was envisaged, particularly for the determination of the rate of profit. Profits depended on wages alone. Further, an increase in capital may be accompanied by a reduction of demand for labour (as in the machinery question). Secondly, as noted above, the effect of accumulation on the natural wage depends, according to Ricardo, on the conditions of production of the wage goods alone.

In the period after Ricardo, when his theory was already facing opposition, the Ricardians (James Mill and John Stuart Mill, in particular) appear to have gradually subordinated the notion of natural wage to the idea that wage is determined by the proportions of capital to labour. James Mill, in his *Elements*, discussed only the variations in wages caused by the disproportionality between population and capital, without any reference in the discussions to natural wage. The notion of wages fund (which began initially with the idea that the demand for labour was limited by the agricultural surplus available for 'advances') was developed as a proxy for capital, representing demand for labour and ultimately culminated into the wages fund doctrine which argued, on the basis of a *fixed* wage fund, that the only lasting means of improving the conditions of labour (i.e. a sustained rise in wages) was through constraints on the growth of the labouring poor. In his later years, J.S. Mill recanted his position.

Marx carried forward and extended in new directions the basic framework of value and distribution of Ricardo whose critical clarification had become necessary particularly since the later 'modifications' and 'extensions' by the Ricardians has obfuscated and corroded that structure. While continuing to hold allegiance to the idea of a given wage, Marx emphasized the influence of the historical elements in its determination. He savagely attacked the Malthusian population dynamics (which was raising its head in the wage fund doctrine) and instead focused on the historical process by which labour-power becomes a 'free' commodity, in the dual sense: freed of personal bondage and also freed of the means of sustenance and production. This situation of the capitalist, in complete control of the means of production and labour, possessing nothing but labour-power to sell, engenders the inequitous capital-labour relation, with the capitalist in command of the labour-process. The wage therefore is influenced by the state of class struggle. Marx displaces the importance of 'population adaptations' in the earlier theories by his concept of the 'reserve army of the unemployed'. He recognizes thereby that the primitive accumulation process that turns labour into a commodity generates a chronic but fluctuating pool of the unemployed and the size of this reserve army not only acts on the supply side of labour but the capitalist strategy of controlling the capital–labour relation is influenced by the size of the reserve army; it being a potential instrument for weakening the bargaining strength of the workers. Marx discusses the various strategies that the capitalists employ in order to strengthen the control over the labour process and maximize the difference between labour productivity and the wage paid out. The strategies discussed are in terms of mechanization, organizational systems, wage systems etc. Not only is the wage therefore not functionally linked to productivity but there are forces that precisely play on their differences. Marx, with his focus on changes in methods of production and on the process of accumulation probed more deeply on the interaction between these and wages. The process of capitalist accumulation was crisis-ridden and Marx visualized a number of contradictions arising in the system which could be potential causes of the ultimate breakdown. For example, the increasing relative immiserization of labour could create a realization problem. He also visualized the 'anarchy' of capitalist production leading to a crisis of disproportionalities. A long-term decline in the rate of profit could also threaten the system. These suggestions were neither worked out fully and rigorously, nor were their mutual compatibilities examined closely. This is partly unavoidable in a complex analysis of the interactions among distribution, accumulation and technology. These are bound to be influenced by a variety of forces and patterns of interdependence among variables specific to particular junctures. It would be precisely for this reason that the simple analytical core of the value and distribution theory needed to be firmly based in order to make sorties into the more complex analyses. Marx did demonstrate that, even with the more limited analytical tools at his disposal, he could venture a long distance. This was evident in his masterly analysis, in *Capital*, Vol. I, of the dynamics of the capital–labour relations and the evolution of wages and profits during the various stages of the growth of the capitalist system.

Krishna Bharadwaj

See also CLASSICAL ECONOMICS.

BIBLIOGRAPHY
Marx, K. 1890. *Capital.* 4th edn. London: Pelican, Marx Library, 1976.
Mill, J. 1821. *Elements of Political Economy.* London: Baldwin, Craddock & Joy.
Mill, J.S. 1848. *Principles of Political Economy.* Ed. W. Ashley, London: Longman, Green & Co., 1909.
Ricardo, D. 1821. *Principles of Political Economy.* In *The Works and Correspondence of David Ricardo*, ed. P. Sraffa and M.H. Dobb, Cambridge: Cambridge University Press, 1951.
Smith, A. 1776. *An Inquiry into the Nature and Causes of the Wealth of Nations.* Ed. E. Cannan, New York: Modern Library, 1937.
Sraffa, P. 1951. Editorial introduction to Vol. I of *The Works and Correspondence of David Ricardo.* Cambridge: Cambridge University Press.
Sraffa, P. 1960. *Production of Commodities by Means of Commodities.* Cambridge: Cambridge University Press.

Wagner, Adolph Heinrich Gotthelf (1835–1917). Adolph Wagner was born in Erlangen (Franconia), the son of a professor of physiology. Studied in Heidelberg and Göttingen and taught between 1858 and 1870 in Vienna, Hamburg, Dorpat (today Tartu, Estonia) and Freiburg (Breisgau). In 1870 he was appointed professor of political economy at the University of Berlin, a position which he was to hold for 46 years, and where he became one of the most important economists of the German Reich.

Wagner tried to steer a middle course between the historical school and its theoretically oriented opponents. At a time when economic theory was neglected in Germany, it was to Wagner's merit that he helped avoid its almost complete disappearance from economic discussion. His important *Grundlegung* (1876) included numerous sociological elements. It emphasized institutional patterns, historical-legal categories and various aspects of the different forms of private and public property. Moreover, he focused on the role of the state, on the psychological motivations of the individual, and on population development, where he had adopted Malthusian views.

Wagner had started his career as an expert on money and banking (Wagner, 1857). But his lasting and outstanding achievement was his work on Public Finance (1871–2), which he freed from its previous fiscal administrative orientation and incorporated into the framework of political economy. In this work the role that Wagner assigned to the state was of primary importance-a concept which has to be seen within the wider context of a particular social philosophy which he himself called 'state socialism' (Wagner, 1887; 1912). This notion ought to be understood as a specifically German type of social conservatism, based on an organic concept of the state and on the rejection of laissez-faire liberalism. 'State socialism' aimed at the integration of the working classes into the monarchic state and was thus directed against the growing social democratic party. This goal was to be achieved by a gradual transformation of liberal capitalism into a state interventionist economy-on which Wagner took a firmer stand than most of the social-reform oriented German professors, the so-called 'Socialists of the chair' (Kathedersozialisten). He advocated the nationalization of sectors that showed a high degree of monopolization, especially transport, utilities, banking and insurance (Wagner, 1887, pp. 43–4). He also favoured the abolition of private real estate property. Moreover, the State was to intervene in the market through a paternalist social policy and a redistributional tax policy. As a result of what he called the social-welfare principle of taxation Wagner advocated progressive income taxation, wealth, inheritance, luxury and capital gains taxes (Wagner [1871–2] 1880, pp. 282–92). He formulated a historical 'law' of 'growing public and state activities' as a general consequence of cultural development (Wagner [1876], 1892–3, pp. 892–908).

It was characteristic of this ideology that Wagner, who referred to Kaiser Wilhelm I and Bismarck as 'state socialists' (Wagner, 1912, p. 24), was at the time a deeply conservative Prussian nationalist. Like many other German conservatives, he was deeply sceptical towards industrial and capitalist development (Wagner, 1901) and antisemitic, which attenuated during his later years. Wagner joined Adolf Stöcker's reactionary and antisemitic Christian Social party, became its vice-president and member in the lower house of the Prussian Diet (1882–5), and was an active member of the Evangelical Social Congress. When the Nazis came to power, Wagner was praised as a precursor of National Socialism (Vleugels, 1935). However, there is still a far way to go from Wagner's type of conservatism to Nazi fascism.

HERMANN REICH

SELECTED WORKS
1857. *Beiträge zur Lehre von den Banken.* Reprinted, Vaduz: Topos, 1977.
1871. Speech on the social question. In *Social Reformers: Adam Smith to John Dewey*, ed D.O. Wagner, New York: Macmillan, 1934.
1871–2. *Finanzwissenschaft.* 4 vols, Leipzig and Heidelberg: Winter. First published as a revision of Rau, K.H., *Lehrbuch der Finanzwissenschaft.* Vol. 1: *Einleitung. Ordnung der Finanzwirtschaft. Finanzbedarf. Privaterwerb*; 3rd edn, 1883. Vol 2: *Gebühren und Allgemeine Steuerlehre*, 1880. For a translation of excerpts, see *Classics in the Theory of Public Finance*, ed. R.A. Musgrave and A.T. Peacock, London and New York: Macmillan, 1958, 1–15. Vol 3 and 4: *Specielle Steuerlehre*, 1889 and 1899–1901.
1876. *Grundlegung der politischen Oekonomie.* Pt. I: *Grundlagen der Volkswirthschaft*; 3rd edn, Leipzig: Winter, 1892–3.
1886. Systematische Nationalökonomie. *Jahrbücher für Nationalökonomie und Statistik*, NF 12. Partially translated as 'Wagner on the present state of political economy', *Quarterly Journal of Economics*, October 1886.
1887. *Finanzwissenschaft und Staatssozialismus.* Sozialökonomische Texte No. 15, ed. A. Skalweit, Frankfurt: Vittorio Klostermann.
1891. Marshall's Principles of Economics (Book Review). *Quarterly Journal of Economics*, April.
1901. *Agrar- und Industriestaat.* 2nd edn, Jena: Gustav Fischer, 1902.
1907–9. *Theoretische Sozialökonomik.* 2 vols, Leipzig: Winter.
1912. *Die Strömungen in der Sozialpolitik und der Katheder- und Staatssozialismus.* Berlin: Volkstümliche Bücherei.

BIBLIOGRAPHY
Clark, E.A. 1940. Adolph Wagner: from national economist to national socialist. *Political Science Quarterly* 55.
Heilman, M. 1980. *Adolph Wagner – ein deutscher Nationalökonom im Urteil der Zeit.* Frankfurt and New York: Campus.
Hutter, M. 1982. Early contributions to law and economics: Adolph Wagner's 'Grundlegung'. *Journal of Economic Issues* 16(1), March, 131–47.
Vleugels, W. 1935. Adolph Wagner: Gedenkworte zur hundertsten Wiederkehr des Geburtstages eines deutschen Sozialisten. *Schmollers Jahrbuch für Gesetzgebung, Verwaltung und Volkswirtschaft im Deutschen Reich*, April.

waiting. The term 'waiting' was introduced by MacVane (1887) to replace the term 'abstinence' used by earlier economists. Both terms are so closely related that they will be discussed together.

Despite some misgivings, Senior adopted the term 'abstinence' because 'there is no familiar term to express the act, the conduct, of which profit is the reward, and which bears the same relation to profit which labour does to wages' (1836, p. 89). The idea that saving implies to abstain from the use of existing goods for consumption purposes had earlier been expressed by Adam Smith ([1759] 1976, pp. 189–90), T.R. Malthus (1820, p. 314), G.P. Scrope (1833, p. 146) and especially John Rae, who had argued explicitly that men 'sacrifice a certain amount of present goods to obtain another, greater amount of goods at some future period' (1834, p. 119). Senior, however, combined saving with investing, and denoted by 'abstinence' both a form of economic activity and its result: 'By the work abstinence we wish to express the agent distinct from labour and the agency of nature the concurrence of which is necessary to the existence of capital' (1836, p. 59); or again 'abstinence expresses both the act of abstaining from the unproductive use of capital, and also the similar conduct of a man who devotes his labour to the production of remote rather than of immediate results' (1836, p. 89). Considered as an 'instrument of production', abstinence was not, however, independent: 'although human labour and the agency of nature independently of that of man are the primary productive powers, they require the concurrence of a third productive principle to give them complete efficiency' (1836, p. 58) because without it time-consuming production is not possible. Abstinence is thus associated by Senior with the idea that production takes time. As 'to abstain from the enjoyment which is in our power, or to seek distant rather than immediate results, are among the most painful exertions of the human will' (1836, p. 60), abstinence commands a price as a scarce factor of production which puts it on a par with the other, primary factors of production.

As a term denoting saving and investing, i.e. a form of economic activity which commands a reward, 'abstinence' was adopted by J.S. Mill, Cairnes and Jevons, Bastiat and Cherbuliez, Hermann and Roscher, and soom became part of established theory. Its general and rapid adoption indicates both the inadequacy and the end of a pure cost of production theory of value. Lassalle castigated and ridiculed it by comparing the sacrifices of millionaires to those of small savers (1864, pp. 110). This critique was answered by Loria (1880, pp. 610–24) and later by Macfarlane (1899) with the argument that the savings of millionaires were intramarginal, and that their rewards benefited from savers' surplus. It was probably for that reason that the term continued to be used for the act of saving and investing. Thus J.B. Clark (1899, p. 134) wrote: 'abstinence is the relinquishment, once and for all, of a certain pleasure of consumption and the aquisition of a wholly new increment of capital'. Yet more and more the term was considered unsatisfactory. Cairnes (1874, pp. 88–95) had unsuccessfully proposed the term 'postponement' in its place. By contrast, MacVane's suggestion (1887) to replace it by 'waiting' was taken up by Marshall, and later by Cassel and others, and subsequently adopted generally.

Marshall equated 'waiting' with 'postponement of enjoyment' (1920, p. 233) or 'saving' (1920, p. 830) and argued that 'the growth of wealth involves in general a deliberate waiting for pleasure which a person has ... the power of commanding in the immediate present' (1920, p. 234). In a similar way Carver (1893) associated 'abstinence' with the disutility of saving when he argued that the rate of interest is determined jointly by a falling marginal productivity of capital schedule and a rising marginal abstinence schedule. Carver showed also that abstinence is related to, but not the same as, the rate of time preference. Both Marshall and Carver thus distinguished between saving and investing, reserving the term 'waiting' (or 'abstinence') for saving.

Marshall also took up Senior's association of abstinence with time-consuming production, and extended it to consumption. Production, if it takes time, requires waiting because most outputs will appear only after most inputs have gone into the process. Similarly, durable consumer goods involve waiting because their services extend over time. The exertions, efforts and sacrifices involved in such economic behaviour in production Marshall counted among the real costs of production; where durable consumer goods are involved, they were counted among the real benefits of their use (1920, p. 339).

In this form, the 'abstinence theory' was severely criticized by Böhm-Bawerk (1921, vol. I, ch. 9 and appendix pt. 4). Based in effect on Senior's denial that capital was an independent factor of production, Böhm-Bawerk maintained that abstinence or waiting could not be counted among the real costs of production. Instead of adding the rewards for abstinence or waiting to the expenses of production the correct way was in his view to take account of the under-valuation of future benefits as reflected in such rewards and count among the (money) costs of production only the rewards of 'primary' factors.

The debate which followed this critique was obfuscated by Cassel because he changed the meaning of the term 'waiting'. Situating his discussion in the context of a price theory, Cassel identified the 'supply of waiting' with savings, thus changing the emphasis from a form of economic behaviour to its results (in money rather than in real terms). At the same time, Cassel resurrected Senior's association of saving with investing, and abstinence with a factor of production, and identified the 'demand for waiting' with the total money value of capital invested (1903, chs 3 and 4). While Cassel's procedure had the advantage of interpreting the price of waiting as the price of keeping a particular stock of capital in use, his adoption of a money value measure of capital (which was not discussed in detail) was confusing if not confused. It did, however, prepare the ground for the debates about saving and investment and their determinants which dominated macroeconomic discussions in the 1930s. In his later treatise (1918) Cassel tended to use the term 'use of capital' (*Kapitaldisposition*) in place of 'waiting'; this indicates that he discussed other issues than the microeconomic ones which had dominated the debates from Senior to Marshall and Böhm-Bawerk.

From Senior to Marshall, abstinence or waiting was associated primarily with the idea that saving involves sacrificing goods available in the present for consumption in order to invest them, and that profits can be regarded as reward for such economic activity. Yet as Rae had shown before the terms were coined, and Carver showed later, the reward for such intertemporal (re-)allocations depends not only on the characteristics of saving behaviour, but also on the productivity, or profitability, of the investment opportunities open to those willing to save. To that extent, therefore, the notion of abstinence for waiting as the activity which is rewarded by profits is misleading. Nor are such terms required to characterize economic behaviour concerned with intertemporal allocations.

From Senior to Böhm-Bawerk, abstinence or waiting was also associated with the notion that the use of durable goods in production as well as in consumption results in time-consuming economic processes, and that profit or interest is in some sense the reward for or price of the capital tied up in such processes. Yet while it is correct that time-consuming economic processes involve 'waiting' or abstinence from immediate consumption, it is not at all clear why such a characteristic of production processes should be given the status of a factor of production. Insofar as Böhm-Bawerk's critique is pertinent (see Fraser, 1937, ch. 14). Nor has it proved possible, in view of the many possible temporal structures such processes can assume, to define measures for the waiting or abstinence involved in them which are such that one can speak of profits or interest as reward or price of such a factor of production (see Haavelmo, 1960; Hicks, 1979). In spite of recent attempts to revive the notion (see Yeager, 1976) 'abstinence' or 'waiting' do not seem to be terms which are useful in economic theory beyond denoting, in a rather general manner, a characteristic feature of time-consuming economic processes.

K.H. Hennings

See also abstinence; impatience; time preference.

BIBLIOGRAPHY

Bastiat, F. 1850. *Harmonies économiques*. Paris: Guillaumin. *Economic Harmonies*, London: Murray, 1860.

Böhm-Bawerk, E. von. 1921. *Kapital und Kapitalzins*. Erste Abteilung: *Geschichte und Kritik der Kapitalzins theorien*. 4th edn, Jena: Fisher. Trans. as *Capital and Interest*, Vol. 1: *History and Critique of Interest Theories*, South Holland, Ill.: Libertarian Press, 1959.

Cairnes, J.E. 1874. *Some Leading Principles of Political Economy Newly Expounded*. London: Macmillan.

Carver, T.N. 1893. The place of abstinence in the theory of interest. *Quarterly Journal of Economics* 8, 40–61.

Cassel, G. 1903. *The Nature and Necessity of Interest*. London: Macmillan.

Cassel, G. 1918. *Theoretische Sozialökonomie*. Leipzig: Deichert. 4th edn. 1927: *Theory of Social Economy*, London: Unwin, 1923. New edn, London, Bern, 1932.

Cherbuliez, A.-E. 1862. *Précis de la Science Economique*. Paris: Guillaumin.

Clark, J.B. 1899. *The Theory of Distribution*. New York: Macmillan.

Fraser, L.M. 1937. *Economic Thought and Language*. London: Black.

Goss, B.A. 1980. Adam Smith on Abstinence. *Australian Economic Papers* 19, 16–21.

Haavelmo, T. 1960. *A Study in the Theory of Investment*. Chicago: Chicago University Press.

Hermann, F.B.W. von. 1874. *Staatswirtschaftliche Untersuchungen*. 2nd edn, Münich: Ackermann.

Hicks, J.R. 1979. Is interest the price of a factor of production? In J.R. Hicks, *Classics and Moderns*, Collected Essays Vol. III, Oxford: Blackwell, 1983.

Jevons, W.S. 1871. *The Theory of Political Economy*. London: Macmillan, 1970.

Lassalle, F. 1864. *Herr Bastiat-Schultze von Delitzsch der ökonomische Julian, oder Kapital und Arbeit*. Berlin: Schlingmann.

Loria, A. 1880. *La rendita fondiaria*. Milan: Hoepli.

Macfarlane, C.W. 1899. *Value and Distribution*. Philadelphia: Lippincott.

MacVane, S.M. 1887. Analysis of cost of production. *Quarterly Journal of Economics* 1, 481–7.

Malthus, T.R. 1820. *Principles of Political Economy*. 2nd edn, London: Murray, 1836.

Marshall, A. 1920. *Principles of Economics*. 8th edn. 9th (Variorum) edn, London: Macmillan, 1961.

Mill, J.S. 1848. *Principles of Political Economy*. London: Parker.

Rae, J. 1934. *Statement of Some New Principles on the Subject of Political Economy*. Boston: Hilliard, Gray and Co.

Roscher, W. 1854. *Grundlagen der Nationalökonomie*. Stuttgart: Cotta.

Scrope, G.P. 1833. *Principles of Political Economy*. London: Longman, Rees, Orme, Brown, Green and Longman.

Senior, W.N. 1836. *Outlines of the Science of Political Economy*. London: Longman, 1850.

Smith, A. 1759. *Theory of Moral Sentiments*. Oxford: Clarendon Press, 1976.

Yeager, L.B. 1976. Toward understanding some paradoxes in capital theory. *Economic Inquiry* 14, 313–46.

Wakefield, Edward Gibbon (1796–1862). Wakefield was born in London on 20 March 1796, the eldest son of Edward Wakefield, a radical Quaker philanthropist, statistician, and author of a standard work on Ireland which was highly regarded by Ricardo, James Mill and other members of the philosophic radical circle. His son was to become one of the more colourful characters to inhabit the margins of the history of economic debate, and can be variously described as a publicist, politician and author. Apart from his practical and frequently controversial contributions to the development of Australia, Canada and New Zealand, he left a distinctive mark in the annals of classical political economy during the middle third of the 19th century.

After a chequered education at Westminster School and Edinburgh High School, from which he was expelled in 1811, Wakefield first read for the Bar and later served as secretary to the British envoy to the Court of Turin (1814–20). In 1816 he successfully eloped with a 16-year-old Ward-in-Chancery who died in childbirth in 1820. From 1820 to 1825 he served with the British legation in Paris and entertained ambitions of entering Parliament. In 1826 he made an attempt to acquire a rich wife by the most direct means available: he abducted the daughter of a wealthy family from her school and married her at Gretna Green. He was apprehended by her family at Calais and subsequently given a three-year sentence which he spent studying capital punishment and transportation, writing a powerful pamphlet condemning the former, and turning the latter into what was to become a lifetime's preoccupation with colonization. His first work on the subject, *A Letter from Sydney* (1829), purporting to be the reflections of a disillusioned settler on the poor prospects for Australian social and economic development, was actually written from Newgate prison. After his release Wakefield produced a spate of books, articles and prospectuses on the subject of colonization which led to the formation of the National Colonization Society in 1830 – a society which obtained the support of a number of Members of Parliament and of the youthful John Stuart Mill. Although most of his writings dealt with colonization in one form or another, his work on *England and America; A Comparison of the Social and Political State of Both Nations* (1833) is of wider interest for its diagnosis of the cause of the 'uneasiness of the middle classes' and for its economic interpretation of slavery. Wakefield also produced an edition of the *Wealth of Nations* (1835–9) which has some interesting editorial comments.

Wakefield's views on colonization were based on a dual analysis of Britain's need for an outlet for its surplus capital and population and a diagnosis of the causes of weak economic development in colonies of new settlement enjoying access to abundant land. His own schemes for 'systematic colonization' were intended as an almost self-regulating solution to both of these problems. Making use of ideas derived from the work of Robert Gourlay, Wakefield advanced a theory of growth in new countries which was designed to support a plan of optimal development. Contrary to the received view, he maintained that access to free or cheap land was responsible for population dispersion, scarcity of labour for hire, and consequent inability to reap the benefits of economies of scale through market concentration and the combined efforts of capital and labour. Under these circumstances the 'natural' pattern of development led to stagnation. Convict labour in Australia and slavery in the American South were both unsatisfactory expedients adopted to deal with a problem that could only be overcome by charging a 'sufficient price' for public or waste land which would deter premature dispersion, stabilize a revolving wage-labour force, and create a fund that could be used to subsidize immigration. The price was defined as one that was high enough to delay land acquisition by newly arrived immigrants without capital of their own, and low enough not to discourage voluntary immigration by reducing real wages and the return on capital.

Colonization on this plan required a new beginning in a colony that was not contaminated by convict labour; and for this purpose Wakefield initially chose South Australia, forming an association for this purpose in 1834. When his proposals were diluted in operation by the founders of the colony (among them another political economist, Robert Torrens), Wakefield turned his attention to New Zealand, serving as the Director of the New Zealand Colonization Company from 1839 to 1846. In 1838 he accompanied Lord Durham on his mission to Canada and wrote the appendix on land disposal to the resulting Durham report.

Wakefield's ideas are of interest for a number of reasons. He belongs to the non-Ricardian underworld by virtue of his attack on Say's Law, the wage-fund doctrine, and the associated idea that capital and labour could never be in surplus together – a mirror image of the problem in colonies where both were scarce. Yet his success in convincing John Stuart Mill and other economists of the correctness of his diagnosis of British and colonial problems gave new significance to the export of capital and labour to colonies and hence to the whole subject of colonization and the development of new countries as a topic within orthodox political economy.

Wakefield also plays a part in the Marxian tradition, or rather its demonology, as a result of Marx's decision to devote a chapter of *Capital* (vol. I, chapter 23) to showing how Wakefield, under colonial conditions of labour scarcity, had been forced to reveal the underlying logic of capitalist exploitation. What could be achieved quite naturally under European conditions had to be created artificially in new colonies, with the additional subtlety that having served a term of exploitation, the wage-labourer had to pay for his replacement. One could also claim that Wakefield, less unwittingly, anticipated Hobson and Lenin in providing an economic interpretation of imperialism as a necessary response to stagnation in mature capitalist economies.

In 1853 Wakefield finally practised what he had been preaching by emigrating to New Zealand, where he died in 1862.

DONALD WINCH

See also COLONIES.

SELECTED WORKS *The Collected Works of Edward Gibbon Wakefield.* Ed. M.F. Lloyd Prichard, London: Collins, 1968.

BIBLIOGRAPHY

Mills, R.C. 1915. *The Colonization of Australia, 1829–42: The Wakefield Experiment in Empire Building*. London: Sidgwick & Jackson.

Winch, D. 1965. *Classical Political Economy and Colonies*. London: Bell & Sons.

Wald, Abraham (1902–1950). Born in Cluj, Rumania, Wald came to Vienna in 1927 to study mathematics with Karl Menger, the geometer and son of the economist Carl Menger. Menger introduced Wald to the active mathematical group in Vienna, and secured for him a position as mathematical tutor to the economist Karl Schlesinger. This led to Wald's producing the first proofs of existence for models of general equilibrium; his analysis was based on Cassel's restatement of the Walrasian model, as modified by Schlesinger's treatment of free goods. These works were published in the proceedings of Menger's mathematical colloquium, and a summary was published in the *Zeitschrift für Nationalökonomie* in 1936. These papers were remarkable for their time and, with von Neumann's paper on equilibrium in a model of an expanding economy, are the first significant contributions to the mathematical analysis of general equilibrium models in economics. Wald is the link between the early work by Walras and the later work by Kenneth Arrow, Gerard Debreu and Lionel McKenzie on the existence of competitive equilibria.

A fine mathematician, Wald was nevertheless prevented from gaining a regular academic position because of Viennese anti-semitism. Menger helped Wald secure a consultancy position with Oskar Morgenstern who directed the Institut für Konjunkturforschung, where Wald took an interest in the statistical problems that were associated with the analysis of business cycles. Wald's book on seasonal adjustment of time series was a result of his work at Morgenstern's Institut.

Wald was able to escape from Vienna when the Nazis arrived, and made his way to the United States where he initially secured a fellowship, in 1938, at the Cowles Commission which was then at Colorado Springs. When the Commission moved to Chicago, Wald obtained a position, on a Carnegie grant, as Harold Hotelling's assistant at Columbia University. He moved to a faculty post at Columbia in 1941, and was promoted to Associate Professor in 1943 and Professor in 1944.

Wald's contributions to statistics are immense. His most significant paper appeared in 1939 in the *Annals of Mathematical Statistics* as 'Contributions to the theory of statistical estimation and testing hypotheses' (in Wald, 1955). This paper, written before modern decision theory was developed, contained notions of decision space, weight and risk functions, and minimax solution (based on von Neumann's 1928 paper on game theory). Wald's paper was not appreciated at the time, much as was the case with his papers on general equilibrium theory. He did not return to statistical decision theory until 1946, after von Neumann and Morgenstern had presented the theory of games.

During World War II, Wald worked with the Statistical Research Group and developed much of the theory of sequential analysis. Although he did not create the idea of taking observations sequentially, Wald did invent the sequential probability ratio test. This original material was published in 1947 after wartime restrictions were lifted.

In 1950, at the height of his powers, Wald and his wife died in a plane crash in India.

E.R. WEINTRAUB

See also EXISTENCE OF GENERAL EQUILIBRIUM; MONOTONE MAPPINGS; REVEALED PREFERENCE THEORY; STATISTICAL DECISION THEORY.

SELECTED WORKS

In 1952 *The Annals of Mathematical Statistics* devoted the first part of its Volume 23 to a memorial to Wald. Articles on Wald by Jacob Wolfowitz, Karl Menger, and Gerhard Tintner were followed by a complete bibliography of Wald's writings. Wald's professional correspondence, and papers from his Viennese days, cannot be located, though it is possible that Karl Menger's archives, currently closed to examination, may contain some material on Wald.

1934. Über die eindeutige positive Lösbarkeit der neuen Produktions gleichungen I. In *Ergebnisse eines mathematischen*

Kolloquiums, 1933–34, ed. K. Menger. Trans. by W. Baumol as 'On the unique non-negative solvability of the new production equations, part I', in *Precursors in Mathematical Economics*, ed. W.J. Baumol and S.M. Goldfeld, London School of Economics Series of Reprints of Scarce Works on Political Economy No. 19, London: London School of Economics, 1968.

1935. Über die Produktionsgleichungen der ökonomischen Wertlehre II. In *Ergebnisse eines mathematischen Kolloquiums*, 1934–35, ed. K. Menger. Trans. by W. Baumol as 'On the production equations of economic value theory, part II', in *Precursors in Mathematical Economics*, ed. W.J. Baumol and S.M. Goldfeld, London School of Economics Series of Reprints of Scarce Works on Political Economy No. 19, London: London School of Economics, 1968.

1936. Über einige Gleichungssysteme der mathematischen Ökonomie. *Zeitschrift für Nationalökonomie*. Trans. by O. Eckstein as 'On some systems of equations in mathematical economics', *Econometrica* 19(4), October 1951, 368–403.

1947. *Sequential Analysis*. New York: John Wiley.

1950. *Statistical Decision Functions*. New York: John Wiley.

1955. *Selected Papers in Statistics and Probability*. New York: McGraw-Hill.

Walker, Francis Amasa (1840–1897). Internationally the most widely known and esteemed American economist of his generation, Walker had a varied and distinguished public career. After obtaining his AB at Amherst in 1860, he studied law for one year before joining the Northern army and was successively a Civil War general, deputy to David A. Wells in the Budget Office, chief of the US Treasury's Bureau of Statistics, Superintendent of the Census of 1870 and 1880, Professor of Political Economy and History at Yale's Sheffield Scientific School, and also occasionally at Johns Hopkins, and President of the Massachusetts Institute of Technology, 1881–97. At home Walker was primarily known as an outstanding educational administrator and statistician, for he permanently raised the standards of government statistics, helped to create a permanent Bureau of the Census, and served as President of the American Statistical Association from 1882–97. Abroad, he was recognized more as an economic theorist, especially for his work on wages, money and currency policy.

His attack on the wages fund and formulation of a residual claimant theory of wages attracted widespread attention, though it gained few adherents. His writings on money, and a textbook on political economy, were also well regarded, and his support for bimetallism, which involved the monetization of silver, represented an important contribution to a highly controversial current policy debate. In 1878 Walker was appointed US Commissioner to the Paris International Monetary Conference, but in later years he refused comparable invitations as he became disenchanted with the slow progress of international negotiations.

A moderate critic of the ruling classical laissez-faire orthodoxy, Walker responded sympathetically to the rising young generation of German-trained American economists, hence he was both an obvious and in practice ideal choice as first President of the American Economic Association, from 1885 to 1892. His Presidential addresses provide revealing insights into the condition of the subject and the emerging economics profession during those critical years. Walker was an open-minded man, forthright in expression but fair in controversy. He believed in competition while recognizing its imperfections. An undoctrinaire free trader, he was concerned about the growth of immigration and the decline in the native birth rate. An advocate of moderate reductions in hours of work, he was one of the first American economists to recognize entrepreneurial gains as rents of ability. Fifty years after his death, Walker's eminence was acknowledged when the American Economic Association selected his name for its most distinguished award, the Walker Medal.

A.W. Coats

SELECTED WORKS

1876. *The Wages Question: A Treatise on Wages and the Wages Class*. New York: H. Holt, 1906.

1878. *Money*. London: Macmillan; New York: H. Holt, 1891.

1879. *Money in its Relations to Trade and Industry*. New York: H. Holt, 1907.

1883a. *Land and its Rent*. Boston: Little, Brown, 1891.

1883b. *Political Economy*. New York: H. Holt. 3rd revised and enlarged edn, 1911. Abridged, 1912.

1896. *International Bimetallism*. London: Macmillan; New York: H. Holt, 1897.

1899. *Discussions in Economics and Statistics*. 2 vols, ed. D.R. Dewey, New York: H. Holt.

1899. *Discussions in Education*. Ed. J.P. Munroe, New York: H. Holt.

BIBLIOGRAPHY

Newton, B. 1968. *The Economics of Francis Amasa Walker: American Economics in Transition*. New York: Kelley.

Wallace, Alfred Russel (1823–1913). Wallace discovered independently the principle of natural selection which he and Charles Darwin co-published in 1858. Wallace's speciality was zoogeography, consonant with his early work as a surveyor and his later on land policy. 'Wallace's Line' through the Makassar Straits dividing Indo-Malayan from Austro-Malayan fauna is an enduring, if modified monument. His *Geographical Distribution of Animals* (1876) has dominated the field.

The acclaim given to natural selection gave new authority to the natural scientist, shaping ideas of social conduct based on new insights into man and nature. For Wallace it was *land*, man and nature. He was influenced by the young Herbert Spencer of *Social Statics* (1850) who wrote then of equal rights to land.

'Survival of the fittest' (Spencer's apothegm) lent itself easily to legitimize predation among humans, reinforcing the dismal doctrines of Malthus. 'Social Darwinism' as articulated by the later Spencer, T. H. Huxley, W. G. Sumner and others became a materialistic, evolution-minded elitism. But Wallace saw mental, social and spiritual factors guiding human evolution. He put his scientist's prestige on the popular side of social issues.

Land policy was aflame with strife. Wallace was outraged by the clearances of the times, and past enclosures, and Irish landlordism, and slums where evictees huddled. In *The Malay Archipelago* (1869) he digressed from natural science to laud primitives as civilized, and score Britain as barbaric. John Stuart Mill sought Wallace out to join the Land Tenure Reform Association which occupied Mill's last years, 1871–3.

Mill's object was to nationalize future increments of land value (or perhaps of rent). Wallace deferred to Mill, but later grew more radical, moved by the Irish land agitation. In 1880 he criticized Parnell's programme for Irish peasant proprietorship as not abolishing privilege, but merely reshuffling some titles.

In 1881 The Land Nationalization Society was formed on Wallace's lines, with him as president. In *Land Nationalization* (1882) he laid out his programme. The state was to assume title to all land, compensating holders with an annuity for the duration of lives in being, based on the same net income from the land derived before nationalization. All men could now lease parcels for use, consummating the natural relation of man to nature, alternating between industry and agriculture.

Land nationalization was not collectivist. Lessees were to have secure tenure and tenant-rights to improvements. Rents to the state would be based on the assessed 'inherent value', dependent only on natural conditions. As a surveyor and a biogeographer Wallace readily distinguished inherent value from man's improvements to land, which he saw as transitory.

Present holders would lose the right to sell; to bequeath; and to let land. They could only hold what they occupied and used themselves. Wallace saw land inheritance as a dysgenic factor in human evolution, giving an artificial advantage to unfit heirs both individually and in their collective power to control social evolution.

Wallace held that man's mind overrode the action of natural selection on his body. The mind understood and controlled natural forces. Without inheritance natural selection would be based on individual merit. Universal education would delay marriage; social reform would reduce male death rates, and female choice would replace Malthusian frightfulness as the engine of selection to improve the race.

Wallace's view was kindred in spirit to Henry George's *Progress and Poverty* (1879), although Wallace had less regard for the market. Both saw man as needing land. Their mutual disapproval of Parnellism brought them together, and both submerged methodological differences to further their common concept. Wallace gave him a platform when George toured Britain. Wallace cast George as a theorist who confirmed Wallace's inductive argument, perhaps underrating George's journalistic background. For many years single tax and land nationalization were closely linked by friend and foe. To Liberal Prime Minister Herbert Asquith they were two arms of a pincers, driven together by valuation: 'Tax or Buy' was his slogan.

In later years Wallace went socialist, but continued to support single tax, which from 1895 to 1914 dominated land reform efforts in Britain. But land reform when it came in the Town and Country Planning Act (1947), although neither would have owned it, evinced more Wallace than George.

MASON GAFFNEY

See also GEORGE, HENRY.

SELECTED WORKS

1882. *Land Nationalization*. London: Swan Sonnenschein.
1869. *The Malay Archipelago*. 2 vols, London: Macmillan.
1905. *My Life: A Record of Events and Opinions*. 2 vols, London: Chapman & Hall.

BIBLIOGRAPHY

Bannister, R.C. 1979. *Social Darwinism*. Philadelphia: Temple University Press.
Clements, H. 1983. *Alfred Russel Wallace, Biologist and Social Reformer*. London: Hutchinson.
Durant, J.R. 1979. Scientific naturalism and social reform in the thought of Alfred Russel Wallace. *British Journal for the History of Science* 12, 31–58.
Fichman, M. 1981. *Alfred Russel Wallace*. Boston: Twayne Publishers.
Lawrence, E.P. 1957. *Henry George in the British Isles*. East Lansing: Michigan State University Press.

Wallich, Henry Christopher (born 1914). Wallich was born in Germany in 1914 and became a citizen of the United States in 1944. He did his graduate work in economics at Harvard University and wrote his doctoral dissertation, later his first published book, on the monetary problems of a small open economy.

The blending of theoretical insights with practical knowledge and policy judgements, begun in his dissertation, has been a hallmark of Wallich's career and work. His early experience and background contributed to this approach. As a young man, he worked first in the export business in Latin America and then as a securities analyst in New York. His tenure as head of the Foreign Research Division of the Federal Reserve Bank of New York in the late 1940s included missions advising less developed countries on central banking and fiscal policy issues.

Wallich's subsequent academic and public careers focused mainly on major domestic and international monetary questions and other practical economic issues, including aspects of tax policy. As Professor of Economics at Yale University from 1951 to 1974, he taught graduate courses in money and banking, published widely, took time off to act first as Assistant to the Secretary of the Treasury and then as a member of the President's Council of Economic Advisers, and wrote (alternately with Milton Friedman and Paul Samuelson) a well-respected column on economics for a national weekly. He became a member of the Board of Governors of the Federal Reserve System in 1974, where his particular responsibilities have largely been in the international area.

Wallich's approach to macroeconomics has encompassed an understanding of both the importance of budgetary and tax policy and the critical role played by money, particularly in the process of containing inflation. He has stressed the desirability of international coordination and cooperation. He has also emphasized the need for an efficient micro economy, with appropriate market incentives to minimize rigidities that might lead to unfavourable macroeconomic trade-offs as between, say, unemployment and prices. When market incentives were working imperfectly, Wallich has favoured remedial action consistent with retaining the flexibility and efficiencies of a market price system, such as tax incentives to restrain wage increases.

STEPHEN H. AXILROD

SELECTED WORKS

1946. Debt management as an instrument of economic policy. *American Economic Review* 36, June, 292–310.
1950. *Monetary Problems of an Export Economy*. Cambridge, Mass.: Harvard University Press.
1955. *Mainsprings of the German Revival*. New Haven: Yale University Press. Also in German.
1956. Conservative economic policy. *Yale Review* 46(1), Autumn, 63–73.
1960. *The Cost of Freedom*. New York: Harper & Brothers. Also in German, Spanish and Portuguese.
1968. Monetary and fiscal policies in open economies under fixed exchange rates. *Journal of Political Economy* 76(4), Pt II, July–August, 951–2.
1971. (With S. Weintraub.) A tax-based income policy. *Journal of Economic Issues* 5(2), June, 1–19.
1981. *Monetary Policy and Practice*. Lexington, Mass.: Lexington Books.

Walras, Antoine Auguste (1801–1866). Amateur economist whose writings have received some limited attention, chiefly because some of his views and economic concepts influenced his son, Léon. Auguste Walras was born in Montpellier, France, on 1 February 1801, and died in Pau on 18 April 1866. He studied at the Ecole Normale of Paris (1820–23); was a tutor in Paris (1823–31); a secondary school teacher (1823, 1831–5); a professor of philosophy first at the Royal College in Lille (1839) and then at the Royal College in Caen (1840–47); and a regional school superintendent (1847–62).

Believing that an understanding of property requires a sound theory of value, Auguste Walras developed the unoriginal and unsatisfactory thesis, primarily on the basis of admittedly metaphysical considerations, that economic value depends upon scarcity (*rareté*). This he defined as the relation between the quantity of a commodity and the number of people that have need for it. He concluded that only scarce things are appropriated and constitute property (Walras, 1831). He then argued that natural law dictates that the state, like the individual, has the right to own property, and that land in particular should belong exclusively to society as a whole. Developing an explanation of the current ownership of land, he pointed out that it is a consequence of social institutions and historical events. During the feudal era, it was placed by the king under the suzerainty of individuals in return for their military services, and their descendants subsequently ruled it as public officials. Since the need for their feudal functions has disappeared, so also has their right to the use of land, and they have become parasites who benefit from economic growth without contributing to it. The class struggle is therefore between landowners and the rest of society, and social justice requires that it be resolved in favour of society as a whole. Believing in conciliation and rejecting revolutionary action, he argued that the state should acquire all land by purchasing it, and should rent it to private users. During the period before complete nationalization the increments in pure land rent arising from the progress of society should be taxed away, and there should be heavy taxes on transfers of land. Since individuals have the right to own what they make, taxation of produced wealth, as distinct from rent, is unjust. It is therefore an advantage of land nationalization that the state would be supported by the rent it earns and taxation could be eliminated (Walras, 1848). He regarded this proposal as being founded upon scientific analysis and described himself as a socialist, but it is clear that his interpretation and solution of 'the social problem' – the problem of the poverty of the working class during the 19th century – was highly coloured by his normative views and was bourgeois in character.

Auguste Walras also studied the function of precious metals in the growth of social wealth, in the measurement of value, and in exchange; argued that the increase of wealth is the object of economic science; made a distinction between capital and income, and between the market for services and the market for products; introduced the entrepreneur as a person who buys factors of production and sells products; and devised the concept of a *numéraire* (Walras, 1849). He did not fully develop these ideas nor integrate them into a theory of economic behaviour. His main concern in all his work was to buttress his theory of property and his solution to the social problem.

DONALD A. WALKER

SELECTED WORKS

1831. *De la nature de la richesse et de l'origine de la valeur*. Paris: Alexandre Johanneau; Evreux: Imprimérie d'Ancelle Fils. Ed. G. Leduc, Paris: Alcan, 1938.

1848. *La vérité sociale, par un travailleur*. Extracts of MS in Leroy (1928).

1849. *Théorie de la richesse sociale our résumé des principes fondamentaux de l'économie politique*. Paris: Guillaumin.

BIBLIOGRAPHY

Jaffé, W. 1984. The antecedents and early life of Léon Walras. *History of Political Economy* (ed. Donald A. Walker) 16(1), Spring, 1–57.

Leroy, L.M. 1928. *Auguste Walras, économiste; sa vie, son oeuvre*. Paris: Librairie Générale de Droit et de Jurisprudence.

Walras, L. 1908. Un initiateur en économie politique, A.A. Walras. *Revue du Mois* 6, August, 170–83.

Walras, Léon (1834–1910). Léon Walras was the founder of the modern theory of general economic equilibrium. He was born on 16 December 1834 in Evreux, which is in the Department of Eure in France, and christened Marie Esprit Léon. He died on 5 January 1910 in Clarens, Switzerland. His father was Antoine Auguste Walras, a secondary school administrator and an amateur economist; his mother was Louise Aline de Sainte Beuve, the daughter of an Evreux notary. After studying at the College of Caen from 1844 to 1850, he entered the Lycée of Douai, where he received the bachelier-ès-lettres in 1851 and the bachelier-ès-sciences in 1853. He entered the School of Mines of Paris in 1854, but finding the course of preparation of an engineer not to his liking, he gradually abandoned his academic studies in order to cultivate literature, philosophy and social science. Although those efforts resulted in a short story and a novel, *Francis Sauveur* (Walras, 1858), it rapidly became apparent to him that his true interests lay with social science. Accordingly, in 1858 he agreed to his father's request to devote himself to economics and promised to continue his father's investigations (Jaffé, 1965, vol. 1, pp. 1–2).

During his youth in Paris, Walras became a journalist for the *Journal des Economistes* and *La Presse* from 1859 to 1862; the author of a refutation on philosophical grounds of the normative economic doctrines of P.-J. Proudhon (Walras, 1860); an employee of the directors of the Northern Railway in 1862; and managing director of a cooperative association bank in 1865. He gave public lectures on cooperative associations in 1865; was co-editor and publisher with Léon Say of the journal *Le Travail*, a review devoted largely to the cooperative movement, from 1866 to 1868; and, during those years, gave public lectures on social topics (Walras, 1868) in which he advocated Victor Cousin's doctrine of compromise between economic classes. After the failure of the association bank in 1868, he found employment with a private bank until 1870 (Jaffé, 1965, vol. 1, pp. 3–4). During the 1860s he tried intermittently to obtain an academic appointment in France, but he lacked the necessary educational credentials, and the eleven economics positions in higher education in France were monopolized by orthodox economists who, he complained, passed their chairs on to their relatives (ibid., p. 3). His fortunes ultimately changed as a result of his participation in 1860 in an international congress on taxation in Lausanne, for that drew him to the attention of Louis Ruchonnet, a Swiss politician who secured his appointment in 1870 to an untenured professorship of economics at the Academy (subsequently University) of Lausanne in Switzerland. He was made a tenured professor there in 1871, and held that position throughout his teaching career.

Walras's personal life was initially unconventional. He and Célestine Aline Ferbach (1834–79) formed a common law union in the late 1850s. She had a son, Georges, by a previous liaison, and she and Walras had twin daughters in 1863, one of whom died in infancy. In 1869 he married Célestine, thereby legitimizing their daughter, Marie Aline, and adopted

Célestine's son. A long illness of Celestine's and the meagerness of Walras's salary made life very difficult for him for several years. His time and energy were sorely taxed not only by the need to care for his wife but by the need to supplement his salary by teaching extra classes, contributing to the *Gazette de Lausanne* and the *Bibliothèque Universelle*, and working as a consultant for La Suisse insurance company. Five years after Célestine's death in 1879, Walras married Léonide Désirée Mailly (1826–1900). The marriage was a happy one. Her annuity relieved his financial distress, and his situation was further improved in 1892 by an inheritance of 100,000 francs from his mother, which enabled him to pay debts incurred in publishing and disseminating his works, and to buy an annuity of 800 francs.

Walras's professional life was devoted to research and teaching. He frequently asserted that his research was a development of his father's, and that was true in some respects. It was under the influence of his father's classification of economic studies that Léon, as early as 1862, planned the division of his life's work into the study of pure theory, economic policies, and normative goals (Walras to Jules du Mesnil Marigny, 23 December 1862, L 81; the 'L' stands for 'letter', and, like all correspondence cited in this entry, the letter is in Jaffé, 1965), the areas of study that were ultimately set forth respectively in the *Eléments d'économie politique pure* (1874, 1877), the *Etudes d'économie social* (1896b) and the *Etudes d'économie politique appliquée* (1898). Léon adopted his father's classification of the factors of production into the services of labour, land and capital goods, regarding the source of each service as a type of capital. He adopted his father's definitions of capital as wealth that can be used more than once and of income as wealth that can be used only once, and adopted his father's vague term 'extensive utility', clarifying it by using it to mean the quantity-axis intercept of a market demand curve. The topic of utility had been treated in French thought by writers such as F. Galiani (a Neapolitan diplomat at Versailles) and E.B. de Condillac, and it was given further development under the name *rarété* by Auguste Walras, who thus bequeathed to Léon an interest in the concept of utility in relation to the value of commodities and an awareness of its dependence upon scarcity, an interest that ultimately led him to define *rareté* as marginal utility. Auguste used the word *numéraire* to mean an abstract unit of account, and Léon adapted the meaning of the word to his purposes. Auguste's philosophy of social justice and his belief in the desirability of nationalizing land were advocated by Léon throughout his adult life. Léon's major economic theories, however, were derived from his own original inspiration and from sources other than his father. Auguste's greatest contributions to Léon's development as an economist were to encourage him to study economics, to suggest that it should be a mathematical science (A.A. Walras, 1831, ch. 18; Jaffé, 1965, vol. 1, p. 493), and to give him access to a library of books on economics.

In that library was A.A. Cournot's *Recherches sur les principes mathématiques de la théorie des richesses* (1838), which Léon Walras credited with having demonstrated that economics could and should be expressed in mathematical form (Walras to Cournot, 20 March 1874, L 253; Walras to H.L. Moore, 2 January 1906, L 1614; Walras, 1905a). Cournot's work introduced Walras to the mathematical formulation of exchange between two locations, the theory of monopoly and the associated conditions for profit maximization, the analysis of how prices are repeatedly changed in a search for equilibrium in a purely competitive market, and the demonstration of the effect of large numbers of traders upon the determinacy of price, all topics that Walras developed in his own work (Walras, 1954, pp. 370–72, 434–40, 443). The first demand curve that Walras beheld was Cournot's, and he found it immensely suggestive. He was critical of it, however, because he perceived that Cournot's postulate that the quantity demanded of a commodity is a function only of its own price is inaccurate if more than two commodities are exchanged, and that Cournot did not provide a theoretical rationale for the demand function. Those perceptions, Walras observed, were the starting point for his own inquiries (Jaffé, 1965, vol. I, p. 5; 1905a).

Other ingredients that went into the composition of Walras's theories were provided by Adam Smith, John Stuart Mill, François Quesnay, A.R.J. Turgot and Jean-Baptiste Say. Smith had revealed many of the consequences of unfettered competition and had formulated the concept of normal value. Mill had provided a supplement to and reinforcement of Cournot's and Smith's analyses of competitive pricing (Walras to Ladislaus von Bortkiewicz, 27 February 1891, L 999), and also an extension and grand synthesis of classical doctrines that served Walras as a catalyst for critical studies (Walras, 1954, pp. 404–5, 411, 419, 423). Quesnay, in his *tableau économique*, had expressed the concept of a circular flow of income and of the interdependence of the various parts of the economy. Turgot had clearly delineated the idea of the simultaneous and mutually determined general equilibrium of those parts. Say (1836) had suggested the distinction between the capitalist and the entrepreneur, had portrayed the entrepreneur as an intermediary between the market for productive services and the market for outputs, and, in that analysis and in his law of markets, had adumbrated the interdependence between the incomes of the factors of production and the demand for commodities. Walras sharpened those ideas and made them a fundamental part of his general equilibrium model.

A.N. Isnard's *Traité des richesses* (1781), a book that Leon owned and that may have been in his father's library, was probably an important source of some of Walras's constructions (Jaffé 1969). Like Walras, Isnard was interested in determining equilibrium price ratios, set up a system of simultaneous equations of exchange showing the dependence of the value of each commodity upon the values of the others, stressed the necessity of having as many independent equations as unknowns, and perceived that the use of a *numéraire* rendered his system determinate. Anticipating Walras's treatment of production, Isnard assumed given ratios of the inputs in a mathematical model and expressed the costs of production in equation form. Also like Walras, Isnard studied the allocation of capital among different uses, coming to the conclusion, as did Walras, that in equilibrium the net rate of income of different capital goods is the same.

Finally, Louis Poinsot's *Eléments de statique* (1803) exerted a powerful influence upon Walras. He first read that book when he was nineteen and kept it at his bedside for decades (Walras to Melle Dick May, 23 May 1901, L 1483). Poinsot painted a picture of the mutual interdependence of a vast number of variables, of how the dynamic forces in physical systems eventuate in an equilibrium in which each object is sustained in its path and relative position. Electrified by the implications of Poinsot's work, Walras conceived a magnificent project. He would emulate Poinsot's vision and analysis in reference to the general equilibrium of the economic universe! That he carried out that plan can be inferred from the striking similarity of the form of his work to Poinsot's, with its careful delineation of functional dependences and parameters, its sets of simultaneous equations and its equilibrium conditions.

Equipped, therefore, with ideas that he could take as building blocks and points of departure, with enough geometry and algebra to put together mathematical statements of economic relationships and conditions – his use of calculus in the *Eléments* came after the first edition – and with the explicit objective of developing a mathematical theory of general equilibrium, Walras began his scholarly activity in Lausanne in 1870. In a period of great creativity that lasted until 1878, he developed most of the foundations of the theory of general equilibrium that appeared in the first edition of the *Eléments*. Walras insisted to his publisher that the first part appear in 1874, before the second part (Walras, 1877b) was completed, because he learned in May of that year that W.S. Jevons had published a mathematical theory of utility and exchange that was similar to his own (J. d'Aulnis de Bourouill to Walras, 4 May, 1874, L 267), and he was anxious to establish the independence of his discoveries and his priority in regard to most of them. For those same reasons, he published four brilliantly original memoirs containing the heart of his theory of general equilibrium during 1874, 1875 and 1876 (Walras, 1877a), paid for the costs of publication of his books, and sent copies of them and of his articles to his many correspondents. From 1878 to 1901, Walras significantly extended, refined, and altered his system, particularly in regard to capital, money, and equilibrating mechanisms, and composed numerous essays on applied and normative economics. After 1900 he made no theoretical contributions but wrote some articles and, in late 1901 and 1902, made some inconsequential changes to the *Eléments* which were ultimately incorporated into the text of the fourth edition (1900) to produce the *édition définitive* of 1926.

Walras was an extremely conscientious teacher, but he was an uninspiring lecturer (Jaffé, 1965, vol. 2, p. 560), and the students at Lausanne were interested in careers in law, not in economics, so he failed to develop disciples among them. Moreover, he was with increasing frequency afflicted by bouts of mental exhaustion and irritability that made it difficult for him to lecture and to read and write. In 1892 he took a leave to regenerate his strength in order to be able to continue teaching, but soon realized he would find the strain of returning to his tasks insupportable and retired in that year, being at that time 58 years of age.

ECONOMIC THEORIES

Walras's subject matter and method. Walras recognized that there were imperfectly-competitive market structures and developed a theory of monopoly to take account of an important class of such phenomena (Walras, 1954, lesson 41). Realizing, however, that the incorporation of non-competitive elements into his general equilibrium model was beyond his powers (p. 256) and believing that a high degree of competition was 'almost universal' and deserved to be treated as the general case (Walras to Ladislaus von Bortkiewicz, 27 February 1891, L 999), he devoted most of his energies to working out a theory of 'freely competitive' markets, the aspect of his theoretical work with which this entry is concerned. Competition was most effective, he noted, in organized auction markets, and he assumed that markets are of that type (Walras, 1954, pp. 83–4), but he also regarded his analysis as applicable in a general way to less highly organized competitive markets (p. 84). The first kind of competitive model with which he dealt will be called his formal general equilibrium model. In it he assumed that preferences, the number of workers, the amounts of natural resources and technology are constant. The second kind, which Walras did not develop in any detail, expresses his ideas about economic growth. Within his formal general equilibrium model, Walras constructed the four sequential and cumulative theories (or models, as they will be interchangeably called) of exchange, production, capital formation and credit, and money and circulation. Each of them has four parts.

The first part is the structure of the market, in which Walras identified the participants and their economic characteristics, their objectives and how they try to achieve them, the types of commodities that are traded, the important institutional features and rules of the market, and the relevant supply and demand functions.

The second part is the dynamic process by which the market undergoes adjustments when it is in disequilibrium, the exposition of which Walras regarded as 'the object and proper goal of pure economics' because he realized that without a demonstration of the stability of a purely competitive system, the solutions to his equations could not be regarded as values to which the variables of his model tend (Walras to Bortkiewicz, 17 October 1889, L 927; Walras to Charles Gide, 3 November 1889, L 933). He also recognized that the dynamic functioning of markets depends on the economic agents, institutions, and conditions identified in the first part of each model, and to portray disequilibrium behaviour he accordingly discussed the activities and interactions among diverse economic agents in trade and production, the generation and elimination of profits and losses, the operation of the stock market and many other details of behaviour drawn from economic life. Thus the allegation, perpetuated by generations of commentators (e.g. Jaffé, 1971, p. 281; 1981, pp. 252–61), that Walras devoted his attention almost exclusively to the conditions of static equilibrium in an abstract model devoid of institutional detail, economic facts and dynamic behaviour, is a misrepresentation of his work.

Walras was partially responsible for that misrepresentation, because he sometimes referred to his general equilibrium model as 'static' without qualification, and contrasted it with what he called 'the dynamic point of view', by which he sometimes meant the view taken in considering economic growth (Walras, 1954, p. 318). On the other hand, he also stated on many occasions that a dynamic theory is contained in his formal model of general equilibrium, and his usage will be followed in this essay. The 'static theory of exchange', he wrote, 'may be defined as the exposition of the equilibrium formula'. The 'dynamic theory', in contrast, which Walras claimed to have been the first to explore, is 'the demonstration of the attainment of that equilibrium through the play of the raising and lowering of prices' (Walras [1895], 1965, vol. 2, p. 630). Similarly, in responding to Irving Fisher's criticism that he had not considered time, Walras pointed out that that was true only of his exposition of the conditions of static equilibrium, and that his theory of production, for example, is given a dynamic treatment in lesson 20 (Walras, 1889) of the *Eléments* (Walras to Fisher, 28 July 1892, L 1064). In his first model of the dynamics of production, which he espoused from 1873 to 1899, disequilibrium production and use of consumer commodities and new capital goods occur during the course of the equilibrating process and are part of it. That he never abandoned most of the language describing this model explains why the 1926 edition of the *Eléments* can be cited in reference to it. In the second model, introduced in 1899 (Walras, 1899, p. 103) and inserted into the *Eléments* in 1900, he excluded those disequilibrium phenomena. In both models, and in all his work, he described the equilibrating process as one of *tâtonnement*, which means 'groping', to emphasize that the equilibrium magnitudes of prices and quantities are not known by the participants during the disequilibrium phase but are found by repeated experiments. His use of the word in all contexts, followed in this essay, was made possible by its neutrality with respect to the presence or absence of disequilibrium transactions or production.

The third part of each of Walras's models is its conditions of equilibrium, and the fourth is its comparative statics.

Theory of exchange. Walras was concerned in this theory with the determination of the equilibrium prices of commodities and the quantities of commodities exchanged. Setting forth the structure of exchange markets, he assumed that the preferences of the traders and the aggregate amounts of the commodities they hold in each market are given. Until constructing his fourth model, he abstracted from the use of money and assumed that commodities are exchanged directly for each other. The participants in exchange markets include brokers, agents, professional traders, retailers, wholesalers, the owners of the factors of production in their capacities as demanders of commodities, and entrepreneurs, who supply and demand commodities. The supply and demand functions are reciprocally related (Walras, 1954, pp. 96–7). Given a trader's demand curve for A, its price times the related number of units he wants to buy is his supply of B expressed as a function of the price of A in terms of B. Observing what happens to the areas of the rectangles under the demand curve for A as its price rises, Walras deduced that the quantity supplied of B initially rises and then falls. In the same way, a trader's supply of A can be derived from his demand for B. Walras summed the individual demand and supply curves respectively in the market for A to obtain the market curves, and similarly for B. It will be seen that he adapted and extended this analysis of the dependence of the supply of one commodity upon the demand for another when he took up the question of multi-commodity exchange. Walras also assumed that, as in the 19th-century bourse, in each market the rule is enforced that disequilibrium transactions are not allowed (Walras, 1880a, p. 461; 1880b, p. 78; 1954, p. 85).

To explain demand and infuse his model of exchange (Walras, 1869/1870) with purposive action, Walras developed a theory of preferences shortly before 1872 in which he assumed that traders want to maximize utility, that utilities are independent and additive, and that the marginal utility of a commodity is a decreasing function of the quantity acquired or consumed. Nevertheless, he was floundering in his attempts to relate utility to market behaviour, so he appealed for help to Antoine Paul Piccard, a professor of industrial mechanics at the Academy of Lausanne, who responded in 1872 by developing a model of utility maximization and deriving the individual demand function within it (Jaffé, 1965, vol. 1, pp. 308–11), thus meriting a part of the credit that has previously been given to Walras for that achievement. Everything then fell into place for Walras, and he proceeded to develop the view of economizing and maximizing behaviour that he imprinted on Continental neoclassical economics, extending the technique shown in the model to obtain the equilibrium conditions of the participants in a multi-commodity system (Walras 1954, lesson 12), and making utility maximization the driving force in each of his models.

The dynamic behaviour of Walras's exchange model is an automatic *tâtonnement* process in the sense that the path of the price is the unplanned outcome of market forces, but the process does not result from unconstrained human nature. It depends upon the rules, institutions and conditions devised and enforced by market authorities and by government (Walras, 1880a, 1880b; [1895], vol. 2, p. 632; and see 1954, p. 474). A price is initially cried at random (*crié au hasard*) (Walras 1877b, p. 127; 1954, p. 169), presumably by any of the traders or by a price-setter, and the participants subsequently follow the Walrasian pricing rule, namely that the price is changed in the same direction as the sign of the market excess demand for the commodity. Since preferences are constant, and since the rule against disequilibrium transactions ensures that the asset distribution remains unchanged during the equilibrating process, the initial supply and demand functions and, consequently, the equilibrium values of the system, are not affected by the disequilibrium behaviour of the traders. In an isolated market for two commodities the *tâtonnement* process therefore leads to the price and quantity that are the solutions to the market supply and demand equations that depend upon the traders' initial utility functions and initial asset holdings, whereupon the equilibrium amounts of each commodity are exchanged (Walras, 1954, p. 106, lessons 6, 9).

Markets are not isolated, however, in recognition of which Walras introduced the central feature of his contribution to economic science, namely an account, in his theory of exchange and in his other models, of the interrelationships among the markets for different commodities. If a trader has a commodity that he wants to trade for several others, the amount that he offers in any market is related to the amounts that he offers in the other markets, so the amount that he wishes to purchase or sell of any commodity is seen to be a function not only of his preferences, his income and the price of that commodity but, in principle, of the price of every other commodity; consequently, the market supply and demand quantities and the price in any market are dependent in part upon the prices in other markets (lesson 12). Moreover, Walras perceived that because a trader's demand for any commodity implies the offer of commodities in exchange for it, the sum of the values of a trader's planned purchases must equal the sum of the values of his planned sales. That relation is one way of stating the individual budget equation. By summing those equations, Walras also perceived that the sum of the net quantities demanded by all traders in a market times the price of the commodity, summed over all markets, is equal to the sum of the net quantities supplied by all traders in a market times the price of the commodity, summed over all markets. He therefore saw that the sum of the individual positive and negative excess demand quantities in all markets is identically zero, a relation that has come to be known as Walras's Law (p. 170, and §§ 118, 210, 244). He was able to identify that fundamental statement of the way that markets are interrelated in part because the device of the *numéraire*, a commodity in terms of which the values of all commodities are expressed (p. 161), made clear to him, as it had to Isnard, that there is exactly the right number of excess demands: in a system with n commodities, there are only n–1 independent market equations involving n–1 price ratios, but also only n–1 unknowns, because the price of the *numéraire*, the nth commodity, in terms of itself is unity (pp. 161–2, 241).

The interdependence of markets, Walras explained, gives rise to the major problem of general equilibrium analysis, which is whether a system of markets that is initially in disequilibrium will tend towards a position of equilibrium. As the price is, for example, adjusted downwards in the market for one commodity when there is initially a negative excess demand for it, the excess demands for other commodities will be affected. Do their markets then become closer to equilibrium or further from it? When their prices change in response to the altered conditions, the equilibrium in the first market will be disrupted. Will its subsequent adjustment aid or impede the equilibrating process taking place in other markets? Walras claimed that he had shown that the answer to those questions is that the market system converges to general equilibrium as a result of the Walrasian pricing rule (pp. 172, 179–80).

Walras then specified the conditions that prevail in the static equilibrium of exchange of a multi-market system. The ratio of the *raretés*, or marginal utilities, of any two commodities is equal to the ratio of their prices, and the price of any commodity in terms of another commodity is equal to the ratio of the prices of those two commodities in terms of any third commodity (p. 157). Those conditions are satisfied when the quantities supplied and demanded of each commodity are equal (p. 172).

Finally, Walras briefly examined some features of the comparative statics of the exchange model (pp. 147–9). He shifted the utility curves for a commodity and determined that its equilibrium price changes in the same direction as the shift in the curves. He then successively increased and decreased the traders' endowments of a commodity and determined that its equilibrium price successively decreases and increases.

Theory of production. In this model Walras was concerned with the determination of the equilibrium prices of productive services and the equilibrium rates of output of the quantities of consumer commodities. Setting forth the structure of the model, Walras first identified the market for productive services, in which he assumed that the amounts of economic resources and their services are given. The demanders of productive services are the entrepreneurs. Their ultimate aim is to maximize utility, which they achieve through maximizing profits. In their capacities as managers of firms, they combine productive services and materials in proportions that are determined by what Walras called the technical coefficients of production. The coefficients, which he assumed to be fixed in his formal general equilibrium theory, indicate the amount of each of the inputs that is used to make a unit of output. With fixed coefficients and given prices of the productive services, the average cost is constant as the firm's output varies. If any of those prices change, the average cost curve shifts in the same direction. The suppliers of productive services are workers, who own personal faculties; landlords, who own natural resources; and capitalists, who own capital goods or provide capital funds (Walras, 1877b, p. 218; 1954, pp. 214–15). Their aim is to maximize utility, which motivates them to demand income from the entrepreneurs. Capital goods are specific items of real capital; capital funds, raised by the sale of shares on the bourse, constitute fluid and mobile purchasing power which can be used to acquire economic resources to construct different kinds of particular physical capital (Walras, 1954, pp. 270, 311). Walras referred to the three sources of services as different types of capital because they all endure through time and produce a flow of services, but in this entry the unqualified word 'capital' or the term 'capital goods' will mean durable, man-made, inanimate instruments of production.

Walras then identified the market for consumer commodities. The suppliers of these are the entrepreneurs. The demanders are the workers, landlords, and capitalists acting in their roles as consumers, motivated in their purchases by the desire to maximize utility. They pay for them with the incomes that they have been paid by the entrepreneurs. Walras assumed that in the markets for productive services and consumer goods all resources are highly mobile, and that entrepreneurs have good knowledge of the profitability or unprofitability of producing any particular commodity.

The *tâtonnement* in the production model is principally the outcome of the actions of entrepreneurs, who are purely intermediaries that buy productive services, semi-finished goods and raw materials, and sell services and finished goods to consumers (lesson 21, and pp. 426–7; Walker, 1986). The payment that they receive in disequilibrium for their entrepreneurial activity is profit, which Walras defined on a per unit basis as the price of output minus its average cost. An entrepreneur may undertake the functions of other factors of production – he may also, for example, be a capitalist or a manager of the firm – and ordinarily he has to do so, but his role as buyer and seller is a distinct one (Walras, 1954, p. 222). One aspect of the *tâtonnement* occurs in the production and sale of consumer goods. It converges to equilibrium as entrepreneurs increase or decrease their output (p. 247) because the change in the output of a product has a direct effect on its price that is unidirectional, whereas the unidirectional changes that it induces in the output of other products has only indirect effects on its price, and because the latter more or less cancel each other out by being some in one direction and some in another (p. 246). 'The [resulting] system of new quantities of manufactured products and of new selling prices is thus closer to equilibrium than the old one; and we have only to continue the process of groping to approach still more closely to equilibrium' (p. 246). The other aspect of the *tâtonnement* occurs in the market for productive services and is a process of groping for the equilibrium amounts of resources employed in different industries. Disequilibrium quantities of productive services are hired and used during the process, and disequilibrium quantities of consumer goods are produced (Walras, 1877b, pp. 254, 264; 1889, pp. 234–5, 240–1, 249–50, 280; 1896a, pp. 235, 240–1, 249–50, 280). As long as the quantities supplied and demanded are unequal, prices and rates of production continue to be changed.

The *tâtonnements* in the markets for productive services and for consumer goods are interrelated. If the consumers' demand for a commodity increases, the quantities demanded and supplied become equal at a high price because the supply is initially highly inelastic. The price of the product then exceeds its cost of production, so the entrepreneurs in the industry make profits. Attracted by the prospect of doing the same, other entrepreneurs enter it, and existing firms increase their output. As the demands for productive services increase, their prices are bid up, which raises the average cost of production. As the supply of output function changes so that more output would be offered at each possible price, the price in the exchange market for the commodity is lowered by the entrepreneurs in an effort to dispose of the entire flow of output. Thus the average cost rises and the price falls (Walras, 1954, p. 253). If demand decreases for a commodity, its price falls below the average cost of production and the entrepreneurs make losses. This leads some of them to leave the industry and some of them to diminish the output of their firms. The prices of the productive services fall as the demand for them decreases, which lowers the average cost of production. As less output is offered, its price tends to be forced up. Thus the average cost falls and the price rises (p. 253).

Walras concluded that whether the demand for a commodity increases or decreases, the average cost of production and the price of the commodity become equal, whereupon equilibrium is reached and the *tâtonnement* ends. It follows that in the equilibrium of production the entrepreneur obtains neither profit nor loss (Walras, 1877b, p. 232; 1954, p. 225). This is Walras's concept of the zero-profit entrepreneur. The equilibrium, Walras stressed, is a theoretical notion. It is the normal state of the market in the sense that it is the one to which the variables perpetually and automatically tend in a regime of free competition (Walras, 1954, p. 224). Since it implicitly contains the equilibrium of exchange (p. 224), it is characterized by the additional conditions that the quantities supplied and demanded of each consumer commodity are equal and that the quantities supplied and demanded of each productive service are equal. A stable circular flow is established in which the total cost equals the total revenue in each firm, the incomes received from the entrepreneurs by the owners of the factors of production equal the revenues earned by the firms, and those incomes are spent on consumer goods by the owners of the factors of production. Walras's theory of production therefore showed how input and output markets are linked together.

Walras then considered variations in some of the parameters of the production model. If the marginal utility curves for a commodity shift up, he reasoned, its price in terms of the *numéraire* increases. If the marginal utility curves shift down, the opposite occurs. If the quantity of a product or service possessed by the holders changes, its price changes in the opposite direction (p. 260).

Theory of capital formation and credit. In this theory Walras first examined the determination of the prices of land and personal faculties, as distinct from the prices of their services. The aggregate supply of land is perfectly inelastic, and its price is simply its gross income divided by the rate of net income (pp. 270, 309). The number of workers is a given condition so far as economic science is concerned, and the price of a worker is equal to his gross income minus the cost of replacing and insuring him, divided by the rate of net income. Workers are not bought and sold, however, so their prices are virtual (p. 271). Since the prices of the services of capital goods are explained in Walras's production model, and since he assumed a fixed relationship between capital goods and the amounts of their services, his theory of capital is concerned with the determination of the amounts and prices of capital goods themselves and the determination of their rate of net income. Capital is formed by capitalists saving funds and, most commonly, lending them to entrepreneurs (p. 270), who purchase capital goods, earn revenue from their use and repay the loans (Walras, 1883, p. 113; 1954, p. 290, §§ 190, 208, 235). Walras's identification of that process explains why he inserted the word 'credit' into the name of his capital-goods model, but obviously he did not develop a true theory of credit within it, because he did not introduce credit extended by banks. Some capitalists prefer to own capital goods, so Walras assumed occasionally that they acquire them directly in physical form (Walras, 1954, p. 289), and assumed frequently that they acquire them through buying stock certificates (p. 289). In each case, the physical capital is used by entrepreneurs, so 'the demand for new capital goods comes from entrepreneurs who manufacture products and not from capitalists who create savings' (p. 270). The entrepreneurs purchase the particular kinds of capital goods that are profitable, with the result that the kinds that are produced and used reflect the structure of demand for consumer commodities (pp. 225, 276, 303; 1871, p. 36).

The net saving of the capitalists equals aggregate income minus aggregate consumption, minus the depreciation and insurance costs of capital goods. A positive, zero or negative excess of aggregate income over aggregate consumption was introduced by Walras into his capital-goods model in 1900 through the concept of a fictional commodity (E) constituted of perpetual annuity shares, a concept that he added without eliminating his references to the purchasing of stock certificates and commercial paper. Apart from the latter, it appears that Walras therefore wished to express aggregate savings as a single homogenous quantity – the demand for E – whereas he treated investment as the construction of heterogenous capital goods and viewed it as reaching equilibrium through adjustments in the markets for those different capital goods (pp. 275–6, 308). Each perpetual share pays one unit of *numéraire* per year, and its price, determined by supply and demand, is the reciprocal of the rate of interest. If people want an additional amount of interest income, they provide savings through purchasing new perpetual shares, and the *numéraire*-capital that they pay for them is used by entrepreneurs to buy productive services and materials that are transformed into new capital goods (274–6, 309); and if net saving is positive, the economy grows.

The *tâtonnement* in the capital-goods market is a disequilibrium-production process (Walras, 1877b, pp. 295–7, 300, 304; 1889, pp. 280, 284–94; 1896a, pp. 280, 284–94; 1954, pp. 287–91, §§ 258–60), one aspect of which takes place in the stock market and the other in the course of the production of capital goods. In the stock market, which is the market for new capital goods, each capitalist attempts to maximize utility by saving and acquiring more stocks that have relatively high yields and less of those with lower yields (Walras, 1954, p. 289), with the result that the total value of new capital goods and the excess of income over consumption both move in the same direction as prices. It follows, Walras maintained, that the tendency of the change in prices to destroy the equality between the total value of new capital goods and the excess of income over consumption is weaker than the tendency of the change in the rate of net income to bring the total value of new capital goods and the excess of income over consumption into equality with each other. 'Thus the system involving the new rate of net income and the new prices will be closer to equilibrium than the old system; and it is only necessary to continue the process of groping for the system to move still more closely to equilibrium' (p. 288).

In the production of capital goods, entrepreneurs acquire more capital goods that yield relatively high returns, and diminish their use of capital goods that yield lower returns. As a consequence, during the *tâtonnement* the net rate of return on all capital goods tends toward equality (p. 273). If profits are being made from the production of capital goods in an industry, new entrepreneurs enter it, and those already in it increase their rate of production. As a result they drive up the prices of productive services, which causes the average cost to rise towards equality with the price of the capital good. If losses are incurred, entrepreneurs diminish production. As a result, they drive down the prices of productive services, which causes the average cost to fall toward equality with the price of the capital good (pp. 292–3). It is probable, Walras maintained, that the effects of changes in the output of a new capital good that tend to cause equality between its average cost and its price will be stronger than the contrary effect of interrelated changes in the output of other capital goods, so the process converges to equilibrium (p. 293).

The equilibrium conditions in the formation of new capital goods are expressed in the lengthy analysis that Walras called the theorem on the maximum utility of new capital goods, which he regarded as crowning and confirming his entire theoretical system (Walras to H.S. Foxwell, 16 December 1888, L 859; see Walker, 1984b). He initially assumed that new capital goods do not require amortization or insurance, but then he made the realistic assumption that capital goods wear out and are subject to accidents. The net rate of income to a particular capital good is then given by the gross income it earns minus amortization and insurance costs, divided by the price of the capital good. In equilibrium each trader maximizes utility by holding the quantities of capital goods that make the ratio of the marginal utility of each capital good to its price equal for all his capital goods, a single price for any type of capital good prevails, and because of the adjustment of yields and capital good prices, the net rate of income derived from every capital good is the same (Walras, 1889, p. 306; and see 1954, p. 305). That rate is the rate of interest, and its equilibrium value equates aggregate saving and investment (Walras, 1889, p. 280; 1954, pp. 276, 281, 300, 305). Through this analysis Walras believed he had seen behind the veil of money or *numéraire* and discovered the real determinants of that rate. It is manifested in the banking system, he argued, but it is determined in the stock market. It is the ratio of net profit to the price of a share of stock, which in equilibrium equals the common ratio of the net price of capital services to the price of the good that yields them (Walras, 1954, p. 290). In equilibrium the prices of well-maintained old capital goods are equal to the prices of the same kinds of new capital goods, so the equilibrium prices of all capital goods are equal to the ratios of their net incomes to the rate of net income. Finally, the price of every capital good equals its average cost (pp. 301–5, 309).

Walras then turned to the comparative statics of the capital goods market (lesson 28). If the price that has to be paid for the services of a capital good increases or decreases as a result of a parametric change, the price of the capital good itself increases or decreases. Its price also varies inversely with the rate of depreciation and with the rate of the insurance premium. If the rate of net income changes, the prices of all capital goods change in the same direction (pp. 309–10). If the utility curves for net income shift up or down, the rate of net income changes in the opposite direction. If the quantity of net income varies, the rate of net income varies in the same direction. If utility functions and the quantity of net income both vary in such a way that the marginal utilities remain unchanged, the rate of net income also remains unchanged (p. 307).

Theory of money and circulation. Walras wanted to design the structure of this model on 'exactly the same terms and in precisely the same way' as in the models of exchange, production and capital formation (p. 42). He therefore described the functions of money and the formation of money prices on the assumption that there is no uncertainty in equilibrium, and consequently that the dates and monetary value of future purchases and sales are known (pp. 317–18). Money is one type of circulating capital; the other is circulating physical capital. Replacing his initial formulation in terms of an equation of exchange that had anticipated Irving Fisher's (Walras, 1877b, pp. 180–81), Walras asserted that circulating physical capital yields utility from its 'service of availability' – that is, by being readily available – and money provides, by proxy, the same service of availability as the commodity that it is destined to purchase and yields the same utility as that service. All economic agents try to hold utility-maximizing amounts of money and circulating physical capital (Walras, 1954, pp. 320–1). The latter, held by consumers and entrepreneurs, is acquired with money, so the essential concern of Walras's model of circulating capital reduces to the demand for and supply of money and its price: an individual has utility functions for the services of availability of commodities and perpetual net income, 'not *in kind*, but *in money*' (p. 320). Entrepreneurs and some consumers have net demands for cash balances because of the non-synchronization of payments and receipts (pp. 319, 321; 1886, pp. 40–44); that is, income received between the present and the date of a future payment is for many firms and people insufficient to provide enough cash for it. Savers make some of their balances available as loans through buying commercial paper or common stocks or perpetual annuity shares or through deposits in banks (Walras, 1954, pp. 318–20). The aggregate gross supply of money is the total stock issued by the monetary authority in the case of a fiat money economy, and is the amount of circulating coin in the case of a commodity-money economy (pp. 321–4).

If money is the *numéraire*, which is in fact the case, its price is unity and the price of its service is the rate of interest (pp. 320, 327). In one passage the latter was defined by Walras as the price of the service of cash balances held for the acquisition of fixed capital, and the rate of discount as the price of the service of cash balances held for the acquisition of circulating physical capital (p. 332), but he did not develop that analysis nor modify the rest of his exposition in the light of it. Accordingly, Walras's position was that, given the flows of receipts and purchases, the individual gross and net demand for cash balances and the individual net supply of them are functions of the rate of interest. The sum of the individual net demands for money is the aggregate demand function, and the sum of the individual net supplies of money is the aggregate supply function (pp. 320–21).

The *tâtonnement* in the money market explains how the rate of interest and the equilibrium aggregate net quantities of cash balances supplied and demanded are determined (pp. 325, 327). The rate of interest changes according to the Walrasian pricing rule. When the excess quantity demanded of cash balances is positive, the rise in the rate decreases the quantity demanded of cash balances by consumers and entrepreneurs by increasing the cost of the service of availability that money provides, and also decreases the quantity demanded by entrepreneurs by causing a fall in profits and hence in the desired rate of production. The rise in the rate of interest also causes the net quantity of cash balances that savers want to supply to increase. If the desired supply of cash exceeds the desired demand at the current rate of interest, the opposite effects occur (p. 333). The *tâtonnement* continues until the equilibrium price of the service of availability of money is found – namely, the price that equates the net and therefore the gross quantities supplied and demanded of cash balances – whereupon the money market reaches equilibrium (Walras, 1889, pp. 379–81; 1899, p. 96; 1900, pp. 297–319; 1954, pp. 315–33). The equilibrium prices of all commodities in terms of money are given by its role as *numéraire* and by the workings of the entire model that determine the ratio of exchange between each commodity and the *numéraire*. In general equilibrium, the price of all money held by different individuals for different purposes is the same (Walras, 1954, p. 326). Moreover, because an underlying influence upon the rate of interest on money is the value productivity of physical capital, an influence exerted through variations in the volume of funds invested, the equilibrium rate on money is the same as the equilibrium rate of net income determined in the market for capital. There is therefore equality in the rate of net income from all capital goods and real and monetary circulating capital (p. 323).

Walras then considered the comparative statics of the model. He changed the utility functions for the service of money and deduced that the *rareté* or value of the service of money changes in the same direction. He changed the quantity of money and deduced that the *rareté* or value of the service of money changes in the opposite direction, and that all prices change in the same direction without any alterations in relative prices (p. 333). The remainder of Walras's discussion of monetary comparative statics is concerned with a commodity-money economy, taking up such topics as the mining of precious metals and the melting of coins.

The elimination of irrevocable disequilibrium behaviour. A problem of internal consistency in Walras's disequilibrium-production model is that the production of consumer goods and capital goods at disequilibrium prices changes some of the conditions that he postulated are constant in constructing the equations of general equilibrium, namely the stocks of goods in exchange and the amounts of capital goods and services. The consequences of those changes spread throughout Walras's model. With each different distribution of the stocks of consumer goods produced during the course of the disequilibrium-production *tâtonnement*, the traders' net supply and demand functions change. No disequilibrium transactions occur in exchange, but each batch of commodities traded in each particular market while the economy is undergoing adjustments in production ordinarily has a different price, and frequently the equilibrating process in a particular market is interrupted by the appearance of new stocks. Each different disequilibrium rate of production and sales of capital goods changes their prices and the amounts of capital-good services that are offered and their prices, and therefore changes average costs, profits and the rate of net income. Disequilibrium hiring of productive services results in the payment of disequilibrium incomes, which changes the demand for consumer goods and, adding its impact to that of the varying rate of interest, changes the supply of saving. The result of these and other disequilibrium phenomena is that the model proceeds along a path of growth that has no relation to the values determined by Walras's equation system.

Walras's solution to this problem was to eliminate disequilibrium production by devising a *tâtonnement* of *ex ante* behaviour in which the intentions of economic agents are reconciled. He assumed that at any quoted price the suppliers and demanders of productive services and capital goods write down their offers on pieces of paper. These markers are *good for* the indicated amounts if the market quantities supplied and demanded are equal, just as a bond carries a pledge, and so Walras called them *bons*, or pledges. Although he did not describe the mechanism of ascertaining the market supply and demand quantities, he asserted that if the aggregate desired quantities are not equal, another price is cried in accordance with the Walrasian rule, and the participants revise their pledges (Walras, 1899, p. 103; 1900, pp. 215, 260; 1954, pp. 242, 282). Walras's model of exchange already contained pledging behaviour, inasmuch as the traders' offers are pledges to trade particular amounts provided that the price that is cried is one at which the quantities supplied and demanded are equal, although the traders, being face to face in each particular market, have no need to write their offers down. To call the entire formal general equilibrium model that Walras presented in 1900 his *pledges model* is therefore consistent with the character of its various parts. Since in it Walras eliminated disequilibrium production and acquisition of consumer goods and new capital goods, and since he had never permitted disequilibrium transactions in exchange, none of the parameters of his system of equations of general equilibrium undergoes endogenously induced changes during the *tâtonnement* phase of behaviour. Walras believed that the equilibrium is therefore the one given by the solutions to that system, and that his new version of *tâtonnement* in production converges to it for the same general reasons as the old one.

Another problem of consistency in Walras's work arises from his assumption that there is aggregate net saving and investment. On the one hand, his equations are constructed on the assumption that the amount of capital services is the fixed amount with which the economy, initially in disequilibrium, embarks upon its equilibrating path, an amount that is a fixed proportion of the constant amount of capital goods in use during the *tâtonnement* process. On the other hand, the use of net additions to the stock of capital goods, even if there is no production during the *tâtonnement* process, changes the capital-goods and services component of the economic resources parameter, with ramifications that alter some of the other nominal parameters and all the variables of the model, thus preventing the solutions of Walras's equations from materializing as its equilibrium values.

Walras's solution to this problem was to assume that new capital goods are not used. This led him to define three phases of the economy. First, there is 'the phase of preliminary gropings towards the establishment of equilibrium in principle' (Walras, 1954, p. 319). Second, there is 'the static phase in which equilibrium is effectively established *ab ovo* as regards the quantity of productive services and products made available during the period considered, under the stipulated conditions, and without any changes in the data of the problem' (p. 319). This means that the economy 'remains [for the time being] *static* because of the fact that the new capital goods play no part in the economy until later in a period subsequent to the one under consideration' (p. 283). Third, there is 'a dynamic phase in which equilibrium is constantly being disturbed by changes in the data and is constantly being re-established' (p. 319). The new capital goods, both fixed and circulating, Walras wrote, 'are made available during the second phase' but 'are not put to use until the third phase'. When they are used, however, 'the first change in the data of our problem' occurs (p. 319), and the economy begins to grow, tracing out a moving equilibrium to which Walras's formal general equilibrium model is seen as a prelude.

Economic growth. Walras did not develop a complete model of economic growth, but he examined two aspects of the topic. One was the possible dynamization of his formal general equilibrium model in the sense of introducing endogenous variations in its parameters. He was led to speculate about that subject by the consideration that the equilibrium identified in his formal theory is never reached in reality because *tâtonnement* takes time, and consequently parameters such as preferences and the amount of labour change before equilibrium is reached (p. 380; and see p. 224). In order to take account of this situation:

> we need only suppose the data of the problem, viz. the quantities possessed, the utility or want curves, etc., to vary as a function of *time*. The *fixed* equilibrium will then be transformed into a *variable* or *moving* equilibrium, which re-establishes itself automatically as soon as it is disturbed (p. 318).

Walras did not analyse that moving equilibrium or 'continuous market' (p. 380), but he briefly explained that when the parameters become variables, annual production and consumption change continually with them. Money, workers and goods are used up and are produced. Net new capital goods come into existence and are put to use, and circulating capital is borrowed by entrepreneurs from the capitalists in the form of short-term loans of money that mature immediately after the sale of the products (p. 319).

The other aspect of growth that Walras examined was 'the laws of the variation of prices in a progressive economy'

(p. 382), or some of the features of alternative paths of economic growth. For this task he first defined economic progress as the substitution of capital services in place of land services in given production functions (p. 383). The substitution implies variable coefficients of production, and to introduce these Walras used the theory of marginal productivity. He did not originate that theory nor claim to have done so. In fact, Hermann Amstein, a mathematician at Lausanne, developed it in 1877 (Amstein to Walras, 6 January 1877, L 364; translated by Walker, 1983, pp. 205–6). Walras did not understand or use Amstein's work, however, and the major credit for the theory of marginal productivity that first appeared in the *Eléments* in 1896 (Appendix III) must be given to Enrico Barone (1895). Walras then defined technical progress as changes in production functions, including the introduction of entirely new processes, but he did not analyse it, beyond concluding that it contributes, along with economic progress, to ensuring that output increases without limit in a progressive economy (Walras, 1954, p. 387). He also examined, in a highly general way, how the prices of products and services vary with different amounts of capital and magnitudes of the population (pp. 389–91). His principal conclusion was that the rate of net income falls as the stock of capital grows, the proximate causes of the process being rising rents and falling prices of capital services.

ECONOMIC POLICIES

Walras was greatly interested in the economic problems of his day and in socio-economic reform. His normative convictions, derived from his father's philosophy of society and justice, were a mixture of conventional 19th-century liberalism and the doctrine of state interventionism (Walras, 1896b, pp. 3–263). Like many writers, each with different views, he bestowed the title of 'natural law' upon the principles of justice that he considered desirable, and so he might be called a natural-law philosopher or casuist. Nevertheless, he was not a natural-law economist. He did not believe that behind observable facts is a structure of economic laws that are divinely ordained, or that are peculiarly in tune with the structure of the universe and human aspirations, or that are ceaselessly at work so that violations of them can only result in friction. Nor did he construct his economic model with the conscious intention of expressing his normative views. Sharply distinguishing normative and positive economics, he designed his theories for the purpose of understanding economic reality (Walker, 1984a) and presented his normative work explicitly as such and carefully segregated it from his economic theories (Walras, 1896b, 1898).

Walras's policy recommendations ranged over natural monopolies, which he believed should be nationalized; prices, which he believed should be stabilized by a monetary authority; bimetallism, which he believed had both advantages and disadvantages; the stock market, which he believed should be regulated by the state in order to improve its organization and ensure its integrity; taxes, which he believed were unjust and confiscatory and should be abolished; and land, which he believed should be purchased by the state and rented to private users, thereby providing it with revenue (Walras, 1905b, pp. 272–3). Arguing that his advocacy of nationalization of land and natural monpolies was based upon a scientific analysis, Walras called himself a 'scientific socialist'.

EVALUATION

The first major criticism of Walras's work relates to the structure and dynamic behaviour of his pledges model. In it, in disequilibrium, entrepreneurs consult the market aggregates of pledges to buy and sell and move from industry to industry and plan to create firms or to expand or contract their existing firms without actually hiring or spending or producing at all. Owners of productive services are imagined to offer their services repeatedly at disequilibrium prices without actually earning any income or consuming any goods or services. The entire system of interrelated markets is imagined to go through complex costless processes of information acquisition, price changes and changes in the demand and supply quantities that are pledged, all without anyone being allowed to agree to a single actual transaction or act of production or consumption, until the equilibrium set of prices has been found. An additional aura of unreality is imparted to this scheme by Walras abstracting from money throughout his theories of exchange, production and capital formation, and then by introducing it in such a way that it does not change their characteristics (Walras, 1954, pp. 319–24). In particular, by excluding uncertainty he eliminated consideration of much of the behaviour associated with money and portrayed it as making no difference in the properties of his model. That is not true of the role of money in the economy, a fact of which his writings on monetary policy reveal him to have been perfectly cognizant. Moreover, his concept of fictional perpetual annuity shares is a superfluity that further detracts from the verisimilitude of his models of capital formation and money. He should instead have elaborated upon the behaviour related to some of the major financial assets in which people actually invest. These various assumptions result in a model of a purely hypothetical economy that is so radically unlike any past or present economy as to fail to be useful as even a highly abstract analysis of economic behaviour. The reason for this situation is that the pledges model is designed to be consistent with certain mathematical conditions – that is, with the solutions of a set of equations – rather than being a set of assumptions and mathematical conditions designed to explain economic behaviour. It is a pity that Walras and most subsequent general equilibrium theorists adopted the pledges model and abandoned his robust and more realistic disequilibrium production model, for through its development lies the way to a more useful general equilibrium theory.

The second major criticism is that Walras was wrong to assert that he had proved that equilibrium exists and proved that the *tâtonnements* of his models converge to equilibrium. He should have been chided gently for making those erroneous claims but not castigated for his failure to give the proofs, because they were beyond the technical ability of any 19th-century economist (see Weintraub, 1983; van Daal, Henderiks and Vorst, 1985).

The third major criticism is that the alleged equilibrium of Walras's formal model is logically flawed. This has already been indicated with reference to his disequilibrium-production model of *tâtonnement*, and the present criticism refers to his pledges model. To construct a model with a genuine static equilibrium, which was his intention, Walras should have assumed that the capital stock is maintained but that there are no net additions to it. He could not, incidentally, have salvaged the solutions of his equations by supposing that the net addition to the capital stock in any year is so small relative to the previously existing stock that its effects in any year are negligible, because many of the economic processes within his model are long-run phenomena. Since he assumed that there are net additions to the capital stock, the equilibrium of his pledges model is of no significance because it cannot be actualized. It is factitious, existing only transitorily while his model is held in a state of arbitrarily suspended animation by the posulate that additions to the capital stock are not used – a *deus ex machina* that interrupts the incomplete workings of its endogenous processes. The instant the postulate is removed, the 'equilibrium' is ruptured and, through a dynamic process that is the antithesis of true equilibrium, many of the nominal parameters and all the variables of the model change, in the way indicated earlier in the discussion of the consequences of the use of net new capital goods. Any stationary equilibrium that the system may eventually reach is quite unlike the solutions to Walras's equations of general equilibrium, and if net new capital goods continue to be produced, the system follows a path of growth. Proofs of the existence of static equilibrium in pledges models in which net investment occurs are therefore invalid.

The fourth major criticism is that Walras's treatment of comparative statics was unsatisfactory because he did not consider some important parametric changes and did not adequately trace the consequences of the parametric changes that he did make, and therefore failed to explore the ramifications that his general equilibrium model was intended to identify. For example, in his theory of production he did not consider alternative values of the fixed coefficients of production, nor changes in the work and income preferences of the workers, nor in their numbers; and in his formal theory of the capital market he did not make parametric changes in the stock of capital goods that exists initially.

These criticisms cannot obscure the greatness of Walras's contribution. When he began his investigations in 1868, economics on the Continent was hardly a scientific pursuit but rather a mixture of normative prescriptions, classical theories expressed alongside protectionist doctrines, and commercial law. In England it was in the state exemplified by the work of J.S. Mill – with much that could be used as a basis for future investigations, but also without a clear view of the relationships of distribution and production, limited by a cost of production theory of value, and lacking a theory of supply and demand in multiple markets. The attitude of most of Walras's contemporaries was that, since economic behaviour involves preferences and the human will, it cannot be expressed in a rigid and deterministic set of algebraic relations. Walras changed all that, transforming economics and propelling it forward in a gigantic intellectual leap.

His contribution can be divided into two interrelated parts. One was that he constructed or refined or adapted to his purposes many of the fundamental building blocks of modern economic theory. Putting his pledges model aside, it can be seen that in this effort he accomplished an enormous amount of highly creative economic analysis, brilliantly structuring economic reality to bring many of its essential features into clear relief, in eight major original contributions to economic theory. First, he went far beyond the work of the other developers of the marginal utility theory by using it to analyse the behaviour and equilibrium in multiple markets of a variety of participants undertaking different economic functions, rather than confining the theory to the investigation of consumption and simple exchange. Second, he had clear priority in constructing the theory of exchange in multiple competitive markets. In that regard, his work was greatly in advance of his predecessors' and was replete with fruitful constructions, theorems and postulates, like the reciprocal relation of supply and demand, the device of a *numéraire*, the individual budget equation, Walras's Law, the theorem of equivalent distributions, and the laws of change of prices. Third, he constructed a theory of the firm and of market supply in which he appears to have developed independently the modern idea of a firm's production function, derived the equation for a firm's average cost, expressed the firm's offer of output mathematically, and aggregated the firm's supply functions to obtain the market supply in a particular industry. Fourth, he was the first to examine the question of the existence of equilibrium in a competitive multi-market system of exchange and production. Fifth, in his work on *tâtonnement* he initiated the study of the problem of the stability of competitive general equilibrium and contributed significantly to its understanding, with his most successful theorizing on the topic relating to a disequilibrium production economy. There is nothing in the literature before Walras's time nor until the time that his work was discussed by others that is even remotely like his examination of the process of convergence to equilibrium of a competitive multi-market system. Sixth, he developed a theory of the entrepreneur, of profits and of the allocation of resources that became the basis of Continental work on those topics (Pareto, 1896/7 passim; Pareto 1906/9, passim; Barone 1896, p. 145; Schumpeter [1911/26] 1961, p. 76; Schumpeter, 1954, p. 893; Walker, 1986). Seventh, Walras created a fruitful theory of capital, achieving an early formulation of the conditions for a Pareto optimum in capital markets. As in a number of his other investigations, his characteristic contribution was not to be the first to think of the problem but to be the first to structure it thoroughly and to provide a mathematical demonstration of the equilibrium conditions. Eighth, he developed a cash-balances theory of money which had great originality and has stimulated much valuable research (Marget, 1931; Marget, 1935; and see Walker, 1970, p. 696). Those eight areas of analysis were the core of neoclassical microeconomic theory and thus constituted much of the structure of knowledge that was the starting place for 20th-century economics.

The second part of Walras's contribution was his idea of the general equilibrium of the economic system and his concrete implementation of that idea through devising a system of equations to express it. By his work Walras demonstrated that it is possible in principle to set up a system of equations to describe the functional relationships and static equilibrium of a multi-market economy in which complex economic processes occur, thus accomplishing by the mid-1870s far more than any other economist had done in regard to building a model of the economic system as a whole, and more single-handedly in that regard than any other economist in the history of the discipline. He therefore provided a substantial beginning for the mathematical analysis of the interrelationships of all parts of the economy as it has developed since the 19th century.

The two parts of Walras's contribution are complementary aspects of a single theoretical whole. Other economists had helped in fashioning the building blocks that he used, but Walras's achievement was not only to develop them but to integrate them into a comprehensive model. To do him complete justice, it is necessary to appreciate the richness of the texture of his work resulting from the many aspects of economic life that he analysed, for without them his general equilibrium theory would be an empty and sterile mathematical shell; and it is necessary to appreciate the mathematical structure that he devised for the purpose of supporting and weaving together those accounts of economic processes, for without it their significance and place in the economic system would not have been fully revealed.

INFLUENCE

Walras's work was hardly noticed in France during the twenty-five years after 1874, and as late as 1934 his centennial elicited no conference on his work there. By the 1950s, however, the French attitude had changed towards Walras, as was ultimately symbolized by the creation in 1984 of the Centre Auguste et Léon Walras at the Université Lyon II. With the English, Walras's experience was also disappointing. His initial cordiality towards W.S. Jevons, as a fellow pioneer in mathematical economics, was dissipated by Jevons's failure to recognize Walras's contributions to the theory of exchange and to the construction of a complete theory of a competitive economy, and eventually Walras, quite unreasonably, came to regard Jevons as a plagiarist of his work (Walras to M. Pantaleoni, 17 August 1889, L 909). Similarly, Walras's relations with P.H. Wicksteed began well (Wicksteed to Walras, 1 December 1884, L 619) but deteriorated sharply when Wicksteed failed to give credit to those whom Walras considered to be the true originators of the theory of marginal productivity (Jaffé, 1965, L 1220, n. 3; Walras, 1896a, pp. 490–92). Walras felt neglected by Alfred Marshall, who mentioned him only thrice in the briefest of comments in the *Principles* (Marshall, 1890, 1920) and wrote not a word about Walras's development of general equilibrium theory. Walras also came to dislike Edgeworth for criticizing his theories of *tâtonnement*, capital goods and the entrepreneur (Walras to Gide, 3 November 1889, L 933, and 11 April 1891, L 1000; Walras to Pantaleoni, 5 January 1890, L 953). In general, Walras believed, the English had closed their minds to his theories and had become spiteful in their treatment of them (see Walker, 1970, pp. 699–70).

The extremity of the language with which Walras characterized the English was unjustified, because, although he had reason for disappointment with their neglect of his general equilibrium theory, Jevons (1879, preface) and Edgeworth (1889) had recognized valuable elements in his work, and he was the only living economist included in the first edition of Palgrave's *Dictionary of Political Economy* (Sanger, 1899). The fact is that Walras grew hypersensitive about the motives of his critics, the failure of the majority of economists to recognize the value and priority of his contributions, and the possibility of plagiarism of his ideas during the 1880s and 1890s. There had been two periods in his life, he complained, 'one during which I was a madman, and one during which everyone made my discoveries before me' (Walras, undated, in Walker, 1983, p. 203, n.54).

This account of Walras's disappointments should be balanced by a realization that his scientific labours had afforded him, 'up to a certain point, pleasures and joys like those that religion provides to the faithful' (Walras to Marie de Sainte Beuve, 15 December 1899, L 1432), and a recognition of the professional satisfactions that he increasingly experienced in the last two decades of his life. Maffeo Pantaleoni (1889), Enrico Barone ([1895], 1983, p. 186; 1896), and Vilfredo Pareto (Pareto to Walras, 15 October 1892, L 1077) contributed greatly toward giving Walras's work a secure place in Continental economics and thus ultimately in economics everywhere. In 1895 Pareto's appointment as Walras's successor to the chair of economics at Lausanne assured Walras that his doctrines would be perpetuated and developed, and the accessible literary presentations of Walras's ideas in Pareto's books (1896/7, 1906/9) began their widespread dissemination. Pareto borrowed most of the ideas of Walras that have been mentioned in this essay, using them as the basis for his contributions to the theories of general equilibrium, the monopolistic entrepreneur, capital, and production. Wilhelm Lexis, Ladislaus von Bortkiewicz and Eugen von Böhm-Bawerk gave Walras's theories serious attention. Knut Wicksell based his theory of price determination squarely upon Walras's work (J.G.K. Wicksell to Walras, 6 November 1893, L 1168), as did Karl Gustav Cassel (1903, 1918). Walras was given recognition in the United States: in 1892 he was made an honorary member of the American Economic Association, Irving Fisher praised his work (Fisher, 1892, p. 45; 1896), and H.L. Moore became his avowed disciple and explicator (Moore to Walras, 19 May 1909, enclosure to L 1747; Moore, 1929).

These manifestations of acceptance led Walras to believe he would ultimately triumph, and that enabled him to achieve a mental calmness (Walras to Marie de Sainte Beuve, 15 December 1899, L 1432; Walras to A. Aupetit, 28 May 1901, L 1485). 'Be assured of my serenity', he wrote to old friends in 1904, 'I have not the least doubt about the future of my method and even of my doctrine; but I know that success of this sort does not become clearly apparent until after the death of the author' (Walras to G. and L. Renard, 4 June 1904, L 1574). A strong indication of what the future would hold for his theories was given by the celebration of his jubilee in 1909 by the University of Lausanne, in the course of which he was honoured as the first economist to establish the conditions of general equilibrium, thus founding the School of Lausanne (Jaffé, 1965, L 1696, n. 5). His achievements were praised in a statement signed by 15 leading French scholars, including Charles Gide, Charles Rist, Georges Renard, Alfred Bonnet, A. Aupetit and François Simiand (enclosure to L 1747), and in communications from many others (Pareto to the Dean of the Faculty of Law of the University of Lausanne, 6 June 1909, L 1755; Schumpeter to Walras, 7 June 1909, L 1756). It is now clearly apparent that his prediction of great success was accurate, because his theory of general equilibrium, as improved by his contemporaries, has been given a great deal of attention and further development in the 20th century by writers such as Henry Schultz, John von Neumann, Abraham Wald, John R. Hicks, Oscar Lange, Paul A. Samuelson, Lionel McKenzie, Gerard Debreu, Don Patinkin, Kenneth Arrow, Frank Hahn and Michio Morishima (see Weintraub, 1983, 1986), and the filiations of Walras's ideas have become so numerous and dense as to be an integral and central part of the mainstream of modern economics. Thus his twofold achievement of developing particular theories and binding them together in a model of an entire economic system has given his work an influence on economic theory that has been durable and immense. For sheer genius and intuitive power in penetrating the veil of the chaos of immediately perceived experience and divining the underlying structure of fundamental economic relationships and their extensive interdependencies and consequences, Walras has been surpassed by no one.

DONALD A. WALKER

See also GENERAL EQUILIBRIUM; TÂTONNEMENT AND RECONTRACTING.

SELECTED WORKS

1858. *Francis Sauveur*. Paris: E. Dentu.

1860. *L'Economie politique et la justice*. Paris: Guillaumin.

1868. *Recherche de l'idéal social: Leçons publiques faites à Paris*. Paris: Guillaumin; and in Walras (1896).

1869–70. 2ᵉ tentative, 1869–1870. In Jaffé (1965), vol. 1, pp. 218–19.

1871. *Discours d'installation. Séance académique du 20 Octobre*. Lausanne: Académie de Lausanne.

1877a. *Théorie mathématique de la richesse sociale: quatre mémoires*. Paris: Guillaumin.

1874, 1877b. *Eléments d'économie politique pure; ou théorie de la richesse sociale*. 2 parts. Lausanne: L. Corbaz; Paris: Guillaumin; Bâsle: H. Georg.

1880a, b. La bourse, la spéculation et l'agiotage. *Bibliothèque Universelle et Revue Suisse* 5, March 1880a, 452–76; 6, April 1880b, 66–94.

1886. *Théorie de la monnaie*. Lausanne: Corbaz.
1889. *Eléments d'économie politique pure*. 2nd edn, Lausanne: F. Rouge; Paris: Guillaumin; Leipzig: Duncker & Humblot.
1893, 1904, 1909. Notice autobiographique. In Jaffé (1965), vol. 1, pp. 1–15.
1895. Enclosure by Léon Walras to Vilfredo Pareto. In Jaffé (1965), vol. 2, 628–32.
1896a. *Eléments d'économie politique pure*. 3rd edn, Lausanne: F. Rouge; Paris: F. Pichon; Leipzig: Duncker & Humblot.
1896b. *Etudes d'économie sociale (Théorie de la répartition de la richesse sociale)*. Lausanne: F. Rouge; Paris: F. Pichon.
1898. *Etudes d'économie politique appliquée (Théorie de la production de la richesse sociale)*. Lausanne: F. Rouge; Paris: F. Pichon.
1899. Equations de la circulation. *Bulletin de la Société Vaudoise des Sciences Naturelles*, June.
1900. *Eléments d'économie politique pure*. 4th edn. Lausanne: F. Rouge; Paris: F. Pichon.
1905a. Cournot et l'économique mathématique. *Gazette de Lausanne*, 13 July; and, except for a few deletions, in *Revue d'Economie Politique*, January–February, 1962.
1905b. Draft of a recommendation for a Nobel Peace Prize. In Jaffé (1965), vol. 3, 270–4.
1926. *Eléments d'économie politique pure*. Definitive edn. Paris: R. Picon & R. Durand-Auzias; Lausanne: F. Rouge.
1954. *Elements of Pure Economics*. Trans. and annotated by William Jaffé, Homewood, Ill.: Richard D. Irwin; London: Allen & Unwin.

BIBLIOGRAPHY

Barone, E. 1895. On a recent book by Wicksteed. Manuscript translated into English in Walker (1983), pp. 182–6.
Barone, E. 1896. Studi sulla distribuzione. *Giornale degli Economisti* 12, February, 107–55, 235–52.
Bertrand, J. 1883. Théorie des richesses. *Journal des Savants*, September.
Cassel, G. 1903. *Nature and Necessity of Interest*. London: Macmillan.
Cassel, G. 1918. *Theory of Social Economy*. New York: Harcourt, 1932.
Cournot, A.A. 1838. *Recherches sur les principes mathématiques de la théorie des richesses*. Paris: Hachette.
Edgeworth, F.Y. 1889. The mathematical theory of political economy. [Review of] *Eléments d'économie politique pure* by Léon Walras, *Nature* 40, 4 September, 434–6.
Fisher, I. 1892. Translator's note to Léon Walras, 'Geometrical theory of the determination of prices'. *Annals of the American Academy of Political and Social Science* 3, July, 45–7.
Fisher, I. 1896. [Review of] *Eléments d'économie politique pure. Troisième édition. Par Léon Walras....* [and of] *An Essay on the Co-ordination of the Laws of Distribution. By Philip H. Wicksteed.... Yale Review* 5(1), August, 222–3.
Isnard, A.N. 1781. *Traité des richesses, contenant l'analyse de l'usage des richesses en général et de leurs valeurs*. London and Lausanne: Grasset.
Jaffé, W. 1964. New light on an old quarrel: Barone's unpublished review of Wicksteed's 'Essay on the coordination of the laws of distribution and related documents.' *Cahiers Vilfredo Pareto* 3, 61–102; where necessary translated into English by Walker (1983).
Jaffé, W. (ed.) 1965. *Correspondence of Léon Walras and Related Papers*. 3 vols, Amsterdam: North-Holland.
Jaffé, W. 1969. A.N. Isnard, progenitor of the Walrasian general equilibrium model. *History of Political Economy* 1(1), Spring, 19–43; and in Walker, 1983.
Jaffé, W. 1971. Reflections on the importance of Léon Walras. In the P. Hennipman festschrift, *Schaarste en Welvaart*, ed. A. Heertje et al., Amsterdam: Stenfert Kroese, pp. 87–107; and in Walker (1983).
Jaffé, W. 1981. Another look at Léon Walras's theory of *tâtonnement*. *History of Political Economy* 13(2), Summer, 313–36; and in Walker (1983).
Jevons, W.S. 1879. *The Theory of Political Economy*. 2nd edn. London: Macmillan.
Marget, A.W. 1931. Léon Walras and the 'cash-balance approach' to the problem of the value of money. *Journal of Political Economy* 39(5), October, 569–600.
Marget, A.W. 1935. The monetary aspects of the Walrasian system. *Journal of Political Economy* 43(2), April, 145–86.
Marshall, A. 1890. *Principles of Economics*. London: Macmillan.
Moore, H.L. 1929. *Synthetic Economics*. New York: Macmillan.
Pantaleoni, M. 1889. *Principii de economia pura*. Florence: Barbèra.
Pareto, V. 1896–7. *Cours d'économie politique*. 2 vols, Lausanne: F. Rouge. Ed. G.-H. Bousquet and G. Busino, Geneva: Librairie Droz, 1964.
Pareto, V. 1906. *Manuale di economia politica*. Milan: Societá Editrice Libraria. Trans. from the Italian as *Manuel d'économie politique*. by Alfred Bonnet. Paris: V. Giard and E. Brière, 1909.
Poinsot, L. 1803. *Eléments de statique*. 8th edn, Paris: Bachelier, 1842.
Sanger, C.P. 1899. Walras, Marie Esprit Léon. In *Dictionary of Political Economy*, ed. R.H. Inglis Palgrave, London: Macmillan, vol. 3.
Say, J.-B. 1836. *Cours complet d'économie politique pratique, suivi des Melanges, Correspondance et Catéchisme d'économie politique*. 3rd. edn, Bruxelles: H. Dumont.
Schumpeter, J.A. 1912, 1926. *The Theory of Economic Development: An Inquiry into Profits, Capital, Credit, Interest, and the Business Cycle*. Trans. from the German by Redvers Opie, Cambridge, Mass.: Harvard University Press, 1934; reprinted New York: Oxford University Press, 1961.
Schumpeter, J.H. 1954. *History of Economic Analysis*. New York: Oxford University Press.
Van Daal, J., Henderiks, R.E.D. and Vorst, A.C.F. 1985. On Walras' model of general economic equilibrium. *Zeitschrift für Nationalökonomie* 45(3), 219–44.
Walker, D.A. 1970. Léon Walras in the light of his correspondence and related papers. *Journal of Political Economy* 78(4), Part I, July–August, 685–701.
Walker, D.A. (ed.) 1983. *William Jaffé's Essays on Walras*. Cambridge, New York: Cambridge University Press.
Walker, D.A. 1984a. Is Walras's theory of general equilibrium a normative scheme? *History of Political Economy* 16(3), Fall, 445–69.
Walker, D.A. 1984b. Walras and his critics on the maximum utility of new capital goods. *History of Political Economy* 16(4), Winter, 529–54.
Walker, D.A. 1986. Walras's theory of the entrepreneur. *De Economist* 134(1), 1–24.
Walras, A.A. 1831. *De la nature de la richesse et de l'origine de la valeur*. Paris: Johanneau.
Weintraub, E.R. 1983. On the existence of a competitive equilibrium: 1930–1954. *Journal of Economic Literature* 21(1), March, 1–39.
Weintraub, E.R. 1986. *General Equilibrium Analysis: Studies in Appraisal*. Cambridge: Cambridge University Press.

Walras's Law. Walras's Law (so named by Lange, 1942) is an expression of the interdependence among the excess-demand equations of a general-equilibrium system that stems from the budget constraint. Its name reflects the fact that Walras, the father of general-equilibrium economics, himself made use of this interdependence from the first edition of his *Eléments d' économie politique pure* (1874, §122) through the fourth (1900, §116), which edition is for all practical purposes identical with the definitive one (1926). I have cited §116 of this edition because it is the one cited by Lange (1942, p. 51, n.2), though in a broader context than Walras's own discussion there (see below). In this section, Walras presents the argument for an exchange economy. In accordance with his usual expository technique (cf. his treatment of the *tâtonnement*), he repeats the argument as he successively extends his analysis to deal first with a simple production economy and then with one in which capital formation also takes place (ibid., §§206 and 250, respectively).

For reasons that will become clear later, I shall derive Walras's Law in a more general – and more cumbersome – way than it usually has been. Basically, however, the derivation follows that of Arrow and Hahn (1971, pp. 17–21), with an admixture of Lange (1942) and Patinkin (1956, chs I–III and Mathematical Appendix 3:a).

Let x_i^h be the decision of household h with respect to good $i\ (i = 1, \ldots, n)$, where 'goods' also include services and financial assets (securities and money). If $x_i^h \geqslant 0$, it is a good purchased by the household; if $x_i^h < 0$, it is a good (mainly, labour or some other factor-service) sold. Similarly, let y_i^f be the decision of firm f with respect to good i; if $y_i^f \geqslant 0$, it is a good produced and sold by the firm (i.e., a product-output); if $y_i^f < 0$, it is a factor-input.

Assume that firm f has certain initial conditions (say, quantities of fixed factors of production) represented by the vector $\mathbf{k}^f$ and operates in accordance with a certain production function. Following Patinkin (1956), let us conduct the conceptual individual-experiment of confronting the firm with the vector of variables $\mathbf{v}$ (the nature of which will be discussed below) while keeping $\mathbf{k}^f$ constant and asking it to designate (subject to its production function) the amounts that it will sell or buy of the various goods and services. By repeating this conceptual experiment with different values of the respective elements of $\mathbf{v}$, we obtain the behaviour functions of firm f,

$$y_i^f = y_i^f(\mathbf{v}; \mathbf{k}^f) \quad (i = 1, \ldots, n). \tag{1}$$

For $y_i \geqslant 0$, this is a supply function; for $y_i < 0$, it is a demand function for the services of factors of production. Profits (positive or negative) of firm f are then

$$R^f = \sum_i p_i y_i^f(\mathbf{v}; \mathbf{k}^f), \tag{2}$$

Let d^{hf} represent the proportion of the profits of firm f received by the household h. Its total profits received are then $\Sigma_f d^{hf} R^f$ and its budget constraint is accordingly

$$\sum_i p_i x_i^h = \sum_f d^{hf} R^f, \tag{3}$$

which assumes that households correctly estimate the profits of firms (cf. Buiter, 1980, p. 7; I shall return to this point below). As with the firm, let us, *mutatis mutandis*, conduct individual-experiments with household h (with its given tastes), subject to its budget constraint (3) by varying the elements of $\mathbf{v}$, while keeping its initial endowment (represented by the vector $\mathbf{e}^h$) constant. This yields the behaviour functions

$$x_i^h = x_i^h(\mathbf{v}; \mathbf{e}^h) \quad (i = 1, \ldots, n). \tag{4}$$

For $x_i \geqslant 0$, this is a demand function for goods; for $x_i < 0$, it is a supply function (e.g., of factor-services).

Substituting from (2) and (4) into (3) then yields

$$\sum_i p_i x_i^h(\mathbf{v}; \mathbf{e}^h) = \sum_f d^{hf} \sum_i p_i y_i^f(\mathbf{v}; \mathbf{k}^f), \tag{5}$$

which holds identically for all $\mathbf{v}$, $\mathbf{e}^h$, $\mathbf{k}^f$ and p_i. Summing up over all households then yields

$$\sum_h \sum_i p_i x_i^h(\mathbf{v}; \mathbf{e}^h) = \sum_h \sum_f d^{hf} \sum_i p_i y_i^f(\mathbf{v}; \mathbf{k}^f), \tag{6}$$

which we rewrite as

$$\sum_i p_i \sum_h x_i^h(\mathbf{v}; \mathbf{e}^h) = \sum_i p_i \sum_f \left(\sum_h d^{hf}\right) y_i^f(\mathbf{v}; \mathbf{k}^f). \tag{7}$$

On the assumption that firm f distributes all its profits,

$$\sum_h d^{hf} = 1 \quad \text{for all } f, \tag{8}$$

so that (7) reduces to

$$\sum_i p_i[X_i(\mathbf{v}; \mathbf{E}) - Y_i(\mathbf{v}; \mathbf{K})] = 0 \tag{9}$$

identically in all $\mathbf{v}$, $\mathbf{E}$, $\mathbf{K}$ and p_i, where

$$X_i(\mathbf{v}; \mathbf{E}) = \sum_h x_i^h(\mathbf{v}; \mathbf{e}^h) \quad \text{and} \quad Y_i(\mathbf{v}; \mathbf{K}) = \sum_f y_i^f(\mathbf{v}; \mathbf{k}^f) \tag{10}$$

represent the aggregate demand and supply functions, respectively, for good i; $\mathbf{E}$ is a vector containing all the $\mathbf{e}^h$; and $\mathbf{K}$ a vector containing all the $\mathbf{k}^f$. If $X_i(\mathbf{v}; \mathbf{E}) - Y_i(\mathbf{v}; \mathbf{K}) > 0$, an excess demand is said to exist in the market; if $X_i(\mathbf{v}; \mathbf{E}) - Y_i(\mathbf{v}; \mathbf{K}) < 0$, an excess supply; and if $X_i(\mathbf{v}; \mathbf{E}) = Y_i(\mathbf{v}, \mathbf{K})$, equilibrium.

Equation (9) is a general statement of Walras's Law. Its most frequent application in the literature has been (as in Walras's *Eléments* itself) to the general-equilibrium analysis of a system of perfect competition, in which the behaviour functions of firms are derived from the assumption that they maximize profits subject to their production function; and those of households are derived from the assumption that they maximize utility subject to their budget constraint. In this context, the vector $\mathbf{v}$ is the price vector $(p_1, \ldots, p_{n-1})$, with the nth good being money and serving as numéraire (i.e., $p_n = 1$), so that there are only $n - 1$ prices to be determined. Ignoring for simplicity vectors $\mathbf{E}$ and $\mathbf{K}$, which remain constant in the conceptual market-experiment, equation (9) then becomes

$$\sum_{i=1}^{n} p_i[X_i(p_1, \ldots, p_{n-1}) - Y_i(p_1, \ldots, p_{n-1})] = 0 \quad \text{identically in the } p_i. \tag{11}$$

(Though it does not bear on the present subject, I should note that under the foregoing assumptions, and in the absence of money illusion, each of the demand and supply functions is homogeneous of degree zero in $p_1, \ldots, p_{n-1}$ and in whatever nominal financial assets are included in $\mathbf{E}$ and $\mathbf{K}$ (e.g., initial money holdings).) Thus Walras's Law states that no matter what the p_i, the aggregate value of excess demands in the system equals the aggregate value of excess supplies. This is the statement implicit in Lange's presentation (1942, p. 50).

Walras himself, however, sufficed with a particular and narrower application of this statement, and was followed in this by, *inter alia*, Hicks (1939, chs. IV: 3 and XII: 4–5), Modigliani (1944, pp. 215–16) and Patinkin (1956, ch. III: 1–3). Assume that it has been shown that a certain price vector $(p_1^0, \ldots, p_{n-1}^0)$ equilibrates all markets but the jth. Since (11) holds identically in the p_i, it must hold for this price vector too. Hence substituting the $n - 1$ equilibrium conditions into (11) reduces it to

$$p_j^0[X_j(p_1^0, \ldots, p_{n-1}^0) - Y_j(p_1^0, \ldots, p_{n-1}^0)] = 0. \tag{12}$$

Thus if $p_j^0 > 0$, the price vector $(p_1^0, \ldots, p_{n-1}^0)$ must also equilibrate the jth market, which means that only $n - 1$ of the equilibrium equations are independent. In this way Walras (and those who followed him) established the equality between the number of independent equations and the number of price-variables to be determined. (Though such an equality is not a sufficient condition for the existence of a unique solution with positive prices, it is a necessary – though not sufficient – condition for the peace-of-mind of those of us who do not aspire to the rigour of mathematical economists.)

It should however be noted that at the end of §126 of Walras's *Eléments* (1926), there is a hint of Lange's broader statement of the Law: for there Walras states that if at a certain set of prices 'the total demand for some commodities is greater (or smaller) than their offer, then the offer of some of the other commodities must be greater (or smaller) than the demand for them'; what is missing here is the quantitative statement that the respective aggregate values of these excesses must be equal.

Since the contrary impression might be gained from some of the earlier literature (cf., e.g., Modigliani, 1944, pp. 215–16), it should be emphasized that no substantive difference can arise from the choice of the equation to be 'dropped' or 'eliminated' from a general-equilibrium system by virtue of Walras's Law. For identity (11) can be rewritten as

$$X_j(p_1,\ldots,p_{n-1}) - Y_j(p_1,\ldots,p_{n-1})$$

$$= -\frac{1}{p_j}\sum_{\substack{i=1\\ i\neq j}}^{n} p_i[X_i(p_1,\ldots,p_{n-1}) - Y_i(p_1,\ldots,p_{n-1})]$$

$$\text{identically in the } p_i. \qquad (13)$$

Thus the properties of the 'eliminated' equation are completely reflected in the remaining ones. Correspondingly, no matter what equation is 'eliminated', the solution for the equilibrium set of prices obtained from the remaining equations must be the same. (From this it is also clear that the heated 'loanable-funds *versus* liquidity-preference' debate that occupied the profession for many years after the appearance of the *General Theory*, was largely misguided; see Hicks, 1939, pp. 157–62; see also Patinkin, 1956, ch. XV: 3, and 1958, pp. 300–302, 316–17.)

In his influential article, Lange (1942, pp. 52–53) also distinguished between Walras's Law and what he called Say's Law, and I digress briefly to discuss this. As before, let the first $n-1$ goods represent commodities and the nth good money. Then Say's Law according to Lange is

$$\sum_{i=1}^{n-1} p_i X_i(p_1,\ldots,p_{n-1}) = \sum_{i=1}^{n-1} p_i Y_i(p_1,\ldots,p_{n-1})$$

$$\text{identically in the } p_i. \qquad (14)$$

That is, the aggregate value of commodities supplied at any price vector $(p_1,\ldots,p_{n-1})$ must equal the aggregate value demanded: supply always creates its own demand.

On both theoretical and doctrinal grounds, however, I must reject Lange's treatment of Say's Law. First of all, Lange himself demonstrates (ibid., p. 62) that identity (14) implies that money prices are indeterminate. In particular, subtracting (14) from (11) yields

$$X_n(p_1,\ldots,p_{n-1}) = Y_n(p_1,\ldots,p_{n-1}) \quad \text{for all } p_i. \qquad (15)$$

That is, no matter what the price vector, the excess-demand equation for money must be satisfied, which in turn implies that money prices cannot be determined by market forces. But it is not very meaningful to speak of a money economy whose money prices are indeterminate even for fixed initial conditions as represented by the vectors **E** and **K**. So if we rule out this possibility, we can say that Say's Law in Lange's sense implies the existence of a barter economy. Conversely, in a barter economy (i.e., one in which there exist only the $n-1$ commodities) Say's Law is simply a statement of Walras's Law. Thus from the above viewpoint, a necessary and sufficient condition for the existence of Say's Law in Lange's sense is that the economy in question be a barter economy: it has no place in a money economy (Patinkin, 1956, ch. VIII: 7).

Insofar as the doctrinal aspect is concerned, identity (14) cannot be accepted as a representation of Say's actual contention. For Say's concern was (in today's terminology) not the short-run viewpoint implicit in this identity, but the viewpoint which denied that in the long run inadequacy of demand would set a limit to the expansion of output. In brief, and again in today's terminology, Say's concern was to deny the possibility of secular stagnation, not that of cyclical depression and unemployment. Thus, writing in the first quarter of the 19th century, Say (1821a, p. 137) adduces evidence in support of his thesis from the fact 'that there should now be bought and sold in France five or six times as many commodities, as in the miserable reign of Charles VI' – four centuries earlier. Again, in his *Letters to Malthus* (1821b, pp. 4–5) Say argues that the enactment of the Elizabethan Poor Laws (codified at the end of the 16th century) proves that '*there was* no employ in a country which since then has been able to furnish enough for a double and triple number of labourers' (italics in original). Similarly, Ricardo, the leading contemporary advocate of Say's *loi des débouchés*, discusses this law in chapter 21 of his *Principles* (1821), entitled 'Effects of Accumulation on Profits and Interest'; on the other hand, he clearly recognizes the short-run 'distress' that can be generated by 'Sudden Changes in the Channels of Trade' (title of ch. 19 of his *Principles*. For further discussion see Patinkin, 1956, Supplementary Note L.).

Let me return now to the general statement of Walras's Law presented in equation (9) above. This statement holds for any vector **v** and not only for that appropriate to perfect competition. *In particular, Walras's Law holds also for the case in which households and/or firms are subject to quantity constraints.* In order to bring this out, consider the analysis of a disequilibrium economy presented in chapter XIII:2 of Patinkin (1956) and illustrated by Figure 1. In this figure, w is the money wage-rate, p the price level, N the quantity of labour, $N^d = Q(w/p, K_0)$ the firms' demand curve for labour as derived from profit-maximization as of a given stock of physical capital K_0; and $N^s = R(w/p)$ is the supply curve of labour as derived from utility maximization subject to the budget constraint (these perfect-competition curves are what Clower (1965, p. 119) subsequently denoted as 'notional curves'). Assume that because of the firms' awareness that at the real wage rate $(w/p)_1$ they face a quantity constraint and will not be able to sell all of the output corresponding to their profit-maximizing input of labour N_1, they demand only N_2 units of labour, represented by point P in Figure 1. This constraint also operates on workers, who can sell only the foregoing quantity of labour instead of

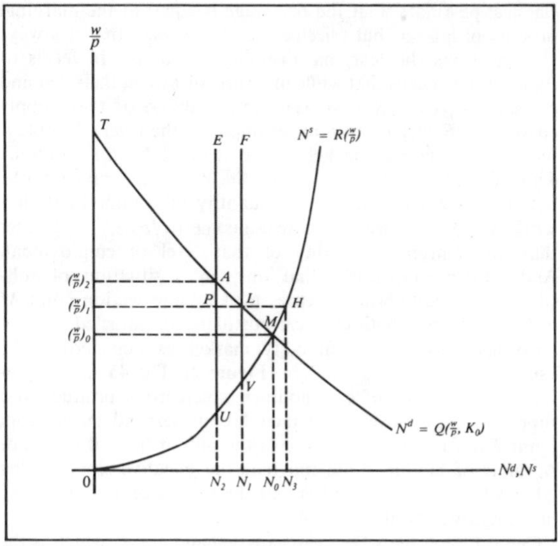

Figure 1

their optimal one N_3, represented by point H. In brief, at point P, both firms and workers are off their notional curves. In order to depict this situation, the notional curves must accordingly be replaced by quantity-constrained ones; namely, the kinked demand curve TAN_2 and kinked supply curve OUE. Note that for levels of employment before they become kinked, the curves coincide respectively with the notional ones (but see Patinkin, ch. XIII: 2, n. 9, for a basic analytical problem that arises with respect to the kinked demand curve TAN_2).

The obverse side of these constraints in the labour market are corresponding constraints in the commodity market. In particular, as Clower (1965, pp. 118–21) has emphasized, the demands of workers in this market are determined by their constrained incomes. Clower also emphasizes that it is this quantity constraint which rationalizes the consumption function of Keynes's *General Theory*, in which income appears as an independent variable. For in the absence of such a constraint, the individual's income is also a dependent variable, determined by the optimum quantity of labour he decides to sell at the given real wage rate in accordance with the labour-supply function $N^S = R(w/p)$ in Figure 1; and he makes this decision simultaneously with the one with respect to the optimum quantities of commodities to buy. If, however, his income is determined by a quantity constraint which prevents him from selling his optimum quantity of labour, the individual can decide on his demands for commodities only after his income is first determined. This is the so-called 'dual decision hypothesis' (Clower, ibid.). To this I would add (and its significance will become clear below) that the quantity constraint also rationalizes the form of Keynes's liquidity preference function, for this too depends on income (*General Theory*, p. 199). Furthermore, if the behaviour functions in the markets for labour, commodities, and money balances are thus quantity-constrained, so too (by the budget constraint) will be that for bonds – the fourth market implicitly (and frequently explicitly) present in the Keynesian system. (The theory of the determination of equilibrium under quantity constraints – inbrief, disequilibrium theory – has been the subject of a growing literature, most of it highly technical; for critical surveys of this literature, see Grandmont, 1977; Drazen, 1980; Fitoussi, 1983; and Gale, 1983, ch. 1.)

In the *General Theory* (ch. 2), Keynes accepted the 'first classical postulate' that the real wage is equal to the marginal product of labour, but rejected the second one, that it always also measures the marginal disutility of labour. In terms of Figure 1 this means that while firms are always on their demand curve $N^d = Q(w/p, K_0)$, workers are not always on their supply curve $N^s = R(w/p)$. Thus, for example, at the level of employment N_2, the labour market will be at point A on the labour-demand curve, corresponding to the real wage rate $(w/p)_2$; but the marginal utility of the quantity of commodities that workers then buy with their real-income $(w/p)_2 \cdot N_2$ is greater than the marginal disutility of that level of employment. And Keynes emphasizes that only in a situation of full-employment equilibrium – represented by intersection point M in Figure 1 – will both classical postulates be satisfied.

Consider now the commodity market as depicted in the usual Keynesian-cross diagram (Figure 2). The 45° line represents the amounts of commodities which firms produce and supply as they move along their labour-demand curve from point T to M. Thus Y_0 represents the output (in real terms) of N_0 units of labour. Note too that the negative slope of the labour-demand curve implies that the real wage declines as we move rightwards along the 45° line.

Curve E represents the aggregate demand curve, which is the vertical sum of the consumption function of workers (E_L) and capitalists (E_C), respectively, and of the investment function (I). For simplicity, these last two are assumed to be constant. The fact that curve E does not coincide with the 45° line reflects Keynes's assumption that in a monetary economy, Say's Law (in Keynes's sense, which is the macroeconomic counterpart of Lange's subsequent formulation) does not hold (ibid., pp. 25–6).

Consider now the consumption function of workers. The income which they have at their disposal is their constrained income as determined by the labour-demand curve in Figure 1. Thus assume that Y_1 and Y_2 in Figure 2 are the outputs corresponding to the levels of employment N_1 and N_2, respectively. The corresponding incomes of workers at these levels are $(w/p)_1 \cdot N_1$ and $(w/p)_2 \cdot N_2$. On the assumption that the elasticity of demand for labour is greater than unity, the higher the level of employment the greater the income of workers and hence their consumption expenditures. From Figure 2 we see that at income Y_2 there is an excess demand for commodities. This causes firms to expand their output to, say, Y_1, and hence their labour-input to, say, N_1, thus causing the constrained labour-supply curve to shift to the right to the kinked curve $OUVLF$. By construction, Y_1 is the equilibrium level of output.

What must now be emphasized is that Walras's Law holds in this situation too – *provided we relate this Law to excess-demand functions of the same type*. Thus if within our four-good Keynesian model we *consistently* consider notional behaviour functions, the excess supply of labour LH in Figure 1 corresponds to an excess demand for commodities which is generated by workers' planned consumption expenditures at the real wage rate $(w/p)_1$ and level of employment N_3 as compared with firms' planned output at that wage rate and lower level of employment N_2; and there will generally also exist a net excess planned demand for bonds and money. Alternatively, if we *consistently* consider constrained functions, then constrained equilibria exist in both the labour market (point L), the commodity market (point L'), the bond market, and the money market. Similarly, the broader form of Walras's Law states that a constrained (say) excess supply in the commodity market corresponds to a constrained net excess

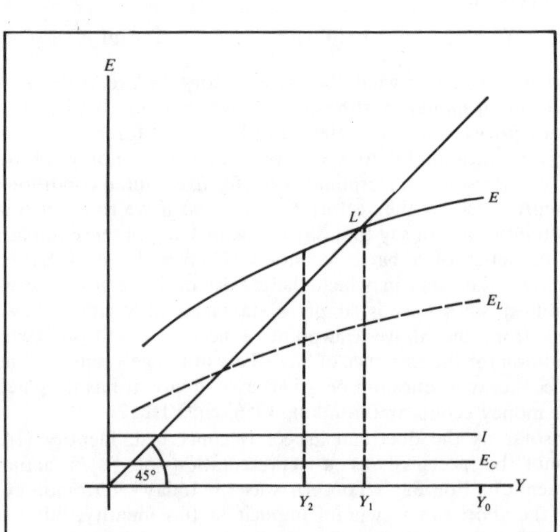

Figure 2

demand in the bond and money markets, while the labour market is in constrained equilibrium. In brief, a sufficient condition for the validity of Walras's Law is that the individual's demand and supply functions on which it is ultimately based are all derived from the same budget constraint, whether quantity-constrained or not. (This is the implicit assumption of Patinkin's (1956, p. 229; 1958, pp. 314–16) application of Walras's Law to a disequilibrium economy with unemployment, and the same is true for Grossman (1971) and Barro and Grossman (1971; 1976, p. 58).)

I must admit that the validity of Walras's Law in this Keynesian model depends on our regarding the kinked curve *OUVLF* as a labour-supply curve, and that this is not completely consistent with the usual meaning of a supply curve or function. For such a function usually describes the behaviour of an agent under constraints which leave him some degree of freedom to choose an optimum, whereas no such freedom exists in the vertical part of *OUVLF*. However, I prefer this inconsistency to what I would consider to be the logical – and hence more serious – inconsistency that lies at the base of the rejection of Walras's Law, and which consists of lumping together behaviour functions derived from different budget constraints.

It is thus clear that the foregoing constrained equilibrium in the labour market is not an equilibrium in the literal sense of representing a balance of opposing market forces, but simply the reflection of the passive adjustment by workers of the amount of labour they supply to the amount demanded by firms (cf. Patinkin, 1958, pp. 314–15). From this viewpoint, the constrained equilibrium in the labour market always exists and simply expresses the fact that, by definition, every ex post purchase is also an ex post sale. In contrast, as we have seen in the discussion of Figure 2 above, the corresponding constrained equilibrium in the commodity market is a true one; for, in accordance with the usual Keynesian analysis, were the level of Y to deviate from Y_1, automatic market forces of excess demand or supply would be generated that would return it to Y_1. And a similar statement holds, *mutatis mutandis*, for the constrained equilibria in the bond and money markets.

Note, however, that in the commodity market too there is an ex post element. This element is a basic, if inadequately recognized, aspect of the household behaviour implied by Clower's 'dual decision hypothesis': namely, that households' constrained decisions on the amount of money to spend on commodities is based on their ex post knowledge of the amount of money received from the constrained sale of their factor services. And to this I again add that a similar statement holds for their constrained decisions with reference to the amounts of bonds and money balances, respectively, that they will want to hold. (Note that an analysis in terms of constrained decisions can also be applied to the case in which households do not correctly estimate firms' profits in equation (3) above, and are thus forced to base their effective (say) consumption decisions on the ex post knowledge of these profits.)

In his treatment of an economy with constrained functions, Clower (1965, pp. 122–3) has claimed that under these conditions Walras's Law does not hold. This is not true for the Law as hitherto discussed. What Clower seems to have in mind, however, is that though the excess supply of labour *LH* in Figure 1 is notional, it nevertheless exerts pressure on workers to reduce their money wages; in contrast, the notional excess demand for commodities corresponding to *LH* (see above) cannot – because of their constrained incomes – lead households to exert expansionary pressures on the commodity market. Thus there exists no *effective* excess demand for commodities to match the *effective* excess supply of labour. Accordingly, no 'signal' to the market is generated that will lead to the expansion of output and consequent reduction of unemployment (cf. also Leijonhufvud, 1968, pp. 81–91). And it is the absence of such a 'signal' that Leijonhufvud (1981, ch. 6) subsequently denoted as 'effective demand failure'.

This 'failure', however – and correspondingly the failure of Walras's Law to hold in Clower's sense – is not an absolute one: for though there is no direct signal to the commodity market, an indirect one may well be generated. In particular, the very fact that the constrained equilibrium in the labour market does not represent a balancing of market forces means that the unemployed workers in this market are a potential source of a downward pressure on the money wage rate. And if this pressure is to some extent effective, the resulting decline in money wages will generate an increase in the real quantity of money, hence a decrease in the rate of interest, hence an increase in investment and consequently in aggregate demand – and this process may be reinforced by a positive real-balance effect (see chapter 19 of the *General Theory*, which, however, also emphasizes how many weak – and possibly perverse – links there are in this causal chain). Thus a sufficient condition for absolute 'effective demand failure' is the traditional classical one of absolute rigidity of money wages and prices.

An analogy (though from a completely different field) may be of help in clarifying the nature of the foregoing equilibrium in the labour market. Consider a cartel of (say) oil-producing firms, operating by means of a Central Executive for the Production of Oil (CEPO) which sets production quotas for each firm. The total quantity-constrained supply so determined, in conjunction with the demand conditions in the market, will then determine the equilibrium price for crude oil, and that equilibrium position is the relevant one for Walras's Law. But this will not be an equilibrium in the full sense of the term, for it coexists with market pressures to disturb it. In particular, the monopolistic price resulting from CEPO's policy is necessarily higher than the marginal cost of any individual member of the cartel. Hence it is to the interest of every firm in the cartel that all other firms adhere to their respective quotas and thus 'hold an umbrella' over the price, while it itself surreptitiously exceeds the quantity constraint imposed by its quota and thus moves closer to its notional supply curve as represented by its marginal-cost curve. And since in the course of time there will be some firms who will succumb to this temptation, a temptation that increases inversely with the ratio of its quota to the total set by CEPO, actual industry output will exceed this total, with a consequent decline in the price of oil. Indeed, if such violations of cartel discipline should become widespread, its very existence would be threatened.

This analogy is, of course, not perfect. First of all, unlike workers in the labour market, the member-firms of CEPO have themselves had a voice in determining the quantity constraints. Second, and more important, any individual firm knows that by 'chiselling' and offering to sell even slightly below the cartel price, it can readily increase its sales. But analogies are never perfect: that is why they remain only analogies.

A final observation: the discussion until now has implicitly dealt with models with discrete time periods. In models with continuous time, there are two Walras's Laws: one for stocks and one for flows: one for the instantaneous planned (or constrained) purchases and sales of assets (primarily financial assets) and one for the planned (or constrained) purchases and sales of commodity flows (cf. May, 1970; Foley and Sidrauski, 1971, pp. 89–91; Sargent, 1979, pp. 67–69; Buiter, 1980). On the other hand, in a discrete-time intertemporal model, in which there exists a market for each period, there is only one

Walras's Law: for in such a model, all variables have the time-dimension of a stock (see Patinkin, 1972, ch. 1).

DON PATINKIN

See also GENERAL EQUILIBRIUM; MONETARY DISEQUILIBRIUM AND MARKET CLEARING; RATIONED EQUILIBRIA; TEMPORARY EQUILIBRIUM

BIBLIOGRAPHY

Arrow, K.J. and Hahn, F.H. 1971. *General Competitive Analysis*. San Francisco: Holden-Day; Edinburgh: Oliver and Boyd.

Barro, R. and Grossman, H.I. 1971. A general disequilibrium model of income and employment. *American Economic Review* 61, March, 82–93.

Barro, R. and Grossman, H.I. 1976. *Money, Employment and Inflation*. Cambridge: Cambridge University Press.

Buiter, W.H. 1980. Walras's law and all that: budget constraints and balance sheet constraints in period models and continuous time models. *International Economic Review* 21 (Feb): 1–16.

Clower, R. 1965. The Keynesian counterrevolution: a theoretical appraisal. In *The Theory of Interest Rates*, ed. F.H. Hahn and F.P.R. Brechling, London: Macmillan, 103–25.

Drazen, A. 1980. Recent developments in macroeconomic disequilibrium theory. *Econometrica* 48, March, 283–306.

Fitoussi, J.P. 1983. Modern macroeconomic theory: an overview. In *Modern Macroeconomic Theory* ed. J.P. Fitoussi, Oxford: Basil Blackwell, 1–46.

Foley, D.K. and Sidrauski, M. 1971. *Monetary and Fiscal Policy in a Growing Economy*. London: Macmillan.

Gale, D. 1983 *Money: in Disequilibrium*. Cambridge: Cambridge University Press.

Grandmont, J.M. 1977. Temporary general equilibrium theory. *Econometrica* 45, April, 535–72.

Grossman, H.I. 1971. Money, interest, and prices in market disequilibrium. *Journal of Political Economy* 79 September–October, 943–61.

Hicks, J.R. 1939. *Value and Capital*. Oxford: Clarendon Press.

Keynes, J.M. 1936. *The General Theory of Employment, Interest and Money*. London: Macmillan.

Lange, O. 1942. Say's Law: A restatement and criticism. In *Studies in Mathematical Economics and Econometrics*, ed. Oscar Lange et al., Chicago: University of Chicago Press, 49–68.

Leijonhufvud, A. 1968. *On Keynesian Economics and the Economics of Keynes*. New York: Oxford University Press.

Leijonhufvud, A. 1981. *Information and Coordination: Essays in Macroeconomic Theory*. Oxford: Oxford University Press.

May, J. 1970. Period analysis and continuous analysis in Patinkin's macroeconomic model. *Journal of Economic Theory* 2, 1–9.

Modigliani, F. 1944. Liquidity preference and the theory of interest and money. *Econometrica* 12, January, 45–88. As reprinted in *Readings in Monetary Theory*, ed. F.A. Lutz and L.W. Mints, Philadelphia: Blakiston, for the American Economic Association, 1951, 186–240.

Patinkin, D. 1956. *Money, Interest, and Prices*. Evanston, Ill.: Row, Peterson. (The material referred to appears unchanged in the second, 1965 edition.)

Patinkin, D. 1958. Liquidity preference and loanable funds: stock and flow analysis. *Economica* 25, November, 300–318.

Patinkin, D. 1972. *Studies in Monetary Economics*. New York: Harper & Row.

Ricardo, D. 1821. *On the Principles of Political Economy and Taxation*, 3rd edn. As reprinted in *The Works and Correspondence of David Ricardo*, Vol. I, ed. P. Sraffa, Cambridge: Cambridge University Press, 1951.

Sargent, T.J. 1979. *Macroeconomic Theory*. New York: Academic Press.

Say, J.B. 1821a. *Traité d'économie politique*, 4th edn, Paris: Deterville. As translated by C.R. Prinsep under the title *A Treatise on Political Economy*, Philadelphia, Grigg R. Elliot: 1834.

Say, J.B. 1821b. *Letters to Thomas Robert Malthus on Political Economy and Stagnation of Commerce*. London. As reprinted with an Historical Preface by H.J. Laski, London: George Harding's Bookshop, 1936; Wheeler Economic and Historical Reprints No. 2.

Walras, L. 1874. *Eléments d'économie politique pure*. Paris: Guillaumin (Sections I–III of the work).

Walras, L. 1900. *Eléments d'économie politique pure*. 4th edn, Paris: F. Pichon.

Walras, L. 1926. *Eléments d'économie politique pure*. Definitive edition. Paris: F. Pichon (for our purposes, identical with 4th edition). As trans. by William Jaffé under the title *Elements of Pure Economics*, London: George Allen and Unwin, 1954.

Walras's theory of capital. The extension of Walras's (1874–7) analysis from non-capitalistic production to the case of capitalistic production involved him in the introduction of four new sets of variables: the rate of net income, i; the l prices of the capital goods, P_k, the l quantities of capital goods demanded, D_k, and the total value of saving (in terms of the numéraire), E.

The rate of net income is defined as the ratio of the rental of a unit of capital good service p_k, less charges for depreciation (μ) and insurance (ν) (both of which are expressed as percentages per annum of the value of the capital good) to the value of the capital good:

$$i = \frac{p_k - (\mu + \nu)P_k}{P_k} \tag{1}$$

Thus the value of each capital good is equal to the net price of a unit of its service divided by the rate of net income plus charges for depreciation and insurance. In competitive equilibrium the rate of net income is equal on all capital goods, but μ and ν may differ from one capital good to another. In what follows, it will be assumed for simplicity that $\mu = \nu = 0$.

Walras expresses the volume of saving as the outcome of demand for an imaginary commodity (E), a unit of which yields perpetual net income at the rate i which is to be determined. In consequence the price of a unit of (E), $p_e = 1/i$. The total volume of saving derives from individuals' utility maximizing choices between units of (E) and units of other commodities.

Summing over individual demands for (E) total demand for (E) is

$$D_e = F_e(p'_k, p'_n, p'_c, i)$$

and hence the total value of saving, E, in terms of the numéraire is

$$E = D_e p_e = G_e(p'_k, p'_n, p'_c, i) \tag{2}$$

where p_n are rentals of non-producible factors and p_c prices of consumer goods. Thus saving is defined as a fluid homogeneous magnitude – 'savings in general'. Walras regarded the market for capital as *finance* as equivalent, in the determination of net income, to the market for capital goods. But even in his examination of the latter saving is always expressed as a quantity of value (in terms of the numéraire), whilst the quantities of particular capital goods produced are expressed in terms of their peculiar physical units. The sum of the values of new capital goods demanded equals the value of saving

$$E = P'_k D_k \tag{3}$$

Although Walras labelled as capital 'all forms of social wealth which are not used up at all or used up only after a lapse of time' the determination of the rate of net income concerns only 'mobile capitals', i.e. reproducible means of production. The essential characteristic of the stock of reproducible means of production is that its composition is determined by economic forces:

> Capital assets are destroyed and vanish, like persons; and like persons they re-appear, not, however, as a result of a natural reproduction, but as a result of economic production. (p. 217)

The essence of 'economic production' is that like all other produced commodities, capital goods

> are subject to the law of cost of production.... In equilibrium their selling prices and their cost of production are equal. (p. 171)

Thus

$$P_k = Ap_k + Mp_n \quad (4)$$

where A is the $l \times l$ matrix of input coefficients of capital goods into capital goods, and M the $l \times m$ matrix of input coefficients of non-reproducible inputs into capital goods.

Walras' complete system may be set out as follows (the lower case roman numeral identifies the equations, the preceding letter (or number) indicates the number of equations in each set):

$$D_c = F_c(p'_k, p'_n, p'_c, i) \quad (n) \quad \text{(i)}$$

$$D_e = F_e(p'_k, p'_n, p'_c, i) \quad (1) \quad \text{(ii)}$$

$$E = D_e p_e = G_e(p'_k, p'_n, p'_c, i)$$

$$O_n = N'D_c + M'D_k \quad (m) \quad \text{(iii)}$$

$$O_k = B'D_c + A'D_k \quad (l) \quad \text{(iv)}$$

$$O_n = Q_n \quad (m) \quad \text{(v)}$$

$$O_k = Q_k \quad (l) \quad \text{(vi)}$$

$$p_c = Bp_k + Np_n \quad (n) \quad \text{(vii)}$$

$$P_k = Ap_k + Np_n \quad (l) \quad \text{(viii)}$$

$$P_k = \frac{p_k}{i} \quad (l) \quad \text{(ix)}$$

$$E = P'_k D_k \quad (1) \quad \text{(x)}$$

a total of $2n + 2m + 4l + 2$ equations to determine the similar number of unknowns, $(D_c, p_c, O_n, p_n, O_k, D_k, p_k, P_k, E, i)$. By Walras's Law one of the equations is redundant. Similarly prices are only determined up to a multiplicative constant, and hence the price of a consumption good (A) is set equal to 1.

Walras has introduced $2l + 2$ new equations ((viii), (ix), (ii) and (x)) to determine the $2l + 2$ additional unknowns (P_k, D_k, E, i) which are required to complete his model of competitive capitalism.

Walras clearly regards the new equations and variables as an attachment to the equations of a-capitalistic production and exchange which does not disturb the solutions of those latter equations in any significant way. Thus the determination of equilibrium conditions in the theory of capital formation is expressed solely in terms of the saving function and the total value and quantities of new capital goods produced:

> With these additional data, we have all the elements necessary for the solution of our problem. New capital goods are exchanged against the excess of income over consumption: and the condition of equality between the value of the new capital goods and the value of the excess gives us the equation required for the determination of the rate of net income and consequently for the determination of the prices of capital goods. Moreover, new capital goods are products; and the condition of equality between their selling price and their cost of production gives us the equations required for the determination of the quantities manufactured. (pp. 269–70)

A peculiarity of Walras's approach to the problem of capitalistic production is that the existence of *positive* net saving plays an important role in his analysis of the determination of the rate of net income; to the extent that he even suggests that the rate of net income can only be determined in a progressive economy (pp. 269 and 479). The rationale of this odd position will become clear as we proceed.

Walras's attempt to embed the concept of 'saving in general', and an analysis of the determination of a uniform rate of net income on the value of capital goods, within the framework he had developed in the analyses of pure exchange and of a-capitalistic production lead was to prove unsuccessful, as was demonstrated by Garegnani (1960).

The source of the problem, which is examined in the next section, may be summarized as follows. The technique Walras had developed in the preceding lessons required that the stocks of means of production, expressed in their individual physical units, should be part of the (arbitrary) data of the problem. So the rentals paid for the services of these means of production will be determined by the demands for the available stocks. In the case of produced means of production the demand-prices of new capital goods will depend on the prices of their services in relation to the rate of net income (equation (ix)). And, since currently produced capital goods are *not* available for use in the period under consideration – if they were, the stock of capital would be unbounded! (pp. 282–3) – the demand price of any new good is determined solely by the demand for the stock of its services currently available – it will not be affected by changes in the output of that good except to the extent that it is used in its own production.

For any given set of prices each type of capital good has a particular rate of return over its cost of production. If the requirement of a uniform rate of net income is imposed on the model, the value (cost of production) of each capital good must be such as to yield that rate of return.

The cost of production of new capital goods may be altered by variations in the composition of the output of new capital goods if these variations lead to changes in the demands for stocks of services. The degree of variation in the cost of production will be determined by the differences in techniques which may be used for the production of the various capital goods, and the total value of savings which may be allocated between the capital goods. Thus, variation in the composition of capital good output will determine both the cost of production and the demand price of each new capital good, whilst the volume of saving will determine the range of that variation. Given the total value of saving the equality between the cost of production and the demand price of each capital good is the condition of equilibrium, and variation in the composition of the output of new capital goods is the only means whereby this condition may be satisfied. Thus this composition must not be fixed by any condition outside the system (i)–(x). For example, if demand functions for capital goods (as functions of all prices and i) were added to the system it would be *overdetermined*, for this would involve adding extra equations to the system without the addition of unknowns. Similarly, if net savings were zero, the composition of output would be determined by the requirements of replacement, and the equations are, once again, overdetermined. Walras, by confining the analysis to an economy in which net saving is positive, obscures this difficulty. Walras's system can only admit of 'saving in general' as demand for the total value of new capital goods produced. It cannot accommodate demand functions for individual capital goods. Even so, the system is generally inconsistent.

EXISTENCE OF A SOLUTION TO THE EQUATIONS OF CAPITAL FORMATION. The conditions which must be satisfied if there is to be a solution to Walras's equations of capital formation, and the rate of net income determined, will now be investigated under a simplifying – but none the less general – assumption.

The endowment of the economy is assumed to consist solely of stocks of reproducible means of production, these stocks being of arbitrary size. Only one technique of production is available to produce each commodity. Thus the equation system (i)–(x) above must be modified by the elimination of all reference to prices or quantities of non-produced means of production.

Since i is uniform, from equations (viii) and (ix) this rate must be such that

$$Ap_k i = p_k \tag{5}$$

and hence

$$0 = [I\lambda - A]p_k \tag{6}$$

where $\lambda = 1/i$. By the Frobenius theorem it is known that since A is non-negative and (we presume) indecomposable, there is only one value of the characteristic roots λ_i with which a positive eigenvector p_k is associated. All other λ_i are associated with vectors which contain negative prices and are therefore economically meaningless. Thus there can be only one value of i, and only one vector of rentals of the services of capital goods, p_k, consistent with the existence of a uniform i on all produced means of production. Once i and p_k are determined, then by equation (vii) p_c are also determined, as are D_c, E and P_k by equations (i), (ii) and (ix).

Only the demands for capital goods remain to be determined, and only the equations expressing the equality between the endowment of capital goods and the demand for new capital goods (iv) and the equation expressing equality between the value of gross saving and the value of new capital goods produced (x) remain to be satisfied. It should be noted that in equilibrium the demand for each stock of capital goods (i.e. for each stock of capital goods services) must be equal to the size of the stock, since all p_k are positive.

By Walras's Law

$$p_c' D_c + E = p_k' Q_k \tag{7}$$

i.e. the amount spent (measured in terms of the numéraire) on consumption goods, plus the amount saved, must be equal to the income earned on the endowment of means of production. Since, by equations (vii) consumption goods' prices are equal in equilibrium to their costs of production, then the total value of the output of consumption goods is equal to the value of the services used in their production.

$$p_c' D_c = p_k' Q_k^c \tag{8}$$

where Q_k^c denotes the vector of quantities of means of production used in the production of consumption goods. Hence

$$E = p_k' Q_k - p_k' Q_k^c = p_k' Q_k^a \tag{9}$$

the value of saving is equal to the total value of the services yielded by the amounts of the initial endowments *available* for the construction of new capital goods (Q_k^a), once the requirements of consumption goods production have been deducted from the original stocks.

The stock of capital–good services *required* for the construction of new capital goods (Q_k^i) may be determined from the two conditions:

$$E = P_k' D_k \quad \text{and} \quad Q_k^i = A' D_k,$$

Walras's equations are consistent only if $Q_k^i = Q_k^a$; that is if there exists a vector of demands for new capital goods D_k such that this latter condition is satisfied. All elements of D_k must be non-negative, and, in turn, all input requirements are non-negative;

$$D_k = (A')^{-1} Q_k^i \geqslant 0; \qquad Q_k^i \geqslant 0 \tag{10}$$

However, there is nothing in the specification of the model to ensure that $Q_k^a \geqslant 0$. The original endowment Q_k must be non-negative. But the solution may imply that the amount of any one element of the endowment available for the production of new capital goods is negative, to the extent of

$$-\sum_c b_{jc} D_c,$$

the quantity of capital good j used in the production of consumption goods. Indeed, only one element of Q_k^a need be positive (this is essential if E is to be positive). Thus the set Q_k^a is bounded from below by the condition $Q_k^a \geqslant -B'D_c$. So if any element of Q_k^a is less than zero, a condition that is as likely as its converse, then the data and the equations are unequivocally inconsistent. Consistency can be attained only by chance. This is a sufficient criticism of Walras' system.

Moreover, even if Q_k^a should be non-negative, condition (10) may render the system inconsistent. The vectors Q_k^i which satisfy (10) lie in a convex cone within the positive orthant, for these vectors must be non-negative linear combinations of the columns of A'. In general, this cone will not be the entire positive orthant – this would only be the case when each productive service appeared only once as the sole input into the production of a single capital good. Hence, in general, some $Q_k^a \geqslant 0$ cannot be equated with a vector Q_k^i which satisfies (10).

This analysis is unaffected if it is assumed that there is more than one technique available for the production of each commodity. The technique which will be chosen is that which yields the highest rate of net income. This technique will be used whatever may be the composition of demand or of the endowment.

The rationale of this result is that there is no reason to suppose that prices paid for the services of the stocks of reproducible means of production will correspond to those prices which would result in a uniform rate of net income, the condition of long-run equilibrium.

Including non-produced means of production in the analysis will not render the model consistent. The vector of rentals which clears the markets for non-produced factors will have associated with it a vector of rentals for capital goods which would be compatible with a uniform rate of net income. Except by a fluke, this vector of capital goods rentals will not be market clearing.

AN ALTERNATIVE SOLUTION. Walras himself became aware, in the 4th, definitive, edition of the *Elements*, that his equations of capital formation might not admit of a solution:

> If we suppose that all fixed capital goods proper . . . are already found in the economy in quantities Q_k . . . and that their gross and net incomes are paid for at prices determined by the system of production equations and by the rates of depreciation and insurance, it is not at all certain that the amount of savings E will be adequate for the manufacture of new fixed capital goods proper in just such quantities as will satisfy the last l equations of the above system (p. 308).

His solution was, however, an evasion of the real problem:

> On the other hand, in an economy in normal operation which has only to maintain itself in equilibrium, we may suppose the last equations to be satisfied (p. 308).

i.e. being in equilibrium we may hope for the attainment of equilibrium!

But Walras also recommended a way out of the dilemma

> All we could be sure of, under these circumstances of insufficient savings to ensure equilibrium is (1) that the utility of new capital goods would be maximized if the first new capital goods to be manufactured were those yielding the highest rate of net income, and (2) that this is precisely the order in which new capital goods would be manufactured under a system of free competition (p. 308).

If we take up this proposal the equations (viii) in Walras' system should be modified, the equality between cost of production and demand price being replaced by the inequality:

$$P_k \leqslant Ap_k + Mp_n \qquad \text{(viii)}'$$

i.e. demand price is less than or equal to cost of production – with the proviso that in the cases of those capital goods for which the inequality holds output will be zero.

The important role which the replacement of equalities by inequalities plays in the establishment of an economically meaningful solution to the equations of exchange and of a-capitalistic production and exchange is well known. In the case of consumption goods a demand price which is less than the cost of production for any positive output means that output of that good must be zero. In the case of non-producible inputs an endowment which is greater than the quantity demanded at any positive price results in the price of that input being zero. Both these circumstances have a clear economic meaning. Reproducible means of production share characteristics of both and the economic meaning of the use of the inequality is less clear. The services of the stock of a reproducible input may command a positive price and yet new units will not be produced for the demand price of that commodity is less than its cost of production. The rate of net income earned in the production of such a commodity, calculated at the ruling prices, will be less than the ruling rate. But a situation in which the rate of net income is not the same on all produced means of production does not conform to the conventional notion of long-run equilibrium. An 'equilibrium' defined with inequalities between demand price and cost of production of some capital goods is a curious hybrid, for although the prices of all non-produced means of production are uniform throughout the economy (a long-run equilibrium condition), the rate of net income is not uniform (a short-run condition). This hybridization cannot be justified by considerations affecting the relative mobility of resources in the two classifications, since mobility of non-reproducible inputs between uses is customarily attained by changes in the structure of the stock of producible inputs with which they are combined. This situation arises not from any particular view of the actual operation of a capitalistic economy but is dictated by the necessity, in Walras' theory, of expressing the stock of reproducible means of production as a set of arbitrary (physical) magnitudes.

In a Note to Chapter III of his *Equilibrium, Stability and Growth*, Michio Morishima has adopted Walras's strategem and demonstrated (with the aid of some additional assumptions) that a solution to the modified system exists. His proof follows the mathematical procedures developed by Wald, and Arrow and Debreu, adapted to the case of capital formation. The technique developed above in the analysis of Walras's equations of capital formation will be used to investigate Morishima's analysis.

The investigation will be conducted under the assumption that all means of production are reproducible, and that only one technique is available for the production of each produced commodity (consumption goods and capital goods). At least one input coefficient is positive for any output. These assumptions are made solely in the interests of simplicity. It will be evident from what follows that the argument could readily be extended to include non-reproducible means of production and many possible techniques.

Suppose that all capital goods are produced and that the price system is that which corresponds to a uniform rate of net income. Then, for the reasons outlined above there will in general be a discrepancy between the stocks of capital goods' services available for the production of new capital goods, and the set of possible combinations of stocks required if all saving is to be absorbed and the outputs of new machines are to be non-negative. Some elements of the difference $Q_k^a - Q_k^i$ (for any Q_k^i selected from the set of possible alternatives) will be positive and others negative. Those elements which are positive relate to an endowment which is greater than that which is absorbed in the production of both consumption goods and capital goods at existing prices. Those elements which are negative relate to an endowment smaller than demand for its services at existing prices.

To attempt to remove the discrepancies select the good for which the ratio $(q_j^a - q_j^i)/q_j$ is greatest, and set the output of the good at zero. The price of its services (which will be denoted by π_j) may now be set anywhere in the range between zero and its price when produced (p_j). The inequality in (viii)′ will therefore hold for good j. Since there was previously an excess supply of this good then it might be expected that π_j set lower than p_j would tend to reduce that excess by encouraging substitution in consumption toward j intensive goods. Such changes may also supplement the available stocks of those services for which there was previously an excess demand. Any value of $\pi_j < p_j$ will result in a higher rate of net income implicit in the price equations of those capital goods which are produced; this may, in turn, tend to increase saving and hence available stocks of all capital goods for capital good production. As good j is not produced it acquires the role in price system of a non-producible means of production, and the analysis may be pursued once more in the manner outlined above; i.e. by relating the intersection of the set $Q_k^i (k \neq j)$, which for all possible pairs $i, \pi_j (\pi_j < p_j)$ results in the absorption of saving, with the set of Q_k^i which satisfy the condition

$$q_j^a \geqslant q_j^i$$

(if the inequality holds $\pi_j = 0$), to the set Q_k^a defined by

$$E - \pi_j q_j^a = p_k' Q_k^a \qquad (k \neq j)$$

There is no reason to believe that the discrepancy will disappear, and so the procedure may be repeated; the production of the capital good for which the value of $(q_k^a - q_k^i)/q_k$ is the greatest should be set equal to zero, and π_k set below p_k. The analysis is then conducted as if there were two non-produced inputs.

The quantity available for capital good production of a capital good previously eliminated from production may fall below zero for all $\pi_j < p_j$ as the structure of production changes with successive eliminations (p_j being calculated as the cost of production of good j at the prices ruling at the stage of the analysis under consideration, not at the stage at which it was eliminated). In such circumstances the price of j must be raised to p_j, which means that it is reintroduced into production, a different good is selected for elimination, and the process continues in the same manner as before.

At each stage of the process of elimination it may happen that there is a set of Q_k^i (of those capital goods still in production), appropriate to the prices associated with a uniform rate of net income on the goods produced. But this event is similar to the attainment of a uniform rate of net income when all capital goods are produced, that is, a configuration of the endowment which happens to result in a Q_k^a which falls in the subset Q_k^i. Since the initial endowment is arbitrary it cannot be claimed that in such a case the existence of an equilibrium to the equations has been proven – since in general, for all circumstances, it has not. A configuration of the endowment can always be found which would result in the elimination being taken a stage further. Each stage of the elimination merely recreates this situation, and thus there is no reason to believe that the process will cease.

The process of elimination may thus continue until only two capital goods remain in production, and $l-2$ capital goods are consigned to the category of non-produced means of production. There is still no necessity that Q_k^a should equal a feasible Q (k not including the $l-2$ eliminated goods). That good which is in excess supply should be eliminated. The system now only contains *one* produced means of production, and the savings function (ii) is, in effect, the demand function for that good alone. No constraints are now imposed on the configuration of prices by the condition that the rate of net income on the produced means should be uniform – for since only one capital good is produced there can only be one value of the rate of net income.

The only case in which there must necessarily be a solution to the system is that in which only one capital good is produced. Condition (viii)′ will hold with just one equality.

Thus, apart from the chance case in which the elimination process is halted with more than one capital-good in production, a maximum uniform rate of net income is attained only when just one capital-good is produced. The rate of net income defined in the production of the single good produced is used to capitalize the value of non-produced capital goods and hence these 'earn' the rate of net income by definition. Morishima's model is thus yet another example of the use in neoclassical models of the 'one-produced input world' assumption, input is to be the one produced is endogenous to the model.

Walras' analysis of capital formation and credit, far from being the triumphant confirmation of his theory of pure economics, is a failure which brings his whole system into question. He is unable to overcome the contradiction between saving in general as a homogeneous fluid magnitude and the heterogeneity of capital goods. This contradiction could be overcome by expressing the endowment of capital goods as a single magnitude – their value. But the value of the endowment cannot be part of the data of the problem without engendering circular reasoning. Walras, in avoiding this circularity, constructed a system in which whilst the method of specifying the data is logically sound, the equations are inconsistent.

JOHN EATWELL

See also ARROW–DEBREU MODEL; GENERAL EQUILIBRIUM.

BIBLIOGRAPHY

Garegnani, P. 1960. *Il capitale nelle teoria della distribuzione*. Milan: Guiffre.

Morishima, M. 1964. *Equilibrium, Stability and Growth*. Oxford: Clarendon Press.

Walras, L. 1874–7. *Eléments d'économie politique pure*. Trans. and ed. W. Jaffé as *Elements of Pure Economics*, London: Allen & Unwin, 1954.

wants. To be in want is not to have. The obverse of want is satisfaction or having the wherewithal for happiness. Much Eastern philosophy recommends happiness based on few wants, just as much of Western philosophical comment condemns excessive wants. The economists' view is different. They tend to worry when an economy comes to rest at a low level of wants and to feel more sanguine when the demand for new possessions goes up, even if they become worried again if demand is inflationary. They are clearly interested in wants. Yet the way that demand for goods is treated within economic theory blocks their curiosity about how wants are generated. This is not to say that distinguished economists have not seriously pondered the subject. Many have produced catalogues of wants, sometimes contrasting material with spiritual satisfications, sometimes comparing long-term with short-term wants, or psychic joys (such as music or affection) with physical requirements (such as food and warmth). Such lists tend to dangle free of theoretical constraints. They remain mere lists whose parts do not mesh into any theory.

Anthropology is in no state to supplement this missing element in economics. Both disciplines have an explicit theory about the circulation of goods but only an implicit theory of wants. In economics the implicit assumption is that the origin of wants is to be found inside the individual's physical and psychic constitution. In anthropology, the implicit assumption is that wants are defined and standardized in social interaction. This latter view makes a better start for thinking about wants because it integrates the choices of the individual agent within a model of the whole economy, whereas economics leaves the choices unexplained except in regard to price. To get into such a starting position economics would need to modify the concept of the consumer as an independent rational agent choosing to satisfy personal needs. It would also need to take an interest in what happens to goods after purchase. The word consumption implies that the goods are destined to be used up in the purchaser's home. Once in the shopping basket they hold little interest for economic theory, but that is the point at which the anthropologist's interest begins. Most goods are likely to be widely shared or passed from hand to hand over a certain span of time. Instead of someone who buys for private purposes the consumer would have to be seen as someone engaged in long-term interactions with other social beings and using goods to promote the particular social patterns that he values.

For the anthropologist, wants are primarily generated in social life; if this is so, when the pace of social interaction slackens, demand for possessions will go down. This approach began with Malinowski's account (1922) of Trobriand Islanders going in canoes to exchange shell ornaments and other products through vast reaches of the Pacific. These people made a clear distinction between trade and gift, and used both to build up partnerships which were not only profitable but supported their intentions within their local political systems. Marcel Mauss (1925) extended these insights to a general theory of solidarity based on reciprocal obligation. From these beginnings, succeeding generations of anthropologists came to study all kinds of transfers of rights and property as flows marking the important channels of social obligation. The focus on types of reciprocity as the basis of solidarity was formalized by Claude Lévi-Strauss in a general theory of kinship. One kind of repeated marriage patterns can produce long lines of exchange embracing everyone in the community and all generations in a generalized system of transfers; another has more restricted effects, linking only two or three descent lines; endogamy is the limit case of marrying-in at the expense of a wider solidarity. Such variations have direct implication for the political system and for the economy. Marrying or procreating appear as part of the total system of reproduction. It has generally been assumed that this kind of analysis applies only to societies in which market organization is weakly developed. However, it can be argued that the sharp disjunction between market and non-market is an artifact of economic theory and one which makes theorizing about demand peculiarly difficult.

The implicit assumption in anthropology is that individual wants are standardized by the same processes that establish social solidarity. Put crudely, the reason anyone wants anything (physical needs apart) is for sharing with or showing or giving to someone else in recognition of similar gestures, gifts or services received in the past. On this assumption, being severely in want means being unable to take part in the major reciprocal exchanges by which future entitlements are conferred. This is no trivial matter. Lacking entitlement is equivalent to becoming a third-class citizen or even to losing civic status. Anyone who exerts no claims on the rest of society finds that his sons and daughters are not sought in marriage; he wants for protection and can expect an indigent old age. Such a theory of wants is capable of being made explicit and generalized beyond the range of societies the anthropologists usually study. It would enable economic theory to integrate social life, family structure, demography and the labour market into the rest of the economy. The obstacle lies in the way that the theory of demand has been formulated.

The original utilitarian philosophy presupposed that wants are in some sense commensurable. Mathematical treatments of wants based on this assumption were already being applied to economic analysis when the theory of diminishing marginal utility was worked out independently in 1871 by Carl Menger and W.S. Jevons; Walras also arrived at it in the same year and independently, though he published a little later. Such a simultaneous convergence upon an intricate idea would be quite impossible if the common infrastructure of theory was not already in place. The relevant point for an article on wants is that the problem to which they all found the same answer was not how to formulate a theory of wants, not at all. The problem was how to formulate the concept of demand so as to harmonize this part of economic theory with the rest of the theory of supply and demand. Diminishing marginal utility means that an individual purchaser gets marginally less satisfaction from each additional increment of a commodity. The underlying metaphor is physical: more and more bread or beer or beef give less benefit to the eater and bigger and bigger doses of a medicine may actually harm instead of curing the patient. By incorporating diminishing marginal satisfaction for the consumer, demand theory matches the theory of supply according to which marginal costs increase with increase in the volume of production. Beyond a certain point, rising costs mean that the price must rise to encourage extra output. As the marginal utility to the consumer falls, he becomes less willing to spend his income on it. The rising supply curve cuts the falling demand curve and the see-saw comes to rest.

Whereas the theories of production, exchange and capital formation drawn up on this model only had to face technical criticism, when the model was applied to wants, philosophical and political objections appeared. How can human wants be given numerical expression? How can one person's wants be compared with another's? How can such comparisons not carry a load of political prejudice?

In the history of science it often happens that a theory does not apply well to the behaviour it is supposed to explain, because its coherence within a larger theory prevents the bad fit with data being taken seriously. In this case the theory of demand cannot give an account of wants simply because this is not what it was designed for. The very completeness of its embedding in the larger, unified theory makes it incapable of focusing on its nominal subject matter. It gives a gravely misleading account of wants for the following reasons.

First, violence is done to the concept of the individual consumer by making it parallel to the concept of the individual firm. The consumer's wants do not correspond to the profit maximizing objectives of the firm. This is essentially because the consumer is not an individual among other consumers as the firm is an individual in the market. In order to live in a society the individual consumer has to develop categories of thought and tastes conformable with those of his fellows. The processes of standardization which should be at the centre of a theory of wants are ignored by economic theory. In default of a theory of how wants are collectively generated, it falls back on hidden assumptions about the priority of physical needs. As a result of this heavy disadvantage in thinking about wants, the threat of famine tends to be perceived as a physical failure of the supply of physical necessities, not as a failure of demand. It is true that in a famine the would-be buyers have nothing to offer in exchange for the food they need. But to know how they got into that situation is to see how demand is generated by a variety of reciprocal exchanges which guarantee future entitlements. A.K. Sen (1981) has argued that the misdiagnosis of the causes of major famines is due to inability to see how individuals enter the economic system and stay in it. Without what he calls exchange entitlements, individuals and their dependents are vulnerable to shocks in the economic system. Such a systemic view of the way that wants enter the economy and are shaped by social and legal processes is necessary if the anthropological approach is to be joined with economics in a general theory of wants. In this perspective the pattern of wants is the surface appearance of a pattern of social relations and social opportunities. Goods are needed as aids to interaction and as clues for constructing intelligible worlds. The consumer is engaged in a continual task of grading goods and occasions and matching them appropriately, as every market researcher knows. It should be useful for a theory of demand to take the social pressures into account. The more isolation and segregation, the more is demand dampened, the more the interaction, the more the need for a symbolic system articulated by finely graded patterns of consumption.

Third, the theory makes one connection (price) between consumption and production but misses another. It treats tastes as personal and subjective and so uninfluenced by the organization of work. But tastes depend upon shared consumption, so the timing of work, the location of homes, the life cycle expectations which are engendered by different occupations, all these and other aspects of the labour market influence the standardization of wants.

To correct these weaknesses in the only theory that claims to be a theory of wants would involve taking much more interest in shared cultural categories that characterize a community. Economists expect to apply their theories to public policy. But whenever they are tempted to speak of what is good for a community, their theory leads to contradiction. As Arrow's theorem proves, the ranked preferences of several individuals cannot necessarily be aggregated into a single ordered set for them all unless, of course, they happen to have the same preferences. In respect of material things they very frequently do. But there is no theory about how this comes to pass. So the theory is at a loss when it comes to thinking about community welfare. Starting from incommensurable, subjective, individual preferences it cannot proceed to theorize about what a community wants. Yet, there seems to be no inherent reason why a theory of wants, which gives credit to their social origins and their social definition and to their community-imposed character, should not serve the needs of economic theory as well as, better than, the one which has historically developed from the concept of the individual as a surrogate for the firm.

MARY DOUGLAS

See also ECONOMIC ANTHROPOLOGY; SOCIAL CHOICE.

BIBLIOGRAPHY

Douglas, M. and Isherwood, B.C. 1979. *The World of Goods*. New York: Basic Books.

Edgeworth, F.Y. 1881. *Mathematical Psychics. An Essay on the Application of Mathematics to the Moral Sciences*. London: Kegan Paul.

Lévi-Strauss, C. 1949. *Les structures élémentaires de la parenté*. Paris: Presses Universitaires.

Mackenzie, D. 1981. *Statistics in Britain, 1865–1930*. Edinburgh: Edinburgh University Press.

Malinowski, B. 1922. *Argonauts of the Western Pacific*. London: Routledge & Kegan Paul.

Mauss, M. 1925. Essai sur le don. *L'année sociologique*, 2nd Series, Vol. 1, 23–4. Trans. as *The Gift*, London: Cohen and West.

Sen, A.K. 1981. *Poverty and Famines: An Essay on Entitlement and Deprivation*. Oxford: Clarendon Press.

Warburton, Clark (1896–1979). American economist; pioneer, before Milton Friedman, in research later labelled 'monetarist', and a critic of Keynesianism during the years when that doctrine was crowding out attention to money.

Warburton was born on 27 January 1896 near Buffalo, New York, and died on 18 September 1979 in Fairfax, Virginia. After overseas military service during World War I, he earned bachelor's and master's degrees from Cornell University. He published his 1932 Columbia PhD dissertation as *The Economic Results of Prohibition*. He held teaching positions in India and the United States in the 1920s and early 1930s and worked at the Brookings Institution from 1932 to 1934, coauthoring *America's Capacity to Consume*. He then joined the newly organized Federal Deposit Insurance Corporation. Although routine FDIC work consumed much of his time (as his files reveal), he still managed to publish over 30 papers on monetary economics, most of them empirically oriented, from 1943 to 1953. Altered FDIC policy then impeded his research and publication until about 1962, when he took a brief leave to serve with the Banking and Currency Committee of the US House of Representatives. He was elected President of the Southern Economic Association for 1963–4. After retiring from the FDIC in 1965, he taught briefly at the University of California, Davis.

Warburton originally accepted a 'real' theory of the business cycle, but scrutiny of statistical and qualitative history changed his views. Using quarterly as well as annual data, he found that deviations from trend of the quantity of money generally preceded turning points in business conditions (and velocity deviations followed). While accepting a quantity-of-money theory of the price level in the long run, he recognized how elements of wage and price stickiness cause monetary disturbances to impinge on output first; he espoused a 'monetary disequilibrium theory' (which, despite its venerability, has ironically been mislabelled 'Keynesian' in recent years). He understood that disequilibrium does not necessarily imply irrational behaviour by individuals.

Warburton emphasized the role of money and inadequate monetary policy in the Great Depression of the 1930s. He continued to criticize the Federal Reserve for deficiencies in its economic theory and research and, in particular, for relying on interest rates in deciding and implementing policy. He believed that pure fiscal policy, unsupported by changes in the quantity of money, is ineffective as a tool of demand management. Skeptical of the authorities' ability to fine-tune the economy, he recommended a policy of steady growth in the quantity of money at a moderate rate appropriate to trends in the labour force, productivity, and velocity.

For Warburton, monetarism was an interpretation reached inductively, not a comprehensive ideology. (So far as any ideology came across in conversations, it was a rather conventional New Deal reformism or liberalism with humanitarian underpinnings.)

Nineteen of Warburton's papers dating from 1945 to 1953 are reprinted, along with a new introduction, in *Depression, Inflation, and Monetary Policy* (1966). Up to his death, Warburton pursued research not only in substantive economics but also in the history of monetary doctrines. These continuing interests are manifest in his last article (published posthumously in *History of Political Economy*, 1981) and in voluminous manuscripts now deposited in the library of George Mason University, Fairfax, Virginia. Plans exist for editing and publishing much of this material.

L. YEAGER

See also QUANTITY THEORY OF MONEY.

SELECTED WORKS

1934. (With M. Leven and G. Moulton.) *America's Capacity to Consume*. Washington, DC: Brookings Institution.

1966. *Depression, Inflation, and Monetary Policy: Selected Papers, 1945–1953*. Baltimore: Johns Hopkins Press.

1981. Monetary disequilibrium theory in the first half of the twentieth century. *History of Political Economy* 13(2), Summer, 285–99.

Ward, Barbara (1914–81). Barbara Ward was born on 23 May 1914 and died in Sussex on 31 May 1981. After graduating from Somerville College, Oxford, she moved rapidly from teaching and research to journalism, becoming assistant editor of *The Economist* in 1940 and later foreign editor. Although she later held appointments at Harvard and Columbia (from 1957 to 1973) and received numerous honorary degrees, the considerable influence she exercised over four decades on international development thinking and policy was primarily due to her masterful skills in popular communication as journalist, broadcaster, outstanding public speaker and author of a score of best-selling books.

Her contributions to development literature were built around three successive and evolving themes. In *The Rich Nations and the Poor Nations* (1961), she dramatized the wide economic and social gap between the industrial and 'under-developed' countries, and underlined the urgent need for international action to bridge it, action for which she argued the Western interest was no less than the interests of the poorer countries themselves. *The Widening Gap* (1971) was a critique of the Pearson Commission report *Partners in Development* (1969), arguing that not only aid but more fundamental changes in international trade, financial arrangements and other economic relationships were also needed. In this respect, *The Widening Gap* laid some of the intellectual foundations for the North–South dialogue of the 1970s and of the subsequent Brandt Commission Report, *North–South: a Programme for Survival* (1979).

Barbara Ward's second contribution is well captured by her concept of 'spaceship earth', her evolving preoccupation with the physical unity and fragility of the planet and what this requires of national and international policy. She emphasized the need for a global perspective of 'human ecology', conservation, the risks of rising armaments and the broader issues of development strategy. These themes were most coherently developed in *Only One Earth: the Care and Maintenance of a Small Planet* (1972) an unofficial report prepared for the United Nations Stockholm Conference on the Human Environment. They also underlay the *Home of Man* (1975) and *Progress for a Small Planet* (1979). Indeed, four or five of the major United Nations' conferences on global issues of the 1970s owed an important part of their intellectual vision and vitality to Barbara Ward.

The third and most persistent characteristic of her contribution to development thinking was the need for vision and the optimistic conviction that enlightened action was almost always possible and could be made politically realistic. The Marshall Plan of 1948–52, was to her a supreme example of such vision and enlightened leadership. Under this plan, the United Stated had for four years transferred some 2 ½% of its GNP on grant terms for the postwar reconstruction of Western Europe. Barbara Ward had eloquently praised this at the time in *The Economist* and she returned to a parallel message in the 1980s when she called for a '20 year Marshall Plan for the Third World'. The call for enlightened leadership, a commitment to morality and idealism in international policy pervaded all Barbara Ward's writings, giving them a cutting edge of practical appeal and inspiration which combined economic liberalism with political radicalism.

RICHARD JOLLY

SELECTED WORKS

1962. *The Rich Nations and the Poor Nations.* New York: Norton.

1971. (With J.D. Runnalls and L. D'Anjou, eds) *The Widening Gap: Development in the 1970's.* New York: Columbia University Press.

1972. (With R. Dubos.) *Only One Earth: The Care and Maintenance of a Small Planet.* New York: Norton.

1976. *The Home of Man. New York.* New York: Norton.

1979. *Progress for a Small Planet.* New York: Norton.

BIBLIOGRAPHY

Brandt, W. 1980. *North–South: Program for Survival.* Report of the Independent Commission on International Development Issues, Cambridge, Mass.: MIT Press.

Pearson, L. 1969. *Partners in Development: Report of the Commission on International Development.* New York: Praeger.

war economy. In wartime, many markets are suspended. When survival is at stake, governments arrogate the task of setting priorities and the power to allocate resources. The problems of wartime allocation are typically those of management and politics, and have to be resolved ad hoc. The majority of wars since 1945 have taken place in less-developed economies, often in the form of insurgencies or civil wars; but this experience and its literature are both fragmented. What follows is based largely on the experience of Germany, Britain and the United States in the First and Second World Wars, in Korea and in Vietnam.

Wartime priorities, even the choice of war as a policy, reflect the constraints of the economy's endowments. At the pre-war stage of power-building, leaders assess their prospective opponents and choose the most appropriate forms of power: whether it should be intensive in capital, labour, enterprise or land. Economic choices are made between bayonets, warships and aircraft, between numbers and quality, home procurement and imports, firepower and mobility, regular war and insurgency, paid armies, voluntary forces or conscription, human capital versus technology and material, defensive versus offensive, fortification versus manoeuvre, 'total war' versus 'limited liability'. Productivity varies in destruction as well as production, and combatants use similar resources with different results. Enterprise, skill and motivation are even more decisive than they are in peacetime. If strategies are influenced by factor endowment, the choice of strategy, in its turn, determines the nature of the economic problem.

One strategic option that has been attractive in the 20th century is economic warfare. This consists of an attempt to identify and destroy vital links in the enemy's economy. World War I the Allied blockade of Germany helped to bring about the collapse of the food supply system, while Britain narrowly avoided the same fate in both world wars. Britain and the United States (but not Germany and Russia) developed doctrines of strategic bombing and dedicated bomber forces to attack the German and Japanese economies. American bomber forces concentrated on economic bottlenecks, and shifted their attack in sequence from key industrial plants to the oil distribution and the transport systems. Britain's Bomber Command, operating at night with less precision, took whole cities as its targets, in the hope of destroying the housing stock and civilian motivation. The flexibility and range of substitutions available in a economy meant that none of these efforts was decisive on its own, and the contribution of economic warfare to Germany's collapse is still debated.

In a war economy the state typically controls a much higher proportion of the national product than in peacetime. One half or more of output can be diverted to military uses. Business rarely continues as usual: instead, government acquires legal powers to direct production, distribution and exchange. But its ability to do so effectively only develops gradually. By taking up idle resources war management can raise the level of output considerably; civilian consumption, especially of durables, is also easy to sacrifice. The existing economic shell remains in place, to make use of production and managerial skills. It is important to reduce duplication of effort, but competition helps to maintain innovation, so firms receive large and secure contracts but retain some independence. War production was largely amenable to the methods of mass production, and often exceeded the scale achieved (or indeed conceivable) in civilian market production. Cost was a secondary consideration. Working at full capacity to produce standard articles at guaranteed prices allowed manufacturers to retain large profits and invest in new plant. Where the difficulties of production exceeded the capacity of private industry (in the case of explosives in the UK, and atomic weapons in America) the government set up or expanded its own arsenals. Much of the new capacity was not easily converted to market production and remained a burden on postwar balance sheets.

Large corporations in America had already undertaken the central management of diversified enterprises before World War I. These methods were adapted to industry-wide management boards in all three countries. Businessmen came forward to manage whole sectors of the economy, often affirming their primary allegiance by refusing to take more than 'a dollar a year'. Such boards commonly governed transport, mining, metals, shipping and food and raw material distribution. The methods used combined delivery quotas, physical resource allocation, price fixing and market incentives. This symbiosis of business and government was known, ironically, as 'war socialism'.

Military tactics in the two world wars were manpower-intensive, and labour was a more crucial factor than capital. The choice between productive and military employment was stark. On the continent of Europe conscription was established in the 19th century and still remains the rule. Britain entered the first war with a professional army, went over to volunteers, and finally, like its allies overseas (except Australia) introduced conscription. All manpower systems gave preference to military over civilian requirements, often to the detriment of efficiency: skilled technicians sometimes served as riflemen. But much of the labour taken up by the armies could be replaced by women, and mass production lent itself to the dilution of skills. In both world wars manpower became a serious constraint on the combatants, especially Germany, which ran short in the trenches, the factories and the farms; in World War II Germany pressed in millions of forced labourers from prison camps and occupied territories. Full employment in large-scale industry is conductive to trade union organization, and memberships rose to record levels. For their part, unions had to remove restrictive practices and repudiate strikes. In return, the membership was shielded from industrial and often military conscription, while the leadership got recognition, incorporation and even partnership in government. Such accommodations weakened the hold of unions over their members, and when wages and working conditions failed to keep up with prices, unauthorized stoppages and unrest kept recurring; in World War I, unrest was transformed into revolution in the wake of military defeat.

War increases the consumption of foods, fibres, other raw materials and metals. It diverts resources from manufacturing and agriculture and creates a general state of material shortages. Agriculture presents some of the most difficult problems of management. Its manpower and draft animals were mobilized by the military, and in Europe it suffered from shortages of imported fodder and fertilizer and breakdowns in transport. In Germany, the official reaction to food shortages was to impose maximum consumer prices and delivery quotas, which helped to reduce shipments to well below peacetime levels, as producers chose to consume more of the output themselves. In contrast, in English-speaking countries farmers got minimum prices, delivered record harvests and achieved a good balance between livestock and arable products. All combatants adopted rationing. In the name of solidarity and fairness, rationing systems tended to equality; often as in the case of Germany, to the point of ignoring physiological inequalities. Rationing, not only of food but of most other consumer commodities, has called for major efforts of administration, which were sometimes tainted by corruption. Extensive black markets restored differentials by offering restricted goods illegally at high prices. With housebuilding at a standstill, all combatants kept inflation and unrest down by holding dwelling rents below market prices. These controls often persisted years beyond the end of the war, distorted pre-existing housing supply systems and affected the structure of the industry.

International trade assumes a peculiar quality in wartime. Transactions become one-sided and unequal, and commodities trade for political assets and capital transfers. In both world wars Britain ran up very large deficits overseas and also liquidated many of its overseas investments. In its turn, Britain supported its allies extensively, while American economic aid underpinned British survival in both world wars. In the First World War, and more systematically in the Second, Germany plundered its occupied territories. The large imbalances of international trade broke down the convertibility of currencies, and placed obstacles on the road to recovery.

Transport is a weak link. Railways are rigid and not easily adapted to wartime freight flows, while shipping is a very lumpy form of capital, which was destroyed and reproduced wholesale in the two world wars. In the second, railways were also disrupted from the air. Transport equipment competed with munitions for the same scarce labour, machinery and materials. In consequence, transport bottlenecks hampered both the military and civilian war efforts. Like other consumer durables, the manufacture of motor cars almost ceased and petrol was strictly rationed, thereby imposing further handicaps on the transport system.

Arms races are a permanent fixture of the 20th century, and the competition of weapons accelerates in wartime. This stimulates technical innovation, and war is a fertile source of practical and impractical inventions. Shortages have prompted technological substitutions like air-fixed nitrogen and synthetic foodstuffs, and social ones like daylight saving. War also effected technology transfers as patents were suspended for the duration, and often for several years beyond.

Finance is a key problem of economic management. The origins of central banking and national debts lie in the war finance of the 18th century. The problem is simply stated, if not so simply resolved. The state withdraws labour and commodities from the economy, and pays with liquid funds. An increased supply of money raises the prices of a depleted flow of civilian goods and services. To keep inflation in check, the state has to withdraw liquidity as fast as it pumps it in. Taxation rises, but its effectiveness depends on civilian motivation, and war governments have preferred to raise most of their funds by borrowing; some of it absorbs purchasing power from individuals and firms, while borrowing from the central and commercial banks increases liquidity. Requisition and confiscation are less efficient and are only used in exceptional circumstances. In both world wars direct taxes rose by an order of magnitude, while war loans paid rates of interest well above prewar levels. Direct taxation penetrated down the social scale, and one of the best British innovations of World War II was deferred wages. As wars progressed, businessmen were made to pay special taxes on their superprofits.

None of these measures could square the circle. In World War I prices more than doubled in four years. Inflation ran completely out of control in the defeated countries and was only arrested in allied countries by savage deflation in 1920–21. The lesson was learned, and in World War II inflation was largely kept in check by measures of forced saving. National debts increased by an order of magnitude. In World War I, the combatants also pinned some hopes on a large indemnity, for which the Franco–Prussian war of 1870–71 provided a precedent. But reparations proved to be a mirage, and neither the allies, nor the Americans who supported them, managed to effect a sufficiently large transfer from debtors to creditors in the inter-war years. After World War II the effort was not repeated; the United States pumped loans and grants into Western Europe during the reconstruction period. This allowed a very rapid recovery in Germany and Japan, which was also assisted by the destruction of their obsolete industrial plant.

20th-century wars have had considerable distributional effects, both international and domestic. From an economic point of view both world wars have favoured the United States, allowing it to capture new markets, wiping out debt in the First World War and pulling the economy out of depression in the Second. Two subsequent American wars, in

Korea and Vietnam, were not so beneficial: with the economy already close to full capacity, they fuelled inflation and may have crowded out domestic projects. Domestically, wartime favours the productive sectors: Industrialists, skilled factory workers and farmers found themselves in positions of relative strength. Labour benefited: after a short period of frictional unemployment at the outset, full employment ensued; even if wages failed to keep up with prices, family earnings usually ran well ahead, with longer hours and higher participation rates, male and especially female. Rationing did not prevent a substantial improvement in working-class nutrition in Britain, while in Germany, for example, a slight relative improvement was wiped out by the absolute immiseration of civilian society. The inter-war settlement in Britain effected a redistribution to capital as women withdrew from the workforce, unemployment reappeared and a large share of tax revenue was transferred to the owners of the national debt. In Germany and central Europe inflation wiped out financial assets and the national debt altogether, and impoverished the owners of fixed-interest securities. It is often argued that wartime laid the ground for a more generous welfare policy post-war, in a number of ways. It began in the form of transfers to servicemen's families and continued as veterans' benefits. More debatable is the claim that mass-participation wars give rise to expectations of reward. 'Homes fit for Heroes', the World War I slogan, captures this expectation; a commitment to full employment followed World War II in both Britain and America. But government expenditure post-war merely takes up the prewar trend, albeit at higher levels. Certainly wars work to raise acceptable tax levels and involve the State in extensive areas of social policy.

War economies build up before the shooting begins and they continue after it subsides. After World War I government share of GNP fell in most combatant economies, although taxation remained high. Government expenditure picked up during the rearmament phase of the 1930s in Germany and Britain. After the end of World War II America and Russia remained in a state of semi-mobilization. One feature is a high share of defence expenditure as a share of GNP; in the United States this is about seven times the inter-war level. Another is conscription, which remains universal in continental Europe, and was only dismantled in the United States after Vietnam. It is argued that defence technology 'crowds out' civilian enterprise, as a good part of scientific manpower works in military research. High defence expenditures continue to exert inflationary pressure. Another, more debatable aspect, is the continuing welfare orientation of advanced economies, which perhaps owes something to wartime solidarity, tax levels and governmental powers. Business symbiosis with defence continues. In America the heads of both General Motors and Ford became Secretaries of Defense, and some large corporations depend heavily on military budgets. One persistent feature of wartime economy in peace are stockpiles of strategic commodities, which are sometimes used to regulate production and prices. Farm support programmes hark back to the experience and apprehensions of the war economy. Limitations on technology transfer are justified not merely by commercial expediency, but by national security.

The command economy of Soviet Russia was formed under the shadow of military threat and consequently has many features of a war economy: a very large military sector, conscription, shortage of consumer goods and housing coupled with strictly controlled prices, high female participation rates, a tendency to autarky, extensive (but low-quality) welfare services and low unemployment. On the other hand it has successfully controlled inflation by means of price and wage controls, and by retaining financial assets almost entirely in state hands.

War is common enough as a policy choice, but is really too uncertain to be approached entirely as a rational undertaking. The stakes and imponderables are very large. Both sides (if there are only two) assume in advance that fighting is worthwhile and at least one of them is wrong. Economic theory has consequently not found much application in war, although the use of price incentives by American and British war administrators have, on the whole, proved sounder than the physical and administrative controls of the Germans. World War II saw the attempts to optimize military decisions by means of operations research and empirical survey. An attempt to manage war with economic tools and systematic analysis of costs, risks and benefits was started at the American Department of Defense under Robert McNamara in the 1960s. Suffice it to say that the best available theory and the world's most powerful economy were not equal to the task.

AVNER OFFER

See also DEFENCE ECONOMICS; MILITARY EXPENDITURE; PRICE CONTROL.

BIBLIOGRAPHY

Carnegie Endowment for International Peace. *Economic and Social History of the War*. (Many vols, covering most of the European combatants and some neutrals in World War I. This is the largest body of published research on war economies.)

Chester, D.N. (ed.) 1951. *Lessons of the British War Economy*. Cambridge: Cambridge University Press.

Clarkson, G.B. 1923. *Industrial America in the World War: The Strategy Behind the Line 1917–1918*. New York: Houghton Mifflin.

Enthoven, A.C. and Smith, K.W. *How Much is Enough? Shaping the Defense Program, 1961–1969*. New York: Harper & Row.

Hancock, W.K. and Gowing, M.M. 1949. *The British War Economy*. London: HMSO. (See also other volumes in the British Official History of the Second World War, Civil Series.)

Hardach, G. 1978. *The First World War 1914–1918*. London: Allen Lane.

Hoffman, F.S. 1959. The economic analysis of defense: choice without markets. *American Economic Review* 49(2), May 368–76.

Kennedy, G. 1983. *Defense Economics*. New York: St Martin's Press.

Keynes, J.M. 1940. *How to Pay for the War*. London: Macmillan.

Klein, G.H. 1959. *Germany's Economic Preparations for War*. Cambridge, Mass.: Harvard University Press.

Knorr, K. 1956. *The War Potential of Nations*. Princeton: Princeton University Press.

Koistinen, P.A.C. 1980. *The Military-Industrial Complex: A Historical Perspective*. New York: Praeger.

Lloyd, E.H.M. 1924. *Experiments in State Control at the War Office and the Ministry of Food*. Carnegie Endowment for International Peace, Economic and Social History of the War, British series, New Haven: Yale University Press.

Milward, A. 1967. *The German Economy at War*. London: Athlone Press.

Milward, A. 1976. *War, Economy and Society 1939–1945*. London: Allen Lane.

Olson, M., Jr. 1963. *The Economics of Wartime Shortage. A History of British Food Supplies in the Napoleonic War and in World Wars I and II*. Durham: Duke University Press.

Scitovsky, T., Shaw, E. and Tarshis, L. 1951. *Mobilizing Resources for War: The Economic Alternatives*. New York: McGraw-Hill.

Skalweit, A. 1927. *Die Deutsche Kriegsernahrungswirtschaft*. Carnegie Endowment for International Peace, Economic and Social History of the War, German series. Stuttgart: Deutsche Verlagsanstalt.

United States Strategic Bombing Survey. *The Effects of Strategic Bombing on the German War Economy*. Washington: GPO.

Warming, Jens (1873–1939). Jens Warming was born on 9 December 1873 and died on 8 September 1939.

After graduating in law, Warming took up economics. In 1919 he became Professor in Applied Statistics at the University of Copenhagen, following more informal attachments to the university. Along with his teaching he produced a number of books describing empirically a wide variety of aspects of the Danish economy. In a way he created the field 'Applied Statistics' as an academic discipline in Denmark. He not only presented figures, but he surrounded them with reasoning, sometimes naive and not very well articulated, often full of wisdom. One example is his warning of the danger of overfishing because no rent is collected (Warming, 1931b). Another most important example is his discovery of the multiplier process, which he presented as early as 1928 and again in 1929–30 and 1931. These important contributions in economic theory were quite often formulated in a somewhat odd way, and they certainly did not attract his fellow economists in Scandinavia.

Warming's formulation of the multiplier runs as follows: assume a closed economy (an assumption he later modified) and consider an investment of, say, 100 units in a railway. This creates an income of equal size, part of it appearing as an increase in savings, but another part as consumption, that latter creating new incomes. This process, he argues will go on until voluntary savings will increase, so that the newly-constructed railway 'gets an owner' (1929–30). This clearly means that the total voluntary savings in the end equal the impulse, i.e. 100 units. An investment will 'finance itself', as he argued at length. However, it does not seem as if Warming was considering the multiplier as part of a more general theory of employment.

P. Nørregaard Rasmussen

SELECTED WORKS

1924. *Valutasprøgsmålet* (The problem of foreign exchange).

1928. Beskæftigelsesproblemet (The employment problem). *Gads Danske Magasin.*

1929–30. *Danmarks Erhvervs- og Samfundsliv* (Denmark's economic and social life). Copenhagen.

1931a. Tilpasning (Adaptation). *Gads Danske Magasin.*

1931b. Aalegaardsretten. *Nationalkonomisk Tidsskrift.*

1932. International difficulties arising out of financing of public works during depression. *Economic Journal* 42, June, 211–24.

1939. *Danmarks Erhvervs- og Samfundsliv* (Denmark's economic and social life). 2nd edn, Copenhagen: G.E.C. Gad. (This edition was never completed.)

BIBLIOGRAPHY

Boserup, M. 1969. A note on the prehistory of the Kahn multiplier. *Economic Journal* 79, September, 667–9.

Gelting, J. H. 1964. Jens Warming. *Nationalkonomisk Tidsskrift.*

Hegeland, H. 1954. *The Multiplier Theory.* Lund: Gleerup.

Kahn, R.F. 1931. The relation of home investment to unemployment. *Economic Journal* 41, June, 173–98.

warranted growth. *See* NATURAL AND WARRANTED RATES OF GROWTH.

warrants. *See* OPTION PRICING; OPTIONS.

waste products. *See* ENVIRONMENTAL ECONOMICS; POLLUTION.

water resources. Interest in the economics of water resources had its inception in the United States upon the passage of the Flood Control Act of 1936. That legislation specified that '... benefits to whomsoever they may accrue, exceed the costs' to justify project development. That statement both implied an efficiency criterion and anticipated the Hicks–Kaldor compensation principle. Thereafter, the newly created Subcommittee on Benefits and Costs of the Interagency River Basin Committee began to elaborate the economic implications of this section of the legislation. Attention was initially focused on getting an appropriate investment criterion, which addressed not only the issues of optimally designing, sizing and timing projects, but also questions of estimating the value of non-priced services such as flood damage reduction and the value of a user-free waterway for barge traffic. In addressing these issues the Subcommittee on Benefits and Costs had to deal practically with several issues that had attracted, or were to attract, the attention of the economics profession.

One of these was to the measurement of the contribution of a project to consumer well-being, when services are not marketed or outputs are large relative to a market. On the larger rivers the site for an impoundment, if developed to a scale that would minimize unit costs, often produced a facility having an output that was large in relation to the existing market (for the the pre-World War II United States economy) not unlike current circumstances in developing countries. Making up a large share of total system capacity, the output of a hydroelectric facility, for example, would have to be sold at a substantial reduction in pre-project price in order to clear the market. Whether from pragmatic considerations, or simple intuition, the Subcommittee recommended that the block of energy be valued at neither the price that ruled before the event, nor at the new market-clearing price, but rather by a price midway between the pre- and post-project prices. Now if the demand for power could be taken to be approximated by a linear function, we observe that this is virtually equal to the area under the demand curve, an accurate measure of the willingness to pay for the service. This issue was treated more precisely in Eckstein's later work (1958).

Another issue addressed by the Subcommittee was the problem of estimating the value of project outputs which are public goods. It is a characteristic of flood management using reservoir storages, that if the system is managed to provide flow regulating services for one occupant in the flood plain, it simultaneously provides damage reduction services for all occupants in the flood plain. And the value of the damage reduction enjoyed by any occupant does not diminish the value of the service to other flood plain occupants. In short, flood stage reducing services of storage reservoirs have the characteristics of a public good. This was discovered as a practical matter before the economic treatment of the problem by Samuelson (1954). In spite of the potential difficulties stemming from non-revelation of preferences for public goods, an estimate of flood control benefits was obtained indirectly by estimates of the demand for substitute market goods in the manner detailed by Karl-Göran Mäler (1974). That is, given the hydrologists' estimates of the recurrence interval of various flood stages with and without the flood control projects, and the difference in damages to facilities in the flood plain that would occur under two regimes, an estimate of the value of the flood management services could be obtained. This procedure was employed to estimate the value of flood control facilities of the Tennessee Valley Authority throughout the 1930s and by the US Corps of Engineers in the remainder of the country.

In addition to awareness of project valuation problems associated with indivisible inputs and outputs, direct or physical interdependence among facilities, a pervasive phenomenon in the natural resource sector, was also recognized early. The value of downstream hydroelectric facilities also was known to be linked to the presence of upstream storage and thus direct interdependence received early attention in planning and valuing water resource systems. This is additional to the wide variety of measurable externalities which were treated routinely in river basin planning.

The conceptual framework that supported the work carried on during the 1930s and 1940s was largely the contribution of the planning engineers assisted by the work of the Subcommittee on Benefits and Costs. Where irrigation agriculture was involved, as it was in all of the arid western states, agricultural economists with the United States Department of Agriculture (USDA) Bureau of Agricultural Economics (BAE) (now the Agricultural Research Service) were notably present. Perhaps the most prominent for his contribution to this area was Mark Regan. The dean of the academic agricultural economists whose contribution was substantial was Professor S.V. Ciriacy-Wantrup of the University of California, Berkeley. It should be mentioned that during the twenty years following the Flood Control Act of 1936, there was little interest in the economics of water resources by academic economists, except for a small number in the agricultural colleges in the western United States where irrigation agriculture was extensively practised.

During the mid- to late 1950s, however, the environment changed dramatically. The water resource ventures in the 1930s and 1940s were an expression of President Roosevelt's New Deal philosophy. In 1952 there was the first change in political parties to head up the national administration in twenty years. The new administration had a pronounced tilt toward using the market and private ventures to substitute for practically all public ventures. Along with this change in policy went a reduction in budgets for public sector expenditures. This change of emphasis in Washington created an environment in which both public and private development had to be justified. The new emphases of this changed environment stimulated a number of economic inquiries by academic economists.

At the end of the 1950s, three studies with somewhat different emphases emerged almost simultaneously. One, by Otto Eckstein (1958), addressed the subject matter of the Subcommittee on Benefits and Costs (1950), providing a more rigorous theoretical structure for the evaluation of water resource projects, including investment criteria to cover the constrained budget case. A second study by Krutilla and Eckstein (1958) addressed the question of the relative efficiency of public and private development of water resource systems, identifying cases in which, under the then current institutional arrangement (Federal Power Act and related legislation) each alternative had the advantage. While this study was undertaken in the spirit of the Hicks–Kaldor compensation criterion it nonetheless undertook the first significant study of the distributional aspects of a public works expenditure. The third volume by McKean (1958) attempted to bring advances in weapon systems evaluation methodology developed at the Rand Corporation to investment analysis in the water resources field. All of these studies, without being explicit, nonetheless relied heavily on old fashioned neoclassical welfare economics.

Perhaps the most comprehensive single study of water resource economics was provided by Hirshleifer, De Haven and Milliman (1960). This study addressed the issue of more efficient allocation of existing supplies as one option to more extensive development of additional sources. The volume, incidentally, represented a thorough-going critique of water resource policies, laws and institutions.

The terminal study of this generation of water studies is the voluminous 'report' of the Harvard Water Resource Seminar, a multi-year seminar that was conducted by members of the Harvard political science, economics and engineering faculties and hosted among its students, practicing public sector professionals regularly engaged in various roles in public water resource agencies.

The combination of analytic vigour and field experience present in the Harvard study served to reveal the interstices between theory and application and make more evident the significance of distributional considerations that constrain the politically feasible optimization prescriptions. The concern with distributional considerations was not confined to the deliberations of the Harvard Water Resources Seminar (Maass et al., 1962). Krutilla and Eckstein (1958) had already addressed the distributional consequences of public expenditures. This was done, however, as a descriptive, rather than as an explicit policy analytic, exercise. The Harvard seminar, the work of Haveman (1965), Freeman (1967), Haveman and Krutilla (1968) and Tolley (1959) investigated the distributional consequences as policy issues bringing up more prominently the significance of distributional considerations than had been done previously.

As the water resource economics field matured the nature of the studies tended to specialize to the various individual functions that water resources development provides. A partial accounting of these would include: for irrigated agriculture, Ruttan (1965), Frederick (1975), Crosson, Cummings, and Frederick (1978); for interbasin transfers, Howe and Easter (1971), Cummings (1974), Hartman and Seastone (1975); for hydropower and flood control development on an international stream, Krutilla (1967) and Lind (1967); and for inland waterway transportation, Howe and associates (1969).

Another study carried out in the same spirit and addressing qualitative aspects of streamflows was the seminal work by Allen Kneese (1964) which brought a whole new dimension to water resources research. It introduced to economic analysis the field of environmental economics, and indeed most of the work in water resources for the next two decades addressed environmental issues of various kinds.

The general field of water resources appeared to many to offer important opportunities to apply welfare economics to practical problems. In this regard, while many of the studies contented themselves with meeting the Hicks–Kaldor compensation criterion, others attempted to implement Little's dictum that the income redistribution of such public undertakings be 'good' (1950). It may be wondered how the present essay can be written without reference to Little's own work applying many of the same analytical techniques in a somewhat similar environment – industrial investment projects in the developing countries. But the work of Little and Mirrlees (1968, 1969) was not specifically related to investments in water resource projects, nor was the work of Mishan (1972) and Squire and Van der Tak (1975). Nevertheless, they all addressed a common genre of problems in an environment where new capacity involved lumpiness, where the outputs involved public goods in part and where externalities similarly bedevilled market indices of value.

JOHN V. KRUTILLA

See also NATURAL RESOURCES; USER FEES.

BIBLIOGRAPHY

Ciriacy-Wantrup, S.V. 1955. Benefit–cost analysis and public resource development. *Journal of Farm Economics* 37(4), November, 676–89.

Ciriacy-Wantrup, S.V. 1964. Concepts used as economic criteria for a system of water rights. In *Economics and Public Policy in Water Resources Development*, ed. S.C. Smith and E.N. Castle, Ames, Iowa: Iowa State University Press.

Crosson, P.R., Cummings, R.C. and Frederick, K.D. (eds) 1978. *Selected Water Management Issues in Latin American Agriculture*. Baltimore and London: Johns Hopkins University Press for Resources for the Future.

Cummings, R.G. 1974. *Interbasin Water Transfers: A Case Study in Mexico*. Washington, DC: Resources for the Future.

Eckstein, O. 1958. *Water Resources Development: The Economics of Project Evaluation*. Cambridge, Mass.: Harvard University Press.

Frederick, K.D. 1975. *Water Management and Agricultural Development: A Case Study of the Cuyo Region of Argentina*. Baltimore: Johns Hopkins Press for Resources for the Future.

Freeman, A.M. 1967. Income distribution and public investment. *American Economic Review* 57(3), June, 495–508.

Hartman, L.M. and Seastone, D. 1975. *Water Transfers, Economic Efficiency and Alternative Institutions*. Baltimore: Johns Hopkins University Press for Resources for the Future.

Haveman, R.H. 1965. *Water Resource Investment and the Public Interest*. Nashville: Vanderbilt University Press.

Haveman, R. and Krutilla, J.V. 1968. *Unemployment, Idle Capacity, and the Valuation of Public Expenditures: National and Regional Analyses*. Baltimore: Johns Hopkins University Press for Resources for the Future.

Hirshleifer, J., Dehaven, J.C. and Milliman, J.W. 1960. *Water Supply Economics, Technology and Policy*. Chicago: University of Chicago Press.

Howe, C.W. and Easter, K.W. 1971. *Interbasin Transfer of Water: Economic Issues and Impacts*. Baltimore: Johns Hopkins University Press for Resources for the Future.

Howe, C.W., Carroll, J.L., Hurter, A.P., Jr., Leininger, W.J., Ramsey, S.G., Schwartz, N.L., Silberberg, E.A. and Steinberg, R.M. 1969. *Inland Waterway Transportation: Studies in Public and Private Management and Investment Decisions*. Washington, DC: Resources for the Future.

Kneese, V. 1964. *The Economics of Regional Water Quality Management*. Baltimore: Johns Hopkins University Press for Resources for the Future.

Krutilla, J.V. 1961. Welfare aspects of benefit–cost analysis. *Journal of Political Economy* 69(3), June, 226–35.

Krutilla, J.V. 1967. *The Columbia River Treaty: The Economics of an International River Basin Development*. Baltimore: Johns Hopkins University Press for Resources for the Future.

Krutilla, J.V. and Eckstein, O. 1958. *Multiple Purpose River Development: Studies in Applied Economic Analysis*. Baltimore: Johns Hopkins University Press for Resources for the Future.

Lind, R.C. 1967. Flood control alternatives and economics of flood protection. *Water Resources Research* 3(2).

Little, I.M.D. 1950. *A Critique of Welfare Economics*. Cambridge: Cambridge University Press.

Little, I.M.D. and Mirrlees, J.A. 196. *Manual of Industrial Project Analysis in Developing Countries*. Vols I and II, Paris: Development Centre of the Organization of Economic Co-operation and Development.

Maass, A., Hufschmidt, M.H., Dorfman, R., Thomas, H.A., Jr., Marglin, S. and Fair, G.M. 1962. *The Design of Water-Resources Systems*. Cambridge, Mass.: Harvard University Press.

Mäler, K.-G. 1972. *Environmental Economics*. Baltimore: Johns Hopkins University Press for Resources for the Future.

McKean, R.N. 1958. *Efficiency in Government Through Systems Analysis, with Emphasis on Water Resource Development*. New York: John Wiley & Sons.

Mishan, E.J. 1972. *Economics for Social Decisions; Elements of Cost-benefit Analysis*. London: George Allen & Unwin.

Ruttan, V.W. 1965. *The Economic Demand for Irrigated Acreage: New Methodology and Some Preliminary Results, 1954–1980*. Baltimore: Johns Hopkins University Press for Resources for the Future.

Samuelson, P.A. 1954. The pure theory of public expenditures. *Review of Economics and Statistics* 36, November, 387–9.

Squire, L. and Van der Tak, H.G. 1975. *Economic Analysis of Projects*. Baltimore: Johns Hopkins University Press for the World Bank.

Steiner, P.O. 1959. Choosing among alternative public investments in the water resources field. *American Economic Review* 49(5), December, 893–916.

Subcommittee on Benefits and Costs. 1950. Report to the Federal Interagency River Basin Committee, *Proposed Practices for Economic Analysis of River Basin Projects*.

Tolley, G. 1959. Reclamations influence on the rest of agriculture. *Land Economics* 35(2), May, 176–80.

wealth. Wealth is a fundamental concept in economics – indeed, perhaps the conceptual starting point for the discipline. Despite its centrality, however, the concept of wealth has never been a matter of general consensus. Although wealth has not become a focus of heated controversy comparable to that of value (despite the fact that the two terms are inextricably conjoined, as we shall see), conceptions of wealth have clashed profoundly and even irreconcilably. The result has been a continuing discussion of deep importance for economics – not only for its intrinsic interest, but because it calls into question the very scope and content of the discipline itself.

At the root of the long history of disagreement about wealth lie two conflicting conceptions of what the word implies. One of these, far more ancient than the formal study of economics and still very much in general use, is the idea of wealth as tangible possessions. For over a century, however, this conception has been challenged by another, which has identified the nature of wealth in the pleasures or 'utilities' generated by tangible goods, rather than the goods themselves. In the differing implications arising from these 'objective' and 'subjective' conceptions of wealth lie consequences of great significance for a discipline that has traditionally considered itself to be concerned with the study of wealth.

The objective conception of wealth is as old as written history, but the economist has not been interested in records of slaves and land and gold, other than to remark (usually as an economic anthropologist) on the extraordinary variety of objects that have been utilized as embodiments of wealth. The analytic problem to which economists have been drawn has been the attempt to establish a common denominator in which to sum up the value represented by a heterogenous collection of objects. 'The entire study of wealth is, indeed, meaningless unless there be a unit for measuring it;' wrote J. B. Clark, 'for the questions to be answered are quantitative. How great is the wealth of a nation?' (Clark, 1895, p. 375).

In ordinary discourse, this common denominator has always been money, and we will later consider the cogency of this common sense rule. For the economist, however, the challenge has been to discover some metric less arbitrary and unstable than a monetary sum. Thus the idea of objective wealth becomes inextricably entwined with the need to discover a standard – an embodiment of 'value' – by which its extent can be calculated. In the late mercantilist period this measure of extent was conceived by Petty and Cantillon to be the 'amounts' of land and labour that entered into the production of things – a considerable advance over earlier ideas that gold and silver possessed intrinsic value. This dual standard was subsequently reduced by Adam Smith to labour alone .'It was not by gold or silver, but by labour that all the wealth of the world was originally purchased,' he wrote in *The Wealth of Nations*, 'and its value, to those who possess it and who want to exchange it for some new productions, is precisely equal to the quantity of labour which it can enable them to purchase or command' (Smith, [1776], p. 48).

The choice of an objective standard of wealth – in Smith's case the labour 'commanded' by goods – focused the discipline of economics on the processes by which these embodiments of wealth were amassed. By the 17th century, the rise of a market organization of trade and production had already brought to the fore the distinctively 'economic' problem of wealth – namely, the need to explain its accumulation as the outcome of impersonal processes rather than as the spoils of power. From Smith's physiocratic predecessors through John Stuart Mill, the principal aim of political economy was accordingly to investigate the consequences of a competitive struggle for wealth, both with respect to its distribution among individuals and social classes, and to its effect on the development of the system as a whole.

Almost from the outset, however, the conception of wealth as an objective element in the economic process posed troublesome questions. One of these was the appropriate treatment of labour that produced services rather than tangible goods. Because services are flows, they cannot be included in wealth, if the latter is defined as a tangible stock. The difference, as Cassel explained, involves *time*: stocks are present in their entirety at a moment in time; flows require the passage of time (Cassel [1918], p. 31). A second difficulty concerned the classification of different kinds of labour. Smith, for example, differentiated between productive and unproductive labour, calling 'productive' only the labour whose product could be sold to replenish the working capital of the manufacturer, and designating as 'unproductive' all services – 'how honourable, how useful, or how necessary soever' – because these activities consumed, but did not renew, the fund of circulating capital whence they derived their subsistence (Smith [1776], p. 331).

In addition, Smith and Ricardo recognized that labour was itself a heterogenous rather that a simple 'substance', and that some means would have to be found to reduce its complexity to a uniform basis. Both consigned the solution of the problem to the workings of the market. This may have been adequate for a rough and ready explanation of wage differentials originally established by market considerations and subsequently perpetuated by social inertia, but it concealed the deeper problem of reducing a spectrum of labour skills to a common denominator of 'simple' labour without recourse to market forces – that is, to supply and demand.

Finally, as Marx was to point out, the classical economists did not perceive that labour was a concrete activity – the labour of Ricardo's deer hunter not being substitutable for that of his salmon fisherman – so that a level of 'abstract' labour had to be posited if labour was to serve as a universal equivalent, or measuring rod, for wealth. Although the full difficulty of reducing labour to its abstract essence escaped Marx himself, for all these reasons the concept of labour as a simple and self-evident metric became increasingly difficult to accept.

In accounting for the decline of the objective view of wealth, however, it is likely that the difficulties enumerated above did not play so important a role as another, quite separate, objection. This was the awareness that wealth as an objective entity did not express the attribute of goods that seemingly endowed them with desirability, namely their capacity to yield pleasure or utility to their possessors or beneficiaries. Oddly enough, we can also trace this view of wealth to Smith, who declared that 'Every man is rich or poor according to the degree in which he can afford the necessaries, conveniencies, and amusements of human life', (Smith [1776], p. 47).

It was Ricardo who first pointed out the inconsistency in Smith's views, in that the subjective enjoyments yielded by wealth – its 'riches' – were not the same as the expenditure of labour power required for its creation – its 'value'. Thus for Ricardo, two countries might be equally 'rich' in necessaries and conveniences, but the value of the riches of one would be larger than that of the second if they required more labour to produce (Ricardo, 1821, ch. 20).

Ricardo's distinction between riches and value marks a sharp distinction between subjective (enjoyment) and objective (embodiment) conceptions of wealth, but Ricardo himself did not pursue the analytic and conceptual horizons opened up by the subjective view. That was to be the work of the post-classical period, culminating in the marginalist 'revolution' of the 1870s. Although this episode is famous for its shift in the concept of value from labour to utility, it is apparent that this shift entailed an equally deep-seated and far-reaching change in the conception of wealth, and as a consequence, in the study of economics. The works of Gossen, Menger, Jevons, and Walras – the pioneers in this redirection of economics – display considerable variations in their internal details but not in their underlying depiction of the task of economics. This was now seen as an examination of the conditions for the optimization of enjoyments (utilities), not for the maximization of tangible wealth (capital). Thus Jevons wrote in *The Theory of Political Economy*, 'The problem of economics may, as it seems to me, be stated thus: Given, a certain population, with various needs and powers of production, in possession of certain lands and other sources of material: required, the mode of employing their labour which will maximize the utility of the produce' (Jevons [1871], p. 254, original in italics).

A striking consequence of this shift was the necessary divorce of economics from any quantitative estimation of the extent of wealth. Utility in the post-classical sense was not the same as the 'use-values' that had always been recognized by Smith or Ricardo or Marx as the prerequisites of exchangeability. Their use-values referred to *objective* attributes of goods – the hardness of diamonds, the softness of cloth – from which was derived the capacity of commodities to yield subjective satisfactions. The utilities of the marginalists, on the other hand, referred exclusively to the states of mind induced by the possession or use of objects. Unlike use-values, therefore, utilities were subject to continual, possibly radical shifts, induced by changes in tastes or income or the relative scarcities of objects – in all cases, changes in the relation between possessors and objects, and not changes in the physical character of the goods themselves.

From this perspective, utility therefore had no objective existence whatsoever. 'We can never say absolutely that some objects have utility and others have not,' Jevons wrote; and following in that line, Robbins declared in *The Nature and Significance of Economic Science* (1932, p. 47) that 'wealth is not wealth because of its substantial qualities. It is wealth because it is scarce'.

The emphasis on the psychological element of wealth and on the role of scarcity in conferring desirability to goods clarified many questions, for example the ancient water–diamonds paradox. In addition the utility approach appeared to resolve the problem of valuation at a level of greater generality than labour. It could be used, for example, to explain exchange value in the case of goods that required little or no labour, such as Ricardo's 'rare statues and pictures', within the same analytic framework as in the case of goods in which labour constituted a major element of cost. Thus the rise of a subjective orientation to wealth and value – we can by now surely appreciate their inextricable association – seemed an immense liberation to economists who had struggled within the constraints of an objective theory of wealth and value, whether exclusively denominated in labour or not.

The new orientation was not, however, without its problems. In so far as marginal utility is normally a direct function of scarcity, its adoption as the metric of wealth entailed the awkward conclusion that wealth as a sum of enjoyments and conveniences might well *increase* as a consequence of the *diminution* of material abundance. Some of the marginalists accepted this result; others, such as Menger, called it only an 'apparent' paradox, on the grounds that the continual augmentation of goods would gradually remove them from the category of 'economic' goods, thereby excluding them from consideration as wealth (Menger [1871], 111). This seems a question-begging resolution. In addition, the replacement of an objective by a subjective standard of wealth led to the even more awkward conclusion that the aggregation of the wealth of individuals was impossible on the same grounds as the aggregation of their feelings or experiences. It was such considerations that led Robbins to declare in his influential essay mentioned above that 'in any rigid determination of Economics, the term wealth should be avoided' (Robbins, 1932, p. 47n).

All attempts to define wealth have therefore led to difficulties and even paradoxes. The conceptual and mensurational problems of an objective approach denominated in labour have been equalled, perhaps even surpassed, by those of a subjective approach denominated in utilities. Notwithstanding Robbins's reservations, however, economists have not abandoned the use of wealth as a fundamental constitutive element of economics, nor have they given up attempts to measure it. Here we can trace the general line of development once more to Adam Smith, this time to his famous abandonment of the category of labour as the measuring rod of value and his substitution of a cost of production measure which simply added up the income flows – wages, rents, and profits – accruing to the three major classes.

From Ricardo on, Smith has been accused of circularity or inconsistency in this choice of an 'adding-up' approach to value, in which no attempt was made to discover a common denominator of wealth. But as a practical solution to the problem of measuring a concept that was universally regarded as real and important, whatever its intrinsic difficulties, Smith's approach was not without merit. The cost of production, or adding-up, approach to national wealth provided a common sense basis for the representation of national power or collective wellbeing, regardless of the unexamined problems behind these representations.

At all events, in modern times the measurement of wealth has become a major preoccupation for virtually all advanced nations. In *The Statistical Abstract of the United States*, for example, we find time series of various stocks and flows that have been selected as being of particular significance for the measurement of national wealth. The stocks include such items as estimates of financial and real assets, business and residential capital, consumers' stocks of durables, land and selected government assets; while the flows concentrate on gross national product and its components. These items have been selected partly on the basis of the availability of data and partly on the basis of their importance for national economic policy. They are neither a complete nor a consistent set of accounts, a number of important stocks and flows being absent, such as the stock of human capital, or the flow of unpaid labour in household work. The method of valuing both stocks and flows also differs from the public to the private sector, since the standard valuation is that of 'market values', which cannot apply to public goods or services. This is not the place to discuss the problems of national accounting, but it is worth noting that the same standard of practicality is applied as we find in Adam Smith, as well as the same absence of any firm conceptual foundation.

There remains another aspect to the concept of wealth. It is expressed with his usual vigour by John Bates Clark in *The Distribution of Wealth*: 'Amounts of wealth are usually stated in money ... The thought in the minds of men who use money as a standard of value runs forward to the power that resides in the coins. The intuitions that are at the basis of this popular mode of speech are nearer to absolute truth than much of economic analysis. They discern a power of things over men ...' (1908, p. 376).

The aspect of wealth to which Clark directs attention is once more anticipated by Smith, who writes, 'Wealth, as Mr. Hobbes says, is power ... the power of purchasing; a certain command over all the labour, or over all the produce of labour which is then in the market' (Smith [1776], p. 48). This definition contains an insight of great significance. To the extent that wealth is a form of power, its inadequate denomination in terms of labour commanded or utilities generated becomes explicable by virtue of the inapplicability of either metric to the 'substance' in which power must be measured.

What might that substance be? Smith and other early investigators of the nature of wealth-seeking society assumed it to be the expression of a universal desire to be admired. 'The rich man glories in his riches, because he feels that they naturally draw upon him the attention of the world ... and he is fonder of his wealth, upon this account, than for all the other advantages it procures him', Smith wrote in *The Theory of Moral Sentiments* ([1759], pp. 50–51).

What was unknown to Smith, or to others, like Senior, who followed his general lead in the psychology of wealth, is that prestige and wealth do not seem to be universally conjoined. Contemporary anthropologists emphasize that wealth differs in a crucial respect from prestige in that the defining characteristic of wealth is its ability to confer social power on its possessors, whereas the enjoyment of prestige carries no such intrinsic rights. As a consequence, we find that in primitive societies, where there is universal access to the resources needed for subsistence, wealth does not exist as a social category, in that no individual or group enjoys command over the labour or the product of others, save for the claims conferred by relations of kinship or communal obligation (Sahlins, 1972; Fried, 1976).

From the anthropological viewpoint, then, primitive societies enjoy Ricardian riches, but no Smithian or Marxian value. From this vantage point, 'wealth' ceases to appear as an eternal attribute of human society, whether as tangible goods or the utilities enjoyed by their beneficiaries. Rather, the crucial element in the conception of wealth, and in the constitution of economics as its study, lies in the historical advent of the institution of property, construed as the right to exclude others from the material or other resources to which legal title has been gained. From this perspective, the fundamental problem posed by wealth is that of tracing the evolution of the social stratification characteristic of all post-primitive societies. Wealth is the economic face of that political stratification, lodged in the hands of a class whose ability to grant or deny access to resources becomes the 'economic' basis for both prestige and power.

ROBERT L. HEILBRONER

See also CAPITALISM; SOCIALISM.

BIBLIOGRAPHY
Cassel, G. 1918. *Theory of Social Economy*. New York: Harcourt Brace & Co., 1932.
Clark, J.B. 1899. *The Distribution of Wealth*. Boston: Ginn & Company, 1908.
Fried, M. 1967. *The Evolution of Political Society*. New York: Random House.
Jevons, W.S. 1871. *The Theory of Political Economy*. Ed. R.D. Collison Black, Harmondsworth: Penguin, 1970.
Menger, C. 1871. *Principles of Economics*. New York: New York University Press, 1981.
Ricardo, D. 1821. *On the Principles of Political Economy and Taxation*. Ed. P. Sraffa, Cambridge: Cambridge University Press, 1951.
Robbins, L. 1932. *An Essay on the Nature of Significance of Economic Science*. London: Macmillan.
Sahlins, M. 1972. *Stone Age Economics*. Chicago: Aldine.
Smith, A. 1759. *The Theory of Moral Sentiments*. Ed. D.D. Raphael and A.L. Macfie, Oxford: Clarendon Press, 1976.
Smith, A. 1776. *An Inquiry into the Nature and Causes of the Wealth of Nations*. Ed. R.H. Campbell, A.S. Skinner and W. B. Todd, Oxford: Clarendon Press, 1976.

wealth constraint. Consumer theory, and thus general equilibrium theory, sees agents as making transactions subject to a wealth constraint, that is, subject to the value of their purchases not exceeding that of their sales.

The wealth constraint first appears explicitly in the writings of the neoclassical school, and particularly in the work of Walras (1874–7). However, it is first made use of rigorously by Slutsky (1915) and then Hicks (1946). In the present discussion we first specify the constraint in the pure exchange case, where borrowing and lending are only implicit, then introduce time, and finally examine the constraint in a monetary economy, where borrowing and lending become explicit.

An agent in an economy with n commodities is represented by his preferences for and endowment of these commodities. His preferences are represented by a complete preordering on the commodity space R^n_+, and his endowment by a point e in $S = R^n_+ - 0$. At any given price system p in S the agent chooses a most preferred point $x(p)$ in R^n_+ subject to the value of this not exceeding the value of his endowment, that is $p \cdot x(p) \leqslant p \cdot e$. This constraint, which we may also write as $p \cdot g(p) \leqslant 0$, where $g(p) = x(p) - e$ is excess demand, is his wealth constraint.

Two aspects of this require comment. The first is that the constraint is not affected if prices are multiplied by any positive scalar. The second is that, provided that all commodities are desirable, the constraint will always be binding. The relevance of these observations is apparent if we aggregate excess demands of individual agents to obtain aggregate excess demand, $f(p)$. The first aspect implies that f is homogeneous, that is, $f(tp) = f(p)$ for all positive t, while the second implies that f obeys Walras's Law, that is $p \cdot f(p) = 0$ for all p.

The interpretation of the budget constraint, that the agent cannot spend more than his wealth, raises the question of his borrowing (or lending). This question may be avoided by defining commodities in such a way that they are distinguished by date, that is, the time at which they are available, as well as on the basis of their physical nature. Thus not only is wheat distinguished from oats, but wheat available today is also distinguished from wheat available tomorrow. In this framework the agent borrows by selling wheat today for delivery tomorrow, and lends by buying wheat today for delivery tomorrow.

A further extension of the way in which commodities are defined can deal with the problem that future endowments may be uncertain. Under this extension commodities are also distinguished by the state of nature in which they are available. Such a state is a complete specification of everything that may affect prices, being defined in such a way that exactly one state must occur. Then if an agent will have as part of his endowment one unit of wheat tomorrow if it is not raining, and nothing if it rains, his wealth is simply the price (today) of wheat tomorrow if it is not raining. Thus although his future endowments are uncertain his wealth constraint is certain (Debreu, 1959).

However, this depends on the existence of suitable contingent markets, and for reasons such as differential information, and indeed transaction costs, such markets may not exist. If they do not then the agent's intertemporal wealth constraint is uncertain: or in other words, he faces two separate constraints – one for today and one for tomorrow.

A similar problem arises if capital markets are imperfect, that is, if there is no market for a machine, say, that produces goods (even with certainty) both today and tomorrow. Again then, the agent faces separate constraints for each period. Equivalently, we may say that he has a sequence of income constraints rather than one wealth constraint.

Lying behind these problems are, implicitly, restrictions on borrowing and lending. These activities become explicit if we introduce money into the economy. Exchange without money may be cumbersome, and involve an agent who plans to exchange oats for wheat finding one agent who both wants to acquire oats and surrender wheat. With money, however, he need only find some agent who plans to buy oats (that is, exchange money for oats) and some, usually different, agent who plans to sell wheat (that is, exchange wheat for money).

The essential aspect of money (or rather economies in which all exchanges must be for money) follows from this: an agent who plans to exchange oats for wheat must sell his oats before he can buy his wheat (unless he has a sufficient reserve of money), and if he cannot sell his oats then he cannot buy wheat. Thus planned demands only become effective if they are backed by money (Clower, 1967).

As is well known, this may lead to effective excess demands for all commodities being zero at the same time as planned excess demands are substantial, that is, to a state of chronic excess demand or supply (such as unemployment). However, this will not occur if borrowing and lending can occur freely, when the wealth constraint again becomes the only restriction on preferences.

MICHAEL ALLINGHAM

See also GENERAL EQUILIBRIUM.

BIBLIOGRAPHY
Clower, R.W. 1967. A reconsideration of the microfoundations of monetary theory. *Western Economic Journal* 6, December, 1–8.
Debreu, G. 1959. *Theory of Value*. New York: Wiley.
Hicks, J.R. 1946. *Value and Capital* (2nd edn). Oxford: Clarendon Press.
Slutsky, E. 1915. Sulla teoria del bilancio del consumatore. *Giornale degli Economisti* 51, July, 1–26.
Walras, L. 1874–7. *Eléments d'économie politique pure*. Definitive edn, Lausanne, 1926. Trans. W. Jaffé as *Elements of Pure Economics*, London: George Allen & Unwin, 1954.

wealth effect. Wealth is ubiquitous in economic analysis; so it is not surprising that the term 'the wealth effect' has been used by different authors and even the same author to refer to many distinct concepts. This brief entry is concerned with only the wealth effect in terms of aggregate consumption. Even in this limited field several distinct usages must be considered.

Haberler (1939), Pigou (1943), and Patinkin (1956) pioneered the idea that variations in money balances will cause movements, *ceteris paribus*, in aggregate consumer expenditures. This wealth effect is often referred to as the Pigou effect or real balance effect. If such a positive relationship between consumption and real money balances were to exist, these authors argued, it would profoundly affect the Keynesian analysis of underemployment equilibrium.

Recall that an underemployment equilibrium was supposed to occur if, in Hicksian terms, the IS curve intersected the LM curve in the liquidity-trap region at an income y less than full-employment income y_F. This is illustrated in figure 1(a) where the initial LM curve is LM_0. If prices fall because of the depressed conditions, this increases real money balances, and shifts the LM curve out to $LM_1, LM_2, \ldots$, but the interest rate remains fixed at the minimum rate r_{min} so that lower prices do not alleviate the depression.

Now, suppose that higher real money balances increase consumption, *ceteris paribus*. If the price level falls and real money balances rise, the IS curve shifts out to $IS_1, IS_2, \ldots$. As illustrated in figure 1(b), this progressively increases real income until IS_3 and LM_3 intersect to determine $y_3 = y_F$. Thus there are market forces which tend to restore real income to full employment levels. Other, stronger forces eliminating underemployment have been recognized subsequently, but the real balance effect was the first effective challenge to the Keynesian structure.

The source of the wealth effect is a more controversial issue than its implications. The modern theory of the consumption function views wealth as the principal determinant of aggregate consumption. Since money balances are a component of wealth, it appears that a change in real money balances should have the same effect on consumption as an increase in wealth reflecting, say, a higher capital stock. Uncertainties arise, however, in regard to what portion of money is an element of wealth and the extent, if any, that the implicit service stream from money should be deemed consumption analogously to the service stream from a consumer's automobile. In addition, a portfolio adjustment element may play a significant role in the real balance effect in disequilibrium.

The first set of issues concerns whether only outside money (commodity of non-interest-bearing government money) should be included in wealth. The remaining inside money is offset on banks' books by debts which increase in real value at the same time a fall in prices or increase in nominal quantity increases the real value of inside money. Accordingly, for society as a whole increases in inside money are not a source of increases in wealth, and the wealth effect is confined to outside money.

A possible measure of wealth is outside money plus physical capital plus a fraction λ of government debt where λ varies from 1 to 0 according to the extent that individuals see through the veil of government. If government bonds are not net wealth, an open market purchase of bonds with new outside money increases wealth so that both the IS and LM curves shift to the right. Thus monetary policy is strengthened by the wealth effect. However, the effect of a lower price level in shifting the IS curve to the right is strongest if λ is close to 1 since then the higher real values of both money and government bonds increases consumer spending. Evidence that λ lies near or at 0 thus favours the effectiveness of monetary policy but reduces the probable significance of price variations for aggregate consumption.

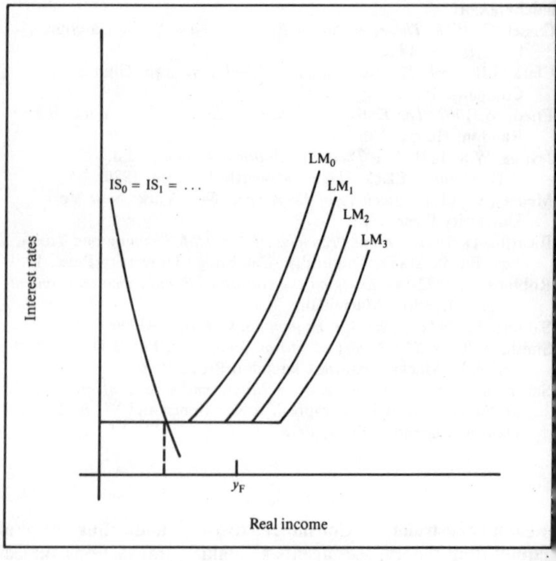

Figure 1 (a) No wealth effect.

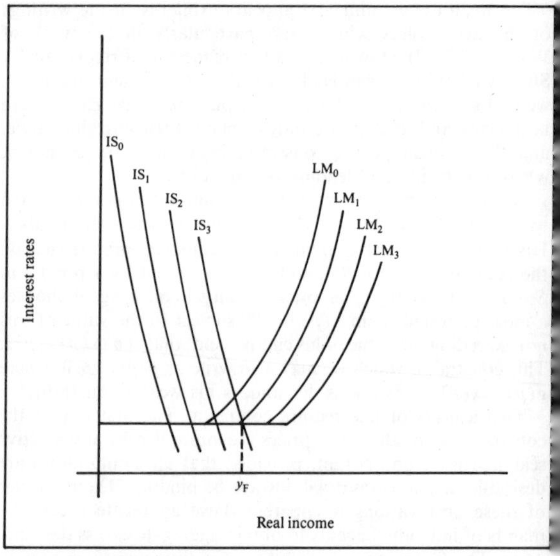

Figure 1 (b) With wealth effect.

Money – particularly outside money – is very much like a durable good: its primary yield is in the form of a service stream. To the extent that outside money is held by consumers, this stream may be counted as a form of consumption. Accordingly, the increase in aggregate consumption associated with an increase in real outside money may be somewhat less than that associated with an increase in the capital stock which is held for its pecuniary income stream.

A final difficulty with interpreting the real balance effect is that higher real money balances may increase consumer expenditures by a much greater amount than pure consumption via a portfolio adjustment channel in disequilibrium.

Since purchases of consumers' durable goods can be considered saving and investment by households, accelerating (retarding) these purchases may be a convenient way of reducing (increasing) cash balances greater (less) than their long-run desired value.

This disequilibrium view was suggested by Friedman and Schwartz (1963). It rationalizes both an effect for inside as well as outside money and also coefficients on real money which are large relative to any reasonable real yield on wealth (see, for example, Darby, 1977–8).

In conclusions, the wealth effect on aggregate consumption has concerned macroeconomists for half a century. Unresolved questions reflect the unsettled issues of the consumption function: Is consumer behaviour described as reflecting Ricardian equivalence? What determines variations in consumers' purchases of durable goods as opposed to the consumption of their services? High nominal deficits in the 1980s have stimulated interest and provided data which may ultimately reduce our uncertainty about the first of these questions. This in turn may simplify the analysis of the second.

MICHAEL R. DARBY

See also IS–LM ANALYSIS

BIBLIOGRAPHY

Darby, M. 1977–8. The consumer expenditure function. *Explorations in Economic Research* 4(5), Winter–Spring, 645–74.

Friedman, M. and Schwartz, A.J. 1963. Money and business cycles. *Review of Economics and Statistics* 45(1), February, Supplement, 32–64.

Haberler, G. 1939. *Prosperity and Depression*. 2nd edn, Geneva: League of Nations.

Patinkin, D. 1956. *Money, Interest, and Prices*. Evanston: Row, Peterson & Co.

Pigou, A.C. 1943. The classical stationary state. *Economic Journal* 53, December, 343–51.

wealth taxes. *See* TAXATION OF WEALTH.

Webb, Beatrice (1858–1943) and **Sidney** (1859–1947). Beatrice and Sidney Webb were the primary authors of the political economy of Fabian socialism. Their work together spanning half a century left an indelible mark on the evolution of opinion and legislation on trade unionism, local government, the relief of poverty, and theories of the transition to socialism.

The appropriate context in which to place the work of the Webbs is in the intellectual history of the labour movement. Judged by European standards, the role of intellectuals in the British labour movement has not been particularly distinguished. There are no figures in this country's past to match the stature of Jaurès, Kautsky or Gramsci, and as is well known, the debate over revisionism largely (but not completely) bypassed English labour. Partly because of their own social distance from organized labour, and partly because of *ouvrieriste* suspicions of their middle-class manners, labour's intellectuals were more isolated and politically marginalized in 19th- and 20th-century Britain than in any other European country.

The Webbs succeeded only in part in overcoming these obstacles. They chose two characteristic forms for their work: scholarship and 'permeation', by which they meant the slow and subtle conversion of men of power to their views.

First, their scholarship. One of the Webbs' major achievements was to provide the British labour movement with a record and a sense of its history. One of the primary challenges which have faced the leaders and rank-and-file of organized labour in Britain all too regularly in this century has been how to deal with political failure. What the Webbs and other historians of labour, such as G.D.H. Cole and R.H. Tawney, have offered is a way of coping with political despair, a means of surviving reversals by locating them within a long and complex experience, the parameters and outcomes of which are always bound to remain obscure to contemporaries. The retrieval of lost strikes, abortive insurrections, and collapsed Utopian experiments can give heart to today's activists by showing them how other men and women in the past faced similar defeats and still managed to retain their convictions. Labour history, largely pioneered by the Webbs, was (and remains) an assertion of the dignity of defiance.

The academic study of the subject of industrial relations was largely begun by the Webbs. Their *History of Trade Unionism* appeared in 1894 and was reissued in four subsequent extended and revised editions in 1896, 1902, 1911, and 1920. This book was followed in 1897 by *Industrial Democracy*, which the authors claimed was not history at all, but rather an account of the structure, function and theory of contemporary trade-union organization. The nine mammoth tomes of the *History of English Local Government* appeared between 1906 and 1929. In this monumental work, they traced the evolution of parochial and county administration from the medieval period to 1929, when authority over public assistance was finally transferred from boards of guardians to county and county borough councils. In a sense, this history is a circular grand tour of the evolution of collective provision for the poor: from parish control in the medieval period, to the reduction of local government to the barren application of the principle of less eligibility in the 19th century, to the 20th-century return of local authorities to their prior position as integrated agencies of social provision.

The two sides of their historical work reflect clearly aspects of their socialist political economy. In the Webbs' political theory, men are considered first of all as consumers, and only secondarily as producers. They never fully explored the implications of this distinction, but it is at the heart of their position. On the one hand, they were the chroniclers *par excellence* of workplace loyalties and organizations. But on the other hand, they argued that the first interest of all inhabitants is the provision of consumer needs. The function of government is to provide a framework within which men can obtain the necessities of daily life. Hence they defined the state as the 'national association of consumers' engaged in 'housekeeping on a national scale'.

The collective ownership of the means of production was a means to fulfill that function in such a way as to ensure that public service rather than private profit governed the economic life of the nation. Thus their work in socialist politics was an outgrowth of their political economy, adumbrated in pamphlets and articles for the Fabian Society, which Sidney helped found in 1884, and the Labour party, the reconstruction of which in 1918, with a commitment to nationalization as a goal, was largely Sidney's major political achievement. He served as President of the Board of Trade in the 1924 Labour government and as Secretary for the Colonies and Dominions from 1929 to 1931, but without distinction in either role.

After the onset of the world economic crisis, the Webbs turned away from many of their earlier commitments and followed a disastrously misguided inclination to believe that Stalin had inaugurated a 'new civilization' in the Soviet Union in the 1930s. But even this misperception – in which the Webbs were not by any means alone – did not obscure the range and depth of the influence of their previous work. This was primarily in the field of political theory and history, rather than in economic theory, the characteristics of large tracts of which they remained blissfully ignorant for most of their lives. It was not for any incisive critique of Marx or Marshall that the Webbs will be remembered, but rather for a lifetime of service to Fabian socialism.

The legacy of their ideas, their writing and their administrative and political efforts was subtle and indirect. But, in essence, it was to provide an intellectual justification for the transition to socialism in Britain, rooted not in class struggle but in the slow, but in their view inexorable, reconstruction of the state as the servant of the basic needs of the community as a whole.

Aside from Clause Four of the Labour party constitution, the most enduring monument to the Webbs' influence is the London School of Economics. Founded in 1895, as Beatrice noted, 'on the lines of the Ecole Libre des Sciences Politique in Paris', the School was devoted not to the study of socialism, but rather (in the words of its first prospectus) to further 'the study and investigation of the concrete facts of industrial life and the actual working of economic and political institutions as they exist or have existed, in the United Kingdom or in foreign countries'. Such impartial and scientific study of social questions would, Sidney believed, inevitably further the cause of socialism; hence there was no need to insist upon doctrinal purity among the academic staff of the School. In fact, the first director, W.A.S. Hewins, was an economist who shared none of the Webbs' assumptions, and in subsequent years, this tradition of political heterogeneity among the directors and lecturers of the School has never been challenged.

It is perhaps best to see this aspect of the Webbs' work – 'the biggest single enterprise of Our Partnership', as Beatrice put it – as reflecting two themes. The first is their lifelong interest in questions of educational provision, a subject to which Sidney devoted considerable attention during his period on the London County Council in the 1890s. The second is as part of their Fabian commitment both to the systematic analysis of contemporary social problems and to the creation of the administrative class which, they believed for most of their lives, would lead Britain out of the morass of industrial capitalism.

J.M. Winter

See also FABIAN ECONOMICS.

SELECTED WORKS

1894. *History of Trade Unionism*. London: Longmans & Co.
1897. *Industrial Democracy*. London: Longmans & Co.
1898. *Problems of Modern Industry*. London: Longmans & Co.
1906–29. *English Local Government from the Revolution to the Municipal Corporations Act*. 8 vols, London: Longmans & Co.
1920. *A Constitution for the Socialist Commonwealth of Great Britain*. London: Longmans & Co.
1923. *The Decay of Capitalist Civilisation*. London: Allen & Unwin.
1935. *Soviet Communism. A New Civilisation?* 2 vols, London: Longmans.
1978. *The Letters of Sidney and Beatrice Webb*. 3 vols, ed. N. MacKenzie, Cambridge: Cambridge University Press for the London School of Economics.
1982–4. *The Diary of Beatrice Webb*. 3 vols, ed. N. and J. MacKenzie, London: Virago in association with the London School of Economics and Political Science.

BIBLIOGRAPHY

Cole, M.I. (ed.) 1949. *The Webbs and their Work*. London: Frederick Muller.

Weber, Alfred (1868–1958). German economist and cultural sociologist, born 30 July 1868 in Erfurt; died 2 May 1958 in Heidelberg. He studied in Berlin and was Privatdozent there 1900–1904, Professor in Prague 1904–7 and in Heidelberg from 1907 until his death, interrupted by voluntary retirement between 1933 and 1945.

Weber's *Reine Theorie des Standorts* (1909) established him as the leading location theorist since Von Thünen, although his theoretical model had been anticipated by Wilhelm Launhardt (1882). Weber's interest in the location of the emerging modern industries arose from his earlier study of home industries, their struggle for survival, and the resulting social conditions of those working under the putting out system. Only Part I was published, an intended empirical Part II never appeared. Under Alfred Weber's guidance several theses were written on particular industries. Alfred Weber's article in the *Grundriss der Sozialoekonomik*, Part VI (1922) is a restatement of his book.

After World War I, Weber turned to 'cultural sociology as cultural history' (1935). This work, while overshadowed by that of his more famous brother, Max (1864–1920), and lacking its precision, provides a fresh perspective of the development of Western civilization.

Alfred Weber, although not an impressive speaker, was a highly influential teacher. Together with Karl Jaspers he re-established academic traditions of excellence at the University of Heidelberg in the post World War II years.

The location of industries according to Weber is governed by cost minimization. When production costs are independent of location, this means the minimization of transportation costs. In the case of two resource deposits and one market, the optimal location may fall inside the triangle spanned by the three given locations. Economies of joint location, based on the exchange of intermediate goods or the joint use of indivisible facilities induce 'agglomeration' of industrial activities in large centres.

Martin Beckmann

See also LOCATION THEORY; THÜNEN, HEINRICH VON.

SELECTED WORKS

1909. *Reine Theorie des Standorts*. Trans. by C.J. Friedrichs as *Theory of the Location of Industries*, Chicago: University of Chicago Press, 1929.
1938. *Kulturgeschichte als Kultursoziologie*. 2nd edn. Munich: Piper, 1950.

BIBLIOGRAPHY

Salin, E. 1958. Obituary. *Kyklos* 11(3), 318–40.

Weber, Max (1864–1920). Max Weber was born in 1864 at Erfurt and died in 1920 at Munich. After early studies in the history of commercial law, he established himself as one of the leading figures in a new generation of historical political economists in the Germany of the 1890s. He was appointed to chairs in political economy at Freiburg in 1894 and at Heidelberg in 1896. A nervous breakdown commencing in 1898 led to his withdrawal from academic teaching, but did little to impair the flow of his writing. In 1904 he took over the editorship of the *Archiv für Sozialwissenschaft und Sozialpolitik*, the leading academic journal in 'social economics', devoted to the exploration of the interrelationship between economy on the one hand, and law, politics and culture on the other. This interconnection formed the main site of Weber's own research, whose focus became increasingly wide-ranging and theoretical, involving an elucidation of the character and presuppositions of modern Western rationalism, as applied to the basic structures of economy and society. Weber was also actively and often controversially involved in the political issues of Wilhelmine Germany, from a progressive national-liberal standpoint, and during the war was one of the leading polemicists for a democratization of the constitution. Such involvement gave particular sharpness to his discussions of social science methodology, the role of value judgements and the relation between academic analysis and political practice. It was only comparatively late in his life that he came to think of his work as 'sociology', though it is as one of the 'founding fathers' of sociology that he is now known. He resumed fulltime teaching activity as professor at Munich in 1919 only shortly before his death.

Weber's early work in political economy can best be understood as reflecting the distinctive concerns of a younger generation of the historical school (including Schulze-Gävernitz, Sombart, Max and Alfred Weber). At the methodological level they sought to resolve the controversy between the theoretical and historical schools by demonstrating the theoretical character of the concepts used in historical economics on the one hand, and the historical presuppositions of theory on the other (*see* IDEAL TYPE). An important element in this resolution was to secure the acceptability of the Marxian concept of 'capitalism' as a valid concept for economic analysis, despite the untenability (as they saw it) of the labour theory of value, and exaggerated claims made for the materialist conception of history.

The recognition of the conflict between labour and capital as a systemic property of capitalism was central to Weber's early work. In his study of the impact of capitalist organization on the agricultural estates east of the Elbe, it supported his conclusion that class conflict had permanently undermined the economic basis of Junker political dominance in the Reich (Weber, 1892). From it he also derived a position on social policy which was critical of the paternalism of the 'Kathedersozialisten', arguing instead that trades unions should be given a secure legal status so that they could bargain for themselves on a more equal footing with capital. The distinctive Weberian conception of class conflict under capitalism was theorized neither in the Marxist terms of 'exploitation' nor in the neoclassical terms of 'factor demand', but in terms of a systematic competition for the social product on the basis of a power relation between the classes that was adjusted and underwritten at the political level.

If the incorporation of Marxian insights into the mainstream of social economics required that the analysis of class conflict be freed from the doctrine of surplus value, it also required a critique of the one-sided assumptions of historical materialism. This Weber offered in his most famous study *The Protestant Ethic and the Spirit of Capitalism* (1904). The argument of this work was that the profit-maximizing behaviour so characteristic of the bourgeoisie, which could be explained under fully developed capitalist conditions by its sheer necessity to survival in the face of competition, could not be so explained under the earlier phases of capitalist development. It was the product of an autonomous impulse to accumulate far beyond the needs of personal consumption, an impulse which was historically unique. Weber traced its source to the 'worldly asceticism' of reformed Christianity, with its twin imperatives to methodical work as the chief duty of life, and to the limited enjoyment of its product. The unintended consequence of this ethic, which was enforced by the social and psychological pressures on the believer to prove (but not earn) his salvation, was the accumulation of capital for investment.

Early critics of Weber's thesis misunderstood it as a purely cultural explanation for capitalism, as if 'a Siberian Baptist or a Calvinist inhabitant of the Sahara' must inevitably become a successful entrepreneur. Weber was in fact well aware both of the material preconditions for capitalist development, and of the social interests that are needed to support the dissemination of new ideas. The crucial question about his thesis is whether the employment of wage labour that made unlimited accumulation possible in principle, also made it inevitable in practice; whether, that is, the Protestant ethic should be seen as providing a necessary motivation for capitalist accumulation, or rather a *legitimation* for it in the face of prevalent values favouring conspicuous consumption on the part of a leisured class. Weber himself saw it as both. His work is the most sophisticated in a long tradition of exploration of the cultural preconditions for capitalist accumulation, from Adam Smith's celebration of 'parsimony', to recent explanations of Britain's economic decline in terms of the gentrification of its entrepreneurial spirit.

At one level the 'Protestant ethic thesis' can thus be read as a critique of historical materialism, with its explanation of capitalist development as the necessary outcome of the feudal order, rather than as the result of a unique conjunction of favourable historical conditions, cultural and political as well as economic. At another level it can be read as an extended critique of the ahistorical theorizing of Carl Menger and the Austrian school. In Weber's view the methodical, calculating, welfare-maximizing behaviour of the neoclassical models was not a universal characteristic of human rationality as such, but a product of modern Western rationalism. His subsequent studies of the economic ethic of the major world religions (Confucianism, Hinduism, Buddhism, ancient Judaism; collected in Weber, 1921) were designed to elucidate this distinctive cultural complex. They showed that, while instrumental rationality was a universal category of social action, only in the modern West had the goal-maximizing calculation of the most efficient means to given ends become generalized. And while other cultures had attempted to make the world intelligible through the development of elaborate theodicies, or to create internally consistent systems of ethics or law, the distinctive features of Western rationalism were the scientific assumption that all things could be comprehended by reason, together with the attitude of practical mastery which sought to subject the world to human control rather than merely adjust oneself to it. In Weber's major unfinished theoretical work, *Economy and Society* (1922), capitalism was shown to be simply one expression, rather than the unique locus, of this 'rationalization' process. The work is structured around the antithesis between 'traditional' and 'rationalized' forms of action and organization in all spheres of social life, and the transition between the two provides the key to the Weberian theory of modernization.

The conclusion of Weber's mature work, the capitalism was to be understood as part of a wider 'rationalization' process, coincided with his analysis of its most advanced forms in contemporary Germany. According to this analysis, the distinctive feature of capitalist concentration was the change in its internal mode of organization: the adoption of a complex technical division of labour and a hierarchical structure of administration that increasingly resembled the bureaucratic type already established in the political sphere. For Weber, the bureaucratic model of administration was becoming generalized throughout all sectors of contemporary society, because of its efficiency in performing complex organizational tasks.

Along with it went the emergence of a new middle class, whose distinctive position in the class structure depended neither on property ownership (capital) nor its absence (labour), but on the possession of technical and organizational skills, and on its authority position within a bureaucratic hierarchy.

Some commentators have seen Weber as an early forerunner of the 'managerial revolution' thesis. Certainly he was among the earliest to identify technical knowledge and organization as crucial sources of social power in modern societies. But to Weber no manager could be a substitute for the risk-taking entrepreneur who stood at the head of large capitalist organizations. The bureaucratic system, with its secure career and promotion prospects, represented a conservative principle in social life, in contrast to the dynamic principle of the market. Like his junior colleague, Joseph Schumpeter, Weber saw the major source of economic innovation to be provided by the captains of industry, ready to chance their judgement in the competition of the market place. This was directly paralleled in the political sphere by his theory of competitive leadership democracy, according to which the leaders of mass parties with their bureaucratic machines competed for support in the electoral market place. If the creative force of individualism, deriving from the Protestant ethic, had itself unintentionally produced the age of organization, in which competition at the individual level was eliminated, nevertheless the role of indivualism was reasserted in Weberian social theory at the head of organizations, in the form of 'charismatic' leadership.

Weber's theory of bureaucracy also provided the basis for a thoroughgoing critique of socialist planning, as prefigured in the wartime German economy. Weber was quick to echo von Mises' contention that a coherent system of allocation was impossible without market indicators, since it confirmed his own historical analysis of the preconditions for rational economic calculation. However, his distinctive criticisms of socialist planning derived from the massive extension of bureaucratic coordination he believed it would entail. Without market competition, he argued, the economy would simply stagnate. Yet the workers would remain subordinate to the same hierarchy of authority at the work place, since this was determined by the technical requirements of production, not by the particular system of ownership. Indeed, their subordination would become a new form of slavery, since the separate hierarchies of the economic, legal and political spheres would be fused into a single, all-embracing structure of power. It was the dictatorship of the official, he concluded, not of the worker, that was on the march (Weber, 1918).

Overall, the progressive widening in the focus of Weber's theoretical concerns, from the conditions for economic rationality to the general theme of 'rationalization', and the subsumption of capitalism itself into the wider category of bureaucratic organization, reflected a shift in his disciplinary focus of interest from political economy to sociology. This was not just a personal development of Weber's, but one typical of the period in which he lived. With the narrowing of theoretical focus represented by neoclassical economics, it was left to the nascent discipline of sociology to take over some of the wider concerns of political economy. The rich tradition of the German historical school, and the methodological debates which it had aroused, made German sociology particularly well placed for this enterprise. It was also particularly urgent in a country where the claims of Marxism to provide a convincing overall theory of society were widely accepted within the labour movement. It was no accident, therefore, that the most sustained rebuttal of these claims should come from the same context. As suggested above, however, Weber's approach to Marxism was not one of outright rejection, but of incorporating its insights into a different theoretical framework which left the validity of private property ownership intact. If the general presuppositions of liberalism had been thematized in the form of political philosophy in the 18th century, and of political economy in the 19th, they can be said to have received their distinctive 20th–century expression in the form of Weberian sociology.

DAVID BEETHAM

See also BUREAUCRACY; IDEAL TYPE..

SELECTED WORKS

1892. Die Lage der Landarbeiter im ostelbischen Deutschland. In *Max Weber Gesamtausgabe*, Vol. 1/3, ed. M. Riesebrodt, Tübingen: J.C.B. Mohr, 1984.
1904. *The Protestant Ethic and the Spirit of Capitalism*. London: Allen & Unwin, 1930.
1918. Socialism. In *Weber Selections in Translation*, ed. W.G. Runciman, Cambridge: Cambridge University Press, 1978.
1921. *Gesammelte Aufsätze zur Religionssoziologie*. Tübingen: J.C.B. Mohr.
1922. *Economy and Society*. New York: Bedminster Press, 1968.

weighted least squares. *See* LEAST SQUARES.

Weintraub, Sidney (1914–1983). Weintraub was born in Brooklyn, New York, on 28 April 1914 and died in Philadelphia, Pennsylvania, on 19 June 1983. Professor at the University of Pennsylvania from 1950 until his death, Weintraub was widely known as the originator (with Henry Wallich) of Tax-based Incomes Policy (TIP); his professional reputation is based on his early criticism (1959b) of the 'neoclassical synthesis' of Keynes's macroeconomics and Walrasian general equilibrium and his own highly original attempts to produce a microeconomics compatible with Keynes's macroeconomic theory.

A postgraduate year (1938–9) at the London School of Economics convinced him of the implications of Keynes's *General Theory* for price theory. His PhD dissertation ('Monopoly and the Economic System', St Johns, 1941) and a series of articles on the formulation of demand in conditions of imperfect competition and imperfect information produced his innovative *Price Theory* (1949).

After the war, Weintraub concentrated on producing a microtheory compatible with Keynes's theory of the endogeneous determination of the equilibrium level of output at less than full employment. His earlier work was extended to the demand for labour and the micro-foundations of the aggregate demand and supply curves. Although this work, summarized in *An Approach to the Theory of Income Distribution* (1958), reached similar conclusions to the aggregate distribution theories then being worked out by Kaldor and Robinson its inspiration was the formulation of a 'Keynesian' microeconomics rather than growth theory.

Evidence of the stability of the mark-up of prices over wage costs presented in *A General Theory of the Price Level* (1959a) led to a 'Watchtower Approach' to wage policy which preceded the widely discussed, but never applied, TIP proposal (1971a, 1971b).

Weintraub's prolific writing and lecturing activities were complemented in 1978 by the founding and editing (with Paul Davidson) of *The Journal of Post Keynesian Economics*.

J.A. KREGEL

See also POST-KEYNESIAN ECONOMICS.

SELECTED WORKS
1942. The foundations of the demand curve. *American Economic Review* 32, September, 538–52.
1946. Monopoly pricing and unemployment. *Quarterly Journal of Economics* 61, November, 108–24.
1949. *Price Theory*. New York: Pitman.
1956. A macroeconomic approach to the theory of wages. *American Economic Review* 46, December, 845–56.
1957. The micro-foundations of aggregate demand and supply. *Economic Journal* 67, September, 455–70.
1958. *An Approach to the Theory of Income Distribution*. Philadelphia: Chilton.
1959a. *A General Theory of the Price Level*. Philadelphia: Chilton.
1959b. *Classical Keynesianism, Monetary Theory and the Price Level*. Philadelphia: Chilton.
1966. *A Keynesian Theory of Employment Growth and Income Distribution*. Philadelphia: Chilton.
1971a. An incomes policy to stop inflation. *Lloyds Bank Review* (99), January, 1–12.
1971b. (With H.C. Wallich.) A tax-based incomes policy. *Journal of Economic Issues* 5(2), June, 1–19.
1978. *Keynes, Keynesians and Monetarists*. Philadelphia: University of Pennsylvania Press.

welfare economics. In 1776, the same year as the American Declaration of Independence, Adam Smith published *The Wealth of Nations*. Smith laid out an argument that is now familiar to all economics students: (1) The principal human motive is self-interest. (2) The invisible hand of competition automatically transforms the self-interest of many into the common good. (3) Therefore, the best government policy for the growth of a nation's wealth is that policy which governs least.

Smith's arguments were at the time directed against the mercantilists, who promoted active government intervention in the economy, particularly in regard to (ill-conceived) trade policies. Since his time, his arguments have been used and reused by proponents of *laissez-faire* throughout the 19th and 20th centuries. Arguments of Smith and his opponents are still very much alive today: The pro-Smithians are those who place their faith in the market, who maintain that the provision of goods and services in society ought to be done, by and large, by private buyers and sellers acting in competition with each other. One can see the spirit of Adam Smith in economic policies involving deregulation of industries, tax reduction, and reduction in government growth in the United States; in policies of denationalization in the United Kingdom, France and elsewhere, and in the deliberate restoration of private markets in China. The anti-Smithians are also still alive and well; mercantilists are now called industrial policy advocates, and there is an abundance of intellectuals and policy makers, aside from neomercantilists, who believe that: (1) economic planning is superior to *laissez-faire*; (2) markets are usually monopolized in the absence of government intervention, crippling the invisible hand of competition; (3) even if markets are competitive, the existence of external effects, public goods, information asymmetries and other market failures ensure that *laissez-faire* results in the common bad rather than the common good; (4) and in any case, *laissez-faire* produces an intolerable degree of inequality.

The branch of economics called welfare economics is an outgrowth of the fundamental debate that can be traced back to Adam Smith, if not before. The theoretical side of welfare economics is organized around three main propositions. The first theorem answers this question: In an economy with competitive buyers and sellers, will the outcome be for the common good? The second theorem addresses the issue of distributional equity, and answers this question: In an economy where distributional decisions are made by an enlightened sovereign, can the common good be achieved by a slightly modified market mechanism, or must the market be abolished altogether? The third theorem focuses on the general issue of defining social welfare, or the common good, whether via the market, via a centralized political process, or via a voting process. It answers this question: Does there exist a reliable way to derive from the interests of individuals, the true interests of society, regarding, for example, alternative distributions of wealth?

This entry focuses on theoretical welfare economics. There are related topics in practical welfare economics which are only mentioned here. A reader interested in the practical problems of evaluating policy alternatives can refer to entries on CONSUMERS' SURPLUS, COST-BENEFIT ANALYSIS and COMPENSATION PRINCIPLE, to name a few.

I. THE FIRST FUNDAMENTAL THEOREM, OR LAISSEZ-FAIRE LEADS TO THE COMMON GOOD

> 'The greatest meliorator of the world is selfish, huckstering trade.' (R.W. Emerson, *Work and Days*)

In *The Wealth of Nations*, Book IV, Smith wrote: 'Every individual necessarily labours to render the annual revenue of the society as great as he can. He generally indeed neither intends to promote the public interest, nor knows how much he is promoting it … . He intends only his own gain, and he is in this, as in many other cases, led by an invisible hand to promote as end which was no part of his intention.' The philosophy of the First Fundamental Theorem of Welfare Economics can be traced back to these words of Smith. Like much of modern economic theory, it is set in the context of a Walrasian general equilibrium model, developed almost a hundred years after *The Wealth of Nations*. Since Smith wrote long before the modern theoretical language was invented, he never rigorously stated, let alone proved, any version of the First Theorem. That honour fell upon Lerner (1934), Lange (1942) and Arrow (1951).

To establish the First Theorem, we need to sketch a general equilibrium model of an economy. Assume all individuals and firms in the economy are price takers: none is big enough, or motivated enough, to act like a monopolist. Assume each individual chooses his consumption bundle to maximize his utility subject to his budget constraint. Assume each firm chooses its production vector, or input–output vector, to maximize its profits subject to some production constraint. Note the presumption of self-interest. An individual cares only about his own utility, which depends on his own consumption. A firm cares only about its own profits.

The invisible hand of competition acts through prices; they contain the information about desire and scarcity that coordinate actions of self-interested agents. In the general equilibrium model, prices adjust to bring about equilibrium in the market for each and every good. That is, prices adjust until supply equals demand. When that has occurred, and all individuals and firms are maximizing utilities and profits, respectively, we have a competitive equilibrium.

The First Theorem establishes that a competitive equilibrium is for the common good. But how is the common good defined? The traditional definition looks to a measure of total value of goods and services produced in the economy. In

Smith, the 'annual revenue of the society' is maximized. In Pigou (1920), following Smith, the 'free play of self-interest' leads to the greatest 'national dividend'.

However, the modern interpretation of 'common good' typically involves Pareto optimality, rather than maximized gross national product. When ultimate consumers appear in the model, a situation is said to be *Pareto optimal* if there is no feasible alternative that makes everyone better off. Pareto optimality is thus a dominance concept based on comparisons of vectors of utilities. It rejects the notion that utilities of different individuals can be compared, or that utilities of different individuals can be summed up and two alternative situations compared by looking at summed utilities. When ultimate consumers do not appear in the model, as in the pure production framework to be described below, a situation is said to be *Pareto optimal* if there is no alternative that results in the production of more of some output, or the use of less of some input, all else equal. Obviously saying that a situation is Pareto optimal is not the same as saying it maximizes GNP, or that it is best in some unique sense. There are generally many Pareto optima. However, optimality is a common good concept that can get common assent: No one would argue that society should settle for a situation that is not optimal, because if A is not optimal, there exists a B that all prefer.

In spite of the multiplicity of optima in a general equilibrium model, most states are non-optimal. If the economy were a dart board and consumption and production decisions were made by throwing darts, the chance of hitting an optimum would be zero. Therefore, to say that the market mechanism leads an economy to an optimal outcome is to say a lot. And now we can turn to a modern formulation of the First Theorem:

> *First Fundamental Theorem of Welfare Economics*: Assume that all individuals and firms are selfish price takers. Then a competitive equilibrium is Pareto optimal.

To illustrate the theorem, we focus on one simple version of it, set in a pure production economy. For a general version of the theorem, with both production and exchange, the reader can refer to Malinvaud (1972).

In a general equilibrium production economy model, there are K firms and m goods, but, for simplicity, no consumers. Given a list of market prices, each firm chooses a feasible input–output vector y_k so as to maximize its profits. We adopt the usual sign convention for a firm's input–output vector y_k: $y_{kj} < 0$ means firm k is a net *user* of good j, and $y_{kj} > 0$ means firm k is a net *producer* of good j. What is feasible for firm k is defined by some fixed production possibility set Y_k. Under the sign convention on the input–output vector, if p is a vector of prices, firm k's profits are given by

$$\pi_k = p \cdot y_k.$$

A list of feasible input–output vectors $y = (y_1, y_2, \ldots y_k)$ is called a *production plan* for the economy. A *competitive equilibrium* is a production plan $\hat{y}$ and a price vector p such that, for every k, $\hat{y}_k$ maximizes π_k subject to y_k's being feasible. (Since the production model abstracts from the ultimate consumers of outputs and providers of inputs, the supply equals demand requirement for an equilibrium is moot).

If $y = (y_1, y_2, \ldots, y_K)$ and $z = (z_1, z_2, \ldots, z_K)$ are alternative production plans for the economy, z is said to *dominate* y if the following vector inequality holds:

$$\sum_k z_k \geqslant \sum_k y_k.$$

Finally, if there exists no production plan that dominates y, y is *Pareto optimal.* (The notational conventions are very important for this model; note for example that $y_{11} + y_{21} + \cdots + y_{K1}$ represents an aggregate amount of good 1 produced in the economy, if positive, and an aggregate amount of good 1 used, if negative. Note also that some y_{k1}'s might be positive and some negative, and that the direction of the vector inequality is 'right' whether good 1 is an input, in the aggregate, or an output).

We now have the apparatus to state and prove the First Theorem in the context of the pure production model:

> *First Fundamental Theorem of Welfare Economics, Production Version.* Assume that all prices are positive, and that $\hat{y}, p$ is a competitive equilibrium. Then $\hat{y}$ is Pareto optimal.

To see why, suppose to the contrary that a competitive equilibrium production plan $\hat{y}_1, \hat{y}_2, \ldots, \hat{y}_K$ is not optimal. Then there exists a production plan $z_1, z_2, \ldots, z_K$ that dominates it. Therefore

$$\sum_k z_k \geqslant \sum_k \hat{y}_k.$$

Taking the dot product of both sides with the positive price vector p gives

$$p \cdot \sum_k z_k > p \cdot \sum_k \hat{y}_k.$$

But this implies that, for at least one firm k,

$$p \cdot z_k > p \cdot \hat{y}_k,$$

which contradicts the assumption that $\hat{y}_k$ maximizes firm k's profits.

II. FIRST FUNDAMENTAL THEOREM DRAWBACKS, AND THE SECOND FUNDAMENTAL THEOREM

> 'That amid our highest civilization men faint and die with want is not due to niggardliness of nature, but to the injustice of man.' (Henry George, *Progress and Poverty*)

The First Theorem of Welfare Economics is mathematically true but nevertheless objectionable. Here are the commonest objections: (1) The First Theorem is an abstraction that ignores the facts. Preferences of consumers are not given, they are created by advertising. The real economy is never in equilibrium, most markets are characterized by excess supply or excess demand, and are in a constant state of flux. The economy is dynamic, tastes and technology are constantly changing, whereas the model assumes they are fixed. The cast of characters in the real economy is constantly changing, the model assumes it fixed. (2) The First Theorem assumes competitive behaviour, whereas the real world is full of monopolists. (3) The First Theorem assumes there are no externalities. In fact, if in an exchange economy person 1's utility depends on person 2's consumption as well as his own, the theorem does not hold. Similarly, if in a production economy firm k's production possibility set depends on the production vector of some other firm, the theorem breaks down.

In a similar vein, the First Theorem assumes there are no public goods, that is, goods like national defence or lighthouses, that are necessarily non-exclusive in use. If such goods are privately provided (as they would be in a completely *laissez-faire* economy), then their level of production will be sub-optimal. (4) The most troubling aspect of the First Theorem is its neglect of distribution. *Laissez-faire* may produce a Pareto optimal outcome, but there are many different Pareto optima, and some are fairer than others. Some people are endowed with resources that make them rich, while others, through no fault of their own, are without. The First Theorem ignores basic distributional questions: How should unfair distributions of goods be made fair? And on the production side, how should production plans that give heavy weight to luxury items for the rich, and little or no weight to food, housing and medical care for the poor, be put right?

The first and second objections to the First Theorem are beyond the scope of this entry. The third, regarding externalities and public goods, is one that economists have always acknowledged. The standard remedies for these market failures involve minor modifications of the market mechanism, including Pigovian taxes (Pigou, 1920) on harmful externalities, or appropriate Coasian (Coase, 1960) legal entitlements to, for example, clean air.

The important contribution of Pigou is set in a partial equilibrium framework, in which the costs and benefits of a negative externality can be measured in money terms. Suppose that a factory produces gadgets to sell at some market-determined price, and suppose that, as part of its production process, the factory emits smoke which damages another factory located downwind. In order to maximize its profits, the upwind factory will expand its output until its marginal cost equals price. But each additional gadget it produces causes harm to the downwind factory – the marginal external cost of its activity. If the factory manager ignores that marginal external cost, he will create a situation that is non-optimal in the sense that the aggregate net value of both firms' production decisions will not be as great as it could be. That is, what Pigou calls 'social net product' will not be maximized, although 'trade net product' for the polluting firm will be. Pigou's remedy was for the state to eliminate the divergence between trade and social net product by imposing appropriate taxes (or, in the case of beneficial externalities, bounties). The Pigovian tax would be set equal to marginal external cost, and with it in place the gap between the polluting firm's view of cost and society's view would be closed. Optimality would be re-established.

Coase's contribution was to emphasize the reciprocal nature of externalities and to suggest remedies based on common law doctrines. In his view the polluter damages the pollutee only because of their proximity, e.g., the smoking factory harms the other only if it happens to locate close downwind. Coase rejects the notion that the state must step in and tax the polluter. The common law of nuisance can be used instead. If the law provides a clear right for the upwind factory to emit smoke, the downwind factory can contract with the upwind factory to reduce its output, and if there are no impediments to bargaining, the two firms acting together will negotiate an optimal outcome. Alternatively, if the law establishes a clear right for the downwind factory to recover for smoke damages, it will collect external costs from the polluter, and thereby motivate the polluter to reduce its output to the optimal level. In short, a legal system that grants clear rights to the air to either the polluter or pollutee will set the stage for an optimal outcome, provided that transactions are costless.

With respect to public goods, since Samuelson (1954) derived formal optimality conditions for their provision, the issue has received much attention from economists; one especially notable theoretical question has to do with discovering the strengths of people's preferences for a public good. If the government supplies a public judicial system, for instance, how much should it spend on it (and tax for it)? At least since Samuelson, it has been known that financing schemes like those proposed by Lindahl (1919), where an individual's tax is set equal to his marginal benefit, provide perverse incentives for people to misrepresent their preferences. Schemes that are immune to such misrepresentations (in certain circumstances) have been developed in recent years (Clarke, 1971; Groves and Loeb, 1975).

But it is the fourth objection to the First Theorem that is most fundamental. What about distribution?

There are two polar approaches to rectifying the distributional inequities of *laissez-faire*. The first is the command economy approach: a centralized bureaucracy makes detailed decisions about the consumption decisions of all individuals and production decisions of all producers. The main theoretical problems with the command approach are that it requires the bureaucracy to obtain and act upon superhuman quantities of information, and that it fails to create appropriate incentives for individuals and firms. On the empirical side, the experience of Eastern European and Chinese command economies suggest that highly centralized economic decision making leaves much to be desired, to put it mildly.

The second polar approach to solving distribution problems is to transfer income or purchasing power among individuals, and then to let the market work. The only kind of purchasing power transfer that does not cause incentive-related losses is the lump-sum transfer. Enter at this point the standard remedy for distribution problems, as put forward by the market-oriented economist, and our second major theorem.

The Second Fundamental Theorem of Welfare Economics establishes that the market mechanism, modified by the addition of lump-sum transfers, can achieve virtually *any* desired optimal distribution. Under more stringent conditions than are necessary for the First Theorem, including assumptions regarding quasi-concavity of utility functions and convexity of production possibility sets, the Second Theorem asserts the following:

> *Second Fundamental Theorem of Welfare Economics.* Assume that all individuals and producers are selfish price takers. Then almost any Pareto optimal equilibrium can be achieved via the competitive mechanism, provided appropriate lump-sum taxes and transfers are imposed on individuals and firms.

One version of the Second Theorem, restricted to a pure production economy, is particularly relevant to an old debate about the feasibility of socialism, see particularly Lange and Taylor (1939) and Lerner (1944). Anti-socialists including Von Mises (1937) argued that informational problems would make it impossible to coordinate production in a socialist economy; while pro-socialists, particularly Lange, argued that those problems could be overcome by a Central Planning Board, which limited its role to merely announcing a price vector. This is called 'decentralized socialism'. Given the prices, managers of production units would act like their capitalist counterparts; in essence, they would maximize profits. By choosing the price vectors appropriately, the Central Planning Board could achieve any optimal production plan it wished.

In terms of the production model given above, the production version of the Second Theorem is as follows:

> *Second Fundamental Theorem of Welfare Economics, Production Version.* Let $\hat{y}$ be any optimal production plan for the economy. Then there exists a price vector p such that $\hat{y}$, p is a competitive equilibrium. That is, for every k, $\hat{y}_k$ maximizes $\pi_k = p \cdot y_k$ subject to y_k being feasible.

The proof of the Second Theorem requires use of Minkowski's separating hyperplane theorem, and will not be given here.

III. TINKERING WITH THE ECONOMY AND VOTING ON DISTRIBUTIONS

The logic of the Second Theorem suggests that it is all right, perhaps even morally imperative, to tinker with the economy. And after all, is not tinkering what is done by policy makers and their economic advisers? How often do we choose between a *laissez-faire* economy and a command economy? Our choices are usually more modest. When choosing among alternative tax policies, or trade and tariff policies, or antimonopoly policies, or labour policies, or transfer policies, what shall guide the choice? The applied welfare economist's advice is usually based on some notion of increasing total output in the economy. The practical political decision, in a Western democracy, is normally based on voting.

Applied welfare economics. The applied welfare economist usually focuses on ways to increase total output, 'the size of the pie', or at least to measure changes in the size of the pie. Unfortunately, theory suggests that the pie cannot be measured. This is so for a number of reasons. To start, any measure of total output is a scalar, that is, a single number. If the number is found by adding up utility levels for different individuals, illegitimate interpersonal utility comparisons are being made. If the number is found by adding up the values of aggregate net outputs of all goods, there is an index number problem. The value of a production plan will depend on the price vector at which it is evaluated. But in a general equilibrium context, the price vector will depend on the aggregate net output vector, which will in turn depend on the distribution of ownership or wealth among individuals. Economists have always agreed that if q^1 and q^2 are alternative aggregate net output vectors, and if p^1 and p^2 are the corresponding price vectors, then $p^1 \cdot q^1 < p^2 \cdot q^2$ has no welfare implications. Unfortunately they now also agree that if there are two or more individuals in the economy, even $p^2 \cdot q^1 < p^2 \cdot q^2$ may not signify q^2 is an improvement in welfare over q^1.

An early and crucial contribution to the analysis of whether or not the economic pie has increased in size was made by Kaldor (1939), who argued that the repeal of the Corn Laws in England can be justified on the grounds that the winners could in theory compensate the losers: 'it is quite sufficient [for the economist] to show that even if all those who suffer as a result are fully compensated for their loss, the rest of the community will still be better off than before'. Unfortunately, Scitovsky (1941) quickly pointed out that Kaldor's compensation criterion (as well as one proposed by Hicks) was in theory inconsistent: it is possible to judge situation B Kaldor superior to A and simultaneously judge A Kaldor superior to B. The Scitovsky paradox can be avoided via a two-edged compensation test, according to which situation B is judged better than A if (1) the potential gainers in the move from A to B could compensate the potential losers, and still remain better off, and (2) the potential losers could not bribe the gainers to forego the move.

Scitovsky's two-edged criterion has some logical appeal, but it, like the single-edged Kaldor criterion, still has a major drawback: it ignores distribution. Therefore, it can make no judgement about alternative distributions of the same size pie. And worse, as was pointed out by Little (1950), either criterion would approve a change that would make the wealthiest man in England richer by £1,000,000,000, while making each of the 1,000,000 humblest men poorer by £900. In Little's view, the applied welfare economist should adopt Scitovsky's two-edged criterion and *also* requires that the change from A to B not result in a worse distribution of welfare. Unfortunately, what constitutes a worse distribution is, as Little concedes, purely a value judgement – a matter of personal opinion.

Another important tool for measuring changes in the economic pie is the concept of consumer's surplus, which Marshall (1920) defined as the difference between what an individual would be willing to pay for an object, at most, and what he actually does pay. With a little faith, the economic analyst can measure aggregate consumers' surplus (note the new position of the apostrophe), by calculating an area under a demand curve, and this is in fact commonly done in order to evaluate changes in economic policy. The applied welfare economist attempts to judge whether the pie would grow in a move from A to B by examining the change in consumers' surplus (plus profits, if they enter the analysis). Faith is required because consumers' surplus, like the Kaldor criterion, has been shown to be theoretically inconsistent; see for example Boadway (1974).

In short, although the tools of applied welfare economics are crucially important in practice, theory says they must be viewed with suspicion.

Voting

'A minority may be right, a majority is always wrong.' (Henrik Ibsen, *An Enemy of the People*)

In most cases, interesting decisions about economic policies are made either by bureaucracies that are controlled by legislative bodies, or by legislative bodies themselves, or by elected executives. In short, either directly or indirectly, by voting. The Second Theorem itself raises questions about distribution that many would view as essentially political: How should society choose the Pareto-optimal allocation of goods that is to be reached via the modified competitive mechanism? How should the distribution of income be chosen? How can the best distribution of income be chosen from among many Pareto optimal ones? Majority voting is the most commonly used method of political choice in a democracy.

The practical objections to voting, the fraud, the deception, the accidents of weather, are well known. To quote Boss Tweed, the infamous chief of New York's Tammany Hall: 'As long as I count the votes, what are you going to do about it?' But let us turn to the theoretical problems.

The central theoretical fact about majority voting has been known since the time of Condorcet's *Essai sur l'application de l'analyse à la probabilité des décisions rendues à la pluralité des voix*, published in 1785: Voting may be inconsistent. The now standard Condorcet voting paradox assumes three individuals 1, 2 and 3, and three alternatives x, y and z, where the three voters have the following preferences:

1: x y z

2: y z x

3: z x y

(Following an individual's number the alternatives are listed in his order of preference, from left to right.) Majority voting between pairs of alternatives will reveal that x beats y, y beats z, and, paradoxically, z beats x.

Recently it has become clear that such voting cycles are not peculiar; they are generic, particularly when the alternatives have a spatial aspect with two or more dimensions (Plott, 1967; Kramer, 1973.) This can be illustrated by taking the alternatives to be different distributions of one economic pie. Suppose, in other words, that the distributional issues raised by the First and Second Theorems are to be 'solved' by majority voting, and assume for simplicity that what is to be divided is a fixed total of wealth, say 100 units worth.

Now let x be 50 units for person 1, 30 units for person 2 and 20 units for person 3. That is, let $x=(50, 20, 30)$. Similarly, let $y=(30\ 50, 20)$ and $z=(20, 30, 50)$. The result is that our three individuals have precisely the voting paradox preferences. Nor is this result contrived, it turns out that *all* the distributions of 100 units of wealth are connected by endless voting cycles (see McKelvey, 1976). The reader can easily confirm that for any distributions u and v that he may choose, there exists a voting sequence from u to v, and another back from v to u!

The reality of voting cycles should give pause to the economist who studies or recommends tax bills. And it is most disturbing for the economist looking for a political basis for judging among alternative distributions.

IV. SOCIAL WELFARE AND THE THIRD FUNDAMENTAL THEOREM

How then might the distribution problem be solved? One potential answer is to assert the existence of a Bergson (1938) Economic Welfare Function $E(\cdot)$, that depends on the amounts of non-labour factors of production employed by each producing unit, the amounts of labour supplied by each individual, and the amounts of produced goods consumed by each individual. Then solve the problem by maximizing $E(\cdot)$. If necessary conditions for Pareto optimality are derived that must hold for any $E(\cdot)$, this exercise is harmless enough; but if a *particular* $E(\cdot)$ is assumed and distributional implications are derived from it, then an objection can be raised: Why that $E(\cdot)$ and not another one?

De V. Graaff (1957) focuses Bergson's approach by analysing welfare functions of the 'individualistic' type: these can be written $W(u^1, u^2, \ldots, u^n)$ where u^i represents person i's utility level. Graaff makes clear that maximizing a too broadly defined $W(\cdot)$ simply rediscovers the conditions for Pareto optimality, whereas maximizing a too narrowly defined $W(\cdot)$ simply rediscovers the preferences of the economist who invents $W(\cdot)$! Thus a good $W(\cdot)$ is neither too broadly nor too narrowly defined; rather it captures some widely shared judgements about which distributions are desirable and which are not. Maximizing such a welfare function implies both Pareto optimality and an appropriate distribution of wealth. But can a good $W(\cdot)$ function be discovered? Graaff is optimistic that the members of society can agree on the degree of equality to be incorporated in $W(\cdot)$. However, $W(\cdot)$ must also incorporate assumptions about an appropriate horizon (do we include unborn children?), as well as attitudes towards uncertainty, time discounting, and so on. And on these issues, he believes it extremely unlikely that enough agreement can be found to build a $W(\cdot)$. So, at the end of an illuminating book on normative economics, Graaff recommends that we all try positive economics. Which still leaves us with the Bergson social welfare function dilemma: Where do they come from?

In his classic monograph *Social Choice and Individual Values* (1963), Arrow brings together both the economic and political streams of thought sketched above. Arrow's theorem can be viewed in several ways: it is a statement about the distributional questions raised by the First and Second Theorems; it is a remarkable logical extension of the Condorcet voting paradox; and it is a statement about the logic of choice of Bergson welfare functions, and about the logic of compensation tests, consumers' surplus tests, and indeed all the tools of the applied welfare economist. Because of its importance, Arrow's theorem can be justifiably called the Third Fundamental Theorem of Welfare Economics.

Arrow's analysis is at a high level of abstraction, and requires some additional model building. We now assume a given set of alternatives, which might be allocations in an exchange economy, distributions of wealth, tax bills in a legislature, or even candidates in an election. The alternatives are written x, y, z, etc. We assume there is a fixed society of individuals, numbered $1, 2, \ldots, n$. Let R_i represent the preference relation of individual i, so xR_iy means person i likes x as well as or better than y. A preference profile for society is a specification of preferences for each and every individual, or symbolically, $R_1, R_2, \ldots, R_n$. We shall write R for *society's* preference relation, arrived at in a way yet to be specified. R is, of course, a much modernized version of Bergson's $E(\cdot)$, appearing here as a binary relation rather than as a function.

Arrow was concerned with the logic of how individual preferences are transformed into social preferences. That is, how is R found? Symbolically we can represent the transformation this way:

$$R_1, R_2, \ldots, R_n \rightarrow R.$$

Now if society is to make decisions regarding distributions, it must 'know' when one alternative is as good as or better than another, even if both are Pareto optimal. To ensure it can make such decisions, Arrow assumes that R is *complete*. That is, for any alternatives x and y, either xRy or yRx (or both, if society is indifferent between the two). If society is to avoid the illogic of cyclical voting, its preference ought to be *transitive*. That is, for any alternatives x, y and z, if xRy and yRz, then xRz. Following Sen (1970), we call a transformation of individual preference relations into a complete and transitive social preference relation an Arrow Social Welfare Function, or more briefly, an Arrow function.

Anyone can make up an Arrow function, just as anyone can make up a Bergson function, or for that matter a judgement about when one distribution of wealth is better than another. But arbitrary judgements are unsatisfactory and so are arbitrary Arrow functions. Therefore, Arrow imposed some reasonable conditions on his function. Following Sen's (1970) version of Arrow's theorem, there are four conditions: (1) *Universality*. The function should always work, no matter what individual preferences might be. It would not be satisfactory, for example, to require unanimous agreement among all the individuals before determining social preferences. (2) *Pareto consistency*. If everyone prefers x to y, then the social preference ought to be x over y. (3) *Independence*. Suppose there are two alternative preference profiles for individuals in society, but suppose individual preferences regarding x and y are exactly the same under the two alternatives. Then the social preference regarding x and y must be exactly the same under the two alternatives. In particular, if individuals change their minds about a third 'irrelevant' alternative, this should not affect the social preference regarding x and y. (4) *Non-dictatorship*. There should not be a dictator. In Arrow's abstract model, person i is a *dictator* if society always prefers exactly what he prefers, that is, if the Arrow function transforms R_i into R.

An economist or policy maker who wants an ultimate answer to questions involving distribution, or questions involving choices among alternatives that are not comparable under the Pareto criterion, could use an Arrow Social Welfare Function for guidance. Unfortunately, Arrow showed that imposing conditions 1 to 4 guarantees that Arrow functions *do not exist*:

> *Third Fundamental Theorem of Welfare Economics*. There is no Arrow Social Welfare Function that satisfies the conditions of universality, Pareto consistency, independence, non-dictatorship.

In order to illustrate the logic of the theorem, we will use a somewhat stronger assumption than independence. This assumption is called N–I–M, or *neutrality–independence–monotonicity*: Let V be a group of individuals. Suppose for some preference profile and some particular pair of alternatives x and y, all members of V prefer x to y, all individuals *not* in V prefer y to x, and the social preference is x over y. Then for *any* preference profile and *any* pair of alternatives x and y, if all people in V prefer x to y, the social preference must be x over y. In short, if V gets its way in one instance, when everyone opposes it, then it must have the power to do it again, under other possibly less difficult circumstances.

A group of individuals V is said to be *decisive* if for all alternatives x and y, whenever all the people in V prefer x to y, society prefers x to y. Assumption N–I–M asserts that if V prevails when it is opposed by everyone else, it must be a decisive group. If the social choice procedure is majority rule, for example, any group of $(n+1)/2$ members, for n odd, or $(n/2)+1$ members, for n even, is decisive. Moreover, it is clear that majority rule satisfies the N–I–M assumption, since if V prevails for a particular x and y when everyone outside of V prefers y to x, then V must be a majority, and must always prevail. (Majority rule is just one example of a procedure that satisfies N–I–M: there are countless other procedures that also do so.)

Now we are ready to turn to a short version of the Third Theorem

> *Third Fundamental Theorem of Welfare Economics, Short Version.* There is no Arrow Social Welfare Function that satisfies the conditions of universality, Pareto consistency, neutrality–independence–monotonicity, and non-dictatorship.

The logic of the proof is as follows: First, there must exist decisive groups of individuals, since by the Pareto consistency requirement the set of all individuals is one. Now let V be a decisive group of minimal size. If there is just one person in V, he is a dictator. Suppose then that V includes more than one person. We show this leads to a contradiction.

If there are two or more people in V, we can divide it into non-empty subsets V_1 and V_2. Let V_3 represent all the people who are in neither V_1 nor V_2. (V_3 may be empty). By universality, the Arrow function must be applicable to any profile of individual preferences. Take three alternatives x, y and z and consider the following preferences regarding them:

For individuals in V_1: $x \;\; y \;\; z$

For individuals in V_2: $y \;\; z \;\; x$

For individuals in V_3: $z \;\; x \;\; y$

(At this point the close relationship between Arrow and Condorcet is clear, for these are the voting paradox preferences!)

Since V is by assumption decisive, y must be socially preferred to z, which we write yPz. By the assumption of completeness for the social preference relation, either xRy or yPx must hold. If xRy holds, since xRy and yPz, then xPz must hold by transitivity. But now V_1 is decisive by the N–I–M assumption, contradicting V's minimality. Alternatively, if yPx holds, V_2 is decisive by the N–I–M assumption, again contradicting V's minimality. In either case, the assumption that V has two or more people leads to a contradiction. Therefore V must contain just one person, who is, of course, a dictator!

Since the Third Theorem was discovered, a whole literature of modifications and variations has been spawned. But the depressing conclusion has remained more or less inescapable: there is no logically infallible way to aggregate the preferences of diverse individuals. By extension, there is no logically infallible way to solve the problem of distribution.

Where does welfare economics stand today? The First and Second Theorems are encouraging results that suggest the market mechanism has great virtue: competitive equilibrium and Pareto optimality are firmly bound. But measuring the size of the economic pie, or judging among divisions of it, leads to the paradoxes and impossibilities summarized by the Third Theorem. And this is a tragedy. We feel we know, like Adam Smith knew, which policies would increase the wealth of nations. But because of all our theoretic goblins, we can no longer prove it.

ALLAN M. FELDMAN

See also COMPENSATION PRINCIPLE; PIGOU, ARTHUR CECIL; PUBLIC FINANCE; SOCIAL CHOICE.

BIBLIOGRAPHY

Arrow, K.J. 1951. An extension of the basic theorems of classical welfare economics. *Second Berkeley Symposium on Mathematical Statistics and Probability*, ed. J. Neyman, Berkeley:University of California Press, 507–32.

Arrow, K.J. 1963. *Social Choice and Individual Values*. 2nd edn, New York: John Wiley and Sons.

Bergson, A. 1938. A reformulation of certain aspects of welfare economics. *Quarterly Journal of Economics* 52, 310–34.

Boadway, R. 1974. The welfare foundations of cost-benefit analysis. *Economic Journal* 84, 926–39.

Clarke, E.H. 1971. Multipart pricing of public goods. *Public Choice* 11, 17–33.

Coase, R.H. 1960. The problem of social cost. *Journal of Law and Economics* 3, 1–44.

Graaff, J. de V. 1957. *Theoretical Welfare Economics*. Cambridge University Press.

Groves, T. and Loeb, M. 1975. Incentives and public inputs. *Journal of Public Economics* 4, 211–26.

Kaldor, N. 1939. Welfare propositions of economics and interpersonal comparisons of utility. *Economic Journal* 49, 549–52.

Kramer, G.H. 1973. On a class of equilibrium conditions for majority rule. *Econometrica* 41, 285–97.

Lange, O. 1942. The foundations of welfare economics. *Econometrica* 10, 215–28.

Lange, O. and Taylor, F.M. 1939. *On the Economic Theory of Socialism*. Minneapolis: University of Minnesota Press.

Lerner, A.P. 1934. The concept of monopoly and the measurement of monopoly power. *Review of Economic Studies* 1, 157–75.

Lerner, A.P. 1944. *The Economics of Control*. New York: The Macmillan Company.

Lindahl, E. 1919. Just taxation – a positive solution. Translated and reprinted in *Classics in the Theory of Public Finance*, ed. R.A. Musgrave and A.T. Peacock, New York: Macmillan, 1958.

Little, I.M.D. 1950. *A Critique of Welfare Economics*. Oxford: Oxford University Press.

Malinvaud, E. 1972. *Lectures on Microeconomic Theory*. Amsterdam: North-Holland.

Marshall, A. 1920. *Principles of Economics*. 8th edn, London: Macmillan, ch. VI.

McKelvey, R. 1976. Intransitivities in multidimensional voting models and some implications for agenda control. *Journal of Economic Theory* 12, 472–82.

Mises, L. von. 1922. *Socialism: An Economic and Social Analysis*. 3rd edn, trans., Indianapolis: Liberty Classics, 1981.

Pigou, A.C. 1920. *The Economics of Welfare*. London: Macmillan, Part II.

Plott, C.R. 1967. A notion of equilibrium and its possibility under majority rule. *American Economic Review* 57, 787–806.

Samuelson, P.A. 1954. The pure theory of public expenditure. *Review of Economics and Statistics* 36, 387–9.
Scitovsky, T. 1941. A note on welfare propositions in economics. *Review of Economic Studies* 9, 77–88.
Sen, A.K. 1970. *Collective Choice and Social Welfare*, San Francisco: Holden-Day.

welfare state. The term 'welfare state' first entered the English language in 1941 when Archbishop Temple coined the phrase to differentiate wartime Britain from the 'warfare' state of Nazi Germany. It quickly entered the vocabulary associated with the Beveridge Report (1942), which propounded state responsibility for individual welfare 'from the cradle to the grave'. Paradoxically, however, it was Germany which pioneered both modern social insurance in the 1880s and the concept of *Wohlfahrstaat* in the 1920s. It is not easy to define the welfare state; for one reason the term refers both to goals (the idea of state responsibility for welfare) and to means (the institutions and practices through which the idea is given effect). Let us begin with goals and a well-known definition by Briggs (1961, p. 228):

> A 'Welfare State' is a state in which organised power is deliberately used (through politics and administration) in an effort to modify the play of market forces in at least three directions – first, by guaranteeing individuals and families a minimum income irrespective of the market value of their property; second by narrowing the extent of insecurity by enabling individuals and families to meet certain 'social contingencies' (for example, sickness, old age and unemployment) which lead otherwise to individual and family crises; and third by ensuring that all citizens without distinction of status or class are offered the best standards available in relation to a certain agreed range of social services.

This has the merit of defining the welfare state as one form of state intervention in a capitalist, market economy. It then specifies those interventions which have as their aim the elimination of poverty and insecurity, and the guaranteeing of 'best available' standards of certain services in kind. Dispute still ensues, however, as to whether those are the defining goals of a welfare state. Some argue that it normally refers only to the provision of a minimum income 'floor' or minimum standards in certain areas of need (e.g. Wilensky and Lebeaux, 1965). Others argue that social policies can serve other goals; for example, meritocratic education policies (Flora and Heidenheimer, 1981). Gough (1979, pp. 44–5) goes further and defines the welfare state as 'the use of state power to modify the reproduction of labour power and to maintain the non-working population in capitalist societies'. Hence a wide range of goals, motives and functions is attributed to the contemporary welfare state, but perhaps there is general agreement that the welfare state signifies the responsibility of the state for the well-being of all individuals on the basis of citizenship rights.

Turning to means, the minimum range of services included within the rubric of the welfare state is that adopted by the ILO, which comprises all cash benefits to individuals (social insurance, social assistance and universal benefits) together with public health services. As Wilensky suggests above, however, this list is usually extended to include education, personal social services and housing. Beyond this core the boundaries of the welfare state are disputed. Mishra (1984) would include full employment policies; Titmuss (1963) the range of tax expenditure he calls 'fiscal welfare' and even the occupational welfare schemes of corporations; Gough (1979) the state regulation of private activities of individuals and corporate bodies which affect the conditions of life of individuals and groups.

Notwithstanding these grey areas, there is general agreement that the welfare state was inaugurated in the mid-19th century with the provision of public elementary education, and more specifically in 1883 when the first of Bismarck's social insurance schemes was enacted. Before this time public assistance and poor relief existed but was based on the punitive criterion of 'less eligibility' and/or was coupled with the loss of citizenship rights (see Rimlinger, 1971, for the 'prehistory' of the welfare state). Developments since this time have been charted by Flora and Heidenheimer (1981) for selected Western countries (Table 1). Two general conclusions can be drawn from this survey of landmarks. First, except for elementary education and some pioneering legislation, the welfare state is essentially a product of the 20th century. Second, countries display marked variations in the vintage and

TABLE 1

Year of Introduction of:	Germany	UK	Sweden	France	Italy	USA	Canada
Social insurance for:							
Industrial accidents	1884	1906	1901	1946	1898	1930	1930
Sickness insurance	1883	1911	1910	1930	1943	—	1971
Pensions	1889	1908	1913	1910	1919	1935	1927
Unemployment insurance	1927	1911	1934	1967	1919	1935	1940
Family allowances	1954	1945	1947	1932	1936	—	1944
Health insurance/service	1880	1948	1962	1945	1945	—	1972
General personal income tax operated uninterruptedly from:	1920* (1873)	1918	1903	1960	1923	1913	N/A
Education:							
Adult illiteracy first <20%	1850	1880	1880	N/A	N/A	1870	N/A
Secondary school enrolment first >10%	1925	1923	1937	N/A	N/A	1915	N/A
University enrolment first >10%	1975	1973	1968	N/A	N/A	1946	N/A

Notes: 'Social insurance' refers to compulsory state insurance, not employers' liability laws or social assistance schemes for specific groups.
*Introduced in Prussia in 1873.
Source: Flora and Heidenheimer (1981), tables 3.1, 6.1, 8.1–4.

scope of their welfare systems; compare, for example, the exceptional position of the USA as pioneer in education yet laggard in the rest of social policy. This will be returned to below.

The scope of the welfare state has expanded dramatically in the 20th century as measured by the share of social service spending in GNP. In Britain social service spending as a share of GNP rose from 4 per cent in 1910 to 29 per cent in 1975, notably in bursts after the two world wars followed by a prolonged period of expansion from the early 1960s to the mid-1970s. This third state of growth was near-universal in OECD countries, the elasticity of growth rates of expenditure to GDP for the OECD as a whole over this period being 1.75 for health, 1.42 for income maintenance and 1.38 for education. The welfare state has been the most dynamic postwar factor increasing the share of the public sector as a whole in GDP. In all major OECD countries except the UK social expenditure exceeded 50 per cent of total public expenditure in the late 1970s. Despite attempts by many governments to stop or reverse this trend after 1973, it continued to rise into the 1980s. By 1981 social expenditure exceeded one-third of GDP in the Netherlands, Denmark, Sweden and West Germany amongst others. Similar results are found by measuring social service employment and the share of household income accounted for by public transfers and employment.

At the same time national variations in the size of the welfare state are wide and persistent: there is no tendency towards convergence over time (Alber, 1983). On all rankings, Japan and the USA come near the bottom whilst Sweden, the Netherlands and Denmark are at the top. The UK is now below average in social expenditure among OECD countries. In Eastern Europe social expenditure exhibits a slower growth and a somewhat lower claim on resources than in Western Europe (though higher than in the USA and Japan).

In the face of such a massive transformation of capitalist economies, it is not surprising that the *causes* and *consequences* of the modern welfare state are disputed. Nor is it surprising that a shift in the respective roles of the economy, the state and civil society has attracted the attention not only of economists but also of sociologists and political scientists amongst others. Theories of the causes of welfare state development can be grouped into three: collective choice theories, modernization theories and Marxist theories.

The economic theory of politics as applied to the welfare state has not been spelt out in definitive form, but Mishra (1984) provides a good overview. It explains the universal growth of welfare spending in terms of political competition for votes, the lack of a cost constraint on voters' behaviour due to the low salience of taxes, the pressure of interest groups outside the state, notably trade unions and professionals, and the operation of budget–maximizing bureaucracies within the state. These forces, buttressed since World War II, by Keynesian economic theory, have exerted an upward 'ratchet' effect on welfare programmes and expenditure, which in turn are predicted to expand faster than tax resources. The theory would appear to explain the expansion of the welfare state since World War II, but is less successful in explaining the wide national disparities in welfare provision noted above.

By contrast, sociological theories (e.g. Wilensky and Lebeaux, 1965; Wilensky, 1975; Flora and Heidenheimer, 1981) have interpreted the welfare state as a response to the structural requirements of modernization. Economic development increases the division of labour and undermines the 'security functions' previously performed by families and communities; this generates new societal problems and requirements which call forth the widening responsibility of the state. Two schools of thought can be distinguished within this theoretical framework. The first emphasizes the role of social policy in adapting the labour force and other social institutions to the requirements of the economy; for example, via changes in the education system. The second, following Durkheim, emphasizes the need for new modes of social integration and explains the welfare state as the response to this societal need. T.H. Marshall's (1963) theory in which the welfare state is perceived as the culmination of citizenship rights, is the most notable example of this school. Both variants of modernization theory are able to theorize the universal expansion of the welfare state, but they suffer from two related problems. First, they offer 'functionalist' explanations of the process which are now discredited, on the familiar grounds that one cannot explain the origin or persistence of a policy in terms of its consequences – whatever they are (Goldthorpe, 1962). Second, they cannot satisfactorily explain historical and contemporary disparities in welfare state development – why, for example, Germany introduced national sickness insurance in 1883 yet the USA (at the time of writing) still has not followed suit.

Marxist theories relate the form and development of the welfare state to the structure and development of the capitalist mode of production. Offe (1975) has shown how the capitalist state is constrained by the fact that it does not control investment decisions and the process of accumulation, yet depends on a healthy capitalist sector for its tax revenues. Hence, whatever the nature of the party in power, it is constrained from pursuing welfare policies harmful to broad capitalist interests. In the hands of some writers, this has resulted in a Marxist version of functionalist modernization theories. Others, however, stress the existence of exploitative class relations and endemic class conflict which generate the modern labour movement which seeks to utilize the state to modify market processes. Thus O'Connor (1973) argues that the state must try to fulfil two basic and often contradictory functions: accumulation and legitimation (the latter to maintain the conditions for social harmony). Gough (1979) interprets the welfare state as the outcome of two sets of forces: on the one hand, the ability of the capitalist welfare state to adapt the population and policy framework to the changing requirements of capital; on the other hand, the pressure exerted by the working class to modify the play of market forces to improve need-satisfaction and levels of welfare. Stephens (1979) and Therborn (1984) argue that measures of labour movement strength correlate well with national and temporal variations in social expenditure. Thus Marxist theories offer some explanation of contemporary welfare variations; nevertheless, they lack an explanation of the citizenship-rights *form* of contemporary welfare policies.

Lastly, we turn to different interpretations of the *consequences* of the welfare state for modern capitalist economies. We can distinguish two interpretations here which we shall label the compatibility and the incompatibility theses. The first has been argued by Keynesian economists (the welfare state as an agency of demand management), and by modernization theorists and radical functionalists, both of whom stress the economic and integrative roles of the welfare state. The view that the welfare state and capitalism form a harmonious partnership was widespread over the postwar decades of economic growth and political stability. The onset of economic crisis in 1973 however has undermined this position.

The opposing incompatibility thesis is argued on the right and left of the political spectrum. On the right it is argued that the extent of contemporary welfare activities has led to government 'failure' and 'overload'. Among the unintended consequences of government action are cited increasing inflation, the failure of social programmes to meet their goals and the erosion of individual responsibility and independence. The responsibilities of the welfare state expand alongside the expectations of citizens, and the result is the political destabilization of democracies (summarized in Mishra, 1984). This version of the incompatibility thesis was one foundation of the Thatcher and Reagan governments' adoption of monetarist and supply-side economic policies designed to reduce government welfare expenditure and taxation. On the left the incompatibility thesis is argued by O'Connor (1973), Offe (1984) and Habermas (1976). Systemic failures result from the central contradiction of capitalist welfare states: the necessity of the welfare state to both commodify and decommodify the economy. 'Commodification' is necessary to permit market mechanisms to operate to ensure economic growth, but 'decommodification' (collective regulation) of the economy is also necessary to cope with the ensuing problems of an economic system which it cannot control.

Though popular since the mid-1970s, incompatibility theories have been criticized on theoretical and empirical grounds. The former essentially reiterate the positive consequences of welfare state activity noted earlier. An empirical survey of the impact of the welfare state by George and Wilding (1984) concludes that its negative economic consequences have been much exaggerated and may be outweighed by its positive effects, whilst the welfare state is also a positive source of political stability.

Incompatibility theories have predominantly been articulated and their policy implications implemented, within the English-speaking countries. In Europe, countries such as Sweden and Norway continued to pursue both full employment and expansionary welfare policies after the mid-1970s (Himmelstrand et al., 1981). Future research is needed on the comparative differences between capitalist socio-economic systems, their welfare states and their economic performance. It is likely to demonstrate, first, that incompatibility theories are not generalizable, and second, that the welfare state signals an historic, irreversible and progressive transformation of advanced capitalist societies.

I. GOUGH

See also ECONOMIC THEORY OF THE STATE.

BIBLIOGRAPHY

Alber, J. 1983. Some causes of social security expenditure development in Western Europe, 1949–1977. In *Social Policy and Social Welfare*, ed. M. Loney et al., Milton Keynes: Open University Press.

Beveridge, W.H. 1942. *Social Insurance and Allied Services*. Cmnd 6404, London: HMSO.

Briggs, A. 1961. The welfare state in historical perspective. *Archives européennes de Sociologie* 2(2), 221–59.

Flora, P. and Heidenheimer, A.J. (eds) 1981. *The Development of Welfare States in Europe and America*. New Brunswick: Transaction Books.

George, V. and Wilding, P. 1984. *The Impact of Social Policy*. London: Routledge & Kegan Paul.

Goldthorpe, J.H. 1962. The development of social policy in England, 1880–1914. *Transactions of the Fifth World Congress of Sociology* 4, 41–56.

Gough, I. 1979. *The Political Economy of the Welfare State*. London: Macmillan.

Habermas, J. 1976. *Legitimation Crisis*. London: Heinemann.

Himmelstrand, U. et al. 1981. *Beyond Welfare Capitalism*. London: Heinemann.

Marshall, T.H. 1963. Citizenship and social class. In T.H. Marshall, *Sociology at the Crossroads and Other Essays*, London: Heinemann.

Mishra, R. 1984. *The Welfare State in Crisis*. Brighton: Wheatsheaf Books.

O'Connor J. 1973. *The Fiscal Crisis of the State*. New York: St Martin's Press.

Offe, C. 1975. The theory of the capitalist state and the problem of policy formation. In *Stress and Contradiction in Modern Capitalism*, ed. L. Lindberg et al., London and Lexington, Mass.: D.C. Heath.

Offe, C. 1984. *Contradictions of the Welfare State*. Ed. J. Keane, London: Hitchinson.

Rimlinger, G.V. 1971. *Welfare Policy and Industrialization in Europe, America and Russia*. New York: Wiley.

Stephens, J.D. 1979. *The Transition from Capitalism to Socialism*. London: Macmillan.

Therborn, G. 1984. The prospects of labour and the transformation of advanced capitalism. *New Left Review* (145), May–June, 5–38.

Titmuss, R. 1963. The social division of welfare. In R. Titmuss, *Essays on 'The Welfare State'*, 2nd edn, London: Allen & Unwin.

Wilensky, H.L. 1975. *The Welfare State and Equality*. Berkeley: University of California Press.

Wilensky, H.L. and Lebeaux, C.N. 1965. *Industrial Society and Social Welfare*. New York: Free Press.

Wells, David Ames (1828–1898). Wells was born on 17 June 1828 in Springfield, Massachusetts, and died on 5 November 1898 in Norwich, Connecticut. Trained at Williams College and Lawrence Scientific School at Harvard, Wells first taught and published as a geologist and chemist. After newspaper work, Wells turned to economics in his mid-forties. After publishing on the national debt, he was appointed to a series of federal and state tax positions, where he issued influential reports, revised tax laws, and originated the stamp system for collecting taxes on tobacco and liquor. He lectured in economics at Yale, Harvard and elsewhere, succeeded John Stuart Mill in 1874 as foreign associate of the French Academy, was president of the American Social Science Association, and received honorary degrees from Oxford, Harvard and Williams. His economic interests were practical and empirical, rather than theoretical; his place was transitional between the popular writer and the technically trained professional investigator.

Politically active, he was a leading exponent of laissez faire doctrine, which he equated with individualism (in the manner of William Graham Sumner, with whom he was associated), free trade and the gold standard. Although an early protectionist disciple of Henry C. Carey, he later actively wrote and campaigned in favour of free trade. He opposed fiat money, the greenbacks and free silver. At one point he proposed the conversion of the greenbacks to interest-bearing government bonds; at another, he advocated a 'cremation theory of specie resumption', with the Secretary of the Treasury to burn a volume of greenbacks each day until they attained parity with gold.

Considered by some to be so doctrinaire as to be impervious to the stresses brought by industrialization in the late 19th century, he was none the less concerned with economic instability. Here he departed from orthodox doctrine, emphasizing the existence of unemployment due to both technology and overproduction relative to present demand, aggravated by the decline of available public lands as an alternative open to labour. His remedy was freer trade.

Through his will, he established the David Ames Wells Prizes in economics at Harvard University. Recipients have included

John H. Williams, Jacob Viner, James W. Angell, Seymour E. Harris, Edward Chamberlin, Robert Triffin, Paul Samuelson, Lloyd Metzler, Robert Solow, Peter Kenen, Lester Thurow, and Donald McCloskey.

WARREN J. SAMUELS

SELECTED WORKS

1864. *Our Burden and Our Strength.* New York: Loyal Publication Society.
1875. *The Cremation Theory of Specie Resumption.* New York: Putnam's.
1876. *Robinson Crusoe's Money.* New York: P. Smith.
1877. *The Silver Question.* New York: Putnam's.
1884a. *A Primer of Tariff Reform.* New York: New York State Revenue Reform League.
1884b. (With W.G. Sumner.) *Political Economy and Political Science.* New York: Society for Political Education.
1885. *Practical Economics.* New York: Putnam's.
1888. *Relation of The Tariff to Wages.* New York: Putnam's.
1889. *Recent Economic Changes.* New York: D. Appleton.
1900. *The Theory and Practice of Taxation.* New York: D. Appleton.

BIBLIOGRAPHY

Joyner, F.B. 1939. *David Ames Wells: Champion of Free Trade.* Cedar Rapids: Torch Press.

West, Edward (1782–1828). Edward West is remembered – if he is remembered at all – for having stated the theory of differential rent based on the principle of diminishing returns in a long pamphlet just before Ricardo did so, and in virtually the same form and language. This has earned West the title of 'the first, though not the name-father and greatest of the "Ricardian" school' (Cannan, 1893, p. 219). However, it appears that Ricardo developed the principle of diminishing returns independently of West and even of Malthus (who also published the idea more or less simultaneously) and at any rate Ricardo's exposition in his *Essay on Profits* (1815) was clearer then anyone else's, was more carefully set out and went beyond West in spelling out its implications for the distribution of income between wages, profits and rent. In addition to his *Essay on the Application of Capital to Land, with Observations Shewing the Impolicy of any Great Restriction of the Importation of Corn* (1815), West only wrote one other work on economics, a short book entitled *Price of Corn and Wages of Labour, with Observations upon Dr. Smith's, Mr. Ricardo's, and Mr. Malthus's Doctrines Upon those Subjects* (1826). At the time of his death, he was working on a treatise in political economy, the manuscript of which has been lost.

West was born in 1782 near London, educated at Harrow and University College, Oxford (where he studied classics and mathematics), and then went on to study law. In 1817, two years after the *Essay on the Application of Capital to Land*, he published a major treatise on the law of 'extents' (indemnities against direct or indirect debts to royality), which was instrumental in reforming the use of extents in the Courth of Chancery. In 1822 he was knighted and appointed Recorder of Bombay, followed two years later by the post of Chief Justice of the Crown in the Bombay province of India. The publication of his book on the *Price of Corn* in 1826 showed that he maintained his interests in economics until his death in India in 1828.

The similarity between the way in which both West and Ricardo expressed the principle of diminishing returns in agriculture – in terms of diminishing average rather than marginal products of composite doses of capital-and-labour applied to a fixed quantity of heterogeneous land and inclusive, not exclusive, of technical progress in agriculture – is startling, and so is the fact that both of them employed it to deduce a falling rate of profit on capital that could be postponed, but not permanently reversed, by the abolition of the Corn Laws. The only striking difference between the two 1815 pamphlets lay in the implications the two authors deduced from diminishing returns: Ricardo inferred that rents per acre would rise as more capital and labour were applied to ever inferior land, while West inferred that rents would fall, so that free trade would benefit landlords as well as capitalists and workers. This was a point on which West later changed his mind: in the *Price of Corn*, he agreed with Ricardo's inference about both rents per acre and the rental share. Unlike Ricardo, West realized that free trade would not imply complete specialization as between manufacturing in Britain and agriculture in Britain's trading partners: diminishing returns would operate abroad to raise the price of exported corn even as free trade would diminish the pressure on the costs of raising corn at home, so that eventually 'the actual price of both in the market must meet'. In this way, he met what was at the time a critical objection to the notion of free trade, namely that it would make Britain for ever dependent on foreign food supplies.

West's *Price of Corn* is a notable book if only because it was virtually the first work to attack the wages fund doctrine embedded in the writings of Adam Smith and Ricardo. 'The opinion that the demand for labour is regulated solely by the amount of capital', West asserted, 'has led perhaps to more false conclusions in the science than any other cause'. The demand for labour, he insisted, is not governed by the stock of wage goods inherited from the past but by the total level of private and public investment and consumption spending in the economy. It followed, he concluded, that 'the demand for the money wages of labour may be increased without any increase of the capital of the country'. The book contained a number of other insights, although opinions must differ as to how original these really were. There was the idea that price is determined by demand and supply, each of them considered as schedules of quantities at various hypothetical prices (an idea also found in Malthus); that the long-run 'natural' price of commodities is equal to average costs, including normal profits; that all manufacturing firms have identical cost functions; that the short-run market price of industrial goods cannot fall below average variable costs; and that the effect of a change in agricultural output on the price of corn depends on both the price and income elasticity of demand for corn. For some commentators these insights make him a 'Marshallian before Alfred Marshall' rather than a Ricardian before Ricardo (Grampp, 1970).

MARK BLAUG

BIBLIOGRAPHY

Cannan, E. 1893. *A History of the Theories of Production and Distribution in English Political Economy from 1776 to 1848.* London: Staples Press, 1953.

Grampp, W.D. 1970. Edward West reconsidered. *History of Political Economy* 2(2), Fall, 316–43.

Westergaard, Harald Ludvig (1853–1936). Westergaard was born on 19 April 1853 in Copenhagen. At the University of Copenhagen he took degrees in mathematics (1874) and economics (1877). He studied in Britain and Germany (1877–8), taught statistics and economics at his alma mater from 1883 to 1924, and died on 13 December 1936 in Copenhagen.

As an economist, Westergaard rejected English classical theory on two grounds. First, his warm heart reacted against a dismissal of social reform as futile. Like his German historical colleagues, Westergaard became an early champion of *Sozialpolitik*. Second, his keen mind reacted against a dismissal of the demand side. In his *Indledning* (1891) he introduced the post-1870 revolution of economic theory in the form received from his friend Jevons. His first article (1876) had accepted cardinal utility to the point of making interpersonal utility comparisons: equalizing the distribution of wealth would increase community utility. Westergaard urged Jevons (1879: preface) to derive the Jevonian marginal equalities simply as the first-order conditions for an individual utility maximum, but Jevons was not up to it.

Jevons never reached a fully general economic equilibrium: his households were do-it-yourself households engaged in barter. By contrast, Walras separated households from industry, found physical quantities of outputs supplied by industry and demanded by households, physical quantities of inputs supplied by households and demanded by industry, and relative prices at which all such outputs and inputs were transacted. By introducing the post-1870 revolution in its Walrasian form, Wicksell and Cassel gave Sweden a clear head-start. After Westergaard, the first Danish generation (Birck) remained Jevonian, and it took yet another generation (Zeuthen) for Walras to reach Denmark.

As a statistician, Westergaard did his most original work. His *Lehre* (1882) and his *Grundzüge* (1890) enjoyed international fame. A 50-page English-language summary, 'Scope' (1916), was published by the American Statistical Association. Westergaard's tools were the binomial and normal distributions combined with a deep analysis of the data divided into rational subgroups. He used his tools to the hilt on demographic and anthropometric data but was always less interested in mathematical rigour than in finding what was hiding behind his data and his errors of measurement. In the fine art of listening to the voice of numbers, few practitioners have had an ear as sensitive as his.

Westergaard's normal distribution was at home in demography and anthropometry, and he was always reluctant to move on to less friendly habitats. Although trained in the triad, then unique, of economic theory, mathematics and statistics, he never became an econometrician: to let economic theory suggest possible forms of a regression equation, to estimate the parameters of each form, and to let correlation analysis decide the choice among forms seemed frivolous to him. Eight years ahead of Moore, Westergaard's doctoral candidate Mackeprang (1906) estimated demand functions for 24 commodities. Westergaard was unimpressed and in his farewell lecture in 1924 still considered correlation analysis a fad.

Out of sympathy with the trends of his chosen field, Westergaard turned to its history and gave us his only English-language full-length book, his *Contributions* (1932). Wide coverage, lucid restatement, and historical accuracy made it a classic.

HANS BREMS

SELECTED WORKS

1876. Den moralske Formue og det moralske Haab (Moral fortune and moral expectation). *Tidsskrift for Matematik*.

1882. *Die Lehre von der Mortalität und Morbilität*. Jena: Fischer. 2nd enlarged edn, 1901.

1890. *Die Grundzüge der Theorie der Statistik*. Jena: Fischer. 2nd much enlarged edn, 1928.

1891. *Indledning til Studiet af Nationalkonomien* (Introduction to the study of political economy). Copenhagen: Philipsen.

1916. Scope and method of statistics. *Quarterly Publications of the American Statistical Association* 15.

1932. *Contributions to the History of Statistics*. London: King.

BIBLIOGRAPHY

Jevons, W.S. 1879. *The Theory of Political Economy*. 2nd edn, London: Macmillan.

Kaergård, N. 1983. Marginalismens gennembrud i Danmark og mændene bag (The breakthrough of marginalism in Denmark and the men behind it). *Nationaløkonomisk Tidsskrift* 1.

Kaergård, N. 1984. The earliest history of econometrics: some neglected Danish contributions. *History of Political Economy* 16(3), Fall, 437–44.

Mackeprang, E. 1906. *Pristeorier* (Price theories). Copenhagen: Bagge.

Rander Buch, K. 1968. Harald Westergaard. In *International Encyclopedia of the Social Sciences*, New York: Macmillan, Vol. 16, 528–9.

Royal Statistical Society (anonymous). 1937. Obituary. Harald Westergaard, 1853–1937. *Journal of the Royal Statistical Society* 100, 149–50.

Whately, Richard (1787–1863). Whately was Fellow of Oriel College, Oxford, 1811–22; rector of Halesworth, Suffolk, 1822–5; principal of St Alban's Hall, 1825–31; Drummond Professor of Political Economy in the University of Oxford, 1829–31; and Archbishop of Dublin, 1831–63.

In the one course of lectures on political economy which he published, Whately displayed flashes of originality, as in his famous aphorism on the labour theory of value, 'It is not that pearls fetch a high price *because* men have dived for them, but on the contrary men dive for them because they fetch a high price', and in his suggestion to re-name the subject 'Catallactics, or the science of exchanges' (1832, pp. 6 and 253). In later years his *Easy Lessons on Money Matters*, the first attempt to present classical political economy in a primary school book, went through 16 editions and was translated into at least three languages.

Although Whately's period as a professor of political economy was only a brief interlude in a long career as theologian and churchman, he exerted a continuing influence on the subject in a variety of ways apart from his writings. He was a lifelong friend of Nassau Senior, his Oxford contemporary and predecessor in the Drummond chair; each influenced the other's thinking on matters of both economic theory and policy.

After his move to Dublin, Whately founded and personally financed the chair of political economy in Trinity College, basing it on the Oxford model and examining the candidates himself. A liberal on matters of social policy, he opposed the introduction of the workhouse system in to Ireland, urging wider measures of economic development.

R.D. COLLISON BLACK

SELECTED WORKS

1831. *Introductory Lectures on Political Economy*. London: B. Fellowes. 2nd edn (including an additional lecture), 1832.

1833. *Easy Lessons on Money Matters, for the use of young people*. London: J.W. Parker for the Society for the Promotion of Christian Knowledge.

BIBLIOGRAPHY

Goldstrom, J.M. 1966. Richard Whately and political economy in school books, 1833–80. *Irish Historical Studies* 15, 131–46.

Whately, E.J. 1866. *Life and Correspondence of Richard Whately*. 2 vols, London.

Wheatley, John (1772–1830). Lawyer and economist, Wheatley was born in Erith, Kent, of a prominent landed and military family, and died at sea on a voyage from South Africa to England. A memorial plaque to him is in the Wheatley chapel of the Erith parish church. At Oxford he was a member of Christ Church, and after receiving his BA in 1793 was admitted to Lincoln's Inn, but his activity in the law was limited, and his life was devoted largely to writing on economics and playing a small part in Whig politics. With him at Christ Church was Charles Watkin Williams Wynn, nephew of Lord Grenville, and Wheatley was active in support of Grenville's successful campaign in 1809 for Chancellor of Oxford University; he had correspondence with Wynn in 1812 about running for Parliament on the Whig ticket, but nothing came of this; a book of 1816 took the form of a letter to Lord Grenville, and his pamphlet of 1823 was a letter to Wynn.

Wheatley published ten books and brochures, two of these in India and one in South Africa. He lived in these two countries for the last nine years of his life, evidently to escape creditors. His works published in India and South Africa received little contemporary attention, and today are extremely rare. Of the others, *Remarks on Currency and Commerce* (1803), and the first volume of *An Essay on the Theory of Money and Principles of Commerce* (1807) received the most contemporary attention, and best stated his theoretical position on the monetary controversy that followed the suspension of cash payments by the Bank of England in 1797. Wheatley stated, in an even more extreme way than Ricardo did later, that exchange fluctuations were due exclusively to domestic price changes, and that the Bank of England, through its credit policy, could control prices, and thus exchange rates. These books of 1803 and 1807 criticized the Bank for its monetary expansion, but following the resumption of specie payments in 1821 Wheatley in his book of 1822 had become a severe critic of both the Bank and of the Tory government for the price deflation. His efforts, both in his book and in correspondence with Whig leaders, to launch an attack on the government's monetary policy, made no headway. In several publications he stressed the danger, for monetary stability, of permitting the issue of notes by banks other than the Bank of England. No economist of his period so well anticipated the note issue provisions of the Bank Act of 1844, which led to the elimination of all notes other than of the Bank of England.

Wheatley's views on political issues were something of a paradox. As a Whig he was frequently a voice for reform; with the background of the landed gentry he sometimes disagreed with Whig positions that threatened the supremacy of the landed aristocracy. He supported free trade, a commercial union with France, removal of restrictions on West Indian trade, and the abolition of slavery. He favoured primogeniture, maintenance of great landed estates, the political supremacy of the landed gentry, and an unreformed Parliament. In foreign policy his imperialist views foreshadowed the idea of the 'white man's burden.'

FRANK WHITSON FETTER

SELECTED WORKS

1803. *Remarks on Currency and Commerce*. London.

1805. *Thoughts on the Object of a Foreign Subsidy*. London.

1807–22. *An Essay on the Theory of Money and Principles of Commerce*. Vol. I, London, 1807; Vol. II, London, 1822.

1807. *A Letter to Lord Grenville, on the Distress of the Country*. London.

1819. *A Report on the Reports of the Bank Committee*. Shrewsbury.

1821. *A Plan to Relieve the Country from Its Difficulties*. Shrewsbury. This short pamphlet is an extract from the book of 1822 that appeared shortly afterwards.

1823. *Letter to the Rt. Hon. Charles Watkin Williams Wynn, President of the Board of Control, on the Latent Resources of India*. Calcutta.

1824. *A Letter to his Grace the Duke of Devonshire on the State of Ireland, and on the General Effects of Colonization*. Calcutta.

1828. *Tempora praeterita: Or, More Currency and More Corn*. Cape Town. This was published anonymously, but in correspondence Wheatley admitted authorship.

The Wheatley letters to Lord Grey are in the Grey of Howick papers at the University of Durham; the Wheatley letters to Charles Watkin Williams Wynn are at the National Library of Wales át Aberystwyth.

BIBLIOGRAPHY

Fetter, F.W. 1942. The life and writings of John Wheatley. *Journal of Political Economy*50, June, 357–76.

Viner, J. 1937. *Studies in the Theory of International Trade*. New York: Harper & Brothers, 138–41, 295–7.

Whewell, William (1799–1866). Whewell was born in Lancaster and died in Cambridge. He received his early education at Lancaster Grammar School and Heversham School, Westmoreland, and in 1812 he went up to Trinity College, Cambridge. In 1817 he became a Fellow of the College, in 1823 a Tutor. In 1841 he was made Master, an appointment which he held until his death.

Whewell was at the centre of a 'network' of Cambridge scientists and exercised considerable influence upon scientific and philosophic circles in Victorian England. In 1820 he became a Lecturer in Mathematics, in 1828 he was appointed Professor of Mineralogy and in 1838 Professor of Moral Philosophy. He was active as an honorary member of twenty-five scientific, historical and philosophical societies in several countries. To mention a few of the most important in England: he was one of the founders of the Cambridge Philosophical Society in 1818; in 1820 he was elected a Fellow of the Royal Society; in 1831 he became a member of the British Association and in 1841 was appointed President.

Whewell was primarily a philosopher and mathematician, and he published his major works in these fields (Whewell, 1837 and 1840). Political economy was one of the many other subjects dealt with by him. However, his contributions in this field – written over the whole period from 1829 to 1862 – give clear proof that his interest in economics was lifelong. Whewell's major works in political economy were four papers on mathematical economics which were read before the Cambridge Philosophical Society (Whewell, 1829; 1831; 1850a and 1850b) and a book – *Six Lectures on Political Economy* (1862) – which was composed for the edification of the Prince of Wales, the future Edward VII. In the *Six Lectures* Whewell presented, in a very elementary way, the principal ideas of Smith, Ricardo and Jones.

Whewell's four papers represent the earliest *systematic* application of mathematical symbols of political economy in England. Whewell believed that the arithmetic used by classical economists was inadequate, and that the more general language of algebra should take its place. He pointed out that the adoption of a mathematical method had two main advantages. Firstly, that many aspects of political economy could be presented in a more simple, clear and systematic form. Secondly – and more importantly – the use of mathematics could help to avoid the danger of drawing false conclusions for assumptions made. To illustrate this point, in his 1829 paper Whewell used mathematics to discuss Ricardo's theory of the incidence of a tax on wages. Ricardo had argued

– against Smith – that a rise in the prices of goods due to a rise in wages would in turn affect wages and 'the action and reaction first of wages on goods and then of goods on wages, will be extended without any assignable limits' (Ricardo, 1821, p. 225). Whewell, on the contrary, showed that if Ricardo had considered the mathematical implications of his theory, he would have found that an unlimited rise in prices and wages was impossible. Indeed, if it is assumed that only a part of the value of goods is wages, and only a part of the labourer's consumption consists of manufactured goods, then the paths that both prices and wages follow take the form of geometric series which converge.

But Whewell's most notable contribution to political economy was his mathematical formulation of Ricardo's theory, and in particular his analysis of fixed capital (Whewell, 1831). This analysis is important not only because it represents the first mathematical treatment of machinery in Ricardo's model, but also and mainly because it constitutes an original contribution to the subject. In 1831 Whewell had already provided an exact formulation for the reduction of fixed capital to dated quantities of labour. He also worked out a simple model to quantify the substitution effect between labour and machinery. Finally, through the annuity formula, he arrived at the equation which defines the production price in the presence of fixed capital.

These results also suggest that the dating of the genesis of fixed capital models may need to be reappraised, for it is usually thought that Bortkiewicz (1907) – on the basis of Dmitriev's contribution (1904) – was the first economist to treat fixed capital mathematically within the theory of production price.

Whewell has been consistently neglected in the history of economic analysis. The few authors who were acquainted with Whewell's work – of whom the most authoritative were Jevons (1871) and Schumpeter (1954) – considered his analysis as purely derivative: supposedly he merely translated into algebraic form results which others had previously expressed in non-mathematical language. The only exception was Walras, who regarded Whewell's contribution as 'really remarkable' (Walras, 1875, p. 32). Whewell was in fact more than a translator: he was a major contributor to the early development of mathematical economics in England, and above all a pioneer in the general debate on fixed capital.

G. Campanelli

SELECTED WORKS

1829. *Mathematical Exposition of Some Doctrines of Political Economy*. Cambridge: Cambridge Philosophical Society, 1830, Transaction 3.

1831. *Mathematical Exposition of Some of the Leading Doctrines of Political Economy: Second Memoir*. Cambridge: Cambridge Philosophical Society, 1833, Transaction 4.

1837. *History of the Inductive Sciences, From the Earliest to the Present Time*. 3rd edn, New York: Appleton, 1890.

1840. *The Philosophy of the Inductive Sciences, Founded Upon their History*. 2nd edn, London: Parker, 1847.

1850a. *Mathematical Exposition of Some Doctrines of Political Economy: Second Memoir*. Cambridge: Cambridge Philosophical Society, 1856, Transaction 9, Part I.

1850b. *Mathematical Exposition of Certain Doctrines of Political Economy: Third Memoir*. Cambridge: Cambridge Philosophical Society, 1856, Transaction 9, Part II.

1862. *Six Lectures on Political Economy*. Cambridge: Cambridge University Press.

1971. *Mathematical Exposition of Certain Doctrines of Political Economy*. New York: A. M. Kelley. A reprint of Whewell's four papers on mathematical economics (Whewell 1829, 1831, 1850a and 1850b).

BIBLIOGRAPHY

Bortkiewicz, L. 1907. Wertrechnung und Preisrechnung im Marxschen System. *Archiv für Sozialwissenschaft und Sozialpolitik*, Vol. 25. The second and the third parts are translated into English as 'Value and price in the marxian system', *International Economic Papers* No. 2, 1952, 5–60.

Dmitriev, V.K. 1904. *Economic Essays on Value, Competition and Utility*. Ed. D.M. Nuti, Cambridge: Cambridge University Press, 1974.

Jevons, W.S. 1871. *The Theory of Political Economy*. London and New York: Macmillan.

Ricardo, D. 1821. *On the Principles of Political Economy and Taxation*. Ed. P. Sraffa, Cambridge: Cambridge University Press, 1951

Schumpeter, J.A. 1954. *History of Economic Analysis*. New York: Oxford University Press.

Walras, L. 1875. Une branche nouvelle de la mathématique: de l'application des mathématiques à l'économie politique. Italian trans. as 'Un nuovo ramo della matematica. Dell'applicazione della matematiche alla economia politica', *Giornale degli Economisti* 3, 1876.

Wicksell, Johan Gustav Knut (1851–1926).

LIFE AND CAREER

Johan Gustav Knut Wicksell was born in Stockholm on 20 December 1851, the youngest of six children of Johan and Christina Wicksell. One child died in infancy, so Knut grew up with three sisters a few years older than he, and a brother, Axel, one year older.

Knut's mother died when he was not quite seven, an event that greatly affected the sensitive boy. His father, a produce dealer, remarried in 1861 but died five years later when Knut was fifteen. After that the children moved to live for a time with an aunt and their maternal grandmother. In the last decades of his life Knut's father had become moderately well-to-do by investing profits from his grocery business in rental properties. The estate that was left at his death yielded an income sufficient to provide for the children and their education through gymnasium (high school), and for the two boys a start at the University of Uppsala.

At the gymnasium Knut had already shown considerable aptitude for languages and an unusual ability at mathematics. Thus when he enrolled at Uppsala University 1869, it was with the intention of becoming a mathematician with physics as a second field of study.

From about age fifteen Knut came increasingly under the influence of a pietistic pastor of the Swedish Lutheran Church. This religious phase lasted about seven years, in the course of which he became a devout Christian; he withdrew from most social activities to study the Bible and meditate. At the same time he made rapid progress in his studies of mathematics, physics and astronomy, earning his first degree, BS *cum laude*, in 1871, after only two rather than the usual four years at the university, and then proceeding to graduate studies.

However, doubts had begun to assail his faith, and in spring 1874 he had an emotional crisis from which he emerged, and for the rest of his life remained, a free thinker. He became a strictly a-religious philosophical rationalist who, later on, became known as an outspoken and witty critic of the Christian religion in all its forms.

Until 1873 Wicksell maintained himself at the university on the modest annual income he received as his share of his father's estate, on a small inheritance from his grandmother, and on a succession of grants from private foundations. Now the last were drying up and the money from his grandmother was nearly gone. To add to his scant resources, he filled a vacancy as a teacher at a secondary school at Uppsala, 1873–4. The year after that he worked as a private tutor to the son of an ironmaster. Also from time to time he borrowed various amounts from one of his sisters who had established herself in Stockholm as a physiotherapist.

In fact, Wicksell's financial condition remained precarious and often severely strained, except for the years 1885 and 1888–9 when he was studying abroad largely supported by grants, for most of his adult life until 1901. Then, at age fifty and supporting his wife and two school-age sons, he was finally appointed professor extraordinarius (about equivalent to associate professor) at Lund University, and then, from 1904, he served there as ordinarius or full professor for twelve years, until his retirement in 1916.

In 1875 he passed two of three required examinations for the degree *philosophiae licentiatus* in mathematics (the *phil. lic.* is a graduate degree taken prior to the student's beginning work on the doctoral dissertation). Soon after that he began to doubt that he would be able to make any significant contributions to mathematics. While contemplating a change of career either to humanities or to the emerging social sciences, he immersed himself, over a long transition period, in the activities of the students' organization, the Student Corps. He was elected as its curator, 1877–9. In that post he became well known for his critical social views and for his surprising effectiveness as a speaker. At this time he also wrote some 'social indignation' poetry as well as some plays, one of which proved popular and was performed at Uppsala and also in some other towns.

In 1879 two events, in themselves inconspicuous, occurred which strongly influenced Wicksell's subsequent career. He moved to share an apartment with two advanced graduate students, H. Ohrvall in medicine, and T. Frölander in law, and he acquired a book just recently released in Swedish translation, G. Drysdale's tome, *The Elements of Social Science*, with its challenging subtitle, 'Physical, Sexual, and Natural Religion; An Explanation of the True Causes and Cure of the Three Primary Evils of Society – Poverty, Prostitution, and Celibacy'. This work published in England 1854, became very popular in the Swedish translation of 1878, and went through over thirty reprintings over the years.

The three men, whose outlook on society was in several respects similar, became lifelong friends. What cemented their friendship was that they set about on their own and jointly to study Drysdale's thoroughly neo-Malthusian treatise. It discussed frankly several subjects then regarded as unmentionable in 'polite society', such as sex, methods of birth control, the allegedly harmful psychological effects of celibacy if continued for a decade or more past puberty, prostitution as the only alternative for the young among the poor, the need for family planning, and the need to limit population growth in order to raise the standard of living for the working class above bare subsistence.

Wicksell treated this book as a revelation. It focused his mind on 'the social question', i.e. on the social sciences toward which his inclination guided him more and more. As an early result of studying Drysdale, supplemented by some writings of J.S. Mill, in February 1880 he gave a lecture to a temperance lodge at Uppsala on 'The Most Common Causes of Habitual Drunkenness and How to Remove Them'. His address got a mixed reception but was reported in the local newspaper, which led to an insistent demand for him to repeat his lecture two weeks later in a much larger hall which was filled to overflowing.

There he attributed alcoholism, widespread among factory workers, to the poverty and monotony of their lives, with wife and children crammed into crowded and often insanitary housing. For this the local inn offered almost the only relief and relaxation available. And with the young workers this led to the use of the services of prostitutes since these workers for years earned too little to marry and start a family. The remedies he urged were for the medical profession to be assigned the duty of disseminating information about birth control techniques, and for the public health authorities to set and enforce standards of sanitation and room space per occupant in housing in the factory districts of cities and towns.

The reaction to his lecture was strong. Papers by the Young Socialists and by some student organizations praised him. Medical and temperance organizations either reviled or ridiculed him, and several newspapers questioned his competence to pronounce on some of the sensitive issues he had covered.

From now on the die was cast. There would always be one or more reporters present at his future appearances, because these were certain to be newsworthy. Reporters would summarize his talks and write longer accounts about how his audience reacted, especially the critics and opponents among them, and how he, in turn, responded to critics. Most of the reportage depicted him as a non-revolutionary radical social reformer, and that was how public opinion came to view him. We may add that he himself did nothing to modify and much to strengthen that impression.

Later in 1880 he issued his lecture as a tract of some ninety pages and along with it a pamphlet, 'Answers To My Critics', both of which sold in several thousand copies. In fact, this became something of a pattern. Between 1880 and 1885, and again in 1886–7, after his return from his first stay abroad, Wicksell had in substance turned into a radical public lecturer and journalist. This was how he earned his spartan maintenance, by paid public lectures sometimes followed by publishing tracts based on them, and by paid articles written in neo-Malthusian spirit on various 'social questions' for several, sometimes in a given week for as many as ten, different city and town newspapers.

In 1885 he set aside his journalistic work for a time and completed the last requirement for the *phil. lic.* degree in mathematics by a research paper, the other requirements he had met in 1875. Now, however, he wanted to shift into the social sciences rather than go on for a doctorate in mathematics. To do that at any level higher than the elementary meant study abroad, for at that time the social science disciplines were not separate fields but were elements of the curricula in law, philosophy, the humanities or theology in Sweden's universities. But he had no funds for going abroad. Then help came unexpectedly.

His sisters had an opportunity to sell the rental properties of the Johan Wicksell estate to a buyer at a favourable price if Knut and his brother, Axel, who had emigrated to the United States, would agree, as they did. Knut's share of the proceeds was sufficient to pay off his old debts and also to maintain him for about a year abroad, and so, in autumn 1885 he went to London.

In London Wicksell spent his days studying some of the classical economists and treatises by Cairnes, Jevons, Walras and Sidgwick, his first exposure in depth to economics, and his weekends in meetings with persons to whom he was introduced by Charles Drysdale, an engineer who continued the neo-Malthusian activities his father, George Drysdale, had initiated. Thus he met prominent British neo-Malthusians, Annie Besant among them, Karl Kautsky and some labour leaders, and the leading Fabians.

By summer 1886 he returned to Uppsala and Stockholm to resume his public lecturing, writing for several newspapers, and composing tracts. This was now a matter of necessity, for he had used up his patrimony during his stay in Britain. In 1886–7 he delivered forty-two public lectures in towns in central Sweden, in Copenhagen and Christiania, for fees which paid very little above his travel and maintenance expense. The subjects he spoke on were as follows:

Marriage	14 lectures
Population Control	10 lectures
Socialism	6 lectures
Prostitution	5 lectures
Spiritualism	2 lectures
Why Not A Free-Thinker?	2 lectures
Religion	1 lecture
Euthanasia	1 lecture
Impressions of Britain	1 lecture

At the end of 1885 Victor Lorén, a wealthy young man, greatly interested in promoting the social sciences after studying them in Germany with Roscher, bequeathed his estate to a foundation bearing his name, with instructions that it should be used for the promotion of studies and research and publications by scholars devoted to economics and related social sciences. Wicksell was still in London when early in 1886 he was informed that the Lorén Foundation was awarding him a grant for up to three years to study economics at universities in Germany and Austria. Lorén's relatives unsuccessfully contested his will in court, but this held up the grant until the summer of 1887, when the suit was settled.

If the Lorén Foundation had not given him that large grant (and later smaller ones for each of the five treatises he published between 1893 and 1906) Wicksell could hardly have become an economist, much less a major figure in this discipline. As it was, he went first to London to renew acquaintances. In October 1887 he went to the University of Strassburg to follow lectures by Brentano on labour economics, on money and credit by both Brentano and Knapp, and on economic distribution by Singer.

In spring 1888 he was in Vienna to listen to Carl Menger's lectures. In July he returned for a short stay in Sweden. On his way there he met Anna Bugge, a Norwegian gymnasium teacher, who later became his wife. By autumn 1888 he was at the University of Berlin to follow the lectures of Adolph Wagner on public finance. In spring 1889 he returned to Sweden to seek a lectureship in economics at the University of Stockholm. He was turned down as being 'too notorious' a person. Summer 1889 he decided to spend the rest of his grant studying economics in Paris. Before going there he took a trip to Christiania to see Anna Bugge, with whom he had corresponded while in Germany. There he proposed a common-law marriage to her, but out of consideration for her parents she turned him down, whereupon he left in a huff for Paris.

A word may be needed here about the romantic side of Wicksell's life. It is known that he was infatuated in his early twenties with two young ladies. But he was always shy and very hesitant in socializing with young women. So the first young woman moved to Switzerland and married there. The second one was a case of love at a distance, for he failed even to make contact with her. The third and last incident occurred years later. For a part of the summer 1886 he was invited to stay in his friend Frölander's household in Stockholm, where he gave most of his lectures. But there he soon found himself becoming infatuated with his friend's wife. So before he might say or do something to jeopardize their friendship, he made the proper excuses and returned to his lonely lodgings in Uppsala.

Anna, however, did not want to give up Knut. She decided she would be happier with than without him even at the cost of estrangement from her parents. She joined him in Paris that summer; he was then 37 and she 26.

In Paris he attended lectures on public finance by Leroy-Beaulieau and on population theory by Desmoulin, and he began to publish in economics. His first article, the translated title of which is 'Empty Stomachs – Full Stores' came out in a Norwegian journal *Samtiden* in 1890. His second article, 'Überproduktion oder Überbevölkerung' (Excess Production or Excess Population) appeared in *Zeitschrift für die gesamten Staatswissenschaften*, also in 1890. In both he argued that it was fluctuations in capital formation that made the difference between prosperity and depression. In recovery a rate of capital formation is generated which fails to be sustained because consumption demand, though rising, lags behind the rate at which productive capacity expands on a growing capital base.

In summer he and Anna returned to Stockholm. Though soon to be a father (their first son, Sven, was born in October 1890, and a second son, Finn, in 1893), Wicksell had no settled way of earning a living. Economics was then taught only in the faculties of law. Those teaching it in addition to a doctorate in economics also had to have at least an undergraduate degree in law in order to give courses on law and economics as related mainly to taxation and public finance. So he had no alternative but to return to being a free-lance journalist and public lecturer.

During the years 1890–99 Wicksell had more trials and tribulations, only a few of which can be related here. He gave rather few public lectures, but some had a very negative effect on his public image.

In 1892 the government wanted to increase the duration of the compulsory military service to strengthen the country's defences. In November Wicksell lectured in Stockholm on the question, 'Can Sweden Protect her Independence?' He argued, and most of his listeners might have agreed with him, that no matter how long the draft were extended, it would not be adequate for defending Sweden against attack by a major military power. But they disagreed vehemently when he went on to say that since the country could not defend itself on its own resources, it would make better sense to disarm and use the resources set free from defence for other domestic purposes. Then Sweden ought to negotiate for incorporation into the Russian empire with its much greater military resources. In return for the protection thus provided, the Swedes with their long traditions of democracy ought then to play a civilizing role within and for the Russian empire.

This performance earned him the sobriquet of 'defence nihilist', which did not deter him twelve years later when another draft extension was proposed from repeating this same lecture, May Day 1904. At that time it occasioned even greater offence and ridicule than in 1892.

His article 'Kapitalzins und Arbeitslohn' (Interest and Wages), published in the *Jahrbücher für Nationalökonomie und Socialwissenschaft und Statistik* 1892, formed the basis for the marginal productivity theory of distribution – one of Wicksell's main contributions to economic theory – which he developed in his first treatise, *Uber Wert Kapital und Rente* 1893 (*Value, Capital and Rent*, translated 1934). This remarkable work received initially almost no attention in Sweden, but was favourably reviewed by both Böhm-Bawerk and Walras.

Next he turned to an examination of Sweden's taxes in his

popular tract, *Our Taxes–Who Pays and Who Ought to Pay Them*? (99 pp., 1894), issued under the pseudonym of Sven Trygg. He was outraged at the regressiveness of the country's taxes. That, he concluded, had to be a consequence of the fact that only the well-to-do could vote, as income and property qualifications for the franchise excluded almost all the workers and most of the small farmers.

The analysis of that tract was extended and refined in his second treatise, *Finanztheoretische Untersuchungen* (Studies in the Theory of Public Finance), 1896. There he urged that the major part of the revenue burden be shifted from indirect to direct progressive taxes on income and wealth. That treatise also embodied his design on an 'equitable' tax system based on an application of marginal utility theory to the public sector, and a methodology (essentially marginal cost pricing) for pricing pure and less than pure public goods, the services of public utilities, and the products of market-sharing oligopolies and cartels.

In fall 1894, Wicksell applied at Uppsala University to have *Value, Capital and Rent* evaluated as a doctoral dissertation. The answer was no, with the added advice to use it for a *viva voce* examination of a *phil. lic.* degree in economics. David Davidson was appointed examiner and Wicksell passed with high marks in May 1895. Next he needed the doctorate. In 1896 he submitted the first part of his *Finanztheoretische Untersuchungen*, 'Theory of Incidence of Taxation', as a dissertation. Again Davidson was chief examiner, and the degree was awarded Wicksell *magna cum laude*.

That done, he began research on monetary theory and policy, which he completed as his third treatise, *Geldzins und Güterpreise*, 1898 (*Interest and Prices*, translated 1936), the home of the Wicksellian 'cumulative price level fluctuations or processes', allegedly generated by a divergence between the rate of return on newly created real capital and the bank-dominated market rate of interest.

Now he applied both at Stockholm and Uppsala universities for a docentship but was rebuffed because he lacked a degree in law. From 1890 into 1897 he had maintained his family slightly above subsistence level by earnings from his newspaper articles and tracts and from a succession of Lorén grants. However, in autumn 1897 he decided at real hardship, with no more Lorén money, to move from Stockholm to Uppsala to devote his entire energy to cramming through law courses as fast as possible to a *juris candidatus* of LL.B. degree. To do this he had to maintain his family by borrowing from his friends Ohrvall, a physician, and Frölander, a banker-lawyer, both of whom were doing well. In 1899, in less than two years, he had earned his law degree, which usually takes undergraduates four years. He was appointed a docent at Uppsala University but without fixed salary. Consequently his income depended on how many law students came at a given fee per head to attend his tutorials.

At the Lund University faculty of law a professorial vacancy was created when an older professor's post, viewed as overloaded, was split to shift its courses in tax law and economics from the old position to the new one. But Parliament, in approving this, had voted less money for it than a full professor's salary. Wicksell and three others, including Gustav Cassel, competed for this post of professor extraordinarius. As the other candidates, (Cassel for lack of a law degree) were eliminated as not sufficiently qualified, the appointment was offered to Wicksell in January 1900. For complex reasons the upgrading of this to ordinary or full professorship was delayed until January 1904, when Wicksell, at the age of 53, was finally securely established as a full professor.

At Lund, where his teaching of tax law courses required much more preparation than economics, he still found time to write *Föreläsningar i Nationalekonomi* (*Lectures on Political Economy I*, 1901, translated 1934). *Lectures I* were an expansion and improvement, especially in capital theory, over what he had presented in *Value, Capital, and Rent*.

His courses in law as related to taxation were well attended but those in economics attracted very few students, it being an elective subject. He soon found out that the students lacked the background to get much out of a semester on *Value, Capital, and Rent* and another on *Interest and Prices*. So he shifted his presentation from pure to applied economics to subjects such as agriculture and industry, commerce and consumption, social movements, social insurance, economic crises and inflation.

He had good relations with students. His approach to them was friendly. They, in turn, liked or were amused by his idiosyncrasies, and they admired his courage to fight for his convictions.

Unlike most professors, who at that time lectured in formal dress, swallowtail coats and all, Wicksell appeared in ordinary, rarely well-pressed, street clothing. Instead of a top hat or a Derby he wore a visored cap, much like a fisherman's. Since he lived some distance from the university, he did the family's marketing at the nearby open-air market before his morning lectures. Consequently, as he strode in to the lecture room, he would adorn one side of the lectern or the other with his market basket filled with produce, meats and fruits.

In 1905 he issued one of his best and last tracts, *Socialiststaten och nutidssamhället* (The Socialist State and Contemporary Society, 40 pp.). He restated more systematically his perspective on socialism which he had lectured on in the 1880s. First he made it clear he considered a limited but not a complete achievement of a socialist economy (with all means of production other than labour collectively owned and administered) to be inevitable in the future. Under universal adult suffrage the workers would be the political majority. As such, they would not for long tolerate the great inequalities of income and wealth and the economic instability (of employment and economic insecurity and dependence in old age) of *laissez faire* capitalism without seeking and taking remedial measures.

He warned against drastic measures of income redistribution taken by a workers' government suddenly come to power. That would only yield a temporary gain followed by loss as private capital accumulation would all but cease before the workers' regime would have developed the means to replace it by public accumulation. A socialist economy is best built gradually by peaceful means and under democratic governance. Nationalization initially of natural monopolies and cartels might suffice if followed by substantial expansion of tax supported, social security and social insurance schemes. For the sake of efficiency, he held it was best to leave farming and most varieties of genuinely competitive enterprises in private and/or cooperative ownership.

Consequently he argued for a form of market socialism with a well developed welfare state. It is surprising to recognize the great extent to which his social vision has become a reality in Sweden (and in Scandinavia as a whole) after nigh on fifty years of Social Democratic rule.

In 1906 Wicksell published *Lectures on Political Economy II*, the volume on money and credit. In part an expansion and revision of what he had put forth in *Interest and Prices*, yet *Lectures II* was much more than that. They were epoch-making less for their particular findings than for the broad framework and methodology they provided for analysis of money and credit. *Lectures II* were translated first into German in 1922 when, in the midst of the German hyperinflation they were read with greater than usual interest, and into English in 1935.

Wicksell's years at Lund were very productive. He wrote about fifty articles and took an active part in the tax reform of 1910, in the national pension legislation of 1913, and, after the outbreak of World War I, along with Davidson, he played an important role in the legislation and policies relating to banking, currency, and exchange controls.

His work had continued in a tranquil manner until 1908. Then a young 'anarchist agitator' was sentenced to prison for 'disturbing the religious peace' by public blasphemy. He had published a parody of the Wedding at Cana in a socialist newspaper. His case, and two or three similar ones that had occurred earlier, impressed Wicksell as infringements by the courts of freedom of speech and press, guaranteed by the Swedish constitution. Against better advice he decided to make a test case of himself. Accordingly in November 1908 at Stockholm he lectured to a large audience on 'The Throne, the Altar, the Sword, and the Bag of Money' in which, inter alia, he satirized the story of the Immaculate Conception. He raised and answered the question:

> Why was not Joseph, the betrothed of the Virgin Mary, rather than the Holy Ghost allowed to father Jesus? Because then the world could not have been saved! Joseph's rights as an individual had to be set aside for the salvation of the many millions of souls in past centuries who would otherwise have gone to perdition and the further millions now and for all time to come until the Last Judgement.

Wicksell was tried and sentenced, against the protests of Social Democrats, organized workers and liberals, to two months in prison. He was allowed to select the jail where he would serve his time. Early in 1910, after a higher court had sustained the lower court's decision, he chose the jail, known to be better than most, at the small fisherman's town of Ystad in southern Sweden. There he suffered no hardship. His university salary was withheld as long as he was a guest of the government. He used his time to advantage by writing his last tract, *Laran om befolkningen, dess sammansättning, och förändringar* (The Theory of Population, Its Composition, and Models of Change, 1910, 52 pp.).

There, apart from the clear demographic analysis it presented, he reiterated the conclusion from his public lectures of the 1880s, that, because of partial depletion and increasing scarcity of natural resources (in Sweden's case primarily timber and iron ore), the country's optimum population should be three instead of its five million inhabitants, and for Europe a reduction to three quarters of its population as of 1910. Like Malthus and many other writers on Population, while he acknowledged the productivity increasing effect of technological progress, he failed to see and greatly underestimated that some of the new technology virtually adds to existing resources, in part by turning former waste products to productive uses, in part by increasing the number of uses to which existing resources can be turned.

Wicksell's remaining years at Lund passed quietly. But as his retirement was approaching it threatened renewed hardships for him and Anna. Before coming to Lund they had no savings, and when leaving, they had very little more than their household effects in rented housing. Since Wicksell had served only sixteen years at the university, compared with colleagues who at age 65 had usually served 25 or more years, he was barely entitled to two-thirds of the usual professorial pension. At the World War I inflated prices, especially in Stockholm to which city he and Anna insisted on moving, two-thirds pension would not pay for much more than house rent.

Two of his friends who were members of parliament succeeded on a motion to obtain a supplementary allowance for him which raised his pension to 90 per cent of the usual amount. There still remained the problem of housing, which had become very expensive in the capital. So his two parliamentarian and several other close friends, including David Davidson and Eli Heckscher, gathered together and by their personal contributions they raised enough money to buy a lot for a house and garden in Mörby, a suburb of Stockholm, and to initiate construction to Anna's specifications. To complete the building of the house, Wicksell negotiated a small mortgage. By Christmas 1916 he and Anna moved into the first house they could call their own.

Now, in his last decade, a new phase of life began for both of them. Anna, who had taken a law degree in 1911 at Lund and had become a leader in the suffrage movement and later the peace movements, now had greater opportunity to be effective than at Lund. Wicksell, freed both from financial worries and the teaching of law courses, could devote himself full time to research and professional activities as an economist with the much greater resources at his disposal for research and opportunities for consultation of Stockholm as compared with Lund. The years 1917–26 were probably the most satisfactory and happiest in their lives.

Wicksell soon became very active. He wrote twenty-nine articles from Mörby on wartime inflation and how to roll it back, on Scandinavia's postwar monetary problems, and on capital theory. From 1915 he had been a consultant to the governor of the Bank of Sweden. In 1916 he and Davidson were appointed to a parliamentary committee on Banking and Credit. Wicksell's involvement with its work and that of its successor committees lasted until his death. He and Davidson were both appointed as experts to another parliamentary committee on Taxation of Income and Property which remained active from 1918 to 1922. These assignments improved Wicksell's finances, for he was paid somewhat more than his pension for his work with these committees.

Among achievements attributable to Wicksell's and Davidson's collaboration in these councils was the adoption in 1916 of the 'gold exclusion policy' for the Bank of Sweden (to limit inflation the Bank was relieved of obligation to issue currency at the pre-war mint ratio to gold turned in to it from Sweden's export surplus, and was given power to lower the price of gold in terms of currency). A second achievement was a thorough revision and improvement of the country's taxation of income and wealth.

In this decade, Wicksell also became a much sought after adviser to young economists about their dissertations. At Lund he had only had three students in economics who took the intermediate graduate degree of *phil. lic.* under his guidance. In Stockholm, as a very active member of the Swedish Economics Association, and an indefatigable participant in the Economy Club, its inner circle of economists (as distinct from such members as bankers and industrialists), he had easy access to the club members' graduate students. He was made president of that club, 1917–22. It was a source of satisfaction for him to be sought out to share in the problems of the young men.

Thus his teaching did not stop with his retirement, for Emil Sommarin, Erik Lindahl, the brothers Gustav and Johan Åkerman, Bertil Ohlin, and probably others such as Palander, Lundberg and Hammarskjöld, consulted him about their dissertations in addition to benefiting from studying his treatises.

In the 1930s these persons, self-confessed 'Wicksellians', formed the core of the 'Stockholm School of economists'. However, he remained estranged from Gustav Cassel, the third of Sweden's leading economists in the 1920s. This had nothing to do with Cassel's competition with him for the position at Lund in 1900; it was due to Cassel's character. Wicksell found him to be intellectually arrogant, rarely acknowledging the contributions or predecessors whose works he was using, and acting as if economics had been in its infancy prior to Cassel. Wicksell found some of his work to be superficial and his interpretations of several points in economic theory to be misleading. This he expressed clearly in his rather severe review in 1919, of Cassel's *magnum opus, The Theory of Social Economy* (1918).

After that the breach between them was complete. Cassel never replied to Wicksell's review. As a result, Cassel remained an outsider to 'the Stockholm School', although he was the mentor of one of its leading members, Gunnar Myrdal.

In spring 1926, Wicksell was working on an article 'Zur Zinstheorie' (On the Theory of Interest) for a Festschrift for Friedrich von Wieser, when he fell ill with a stomach disorder which was further complicated by pneumonia. He died on 2 May 1926, at age 74.

His widow Anna, then a delegate from Sweden to the League of Nations, survived him until 1928. Their eldest son, Sven, became a professor of statistics at Lund University and died in 1939. Their young son, Finn, died in an accident in 1913 at the age of 19, when a medical student at Lund University.

Knut Wicksell would doubtless have objected to the elaborate funeral that was arranged for him, evidently with his widow's consent. Throughout life he had steadfastly rejected as meaningless and offensive to his sense of rationality all pomp and circumstance, academic formalities along with marriage ceremonies, baptism and confirmation for his children.

CONTRIBUTIONS TO ECONOMICS

In his own lifetime Wicksell did not receive much recognition for his creative work, not even in Scandinavia. It was not until the 1930s, when at the initiative of R.F. Kahn and J.M. Keynes, *Geldzins* as *Interest and Prices* and *Vorlesungen* as *Lectures on Political Economy I and II* were translated, that economists generally heard of Wicksell. Yet is it clear that his stature in the annals of economics has grown steadily over the last fifty-sixty years. In summary form, his main contributions were:

In *Value, Capital, and Rent* he performed a remarkable labour of synthesis. He adopted the marginal utility marginal productivity theory of value of Jevons, Menger and Marshall, added to it the Böhm-Bawerk analysis of capital, and fused the result in a Walrasian comparative static general equilibrium framework. In this process he became a founder of the marginal productivity (product exhausting) theory of distribution shortly ahead of Wicksteed. In his *Studies in the Theory of Public Finance* he pioneered a marginal utility approach to the public sector, synthesizing the benefit and ability principles of taxation, and urging that services of public sector enterprises and natural monopolies be provided on a marginal cost pricing basis.

In *Lectures I* he completed the restructuring, begun in *Value, Capital, and Rent*, of Böhm-Bawerk's theory of capital and interest. He reduced Böhm's trinitarian 'grounds' for interest to the simpler, more realistic explanation as the marginal productivity of waiting. He relaxed Böhm's quantification of capital as an average period of production by a concept of capital as the time structure of inputs invested for various terms in production. He showed that this structure was capable of change in at least two dimensions, width and height. He endeavoured with partial success (on problems still unresolved about 'Wicksell effects' and 'switching of techniques') to develop a theory of the modes of change of this time structure of production, how it changes and interacts with variations in wages, rent, and interest, in conditions both of capital accumulation and technological change. He extended his treatment of these relationships from comparative static to dynamic analysis, using clear mathematical models for this purpose.

The greatest contribution to monetary analysis, both in terms of novelty back in 1898 and 1906, and in terms of eventual influence by fortifying the related analysis, independently worked up by J.M. Keynes three decades later in his *Treatise on Money* (1930), was Wicksell's work on monetary theory in *Interest and Prices* and especially in *Lectures on Political Economy II*.

Wicksell was a pioneer of applying an aggregate demand-supply approach with emphasis on the relations between investment and saving, to explain variations in value of money or fluctuations in prices: 'Any theory of money worthy of the name must be able to show why pecuniary demand for goods exceeds or falls short of the supply of goods in given conditions' (*Lectures II*, p. 160).

Most versions of the quantity theory had the price level varying directly and proportionately to changes in the quantity of money. In that theory there was no link from the elasticity, as affected by bank credit, and quantity of money with individual income dispositions and entrepreneurial production decisions. Wicksell provided such a link in his hypothesis that in the absence of certain disturbances over which central banks have no control (such as large influx or efflux of gold, internal cash drains, large government deficits financed by loans from the central bank, fiat issues of inconvertible currencies, sudden and large changes in productivity or supply of goods), price level fluctuations were due to a persistent divergence between the bank rate or market rate of interest and the real rate, defined as the expected rate of return on newly produced capital goods.

> The fluctuations of commodity prices, which are *not* due to a change in gold production [a gold standard currency is assumed here] ... have another cause ... changes in the real rate of interest ... [to which] ... the loan-rate does not adapt itself quickly enough (*Lectures II*, p. 205).

Thus Wicksell's analysis showed, contrary to that of the simple quantity theory, that it was the quantity of money that adapted itself to the movement of the price level, and in doing so affected the distribution of income and the dispositions to invest and save in the process.

In his analysis monetary equilibrium and stability of prices required the simultaneous fulfilment of the conditions that: (i) the money rate of interest correspond to the real rate; (ii) at that money rate demand for loans for investment and for cash for real balances equal the supply of savings by individuals and business enterprises; and (iii) that interest rate must be neutral in its effect on prices. Then: ' ... equilibrium must *ipso facto* obtain – if not disturbed by other causes – in the market for goods and services, so that wages and prices will remain unchanged' (*Lectures II*, p. 193).

The consistency and compatibility of Wicksell's three criteria for monetary equilibrium and a critique of them in conditions of changing productivity by Davidson were given a thorough exegesis and analysis in the later 1920s and early 1930s by Lindahl, Myrdal, and Ohlin. Their work combined with the efforts of younger colleagues such as Lundberg, Hammarskjold, and Svennilson greatly expanded the heritage of Wicksellian economic theory and gave rise to the doctrines associated with the Stockholm school of economics.

C.G. Uhr

See also STOCKHOLM SCHOOL.

Section I above relies heavily on both Blaug (1985) and Gårdlund (1958) and in addition on information obtained in correspondence with the late Professors Erik Lindahl and Emil Sommarin.

SELECTED WORKS

1890a. Tomme maver – og fulde magasiner (Empty stomachs and full stores). *Samtiden* (Contemporary Times, a Norwegian periodical), 245–7, 293–320.

1890b. Überproduction oder Überbevölkerung (Excess production or excess population). *Zeitschrift für die gesamten Staatswissenschaften* 46.

1892. Kapitalzins und Arbeitslohn (Interest and capital). *Jahrbücher für Nationalökonomie* 59, 552–74.

1893. *Über Wert, Kapital, und Rente*. Jena: G. Fischer. Trans. by S.H. Frowein as *Value, Capital and Rent*, London: Allen & Unwin, 1954. Reprinted, New York: Augustus M. Kelley, 1970.

1894. Våra skatter: hvilka betalar dem, och hvilka border betala? (Our taxes: who pays them, and who ought to pay them?) Stockholm. This was one of Wicksell's early and very popular tracts, written under the pseudonym of Sven Trygg. It provides non-technical background and may be viewed as an introduction to Wicksell (1896).

1896. *Finanztheoretische Untersuchungen nebst Darstellung und Kritik des Steuerewesens Schwedens*. Jena: G. Fischer. iv–vi, 76–87 and 101–59 trans. by J.M. Buchanan as ch. 6 of *Classics of Public Finance*, ed. R.A. Musgrave and A.T. Peacock, London: Macmillan, 1958; 2nd edn, 1967. This treatise has only been translated in part; the untranslated sections deal with an histori cal sketch of the development of Sweden's system of taxation from the early 16th century up to the 1890s.

1898. *Geldzins und Güterpreise bestimmenden Ursachen*. Jena: G. Fischer. Trans. by R.F. Kahn as *Interest and Prices. A Study of the Causes Regulating the Value of Money*, London: Macmillan, 1936.

1900. Om gränsproduktiviteten såsom grundval för den nationalekonomiska fördelningen. *Ekonomisk Tidskrift* 2, 305–37. Trans. as 'Marginal productivity as the basis for distribution in economics', in *Selected Papers on Economic Theory by Knut Wicksell*, ed. E. Lindahl, London: Allen & Unwin, 1958, 93–121.

1901. The theory of exchange in its final form. In *Föreläsningar i nationalekonomi. Häft I*, Stockholm, Lund: Fritzes, Berlingska. The 3rd Swedish edn (1928) of this vol. trans. by E. Classen as *Lectures on Political Economy*. Vol. 1: General Theory, London: Routledge & Kegan Paul, 1934.

1902. Till fördelningsproblemet. *Ekonomisk Tidskrift* 4, 424–33. Translated as 'On the problem of distribution', in *Selected Papers on Economic Theory by Knut Wicksell*, ed. E. Lindahl (1958), 121–30.

1904. Mål och medel i nationalekonomien. *Ekonomisk Tidskrift* 6, 457–74. Translated as 'Ends and means in economics', in *Selected Papers on Economic Theory by Knut Wicksell*, ed. E. Lindahl (1958), 51–66.

1905. Socialiststaten och nutidssamhället (The socialist state and contemporary society). Stockholm (a popular tract, 40 pp.).

1906. *Föreläsningar i nationalekonomi. Häft II: Om penningar och kredit*. Stockholm and Lund: Fritzes, Berlingska. The 3rd Swedish edn (1929) trans. by E. Classen, ed. L. Robbins, as *Lectures on Political Economy*. Vol. 2: Money, London: Routledge & Kegan Paul, 1935; reprinted 1946.

1907. Krisernas gåta. *Statsekonomisk Tidskrift* (Oslo). Trans. by C.G. Uhr as 'The enigma of business cycles', in *International Economic Papers* No. 3, 1953, 58–74. This article expands on and lifts to a higher level of analysis the rather primitive treatment of business cycles presented in Wicksell (1890a and 1890b) and in Wicksell's brief 'Note on trade cycles and crises', 209–15 in *Lectures on Political Economy*, Vol. II.

1910. *Läran om Befolkningen, dess Sammansättning och Förändringar* (Theory of population, its composition, and modes of change). Stockholm: A. Bonniers, 92 pp. A popular tract written while Wicksell served a two-month jail sentence in southern Sweden for disturbing the religious peace by public blasphemy in a public lecture he had given in Stockholm in 1908.

1919a. Växelkursernas gåta. *Ekonomisk Tidskrift* 21, 87–103. Trans. as 'The riddle of the foreign exchanges', in *Selected Papers on Economic Theory by Knut Wicksell*, ed. E. Lindahl (1958), 229–50.

1919b. Professor Cassels ekonomiska system. *Ekonomisk Tidskrift* 21, 195–226. This article, highly critical of several of Cassel's interpretations and formulations of economic theory, has been translated and added as Appendix 1 in *Lectures on Political Economy*, Vol. I (1934), 219–57.

1923. Realkapital och kapitalränta. *Ekonomisk Tidskrift* 25, 145–80. A review and a mathematical elucidation of the analysis in G. Åkerman's doctoral dissertation *Realkapital und Kapitalzins*, Lund, 1923. It has been translated and added to *Lectures on Political Economy*, Vol. I, as Appendix 2, 'Real capital and interest', 258–99. Among other things, this article features demonstrations of both the 'Wicksell Effect' and the reversal of that 'Effect' in an effort to determine the relationship between the optimum durability of fixed capital and the rate of interest. As such, this article, long after Wicksell's death, has played an important role in the controversy over capital theory between the Cambridge (England) and Cambridge (Massachusetts) economists.

1925. Valutaspörsmålet i de skandinaviska länderna. *Ekonomisk Tidskrift* 27, 103–25. This article has been translated and added to *Interest and Prices* as an Appendix as 'The monetary problem of the Scandinavian countries', 199–219. It represents the several qualifications Wicksell was moved to add to his norm of price level stabilization for monetary policy, qualifications both to meet Davidson's criticism of this norm and to incorporate lessons from the monetary experiences and upheavals of World War I and its aftermath in the early 1920s. The qualifications were introduced to make allowance for significant increases in productivity, and for something like its opposite, severe commodity shortages due to wartime blockades, crop failure and also for significant issues of fiat money by governments running large deficit budgets, and so on.

A full-scale bibliography of all of Wicksell's published writings is now available. Its author is Dr. E.D. Knudtson, who has written *Knut Wicksells Tryckta Skrifter 1868–1950* (The Published Writings of Knut Wicksell, 1868–1950) edited by T. Hedlund-Nyström, and issued in the series Acta Universitatis Lundensis, Section I, Theologia-Juridica-et-Humaniora, No. 25, and published by the C.W.K. Gleerup Publishing House, Lund, Sweden, 1976. This bibliography runs to slightly more than 100 pages and accounts for 889 titles or items dating from Wicksell's student days in the later 1860s through his entire career, inclusive of his many popular articles for Sweden's leading newspapers, and beyond, to include also listings of the translations of his major works and reviews of these translations, which appeared between the decade or two after Wicksell's death.

BIBLIOGRAPHY

Blaug, M. 1985. *Economic Theory in Retrospect*. 4th edn, Cambridge: Cambridge University Press. Chapter 12, especially 'Reader's guide to *Lectures on Political Economy*, vol. I', 546–565: see also some of the earlier part of this chapter, 498–519. Chapter 15, 'Reader's guide to Wicksell's *Lectures* vol. II', 646–51, and also in the earlier part of this chapter, 637–45.

Gårdlund, T. 1958. *The Life of Knut Wicksell*. Stockholm: Almqvist & Wiksell. The original Swedish version of this biography; *Knut Wicksell–Rebell i Det Nya Riket* (Rebel in a New Realm), Stockholm, 1956, is somewhat longer than the English version, largely because it contains, but the English omits, notes on source materials and valuable bibliographical data, 374–405.

Hedlund-Nyström, T. and Jonung, L. 1986. Knut Wicksell's opublicerade manuscript. 2 vols, Mimeo, Department of Economics, University of Lund.
Jonung, L. 1987. Knut Wicksell's unpublished manuscripts. Mimeo, Department of Economics, University of Lund.
Uhr, C.G. 1951. Knut Wicksell – a centennial evaluation. *American Economic Review* 41(5), December, 829–60.
Uhr, C.G. 1960. *Economic Doctrines of Knut Wicksell.* Berkeley: University of California Press.

Wicksell and neoclassical economics. Knut Wicksell was long known as Scandinavia's Alfred Marshall, the leading economist of that region, whose microeconomics married Böhm-Bawerk's time-phased interest theory with Walras's mathematical general equilibrium. His macroeconomics was thought to foreshadow Keynes's 1936 *General Theory*, even though it emphasized that the discrepancy between investment and saving is the cause merely of an inflationary trend in the general price level.

Usually when a great economist is translated into English, reputation is deflated. Not so with Wicksell: the 1930s appearance of his 1898 *Interest and Prices* (Wicksell, 1936) and of his *Lectures on Political Economy*, Volume I ('micro') and Volume II (money), which appeared in Swedish and German editions between 1901 and 1928 and was translated into English in 1934 (Wicksell, 1934), sent his reputation soaring over his neoclassical contemporaries, Alfred Marshall in England and his great Swedish rival Gustav Cassel. Just below the pure-theory throne of Léon Walras sits Knut Wicksell: anyone who reads Hicks's seminal *Theory of Wages* (1932) will realize that Wicksell brings analysis to bear on the recurrent problems of our own age: as an example, his explication of how technical innovation can affect the distribution of income and the real-wage level is a quantum leap in sophistication over Ricardian and Marxian paradigms.

A decade after Wicksell's death in 1926, it was his saving–investment macroeconomics that economists most prized. All Scandinavians were neo-Wicksellians in the interval between Keynes's 1930 *Treatise on Money* and *The General Theory of Employment, Interest and Money* (1936): on the continent, Austrians such as Ludwig von Mises, Friedrich von Hayek, and Gottfried von Haberler thought in the same mode; in America, the young Alvin Hansen was a Wicksellian fellow traveller in the period before his trek on the road to the Damascus of Keynes's *General Theory*. Although neo-Wicksellianism did weaken faith in Say's Laws, not much of it lives on in present-day economics. Now we realize that Gunnar Myrdal and Erik Lindahl were not anticipating in their Wicksellian debates of the early 1930s any general theory of *output as a whole*. Like the *Treatise on Money* and Dennis Robertson's monetary paradigms, their primary focus was on the *price* level as the macrovariable of their equilibrium theory. True, Bertil Ohlin and Ragnar Frisch wrote presciently about induced changes in aggregate output as the Great Depression deepened and as efficacious fiscal and monetary policies were advocated. And in this they were mindful of Wicksell's grapplings with macroeconomics. But, as Don Patinkin (1982) has documented, these sage writers articulated no formal paradigm of effective demand comparable to that of the 1936 *General Theory* (or of Michal Kalecki's concomitant partial formulation of an aggregate–output model).

Before concentrating on the Wicksellian microeconomics that moderns see as the jewel in his crown, I should devote a few words to Wicksell's macroeconomics. Wicksell affirmed, rather than denied, that germ of truth in the Quantity Theory of Money and Prices which holds that raising in balance *all* nominal prices of goods, services and assets can leave all *real* supplies and demands and all relative prices intact. Actually, Wicksell's own theory of the business cycle was not a saving–investment analysis but rather an exogenous-shock theory emphasizing the innovations and technical changes that were emphasized by Joseph Schumpeter, Arthur Spiethoff, Gustav Cassel, and by the young Dennis Robertson and young Alvin Hansen. Wicksell's image of a rocking horse, which can be set into quasi-periodic motions even by random hammer blows, was later revived to good effect by Ragnar Frisch and Jan Tinbergen.

Wicksell's saving and investment paradigm was essentially a theory of how the total supply of money will be driven secularly upward or downward by a Central Bank that insists on setting the market interest rate persistently below the *real* (or 'natural') interest rate defined neoclassically by the system's time-phased technology and time-phased consuming preferences. If M grows secularly at 5 per cent per year above the trend growth rate of output – because of persistent perverse pegging of the market interest rate too low – then P in aggregate PQ grows at about 5 per cent with Q limited (over the business cycle) to about its same approximation to high-employment potential-output. In opposition to Wicksell's insistence on the goal of stability for the price level, his great Swedish contemporary David Davidson espoused a price level that fell proportionately to society's gain in productivity, an arguable thesis if we put aside pragmatic frictions. The Wicksell who uncharacteristically made a fetish of honouring prewar 1914 price levels could only with poor consistency make light of real-world frictions.

Wicksell's device of an interest rate specified by the bank-credit system was perhaps 'too clever by 'arf' and did mischief later in delaying decay of the Model T Keynesianism that dogmatically downplayed the potency of M-changes to affect real Q. The middle-aged Bourbons who fabricated the Radcliffe Committee Report in Britain (Radcliffe, 1959), with its antiquated refusal to forget about great-depression liquidity traps, had their minds frozen in their salad days of 1936–39 along Wicksellian modes of thought in which halvings in the general price and wage level merely halved the total money supply – and in which singular versions of the Keynesian systems were invoked, implicitly or explicitly, that hypothesized the near-vanishing of $\partial(MV)/\partial M$.

For a neoclassical economist, the time to be born was by 1840, the epoch of Jevons, Walras and Menger. Vilfredo Pareto, Marshall, Wicksell and Cassel came too late for the feast – to say nothing of A.C. Pigou, Frank Knight and Jacob Viner. Besides, Wicksell was a late bloomer, whose degree in mathematics was followed by a bohemian existence of preoccupation with anti-religion, anti-sexual puritanism, anti-alcoholism, anti-monarchism and anti-militarism. Just as birth control was beginning to catch hold in Europe, Wicksell was obsessed with Malthusian overpopulation and the law of diminishing returns.

By good luck and genius, this self-taught and unemployed post-Doc wrote in his forties a splendid synthesis of Böhm-Bawerk's capital theory with Walras's general equilibrium. See *Über Wert, Kapital und Rente* (1893), translated as *Value, Capital and Rent* (1954), in which Wicksell builds a Jevons–Böhm model where output is increased when the time interval is enlarged between application of inputs and harvest of output. This marginal-productivity-of-time paradigm for a positive interest rate is second in importance only to Irving Fisher's 20th-century general equilibrium reformulation of Böhm-Bawerk's insights.

Only for singularly special technologies is it true that the interest rate equals the derivative of the value of total output with respect to the value of total capital, $\partial(\Sigma PQ)/\partial(\Sigma PK)$ – as Wicksell pointed out with reference to the technology of maturing wine. (His accusation (Wicksell, 1954, pp. 141–2) that Thünen erred on this point is refuted in Samuelson's (1983, Equation A11) demonstration.) Such a discrepancy between the interest rate and this derivative is called a 'Wicksell effect' in the modern literature. Recognizing Wicksell effects is important to correct over-simple neoclassical parables, yes; but this is not to agree with the frequently met notion that, in consequence, the steady-state interest rate of perfect competition can lack *intertemporal Pareto-optimality* when Wicksell effects are present. Actually, no matter what 'reswitchings' or Wicksell effects are present, the competitive equilibrium does support *intertemporal production-and-consumption 'efficiency'*.

Fruitful critiques have been made in our time by Joan Robinson (1956) and Pierro Sraffa (1960) of the simple parable that lower steady-state interest rates *must* be associated with 'more-roundabout' modes of production. What remains intact is only this: (1) if a stationary population is endowed with capital goods that cannot support a golden-rule state of maximal per capita consumption, it can evolve into that golden-rule state *only by transiently sacrificing some current consumption in return for permanently enhanced consumption*; (2) for each specified interest rate, there is a convex tradeoff frontier between steady-state real factor prices (real wage, real rent of land, etc.), and any increase in that interest rate must shift downward that tradeoff frontier.

This first 1893 work illustrates Wicksell's virtues: his generosity in recognizing contributions of others; his confession that specified problems remain unsolved, or fail to be solved to the satisfaction of his scientific conscience; his depth of insight into the essence of an economic situation. Four decades before the mathematician Abraham Wald used inequalities and zero prices to ensure existence of a competitive equilibrium, Wicksell (1893, p. 84, n.1) adumbrates the duality equalities-inequalities that common sense of economics requires. Wicksell (1934, pp. 180–81) gives pictures and words of a 'switch point', where two different activities that are coexistable are combined in any weighting just as ice and water coexist in any proportions at the freezing point. In his seventy-third year, Wicksell (1954) works out how fixed capital can be added to the Austrian models of circulating capital, an exposition that could be improved on only if he had replaced straight-line depreciation by the more convenient exponential depreciation.

Wicksell was an important creator of the neoclassical theory of the distribution of income according to the principles of marginal productivity. His work postdated J.B. Clark's breakthrough of the late 1880s; Phillip Wicksteed's conscious articulation in the early 1890s of first-degree-homogeneous production functions whose marginal products do exactly 'exhaust' the output; Léon Walras's mid-1890s generalization to infinite-many substitutable techniques of production, from his first edition's single technique and his second edition's finite-number of activities, a generalization that Walras could achieve only with the prior help of Pareto and Enrico Barone. If 'marginalism' is the essence of neoclassicism – and it is surely one important component – then Wicksell forms a trio with Johann Heinrich von Thünen (1826, 1850) and J.B. Clark (1899) as an archetypal neoclassicist.

Moreover, Wicksell's turn-of-century marginal productivity utilized the macromodel methodology of his 1893 capital theory: a simple general-equilibrium for society is envisaged with a single good and its production function. This is not macroeconomics in the modern Keynesian sense involving general price levels and elements of effective demand (the sense in which, up until now in this article, the word macroeconomics has been used). Rather, it is macroeconomics in the secondary sense that the word connoted in the mid-1940s when it early appeared in the literature: the sense of Cobb–Douglas aggregate production functions; the sense of a Clarkian aggregate produced by aggregate labour and one idealized total of homogeneous capital. Indeed, the so-called 1927 Cobb–Douglas production function, $Q = L^k C^{1-k}$, was already buried in Wicksell's earlier writings of the Victorian era. (See also Wicksell, 1934, pp. 125, 286.)

David Ricardo shocked his followers and contemporaries with a new chapter in the last edition of his *Principles*, which asserted that invention of machinery could harm wages and cause total production of society to shrink. A Wicksellian exposition, in which $Q(L, C)$ denotes output and $\partial Q(L, C)/\partial L$ denotes the real wage, clearly exposes the possibility that a viable invention which raises Q for fixed L and C can most certainly lower absolute $\partial Q(L, C)/\partial L$.

Uncharacteristically, Wicksell (1934, p. 137) blundered in falsely accusing Ricardo of error: under Ricardo's classical hypothesis that labour supply adjusts to keep the real wage near a constant level of subsistence, total Q could indeed be induced to shrink by a technology parameter's shift that lowered $\partial Q(L, C)/\partial L$ – as when raising the technical parameter T somewhat above unity near $(L, C, T) = (1, 1, 1)$ definitely does depress Q in $Q = 1.5(T-1)C + T^{-1}(LC)^{1/2}$ when the real wage is kept constant by downward adjustments of the labour supply.

Wicksell has good company in making this error: such eminent modern economists as Nicholas Kaldor and George Stigler, rightly impressed with the Pareto-optimality of competition's Invisible Hand in selecting viable inventions, wrongly infer that Ricardo's asserted drop in Q would contradict this Pareto Optimality and hence wrongly judge that there has to be an error on Ricardo's part. Since Ricardo is envisaging an induced drop in L, he is correct to assert that Q may well be decreased by the invention.

Of all the neoclassicists Wicksell is the most humanitarian, the least conservative. During his sixth decade of life he went to jail for the crime of blasphemy. A friend of the *avant garde* August Strindberg, Knut Wicksell espoused redistribution from rich to poor at whatever cost to his own career. No writer of the Edwardian age came closer to the New Deal ideology of 1933–65 and to that of modern social democracy than did Wicksell. Yet, using the words '... the Hegelian darkness – and conceit of Karl Marx ...', Wicksell (1893, Preface, p. i) explicitly rejected Marxism as a paradigm to diagnose and understand the laws of motion of capitalism and as an erroneous programme for improving the welfare of the worker and peasant classes. His rejection of Marxism was based on knowledge of Marx's analysis and not on *a priori* prejudice; actually honesty in this regard inflicted a cost in terms of Wicksell's popularity, since Scandinavia was no exception to the rule that Marxism generated much political appeal in the three decades before World War I, the epoch just after Karl Marx's own death.

Despite his admiration for Ricardo, Wicksell denounced the unrealism of that writer's labour theory of value. Even the great editor of Ricardo, in Sraffa (1951, p. xxiii), lets that writer get away with transparent murder in fallaciously claiming to be able to 'get rid of [the complication of land and] rent' by setting each good's price to its labour cost on extensive-margin zero-rent land. Wicksell (1934, p. 24) points out that where the extensive margin for land will fall is itself an *endogenous* variable that is changed when the composition of demand alters away from land-intensive corn and toward labour-intensive cloth. Along with dozens of other self-contradictions in Ricardo's writings, there is clear recognition in his new chapter on machinery that a wartime shift of demand toward labour services of soldiers rather than toward rural produce would alter the distribution of income – a passage which is the root source for J.S. Mill's later overblown doctrine that 'demand for goods is not demand for labour'. If taste changes can alter distributive shares, then hopeless is Ricardo's attempt to separate distribution theory from value theory – and Wicksell was not loathe to call a spade a spade and a hopeless task hopeless.

One is left, most of all, with an impression of Wicksell's depth and breadth. Except for the Åkermans and Lindahl, Wicksell in his brief end-of-life professorship at Lund had almost no career-economist pupils. But it is no accident that Eli Heckscher and Bertil Ohlin should have originated the paradigm of factor–price equalization by free trade in goods. For, in his post-retirement years back at Stockholm, Knut Wicksell was a national treasure who inspired a generation of younger economists (and succeeded, partially, in keeping Gustav Cassel scientifically honest).

One of the many harvests of his versatility is the 'voluntary exchange' (or 'benefit') theory of public finance and taxation. Wicksell [1896] began this Wicksell–Lindahl–Musgrave–Samuelson–Vickrey theory of pure public goods and the work of his pupil, Erik Lindahl (1919), created its foundation. When private goods consumed by a single person only are supplemented by a public good that is simultaneously enjoyed by many people, Pareto optimality requires that production of the public good be carried to a point where its marginal (opportunity) cost just equals the sum of all citizen's marginal-rates-of substitution between the public good and any private good. Relying on a hoped-for Scandinavian consensus or 'unanimity', Wicksell perhaps worried too little about the 'free rider' problem (that results from the fact that every citizen in a Lindahl market is tempted to pretend not to much want the public good).

Finally, Wicksell's civility towards his great rival Gustav Cassel sets us all a noble example. Cassel had every gift except the gift of 'maybe'. Tutor to the King, Cassel pleased the Establishment and, prior to the post-1930 age of Keynes, was the economist most quoted by the international press. Although Schumpeter called Cassel '90% Walras and 10% water', I judge him to be a creative scientist, underrated today because of his egotistical failures to acknowledge doctrinal borrowings. (When his secretary wrote his biography, she alibied for this failing on the grounds that friction with his father blotted out from Cassel's memory all writers from whom he learned in early life!)

Wicksell (1934, pp. 219–52) gives his final reckoning with Cassel. His verdicts are unsparing, often harsh, but by no means malicious. Moreover, by modern standards, often it is Wicksell who must be judged to have the weaker case. Cassel (1918) brilliantly anticipated the Harrod–Domar mode of balanced exponential growth, and deserves praise not blame for soft-pedalling diminishing returns to land in modern Europe. Cassel, like Pareto, was right to downplay cardinal-measurable marginal utility even though he went too far in hypothesizing reduced-form, positivistic demand functions. Wicksell was not wrong in wishing for individual tastes to underlie welfare economics; but, as Abram Bergson (1938) was later to demonstrate, ordinal welfare economics does not necessarily require independently addable Benthamite utility functions for individuals. Wicksell, better than Marshall or Mises or Walras, realized from the beginning that competitive equilibrium of *laissez faire* does not necessarily achieve or approximate to a state of maximal social welfare or equity. He recognized, dimly, that the algorithm of perfect competition (not to be confused with *laissez faire*) does achieve the efficiency of production and exchange that we have since 1950 called 'Pareto optimality'; so, with the aid of feasible-best prior redistribution of people's endowments, the competitive market mechanism might be used to contrive a state of ethical optimality. Better to see obscurely in 1893 what we came to understand only after 1938. But, short of that, better for Wicksell to stubbornly insist that the emperor of market competition wore no ethical clothes than fall in with capitalistic apologias.

Wicksell's economics, because of its eclecticism and generality, adapts well to the present post-neoclassical age. As with Cournot, his writings speak eloquently to readers of a later century.

PAUL A. SAMUELSON

BIBLIOGRAPHY

Bergson, A. 1938. A reformulation of certain aspects of welfare economics. *Quarterly Journal of Economics* 52, February, 310–34.

Cassel, G. 1918. *Theory of Social Economy*. Trans., New York: Harcourt, Brace & Co., 1932.

Clark, J.B. 1899. *The Distribution of Wealth*. New York: Macmillan.

Gårdlund, T. 1956. *The Life of Knut Wicksell*. Trans. N. Adler, Stockholm: Almqvist & Wiksell, 1958.

Hicks, J.R. 1932. *The Theory of Wages*. London: Macmillan.

Patinkin, D. 1982. *Anticipations of the General Theory? and Other Essays on Keynes*. Chicago: University of Chicago Press.

Radcliffe, Lord (Chairman). 1959–60. *Committee on the Working of the Economy: Report, Minutes of Evidence, and Memoranda*. London: HMSO.

Robinson, J. 1956. *The Accumulation of Capital*. London: Macmillan.

Samuelson, P.A. 1983. Thünen at 200. *Journal of Economic Literature* 21, December, 1468–88.

Stigler, G.J. 1941. *Production and Distribution Theories: The Formative Period*. New York: Macmillan.

Sraffa, P. 1960. *Production of Commodities by Means of Commodities*. Cambridge: Cambridge University Press.

Sraffa, P. (With the collaboration of M.H. Dobb.) 1951. General Preface to D. Ricardo, *On the Principles of Political Economy and Taxation*, Cambridge: Cambridge University Press for the Royal Economic Society.

von Thünen, J.H. 1826, 1850. *Der Isolierte Staat*, Pts I and II.

Wicksell, K. 1893. *Über Wert, Kapital und Rente*. Jena: Gustav Fischer. Trans. as *Value, Capital and Rent*, London: George Allen & Unwin, 1954. This contains a fairly complete Wicksell bibliography, on pp. 169–75, completed by Arne Amundsen.

Wicksell, K. 1896. *Finanztheoretische Untersuchungen nebst Darstellung und Kritik des Steuerwesens Schwedens*. Jena: Gustav Fischer.

Wicksell, K. 1898. *Interest and Prices*. Trans., London: Macmillan, 1936.

Wicksell, K. 1934. *Lectures on Political Economy*. Vol. I: *General Theory*; Vol. II: *Money*. London: George Allen & Unwin.

Wicksell effects. In realistic economic models with n different types of capital goods, the value of the capital stock is

$$V = \sum_{i=1}^{n} P_i K_i \qquad (1)$$

where P_i is the price of the ith capital good in terms of some *numéraire*. The value of capital, however, is not an appropriate measure of the 'aggregate capital stock' as a factor of production except under extremely restrictive conditions.

Wicksell (1893, 1934) originally recognized this fact, which subsequently was emphasized by Robinson (1956).

If attention is restricted to alternative steady-state comparisons, in constant-returns-to-scale economies without joint production V is a function of the interest rate, r; see, for example, Burmeister and Dobell (1970). The *Wicksell effect* is the change in the value of the capital stock from one steady state to another, namely

$$\frac{\mathrm{d}V}{\mathrm{d}r}. \tag{2}$$

The term 'Wicksell effect' was introduced by Uhr (1951), but its importance was not widely recognized until the writings of Robinson (1956) and Swan (1956).

The Wicksell effect is the sum of the *price Wicksell effect* (which is the revaluation of the inventory of capital goods due to new prices) and the *real Wicksell effect* (which is the price-weighted sum of the changes in the physical quantities of different capital goods):

$$\frac{\mathrm{d}V}{\mathrm{d}r} = \sum_{i=1}^{n} \frac{\mathrm{d}P_i}{\mathrm{d}r} K_i + \sum_{i=1}^{n} P_i \frac{\mathrm{d}K_i}{\mathrm{d}r}. \tag{3}$$

Numerical examples show that the price Wicksell effect can be negative, i.e.,

$$\sum_{i=1}^{n} P_i \frac{\mathrm{d}K_i}{\mathrm{d}r} < 0 \tag{4}$$

is possible, even when (i) the total Wicksell effect is positive [$\mathrm{d}V/\mathrm{d}r > 0$], or (ii) particular capital stocks are increasing with $\mathrm{d}K_i/\mathrm{d}r > 0$ for some but not all i; see Burmeister and Dobell (1970, pp. 289–93). In neoclassical models with only one capital good ($n = 1$), the real Wicksell effect is always negative. Moreover, the sign of the price Wicksell effect depends upon the choice of *numéraire*, and hence so does the total Wicksell effect given by (3). The sign of the real Wicksell effect, however, is independent of the choice of *numéraire*.

One central issue of the Cambridge controversies in capital theory involves Wicksell effects. Does a decrease (increase) in the steady-state interest rate always imply a rise (fall) in per capita steady-state consumption provided the rate of interest is greater (less) than the rate of growth of labour? In one-capital good models, the answer to this question is, 'Yes'. In general, the answer is, 'Yes', if and only if the real Wicksell effect is negative; see Burmeister and Turnovsky (1972) and Burmeister (1976).

To establish this relationship between the behaviour of per capita consumption and the real Wicksell effect, consider a technology which can be represented by a *production possibility frontier*

$$Y_1 = T(Y_2, \ldots, Y_n; L, K_1, \ldots, K_n) \tag{5}$$

where Y_i is the output of commodity i, L is the labour which grows at the exogenous rate g, and K_i is the stock of commodity i used as a capital input.

It is assumed further that $T(\cdot)$ is twice continuously differentiable, exhibits constant returns to scale, and has a Hessian matrix $[T_{ij}]$ that is negative semi-definite and whose rank varies with the degree of joint production in the economy; see Samuelson (1966), Burmeister and Turnovsky (1971), and Kuga (1973). The analysis which follows can be generalized to non-differentiable technologies as in Burmeister (1976), but for simplicity only differentiable technologies are considered here.

In steady-state equilibria all quantities grow at the rate g, implying that the output of every commodity must satisfy

$$Y_i \equiv C_i + \dot{K}_i = C_i + gK_i, \qquad i = 1, \ldots, n, \tag{6}$$

where C_i denotes the consumption of commodity i. Substituting these steady-state restrictions into (5) and using lower-case letters to denote per capita quantities, we have

$$c_1 + gk_1 = T(c_2 + gk_2, \ldots, c_n + gk_n; 1, k_1, \ldots, k_n). \tag{7}$$

Let the prices of commodities and the rental rates for capital goods, both in terms of the wage rate as *numéraire*, be denoted by p_i and w_i, respectively, $i = 1, \ldots, n$; also let r denote the interest or profit rate. It is well-known that intertemporal profit maximization and/or efficiency necessitates that

$$\frac{\dot{p}_i}{p_i} + \frac{w_i}{p_i} = r, \qquad i = 1, \ldots, n. \tag{8}$$

Imposing the steady-state requirement that relative prices remain constant, (8) implies that

$$w_i = rp_i, \qquad i = 1, \ldots, n. \tag{9}$$

Using the well-known marginal conditions

$$\frac{\partial T}{\partial(c_i + gk_i)} = -\frac{p_i}{p_1} \quad \text{and} \quad \frac{\partial T}{\partial k_i} = \frac{w_i}{p_1}, \qquad i = 1, \ldots, n, \tag{10}$$

we see that a vector

$$(c^*, k^*; r^*, p^*) = (c_1^*, \ldots, c_n^*; r^*, p_1^*, \ldots, p_n^*) \geqslant 0 \tag{11}$$

satisfying (7) and (10) represents a steady-state solution at the growth rate g. It thus follows immediately from differentiation of (7) that almost everywhere

$$\sum_{i=1}^{n} P_i \left(\frac{\mathrm{d}c_i}{\mathrm{d}r}\right)\bigg|_{(r^*, p^*)} = (r - g) \sum_{i=1}^{n} P_i \left(\frac{\mathrm{d}k_i}{\mathrm{d}r}\right)\bigg|_{(r^*, p^*)}; \tag{12}$$

see Burmeister (1976) for details.

Now let v denote the per capita value of capital in terms of the wage rate as *numéraire:*

$$v = \sum_{i=1}^{n} p_i k_i. \tag{13}$$

The change in the per capita value of capital across alternative steady-state equilibria is obtained by differentiating (13); thus almost everywhere the per capita Wicksell effect is

$$\frac{\mathrm{d}v}{\mathrm{d}r}\bigg|_{(r^*, p^*)} = \sum_{i=1}^{n} \left(\frac{\mathrm{d}p_i}{\mathrm{d}r}\right)\bigg|_{(r^*, p^*)} \cdot k_i + \sum_{i=1}^{n} p_i \cdot \left(\frac{\mathrm{d}k_i}{\mathrm{d}r}\right)\bigg|_{(r^*, p^*)} \tag{14}$$

Comparing (14) and (12), it is seen that it is the real Wicksell effect which determines whether or not 'consumption' is well-behaved across steady-state equilibria. That is, if the real Wicksell effect is negative and

$$\sum_{i=1}^{n} p_i \cdot \left(\frac{\mathrm{d}k_i}{\mathrm{d}r}\right)\bigg|_{(r^*, p^*)} < 0, \tag{15}$$

then almost everywhere

$$\sum_{i=1}^{n} P_i \left(\frac{\mathrm{d}c_i}{\mathrm{d}r}\right)\bigg|_{(r^*, p^*)} \gtreqless 0 \quad \text{as} \quad r \gtreqless g. \tag{16}$$

In particular, when $c_2 = c_3 = \cdots = c_n$ and only commodity 1 is consumed, consumption as measured by c_1 rises (falls) as r is increased from r^* to $r^* + \Delta r^*$ when r^* is greater (less) than g. (The familiar Golden Rule condition giving maximum per capita steady-state consumption holds at $r^* = g$.)

It follows, then, that a negative real Wicksell effect is the appropriate concept of 'capital deepening' in a model with many heterogeneous capital goods. That is, when (15) and hence (16) hold, an economy with a low interest rate (but exceeding g) has 'more capital' than one with a higher interest rate in the sense that it is capable of providing more steady-state per capita consumption. Although (15) and (16) always hold in a neighbourhood of $r^* = g$, examples show that they do not generally hold everywhere. This possibility – that (16) does not hold everywhere – is perhaps the most interesting conclusion to emerge from the Cambridge controversies and has been termed a 'paradox'. However, the 'paradox' involves comparisons of alternative steady-states rather than comparisons of alternative feasible paths; Bliss (1975) provides a lucid explanation of why such 'paradoxes' are in fact not surprising or damaging to the neoclassical paradigm.

Imposing some set of conditions on the technology $T(\cdot)$ should be sufficient to assure that the real Wicksell effect is always negative. Such conditions would be of interest – especially if they could be empirically tested – since they would validate the qualitative conclusions derived from the one-good models often used in macroeconomics without any theoretical justification for ignoring capital aggregation problems. Moreover, Burmeister (1977, 1979) has proved that a negative real Wicksell effect is a necessary and sufficient condition for the existence of an index of capital, κ, and a neoclassical aggregate production function $F(\kappa)$ defined across steady-state equilibria such that (i) $c = F(\kappa)$, (ii) $r = F'(\kappa)$, and (iii) $F''(\kappa) < 0$. Unfortunately, no set of such sufficient conditions is known, but the literature on capital aggregation suggests that they would impose severe restrictions on the technology.

EDWIN BURMEISTER

See also CAPITAL THEORY: PARADOXES; RESWITCHING OF TECHNIQUE; REVERSE CAPITAL DEEPENING.

BIBLIOGRAPHY

Bliss, C. 1975. *Capital Theory and the Distribution of Income.* Amsterdam: North-Holland.

Burmeister, E. 1976. Real Wicksell effects and regular economies. In *Essays in Modern Capital Theory*, ed. M. Brown, K. Sato and P. Zarembka. Amsterdam: North-Holland.

Burmeister, E. 1977. On the social significance of the reswitching controversy. *Revue d'économie politique* 87(2), March–April, 330–50.

Burmeister, E. 1979. Professor Pasinetti's 'unobtrusive postulate', regular economies, and the existence of a well-behaved aggregate production function. *Revue d'économie politique* 89(5), September–October, 644–52.

Burmeister, E. and Dobell, A.R. 1970. *Mathematical Theories of Economic Growth.* New York: Macmillan.

Burmeister, E. and Turnovsky, S.J. 1971. The degree of joint production. *International Economic Review* 12, February, 99–105.

Burmeister, E. and Turnovsky, S.J. 1972. Capital deepening response in an economy with heterogeneous capital goods. *American Economic Review* 62, December, 842–53.

Kuga, K. 1973. More about joint production, *International Economic Review* 14(1), February, 196–210.

Robinson, J. 1956. *The Accumulation of Capital.* London: Macmillan.

Samuelson, P.A. 1966. The fundamental singularity theorem for non-joint production. *International Economic Review* 7, January, 34–41.

Swan, T. 1956. Economic growth and capital accumulation. *Economic Record* 32, November, 334–61.

Uhr, C.G. 1951. Kunt Wicksell, a centennial evaluation. *American Economic Review* 41, December, 829–60.

Wicksell, K. 1893. *Value, Capital and Rent.* Reprinted New York: Augustus M. Kelley, 1970.

Wicksell, K. 1934. *Lectures on Political Economy.* 3rd edn, London: George Routledge and Sons Limited, 1938.

Wicksell's theory of capital. Wicksell first developed his real theory of capital on 'the purely imaginary assumption' that the phenomena of capital and interest could take place without the intervention of money or credit; he then endeavoured to bring to light the modifications that are called for by the appearance of money, and by so doing he laid the foundation of this century's dominant approach to money and real magnitudes. Wicksell's theory can actually be said to have established the basis of mainstream long-period analysis of the economy, with its explanation in real terms of the equilibrium rate of interest and the conception of money as a factor that may be important to the gravitation of the economy towards its equilibrium position but not as a determinant of that position.

Wicksell's general equilibrium – what he calls 'The Theory of Exchange Value in its Final Form' (1901, p. 196) – consists of a system of equations by which relative prices are determined simultaneously with normal outputs, factor uses and the equilibrium prices of factor services (that is, distribution), on the basis of given consumer tastes, technical conditions of production and factor endowments. 'Capital' enters *twice* into the picture: first, when the quantity produced in the economy of each final article is expressed as a function of all the quantities of factors employed, according to given 'production functions' reflecting the given technical conditions; secondly, in the relations expressing the condition that the supply of each factor of production annually available in the economy must be equal to the quantity of it annually employed (i.e. demanded). On the basis of these conditions, the equilibrium prices of factor services depend on their relative scarcities; the equilibrium rate of interest, in particular, depends on the relative scarcity of the whole available capital and is the same on all capital (Wicksell, 1901, pp. 144–6). Wicksell's system thus depicts a 'long-run' equilibrium, which ultimately reflects the idea, common to the original versions of the marginal theory, that the competitive tendency towards a uniform rate of interest (profit) would deprive of any significance, as centres of gravitation of the economy, quantities and prices determined for situations in which each particular capital-good gave a different rate of return over its cost. (The same idea explains Wicksell's attention being focused throughout his main writings on *circulating* capital, for which the equilibrium condition represented by a uniform rate of return tends rapidly to impose itself through changes in the proportions amongst the different kinds of capital-goods annually employed in the economy. As for the treatment of durable or fixed capital, see Wicksell, 1923.)

The important point to be noticed about Wicksell's 'production functions' is that the capitalist element is expressed in them not by means of *value* magnitudes but in 'technical units'. He was fully aware that the partial derivatives of any such function in which 'capital' appears in value terms can be of no use for determining the 'productive contribution' of the different productive factors, and hence distribution. (An increase in the value of capital may simply reflect a rise of wages and rent, possibly without causing any change in the magnitude of the return; the additional product of the new capital may thus be nil, but this would give no information at all about the new level of the rate of interest: see Wicksell, 1893, pp. 25, 115–19; 1901, p. 148.)

In *Value, Capital and Rent* Wicksell used Böhm-Bawerk's 'average period of production' (Böhm-Bawerk, 1889, vol. II, bk. II, ch. II) so that the role of capital was seen as making possible the introduction of a longer period of time between the beginning and the conclusion of the process of production 'and consequently the adoption of a more roundabout method of production than would be possible if production were less strong in capital or totally devoid of capital'. He maintained, accordingly, that the greater the amount of capital employed, 'that is to say, the lengthier the average period of production that can be applied, the greater will be the annual production of finished consumption goods, provided the same number of workers and the same area of the country are involved' (1893, p. 116).

Wicksell realized, however, that the average period of production made it necessary to have recourse to calculation with simple interest (1893, pp. 125–6; 1901, p. 205 and Preface to the 2nd edn); so in the *Lectures* (1901), while still adhering to Böhm-Bawerk's view of the role of capital, Wicksell moved to a conception of capital in the production functions as a *complex* of variables: dated quantities of labour and land (or 'saved-up labour and saved-up land' as he called them to indicate that instead of being quantities of current labour and land *directly* employed in the production of consumption goods, they are employed in the production of capital goods). Wages and rents actually paid to those quantities of labour and land remain 'invested' in production from the moment they are paid until the conclusion of the process of production of the consumption good concerned; on the other hand, their marginal productivities are greater than those of current labour and land directly employed in production – the idea being that the productivity of original factors becomes greater if they are employed for distant ends than if they are employed in the immediate production of consumption goods: this difference in productivity constitutes the very source of interest (1901, p. 154).

Now, for the *rate* of interest to be same on all kinds of investment (in labour-capital or in land-capital, for a single year or for a period of years), the marginal productivities of the dated quantities of original factors – that is, the partial derivatives of the production function with respect to each of the variables included in it – must stand in a certain relation to each other, 'corresponding to that which exists in a calculation with compound interest' (p. 160). Full equilibrium determination then entails that the dated quantities of labour and land appearing in the production functions cannot be taken as given, but must be included amongst the unknowns of the system (pp. 203–5).

We can sum up the above by saying that the notion of marginal productivity is never applied by Wicksell directly to capital or capital goods; it is applied (in his chief work) to dated quantities of the two original 'factors of production'. Each commodity is seen as ultimately resolving itself into labour and land employed in different years – current labour and land, and 'saved-up' labour and land; they are remunerated according to their marginal productivities and are employed in the proportions demanded by the equilibrium condition of a uniform rate of interest. The equilibrium level of the rate of interest ultimately reflects the relative scarcity of saved-up original factors:

> the marginal productivity of the latter is greater, simply because current labour and land exist in relative abundance for the purposes for which they can be employed, whilst saved-up labour and land are not adequate in the same degree for the many purposes in which they have an advantage. This again is to be explained by the circumstances which limit the accumulation of capital (p. 155).

The explanation of the equilibrium rate of interest by the scarcity of capital, and as the reward for 'waiting', is one and the same thing as the conception of the rate of interest as the variable that brings to equality the supply of and the demand for capital. To this equality we now turn our attention.

In the relations expressing the equality between the supply of and the demand for each factor of production, together with the total quantities of labour and land, the total quantity of capital annually available in the economy is taken as given; it is a single magnitude, so that what Wicksell actually takes as given to solve the system is the total *exchange value* (measured in terms of one of the final products) of the capital available in the economy (pp. 204–5). A value magnitude is thus included amongst the determinants of distribution and prices. In criticizing Walras for having taken the physical quantities of the different kinds of capital goods as given, Wicksell argued that we need 'a unified treatment of the role of capital in production ... in order to calculate the rate of interest, which in equilibrium is the same on all capital' (p. 149). Accordingly, the quantity of capital available in the economy is conceived in his system as a single magnitude, a value magnitude taken as given, whilst, as we saw above, its physical composition, the relative quantities of its different technical constituents, is left free to change during the process of adjustment to equilibrium in order to satisfy the condition of a uniform rate of interest.

If the quantity of capital available in the economy is increased by 'real, productive, saving' (i.e. 'by restricting or postponing consumption'), then, *ceteris paribus*, the equilibrium rate of interest must fall. At the old rate the supply of capital now exceeds the quantity of it annually employed in the various industries; competition amongst capitalists presses the rate of interest downwards, thereby causing more roundabout processes, which were previously unremunerative, to become profitable. In Wicksell's view, not only does the process of production of each consumption good tend to become more 'capitalistic', through increases in 'saved-up' labour and land relative to current labour and land used in the course of a year and the introduction of 'longer-dated' investments, but also the composition of final demand and output tends to change in favour of more 'capitalistic' consumption goods, through the relative cheapening of such goods brought about by the fall in the rate of interest. Following, therefore, an increase in the supply of capital, substitution amongst alternative methods of production and amongst alternative consumption goods would ensure a new equality between supply of and demand for capital at a new lower level of the rate of interest. It may conveniently be added that if only circulating capital is taken into consideration – as Wicksell actually did by centering his theory of capital upon the case of capital goods that last only one year in an economy where production takes place in yearly cycles – then there is no need to distinguish, in the determination of interest, between supply of and demand for capital as a stock and as an annual flow; one may simply refer to the equilibrium rate of interest as being determined by supply and demand for gross saving.

This explanation of the 'real capital rate', with the essential role played in it by the interest elasticity of demand for saving, constitutes the basis of Wicksell's theory of money and prices (1898a, 1898b, 1906). We shall here refer to its more mature version, contained in volume II of the *Lectures* (1906).

In Wicksell's opinion, 'any theory of money worthy of the name must be able to show how and why the monetary or pecuniary demand for goods exceeds or falls short of the supply of goods in given conditions'. He contended that the advocates of the Quantity Theory, in postulating the price-level as an increasing function of the quantity of money, failed to show 'why such a change of price must always follow a change in the quantity of money and to describe what happens' (1906, p. 160). In the solution he put forward, the primary cause of price fluctuations is singled out as the difference between the actual money or loan rate and the normal or natural real rate of interest, determined by the scarcity of capital (saving).

As we saw above, *ceteris paribus* a lowering of the real rate unconditionally demands increased saving. The same applies to a lowering of the loan rate in the case of 'simple credit between man and man'; the loan market would directly reflect in such a case the supply of and demand for saving, so that there would be an immediate connection between the money rate and the real capital rate. Changes in the loan rate would take place simultaneously and uniformly with corresponding changes in the real rate, with the result that no change in the level of commodity prices could occur. Things are different when the activity of the banks is taken into consideration: banks 'possess a fund for loans which is always elastic and, on certain assumptions [i.e. with a pure credit system], inexhaustible', with the consequence that the immediate connection between the money rate and the real natural rate disappears. 'In our complex monetary system', says Wicksell, 'there exists no other connection between the two than the *variations in commodity prices* caused by the difference between them' (1906, pp 194, 206).

Thus, starting from an equilibrium situation and no changes occurring in the circumstances upon which the real natural rate depends, a reduction of the rate of interest on the part of the banks will lead to an increase in monetary demand: owing to the increased demand for loan capital and the expansion of credit, on the one hand, and to a reduced supply of saving, on the other, an excess of investment spending over saving decisions will arise. Since the normal or equilibrium situation of the economy is characterized by the full employment of all productive factors, the increased monetary spending will result in a rise in prices, both of production and of consumption goods. As the parallel rise in money prices and incomes tends to leave the real capital rate unaffected, at the new higher price level an excess of investment spending over saving decisions will present itself again – so that the inflationary process is bound to continue as long as the money rate is kept below the real rate. The opposite would occur if banks maintained the rate of interest above its natural level. In both cases, in order to re-establish monetary equilibrium – the stability of the price level – banks would have to bring the money rate of interest back to the level of the 'real natural rate'. The conclusion then is that by virtue of the 'connecting link' of price-movements, the money rate will gravitate towards the real rate, even if such a gravitation process will not be of an automatic-spontaneous nature. (We may add that persistent full employment does not seem to be essential to the Wicksellian notion of a non-automatic gravitation of the actual money rate towards the normal natural rate. If, in the face of a money rate of interest that is higher than the natural rate, rigid money wages are assumed, then the role of 'connecting link' between the two rates might be played not only by reductions in prices but also by the fall in employment.)

So, in this picture it is maintained that a low rate of interest causes prices to rise, and vice versa. But Wicksell recognizes that in actual experience rising prices very rarely coincide with low or falling interest rates, and that the opposite is the general rule. He argues that this 'apparently crushing objection' to his theory ('an objection which the members of the Tooke School have triumphantly produced at every opportunity as a support for their theory') is indeed perfectly consistent with his view of the influence of the rate of interest on prices: instead of assuming a lowering of the rate of interest by the banks, other things being equal, one has simply to make the more realistic assumption that the difference between the two rates arises because the natural rate rises or falls whilst the money rate remains unchanged and only tardily follows it. The *primum movens*, that is to say, generally consists in changes in the natural real rate of interest: a rise (fall) in the natural rate will result in a rise (fall) in prices which, in its turn, will sooner or later force up (down) the money rate (1906, pp. 202–8; see Keynes's identical explanation in *A Treatise on Money*, 1930, vol. I, p. 196n. and vol. II, pp. 198, 203).

The critique of the marginalist notion of capital which was stimulated by the work of Piero Sraffa (1960) applies also to Wicksell's theory. Amongst the numerous relevant contributions, we shall recall here the careful critical analysis of Wicksell's theory of capital contributed by Garegnani (1960, chs. 4–6, see also Garegnani, 1970), and the symposium on capital theory in the *Quarterly Journal of Economics* (1966) with the contributions by Pasinetti, Samuelson, Morishima, Burmeister and others.

As we saw above, in Wicksell's system the quantity of capital annually available in the economy is taken as given in terms of a single magnitude, which is thus included amongst the determinants of general equilibrium. At the same time, a decreasing demand function for capital (saving) is postulated, based on the 'substitution' principle – the principle according to which a fall in the rate of interest cheapens the more capital-intensive processes of production relative to the others, thereby raising the proportion of capital to the other productive factors in the economy. Such a demand function is essential to the idea that, *ceteris paribus*, increased saving will result in a reduced natural rate of interest, hence to the explanation of interest by the scarcity of capital.

Both these aspects of the marginalist analysis of capital have been found faulty on logical grounds, the main ingredients of the critique having been provided by Sraffa (1960). By studying the movement of relative prices consequent upon changes in distribution, he found that, in the face of unchanged methods of production, *reversals* in the direction of that movement may occur – a phenomenon which 'cannot be reconciled with *any* notion of capital as a measurable quantity independent of distribution and prices' (1960, p. 38); that is, of the very unknowns that the quantity of capital available in the economy should contribute to determine. (No such reversals could possibly occur if a single magnitude existed which was both independent of distribution and prices *and* representative of capital. Böhm-Bawerk's average period of production, for example, is independent of distribution and prices, but is not representative of the quantity of capital: if it were, then, assuming an average period of production of commodity A greater than that of commodity B, p_a would *continuously* rise relative to p_b with the rising of the rate of interest, contrary to what is shown by Sraffa (para. 48).) Moreover, the reversals in the direction of the movement of relative prices and the analogous phenomenon of 'reswitching' of methods of production (ch. XII) entail that no demand function for capital (saving) can be deduced from the existence of alternative methods of production and alternative consumption goods, except in very restrictive hypotheses.

We pointed out above the crucial role played in Wicksell's theory by the concept of a natural real rate of interest. The same concept plays a significant role also in Keynes's writings. This is clearly so in the *Treatise*; but also in the *General Theory*, notwithstanding the author's statement that he no longer regards the concept as 'a most promising idea' (Keynes,

1936, p. 243), yet the 'natural rate' is still there, as the rate of interest that would ensure equality between full employment saving and investment decisions. Keynes's underemployment equilibrium is ultimately the result of the presence in the economic system of factors that hinder the possibility of bringing the actual rate of interest down to its 'natural' or full employment level – it is the result, in other words, of a limited flexibility of the money rate of interest. If one takes into account that also in Wicksell there is no automatic gravitation of the money rate towards the level of the natural real rate (banking policy having to perform the task; see above), then the difference between the two authors will not appear so marked: they both share, in particular, the idea of an inverse relation between the rate of interest and investment decisions, whilst the contrast of opinion is essentially centred upon the degree of (non-automatic) flexibility of the rate of interest in the face of discrepancies between full employment saving and investment decisions. We believe that largely in the light of such a comparison the thesis was successfully laid down that, far from constituting *the* general theory, 'The General Theory of Employment is the Economics of Depression' (Hicks, 1937, p. 154). So our point here is that a better knowledge of Wicksell's work would have greatly facilitated the singling out of the traditional premises in *The General Theory* that aided the subsequent 'neoclassical synthesis', thereby helping to realize the importance of the critique of the marginal theory of capital and interest for establishing Keynes's principle of effective demand on firmer ground.

MASSIMO PIVETTI

See also AUSTRIAN SCHOOL OF ECONOMICS; BÖHM-BAWERK, EUGEN VON; QUANTITY OF CAPITAL.

BIBLIOGRAPHY

Böhm-Bawerk, E. von. 1889. *Capital and Interest: a critical history of economic theory*. Trans. W. Smart, New York: Stechert, 1932.

Burmeister, E. 1976. Real Wicksell effects and regular economies. In *Essays in Modern Capital Theory*, ed. M. Brown, K. Sato and P. Zarembka, Amsterdam: North-Holland.

Garegnani, P. 1960. *Il capitale nelle teorie della distribuzione*. Milan: Giuffrè.

Garegnani, P. 1970. Heterogeneous capital, the production function and the theory of distribution. *Review of Economic Studies* 37(3), 407–36.

Hicks, J.R. 1937. Mr. Keynes and the 'classics': a suggested interpretation. *Econometrica* 5(2), 157–9.

Keynes, J.M. 1930. *A Treatise on Money*. London: Macmillan.

Keynes, J.M. 1936. *The General Theory of Employment, Interest and Money*. London: Macmillan.

Pasinetti, L., Levhari, D., Samuelson, P.A., Morishima, M., Bruno, M., Burmeister, E., Sheshinski, E. and Garegnani, P. 1966. Paradoxes in capital theory: a symposium. *Quarterly Journal of Economics* 80(4), 503–83.

Sraffa, P. 1960. *Production of Commodities by Means of Commodities: prelude to a critique of economic theory*. Cambridge: Cambridge University Press.

Wicksell, K. 1893. *Über Wert, Kapital und Rente*. Jena: G. Fisher. Trans. by S. H. Frowein as *Value, Capital and Rent*, London: Allen & Unwin, 1954; reprinted, New York: Kelly, 1970.

Wicksell, K. 1898a. *Geldzins und Güterpreise bestimmenden Ursachen*. Jena: G Fischer. Trans. by R.F. Kahn as *Interest and Prices: A Study of the Causes Regulating the Value of Money*, London: Macmillan, 1936.

Wicksell, K. 1898b. The influence of the rate of interest on commodity prices. In K. Wicksell, *Selected Papers on Economic Theory*, London: Allen & Unwin, 1958.

Wicksell, K. 1901. *Föreläsningar i nationalekonomi. Häft I*. Stockholm, Lund: Fritzes, Berlingska. The 3rd Swedish edn (1928) of this volume trans. by E. Classen, ed. L. Robbins, as *Lectures on Political Economy*, Volume I: *General Theory*, London: Routledge & Kegan Paul, 1934.

Wicksell, K. 1906. *Föreläsningar i nationalekonomi. Häft II: Om penningar och kredit*. Stockholm, Lund: Fritzes, Berlingska. The 3rd Swedish edn (1929) trans. by E. Classen, ed. L. Robbins, as *Lectures on Political Economy*, Volume II: Money, London: Routledge & Kegan Paul, 1935.

Wicksell, K. 1923. Realkapital och kapitalränta. *Economisk Tidskrift* 21, 45–80. Trans. by S. Adler as *Real Capital and Interest* as Appendix 2 to Volume I of the *Lectures*, London: Routledge & Kegan Paul, 1934.

Wicksteed, Philip Henry (1844–1927). Wicksteed was born in October 1844 in Leeds, where his father, Charles Wicksteed, was a Unitarian minister. He died, at the age of 83, in March 1927, at Childrey in Berkshire. He attended Ruthin Grammar School in North Wales and then University College School, London, before studying at University College London (1861–4) and at Manchester New College (1864–7) in Gordon Square nearby. He received his master's degree, with a gold medal for classics, in 1867. Wicksteed then became a Unitarian minister, first at Taunton in Somerset (1867–9), then at Dukinfield, east of Manchester (1870–74), and finally at Little Portland Street Chapel, London (1874–97). He left the ministry in 1897 and thereafter earned his living by writing and lecturing. From 1887 to 1918 Wicksteed was a most active University Extension Lecturer, lecturing on Wordsworth, Dante, Greek tragedy, Aristotle and Aquinas – and economics. He never held a university post.

The great breadth of Wicksteed's intellectual activity was far from being confined to his Extension lecturing. He had a considerable linguistic talent; whilst a minister in Dukinfield, for example, he learned Dutch for the express purpose of translating into English Oort and Hooykaas's *Bible for Young People* (six volumes, 1873–9). And he completed a translation, with F.M. Cornford, of Aristotle's *Physics* only days before his death. Yet it was as a translator, expounder and interpreter of Dante that he became most widely known; his work as a Dante scholar, which extended over more than forty years, included translations of and commentaries on the *Vita Nuova*, the *Convivio*, *De Monarchia* and the *Divina Commedia*. Combined with his theological and philosophical interests, this study of Dante led Wicksteed to Aquinas and thus to the writing of his *Dante and Aquinas* (1913) and his *Reactions between Dogma and Philosophy, illustrated from the Works of S. Thomas Aquinas* (1920). That a study of Aquinas' thought by a former Unitarian minister could be reviewed favourably in the *Blackfriars Review* is perhaps an indication of the catholicity of Wicksteed's interests and capacities. Nor did those interests extend only to the past; for example, Wicksteed publicly defended the poetry and drama of Ibsen at a time when Ibsen's work was the object of considerable hostility in England. And Wicksteed's numerous contributions to the *Inquirer*, the Unitarian newspaper, over a span of some fifty years, relate not only to theological and literary matters but also to many economic and political issues.

While he had earlier been influenced by the thought of Comte and of Ruskin, Wicksteed's first direct contact with political economy took the form of reading Henry George's *Progress and Poverty*, of corresponding with George in 1882 and 1883 and of being a co-founder, in 1883, of the Land Reform Union, which supported George's lecture tour of England and Scotland in 1883–5. (He continued to support some form of land nationalization long after this time.) It was probably late in 1882 that Wicksteed began to study the work of Jevons and thus to become 'Jevons's only disciple'. By early 1884, however, he was playing an active role in promulgating

Jevonian theory in the Economic Circle, which met until 1888 or 1889 (to be followed by the Economic Club and the British Economic Association, later to become the Royal Economic Society). Wicksteed became a close friend of George Bernard Shaw and of Graham Wallas, and was well-informed about Fabian and other aspects of the 'social movements' of the 1880s and 1890s, but was generally an acute and sympathetic observer, rather than a direct participant in those movements. He was, however, a founder member, in 1891, of the Labour Church movement and continued to give that movement strong support even after other early supporters had withdrawn their active sympathy.

Wicksteed published three books in the field of economics. The first, *The Alphabet of Economic Science, Part I. Elements of the Theory of Value or Worth*, was published in 1888; the second, *An Essay on the Co-ordination of the Laws of Distribution*, was published in 1894, and the third work, *The Common Sense of Political Economy*, was first published in one volume in 1910; a second edition in two volumes, edited by L. Robbins and containing various papers and reviews by Wicksteed, was published in 1933.

Of Wicksteed's other writings in economics, the most important are probably his critique of *Das Kapital*, published in the socialist journal *To-Day* in 1884; his article on Jevons's *Theory of Political Economy* (1889); his various contributions to the first (1894) and second (1925) editions of *Palgrave's Dictionary of Political Economy*; and his 'Scope and Method of Political Economy' paper (1914), which originated as Wicksteed's Presidential Address to Section F of the British Association for the Advancement of Science in 1913. (All of these papers appear in the Robbins edition of the *Common Sense*.)

There are a few extant letters (Sturges, 1975, p. 128) and some handwritten sermons and letters at Manchester College, Oxford, but Wicksteed wrote to a correspondent (J.M. Connell) that 'I have never kept careful records of my life and have next to no documents.' As to secondary material, the following may be consulted: Herford's full biography (1931); Robbins's editorial introduction (1933); the relevant chapters in Hutchison (1953) and Stigler (1941); Steedman's editorial introduction (1986); and the relevant entries in the *Encyclopaedia of the Social Sciences* (by H.E. Batson, vol. XV, 1935) and in the *International Encyclopedia of the Social Sciences* (by W.D. Grampp, vol. 16, 1968).

WORKS AND MAIN CONTRIBUTIONS

Wicksteed's first contribution to economic theory was his October 1884 critique of *Das Kapital, Volume I.* Resulting perhaps from a Fabian challenge within the Economic Circle, it was published in *To-Day*, which, in 1884, carried articles by many of the leading socialists of the time. Wicksteed's critique certainly converted George Bernard Shaw from the Marxian to the Jevonian theory of value and, since no effective reply was published, may have had a wider influence on the theory adopted by British socialists: some writers have regarded Böhm-Bawerk's later attack on the labour theory of value, of 1896, as inferior to that of Wicksteed. Displaying a firm grasp of many of the specific features of Marx's argument, Wicksteed was able to focus clearly on two central issues. Is the exchange-value of ordinary commodities determined by labour time? And does Marx's argument apply to 'labour force' (as Wicksteed called it)?

With respect to the first question, Wicksteed follows Marx in saying that if two commodities are exchanged they must simultaneously differ from one another, to motivate the exchange, and have something in common, to make them commensurable. But he then seizes on Marx's point that labour time only 'counts' when producing something useful and argues that it was merely arbitrary for Marx to assert that commodities have only 'abstract labour' in common. On the contrary, Wicksteed insists, all commodities have 'abstract *utility, i.e.*, power of satisfying human desires' in common; moreover, this is just as true of exchangeable objects which are not freely reproducible. Thus, in a neat twist of the argument, he proposes '*abstract utility* as the measure of value'. Wicksteed argues, nevertheless, that for freely reproducible commodities equilibrium relative prices will *coincide* with relative labour costs – but this is not because labour quantities determine prices but because labour will be so allocated as to produce those quantities of the commodities which imply marginal utilities proportional to the given labour costs. For old masters, the products of monopolized industries, etc. even this coincidence will not hold.

Turning to 'the value of labour-force', Wicksteed then observes that, in a non-slave society, labour is not allocated to the production of 'labour-force' under competitive pressures. He deduces that there is no reason to expect that the ratio of the money wage rate to the labour value of the necessary wage goods will be equal to the money price-embodied labour ratio for ordinary commodities. Consequently, he concludes, Marx has failed to show that 'surplus labour' is the source of profit. Neither George Bernard Shaw nor any other contributor to *To-Day*, or to the other British socialist periodicals of the period, provided a remotely effective reply to Wicksteed's argument.

The Alphabet. Wicksteed's *Alphabet of Economic Science*, of 1888, was dedicated to members of the Economic Circle who had 'met to discuss the principles set forth in these pages'. Both the subtitle of the volume and certain remarks in Wicksteed's Introduction suggested that there might be successor volumes but this proved not to be the case. Although the work received the approbation of both Edgeworth and Pareto, it did not find a wide audience, which is perhaps not surprising given that it was simultaneously introductory and somewhat mathematical. As in his other books, Wicksteed disclaimed originality but showed himself to be, at the very least, a most careful and detailed thinker and expositor; in the case of the *Alphabet* a great many vivid examples are used to reinforce the reader's firm grasp of marginal principles. (The book's only index is indeed an index of examples.) As in his earlier reply to G.B. Shaw, of 1885, and in the subsequent *Co-ordination of the Laws of Distribution*, of 1894, Wicksteed emphasized the importance of the mathematical expression of marginal economic theory.

For Wicksteed, the theory of value – or 'worth' – means essentially the theory of demand (the theory of supply he refers to as that of production – or 'making'). In both the discussion of 'individual worth' (pp. 1–67) and that of 'social worth' (pp. 68–138), stress is firmly laid on the distinction between total and marginal utility. (Wicksteed uses the latter term and avoids Jevons's 'final utility' and 'final degree of utility'.) While the analysis is based on utility rather than on choice or preference – and 'hedonistic value' is referred to (p. 54) – Wicksteed's later stress on choice between satisfactions which are rendered comparable at the margin is already foreshadowed in the *Alphabet*. It is suggested that all marginal utilities and disutilities, for an individual, may be measured in terms of the hedonistic value, to that individual, of foot-pounds of lifting work or perhaps of one hour of correcting examination papers. Although the exposition is elementary throughout the book, the careful reader will notice Wicksteed's remarks on indivisible commodities and marginal analysis, on the acquiring of preferences, on minimum perceived differences, on traditions and habits, on the desire to impress or to give to others, and on negative marginal (and even total) utilities.

Turning to 'social worth', Wicksteed asserts at once that interpersonal comparisons of utility are impossible; all that can be said is that the ratio of the marginal utilities of any two commodities is the same for any two individuals who possess some of each commodity. (Wicksteed gives a particularly clear account of why this proportionality rule does not hold for an individual whose possession of one or both of the commodities is zero.) Yet he is still ready to argue, on grounds of 'averages' and probabilities, that a more equal distribution of income will probably make the objective social scale of relative prices a more reliable guide to the relative social importance, at the margin, of the various commodities. Wicksteed then discusses the market demand curve, the law of indifference (i.e. of one price) and various kinds of price discrimination.

As indicated above, Wicksteed considers that 'Strictly speaking [the allocation of productive resources] does not come within the scope of our present inquiry' (p. 109) but he nevertheless devotes pp. 109–24 to the allocation of 'the labour (and other efforts or sacrifices, if there are any others) needful to production' (p. 109). As in the *To-Day* essay of 1884, he argues that the relative prices of freely reproducible commodities will, in equilibrium, be equal to their relative effort-and-sacrifice costs but that this is *not* because production costs give commodities their exchange value. Rather it is because resources are reallocated until the commodities are produced in those quantities for which the marginal utilities – which *are* the sources of exchange value – will be proportional to the constant costs. Given that Wicksteed argues here in terms of 'a unit of effort-and-sacrifice' or 'a unit of productive force' (p. 112 and n.), it is not surprising that no theory of distribution is offered or, indeed, even hinted at.

Co-ordination of the Laws of Distribution. Wicksteed's *QJE* article of the following year, 1889, nevertheless contained an important passage criticizing and extending Jevons's marginal productivity theory of the interest rate, and distribution theory became more prominent in Wicksteed's lectures in the following years. This development culminated with the publication, in 1894, of his famous *Essay on the Co-ordination of the Laws of Distribution*. A number of writers in the early 1890s began to extend the marginal theory of intensive rent into a more general theory of distribution but it was Wicksteed's *Essay* which most clarified the issues involved. He noted that the traditional exposition of intensive rent theory, in which varying amounts of 'capital-and-labour' were applied to a fixed amount of land, had two crucial properties. First, that the argument essentially concerned only the *proportions* between inputs, and not their absolute levels, and second that the whole argument was *reversible* – the logic is quite unchanged if varying amounts of land are applied to a fixed quantity of 'capital-and-labour'. It was thus a mere matter of historical accident, Wicksteed argued, that the conventional diagram made one factor return appear as a 'marginal product' and the other as a 'surplus'.

Having argued that it was in any case self-evident that a profit-maximizing entrepreneur would hire each input up to the point at which its marginal value product equalled its (given) price, Wicksteed set himself the task of demonstrating that marginal product pricing of all inputs would entail product exhaustion. (He did not show that there would be any objection in principle to a theory in which *one* return was determined residually – nor could he have done so.) This he did by a long and inelegant mathematical argument, which amounts to no more (and no less) than a proof of Euler's Theorem for homogeneous functions, in the two-variable case. (As was quickly pointed out by Flux in a review in the *Economic Journal* for June 1894; there is some evidence to suggest that Wicksteed was completely unaware of Euler's Theorem before reading Flux's review.) More interesting than the inelegance of Wicksteed's proof, however, is that he was not satisfied with the argument, for while he considered it to be a 'truism' that there are constant returns to scale in physical production, he insisted that there might well not be constant returns in terms of revenue. Even if such 'commercial' factors as 'goodwill', 'travelling' and 'notoriety' could be increased in the same proportion as all the inputs to physical production, he argued, total revenue might increase in a smaller proportion. Wicksteed was thus led first to consider a monopolist (and to present quite explicitly the marginal revenue formula – already known to Cournot – of the imperfect competition theory of some forty years later) and then to show how, as the number of firms in an industry becomes ever larger, the product exhaustion theorem will become 'virtually' correct. In his later review of Pareto's *Manuale* (*EJ*, 1906) and in the *Common Sense* (1910, p. 373, n. 1) Wicksteed appeared to withdraw the sixth section of the *Essay* dealing with product exhaustion in the presence of monopoly, etc. (although not the *Essay* as a whole) but there has been considerable discussion of just how that apparent withdrawal ought to be interpreted. (*See also* ADDING-UP PROBLEM for the contemporary reception of Wicksteed's *Essay*.)

Wicksteed's *Essay* constituted a major contribution to marginal productivity theory, by raising and discussing the product exhaustion question and by setting the theory very firmly in a multi-product, multi-input setting. (The practice of treating capital, or 'capital-and-labour', as a single sum of value is sharply criticized.) It is to be clearly noted, however, that the *Essay* presented *partial* equilibrium analysis throughout; Wicksteed always takes input prices as given and, contrary to some commentators, he never asserts that input supplies are exogenously determined. The *Essay* is a major text in partial analysis; it does not present a general equilibrium argument.

The Common Sense. From 1894 to 1910 Wicksteed published very little in the field of economics but in 1906 he was ready to begin work on his magnum opus *The Common Sense of Political Economy*, published in 1910. In this 700-page book, he sought to expound in minute detail the consequences of 'the revolution that has taken place' (p. 2) in economic theory. Disclaiming originality yet again, as he had done in 1888 and in 1894, and making very few *explicit* references to the work of others, Wicksteed presented a consistently subjective approach to all aspects of economic life. (Just five years earlier, in the *Economic Journal* (1905, p. 435), he had written that 'The school of economists of which Professor Marshall is the illustrious head may be regarded from the point of view of the thorough-going Jevonian as a school of apologists.') Ranging from behaviour at the dining table to the significance of the division of labour in an advanced society, Wicksteed argued that attention to *selection between alternatives* was the key to understanding *all* aspects of allocation – whether of bread, of bricks, of friendship, of charity, of labour time or of prayers. Indeed he even saw an intimate connection between careful marginal allocations and 'the law formulated by Aristotle with reference to virtue', that of the mean. The following discussion of Wicksteed's long, immensely detailed and occasionally prolix work will have to centre on his positive contributions and no reference will be made to weaker parts of his analysis (for example, that on increasing and diminishing returns in Book II, Chapter V) or to his discussion of distribution theory, already referred to above in relation to the *Essay* of 1894. (Wicksteed's famous 'Scope and Method' paper, of 1914, presents an incisive epitome of the central themes of the *Common Sense* and may serve as an introduction to it.)

Wicksteed's analysis of choice, in the *Common Sense*, is firmly based on the concept of a scale of preferences, diminishing marginal significance and equivalence at the margin; it has been freed from the notions of utility and marginal utility as quantities, which are still evident in the earlier *Alphabet*. Moreover, while there is some room for doubt, in the *Alphabet*, whether the 'marginal utility' of a commodity depends only on the quantity of that commodity or on the quantities of all the commodities possessed, it is completely clear, in the *Common Sense*, that the 'marginal significance' of a quantity of a particular commodity depends on all the quantities in question. Indeed it depends not only on all those quantities but on all the circumstances of the choosing individual, for Wicksteed is insistent throughout that *all* objects of choice, and not just marketable commodities, have a bearing on each choice. The principles at work in the allocation of money between potatoes and milk are the same as those involved in the allocation of time between friendship and prayer: 'whatever our definition of Economics and the economic life may be, the laws which they exhibit and obey are not peculiar to themselves, but are laws of life in its widest extent' (p. 160). Wicksteed's firm refusal to draw boundaries is more readily understood when account is taken of his conviction that 'these things, of which money gives us command, are, strictly speaking, never the ultimate objects of deliberate desire at all ... as soon as we deliberately desire possession of any external object, it is because of the experiences or the mental states and habits which it is expected to produce or to avert' (p. 152). In modern terms, the underlying preference ordering is over mental experiences, not over commodities, and there is no reason to expect that 'economic' choices will fall under different principles than do 'other' choices.

The individual's preference ordering, Wicksteed argues, will be complete but will not always be consistent (transitive), although reflection will increase its consistency. The ordering often will not be, and will not need to be, fully present to the agent's consciousness. Apparently 'irrational' behaviour based on impulse, habit or tradition certainly occurs but does not undermine the fundamental principles of rational behaviour; 'Habit or impulse perpetually determines our selection between alternatives ... But if [the terms on which alternatives are offered us] are altered beyond a certain point the habit will be broken or the unconscious impulse checked' (pp. 28–9). Expectations, uncertainty and consumption loans are all discussed by Wicksteed, as is the fact that rational administration of one's resources is itself costly, in terms of time and effort, and thus should not be pursued beyond a certain point. Throughout his analysis of choice between alternatives Wicksteed returns repeatedly to the idea that the most heterogeneous of satisfactions not only can be but actually are compared at the margin. He is thus led to consider how this analysis can represent 'the martyr who has borne the rack [and] is ready to be burnt to death sooner than depart a hair's breadth from the formula of his confession' (p. 404) or the man for whom there are 'certain things which he would not do for any amount of money, however large' (p. 405). Wicksteed's answer, in terms of all other considerations falling below a *minimum sensible* in such cases, appears to do little more than provide a polite reconciliation between his equality of marginal satisfactions and the presence of a *lexicographic* priority of honour over money, or of keeping the faith over escaping torture. Indeed it is not clear how Wicksteed could maintain his own insistence that ethical considerations have priority over others (pp. 123–4), without allowing for at least some element of lexical ordering of alternatives. That said, Wicksteed's many subtle illustrations of how often disparate satisfactions *are* compared and equated at the margin remain highly instructive.

That Wicksteed pursued to the limit the concept of the rational maximizing individual is far from meaning that he had an asocial or 'atomistic' view of individual agents, or that he subscribed to the methodological fiction of the 'economic man'. On the contrary, his most important contribution to marginal theory perhaps lies in his forceful rejection of the 'economic man' concept and his closely related demonstration that the marginal analysis of individual action is entirely compatible with the recognition of the intrinsically social nature of many, even most, of the individual agent's purposes and concerns. Whilst the whole of the *Common Sense* contributes powerfully to this 'double' argument, it is in Book I, Chapter V, 'Business and the Economic Nexus', that these issues are confronted most directly. 'But when we pass ... to the phrase "the economic motive" ... we are in the presence of one of the most dangerous and indeed disastrous confusions that obstruct the progress of Economics' (p. 163), Wicksteed argues, for there can be no non-arbitrary way of distinguishing motives and considerations which do influence economic actions from those which do not. There are thus two coherent alternatives; 'We may either ignore motives altogether, or may recognise all motives that are at work, according to the aspect of the matter with which we are concerned at the moment; but in no case may we pick and choose between the motives we will and the motives we will not recognise as affecting economic conditions' (p. 165). (In fact Wicksteed very seldom adopts the former, external or behaviouristic analysis, even if there is one passage (p. 34) which strongly evokes the later 'revealed preference' approach.) If all motives are to be considered by the economic theorist, it follows, of course, that 'The proposal to exclude "benevolent" or "altruistic" motives from consideration in the study of Economics is ... wholly irrelevant and beside the mark' (p. 179); the interests which an agent seeks to pursue may or may not be directly his own. (And motivations can very well be mixed).

But if all motives are to be taken into account, and if the principles guiding economic activity are simply the principles guiding all human activity, what defines the particular object of study of the Economist? For Wicksteed, the answer lies in the concept of '*economic relations*'; 'economic investigation is concerned [with] the things a man can give to or do for another independently of any personal and individualised sympathy with him or with his motives or reasons' (pp. 4–5). When persons A and B stand in an economic relation to one another, they may well be furthering each other's purposes in fact but A enters the relation with no thought or intention of promoting B's ends and B, likewise, is motivated by no desire to further the purposes of A; however rich and complex may be the motivations of A and of B, the economic relation between them is an impersonal one. 'The economic relation does not exclude from my mind every one but me, it potentially includes every one but you' (p. 174). To stress this point Wicksteed introduced the term 'non-tuism', which serves to focus attention upon the fact that, in an economic relation, A's lack of concern for the purposes of B (and vice-versa), by no means entails that A acts from selfish motives. 'The specific characteristic of an economic relation is not its "egoism" but its "non-tuism"' (p. 180).

With respect to the 'supply side' – a term which he might well have rejected – Wicksteed's central contributions lay in his stress on the conception of costs as opportunity costs and in his related views on reservation price and the supply curve as a 'reverse' demand curve. Wicksteed laid considerable emphasis on the idea that, no matter how indispensable productive inputs might be, 'within limits, the most apparently unlike of these factors of production can be substituted for each other at the margins' (p. 361). (Although it is noteworthy that, in the *Essay* of 1894, he had explicitly drawn attention to the possibility of completely dispensable inputs, p. 37, n.1.) This emphasis no doubt facilitated – but did not, of course, entail – his insistence on the opportunity costs view of cost of production. 'Cost of production', he wrote, 'is simply and solely "the marginal significance of something else"' (p. 382) or, less abstractly, 'By cost of production, or cost price, when the phrase is used without qualification, I mean the estimated value, measured in gold, of all the alternatives that have been sacrificed in order to place a unit of the commodity in question upon the market' (p. 385). As he had done in 1884 and 1888, Wicksteed argued that 'there is a constant tendency to equality between price and cost of production, but not because the latter determines the former' (p. 358). The central thrust of the opportunity cost doctrine was thus directed against the 'real cost' doctrines. In his 1905 attack on the 'apologetic' school headed by Professor Marshall (referred to above), Wicksteed had written that 'To scholars of this school the admission into the science of the renovated study of consumption leaves the study of production comparatively unaffected. As a determining factor of normal prices, cost of production is co-ordinate with the schedule of demands registered on the "demand curve".' His conclusion in 1910 was more explicit: 'The only sense, then, in which cost of production can affect the value of one thing is the sense in which it is itself the value of another thing. Thus what has been variously termed utility, ophelemity, or desiredness, is the sole and ultimate determinant of all exchange values' (p. 391). This was naturally a striking and challenging conclusion but Wicksteed did not give adequate consideration to the implications for the opportunity cost doctrine of limitations to factor mobility or of the presence of nonpecuniary benefits. (See the entry RESERVATION PRICE for further discussion of Wicksteed's 'rejection' of the supply curve.)

If Wicksteed's *Common Sense* is not flawless, it remains a brilliant demonstration that a writer who had a strongly 'social' conception of the individual agent, who was friendly to the socialist and labour movements of his time, and who was sometimes a sharp critic of the market system, could yet be a purist of marginal theory.

IAN STEEDMAN

SELECTED WORKS

1884. *Das Kapital:* a criticism. *To-Day* NS 2, October. Reprinted in *Common Sense* (1933).

1888. *The Alphabet of Economic Science*. Part I: *Elements of the Theory of Value or Worth*. London: Macmillan. Reprinted, New York: Augustus Kelley, 1955.

1889. On certain passages in Jevons's Theory of Political Economy. *Quarterly Journal of Economics,* April. Reprinted in *Common Sense* (1933).

1894a. *An Essay on the Co-ordination of the Laws of Distribution*. London: Macmillan. Reprinted as No. 12 in LSE Series of Reprints of Scarce Tracts in Economic and Political Science, 1932. Reprinted, ed. I. Steedman, London: Duckworth, 1987.

1894b. Degree of utility; Dimensions of economic quantities; Final degree of utility; W.S. Jevons; Political economy and psychology. Entries in *Palgrave's Dictionary of Political Economy*, London: Macmillan. All reprinted in *Common Sense* (1933).

1905. Note on Jevons's economic work. *Economic Journal* 15, September. Reprinted in *Common Sense* (1933).

1906. Review of Pareto's *Manuale di Economia Politica. Economic Journal* 16, December. Reprinted in *Common Sense* (1933).

1910. *The Common Sense of Political Economy*. London: Macmillan. 2nd edn, 2 vols., ed. L. Robbins, London: Routledge & Kegan Paul, 1933.

1914. The scope and method of political economy in the light of the 'marginal' theory of value and distribution. *Economic Journal* 24, March. Reprinted in *Common Sense* (1933).

1925. Final utility. Entry in *Palgrave's Dictionary of Political Economy*, 2nd edn., ed. H. Higgs, London: Macmillan. Reprinted in *Common Sense* (1933).

BIBLIOGRAPHY

Encyclopaedia of the Social Sciences, Vol. XV Ed. E.R.A. Seligman and A. Johnson, London: Macmillan, 1935.

Flux, A.W. 1894. Review of Wicksell's *Über Wert, Kapital und Rente* and of Wicksteed's *Essay*. *Economic Journal* 4, June, 305–13.

Herford, C.H. 1931. *Philip Henry Wicksteed: His Life and Work*. London: Dent & Sons.

Hutchison, T.W. 1953. *A Review of Economic Doctrines, 1870–1929* Oxford: Clarendon Press.

International Encyclopedia of the Social Sciences, Vol. 16 Ed. D.L. Sills, London and Glencoe: Macmillan and the Free Press, 1968.

Robbins, L. 1933. Editorial Introduction to Wicksteed (1910).

Steedman, I. 1987. Editorial Introduction to Wicksteed (1894a).

Stigler, G.J. 1941. *Production and Distribution Theories: The Formative Period.* New York: Agathon Press, 1968.

Sturges, R.P. 1975. *Economists' Papers 1750–1950*. London: Macmillan.

widow's cruse. The miracle of the widow's cruse (II Kings iv) was one of the most famous parables used by Keynes to present the conclusions of an analysis in the form of paradoxes.

In the *Treatise on Money*, the Fundamental Equations express the formulae for determining the price level of consumption goods and the price level of output as a whole (p. 123). The equilibrium of this two-equation system (associated with a stable price level) occurs when saving and investment balance, and is characterized by the full employment of capital and labour. To turn these 'mere identities' into cause-effect relationships. Keynes used the traditional approach of divergences between the 'natural' and 'market' rates of interest as the factors which create 'profits' (or 'losses') by upsetting the balance between current investment and saving. On the strength of this set of assumptions, Keynes maintained that such an excess of investment over saving would be felt through an alteration in the general level of prices *only*. Hence,

> if entrepreneurs choose to spend a portion of their profits on consumption,... the effect is to *increase* the profit on the sale of consumption goods by an amount exactly equal to the amount of profits which have been thus expanded ... . Thus, however much of their profits entrepreneurs spend on consumption, the increment of wealth belonging to entrepreneurs remains the same as before ... . Thus profits, as a source of capital increment for entrepreneurs, are a widow's cruse which remains undepleted however much of them may be devoted to riotous living ... (p. 125).

On the other hand, when saving exceeds investment and entrepreneurs make 'losses', the widow's cruse becomes a *Danaid jar* which can never be filled.

After the publication of the *Treatise*, Keynes was quick to concede that for this result to be the *only* possible effect, an assumption of *constant output* had to be added. Indeed, and partially thanks to the relaxation of this constant output assumption, Keynes managed to move away progressively from quantity adjustments grafted onto the *Treatise* argument (in which variations in the rate of interest ensure the equilibrium of planned savings and planned investment) towards changes in the level of output as *the* adjustment mechanism between saving and investment (i.e. the analytical core of the *General Theory*).

P. BRIDEL

See also KEYNES, JOHN MAYNARD.

BIBLIOGRAPHY

Keynes, J.M. 1930. *A Treatise on Money*. Vol. I: *The Pure Theory of Money*. As in *The Collected Writings of John Maynard Keynes*, Vol. V, London: Macmillan, 1971.

Wiener process. Brownian motion is the most renowned, and historically the first stochastic process that was thoroughly investigated. It is named after the English botanist, Robert Brown who in 1827 observed that small particles immersed in a liquid exhibited ceaseless irregular motion. Brown himself mentions several precursors starting at the beginning with Leeuwenhoek (1632–1723). In 1905 Einstein, unaware of the existence of earlier investigations about Brownian motion, obtained a mathematical derivation of this process from the laws of physics. The theory of Brownian motion was further developed by several distinguished mathematical physicists until Norbert Wiener gave it a rigorous mathematical formulation in his 1918 dissertation and in later papers. This is why the Brownian motion is also called the Wiener process. For a brief history of the scientific developments of the process see Nelson (1967).

Having made these remarks we now define the process. A *Wiener process* or a *Brownian motion process*

$$\{Z(t,\omega):[0,\infty)\times\Omega\to R\}$$

is a stochastic process with index $t\in[0,\infty)$ on a probability space Ω, and mapping to the real line R, with the following properties:

(1) $Z(0,\omega)=0$ with probability 1, that is by convention we assume that the process starts at zero.

(2) If $0\leqslant t_0\leqslant t_1\leqslant\cdots\leqslant t_n$ are time points then for any real set H_i

$$P[Z(t_i)-Z(t_{i-1})\in H_i \text{ for } i\leqslant n] = \prod_{i\leqslant n} P[Z(t_i)-Z(t_{i-1})\in H_i].$$

This means that the increments of the process $Z(t_i)-Z(t_{i-1})$, $i\leqslant n$, are independent variables.

(3) For $0\leqslant s<t$, the increment $Z(t)-Z(s)$ has distribution

$$P[Z(t)-Z(s)\in H] = (1/\sqrt{2\pi(t-s)})\int_H \exp[-x^2/2(t-s)]\,dx.$$

This means that every increment $Z(t)-Z(s)$ is normally distributed with mean zero and variance $(t-s)$.

(4) For each $\omega\in\Omega$, $Z(t,\omega)$ is continuous in t, for $t\geqslant 0$.

Note that condition (4) can be proved mathematically using the first three conditions. Here it is added because in many applications such continuity is essential. Although the sample paths of the Wiener process are continuous, we immediately state an important theorem about their differentiability properties.

Theorem. (Non-differentiability of the Wiener process). Let $\{Z(t), t\geqslant 0\}$ be a Wiener process in a given probability space. Then for ω outside some set of probability 0, the sample path $Z(t,\omega)$, $t\geqslant 0$, is nowhere differentiable.

Intuitively, a nowhere differentiable sample path represents the motion of a particle which at no time has a velocity. Thus, although the sample paths are continuous, this theorem suggests that they are very kinky, and their derivatives exist nowhere. The mathematical theory of the Wiener process is briefly presented in Billingsley (1979) and more extensively in Knight (1981).

The first application of Brownian motion or the Wiener process in economics was made by Louis Bachelier in his dissertation 'Théorie de la spéculation' in 1900. Cootner (1964) collects several papers and cites additional references on the application of the Wiener process in describing the random character of the stock market. In the early 1970s Merton, in a series of papers, established the use of stochastic calculus as a tool in financial economics. The Wiener process is a basic concept in stochastic calculus and its applicability in economics arises from the fact that the Wiener process can be regarded as the limit of a continuous time *random walk* as step sizes become infinitesimally small. In other words, the Wiener process can be used as the cornerstone in modeling *economic uncertainty* in continuous time. For purposes of illustration consider the stochastic differential equation

$$dX(t)=\mu(t,x)\,dt+\sigma(t,x)\,dZ(t) \qquad (1)$$

which appears in the economic literature describing asset prices, rate of inflation, quantity of money or other variables. In (1), changes in the variable $X(t)$, denoted as $dX(t)$, are described as a sum of two terms: $\mu(t,x)$ which is the *expected* instantaneous change and $\sigma(t,x)\,dZ(t)$ which is the *unexpected* change. Furthermore, this unexpected change is the product of the instantaneous standard deviation $\sigma(t,x)$ and uncertainty modelled by increments in the Wiener process. See Merton (1975) for a methodological essay on continuous time modelling and Malliaris and Brock (1982) or Harrison (1985) for numerous applications of the Wiener process in economics and business.

Economists have constructed various processes based on the Wiener process. Let $\{Z(t), t\geqslant 0\}$ be a Wiener process and use it to construct a process $\{W(t), t\geqslant 0\}$ defined by $W(t)=Z(t)+\mu t$, $t\geqslant 0$, where μ is a constant. Then we say that $\{W(t), t\geqslant 0\}$ is a *Wiener process* or *Brownian motion process with drift* and μ is called the drift parameter. In this case the only modification that occurs in the definition of a Wiener process is in property (3) where $W(t)-W(s)$ is normally distributed with mean $\mu(t-s)$ and variance $(t-s)$. Finally, let $W(t)$ be a Wiener process with drift as just defined. Consider the new process given by $Y(t)=\exp[W(t)]$, $t\geqslant 0$. Then $\{Y(t), t\geqslant 0\}$ is called a *geometric Brownian motion* or *geometric Wiener process.*

The availability of an extensive mathematical literature on the Wiener process and the economists' fundamental goal to model economic uncertainty in continuous time suggest that this process will continue to be an important tool for economic theorists.

A.G. MALLIARIS

See also CONTINUOUS-TIME STOCHASTIC PROCESSES; MARTINGALES.

BIBLIOGRAPHY

Billingsley, P. 1979. *Probability and Measure*. New York: John Wiley.

Cootner, P.H. 1964. *The Random Character of Stock Market Prices*, Cambridge, Mass. MIT Press.

Harrison, J.M. 1985. *Brownian Motion and Stochastic Flow Systems*. New York: John Wiley.

Knight, F.B. 1981. *Essentials of Brownian Motion and Diffusion*. Mathematical Surveys, Number 18. The American Mathematical Society, Providence, Rhode Island.

Malliaris, A.G. and Brock, W.A. 1982. *Stochastic Methods in Economics and Finance*. Amsterdam: North-Holland Publishing Company.

Merton, R.C. 1975. Theory of finance from the perspective of continuous time. *Journal of Financial and Quantitative Analysis* 10, 659–74.

Nelson, E. 1967. *Dynamical Theories of Brownian Motion*. Princeton, New Jersey: Princeton University Press.

Wieser, Friedrich, Freiherr von (1851–1926). Wieser is commonly cited together with his senior, Carl Menger, and his exact contemporary, Eugen Böhm von Bawerk, as one of the founding trio of the Austrian School of Economics in the last quarter of the 19th century. The exact nature of his achievement, however, seems now practically forgotten: possibly because he produced an intractable mixture of deep and influential insights, very distinctly his own, intermingled with oratorical prose and often unpalatable value judgements; he was extremely successful in his own generation but appeared outdated in his attitudes half a century later.

Wieser was born on 10 July 1851, in Vienna. His father was Commissary-General of the Austrian army in the war of 1859, for which service he was ennobled, later becoming Vice-President of the Austrian Court of Audit, a baron and a privy councillor (Geheimrat). But this high social status was only acquired after Friedrich Wieser's birth and very little money went with it so that the family lived in modest circumstances. Wieser went to the Benedictine Schottengymnasium in Vienna, one of the city's three elite schools. His classmate was Eugen Böhm von Bawerk, who became his close friend and brother-in-law. Together the two studied at Vienna University Law Faculty (which included courses in economics), together they entered the civil service in the fiscal division, and together they went on a two-year leave of absence to perfect themselves in economics at Heidelberg, Leipzig, and Jena, with Knies, Roscher and Hildebrand. A little after Böhm, Wieser passed his 'Habilitation' in economics with Menger in 1883, was appointed associate professor in 1884 and full professor in 1889 at the University of Prague and was that university's Vice Chancellor in 1901–2. In 1903, he succeeded Menger in the chair of economic theory at Vienna University Law Faculty on the latter's early retirement, Böhm again joining him only a year later as extraordinarily appointed additional full professor. Böhm, Menger, and finally also Wieser, served as members of the Austrian House of Lords (Herrenhaus). Wieser became Minister of Commerce in 1917, holding this office up to the end of the monarchy in 1918. He died on 23 July 1926.

Apart from the short ministerial interlude Wieser thus taught from 1884 to 1926 at the largest universities of Austria. Basically, he must be considered the most successful teacher (especially of undergraduates) and the orator of the trio. His influence was pervasive through his lecturing to tens of thousands of law students, many of whom he examined in person, and at second and third remove on even vaster numbers in the intellectual melting pot of Vienna. In a true oral tradition Wieser influenced present-day economics through what these frequently very young students – an appreciable percentage of whom later became themselves important in Western intellectual life – picked up in a kind of intellectual osmosis, mostly without realizing it and therefore usually without attributing the ideas to their teacher.

Wieser's main works are: his thesis of 'Habilitation' (Wieser, 1884), which encompasses a large part of his original thought, particularly the marginal productivity valuation of factors of production and his cost theory; Wieser (1889), mainly an elaboration of the former together with an attempt to give the marginal utility concept normative distributional content; Wieser (1914), the definitive textbook of the Austrian School and (with its rival, G. Cassel's more up-to-date *Theoretische Sozialökonomie*, 1918) one of the two main theoretical textbooks in German of the early interwar period, a book still worth reading, especially the less well-known institutional chapters on large corporations and money and banking; finally Wieser (1926), a sociophilosophical tract in abject adulation of power (power being justified by mere 'success'), whose lack of judgement can only be justified by the effect of the total breakdown of all established social and political order after World War I on Wieser's own moral fibre.

Wieser prided himself on the invention of telling phrases, particularly the term 'Grenznutzen' in Wieser (1884), wherefore Marshall credits him, perhaps unjustly, with originating the term 'marginal utility'. During his leadership the Austrian School had to sail under the flag 'Grenznutzenschule'. In contrast to the purely analytic usage by the other members of the trio, 'Grenznutzen' had for Wieser a near mystic connotation and certainly normative content: more precisely, it is the average marginal utility in a competitive society with equality of incomes, which is the 'natural value' of Wieser (1889). 'Grenznutzen' thus served Wieser, who was (unusual for an Austrian economist) a paternalistic interventionist, as a yardstick of policy evaluation.

In contrast to Menger and Böhm, Wieser was not a clear logical analyst but had influential visions. He was clearest in his cost and production theory, frequently being credited with introducing the opportunity cost principle that all costs are only utilities foregone, though Wieser's actual advance over Menger appears slight. Wieser certainly, however, gave what appears to be the first account of the principles of efficient production, which Menger had ignored (Wieser, 1884). Production is undertaken in expectation of the price the marginal valuation of consumers will allow, Wieser (1884) first formulating the equimarginal principle in production: the marginal product of each factor (or its cost) must be the same in all its different uses and as high as the least important marginal utility achievable from its given supply (Wieser's Law of Cost). In Wieser (1914) this is extended (contemporaneously with Wicksteed, *Commonsense of Political Economy*, 1910) to an analysis of differential quality rents on the lines of Ricardo: any more efficient factor earns as rent the additional value added over the least efficient equivalent factor. Some of his insights into capital and efficient production Wieser probably owes, as the terminology suggests, to Marx (Wieser never gives his authorities, apart from sparse references in Wieser, 1914): for example that the value of factors of production must reflect the socially necessary cost of production (the use of the best generally known technique); or that innovation brings extra profits to the innovator, without changing the value of the (other) factors. (Marx, Engels, Ricardo, Jevons, and

Menger are the five authors Wieser acknowledges as inspiration in the Introduction to Wieser, 1884.) As to distribution, Wieser first posed the problem whether the marginal product reward of all factors of production would exactly exhaust the product ('Zurechnungsproblem', the problem of imputation), without being, despite many attempts, able to solve it.

These ideas were, however, all on the point of being discovered by others. Uniquely his own is the repeated stress, already in Wieser (1884), of the paramount importance of economic calculation and the need to have an economic measuring rod for all rational 'planning' for the future. (One is tempted to suspect this to be an obsession of the son of the Vice-President of the Court of Audit.) The measuring rod for Wieser is marginal utility in its wide sense; but it was a small step, taken by Mises and Hayek, to make out of this need for a measuring rod in all economic planning the concept of the informative nature of prices. Economics may even owe the (then uncommon) term 'planning' for the rational activity in economics on the individual as well as the societal level to Wieser via Mises. Wieser already stated repeatedly that even a socialist economy would have to use the same economic measuring rod and basically the same principles of 'planning' as a capitalist one: out of which Mises developed the idea that, lacking prices, a socialist society could not plan rationally.

Besides his production and distribution-oriented ideas Wieser had a second influential vision: the importance of the creative individual in all economic processes. He felt deeply the basically contradictory nature of his two visions, the impersonal mass effects of efficient production on the one hand, an idea which he curiously traced to the influence of Herbert Spencer, and the elitist idea of the effects of the outstanding individual, which he attributed to the hero-worshipping teaching of history in the Schottengymnasium. In this vein, which he cultivated in his later years, he was again, above all, influential through the forceful and suggestive use of words, the terms 'Führer', 'Pionier', 'Neuerung' (German for innovation) being of his creation. Schumpeter adopted virtually all the terminology for his *Theory of Economic Development* from his acknowledged teacher Wieser and also the idea that economic 'dynamics' (in contrast to statics) is due to individual leadership activity. Wieser himself had developed relatively few concrete conclusions out of his leadership rhetoric, apart from remarks about the countervailing power of trade unions and the administrative and even innovative efficiency of large corporations in Wieser (1914), an idea taken up by Schumpeter only later. Wieser's second vision degenerated into the lurid prose of Wieser (1926), where, for example, the 'Führer' (a pet word of Wieser's), Adolf Hitler, is chided (in 1926!) for not quite making the grade. For Wieser, again in sharp contrast to the staunch liberal principles of Menger and Böhm, tended, in spite of his basic Catholic-conservative outlook, to flirt with any social movement that was new and appeared 'great', making commendatory references to socialism in his youth and to German nationalism and fascism in his old age.

E. STREISSLER

See also AUSTRIAN SCHOOL OF ECONOMICS.

SELECTED WORKS

1884. *Über den Ursprung und die Hauptgestze des wirtschaftlichen Werthes.* Vienna: Hölder.

1889. *Der Natürliche Werth.* Vienna: Hölder. Trans. as *Natural Value* ed. W. Smart, London: Macmillan, 1893. Reprinted, New York: Kelley & Millman, 1956.

1914. Theorie der gesellschaftlichen Wirtschaft. In *Grundriss der Sozialökonomik*, Vols 1 and 2, Tübingen: Mohr-Siebeck. 2nd edn, 1923. Trans. as *Social Economics*, New York: Greenberg, 1927.

1926. *Das Gesetz der Macht.* Vienna: Springer.

BIBLIOGRAPHY

Mayer, H. 1929. Friedrich Freiherr von Wieser. In *Neue österreichische Biographie*, Vol. 6, Vienna: Amalthea, 180 ff.

Schumpeter, J.A. 1912. *The Theory of Economic Development. An inquiry into profits, capital, credit, interest, and the business cycle.* Trans. R. Opie, Cambridge, Mass.: Harvard University Press, 1934.

Stigler, G.J. 1941. *Production and Distribution Theories: The Formative Period.* New York: Macmillan.

Streissler, E.W. 1986. Arma virumque cano – Friedrich von Wieser, the bard as economist. In *Die Wiener Schule der Nationalökonomie*, ed. N. Leser, Vienna: Hermann Böhlau.

Williams, John Henry (1887–1980). John H. Williams was a member of the US delegation to the Preparatory Committee for the World Monetary and Economic Conference of 1932–3; Nathaniel Ropes Professor of Political Economy, 1933–57 and Dean of the Graduate School of Public Administration, Harvard University, 1937–47; Vice President and, subsequently, Economic Adviser, Federal Reserve Bank of New York, (1936–56) and President of the American Economic Association in 1951.

Williams was a rare combination of the scholar and the practitioner of the art of central banking. Familiar with the evolution of economics, his career was devoted to the application of that discipline to public policy.

In doing so, he saw value, as well as danger, in theory. Without theory, as Keynes had said, we are 'lost in the woods'. But theory inevitably simplifies reality. Moreover, the most influential theories originate in unique circumstances and in views about policies to deal with them. Since circumstances change, he warned that those who prescribe glibly from theory are dangerous as policy-makers.

His views about theory were applied with the greatest effect in the international monetary sphere. He particularly questioned conventional views about the gold standard. The classical specie flow mechanism was a beautiful intellectual construct. However, the pre-1914 reality was that Britain maintained a gold standard while related countries based their currencies on sterling. With the subsequent rise of rival centres, the maintenance of international monetary stability boiled down to negotiating mutually acceptable relations between the 'key currencies', and then maintaining those relations – stable but not immutable – through appropriate domestic policies in the centre countries. Such views clearly influenced the negotiation of the Tripartite Agreement of 1936. They were also the basis for Williams' reservations, a few years later, about the International Monetary Fund.

A selection of Williams's more important works is published in his *Postwar Monetary Plans and Other Essays* (1945).

STEPHEN V.O. CLARKE

SELECTED WORKS

1945. *Postwar Monetary Plans and Other Essays.* New York: Knopf.

Wilson, Edwin Bidwell (1879–1964). While primarily a mathematician, Wilson's relatively few contributions to economics in the interwar years, particularly two short papers on demand theory (1935 and 1939) and one on business cycles (1934), were not without their influence in Harvard economic circles of the day. Schumpeter drew on the arguments of Wilson's paper on the periodicity of US business cycles in his *Business Cycles* and Samuelson's *Foundations* contains an acknowledgement to Wilson (with Schumpter and Leontief) in its preface, and credits him with the suggestion of utilizing the Le Chatelier principle in economic analysis.

The essay on cyclical fluctuations in business activity was an attempt to make deeper analytical use of the monthly index of US business activity prepared by Leonard Ayers and published in 1931. Using the device of the 'periodogram', invented by Arthur Schuster, Wilson is able to extract from Ayers' data 'hidden' cycles of different periodicities. The idea that behind any given aggregative series there might lurk different patterns of cyclical movement was, no doubt, a spur to Schumpter's consideration of the simultaneous operation of Juglar, Kitchin and Kondratieff cycles in *Business Cycles*.

The two short essays on demand theory (1935 and 1939) are concerned with the derivation of the law of demand – that is, the inverse relationship between price and quantity demanded. The first generalizes Pareto's proof of the proposition, which had assumed additively separable utility functions. Wilson assumes instead only that $U_i(x_1 \ldots x_n)$ may take the form $U_i(\mathrm{x}_1)+U_i(x_2 \ldots x_n)$, and derives from this the law of demand. The second paper is designed to show that Marshall's assumption of a constant marginal utility of money gave only a special case of the law of demand, and that the same result could be obtained without it. As Wilson observed, this 'forces us over from the "index of ophelimity" to a utility definite except for a linear transformation, i.e., except for scale and origin' (1939, p. 649). The importance of this result, especially given its relation to the Hicks–Allen theory of demand, for the subsequent debates over cardinal versus ordinal utility is readily apparent.

Wilson was born at Hartford, Connecticut, on 25 April 1879. After graduating from Harvard in 1899, he took his PhD from Yale in 1901. From 1907 until 1922 he was on the faculty at MIT, first as professor of mathematics and later as professor of mathematical physics. From that date until his retirement, he was professor of vital statistics at the Harvard School of Public Health. He served as president of the American Statistical Association (1929), was vice-president of the National Academy of Sciences (1949–53), and was an honorary fellow of the Royal Statistical Society. He died on 28 December 1964.

MURRAY MILGATE

SELECTED WORKS

1912. *Advanced Calculus*. Boston and New York: Ginn & Co.

1934. The periodogram and American business activity. *Quarterly Journal of Economics* 48(3), May, 375–417.

1935. Generalization of Pareto's demand theorem. *Quarterly Journal of Economics* 49(4), August, 715–17.

1939. Pareto versus Marshall. *Quarterly Journal of Economics* 53(4), August, 645–50.

Wilson, James (1805–1860). Politician, political economist, founder and owner of *The Economist* and father-in-law of Walter Bagehot, James Wilson was born at Hawick, Scotland, the son of a millowner. After a personal financial crisis in 1837 Wilson turned to pamphleteering against the Corn Laws, which in 1839 he claimed benefited the agricultural interest no more than manufacturers or workers. In two later pamphlets, 1840 and 1842, he traced business fluctuations to the artificial influence of the corn laws and advised increased direct taxation and reduced customs and excise duties to restore prosperity. Until Sir Robert Peel, following the main thrust of this policy, repealed the Corn Laws in 1846, Wilson worked closely with Richard Cobden and the Anti-Corn Law League. *The Economist*, the first number of which, written mainly by Wilson, appeared on 2 September 1843, was a free-trade advocate which soon attracted a regular business readership as an internationally known journal of fact and opinion. In 1847, when Wilson was returned to Parliament, he published 'Capital, Currency and Banking', pleading for a 'sound currency' and opposing sections of Peel's Bank Charter Act of 1844. He also argued for the repeal of the Navigation Laws. Soon given government office in 1848, Wilson was an able Financial Secretary to the Treasury from 1853 to 1858; and in 1859, after briefly holding the Vice-Presidency of the Board of Trade, he served in India as first financial member of the Viceroy's Council with the task of reforming finances. His 1860 budget introduced a controversial income tax and later in the year, just before his death, he established a paper currency.

ASA BRIGGS

Wilson, Thomas (1525–1581). English lawyer and man of letters, Wilson is remembered in the history of economics for his *Discourse on Usury*, published in 1572. Wilson lived in England during his youth and early manhood. After the accession of Queen Mary I, Wilson, a Protestant, went into exile on the Continent, where he earned a doctorate in civil law. On his return in 1560 he held a number of high offices as a Member of Parliament, judge, diplomat and Secretary of State.

Wilson wrote the *Discourse on Usury* at a time when the public attitude to interest-taking underwent a profound change. During the Middle Ages the usury rule, which outlawed interest, had prevailed. After the break with Rome, legislation was passed in England in 1546 which allowed interest up to a rate of 10 per cent. After some wavering the legislation of 1546 was confirmed in 1571. When the latter bill was passed in Parliament, Wilson was one of the two members who voted against it; he was part of a minority then on its way out. His *Discourse* contains a belated argument in favour of the medieval prohibition of interest, an argument that he supported with copious references to the Scholastic literature. He gave a respectful hearing to the divergent views of such reformers as Calvin and Bucer, but felt unable to accept them in view of the condemnation of interest in the Bible.

Wilson's opposition to interest cannot be explained by a lack of wordly wisdom on his part. His career attests to his familiarity with the world of affairs, but his strong religious and moral convictions and aversion to the hustle and bustle of commerce made him feel not at home in this world.

The *Discourse* was reprinted in 1926, edited with an historical introduction by R.H. Tawney (London: Bell). Tawney's noteworthy introduction of some 170 pages supplies further detail about Wilson's career and his work.

HENRY W. SPIEGEL

windfalls. *See* AGGREGATE DEMAND AND SUPPLY ANALYSIS.

Withers, Hartley (1867–1950). British financial journalist and editor of the *Economist* from 1916 to 1921, Withers was born at Liverpool on 15 July 1867. After Westminster School and Christ Church, Oxford, he joined the staff of *The Times* in 1894 rising to become head of its City office in 1905. In 1910 he took over the City editorship of the *Morning Post*, but in 1911 moved to a position with a company of merchant bankers in the City of London. During World War I he returned to journalism at the *Economist*. These close links with the financial sector led him to colour most of his writings with a rather rosy hue when it came to assessing the role of the City of London in promoting national and international economic development. For example, in his first book, *The Meaning of Money* (1909), he concluded that 'a credit system has thus been evolved of extraordinary elasticity and perfection, so perfect in fact that its perfection is its only weakness' (pp. 295–6). In *International Finance* (1916) he professed a 'weakness for financiers' (p. 94), defending them, in particular, against charges made by the British socialist politician Philip Snowden that their interests were in war not peace and, more generally, against the traditional socialist challenge to the influence of finance capital in the economy as a whole. This argument was extended in his *Case for Capitalism* (1920), where he claimed that the system of private property and private enterprise was necessary for civilization.

In so far as his numerous books treated matters of economic theory, probably the most interesting fact is that Withers was an early proponent of what was to become known as the Cambridge cash balance approach to the quantity theory of money. He also drew the practical distinction between the activities of saving and finance, but failed to draw the analytical distinction between them which was to be so important in Keynes's work in the late 1920s and early 1930s. Although the finance of industry and trade was seen by Withers to be essentially an independent activity, he maintained that it was limited by available capital, itself accumulated by 'the quiet, prosaic, and often rather mean and timorous people who have saved their money for a rainy day' (1916, p. 83). Withers held to the traditional idea that there was a necessary trade-off between consumption and capital accumulation (investment), and invoked this to dismiss what he called 'socialistic' claims to the effect that under a different system of economic organization and management both consumption and investment might be expanded simultaneously.

It would be incorrect, however, to view Withers as being entirely uncritical of the financial system. He was, for example, alert to what he felt to be the dangers of financial instability in the world economy; a factor which led to his advocacy of world peace and his vigorous support for the League of Nations, whose efforts to secure international cooperation rather than conflict he saw as being the only constructive international economic policy (1918). Moreover, and perhaps simply illustrating that there is nothing new under the sun, Withers was concerned with the possible consequences of any large expansion of international indebtedness. When loans went to economies whose capacity to repay was not properly assessed, there was a very real danger of default and so international monetary instability. Withers illustrated his point with the case of British loans to Honduras in the 19th century, and international loans to Brazil and Mexico in the early 20th century. Discussing phenomena which some economists of the 1970s and 1980s thought to be entirely new in their generation, Withers (1916) noted the fragility of the financial position of borrowers whose principal source of export earnings relied on primary products whose prices in international markets were subject to wide variation. Withers attributed Brazilian problems to recent dramatic falls in its then staple export, rubber. The case of the Mexican default, with its then recent revolution, arose (according to Withers) from taking insufficient account of the factor of political stability in international lending. He also discussed what is now commonly called re-scheduling of debt, insisting on terms (so familiar to debtor nations of the late 20th century) which ensured budgetary stringency at home. He opposed lending designed simply to finance domestic deficits.

His last work, *The Defeat of Poverty* (1939), was a contribution to the literature of recovery from depression. He died at Colchester on 21 March 1950.

MURRAY MILGATE AND ALASTAIR LEVY

SELECTED WORKS

1909. *The Meaning of Money*. London: Smith, Elder & Co.
1910. *Stocks and Shares*. London: Smith, Elder & Co.
1913. *Money Changing*. London: Smith, Elder & Co.
1914. *Poverty and Waste*. London: Smith, Elder & Co.
1915. *War and Lombard Street*. London: Smith, Elder & Co.
1916. *International Finance*. London: Smith, Elder & Co.
1918. *The League of Nations: Its Economic Aspect*. Oxford: Oxford University Press.
1920. *The Case for Capitalism*. London: Eveleigh Nash.
1939. *The Defeat of Poverty*. London: Jonathan Cape.

Witte, Edwin Emil (1887–1960). Witte was Professor of Economics at the University of Wisconsin (1933–57), President of the American Economic Association (1955), first President of the Industrial Relations Research Association (1948), and Chief of the Wisconsin Legislative Reference Service (1922–33). His primary field was labour and social legislation. A student of John R. Commons, he was an institutional economist and a pragmatic social reformer.

His outstanding contribution was his significant role as Executive Director of President Franklin D. Roosevelt's Cabinet Committee on Economic Security (1934–5) which drafted the legislation that became the Social Security Act of 1935. Witte prepared the Committee's report and recommendations to the President. His *The Development of the Social Security Act* (1963) recounting the legislative history of the Act is an outstanding model of its type.

Witte published *The Government in Labor Disputes* (1932), assisted in the formulation of the Norris–LaGuardia Act (1932) restricting injunctions in labour disputes and he was Regional Director of the War Labor Board in Detroit (1942–5).

Witte received his PhD in economics from the University of Wisconsin (1927) and was Chairman of the Department of Economics (1936–41 and 1946–57). Except for temporary assignments, he lived in Wisconsin all his life. He had a practical outlook on economic and political issues, coloured by LaFollette progressive populism.

W. COHEN

SELECTED WORKS

1932. *The Government in Labor Disputes*. New York and London: McGraw-Hill.
1936. *The Development of the Social Security Act; a memorandum on the history of the Committee on Economic Security and the drafting and legislative history of the Social Security Act*. Washington, DC. Reprinted, with a foreword by Frances Perkins, Madison: University of Wisconsin Press, 1962.

BIBLIOGRAPHY

[Anon.] 1960. Edwin E. Witte (1887–1960). Father of social security. *Industrial and Labor Relations Review* 14(1), October, 7–9.
Schlabach, T.F. 1969. *Edwin E. Witte: Cautious Reformer*. Madison: State Historical Society of Wisconsin.

Wold, Herman O.A. (born 1908). Wold was born at Skien in Norway on 25 December 1908 but the family migrated to Sweden in 1912. His university education was at Stockholm, where he took his doctoral degree in 1938, under H.A. Cramér. He became Professor of Statistics at Uppsala in 1942, moved to Gothenburg in 1970, and retired in 1975.

His doctoral thesis (Wold, 1934) dealt with the theory of stationary time series. Two theorems first proved in it are of lasting value. The first is the Wiener–Khintchine relation for a discrete-time series, but probably more important was the Wold Decomposition Theorem, which represents a stationary time series as the sum of an (infinite) moving average of past innovations (linear prediction errors) and a perfectly predictable component. Wold was also influential in time series analysis through his student, P. Whittle.

However, most of Wold's later work has been in econometrics. Membership of a 1938 committee to study consumer demand, rationing in case of war being the motivating force, led him to the study of general economic modelling. His work on consumer demand culminated in Wold and Juréen (1952). Economic modelling, in turn, led him to the work of Tinbergen (1939) on the statistical measurement of business cycles. Tinbergen's model was linear and connected a vector, $y(t)$, of endogenous variables to a vector, $z(t)$, of exogenous variables and lagged endogenous variables by an equation

$$y(t) = By(t) + Gz(t) + \epsilon(t), \qquad E\{\epsilon(s)\epsilon(t)'\} = \delta_{s,t}\Omega \qquad (1)$$

where the $\epsilon(t)$ are errors. Wold observed that Tinbergen's equations were recursive in that after a rearrangement of the rows of (1) the matrix B was lower triangular with zeros along the diagonal. If Ω is diagonal then (1) may be validly estimated by least squares and this will be the maximum likelihood method if the $\epsilon(t)$ are also Gaussian. Wold sought to promote recursive modelling in contrast to the non-causal modelling that became influential in econometrics following Haavelmo (1944). The recursive models are causal since, after the rearrangement of rows, elements of $y(t)$ can be regarded as arranged in a causal hierarchy. Wold's view does not seem to have prevailed. The complexity of economic phenomena, including the non-linearity of economic behaviour, the poor quality of much data, and the large amount of aggregation, together with auto-correlation of $\epsilon(t)$, make the issue seem somewhat removed from reality.

Wold (1959) also emphasized the distinction between prediction and structural estimation and has proposed an iterative estimation of (1), oriented towards prediction, where $y(t)$ on the right is replaced by $(I - \hat{B})^{-1}(\hat{G}z(t))$, with $\hat{B}, \hat{G}$ obtained from a previous iteration.

E.J. Hannan

SELECTED WORKS

1934. *A Study in the Analysis of Stationary Time Series*. Stockholm: Almqvist and Wiksell.

1959. Ends and means in econometric model building: basic considerations reviewed. In *Probability and Statistics*, The Harald Cramér volume, ed. U. Grenander, Stockholm: Almqvist and Wiksell, 355–434.

1960. *Forecasting on a Scientific Basis*. Lisbon: Gulbenkian Foundation.

1965. *Bibliography of Time Series and Stochastic Processes*. Edinburgh: Oliver & Boyd.

1980. *The Fix-Point Approach to Interdependent Systems*. Amsterdam: North-Holland.

1952. (With L. Juréen.) *Demand Analysis: A Study in Econometrics*. New York: John Wiley.

BIBLIOGRAPHY

Bentzel, R. and Wold, H. 1946. On statistical demand analysis from the viewpoint of simultaneous equations. *Skand. Aktuarietidskrift* 29, 95–114.

Haavelmo, T. 1944. The probability approach in econometrics. *Econometrica* 12, supplement.

Tinbergen, J. 1939. *Statistical Testing of Business Cycle Theories, Vol. II: Business Cycles in the USA. 1919–9132*. Geneva: League of Nations.

women and work. Why is 'women and work' an issue? In the past, as in the present, most women, like most men, have worked for a living. But women's work, its particular historic development, its current content and location, and its meaning to its subjects and objects, is different from the work of men. Work is a gendered experience.

Women's work is distinguished primarily, though not exclusively, by their responsibility for certain tasks associated with daily and intergenerational reproduction. The cooking, cleaning, childcare, nursing and nurturing involved is a distinct labour in many ways: not least because it is unpaid. It has remained privatized even in advanced industrial economies whether organized by a plan or by the market, and in societies where planners' preferences or market prices index value, work which is neither planned nor marketed is undervalued, indeed often to the point of invisibility. It is not deemed to be work at all.

The differences between men's and women's work does not stop here. Paralleling the division of labour between men and women in unpaid work in the home is a division of labour by sex in paid work. Men and women are not randomly distributed across the employment structure. Rather there are men's jobs in which primarily men are engaged and women's jobs where the labour force is overwhelmingly female. There are few mixed occupations where men and women can be found in the same proportions as in the labour force as a whole.

A third significant dimension of women's jobs concerns their terms and conditions. They are less likely to be complemented by expensive capital equipment, thus less productive, more likely to be temporary and insecure, less likely to be organized, and less associated with prospects for promotion. Above all they are less well paid.

The implications of these characteristics for the economic position of women are clearly pernicious. In the home women are unpaid and unappreciated; in the workplace their relatively low wages make them vulnerable to poverty and deny them independence from state or family subsidies which are desperately needed if there are others dependent on their wages. Their higher labour market flows and sometimes disproportionate representation in unstable jobs make them especially subject to recession-enforced periods of nonparticipation or unemployment.

Massive empirical evidence documents these characteristics of women's work as universals within the advanced industrial world (OECD, 1985; ILO, 1985). There are outliers. Modern Sweden, the USSR, and most countries during wartime have achieved extraordinary female involvement in paid production. Ireland is out at the opposite extreme. Eastern European countries have less sexual segmentation and different jobs are feminized, but a sexual division of labour exists nonetheless. The deployment of women in some countries has to be seen as mediated by religion, but this usually compounds rather than mitigates the privatization, segmentation and subordination suggested here as universals.

The history of women's work can also be characterized in terms of stylized facts. Thus the painful and problematic transition of women from production for use to waged work, closely documented in the British case, can and has been paralleled in other national experiences (Pinchbeck, 1930; Tilly and Scott, 1978). Even countries at very different levels of development can be interpreted as exhibiting aspects of the same sexual divisions of labour if the comparison is with the historical experience of the now economically advanced countries.

So overwhelming is the evidence of a *generic* women's experience of work in both the past and the present that it has prompted explanations in terms of some universal, cross–cultural, historical model of female subordination often described as patriarchy. This and other sometimes integrated universalist explanations appealing to biological or psychological differences between the sexes constitutes the first explanatory framework reviewed below.

MODELS OF EXPLANATION

Patriarchy. Patriarchal models of explanation see male dominance and female subordination as an enduring characteristic of all societies, hence readily explaining the commonalities of experience. An important move here is the detachment of patriarchy from other class systems of dominance and subordination and the denial, in opposition to classical marxism, of the former's dependence logically and historically on private property (Delphy, 1977; Hartmann, 1976).

Much of the empirical debate has been anthropological, involving the operational definition of patriarchy and its identification in preclass societies. One question of interest here is whether a sexual division of labour in work itself constitutes patriarchy, or if separate but equal roles for men and women are feasible.

The enormous changes that have taken place in women's political, legal and economic status suggest that an immutable patriarchy is indefensible, and most recent presentations within this framework argue that while patriarchal power relations remain a constant their particular expressions, and perhaps their intensity, change with economic and social development. Much of this literature is concerned to specify the form of interaction between patriarchal power relations and class society while retaining the essential autonomy of male authority and control. Adherents of this model of explanation must argue that the subordination of women in advanced capitalism is explained not by the dominant mode of production but by patriarchal power relations operating through the family and the political system and within the social relations of production. Capitalism may exploit the divisions among the working class arising from patriarchy, but above all capitalism must adapt itself to a given system of sexual hierarchy. Thus the conditions of women's employment are primarily determined by the dominance of men and capital must adapt to a sex-differentiated wage hierarchy so that men's power in the domestic and political spheres is not contradicted in the workplace. Adaptation takes place despite the interests of capital in eroding male power and establishing a homogeneous competitive labour force. Alleged mechanisms of control have received attention: ideology and socialization as well as concrete institutions like schools and trade unions.

One of the major criticisms of patriarchy as an explanatory framework is that it contains no material explanation of women's position and ultimately the argument must devolve on biologism, psychoanalytic theory or cultural catalepsy. Another possibility is to see patriarchy itself as an economic class system with men as the appropriators of female labour-time: a prospectively rich but empirically underdeveloped approach that is unfortunately thwarted by the suspicion that much of women's potentially alienable labour time benefits children rather than fathers.

Whatever the origins of patriarchy, they are clearly independent of the capitalist mode of production. There is therefore truth in the argument that women's economic subordination has its roots in precapitalist forms and cannot be explained solely by functionalist reference to capitalism. The third conceptual framework reviewed below owes much to this challenge to classical marxism.

Neoclassical economics. Neoclassical economic theory tries to explain women's economic subordination in terms of rational utility-maximizing behaviour. The emphasis has been on the narrowly economic issues of women's labour supply, occupational distribution and relative pay. Neoclassical analysis of labour supply postulates an individual allocating his/her time between work and leisure. Leisure here is a catch-all term for all uses of time other than paid work but it is a peculiarly male label in view of the reality of domestic labour and the latter's impact on women's 'leisure'. Indeed, much of the neoclassical interest in female labour supply has occurred precisely because the question 'Why do paid work?' can meaningfully be asked of women, for they have the option of work in the home. The added dimension to women's choice set challenged neoclassical economists, who soon realized that female labour supply could not be modelled analogously to that of men and significant innovations with widespread repercussions for mainstream economics followed. Two relevant developments are sketched below.

First, recognition that simple reduced form models of female labour supply, drawing only on samples of working women, involved serious biases, prompted the development of structural models in which labour supply decisions were modelled as involving discrete quantitative choices about whether or not to work and how many hours to work. These second generation labour-supply models involved new techniques for handling discrete choices (logit, probit and tobit) and the introduction of the shadow or imputed wage to capture the influence of unobservable but relevant returns, for example, to non-market activities (Heckman, 1974; Heckman, Killingsworth and MaCurdy, 1981; Killingsworth, 1983).

As longitudinal data have become increasingly available, particularly in the United States, investigation has focused on lifetime experience and appropriate techniques for handling analyses of attachment to the labour force over the whole life cycle have been developed. Much empirical work has now been undertaken for the USA and UK providing important information regarding female labour supply.

However, the widespread use of personal characteristics and family circumstances as proxies for the tastes of individuals or the shadow wage of domestic work, indicates the limitations of the approach (Greenhalgh and Mayhew, 1981). Belief that these variables genuinely represent exogenous tastes or comparative advantages surely involves some dubious propositions about sex and race-linked biological endowments! However, the attachment of certain behavioural proclivities to variables like race, sex and the presence of small children may simply reflect rational expectations about discrimination or family opposition to waged work, or even historical differences in the relative earnings potential of men and women. Then labour supply cannot be taken as independent of demand-side variables or the organization of the family and a historic and interactive analysis between production and social reproduction must be undertaken.

A second development stemmed from recognition that husbands' and wives' decisions about work, leisure and homeproduction are interdependent, which contested the basis of neoclassical economic theory in the individual decision-maker. Simultaneously neoclassical economists, looking for new areas of behaviour to subject to their choice theoretic framework, lighted on fruitful terrain: the household. Becker's (1965) analysis of household decisionmaking in terms of his theory of the allocation of time produced the New Household Economics (NHE).

The NHE views the household as a production unit and consumption decisions as dictated by the drive to maximize utility. Various activities can contribute to utility and these activities require inputs of time and other goods. The ultimate product is the utility derived. All kinds of household decisions from the mundane to the consideration of whether to have children of certain qualities and quantities, have been cast in this framework. Economists' techniques can then be mobilized to describe the optimal allocation of time under certain assumptions about tastes and relative costs.

The value of the NHE lies in its explication of the link between labour supply decisions and consumption decisions and therefore between women's primary responsibility for work in the home and their partial and discontinuous involvement in paid work. Unfortunately the insight is not maintained. Other relevant problems are sidestepped or trivialized: for example, the deep difficulties involved in synthesizing a collective preference ordering from individuals' preferences are not addressed here despite the move from the individual to the household. One way out is to postulate a set of rules for aggregating and weighting individuals' preferences; another is to understand the collectivity's preference ordering as 'given' by an *individual* representative: 'the benevolent dictator' of welfare economics. Both methods abstract from the conflicts and complementarities among household members and, essentially, collapse household and individual decision-making. Moreover, feminists see the benevolent dictator as mirroring the dominant patriarchal form of family organization in society and, not surprisingly, are leery of closing the model by accepting the very hierarchy of authority that they want to question. Perhaps the recent interest in bargaining models of family relations (Pollak, 1985) will eventually help with these difficulties.

More importantly, the NHE cannot explain why the most efficient allocation of time by family members should involve a sexual division of labour between paid and unpaid work. Specialization is explained by comparative advantage, but the latter's suggested origins often make the argument circular: women hiring men as breadwinners because they earn more, but women earning less because they leave the labour market to have children (Becker, 1981). Alternatively the argument is sometimes shored up here by biologism: higher productivity in domestic labour simply being read off the female sex, or women's prior investment in children, since they carry them in the womb, being held to make them more inclined to further childcare investment (ibid). So comparative advantage is deduced from the existing sexual division of labour and then used to explain that division.

Neoclassical economics' treatment of the occupational distribution of women workers and their relative terms and conditions, suffers from similar defects. Briefly both occupational choice and relative wages are viewed as the outcomes of rational utility–maximizing behaviour. Indeed the former is often held as an 'explanation' of the latter as women's disproportionate representation in poorer paying jobs accounts for a substantial part of the male–female wage differential. Sometimes occupational choice and relative wages are analysed in the framework which subsumes them both into sex specific choices about levels of investment in human capital. Employers' discrimination has usually entered the argument only to explain the residual after the impact of other sex specific worker characteristics have been deducted.

Why do women choose certain occupations in preference to alternatives despite the fact that the resulting occupational distribution is (demonstrably) a major factor in their relatively low pay and poor terms of employment? An obvious defensive manoeuvre, and one which neoclassical economists have not ignored, despite its disturbing implications for the premise of rational-maximizing behaviour, is to cite pre–market discrimination as engineering women's choices, or cultural predispositions to study certain subjects as leading girls into less well-paid jobs. But these arguments are *non sequiturs* as far as economic explanations of women's subordination are concerned.

Human capital theory has also been used to explain such seemingly paradoxical choices as rational-maximizing behaviour. Polachek (1975, 1976) has argued that women *choose* occupations for which earnings losses during spells of non-participation are minimized. Since women plan intermittent paid work because of intended childrearing, they prefer occupations where skills depreciate only slowly when not employed. Women's primary responsibility for children is assumed in this model, as are differences in the rates of decay of human capital across occupations. Polachek's work has been subject to both theoretical and empirical criticism internal to his own paradigm (England, 1982; Beller, 1982). Radical reservations have also been expressed about the notion of productivity embedded in human capital theory. It is essentially a sexist concept since it only counts as productive those skills which the market rewards and many skills which women have go unrecognized (Dex, 1985).

To summarize: neoclassical economic theory confuses *descriptions* with *explanations* of the subordination of women. Moreover, cultural and even biological factors have sometimes been used as prime movers in the argument, despite the inconsistency of this procedure with a belief in the prime explanatory power of rational maximizing behaviour. This is not to deprecate the value of much neoclassical work on female labour supply, or the insights of the NHE, but as a model of explanation of either women's specialization in the home or the sexual division of labour in paid work, the approach is ultimately nugatory.

Neo-marxist economics. The neo-marxist approach developed out of the challenge to classical marxism's treatment of women's subordination posed by the persistence of patriarchal social relations. Interest was initially focussed on the articulation of unpaid work in the home to production relations in a capitalist economy and the meaning of the former for value categories: the domestic labour debate (Dalla Costa and James, 1972). How domestic labour should be integrated into value accounting represented a challenge to marxian value theory and to classical analyses of the natural price of labour (Himmelweit and Mohun, 1977). The domestic labour debate's attention to work done to reproduce workers and their labour power promoted new interest in the process of *social reproduction* more broadly defined (Kuhn and Wolpe, 1978). Consequently developments in the theory of the family have both drawn on and contributed to developments in the theory of the state Both have contributed to significant progress in neo-marxist understanding of advanced capitalism. It is interesting to note that neo-marxist interest too is now turning to bargaining models of the family.

Attention also spread to analyses of the relationship between women's primary responsibility for the reproductive work of the home and their position in paid labour. Concepts for classical marxism, such as the reserve army of labour, as well as from contemporary labour economics, such as labour market segmentation, have been especially useful in analyses of the impact of secular restructuring and the business cycle on women workers. Recent studies have tried to test whether women do constitute a buffer labour reserve over the business cycle or if their segregation in the less volatile sectors and occupations affords them relative protection in hard times (Bruegel, 1979). A third hypothesis which has received attention is whether women's cheapness in conjunction with their predominance in growing sectors is causing women to be substituted cyclically and secularly for men (Rubery, 1987).

These studies have developed a dual systems theoretic approach which sees women's economic subordination as the outcome of interaction between social reproduction and production. Although debate continues as to the precise specification of this interaction, key characteristics of the neo-marxist approach to understanding women's work include: (1) an insistence that social reproduction be taken seriously as work and as an integral part of the economy; (2) a conviction that social reproduction is relatively independent of the organization of production and does not respond smoothly, accommodatingly or predictably to the needs of the economy; (3) the deduction therefore that the relationship between the spheres of production and social reproduction can only be understood historically and is not predetermined; and (4) also that the relationship must be analysed within a nonfunctionalist perspective (Humphries and Rubery, 1984).

The approach is less methodologically hidebound and much more open-ended than that of neoclassical theory. Nevertheless developments within this literature have both drawn from and fed back into neoclassical economics. Moreover both approaches are forced to respond to the contemporary dramatic increases in female participation rates in advanced industrial economies and attempt to predict the implications for the unequal burden of domestic work, for occupational segregation, and for the terms and conditions of women's work.

CONCLUSION

As suggested above, interest in women's work is not only analytical. Social commentators of the past, as well as of the present, have attributed major significance to shifts in the allocation of women's labour time between the home and the workplace, though not always in agreement as to their implications. Contrast the oft-quoted view of Engels that 'The emancipation of women will only be possible when women can take part in production on a large social scale, and domestic work no longer claims anything but an insignificant amount of her time' (1891, p. 221) with the more traditional position of Marshall: 'If we compare one country of the civilized world with another, or one part of England with another, or one trade ... with another, we find that the degradation of the working classes varies almost uniformly with the amount of rough work done by women' (1961, p. 565).

Perhaps the reconciliation of these two distinguished views lies in consideration of the terms and conditions of women's paid work and how it is coordinated with childcare and domestic labour. Significantly it is college-educated women with their more interesting, better-paid jobs, who are able to purchase domestic help and high-quality childcare, who find work most enriching. For women as for men, one objective must be more interesting work. More contentious, in terms of the distribution of necessary labour time between the sexes, is the target of a more equal distribution of domestic responsibilities.

JANE HUMPHRIES

See also GENDER; LABOUR MARKET DISCRIMINATION.

BIBLIOGRAPHY

Becker, G. 1965. A theory of the allocation of time. *Economic Journal* 75, September, 493–517.

Becker, G. 1981. *A Treatise on the Family*. Cambridge, Mass.: Harvard University Press.

Beller, A. 1982. Occupational segregation by sex: determinants and changes. *Journal of Human Resources* 17(3), Fall, 371–92.

Bruegel, I. 1979. Women as a reserve army of labour: a note on recent British experience. *Feminist Review* (3), Autumn, 12–23.

Dalla Costa, M. and James, S. 1972. *The Power of Women and the Subversion of the Community*. Bristol: Falling Wall Press.

Delphy, C. 1977. *The Main Enemy: A Materialist Analysis of Women's Oppression*. London: Women's Research and Resources Centre.

Dex, S. 1985. *The Sexual Division of Work*. Brighton: Wheatsheaf.

Engels, F. 1891. *The Origin of the Family, Private Property and the State*. 4th edn. New York: International Publishers, 1972.

England, P. 1982. The failure of human capital theory to explain occupational sex segregation. *Journal of Human Resources* 17(3), Fall, 358–70.

Greenhalgh, C. and Mayhew, K. 1981. Labour supply in Great Britain: theory and evidence. In *The Economics of the Labour Market*, ed. Z. Hornstein, J. Grice and A. Webb, London: HMSO.

Hartmann, H. 1976. Capitalism, patriarchy and job segregation by sex. *Signs: Journal of Women in Culture and Society* 1(3), Pt 2, Spring, 137–69.

Heckman, J. 1974. Shadow prices, market wages and labor supply. *Econometrica* 42(4), July, 679–94.

Heckman, J., Killingsworth, M. and MacCurdy, T. 1981. Empirical evidence on static labour supply models. In *The Economics of the Labour Market*, ed. Z. Hornstein, J. Grice and A. Webb, London: HMSO.

Himmelweit, S. and Mohun, S. 1977. Domestic labour and capital. *Cambridge Journal of Economics* 1(1), March, 15–31.

Humphries, J. and Rubery, J. 1984. The reconstitution of the supply side of the labour market: the relative autonomy of social reproduction. *Cambridge Journal of Economics* 8(4), December, 331–46.

ILO. 1985. *World Labour Report*, Volume II. Geneva: ILO Publications.

Killingsworth, M. 1983. *Labour Supply*. Cambridge: Cambridge University Press.

Kuhn, A. and Wolpe, A. (eds) 1978. *Feminism and Materialism*. London: Routledge & Kegan Paul.

Marshall, A. 1961. *Principles of Economics*. 9th edn, London: Macmillan.

OECD. 1985. *The Integration of Women into the Economy*. Paris: OECD.

Pinchbeck, I. 1930. *Women Workers in the Industrial Revolution, 1750–1850*. London: Frank Cass, 1969.

Polachek, S. 1975. Discontinuities in labour force participation and its effects on women's earnings. In *Sex Discrimination and the Division of Labor*, ed. C. Lloyd, New York: Columbia University Press.

Polachek, S. 1976. Occupational segregation: an alternative hypothesis. *Journal of Contemporary Business Studies* 5(1), 1–12.

Pollak, R. 1985. A transaction cost approach to families and households. *Journal of Economic Literature* 23(2), June, 581–608.

Rubery, J. (ed.) 1987. *Women and Recession*. London: Routledge & Kegan Paul.

Tilly, L. and Scott, J. 1978. *Women, Work and Family*. New York: Holt, Rinehart & Winston.

women's wages. Women's average wages are consistently lower than men's average wages in all countries, even after adjustments for differences in working hours. These lower wages cannot be simply explained by differences in the productivity of women workers, or by the segregation of women into different jobs: they are related to the role of women in the social reproduction sphere, that is to their expected contributions to domestic labour and to family income. However, women's wages should not be identified as a separate issue; to do so suggests that it is women's wages that do not conform to a competitive norm and therefore require separate analysis as an anomaly. Women form too large a segment of the labour force for this 'anomaly' not to affect the other segment, 'male labour', and men's role in social reproduction has an equal and specific impact on their characteristics as wage labour. There is nevertheless an argument on social and political grounds for singling out women's wages for special study. Women's wages are not only low at the average or macro level, but also are consistently lower than men's at the micro level of the occupation, firm or industry. Women account for overwhelmingly the largest share of low-paid adult workers in the UK, so that ten years after the Equal Pay Act it is still reasonable to talk of a separate set of wages for women to that available to the majority of men.

NEOCLASSICAL EXPLANATION OF WOMEN'S WAGES. There are three different types of hypotheses that have been put forward within a neoclassical framework to explain women's lower wages. The first is the wage discrimination hypothesis, associated with Becker's (1971) work on racial discrimination, under which women are paid less than their marginal products to compensate either employers or co-workers for their distaste for female workers. The second and third hypotheses assume that women are paid relative to their actual marginal products; according to the second hypothesis women are less productive employees than male employees, and under the third hypothesis, women are employed in less productive jobs than men, but not necessarily because they are inherently less productive workers. The discrimination hypothesis of Becker was found to be rather difficult to reconcile with neoclassical theory unless one could assume all employers were equally discriminatory. A less or non-discriminating employer would be able to compete successfully against the established group of discriminating employers.

The second hypothesis is associated with human capital theory; women's lower wages are attributed to lower levels of educational training and perhaps more significantly, to their lack of continuous work experience which develops skills and also renews and updates them. Pre-market discrimination, in-market discrimination or personal and household preferences could all account for these different patterns of human capital acquisition, but whatever the cause the lower wages are taken to result directly from women's lack of skills relative to men's. Women's role as wives and mothers may have an indirect effect on productivity through lowering human capital acquisition, but there may also be a direct effect if women take prime responsibility for the family and they behave in ways which make them less committed and less productive workers, such as working only part-time hours or having a higher tendency to absenteeism or to voluntary quits.

One of the consequences of such characteristics might be that women are in fact confined to lower-productivity jobs, because of the difficulties of adjusting all jobs to meet different behaviour patterns and characteristics of workers. This 'confinement' may be a demand side phenomenon, employers making assumptions about women's behaviour patterns, or a supply-side phenomenon, women choosing jobs which allow them to carry out their domestic responsibilities. The origins of these different preferences or 'tastes' are taken either to be exogenous to the economy and outside the sphere of economics, or as in the New Household Economics, to arise out of the process of welfare maximization for the household, instead of for the individual. Thus one explanation of the third hypothesis, job segregation, is women's role in social reproduction.

Segregation may also be held to result because of either prejudice, based on custom and practice, about which jobs are suitable for women, or thirdly, because women have essentially different attributes or skills to those of men. All three versions of the job segregation hypothesis are compatible with a view that the jobs women do are low skilled, low productivity jobs, but with the latter two versions it could be the over-supply of women to a relatively narrow range of jobs which results in lower supply prices, more labour-intensive technology and consequently lower-marginal products (Mill, 1848; Bergman, 1971). According to these two versions if demand for labour in these types of jobs rose, women's wages would be expected to rise accordingly, but under the first social reproduction hypothesis, an increase in demand for labour in these type of jobs could stimulate substitution of women by more 'committed' and 'productive' workers. The hypothesis of job segregation through prejudice is open to the same objections as were raised against Becker's hypothesis; unless the basis for segregation is real differences in skills then it would be broken down eventually by non-prejudiced employers. The 'economics of information costs' has helped to restore this hypothesis by suggesting that it may be rational for employers to use cheap 'screens' such as sex in their recruitment decisions, to avoid hiring and firing costs. Women may be excluded from a segment of the labour market either because on average women have less desirable characteristics than men (Phelps, 1972), or because no women think it worthwhile to acquire the skills for entry into this segment, so the employers' beliefs remain untested (Spence, 1973).

It is, nevertheless, more comfortable for neoclassical economists to attribute low wages for women to supply-side characteristics, to differences in attributes or preferences arising out of biological or social and cultural factors, than to place the burden of explanation on demand-side imperfections which prevent the equalization of returns to productivity. Under neoclassical analysis the forces of competition will always be working towards undermining these demand-side constraints, but as economists offer no analysis of the forces of social and biological change, persistence of inequality can be more readily accounted for, and changes in the economic status of women can be attributed to exogenous changes in tastes. However it is this procedure that also reveals the weakness of neoclassical analysis (Humphries and Rubery, 1984); by eschewing the need to develop an analysis of the historical relationship between the organization of production and the organization of social reproduction, neoclassical theorists make adjustments to the preference functions in their models, not to take account of changes they have identified in the organization of social reproduction but to find a better fit for their model when the previous preference function fails to perform adequately. There is thus no theoretical basis for making these changes (Tarling, 1981). This critique of neoclassical methodology suggests that it may be more appropriate to consider women's preferences in the labour market as conditioned by past historical experience and responses to current opportunities than as an independent cause of low wages.

A second major problem with the neoclassical analysis of women's wages arises from its assumptions that relative wages reflect relative marginal products, so that the issue to be explained is why women workers have low marginal products. Clearly, therefore, all the critiques which apply to the marginal productivity approach to wage determination also apply here to the specific issues of women's wages. However this issue also highlights some of the deficiencies of the neoclassical approach. For example, the analytical framework is based on competitive wage determination, with market clearing, but historical and cross cultural empirical evidence suggests that the female wage labour market is rarely if ever cleared. Surveys indicate a high level of hidden unemployment amongst economically inactive women, so that there are still large supplies of labour available at current wage rates. Secondly, the neoclassical approach implies that wage relativities should reflect relative skills and relative efficiencies of labour. Women's wages are in practice remarkably uniform, displaying much lower dispersion at micro and macro levels than male wages. The exclusion of women from more skilled work only provides a partial explanation, as the usual practice is to place all women's jobs whatever their characteristics, and all women, regardless of their skill or experience, within a narrow band of pay at the bottom of the pay hierarchy (Craig et. al, 1985). Thirdly, if marginal products influence wages, changes in the ratio of female to male pay should come about as a result either of a change in the distribution of women within the labour market, or as a result of changes in demand or supply in the female labour market. In practice changes in the ratio have been associated, at least in Britain, more with social and institutional forces than with changes in labour market opportunities.

These considerations suggest that women's lower wages may be determined to some extent prior to the allocation of women to jobs, and independently of their characteristics and attributes. This proposition is taken up by two of the three non-neoclassical theories examined below, that is the patriarchy theory and the family wage theory. This type of approach was rejected by neoclassical theorist because it is not easily compatible with theories of competitive equilibrium. Segmentation theory, the other non-neoclassical perspective examined below, argues that there is in fact no necessary tendency for the system of competition to bring about equalization of returns to productivity for the labour employed.

NON-NEOCLASSICAL EXPLANATIONS OF WOMEN'S WAGES. Patriarchal theories of women's wages start from the assumption that the fundamental explanation of women's inferior position in the economic system is their inferior position in the social and cultural system. Patriarchal social relations existed prior to capitalism and capitalism has had to adapt to a patriarchal system (Hartman, 1979). Women earn lower wages than men in order that there should be no challenge to the system of authority within the family and the social and political structure. Employers share the patriarchal values of society, so that the system is not subject to challenge by profit-seeking entrepreneurs. Inequality in pay may be reinforced by the subordination of women in inferior or 'feminine' jobs, but the low wages do not arise out of the characteristics of the jobs but out of the characteristics of women's position in a patriarchal society.

In contrast, the labour market segmentation approach, in its simple form, locates the causes of female inequality in the process of uneven development of the capitalist economy. Women are concentrated in particular sections of the labour market, but unlike the neoclassical model of dualism, the origins of the division between the so-called 'primary' and 'secondary' sectors are not social and institutional imperfections which distort the market, but the requirements of the economic system itself (Doeringer and Piore, 1971). Primary employment sectors develop in order to maximize advantages from operating at efficient levels of capacity with a stable and fully-trained labour force. Fluctuations in demand are dealt with by subcontracting to secondary employment sectors. In addition, whole industries are located in the secondary sector if the demand for the product is generally variable and unstable. The explanation of the divergence between returns to labour in the two sectors is rooted in the operation of the economic system, but in this dual labour market model, the explanation of why women are concentrated in the secondary sector has to be looked for elsewhere. The radical version of labour market segmentation theory (Edwards, Gordon and Reich, 1975) provides an explanation both of the structuring of the labour market into primary and secondary sectors and of the allocation of women to the secondary portion. To forestall the development of class consciousness, capitalists, it is argued, segmented or divided the labour force by creating 'artificial' hierarchies or divisions. In order to minimize the likelihood of alliances being formed across these divides, workers with different social characteristics were allocated to different segments: hence the concentration of women and ethnic minorities in secondary segments.

In the family-wage approach the analysis of women's position in the family and social system is linked directly to the analysis of the forces of production (Humphries, 1977; Beechey, 1978). Reliance simply on Marx cannot provide an adequate theory of women's wages because of the absence of a theory of the family. In contrast to the predictions of Engels, the nuclear family failed to 'wither away' to produce a wage labour market of undifferentiated individuals. Instead individuals on the labour market are still reproduced within a sex-differentiated social and family system and within a social reproduction system which provides forms of income support to non-wage labour. It is the differences in men's and women's relationships to the social reproduction system that leads to their labour being supplied on different terms. Men's wages are based on the cost of their own social reproduction and that of their dependents, but women's wages are based on only part of the cost of their own reproduction, on the assumption that they have access to support from either their husbands or their fathers, an assumption which is reinforced by social security systems which deny married women access to income support in their own right.

The tendency for women's labour to be supplied at below the value of labour power (that is below the average cost of reproduction) has specific consequences for the mobilization and utilization of female labour within the productive system. Female labour will tend to be mobilized at times when there are strong competitive pressures on capital to restore the falling rate of profit and female labour will tend to be concentrated in those sectors where capital is under particular pressure to force the cost of labour down below the value of labour power. Individual households do not in fact exercise 'choice' over their sexual division of labour as women are confined to jobs which offer wages below the cost of average adult subsistence. Thereby the structure of wages in the productive sphere serves to reinforce the system of social organization on which it is founded.

Under this family wage hypothesis, therefore, the lower wages that women are paid derive primarily from their own social characteristics, in particular from their position in the family income system, and not from the characteristics of the jobs that they perform. Women's low wages are thus assumed in some sense to be independent of the jobs they perform, as in the patriarchy argument. However, contrary to the simple patriarchy notion, women's lower wages are identified as having a materialist base which relates both to their role in social reproduction and to their role in production. The lower wages are used not simply to reproduce patriarchal values but to serve competitive objectives. Thus even though low wages for women are not caused by different patterns of job allocation they may themselves lead to different patterns of female labour throughout the economy.

In order to develop a fully adequate theory of women's wages it is necessary to combine the insights of the family-wage hypothesis with the perspectives on job segregation offered respectively by the patriarchy and labour market segmentation approach. There is now a considerable body of empirical research which suggests that, at least in the UK, women's low wages cannot be explained by the characteristics of the jobs they perform. Many women's jobs require skills and experience, but these factors are not reflected in pay or grading of the jobs (West, 1982; Craig et al. 1985). Moreover, work carried out within the context of the labour process debate suggests that there is no direct relationship between the skill of a job, however measured, and its pay and status. The characteristics and the bargaining power of the workers employed are more important explanatory variables. Indeed in order to 'deskill' a job it may be necessary to employ workers of lower status and bargaining power. However the substitution of women for men in order to deskill jobs has not been a universal process, so we need to understand the limits to this process. It is here that patriarchal relations may play an important role in setting up boundaries between men's work and women's work which are only breached when economic or other social forces are strong enough to break down the customary division of labour by sex. Moreover when the old division of labour is broken down and a new division established, newly feminized jobs are quickly redefined as only suitable for women, and the new division of labour is rigidified by these social values and by the continuing differentials in male and female pay.

Segmentation theory helps to explain why the utilization of women within the production sphere is concentrated in specific areas. Within this approach, it is argued that capitalism is subject to a process of uneven development, with different systems of competition prevailing in and between different sectors of the economy. As competition cannot be reduced to simply cost minimization, there is no necessary tendency for the incentives to substitution to be such as to ensure equalization of wage costs between firms or categories of labour. However, once a firm or sector becomes organized around low wage labour that cost structure becomes built into its system of organization.

The incentive to substitute low wage labour for higher paid labour is constrained by the firm's other objectives; such substitution might endanger the overall efficiency of the firm, by increasing the likelihood of instability among the experienced labour force or by reducing overall cohesion and cooperation. Moreover labour markets are also regulated by trade union organization and government employment policy which reduce firms' discretion in both wages and employment decisions. The actual form of trade union organization and government labour regulations differ considerably between countries and have a major impact both on the established norm for female wages and on the specific ways in which female labour is utilized in the economy. Thus trade union wage policies, the type of legal minimum wage system and the employment protection and benefits associated with part-time work have an impact on the terms and conditions under which women are employed which is relatively independent of the characteristics of the jobs that they perform in any particular country.

Women's wages cannot be explained solely by reference to women's family position, as the wage levels are also influenced by the system of wage determination and employment protection that prevails in the labour market. It is significant that it is countries with more egalitarian trade union wage policies or more effective minimum wage policy that tend to have a higher earnings ratio for women to men although these always stop short of unity.

These higher ratios automatically raise women's contribution to family income, and as these higher pay levels become permanently established, so the dependence of the family on women's income is strengthened. However it is not clear whether differences in systems of family organization between countries are themselves a cause of differences in labour market earnings for women or an outcome of these differences. This issue raises important questions over the ways in which women's pay inequality could be reduced. It could be argued that as women's inferior economic status can be attributed primarily to their historical role as dependents in the family system, then it is to changes in family organization that we must look before any real progress in women's position can be made. If women were to become reliant on their own earnings for their subsistence, the 'natural price' of female labour would change in theory; however it is possible that this change would reduce the standard of living of many women unless there are mechanisms by which the necessary real wages to maintain current consumption standards could be secured in the labour market. Indeed it could be argued that increasing numbers of American women have been thrown into poverty because a change in family organization towards more single parent families has preceded the development of any effective mechanisms for women to improve upon the wage levels which relate to an outdated system of family organization. If instead gains for women are secured through trade union organization, government labour market regulations or other means, then these are likely to be relatively easily and quickly translated into a new family budget structure which then becomes a material basis for changes in women's social and family roles.

J. Rubery

See also GENDER; INEQUALITY BETWEEN THE SEXES; LABOUR SUPPLY OF WOMEN.

BIBLIOGRAPHY

Becker, G. 1971. *The Economics of Discrimination*. 2nd edn, Chicago: Chicago University Press.

Beechey, V. 1978. Women and Production: a critical analysis of some sociological theories of women's work. In *Feminism and Materialism*, ed. A. Kuhn and A.M. Wolpe, London: Routledge and Kegan Paul, 155-97.

Bergmann, B.R. 1971. The effect on white incomes of discrimination in employment. *Journal of Political Economy* 71(2) Mar-Apr., 294–313.

Craig, C. Garnsey, E. and Rubery, J. 1985. *Payment Structures in Smaller Firms: Women's Employment in Segmented Labour Markets*. Department of Employment Research Paper no. 48, London.

Doeringer, P. and Piore, M. 1971. *Internal Labour Markets and Manpower Analysis*.Lexington, Mass.: D.C. Heath.

Edwards, R. Reich, M. and Gordon, D.M. (eds.) 1975. *Labour Market Segmentation*. Lexington, Mass.: D.C. Heath.

Hartman, H. 1979. The unhappy marriage of Marxism and feminism: towards a more progressive union. *Capital and Class* 8, Summer, 1–33.
Humphries, J. 1977. Class struggle and the persistence of the working-class family. *Cambridge Journal of Economics* 1(3), September, 241–58.
Humphries, J. and Rubery, J. 1984. The reconstitution of the supply-side of the labour market: the relative autonomy of social reproduction. *Cambridge Journal of Economics* 8(4), 331–46.
Mill, J.S. 1848. *Principles of Political Economy*. 1st edn, London.
Phelps, E.S. 1972. The statistical theory of racism and sexism. *American Economic Review* 62(4) September, 659–61.
Spence, A.M. 1973. Job market signalling. *Quarterly Journal of Economics* 87(3), August, 355–74.
Tarling, R. 1981. The relationship between employment and output: where does segmentation theory lead us? In *The Dynamics of Labour Market Segmentation*, ed. F. Wilkinson, London: Academic Press, pp. 281–90.
West, J. (ed.) 1982. *Work, Women and the Labour Market*. London: Routledge & Kegan Paul.

Wood, Stuart (1853–1914). A member of a prominent Philadelphia Quaker family, Wood was briefly active in economics twice in his life. The first period was 1873–5, when he received at Harvard the first PhD in economics in the United States. The second period was 1888–90, when he wrote three first-class articles on wage theory. His primary interests during his adult life were in business and finance.

In the two years Wood was at Harvard he took courses in economics and its history, chiefly from Professor Charles Dunbar, and wrote an essay on 'A Review of the "Principles of Social Science" by Henry C. Carey'. It was not an impressive piece, even allowing for the time, the age (21) of the writer and the extreme vulnerability of the target.

It is all the more impressive that thirteen years later he wrote two fine articles on the marginal productivity theory and one on the history of the wages-fund theory. Wood must be acknowledged to be an independent discoverer of the marginal productivity theory, an honour he shares with Marshall, Edgeworth, Barone, Wicksell, Clark and other major economists. Wood's version was not mathematical, but it synthesized two important dimensions of substitution between capital and labour: the substitution between industries with different capital–labour ratios, and the substitution within enterprises. The formulation was a skilful synthesis incorporating consumer demands and factor supplies as well as technological substitution.

Wood's final contribution was a history of the wages-fund doctrine (which was to be treated no more penetratingly by Harvard's second PhD in economics, F.W. Taussig). Perhaps one should mention one other, involuntary role Wood played in the study of the history of economics: he was the victim of a thinly disguised, utterly unfounded charge of plagiarism (of Lord Lauderdale) in *The Journal of Political Economy* in 1894.

George J. Stigler

SELECTED WORKS

1888–9. A new view of the theory of wages. Pts I-II. *Quarterly Journal of Economics* 3, 60–86; 462–80.

1889. The theory of wages. *Publications of the American Economic Association* 4, 5–35.

1890. A critique of wage theories. *Annals of the American Academy of Political and Social Science* 1, 426–61.

BIBLIOGRAPHY

Stigler, G.J. 1947. Stuart Wood and the marginal productivity theory. *Quarterly Journal of Economics* 61, August, 640–49.

worker-managed economies. *See* LABOUR-MANAGED ECONOMIES.

Woytinsky, Wladimir Savelievich (1885–1960). Wladimir Woytinsky was born in St Petersburg, Russia, on 12 November 1885, the son of a professor of mathematics at a polytechnic college. Tutored at home until he was fourteen, at high school he was a brilliant student and in 1904 entered St Petersburg University to read law.

While still in high school he had written *Market and Prices*, which was published with a foreword by Tugan-Baranovsky (it gained another foreword, by Jacob Marschak, when it was translated and published four years after his death). As a subjectively original contribution to neoclassical economic theory its long technical discussion of demand theory and spatial competition made it respectable but unremarkable, but as a schoolboy's performance it was quite extraordinary.

By the time the book was published in 1906 'I turned the pages as though they had been written by a complete stranger' (1962, p. 9). The bloody riots of 1905 had shocked Woytinsky into revolutionary activity as a member – 'Sergei Petrov' – of the Bolshevik wing of the Social Democrats (S-D), though he seems never to have been a full marxist in his economics. He was in and out of Tsarist prisons for the next several years (including the notorious Ekaterinoslav Castle) and in the intervals continued his S-D activity, such as organizing public works for the unemployed in St Petersburg. Eighteen months after his last arrest he was sentenced in the summer of 1909 to four years of forced labour, to be followed by deportation for life to Siberia.

Most of his time in Siberia was spent out of jail, and in 1916 he met and married an energetic young woman, Emma Shadkhan, who became his devoted assistant and co-author for the rest of his life. When the Revolution broke out in 1917 he returned to Petrograd and began to work for the Menshevik wing of the S-D, influenced in particular by Tseretelli. He spent some time as an editor of Izvestia and then became the Provisional Government's Commissar on the Northern Front. After the fall of that Government in November he was arrested by Trotsky himself but released early in 1918. In disguise, he and his wife fled with Tseretelli to Georgia, where Woytinsky was asked to edit the political newspaper *Bor'ba*.

In August 1920 he became economic adviser to a Georgian delegation to the countries of Western Europe, and he travelled with them until soon after Georgia was absorbed into the USSR in 1921. He settled in Germany in 1922, began work as a private economic journalist, and with Ladislaus von Bortkiewicz as editorial adviser, produced the massive *Die Welt in Zahlen* (The World in Figures), which established his reputation in Germany. In 1928 he was asked to direct the statistical department of the General Federation of Labour Unions and to act as its economic consultant, which brought him into contact with many German Social Democrats. With the onset of the Great Depression his advocacy of public works financed by budget deficits received approval from economists such as Gerhard Colm but met with considerable opposition in the party, especially from Rudolf Hilferding.

Hitler's mass arrest of union leaders in 1933 convinced Woytinsky to leave Germany. 'I was a foreigner, a Russian Jew active in the German labour movement' (1961, p. 477). After brief stops in Switzerland and France he joined the International Labour Office (I.L.O) in Geneva for a year and then, in 1935, the couple left for the United States, where he worked for the Central Statistical Board (1935–6), the

Committee on Social Security of the Social Science Research Council (1936–41), and finally the Social Security Administration itself (1941–7). His career ended as a research director for the Twentieth Century Fund, combined with a research professorship at Johns Hopkins University. He died on 10 June 1960, in Washington, DC.

Woytinsky's main professional output consisted of massive compendia of economic statistics produced mostly by him and his wife working alone, a form of work and publication that for better or worse is now quite out of fashion in economics. His other published studies were mostly concerned with current economic and social policy and their interest was largely ephemeral. So his work seems unlikely to be remembered; but his life exemplifies what can happen in this terrible century to an intellectual with a social conscience.

PETER NEWMAN

SELECTED WORKS

1906. *Rynok i tsieny*. St. Petersburg, with a foreword by M.I. Tugan-Baranowsky. Translated by Emma Woytinsky as *Market and Prices. Theory of Consumption, Market and Market Prices*, with an additional foreword by Jacob Marschak, New York: Augustus M. Kelley, 1964. (Curiously, this translation nowhere contains the Russian title of the original book, either transliterated or in cyrillic.)

1925–8. *Die Welt in Zahlen*. 7 vols, Berlin: R. Mosse.

1926. *Die vereinigten staaten von Europa*. Berlin: J.H.W. Dietz nachf.

1935. *Three Sources of Unemployment*. Geneva: ILO.

1936. *The Social Consequences of the Economic Depression*. Geneva: I.L.O.

1939. *Seasonal Variations in Employment in the United States*. Washington, DC: Social Science Research Council.

1942. *Three Aspects of Labor Market Dynamics*. Washington, DC: Social Science Research Council.

1943. *Earnings and Social Security in the United States*. Washington, DC: Social Science Research Council.

1953. (With associates.) *Employment and Wages in the United States*. New York: Twentieth Century Fund.

1955. (With E.S. Woytinsky.) *World Commerce and Governments; Trends and Outlook*. New York: Twentieth Century Fund.

1962. *Stormy Passage*. Introduction by A.A. Berle. New York: Vanguard Press.

BIBLIOGRAPHY

Woytinsky, E.S. (ed.) 1962. *So Much Alive; The Life and Work of Wladimir S. Woytinsky*. New York: Vanguard Press.

X

X-efficiency theory. One has to distinguish the X-efficiency concept from the theory intended to explain it. As a concept X-inefficiency is similar to technical inefficiency. Leibenstein originated the concept of X-inefficiency because of a belief that there is nothing technical about the most substantial sources of non-allocative inefficiencies in organizations. At the time of the original article (Leibenstein, 1966), it seemed that no available concept, such as organizational inefficiency or motivational inefficiency, implied all the elements that could be involved in non-allocative inefficiencies. Hence, the comprehensive term, 'X-inefficiency', was used.

X-efficiency theory represents a line of reasoning based on postulates that differs from standard micro theory. A brief statement of the postulates and other elements of the theory follows. (a) *Relaxing Maximizing Behaviour*: it is assumed that some forms of decision making, such as habits, conventions, moral imperatives, standard procedures, or emulation, can be and frequently are of a non-maximizing nature. They do not depend on careful calculation. Other decisions attempt at maximizing utility. In order to deal with the max/non-max mixture we use a psychological law, the Yerkes–Dodson Law, which essentially says that at low pressure levels individuals will not put much effort into carefully calculating their decisions, but as pressure builds they move towards more maximizing behaviour. At some point too much pressure can result in disorientation and a lower level of decision performance. (b) *Inertia*: we assume that functional relations are surrounded by inert areas, within which changes in certain values of the independent variables do not result in changes of the dependent variable. (c) *Incomplete Contracts*: we assume the employment contract is incomplete in that the payment side is fairly well specified but the effort side remains mostly unspecified. (d) *Discretion*: we assume both that employees have effort discretion within certain boundaries, and that the firm, through its top management, has discretion with respect to working conditions and some aspects of wages.

Under these postulates the firm does not control all of the variables. Rather, the variables are controlled by employees on the one side, and management on the other; both jointly determine the outcome. Thus, this is a standard game-theory type problem. Given the postulates it is easy to suggest that a latent Prisoner's Dilemma problem exists. Employees have an incentive to move towards the minimum-tolerated effort level (E) and the firm has the incentive to move towards the minimum-tolerated working-condition-wage level (W). This is illustrated in Figure 1, where the discretionary effort options run from E_1 to E_n, $E_1 < E_i \cdots < E_n$, and the discretionary working-condition – wage options run from W_1 to W_n, $W_1 < W_i \cdots < W_n$. Under individual maximizing behaviour employees would want to end up at E_1, and the firm would want to offer W_1. This is the Prisoner's Dilemma solution. The optimal solution is $E_n W_n$. However, the theory argues that in general the Prisoner's Dilemma solution will be avoided. The reason is that a system of conventions, which depends on the history of human relations within the firm, is likely to lead to an outcome that is usually intermediate between the Prisoner's Dilemma outcome and the optimal solution. In Figure 1 the line with the arrow *MG* represents a locus (one of many) of 'mutual gain' situations. That is, for any point on the locus there is a point further up in the direction of the arrow that involves greater effort, greater firm revenues, and a division of the increase in quasi-rents such that both wages and profits are improved. In other words, both the employees and the firm can gain.

We should note that for every effort option that employees choose the firm will want to choose the minimum wages and working conditions, W_1. Similarly, for every W the firm chooses the employees will want to choose E_1. This is the Prisoner's Dilemma outcome, which the arguments that follow will suggest is not likely to occur. However, this adversarial-relations problem between employees and managers is compounded by another free-rider problem. Every employee has a free-rider incentive to move to the tolerated minimum level E_1, even though he or she might want others to work effectively. Since all employees and managers face these incentives, overall effort would be reduced to the minimum if they all followed their individual self-interest. Clearly, in this organizational situation individual rationality cannot solve the Prisoner's Dilemma problem. Something akin to 'group rationality' (see Rapoport, 1970) is required to achieve an improved solution.

A formal theory of conventions (social norms) has been developed in recent years based on the work of T. Schelling, D. Lewis, and E. Ullman-Margalit. The basic ideas are that conventions should be viewed as solutions to multi-equilibrium, coordination problems, and that conventions can provide superior solutions to the Prisoner's Dilemma outcome. An example is whether automobiles should be driven on the left or the right. Everyone driving on the right is a desired outcome, and everyone driving on the left is a desired outcome, but a mixture of left-hand and right-hand driving has a negative payoff. Obviously, a convention is required to choose between all left-hand or all right-hand driving. A coordinated solution is superior to an uncoordinated outcome. However, the various coordinated solutions that are possible need not be equally good. Thus, different times of starting work may not be equally preferred, but a coordinated time may still be preferred to an uncoordinated time. Hence, the conventional hours of starting work need not be optimal.

The point of all this is that effort conventions and working-condition conventions can bring about a non-Prisoner's Dilemma solution. This is shown by the point C in Figure 1. The circle surrounding the point represents the inert area surrounding the solution. The distance between C and $E_n W_n$ represents the degree of X-inefficiency in the system. Thus, the effort convention is a coordinated solution that is superior to uncoordinated individual behaviour. Similar remarks hold for managerial decisions. Of course, the value of

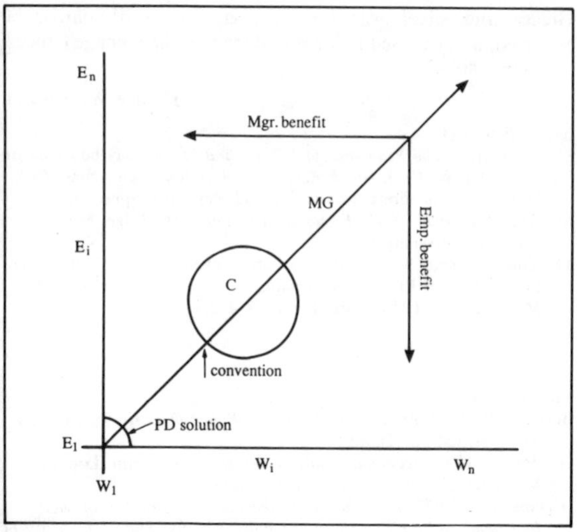

Figure 1

W has to be viable in the sense that it must represent a long-run profitable outcome, although not necessarily the maximum profit level.

There is a difference between the creation of a convention and adherence to it. The creation may come about through various means, such as the leadership of some managers, or some employees, or by some initial effort levels being chosen arbitrarily. Once established, a convention reduces the flexibility of employees' behaviour. Thus, new employees will adhere to the convention, and possibly support it through sanctions on others.

Although stable to small changes of its independent variables, an effort convention need not stay at its initial level indefinitely. The concept of inert areas suggests that a large enough shock can destabilize a convention. Once destabilized it is no longer clear whether the dynamics of readjustment will lead to a superior or inferior situation for both sides, or a situation under which one side gains at the expense of the other. Such considerations (and fears) help to stabilize the convention.

It is of interest to note that under low-pressure conditions the postulate of non-maximizing behaviour enables us to recognize and understand why firm members may stick with their conventions and impose supporting sanctions even in situations where they would be better off not doing so. Non-calculating, situation-response behaviour helps to shore up the convention-solution to the Prisoner's Dilemma problem, and to shore up the persistence of nonoptimal conventions. This helps to explain the existence and persistence of X-inefficient behaviour.

An illustration of X-inefficient behaviour was described in an article in the *New York Times* (13 October 1981) that compared two identically designed Ford plants, one in the UK and one in Germany, both designed to produce the identical automobile utilizing the same manpower and equipment. Nevertheless, the German plant produced 50 per cent more automobiles than its UK counterpart with 22 per cent *less* labour. Despite the identical plant design, the different effort conventions help to explain the X-inefficient result in the UK plant.

The theory permits a number of inferences to be drawn, some of which (stated without proof) are as follows. Firms generally operate *within* rather than *on* their production frontiers. Given the output, costs per unit are generally not minimized. Innovations are generally not introduced when it is optimal to do so. Less output is not necessarily associated with more desired leisure. The price of the product can have an influence on the cost of production.

There have been a number of measurements of X-inefficiency and empirical tests of its inferences. Professor Roger Frantz (1987) has estimated that over fifty empirical studies exist that either measure the degree of X-inefficiency or provide econometric results that help to confirm the theory.

HARVEY LEIBENSTEIN

BIBLIOGRAPHY

Frantz, R. 1987. *X-Efficiency: Theory, Evidence, and Applications.* New York: Kluwer-Nyhoff.

Leibenstein, H. 1966. Allocative efficiency vs. 'X-efficiency'. *American Economic Review* 56, June, 392–415.

Leibenstein, H. 1976. *Beyond Economic Man.* Cambridge, Mass.: Harvard University Press.

Leibenstein, H. 1982. The Prisoner's Dilemma in the invisible hand: an analysis of intrafirm productivity. *American Economic Review* 72(2), May, 92–7.

Leibenstein, H. 1987. *Inside the Firm: The Inefficiencies of Hierarchy.* Cambridge, Mass.: Harvard University Press.

Lewis, D. 1969. *Convention: A Philosophical Study.* Cambridge, Mass.: Harvard University Press.

Rapoport, A. 1970. *N-Person Game Theory.* Ann Arbor: University of Michigan Press.

Schelling, T. 1960. *The Strategy of Conflict.* Oxford: Oxford University Press.

Ullman-Margalit, E. 1977. *The Emergence of Norms.* New York: Oxford University Press.

Xenophon (*c*430 BC–*c*355 BC). Xenophon was a disciple of Socrates who made a name for himself as a military and political leader. Although he was a man of action rather than a philosopher, he wrote on many subjects and some of his writings touch on economic matters – the division of labour, management, the nature of wealth, public finance, and the relationship between gold and silver. In the *Cyropaedia*, a work ostensibly devoted to the education of a prince, Xenophon comments on the excellence of the king's table, where everything is prepared by specialists. He then goes on to elaborate this thought, stresses the advantages of the division of labour as far as the quality of goods is concerned, and makes the division of labour limited by the extent of the market:

> In small towns, the same workman makes chairs and doors and plows and tables, and often this same artisan builds houses, and even so he is thankful if he can only find employment enough to support him. And it is, of course, impossible for a man of many trades to be proficient in all of them. In large cities, on the other hand, inasmuch as many people have demands to make upon each branch of industry, one trade alone, and very often even less than a whole trade, is enough to support a man (Book VIII, s. ii, 4–6).

Xenophon's reference to the matter differs from that of Plato in that he does not relate the division of labour to human inequality and the stratification of society. Marx, who was of the opinion that Adam Smith had not contributed anything new about the division of labour (*Capital*, Vol. 1, ch. 12, s. 3), cited Xenophon's passage in full (ibid., s. 5).

Xenophon, a soldier and gentleman farmer, assembled thoughts on the management of farms and households in *The*

Economist, the opening chapter of which contain an enquiry into the meaning of wealth. According to Xenophon, a man's wealth is only what benefits him or what he knows to use. A true gentleman should engage in agriculture and war, not in mechanical arts, which do damage to mind and body. John Ruskin found much to praise in this work, especially the view about wealth (1876, p. xxxix), which has parallels also in J.A. Hobson's *Work and Wealth* (1914).

Xenophon is also credited – although not unanimously – with the authorship of *Ways and Means to Increase the Revenues of Athens*, an early essay in the field of public finance, in which numerous suggestions are made to realize the goal indicated in the title. Xenophon proposes to admit a larger number of guest workers, improve the port facilities, construct markets and inns for visitors, establish a government-owned merchant fleet, increase the production of silver by the government-owned mines, and have the city acquire slaves to be hired out to private users. His plea for government enterprise has occasionally been commented upon and he has been called a mercantilist. Opportunity for comment is also provided by his view about the respective merits of gold and silver. Silver, he states, will never lose its value, while an abundance of gold will cause its value to fall and that of silver to rise. Implied here are visions of demand and supply and of an equilibrating mechanism; as for the substance of his view about gold and silver, modern authorities accept it as plausible in the light of the conditions of the time, when Persian gold coins circulated more freely in Greece and silver was apt to disappear into hoards, be exported, and exposed to wear and tear on the coinage (Burns, 1927, pp. 467–72).

HENRY W. SPIEGEL

SELECTED WORKS

Selections from *The Economist* and *Ways and Means* may be found in:

Laistner, M.L.W. 1923. *Greek Economics*. London: Dent; New York: Dutton. Translations from the second work also appear in:

Monroe, A.E. 1924. *Early Economic Thought*. Cambridge, Mass.: Harvard University Press.

The complete texts with translations are conveniently available in the Loeb Classical Library, Xenophon, *Works*, 7 vols, Cambridge, Mass.: Harvard University Press, 1914–25.

BIBLIOGRAPHY

Burns, A.R. 1927. *Money and Monetary Policy in Early Times*. New York: Alfred A. Knopf.

Gordon, B. 1975. *Economic Analysis Before Adam Smith*. London: Macmillan; New York: Barnes & Noble.

Higgins, W.E. 1977. *Xenophon the Athenian: The Problem of the Individual and the Society of the Polis*. Albany: State University of New York Press.

Lowry, S.T. 1987. *The Archeology of Economic Ideas*. Durham, North Carolina: Duke University Press.

Ruskin, J. (ed.) 1876. *Xenophon's The Economist*. Trans. A.D.O. Wedderburn and W.G. Collingwood, *Bibliotheca Pastorum*, Vol. 1, London: Allen & Unwin.

Tozzi, G. 1961. *Economisti greci e romani*. Milan: Feltrinelli.

Y

Yntema, Theodore O. (1900–1985). Yntema was born on 8 April 1900 and died on 18 September 1985. He distinguished himself in the academic world as well as in the worlds of public policy and of business. His training was as varied as his career: he received an AM degree in chemistry in 1922, became a CPA in 1924, an AM in business in 1924, and a PhD in economics in 1929. His PhD thesis, *A Mathematical Reformulation of the General Theory of International Trade* – still in print in 1985 – is an elegant mathematical extension to the field of international trade, of Alfred Marshall's price theory for a domestic economy. The year after receiving his Master's degree in chemistry he began a 25-year academic career at the University of Chicago. After one decade in accounting, he served a second decade as Professor of Statistics, a post which for three years he combined with that of Director of Research of the Cowles Commission for Research in Economics. The last five years he served as Professor of Business and Economic Policy, an area in which he could draw upon his wide experience as economic consultant to United States Government agencies and to private companies. During 1942–9 he served as Director of Research, and, in 1961–7, as Chairman of the Research and Policy Committee, of the Committee for Economic Development (CED), shaping it into one of the most influential public organizations in the field of economic and social policy. In 1949 he embarked upon a new career, going to the Ford Motor Company as Vice-President and Director, and serving as Chairman of its Finance Committee during 1961–5. In that capacity, he was responsible for introducing highly innovative systems of financial management and for the recruitment and supervision of a group of so-called 'whiz kids' who helped to revitalize the company, two of whom subsequently became Presidents of the company.

JACOB L. MOSAK

Young, Allyn Abbott (1876–1929). Allyn Young's career presents a puzzle. He is best known to modern readers, if at all, as the author of one much-reprinted article on 'Increasing Returns and Economic Progress' (1928). With such a narrow base his present fame can of course hardly compare with that of some other leading American economists of his day, such as Irving Fisher, Frank Knight, Wesley Mitchell and Thorstein Veblen. Yet during his life he was very highly regarded indeed, and not just by a US economics profession more insular then than now. To Schumpeter, 'his published work ... [does] ... not convey any idea of the width and depth of his thought and still less of what he meant to American economics' (1954, p. 875, n23). To Keynes, in a letter of consolation to Young's widow, 'His was the outstanding personality in the economic world and the most lovable' (Blitch, 1983, p. 22). To Ohlin, he was 'a man, who knew and thoroughly understood his subject – economics – better than anyone else I have ever met' (ibid., p. 14). The London School of Economics, in the mid-1920s flush with Rockefeller money and looking to make an 'appointment to the new chair [that] should be so eminent as to be the basis of a major expansion', chose Young 'after a prolonged search of the English-speaking world' (Robbins, 1971, p. 119).

Unlike those other American economists, he never wrote a book. Although he was an incorrigible contributor to such general compendia as the *Encyclopaedia Britannica* and *The Book of Popular Science*, and to such lesser magazines as the *Annalist* and *The Cornell Civil Engineer*, he wrote few major articles. One reason might have been that, as Keynes remarked in the same letter, he 'would always share with others all his best ideas ... it was his own work ... which always came last' (Blitch, 1983, pp. 22–3). Indeed, much of his best work was done through others, two of the great books in economic theory in the first half of this century, Knight (1921) and Chamberlin (1933), originating as doctoral dissertations written under his supervision. Thus like R.F. Kahn, though in the other Cambridge, Young remained an 'elusive figure who hides in the prefaces of Cambridge books' (Samuelson, 1947, p. 329).

His peculiar choices of what and how to publish are therefore one explanation of why today he is a minor figure; but they are not the whole, nor perhaps even the major, explanation.

LIFE. Allyn Abbott Young was born in Kenton, Ohio, on 18 September 1876, the eldest child of two schoolteachers; his given names were the surnames of his two grandmothers. His father was also a lawyer, and active in the midwestern debates on 'free silver' which were part of the political phenomenon that was William Jennings Bryan (see Blitch, 1983, to whose article most of these biographical details are due; Dorfman (1959, pp. 222–33) is also useful, but sometimes inaccurate). A prodigy, Young entered Hiram College in Ohio at 14 and graduated at 17, having studied languages as well as mathematics and physical sciences. After graduation he worked as a printer for some years in Ohio and Minnesota and saved enough money to further his education, so it was perhaps no accident that the chief example in his famous article (1928) was the printing trades.

In the fall of 1898 he entered the graduate programme in economics at the University of Wisconsin, then and for many years later a major centre of institutional economics. Richard Ely, his chief teacher, was so impressed by Young's ability that in 1899 he secured for him a 15 months' internship with the staff of the Twelfth Census in Washington, where he met and formed fast friendships with, among others, Wesley Mitchell and Walter Willcox, a professor at Cornell. In the fall of 1900 he returned to Madison and two years later obtained the PhD with a thesis on 'age statistics'. Two years after that he married a girl from Madison.

Young was unusually restless for the whole of his academic career, which began in 1902. He first spent two years at Western Reserve University in Cleveland, then one at

Dartmouth College, one back at Wisconsin, four at the new Stanford University (where he was the first chairman but failed twice to persuade President Jordan that Veblen should be promoted to full professor), one as a visitor at Harvard, and two as chairman at Washington University in St Louis. The pace slowed somewhat with his appointment in 1913 at Cornell, but even there he took leave of absence for two years in 1918–19 to work with the Wilson Administration on preparations for the peace conference (Blitch has a long account of this episode). He received the traditional 'call from Harvard' in 1920 but instead returned dutifully to Cornell. However, the next year he yielded to the renewed invitation of the Harvard department and soon became one of its most popular and respected members, among faculty and graduate students alike.

But Young was too complex a man to stay long even at Harvard, that absorbing barrier of so many academic random walks. Instead, he accepted the attractive offer from London, for a period of three years and at a salary well above the usual English professorial level (Blitch says that 'It was the first time that a chair in a British university had been offered to an American'). Unfortunately, according to Robbins (1971, 121), Young 'gave ... the impression of a profoundly unhappy man' in the job, and in fact decided to return to Harvard when his three years were up, in spite of a handsome offer from Chicago. Tragically, in the winter of 1928–9 he became a victim of a severe influenza epidemic and very quickly succumbed to pneumonia, dying in London on 7 March 1929 at the early age of 52.

CHARACTER. In appearance Young was tall and thickset, looking according to E.S. Mason 'more of a poet than an economist' (Blitch, 1983, p. 13). He was well-read in his own subject and many others, a musician, 'singularly unworldly', and famously absent-minded, sometimes having to be summoned to his lectures by colleagues or students.

His reputation stood very high as a teacher, but perhaps more as a supervisor of dissertations and discussant of work in progress than as a formal lecturer, where apparently he was given to long silences while he puzzled out what he wanted to say. Lauchlin Currie said that he 'gave the impression of *thinking* as he went along' (Blitch, 1983, p. 14). Such teaching was more suited to graduates or brilliant undergraduates like Kaldor than to an average undergraduate audience, and Robbins's report of the same style as Young practised it in England was distinctly cool: 'The more frivolous spirits ... would compile betting books on the length in seconds of the longest interval.' He was still harsher on Young's poor administrative ability: 'after his untimely death ... [there was] ... a condition of almost unimaginable confusion, no order or system anywhere' (1971, p. 120).

In spite of this alleged lack, Young seems to have been a successful chairman at Stanford and in St Louis. Moreover, he was a loyal member of his profession, serving as Secretary of the American Economic Association (AEA) from 1914 until 1920, as President of the American Statistical Association in 1917, and in 1925, after Veblen had refused the position (Dorfman, 1934, 491–2), as President of the AEA. His most famous paper (1928) was actually delivered as the Presidential Address of Section F of the British Association, 'the first American to be so honored' (Blitch, 1983, p. 18).

His feelings of loyalty may on occasion have affected his judgement. As a member of Wilson's delegation to the Peace Conference in 1919 he had independently arrived at much the same position towards the Treaty that Keynes developed with such force in *The Economic Consequences of the Peace*, but unlike Keynes could not bring himself to make a clean break with his government. On his return to the US he reviewed Keynes' book in the *New Republic* (1919–20), and privately protested to Keynes at the latter's account of Wilson's behaviour. Keynes wrote a placatory reply, saying that 'I still believe that essentially the President played a nobler part at Paris than any of his colleagues' (1977, p. 45). In what he later called 'an indiscretion which I regret' (ibid., p. 48), at a public debate Young quoted without permission from Keynes's letter, inadvertently making it appear that in the *Consequences* Keynes had consciously distorted the truth about Wilson for his own propagandist purposes. Keynes was furious – 'Young was very wrong ... to make reference to a private letter' – and threatened to publish the whole correspondence. However, Young finally wrote a letter of apology to the New York *Evening Post*, which to Keynes seemed 'quite satisfactory ... I am now quite content to let the matter drop' (ibid., p. 49).

Forgiven, then; but not forgotten. In *A Revision of the Treaty* (1922, p. 3n) Keynes first quoted the reference in Young's original review to the Treaty's 'timorous failure to reckon with economic realities', and then scathingly remarked: 'Yet Professor Young has thought right, nevertheless, to make himself a partial apologist of the Treaty, and to describe it as a "forward-looking document".' Young reviewed the new book, wrote an irenic letter to Keynes (Harrod, 1951, p. 312) and the episode finally closed, apparently (to judge from Keynes's letter to Young's widow) without seriously affecting their mutual regard.

WORKS. Young's range as an economist was unusually wide, even in an age when it was easier to be at the frontier of research in several fields than it is now. Beginning in what would now be called demography (1900–1901), he worked and published in several areas of applied economics, such as public utility regulation, anti-trust policy, banking, index-numbers, public finance, income distribution, and problems of war finance and reparations (e.g. 1922–3). In the nature of the case however, little of this applied work was of lasting importance, and so rather unjustly it will be his work in theory and doctrine that receives attention here.

It is typical of him that Young should have made his first major theoretical impact with two review articles, rather than with independently original work. The first, appearing in 1912 when he was already 36 and an established member of the profession, was a review of the Fourth Edition of Jevons's *Theory of Political Economy*, appearing 40 years after the original edition of 1871. Thus Young's review (reprinted in 1927) was perforce an essay in the history of economic thought rather than current economics. As such it was a penetrating contribution, well worth reading today and by no means inferior to some modern assessments of Jevons.

Matters were quite different with the second review article (1913), on Pigou's recently published *Wealth and Welfare*. It was this that made Young's international reputation, for he was the first to point out a basic flaw in Pigou's reasoning. The excess of 'marginal supply price' over supply price that Pigou saw as a reason for taxing decreasing returns industries, turned out to be in Young's argument almost entirely a matter of those increases in rents of the relatively scarcer factors by which necessary transfers of resources are accomplished, and certainly does not correspond to increased real usage of resources. The international impact of this fundamental criticism was probably all the greater because at that time one did not look for such subtle general equilibrium reasoning to come from the heavily empirically-minded US profession. However, for reasons which were hardly Young's fault, it failed to sweep away as it should all arguments of the Pigovian kind, so that later Young's student Knight (1924) felt impelled to repeat essentially the same point, in an article that is today much better known than Young's original criticism (see RISING SUPPLY PRICE).

It is curious that Young did not see fit to reprint this article in his collection (1927), which included far inferior pieces. A kind and modest man, possibly he did not want to upstage his friend Knight's recently published article on the same subject. It is far more likely however, that he did not want to give renewed currency to a view which, in 1927, he almost certainly no longer held. To Pigou's claim (1912, p. 177) that 'Provided that certain external economies are common to all the suppliers jointly, the presence of increasing returns in respect of all together is compatible with the presence of diminishing returns in respect of the special work of each severally', Young had in 1913 made the terse dismissive comment that 'I cannot imagine "external economies" adequate to bring about this result' (p. 678n). But it was precisely Young's vivid and convincing vision of such external economies as the main vehicle of increasing returns and economic progress that was the centrepiece of his famous article a year later, in 1928.

Between 1913 and 1928 Young contributed no major articles in economic theory. One reason may have been his work on Ely's *Outlines of Economics*, which with Thomas Adams and Max Lorenz he had helped to revise in 1908 and whose revisions he supervised in 1916 and 1923, writing the whole of ten chapters and parts of others (Dorfman, 1959, p. 222 n 2). This work was by far the most popular college textbook in economics in America, selling a total of 350,000 copies and outstripping its chief rival (Taussig's *Principles*) by two to one (ibid., p. 211n). Of much greater importance must have been his work arising from the Peace Conference, which seems to have preoccupied him for several years from 1918 on.

His paper of 1928 is not quite the isolated phenomenon that it appears. Several of his contributions to the great 14th edition (1929) of the *Encyclopaedia Britannica* are consistent with the approach taken in (1928), particularly his entry on Capital. This is not surprising, for the chief analytical innovation in (1928), as distinct from its new 'vision' of economic progress, was to make the degree of roundaboutness depend primarily not on the rate of interest but on the scale of production, taken in a broad sense.

Although no brief summary can do justice to Young's vision and its details as set out in (1928), the following passage taken from the essay on Capital (1929, Vol. 4, p. 796) is a modest if inadequate substitute for reading the paper itself:

> There is nothing inherently economical in roundabout methods, but the most economical methods often happen to be roundabout. The degree of roundaboutness which is most economical generally depends upon the amount of a particular kind of work which is to be done. And also the making and use of instruments involves an extension of the principle of the division of labour, and the division of labour, as Adam Smith observed, depends upon the extent of the market. The use of capital on a large scale in industry came later than its use in commerce, for the reason that not until there were markets which were able to absorb large outputs of standard types of goods was it profitable to make any extensive use of roundabout methods of production. Once established, however, industrial capitalism showed that it had within itself the seeds of its own growth. Cheaper goods, improved means of transport, and the increased advantages of specialization led to larger markets, so that the economies of industrial capitalism grew in a cumulative way. The increasing division of labour, by breaking up complex industrial processes into simpler parts, not only invited a larger use of instruments, but also prompted the invention of new types of instrument.

Apart from an interesting discussion by Marx (see INCREASING RETURNS) Young's article was the first serious advance beyond Adam Smith on the relations between increasing returns and economic growth. However, the problems of formalizing that persuasive vision into a tractable model have proved formidable indeed, the chief technical problems being those of nonconvex technologies and the introduction of new intermediate commodities. So, old as it is, his paper remains important for us precisely because there is not much else. Although there have recently been some encouraging signs that this long drought may be coming to an end, these are not yet sufficient either in number or in quality to predict definitely that it will.

CONCLUSION. As a critic, Young was knowledgeable and perceptive and possessed of that rare ability of entering into and appreciating minds that were quite unlike his own. This can be seen not only in his reviews of Jevons and Pigou and Edgeworth (1925) and his work with countless graduate students (not just stars like Knight and Chamberlin), but in a wider perspective. Thus although he had a populist upbringing in the Midwest and was trained in the very citadel of institutional economics, it is clear from his writings that by nature he had much greater affinities with the modes of thought of traditional economic theory. To that extent he was seriously handicapped in living in a time and place that was at best atheoretical. Nevertheless, his sympathies were so far extended that he could refer to Veblen as 'the most gifted man I have known' (Dorfman, 1961, p. 299) and could review much too kindly the institutionalist manifesto edited by Tugwell (1924), trying hard to see the mazy merits of its case.

Perhaps that is the key to the puzzle about Allyn Young. He was above all a great critic, and great critics, like great journalists and great wits, seldom survive into posterity.

PETER NEWMAN

See also CUMULATIVE CAUSATION; DIVISION OF LABOUR; INCREASING RETURNS.

SELECTED WORKS

1900–1901. The comparative accuracy of different forms of quinquennial age groups. *Publications of the American Statistical Association* 7, 27–39.

1908. (With T.S. Adams and M.O. Lorenz) Revised edition of R.T. Ely, *Outlines of Economics*, New York: Macmillan. Subsequent revisions in 1916, 1923 and 1930.

1913. Pigou's Wealth and Welfare. *Quarterly Journal of Economics* 27, 672–86.

1919–20. The economics of the treaty. *New Republic* 21, 388–9.

1922–3. The United States and reparations. *Foreign Affairs* 1, 35–47.

1925. Papers relating to political economy. *American Economic Review* 15, 721–4.

1927. *Economic Problems New and Old.* Boston: Houghton Mifflin. (This contains 14 papers, dated 1911 through 1927, that are not included in the present list.)

1928. Increasing returns and economic progress. *Economic Journal* 38, 527–42.

1929. Eleven articles, published posthumously: Capital; Economics; Labour; Land; Price; Rent; Supply and Demand; Utility; Wages; Wealth; Value. In *The Encyclopaedia Britannica*, 14th edn, London: Encyclopaedia Britannica Company.

BIBLIOGRAPHY

Blitch, C.P. 1983. Allyn A. Young: a curious case of professional neglect. *History of Political Economy* 15, 1–24.

Chamberlin, E.H. 1933. *The Theory of Monopolistic Competition.* Cambridge, Mass.: Harvard University Press.

Dorfman, J. 1934. *Thorstein Veblen and his America.* New York: Viking Press. Reprinted with new appendices, New York: Augustus M. Kelley, 1961.

Dorfman, J. 1959. *The Economic Mind in American Civilization.* Vol. 4, New York: Viking Press.

Harrod, R.F. 1951. *The Life of John Maynard Keynes.* London: Macmillan.

Keynes, J.M. 1919. *The Economic Consequences of the Peace.* London: Macmillan.

Keynes, J.M. 1922. *A Revision of the Treaty.* London: Macmillan.

Keynes, J.M. 1977. *Activities 1920–1922: Treaty Revision and Reconstruction.* Ed. E. Johnson. In *The Collected Writings of John Maynard Keynes*, Vol. XVII, London: Macmillan for the Royal Economic Society.

Knight, F.H. 1921. *Risk, Uncertainty, and Profit.* Boston: Houghton Mifflin.

Knight, F.H. 1924. Some fallacies in the interpretation of social cost. *Quarterly Journal of Economics* 38, 582–606.

Pigou, A.C. 1912. *Wealth and Welfare.* London: Macmillan.

Robbins, L. 1971. *Autobiography of an Economist.* London: Macmillan.

Samuelson, P.A. 1947. 'The General Theory'. In *The New Economics: Keynes' Influence on Theory and Policy*, ed. S. Harris, New York: Alfred A. Knopf.

Schumpeter, J.A. 1954. *History of Economic Analysis.* New York: Oxford University Press.

Tugwell, R.G. (ed.) 1924. *The Trend of Economics.* New York: Alfred A. Knopf.

Young, Arthur (1741–1820). Born into a Suffolk clerical family in 1741, Arthur Young began his literary career at seventeen, writing novels and pamphlets. He began farming in his early twenties, and in 1767 he took on the tenancy of an Essex farm which was however beyond his means. Exchanging this tenancy for a smaller farm in Hertfordshire which proved equally unrewarding, his income during the 1770s was drawn as much from writing as farming. The publication of his accounts of travels in England and Ireland met with great success, but the long absences and expense involved led to the neglect of his farm. His response was to extend his literary activities, in 1784 he launched the *Annals of Agriculture*, a journal which rapidly gained international recognition. During the later 1780s he toured the Continent, and his observations of France on the eve of the Revolution remain a valuable source. On the establishment of the Board of Agriculture in 1793 Young became its Secretary, and it was his descriptive methods which were followed by the writers of the County Surveys for which the Board is best known. In 1811 Young became blind, and he died in 1820, leaving behind an autobiography which provided a social and personal record of a life devoted to farming and literary activities.

Young worked until his death on a book entitled *Elements of Agriculture*, a general survey of agricultural method and practice; but the work was never published, and indeed it is evident that Young's strength lay in his observational method and his systematic appraisal of rational agriculture, rather than his ability to produce a general survey of agricultural conditions. This is evident from his *Political Arithmetic* of 1774, which, while combining an account of the agricultural state of England with commentary on the writings of Steuart, Davenant and the Physiocrats, lacks the originality of his agricultural writings. Even in the first of these writings, *The Farmer's Letters* (1767), he supports arguments for progressive husbandry and agrarian reform with the construction of 'model farms' which postulate ideal combinations of land, labour and capital for differing conditions of fertility and husbandry. This pattern was repeated in his *Six Weeks' Tour* (1768) and also in many subsequent works which record and comment upon the condition of farms and estates encountered on his route. Experiments carried out on his farm were also written up, while in *The Farmer's Guide* he produced a handbook for the establishment and conduct of a tenant farm – together with his *Rural Oeconomy*, an outline of capitalist farm management.

Visitors to Young's own farm were often struck by his failure to follow his own recommended 'best practice' – instead of order and efficient supervision, they found disarray and confusion. It may be that Young devoted too much time to writing to properly supervise the work of the farm (the true business of the farmer in his view), or he may simply have lacked the application necessary; but his practical shortcomings do not diminish his real achievement – the establishment of a system of agricultural observation which was a model for 19th-century studies of agricultural production.

K. TRIBE

SELECTED WORKS

1767. *The Farmer's Letters to the People of England.* London.

1768. *A Six Weeks' Tour through the Southern Counties of England and Wales.* London.

1770a. *The Farmer's Guide in Hiring and Stocking Farms.* 2 vols, London.

1770b. *A Course of Experimental Agriculture.* 2 vols, London.

1770c. *Rural Oeconomy.* London.

1771a. *The Farmer's Tour through the East of England.* 4 vols, London: W. Strahan.

1771b. *The Farmer's Calendar.* London.

1774. *Political Arithmetic.* Pt I, London: W. Nicoll. Pt II, London: T. Cadell, 1779.

1780. *A Tour in Ireland.* London.

1784–1815. *Annals of Agriculture* (1784–1815). 46 vols.

1792. *Travels during the Years 1787, 1788 and 1789 … in France.* Bury St. Edmunds.

1794–1809. *General View of the Agriculture of the County of Suffolk.* (1794); also on Lincoln (1799), Hertfordshire (1804), Norfolk (1804), Essex (1807), Oxford (1809). London: Board of Agriculture.

1808. *General Report on Enclosures.* London: Board of Agriculture.

1809. *On the Advantages which have resulted from the Establishment of the Board of Agriculture.* London.

1898. *The Autobiography of Arthur Young.* Ed. M. Betham-Edwards, London: Smith, Elder & Co.

Z

Zawadzki, Wladyslaw Marian (1885–1939). The Polish economist W.M. Zawadzki, was born in Vilno, historic capital of Lithuania, and studied mathematics and social sciences in Moscow, Leipzig and Paris.

His first major work, *Les Mathématiques appliquées à l'économie politique*, was published in 1914 in Paris. After World War I this book was recognized as a significant contribution to the development of general equilibrium theory as conceived by Vilfredo Pareto. At the beginning of his academic career, Zawadzki was also involved in the study of the role of theories of value in the history of economic thought. He came to the conclusion that, contrary to the prevailing view of the time, the idea of exchange value as something different from market prices should be discarded. This point of view is further developed in the book on 'Value and Price', containing extracts from the works of various economists and published in Polish under the editorship of Zawadzki in 1919. When the Econometric Society was founded in 1931 Zawadzki became one of its original members and was elected to the first Committee of the Society.

In 1919 Zawadzki contributed to the reestablishment of the ancient University of Vilno, closed down eighty years before by the Russians, and became there the Professor of Political Economy. At that time Zawadzki following the example of Vilfredo Pareto turned his attention to the problems of economic sociology. This found expression in his second major work *The Theory of Production*, published in 1923 in Polish and in 1925, with certain abbreviations, in French – an extensive study of production in various social, cultural and technical environments. Zawadzki distinguishes five types of environments in which regular production can take place: primitive, partriarchal, individualistic, based on compulsion and collectivist. The main part of the book is devoted to the analysis of the conditions of production in an individualistic environment. While admitting the feasibility of regular production in a collectivist society, Zawadzki is sceptical about the Marxist view that the conditions for collectivist systems can gradually emerge in the course of development of individualistic society. But he admits the possibility of a revolutionary transition to collectivism as preached by George Sorel and the French syndicalist revolutionaries.

Zawadzki was the Polish Minister of Finance in 1931–5 and was to a very great extent responsible for keeping his country on the gold standard in spite of the abandonment of that system by Britain and the USA.

From 1936 until his death in 1939 Zawadzki was Professor of Economics in the Central School of Commerce, Warsaw. During that period he worked mainly in the field of monetary theory and had considerable influence as a teacher – several young economists adopted his ideas and tried to develop them.

STANISLAW SWIANIEWICZ

SELECTED WORKS

1914a. *Les mathématiques appliquées à l'économie politique*. Paris.

1914b. *Zastosowanie matematyki do ekonomji politycznej* (The application of mathematics to political economy). Wilno.

1919. *Wartosc i cena. Wypisy* (Value and price. An economic selection). Warsaw.

1923. *Teorja produkcji* (The theory of production). Warsaw.

1927. *Esquisse d'une théorie de la production*. Paris.

1938. *Manipulowanie pieniadzen jako narzedzie polityki gospodarczej* (The manipulation of money as an instrument of economic policy). Krakow.

zero-profit condition. The profit-function for a competitive firm may be defined as

$$\pi(p, w) = \max p \cdot f(x) - w \cdot x$$

where p, w are the prices of the output, $y = f(x)$, and inputs, respectively. If f displays increasing returns to scale π will not be defined. If f displays constant returns to scale π may not be defined.

Suppose profits for the optimal inputs for a given output are strictly positive

$$p \cdot f(x^*) - w \cdot x^* = \pi > 0.$$

Increasing the scale of operation by a factor t will result in yet greater profits:

$$p \cdot f(tx^*) - w \cdot tx^* \geqslant tp \cdot f(x^*) - w \cdot tx^* = t\pi > \pi$$

whenever $s \geqslant 1$ in

$$t^s y = f(tx)$$

Profits are unbounded, and no maximal profit equilibrium exists for the competitive firm. Hence, the only meaningful competitive equilibrium requires that the technology display constant returns to scale, and that profits are maximized at zero.

This necessary condition of competitive equilibrium has caused some confusion in the literature. This confusion has been, in part, a matter of vocabulary. The use of the term 'profit' in the zero-profit condition has been confused with the profit which is a revenue to capital goods. In equilibrium capital goods which are not free-goods will receive positive rentals, and in long-run equilibrium these rentals will be proportionate to the cost of reproduction of capital goods forming a positive long-run rate of profit. The zero-profit condition applies not to the revenue of factors, but to the short-run excess profits which may be acquired out of equilibrium. Marshall (1890) clarified the vocabulary of the problem by labelling these excess-profits as one category of 'quasi-rents' and distinguishing between 'quasi-rents which do not, and the profits which do, directly enter into the normal supply prices of produce ...' (p. 636n).

This confusion in vocabulary has extended to analytic confusion. Edgeworth found the zero-profit condition confusing. Walras (1874–7, ch. 18), whilst differentiating clearly between the rate of net income which is the return on capital, and the equilibrium condition of zero excess profits, nonetheless regarded excess profits as the reward to entrepreneurship and hence argued that in equilibrium, the return to entrepreneurship would be zero – 'les entrepreneurs ne font ni bénéfice ni perte' (p. 225). Listing entrepreneurial talents amongst those factors of production which earn a competitive rental would have eliminated this anomaly.

John Eatwell

See also GENERAL EQUILIBRIUM; WALRAS, MARIE-ESPRIT LÉON.

BIBLIOGRAPHY

Marshall, A. 1890. *Principles of Economics*. 9th (Variorum) edn, London: Macmillan, 1961.

Walras, L. 1874–7. *Elements of Pure Economics*. Trans. and ed. W. Jaffe, Homewood, Ill.: Irwin, 1954.

zero-sum games. Zero-sum games are to the theory of games what the twelve-bar blues is to jazz: a polar case, and a historical point of departure. A *game* is a situation in which (i) each of a number of agents (*players*) has a set of alternative courses of action (*strategies*) at his disposal; (ii) there are outcomes which depend on the *combination* of the players' actions and give rise to preferences by the players over these combinations; (iii) the players know, and know that each other knows, these preferences. (Strictly, such a situation is a game of *complete information* in *normal form*: these qualifications should henceforth be understood.) In the case which dominates the literature of zero-sum games there are two players, A and B say, each with a finite set of strategies, and their preferences can be represented by von Neumann–Morgenstern utilities. The preference structure can then be displayed in a *payoff matrix*, whose (i, j)th entry (u_{ij}, v_{ij}) gives the expected utilities or *payoffs* of A and B respectively for A using his ith strategy and B using his jth. A game of this type in which $u_{ij} + v_{ij} = 0$ for all i, j is known as a *zero-sum matrix game* (henceforth simply *zero-sum game*). In a zero-sum game the players have exactly opposed preferences over strategy-pairs. Hence there is no scope for the pair of them to act *as* a pair – there is nothing for them to cooperate about. The theory of cooperative zero-sum games is thus an empty box; zero-sum games are non-cooperative games, and each player must choose in uncertainty of the other's choice.

Figure 1 shows the payoff matrix of a zero-sum game ('The Battle of the Bismarck Sea'). As is conventional with zero-sum games, only the 'row-chooser's' payoff is shown. General Kenney (A) must decide whether to reconnoitre to the north, where visibility is poor (α_1) or to the south (α_2); the Japanese commander (B) whether to sail north (β_1) or south (β_2). Kenney's payoff is the expected number of days for which he will bomb the enemy fleet.

The theory of games was introduced by von Neumann and Morgenstern (1944) as part of the theory of rational action. It was to be the part that dealt with *social* contexts, in which the outcomes of concern to agents are radically dependent on each other's decisions. In such contexts characterizing the rational

A's strategies		B's strategies	
		β_1	β_2
	α_1	2	2
	α_2	1	3

is problematical, as von Neumann and Morgenstern were acutely aware. The central theoretical problem is to say what A and B will do if each does what is best for him. But what is best for A depends on what B *will* do, and so, in any answer, on what is best for B. We are entrammelled in regress. To this deep problem von Neumann and Morgenstern believed they had discovered a satisfactory answer in the special case of zero-sum games. It is this answer which has made zero-sum games famous.

The power of von Neumann and Morgenstern's proposal lies in their demonstration that over a wide class of zero-sum games each of two quite independent principles of rational action gives the same answer to the question of what the players should do – and an essentially determinate one. This high degree of coherence in the theory, the reciprocal support of its postulates, may perhaps have led to too charitable a view of their individual merits. The two principles of rational action are the Equilibrium Principle and the Maximin Principle. The Equilibrium Principle says that the strategies α^* and β^* are rational only if each is a *best reply* to the other, that is, α^* maximizes $u(\alpha, \beta^*)$ and β^* maximizes $v(\alpha^*, \beta)$, where $u(\alpha, \beta)$, $v(\alpha, \beta)$ denote the payoffs of A and B respectively for the strategy-pair (α, β). 'Reply' here is metaphorical, for there is no communication. Such a pair is called a *non-cooperative* or *Nash equilibrium* in game theory. Here, since $v(\alpha, \beta) = -u(\alpha, \beta)$, it is often called a *saddle-point*, for it locates a maximum of u over α and a minimum of u over β. The Equilibrium Principle has often been too casually accepted, but it has also been carefully defended (see e.g. Johansen, 1981). Von Neumann and Morgenstern saw with clarity that it can be no more than a necessary condition on rational choices by the players: *if* such choices exist they must, arguably, satisfy it, but some independent argument for this existence is needed (von Neumann and Morgenstern, 1944, section 17.3).

The Maximin Principle says that A should maximize over α the minimum over β of $u(\alpha, \beta)$ – he should 'maximin' u; and B should maximin v, or, what is equivalent, 'minimax' u. In other words, A should maximize his *security level*, where the security level of a strategy α is defined as $\min_\beta u(\alpha, \beta)$, the worst that α can bring him; and B should minimize his *hazard level* $\max_\alpha u(\alpha, \beta)$, the best that β can bring his adversary. This principle has been much criticized, and the qualified acceptance it has enjoyed owes something to its protective alliance with other elements of von Neumann and Morgenstern's theory. Their own arguments for it were suggestive rather than apodictic. It is claimed to express a rational caution in a situation in which a player has no valid basis for assigning probabilities to his opponent's decision. A second argument is also advanced, unworthy of them and justly attacked by Ellsberg (1956), according to which it is rational for A to choose by supposing he is playing the 'minorant game' associated with the payoff matrix: in this game A chooses first and B second in knowledge of A's choice (so that A is a Stackelberg 'leader'). In *this* situation rock-hard principles of decision under certainty make it rational for A to maximin. But convincing reasons for A to assume that it obtains are missing.

In the Bismarck Sea game it is readily seen that the set of maximin strategy-pairs and the set of saddle-points are the same. This fact instantiates a general fact (Theorem 1): In a zero-sum game which has a saddle-point, a strategy-pair is a saddle-point if and only if it is a maximin pair. Theorem 1 expresses the agreement of the two principles of choice. They are also effectively determinate, for we also have (Theorem 2): In a zero-sum game with a saddle-point, all maximin strategies of one player yield the same payoffs when paired with given a maximin strategy of the other player.

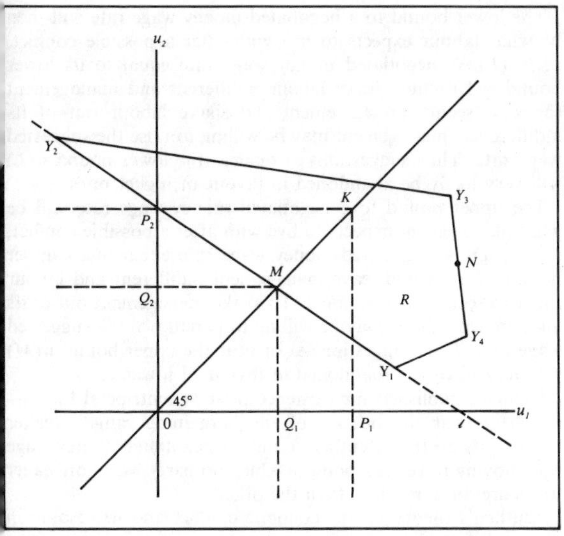

Figure 2

The significance of these results is impaired by their limitation to games which have saddle-points. Plenty do not. Von Neumann and Morgenstern's response was to seek a modest enlargement of the strategy-sets of the players of an arbitrary zero-sum game which would ensure a saddle-point. The ingenious mode of enlargement they propose is to provide the players with roulette wheels. More formally, if a player has strategies $\alpha_1, \ldots, \alpha_m$ at his disposal, it is supposed that he also has the strategy 'with probability p_1 do α_1 and ... and with probability p_m do α_m', where $p_1 + \cdots + p_m = 1$. The original strategies $\alpha_1, \ldots, \alpha_m$ are called *pure* strategies and the new ones *mixed* strategies. Now it may be shown that (Theorem 3): In any zero-sum game, $\max_\alpha \min_\beta u(\alpha, \beta) \leqslant \min_\beta \max_\alpha u(\alpha, \beta)$, with equality if and only if the game has a saddle-point. So a strategy-set enlargement which raises A's highest security level is a move towards ensuring a saddle-point. Allowing A to 'mix' his strategies is a hedging device which has just this effect. The security level of a strategy α is what A would get from it against a prescient opponent. But even such a being can only adopt one strategy. Generally, mixing raises A's security levels since, whatever that strategy is, with some probability it fails to inflict maximal damage.

The success of von Neumann and Morgenstern's manoeuvre is recorded in what is the most celebrated theorem in game theory, the so-called Minimax Theorem: Every zero-sum (matrix) game with mixed strategies has a saddle-point. The Minimax Theorem duly yields, as desired, counterparts of Theorems 1 and 2 for the class of all 'mixed' zero-sum games. The early proofs of the Minimax Theorem employed fixed-point theorems, but it may also be proved by a constructive method based on the properties of convex sets (see e.g. Gale, 1951). The main lines of this method may be gleaned from Figure 2 for the case in which A has two pure strategies.

Let A's pure strategies be α_1, α_2 and B's be $\beta_1, \ldots, \beta_n$. Let $\mathbf{q} = (q_1, \ldots, q_n)$ denote the mixed strategy in which B does β_j with probability $q_j (j = 1, \ldots, n)$. Figure 2 shows a case in which $n = 4$. The axes measure A's payoffs to α_1, α_2 respectively. A vertex Y_j of the region R shows A's two payoffs if B chooses the pure strategy β_j, the other points of R his two payoffs against mixed strategies of B (e.g. the abscissa of the point N is $u(\alpha_1, \mathbf{q})$ for $\mathbf{q} = (0, 0, \frac{1}{2}, \frac{1}{2})$. At any point on a line like P_1KP_2, B's hazard level is constant; hence B minimizes his hazard level at M (in other cases, not illustrated, the minimum-hazard point is along a side of a line of type P_1KP_2 and at a *vertex* of R). At M, B is using the mixed strategy $\mathbf{q}^* (q^*, 1 - q^*, 0, 0)$, where $q^* = MY_2/Y_1Y_2$; and A receives the payoff u^* say $(= OQ_1)$ whatever pure (or mixed) strategy he uses. The region whose north-east border is Q_1MQ_2 and the region R are both convex. Consider their separating line ℓ – the extension of Y_1Y_2. It may be written $p^*u_1 + (1 - p^*)u_2 = u^*$, where $0 \leqslant p^* \leqslant 1$. Then if $\mathbf{p}^*$ is the mixed strategy in which A does α_1 with probability p^*, $(\mathbf{p}^*, \mathbf{q}^*)$ is the claimed saddle-point. For on one hand since all A's strategies give the same payoff against $\mathbf{q}^*$, $\mathbf{p}^*$ maximizes it. On the other hand, since ℓ is the specified separating line, $p^*u_1 + (1 - p^*)u_2 \geqslant u^*$ for all (u_1, u_2) in R, that is, A's payoff from $\mathbf{p}^*$ is at least u^* for all the strategies available to B.

The Minimax Theorem establishes that the agreement of von Neumann and Morgenstern's two principles of rational choice holds in all zero-sum games provided players may mix their strategies. The mixability assumption, unfortunately, is far from innocuous. Not only may randomization be excluded by the rules of a game or by physical constraint, but the idea that rational players employ it threatens downright contradiction. For the pure strategy picked out by the wheel may have a lower security level than its alternatives, so that a maximinning agent has a motive to go back on his decision. This, moreover, he is in a position to anticipate.

It is worth considering briefly the empirical evidence about whether people play zero-sum games in the von Neumann–Morgenstern manner. The most important evidence is from laboratory experiments. Typically, the game situation is presented to the subjects in words, and they are invited to play a series of trials of the game for points or for small or fictitious reward: in some experiments subjects play against each other, in others against a programme. A fundamental difficulty is to make sure that subjects are solely motivated by the payoffs of the presented game, and do not 'import utilities', for example deriving utility from their opponents' payoffs. In most experiments subjects clearly have failed to choose in accordance with the theory, though sometimes a tendency has been noted for them to do so more nearly as trials progress. It should be noted that departure from saddle-point behaviour may be rational if it is rational to think that one's opponent is deviating from it. However, subjects have also typically failed to exploit programmed non-saddle-point play. They have declined, too, to avail themselves of randomizing facilities.

These experiments addressed an empirical question rather than the question to which von Neumann and Morgenstern claimed to have found an answer, that of how it is *rational* to act in zero-sum games. To the solution of the latter problem these authors made a revolutionary contribution which, however, did not dispose of it. Against the elegance, the formal satisfyingness, and the pregnant originality of the von Neumann–Morgenstern theory must be set as yet unresolved doubts as to the adequacy of the pure theory of rational decision which it embodies.

MICHAEL BACHARACH

See also GAME THEORY; SADDLEPOINTS.

BIBLIOGRAPHY

Colman, A. 1982. *Game Theory and Experimental Games*. Oxford: Pergamon.
Ellsberg, D. 1956. Theory of the reluctant duelist. *American Economic Review* 46, December, 909–23.

Gale, D. 1951. Convex polyhedral cones and linear inequalities. In *Activity Analysis of Production and Allocation*, ed. T.C. Koopmans, New York: Wiley.
Johansen, L. 1981. Interaction in economic theory. *Economie appliquée* 34(2–3), 229–67.
Von Neumann, J. and Morgenstern, O. 1944. *Theory of Games and Economic Behavior*. Princeton: Princeton University Press.

Zeuthen, Frederik Ludvig Bang (1888–1959). Zeuthen was born on 9 September 1888 in Copenhagen. He took a degree in economics at the University of Copenhagen in 1912 and spent the next eighteen years in the service of the Danish social security system. That system, already then full-fledged by American standards, was the subject matter of a large number of books and articles published by Zeuthen in the period 1912–28. But then, at 40, Zeuthen published his *Fordeling* (1928) in which is found, among other things, his use of inequalities in a Walras system as well as his theory of collective bargaining. The following year he published his article (1929) on product differentiation under monopolistic competition. Zeuthen's treatment of collective bargaining and monopolistic competition appeared in English (1930) with a preface by Schumpeter, who called it a 'bold raid into new and difficult country'. The new country would soon become part of mainstream economic theory. Also in English (1957), Zeuthen gave us his mature views on all this. He taught theory, labour economics and social security at his alma mater from 1930 to 1958 and died on 24 February 1959 in Copenhagen.

INEQUALITIES IN A WALRASIAN SYSTEM. In a Walrasian system with fixed input-output coefficients, Zeuthen ([1928, p. 27] 1932–3, pp. 2–3) saw that feasibility would require the sum of all inputs of any good absorbed in all processes to be smaller than or equal to the sum of all outputs of it supplied in all processes. By introducing a new variable, i.e., the unused portion, Zeuthen could then turn his inequality into an equality and say that either the unused portion of the input or the price of the input would be equal to zero.

In a short paper Schlesinger (1935) agreed, but neither Zeuthen nor Schlesinger attempted to prove the existence of a general equilibrium. Wald (1935, 1936) made the attempt for a stationary economy, and von Neumann (1937) succeeded for a growing one. Von Neumann formulated a primal and a dual problem. His primal problem was to maximize the rate of growth subject to the constraint that excess demand for any good must be non-positive. That constraint was what Zeuthen and Schlesinger had seen and Wald had worked on.

Von Neumann's dual problem was this. We must minimize the rate of interest subject to the constraint that in any time-consuming process profits must be nonpositive. That constraint was seen by neither Zeuthen nor Schlesinger. Taking his primal and his dual together, von Neumann found his familiar existence proof in which the maximized rate of growth equalled the minimized rate of interest.

COLLECTIVE BARGAINING. Inherent in labour–management bargaining is the threat of conflict. Zeuthen's ([1928] 1930, pp. 104–50) point of departure was the net outcome of a possible conflict as expected by labour and management, respectively.

As seen by labour, let the net outcome be $w(L)$ defined as the money wage rate after conflict reduced by labour's cost of conflict, i.e. lost wages. As seen by management, let the net outcome be $w(M)$ defined as the money wage rate after conflict raised by management's cost of conflict, i.e., lost orders.

The lower bound to a negotiated money wage rate will then be what labour expects to live with after a possible conflict, i.e., $w(L)$. A negotiated money wage rate equal to its lower bound w(L) would leave labour indifferent and management eager to secure an agreement. To shake labour out of its indifference, management may be willing to raise the suggested wage rate. Thus suggestions at or near the lower bound $w(L)$ will very likely be abandoned in favour of higher ones.

The upper bound to a negotiated money wage rate will be what management expects to live with after a possible conflict, i.e., $w(M)$. A negotiated money wage rate equal to its upper bound $w(M)$ would leave management indifferent and labour eager to secure an agreement. To shake management out of its indifference, labour may be willing to pare down the suggested wage rate. Thus suggestions at or near the upper bound $w(M)$ will very likely be abandoned in favour of lower ones.

Having established the existence of such centripetal forces – powerful near the bounds of the bargaining range, weaker towards its centre – Zeuthen found his negotiated money wage rate moving towards a point in which no party was more eager to secure an agreement than the other.

Zeuthen's theory of an economic conflict and its resolution may well have been the first ever.

PRODUCT DIFFERENTIATION. Like Bertrand, Zeuthen ([1929] 1930, pp. 24–5) assumed his duopolists to have a price policy but cautiously removed Cournot's and Bertrand's assumption of '*qualité identique*'. Zeuthen's product differentiation consisted in differences in product quality, geographical location, or advertising-generated image. Such product differentiation was not strong enough to protect a duopolist failing to match a price cut but strong enough to allow a duopolist matching any price cut to keep his old customers. Like Cournot and Bertrand duopolists, Zeuthen's duopolists would always sell at a common price but could attract new customers by lowering it. A 'coefficient of expansion' measured a duopolist's ability to attract them by differences in product quality, geographical location, or advertising-generated image.

Unlike Joan Robinson's one-firm model three years later, Zeuthen's model had two firms interacting in a group equilibrium. Unlike Edward Chamberlin's group equilibrium three years later, Zeuthen's group equilibrium did not assume equal market shares: the more successful firm had the larger coefficient of expansion, hence the larger market share.

HANS BREMS

See also BARGAINING.

SELECTED WORKS

1928. *Den konomiske Fordeling* (Economic distribution). Copenhagen: Busck.
1929. Mellem Konkurrence og Monopol (Between competition and monopoly). *Nationalkonomisk Tidsskrift* 67, 265–305.
1930. *Problems of Monopoly and Economic Warfare*. With a preface by J.A. Schumpeter, London: Routledge.
1932–3. Das Prinzip der Knappheit, technische Kombination und ökonomische Qualität. *Zeitschrift für Nationalökonomie* 4, 1–24.
1957. *Economic Theory and Method*. Cambridge, Mass.: Harvard University Press.

BIBLIOGRAPHY

Baumol, W.J. and Goldfeld, S.M. (eds) 1968. *Precursors in Mathematical Economics: an anthology*. London: London School of Economics and Political Science.

Neumann, J. von. 1937. Über ein ökonomisches Gleichungssystem und eine Verallgemeinerung des Brouwerschen Fixpunktsatzes. *Ergebnisse eines mathematischen Kolloquiums* 8. Trans. by G. Morgenstern in Baumol and Goldfeld (eds, 1968).
Schlesinger, K. 1935. Über die Produktionsgleichungen der ökonomischen Wertlehre. *Ergebnisse eines mathematischen Kolloquiums* 6. Trans. by W.J. Baumol in Baumol and Goldfeld (eds, 1968).
Wald, A. 1935. Über die eindeutige positive Lösbarkeit der neuen Produktionsgleichungen. *Ergebnisse eines mathematischen Kolloquiums* 6. Trans. by W.J. Baumol in Baumol and Goldfeld (eds, 1968).
Wald, A. 1936. Über die Produktionsgleichungen der ökonomischen Wertlehre. *Ergebnisse eines mathematischen Kolloquiums* 7. Trans. by W.J. Baumol in Baumol and Goldfeld (eds, 1968).

Ziber, Nikolaj Ivanovich (1844–1888). Ziber was born in Sudak (Tavrik, Crimea) on 10 March 1844. He died in Yalta on 28 April 1888. His intellectual standing and achievements grant him a distinguished position among writers in the tradition of classical political economy.

Ziber was born in a family of Swiss origin that had settled in Russia. (The original family name was Sieber, and under this name Ziber was sometimes known to his contemporaries.) After attending the Gymnasium at Simferopol', he entered the Law Faculty of Kiev University (1864). After concluding his law course, Ziber became judicial mediator in the Volinskij province. Eventually, however, Friedrich George Bunge, his economics professor at Kiev, obtained for him a scholarship at Kiev University which permitted him to undertake full-time research in political economy. His doctoral dissertation on Ricardo's theory of value and capital (examined 'in relation to the latest additions and explanations', as the subtitle explicitly states) was ready by 1871 (Ziber, 1871). It presents a detailed reconstruction of the classical theories of value and capital, and compares them with subsequent developments in economic literature, both in the 'classical' and the 'subjectivist' traditions. Ziber's dissertation also attempted an assessment of Marx's theoretical contribution in *Das Kapital*, Book I (1867) within the framework of Ricardian economics. This work, almost immediately after publication, drew the attention of Marx, who mentioned it with praise in the afterword to the second German edition of *Das Kapital*, Book I:

> As early as 1871, N. Sieber, Professor of Political Economy in the University of Kiev, in his work 'David Ricardo's Theory of Value and Capital', referred to my theory of value, of money and of capital, as in its fundamentals a necessary sequel to the teaching of Smith and Ricardo. That which astonishes the Western European in the reading of this excellent work, is the author's consistent and firm grasp of the purely theoretical position (Marx [1872] 1983, p. 26).

After receiving his doctorate, Ziber was sent on study leave to Western Europe. There he remained for approximately two years, travelling extensively through Germany, Switzerland, Belgium and England. During this period he attended courses at leading universities (such as Heidelberg and Leipzig). He also visited factories, cooperative societies and statistical offices, gaining a first-hand acquaintance of the social conditions in the most developed countries of his time. In 1873 Ziber took up the chair of political economy and statistics at Kiev University. In this period, he was occupied with research on classical political economy (Ziber, 1873a, 1873b; 1875) and on economic statistics.

Dissatisfied with the cultural and political environment that he had found in Kiev after returning from Western Europe, in 1875 he left his academic position and country, settling in Bern (Switzerland). There he undertook research in economic theory, applied economics, sociology and economic anthropology, by focusing on the following issues: (i) the social institutions and problems of a modern industrial economy; (ii) the economic and social conditions of contemporary Russia; (iii) the economic structure of 'primitive' communities; (iv) classical and Marxian political economy, particularly in their connection with legal institutions and economic anthropology (Ziber, 1876–78, 1879–80, 1883a).

In this period, Ziber also edited a Russian edition of Ricardo's works, to which he contributed substantial comments (Ziber, 1882). In 1883 he published *Ocherki pervobytnoĭ êkonomicheskoĭ kult'ury* (Essays on primitive economic culture). Here, Ziber outlines a general theory of primitive economic systems, on the assumption that the study of such systems provides a deeper insight into the community structures that are also at the basis of more modern and 'complex' types of economic organisation.

In 1884 poor health persuaded Ziber to go back to his native country and family. In 1885 he published *David Rikardo i Karl Marks*, a volume based on his doctoral dissertation and subsequent work on Marx's theory.

Ziber's contribution to economic theory is characterized by a clear perception of the specific features of Ricardian economics with respect to other classical and post-classical theories. In particular, he stressed the originality of Ricardo's methodological standpoint, which he identified with the idea that political economy should be concerned with macro-social laws and use an 'average period' as the basic unit of time. He also stressed that the analytical core of classical political economy (from Smith to McCulloch, including Ricardo) is 'a theoretical framework in which production is considered the most important economic factor, and exchange a secondary, subordinate factor' (Ziber, 1871, p. 3). This approach led Ziber to criticize, on the basis of an early remark by Storch (1823, vol. I, p. 422n.) and of later criticism by Thünen (1857) and Komorzynski (1869), Adam Smith's 'adding up' theory of price determination. In particular, Ziber thought that the 'circularity' of Smith's argument could be overcome by stressing the special position of wage (its 'external foundation') in the theory of the cost of production.

Ziber also extended Ricardo's theory in a number of points. He formulated an 'objective' theory of utility by insisting that no meaningful comparison among goods can be made on the basis of their relative utility. Given that the vast majority of goods are related with specific needs, 'preference' appears to be the expression of the principle that 'until the need is satisfied, two units [of the relevant good] are more valuable than one' (Ziber, 1871, p. 29). In Ziber's view, this is hardly an instance of subjective preference and rational choice. Diminishing marginal utility is criticized on similar grounds: 'within the limits of the existing need, an additional unit of product is associated with an additional unit of utility; beyond such limits, the product is completely useless and total utility is unchanged' (p. 38). He then formulated an alternative explanation of the association between diminished supply and higher market price: 'if we now diminish the number of products, their *utility* is not increased because part of demand is not satisfied; what is increased is only the *fear* that a certain share of demand might not be satisfied' (p. 39).

Ziber also distanced himself from Ricardo and Marx by adopting a view of the productive system by vertically integrated sectors: '*the series of operations* performed on skin by the butcher, the tanner, the shoemaker, from the point of view of the social economy are nothing but a direct, *single operation of boot production*' (Ziber, 1871, p. 228). This view is a result of the method of 'social averages': in any average period of time, the economic system would be performing, for all produced commodities, all the different stages of the production process. Ziber also maintained that different proportions of capital in different industries may be made compatible with the pure labour theory of value provided the method of the 'social economy' (as distinguished from that of the 'private economy') is consistently adopted (see also Scazzieri, 1987).

Ziber's interpretation of the relationship between Ricardo and the other classical economists, and between Ricardo and Marx, exerted considerable influence on Russian economic theorists, and is an important factor in explaining the persistence of classical themes in the economic literature of that country well into the first part of this century.

R. SCAZZIERI

SELECTED WORKS

1871. Teoriia tsennosti i kapitala D. Rikardo, v sviazh s pozdnieshimi dopolneniiami i raz'iasneniiami (Ricardo's theory of value and capital, in relation to the latest additions and explanations). *Universitetskie Izviestiia* (University News) (Kiev), Nos 1–2 and 4–11.

1873a. (ed.) *Nachala politicheskoi ekonomii* (Principles of Political Economy), by David Ricardo, translation of the first part. *Universitetskie Izviestiia* (University News) (Kiev), Nos 1–10.

1873b. Zhizn' i trudy Davida Rikardo (The life and works of David Ricardo). *Universitetskie Izviestiia* (University News) (Kiev), No. 9.

1875. Tsena truda (The cost of labour). *Universitetskie Izviestiia* (University News), No. 2.

1876–8. Ekonomicheskaia teoriia Karla Marksa (The economic theory of Karl Marx). *Znanie* (Knowledge) (1876), Nos 10, 12; *Znanie* (1877), No. 2; *Slovo* (The Word) (1878), Nos. 1, 3, 9, 12.

1879–80. Mysli ob otnoshenii mezhdu obshchestvennoiu ekonomiki i pravom (Thoughts on the relationship between general economics and law). *Slovo* (The Word) (1879). No. 2; *Slovo* (1880), No. 6.

1882. (ed.) *Sochineniia Davida Rikardo* (Works of David Ricardo). With translator's supplements, St Petersburg.

1883a. Obshchestvennaia ekonomiia i pravo (General economics and law). *Iuridicheskii Vestnik* (Legal Bulletin), Nos 5, 9, 10.

1883b. *Ocherki poervobytnoi ekonomicheskoi kult'uri* (Essays on primitive economic culture). Moscow: Izd. K.T. Soldatenkova.

1885. *David Rikardo i Karl Marks v ikh obshchestvenno-ekonomicheskikh issledovaniiakh* (David Ricardo and Karl Marx in their social-economical researches). St Petersburg: Tip. M.N. Stasiulevicha.

BIBLIOGRAPHY

Komorzynski, J. von. 1869. Ist auf Grundlage der bisherigen wissenschaftlicher Forschung die Bestimmung der natürlichen Höhe der Güterpreise möglich? *Zeitschrift für die gesamte Staatswissenschaft* 25, 189–238.

Marx, K. 1867. *Capital. A Critique of Political Economy*. Book One: *The Process of Production of Capital*. (Afterword to second German edition first published in 1872.) London: Lawrence & Wishart, 1983.

Ricardo, D. 1817–21. *On the Principles of Political Economy and Taxation*. Vol. I of *Works and Correspondence of David Ricardo*, ed. P. Sraffa with the collaboration of M.H. Dobb, Cambridge: Cambridge University Press, 1951.

Scazzieri, R. 1987. Ziber on Ricardo. *Contributions to Political Economy* 6, March.

Storch, H. 1823. *Cours d'économie politique, ou exposition des principes qui déterminent la prosperité des nations* (1815). Paris: J.P. Aillaud, Bossange père, Rey et Gravier.

Thünen, J.H. von. 1850. *Le salaire naturel et son rapport au taux de l'intérêt*. Paris: Guillaumin et Cie, 1857.

zoning. *See* TIEBOUT HYPOTHESIS; URBAN ECONOMICS.

Appendix I

Entries in *The New Palgrave*, by Author

The following is a list of entries in *The New Palgrave* arranged by author. Entries with joint authors appear under the name of each author. Authors who contributed to *Palgrave's Dictionary of Political Economy* are shown in square brackets, e.g. [F.Y. Edgeworth].

Sam Aaronovitch
- Burns, Emile (1889–1972)

M. Abdel-Fadil
- colonialism

Andrew B. Abel
- Ricardian equivalence theorem

F. Gerard Adams
- satellite models

Walter Adams
- countervailing power

Irma Adelman
- factor analysis
- Fellner, William John (1905–1983)
- Scitovsky, Tibor (born 1910)
- simulation models

S.N. Afriat
- Lagrange multipliers

Dennis J. Aigner
- latent variables

Joshua Aizenman
- wage indexation

Armen A. Alchian
- Kessel, Reuben Aaron (1923–1975)
- property rights
- rent

Robert Z. Aliber
- exchange rates

Maurice Allais
- Allais Paradox
- economic surplus and the equimarginal principle
- Roy, René François Joseph (1894–1977)

William R. Allen
- mercantilism
- specie-flow mechanism

Michael Allingham
- excess demand and supply
- numéraire
- uniqueness of equilibrium
- wealth constraint

William Alonso
- gravity models

Edward J. Amadeo
- multiplier analysis

Takeshi Amemiya
- discrete choice models
- limited dependent variables

Samir Amin
- nationalism

Alice H. Amsden
- appropriate technology
- imperialism
- Tarbell, Ida Minerva (1857–1944)

F.J. Anscombe
- residuals

M. Anyadike-Danes
- Gaitskell, Hugh Todd Naylor (1906–1963)
- Robertson, Dennis (1890–1963)

Andrew Arato
- Marxism

G.C. Archibald
- firm, theory of the
- monopolistic competition

H.W. Arndt
- Clark, Colin Grant (born 1905)

Richard Arnott
- spatial economics

Kenneth J. Arrow
- Arrow's Theorem
- economic theory and the hypothesis of rationality
- Hotelling, Harold (1895–1973)

Michael Artis
- deficit spending
- income–expenditure analysis

Joseph Ascheim (with George S. Tavlas)
- Del Mar, Alexander (1836–1926)

[W.J. Ashley]
- socialists of the chair

Tony Aspromourgos
- 'neoclassical'

P.S. Atiyah
- Chadwick, Sir Edwin (1800–1890)
- common law

A.B. Atkinson
- poverty

Alan J. Auerbach
- taxation of income
- taxation of wealth

R.J. Aumann
- game theory

H.A. Averch
- Averch–Johnson effect

Stephen H. Axilrod
- Wallich, Henry Christopher (born 1914)

Stephen H. Axilrod (with Henry C. Wallich)
- open-market operations

Costas Azariadis
- implicit contracts

Michael Bacharach
- zero-sum games

Amiya Kumar Bagchi
- Chayanov, Alexander Vasil'evich (1888–1939)
- development planning
- industrialization

Egon Balas
- integer programming

Y. Balasko
- catastrophe theory

Bela Balassa
- economic integration

Pietro Balestra
- dummy variables
- seasonal variation

Ernst Baltensperger
- credit

M. Baranzini
- distribution theories: Keynesian

Ingo Barens
- Spiethoff, Arthur August Kaspar (1873–1957)

Robin Barlow
- declining population

A.P. Barten
- household budgets
- Koyck [Koijck], Leendert Marinus (1918–1962)

J.R. Barth (with P.A.V.B. Swamy)
- random co-efficients

H. Bartoli
- Proudhon, Pierre Joseph (1809–1865)

R.L. Basmann
- maximum likelihood

[C.F. Bastable]
- experimental methods in economics (i)

Kaushik Basu
- Nurkse, Ragnar (1907–1959)

Charles E. Bates
- instrumental variables

Francis M. Bator
- fine tuning
- functional finance

Peter Bauer
- marketing boards

[S. Bauer]
- balance of trade, history of the theory

William J. Baumol
indivisibilities
performing arts
Ramsey pricing

Peter Bearman
Durkheim, Emile (1858–1917)

Giacomo Becattini
internal economies
Marshall, Mary Paley (1850–1944)
Pantaleoni, Maffeo (1857–1924)

Gary S. Becker
family

Wilfred Beckerman
limits to growth
national income

Martin J. Beckmann
assignment problem
location of economic activity
rank
Weber, Alfred (1868–1958)

David Beetham
ideal type
Weber, Max (1864–1920)

Jere R. Behrman
agricultural supply

Clive Bell
development economics

R.P. Bellamy
Cattaneo, Carlo (1801–1861)
Croce, Bendetto (1866–1952)
Hegelianism

Bernard Belloc (with Michel Moreaux)
Allais, Maurice (born 1911)

David A. Belsley
Kuh, Edwin (1925–1986)

Jean-Pascal Benassy
disequilibrium analysis
rationed equilibria

B. Berch
Breckenridge, Sophonisba Preston (1866–1948)
Gilman, Charlotte Perkins (1860–1935)

Maxine Berg
Babbage, Charles (1791–1871)
Barton, John (1789–1852)

James O. Berger
randomization
sequential analysis
statistical decision theory

Ted Bergstrom
free disposal

Richard A. Berk
household production

[Angelo Bertolini]
Genovesi, Antonio (1712–1769)

Roger Betancourt
capital utilization

Amit Bhaduri
disguised unemployment
golden age
moneylenders

Jagdish N. Bhagwati
directly unproductive profit-seeking (DUP) activities
immiserizing growth
smuggling

Krishna Bharadwaj
natural wage
subsistence
vulgar economy
wages in classical economics

R.J. Bigg
Andreades, Andreas (1876–1935)
Crowther, Geoffrey (1907–1972)
Gregory, Theodore Emanuel Gugenheim (1890–1970)
Hawtrey, Ralph George (1879–1975)

R.D. Collison Black
Banfield, Thomas Charles (1800–?1882)
Cairnes, John Elliott (1823–1875)
Collet, Clara Elizabeth (1860–1948)
Ingram, John Kells (1823–1907)
Jenkin, Henry Charles Fleeming (1833–1885)
Jennings, Richard (1814–1891)
Jevons, William Stanley (1835–1882)
Longfield, Mountifort (1802–1884)
utility
Whately, Richard (1787–1863)

S.W. Black
international monetary institutions
seignorage

C. Blackorby
lexicographic orderings
orderings
preorderings

Douglas Blair
acyclicity

Olivier Jean Blanchard
crowding out
leads and lags
neoclassical synthesis

Francine D. Blau
gender

Mark Blaug
circulating capital
classical economics
Hermann, Friedrich Benedict Wilhelm von (1795–1868)
Hutchison, Terence Wilmot (born 1912)
iron law of wages
productive and unproductive consumption
Storch, Heinrich Friedrich von (1766–1835)
West, Edward (1782–1828)

Michael Bleaney
Mummery, Albert Frederick (1855–1895)
over investment
over saving

Mario I. Blejer (with Jacob A. Frenkel)
monetary approach to the balance of payments

Christopher Bliss
distribution theories: neoclassical
equal rates of profit
Farrell, Michael James (1926–1975)
Hicks, John Richard (born 1904)

C.A. Blyth
Phillips, Alban William Housego (1914–1975)
wage fund doctrine

Luciano Boggio
centre of gravitation

Peter Bohm
external economies
Lindahl on public finance
second best

Volker Böhm (with Hans Haller)
demand theory

Marcel P. Boiteux
Massé, Pierre (born 1898)

Lawrence A. Boland
methodology
stylized facts

Gottfried Bombach
Schneider, Erich (1900–70)

[James Bonar]
examples
Fichte, Johann Gottlieb (1762–1814)
Paley, William (1743–1805)

[James Bonar (with S. Olivier and J.D. Rogers)]
labour exchange

Karl H. Borch
Johansen, Leif (1930–1982)
life insurance

Michael D. Bordo
bimetallism
equation of exchange
Law, John (1671–1729)

V.K. Borooah
politics and economics

E. Boserup
agricultural growth and population change
inequality between the sexes

Tom Bottomore
Bauer, Otto (1881–1938)
Bernstein, Eduard (1850–1932)
Dühring, Eugen Karl (1833–1921)
Lassalle, Ferdinand (1825–1864)

Kenneth E. Boulding
assets and liabilities
Bertalanffy, Ludwig von (1901–1972)
general systems theory

Mary Jean Bowman
Reid, Margaret Gilpin (born 1896)
Schultz, Theodore Wilhain (born 1902)

Robert Boyer
régulation

Vladimir Brailovsky
international indebtedness

Margaret Bray
perfect foresight

D. Breeden
intertemporal portfolio theory and asset pricing

Hans Brems
Birck, Laurito Vilhelm (1871–1933)
Ohlin, Bertil Gotthard (1899–1979)
Westergaard, Harald Ludvig (1853–1936)
Zeuthen, Frederik (1888–1959)

M.J. Brennan
capital asset pricing model

Robert Brenner
feudalism
Postan, Michael Moïssey (1899–1981)

Stephen Breyer (with Paul W. MacAvoy)
regulation and deregulation

James A. Brickley (with John J. McConnell)
dividend policy

P. Bridel
Chevalier, Michel (1806–1879)
credit cycle
Ganilh, Charles (1785–1836)
Goschen, George Joachim, Viscount (1831–1907)
Lavington, Frederick (1881–1927)
Montchrétien, Antoyne de (1575–1621)
price level
public works
saving equals investment
widow's cruse

Asa Briggs
Bagehot, Walter (1826–1877)
Wilson, James (1805–1860)

John A. Bristow
Bastable, Charles Francis (1855–1945)

W.A. Brock
optimal control and economic dynamics

A. Brody
prices and quantities

M. Bronfenbrenner
employment, theories of

Brendan Brown
capital flight
Einzig, Paul (1897–1973)
hot money

Clair Brown (with Amelia Preece)
housework

E. Cary Brown
Domar, Evsey David (born 1914)

Henry Phelps Brown
inequality of pay
trade unions
wages, real and money

Murray Brown
Cobb-Douglas functions

William Brown
collective bargaining

Irene Bruegel
labour market discrimination

Karl Brunner
high-powered money and the monetary base
money supply

W. Brus
market socialism

James M. Buchanan
constitutional economics
opportunity cost
public debt

David Burchell
Strachey, John (1901–1963)

Edwin Burmeister
linear models
saddlepoints
Wicksell effects

G. Busino
Pareto, Vilfredo (1848–1923)

F. Caffè
Barone, Enrico (1859–1924)
Einaudi, Luigi (1874–1961)
Ferrara, Francesco (1810–1900)
Mazzola, Ugo (1863–1899)
Papi, Giuseppe Ugo (born 1893)
Vecchio, Gustavo del (1883–1972)
Viti de Marco, Antonio de (1858–1943)

Phillip Cagan
hyperinflation
monetarism

Nilüfer Çağatay
beggar-thy-neighbour
quotas and tariffs

Glen G. Cain
segmented labour markets

Bruce J. Caldwell
positivism

Guillermo A. Calvo
hierarchy
tulipmania

Gordon C. Cameron
central place theory
Christaller, Walter (1894–1975)

G. Campanelli
Tozer, John Edward (1806–1877)
Whewell, William (1799–1866)

Robert W. Campbell (with Holland Hunter)
Novozhilov, Viktor Valentinovich (1892–1970)

Antonietta Campus
marginalist economics

[Edwin Cannan]
Christian Socialism
Marcet, Jane (1769–1858)
Ortes, Giammaria (1713–1790)

Dennis R. Capozza (with Robert Van Order)
spatial competition

Mark Casson
entrepreneur

[E. Castelot]
Knights Templar
laissez-faire, laissez-passer, history of the maxim
Say, Louis Auguste (1774–1840)

George Catephores
alienation

Filippo Cesarano
Galiani, Ferdinando (1728–1787)

Sukhamoy Chakravarty
cost–benefit analysis
Mahalanobis, Prasanta Chandra (1893–1972)
optimal savings
Tinbergen, Jan (born 1903)

[M.D. Chalmers]
quasi-contract

Christophe Chamley
taxation of capital

D.G. Champernowne
divided populations and stochastic models

S.G. Checkland
industrial revolution

Hollis Chenery
foreign aid

Steven N.S. Cheung
Alchian, Armen Albert (born 1914)
Coase, Ronald Harry (born 1910)
common property rights
economic organization and transactions costs

S.H. Chew
mean values

Victoria Chick
Coddington, Alan (1941–1982)
finance and saving
Gesell, Silvio (1862–1930)
Townshend, Hugh (1890–1974)

John S. Chipman
Bickerdike, Charles Frederick (1876–1961)
compensation principle
Haberler, Gottfried (born 1900)
international trade
Machlup, Fritz (1902–1983)

Gregory C. Chow
hypothesis testing

Carl F. Christ
government budget restraint

Carl F. Christ (with Leonid Hurwicz)
Koopmans, Tjalling Charles (1910–1985)

Gregory Claeys
utopias

Colin G. Clark
Coghlan, Timothy A. (1855–1926)
Douglas, Paul Howard (1892–1976)
Jones, George Thomas (1902–1929)
Nef, John Ulric (born 1899)

Colin W. Clark
bioeconomics
fisheries
renewable resources

David Clark
Bakunin, Mikhael Alexandrovitch (1814–1876)
Douglas, Clifford Hugh (1879–1952)
monetary cranks

[J.B. Clark]
distribution, ethics of
distribution, law of

Robert L. Clark
ageing populations

Peter Clarke
Hobson, John Atkinson (1858–1940)
Stephen V.O. Clarke
Williams, John Henry (1887–1980)
Wolfgang-Dieter Classen
fascism
Schacht, Horace Greeley Hjalmar (1877–1970)
Simone Clemhout (with Henry Y. Wan, Jr.)
differential games
J.A. Clifton
competitive market processes
Ansley J. Coale
demographic transition
stable population theory
Ronald H. Coase
Plant, Arnold (1898–1978)
Ken Coates
co-operatives
A.W. Coats
Adams, Henry Carter (1851–1921)
American Economic Association
Bullock, Charles Jesse (1869–1941)
Carver, Thomas Nixon (1865–1961)
Dunbar, Charles Franklin (1830–1900)
Ely, Richard Theodore (1854–1943)
Hollander, Jacob Harry (1871–1940)
Moore, Henry Ludwell (1869–1958)
Patten, Simon Nelson (1852–1922)
Royal Economic Society
Seligman, Edwin Robert Anderson (1861–1939)
Walker, Francis Amasa (1840–1897)
Thomas C. Cochran
Gras, Norman Scott Brien (1884–1956)
Robert M. Coen (with Robert Eisner)
investment
Joel E. Cohen
Lotka, Alfred James (1880–1949)
W. Cohen
Burns, Eveline Mabel (1900–1985)
Witte, Edwin Emil (1887–1960)
D.C. Coleman
Colbert, Jean-Baptiste (1619–1683)
Colbertism
James S. Coleman
equality
David Collard
Dickinson, Henry Douglas (1899–1969)
Stefan Collini
Stephen, Leslie (1832–1904)
Gregory Connor
hedging
Robert D. Cooter
Coase theorem
Thomas E. Copeland (with J. Fred Weston)
asset pricing
W.M. Corden
effective protection
Wilfred Corlett
bunch maps
multicollinearity
John Cornwall
inflation and growth
long cycles
stagflation
total factor productivity
B.A. Corry
Attwood, Thomas (1783–1856)
Bowley, Marian (born 1911)
overproduction
Robbins, Lionel Charles (1898–1984)
Torrens, Robert (1780–1864)
A. Cosh
diversification of activities
retention ratio
Stephen R. Cosslett
semiparametric estimation
[A. Courtois]
Babeuf, François Noel (1764–1797)
Bodin, Jean (1530–1596)
Laveleye, Emile de (1822–1892)
Meynieu, Mary (died 1877)
Necker, Jacques (1732–1804)
K.J. Coutts
average cost pricing
foreign trade multiplier
F.A. Cowell
Champernowne, David Gawen (born 1912)
redistribution of income and wealth
D.R. Cox
transformation of statistical variables
N.F.R. Crafts
economic history
empty boxes
John G. Cragg
Monte Carlo methods
J.S. Cramer
velocity of circulation
A.B. Cramp
bank rate
liquidity
Sayers, Richard Sydney (born 1908)
sound money
tight money
Vincent P. Crawford
fair division
A.D. Crockett
international liquidity
J.P. Croshaw
Edgeworth, Maria (1767–1849)
J.-P. Crouzeix
homogeneous and homothetic functions
quasi-concavity
Camilo Dagum
Gini, Corrado (1884–1965)
Gini ratio
Ralf Dahrendorf
Erhard, Ludwig (1897–1977)
liberalism
George Dalton
Herskovits, Melville Jean (1895–1963)
Polanyi, Karl (1886–1964)
Eric van Damme
extensive form games
George B. Dantzig
linear programming
simplex method for solving linear programs
Michael R. Darby
consumption function
wealth effect
William Darity, Jr.
Postlethwayt, Malachy (1707?–1767)
Partha Dasgupta
project evaluation
Ednaldo Araquem da Silva
absolute rent
unequal exchange
Paul Davidson
aggregate supply function
user cost
Richard B. Day
Trotsky, Lev Davidovich (1879–1940)
Paul de Grauwe
international monetary policy
Phyllis Deane
Ashton, Thomas Southcliffe (1889–1968)
Clapham, John Harold (1873–1946)
Cohen, Ruth Louisa (born 1906)
Fawcett, Henry (1833–1884)
Keynes, John Neville (1852–1949)
King, Gregory (1648–1712)
political arithmetic
Power, Eileen Edna (1889–1940)
Sidgwick, Henry (1838–1900)
Angus Deaton
consumers' expenditure
Stone, John Richard Nicholas (born 1913)
Gerard Debreu
existence of general equilibrium
mathematical economics
S. de Brunhoff
fictitious capital
Marcello de Cecco
gold standard
Roger Dehem
Aupetit, Albert (1876–1943)
Gide, Charles (1847–1932)
Pirou, Gaetan (1886–1946)
Rist, Charles (1874–1955)
Rueff, Jacques (1896–1978)
Neil de Marchi
abstinence
non-competing groups
paradoxes and anomalies
Senior, Nassau William (1790–1864)
E. Denison
Goldsmith, Raymond William (born 1904)
Goldsmith, Selma (née Selma Evelyn Fine) (1912–1962)
growth accounting
Jaszi, George (born 1915)

Ray C. Fair
macroeconometric models

M. Falkus
backwardness
Chernyshevskii, Nikolai Gavrilovich (1828–1889)
Plekhanov, Georgii Valentinovich (1856–1918)
Rodbertus, Johann Karl (1805–1875)

C.H. Feinstein
measurement of economic growth

Allan M. Feldman
equity
welfare economics

Frank Whitson Fetter
Wheatley, John (1772–1830)

Ronald Findlay
comparative advantage
free trade and protection
Lewis, W. Arthur (born 1915)
terms of trade

M.I. Finley
Aristotle (BC 384–322)
chrematistics

Massimo Finoia
Fasiani, Mauro (1900–1950)

Stanley Fischer
new classical macroeconomics
Samuelson, Paul Anthony (born 1915)
Sidrauski, Miguel (1939–1968)

Peter C. Fishburn
interdependent preferences
representation of preferences
utility theory and decision theory

Anthony C. Fisher
natural resources

Franklin M. Fisher
adjustment processes and stability
aggregation problem

Malcolm R. Fisher
life cycle hypothesis
Salter, Wilfred Edward Graham (1929–1963)

Walter D. Fisher
aggregation of economic relations

Albert Fishlow
Gerschenkron, Alexander (1904–1978)
inequality between nations

J.P. Fitoussi
Shonfield, Andrew Akiba (1917–1982)

E.V.K. FitzGerald
land reform
latifundia

Diane Flaherty
Erlich, Alexander (1913–1985)
radical political economy

Roderick Floud
cliometrics

[A.W. Flux]
plutology

D. Foley
money in economic activity

Robert Forster
Bloch, Marc (1886–1944)
Braudel, Fernand (1902–1985)
Lefebvre, Georges (1874–1959)
Mantoux, Paul (1877–1956)
peasants

J. Foster
bourgeoisie
class
Kuczynski, Jurgen Peter (born 1904)

John Bellamy Foster
Sweezy, Paul Malor (born 1910)

Karl A. Fox
agricultural economics
Nicholls, William Hord (1914–1978)
Roos, Charles Frederick (1901–1958)
Tintner, Gerhard (1907–1983)

S. Herbert Frankel
Lehfeldt, Robert Alfred (1868–1927)
Simmel, Georg (1858–1918)

C. Freeman
innovation
long swings in economic growth
structural unemployment

R.B. Freeman
Dunlop, John Thomas (born 1914)
labour economics

R.D. Freeman
Arndt, Heinz Wolfgang (born 1915)

Xavier Freixas
certainty equivalent

Jacob A. Frenkel
Johnson, Harry Gordon (1923–1977)

Jacob A. Frenkel (with Mario I. Blejer)
monetary approach to the balance of payments

Jacob A. Frenkel (with Richard M. Levich)
spot and forward markets

A.L. Friedman
de-skilling
Taylorism

Benjamin M. Friedman
capital, credit and money markets

David D. Friedman
just price
law and economics

James W. Friedman
bilateral monopoly
duopoly

Milton Friedman
Laughlin, James Laurence (1850–1933)
Newcomb, Simon (1835–1909)
quantity theory of money

Richard Fry
financial journalism

Victor R. Fuchs
health economics

Daniel R. Fusfeld
Methodenstreit
Taylor, Fred Manville (1855–1932)

Melvyn A. Fuss
production and cost functions

Mason Gaffney
Brown, Harry Gunnison (1880–1975)
George, Henry (1839–1897)
land tax
single tax
Wallace, Alfred Russel (1823–1913)

J.K. Galbraith
Berle, Adolf Augustus, Jr. (1895–1971)
Harris, Seymour Edwin (1897–1975)
Nathan, Robert Roy (born 1908)
price control

A. Ronald Gallant
non-linear methods in econometrics

Giancarlo Gandolfo
Amoroso, Luigi (1886–1965)
Ceva, Giovanni (1647/48–1734)
de Finetti, Bruno de (1906–1985)
Ricci, Umberto (1879–1946)
Slutsky, Eugen (1880–1948)
stability
Volterra, Vito (1860–1940)

Pierangelo Garegnani
surplus approach to value and distribution

Roger W. Garrison (with Israel M. Kirzner)
Hayek, Friedrich August von (born 1899)

Joseph L. Gastwirth
non-parametric statistical methods

David E.R. Gay
Divisia, François Jean Marie (1889–1964)
Gibrat, Robert Pierre Louis (1904–1980)

John Geanakoplos
Arrow–Debreu model of general equilibrium
overlapping generations model of general equilibrium

J.M.A. Gee
Anderson, James (1739–1808)

Ernest Gellner
economic interpretation of history

K.D. George
rationalization of industry

Nicholas Georgescu-Roegen
entropy
Manoïlescu, Mihail (1891–?1950)
ophelimity
Oppenheimer, Franz (1864–1943)

Vincent J. Geraci
errors in variables

John Geweke
endogeneity and exogeneity

Gilbert R. Ghez
Bowman, Mary Jean (born 1908)

A.K. Ghose
famine

[H. de B. Gibbins]
Stirner, Max (1806–1856)

[C. Gide]
Secrétan, Charles (1815–1895)
solidarity

Peter Holmes
indicative planning
J.K. Horsefield
fiduciary issue
B. Horvat
labour-managed economics
George Horwich (with John Pomeroy)
Metzler, Lloyd Appleton (1913–1980)
H.S. Houthakker
Engel, Ernst (1821–1896)
Engel curve
Engel's Law
futures trading
Peter Howitt
macroeconomics: relations with microeconomics
money illusion
optimum quantity of money
Susan Howson
cheap money
dear money
Cheng Hsiao
identification
Ch-fu Huang
continuous-time stochastic processes
Gur Huberman
arbitrage pricing theory
Alan Hughes
competition policy
conglomerates
managerial capitalism
Charles R. Hulten
amortization
Divisia index
Paul W. Humphreys
induction
Jane Humphries
women and work
E.K. Hunt (with Mark Glick)
transformation problem
Holland Hunter (with Robert W. Campbell)
Novozhilov, Viktor Valentinovich (1892–1970)
Hillard G. Huntington
energy economics
Leonid Hurwicz (with Carl F. Christ)
Koopmans, Tjalling Charles (1910–1985)
A. Hussain
commodity fetishism
Yuji Ijiri
birth-and-death processes
Jonathan E. Ingersoll, Jr.
interest rates
option pricing theory
Michael D. Intriligator
non-linear programming
Shigeru Ishikawa
structural change
Richard Jackman
wage flexibility
Dwight M. Jaffee
credit rationing
R. Jessop
economic theory of the state
mode of production
T. Johnston
Gray, Alexander (1882–1968)
Richard Jolly
Ward, Barbara (1914–81)
B.L. Jones
Currie, Lauchlin Bernard (born 1902)
Ronald W. Jones
Heckscher–Ohlin trade theory
Dale W. Jorgenson
production functions
vintages
P.N. Junankar
acceleration principle
A. Kadish
Toynbee, Arnold (1852–1883)
R.F. Kahn
Rostas, Laslo (1909–1954)
Shove, Gerald Frank (1888–1947)
Nanak Kakwani
Lorenz curve
Morton I. Kamien
calculus of variations
limit pricing
market structure and innovation
Ravi Kanbur
buffer stocks
North–South economic relations
shadow pricing
Ravi Kanbur (with J. McIntosh)
dual economies
Leonid Kantorovich (with Victor Polterovich)
functional analysis
Edi Karni
fraud
preference reversals
state-dependent preferences
A.F. Karr
martingales
M.C. Kaser
Nemchinov, Vasily Sergeevich (1894–1964)
Strumilin, Stanislav Gustavovich (1877–1974)
Struve, Pyotr Berngardovich (1870–1944)
Voznesensky, Nikolai Alekseevich (1903–1950)
Donald W. Katzner
integrability of demand
supply functions
Masahiro Kawai
backwardation
optimum currency areas
John Kay
consumption taxation
direct taxes
indirect taxes
T.J. Kehoe
comparative statics
Murray C. Kemp
correspondence principle
elasticities approach to the balance of payments
gains from trade
Marshall–Lerner conditions
trade subsidies
Charles Kennedy
biased and unbiased technological change
P. Kenway
crises
realization problem
P. Kerr
Abbott, Edith (1876–1957)
Albert Kervyn
Triffin, Robert (born 1911)
Nathan Keyfitz
demography
life tables
[J.N. Keynes]
relativity, principle of, in political economy
Leon H. Keyserling
Means, Gardiner Coit (born 1896)
pump priming
Tugwell, Rexford Guy (1891–1979)
M. Ali Khan
correspondences
Court, Louis Mehel
Harris–Todaro model
perfect competition
B.F. Kiker
Nicholson, Joseph Shield (1850–1927)
Mark R. Killingsworth
labour supply of women
Charles P. Kindleberger
bubbles
financial crisis
Sohmen, Egon (1930–1977)
Robert G. King (with Michael Dotsey)
business cycles
A.P. Kirman
Antonelli, Giovanni Battista (1858–1944)
atomistic competition
combinatorics
graph theory
measure theory
Pareto as an economist
Israel M. Kirzner
Austrian school of economics
economic harmony
Israel M. Kirzner (with Roger W. Garrison)
Hayek, Friedrich August von (born 1899)
Kurt Klappholz
ideology
rent control
T. Kloek
principal components
J. Kmenta
heteroskedasticity
Allen V. Kneese (with Clifford S. Russell)
environmental economics

Jack L. Knetsch
recreation
Serge-Christophe Kolm
public economics
Gerard M. Koot
Foxwell, Herbert Somerton (1849–1936)
Richard F. Kosobud
relative income hypothesis
Laurence J. Kotlikoff
social security
Y. Kotowitz
moral hazard
Tadeusz Kowalik
central planning
Kautsky, Karl (1854–1938)
Lange, Oskar Ryszard (1904–1965)
Lange–Lerner mechanism
Luxemburg, Rosa (1870–1919)
William S. Krasker
outliers
Irving B. Kravis
Gilbert, Milton (1909–1979)
international income comparisons
J.A. Kregel
effective demand
natural and warranted rates of growth
output and employment
rentier
Weintraub, Sidney (1914–1983)
Wilhelm Krelle
Stackelberg, Heinrich von (1905–1946)
David M. Kreps
Nash equilibrium
Ronald J. Krumm (with George S. Tolley)
regional economics
John V. Krutilla
water resources
Robert E. Kuenne
Chamberlin, Edward Hastings (1899–1967)
O. Kurer
Ashley, Sir William James (1860–1927)
Cunningham, William (1849–1919)
Maine, Sir Henry James Sumner (1822–1888)
Rogers, James Edwin Thorold (1823–1890)
Heinz D. Kurz
capital theory: debates
factor-price frontier
Mordecai Kurz
myopic decision rules
J.J. Laffont
externalities
revelation of preferences
David Laidler
Boyd, Walter (1754–1837)
Bullionist Controversy
Thornton, Henry (1760–1815)
Sanjaya Lall
transfer pricing
Robert J. Lampman
transfer payments

K.J. Lancaster
Makower, Helen (born 1910)
non-price competition
product differentiation
Vickrey, William Spencer (born 1914)
K. Laski
Kalecki, Michal (1899–1970)
Rothschild, Kurt Wilhelm (born 1914)
Steindl, Josef (born 1912)
Marie Lavigne
East–West economic relations
Edward P. Lazear
incentive contracts
William Lazonick
labour process
Ure, Andrew (1778–1857)
Stephen F. LeRoy
present value
Edward E. Leamer
Leontief paradox
specification problems in econometrics
J. Lecaillon
Marchal, Jean (born 1905)
Marczewski, Jean (born 1908)
John O. Ledyard
incentive compatibility
market failure
Ronald Lee
population cycles
Sauvy, Alfred (born 1898)
Harvey Leibenstein
X-efficiency theory
Axel Leijonhufvud
IS–LM analysis
natural rate and market rate
Wassily Leontief
input–output analysis
Richard M. Levich (with Jacob A. Frenkel)
spot and forward markets
Alastair Levy (with Murray Milgate)
Angell, James Waterhouse (1898–1986)
Bonar, James (1852–1941)
Fawcett, Millicent Garrett (1847–1929)
Fay, Charles Ryle (1884–1961)
Gonner, Edward Carter Kersey (1862–1922)
Layton, Walter Thomas (1884–1966)
Macleod, Henry Dunning (1821-1902)
Thompson, Thomas Perronet (1783–1869)
Withers, Hartley (1867–1950)
Haim Levy
stochastic dominance
Assar Lindbeck
Lundberg, Erik Filip (born 1907)
D.V. Lindley
Bayes, Revd Thomas (1702–1761)
regression and correlation analysis
statistical inference
David E. Lindsey (with Henry C. Wallich)
monetary policy

Steven A. Lippman
dynamic programming and Markov decision processes
Robert Lipsey
Schwartz, Anna Jacobson (born 1915)
I.M.D. Little
Crosland, Anthony (1918–1977)
B. Lockwood
Pareto efficiency
Peter A. Loeb (with Salim Rashid)
Lyapunov's theorem
non-standard analysis
Michael C. Lovell
inventory cycles
R. Duncan Luce (with Louis Narens)
meaningfulness and invariance
measurement, theory of
W.A.J. Luxemburg
Robinson, Abraham (1918–1974)
Esfandiar Maasoumi
information theory
Paul W. MacAvoy (with Stephen Breyer)
regulation and deregulation
Kenneth R. MacCrimmon
critical path analysis
Louis J. Maccini
adjustment costs
inventories
Mark J. Machina
expected utility hypothesis
Mark J. Machina (with Michael Rothschild)
risk
C.B. Macpherson
Burke, Edmund (1729–1797)
Hobbes, Thomas (1588–1679)
individualism
G.S. Maddala
censored data models
[F.W. Maitland]
Domesday Book
Mukul Majumdar
multisector growth models
V. Makarov
Kantorovich, Leonid Vitalievich (1912–1986)
V. Makarov (with A. Rubinov)
Von Neumann technology
Louis Makowski
imperfect competition
E. Malinvaud
capital gains and losses
decentralization
intertemporal equilibrium and efficiency
Landry, Adolphe (1874–1956)
Burton G. Malkiel
efficient market hypothesis
term structure of interest rates
A.G. Malliaris
stochastic optimal control
Wiener process

J. Maloney
Cliffe Leslie, Thomas Edward (1827–1882)
English historical school
real cost doctrine

Ernest Mandel
communism
Marx, Karl Heinrich (1818–1883)

Benoit B. Mandelbrot
Bachelier, Louis (1870–1946)

Edwin Mansfield
diffusion of technology
Gibrat's Law
transfer of technology

Stephen A. Marglin
investment and accumulation

Harry M. Markowitz
mean-variance analysis

R.L. Marris
corporate economy
Penrose, Edith Tilton (born 1914)

Thomas Marschak
organization theory

Peter Marshall
Godwin, William (1756–1836)

Béla Martos
control and coordination of economic activity

L. Maruszko (with M.P. Todaro)
international migration

A. Mas-Colell
cooperative equilibrium
non-convexity

Pierre B. Massé
public utility pricing

Gautham Mathur
depreciation

John J. McCall
insurance, economics of
replacement policy

Bennett T. McCallum
inflationary expectations

Bennett T. McCallum (with Marvin S. Goodfriend)
demand for money: theoretical studies

Donald N. McCloskey
continuity in economic history
counterfactuals
fungibility
Hamilton, Earl Jefferson (born 1899)
Kindleberger, Charles Poor (born 1910)
open field system
rhetoric

J.S.L. McCombie
Verdoorn's Law

John J. McConnell (with James A. Brickley)
dividend policy

Martin C. McGuire
clubs
defence economics

J. McIntosh (with Ravi Kanbur)
dual economies

Lionel W. McKenzie
general equilibrium
gross substitutes
turnpike theory

Paul J. McNulty
competition: Austrian conceptions

M. McPherson
changes in tastes
Hirschman, Albert Otto (born 1915)

A. Medio
multiplier–accelerator interaction
trade cycle

G. Meeks
mergers

J. Meenan
O'Brien, George (1892–1973)

Gerald M. Meier
infant industry

Luca Meldolesi
Bortkiewicz, Ladislaus von (1868–1931)

Jean-François Mertens
repeated games
supergames

Robert C. Merton
continuous-time stochastic models
options

S. Metcalfe
technical change

Peter Mieszkowski
Musgrave, Richard Abel (born 1910)
taxation of corporate profits
urban economics

Deborah Duff Milenkovitch (with Andrew Zimbalist)
socialist economics

Murray Milgate
Cannan, Edwin (1861–1935)
Carlyle, Thomas (1795–1881)
equilibrium: development of the concept
Florence, Philip Sargent (1890–1982)
Giffen, Robert (1837–1910)
goods and commodities
Higgs, Henry (1864–1940)
Juglar, Clémont (1819–1905)
Keynes's *General Theory*
Massie, Joseph (died 1794)
neo-Ricardianism
Novalis [Georg Friedrich Philipp von Hardenberg] (1772–1801)
Palgrave, Robert Harry Inglis (1827–1919)
Palgrave's Dictionary of Political Economy
Pennington, James (1777–1862)
Smart, William (1853–1915)
Staehle, Hans (1903–1961)
Tiebout, Charles Mills (1924–1968)
Titmuss, Richard Morris (1907–1973)
Twiss, Travers (1809–1897)
Wilson, Edwin Bidwell (1879–1964)

Murray Milgate (with Alastair Levy)
Angell, James Waterhouse (1898–1986)
Bonar, James (1852–1941)
Fawcett, Millicent Garrett (1847–1929)
Fay, Charles Ryle (1884–1961)
Gonner, Edward Carter Kersey (1862–1922)
Layton, Walter Thomas (1884–1966)
Macleod, Henry Dunning (1821-1902)
Thompson, Thomas Perronet (1783–1869)
Withers, Hartley (1867–1950)

Paul Milgrom
predatory pricing

Nicholas R. Miller
voting

Edwin S. Mills
user fees

Ravi Mirchandani
Habakkuk, John Hrothgar (born 1915)

Leonard J. Mirman
perfect information

D.E. Moggridge
fundamental disequilibrium
Tarshis, Lorie (born 1911)

Josef Molsberger
Eucken, Walter (1891–1950)
Röpke, Wilhelm (1899–1966)

D.H. Monro
self-interest

[F.C. Montague]
optimism and pessimism

Guido Montani
extensive and intensive rent
productive and unproductive labour
scarcity

Barry Moore (with John Rhodes)
regional distribution of economic activity

Geoffrey H. Moore
Burns, Arthur Frank (1904–1987)
Fabricant, Solomon (born 1906)
Mitchell, Wesley Clair (1874–1948)

James C. Moore
cost and supply curves

Michel Moreaux (with Bernard Belloc)
Allais, Maurice (born 1911)

James N. Morgan
Katona, George (1901–1981)
survey research

Jacob L. Mosak
Schultz, Henry (1893–1938)
Yntema, Theodore O. (1900–1985)

John Muellbauer
consumer durables

Peter Mueser
discrimination
internal migration

Alicia H. Munnell (with Joseph B. Grolnic)
indexed securities

[E.C. Munro]
principal and agent (i)

Richard A. Musgrave
Hansen, Alvin (1887–1975)
merit goods
public finance
H. Myint
vent for surplus
G. D. Myles (with W. M. Gorman)
characteristics
M. Ishaq Nadiri
joint production
production: neoclassical theories
Tsuneo Nakauchi
Tsuru, Shigeto (born 1912)
Louis Narens (with R. Duncan Luce)
meaningfulness and invariance
measurement, theory of
Robert R. Nathan
Hagen, Everett Einar (born 1906)
J.P. Neary
rationing
Takashi Negishi
monopolistic competition and general equilibrium
tâtonnement and recontracting
P.A. Neher
forests
Edward J. Nell
accumulation of capital
Lowe, Adolph (born 1893)
Neisser, Hans Philipp (1895–1975)
Forrest D. Nelson
logit, probit and tobit
Marc Nerlove
Liu, Ta-Chung (1914–1975)
Marc Nerlove (with Francis X. Diebold)
autoregressive and moving-average time-series processes
estimation
time series analysis
David M. Newbery
futures markets, hedging and speculation
Ramsey model
John L. Newman
fecundity
Peter Newman
consumption sets
convexity
cost minimization and utility maximization
Donisthorpe, Wordsworth (1847–?)
duality
Edgeworth, Francis Ysidro (1845–1926)
elasticity
Euler's Theorem
gauge functions
Gray, Simon (*fl.* 1795–1840)
indirect utility function
inequalities
monotone mappings
optimality and efficiency
Ramsey, Frank Plumpton (1903–1930)
rising supply price
Shaw, George Bernard (1856–1950)
substitutes and complements
Woytinsky, Wladimir Savelievich (1885–1960)
Young, Allyn Abbott (1876–1929)
Jürg Niehans
Auspitz, Rudolf (1837–1906)
Gossen, Hermann (1810–1858)
Launhardt, Carl Friedrich Wilhelm (1832–1918)
Lieben, Richard (1842–1919)
Lutz, Friedrich August (1901–1975)
Oncken, August (1844–1911)
overshooting
Thünen, Johann Heinrich von (1783–1850)
transaction costs
Hukukane Nikaido
fixed point theorems
Hawkins–Simon conditions
Perron–Frobenius theorem
Peter Nolan
Bettelheim, Charles (born 1913)
collective agriculture
Mao Zedong [Mao Tse-Tung] (1893–1976)
Roger G. Noll
communications
Neville R. Norman
protection
Rudolf Nötel
Varga, Evgeny (Jenö) (1879–1964)
Alec Nove
planned economy
socialism
Tugan-Baranovsky, Mikhail Ivanovich (1865–1919)
D.M. Nuti
co-determination and profit-sharing
cycles in socialist economies
Dmitriev, Vladimir Karpovich (1868–1913)
pay-off period
D.P. O'Brien
Chalmers, Thomas (1780–1847)
Colquhoun, Patrick (1745–1820)
McCulloch, John Ramsay (1789–1864)
Newmarch, William (1820–1882)
Overstone, Lord (1796–1883)
Ravenstone, Piercy
R. O'Donnell
real and nominal quantities
William H. Oakland
value-added tax
Wallace E. Oates
property taxation
Maurice Obstfeld
international finance
Avner Offer
war economy
Lawrence H. Officer
Malynes, Gerard de (*fl.* 1586–1623)
Walter Y. Oi
fixed factors
N. Okishio
choice of technique and rate of profit
constant and variable capital
[S. Olivier (with James Bonar and J.D. Rogers)]
labour exchange
Mancur Olson
bureaucracy
collective action
Peter M. Oppenheimer
external debt
fixed exchange rates
Guy H. Orcutt
simulation of microanalytic systems
Robert Van Order (with Dennis R. Capozza)
spatial competition
G. Orosel
period of production
Dale K. Osborne
transformations and invariance
Joseph M. Ostroy
money and general equilibrium theory
U. Pagano
Gioia, Melchiorre (1767–1829)
Morton Paglin
Lauderdale, Eighth Earl of [James Maitland] (1759–1839)
J.G. Palma
dependency
Prebisch, Raul (1901–1986)
structuralism
Carlo Panico
'effectual demand' in Adam Smith
interest and profit
liquidity preference
Carlo Panico (with John Eatwell)
Sraffa, Piero (1898–1983)
Carlo Panico (with Fabio Petri)
long-run and short-run
John C. Panzar
competition and efficiency
Gustav F. Papanek
Mason, Edward Sagendorph (born 1899)
Derek Parfit (with James Griffin)
hedonism
William N. Parker
Usher, Abbot Payson (1884–1965)
Michael Parkin
adaptive expectations
inflation
William Parry
ergodic theory
Donald O. Parsons
minimum wages
B. Peter Pashigian
cobweb theorem
Luigi L. Pasinetti
Kahn, Richard Ferdinand (born 1905)
Robinson, Joan Violet (1903–1983)
Luigi L. Pasinetti (with Roberto Scazzieri)
capital theory: paradoxes
structural economic dynamics

Stephen M. Robinson
convex programming
J.E. Roemer
Marxian value analysis
[J.D. Rogers]
Swift, Jonathan
[J.D. Rogers (with S. Olivier and James Bonar)]
labour exchange
Alessandro Roncaglia
Petty, William (1623–1687)
Jaime Ros
growth and international trade
Hugh Rose
aggregate demand and supply analysis
Susan Rose-Ackerman
bribery
Sherwin Rosen
human capital
N. Rosenberg
Mandeville, Bernard de (1670–1733)
Schmookler, Jacob (1918–1967)
Mark R. Rosenzweig
family planning
Stephen A. Ross
finance
Stephen A. Ross (with Philip H. Dybvig)
arbitrage
Murray N. Rothbard
catallactics
Fetter, Frank Albert (1863–1949)
imputation
Mises, Ludwig Edler von (1881–1973)
time preference
Thomas J. Rothenberg
full and limited information methods
simultaneous equations models
Kurt W. Rothschild
degree of monopoly
Michael Rothschild (with Mark J. Machina)
risk
Eugene Rotwein
Hume, David (1711–1776)
Guy Routh
Phelps Brown, (Ernest) Henry (born 1906)
Charles K. Rowley
Borda, Jean-Charles de (1733–1799)
J. Rubery
women's wages
A. Rubinov
von Neumann ray
A. Rubinov (with V. Makarov)
von Neumann technology
Nancy D. Ruggles
social accounting
Clifford S. Russell (with Allen V. Kneese)
environmental economics
Alan Ryan
liberty
Mill, John Stuart (1806–1873)
property
Paul Ryan
primary and secondary labour markets

Zvi Safra
contingent commodities
strategic reallocations of endowments
M. Saito
Aoyama, Hideo (born 1910)
Massimo L. Salvadori
Gramsci, Antonio (1891–1937)
Neri Salvadori
basics and non-basics
non-substitution theorems
Warren J. Samuels
Ayres, Clarence Edwin (1891–1972)
Clark, John Maurice (1884–1963)
Commons, John Rogers (1862–1945)
Davenport, Herbert Joseph (1861–1931)
Homan, Paul Thomas (1893–1969)
institutional economics
Johnson, Alvin Saunders (1874–1971)
Sumner, William Graham (1840–1910)
Taussig, Frank William (1859–1940)
Wells, David Ames (1828–1898)
Paul A. Samuelson
Sraffian economics
Wicksell and neoclassical economics
Agnar Sandmo
Haavelmo, Trygve (born 1911)
public goods
Thomas J. Sargent
rational expectations
Kazuo Sato
ideal indexes
Ryuzo Sato
CES production function
group (Lie group) theory
Mark A. Satterthwaite
strategy-proof allocation mechanisms
I. Richard Savage
random variables
Savage, Leonard J. (1917–1971)
John Saville
combinations
N.E. Savin
rational expectations: econometric implications
two-stage least squares and the k-class estimator
M. Sawyer
autonomous expenditures
kinked demand curve
Herbert E. Scarf
computation of general equilibria
Roberto Scazzieri
reswitching of technique
reverse capital deepening
Ziber, Nikolai Ivanovich (1844–1888)
Roberto Scazzieri (with Luigi L. Pasinetti)
capital theory: paradoxes
structural economic dynamics

Bertram Schefold
Brentano, Lujo (Ludwig Josef) (1844–1931)
Bücher, Karl Wilhelm (1847–1930)
joint production in linear models
Knapp, Georg Friedrich (1842–1926)
Knies, Karl Gustav Adolf (1821–1898)
Roscher, Wilhelm Georg Friedrich (1817–1894)
Salin, Edgar (1892–1974)
Schmoller, Gustav von (1838–1917)
Sombart, Werner (1863–1941)
Spann, Othmar (1878–1950)
Thomas C. Schelling
value of life
F.M. Scherer
market structure
selling costs
Robert J. Schiller
expectations
F. Schinzinger
German historical school
Richard Schmalensee
advertising
industrial organization
David Schmeidler (with Peter Wakker)
expected utility and mathematical expectation
K. Schmidt
Helfferich, Karl (1872–1924)
Sax, Emil (1845–1927)
Michael Schneider
underconsumption
[E. Schuster]
gaming contracts
Anna J. Schwartz
Banking School, Currency School, Free Banking School
Gayer, Arthur David (1903–1951)
Joplin, Thomas (*c*1790–1847)
Palmer, John Horsley (1779–1858)
G. Schwödiauer
Menger, Karl (1902–1985)
Schlesinger Karl (1889–1938)
T. Scitovsky
balanced growth
Lerner, Abba Ptachya (1905–1982)
tariffs
Anthony Scott
Faustmann, Martin (1822–1876)
T. Sekine
Uno, Kozo (1897–1977)
Willi Semmler
competition: marxian conceptions
Amartya Sen
Dobb, Maurice Herbert (1900–1976)
justice
rational behaviour
social choice
Wayne Shafer
community indifference curves
transitivity

Anwar Shaikh
abstract and concrete labour
capital as a social relation
exploitation
humbug production function
market value and market price
organic composition of capital
surplus value
Matthew D. Shapiro
supply shocks in macroeconomics
William W. Sharkey
natural monopoly
subadditivity
Karl Shell
hamiltonians
sunspot equilibrium
G. Shelton
Tucker, Josiah (1713–1799)
William G. Shepherd
Bain, Joe Staten (born 1912)
concentration ratios
Herfindahl index
market share
Anthony F. Shorrocks
inequality between persons
John B. Shoven
tax incidence
Martin Shubik
Bertrand, Joseph Louis François (1822–1900)
co-operative games
Cournot, Antoine Augustin (1801–1877)
fiat money
Morgenstern, Oskar (1902–1977)
[Henry Sidgwick]
economic science and economics
Eugene Silberberg
envelope theorem
marginal utility of money
Z.A. Silberston
Jewkes, John (born 1902)
patents
Robinson, Edward Austin Gossage (born 1897)
Joaquim Silvestre
economies and diseconomies of scale
fixprice models
N.E. Simmonds
natural law
Herbert A. Simon
behavioural economics
bounded rationality
causality in economic models
Evans, Griffith Conrad (1887–1973)
satisficing
Christopher A. Sims
continuous and discrete time models
multivariate time series models
H.W. Singer
terms of trade and economic development
Ajit Singh
manufacturing and deindustrialization

Andrew S. Skinner
Buchanan, David (1779–1848)
Hutcheson, Francis (1694–1746)
Macfie, Alec Lawrence (1898–1980)
Meek, Ronald Lindley (1917–1978)
Rae, John (1845–1915)
Scott, William Robert (1868–1940)
Smith, Adam (1723–1790)
Steve Smale
global analysis
Clifford W. Smith, Jr.
agency costs
R.M. Smith
Farr, William (1807–1883)
Graunt, John (1620–1674)
R.P. Smith
arms races
military expenditure
Vernon L. Smith
auctions
experimental methods in economics
hunting and gathering economies
Matthew J. Sobel
queueing theory
E. Solomon
capital budgeting
S.N. Solomou
Kitchin, Joseph (1861–1932)
Kondratieff, Nikolai Dmitrievich (1892–?1931)
Kondratieff cycle
Kuznets swings
Hugo Sonnenschein
aggregate demand theory
oligopoly and game theory
Thomas Sowell
Say, Jean-Baptiste (1767–1832)
Say's Law
Sismondi, Jean Charles Leonard Simonde de (1773–1842)
Stigler, George Joseph (born 1911)
Veblen, Thorstein (1857–1929)
Henry W. Spiegel
Bresciani-Turroni, Costantino (1882–1963)
Burns, Arthur Robert (1895–1981)
Carey, Henry Charles (1793–1879)
Carey, Mathew (1760–1839)
Colwell, Stephen (1800–1871)
Dorfman, Joseph (born 1904)
Franklin, Benjamin (1706–1790)
Hamilton, Alexander (1755–1804)
Jefferson, Thomas (1743–1826)
Johannsen, Nicolas August Ludwig Jacob (1844–1928)
national system
Perroux, François (1903–1987)
Pownall, Thomas (1722–1805)
Raymond, Daniel (1786–1849)
scholastic economic thought
Spengler, Joseph John (born 1902)
Tucker, George (1775–1861)
usury
Viner, Jacob (1892–1970)
Wilson, Thomas (1525–1581)
Xenophon (*c*430 BC – *c*355 BC)

T.N. Srinivasan
distortions
H. Stanback
race and economics
F. Stanković
conspicuous consumption
leisure class
Ross M. Starr
sequence economies
Shapley–Folkman theorem
Gareth Stedman Jones
dialectical reasoning
Engels, Friedrich (1820–1895)
Ian Steedman
adding-up problem
foreign trade
free goods
reservation price and reservation demand
Wicksteed, Philip Henry (1844–1927)
Otto Steiger
ex ante and ex post
Lindahl, Erik Robert (1891–1960)
monetary equilibrium
Herbert Stein
Simons, Henry C. (1899–1946)
P.G. Stein
Grotius (de Groot), Hugo (1583–1645)
jurisprudence
Pufendorf, Samuel von (1632–1694)
Josef Steindl
Grossmann, Henryk (1881–1950)
Pareto distribution
stagnation
Strigl, Richard von (1891–1942)
Hillel Steiner
entitlements
N.H. Stern
optimal taxation
peasant economy
George J. Stigler
competition
Knight, Frank Hyneman (1885–1962)
Wood, Stuart (1853–1914)
Stephen M. Stigler
Edgeworth as a statistician
Joseph E. Stiglitz
principal and agent
sharecropping
S.C. Stimson
Rousseau, Jean Jacques (1712–1778)
social democracy
Swift, Jonathan (1667–1745)
George N. Stolnitz
mortality
Wolfgang F. Stolper
Lösch, August (1906–1945)
J.R.N. Stone
Allen, Roy George Douglas (1906–1983)
Bowley, Arthur Lyon (1869–1957)
Geary, Robert Charles (1896–1983)
Kendall, Maurice George (1907–1983)
matrix multiplier
Rothbarth, Erwin (1913–1944)
Stamp, Josiah Charles (1880–1941)

D.K. Stout
competition in international trade
Heinrich L. Strecker
Anderson, Oskar Nikolayevich (1887–1960)
Paul Streeten
Balogh, Thomas (1905–1985)
Myrdal, Gunnar (1898–1987)
E. Streissler
Weiser, Friedrich Freiherr (Baron) von (1851–1926)
Myra H. Strober
occupational segregation
D.J. Struik
Ryazanov, David (1870–1938)
P. Sturges
economics libraries and documentation
Shiro Sugihara
Shibata, Kei (1902–1986)
Patrick Suppes
axiomatic theories
Kotaro Suzumura
social welfare function
P.A.V.B. Swamy (with J.R. Barth)
random co-efficients
Paul M. Sweezy
Baran, Paul Alexander (1910–1964)
monopoly capitalism
Stanislaw Swianiewicz
Zawadzki, Wladyslaw Marian (1885–1939)
P. Sylos-Labini
oligopoly
Akira Takayama
consumer surplus
R. Tarling
labour markets
L. Tarshis
Keynesian revolution
Paul Taubman
Friend, Irwin (born 1915)
[F.W. Taussig]
stationary state
George S. Tavlas
Persons, Warren Milton (1878–1937)
Snyder, Carl (1869–1943)
George S. Tavlas (with Joseph Aschheim)
Del Mar, Alexander (1836–1926)
John B. Taylor
involuntary unemployment
[H.R. Tedder]
Asgill, John (1659–1738)
Vansittart, Nicholas, Lord Bexley (1766–1851)
A.P. Thirlwall
expenditure tax
Gerald L. Thompson
von Neumann, John (1903–1957)
N.W. Thompson
Bray, John (1809–1897)
Cobbett, William (1763–1835)
Gray, John (1799–1883)
Hodgskin, Thomas (1787–1869)
Owen, Robert (1771–1858)
Thompson, William (1785–1833)

Ross Thomson
primitive capitalist accumulation
Rosemary Thorp
Seers, Dudley (1920–1983)
Lester C. Thurow
declining industries
Eckstein, Otto (born 1927)
Galbraith, John Kenneth (born 1908)
W.O. Thweatt
Spiegel, Henry (born 1911)
C. Peter Timmer
nutrition
Jan Tinbergen
targets and instruments
James Tobin
financial intermediaries
Fisher, Irving (1867–1947)
Okun, Arthur M. (1928–1980)
M.P. Todaro (with L. Maruszko)
international migration
George S. Tolley (with Ronald J. Krumm)
regional economics
J. Tomlinson
finance capital
K. Tribe
Defoe, Daniel (1660–1731)
Eden, Frederick Morton (1766–1809)
Justi, Johannn Heinrich Gottlob von (1720–1771)
List, Friedrich (1789–1846)
Saint Simon, Claude-Henri de Rouvroy (1760–1825)
Sonnenfels, Joseph von (1733–1817)
Young, Arthur (1741–1820)
Jack E. Triplett
hedonic functions and hedonic indexes
S.C. Tsiang
Fleming, John Marcus (1911–1976)
loanable funds
Polak, Jacques Jacobus (born 1914)
Gordon Tullock
biological applications of economics
public choice
rent seeking
Insan Tunali
path analysis
Lynn Turgeon
Keyserling, Leon Hirsch (born 1908)
Carl G. Uhr
Davidson, David (1854–1942)
Heckscher, Eli Filip (1879–1952)
Wicksell, Johan Gustav Knut (1851–1926)
Lloyd Ulman
industrial relations
Peter Urbach
paradigm
J. Urry (with C.A. Gregory)
Armstrong, Wallis Edwin (1892–1980)
D. Usher
income
real income
H. Uzawa
models of growth
two-sector models

G. Vaggi
advances
market price
natural price
necessaries
Physiocrats
produit net
Quesnay, François (1694–1774)
Hal R. Varian
fairness
microeconomics
Paolo Varri
fixed capital
net product
Spyros Vassilakis
increasing returns
learning-by-doing
Karen I. Vaughn
invisible hand
Locke, John (1632–1704)
Menger, Carl (1840–1921)
Arthur F. Veinott, Jr.
inventory policy under certainty
K. Velupillai
Åkerman, Johan Gustav (1888–1959)
Åkerman, Johan Henrik (1896–1982)
Raymond Vernon
product cycle
Ilan Vertinsky
operations research
Fernando Vianello
labour theory of value
J. Vichniac
Neumann, Franz (1900–1954)
Douglas Vickers
Barbon, Nicholas (1637/40–?1698)
Child, Sir Josiah (1630–1699)
Gee, Joshua (*fl.*1725–1750)
Martin, Henry (died 1721)
Misselden, Edward (*fl.* 1608–1654)
North, Sir Dudley (1641–1691)
William Vickrey
marginal and average cost pricing
progressive and regressive taxation
Shoup, Carl Sumner (born 1902)
David Vines
absorption approach to the balance of payments
crawling peg
inflationary gap
Meade, James Edward (born 1907)
stabilization policy
Rajiv Vohra
planning
Peter Wakker (with David Schmeidler)
expected utility and mathematical expectation
Donald A. Walker
Giffen's paradox
Jaffé, William (1898–1980)
Marget, Arthur William (1899–1962)
Walras, Antoine Auguste (1801–1866)
Walras, Léon (1834–1910)
[G. Wallace]
chartism: the points of the Charter

Immanuel Wallerstein
periphery
Henry C. Wallich (with David E. Lindsey)
monetary policy
Henry C. Wallich (with Stephen H. Axilrod)
open-market operations
Vivian Walsh
Cantillon, Richard (1697–1734)
models and theory
philosophy and economics
Alan A. Walters
Bauer, Peter Tamas (born 1915)
congestion
currency boards
Friedman, Milton (born 1912)
transport
Henry Y. Wan, Jr. (with Simone Clemhout)
differential games
Terry Ward
fiscal stance
full-employment budget surplus
public sector borrowing
Harold W. Watts
negative income tax
Roger N. Waud
Almon, Shirley Montag (1935–1975)
Almon lag
R.K. Webb
Martineau, Harriet (1802–1876)
Place, Francis (1771–1854)
Robert J. Weber
games with incomplete information
E.R. Weintraub
Bronfenbrenner, Martin (born 1914)
Wald, Abraham (1902–1950)
D.R. Weir
Malthus's theory of population
Burton A. Weisbrod
non-profit organizations
Leonard W. Weiss
cartels
C. Welch
utilitarianism
Edwin G. West
monopoly
J. Fred Weston
Durand, David (born 1912)
Lintner, John Virgil (1916–1983)
J. Fred Weston (with Thomas E. Copeland)
asset pricing
J.K. Whitaker
Berry, Arthur (1862–1929)
ceteris paribus
Cunynghame, Sir Henry Hardinge (1848–1935)
demand price
derived demand
Flux, Alfred William (1867–1942)
Marshall, Alfred (1842–1924)
Sanger, Charles Percy (1871–1930)
Halbert White
least squares
Harrison C. White (with Robert G. Eccles)
producers' markets
M.V. White
Hearn, William Edward (1826–1888)
Robinson Crusoe
G. Whittington
accounting and economics
historical cost accounting
inflation accounting
P. Whittle
prediction
[P.H. Wicksteed]
degree of utility
dimensions of economic quantities
final degree of utility
final utility
political economy and psychology
P.J.D. Wiles
administered prices
convergence hypothesis
economic war
full communism
Nove, Alexander (Alec) N. (born 1915)
Frank Wilkinson
low pay
Alan Williams
public health
state provision of medical services
John Williamson
international capital flows
Oliver E. Williamson
anti-trust policy
vertical integration
T. Williamson
common land
Robert D. Willig
contestable markets
Charles Wilson
adverse selection
incomplete markets
Robert Wilson
bidding
exchange
Donald Winch
colonies
Horner, Francis (1778–1817)
Merivale, Herman (1806–1874)
Mill, James (1773–1836)
Wakefield, Edward Gibbon (1796–1862)
Gordon C. Winston
leisure
J.M. Winter
Tawney, Richard Henry (1880–1962)
Webb, Beatrice (1858–1943) and Sidney (1859–1947)
Sidney G. Winter
competition and selection
natural selection and evolution
Jack Wiseman
peak-load pricing
Charles Wolf, Jr.
present value of the past
J. Wolff
Blanc, Louis Joseph Charles (1811–1882)
Fourier, François Marie Charles (1772–1837)
Helvetius, Claude Adrien (1715–1771)
K. Wolpin
infant mortality
Stanley Wong
positive economics
Adrian Wood
Kaldor, Nicholas (1908–1986)
John Wood
advisers
George Woodcock
anarchism
A.D. Woodland
tradeable and non-tradeable commodities
J.E. Woods
invariable standard of value
G.D.N. Worswick
demand management
full employment
Schumacher, E.F. (Fritz) (1911–1977)
Anthony Wright
Cole, George Douglas Howard (1889–1959)
Hyndman, Henry Mayers (1842–1921)
Erik Olin Wright
inequality
Georg Henrik von Wright
preferences
Basil S. Yamey
double-entry book-keeping
overhead costs
L. Yeager
Warburton, Clark (1896–1979)
S.L. Zabell
Bernoulli, Daniel (1700–1782)
Johnson, William Ernest (1858–1931)
Lexis, Wilhelm (1837–1914)
Stefano Zamagni
economic laws
Georgescu-Roegen, Nicholas (born 1906)
Ricardo–Hayek effect
Paul Zarembka
transformation of variables in econometrics
V. Zarnowitz
indicators
M.I. Zelikin
Pontryagin's principle of optimality
Arnold Zellner
Bayesian inference
Itzhak Zilcha
intergenerational models
Andrew Zimbalist (with Deborah Duff Milenkovitch)
socialist economics

Appendix II

Biographies included in the 1925 edition of *Palgrave's Dictionary of Political Economy*, but omitted from *The New Palgrave*

Where the date of birth or death is uncertain, the abbreviation *c* (*circa*) precedes the approximate year. Where the date of death is unknown, *fl.* (*flourit*) has been used to indicate the subject's most productive period of authorship. The dates following *fl.* should, however, be treated only as a guide and not as a definitive statement of the duration of the individual's career.

Abbott, Charles, Lord Colchester (1757–1829)
Abeille, Louis Paul (1719–1807)
About, Edmond (1828–1885)
Achenwall, Gottfried (1719–1772)
Acland, Rev. John (1699–*c*1796)
Adams, Charles Francis (1807–1886)
Addison, Joseph (1672–1719)
Agazinni, Michele (*fl.*1822–1835)
Aickin, Rev. Joseph (*fl.*1693–1699)
Aikin, John (1747–1822)
Aislabie, John (1670–1742)
Alcock, Rev. Thomas (1709–1798)
Algarotti, Francis (1712–1764)
Alison, Sir Archibald (1792–1867)
Alison, William Pulteney (*fl.*1844–1850)
Althusius, Johannes (1557–1638)
Anderson, Adam (*c*1692–1765)
Ansell, Charles (1794–1881)
Antonius, St. (1389–1459)
Appleton, Nathan (1779–1861)
Arbuthnot, John (1667–1735)
Arbuthnot, John of Mitcham (*fl.*1773)
Arco, Gherardo Giambattista, Conti d'Arco (1739–1791)
Argenson, Réné Louis de Voyer de Paulmy (1694–1757)
Armstrong, Clement (*fl.*1530)
Arnd, Karl (1788–1877)
Arnould, Ambroise-Marie (1750–1812)
Arrivabene, Giovanni, Count (1787–1881)
Ashburton, Alexander Baring (1774–1848)
Ashley, John (died 1751)
Atkinson, Edward (1827–1905)
Atkinson, William (*c*1800–*c*1844)
Auckland, William Eden, Lord (1744–1814)
Audiffret, Ch. L.G., Marquis d' (1787–1878)
Audiganne, Amand (1814–1875)
Augustinis, Matteo de (*fl.*1833–1844)
Auxiron, Claude François Jospeph d' (1728–1778)
Aves, Ernest (1857–1917)
Bacon, Francis, Viscount St. Albans (1560/61–1626)
Baily, Francis (1774–1844)
Baines, Edward (1774–1845)
Baines, Sir Edward (1800–1890)
Baines, Thomas (1806–1881)
Balbi, Adriano (*fl.*1820–1845)
Baldwin, Loammi (1780–1838)
Balsamo, Paolo (1763–1816)
Bamford, Samuel (1788–1872)
Bandini, Salustio Anotonio (1677–1760)
Baring, Sir Francis (1740–1810)
Barnard, Sir John (1685–1764)
Barrington, Shute, Bishop (1734–1826)
Batbie, Anselme Polycarpe (1828–1887)
Baudie, Carlo di Vesma (1809–1877)
Baudrillart, Henri Joseph Léon (1821–1892)
Baumstark, Edward (1807–1889)
Baxter, Robert Dudley (1827–1875)
Bazard, Saint-Armand (1791–1832)
Becher, Johann Joachim (*c*1625–1685)
Beckmann, Johann (1739–1811)
Beldam (*fl.*1772)
Bell, William (1731–1816)
Bellers, John (*c*1654–1725)
Bellitti, Giacinto (*fl.*1791)
Belloni, Girolamo (*fl.*1750–1757)
Bernard, Sir Thomas (1750–1818)
Bernhardi, Theodor von (1802–1887)
Besold, Christoph (1577–1638)
Bianchini, Ludovico (1803–1871)
Biblia, Fabrizio (*fl.*1621)
Biddle, Nicholas (1786–1844)
Biel, Gabriel (*c*1430–1495)
Bigelow, Erastus Brigham (1814–1879)
Biundi, G. (*fl.*1853–1867)
Black, David (*fl.*1706)
Block, Maurice (1816–1901)
Bocchi, Romeo (*fl.*1621)
Böckh, August (1785–1867)
Boecler, Johann Heinrich (1611–1672)
Boileau (or Boyleau), Etienne (*c*1200–1272)
Bolles, John A. (1809–1878)
Bollman, Justus Erick (1764–1821)
Boncerf, Pierre-François (*c*1745–1794)
Bonnet, Victor (1814–1889)
Booth, Charles (1840–1916)
Bornitz, Jacob (*fl.*1608–1625)
Bosanquet, Charles (1769–1850)
Bosellini, Carlo (1765–1823)
Botero, Giovanni (1540–1617)
Boulainvilliers, Henri de (1658–1722)
Bowen, Francis (1811–1890)
Boxhorn, Marcus Zuerius (1602–1653)
Bradlaugh, Charles (1833–1891)
Brassey, Thomas (1805–1870)
Bray, Charles (1811–1884)
Breck, Samuel (*fl.*1843)
Brewster, Sir Francis (*fl.*1674–1702)
Briganti, Filippo (1725–1804)
Brindley, James (1716–1772)
Briscoe, John (*fl.*1694–1696)
Brissot de Warville, Jean-Pierre (1754–1793)
Broggia, Antonio (*c*1683–*c*1767)
Brown, John (1715–1766)
Buchez, Philippe Joseph Benjamin (1796–1865)
Bülau, Friedrich von (1805–1859)
Buonarroti, Philippe (1761–1837)
Buquoy, Georg Franz, Count (1781–1851)
Buret, Antoine Eugène (1810–1842)
Burlamaqui, Jena Jacque (1694–1748)
Burton, John Hill (*see* Hill Burton, J.)
Büsch, Johann Georg (1728–1800)
Büsching, Anton Frederick (1724–1793)
Butel-Dumont, George Marie (*fl.*1753–1771)
Butt, Isaac (1813–1879)
Cabet, Etienne (1788–1856)
Cadet, Félix (1827–1888)
Cagnazzi, Luca Samuele (1764–1852)
Caird, Sir James (1816–1892)
Calonne, Charles Alexandre de (1734–1802)
Calvin, Jean (1509–1564)
Cambon, Pierre Joseph (1756–1826)
Cambreleng, Churchill C. (1786–1862)
Camerarius, Jocham (1500–1574)
Campanella, Tommaso (1568–1639)
Campomanes, Pedro Rodriguez (1723–1802)
Cancrin, George (1774–1845)
Canning, George (1770–1827)
Cantalupo, Domenico (*fl.*1783–1795)
Capello, Pier Andrea (*fl.*1752)
Caraccioli, Domenico (1715–1789)
Carafa, Diomede (died 1487)
Cardozo, Isaac N. (1786–1850)
Carli, Gian Rinaldo (1720–1795)
Cary, John (died *c*1719)
Casaregis, Josephus Laurentius Mariade (1670–1737)
Cavour, Count Camillo Benso di (1810–1861)
Cayley, Edward (*fl.*1826)
Cernuschi, Henri (1821–1896)
Cesare, Carlo de (1824–1882)
Chalmers, George (1742–1825)
Chamberlayne, Edward (1616–1703)
Chamberlen, Hugh (1664–1728)
Chamillart, Michel de (1653–1721)
Chastellux, François Jean, Marquis de (1734–1788)
Chickering, Jesse (1797–1855)
Chitti, Luigi (*fl.*1833–1839)
Cibrario, Giovanni Antonio Luigi, Count (1802–1870)
Clamageran, Jean Jules (1827–1904)
Clarkson, Thomas (1760–1846)
Clay, Henry (1777–1852)
Clayton, David (*fl.*1719)
Clément, Ambroise (1805–1886)
Clément, Pierre (1809–1870)
Clement, Simon (1695–1720)
Cochut, Pierre André (1807–1890)
Cognetti de Martis, Salvatore (1844–1891)
Cohn, Gustav (1846–1919)
Coke, Roger (1643–1696)

Colton, Rev. Calvin (1789–1857)
Comte, Charles (1782–1837)
Conduitt, John (1688–1737)
Conigliani, Carlo Angelo (died 1901)
Conring, Hermann (1606–1681)
Considérant, Victor Prosper (1808–1893)
Cooper, Thomas (1759–1840)
Cooper, Thomas (1805–1892)
Copernicus, Nicolaus (1473–1543)
Copleston, Edward (1776–1849)
Coquelin, Charles (1805–1852)
Corbetta, Eugenio (*fl.*1872)
Corniani, Giambattista (1742–1813)
Corti, Adolfo (*fl.*1829)
Corvaia, Baron (*fl.*1844)
Corvetto, Louis-Emmanuel, Comte de (1756–1821)
Cotterill, Charles Foster (*fl.*1831)
Cotton, Sir Robert Bruce (1570–1631)
Courcy, Alfred de (1816–1888)
Court, Pieter de la (1618–1685)
Courten, Sir William (1572–1636)
Courtney, Leonard Henry, Baron (1832–1918)
Cowell, John Welsford (*fl.*1843–1858)
Coxe, Tench (1755–1824)
Cradocke, Francis (*fl.*1660–1661)
Craig, John (*fl.*1814–1821)
Crombie, Alexander (1762–1842)
Crome, August Friedrich Wilhelm (1753–1833)
Crumpe, Samuel (1766–1796)
Custodi, Pietro (1771–1846)
Daire, Eugène (1798–1847)
Dalbiac, General Sir James Charles (1776–1848)
Dalrymple, Sir John (1726–1810)
Dameth, Henri (1812–1884)
Danguel, Marquis de Plumart (*fl.*1750–1756)
Danson, John Towne (1817–1898)
Davidson, John (died 1905)
Davies, David (died *c*1819)
Dávila, El Padre Báutista (*fl.*1651)
Dávila, y Lugo, Don Francisco (*fl.*1636)
De Brouckère, Charles (1796–1860)
De Cardenas di Maqueda, Diego Raffaele (*fl.*1784)
Decker, Sir Matthew (1679–1749)
De Lajonchère (*fl.*1718–1720)
De La Mare, Nicolas (1639–1723)
Delfico, Melchiorre (died *c*1835)
De Luca, Giovanni Battista (1614–1683)
De Metz-Noblat, Alexandre (1820–1871)
Denny, William (1847–1887)
Deparcieux, Antoine (1703–1768)
De Parieu, Esquirol de (*see* Parieu, Esquirol de)
De Sanctis, Marco Antonio (*fl.*1605–1613)
Desmarets, Nicolas (1648–1721)
Devas, Charles Stanton (1848–1900)
De Vio, F. Tommas (1470–1534)
Dew, Thomas Roderick (1802–1846)
Dickinson, John (1732–1808)
Dickson, Rev. Adam (1721–1776)
Dieterici, Karl Friedrich Wilhelm (1790–1859)
Digges, Sir Dudley (1583–1639)
Diodati, Domenico (*fl.*1788)
Diodati, Luigi (*fl.*1790–1794)
Dirom, Major Alexander (*fl.*1796)
D'Ivernois, Sir Francis (1757–1842)
Dobbs, Arthur (1689–1765)
Dombasles, Alexandre Mathieu (1777–1843)
Donato, Nicolas (*fl.*1753)
Doria, Paolo Matt. (1675–1743)
Dormer, Diego José (*fl.*1684)
Doubleday, Thomas (1790–1870)
Douglass, William (*c*1691–1752)
Dove, Patrick Edward (1815–1873)
Dowell, Stephen (1833–1898)
Dragonetti, Giacinto (*fl.*1767)
Dragonetti, Luigi (*fl.*1820)
Drake, James (1667–1706/7)
Droz, Joseph (1773–1850)
Droz, Numa (1844–1899)
Dubos, Abbé Jean Baptiste (1670–1742)
Duchatel, Comte Tanneguy (1803–1867)
Ducpetiaux, Edouard (1804–1868)
Dufau, F.P. (*fl.*1840–1847)
Duhamel du Monçeau (1700–1781)
Dumoulin, Charles (*see* Molinaeus, Carolus)
Duncan, Henry (1774–1846)
Duncan, John (*fl.*1815)
Duncan, Jonathan (1799–1865)
Dundas, Henry (1742–1811)
Dunning, Richard (*fl.*1685–1698)
Dupin, Baron Charles (1784–1873)
Dupin, Claude (died 1769)
Dupont-White, Charles (1807–1878)
Dupré de Saint-Maur, Nicolas François (*c*1695–1774)
Duquesnoy, Adrien Cyprien (1763–1808)
Dussard, Hippolyte (1798–1876)
Dutens, Joseph Mical (1765–1848)
Dutot (*fl.*1718–1738)
Duvillard de Durand, Etienne (1755–1832)
Eaton, Daniel Isaac (*c*1752–1814)
Ebaudy de Fresne (*fl.*1788–1790)
Eck, Johann (1486–1543)
Edmonds, Thomas Rowe (1803–1889)
Edwards, Bryan (1743–1800)
Edwards, George (1752–1823)
Egron, Adrien César (*fl.*1844–1847)
Einert, Carl (1777–1855)
Eisdell, Joseph Salway (*fl.*1839)
Eiselen, Johann Friedrich Gottfried (1785–1865)
Elder, William (1806–1885)
Elibank, Patrick Murray (1703–1778)
Eliot, Francis Perceval (*c*1756–1818)
Elking, Henry (*fl.*1720–1723)
Elliott, Ebenezer (1781–1849)
Ellis, William (died 1758)
Ellis, William (1800–1881)
Ellman, John (1753–1832)
Emerson, Gouverneur (1796–1874)
Emmery de Sept Fontaines, Henri Charles (1789–1842)
Enfantin, Prosper (1796–1864)
Ensenada, Zenon de Somodevilla y Bengoechea, Marquis de la (1702–1782)
Estcourt, Thomas (*fl.*1784–1806)
Esterno, (Henri) Philippe, Comte d' (1805–1883)
Evans, David Morier (1819–1874)
Evans, Thomas (*fl.*1798–1816)
Evelyn, John (1620–1706)
Evelyn, John (*fl.*1830)
Everett, Alexander Hill (1792–1847)
Everett, George (*fl.*1693–1698)
Eyton, Robert William (1815–1881)
Fabbroni, Giovanni (1752–1822)
Fajordo or Faxardo, Count Diego de Saavedra Faxardo (1584–1648)
Fallati, Johannes (1809–1855)
Farrer, Thomas Henry, Lord (1819–1899)
Faucher, Julius (1820–1878)
Faucher, Léon (1803–1854)
Fauquier, Francis (*c*1704–1768)
Favre, Antoine (1587–1624)
Felt, Joseph B. (1789–1869)
Fénelon, François de Salignac de la Mothe (1651–1715)
Ferrari, Jacopo (*fl.*1623)
Ferretti, Julius (*fl.*1541)
Ferroni, Pietro (*fl.*1804)
Fielding, Henry (1707–1754)
Filangieri, Gaetano (1752–1788)
Filiucci, Vincenzo (*fl.*1622)
Fineschi, F. Vincenzo (*fl.*1767)
Finlaison, John (1783–1860)
Fiorentino, Nicola (*fl.*1794)
Firmin, Thomas (1632–1697)
Fitzherbert, Sir Anthony (1470–1538)
Fix, Théodore (1800–1846)
Fleetwood, William (1656–1723)
Fletcher, Andrew (1655–1716)
Florez Estrada, Alvaro (1765–1853)
Florida-Blanca, José Moñino, Count (1728–1808)
Folkes, Martin (died 1754)
Fonfrède, Henri (1788–1840)
Fontanelli, Carlo (died 1886)
Fonteyraud, Alcide (1822–1849)
Ford, Sir Edward (1605–1670)
Formaleoni, Vincenzo (*fl.*1785–1791)
Foronda, Valentin de (*fl.*1787–1801)
Foronda, Valentino (*fl.*1789)
Forster, Nathaniel (1726/7–1790)
Forti, Eugenio (*fl.*1875–1878)
Fortrey, Samuel (1622–1681)
Fortunato, Nicolo (*fl.*1760)
Fortune, E.F. Thomas (*fl.*1796–1808)
Fossambroni, Vittorio, Count (*fl.*1804)
Foster, John Leslie (died 1842)
Foucquet, Nicolas (1615–1680)
Fourier, Charles (1772–1837)
Frachetta, Girolamo (*fl.*1597–1599)
Franchi, Carlo (*fl.* *c*1753)
Francis, John (1810–1886)
Francis, Peter (1740–1818)
Fregier, A. (1789–*c*1850)
Friedrich, Margrave Karl (*see* Karl Friedrich)
Fürstenau, Karl Gottfried (1734–1803)
Fustel de Coulanges, Numa Denis (1830–1889)
Gaëta, Duke of, Martin Michel Charles Gaudin (1756–1841)
Galanti, Giuseppe M. (1743–1799)
Galdi, Matteo (*fl.*1790)
Galitzin, Dimitri, Prince (1730–1803)
Gambrini, Francesco (*fl.*1819)
Gardiner or Gardner, Ralph (*fl.*1650–1655)
Garelli, della Morea, Giusto Emanuele (died 1893)
Garfield, James Abram (1831–1881)
Garnier, Comte Germain (1754–1821)
Garrati, Martino (*fl.* *c*1438)
Garve, Christian (1742–1798)
Gaskell, P. (*fl.*1833–1836)
Gasparin, Adrien Etienne Pierre, Count of (1783–1862)
Gasparino, Bartolomeo (*fl.*1634)
Gasser, Simon Peter (1676–1745)
Geijer, Eric Gustav (1783–1847)
Geissler, Adolf (*c*1834–1902)
Gemilli, Francesco (*fl.*1776)
Gentleman, Tobias (*fl.*1614)
Gentz, Friedrich von (1764–1832)
Gérando, Joseph Maria, Baron de (1772–1842)
Gerson, Jean Charlier de (1363–1429)
Ghent, Henry of (*c*1217–1293)
Ghetti, Ludovico (15th century)

Gianni, Francesco Maria (1728–1821)
Gibbins, Rev. Henry de Beltgens (1865–1907)
Gibbons, James Sloan (*fl.*1859–1867)
Giginta, Miguel de (*fl.*1579–1586)
Gilbart, James William (1794–1863)
Gilbert, Thomas (1720–1798)
Giogalli, Simone (*fl.*1619)
Girardin, Emile de (1806–1886)
Giustiniani, D. Bernardo (*fl.*1619)
Glanvill, Ranulf (died 1190)
Glock or Glocke (*see* Klock, Kaspar)
Godfrey, Michael (died 1695)
Godin, Jean Baptiste André (1817–1888)
Gogel, Isaac Jan Alexander (1765–1821)
Googe, Barnaby (1540–1594)
Gouge, William M. (1796–1863)
Gould, Sir Nathaniel (died 1728)
Graham, Sir James George Robert (1792–1861)
Gramont, Scipion de (died *c*1638)
Grant, James (*fl.*1790)
Grant, Sir Robert (1779–1838)
Graslin, Louis François (1727–1790)
Graswinckel, Dirck (1600–1660)
Graumann, Johann Philip (1690–1762)
Greeley, Horace (1811–1872)
Greg, William Rathbone (1809–1881)
Grenville, George (1712–1770)
Greville, William Wyndham, Baron Grenville (1759–1834)
Grundler, Christian Gottlob (*fl.*1787–1788)
Guarini, G.B. (*fl.*1668)
Guérard, Benjamin (1797–1854)
Guerry de Champneuf, Jacques (1788–1852)
Guicciardini, Francesco (1482–1540)
Guicciardini, Luigi (1523–1589)
Guillaumin, Urbain Gilbert (1801–1864)
Hagen, Karl Heinrich (1785–1856)
Haines, Richard (*fl.*1674–1681)
Hale, Sir Matthew (1609–1676)
Hale, Nathan (1784–1863)
Hales, John (*fl.*1548)
Halifax, Charles Montague, Earl of (1661–1715)
Hall, Charles (*c*1745–*c*1825)
Hall, Van (*see* Van Hall)
Haller, Karl Ludwig von (1768–1854)
Halley, Edmund (1656–1742)
Hamilton, Robert (1743–1829)
Hancock, William Neilson (1820–1888)
Hanssen, Georg (1809–1894)
Hanway, Jonas (1712–1786)
Harcourt, François Eugène Gabriel, Duke of (1786–1865)
Hardenberg, Karl August, Prinz von (1750–1822)
Harrington, James (1611–1677)
Harris, Joseph (1702–1764)
Harrison, William (1534–1593)
Harte, Rev. Walter (1709–1774)
Hartlib, Samuel (died *c*1670)
Hassia, Henricus de (*see* Langenstein)
Hawkins, Edward (1780–1867)
Hawkins, Sir John (1719–1789)
Hayes, John L. (1813–1887)
Hayne, Samuel (*fl.*1630–1660)
Haynes, Christopher (*fl.*1713)
Haynes, John (*fl.*1706–1715)
Haxthausen, August Franz, Freiherr von (1792–1866)
Heathfield, Richard (*c*1775–1859)
Heeren, Arnold Hermann Ludwig (1760–1842)
Hegel, Georg Wilhelm Friedrich (1770–1831)
Held, Adolf von (1844–1880)
Helm, Elijah (1837–1904)
Henley, Walter of (*c*1200–1250)
Henry of Ghent (*see* Ghent, Henry of)
Herbert, Claude-Jacques (1700–1758)
Herrenschwand (*fl.*1786–1797)
Herrera, Cristobal Perez de (*fl.*1595–1608)
Herries, John Charles (1778–1855)
Herrmann, Emanuel (1839–1902)
Heuschling, Philippe F. Xavier Theodore (1802–1883)
Heysham, John (1753–1834)
Hildreth, Richard (1807–1867)
Hill, Sir Roland (1795–1879)
Hill-Burton, John (also known as Burton, John Hill) (1809–1881)
Hitchcock, Robert (*fl.*1580)
Hock, Baron Karl von (1808–1869)
Hodgson, James (1672–1755)
Hodgson, William Ballantyne (1815–1880)
Hoeck, Johann Daniel Albrecht (1763–1839)
Hofacker, Johann Daniel (1788–1828)
Hoffmann, Johann Gottfried (1765–1847)
Hogendorp, Gysbert, Karel van (1762–1834)
Holland, John (died 1722)
Holyoake, George Jacob (1817–1906)
Hooke, Andrew (*fl.*1750)
Horn, Ignace Einhorn (also known as Edward Horn) (1825–1875)
Horne, Andrew (died 1328)
Horneck, Philipp Wilhelm von (*c*1638–1713)
Horsley, William (*c*1701–*c*1776)
Horton, Samuel Dana (1844–1895)
Houghton, John (*fl.*1692–1703)
Howard, John (1727–1790)
Howe, John Badlam (1813–1882)
Howlett, John (1731–1800)
Hübner, Otto (1818–1877)
Huc, E., Abbé (1813–1860)
Huet, François (1816–1865)
Huet, Pierre Daniel (1630–1721)
Hufeland, Gottlieb (1761–1817)
Hüllmann, Karl Dietrich (1765–1846)
Humboldt, Alexander von, Baron (1769–1859)
Humboldt, Wilhelm von (1767–1835)
Hume, James Deacon (1774–1842)
Hume, Joseph (1777–1855)
Hutcheson, Archibald (died 1740)
Hutchinson, John Hely (1724–1794)
Huysers, Arien (died 1806)
Iddesleigh, Earl of (also known as Sir Stafford Northcote) (1818–1887)
Invrea, Fabio (*fl.*1846)
Iselin, Isaak (1728–1782)
Isola, Francesco (*fl.*1811)
Invernois, Sir Francis d' (1757–1842)
Jacini, Count Stefano (1837–1891)
Jacob, William (*c*1762–1851)
Jakob, Ludwig Heinrich von (1759–1827)
Jannet, Claudio (1844–1894)
Janssen, Sir Theodore (died 1748)
Jarrold, Thomas (1770–1853)
Jarvis, Edward (1803–1884)
Jenyns, Soame (1704–1787)
Jobard, Jean Baptiste Ambroise-Marcelin (1796–1861)
Johnson, Samuel (1709–1784)
Jones, David (1806–1854)
Jones, Ernest Charles (1819–1869)
Jourdan, Alfred (1825–1892)
Jovellanos, Gaspar Melchoir de (1744–1811)
Joyce, Jeremiah (1763–1816)
Jung Stilling, Johann Heinrich (1740–1817)
Justice, Alexander (*fl.*1705–1707)
Kane, Sir Robert John (1809–1890)
Kant, Immanuel (1724–1804)
Karl Friedrich, Grand Duke of Baden (1728–1811)
Kay-Shuttleworth, Sir James Phillips (1804–1877)
Kelley, Wiliam D. (1814–1890)
Kellogg, Edward (1790–1858)
Kemper, Jerommo de Bosch (1808–1876)
Kersseboom, Willem (1691–1771)
King, Charles (*fl.*1713–1721)
King, Peter, Lord (1776–1833)
Kingsley, Charles (1819–1875)
Klock, Kaspar (also Glock and Glocke) (1583–1655)
Knox, John J. (1828–1892)
Kops, J.L. de Bruyn (1822–1887)
Kosegarten, Wilhelm (1792–1868)
Kraus, Christian Jakob (1753–1807)
Kröncke, Klaus (1771–1843)
Krug, Johann Leopold (1770–1843)
Kuricke, Rein (*fl.*1667)
Laborde, Alexandre, Comte de (1774–1842)
Laboulaye, Edouard René Lefebvre (1811–1883)
Laboulinière, Pierre (*fl.*1803–1821)
Lacroix, Emeric de (in Latin, Cruceus) (*fl.*1623)
La Farelle, François Felix (1810–1872)
Laffemas, Barthélémy de (1545–1612)
Laffemas, Isaac de, Sieur de (*fl.*1606)
Laffitte, Jacques (1767–1844)
Lagrange, Joseph Louis (1736–1813)
Laing, Samuel (1780–1868)
La Jonchère, de (*see* De La Jonchère)
Lalor, John (1814–1856)
La Luzerne, César-Guillaume de (1738–1821)
La Mare, de (*see* De La Mere)
Lambe, Samuel (*fl.*1657)
Lambin de Saint Félix (*see* Lottin, A.P.)
Lamond, Elizabeth (1860–1891)
Lampredi, Giovanni Maria (*fl.*1756–1761)
Lange, Friedrich Albert (1828–1875)
Langenstein, Henry of (1325–1397)
La Rochefoucauld Liancourt, Alexandre Frédéric, Duc de (1747–1827)
La Rochefoucauld Liancourt, Frédéric Gaetan, Marquis de (1779–1850)
Larruga, Eugenio de (*fl.*1785–1800)
Lastri, Marco (*fl.*1785)
Latimer, Hugh (1472–1555)
Lavergne, Louis Gabriele Léonce Guilhaud de (1809–1880)
Lavoisier, Antoîne Laurent (1743–1794)
Lawson, James Anthony (1817–1887)
Leake Stephen Martin (1702–1773)
Leber, Constant (1780–1859)
Leblanc, François (died 1698)
Leclaire, Edmé-Jean (1801–1872)
Lefèvre de Beaudvray, Pierre (1724–1790)
Le Gendre, François (*fl.*1646)
Legoyt, Alfred (1815–1885)
Le Hardy de Beaulieu, Charles (1816–1871)
Leib, Johann Georg (1670–1727)
Leibniz (Leibnitz), Baron Gottfried Wilhelm von (1646–1716)
Lemonnier, Charles (*fl.*1843–1859)
Lenzi, Domenico (*fl.*1320–1335)
Léonce de Lavergne, Louis Gabriel Léonce Guilhard de (*see* Lavergne, L.G.L.G. de)
Le Play, Pierre, Guillaume Frédéric (1806–1882)
Leroux, Pierre (1797–1871)

Levi, Leone (1821–1888)
Lewis, Sir George Cornewall (1806–1863)
Lewis, Matthew or Mark (*fl.*1677–1678)
Leymarie, Achille (1812–1861)
Linguet, Simon Nicolas Henri (1736–1794)
Lips, Alexander (1779–1838)
Lith, Johann Wilhelm von der (1709–1775)
Liverpool, Charles Jenkinson, First Earl of (1727–1808)
Liverpool, Robert Banks Jenkinson, Second Earl of (1770–1828)
Loch, Sir Charles Stewart (1849–1923)
Locré, Jean Guillaume, Baron de Roisey (1758–1840)
Loménie de Brienne, Etienne Charles, Comte de Brienne (1727–1794)
Lord, Eleazar (1788–1871)
Lottin, Antoîne Prosper (1739–1812)
Lotz, Johann Friedrich Eusebius (1771–1838)
Louis, Dominique, Baron (1755–1837)
Lowe, Joseph (*fl.*1807)
Lowe, Robert (*see* Sherbrooke, Viscount)
Lowndes, William (1652–1724)
Lubbock, Sir John William (1803–1865)
Lucas, Charles Jean Marie (1803–1889)
Luder, August Ferdinand (1760–1819)
Ludewig, Johann Peter (1670–1743)
Lunetti, Vittorio (*fl.*1630–1660)
Lupo, Giambattista (*fl.*1577)
Luther, Martin (1483–1546)
Luzac, Elie (1723–1796)
Mably, Gabriel Bonnot, Abbé de (1709–1785)
Macadam, John Loudon (1756–1836)
Macanaz, Melchoir de (died *c*1788)
Macdonnel, Sir John (1846–1921)
M'Farlan, John (*fl.*1767–1782)
Macgregor, John (1797–1857)
Machault d'Arnouville, Jean Baptiste (1701–1794)
Maclean, John Hugh (*fl.*1825)
M'Lennan, John F. (1827–1881)
Macnab, Henry Grey (1762–1823)
Macpherson, David (1746–1816)
Madison, James (1751–1836)
Madox, Thomas (1666–1727)
Maffei, Scipione (1675–1755)
Magens, or Magen or Meggens, Nicholas (died 1764)
Magliani, Agostino (1825–1891)
Maizières, Phillipe de (1312–1405)
Major, John (*c*1469–*c*1549)
Malchus, Karl August von (1770–1840)
Malebranche, Nicolas (1638–1715)
Malesherbes, Chrétien Guillaume de Lamoignon de (1721–1794)
Malestroit, Seigneur de (*fl.*1566)
Mallet, Jean-Roland (died 1736)
Mallet, Sir Louis (1823–1890)
Mallet Du Pan, Jacques (1749–1800)
Mallet, Paul Henri (1730–1807)
Malon, Benoît (1841–1893)
Malouet, Pierre-Victor, Baron (1740–1814)
Mancini, Celso (died 1612)
Manley, Thomas (*fl.*1669–1677)
Mansfield, William Murray, First Earl of (1705–1793)
Mantellier, Philippe (1811–1884)
Manzoni, Alexander (1784–1873)
Marachio, Massimo (*fl.*1794)
Marescotti, Angelo (1815–1892)
Mariana, Juan de (1536–1623)
Marlo, Karl (pseudonym of Karl Georg Winkelblech) (1810–1865)
Marmontel, Jean François (1723–1799)
Marogna, Conte Gian Giuseppe (*fl.*1792)
Marperger, Paul Jacob (1656–1730)
Marshall, William (1745–1818)
Martin, Frederick (1830–1883)
Martin, Robert Montgomery (1803–1868)
Martinez de la Mata, Francisco (*fl.* *c*1650)
Marulli, Vicenzo (*fl.*1804)
Maseres, Francis (1731–1824)
Maslov (*fl.*1820)
Masselin, Jean (died 1500)
Mastrofini, Marco (*fl.*1831)
Mathias de Saint Jean, Jean Eon (1600–1681)
Mattia (Di), Nicola (*fl.*1805)
Maugham, Robert (died 1862)
Maurice, John Frederic Denison (1805–1872)
Mauvillon, Jakob (1743–1794)
Medina, Fray Juan de (*fl.*1545)
Meek, Sir James (1778–1856)
Mees, Willem Cornelis (1813–1885)
Melanchthon, Philip (1497–1560)
Melon, Jean François (died 1738)
Mengotti, Francesco (1749–1830)
Menier, Emile Justin (1826–1881)
Mercier, Louis Sébastien (1740–1814)
Meredith, Sir William (1724–1790)
Merello, Michele (*fl.*1607)
Merenda, Antonio (*fl.*1645)
Mesnil Marigny, Jules de (1810–1885)
Messance, M. (*fl.*1763–1788)
Messedaglia, Angelo (1820–1901)
Meyer, Hermann Rudolph (1839–1899)
Mézagues, Vivant de (*fl.*1754–1766)
Michaelis, Otto (1826–1890)
Michel, Francisque (1809–1887)
Miklashevsky, Ivan (1858–1901)
Milles, Thomas (*c*1500–*c*1630)
Milne, Joshua (1776–1851)
Milner, James (died 1721)
Minghetti, Marco (1818–1886)
Mirabeau, Victor Riquetti (1715–1789)
Miro, Vicenzo de (*fl.*1718–1731)
Moffat, Robert Scott (*fl.*1878)
Moheau (*fl.*1774–1778)
Mohl, Robert von (1799–1875)
Molesworth, Sir William (1810–1855)
Molina, Ludovicus (1535–1600)
Molinaeus, Carolus (1500–1566)
Mollien, François Nicolas (1758–1850)
Molster, Johannes Adrien (1827–1889)
Moncada, Sancho de (*fl.*1619)
Montaigne, Michel de (1533–1592)
Montanari, Geminiano (1633–1687)
Montesquieu, Charles de Secondat Baron de la Brède et de Montesquieu (1689–1755)
Montyon, Antoine Robert Auget, Baron de (1733–1820)
Monypenny, David (*fl.*1834–1840)
Moore, Adam (*fl.*1650)
More, Sir Thomas (*c*1478–1535)
Moreau de Beaumont, Jean Louis (1715–1785)
Moreau de Jonnès, Alexandre (1778–1870)
Morel Vindé, Charles Gilbert, Vicomte de (1759–1842)
Morellet, Abbé André (1727–1819)
Morelly (*fl.*1750–1760)
Morgan, Augustus de (1806–1871)
Morgan, William (1750–1833)
Morhof, Daniel Georg (1639–1691)
Morpurgo, Emilio (1836–1889)
Morris, Corbyn (died 1779)
Morstadt, Eduard (1792–1850)
Mortimer, Thomas (1730–1810)
Möser, Justus (1720–1794)
Moser, Friedrich Karl von (1723–1798)
Moser, Johann Jacob (1701–1785)
Mosse or Moses, Miles (*fl.*1580–1614)
Muñoz, Antonio (*fl.*1769)
Munro, Joseph Edward Crawford (1849–1896)
Münster, Sebastian (1489–1552)
Muratori, Ludovico Antonio (1672–1750)
Murray, Robert (*fl.*1676–1696)
Murray, William (*see* Mansfield, First Earl)
Mushet, Robert (1782–1828)
Nasse, Erwin (1829–1890)
Navarrete, Pedro Fernandez (*fl.*1626)
Navarrus de Azpilcueta, Martinus (died 1586)
Naveau, Jean Baptiste (1716–1762)
Naville, François Marc Louis (1784–1846)
Nazzani, Emilo (1832–1904)
Neale, Edward Vansittart (1810–1892)
Nebenuis, Karl Friedrich (1784–1857)
Neri, Pompeo (1707–1777)
Neumann Spallartm, Franz Xavier (1837–1888)
Neves, Jose Accursio das (1766–1834)
Newbury, Jack of (died 1520)
Newenham, Thomas (1762–1831)
Newton, Sir Isaac (1642–1727)
Nicéron, Jean Pierre (1685–1738)
Nicholls, Sir George (1782–1865)
Nicolai (*fl.*1803)
Nifo, Agostino (1473–1538)
Niles, Hezekiah (1777–1839)
Nitzsch, Karl Wilhelm (1818–1880)
Norman, G. Warde (1793–1882)
Normante Y. Carcaviella, Doctor Lorenzo (*fl.*1784–1786)
North, The Hon. Roger (1650–1733)
Northcote, Sir Stafford (*see* Iddlesleigh, Earl of)
Noy, William (1577–1634)
Nuytz, Gaetano (18th–19th century)
Oastler, Richard (1789–1861)
Obrecht, George (1547–1612)
Oddy, J. Jepson (died 1814)
Ogilvie, William (1736–1819)
Oliphant, Charles (*fl.*1824–1825)
Olivares, Damian de (*fl.*1620)
Olmsted, Frederick Law (1822–1903)
Olufsen, Oluf Christian (*fl.*1797–1820)
Onely, Rev. Richard (1723–1787)
Opdyke, George (1807–1880)
Ortiz, José Alonso (*fl.*1794–1796)
Ortiz, Luis (*fl.*1558)
Oscar I, King of Sweden (1799–1859)
Ouvrard, Gabriel Julien (1770–1846)
Owen, Robert Dale (1801–1877)
Pacioli or Paciolo, Fra Luca (*fl.*1485)
Pagano, Francesco Mario (1748–1799)
Page, Frederic (1769–1834)
Paget, Amédée (died *c*1850)
Pagnini, Giovanni Francesco (1715–1789)
Paine, Thomas (1737–1809)
Palissy, Bernard de (1500–1589)
Palmeri, Nicolo (died 1837)
Palmieri, Giuseppe (1721–1794)
Palmieri, Matteo (1405–1475)
Paoletti, Ferdinando (1717–1801)
Paolini, Giovano Battista (*fl.*1785)
Paolini (1st half of 14th century)
Paradisi, Agostino (1736–1783)
Pardessus, Jean Marie (1772–1853)
Pare, William (1805–1873)
Parieu, Felix Esquirol de (1815–1893)

Pâris-Duverney, Joseph (died 1770)
Park, James Alan (1763–1838)
Parker, Henry (1604–1651)
Paruta, Paolo (1640–1698)
Pascoli, Leone (*fl.*1728)
Pashley, Robert (1805–1859)
Pasley, Lieut.-General Sir C.W. (1780–1861)
Passy, Frederic (1822–1912)
Passy, Hippolyte Philibert (1793–1880)
Paterson, Thomas (1828–1882)
Paterson, William (1658–1719)
Patrizi, Francesco (1412–1494)
Paulus Julius (*fl.* *c*3rd century AD)
Peacock, George (1791–1858)
Pearson, Charles Henry (1830–1894)
Pechhio, Guiseppe (1785–1835)
Pecqueur, Constantin (1801–1859)
Pedregal, Manuel (died 1896)
Peel, Sir Robert (1788–1850)
Péravy, de (*see* St. Péravy)
Perceval, Spencer (1762–1812)
Perdiguier, Agricol (1805–1875)
Pereira, Gregorio Pietro (*fl.*1757)
Periere, Emile (1800–1875)
Periere, Isaac (1806–1880)
Peri, Giovanni Domenico (*fl.*1638)
Périer, Casimir (1777–1832)
Perry, Arthur Latham (1830–1905)
Pescatore, Matteo (1813–1879)
Pestel, Friedrich Wilhelm von (1724–1805)
Petitti di Roreto, Carlo Ilarione (1790–1850)
Pfeiffer, Johann Friedrich von (1718–1787)
Philips, Erasmus (died 1743)
Phillips, Willard (1784–1873)
Pickering, John (*fl.*1847)
Pietro Da Ancarano (end of 16th century)
Pigeonneau, Henri (1834–1892)
Pillet-Will, Count (1781–1860)
Pinkerton, John (1758–1826)
Pinto, Isaac (1715–1787)
Pitt, William (1759–1806)
Plato (427–347 BC)
Plumart, Marquis de (*see* Dangeul)
Pococke, Richard (1704–1765)
Pontano, Giovanni (1426–1503)
Porphyry (233–*c*303 AD)
Porter, George R. (1792–1855)
Postlethwayt, James (died 1761)
Pothier, Abbé Remy (1727–1812)
Pothier, Robert Joseph (1699–1772)
Potter, Thomas Bayley (1817–1898)
Potter, William (*fl.*1650–1651)
Poullain, Henry (*fl.*1621)
Pratt, J. Tidd (1797–1870)
Prentice, Archibald (1792–1857)
Price, Bonamy (1807–1888)
Price, Dr. Richard (1723–1791)
Prince-Smith, John (1809–1874)
Prinsep, Charles Robert (1789–1864)
Prior, Thomas (1682–1751)
Ptolemy of Lucca (1236–1327)
Quetelet, Lambert Adolphe Jacques (1796–1874)
Rabbeno, Ugo (1864 1897)
Rae, George (1817–1902)
Raguet, Condy (1784–1842)
Raiffeisen, Friedrich Wilhelm (1818–1888)
Ralegh, Sir Walter (1552–1618)
Ramos, Enrique (*see* Muñoz)
Ramsey, Sir George (*fl.*1836–1862)
Raper, Matthew (*fl.*1771)
Rapp, George (1770–1847)
Raudot, Claude Marie (1801–1879)
Raynal, Guillaume Thomas François (1713–1796)
Recorde, Robert (*c*1510–1558)
Rees, Otto van (died 1868)
Renaudot, Théophraste (1584–1653)
Renny, Robert (*fl.*1807)
Renouard, Augustin Charles (1794–1878)
Ressi, Adeodato (*fl.*1811–1820)
Reybaud, Marie Roch Louis (1799–1879)
Ricca-Salerno, Guiseppe (1853–1903)
Ricci, Ludovico (1742–1799)
Richard des Glanières (*fl.*1774–1776)
Richelieu, A.J. du Plessis, Cardinal Duc de (1585–1642)
Ridolfi, Cosimo (1794–1865)
Riley, Henry Thomas (1816–1878)
Ritchie, David George (1853–1903)
Roberts, Lewes (died 1641)
Robertson, George (*c*1765–*c*1829)
Robinson, Henry (*fl.*1641–1656)
Rodriguez de Colmenar (*see* Colmenar, Rodriguez de)
Roederer, Pierre Louis, Comte (1754–1835)
Roesler, Karl Friedrich Hermann (1831–1895)
Rohr, Julius Bernhard von (1683–1742)
Rolt, Richard (1725–1770)
Romagnosi, Gian Domenico (1761–1835)
Rooke, John (1780–1856)
Rose, Right Hon. George (1744–1818)
Rösler (*see* Roesler, Karl F.H.)
Rota, Pietro (1846–1875)
Rouband, Pierre Joseph André, Abbé (1730–1791)
Royer, Charles Edouard (1810–1847)
Ruding, Rev. Rogers (1751–1820)
Ruffin, Edmund (1794–1865)
Ruge, Arnold (1802–1880)
Ruggles, Thomas (1745–1813)
Rümelin, Gustav von (1815–1889)
Saavedra-Faxardo (*see* Fajardo)
Sadler, Michael T. (1780–1835)
Saint-Aubin, Camille (1758–1820)
Saint Chamans, Vicomte Auguste de (1777–1861)
Saint Haippy, M. de (*see* Lottin, A.P.)
Saint-Marc, Henri (1854–1896)
Saint Péravy, Jean Nicholas Marcellin Guérineau de (1732–1789)
Saint-Pierre, Charles Irénée Castel, Abbé de (1658–1743)
Salmasius (Claude de Salmasius) (1588–1653)
Salmour, Ruggero G., Count of (died 1878)
Sanctis, M.A. (*see* De Sanctis)
Sandelin, Pieter Alexander (1777–1861)
Sander (or Sanders), Nicholas (*c*1527–1582)
San Salvatore (di), Padre Antonio (*fl.*1623)
Sansovino, Francesco (1521–1586)
Sarchiani, Giuseppe (1746–1835)
Sartorius, Georg Friedrich (1766–1828)
Sassetti, Filippo (1540–1588)
Saunders, N. (*see* Sander, N.)
Saunders, Robert (*fl.*1799–1802)
Savary Family – Savary, Jacques (1622–1690
Savary des Brulons, Jacques (1657–1716
Savary, Louis Philémon, Abbé (1654–1727)
Savigny, Friedrich Carl von (1779–1861)
Scaccia, Sigismonde (*fl.*1619)
Scaruffi, Gasparo (1519–1584)
Schlettwein, Johann August (1731–1802)
Schloss, David Frederick (1850–1912)
Schlözer, August Ludwig von (1735–1809)
Schmalz, Theodor Anton Heinrich (1760–1831)
Schmeitzel, Martin (1679–1747)
Schmidt, Caspar (*see* Stirner, Max)
Schoenhof, Jacob (1839–1903)
Schön, Heinrich Theodor von (1773–1856)
Schröder, Wilhelm Freiherr von (died 1689)
Schulze-Delitzsch, Franz Hermann (1808–1883)
Schwab, John Christopher (1865–1916)
Scialoja, Antonio (1817–1877)
Scola, Giovanni (*fl.*1787)
Scott, William (*fl.*1635)
Scrofani, Saverio (1756–1837)
Seaman, Ezra Champion (1805–1880)
Seckendorf, Veit Ludwig von (1626–1692)
Seebohm, Frederic (1833–1912)
Segni, Giovan Battista (*fl.*1602)
Selkirk, Thomas Douglas, Fifth Earl of (1771–1820)
Sella, Quintino (1827–1884)
Sempere y Guarinos, José (1754–1839)
Sénac de Meilhan, Gabriel (1736–1803)
Seneca, Luccius Annaeus (*c*4 BC–65 AD)
Seyd, Ernest (1833–1881)
Shattuck, Lemuel (1793–1859)
Sheffield, John Baker Holroyd, Earl of (1741–1821)
Sherbrooke, Viscount (Robert Lowe) (1811–1892)
Short, Thomas (1734–1772)
Silio, Guglielmo (*fl.*1792)
Simon, James (*fl.*1757)
Simpson, Stephen (1789–1854)
Sinclair, Sir John (1754–1835)
Skidmore, Thomas (died 1832)
Smith, Charles (1713–1777)
Smith, Edouard (1789–1852)
Smith, Erasmus Peschine (1814–1882)
Smith, Henry (1550–*c*1592)
Smith, John (*fl.*1661–1670)
Smith, Joshua Toumlin (1816–1869)
Smith, Prince (*see* Prince-Smith)
Smith, Sir Thomas (1514/5–1577)
Snelling, Thomas (1712–1773)
Soden, Friedrich Julius Heinrich Reichsgraf von (1754–1831)
Soetbeer, Adolph (1814–1892)
Spence, Thomas (1750–1814)
Spence, William (1783–1860)
Spooner, Lysander (1808–1887)
Springer, Johann (1727–1798)
Stafford, William (*fl.*1581)
Stair, John Dalrymple, Fifth Earl of (died 1789)
Stein, Heinrich Friedrich Karl Freiherr von (1757–1831)
Stein, Lorenz von (1815–1890)
Stephen, James (1759–1832)
Stirling, Patrick James (1809–1891)
Story, Joseph (1779–1845)
Stracca, Benvenuto (1509–1578)
Struzzi, Alberto (*fl.*1624)
Sugden, Edward Burtenshaw, Baron St Leonards (1781–1866)
Sully, Maximillien de Béthune, Duc de (1560–1641)
Süssmilch, Johann Peter (1706–1767)
Swann, Colonel James (1754–1835)
Tacitus, C. Cornelius (*c*61–*c*117 AD)
Tapia, Carlo (di) Marchese di Belmonte (*fl.* *c*1638)
Targioni Luigi (*fl.*1786–1814)
Tatham, William (1752–1819)

Temple, Sir William (1628–1699)
Temple, William (*fl.*1758)
Tesauro, Gaspare Antonio (*fl.*1609)
Thackrah, Charles Turner (1795–1833)
Thellusson, Peter (died 1797)
Thiers, Louis Adolphe (1797–1877)
Thomas, Pierre Emile (1822–1880)
Thomasius, Christian (1655–1728)
Thonissen, Jean Joseph (1816–1891)
Tompkins, Daniel Augustus (1851–1914)
Torre, Raffaele della (*fl.*1641)
Torri, Luigi (1719–1814)
Townsend, Rev. Joseph (1739–1816)
Treitschke, Heinrich von (1834–1896)
Trotter, Sir Coutts (1767–1837)
Turboli, Gian Donato (*fl.*1616–1629)
Turton, Thomas (1764–1844)
Tusser, Thomas (*c*1525–1580)
Tydeman, Hendrick Willem (1778–1863)
Ulloa, Bernardo de (*fl.*1740)
Usselincx, William (*fl.*1608)
Uztáriz, Jéronmio de (*fl.*1724–1757)
Van Hall, Floris Adrian (1791–1866)
Vandermonde, Alexandre Théophile (1735–1796)
Varro, M. Terentius (116–28 BC)
Vasco, Giovan Battista (1733–1796)
Vauban, Sebastian le Prestre, Seigneur de (1633–1707)
Vaughan, Rice (*fl.*1643–1660)
Vauvenargues, Luc de Clapiers, Marquis de (1715–1747)
Venturi, Giambattista (1746–1822)
Venusti, M. Antonio Maria (*fl.*1591)
Vergani, Paolo (*fl.*1794)
Vethake, Henry (1792–1866)
Vico, Giambattista (1668–1744)
Vidal, François (*fl.*1846–1848)
Vigano, Francesco (1807–1891)
Villano, Fillipo (*fl.*1768–1770)
Villeneuve-Bargemont, Vicomte Alban de (1784–1850)
Villermé, Louis René (1782–1863)
Villiaume, Nicolas (1818–1877)
Violet, Thomas (*fl.*1635–1662)
Virgilio, Jacopo (1824–1891)
Vissering, Simon (1818–1888)
Vivant de Mézagues (*see* Mézagues)
Vives, Juan Luis (1492–1540)
Vivorio, Agostino (1744–1822)
Voltaire, François Marie Arouet de (1694–1778)
Vuitry, Adolphe (1803–1883)
Wakefield, Daniel (1776–1846)
Wakefield, Edward (1774–1854)
Wales, William (died 1798)
Walker, Amasa (1799–1875)
Walker, Sir Byron Edmund (1848–1924)
Walker, Robert J. (1801–1869)
Wallace, Robert (1697–1771)
Wallace, Thomas (1769–1844)
Walpole, Sir Robert (Earl of Oxford) (1676–1745)
Walsh, Sir John Benn (1798–1881)
Walsh, Richard Hussey (1825–1862)
Ward, Bernardo (died *c*1760)
Ware, Nathaniel (1780–1854)
Warren, Josiah (1799–1874)
Warville (*see* Brissot de Warville)
Watteville, Adolphe de Grabe, Baron de (1799–1866)
Wayland, Francis (1796–1865)
Weber, Friedrich Benédict (1774–1848)
Webster, Daniel (1782–1852)
Webster, Pelatiah (1725–1795)
Weitling, Wilhelm (1808–1871)
Weston, George Melville (*fl.*1856–1882)
Weyland, John (*fl.*1807–1816)
Wheeler, John (*fl.*1601)
White, Horace (1834–1916)
Whittington, Sir Richard (*c*1350–1423)
Will, Georg Andreas (1727–1798)
Wilson, Glocester (*fl.*1811–1821)
Winchcombe, John (*see* Newbury, Jack of)
Winkleblech, K.G. (*see* Marlo, Karl)
Witt, Johan de (1623–1672)
Wolff, Christian von (1679–1754)
Wolowski, Louis François Michel Raymond (1810–1876)
Wood, W. (*fl.*1724)
Worlidge, John (*fl.*1669)
Wright, Carroll D. (1840–1909)
Wright, Frances (Mme D'Arusmont) (1795–1852)
Yarranton, Andrew (*c*1616–1685)
Young, Major Gavin (*fl.*1817–1832)
Zacchia, Lanfranco (*fl.*1658)
Zacharias, Otto (*fl.*1880)
Zanon, Antonio (1696–1770)
Zecchi, Lelio (1532–1610)
Zerbi, Giovanni Anotonio (*fl.*1593–1599)
Zincke, Rev. Foster Barham (1817–1893)
Zincke, Georg Heinrich (1692–1769)
Zuccolo, Lodivico (*fl.*1625)

Appendix III

Entries in *Palgrave's Dictionary of Political Economy*, by Author

NOTE: A dagger (†) indicates that the entry appeared only in the second edition, edited by Henry Higgs (1925–7). An asterisk (*) indicates that the entry in the second edition is a continuation of a similarly titled entry in the first edition.

Abrahams, B. Lionel. Jews in England; Jews, Exchequer of the; Jews, Houses of Converted; Poor relief among the Jews of England.

Akworth, W.M. Railways; Transport* (Inland, other than Railway).

Allum, F.E. Angel; Anna; As; Ban; Bezants; Candareen; Carolus (English); Carolus dollar; Cash. Money: Circulation: Currency; Cent, Centesimo or Centavo; Centesimi; Centimes; Centimos; Copper money (England); Copper money (Sweden); Cowrie; Crown [coin]; Crusade; Daric; Decime; Demonetisation; Denarius; Denier (Coin); Dime; Dinar; Dollar, (South and Central American Republics); Dollar, (United States); Dollar, Hard (Spanish); Dollar, Maria Theresa, or Levantiner Thaler; Dollar, Mexican, or Peso; Dollar, Trade (United States); Double-Florin; Doubloon; Drachma; Ducat (Modern); Eagle; Ecu; Eight-piece; Escudo; Farthing; Five-franc piece; Five-pound piece; Florin (Austrian), or Gulden; Florin (Dutch), or Gulden; Florin (English), Gold; Fourpence or Groat; Fractional currency; Franc, coin; Garbled coin; Gourde; Groschen; Half-crown; Half-sovereign; Halfpenny; Hall-marking; Hard-dollar; Heller; Imperial; Ingot; Iron and steel as money; Journey (Mint); Kopeck; Kreutzer; Light gold and silver coin; Louis d'or; Mace; Mark (German); Markka (Finland); Maundy money; Medjidie; Milreis; Mohur; Money of account; Napoleon (Coin); Ochr-el-guerch; Ora; Ore; Ounce; Penni; Penny; Pfennig; Piastre; Pie; Pistole; Pound sterling; Pound, Egyptian; Quartillo or Cuartillo; Real; Rei; Remedy (Mint); Rixdaler (Dutch); Rouble; Schilling or Skilling; Seignorage; Sequin; Shilling; Sixpence; Sol; Soldo; Sovereign; Stotinki; Sycee; Tael; Talent, Greek; Talent, Hebrew; Threepence; Tical; Toman; Trial plate (assay); Unite; Worseness; Yen.

Andreades, A. Aristotle*; Xenophon*

Andrews, Charles M. Land system in the American colonies; Manor, The (Historical); Mark system.

Andrews, Clement Walker. Economic libraries†

Ashley, W.J. Aquinas, St. Thomas; Benefice (1); Damnum Emergens; Eck, Johann; Economic history; Fathers, The; their economic teaching and influence; Feudalism; Fleetwood, William; Freeman; Hill, Sir Rowland; Historical School of Economics; Intercursus Magnus; Intercursus Malus; Journeyman; Journeymen's societies; Justum pretium; Kind, Payments in; Livery companies; Livery; Liverymen; Loan (Mutuum), Canonist definition of; Lucrum cessans; Luther, Martin; Major, John; Market as place of sale; Marshall, William; Melanchthon, Philip; Mercers; Merton, The Statute (or Provisions) of; Molina, Ludovicus; Molinaeus, Carolus; Montchretien, Antoyne de; National economy; Navarrus de Azilcueta, Martinus; Newbury, Jack of; Nitzsch, Karl Wilhelm; Oresme; Partnership, Canonist Theory; Partnership, Medieval; Ptolemy of Lucca; Rent-charge, Medieval; Riley, Henry Thomas; Rogers, Kames Edwin Thorold; Smith, Joshua Toulmin; Socialists of the chair; Steelyard, the; Taylors, Merchant; Towns, Policy of the (medieval); Tronage; Tusser, Thomas; Vives, Juan Luis; Zunft.

Atterbury, Frederick. Forced labour, instances of; Indirect taxation; Inhabited house duty; Land tax; Stamp duties; Taxation.

Avebury, Lord Municipal and government trading†.

Baker, E.N. Opium, as a state monopoly.

Barnett, R.W. Clearing system: Clearing houses; Denominations of banknotes; Deposit (Deposits); Discount; Divisibility of money. Divisions of money; Drain of bullion; Exchange, Internal; Futures; Gold points in foreign exchanges; Grading; Hoarding; Investment; Kite; Liquid assets; Margin (in monetary transactions); Marked cheque; Metropolis, Management of; Minimum (Rate of Discount); Mint par of exchange; Mint price of bullion; Options; Par; Parity of value; Pound. Tower, troy, avoirdupois; Premium; Price of gold and silver; Promoter; Prompt; Qualification; Quorum; Quota; Quotation; Realise; Rebate; Recoup; Recourse; Remittance; Reserves (Banking); Retire a Bill; Securities; Settling day; Short exchange; Sight (=Demand); Standard gold and silver; Stringency in the money market; Suspense account; Suspension of specie payments; Trade coins.

Barton, Dora M. Female labour*; Females, Earnings of*.

Bastable, C.F. Commerce, British (History of); Distribution of the precious metals; Equalisation of international demand; Experimental methods in economics; Fair rents; Fair trade; Farming taxes, Principle of; Finances –General principles; Food, Taxes on; Free trade, Theory of; Gale and hanging gale; Griffith's valuation; International trade; International value, Theory of; Local government; Pale (Ireland); Progress, Influence of, on value; Protection, and protective system; Salt, Taxes on; Ulster tenant right; Wood, W.

Bateman, A.E. Coasting trade.

Bauer, Stephan. Althusius, Johannes; Arbuthnot, John, of Mitcham (Surrey); Arithmetic, Political. History of; Armstrong, Clement; Arnd, Karl; Arnould, Ambroise-Marie; Atkinson, William; Balance of trade (History of the theory); Barbon, Nicholas, M.D; Barrington, Shute; Barton, John*; Bell, William; Bernard, Sir Thomas, Bart; Black, David; Boecler, Johann Heinrich; Boncerf, Pierre-Francois; Boulainvilliers, Henri de; Bray, Charles; Bray, J.F; Brewster, Sir Francis; Brissot de Warville, Jean-Pierre; Brown, John; Butel-Dumont, George Marie; Cantillon, Richard; Danguel, Marquis de Plumart; Diderot, Denis; Drake, James; Ephemerides; Ogilvie, William.

Beazley, R.C. Futures in cotton.

Beck de Madaras, Gyula. Lotteries, Continent of Europe.

Bellot, Hugh L.L. Arbitration, International†; Declaration of London 1909†; Drago doctrine†; Hague conferences (1899–1920)†; International law, private* –uniformity of laws; International law, private*; International law*.

Bemis, E.W. Trades unions (United States).

Bertolini, Angelo. Fabroni, Giovanni; Ferrari, Jacopo; Ferretti, Julius; Ferroni, Pietro; Filangieri, Gaetano; Filiucci, Vincenzo; Fineschi, F. Vincenzo; Fiorentino, Nicola; Fontanelli, Carlo; Formaleoni, Vincenzo; Foronda, Valentino; Forti, E; Fortunato, Nicola; Fossombroni, Vittorio; Frachetta, Girolamo; Franchi, Carlo; Fuoco, Francesco; Gaito, Giovanni Domenico; Galanti, Giuseppe M; Galdi, Matteo; Galiani, Ferdinando; Gambrini, Francesco; Garelli della Morea, Giusto Emanuele; Garrati, Martino; Gasparino, Bartolomeo; Gemelli, Francesco; Genovesi, Antonio; Ghetti, Ludovico; Gianni, Francesco Maria; Giogalli, Simone; Gioja, Melchiorre; Guarini, G.B; Intieri, Bartolomeo; Invrea, Fabio; Isola, Francesco; Jacini, Count Stefano; Pagnini, Giovanno Francesco; Palmeri, Nicolo; Paoletti, Ferdinando; Paolino; Patrizi, Francesco; Paulus Julius; Peri, Giovanni Domenico.

Bewes, Wyndham A. Lawful hours*; Lease property*; Lease*.

Blain, W. Rupee, History of.

Bonar, J. Abbot, Charles; Abeille, Louis Paul; Abundance; Advances; Aikin. John, M.D; Alison, William Pulteney, M.D; Anderson, James (No. 2); Angarie, Droit d'; Anti-rent agitations; Appanage; Aristocracy; Artel; Auncel, or Handsal; Austrian School of Economists; Babbage, Charles; Baines, Edward; Baines, Thomas; Bamford, Samuel; Banfield, Thomas C; Beckmann, Johann; Bentham, Jeremy; Board of Agriculture (1793); Bosanquet, Charles; Bourgeois; Bradlaugh, Charles; Bray, J.F; Bubble act; Bureau of Labour; Canning, George; Canon law; Carlyle, Thomas; Cartel; Chaffer; Chalmers, Thomas; Chamberlen, Hugh; Classical economists; Cobbett, William; Cobden, Richard; Complementary goods; Comte, Aug., and English Political Economy; Concession; Conjunctur; Copleston, Edward; Crombie, Alexander; Custom (Habit) –its place in economics; Dalbiac, General Sir James Charles; Denny, William; Development; Dirom, Major Alexander; Distribution, Uses of the term; Doubleday, Thomas; Dove, Patrick Edward; English School of Political Economy –Modern Economics; Equality; Examples; Fichte, Johann Gottlieb; Francis, Philip; Friction in economics; German School of Political Economy –Period III; Godwin, William; Goods, Economic; Held, Adolf von; Hermann, Friedrich Benedict Wilhelm; Hill-Burton, John; Jarrold, Thomas; Kant, Immanuel; Locke on currency; Mathus, Thomas Robert; Paley, William; Population: Economic theory; Population*; Positive law; Positive theory of capital; Read, Samuel; Rolt, Richard; Smith, Adam; Socialism*; Tavereel (or Tafereel); Treitschke, Heinrich von; Vert.

Bonney, Rev. T.G. Mines and minerals.

Bourne, Stephen. Conventional value; Declared and real values; Entrepots; Entry, Bill of; Warehousing system.

Bower, E.E.N. Income tax in the United Kingdom; Income tax in the United Kingdom* [since 1896].

Bowley, A.L. Prices, History of*; Wages, Nominal and real; Wages, Nominal and real,* changes in, in the U.K. since 1850; Workmen's budgets.

Brabrook, E.W. Building Societies*; Friendly Societies*; Friendly societies, their numbers and constitution.

Brooks, John Graham. Gothenburg system, The; Insurance, State (Germany).

Butlin, F.M. Transportation, The economic effect of.

Buxton, Sydney C. Budget, The.

Caldecott, A. Bounties; Colonies:; Coolie system; Emancipation; Production, Instruments of; Produit net; Sinecures, Colonial; Tithes.

Cannan, Edwin. Amana Society; Anarchism; Arithmetic ratio or progression; Bakounin, Michael; Bounarroti, Philippe; Brands and other certificates of quality, Government; Capital; Christian socialism; Collectivism; Commune of Paris, 1871; Communism; Darwinism; Definitions; Diffusion theory of taxation; Diminishing returns; Distribution; Distributive justice; Employment; Exchange; Expenditure or spending; Exploit; Fauquier, Francis; Fortrey, Samuel; Geometrical ratio or progression; Glut; Good for trade; Gross and net; Hire; Ideal, The Economic; Increasing returns; Investment; Marcet, Mrs. Jane; Produce; Production; Profit; Saving.

Castelot, E. Baudrillart, Henri Joseph Leon†; Block, Maurice†; Bounties on sugar; Clamageran, Jean Jules†; Davila y Lugo, Don Francisco; Davila, el Padre Bautista; De Lajonchere; De la Mare, Nicolas; Dombasles, Alexandre Mathieu de; Dormer, Diego Jose; Dubos, Abbe J.B; Ducpetiaux, Edouard; Dufau, F.P; Duhamel du Monceau, Henri Louis; Dupin, Claude; Duquesnoy, Adrien Cyprien; Duvillard de Durand, Etienne; Ebaudy de Fresne; Egron, Adrien Cesar; Emmery de Sept Fontaines, Henri Charles; Encabezamiento; Encomienda; Ensenada, Zenon de Somodevilla y Bengoechea, Marquis de la; Escusado; Etats Generaux, The; Fajardo or Faxardo, Count Diego de Saavedra Faxardo; Favre, Antoine; Finances –Belgium; France; Florez Estrada, Alvaro; Florida-Blanca, Jose Monino, Count; Fonfrede, Henri; Foronda, Valentin de; Foucquet, Nicolas; Fregier, A; Furstenau, Karl Gottfried; Gaeta, Duke of, Martin Michel Charles Gaudin; Galeon; Galitzin, Dimitri, Prince; Garve, Christian; Gasparin, Adrien Etienne Pierre; Gasser, Simon Peter; Giganti, Miguel de; Gild system in Spain; Gournay, Jean Claude Marie Vincent de; Gramont, Scipion de; Graslin, Louis Francois de; Graumann, Johann Philip; Guerard, Benjamin; Guerry de Champneuf, Jacques; Haller, Karl Ludwig von; Harcourt, Francois Eugene Gabriel, Duke of; Heeren, Arnold Hermann Ludwig; Helvetius; Herbert, Claude-Jacques; Herrenschwand,; Herrera, Cristobal, Perez de; Heuschling, Philipp F. Xavier Theodore; Hock, Baron Karl von; Hoeck, Johann Daniel Albrecht; Hubner, Otto; Huc, E., Abbe; Huet, Pierre Daniel; Hullman, Karl Dietrich; Humboldt, Alexander von, Baron; Huysers, Arien; Impot unique (or single tax); Internal customs and tolls; Isnard, Achille Nicolas; Jannet, Claudio; Jobard, Jean Baptiste Ambroise-Marcelin; Jourdan, Alfred; Jovellanos, Gaspar Melchior de; Juglar, Clement†; Jung Stilling, Johann Heinrich; Juros; Klock, Kaspar; Kosegarten, Wilhelm; Kries, Karl Gustav; Kroncke, Klaus; Krug, Johann Leopold; Kuricke, Rein; La Rochefoucauld Liancourt, Alexandre Frederic, Duc de; La Rochefoucauld Liancourt, Frederic Gaetan, Marquis de; Labouliniere, Pierre; Lacroix, Emeric de; Laffemas, Barthelemy de; Laffemas, Issac de, Sieur de; Lagrange, Joseph Louis; Laissez-faire, laissez-passer, History of the Maxim; Land, Domaine Congeable; Langenstein, Henry of; Larruga, Eugenio de; Le Gendre, Francois; Leber, C; Lefevre de Beauvray, Pierre; Leib, Johann Georg; Lenda; Leymarie, Achille; Linguet, Simon Nicolas Henri; Lips, Alexander; Lith, Johann Wilhelm von der; Livre de raison; Lomenie, Louis de; Lottin, Antoine Prosper; Lucas, Charles Jean Marie; Ludewig, Johann Peter; Macanaz, Melchior de; Maizieres, Philippe de; Majorat; Malchus, Karl August von; Malesherbes, Chretien Guillaume de Lamoignon de; Malestroit, Seigneur de; Malon, Benoit; Mantellier, Philippe; Mariana, Juan de; Marperger, Paul Jacob; Martinez de la Mata; Masselin, Jean; Mathias de Saint Jean, Jean Eon; Media Anata; Medina, Fray Juan de; Menier, Emile Justine; Mercier, Louis Sebastien; Mesnil Marigny, Jules du; Mesta; Michaelis, Otto; Michel, Francisque; Millones y cientos; Minorat; Mohl, Robert von; Molster, Johannes Adriaan; Moncada, Sancho de; Moneda Forera; Moneda, Pedidos, or Servicios; Monedage; Montaigne, Michel de; Montazgo; Monts de Piete; Morcellement; Moreau de Beaumont; Moreau, Cesar; Morel Vinde, Charles Gilbert; Morhof, Daniel Georg; Morstadt, Eduard; Moser, Friedrich Karl von; Moser, Johann Jacob; Municipal Government in Belgium; Municipal Government in France; Municipal Government in Italy; Munoz, Antonio; Munster, Sebastian; Navarrete, Pedro Fernandez; Naveau, Jean Baptiste; Niceron, Jean Pierre; Nicholls, Chevalier; Normante y Carcaviella, Doctor Lorenzo; Notables commercants; Notables, Assemblees des; Octroi; Olivares, Damian de; Olufsen, Oluf Christian; Orbrecht, George; Ortes, Giammaria; Ortiz, Jose Alonso; Ortiz, Luis; Pacioli or Paciolo, Fra Luca; Paget, Amedee; Palissy, Bernard de; Pardessus, Jean Marie; Patronage (in the French sense); Peasant proprietors; Perdiguier, Agricol; Pereire, Emile; Pereire, Issac; Perier, Casimir; Pietro de Ancarano; Pigeonneau, H; Pillet-Will, Count; Portazgo, Pontazgo and Barcage; Pothier, Robert Joseph; Pothier, The abbe Remy; Poullain, Henry; Propios y arbitrios; Pufendorf, Samuel; Quintos; Raynal, Guillaume Thomas Francois; Regie; Renaudot, Theophraste; Rentas Estancadas; Retenue; Richard des Glanieres; Rohr, Julius Bernhard von; Roturier; Royer, Charles Edouard; Ruge, Arnold; Rumelin, Gustav von; Saint Peravy (Jean Nicholas Marcellin Guerineau de); Sandelin, Pieter Alexander; Sansovino, Francesco; Say, Horace Emile; Say, Leon; Say, Louis Auguste; Schmeitzel, Martin; Scrofani, Saverio; Sempere y guarinos, Jose; Senac de Meilhan, Gabriel; Seneuil, Jean Gustave Courcelle-; Servicio (or Pedido); Sisa; Smith, Edouard; Sou; Sous de cloche; Spanish School of Political Economy; Springer, Johann; Struzzi, Alberto; Tante; Taula de cambi; Templars, The Knights; Tercias Reales; Tercio Diezmo; Thomas, Pierre Emile; Transhumance; Tydeman, Hendrik; Ulloa, Bernardo de; Uztariz, Jeronimo de; Vales Reales; Vauvenargues, Luc de Clapiers, Marquis de; Vavasseur; Viriculture; Voltaire, Francois Marie Arouet de; Ward, Bernardo; Weber, Friedrich Benedict; Will, Georg Andreas; Yantar.

Chalmers, M.D. Acceptance; Accommodation bill; Bankruptcy law and administration;

Bill of Exchange, Law of; Bills of Exchange Act 1882†; Cheques, Law of; Debt; Discharge in bankruptcy; Dividend (in bankruptcy); Dividend warrant; Factors' acts; Fictitious payee; Floating policy; Fraud; Fraudulent preference (in bankruptcy); Honour (Payment for); Instrument, Negotiable; Insurance, Marine; Insurance, Mutual; Maker (of promissory note); Market overt; Merchantableness, Implied warranty of; Money bill; Moneys to be provided by parliament; Moratory law; Negotiable instrument; Not negotiable; Noting of bills; Obligation; Open policy; Order; Payment; Pledge; Price; Procuration by signature (bills of exchange); Promissory note; Protest (of bills); Provable debt; Proxy; Public policy; Qualified acceptance; Quasi-contract; Restraint of trade (law of).

Chalmers, Robert. Colonies: Currency in British Colonies; Dollar, History of; Doubloon, History of; Mohur, History of; Pagoda, History of; Pistareen, History of

Chapman, Sir S.J. Unemployed†; Workmen's insurance†.

Chisolm, G.G. with R. Lodge. Commercial routes*.

Clare, George. Exchange, Foreign, practical working of; Exchange, as Bourse; Exchange, broker.

Clark, A.B. Poor law, Scotch.

Clark, J.B. Distribution, Ethics of; Distribution, Law of; Labour, Mobility of; Labour, Skilled; Labour; Legal tender; Lewis, Sir George Cornewall; Localisation of industry; Mechanics of industry.

Cohen, J.L. National health insurance†; Pensions*; Poor law*; Poor relief among the Jews of England*; Social insurance†; Unemployment insurance†; Unemployment†; Workmen's compensation†.

Colby, C.W. Walker, Sir Bryon Edmund†.

Collet, Clara E. Booth, Charles†; Edgeworth, Marie; Female labour; Females and children, Earnings of; Schloss, David Frederick†.

Connell, A.K. Cite Ouvriere; City: Ancient, Medieval, Modern; Free towns; Geography, Commercial (Connected with Great Britain).

Cook, E.T. Ruskin, John†.

Corbett, W.J. Debasement of coin.

Courtois, A., fils. Argenson, Rene Louis de Voyer de Paulmy; Audiffret, Ch. L.G., Marquis d'; Audiganne, Amand; Babeuf, Francois Noel; Batbie, Anselme Polycarpe; Baudeau, Nicolas, Abbe; Bazard, Saint-Amand; Blanc, Jean Joseph Louis; Bodin, Jean; Boisguillebert, alias Boisquilbert, Pierre le Pesant; Bonnet, Victor; Buchez, Philippe Joseph Benjamin; Buret, Antoine Eugene; Cabet, Etienne; Cadet, Felix; Calonne, Charles Alexandre; Chastellux, Francois Jean; Cherbuliez, Antoine Elysee; Chevalier, Michel; Clement, Ambroise; Clement, Pierre; Cochut, Pierre Andre; Colbert, Jean Baptiste; Comte, Auguste; Comte, Charles; Condillac, Etienne Bonnot de; Condorcet, Marie Caritat, Marquis de; Courcy, Alfred de; Daire, Eugene; Dameth, Henri; De Brouckere, Charles; De Metz-Noblat, Alexandre; Destutt de Tracy, Antoine Louis Claude, Comte; Droz, Joseph; Duchatel, Comte Tanneguy; Dunoyer, Charles; Dupin, Baron Charles; Dupont-White, Charles; Dupre de Saint-Maur, Nicolas Francois; Dussard, Hipp; Dutens, Joseph Michel; Dutot; Enfantin, Prosper; Esterno, Phil., Comte d'; Faucher, Leon; Fenelon, Francois de Salignac de la Mothe; Fix, Theodore; Fonteyraud, Alcide; Forbonnais, Francois Veron de; Fourier, Charles; Gaeta, Duke of, Martin Michel Charles Gaudin; Garnier, Comte Germain; Garnier, Joseph; Gautier, Jules; Gerando, Joseph Maria; Girardin, Emile de; Guillard, Achille; Guillaumin, Urbain Gilbert; Horn, Ignace Einhorn; La Farelle, Francois Felix; Laborde, Alexandre, Comte de; Laboulaye, Edouard Rene Lefebvre; Laffitte, Jacques; Laveleye, Emile de; Lavergne, Louis Gabriel Leonce Guilhaud de; Lavoisier, Antoine Laurent; Le Hardy de Beaulieu, Charles; Leroux, Pierre; Letrosne (or Letrone) Guillaume Francois; Louis, Dominique, Baron; Mably, Gabriel Bonnot; Machault d'Arnouville, Jean Baptiste; Melon, Jean Francois; Mercier (alais Lemercier) de la Riviere, Paul Pierre; Meynieu, Madame Mary; Mirabeau, Honore Gabriel Riquetti; Mollien, Francois Nicolas; Montesquieu, Charles de Secondat; Montyon, Antoine Robert Auget; Morellet, Abbe Andre; Morelly; Morreau de Jonnes, Alexandre; Naville, Francois Marc Louis; Necker, Jacques; Parieu, Felix Esquirou de; Paris-Duverney, Joseph; Passy; Pecqueur, Constantin; Pinto, Isaac; Quesnay, Francois; Quetelet, Lambert Adolphe Jacques; Raudot, Claude Marie; Renouard, Augustin Charles; Reybaud, Marie Roch Louis; Roederer, Pierre Louis; Rossi, Pellegrino Luigi Edoardo; Rouband, Pierre Joseph Andre, Abbe; Saint Chamans, Vicomte Auguste de; Saint-Aubin, Camille; Saint-Pierre, Charles Irenee Castel; Savary Family; Sismondi, Jean Charles Leonard Simonde de; Systeme; Thiers, Louis Adolphe; Thonissen, Jean Joseph; Vandermonde, Alexandre Theophile; Villeneuve-Bargemont, Vicomte Alban de; Villerme, Louis Rene; Visa; Vuitry, Adolphe; Watteville; Wolowski, Louis Francois Michel Raymond.

Craigie, P.G. Chambers of agriculture; Chambers of commerce.

Crowly, J.P. Pensions.

Crump, C.G. Amercements; Aubaine, Droit d'; Badger; Bede; Chapman; Chevage; Chiminage; Cornage; Corvee; Detraction; Edwards, Bryan; Edwards, George; Elliott, Ebenezer; Estcourt, Thomas; Evans, Thomas; Forced labour, Common characteristics of; Fustel de Coulanges, Numa Denis.

Crump, Norman. Rupee*.

Cunningham, Rev. W. Civilisation; Enclosures; Hales, John; Henley, Walter of; Johnson, Samuel; Lamond, Elizabeth; Latimer, Hugh; Luddites.

Daniell, A. Acceptilation; Accretion; Act of bankruptcy; Arbitration; Scotch; Assythment; Bankruptcy in Scotland; Banks, Chartered (Scotland); Cash credit; Caution; Cess; Code Napoleon; Commandite, Societe en; Common good; Commonty; Companies: English and Scotch law; Compromise; Concourse; Concurrence; Confirmation of executor; Consideration; Courts (Scotland); Damnum fatale; Davach; Dead freight; Dead's part; Deadly, Warrandice against all; Debitum fundi; Decree of registration; Deed; Del Credere; Discharge; Discussion; Dishonour of a bill; Disposition; Docquet; Domicile, Scotland; Donation; Factor; Fee (Scots law); Ferries; Feu; Fiars prices; Fixtures; Fugae warrant; Goodwill; Ground-annual; Heritable and moveable; Heritable securities; Holograph; Hypothec; Inhibition; Interdict; Interdiction (Scots law); Irritancy; Judicial factor; Jurisdiction, Scotch; Jury (England); Jury (Scotland); Jus ad rem: Jus in re; Jus relictae; Keys, Queen's; Master and servant; Ploughgate; Poinding of the ground; Prescription (Scots law); Sasine (Scots law); Succession (Scots law); Teinds; Warrandice.

Davids, T.W. Rhys. Caste.

Davidson, Mark G. Depression of trade; Division of labour; Drawbacks; Earnings of management; Economic freedom; Economic harmony; Economic law; Equilibrium; Fair price; Fixed and floating capital; Flow of capital; Friction in economics; Home industries; Hutcheson, Francis; Industry, Organisation of; Legitim.

Dawson, W. Harbutt. Oncken, August†; Philippovich, Eugen von†; Pierson, Nicolas Gerard†; Rae, George†; Rae, John (1845–1915)†; Rae, John (1796–1872)*; Schaffle, Albert Eberhard Friedrich†; Seebohm, Frederic†; Smart, Wiliiam†; Syndicalism†.

Dearle, N.B. Geissler, Adolf†; Herrmann, Emanuel†.

Deverell, Edith M. Trunk acts.

Devine, E.T. Production and consumption; Single tax; Smith, Erasmus Peschine; Vethake, Henry; Walker, Robert J; Webster, Daniel.

Dewey, D.R. Adams, Charles Francis; Appleton, Nathan; Baldwin, Loammi; Bigelow, Erastus Brigham; Bolles, John A; Bollman, Justus Erick, M.D; Breck, Samuel; Cambreleng, Churchill C; Cardozo, Isaac N; Chickering, Jesse; Clay, Henry; Colton, Rev. Calvin; Colwell, Stephen; Coxe, Tench; Dew, Thomas Roderick; Douglass, William; Elder, William; Emerson, Gouverneur; Everett, Alexander Hill; Factory laws in the United States; Felt, Joseph B; Fiat money; Franklin, Benjamin; Garfield, James Abram; Gibbons, James Sloan; Gold certificates; Gold notes; Gouge, William M; Grangers and Granger laws; Greeley, Horace; Greenback; Hale, Nathan; Hamilton, Alexander; Hard money; Hayes, John L; Hildreth, Richard; Howe, John Badlam; Income tax in the United States; Industrial education in the United States; Internal revenue taxes in the United States; Jarvis, Edward; Kelley, William D; Kellog, Edward; Knox, John J; Land, Public, of the United States; Mint, United States; Nationalist (U.S.A); Phillips, Willard; Reciprocity in the United States; Repudiation, United States; Silver legislation in the United States; Treasury Department of the United States; Tucker, George; Warehousing system, United States.

Dixon, E. Leake, Stephen Martin; Lewis, Matthew or Mark; Massie, Joseph; Maugham, Robert; Milles, Thomas; Morris, Corbyn; Murray, Robert.

Dunbar, C.F. Banks, National (United States of America); Carey, Henry Charles; Free banking; Horton Samuel Dana; Walker, Francis Amasa.

Edgeworth, F.Y. Absentee; Agents of production; Aickin, Rev, Joseph; Aleatory; Antoninus, St; Attwood, Thomas and the Birmingham School; Auxiron, Claude Francois Joseph d'; Average; Averages*; Bailey, Samuel, on value; Barter and exchange; Bastiat as a theorist; Baxter, Robert Dudley; Beldam; Berkeley, George; Birth-rate*; Birthrate; Blake, William; Bounties, Abstract theory of; Brassey, Thomas; Bright, John; Brindley, James; Briscoe; Brougham, Henry; Buckle, Thomas Henry; Buquoy, Georg Franz; Buridan, Jean; Burke, Edmund; Burlamaqui, Jean Jaques; By-products, Theory of value of; Camerarius, Joachim; Campanella, Tommaso; Canard, Nicholas Francois; Cantillon, Richard; Cary, John; Cayley, Edward; Census; Census*; Child, Sir Josiah; Clarkson, Thomas; Clayton, David; Colquhoun, Patrick; Competition and regulation; Conditt, John; Coquelin, Charles; Corbet, Thomas; Cotton, Sir Robert Bruce; Cournot, Antoine Augustin; Cowell, John Welsford; Cradocke, Francis; Craig, John; Crumpe, Samuel; Culpeper, Sir Thomas the elder (1578–1662); Culpeper, Sir Thomas the younger (1626–1697); Curves; Curves*; De Quincey, Thomas; Death-rate; Debasement of coin; Deferred payments; Demand curves; Demoivre (or De Moivre), Abraham; Denominator, Common; Deparcieux (or De Parcieux), Antoine; Depreciation of monetary standard; Dieterici, Karl Friedrich Wilhelm; Difficulty of attainment; Distance in time as an element of value; Doctrinaire; Doses (of capital); Dupont, Pierre Samuel; Dupuit, A.J. Etienne-Juvenal; Duration of life (as an element of well-being); Economics, teaching at Oxford†; Eden, Sir Frederick Morton; Efficiency of money; Elasticity; Eliot, Francis Perceval; Ellis, William (1800–1881); Error, Law of; Error, Law of*; Exchange, Value in; Expectation of life; Facts; Fallacies; Fixed incomes; Forced currency; Fullarton, John; Functions; Gossen, Hermann Heinrich; Growth, Proportionate; Hagen, Karl Heinrich; Hearn, William Edward; Helferich, Johannes a Renatus von; Higgling; Ideal money; Income; Inconvertible currency; Index numbers; Index numbers*; Indifference, Law of; Intrinsic value; Jenkin, Henry Charles Fleeming; Jennings, Richard; Joint production –Joint products; Jones, Richard; King, Peter, Lord; Least squares, Method of; Luck; Luxury; Margin (in economics); Marriage-rate; Mathematical method in political economy; Maximum satisfaction; Mean; Means, Method of; Mill, James; Mill, John Stuart; Mistery; Moffat, Robert Scott; Monopoly; Multiplication of services; Negative quantities; Numerical determination of the laws of utility; Over-production; Pantaleoni, Maffeo†; Pareto's law†; Pareto, Vilfredo†; Peacock, George; Playfair, William; Pleasure and pain; Porphyry; Present goods; Probability and calculus of probabilities; Rae, John; Risk; Supply-curves; Total utility; Unit of value; Utility; Wealth; Wilson, Glocester.

Egerton, Hugh E. Gaskell, P; Godwin, William; Gray, John (18th cent.); Hall, Charles; Hodgskin, Thomas; Horsley, W; Hume, David; Hume, James Deacon; Ivernois, Sir Francis d'; La Luzerne, Cesar-Guillaume de; Lauderdale, Eighth Earl of; Leclaire, Edme-Jean; Lemonnier, Charles; Locre, Jean Guillaume, Baron de Roisey; Longfield, Mountifort; Loyd, Samuel Jones; MacFarlan, John; Maclean, J.H; Macnab, Henry Grey; Macpherson, David; Maddison, Sir Ralph; Madison, James; Magens; Mallet, P.H; Mandeville, Bernard de; Martin, Frederick; Martineau, Harriet; Maseres, Francis; Maslov; Maurice, John Frederick Denison; McLennan, John F; Meek, Sir James; Merchants' petition of 1820, The; Meredith, Sir William; Millar, John; Milne, Joshua; Molesworth, Sir William; Moore, Adam; Morgan, William; Mortimer, Thomas; Mosse or Moses, Miles; Mushet, Robert; Newenham, Thomas; Nicholls, Sir George; North, Sir Dudley; Noy, William; Oddy, J. Jepson; Oliphant, Charles; Onely, Rev. Richard; Ouvrard, G.J; Page, Frederic; Palmer, J. Horsley; Park, James Alan; Paterson, William; Pennington, James; Philips, Erasmus; Pitt, William; Playfair, William; Porter, George R; Price, Richard; Profit sharing; Progressive wage; Sadler, Michael T; Senior, William Nassau; Settlement, Poor law; Thornton, Henry; Thornton, William Thomas; Tooke, Thomas; Whately, Richard.

Elliott, T.H. Audit office; Bonded warehouses; Cadastral survey; Capitation taxes; Centralisation; Commissions of enquiry; Consular reports; Consumption, Taxes on; Contraband; Conversion of British National Debt; Cost of collection of taxes; Countervailing duty; Custom –customs duties; Deadweight Annuity; Death duties; Debts, Public; Deficiency advances; Deficiency bills; Deficit; Department (France); Department; Direct taxation; Discriminating of differential duties.

Ellis, A. Account; Arbitrage (Stock Exchange); Backwardation; Bear; Bearer; Bonus; Boom; Broker, General; Bull; Buying in; Call; Carrying over; Cash, Sale for; Cedula; Certificate, Share; Client, Stockbroker's; Continuation or contango; Contract note; Corner on Stock Exchange; Cum dividend; Dealer (Stock Exchange); Deferred stock; Delivery, Good; Discount, French Stock Exchange; Dollar of account; Dollar, Hard (Stock Exchange use of word); Drawing; Enfaced paper or rupee paper; Ex. all; Ex. dividend; Ex. drawing; Ex. new; Exchange, Stock; Exchequer bond; Forestall; Inscribed stock; Instalment; International securities; Jobber; Letter of allotment; Letter of application; Making-up; Market; Maturity of bonds; Middle price; Mortgage bond.

Ely, R.T. Farmers' Organisations in the United States.

Escreet, H.C. Children's employment†; Factory acts*.

Faraday, Ethel R. Paine, Thomas; Productive and unproductive labour; Produit net; Restrictions on labour.

Faraday, F.J. Political Economy, Recent developments of; Produce clearing.

Fass, H.E. Budget*.

Fitzmaurice, Lord Edmond. Petty, Sir William.

Floud, Sir F.L.C. Small holdings*.

Flux, A.W. Diagrams; Graphic method; Interest, Theory of; Laws of political economy –examples; Laws of political economy –general principles; Plutology; Polegraphy; Political Economy, Postulates of; Prices and money; Prices, History of; Prices, Short-period supply and long-period supply; Productive, The terms; Productivity of capital; Rent does not enter into cost of production; Rent, Basis of; Satiety price; Saturate; Statistics; Surplus; Value; Wages, Purchasing power of; Weighted observations.

Foley, Caroline A. Fallati, Johannes; Famine; Fashion, Economic influence of; Faucher, Julius; Fibonacci, Leonardo Pisano; Fielding, Henry; Francis, John; Gee, Joshua; Gerson, Jean Charlier de; Leibniz, Baron Gottfried Wilhelm von; Malebranche, Nicolas; Ralegh, Sir Walter; Rent of ability; Rousseau, Jean Jacques; Science, Economic, as distinguished from art; Statics, Social and social dyanmics; Vanderlint, Jacob.

de Foville, A. About, Edmond; Bastiat, Frederic; Blanqui. Jerome Adolphe.

Fowler, William.. Bill broking; Crises, 1857–1866–1890.

Fox, Stephen N. Foreign labour.

Foxwell, H.S. The Goldsmith's Company's Library of Economic Literature†.

Gibbins, Rev. H. de B. Goldsmiths; goldsmiths' notes; Government regulation of industry, earlier history; Oastler, Richard; Pre-roman industry in Britain; Stirner, Max.

Gibson, T.G. and A.A. Uthwatt. Companies, Increase of*.

Gibson, T.G. Commercial intelligence (United Kingdom)†; Consular reports,* British; Consuls, British, Duties of†.

Giddings, F.H. Future goods and services.

Gide, C. Christianity and economics: Roman Catholic School; French School of Political Economy; French School of Political Economy*; Metayage; Proudhon, Joseph; Say, Jean Baptiste; Secretan, Charles; Solidarity; St. Simon (St. Simonism) Claude-Henri, Comte de; Sully, Maximilien de Bethune, Duc de; Vauban, Sebastian Le Prestre; Vidal, Francois; Villiaume, Nicolas.

Glover, John. Freight.

Gonner, E.C.K. Black Death, The; Buchanan, David; Cameralistic science; Carucage; Chalmers, George; Chamberlayne, Edward; Champion and severalty; Chartism; Ciompi; Colonies: Systems of colonisation; Commerical science; Companies, Staple; Decker, Sir Matthew; Discoveries, Geographical (Influence on trade of); East

India Company; Eastland Company; Education, Economic Aspects of; Exchanger, Royal; Foreign traders and their rights, History of; Ganilh, Charles; Greenland Company; Greg, William Rathbone; Harrison, William; Howlett, John; Hudson's Bay Company; Huskisson, William; Nasse, Erwin; Ricardo, David.

Gray, F.W. Conversion of British National Debt*; Currency (or Treasury) notes†; Drain of bullion*; State notes*; Stringency in the money market* 1906–1907; [Banking], Banks*.

Greening, E.O. Co-operation: Co-operative Farming; Co-operation: Co-operative Workshops.

Greven, H.B. Dutch School of Economics; Finances –The Netherlands.

Gross, Chas. Convention of Royal Burghs of Scotland; Gilds: Early history, religious gilds, gild merchant, craft gilds; Hanse of London; Madox, Thomas; Scot and lot.

van Gyn, Ant. Finances, The Netherlands*.

Hadley, A.T. Interstate commercial law (U.S.A); Pool; Transport, Cost of Inland

Hall, Hubert. Church-seed; Day, day work, and diet; Denarius dei; Deniers de Calais; Deodand; Depopulation (Term); Depopulation, in relation to Economic History; Deputy; Derelict; Dica; Dividend, Medieval; Doitkin; Dole-fish; Drengage; Drofland, or Dryfland; Dry Exchange; Dry rent; Due; Emption; Pipe rolls.

Hargreaves, Eric L. Atkinson, Edward†; Auspitz, Rudolph†; Board of trade*; Bounties on sugar*; Caird, Sir James†; Canals*; Cohn, Gustave†; Conigliani, Carlo Angelo*; Considerant, Victor Prosper†; Courcelle-Seneuil, Jean Gustave†; Courtney, Leonard Henry Baron†; Devas, Charles Stanton†; Docks*; Droz, Numa†.

Harris, C.A. African companies, early; African companies, recent; Colonies: Denominational currency; Colonies: Government of colonies by companies; Colonies: Government of, by Companies*; Emigration –its effects on the country of origin; Exports, Duties on; Finances –Imperial; local; colonial and Indian; Foreign dividends; Foreign investments; Free list; Funding system; Gauger; Gold, Distribution and production of; Good; Gresham's law; Hours of labour; Import duties, Free exports; Import duties, Imports and exports, freedom and restraint for; Import duties; Imports and exports; Imports, Restraint on; Imprest; Industrial regime; International coinage; Irish currency; Irregularity of employment; Joe; Johannes; Kernetty; Khran; King's cattle; Lakh or Lac; Land companies; Landing-waiter; MacGregor, John; Macuta; Manifest; Martin, Robert Montgomery; Metayer, in West Indies; Moidore (Portuguese); National debt; National debt*; Navigation clause; Navigation laws; New subsidy; Official values; Parnell, Henry Brooke; Peseta; Plantation duties; Plantation; Quadruple; Quarantine; Quattie; Rapidity of circulation; Reciprocity; Scudino; Scudo; Search, Right of; Sinking fund; Sinking fund*; Slavery; Sorchin; Spendings; Story, Joseph; Supplementary estimate; Tariff; Termon lands; Tillage duties; Torrens act; Torrens, Robert, Colonel; Torrens, Sir Robert Richard; Treasury; Treasury note†; Vellon; Wakefield, Edward Gibbon; Zollverein.

Helm, Elijah. Children's labour; Cotton famine (1861–1865); Manchester School, The.

Hendriks, F. Farr, William; Jones, David; Metric system –England; Morgan, Augustus de [footnote]; Newmarch, William; Terminable annuities; Actuary; Annuity; Average (Maritime); Billon; Bottomry, Loan on; Brydges, Sir Egerton, Bart; Chadwick, Sir Edwin; Conventional tariff; Decimal system; Demography; Duodecimal system.

Herkner, H. Schmoller, Gustav†; Wagner, Adolf†.

Hewins, W.A.S. Apprenticeship, Statute of; Clement, Simon; Coke, Roger; Companies (City of London); Digges, Sir Dudley; Dunning, Richard; Elking, Henry; English early economic history; Evelyn, John (fl. 1830); Evelyn, John F.R.S. (1620–1706); Everett, George; Exchequer, Closing of the (1672); Firmin, Thomas; Fletcher, Andrew; Ford, Sir Edward; Free trade, Early history of; Gardiner or Gardner, Ralph; Gentleman, Tobias; Googe, Barnaby; Gould, Sir Nathaniel; Graunt, John; Hartlib, Samuel; Hayne, Samuel; Haynes, Christopher; Haynes, John; Interlopers; Janssen, Sir Theodore; King, Charles; King, Gregory; Lambe, Samuel; Law, John; Legislation (Elizabethan); Lowndes, William; Mercantile system; Milner, James; Mun, Thomas.

Hibbard, Benjamin H. Farmers' organisations in the United States*.

Higgs, Henry [attributed contributions]. Appropriation (Public Finance)†; Census of production†; Craig, John*; Farrer, Thomas Henry, Lord†; Giffen, Sir Robert†; Leroy-Beaulieu, Paul†; Leroy-Beaulieu, Pierre†; MacDonell, Sir John†; Marshall, Alfred†; Molinari, Gustave de†; Passy, Frederic†; Saint-Pierre, Abbe de*.

Higgs, Henry as editor [i.e. unattributed]. Average, weighted (in statistics)†; Butt, Isaac†; Cernuschi, Henri†; Copartnership†; Cossa, Luigi†; Cotterhill, Charles Foster†; Danson, J.T.†; Dowell, Stephen†; Engel, Ernst†; Engels, Friedrich†; Engineering and allied industry agreements†; Exports, invisible†; Gibbins, Rev. Henry de Beltgens†; Gonner, Sir Edward C.K.†; Goschen, George Joachim†; Hanssen, Georg†; Ingram, John Kells†; Interpolation†; Knies, Karl†; Lexis, Wilhelm†; Lloyd, Rev. William Foster†; Longfield,* Mountifort; Martin, John Biddulph†; Mean,* frequential; Meyer, Hermann Rudolph†; Miklashevsky, Ivan†; Mode (in Statistics)†; Munro, J.E.C.†; Octroi*; Pedregal, Manuel†; Potter, Thomas Bayley†; Ravenstone, Percy†; Ricca-Salerno, Giuseppe†; Rooke, John†; Saint-Marc, Henri†; Social conditions: The Need of Trained Inquirers into†; Torrens, Col. Robert*; Treasury of the United States, The†; Unbiassed error†; Walras, Marie Esprit Leon†.

Higgs, Henry. Ateliers Nationaux; Boileau (or Boyleau) Etienne; Bourse du Travail; Cantillon, Philip; Cantillon, Richard; Chamillart, Michel de; Corvetto, Louis-Emmanuel, Comte de Corvetto; Debouches, Theorie des; Dickinson, John; Dwellings, Model, of working classes in France; Economistes; English School of Political Economy –before A. Smith; Familistere; Family budget; Farmer-general Godin, Jean Baptiste Andre; Le Play, Pierr Guillaume Frederic; Mirabeau, Victor Riquetti; Turgot, Anne Robert Jacques Turgot.

Hirst, Francis W. Tabular standard.

Hodgkin, Howard. Neale, Edward Vansittart.

Hollander, J.H. Adams, Henry Carter†; American School of Political Economy*.

Holme, L.R. Regulated companies; Rundale; Steelbow tenants; Thirlage; Victual brethren.

Hooker, Reginald H. Ferguson, Adam; Geijer, Eric Gustav; Gilbart, James William; Godfrey, Michael; Gold as consumed in industry; Grundler, Christian Gottlob; Guicciardini, Luigi; Hawkins, Sir John; Heathfield, Richard; Heysham, John; Hitchcock, Robert; Hodgson, James; Hofacker, Johann Daniel; Hoffmann, Johann Gottfried; Hooke, Andrew; Horne, Andrew; Horner, Francis; Howard, John; Insurance, History; Jacob, William; Jenyns, Soame; Jones, Ernest Charles; Mezagues, Vivant de.

Hooper, Wynnard. Co-operation: Co-operative associations; Credit. Influence on prices; Legoyt, Alfred; Loans, public; Middleman; Money market; Neumann Spallart, Franz Xavier; Pressure, Monetary; Prices, Real and nominal; Revival, Trade; Social science (sociology); Sussmilch, Johann Peter; Time bargains.

Howlett, Richard. Guicciardini, Francesco; Hansards; Hanse towns; Hanseatic league; Jus naturae; Latifundium; Leblanc, Francois; Liber homo; Libere tenenties; Lotteries, English; Mansus (Mansum); Manuoperationes (Manopera); Maritagium; Marriage (Feudal system); Mayor; Mensarius; Operarius; Paragium; Parceners; Piepowder court; Pyx, Trial of; Pyx; Quinarius; Radmanni; Recognitions; Recovery; Reeve; Sceatta; Scythe-penny; Seneca, Lucius Annaeus; Serf (Serfdom); Services, Predial and military; Servitudes; Servus (Roman law); Socmen; Soke; Sokemanemot; Tacitus, C. Cornelius; Territorium; Tertius denarius; Testa de Nevill; Thrall; Three-field system; Thrymsa; Tithing; Tokens, History of; Towns, Decay of (medieval); Township; Tributarius; Udal tenure; Usucapio; Varro, M. Terentius; Village communities; Villanus; Villein tenure; villenage; Virga; Virgate; Ward-penny; Wards; Wayland, Francis; Waynage; Week-work; Yardland; Yardling or yerdling.

Hughes, A. Cambage, Droit de; Collegium; Compagnonnages; Davenant, Charles; Elibank, Patrick Murray; Ellman, John; Essart, Exart; Evans David Morier; Expeditation; Eyton, Robert William; Faldage.

Hunt, G.H. Exchequer bill; Exchequer bond, History of.

Ilbert, Lettice. Pensions, Old age.

Ingram, J.K. Achenwall, Gottfried; Adventurers, Merchants; Alcavala; Baks, Early European; Baumstark, Edward; Becher, Johann Joachim; Bernhardi, Theodor Von; Besold, Christoph; Biel, Gabriel; Bockh, August; Bornitz, Jacob; Bulau, Friedrich von; Busch, Johann Georg; Busching, Anton Friedrich; Campomanes, Pedro Rodriguez; Cancrin, George; Carrying trade; Chambre ardente; Chrematistic; Conring, Hermann; Copernicus, Nicolaus; Corporations of arts and trades: England, France, Germany; Crome, August Friedrich Wilhelm; Gentz, Friedrich von; Hardenberg, Karl August, Prinz von; Haxthausen; Held, Adolf von; Hermann, Friedrich Benedict Wilhelm; Hoffmann, Hohann Gottfried; Horneck, Philipp Wilhelm von; Hufeland, Gottlieb; Humboldt, Wilhelm von; Jakob, Ludwig Heinrich von; Justi, Johann Heinrich Gottlob von; Karl Friedrich; Kraus, Christian Jakob; Lange, Friedrich Albert; Lassalle Ferdinand; Leslie, Thomas Edward Cliffe; List, Friedrich; Lotz, Johann Friedrich Eusebius; Luder, August Ferdinand; Mangoldt, Hans Karl Emil von; Marlo, Karl; Marx, Heinrich Karl; Medici, The; Moser, Justus; Muller, Adam Heinrich; Nasse, Erwin; Nebenius, Karl Friedrich; Pare, William; Positivism; Prince-Smith, John; Raiffeisen, Friedrich Wilhelm; Rau, Karl Heinrich; Right to labour; Rodbertus, Karl Johann (Rodbertus-Jagetzow); Roesler, Karl Friedrich Hermann; Sartorius, Georg Friedrich; Schlozer, August Ludwig von; Schmalz, Theodor Anton Heinrich; Schon, Heinrich Theodor von; Schulze-Delitzsch, Franz Hermann; Soden, Friedrich Julius Heinrich Reisgraf von; Sonnenfels, Joseph Reichsfreiherr von; Spence, Thomas; Stein, Heinrich Freidrich Karl Freiherr vom; Stein, Lorenz von; Steuart, Sir James; Stewart, Dugald; Storch, Heinrich Friedrich von; Survival of the fittest; Thompson, William; Thunen, Johann Heinrich von; Vico, Giambattista; Walsh, Richard Hussey; Weitling, Wilhelm; Zincke, Georg Heinrich.

Innes, J.W. Brodie. Entail (Scotland); Exchequer (Scotland); Executor; Executry; Exercitor.

Jenks, J.W. Homestead and exemption laws of the United States; Local government in the United States; Monopolies in the United States; Naturalization in the United States; Naturalization in the United States*; Pensions in the United States; Pensions in the United States*; Tammany Hall; Township and towns in the United States.

Jeze, Gaston. Finances, France*.

Johnson, W.E. Economic man; Goods, Classification of; Hypothesis; Logic and political economy; Method of political economy; Motives, Measurable; Political economy, Applications of logical conceptions to; Producers' goods; Producers' rent; Services: Material and personal; Supply and demand; Supply; Synthesis and synthetic method; Theory.

Johnstone, E. Companies: Their Influence on Business.

Jones, J.H. Davidson, John†; George, Henry†; Helm, Elijah†; Ritchie, David George†.

Kaufmann, M. Christianity and economics: Protestantism; Encyclical; Huet, Francois; Humanism, its influence on economics; Nihilism (Russian); Socialism; Utopias.

Keynes, J.N. A Priori; A posteriori; Abstract political economy; Analytical method; Applied economics; Art of political economy; Cairnes, John Elliot; Catallactics; Collective goods; Consumers' goods (or Consumption Goods); Consumers' rent; Deductive method; Demand; Discommodity; Gratuitous utility; Relativity, Principle of, in political economy; Sidgwick, Henry†.

Kiddy, A.W. Palgrave, Sir R.H. Inglis†.

King, George. Insurance, Life, Theory of.

Kinnear, John Boyd. Farming; Gamelaws.

Kitchin, Joseph. Gold, distribution and production of*; Gold, increase in the production of†.

de Laveleye, E. Commune.

Law, Alice. Hutcheson, Archibald; Hutchinson, John Hely; Industrial education in England; Joyce, Jeremiah; Kane, Sir Robert John; Kay-Shuttleworth, Sir James Phillips; Labour statutes; Laing, Samuel; Lalor, John; Lampredi, Giovanni Maria; Lawson, James Anthony; Lord, Eleazar; Lowe, Joseph; Macadam, John Loudon; Mallet, Jean-Roland; Malouet, Pierre-Victor; Malynes, Gerard de; Manley, Thomas; Mansfield, William Murray; Manzoni, Alexander; Marmontel, Jean Francois; Merivale, Herman; Messance, M; Mir; Misselden, Edward; Moheau; Monypenny, David; Morgan, Augustus de; Norman, G. Warde; North, The Hon. Roger; Pashley, Robert; Pasley, Lieut.-General Sir C.W; Personal services; Petty bag; Pinkerton, John; Place, Francis; Pococke, Richard; Pollards and crockards; Potter, William; Pownall, Thomas; Pratt, J. Tidd; Prentice, Archibald; Prinsep, Charles Robert; Ramsay, Sir George; Renny, Robert; Residual and waste products (by-products); Ring money; Selkirk, Thomas Douglas; Sheffield, John Baker Holroyd; Shoddy; Short, Thomas; Smith, John (18th century); Stephen, James; Sugden, Edward Burtenshaw; Swan, Colonel James; Tally trade; Turkey company; Whittington, Sir Richard.

Lawrence, Rev. T.J. Declaration of Paris; International law; Licenses (Continental war); Monroe doctrine; Most favoured nation clause; Nation; Nationality; Neutral markets; Neutral property; Paper blockade; Queen Anne's bounty; Recognition; Sovereignty; Spoils system; Truce of God; Twiss, Sir Travers; Whewell, William.

Leadam, I.S. Interest and usury; Licenses, History of; Marque, Letters of; Merchants, Alien; Merchants, History of English; Mines; Stannaries; Statute of merchants; Subsidies; Virginia company, The.

Leathes, Sir Stanley M. Bureau of labour in the United States*; Dearness, Artificial; Gold as standard.

Legge, J.G. Prison labour.

Leser, Emanuel. Finances –German empire and Prussia.

Lethbridge, Sir Roper. Opium* as a State Monopoly.

Leyden, A.F. v. Ackersdyk, John; Boxhorn, Marcus Zuerius; Court, Pieter de la; Gogel, Isaac Jan Alexander; Graswinckel, Dirck; Hogendorp, Gysbert, Karel van; Kemper, Jerommo de Bosch; Kops, J.L. de Bruyn; Luzac, Elie; Mees, Willem Cornelis; Pestel, Friedrich Wilhelm von; Rees, Otto van; Salmasius (Claude de Saumaise); Vissering, Simon.

Lindsay, S. McC. Gold bullion, as a commodity at the mints; Hildebrand, Bruno; Latin union; Monetary conferences (International); Precious metals; Prices, History of (1850–1896); Prices, Theory of; Silver, as standard; Soetbeer's table of prices; Soetbeer, Adolph; Walker, Amasa.

Loch, C.S. Industrial colonies (Germany); Ruggles, Thomas; State-aided pensions; Townsend, Rev. Joseph; Union, Poor law; Vagrancy; Workhouse test; Workhouse.

Lodge, R. and G.G. Chisholm. Commercial routes*.

Lodge, R; Aides, Cour des Ale-taster; Alod, Alodial Land; Annates; Armed Neutrality; Augmentations, Court of; Aulnager; Banalites; Banvin, Droit d'; Bate's Case, or the Case of Impositions; Blairie, Droit de; Bocland; Boston Port Bill; Brehon Law; Capitation (in France); Casuel; Catasto; Cens; Champart; Commerical routes, History of; Comptes, Chambre des; Continual system; Coshery; Cottiers; Crusades, Economic Effects of; Danegeld; Darien Company; Decimes; Denier (Tax); Dialogus de Scaccario; Dime Royale; Dizain; Domaine; Don Gratuit; Douane; Drapier's letters; Easterlings; Ecu; Elus; Enumerated commodities; Epices; Escheat (historical); Estimo; Farming of taxes; Feormfultum; Ferm or Firma; Folkland; Formariage, Droit de; Fouage or Feuage; Franc, History of; Francfief, Droit de; Frankalmoign; Frankpledge; Fyrd; Gabelle; Gavelkind; Generalite; Greniers a sel; Heriot; Hidage; Hide; Hundred; Jurande; Knight's fee; Knighthood, Distraint of; Laenland; Liard; Livre; Loans, Forced; Louis d'Or, History of; Malatolta, Maletoute, Maltolte; Metheun treaty; Morton's fork; Murdrum; Orders in council; Paulette; Provisors, Statute of; Purveyance; Regale; Relief; Residual share (wages); Richelieu, A.J. du Plessis, Cardinal duc de; Sheriff; Ship-money; Socage; Taille; Tallage; Vingtieme.

Longhurst, T. Change (Agents de); Coulisse; Credit Foncier of France; Denier (as denoting price); Depots et consignations; Enregistrement; Expertise; Grand livre; Greniers d'Abondance; Homologation; Immeubles; Indemnite; Inscription Maritime (France); Jetons de presence; Livret; Mandat; Metric system (France etc.); Pacotille; Parquet; Passe-debout; Patente; Prescription (Fr.); Prestation (Fr.); Prime: Fr. (1) Bourse; (2) Commerce; Proces verbal; Prud'hommes; Quotite and repartition; Quotite disponible; Railways (French); Rehabilitation (Fr.); Rente (Fr.); Ristourne; Seign prive; Societes commerciales; Surenchere; Syndicats professionels.

Longstaff, G.B. Depopulation (Causes).

Loria, Achille. Italian School of Economists; Italian School of Economists* in the last 25 years.

Lotz, Wilhelm. Finances, Germany*; German School of Political Economy* Period IV.

Lupton, Walter. Ducat, History of.

MacDonell, Sir John. Socialism*.

MacGregor, D.H. Insurance* (Unemployment); Labour exchanges†.

Mackay, T. Poor-law, History of; Saunders, Robert.

Mackenzie, J.S. Historical method; Inductive method.

Maitland, F.W. Court rolls, manorial accounts and extents; Domesday Book.

Mallet, Bernard and J.C. Stamp. Income tax statistics –in Estimating National Income†.

Marshall, Alfred. Economics, Teaching of: general, Cambridge†.

Martin, J.B. Respondentia bonds.

Martin, J.H. Aves, Ernest† H; Loch, Sir Charles Stewart†.

Martin, Mary Trice. Forests, Medieval; Knight's service; Lombards; Malt silver; Staple, The staple system; Sumptuary laws; Trade, Foreign, regulations of.

Martin, R. Holland. Clearing House, The London Bankers'*.

Mathieson, Ewing. Depreciation.

Mavor, James. Dock.

Mayo-Smith, Richmond. Bureau of labor in the United States; Census, United States; Immigration; Resumption (in U.S.A); Statistical method; Wages, Statistics of (in the United States of America); Workmen's budgets.

McArthur, Ellen A. Exchequer, Early History of; Fitzherbert, Sir Anthony; Freedom of the city of London; Hawkins, Edward; Holland, John; Kingsley, Charles; Peasants' revolt; Periculum sortis; Russia company; Sanctuary, Economic aspects of; South sea company (South sea bubble); Tellers of the exchequer.

McKillop, J. Self-interest.

Miklachewsky, Ivan. Russian School of Political Economy.

Miller, A.C. Biddle, Nicholas.

Milner, Viscount. Colonial policy –recent developments†.

Mitchell, Broadus. Newcomb, Simon†; Niles, Hezekiah†; Olmsted, Frederick Law†; Opdyke, George†; Owen, Robert Dale†; Patten, Simon Nelson†; Perry, Arthur Latham†; Pickering, John†; Raguet, Condy†; Ruffin, Edmund†; Schoenhof, Jacob†; Schwab, John Christopher†; Seaman, Ezra Champion†; Shattuck, Lemuel†; Simpson, Stephen†; Skidmore, Thomas†; Spooner, Lysander†; Tompkins, Daniel Augustus†; Ware, Nathaniel†; Weston, George Melville†; White, Horace†; Wright, Carroll D.†; Wright, Frances (Mme. D'Arusmont)†.

Mitchell, E.L. Allotment*; Tithes*.

Montagu, Samuel. Exchange, Foreign.

Montague, F.C. Administration, Letters of; Administration; Citizen; Classification; Commissions, Judicial; Decentralisation; Defalcation; Defoe, Daniel; Deposition; Distress (Legal Term); Dogma; Dower; Egoism; Eject, Ejectment, Ejection; Embezzlement; Empiricism; Employers' liability act; Emulation; Entail, Law of; Eviction; Excambion; Experience; Expert; Expropriation; F's, The three; Fealty; First-fruits and tenths; Flotsam and jetsam; Forethought; Forfeiture; Forgery; Frauds, The Statute of; Freehold, Historical; Freehold, Legal; Goverment regulation of industry in the 19th century; Government, Economic effects of; Hedonism; Heredity; Hobbes, Thomas; Holidays; Idealist; Idealogue; Impressment; Incorporeal property; Increment, The unearned; Land legislation, Irish; Land registration; Land tenures; Land, Law relating to; Land, Nationalisation of; Lapse of time as creating or extinguishing rights; Merger; Minimum of subsistence; Morality, Systems of, in relation to political economy; Municipality; Observation and experiment; Optimism; Overseers (of the poor); Parish; Parliament, Rolls of; Particular estate; Perpetuities, Rule against; Personal property; Pessimism; Pignus; Pre-emption, Right of; Primogeniture; Property; Publicani; Rate in aid; Rate; Res nullius; Roundsman; Sciences, Moral and political; Settlment (Land); Simple contract; Sinecure; Small holdings act 1892; Social contract, The; Tenant right; Tenant-at-will; Thrift; Tocqueville, Alexis Charles Henri Clerel de; Toynbee, Arnold; Trade mark; Trespass; Trust and trustee; Turnpike trusts; Uses, Charitable, (History of Law as to); Valuable consideration; Vicesima hareditatum; Voluntary deed; Xenophon.

Mozley, J.R. Price, Bonamy.

Munro, J.E.C. Abstract of title; Ademption of legacy; Adjustment, Average; Alba Firma; Allotment; Apportionment (No. 1); Appropriation; Artisan; Assessment; Assiento treaty; Barter; Benefice (2); Benevolences; Bequest, Power of; Blockade; Board; Body corporate or corporation; Bona notabilia; Bona vacantia; Book of rates; Booty; Bull of Borgia; Canals; Carrier, Common; Cattle plague orders; Caveat emptor; Charging order; Charter; Choses in action; Choses in possession; Cinque ports; Clipped money; Cloff or Clough; Combination laws; Combination; Commercial law; Common assurance; Common employment; Compensation; Compound interest; Compulsory pilotage; Compulsory preference; Compulsory taking of land; Conflict of laws; Conquest; Conscription; Conspiracy, Common law doctrine of; Consul; Coparceners; Copyright; Corn returns; Corporation, Aggregate; Corporation, Municipal; Cost book; Cotton lists; County borough; County council; County rate; Coverture; Crown debts; Crown lands; Curator bonis; Damages, Measure of; Darg; Dead rent; Debit; Declaration of war; Deed poll; Demonstrative legacy; Denizen; Descent of property; Designs, Copyright in; Dormant (or Sleeping) partner; Droits of admiralty; Enemy goods; Equitable assets; Equitable estate; Equitable execution; Equitable mortgage; Equitable waste; Equity of redemption; Equity to a settlement; Fee simple; Fee; Feod or Feud; Feoffment; Foreclosure; Free bench; Garnishee; Heirlooms; Hiring; Illegal contract; Immovables; Impeachment of waste; Interesse termini; Joint tenancy; Jointure; Laches; Lawful hours; Lay days; Legacy; Liquidated damages; Liquidation; Liquidator; Movables; Notice; Novation; Nudum pactum; Occupation; Official receiver; Order and disposition; Outlaw; Packman; Partnership, Form of, as commandite; Pawn; Payee; Pedlar; Permit; Prescriptive right; Price (rate of wages in cotton trade); Principal and agent; Probate; Rack rent; Receipt; Receiver; Regalia; Restraint of anticipation; Salvage; Sample; Seisin; Separate estate; Sequestration; Servitude, Natural; Slip; Stoppage in transitu; Subinfeudation; Surety; Tenement; Underwriter; Underwriting; Warranty; Waste.

Nash, Vaughan. Co-operation: Social aspects of co-operation; Federal Co-operation.

Nicholson, J.S. Abolitionist; Abstinence; Accumulation; Agricultural community; Altruism; Balance of trade; Board; Bubbles (History of); Capital; Certainty; Checks on population; Commercial system; Commercial treaties; Consumption; Cost (comparative and relative); Cost of production; Credit; Hodgson, William Ballantyne.

Nisbet, J. Forests, Economic aspects of.

Ogilvie, Sir Andrew. Post Office, The.

Olivier, Sydney. Labour exchange.

Oncken, A. German School of Political Economy –periods I and II; Iselin, Isaak; Mauvillon, Jakob; Pfeiffer, J.F. von; Roscher, William; Schlettwein, Johann August; Schroder, Wilhelm Freiherr von; Seckendorff, Veit Ludwig von; Thomasius, Christian; Von Bielfeld, Jakob Friedrich.

Osborn, E.B. Co-operation, Partial (Oldham Cotton-Spinning Companies).

Paget, J.R. Contract; Partnership*: Limited Partnerships Act 1907; Public Trustee Act 1906†.

Palgrave, R.H. Inglis. Abrasion; Acceptor; Ad valorem duty; Addison, Joseph; Adulteration; Advice; Agiotage, or Agio; Agricultural systems; Aid, Auxilium; Allonge; Allowance system; Allowance; Alternative standard; Amortisation; Annual rent; Appraisers; Appreciation of standard; Approved bill; Arithmetic, Political; Arles or Arrhes; Arrears; Arrestment (Scots law); Articles of roup; Assessed taxes; Assets; Assignat; Assignation; Assignee; Assignment; Assignor; Assize of weights and measures; Assumption, Deed of; Attestation; Attorney, Power of; Auction, Ordinary; Audit (Scots law); Auditor of the court of session; Autumnal drain; Back-bond; Bacon, Francis; Bagehot, Walter; Bailee; Baines, Sir Edward; Balance sheet; Banco; Banknote, Regulations in different countries; Banks, Popular (Germany); Banks, Popular (Italy); Banks, Savings; Banks; Bazaar; Beneficium cedendarum actionum; Bi-metallism; Bill of exchange; Bland act; Blank credit; Blank endorsement; Blench; Board of agriculture (1889); Board of trade; Bond and disposition in security; Bond of corroboration; Bond of relief; Book account credit; Brassage; Breach of trust (Scots criminal law term); Brevi manu traditio; Brokerage; Bullion Committee, Report of; Bullion; Bureaucracy; Butlerage; Cancel, Cancellation; Capitainerie; Capital; Carbonari; Cartogram; Cash account; Cashier; Chorogram; Chronogram and hexogram; Circulating medium; Civil list; Clearing system: cotton clearing; Clergy, Benefit of; Coinage, The Right of; Commerce; Commodatum; Commodity; Communication, Means of; Conditioning; Consignee; Consolidated fund; Consols; Consumptibles; Conversion, colonial and foreign stocks; Convertibility of bank notes; Cooper, Thomas (1805–1892); Corner on stock exchange; Cost, in the Sense of Price; Council bills (India Council Drawings); Criminal prosecution; Crises, Commercial and financial; Cross drawing; Crossed cheque; Currency doctrine or principle; Currency; Davenant, Charles; Debt, Public, Local, Great Britain and Ireland; Debt, Public, Statement of (Government indebtedness); Destutt de Tracy and Ricardo; Dock labour; Elevator; Elizabethan legislation; Enfacement; Enfranchisement of land from copyhold and similar tenures; Exchange between Great Britain and British India; Exchange of notes; Exchange, Stock, Provincial, in Great Britain and Ireland; Exchequer, Present Constitution of; Excise Scheme, The; Excise, The; Fairs and markets; Folkes, Martin; Freedom in the middle ages; Ganilh, Charles; Gilbert, Thomas; Gilds of Newcastle-upon-tyne; Gray, John (19th cent.); Guarantyism; Habit; Hedgmint; Hide; Indirect utility; Inflation, Great Britain; Kacorawns; Labour exchange; Land, Nationalisation of [comment]; Law; Lepta; Letrosne (or Letrone) Guillaume Francois; Lira; Little goes; Lloyd's; Lombard Street; Lomenie de Brienne, Etienne Charles, Comte de Brienne; Lubbock, Sir John William; Mean afterlifetime; Mechanics of industry; Mil; Mintage, Free; Months, Fourths of; Neves, Jose Accursio das; New customs; New impost; Note circulation; One pound note; Orthodox economists; Oscar I; Political economy, Authorities on; Populist movement in the United States; Postlethwayt, James; Postlethwayt, Malachy; Profit and loss account; Redemption of national debt; Reserve; Rest, The (Bank of England); Rin; Seyd, Ernest; Soft money; Spence, William; Stafford, William; Standard of value; Tack, Tacking; Tontine; Tribal system; Twiss, Sir Travers; Unit of account; Usselincx, William; Wages and prices of commodities; Wallace, Robert; Wallace, Thomas; Weyland, John; White bonnet; Yen; Zacharias, Otto.

Palgrave, Reginald. Supply, Parliamentary.

Pantaleoni, M. Agazzini, Michele; Algarotti, Francis; Arco, Gherardo Giambattista dei Conti d'Arco; Arrivabene, Giovanni; Augustinis, Matteo de; Azuni, Domenico Alberto; Balbi, Adriano; Balsamo, Paolo; Bandini, Salustio Antonio; Baudi, Carlo, di Vesme; Beccaria, Cesare Bonesana; Bellitti, Giacinto; Belloni, Girolamo; Bianchini, Ludovico; Biblia, Fabrizio; Biundi, G; Boccardo, Girolamo†; Bocchi, Romeo; Bosellini, Carlo; Botero, Giovanni; Briganti, Filippo; Broggia, Antonio; Cagnazzi, Luca Samuele; Cantalupo, Domenico; Capello, Pier Andrea; Caraccioli, Domenico; Carafa, Diomede; Carli, Gian Rinaldo; Casaregis, Josephus Laurentius Maria de; Cattaneo, Carlo; Cavour, Count Camillo Benso di; Cesare, Carlo de; Ceva, Giovanni; Chitti, Luigi; Cibrario, Giovanni Antonio Luigi; Cognetti de Martiis, Salvatore†; Corbetta, Eugenio; Corniani, Giambattista; Corti, Adolfo; Corvaia, Baron; Custodi, Pietro; Davanzati, Bernardo; De Cardenas di Maqueda, Diego Raffaele; De Luca, Giovanni Battista; De Sanctis, Marco Antonio; De Vio, F. Tommaso; Delfico, Melchiorre; Diodati, Domenico; Diodati, Luigi; Donato, Nicolo; Doria, Paolo Matt; Dragonetti, Giacinto; Dragonetti, Luigi; Ferrara, Francesco†; Macinato; Mazzola, Ugo†; Messedaglia, Angelo†; Nazzani, Emilio†; Rabbeno, Ugo†.

Parkin, G.R. Federation, Commercial.

Patrick, William. Calvin, Jean; Duncan, Henry; Dundas, Henry.

Peirson, J. Book-keeping.

Phelps, Rev. L.R. Boarding-out system; Charitable foundations; Charitable institutions; Charity organisation; Charity, State; Charity; Competition and custom; Consumptibles. A Term employed by the Schoolmen; Distress; Doles; Dwellings (Regulation by the State in England); Endowments; Foundling hospitals; Fungibles; Gilbert's act; Guardians of the poor; Industrial colonies; Mendicity; Pauperism; Poor law, Administration of; Poor; Poverty; Public assistance.

Pigou, A.C. Economics, Teaching of: Cambridge (Economics Tripos)†.

Pollock, Frederick. Eminent domain.

Poole, R.L. Christianity and economics: Church, the Medieval.

Powell, Eleanor G. Eaton, Daniel Isaac; Ellis, William (died 1758); Extraneus; Factories; Fald-silver; Fastnyngseed; Ferdel or Ferling; Field systems; Finlaison, John; Fisc; Fish-silver; Fleyland; Florin, History of the English gold; Food-rents; Forster, Nathaniel; Fortune, E.F. Thomas; Foster, John Leslie; Fuggers; Gablatores; Gafol, Gabel or Gable; Gebur; Glanvill, Ranulf; Grant, James; Grant, Sir Robert; Gray, Simon; Gresham, Sir Thomas; Guinea trade; Haines, Richard; Hale, Sir Matthew; Halley, Edmund; Hamilton, Robert; Hancock, William Neilson; Hanway, Jonas; Harris, Joseph; Harte, Rev. Walter; Hearth-money or Hearth-tax; Holdings of land; Honour; Houghton, John; Justice, Alexander; Kelp, Rent of; Lammas-lands, Lammas-meadows; Landgafol; Landsettus; Lathes; Leet court; Lodland; Lundinarium; Lushboroughs; Mancus; Mark (English money); Merchet; Messor; Molmen; Moneyers; Monthly assessments; Noble of Raymond Lully; Noble; Owlers; Paper, Taxes on; Plough-team; Portreeve; Praepositus; Primer seisen; Proclamations; Rent, Labour (Medieval); Roberts, Lewes; Robertson, George; Rose, Right Hon. George; Ruding, Rev. Rogers; Sander (or Sanders), Nicholas; Sinclair, Sir John; Smith, Henry; Smith, John; Smith, Sir Thomas; Stair, John Dalrymple; Stint; Temple, William; Tithes; Wheeler, John; Wilson, Thomas; Worlidge.

Powers, H.H. Harmonies of economics; Immaterial capital amd immaterial wealth; Individualism.

Pownall, G.H. Crises, Periodicity of.

Price, L.L. Apprenticeship; Arbitration between employers and employed; Comfort, Standard of; Conciliation, Boards of; Conseils de Prud'hommes; Domestic system of industry; Earnings and interest fund; Employers and employed; Employing class; Entrepreneur; Fawcett, Henry; Industrial partnership; Industrial revolution; Industries, Large and small; Industry, Captains of; International working men's association, The; Labour and capital; Lock-out; Monometallism; Trade, Large and small.

Prothero, R.E. Agriculture in England; Arable land, Conversion to pasture in Great Britain; Commons; Conversion of arable land into pasture in England; Culture, large and small; Depression, agricultural.

Rabbeno, Ugo. Giustiniani, D. Bernardo; Lastri, Marco; Lenzi, Domenico; Lunetti, Vittorio; Lupo, Giambattista; Maffei, Scipione; Magliani, Agostino; Mancini, Celso; Marachio, Massimo; Marescotti, Angelo; Marogna, Conte Gian Giuseppe; Marulli, Vicenzo; Mastrofini, Marco; Mattia (di), Nicola; Mengotti, Francesco; Merello, Michele; Merenda, Antonio; Minghetti, Marco; Miro, Vincenzo de; Montanari, Geminano; Morpurgo, Emilio; Muratori, Ludovico Antonio; Neri, Pompeo; Nicolai; Nifo, Agostino; Nuytz, Gaetano; Ortes, Giammaria; Pagano, Francesco Mario; Palmieri, Guiseppe; Palmieri, Matteo; Paolini, Giovano Battista; Paradisi, Agostino; Paruta, Paolo; Pascoli, Leone; Pecchio, Giuseppe; Pereira, Gregorio Pietro; Pescatore, Matteo; Petitti de Roreto, Carlo Ilarione; Pontano, Giovanni; Ressi, Adeodato; Ricci, Ludovico; Ridolfi, Cosimo; Romagnosi, Gian Domenico; Rota, Pietro; Salmour, Ruggero G; San Salvatore (Di), Padre Antonio; Sarchiani, Giuseppe; Sassetti, Filippo; Scaccia Sigismonde; Scaruffi, Gasparo; Scialoja, Antonio; Scola, Giovanni; Segni, Giovan Battista; Sella, Quintino; Serra, Antonio; Silio, Guglielmo; Stracca, Benvenuto; Tapia, Carlo (Di) Marchese di Belmonte; Targioni, Luigi; Tesauro, Gaspare Antonio; Torre, Raffaele Della; Torri, Luigi; Turboli, Gian Donato; Valeriani, Luigi Molinari; Vasco, Giovan Battista; Venturi, Giambattista; Venusti, M. Antonio Maria; Vergani, Paolo; Verri, Pietro; Vigano, Francesco; Villano, Filippo; Virgilio, Jacopo; Vivorio, Agostino; Zacchia, L; Zanon, Antonio; Zecchi, Lelio; Zerbi, Giovanni Antonio; Zuccolo, Ludovico.

Rae, John. Efficiency of labour; Eight hours movement; Enfranchisement.

Raleigh, T. Civil law; Land.

Rew, R.H. Food supply of the United Kingdom†.

Rigg, E. Free coinage; Guinea. Introduction and rating of; Mint; Newton, Sir Isaac; Periot (or Perit).

Ritchie, D.G. Aristotle; Grotius, Hugo; Jus Naturalae, Jus Gentium, Jus Divinum, Jus Humanun; Locke, John; Plato.

Roberts-Austen, W. Alloy; Annealing; Assay; Betterness; By-product; Fineness of coins.

Rogers, J.D. Intensive cultivation; Laissez-faire in England; Law merchant; More, Sir Thomas; Naturalization; Owen, Robert; Parker, Henry; Paterson, Thomas; Pearson, Charles Henry; Police; Pollexfen; Quia emptores; Raper, Matthew; Rate; Rates, Incidence of; Recoinages; Referendum; Remonetisation; Rent of land; Retaliation; Ricardo, David; Ring; Robinson, Henry; Ryot; S.W., Gent; Savigny, Friedrich Carl von; Scott, William; Serjeanty, Petit; Sestertius; Silver, Discoveries of; Simon, James; Smith, Charles; Snelling, Thomas; Social science; Solidus; State notes; Stiver; Sub-contract; Swift, Jonathan; Tatham, William; Temple, Sir William; Testoon; Thackrah, Charles Turner; Thompson, Thomas Perronet; Tucker, Josiah; Turton, Thomas; Utopias and modern socialism; Vaughan, Rice; Vaughan, Robert; Vend, Newcastle; Vendor and purchaser; Violet, Thomas; Wakefield, Daniel; Wakefield, Edward; Wales, William; Walsh, Sir John Benn; Warren, Josiah; Wheatley, John; Witt, Johan de; Wolff, Christian von; Yeomen; Young, Arthur; Zemindar.

Rogers, J.E. Thorold. Anti-corn-law league; Assize of bread and beer; Cobden, Richard; Corn laws; Corn rents.

Rose, T.K. Alloy*; Remedy (Mint)*; Seignorage*; Silver legislation in the United States*; Silver, Discoveries of*; Standard gold and silver*.

Rosewater, Victor. Laissez-faire (from American point of view).

Rossi, G. Book-keeping.

Rowe, Leo S. Municipal government in Prussia; Municipal government in United States of America.

Sanger, C.P. Walras, Antoine Auguste; Walras, Marie Esprit Leon.

Schelle, Gustave. Physiocrats, The.

Schuster, E. Abatement or rebate; Accessio; Accrue; Acknowledgment; Acquittance; Actus; Administrator; Agency, Law of; Agio; Agnati (Adgnati); Agricultural holdings act; Alieni juris; Aliens; Anatocismus; Antedate; Antichresis; Apportionment (No. 2); Arbitrage (Exchange); Arbitrage (General Business); Argentarii; Arrangement, Deed of; Arrest; Articles of apprenticeship; Articles of association; Assignment, Deed of; Attachment; Attornment; Award; Barrator; Beneficium Competentiae; Beneficium Excussionis; Beneficium Inventarii; Betterment; Bill of lading; Bill of sale; Blackleg; Blank transfer; Bon; Bona fide; Bonarum Possessio; Bond; Borough English; Borough; Bourse; Boycotting; Breach of trust; Bubble act; Building societies; Burgh; By-law, Byelaw; Cable transfer; Caisse; Capital; Casus; Caution; Caveat; Change; Charter party; Chattel or Chattel Personal; Citation; Codicil; Collect; Commercial instrument; Commission agent; Committee of inspection; Committee; Communio; Companies: Increase of; Conflict of laws; Confusio; Consolidatio; Constitutum Debiti; Constitutum Possessorium; Contract, Law of; Contractors; Conveyance; Coparceners; Copyhold; Corporation, Sole; Coupon; Courts (Ireland); Courts (Scotland); Courts of law (England); Credit, Letter of; Culpa; Custodia; Damages; Date of drawing; Days of grace; Debenture stock; Debenture; Defence; Delegation; Delictum; Delivery (of Chattels); Demesne; Demise; Demurrage; Deposit (Sales of land); Depositum; Derelictio; Devise; Diligence; Diligentia; Directors, Legal duty of; Disabilities of aliens; Disabilities of infants; Disabilities of lunatics and drunkards; Disabilities of married women; Disclaimer; Discovery in actions; Distribution, Statutes of; Distringas; Dividend on stock and shares; Dock warrant; Dolus; Domicil or Domicile; Domiciled bill; Dominium; Donatio mortis causa; Dos; Drawer of a bill of exchange; Drunkards, Legislation respecting; Due date (Bill of exchange); Earnest money; Easement; Effects; Election; Elegit (Writ of); Embargo; Emblements; Empanel; Emphyteusis; Entry, Right of; Equity; Error excepted; Escheat (Modern law); Estate; Estoppel; Estovers; Execution; F.O.B; Face value; Fee tail; Fiduciary; Fieri facias, Writ of; Fine; Firm; Floating charge; Floating debt; Foreign law in English courts; Forestallers and regrators; Forged transfer; Franchise; Fraudulent conveyance; Freight is the mother of wages; Funded debt; Gaming contracts; Gazette; Gift; Good delivery; Goods and chattels; Ground rents; Growing crops; Guarantee; Hegel, G.W.F; Heir; Hereditament; Heriot; Hire and purchase agreements; Holder of a bill of exchange; Hotchpot; Hundred; Husband (as to wife's property); Hypothecation; I.O.U; Illegitimacy; Impound; Income tax on the continent of Europe; Incorporation of companies; Indemnity; Indenture; Infants; Inheritance, Estate of; Insurance, Life, Law and Practice; Interdiction; Interpleader; Intestacy (England); Invoice; Joint debtors; Joint ownership; Joint-stock companies; Judgement debtor; Judgement; Jurisdiction; King's peace; Landes-creditkassen; Lease; Leasehold property; Lex loci contractus; Liabilities on shares; Liability, Limited; Lien; Limitation, Statutes of; Lloyd's bonds; Lombard loan; Lunacy, Law of; Marriage settlement; Medieval fairs; Meeting, Company; Memorandum of association; Mortgage banks; Mortgage debenture; Mortgage; Mortgagee; Mortgages, registration of; Mortgagor; Notes, Bought and sold; Onerous property; Particular average; Partnership (Law of); Partnership, History of; Patent and patent law; Patronage; Pawnbroking; Preference shares; Principal; Procuration by signature (mercantile usage generally); Prospectus; Put and call; Re-entry; Real property; Receiving order; Referee; Release; Rent sec; Rent-charge; Roman law; Sale of goods; Scire facias; Scrip; Set-off; Shareholders; Shares; Speciality debt; Specific performance; Stock; Style or trade name; Syndicate; Talon; Telegraphic transfers; Term of years; Time bargains; Tort; Trade disputes, Law as to; Transfer days; Transfer or 'Deed of transfer'; Trustee (judicial); Trusts, Charitable (Present law as to); Trusts; Ultra vires; Usance; Visa (as to a passport); Voluntary deed; Wager policy; Warrants; Watering stock; Way, Right of; Will, Bequest by; Winding-up; Writ

Scott, W.R. Cunningham, William†.

Seligman, E.R.A. Dunbar, Charles Franklin†; Economic teaching in the United States†; Finances –The United States; Graduated taxation; Wells, David Ames†.

Shaw, W.A. Land banks, Schemes of, in England.

Sidgwick, Henry. Economic science and economics; Political economy and ethics; Political economy: Method; Political economy: Scope.

Smart, William. Diseases of animals acts and their administration†; Living wage; Sliding scale (Wages); Stirling, Patrick James; Wages of women.

Smith, A.L. Yarranton, Andrew.

Smith, G. Barnett. Free trade, Modern history of; Graham, Sir James George Robert; Grenville, George; Grenville, William Wyndham, Baron Grenville; Halifax, Charles Montague, Earl of; Harrington, James; Herries, John Charles; Hume Joseph; Iddesleigh, The Earl of; Levi, Leone; Liquor laws; Liverpool, Charles Jenkinson; Liverpool, Robert Banks Jenkinson; Local option; McCulloch, John Ramsy; Peel, Sir Robert; Perceval, Spencer; Plymouth adventurers; Poynings' act; Rapp, George; Scrope, G. Poulett; Sherbrooke, Viscount (Robert Lowe); Thellusson, Peter; Wapole, Sir Robert.

Smith, John. Deed of arrangement.

Smith, William H. Local finance.

Spencer, A.J. Agricultural holdings acts*.

Spooner, Rev. W.A. Socialism, State; Unproductive consumption; Wages fund.

Spyers, T.G. Alien immigration†; Labour department; Labour in relation to the law; Masters' associations; Strikes; Trade unions; Trade unions* and strikes; Truck system; Truck; Wages statistics.

Stamp, A.E. Farm, of the counties; Feodary; Fifteenths and tenths; Foreshore; Fosterland; Gainage or wainage; Glebe land; Guard rents, Castle-guard rents; Hanaper; Hundred rolls; Incrementum or crementum; Integral and differential calculus; Justice or Justiciare; Manumission; Maritima angliae; Measures and weights; Messuage; Monopolies; Mortmain; Pannage; Pells; Peter's pence; Pontage; Prescription; Prior, Thomas; Promissum; Quayage; Queen gold; Quit rent; Quittance; Remainder; Royalty; Saltsilver; Tale; Tallies; Tanistry; Tare and tret; Thistle rent; Tonnage and poundage.

Stamp, Josiah C. and B. Mallet. Income tax statistics –in Estimating National Income†.

Starr, Harris E. Sumner, William Graham†.

Steele, F.E. Distribution of the precious metals.

Stephens, H. Morse. Cambon, Pierre Joseph.

Stephenson, W. Tetley. Railways*.

Steffen, Gustav F. Exchange, Value in. History of growth of theory.
Stuart, C.A. Verrijn. Kersseboom, Willem; Van Hall, Floris Adrian.
Symes, J.E. Revolution, French (economic aspects of).
Taussig, F.W. American School of Political Economy; Bigelow, Erastus Brigham; Bowen, Francis; Carey, Matthew; Cooper Thomas (1759–1840); Gallatin, Albert; Inflation, United States; Stationary state.
Taylor, R.W. Cooke. Factory acts; Factory system; Manufacture; Mill; Retail and wholesale; Sampling (Conditioning); Sweating; Tool rent; Tool; Trade; Trader; Workshop.
Tedder, H.R. Ackland, Rev. John; Aislabie, John; Alcock, Rev. Thomas; Alison, Sir Archibald; Anderson, Adam; Anderson, James; Ansell, Charles; Arbuthnot, John, M.D; Asgill, John; Ashburton, Alexander Baring; Ashley, John; Attwood, Thomas; Auckland, Willam Eden; Bailey, Samuel; Baily, Francis; Baring, Sir Francis; Barnard, Sir John; Barton, John; Beeke, Rev. Henry; Bellers, John; Dalrymple, Sir John; Davies, David; Desmarets, Nicolas; Dickson, Rev. Adam; Dobbs, Arthur; Drummond, Henry; Duncan, John; Duncan, Jonathan; Edmonds, Thomas Rowe; Einert, Carl; Eisdell, Joseph Salway; Eiselen, Johann Friedrich Gottfried; Ghent, Henry of; Holyoake, George Jacob†; Macleod, Henry Dunning†; Mallet, Sir Louis; Mallet du Pan, Jacques; Recorde, Robert; Spencer, Herbert†; Trotter, Sir Coutts; Vansittart, Nicholas, Lord Bexley; West, Hon. Sir Edward; Wilson, Rt. Hon James; Young, Major Gavin; Zincke, Rev. Foster Barham.
Turner, G.I. Recta prisa; Standards; Triple assessment; Villes franches and chartered towns; Villes neuves; Waif.
Uthwatt, A. Andrews and T.G. Gibson. Companies, Increase of*.
Uthwatt, A. Andrews. Patent*; Prospectus*; Style or trade name*.
Van Den Berg, N.P. Exchange between Holland and Dutch India.
Vince, Charles Anthony. Tariff Reform Movement, The (1903–1919)†.
Walker, B.E. Banks, Canada.
Walker, F.A. Money; Quantity theory of money; Webster, Pelatiah.
Wallas, Graham. Chartism. The Points of the Charter.
Warner, Henry Lee. Gangs, Agricultural.
Waterhouse, E. Audit; Balance-sheet.
Waterhouse, Paul. Dwellings, Industrial.
Webb, Sidney and Beatrice. Standard rate (of wages).
Westlake, J. International law, Private.
Whittuck, E.A. Client; Colonies: Methods of Government; Emptio-venditio; Exhereditatio; Falsa demonstratio non nocet; Fideicommissum; Fides, Bona, Mala; Fiscus; Foenus Nauticum; Hereditas; Hypotheca; Inofficium testamentum; Institoria actio; Interdictio aquae et ignis; Interdictum; Invecta et illata; Jactus navis levandi gratia; Joint family; Justa causa; Legatum; Libertus; Majestas; Mancipatio; Mandatum; Mora; Mos; Mutuum; Necessarii Heredes; Novatio; Obligatio; Occupatio; Patronus; Pauperies; Possession; Possessio; Postliminium; Praescriptio; Precarium; Prodigus; Relegatio; Restitutio in integrum; Servitus; Societas; Solutio; Stipulatio; Testamentum; Usus; Uti possidetis; Vacantia bona; Vertigales agri.
Wicksteed, Rev. P.H. Degree of utility; Dimensions of economic quantities; Final Utility*; Final degree of utility; Jevons, William Stanley; Political economy and psychology.
Wieser, F. Austrian School of Economics, The*; Bohm-Bawerk, Eugen von†; Hock, Carl*; Menger, Anton†; Menger, Carl†.
Wilkinson, Spenser. Defence, Cost of.
Willcox, W.F. Immigration*.
Williams, C.R. Agriculture and fisheries†.
Willink, Henry George. Industrial Colonies (Belgium); Industrial Colonies (Holland).
Willis, Henry Parker. Bank note (United States of America)*.

Appendix IV

Subject Index

Note: Each entry appears once, and once only, in the lists below. The biographical entries are classified according to the country where the subject spent the most significant years of his career, rather than country of origin.

Macroeconomic Theory
autonomous expenditures
consumption function
cost-push inflation
crowding out
demand-pull inflation
equilibrium: an expectational concept
expectations
forced saving
government budget constraint
income–expenditure analysis
inflation
inflationary expectations
inflationary gap
IS–LM analysis
leads and lags
life-cycle hypothesis
macroeconomics: relations with microeconomics
neoclassical synthesis
new 'classical' macroeconomics
Phillip's curve
price level
rational expectations
relative income hypothesis
stagflation
stocks and flows
supply shocks in macroeconomics
tulipmanias
wealth effect

Macroeconomic Policy
budgetary policy
built-in stabilizers
dear money
deficit financing
deficit spending
demand management
fine tuning
fiscal stance
full employment budget surplus
functional finance
incomes policies
indexed securities
monetarism
monetary policy
open-market operations
public sector borrowing
public works
pump priming
régulation
sound money
stabilization policy
tight money
wage indexation

Keynesian economics
aggregate supply function
balanced budget multiplier
bastard Keynesianism
effective demand
finance and saving
imperfectionist models
Keynes's *General Theory*
Keynesianism
Keynesian revolution
liquidity preference
marginal efficiency of capital
multiplier analysis
output and employment
propensity to consume
saving equals investment
user cost
widow's cruse

VIII. DYNAMICS, GROWTH AND DEVELOPMENT

Investment
adaptive expectations
adjustment costs
choice of technique and the rate of profit
foreign investment
internal rate of return
inventory policy under certainty
investment
investment and accumulation
investment decision criteria
investment planning
overinvestment
pay-off period
replacement policy

Cycles
acceleration principle
aggregate demand and supply analysis
buffer stocks
business cycles
cobweb theorem
credit cycle
cumulative processes
growth and cycles
indicators
inventory cycles
Kondratieff cycle
Kuznets swing
long cycles
multiplier-accelerator interaction
oversaving
political business cycle
trade cycle
underconsumption

Economic Growth
classical growth models
cumulative causation
golden age
Harrod–Domar model
inflation and growth
limits to growth
long swings in economic growth
measurement of economic growth
models of growth
multisector growth models
natural and warranted rates of growth
neoclassical growth theory
optimal savings
Ramsey model
stagnation
structural economic dynamics
turnpike theorems
two-sector models
von Neumann ray
von Neumann technology

Technical Change
biased and unbiased technological change
creative destruction
diffusion of technology
Gibrat's Law
growth accounting
innovation
learning-by-doing
market structure and innovation
patents
productivity: measurement problems
structural change
technical change
total factor productivity
transfer of technology
Verdoorn's law
vintages

Development
absorptive capacity
advisers
agriculture and economic development
appropriate technology
balanced growth
colonialism
cost-benefit analysis
dependency
development economics
development planning
disguised unemployment
dual economies
famine
fiscal and monetary policies in developing countries
foreign aid
Harris–Todaro model
import substitution and export-led growth
industrialization
inequality between nations
labour surplus economies
linkages
marketing boards
moneylenders
North–South economic relations
nutrition
peasant economy
periphery
poles of development
project evaluation
shadow pricing
sharecropping
structuralism
terms of trade and economic development
uneven development

International Trade
autarky
beggar-thy-neighbour
comparative advantage
competition in international trade
countertrade
customs unions
dumping
East–West economic relations
economic integration
effective protection
foreign trade
free trade and protection
gains from trade
growth and international trade
Heckscher–Ohlin trade theory
immiserizing growth
infant industry
international trade
Leontief paradox
Marshall–Lerner conditions
national system
offer curves or reciprocal demand curve
optimal tariffs
product cycles
quotas and tariffs
smuggling
tariffs
terms of trade
tradeable and nontradeable commodities
trade subsidies
transfer pricing
vent for surplus

Spatial Economics
basing point systems
central place theory
gravity models
location of economic activity
monocentric models in urban economics
regional development
regional distribution of economic activity
regional economics
spatial competition
spatial economics
Tiebout hypothesis
urban economics

Buckle, Thomas Henry
Burke, Edmund
Burns, Emile
Cairnes, John Elliott
Cannan, Edwin
Cantillon, Philip
Carlyle, Thomas
Carroll, Lewis
Cazenove, John
Chadwick, Edwin
Chalmers, Thomas
Champernowne, David Gawen
Child, Josiah
Clapham, John Harold
Clark, Colin Grant
Cliffe Leslie, Thomas Edward
Cobbett, William
Cobden, Richard
Coddington, Alan
Cohen, Ruth Louisa
Cole, George Douglas Howard
Collet, Clara Elizabeth
Colquhoun, Patrick
Crosland, C. Anthony
Crowther, Geoffrey
Cunningham, William
Cunynghame, Henry
Dalton, Hugh
Davenant, Charles
Defoe, Daniel
De Moivre, Abraham
De Quincey, Thomas
Dickinson, Henry Douglas
Dobb, Maurice Herbert
Donisthorpe, Wordsworth
Douglas, Clifford Hugh
Durbin, Evan Frank
Eden, Frederick Morton
Edgeworth, Francis Ysidro
Edgeworth, Maria
Einzig, Paul
Farr, William
Farrell, Michael James
Fawcett, Henry
Fawcett, Millicent Garrett
Fay, Charles Ryle
Ferguson, Adam
Finley, Moses
Fisher, Ronald Aylmer
Fleming, John Marcus
Florence, Philip Sargent
Flux, Alfred William
Foxwell, Herbert Somerton
Fullarton, John
Gaitskell, Hugh Todd Naylor
Geary, Robert Charles
Gee, Joshua
Gervaise, Isaac
Giffen, Robert
Godwin, William
Gonner, Edward Carter Kersey
Goschen, George Joachim, Viscount
Graunt, John
Gray, Alexander
Gray, John
Gray, Simon (alias George Purves LLD)
Gregory, Theodore Emanuel Gugenheim
Gresham, Thomas
Habakkuk, John Hrothgar
Hammond, John Lawrence Le Breton and Lucy Barbara
Harrod, Roy Forbes
Hawtrey, Ralph George
Henderson, Alexander
Henderson, Hubert Douglas
Hicks, John Richard
Hicks, Ursula Kathleen
Higgs, Henry
Hill, Polly
Hobbes, Thomas
Hobson, John Atkinson
Hodgskin, Thomas
Horner, Francis
Hume, David
Huskisson, William
Hutcheson, Francis
Hutchison, Terence Wilmot
Hyndman, Henry Myers
Ingram, John Kells
Jenkin, Henry Charles Fleeming
Jennings, Richard
Jevons, William Stanley
Jewkes, John
Johnson, William Ernest
Jones, George Thomas
Jones, Richard
Joplin, Thomas
Kahn, Richard Ferdinand
Kaldor, Nicholas
Kendall, Maurice George
Keynes, John Maynard
Keynes, John Neville
King, Gregory
Lardner, Dionysius
Lauderdale, Eighth Earl of
Lavington, Frederick
Law, John
Layton, Walter Thomas
Lloyd, William Forster
Locke, John
Longe, Francis Davy
Longfield, Samuel Mountifort
McCulloch, John Ramsay
Macfie, Alec Lawrence
Macleod, Henry Dunning
Maine, Henry James Sumner
Makower, Helen
Malthus, Thomas Robert
Malynes, Gerard de
Mandeville, Bernard de
Marcet, Jane
Marshall, Alfred
Marshall, Mary Paley
Martin, Henry
Martineau, Harriet
Massie, Joseph
Meade, James Edward
Meek, Ronald Lindley
Merivale, Herman
Mill, James
Mill, John Stuart
Millar, John
Misselden, Edward
Mummery, Albert Frederick
Mun, Thomas
Newmarch, William
Nicholson, Joseph Shield
North, Dudley
Nove, Alexander
O'Brien, George
Overstone, Lord
Owen, Robert
Paley, William
Palgrave, Robert Harry Inglis
Palmer, J. Horsley
Parnell, Henry Brooke
Pennington, James
Penrose, Edith Tilton
Petty, William
Phelps Brown, Ernest Henry
Pigou, Arthur Cecil
Place, Francis
Plant, Arnold
Playfair, William
Postan, Michael Moïssey
Postlethwayt, Malachy
Power, Eileen Edna
Pownall, Thomas
Price, Langford Lovell Frederick
Rae, John (1796–1872)
Rae, John (1845–1910)
Ramsey, Frank Plumpton
Ravenstone, Piercy
Read, Samuel
Reddaway, William Brian
Ricardo, David
Robbins, Lionel Charles
Robertson, Dennis
Robinson, Edward Austin Gossage
Robinson, Joan Violet
Rogers, James Edward Thorold
Rostas, Laszlo
Rothbarth, Erwin
Ruskin, John
Sanger, Charles Percy
Sayers, Richard Sidney
Schumacher, E.F. (Fritz)
Scott, William Robert
Scrope, George J. Poulett
Seers, Dudley
Senior, Nassau William
Shackle, George Lennox
Shaw, George Bernard
Shonfeld, Andrew Akiba
Shove, Gerald Frank
Sidgwick, Henry
Smart, William
Smith, Adam
Spencer, Herbert
Sraffa, Piero
Stamp, Josiah Charles
Stephen, Leslie
Steuart, Sir James
Stewart, Dugald
Stone, John Richard Nicholas
Strachey, John
Swift, Jonathan
Tawney, Richard Henry
Taylor, Harriet
Thompson, Thomas Perronet
Thompson, William
Thornton, Henry
Thornton, William Thomas
Titmuss, Richard Morris
Tooke, Thomas
Torrens, Robert
Townshend, Hugh
Toynbee, Arnold
Tozer, John Edward
Tucker, Josiah
Twiss, Travers
Ure, Andrew
Vanderbilt, Jacob
Vansittart, Nicholas
Wakefield, Edward Gibbon
Wallace, Alfred Russel
Ward, Barbara
Webb, Beatrice and Sidney James
West, Edward
Whately, Richard
Wheatley, John
Whewell, William
Wicksteed, Philip Henry
Wilson, James
Wilson, Thomas
Withers, Hartley
Young, Arthur

France

Aftalion, Albert
Allais, Maurice
Aupetit, Albert
Babeuf, François Noël
Bachelier, Louis
Bastiat, Claude Frédéric
Baudeau, Nicolas
Bertrand, Joseph Louis François
Bettelheim, Charles
Blanc, Jean Joseph Louis
Blanqui, Jerome Adolphe
Bloch, Marc
Bodin, Jean
Boisguillebert, Pierre le Pesant, Sieur de
Borda, Jean-Charles de
Braudel, Fernand

Germany, Austria and the Low Countries

Italy and Southern Europe

Scandinavia

Eastern Europe

Chayanov, Alexander Vasil'evich
Chernishevskii, Nikolai Gavrilovich
Dmitriev, Vladimir Karpovich
Fel'dmann Gregorii Alexandrovich
Kalecki, Michal
Kantorovich, Leonid Vitalievich
Kondratieff, Nikolai Dmitrievich
Konyüs, A.A.
Lange, Oskar
Lenin, Vladimir Ilich
Manoïlesco, Mihail
Nemchinov, Vasily Sergeevich
Novozhilov, Viktor Valentinovich
Plekhanov, Georgi Valentinovich
Preobrazhensky, Evgeny
Polak, Jacques Jacobus
Polanyi, Karl
Preobrazhensky, Evgeny Alexeyevich
Ryazanov, David
Slutsky, Eugen
Stalin, Joseph Vissaronovich
Storch, Heinrich Friedrich von
Strumilin, Stanislav Gustavovich
Struve, Pyotr Berngardovich
Trotsky, Lev Davidovich
Tugan-Baranovsky, Mikhail Ivanovich
Varga, Evgeny
Vosnesenski, Nikolai Alekseevich
Zawadzki, Wladyslaw Marian
Ziber, Nikolia Ivanovich

North America
Abbott, Edith
Abramovitz, Moses
Adams, Henry Carter
Alchian, Armen Albert
Almon, Shirley Montag
Angell, James Waterhouse
Ayres, Clarence Edwin
Bain, Joe Staten
Baran, Paul Alexander
Bergson, Abram
Berle, Adolph Augustus, Jr.
Bertalanffy, Ludwig von
Boulding, Kenneth Ewart
Bowman, Mary Jean
Brady, Dorothy Stahl
Braverman, Harry
Breckenridge, Sophinisba Preston
Bronfenbrenner, Martin
Brown, Harry Gunnison
Bullock, Charles Jesse
Burns, Arthur Frank
Burns, Arthur Robert
Burns, Eveline Mabel
Carey, Henry Charles
Carey, Matthew
Carver, Thomas Nixon
Chamberlin, Edward Hastings
Clark, John Bates
Clark, John Maurice
Coase, Ronald Harry
Colwell, Stephen
Commons, John Rogers
Court, Louis Mehel
Currie, Lauchlin Bernard
Davenport, Herbert Joseph
Del Mar, Alexander
Domar, Evsey David
Dorfman, Joseph
Douglas, Paul Howard
Dunbar, Charles Franklin
Dunlop, John Thomas
Durand, David
Eckstein, Otto
Ellet, Charles, Jr.
Ely, Richard Theodore
Erlich, Alexander
Evans, Griffith Conrad
Fabricant, Solomon
Fellner, William John
Fetter, Frank Albert
Fetter, Frank Whitson
Fisher, Irving
Franklin, Benjamin
Friedman, Milton
Friend, Irwin
Galbraith, John Kenneth
Gayer, Arthur David
George, Henry
Georgescu-Roegen, Nicholas
Gerschenkron, Alexander
Gilbert, Milton
Gilman, Charlotte Perkins
Goldsmith, Raymond William
Goldsmith, Selma
Gordon, Robert Aaron
Graham, Frank Dunstone
Gras, Norman Scott Brien
Hadley, Arthur Twining
Hagen, Everett Einar
Hamilton, Alexander
Hamilton, Earl Jefferson
Hansen, Alvin Harvey
Hardy, Charles Oscar
Harris, Seymour Edwin
Hart, Albert Gailord
Heller, Walter
Herskovitz, Melville Jean
Hirschman, Albert Otto
Hollander, Jacob Harry
Homan, Paul Thomas
Hotelling, Harold
Hymer, Stephen
Innis, Harold Adams
Jaffé, William
Jaszi, George
Jefferson, Thomas
Johannsen, Nicolaus
Johnson, Alvin Saunders
Johnson, Harry Gordon
Katona, George
Kelley, Augustus Maverick
Kemmerer, Edwin Walter
Kessel, Reuben Aaron
Keyserling, Leon Hirsch
Kindleberger, Charles Poor
Kitchin, Joseph
Knight, Frank Hyndman
Koopmans, Tjalling Charles
Kuh, Edin
Kuznets, Simon
Laughlin, James Laurence
Leontief, Wassily
Lerner, Abba Ptachya
Lintner, John Virgil
Lotka, Alfred James
Machlup, Fritz
Marget, Arthur William
Marschak, Jacob
Mason, Edward Sagendorph
Means, Gardiner Coit
Metzler, Lloyd Appleton
Mitchell, Wesley Clair
Moore, Henry Ludwell
Morgenstern, Oskar
Musgrave, Richard Abel
Nathan, Robert Roy
Nef, John Ulric
Newcomb, Simon
Nicholls, William Hord
Okun, Arthur M.
Parsons, Talcott
Patten, Simon Nelson
Perlman, Selig
Persons, Warren Milton
Rae, John
Raymond, Daniel
Reid, Margaret
Robinson, Abraham
Roos, Charles Frederick
Rosenstein-Rodan, Paul Narcyz
Samuelson, Paul Anthony
Savage, Leonard James
Schmookler, Jacob
Schultz, Henry
Schultz, Theodore William
Schwartz, Anna Jacobson
Schwartz, Nancy Lou
Scitovsky, Tibor
Seligman, Edwin Robert Anderson
Shephard, Ronald W.
Shoup, Carl Sumner
Sidrauski, Miguel
Simons, Henry Calvert
Slichter, Sumner Huber
Smithies, Arthur
Snyder, Carl
Spengler, Joseph John
Spiegel, Henry William
Stigler, George Joseph
Sumner, William Graham
Sweezy, Paul Malor
Tarbell, Ida Minerva
Tarshis, Lorie
Taussig, Frank William
Taylor, Fred Manville
Tiebout, Charles Mills
Tintner, Gerhard
Triffin, Robert
Tucker, George
Tugwell, Rexford Guy
Usher, Abbott Payson
Veblen, Thorstein
Vernon, Raymond
Vickrey, William Spencer
Viner, Jacob
Von Neumann, John
Wald, Abraham
Walker, Francis Amasa
Wallich, Henry Christopher
Warburton, Clark
Weintraub, Sidney
Wells, David Ames
Williams, John Henry
Wilson, Edwin Bidwell
Witte, Edwin Emil
Wood, Stuart
Woytinsky, Wladimir Savelievich
Yntema, Theodore
Young, Allyn Abbott

Asia
Liu, Ta-Chung
Mahalanobis, Prasantha Chandra
Mao Zedong

Australia and New Zealand
Arndt, Heinz Wolfgang
Coghlan, Timothy A.
Copland, Douglas Berry
Giblin, Lyndhurst Falkiner
Hearn, William Edward
Phillips, Alban William Housego
Salter, Wilfred Edward Graham

Japan
Aoyama, Hideo
Shibata, K.
Tsuru, Shigeto
Uno, Kozo

South Africa
Lehfeldt, Robert Alfred

South America and the Caribbean
Lewis, W. Arthur
Prebisch, Raul

Index

The index is confined to significant discussions of key subjects that occur throughout *The New Palgrave*. Page numbers refer to the opening of the discussion and do not give the complete page span of the discussion. Duplication of material has been avoided wherever possible; where *see also* appears at the end of an index entry the reader should consult the index entries listed there for further amplification. Additional guidance will be found in the Introductory Notes in Volume I, p. xvii.